Florida

Published by:
AAA Publishing
1000 AAA Drive
Heathrow, FL 32746-5063
Copyright AAA 2000

Send Written Comments to:
AAA Member Comments
1000 AAA Drive, Box 61
Heathrow, FL 32746-5063

**Advertising Rate and Circulation
Information**
Call: (407) 444-8280

Printed in the USA by Quebecor
World, Buffalo, NY

 Printed on recyclable paper.
Please recycle whenever possible.

Stock #4609

Florida

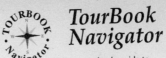

TourBook Navigator

Featured Information

MAPS

The sign it's time to pull off the road.

 After a day of traveling, few sights are more welcome than a Hampton.™ Because if you have a AAA card, you're entitled to savings at over 1,000 locations nationwide. You'll also enjoy a free breakfast bar and our 100% Satisfaction Guarantee, and you can earn Hilton HHonors® hotel points and airline miles throughout your stay. So come join us. When you're on the road, there's no better place to stay.

We're with you all the way. Hampton Inn Hampton Inn & Suites

Call 1-800-456-7793 for reservations.

EVERY KNIGHT.
JUST RIGHT.®
Stay with us from coast to coast—
and get a great night's rest at a
great Knights rate at over 235 locations.
The right place.
The right people.
The right price.
Knights Inn
For AAA discounts,
call 1-800-THE KNIGHTS
(800-843-5644) and ask
for the S3A rate.*
Visit our Web site at
KNIGHTSINN.COM
*Rates based on availability. Not valid with other discounts.
All Knights Inn® hotels are independently owned and
operated. ©Knights Franchise Systems, Inc. 2000.

Trust the AAA TourBook® guide for objective travel information.

Follow the pages of the TourBook Navigator to thoroughly understand this unique member benefit.

Making Your Way Through the AAA Listings

Attractions, lodgings and restaurants are listed on the basis of merit alone after careful evaluation, approval and rating by one of our full-time Tourism Editors or, in rare cases, a designated representative. Annual lodging evaluations are unannounced and conducted on site by random room sample.

Those lodgings and restaurants listed with an (fyi) icon have not gone through the same evaluation process as other rated properties. Individual listings will denote the reason why this icon appears. Bulleted recreational activity listings are not inspected but are included for member information.

An establishment's decision to advertise in the TourBook guide has no bearing on its inspection, evaluation or rating. Advertising for services or products does not imply AAA endorsement.

How the TourBook is

Organized

Geographic listing is used for accuracy and consistency. This means attractions, lodgings and restaurants are listed under the city in which they physically are located—or in some cases under the nearest recognized city. The Comprehensive City Index located in the back of the book contains an A-to-Z list of cities. Most listings are alphabetically organized by state or province, city, and establishment name. A color is assigned to each state or province so that you can match the color bars at the top of the page to switch from ❶ Points of Interest to ❷ Lodgings and Restaurants.

Destination Cities and Destination Areas

The TourBook guide also groups information by destination city and destination area. If a city is grouped in a destination vicinity section, the city name will appear at its alphabetical location in the book, and a handy cross reference will give the exact page on which listings for that city begin. Maps are placed at the beginning of these sections to orient you to the destinations.

❸ Destination cities, established based on government models and local expertise, are comprised of metropolitan areas plus nearby vicinity cities.

Destination areas are regions with broad tourist appeal. Several cities will comprise the area.

All information in this TourBook guide was reviewed for accuracy before publication. However, since changes inevitably occur between annual editions, we suggest you contact establishments directly to confirm prices and schedules.

Points of Interest Section

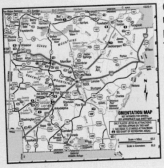

Orientation maps
near the start of each Attractions section show only those places we call points of interest. Coordinates included with the city listings depict the locations of those cities on the map. A GEM symbol (⬡) accents towns with "must see" points of interest which offer a *Great Experience for Members*. And the black ovals with white numerals (**22** for example) locate items listed in the nearby Recreation Areas chart.

Destination area maps
illustrate key travel areas defined by local travel experts. Communities shown have listings for AAA approved attractions.

National park maps
represent the area in and around the park. Some campground sites and lodges spotted on the maps do not meet AAA/CAA criteria, but are shown for members who nevertheless wish to stay close to the park area.

Walking or self-guiding tour maps
correspond to specific routes described in TourBook guide text.

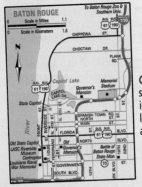

City maps
show areas where numerous points of interest are concentrated and indicate their location in relation to major roads, parks, airports and other landmarks.

Lodgings & Restaurants Section

Destination area maps
illustrate key travel areas defined by local travel experts. Communities shown have listings for AAA-RATED® lodgings and/or restaurants.

Spotting maps
show the location of lodgings and restaurants. Lodgings are spotted with a black background (**22** for example); restaurants are spotted with a white background (**23** for example). Spotting map indexes have been placed immediately after each map to provide the user with a convenient method to identify what an area has to offer at a glance. The index references the map page number where the property is spotted, indicates if a property is an Official Appointment and contains an advertising reference if applicable. It also lists the property's diamond rating, high season rate range and listing page number.

Downtown/city spotting maps
are provided when spotted facilities are very concentrated. GEM points of interest also appear on these maps.

Vicinity spotting maps
spot those properties that are outside the downtown or city area. Major roads, landmarks, airports and GEM points of interest are shown on vicinity spotting maps as well. The names of suburban communities that have AAA-RATED® accommodations are shown in magenta type.

Featured Information Section

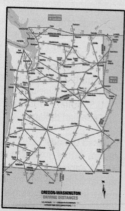

Driving distance maps
are intended to be used only for trip-distance and driving-time planning.

Sample Attraction Listing

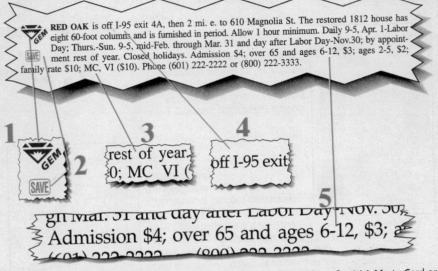

RED OAK is off I-95 exit 4A, then 2 mi. e. to 610 Magnolia St. The restored 1812 house has eight 60-foot columns and is furnished in period. Allow 1 hour minimum. Daily 9-5, Apr. 1-Labor Day; Thurs.-Sun. 9-5, mid-Feb. through Mar. 31 and day after Labor Day-Nov.30; by appointment rest of year. Closed holidays. Admission $4; over 65 and ages 6-12, $3; ages 2-5, $2; family rate $10; MC, VI ($10). Phone (601) 222-2222 or (800) 222-3333.

1

2

3 rest of year. 0; MC VI (

4 off I-95 exit

5

gh Mar. 31 and day after Labor Day-Nov. 30;
Admission $4; over 65 and ages 6-12, $3; a
(601) 222-2222 — (800) 222-3333

1 SAVE Participating attractions offer AAA/CAA cardholders or holders of a AAA MasterCard or AAA Visa Card and up to six family members at least 10% off the attraction's standard admission for the validity period of the TourBook guide; members should inquire in advance concerning the validity of the discount for special rates. Present your card at the admissions desk. A list of participating points of interest appears in the Indexes section of the book. The SAVE discount may not be used in conjunction with other discounts. Attractions that already provide a reduced senior rate may not honor the SAVE discount for this age group. Discounts may not apply during special events or particular days or seasons.

2 This attraction is of exceptional interest and quality and therefore has been designated a AAA GEM—offering a *Great Experience for Members.*

3 AE = American Express   JC = Japanese Credit Bureau
CB = Carte Blanche   MC = MasterCard
DI = Diners Club   VI = VISA
DS = Discover
Minimum amounts that may be charged appear in parentheses when applicable.

4 Unless otherwise specified, directions are given from the center of town, using the following highway designations: I (interstate highway), US (federal highway), Hwy. (Canadian highway), SR (state route), CR (county road), FM (farm to market road), FR (forest road), MM (mile marker).

5 Admission prices are quoted without sales tax. Children under the lowest age specified are admitted free when accompanied by an adult. Days, months and age groups written with a hyphen are inclusive. Prices pertaining to points of interest in the United States are quoted in U.S. dollars; prices for Canadian province and territory points of interest are quoted in Canadian dollars.

Bulleted Listings: Casino gambling establishments are visited by AAA personnel to ensure safety; casinos within hotels are presented for member information regardless of whether the lodging is AAA approved. Recreational activities of a participatory nature (requiring physical exertion or special skills) are not inspected. Wineries are inspected by AAA Tourism Editors to ensure they meet listing requirements and offer tours. All are presented in a bulleted format for informational purposes.

Attraction Partners

AAA. Every Day.

These Show Your Card & Save® partners provide the listed member benefits. Admission tickets that offer greater discounts may be available for purchase at the local AAA/CAA club. A maximum of six tickets is available at the discount price.

UNIVERSAL Orlando
Universal Studios Hollywood

SAVE Save $3 on 1-day admission at Universal Studios Hollywood; $4 on 2-day admission and $5 on 3-day admission at Universal Orlando's theme parks. These savings apply to tickets purchased at the gate.

SAVE Save 10% on selected souvenirs and dining in both parks and at CityWalk, Universal Orlando.

SeaWorld/Busch Gardens

SAVE Save at SeaWorld, Busch Gardens, Sesame Place, Water Country USA and Adventure Island

SAVE Save 10% on general admission

Six Flags Adventure Parks

SAVE Save $4 on admission at the gate

SAVE Save $12 on admission at the gate each Wednesday

SAVE Save 10% on selected souvenirs and dining (check at main gate for details)

Golden Passports – National Parks Pass

Citizens or permanent residents of the United States who are 62 and older can obtain Golden Age Passports for a one-time $10 fee. Golden Access Passports are free to citizens or permanent residents of the United States (regardless of age) who are medically blind or permanently disabled.

Both cover entrance fees for the holder and accompanying private party to all national parks, historic sites, monuments and battlefields within the U.S. national park system, plus half off camping and other fees. Apply in person at most federally operated areas.

The Golden Eagle Passport is available to everyone, despite country of origin. It costs $65 annually and covers entrance fees for the holder and accompanying private party to all federally operated areas. Obtain the pass in person at any national park or regional office of the U.S. park service or forest service.

The National Parks Pass, valid for 1 year from the date of purchase, allows unlimited admissions to all U.S. national parks. The $50 pass covers all occupants of a vehicle at parks where the entrance fee is per vehicle. At parks with individual entry fees, the pass covers the pass holder, spouse, parents and children.

As a result of a partnership with the National Park Service, AAA members may purchase the pass for $48, either through AAA's Internet site (www.aaa.com) or by phoning or visiting a participating AAA office. Nonmembers may purchase the pass through AAA for the full $50 price.

The passes are personalized at a distribution center and are mailed directly to the purchaser.

Sample Lodging Listing

1 Ⓐ or Ⓒ indicates our Official Appointment (OA) lodgings. The OA program permits properties to display and advertise the Ⓐ or Ⓒ emblem. We highlight these properties with red diamonds and classification. Some OA listings include special amenities such as free continental breakfast; early check-in/late check-out; free room upgrade or preferred room, such as ocean view or poolside (subject to availability); free local phone calls; and free daily newspaper. This does not imply that only these properties offer these amenities. The Ⓐ or Ⓒ sign helps traveling members find accommodations that want member business.

▼▼▼ or ▼▼▼▼ The number of diamonds—not the color—informs you of the overall level of quality in a lodging's amenities and service. More diamond details appear on page 14.

Motel or Motel: Diamond ratings are applied in the context of lodging type, or classification. See pages 20-21 for our Lodging Classifications.

Discounts

SAVE Official Appointment properties guarantee members a minimum 10% discount off the standard room rates published in TourBook guides.

SAVE AAA's Show Your Card & Save® chain partners provide special values to our members: Select Choice hotels, Days Inn, Hampton Inn, Hilton, Hyatt, and La Quinta. Individual properties in these chains appearing in the TourBook guides have been evaluated and approved by AAA. Be sure to read about the specific member benefits on page 18.

Sᴅ Establishments offer a minimum senior discount of 10% off the listed rates. This discount is available to members 60 or older.

ASK Many TourBook guide properties offer discounts to members even though the lodgings do not participate in a formal discount program. The ASK is another reminder to inquire about available discounts when making your reservations or at check-in.

To obtain published rates or discounts, you must identify yourself as a AAA or CAA member and request AAA rates when making reservations. The SAVE or senior discount may not be used in conjunction with other discounts. Be sure to show your card at registration and verify the room rate

Discounts normally offered at some lodgings may not apply during special events or holiday periods. Special rates and discounts may not apply to all room types.

The rates listed for approved properties are provided to AAA by each lodging and represent the regular (rack) rate for a standard room. Printed rates, based on rack rates and last room availability, are rounded to the nearest dollar. Rates do not include taxes and discounts. U.S. rates are in U.S. dollars; rates for Canadian lodgings are in Canadian dollars.

2 Rate Lines
Shown from left to right: dates the rates are effective; rates for 1 person or 2 persons; extra person charge (XP); and any applicable family plan indicator.

Rates Guaranteed
AAA/CAA members are guaranteed that they will not be charged more than the maximum regular rate printed in each rate range for a standard room. Rates may vary within the range depending on season and room type. Listed rates are based on last standard room availability.

Exceptions
Lodgings may temporarily increase room rates, not recognize discounts or modify pricing policies during special events. Examples of special events range from Mardi Gras and Kentucky Derby (including pre-Derby events) to college football games, holidays, holiday periods and state fairs. Although some special events are listed in AAA/CAA TourBook guides, it is always wise to check, in advance, with AAA travel counselors for specific dates.

Discounts
Member discounts will apply to rates quoted, within the rate range, applicable at the time of booking. Special rates used in advertising, and special short-term, promotional rates lower than the lowest listed rate in the range, are not subject to additional member discounts.

3 Meal Plan Indicators
The following types of meal plans may be available in the listed room rate:
AP = American Plan of three meals daily
BP = Breakfast Plan of full hot breakfast
CP = Continental Plan of pastry, juice and another beverage
ECP = Expanded Continental Plan, which offers a wider variety of breakfast items
EP = European Plan, where rate includes only room
MAP = Modified American Plan of two meals daily

Check-in times are shown in the listing only if they are after 3 p.m.; check-out times are shown only if they are before 10 a.m.

Parking is on the premises and free unless otherwise noted.

4 Family Plan Indicators
F = Children stay free
D = Discounts for children
F17 = Children 17 and under stay free (age displayed will reflect property's policy)
D17 = Discount for children 17 and under

5 Lodging Locators
Numerals are used to locate, or "spot," lodgings on maps we provide for larger cities.

The lodging listings with **fyi** in place of diamonds are included as an "information only" service for members. The icon indicates that a property has not been rated for one or more of the following reasons: too new to rate; under construction; under major renovation; not evaluated; or may not meet all AAA requirements. Listing prose will give insight as to why the **fyi** rating was assigned.

The Lodging Diamond Ratings

AAA Tourism Editors evaluate and rate each lodging based on the overall quality and services offered at a property. The size, age and overall appeal of an establishment are considered as well as regional decorating and architectural differences.

While guest services are an important part of all diamond ratings, they are particularly critical at the four and five diamond levels. A property must provide a high level of service, on a consistent basis, to obtain and support the four and five diamond rating.

Properties are world-class by definition, exhibiting an exceptionally high degree of service as well as striking, luxurious facilities and many extra amenities. Guest services are executed and presented in a flawless manner. The guest is pampered by a professional, attentive staff. The properties' facilities and operation help set industry standards in hospitality and service.

Properties are excellent and display a high level of service and hospitality. They offer a wide variety of amenities and upscale facilities in the guest rooms, on the grounds and in the public areas.

Properties offer a degree of sophistication. Additional amenities, services and facilities may be offered. There is a noticeable upgrade in physical attributes, services and comfort.

Properties maintain the attributes offered at the one diamond level, while showing noticeable enhancements in room decor and quality of furnishings.

Properties offer good but modest accommodations. Establishments are functional, emphasizing clean and comfortable rooms. They must meet the basic needs of comfort and cleanliness.

Guest Safety

Room Security

In order to be approved for listing in AAA/CAA TourBook guides for the United States and Canada, all lodgings must comply with AAA's guest room security requirements.

In response to AAA/CAA members' concern about their safety at properties, AAA-RATED® accommodations must have dead-bolt locks on all guest room entry doors and connecting room doors.

If the area outside the guest room door is not visible from inside the room through a window or door panel, viewports must be installed on all guest room entry doors. Bed and breakfast properties and country inns are not required to have viewports. Ground floor and easily accessible sliding doors must be equipped with some other type of secondary security locks.

Tourism Editors view a percentage of rooms at each property since it is not feasible to evaluate every room in every lodging establishment. Therefore, AAA cannot guarantee that there are working locks on all doors and windows in all guest rooms.

Fire Safety

Because of the highly specialized skills needed to conduct professional fire safety inspections, AAA/CAA Tourism Editors cannot assess fire safety.

All U.S. and Canadian lodging properties must be equipped with an operational, single-station smoke detector, and all public areas must have operational smoke detectors or an automatic sprinkler system. A AAA/CAA Tourism Editor has evaluated a sampling of the rooms to verify this equipment is in place.

For additional fire safety information read the page posted on the back of your guest room door, or write:

National Fire Protection Association
1 Batterymarch Park
P.O. Box 9101
Quincy, MA 02269-9101

Access for Travelers with Disabilities

Qualified properties listed in this guide have symbols indicating they are fully accessible, semi-accessible or meet the needs of the hearing-impaired. This two-tiered mobility standard was developed to meet members' varying degrees of accessibility needs.

🛦 Fully accessible properties meet the needs of those who are significantly disabled and utilize a wheelchair or scooter. A fully accessible lodging will provide at least one guest room meeting the designated criteria. A traveler with these disabilities will be able to park and access public areas, including restrooms, check-in facilities and at least one food and beverage outlet. A fully accessible restaurant indicates that parking, dining rooms and restrooms are accessible.

🛦 Semi-accessible properties meet the needs of those who are disabled but do have some mobility. Such travelers would include people using a cane or walker, or a disabled individual with good mobility but a limited arm or hand range of motion. A semi-accessible lodging will provide at least one guest room meeting the designated criteria. A traveler with these disabilities will be able to park and access public areas, including restrooms, check-in facilities and at least one food and beverage outlet. A semi-accessible restaurant indicates that parking, dining rooms and restrooms are accessible.

🖉 This symbol indicates a property with the following equipment available for hearing impaired travelers: TDD at front desk or switchboard; visual notification of fire alarm, incoming telephone calls, door knock or bell; closed caption decoder available; text telephone or TDD available for guest room use; telephone amplification device available, with shelf and electric outlet next to guest room telephone.

The criteria used by AAA/CAA do not represent the full scope of the Americans With Disabilities Act of 1990 Accessibility Guidelines (ADAAG); they are, however, consistent with the ADAAG. Members can obtain from their local AAA/CAA club the AAA brochure, "AAA Accessibility Criteria for Travelers with Disabilities," which describes the specific criteria pertaining to the fully accessible, semi-accessible and hearing-impaired standards.

The Americans With Disabilities Act (ADA) prohibits businesses that serve the public from discriminating against persons with disabilities who are aided by service animals. Some businesses have mistakenly denied access to their properties to persons with disabilities who use service animals. ADA has priority over all state and local laws, as well as a business owner's standard of business, that might bar animals from the premises. Businesses must permit guests and their service animal entry, as well as allow service animals to accompany guests to all public areas of a property. A property is permitted to ask whether the animal is a service animal or a pet, or whether a guest has a disability. The property may not, however, ask questions about the nature of a disability or require proof of one.

No fees or deposits (even those normally charged for pets) may be charged for the service animal.

AAA/CAA urges members with disabilities to always phone ahead to fully understand the accommodation's offerings. Some properties do not fully comply with AAA/CAA's exacting accessibility standards but may offer some property design standards that meet the needs of some guests with disabilities.

AAA/CAA does not evaluate recreational facilities, banquet rooms or convention and meeting facilities for accessibility. Phone a property directly to inquire about your needs for these areas.

What The Icons Mean

Member Values

(AAA) or (CAA) Official Appointment

[SAVE] Offers minimum 10% discount

[SAVE] Show Your Card & Save partners

[ASK] May offer discount

[S$] Offers senior discount

[fyi] Informational listing only

Member Services

[✈] Airport transportation

[🐾] Pets allowed

[🍽] Restaurant on premises

[🍽+] Restaurant off premises (walking distance)

[24🍽] 24-hour room service

[🍸] Cocktail lounge

[👶] Child care

Accessibility Features

[♿] Fully accessible

[♿] Semi-accessible

[♿] Roll-in showers

[👂] Hearing impaired

Leisure Activities

[🏊] Outdoor pool

[🏊] Indoor pool

[🏊] Indoor/outdoor pool

[💪] Health club on premises

[💪] Health club off premises

[🎿] Recreational activities

In-Room Amenities

[🚭] Non-smoking rooms

[AC] No air conditioning

[☎] No telephones

[CTV] No cable TV

[🎬] Movies

[VCR] VCR

[📻] Radio

[▭] Coffee maker

[▭] Microwave

[▮] Refrigerator

[DATA PORT] Data port/modem line

Availability

If an in-room amenity is available only on a limited basis (in some but not all rooms), the term "SOME UNITS" will appear above those icons.

SOME UNITS
[♿] [👂] [🎬] [VCR] [▭] / [▮] [DATA PORT] [🚭] /

Additional Fees

Fees may be charged for some of the services represented by the icons listed here. The word "FEE" will appear below each icon when an extra charge applies.

SOME UNITS
[♿] [👂] [🎬] [VCR] [▭] / [▮] [DATA PORT] [🚭] /
         FEE FEE   FEE

Preferred Lodging Partners

Phone the member-only toll-free numbers below or your AAA/CAA club to get these member benefits. Have your membership card on hand when calling.

GUARANTEED LOWEST RATES - The lowest public rate will automatically be offered to you when calling any of these numbers for reservations, except Choice Hotels International which offers a 10-20% discount available all the time. Your club code, found on your membership card, must be provided at the time of reservation.

SATISFACTION GUARANTEE - If you are not satisfied with a part of your stay, please provide the property the opportunity to correct any fault during your stay. If it cannot be corrected, your stay is free. Rules vary slightly by chain.

Choice Hotels International

(800) 228-1222

(800) 432-9755

(800) 532-1496

(800) 916-2221

(800) 221-4731

(800) 456-7793

Making Reservations

Give Proper Identification

When making reservations, you must identify yourself as a AAA/CAA member. Give all pertinent information about your planned stay. Request written confirmation to guarantee: type of room, rate, dates of stay, and cancellation and refund policies. Note: Age restrictions may apply.

Confirm Deposit, Refund and Cancellation Policies

Most establishments give full deposit refunds if they have been notified at least 48 hours before the normal check-in time. Listing prose will note if more than 48 hours notice is required for cancellation. However, when making reservations, confirm the property's deposit, cancellation and refund policies. Some properties may charge a cancellation or handling fee.

When this applies, "cancellation fee imposed" will appear in the listing. If you cancel too late, you have little recourse if a refund is denied.

When an establishment requires a full or partial payment in advance, and your trip is cut short, a refund may not be given.

When canceling reservations, phone the lodging immediately. Make a note of the date and time you called, the cancellation number if there is one, and the name of the person who handled the cancellation. If your AAA/CAA club made your reservation, allow them to make the cancellation for you as well so you will have proof of cancellation.

Review Charges for Appropriate Rates

When you are charged more than the maximum rate listed in the TourBook guide for a standard room, question the additional charge. If management refuses to adhere to the published rate, pay for the room and submit your receipt and membership number to AAA/CAA within 30 days. Include all pertinent information: dates of stay, rate paid, itemized paid receipts, number of persons in your party, the room number you occupied, and list any extra room equipment used. A refund of the amount paid in excess of the stated maximum will be made if our investigation indicates that unjustified charging has occurred.

Get the Room You Reserved

When you find your room is not as specified, and you have written confirmation of reservations for a certain type of accommodation, you should be given the option of choosing a different room or finding one elsewhere. Should you choose to go elsewhere and a refund is refused or resisted, submit the matter to AAA/CAA within 30 days along with complete documentation, including your reasons for refusing the room and copies of your written confirmation and any receipts or canceled checks associated with this problem.

How to Get the Best Room Rates

You'll find the best room rate if you book your reservation in advance with the help of a travel counselor or agent at your local AAA/CAA office.

If you're not yet ready to make firm vacation plans or if you prefer a more spontaneous trip, take advantage of the partnerships that preferred hotel chains have arranged with AAA. Phone the toll-free numbers on the previous page that have been set up exclusively for members for the purpose of reserving with these Show Your Card & Save® chain partners.

Even if you were unable to make a reservation, be sure to show your membership card at the desk and ask if you're being offered the lowest rate available for that time. Many lodgings offer reduced rates to members.

Lodging Classifications

AAA Tourism Editors evaluate lodgings based on classification, since all lodging types by definition do not provide the same level of service and facilities. Thus, hotels are rated in comparison to other hotels, resorts to other resorts—and so on. A lodging's classification appears beneath its diamond rating in the listing.

Hotel — *full service*
Usually high-rise establishments, offering a wide range of services and on-premise food/beverage outlets, shops, conference facilities and recreational activities.

Motel — *limited service*
Low-rise or multi-story establishment offering limited public and recreational facilities.

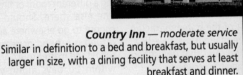

Country Inn — *moderate service*
Similar in definition to a bed and breakfast, but usually larger in size, with a dining facility that serves at least breakfast and dinner.

Resort — *full service*
Offers a variety of food/beverage outlets and an extensive range of recreational and entertainment programs—geared to vacation travelers.

Bed & Breakfast — *limited service*
Usually smaller, owner-operated establishments emphasizing an "at home" feeling. A continental or full, hot breakfast is served and included in the room rate.

Condominium — *limited service*
Apartment-style units or homes primarily owned by individuals and available for rent. A variety of room styles and decor treatments, as well as limited housekeeping service, is typical.

Motor Inn — *moderate service*
Single or multi-story establishment offering on-premise food/beverage service, meeting and banquet facilities and some recreational facilities.

Complex — *service varies*
A combination of two or more types of lodging classifications.

NAVIGATOR · *Lodgings*

Lodge — *moderate service*
Typically two or more stories with all facilities in one building. Rustic decor is common. Usually has food/beverage service.

Apartment — *limited service*
Primarily offers temporary guest accommodations with one or more bedrooms, a living room, a full kitchen and an eating area. Studio apartments may combine the sleeping and living areas into one room.

Cottage — *limited service*
Primarily individual housing units that may offer one or more separate sleeping areas, a living room and cooking facilities.

Ranch — *moderate service*
Often offers rustic decor treatments and food/beverage facilities. Entertainment and recreational activities are geared to a Western theme.

Lodging Subclassifications

The following are subclassifications that may appear along with the classifications listed above to provide a more specific description of the lodging.

Suite
One or more bedrooms and a living room/sitting area, closed off by a full wall. Note: May not have a partition bedroom door.

Extended Stay
Properties catering to longer-term guest stays. Will have kitchens or efficiencies and may have a separate living room area, evening office closure and limited housekeeping services.

Historic
Properties must meet one of the following criteria:
- Be listed on the National Register of Historic Places
- Be designated a National Historic Landmark
- Be located in a National Register Historic District

Classic
Renowned and landmark properties, older than 50 years, known for their unique style and ambience.

Sample Restaurant Listing

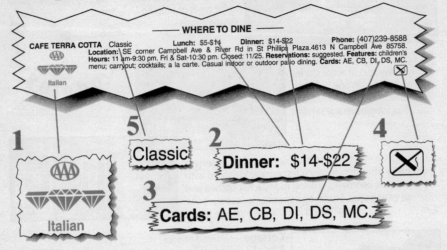

— WHERE TO DINE —

CAFE TERRA COTTA Classic **Lunch:** $5-$14 **Dinner:** $14-$22 **Phone:** (407)239-8588
Location: SE corner Campbell Ave & River Rd in St Phillips Plaza.4613 N Campbell Ave 85758.
Hours: 11 am-9:30 pm. Fri & Sat-10:30 pm. Closed: 11/25. **Reservations:** suggested. **Features:** children's menu; carryout; cocktails; a la carte. Casual indoor or outdoor patio dining. **Cards:** AE, CB, DI, DS, MC.

Italian

1

5 Classic

2 Dinner: $14-$22

4

3 Cards: AE, CB, DI, DS, MC.

Italian

1 ⬥⬥⬥ or ⬥⬥ indicates our Official Appointment (OA) restaurants. The OA program permits properties to display and advertise the ⬥⬥⬥ or ⬥⬥ emblem. We highlight these properties with red diamonds and cuisine type. The ⬥⬥⬥ or ⬥⬥ sign helps traveling members find restaurants that want member business.

⬥⬥⬥⬥ or ⬥⬥⬥ The number of diamonds—not the color—informs you of the overall level of quality for food and presentation, service and ambience.

A cuisine type is assigned for each restaurant listing. AAA currently recognizes more than 90 different cuisine types.

2 The dinner price range is approximate and includes a salad or appetizer, an entree, a vegetable and a non-alcoholic beverage for one person. Taxes and tip are not included. Some listings include additional information such as the availability of a senior citizen menu, children's menu or "early bird specials," if offered at least 5 days a week.

3 AE = American Express
CB = Carte Blanche
DI = Diners Club

DS = Discover
JC = Japanese Credit Bureau

MC = MasterCard
VI = VISA

Minimum amounts that may be charged appear in parentheses when applicable.

4 This icon indicates that the restaurant has a designated non-smoking section or is entirely smoke-free.

5 If applicable, restaurants may be further defined as:
Classic—renowned and landmark properties, older than 25 years, known for unique style and ambience.
Historic—properties must meet one of the following criteria:
- Be listed on the National Register of Historic Places
- Be designated a National Historic Landmark
- Be located in a National Register Historic District

fyi The restaurants with **fyi** in place of diamonds are included as an "information only" service for members. This designation indicates that the restaurant has not been evaluated.

The Restaurant Diamond Ratings

AAA Tourism Editors are responsible for determining a restaurant's diamond rating based on established criteria.

These criteria were established with input from AAA trained professionals, members and restaurant industry experts. They are purposely broad to capture what is typically seen throughout the restaurant industry at each diamond rating level.

Often renowned, these establishments impart a world-class and opulent, adult-oriented experience. This is "haute cuisine" at its best. Menus are often cutting edge, with an obvious dedication to use of only the finest ingredients available. Even the classic dishes become extraordinary under the masterful direction of highly acclaimed chefs. Presentations are spectacular, reflecting impeccable artistry and awareness. An expert, formalized staff continuously anticipates and exceeds guest expectations. Staff members' unfailing attention to detail appears effortless, well-rehearsed and unobtrusive. Undoubtedly, these restaurants appeal to those in search of the ultimate dining experience.

Examples include renowned dining rooms associated with luxury lodgings, or exclusive independent restaurants often found in metropolitan areas.

These establishments impart a luxurious and socially refined experience. This is consistent fine dining. Menus typically reflect a high degree of creativity and complexity, featuring elaborate presentations of market-driven or traditional dishes. A cultured, professional and highly proficient staff consistently demonstrates a profound desire to meet or exceed guest expectations. Restaurants of this caliber are geared to individuals with an appetite for an elite, fine-dining experience.

Examples include dining rooms associated with luxury lodgings, or exclusive independent restaurants often found in metropolitan areas.

These establishments impart an increasingly refined and upscale, adult-oriented experience. This is the entry level into fine dining. Creative and complex menus offer a blend of traditional and trendy foods. The service level is typically semi-formal with knowledgeable and proficient staff. Routinely these restaurants appeal to the diner in search of an experience rather than just a meal.

Examples include high-caliber, chic, boutique and conventional restaurants.

These establishments provide for dining needs that are increasingly complex, but still reasonably priced. They typically exhibit noticeable efforts in rising above the ordinary in many aspects of food, service and decor. Service is typically functional yet ambitious, periodically combining informal style with limited self-service elements. Often well-suited to traditional, special occasion and family dining.

Examples include a varied range of specific concept (theme) and multi-purpose establishments.

These establishments appeal to a diner seeking good, wholesome, no-nonsense eating at an affordable price. They typically provide simple, familiar and unadorned foods served in a sensible, casual or self-service style. Often quick service and family oriented.

Examples include coffee shops, diners, cafeterias, short order and modest full service eateries.

The Smart Solution for Your Family's Financial Future

Y our family's financial needs change throughout life. Now you can trust AAA to bring you a full array of financial products and services to meet your needs at every stage. With AAA Financial Services' great rates and hassle-free service, you're covered for life. Call us today!

Exclusively for AAA members

- ◆ AAA *Platinum Plus*[sm] Visa® Credit Card

1-800-523-7666

- ◆ Auto Loans
- ◆ Home Equity Loans & Lines of Credit[1]
- ◆ Money Market Index Accounts
- ◆ Certificates of Deposit[2]

1-877-481-4AAA

Financial Services

AAA. Every Day.™
24 Hours A Day. 7 Days A Week.
www.aaa.com

THINK YOU CAN'T FIT ANOTHER SOUVENIR IN YOUR SUITCASE?

No matter how many mementos you plan on packing, there's always room for a Florida Lottery ticket. You can try your luck at five exciting online games, as well as a variety of scratch-off tickets. With our Advance Play option, you can play your favorite numbers even after your vacation in the Sunshine State ends. Who knows, you may go home with a lot more than fond memories. For winning numbers, visit our website at www.flalottery.com.

Florida

Sandy Beaches

Sun and fun are found in abundance along the expansive coast

Theme Park Adventures

Amusements range from water slides to roller coasters

Manatees & Alligators

Placid waters harbor Florida's native creatures

Relaxing in the Keys

Clear water and coral characterize this diving paradise

Journey into Space

Awesome launches light up the sky at Cape Canaveral

a whimsical paradise

W hen you hear the word "Florida," there's a good chance that you conjure a vivid mental picture.

It probably includes swaying palms, sandy beaches and piercing rays of sunlight reflecting off the surface of the ocean.

Perhaps you envision the emerald-green waters that caress the Gulf beaches at Pensacola. Or the sharks' teeth sprinkled across the sand in Venice. Or the colorful varieties of seashells blanketing the coast on the islands of Captiva and Sanibel. Or the rolling waves lapping at the sugary shore at Ponce Inlet.

Without a doubt, the state's seascapes are spectacular. But Florida boasts an appeal that stretches far beyond its handsome coast.

Images of lush inland landscapes are just as plentiful. Towering pine trees and stolid oaks rise from dense thickets of palmettos in the Apalachicola, Ocala and Osceola national forests. Prairies of sawgrass interrupt mangrove stands and mazes of gnarled cypress roots that emerge from the murky swampland in the Everglades.

And Florida's most notable man-made enticements can't be overlooked: Glittery theme parks encourage young and old to make time for a day of play beneath a sun that almost always shines.

Florida is as close as you can get to seeing the world through the eyes of an artist with a mischievous sense of humor and a wildly creative genius.

The Sunshine State is a place of stunning extremes—a place where the sun shines brighter, the water runs bluer, the slash pines reach higher, the sands feel softer.

It's a place in which the Northerners live way down south around Miami and Fort Lauderdale and where twangy Southern accents ring out from such northern enclaves as Pensacola and Tallahassee.

Weird creatures inhabit the water, the land and the air. Oafish manatees—thought to have given rise to the legend of the mermaid—ply the waters of coastal waterways and placid springs. Garish roseate spoonbills, whose showy pink plumes topped the chapeaus of many a society matron in the early 1900s, grace shorelines once dotted with flocks of flamingos.

Dog-sized Key deer skirt the brush on Big Pine Key. Libidinous lovebugs, known for their mating-while-flying rendezvous, make their impact as they smash two-by-two into the windshields of passing cars.

Exotic plants enliven the landscape with splashes of vivid color—the purple of the spiky pontederia, the fiery crimson of the hibiscus and poinciana, the violet-bluish cast of the Blewit mushroom, the orange, yellow and green of the citrus growing in the state's ubiquitous groves.

They Came with a Dream

This naturally varied canvas has reached out like a beckoning finger to visionaries far and wide.

Juan Ponce de León, who came in search of the legendary Fountain of Youth, blazed a trail for the conquistadores who followed in his footsteps. A pair of Henrys—Flagler and Plant—laid the framework, or rather the railroad tracks, that enabled the state to become a major vacation destination.

Building on that framework: An entrepreneur named Walt Disney, the man who turned a central Florida cow pasture into the home of the rodent with arguably the state's most recognized face—if not surely its most recognized pair of ears.

The stylistic touches left behind by architects of many eras give Florida a rich sense of texture. A Spanish flair prevails in

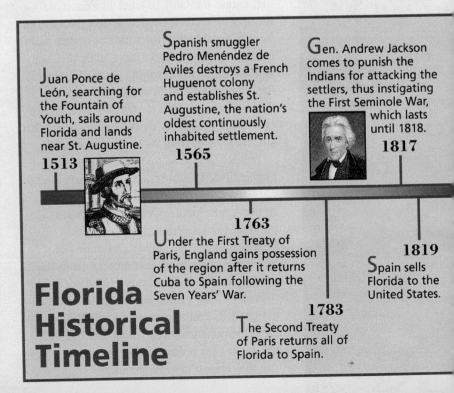

Florida Historical Timeline

Juan Ponce de León, searching for the Fountain of Youth, sails around Florida and lands near St. Augustine.
1513

Spanish smuggler Pedro Menéndez de Aviles destroys a French Huguenot colony and establishes St. Augustine, the nation's oldest continuously inhabited settlement.
1565

Gen. Andrew Jackson comes to punish the Indians for attacking the settlers, thus instigating the First Seminole War, which lasts until 1818.
1817

1763
Under the First Treaty of Paris, England gains possession of the region after it returns Cuba to Spain following the Seven Years' War.

1783
The Second Treaty of Paris returns all of Florida to Spain.

1819
Spain sells Florida to the United States.

historic St. Augustine, where buildings are distinguished by walled patios, stately arches and roofs of burnt-orange clay tile. Ybor City's showier flourishes—wrought-iron balconies, sidewalk cafes and plazas—point to a profoundly Latin influence. Synthetic materials, pastel hues and recti-linear forms characterize the art deco hotels along Ocean Drive in Miami's trendy South Beach.

As diverse as the state's architecture are the people who call Florida home. Sharing a place under the sun is a seemingly hap-hazard mix of retirees, jet setters, refugees and adventurers, of young and old, of "conch" fishermen, business tycoons and developers, and of tourists who came to visit but decided to stay.

Endless Days of Sunshine

One of the state's very few constants is its weather. Florida's climate is sultry, whether you visit in February or August. Its thermostat has but two settings: warm and hot.

For the most part Mother Nature smiles kindly, although she is prone to excess when angered. Hurricanes, tornadoes, floods and fires are among the punishments mercilessly inflicted when she unleashes sporadic fits of fury.

But Floridians take it all in stride. It's considerably easier in a state that simply refuses to take itself too seriously.

As much as Florida is rolling oceans, sawgrass prairies and mangrove and cy-press swamps, it is bicycle-riding birds, leaping alligators, and sea lions and wal-ruses masquerading as actors.

As much as you can make a living here growing sugar cane, catching fish or manu-facturing semiconductors, you can pull on a tail to perform as a mermaid, choose a sunny sidewalk spot from which to draw caricatures of passersby or stroll through gardens bedecked as a prim Southern belle.

What other state's identity ties so closely to the unabashedly seedy treasures that lurk behind signs of brash neon? Plastic yard flamingos, seashell figurines with glued-on rolling eyes, the simple word "Florida" set amid the chaos of unrestrained tie-dye on a 50/50 cotton blend T-shirt—like no other state, Florida has its kitsch in sync.

It's a place that brings forth smiles and laughter and lets us see things in a different light. A whimsical light. A humorous light.

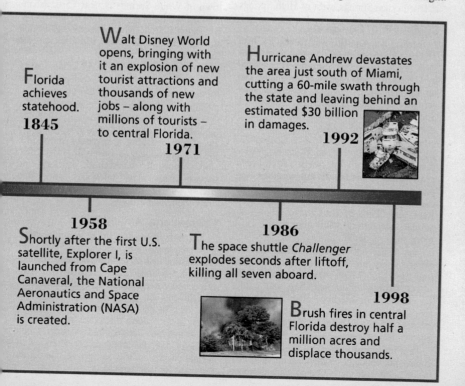

Florida achieves statehood.
1845

Walt Disney World opens, bringing with it an explosion of new tourist attractions and thousands of new jobs – along with millions of tourists – to central Florida.
1971

Hurricane Andrew devastates the area just south of Miami, cutting a 60-mile swath through the state and leaving behind an estimated $30 billion in damages.
1992

1958
Shortly after the first U.S. satellite, Explorer I, is launched from Cape Canaveral, the National Aeronautics and Space Administration (NASA) is created.

1986
The space shuttle *Challenger* explodes seconds after liftoff, killing all seven aboard.

1998
Brush fires in central Florida destroy half a million acres and displace thousands.

Recreation

Water, water everywhere, and most is great for play. Recreation is a way of life in the Sunshine State, and what better way to catch some rest 'n' relaxation than to get wet.

Not only is Florida nearly surrounded by ocean and gulf waters, but it also harbors thousands of lakes and hundreds of miles of rivers and canals. The prevalence of boat ramps and the impressive facilities of municipal marinas testify to the popularity of **boating**. Boaters should take caution to watch for endangered manatees in springs and coastal waterways.

To appreciate the beauty of the Everglades' narrow creeks and shallow bays, set out on a **canoeing** adventure. A tranquil weeklong escape awaits serious paddlers who tackle the 100-mile-long Wilderness Waterway. Although the Turner River and Mud Lake Loop trails are considerably shorter, the scenery is no less spectacular. Also worth navigating are the myriad rivers, lakes and ponds of the Apalachicola and Ocala national forests.

Looking for a lazy way to pass the day? Grab a tube and go **river floating** at Coldwater Creek in Blackwater River State Forest or at Ichetucknee Springs, west of High Springs.

In Motion in the Ocean

Surfing is a sure-fire way to beat the heat. The best waves crash on the Atlantic beaches, most notably from New Smyrna Beach south to Sebastian Inlet. Swells occasionally kick up south of Mayport Naval Base near Jacksonville and around Deerfield Beach and South Beach in south Florida.

Off the Miami coast, shipwrecks and other sunken items—such as a Boeing 727 jet lowered to the ocean floor in 1993—function as artificial reefs. Rich coral growth makes **scuba diving** ventures here particularly attractive. **Snorkeling**, especially popular at John Pennekamp Coral Reef State Park in Key Largo, allows for similar encounters with marine life at a more shallow depth.

The nearly 600 varieties of fish that live off the coast lure anglers to cast their lines into the brine. Many marinas provide **saltwater fishing** equipment, bait and guides for deep-sea or offshore charters. Record-size specimens also swim in the state's rivers and lakes, making **freshwater fishing** equally rewarding.

Don't neglect to pick up a license from the county tax collector or a subagent, such as a tackle shop, fish camp or hardware or sporting goods store. Saltwater licenses, required for all anglers ages 16 to 64, cost nonresidents $6.50 for 3 days, $16.50 for 7 days or $31.50 for 1 year; a resident license costs $13.50 for 1 year. Stamps that allow you to reel in snook and crawfish cost an additional $2 each. Freshwater licenses cost nonresidents $16.50 for 7 days or $31.50 for 1 year; a 1-year resident license costs $13.50.

Taking to the Terrain

Set out on foot to explore the more than 1,100 miles of **hiking** trails that comprise the Florida Trail; write the Florida Trail Association, P.O. Box 13708, Gainesville, FL 32604, or phone (352) 378-8823, or (800) 343-1882 in Fla. Supplement your strides with spectacular ocean views by walking along the coastline at Canaveral National Seashore; the Klondike stretch is open only to hikers. Leashed pets are welcomed at Smyrna Dunes Park, at the northern tip of the New Smyrna Beach peninsula.

If you prefer your exertion on the easy to moderate end of the spectrum, catch a breeze while **bicycling** on the relatively flat Florida terrain. Although you won't experience many downhill thrills, you won't grunt through many uphill struggles either. The town of White Springs is near 15 trails, including the looping Gar Pond Trail and the Big Shoals Trail, which passes one of the state's scant white-water stretches on the Suwannee River.

For information about Florida's many **camping** areas, both public and private, *see the AAA Southeastern CampBook.*

Public and semiprivate courses all over the state make **golf** immensely popular. And there's a good chance you'll work up a sweat just watching a spectator sport. Major and minor league **baseball** and professional **football, basketball, hockey** and **soccer** teams play statewide, while **dog racing, horse racing, jai alai** and **polo** draw their own crowds.

Recreational Activities

Throughout the TourBook, you may notice a Recreational Activities heading with bulleted listings of recreation-oriented establishments listed underneath. Since normal AAA inspection criteria cannot be applied, these establishments are presented only for information. Age, height and weight restrictions may apply. Reservations often are recommended and sometimes are required. Visitors should phone or write the attraction for additional information; the address and phone number are provided for this purpose.

Fast Facts

POPULATION: 14,653,900.

AREA: 58,560 square miles; ranks 22nd.

CAPITAL: Tallahassee.

HIGHEST POINT: 345 ft., Walton County.

LOWEST POINT: Sea level, Atlantic Ocean.

TIME ZONES: Eastern/Central. DST.

MINIMUM AGE FOR DRIVERS: 16; 15 with a restricted license.

MINIMUM AGE FOR GAMBLING: 18.

SEAT BELT/CHILD RESTRAINT LAWS: Seat belts required for driver, front-seat passengers and back-seat passengers under 16; child restraints required for under 6.

HELMETS FOR MOTORCYCLISTS: Optional for drivers and passengers over 21 provided they meet minimum insurance coverage requirement.

RADAR DETECTORS: Permitted.

FIREARMS LAWS: Vary by state and/or county. Contact the Florida Department of State, Division of Licensing, P.O. Box 6687, Tallahassee, FL 32314-6687; phone (850) 488-5381.

HOLIDAYS: Jan. 1; Martin Luther King Jr.'s Birthday, Jan. (3rd Mon.); Memorial Day, May (4th Mon.); July 4; Labor Day, Sept. (1st Mon.); Veterans Day, Nov. 11; Thanksgiving, Nov. (4th Thurs.); Dec. 25.

TAXES: Florida's statewide sales tax is 6 percent, with counties allowed to levy up to an additional 1 percent. Counties also may levy on accommodations and meals a Tourist Development Tax or a Tourist Impact Tax of varying increments.

STATE WELCOME CENTERS can be found just south of the Florida/Georgia border on US 231 at Campbellton, south of the Florida/Georgia border off I-75 near Jennings, near the Florida/Alabama border off I-10 16 miles west of Pensacola, south of the Florida/Georgia border off I-95 near Yulee, and in the Capitol in Tallahassee.

SPECIAL REGULATIONS: All motorists who drive trucks or pull trailers must stop at road guard agricultural inspection stations. Recreational vehicles and private passenger vehicles without trailers are not required to stop at these stations.

Permanently disabled persons with "handicapped" license plates from any state receive special parking privileges in Florida.

SPECIAL NOTE: Lovebugs are unlovely insects that swarm during daylight hours April through May and September through October, often clogging car radiators and smearing windshields. These insects are extremely sticky and contain an acid which, if allowed to remain on a car, can corrode the finish.

To lessen the problems posed by these insects, place a screen in front of your car's radiator, restrict travel to the early morning or late afternoon hours and drive at slower speeds.

NATIONAL FOREST INFORMATION:
Supervisor's Office
325 John Knox Rd., Bldg. F100
Tallahassee, FL 32303-4160
(850) 942-9300
(877) 444-6777 (reservations)

FISHING AND HUNTING REGULATIONS:
Freshwater:
Game and Freshwater Fish Commission
620 S. Meridian St.
Tallahassee, FL 32399-1600
(850) 488-4676
Saltwater:
Fish and Wildlife Conservation Commission
Office of Fisheries Management and
 Assistance Services
Division of Saltwater Fisheries
2590 Executive Center Cir.
Tallahassee, FL 32301
(850) 488-6058

RECREATION INFORMATION:
Department of Environmental Protection
Office of Recreation and Parks
3900 Commonwealth Blvd.
Mail Stop 536
Tallahassee, FL 32399-3000
(850) 488-9872

FURTHER INFORMATION FOR VISITORS:
Visit Florida Inc.
P.O. Box 1100
Tallahassee, FL 32302
(850) 488-5607
(888) 735-2872

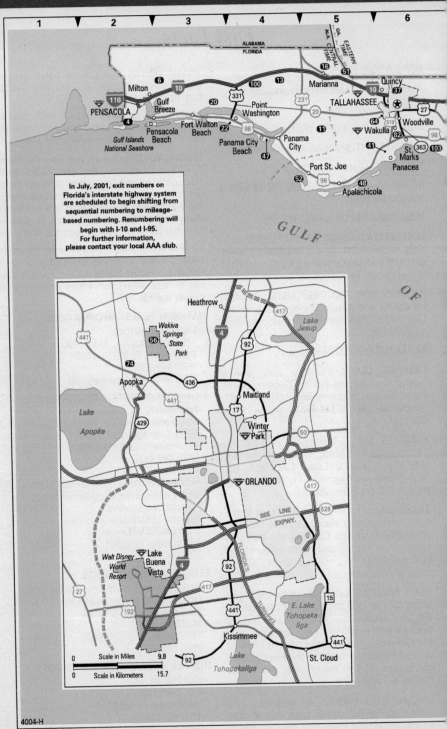

In July, 2001, exit numbers on Florida's interstate highway system are scheduled to begin shifting from sequential numbering to mileage-based numbering. Renumbering will begin with I-10 and I-95. For further information, please contact your local AAA club.

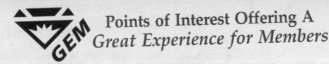

Points of Interest Offering A
Great Experience for Members

Daytona Beach (C-10)

DAYTONA USA—Interactive displays, a movie and trivia games chronicle the city's racing heritage. See p. 52.

Everglades National Park (H-10)

EVERGLADES NATIONAL PARK—Labyrinthine waters creep through salt prairies, hardwood hammocks and stands of mangroves and cypress trees. See p. 56.

Gainesville (C-8)

FRED BEAR MUSEUM—The museum presents a collection of trophies, tools, decorations and weapons Fred Bear collected on his bowhunting adventures around the world. See p. 86.

Jacksonville (B-9)

CUMMER MUSEUM OF ART & GARDENS—Noteworthy gallery features include Meissen porcelain tableware and a formal garden extending to the river. See p. 93.

Kennedy Space Center (D-11)

ASTRONAUT HALL OF FAME—The hall of fame honors America's space pioneers and traces the development of space exploration. See p. 97.

ASTRONAUT MEMORIAL: SPACE MIRROR—The black granite memorial pays tribute to American astronauts who died in the line of duty. See p. 99.

KENNEDY SPACE CENTER—The center operates as America's center of space operations. See p. 97.

KENNEDY SPACE CENTER VISITOR COMPLEX—The complex features multimedia displays about the American and Russian space programs, IMAX theaters and actual spacecraft. See p. 97.

Key West (I-9)

CONCH TOUR TRAINS—Narration centers on area history as the trains navigate old and new Key West. See p. 67.

Lake Buena Vista (G-2)

WALT DISNEY WORLD® RESORT—The sprawling complex includes the Magic Kingdom® Park, Epcot®, Disney-MGM Studios, Disney's Animal Kingdom® Theme Park and three water parks as well as numerous additional attractions and shopping and dining facilities. See p. 162.

Lake Wales (E-9)

BOK TOWER GARDENS—Landscaped gardens surround the marble and coquina stone tower, which contains 57 bronze bells. See p. 101.

Miami-Miami Beach (H-11)

THE HOLOCAUST MEMORIAL—The 6 million Jews who died at the hands of the Nazis are remembered here. See p. 114.

METRO-DADE CULTURAL CENTER—The center comprises a museum that outlines the history of south Florida; a museum that features the artwork of international contemporary artists; and a library. See p. 114.

METROZOO—Animal shows complement cageless environments inhabited by species of African, Asian and European animals. See p. 115.

PARROT JUNGLE AND GARDENS—Parrots and other exotic birds thrive in this subtropical flowery paradise. See p. 116.

VIZCAYA MUSEUM AND GARDENS—Opulent furnishings in the impressive 34-room villa represent the renaissance, baroque, rococo and neoclassical eras. See p. 116.

Ocala (C-9)

THE APPLETON MUSEUM OF ART—The museum is a showcase for European, pre-Columbian, West African and Asian art as well as antiquities. See p. 130.

FLORIDA'S SILVER SPRINGS—Glass-bottom boats cruise along the clear artesian springs, offering views of underwater life as far as 40 feet below the water's surface. See p. 131.

Orlando (D-9)

DISCOVERY COVE—Swim with the sharks and hug dolphins at this resort-style park geared towards intimate, safe and unforgettable encounters between humans and animals. See p. 142.

SEAWORLD ORLANDO—The theme park lets visitors experience marine life up close through varied displays and shows, such as the one featuring the famed Shamu. See p. 146.

UNIVERSAL ORLANDO—The park features Universal

Studios, where rides and shows are based on popular films and TV shows; Islands of Adventure, with five lands representing legendary characters and super heroes; as well as an entertainment section with restaurants and clubs. See p. 149.

Palm Beach (F-12)

FLAGLER MUSEUM—This Gilded-Age mansion, furnished in original and period pieces, contains historical exhibits. See p. 178.

Palm Coast (C-10)

WASHINGTON OAKS STATE GARDENS—Covering more than 400 acres of Florida coastal scenery, the gardens feature exotic plants from around the world. See p. 178.

Pensacola (B-2)

NATIONAL MUSEUM OF NAVAL AVIATION—Highlights of the museum collection are an NC-4 Flying Boat; the World War II fighter F6F Hellcat; and the Skylab Command Module. See p. 181.

St. Augustine (B-10)

CASTILLO DE SAN MARCOS NATIONAL MONUMENT—The Spanish fortress, which features massive diamond-shaped bastions at each corner, defended the city until the mid-18th century. See p. 184.

GOVERNMENT HOUSE MUSEUM—American Indian artifacts, treasure from Spanish shipwrecks and religious items are among the exhibits detailing area history. See p. 186.

HISTORIC OLD JAIL COMPLEX—The complex comprises a museum that depicts Florida's growth; the jail, which displays weaponry and outlines prison life; and a tour company. See p. 189.

LIGHTNER MUSEUM—Tiffany stained glass, Oriental art and art nouveau works are noteworthy in the Lightner collection. See p. 186.

OLDEST HOUSE—Also known as the González-Alvarez House, the structure is home to two museums: one tracing city history and one devoted to Florida's army. See p. 187.

ST. AUGUSTINE ALLIGATOR FARM—All 22 crocodilian species are represented at the farm, which also features tropical birds, monkeys and other exotic creatures. See p. 190.

SPANISH QUARTER VILLAGE—Costumed guides depict the 1740s lifestyle in this quarter of restored and reconstructed buildings. See p. 187.

WORLD GOLF VILLAGE AND HALL OF FAME—The showcase for this sport honors golfing legends in a hall of fame and along a Walk of Champions; an IMAX theater is part of the complex. See p. 191.

St. Petersburg (E-8)

THE FLORIDA HOLOCAUST MUSEUM AND EDUCATIONAL CENTER—Tolerance and understanding are the lessons taught at this museum commemorating the millions who perished during this tragic period. See p. 208.

SALVADOR DALI MUSEUM—The Spanish artist's creative diversity is captured in works ranging from small impressionistic pieces to gigantic surrealistic montages. See p. 213.

Sanibel (G-9)

THE BAILEY-MATTHEWS SHELL MUSEUM—Seashells from the nearby beaches of Sanibel and Captiva islands as well as locations around the world are displayed. See p. 192.

Sarasota (F-8)

THE JOHN AND MABLE RINGLING MUSEUM OF ART—An extensive collection of pieces by Peter Paul Rubens is the centerpiece of the Italian Renaissance museum. See p. 194.

Sebring (F-10)

HIGHLANDS HAMMOCK STATE PARK—Lush vegetation flourishes in the dense jungle and swampland in this easy-to-explore park. See p. 196.

Tallahassee (B-5)

ALFRED B. MACLAY STATE GARDENS—Colorful azaleas, camellias and Oriental magnolias decorate the grounds of this Southern estate. See p. 197.

Tampa (E-8)

BUSCH GARDENS TAMPA BAY—A late 19th-century African motif punctuates the rides, entertainment, animal exhibits and shows in the park. See p. 213.

THE FLORIDA AQUARIUM—Florida's ecosystem and aquatic habitats are detailed in aquarium exhibits. See p. 215.

MUSEUM OF SCIENCE & INDUSTRY (MOSI)—In addition to a planetarium and an IMAX Dome theater, the museum presents displays that explain aspects of science and technology. See p. 217.

Wakulla (B-6)

EDWARD BALL WAKULLA SPRINGS STATE PARK—The clear, deep springs are believed to have been discovered by Ponce de León, who claimed them to be the "fountain of youth." See p. 230.

Winter Haven (E-9)

CYPRESS GARDENS—In addition to being home to more than 8,000 varieties of plants and flowers from around the world, the state's first theme park is popular for its shows and lovely Southern belles. See p. 235.

Winter Park (F-4)

CHARLES HOSMER MORSE MUSEUM OF AMERICAN ART—Most noteworthy in the museum is an extensive collection of works by art nouveau master Louis Comfort Tiffany, whose stained glass gained him fame. See p. 176.

RECREATION AREAS

	MAP LOCATION	CAMPING	PICNICKING	NATURE TRAILS	BOATING	BOAT RAMP	BOAT RENTAL	FISHING	SWIMMING	PETS ON LEASH	BICYCLE TRAILS	SKIN/SCUBA	VISITOR CENTER	LODGE/CABINS	FOOD SERVICE
NATIONAL PARKS *(See place listings)*															
Biscayne (H-12) 180,000 acres. Scenic.		●	●	●	●	●		●	●			●	●		
Dry Tortugas (I-8) 64,657 acres. Scenic.		●	●		●	●		●	●			●	●		
Everglades (H-10) 1,506,539 acres. Scenic.		●	●	●	●	●	●	●					●	●	●
Chekika (H-11) 640 acres 18 mi. n.w. of Homestead off SR 997.	9	●	●	●					●						
NATIONAL FORESTS *(See place listings)*															
Apalachicola 565,543 acres. Northwestern Florida.		●	●	●	●	●		●	●						
Ocala 383,573 acres. North-central Florida. Horse rental.		●	●	●	●	●	●	●	●	●	●	●	●		●
Osceola 198,484 acres. Northeastern Florida. Horse rentals and trails.		●	●	●	●	●		●	●				●		
NATIONAL SEASHORES *(See place listings)*															
Canaveral (D-10) 57,000 acres. East-central Florida.		●	●	●	●	●		●	●				●		
Gulf Islands (B-2) 137,000 acres. Northwestern Florida.		●	●	●	●			●	●		●	●	●		
ARMY CORPS OF ENGINEERS															
Lake Oklawaha (C-9) 10 mi. s.w. of Palatka off SR 19 access roads. Horse trails.	79	●	●	●	●			●							
Ortona Lock (G-10) e. of La Belle off SR 80.	80	●	●		●	●		●							
St. Lucie Lock (F-11) 140 acres 8 mi. s.w. of Stuart off SR 76.	81	●	●	●	●	●		●							
STATE															
Alfred B. Maclay State Gardens (A-6) 307 acres 5 mi. n.e. of Tallahassee on US 319. Scenic. Horse trails. *(See Tallahassee p. 197)*	37		●	●	●			●	●				●		
Anastasia (B-10) 1,035 acres at St. Augustine Beach off SR A1A at SR 3.	1	●	●	●	●			●	●						●
Bahia Honda (I-10) 276 acres on Bahia Honda Key off US 1 at mile marker 35.	2	●	●	●	●	●	●	●	●			●		●	●
Big Lagoon (B-2) 700 acres 10 mi. s.w. of Pensacola on SR 292A.	4	●	●	●	●			●	●						
Bill Baggs Cape Florida (H-11) 900 acres off US 1 on Key Biscayne. Historic.	5		●					●	●		●	●	●		●
Blackwater River (A-3) 590 acres 15 mi. n.e. of Milton off US 90. Historic. Canoe rentals.	6	●	●	●	●				●						
Blue Spring (D-9) 518 acres 2 mi. w. of Orange City off US 17/92 on W. French Ave. *(See Orange City p. 132)*	7	●	●	●	●			●	●				●	●	●
Bulow Plantation Ruins (C-10) 109 acres 9 mi. s.e. of Bunnell off CR 2001 (Old Kings Rd.), between SR 100 and Old Dixie Hwy. Historic. Interpretive center. Canoeing. *(See Bunnell p. 49)*	92		●	●	●	●		●		●					
Caladesi Island (G-7) 653 acres in the Gulf of Mexico w. of Dunedin. Bird-watching. *(See Dunedin p. 226)*	8	●	●	●	●				●			●			●
Cayo Costa (G-8) 2,506 acres accessible by boat from Boca Grande or Fort Myers. Bird-watching.	93	●						●	●				●		
Collier-Seminole (H-9) 6,423 acres 17 mi. s. of Naples on US 41. Historic. Bird-watching. *(See Naples p. 128)*	10	●	●	●	●	●	●	●		●	●		●		●
Dead Lakes (B-5) 83 acres .5 mi. n. of Wewahitchka on SR 71.	11	●	●	●	●	●		●							
De Leon Springs (C-9) 443 acres 1 mi. s. of DeLeon Springs on SR 181. Canoe rentals.	46		●	●	●	●	●	●	●				●		●

RECREATION AREAS

	MAP LOCATION	CAMPING	PICNICKING	NATURE TRAILS	BOATING	BOAT RAMP	BOAT RENTAL	FISHING	SWIMMING	PETS ON LEASH	BICYCLE TRAILS	SKIN/SCUBA	VISITOR CENTER	LODGE/CABINS	FOOD SERVICE
Delnor-Wiggins Pass (G-9) 166 acres 11 mi. n.w. of Naples off SR 846. Shell gathering, turtle watching in nesting season; boardwalks, observation tower. *(See Naples p. 127)*	12		•	•	•	•		•	•	•					
Don Pedro Island (F-8) 115 acres accessible only by boat.	94		•	•	•			•	•	•					
Econfina River (B-6) 3,377 acres s. of Lamont at the end of CR 14. Horse trails.	103		•	•	•	•		•		•					
Edward Ball Wakulla Springs (B-6) 2,860 acres .5 mi. e. of Wakulla Springs at jct. SRs 61 and 267. Boat tours, bird-watching; hiking trails. *(See Wakulla p. 230)*	82		•	•					•	•				•	•
Falling Waters (A-4) 155 acres 3 mi. s. of Chipley off SR 77.	13	•	•	•					•						
Fanning Springs (C-7) 188 acres on US 19/98 on the e. bank of the Suwanee River in Fanning Springs.	104		•	•	•			•	•				•		
Faver-Dykes (B-9) 752 acres 15 mi. s. of St. Augustine off US 1.	14	•	•	•	•	•		•							
Florida Caverns (A-5) 1,280 acres 3 mi. n. of Marianna on SR 166. Bird-watching; horse trails. *(See Marianna p. 102)*	16	•	•	•	•	•	•	•	•				•		
Fort Clinch (A-9) 1,153 acres 2 mi. e. of Fernandina Beach on SR A1A at n. end of Amelia Island. Historic. Bird-watching. *(See Fernandina Beach p. 96)*	17	•	•	•				•	•	•		•	•		
Fort Cooper (D-8) 707 acres 2 mi. s. of Inverness off US 41. Historic.	67		•	•				•	•						
Fort Pierce Inlet (F-11) 340 acres 3 mi. e. of Fort Pierce on SR A1A. Bird-watching. *(see Fort Pierce p. 83)*	18		•	•				•	•	•	•	•			
Fort Zachary Taylor (I-9) 78 acres at the s.w. end of Key West via Southard St. Historic. *(See Key West p. 67)*	88		•	•				•	•				•		•
Fred Gannon Rocky Bayou (B-3) 357 acres 5 mi. e. of Niceville on SR 20.	20	•	•	•	•	•		•							
Gamble Rogers Memorial State Recreation Area (C-10) 145 acres .5 mi. s. of Flagler Beach on SR A1A.	15	•	•	•	•	•		•	•						
Gasparilla Island (G-8) 144 acres 3 mi. s. of Placida on CR 775. Historic. Interpretive center. Lighthouse.	95							•	•	•			•		
Grayton Beach (B-3) 365 acres adjacent to Grayton Beach on SR 30A.	22	•	•	•	•	•	•	•	•	•					
Guana River (B-9) 2,400 acres on SR A1A 10 mi. s. of Ponte Vedra Beach. Bird-watching.	105			•	•			•				•			
Highlands Hammock (F-9) 8,133 acres 3.5 mi. w. of US 27 on CR 634. Scenic. Museum. Bird-watching; horse trails. *(See Sebring p. 196)*	23	•	•	•									•	•	•
Hillsborough River (E-8) 2,990 acres 6 mi. s. of Zephyrhills off US 301. Living-history program.	24	•	•	•			•	•	•						
Honeymoon Island (G-7) 450 acres 3 mi. n. of Dunedin on SR 586, w. of US 19A. Bird-watching. *(See Dunedin p. 226)*	84		•	•				•	•	•			•		
Hontoon Island (C-9) 1,649 acres 6 mi. w. of DeLand off SR 44.	25	•	•	•	•			•						•	
Hugh Taylor Birch (G-11) 180 acres at Sunrise Blvd. and SR A1A in Fort Lauderdale.	26		•	•	•			•	•	•	•				
Ichetucknee Springs (B-7) 2,241 acres off US 27 .5 mi. e. of Hildreth. Scenic. Bird-watching; tubing. *(See High Springs p. 87)*	68		•	•	•				•	•			•	•	

RECREATION AREAS

Recreation Area	Map Location	Camping	Picnicking	Nature Trails	Boating	Boat Ramp	Boat Rental	Fishing	Swimming	Pets on Leash	Bicycle Trails	Skin/Scuba	Visitor Center	Lodge/Cabins	Food Service
John D. MacArthur Beach (F-12) 760 acres on SR A1A, 2.8 mi. s. of jct. US 1 on Singer Island. Bird-watching. *(See Singer Island p. 196)*	96		•	•				•	•	•		•	•		
John Pennekamp Coral Reef (I-11) 178 nautical miles on US 1 near Key Largo mile marker 102.5. *(See Key Largo p. 66)*	27	•	•	•	•	•	•	•	•	•		•	•		•
John U. Lloyd Beach (G-11) 244 acres 3 mi. s. of Fort Lauderdale on SR A1A.	28		•	•	•	•	•	•	•	•		•			•
Jonathan Dickinson (F-11) 10,328 acres 6 mi. n. of Jupiter on US 1. Historic. Scenic. Bird-watching; bicycle rental, horse trails. *(See Jupiter p. 97)*	29	•	•	•	•	•	•	•	•		•			•	•
Koreshan (G-9) 139 acres .5 mi. s. of Estero on US 41. Historic. Bird-watching. *(See Estero p. 55)*	30	•	•		•	•		•							
Lake Griffin (D-9) 423 acres 1 mi. e. of Fruitland Park off US 27.	31	•	•	•	•	•		•							
Lake Kissimmee (E-9) 5,027 acres 8 mi. e. of Lake Wales via SR 60, 4 mi. n. on Boy Scout Rd., then 5 mi. n. on Camp Mack Rd. following signs. Living-history program. Bird-watching; horse trails. *(See Lake Wales p. 101)*	32	•	•	•	•	•		•							
Lake Louisa (D-9) 1,790 acres 7 mi. s.e. of Clermont on Lake Nellie Rd. Horse trails. *(See Clermont p. 160)*	33		•		•			•	•						
Lake Manatee (F-8) 556 acres 14 mi. e. of Bradenton on SR 64. Bird-watching.	34	•	•	•	•	•	•	•	•	•	•				
Little Manatee River (E-8) 2,020 acres 5 mi. s. of Sun City off US 301. Equestrian camping; horse trails.	85	•	•	•	•			•							
Little Talbot Island (A-9) 2,500 acres 17 mi. n.e. of Jacksonville on SR A1A. Pier.	35	•	•	•				•	•			•			
Long Key (I-10) 849 acres on Long Key at Layton on US 1.	36							•	•			•			
Lover's Key State Recreation Area (G-9) 267 acres on CR 865, 2 mi. s. of Big Carlos Pass on Lover's Key. *(See Fort Myers Beach p. 82)*	89		•	•	•			•	•						
Manatee Springs (C-7) 1,075 acres 6 mi. w. of Chiefland on SR 320. Bird-watching.	38	•	•	•	•	•		•				•	•		•
Mike Roess Gold Head Branch (B-9) 1,414 acres 6 mi. n.e. of Keystone Heights on SR 21. Bird-watching; bicycle, canoe and paddleboat rentals.	39	•	•	•	•	•		•	•	•		•		•	
Myakka River (F-8) 28,875 acres 17 mi. e. of Sarasota on SR 72. Airboat and safari tram tours, bird-watching; bicycle rentals, hiking and horse trails. *(See Sarasota p. 194)*	40	•	•	•	•	•	•	•			•		•	•	•
Ochlockonee River (B-6) 392 acres 4 mi. s. of Sopchoppy on US 319.	41	•	•	•	•	•	•	•	•						
O'Leno (B-8) 6,700 acres 6 mi. n. of High Springs off US 41. Historic. Bird-watching. *(See High Springs p. 87)*	42	•		•	•			•	•	•	•		•		
Oleta River (H-11) 90 acres at 3400 N.E. 163rd St. in North Miami Beach.	83		•	•	•			•	•			•			•	•
Oscar Scherer (F-8) 1,383 acres 2 mi. s. of Osprey on US 41. Bird-watching.	43	•	•	•	•			•	•	•					
Paynes Creek (E-9) 400 acres .5 mi. e. of Bowling Green at 888 Lake Branch Rd. Historic. Interpretive center. Bird-watching, canoeing.	99		•	•				•		•				•		
Paynes Prairie Preserve (C-8) 21,000 acres 1 mi. n. of Micanopy on US 441. Bird-watching; horse trail. *(See Micanopy p. 127)*	45	•	•	•	•	•		•		•			•		

RECREATION AREAS

Recreation Area	Map Location	Camping	Picnicking	Nature Trails	Boating	Boat Ramp	Boat Rental	Fishing	Swimming	Pets on Leash	Bicycle Trails	Skin/Scuba	Visitor Center	Lodge/Cabins	Food Service
Ponce de Leon Springs (A-4) 441 acres .5 mi. s. of Ponce de Leon on US 90.	100		•	•					•	•					
Rainbow Springs (C-8) 1,000 acres 3 mi. n. of Dunnellon on US 41. Waterfalls. Tubing.	21	•	•		•				•				•		
St. Andrews (B-4) 1,260 acres 3 mi. e. of Panama City Beach via SR 392. *(See Panama City Beach p. 180)*	47	•	•	•	•	•	•	•	•	•			•		•
St. George Island (C-5) 1,833 acres off US 98 via CRs G1A and 300 on St. George Island. Bird-watching.	48	•	•	•	•	•		•	•	•			•		
St. Lucie Inlet (F-11) Accessible by boat from Port Salerno on the Intracoastal Waterway. Bird-watching.	87			•				•	•						
Sebastian Inlet (E-11) 578 acres 15 mi. s. of Melbourne Beach on SR A1A. Museum. Bird-watching. *(See Sebastian p. 195)*	49	•			•	•		•	•				•		•
Suwannee River (B-7) 1,831 acres 13 mi. w. of Live Oak on US 90. Historic.	50	•	•	•	•			•	•						
Three Rivers (A-5) 682 acres 2 mi. n. of Sneads off US 90.	51	•	•	•	•	•		•	•						
T.H. Stone Memorial (St. Joseph Peninsula) (C-4) 2,500 acres 20 mi. s.w. of Port St. Joe. Bird-watching.	52	•	•	•	•	•	•	•	•	•					
Tomoka (C-10) 915 acres 3 mi. n. of Ormond Beach. Museum.	53	•	•	•	•	•		•	•				•		
Tosohatchee State Preserve (D-10) 28,000 acres 4 mi. s. of Christmas on SR 50. Bird-watching; hiking and horse trails. *(See Christmas p. 159)*	3	•						•			•				
Washington Oaks (C-10) 400 acres at 6400 Oceanshore Blvd. Interpretive center. *(See Palm Coast p. 178)*	55		•	•					•	•			•		
Wekiwa Springs (E-2) 6,396 acres 4 mi. n.w. of I-4, off US 441 near Apopka. Bird-watching; horse trails.	56	•	•	•	•			•	•	•					•
OTHER															
Alexander Springs (C-9) 30 acres 13 mi. n.e. of Umatilla via SR 19 and CR 445. *(See Ocala National Forest p. 132)*	57	•	•	•	•			•	•	•	•				
Avon Park Air Force Range (E-9) 84,000 acres on SR 64 in Avon Park.	66	•	•	•	•	•		•							
C.B. Smith (G-11) 320 acres at Flamingo Rd. and Hollywood Blvd. in Pembroke Pines. Miniature golf, tennis; waterslide.	58	•	•		•	•	•	•	•	•					
Everglades Holiday (H-11) 10 acres 20 mi. w. of Dania off Griffin Rd. Airboat rides.	71	•			•	•	•	•							
Fort De Soto (F-8) 1,136 acres off I-275 exit 4 at Pinellas Bayway. Historic. *(See St. Petersburg p. 209)*	59	•	•	•	•	•		•	•	•		•	•		•
Ginnie Springs (C-8) 200 acres 7 mi. w. of High Springs off CR 340. Canoeing. *(See High Springs p. 87)*	72	•	•	•	•		•	•	•			•		•	•
Juniper Springs (C-9) 47 acres 28 mi. e. of Ocala on SR 40. *(See Ocala National Forest p. 132)*	60	•	•	•				•	•	•					
Kathryn Abbey Hannah (B-9) 450 acres next to Mayport Naval Station off SR A1A in Jacksonville Beach. Canoeing, horseback riding; horse rentals.	73	•	•					•	•	•			•		
Kelly Park (E-2) 200 acres 6 mi. n. of Apopka on SR 435. Tubing. *(See Apopka p. 159)*	74	•	•	•					•		•				
Lake Dorr (D-9) 10 acres 5 mi. n. of Umatilla on SR 19. *(See Ocala National Forest p. 132)*	61	•	•		•	•		•	•						
Lakes Park (G-9) 279 acres 6 mi. s.w. of I-75 exit 21, via Six Mile Cypress. Bicycle rental, jogging trails.	90		•	•				•	•	•					•

RECREATION AREAS

	Map Location	Camping	Picnicking	Nature Trails	Boating	Boat Ramp	Boat Rental	Fishing	Swimming	Pets on Leash	Bicycle Trails	Skin/Scuba	Visitor Center	Lodge/Cabins	Food Service
Maximo Park (I-8) 65 acres in St. Petersburg at 34th St. and Pinellas Point Dr. S. Observation tower, playground.	101		•	•	•	•		•		•					
Okeeheelee (G-11) 1,000 acres in Palm Beach, 6 mi. w. of I-95 on Forest Hills Blvd. Ball fields, water-skiing course.	75		•	•	•	•		•	•						
Olustee Beach (B-8) 15 acres .25 mi. n. of Olustee on CR 231.	63		•					•	•	•					
Poe Springs Park (B-8) 202 acres 3 mi. w. of High Springs on CR 340.	102		•	•	•			•	•						
Quiet Waters (G-12) 427 acres 2 mi. w. from I-95 via SR 810, then .25 mi. s. on SR 845 in Deerfield Beach. Cable water skiing; canoe, paddleboat and bicycle rentals. *(See Deerfield Beach p. 77)*	69	•	•					•	•	•	•				•
Silver Lake (B-5) 25 acres 8 mi. w. of Tallahassee off SR 20.	64	•	•	•	•	•			•						
Topeekeegee Yugnee (T-Y) (H-11) 150 acres .5 mi. w. of I-95 on Sheridan St. (SR 822) in Hollywood. Miniature golf; canoe and paddleboat rentals, waterslide.	77	•	•				•	•	•	•					•
Tradewinds (G-11) 90 acres at 3600 Sample Rd. in Coconut Creek. Museum. Botanical gardens, horse rental, pony and hay rides.	65		•	•			•	•		•	•		•		
Tree Tops (G-11) 256 acres at 3900 S.W. 100th Ave. in Davie. Canoe, horse and paddleboat rentals.	78		•	•			•	•		•			•		

Florida Temperature Averages
Maximum / Minimum
From the records of the National Weather Service

	JAN	FEB	MAR	APR	MAY	JUNE	JULY	AUG	SEPT	OCT	NOV	DEC
Jacksonville	65/44	67/46	72/50	79/57	85/64	88/70	90/72	90/72	86/70	79/62	71/51	66/45
Key West	76/66	77/66	79/69	82/74	85/76	88/79	89/80	89/80	88/79	84/75	80/71	76/67
Miami	76/59	77/59	79/63	83/67	85/71	88/74	89/75	90/76	88/75	85/71	80/64	77/60
Orlando	70/50	72/51	76/56	81/61	87/66	89/71	90/73	90/73	88/72	82/66	76/57	71/51
Tallahassee	64/41	66/43	72/48	80/56	87/63	90/70	91/72	90/72	87/69	81/58	71/46	65/41
Tampa	71/50	72/52	76/56	82/62	87/67	90/72	90/74	90/74	89/73	84/65	77/56	72/51
West Palm Beach	75/56	76/56	79/60	83/65	86/69	88/72	90/74	90/74	88/75	84/70	79/62	76/57

Your **key to savings** is actually a card.

www.hilton.com
1-800-916-2221

Hilton offers special room rates to all AAA members. Wherever you travel in the United States, there's a Hilton or Hilton Garden Inn® (HGI) hotel or resort waiting to serve you. And now, AAA members can receive members-only room rates when you Show Your Card & Save® at Hiltons.

It happens at the Hilton.™

FLORIDA:

Cocoa Beach Oceanfront

Daytona Beach Resort

Deerfield Beach/Boca Raton

Destin/Sandestin Beach Resort

Fort Lauderdale Airport

Fort Lauderdale/Sunrise

Hilton Clearwater Beach Resort

Jacksonville JTB/Deerwood Park, HGI

Jacksonville Riverfront

Key West Resort

Key West Resort/
   Sunset Key Guest Cottages

Marco Island Resort

Melbourne Airport

Melbourne Beach/Indialantic

Miami Airport & Towers

Miami Beach,Fontainebleau Resort

Naples & Towers

Ocala

Orlando Airport, HGI

Orlando,WALT DISNEY WORLD® Resort

Orlando/Altamonte Springs

Orlando/Lake Mary, HGI

Palm Beach Airport

Palm Beach Resort

Sarasota/Longboat Key Resort

Singer Island Oceanfront Resort

St. Augustine Beach, HGI

St. Petersburg

Tallahassee, HGI

Tampa Airport

Tampa Bay/North Redington Beach Resort

Tampa Ybor Historic District, HGI

Points of Interest

AMELIA ISLAND—
see Jacksonville p. 95.

APALACHICOLA (C-5)
pop. 2,600, elev. 17'

Apalachicola is a Hitchiti Indian word meaning "people on the other side." More than 80 percent of the state's oyster crop (10 percent of the nation's total) is cultivated in Apalachicola's more than 6,000 acres of oyster beds.

Apalachicola Bay Chamber of Commerce: 99 Market St., Suite 100, Apalachicola, FL 32320-1776; phone (850) 653-9419.

JOHN GORRIE STATE MUSEUM, at Sixth St. and Ave. D, is 1 blk. e. of US 98 on Gorrie Square. Historical and scientific exhibits pertain to the Apalachicola area and to Dr. John Gorrie, inventor of man-made ice, refrigeration and air conditioning. Allow 30 minutes minimum. Thurs.-Mon. 9-5; closed Jan. 1, Thanksgiving and Dec. 25. Admission $1, under 6 free. Phone (850) 653-9347.

APALACHICOLA NATIONAL FOREST

Elevations in the forest range from 10 ft. to 100 ft.

Apalachicola National Forest, the largest of Florida's three national forests, encompasses 565,543 acres in four northwestern counties. Its varied terrain includes pine flatwoods, hardwood hammocks, swamp rivers, lakes and two wilderness areas, Bradwell Bay and Mud Swamp/New River. Secluded lakes and streams and canoe trails on the Sopchoppy and lower Ochlockonee rivers make this area popular with canoeists. Several lakes have campgrounds and hiking trails. Hunting and fishing also are popular activities.

A portion of the Florida National Scenic Trail, a scenic hiking route through the state, passes through the forest, showcasing a wide variety of plants and wildlife native to the area. Hikers may catch glimpses of such rare and endangered species as Florida alligators, red-cockaded woodpeckers, indigo snakes and southern bald eagles.

One of the forest's special features is Trout Pond, a recreational facility designed for the physically limited. It offers a fishing pier and an interpretive trail. Further information about the forest can be obtained at the district headquarters offices in Crawfordville, (850) 926-3561, and in Bristol, (850) 643-2282. *See Recreation Chart.*

APOLLO BEACH—
see Tampa Bay p. 225.

APOPKA—*see Orlando p. 159.*

BARBERVILLE (C-9) pop. 400, elev. 44'

THE PIONEER SETTLEMENT FOR THE CREATIVE ARTS is just w. of jct. US 17 on SR 40. Guided tours take visitors through buildings from the early 1900s. Many of the houses, stores and barns are Florida originals which have been relocated to the site. During events the settlement features music, crafts and art from the turn of the 20th century. Allow 2 hours minimum. Mon.-Fri. 9-4, Sat. 9-2; closed holidays. Last weekday tour begins at 3. Admission $2.50; ages 5-12, $1.50. Phone (904) 749-2959.

BIG CYPRESS NATIONAL PRESERVE (H-10)

Big Cypress National Preserve is part of Big Cypress Swamp, which encompasses more than

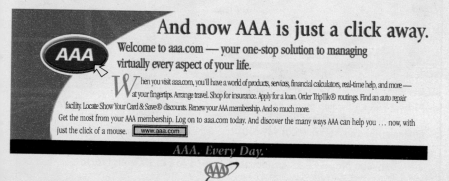

2,400 square miles of south Florida. These areas are a major source of water for the fragile Everglades and the southwestern part of the state. Big Cypress National Preserve protects this valuable resource and provides sanctuary for varied wildlife, including alligators, herons, egrets, woodpeckers, bald eagles, deer and the endangered Florida panther.

Although referred to as a swamp, the preserve has marshlands, dry prairies, estuarine mangrove forests and islands of hardwoods. Its most distinctive feature is the broad belts of bald and dwarf cypress trees lining the sloughs and wet prairies. Two major highways, Alligator Alley (SR 84) and scenic Tamiami Trail (US 41), cross the preserve and make it accessible from both coasts.

Big Cypress Visitor Center, 20 miles east of Ochopee on US 41, presents a 13-minute film about the preserve as well as exhibits about natural resources and native animal and plant life; phone (941) 695-4111. Hunting and fishing are permitted under special regulations; licenses are required.

The visitor center is open daily 8:30-4:30; closed Dec. 25. Free. For further information contact the Superintendent, Big Cypress National Preserve, HCR 61, Box 11, Ochopee, FL 34141; phone (941) 695-2000.

BIG CYPRESS SEMINOLE INDIAN RESERVATION (G-10)
pop. 500

AH-TAH-THI-KI MUSEUM, 17 mi. n. of I-75 exit 14 on CR 833, tells the story of Florida's Seminole Indians. A short movie details the history of the tribe. Life-size figures in native costume depict how the Seminoles hunted, danced, played and lived. Among exhibits are baskets, utensils, clothing and jewelry. A boardwalk traverses the site. Allow 1 hour, 30 minutes minimum. Tues.-Sun. 9-5; phone for holiday hours. Admission $6; over 55, ages 6-17 and students with ID $4. AE, CB, DI, DS, MC, VI. Phone (863) 902-1113. *See color ad.*

SAVE **BILLIE SWAMP SAFARI,** 19 mi. n. of I-75 exit 14, gives 25-minute airboat tours and 60-minute "swamp buggy" eco-tours of Big Cypress. Views of such wildlife as panthers, alligators, snakes, razorback hogs and crocodiles are common. Day and overnight safaris also are offered by reservation. Food is available. Tours depart daily 8:30-6:30; closed Dec. 25. Airboat tour $10. Eco-tour $20; over 54, $18; ages 6-12, $10. AE, DS, MC, VI. Phone (863) 983-6101 or (800) 949-6101. *See color ad.*

BIG PINE KEY—
see The Florida Keys p. 64.

BOCA RATON (G-12)
pop. 61,500, elev. 15′

Long a haven for the wealthy, Boca Raton has become a center for commerce, finance and technology. Strictly enforced regulations help to maintain the city's "small-town" appeal.

The city's oldest unaltered wooden structure, built in 1911 with timber found on the beach, now houses Singing Pines Museum. The museum, on Crawford Boulevard, features changing exhibits for children.

The Gulf Stream comes closest to the Florida shore at Boca Raton, making the climate ideal for sports and recreation.

Greater Boca Raton Chamber of Commerce: 1800 N. Dixie Hwy., Boca Raton, FL 33432; phone (561) 395-4433.

Shopping areas: Boca Center, at Military Trail and Town Center Road, offers boutiques, art galleries and restaurants. Mizner Park, on Federal Highway between Palmetto Park and Glades roads, is an outdoor mall with an amphitheater. Royal Palm Shopping Plaza, US 1 and Mizner Boulevard, features boutiques and specialty shops in a Mediterranean setting. Town Center, .5 mile west of I-95 on Glades Road, contains 187 stores including Bloomingdales, Burdines, Lord & Taylor, Saks Fifth Avenue and Sears.

BOCA RATON HISTORICAL SOCIETY, on US 1 at Palmetto Park Rd., is housed in the restored 1927 Town Hall, noted for its gold dome. The Mediterranean Revival-style building, designed by Addison Mizner, has such architectural features as cypress millwork, a pecky cypress ceiling, fan-lit windows and a gilded dome. Changing art and history exhibits are shown regularly. Allow 30 minutes minimum. Tues.-Fri. 10-4; closed holidays. Free. Phone (561) 395-6766.

BOCA RATON MUSEUM OF ART, 1 mi. e. off I-95 exit 38 at 801 W. Palmetto Park Rd., houses changing exhibits of varied art media. The permanent collection contains late 19th- and early 20th-century works, including pieces by Edgar Degas, Henri Matisse and Pablo Picasso. An outdoor sculpture garden with contemporary works and a photography collection dating from the 19th century are among the museum's highlights.

Allow 1 hour minimum. Tues.-Fri. 10-4 (also Wed. 4-8, Sept.-May), Sat.-Sun. noon-4; closed holidays. Admission $3; students with ID $2; over 64, $1; under 12 free; free to all Wed. Phone (561) 392-2500.

GUMBO LIMBO NATURE CENTER, 1 mi. n. of Palmetto Park Rd. on SR A1A, has examples of native plants and animals in a variety of habitats, including coastal dune, tropical hardwood hammock, sabal palm hammock and mangrove wetlands. Also featured are outdoor seawater tanks, a boardwalk with a viewing tower and a nature

trail. Allow 30 minutes minimum. Mon.-Sat. 9-4, Sun. noon-4; closed holidays. Donations. Phone (561) 338-1473.

INTERNATIONAL MUSEUM OF CARTOON ART, off US 1 at 201 Plaza Real in Mizner Park, is home to more than 160,000 works by more than 1,000 artists. Exhibits include comic strips and books, editorial cartoons, animations, caricatures, illustrations, graphic novels and greeting cards. Spanning more than 100 years, the collection ranges from cartoons by Thomas Nast and Richard Outcault to original cels and sketches for the Road Runner, Bugs Bunny, Donald Duck and Goofy. The Hearst Cartoon Hall of Fame features noted works. Food is available.

Allow 1 hour minimum. Tues.-Sat. 10-6, Sun. noon-6; closed Dec. 25. Admission $6; over 61, $5; students with ID $4; ages 6-12, $3. AE, MC, VI. Phone (561) 391-2200.

[SAVE] **SPORTS IMMORTALS MUSEUM,** 1 mi. n. of Yamato Rd. to 6830 N. Federal Hwy. (US 1), features rotating displays from a collection of more than a million mementos. Among memorabilia are racing helmets, autographed baseballs, uniforms, World Series pins and varied equipment used by sporting greats. Mon.-Fri. 10-6, Sat. 10-5. Admission $5; under 12, $3. MC, VI. Phone (561) 997-2575.

BOKEELIA (G-8) pop. 1,700, elev. 5′

TROPIC STAR CRUISE BOAT, 6 mi. n. of jct. SR 78 and CR 767 at 16499 Porto Bello St., offers full-day narrated cruises through the protected waters of Pine Island Sound to Cabbage Key and a rustic state park on Cayo Costa; a tram carries visitors to the beach. Visitors can view porpoises and birds as well as explore islands accessible only by boat. Picnicking is allowed on Cayo Costa. Allow a full day. Cruises depart daily at 9:30 and return at 4. Fare $25; ages 2-12, $15. State park fee including tram $1. Reservations are required. Phone (941) 283-0015.

BONITA SPRINGS (G-9)
pop. 13,600, elev. 12′

At the edge of Cypress Swamp, Bonita Springs offers good fishing in both the Gulf of Mexico and the Imperial River. Greyhound racing is the focus of attention at The Naples-Fort Myers Greyhound Track; phone (941) 992-2411.

Note: Policies vary concerning admittance of children to pari-mutuel betting facilities. Phone for information.

Bonita Springs Area Chamber of Commerce and Visitor Center: 25071 Chamber of Commerce Dr., Bonita Springs, FL 34135; phone (941) 992-2943 or (800) 226-2943.

EVERGLADES WONDER GARDENS, 27180 Old US 41, was opened in 1936 as a refuge for injured animals. The facility since has grown and now is home to exotic birds, panthers, alligators, flamingos, bears and otters. The grounds include botanical gardens and trees from around the world. A natural history museum also is on the premises. Guided tours are available. Allow 1 hour, 30 minutes minimum. Daily 9-5. Last tour begins 1 hour before closing. Admission $9; ages 3-12, $5. Phone (941) 992-2591.

BRADENTON (F-8)
pop. 43,800, elev. 21'

See map page 193.

Nearby Gulf beaches attract visitors to Bradenton (BRAY-den-ton), on Florida's west coast. The Art League of Manatee County, 209 Ninth St. W., displays works of local artists. Classes, demonstrations and workshops are offered September through July; phone (941) 746-2862.

Pirate City, 1701 27th St. E., is spring training camp for the Pittsburgh Pirates baseball team. Games are played at McKechnie Field, Ninth Street and 17th Avenue W., from early March to early April; phone (941) 748-4610. Bradenton also is the home of Pittsburgh's teams in the Gulf Coast Rookie League and the Florida Instructional League, providing baseball games from June to mid-October; phone (941) 747-3031.

Bradenton Area Convention & Visitors Bureau: P.O. Box 1000, Bradenton, FL 34206; phone (941) 729-9177 or (800) 462-6283.

Shopping areas: De Soto Square Mall, US 41 and Cortez Road, features Burdines, Dillard's, JCPenney and Sears among its 106 stores.

DE SOTO NATIONAL MEMORIAL —
see place listing p. 54.

HUNSADER FARMS is 10 mi. e. of I-75 exit 41 on SR 70, then 3 mi. n. to 5500 CR 675. Geared toward educating children about farming and farm life, the farm features displays of agricultural machinery and equipment and a petting zoo with chickens, cows, ducks, emus, goats, llamas, pheasants, pigs and turkeys. Hayrides and pony rides are available. Picnicking is permitted. Allow 1 hour minimum. Mon.-Sat. 8-4, Sept. 15-June 15; closed holidays. Free. Phone (941) 322-2168.

MANATEE VILLAGE HISTORICAL PARK is on SR 64, 1 mi. e. of US 41 at jct. Sixth Ave. E. and 15th St. E. The park includes an 1860 courthouse, 1887 church, 1912 settler's house, 1903 general store and 1908 one-room schoolhouse. Other highlights include a replica of a typical Florida barn as well as a boat exhibit, restored smokehouse and sugar cane mill. Visitors can tour the 1850 Old Manatee Burial Grounds by appointment. Picnicking is permitted. Allow 2 hours minimum. Mon.-Fri. 9-4:30, Sun. 1:30-

4:30, Sept.-June; Mon.-Fri. 9-4:30, rest of year. Free. Phone (941) 749-7165.

[SAVE] **SOUTH FLORIDA MUSEUM, BISHOP PLANETARIUM AND PARKER MANATEE AQUARIUM,** 201 10th St. W., shows varied aspects of southwest Florida history, including collections of Stone Age relics, Civil War memorabilia and pioneer artifacts. A medical wing has an old-time doctor's office, dentist's office and pharmacy. Snooty and Mo, a pair of manatees, share a 60,000-gallon aquarium and are fed daily at 12:30, 2 and 3:30.

Allow 1 hour, 30 minutes minimum. Museum open Mon.-Sat. 10-5, Sun. noon-5, Jan.-Apr. and in July; Tues.-Sat. 10-5, Sun. noon-5, May-June, in Aug. and mid-Sept. to Dec. 31. Closed Jan. 1, Easter, Veterans Day, Thanksgiving and Dec. 25. Observatory open Fri.-Sat. 8:30-10 p.m. (weather permitting). Planetarium shows are given daily at 1 and 4. Laser sound-and-light shows are presented daily at 2:30 (also Fri.-Sat. at 9 and 10:30). A live astronomy presentation is given Fri.-Sat. at 7 p.m.

Museum (including daytime planetarium shows) $7.50; over 59, $6; ages 5-12, $4. Laser show Fri.-Sat. evening $5.50; under 13, $3.50. Laser show included with general admission other times. Astronomy presentation (includes observatory) $3; under 12, $1.50. Only observatory $1. MC, VI. Phone (941) 746-4131.

BROOKSVILLE (D-8)
pop. 7,400, elev. 126'

The rolling terrain surrounding Brooksville is rich in limestone, making its quarrying and distribution the city's major industry. The limestone also makes this a fertile agricultural and grazing area, as evidenced by the number of cattle ranches and horse farms. The founding of Brooksville predates the Civil War, and many of its residential streets are lined with turn-of-the-20th-century Victorian homes.

In the center of town, Hernando Park has an outdoor band shell, a playground and recreational facilities. The park also is the site of arts and crafts shows. Winding through nearby countryside are miles of hiking and biking trails, including those of nearby Withlacoochee State Forest.

Tourist Development Department: 16110 Aviation Loop Dr., Brooksville, FL 34609; phone (800) 601-4580.

MAY STRINGER HERITAGE MUSEUM is at 601 Museum Ct., 1 blk. n. of jct. SRs 50 and 41. Costumed guides conduct tours of the four-story gabled building, which was built in the mid-19th century. Furnished rooms and a re-created schoolroom depict area history. Also featured is a collection of period medical equipment. Allow 1 hour minimum. Tues.-Sat. noon-3, Sept.-July. Donations. Phone (352) 799-0129.

ROGERS' CHRISTMAS HOUSE VILLAGE is at 103 Saxon Ave. The main house is decorated in a Christmas theme and displays gift items from around the world. Country Cottage, Magnolia House and Little House Under the Oak Tree also feature decorations and gifts. Storybook Land, next to the main house, has animated displays. Daily 9:30-5; closed Dec. 25. Free. Phone (352) 796-2415.

BUNNELL (C-9) pop. 1,900, elev. 25′

BULOW PLANTATION RUINS AND STATE HISTORIC SITE, 9 mi. s.e. on CR 2001 (Old Kings Rd.), following signs, are the remnants of Bulowville, a territorial period sugar mill and plantation destroyed by Seminoles in 1836. Interpretive center exhibits relate the story of the plantation and its destruction. The 109-acre site features a canoe trail, picnic and playground facilities and the preserved remains of original boat slips. Canoe rental is available. Freshwater and saltwater fishing is permitted with a license.

Allow 30 minutes minimum. Daily 9-5. Admission $2 per private vehicle. Phone (904) 517-2084. *See Recreation Chart.*

BUSHNELL (D-8) pop. 2,000, elev. 75′

Rural Bushnell, where the Withlacoochee River flows through a cypress swamp as a small stream, features small lakes once fished by American Indians and Spanish explorers. Most are still popular with anglers today, as is Lake Panasoffkee, to the north. Withlacoochee State Forest which covers 113,000 acres in three units, is west of town.

Florida National Military Cemetery, off I-75 exit 62 on SR 476B, is among the largest in the nation. On SR 471 in nearby Webster shoppers enjoy Monday events at the Webster Flea Market, one of the largest flea markets in the country.

Sumter County Chamber of Commerce: 223 N. Main St., P.O. Box 550, Bushnell, FL 33513; phone (352) 793-3099.

DADE BATTLEFIELD STATE HISTORIC SITE, 1.5 mi. e. off I-75 exit 63 or 1 mi. w. of US 301 on CR 603, commemorates the massacre of Maj. Francis L. Dade and his troops, who were ambushed by Seminole Indians the morning of Dec. 28, 1835. Highlights of the 80-acre park include reproductions of the log breastworks used in the battle and monuments to the valor of Dade and his men. A visitor center has exhibits and artifacts, and an interpretive trail marks the military road and battlefield. Picnic facilities are available.

Allow 1 hour minimum. Grounds open daily 8-dusk. Visitor center open daily 9-5. Admission $2 per private vehicle (maximum eight people), $1 per person arriving by bicycle or on foot. Phone (352) 793-4781.

CANAVERAL NATIONAL SEASHORE (D-10)

Canaveral National Seashore lies north of the Kennedy Space Center. This 57,000-acre wilderness area encompasses 24 miles of unspoiled barrier beaches, shallow lagoons and dunes. Alligators, turtles, manatees and a variety of birds are among the abundant wildlife.

Swimming, boating, surf fishing and ranger-led activities can be enjoyed at Playalinda Beach at the southern tip of the seashore and at Apollo Beach at the area's northern end. The Merritt Island National Wildlife Refuge *(see Titusville p. 230)* adjoins the national seashore. An information center at 7611 S. Atlantic Ave. in New Smyrna Beach is open daily; phone (904) 428-3384.

The seashore is open daily 6 a.m.-8 p.m., late Apr.-late Oct.; 6-6, rest of year. Playalinda Beach is closed 3 days before a shuttle launch and re-opens the following day. Admission $5 per vehicle. An annual pass is $28. For further information contact the Superintendent, Canaveral National Seashore, 308 Julia St., Titusville, FL 32796; phone (321) 267-1110. For a recorded daily beach report, phone (321) 867-0677. *See Recreation Chart.*

CAPE CORAL (G-9) pop. 75,000, elev. 5′

[SAVE] **THE CHILDREN'S SCIENCE CENTER**, .5 mi. w. of US 41 at 2915 N.E. Pine Island Rd. (SR 78), offers hands-on exhibits dealing with science, math and technology. Visitors can experiment with optical illusions, mazes, holographs and various inventions. Allow 1 hour minimum. Mon.-Fri. 9:30-4:30, Sat.-Sun. noon-5; closed Jan. 1, Easter, July 4, Thanksgiving and Dec. 25. Admission $4; ages 3-16, $2. MC, VI. Phone (941) 997-0012.

[SAVE] **SUN SPLASH FAMILY WATERPARK**, off I-75 exit 22, w. on Colonial Blvd., then n. to 400 Santa Barbara Blvd., offers 12 acres of recreational activities, including giant waterslides, activity and family pools, otter slides, an inner tube river, a children's play area and a game arcade. Food is available. Allow 2 hours minimum. Daily 10-5, mid-Mar. through Oct. 1; otherwise varies. Admission $9.95, under 48 inches tall $7.95, under age 2 free. Parking $1. AE, DS, MC, VI. Phone (941) 574-0558.

CAPTIVA ISLAND—*see Sanibel p. 191.*

CASTILLO DE SAN MARCOS NATIONAL MONUMENT—
see St. Augustine p. 184.

CEDAR KEY (C-7) pop. 700, elev. 8′

Due to its location on a small barrier island off the Gulf Coast of Florida, Cedar Key was a strategic point from which blockade runners exported cotton and lumber and imported food and supplies for the Confederacy during the Civil War. Following the war, lumbering and then fishing and shipbuilding formed the town's economic base.

An 1896 hurricane leveled the original town. Now primarily a resort area, the town relies on commercial fishing, crabbing, clam farming, oystering and tourism to sustain its economy. Cedar Key is home to many artists and its surrounding area is popular with bird-watchers.

Cedar Key Area Chamber of Commerce: P.O. Box 610, Cedar Key, FL 32625; phone (352) 543-5600.

Self-guiding tours: The Cedar Key Historical Society (see attraction listing) offers brochures with tours of the city.

CEDAR KEY HISTORICAL SOCIETY MUSEUM, on SR 24 at Second St., depicts the town's history through photographs dating back to 1850. Other displays include Seminole and Timucuan Indian artifacts, minerals and woodworking tools. Allow 30 minutes minimum. Mon.-Sat. 11-5, Sun. 2-5, Nov.-Apr.; Sun.-Thurs. 2-5, Fri.-Sat. 11-5, rest of year. Closed Jan. 1, Thanksgiving and Dec. 25. Admission $1; ages 12-18, 50c. Phone (352) 543-5549.

CEDAR KEY STATE MUSEUM, 1.75 mi. n. of SR 24 following signs, exhibits household articles from the past, historical dioramas and a shell collection said to be one of the most complete collections ever assembled. Allow 30 minutes minimum. Thurs.-Mon. 9-5. Admission $1, under 6 free. Phone (352) 543-5350.

CHIEFLAND (C-7) pop. 1,900, elev. 40′

LOWER SUWANNEE NATIONAL WILDLIFE REFUGE, 17 mi. s. on CR 347, is home to more than 90 species of birds that make their nests in the refuge's 51,340 acres. Hikers may spot such wildlife as bald eagles, white-tailed deer, wood ducks, blue-winged and green-winged teals and alligators. The .4-mile River Trail offers visitors a view of the Suwanee River and the cypress trees and hardwood swamps that surround it. The refuge is open daily 24 hours; the refuge office is open Mon.-Fri. 7:30-4. Free. Phone (352) 493-0238.

CHRISTMAS — see Orlando p. 159.

CLEARWATER — see Tampa Bay p. 225.

CLERMONT — see Orlando p. 160.

COCOA (D-10) pop. 17,700, elev. 25′

ASTRONAUT MEMORIAL PLANETARIUM & OBSERVATORY is 2.5 mi. e. of I-95 exit 75 on SR 520, then 1.75 mi. n. on SR 501 to 1519 Clearlake Rd. Visitors can look through a 24-inch telescope to see objects in the solar system and deep space. The planetarium's International Hall of Space Explorers honors the men and women from around the world who have flown in space. The Science Quest Demonstration Hall features hands-on exhibits relating to space science. Other options include presentations in the planetarium theater, large-format films in the IWERKS Discovery Theatre and a laser show.

Tues. and Fri.-Sat. 6:30-9:30. Days and times may vary; phone ahead. Film or planetarium show $5; over 59, $4; under 12, $3. Film and planetarium show $9; over 59, $7; under 12, $5. Laser show $6. Three shows $12. Rooftop observatory free. MC, VI. Phone (321) 634-3732 or 632-1111.

COCOA BEACH (D-11)
pop. 12,100, elev. 12′

Long a popular spot with locals, Cocoa Beach also is known for its location at the heart of the Space Coast. Cocoa Beach Pier extends 800 feet into the Atlantic, affording opportunities for fishing, surfing, dining and dancing. An 850-foot promenade leads to the beach and an observation deck overlooking the ocean.

Cocoa Beach Area Chamber of Commerce: 400 Fortenberry Rd., Merritt Island, FL 32952; phone (321) 459-2200.

COCONUT CREEK—
see Fort Lauderdale p. 77.

COCONUT GROVE—
see Miami-Miami Beach p. 125.

CORAL GABLES—
see Miami-Miami Beach p. 125.

CORAL SPRINGS—
see Fort Lauderdale p. 77.

CROSS CREEK (C-9) elev. 69′

MARJORIE KINNAN RAWLINGS STATE HISTORIC SITE, on CR 325, 4 mi. w. of jct. US 301 next to the county park, is the restored home of Marjorie Kinnan Rawlings, author of the Pulitzer Prize-winning novel "The Yearling." This area was the setting for several of Rawlings's books. Grounds open daily 9-5. Guided house tours are given Thurs.-Sun. at 10, 11, 1, 2, 3 and 4, Oct.-July; closed Jan. 1, Thanksgiving and Dec. 25. Grounds free. Tours $3; ages 6-12, $2. Phone (352) 466-3672.

CRYSTAL RIVER (D-8)
pop. 4,000, elev. 4′

Crystal River denotes both a town and the river that runs through it into Kings Bay. The waters accommodate anglers and scuba divers.

Citrus County Chamber of Commerce at Crystal River: 28 N.W. US 19, Crystal River, FL 34429-3900; phone (352) 795-3149.

CRYSTAL RIVER STATE ARCHEOLOGICAL SITE, 2.5 mi. w. off US 19N on N. Museum Point, preserves the ceremonial mound complex built by American Indians who occupied the site from 200 B.C. to 1400. In addition to temple and burial mounds, there are middens, or refuse mounds, formed in part by the empty shells of the seafood that was an important part of the Indians' diet. The visitor center displays artifacts and information about these pre-Columbian Mound Builders.

Allow 1 hour, 30 minutes minimum. Grounds open daily 8-dusk. Visitor center open daily 9-5. Admission $2 per private vehicle (maximum eight people), $1 per person arriving by bicycle, motorcycle or on foot. Phone (352) 795-3817.

THE POWER PLACE ENERGY INFORMATION CENTER is 4 mi. n. on US 19 then 4 mi. w. on Powerline St., in the site administration building of the energy complex. Exhibits deal with current and future methods of generating electricity. Mon.-Fri. 9:30-4. Free. Phone (352) 563-4490.

◆ CYPRESS GARDENS—
see Winter Haven p. 234.

DADE CITY—*see Tampa Bay p. 226.*

DANIA BEACH—
see Fort Lauderdale p. 77.

DAVIE—*see Fort Lauderdale p. 77.*

DAYTONA BEACH (C-10)
pop. 61,900, elev. 10′

Daytona Beach was more speedway than beach in the early days of the automobile. Between 1902 and 1935 some 13 speed records were set by Barney Oldfield, Sir Henry Segrave and Sir Malcolm Campbell. The tradition continues at Daytona International Speedway *(see attraction listing)* with such races as the Daytona 500 in February and the Pepsi 400 in July. For ticket information phone (904) 253-7223.

White sand beaches stretch for 23 miles; during the day cars may be driven on most of the hard-packed sand along the water's edge. For safety, beach driving should be done during a low or outgoing tide and never in the water, however shallow.

Drivers should heed signs noting conservation areas. Overnight parking or camping is not permitted on the beach. The beach is not open to motor vehicles from Sea Breeze to International Speedway boulevards and south of the Emelia Avenue beach approach in Daytona Beach Shores to the Beach Street approach in Ponce Inlet, at Lighthouse Point Park in Ponce Inlet or north of the Granada Boulevard beach approach in Ormond Beach. A daily beach access toll

Safety At Florida's Beaches

Florida's expansive coastline provides numerous opportunities for fun in the sun, but it also requires an extra degree of caution when taking a dip: A large number of Florida beaches are unguarded. Swimming at an unguarded beach presents a risk to swimmers not only through injury or drowning, but also through the dangers of rip currents, dangerous or poisonous marine animals and other hidden hazards.

However, many Florida beaches are guarded by trained,  certified ocean lifeguards. To ensure your safety and that of your family, be sure to swim only when ocean lifeguards are present. A list of guarded beaches is available from the United States Lifesaving Association and the Florida Beach Patrol Chiefs Association, 340 S. Ocean Blvd., Delray Beach, FL 33483; phone (561) 243-7352.

of $5 per vehicle is charged February through November. Toll booths are at each approach. The speed limit on the beach is 10 miles per hour. For beach information phone (904) 239-7873.

A wide promenade along the ocean is the center of the amusement area near the fishing pier. Featured are a sightseeing tower and sky ride. The bandshell in Oceanfront Park, at the north end of the promenade, is the setting for events.

A scenic portion of SR A1A extends along the ocean from Daytona Beach north to Fernandina Beach, a distance of 105 miles.

Ocean lovers enjoy sailing, surfing and riding personal watercraft; the Halifax River is a popular boating, water skiing and sailboarding destination. Greyhounds race at Daytona Beach Kennel Club, next to the speedway; phone (904) 252-6484.

Note: Policies vary concerning admittance of children to pari-mutuel betting facilities. Phone for information.

Daytona Beach Area Convention and Visitors Bureau: 126 E. Orange Ave., Daytona Beach, FL 32115; phone (904) 255-0415 or (800) 854-1234. *See color ad & p. 149.*

Shopping areas: Daytona Flea Market, 1 mile west of Daytona Speedway at the junction of I-95 and US 92, provides weekend browsing. Fresh produce, citrus and seafood are available at the Farmers Market, downtown on City Island. Volusia Mall, 1700 International Speedway Blvd. (US 92), features Burdines, Dillard's, JCPenney and Sears among its 120 stores.

ANGELL & PHELPS CHOCOLATE FACTORY TOUR, just s. of US 92 at 154 S. Beach St., offers tours of a working factory where visitors can watch handmade chocolates being created. Allow 30 minutes minimum. Mon.-Fri. 10-3. Free. Phone (904) 257-2677.

DAYTONA INTERNATIONAL SPEEDWAY is 1 mi. e. of I-95 exit 87A (southbound) or exit 87 (northbound) on US 92. The track is accessible to visitors for self-guiding tours through the entrance to Daytona USA. Guided tram tours of the racetrack, infield, pit and garage areas are offered by Daytona USA *(see attraction listing).* Sections of the grandstands are named for well-known racers. The speedway features eight weekends of racing each year, including stock cars, sports cars, motorcycles and go-carts.

Track open daily 9-5:30 (weather and track schedule permitting). Self-guiding tours free. Phone (904) 253-7223 for tickets, or TDD (904) 947-6700. *See color ad p. 53.*

DAYTONA USA is 1 mi. e. of I-95 exit 87A (southbound) or exit 87 (northbound) on the grounds of Daytona International Speedway. Visitors enter through a replica of the raceway's famed twin tunnels and are greeted by "The Heritage of Daytona," an exhibit that offers a chronological look at racing history.

Through interactive displays guests can broadcast a race, electronically interact with eight of racing's drivers, test their motor sports knowledge at a six-station trivia game, computer-design their own race car and participate in a timed pit stop. Visitors can experience the thrill of being in the driver's seat by watching "The Daytona 500," a 14-minute audiovisual presentation that captures the excitement of stock car racing. Viewers exit the theater to step into Victory Lane, where the winning car from the current Daytona 500 is displayed.

A 30-minute tram tour of the speedway features stops at Pit Road, the Start/Finish Line, the 31-degree banking on Turn Four and Victory Lane. Food is available. Allow 1 hour, 30 minutes minimum. Daily 9-7; closed Dec. 25. Speedway tour daily (weather and track schedule permitting) 9:30-4:30. Admission $12; over 59, $10; ages 6-12, $6. Speedway tour $6, under 6 free. Admission and tour $16; over 59, $14; ages 6-12, $11. MC, VI. Phone (904) 947-6800.

HALIFAX HISTORICAL SOCIETY AND MUSEUM is 2 blks. s. of US 92 at 252 S. Beach St. Housed in the restored 1911 Merchants Bank building, the museum's displays include historic photographs, postcards, American Indian and plantation era artifacts and memorabilia from the early days of automobile racing. Noteworthy is

the elaborate miniature replica of the boardwalk circa 1938; it depicts the bandshell with concertgoers, underground walkways and vintage automobiles.

Allow 1 hour minimum. Tues.-Sat. 10-4; closed Jan. 1, Thanksgiving and Dec. 25. Admission $3; under 12, $1; free to children under 12 on Sat.; Thurs. after noon by donations. Phone (904) 255-6976.

KLASSIX AUTO ATTRACTION is .5 mi. s.w. of I-95 exit 87B on US 92 to 2909 W. International Speedway Blvd. The museum features a large assortment of classic automobiles and muscle cars as well as vehicles used in television shows and movies. Also presented are motorcycles and racing memorabilia. Food is available. Allow 1 hour, 30 minutes minimum. Daily 9-6. Admission $8.50; over 55, $7.50; ages 7-12, $4.25. AE, DS, MC, VI. Phone (904) 252-3800.

MUSEUM OF ARTS AND SCIENCES is .25 mi. w. of Nova Rd. (SR 5A) and .75 mi. s. of jct. US 92 at 1040 Museum Blvd. Collections include Cuban and Florida art, American and European fine and decorative arts, pre-Columbian and African artifacts, Pleistocene fossils and displays about Florida's cultural and natural history. The museum also houses changing art and science exhibits and maintains a planetarium, library and a sculpture garden.

Allow 1 hour minimum. Museum open Tues.-Fri. 9-4, Sat.-Sun. noon-5; closed major holidays. Planetarium star shows Tues.-Fri. at 2, Sat.-Sun. at 1 and 3 and the first Tues. of each month at 2 and 7. Museum admission $5, students with ID $1, under 7 free. Planetarium admission an additional $3, children $2. Phone (904) 255-0285.

SOUTHEAST MUSEUM OF PHOTOGRAPHY is at 1200 W. International Speedway Blvd., Building 37, on the Daytona Beach Community College campus. The gallery of changing photography exhibits features both early and contemporary selections. Allow 30 minutes minimum. Mon.-Fri. 9:30-4:30 (also Tues. 4:30-7), Sat.-Sun. noon-4;

closed holidays. Donations. Phone (904) 254-4475.

A TINY CRUISE LINE departs from the Halifax Harbor Marina "Showdock" at 425 S. Beach St. Narrated cruises along the Halifax River are aboard a replica of an 1890s excursion boat. A 2-hour midday waterway trip offers chances to see dolphins and wildlife. One-hour cruises travel past riverfront estates or historic downtown. Sunset cruises also are available April through October.

Two-hour waterway cruise departs Mon.-Sat. at 11:30. One-hour riverfront estate cruise departs Mon.-Sat. at 2; historic downtown trip departs Mon.-Sat. at 3:30. Fare for 1-hour cruises $9.66; ages 4-12, $6.12. Fare for 2-hour cruise $14.37; ages 4-12, $8. Reservations are required for sunset cruises. Phone (904) 226-2343.

DEERFIELD BEACH—
see Fort Lauderdale p. 77.

DELAND (C-9) pop. 16,500, elev. 27′

The stately oaks lining the streets of DeLand are the result of the arboreal interests and endeavors of Henry A. DeLand, who founded the city in 1876. Another local entrepreneur was Chinese emigrant Lue Gim Gong, who produced highly successful strains of oranges and grapefruit in the late 1800s.

DeLand Museum of Art presents changing exhibits; phone (904) 734-4371. Stetson University, established in 1886 by DeLand and named for hat magnate John Stetson, contains Gillespie Museum of Minerals and Duncan Gallery of Art; phone (904) 822-7000. Both attractions are on N. Woodland Boulevard. A booklet describing a campus walking tour is available at the public relations office.

Bill Dreggors Park on Stone Street is a popular picnic spot; phone (904) 734-5333.

West Volusia Visitors Bureau: 101 N. Woodland Blvd., DeLand, FL 32720; phone (904) 734-0575 or (800) 749-4350.

THE AFRICAN AMERICAN MUSEUM OF THE ARTS, off US 17/92 at 325 S. Clara Ave., presents permanent displays of more than 150 artifacts including masks and carvings, as well as a photo gallery of famous African-Americans and changing exhibits from established and emerging artists. Allow 30 minutes minimum. Wed.-Sat. 10-4. Free. Phone (904) 736-4004.

CULTURAL ARTS CENTER, .5 mi. n. of jct. US 17/92 and SR 44 at 600 N. Woodland Blvd., offers changing exhibits in two galleries. Plays, concerts and children's shows are presented in the 240-seat theater. Allow 30 minutes minimum. Tues.-Sat. 10-4, Sun. 1-4; closed holidays. Donations. Phone (904) 736-7232.

HENRY A. DeLAND HOUSE MUSEUM, 137 W. Michigan Ave., was built in 1886 on land purchased from city founder Henry A. DeLand. The home was built by attorney George Hamlin, developer of the Hamlin orange, and is filled with period furnishings and collectibles. An extensive collection of period photographs is on display. Guided tours are available. Allow 1 hour minimum. Tues.-Sat. noon-4; closed holidays. Donations. Phone (904) 740-6813.

MANATEE SEEKER SCENIC CRUISE departs from Pier 44 Marina, 5 mi. w. on SR 44. Two-hour narrated cruises along the St. Johns River offer insights into the history of Florida and the river. Native wildlife such as manatees, alligators, otters, ospreys, bald eagles and egrets may be sighted in their natural environment. Cruises depart daily at 10, 12:30 and 3; closed the last 2 weeks in May and Dec. 20-26. Fare $20; over 65 and ages 6-11, $16; under 6, $10. Reservations are recommended. Phone (800) 587-7131.

DELRAY BEACH (G-12)
pop. 47,200, elev. 20′

A resort community, Delray Beach offers its residents simplicity and a relaxed pace. The city supports a variety of light industries.

Greater Delray Beach Chamber of Commerce: 64 S.E. Fifth Ave., Delray Beach, FL 33483; phone (561) 278-0424.

ARTHUR R. MARSHALL LOXAHATCHEE NATIONAL WILDLIFE REFUGE is on US 441/SR 7, 2 mi. s. of jct. SR 804 (Boynton Beach Blvd.) or 3 mi. n. of jct. SR 806 (Atlantic Ave.). The 147,000-acre refuge is home to endangered and threatened species such as the snail kite, the wood stork and the American alligator. Migrating waterfowls flock in the winter. The refuge offers facilities for fishing, boating and bird-watching. Other features include an observation tower, nature trails, a 12-mile bicycle trail, a 5.5-mile canoe trail and a visitor center with exhibits and a videotape presentation about the area.

Refuge open daily 6 a.m.-dusk. Visitor center open Mon.-Fri. 9-4, Sat.-Sun. 9-4:30, mid-Oct.

through Apr. 30; Wed.-Fri. 9-4, Sat.-Sun. 9-4:30, rest of year. Closed Dec. 25. Admission $5 per private vehicle or $1 per person arriving by bicycle or on foot. MC, VI. Phone (561) 734-8303.

SAVE **THE MORIKAMI MUSEUM AND JAPANESE GARDENS** are 3.5 mi. w. of I-95 exit 41 on Linton Blvd., 1 mi. s. on Jog Rd., then .5 mi. w. on entrance road to 4000 Morikami Park Rd. Dedicated exclusively to the living culture of Japan, the museum explores modern and traditional Japanese culture and the history of Florida's Yamato Colony, an early 20th-century farming settlement. Two museum buildings house permanent and changing exhibits. On the grounds are a 200-acre park, ponds, Japanese and bonsai gardens and a nature trail. Picnicking is permitted. Food is available.

Allow 1 hour, 30 minutes minimum. Tues.-Sun. 10-5; closed holidays. Admission $5.25; over 65, $4.75; ages 6-18, $3. Phone (561) 495-0233.

OLD SCHOOL SQUARE CULTURAL ARTS CENTER AND NATIONAL HISTORIC SITE is 5 blks. w. of US 1 at 51 N. Swinton Ave., or 1 mi. e. of I-95 on Atlantic Ave. The center contains three early 20th-century school buildings: a reception hall, Crest Theatre and Cornell Museum of Art & History. Crest Theatre presents music, theater and dance productions, while the museum features changing art exhibits.

Allow 30 minutes minimum. Tues.-Sat. 11-4, Sun. 1-4 Oct.-Apr.; Tues.-Sat. 11-4, rest of year. Closed holidays. Admission $3; ages 6-11, $1. AE, MC, VI. Phone (561) 243-7922, or 243-3183 for theater reservations.

DE SOTO NATIONAL MEMORIAL (F-8)

De Soto National Memorial is on the south shore of the Manatee River, 5 miles west of Bradenton on SR 64, then 2 miles north on 75th Street N.W. The memorial commemorates the first major European exploration of what is now the southeastern United States.

The expedition began in 1539 when Hernando de Soto and about 600 Spanish soldiers landed somewhere in the Tampa Bay area. Marked by many Indian battles, the expedition covered 4,000 miles to the north and west. De Soto crossed the Mississippi River in 1541 and was buried in it when he died a year later. About half the group survived the 4-year ordeal.

The visitor center contains artifacts and exhibits explaining the expedition's effect on American Indians. A 21-minute film depicting the expedition is shown hourly. Talks by costumed rangers as well as crossbow and arquebus (matchlock musket) demonstrations are given hourly 10:30-3:30, mid-December to early April. There also is a nature trail. Allow 1 hour minimum. Daily 9-5. Free. Phone (941) 792-0458.

DISNEY WORLD, WALT—
see Lake Buena Vista in Orlando p. 162.

DRY TORTUGAS NATIONAL PARK—*see The Florida Keys p. 64.*

DUNEDIN—*see Tampa Bay p. 226.*

ELLENTON (F-8) pop. 1,600, elev. 11′

Ellenton, a popular retirement community on the Manatee River, offers fine fishing opportunities, nearby white sandy beaches and a climate favorable to agricultural endeavors.

Manatee County Tourist Information Center: 5030 US 301 N., Ellenton, FL 34222; phone (941) 729-7040.

Shopping areas: Prime Outlets Ellenton, off I-75 exit 43, features 135 factory outlet stores, including Gap, Naturalizer, Samsonite and Tommy Hilfiger.

GAMBLE MANSION AND JUDAH P. BENJAMIN CONFEDERATE MEMORIAL STATE HISTORIC SITE, on US 301, was a prosperous 3,500-acre sugar plantation from about 1845 to the late 1850s. The antebellum mansion is furnished in period. At the end of the Civil War, Judah P. Benjamin, secretary of state of the Confederacy, found refuge here before escaping to England. Picnicking is permitted. Allow 1 hour minimum. Tours are given Thurs.-Mon. at 9:30, 10:30, 1, 2, 3 and 4. Admission, which is only by guided tour, $3; ages 6-12, $1.50. Phone (941) 723-4536.

EPCOT—
see Lake Buena Vista in Orlando p. 164.

ESTERO (G-9) pop. 200, elev. 11′

KORESHAN STATE HISTORIC SITE, US 41 at Corkscrew Rd. on the banks of the Estero River, was the site of the religious community established in 1894 when Cyrus Reed Teed and his followers, members of the Koreshan Unity, arrived from Chicago. Restored historical buildings and gardens occupy the site. Carry insect repellent. Camping is available; reservations are recommended. Fireside programs for campers are available by seasonal demand.

Allow 1 hour minimum. Park open daily 8-dusk. Self-guiding walking tours can be taken daily 8-5. Admission $3.25 per private vehicle (maximum eight people), $1 per person arriving by bicycle or on foot. AE, DS, MC, VI. Phone (941) 992-0311. *See Recreation Chart and the AAA Southeastern CampBook.*

EVERGLADES CITY (H-10)
pop. 300, elev. 3′

Because of its location at the northwest corner of the Everglades, Everglades City is a popular point of departure for fishing trips into Everglades National Park. Some hotels will send a box lunch with the angler and also will prepare the day's catch for the evening meal.

Everglades Area Chamber of Commerce: P.O. Box 130, Everglades City, FL 34139; phone (941) 695-3941 or (800) 914-6355.

EDEN OF THE EVERGLADES, 2 mi. s. of jct. US 41 on SR 29, has an elevated boardwalk that winds through a mangrove forest. Forty-five-minute pontoon boat trips tour the waterways of the Ten Thousand Islands area. Airboat rides also are available. Carry insect repellent. Daily 9-5. Admission $13.95; ages 3-10, $8. MC, VI. Phone (941) 695-2800 or (800) 543-3367.

E.J. HAMILTON OBSERVATION TOWER, s. on SR 29 following signs, offers a panorama of the Everglades and the Ten Thousand Islands. The wooden tower is 80 feet tall and has 180 steps. A boardwalk leads through a small portion of mangrove swamp to a waterway where marine birds can be seen. Daily 24 hours. Admission $1. Phone (941) 695-2073.

EVERGLADES EXCURSIONS—
see Naples p. 129.

EVERGLADES NATIONAL PARK BOAT TOURS leave from the park's ranger station .5 mi. s. on CR 29. The Mangrove Wilderness tour cruises past Calusa Indian shell mounds to native mangrove forests, and the Ten Thousand Islands tour cruises through this island group bordering the Gulf of Mexico. Both tours offer bird and wildlife sightings. For reservations and schedule information write P.O. Box 119, Everglades City, FL 34139. Cruises depart at intervals daily 8:30-5. Fare $16; ages 6-12, $8. AE, DS, MC, VI. Phone (941) 695-2591, or (800) 445-7724 in Fla.

DID YOU KNOW

Amelia Earhart departed from Hialeah in her attempt to fly around the world.

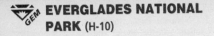

EVERGLADES NATIONAL PARK (H-10)

Elevations in the park range from sea level to 8 ft.

Everglades National Park, the largest remaining subtropical wilderness in the nation, is a diverse and intricately linked series of habitats sheltering a variety of plants and animals, many of them threatened or endangered. The park contains more than 1.5 million acres of natural habitat, half of them water, including Cape Sable, the southernmost point on the U.S. mainland. From Cape Sable the park extends 45 miles north along the Gulf of Mexico and 30 miles east, including Florida Bay.

The Everglades is essentially a slow-moving freshwater river, 50 miles wide and a few inches deep, fed by Lake Okeechobee. Much of the region is a labyrinth of mangrove waterways and sawgrass marsh dotted with hammocks and salt prairies. Except for the pinelands and the highest hammocks, any spot can become a swamp in the rainy season.

Increased development in southern Florida imperils the area. Canals alternately drain and flood the region to meet the water demands of nearby cities, but in doing so they reverse the natural wet and dry cycles of the Everglades. Although fire occurs naturally in this environment, drought and canal drainage have magnified its destructive impact.

The land areas are not more than 8 feet above mean sea level, and bay bottoms are not more than 16 feet below mean sea level. The Ten Thousand Islands area conceals a strange kind of beauty and tranquility within its tide-swept maze of islets, oyster bars and mud shallows.

Trees and flowers are much the same as those found in Cuba and the West Indies. At least six species of palms grow within the park. The stately royal palm is found in greatest numbers at the Royal Palm Visitor Center. In addition to the tropical and semitropical trees and shrubs, there are at least four species belonging to the temperate zone and multitudes of ferns, orchids and air plants. Beware of the sawgrass; its sharp barbs can easily slash bare skin and thin clothing.

The park is home to more than 350 species of birds, 60 percent of which leave during summer.

2079-H

Among those that stay are two species found only in the southernmost tip of the Florida peninsula: the Cape Sable sparrow and the great white heron. One species that does proliferate is the mosquito; strong insect repellent is a necessity from May to November and is recommended all year.

The Everglades is among the few remaining places where the manatee, or sea cow, and the rare American crocodile are assured a permanent sanctuary. Along with more than 600 species of fish, alligators, snakes and sea turtles are common. Bottlenose dolphins occasionally are seen. A fishing license is required for all fishing areas, and bag limits are strictly enforced for both freshwater and saltwater fishing.

General Information and Activities

Everglades National Park is open all year. The park's main entrance is reached via SR 9336 from US 1 at Florida City. From the headquarters and visitor center at the main entrance, this road continues to Flamingo. The Tamiami Trail (US 41) skirts the park's northern border and leads to the Shark Valley and Everglades City entrances.

Few people really know the waterways of the Everglades. Most of the waters have been charted by the U.S. Coast and Geodetic Survey, and visitors traveling by boat should obtain these charts at area bait and tackle shops before starting their trips. Permits, obtainable at ranger stations, are required for overnight camping and as a safety precaution, park officials urge boaters to file trip plans before their departures.

Four marked canoe trails offer 4- to 22-mile round trips from the Flamingo area, and the 99-mile Wilderness Waterway winds between Flamingo and Everglades City. The Shark River is navigable for most small boats. Canoe rentals are available at outfitters in Flamingo and Everglades City; visitor centers distribute trail maps.

Along the main park road between park headquarters and Flamingo are five major boardwalk or blacktop nature trails *(see Points of Interest)*. Flamingo has accommodations, restaurants, sightseeing and charter fishing boats, a service station, marina, campground and visitor center. A ranger station on the south side of Everglades City on SR 29 is open daily 7:30-5, Nov.-Apr.; 8-4:30, rest of year; phone (941) 695-3311. *See Recreation Chart and the AAA Southeastern CampBook.*

Sightseeing opportunities are abundant. Boat trips through a portion of the Ten Thousand Islands area leave from nearby cities *(see Everglades City p. 55 and Naples p. 129)*. Other sightseeing trips are available from Flamingo, within the park. Self-guiding bicycle, kayak and canoe trips originate in Flamingo; phone (941) 695-3101.

Boat tours depart from Flamingo Lodge. The 2-hour Backcountry cruises leave daily at 9, noon and 1:30, late Dec. to mid-Apr.; schedule varies rest of year. A 1.5-hour Florida Bay Cruise is offered daily at 2:30 and sunset, late Dec. to mid-Apr.; schedule varies rest of year. Boarding is 10 minutes before departure. Boat tours also leave from the visitor center in Everglades City.

Backcountry cruise $16; ages 6-12, $8. Florida Bay Cruise $10; ages 6-12, $5. Reservations are recommended for all boat tours. For further information about all boat tours phone the lodge at (941) 695-3101.

Airboat rides, available outside the park, are offered by private operators along the Tamiami Trail (US 41) west of Miami.

VISITOR CENTERS offer information that can enhance a visit to the park.

Ernest Coe Visitor Center, at the entrance at 40001 SR 9336, has exhibits about the park. Naturalists are on duty daily 8-5. Free. Phone (305) 242-7700.

Flamingo Visitor Center, 38 mi. s.w. of the main park entrance via SR 9336, has natural history exhibits and a marina opening onto Florida Bay. Rentals are available. Daily 8-5. Free. Phone (941) 695-2945.

Gulf Coast Visitor Center, in Everglades City in the northwest corner of the park, contains natural-history exhibits. Daily 8:30-5. Free. Phone (941) 695-3311.

Royal Palm Visitor Center is 4 mi. inside the park, off the main park road. The center provides park information and, in winter, naturalist-led walks and illustrated talks. Daily 8-4:15. Free. Phone (305) 247-6211.

ADMISSION to the park is $10 per private vehicle or $5 per person arriving by bicycle, motorcycle or on foot.

PETS are permitted only in the park campgrounds and only if they are leashed, crated or otherwise physically restrained at all times. They are not allowed on developed trails, in the backcountry or in the visitor centers.

ADDRESS inquiries to the Superintendent, Everglades National Park, 40001 SR 9336, Homestead, FL 33034; phone (305) 242-7700.

Points of Interest

ANHINGA TRAIL, beginning at the Royal Palm Visitor Center, follows an elevated boardwalk. During the winter, alligators, snowy egrets, water turkeys and garfish can be seen.

CHEKIKA, 18 mi. n.w. of Homestead off SR 997, offers 640 acres of hardwood hammocks and wetlands with more than 100 species of birds. Admission $8 per private vehicle or $4 per person arriving by bicycle or on foot (fee deductible from entrance fee to Everglades National Park). For information phone (305) 242-7700. *See Recreation Chart.*

GUMBO LIMBO TRAIL, starting from Royal Palm Visitor Center, penetrates the interior of Paradise Key hammock, where many species of native plants can be seen.

LONG PINE KEY AREA, 7 mi. from the entrance station, contains camping and picnic facilities, and nature and hiking trails. *See the AAA Southeastern CampBook.*

MAHOGANY HAMMOCK, 19.5 mi. from the park entrance, is a region of mahogany trees and many other subtropical plants labeled for easy identification. An elevated boardwalk winds through the forest.

MANGROVE TRAIL, 30.5 mi. from the park entrance station at West Lake, extends through a mangrove forest on an elevated boardwalk. The trail, badly damaged by a hurricane in 1960, shows the devastation such storms can cause.

PA-HAY-OKEE OVERLOOK is 12.5 mi. from the park entrance. The overlook consists of a 12-foot tower at Shark River Basin which affords views of the vast sawgrass wilderness.

PINELANDS TRAIL, 6.5 mi. from the park entrance, extends into an area of southern pines, scrub palmetto and related plants.

SHARK VALLEY, off US 41, has several short self-guiding trails that explore the area. Bobcat Hammock Trail passes through a variety of habitats, while Otter Cave Trail leads through limestone formations and a tropical hammock. Self-guiding bicycle trails and bicycle rentals are available. A visitor center is open daily 8:30-5:15. Admission $8 per private vehicle, $4 per person arriving by bicycle, motorcycle or on foot (fee deductible from entrance fee to Everglades National Park). Phone (305) 221-8776.

The Shark Valley Tram Tour departs from Shark Valley off US 41. The 2-hour, 15-mile excursion explores the sawgrass wilderness of Shark Valley and includes a 20-minute stop at the observation tower at the southern end of the valley. Tours operate daily 9-4, Dec.-Apr.; 9:30-3, rest of year (weather permitting). Fare $9.50; over 62, $8.35; under 12, $5.15. Reservations are required 1 to 3 weeks in advance Nov.-Apr. AE, DS, MC, VI. Phone (305) 221-8455.

FERNANDINA BEACH—
see Jacksonville p. 95.

FLORIDA CITY—
see Miami-Miami Beach p. 125.

◤GEM◥ FLORIDA'S SILVER SPRINGS—*see Ocala p. 131.*

FORT GEORGE ISLAND—
see Jacksonville p. 96.

Only AAA offers an integrated travel information system that is tailored to your individual needs.

*O*ur highly trained counselors can assist you with all facets of planning your trip, from designing the route to making reservations. In addition, only AAA travel counselors can provide our exclusive collection of travel materials selected especially for you.

TourBook® guides are comprehensive travel guides listing AAA Approved attractions, lodgings and restaurants. In addition to the coveted Diamond Ratings, you'll find descriptions of towns and cities and information on discounts available only to AAA members. TourBooks are updated annually and cover every state and province in the United States and Canada.

TripTik® routings trace your route mile-by-mile and are clearly marked with the vital information you need while on the road, such as highway exits and rest stops. These handy maps are custom-configured by your AAA travel counselor and can highlight the quickest, shortest or most scenic routes, as well as highway construction projects along the way.

Sheet maps are updated annually and cover every state and province, plus regional areas throughout North America. An extensive network of road reporters and club staff works with AAA cartographers to ensure that AAA maps are the most detailed and accurate maps available.

CampBook® guides list AAA Approved camping and RV facilities, both public and private, throughout the United States and Canada.

So the next time you're planning a trip, remember to visit your local AAA travel counselor.

***Travel With Someone
You Trust*** ®

The Florida Keys

A watercolor sky glows lavender, cobalt, carmine, sienna—another sunset. The street performers pause. The audience applauds.

And then, on with the show. Back to shuffling for a better spot to watch the cartwheeling cats, pirouetting pig, painted human "statue" and tip-pleading tightrope walker. Back to dodging oncoming onlookers, observing the people parade and eyeing vendors' wares. Back to the raucous ritual.

End the Beginning

You could only be in Key West, Florida's accessible slice of island spice. The final course in The Florida Keys' full menu of fun.

Imbued with a tropical flavor that extends to its ubiquitous dishes—conch chowder, conch fritters and, of course, Key lime pie—this tiny town at The End of the Road is a slightly sugary, slightly tart, somehow sublime little custard of sights, sounds, tastes and tempos. As impious as eating dessert first, it's perfectly placed to introduce this curving island chain's curious charisma.

Like its sister Keys that Henry Flagler's railroad linked, Key West's influences have been Bahamian, Cuban, military, visionary. Its industries have ranged from shipwreck salvaging to turtle hunting to cigar making to tourism. Its wealth has been vast (in the 1880s, before lighthouses helped treasure-laden ships avoid treacherous reefs) and lost (in the 1930s, after 42 miles of railroad succumbed to storm-tossed seas).

Its Old Town historic district—pedestrian-friendly and architecturally rich—is where wreckers' and shipbuilders' hybrid homes are now high-end bed-and-breakfasts admired for their tin roofs, gingerbread trim, signature shutters and wraparound verandas. Where former hangouts of hard-drinking heroes and hippies are now vacation-photo backdrops for families *and* frat boys. Where fierce, fighting roosters' docile descendents quaintly roam free, legally protected. That's Key West: tradition with a Key lime twist.

But of all its aspects, the self-nicknamed Conch Republic is arguably best known for having perpetuated a simple habit of nightly saluting the blazing horizon, albeit with an atmosphere increasingly more theme park than Thoreau.

In fact, if you strayed there straight from the airport or cruise ship, today's Mallory Square sundown scene could cause culture shock. Amid the pet-toting locals

and souvenir T-shirt masses, first-timers tend to feel a bit like bit players on a crowded movie set. But for those who've been before, or who drove in through all those other quirky Keys, well, you've seen enough to know it's all for real. Surreal as it may be.

Driving the mostly two-lane Road That Went to Sea from Miami to Key West is like backtracking to the days predating endless exit ramps. Through the car windows—interspersed with mangroves, cattails and "passing lane 3 miles" signs—appear pirates posed in full regalia, monster lobsters, towering mermaid cutouts, lots of crusty cannons, a few giant anchors. Conspicuously placed as if to encourage a pull-off photo op, followed by a stop inside the air-conditioned comfort of whatever restaurant or shop sits close by, such oddities lend the landscape an innocent charm.

Then there are the signs: "Seafood" spelled in seashell mosaic; a neon turtle; even a rhinoceros-topped billboard. After many miles of this sort of scenery, one reaches the landlocked concrete buoy emblazoned "Southernmost Point" a little more prepared for Key West's mystique.

But don't think you have to head all the way to that oft-photographed red, yellow and black landmark to have *arrived.* Simply stop at almost any populated Key (taken from the Spanish *cayo,* or "small island") along the way and you'll usually be well fixed with great R & R opportunities. A good number of Florida Keys vacationers do just that, making family traditions out of annual stays at tuck-away campgrounds, easygoing efficiencies, "botels"—lodgings where marinas replace parking lots—or sport-fishing hot spots flush with charter boats, guides and all-inclusive resorts.

Getting There *Is* Half the Fun

In the Upper Keys, where most of the kitsch is confined, Key Largo and the unparalleled John Pennekamp Coral Reef State Park beckon snorkelers and scuba divers. Here, experienced divers can find everything needed to explore the fantastically diverse and extremely fragile reef system several miles offshore. But amateurs aren't left out; many lodgings offer on-site diving instruction. The park's main beach even has a staged shipwreck that especially delights children, who can be heard shouting to shore their discovery of what surely is the long-lost cannon of an unfortunate Spanish galleon.

Anchoring the Upper Keys stretch is sport-fishing-focused Islamorada, boasting one of the region's largest concentrations of charter boats as well as the midwaylike atmosphere of lively Holiday Isle; complete with beach, pools, shops, boardwalk and marina, the resort is famous for appealing to a festive crowd. Nearby, The Museums of Crane Point Hammock offers an educational look at area animals, marine life

(continued on p. 64)

Destination The Florida Keys

Blame Henry Flagler. He laid the track that became the roadbed that put the Keys in easy reach.

Now, millions visit. Some drop in, some drop out, some just drop anchor. And why not? With its warm breezes, top-notch water sports and weekend way of life, this enigmatic island chain is hard to resist.

Ernest Hemingway Home and Museum, Key West. Six-toed cats and gracious grounds complete a must-see scene at the famous author's former home. (See listing page 67)

Southernmost Point, Key West. Slip on your flip-flops and strike a pose—it's the landmark that lands in nearly every visitor's vacation-photo album. (See mention page 66)

Key
West

Sugarloaf
Key

Big
Pine
Key

Places included in this AAA Destination Area:

Conch Tour Trains, Key West.
Sit back, enjoy the sights and
learn a little about the locale on
a narrated tour through town.
(See listing page 67)

9336

1

*Key
Largo*

Islamorada

1

Marathon

Florida Keys

*John Pennekamp
Coral Reef State Park,
Key Largo.*
In addition to its
natural wonders,
this scuba diver's
delight also is home
to the serene statue
"Christ of the Deep."
(See listing page 66)

Key West Lighthouse Museum.
Climb the stairs if you dare,
or just enjoy the historical
exhibits and life-size lens that
accompany this 1847 structure.
(See listing page 68)

and ecosystems. If time allows, a kayak jaunt through the Florida Bay "backcountry" can provide a fascinating close-up glimpse of similar sights; rentals are readily available.

Marathon, in the Middle Keys, combines residential side roads, numerous fishing tournaments and several resorts ideal for tropical retreats, and the sunset's just as pretty from here.

Once over the Seven Mile Bridge, be sure to visit Bahia Honda State Park. A sandy beach and walkable segment of old bridge—providing incredible views of the new bridge—make this a must-see spot to stretch your legs *and* shift your perspective into "island time."

Back in the car now and heading to the Lower Keys, you're in the homestretch. Be sure to slow for the endangered Key deer in Big Pine Key; it's the law. Then prepare for the sameness of mangroves, scrub, Australian pines and power lines, sights whose monotony instills an antsy appetite for what lies ahead.

The feeling heightens as you close in on Key West proper. You may know you're there by the sound of Navy fighter jets shredding air overhead; Naval Air Station Key West, on nearby Boca Chica Key, is one of the Navy's premier pilot-training facilities. Or by the "T" where U.S. 1 hits Roosevelt Boulevard (and New Town's jumble of condos and commerce commences). Or perhaps it won't fully register till you've reached Old Town itself and done the obligatory "Duval crawl"—head swiveling from T-shirt shop to tavern to tree-shaded courtyard eatery.

However you reach it, once that mile-marker-zero mentality finally hits, you'll know The End of the Road—just like the sunset that closes every Key West day—is only the beginning of the bar-hopping, souvenir-shopping, conch-fritter-popping party more than a million visitors a year sojourn here to savor. On with the show.

Destinations in this region listed under their own names are Big Pine Key, Dry Tortugas National Park, Islamorada, Key Largo, Key West, Marathon and Sugarloaf Key.

BIG PINE KEY (I-10)
pop. 4,200, elev. 5′

Big Pine Key, between Marathon and Key West, is home to the Key deer, a miniature species maturing to the size of a large dog. By the 1950s hunting had almost annihilated this subspecies of the Virginia whitetail. With only 800 of the animals remaining, the deer still is an endangered species.

Many deer have collided with vehicles and been injured or killed. Visitors are asked to observe the speed limit and not pull over to feed or photograph deer, as doing so encourages them to approach the road.

Great White Heron and Key West national wildlife refuges also preserve area bird life. The Key West refuge also provides a safe haven for sea turtle nests. Both are accessible only by boat.

The headquarters for both wildlife refuges—in Big Pine Shopping Plaza, .5 miles north of US 1 on Key Deer Boulevard at mile marker 30.5 at the traffic light—is open Mon.-Fri. 8-5.

Many reefs and their undersea inhabitants are protected in the Florida Keys National Marine Sanctuary, at nearby Looe Key. Characterized by coral reefs and clear water, the sanctuary is a delight to divers. Snorkel and scuba trips can be arranged from Looe Key Diving Center on Ramrod Key at mile marker 27.5; phone (305) 872-2215 or (800) 942-5397.

Lower Keys Chamber of Commerce: P.O. Drawer 430511, Big Pine Key, FL 33043-0511; phone (305) 872-2411 or (800) 872-3722.

NATIONAL KEY DEER REFUGE, headquarters at mile marker 30.5 on US 1, is a designated sanctuary for the endangered diminutive deer. It encompasses approximately 2,300 acres. Blue Hole, 1.25 miles north of Key Deer and Watson boulevards, is a freshwater pond in a former quarry. It attracts such wildlife as alligators and turtles. A .7-mile self-guiding nature trail begins off Key Deer Boulevard, north of the Blue Hole, and winds through the refuge area. Early morning and evening hours are the best times to view the deer. Daily dawn-dusk. Free. Phone (305) 872-2239.

DRY TORTUGAS NATIONAL PARK (I-8)

Elevations in the land portion
of the park are at sea level. Most
of the park is water.

The seven Tortugas Keys, or Dry Tortugas Islands, and the surrounding waters in the Gulf of Mexico constitute Dry Tortugas National Park. Discovered by Ponce de León in 1513 and named Las Tortugas for their great number of turtles, the islands are called Dry Tortugas because they lack fresh water. The Tortugas are 68 nautical miles west of Key West.

For centuries the islands were inhabited by pirates who were protected from detection by passing vessels by the rocks and shallow waters. Lighthouses were built on Garden Key in 1825 and on Loggerhead Key in 1856. Discoveries of sunken Spanish treasure ships nearby bear witness to the shipwrecks that occurred along these shoals.

Strategically located between the United States and South America, the Tortugas attract many species of migratory birds. The most noted inhabitant is the sooty tern, which breeds on Bush Key between March and September. Another familiar inhabitant is the sea turtle, four endangered species of which nest in the park.

Access to the park is by boat or seaplane. Seaplanes of Key West Inc., in Key West International Airport, provides daily half- and full-day trips to Fort Jefferson in the park; reservations are required. The 40-minute low-altitude flights allow good views of marine life, shipwrecks and treasure-salvaging operations. Phone (800) 950-2359.

Fort Jefferson was begun on Garden Key in 1846, but after 30 years of construction it was still incomplete. Intended to protect vital shipping access to the Gulf, its 8-foot-thick walls and 450 guns were never tested. During the Civil War Federal troops occupied the fort, but by 1866 the introduction of rifled cannon and the fall of Fort Pulaski had made brick and masonry forts obsolete.

In 1861 Fort Jefferson became a prison for army deserters and in 1865 received the four "Lincoln Conspirators," condemned for their part in the assassination of President Abraham Lincoln. The fort was abandoned in 1874 following a hurricane and a second yellow fever outbreak. The Navy used it as the site for a wireless station in the early 1900s, then as a seaplane base in World War I. In 1935 President Franklin Roosevelt proclaimed the area a national monument.

Dry Tortugas National Park is open daily 24 hours. Fort open daily 9-5. Park free. A fee is charged for camping. A brief audiovisual presentation is available in the visitor center. Camping is permitted on the fort's grassy apron, and its shores lend themselves to swimming and snorkeling. No fresh water, food, fuel, supplies or public telephones are available. For further information contact the Superintendent, Everglades National Park, 40001 SR 9336, Homestead, FL 33034; phone (305) 242-7700. *See Recreation Chart.*

ISLAMORADA (I-11) pop. 1,200, elev. 5′

Islamorada (I-lah-mor-AH-dah) is a fishing resort spread over the islands of Lower Matecumbe Key, Plantation Key, Upper Matecumbe Key and Windley Key. Its purplish appearance from a distance caused the Spanish to call it the "purple isle" *(isla morada).* The wreck of the galleon *Herrera,* 2.5 miles off Whale Harbour Bridge, offers opportunities for underwater exploration and photography.

Indian Key State Historic Site, .5 mile southeast of Lower Matecumbe Key, is a 10-acre uninhabited island. This lavish paradise of notorious wrecker Capt. Jacob Housman was destroyed in 1840 when the captain's misuse of power prompted an Indian uprising. The ruins of houses and cisterns are now choked by vegetation planted by physician and botanist Dr. Henry Perrine, who conducted plant experiments at the settlement in 1838. The site is accessible only by

private or chartered boat. For information phone (305) 664-2540 or (800) 322-5397.

Lignumvitae Key State Botanical Site can be reached only by private or chartered boat from the marinas at the western end of Islamorada. Because of its high elevation and the sensitive management of former owner William Matheson, the island retains a singular plant community and is a fine example of a West Indian hardwood hammock. Indigenous and introduced trees blossom at various times but are best viewed in spring or early summer.

Matheson House, built of coral in 1919 and furnished in 1930s styles, remains unchanged. A stone wall, possibly built by Spanish explorers as a navigation aid, extends the length of the island. Walking shoes and mosquito repellent are musts. For information phone (305) 664-2540.

Islamorada Chamber of Commerce: P.O. Box 915, Islamorada, FL 33036; phone (305) 664-4503 or (800) 322-5397.

KEY LARGO (I-11) pop. 11,300, elev. 6′

At 30 miles, Key Largo is the longest of the Florida Keys. Linked to the mainland by the first of 42 bridges along the Overseas Highway—the scenic 113-mile section of US 1 between the Florida mainland and Key West—Key Largo introduces the lifestyle of the keys with its marinas and diving and tackle shops.

Key Largo Chamber of Commerce: 106000 Overseas Hwy., Key Largo, FL 33037; phone (305) 451-1414 or (800) 822-1088.

JOHN PENNEKAMP CORAL REEF STATE PARK, on US 1 at mile marker 102.5, combines a land area with 178 nautical miles of protected ocean waters. Features include a portion of a living coral reef and the underwater, 9-foot bronze statue, "Christ of the Deep," which can be viewed by snorkel or scuba tours. It also is possible to view the statue from a boat if water conditions are favorable.

A boardwalk provides access to a mangrove area. A visitor center displays aquariums and offers films and interpretive programs. Glass-bottom boat, sail-and-snorkel or snorkel tours, which range from 2.5 to 4 hours, are available.

Park open daily 8-dusk (weather permitting). Visitor center open daily 8-5. A 2.5-hour glass-bottom boat tour departs daily at 9:15, 12:15 and 3. A 2.5-hour snorkel tour departs daily at 9, noon and 3. The 4-hour sail-and-snorkel tour departs daily at 9 and 1:30. Visitors must be at the boat 1 hour before departure.

Admission $4 per private vehicle and driver plus 50c per person; $1.50 per person arriving by bicycle, bus or on foot. Glass-bottom boat tours $18; ages 3-11, $10. Snorkeling tour $24.95; under 18, $19.95. Sail-and-snorkel tour $31.95; under 18, $26.95. Reservations are recommended.

Phone (305) 451-1202, or (305) 451-1621 for tour information and reservations. *See Recreation Chart and the AAA Southeastern CampBook.*

MARITIME MUSEUM OF THE FLORIDA KEYS, 102670 US 1, at mile marker 102 across from John Pennekamp Coral Reef State Park *(see attraction listing),* exhibits objects recovered from sunken wrecks dating from the 17th century. Among artifacts is the rare Haskins Capitana Medallion, one of the oldest pieces found. A reconstruction of a shipwreck site illustrates underwater archeology as well as recovery techniques. Allow 1 hour minimum. Fri.-Mon. 10-4. Admission $5; over 55, $4.50; ages 6-12, $3. Phone (305) 451-6444.

CASINOS

• **Sun Cruz Casino Cruises**, on US 1 at Holiday Inn Key Largo Resort and Marina at mile marker 100. Departures Sun.-Thurs. at 2, 5, 7, 9 and 11 (last return to shore 2 a.m.), Fri.-Sat. 2-12:30 a.m. (last return to shore 3 a.m.). After the initial 2 p.m. sailing, guests are shuttled out to the ship on a water taxi. Phone (800) 474-3423.

KEY WEST (I-9) pop. 24,800, elev. 22′

To its rocky shores, sandy beaches and weathered homes reminiscent of a coastal New England town, Key West adds another feature: its subtropical climate, which nourishes lush vegetation, especially palm trees, hibiscus and bougainvillea. Ship carpenters, using wooden pegs instead of nails, built many of the older houses, which are predominantly Bahamian in architecture.

The southernmost city in the continental United States, Key West once served as a base of operation against pirates; today it is the southern terminus of the scenic Overseas Highway (US 1). The prosperity of mid-19th century Key West was based on the thriving salvage business. At one time these enterprises provided the town with the highest per capita income in the nation.

Because of its proximity to Havana, about 90 miles south, the town was later a haven for Cuban political exiles. San Carlos Institute on Duval Street dates from the late 19th century, when it was used as a meeting place for the local Cuban community. City Cemetery on Margaret Street is the gravesite of the victims of the USS *Maine,* whose sinking precipitated the Spanish-American War.

Home at various times to Ernest Hemingway, Tennessee Williams and Robert Frost, Key West remains a popular retreat for artists and writers.

Although turtle hunting was once a major industry, federal laws protecting the endangered reptiles were enacted in the 1970s. The remains of a turtle-canning factory stand behind Turtle Kraals Bar and Restaurant on the harborfront at the north end of Margaret Street.

Donkey Milk House Museum, 613 Eaton St., derives its name from the alley in back where donkeys used to pull milk delivery carts. The restored 1860s home is open by appointment only; phone (305) 296-1866.

Of Key West's many natural attractions, its sunsets are among the most popular. Every night, weather permitting, more than two dozen street vendors and performers gather at Mallory Square Dock in Old Town off Duval Street. Jugglers, palm readers, contortionists, musicians and other entertainers vie for the attention and donations of the many spectators who begin gathering about an hour before sunset.

Nature also puts on a show in the shady confines of Nancy Forrester's Secret Garden at 1 Free School Ln., off Simonton Street, where an extensive collection of rain forest plants creates a junglelike atmosphere complete with (caged) parrots; phone (305) 294-0015.

The Caribbean influence extends to the town's cuisine. Along Duval Street and its side streets, imaginative cafes and open-air restaurants serve foods ranging from gourmet specialties to ethnic snacks.

Various types of cruises, including those offering sailing, snorkeling and reef diving, depart from several private and city marinas. Deep-sea fishing trips leave from City Marina on Garrison Bight off Roosevelt Boulevard. Seaplanes of Key West Inc. provides transportation to Dry Tortugas National Park *(see place listing p. 64)*, 68 miles west.

Note: Parking regulations are strictly enforced throughout the city. There is no street parking available for recreational vehicles; follow signs to designated RV parking areas.

Key West Chamber of Commerce: Mallory Square, 402 Wall St., Key West, FL 33040; phone (305) 294-2587 or (800) 527-8539.

Self-guiding tours: Pelican Path—a route marked with pelican signs—leads visitors through historic Key West. A descriptive brochure outlining the tour and its sights can be picked up at the chamber of commerce.

SAVE **AUDUBON HOUSE AND GARDENS,** 205 Whitehead St., is where John James Audubon stayed while painting the wildlife of the Florida Keys in 1832. Chippendale furniture, a rare collection of porcelain birds and 1820 Staffordshire pottery are among the 18th- and 19th-century furnishings found in the restored home of noted harbor pilot and wrecker Capt. John Geiger. Original engravings by Audubon are displayed. Tours include the house and tropical gardens, which feature exotic native plants. Allow 1 hour minimum. Daily 9:30-5. Admission $8.50; ages 6-12, $3.50. AE, MC, VI. Phone (305) 294-2116.

GEM **CONCH TOUR TRAINS** leave from two depots—Mallory Square and 3850 N. Roosevelt Blvd. The 90-minute, 10-mile tour through old and new Key West features an informative narration about area history. Local points of interest along the tour include Old Town, Hemingway's house, Duval Street, Southernmost Point and the waterfront. Trains depart daily every half-hour 9-4:30. Fare $18; ages 4-12, $9. DS, MC, VI. Phone (305) 294-5161.

ERNEST HEMINGWAY HOME AND MUSEUM is at 907 Whitehead St. Hemingway bought the 1851 Spanish colonial-style mansion in 1931. Among works written here is "For Whom the Bell Tolls." The house, set in a lush tropical garden planted by the author, is home to more than 50 cats, descendants of Hemingway's felines. Of interest is the penny embedded in the concrete at the head of the pool—it supposedly was tossed there when Hemingway discovered the pool's $20,000 price tag. Allow 30 minutes minimum. Daily 9-5. Admission $7.50; ages 6-12, $4.50. AE, MC, VI. Phone (305) 294-1575.

FORT ZACHARY TAYLOR STATE HISTORIC SITE, at the s.w. end of the island via Southard St. past the Truman Annex, was built 1845-66 as part of Florida's coastal defense system. The cannons within the walls constitute one of the largest collections of Civil War armaments. Swimming, fishing and picnicking on a tropical beach are among the recreational activities available. Guided tours are available.

Allow 3 hours minimum. Daily 8-dusk. Tours are given daily at noon and 2. Admission $4 per vehicle (maximum eight people); $1.50 per person arriving by bicycle, bus or on foot. Phone (305) 292-6713. *See Recreation Chart.*

KEY WEST AQUARIUM, at the foot of Whitehead St. on Mallory Sq., was one of the first open-air aquariums when it opened in 1934. Shark and turtle feedings take place daily, and a touch tank lets visitors interact with the marine life. Guided tours are available. Allow 1 hour minimum. Daily 10-6. Admission $8; ages 4-12, $4. Phone (305) 296-2051.

KEY WEST LIGHTHOUSE MUSEUM, 938 Whitehead St., recounts Florida lighthouse history through exhibits featuring historical items, including a complete light assembly. The museum is in the former keeper's quarters. A spiral staircase leads to the top of the 1847 Key West Lighthouse. Allow 30 minutes minimum. Daily 9:30-4:30; closed Dec. 25. Admission $8; over 64, $6; ages 7-17, $4. AE, MC, VI. Phone (305) 294-0012.

KEY WEST SHIPWRECK HISTOREUM, 1 Whitehead St. in Old Mallory Square, is housed in a reproduction of the wreckers warehouse that originally stood on the site. Costumed actors interact with visitors and recreate the events of the wreck and salvage of the *Isaac Allerton,* which sank in 1856. Artifacts from the shipwreck are on display and videotapes are shown. A 65-foot observation tower provides a magnificent view of the Atlantic Ocean and the Gulf of Mexico. Allow 1 hour minimum. Daily 9:45-4:45. Admission $8; ages 4-12, $4. AE, DS, MC, VI. Phone (305) 292-8990.

SAVE **THE LIBERTY FLEET OF TALL SHIPS** departs from Hilton Resort and Marina, jct. Front and Greene sts. The schooner cruises around Key West and allows passengers the chance to steer and sail. Brunch and dinner cruises also are available. Cruises depart daily at 11, 2:30 and 6:30, Oct. 21-Memorial Day weekend. Fare for 11 and 2:30 cruises $25; under 12, $12.50. Fare for 6:30 cruise $35; under 12, $18. Reservations are required. DS, MC, VI. Phone (305) 292-0332.

LITTLE WHITE HOUSE MUSEUM, 111 Front St. inside the Truman Annex, is the vacation retreat that Presidents Harry Truman, Dwight Eisenhower and John F. Kennedy used during their administrations. The house has been restored to its 1948 appearance. A 10-minute videotape introduces visitors to Truman, and a 40-minute guided tour gives insight into both his experiences in Key West and his presidency. Allow 1 hour minimum. Daily 9-5. Admission $8; ages 6-12, $4. MC, VI. Phone (305) 294-9911.

MARTELLO TOWERS, on the south side of the island, are reached via SR A1A (S. Roosevelt Blvd.). The two brick fortifications were begun in 1858 by Union engineers to protect the defenses east of Fort Zachary Taylor.

East Martello Gallery and Museum, 3501 S. Roosevelt Blvd. at the airport entrance, exhibits Key West memorabilia relating to trade and the development of the island, including shipbuilding tools, treasure chests and boat models. The works of Mario Sanchez, a local artist and woodcarver, and metal sculpture by folk artist Stanley Papio are displayed. Allow 30 minutes minimum. Daily 9:30-5; closed Dec. 25. Admission $6; ages 7-12, $2. AE, MC, VI. Phone (305) 296-3913.

Key West Garden Center is on a county beach on Atlantic Blvd. and White St. Tropical plants grow among the ruins of the west tower. Tues.-Sat. 9:30-3:15. Donations. Phone (305) 294-3210.

MEL FISHER MARITIME MUSEUM, Greene and Front sts., displays both precious and functional artifacts recovered from the wreckage of two Spanish galleons. While en route to Spain from Havana, the ships sank 40 miles off Key West in a hurricane Sept. 6, 1622. Highlights of the collection include a 77.76-carat emerald as well as gold and silver religious objects. Informative exhibits illustrate techniques of underwater archeology. Allow 1 hour minimum. Daily 9:30-5. Admission $6.50; students with ID and ages 13-18, $4; ages 6-12, $2. AE, MC, VI. Phone (305) 294-2633.

OLD TOWN TROLLEY tours leave from Mallory Square downtown or can be joined at any of the 14 stops as the trolley tours the island. The 1-hour, 30-minute tours of old Key West provide a narrated introduction to the history, legends and geography of the island. Points of interest along the tour include Key West Aquarium, Duval Street and Ernest Hemingway's house. Frequent departures daily 8:56-4:30. Fare $18; ages 4-12, $9. Tickets include one full loop around the island. AE, DS, MC, VI. Phone (305) 296-6688.

SAVE **RIPLEY'S BELIEVE IT OR NOT! ODDITORIUM,** 527 Duval St. between Fleming and Southard, exhibits humorous and bizarre articles collected from around the world. Audiovisual presentations and films feature unusual stunts and people. Allow 1 hour minimum. Daily 9 a.m.-11 p.m. Admission $10.95; ages 4-12, $8.95. AE, DS, MC, VI. Phone (305) 293-9686.

STARS & STRIPES—KEY WEST, departing from Land's End Marina at Caroline and Margaret sts., offers trips aboard a 54-foot catamaran. A full-day excursion includes snorkeling and beachcombing as well as undersea viewing through the glass-bottomed hull. A 2-hour sunset cruise offers a full view of Key West's legendary sunsets; complimentary refreshments are served.

Full-day trip departs daily at 9:30. Sunset cruise departs daily; times vary according to season. Boarding is 30 minutes before departure. Full-day fare (includes snorkel gear, instruction and food) $75; ages 7-17, $40. Sunset sail $35; ages 7-17, $17.50. Reservations are recommended. AE, MC, VI. Phone (305) 294-7877 or (800) 634-6369.

WRECKERS' MUSEUM/OLDEST HOUSE, 322 Duval St., is said to be the oldest house in south Florida. The construction of the 1829 house includes horizontal wall boards, a ship's hatch in the roof and the "landlubber's tilt" in the office. Furnished with American antiques, the house contains maritime documents, ship models, undersea artifacts and displays about the history of 19th-century ship wrecking. The garden has a separate cookhouse and an exhibit pavilion. Allow 30 minutes minimum. Daily 10-4. Admission $5; ages 3-12, $1. DS. Phone (305) 294-9502.

RECREATIONAL ACTIVITIES
Fishing
- **Déjà Vu Custom Charters**, departs from Land's End Marina at the end of Margaret St. Write 815 Catherine St., Key West, FL 33040. Other activities are offered. Full- and half-day excursions depart daily. Phone (305) 294-9560.

MARATHON (I-10) pop. 8,900

Marathon Key, named for the lament of an East Coast Railroad engineer when told to continue the line still farther, is the commercial and sport fishing center of the Middle Keys.

MUSEUMS OF CRANE POINT HAMMOCK, gulfside at mile marker 50.5, features models of marine life, animals and birds in naturalistic settings. Also on site are a children's area with touch tanks and a model ship's deck, nature trails and an early Bahamian homestead. Allow 1 hour minimum. Mon.-Sat. 10-4:15, Sun. noon-4:15. Tours are given Mon.-Thurs. at 10, 11, 1:30 and 2:30, Fri. at 10 and 11. Admission $7.50; over 65, $6; students with ID $4; under 7 free. Phone (305) 743-9100.

SUGARLOAF KEY (I-9)

Sugarloaf Key gained its name from the sugarloaf pineapples once grown in the area. Just north of US 1 at the airport entrance is Bat Tower, an island landmark and a monument to a futile attempt to manipulate nature. Built in 1929 by fishing resort owner R.C. Perky, the tower was to become home to a colony of bats intended to feed on the resident mosquito population; once the bats were released they flew away, and the mosquitoes remained.

This ends listings for The Florida Keys.
The following page resumes the alphabetical listings
of cities in Florida.

Fort Lauderdale

Honeycombed by rivers, bays, inlets and canals, Fort Lauderdale is a city of islands, where the boat rivals the automobile as a mode of transportation. One-tenth of the city surface is water; 165 miles of navigable waters provide either home or temporary port for boats of all sizes. The city's abundance of waterways bolsters its claim of having the country's largest yacht basin.

Fort Lauderdale is primarily residential; with the exception of the waterfront and beach areas, it does not give the appearance of a resort community. The canals and waterways furnish a striking setting for many beautiful homes, the most lavish of which are east of US 1. However, residential does not necessarily mean sedate—Fort Lauderdale's clubs and discotheques offer a flourishing nightlife.

Although settled in 1838 by Maj. William Lauderdale, the resort did not begin to grow until after its incorporation in 1911. In Fort Lauderdale proper almost all hotels, motels and stores are just west of SR A1A. The beach to the east provides a 3-mile-long strip of sand that has proven to be one of Fort Lauderdale's foremost attractions.

Miles of lagoons, waterways and beaches make Fort Lauderdale one of the most popular areas on the Gold Coast.

In addition to being a leading resort area, Fort Lauderdale also is an active commercial center. The marine industry and citrus groves play important roles. Port Everglades, 2 miles south, has one of the deepest harbors south of Norfolk, Va. The 10 modern terminals provide facilities for Caribbean-bound luxury liners as well as for the handling of millions of tons of cargo each year.

Approaches
By Car

SR A1A, US 1, Florida's Turnpike (toll), I-95 and US 441 are the major approaches to Fort Lauderdale from the north, while I-75/I-595 is the major western approach. The roads are well-marked; the only trouble drivers might have is with US 1, variously posted as US 1 and Federal Highway. Downtown this route is known as N.E. or S.E. Sixth Avenue.

Getting Around
Street System

The street plan of Fort Lauderdale is a fairly simple grid. Broward Boulevard and Andrews Avenue divide

the city into quadrants (N.E., S.W., etc.). Boulevards, courts, drives and streets run east and west; avenues, terraces and ways run north and south.

The speed limit is 25 mph or as posted. Do not try to follow an unfamiliar route during rush hours (7 to 9 a.m. and 4:30 to 6 p.m.) or during lunch time.

Parking

Parking on downtown streets is metered; there are ample lots at rates of 75c per hour. Municipal parking in the beach areas costs $3-$6 per day. No parking is available along SR A1A. Parking along side streets costs 25c-75c per hour.

What To See

BONNET HOUSE, 900 N. Birch Rd., just s. of Sunrise Blvd., is a 35-acre beachfront estate that was the winter home of two artists, Frederic and Evelyn Bartlett. Built during the 1920s, the estate features lagoons, gardens and an art gallery. Also of note are pieces of artwork and hand-painted ceilings created by the Bartletts. Allow 1 hour, 30 minutes minimum. Tours given Wed.-Fri. 10-1:30, Sat.-Sun. noon-2:30; closed holidays. Schedule may vary; phone ahead. Admission $9; over 60, $8; ages 6-18, $7. AE, MC, VI. Phone (954) 563-5393.

FORT LAUDERDALE HISTORICAL MUSEUM, 231 S.W. Second Ave., houses local artifacts from the Seminole Wars period to the present and includes an extensive photograph collection. The changing exhibits, archives and library offer information about local and regional history. Historical walking, river and city bus tours are offered; a fee is charged. Allow 1 hour minimum. Tues.-Sat. 10-5, Sun. noon-5; closed Jan. 1, Thanksgiving and Dec 25. Admission $4; ages 7-12, $2. Phone (954) 463-4431.

INTERNATIONAL SWIMMING HALL OF FAME is 1 blk. s. of Las Olas Blvd., just w. of SR A1A at 1 Hall of Fame Dr. The hall highlights the achievements of notable swimmers and contains aquatic artifacts dating to the 15th century. An art gallery features aquatic art from around the world. The Hall of Fame swimming pools adjoin the museum.

Allow 1 hour minimum. Museum daily 9-7. Art gallery Mon.-Fri. 9-5. Pool daily 8-4 (also Mon.-Fri. 6-8 p.m.); closed during swim meets. Museum and art gallery admission $3; over 55, $1; under 12 free; family rate $5. Pool $3; senior citizens, military and students with ID $2. Parking $1 per hour. Phone (954) 462-6536, or (954) 468-1580 for the pool.

MUSEUM OF ART, 1 E. Las Olas Blvd., features a permanent collection of 20th-century European and American art including works by Moore, Picasso, Stella and Warhol. The museum also contains an

(continued on p. 74)

The Informed Traveler

City Population: 149,400

Elevation: 7 ft.

Sales Tax: The sales tax in Broward County is 6 percent. A tourist development tax of 5 percent is levied on rental accommodations.

WHOM TO CALL

Emergency: 911

Police (non-emergency): (954) 761-5700; sheriff (954) 765-4321.

Fire: (954) 761-5700

Time and Temperature: (954) 748-4444

Hospitals: Broward General Medical Center, (954) 355-4400; Imperial Point Medical Center, (954) 776-8500.

WHERE TO LOOK

Newspapers

The Fort Lauderdale *Sun Sentinel* is published daily. The daily *Miami Herald* is available throughout the city. Many weekly publications supplement these papers.

Radio

Fort Lauderdale radio station WINZ (940 AM) is an all-news/weather station; WLRN (91.3 FM) is a member of National Public Radio.

Visitor Information

The Greater Fort Lauderdale Chamber of Commerce distributes maps, brochures and a variety of other local information Mon.-Fri. 8-5. For further information contact the chamber at 512 N.E. Third Ave., Fort Lauderdale, FL 33301; phone (954) 462-6000.

The Greater Fort Lauderdale Convention and Visitors Bureau *(see card insert)*, open Mon.-Fri. 8:30-5, is at 1850 Eller Dr., Suite 303; phone (954) 765-4466 or (800) 356-1662, events hotline (954) 357-5700. The Fort Lauderdale Parks and Recreation events hotline is (954) 761-5363.

TRANSPORTATION

Air Travel

The Fort Lauderdale-Hollywood International Airport is between I-95 and US 1, just south of SR 84. Friendly Checker Cab, (954) 923-2302, provides service to the airport from downtown; the fare is approximately $10.

Rental Cars

Hertz, 3030 Holiday Dr. in Marriott Harbor Beach Hotel, (800) 654-3080, and at the airport, (954) 764-1199 or (800) 654-3080, offers discounts to AAA members. Many car rental agencies are listed in the telephone directory.

Rail Service

The Amtrak station is at 200 S.W. 21st Terr. For arrival information phone (954) 587-6692; for reservations and other information phone (800) 872-7245.

Buses

The bus terminal serving the city is Greyhound Lines Inc., 513 N.E. Third St.; phone (954) 764-6551, or (800) 231-2222 for schedule and rate information.

Taxis

Cabs are plentiful. Fares are metered and are $2.45 for the first mile and $1.75 for each additional mile. The largest company is Yellow Cab, (954) 565-5400; consult the telephone directory for others.

Public Transport

Broward County Transportation Authority, (954) 357-8400, provides transportation to all sections of Fort Lauderdale and its outlying areas. Buses also are available between the downtown area and the beach. Free shuttle buses operate downtown on weekdays; for information phone (954) 761-3543.

Destination Ft. Lauderdale

*C*asual and laid-back. Sophisticated and energetic. Contradictory terms, but all appropriate for describing Fort Lauderdale.

*B*reezy resortwear is perfect for a day at the beach, a riverfront stroll or a museum visit. Or indulge in a little haute couture, fast-paced jai alai or Thoroughbred action. Set your own style and pace in Fort Lauderdale.

Riverwalk, Fort Lauderdale.
Lushly landscaped, this 1.5-mile-long park downtown along the New River is lined with restaurants, shops and museums. (See listing page 74)

Las Olas shopping, Fort Lauderdale.
You can shop 'til you drop (or just window shop) at the boulevard's fashionable boutiques and galleries.

Butterfly World, Coconut Creek. Colorful free-flying butterflies issue a fluttering welcome to visitors. (See listing page 77)

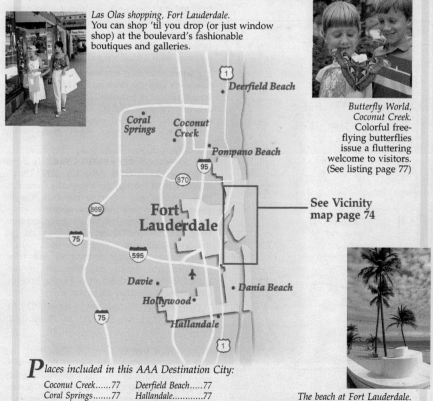

See Vicinity map page 74

The beach at Fort Lauderdale.
Palm trees and decorative street lamps line Fort Lauderdale's beachfront promenade.

*P*laces included in this AAA Destination City:

extensive collection of American Impressionist William Glacken's works as well as art from the CoBrA movement and important African, South Pacific and contemporary Cuban art.

Allow 2 hours minimum. Tues.-Sat. 10-5 (also Fri. 5-8), Sun. noon-5; closed holidays. Admission $10; over 64, $8; students ages 19-25 with ID $6; ages 6-18, $2. Parking is available for a fee in nearby City Garage. An additional fee may be charged for special exhibits. Phone (954) 525-5500.

[SAVE] **MUSEUM OF DISCOVERY AND SCIENCE AND BLOCKBUSTER IMAX 3D THEATER,** 401 S.W. Second St., is a hands-on science center featuring seven interactive exhibit areas. Gizmo City offers visitors a chance to play virtual volleyball and explore the Internet. Florida EcoScapes, focusing on the state's native ecology, has live sea turtles, sharks, alligators and an Atlantic coral reef. The Discovery Center offers a scientific playground for young children, while Space Base features a manned maneuvering unit (MMU) ride that simulates a space flight.

No Place Like Home is a cutaway of a house designed to explore issues of construction and conservation. The Sound exhibit illustrates the principles of sound and hearing. Choose Health presents the facts about nutrition, drugs and the human body. The Great Gravity Clock is a 52-foot-tall kinetic energy sculpture. Traveling exhibits also are featured. The 300-seat Blockbuster IMAX 3D Theater presents films on a five-story screen; headsets enhance the experience. Food is available.

Allow 2 hours minimum. Mon.-Sat. 10-5, Sun. noon-6; closed Dec. 25. IMAX shows are presented daily; schedule varies with each film. Museum admission $6; over 64 and ages 3-12, $5. Theater admission $9; over 64, $8; ages 3-12, $7; no charge for babies held on an adult's lap. Combination ticket $12.50; over 64, $11.50; ages 3-12, $10.50. Metered parking is available. AE, MC, VI. Phone (954) 467-6637 for museum or 463-4629 for theater.

RIVERWALK, downtown, is a multifaceted promenade along the New River featuring tropical landscaping and interactive displays. A weather station displays a barometer and rain gauges, while a gazebo holds a telescope and kaleidoscope.

Plaques describing renowned scientists and astronomers ring the lawn area, which contains a human sundial in its center. Of particular interest are the "whisper dishes," satellite-like dishes that amplify whispered messages from 25 feet away. Daily 24 hours. Free. Phone (954) 468-1541.

[SAVE] **SAWGRASS RECREATION PARK** is 2 mi. n. of jct. I-75 at 5400 US 27N. Thirty-minute airboat tours of the Everglades feature an environmental and historical narration. Guides point out native flora and fauna; alligators sometimes can be seen. An Indian guide explains tribal customs and history as visitors are led through a replica of a typical Seminole village with clothing, musical instruments and other tribal artifacts. Snakes and alligators are displayed in separate exhibit areas. Fishing licenses, guides and boat rentals are available.

Daily 9-5. Admission $15; over 60, $13.50; ages 4-12, $7.15. AE, DS, MC, VI. Phone (954) 389-0202, 426-2474 or (800) 457-0788.

STRANAHAN HOUSE is at Las Olas Blvd. and S.E. Sixth Ave. Owned by one of Fort Lauderdale's founding families, this 1901 building has served as a trading post, restaurant and private home. Guided tours are available. Events are held throughout the year. Allow 30 minutes minimum. Wed.-Sat. 10-4, Sun. 1-4; closed major holidays. Guided tours are given on the hour. Last tour begins 30 minutes before closing. Admission $5; under 12, $2. Phone (954) 524-4736.

© AAA

FORT LAUDERDALE

To West Palm Beach

Scale in Miles   0 — 1.5
Scale in Kilometers   0 — 2.4

2068-H

What To Do

Sightseeing

Boat Tours

[SAVE] Discovery Cruise Line, in Port Everglades, offers day cruises. Food, casino gambling and entertainment are featured. Departures all year; times vary. Phone (800) 937-4477 in Fla. or (800) 866-8687 out of Fla.

SeaEscape offers 1-day cruises; phone (954) 925-9700.

Sightseeing cruises along the Intracoastal Waterway and the New River are available aboard the Water Taxi. The taxis also offer transportation to restaurants, hotels, shops and attractions. For schedules and information phone (954) 467-6677.

JUNGLE QUEEN SIGHTSEEING CRUISE, s. side of Bahia-Mar Yacht Basin on SR A1A, offers a 3-hour sightseeing cruise down the New River past luxurious homes and downtown Fort Lauderdale. A dinner/entertainment cruise also is available. Cruises depart daily at 10 and 2; closed Dec. 25. Fare $11.50; ages 2-10, $7.75. Reservations are required. Phone (954) 462-5596. *See color ad.*

RIVERFRONT CRUISES, New River dock at Las Olas Riverfront Marketplace, 1 blk. w. of Andrews Ave., offers a 90-minute cruise along the New River and Intracoastal Waterway to the mansion-lined canals nicknamed "The Venice of America." Cruises depart daily at 10:30, 12:30, 2:30, 4:30, 6:30 and 8:30 (also Sat.-Sun. at 10:30 p.m.). Fare $14; ages 4-10, $8. AE, MC, VI. Phone (954) 267-3699.

Sports and Recreation

Fort Lauderdale has a public beach and excellent inland and ocean **fishing** waters. Many species of fish are caught in the "inside" waters, and the deep-sea fishing ranks with the best in Florida. Fishing boats can be rented at Bahia-Mar, Marina del Americana and Pier 66. Area piers are good spots for fishing; bait, tackle and food are available.

Boating is another popular sport. There are numerous canals to be explored, and sailing around the barrier islands is a favorite pastime. Most marinas rent boats.

Scuba diving is rewarding along three lines of reefs, where clear water permits views of sea fans, branched coral and tropical fish. Many firms offer instruction and rental equipment; consult the telephone directory.

Water skiing is popular on the city's protected waterways and canals. The McGinnis School, 2421 S.W. 46th Ave., offers instruction; phone (954) 321-0221.

Landlubbers may enjoy the many recreation programs offered at most of the community centers. Activities range from bridge for beginners to instruction in shellcraft. For a schedule phone the Parks and Recreation Department at (954) 761-5383.

The Baltimore Orioles head south each year for **baseball** spring training in Fort Lauderdale. **Hockey** comes to sunny South Florida in October when the Florida Panthers of the National Hockey League take to the ice at National Car Rental Center in Sunrise; phone (954) 835-7000, or 835-8326 for tickets.

Golf in the area is excellent. Most courses are semiprivate, with play governed by local regulations. Many hotels have agreements allowing guests to play on certain courses; check with your hotel manager.

Tennis is popular throughout the area; many hotels and motels have their own courts. Supplementing these are the public courts at George English Park, 1101 Bayview Dr., (954) 396-3620; Holiday Park, 701 N.E. 12th Ave., (954) 761-5378; and Joseph C. Carter Park, 1450 W. Sunrise Blvd., (954) 761-5411.

Shopping

Broward County shopping is diverse and plentiful. The two-story Galleria, 2414 E. Sunrise Blvd., features 150 shops including anchors Burdines, Dillard's, Lord & Taylor, Neiman Marcus and Saks Fifth Avenue. In nearby Plantation are Broward Mall, University Drive and Broward Boulevard, and Fashion Mall at Plantation, 321 N. University Dr. Lauderhill Mall, US 441 and N.W. 40th Avenue, is in Lauderhill.

Offerings in the northern suburbs include Coral Square Mall, 9469 W. Atlantic Blvd. in Coral Springs, and Pembroke Lakes Mall, 11401 Pines Blvd. in Pembroke Pines. South of the city is Oakwood Plaza, 2900 Oakwood Blvd. in Hollywood.

The shops along Las Olas Boulevard between Federal Highway and the beach offer a unique experience. Specialty shops line US 1 at both the north and south entrances to the city.

DID YOU KNOW

Harriet Beecher Stowe, author of *Uncle Tom's Cabin*, had a winter home on the St. John's River 1867-84.

More than 270 outlet stores comprise Sawgrass Mills, 12801 W. Sunrise Blvd. in Sunrise.

True bargain hunters may enjoy the Swap Shop, 3291 W. Sunrise Blvd. The 80-acre flea market features more than 2,000 vendors with wares ranging from brand-name electronics to antiques.

Theater and Concerts

Parker Playhouse, in Holiday Park at US 1 and N.E. Eighth Street, offers Broadway shows from Nov. 15 through May 1; phone (954) 763-2444. Sunrise Musical Theater, at Commercial Boulevard and N.W. 95th Avenue in Sunrise, operates daily. Tickets vary with the performer and the presentation; phone (954) 741-7300.

Broward Center for the Performing Arts, 201 S.W. Fifth Ave. on the New River, is the setting for events including ballet, opera, Broadway shows, children's theater and concerts; phone (954) 522-5334 or 462-0222.

War Memorial Auditorium, at 800 N.E. Eighth St. in Holiday Park, seats 2,100 people. Plays, operas, concerts, sports events and exhibitions are presented throughout the year; phone (954) 761-5380.

Broward County supports an opera company, symphony orchestra and ballet, as well as other dance and musical programs. For performance information contact the Arts and Entertainment Hotline, (954) 357-5700, or (800) 249-2787 out of Fla.

Special Events

During January and February artists from across North America show their efforts at the Las Olas Art Fair. Canada Fest and Florida Renaissance Festival are held during February. In mid-February the Seminole Tribal Fair takes place in nearby Hollywood.

March brings the PGA Honda Golf Classic and Art on the Boulevard. The Fort Lauderdale Spring Boat Show and the Fort Lauderdale Seafood Festival are held in April.

The Fort Lauderdale Air & Sea Show, featuring demonstrations of military aircraft along 4 miles of the city's beachfront, takes place in early May. The Pompano Fishing Rodeo also is in May.

The Riverwalk Fall Arts Show takes place in October. The Fort Lauderdale International Boat Show is held in late October and early November. During the Fort Lauderdale International Film Festival in November celebrities flock to town to preview films from around the globe.

Also in November is the Riverwalk Blues Festival, a 2-day event featuring local and nationally known blues artists; and the Hollywood Jazz Festival. Mid-November through January Tradewinds Park dresses up for the Holiday Fantasy of Lights.

On a mid-December Saturday yachts at Port Everglades don holiday lights in preparation for a night's cruise up the Intercoastal Waterway—the spectacular and festive Winterfest Boat Parade. For further event information phone (954) 767-0686.

The Fort Lauderdale Vicinity

COCONUT CREEK (G-11)
pop. 29,200, elev. 17′

BUTTERFLY WORLD, in Tradewinds Park South at 3600 W. Sample Rd., includes a breeding laboratory, a butterfly museum and an insectarium with displays of unusual insects and butterflies from around the world. Also featured are a botanical vine walk and an English rose garden. Two-story aviaries present gardens and a simulated tropical rain forest in which butterflies live restricted only by the buildings' screen construction.

Allow 1 hour minimum. Mon.-Sat. 9-5, Sun. 1-5; closed Thanksgiving and Dec. 25. Last admission 1 hour before closing. Admission $12.95; ages 4-12, $7.95 Park entrance fee on weekends and holidays $1 per person. AE, MC, VI. Phone (954) 977-4400.

CORAL SPRINGS (G-11) pop. 79,400

[SAVE] **CORAL SPRINGS MUSEUM OF ART,** off SR 868 exit 8, 1.5 mi. e. on Sample Rd., then .5 mi. n. to 2855 Coral Springs Dr., displays paintings, sculpture and mixed-media works by local and regional artists. Allow 1 hour minimum. Tues.-Sat. 10-5, Sun. noon-5. Admission $3, under 18 free. AE, MC, VI. Phone (954) 340-5000.

DANIA BEACH (G-12)
pop. 13,000, elev. 11′

Dania Beach is a winter beach resort. Jai alai is played year-round at Dania Jai Alai Fronton on Dania Beach Boulevard, one-half mile east of US 1; for schedule phone (954) 927-2841.

Note: Policies vary concerning admittance of children to pari-mutuel betting facilities. Phone for information.

Shopping areas: Antique hunters will find remembrances of early Americana in the shops along Federal Highway.

[SAVE] **GRAVES MUSEUM OF ARCHAEOLOGY AND NATURAL HISTORY,** 2.5 mi. e. of I-95 exit 24 on SR 822 (Sheridan St.), then .7 mi. n. on US 1 (Federal Hwy.) to 481 S. Federal Hwy., features a wide array of artifacts, fossils and other objects including remains of a rare Bambiraptor dinosaur, African tribal art, South Florida minerals, pre-Columbian ceramics and salvage from shipwrecks. Allow 2 hours minimum. Tues.-Sat. 10-4 (also Sat. 4-6), Sun. noon-6. Admission $7; senior citizens and students with ID $6 only on Tues.; ages 4-12, $5. AE, MC, VI. Phone (954) 925-7770, ext. 212.

DAVIE (G-11) pop. 49,700, elev. 5′

BUEHLER PLANETARIUM, on the central campus of Broward Community College, 1 mi. s. of I-595 at 3501 S.W. Davie Rd., offers programs with time and space travel themes. Allow 1 hour minimum. Main features Fri.-Sat. at 7 p.m. Family features Sat.-Sun. at 1:30 and 3. Phone ahead for laser light show schedule. Doors to the shows close on time. Main feature tickets $5; family show tickets $4. For information phone (954) 475-6680.

FLAMINGO GARDENS, w. on I-595 to exit 2, then 3 mi. s. to 3750 Flamingo Rd., contains trees indigenous to subtropical forests throughout the world. A 1.5-acre free-flight aviary features a large collection of wading birds. Other features include a wetlands area, Flamingo Island Habitat, a crocodile lagoon, the Wray Historical Home, a tropical plant house and a 1.5-mile narrated tram ride through hammocks, wetlands and citrus groves.

Allow 2 hours, 30 minutes minimum. Daily 9:30-5:30, Oct.-May; Tues.-Sun. 9:30-5:30, rest of year. Last tram ride leaves 1 hour, 30 minutes before closing. Admission $10; over 65, $8; ages 4-11, $5.50. Tram $2; ages 4-11, $1. Phone (954) 473-2955.

YOUNG AT ART CHILDREN'S MUSEUM is off I-595 exit 3, then just s. to 11584 SR 84. Geared to children 2-11, this hands-on museum includes a recycled-arts center where kids make sculptures from donated materials, a music space, finger-painting center, multicultural "village" and toddler play area. Mon.-Sat. 10-5, Sun. noon-5. Admission $4; over 60, $3.50; under 2 free. MC, VI. Phone (954) 424-0085.

DEERFIELD BEACH (G-12)
pop. 46,300, elev. 16′

QUIET WATERS COUNTY PARK, 401 S. Powerline Rd., is 2 mi. w. from I-95 via SR 810 (Hillsboro Blvd.), then .25 mi. s. on SR 845 (Powerline Rd.). Within its 427 acres this water-oriented park offers canoeing, paddleboating, swimming, camping, picnicking, bicycling and a mechanical water ski tow. For tow schedule and prices phone (954) 429-0215. Daily 8-7:30, Apr.-Sept.; 8-6, rest of year. Park admission Mon.-Fri. free; Sat.-Sun. and holidays $1 for vehicle driver and per passenger over age 4. Phone (954) 360-1315. *See Recreation Chart.*

HALLANDALE (H-12)
pop. 31,000, elev. 10′

Primarily a retirement community, Hallandale is the home of Gulfstream Park and the Hollywood Greyhound Dog Track. The dog track presents races December through May; phone (954) 454-9400. Gulfstream Park, at US 1 and Hallandale Beach Boulevard, is open for horse racing from early January to mid-March; phone (954) 454-7000.

Note: Policies vary concerning admittance of children to pari-mutuel betting facilities. Phone for information.

HOLLYWOOD (G-12)
pop. 121,700, elev. 7'

A resort and residential city north of Miami, Hollywood is bordered with palm-lined ocean beaches. The municipal bandshell in Young Circle Park and Theater Under the Stars offer free evening entertainment throughout the year. The Broward County Brian Piccolo Velodrome in nearby Cooper City consists of two tracks: one for competitive bicycle racing and one for recreational riding and in-line skating; phone or (954) 437-2626.

Greater Hollywood Chamber of Commerce: 330 N. Federal Hwy., Hollywood, FL 33020; phone (954) 923-4000 or (800) 231-5562.

ANN KOLB NATURE CENTER is off I-95 exit 24, then 2.8 mi. e. to 751 Sheridan St. The center has nature trails, interactive bird-call displays and an observation tower overlooking a mangrove estuary. An exhibit hall houses a research center and three aquariums. Allow 1 hour minimum. Park open Mon.-Fri. 8-5:30. Exhibit hall open Mon.-Fri. 9-5. Admission $3; ages 6-12, $1.50. Phone (954) 926-2415.

ART AND CULTURE CENTER OF HOLLYWOOD, 1650 Harrison St., presents exhibits of sculpture, photography, jewelry and antiques as well as cul-

tural and educational programs. Short plays and concerts are presented occasionally. Allow 1 hour minimum. Tues.-Sat. 10-4, Sun. 1-4; closed holidays. Admission $3. Phone (954) 921-3275.

POMPANO BEACH (G-12)
pop. 72,400, elev. 13'

Settled in 1880 and named for a local fish, Pompano Beach is known for its abundant sunshine and variety of recreational opportunities. Tourism became the city's focus in the 1920s after the Dixie Highway was completed. Warmed by the Gulf Stream, Pompano Beach is a popular resort. The city has approximately 20 parks, many of which are equipped for tennis, softball and swimming.

Horse racing takes place at Pompano Park Racing, west of I-95 on Powerline Road (Race Track Road), October through August; phone (954) 972-2000.

Note: Policies vary concerning admittance of children to pari-mutuel betting facilities. Phone for information.

Greater Pompano Beach Chamber of Commerce: 2200 E. Atlantic Blvd., Pompano Beach, FL 33062; phone (954) 941-2940.

Shopping areas: Pompano Square Mall, 1 Pompano Sq. at the corner of Federal Highway and Copans Road, counts Burdines, JCPenney and Sears among its 100 stores. Festival Flea Market, 2900 W. Sample Rd. in Pompano, offers more than 600 vendors selling bargains Wednesday through Sunday.

This ends listings for the Fort Lauderdale Vicinity.
The following page resumes the alphabetical listings
of cities in Florida.

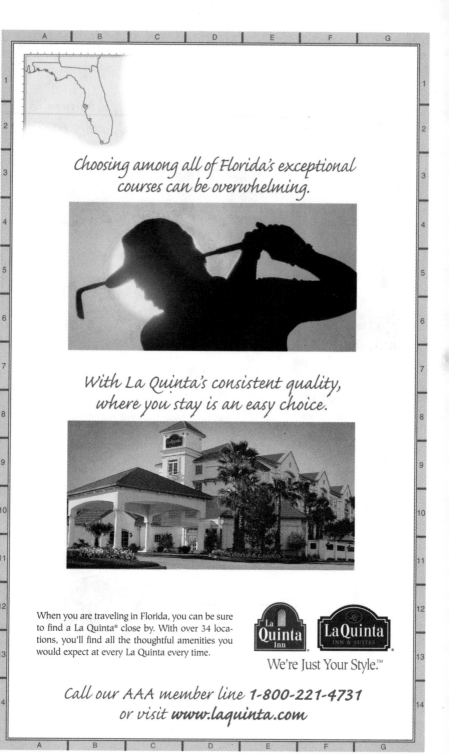

No matter where the road takes you, you'll be sure to find generous rooms at every La Quinta®, every time.

Show Your Card & Save

AAA. Everyday.
14-yr partner

100% satisfaction guarantee
Guaranteed lowest rate
100% AAA three-diamond rating

With so many locations in the area, AAA members can enjoy La Quinta® hospitality in all the best places. You can be sure to find a relaxing place to stay, filled with all the thoughtful amenities you would expect. And more.

- Free local calls
- Free breakfast and in-room coffeemakers
- 25" TVs with movies on demand and Nintendo®
- Sparkling swimming pools
- Children 18 and under stay free in parents' room

- More deluxe Inn & Suites also offer king rooms and two-room suites with microwaves and refrigerators
- Spas and fitness centers

We're Just Your Style.™

Call our AAA member line 1-800-221-4731 or visit www.laquinta.com

FORT MATANZAS NATIONAL MONUMENT (B-10)

Fort Matanzas National Monument includes the southern tip of Anastasia Island and the northern third of Rattlesnake Island. The fort from which the monument took its name is on Rattlesnake Island, off SR A1A 14 miles south of St. Augustine. There is ferry service to the fort every hour on the half hour daily 9:30-4:30; to determine if the ferry is operating phone (904) 471-0116. The fort can be seen from the dock on Anastasia Island.

Built of coquina 1740-42 by the Spaniards, Fort Matanzas replaced temporary watch stations that had guarded the southern approach to St. Augustine since 1569. During the 16th century French Huguenots established bases in the area, threatening the Spaniards with territorial encroachment and what the latter considered to be religious heresy. The fort became United States property in 1821.

In 1565 Pedro Menéndez de Avilés set up his headquarters at what later became known as St. Augustine; in a hurricane which scattered the French ships, he captured the enemy base about 35 miles north of St. Augustine. Upon returning to St. Augustine, Menéndez located the shipwrecked survivors of the French fleet some 14 miles south of town, where most of them surrendered and were killed. This engagement led the Spaniards to christen it the site of *matanzas,* or "slaughters."

A small visitor center on Anastasia Island contains exhibits pertaining to the fort's history. Swimming east of SR A1A at Matanzas Inlet is dangerous because of the currents. Grounds open daily 8:30-5:30. Visitor center open daily 9-4:30. Closed Dec. 25. Free. Phone (904) 471-0116.

FORT MYERS (G-9)
pop. 45,200, elev. 9′

Majestic royal palms line the streets of Fort Myers, a city with more than 70 varieties of palms and a profusion of exotic flowers and tropical fruit. March through early April Fort Myers is the spring training home of the Boston Red Sox and the Minnesota Twins. The Red Sox play exhibition games at City of Palms Park, 2201 Edison Ave.; phone (941) 334-4700. The Twins play their games at Lee County Sports Complex off Daniels Road and Six Mile Cypress; phone (941) 768-4270 or (800) 338-9467.

Another sporting option is the Florida Everblades, who play their East Coast Hockey League home games at Everblades Arena, at I-75 exit 19 (Corkscrew Road); phone (941) 948-7825. The hockey season is mid-October through April.

The City Yacht Basin area is the town's boating center. Boating is popular on the Caloosahatchee River; a tropical cruise leaves from the yacht basin regularly.

During colder months, the Orange River is frequented by manatees. At Lee County Manatee Park, off I-75 exit 25 then 1.5 miles east to 10901 S.R. 80, an observation platform and education programs allow visitors to learn more about these gentle creatures; phone (941) 694-3537 for updates on best viewing times.

Greater Fort Myers Chamber of Commerce: 2310 Edwards Dr., P.O. Box 9289, Fort Myers, FL 33902; phone (941) 332-3624 or (800) 366-3622.

Shopping areas: Edison Mall, 4125 Cleveland Ave. (US 41), features Burdines, Dillard's, JCPenney and Sears among its 155 stores. Bell Tower Shops, 13499 US 41 S.E., includes Saks Fifth Avenue and upscale boutiques. Royal Palm Square, 1400 Colonial Blvd., offers many boutiques and restaurants. Outlet shoppers will find more than 55 stores at Tanger Sanibel Factory Stores, between McGregor Boulevard and Summerlin Road, and more than 45 shops at Miromar Outlets, I-75 and Corkscrew Road (exit 19).

BURROUGHS HOME, Fowler and First sts. (SR 80) at 2505 First St., is a riverside home built in 1901 for a wealthy businessman. Of Georgian Revival architecture, the three-story home is furnished with original family pieces. Tour guides portray characters from the history of Fort Myers. Allow 30 minutes minimum. Tours are given on the hour. Tues.-Fri. 11-3, Dec.-May; by appointment only, rest of year. Admission $6; ages 6-12, $3. Free parking is available at the adjacent Amtel Marina Hotel. Phone (941) 332-6125.

SAVE **CALUSA NATURE CENTER AND PLANETARIUM** is .5 mi. w. of I-75 exit 22 on SR 884, then n. to 3450 Ortiz Ave. In addition to being home to snakes, turtles, alligators and crocodiles, the center offers a learning area for children, nature trails, an aviary, a reproduction of a Seminole Indian village and planetarium shows.

Allow 2 hours, 30 minutes minimum. Nature center open Mon.-Sat. 9-5, Sun. 11-5; closed Jan. 1, July 4, Labor Day, Thanksgiving and Dec. 25. Planetarium open Wed.-Sun. Planetarium show schedule varies; phone ahead. Admission $4; ages 3-12, $2.50. Planetarium show $3; ages 3-12, $2. MC, VI. Phone (941) 275-3435.

ECHO is off I-75 exit 26, then 1 mi. e. on SR 78 to 17391 Durrance Rd. ECHO, Educational Concerns for Hunger Organization, is a 21-acre farm devoted to the development of Third World farming techniques. One greenhouse simulates rain forest conditions and another greenhouse has a semi-arid environment; these greenhouses allow the workers to experiment with nutrient-rich plants that would thrive in such environments. Gardens in old tires and on rooftops grow throughout the farm, exhibiting the capacity to grow food in unusual locations.

Allow 1 hour, 30 minutes minimum. Landscape nursery open Mon.-Sat. 9-noon; closed holidays. Tours are given Tues. and Fri.-Sat. at 10. Donations. Phone (941) 543-3246.

EDISON-FORD WINTER ESTATES, 1 mi. s.w. on SR 867 at 2350 McGregor Blvd., contains the adjacent winter homes of two of America's most famous early 20th-century industrialists. Another highlight is a banyan tree said to be the largest in the continental United States, a 1925 gift from Harvey Firestone to Thomas Edison. Admission is only by guided tour. A replica of the *Reliance*, Edison's battery-powered boat, offers cruises on the Caloosahatchee River.

Estate tours depart continuously Mon.-Sat. 9-4, Sun. noon-4; closed Thanksgiving and Dec. 25. River cruises depart every 30 minutes Mon.-Fri. 9-3:10 (weather permitting). Admission Jan.-Apr. (includes both estates) $12; ages 6-12, $5.50. Admission rest of year $11; ages 6-12, $5.50. River cruise $4. MC, VI. Phone (941) 334-3614. *See color ad p. 80.*

Henry Ford Winter Home, "Mangoes," has been restored and furnished in the style of the 1920s, using photographs and records of the house. Bought by Ford in 1916 because of its proximity to his good friend Edison, this winter residence of the world's first billionaire features grounds planted with citrus, bamboo and tropical foliage. A garage houses three antique cars in operating condition. Allow 1 hour minimum. *See color ad p. 80.*

Thomas A. Edison's Winter Home, "Seminole Lodge," is where the inventor spent his "working vacations" from 1886 until his death in 1931. Here he perfected such earlier inventions as the incandescent light bulb, the phonograph, the mo-

tion picture camera and the storage battery. He also cultivated a 14-acre tropical garden. Tours include the furnished home, a guest house, the laboratory and workshops, a museum containing a large collection of his inventions and the garden. Allow 1 hour, 30 minutes minimum. *See color ad p. 80.*

FORT MYERS HISTORICAL MUSEUM is 1.5 mi. e. of US 41 on Dr. Martin Luther King Blvd., then 1 blk. s. on Jackson to 2300 Peck St. In a restored railroad depot, artifacts depict the history of Fort Myers and southwest Florida, focusing on Calusa and Seminole Indian cultures, Spanish exploration and early settlers. Also displayed is *The Esperanza,* the longest and the last-built Pullman private railroad car. Tues.-Sat. 9-4; closed holidays. Admission $6; over 64, $5.50; ages 2-11, $3. MC, VI. Phone (941) 332-5955.

IMAGINARIUM HANDS-ON MUSEUM AND AQUARIUM, 2000 Cranford Ave., contains interactive exhibits that allow visitors to explore Southwest Florida's environment as well as topics such as physics, anatomy and the weather. An outdoor area offers a lagoon with koi, a touch pool and walking paths, while aquariums and a theater with a 3-D movie are indoor diversions.

Allow 1 hour, 30 minutes minimum. Tues.-Sat. 10-5; closed Thanksgiving and Dec. 25. Admission $6; over 55, $5.50; ages 3-12, $3. Under 13 must be with an adult. MC, VI. Phone (941) 337-3332.

J.C. SIGHTSEEING BOAT CRUISES, at the foot of Lee St. at the Fort Myers Yacht Basin, offers jungle cruises aboard 80-passenger *The Wofford* and several other cruises, including lunch and

dinner cruises, aboard the triple-decked, 600-passenger paddlewheeler *The Capt. J.P.* The boats take passengers by historic sites and lush wooded areas. Exotic birds, manatees, alligators and other tropical fauna can be seen in their native habitat.

Allow 2 hours minimum. Jungle cruises depart Tues.-Thurs. at 10 and 2, Sun.-Mon. and Fri. at 2, Nov.-Apr.; Tues. and Thurs. at 10, Sun. at 2, rest of year. Day and evening cruises aboard the *Capt. J.P.* available daily, late Oct.-April 15. Schedule may vary; phone ahead. Arrive 30 minutes before departure. Fares for *Capt. J.P.* $15-$75; ages 3-11, $8-$38. Jungle cruise $12; ages 3-11, $6. Reservations are required. MC, VI. Phone (941) 334-7474.

SEMINOLE GULF RAILWAY departs from Colonial Station, 3.5 mi. w. of I-75 exit 22 on Colonial Blvd. The 75-minute Riverview Special and the 105-minute Bayshore Express excursions travel north to the Caloosahatchee trestle and back in vintage coaches while a narrator recounts information about railroad history, animals and plant life. Dinner trips also are available.

Allow 1 hour, 30 minutes minimum. Riverview Special departs Wed. and Sat. at 10 and 2, Sun. at 2. Bayshore Express departs Wed. and Sat.-Sun. at noon. Riverview Special fare $7.95; ages 3-12, $4.95. Bayshore Express fare $11.95; ages 3-12, $6.95. DS, MC, VI. Phone (941) 275-8487 or (800) 736-4853.

SIX MILE CYPRESS SLOUGH PRESERVE is 4 mi. w. of I-75 exit 21 on Daniels Pkwy., then 1.8 mi. n. on Ben Pratt-Six Mile Cypress Pkwy. While walking along a milelong boardwalk trail visitors can explore the wetland and observe such inhabitants as turtles, wading birds and alligators. Allow 1 hour minimum. Daily 8-8, Apr.-Sept.; 8-5, rest of year. Closed Dec. 25. Tours are given daily at 9:30

DID YOU KNOW

Except for their cream-colored bellies, alligators are black, not green.

and 1:30, Jan.-Apr.; daily at 9:30, Nov.-Dec.; Wed. and Sat. at 9:30, rest of year. Free. Parking 75c an hour or $3 a day. Phone (941) 432-2004.

FORT MYERS BEACH (G-9)
pop. 9,300, elev. 8′

Fort Myers Beach traces its history from 1513, when Ponce de León passed this way. The town comprises part of the mainland and two islands: Estero Island and San Carlos Island. A barrier island on the Gulf of Mexico, Estero Island includes seven miles of white sand beaches. Recreational activities include golf, tennis, scuba diving and fishing.

Lynn Hall Memorial Park, south of Matanzas Pass Bridge, offers a public beach area with picnic facilities. On the north end of Estero Island, Bowditch Point Park is accessible by foot, bicycle or trolley. On the south end are Lover's Key State Recreation Area *(see Recreation Chart)* and Carl Johnson Park.

To facilitate beach traffic, public transportation is provided for a fee; phone (941) 275-8726.

Greater Fort Myers Beach Area Chamber of Commerce: 17200 San Carlos Blvd., Fort Myers Beach, FL 33931-5306; phone (941) 454-7500 or (800) 782-9283.

CASINOS

- **Europa SeaKruz,** s. on San Carlos Blvd., over Matanzas Bridge to Snug Harbor. Departures daily. Reservations are required. Phone (941) 463-5000 or (800) 688-7529.

FORT PIERCE (E-11)
pop. 36,800, elev. 16′

Beef, citrus and vegetables from nearby ranching and farming areas find a market in Fort Pierce, which developed on the site of a U.S. Army post established in 1838 as a defense against the Seminoles. Native trees, flowers and colorful birds can be seen along Indian River Drive, which follows the river's west shore toward Jensen Beach.

The world's fastest ball game can be seen at Fort Pierce Jai Alai, 1750 S. Kings Hwy. (SR 713). Evening and matinee games are scheduled January through May 1; phone (561) 464-7500 or (800) 524-2524.

Note: Policies vary concerning admittance of children to pari-mutuel betting facilities. Phone for information.

Ball games of a different kind are played at Thomas J. White Stadium in nearby Port St. Lucie. In early February this stadium becomes the spring training site for the New York Mets, and the St. Lucie Mets play minor league baseball here April through September; for further information phone (561) 871-2100.

The Indian River Community College McAlphin Fine Arts Center presents live performances throughout the year; phone (561) 462-4750.

East of Fort Pierce on SR A1A, Fort Pierce Inlet State Recreation Area includes Jack Island, a bird and wildlife refuge accessible by footbridge, as well as recreational facilities *(see Recreation Chart)*.

St. Lucie County Chamber of Commerce: 2200 Virginia Ave., Fort Pierce, FL 34982; phone (561) 595-9999.

FPL'S ENERGY ENCOUNTER, on Hutchinson Island at 6501 S. Ocean Dr. at the St. Lucie nuclear power plant (Gate B), offers interactive displays and exhibits pertaining to the history of energy production. Highlights include an energy treasure hunt, computer games and a transparent nuclear reactor model. Also at the site is a self-guiding nature trail that winds through three habitats of a coastal barrier island—beach/dune, mangrove and a tropical hammock.

Allow 1 hour minimum. Energy Encounter and nature trail open Sun.-Fri. 10-4; closed holidays. Free. Phone (561) 468-4111 or (877) 375-4386.

HARBOR BRANCH OCEANOGRAPHIC INSTITUTION, 1 mi. n. on US 1 from jct. SR 614 to 5600 US 1N, then e. to visitor center, is devoted to the research and study of the marine environment. Two tours are available, a facility tour and a 90-minute boat trip up the Indian River lagoon to explore wildlife.

Allow 2 hours minimum. Facility tours Mon.-Sat. at 10, noon and 2, Thanksgiving-Easter; noon and 2 rest of year. Boat tours Mon.-Sat. at 10, 1 and 3, Thanksgiving-Easter; at 1 and 3, rest of year. Facility tour $10; ages 6-12, $6. Boat trip $19; ages 6-12, $12. Reservations are suggested for boat trips. AE, MC, VI. Phone (561) 465-2400, ext. 517.

HEATHCOTE BOTANICAL GARDENS, between Virginia Ave. and Edwards Rd. at 210 Savannah Rd., showcases varied gardens, including a Japanese and herb garden. Flowers and foliage of the subtropics, palm trees and memorial and children's gardens also are featured. A self-guiding tour is available. Events are held throughout the year. Allow 1 hour minimum. Tues.-Sat. 9-5, Sun. 1-5, Nov.-Apr.; Tues.-Sat. 9-5, rest of year. Closed major holidays. Admission $3; ages 6-12, $1. Phone (561) 464-4672.

ST. LUCIE COUNTY HISTORICAL MUSEUM, 414 Seaway Dr. (S. SR A1A), is at the east end of South Beach Bridge. Spanish shipwreck treasures, artifacts from the 1837 Old Fort Pierce and Seminole relics are on display. The complex also includes a restored 1919 American LaFrance fire engine, a restored 1907 early Florida home, a memorial garden and changing exhibits. Allow 1 hour minimum. Tues.-Sat. 10-4, Sun. noon-4; closed holidays. Admission $3; ages 6-11, $1.50. Phone (561) 462-1795.

UDT—SEAL MUSEUM, 3 mi. n.e. of US 1 at 3300 N. SR A1A, depicts the history and development of the U.S. Navy's UDTs (Underwater Demolition Teams), SEALs (Sea, Air, Land Teams), Naval Combat Demolition Units, Scouts and Raiders through photographs and artifacts. The collection features weapons, equipment and suits used by UDT and SEAL members. A

Manatees

If you see a manatee while in Florida, both you and the manatee are lucky. You would be lucky to see one of Florida's most endangered animals, and the manatee will be lucky simply to exist. Despite protection efforts, the large gray mammals that inspired the legend of mermaids are threatened by human activity, and their future is uncertain.

Also called sea cows, manatees once ranged from North Carolina to Texas but now live almost exclusively in Florida. In winter they gather in the Crystal and Homosassa rivers,  near Sanibel Island and Fort Myers, throughout the tip of the peninsula and along the St. Johns River. Blue Spring State Park in Orange City is a manatee refuge, and the animals are protected by state and federal law.

Manatees can be 8 to 10 feet long and almost 2,000 pounds. They have round bodies, two front appendages, a large round tail and a square, whiskery snout. Since each eats 50 to 100 pounds of vegetation a day, they act as underwater lawnmowers, helping keep waterways open.

Although they have no natural predators, pollution and development can destroy their habitats. Manatees must be near the surface to breathe, but they have poor eyesight and move too slowly to avoid motorboats, the greatest cause of injury and death. Motorboat propellers kill up to 50 manatees per year.

Females take 2 to 3 years to bear and raise a calf, and the population grows slowly. Manatees are bred in captivity at the Miami Seaquarium in the hope that those calves can be released into the wild to benefit future generations of manatees and humans.

videotape presentation details the arduous training process. Outdoor displays include small landing craft, a helicopter and Apollo training modules.

Allow 1 hour minimum. Mon.-Sat. 10-4, Sun. noon-4, Jan.-Apr.; Tues.-Sat. 10-4, Sun. noon-4, rest of year. Closed major holidays. Admission $4; ages 6-11, $1.50. Phone (561) 595-5845.

FORT WALTON BEACH (B-3)
pop. 21,500, elev. 18′

Warm Gulf waters and a wide variety of recreational activities make Fort Walton Beach a popular area for family vacations. The sugar white sand beaches have attracted people since 500 B.C., when various Indian tribes conducted ceremonies in the area.

Just north is Eglin Air Force Base, where Gen. Jimmy Doolittle's "Raiders" trained and which is the headquarters of the Air Force Development Test Center and home of the climatic laboratory.

Greater Fort Walton Beach Chamber of Commerce: 34 S.E. Miracle Strip Pkwy., P.O. Drawer 640, Fort Walton Beach, FL 32549; phone (850) 244-8191.

AIR FORCE ARMAMENT MUSEUM is 6 mi. n. of US 98 on SR 85, just outside Eglin Air Force Base's west gate. The museum exhibits nearly 30 restored aircraft including B-52 and B-17 bombers, a SR-71 Blackbird spy plane, an F-16 jet fighter and a Soviet MiG. The armament collection features missiles, bombs and rockets. Noteworthy among an extensive collection of antique pistols are flintlock dueling pistols and Western six-shooters. A videotape depicts the history and development of Eglin Air Force Base. Daily 9:30-4:30; closed federal holidays. Free. Phone (850) 882-4062.

[SAVE] **GULFARIUM,** 1 mi. e. on US 98, presents the Living Sea, where sharks, moray eels and sea turtles can be seen in their natural habitat through a glass-enclosed tank. Penguins, otters and alligators are featured in separate exhibits. Live shows present the antics of dolphins and sea lions. Daily 9-dusk; closed Thanksgiving and Dec. 25. Shows are given at 10, noon, 2 and 4 (also at 6, May 15-Sept. 15). Admission $16; over 55, $14; ages 4-11, $10. MC, VI. Phone (850) 244-5169.

INDIAN TEMPLE MOUND MUSEUM, 139 Miracle Strip Pkwy., depicts 10,000 years of Indian occupation of the northwest Florida coast as well as the history of European exploration and settlement in the area. The museum houses one of the largest collections of Woodland pottery in the Southeast. The temple mound, next to the museum, is topped by a replica temple. The mound was constructed around 1400 A.D.

Allow 30 minutes minimum. Mon.-Sat. 9-4:30, Sun. 12:30-4:30, June-Aug.; Mon.-Fri. 11-4, Sat.

Florida's **EMERALD** *Coast*

Enjoy refreshing walks and create new memories along 24 mile. waters of Florida's Emerald Coast. Call 1-800-322-3319 o

9-4, rest of year. Admission $2; ages 6-17, $1. Phone (850) 833-9595.

GAINESVILLE (C-8)
pop. 84,800, elev. 170'

Gainesville was founded in 1854 and named for Revolutionary War general Edmund Gaines. Both an agricultural and educational center, the community is home to the University of Florida and Santa Fe Community College. A map of the University of Florida campus can be obtained from the AAA office at 1201 N.W. 13th St. or by contacting the university at (352) 392-2241.

Opportunities to observe wildlife and geological formations are within a few miles of town. To the northwest is the 6,500-acre San Felasco Hammock State Preserve; a nature trail on SR 232 (Millhopper Road) at the I-75 overpass enters the area. Ranger-guided weekend activities are offered October through April. Activities include walks, hikes, overnight trips and classes in wilderness orientation; reservations are required. Phone (352) 462-7905.

In nearby Micanopy (see place listing p. 127) is the 20,000-acre Paynes Prairie State Preserve (see Recreation Chart). The Gainesville to Hawthorne Rail Trail, a 17-mile trail designed for walking, bicycling and horseback riding, extends from Gainesville's Historic Boulware Springs Park at Paynes Prairie through Lochloosa Wildlife Management Area to the town of Hawthorne.

Gainesville Raceway, on CR 225, is where to go for automobile racing.

Hippodrome State Theatre, one of Florida's four state theaters, offers performances in the original Gainesville Post Office. The theater also offers a cinema series and a gallery which displays the work of local artists.

Alachua County Visitors and Convention Bureau: 30 E. University Ave., Gainesville, FL 32601; phone (352) 374-5231. See color ad p. 413.

Shopping areas: Among the 175 stores at Oaks Mall, 6419 Newberry Rd., are Belk Lindsey, Burdines, Dillard's, JCPenney and Sears.

DEVIL'S MILLHOPPER STATE GEOLOGICAL SITE is at 4732 Millhopper Rd. (SR 232), following signs. Measuring 120 feet deep and 500 feet across, this sinkhole formed as early as 10,000 years ago. The area is home to plants and animals normally found in the ravines of the Appalachian Mountains. A half-mile walking path circles the sinkhole while a 232-step wooden walkway descends it. An interpretive center houses exhibits about the natural history of the site as well as an audiovisual presentation about sinkholes. Picnic facilities are available.

Allow 30 minutes minimum. Mon.-Fri. 9-5, Sat.-Sun. 9-dusk, Apr.-Sept.; daily 9-5, rest of

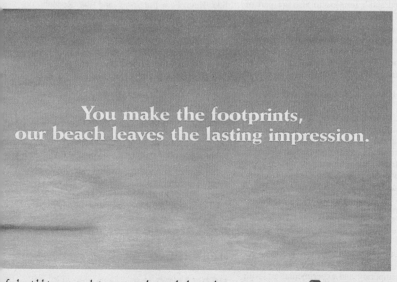

year. Guided tours depart Saturday at 10. Admission $2 per private vehicle, $1 per person arriving by bicycle, bus or on foot. Phone (352) 955-2008.

FLORIDA MUSEUM OF NATURAL HISTORY, Hull Rd. and S.W. 34th St. on the University of Florida campus, exhibits a full-size North Florida limestone cave replica, a 14-foot-tall mammoth skeleton and more than 25 million archeological specimens. Allow 1 hour minimum. Mon.-Sat. 10-5, Sun. and holidays 1-5; closed Thanksgiving and Dec. 25. Free. Phone (352) 846-2000.

FRED BEAR MUSEUM, 1 blk. w. of I-75 on Fred Bear Rd. at Archer Rd., features natural history exhibits, archery artifacts, bowhunting trophies and items Fred Bear collected on his bowhunting adventures around the world. The many animals displayed include an elephant, lion, kodiak bear, polar bear, brown bear, American buffalo and moose. Indian, Eskimo and tribal African items can be seen as well as ancient tools, weapons, charms and decorations.

Allow 1 hour minimum. Daily 10-6; closed Jan. 1, Easter, Thanksgiving and Dec. 25. Admission $5; senior citizens $4; ages 6-12, $3; family rate (two adults and children under 12) $12. Phone (352) 376-2411.

KANAPAHA BOTANICAL GARDENS is 1 mi. w. off I-75 exit 75 (SR 24) at 4700 S.W. 58th Dr. This 62-acre facility features a 1.5-mile paved walkway through butterfly, hummingbird, vinery, bamboo, wildflower, medicinal herb, palm, rock, carnivorous plant, sunken and rock gardens. A water lily pond and a fern grotto also are part of the gardens. Demonstrations of a water reclamation facility are presented. Picnic facilities are available. Pets on leash are permitted. Allow 1 hour minimum. Wed. and Sat.-Sun. 9-dusk, Mon.-Tues. and Fri. 9-5. Admission $3; ages 6-13, $2. Phone (352) 372-4981.

SAMUEL P. HARN MUSEUM OF ART, on the University of Florida campus at jct. S.W. 34th St. and Hull Rd., houses a diverse collection of art from varied cultures of the Americas, Asia, Africa and Europe. Permanent exhibits include American paintings, contemporary art and art from West Africa. Changing exhibits also are displayed. Allow 1 hour minimum. Tues.-Fri. 11-5, Sat. 10-5, Sun. 1-5; closed state holidays. Guided tours are given Wed. at 12:30, Sat.-Sun. at 2. Last admission 15 minutes before closing. Free. Phone (352) 392-9826.

UNIVERSITY GALLERY is in the College of Fine Arts at the University of Florida at the intersection of S.W. 13th St. and 4th Ave. The gallery displays contemporary and experimental art, with an emphasis on the works of emerging, mid-career and senior artists. Allow 1 hour minimum. Tues.-Fri. 10-5 (also Tues. 5-8), Sat. 1-5; closed holidays. Free. Phone (352) 392-0201.

GULF BREEZE (B-3)
pop. 5,500, elev. 14'

Incorporating miles of bays and lagoons, this peninsula 1 mile from the Gulf of Mexico offers a variety of recreational activities including swimming, boating, skiing, sailing, fishing, diving and golfing.

Gulf Breeze Area Chamber of Commerce: 1170 Gulf Breeze Pkwy., P.O. Box 337, Gulf Breeze, FL 32562; phone (850) 932-7888.

SAVE **THE ZOO,** 8 mi. e. on US 98 at 5701 Gulf Breeze Pkwy., is home to more than 700 animals in naturalistic habitats. Highlights include Japanese gardens, Gorilla Island, a children's petting zoo and an outdoor amphitheater featuring elephant and wildlife demonstrations. Visitors ride the Safari Line train through a 30-acre wildlife park with free-roaming animals. Daily 9-6, Apr.-Sept. (weather permitting); 9-4, rest of year. Closed Thanksgiving and Dec. 25. Last admission 1 hour before closing. Admission (includes train) $16; over 62, $15; ages 3-11, $12. AE, DS, MC, VI. Phone (850) 932-2229.

GULF ISLANDS NATIONAL SEASHORE (B-2)

Stretching west 150 miles from Fort Walton Beach to Ship Island off Gulfport, Miss., Gulf Islands National Seashore covers more than 137,000 acres, 80 percent of which are submerged lands. Most of Florida's portion is accessible by car and includes Naval Live Oaks Reservation; part of Perdido Key; Fort Barrancas and the Redoubt on Pensacola Naval Air Station; the Okaloosa area near Fort Walton beach; and portions of Santa Rosa Island including the Fort Pickens area.

Guided tours of Fort Pickens are offered daily, and tours of restored Fort Barrancas *(see Pensacola p. 182)* and other forts are offered seasonally. A visitor center at Naval Live Oaks Reservation features a picnic area, interpretive trail and exhibits.

On the bay side of Santa Rosa Island is a recreation area with picnic facilities. Entrance fees are charged at Perdido Key, Fort Pickens and Santa Rosa areas.

For further information contact Gulf Islands National Seashore, 1801 Gulf Breeze Pkwy., Gulf Breeze, FL 32561; phone (850) 934-2600. *See Recreation Chart and the AAA Southeastern CampBook.*

HALLANDALE—*see Fort Lauderdale p. 77.*

HEATHROW—*see Orlando p. 160.*

HERNANDO (C-8) pop. 2,100, elev. 50'

SAVE **TED WILLIAMS MUSEUM AND HITTERS HALL OF FAME** is 3.2 mi. w. of jct. US 41 on CR 486 in The Villages of Citrus Hills. Built in the shape of a baseball diamond, the museum houses photographs, artwork, a bat collection and other items from the life and career of Ted Williams, one of baseball's greatest hitters. The museum includes a library and a separate stadium room featuring "The 20 Greatest Hitters," a videotape narrated by Williams.

Allow 1 hour, 30 minutes minimum. Tues.-Sun. 10-4; closed holidays. Admission $5; under 13, $1. MC, VI. Phone (352) 527-6566.

HIGH SPRINGS (C-7)
pop. 3,100, elev. 69'

High Springs, once a mining and railroad town, now offers antiquing and recreational opportunities in a small-town atmosphere. The downtown business section, representative of old Florida, features antique shops and several historic buildings.

O'Leno State Park, one of the first state parks developed in Florida, is 6 miles north and offers primitive camping, swimming, boating, fishing, nature trails, horseback riding trails, bicycle trails and a playground. For the adventurer, Ginnie Springs and Ichetucknee Springs offer swimming, tubing, canoeing and underwater cave exploration. *See Recreation Chart and the AAA Southeastern CampBook.*

High Springs Chamber of Commerce: P.O. Box 863, High Springs, FL 32643; (904) 454-3120.

RECREATIONAL ACTIVITIES
Canoeing
• **Santa Fe Canoe Outpost**, US 441 at the Santa Fe River Bridge, P.O. Box 592, High Springs, FL 32643. Daily year-round. Phone (904) 454-2050.

HOLLYWOOD—
see Fort Lauderdale p. 78.

HOMESTEAD—
see Miami-Miami Beach p. 126.

HOMOSASSA SPRINGS (D-8)
pop. 6,300, elev. 6'

HOMOSASSA SPRINGS STATE WILDLIFE PARK is on US 19, 6 mi. n. of jct. US 19/98, following signs. Source of the Homosassa River, the freshwater spring emits millions of gallons each hour at a constant temperature of 72 F. Saltwater and freshwater fish inhabit the spring and can be watched through a floating glass observatory. Pontoon boats make scenic shuttle runs from US 19 to the park.

A trail through woodlands and wetlands allows visitors to observe native wildlife, including black bears, bobcats, river otters, alligators, cougars, white-tailed deer and crocodiles. Daily educational programs feature manatees, alligators, crocodiles, a hippopotamus, birds of prey, tortoises and native snakes. Food is available.

Allow 3 hours minimum. Daily 9-5:30. Last admission and boat departure 1 hour, 30 minutes before closing. Admission $8.95; ages 3-12, $4.95. AE, DS, JC, MC, VI. Phone (352) 628-2311.

YULEE SUGAR MILL STATE HISTORIC SITE is 2.5 mi. w. of US 19/98 via CR 490A and Fish Bowl Dr. Now a ruin, the 1851 mill was built by Florida's first U.S. senator, David Levy Yulee, as part of a 5,100-acre sugar plantation. During the Civil War the mill supplied the Confederate Army with sugar products. Picnic facilities are available. Daily 8-dusk. Free. Phone (352) 795-3817.

INDIAN ROCKS BEACH—
see Tampa Bay p. 226.

INDIAN SHORES— *see Tampa Bay p. 227.*

INVERNESS (D-8) pop. 5,800, elev. 38'

WILD BILL'S AIRBOAT TOURS & WILDLIFE PARK is on SR 44, 6.3 mi. e. of jct. US 41. Narrated 45-minute airboat rides on the Withlacoochee River provide local history as well as sightings of native wildlife, including birds and alligators. A wildlife park allows visitors to meet leopards, otters, deer, cougars, ospreys, lions, monkeys, alligators, goats and miniature donkeys.

Allow 1 hour, 30 minutes minimum. Daily 10-5; closed Dec. 25. Admission $12.95; ages 3-11, $8.95. AE, DS, MC, VI. Phone (352) 726-6060.

ISLAMORADA—
see The Florida Keys p. 65.

DID YOU KNOW

The Gulf Between It, the first film to be shot in Technicolor, was filmed in Jacksonville in 1917.

Jacksonville

Jacksonville is in the great double loop of the St. Johns River, the nation's longest north-flowing river. A busy seaport, it is one of Florida's major cultural, financial, industrial, transportation and commercial centers. The city also is a wholesale lumber market and coffee importation port and is home to a naval stores yard.

The city's history began in 1562, decades before the English settled Jamestown, when French Protestants known as Huguenots founded a colony on the banks of the St. Johns River. Named Fort Caroline, the ill-fated settlement was destroyed just 3 years later by Spanish troops from the garrison at nearby St. Augustine, and for the next 200 years Spain controlled Florida.

Spanish rule ended in 1763 when Spain traded Florida to Britain in return for Havana, which the British had conquered the year before. Ownership by Britain lasted only 20 years, but during that time The King's Road between Savannah, Georgia, and St. Augustine was completed. A settlement developed where the road crossed the St. John's River, roughly where downtown Jacksonville is today.

As a result of the 1783 Treaty of Paris which officially ended the American War of Independence, Britain returned Florida to Spain. But despite Spanish ownership, citizens of the new United States of America began settling in northern Florida, and during the War of 1812 both British and American forces made several incursions into the region.

To contend with the threat of American expansionism, Spain struck a deal with the United States in 1819 trading its interests in the Oregon Country and Florida in exchange for recognition of Spanish sovereignty over Texas.

After the United States took formal possession of Florida in 1821, settlers poured into the territory. The next year residents founded Jacksonville and named it after Gen. Andrew Jackson, the first military governor of the territory.

The town prospered as a port of entry until the Civil War, during which it was burned and abandoned several times. A major yellow fever outbreak killed hundreds of citizens in the late 1880s and forced many more to flee. In 1901 tragedy visited the city yet again when a fire destroyed nearly the entire downtown area.

The resurrected town became the leading metropolitan area in Florida for the next 40 years thanks to the railroad and the wealthy tourists who flocked to the

city each winter. During these years several movie studios opened in the area, giving Jacksonville the nickname, "the World's Winter Film Capital." Naval bases built during World War II contributed to the city's further growth, and later, banking and insurance became important parts of the local economy.

City and county governments were consolidated in 1968 which made Jacksonville the largest U.S. city in land area at the time. In 1996 the metropolitan area's population passed the 1 million mark, and today Jacksonville remains a major port, financial center, site of military bases and a health center that continues to grow rapidly.

Approaches

By Car

Two important interstate highways, I-95 and I-10, intersect in Jacksonville's downtown area. I-95 traverses the United States from north to south beginning in Maine and ending in Miami. It is frequently congested as it approaches downtown.

I-10 connects Jacksonville on the East Coast with Los Angeles by way of New Orleans, Houston, San Antonio, Tucson and Phoenix.

I-295 arcs northeast and southwest of downtown, connecting with I-95 both south and north of downtown. I-295 also intersects with I-10 directly west of the city.

A more scenic approach is SR A1A which follows the coastline through Jacksonville. Northeast of the city, SR A1A travels through historic Fernandina Beach.

US 1 is another important route. This highway runs the length of America's east coast, from Lubec, Maine, to Key West, Fla. US 17 approaches from the west and provides yet another route into Jacksonville.

Getting Around

Street System

Like most newer cities, the street system of downtown Jacksonville is a simple grid. Bay Street divides the city north-south, while Main Street is the east-west divider. The city does not adhere to a street naming convention, and thus a road's name (that is, whether it is called a street, avenue or boulevard) does not indicate its compass orientation.

The downtown speed limit is 30 mph. Traffic is most congested 7 to 9 a.m. and 4 to 6 p.m.

Parking

Both on-street parking and several parking garages are available downtown. A parking area under the Main Street bridge is convenient to Jacksonville Landing and other businesses. Parking meters require 25c per half hour.

(continued on p. 93)

The Informed Traveler

City Population: 635,200

Elevation: 20 ft.

Sales Tax: The sales tax is 7 percent in Clay and Nassau counties, 6.5 percent in Duval County and 6 percent in St. Johns County. A 6 percent bed tax is levied in Duval and St. Johns counties; the tourist development tax in Clay County is 2 percent.

WHOM TO CALL

Emergency: 911

Police (non-emergency): (904) 630-0500

Fire: (904) 630-0529

Time and Temperature: (904) 358-1212

Weather: (904) 741-4311

Hospitals: Baptist Medical Center, (904) 202-2000; Columbia Memorial Hospital Jacksonville, (904) 399-6111; St. Vincent's Medical Center, (904) 308-7300; Shands Jacksonville Medical Center, (904) 549-5000.

WHERE TO LOOK

Newspapers

Jacksonville's daily paper is *The Florida Times-Union*, distributed in the morning.

Radio

Radio station WZNZ (1460 AM) is an all-news station; WJCT (89.9 FM) is a member of National Public Radio.

Visitor Information

Visitor information is available from the Jacksonville and the Beaches Convention and Visitors Bureau, 3 Independent Dr., Jacksonville, FL 32202; phone (904) 798-9111 or (800) 733-2668.

TRANSPORTATION

Air Travel

More than a dozen major and regional carriers serve Jacksonville International Airport, which is about 13 miles north of downtown near the northern junction of I-95 and I-295.

Several taxi and limousine companies serve the airport, although the baggage claim area is served exclusively by Gator City Taxi, (904) 355-8294. Taxi fares to downtown average $20.

Rental Cars

Hertz, at the airport, offers discounts to AAA members; phone (904) 741-2151 or (800) 654-3080. For listings of other agencies check the telephone directory.

Rail Service

The Amtrak station is at 3570 Clifford Ln., 5 miles northwest of downtown. For arrival information phone (904) 766-5110; for reservations and information phone (800) 872-7245.

Buses

The main Greyhound Lines Inc. bus terminal is at 10 Pearl St.; phone (904) 356-9976. A sub-station is at the Naval Air Station; phone (904) 772-3209. For rate and schedule information phone (800) 231-2222.

Taxis

Major cab companies include Checker Cab Co., (904) 764-2472; Gator City Taxi, (904) 355-8294; and Yellow Cab Co., (904) 260-1111. Base fare is $1.25 with a rate of $1.25 per mile.

Public Transport

Jacksonville Transportation Authority operates city buses. Stops include the transfer center at Florida Community College Jacksonville and the South Bank area. Fare for buses on the beaches is $1.35; town routes are 75c. For information phone (904) 630-3100. The Automated Skyway Express (ASE) provides transportation between Florida Community College's downtown campus and the San Marco area across the river for 35c; phone (904) 630-3181.

Boats

River taxi service between points along the St. Johns River is available from S.S. Marine Taxi, (904) 733-7782.

Destination Jacksonville

*F*or many visitors heading south Jacksonville is, geographically at least, Florida's unofficial welcome center—and the city is a fine example of what the Sunshine State is all about.

*T*ake beaches for example. Jacksonville and its environs have miles of sand to wiggle your toes in. Add to that an assortment of museums to suit individual tastes, professional sports and abundant recreational activities.

Cummer Museum of Art and Gardens, Jacksonville.
Riverfront gardens grace the grounds of this museum, while fine and decorative arts adorn its galleries. (See listing page 93)

Horseback riding, Amelia Island. The barrier island's quartz beaches are ideal for weekend rides along the surf.

Museum of Science and History, Jacksonville.
Civil War memorabilia and the area's cultural and natural history are the focus here, while a planetarium invites budding stargazers. (See listing page 93)

Fernandina Beach
Amelia Island
Fort George Island
Mayport
Jacksonville
Jacksonville Beach

See Vicinity map page 92

Jacksonville Jaguars. Legions of fans flock to Alltell Stadium for the excitement and thrill of NFL action. (See mention page 94)

*P*laces included in this AAA Destination City:

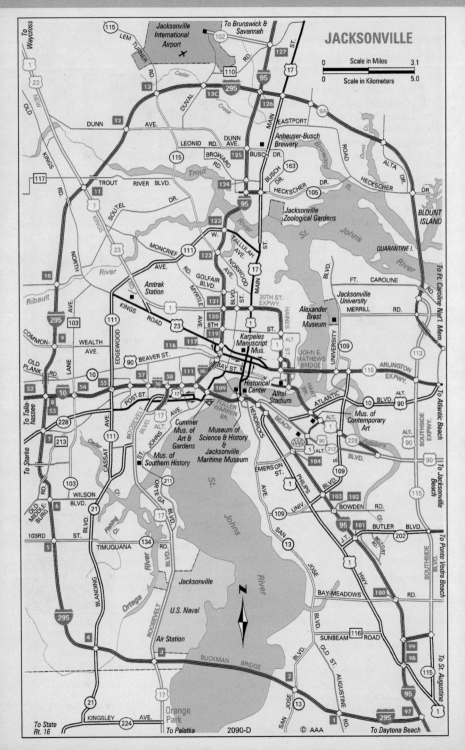

What to See

ALEXANDER BREST MUSEUM, 6 mi. n. on the Jacksonville University campus at 2800 University Blvd. N., features a permanent collection of decorative arts, pre-Colombian objects and Chinese porcelain, in addition to works by guest artists, faculty and students. Mon.-Fri. 9-4:30. Free. Phone (904) 745-7371.

CUMMER MUSEUM OF ART & GARDENS, 829 Riverside Ave., contains an impressive array of decorative and fine arts dating from 2000 B.C. Of interest is a collection of early 18th-century Meissen porcelain tableware. Changing exhibits complement the permanent collection. A formal garden, modeled after the gardens of Villa Gamberaia in Florence, Italy, extends from the museum to the river. Art Connections, in the Art Education Center, features an interactive teaching gallery.

Allow 2 hours minimum. Tues.-Sat. 10-5 (also Tues. and Thurs. 5-9), Sun. noon-5; closed holidays and for 2 weeks in Apr. Admission $6; senior citizens and military with ID $4; students with ID $3; under 6, $1; free to all Tues. 4-9. Phone (904) 356-6857.

FORT CAROLINE NATIONAL MEMORIAL, 13 mi. e. near jct. Monument and Fort Caroline rds., is within the Timucuan Ecological and Historic Preserve. The memorial marks the site near which French colonial adventurers established a settlement in 1564. A year later Spaniards massacred many of them at Matanzas Inlet. A model of the fort is reached by a .25-mile path through oak woods. Ribault Monument, .5 miles east of the fort, is an obelisk that commemorates the first landing at St. Johns in 1562. A 1-mile trail helps explain the site's history. Trails also lead to other areas within the preserve.

The visitor center, which also serves as the chief interpretive center for the Timucuan Ecological and Historic Preserve, has displays about the area's marine environment, the Timucuan Indian era, early attempts at colonization and a satellite image of present-day northeast Florida. Allow 1 hour minimum. Daily 9-5; closed Dec. 25. Free. Phone (904) 641-7155.

FORT GEORGE ISLAND—
see place listing p. 96.

JACKSONVILLE HISTORICAL CENTER, on S. Riverwalk just e. of Main St. Bridge, features displays depicting Jacksonville's history. Daily 11-5; closed Jan. 1, Thanksgiving and Dec. 25. Donations. Phone (904) 398-4301.

JACKSONVILLE MARITIME MUSEUM, on the s. bank of the Riverwalk at 1015 Museum Cir., promotes the nautical history of the area. The importance of the St. Johns River and the port of Jacksonville is emphasized. Among displays are scale-model ships, paintings and photographs.

Mon.-Sat. 10:30-3:30, Sun. 1-5. Admission $2, under 13 free. Phone (904) 398-9011.

JACKSONVILLE ZOOLOGICAL GARDENS, SAVE I-95 exit 124A, off Heckscher Dr. at 8605 Zoo Rd., has more than 800 mammals, birds and reptiles. Okavango Village features a petting zoo, a pinewood trail, a walk-through aviary and a pier on the Trout River. The African Veldt features elevated walkways past lion exhibits to the African Savannah. Great Apes of the World features gorillas, baboons, chimpanzees and pygmy marmosets. A group of meerkats is housed in its own habitat. A petting zoo train ride and a play area also are available. Picnic facilities and wheelchairs are available.

Allow 2 hours minimum. Daily 9-5; closed Thanksgiving and Dec. 25. Admission $8; over 65, $6.50; ages 3-12, $5. Additional fee for train ride. AE, DS, MC, VI. Phone (904) 757-4462.

KARPELES MANUSCRIPT MUSEUM, 101 W. First St., has changing exhibits of historic and significant documents. Displays, which rotate between the Karpeles museums, may include letters by Napoleon Bonaparte and George Washington, the musical notations of Ludwig van Beethoven, Wolfgang Amadeus Mozart or Richard Wagner, or such documents as constitutions and treaties. A highlight of the collection is the Emancipation Proclamation signed by Abraham Lincoln. Allow 1 hour minimum. Mon.-Sat. 10-3. Free. Phone (904) 356-2992.

KINGSLEY PLANTATION—
see Fort George Island p. 96.

MUSEUM OF SCIENCE AND HISTORY is at 1025 Museum Cir. A Civil War collection is among the museum's permanent displays. Other exhibits cover dolphins and manatees and 12,000 years of Jacksonville and northeast Florida history. Hands-on exhibits encourage interaction between parents and children. Physical science shows are held in the science theater and multimedia shows are presented in Alexander Brest Planetarium.

Mon.-Fri. 10-5, Sat. 10-6, Sun. 1-6; closed Jan. 1, Easter, Thanksgiving and Dec. 25. Admission $6; senior citizens and military with ID $4.50; ages 3-12, $4. AE, MC, VI. Phone (904) 396-7061.

MUSEUM OF SOUTHERN HISTORY is off I-10 exit 55, 3 mi. s. on Cassat Ave., 1.5 mi. e. on San Juan Ave., then just n. to 4304 Herschel St. The museum houses an extensive collection of artifacts, clothing and memorabilia from the Civil War era, in addition to a 2,500-volume research library and genealogical records. Allow 1 hour minimum. Tues.-Sat. 10-5. Admission $1, under 16 free. Phone (904) 388-3574.

What To Do
Sightseeing
Industrial Tours

ANHEUSER-BUSCH BREWERY, 111 Busch Dr., offers self-guiding and guided tours. Visitors may view the brewing and bottling processes and then sample products in the hospitality room. Allow 1 hour minimum. Mon.-Sat. 9-4; closed major holidays. Guided tours are given on the hour. Free. Phone (904) 751-8116.

Sports and Recreation

The intricate chain of barrier islands off the coast adjacent to Jacksonville offers more than 50 miles of white sandy beaches that are great for **swimming**. Just 20 miles northeast of the city are the pristine beaches and wild natural beauty of Little Talbot Island State Park and Fort George Island State Cultural Site. The beach communities of the area—Atlantic Beach, Neptune Beach, Jacksonville Beach and, to the south, Ponte Vedra Beach—combine surf and sand with the amenities of hotels and restaurants.

With Jacksonville's access to water, **boating** is a popular pastime in the area. The city operates docks at the following locations: Huguenot Memorial Park, Kathryn Abbey Hanna Park, Metropolitan Park and Southbank Riverwalk.

Fishing can be enjoyed along the St. Johns River and Intracoastal Waterway and in the Atlantic Ocean. Speckled trout, striped bass, bluefish, redfish, flounder and whiting are a few of the fish frequently caught at Little Talbot Island State Park. Anglers heading to another popular fishing spot—the 983-foot-long Jacksonville Beach Fishing Pier—will find a newly rebuilt structure awaiting them after Hurricane Floyd's effects are repaired; re-opening is expected by spring 2001. Saltwater fishing and more than 60 acres of freshwater fishing lakes are available at Kathryn Abbey Hanna Park.

Golf and Florida's balmy climate go together perfectly, and Jacksonville has courses in abundance. Courses include Baymeadows Golf Club at 7981 W. Baymeadows Cir., (904) 731-5701; Deerfield Lakes Golf Club off Lem Turner Road, (904) 359-0404; Fernandina Municipal Golf Club at 2800 Bill Melton Rd., (904) 277-7370; Golf Club of Jacksonville at 10440 Tournament Ln., (904) 779-0800; and Jacksonville Beach Golf Club at 605 S. Penman Rd., (904) 247-6184.

Tennis courts can be found throughout the Jacksonville area. The Association of Tennis Professionals (ATP) Tour is headquartered in Ponte Vedra.

Timucuan Ecological & Historic Preserve, 12713 Fort Caroline Rd., offers numerous **hiking** trails through several distinct ecological communities; phone (904) 641-7155. Three self-guiding nature trails are at the University of North Florida Nature Preserve. Bird-watching is a popular pastime along the hiking trails of both Big and Little Talbot islands. Tree Hill Nature Center, at 7152 Lone Star Rd., offers 40 acres of undeveloped land and several nature trails in the middle of suburbia; phone (904) 724-4646.

Local fans of professional **football** were given a gift in 1993 when the city was awarded a National Football League franchise. The Jacksonville Jaguars play at Alltel Stadium, One Alltel Stadium Place; phone (904) 633-2000. The Jacksonville Tomcats play arena football in spring and summer at Jacksonville Veterans Memorial Coliseum; phone (904) 358-7825.

The Jacksonville Suns, a farm team of the Detroit Tigers, play AA Southern League **baseball** at Wolfson Park, 1201 E. Duval St.; phone (904) 358-2846. **Hockey** fans can watch two teams play in Jacksonville: The Southern Hockey League's Bullets are a farm team for the Detroit Red Wings, and the East Coast Hockey League's Lizard Kings play at Jacksonville Veterans Memorial Coliseum; phone (904) 630-3900.

Greyhound racing takes place at Orange Park Kennel Club from early September to mid-April and at Jacksonville Kennel Club from mid-April through early September. For more information about either track, phone (904) 646-0001.

Note: Policies vary concerning admittance of children to pari-mutuel betting facilities. Phone for information.

Shopping

In addition to major shopping malls, a multitude of small shopping centers and an array of antique stores and flea markets, the city boasts Jacksonville Landing, on Independent Drive along the St. Johns River. This downtown marketplace features shops, riverfront cafes and restaurants. A water taxi takes patrons across the river to the Riverwalk.

Avenues Shopping Mall, 10300 Southside Blvd., has 110 stores including Belks, Dillard's, JCPenney, Parisian and Sears. Orange Park Mall, 1910 Wells Rd., counts Belks, Dillard's, JCPenney and Sears among its 134 stores. Regency Square, 9501 Arlington Expwy., has 160 stores including Belks, Dillard's, JCPenney and Sears.

Theater and Concerts

The Jacksonville Symphony Orchestra presents performances throughout the year including a guest artist series, an outdoor concert series and smaller group concerts. Times-Union Center for the Performing Arts, 300 Water St., is a state-of-the-art performance venue overlooking the St. Johns River downtown. Its three halls include Robert E. Jacoby Hall, home of the Jacksonville Symphony Orchestra; Moran Theater, which can accommodate large-scale concerts and Broadway touring shows; and Terry Theater, which is used for smaller performances. For more information phone (904) 630-3900.

The Florida Community College at Jacksonville Artist Series brings Broadway productions along with national and international ballet, opera and contemporary dance companies; phone (904) 632-3373.

Located downtown, the lavish Florida Theater was built in 1927 and serves as a performing arts center; phone (904) 355-5661 for information or 355-2787 for tickets. Seawalk Plaza in Jacksonville Beach has a scenic two-stage pavilion and an amphitheater used for arts and crafts festivals as well as entertainment.

Special Events

Jacksonville is host to exciting events throughout the year. College football fans celebrate the new year with the Gator Bowl, which is played on the Saturday nearest Jan. 1 and is one of the city's top sporting events.

In March the GATE River Run attracts 9,000 runners for a 15-kilometer race along the city's roads and bridges. Also taking place in March is The Players Championship golf tournament, the Professional Golf Association's premier spring

event. In late April, Beaches Festival Weekend is celebrated at Metropolitan Park, on the riverfront next to Jacksonville Municipal Stadium.

In May the Kuumba Festival celebrates African-American heritage with parades, music and food at Clanzel Brown Park. The Greater Jacksonville Kingfish Tournament features prizes, a fish fry, seafood festival and entertainment in July.

The Greater Jacksonville Agricultural Fair in October offers livestock, a petting zoo, horticultural exhibits, arts and crafts, carnival rides and country entertainment. In early November jazz enthusiasts gather for the Jacksonville Jazz Festival, an important international festival and competition.

Ring in the new year during the Jacksonville Landing "Down Town" Countdown.

The Jacksonville Vicinity

AMELIA ISLAND (A-9)

Miles of Appalachian quartz beaches and towering sand dunes distinguish Amelia Island, a picturesque island off the northeast tip of Florida's Atlantic coast. Formerly a haven for smugglers of slaves, liquor and foreign goods, in the mid-19th-century the island became the site of Florida's first cross-state railroad and, consequently, the state's first resort. The many Victorian buildings in Fernandina Beach, the island's only city (see place listing p. 95), remain a testament to the island's "Golden Age."

Ironically, another railroad—Henry Flagler's Florida East Coast Railway—soon lured tourists farther south, locking the island in its Victorian atmosphere. Once thought a disaster, this development is now heralded as a blessing, as visitors seek relief from the modern world in Amelia Island's old-fashioned charm and pace.

A popular resort area, the island offers many recreational opportunities including golf, swimming and horseback riding. At the southern end of the island is American Beach, one of the country's last predominately African-American beaches. The town of American Beach was founded in the 1930s, an era during which many beaches were closed to African-Americans.

Amelia Island/Fernandina Beach/Yulee Chamber of Commerce: P.O. Box 472, Fernandina Beach, FL 32035-0472; phone (904) 261-3248 or (800) 226-3542.

RECREATIONAL ACTIVITIES
Horseback Riding

• **Kelly Seahorse Ranch**, 7500 First Coast Hwy., Amelia Island, FL 32034. Rides daily at 10, noon, 2 and 4. Reservations are recommended. Phone (904) 491-5166.

FERNANDINA BEACH (A-9)
pop. 8,800, elev. 10'

Fernandina Beach is the northern terminus for a portion of scenic highway extending 105 miles south via SR A1A to Daytona Beach. Once called a "festering fleshpot" by President James Monroe because of the pirates and smugglers who anchored here, the town later became Florida's first resort.

This centuries-old town on Amelia Island features a variety of architectural styles. The Victorian district is scattered across 50 blocks, including residential and commercial buildings and a popular shopping area. On Centre Street at Second Avenue is the Palace Saloon, built in 1878 and reputedly the oldest in the state. A hand-carved, 40-foot mahogany bar and hand-painted murals decorate the interior.

The first week in May the town celebrates the local shrimping industry and its early days under the flags of eight nations with the Isle of Eight Flags Shrimp Festival.

Amelia Island/Fernandina Beach/Yulee Chamber of Commerce: P.O. Box 472, Fernandina Beach, FL 32035-0472; phone (904) 261-3248 or (800) 226-3542.

Self-guiding tours: A brochure outlining a tour of the historic district is available from the chamber of commerce.

AMELIA ISLAND MUSEUM OF HISTORY, 233 S. Third St., is in Nassau County's former jailhouse. The second floor of the museum depicts the history of Amelia Island through photographs and artifacts. One-hour guided tours of the first floor exhibit hall depict the island's past and tell of the eight nations whose flags have flown over its harbor. Allow 1 hour minimum. Museum open Mon.-Fri. 10-5, Sat. 10-4; closed holidays. Guided tours are given Mon.-Sat. at 11 and 2. Admission $4, students with ID $2. Phone (904) 261-7378.

FORT CLINCH STATE PARK, 2 mi. e. on SR A1A at the n. end of Amelia Island, comprises 1,153 acres. The brick and masonry fort was begun in 1847 but never completed. Occupied by Federal forces in 1862, it was instrumental in introducing Northerners to Florida's warm climate, which resulted in a tourist boom after the Civil War. The interpretation center traces the history of the fort. Rangers dressed in Union uniforms carry out the daily chores of garrison soldiers of the Civil War era.

Park open daily 8-dusk. Fort open daily 9-5; candlelight tours Fri.-Sat., early May-Labor Day. Park admission $3.25 per private vehicle (maximum eight people), $1 per person arriving by bicycle or on foot. Fort admission $1, under 6 free. Candlelight tours $2. Phone (904) 277-7274. *See Recreation Chart and the AAA Southeastern CampBook.*

FORT GEORGE ISLAND (A-9)

In the 16th century the Spanish established a blockhouse and the mission San Juan del Porto on Fort George Island. By 1736 Gen. James Oglethorpe had turned the island into a base for forays against the Spanish. About 25 miles northeast of Jacksonville, the island is accessible from the beaches on SR A1A and by ferry from Mayport. The Dames Point Bridge provides access to the island via SR 105.

KINGSLEY PLANTATION, .5 mi. n. of the St. Johns River Ferry on SR A1A, then 2.5 mi. w. on Fort George Rd., is part of the Timucuan Preserve. This 19th-century cotton plantation was operated 1813-39 by Zephaniah Kingsley. It is one of the last remaining examples of the plantation system of territorial Florida. The main lodge and the remains of 23 slave cabins are visible. Interpretive displays reflect 19th-century plantation life. Daily 9-5; closed Dec. 25. Free. Phone (904) 251-3537.

JACKSONVILLE BEACH (B-10)
pop. 17,800, elev. 14′

ADVENTURE LANDING, 1 mi. w. of SR A1A at 1944 Beach Blvd., features an uphill water coaster, a wave pool and a pirate play village with 12 slides and more than 200 spray nozzles. Among other amusements are go-karts, laser tag and miniature golf. Amusement park open Mon.-Thurs 11-10, Fri. 11 a.m.-midnight, Sat. 10 a.m.-midnight, Sun. 10-10. Water park open daily 10-8, mid-Apr. to mid-Oct. Admission $18.99, under 42 inches tall $14.99, under 3 free when accompanied by an adult. After 4 p.m. $12.99. AE, DS, MC, VI. Phone (904) 246-4386.

MAYPORT (B-9) elev. 10′

CASINOS

- **La Cruise Casino,** 4738 Ocean St. Tues.-Sat. 7 p.m.-midnight (also Wed. and Sat. 11 a.m.-4 p.m.); Sun. 1-6. Phone (904) 241-7200 or (800) 752-1778.

This ends listings for the Jacksonville Vicinity. The following page resumes the alphabetical listings of cities in Florida.

JUPITER (F-11) pop. 24,900, elev. 28′

Once the transportation hub of southeastern Florida, Jupiter was the starting point for the Celestial Railroad, which ran through Mars, Venus, Neptune and Juno to Lake Worth. The town since has become a center for recreation and light industry while retaining its quaint atmosphere.

The Montréal Expos and the St. Louis Cardinals both take up residence in Jupiter during spring training. Exhibition baseball games are played in March at Roger Dean Stadium, 4751 Main St.; phone (561) 775-1818.

Jupiter-Tequesta-Juno Beach Chamber of Commerce: 800 N. US 1, Jupiter, FL 33477-4440; phone (561) 746-7111.

FLORIDA HISTORY CENTER & MUSEUM, s. of jct. SR A1A at 805 N. US 1 in Burt Reynolds Park, presents photographs and memorabilia depicting Florida history. Conservation of the coastline and the impact of the Florida East Coast Railroad are explored through the exhibits, which include fossil shells and Seminole artifacts. Changing displays also are featured. Tours of the nearby 1896 DuBois Pioneer Home and 1860 Jupiter Inlet Lighthouse Museum are available.

Allow 1 hour minimum. Museum open Tues.-Fri. 10-5, Sat.-Sun. noon-5; closed major holidays. Tours of the DuBois Home are given Wed. and Sun. 1-4. Admission $5; over 55, $4; ages 6-18, $3. AE, MC, VI. Phone (561) 747-6639.

JONATHAN DICKINSON STATE PARK, 6 mi. n. on US 1, comprises 12,000 acres, including the Loxahatchee River. Bald eagles, scrub jays and sandhill cranes are among the birds that thrive amid the park's abundant plant life. Guided tours depart to Trapper Nelson Interpretive Center on the river; it is accessible only by boat. Canoe rentals are available. A 2-hour river tour is available on the *Loxahatchee Queen*; phone (561) 746-1466.

Park open daily 8-dusk. River tours depart daily at 9, 11, 1 and 3. Admission $3.25 per private vehicle (maximum eight people), $1 per person arriving by bicycle, bus or on foot. River tour fare $12; ages 6-12, $7. Phone (561) 546-2771. *See Recreation Chart.*

JUPITER INLET LIGHTHOUSE is .5 mi. n. on US 1, .1 mi. e. on Beach Rd., then .25 mi. s. on Captain Armours Way. Completed in 1860, the lighthouse still guides ships approaching the Florida coast with a beam that is visible from 18 miles at sea. On 45-minute guided tours, visitors can climb 108 feet for a view of the Atlantic Ocean (maximum 15 people per tour). Allow 1 hour minimum. Sun.-Wed. 10-4. Last admission 45 minutes before closing. Admission $2, climbing tour $5. Under 48 inches tall not permitted on tour. Phone (561) 747-8380.

KENNEDY SPACE CENTER (D-11)

Kennedy Space Center and Cape Canaveral Air Station are the country's center of space operations. Forty-seven miles east of Orlando via the Bee Line Expressway (toll) or SR 50, the 140,000-acre center is accessible from the mainland off US 1, 6 miles across the SR 405 causeway over the Indian River, or from the beaches across the SR 520 or 528 causeways to Merritt Island, then north on SR 3.

Early launches from Cape Canaveral Air Station included the May 5, 1961, suborbital space flight of Navy Cmdr. Alan B. Shepard Jr. and America's first manned orbital flight by Marine Lt. Col. John H. Glenn Jr. on Feb. 20, 1962.

Following construction of Kennedy Space Center on adjacent Merritt Island, moonbound U.S. spacecraft blasted off from two massive launch pads; on July 20, 1969, Neil A. Armstrong and Edwin E. Aldrin became the first men to walk the moon's surface. Kennedy Space Center also is the primary home for the *Atlantis, Columbia, Discovery* and *Endeavour* space shuttles.

Cape Canaveral Air Station, east of the space center, is the site of NASA's unmanned launches. The most current shuttle information can be obtained from NASA's shuttle hotline; phone (321) 867-4636 or (800) 572-4636. Missile launches can be viewed from Cocoa Beach or along the Indian River in Titusville. The Cocoa Beach Pier, 1 mile north of the SR 520 causeway, is a favorite spot, as is Jetty Park in Port Canaveral and Merritt Island National Wildlife Refuge. With the purchase of a $15 Launch Transport Ticket, visitors parking at the Kennedy Space Center Visitor Complex can board shuttle buses to a viewing site at the NASA causeway. For additional information phone (321) 452-2121.

ASTRONAUT HALL OF FAME is at 6225 Vectorspace Blvd., w. on SR 405. Dedicated to honoring America's space pioneers, the Astronaut Hall of Fame traces the development of space exploration through video footage, personal memorabilia and historical artifacts. Simulators let visitors experience aerial acrobatics and astronaut training, squeeze inside a Mercury spacecraft and take a multimedia ride aboard a space shuttle mock-up. Visitors also may observe children training in space camp.

Allow 3 hours minimum. Daily 9-5, with extended summer hours; closed Dec. 25. Admission $13.95; ages 6-12, $9.95. AE, MC, VI. Phone (321) 269-6100. *See color ad p. 99.*

KENNEDY SPACE CENTER VISITOR COMPLEX, 11 mi. e. of I-95 on SR 405, is part of Merritt Island National Wildlife Refuge. The U.S. space program is explored here through multimedia displays, IMAX films, Astronaut Encounter programs and a bus tour of the space center.

Highlights at the visitor complex include a moon rock, actual spacecraft, a shuttle replica and the Rocket Garden, where space equipment traces the program's development. A wildlife exhibit focuses on the wonders of nature. The Universe Theater shows a 15-minute film about the possibility of life on other planets. Robot Scouts is an exhibit about NASA's robotic space exploration. Other exhibits provide information about NASA's ongoing Mars missions.

Two IMAX theaters, both equipped with 5½-story screens, present "The Dream is Alive," featuring footage taken by astronauts in space; "L5: First City in Space," a depiction of a space city of the future; and "Mission to Mir," an explanation of what life was like for the astronauts aboard the Russian space station.

An Astronaut Encounter show allows visitors to greet men and women involved in the space program, and hear tales of their experiences.

The self-paced bus tour includes stops at Launch Complex 39, where the 60-foot LC 39 Observation Gantry tower provides views of KSC's shuttle launch pads; the International Space Station Center, where visitors can walk through full-size models of space station modules and watch space station components being readied for use; and the Apollo/Saturn V Center, featuring an audiovisual presentation, interactive displays and a 363-foot moon rocket. Tour buses make continuous rounds until approximately 2 hours before closing, allowing visitors to explore each leg of the tour at their own pace.

The Air Force Space and Missile Museum at Cape Canaveral Air Station, which features a collection of rockets used in the early days of space exploration, can only be visited as part of the Cape Canaveral: Then & Now tour. Stops include the hangar where Mercury astronauts lived and worked, the Air Force Space and Missile Museum, Cape Canaveral Lighthouse and launch pads used for Mercury, Gemini and Apollo missions. Some portions of the tour may be off-limits during special operations.

Allow 5 hours minimum to see the visitor complex and take the KSC bus tour. To avoid crowds arrive early. Free kennels are available. Daily 9-dusk; closed Dec. 25 and during certain periods on launch days. Cape Canaveral tour hours vary; phone ahead. KSC admission (includes bus tour and IMAX films) $24; ages 3-11, $15. Combination ticket with Cape Canaveral tour $44; ages 3-11, $35. AE, DI, DS, MC, VI. Phone (321) 449-4400. *See color ad p. 98.*

Astronaut Memorial: Space Mirror, accessible through the entrance to the Kennedy Space Center Visitor Complex, is visible from SR 405. Dedicated to American astronauts who died in the line of duty, this black granite memorial has reflective panels behind the

carved name of each. Computers keep the monument's turntable constantly aimed at the sun so that its light shines through the names of the men and women. Allow 30 minutes minimum. Daily 9-dusk; closed Dec. 25 and during certain periods on launch days. Free. Phone (321) 452-2887.

KEY BISCAYNE—
see Miami-Miami Beach p. 126.

KEY LARGO—*see The Florida Keys p. 66.*

KEY WEST—*see The Florida Keys p. 66.*

KISSIMMEE—*see Orlando p. 160.*

LAKE BUENA VISTA—
see Orlando p. 162.

LAKE CITY (B-7) pop. 10,000, elev. 188′

Once named Alligator after a Seminole Indian chief, Lake City is south of the Georgia state line at the intersection of I-75 and US 90.

Lake City Chamber of Commerce: 106 S. Marion St., Lake City, FL 32025; phone (904) 752-3690.

FLORIDA SPORTS HALL OF FAME AND MUSEUM OF FLORIDA SPORTS HISTORY, .25 mi. w. on US 90 from jct. I-75, then .25 mi. n. on Hall of Fame Dr., offers exhibits honoring athletes with a tie to Florida. Featured are videotape presentations, interactive games and exhibits about 25 sports played by high school as well as professional athletes and teams. Allow 1 hour minimum. Mon.-Sat. 9-4; closed Dec. 25. Admission $3; over 54, $2; under 12 free with an adult. MC, VI. Phone (904) 758-1310.

LAKELAND (E-9) pop. 70,600, elev. 227′

Lakeland encompasses 13 lakes providing ample opportunities for fishing, boating and water skiing. The area also offers pleasant surroundings for such sports as golf and tennis. The city is a processing and distribution center for citrus fruits and other agricultural products. A majority of the world's phosphate, the primary ingredient in fertilizer, is mined in the Lakeland area.

The world's largest group of buildings designed by Frank Lloyd Wright is on the Florida Southern College campus at Ingraham Avenue and McDonald Street. The 1938 Annie Pfeiffer Chapel was the first structure here; others were patterned after its theme. Maps for a self-guiding tour are available outside the administration building.

During March the city is the spring-training camp for baseball's Detroit Tigers, and from April through August it is the home of the Lakeland Tigers. Exhibition games are played at Joker Marchant Stadium; phone (863) 499-8229. Ice hockey games, concerts, ballet performances and trade shows are among the entertainment presented at The Lakeland Center, 700 W. Lemon St.

Lakeland Chamber of Commerce: 35 Lake Morton Dr., Lakeland, FL 33801; phone (863) 688-8551.

Self-guiding tours: Information about tours of the downtown historic district is available from the chamber of commerce.

Shopping areas: Lakeland Square, on US 98 at I-4, contains Belk Lindsey, Burdines, Dillard's, JCPenney and Sears. Antique lovers can find more than 60 shops and dealers in the city's antiques district, located 2 blocks north of Main Street along Kentucky Avenue and Pine Street.

EXPLORATIONS V CHILDREN'S MUSEUM, 125 S. Kentucky Ave., offers changing hands-on exhibits, materials and activities allowing children ages 2-12 to explore the realms of nature, science, the continents, business and fantasy. The interactive programs are designed to promote learning and cultural growth. Allow 1 hour minimum. Wed.-Sat. 9-4, Sun. 1-4, Mon.-Tues. 9-1; closed holidays. Ages 2-15, $3.50; over 15, $1.50. Phone (863) 687-3869.

POLK MUSEUM OF ART, 800 E. Palmetto St. just off Lake Morton Dr., has changing exhibits of contemporary and historical art. The museum's permanent collection includes pre-Columbian artifacts;

Oriental ceramics, ivory and fabrics; European ceramics; Georgian silver; and American art of the 19th and 20th centuries. Allow 1 hour minimum. Tues.-Fri. 9-5, Sat. 10-4, Sun. 1-5; closed holidays. Free. Phone (863) 688-7743.

LAKE WALES (E-9)
pop. 9,700, elev. 252′

On North Wales Drive at North Avenue in Lake Wales a bizarre phenomenon occurs: Through optical illusion, cars appear to roll uphill. To experience this mystery, park your car at the bottom of the incline known as Spook Hill and release the brake.

It is said that the Spook Hill mystery stems from a Seminole legend in which Chief Cufcowellax and his tribe settled on Lake Wales. Soon a huge bull alligator moved into the lake and regularly attacked the Indians. Aided by the Great Spirit, the chief stalked the beast and engaged him in a monthlong battle, after which the chief rose from the water in victory.

During the battle a small lake, now North Lake Wales, appeared next to the big one. The chief was later buried on the shores of the new lake. Some attribute the Spook Hill enigma to the alligator seeking revenge, while others speculate that Cufcowellax has returned to defend his homeland from encroachment.

Lake Wales Area Chamber of Commerce: 340 W. Central Ave., P.O. Box 191, Lake Wales, FL 33859-0191; phone (863) 676-3445.

Shopping areas: Eagle Ridge Mall, 5 miles north on US 27, has Dillard's, JCPenney and Sears as its anchor stores.

BOK TOWER GARDENS, 3 mi. n. off CR 17A (Burns Ave.), is surrounded by 200 acres of landscaped gardens, much of which was designed by Frederick Law Olmstead, Jr. The marble and coquina stone tower contains 60 bronze bells weighing from 17 pounds to more than 11 tons. Carillon recitals are given daily at 3 (some days a recorded recital); selections are played every 30 minutes daily beginning at 10. Special recitals are announced in advance. The bells are best heard at a distance of about 200 yards.

The tower and gardens were dedicated to the American people by founder Edward Bok, a Dutch immigrant. A self-guiding tour leads visitors through walkways graced by thousands of native and exotic plants. Swans and ducks can be seen in the Reflection Pool, while foxes, raccoons, bobcats and many rare plant species abound in The Pine Ridge Nature Reserve. The reserve includes Window by the Pond, a nature observatory.

An audiovisual tour of the garden and tower is presented in the theater at the Education and Visitor Center; the center also houses art exhibits and exhibits about Bok, the tower, carillon and an endangered species program. Guided nature walks depart from the visitor center daily. Picnic

facilities and food are available. Gardens open daily 8-6. Last admission 1 hour before closing. Visitor center open daily 9-5. Admission $6; ages 5-12, $2. Phone (863) 676-1408. *See ad.*

THE DEPOT—LAKE WALES MUSEUM AND CULTURAL CENTER, 325 S. Scenic Hwy. (US 27A), is the former 1928 Atlantic Coast Line train depot. A turn-of-the-20th-century Pullman car is the highlight of the center's displays, which include photographs and memorabilia pertaining to local history and the railroad, cattle, citrus and turpentine industries. Also featured are a 1926 restored caboose, a 1944 engine and changing exhibits. The adjacent 1916 Lake Wales depot is restored as a train museum. Allow 30 minutes minimum. Mon.-Fri. 9-5, Sat. 10-4; closed some holidays. Free. Phone (863) 678-4209.

LAKE KISSIMMEE STATE PARK is 8 mi. e. via SR 60, 4 mi. n. on Boy Scout Rd., then 5 mi. n. on Camp Mack Rd. following signs. Wildlife abounds in this part of Florida's Osceola Plain between lakes Kissimmee, Rosalie and Tiger, an area that forms the headwaters of the Everglades. During the ice ages this plain lay beneath the sea; the ancient shoreline and beach dunes still are recognizable in the form of a rise and dips on Camp Mack Road.

Thirteen miles of hiking trails wind through the park. An observation tower provides a good view. Daily 7-dusk. Admission $3.25 per vehicle (maximum eight people), $1 per person arriving by bicycle or on foot. Phone (863) 696-1112. *See Recreation Chart and the AAA Southeastern CampBook.*

Kissimmee Cow Camp, 14248 Camp Mack Rd., is a living-history representation of the area's frontier cattle country days in 1876. Sat.-Sun. and major holidays 9:30-4:30. Admission included in park entrance fee.

LAKE WORTH (G-12)
pop. 28,600, elev. 19′

Development of Lake Worth began in the 1900s when lakeshore lots were offered as giveaways to those who bought nearby tracts of fruit and truck land. The area became so popular that land to the west intended for development was virtually abandoned until the late 1930s, while the lake settlement expanded and was named for Gen. William Jenkins Worth of Seminole Indian Wars fame.

Visitors and residents alike enjoy a variety of activities, including golf, concerts in the park, shuffleboard, tennis, boating and performances by a theater group. Concerts are held at Watson B. Duncan III Theater on the Palm Beach Community College campus; phone (561) 439-8141.

Lake Worth offers fine fishing. Freshwater varieties are caught in Lake Osborne at the city's western edge and from bridges spanning Lake Worth; saltwater species are snagged from one of Florida's longest municipally owned Atlantic Ocean piers as well as from charter craft for deep-sea and reef fishing. A trackless trolley provides service to the beach, shopping areas, parks and downtown businesses.

Lake Worth Chamber of Commerce: 807A Lucerne Ave., Lake Worth, FL 33460; phone (561) 582-4401.

LARGO— *see Tampa Bay p. 227.*

MADEIRA BEACH—
see Tampa Bay p. 227.

MAITLAND— *see Orlando p. 174.*

MARATHON— *see The Florida Keys p. 69.*

MARCO ISLAND (H-9)

At the northern tip of the Ten Thousand Islands, Marco Island is reached from US 41 via either SR 92 or 951; both bridges are free. This shell-gatherer's paradise on Florida's southern Gulf Coast has been transformed from a fishermen's retreat into a lively resort community. Golf, tennis, swimming and surfing are among the recreational activities.

Marco Island Area Chamber of Commerce: 1102 N. Collier Blvd., Marco Island, FL 34145; phone (941) 394-7549.

Shopping areas: Prime Outlets at Naples, 5 miles north on SR 951, offers 40 outlet shops representing manufacturers such as Bass Shoes, Dansk, Geoffrey Beene, Liz Claiborne and Mikasa.

MARCO ISLAND TROLLEY TOURS, boarded at most accommodations on Marco Island, provides a 90-minute narrated tour of the island's historic sites, including seashell mounds built by Calusa Indians. Departures daily 10-4:45. Last boarding at 3:15. Fare (includes an all-day boarding pass) $14; ages 1-12, $7. Phone (941) 394-1600.

MARIANNA (A-5) pop. 6,300, elev. 89′

FLORIDA CAVERNS STATE PARK, 3 mi. n. on SR 166, has extensive limestone caverns with calcite formations, a museum, natural rock gardens and a horse trail (no horse rental). The Chipola River Canoe Trail, part of the Florida Canoe Trail System, begins here. Guided cavern tours cover a lighted passageway.

The park is open daily 8-dusk. Cavern tours are conducted daily 9-4. Park admission $3.25 per private vehicle (maximum eight people), $1 per person arriving by bicycle or on foot. Cavern admission $4; ages 3-12, $2. Canoe rental $10 per half-day, $15 per full day. Phone (850) 482-9598 for recorded information or 482-1228 for reservations. *See Recreation Chart and the AAA Southeastern CampBook.*

MAYPORT— *see Jacksonville p. 96.*

MELBOURNE (E-11)
pop. 59,600, elev. 21′

Melbourne's first residents were black freedmen who established a settlement in the area in the 1860s. The town was named Melbourne, after the Australian postmaster's hometown, in 1879. The arrival of the Florida East Coast Railroad in 1894 brought economic growth to the small community.

The introduction of another innovative form of travel—space flight—has led to the development of high-tech and electronics industries, an additional benefit of the city's proximity to the Kennedy Space Center *(see place listing p. 97).* Space Coast Stadium is home to baseball's Florida Marlins during spring training.

Melbourne-Palm Bay Area Chamber of Commerce: 1005 E. Strawbridge Ave., Melbourne, FL 32901-4782; phone (321) 724-5400 or (800) 771-9922.

Shopping areas: Melbourne Square Mall, on US 192, 2 miles east of I-95, contains Belk Lindsey, Burdines, Dillard's and JCPenney.

BREVARD MUSEUM OF ART AND SCIENCE, 2 blks. e. of US 1 at 1463 Highland Ave., presents changing exhibits of works by local, national and international artists. Workshops and demonstrations are presented on a regular basis. The Ruth Cote Clemente Children's Science Center offers more than 35 interactive exhibits. Allow 1 hour minimum. Tues.-Sat. 10-5, Sun. 1-5; closed holidays. Admission $5; over 64, $3; students with ID $2; free to all Thurs. after 1. AE, MC, VI. Phone (321) 242-0737.

BREVARD ZOO, .5 mi. e. of I-95 exit 73 to 8225 N. Wickham Rd., features more than 400 animals representing some 100 species. From shaded boardwalks visitors can view such animals as alligators, giant anteaters, jaguars, river otters and exotic birds. Paws-on is an interactive learning area for children. Australia is home to red kangaroos, wallabies, emus and kookaburras. The Wetlands Outpost explores the native Florida environment on 160 feet of raised boardwalk traversing 22 acres of wetland habitat; 25-minuted guided kayak tours also are available. A train ride and food are available.

Allow 2 hours minimum. Daily 10-5; closed Thanksgiving and Dec. 25. Kayak tours daily 10-1 and 2-3:30. Last admission 45 minutes before closing. Admission $6.50; over 59, $5.50; ages 2-12, $4.50. For kayak tours, under 11 must be with an adult; under 4 are not permitted. AE, DS, MC, VI. Phone (321) 254-3002.

AAA Accessibility Criteria for Travelers With Disabilities

*A*ccessibility is an important issue for travelers with disabilities. In an effort to provide this imperative information to our members with disabilities, AAA has created ***AAA Accessibility Criteria for Travelers With Disabilities***, a brochure that outlines the criteria used by our tourism editors to determine if a AAA Rated® property is considered accessible.

Once all applicable criteria have been met, the appropriate icons indicating a property's level of accessibility can be found in the lodging listings of the TourBook® guides.

For more information or to receive a copy of this brochure, call or stop by your local AAA Club.

Miami-Miami Beach

Population:
Miami 358,500   Miami Beach 90,200
Miami Elevation: 20 ft.

Popular Spots:

Metrozoo ....(see p. 115)
Vizcaya Museum and Gardens...(see p. 116)

Cultivated from a tropical wilderness, Miami celebrated its centennial in 1996. Even Julia Tuttle and Henry Flagler, the visionaries who saw the potential of this seemingly inhospitable portion of south Florida, would be amazed to see the transformation the area has undergone. The former wilderness is now a thriving, colorful city, young and vibrant despite its 100 years. Mediterranean architecture and a contemporary skyline blend with art deco styling, just as the smell of orange blossoms now coexists with the scent of *arroz con pollo.*

Then there are the colors: flamingo pink, lime green, Caribbean blue. The landscape is punctuated with marzipan hues, predominant in the tropical deco of hip Miami Beach. And it is surely the image of a fuzzy orange Miami sun, green palms and azure waters that draw some 13 million vacationers annually to this new Casablanca.

Miami and Miami Beach, interchangeable in the minds of most tourists, in reality are vastly different. Miami is a larger and more diverse metropolis that caters to tourism but also supports light industry. Miami Beach, almost exclusively tourist-oriented, consists mostly of condos and hotels. In fact, squeezed into an area of only 7.5 square miles, sandwiched between the Atlantic Ocean and Biscayne Bay, is a dazzling array of hotels that can accommodate three times the city's usual population.

One of the first to recognize Miami's potential was Julia Tuttle. The Chicagoan arrived in 1891, enchanted by the sunshine and mild ocean breezes. South Florida then was frontier territory and Miami amounted to little more than the ruins of a U.S. army outpost and a few plantations.

But the coastal location and commercial promise of the Miami River led to Tuttle's bold prediction—that the area would become one of the world's busiest seaports and a vital link for trade with the Americas and the Caribbean.

Tuttle unsuccessfully tried to persuade millionaire industrialist Henry Morrison Flagler to extend his rail line south from West Palm Beach. Then, in a fateful twist, an 1895 freeze destroyed most of Florida's northern citrus crop. Tuttle sent a bouquet of orange blossoms to Flagler, proof of a frost-free Miami. It was enough to change Flagler's mind: The Florida East Coast Railroad arrived in April 1896, and the city of Miami was incorporated 3 months later.

Among the first of the tourists and Northern transplants was New Jersey businessman John Collins, who had bought, sight unseen, a coconut plantation on one of Miami's barrier islands. Collins sought to link the isles with the mainland by building a bridge, but ran out of money before finishing the project.

Exclusive Fisher Island is named for the businessman who came to Collins' aid. Carl Fisher, inventor of the automobile headlight and owner of the Indianapolis Speedway, traded completion

Getting There —starting on p. 110

Getting Around — starting on p. 111

What To See —starting on p. 112

What To Do — starting on p. 117

Where To Stay — starting on p. 487

Where To Dine — starting on p. 490

of the bridge for part of Collins' island property—and Miami Beach was born. Dredging Biscayne Bay to build up the narrow, sandy stretch, Collins sculpted paradise, constructing golf courses, hotels, tennis courts and polo fields, beginning the halcyon days of winter retreats and sun-splashed resorts.

The first real estate boom was barely in full swing when it rocked out of control. Property sold for mere pennies, hawked on street corners by binder boys who would bind the sale with a slip of paper. Speculation was such that entire communities were designed and auctioned without so much as a brick laid, though there might be an imposing archway leading nowhere.

The whimsical, pastel-painted art deco hotels on South Beach today are gentle reminders of a reawakening city after the dismal Depression era. Created in the streamlined moderne style, lodgings sported the mixture of austere and cheerful favored by designers of the day. Charmed by the look and Miami's affordability, vacationers, retirees and Northern transplants flocked to the area in the 1930s and '40s.

Miami's modern expansion saw a changing social climate and a growth of business opportunities. A second building boom was on, as servicemen who trained in Miami Beach during World War II returned with their families after the war. And the advent and increasing popularity of commercial aviation brought the city its first flush of international sun worshippers.

There were other firsts, such as the bittersweet press reviews of the 1950s when the city made national headlines during the U.S. Senate committee hearings on organized crime. Miami had attracted

mafiosi, including the infamous Al Capone. The '50s were, nonetheless, heydays, as Arthur Godfrey and Jackie Gleason televised nationally from Miami studios and high fashion held sway in such stores as Saks Fifth Avenue, Bonwit Teller and Cartier. Few could conceive the turning point of 1959 and its profound implications.

When Fidel Castro overthrew Fulgencio Batista Zaldivar on Jan. 1, 1959, the first Cubans exiled to Miami were the deposed dictator's political and military henchmen. Wealthy Havana citizens and a brain drain of professionals—doctors, journalists, lawyers, conservative politicians—followed, suspicious of Castro's socialist drift. When widespread disillusion with the regime set in, an exodus began, and Miami's Cuban population swelled to 300,000 before the freedom flights ended in 1973.

By sheer numbers, Cuban expatriates transformed Miami; their entrepreneurial skills and desire for a new life formed the basis for a multinational society. Although the changing face of the city brought with it ethnic tensions, industry flourished. The next decade saw Miami's harbor become the world's largest cruise ship port.

Events in Cuba once again changed the face of the city. When Castro opened the port of Mariel, 140,000 Cuban refugees arrived in 1980. Liberty City and other overcrowded areas erupted in violence, and longtime residents, disheartened by the crime and commotion, headed north out of Miami-Dade County.

But Miami surmounted its crisis in a timely and spectacular fashion. The criminal-justice system worked to blot up hard-core criminals, and a $3 billion building boom downtown resulted in the glass skyscrapers and fanciful architecture along Biscayne Bay's boulevards.

Other Spanish-speaking groups also have made Miami their home, and Spanish is heard everywhere. Whether street signs and billboards are in English or Spanish first (nearly all display both) depends on how close they are to "Little Havana," the Latin district centering on S.W. Eighth Street, or *Calle Ocho*.

When producers discovered the city's unpredictable shapes and dazzling colors, Miami became the locale of a new television series. "Miami Vice" premiered in 1984, transforming the city into a cool, hip, hot metropolis. Property values rose, tourism boomed and investors rushed in. When "Miami Vice" ended in 1989, the city's international reputation had been set, and city leaders looked forward to capitalizing on the resulting mystique. They did not, of course, anticipate the devastating results of Hurricane Andrew, which demolished billions of dollars worth of real estate in 1992. But Miami survived.

As the cultural complexion of Miami continues to evolve, Hispanics, Central and South Americans and those of Caribbean heritage are joined by Asians and Europeans, transforming the city's social and economic fabric. Nowhere is this more apparent than in South Beach, where the art deco gems of yesterday are now the ultra-hip backdrop for America's Riviera.

Though much of the action is centered around the art deco district's refurbished landmarks, sidewalk cafes, nightclubs and beaches, the mainland is thriving as well. Little Havana and Little Haiti are reminders of Miami's cultural heritage, while downtown the highest concentration of international banks in the Southeast adds muscle to Miami's transcontinental economy.

Central to Miami-Dade County's worldwide air, sea and ground transportation networks is the Port of Miami, handling more than 5 million tons of containerized cargo annually. Miami International Airport ranks first among U.S. airports for international cargo, moving more than 1 million tons each year.

As America's new Ellis Island, Miami may very well be the most foreign of U.S. cities. The entrepreneurial spirit, however, that fostered its evolution from swampy wetland to diverse, international metropolis is distinctly American. The intriguing contrasts of hedonism and hardship are unmistakably Miami.

The Informed Traveler

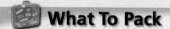 Whom To Call

Emergency: 911

Police (non-emergency): (305) 595-6263 (Miami-Dade County) or (305) 579-6111 (Miami)

Fire: (305) 595-6263 (Miami-Dade County) or (305) 579-6231 (Miami)

Time and Temperature: (305) 324-8811

Weather: (305) 229-4522

Hospitals: Baptist Hospital of Miami, (305) 596-1960; Jackson Memorial Hospital, (305) 585-5400.

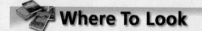 Where To Look

Newspapers

Miami's two papers are: the *Miami Herald* (morning) and *Diario Las Americas* (Spanish, afternoon). Miami Beach has the *Miami Beach Sun Post* (weekly).

Radio

Miami radio station WINZ (940 AM) is an all-news/weather station; WLRN (91.3 FM) is a member of National Public Radio.

Visitor Information

The Greater Miami Convention and Visitors Bureau distributes information Mon.-Fri. 8:30-5. Write 701 Brickell Ave., Suite 2700, Miami, FL 33131; phone (305) 539-3000. *Miami/South Florida,* a monthly magazine, lists daily events.

What To Pack

Miami's average annual temperature is a balmy 76 degrees. December through March is delightful, with daytime highs in the mid-70s, comfortable lows around 60 and little rain. Miami is hot and humid the rest of the year. June through September can be sweltering, with daytime temperatures averaging around 90. Ocean breezes temper the heat along the coast.

The sun's ultraviolet rays are insidiously strong, especially when reflected off the water. Wear sunscreen—an SPF rating of at least 15 is recommended—and a hat.

Thunderstorms are common from May through October; carry an umbrella to be prepared for sudden showers. Severe storms and hurricanes are unlikely but do occur; Hurricane Andrew is the most recent example. The hurricane season lasts from

June through November. *For additional information see temperature chart p. 43.*

Lightweight resort wear is appropriate almost everywhere although there are ample opportunities to dress up. A light sweater is handy in some air-conditioned interiors.

Sales Tax: Miami-Dade County sales tax is 6.5 percent. Additional taxes total 3 percent in Bal Harbour; 4 percent in Surfside; and 6 percent in the rest of Miami-Dade County.

Destination Miami

The Ericsson Open, Key Biscayne. Elite players in the world of tennis compete every March at Crandon Park Tennis Center.

*L*inked by causeways and an easygoing lifestyle, Miami and Miami Beach are an energizing mix of natural beauty and contemporary entertainment.

*S*napshots of swaying palm trees and gently breaking waves share space in vacation albums with souvenir programs from professional sporting events. And reminiscences of exotic bougainvillea and hibiscus linger with memories of performing dolphins and rare wildlife.

See Vicinity
map page 113

Miami Seaquarium. Flipper and friends frolic during daily performances at this Miami landmark (hint: don't sit too close if you don't want to get wet). (See listing page 115)

Metro-Dade Cultural Center, Miami. This downtown destination offers two museums, a library and a spacious, sunny courtyard. (See listing page 114)

*P*laces included in this AAA Destination City:

Homestead ●

Florida City

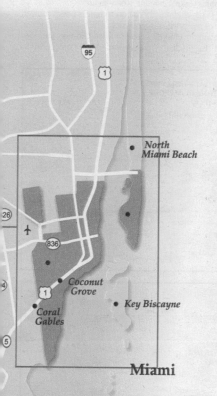

North
Miami Beach

95

1

26

836

4

1

Coconut
Grove

Coral
Gables

5

Key Biscayne

Miami

Beach and palm trees,
Miami Beach is known
worldwide for its
sunny days and
sandy beaches.

Metrozoo,
Miami.
Animals
native to
Asia, Africa
and Europe
roam in
cageless
surroundings
similar to
their native
habitats.
(See listing
page 115)

Getting There

By Car

Moving from the coast inland, the major north-south routes are SR A1A, US 1, I-95, US 441 and Florida's Turnpike. The coastal route—SR A1A—is by far the most scenic but is slow. It is the only approach to Miami Beach from the north. US 1 travels through cities and commercial areas. I-95 is a congested four- to six-lane freeway. Two- to four-lane US 441 traverses developed and industrial land with heavy traffic.

From farther north, through the central part of the state, comes Florida's Turnpike (toll), which swings in a wide arc to the west around Miami; it also is linked directly with the I-95 connection into downtown. SR 826 (Palmetto Expressway) provides another western bypass closer to the city limits.

From the west come I-75, US 27 and US 41 (Tamiami Trail), all of which become congested as they approach the city limits.

Seven causeways span Biscayne Bay to link Miami and Miami Beach: MacArthur (US 41 and SR A1A), Venetian (toll), Julia Tuttle (I-195), 79th Street, Broad (96th Street), 163rd Street and William Lehman (SR 856).

Air Travel

Miami International Airport, northwest at Le Jeune Road and N.W. 36th Street, is centrally located 7 miles from downtown. It ranks ninth in the United States and 14th in the world for total passenger traffic, serving approximately 34 million travelers annually. A $5.4 billion airport expansion is expected to be completed in 2010.

Exit the airport on Central Boulevard east to Le Jeune Road (S.W. 42nd Avenue). To go directly downtown, take Le Jeune Road south to SR 836 East. For points north, take Le Jeune Road north to SR 112 (Airport Expressway) and I-95 north. For Miami Beach, take Le Jeune Road north to SR 112, following the signs for I-195 and the 36th Street (Julia Tuttle) Causeway.

Kendall, West Miami and other points west are accessed by taking Le Jeune Road south to SR 836 (Dolphin Expressway). SR 836 crosses northbound/southbound SR 826 (Palmetto Expressway). To reach Coconut Grove and Coral Gables, take Le Jeune Road south.

Taxis offer transportation to hotels but at almost twice the price of limousines, which may not leave the airport until all seats are filled and may stop often to discharge passengers. Some hotels offer

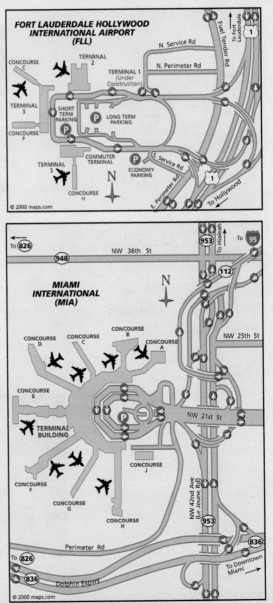

FORT LAUDERDALE HOLLYWOOD INTERNATIONAL AIRPORT (FLL)

MIAMI INTERNATIONAL (MIA)

© 2000 maps.com

shuttles for their guests; the shuttles stop only at departure level airport entrances. Airport limousine service to most locations in Miami-Dade and Broward counties may be charged at a flat rate; return trip rates usually are less.

The Fort Lauderdale-Hollywood International Airport, between I-95 and US 1, just south of SR 84, is a convenient option for those traveling to the northern portions of the Miami-Miami Beach area. The airport is approximately 45-minutes to 1-hour north of Miami via I-95, US 1 or Florida's Turnpike.

Miami and Miami Beach are served by many major car rental agencies. Arrangements should be made before you leave on your trip; your local AAA club office can provide this assistance or additional information. Hertz, (800) 654-3080, or (305) 871-0300 at Miami International Airport, and (305) 534-4661 inside the Fontainebleau Hilton in Miami Beach, offers discounts to AAA members.

Rail Service

The Amtrak Station is at 8303 N.W. 37th Ave. For arrival information phone (305) 835-1221; for reservations and other information phone (800) 872-7245.

Buses

Greyhound Lines Inc. stations are at 4111 N.W. 27th St. and 700 Biscayne Blvd. in Miami; at 16560 N.E. Sixth Ave. in North Miami.

Getting Around

Street System

Negotiating the streets of Miami can be mastered easily despite its sprawling layout. Two helpful points of reference are the city's cluster of skyscrapers, downtown at the geographical center, and Biscayne Bay, always to the east.

Miami is divided into four quadrants: Northeast, Northwest, Southeast and Southwest. Should you be looking for a particular address within the city, the section designation (N.E., N.W., S.E., S.W.) is an important factor.

Flagler Street divides the city north-south, while Miami Avenue is the east-west divider. Avenues, courts and places run north and south; streets and terraces run east and west. Except for the communities of Hialeah and Coral Gables, which have their own numbering systems, all

street numbers start at Flagler Street and at Miami Avenue.

Unless otherwise posted, the speed limit is 30 mph in business and residential areas and 55 mph on highways. It is 65 or 70 mph on Florida's

Turnpike and other designated highways. Miami has a typical big city rush hour (7 to 9 a.m. and 4:30 to 6 p.m.). Expressway traffic is particularly slow. Right turns on red are permitted after a complete stop, unless otherwise posted. Left turns on red are permitted from a one-way street onto another one-way street after a complete stop. U-turns are permitted except where otherwise posted.

The primary point of reference in Miami Beach is Collins Avenue (SR A1A), the city's major north-south through street. Along or near this thoroughfare is the famed string of hotels and motels, with the residential area lying west to Bay Road.

In both cities the speed limit is 25 mph or as posted. Motorists should not try to follow an unfamiliar route during rush hours. The lunch hour also is busy.

Directional signs sporting an orange sunburst on a blue background begin at the airport and guide motorists to some of the more popular destinations within the Miami area as well as pointing out the quickest routes to such resort areas as Orlando and Key West.

Parking

Both Miami and Miami Beach have downtown, on-street metered parking, parking lots and garages. Downtown metered street parking is available in Miami at the rate of $1 per hour.

Miami has four municipal parking garages: at 40 N.W. Third, 190 N.W. Third, 90 S.W. First and 100 S.E. Second streets. Rates at the former two are $1.25 per 30 minutes to a daily maximum of $9.50; at the latter two the rates are $2 and $3 respectively per half-hour with daily maximums of $14.50 (on S.W. First) and $21 (at S.E. Second). Some specialty districts, such as Bayside Marketplace, have their own lots and fee schedules. Lot rates vary according to location, but they generally start at about 50c to $1 for the first hour and about 50c for each additional half-hour. Bayside Marketplace charges $2 per hour for parking after 9 a.m.

On-street parking in Miami Beach often is difficult to find. Visiting drivers should look carefully for signs when parking on Miami Beach streets due to the number of areas where parking is restricted.

Metered parking is available throughout Miami Beach at the rate of 25¢ per 15 minutes to half-hour. There are four municipal parking garages: at 42nd Street between Sheridan and Royal Palm avenues; 17th Street between Penna and Meridian avenues; Collins Avenue at 13th Street; and Drexel Avenue at 12th Street.

There are also numerous public parking lots in the Miami Beach area. Rates vary by lot and location. Lots with daily rates generally charge $4 during the week and $6 on weekends (including Fridays). Some lots are served by electronic meters that charge the standard metered rate; these lots offer a daily rate only during events.

Taxis & Limousines

Cabs are plentiful and operate on the meter system. Fares are $1.50 base fee plus $2 per mile and 30c for each minute of waiting. The largest companies are Yellow Cab Co., (305) 444-4444, and Metro Taxi, (305) 888-8888. Consult the telephone directory for others.

Private limousine service is $40 to $60 an hour, with a 2-hour minimum; most companies add a 20 percent driver gratuity.

Public Transportation

The Miami-Dade County Transit Agency links greater Miami with buses, Metrorail and Metromover. Metrorail is an elevated rail system serving downtown Miami; it also runs north and west to Hialeah and south to Kendall. Metromover is a 4.4-mile elevated rail system that loops around downtown.

Buses operate countywide. The fare is $1.25, plus 25c for a transfer to another bus or to Metrorail; transfers to Metromover are free. Express bus fare is $1.50. Exact change is required.

Metrorail fare is $1.25; exact change is required. Bus transfers are 25¢; transfers to Metromover are free. Regular Metromover fare is 25¢; there is a $1 fee to transfer from Metromover to a bus or Metrorail. Both trains operate daily 6 a.m.-midnight. Metromover trains arrive every 90 seconds; Metrorail trains arrive approximately every 20 minutes. For schedules and route information about both systems phone (305) 770-3131.

What To See

THE AMERICAN POLICE HALL OF FAME AND MUSEUM, 3801 Biscayne Blvd. (US 1), 2 blks. n. of jct. I-195, displays more than 10,000 items relating to law enforcement. Exhibits include a mock crime scene, execution equipment, specialty cars and replicas of jail cells. A memorial lists the names of U.S. police officers killed in the line of duty since 1960. Allow 1 hour minimum. Daily 10-5:30; closed Dec. 25. Admission $6; over 65, $4; ages 6-11, $3; out-of-state police officers $1; Florida police officers 25c. MC, VI. Phone (305) 573-0070.

BASS MUSEUM, 2121 Park Ave. in Miami Beach, features a permanent collection of Old Master paintings and sculpture, contemporary art and architecture. Temporary exhibits in the art deco building include contemporary and historical art from throughout the world. **Note:** The museum will be closed as it undergoes expansion and renovation; Reopening is scheduled for November 2000; phone ahead for hours.

Allow 1 hour minimum. Tues., Thurs.-Sat. and first and third Wed. of the month 10-5, second and fourth Wed. of the month 1-9, Sun. 1-5; closed holidays. Admission $5, senior citizens and students with ID $3, under 6 free. Admission is charged during special exhibitions. AE, MC, VI. Phone (305) 673-7530.

CARL FISHER MONUMENT is in Fisher Park at Alton Rd. and Surprise Ave. in Miami Beach.

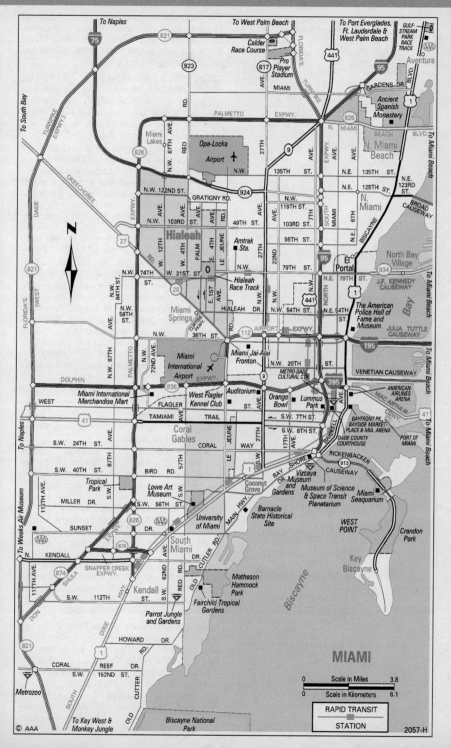

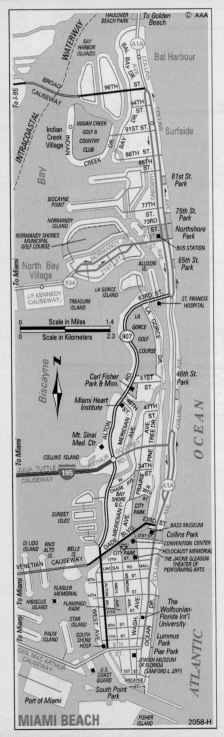

The monument, which consists of a bust of Fisher mounted on a large keystone, commemorates the man who helped to establish Miami Beach and who deeded many public beaches and parks to the city.

THE HOLOCAUST MEMORIAL, 1933-1945 Meridian Ave., is dedicated to the memory of the 6 million Jews who suffered and died at the hands of the Nazis during their rule of Germany from Jan. 30, 1933, until the Germans surrendered May 7, 1945.

The focus of the memorial is a 42-foot-high bronze arm rising from the ground; sculptured people climb it, looking for an escape. Other features include a memorial wall with black granite panels etched with names of victims; a series of vignettes displaying victims helping victims; a meditation garden; and the Dome of Contemplation with an eternal flame. Guided tours are available by reservation. Allow 30 minutes minimum. Daily 9-9. Free. Phone (305) 538-1663.

JEWISH MUSEUM OF FLORIDA (SANFORD L. ZIFF), 2 blks. s. of Fifth St. at 301 Washington Ave., is housed in a restored art deco synagogue. The core exhibit depicts more than 200 years of Jewish life in Florida. Temporary exhibits change three times annually. Films and public programs are presented. Allow 1 hour minimum. Tues.-Sun. 10-5; closed Jewish holidays. Admission $5; over 65 and students with ID $4; under 6 free; family rate $10; free to all Sat. Phone (305) 672-5044.

METRO-DADE CULTURAL CENTER, 101 W. Flagler St. at First Ave., comprises three Spanish-style buildings with arched windows, tile roofs and wrought-iron fixtures surrounding a large plaza.

Allow 1 hour, 30 minutes minimum. Combination ticket to the Miami Art Museum and the Historical Museum of Southern Florida $6. Visitors can get a parking discount at the three garages to the west and south of the center if they get their parking stubs validated at either museum.

Historical Museum of Southern Florida uses artifacts, dioramas, audiovisual displays, photographs and other media to illustrate the past 10,000 years of the region's history and development. Highlights include a replica of a pioneer house and a 1920s trolley car. Mon.-Sat. 10-5 (also Thurs. 5-9), Sun. noon-5; closed Jan. 1, Thanksgiving and Dec. 25. Admission $5; ages 6-12, $2. Phone (305) 375-1492.

Main Library of the Miami-Dade Public Library System offers a lecture and concert series. Mon.-Sat. 9-6 (also Thurs. 6-9 p.m.), Sun. 1-5, Oct. 1-weekend before Memorial Day; Mon.-Sat. 9-6 (also Thurs. 6-9 p.m.), rest of year. Closed holidays. Free. Phone (305) 375-2665.

Miami Art Museum offers two stories of works by international artists, including major touring exhibitions focusing on contemporary art since 1945. Tues.-Fri. 10-5 (also third

Thurs. of the month 5-9), Sat.-Sun. noon-5; closed Jan. 1, Thanksgiving and Dec. 25. Admission $5, over 65 and students with ID $2.50, under 12 free; by donation Tues.; free to all third Thurs. of month 5-9 and to families on second Sat. of month. Phone (305) 375-3000.

METROZOO is at 12400 S.W. 152nd St. (Coral Reef Dr.), .25 mi. w. of jct. SR 821 (Florida's Tpke.). Metrozoo is a cageless zoo where animals roam in settings similar to their natural habitats. The spacious exhibits cover the continents of Africa, Asia and Europe with such inhabitants as chimpanzees, orangutans, elephants, bongo antelopes, Malayan sun bears and Siamese crocodiles.

Asian River Life is home to small-clawed otters, clouded leopards, Malayan water monitors and blood pythons. Winding paths and tunnels separate the animals from the visitors in this jungle exhibit. Also featured are rare white Bengal tigers, whose island replicates an Asian temple; an African plains exhibit, where giraffes, zebras and ostriches coexist as they do in the wild; and a gorilla family.

Animal shows are presented three times daily. An air-conditioned monorail provides an overview of the zoo's 290 acres. Viewing caves are offered. The Children's Zoo has an ecology theater and a petting zoo. Food is available.

Allow 3 hours minimum. Daily 9:30-5:30. Last admission 1 hour, 30 minutes before closing. Admission $8; ages 3-12, $4. AE, MC, VI. Phone (305) 251-0400.

SAVE **MIAMI SEAQUARIUM,** 4400 Rickenbacker Cswy., offers shows and presentations as well as numerous marine exhibits. Divers hand feed reef fish and moray eels in a 750,000-gallon saltwater aquarium. Popular shows involve the funny exploits of Salty the Sea Lion and his friends and the graceful beauty of the Pacific white-sided dolphins that perform with Lolita the killer whale. Other features include sharks and endangered manatees and green sea turtles. Kennels and food are available.

Allow 4 hours, 30 minutes minimum. Daily 9:30-6. Last admission 1 hour, 30 minutes before closing. Admission $21.95; over 55, $19.95; ages 3-9, $16.95. Parking $4. AE, MC, VI. Phone (305) 361-5705. *See color ad.*

SAVE **MONKEY JUNGLE** is 22 mi. s.w. on US 1, then 3 mi. w. at 14805 S.W. 216th St. Primates roam freely within large enclosures simulating their natural habitat while visitors stroll through enclosed walkways. South American monkeys inhabit a re-creation of an Amazonian rain forest complete with more than 100 native species of plants. Various shows are presented daily. Allow 2 hours, 30 minutes minimum.

THREE TONS OF KILLER POWER!

Visit Miami's premier attraction—home of *Lolita* the Killer Whale and TV Superstar *Flipper*. Enjoy great shows and dozens of marine life exhibits. Come spend a fun-filled day at Miami Seaquarium,® just ten minutes from downtown and the port of Miami. **For information, telephone 305-361-5705.**

PRESENT YOUR AAA CARD AND RECEIVE 15% OFF REGULAR ADMISSION.

Miami Seaquarium®

©1999 Miami Seaquarium

Take I-95 south to Key Biscayne on Rickenbacker Causeway. Offer not valid with any other offers, discounts or 12-Month Pass purchases.

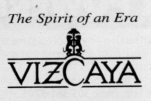
Daily 9:30-5. Last admission 1 hour before closing.
Admission $13.50; over 65, $10.50; ages 4-12, $8.
AE, DI, DS, MC, VI. Phone (305) 235-1611.

**MUSEUM OF SCIENCE AND SPACE TRANSIT
PLANETARIUM,** 3280 S. Miami Ave., can be
reached via the pedestrian overpass from the Vizcaya Metrorail station.

[SAVE] **Miami Museum of Science** presents robotic dinosaurs, virtual-reality basketball
and nearly 150 hands-on exhibits that illustrate
principles of physics, electricity, light and sound.
The outdoor Wildlife Center is a rehabilitation
facility for injured birds of prey and reptiles;
more than 75 animals can be viewed. Science
and wildlife demonstrations are held daily.

Daily 10-6; closed Thanksgiving and Dec. 25.
Last admission 1 hour before closing. Admission
(including Space Transit Planetarium) $9; over
61 and students with ID $7; ages 3-12, $5.50;
half-off admission Mon.-Fri. after 4:30. AE, MC,
VI. Phone (305) 646-4200.

[SAVE] **Space Transit Planetarium** presents multimedia laser and star shows daily; phone for
schedule. Allow 1 hour, 30 minutes minimum.
Planetarium open daily 10-6. Observatory open
Fri. 8-10 p.m. (weather permitting); free star
show Fri. at 7:30 p.m. A recorded Spanish trans-
lation is available with deposit. Admission (including Miami Museum of Science) $9; over 61
and students with ID $7; ages 3-12, $5.50. Laser
show $6. AE, MC, VI. Phone (305) 646-4270, or
646-4420 for show information.

[GEM] **PARROT JUNGLE AND GARDENS** is at
11000 S.W. 57th Ave., 11 mi. s.w. at jct.
Red Rd. (S.W. 57th Ave.) and Killian Dr.
[SAVE] (S.W. 112th St.). The facility presents a
large collection of parrots and other exotic birds in
a subtropical jungle with orchids, bromeliads and
flowering trees and shrubs. Macaws, parrots and
cockatoos perform in the Trained Parrot Show. A
large flock of Caribbean flamingos resides at Flamingo Lake in the Garden Section. Visitors can
hand-feed parrots and walk through an aviary.

Shows include Creatures in the Night, a noc-
turnal animal show; trained primates performing
in Monkey See, Monkey Do; and Dragons and
Monsters—A Reptile Encounter, featuring a rare
albino alligator. A playground with a petting zoo
is available. Allow 4 hours minimum. Daily
9:30-6. Last admission 1 hour before closing.
Admission $14.95; over 65, $12.95; ages 3-10,
$9.95. AE, MC, VI. Phone (305) 666-7834.

[GEM] **VIZCAYA MUSEUM AND GARDENS,**
3251 S. Miami Ave., is an Italian
Renaissance-style villa. Formerly the estate of industrialist James Deering, the 10-acre villa is
now a museum featuring 34 rooms lavishly furnished with European decorative arts representing the Renaissance, baroque, rococo and
neoclassic eras. The once open-air home has
been enclosed unobtrusively with glass to protect

the valuable furnishings from the weather. The use of cameras within the house is prohibited.

Hedges and walls divide the estate into many small gardens. Extensive formal gardens with pools and fountains contain sculptures from France and Italy. At the foot of the steps leading to Biscayne Bay, an unusual sculptured barge creates an area of calm water.

Allow 2 hours minimum. House open daily 9:30-5. Gardens open daily 9:30-5:30. Closed Dec. 25. Last admission at 4:30. Admission $10; ages 6-12, $5. AE, MC, VI. Phone (305) 250-9133. *See ad p. 116.*

SAVE **WEEKS AIR MUSEUM,** 14710 S.W. 128th St., occupies a hangar at Kendall-Tamiami Airport. Dedicated to the preservation and restoration of aircraft, the museum displays planes, many in flying condition, along with collections of engines, propellers and models. A video booth features actual footage of war planes in action. Allow 1 hour minimum. Daily 10-5; closed Thanksgiving and Dec. 25. Admission $9.95; over 65, $6.95; ages 5-12, $5.95. AE, MC, VI. Phone (305) 233-5197.

THE WOLFSONIAN—FLORIDA INTERNATIONAL UNIVERSITY is at 1001 Washington Ave. in Miami Beach's Art Deco District. Housed in a renovated 1920s Mediterranean-style warehouse, the museum features furniture, paintings, ceramics, architectural models, posters, books and memorabilia that depict the history, art, architecture and design of the late 19th and early 20th centuries.

Allow 1 hour minimum. Mon.-Tues. and Thurs.-Sat. 11-6 (also Thurs. 6-9 p.m.), Sun. noon-5; closed Jan. 1, July 4, Thanksgiving and Dec. 25. Admission $5, senior citizens and students with ID $3.50, under 6 free; free to all Thurs. 6-9 p.m. Phone (305) 531-1001.

What To Do

Sightseeing

Driving Tours

Main and Ingraham highways and Old Cutler Road, south from Coconut Grove, offer scenic drives through Coconut Grove and Coral Gables. Old Cutler Highway passes Matheson Hammock Park and Fairchild Tropical Gardens *(see Coral Gables p. 125).* To reach Parrot Jungle, continue to Red Road, then bear right for about a half mile.

South Miami Avenue, between 15th Road and Dixie Highway, is lined with royal poinciana

trees. During late May and June the trees are ablaze with red flowers.

An interesting drive in Miami Beach is along Collins Avenue, with its hotels and motels. Also of interest are the magnificent homes and estates, which run the architectural gamut from Spanish-Mediterranean to bold modern. Although not open to the public, these can be seen by driving around some of the private islands accessible from the MacArthur, Venetian, North Bay and Broad causeways.

Walking Tours

There are several opportunities for exploration on foot. Coconut Grove, with its varied architecture and bohemian air, is particularly appealing.

The Art Deco District in Miami Beach is a showcase for the movement's characteristic architectural touches: porthole windows, geometric patterns, rounded corners and glass-block construction as well as walls bathed in fuchsia, turquoise, chartreuse and lavender. The Miami Design Preservation League offers a 90-minute tour of the area Thursdays at 6:30 p.m. and Saturdays at 10:30 a.m. The tour begins and ends at the Art Deco Welcome Center at Ocean Front Auditorium, 1001 Ocean Dr. in Miami Beach; phone (305) 672-2014. The fee is $10. The organization also arranges other Miami Beach area tours and provides audiotapes for self-guided tours.

Little Havana, S.W. 12th Avenue to S.W. 27th Avenue, has open-air markets, music, shops, restaurants and a plaza, all of which reflect the Cuban culture. For information about the area contact the Little Havana Development Authority Inc., 970 S.W. First St., Suite 408, Miami, FL 33130; phone (305) 324-8127.

Spectator Sports

In addition to year-round sunshine and white, sandy beaches, Miami is blessed with an abundance of professional sport offerings, including four major-league teams. No matter what your preference might be, you'll find a venue and a crowd of like-minded fans ready to cheer on their favorites.

Auto Racing

The 5,000-seat stadium at **Hialeah Speedway**, 3300 Okeechobee Rd., holds weekly stock-car races in five divisions; phone (305) 821-6644.

The **Homestead-Miami Speedway**, 1 Speedway Blvd. in Homestead, has a 1.5-mile oval track that is negotiated by some of the sport's top names. For information phone (305) 230-7223.

Baseball

The National League **Florida Marlins** are one of baseball's newest expansion teams, passionately supported during their home games at **Pro Player Stadium**, 2269 199th St., east of 27th Avenue in North Miami; phone (305) 626-7400. The Marlins brought the World Series title home to Miami in 1997. The national pastime also is played locally in the college ranks when the **University of Miami Hurricanes** take the field on the UM campus at **Mark Light Stadium**.

Basketball

The Atlantic division champion **Miami Heat** have been a hot ticket in town since their November 1988 debut. During their November to April season, the Heat play at the new **American**

Airlines Arena, downtown on Biscayne Boulevard adjacent to Bayside Marketplace; phone (305) 960-8500 for information.

Football

Backed by legions of "dolfans," the **Miami Dolphins** suit up for battle at the 75,000-seat Pro Player Stadium; phone (305) 626-7426 for the Dolphins or (305) 623-6100 for the stadium. The **Orange Bowl** stadium at 1501 N.W. Third St. is home turf for the University of Miami Hurricanes; phone (305) 643-7100. Despite three national championship titles, the 'Canes seldom fill up the stadium, so tickets are not difficult to come by.

Greyhound Racing

The dogs average a swift 40 mph at ⟨SAVE⟩ **Flagler Greyhound Track**, 401 N.W. 38th Ct., from June through November; phone (305) 649-3000.

Horse Racing

Thoroughbreds run to the roar of the crowd at **Gulfstream Park,** 901 S. Federal Hwy. in nearby Hallandale *(see Hallandale p. 77)*, about a half-hour drive north from downtown Miami. The scenic track, encircling an artificial lake, is host to numerous major races; phone (305) 931-7223. The grandeur of old-fashioned stands distinguishes **Hialeah Park**, 2200 E. 4th Ave. in Hialeah; phone (305) 885-8000.

The usual March-to-May season is extended at **Calder Race Course**, just south of County Line Road (SR 852) at 21001 N.W. 27th Ave., where the horses run from late May to early January on a 1-mile course in a glass-enclosed, air-conditioned sports facility. Phone (305) 625-1311 for specific starting and wrap-up dates.

Jai Alai

In this high-speed, indoor version of lacrosse, players climb the walls to catch and hurl balls *(pelotas)* with woven baskets *(cestas)*. Spectators place bets on the evening's players from behind a protective wall of glass. See the action for yourself at America's oldest jai alai arena *(fronton)*, the **Miami Jai Alai Fronton**, 3500 N.W. 37th Ave.; phone (305) 633-6400.

Note: Policies on admitting children to parimutuel betting facilities vary. Phone in advance for specific information.

Recreation

A wealth of clear blue skies and a climate conducive to outdoor activity any time of the year make Miami a "hot" spot for those in search of fun in the sun. This tropical playground, with an average annual temperature of 76 F, comes equipped with aquamarine waters and more than enough land-based activities to suit all tastes.

Bicycling

Few places offer such diverse cycling environments as Miami. Pedal the hard-packed sands of

Miami Beach while enjoying the sun and sights, or take the bicycle path that winds beneath a canopy of trees in **Coconut Grove,** where you can hop off and cruise through the neighborhood's colorful downtown area. Slightly more removed is the tropical escape of **Key Biscayne.** Here, on an island just 7 miles long and 2 miles wide, are 12 miles of bicycling trails. Bicycle rentals are available at all of the above locations; helmets are required for those under 17.

Experienced bicyclists desiring more extensive routes can contact the Miami-Dade Bicycle Pedestrian Program, which distributes maps about bicycling and bicycling safety and outlines some of Miami's more than 138 miles of bicycle trails; phone (305) 375-4507. A color-coded map of Miami-Dade County's 4,000 miles of suitable roads also is available.

Fishing

An abundance of water naturally brings plenty of fishing opportunities, and the popularity of bridge fishing, seen all over Miami, is just a prelude to the opportunities available in a city where fishing is serious business. Both **South Pointe Park** in south Miami Beach and **Haulover Beach Park** at Collins Avenue and 105th Street offer excellent surf casting. Although bridge fishing is generally not allowed, it is permitted on the old **Rickenbacker Causeway,** which was left standing for that purpose when the new bridge was constructed for automobile traffic. Several piers in Miami Beach, as well as the **Tamiami Canal,** also are favorites of anglers.

Numerous marinas offer deep-sea fishing excursions, where avid anglers haul in prizes that range from snapper and bonita to big game catches like sailfish, tarpon and bluefish. **Kelley Fishing Fleet,** 10800 Collins Ave. at Haulover Marina, provides party boats for half-day or full-day excursions out of Miami Beach; phone (305) 945-3801. Private charter boats abound at Haulover, with many offering 2-, 3- and 4-day fishing trips to the Bahamas; make the rounds and choose the one that suits your needs.

Licenses, required for freshwater fishing, are available at bait and tackle shops, sporting goods and discount department stores, as well as the county tax collector's office in the Miami-Dade County Courthouse, 140 W. Flagler St., Miami, FL 33130. Licenses also are available by mail; phone (888) 347-4356 (a credit card is required).

Golf

More than 30 golf courses provide a wide choice of greens for hackers and seasoned golfers alike. Crandon Park Golf Course, 6700 Cran-

don Blvd. in Key Biscayne, (305) 361-9129, is recognized by most Florida golfers as the No. 1-ranked public course in the state; it also is among the top public links in the country. All courses listed below offer at least 18 holes and are open to the public.

Sites in the Miami area include Bayshore, 2301 Alton Rd. in Miami Beach, (305) 532-3350; Biltmore, 1210 Anastasia in Coral Gables, (305) 460-5364; Don Shula's Hotel and Golf Club, 15255 Bull Run Rd. in Miami Lakes, (305) 821-1150; Doral Park Golf and Country Club, 5001 N.W. 104th Ave., (305) 591-8800; Golf Club of Miami, 6801 Miami Gardens Dr., (305) 829-8449; Killian Green, 9980 S.W. 104th St., (305) 271-0917; Melreese Golf Course, 1802 N.W. 37th Ave., (305) 633-4583; Miami National, 6401 Kendall Lakes Dr., (305) 382-3930; and Miami Springs Golf Course, 650 Curtiss Pkwy. in Miami Springs, (305) 863-0980.

The two city-owned Miami Beach courses welcome guests, and many hotels and motels have arrangements with private and semiprivate courses that allow guests to play.

Tennis

Miami's balmy climate allows for year-round tennis dates, and nearly 500 public courts cater to the racket. A majority of the hotels and motels in Miami and Miami Beach have private tennis facilities for their guests. Nearly all charge an hourly fee for use by nonresidents.

Best bets include the **Tennis Center at Crandon Park,** 7300 Crandon Blvd. in Key Biscayne, with hard courts; phone (305) 365-2300. Miami Beach's **Flamingo Tennis Center,** at Meridian and 11th streets, offers nearly 20 well-maintained clay courts; phone (305) 673-7761. For additional information about public courts phone the Miami-Dade County Parks Department at (305) 755-7800.

Water Sports

Whether you like zipping across its surface or exploring the world below it, everything you need to enjoy the water can be found in Miami, and all of it can be rented—from kayaks, windsurfers and boogie boards to catamarans, sailboats, personal watercraft and scuba equipment.

Many scuba and sail shops offer day-trip packages that include rental equipment and lessons for windsurfing, scuba diving and snorkeling. There are many sunken hulls, reefs and underwater gardens that provide excellent opportunities for photography or exploration. North of Snapper Creek and south of Matheson Hammock Park is one of the better snorkeling sites. Another favorite location is near **Fowley Rocks Light** just south of Key Biscayne.

Boating is popular in Miami. Boats of all sizes and descriptions are for hire, whether for pleasure cruising, fishing or water skiing. **Dinner Key** and waterfront Coconut Grove are pristine and popular sites for launching sailboats. Other locations for sailboat rentals are available around the bay and on the **Miami River.** Boating events, whose locations and schedules are printed in area newspapers, take place throughout the year.

Powerboat rentals are available from **Club Nautico** at several locations: at Monty Trainer Restaurant, 2560 S. Bayshore Dr. in Coconut Grove, (305) 858-6258; at Crandon Park Marina in Key Biscayne, (305) 361-9217; and at Miami Beach Marina, in Miami Beach, (305) 673-2502. Renters must be at least 21 years of age.

Water skiing and windsurfing instruction and equipment are available throughout the area. Many shops are clustered around the 79th Street Causeway (North Bay). Skiing is good all along the bay. Personal watercraft also can be rented.

Surfing, while not the best in the country, attracts many enthusiasts. Two of the best spots are **South Beach** and **Haulover Beach.**

Some of the most popular white sand beaches in the Miami area are at **Bill Baggs Cape Florida State Recreation Area** and **Crandon Park.** Miami Beach's oceanfront restoration program added 150 to 200 feet to the width of the city's 10.5-mile stretch of beach, southward from 87th Terrace to the south end of Miami Beach.

Shopping

Greater Miami can easily accommodate those with a shop-'til-you-drop mentality. Although big city congestion can mean rare parking spaces and a frenzied atmosphere, such inconveniences are quickly forgotten by those who browse the shops' enticements. And, because of Miami's tourist orientation, the area is a treasure trove of souvenirs, from technicolor T-shirts to opulent *objets d'art.*

Antiques

Miami's antique tastes are far from mainstream. Shops are hidden around the region, to be uncovered like sunken treasure. Fine European furniture, clocks, bronzes and art glass are at **Alhambra Antiques Center**, 3640 Coral Way. **Olde Tyme Shoppe**, 1423 Ponce de Leon Blvd. in Coral Gables, offers vintage pocket watches, chiming watches, clocks and other unique collector pieces. And, of course, where else would you expect to find a wealth of art deco wares but in the heart of the trendy art deco district?

Malls

More than 160 specialty shops fill the spacious **Dadeland Mall**, 7535 N. Kendall Dr. in Kendall. Anchored by Florida's largest Burdines department store, Dadeland features JCPenney, Lord & Taylor and Saks Fifth Avenue. Also in Kendall, the open-air **The Falls**, 8888 S.W. 136th St., has Miami's only Bloomingdale's department store as well as more than 50 ritzy shops in a lush, tropical setting.

Just west of the airport, **Miami International Mall**, 1455 N.W. 107th Ave., has Burdines, JCPenney, Mervyn's and Sears in addition to 150 smaller stores. Off the Palmetto Expressway at the N.W. 103rd Street exit in Hialeah is **Westland Mall**. Burdines, JCPenney and Sears join 100 smaller shops. Closer to downtown is the 85-store **Omni International Mall**, at 1601 Biscayne Blvd.; children love the old-fashioned carousel here.

At 19501 Biscayne Blvd. in Aventura, a short hop off the William Lehman Causeway (SR 856), **Aventura Mall** is anchored by JCPenney, Lord & Taylor, Macy's and Sears. Specialty boutiques are among the mall's 200 shops and restaurants. **Cutler Ridge Mall**, US 1S and Caribbean Boulevard, has Burdines, JCPenney, Luria's, Mervyn's and Sears among its 101 stores.

Specialty Districts

In addition to a multitude of malls, Miami also features upscale and themed shopping districts. The boutique district along **Collins Avenue** in South Beach features Armani Exchange, Banana Republic and Nicole Miller. Continental cafes and the boutiques of Bulgari, Cartier, Gucci, Louis Vuitton, Tiffany & Co. and Ungaro, to name a few, give credence to the internationally renowned status of **Bal Harbour Shops,** 9700 Collins Ave. in Bal Harbour; the shops also claim Florida's largest Neiman Marcus store. In this area it is not just business as usual; gracious transactions and outstanding service are customary in Bal Harbour's elegant setting.

The 50 swanky boutiques in the European-styled **Streets of Mayfair,** 2911 Grand Ave. in Coconut Grove, proffer exclusive gifts, art, antiques and apparel; late-night clubs and trendy restaurants are nestled around the palm trees and waterfalls as well. VIP services for shopping, mailing or wrapping add the extra touch for which Mayfair is known.

Fun, funky and favored for drinks by an after-work crowd, the **Bayside Marketplace,** 401 Biscayne Blvd., is a downtown shopping, dining and entertainment mecca on Biscayne Bay. Designed after the historic Faneuil Hall Marketplace in Boston, the waterfront arcade combines more than 150 specialty boutiques, street performers, restaurants and outdoor eateries, and nightly open-air concerts to create a festive atmosphere. The **Pier 5 Market,** part of the complex, showcases the works of local artisans, entrepreneurs and inventors.

Rustic outdoor push carts, avant-garde clothing stores and lavishly decorated plazas are the hallmarks of **Coconut Grove,** Miami's tropical, pedestrian-friendly shopping and dining village. A smorgasbord of funky import shops, European salons and vintage clothing boutiques, the Grove is centered around Main Highway and Grand Avenue. At its heart is **CocoWalk,** 3015 Grand Ave., a colorful, casual open-air shopping center that includes cafes and trendy nightspots.

Some of the region's finest boutiques, gourmet restaurants and art galleries line the famed **Miracle Mile** in Coral Gables. The neighborhood's central boulevard and an integral part of George Merrick's original city plan, Miracle Mile is actually a half mile, between 37th and 42nd avenues, of small, picturesque 1970s storefronts along a wide, tree-lined boulevard. The significance here is historical as well as commercial.

A unique assortment of art galleries, antique shops and offbeat boutiques provides blocks of inspired browsing along South Miami Beach's

Lincoln Road. This 7-block pedestrian mall near the north end of the art deco district is the center of the city's happening art scene. It is surrounded by the district's two main commercial arteries, Collins and Washington avenues.

Performing Arts

The 1981 development of the National Foundation for the Arts was the springboard for cultural evolution in south Florida. Patrons of the arts enjoy an expanding array of performing arts

venues. Included are the handsomely refurbished **Colony Theater** on Lincoln Road in south Miami Beach, (305) 674-1026; the 1,700-seat, Moorish-styled **Gusman Center for the Performing Arts,** on E. Flagler Street in downtown Miami, (305) 374-2444; and the art deco **Jackie Gleason Theater of the Performing Arts** (known as "TOPA") on Washington Avenue in south Miami Beach, (305) 673-7300.

Dance

Among the professional dance troupes in the Miami area is the **Miami City Ballet,** Florida's first fully professional resident ballet company. Artistic director Edward Villella premiered in the New York City Ballet under George Balanchine; works by Balanchine are included in the company's repertoire. Performances take place October through March at the Jackie Gleason Theater of the Performing Arts and at other venues throughout south Florida; phone (305) 929-7010 for ticket information.

The professional dance company **Ballet Flamenco La Rosa** moves to a flamenco and Latin-style beat; for ticket and schedule information phone (305) 672-0552.

Music

Although Miami does not have a resident symphony orchestra, the void is filled by the **New World Symphony.** Conductor Michael Tilson Thomas created the only advanced-training orchestra in the world as an interim step for young musicians who have completed their academic instruction. For subscriptions, season or single tickets phone (305) 673-3331, or phone the main office at (305) 673-3330.

Lovers of classical music appreciate the high-caliber offerings of the **Concert Association of Florida**. The long-running series features such luminaries as Itzhak Perlman and Andre Watts; phone (305) 532-3491.

Performing primarily at Gusman Center for the Performing Arts downtown, the **Florida Philharmonic** maintains its main office at 3401 N.W. 9th Ave. in Fort Lauderdale. Under the direction of James Judd, south Florida's premier symphony orchestra presents a full season of recitals, including children's programs; phone (954) 561-2997 or (800) 226-1812 for schedule and ticket information.

Opera

The celebrated **Florida Grand Opera**, 2901 W. Flagler St., which has provided South Florida with operatic performances since the early 1940s, offers five productions annually in the **Dade County Auditorium**, at Flagler Street and 29th Avenue; phone (305) 547-5414. Included among those honored during the opera's International Series are Placido Domingo and Luciano Pavarotti. Promising singers make their mark in lead roles during the lower-priced National Series.

Theater

Housed in a lovely Spanish rococo-style palace, **Coconut Grove Playhouse**, 3500 Main Hwy. in Coconut Grove, has been one of Mi-

ami's most respected theaters since its inception in 1956, offering star casts in hit shows. Check the local newspapers for rates and schedules or phone (305) 442-4000. Broadway-bound plays and musical reviews are staged in its 1,100-seat main section; the playhouse also presents experimental productions in the intimate **Encore Room**.

Area Stage Company presents off-Broadway plays throughout the year. **Actor's Playhouse** offers year-round productions for adults and children and is host to the National Children's Theater Festival.

Special Events

On New Year's Day Miami honors the orange with the **Orange Bowl Festival**. The festival is capped that night by the **Orange Bowl** football game. Runners join in the celebration during the **Orange Bowl 5K/10K**. The **Junior Orange Bowl Festival**, held in December, is a children's counterpart to the Orange Bowl festivities and features arts and crafts shows and competitions in football, tennis, soccer, golf and bowling.

Art Deco Weekend, a 3-day festival in mid-January where South Beach's fanciful architecture takes center stage, celebrates the Miami Beach historic district with a street fair, a 1930s-style ball, a film series, lectures, entertainment and a parade. The **Royal Caribbean Classic** golf tournament beckons devotees of that sport late January to early February.

The February calendar is filled with such events as the **Miami/Coconut Grove Art Festival**, one of the state's largest, offering works in almost every medium; the **Miami International Boat Show** at Miami Beach Convention Center; and the **Mid-Winter Sailing Regatta**. Miami-bound foreign and independent film fans will enjoy the **Miami International Film Festival**, which takes place during 10 days in February at Gusman Center for the Performing Arts. This increasingly important affair attracts more than 45,000 cinema aficionados. In late February or early March, engines and crowds roar during the **Miami Grand Prix**, while galleries of fans hush at the **Doral Ryder Open**.

In the jubilant tradition of Rio de Janeiro, 9 days of merrymaking begin with the pageantry of **Carnival Miami**, said to be the nation's largest Hispanic celebration and Miami's largest event. This weeklong Cuban celebration in early March has parades, concerts, fireworks and entertainment. Festivities culminate in the famous **Calle Ocho**, where more than 1 million people, mostly of Latin American descent, fill a 23-block area along S.W. Eighth Street in the heart of the Cuban district to enjoy music, food and each other's company.

Villa Vizcaya fills with period costumes, food and craft vendors, music and performances at the **Italian Renaissance Festival** in mid-March. In

June the **Royal Poinciana Festival** coincides with the blooming of the trees in Bayfront Park. Also in June, the **Miami-Bahamas Goombay Festival** celebrates the city's ties to Caribbean culture with street dances and other entertainment; this event takes place in Coconut Grove.

Handmade arts and crafts, alligator wrestling, food and American Indian music are all part of the festivities that take place in late July at the Miccosukee Indian Village during the **Everglades Music and Craft Festival**. Amid more than 150 exhibits of arts, crafts and novelties, south Florida jazz musicians perform on three stages in mid-September at **Taste of Art and Jazz** in Miami Lakes.

Cultural heritage comes to the forefront at three fall events. At the beginning of October is the **West Indian American Way Carnival Extravaganza**, a celebration of the Caribbean, featuring concerts, arts and crafts, food, costumed galas and street festivals. **Caribbean Carnival**, also in October, is a celebration of the Caribbean people and cultures, featuring concerts, arts and crafts, food, costumed galas and street festivals, all taking place at Hialeah Park race track in Hialeah. The **Sun Street Festival** in November celebrates African-American culture with gospel and talent shows, parades and street festivals.

In November the **Marion Edwards Jr. Memorial Race** for late-model stock cars is held at the Hialeah Speedway, and the **NASCAR Winston Cup Series Pennzoil 400** and the **NASCAR Busch Series Miami 300** are run at the Homestead-Miami Speedway. The **Harvest Festival**, a popular craft extravaganza, includes historical re-enactments, music, a quilt sale and antique cars in mid-November.

In a zany spoof of the beloved King Orange Jamboree Parade, the **King Mango Strut** on Dec. 26 features such wacky entries as the Precision Briefcase Drill Team and the Marching Freds. To round out the year the **Big Orange New Year's Eve Celebration and Parade** snakes along Biscayne Bay to kick off a weekend of New Year's celebrations.

The Latin Chamber of Commerce (CAMACOL) sponsors Hispanic festivals throughout the year. For information contact the chamber at 1417 W. Flagler St., Miami, FL 33135; phone (305) 642-3870.

Nightlife

Generally, Miami's native night owls balance a feverish club scene with simple evenings spent dockside. **Sundays on the Bay,** 5420 Crandon Blvd. in Key Biscayne, is one of numerous hot spots where locals enjoy a breathtaking view and live band sounds under the stars; phone (305) 361-6777. **Shuckers,** in the Best Western Bayfront at 1819 79th St. Cswy., is another bayfront bar, adding volleyball and late-night dancing to its casual but raucous atmosphere; phone (305) 866-1570.

Roadhouse-style blues, reggae and salsa are easy to find around town, as is mainstream pop and rock. Gentler souls who desire the sounds of jazz piano or the quiet tempo of a Latin ballad are especially gratified in this city, often finding solace in the cool, lush intimacy of a hotel lounge. Diversity is Miami's strong suit, but there is one exception: Country and folk music fans will have to look hard and be lucky—such acts are infrequently booked at area clubs.

Dance Clubs

The dance club scene in Miami is centered within South Beach's art deco district. Clubs—gay and straight—are constantly being reinvented, keeping South Beach at the pinnacle of the city's hot spots. Weekends are jammed with fashionable partyers making the Washington Avenue venues. A current favorite is Sean Penn's **Bash,** 655 Washington Ave., for dancing and enjoying tapas on an intimate patio; phone (305) 538-2274.

The **Cameo Theatre,** 1445 Washington Ave., is still decorated with remnants of its grand days as a 1930s theater. The spacious interior pulses with disco, alternative and progressive sounds, and Sunday is always disco night; phone (305) 532-0922. Also popular are the intimate **Groove Jet,** 323 23rd. St., and the trendy **Liquid,** 1439 Washington Ave.; phone (305) 532-2002 and (305) 532-9154, respectively.

Entertainment Complexes

The pub-hopping crowd finds a mix of upbeat and laid-back entertainment downtown at **Bayside Marketplace,** 401 Biscayne Blvd., where

Hooters, the Hard Rock Cafe, Snapper's Bar and Grill, Bubba Gump Shrimp Co. and Mambo Cafe all serve a happy, loud bunch; phone (305) 577-3344. **Let's Make a Daiquiri,** an outdoor bar, presents live jazz, rock, reggae and calypso music, along with bay breezes and glimpses of ocean liners as they make their way to and from the Port of Miami; phone (305) 372-5117.

In Coconut Grove locals and out-of-towners rendezvous at **CocoWalk,** 3015 Grand Ave., (305) 444-0777, a multilevel open mall with a combination of popular clubs including Cafe Tu Tu Tango, Fat Tuesdays, Hooters and Cafe Med.

Jazz & Blues

In the Miami area the urban roadhouse of long standing is **Tobacco Road,** 626 S. Miami Ave. Opened in 1912, this one-time Prohibition speakeasy sings the blues downtown, with local and national bands performing Friday and Saturday nights; past performers have included Albert Collins, James Cotton and John Lee Hooker. Jazz jams take place on Wednesday nights; phone (305) 374-1198.

You also can enjoy the rhythms of jazz and blues at **Jazid,** in Miami Beach at 1342 Washington Ave., (305) 673-9372; at the upscale **Martini Bar,** 3390 Mary St. on the third floor of Streets of Mayfair, (305) 444-5911; performed nightly by both local and national artists at **Satchmo Blues,** 60 Merrick Way in Coral Gables, (305) 774-1883; and **Upstairs at the Van Dyke,** in Miami Beach, at 846 Lincoln Rd., (305) 534-3600.

Latin Clubs

Snappy rhythms, swirling partners, the click of heels on a parquet floor ... now that's Miami. At the city's heart is a Latin beat, and the Fontainebleau Hilton Resort & Towers, 4441 Collins Ave., offers **Club Tropigala,** a jungly four-tier cabaret featuring a Latin orchestra Wednesday through Sunday nights; phone (305) 672-7469.

Similar smaller venues are scattered throughout the city. **Studio 23,** 247 23rd St. in Miami Beach, is a lively disco that reverberates to the sounds of salsa and merengue; phone (305) 538-1196. Another hot spot for Latin and salsa beats is **Alcazaba,** 50 Alhambra Plaza, in the Hyatt Regency Coral Gables; phone (305) 441-1234.

Rock

Miamians in search of hard-driving rock 'n' roll head to **Penrod's,** 1 Ocean Dr. in south Miami Beach, where live music by the pool is a weekend tradition; phone (305) 538-1111.

The Miami-Miami Beach Vicinity

BISCAYNE NATIONAL PARK (H-12)

Elevations in the land portion
of the park are at sea level.
Ninety-five percent of the park
is water.

Biscayne National Park encompasses a huge part of southeast Florida. Reached via Florida's Turnpike (exit 2, Campbell Drive) and S.W. 328th St. (North Canal Drive), the park offers a look at an unspoiled part of Florida. Only 4,370 of its 180,000 acres are land; the rest are water, and there is as much to see below its surface as there is above it.

Biscayne National Park has four biological systems: the mainland mangrove forests, Biscayne Bay, the upper Florida Keys and the underwater reefs. Shallow Biscayne Bay, which is between the coast and the northernmost Florida Keys, has clear water and is home to sponges, crabs, dolphins and manatees, endangered mammals that favor the bay's warm waters.

The undeveloped upper Florida Keys are the result of many thousands of years of construction by the tiny animals collectively known as coral. The 20 miles of the park's reefs were formed by more than 100 species of coral and harbor more than 200 different kinds of fish, including brilliantly colored parrotfish, angelfish and wrasses. Moray eels also inhabit many of the underwater crevices.

To preserve the fragile reefs, visitors must anchor boats in the sandy bottoms, not on the coral. Do not touch the coral; doing so will kill it. Also, do not sit or stand on the coral, as it breaks easily and can cause painful cuts. Collecting coral, plants, animals, shipwreck artifacts or any other "souvenir" is prohibited.

The upper keys support other endangered species. Bald eagles, ospreys, pelicans, egrets and other large birds find refuge in the dense vegetation. Arsenicker and West Arsenicker keys are important nesting areas and therefore are closed to the public.

The islands feature many tropical plants that originated from seeds either blown here by West Indian winds or deposited by birds. On the mainland are forests of mangroves, easily recognized by their twisted roots, which trap and filter out sediment that would otherwise harm the water and its inhabitants. The mangrove roots provide excellent hiding places and food sources for young fish—another function vital to the region's food chain.

Biscayne National Park is an undeveloped wilderness. Camping is permitted only on Elliott Key and Boca Chiton Key, which can be reached only by boat. Because the park is accessible primarily by boat, it is helpful to get a tour boat schedule from the headquarters on Convoy Point, 9 miles east of Homestead on S.W. 328th Street. The facility is open daily 8:30-5; closed Dec. 25.

Canoe rentals also are available. Reservations are required for all trips and rentals and must be confirmed before departure; phone (305) 230-1100.

For further park information contact Biscayne National Park, 9700 S.W. 328th St., Homestead, FL 33033-5634; phone (305) 230-7275. *See Recreation Chart and the AAA Southeastern CampBook.*

Biscayne National UnderWater Park Inc., whose trips depart from Convoy Point Visitor Center on S.W. 328th St., offers 3-hour glass-bottom boat tours on a 53-foot vessel and snorkeling and scuba diving excursions on a 45-foot catamaran.

Glass-bottom boat trips depart daily at 10. Snorkeling trips depart daily at 1:30. Scuba diving trips depart Wed.-Fri. 9-1, Sat.-Sun. 8:30-1 (weather permitting). Glass-bottom boat fare $19.95; under 13, $9.95. Snorkeling fare (includes equipment) $27.95. Scuba fare $35. Reservations are required. AE, MC, VI. Phone (305) 230-1100.

COCONUT GROVE (H-11) elev. 10′

BARNACLE STATE HISTORICAL SITE is at 3485 Main Hwy. Commodore Ralph Munroe, an area pioneer and noted designer of shallow-draft ships, built the cottage in 1891 and later enlarged it by raising the seven rooms to accommodate another floor underneath. Most furnishings belonged to Munroe, and many of his photographs are displayed. A boat house also is on the property. The cottage may be viewed only by guided tour.

Allow 1 hour minimum. Grounds open Fri.-Mon. 9-4; closed Jan. 1 and Dec. 25. Guided tours of the cottage are given at 10, 11:30, 1 and 2:30. Admission $1, under 10 free. Phone (305) 448-9445.

CORAL GABLES (H-11)
pop. 40,100, elev. 11′

A planned community, Coral Gables is noted for its landscaped plazas and parkways, gateways of coral rock and royal poinciana trees. Spanish, Mediterranean and contemporary architecture blend in the downtown area. Many estates are in the older section of the city; modern mansions line the bayfront. Coral Gables House, 907 Coral Way, was the home of founder George Merrick, who named the city after his family home.

The Spanish architecture, lagoons and grottoes of the Venetian Pool, a public swimming pool at 2701 DeSoto Blvd., reflect the lavish Coral Gables lifestyle of the 1920s. Also of interest are the Dutch-South African, Chinese and French villages.

Coral Gables is home to the University of Miami.

Coral Gables Chamber of Commerce: 50 Aragon Ave., Coral Gables, FL 33134; phone (305) 446-1657.

[SAVE] **FAIRCHILD TROPICAL GARDENS,** next to Matheson Hammock Park at 10901 Old Cutler Rd., is an 83-acre tropical botanical garden with vistas, a rain forest and a conservatory. Free guided walking tours are offered. Narrated tram tours depart hourly. Food is available. Gardens open daily 9:30-4:30; closed Dec. 25. Tram tours Mon.-Fri. 10-3, Sat.-Sun. 10-4. Admission (includes tram tour) $8, under 13 free with an adult. AE, DS, MC, VI. Phone (305) 667-1651.

LOWE ART MUSEUM, w. of jct. US 1 and Stanford Dr. at 1301 Stanford Dr., is on the University of Miami campus. Renaissance paintings and furniture as well as 20th-century works are displayed. The museum also presents changing exhibits from collections of Asian, African, American, baroque, pre-Columbian, southwest American Indian and contemporary artworks.

Allow 1 hour minimum. Tues.-Wed. and Fri.-Sat. 10-5, Thurs. noon-7, Sun. noon-5; closed Jan. 1, July 4, Thanksgiving and Dec. 25. Admission $5, over 65 and students with ID $3, under 13 free. AE, DS, MC, VI. Phone (305) 284-3535.

MATHESON HAMMOCK PARK, 9610 Old Cutler Rd., is a man-made atoll pool separated from Biscayne Bay by a walkway. Trails wind among native shrubs and virgin forest. A boat ramp, bathhouse and picnic areas are available. Daily 6 a.m.-dusk. Admission $3.50. Parking $3.50 for automobiles, $6 for recreational vehicles or buses, $8 for boats. Phone (305) 665-5475.

FLORIDA CITY (H-11)
pop. 5,600, elev. 6′

Florida City is surrounded by agricultural fields often referred to as the nation's "winter vegetable basket." Snap and pole beans, zucchini and squash are winter crops, while okra, limes, avocados and mangoes grow during the summer. Florida City State Farmer's Market, 300 N. Krome Ave. west of the junction of US 1 and Florida's Turnpike, is a wholesale and retail outlet. The retail outlet is open November through June, the wholesale outlet year-round; phone (305) 246-6334.

Greater Homestead-Florida City Chamber of Commerce: 43 N. Krome Ave., Homestead, FL 33030; phone (305) 247-2332.

Shopping: Prime Outlets at Florida City, junction SR 821 (Florida's Turnpike) and US 1 at

250 E. Palm Dr., offers 60 outlet shops including Bass, Mikasa and Nike.

HOMESTEAD (H-11)
pop. 26,900, elev. 9'

The center of south Florida's fruit and nursery production, Homestead serves as a gateway to Everglades National Park *(see place listing p. 56)*, Biscayne National Park *(see place listing p. 124)* and The Florida Keys *(see place listing p. 60)*.

Homestead-Miami Motorsports Complex, 1 Speedway Blvd., offers scheduled races throughout the year. For ticket information phone (305) 230-7223. The city's historic district offers shops and restaurants in a landscaped setting.

Tropical Everglades Visitor Center: 160 US 1, Florida City, FL 33034; phone (305) 245-9180 or (800) 388-9669.

[SAVE] **CORAL CASTLE OF FLORIDA,** 2 mi. n. on US 1, is built of massive blocks of handhewn coral rock. Using primitive tools, Latvian immigrant Ed Leedskalnin worked alone 1923-40 to build the structure and its furnishings. Audiotapes are available for self-guiding tours. Allow 1 hour minimum. Daily 9-6; closed Dec. 25. Admission $7.75; over 62, $6.50; ages 7-12, $5. AE, DS, MC, VI. Phone (305) 248-6344.

FRUIT AND SPICE PARK, 5 mi. w. of US 1 on S.W. 248 St., encompasses 35 acres with more than 500 species of fruit, nut and spice trees from throughout the world. Features include an herb and vegetable garden and a banana grove. Picnic facilities are available. Daily 10-5; closed Dec. 25. Admission $3.50; ages 4-12, $1. Phone (305) 247-5727.

KEY BISCAYNE (H-12)
pop. 8,900, elev. 5'

CRANDON PARK, 4000 Crandon Blvd., is reached via the Rickenbacker Causeway over Biscayne Bay; toll $1. A scenic park, it has landscaped picnic areas and a 2.5-mile public beach. Allow 1 hour minimum. Daily 8-dusk. Admission $3.50 per car, $6 per bus or recreational vehicle. Phone (305) 361-5421.

NORTH MIAMI BEACH (H-11)
pop. 35,400, elev. 10'

ANCIENT SPANISH MONASTERY (Episcopal) is at 16711 W. Dixie Hwy. Built in 12th-century Spain, the structure was dismantled and shipped to the United States in 1925. The monastery was rebuilt in 1952 and now houses ancient artworks and furniture. Allow 2 hours minimum. Mon.-Sat. 10-4, Sun. 1-5; closed Easter, Thanksgiving and Dec. 25. Admission $4.50; over 65, $2.50; under 12, $1. Phone (305) 945-1461.

This ends listings for the Miami-Miami Beach Vicinity.
The following page resumes the alphabetical listings of cities in Florida.

MICANOPY (C-8) pop. 600, elev. 100'

The former site of a Timucuan Indian village, Micanopy (MIK-uh-no-pee) is the state's oldest inland town. Many antique, art and curio shops help to create an atmosphere of a small Florida village during the 19th century.

PAYNES PRAIRIE STATE PRESERVE, 1 mi. n. on US 441, encompasses 21,000 acres of freshwater marsh, hammocks, pine flatwoods, swamps and ponds. More then 20 miles of trails are available to explore these areas. Visitor center exhibits interpret the natural and cultural history of this important ecological area. An audiovisual program explains the preservation of the basin's natural landscape. A 50-foot observation tower stands near the center of the preserve and a recreation area is at Lake Wauberg. Camping is permitted.

Ranger-led activities are available November through April by reservation; phone (352) 466-4100. Allow 1 hour minimum. Park open daily 8-dusk. Visitor center open daily 9-5. Admission $3.25 per private vehicle (maximum eight people), $1 per person arriving by bicycle or on foot. Phone (352) 466-3397. *See Recreation Chart and the AAA Southeastern CampBook.*

MILTON (A-2) pop. 7,200, elev. 15'

A heavy growth of briars along the Blackwater River elicited Milton's early name, Scratch Ankle. The Blackwater, one of the state's most pristine rivers, has retained its importance to modern Milton as a carrier of recreational canoeists rather than commerce; canoes and tubes can be rented in the area. Blackwater River State Park *(see Recreation Chart)* and Blackwater River State Forest are northeast. Historic old homes date back to the Civil War days. Whiting Field Naval Air Station is north on SR 87.

Santa Rosa County Chamber of Commerce: 5247 Stewart St., Milton, FL 32570; phone (850) 623-2339.

RECREATIONAL ACTIVITIES
Canoeing
- **Adventures Unlimited,** 12 mi. n. on SR 87, then 4 mi. e. following signs. Write Route 6, Box 283, Milton, FL 32570. Other activities are offered. Daily 8-6, Mar.-Sept.; 8-4, rest of year. Closed Thanksgiving and Dec. 25. Phone (850) 623-6197 or (800) 239-6864.

MULBERRY (E-9) pop. 3,000, elev. 140'

Long known as the center of phosphate production in Central Florida, Mulberry was founded in 1901. The city today covers about 6 square miles.

MULBERRY PHOSPHATE MUSEUM, 1 blk. s. of jct. SRs 37 and 60 at 101 S.E. First St. (SR 37),

features a collection of fossilized remains of prehistoric animals, area memorabilia and exhibits related to the phosphate industry. A phosphate train also is displayed. Allow 1 hour minimum. Tues.-Sat. 10-4:30. Donations. Phone (863) 425-2823.

NAPLES (G-9) pop. 19,500, elev. 9'

Naples quickly is becoming the Palm Beach of Florida's west coast; its Fifth Avenue corridor contains trendy boutiques, art galleries, cozy restaurants and other upscale accouterments. This image is a far cry from the days in 1885 when development began and the area was accessible only by water. The Naples Pier is a relic of that period.

Naples' greatest treasures are not found in the shops and malls—the city has long been famous for its 10 miles of public beaches. Shell gathering and other beachfront activities are available at Delnor-Wiggins Pass State Recreation Area *(see Recreation Chart),* 11 miles northwest via SR 846.

Rookery Bay, 5 miles south, is an area of mangrove islands that shelter rare birds and marine life. Maintained as a national estuarine research reserve, it is reached by a half-mile boardwalk that explores the upland areas. The reserve also features Briggs Nature Center *(see attraction listing p. 129).* The mainland portions

are accessible from Shell Island Road, off SR 951 in East Naples.

Golfing is popular in the Naples area, as is swamp buggy racing. Swamp buggy races, first held in 1949, are occasionally held off SR 951 at the Florida Sports Park; phone (800) 897-2701.

Philharmonic Center for the Arts, at 5833 Pelican Bay Blvd., presents varied entertainment; phone (941) 597-1900 or (800) 597-1900.

Naples Visitors Center: 895 Fifth Ave. S., Naples, FL 34102; phone (941) 262-6141.

Shopping areas: Among the 140 stores at Coastland Center, 1900 N. Tamiami Tr., are Burdines, Dillard's, JCPenney and Sears. Old Marine Marketplace at Tin City, at the corner of US 41 (Tamiami Trail) and SR 851 (Goodlette-Frank Road), is restored to capture the flavor of pioneer-era Naples. The Village on Venetian Bay, 4200 Gulf Shore Blvd. N., offers boutiques, restaurants and galleries in a Mediterranean setting.

Waterside Shops, US 41 and Seagate Drive, has a wide selection of shops including Banana Republic, Jacobsons and Saks Fifth Avenue. The Third Street South Shopping Area in the historic district of Old Naples, just 2 blocks from the Naples Pier, has more than 100 shops, galleries, restaurants and cafes.

CARIBBEAN GARDENS, 1590 Goodlette Rd., is 1.75 mi. n. via US 41, then .5 mi. e. The pre-serve and botanical garden features a petting zoo and a self-guiding trail that winds through a tropical setting populated by birds and animals. Visitors to Safari Canyon can watch an animal show complemented by wildlife footage and graphics displayed on television monitors. A 20-minute boat cruise lets visitors view primates roaming freely in an island habitat. Alligator feedings and other activities are scheduled. Picnicking is permitted.

Allow 4 hours minimum. Daily 9:30-5:30; closed Easter, Thanksgiving and Dec. 25. Last admission 1 hour before closing. Admission $14.95; ages 4-15, $9.95. MC, VI. Phone (941) 262-5409.

COLLIER COUNTY MUSEUM is at jct. US 41E and Airport Rd., in the County Government Center. Exhibits trace the history of Collier County from the Calusa Indian period to the present. A steam logging locomotive also is featured. Allow 30 minutes minimum. Mon.-Fri. 9-5; closed holidays. Free. Phone (941) 774-8476.

COLLIER-SEMINOLE STATE PARK BOAT TOURS is 17 mi. s. on US 41 at 20200 E. Tamiami Tr. Hourlong tours aboard a pontoon boat take passengers along the Black Water River, which runs through Collier-Seminole State Park. Narration is provided about the early settlements and pioneers of the area as well as the animals and plants that populate the Everglades.

Departures daily at 9:30, 11, 12:30, 2 and 3:30; closed Dec. 25. Departures require a minimum of four adults. Fare $10; ages 6-12, $7.50. MC, VI. Phone (941) 642-8898. *See Recreation Chart and the AAA Southeastern CampBook.*

THE CONSERVANCY—NAPLES NATURE CENTER, off Goodlette-Frank Rd. at 1450 Merrihue Dr., features a wildlife rehabilitation center, nature trails, canoe and kayak rentals and an outdoor aviary. A Museum of Natural History features snakes, a loggerhead sea turtle, a marine aquarium with an exhibit tank and a touch tank, a manatee videotape presentation and hands-on displays. Among the highlights is a free 45-minute narrated boat tour of a mangrove forest and lagoon.

Allow 1 hour minimum. Mon.-Sat. 9-4; closed Jan. 1 and Dec. 25. Center $6; ages 3-12, $2. Grounds free. Phone (941) 262-0304.

Briggs Nature Center, in Rookery Bay National Estuarine Research Reserve between Naples and Marco Island, offers nature exhibits, canoe rides, boat trips and nature excursions. A .5-mile boardwalk explores a butterfly garden and the upland areas. Admission $3; ages 3-12, $1. Phone (941) 775-8569.

CORKSCREW SWAMP SANCTUARY, on Sanctuary Rd. 16 mi. e. of I-75 exit 17 via Immokalee Rd., is an 11,000-acre wilderness area and wildlife sanctuary of the National Audubon Society. A large colony of American wood storks nests here from November through April. The sanctuary contains the largest known stand of virgin bald cypress in North America; some trees are said to be more than 700 years old. Alligators can be seen regularly from the boardwalk on the 2.25-mile self-guiding tour.

Allow 1 hour minimum. Daily 7-5, Dec.-Apr.; 8-5, rest of year. Admission $8; students with ID $5.50; ages 6-18, $3.50. MC, VI. Phone (941) 348-9151.

DOUBLE SUNSHINE, departing from Tin City on US 41, offers 90-minute narrated sightseeing cruises of Naples Bay. Passengers can enjoy views of mangrove-lined islands as well as dolphins, manatees and such birds as bald eagles and pelicans. Shelling trips visit Keewaydin Island. Deep-sea fishing trips aboard the *Lady Brett* also are available.

Sightseeing cruises depart daily at 10, noon, 2, 4 and 1 hour before dusk. Shelling trips depart daily at 1. Sightseeing fare $20; under 12, $10. Shelling fare $30; under 12, $20. Reservations are recommended. Phone (941) 263-4949.

EVERGLADES EXCURSIONS, departing from hotels in Naples and Marco Island, offers full- and half-day excursions throughout the Everglades. Highlights include a narrated cruise through sawgrass prairies and mangroves, a visit to Everglades City, an airboat ride through the Ten Thousand Islands and a tour of Fakahatchee Strand State Preserve and Big Cypress Swamp.

Allow 4 hours minimum. Everglades trips depart daily at 8; closed Dec. 25. Half-day Everglades fare $59; ages 4-12, $49. Full-day fare (including lunch) $79; ages 4-12, $64. Reservations are required. AE, DS, MC, VI. Phone (941) 262-1914 or (800) 592-0848. *See color ad.*

NAPLES DEPOT CIVIC AND CULTURAL CENTER, 1051 Fifth Ave. S., downtown, is a renovated 1927 train station which serves as a civic and cultural center. A baggage car stands beside the depot, and a collection of railroad memorabilia, including an operating Lionel train, is displayed in the depot. Mon.-Fri. 10-4. Free. Phone (941) 262-1776.

NAPLES TROLLEY TOURS, boarded at Old Naples General Store & Trolley Depot, downtown, and at many stops along the route, offers 1.75-hour tours of the area's historic sites, shopping areas and residential sections. The historical narration covers Naples' history on a route including Naples Pier, Palm Cottage, 5th Avenue S. and Tin City. Daily 8:30-5:30. Fare (includes an all-day reboarding pass) $15; ages 4-12, $7. AE, DS, MC, VI. Phone (941) 262-7300 or (800) 592-0848. *See color ad.*

THE TEDDY BEAR MUSEUM OF NAPLES, 1 mi. w. of I-75 exit 16 at 2511 Pine Ridge Rd., displays almost 4,000 teddy bears, ranging in size from less than 1 inch to larger than life. The collection includes bears made of fabric, marble and bronze as well as antique and limited-edition bears. Teddy bear art and memorabilia also are featured, and teddy bear-making classes are available seasonally. Allow 30 minutes minimum. Mon. and Wed.-Sat. 10-5, Sun. 1-5, Dec.-Apr.; Wed.-Sat. 10-5, Sun. 1-5, May-Oct. and mid-Nov. through Nov. 30. Closed major holidays. Admission $6; over 60, $4; ages 4-12, $2. DS, MC, VI. Phone (941) 598-2711.

NEW SMYRNA BEACH (C-10)
pop. 16,500, elev. 10'

Automobiles may be driven along the stretch of firm white sand from the inlet south to 27th Avenue. Drivers should heed signs noting unsafe areas. Overnight parking or camping are not permitted on the beach. A daily driving toll of $5 per car is charged; season passes are available for both residents ($20) and nonresidents ($40). Toll booths are at each approach.

The foundations of the Turnbull Ruins/Old Fort, built of coquina, are on N. Riverside Drive between Washington and Julia streets. These ruins, made of walls 3 feet thick, represent a local mystery—it has never been established if the foundation is the unfinished remains of a Spanish fort or the incomplete beginnings of a mansion for the Turnbull family. West of town off Mission Road is the New Smyrna Sugar Mill Ruins State Historic Site, the ruins of a large plantation's sugar mill, which was built in the 1830s and destroyed during the Second Seminole War.

The Atlantic Center for the Arts, 1414 Art Center Ave., features an art gallery and various performances and exhibitions by the resident artists; phone (904) 427-6975.

Southeast Volusia Chamber of Commerce and Visitor Information Center: 115 Canal St., New Smyrna Beach, FL 32169; phone (904) 428-2449 or (800) 541-9621. *See color ad.*

[SAVE] **FLORIDA COASTAL CRUISES** departs from Sea Harvest Marina between North and South causeways in New Smyrna Beach and from Inlet Harbor Marina & Restaurant in Ponce Inlet. Narrated cruises aboard the *Manatee* navigate the protected wetland and scenic mangrove shores on the Indian River. Sights include Ponce de Leon Lighthouse and native wildlife, such as dolphins. Lunch and dinner cruises also are available. Narrated cruises depart daily; times vary. Boarding is 15 minutes before departure. Fare $15; under 12, $12. Reservations are required. Phone (904) 428-0201 or (800) 881-2628.

NORTH MIAMI BEACH—
see Miami-Miami Beach p. 126.

OCALA (C-9) pop. 42,000, elev. 104'

An agricultural and manufacturing city, Ocala (oh-KAL-a) has moss-draped oaks and stately old Southern homes along many of its streets. The surrounding area is considered to be the heartland of Florida's Thoroughbred industry. Tours of some area horse farms are available. Particularly scenic segments of two highways approach Ocala: US 301 from Waldo and US 27 from Williston.

Ocala-Marion County Chamber of Commerce: 110 E. Silver Springs Blvd., Ocala, FL 34470; phone (352) 629-8051.

Shopping areas: Paddock Mall, a half-mile east of I-75 on SR 200, features 90 stores, including Belk Lindsey, Burdines, JCPenney and Sears.

[GEM] [SAVE] **THE APPLETON MUSEUM OF ART,** 4333 N.E. Silver Springs Blvd., houses European paintings, sculpture and decorative arts and pre-Columbian, West African and Asian art as well as antiquities. The Edith-Marie Appleton wing features a library, a workshop and additional galleries. Lectures, films and concerts also are offered. Allow 1 hour minimum. Daily 10-6; closed Jan. 1, Easter and

Dec. 25. General admission $6, over 54, $5; students with ID $2, under 18 free. Permanent exhibits only $3. MC, VI. Phone (352) 236-7100.

E-ONE FACTORY TOURS is .5 mi. e. of I-75 exit 69 on SR 40, .5 mi. s. on S.W. 33rd Ave., then 1 mi. s.w. on S.W. Seventh St. to 1601 S.W. 37th Ave. Guided tours of three factories where fire trucks are manufactured are offered. Tours cover 2 miles of walking and safety goggles are provided; the tour can be noisy and hot during the summer.

Allow 1 hour, 30 minutes minimum. Tours offered Mon.-Fri. at 1 and 3 (weather permitting); closed holidays and Dec. 26-31. Phone for availability of morning tours. Admission $6; over 55, $4; fire service members and under 12 free. Under 6 are not allowed on the factory tour, but may take an abbreviated tour of the Vehicle Delivery Center which includes sitting in the cab of a fire truck and a demonstration of the vehicle's lights and sirens. Phone (352) 861-3524.

FLORIDA'S SILVER SPRINGS, on SR 40, is reputedly the world's largest formation of clear artesian springs. One major spring, 65 feet long and 12 feet high, and more than a dozen minor springs form the headwaters of the crystalline Silver River, part of the inland waterway that links the springs to the St. Johns River and Jacksonville. The springs release more than 550 million gallons every 24 hours.

The narrated Glass-Bottom Boat Cruise offers a clear view of underwater life as far as 40 feet below the surface. During the Jungle Cruise visitors can spot more than 22 species of animals—including zebras, giraffes and ostriches—from six continents. Jeep Safari is a four-wheel adventure through a 35-acre area where sloths, Brazilian tapirs and oryxes roam free. The safari also takes visitors through a 3-foot-deep alligator pond.

Among other features are World of Bears, home to five bear species; Panther Prowl, an outdoor habitat with Florida panthers and western cougars; Big Gator Lagoon; Lost River Voyage; and live animal shows. Concerts are presented on the Twin Oaks Mansion stage seasonally. Free pet kennels are available. Picnicking is permitted only in the picnic area.

Allow 5 hours minimum. Daily 10-5. Last admission 1 hour before closing. All-inclusive admission $30.95; ages 3-10, $21.95. Combination ticket with Silver Springs Wild Waters $31.95; ages 3-10, $22.95. AE, DS, MC, VI. Phone (352) 236-2121. *See color ad.*

Silver Springs Wild Waters is a water park with a wave pool; waterslide flumes including the Twin Twister; and Cool Kids Cove, a children's play area. Picnic and volleyball facilities are available. Daily 10-7 (also Wed. and Fri. 7-9 p.m.) May 21-Aug. 6; Thurs.-Sun 10-5, rest of year. Hours may vary; phone ahead. Admission $21.95; ages 3-10, $19.95. Parking $4. Phone (352) 236-2121.

GARLITS' AUTO ATTRACTIONS, 8 mi. s. at 13700 S.W. 16th Ave., is .25 mi. e. on CR 484 off I-75 exit 67, then .25 mi. s. on CR 475A. In addition to displaying 100 antique automobiles in a separate building, the museum traces the evolution of the sport of drag racing through the 30-year collection of "Big Daddy" Garlits' drag racing cars and artifacts.

Allow 1 hour minimum. Daily 9-5; closed Dec. 25. Drag racing museum and antique car museum each $8; over 55 and students age 13-18 with ID $6; ages 5-12, $3. Combination ticket $12; over 55 and students age 13-18 with ID $10; ages 5-12, $3. Under 13 must be with an adult. MC, VI. Phone (352) 245-8661.

OCALA NATIONAL FOREST

Elevations in the forest range
from 10 ft. to 125 ft.

The predominant trees in Ocala National Forest are the state's largest stand of sand pine, as well as longleaf, slash and other pine, cypress and hardwoods. The forest, with more than 430,000 acres, contains numerous species of vegetation and hundreds of clear lakes and streams.

In addition to several shorter trails, a well-traveled section of the Florida Trail which winds its way through the forest is popular with hikers. Hunting is allowed by permit.

Developed recreation sites include Alexander Springs, Juniper Springs, Lake Dorr, Fore Lake, Mill Dam, Clearwater Lake, Salt Springs and Silver Glen Springs. Juniper Prairie Wilderness is home to Pat's Island, where parts of the movie "The Yearling" were filmed. Juniper Springs was constructed in 1935 by the Civilian Conservation Corps. Phone (352) 625-2520. *See Recreation Chart.*

Brochures and information on forest recreational opportunities are available at Ocklawaha Visitor Center on SR 40 at SR 315, between Silver Springs and the Ocklawaha River; phone (352) 236-0288. The center is open daily 9-5.

OKEECHOBEE (F-10)
pop. 4,900, elev. 29'

At the crossroads of SR 70, US 98 and US 441, Okeechobee serves as a center for such outdoor activities as fishing, camping and air boat rides. The town also is a commercial center for cattle which is evident in the several rodeos that take place throughout the year.

Okeechobee Chamber of Commerce: 55 S. Parrott Ave., Okeechobee, FL 34974; phone (863) 763-6464 or (800) 871-4403.

LAKE OKEECHOBEE, covering approximately 750 square miles, is the second largest freshwater lake in the continental United States. Its greatest depth is 24 feet, but the water is so shallow in most places that birds can be seen wading a mile from shore. A lighted pier at Lock 7 (US 441 and SR 78) provides day and night fishing. A hiking and biking trail—part of the Florida National Scenic Trail—winds 110 miles along a levee which surrounds the entire lake to protect adjacent rich lands from overflow. Recreational facilities are available.

OLUSTEE (B-8) elev. 140'

OLUSTEE BATTLEFIELD STATE HISTORIC SITE, about 2.5 mi. e. on US 90, marks the site of the largest Civil War battle on Florida soil. Union forces were defeated decisively at the site on Feb. 20, 1864; the battle is re-enacted every February. Highlights include a museum featuring Civil War artifacts. Site open daily 8-5. Museum open Thurs.-Mon. 9-5. Site and museum free. Phone (904) 758-0400.

ORANGE CITY (D-9)
pop. 5,300, elev. 43'

Orange City's early residents were the Timucuan Indians, who lived along the St. Johns River and ate the snails that inhabited the river's sandbars. The mound formed by the accumulation of centuries of snail shells later served as a foundation for the area's first permanent home, the 1872 Thursby House.

Today the residence is preserved in Blue Spring State Park, a winter habitat of the endangered manatee.

Greater Orange City Area Chamber of Commerce: 520 N. Volusia Ave., Orange City, FL 32763; phone (904) 775-2793.

BLUE SPRING STATE PARK, 2 mi. w. off US 17/92 on W. French Ave., contains a spring run that maintains a temperature of 72 degrees Fahrenheit. Manatee season is November through March, although the sea cows also can be seen here when they come to escape the cooler waters of the St. Johns River. A manatee-viewing platform and ranger interpretation programs, including a slide presentation, introduce visitors to these gentle creatures. Visitors may not swim with or feed the manatees.

Allow 2 hours minimum. Park daily 8-dusk. Slide presentation shown Mon.-Fri. at 1:30, 2:30 and 3:30, Sat.-Sun. at 11, 1:30, 2:30 and 3:30, Nov.-Mar. Admission $4 per private vehicle (maximum eight people), $1 per person arriving by bicycle or on foot. Phone (904) 775-3663. *See Recreation Chart and the AAA Southeastern CampBook.*

SAVE **ST. JOHNS RIVER ECOTOURS, INC.,** 2100 W. French Ave., offers narrated cruises and nature tours along the St. Johns River. Allow 2 hours minimum. Cruises depart daily at 10 and 1. Fare $14; over 60, $12; ages 3-12, $8. Reservations are required. AE, MC, VI. Phone (407) 330-1612 or (904) 917-0724.

DID YOU KNOW

Stephen Crane wrote his short story "The Open Boat" after he spent 51 hours in a boat off New Smyrna Beach.

Disney and AAA...
Making Membership Magic

*L*et AAA help plan your next *Disneyland*®
Resort vacation and receive these
AAA member benefits.

- Special savings and
  benefits on selected
  AAA Vacations® travel
  packages to the
  Disneyland Resort
- *AAA Vacations Disneyland*
  packages include
  AAA exclusive FREE parking
  at Disneyland® Park
- Ask about *AAA Vacations*
  travel packages to
  San Diego or
  San Francisco, and
  experience all that
  California has to offer.

Call your nearest AAA travel office today to
find out more about AAA member benefits at the
Disneyland Resort!

While at Disneyland Park,
visit the AAA Touring & Travel Services Center
operated by the Automobile Club of Southern California.

All packages and offers are date specific and subject to
limited availability. Certain restrictions apply.

Orlando

Population: 173,900   **Elevation:** 111 ft.

Popular Spots:

SeaWorld Orlando ....(see p. 146)

Universal Orlando................(see p. 149)

Walt Disney World Resort......(see p. 162)

Walt Disney World. It is the dream destination of every young child, the first stop on a Super Bowl champion's victory tour. It conjures up images of azure swimming pools, life-size cartoon characters and a fantasy castle where dreams come true. And it has made the young city of Orlando the world's most popular vacation spot.

Central Florida's Disney story began in the mid-1960s, when entertainment visionary "Uncle Walt" Disney paid a series of hush-hush visits to the swamplands of southwest Orange County. Secretive property deals soon followed, piquing locals' interest and sparking questions about the mysterious doings south of town. The answer—and instant fame—came in 1971 when the Magic Kingdom became the area's first theme park.

Bolstered by Walt Disney World's phenomenal success, Orlando began a rapid growth spurt. Hotels and restaurants sprang up around the park practically overnight, swiftly followed by a legion of souvenir shops and tourist strips. A diverse mix of people flocked to the area, lured by Disney's magic spell and the promise of easy living in the nation's new vacation capital.

But while Disney is the centerpiece of Orlando's appeal, the City Beautiful offers more than just theme parks. Summer rainstorms and a warm climate promote lush vegetation. Pines, palms and oaks draped with Spanish moss line the streets, and landscaped gardens display many varieties of flowers.

In the midst of the state's lake country, central Florida offers more than 1,200 lakes and dozens of parks in which to hike, lounge, bike or engage in water sports. Even in the throes of rapid growth, the downtown streets, many of them brick, seem clean and friendly, the skies are smog-free and subtropical vegetation graces almost every view.

Of course, success breeds risks along with rewards. New residents arrive by the thousands each year, and as a result, Orlando natives make up less than half the population and the best-known citizens are the mascots of the local theme parks.

Surprisingly, Orlando is no stranger to the boomtown hustle and bustle, having experienced several boom-and-bust cycles in its short but tumultuous past. The city began as a small settlement founded by brothers Aaron and Isaac Jernigan, who in 1843 established a cattle ranch and trading post on what is now Lake Holden.

More than one story explains the origin of the town's name, but the most reliable claims it honors a member of a company of U.S. soldiers and volunteers, Orlando Reeves. One night in 1835 Reeves was at his post as sentry along Sandy Beach—the shores of today's Lake Eola—when he noticed a "log" in the lake. Realizing it was an Indian creeping toward the camp, Reeves gave the alarm to warn his company.

The frontier outpost grew quickly, and by the 1860s cattle ranches and cotton plantations were a common sight. By virtue of its remote location, Orlando was far removed from the ravages of the Civil War. It was very much a Confederate city,

Getting There —starting on p. 140

Getting Around — starting on p. 141

What To See — starting on p. 142

What To Do — starting on p. 152

Where To Stay — starting on p. 572

Where To Dine — starting on p. 578

however, and so became a haven for displaced Southerners. They came seeking a fresh start among the thriving cattle herds and the thick groves of a new industry: citrus production.

The first success story belonged to William Harrison Holden, who in 1875 planted a commercial orange grove on the shore of the lake that would later take his name. Countless would-be citrus kings followed his lead, and soon lemons, oranges and grapefruit constituted the area's leading business.

The pioneer period came to a close in 1880 with the completion of the South Florida Railroad, which offered a link to the North. The advent of rail travel was a defining moment for the city: Along with increased commercial opportunities came multitudes of sun-seeking tourists escaping harsh Northern winters.

By 1890 the cowtown had become a real town, with all the trappings of 19th-century success. Stores and businesses prospered along the main thoroughfare, Orange Avenue, and Orlando's first population boom was well under way. Even a minor freeze in 1886—a harbinger of larger disasters to come—had little effect on the growth of the citrus and real estate industries.

Those heady days ended soon enough. Another, more devastating freeze gripped central Florida during the winter of 1894-95, destroying crops and ruining growers' fortunes overnight. A gradual recovery eventually offset the losses, and citrus production continued to be an economic staple through the 1950s. But increasing urbanization and colder winters steadily pushed the industry south into warmer, more rural areas, and Orange County's once-abundant groves now are a distant memory.

In the waning years of the 1920s, growth had escalated to unsupportable levels and the local economy destabilized. A serious fruit fly infestation in 1929 derailed the citrus business, leading to an eerily prophetic crash. As the boom ground to a halt, the Great Depression struck a heavy blow, leaving the city and its residents in dire financial straits.

World War II brought defense manufacturing and related businesses, helping to erase the effects of the Depression. But it was the postwar period that ushered in the region's most dynamic growth. Defense build-ups and the space race—the major fronts of the Cold War—soon became central Florida's primary industries. The Martin Co. (now Lockheed Martin Corp.) opened its first Orlando plant in 1957, bringing in hundreds of workers from the North and creating thousands of jobs for locals. The Kennedy Space Center soon followed, and the resulting economic activity spawned numerous supporting businesses, attracting a tremendous influx of new residents.

These developments were spurred in large part by the area's most rewarding transaction: Walt Disney's purchase of the land where he would build the Walt Disney World Resort. When plans for developing the site were formally announced late in 1965, they fueled yet another land rush. Real estate prices skyrocketed as speculators bought their own piece of the action. In an unprecedented move, the state legislature granted the company the autonomy to rule itself. Disney promptly set up its own government within an area called the Reedy Creek Improvement District, complete with taxing privileges and municipal services.

The Magic Kingdom's price tag topped $400 million at its Oct. 1, 1971, opening. Though Disney himself was not alive to see it, the park quickly exceeded all expectations and remains one of the world's most popular destinations. In fact, Walt Disney World's allure helped make Orlando something of a theme park mecca. In the decades since the first guests walked through the turnstiles, such attractions as SeaWorld Orlando, Epcot, Disney-MGM Studios and Universal Orlando have opened their gates to the visitors thronging Mickey Mouse's hometown. Gone are the quiet days of orange groves and rural simplicity.

Today Orlando is a far cry from the small Southern town it was in the 1840s. The perennial boomtown is well on its way to becoming a major international city. The Orlando International Airport has undergone a series of renovations and expansions that have made it an important transportation center. The Orlando Arena (renamed T.D. Waterhouse Centre in 2000) opened in 1989, mainly to serve as home court for the city's popular NBA expansion team, the Orlando Magic. The area also has attracted new businesses, even as others like Lockheed Martin began to downsize.

With the coming of two major players in the entertainment market, Universal and Disney-MGM, Orlando has emerged as an up-and-coming center for the motion picture industry. Technology also remains a key component in Orlando's business picture. Although defense has taken a big hit, the high-tech fields of software, telecommunications, lasers and electro-optics may soon fill the gap.

Recent developments indicate that the city's growth shows no signs of ending any time soon. Despite the Navy's decision to close the city's Naval Training Center, Orlandoans are optimistic about plans to convert the site to other, equally productive uses. The University of Central Florida (UCF), founded in 1968, continues to grow and now has one of the region's finest technology programs. Disney's planned residential community, Celebration, is patterned after the progressive village that Walt himself envisioned as the solution to modern urban problems.

The Informed Traveler

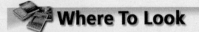 Whom To Call

Emergency: 911

Police (non-emergency): (407) 246-2414; Sheriff (407) 737-2400

Fire: (407) 422-7121

Time and Temperature: (407) 646-3131

Hospitals: Florida Hospital, (407) 896-6611; Orlando Regional Health Care System, (407) 841-5111.

Where To Look

Newspapers

The Orlando Sentinel is distributed in the morning. Friday's *Calendar* section summarizes the coming week's events.

Radio

Radio station WWNZ (740 AM) is an all-news/talk station; WDBO (580 AM) is an all-talk/weather station; WMFE (90.7) is a member of National Public Radio.

Visitor Information

Orlando/Orange County Convention and Visitors Bureau distributes a variety of information. The Official Visitor Center on International Dr. is open daily 8-7. Write 8723 International Dr., Orlando, FL 32819; phone (407) 363-5871. *See color ad p. 150.*

The Greater Orlando Chamber of Commerce distributes information Mon.-Fri. 8:30-5. Write 75 S. Ivanhoe Blvd., Orlando, FL 32804; phone (407) 425-1234.

A free monthly magazine titled *See Orlando* is distributed at hotels and motels throughout the city.

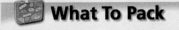 What To Pack

Orlando is as renowned for its warm weather as for its theme parks. The winter months especially are a relief from colder climes, with lows generally in the 50s and highs in the 70s. Sudden cold snaps lend a certain unpredictability to central Florida winters, but these usually are short-lived.

Summer months tend to be hot and muggy, with temperatures routinely in the 90s. The intense humidity is alleviated many afternoons by brief, violent thunderstorms. These sudden storms are the worst facet of Orlando's weather. (Note: Seek shelter indoors to wait out storms, as lightning strikes and pounding rain pose serious hazards, especially to the uninitiated driver. If you can't pull over safely, turn on your headlights and proceed with extreme caution.)

It is always a good idea to wear sunblock if you will be outdoors for any length of time, as the strong Florida sun can burn unprotected skin even on cool or overcast

days. *For additional information see temperature chart p. 43.*

Comfort is the driving fashion force in Florida, and Orlando is a typically casual city. Shorts and sandals are acceptable in all but the most exclusive restaurants. Winters are fairly mild, but cold snaps necessitate sweaters, jackets or light coats from December through February.

A word to the wise: Warm temperatures outside often make for cold temperatures inside, as air conditioners are turned full blast against the summer heat.

Sales Tax: In Orange and Osceola counties the sales tax is 6 percent; in Lake and Seminole counties it is 7 percent. Orange and Osceola counties levy a 4 percent resort tax, while in Lake and Seminole counties the tax is 2 percent.

Destination Orlando

*I*t all started with a mouse—the emergence of Orlando as everyone's favorite vacation destination, that is.

*O*nce a quiet town surrounded by citrus groves, Orlando was almost overnight transformed into a tourist mecca. Other attractions followed Mickey, and Orlando soon grew into a vibrant metropolitan area with world-class cultural offerings.

Medieval Times Dinner and Tournament, Kissimmee.
Knights on horseback compete while spectators feast on a four-course meal at one of Orlando's dinner shows.
(See listing page 161)

Cinderella Castle at The Magic Kingdom® Park, Lake Buena Vista.
The castle is recognized around the world as the focal point of the Walt Disney World® Resort.
(See listing page 174)

©Disney

*P*laces included in this AAA Destination City:

Charles Hosmer Morse Museum of American Art,
Winter Park.
One of the world's largest collections of Louis
Comfort Tiffany's stained-glass masterpieces
grace the museum's galleries.
(See listing page 176)

Southern Ballet
Theatre, Orlando.
Orlando's cultural
scene is diverse and
well-rounded.

See Vicinity map page 143

Islands of Adventure,
Universal Orlando.
The Incredible Hulk Coaster is
among the rides and shows at this
park based on myths,
legends and super heroes.
(See listing page 150)

Getting There

By Car

Orlando is laced with busy thoroughfares. Primary among these is I-4, a trans-Florida route that combines direct travel through the city with strategic controlled access. From the Daytona Beach area it forks off I-95 and enters Orlando on the northeast side; from the Gulf Coast it comes from Tampa and St. Petersburg, passing Walt Disney World and entering town from the southwest.

Florida's Turnpike (toll) links Orlando with the resort areas of southeastern Florida. About 35 miles to the northwest it connects with I-75, a major north-south freeway. Florida's Turnpike interchanges with I-4 at the southwestern city limits.

I-4 and Florida's Turnpike form an X across central Florida. Two older routes, US 17/92 and US 441, also cross at Orlando, traversing different portions of the area.

SR 528, more commonly known as the Bee Line Expressway (toll), passes south of the city. It channels traffic between Orlando and the Cape Canaveral area and connects with routes leading downtown.

SR 50 (Colonial Drive) is an east-west route that passes through downtown and connects smaller communities near the Gulf with Atlantic coast areas. To avoid traffic an alternative is SR 408, the East-West Expressway (toll), which links with SR 50 both east and west of downtown. The expressway also connects with the Central Florida Greeneway (SR 417) just south of SR 50. An expansion to the eastern terminus brings the toll road to US 17/92 in Sanford; other eastern and western expansions are planned and sections of the expressway may be undergoing construction.

SR 436 (Semoran Boulevard) swings in a wide northwesterly arc from the airport and Bee Line Expressway southeast of town to US 441 northwest at Apopka and offers an alternative—although often busy—route to I-4.

Air Travel

The Orlando area is served by two airports: Orlando International Airport (OIA), at SR 436 and the Bee Line Expressway, and Orlando Sanford Airport in Sanford, which serves commercial and private aircraft. OIA, about 15 miles from both downtown and the tourist district, is a primary destination for many major domestic and international airlines. Serving more than 27 million passengers in 1999, it is one of the world's fastest growing major airports. Its three satellite terminals are linked to the main terminal by automated people movers, making it easy to navigate. (**Note:** Orlando's tourist volume often leads to traffic congestion during peak vacation seasons. Allow plenty of transit time—coming and going—between the airport and your destination.)

To reach downtown Orlando, follow Airport Boulevard north as it merges into SR 436. Though heavily traveled, SR 436 offers direct access to central, east and north Orlando via SRs 50 or 408 (toll). To reach the International Drive area, take Airport Boulevard to SR 528 (toll), then head west to SR 482, which intersects International just east of I-4. Take Airport Boulevard south to SR 417 (toll) to go to the Disney resort via SR 536 or to reach Kissimmee via US 17/92/441.

Cab fares from the Orlando airport to downtown or International Drive average $25; limousines are approximately $75; shuttle vans are $15; and public transportation is $1. Cab fare to the Disney resort averages $42. Many hotels and motels have courtesy car service.

Orlando is served by several major rental car agencies. Arrangements should be made before you depart especially during peak seasons. Your local AAA club can provide this service or additional information. Hertz, (407) 859-8400 or (800) 654-3080, offers discounts to AAA members.

Rail Service

Amtrak provides train service to four stations in the metro area. Passenger-only trains stop at the stations at 1400 Sligh Blvd. in downtown Orlando and 150 W. Morse Blvd. in downtown Winter Park; Kissimmee's passenger station is at 111 Dakin St. The AutoTrain, which runs south

from Lorton, VA, stops at the Sanford station at 800 Persimmon Ave. Phone (800) 872-7245 for both rail services.

Buses

A Greyhound Lines Inc. terminal, (407) 292-3422, (800) 231-2222, or (800) 531-5332 for Spanish-speaking persons, is off SR 50 (Colonial Drive) at 555 N. John Young Pkwy.

Getting Around

Street System

Because much of Orlando's growth occurred during the 1960s and '70s, the city is remarkably car-friendly. Roads are generally in good shape, although construction caused by near-constant expansion is a fact of life around the tourist district and downtown. Points of interest are usually on or near the main thoroughfares, most of which are accessible via I-4. For a small city, Orlando has surprisingly lengthy rush-hour periods, 6:30-9 a.m. and 4-6:30 p.m. Try to avoid traveling on I-4, US 17/92, SR 50 and SR 436 during these times.

Downtown Orlando is basically a grid, with several one-way streets. All street numbering begins at the intersection of Central Boulevard and Orange Avenue, the main strip through downtown. Orange is a one-way road south through the downtown core; its northbound counterpart is Rosalind Avenue. East-west roads accessing important downtown sites include Amelia Street (T.D. Waterhouse Centre), Livingston Street (Bob Carr Performing Arts Center, Expo Center), Robinson Street (Lake Eola), Central (Orlando Public Library, Lake Eola), Church Street (Church Street Market/Station/Exchange, Downtown Farmer's Market) and South Street (City Hall).

International Drive, the heart of the tourist area, is south Orlando's busiest road. A profusion of hotels, shopping centers, outlet stores, restaurants, strolling vacationers and cruising teenagers usually combine to create crowded conditions and frequent delays.

Unless otherwise posted, the speed limit on most streets is 30 mph. Rush-hour traffic, 6:30 to 9 a.m. and 4 to 6:30 p.m., should be avoided. Unless otherwise posted, right turns are permitted on red after a complete stop.

Parking

Metered street parking downtown is available at 75¢ per hour, but spaces are generally hard to find at peak periods, which are on weekdays and weekend evenings. The most convenient parking for Church Street Station—downtown's big attraction—is an open-air lot underneath I-4 on

Garland Avenue between Central Boulevard and Pine Street.

Municipal garages can be found throughout downtown, including at Amelia Street, between Revere Street and Hughey Avenue; Church Street, between Division and Hughey avenues; Pine Street, between Garland and Orange avenues; Central Boulevard, between Garland and Orange avenues; and Central Boulevard, between Rosalind and Magnolia avenues. Rates average $1 per half-hour or $12 per day.

Winter Park has free parking along Park Avenue, but spaces can be hard to come by during peak hours. Public lots are located just west of Park Avenue off New England Avenue, Morse Boulevard and Canton Avenue.

Most attractions and shopping centers have ample parking, but parking fees for the major theme parks can run as high as $5 per day. Check with your hotel to see if it offers free shuttle service to the theme parks.

Taxis and Limousines

Local taxis are metered and charge $3 for the first mile, $1.50 for each additional mile. Major cab companies are Ace Metro, (407) 855-0564; Checker, (407) 699-9999; City, (407) 422-5151; and Yellow, (407) 422-4455.

Limousine service is available throughout most of the city; the ride from the airport to downtown Orlando or International Drive is about $75.

Public Transportation

Brightly painted buses are a colorful sight in the metro area, thanks to LYNX, the transit authority for Orange, Osceola and Seminole counties, which operates more than 200 buses on 50-plus routes. The main transit station is hard to miss—it is painted bubblegum-pink and is located in the heart

of downtown on Central Boulevard between Garland and Orange avenues.

Bus stops, called Links, are marked by fuchsia paw-print signs listing all the routes that are immediately accessible from that stop. The system serves most of the city, including downtown, the tourist district and major shopping centers. Main routes are 4, between south Orlando and Kissimmee; 10, through Kissimmee; 38, downtown to the International Drive area; 41, between SR 436 and the airport; 42, between Dr. Phillips Boulevard and the airport; and 50, between downtown to the Walt Disney World Resort.

I-Ride Trolleys cater exclusively to tourist traffic along International Drive from 7 a.m.-midnight; the wait is 15 minutes. Trolley fare is 75c; over 65, 25c; under 13 free with adult. LYNX also offers Lymmo, a free bus service that uses a bus-only lane to transport passengers throughout the downtown area, including stops at city hall and T.D. Waterhouse Centre. Lymmo runs Mon.-Thurs. 6 a.m.-10 p.m., Fri. 6 a.m.-midnight, Sat. 10-midnight, Sun. 10-10.

LYNX fare is $1; transfers are an extra 10c. Exact change is required. Buses run Mon.-Fri. 5 a.m.-12:15 a.m., Sat. 5:30-a.m.-7:15 p.m., Sun. 6:15-6:15; holiday schedules may vary. For additional information about routes and schedules phone (407) 841-8240 or 423-0787.

What To See

DISCOVERY COVE is at 6000 Discovery Cove Way next to SeaWorld Orlando. The park allows visitors to encounter a variety of animals up-close and in a lush island resort setting. The centerpiece pool is home to playful dolphins with which guests, under the supervision of trainers, can swim and have their pictures taken. An artificial lagoon beckons snorkelers with its realistic reef and colorful tropical fish. Nearby, swimmers, protected by clear underwater partitions, come face-to-face with sharks and barracudas. A lazy river lets guests float through a free-flight aviary where they can hand-feed exotic birds. Sting rays, sloths and anteaters are among the other touchable creatures at the park.

Allow a full day. Daily 9-5:30. Admission, including dolphin swim, $179; without dolphin swim, $89; under age 3 free. Admission to Discovery Cove includes SeaWorld Orlando admission, one meal and all gear rental. Children under 6 are not permitted to swim with the dolphins. Reservations are required. AE, DS, MC, VI. Phone (877) 434-7268. *See color ad p. 148.*

EPCOT—*see Lake Buena Vista p. 164.*

SAVE **GATORLAND,** 8 mi. s. of the Bee Line Expwy. (SR 528) on US 17/92/441 at 14501 S. Orange Blossom Tr., has thousands of alligators, crocodiles, snakes and other reptiles. Shows—including Gator Jumparoo Show, with leaping alligators; a snake show; Jungle Crocs Show; and Gator Wrestlin'—are presented several times daily. A boardwalk winds through a cypress swamp, and a three-story observation tower overlooks the alligator breeding marsh. Picnicking is permitted. Food is available.

Allow 3 hours minimum. Daily 9-dusk. Admission $16.93; senior citizens $13.54; ages 3-12, $7.48. AE, MC, VI. Phone (407) 855-5496 or (800) 393-5297.

HARRY P. LEU GARDENS is at 1920 N. Forest Ave.; I-4 exit 43 to Princeton Ave., s. on Mills Ave., then .5 mi. e. via Virginia Dr. The Leu House Museum, dating from the 1880s, can be viewed by guided tour. The garden's 50 acres feature paved walkways, camellias, one of the largest formal rose gardens in Florida and the Orchid House. A wooded deck overlooks Lake Rowena. Allow 1 hour, 30 minutes minimum. Gardens open Mon.-Sat. 9-8, Sun. 9-6, Apr.-Oct.; daily 9-5, rest of year. Closed Dec. 25. House tours are given daily 10-3:30. Admission $4; ages 5-18, $1. Phone (407) 246-2620.

LAKE EOLA PARK, 3 blks. from the center of town on E. Central Blvd., has stately trees and flowering plants and shrubs. In the center of

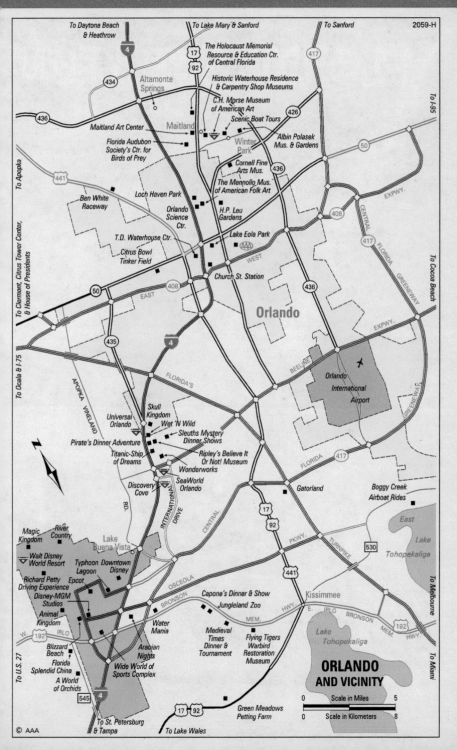

2059-H

To Daytona Beach & Heathrow

To Lake Mary & Sanford

To Sanford

The Holocaust Memorial Resource & Education Ctr. of Central Florida

Altamonte Springs

Historic Waterhouse Residence & Carpentry Shop Museums

C.H. Morse Museum of American Art

Scenic Boat Tours

Maitland Art Center

Maitland

Winter Park

Albin Polasek Mus. & Gardens

Florida Audubon Society's Ctr. for Birds of Prey

Cornell Fine Arts Mus.

The Mennollo Mus. of American Folk Art

Ben White Raceway

Loch Haven Park

Orlando Science Ctr.

H.P. Leu Gardens

To Apopka

T.D. Waterhouse Ctr.

Lake Eola Park

To Clermont, Citrus Tower Center, & House of Presidents

Citrus Bowl Tinker Field

Church St. Station

WEST

Orlando

EAST

To Ocala & I-75

To Cocoa Beach

CENTRAL FLORIDA GREENEWAY

EXPWY.

BEELINE

Orlando International Airport

FLORIDA'S

APOPKA VINELAND

Skull Kingdom

Universal Orlando

Wet 'N Wild

Sleuths Mystery Dinner Shows

Pirate's Dinner Adventure

Titanic-Ship of Dreams

Ripley's Believe It Or Not! Museum

Wonderworks

Discovery Cove

SeaWorld Orlando

Gatorland

Boggy Creek Airboat Rides

East Lake Tohopekaliga

INTERNATIONAL DRIVE

RD.

CENTRAL

Magic Kingdom

River Country

Lake Buena Vista

Walt Disney World Resort

Typhoon Lagoon

Downtown Disney

Richard Petty Driving Experience

Epcot

Disney-MGM Studios

Animal Kingdom

OSCEOLA

BRONSON

PKWY.

TURNPIKE

To Melbourne

Capone's Dinner & Show

Jungleland Zoo

Kissimmee

Blizzard Beach

Water Mania

Medieval Times Dinner & Tournament

Flying Tigers Warbird Restoration Museum

MEM.

E. IRLO BRONSON MEM. HWY.

To Miami

Florida Splendid China

A World of Orchids

Arabian Nights

Wide World of Sports Complex

Lake Tohopekaliga

To U.S. 27

To St. Petersburg & Tampa

Green Meadows Petting Farm

To Lake Wales

© AAA

ORLANDO AND VICINITY

Scale in Miles 0 — 5

Scale in Kilometers 0 — 8

FLORIDA SUN & FUN

...FOR EVERYONE!

After a fun-packed day in Florida's famous sun, the good times roll on...at Travelodge®! That's right. Because when you stay with us, you'll get more than just a clean, comfortable room at an affordable rate. You'll enjoy fantastic FREE amenities that will make every member of the family feel more at home. Like a convenient in-room coffee maker, no-charge long distance access to help you stay in touch and even a weekday lobby newspaper.* But the good news doesn't end there. The kids can have a place of their own in one of Sleepy Bear's Den rooms, complete with VCR and a super selection of family-friendly videos available at the front desk.** And you can earn valuable merchandise as a member of our Travelodge Miles guest rewards program. With all that, you can see why Travelodge is the perfect stay for everyone!

**For reservations call 1-800-578-7878
or visit us at www.Travelodge.com
and ask for the
AAA discount/S3A rate code.**

Lake Eola is the colorfully lighted Clinton Allen Fountain. Swan paddleboats, a playground and food are available. Paddleboats available daily 11-dusk; under 14 must be with an adult. Playground open daily 8 a.m.-10 p.m. Park and playground free. Paddleboats $7 per half-hour (three people per boat). Phone (407) 246-2827 or 839-8899 for paddleboat information.

LOCH HAVEN PARK, bounded by Mills (US 17/92) and Orange aves. and bisected by Princeton St., contains three museums and a theater. The Civic Theatre of Central Florida stages productions. *(See What To Do, Theater and Concerts.)* Phone (407) 896-7365.

Orlando Museum of Art, 2416 N. Mills Ave., maintains a permanent collection of American art. Other displays include African objects and pre-Columbian artifacts. The Art Encounter offers a hands-on exhibition for children. Changing exhibits also are featured. Allow 1 hour minimum. Tues.-Sat. 10-5, Sun. noon-5; closed holidays. Admission $6; over 55 and students with ID $4; ages 4-11, $2. Phone (407) 896-4231.

Orlando Science Center, 777 E. Princeton St., features interactive exhibits that focus on the sciences, mathematics and applied technologies. Visitors can watch as a sinkhole swallows a house, become a particle of food as it travels through the body, and travel to other planets or the Earth's core. Large-format films and planetarium presentations can be viewed in the eight-story CineDome.

Allow 2 hours minimum. Tues.-Sat. and Mon. holidays 9-5 (also Fri.-Sat. 5-9), Sun. noon-5; closed Thanksgiving and Dec. 25. Hours may vary; phone ahead. Admission to exhibits $9.50; over 54, $8.50; ages 3-11, $6.75. Exhibits and one CineDome show $12.50; over 54, $11.50; ages 3-11, $9.25. Exhibits and two CineDome shows $14.25; over 54, $13.25; ages 3-11, $11. Parking $3.50. Phone (407) 514-2000 or (888) 672-4386.

THE MENNELLO MUSEUM OF AMERICAN FOLK ART, .5 mi. e. off I-4 Princeton St. exit, next to Orlando Science Center's parking garage,

houses a permanent collection of the works of Earl Cunningham, a prominent 20th-century American folk artist. Traveling exhibits are also featured. Allow 30 minutes minimum. Tues.-Fri. 11-5 (also Thurs. 5-8), Sat. 11-5, Sun. noon-5. Admission $2, over 54 and students with ID $1; under 12 free. Phone (407) 246-4278.

[SAVE] **PIRATE'S DINNER ADVENTURE,** .25 mi. s. of International Dr. at 6400 Carrier Dr., is a musical dinner show that includes stunts, special effects and aerial acts that take place aboard a galleon. After the show, guests may attend the Buccaneer Bash dance party. Performance daily at 7:45. Admission $38.95; ages 3-11, $23.95. Reservations are recommended. AE, CB, DS, MC, VI. Phone (407) 248-0590 or (800) 866-2469.

[SAVE] **RIPLEY'S BELIEVE IT OR NOT! MUSEUM,** 8201 International Dr., .5 mi. s.e. of I-4 exit 29, offers hundreds of displays ranging from the unusual to the macabre. Thematic galleries feature global curiosities, interactive exhibits and audiovisual presentations. Particularly interesting is a "mobile" wooden bridge—the bridge actually is stationary, but moving pictures on the walls create the illusion of motion. Allow 1 hour minimum. Daily 9 a.m.-1 a.m. Last admission 1 hour before closing. Admission $12.95; ages 4-12, $8.95. AE, DS, MC, VI. Phone (407) 345-0501.

[GEM] **SEAWORLD ORLANDO** is at 7007 Sea World Dr., at jct. I-4 and SR 528 (Bee Line Expwy.). SeaWorld Orlando is a [SAVE] marine life adventure park featuring sea-themed shows, up-close marine animal encounters, attractions and rides.

Kraken, a "floorless" roller coaster, combines a 15-story ascent with three underground loops—one of them underwater through a mythical serpent's lagoon. Journey to Atlantis is a water coaster thrill ride that plunges visitors into the middle of a clash for the lost city of Atlantis.

A rocky, simulated helicopter ride transports visitors to Wild Arctic!, where beluga whales, walruses and polar bears coexist.

Shows include The Shamu Adventure, a killer whale show featuring an eagle and video host and animal expert Jack Hanna; Clyde and Seamore Take Pirate Island, featuring sea lions, walruses, otters and harbor seals searching for a lost treasure map; Pets on Stage, which is a showcase for four-legged celebrities adopted from animal shelters; Cirque de la Mer, which blends athleticism, dance, music and special effects into a nontraditional circus; and The Intensity Games Water Ski Show, a performance of wakeboarding, skiing and water stunts.

Dive into a New Dimension of SeaWorld Fun!

**AAA. Every Day.
AAA Members Can
Save Two Ways!**
SAVE when you pre-purchase
tickets at your local participating
AAA, or Show Your Card &
Save® 10% off one-day
general admission at the
front gate. Be sure to visit
our other Anheuser-Busch
Adventure Parks in Central
Florida: Busch Gardens® Tampa Bay
and Adventure Island® *(See the Tampa
section for more information.)*

SeaWorld.
ADVENTURE PARK
Orlando

www.seaworld.com
©2000 Busch Entertainment Corporation. All rights reserved.

Show Your Card & Save

AAA. Every Day.

No barriers.

No crowds.

No lines.

Imagine a tropical paradise you and your family can call your own. Swim with dolphins, rays and thousands of tropical fish. No barriers. No crowds. No lines. New Discovery Cove. Right in the heart of Orlando. Come spend a day. And be touched forever.

By reservation only, call 1-877-4-DISCOVERY or book online at discoverycove.com

DISCOVERY COVE.

ORLANDO

Key West at Sea World features live bands and entertainment, close-up encounters with sea turtles and opportunities to touch and feed dolphins and stingrays. Manatees: The Last Generation? explores the underwater world of the endangered manatee, and Pacific Point Preserve is home to California sea lions and harbor and fur seals. Playful bottlenose dolphins and false killer whales are the focus of Key West Dolphin Fest.

Other features include Shamu's Happy Harbor, a 3-acre children's play area; Penguin Encounter, home to hundreds of arctic birds; Dolphin Nursery, with new moms and calves; Tropical Reef, which is a showcase for sea creatures in jewel aquariums; Terrors of the Deep, with sharks and other feared ocean dwellers; and The Anheuser-Busch Hospitality Center, featuring beautiful Clydesdales.

Available for an additional fee are rides on the 400-foot sky tower; behind-the-scenes tours; educational classes; and the Dolphin Interaction Program. The 5.5-hour Adventure Express includes reserved seating and no waiting in line at certain shows and attractions; feeding opportunities; and guide service. Other guided tours also are available. Kennels, strollers, lockers and wheelchair rentals are available.

Allow a full day. Park generally open daily at 9; closing times vary. Last admission 1 hour before closing. Admission $46; ages 3-9, $37. Two-day pass $56; ages 3-9, $47. Adventure Express $55; ages 3-9, $50. Guided tours $6.95; ages 3-9, $5.95. Sky tower $3. Wild Card Pass, including unlimited admission to Busch Gardens Tampa Bay *(see Tampa Bay p. 213)* and SeaWorld Orlando for 1 year, $124.95; over 54 and ages 3-9, $109.95.

AAA members can buy a combination park ticket that gives 7 consecutive days admissions to SeaWorld Orlando, Universal Studios, Islands of Adventure and Wet 'n Wild. If Busch Gardens Tampa Bay is included, the pass is valid for 10 consecutive days. Parking $6 for automobile, $8 for recreational vehicle or camper.

Check with the attractions or your AAA club for more details about the combination park ticket. DS, MC, VI. Phone (407) 351-3600. *See color ad p. 147.*

SKULL KINGDOM, off I-4 exit 30A at 5933 American Way, is a haunted castle complete with special effects and robotics as well as ghouls and demons. Sudden encounters and gruesome scenes await visitors as they make their way through two floors of mazes and caverns. Daily noon-11, July-Aug. and major holidays; Mon.-Fri. 6 p.m.-11 p.m., Sat.-Sun. noon-11, rest of year. Admission $12.50. Not recommended for under 8. AE, CB, DS, JC, MC, VI. Phone (407) 354-1564.

SLEUTHS MYSTERY DINNER SHOWS, 2 blks. e. of International Dr., jct. of Univer-

sal Blvd. and Carrier Dr. at 7508 Universal Blvd., offers dinner shows featuring a comedy/murder mystery. The audience participates in solving the mystery. Allow 3 hours minimum. Shows daily at 6, 7:30 and/or 9 p.m. Show times vary; phone ahead. Tickets $39.95; ages 3-11, $23.95. Reservations are required. AE, DI, DS, MC, VI. Phone (407) 363-1985 or (800) 393-1985.

TITANIC—SHIP OF DREAMS, off I-4 exit 29, just e. on SR 482 (Sand Lake Rd.), then .5 mi. s., in The Mercado Shopping Village, features recreations of the Grand Staircase and other ship interiors, artifacts and a gallery devoted to movies and plays about the vessel. A 30-minute guided tour features costumed actors interacting with visitors. Allow 1 hour minimum. Daily 10-9. Admission $16.95; ages 6-12, $11.95. AE, CB, DI, DS, MC, VI. Phone (407) 248-1166.

UNIVERSAL ORLANDO is off I-4 exit 30A (eastbound) or 29B (westbound), following signs. The complex brings movies to life through rides and shows at Universal Studios, visits the universe of myths, legends and super heroes at Islands of Adventure, and offers CityWalk for shopping, dining and entertainment.

The theme parks, entertainment area and on-site resorts are within walking distance of each other. All shopping, dining and entertainment facilities also are available to day guests. Because of the popularity of the parks, large crowds and long lines can be expected, especially during holiday periods. Strollers, wheelchairs and electric carts can be rented. Kennels are available.

The theme parks open daily at 9; closing hours vary by season. CityWalk open daily 11 a.m.-2 a.m.

A 1-day pass to either Universal Studios or Islands of Adventure is $46; ages 3-9, $37. Two- and 3-day passes provide unlimited admission to both parks on the same day. Multi-day passes also include early admission to the parks and access to all clubs at CityWalk. Two-day pass $84.95; ages 3-9, $69.95. Three-day pass $99.95; ages 3-9, $79.95. Multi-day passes do not expire until all days are used. AAA members can buy a combination park ticket that gives 7 consecutive days admissions to SeaWorld Orlando, Universal Studios, Islands of Adventure and Wet 'n Wild. If Busch Gardens Tampa Bay is included, the pass is valid for 10 consecutive days. Check with the attractions or your AAA club for more details.

Parking $6; valet parking $12. Special discounts are available to AAA members. See page 11 for more information. AE, DS, MC, VI. Phone (407) 363-8000.

CityWalk, off I-4 exit 30A (eastbound) or 29B (westbound), is an entertainment complex featuring dining in celebrity-themed restaurants, specialty shopping and movie theaters. Live performances at restaurants and nightclubs are evening highlights. Daily 11 a.m.-2 a.m. Evening cover charges vary by club. A pass covering evening admission to all clubs is $7.95, or $11.95 with cineplex admission included. AE, DS, MC, VI. Phone (407) 224-2600.

Islands of Adventure, off I-4 exit 29B (westbound) or 30A (eastbound), following signs, is a theme park that presents five themed islands with rides and shows based on such popular and legendary characters as The Cat in the Hat, Spider-Man, Popeye, The Incredible Hulk, Sindbad and the dinosaurs of "Jurassic Park." The Port of Entry, with food and shops, serves as an introduction to the park.

Flying Unicorn takes younger visitors on a flight through an enchanted forest in The Lost Continent, while at Marvel Super Hero Island children can help Storm battle the villainous Magesto.

The whimsical characters of Theodor "Dr. Seuss" Geisel's popular books come to life at Seuss Landing. The Cat In The Hat takes visitors on a couch ride through Dr. Seuss' childhood classic, and a menagerie of the good doctor's characters serve as steeds on the Caro-Seuss-el.

The younger set will also enjoy the play area If I Ran The Zoo and One Fish, Two Fish, Red Fish, Blue Fish.

Meet some of your favorite characters at Toon Lagoon, where rides and shows are based on cartoons and comic strips. Watch out for splashing water on Dudley Do-Right's Ripsaw Falls log flume ride and Popeye & Bluto's Bilge-Rat Barges white-water raft ride.

Experience the worlds of legendary super heroes and villains at Marvel Super Hero Island. Rides include Doctor Doom's Fearfall, a rocket ride 150 feet straight up—and then back down again; The Amazing Adventures of Spider-Man, a high-tech 3-D thrill ride; and the Incredible Hulk Coaster, a high-speed roller coaster adventure.

The centerpieces of the mysterious island Lost Continent are Dueling Dragons, an inverted double roller coaster, and Poseidon's Fury: Escape From the Lost City, an undersea battle between Zeus and Poseidon. The Eighth Voyage of Sindbad is an action-filled stunt show.

Jurassic Park, based on the popular motion picture and novel, re-creates the land inhabited by prehistoric animatronic creatures. Jurassic Park River Adventure, a raft ride through dinosaur habitats, features a steep water drop, while visitors have an opportunity to create a dinosaur through DNA sequencing at Jurassic Park Discovery Center. Camp Jurassic is an interactive prehistoric play area, and Pteranodon Flyers offers a view of the Jurassic Park area from up high.

Allow a full day. Park opens daily at 9; closing hours vary according to season. One-day admission $46; ages 3-9, $37. Parking $7; valet parking under 2 hours $7, more than 2 hours $14. AE, DS, MC, VI. Phone (407) 363-8000.

Universal Studios, off I-4 exit 30A (eastbound) or 29B (westbound), following signs, is a theme park that takes visitors into the worlds of Hollywood, movies and television. The theme park also is a working studio for television and motion picture production, complete with a back lot and sound stages. Realistic street scenes and special sets include Rodeo Drive, Hollywood Boulevard, Pennsylvania Station, Fifth Avenue, Gramercy Park and Fisherman's Wharf.

Men in Black Alien Attack, based on the movie, is a high-tech ride that gives visitors a chance to save Earth from aliens by zapping the creatures as the ride progresses through the streets of New York.

The multisensory Terminator 2: 3-D Battle Across Time, offers a 3-D cyberadventure. Visitors hurtle through time and space in Back to the Future...The Ride and come face-to-face with a tornado in Twister...Ride It Out. Nickelodeon Studios, The Place Where Nick is Made, offers a firsthand look at live television production.

Now NAPA is giving AAA customers a new set of breaks.

tive days admissions to SeaWorld Orlando, Universal Studios, Islands of Adventure and Wet 'n Wild. If Busch Gardens Tampa Bay is included, the pass is valid for 10 consecutive days. Check with the attractions for more details. AE, DS, MC, VI. Phone (407) 351-1800 or (800) 992-9453.

WONDERWORKS is at 9067 International Dr., .8 mi. n. of SR 528. This interactive entertainment center, in what appears to be an upside down building, features virtual reality experiences, games and exhibits. Simulated earthquakes and hurricane force winds, an anti-gravity chamber and a large laser tag facility are highlights. Food is available.

Allow 1 hour minimum. Daily 9 a.m.-midnight. Admission $14.95; over 55 and ages 5-11, $10.95. Laser tag is additional. Fee for parking. AE, DI, DS, JC, MC, VI. Phone (407) 351-8800.

What To Do

Sightseeing

Balloon Tours

[SAVE] Orange Blossom Balloons, (407) 239-7677, offers aerial views of the area via hot air balloons. The scenic trips include breakfast and champagne.

Bus, Carriage, Limousine or Train Tours

Guided tours are a good way to make the best use of time in Orlando. Many tour packages are provided for both day and evening sightseeing by [SAVE] Gray Line of Orlando; phone (407) 826-9999.

Spectator Sports

From downtown Orlando to Walt Disney World Resort, fans have several venues to choose from when it comes to the city's various professional sports offerings. Orlando's premier sports arena, **T.D. Waterhouse Centre**, 600 W. Amelia St., hosts arena football, basketball and hockey games.

Baseball

Baseball fans can cheer Orlando's minor league team, the **Orlando Rays**, at **Disney's Wide World of Sports**, Osceola Parkway and Victory Way, April through August. Disney's 200-acre multi-purpose sports complex also is the spring training home of the **Atlanta Braves**. For game schedules and ticket information phone (407) 363-6600.

Osceola County Stadium, 1000 Bill Beck Blvd. in Kissimmee, is the site of the **Houston Astros** spring training camp. The **Kansas City Royals** spend camp in **Baseball City**, at the

An 8.3 earthquake hurls fire, flood and even a runaway truck at visitors as their surroundings are leveled in Earthquake...The Big One, while King Kong is on the rampage in Kongfrontation. Jaws subjects visitors to an attack by a 3-ton, 32-foot great white shark.

Woody Woodpecker's KidZone, a special area just for kids, features the Curious George Goes to Town play area, Woody Woodpecker's Nuthouse Coaster, E.T. Adventure, A Day in the Park with Barney, Animal Actors Stage and Fievel's Playland.

Allow a full day. Park opens daily at 9; closing hours vary according to season. One-day admission $46; ages 3-9, $37. Parking $7; valet parking under 2 hours $7, more than 2 hours $14. AE, DS, MC, VI. Phone (407) 363-8000.

WALT DISNEY WORLD— *see Lake Buena Vista p. 162.*

[SAVE] **WET 'N WILD** is off I-4 exit 30A at 6200 International Dr. This water recreation park contains slides and flumes, a wave pool and a cable-operated kneeboard ride. Among the highlights is Surge, a multipassenger slide that races through 600 feet of curves and Fugi Flyer, a four-passenger toboggan ride. A children's playground offers child-size versions of the park's most popular rides. Food, picnic facilities, locker rooms and showers are available.

Allow 6 hours minimum. Open daily; hours vary according to season. Admission $28.95; ages 3-9, $22.95; over 54, $14.47. Parking $5; recreational vehicles $6. Lockers $5. A combination park ticket is available that gives 7 consecu-

junction of US 27 and I-4. For tickets and information phone (407) 933-5500 or (941) 424-2424, respectively.

Basketball

Orlando basketball enthusiasts root for their home team, the NBA's **Orlando Magic**. Fans can attend games at T.D. Waterhouse Centre, where they can also watch the Women's NBA **Orlando Miracle**. The city's two colleges also have basketball teams. For schedule and ticket information phone the Orlando Magic, (407) 916-2400; Rollins College, (407) 646-2663, in Winter Park; and the University of Central Florida Arena, (407) 823-1015, in Orlando.

Football

The **Citrus Bowl** hosts college football games, including the annual CompUSA Florida Citrus Bowl and home games for the Division I **UCF Knights**. The city has an arena football team, the **Orlando Predators**, who contended for the league championship during the 1994 Arena Bowl, held in the T.D. Waterhouse Centre.

Greyhound Racing

Dog racing is a year-round diversion. **Sanford-Orlando Kennel Club**, (407) 831-1600, at 301 Dog Track Rd. in Longwood, holds matinee and evening races from November through early May. **Seminole Greyhound Park**, (407) 699-4510, at 2000 Seminola Blvd. in Casselberry, is open from early May through October.

Note: Policies concerning admittance of children to pari-mutuel betting facilities vary. Phone for information.

Hockey

The T.D. Waterhouse Centre also is the home rink of the IHL **Orlando Solar Bears**, who played in the 1999 Turner Cup finals. For tickets and information phone (407) 872-7825.

Horse Racing

Not far from the horse farms surrounding Ocala, **Ben White Raceway**, at 1905 Lee Rd., is a training facility for harness racing. Training sessions can be observed Monday through Saturday mornings; phone (407) 293-8721.

Note: Policies concerning admittance of children to pari-mutuel betting facilities vary. Phone for information.

Jai alai

Played in only a few states, jai alai is one of Orlando's most unusual offerings. The game is similar to handball, except the athletes field the ball not with their bare hands, but with a curved basket worn on one arm. Pari-mutuel betting adds to the excitement of this fast-paced sport at **Orlando-Seminole Jai Alai Fronton**, (407) 339-6221, in Fern Park on US 17/92.

Note: Policies concerning admittance of children to pari-mutuel betting facilities vary. Phone for information.

Recreation

Lengthy summers and mild winters create ideal recreation conditions in central Florida year-round, and locals make the most of it. The area's many waterways host a wide variety of activities, and drier pastimes abound as well.

Bicycling

Although bicycling is growing in popularity in Orlando, there are few dedicated bike paths in the city, and traffic is always a concern. Exercise caution and obey all traffic laws when bicycling on the street. If possible, ride in a park—both **Turkey Lake** and **Lake Underhill** parks offer trails—or other specially designated area. Locals enjoy the **Cady Way Trail**, running from the Fashion Square Mall on SR 50 to Cady Way in Winter Park, as well as the quiet, tree-lined streets of **Rollins College**, **College Park** and **downtown Orlando**. The **Walt Disney World Resort** offers a variety of trails as well as bicycle rentals.

Fishing

With hundreds of lakes and several rivers to choose from, anglers will have no problem finding a place to cast their lines—bass, bream and catfish are among the available catches. Some favorite spots are **Gaston Edwards Park** on **Lake Ivanhoe** near downtown; **Lake Fairview**, north

of College Park; Lake Underhill Park, east of town off Conway Road; **Lake Cane/Marsha Park** and **Turkey Lake Park**, both just off Conroy-Windermere Rd.; **Wekiwa Springs State Park**, on SR 435 in northwest Orange County; and **Lake Tohopekaliga** in Kissimmee, south of US 192. The Walt Disney World complex also affords angling opportunities for tourists and residents alike. A freshwater license is required for those age 16 or older; phone Fisheries Management, (407) 846-5300, for additional details.

Deep-sea fishing is a popular pastime, and charters are available in many beachfront towns. Anglers age 16 and over must purchase saltwater licenses, which are available at many bait and tackle shops, most Wal-marts and Kmarts and at all tax assessors' offices. For further information phone the Florida Marine Enforcement, (800) 342-5367.

Golf

Golf is a way of life for many Orlando residents; An abundance of courses—more than 125—graces the metropolitan area, from the city-bound links of small municipal properties to the spectacular settings of the luxury resorts. All of the following courses offer at least 18 holes and are open to the public year round: Buena Vista, (407) 828-3741, in Lake Buena Vista; Casselberry, (407) 699-9310, 300 S. Triplet Lake Dr.; Celebration Golf Club, (407) 566-4653, 701 Golf Park Dr.; Dubsdread, (407) 246-3636, 549 W. Par St.; Eastwood Golf Club, (407) 281-4653, 13950 Golfway Blvd.; Hunter's Creek, (407) 240-4653, 14401 Sports Club Way; MetroWest

Country Club, (407) 299-1099, 2100 S. Hiawassee Rd.; Stoneybrook Orlando, (407) 384-6888, 2900 Northampton Ave.; Walt Disney World Golf Complex, (407) 939-4653, in Lake Buena Vista; and Wedgefield Golf and Country Club, (407) 568-2116, 20550 Maxim Pkwy.

Jogging and Walking

Orlando also boasts two scenic, paved recreation trails built on old railway beds. Both provide opportunities for walking and jogging. The 19-mile **West Orange Trail** runs between the Lake/Orange county line through abandoned orange groves to Apopka. For information contact the Orange County Parks and Recreation Department at (407) 836-6200. Closer to downtown Orlando, the 3.5-mile Cady Way Trail connects Winter Park to Fashion Square Mall. For information contact the Transportation Planning Bureau (407) 246-2775.

One can walk or jog just about anywhere in central Florida, but the following spots are exceptionally nice. Downtown Orlando features **Lake Eola**, noted for Centennial Fountain, as well as **Langford Park** on Central Boulevard. Just outside downtown are College Park's charming streets and the serene oasis of Lake Ivanhoe's **Gaston Edwards Park**. **Winter Park** is a good place for a stroll, particularly along popular **Park Avenue** or on the **Rollins College** campus. Other appealing sites include **Mead Gardens** and **Kraft Azalea Gardens and Park** in Winter Park. Due to the relentless Florida sun, early morning and late afternoon are the best times for either activity.

Tennis

Tennis courts are nearly as numerous as lakes in metropolitan Orlando, with more than 800 throughout the area. Many hotels offer court privileges to their guests. The courts at county parks are always open to the general public; for further details phone the City of Orlando Recreation Bureau, (407) 246-2288, or the Orange County Parks and Recreation Department, (407) 836-6200. Some resorts offer public access, including **Cypress Creek Country Club** at 5353 S. Vineland Rd., (407) 351-2187; the **Grand Cypress Racquet Club**, 55 Grand Cypress Blvd., (407) 239-1944; and Kissimmee's **Poinciana Golf & Racquet Resort**, 500 E. Cypress Pkwy., (407) 933-5300.

Water Sports

The plethora of lakes in central Florida—more than 1,200 by some counts—provides endless opportunities for water sports of all kinds, including boating, canoeing, swimming, water skiing and windsurfing. Some of the most popular sites include Lake Ivanhoe; **Lake Fairview**, accessible via either Lee Road or US 441; Lake Underhill; and the **Butler Chain of Lakes** and **Winter Park Chain of Lakes**. For information contact the Orange County Parks and Recreation Department at (407) 836-6200.

Just north of Orlando near Apopka is Wekiwa Springs State Park *(see Recreation Chart and the AAA Southeastern CampBook)*, where swimming in the crystal clear spring water is popular. The Wekiva River is considered one of the state's best canoeing rivers; canoe rental information is available at the marina, (407) 862-1500.

Boating is a favorite recreation; residents have their choice of several inland waterways to explore. The Butler and Winter Park Chain of Lakes are groupings of connected lakes. The Rollins College campus and beautiful homes line the shores of the lakes in Winter Park's chain, and boat tours are available *(see place listing p. 176)*. Another active waterway, the **St. Johns River**, connects nearby Sanford with Jacksonville. Houseboats can be rented on a daily basis in DeLand, allowing visitors to navigate the river in style.

Shopping

With an influx of tourists from all over the world, Orlando's shopping areas must satisfy a variety of tastes and styles. From high fashion and international selections to famous labels at bargain-hunter prices, Orlando has them. Weather-related items such as lightweight sportswear and swimsuits are stocked all year, and area citrus products are sold at many roadside stands.

Antiques

The best antiquing downtown is in the **North Orange Avenue Antique District**, running south from the 2900 block to the 1600 block. This funky strip is lined with stores selling everything from 1930s radios to 19th-century furniture to housewares from the 1950s and '60s. Particularly charming is a little cluster of buildings known as

Ivanhoe Row, along the 1200 block across from Lake Ivanhoe. The College Park section of **Edgewater Drive** and **Fairbanks Avenue** east of I-4 also have a number of antiques dealers. Pricier items can be found at the shops along **Park Avenue** in Winter Park.

Malls

In south Orlando, the massive **Florida Mall**, 8001 S. Orange Blossom Tr., boasts more than 200 shops and a bustling food court anchored by such major retailers as Dillard's, JCPenney, Saks Fifth Avenue and Sears, and including the Adam's Mark Hotel as well. Northeast of downtown is **Orlando Fashion Square Mall**, 3201 E. Colonial Dr., featuring Burdines, JCPenney, Sears, a second-floor food court and 165 smaller stores, including such mall standards as the Limited and the Gap. **Altamonte Mall**, 451 E. Altamonte Dr., offers four anchors—Burdines, JCPenney, Parisian and Sears—along with a food court and two floors containing 175 boutiques from the Banana Republic to the Body Shop.

Sanford's **Seminole Towne Center**, 200 Towne Center Cir., is the northernmost of the area malls. It has about 120 shops, a food court and five department stores: Burdines, Dillards, JCPenney, Parisian and Sears. East of Orlando is the **Oviedo Marketplace** with Dillards and Parisian. West of downtown, **West Oaks Mall** at Clarke Road and SR 50 in Ocoee is anchored by Dillards, JCPenney and Sears.

Outlets

International Drive is a mecca for bargain hunters. In addition to the abundance of souvenir shops, there are outlet stores scattered along the length of the road throughout the tourist area. Goods run the gamut from shoes to cookware,

representing such manufacturers as Corning-Revere, Dansk, Mikasa and Royal Doulton.

The largest conglomeration of outlet stores is at the **Belz Factory Outlet World**, off International Drive on West Oakridge Road. Apparel, electronics, jewelry, shoes, housewares and other items are available from more than 170 vendors; the Annex also offers a food court and a carrousel. Expect to find the likes of Bally, Calvin Klein, Capezio, Etienne Aigner, London Fog and Oneida, among many others. Just south is the **Belz Designer Outlet Centre**, 5211 International Dr., a large plaza ringed with discount shops for Brooks Brothers, Coach, Cole Haan, Fossil, Lenox, Anne Klein, Ruff-Hewn, Saks Fifth Avenue and more. The **Kissimmee Manufacturer's Outlet**, 4673 W. Irlo Bronson Memorial Pkwy., features several dozen stores, including Bass and Nike.

Specialty Districts

Large malls aren't the only game in town—there are many interesting boutiques to be found in the area's themed shopping areas and independent districts. The **Church Street Station Exchange** *(see color ad p. 155)*, downtown at Church Street Station, has a Victorian flair and nearly 50 shops selling goods from new-age crystals to cow memorabilia. The second floor features a food court and the third floor offers **Commander Ragtime's**, an old-fashioned arcade with all the latest video games. A large courtyard is the centerpiece of the neighboring **Church Street Marketplace**. Surrounded by restaurants and specialty stores, the expansive brick plaza has become a gathering place for people of all walks, bringing together shoppers with street performers.

The **Winter Park Farmer's Market** fills Saturday mornings with fresh produce, herbs, baked goods and hot coffee in a refurbished train depot at 200 W. New England Ave. One block east is Winter Park's heart and soul, **Park Avenue**. The European-flavored promenade is lined with an eclectic assortment of boutiques, galleries and eateries ranging from the upscale to the funky, making the avenue a favorite for shopping, browsing or just meandering. Especially interesting are the shops in the courtyards and the **Hidden Garden**. Tired shoppers can take a break across the street in **Central Park** or at one of the many charming cafes along the way.

With five restaurants, 60 stores and live entertainment in the courtyard every night, the **Mercado Mediterranean Shopping Village**, 8445 International Dr., is almost a world unto itself. Boutiques in the Spanish-style complex sell a variety of wares, including beachwear, collectibles, casual clothing and imported goods.

Downtown Disney Marketplace is the place to go for international purchases. Here boutiques filled with items from around the world line the shores of Buena Vista Lagoon, and artisans demonstrate their skills for passersby. Also in the Downtown Disney area on Buena Vista Drive is **Planet Hollywood**, where the fascination with all that is Hollywood is captured in souvenirs ranging from designer T-shirts to key chains to leather jackets. Farther south, near the intersection of I-4 and US 192, is **Disney's Town of Celebration**, a planned community with all the amenities of a small town including a downtown area complete with nearly two dozen shops and restaurants.

Yet another shopping destination on International Drive is **Pointe Orlando**, at 9101 International Dr. near the Orange County Convention Center. This six-building complex features more than 80 shops, restaurants and attractions, including FAO Schwarz, IMAX and conventional theaters, and WonderWorks *(see attraction listing p. 152)*, an entertainment center in what appears to be a three-story, upside-down building.

Flea World, on US 17/92, features merchants, eateries, amusement rides and live entertainment *(see Sanford p. 175)*. A half-hour northwest of Orlando, historic Mount Dora is known for its abundance of antique shops. Hundreds of dealers gather each weekend at **Renninger's Antique Market** on SR 441. Antique lovers also can search for finds in downtown Sanford.

Kissimmee's **Old Town**, 5770 W. Irlo Bronson Memorial Pkwy., evokes a turn-of-the-20th-century atmosphere with brick walkways, a Ferris wheel, a roller coaster and a wooden train exhibit. More than 70 shops offer an extensive selection of wares ranging from music boxes to magic tricks.

Performing Arts

The strength of Orlando's appeal lies mainly with its family-oriented attractions and entertainment. While this is good news for the folks at

Disney and Universal, it has detracted some focus from the city's cultural scene. Arts enthusiasts need not despair, though—local arts groups have begun to expand their presence. Theater offers the most varied slate, with dance and music filling in the gaps. As the film industry gains a foothold in the area, it is likely that the fine arts will enjoy even greater success, attracting new artists to practice their crafts in the City Beautiful.

Dance

The **Southern Ballet Theatre** is Orlando's professional dance company. The season, which lasts from September to May, features concerts and programs ranging from classical to modern. The troupe also stages the Nutcracker ballet every Christmas, accompanied by a live orchestra of local musicians. Performances generally are held at the **Bob Carr Performing Arts Centre**; for information phone (407) 426-1733.

Rollins College brings in some of the dance world's brightest stars, including the Alvin Ailey Repertory and Pilobolus, to the **Annie Russell Theatre** to supplement the **Rollins Dance** student program; phone (407) 646-2145.

Film

Alternative cinema finds a home at the **Enzian Theater**, 1300 S. Orlando Ave., offering filmgoers a varied menu of critically acclaimed American independent and foreign films. The theater itself is unusual—it is set in an old house, with audience seating at tables rather than in an auditorium. For information phone (407) 629-1088.

Music

Despite lacking a full-time professional orchestra, Orlando does have a variety of groups dedicated to making beautiful music. The **Orlando Philharmonic** gives three concert series during the year. Performances are held at both the Bob Carr Performing Arts Centre and the **Orlando Museum of Art**, 2416 N. Mills Ave., in Orlando Loch Haven Park; for additional information phone (407) 896-6700. The **Orlando Celebrity Concert Association (OCCA)**, (407) 896-2451, imports full-size symphonies as well as smaller ensembles for the Festival of Orchestras including such esteemed groups as the Cleveland Orchestra. OCCA guests also play at the Bob Carr.

A favorite local event is the Bach Festival, a celebration of masterworks by Bach and other major composers. Held in late February or early March, the program is performed by the **Bach Festival Choir and Orchestra**, which also offers the Festival Concert Series from October through April. The group performs at the **Knowles Memorial Chapel** at Rollins College; phone (407) 646-2182.

Opera

Opera in central Florida is presented by the **Orlando Opera Company**, staging three major

works from November through March, as well as special programs during the season. Performances are at the Bob Carr Performing Arts Centre with the venue for the company's operettas being the **Dr. Phillips Center for the Performing Arts** at 1111 N. Orange Ave. For season and ticket information phone (407) 426-1717 or 426-1700 for the box office.

Theater

One of the area's most popular theaters is the **Civic Theatre of Central Florida**. In addition to standard theater fare, the company produces children's shows and the offbeat works of the Second Stage Series; phone (407) 896-7365. Another local favorite is the **Orlando Broadway Series**, sponsoring touring Broadway shows at the Bob Carr Performing Arts Centre. Tickets for the biggest hits often require several weeks' notice; phone (800) 448-6322. **Theatre Downtown**, (407) 841-0083, offers avant-garde and mainstream works just north of the city center at 2113 N. Orange Ave. The **Orlando Theatre Project**, (407) 328-2040, puts on a similar mix at **Seminole Community College's Fine Arts Theatre**, 100 Weldon Blvd. in Sanford.

The play's the thing at the **Orlando Shakespeare Festival**, (407) 893-4600, dedicated to staging the bard's timeless plays in innovative ways. The festival, held each April at the **Walt Disney Amphitheater at Lake Eola Park**, produces additional works throughout the year, from classically-inspired independent pieces to the **PlayLab Series**, a selection of experimental plays, presented at the **Orange County Historical Museum Theatre** at Loch Haven Park, 812 E. Rollins Ave.

The University of Central Florida features a full season of performances through **Theatre UCF**, (407) 823-1500. Rollins College also mounts a full season, with four productions at the Annie Russell Theatre running the gamut of theatrical styles; phone (407) 646-2145.

Special Events

On New Year's Day two top college football teams test their skills during the **CompUSA Florida Citrus Bowl** Football Classic. A parade and other related activities precede the big game.

In late January the **Zora Neale Hurston Festival of Arts and Humanities** celebrates the life of

the noted interpreter of Southern rural African-American culture. This culture is celebrated further throughout February at varied events during the **Black History Month Festival**.

Orlando's moderate temperatures are ideal for art festivals. Most popular are the **Mount Dora Arts Festival** in early February; the **Downtown Orlando Arts Festival** in early March; the **Winter Park Sidewalk Art Festival** on the third weekend in March; and the **Maitland Arts & Fine Crafts Festival** in mid-April. A pair of **Fiesta in the Park** celebrations take place in April and November on the shores of Lake Eola.

For 10 days in late April and early May, entertainers from around the world converge on downtown Orlando, treating theatergoers to a variety of unusual and cutting edge performances as part of the **International Fringe Festival**. Towards the end of the following month, more than 200,000 ears of corn are eaten during the **Zellwood Sweet Corn Festival**, also a showcase for big-name country musicians.

Two PGA golf tournaments are on Orlando's calendar of events. In March the **Bay Hill Invitational** is held at Bay Hill Country Club, while the **National Car Rental Golf Classic at Walt Disney**

World is held at the Palm, Osprey and Magnolia courses at Walt Disney World in October.

In early November the **Walt Disney World Festival of the Masters** is held at Downtown Disney Marketplace. During this 3-day event, major American artists display their works. The city of Winter Park rings in the holiday season with **Christmas in the Park**, which combines a concert by the Bach Festival Choir and stunning outdoor displays of lighted Tiffany windows on loan from the nearby Charles Hosmer Morse Museum of American Art.

Nightlife

Before **Church Street Station** *(see color ad p. 155)* opened—and even for some time after—Orlando's evening scene was best described as quiet. But since the downtown renaissance of the 1970s and '80s, downtown has become a hotbed of hot spots, from crowded dance clubs to alternative coffeehouses. And for those who want a theme to go along with their entertainment, Church Street Station along with nightspots at the Walt Disney World Resort and Universal Orlando fit the bill nicely.

A handful of clubs line Church Street from Orange Avenue to the **Church Street Marketplace**, including **Mulvaney's Irish Pub**, (407) 872-3296. The Calendar section of the Friday Orlando Sentinel has the latest information on all the area nightspots.

Country

Line-dancing is popular at the **Crazy Horse Saloon**, 7050 S. Kirkman Rd., (407) 363-0071, but bull-riding is the big draw at downtown's **8 Seconds**, 100 W. Livingston St., (407) 839-4800.

Dance Clubs

Orange Avenue is the main strip for downtown dance clubs, and alternative rock is the music of choice. **Barbarella**, 68 N. Orange Ave., presents live bands playing alternative and underground music; phone (407) 839-0457. Daring types dance the night away to house music at The **Club at the Firestone**, (407) 872-0066, in the former Firestone Tire and Service Center at 578 N. Orange Ave. The old Beacham Theater, 46 N. Orange Ave., houses **Zuma Beach**, (407) 648-8363, a hot spot popular for its mix of disco, high-energy and Top 40 tunes. At the Egyptian-themed **Cairo**, 22 S. Magnolia Ave., music ranges from disco to house; phone (407) 422-3595.

On Disney property in the Wyndham Palace Resort and Spa is the **Laughing Kookaburra Good Time Bar**, (407) 827-3722, also known as "the Kook." International Drive offers **Backstage** at the Clarion Plaza Hotel; phone (407) 996-1719.

Entertainment Complexes

Glowing with lights and bustling with people, Church Street Station, (407) 422-2434, is reminiscent of an old-fashioned street party, complete with turn-of-the-20th-century decor. *Rosie O'Grady's Good Time Emporium* is the granddaddy of the place, featuring Dixieland jazz and cancan dancers in an old-time bar decked in brass. The similarly "antique" look of the *Orchid Garden Ballroom* presents an unusual blend of Victorian furnishings and rock 'n' roll. Cloggers and line dancers stomp to their hearts' delight across the street at the country-themed *Cheyenne Saloon and Opera House*, and high-energy dance and pop music take center stage at *Phineas Phogg's Balloon Works*.

It's always New Year's Eve at **Downtown Disney Pleasure Island**, (407) 934-7781, celebrated every night at midnight with lots of music and fireworks. Baby boomers can indulge their 1970s nostalgia at *8TRAX* while Generation Xers dance the night away to current chart-toppers at *Mannequins Dance Palace*. The *Rock 'n' Roll Beach Club* features live bands covering hits from the '60s through the '90s and *BET Soundstage Club* delivers urban contemporary entertainment. The '30s are the focus of the eccentric players of the *Adventurers Club*, and a troupe of improvisational players brings down the house at the *Comedy Warehouse*. Honkytonkers can line dance until the wee hours of the morning at the *Wildhorse Saloon*, but jazz aficionados will appreciate the mellower stylings of the *Pleasure Island Jazz Company*.

Downtown Disney West Side features the *House of Blues*, serving up some of America's best-loved music with rock 'n' roll, R&B, country, alternative, gospel and the root of it all—blues. Another Lake Buena Vista hot spot, **Disney's BoardWalk**, (407) 939-5101, offers a dance hall and live band at *Atlantic Dance*, dueling pianos at *Jellyrolls*, and the sports-oriented *ESPN Club*.

At the entrance to Universal Orlando is an eye-catching new entrant in the competition for Orlando's late-night revelers and club hoppers: **CityWalk**; phone (407) 224-9255. If variety is the spice of life, then this place is five-alarm chili *hot*. Reggae rules at *Bob Marley-A Tribute to Freedom*, which is housed in a replica of Marley's former home in Jamaica. Performers sing Motown's classic hits every twenty minutes at the *Motown Cafe*, and jazz mementos line the walls at *CityJazz*, which also features live performances. *Pat O'Brien's* is a carbon copy of the New Orleans landmark; pianos duel it out in the raucous piano bar. Wildly decorated period rooms offer retreats from the pounding beat on the dance floor at *the groove*, while the *Latin Quarter* plays host to Salsa, Merengue, Mariachi and Latin Rock bands. Designed to look like Rome's Coliseum, *Hard Rock Live* is a state-of-the-art theater spotlighting some of the biggest names in music.

Jazz & Blues

Locals make the scene downtown at the **Sapphire**, (407) 246-1419, 54 N. Orange Ave. A few doors away at 100 S. Orange Ave. is the bluesy **Tanqueray's Bar & Grille**, (407) 649-8540, set in the cellar of the 1920s Metcalf Building.

Rock

The **Howl at the Moon Saloon**, (407) 841-4695, in the Church Street Marketplace at 55 W. Church St., features dueling pianists covering rock standards and a rowdy crowd welcome to join in the fun. Dueling pianos also provide the spark at **Blazing Pianos**, 8445 International Dr. in the **Mercado Mediterranean Shopping Village**; phone (407) 363-5104.

The Orlando Vicinity

APOPKA (E-2) pop. 13,500, elev. 150'

ROCK SPRINGS AND KELLY PARK are 6 mi. n. on SR 435. Rock Springs, a half-mile east of the park entrance on Kelly Park Road, discharges 26,000 gallons of clear, 68-degree Fahrenheit water per minute into a spring that is popular for tubing and swimming. Picnic grounds, shelters, bathhouses, tube rentals (outside park), hiking trails and camping facilities are available. Daily 9-7, Apr.-Oct.; 8-6, rest of year. Admission $1, under 6 free. Phone (407) 889-4179. *See Recreation Chart.*

CHRISTMAS (D-10) elev. 44'

Every yuletide the town of Christmas receives thousands of pieces of mail, which are stamped with the Christmas postmark and sent on their way. Four miles south on SR 50 is the headquarters of the Tosohatchee State Preserve. The preserve's 28,000 acres of woodlands and wetlands along the St. Johns River offer primitive camping, hiking and nature study *(see Recreation Chart)*.

FORT CHRISTMAS MUSEUM is 2 mi. n. of SR 50 on CR 420 (Fort Christmas Rd.). The museum is a reconstruction of a fort begun Dec. 25, 1837, during the Second Seminole Indian War. Two blockhouses contain exhibits about the Seminole Indian Wars and area pioneers. Guided tours of seven restored pioneer houses are available. Picnic and recreation facilities are available. Allow 1 hour minimum. Tues.-Sat. 10-5,

Sun. 1-5; closed holidays. Tours given Tues.-Sat. 11-3, Sun. 1-3. Free. Phone (407) 568-4149.

[SAVE] **JUNGLE ADVENTURES,** 26205 E. SR 50, lets visitors view alligators in their natural habitat. A swamp cruise on board a pontoon boat; a wildlife show including endangered Florida panthers; and alligator feeding demonstrations are featured. An American Indian village re-creates the lifestyle of native Florida Indians. Guided tours are available. Allow 2 hours, 30 minutes minimum. Daily 9:30-5:30. Admission $14.50; over 60, $11.50; ages 3-11, $8.50. AE, DS, MC, VI. Phone (407) 568-1354.

CLERMONT (D-9) pop. 6,900, elev. 190′

Clermont founder A.F. Wrotnoski named this town of wide, shady streets and rolling hills after his French birthplace. Lake Louisa State Park (*see Recreation Chart*), 7 miles southeast of Clermont on Lake Nellie Road, is one of 13 in a chain of lakes connected by the Palatkahah River.

South Lake Chamber of Commerce: 691 W. Montrose St., P.O. Box 120417, Clermont, FL 32712-0417; phone (352) 394-4191.

[SAVE] **CITRUS TOWER CENTRE** is 1 mi. n. of the SR 50 jct. at 141 N. US 27. Reached by elevator, the 226-foot-tall tower's observation deck provides a panorama of the surrounding lakes and rolling hills. Food is available. Allow 30 minutes minimum. Mon.-Sat. 8-8, Sun. 11-6; closed Jan. 1 and Dec. 25. Admission $3.50; ages 3-15, $1. MC, VI. Phone (352) 394-4061.

HOUSE OF PRESIDENTS, just n. of SR 50 at 123 N. US 27, features changing exhibits of memorabilia related to U.S. presidents. Among displays are campaign and inaugural artifacts, replicas of China place settings, first ladies' evening gowns and the White House duplicated in miniature. A videotape tour of the White House is shown. Allow 2 hours minimum. Daily 9:30-5:30. Admission $7.95; ages 4-11, $3.95. AE, MC, VI. Phone (352) 394-2836.

WINERIES

• **Lakeridge Winery and Vineyards,** 2.5 mi. s. off Florida's Tpke. exit 285 on US 27. Mon.-Sat. 10-5, Sun. 11-5; closed Jan. 1, Easter, Thanksgiving and Dec. 25. Phone (352) 394-8627 or (800) 768-9463.

HEATHROW (D-3) elev. 50′

Heathrow is the site of American Automobile Association's national office. North of Orlando at I-4 and Lake Mary Boulevard, the Heathrow community includes recreational, commercial and residential areas.

KISSIMMEE (H-3) pop. 30,100, elev. 62′

Kissimmee (Kiss-SEM-mee), or "Heaven's Place" in the Calusa Indian language, is near the southern terminus of a scenic portion of Florida's Turnpike extending 65 miles southeast from Wildwood. Many downtown businesses occupy structures dating from the late 1800s; landscaping and renovations preserve the town's old-time aura.

Area industries include plastics, engineering, electronics and agriculture. The Florida Cattlemen's Association and Tupperware International operate headquarters in town. Kissimmee also attracts the sports-minded with the Osceola County Stadium and Sports Complex, where the Houston Astros conduct spring training during March; phone (407) 933-5400, or 933-2520 for Astros ticket information.

Picnic tables and boat ramps are available at Lake Front Park, .25 mile southeast of US 17/92. Also in this park is the Monument of States, a stone pyramid consisting of stones from various states and 22 countries.

Kissimmee-St. Cloud Convention & Visitors Bureau: 1925 E. Irlo Bronson Memorial Hwy., P.O. Box 422007, Kissimmee, FL 34742-2007; phone (407) 847-5000 or (800) 327-9159. *See color ad p. 646.*

Shopping areas: Old Town, just east of I-4 on US 192, features 75 specialty shops as well as restaurants and amusement rides in a re-created turn-of-the-20th-century setting. Hundreds of classic cars cruise the streets of Old Town every Friday and Saturday night.

[SAVE] **ARABIAN NIGHTS,** off I-4 exit 25A at 6225 W. US 192, is a 2-hour dinner show featuring equestrian acts in an indoor arena. The performances include a Wild West act, Lipizzan horses and a Roman chariot race. A three-course dinner is served during the show. Allow 2 hours, 30 minutes minimum. Performances nightly; occasional noon matinee. Admission $36.95; ages 3-11, $23.95. Reservations are recommended. AE, CB, DI, DS, MC, VI. Phone (407) 239-9223, 239-9221 or (800) 553-6116.

[SAVE] **BOGGY CREEK AIRBOAT RIDES** is e. on Osceola Pkwy., just n. on Boggy Creek Rd. (CR 530), then e. 1.5 mi. to East Lake Fish Camp, following signs. The company offers airboat trips through the wetland wilderness around Boggy Creek. Passengers can see eagles, turtles, alligators and other Florida wildlife during the voyage. Allow 30 minutes minimum. Daily 9-5:30. Fare $16.95; ages 3-12, $10. MC, VI. Phone (407) 344-9550.

[SAVE] **CAPONE'S DINNER AND SHOW,** 4740 W. Irlo Bronson Memorial Hwy. (US 192), .7 mi. e. of jct. SR 535, presents a musical dinner show based on the 1930s escapades of gangster Al Capone. Allow 2 hours, 30 minutes minimum. Performances nightly at 8. Admission $39.95; ages 4-12, $23.95. Reservations are suggested. AE, DS, MC, VI. Phone (407) 397-2378.

FLORIDA SPLENDID CHINA is 3 mi. w. of I-4 exit 25B on US 192, then s. via Formosa Garden Blvd. to 3000 Splendid China Blvd. The park lets visitors experience Chinese heritage, culture, geography, architecture and lifestyles while viewing more than 60 miniaturized replicas of such landmarks as the Great Wall, the Terra-cotta Warriors, the Forbidden City, Tibet's Potala Palace and the Stone Forest. Other park features include live entertainment, a playground and cuisine native to various regions of China. A 90-minute dinner show is available. Guided tours are available.

Allow 5 hours minimum. Daily 9:30-7. Dinner show Tues.-Sun. at 6. Admission (includes dinner show) $26.99; over 54, $25.30; ages 5-12, $16.99. Dinner show only $14.95; ages 5-12, $9.95. AE, MC, VI. Phone (407) 396-7111 or (800) 244-6226.

FLYING TIGERS WARBIRD RESTORATION MUSEUM is at 231 N. Hoagland Blvd., 7 mi. e. of I-4 off US 192. The museum specializes in the restoration of World War II aircraft. Displays include antique and World War II planes, equipment, armaments and memorabilia. Guided tours are available. Allow 1 hour, 30 minutes minimum. Daily 9-5:30. Admission $8; over 60, $7; ages 6-11, $6. DS, MC, VI. Phone (407) 933-1942.

GREEN MEADOWS PETTING FARM, 3 mi. e. of I-4 exit 25A on US 192, then 5 mi. s. on Poinciana Blvd., offers guided tours of a 40-acre farm with more than 300 farm animals. The hands-on philosophy encourages learning as visitors milk a cow, ride a pony or hold a chicken. Petting pens with various farm animals are a highlight of the tour. Tractor-drawn hayrides and a train ride are included. Picnic facilities are available.

Allow 2 hours minimum. Daily 9:30-4; closed Thanksgiving and Dec. 25. Last tour begins 1 hour, 30 minutes before closing. Admission $15, under 2 free. DS, MC, VI. Phone (407) 846-0770.

JUNGLELAND ZOO, 4580 W. Irlo Bronson Memorial Hwy. (US 192), is home to hundreds of rare and exotic animals including tigers, bears, leopards, monkeys, alligators and Nala the lioness. Allow 2 hours minimum. Daily 9-6. Alligator presentations are given daily at noon, 2 and 4. Admission $11.95; over 55, $9.95; ages 3-11, $6.95. MC, VI. Phone (407) 396-1012.

LAKE KISSIMMEE STATE PARK—
see Lake Wales p. 101.

SAVE **MEDIEVAL TIMES DINNER AND TOURNAMENT,** 6 mi. e. of I-4 exit 25A at 4510 W. Irlo Bronson Memorial Hwy. (US 192), is in a replica of an 11th-century European-style castle. A four-course dinner is served by staff members costumed in medieval attire. Spectators feast a few feet from the action in the Great Ceremonial Arena, where knights on horseback compete in battles and a jousting tournament and equestrian precision drills are performed.

Allow 2 hours minimum. Performances nightly; show times vary. Admission $41; ages 3-11, $25. Reservations are required. AE, DS, MC, VI. Phone (407) 396-1518, 239-0214 or (800) 229-8300.

Medieval Life is a re-creation of a village where costumed tradesmen and artisans ply their trades using materials and tools of the period. Features include a birds of prey exhibit and a dungeon and torture chamber. Allow 1 hour minimum. Daily 4-8. Admission $8; ages 3-11, $6. Free admission with Medieval Times dinner ticket.

WATER MANIA, .5 mi. e. of I-4 at 6073 W. Irlo Bronson Memorial Hwy. (US 192), is a 36-acre park containing raft rides, waterslides, flumes, a wave pool, a surfing simulator, an inner tube river ride, children's play areas, bumper boats, go-carts and an arcade. Picnic facilities, raft rentals, life vests, showers, changing rooms, lockers and food are available. Allow 4 hours minimum. Daily 10-5, early June to mid-Aug.; otherwise varies rest of year. Admission $25.95; over 54, $20.76. Parking $5. MC, VI. Phone (407) 396-2626 or (800) 527-3092.

SAVE **A WORLD OF ORCHIDS** is 2.5 mi. w. of I-4 exit 25B on US 192, then 1 mi. s. on CR 545 (Old Lake Wilson Rd.). Thousands of exotic orchids are showcased in changing exhibits in an enclosed tropical rain forest setting. Indoor and outdoor gardens feature various varieties of bamboos, palms, ferns and bromeliads. Allow 1 hour minimum. Tues.-Sun. 9:30-4:30; closed Jan. 1, July 4, Thanksgiving, Dec. 25 and the second and third weeks in July. Free. Phone (407) 396-1887.

DID YOU KNOW

In August 1870 it rained for 10 days in Orlando, soaking the town with 53 inches of rain.

General Information

Disney's Magic Kingdom® Park, Epcot® and Disney-MGM Studios open daily generally at 9. Disney's Animal Kingdom® Theme Park opens daily generally at 8. Closing times vary between each park, depending on the season.

Large crowds and long waiting lines are to be expected, especially during holiday periods. FASTPASS, a guest service that allows visitors to obtain a designated ride time for some of the park's most popular attractions, helps avoid long waits in line. Individual park maps are available at Guest Relations Information Centers near the entrance of each park.

Parking and Pets

The entrance road leads to parking (fee $6 per day). Free tram service connects the parking area with the Ticket and Transportation Center, Epcot, Disney-MGM Studios and Disney's Animal Kingdom Theme Park. Transportation also is available to all guest areas. Kennels—at Magic Kingdom Park, Ticket and Transportation Center, Epcot, Disney-MGM Studios, Disney's Animal Kingdom Theme Park and Disney's Fort Wilderness Resort and Campground—charge a nominal fee to care for and feed pets.

Admissions

Park Hopper Plus Pass provides admission to the four theme parks for the number of days purchased plus a set number of visits to Downtown Disney Pleasure Island, Disney's water parks and Disney's Wide World of Sports complex. Five days $236; ages 3-9, $192. Six days $266; ages 3-9, $217. Seven days $296; ages 3-9, $242.

Park Hopper Pass provides unlimited admission to the four theme parks for the number of days on the pass. Four-day pass $176; ages 3-9, $142. Five-day pass $206; ages 3-9, $167.

One-day, One-park ticket covers one day's admission to attractions in one of four theme parks: Magic Kingdom Park or Disney's Animal Kingdom Theme Park or Epcot or Disney-MGM Studios. Admission $46; ages 3-9, $37.

LAKE BUENA VISTA (G-2)
pop. 1,800, elev. 100'

RICHARD PETTY DRIVING EXPERIENCE, off US 192 exit World Dr., following signs to Magic Kingdom, puts race fans in the seat of a Winston-Cup style stock car on a 1-mile, tri-oval track. A ride-along program allows guests 16 and older to ride with a professional instructor at speeds up to 145 mph. A variety of programs for drivers 18 and older include racing lessons and timed laps; reservations and a valid driver's license are required. Allow 1 hour minimum. Daily 8-5; closed Jan. 1 and Dec. 25. Admission free. Ride-along program $89; riders 16-18 must be accompanied by parent or legal guardian. Driving programs start at $349. AE, DS, MC, VI. Phone (407) 939-0130 or (800) 237-3889.

WALT DISNEY WORLD® RESORT is accessible from US 192, Osceola Pkwy. and several exits off I-4 s. of Orlando, depending on the park destination. Covering 30,500 acres, the complex includes the Magic Kingdom® Park; Epcot®; Disney-MGM Studios; Disney's Animal Kingdom® Theme Park; three themed water parks; more than a dozen resorts; Disney's Fort Wilderness Resort and Campground; five championship golf courses; two luxurious spas; Disney's Wide World of Sports™ complex; and the Downtown Disney area, a shopping, dining and entertainment district. The resort is in a near-constant state of expansion and modernization. This process may include enhancements to existing attractions as well as new construction.

Navigating the Walt Disney World property is greatly simplified by clear, concise road signs. Tram service is provided from parking areas to the main entrance of Disney's Animal Kingdom Theme Park, Epcot, Disney-MGM Studios and to the Transportation and Ticket Center near the Magic Kingdom Park. From the Transportation and Ticket Center, ferries and a monorail transport visitors to the Magic Kingdom Park.

The recreational, shopping, dining and entertainment facilities of the resort also are open to day visitors. Monorail, boat and motorcoach transportation are available throughout the resort.

Theme parks open generally at 9; closing times vary. Multi-day ticket options provide admission to all four theme parks and other entertainment areas. One-day, One-park admission $46; ages 3-9, $37. AE, DI, DS, JC, MC, VI. Phone (407) 824-4321. *See color ads starting on p. 165 & color ads p. 680 & p. 681.*

Disney's Animal Kingdom® Theme Park, n. of US 192 on World Dr. then following signs along Osceola Pkwy., offers adventures with creatures from different realms. Visitors can go back in time to encounter dinosaurs, take an African safari amid free-roaming animals, be transported to southeast Asia and come face-to-face with Disney characters in entertaining settings. At the center of the park in Safari Village is the majestic Tree of Life, which reaches 14 stories high and represents the diversity of animal life through intricate carvings of more than 300 animal life forms. Shown deep inside the Tree of Life, a 3-D, special effects adventure offers a bug's-eye view of the world.

DinoLand U.S.A.® is devoted to the drama of the Age of Dinosaurs. The thrill ride Dinosaur blasts back 65 million years to rescue a dinosaur from the edge of extinction as a deadly asteroid speeds toward Earth. The Boneyard is an open-air playground and dig site in which children can help unearth the bones of a giant mammoth.

Africa features a journey into one of the last wild sanctuaries of our planet. Beginning in the modern-day town of Harambe, the Kilimanjaro Safaris® expedition crosses an African savanna where wildlife roams freely. A troop of gorillas interacting in a naturalistic habitat can be observed from the Pagani Forest Exploration Trail.

The land of Asia features white-water adventures at Kali River Rapids, while intrepid explorers encounter tigers, giant fruit bats and Komodo dragons while on the Maharajah Jungle Trek.

Costumed actors and storytellers, puppets, stage floats and live animals entertain in Disney's Animal Kingdom. Festival of the Lion King at Camp Minnie-Mickey combines song, dance and characters from the popular movie. Other shows include Tarzan Rocks!, an array of stunts and aerial acts outside of DinoLand U.S.A.; Flights of Wonder, at the Caravan Stage on the edge of Asia; and Pocahontas and Her Forest Friends, at Camp Minnie-Mickey.

Park generally open daily 8-7. Admission $46; ages 3-9, $37. AE, DI, DS, JC, MC, VI. Phone (407) 824-4321. *See color ads starting on p. 165.*

Disney's Blizzard Beach Water Park, 2 mi. n. of US 192 off World Dr., features a mix of Florida sun and alpine snow. The water park features Summit Plummet, where those who dare can plunge down a 90-foot drop at 60 mph. Tamer offerings include a family raft ride down Teamboat Springs and "icy" bobsled runs. Food is available. Hours vary. Admission $27.95; ages 3-9, $22.50. AE, DI, DS, JC, MC, VI. Phone (407) 560-9283. *See color ads starting on p. 165.*

Disney-MGM Studios, 2 mi. n. of US 192 off World Dr., is a working production studio that features attractions, Broadway-style shows and live entertainment, all centered around popular films, television, music and animation. In addition, Hollywood and Sunset boulevards re-create the glamorous golden age of Hollywood. The focal points of Sunset Boulevard are The Twilight Zone Tower of Terror™, a journey through the haunted hallways of the vintage Hollywood Tower Hotel ending in multiple drops in a runaway service elevator, and Rock 'n' Roller Coaster Starring Aerosmith, a high-speed trip through the streets of Los Angeles.

Fantasmic! is a nighttime water spectacular that takes you inside the dreams of Sorcerer Mickey. The show is a battle of good versus evil in which Sorcerer Mickey's magic creates dancing waters, dazzling lasers, shooting comets, animated fountains, swirling stars, balls of fire and other wonders.

Death-defying stunts are the cornerstone of the Indiana Jones™ Epic Stunt Spectacular. A Broadway-style rendition of "Beauty and the Beast" is performed at the Theater of the Stars, where highlights from that animated

General Information
(continued)

Premium Annual Pass provides unlimited admission to all four theme parks, Disney's three water parks, Pleasure Island and Disney's Wide World of Sports™ Complex for 1 year from date of first use, free parking and other benefits. Admission $434; ages 3-9, $369.

Theme Park Annual Pass provides unlimited admission to all four theme parks for 1 year from date of first use, free parking and other benefits. Admission $324; ages 3-9, $275.

Select Park Hopper and Park Hopper Plus passes are available at participating AAA travel offices.

Tickets are valid during regular hours. Passes include unlimited use of the Walt Disney World transportation system. No refunds for unused tickets are issued for any reason. Tickets are non-transferrable. Some activities or events may be separately priced. **Prices quoted above do not include tax.** Prices and entitlements may change without notice. AE, DI, DS, JC, MC, VI. For ticket information phone (407) 824-4321 or TDD (407) 827-5141.

© Disney

film are presented. Voyage of the Little Mermaid brings the story of Ariel and her colorful undersea world to stage. The Hunchback of Notre Dame—A Musical Adventure captures the power and majesty of the musical story in a live stage event.

Visitors will feel as if they are bursting into outer space aboard Star Tours, a motion simulator ride based on the movie "Star Wars." Disney-MGM Studios Backlot Tour takes riders on a tour of movie sets and includes an explosive journey through Catastrophe Canyon. Guests can travel into classic moments from the movies on The Great Movie Ride as well as see a new show starring Doug from Disney's hit Saturday morning show. Bear and all his friends are ready to sing and laugh with visitors at Bear in the Big Blue House—Live on Stage!

Park opens daily generally at 9; closing times vary. Admission $46; ages 3-9, $37. AE, DI, DS, JC, MC, VI. Phone (407) 824-4321. *See color ads starting on p. 165.*

Disney's River Country Water Park, w. on US 192, n. on World Dr., then e. on Vista Blvd. following signs to Disney's Fort Wilderness Resort and Campground, has water rides, sandy beaches and nature trails. Disney characters frequent the All-American Water Party during the summer. Hours vary. Admission $27.95; ages 3-9, $22.50. AE, DI, DS, JC, MC, VI. Phone (407) 560-9283. *See color ads starting on p. 165.*

Disney's Typhoon Lagoon Water Park, US 192 w. to World Dr., then e. on Buena Vista Dr., recreates a tropical paradise with water slides, family rides and a large wave pool. Admission $27.95; ages 3-9, $22.50. AE, DI, DS, JC, MC, VI. Phone (407) 560-9283. *See color ads starting on p. 165.*

Disney's Wide World of Sports™ Complex, w. on US 192 to World Dr., then e. on Osceola Pkwy., is a state-of-the-art sports venue where amateur athletes hone their skills and compete in their particular sport. It also is the spring-training home of the Atlanta Braves and is the training site of the Harlem Globetrotters.

Guests can test their football skills at the NFL Experience and punt, pass and kick on an interactive playground. Food is available. Admission (includes NFL Experience) $9; ages 3-9, $7. Admission may increase for special events. Some events may require a separate admission charge. Parking is free. AE, DI, DS, JC, MC, VI. Phone (407) 363-6600. *See color ads starting on p. 165.*

Downtown Disney Area, w. on US 192 to World Dr. then e. on Buena Vista Dr., is a 120-acre waterfront shopping, themed dining and entertainment district.

The area is a showplace of celebrity restaurants, music venues, a 24-screen movie theater and specialty shops. DisneyQuest® Indoor Interactive Theme Park is where visitors can design and ride their own roller coaster or battle virtual villains. Other options include the extravagant

theatrical productions of Cirque du Soleil. Specialty shopping includes the LEGO Imagination Center®, an interactive LEGO playground.

For adult nighttime fun Downtown Disney Pleasure Island is a shopping, dining and entertainment complex featuring eight themed clubs, including an improv comedy club; a '70s-themed dance club; Mannequins Dance Palace, with a rotating dance floor; the BET SoundStage™ Club, featuring rhythm & blues and hip-hop; a live jazz club; and Wildhorse Saloon, which has hot country music and cool country dance. A New Year's Eve celebration is held nightly.

An $18.86 entrance fee provides admission to Pleasure Island and all clubs after 7 p.m. An annual pass is $54.95. There may be additional charges for special events. Under 18 must be with a parent or legal guardian for admission after 7 p.m. Under 21 not permitted in Mannequins or BET SoundStage Club. Cirque du Soleil $62; under 10, $38. AE, DI, DS, JC, MC, VI. Phone (407) 934-7781, or 939-7600 for Cirque du Soleil reservations. *See color ads starting on p. 165.*

Epcot® is 3 mi. s. of the Magic Kingdom Park off World Dr. The park encompasses Future World and World Showcase—two major areas designed to combine Disney fun and imagination with the wonders of the real world.

Attractions in Future World include Spaceship Earth, Innoventions, Universe of Energy, Test Track, "Honey I Shrunk the Audience," Journey Into Your Imagination, The Land, Wonders of Life and The Living Seas. These areas explore advances in science and technology in a fun and interactive way. Innoventions lets guests discover the world's latest technology in a constantly-changing, hands-on showcase. Interactive displays include new technologies such as cars of the future, a high-tech home, medical breakthroughs and the future of the Internet. Test Track is based on a General Motors automotive proving grounds and takes guests on a high-speed ride filled with turns, climbs and evasive maneuvers.

World Showcase presents the best of Mexico, China, Norway, Germany, Italy, Japan, France, Morocco, the United Kingdom, Canada and America, all of which can be reached by foot or boat across the World Showcase Lagoon. Guests can experience the cultures, traditions, holidays, architecture, food and entertainment of all 11 countries.

The CircleVision 360 films in the China and Canada showcases and a 180-degree film in the France pavilion celebrate each nation's history and culture. Other showcases spotlight artists performing traditional music, dance and theatrical works. All showcases are staffed by nationals of that country and bilingual Disney cast members. Fanciful puppets more than 20 feet tall, accompanied by drummers and dancers, fill the World Showcase Promenade nightly in a street festival called Tapestry of Nations. IllumiNations: Reflections of Earth features fireworks, original music, lasers and magic every evening. Epcot also is the site of several festivals held throughout the year.

This year, experience the most magical place on earth. Visit the *Walt Disney World* Resort, where magical fantasies and exciting adventures come to life, and live happily ever after in the hearts

Turn your dreams into fun in 2001

of all who enjoy them. It's true. The *Walt Disney World* Resort now features four spectacular theme parks: the *Magic Kingdom* Park, *Disney-MGM Studios*, *Disney's Animal Kingdom* Theme Park and *Epcot*...plus over 70 stores, restaurants and entertainment escapes at the bustling *Downtown Disney* area. Then again, you might want to add an exciting 3- or 4-day *Disney Cruise Line* vacation to your *Walt Disney World* Resort package. So many magical things to do. So many Disney Resorts to choose from. Turn the page and we'll help you make the dream come true.

It's as if the Fairy Godmother, Aladdin's Genie and the Sorcerer's Apprentice all came together to build a magical Theme Park. Then Tinker Bell flew over, sprinkling every square inch of it with

Where fairytale fantasies come to life

golden pixie dust. The *Magic Kingdom* Park at the *Walt Disney World* Resort is such a place. Here fantasy becomes reality as you zip-a-dee do-dah down *Splash Mountain*, step into the *Many Adventures of Winnie the Pooh* (a hunny of a new attraction) and dine in *Cinderella Castle*. Speaking of new attractions, you can also take a trip to infinity and beyond at the new *Buzz Lightyear's Space Ranger Spin*. All your favorite Disney Characters are here... and they can't wait to see you.

Below: *Buzz Lightyear's Space Ranger Spin*
Inset: *Many Adventures of Winnie the Pooh*

Magic Kingdom

DISNEY'S ANIMAL KINGDOM®

Explore the newest of the four *Walt Disney World®* Theme Parks, and expect the unexpected. Fantastic animal adventures abound here in thickly forested Asian jungles, wide-open African savannas

See Disney's wild side

and spectacular prehistoric landscapes. Speaking of the past, that's exactly where you'll go in *DINOSAUR*. Then be sure to experience *Kilimanjaro Safaris,* an unforgettable journey through lands of lions, elephants, hippos, giraffes and who knows what else is out there. And drop into *Tarzan™ Rocks!* This wildly popular stage show features Tarzan, Jane and Terk performing incredible stunts to the swinging sounds of a live concert of hit songs from Disney's animated classic movie. If you're really brave, and don't mind getting wet, take off for the river run of your life on *Kali River Rapids*.

It's the opportunity of a lifetime to experience the glitter and glamour of going backstage and being center stage for all the action. Did someone say "Action?" Time to hop into your stretch

Get into show business

limo and head into the Hollywood night for an up, down and all-around wild ride on the *Rock 'n' Roller Coaster Starring Aerosmith.* Once you're right side up again, come be our guest for a special Broadway-style production of *Beauty and the Beast- Live on Stage.* And if you'd like to know how spectacular show business can be at night, see *Fantasmic!,* the new extravaganza of lights, lasers, dancing waters and special effects starring Sorcerer Mickey, Disney villains and an epic battle of good versus evil. And that's just a sneak preview of all the show biz fun.

Below: *Fantasmic!*
Inset: *Rock 'n' Roller Coaster Starring Aerosmith*

DISNEY-M·G·M STUDIOS

Epcot

Always adding, always changing, the enormously fascinating, one and only *Epcot* offers a thrilling new discovery at every turn. And turns are what you'll find on *Test Track,* the longest, fastest

Discover the world

ride ever created for a Disney Theme Park. Next we turn your attention to a big idea that makes you feel small. It's *Honey, I Shrunk the Audience,* a delightfully delirious 3-D misadventure in which Professor Wayne Szalinski shrinks—get this—the entire theater, including you! Eventually you return to normal size. And just in time too, because an entire world lies ahead: the 11 countries of *World Showcase.* Come nightfall, this is where you'll want to be to see the all-new *IllumiNations: Reflections on Earth,* the famous finale to every *Epcot* day of discoveries.

Disney's FASTPASS

GET A TIME, WHY WAIT IN LINE?™

Only Disney lets you ride some of your favorite attractions without having to wait in line! When you get to the Disney Theme Parks, just look for Disney's complimentary FASTPASS℠ turnstiles at participating

Make the most of every magical moment

attractions. Receive a designated returntime, then go and enjoy the Park. Return at the designated time, and you'll be able to walk past the stand-by line onto the attraction. Disney's FASTPASS℠ service is free, and it's here to help you get the most out of every minute of your magical vacation.

A thriving downtown right in the heart of the *Walt Disney World®* Resort? Come see for yourself. By day, the *Downtown Disney* area bustles with shoppers looking for unique take-home

The heart of a city on a corner of our world

treasures. Or a place to take a fascinating stroll. Be sure to drop into *World of Disney,* the largest collection of Disney merchandise anywhere. At night, the 70 unique shops, restaurants and entertainment venues really brighten the skyline. For a place to party, escape to the *Downtown Disney* area...and indulge yourself beyond imagination.

Below: *Downtown Disney* West Side

ᗡꙆꙅꙒꙄ꙰ CRUISE LINE

Want to see how we can make your dreams come true? Experience our new 7-Night Cruise to the Caribbean including visits to the exotic ports of St. Maarten and St. Thomas, with excursions

Chart a course for a new kind of Disney vacation

to St. John, and Disney's private island paradise, *Castaway Cay*. Or combine 3- or 4-days of fantasy and fun at the *Walt Disney World®* Resort with a 3- or 4-night cruise to Nassau in The Bahamas and Disney's *Castaway Cay* on a 7-Night Land and Sea Vacation. Whichever course you choose, there's something for everyone aboard the spectacular ships of *Disney Cruise Line*. On every cruise, activities abound for children, teens and adults and legendary Disney service, spectacular dining experiences and dazzling adventures come together to create a vacation only Disney could create. Extend your dreams to new horizons with a magical *Disney Cruise Line* vacation.

Ships' Registry: The Bahamas

With a *Disney* **Park Hopper** Ticket in hand, no need to plan once you're on vacation. You can just come and go as you please through all four *Walt Disney*

We have a magical ticket for you

World Theme Parks everyday, even visit more than one park on any single day. And selected *Disney* **Park Hopper** Tickets give you all that plus *Disney's Water Parks, Downtown Disney* Pleasure Island and *Disney's Wide World of Sports* Complex. Don't waste a moment of your vacation time standing in ticket lines. Stop by your participating AAA office and buy your *Disney* **Park Hopper** Tickets before you leave home.

Disney makes it magic.
AAA makes it real.

When Aladdin makes a wish...poof!...he's vacationing at the *Walt Disney World* Resort. Your "genie" is the nearest AAA Travel office. AAA members receive excellent benefits:

- All AAA Vacations® packages include entrance to the AAA VIP Lounge located in the *Magic Kingdom* Park, Preferred Parking in special AAA Diamond lots and the *AAA Vacations® Diamond Card,* which provides additional savings and values on meals, merchandise and recreation at selected locations throughout the *Walt Disney World* Resort.

- Special savings on selected *Walt Disney World* Resort Hotels (based on season and availability).

- Availability of select Disney *Park Hopper* Tickets at participating AAA Travel Offices.

- When you make your Disney Cruise Line vacation arrangements with AAA, you'll receive a framed Disney Cruise Line ship cloisonné pin set, for guests booked in an oceanview stateroom (one per stateroom), or a commemorative picture frame, for guests booked in an inside stateroom (one per stateroom).

See the Disney ad in the Lodging section of this TourBook for the benefits of staying in a *Walt Disney World* Resort Hotel.

For daily entertainment schedules visit Guest Relations. Reservations for lunch or dinner at any full-service restaurant should be made at Guest Relations or by phoning (407) 939-3463. Epcot is connected to the Magic Kingdom Park by an 8-mile monorail circuit.

Future World opens daily generally at 9. World Showcase opens daily at 11. Closing times vary. Admission $46; ages 3-9, $37. AE, DI, DS, JC, MC, VI. Phone (407) 824-4321. *See color ads starting on p. 165.*

Magic Kingdom® Park, US 192 exit World Dr. following signs, is divided into seven themed "lands," all featuring attractions, entertainment, restaurants and shops. The park is entered through Main Street, U.S.A., a representation of a typical late 19th-century boulevard complete with cafes, shops and horse-drawn streetcars. Entertainment schedules and other services are available at City Hall. Main Street, U.S.A., also serves as the starting point for the park's seven lands and is the site of Disney's Magical Moments Parade as well as a nighttime parade.

The park's centerpiece is Cinderella Castle, the gateway to Fantasyland. The adventures in this whimsical land are based on Disney film classics from "Dumbo" to "The Lion King." The Many Adventures of Winnie the Pooh is a journey into the Hundred Acre Wood for encounters with Pooh and friends, while hundreds of dolls in international costumes perform at It's a Small World.

Adjacent to Fantasyland at Mickey's Toon-Town Fair children can visit Mickey's house, Minnie's cottage and Donald's boat, an interactive water fountain. The Barnstormer, a children's roller coaster, is featured at Goofy's Wiseacre Farm.

Tomorrowland features The Timekeeper, a trip through time in CircleVision 360; Space Mountain, a high-speed race through space; Astro Orbiter, a rocket to the stars; the ExtraTERRORestrial Alien Encounter, a sensory thriller; and Buzz Lightyear's Space Ranger Spin, an interactive space fantasy.

Liberty Square depicts early America with riverboat trips and the Hall of Presidents, where Bill Clinton joins his predecessors in animated conversation. Ghosts and ghouls are found in the Haunted Mansion.

Adventureland offers a voyage with the Pirates of the Caribbean. The Enchanted Tiki Room—Under New Management features singing animatronic birds, and Jungle Cruise journeys through four continents and encounters "wild" animals from tropical jungles.

Big Thunder Mountain Railroad, a runaway mine train, is the focus of Frontierland, which also is the site of Splash Mountain, a log flume ride themed after "Song of the South."

Park opens daily generally at 9; closing times vary. Admission $46; ages 3-9, $37. AE, DI, DS, JC, MC, VI. Phone (407) 824-4321. *See color ads starting on p. 165.*

MAITLAND (E-4) pop. 9,100, elev. 91′

FLORIDA AUDUBON SOCIETY'S CENTER FOR BIRDS OF PREY is e. of I-4 exit 46 on Lee Rd., n. on Wymore Rd., e. on Kennedy Blvd., n. on East St., then 1 blk. n. to 1101 Audubon Way. Outdoor cages allow close viewing of up to 22 species of birds of prey in a junglelike setting. The center includes a rehabilitation facility for injured birds. Picnic facilities are available. **Note:** Following renovations, the center is expected to reopen fall 2000; phone ahead for rates and hours. Allow 30 minutes minimum. Tues.-Sun. 10-4; closed holidays. Admission $5; under 12, $4. MC, VI. Phone (407) 644-0190.

HISTORIC WATERHOUSE RESIDENCE AND CARPENTRY SHOP MUSEUMS, .9 mi. n. of SR 423 on US 17/92, then e. to 820 Lake Lily Dr., features the restored 1884 Waterhouse home as well as a carpentry shop where a carpenter demonstrates the woodworking methods of the late 1800s. Allow 30 minutes minimum. Thurs.-Sun. noon-4; closed major holidays. Donations. Phone (407) 644-2451.

THE HOLOCAUST MEMORIAL RESOURCE AND EDUCATION CENTER OF CENTRAL FLORIDA is 1.25 mi. e. of I-4 exit 47A at 851 N. Maitland Ave. (SR 414). The center illustrates key events of the Holocaust through chronological displays, photographs and audiovisual presentations. A memorial wall built of Jerusalem stone remembers the 6 million Jews who died at the hands of the Nazis. Allow 1 hour minimum. Mon.-Thurs. 9-4, Fri. 9-1, Sun. 1-4; closed major national and Jewish holidays. Free. Phone (407) 628-0555.

MAITLAND ART CENTER is 1.5 mi. e. of I-4 exit 47A on SR 414 (Maitland Blvd.), .7 mi. s. on CR 427 (Maitland Ave.), then .2 mi. w. to 231 W. Packwood Ave. Originally an artist's colony founded in the 1930s, the center now has changing exhibits which showcase local, regional and national artists and craftspersons. The complex comprises 23 buildings ornamented with murals, bas-reliefs and carvings in Aztec and Mayan styles. Walkways wind through courtyards and gardens. Guided tours are available. Programs are presented year round.

Allow 1 hour minimum. Mon.-Fri. 9-4:30, Sat.-Sun. noon-4:30; closed major holidays. Donations. Phone (407) 539-2181.

ST. CLOUD (I-5) pop. 12,500, elev. 63′

REPTILE WORLD SERPENTARIUM, 4 mi. e. on US 192, .5 mi. e. of jct. CR 532, houses snakes from around the world in glass display cases. A walled compound contains turtles and a fenced compound houses alligators. Venom programs are given daily at noon and 3. Allow 1 hour, 30 minutes minimum. Tues.-Sun. 9-5:30, Oct.-Aug.; closed Thanksgiving weekend and Dec. 25. Admission $5.50; ages 6-17, $4.50; ages 3-5, $3.50. Phone (407) 892-6905.

SANFORD (D-10) pop. 32,400, elev. 20′

At the head of navigation on the St. Johns River, Sanford was established as a trading post in 1837. Gen. Henry R. Sanford bought 12,000 acres, including the townsite, in 1871 and established citrus groves.

Amtrak's Auto Train transports passengers and their cars to and from Lorton, Va. To reach the station, take SR 46 (I-4 exit 51) east to 400 Persimmon Ave.

Sanford/Seminole Chamber of Commerce: 400 E. First St., Sanford, FL 32771; phone (407) 322-2212.

THE BIG TREE ("The Senator") is 6 mi. s. on US 17/92, then 1.5 mi. w. on Gen. J.C. Hutcheson Pkwy., near Longwood. This giant cypress is one of the largest in the United States and is estimated to be 3,500 years old. It is 138 feet high, with a diameter of 17.5 feet and a circumference of 47 feet.

SAVE **CENTRAL FLORIDA ZOOLOGICAL PARK** is n.w. on US 17/92, .7 mi. s. of I-4 exit 52. The park contains mammals, birds, reptiles and a children's zoo. Picnic facilities are available. Allow 2 hours minimum. Daily 9-5; closed Thanksgiving and Dec. 25. Park free. Zoo admission $7; over 60, $4; ages 3-12, $3. DS, MC, VI. Phone (407) 323-4450.

MUSEUM OF SEMINOLE COUNTY HISTORY is 1 mi. s. on 17/92, then w. to 300 Bush Blvd.

Housed in the former County Old Folks Home built in 1927, the museum features displays about steamships, railroads and the history of the local celery industry. Rooms contain early farm equipment and historical pictures of Seminole County towns in the early 20th century.

Other highlights include a country store, a hospital room, period rooms and an exhibit about the Second Seminole War. Guided tours are available. Allow 30 minutes minimum. Tues.-Fri. 9-noon and 1-4, Sat. 1-4; closed holidays. Free. Phone (407) 321-2489.

RIVERSHIP *ROMANCE*, docked 4 mi. e. of I-4 exit 51, on SR 46 at Monroe Harbour Marina, offers luncheon sightseeing cruises along the St. Johns River aboard a 100-foot, 1940s-style Great Lakes steamer. Dinner/dance cruises also are available. Three-hour luncheon cruise departs Wed. and Sat.-Sun. at 11; 4-hour luncheon cruise departs Mon.-Tues. and Thurs.-Fri. at 11. Three-hour lunch fares start at $35; 4-hour lunch fares begin at $45. Reservations are required. AE, DS, MC, VI. Phone (407) 321-5091 or (800) 423-7401.

THE SANFORD MUSEUM, 520 E. First St., houses exhibits depicting the city's history. Two rooms dedicated to city founder Henry Shelton Sanford include his art collection, books and papers. Tues.-Fri. 11-4, Sat. 1-4; closed holidays. Free. Phone (407) 302-1000.

TAVARES (D-9) pop. 7,400, elev. 66′

CAPTAIN DAVE'S DORA CANAL CRUISES departs from the dock near the intersection of US 441 and Lake Shore Blvd. Captain Dave's offers narrated cruises of Lake Eustis, Lake Dora and the Dora Canal during which passengers can see

a variety of local wildlife. Allow 1 hour, 30 minutes minimum. Cruises depart at 10:30, 1 and 3, mid-Oct. to mid-May. Fare $10. Reservations are required. Phone (352) 343-3889.

WINTER PARK (F-4)
pop. 22,600, elev. 96'

Moss-draped oaks line the residential streets of Winter Park, a community of beautiful homes and picturesque lakes. The campus of Rollins College features brick streets and Mediterranean-style buildings on the shores of Lake Virginia. The small, private college is at the foot of Park Avenue, a popular shopping district with a varied selection of upscale boutiques, galleries and restaurants.

Winter Park Chamber of Commerce: 150 N. New York Ave., P.O. Box 280, Winter Park, FL 32790; phone (407) 644-8281.

ALBIN POLASEK MUSEUM AND GARDENS is 1.3 mi. e. of US 17/92 at 633 Osceola Ave. (SR 426). Three galleries and the gardens display the sculptures and paintings of the Czech-American artist. Noteworthy is a wooden nativity Polasek created at age 15. Tues.-Sat. 10-4, Sun. 1-4, Sept.-June; closed holidays. Donations. Phone (407) 647-6294.

CHARLES HOSMER MORSE MUSEUM OF AMERICAN ART, 445 Park Ave. N., contains a major collection of works by Louis Comfort Tiffany, master of the art nouveau movement. Many of the stained-glass windows on exhibit were installed at Laurelton Hall, Tiffany's mansion on Long Island. A highlight is the chapel Tiffany designed for the 1893 Exposition at the Chicago World's Fair.

The museum houses works of art and historical documents including works by Tiffany's contemporaries, a collection of American art pottery and American paintings from the late 19th century to the early 20th century. Guided tours are available. Allow 1 hour minimum. Tues.-Sat. 9:30-4, Sun. 1-4; closed holidays. Admission $3; students over 12, $1. Phone (407) 645-5311.

CORNELL FINE ARTS MUSEUM, 2.25 mi. e. of I-4 exit 45 at the end of Holt Ave. on the Rollins College campus, displays permanent and changing exhibits of American and European paintings, decorative arts and sculpture. Representative artists include William Merritt Chase, Childe Hassam and Louis Comfort Tiffany. Allow 1 hour minimum. Tues.-Fri. 10-5, Sat.-Sun. 1-5; closed holidays. Free. Phone (407) 646-2526.

SCENIC BOAT TOURS, leaving from the foot of Morse Blvd., provide narrated 1-hour cruises past many of Winter Park's opulent lakeside estates and landmarks. Allow 1 hour, 30 minutes minimum. Departures daily on the hour 10-4; closed Dec. 25. Fare $7; under 12, $3. Phone (407) 644-4056.

This ends listings for the Orlando Vicinity.
The following page resumes the alphabetical listings of cities in Florida.

ORMOND BEACH (C-10)
pop. 29,700, elev. 6'

Charles and Frank Duryea, Barney Oldfield, R.E. Olds, Alexander Winton and others raced cars on the sands of Ormond Beach in the early and mid-1900s, giving the city its reputation as the birthplace of speed.

Ormond Beach Chamber of Commerce: 165 W. Granada Blvd., P.O. Box 874, Ormond Beach, FL 32175; phone (904) 677-6362.

THE CASEMENTS, 25 Riverside Dr., was the winter home of John D. Rockefeller from 1914 until his death in 1937. The house is now a cultural and civic center, with a collection of Hungarian folk art, Boy Scout memorabilia and an exhibit of Rockefeller furnishings and personal items. Changing exhibits are featured. Allow 30 minutes minimum. Mon.-Thurs. 9-9, Fri. 9-5, Sat. 9-noon; closed holidays. Tours Mon.-Fri. 10-2:30, Sat. 10-11:30. Donations. Phone (904) 676-3216.

ORMOND MEMORIAL ART MUSEUM AND GARDENS, 1 mi. e. of US 1 at 78 E. Granada Blvd., contains a 4.5-acre botanical memorial garden with a waterfall, nature trails and turtle ponds as well as changing exhibits of contemporary Florida art and fine crafts. Of note is a collection of symbolic religious paintings by Malcolm Fraser. Allow 30 minutes minimum. Gardens open daily dawn-dusk. Gallery open Mon.-Fri. 10-4, Sat.-Sun. noon-4; closed major holidays. Admission $2; senior citizens and students free. Phone (904) 676-3347.

OSCEOLA NATIONAL FOREST

Elevations in the forest range
from 120 ft. to 180 ft.

Osceola National Forest encompasses 187,000 acres of flat country dotted with ponds and swamps. Fishing is available in numerous creeks and rivers. Hunting is permitted, but a special license is required in the Osceola Wildlife Management Area; for information phone the Florida Fish and Wildlife Conservation Commission at (850) 488-4676. Endangered species in the forest include the red cockaded woodpecker and gray bat. Ocean Pond (see the AAA Southeastern CampBook) and Olustee Beach are major recreation areas within the forest. Phone (904) 752-2577. See Recreation Chart.

OSPREY (F-8) pop. 2,600, elev. 10'

HISTORIC SPANISH POINT, 337 N. Tamiami Trail (US 41), is a 30-acre archeological, historic and environmental site on Little Sarasota Bay featuring the remains of a prehistoric living site, a pioneer family homestead and restored gardens from an early 20th-century estate. A nature trail now leads visitors along the bay past a citrus packing house, a restored pioneer home, a chapel, boat-building exhibits, native plants and formal gardens. Visitors can view an archeology display inside a prehistoric shell mound. An orientation video is shown in the visitors center. Guided tours are available. Picnicking is permitted.

Allow 1 hour, 30 minutes minimum. Mon.-Sat. 9-5, Sun. noon-5; closed Jan. 1, Easter, Thanksgiving and Dec. 25. Admission $7; senior citizens $5 on Mon.; ages 6-12, $3. MC, VI. Phone (941) 966-5214.

PALATKA (B-9) pop. 10,200, elev. 28'

Judge Isaac Bronson, one of Palatka's foremost residents, was a member of the 25th U.S. Congress and was responsible for proposing the act by which Florida became a state. His restored home, Bronson-Mulholland House, 100 Mulholland Park, was built in 1854 and is open to the public.

Putnam County Chamber of Commerce: 1100 Reid St., P.O. Box 550, Palatka, FL 32178; phone (904) 328-1503.

RAVINE STATE GARDENS, on Twigg St., is 1.25 mi. s. off SR 20. Formed by water erosion from the St. Johns River, the steep ravines provide a rich environment for wild plants. Two swinging bridges cross the ravines, and nature trails wind through the 85-acre park, which has been landscaped extensively with azaleas and camellias. Picnic facilities, a preschoolers' playground and a fitness trail are available. Daily 8-dusk. The road is closed to traffic at 4 p.m. Admission $3.25 per private vehicle (maximum of eight people), $1 per person arriving by bicycle, bus, motorcycle or on foot. Phone (904) 329-3721.

PALM BEACH (F-12)
pop. 9,800, elev. 32'

Also see West Palm Beach p. 231.

In 1878 a Spanish brigantine bound from the West Indies to Spain went aground at Palm Beach, spilling its cargo of coconuts along the sandy, barrier island. When Henry Flagler visited the area in the early 1890s, he found a small community of settlers amid a growth of coconut palms. Recognizing the potential of South Florida, he chose Palm Beach for the site of his next luxury hotel and laid out a fashionable resort that has retained the quiet charm and tropical beauty of his original vision. A scenic portion of SR A1A meanders along the ocean as it extends from Palm Beach south to Fort Lauderdale, a drive of 47 miles.

Palm Beach Chamber of Commerce: 45 Cocoanut Row, Palm Beach, FL 33480; phone (561) 655-3282.

Shopping areas: Exclusive shops line tree-shaded Worth Avenue.

BETHESDA-BY-THE-SEA, S. County Rd. and Barton Ave., is an Episcopal church of modified

15th-century Gothic design. Adjacent are the attractive, formally landscaped Cluett Memorial Gardens. Church and gardens open daily 8-5. Free. Phone (561) 655-4554.

FLAGLER MUSEUM is at Cocoanut Row and Whitehall Way. Original and period furnishings and Flagler family memorabilia grace Whitehall, the opulent 1902 Gilded Age mansion railroad magnate Henry Flagler built for his bride. The grandeur of the 55-room house earned it the title "Taj Mahal of North America."

The house was restored as a museum in 1960. Among the highlights are a marble entrance hall, Louis XIV music room and Louis XV ballroom. The museum also features changing exhibits and special programs. Visitors can see Flagler's private railroad car on the south lawn.

Allow 1 hour, 30 minutes minimum. Tues.-Sat. 10-5, Sun. noon-5; closed Jan. 1, Thanksgiving and Dec. 25. Admission $8; ages 6-12, $3. AE, MC, VI. Phone (561) 655-2833. *See ad p. 232.*

HIBEL MUSEUM OF ART, 150 Royal Poinciana Plaza, houses the work of artist Edna Hibel. The collection contains lithographs, paintings and porcelains, including limited-edition plates. Allow 1 hour minimum. Mon.-Sat. 10-5; closed Thanksgiving and Dec. 25. Free. Phone (561) 833-6870.

SOCIETY OF THE FOUR ARTS, Four Arts Plaza just off Royal Palm Way, comprises a library, art gallery, auditorium and sculpture and botanical gardens. Lectures by authors and noted speakers are presented weekly, early December through mid-April. Allow 30 minutes minimum. Gallery open Mon.-Sat. 10-5, Sun. 2-5, Dec. 1 to mid-Apr. Gardens open Mon.-Fri. 10-5 (also Sat. 10-5, Nov.-Apr.). Library open Mon.-Fri. 10-5 (also Sat. 9-1, Nov.-Apr.). Free. Phone (561) 655-7226 or 655-2766 for the library.

PALM COAST (C-10)
pop. 14,300, elev. 10'

WASHINGTON OAKS STATE GARDENS, 6400 N. Oceanshore Blvd., originally was part of Bella Vista Plantation owned by Gen. Joseph Hernandez, a militia general who commanded troops during the Second Seminole War. Extending from the Atlantic Ocean to the Matanzas River, the preserve covers more than 400 acres of Florida coastal scenery. Included are scenic tidal marshes, a scrub community, a beach and a hammock. Coquina rock outcroppings worn into unusual shapes by the sea give the beach area an unearthly appearance. Many species of shorebirds and marine and forest animals make their home in the area.

Formal gardens contain exotic plants from around the world; a history of the area is presented at the Young House. Guided walks are provided on weekends and by request. Picnicking is permitted. Allow 3 hours minimum. Daily

8-dusk. Admission $3.25 per private vehicle. Phone (904) 446-6780. *See Recreation Chart.*

PANACEA (B-6) elev. 5'

GULF SPECIMEN MARINE LABORATORY, just s. of US 98, following signs to 222 Clark Dr., features a 25,000-gallon marine aquarium as well as touch tanks housing sea horses, crabs, rays, sponges, starfish and small sharks. Allow 1 hour minimum. Mon.-Fri. 9-5, Sat. 10-4, Sun. noon-4. Admission $4; ages 2-11, $2. Phone (850) 984-5297.

PANAMA CITY (B-4)
pop. 34,400, elev. 33'

Panama City, county seat of Bay County, is a leading port on St. Andrew Bay off the Gulf of Mexico and is the eastern terminus for a scenic portion of US 98 extending 98 miles to Gulf Breeze, just south of Pensacola. Spanish expeditions visited this site 1516-40, but it was not until 1765 that an English settlement was made at St. Andrew, now part of Panama City.

Once a sleepy fishing village, Panama City is now a progressive industrial and resort town and an increasingly popular spring break destination for college students. The area also is home to Tyndall Air Force Base and Navy Coastal Systems Station. A marina at the foot of Harrison Avenue includes berths for about 400 boats. Fishing boats can be chartered on St. Andrew Bay.

Bay County Chamber of Commerce: 235 W. Fifth St., P.O. Box 1850, Panama City, FL 32402-1850; phone (850) 785-5206.

JUNIOR MUSEUM OF BAY COUNTY, 1731 Jenks Ave., offers child-oriented hands-on exhibits including Body Works, Hands-On Science, Nature Corner, Imagine Me and Discovery Depot. Highlights include the Pioneer Homestead, a re-created farm from the late 1800s, and a nature trail through a forested swamp and forest area. Children may play on a Bayline Railroad locomotive on the museum grounds. Allow 30 minutes minimum. Mon.-Fri. 9-4:30, Sat. 10-4; closed major holidays. Admission $3; ages 2-12, $2. Phone (850) 769-6128.

PANAMA CITY BEACH (B-4)
pop. 4,100, elev. 7'

Powdery white sand beaches and emerald waters of the Gulf of Mexico give Panama City Beach its status as a popular shore resort. The Yucatan Current, part of the Gulf Stream, runs close to the shores of Panama City Beach, bringing with it nutrient-rich Caribbean water and blue marlin, sailfish, big bull dolphin (fish), wahoo and tuna. One fishing pier extends 1,600 feet into the Gulf.

Scuba diving locations in the Gulf of Mexico include shipwrecks and almost 50 artificial reefs. Five championship golf courses are in the immediate area.

WOULD YOU RATHER WORK ON YOUR YARD?

OR WORK ON YOUR TAN?

The affordable Florida beach vacation that's a cut above the rest.
At Panama City Beach, Florida, you'll find 27 miles of newly widened white sand beaches.
You'll also enjoy sensational diving, snorkeling, fishing, golf, tennis, theme parks, dining, shopping
and affordable accommodations. So leave the rest of the world–and your yardwork–behind.

PANAMA CITY BEACH
Convention & Visitors Bureau

For a free Panama City Beach, Florida vacation guide, call **1-800PCBEACH**
or visit us on the web at **www.800pcbeach.com**

St. Andrews State Recreation Area *(see Recreation Chart and the AAA Southeastern CampBook)* flanks the pass separating Panama City Beach from Shell Island, the barrier isle guarding the mouth of St. Andrew Bay. The mainland portion of the park, reached via Thomas Drive, contains a restored turpentine still.

The Shell Island segment, an excellent spot for both swimming and shell gathering, is accessible only by boat. Passage is available from the recreation area and Capt. Anderson's Marina, 5550 N. Grand Lagoon Dr., from March 1 through Labor Day. Shuttles to Shell Island also depart from Treasure Island Marina.

Miracle Strip Amusement Park, 12000 Front Beach Rd., and the adjacent Shipwreck Island, a water theme park, are popular family attractions.

Panama City Beach Convention and Visitors Bureau: P.O. Box 9473, Panama City Beach, FL 32417; phone (850) 233-6503 or (800) 722-3224. *See color ad p. 179.*

CAPTAIN ANDERSON CRUISES, Capt. Anderson's Marina off Grand Lagoon Dr., offers sightseeing cruises to Shell Island and a sunset dolphin watch aboard the *Capt. Anderson III,* a glass-bottom boat. Dinner/dance, gospel music and deep-sea fishing cruises also are available. Shell Island cruises depart daily at 9 and 1, sunset cruise daily at 5:15, Mar.-Oct. Shell Island cruise $12; ages 6-11, $7; ages 2-5, $6. Sunset cruise $7; ages 2-11, $5. MC, VI. Phone (850) 234-3435, or (800) 874-2415 out of Fla.

SAVE **THE MUSEUM OF MAN IN THE SEA,** .25 mi. w. of jct. SR 79 at 17314 Panama City Beach Pkwy. (US 98), illustrates the history of undersea exploration using dioramas and written records. Highlights include rare and antique diving equipment and related displays. Changing exhibits are featured. Allow 1 hour minimum. Daily 9-5; closed Jan. 1, Thanksgiving and Dec. 25. Admission $5; over 65, $4.50; ages 6-16, $2.50. AE, DS, MC, VI. Phone (850) 235-4101.

SAVE **THE OCEAN OPRY SHOW,** 2 mi. w. of Hathaway Bridge on W. US 98A (Front Beach Rd.), presents comedy and country music stage shows in a theater that seats 1,000. Nashville stars can be seen October through March. Food is available. Allow 2 hours minimum.

Performances Mon.-Sat. at 8 p.m., June-Aug. (also Sun. performance weekends before and after July 4); Tues. and Thurs.-Sat. at 7:30 p.m., Jan.-Feb. and Sept.-Oct. (also Sun. performance Labor Day weekend); Tues. and Fri.-Sat. at 7:30 p.m., Mar.-May (also Sun. performance Memorial Day weekend); Tues. and Sat. at 7:30 p.m., rest of year. Admission $18; ages 5-11, $9. Prices vary for special shows. DS, MC, VI. Phone (850) 234-5464 for reservations and schedule.

PENSACOLA (B-2)
pop. 58,200, elev. 39'

Although an attempt was made in 1559 by Don Tristan de Luna, permanent settlement at Pensacola was not established until Fort San Carlos was built in 1698. The town has flown the flags of Spain, France, England, the Confederate States and the United States, and its government has changed hands 13 times.

In 1814 the British used the harbor as a base in their war with the United States, but withdrew when the city was attacked by Gen. Andrew Jackson. Here Jackson completed the transaction by which Spain sold Florida to the United States in 1821. In the city's historic section, Park Square encompasses Plaza Ferdinand VII where the agreement is believed to have been reached. Pensacola was the territorial capital until 1822, and Andrew Jackson was a resident while the first territorial governor of Florida.

The Seville Square historic district, bounded on the north by Government Street and on the east by Alcaniz Street, is an area of restored 19th-century buildings that now houses shops, restaurants, museums and art galleries.

Pensacola's Naval Air Station is a center for electronic warfare and cartographic training as well as headquarters for the Blue Angels precision flying team.

Gulf Islands National Seashore *(see place listing p. 86 and Recreation Chart)* offers miles and

miles of unspoiled sugar-white beaches and emerald waters. Recreational activities include boating, swimming and sun-bathing. Other outdoor activities can be enjoyed on the area's numerous waterways, including the Blackwater and Perdido rivers and Coldwater and Sweetwater-Juniper creeks *(see Milton p. 127).*

The Wildlife Sanctuary of Northwest Florida, 105 N. S St., cares for injured and orphaned wildlife, including foxes, deer, eagles, egrets, herons, owls, pelicans and hawks; for information phone (850) 433-9453.

West of the city on Dog Track Road, Pensacola Greyhound Track presents dog races Tuesday through Wednesday and Friday through Sunday.

Note: Policies vary concerning admittance of children to pari-mutuel betting facilities. Phone for information.

Pensacola Convention and Visitors Center: 1401 E. Gregory St., Pensacola, FL 32501; phone (850) 434-1234 or (800) 874-1234.

Self-guiding tours: The convention and visitors center, at the foot of the 3-mile bay bridge, offers free information about tours of the city.

Shopping areas: Cordova Mall, 5100 N. Ninth Ave., contains 140 stores including Dillard's and Parisian. University Mall, 7171 N. Davis Hwy., features JCPenney, McRaes and Sears among its 70 stores. Old buildings have been transformed into specialty shops at Palafox Place.

CIVIL WAR SOLDIERS MUSEUM, 108 S. Palafox Pl., offers insights into the daily lives of Civil War soldiers from the North and the South through an extensive display of medical artifacts and life-size camp dioramas. Tues.-Sat. 10-4:30; closed Jan. 1, Thanksgiving and Dec. 24-25. Admission $5; military with ID $4; ages 6-12, $2.50. MC, VI. Phone (850) 469-1900.

HISTORIC PENSACOLA VILLAGE is a complex of 19th-century buildings. Allow 1 hour minimum. Mon.-Sat. 10-4; closed holidays. Admission $6; over 65 and military with ID $5; ages 4-16, $2.50. Phone (850) 595-5985.

Charles Lavallé House, 203 E. Church St., is one of the oldest houses in Pensacola. Built in 1810, its architecture is typical of the Gulf Coast Creole cottage popular during the last Spanish period 1781-1872.

Clara Barkley Dorr House, 311 S. Adams St. at Church St., is an example of Classical Revival architecture. Built in 1871, it is furnished with late Victorian pieces.

Julee Cottage, Zaragoza and Barracks sts., was built in 1804 and once belonged to Julee Panton, a free black woman.

Museum of Commerce, next to the Museum of Industry, contains a full-scale replica of late 19th- and early 20th-century Pensacola streets, with a print shop, stores, wagons, buggies, a gas station, train depot and trolley.

Museum of Industry, Zaragoza and Tarragona sts., contains exhibits related to the turn-of-the-20th-century industrial boom in west Florida. Displays focus on the fishing, brickmaking and lumber industries.

T.T. Wentworth Jr. Florida State Museum, 330 S. Jefferson St., in the restored Pensacola City Hall, is a fine example of Italian Renaissance architecture. The museum contains exhibits about the history and natural history of western Florida, Coca-Cola memorabilia and a children's museum. Tues.-Sat. 10-4; closed state holidays. Admission is included in admission price to Historic Pensacola Village. Phone (850) 595-5985.

NATIONAL MUSEUM OF NAVAL AVIATION, on the Naval Air Station, Pensacola, traces the development of American naval aviation from its beginnings to the present. Among the highlights of the collection are the NC-4 Flying Boat, which in 1919 became the first plane to cross the Atlantic; the World War II fighter F6F Hellcat; and the Skylab Command Module in addition to more than 170 other historic naval aircraft. Four A-4 Skyhawks are suspended from the ceiling in formation in the Greater Pensacola Blue Angels Atrium. Bus tours of the flight line feature additional aircraft.

Dioramas portray a World War II carrier hangar bay, South Sea Island forward Marine base and the wartime home front. Other exhibits range from pre-World War I memorabilia to items used by Navy prisoners of war during the Vietnam War.

One wing of the 290,000-square-foot exhibit area showcases a replica of a World War II aircraft carrier island and flight deck with a working elevator. Visitors can take the controls of aircraft trainers and simulators and ride a motion-based simulator. Aviation art and photography also are featured. An IMAX theater presents films every hour. Food is available. Allow 1 hour, 30 minutes minimum. Daily 9-5; closed Jan. 1, Thanksgiving and Dec. 25. Museum free. IMAX movie $5.50; senior citizens, military with ID and ages 4-12, $5. Phone (850) 453-2389 or (800) 327-5002. *See color ad p. 181.*

NAVAL AIR STATION, PENSACOLA, s. end of Navy Blvd., provides maps and visitor information at the front gate, Building 777. For historical maps and base information contact the public affairs office. The air station is open daily; hours vary. Free. Phone (850) 452-2311.

Fort Barrancas is one of several U.S. forts built by the U.S. Corps of Engineers in the 19th century along northwestern Florida's coastline. A dry moat surrounds the inner walls and makes access to the fort possible only by way of a drawbridge. Allow 30 minutes minimum. Daily 9:30-5, Apr.-Oct.; Wed.-Sun. 10:30-4, rest of year. Hours may vary; phone ahead. Closed Dec. 25. Tours are given Sat.-Sun. at 2. Free. Phone (850) 455-5167.

PENSACOLA HISTORICAL MUSEUM, 115 E. Zaragoza St., is in the Arbona Building. Exhibits of local historical items include clothing, silver, bottles, American Indian artifacts and glass from the Colonial era through the Civil War to the present. A resource center maintains genealogical information, maps, government records, photos and manuscripts relating to the area's history. Allow 30 minutes minimum. Museum Mon.-Sat. 10-4:30. Resource center Tues.-Thurs. and Sat. 10-noon and 1-3. Closed holidays. Museum $1. Resource center research fee $5. Phone (850) 433-1559 for museum, or 434-5455 for resource center.

PLAZA FERDINAND VII, S. Palafox St. between E. Government and Zaragoza sts., was part of Pensacola's original Spanish settlement. A statue of Andrew Jackson commemorates the transfer of Florida to the United States.

VETERANS MEMORIAL PARK, at the corner of Bayfront Pkwy. and Romana St., is a half-size replica of the Vietnam Veterans Memorial in Washington, D.C. It contains the names of the Americans lost in Southeast Asia during the Vietnam War. Also on the site are a UH-1M "Huey" helicopter and a World War I veterans memorial. Daily 24 hours. Free. Phone (850) 456-0040.

PENSACOLA BEACH (B-3) elev. 7′

Snow white sand and aquamarine water make Pensacola Beach one of Florida's most beautiful beaches. Bordered by two preserved seashores, the area offers more than 20 miles of beach front covered in sugarlike sand composed of 99 percent pure quartz.

Wide paths parallel beach roads to offer skaters, cyclists, walkers and joggers a place for recreation. Other popular pursuits include fishing, golf and a wide array of water sports.

Pensacola Beach Chamber of Commerce: Visitor Information Center, 735 Pensacola Beach Blvd., Pensacola Beach, FL 32561; phone (850) 932-1500 or (800) 635-4803. *See ad p. 180 & p. 732*

PERRY (B-7) pop. 7,200, elev. 30′

FOREST CAPITAL STATE MUSEUM, 1 mi. s. on US 19/27A/98 at 204 Forest Park Dr., depicts the development of the forest industry. Exhibits illustrate modern forestry, turpentine production, regional wildlife and the cutting of virgin forests, cypress swamps and hardwood hammocks. The adjacent North Florida Cracker Homestead, built in the 1860s, interprets the lifestyle of early settlers. A playground is available. Picnicking is permitted. Allow 30 minutes minimum. Thurs.-Mon. 9-noon and 1-5; closed Jan. 1, Thanksgiving and Dec. 25. Admission $1, under 6 free. Phone (850) 584-3227.

PLANT CITY — *see Tampa Bay p. 228.*

POINT WASHINGTON (B-4) elev. 16′

EDEN STATE GARDENS AND MANSION, in Eden State Park, are 1 mi. n. of US 98 on CR 395. Magnolias, colorful camellias and azaleas, and live oaks draped in Spanish moss surround an 1898 Greek Revival mansion filled with Colonial, Empire and Victorian furnishings. Two Civil War re-enactments, including a Confederate Christmas, are held throughout the year; phone for information. Forty-five minute guided tours of the mansion are offered.

Grounds open daily 8-dusk. Mansion tours Thurs.-Mon. on the hour 9-4. Admission to grounds $2 per private vehicle. Mansion tour $1.50; under 13, 50c. Phone (850) 231-4214.

POLK CITY (D-9) pop. 1,500, elev. 173′

[SAVE] **FANTASY OF FLIGHT,** I-4 exit 21, then .5 mi. n. on SR 559, features vintage aircraft portraying various eras of aviation including the Short Sunderland—purportedly the world's last airworthy civilian four-engine flying boat. A full-scale, walk-through diorama of a World War II bombing mission aboard a B-17 Flying Fortress is complete with films and audiotapes. Fightertown lets visitors experience an aerial dogfight.

Guided tours of the aircraft shop are available. Food is available.

Allow 1 hour, 30 minutes minimum. Daily 9-5. Admission $24.95; over 59, $22.95; ages 5-12, $13.95. AE, MC, VI. Phone (863) 984-3500.

POMPANO BEACH—
see Fort Lauderdale p. 78.

PONCE INLET (C-10)
pop. 1,700, elev. 10'

FLORIDA COASTAL CRUISES—
see New Smyrna Beach p. 130.

PONCE DE LEON INLET LIGHTHOUSE, just w. of SR A1A (S. Atlantic Ave.) at 4931 S. Peninsula Dr., is a restored 175-foot-high brick structure whose light, reactivated in 1982, guided mariners past the shoals 1887-1970. Visitors may climb to the top of the lighthouse for a panorama of the Daytona Beach area. The keepers' cottages are now museums. The generator building houses tools and lighthouse pictures from around the world. A park with picnic tables is next to the lighthouse.

Allow 1 hour minimum. Daily 10-9, day after Labor Day-Apr. 30; 10-5, rest of year. Last admission 1 hour before closing. Admission $4; under 11, $1. Phone (904) 761-1821.

PORT ORANGE (C-10)
pop. 35,300, elev. 20'

SUGAR MILL GARDENS, 1 mi. w. of US 1 off Herbert St. on Old Sugar Mill Rd., encompasses 12 acres of landscaped grounds surrounding the restored ruins of an 1836 English sugar mill burned by Seminole Indians. Four dinosaur statues are along the garden trails. Guided tours are available. Daily dawn-dusk. Tours are given Wed. 9-3. Donations. Phone (904) 767-1735.

PORT ST. JOE (B-5) pop. 4,000, elev. 5'

CONSTITUTION CONVENTION STATE MUSEUM, 1.5 mi. s. on US 98, preserves the site of Florida's first constitutional convention. Exhibits pertain to this event and other local history. Animated talking mannequins provide 2 minutes of closing remarks at the end of the tour. Allow 30 minutes minimum. Thurs.-Mon. 9-noon and 1-5; closed Jan. 1, Thanksgiving and Dec. 25. Admission $1, under 6 free. Phone (850) 229-8029.

PUNTA GORDA (F-9)
pop. 10,700, elev. 61'

Punta Gorda, the county seat, is Charlotte County's only incorporated community. The old city dock, on the banks of the Peace River, has been transformed into Fisherman's Village, a marina and shopping complex. Visual Arts Center houses several galleries and features revolving exhibits.

Octagon Wildlife Sanctuary, I-75 exit 26, provides refuge for injured or unwanted wild and exotic animals; phone (941) 543-1130. Another organization offering assistance to orphaned or injured animals is the Peace River Wildlife Center in Ponce de Leon Park, which attempts to rehabilitate and release native wildlife to their natural habitats; phone (941) 637-3830.

Charlotte County Chamber of Commerce: 326 W. Marion #112, Punta Gorda, FL 33950, phone (941) 639-2222.

BABCOCK WILDERNESS ADVENTURES is at 8000 SR 31; go 1 mi. n. of I-75 exit 29 (southbound) on US 17, 15 mi. e. on SR 74, then 6 mi. s. on SR 31 or 3 mi. e. of I-75 exit 26 (northbound) on SR 78, then 9 mi. n. on SR 31. Visitors get a close look at rare Florida panthers, alligators, snakes, birds, bison and other native fauna and flora during the 1 hour, 30 minute swamp buggy tours through a working cattle ranch and the surrounding cypress swamps. Seasonal off-road bicycle tours also are offered. These 3-hour guided rides explore Florida ecosystems; reservations are required. Food is available.

Allow 2 hours minimum. Swamp buggy tours daily 9-3. Fare $17.95; under 12, $9.95. Reservations are required. AE, DS, MC, VI. Phone (800) 500-5583 for reservations. *See ad p. 81.*

FLORIDA ADVENTURE MUSEUM is 1 blk. n. of US 17, between US 41N and US 41S at 260 W. Retta Esplanade. The museum houses changing exhibits relating to state and local history, science and Florida natural history. Educational programs are available. Allow 30 minutes minimum. Mon.-Fri. 10-5, Sat.-Sun. 10-3; closed major holidays. Admission $2; under 13, $1. Phone (941) 639-3777.

KING FISHER CRUISE LINES, 1200 W. Retta Esplanade in Fisherman's Village, offers day

DID YOU KNOW

Of the 50 states, only Alaska has more islands than Florida.

trips to the offshore islands of Cabbage Key and Cayo Costa. Nature, harbor, sunset, fishing and chartered cruises also are available. Cabbage Key cruises depart Tues.-Thurs. and Sat. at 9. Cayo Costa cruises depart Tues., Thurs. and Sun. at 9. Schedules may vary; phone ahead. Day trips $19.95; under 12, $10. Reservations are recommended. AE, MC, VI. Phone (941) 639-0969.

QUINCY (A-6) pop. 7,400, elev. 187'

Established in 1828, the agricultural town of Quincy owed its early prosperity to the tobacco industry. The Quincy State Bank eventually persuaded its patrons to invest in the fledgling Coca-Cola Co., resulting in economic fortune for both the town and its citizens.

Soldiers from the battles of Natural Bridge and Olustee were treated in Quincy, a medical center during the Civil War. The town also served as a supply commissary for the Confederate Army. In 1868 a fire destroyed more than half the town, leading to an ordinance requiring that all new buildings be constructed of brick.

The 36-block historic district features landscaping, period lighting and Victorian-style buildings. Most structures were built in the late 1880s, although several houses date back to the 1840s.

Gadsden County Chamber of Commerce: 203 E. Jefferson St., P.O. Box 389, Quincy, FL 32353; phone (850) 627-9231.

Self-guiding tours: A brochure outlining a tour of the historic district is available from the chamber of commerce.

ST. AUGUSTINE (B-10)
pop. 11,700, elev. 7'

As the oldest, continuously occupied European settlement in the United States, St. Augustine has played varied and prominent historic roles. Juan Ponce de León, in search of the legendary Fountain of Youth, landed in this area Apr. 3, 1513, and took possession of the region for Spain. In 1565 King Phillip II sent Pedro Menéndez de Avilés to colonize the new territory. Menéndez de Avilés arrived in Florida on the Feast Day of St. Augustine and named the landing site after the saint.

Its coastal location made the town both strategic and vulnerable. Pirates sacked St. Augustine in both the 16th and 17th centuries. Military importance soon came to the forefront as England extended its holdings southward down the coast. Spain responded by starting to build Castillo de San Marcos in 1672.

By the time St. Augustine was ceded to England in 1763, it had served as the seat of government for 30 missions as well as for all Spanish possessions in the regions of Florida and coastal Georgia. British loyalists from adjacent states sought refuge during the Revolutionary War.

In 1783 Florida was traded back to Spain. Encouraged by Spanish land grants, many Americans moved onto property vacated by the English. Florida became a U.S. possession in 1821, and during the Second Seminole War in the 1830s, St. Augustine resumed a military role.

The quiet coastal town came to life in the 1880s when Henry Flagler began to develop the area as a winter resort and playground. With a railway link provided from New York, plush hotels were built and leisure activities such as golf and yachting awaited the city's guests.

Still preserving strong evidence of its Spanish origin, the Old City is being restored to a likeness of its colonial days; much of the historic area north of the Plaza de la Constitución is complete. Typical Spanish houses, with walled patios enclosing Old World gardens, line the many narrow streets.

Tolomato Cemetery, also known as the Old Spanish Cemetery, is at Cordova Street between Orange and Saragossa streets. Formerly the site of the Christian Indian village of Tolomato, the cemetery served as a Catholic burial ground 1784-1892 and is the burial site of Augustin Verot, the first bishop of St. Augustine. The cemetery is only open by request; information is available at the rectory entrance of the Cathedral of St. Augustine on Treasury Street.

South of the city, St. Augustine Beach provides a return to the present. Miles of wide, hard-packed sand beaches afford beach driving, swimming and surfing opportunities. Boating also is popular.

Tours of area attractions by horse-drawn carriage depart from the bayfront area next to Castillo de San Marcos. [SAVE] St. Augustine Scenic Cruise offers sightseeing cruises departing from St. Augustine Municipal Marina; phone (904) 824-1806 or (800) 542-8316.

The Huguenot cemetery, between the City Gate and the Visitor Information Center, is open to the public anytime the gate is unlocked.

Note: Parking regulations are enforced strictly throughout the city. Yellow curbs are no-parking zones.

St. Johns County Visitors and Convention Bureau: 88 Riberia St., Suite 400, St. Augustine, FL 32084; phone (904) 829-1711 or (800) 653-2489. *See color ad p. 186.*

Shopping areas: St. Augustine Outlet Center and Belz Factory Outlet World are both off I-95 exit 95 on SR 16.

The Old City

CASTILLO DE SAN MARCOS NATIONAL MONUMENT, a Spanish fortress, is at Castillo Dr. and Avenida Menéndez. The oldest masonry fort in the United States, it was built 1672-95 of coquina, a soft local shellrock, as part of the defenses along the route of

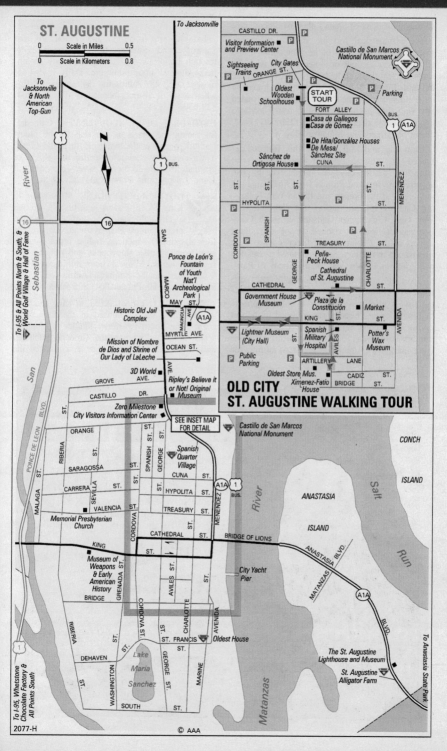

ST. AUGUSTINE

Scale in Miles 0 — 0.5
Scale in Kilometers 0 — 0.8

To Jacksonville

To Jacksonville & North American Top-Gun

CASTILLO DR.

Visitor Information and Preview Center

Castillo de San Marcos National Monument

Sightseeing Trains City Gates ORANGE ST.

Oldest Wooden Schoolhouse

START TOUR

FORT ALLEY

Parking

Casa de Gallegos
Casa de Gómez

De Hita/González Houses
De Mesa/Sánchez Site

Sánchez de Ortigosa House

CUNA ST.

HYPOLITA ST.

SPANISH

CORDOVA

TREASURY ST.

Ponce de León's Fountain of Youth Nat'l Archeological Park

MARCO ST.

MAY ST.

MAGNOLIA AVE.

A1A

MYRTLE AVE.

Historic Old Jail Complex

OCEAN ST.

Mission of Nombre de Dios and Shrine of Our Lady of LaLeche

Peña-Peck House

Cathedral of St. Augustine

CATHEDRAL

GEORGE

CHARLOTTE

Government House Museum

Plaza de la Constitución

Market

KING ST.

Lightner Museum (City Hall)

Spanish Military Hospital

Potter's Wax Museum

AVILES

AVENIDA

Public Parking

ARTILLERY LANE

3D World AVE.

GROVE AVE.

CASTILLO DR.

Ripley's Believe it or Not! Original Museum

Oldest Store Mus.
Ximenez-Fatio House

CADIZ ST.

BRIDGE ST.

Zero Milestone
City Visitors Information Center

SEE INSET MAP FOR DETAIL

OLD CITY
ST. AUGUSTINE WALKING TOUR

ORANGE ST.

Castillo de San Marcos National Monument

CONCH ISLAND

RIBERIA ST.

SARAGOSSA ST.

Spanish Quarter Village

SPANISH ST.

GEORGE ST.

CUNA ST.

ANASTASIA ISLAND

MALAGA ST.

CARRERA ST.

SEVILA ST.

HYPOLITA ST.

MENENDEZ

A1A

BUS. 1

River

VALENCIA ST.

TREASURY ST.

Memorial Presbyterian Church

CORDOVA ST.

CATHEDRAL ST.

BRIDGE OF LIONS

ANASTASIA ISLAND

PONCE DE LEON BLVD.

KING ST.

Museum of Weapons & Early American History

GRENADA ST.

AVILES ST.

City Yacht Pier

ANASTASIA BLVD.

Salt Run

BRIDGE ST.

CORDOVA ST.

CHARLOTTE ST.

AVENIDA

MATANZAS BLVD.

A1A

To Anastasia State Park

RIBERIA ST.

DEHAVEN ST.

Lake Maria Sanchez

ST. FRANCIS

Oldest House

GEORGE ST.

MARINE ST.

The St. Augustine Lighthouse and Museum

St. Augustine Alligator Farm

WASHINGTON ST.

SOUTH ST.

To I-95, Whetstone Chocolate Factory & All Points South

To I-95 & All Points North & South, & World Golf Village & Hall of Fame

San Sebastian River

Matanzas

2077-H

© AAA

the treasure fleets. For many years the fort was the northernmost point of Spain's New World holdings.

The symmetrical fort has massive diamond-shaped bastions at each of its four corners, and 60 to 77 cannons once occupied the gun deck. Its walls, 12 feet thick at the base, 8 feet thick at the top and 33 feet high, are skirted by a moat on three sides. Part of the "Cubo Line," a palisaded city wall, has been rebuilt. A stairway leads to the gun deck overlooking the Old City Gate, quaint old streets and Matanzas Bay.

Until the mid-18th century this fortress defended St. Augustine; after one unsuccessful siege in 1702, the city was burned. The English acquired the fort and Florida from Spain in 1763 at the end of the French and Indian War. Following Charleston's fall during the Revolutionary War, Gen. Christopher Gadsden, a South Carolina patriot, was imprisoned in the fort; three signers of the Declaration of Independence were imprisoned in the city. Spain regained possession of Florida in 1784 as part of the Treaty of Paris.

Upon the acquisition of Florida in 1821, the fortress became part of the U.S. coastal defense system. It also was used as a military prison. Seminole leader Osceola was confined in the fort during the Second Seminole War. The fort's final military use was for imprisonment of some court-martialed American soldiers during the Spanish-American War. It was decommissioned in 1900.

Exhibits trace its history, and cannons are fired Saturday and Sunday from Memorial Day through Labor Day. Metal detectors are prohibited. Allow 1 hour minimum. Daily 8:45-4:45; closed Dec. 25. Admission $4, under 17 free when with a responsible adult. Phone (904) 829-6506.

CATHEDRAL OF ST. AUGUSTINE, on Cathedral St. facing the plaza, is the seat of the oldest Catholic parish in the nation. Built in the 1790s, it was reconstructed after a fire in 1887. The original structure forms the nave. Tours daily at 1 and 3. Donations. Phone (904) 824-2806.

GOVERNMENT HOUSE MUSEUM, 48 King St., illustrates area history through a chronological series of exhibits and presentations. Displays feature an archeological exhibit, American Indian artifacts, treasure from Spanish shipwrecks and military and religious items. Allow 1 hour minimum. Daily 9-6; closed major holidays. Admission $3.50; ages 6-18, $1.50. Phone (904) 825-5033.

LIGHTNER MUSEUM, at King and Cordova sts., is housed in the former Alcazar Hotel, built by Henry Flagler in 1888. In 1948 Otto C. Lightner, the Chicago publisher and editor of *Hobbies* magazine, converted the

empty hotel into a museum to contain his vast collection of art, antiques and other items.

Three floors display furnishings, costumes, Victorian art glass and natural history specimens. One room is devoted to a collection of Tiffany stained glass. Other highlights include Oriental art, art nouveau works and a Victorian village.

Nineteenth-century mechanical musical instruments are demonstrated daily at 11 and 2. The steam baths of the hotel still exist on the second floor. The former indoor swimming pool behind the building, one of the largest of its day, is now an antiques mall. Allow 2 hours minimum. Daily 9-5; closed Dec. 25. Admission $6; ages 12-17, $2. Phone (904) 824-2874.

OLDEST HOUSE, 14 St. Francis St. at the s. end of the seawall, also is known as the González-Alvarez House and is on a site occupied since the early 1600s. The present structure, with coquina walls and hand-hewn cedar beams, dates from the early 1700s. Records dating to 1763 identify Tomás González, an artilleryman at the Castillo de San Marcos, as the owner. Gerónimo Alvarez bought the house in 1790, and it remained in his family for almost 100 years.

During the British period 1763-83, the first of a number of alterations was made which brought the house into its current shape and size, reflecting both Spanish and British architectural styles. The house is furnished to represent its different periods; artifacts unearthed at the site are displayed.

An ornamental garden typifies plants grown by the Spanish, British and American occupants. Within the complex are two museums; one traces the city's history and contains the historical society's gallery, and the other, The Museum of Florida's Army, follows the army's history from 1565 to the present. Guided tours are available.

Allow 1 hour minimum. Daily 9-5; closed Dec. 25. Tours are given daily every half hour. Last admission 30 minutes before closing. Admission $5; over 55, $4.50; students with ID $3. MC, VI. Phone (904) 824-2872.

OLDEST STORE MUSEUM, 4 Artillery Ln., evokes turn-of-the-20th-century life with more than 100,000 items from the store's original stock. Antique vehicles include a steam tractor, a Model T Ford and a Conestoga wagon. Allow 30 minutes minimum. Mon.-Sat. 9-5, Sun. 10-5, June-Aug.; Mon.-Sat. 9-5, Sun. noon-5, rest of year. Closed Dec. 24-25. Admission $5; ages 6-12, $1.50. Children must be with an adult. Phone (904) 829-9729.

OLDEST WOODEN SCHOOLHOUSE, 14 St. George St., was built 1750-60 of cypress and cedar and is among the nation's oldest. Automated mannequins representing the professor and his students dressed in period clothing relate the school's history and explain the barter system,

subjects studied and the use of the dunce cap. Schoolbooks, slates, old maps and other artifacts are displayed. The kitchen, separated from the main building to reduce the risk of fire, is open to the public.

Allow 30 minutes minimum. Daily 9-5; closed Dec. 25. Admission $2.50; over 65 and military with ID $2; ages 6-12, $1.50. Phone (904) 824-0192.

PEÑA-PECK HOUSE, 143 St. George St., was built in the 1740s of native coquina stone. Originally the home of Royal Treasurer Juan Estaban de Peña, Dr. Seth Peck bought the property in 1837. Displays include early Spanish artifacts and Peck family furnishings from the 18th century. Allow 30 minutes minimum. Mon.-Fri. 12:30-4:30, Sat. 10:30-4:30, Sun. noon-4:30; closed Easter, Thanksgiving and Dec. 23-25. Admission $4.50; over 55, $3.50; ages 12-18, $2.50. MC, VI. Phone (904) 829-5064.

PLAZA DE LA CONSTITUCIÓN, bounded by Cathedral, King, Charlotte and St. George sts., was the central square around which the business section of the Old City was built and where the slave market was held. One end overlooks Matanzas Bay and opens into the approach to the Bridge of Lions. Spaniards erected the monument in the center of the plaza in 1813. The public marketplace at the east end is a reconstruction of one built in 1824.

POTTER'S WAX MUSEUM, 17 King St., faces the plaza. More than 170 life-size figures depict historically significant persons and events. In summer visitors may watch the craftspersons at work. Allow 30 minutes minimum. Daily 9-9, June 15-Labor Day; 9-5, rest of year. Closed Dec. 25. Admission $5.95; over 55, $4.95; ages 6-12, $2.75. AE, DS, MC, VI. Phone (904) 829-9056.

SIGHTSEEING TRAINS, 170 San Marco Ave., provides stop-offs at major points of interest, shops and restaurants over a 7-mile loop. Tours depart every 15-20 minutes daily 8:30-5. Fare (good for 3 consecutive days) $12; ages 6-12, $5. Package tours are available. Phone (904) 829-6545 or (800) 226-6545.

SPANISH QUARTER VILLAGE consists of restored and reconstructed buildings that reflect different aspects of Spanish colonial life. The Triay House contains an orientation center with period artifacts and informational displays. Costumed guides demonstrate 1740s crafts and lifestyles; of interest are the blacksmith, woodworker and textile crafts shops. Tickets are available at the Museum Store, 33 St. George St.

Allow 1 hour minimum. Daily 9-6; closed Dec. 25. Admission (includes all buildings except Spanish Military Hospital) $6.50; over 62 and military with ID $5.50; ages 6-18, $4; family rate $13. Phone (904) 825-6830.

Casa de Gallegos, 21 St. George St., is a tabby (oyster shell and lime) house typical of the 1750s. Inside the lifestyles of early Spanish settlers are demonstrated.

Casa de Gómez, 23 St. George St., is a typical wooden house occupied by a Spanish soldier and his family in the 1750s.

De Hita/González Houses, 37 St. George St., are good examples of Spanish colonial homes. The González House presents demonstrations of textile arts. The De Hita House offers hands-on learning activities.

De Mesa/Sánchez Site began as a two-room coquina (shell-rock) house in the mid-18th century. Additions and modifications continued until the end of the 19th century. Much information about the area has been gleaned from the excavation.

Spanish Military Hospital, 4 blks. off St. George St. at 3 Aviles St., is a reconstruction of a military hospital of the second Spanish colonial period. Costumed guides re-enact the daily life of patients and staff in the 18th-century hospital. Five exhibit areas illustrate medical practices of the time and include an apothecary with period artifacts. Allow 30 minutes minimum. Daily 9-5; closed Dec. 25. Admission $2.50; under 18, $1. Phone (904) 825-6830.

XIMENEZ-FATIO HOUSE, 20 Aviles St., is a well-preserved merchant's house and store dating to the Second Spanish Period 1783-1819. The house has been restored to the Territorial Period 1821-45, when it was operated as an inn. Guided tours are offered. Allow 30 minutes minimum. Thurs.-Sat. and Mon. 11-4, Sun. 1-4. Tours are conducted every half-hour. Last tour begins 30 minutes before closing. Donations. Phone (904) 829-3575.

Walking Tour of the Old City

See map page 185.

This tour will take less than 2 hours, allowing for a leisurely pace and stops for photography and plaque reading. Allow more time for stops at the listed attractions. The best way to see the city is to combine the walking tour with stops at the attractions along the way. The names of sites listed in detail in The Old City section are printed in bold type. Even if you do not tour a listed site, reading the attraction listing when you reach that point will make the tour more interesting.

Parking is scarce and the tour does not take one-way streets into account. There are parking facilities at the Visitor Information Center, 10 Castillo Dr. No automobiles are permitted on St. George St. in the restoration area.

In the early 18th century the Old City was approached through the City Gates, and this remains a logical place to start an expedition through Old St. Augustine. Narrow, almost tunnel-like, second-story balconies overhang either side of St. George St., where more than 50 houses and craft shops have been restored or reconstructed.

One of the first structures you will encounter is the **Oldest Wooden Schoolhouse** at 14 St. George. The major part of the restoration area begins as you cross Fort Alley and find the Casa de Gallegos at 21 St. George. **Casa de Gallegos** provides a glimpse into domestic life of the 1750s.

Across the street, Casa de Ribera is decorated with antique furnishings. Next door is **Casa de Gómez,** a Spanish soldier's dwelling. Also in this block, at 41 St. George, is the National Greek Orthodox Shrine, with its St. Photios Chapel decorated with frescoes depicting Greek Orthodox theology. Gold leaf highlights much of the chapel's artwork. Across the street note the **De Hita/González Houses** and **De Mesa/Sánchez Site.** Back on the west side of the street at the corner of Cuna St. is the Sánchez de Ortigosa House.

Cross Cuna and proceed along St. George, enjoying the warm tones of the ancient coquina stonework and the glimpses of courtyards between many of the buildings. At 105 St. George is the Sánchez House, a restored coquina and masonry house. The **Peña-Peck House** occupies

the corner of Treasury and St. George; it was built in the 1690s for the Spanish treasurer. Glance down Treasury St.—one of the narrowest streets in the Old City.

As you continue along St. George, you will come upon the **Plaza de la Constitución,** situated between Cathedral Pl. and King St. The heart of the business district during the Spanish heyday, the Plaza now serves as a setting for the **Cathedral of St. Augustine,** which faces the Plaza on Cathedral St. You can either end your tour here, following Cathedral St. eastward to Charlotte where you will head north to Cuna St. leading back to St. George, or continue into the oldest part of the city.

The **Government House Museum,** on the corner of St. George and King sts., dates back to the 1600s and is home to the St. Augustine Preservation Board. Take a right and proceed down King St. Crossing Cordova St., the Ponce de Leon Hotel will be on your right. Built in 1885 by millionaire developer Henry Flagler, the lavish structure is now home to Flagler College.

Directly across the street, on the corner of King and Cordova sts., is the Alcazar Hotel, home of the **Lightner Museum.** Also built by Henry Flagler in the late 1880s, the former hotel is of Moorish and Spanish architecture. You can deviate from the tour by walking 1 block west on King St. to the **Museum of Weapons and Early American History.** Cross Cordova, heading back down King St., and on your right you will find the Casa Monica Hotel, built in 1888 and purchased by Henry Flagler.

Continue east on King St., take a right on St. George, then head east on Artillery Ln. After experiencing late 19th-century shopping at the **Oldest Store Museum,** continue east to Aviles. Turn right to see the **Ximenez-Fatio House** on the corner of Cadiz and Aviles. This late 18th-century coquina house has been restored and is furnished to reflect an 1850s boarding house.

Stroll back north on Aviles into the center of the art colony. On the left, at 3 Aviles, is the **Spanish Military Hospital,** which houses displays of 18th-century hospital life.

Go right on Cathedral St., then left on Charlotte St. and proceed north. A 3-block stroll up Charlotte past a number of interesting structures leads to Cuna St. Shops line Cuna St. between Charlotte and St. George sts., where you began your tour.

Other Points of Interest

[SAVE] **3D WORLD,** 28 San Marco Ave., presents three 15- to 20-minute 3-D movies, two in motion-simulator theaters and one in a fixed-seating theater. Allow 1 hour minimum. Daily 10-10, May-Aug.; Sun.-Thurs. 10-8, Fri.-Sat. 10-10, rest of year. Admission $10, under 42 inches tall (permitted in fixed-seating theater only) free. AE, DS, MC, VI. Phone (904) 829-9849.

[GEM] **HISTORIC OLD JAIL COMPLEX,** 167 San Marco Ave., encompasses the Florida Heritage Museum, The Old Jail and St. Augustine Historical Tours. Daily 8:30-5; closed Easter and Dec. 24-25. Combination rates are available. Phone (904) 829-3800 or (800) 397-4071.

Florida Heritage Museum depicts Florida's growth from early Indian cultures through the Flagler era. Personal items and pictures of Henry Flagler are displayed along with a model railroad tracing the route he established between Jacksonville and Key West. Additional exhibits include an antique doll and toy collection, Confederate items, 16th-century Spanish weapons, a life-size sunken ship and its treasures, and a replica of an Indian village. Allow 1 hour minimum. Admission $4.25; ages 6-12, $3.25.

The Old Jail contains a large collection of weapons and displays that illustrate prison life in early St. Augustine. Costumed guides portray the sheriff and his wife; visitors may tour the family's living quarters, which were in the same building as the prisoners' cells. Newspapers and photographs depict the history of the jail. Visitors also may sit in a replica of an electric chair (minus the electric hardware). Allow 30 minutes minimum. Admission $4.25; ages 6-12, $3.25.

St. Augustine Historical Tours offers six narrated tours lasting from 2 hours to 2 days. All

visit a variety of sites within the Old City. Transportation is in open-air trolleys. The basic 1-hour tour stops at 16 attractions. Tours depart every 15-20 minutes daily 8:30-4:30. Basic tour $12; ages 6-12, $5. Admission to separate attractions not included in basic tour fee. MC, VI.

MEMORIAL PRESBYTERIAN CHURCH is at Valencia and Sevilla sts. Henry Flagler built the Venetian Renaissance structure in 1890 as a memorial to his daughter. Construction was completed in less than a year, although the stained-glass windows took an additional 11 years to complete. Guides provide a brief overview of the church's history. Allow 30 minutes minimum. Mon.-Sat. 9-4:30, Sun. 12:30-4:30. Donations. Phone (904) 829-6451.

MISSION OF NOMBRE DE DIOS and Shrine of Our Lady of LaLeche are 5 blks. n. of the city gate on San Marco Ave. Pedro Menéndez de Avilés landed here Sept. 8, 1565, and established the first permanent community. A 208-foot stainless-steel cross marks the site of the founding of St. Augustine. A small museum is on site. Allow 1 hour minimum. Grounds daily 7-6. Mission, museum and shrine daily 7-6; closed Easter and Dec. 25. Donations. Phone (904) 824-2809.

MUSEUM OF WEAPONS AND EARLY AMERICAN HISTORY, 81-C King St., displays weapons of all types including cane guns, swords, muskets and unusual firearms. Other exhibits include 18th-century shipwreck items, Indian artifacts, the only known Confederate Florida flag and artifacts relating to American history. Allow 30 minutes minimum. Daily 9:30-5; closed Dec. 25. Admission $4; over 62, $3.50; ages 7-12, $1. Phone (904) 829-3727.

NORTH AMERICAN TOP-GUN, at the St. Augustine Airport on US 1, offers rides and air-to-air combat training in World War II fighter-type aircraft. Passengers can choose sightseeing, aerobatic or fighter pilot flights, most lasting 15 minutes to 1 hour. A videotape of the flight is available. Daily 9-5. Fare $190-$590, depending on length and type of flight; $1,490 for air-

combat courses. Reservations are required. AE, DS, MC, VI. Phone (904) 823-3505 or (800) 257-1636.

PONCE DE LEÓN'S FOUNTAIN OF YOUTH NATIONAL ARCHEOLOGICAL PARK, e. of SR A1A (San Marco Ave.) on Williams St. to 11 Magnolia Ave., is on the site claimed to be Ponce de León's landing place Apr. 3, 1513. The park contains the spring reputed to be the Fountain of Youth; a cross of coquina stones first excavated in 1868 and believed to be Ponce de León's landmark cross; remains of a Timucuan Indian burial ground; and exhibits pertaining to Spanish colonization. Additional features include a planetarium, an audiovisual display of celestial navigation techniques and a two-story, revolving world globe.

Allow 1 hour minimum. Daily 9-5; closed Dec. 25. Admission $5.50; over 60, $4.50; ages 6-12, $2.50. Phone (904) 829-3168 or (800) 356-8222.

RIPLEY'S BELIEVE IT OR NOT! ORIGINAL MUSEUM, 19 San Marco Ave., contains oddities collected by Robert Ripley, including a two-headed calf and an oil painting on a pinhead. Some of his cartoons also are displayed. Allow 1 hour minimum. Daily 9 a.m.-10 p.m. Last admission 2 hours before closing. Admission $9.95; ages 5-12, $5.95. AE, DS, MC, VI. Phone (904) 824-1606. *See ad p. 189.*

ST. AUGUSTINE ALLIGATOR FARM, 1.75 mi. s.e. on SR A1A, on Anastasia Island, features a complete collection of the 22 crocodilian species. An elevated walkway winds through a rookery and over an alligator swamp. Florida wildlife shows are presented hourly. Allow 2 hours minimum. Daily 9-6, June-Aug.; 9-5, rest of year. Admission $11.95; ages 3-10, $7.95. AE, DS, MC, VI. Phone (904) 824-3337. *See color ad p. 188.*

THE ST. AUGUSTINE LIGHTHOUSE AND MUSEUM is 1 mi. s.e. on SR A1A, then n. on Red Cox Dr. on Anastasia Island. The museum is housed in the restored lightkeeper's house. A Victorian period room and maritime artifacts are

among highlights. An interactive computer re-
lates stories of the lighthouse keepers and their
families. Visitors may climb the 219 stairs to the
top of the 165-foot tower, which provides a
panorama of St. Augustine.

Daily 9-6; closed Easter, Thanksgiving and
Dec. 24-25. Lighthouse tower opens 15 minutes
after the museum. Lighthouse and museum
$5.50; over 55, $4; ages 7-11, $2.75. Museum
only $2.75; over 55, $2; under 12 free. Under
age 7 or under 4 feet tall are not admitted to the
lighthouse tower. Phone (904) 829-0745.

WHETSTONE CHOCOLATE FACTORY, 2 Coke
Rd., offers self-guiding tours of its factory. Visitors can see a high-speed molding plant, the
packing room and the specialty room where
chocolates are made. A 15-minute videotape introduces visitors to the factory. Allow 1 hour
minimum. Mon.-Sat. 10-5; closed Thanksgiving
and Dec. 25. Prime production times are 10-2.
Free. Phone (904) 825-1700, ext. 25. *See color
ad p. 190.*

**WORLD GOLF VILLAGE AND HALL OF
FAME,** .5 mi. w. of I-95 exit 95A, is a
showcase for the game of golf. In addition to the
sport's hall of fame, the complex also consists of
the Walk of Champions, an IMAX theater, several golf courses, hotels, a convention center and
shopping.

The hall of fame pays tribute to the history of
the game and honors the world's greatest golfers.
Interactive exhibits allow visitors to test their
golfing skills as well as experience the joy of
sinking a hole-in-one. Collections of golfing artifacts and videotape presentations help explain
the game, while the swing analyzer and putting
areas allow visitors to participate. Guided tours
are available. Food is available.

Daily 10-6. Admission $10; over 49 and stu-
dents with ID $8; ages 5-12, $5. IMAX theater
$9; over 49, ages 3-12 and students and military
with ID $7. Combination tickets are available.
AE, DS, MC, VI. Phone (904) 940-4123.

ZERO MILESTONE is at Castillo Dr. and San
Marco Ave. The coquina ball marks the eastern
terminus of both the Old Spanish Trail, which
linked the missions between St. Augustine and
Pensacola, and the first transcontinental highway
within the United States. Daily 24 hours. Free.

WINERIES

- **San Sebastian Winery,** 157 King St. Mon.-
  Sat. 10-6, Sun. 11-6; closed Jan. 1, Easter,
  Thanksgiving and Dec. 25. Phone (904)
  826-1594 or (888) 352-9463.

ST. CLOUD — *see Orlando p. 174.*

ST. MARKS (B-6) pop. 300, elev. 7'

In 1836 a railroad was built to connect Tallahassee with St. Marks. Now dismantled, the
Tallahassee-St. Marks Historic Railroad State
Trail offers a 16-mile paved trail for bicyclists,
hikers, horseback riders and skaters. For additional information phone (850) 922-6007.

ST. MARKS NATIONAL WILDLIFE REFUGE, off
CR 59 s. of Newport, covers 68,000 acres along
the Gulf of Mexico. The refuge borders
Apalachee Bay and extends from the Aucilla
River to the Ochlockonee River. A portion of the
Florida Trail passes through the refuge. Varied
wildlife can be observed all year; concentrations
of waterfowls can be seen during fall and winter.
In 1521 the Spanish established an early ship-
building yard and smithy at the junction of the
St. Marks and Wakulla rivers. Also within the
refuge is the 1831 St. Marks Lighthouse.

Visitor center open Mon.-Fri. 8-4, Sat.-Sun.
10-5. The refuge is open daily dawn-dusk; closed
federal holidays. Admission $4 per private ve-
hicle, $1 per person arriving by bicycle or on
foot. Phone (850) 925-6121.

**SAN MARCOS DE APALACHEE STATE HIS-
TORIC SITE,** off SR 363, 1 mi. s.w. on Old Fort
Rd., displays Indian, Spanish and Civil War artifacts. The interpretive center is on the site of a
fort built by the Spanish in 1679 at the conflu-
ence of the Wakulla and St. Marks rivers and
later occupied by English, Confederate and Federal troops. Outside are a military cemetery and
the remains of the fort and earthworks. Allow 30
minutes minimum. Thurs.-Mon. 9-5; closed Jan.
1, Thanksgiving and Dec. 25. Grounds free. Museum $1, under 6 free. Phone (850) 925-6216 or
922-6007.

ST. PETE BEACH —
see Tampa Bay p. 228.

ST. PETERSBURG —
see Tampa Bay p. 200.

SANFORD — *see Orlando p. 175.*

SANIBEL (G-9) pop. 5,500, elev. 6'

Sanibel is on a resort island of the same name;
access to the island is by a toll causeway ($3 ac-
cess, free egress) from Punta Rassa. This barrier
island is known for its lighthouse, lush vegetation, extensive beaches, abundant bird life and,
perhaps most of all, seashells. Each tide brings
thousands of shells onto the fine sand beaches.

When Ponce de León discovered the southwest coast of Florida in 1513, he named it *Costa
de Caracoles,* or "Coast of Seashells." The apparently smooth harbor at the southern end of
this chain of islands later was designated on a
Spanish map as *Puerto S. Nibel,* south level port.
S. also is the Spanish abbreviation for *San,* or
saint; through an error, subsequent maps designated this harbor as *Puerto de San Nibel.*

The traditional, and less prosaic, explanation of Sanibel's name is that pirate José Gaspar was so charmed by this lovely island that he named it after Santa Isabella, a beautiful queen of Spain.

The many paved trails beneath overhanging trees make bicycling a favorite mode of transportation. Moped and bicycle rentals are available. Public parking is limited on Sanibel Island and regulations are enforced strictly. For information about designated parking areas contact the Sanibel Visitors Center.

A bridge connects Sanibel Island with Captiva Island. Some historians believe that the incident that gave Captiva its name was one that was similar to that of Pocahontas. In 1528 Juan Ortiz was captured by the Calusa Indians and held captive on the island. Facing execution, Ortiz escaped to a friendly Indian tribe with help from the chief's daughter. In 1539 he was released to Hernando de Soto and became his interpreter. Visitors can see the remains of the ceremonial shell mounds built by the Calusa.

Sanibel Visitors Center: 1159 Causeway Rd., Sanibel, FL 33957; phone (941) 472-1080.

THE BAILEY-MATTHEWS SHELL MUSEUM, 3075 Sanibel-Captiva Rd., features a large collection of seashells from around the world. Displays include locally found shells, land snail shells and shells that once were used as money. Also on display are works of art created using shells including ceremonial masks, mother-of-pearl inlaid furniture pieces, religious objects and jewelry.

A learning lab features hands-on play areas for children and a simulated saltwater environment with indigenous shellfish and snails. A slide presentation is shown. Allow 1 hour minimum. Tues.-Sun. 10-4; closed major holidays. Admission $5; ages 8-16, $3. Phone (941) 395-2233.

CAPTIVA CRUISES departs from South Seas Resort on Captiva Island. Among cruises offered are 1- to 3-hour nature, natural history and sunset cruises, 3-hour shelling trips, 4- to 5-hour cruises to Cabbage Key or Useppa Island, and 5- and 6-hour excursions to Boca Grande or Cayo Costa.

Tours offered daily. Dolphin-wildlife and sunset cruises depart 4 and dusk; shelling trips at 9 and 1; island cruises at 10 and 10:30. Closed Dec. 25. Fare $17.50-$35; ages 4-12, $10-$17.50. Reservations are required. Inquire about policies regarding refunds, inclement weather and minimum number of passengers. AE, MC, VI. Phone (941) 472-5300.

J.N. "DING" DARLING NATIONAL WILDLIFE REFUGE, 1 Wildlife Dr., is named for the editorial cartoonist and pioneer conservationist. The refuge encompasses more than 6,000 acres of wetlands and island uplands on the north side of the island. Facilities include canoe trails, a bird-watching tower, a wildlife drive, an interpretive

trail and marinas. A list of more than 200 bird species that can be viewed is available from the headquarters at the refuge entrance.

Refuge open Sat.-Thurs. 7:30-30 minutes before dusk. Visitor center open daily 9-5, Nov.-Apr.; 9-4, rest of year. Phone for holiday hours. J.N. "Ding" Darling National Wildlife Refuge Drive open Sat.-Thurs. dawn-dusk. Admission $5 per private vehicle, $1 for pedestrians and bicyclists. Phone (941) 472-1100.

Sanibel-Captiva Conservation Foundation, 3333 Sanibel-Captiva Rd., has guided nature trail tours, a butterfly house, an exhibit with a touch tank, and a reception center with displays about the ecology of area wetlands. Mon.-Sat. 8:30-4, mid-Nov. to mid-Apr.; Mon.-Fri. 8:30-3, rest of year. Admission $3, under 17 free. AE, DS, MC, VI. Phone (941) 472-2329.

SANIBEL HISTORICAL VILLAGE AND MUSEUM, 850 Dunlop Rd., exhibits local artifacts and memorabilia in a 1913 Florida "cracker" house. Early photographs and documents trace the history of Sanibel from its pioneer days, while archeological finds document the prehistory of the island. A 1926 post office, a 1927 tearoom and the 1927 Bailey's General Store and Gas Station have been moved to the site and restored in period. A 1926 Model T pickup truck is displayed.

Wed.-Sat. 10-4, Sun. noon-4, Dec. 1-Easter; Wed.-Sat. 10-4, day after Easter-late Aug. and mid-Oct. through Nov. 30. Donations. Phone (941) 472-4648.

SARASOTA (F-8) pop. 51,000, elev. 18′

Although the origin of its name is not clear, the town has been a fixture on Sarasota Bay since the 1700s. The population was augmented by Scottish settlers in the 1880s, and the area became popular as a resort in the early part of the 20th century.

The circus is an integral part of Sarasota's past. In 1927 John Ringling selected the town for his Ringling Brothers and Barnum & Bailey Circus and made it his home. He exerted a major influence on the growth and development of the city because people from all over the world came to Sarasota to star in his show.

Sarasota, including the offshore islands of Lido Key, Longboat Key, St. Armand Key and Siesta Key, is a beach resort and art community. Hotels and residential and commercial areas ring Sarasota Bay, and the islands offer 35 miles of beaches that border the clear waters of the Gulf.

In the mainland section of the city is an array of performing arts groups, including the Asolo Theatre Company, The Players, Sarasota Opera, the Florida West Coast Symphony, Sarasota Ballet of Florida, the Florida String Quartet, Florida Symphonic Band and several vocal and chamber ensembles as well as an active theater district.

Performing arts facilities include the The F.S.U. Center for the Performing Arts *(see attraction listing)* and Van Wezel Hall, 777 N. Tamiami Tr. Golden Apple Dinner Theatre, 25 N. Pineapple St., presents entertainment from drama to musicals.

Since Sarasota is the city where golf was introduced to Florida from Scotland and where the first course was laid out in 1886, it is understandable that the sport remains popular; more than 30 courses are within minutes of downtown.

During March, Ed Smith Sports Complex at 12th Street and Tuttle Avenue is the spring training home for baseball's Cincinnati Reds; phone

(941) 954-4101, ext. 5200. Beginning Dec. 1 and throughout spring training, ticket information for Reds games is available at (941) 954-4464. The Sarasota Red Sox, the class A affiliate of the Boston Red Sox, take to the field April through early September; phone (941) 365-4460.

Sarasota Ski-A-Rees presents a free water ski show each Sunday from late January through the end of April at Ken Thompson Park on City Island near the aquarium; phone (941) 388-1666.

Greyhound racing takes place from late December to mid-April at Sarasota Kennel Club on Old Bradenton Road; phone (941) 355-7744.

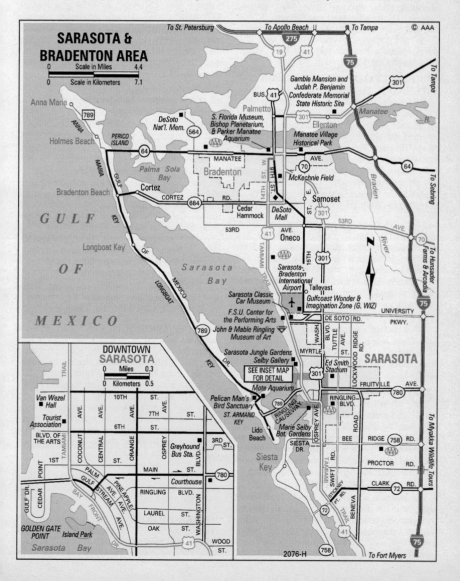

Note: Policies vary concerning admittance of children to pari-mutuel betting facilities. Phone for information.

From January through March Sarasota is home to the Royal Lipizzan Stallions from Austria. These world-renowned horses are trained at Colonel Herrman's Ranch in Manatee County on Singletary Road. Visitors are welcome at the training sessions; phone (941) 322-1501 Jan. 2-April 1.

Visitor Information Center: 655 N. Tamiami Tr., Sarasota, FL 34236; phone (941) 957-1877 or (800) 522-9799.

Shopping areas: Sarasota Square Mall, 8201 S. Tamiami Tr., includes Burdines, Dillard's, JCPenney and Sears among its 90 stores. St. Armands Circle and the vicinity contain more than 150 shops. Dillard's, Burdines and Saks Fifth Avenue are at South Gate Mall, 3501 S. Tamiami Tr.

THE F.S.U. CENTER FOR THE PERFORMING ARTS, 5555 N. Tamiami Tr., is an arts complex whose ornate interior is a reconstruction of a 1903 Scottish opera house. The complex houses the Florida State University teaching conservatory and the acting conservatory as well as the Asolo Theatre Company, which stages matinee and evening performances December through June. Although the schedule varies, tours generally are available Wed.-Sat. 10-noon. For tour information or theater reservations phone (941) 351-8000 or (800) 361-8388.

GULFCOAST WONDER & IMAGINATION ZONE (G.WIZ), 8251 15th St. E. (US 301) at the Airport Mall, encourages learning through hands-on activities. In addition to exploring science, machinery and electricity, visitors can play the laser harp and build a robot. A Tot Science area is aimed at preschoolers. Crafts and educational demonstrations are given Saturday mornings. Picnicking is permitted.

Allow 1 hour minimum. Tues.-Sat. 10-5, Sun 1-5; closed Jan. 1, Easter, Thanksgiving and Dec. 25. Admission $6; over 54, $5; ages 2-18, $4. All children must be with an adult. Phone (941) 906-1851.

THE JOHN AND MABLE RINGLING MUSEUM OF ART is 4 mi. n., just w. of US 41 at Sarasota/Bradenton Airport. The fortune John Ringling derived from his circus and vast real estate investments was well spent on his art museum and early 1920s estate. The 66-acre complex, decorated with statues and dotted with banyan trees and Cuban laurels, offers flower gardens, sitting areas and a view of Sarasota Bay.

The museum was built in Italian Renaissance style, with an inner garden courtyard studded with reproductions of many world-famous sculptures and dominated by a bronze cast of Michelangelo's "David." The collection of paintings includes works from the 14th to 20th centuries, representing Western European cultures and emphasizing the baroque period.

The museum also has a collection of 17th-century Italian paintings, an extensive Peter Paul Rubens collection, modern works and temporary exhibits. Food is available.

Allow 3 hours minimum. Museum open daily 10-5:30; closed Jan. 1, Thanksgiving and Dec. 25. Grounds free. Admission (also includes The Museum of the Circus and Cà d'Zan) $9, senior citizens $8, under 12 free; Florida students and teachers free with ID. AE, MC, VI. Phone (941) 359-5700.

Cà d'Zan (Ringling Winter Residence) is on Sarasota Bay. Completed in 1926 at a cost of $1.5 million, the 30-room, terra-cotta mansion resembles a Venetian palace. Marble, tapestries and elaborately carved and gilded furniture dominate the interior. **Note:** The mansion is undergoing a total restoration; completion is expected in 2001.

The Museum of the Circus consists of displays of gilded parade wagons, calliopes, costumes, posters, photographs and a variety of circus memorabilia as well as changing exhibitions.

[SAVE] **MARIE SELBY BOTANICAL GARDENS,** US 41S at 811 S. Palm Ave., occupies 9 acres of lush gardens. The gardens specialize in epiphytes, or air plants. Among plants featured in the varied gardens are orchids, Amazonian bromeliads, carnivorous pitcher plants, cypress trees, water lilies, succulent plants, giant bamboo and banyan trees. The Baywalk Sanctuary Canopy Walk features an elevated boardwalk that winds through a mangrove swamp. Other features include a butterfly garden, a museum of 18th-century through contemporary botanical art and a learning center. Food is available.

Allow 1 hour, 30 minutes minimum. Daily 10-5; closed Dec. 25. Admission $8; ages 6-11, $4. Phone (941) 366-5731, ext. 10.

MOTE AQUARIUM is on City Island between Longboat Key and St. Armands Key at 1600 Ken Thompson Pkwy. On view in the aquarium's more than 50 exhibits are manatees, sharks, sea turtles, eels and many of Southwest Florida's plants, fish and invertebrates. Visitors can feel stingrays, horseshoe crabs and other marine life in a 30-foot touch tank, and observe Mote Marine Laboratory's aquaculture to learn about the breeding and growing of fish for stock enhancement. Boat tours of local waters are available aboard the *Sarasota Bay Explorer*. Food is available.

Allow 1 hour minimum. Daily 10-5. Admission $10; ages 4-17, $7. Additional fee for boat tours. AE, DS, MC, VI. Phone (941) 388-2451 or (800) 691-6683.

MYAKKA WILDLIFE TOURS, 9 mi. e. of I-75 exit 37 via SR 72, offers narrated tram tours through the wildlife habitats in Myakka River State Park *(see Recreation Chart and the AAA*

Southeastern CampBook). Narrated airboat cruises on Upper Myakka Lake interpret the ecology of the lake and offer views of the animals. Binoculars are suggested.

Allow 1 hour minimum. Tram tours daily at 1 and 2:30, Dec. 16-May 31. Airboat cruises daily at 10, 11:30 and 1 (also at 2:30, Dec. 16-May 31). Fare for each tour $7; ages 6-12, $4. Apply for boarding pass upon arrival. Phone (941) 365-0100.

PELICAN MAN'S BIRD SANCTUARY is s. of Longboat Key at s. end of New Pass Bridge at 1708 Ken Thompson Pkwy., off SR 789. Dedicated to the rehabilitation of sick and injured birds, the sanctuary also serves as an education center. A boardwalk winds through the parklike setting, which contains habitats for a variety of birds including pelicans, herons, storks and sandhill cranes. Hawks, ospreys and owls can be viewed in the Birds of Prey Center. Guided tours are available. Allow 30 minutes minimum. Daily 10-5. Admission $3, children $1. Phone (941) 388-4444.

[SAVE] **SARASOTA CLASSIC CAR MUSEUM** is 3.5 mi. n. at jct. US 41 and University Rd., 1 blk. s. of Sarasota/Bradenton Airport. More than 75 antique and classic automobiles are featured, including four cars owned by John Ringling, Stephen King's "Christine" and John Lennon's Mercedes roadster. Also displayed are a collection of player pianos, music boxes, calliopes and band organs. Allow 1 hour, 30 minutes minimum. Daily 9-6. Guided tours begin every 30 minutes. Admission $8.50; senior citizens $7.65; ages 6-12, $4. AE, MC, VI. Phone (941) 355-6228.

[SAVE] **SARASOTA JUNGLE GARDENS** is .25 mi. w. of US 41 via Myrtle St., at 3701 Bayshore Rd. Trails wind through a 10-acre tropical jungle of palms, flowering shrubs and unusual plants. The Flamingo Lagoon contains flamingos, swans and native waterfowls. Leopards, alligators, wallabies, lemurs, monkeys, cockatoos and macaws are housed along the jungle trails. Reptile and bird shows are presented daily. The Gardens of Christ display hand-carved dioramas depicting the life of Jesus. Children's highlights include a petting area and a playground; pony rides are available on weekends. Food is available.

Allow 2 hours minimum. Daily 9-5; closed Dec. 25. Reptile shows are presented daily at noon, 2 and 4. Bird shows are presented daily on the half-hour. Admission $9; over 62, $8; ages 3-12, $5. AE, DS, MC, VI. Phone (941) 355-5305.

SELBY GALLERY, on the campus of Ringling School of Art and Design on Dr. Martin Luther King Jr. Way, just e. of 2700 N. Tamiami Trail, showcases exhibits by national and international artists and designers. Lectures and films are presented throughout the year. Allow 30 minutes minimum. Mon.-Sat. 10-4; closed holidays and between exhibits. Free. Phone (941) 359-7563.

SEBASTIAN (E-11)
pop. 10,200, elev. 19′

In July 1715 several ships were lost in Sebastian Inlet during a hurricane. The 1,500 men, women and children who survived formed a camp to recover for the Spanish Crown the gold and silver that had been lost to the sea. Their efforts were aided by Ais Indians in the area.

Sebastian River Area Chamber of Commerce: 700 Main St., Sebastian, FL 32958; phone (561) 589-5969.

McLARTY TREASURE MUSEUM, 5.25 mi. n. of CR 510 on SR A1A, is at the s. end of Sebastian Inlet State Recreation Area *(see Recreation Chart).* The museum's historical displays include artifacts and a diorama of the 1715 *Spanish Plate Fleet* and the shipwreck survivors' camp, including salvage materials. An audiovisual presentation highlights the modern-day treasure salvaging operations off the coast. Allow 1 hour minimum. Daily 10-4:30. Last show begins 1 hour, 15 minutes before closing. Admission $1, under 5 free. Phone (561) 589-2147.

SEBRING (F-10) pop. 8,900, elev. 160′

Sebring (SEE-bring) boasts some of the state's largest groves of citrus, lime and avocado trees.

Sebring International Raceway plays host to automobile races; phone (800) 626-7223.

Medal of Honor Park, on US 27 at the Agricultural Center, is an outside memorial dedicated to veterans.

Sebring Chamber of Commerce: 309 South Circle, Sebring, FL 33870; phone (863) 385-8448.

THE CHILDREN'S MUSEUM OF THE HIGHLANDS, 219 N. Ridgewood Dr., has a child-size supermarket complete with shopping carts, a scanner and a cash register. Other hands-on exhibits include a bank and a television station. Children can make music, paint their faces and make huge bubbles using materials provided by the museum. Allow 1 hour, 30 minutes minimum. Tues.-Sat. 10-5 (also Thurs. 5-8); closed Jan. 1, Thanksgiving and Dec. 24-25. Admission $2. Children must be with an adult. Phone (863) 385-5437.

HIGHLANDS HAMMOCK STATE PARK, 3.5 mi. w. of US 27 on CR 634, is a 8,133-acre wilderness of lush vegetation, dense jungle and swamps, all accessible by an excellent system of paved drives and well-marked trails. Trees range in age from more than 400 years to nearly 1,000 years. Ranger-narrated tram tours are available with a minimum of five persons; inquire at the ranger station. The Florida State Civilian Conservation Corps Museum features displays about animals and plants native to the area.

Park rangers conduct nature programs on Thursday evenings, November-April. Slide presentations about a variety of topics are offered on Saturday evenings. Food is available during winter months. Park open daily 8-dusk (also open Fri.-Sat. dusk-10 p.m. for camper check-in, Oct.-May). Museum open daily 8-5. Nature walk Mon. at 10, Nov.-Apr. Admission $3.25 per private vehicle (maximum of eight people), $1 per person arriving by bicycle or on foot. Phone (863) 386-6094. *See Recreation Chart and the AAA Southeastern CampBook.*

SINGER ISLAND (F-12)

Known for its wide beaches and proximity to the Gulf Stream a mile away, Singer Island was owned in the 1920s by Paris Singer, son of the sewing machine magnate. He planned to develop the island as Palm Beach had been, but it became the property of one of Singer's ex-wives, who did not appreciate its potential. The island now supports a resort community.

JOHN D. MACARTHUR BEACH STATE PARK is on SR A1A. The park is 1.75 mi. s. of jct. US 1, SR A1A and SR 786 or 3 mi. n. of jct. US 1, SR A1A and SR 708. Sandwiched between the Atlantic Ocean and Lake Worth, the park features nature trails and a 1,600-foot-long footbridge over a cove to sand dunes. Free tram service from the parking lot to the beach front is avail-

able daily 10-4. Snorkeling (must have a dive flag), swimming, fishing and picnic sites also are available. The nature center has exhibits about ecology and area flora and fauna and presents a movie about this ecosystem.

Allow 1 hour, 30 minutes minimum. Park open daily 8-dusk. Nature center open Wed.-Mon. 9-5. Admission $3.25 per private vehicle (maximum eight people), $1 per person arriving by bicycle or on foot. Phone (561) 624-6950. *See Recreation Chart.*

STARKE (B-8) pop. 5,200, elev. 150'

CAMP BLANDING WORLD WAR II MUSEUM AND MEMORIAL PARK is 8.5 mi. e. of jct. US 301 on SR 16, at the main gate of Camp Blanding. The museum, housed in a refurbished World War II barracks, contains photographs, artifacts and exhibits honoring the camp, which was a major training center during World War II, and those who trained there.

Outdoor exhibits include weapon and vehicle displays as well as monuments and memorials to individuals, groups and divisions who served in World War II and other conflicts during the 20th century. Tours are available. Allow 1 hour minimum. Daily noon-4; closed holidays. Donations. Phone (904) 682-3196.

STUART (F-11) pop. 11,900, elev. 12'

Stuart is known by boating enthusiasts as the eastern terminus of the Okeechobee Waterway, which crosses the state to the Gulf of Mexico. Fishing is excellent in nearby Indian River as well as in the Gulf Stream about 10 miles offshore, where larger species, especially sailfish, are caught.

At nearby Jensen Beach during June and July, approximately 6,000 sea turtles can be observed making their annual nesting journey from ocean to shore and back. The turtles should not be disturbed. The Jensen Beach Chamber of Commerce can make reservations for turtle watches; phone (561) 334-3444.

Stuart/Martin County Chamber of Commerce: 1650 S. Kanner Hwy., Stuart, FL 34994; phone (561) 287-1011.

Self-guiding tours: The chamber of commerce provides a walking tour map of downtown.

ELLIOTT MUSEUM is on Hutchinson Island, 4.5 mi. n.e. of US 1 on SR A1A. The museum houses the many inventions and patents of Sterling Elliott and his son. The Americana Wing contains turn-of-the-20th-century shops, including barber, apothecary and tobacco shops and an ice cream parlor. A hand-carved miniature circus is displayed. Other galleries house antique bicycles, autographed memorabilia from Baseball Hall of Fame members and vintage cars, including a 1926 Bugatti Grand Prix race car.

Allow 1 hour minimum. Daily 10-4; closed Jan. 1, Easter, July 4, Thanksgiving and Dec. 25. Admission $6; ages 6-13, $2. Phone (561) 225-1961.

GILBERT'S BAR HOUSE OF REFUGE MUSEUM, on Hutchinson Island, is 4 mi. n.e. via SR A1A, then 1.25 mi. e. through Indian River Plantation Resort. The restored 1875 lifesaving station houses a museum of nautical and marine history. A restored boathouse contains a maritime exhibit. Allow 30 minutes minimum. Daily 10-4; closed July 4 and Dec. 25. Admission $4; ages 6-12, $2. Phone (561) 225-1875.

SUGARLOAF KEY—
see The Florida Keys p. 69.

TALLAHASSEE (B-5)
pop. 124,800, elev. 216′

Tallahassee (tal-a-HASS-ee) became the site of Florida government in 1823, 2 years after the territory became part of the United States. A convention in 1861 declared Florida an independent nation and a member of the Confederate States of America. In 1865 during the Civil War, Confederate Floridian soldiers repelled Union forces at the Battle of Natural Bridge *(see place listing p. 235)* to protect Tallahassee, making it the only uncaptured Confederate capital east of the Mississippi River.

The oldest building in the city is the Columns, begun in 1830 by wealthy banker William "Money" Williams. It served as the focal point of financial, political and social development in the state's early history and was saved from demolition by being moved to 100 N. Duval St. in 1973.

The Governor's Mansion at Brevard and Adams streets is open for tours during legislative sessions and the Christmas season. Highlights include hollowware from the battleship USS *Florida* and French impressionist paintings. Another historic landmark is Union Bank at 295 Apalachee Pkwy. The oldest surviving bank building in the state, the

restored 1841 structure contains displays about the history of Florida banking and the history of the bank and its restoration.

In a region of rolling hills, live oak forests and rivers, Tallahassee has beautiful gardens and large lakes. The city also is noted for its many canopy roads; Miccosukee, Centerville, Meridian and Old Bainbridge are just a few of the protected roads. In addition to being the home of Florida A&M University, Florida State University is on a 347-acre campus slightly west of downtown.

Tallahassee Little Theatre presents comedic and dramatic productions from September to July. Both evening and matinee performances are offered; phone (850) 224-8474.

The Flying High Circus offers collegiate performances under Florida State University's big top in April.

Tallahassee Area Convention and Visitors Bureau: 106 E. Jefferson St., Tallahassee, FL 32301; phone (850) 413-9200 or (800) 628-2866.

Shopping areas: Among the 140 stores at Governors Square Mall, 1500 Apalachee Pkwy., are Burdines, Dillard's, JCPenney and Sears. Tallahassee Mall, 2415 N. Monroe St., features Dillard's and Parisian among its 90 stores. Antique stores and art galleries line Main Street in downtown Havana, a small town 13 miles north of Tallahassee.

ALFRED B. MACLAY STATE GARDENS, 1 mi. n. of I-10 exit 30 on US 319, consists of 307 acres and is the focal point of a state park. New York businessman Alfred B. Maclay and his wife Louise began the gardens in 1923 on the grounds of their southern estate. The gardens contain colorful azaleas, camellias and Oriental magnolias as well as many native plants. The Maclay House has restored living and dining rooms and serves as a center for information about camellias.

Allow 1 hour minimum. Park open daily 8-dusk. Gardens open daily 9-5. House open

---

daily 9-5, Jan.-Apr. Park admission $3.25 per private vehicle (maximum eight people, $1 extra for every person over the maximum), $1 per person arriving by bicycle, motorcycle or on foot. Gardens (includes house) $3; ages 6-12, $1.50, Jan.-Apr.; free rest of year. DS, MC, VI. Phone (850) 487-4556. *See Recreation Chart.*

BLACK ARCHIVES RESEARCH CENTER AND MUSEUM is on the Florida A&M University campus, off Monroe St. between Gaines St. and Orange Ave. Housed in the 1907 Carnegie Library, the oldest building on campus, the museum contains artifacts, photographs, manuscripts, art works, oral history tapes and rare maps that document the history and culture of Africans and African Americans. A visitor parking permit is available at the campus police department on Wahnish Way. Allow 1 hour minimum. Mon.-Fri. 9-4; closed holidays. Free. Phone (850) 599-3020.

EDWARD BALL WAKULLA SPRINGS STATE PARK — *see Wakulla p. 230.*

FLORIDA STATE CAPITOL, S. Adams St., is a 22-story tower with house and senate chambers on either side, both with public viewing galleries. There is an observation deck on the top floor and a Florida information center just inside the west plaza entrance. Florida's legislature is in session from March through April. Guided tours are available all week. On weekends and holidays visitors must be with a guided tour.

Allow 1 hour minimum. Building open Mon.-Fri. 8-5; closed Jan. 1, Easter, Labor Day, Thanksgiving and Dec. 25. Free. Phone (850) 488-6167.

THE KNOTT HOUSE MUSEUM, 301 E. Park Ave., was built in 1843 as a private home. This stately house has been restored and is fully furnished with the Victorian pieces owned by the Knott family when they bought the house in 1928. After viewing an 8-minute videotape about the history of the house and the Knott family, visitors are taken on a narrated guided tour of the house. Tours are given on the hour Wed.-Fri. 1-4, Sat. 10-4; closed holidays. Free. Phone (850) 922-2459.

LAKE JACKSON MOUNDS STATE ARCHAEOLOGICAL SITE is 2 mi. n. of I-10 at the s. tip of Lake Jackson. The mounds are remains of a ceremonial center that existed A.D. 1200-1500. Six earth temple mounds are within the site. Daily 8-dusk. Admission $2 per private vehicle, $1 per person arriving by bicycle or on foot. Phone (850) 922-6007.

MISSION SAN LUIS is 2 blks. n. of US 90 at 2020 Mission Rd. Marked trails connect re-created dwellings and other structures on this hilly, oak-shaded site, home to a Spanish-Indian village 1656-1704. Mon.-Fri. 9-4:30, Sat. 10-4:30, Sun. and most holidays noon-4:30; closed

Thanksgiving and Dec. 25. Donations. Phone (850) 487-3711.

MUSEUM OF FLORIDA HISTORY, in the R.A. Gray Building at 500 S. Bronough St., has exhibits depicting Florida's colorful past. Visitors can view a mastodon skeleton and a giant armadillo mannequin from the Pleistocene era, gold and silver from Spanish shipwrecks, the actual flags flown during the Civil War, a partial replica of a Florida steamboat and various artifacts from the changing gallery. Special event tours and educational programs also are featured.

Allow 30 minutes minimum. Mon.-Fri. 9-4:30, Sat. 10-4:30, Sun. and holidays noon-4:30; closed Thanksgiving and Dec. 25. Donations. Phone (850) 488-1484.

SAVE **ODYSSEY SCIENCE CENTER AND TALLAHASSEE MUSEUM OF ART,** 350 S. Duval St., houses an art museum and interactive educational displays. The museum portion features a broad range of works from many cultures and time periods, and includes one of the largest collections of artwork by untrained amateurs—often called "outsider" art.

In the science center, children can explore models of a TV weather station and a planetarium, as well as exhibits on energy and the region's hydrology. Museum and science center open Mon.-Sat. 10-5, Sun. 1-5; closed holidays. Museum/science center admission $6; over 61 and under 17, $3.50. Phone (850) 513-0700.

THE OLD CAPITOL, jct. Monroe St. and Apalachee Pkwy., has been restored to its 1902 appearance. Interpretive exhibits depict periods of Florida history, including territorial Florida history, the years between statehood and secession and the Bourbon era. Self-guiding tours of the building cover the house and senate chambers, the governor's suite, the supreme court and the rotunda. Special educational programs also are featured. Allow 30 minutes minimum. Mon.-Fri. 9-4:30, Sat. 10-4:30, Sun. and holidays noon-4:30; closed Thanksgiving and Dec. 25. Donations. Phone (850) 487-1902.

SAVE **TALLAHASSEE MUSEUM OF HISTORY AND NATURAL SCIENCE,** 6.5 mi. s.w. at Lake Bradford, depicts north Florida's natural and human history. A trail winds through 52 acres of woodlands, cypress swamp and old fields, which are home to more than 100 indigenous animals. Also on the grounds are a restored 1880s farm complex; the antebellum home of the great-grandniece of George Washington; a one-room schoolhouse; a church; a gristmill and a caboose. Picnic facilities are available.

Allow 2 hours minimum. Mon.-Sat. 9-5, Sun. 12:30-5. Admission $6; over 62, $5.50; ages 4-15, $4. MC, VI. Phone (850) 576-1636.

Precautions Can Save A Vacation!

*T*ravelers are faced with the task of protecting themselves while in a strange environment. Although there is no way to guarantee absolute protection from crime, the experts—law enforcement officials—advise travelers to take a proactive approach to securing their property and ensuring their safety.

 Make sure the hotel desk clerk does not announce your room number; if he/she does, quietly request a new room assignment.

Ask front desk personnel which areas of town to avoid and what, if any, special precautions should be taken when driving a rental car (some criminals target tourists driving rental cars).

Never open the door to a stranger; use the peephole and request identification. If you are still unsure, call the front desk to verify the identity of the person and the purpose of his/her visit.

Carry money separately from credit cards or use a "fanny pack." Carry your purse close to your body and your wallet in an inside coat or front trouser pocket. Never leave luggage unattended, and use your business address, if possible, on luggage tags.

Beware of distractions staged by would-be scam artists, especially groups of children that surround you, or a stranger who accidentally spills something on you. They may be lifting your wallet.

If using an automatic teller machine (ATM), choose one in a well-lit area with plenty of foot traffic, such as one at a grocery store. Law enforcement officials suggest that machines inside establishments are generally safer to use.

Use room safes or safety deposit boxes provided by the hotel. Store all valuables out of sight, even when you are in the room.

Law enforcement agencies consider card-key (electronic) door locks the most secure.

Tampa Bay
including St. Petersburg and Tampa

Population:
St. Petersburg 238,600   Tampa 280,000
Elevation:
St. Petersburg 45 ft.   Tampa 27 ft.

Popular Spots:

Busch Gardens Tampa Bay .....(see p. 213)

Salvador Dali Museum ....(see p. 213)

With the world's tourism mecca—Orlando—just 70 miles up the road, it's easy to overlook the cities by the bay as major travel destinations. But Tampa, St. Petersburg, Clearwater and their adjoining communities have a great deal to offer the visitor. And yes, there's a theme park here, too: Busch Gardens Tampa Bay preceded Walt Disney's dream by 12 years.

But there are also some things Mickey and friends don't have. Stretching for almost 30 miles from Crystal Beach south to Fort DeSoto Park are the Gulf Coast's broad, graceful, white-sand beaches—some of the prettiest in the country. With varied cultural offerings, water recreation opportunities and savory Spanish- and Cuban-influenced cuisine, Tampa Bay merits a closer look.

Spanish explorer Hernando de Soto apparently agreed when he led a band of men ashore on the southern Pinellas coast in 1539. But de Soto wasn't the first foreign visitor. Fellow countryman Panfilo de Narváez had stopped off 11 years earlier, and some historians believe that Juan Ponce de Léon may have come ashore as early as 1513.

Yet the Timucuan and Tocobega tribes inhabited the area centuries before the first Spaniards arrived. The Pinellas Peninsula takes its name from the Spanish phrase meaning "point of pines," and the city of Clearwater borrowed from the Tocobegan word *pocotopaug,* "clear water."

But the name "Tampa" is a cartographic typo. Local American Indians called their village *Tanpa,* meaning "sticks of fire" (an allusion to the lightning so common in central Florida), but the area's first maps read "Tampa."

During the 18th century the bay belonged to pirates who left a decided influence on the area. One of them, the legendary Jose Gaspar, may have pillaged and kidnapped his way to annual celebrity—Tampa's first Gasparilla Pirate Festival was held in 1904, and the weeklong extravaganza continues each February. The area's NFL team, the Tampa Bay Buccaneers, also takes its name from this era.

In 1824 the U.S. Army arrived to establish Fort Brooke. Tampa was chartered within a decade and became the center of the Florida territory's cattle industry due to nearby pastureland and convenient water transportation. The Civil War interrupted growth; the defenseless settlement was shelled by Union troops and ravaged by a yellow fever epidemic in the early 1870s. Prosperity returned when railroad tycoon Henry B. Plant brought his South Florida Railroad to town in 1884. Plant also built several deep-water piers, setting the stage for the city's development as a port.

Meanwhile, Dr. Odet Philippe arrived on the Pinellas Peninsula in the mid-1830s. Philippe

Getting There —starting on p. 206

Getting Around — starting on p. 207

What To See — starting on p. 208

What To Do — starting on p. 217

Where To Stay — starting on p. 811

Where To Dine — starting on p. 815

brought with him Bahamian citrus stock and planted the area's first groves at what is now Safety Harbor. Nearby Clearwater took shape after the 1841 establishment of Fort Harrison; the town was incorporated in 1891, 3 years after Russian immigrant Peter A. Demens brought his Orange Belt Railroad through en route to St. Petersburg. Following the 1894-95 freeze (which damaged local citrus groves), Plant took over the railroad and in 1896 built the Gulf Coast's first luxury hotel, the Belleview. Shortly thereafter wealthy winter residents built estates overlooking Clearwater Harbor.

St. Petersburg saw its first influx of homesteaders around 1856. Union blockaders forced inhabitants across the bay during the Civil War, yet farmers and fishermen trickled back to the peninsula following the war, and citrus groves were planted. About the time Plant was making tracks to Tampa, Demens' Orange Belt Railroad arrived. He named the city for his Russian birthplace, and St. Petersburg was incorporated in 1892. Although somewhat isolated, it became a popular winter resort.

Tampa, however, maintained a developmental edge. By 1890 the Ybor City cigar industry was booming, and sponge beds were found in gulf waters near Tarpon Springs; Greek immigrants arrived by the hundreds to cultivate them. Railroads stimulated the tourist trade, and the area attracted wealthy Northern vacationers. The exclusive Tampa Bay Hotel, now part of the University of Tampa, was built by Plant in an effort to outdo railroad rival Henry Flagler, who was developing a string of luxury properties southward down Florida's east coast. The hotel's 1891

opening was attended by royalty, financial bigwigs and luminaries.

With the outbreak of the Spanish-American War in 1898 came another group of visitors—the U.S. military. Theodore Roosevelt and his Rough Riders set up camp in Tampa and staged their Cuban invasion from the port on Old Tampa Bay.

Tampa's population grew to nearly 16,000 by 1900—after Jacksonville, it was the state's largest city. The cigar industry peaked shortly before World War I, but cigar makers continued to produce high-quality, handmade Havanas. Most of the '20s roared by in a series of successive land booms. During this period O.H. Platt developed Tampa's first subdivision—the stately Victorian homes comprising Hyde Park, west of the Hillsborough River. David P. Davis, meanwhile, reclaimed the land south of downtown known as the Davis Islands. These man-made islands were a showcase of winding streets, substantial homes and ornamental landscaping.

By 1934 two bridges—the Gandy and the Courtney Campbell—linked Tampa with St.

Petersburg and Clearwater respectively, establishing the Pinellas Peninsula as a major travel destination in its own right. (A third, the Howard Frankland Bridge, opened in 1960.) Tampa's MacDill Air Force Base received its first troops in 1940, and the port became an important shipbuilding center during World War II.

Cigars were once the city's mainstay, and brick and frame buildings housing such companies as the Hav-a-Tampa Cigar Factory and the Cuesta-Rey Cigar Factory provided employment for Spanish and Cuban immigrants who labored at long tables hand-rolling tobacco leaves. Cigars are still produced, but the area business community has diversified. Tourism has the biggest economic impact—visitors spend some $1.9 billion here every year—but varied industries include electronic equipment and biomedical manufacturing, citrus canning, shrimping, paint production, brewing, phosphate mining, transportation and finance and government sectors.

Tampa is the foremost port of Florida's west coast and one of the nation's busiest. The port's strategic location contributes to some 93,000 jobs and $10.6 billion each year to the local economy.

Tampa Bay also is known to some as "Technology Bay." Fifteen percent of Florida's high-tech employees live and work in the bay area at such firms as AT&T Paradyne, General Electric, GTE, Honeywell Avionics, Johnson & Johnson, Verizon and Unisys, and the Home Shopping Network's headquarters are in St. Petersburg. The bay area is home to, in whole or in part,

nearly 200 of the nation's Fortune 500 companies, and 23 percent of Florida's biomedical manufacturing takes place in the Tampa metropolitan area.

Architecturally, Tampa admirably records the different periods of its growth. Older stucco homes with flat roofs, patios and wrought-iron balconies show a marked Spanish influence. Scattered throughout the central city are old frame dwellings and compact single-story bungalows surrounded by moss-draped oaks, towering palms and blooming hibiscus.

Tampa's vertical profile was fairly thin before the building boom of the 1980s and early 1990s. The addition of Tampa Convention Center, Tampa Bay Performing Arts Center (TBPAC) and several office skyscrapers heightened the city's once modest business district to a stature worthy of more established corporate centers. Adding an exotic—albeit low-lying—touch to the lofty skyscrapers are the bulbous silver-domed minarets and intricate Moorish accents of the University of Tampa.

The 1990s have brought further development. A $110 million expansion enhanced the Tampa International Airport, and next door to the Florida Aquarium, the Garrison Seaport Center is taking shape as a dining, shopping and entertainment complex centered on the new cruise ship terminals; a recent addition to the complex is the Seaport Street Terminal.

The Tampa Bay area's blend of big-time industry and leisure pursuits proves to be a combination that works.

The Informed Traveler

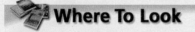

Whom To Call

Emergency: 911

Police (non-emergency): *St. Petersburg:* (727) 893-7780; Sheriff (727) 582-6200. *Tampa:* (813) 273-0770; Sheriff (813) 247-8200.

Fire: *St. Petersburg:* (727) 893-7694; *Tampa:* (813) 227-7015.

Hospitals: *St. Petersburg:* Bayfront Medical Center, (727) 823-1234; St. Anthony's, (727) 825-1100. *Tampa:* St. Joseph's Hospital, (813) 870-4000; Tampa General Healthcare, (813) 251-7000.

Where To Look

Newspapers

The area is served by two daily newspapers, the *St. Petersburg Times* and *The Tampa Tribune*. Several publications with smaller circulations serve local areas; one such paper is the tri-lingual *La Gaceta*.

Radio

WUSF (89.7 FM) is a member of National Public Radio.

Visitor Information

Visitors to **St. Petersburg** can obtain information, maps and brochures from the St. Petersburg Chamber of Commerce at 100 Second Ave. N., St. Petersburg, FL 33701; phone (727) 821-4715. It is open Mon.-Fri. 8-5. An information center at The Pier is open Mon.-Sat. 10-8, Sun. 11-6; phone (727) 821-6164. Suncoast Welcome Center is open daily 9-5; closed Jan. 1, Easter, Thanksgiving and Dec. 25. For information write 2001 Ulmerton Rd., Clearwater, FL 33762; phone (727) 573-1449.

For visitors to **Tampa**, information about touring the area is available Mon.-Sat. 9-5 from Tampa/Hillsborough Convention and Visitors Association, 400 N. Tampa St., Suite 1010, Tampa, FL 33602; phone (813) 223-1111.

What To Pack

Winter temperatures in the Tampa Bay area rarely fall below freezing. Skies are mostly sunny, and humidity is moderate. However, from May into October highs hover around 90 degrees. The "heat index" reading—a combination of heat and the relative humidity—may make it feel more like 100. Afternoon thunderstorms offer relief but can be dangerous, capable of producing high winds, lightning, driving rain,

local flooding, occasional hail and, possibly, tornadoes. *For additional information see temperature chart p. 43.*

Even though **Tampa** is more businesslike than **St. Petersburg** and Clearwater when it comes to attire, dress tends to be informal. Few restaurants require a jacket and tie, and most nightspots are decidedly casual. When sightseeing, dress for comfort.

Sales tax: Sales tax is 6.75 percent in Hillsborough County, 7 percent in Pinellas County and 6 percent in Pasco County. An accommodations tax is 5 percent in Hillsborough County and 4 percent in Pinellas County.

Destination Tampa-St. Petersburg

*T*he Tampa Bay area has all the ingredients for one heck of a vacation.

*T*here are theme and water parks for the active crowd; world-class museums for the culturally inclined; recreational pursuits for athletic types; and shopping and spectator sports for everyone in between.

The Pier, St. Petersburg.
Fishing, boutique shopping, dining, miniature golfing, a panoramic view—this landmark has it all. (See listing page 213)

Bayshore Boulevard, Tampa. Following the curve of Hillsborough Bay, the boulevard's scenic sidewalk is a favorite with joggers, cyclists and inline skaters.

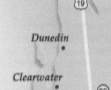

*P*laces included in this AAA Destination City:

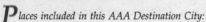

Tarpon Springs

19

Dunedin

Clearwater

60

Indian Rocks Beach

Largo

Indian Shores

Madeira Beach

St. Pete Beach

Salvador Dali Museum, St. Petersburg.
Get surreal! A diverse collection of the
Spanish artist's works is on display.
(See listing page 213)

• *Dade City*

75

301

54

275

301   39

Thonotosassa

75

4   *Plant
City*

60

275

Tampa

*Apollo
Beach*

**St.
Petersburg**

75

Tampa Bay Buccaneers.
The Bucs bring exciting NFL action
to the Tampa Bay area at the new
Raymond James Stadium.

See Vicinity map page 210

Busch Gardens Tampa Bay.
Gwazi, Montu, Kumba—Check out the latest
in roller coasters at this African-themed
family entertainment park.
(See listing page 213)

Getting There

By Car

When approaching *St. Petersburg* from the north, take I-75 and US 19. I-75, the fast freeway route, merges with other routes in Tampa and becomes I-275 as it heads for St. Petersburg over the Howard Frankland Bridge. Divided US 19 and two-lane US 19A diverge at Tarpon Springs to offer a choice of slower approaches from the northern Gulf Coast.

Coming from the south on I-75, US 19 and I-275, enter *St. Petersburg* over the mouth of Tampa Bay via the Sunshine Skyway Bridge (toll). Approaching from the east, I-4 provides direct access to the I-275/ Howard Frankland Bridge into St. Petersburg.

The major direct route to *Tampa* from the north is I-75, which traverses Florida's north-central lake district: The 62-mile stretch south of Wildwood is especially scenic. It is roughly paralleled by US 301 on the east and US 41 on the west. North of downtown I-75 changes to I-275, which merges with I-4 in mid-city. I-75 bypasses the city proper to the east, rejoining I-275 north of Bradenton.

Driving into *Tampa* from the south, US 41 parallels I-75, the main corridor from the southern Gulf Coast. From Daytona Beach in the east, I-4 angles across central Florida through Orlando, while older US 92 runs parallel from Lakeland. SR 60, a four-lane, divided highway, leads from Lake Wales. Running from the Gulf Coast west of Tampa, SR 60 connects to Clearwater, and I-275 travels to St. Petersburg.

Air Travel

Commercial flights entering *Tampa* land at Tampa International Airport. Several commercial airlines and privately-owned planes use St. Petersburg-Clearwater International Airport. Private and corporate planes have access to Albert Whitted Airport in *St. Petersburg*. The Peter O. Knight Airport in Tampa serves general aviation.

Tampa International Airport is on the city's west side along Old Tampa Bay. To reach downtown *Tampa*, take Memorial Highway about a mile

south to I-275 (Tampa Expressway). Then head north on I-275—though you'll actually be traveling east—and take the Ashley Street exit. Past this exit I-275 turns sharply northward, bisecting the city. Continue along I-275 to reach such destinations as the University of South Florida and Busch Gardens Tampa Bay. Exit to I-4 east if you're heading for Ybor City, Plant City or Lakeland. Or take a cab: United and Yellow cabs

© 2000 maps.com

provide service from the airport. Average fare to downtown (about 6 miles) is about $17.

To reach downtown **St. Petersburg**, take Memorial Highway south to I-275 south. Cross the bay on the 7-mile Howard Frankland Bridge and proceed another 10 miles or so due south. From I-275, take I-375 into the northern half of downtown or I-175 into the southern half. Transportation from Tampa International to St. Petersburg is easily acquired. The Limo provides transfers from Tampa International to St. Petersburg and other Tampa Bay-area cities; phone (727) 572-1111. Share Ride limousine fare to St. Petersburg is $15; ages 3-11, $8. Central Florida Limousine, (813) 396-3730, also provides transfers from the airport to most points in Hillsborough and Polk counties.

St. Petersburg-Clearwater International Airport is about 10 miles across the bay from Tampa on SR 686 (Roosevelt Boulevard), near the west side of the Howard Frankland Bridge. Airport traffic exits northwest toward Clearwater or south, providing access to St. Petersburg and Tampa. To reach Clearwater, take SR 686 about 3 miles west to US 19, US 19 another 3 miles north to SR 60 (Gulf-to-Bay Boulevard), then SR 60 a mile or so west into town. Downtown St. Petersburg is about 10 miles due south of the airport via I-275. To get to the interstate, exit south from the airport on SR 686 to SR 688 (Ulmerton Road). Go a mile or so east to another segment of SR 686 and take it a mile south to I-275.

Hertz, which offers discounts to AAA members, is at Tampa International Airport, (813) 874-3232; St. Petersburg-Clearwater International Airport, (727) 531-3774; and at St. Pete Beach, (727) 360-1631; or phone (800) 654-3080. Check the telephone directory for other agencies.

Rail Service

Tampa's Amtrak station is at 601 N. Nebraska Ave. in downtown Tampa, behind historic Union Station. Daily service is offered; phone (813) 221-7600 or (800) 872-7245. Buses from *St. Petersburg* to the Amtrak station leave ParkSide Mall, Suite 324, 7200 US 19N; phone (727) 522-9475 for schedule.

Bus service to Union Station also is available via several HARTLine routes; phone (813) 254-4278. In addition, the Pinellas Suncoast Transit Authority maintains two bus routes to the terminal: The 100X runs from Gateway Mall, Ninth Street N. and 77th Avenue, and the 200X runs from Clearwater Mall, US 19 and Gulf to Bay Boulevard. For schedules phone (727) 530-9911.

Buses

Greyhound Lines Inc. is at 180 Ninth St. N. in *St. Petersburg* and 610 E. Polk St. in *Tampa;* phone (800) 231-2222.

Getting Around

Street System

St. Petersburg's street system is essentially a compass-oriented grid. All avenues, terraces and places run east-west; streets and ways run north-south. Central Avenue (CR 150) is the north-south divider; parallel to Tampa Bay is First Street. Numbering of north-south streets begins at the bay and progresses westward 81 blocks to Boca Ciega Bay on the Gulf.

From I-275, I-375 accesses the northern half of downtown *St. Petersburg* and I-175 the southern half. US 92 (Fourth Street) and SR 689 (Ninth Street) provide downtown access from I-275 as well.

Downtown *Tampa* is bracketed by water and has only a few major access routes. From I-275, take the Ashley Street exit. Also from the north, SR 45 (Nebraska Avenue) and one-way US 41 Bus. Rte. lead into downtown. Cass Street approaches from the west. From the east, use SR 60 (John F. Kennedy Boulevard).

Tampa also is laid out in a basic grid, with a few geographic variations. US 41 Bus. Rte. (Florida Avenue) divides east from west; John F. Kennedy Boulevard/Frank Adamo Drive (SR 60) separates north from south. Many streets in the downtown area are one way.

Five major east-west thoroughfares support cross-town traffic: SR 582 (Fowler Avenue), SR

580 (Busch Boulevard), US 92/US 41 (Hillsborough Avenue), SR 574 (Martin Luther King Jr. Boulevard), and the South Crosstown Expressway (toll). Three others parallel I-275: on the west, SR 597/SR 580/US 92 (Dale Mabry Highway); through the central city, US 41/SR 45 (Nebraska Avenue); and on the east, SR 583 (56th Street).

Besides I-275, US 19 and US 19 Alt. are the main north-south routes on the Pinellas Peninsula. Congested SR 699 (Gulf Boulevard), lined with shops, restaurants and motels, connects the beach communities from Clearwater Beach south to St. Pete Beach. Running east-west are SR 60 (Gulf-to-Bay Boulevard/Courtney Campbell Causeway) to Clearwater, SR 688 (Ulmerton Road) to the beaches, and SR 694/CR 694 (Gandy Boulevard/Park Boulevard) through the communities of Pinellas Park and Seminole to the beaches.

Generally, downtown speed limits for both *St. Petersburg* and *Tampa* are 30 mph or as posted. Unless otherwise posted, a right turn is allowed on a red light after a complete stop. It is best to avoid taking an unfamiliar route during rush hours (about 7 to 9 a.m. and 4:30 to 6 p.m.).

Parking

St. Petersburg and *Tampa* both have limited on-street parking in the downtown business sections and along major thoroughfares. Rates for municipal parking garages start at 90c per hour and range from $5.40 to $7 for 6-24 hours. Metered lot parking and use of the Old Fort Brooke

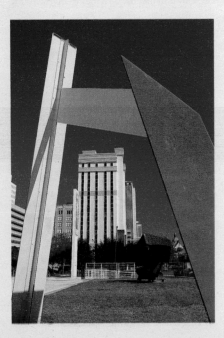

parking garage in Tampa cost $1.25 per hour (if using the garage for 6-24 hours, the rate is $7).

Metered parking at the beaches is available on the street and in lots at 25c-$1 per hour; beach parking is not allowed. For additional parking information phone (813) 274-8179.

Taxis and Limousines

Companies include *Tampa*-based United Cab Co., Tampa Bay Cab and Taxi Plus, all at (813) 253-2424; and Yellow Cab Co., (813) 253-0121 in Tampa and (727) 821-7777 in *St. Petersburg.*

Taxis are metered. Most *St. Petersburg* cabs charge $1.50 to enter and $1.60 per mile; most *Tampa* cabs are $1.25 to enter and $1.75 per mile. Limousine service averages $40-$50 per hour in the Tampa Bay area.

Public Transportation

Pinellas Suncoast Transit Authority serves *St. Petersburg* and Pinellas County; for bus fares and schedules phone (727) 530-9911. HARTLine serves *Tampa* and its immediate suburbs; for fares and schedules phone (813) 254-4278.

What To See

ST. PETERSBURG

See map page 210.

BOYD HILL NATURE PARK, 1101 Country Club Way S., is reached by taking I-275 exit 4, 1.75 mi. e. on 54th Ave. to Martin Luther King St., n. to Country Club Way, then w. 2 blks. This 245-acre preserve on the west side of Lake Maggiore has nature trails and boardwalks. The Nature Center offers interpretive displays, an aquarium and birds of prey exhibits. A 90-minute guided tram tour is offered daily at 1.

Picnic facilities, bicycle trails, nature trails and guided walks are available; nighttime hikes are offered the second Monday of the month. Allow 1 hour, 30 minutes minimum. Daily 9-5 (also Tues. and Thurs. 5-8, during DST); closed Thanksgiving and Dec. 25. Admission $1; under 18, 50c. Tram tour $2; under 18, $1.50. Phone (727) 893-7326.

Lake Maggiore Park, Ninth St. and 30th Ave. S., covers 721 acres around Lake Maggiore. Fishing and picnic facilities as well as bicycle trails are available. Daily dawn-dusk. Free.

THE FLORIDA HOLOCAUST MUSEUM AND EDUCATIONAL CENTER, downtown at 55 Fifth St. S. at jct. First Ave. S., is one of the country's largest Holocaust museums. Eleven eternal flames, symbolizing the 11 million victims of the Nazis, are part of the three-story building's facade. The 12 sections of the permanent exhibit trace the Holocaust's beginnings in eastern Europe through the establishment of the state of Israel. The museum's centerpiece is one of the boxcars used to transport Jews and other prisoners to concentration/death camps; the car rests on a section of railroad track from the Treblinka camp.

Changing exhibits feature art, photography and artifacts related to the Holocaust, tolerance and understanding. Allow 2 hours minimum. Mon.-Fri. 10-5, Sat.-Sun. noon-5; closed Thanksgiving, Dec. 25 and Jewish holidays. Last admission 1 hour before closing. Admission $6; over 60 and students with ID $5; under 18, $2. AE, CB, DS, MC, VI. Phone (727) 820-0100. *See color ad p. 212.*

FLORIDA INTERNATIONAL MUSEUM is at 100 Second St. N. The 300,000-square-foot facility presents major international traveling exhibitions. Permanently displayed are more than 600 items relating to John F. Kennedy and the Kennedy family, as well as a re-creation of the West Wing of the White House. An audiotape tour is available. Garage parking is available at 218 Second Ave. N. Mon.-Sat. 9-6, Sun noon-6. Last admission 90 minutes before closing. Admission $13.95; over 64, $12.95; college students with ID $7.95; ages 6-18, $5.95. Parking $5. MC, VI. Phone (727) 822-3693 or (800) 777-9882. *See color ad p. 212.*

FORT DE SOTO PARK is off I-275 exit 4 at Pinellas Bayway; two toll causeways are crossed en route. The 1,136-acre park occupies five keys: Madeleine, St. Jean, St. Christopher, Bonne Fortune and Mullet. Plants and wildlife are protected; pets must be leashed. Daily dawn-dusk. Nature tours begin at various locations Sat.-Sun. at 10. Free. Toll 85c. Phone (727) 866-2484. *See Recreation Chart and the AAA Southeastern CampBook.*

Fort De Soto, on the southern end of Mullet Key, was begun during the Spanish-American War but was incomplete at war's end. Its guns never were fired in battle. There are walkways around the fort area. A pamphlet outlining a self-guiding tour along the Historical Trail is available. A 90-minute guided walking tour of the fort is offered Sat. at 10.

SAVE **GREAT EXPLORATIONS,** on the third floor of The Pier, 800 Second Ave. N.E., offers six pavilions of hands-on exhibits including Explore Galore, which is geared towards children under 7. VETerinary Office puts children in charge of a toy animal's exam, while Touch Tunnel challenges the senses in a pitch-black, 90-foot maze. Other exhibits focus on health and fitness; touch- and sound-activated art; and international displays. Changing programs and exhibits explore various facets of the arts and sciences.

Allow 1 hour minimum. Mon.-Sat. 10-8, Sun. 11-6. Admission $4; over 55, $2; under 3 free.

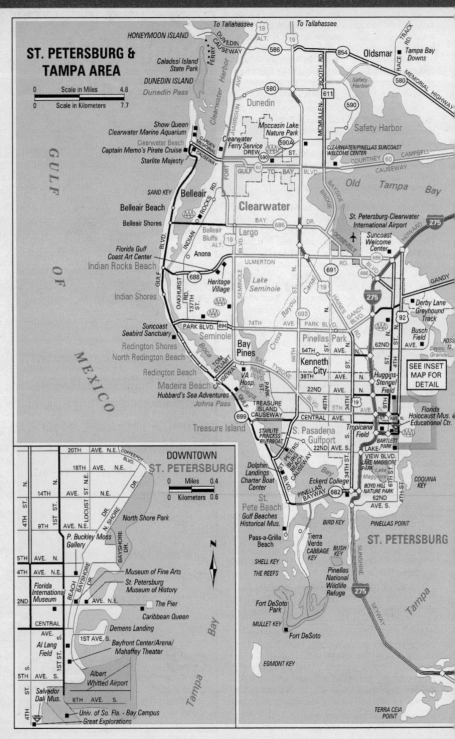

ST. PETERSBURG & TAMPA AREA

Scale in Miles   4.8
Scale in Kilometers   7.7

HONEYMOON ISLAND

To Tallahassee
To Tallahassee

Caladesi Island State Park

DUNEDIN ISLAND
Dunedin Pass

DUNEDIN CAUSEWAY

Oldsmar
Tampa Bay Downs

TRACK
RACE

Show Queen
Clearwater Marine Aquarium
Clearwater Beach
Captain Memo's Pirate Cruise
Starlite Majesty

Safety Harbor

MEMORIAL HIGHWAY

Dunedin

Moccasin Lake Nature Park

CLEARWATER/PINELLAS SUNCOAST WELCOME CENTER

Safety Harbor

Clearwater Ferry Service

CAMPBELL
COURTNEY CAUSEWAY

SAND KEY

Belleair

Belleair Beach

Belleair Shores

Clearwater

Clearwater Bay

Largo

St. Petersburg-Clearwater International Airport

Suncoast Welcome Center

Old Tampa Bay

Florida Gulf Coast Art Center
Indian Rocks Beach

Belleair Bluffs

Anona

Heritage Village

ULMERTON

Lake Seminole

Indian Shores

GANDY

Derby Lane Greyhound Track

Suncoast Seabird Sanctuary

Redington Shores
North Redington Beach
Redington Beach

Seminole

Bay Pines

Pinellas Park

Busch Field

PARK BLVD.
74TH
PARK BLVD.

Kenneth City

Huggins-Stengel Field

ROSS. IS.
Bayou Grande

Madeira Beach
Hubbard's Sea Adventures
Johns Pass

VA Hosp.

38TH

SEE INSET MAP FOR DETAIL

TREASURE ISLAND CAUSEWAY

22ND

Florida Holocaust Mus. Educational Ctr.

Treasure Island

CENTRAL   AVE.

Tropicana Field

Starlite Princess Riverboat

S. Pasadena   Gulfport
22ND AVE. S.

Bartlett Park

LAKE

VIEW BLVD.
LAKE MAGGIORE PARK
Lake Maggiore

COQUINA KEY

DOWNTOWN ST. PETERSBURG

Miles   0.4
Kilometers   0.6

20TH   AVE. N.E.
18TH   AVE. N.E.
14TH   AVE.   N.E.
COFFEEPOT BLVD.

North Shore Park

Dolphin Landings Charter Boat Center

Eckerd College

BOYD HILL NATURE PARK
62ND   AVE. S.

PINELLAS POINT

P. Buckley Moss Gallery

St. Pete Beach
Gulf Beaches Historical Mus.

BIRD KEY

ST. PETERSBURG

5TH   AVE. N.
4TH   AVE. N.E.

Museum of Fine Arts
St. Petersburg Museum of History

Pass-a-Grille Beach

Tierra Verde
CABBAGE KEY
BUSH KEY

Florida International Museum
2ND

The Pier

SHELL KEY

THE REEFS

Pinellas National Wildlife Refuge

CENTRAL   AVE.

Caribbean Queen

Demens Landing

Fort DeSoto Park

Al Lang Field

1ST AVE. S.
Bayfront Center/Arena/ Mahaffey Theater

MULLET KEY

5TH   AVE. S.

Albert Whitted Airport

Fort DeSoto

EGMONT KEY

Salvador Dali Mus.

8TH   AVE.   S.

Univ. of So. Fla. - Bay Campus
Great Explorations

TERRA CEIA POINT

Tampa Bay

SUNSHINE SKYWAY

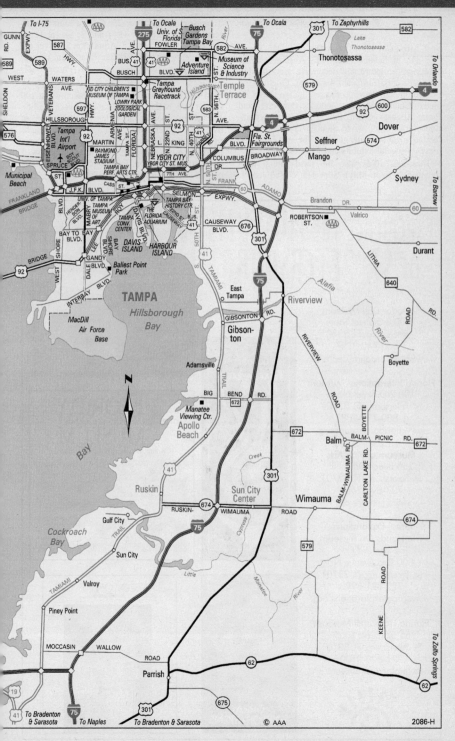

AE, MC, VI. Phone (727) 821-8992. *See color ad p. 212.*

[SAVE] **MUSEUM OF FINE ARTS** is at 255 Beach Dr. at Second Ave. N.E. A showcase for paintings, sculpture and decorative arts, the museum features European, American, Oriental and pre-Columbian artwork. Representative artists include Claude Monet, Georgia O'Keeffe and Pierre Auguste Renoir. Period rooms display antique furnishings, while Steuben crystal is highlighted in a separate gallery. The museum also presents special exhibits and lectures.

Tues.-Sat. 10-5 (also the third Thurs. each month 5-9, Sept.-May), Sun. 1-5; closed Jan. 1, Thanksgiving and Dec. 25. Guided tours are offered Tues.-Fri. at 10, 11, 1 and 2; Sat. at 11, 1, 2 and 3; Sun. at 1 and 2. Admission $6; over 65, $5; students with ID $2; free to all Sun. (except during special exhibits). MC, VI. Phone (727) 896-2667. *See color ad p. 212.*

P. BUCKLEY MOSS GALLERY, downtown at 190 Fourth Ave. N.E., overlooks a small yacht harbor. The gallery houses an extensive collection of paintings, watercolors, etchings and serigraphs by P. Buckley Moss, a contemporary artist focusing on Amish and Mennonite themes. Allow 1 hour minimum. Mon.-Fri. 10-6, Sat. 10-5, Sun. noon-5, Sept.-May; Mon.-Fri. 10-6, Sat. 10-5,

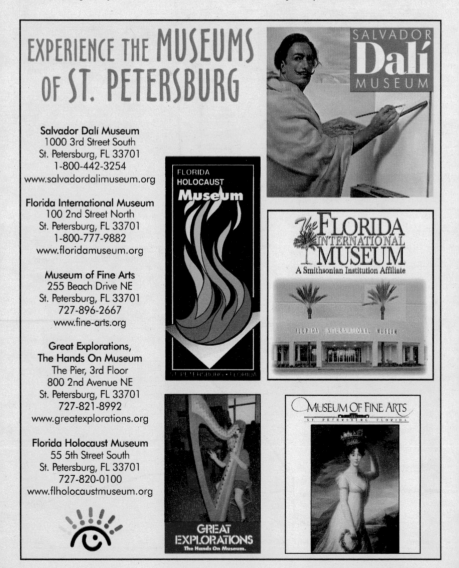

rest of year. Closed major holidays. Free. Phone (727) 894-2899.

THE PIER, extending 2,400 feet into Tampa Bay at the foot of Second Ave. N.E., downtown, is one of the most recognized landmarks on Florida's west coast. The complex is an inverted five-story pyramidal structure that offers fishing, an aquarium, miniature golf, a variety of specialty shops and boutiques, restaurants and entertainment. An information center is on the first floor.

A free trolley runs between the parking lot and the pier. Allow 2 hours minimum. Open Mon.-Sat. at 10, Sun. at 11; closing times vary. Information center open Mon.-Sat. 10-8, Sun. 11-6. Parking $3; $4 for special events. Phone (727) 821-6164.

ST. PETERSBURG MUSEUM OF HISTORY is next to The Pier at 335 Second Ave. N.E. Five thematic exhibit areas use lighting and scenery to depict the area's development from pre-history to the present. Among displays are fossils and primitive shell tools; replicas of an 1880s general store and of the Orange Belt Railway Depot; and a 1910 trolley. The Benoist Pavilion presents the history of commercial aviation. The museum also features rotating exhibits, programs and guided tours.

Allow 1 hour, 30 minutes minimum. Mon.-Sat. 10-5, Sun. 1-5; closed Jan. 1, Thanksgiving and Dec. 25. Admission $5; senior citizens and college students with ID $4; ages 7-17, $2. Phone (727) 894-1052.

SALVADOR DALI MUSEUM, next to the University of South Florida Bayboro Campus at 1000 Third St. S., houses a comprehensive collection of the Spanish artist's works. Dating from 1914-80, Dali's paintings range from small impressionistic works to gigantic surrealistic montages. Sculptures and other objects illustrate Dali's artistic diversity. Guided tours are conducted regularly; phone for schedule.

Allow 1 hour minimum. Mon.-Sat. 9:30-5:30 (also Thurs. 5:30-8), Sun. noon-5:30; closed Thanksgiving and Dec. 25. Admission $9; over 65, $7; students with ID $5; under 10 free. DS, MC, VI. Phone (727) 823-3767. *See color ad p. 212.*

SUNSHINE SKYWAY connects Pinellas and Manatee counties across lower Tampa Bay. The 15-mile bridge is made up of three smaller bridges and a 4-mile concrete skyway and is a vital link of I-275. There are areas for fishing, picnicking and swimming off the roadway. The central section of the southbound span of the original bridge collapsed into the bay when a tanker hit one of the supports in 1980. The original north section now is home to a 1.5-mile fishing pier. Toll $1. Fishing pier $3 per vehicle. There is a separate fishing fee of $2; over 64, $1.50; ages 6-12, $1. Phone (727) 865-0668.

TAMPA

See map page 210.

ADVENTURE ISLAND, .25 mi. n. of Busch Gardens Tampa Bay at 1001 Malcolm McKinley Dr. (40th St.), is a 25-acre water park encompassing slides, water play areas and a beach volleyball complex, all within a Key West atmosphere. Twists, drops, curves and turns can be expected while negotiating the thrill slide Wahoo Run, a tunnel raft ride. Key West Rapids sends rafters cruising down six stories of turns, water mines and pools. Splash Attack is an extensive tree house.

Changing facilities and showers are included with admission; free kennels are available at Busch Gardens. There is an additional fee for locker rental and the games area. Food is available.

Allow 5 hours minimum. Daily Apr.-Aug.; Sat.-Sun., late Feb.-March 31 and Sept.-Oct. Park generally open between 9 and 10; closing times vary. Phone ahead for exact hours. Admission $24.95; ages 3-9, $22.95. Combination ticket with Busch Gardens Tampa Bay $60.45; ages 3-9, $50.75. The Surf 'n Safari Pass includes unlimited admission to Adventure Island and Busch Gardens for 1 year and costs $109.95. Parking $4. Under 8 must be with an adult. AE, DS, MC, VI. Phone (813) 987-5660.

BUSCH GARDENS TAMPA BAY is at 3000 E. Busch Blvd. (SR 580), 2 mi. e. of jct. I-275 exit 33 or 2 mi. w. of I-75 exit 54. The 335-acre African-themed family-entertainment park offers naturalistic animal habitats, thrill rides, live entertainment,

Does this **Look** like a **Garden** to you?

AAA. Every Day.
AAA Members Can Save Two Ways!
SAVE when you pre-purchase tickets at your participating local AAA, or Show Your Card & Save® 10% off one-day general admission at the front gate. Be sure to visit our other Anheuser-Busch Adventure Parks in Central Florida: Adventure Island,® located directly across from Busch Gardens Tampa Bay; and SeaWorld® Orlando.
(See the Orlando section for more information.)

BUSCH GARDENS
Tampa Bay
www.buschgardens.com
©2000 Busch Entertainment Corporation. All rights reserved.

AAA
Show Your Card & Save

AAA. Every Day.

shopping and dining. Nearly 2,700 animals are part of the park's African atmosphere.

Roller coaster thrills can be experienced on Gwazi, a double wooden coaster; Montu, an inverted steel coaster; and the loops and spirals of Kumba. With a world-class zoo as its showcase, Edge of Africa offers an intense safari experience and features naturalistic animal habitats, remote encampments and African villages.

Those who opt for the Serengeti Safari Tour will take a ride on an open, flat-bed truck past free-roaming giraffes, zebras, antelopes and ostriches. Lory Landing is an aviary populated with tropical birds, including lorikeets, hornbills and touracos. Myombe Reserve: The Great Ape Domain allows visitors to observe lowland gorillas and chimpanzees in a naturalistic setting.

World Rhythms on Ice is a Broadway-style show featuring skaters and special effects. Other entertainment options include Akbar's Adventure Tours, a humorous journey through Egypt starring Martin Short, and the marching brass band Mystic Sheiks of Morocco. Food, free kennels, and stroller, wheelchair and locker rentals are available.

Allow a full day. Park open generally daily at 9; closing hours vary. Phone ahead for exact hours. Admission $45.68; ages 3-9, $36.74. Additional fee for Serengeti Safari Tour. The Wild Card Pass includes unlimited admission to Busch Gardens Tampa Bay and SeaWorld Orlando (see Orlando p. 146) for 1 year and costs $124.95; over 54 and ages 3-9, $109.95. AAA members can buy an Orlando FlexTicket that gives 10 consecutive days admissions to Busch Gardens Tampa Bay, SeaWorld Orlando, Universal Studios, Islands of Adventure and Wet 'n Wild; check with the attractions or your AAA club for more details. Parking $6 for automobiles, $7 for recreational vehicles and campers. AE, DS, MC, VI. Phone (813) 987-5082. See color ad p. 214.

▼GEM THE FLORIDA AQUARIUM, 701 Channelside Dr., is a three-story, glass-domed aquarium that features exhibits related to Florida's ecosystem and aquatic habitats. Highlights include the Florida Wetlands Gallery, which displays a cypress swamp, mangrove roots and a river containing live otters; the Florida Bays and Beaches Gallery, which contains freshwater and saltwater displays; and the Florida Coral Reefs Gallery, which showcases many fish, barracudas and colorful coral reefs.

Other plants and animals native to Florida—including alligators and crocodiles—are shown in their natural habitats. Also housed at the aquarium are sharks and rays from around the world and deep-sea creatures from the Gulf of Mexico. Food is available.

Allow 2 hours minimum. Daily 9:30-5; closed Thanksgiving and Dec. 25. Admission $12.95; over 49, $11.95; ages 3-12, $7.95. Parking $4.

AE, DS, MC, VI. Phone (813) 273-4000. See color ad p. 216.

KID CITY CHILDREN'S MUSEUM OF TAMPA, 7550 North Blvd., is next to Lowry Park Zoological Garden. Designed like a child-size city, the museum features stores where children can shop for groceries and streets where they can drive cars and become firefighters. Allow 1 hour minimum. Mon.-Fri. 9-5:30, Sat. 10-5:30, Sun. noon-5:30; closed major holidays. Admission $4, under 2 free. Phone (813) 935-8441.

LOWRY PARK ZOOLOGICAL GARDEN, 7530 North Blvd. on Sligh Ave., is home to more than 350 exotic animal species from four continents. The zoo contains the Asian Domain, Lorikeet Landing, Primate World, Underwater Manatee Adventure, Florida Wildlife, Aviary and a children's petting zoo. Manatee viewing tanks let visitors observe the gentle animals. Also featured are a river otter exhibit with underground viewing pools and habitats for alligators, turtles, freshwater and saltwater fish, amphibians and Florida snakes. Food is available.

Daily 9:30-5. Last admission 15 minutes before closing. Admission $8.50; over 50, $7.50; ages 3-11, $4.95. AE, DS, MC, VI. Phone (813) 935-8552 or 932-0245. See color ad p. 216.

MUSEUM OF SCIENCE & INDUSTRY (MOSI), 4801 E. Fowler Ave., is 3 mi. e. on SR 582 from I-275 exit 34 or 3 mi. w. of I-75 exit 54. The science center contains more than 254,000 square feet of exhibits including hands-on displays; various demonstrations pertaining to science and technology; health and human body exhibits; and flight and space displays.

The Gulf Coast Hurricane simulates the winds of a hurricane, while the Back Woods, a 40-acre wilderness, offers more than 3 miles of trails to explore. Visitors can follow the life cycle of a butterfly in a free-flight butterfly garden, focus on environmental factors of the state in Our Florida, and learn about space and flight in Our Place in the Universe. There also is a special area for children under age 5.

The Saunders Planetarium offer presentations daily; phone for schedule. A high-powered telescope is available on Saturday night. The IMAX Dome Theatre features movie presentations projected on a 10,500-square-foot screen.

Allow 4 hours minimum. Open daily at 9, closing times vary. Admission, including the IMAX theater, $13; over 49, $11; ages 2-13, $9. AE, MC, VI. Phone (813) 987-6300 or 987-6100. *See color ad p. 216.*

TAMPA BAY HISTORY CENTER, I-275 exit 25, then 1.5 mi. e. following signs to 225 S. Franklin St., features artifacts, memorabilia, maps, military uniforms and photographs depicting life in the Tampa Bay region from 12,000 years ago to the present. Changing exhibits also are featured. Allow 1 hour minimum. Tues.-Sat. 10-5; closed holidays. Free. Phone (813) 228-0097.

TAMPA MUSEUM OF ART, 600 N. Ashley Dr., displays permanent and major traveling art exhibits. Permanent collections include Greek and Roman antiquities as well as contemporary art. Tues.-Sat. 10-5 (also Thurs. 5-8), Sun. 1-5; closed major holidays. Admission $5; senior citizens $4; students with ID $3; under 6 free. AE, MC, VI. Phone (813) 274-8130.

UNIVERSITY OF SOUTH FLORIDA occupies 1,695 acres on Fowler Ave. in n.e. Tampa. The campus features a contemporary art museum and botanical gardens. Guided campus tours can be arranged. Phone (877) 873-2855.

UNIVERSITY OF TAMPA, 401 W. Kennedy Blvd., was established in 1931 as a private liberal arts-based institution. Today it offers more than 60 fields of study. Encompassing 80 acres, the campus centers on the former Tampa Bay Hotel, a Victorian-style building complete with Moorish revival architecture featuring minarets, domes and cupolas. The hotel was built in 1891 by Henry B. Plant, the transportation magnate who was instrumental in the reconstruction of the South. The administration and classroom building, Plant Hall, served as Theodore Roosevelt's headquarters in the Spanish-American War.

Allow 30 minutes minimum. University tours are given Tues. and Thurs. at 1:30, Sept.-May; closed Jan. 1, Thanksgiving and Dec. 18-25. Free. Phone (813) 253-3333.

Henry B. Plant Museum, housed in the s. wing of Plant Hall in the former Tampa Bay Hotel, displays elaborate furnishings and gilded art original to the hotel. Exhibits trace the history of the hotel, the Plant transportation system, early tourism and the Tampa area. Tues.-Sat. 10-4, Sun. noon-4. Admission $5; under 13, $2. A fee is charged for the Victorian Christmas Stroll in Dec. Phone (813) 254-1891.

YBOR CITY STATE MUSEUM, 3 blks. s. of I-4 exit 1 at 1818 E. Ninth Ave., is in a former bakery with huge brick ovens still intact. Displays depict Ybor City's founding by Vicente Martinez-Ybor as well as the cigar industry, which brought many nationalities to Tampa. An 1895 cigar worker's cottage, furnished in period, is open by appointment. Allow 30 minutes minimum. Daily 9-5. Admission $2, under 6 free. Phone (813) 247-6323.

What To Do

Sightseeing
Balloon Tours

THE BIG RED BALLOON meets in the Outback Steak House parking lot, on Dale Mabry Rd. between Stall Rd. and Hudson Ln. in Tampa, for

departure to the launch site. Trips offer panoramas of the Tampa landscape. A champagne brunch and a history of ballooning are provided. Rides last approximately 1 hour. All pilots are FAA certified. Trips depart year-round (weather permitting). Fare $160; ages 5-10, $145. Reservations are required. AE, DS, MC, VI. Phone (813) 969-1518.

CRYSTAL MAGIC BALLOON COMPANY meets in the Northdale Shopping Center parking lot on Dale Mabry Rd. just n. of jct. Ehrlich Rd./Bearss Ave. in Tampa, for departure to the launch site. Flights offer views of the Tampa Bay area, and a champagne brunch is provided. Rides last approximately 1 hour. Both pilots are FAA certified. Trips depart year-round (weather permitting). Fare $150; ages 8-12, $135. Under 45 inches tall not permitted. Reservations are required. AE, DS, MC, VI. Phone (727) 536-3005.

Note: The mention of the preceding hot air balloon rides is only for information and does **not** imply endorsement by AAA.

Boat Tours

Tampa Town Ferry provides transportation to *Tampa* attractions along the Hillsborough River. Sunset cruises also are available. For schedules and information phone (813) 223-1522.

CARIBBEAN QUEEN leaves from The Pier at the end of Second Ave. N.E. in downtown *St. Petersburg*. The 1-hour sightseeing excursion

takes passengers into Tampa Bay. A historical narrative is provided as local sights are pointed out. Dolphins are often spotted in the distance. Departures Mon.-Sat. at 11, 1, 3 and 5, Sun. at 1, 3 and 5 (weather permitting), Mar.-Sept.; daily at 1, 3 and 5 (weather permitting), rest of year. Fare $12; over 54 and ages 12-17, $10; ages 3-11, $6. Phone (727) 895-2628.

[SAVE] *STARLITE PRINCESS* RIVERBOAT boards at the St. Pete Beach Causeway at 3400 Pasadena Ave. S. in *St. Petersburg*. The paddlewheel excursion boat offers a variety of sightseeing cruises on scenic inland waterways. Dinner

dance cruises also are offered. Food is available. Two-hour luncheon/sightseeing cruise departs Tues. and Fri.-Sat. at noon. A 3-hour luncheon/sightseeing cruise departs Wed. at noon. Boarding begins at 11:30. Dixieland Jazz cruise departs Sun. at 1. Closed major holidays.

Two-hour luncheon/sightseeing cruise (meal optional) $10.50; ages 3-12, $7.71. Three-hour sightseeing and Dixieland Jazz cruises (meal optional) $12.85; ages 3-12, $9.35. Reservations are required. AE, MC, VI. Phone (727) 462-2628 or (800) 444-4814.

Bus Tours

First Class Coach Martz Group bus tours service the Tampa Bay area; phone (727) 526-9086 or (800) 282-8020 for additional information.

Driving Tours

With its scenic views of Hillsborough Bay, Bayshore Boulevard in *Tampa* is not only a popular hiking area but also a preferred driving route. Among the beautiful residential neighborhoods to explore is Davis Island, built on three man-made islands in the 1920s.

Walking Tours

The 6-mile sidewalk along Bayshore Boulevard in *Tampa,* which skirts the west side of Hillsborough Bay, is an excellent hiking area. The sidewalk is reputedly one of the world's longest continuous walkways.

The Ybor City Chamber of Commerce and Ybor City State Museum offer a guided walking tour of historic Ybor City; the fee is $4. The 1-hour tour departs from Ybor City State Museum Sat. at 10:30. For further information contact the museum at 1818 E. Ninth Ave., Tampa, FL 33605; phone (813) 247-6323.

Spectator Sports

Tampa Bay area fans have the option to root for a home run; slap high-fives after a touchdown; count down the time during a power play; watch dogs chase a stuffed rabbit; or applaud as a favorite horse makes a photo finish. Whatever your pleasure, the following options will have you cheering.

Baseball

Professional baseball is played at several locations. The **Tampa Bay Devil Rays** play major league baseball April through September at **Tropicana Field**, 1 Tropicana Dr. in *St. Petersburg;* phone (727) 825-3250 for general information, or (727) 898-7297 for tickets. The Devil Rays remain in St. Petersburg during the off-season; spring training games take place at Al

Lang Field at **Florida Power Park**, 180 Second Ave. S.E.; phone (727) 822-3384 for ticket information. Both the Devil Rays major and minor league teams train at 7901 30th Ave. N.

The **New York Yankees** major and minor league teams call *Tampa* home in the spring. They play at **Legends Field**, N. Dale Mabry Highway and Martin Luther King Jr. Boulevard. The facility's 10,000-seat stadium is a replica of New York's Yankee Stadium. Play is April to September; for information phone (813) 875-7753.

Two other major league teams hold spring training on the Pinellas Peninsula: the Philadelphia Phillies and the Toronto Blue Jays, both of which have minor league affiliates that play ball locally. In summer the **Clearwater Phillies** train at Clearwater's **Jack Russell Memorial Stadium**, north of Drew Street at 800 Phillies Dr., and the **Dunedin Blue Jays** work out at **Dunedin Stadium**, 311 Douglas Ave. in Dunedin. Both teams play a full minor league schedule; phone (727) 441-8638 for the Phillies and (727) 733-0429 for the Blue Jays.

Plant City Stadium, South Park Road in nearby Plant City, is the world headquarters of the **International Softball Federation.** Both the **Tampa Bay FireStix** and **Florida Wahoos** play here June through August; phone (813) 764-9775 for ticket information.

Football

The NFL's **Tampa Bay Buccaneers** play at **Raymond James Stadium** between N. Dale Mabry Highway and N. Himes Avenue; for ticket information phone (813) 879-2827. The stadium also is the setting for the Outback Bowl game, played on New Year's Day. The **Tampa Bay Storm** play arena football from April to August at the **Ice Palace**, downtown *Tampa* at Channelside Drive and Morgan Street.

Greyhound Racing

The *St. Petersburg* Kennel Club's **Derby Lane** track at 10490 Gandy Blvd. features greyhound racing most evenings and weekends from early January to late June; phone (727) 576-1361. **Tampa Greyhound Track**, 8300 N. Nebraska Ave. at Waters Street in the Sulphur Springs section of *Tampa,* does the same July through December; phone (813) 932-4313.

Note: Policies vary concerning admittance of children to pari-mutuel betting facilities. Phone for information.

Hockey

The NHL's **Tampa Bay Lightning** hits the ice at the Ice Palace October through April. For more information phone (813) 223-6100; for tickets phone (813) 223-1000.

Horse Racing

Horse racing devotees can go to the only Thoroughbred track on Florida's west coast,

Tampa Bay Downs, 11225 Race Track Rd. in Oldsmar. The track holds races mid-December to early May. For more information phone (813) 855-4401.

Note: Policies vary concerning admittance of children to pari-mutuel betting facilities. Phone for information.

Soccer

The **Tampa Bay Mutiny** takes major league soccer to the field in March. All games are played at Raymond James Stadium; phone (813) 289-6811 for schedule and ticket information.

Recreation

The American Medical Association was on to the bay area's bounty of recreational riches back in 1885, when it named St. Petersburg as an ideal location for a "world health city." Near year-round warmth, broad beaches, a varied system of waterways and some 400 public parks and playgrounds make the region a true haven for outdoor enthusiasts.

Bicycling

Tampa's busy roadways generally are not conducive to safe bicycling; however, scenic, 6-mile **Bayshore Boulevard** is a delightful exception. It offers a breezy ride along the western shore of Hillsborough Bay with pretty water views as a backdrop.

The **Friendship Trail Bridge**, once the Old Gandy Bridge connecting *Tampa* and *St. Petersburg*, now serves as an over-the-water recreation trail for bicyclists, in-line skaters and joggers. Phone (813) 289-4400, ext. 303 for information.

Fishing

The central Gulf Coast offers some of the best saltwater fishing in the state. More than 300 species roam these warm waters. Tarpon appear in

late spring and early summer, and kingfish run in spring and fall. Sea trout, bluefish, mackerel, grouper and channel bass (locally called redfish) are commonly caught, and the waters of Hillsborough County yield bass, bream and perch.

Boats can be chartered for inshore and offshore saltwater and freshwater fishing; make arrangements at **Clearwater City Marina, St. Pete Beach** or **Isla del Sol**. Boats equipped for 30-100 passengers venture into deep Gulf waters; they can be rented for half-day or all-day trips, which can cost $20-$40 per person, depending on the amenities offered. For details about what may be caught where and when, pick up a *Guide to Florida Fishing* at local tackle shops.

Lake Thonotosassa, northeast of *Tampa* via SR 582, attracts freshwater fishing enthusiasts. The docks off **Davis Island** and Bayshore Boulevard in Tampa offer ample casting sites. **The Skyway Fishing Pier**, next to the Sunshine Skyway Bridge, extends 3,350 feet into lower Tampa Bay; its northern end has concession stands, showers, picnic tables and parking lots.

Freshwater and saltwater fishing licenses are sold at some tackle shops, sporting goods and discount department stores and at the county tax collector's office. Phone (813) 307-6549 for information.

Golf

With some 50 courses to choose from and weather that allows for year-round play, the bay area is a true golfer's paradise. Some of the public and semiprivate courses in the *St. Petersburg* area are Bardmoor Golf and Tennis Club, 7919 Bardmoor Blvd., (727) 392-1234; Baypointe, 9399 Commodore Dr., (727) 595-2095; Main-

lands, 9445 Mainlands Blvd., (727) 577-4847; Mangrove Bay, 875 62nd Ave. N.E., (727) 893-7800; Tides, 11832 66th Ave. N., (727) 393-8483; and Twin Brooks, 3800 22nd Ave. S., (727) 893-7445. East Bay Golf Club of Largo, 702 Country Club Dr., offers night golf until 11:30 p.m.; phone (727) 581-3333.

Tampa area courses include Babe Zaharias, 11412 Forest Hills Dr., (813) 631-4374; Rocky Point, 4151 Dana Shores Dr., (813) 673-4316; and Rogers Park, 7910 N. 30th St., (813) 673-4396. There are several semiprivate courses, such as Northdale, (813) 962-0428, that let visitors play upon payment of greens and cart fees.

Jogging and Walking

Sunny weather encourages both visitors and locals to enjoy the outdoors. The **Pinellas Trail**, a former railroad corridor stretching 47 miles from Tarpon Springs to *St. Petersburg*, provides opportunities for walking, jogging, bicycling and in-line skating. Many entry and exit points exist along the trail. For information contact the Pinellas County Park Department, 631 Chestnut St. in Clearwater; phone (727) 464-3347.

Some 8 miles of nature trails wind through scenic hardwood hammocks at **Hillsborough River State Park**, about 12 miles northeast of *Tampa* via US 301.

Tennis

The **St. Petersburg Tennis Center**, 650 18th Ave. S., features 15 clay tennis courts and shuffleboard courts; phone (727) 893-7301. For additional information phone the Tampa Recreation Department at (813) 274-7529.

In *Tampa* the city-operated facility at **Hillsborough Community College**, west of Raymond James Stadium, has both hard and soft courts; phone (813) 348-1173. There are eight clay courts at **Marjorie Park**, on Davis Island just south of downtown Tampa; phone (813) 259-1664. There are six clay and two hard courts at the **Treasure Island Golf, Tennis and Recreation Center**, 10315 Paradise Blvd.; phone (727) 360-6062.

Water Sports

The Pinellas Peninsula's many beaches, with their attendant pleasures—swimming, skin diving and water skiing—line the slender offshore islands.

While there are two public beaches on the *Tampa* side of the bay—**Ben T. Davis Beach**, along Courtney Campbell Causeway (SR 60) near the airport, and **Picnic Island Park** near

Port Tampa—it's the gulf beaches that draw water lovers. Some of the popular island towns are **Indian Rocks Beach, Madeira Beach**, St. Pete Beach, **Treasure Island** and **North Redington Beach**.

Water sports of all kinds, including parasailing, are the focal point at **John's Pass Village and Boardwalk**, 140 128th Ave. in Madeira Beach, (727) 391-7373. The **Tackle Shack** in Pinellas Park offers instruction and rentals for windsurfing, water skiing, wakeboarding and scuba diving; phone (727) 546-5080.

Canoeing on area waters is another popular form of recreation. **Canoe Escape**, off I-75 exit 54, then east to 9335 E. Fowler Ave. in Thonotosassa, offers trips of varying distances. Trips weave through streams and creeks adjacent to wooded banks populated with alligators, turtles and birds. Canoers paddle downstream where they are met and shuttled to the point of origin; phone (813) 986-2067.

The Pinellas County park system provides several areas throughout the county where picnicking, boating and swimming can be enjoyed. **Fort De Soto Park**, south of St. Pete Beach, is one of the most developed *(see Recreation Chart and the AAA Southeastern CampBook)*.

Picnic Island Park, near the original encampment of Theodore Roosevelt and his Rough Riders during the Spanish-American War, beckons boaters, swimmers, picnickers and anglers. The park is south of the Gandy Bridge (US 92) near MacDill Air Force Base and accessible via Commerce Street in *Tampa*.

Other Diversions

One of the world's largest shuffleboard clubs is at **Mirror Lake Recreation Park** in downtown *St. Petersburg*. A daily guest membership is available. The **St. Petersburg Lawn Bowling Club**, next to Mirror Lake Recreation Park, provides lawn bowling lanes; phone (727) 822-2083.

Shopping

Tampa Bay's retail front offers a great deal of activity, whether it be expansive malls, factory outlet centers or specialty shopping districts.

Antiques

In *St. Petersburg* the **Gas Plant Antique Arcade**, 1246 Central Ave., offers wares from more than 100 dealers. Unusual shops contain a variety of finds from jewelry to antiques along **Beach Drive**.

An antique district of sorts centers on the shops along **Euclid Avenue** and **El Prado Boulevard** near south *Tampa's* Palma Ceia neighborhood. And **Antique & Decorative Arts**, 917 N. Franklin St., carries European furniture, glassware, rugs, silver jewelry, porcelain and works of art.

Malls

Want to shop until you drop? *St. Petersburg's* selection of malls can get you started. The four anchors at **Tyrone Square Mall**, Tyrone Boulevard and 22nd Avenue N., are Burdines, Dillard's, JCPenney and Sears. The mall also contains more than 150 other stores and restaurants. Other malls include **Crosswinds Shopping Center**, 66th Street and 20th Avenue N., and **ParkSide Mall**, Park Boulevard and US 19.

The largest mall on the Pinellas Peninsula is Clearwater's **Countryside Mall**, US 19N and SR 580, which features Burdines, Dillard's, JCPenney and Sears, in addition to restaurants and more than 160 boutiques and specialty outlets. Countryside also contains the state's only in-mall ice-skating rink.

Clearwater Mall, US 19N and Gulf-to-Bay Boulevard, has Burdines, Dillard's, Gayfers, Montgomery Ward and more than 120 others. If you're heading for the beach and need to pick up a few things, **Seminole Mall**, at the corner of 113th Street and Park Boulevard in Seminole, has a Bealls outlet and some 70 other stores.

There's more shopping across the bay in *Tampa*. **Franklin Street Mall** is in the city center. **Citrus Park Town Center**, off Veterans Expressway and Gunn Highway, is in west Tampa. One of the area's newer malls, built in 1995, is **Brandon TownCenter**, at the intersection of I-75 and SR 60 on Tampa's east side. The major anchor stores are Burdines, Dillard's, JCPenney and Sears, complemented by 120 specialty shops and boutiques.

University Mall, west of the University of South Florida at 2200 E. Fowler Ave., is the region's largest at 1.3 million square feet. Five major stores operate here—Burdines, Dillard's, JCPenney, Montgomery Ward and Sears—along with more than 130 specialty shops and restaurants.

Shoppers at **Tampa Bay Center**, just east of Raymond James Stadium at Himes Avenue and Martin Luther King Jr. Boulevard, have more than 150 stores and restaurants to choose from. Last but not least, **West Shore Plaza**, off I-275 exit 21, opened in 1967 and was the first of *Tampa's* enclosed malls. Burdines, Dillard's and JCPenney anchor the mall, which has more than 100 other stores and an international food court.

Outlets

The area's factory outlets are a good bet for good buys. **Bay Area Outlet Mall**, Roosevelt Boulevard and US 19 in Clearwater, has Bass Shoes, Johnston & Murphy, 9 West, TJ Maxx, Van Heusen and about 60 other stores.

Specialty Districts

The Pinellas side of the bay offers intriguing shopping, much of it with an appropriately waterside theme. At Gulf Boulevard and 128th Avenue in Madeira Beach is **St. John's Pass Village & Boardwalk**, where a fishing village atmosphere permeates more than 100 stores, boutiques and restaurants. The shopping experience is enhanced by a scenic 1,000-foot boardwalk. The **Wagon Wheel Flea Market**, 7801 Park Blvd. in Pinellas Park, has more than 3,000 vendors and is open Sat.-Sun. 7:30-4.

A bit farther down the peninsula, at 5501 Gulf Blvd. in St. Pete Beach, is **Silas Bayside Market**, a small complex of shops and restaurants in a tropical setting. Clearwater's **Boatyard Village**, at 16100 Fairchild Dr. (near St. Petersburg-Clearwater International Airport), is a re-created, 1890s fishing village on Old Tampa Bay; it includes a similar mix of boutiques, restaurants and galleries as well as a playhouse. **The Pier**, at the end of 2nd Avenue N.E. in downtown *St. Petersburg*, has shops, restaurants and a food court, all under one inverted pyramid roof facing Tampa Bay.

The atmosphere is as enticing as the offerings at the bay area's assorted specialty emporiums. Just off Bayshore Boulevard at Swann and Dakota avenues in Hyde Park—a stone's throw from downtown *Tampa*—is **Old Hyde Park Village**, which contains a delightful collection of nearly 60 shops, restaurants and cafes. The area offers an Old World charm complemented by a cosmopolitan tempo. Shoppers can settle at a shady outdoor table after perusing the upscale merchandise at the likes of Brooks Brothers, Jacobson's, Restoration Hardware, The Sharper Image and Williams-Sonoma.

More eclectic offerings are available in Ybor City, *Tampa's* Latin Quarter just northeast of downtown. Shopping and dining establishments are focused around the refurbished former cigar factory of **Ybor Square**, at the corner of 13th Street and 8th Avenue. Other streets in the neighborhood—particularly several blocks along 7th Avenue—are lined with ethnic stores and eateries, art galleries and antique shops.

Performing Arts

Tampa Bay's spectrum of arts encompasses blockbuster Broadway musicals, symphony and chamber music concerts, children's shows and holiday spectaculars. Its keystone is the 300,000-square-foot **Tampa Bay Performing Arts Center** (TBPAC), the largest performing arts facility south of Washington, D.C.'s Kennedy Center. On the east bank of the Hillsborough River in downtown *Tampa*, the TBPAC plays host to a great variety of cultural events at its venues: the 2,557-seat **Carol Morsani Hall**; 1,000-seat **Playhouse**; 300-seat **Jaeb Theater**; and 150-seat **Off Center Theater**. Phone (813) 229-7827 for schedule and ticket information regarding each of these venues.

Be sure to grab a free copy of the *Weekly Planet*, which is available throughout the city. The publication is filled with local news features; sections on restaurants, theater, film and music; and listings of upcoming events.

Film

Downtown's 1,500-seat **Tampa Theatre**, a restored 1926 movie palace at 711 Franklin St. Mall, is a great spot to catch foreign films, cult movies, Hollywood classics and occasional concerts. Tours of the historic building also are offered; phone (813) 274-8981. **Beach Theatre**,

315 Corey Ave. in St. Pete Beach, shows foreign and offbeat, low-budget films; phone (727) 360-6697.

Music

A full season of symphonic presentations is brought to the Tampa Bay area by the **Florida Orchestra Inc.** and by local dance companies. Performances take place at TBPAC; Clearwater's acoustically acclaimed **Ruth Eckerd Hall** in the Richard B. Baumgardner Center for the Performing Arts; and the **Mahaffey Theater** in *St. Petersburg's* Bayfront Center. Schedules are augmented by performance dates from music departments at the University of South Florida and the University of Tampa. Phone (813) 286-2403 or (800) 662-7286 for ticket and schedule information.

Works for voice are presented by the **Master Chorale of Tampa Bay**, (813) 289-9468; **Tampa Oratorio Singers**, (813) 988-2165; **Tampa Bay Gay Men's Chorus**, (813) 837-4485; and **Crescendo: the Tampa Bay Womyn's Chorus**, (813) 930-9055. Performance locations vary.

Free band concerts are held January through March at **Williams Park** in downtown *St. Petersburg*. **Straub Park**, next to the Museum of Fine Arts overlooking the inner harbor, and bayside **Vinoy Park**, adjacent to Straub Park, are settings for many events in St. Petersburg.

Theater

Broadway and off-Broadway plays are a big hit in the bay area. Try the **American Stage Theater**, 211 Third St. S. in *St. Petersburg*, for classical and contemporary plays in an intimate setting; phone (727) 823-7529. The **St. Petersburg Little Theater**, 4025 31st St. S., stages six major productions September through June; phone (727) 866-1973.

The Carrollwood Players, 4333 Gunn Hwy. in *Tampa*, is a little-theater group presenting a variety of productions; phone (813) 265-4000. TBPAC's Off Center Theater features local performing companies and improvisational groups, and the cozy Jaeb Theater presents plays and cabaret shows.

The **Tampa Bay Broadway Series** brings the best of Broadway to TBPAC's Carol Morsani Hall. Productions have included "The Phantom of the Opera," "Kiss of the Spider Woman," "Rent" and "Grease."

Special Events

St. Petersburg recognizes its ethnic groups during the **International Folk Fair** in March; offerings include ethnic foods and folk dances. The **Florida State Shuffleboard Tournaments** take place in February and October.

St. Petersburg's biggest celebration is the **Festival of States**, which is held late March through early April and pays tribute to the city's winter

visitors; waterfront fireworks, an arts festival, music festival, the election of royalty, a ball and a parade fill the agenda.

St. Petersburg also is host to **St. Anthony's Tampa Bay Triathlon**, which takes place in April; **Shakespeare in the Park**, which offers several weeks of professional productions of Shakespeare's works redone in a lighter, humorous mode during early May; and **Tarpon Round-Up**, a popular fishing event held during May and June. To round out the year, the holiday **Lighted Boat Parade** takes place downtown at the waterfront in mid-December.

Tampa's calendar of events begins with **The Outback Bowl** at **Raymond James Stadium** on Dale Mabry Highway. This New Year's Day event matches college football's Southeastern Conference and Big 10 Conference champions.

But of all the goings-on, the **Gasparilla Invasion and Parade of the Pirates** is the biggest, maddest and most colorful of *Tampa's* events. Florida's answer to Mardi Gras, Gasparilla is held the first Saturday in February with the capturing of Tampa by pirates, followed by several parades throughout the city. The festivities continue throughout the month with **Fiesta Day**, a celebration of ethnic diversity in Ybor City, and the 5- and 15-kilometer **Gasparilla Distance Classic**. The **Gasparilla Festival of the Arts** wraps up the celebration the first weekend in March with artists and craftspersons from around the world.

Not to be outdone by "the invasion" and all its associated activities, the **Florida State Fair** in February is the showcase for the state's finest agriculture, handicrafts, arts and industry. A midway,

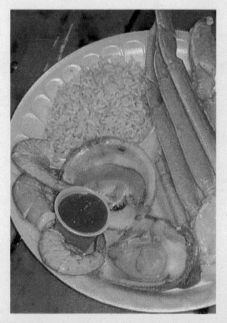

entertainment, shows and exhibits add to the festivities. The **GTE Classic**, held at TPC of Tampa Bay, tees off in mid-February. The **Florida Dance Festival**, sponsored by the University of South Florida, presents performances, classes and workshops that attract dancers and choreographers from around the country. The event takes place during the last two weeks in June; phone (305) 237-3413.

Fall events kick off with **A Taste of Florida** in mid-October, a 3-day food and entertainment festival that features the best that some 40 area restaurants have to offer. **Guavaween**, *Tampa's* Latin-style Halloween celebration, includes a street party, satirical parade, contests and entertainment. The event, held in Ybor City in October, takes its name from a succulent tropical fruit and echoes a Tampa nickname: "The Big Guava."

Celebrate another delicious fruit at the 10-day **Florida Strawberry Festival** in Plant City, where visitors can indulge in strawberry shortcakes and enjoy musical performances. Festivities coincide with the fruit's harvest in early March.

Aficionados of performing arts won't want to miss the **Clearwater Jazz Holiday**. The 4-day festival, held the third weekend in October at downtown's Coachman Park, features performers of national and international acclaim; phone (727) 461-5200.

Nightlife

Evening options in Tampa Bay range from a romantic stroll along a quiet beach under the stars to a night of dancing, where the musical accompaniment could be mellow jazz, twangy country and western, thunderous rock or just about anything in between.

Comedy Clubs

Give your funny bone a workout at **SideSplitters**, 12938 N. Dale Mabry Hwy. at S.W. Fletcher Avenue in *Tampa*. The club presents local talent and national acts; phone (813) 960-1197 for show times and reservations.

Two **Coconuts Comedy Clubs** can be found in the city; phone (727) 797-5653 (Sunset Point Road and US 19 in the Cinema Cafe); or (727) 360-5653 (6100 Gulf Blvd. in the Howard Johnson, St. Pete Beach).

Country

Country music is popular in the bay area, and several area clubs accommodate the genre by offering live and recorded music. In *Tampa* it's the **Round-Up**, 13918 W. Hillsborough Ave. at Race Track Road, a country & western club with a 3,000-square-foot dance floor, free dance lessons and occasional live concerts; phone (813) 855-1464.

Dance Clubs

More than a few spots in the bay area specialize in disco- and alternative-style music. At 420 Park Place Blvd. in Clearwater, **Joe Dugan's** is a restaurant and DJ dance club; phone (727) 796-7867. Another choice is the **Bombay Bicycle Club**, a restaurant featuring dancing and a daily happy hour, at 2721 Gulf-to-Bay Blvd.; phone (727) 799-1841.

Ybor City in downtown *Tampa* has several nightclubs that pack in the crowds. **Club 1509** is at 1509 E. Eighth Ave.; phone (813) 247-6606. **Pleasuredome**, 1430 E. Seventh Ave., caters to a gay and lesbian clientele on Tuesday nights and attracts people of all persuasions Friday and Saturday. The club features high-energy dancing and occasional concerts; phone (813) 247-2711. Nearby is **Masquerade**, 1503 E. Seventh Ave., in the historic Ritz Theatre. The young, dressed-to-thrill crowd grooves to house, techno, underground and alternative music programmed by guest DJs. Live shows tend toward the latest new bands. Masquerade is open Wednesday through Sunday; phone (813) 247-3319.

Jazz & Blues

Tampa Bay retains an active jazz and blues scene. In *St. Petersburg*, check out the **Ringside Cafe**, 2742 Fourth St. N., (727) 894-8465.

Skipper's Smokehouse, at the corner of Skipper Road and Nebraska Avenue in north *Tampa*, offers an eclectic lineup of artists covering blues to reggae to funk to world beat. Most shows start at 8 p.m.; phone (813) 971-0666. Jazz predominates at **Apropos**, 2102 S. Dale Mabry Hwy.; phone (813) 251-8180. Another spot at which to catch the blues is **Blues Ship Cafe**, 1910 E. 7th Ave. in Ybor City; phone (813) 248-6097.

Rock

Classic and contemporary rock in addition to Top 40 and reggae—live as well as recorded—all can be heard around town. Near the gulf beaches, try **Cha Cha Coconuts** at The Pier, 800 2nd Ave. N.E. in *St. Petersburg*; phone (727) 822-6655. Alternative bands take the stage in St. Petersburg at **Jannus Landing**, 200 First Ave. N.; phone (727) 896-2276. Another favorite is **Gasoline Alley**, at 17928 US 19 in Clearwater; phone (727) 532-0265.

The Green Iguana has two locations: at 4029 S. Westshore Blvd. in south *Tampa* and 1708 E. 7th Ave. in Ybor City; phone (813) 837-1234 or 248-9555, respectively. Ybor City also is home to **Harpo's**, 1805 E. 7th Ave.; phone (813) 248-4814.

Current pop, rock and rap acts are booked into the **Sun Dome** at the University of South Florida, 4202 E. Fowler Ave., and **Expo Hall**, on the Florida State Fairgrounds at 4800 Hwy. 301 N.; phone (813) 974-3002 or 621-7821, respectively.

The Tampa Bay Vicinity

APOLLO BEACH (E-8) pop. 6,000

MANATEE VIEWING CENTER, jct. Big Bend (CR 672) and Dickman rds. across from a Tampa Electric power plant, overlooks a manatee sanctuary. The center contains exhibits and videotapes about manatees and the nearby power plant as well as an observation platform. A nature trail along a tidal flat provides closer glimpses of the sea cows, plants and wildlife native to the area. Allow 1 hour, 30 minutes minimum. Daily 10-5, mid-Nov. to mid-Apr.; closed Easter, Thanksgiving and Dec. 25. Free. Phone (813) 228-4289.

CLEARWATER (G-7)
pop. 98,800, elev. 29'

A resort city and popular retirement community on the Pinellas Peninsula, Clearwater overlooks the Gulf of Mexico. Clearwater Beach, which is part of the city, is connected with the mainland by the Clearwater Memorial Causeway, a landscaped, 2-mile drive. The broad, white sand beach attracts both residents and visitors.

Outdoor entertainment is plentiful. The Clearwater Municipal Marina harbors a large sportfishing fleet: Boats for deep-sea fishing can be chartered daily. Sightseeing cruises on the Gulf are available. The Philadelphia Phillies baseball team trains and plays exhibition games at Jack Russell Memorial Stadium from early March to early April; phone (727) 441-8638. Magicians, jugglers, musicians, and craftspeople gather on Pier 60 daily at dusk for Sunsets at Pier 60.

The Clearwater Ferry Service, at Clearwater Municipal Marina, offers the Dolphin Encounter, an opportunity to view dolphins and feed seabirds, and cruises to Caladesi Island State Park. For schedule and fare information phone (727) 442-7433.

Broadway shows, orchestral and jazz performances, ballet, opera and children's theater are staged throughout the year at Ruth Eckerd Hall in Richard B. Baumgardner Center, 1111 McMullen Booth Rd.; phone (727) 791-7400.

Greater Clearwater Chamber of Commerce: 1130 Cleveland St., P.O. Box 2457, Clearwater, FL 33755; phone (727) 461-0011.

Shopping areas: Bay Area Outlet Mall, 15579 US 19 S., offers a variety of shops. Burdines and Montgomery Ward anchor Clearwater Mall, at the junction of US 19 and SR 60. Countryside Mall, 27001 US 19 N., features Burdines, Dillard's, JCPenney and Sears as well as an ice skating rink.

CAPTAIN MEMO'S PIRATE CRUISE, just off SR 60 at Clearwater City Marina, offers 2-hour

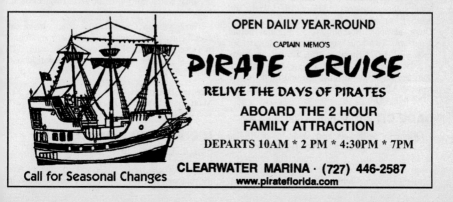

cruises in the Gulf of Mexico aboard a reproduction of a pirate ship. Cruise departs daily at 10, 2, 4:30 and 7 p.m. Boarding is 30 minutes before departure. Schedule may vary; phone ahead. Fare $28 ($30 for 4:30 and 7 p.m. cruises); over 65 and ages 13-17, $22; ages 2-12, $18. Reservations are recommended. AE, DS, MC, VI. Phone (727) 446-2587. *See ad p. 225.*

SAVE **CLEARWATER MARINE AQUARIUM**, 249 Windward Passage, is dedicated to the rescue and rehabilitation of injured marine mammals, river otters and sea turtles. Visitors can view dolphins and sea turtles in large holding tanks. Also available are a mangrove exhibit and a beach tank with sharks and stingrays. Allow 1 hour, 30 minutes minimum. Mon.-Fri. 9-5, Sat. 9-4, Sun. 11-4; closed holidays. Admission $6.75; ages 4-11, $4.25. MC, VI. Phone (727) 441-1790.

MOCCASIN LAKE NATURE PARK: AN ENVIRONMENTAL AND ENERGY EDUCATION CENTER, 2750 Park Trail Ln., is a 51-acre nature preserve. The interpretive center features wildlife, plant and energy exhibits. Nature trails wind through upland hardwoods and wetlands to a 5-acre lake. Allow 1 hour minimum. Tues.-Fri. 9-5, Sat.-Sun. 10-6; closed Jan. 1, July 4, Thanksgiving, day after Thanksgiving and Dec. 25. Admission $2; ages 3-12, $1. Phone (727) 462-6024.

SHOW QUEEN, departing from Clearwater Beach Marina at 25 Causeway Blvd., offers sightseeing cruises along the Clearwater harbor and intracoastal waterway. The open top deck provides opportunities for viewing seabirds and marine life. The captain gives a historical narration. Dinner cruises also are available. Sightseeing cruises depart Mon.-Sat. at noon, Sun. at 1:30 (weather permitting). Sightseeing cruise $8.95; ages 4-10, $5.95. Sightseeing cruise with lunch $16.95; ages 4-10, $7.95. Reservations are recommended. AE, DI, MC, VI. Phone (727) 461-3113.

SAVE *STARLITE MAJESTY*, just off SR 60 at Clearwater Beach Marina, offers 2- and 3-hour sightseeing tours of Clearwater Harbor. Dinner/dance cruises also are available. Two-hour sightseeing tours depart Tues.-Wed. and Fri.-Sat. at noon. Three-hour cruise departs Thurs. at noon. Boarding is 30 minutes before departure. Two-hour sightseeing cruise $10.50; ages 3-12, $7.71 (meals extra). Three-hour cruise $12.85; ages 3-12, $9.35 (meals extra). Reservations are required for luncheon and dinner/dance cruises. AE, MC, VI. Phone (727) 462-2628 or (800) 444-4814.

DADE CITY (D-9) pop. 5,600, elev. 89′

Originally settled as Fort Dade in the 1840s, the settlement's name was changed to Dade City in 1884. The town is the commercial center for nearby citrus growers, cattle ranchers and poultry farmers. Historic Church Avenue, the Old Courthouse and antique shops add to the community's quaint atmosphere.

Greater Dade City Chamber of Commerce: 14112 8th St., Dade City, FL 33525; phone (352) 567-3769.

SAVE **PIONEER FLORIDA MUSEUM** is 1.5 mi. n. via US 301, then e. on Pioneer Museum Rd. Highlights include a one-room pioneer schoolhouse; the 1860s John Overstreet House; Enterprise Methodist Church; the 1896 Trilby Depot, featuring a 1913 Porter steam engine; Cummers Sons Cypress Sawmill Co. buildings; and Bromley Shoe Repair Shop. The museum's permanent collection displays early farm machinery, vintage carriages, American Indian artifacts, Roseville pottery, textiles, and antique toys and dolls.

Allow 2 hours minimum. Tues.-Sun. 1-5; closed holidays. Admission $5; over 54, $4; ages 6-18, $2. Phone (352) 567-0262.

DUNEDIN (G-7) pop. 34,000, elev. 13′

Dunedin, a name closely resembling the Gaelic word from which Edinburgh is derived, traces its Scottish heritage to the town's early days as a seaport and trading center. Its village-like image has been preserved in a rejuvenated downtown, while subtropical surroundings and almost four miles of waterfront account for its tranquil atmosphere. Home of the spring training camp of the Toronto Blue Jays baseball club, exhibition games are played at Dunedin Stadium from early March to early April; phone (727) 733-9302.

Just off the coast, two barrier islands are available to water and nature enthusiasts. The Gulf beaches of Honeymoon Island State Recreation Area, accessible via Dunedin Causeway, are popular for swimming and sunbathing. Caladesi Island State Park is reached by passenger ferry departing from the recreation area at regular intervals; phone (727) 734-5263. *See Recreation Chart.* Both parks are refuges for endangered birds, including egrets, herons and storks. Between the mainland and the islands outdoor enthusiasts can windsurf, sail catamarans and ride personal watercraft on the protected waters of St. Joseph Sound.

Transportation memorabilia and historical documents, photographs and artifacts are found at Dunedin Historical Society and Museum, 341 Main St., in the former railroad depot; phone (727) 736-1176.

Greater Dunedin Chamber of Commerce: 301 Main St., Dunedin, FL 34698; phone (727) 733-3197.

INDIAN ROCKS BEACH (H-7) pop. 4,000, elev. 10′

Indian Rocks Beach is a resort community near the midpoint of Sand Key, a long, narrow island in the Gulf off the Pinellas County coast. It is accessible by SR 688 north of St. Petersburg.

Gulf Beaches Chamber of Commerce: 6990 Gulf Blvd., St. Pete Beach, FL 33706; phone (727) 360-6957 or (800) 944-1847.

INDIAN SHORES (H-7)
pop. 1,400, elev. 5′

SUNCOAST SEABIRD SANCTUARY, on the Gulf Coast at 18328 Gulf Blvd., houses and treats injured pelicans, herons, egrets, owls, hawks and other birds. Rehabilitated birds are released into the wild; those with permanent impairments remain at the sanctuary or are sent to other wildlife parks around the world. Educational programs are presented the first Sunday of each month at 2. Daily 9-dusk. Guided tours and lectures are offered Wed. and Sun. at 2. Donations. Phone (727) 391-6211.

LARGO (H-7) pop. 65,700, elev. 50′

Largo is bordered on three sides by water—the Gulf of Mexico circles around the west and south sides, and Tampa Bay is on the eastern border. In 1905 when it became a city, it had 291 residents and covered 1 square mile.

Greater Largo Chamber of Commerce: 151 3rd St. N.W., P.O. Box 326, Largo, FL 33779; phone (727) 584-2321.

Shopping areas: Largo Mall, on the corner of Ulmerton Road (SR 688) and Seminole Boulevard, has more than 75 stores and restaurants.

FLORIDA GULF COAST ART CENTER, 12211 Walsingham Rd. just s. of Ulmerton Rd., features permanent and changing displays of Florida contemporary art and American crafts as well as a sculpture garden on landscaped grounds. Allow 1 hour minimum. Tues.-Sat. 10-4 (also Thurs. 4-7 p.m.), Sun. noon-4. Free. Phone (727) 518-6833.

HERITAGE VILLAGE is at 11909 125th St. N. Pioneer buildings relocated to this 21-acre site depict life during the early days of Pinellas County. A museum in the center of the complex displays maps and photographs of early Pinellas County. Guides offer tours of some buildings. Tues.-Sat. 10-4, Sun. 1-4; closed major holidays. Last tour begins 30 minutes before closing. Donations. Phone (727) 582-2123.

MADEIRA BEACH (H-7)
pop. 4,200, elev. 6′

Joined to the mainland near St. Petersburg by a free causeway, Madeira Beach offers good swimming and parasailing as well as rentals of personal watercraft. Boats can be chartered from several marinas for fishing in the Gulf of Mexico. Europa Cruise Line offers 6-hour cruises.

Gulf Beaches of Tampa Bay Chamber of Commerce: 6990 Gulf Blvd., St. Pete Beach, FL 33706; phone (727) 360-6957 or (800) 944-1847.

Shopping areas: John's Pass Village and Boardwalk, 12901 Gulf Blvd. E., is a shopping area with a nautical theme; it contains more than 100 gift and specialty shops, restaurants and art galleries.

(SAVE) **HUBBARD'S SEA ADVENTURES,** departing from 150 John's Pass Boardwalk, offers a narrated 2-hour sightseeing trip aboard a catamaran. Passengers can view dolphins and a variety of bird life along the way. Deep-sea fishing trips also are available. Allow 2 hours, 30 minutes minimum. Sightseeing cruise departs daily at 10, 1 and 4; closed Dec. 25. Fare $11.95; ages 3-11, $6. Reservations are suggested. MC, VI. Phone (727) 398-6577.

PLANT CITY (E-8) pop. 22,800, elev. 37'

Plant City is named for Henry B. Plant, a wealthy railroad magnate. The Tampa Bay Polo Club plays at Walden Lake Polo Field Sunday afternoons at 2 from early January through late April; admission $4; phone (813) 752-4495.

The Pioneer/Heritage Museums, in the 1914 Plant City High School Community Center at 605 N. Collins St., have several exhibit rooms with period themes such as clothing, furnishings, medical equipment, farm implements and railroading; phone (813) 757-9226.

City Hall: 302 W. Reynolds St., Plant City, FL 33566; phone (813) 757-9144.

(SAVE) **DINOSAUR WORLD,** off I-4 exit 10, just n. on Branch Forbes Rd., then just w. to 5145 Harvey Tew Rd., features more than 100 life-size fiberglass models of dinosaurs in a tropical outdoor setting. Picnicking and pets are permitted. Allow 1 hour minimum. Daily 9-dusk. Admission $9.75; senior citizens $8.95; ages 3-12, $7.75. AE, DS, MC, VI. Phone (813) 717-9865.

ST. PETE BEACH (I-7)
pop. 9,200, elev. 5'

A resort community on Long Key, St. Pete Beach is connected to the mainland by the St. Pete Beach Causeway and the Pinellas Bayway (toll). The town has good swimming beaches, several fishing piers and charter boat operations.

Gulf Beaches of Tampa Bay Chamber of Commerce: 6990 Gulf Blvd., St. Pete Beach, FL 33706; phone (727) 360-6957 or (800) 944-1847.

Shopping areas: Silas Bayside Market, 5505 Gulf Blvd., features specialty shops in a tropical setting. The historic Corey Avenue area offers varied shops.

DOLPHIN LANDINGS CHARTER BOAT CENTER is at 4737 Gulf Blvd. (SR 699), .5 mi. s. of jct. SRs 693 and 699, in Dolphin Village Shopping Center. The 2-hour dolphin watch cruise on a 37- to 46-foot sailboat affords opportunities for spotting the playful creatures. Other cruises are available, including sunset, snorkeling, fishing and shelling excursions. Allow 2 hours minimum. Dolphin watch departures daily at 9:30, noon and 2:15. Departures require a minimum of two people. Fare $25; under 12, $15. AE, MC, VI. Phone (727) 367-4488.

GULF BEACHES HISTORICAL MUSEUM, 115 10th Ave., is housed in a former 1917 church— the first one built on the barrier island section of Pinellas County. Exhibits portray the history of the area. Allow 1 hour minimum. Thurs. and Sat. 10-4, Sun. and Fri. 1-4; closed major holidays. Free. Phone (727) 360-2491.

TARPON SPRINGS (F-7)
pop. 17,900, elev. 18'

Tarpon Springs became an important center for sponge fishing when Greek divers came to the area in the early 1900s. Although the industry has diminished, the Greek influence still is evident in the remaining sponge boats and in the dock area, where sponge shops and Greek restaurants and bakeries are plentiful. Sponge-diving exhibitions and deep-sea fishing charters are available from the dock area.

A replica of St. Sophia's in Constantinople, the 1943 Greek Orthodox Cathedral of St. Nicholas, at the corner of Pinellas Avenue (US 19A) and Orange Street, is the center of colorful pageantry during Greek festivals.

The ancient craft of brass rubbing, transferring designs from brass engravings to paper, can be attempted at the Medieval Brass Rubbing Centre on Dodecanese Boulevard; phone (727) 934-6760.

Tarpon Springs Chamber of Commerce: 11 E. Orange St., Tarpon Springs, FL 34689; phone (727) 937-6109.

GEORGE INNESS JR. PICTURES, in the Unitarian Universalist Church at Grand Blvd. and Read St., contains 11 religious paintings by George Inness Jr., son of the American 19th-century landscape artist. The paintings depict his extraordinary treatment of light and use of the green tones that were named after him. Guided tours are available. Allow 30 minutes minimum. Tues.-Sun. 2-5, Nov.-May; closed holidays. Last tour begins 30 minutes before closing. Donations. Phone (727) 937-4682.

(SAVE) **KONGER TARPON SPRINGS AQUARIUM** is at 850 Dodecanese Blvd. A simulated coral reef, complete with native plants and tropical fish, illustrates life under the sea in a 120,000-gallon tank. Marine life from the Pacific Ocean is highlighted in the Pacific Jewels Aquarium and South Pacific Predators Tank. Visitors may watch a feeding at the moray eel exhibit, while a tidal pool offers a close look at such sea creatures as starfish and hermit crabs. Small sharks and stingrays can be fed in a petting tank. Allow 30 minutes minimum. Mon.-Sat. 10-5, Sun. noon-5. Admission $4.75; over 55, $4; ages 3-11, $2.75. Phone (727) 938-5378.

SAVE **ST. NICHOLAS BOAT LINE,** .4 mi. w. of jct. Alt. US 19 at 693 Dodecanese Blvd., offers 35-minute, narrated, round-trip cruises through the historic sponge docks of Tarpon Springs. A diver in traditional diving gear provides a demonstration of sponge harvesting. The boat has been used in the filming of several movies and television shows. Allow 1 hour minimum. Departures daily approximately every 45 minutes 10-5; closed Greek Orthodox Easter and Dec. 25. Fare $5; ages 6-12, $2. Phone (727) 942-6425.

SPONGEORAMA EXHIBIT CENTER, on Dodecanese Blvd. off Alt. US 19, includes the Museum of Sponge Diving History and a 30-minute film presentation about sponge diving. Food is available. Allow 1 hour minimum. Mon.-Sat. 10-6, Sun. noon-4. Free. Phone (727) 943-9509.

THONOTOSASSA (E-9)
pop. 19,300, elev. 49′

Fort Foster, on the Hillsborough River in nearby Hillsborough River State Park *(see Recreation Chart),* was used as a battle post and supply depot during the Second Seminole War. Abandoned in 1838 because of disease and the miserable, damp conditions, the fort and the bridge it guarded have been reconstructed on the original site. Canoeing, picnicking and fishing are permitted. Bicycle trails are available. Guided tours are available; phone (813) 987-6771.

RECREATIONAL ACTIVITIES
Canoeing

- **Canoe Escape,** off I-75 exit 54, then .5 mi. e. to 9335 E. Fowler Ave., Thonotosassa, FL 33592. Mon.-Fri. 9-5, Sat.-Sun. 8-6; closed Thanksgiving and Dec. 24-25. Last 2-hour trip departs at 2. Phone (813) 986-2067.

This ends listings for the Tampa Bay Vicinity.
The following page resumes the alphabetical listings of cities in Florida.

TARPON SPRINGS—
see Tampa Bay p. 228.

TAVARES—*see Orlando p. 175.*

THONOTOSASSA—
see Tampa Bay p. 229.

TITUSVILLE (D-10)
pop. 40,000, elev. 18′

Named for founder Col. Henry T. Titus in 1874, Titusville once was a citrus shipping point and commercial fishing port. The establishment of Kennedy Space Center *(see place listing p. 97)* brought the Space Age—and increased tourism—to this small mainland city.

Titusville Area Chamber of Commerce: 2000 S. Washington Ave., Titusville, FL 32780; phone (321) 267-3036.

MERRITT ISLAND NATIONAL WILDLIFE REFUGE, 3.5 mi. e. on SR 402 across the Titusville Cswy., is a habitat for wintering migratory waterfowls. A visitor center offers educational displays, wildlife exhibits and a 20-minute video about the refuge. Behind the center, a boardwalk takes visitors over a pond and through an oak hammock to a freshwater marsh. Special interpretive programs are offered November through March.

Licensed hunting for waterfowls is permitted in season; licensed fishing is available all year. Black Point Wildlife Drive off SR 406 is a 7-mile self-guiding driving tour of major refuge habitats. Oak Hammock Foot Trail off SR 402 identifies the plants of a hammock community. For information contact the Refuge Manager, Merritt Island National Wildlife Refuge, P.O.

DID YOU KNOW

The oldest place name in North America is Florida.

Box 6504, Titusville, FL 32782. Park daily dawn-dusk. Visitor center Mon.-Fri. 8:30-4:30, Sat. 9-5 (also Sun. 9-5, Nov.-Mar.). Free. Phone (321) 861-0667.

VALIANT AIR COMMAND WARBIRD AIR MUSEUM, 6600 Tico Rd. at the Space Coast Regional Airport, following signs, features such aviation memorabilia as model planes, uniforms, controls from various aircraft and a U.S. Navy flight simulator. A hangar and a ramp contain a changing collection of restored planes in running condition. Allow 2 hours minimum. Daily 10-6; closed Jan. 1, Thanksgiving and Dec. 25. Admission $9; over 60 and military with ID $8; ages 4-12, $6. MC, VI. Phone (321) 268-1941.

VENICE (F-8) pop. 16,900, elev. 13′

As its name implies, Venice is crisscrossed by canals. Unlike its famous namesake, however, the town is known as a shark tooth mecca. The pursuit of the teeth, which can range in size from one-eighth-inch to 3 or more inches, is so popular that a Florida "snow" shovel has even been invented to aid in their recovery from sand and shell debris. Fortunately for the collector, the teeth come not from living specimens, but from ancient sharks that have decomposed on the sea floor.

Venice Area Chamber of Commerce: 257 Tamiami Trail N., Venice, FL 34285-1908; phone (941) 488-2236.

VERO BEACH (E-11)
pop. 17,400, elev. 17′

Vero Beach plays host to the Los Angeles Dodgers baseball team during spring training. Exhibition games are played at Holman Stadium from March to early April; phone (561) 569-4900. The Vero Beach Dodgers offer games during their regular season from mid-April to early September.

Indian River County Chamber of Commerce: 1216 21st St., Vero Beach, FL 32960; phone (561) 567-3491.

WAKULLA (B-6)

EDWARD BALL WAKULLA SPRINGS STATE PARK, jct. SRs 61 and 267, was known to early Seminole Indians for its plentiful wildlife and was believed to be discovered by Ponce de León in 1513, who claimed it to be the "fountain of youth." The main spring, with a water temperature of 70 F, is considered one of the state's deepest, having been explored to a depth of 300 feet. The maximum flow was recorded in 1973 at 1.2 billion gallons a day; in 1931 the minimum flow was measured at 16.2 million gallons. The average is 576 million gallons of crystal-clear water daily.

A popular "birding mecca," the park offers hiking, bicycle and nature trails as well as swimming opportunities. Narrated river cruises offer glimpses of a variety of animals in their native habitats, while glass-bottom boat tours provide views of fish, marine plants and mastodon bones. A free sight-and-sound filmed tour offers an underwater view.

Allow 2 hours minimum. Park daily 8-dusk. River cruises depart daily every half hour 9:45-5, during DST; 9:15-4:30, rest of year (weather permitting). Glass-bottom boat cruises depart daily 11-3 (only when the water has clear visibility). Admission $3.25 per private vehicle (maximum eight people), $1 extra for every person over the maximum. Glass-bottom boat or river cruise $4.50; under 13, $2.25. Phone (850) 224-5950. *See Recreation Chart.*

▼ **WALT DISNEY WORLD—**
GEM *see Lake Buena Vista p. 162.*

WEEKI WACHEE (D-8)
pop. 50, elev. 34′G

WEEKI WACHEE SPRINGS WATERPARK, on US 19 at jct. SR 50, is built around a spring that flows at a rate of 170 million gallons a day and maintains a temperature of 74 F. The Wilderness River Cruise explores the flora and fauna of a typical Florida ecosystem. Petti-goat Junction is a petting area featuring goats. "Mermaids" perform in an underwater theater.

A natural spring on the Weeki Wachee River features a white sand beach, three flume rides, a river tube ride and a children's play area. Lockers, picnic facilities, food and kennels are available. Allow 6 hours minimum. Park opens daily at 10; closing times vary. Water park is open seasonally; phone ahead. Last admission 1 hour before closing. Admission $14.95; ages 3-10, $10.95. AE, MC, VI. Phone (352) 596-2062 or (877) 469-3354. *See color ad.*

WELAKA (C-9) pop. 500, elev. 28′

NATIONAL FISH HATCHERY AQUARIUM, on CR 309, displays reptiles and 22 tanks containing specimens of about 50 species of native freshwater fish. Allow 30 minutes minimum. Daily 7-3:30. Free. Phone (904) 467-2374.

WEST PALM BEACH (G-12)
pop. 67,600, elev. 21′

An important commercial city bordering Lake Worth, West Palm Beach has grown into a center for commerce and business. Despite industrial expansion, the city offers abundant opportunities for golf, tennis, fishing and shuffleboard.

Approximately 15 miles west of town in Wellington, polo matches are held on Sunday from

late December to late April. Opportunities to play also are available.

The [SAVE] Palm Beach Kennel Club, Belvedere Road and Congress Avenue, holds greyhound races year round; phone (561) 683-2222.

Note: Policies vary concerning admittance of children to pari-mutuel betting facilities. Phone for information.

Kravis Center for the Performing Arts includes a 2,200-seat concert hall, a "black box" theater, a restaurant and an outdoor amphitheater. Performances range from classical to country and feature well-known entertainers; for information phone (561) 833-8300 or (800) 572-8471.

Palm Beach County Tourist Information Center: 8020 W. Indian Town Rd., Jupiter, FL 33478; phone (561) 575-4636.

Shopping areas: Palm Beach Mall, 1 block east of I-95 exit 53, features Burdines, Dillards, JCPenney, Lord & Taylor and Sears among its 100 stores.

[SAVE] **DREHER PARK ZOO,** e. of I-95 at 1301 Summit Blvd., displays more than 500 animals, including a Florida panther, Bengal tigers, giant tortoises and exotic birds. Wallabies and red kangaroos are the highlights of the Australian Outback exhibit. Also featured is the Cornell Nature Trail, an elevated boardwalk from which deer, shore birds and labeled plant life can be seen. The children's zoo features small animals. Picnic facilities are available.

Allow 2 hours minimum. Daily 9-5. Last admission 45 minutes before closing. Admission $6; over 60, $5; ages 3-12, $4. AE, DS, MC, VI. Phone (561) 533-0887 or 547-9453.

LION COUNTRY SAFARI, 18 mi. w. of I-95 on US 98/441 and SR 80 (Southern Blvd.), is a 500-acre drive-through wildlife preserve in which giraffes, wildebeests, rhinoceroses and other animals roam freely in simulated habitats. Visitors must stay in their cars with doors and windows closed. Convertibles are not permitted; rental cars are available. Other park highlights include an amusement park, a baby animal nursery, a petting zoo, aviaries, reptile habitats and animal demonstrations. A miniature golf course, a carousel, a bird feeding exhibit and a boat ride also are offered. Picnic facilities, food and free kennels are available.

Allow 3 hours minimum. Daily 9:30-5:30. Last vehicle admission 1 hour before closing. Admission $15.50; over 65 and ages 3-9, $10.50. Rental cars $6 per hour. AE, MC, VI. Phone (561) 793-1084. See ad p. 233.

NORTON MUSEUM OF ART is .5 mi. s. of Okeechobee Blvd. on US 1, at 1451 S. Olive Ave. The museum contains an impressive permanent collection of 19th- and 20th-century French paintings by such artists as Paul Cézanne, Paul

Gauguin and Henri Matisse. The American collection focuses on works from the 20th century, including pieces by Edward Hopper and Georgia O'Keeffe. An extensive Chinese art display features a jade, porcelain and Buddhist sculpture collection. Pablo Picasso and Edgar Degas are represented in the landscaped sculpture patio.

Allow 1 hour minimum. Tues.-Sat. 10-5, Sun. 1-5 (also Mon. 10-5, Dec.-Mar.); closed major holidays. Guided tours are given daily at 2, Oct.-Apr. Admission $6; ages 13-21, $2; free to all Wed. 1:30-5. AE, DS, MC, VI. Phone (561) 832-5196.

(SAVE) **SOUTH FLORIDA SCIENCE MUSEUM, PLANETARIUM AND AQUARIUM,** 4801 Dreher Tr. N. in Dreher Park, has a variety of permanent and changing exhibits and interactive displays. The Light and Sight Hall explores visual media, the Native Plant Center presents a nature trail that winds through tropical foliage and the Gibson Observatory features one of the largest telescopes in the state. Several aquariums house Atlantic and Pacific species as well as live corals. The Aldrin Planetarium offers star and laser light shows.

Allow 1 hour minimum. Museum open Mon.-Fri. 10-5 (also Fri. 5-10), Sat. 10-6, Sun. noon-6; closed Thanksgiving and Dec. 25. Planetarium shows daily at 1 and 2 (also Fri. at 7 and 8 p.m.). Laser light shows daily at 3 (also Fri. at 9 and 10 p.m.). Museum $6; ages 3-17, $4. Fees may change for special exhibits. Planetarium shows $2. Laser light shows $4 (Fri. evening $6.50). Phone (561) 832-1988 or 832-2007.

WHITE SPRINGS (B-8)
pop. 700, elev. 125′

Once a health resort, White Springs is built around sulphur springs. Seminole and Timucuan Indians considered the springs sacred and believed their warriors were impervious to attack while recuperating.

STEPHEN FOSTER STATE FOLK CULTURE CENTER, 3 mi. e. of I-75 on US 41, covers 850 acres of wooded land beside the Suwannee

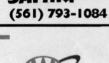

Start Planning
Your Next Vacation

AAA Travel

ℱor more information, call or visit your local
AAA Travel Office today!

River, which the composer immortalized in his song "Old Folks At Home." In the visitor center are animated dioramas depicting Foster's songs. Two other dioramas and period exhibits are in the 200-foot carillon tower; recitals are given daily. An arts and crafts center features "cracker"-style buildings, a two-story craft shop and five studios in which Florida crafts are demonstrated daily. Hiking and bicycling trails are available. Picnicking is permitted.

Allow 4 hours minimum. Park open daily 8-dusk. Buildings open daily 9-5. Admission $3.25 per private vehicle (maximum eight people) or motorcycle, $1 per person arriving by bicycle, bus or on foot. Some events have varying admission charges. Phone (904) 397-2733.

WINTER HAVEN (E-9)
pop. 24,700, elev. 170′

Located 75 miles from both the Atlantic Ocean and the Gulf of Mexico, Winter Haven is surrounded by some of the state's finest citrus groves. Exhibition games for baseball's Cleveland Indians are held in March at Chain of Lakes Stadium; phone (863) 293-3900.

Community theater productions are presented at Theatre Winter Haven, in the Chain of Lakes complex on Cypress Gardens Boulevard; for performance information phone (863) 299-2672.

Fishing is among Winter Haven's popular recreational activities. Spring-fed lakes near the city are connected by canals to form a 30-mile waterway containing numerous game fish. Around Lake Silver, tennis and shuffleboard, an amphitheater, two recreational sport facilities and a beach are available.

Greater Winter Haven Area Chamber of Commerce: 401 Ave. B N.W., P. O. Box 1420, Winter Haven, FL 33882; phone (863) 283-2138. *See color ad p. 234.*

CYPRESS GARDENS is 5 mi. s.e. on SR 540. Founded in 1936, Cypress Gardens was the state's first theme park. More than 8,000 varieties of plants and flowers from 90 countries around the world are showcased in the renowned 208-acre botanical garden. Towering cypress trees provide the backdrop for elaborate displays of bromeliads, bougainvillea, hibiscus and other exotic flora. Special areas include the Mediterranean Waterfall, Big Lagoon, Oriental Gardens and the All-American Rose Garden.

The Cypress Roots Museum displays photographs and memorabilia tracing the park's development. When Radios Were Radios is an exhibit of vintage radios and radio equipment from the 1920s through the 1950s. An elaborate model railroad travels across historic America at Cypress Junction, while Southern Crossroads recreates an antebellum town.

Southern Breeze, a turn-of-the-20th-century paddle-wheel boat, offers daily cruises; dinner cruises are available nightly.

Wings of Wonder is a glass-enclosed, Victorian-style conservatory containing more than 1,000 free-flying butterflies. Plantation Gardens feature rose, herb and scent and fruit and vegetable gardens, as well as a butterfly garden with plants that attract Florida butterflies.

Five animal habitats and an aviary add to the natural enjoyment. Events, including light shows and floral festivals, are held throughout the year.

Among the park's shows are Ski Xtreme, a fast-action water ski show with world-class, champion athletes; Fairy Tales on Ice, which features European skaters in the Ice Palace; European Circus Magic, a variety show with jugglers, acrobats, dancers and clowns; and Calling All Animals, an educational program featuring parrots, birds of prey and exotic reptiles.

The Historical Florida Garden Railway, which includes replicas of the Thomas Edison and Ernest Hemingway houses, Church Street train depot and Bok Tower, focuses on the role of the railway in Florida's growth. Acorns, pine cones, tree bark and leaves are among the materials used to construct the buildings.

No pets are allowed inside the park; a kennel is available at the entrance for a fee. Food is available, as are wheelchair and stroller rentals.

Daily 9:30-5 with extended hours during special seasons. Admission $32.95; ages 6-12, $15.95. DS, MC, VI. Phone (863) 324-2111. *See color ad p. 234.*

WATER SKI MUSEUM AND HALL OF FAME, 799 Overlook Dr. S.E., features videotape presentations that portray the history of water skiing, Cypress Gardens and barefoot skiing. There also are photographs, artifacts and equipment relating to the sport. The Hall of Champions includes displays, paintings and information about water skiing's pioneers and star performers. Allow 1 hour, 30 minutes minimum. Mon.-Fri. 10-5; closed holidays. Donations. Phone (863) 324-2472.

WINTER PARK—*see Orlando p. 176.*

WOODVILLE (B-6) pop. 2,800, elev. 39′

NATURAL BRIDGE BATTLEFIELD STATE HISTORIC SITE is a 6-acre site 6 mi. e. off SR 363. The Battle of Natural Bridge was fought Mar. 6, 1865, to prevent Union troops from capturing the Capitol at Tallahassee. Fishing opportunities and picnic facilities are available. Daily 8-dusk. Free. Phone (850) 922-6007.

Look for our Partners in Savings!

When selecting a AAA Approved lodging, look for properties that participate in our various partnership programs. In addition to actively soliciting AAA business, many of them also offer discounts to AAA members.

- Properties that advertise in the TourBook® guide understand the value of AAA member business and want to provide members with a more complete picture of their property. Please refer to their ads for more details on what these properties have to offer.

- A red SAVE icon in their TourBook guide listing indicates an **Official Appointment** property that offers a minimum 10% discount off published TourBook standard room rates to AAA members.

- A black SAVE icon indicates a chain hotel that participates in the **Show Your Card & Save**® program. SYC&S partners offer a satisfaction guarantee and the lowest available rate for your dates of stay.* Reservations must be made by calling their exclusive AAA member toll-free numbers:

Days Inn 800-432-9755 ■ **La Quinta Inns** 800-221-4731
Hampton Inns 800-456-7793 ■ **Hilton Hotels** 800-916-2221
Hyatt Hotels 800-532-1496
Sleep, Comfort, Quality, Clarion, Econo Lodge, Rodeway
800-228-1222

*Sleep, Comfort, Quality, Clarion, Econo Lodge, Rodeway offer a 10-20% discount.

Florida

Florida Orientation Map to Destinations

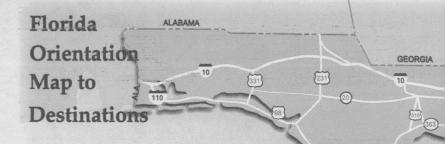

GEORGIA

95

301

17

10

75

10

19

17

95

301

ALT.
27

40

4

75

Jacksonville

Tampa Bay

50

75

19

75

4

Tampa

60

75

St. Petersburg

17

27

70

82

75

29

41

27

50

528

Orlando

192

95

60

95

710

Fort Lauderdale

Miami-Miami Beach

1

1

Florida Keys

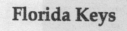

1

Major destinations are color-coded to index boxes, which display vicinity communities you will find listed within that destination's section of the book.
Cities outside major destination vicinities are listed in alphabetical order throughout the book.
Use the *Comprehensive City Index* at the back of this book to find every city's listing locations.

In July 2001, exit numbers on Florida's interstate highway system are scheduled to begin shifting from sequential numbering to mileage-based numbering. For further information, please contact your local AAA club.

ALACHUA pop. 4,500

——— WHERE TO STAY ———

COMFORT INN
[AAA] [SAVE]
♦♦♦♦♦
Motel

Phone: 904/462-2414
All Year · · · · · · 1P: $65-$110 · · · 2P: $75-$150 · · · XP: $5
Location: I-75, exit 78, just e on US 441. 15405 Martin Luther King Blvd 32615. Fax: 904/462-2220. **Facility:** Spacious guest rooms with bright, cheerful decor throughout. 62 units. Some whirlpool units ($110-$150). 2 stories, exterior corridors. **Terms:** 7 day cancellation notice, pets ($10 extra charge, in smoking rooms). **Amenities:** extended cable TV. *Some:* irons, hair dryers. **Guest Services:** coin laundry. **Business Services:** fax. **Cards:** AE, CB, DI, DS, MC, VI. **Special Amenities: free continental breakfast and free news-paper.**
SOME UNITS

[🛏] [🍴] [🏊] [📷] [DATA PORT] / [✕] [🖨] [▣] [▣] [🔌] /

ALTAMONTE SPRINGS —See Orlando p. 625.

AMELIA CITY —See Jacksonville p. 439.

AMELIA ISLAND —See Jacksonville p. 439.

ANNA MARIA pop. 1,700 (See map p. 764; index p. 768)

——— WHERE TO DINE ———

BISTRO AT ISLAND'S END
♦♦♦♦♦
Continental

Dinner: $8-$27 · · · · · · **Phone:** 941/779-2444 · · 65
Location: On north end, jct Gulf Dr and Pine Ave; 3 mi n of jct SR 64. 204 Pine Ave 34216. **Hours:** 5 pm-9:30 pm, Fri & Sat-10:30 pm. Closed: Mon & Tues. **Reservations:** suggested. **Features:** dressy casual; children's menu; carryout; cocktails & lounge; entertainment. Enjoy steak, seafood and pasta in a cozy, bistro-style setting. Excellent presentation, quality ingredients and good flavor are all elements of this superb menu. Wet your appetite with Gulf Coast gumbo, then sample the first-rate grilled salmon. Smoke free premises. **Cards:** AE, CB, DI, DS, MC, VI. [✕]

SANDBAR
♦♦♦♦
Seafood

Lunch: $6-$11 · · · · **Dinner:** $11-$18 · · · · **Phone:** 941/778-0444 · · 66
Location: 2.8 mi n of SR 64 on Gulf Dr, just w. 100 Spring Ave 34216. **Hours:** 11:30 am-10 pm. **Features:** casual dress; children's menu; early bird specials; carryout; cocktails & lounge; entertainment; a la carte. "Old Florida" is the theme of this popular, casual restaurant overlooking the Gulf of Mexico. Vintage photos set a nostalgic mood, and each table is afforded a wonderful view of the bay. Enjoy live entertainment nightly on the outdoor dining deck. **Cards:** AE, CB, DI, DS, MC, VI. [✕]

APALACHICOLA pop. 2,600

——— WHERE TO STAY ———

BEST WESTERN APALACH INN
[AAA] [SAVE]
♦♦♦♦
Motel

Phone: (850)653-2116
All Year · · · · · · 1P: $75-$110 · · · 2P: $85-$120 · · · XP: $8 · · · F14
Location: 1.5 mi w. 249 Hwy 98 32320. Fax: 850/653-9136. **Facility:** Comfortable rooms. 42 units. Some whirlpool units ($90-$110). 2 stories, exterior corridors. **Amenities:** hair dryers. **Cards:** AE, CB, DI, DS, MC, VI. **Special Amenities: free continental breakfast and free local telephone calls.**
SOME UNITS

[SD] [🐾] [🏊] [📷] [🖨] [DATA PORT] / [✕] [▣] /

THE GIBSON INN

(AAA) (SAVE)

▼▼▼▼

Historic Country Inn

All Year   1P: $85-$100   2P: $85-$100   XP: $5

Phone: (850)653-2191   F

Location: On US 98 at west end of bridge. Market St & Ave C 32329 (PO Box 221). Fax: 850/653-3521. **Facility:** Restored National Register inn, built in 1907. Individually decorated rooms with Victorian accent and antiques from around the world. 30 units. *Bath:* combo or shower only. 3 stories (no elevator), interior corridors. **Parking:** street only. **Terms:** pets ($5 extra charge). **Dining:** restaurant, see separate listing. **Business Services:** meeting rooms. **Cards:** AE, MC, VI.

SOME UNITS

[S/D] [icons] / [X] /

RANCHO INN

(AAA) (SAVE)

▼▼▼▼

Motel

All Year   1P: $47-$70   2P: $50-$80   XP: $6

Phone: 850/653-9435   D12

Location: On US 98, 1 mi w. 240 Hwy 98 32320. Fax: 850/653-9180. **Facility:** 32 units. Some suites ($75-$100). 2 stories, exterior corridors. **Terms:** pets ($6 extra charge). **Amenities:** extended cable TV. **Cards:** AE, DS, MC, VI. **Special Amenities:** free local telephone calls and preferred room (subject to availability with advanced reservations).

SOME UNITS

[icons] / [X] [icons] /

——— WHERE TO DINE ———

THE GIBSON INN   Country Inn   Lunch: $6-$10   Dinner: $12-$25   Phone: 850/653-2191

▼▼

American

Location: On US 98 at west end of bridge; in The Gibson Inn. Market St & Ave C 32320. **Hours:** 7:30 am-3 & 6-9 pm, Fri & Sat-10 pm. **Features:** casual dress; children's menu; carryout; cocktails & lounge; street parking. Located in a historic coastal hotel, the restaurant projects a warm, inviting atmosphere with walls of cypress, candlelight and fresh flowers. The menu features delicious creations like sesame yellowfin tuna, coated in seeds and seared in oil. **Cards:** AE, MC, VI.

[X]

APOLLO BEACH —*See Tampa Bay p. 840.*

APOPKA —*See Orlando p. 628.*

ARCADIA pop. 6,500

——— WHERE TO STAY ———

BEST WESTERN ARCADIA INN

▼▼▼

Motel

2/1-4/15	1P: $75-$105	2P: $79-$119	XP: $10 F12
12/1-1/31	1P: $65-$85	2P: $75-$95	XP: $10 F12
10/1-11/30	1P: $55-$75	2P: $65-$85	XP: $10 F12
4/16-9/30	1P: $45-$75	2P: $55-$85	XP: $10 F12

Phone: (863)494-4884

Location: 0.6 mi s of SR 70 on US 17. 504 S Brevard Ave 34266. Fax: 863/494-2006. **Facility:** 37 units, 3 with efficiency. *Bath:* some combo or shower only. 1 story, exterior corridors. **Terms:** small pets only ($15 extra charge, with prior approval). **Amenities:** irons. **Guest Services:** [CP] meal plan available, gift shop. **Cards:** AE, CB, DI, DS, MC, VI.

SOME UNITS

[ASK] [S/D] [icons] / [X] /

FEE

——— WHERE TO DINE ———

ARCADIA TEA ROOM RESTAURANT   Lunch: $4-$8   Phone: 863/494-2424

▼▼▼ ▼▼

American

Location: Downtown on SR 70. 117 W Oak St 34266. **Hours:** 11 am-4 pm, Sun-3 pm. Closed: Mon. **Features:** casual dress; Sunday brunch; carryout; beer & wine only; street parking. Step into history in these quaint dining rooms decorated with lavish antiques. Fresh, home-cooked entrees are offered at reasonable prices, like the hearty classic, liver and onions with real mashed potatoes and savory gravy. **Cards:** DS, MC, VI.

[X]

NAV-A-GATOR GRILLE   Lunch: $3-$24   Dinner: $3-$24   Phone: 941/627-3474

▼▼▼

Seafood

Location: I-75, exit 31, 3.1 mi ne on CR 769, 1.5 mi s on Peace River St. 9700 SW Riverview Cir 34266. **Hours:** 11 am-9 pm, Thur-Sat to 9 pm, Sun-5 pm. Closed: 4/15, 11/22, 12/25. **Features:** casual dress; carryout; beer & wine only. Located on the Peace River in the Desoto Marings, this active and loud restaurant is a local favorite with a menu offering grouper, captains platter, shrimp, gator, seafood baskets and many sandwiches. Enjoy deck dining and watch nature and fisherman bringing in their latest catch or take a stroll through the small museum on site. **Cards:** AE, DS, MC, VI.

[X]

ATLANTIC BEACH —*See Jacksonville p. 442.*

AVENTURA —*See Miami-Miami Beach p. 511.*

AVON PARK pop. 8,000

——— WHERE TO STAY ———

ECONO LODGE

(AAA) (SAVE)

▼▼▼▼

Motel

1/16-3/31	1P: $60-$130	2P: $60-$130	XP: $5 F18
9/1-11/30	1P: $50-$90	2P: $50-$90	XP: $5 F18
12/1-1/15 & 4/1-8/31	1P: $50-$70	2P: $50-$70	XP: $5 F18

Phone: (863)453-2000

Location: US 27, 2.5 mi s of jct SR 17 and 64. 2511 US Hwy 27 S 33825. Fax: 863/453-0820. **Facility:** Overlooking Lake Glenada. 58 units, 4 with efficiency. 2 stories, exterior corridors. **Amenities:** extended cable TV. **Guest Services:** coin laundry. **Cards:** AE, DS, MC, VI.

SOME UNITS

[S/D] [icons] / [X] [icons] /

BALDWIN —*See Jacksonville p. 443.*

BAL HARBOUR —*See Miami-Miami Beach p. 512.*

BELLEAIR BLUFFS —*See Tampa Bay p. 840.*

BELLE GLADE pop. 16,200

———— WHERE TO STAY ————

TRAVELERS MOTOR LODGE
Phone: 561/996-6761

12/1-5/31	1P: $52-$58	2P: $58-$68	XP: $10 F12
6/1-11/30	1P: $48-$52	2P: $58-$62	XP: $10 F12

Motel

Location: 1 mi sw on SR 80. 1300 S Main St 33430. Fax: 561/996-6764. **Facility:** All rooms with at-door parking. 26 units. 1 story, exterior corridors. **Terms:** cancellation fee imposed. **Amenities:** extended cable TV. **Cards:** AE, DS, MC, VI. **Special Amenities:** free local telephone calls and preferred room (subject to availability with advanced reservations).

SOME UNITS

BOCA GRANDE pop. 1,700

———— WHERE TO STAY ————

UNCLE HENRY'S MARINA RESORT
Phone: (941)964-2300

12/1-7/14 & 11/15-11/30	1P: $145-$225	2P: $145-$225
7/15-11/14	1P: $105-$165	2P: $105-$165

Motor Inn

Location: I-75, exit 32, north end of Gasparilla Island, 2 mi s of the cswy toll; in the Courtyard Shopping Center. 5800 Gasparilla Rd 33921 (PO Box 294). Fax: 941/964-2098. **Facility:** Airy, contemporary rooms with high ceilings and private balcony. 18 units. 2 two-bedroom units. Some suites. 2 stories, exterior corridors. **Terms:** 3 day cancellation notice-fee imposed. **Amenities:** extended cable TV, irons, hair dryers. **Leisure Activities:** boat ramp, charter fishing. *Fee:* boating. **Guest Services:** coin laundry. **Business Services:** meeting rooms. **Cards:** AE, DI, DS, MC, VI.   SOME UNITS

FEE

BOCA RATON pop. 61,500

———— WHERE TO STAY ————

BEST WESTERN UNIVERSITY INN
Phone: (561)395-5225

12/1-4/15		2P: $89-$139
4/16-11/30		2P: $59-$139

Motor Inn

Location: US 1, 1 mi n of jct SR 808 (Glades Rd). 2700 N Federal Hwy 33431. Fax: 561/338-9180. **Facility:** Good sized rooms. Pleasant poolside courtyard with breakfast patio. 90 units. 2 stories, interior/exterior corridors. **Terms:** monthly rates available. **Amenities:** voice mail, irons, hair dryers. **Dining:** restaurant, 11 am-11 pm, $5-$12, cocktails. **Leisure Activities:** heated pool, whirlpool, exercise room. **Guest Services:** coin laundry.
Cards: AE, CB, DI, JC, MC, VI. **Special Amenities:** free continental breakfast.   SOME UNITS

BOCA RATON MARRIOTT
Phone: (561)392-4600

1/1-4/30	1P: $184-$239	2P: $184-$239	XP: $15 F18
12/1-12/31	1P: $154-$199	2P: $154-$199	XP: $15 F18
9/16-11/30	1P: $159-$194	2P: $159-$194	XP: $15 F18
5/1-9/15	1P: $129-$164	2P: $129-$164	XP: $15 F18

Hotel

Location: Military Trail; 0.8 mi n of I-95, exit 38 (Palmetto Park Rd). 5150 Town Center Cir 33486. Fax: 561/368-9223. **Facility:** Impressive public areas. Relaxing pool area, rooms with a classic touch. 256 units. Some suites. 11 stories, interior corridors. **Parking:** valet. **Terms:** cancellation fee imposed. **Amenities:** dual phone lines, voice mail, honor bars, irons, hair dryers. *Some:* safes. **Leisure Activities:** heated pool, sauna, whirlpool, exercise room. **Guest Services:** gift shop, valet laundry. **Business Services:** conference facilities, administrative services, PC, fax. **Cards:** AE, CB, DI, DS, MC, VI.   SOME UNITS

FEE   FEE   FEE FEE

BOCA RATON RADISSON SUITE HOTEL

Phone: (561)483-3600

AAA SAVE	12/21-4/14	1P: $209-$235	2P: $229-$255	XP: $10	F18
	10/1-11/30	1P: $155-$185	2P: $175-$205	XP: $10	F18
	12/1-12/20	1P: $145-$175	2P: $165-$195	XP: $10	F18
Suite Motor Inn	4/15-9/30	1P: $139-$169	2P: $159-$189	XP: $10	F18

Location: SR 808, facing Florida Tpke, exit 75; in Arvida Parkway Center. 7920 Glades Rd 33434. Fax: 561/479-2280. **Facility:** Built around atrium with tropical garden and fountain. one-bedroom suites, some with balcony. Situated in Mediterranean-style commercial center. 200 units. 7 stories, interior corridors. **Terms:** cancellation fee imposed, package plans, small pets only ($100 fee). **Amenities:** video games, dual phone lines, voice mail, honor bars, irons, hair dryers. **Leisure Activities:** heated pool, whirlpool, exercise room. **Guest Services:** [BP] meal plan available, gift shop, complimentary evening beverages, area transportation-within 5 mi, valet and coin laundry. **Business Services:** meeting rooms. **Cards:** AE, CB, DI, DS, JC, MC, VI. **Special Amenities: free continental breakfast and free newspaper.** *(See ad below)*

SOME UNITS

COURTYARD BY MARRIOTT

Phone: (561)241-7070

	12/1-4/15	1P: $129-$189
	4/16-5/27 & 10/8-11/30	1P: $129-$159
Motel	5/28-10/7	1P: $109-$139

Location: SR 808 (Glades Rd) at jct I-95, exit 39. 2000 NW Executive Ct 33431. Fax: 561/241-7080. **Facility:** Large upscale rooms. Attractive landscaped courtyard. 152 units. Some suites. 4 stories, interior corridors. **Terms:** cancellation fee imposed. **Amenities:** dual phone lines, irons, hair dryers. **Leisure Activities:** heated pool, whirlpool, exercise room. **Business Services:** meeting rooms. **Cards:** AE, DI, DS, MC, VI. *(See color ad p 242)*

SOME UNITS

DOUBLETREE GUEST SUITES-BOCA RATON

Phone: (561)997-9500

	1/1-4/30	1P: $189-$209	2P: $189-$209	XP: $10	F18
	12/1-12/31	1P: $89-$159	2P: $89-$159	XP: $10	F18
	10/1-11/30	1P: $99-$119	2P: $99-$119	XP: $10	F18
Suite Motor Inn	5/1-9/30	1P: $89-$109	2P: $89-$109	XP: $10	F18

Location: I-95, exit 40 (Yamato Rd), just w; in Arvida Corporate Park. 701 NW 53rd St 33487. Fax: 561/994-3565. **Facility:** Single bedroom, two-room suites with wet bar, built around attractive courtyard. 183 units. 4 stories, exterior corridors. **Terms:** cancellation fee imposed, monthly rates available, package plans, pets ($50 extra charge). **Amenities:** voice mail, irons, hair dryers. **Leisure Activities:** heated pool, whirlpool. **Guest Services:** complimentary evening beverages, area transportation, valet and coin laundry. **Fee:** massage. **Business Services:** meeting rooms. **Cards:** AE, DI, DS, MC, VI.

SOME UNITS

EMBASSY SUITES-BOCA RATON

Phone: (561)994-8200

1/1-4/30	1P: $179-$259	2P: $179-$259	XP: $10	F18
12/1-12/31	1P: $109-$199	2P: $109-$199	XP: $10	F18
10/1-11/30	1P: $109-$149	2P: $109-$149	XP: $10	F18
5/1-9/30	1P: $99-$139	2P: $99-$139	XP: $10	F18

Suite Motor Inn

Location: I-95, exit 40 (Yamato Rd), just w; in Arvida Corporate Park. 661 NW 53rd St 33487. **Fax:** 561/995-9821. **Facility:** Multi-story atrium lobby with tiered room entrance. All suites have separate bedroom and living room. 263 units. 2 two-bedroom units. 7 stories, interior corridors. **Parking:** valet. **Terms:** 3 day cancellation notice-fee imposed, monthly rates available, package plans. **Amenities:** extended cable TV, voice mail, safes, irons, hair dryers. **Leisure Activities:** heated pool, saunas, whirlpool, exercise room. **Guest Services:** gift shop, complimentary evening beverages, area transportation, valet and coin laundry. **Fee:** massage. **Business Services:** meeting rooms. **Cards:** AE, CB, DI, DS, JC, MC, VI.

HAMPTON INN-BOCA RATON

Phone: (561)988-0200

SAVE

12/23-2/28	1P: $159-$189	2P: $169-$199	XP: $10	F10
3/1-4/30	1P: $149-$179	2P: $159-$189	XP: $10	F10
5/1-11/30	1P: $90-$129	2P: $100-$139	XP: $10	F10
12/1-12/22	1P: $119	2P: $99-$139	XP: $10	F10

Motel

Location: Exit 40 from southbound; exit 40B from I-95 N. 1455 Yamato Rd 33431. **Fax:** 561/988-0203. **Facility:** Attractive lobby and pool areas. Rooms are business person friendly. 94 units. Some suites. **Bath:** combo or shower only. 4 stories, interior corridors. **Terms:** 14 day cancellation notice-fee imposed, weekly & monthly rates available. **Amenities:** dual phone lines, voice mail, irons, hair dryers. **Some:** fax. **Leisure Activities:** heated pool. **Guest Services:** [ECP] meal plan available, valet laundry. **Cards:** AE, CB, DI, DS, MC, VI.

HOLIDAY INN BOCA RATON TOWN CENTER

Phone: (561)368-5200

AAA **SAVE**

1/30-3/31		2P: $155	XP: $10	F17
12/1-1/29		2P: $89-$99	XP: $10	F17
4/1-9/30 & 10/1-11/30		2P: $95	XP: $10	F17

Motor Inn

Location: I-95, exit 39, SR 808 (Glades Rd), just w. 1950 Glades Rd 33431. **Fax:** 561/338-9453. **Facility:** Spanish Mediterranean style. Very attractive pool patio. Some suites with separate living room. New room package in 1999 that gives the room light tones of furniture with an attractive room decor. 184 units. Some suites ($129-$209). 3-5 stories, interior/exterior corridors. **Amenities:** voice mail, irons, hair dryers. **Dining:** restaurant, 6:30-11 am, 11:30-2 & 5-10 pm, $11-$18, cocktails. **Leisure Activities:** heated pool, wading pool, whirlpool. **Guest Services:** valet laundry. **Business Services:** meeting rooms. **Cards:** AE, CB, DI, DS, JC, MC, VI. **Special Amenities:** free newspaper.

HOLIDAY INN EXPRESS-DOWNTOWN BOCA RATON

Phone: 561/395-7172

2/1-4/30	1P: $119-$129	2P: $135-$149
12/24-1/31	1P: $109-$129	2P: $119-$139
5/1-11/30	1P: $72-$81	2P: $81-$89
12/1-12/23	1P: $65-$71	2P: $71

Motel

Location: US 1, 1 mi n of jct SR 808 (Glades Rd). 2899 N Federal Hwy 33431. **Fax:** 561/750-7351. **Facility:** Well located for downtown and beach. 48 units. 2 stories, exterior corridors. **Amenities:** extended cable TV, irons, hair dryers. **Guest Services:** [CP] meal plan available, valet laundry. **Business Services:** meeting rooms. **Cards:** AE, CB, DI, DS, MC, VI.

HOLIDAY INN-WEST BOCA

Phone: (561)482-7070

12/1-4/22	1P: $119-$149	2P: $119-$149
4/23-11/30	1P: $78-$90	2P: $78-$90

Motor Inn

Location: SR 808, w of Florida Tpke, exit 75; in Lakeside Centre Shops. 8144 Glades Rd 33434. **Fax:** 561/482-6076. **Facility:** Pete Rose Ballpark Cafe and Sportsbar features memorabilia from this baseball star's career. 97 units. **Bath:** combo or shower only. 2-4 stories, interior corridors. **Terms:** monthly rates available, package plans. **Amenities:** voice mail, irons, hair dryers. **Leisure Activities:** heated pool, game room. **Guest Services:** [BP] meal plan available, valet laundry. **Business Services:** meeting rooms. **Cards:** AE, CB, DI, DS, JC, MC, VI.

HOMESTEAD VILLAGE GUEST STUDIOS

Phone: 561/994-2599

Property failed to provide current rates

Extended Stay Motel

Location: I-95, exit 40C, just w of Congress Ave. 501 NW 77th St 33487. **Fax:** 561/994-2792. **Facility:** Office hours 7 am-9 pm, Sat 9 am-5 pm, Sun noon-8 pm. Spacious rooms. 141 efficiencies. **Bath:** combo or shower only. 22 stories, exterior corridors. **Terms:** pets ($75 fee). **Amenities:** voice mail, irons. **Guest Services:** coin laundry. **Cards:** AE, CB, DI, DS, MC, VI.

THE INN AT BOCA TEECA

Phone: (561)994-0400

12/15-4/15	1P: $125-$135	2P: $125-$135	XP: $10	F17
12/1-12/14 & 4/16-11/30	1P: $59-$69	2P: $59-$69	XP: $10	F17

Resort

Location: I-95, exit 40A (Yamato Rd), 0.5 mi e, 0.5 mi n; in Boca Teeca Country Club. 5800 NW 2nd Ave 33487. **Fax:** 561/998-8279. **Facility:** Most rooms with balcony or patio. 46 units. 3 stories, interior corridors. **Terms:** check-in 4 pm, 3 day cancellation notice, weekly & monthly rates available. **Amenities:** extended cable TV. **Leisure Activities:** heated pool, saunas, whirlpools, 6 tennis courts, exercise room. **Fee:** golf-27 holes. **Guest Services:** coin laundry. **Business Services:** meeting rooms. **Cards:** AE, DI, MC, VI.

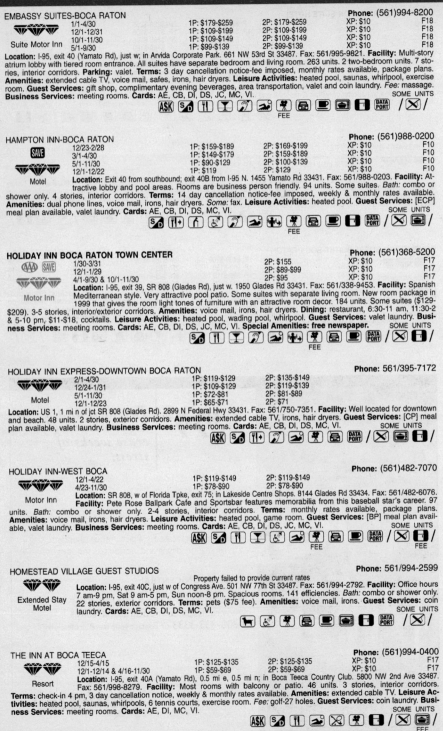

OCEAN LODGE

(AAA) (SAVE)

Motel

2/1-4/16 Wkly	1P: $650-$825	2P: $650-$825	XP: $10	F12
12/19-1/31 Wkly	1P: $525-$825	2P: $525-$825	XP: $10	F12
12/1-12/18 Dly	1P: $350-$500	2P: $350-$500	XP: $10	F12
4/17-11/30 Wkly	1P: $350-$500	2P: $350-$500	XP: $10	F12

Phone: (561)395-7772

Location: SR A1A, 0.5 mi n of jct Palmetto Park Rd. 531 N Ocean Blvd 33432. Fax: 561/395-0554. **Facility:** Comfortable to elegantly furnished rooms. Across the highway to beach. 18 units, 11 with efficiency. 2 stories, exterior corridors. **Terms:** 45 day cancellation notice, monthly rates available. **Amenities:** extended cable TV, video games, voice mail. **Leisure Activities:** heated pool. **Guest Services:** coin laundry. **Cards:** AE, DS, MC, VI. **Special Amenities:** free room upgrade (subject to availability with advanced reservations).

SOME UNITS

RADISSON BRIDGE RESORT OF BOCA RATON

(AAA) (SAVE)

Hotel

12/21-4/17	1P: $245	2P: $255	XP: $10	F16
12/1-12/20 & 4/18-11/30	1P: $149	2P: $159	XP: $10	F16

Phone: (561)368-9500

Location: Just w of SR A1A, 1 mi s of jct SR 798 (Palmetto Park Rd). 999 E Camino Real 33432. Fax: 561/362-0492. **Facility:** Many rooms, pool and cafe area overlook Intracoastal Waterway. Hair salon on property. 121 units. Some suites. **Bath:** combo or shower only. 11 stories, interior corridors. **Parking:** valet. **Terms:** 3 day cancellation notice, in season-fee imposed, package plans. **Amenities:** extended cable TV, video games, voice mail, irons, hair dryers. **Dining:** dining room, restaurant, 6 am-10 pm, Fri & Sat-11 pm; rooftop dining room with extensive Intracoastal view, closed Sun & Mon. Sunday brunch avail roof top 11 am-3 pm, $10-$28, cocktails, entertainment. **Leisure Activities:** heated pool, saunas, exercise room. Fee: boats, bicycles. **Guest Services:** gift shop, complimentary evening beverages, valet laundry. **Business Services:** meeting rooms. Fee: fax. **Cards:** AE, CB, DI, DS, JC, MC, VI. **Special Amenities:** free newspaper and free room upgrade (subject to availability with advanced reservations). *(See ad below)*

SOME UNITS

RAMADA INN

(AAA) (SAVE)

Motor Inn

12/18-4/30	1P: $115-$145		XP: $10	F18
12/1-12/17 & 5/1-11/30	1P: $65-$85		XP: $10	F18

Phone: (561)395-6850

Location: US 1, 1 mi n of jct SR 808 (Glades Rd). 2901 N Federal Hwy 33431. Fax: 561/368-7964. **Facility:** Attractive public areas. Contemporary room decor. 97 units. 2 stories, exterior corridors. **Terms:** cancellation fee imposed, small pets only ($10 extra charge, $100 deposit). *Some:* irons, hair dryers. **Dining:** restaurant, 6:30-10 am, 11-1:30 & 5-10 pm, $9-$18, cocktails. **Leisure Activities:** whirlpool. **Guest Services:** coin laundry. **Business Services:** meeting rooms. **Cards:** AE, CB, DI, DS, MC, VI. **Special Amenities:** free continental breakfast and free room upgrade (subject to availability with advanced reservations).

SOME UNITS

RESIDENCE INN-BY MARRIOTT-BOCA RATON

Phone: (561)994-3222

▼▼▼

| 12/1-4/15 | 1P: $159-$189 | 2P: $159-$189 |
| 4/16-11/30 | 1P: $99-$149 | 2P: $99-$149 |

Apartment

Location: I-95, exit 40C, just w of Congress Ave. 525 NW 77th St 33487. **Fax:** 561/994-3339. **Facility:** Studio and one-bedroom suites with fireplace. Adjacent to small lake. 120 units with kitchen. *Bath:* combo or shower only. 2 stories, exterior corridors. **Terms:** cancellation fee imposed, weekly & monthly rates available, pets ($100-$150 extra charge). **Amenities:** irons, hair dryers. *Some:* voice mail. **Leisure Activities:** heated pool, whirlpools, sports court. **Guest Services:** [BP] meal plan available, complimentary evening beverages: Mon-Fri, area transportation, valet and coin laundry. **Business Services:** meeting rooms.

SOME UNITS

ASK SD [icons] FEE [icons] / X VCR / FEE

SPRINGHILL SUITES BY MARRIOTT

Phone: (561)994-2107

▼▼▼

12/1-4/15	1P: $129-$189	2P: $129-$189	XP: $10	F17
10/1-11/30	1P: $119-$139	2P: $119-$139		
4/16-9/30	1P: $89-$119	2P: $89-$119	XP: $10	F17

Motel

Location: I-95, exit 40 (Yamato Rd), just w; in Arvida Corporate Park. 5130 NW 8th Ave 33487. **Fax:** 561/994-0226. **Facility:** Large suite like rooms. Spacious rooms with a contemporary decor. Relaxing pool area. 146 units. *Bath:* combo or shower only. 5 stories, interior corridors. **Amenities:** extended cable TV, dual phone lines, voice mail, irons, hair dryers. **Leisure Activities:** heated pool, whirlpool, exercise room. **Guest Services:** valet and coin laundry. **Business Services:** meeting rooms, administrative services. **Cards:** AE, DI, DS, JC, MC, VI. *(See color ad p 245)*

SOME UNITS

ASK SD [icons] FEE [icons] / X /

TOWNEPLACE SUITES BY MARRIOTT

Phone: (561)994-7232

▼▼▼

| 12/1-4/15 | 1P: $129-$159 | 2P: $129-$159 |
| 4/16-11/30 | 1P: $59-$79 | 2P: $59-$79 |

Extended Stay Motel

Location: I-95, exit 40 (Yamato Rd), just w; in Arvida Corporate Park. 5110 NW 8th Ave 33487. **Fax:** 561/994-2134. **Facility:** Located at the edge of Arvida Corporate Park. Spacious and well equipped rooms with a colorful contemporary decor. Limited housekeeping. 91 units with kitchen. 19 two-bedroom units. Some suites. *Bath:* combo or shower only. 4 stories, interior corridors. **Amenities:** extended cable TV, video games, dual phone lines, voice mail, irons. **Leisure Activities:** heated pool, exercise room. **Guest Services:** valet and coin laundry. **Business Services:** fax. **Cards:** AE, DI, DS, JC, MC, VI. *(See color ad p 245)*

SOME UNITS

ASK SD [icons] / X /

The following lodging was either not evaluated or did not meet AAA rating requirements but is listed for your information only.

BOCA RATON RESORT & CLUB

Phone: 561/395-3000

[fyi] Not evaluated. **Location:** I-95, exit 38, 2.3 mi e on Palmetto Park Rd to Federal Hwy; 0.5 mi. 501 E Camino Real 33432 (PO Box 2025). Facilities, services, and decor characterize an upscale property.

——— WHERE TO DINE ———

CRAB HOUSE SEAFOOD RESTAURANT

Lunch: $5-$14 **Dinner: $13-$18** **Phone: 561/750-0498**

▼▼ ▼▼

Seafood

Location: Powerline Rd and SW 18th St; in Whiteside Shops. 1.3 mi s of jct Palmetto Park Rd. 6909 SW 18th St 33433. **Hours:** 11:30 am-10 pm, Fri-11 pm, Sat noon-11 pm. Closed: 11/22. **Reservations:** accepted. **Features:** casual dress; children's menu; early bird specials; carryout; salad bar; cocktails & lounge. When you're hungry for seafood but don't want to make a trip to the beach, this popular and busy lakefront restaurant fits the bill. Enjoy a drink at the outside bar before sampling varied crab dishes, seafood offerings and raw bar delicacies. **Cards:** AE, DI, DS, MC, VI.

X

FIREHOUSE RESTAURANT & LOUNGE

Dinner: $10-$25 **Phone: 561/997-6006**

▼▼ ▼▼

Steak & Seafood

Location: US 1, 1 mi n of jct Yamato Rd. 6751 N Federal Hwy 33487. **Hours:** 4 pm-11 pm. Closed: 12/25; also Mon in summer. **Reservations:** suggested. **Features:** dressy casual; children's menu; salad bar; cocktails & lounge. A firehouse-style building is the unusual setting for this eatery, decorated with related memorabilia and antiques. Dine on prime rib, steak and fresh fish caught in local waters. Daily happy hour with complimentary hors d'oeuvres from 4 pm to 7 pm. **Cards:** AE, CB, DI, DS, MC, VI.

X

KATHY'S GAZEBO CAFE

Lunch: $9-$18 **Dinner: $24-$35** **Phone: 561/395-6032**

▼▼▼▼

Continental

Location: US 1, 0.5 mi s of Yamato Rd. 4199 N Federal Hwy 33431. **Hours:** 11:30 am-3 & 5:30-10 pm, Sat & Sun from 5:30 pm. Closed major holidays; also Sun 8/7-9/1. **Reservations:** suggested. **Features:** semi-formal attire; carryout; cocktails; a la carte. This popular, European-style restaurant features fine dining with generous portions of freshly prepared entrees. Subdued lighting, fresh flowers and comfortable booths enhance the intimate, cozy setting. Patio dining is also offered. **Cards:** AE, MC, VI.

X

LA VIEILLE MAISON Historical

Dinner: $18-$42 **Phone: 561/391-6701**

AAA

▼▼▼▼

French

Location: Just w of SR A1A. 770 E Palmetto Park Rd 33432. **Hours:** 6 pm-9:30 pm, to 10 pm in season. **Reservations:** required. **Features:** semi-formal attire; cocktails & lounge; valet parking; a la carte, also prix fixe. This restored Mizner-style mansion with a lovely courtyard is set among lush tropical gardens. Several intimate dining rooms, each tastefully appointed, provide the backdrop for nouvelle and classic French cuisine. An extensive wine list is available. **Cards:** AE, DI, DS, MC, VI.

X

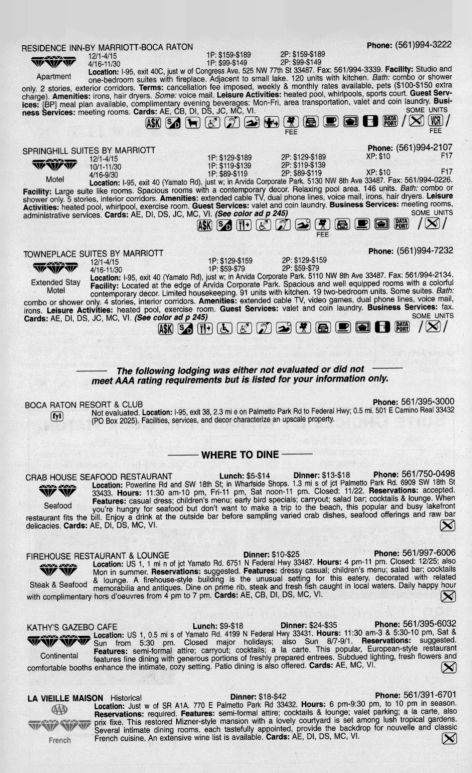

MARK'S AT THE PARK   **Lunch:** $8-$15   **Dinner:** $15-$30   **Phone:** 561-395-0770

Armenian

Location: I-95, exit 39, SR 808 (Glades Rd), e on Glades Rd, 2.2 mi, then 0.4 mi s on N Federal Hwy, then e to Mizner Park, opposite fountains. 344 Plaza Real 33432. **Hours:** 11:30 am-3 & 5:30-11 pm, Fri & Sat-midnight, Sun-10 pm. **Reservations:** suggested. **Features:** dressy casual; Sunday brunch; carryout; cocktails & lounge; valet parking; a la carte. Featuring "New Mediterranean" cuisine. A delicate balance of all the flavors of the different countries of the region with the fresh local ingredients, the foods are wonderful. Try everything, there is something for everyone, fish, poultry, fresh pasta and meat. The atmosphere is modern contemporary with muted colors accented with mild tones. Soft indirect lighting, a chef's counter with a view of the kitchen. Outdoor seating is also available. **Cards:** AE, DI, MC, VI.

NEW YORK PRIME, A STEAKHOUSE   **Dinner:** $25-$39   **Phone:** 561-998-3881

Steak House

Location: I-95, exit 39 (Glades Rd). 2350 NW Executive Center Dr 33431. **Hours:** 5 pm-10 pm. **Reservations:** required. **Features:** No A/C; dressy casual; cocktails & lounge; valet parking; a la carte. Steak is the prime entree and not to be overlooked. There are some other meat selections as well as seafood. The steaks are large and the lobster's are larger. A very upbeat and bustling room. An extensive wine list available. **Cards:** AE, MC, VI.

RED BOWL RICE & NOODLE CO   **Lunch:** $5-$12   **Dinner:** $8-$16   **Phone:** 561-394-6699

English

Location: I-95, exit 38, 2.1 mi w on Palmetto Park Rd, then s on Powerline Rd, then w; in the Palms Plaza. 22191 Powerline Rd 33433. **Hours:** 11:30 am-10:30 pm, Fri-11 pm, Sat 5 pm-11 pm, Sun 5 pm-10:30 pm. Closed major holidays. **Features:** dressy casual; children's menu; carryout; cocktails & lounge; a la carte. Unique decor with a Chinese twist. The cuisine is "Cool Asian" with flavors of Asia and the Pacific Islands. Try the "U Choose Stir Fry," you choose the ingredients and they stir fry. Other favorites also available. **Cards:** AE, DI, DS, MC, VI.

ZEMI   **Lunch:** $8-$15   **Dinner:** $14-$36   **Phone:** 561-391-7177

American

Location: I-95, exit 38, 0.3 mi w of Palmetto Park Rd, 1 mi n on Military Tr; in the Boca Center. 5050 Town Center Circle #245 33486. **Hours:** 11:30 am-2:30 & 6-10:30 pm, Fri-11 pm, Sat 6 pm-11 pm, Sun 6 pm-10 pm. **Features:** semi-formal attire; cocktails & lounge; fee for valet parking; a la carte. They call it "A New Style American Restaurant", serving Eclectic American Cuisine with major influences of Asian and Mediterranean taste. All foods with the freshest of ingredients, brick oven in the back visible from most tables. Large fabric panels soften the bustling setting, large mirrors brighten the room with its soft indirect lighting. Tables on the patio with heaters for that chill. **Cards:** AE, CB, DI, DS, MC, VI.

The following restaurant has not been evaluated by AAA but is listed for your information only.

FLANIGAN'S SEAFOOD BAR & GRILL   **Phone:** 561-395-4699

`fyi`   Not evaluated. **Location:** 45 S Federal Hwy. **Features:** A casual atmosphere that is inexpensive and family friendly. Known for their barbecue baby back ribs, large burgers and fresh local seafood.

BONIFAY pop. 2,600

——— **WHERE TO STAY** ———

TIVOLI INN   All Year   1P: $59-$90   2P: $59-$90   XP: $7   **Phone:** 850/547-4251   F12

Motel

Location: I-10, exit 17, 0.5 mi n. 2004 S Waukesha St 32425. Fax: 850/547-6679. **Facility:** Serene setting. 56 units. 2 stories, exterior corridors. **Terms:** pets ($7 extra charge). **Amenities:** extended cable TV. **Leisure Activities:** jogging. **Guest Services:** [CP] meal plan available, coin laundry. **Business Services:** meeting rooms. **Cards:** AE, CB, DI, DS, MC, VI.

SOME UNITS

BONITA SPRINGS pop. 13,600

——— **WHERE TO STAY** ———

AMERICINN MOTEL & SUITES   **Phone:** (941)495-9255

1/23-4/15	1P: $137-$143	2P: $137-$143	XP: $6	F18
12/21-1/22	1P: $105-$112	2P: $105-$112	XP: $6	F18
12/1-12/20	1P: $73-$79	2P: $73-$79	XP: $6	F18
4/16-11/30	1P: $70-$76	2P: $70-$76	XP: $6	F18

Motel

Location: I-75, exit 18, just s of Bonita Beach Rd on US 41. 28600 Trails Edge Blvd 34134. Fax: 941/495-6448. **Facility:** Newer construction motel units with some spacious suites. 87 units. 9 two-bedroom units. Some suites ($90-$167). **Bath:** combo or shower only. 4 stories, interior corridors. **Amenities:** extended cable TV, irons. **Leisure Activities:** heated pool, exercise room, game room. **Guest Services:** [ECP] meal plan available, gift shop, coin laundry. **Business Services:** meeting rooms. **Cards:** AE, DI, DS, MC, VI. *(See color ad p 818)*

SOME UNITS

COMFORT INN HOTEL   **Phone:** (941)992-5001

1/19-4/21	1P: $99-$109	2P: $104-$114	XP: $5	F17
4/22-11/30	1P: $52-$97	2P: $57-$102	XP: $5	F17
12/1-1/18	1P: $89-$94	2P: $89-$99	XP: $5	F17

Motor Inn

Location: I-75, exit 18, 2.5 mi w on CR 865. 9800 Bonita Beach Rd 34135. Fax: 941/992-9283. **Facility:** Large rooms, all with wet bar; poolside rooms also have queen sleeper sofa. 69 units. 3 stories, interior corridors. **Amenities:** extended cable TV, voice mail, safes. **Leisure Activities:** heated pool, whirlpool. **Guest Services:** [ECP] meal plan available, coin laundry. **Business Services:** meeting rooms. **Cards:** AE, DI, DS, MC, VI. **Special Amenities:** free continental breakfast and free local telephone calls.

SOME UNITS

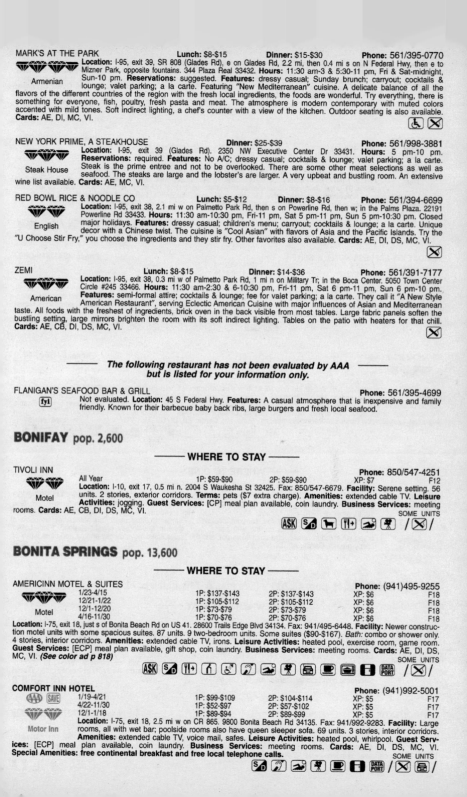

DAYS INN

SAVE

Motel

Phone: (941)947-3366

All Year   1P: $42-$125   2P: $42-$125
Location: I-75, exit 18, just w on CR 865. 28090 Quails Nest Ln 34135. **Fax:** 941/947-6789. **Facility:** Economy rooms. Convenient highway location. 100 units. *Bath:* combo or shower only. 1 story, exterior corridors. **Terms:** check-in 4 pm. **Amenities:** extended cable TV. **Leisure Activities:** heated pool. **Guest Services:** coin laundry. **Cards:** AE, DI, DS, JC, MC, VI.

SOME UNITS

HAMPTON INN

SAVE

Motel

Phone: 941/947-9393

12/17-4/15	1P: $89-$129	2P: $89-$139
12/1-12/16	1P: $64-$69	2P: $69-$74
4/16-11/30	1P: $59-$69	2P: $59-$74

Location: I-75, exit 18, 3.3 mi w on CR 865 at jct US 41 and Bonita Beach Rd. 27900 Crown Lake Blvd 34135. **Fax:** 941/947-3966. **Facility:** Centrally located newer building with very good-sized rooms and contemporary decor. 91 units. *Bath:* combo or shower only. 3 stories, interior corridors. **Terms:** cancellation fee imposed, monthly rates available. **Amenities:** extended cable TV, voice mail, irons, hair dryers. **Leisure Activities:** heated pool. **Guest Services:** [ECP] meal plan available, valet laundry. **Business Services:** meeting rooms. **Cards:** AE, DI, DS, MC, VI.

SOME UNITS

HOLIDAY INN EXPRESS HOTEL & SUITES

Motel

Phone: (941)948-0699

1/1-4/15	1P: $130-$150
12/1-12/31	1P: $119-$140
4/16-11/30	1P: $74-$85

Location: I-75, exit 18, 3.3 mi w on CR 865 at jct US 41 and Bonita Beach Rd. 27891 Crown Lake Blvd 34135. **Fax:** 941/948-0676. **Facility:** 108 units. *Bath:* combo or shower only. 4 stories, interior corridors. **Terms:** 5 day cancellation notice. **Amenities:** extended cable TV, dual phone lines, voice mail, irons, hair dryers. **Leisure Activities:** heated pool. **Guest Services:** [CP] & [ECP] meal plans available, valet and coin laundry. **Cards:** AE, CB, DI, DS, JC, MC, VI.

SOME UNITS

TRIANON BONITA BAY

Motel

Phone: 941/948-4400

4/1-4/30	2P: $115-$300	XP: $10	F18
5/1-11/30	2P: $75-$290	XP: $10	F18
12/1-3/31	2P: $75-$125	XP: $10	F18

Location: I-75, exit 19, just w of US 41, 6 mi s of Corkscrew Rd. 3401 Bay Commons Dr 34134. **Fax:** 941/948-4401. **Facility:** Luxurious guest rooms and public areas. Some rooms with balconies and lake view. 100 units. Some suites. *Bath:* combo or shower only. 4 stories, interior corridors. **Terms:** cancellation fee imposed, package plans. **Amenities:** extended cable TV, voice mail, safes, irons, hair dryers. *Some:* CD players. **Leisure Activities:** heated pool. **Guest Services:** [ECP] meal plan available, valet laundry. **Business Services:** meeting rooms, fax. **Cards:** AE, DI, DS, MC, VI.

SOME UNITS

FEE   FEE

———— WHERE TO DINE ————

ROOFTOP RESTAURANT

Seafood

Dinner: $11-$20   **Phone:** 941/992-0033

Location: SR 865, 4.5 mi w of US 41; in Casa Bonita Plaza. 25999 Hickory Blvd 34134. **Hours:** 5 pm-10 pm, Sun 10:30 am-2 & 5-10 pm. Closed: Mon 5/1-11/30. **Reservations:** suggested. **Features:** casual dress; Sunday brunch; children's menu; carryout; cocktails & lounge; entertainment. This nautical eatery offers a waterfront view and Florida cuisine with pasta, beef, chicken and locally caught seafood. Fresh-baked bread is served in a cute terra cotta flowerpot, and the house salad includes bay shrimp and three types of crispy greens. **Cards:** AE, DI, MC, VI.

BOYNTON BEACH pop. 46,200   (See map p. 710; index p. 712)

———— WHERE TO STAY ————

ATLANTIC LODGE

Motel

Phone: 561/732-4446   68

12/15-4/14	1P: $66	2P: $70-$77	XP: $10 D12
12/1-12/14 & 4/15-11/30	1P: $40	2P: $44-$47	XP: $5 D12

Location: US 1, 0.8 mi s of jct Woolbright Rd. 2607 S Federal Hwy 33435. **Fax:** 561/731-0325. **Facility:** Quiet location. 20 units, 9 with efficiency. *Bath:* combo or shower only. 1 story, exterior corridors. **Terms:** 14 day cancellation notice-fee imposed. **Amenities:** extended cable TV. **Leisure Activities:** heated pool. **Guest Services:** coin laundry. **Cards:** AE, DI, DS, MC, VI.

BOYNTON MOTEL

Motel

Phone: (561)737-3729   67

12/18-4/15	1P: $65	2P: $70	XP: $5 F17
12/1-12/17 & 4/16-11/30	1P: $45	2P: $50	XP: $5 F17

Location: US 1, 0.5 mi s of jct SR 804, Boynton Beach Blvd. 623 S Federal Hwy 33435. **Fax:** 561/731-1612. **Facility:** Quiet location, well kept property. 21 efficiencies. *Bath:* shower only. 1 story, exterior corridors. **Terms:** 3 day cancellation notice, weekly & monthly rates available. **Amenities:** extended cable TV. **Guest Services:** coin laundry. **Cards:** AE, CB, DI, DS, JC, MC, VI.

(See map p. 710)

HAMPTON INN BOYNTON BEACH

[SAVE]

Motel

1/16-5/1	2P: $169-$219	XP: $10	F18
12/21-1/15	2P: $139-$189	XP: $10	F18
12/1-12/20	2P: $129-$169	XP: $10	F18
5/2-11/30	2P: $99-$129	XP: $10	F18

Phone: (561)369-0018 [63]

Location: I-95, exit 44C (Gateway Blvd), 1.2 mi w. 1475 W Gateway Blvd 33426. Fax: 561/738-5235. **Facility:** Very attractive public areas with comfortable conversational seating. A relaxing pool next to a small lake, accented by flowering plants. Rooms are large with furniture of cherry wood finish and classic colors. Attention to detail is a priority. 107 units, 3 with efficiency. Some suites. *Bath:* combo or shower only. 4 stories, interior corridors. **Terms:** weekly & monthly rates available. **Amenities:** extended cable TV, video games, voice mail, irons, hair dryers. **Leisure Activities:** heated pool. **Guest Services:** [ECP] meal plan available, complimentary evening beverages: Mon-Thurs, valet and coin laundry. **Business Services:** meeting rooms. **Cards:** AE, CB, DI, DS, MC, VI.

SOME UNITS

HOLIDAY INN-CATALINA

Motor Inn

1/29-4/28	1P: $169-$199	2P: $169-$199
12/21-1/28	1P: $159-$169	2P: $159-$169
4/29-11/30	1P: $89-$129	2P: $89-$129
12/1-12/20	1P: $89-$109	2P: $89-$109

Phone: (561)737-4600 [64]

Location: SR 807 (Congress Ave), 0.3 mi s of jct SR 806 (Gateway Blvd), adjacent to Catalina Shopping Center. 1601 N Congress Ave 33426. Fax: 561/734-6523. **Facility:** The exterior has a Spanish look. A large pool area with a tropical canopy of trees with flowering plants around the deck. The rooms are spacious with light wood tones. A soft color package. 170 units. 14 two-bedroom units and 18 units with kitchen. Some suites ($110-$275). 4 stories, interior/exterior corridors. **Terms:** package plans. **Amenities:** voice mail, irons, hair dryers. **Leisure Activities:** heated pool, whirlpool, exercise room. **Guest Services:** valet laundry. **Business Services:** conference facilities. **Cards:** AE, CB, DI, DS, MC, VI.

SOME UNITS

HOLIDAY INN EXPRESS I-95

[AAA] [SAVE]

Motel

12/21-11/30	2P: $66-$127	XP: $10	F
12/1-12/20	2P: $95-$112	XP: $10	F

Phone: (561)734-9100 [66]

Location: SR 804, Boynton Beach Blvd at jct I-95, exit 44. 480 W Boynton Beach Blvd 33435. Fax: 561/738-7193. **Facility:** Easy access to interstate. 102 units. 4 stories, interior corridors. **Terms:** weekly & monthly rates available, package plans. **Amenities:** extended cable TV, irons, hair dryers. **Guest Services:** [ECP] meal plan available, complimentary evening beverages, coin laundry. **Business Services:** meeting rooms. **Cards:** AE, DI, DS, JC, MC, VI. **Special Amenities:** free continental breakfast and free local telephone calls.
(See color ad below)

SOME UNITS

FEE FEE

(See map p. 710)

———— WHERE TO DINE ————

HOLIDAY HOUSE
American

Lunch: $4-$6   **Dinner:** $4-$7   **Phone:** 561/732-6841   ㉞
Location: On US 1, 0.3 mi n of jct SR 804 Boynton Beach Blvd. 710 N Federal Hwy 33435. **Hours:** 11 am-3 & 4-8:30 pm. Closed: 12/24 for dinner. **Features:** casual dress; children's menu; carryout; buffet. This family-owned chain of restaurants features a medley of salads, vegetables, and hand-carved roast beef, ham and turkey. Piping-hot garlic bread, triple-layer cakes, homemade pies and cobblers finish off the smorgasbord-style meal. Smoke free premises. **Cards:** AE, MC, VI.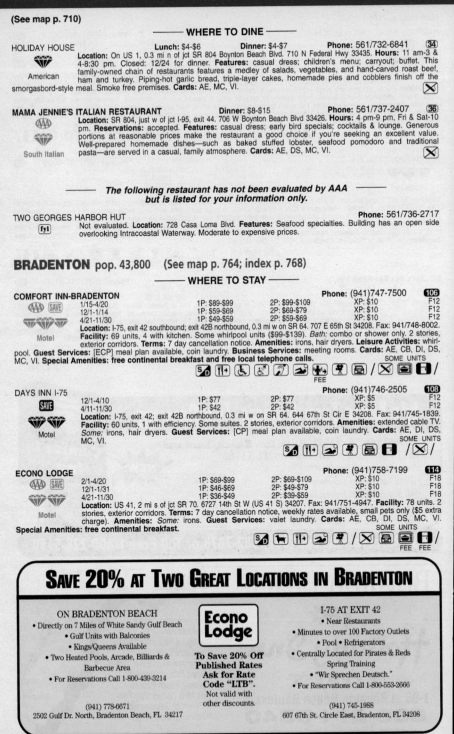

MAMA JENNIE'S ITALIAN RESTAURANT
South Italian

Dinner: $8-$15   **Phone:** 561/737-2407   ㊱
Location: SR 804, just w of jct I-95, exit 44. 706 W Boynton Beach Blvd 33426. **Hours:** 4 pm-9 pm, Fri & Sat-10 pm. **Reservations:** accepted. **Features:** casual dress; early bird specials; cocktails & lounge. Generous portions at reasonable prices make the restaurant a good choice if you're seeking an excellent value. Well-prepared homemade dishes—such as baked stuffed lobster, seafood pomodoro and traditional pasta—are served in a casual, family atmosphere. **Cards:** AE, DS, MC, VI.

———— *The following restaurant has not been evaluated by AAA* ————
but is listed for your information only.

TWO GEORGES HARBOR HUT
fyi

Phone: 561/736-2717
Not evaluated. **Location:** 728 Casa Loma Blvd. **Features:** Seafood specialties. Building has an open side overlooking Intracoastal Waterway. Moderate to expensive prices.

BRADENTON pop. 43,800   (See map p. 764; index p. 768)

———— WHERE TO STAY ————

COMFORT INN-BRADENTON
Motel

Phone: (941)747-7500   ⓐ⓪⓺
1/15-4/20	1P: $89-$99	2P: $99-$109	XP: $10 F12
12/1-1/14	1P: $59-$69	2P: $69-$79	XP: $10 F12
4/21-11/30	1P: $49-$59	2P: $59-$69	XP: $10 F12

Location: I-75, exit 42 southbound; exit 42B northbound, 0.3 mi w on SR 64. 707 E 65th St 34208. Fax: 941/748-8002. **Facility:** 69 units, 4 with kitchen. Some whirlpool units ($99-$139). *Bath:* combo or shower only. 2 stories, exterior corridors. **Terms:** 7 day cancellation notice. **Amenities:** irons, hair dryers. **Leisure Activities:** whirlpool. **Guest Services:** [ECP] meal plan available, coin laundry. **Business Services:** meeting rooms. **Cards:** AE, CB, DI, DS, MC, VI. **Special Amenities: free continental breakfast and free local telephone calls.**

SOME UNITS

DAYS INN I-75
Motel

Phone: (941)746-2505   ⓐ⓪⓼
12/1-4/10	1P: $77	2P: $77	XP: $5 F12
4/11-11/30	1P: $42	2P: $42	XP: $5 F12

Location: I-75, exit 42; exit 42B northbound, 0.3 mi w on SR 64. 644 67th St Cir E 34208. Fax: 941/745-1839. **Facility:** 60 units, 1 with efficiency. Some suites. 2 stories, exterior corridors. **Amenities:** extended cable TV. *Some:* irons, hair dryers. **Guest Services:** [CP] meal plan available, coin laundry. **Cards:** AE, DI, DS, MC, VI.

SOME UNITS

ECONO LODGE
Motel

Phone: (941)758-7199   ⓐ⓵⓸
2/1-4/20	1P: $69-$99	2P: $69-$109	XP: $10 F18
12/1-1/31	1P: $46-$69	2P: $49-$79	XP: $10 F18
4/21-11/30	1P: $36-$49	2P: $39-$59	XP: $10 F18

Location: US 41, 2 mi s of jct SR 70. 6727 14th St W (US 41 S) 34207. Fax: 941/751-4947. **Facility:** 78 units. 2 stories, exterior corridors. **Terms:** 7 day cancellation notice, weekly rates available, small pets only ($5 extra charge). **Amenities:** *Some:* irons. **Guest Services:** valet laundry. **Cards:** AE, CB, DI, DS, MC, VI. **Special Amenities: free continental breakfast.**

SOME UNITS

(See map p. 764)

ECONO LODGE I-75

Phone: (941)745-1988 **113**

	1P: $69-$94	2P: $75-$99	XP: $4	F18
1/31-4/15	1P: $54-$84	2P: $59-$89	XP: $4	F18
12/22-1/30	1P: $49-$59	2P: $51-$68	XP: $4	F18
4/16-11/30	1P: $47-$57	2P: $49-$66	XP: $4	F18
12/1-12/21				

Motel **Location:** I-75, exit 42 southbound; exit 42B northbound, 0.3 mi w on SR 64. 607 67th St Cir E 34208. Fax: 41/746-6983. **Facility:** 53 units. 2 stories, exterior corridors. **Terms:** weekly rates available, package plans - off season. **Amenities:** extended cable TV. **Guest Services:** coin laundry. **Cards:** AE, CB, DI, DS, JC, MC, VI. **Special Amenities:** free local telephone calls. *(See color ad p 250)*

SOME UNITS

HOLIDAY INN EXPRESS

Phone: (941)748-6610 **107**

All Year 2P: $65-$170 XP: $7 F18

Motel **Location:** I-75, exit 42 southbound; exit 42B northbound, 0.3 mi w on SR 64. 648 E 67th Cir 34208. Fax: 941/748-0922. **Facility:** 60 units. Some suites and whirlpool units ($99-$170). *Bath:* combo or shower only. 3 stories, interior corridors. **Terms:** package plans. **Amenities:** extended cable TV, dual phone lines, voice mail, irons, hair dryers. **Guest Services:** [ECP] meal plan available, valet and coin laundry. **Business Services:** administrative services, PC, fax. **Cards:** AE, DI, DS, MC, VI.

SOME UNITS

HOLIDAY INN-RIVERFRONT

Phone: (941)747-8599 **109**

| 1/1-4/30 | 1P: $129 |
| 12/1-12/31 & 5/1-11/30 | 1P: $99 |

Hotel **Location:** W of US 41 and 301, at south side of Hernando Desoto Bridge via 3rd St W. 100 Riverfront Dr W 34205. Fax: 603/559-2127. **Facility:** Many rooms with river view and several suites overlook the courtyard which is extensively landscaped and with attractive fountain, Spanish influenced exterior and public area design. 153 units. Some suites ($98-$134). 5 stories, interior corridors. **Terms:** package plans. **Amenities:** voice mail, irons, hair dryers. **Leisure Activities:** heated pool, whirlpool, fishing, bicycles, exercise room. **Guest Services:** gift shop, valet and coin laundry. **Business Services:** conference facilities, fax. **Cards:** AE, CB, DI, DS, JC, MC, VI.

SOME UNITS

HOWARD JOHNSON EXPRESS INN

Phone: (941)756-8399 **117**

3/1-4/15	1P: $56-$80	2P: $56-$90	XP: $5	F17
1/1-2/28	1P: $40-$80	2P: $40-$90	XP: $5	F17
12/1-12/31 & 4/16-11/30	1P: $33-$45	2P: $33-$50	XP: $5	F17

Motel **Location:** US 41, 1.5 mi s of jct SR 70. 6511 14th (US 41 S) St W 34207. Fax: 941/755-1387. **Facility:** 48 units, 12 with efficiency. 2 stories, exterior corridors. **Terms:** 7 day cancellation notice, weekly rates available, pets ($5 extra charge). **Amenities:** extended cable TV. *Some:* irons, hair dryers. **Leisure Activities:** heated pool, sun decks. **Guest Services:** coin laundry. **Cards:** AE, CB, DI, DS, MC, VI. **Special Amenities:** free continental breakfast and free room upgrade (subject to availability with advanced reservations).

SOME UNITS

PARK INN & SUITES

Phone: (941)795-4633 **110**

| 2/16-4/21 | 1P: $74-$124 | 2P: $74-$124 |
| 12/1-2/15 & 4/22-11/30 | 1P: $64-$94 | 2P: $64-$94 |

Motel **Location:** 2 mi w of jct US 41 and SR 684 (Cortez Rd), just s. 4450 47th St W 34210. Fax: 941/795-0808. **Facility:** 130 units. Some suites and whirlpool units. 3 stories, interior corridors. **Terms:** package plans, small pets only ($10 extra charge). **Amenities:** video games, irons, hair dryers. **Leisure Activities:** heated pool, whirlpool. **Guest Services:** [ECP] meal plan available, complimentary evening beverages, valet laundry. **Business Services:** meeting rooms, fax. **Cards:** AE, CB, DI, DS, JC, MC, VI. **Special Amenities:** free continental breakfast and free newspaper. *(See color ad below)*

SOME UNITS

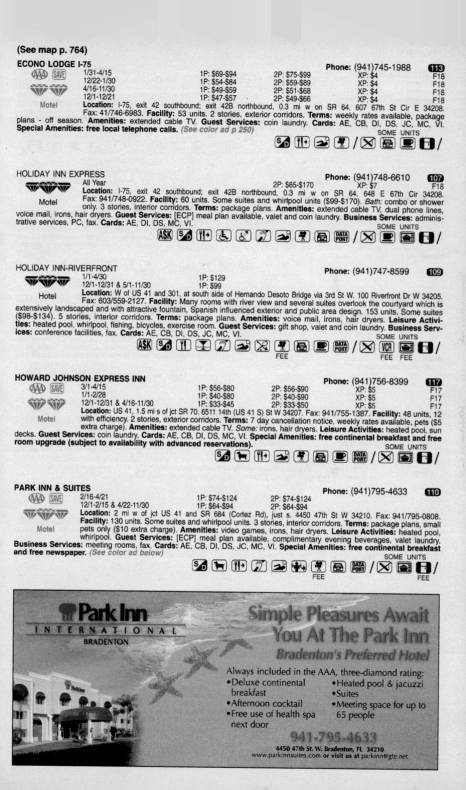

(See map p. 764)

QUALITY INN & SUITES

Phone: (941)747-6465 112

SAVE

Motel

			XP: $5	F16
1/1-4/30	1P: $70-$95	2P: $70-$95	XP: $5	F16
12/1-12/31	1P: $55-$85	2P: $55-$85	XP: $5	F16
5/1-11/30	1P: $45-$65	2P: $45-$65	XP: $5	F16

Location: US 41, 1 mi s of jct SR 64. 2303 1st St E 34208. Fax: 941/747-1070. **Facility:** 186 units. Some suites ($65-$95). 2 stories, exterior corridors. **Terms:** 3 day cancellation notice-fee imposed, monthly rates available, package plans. **Amenities:** extended cable TV. *Some:* irons. **Leisure Activities:** heated pool, 2 tennis courts, playground, shuffleboard. **Guest Services:** [ECP] meal plan available, coin laundry. **Business Services:** fax. **Cards:** AE, DI, DS, MC, VI.

SOME UNITS

SHOREWALK VACATION VILLAS RESORT

Phone: (941)794-9800 111

Condominium

2/1-4/15	1P: $129	2P: $129
12/16-1/31	1P: $99	2P: $99
12/1-12/15 & 4/16-11/30	1P: $89	2P: $89

Location: 2 mi w of US 41 on SR 684 (Cortez Rd), just s on 47th St W. 4601 46th St Ct W 34210. Fax: 941/795-2163. **Facility:** All rooms with 2 baths, kitchen and washer/dryer. 150 two-bedroom units with kitchen. 2 stories, exterior corridors. **Terms:** 14 day cancellation notice-fee imposed, weekly & monthly rates available, package plans. **Amenities:** extended cable TV, irons. *Some:* hair dryers. **Leisure Activities:** 2 heated pools, whirlpools, fishing, 2 lighted tennis courts, recreation program, social program, playground, shuffleboard, volleyball. *Fee:* paddleboats, bicycles. **Guest Services:** complimentary laundry. **Cards:** AE, DS, MC, VI.

SOME UNITS

SUPER 8 MOTEL

Phone: (941)756-6656 116

(AAA) **SAVE**

Motel

2/1-4/20	1P: $69-$89	2P: $79-$99	XP: $10	F15
1/1-1/31	1P: $44-$70	2P: $49-$75	XP: $10	F15
4/21-11/30	1P: $40-$60	2P: $49-$65		
12/1-12/31	1P: $40-$60	2P: $49-$65	XP: $10	F15

Location: US 41, 1.5 mi s of jct SR 70. 6516 14th (US 41 S) St W 34207. Fax: 941/758-3847. **Facility:** 49 units. 2 stories, exterior corridors. **Terms:** weekly rates available, small pets only ($10 fee). **Amenities:** *Some:* irons. **Guest Services:** coin laundry. **Cards:** AE, CB, DI, DS, JC, MC, VI. **Special Amenities:** early check-in/late check-out and free continental breakfast.

SOME UNITS

——— WHERE TO DINE ———

ANNA MARIA OYSTER BAR

(AAA)

Seafood

Lunch: $5-$25 Dinner: $5-$25 Phone: 941-758-7880 52

Location: On US 41 at jct 69th Ave, 2.1 mi s of jct. 6906 14th St W (US 91S) 34207. **Hours:** 11:30 am-10 pm, Fri & Sat-11 pm. **Features:** casual dress; cocktails & lounge; a la carte. Island style dining with contemporary setting. Lots of nautical and island touches for a fun atmosphere. The menu has a multitude of selection from seafood to poultry to meat dishes. The fried shrimp is wonderful. **Cards:** AE, DS, MC, VI.

CATTLE COMPANY CAFE

American

Lunch: $5-$11 Dinner: $5-$11 Phone: 941/758-5643 50

Location: On US 41 at jct Florida Blvd. 6706 14th St W 34207. **Hours:** 11 am-9 pm, Fri & Sat-9:30 pm. Closed: 11/22, 12/25. **Features:** casual dress; children's menu; carryout; salad bar; a la carte, buffet. Very basic but maintained decor. Service line type food line placing order which is then delivered to table. Salad bar is also available with variety of fresh ingredients. The menu offers such items as sirloin steak, sandwiches, seafood, chicken, combination plates, special steaks. **Cards:** MC, VI.

LEVEROCK'S OF PERICO HARBOR

Steak & Seafood

Lunch: $6-$9 Dinner: $9-$21 Phone: 941/794-8900 54

Location: SR 64, on Perico Island, east side of Anna Maria Island Bridge. 12320 Manatee Ave W 34209. **Hours:** 11:30 am-10 pm. Closed: 11/22, 12/25; also Super Bowl for dinner. **Features:** casual dress; Sunday brunch; children's menu; early bird specials; carryout; cocktails & lounge. Atmosphere abounds at this waterfront destination, where busy boat docks and gorgeous sunsets are among the many sights to see. The seafood Martinique, babyback ribs and puffed seafood pastry with cream sauce are particularly tasty. **Cards:** AE, DI, DS, MC, VI.

MILLER'S DUTCH KITCH'N

American

Lunch: $4-$14 Dinner: $4-$14 Phone: 941/746-8253 53

Location: Downtown on US Business Rt 41 at jct 35th Ave W. 3401 14th St W 34205. **Hours:** 11 am-8 pm. Closed major holidays; also Sun. **Features:** casual dress; children's menu; carryout; a la carte. Amish cooking and courteous service are the attractions, with simple meals to remind you of home like pan-fried chicken with potatoes and gravy; or come in for a cup of coffee and a slice of one of 20 made-from-scratch pies, like the rich coconut cream. Smoke free premises. **Cards:** MC, VI.

BRADENTON BEACH pop. 1,700 (See map p. 764; index p. 767)

──────── WHERE TO STAY ────────

ECONO LODGE SURFSIDE
`SAVE`
▼▼▼
Motel
Phone: **941/778-6671** 75

2/1-4/25	2P: $119-$170	XP: $10
12/21-1/31	2P: $99-$155	XP: $10
4/26-11/30	2P: $92-$145	XP: $10
12/1-12/20	2P: $88-$139	XP: $10

Location: On SR 789, 1.2 mi n of jct SR 684. 2502 Gulf Dr N 32417. Fax: 941/778-0360. **Facility:** 53 units. 1 two-bedroom unit and 22 efficiencies. *Bath:* combo or shower only. 3 stories, exterior corridors. **Terms:** weekly & monthly rates available. **Leisure Activities:** heated pool, beach, sun deck, putting green, game room. **Guest Services:** coin laundry. **Business Services:** meeting rooms, fax. **Cards:** AE, CB, DI, DS, MC, VI. *(See color ad p 250)*   SOME UNITS

🛏➕ 🕹 🛥 🖼 💾 📠 / ✕ 💻 /

SUNSET BEACH MOTEL
AAA `SAVE`
▼▼▼
Motel
Phone: **941/778-7900** 76

1/14-4/30	2P: $110-$129	XP: $10
12/22-1/13	2P: $85-$99	XP: $10
5/1-11/30	2P: $62-$89	XP: $10
12/1-12/21	2P: $62-$71	XP: $10

Location: SR 789, 1 mi n of jct SR 684. 2201 Gulf Dr N 34217. Fax: 941/778-0485. **Facility:** Cabana available. Private beach across street. 14 units, 8 with efficiency. 2 stories, exterior corridors. **Terms:** 21 day cancellation notice-fee imposed, weekly & monthly rates available. **Amenities:** extended cable TV. *Some:* irons, hair dryers. **Leisure Activities:** heated pool, shuffleboard, barbecue grill, beach chairs, pool floats, sun deck. **Guest Services:** coin laundry. **Cards:** CB, DI, DS, MC, VI.   SOME UNITS

🛏➕ 🛥 🖼 🖼 💾 / ✕ 💻 /

TORTUGA INN
▼▼▼
Motel
Phone: **(941)778-6611** 79

All Year	2P: $99-$229

Location: SR 789, 0.3 mi n of jct SR 684. 1325 Gulf Dr N 34217. Fax: 941/778-6748. **Facility:** All rooms with private patio; beautifully landscaped grounds and pool area with fountains. 35 units. 13 two-bedroom units and 26 units with kitchen. Some suites ($129-$149) and whirlpool units ($229-$259). *Bath:* combo or shower only. 2 stories, exterior corridors. **Terms:** check-in 4 pm, 7 day cancellation notice-fee imposed, daily & monthly rates available. **Amenities:** voice mail, irons, hair dryers. **Leisure Activities:** heated pool, beach access, boat dock, fishing, exercise room. **Guest Services:** coin laundry. **Cards:** AE, CB, DS, MC, VI.   SOME UNITS

🐾 🛏➕ 🛥 ✕ VCR 🖼 💻 🖼 💾 / ✕ /

TRADEWINDS RESORT
AAA `SAVE`
▼▼▼▼
Apartment
Phone: **(941)779-0010** 77

2/1-4/30	1P: $125-$263	2P: $125-$263	XP: $10	F9
12/1-1/31	1P: $98-$236	2P: $98-$236	XP: $10	F9
5/1-11/30	1P: $79-$210	2P: $79-$210	XP: $10	F9

Location: SR 789, 0.5 mi n of jct SR 684. 1603 Gulf Dr N 34217. Fax: 941/778-6114. **Facility:** Key West style appearance set on Intracoastal Waterway. Designated smoking area. 34 units with kitchen. 1 two-bedroom unit. Some suites. *Bath:* combo or shower only. 1 story, exterior corridors. **Terms:** 2 night minimum stay, 14 day cancellation notice-fee imposed, weekly & monthly rates available, pets ($25 extra charge, in selected rooms). **Amenities:** extended cable TV, irons. *Some:* hair dryers. **Leisure Activities:** heated pool, access to private beach, fishing dock only, video library, picnic tables, barbecue areas. **Guest Services:** coin laundry. **Business Services:** fax. **Cards:** AE, DS, MC, VI.

🐾 🛏➕ 🛥 ✕ VCR 🖼 💻 🖼 💾 📠

BRANDON —*See Tampa Bay p. 840.*

BROOKSVILLE pop. 7,400

──────── WHERE TO STAY ────────

HAMPTON INN
`SAVE`
▼▼▼
Motel
Phone: **(352)796-1000**

12/25-4/15	1P: $69	2P: $69
12/1-12/24 & 4/16-11/30	1P: $64	2P: $64

Location: I-75, exit 61, just w on SR 50. 30301 Cortez Blvd 34602. Fax: 352/796-9170. **Facility:** 75 units. Some suites. *Bath:* combo or shower only. 2 stories, interior/exterior corridors. **Terms:** 7 day cancellation notice-fee imposed. **Amenities:** irons. *Some:* hair dryers. **Guest Services:** [ECP] meal plan available, valet laundry. **Business Services:** meeting rooms, fax. **Cards:** AE, CB, DI, DS, JC, MC, VI.   SOME UNITS

🛏➕ ♿ 🕹 📷 🎥 🖼 💻 📠 / ✕ 🖼 💾 /

HOLIDAY INN
▼▼ ▼▼
Motor Inn
Phone: **352/796-9481**

12/1-4/15	1P: $85	2P: $85
4/16-11/30	1P: $69	2P: $69

Location: I-75, exit 61, just w on SR 50. 30307 Cortez Blvd 34602. Fax: 352/799-7595. **Facility:** 121 units. *Bath:* combo or shower only. 2 stories, exterior corridors. **Terms:** package plans, pets ($20 fee). **Amenities:** irons, hair dryers. **Leisure Activities:** wading pool, playground, exercise room. **Guest Services:** [BP] meal plan available, valet and coin laundry. **Business Services:** meeting rooms. **Cards:** AE, CB, DI, DS, MC, VI.   SOME UNITS

ASK 🐾 🍴 🍽 🕹 🛥 🎥 🖼 💻 📠 / ✕ 🖼 💾 /

VERONA HOUSE B&B
Phone: (352)796-4001

AAA SAVE

Historic Bed & Breakfast

All Year   1P: $77-$100   2P: $77-$100   XP: $10   F18
Location: Downtown; just s of jct 61, 4 mi w on US 98/SR 50. 201 S Main St 34601. Fax: 352/799-0612. **Facility:** Verona model Sears and Roebuck catalog house circa 1925, two story Dutch colonial. On the National Register of Historic Places. Designated smoking area. 4 units. *Bath:* combo or shower only. 2 stories, interior corridors. **Parking:** street only. **Terms:** 7 day cancellation notice, weekly & monthly rates available, package plans. **Amenities:** no TVs. **Leisure Activities:** whirlpool, bicycles, barbecue grill. **Guest Services:** [BP] meal plan available. **Cards:** AE, DI, DS, MC, VI. **Special Amenities:** early check-in/late check-out and free room upgrade (subject to availability with advanced reservations).

SOME UNITS

---------- **WHERE TO DINE** ----------

PAPA JOE'S ITALIAN RESTAURANT   **Lunch:** $5-$16   **Dinner:** $6-$16   Phone: 352/799-3904

Italian

Location: I-75, exit 61, 4 mi w on US 98/SR 50, just s. 6244 Spring Lake Hwy 34601. **Hours:** 11 am-9 pm, Fri & Sat-10:30 pm, Sun noon-8 pm. Closed major holidays. **Features:** casual dress; children's menu; carryout; cocktails. This well-established local favorite offers a wide variety of homemade items. Try the seafood pasta loaded with lobster, crab, shrimp, oysters and scallops in a creamy sauce. A deli, capricci and gift shop appeals to after-dinner browsers. **Cards:** AE, DS, MC, VI.

TONI'S LA BELLA TRATTORIA   **Lunch:** $7-$21   **Dinner:** $7-$21   Phone: 352/799-4733

Italian

Location: I-75, exit 61, just e on SR 50. 31077 Cortez Blvd 34601. **Hours:** 10 am-9 pm, Fri & Sat-9:30 pm. Closed: 4/15, 11/22, 12/25; also Sun. **Features:** casual dress; children's menu; carryout; beer & wine only; a la carte. Authentic Italian specialties such as ravioli, ziti, parmigiana, stromboli, subs, pizza and calzones comprise the tempting menu. Filled with pepperoni, ham, sausage, cheese and tomato sauce, the overstuffed calzone is a delicious family meal in itself. **Cards:** MC, VI.

YE OLDE FIRESIDE INN   **Lunch:** $6-$9   **Dinner:** $12-$23   Phone: 352/796-0293

American

Location: Just ne of jct SR 50 truck route, on US 41. 1175 S Broad St 34601. **Hours:** 11:30 am-9 pm, Fri & Sat-10 pm, Sun-8 pm. Closed: Mon. **Reservations:** suggested. **Features:** casual dress; children's menu; early bird specials; carryout; cocktails & lounge. A rustic feel, characterized by three fireplaces and old photographs, is the trademark of this 1908 home. Settle into the relaxed atmosphere to peruse the predominant beef and seafood selections, such as Iowa prime rib, the centerpiece of the menu. **Cards:** AE, MC, VI.

BUNNELL pop. 1,900

---------- **WHERE TO STAY** ----------

PLANTATION INN
Phone: (904)437-3737

AAA SAVE

Motor Inn

12/1-4/30   2P: $65-$115
10/1-11/30   2P: $65-$85
5/1-9/30   2P: $55-$65
Location: I-95, exit 90. 2251 S Old Dixie Hwy 32110. Fax: 904/437-0290. **Facility:** 100 units, 1 with kitchen (no utensils). 2 stories, exterior corridors. **Terms:** 3 day cancellation notice, small pets only ($10 extra charge). **Amenities:** safes (fee), hair dryers. **Dining:** restaurant, 4:30 pm-9 pm, $5-$12, cocktails. **Leisure Activities:** whirlpool. **Guest Services:** [CP] meal plan available. **Cards:** AE, CB, DI, DS, MC, VI. *(See color ad p 706)*

SOME UNITS

BUSHNELL pop. 2,000

---------- **WHERE TO STAY** ----------

BEST WESTERN GUEST HOUSE INN
Phone: (352)793-5010

AAA SAVE

Motel

12/1-4/30   1P: $49-$69   2P: $49-$79   XP: $4   F12
5/1-11/30   1P: $39-$59   2P: $39-$59   XP: $4   F12
Location: I-75, exit 63, just e. 2224 W SR 48 33513 (PO Box 847). Fax: 352/793-1310. **Facility:** 48 units. 2 stories, exterior corridors. **Terms:** weekly & monthly rates available, small pets only ($5 extra charge). **Leisure Activities:** playground. **Business Services:** fax. **Cards:** AE, CB, DI, DS, MC, VI. **Special Amenities:** early check-in/late check-out and free continental breakfast.

SOME UNITS

FEE

CYPRESS HOUSE BED & BREAKFAST
Phone: 352/568-0909

Bed & Breakfast

12/1-5/1   2P: $60-$80
5/2-11/30   2P: $50-$65
Location: I-75, exit 62, 2 mi n on CR 476 B, just e on 90th Blvd (dirt and gravel road). CR 476 B, 5175 SW 90th Blvd 33513. Fax: 352/793-1808. **Facility:** Rustic setting on 10 acres of farmland. Modern cypress log home with cozy country decor, including handmade quilts and rockers on the veranda. Smoke free premises. 5 units. *Bath:* some shared or private, shower only. 2 stories, interior/exterior corridors. **Terms:** 7 day cancellation notice-fee imposed, weekly rates available, package plans. **Leisure Activities:** hiking trails, horseshoes. *Fee:* horseback riding. **Guest Services:** [BP] meal plan available. **Business Services:** meeting rooms. **Cards:** MC, VI.

SOME UNITS

CAPE CANAVERAL pop. 8,000

-------- WHERE TO STAY --------

CAPE WINDS RESORT

△△△ SAVE
▽▽▽△▽▽
Apartment

Phone: (321)783-6226

All Year   1P: $117-$160   2P: $117-$160   XP: $12   D18
Location: Jct SR 520, 1.8 mi n on SR A1A, 0.3 mi e via Taylor Ave. 7400 Ridgewood Ave 32920. Fax: 321/799-2676. **Facility:** One and two-bedroom apartments with two baths. Most have balcony. Office hours 7 am-11 pm, Sat and Sun 8 am-10 pm. 67 units with kitchen. 46 two-bedroom units. 5 stories, exterior corridors. **Terms:** 3 day cancellation notice-fee imposed, weekly & monthly rates available. **Amenities:** voice mail, irons, hair dryers. **Leisure Activities:** heated pool, sauna, whirlpool, beach, swimming, 2 lighted tennis courts, basketball. **Guest Services:** [CP] meal plan available, coin laundry. **Cards:** AE, DI, DS, MC, VI.

SOME UNITS

🏊 ⊗ VCR 🖨 🖵 DATA PORT / ⊗ /

RADISSON RESORT AT THE PORT

△△△ SAVE
▽▽▽△▽▽
Motor Inn

Phone: (321)784-0000

All Year   1P: $122-$149   2P: $122-$149   XP: $10   F17
Location: A1A. 8701 Astronaut Blvd 32920. Fax: 321/784-3737. **Facility:** Extensively landscaped with tropical palms, flowers, bushes and various plant varieties. All rooms with ceiling fan. 50 evergreen rooms with filtered air and water, extra charge. 200 units. 2 stories, exterior corridors. **Terms:** cancellation fee imposed, package plans. **Amenities:** voice mail, irons, hair dryers. **Dining:** restaurant, daily breakfast buffet & Sun brunch 6:30 am-2 & 5:30-10:30 pm, $10-$21, cocktails. **Leisure Activities:** 2 pools (1 heated), wading pool, whirlpool, lighted tennis court, exercise room, car rental on premise, beauty salon. **Guest Services:** gift shop, area transportation-cruise ships & beach, valet and coin laundry. **Fee:** massage. **Business Services:** conference facilities. **Cards:** AE, CB, DI, DS, JC, MC, VI. **Special Amenities:** free newspaper. *(See ad below)*

SOME UNITS

S/D 🍽 ⊡ ᚛ ⛱ 📹 🖨 🖵 DATA PORT / ⊗ 🖵 📞 /
FEE

ROYAL MANSION RESORT

△△△ SAVE
▽▽▽△▽▽
Apartment

Phone: (321)784-8484

All Year Wkly   1P: $665-$1715   2P: $665-$1715
Location: Jct SR 520, 2.8 mi n on SR A1A, then 1 mi e via Central Blvd. 8600 Ridgewood Ave 32920. Fax: 321/799-2907. **Facility:** Built in French Caribbean style on oceanfront grounds. One- and two-bedroom, two-bath bi-level apartments with balcony or patio. Barbecue grills and picnic area. 108 units with kitchen. 36 two-bedroom units. Some whirlpool units. 2-4 stories, exterior corridors. **Terms:** 7 day cancellation notice, daily & monthly rates available, package plans. **Amenities:** extended cable TV, voice mail, safes (fee), irons, hair dryers. **Leisure Activities:** heated pool, whirlpool, beach, swimming. **Guest Services:** coin laundry. **Cards:** AE, DI, DS, MC, VI. **Special Amenities:** free room upgrade (subject to availability with advanced reservations). *(See color ad p 266)*

S/D ♿ ᚛ 📹 🖨 🖵 🖵 📞

Our Members are Surfing ...
Surfing aaa.com

AAA

When booking your travel plans o n l i n e at **aaa.com**, look for lodgings with an online photo listing. The photographs and descriptive text not contained in standard listings allow you to "virtually" experience the property prior to making your reservations. And with the immediate booking capabilities for many of the properties, you can complete your transaction in one easy site visit!

Properties with photo listings are easily located in the TourBook search section of AAA online. Simply begin your lodging search by entering your trip criteria including destination, Diamond rating preference, dates of stay, and more, and then look for the camera icon in the property listings that meet your selection criteria.

So, the next time you're booking travel plans online at **aaa.com**, be sure to look at the photo listings prior to making your lodging decisions!

CAPE CORAL pop. 75,000

------ WHERE TO STAY ------

CASA LOMA MOTEL

♦♦♦♦ Motel

2/1-3/31	2P: $70-$80	XP: $5
4/1-4/30	2P: $60-$65	XP: $5
12/1-1/31	2P: $45-$60	XP: $5
5/1-11/30	2P: $45-$50	XP: $5

Phone: 941/549-6000

Location: I-75, exit 22, 1.5 mi n of jct Cape Coral Pkwy. 3608 Del Prado Blvd 33904. Fax: 941/549-4877. **Facility:** Spacious, traditional motel rooms; some facing attractive inlet. 49 units. 48 efficiencies and 1 unit with kitchen. *Bath:* combo or shower only. 2 stories, interior/exterior corridors. **Terms:** 7 day cancellation notice. **Amenities:** extended cable TV. **Leisure Activities:** heated pool, sun deck, boat dock, fishing. **Guest Services:** coin laundry. **Cards:** AE, DS, MC, VI. *(See color ad below)* SOME UNITS

QUALITY INN-NAUTILUS

♦♦♦ [SAVE] ♦♦♦♦ Motel

2/1-4/30	1P: $100-$105	2P: $110-$115	XP: $10	F18
12/1-1/31	1P: $70-$80	2P: $75-$85	XP: $5	F18
5/1-11/30	1P: $55-$60	2P: $70-$80	XP: $5	F18

Phone: (941)542-2121

Location: I-75, exit 22, jct Del Prado Blvd. 1538 Cape Coral Pkwy 33904. Fax: 941/542-6319. **Facility:** All rooms newly remodeled, most with private balcony. 142 units. 5 stories, interior corridors. **Terms:** check-in 4 pm, package plans, pets ($10 extra charge, on 1st floor). **Amenities:** *Some:* irons, hair dryers. **Dining:** poolside tiki bar. **Leisure Activities:** heated pool, exercise room, shuffleboard. **Guest Services:** coin laundry. **Business Services:** meeting rooms. **Cards:** AE, DI, DS, JC, MC, VI. **Special Amenities: free local telephone calls and free newspaper.**

SOME UNITS

RAINBOW MOTEL RESORT

♦♦♦ [SAVE] ♦♦ Motel

1/16-3/31	2P: $89	XP: $5	F13
12/1-1/15	2P: $49-$69	XP: $5	F13
4/1-4/17	2P: $69	XP: $5	F13
4/18-11/30	2P: $49	XP: $5	F13

Phone: 941/542-0061

Location: I-75, exit 22, 1.5 mi n of jct Cape Coral Pkwy. 3817 Del Prado Blvd 33904. Fax: 941/542-0061. **Facility:** Good sized rooms with older vintage and some contemporary appointments, set on inlet, dock for boats to 25 feet. 15 units with kitchen. Some suites. 2 stories, exterior corridors. **Terms:** 7 day cancellation notice, weekly rates available. **Amenities:** extended cable TV. **Leisure Activities:** heated pool, boat dock, fishing, gas grills, tiki deck. **Guest Services:** coin laundry. **Cards:** MC, VI.

SOME UNITS

------ WHERE TO DINE ------

ARIANI ITALIAN STEAKHOUSE

♦♦♦♦ Northern Italian

Dinner: $15-$25 **Phone: 941/772-8000**

Location: I-75, exit 26, just e of Del Prado Blvd; in Del Prado Mall. 1529 SE 15th Terr 33990. **Hours:** 5 pm-10 pm. Closed: Sun. **Reservations:** suggested. **Features:** casual dress; carryout; cocktails & lounge; a la carte. Specalizing in northern Italian cuisine. Casually elegant dining room with well attired attentive servers. Wide selection of fresh pasta dishes, grilled and roasted meats, fresh seafood. Specialities include steak, lambuco, Italian sausage, veal scallopine, salmon, tuna, calamari, mussels, shrimp, pork medallions florentine and chicken breast prepared to your taste; alla riveria, marsala mushroom, pizzaiola, milanese or alla parmigana. **Cards:** AE, DI, MC, VI.

BRIGANDS

♦♦ Steak & Seafood

Lunch: $5-$9 **Dinner: $13-$24** **Phone: 941/540-4665**

Location: In Cay West Pavilion. 1708 Cape Coral Pkwy W 33914. **Hours:** 11 am-10:30 pm, Sun from 4 pm. Closed major holidays. **Features:** casual dress; children's menu; early bird specials; carryout; cocktails & lounge. This clean dining room with a nautical decor is tucked away in a small shopping mall. The menu features grilled, fried, broiled or blackened seafood, and other specialties like prime rib and chicken. Love spicy food? Try the Jamaican jerk chicken. **Cards:** AE, MC, VI.

IGUANA MIA ▼▼ ▼▼▲▲

Mexican

Lunch: $6-$10   **Dinner:** $6-$15   **Phone:** 941/945-7755
Location: Cape Coral Pkwy, just e of jct SE 10th Pl (Leonard St). 1027 E Cape Coral Pkwy 33904. **Hours:** 11 am-midnight, Fri & Sat-1 am, Sun-10 pm. **Closed:** 11/22, 12/25. **Features:** casual dress; children's menu; early bird specials; carryout; cocktails & lounge; a la carte. Hop into this lively, yet simple, cantina, where you'll find a good variety of standard favorites such as sour cream chicken, fajitas and beef burritos with black beans. Frozen margaritas and fried ice cream cool the jalapeno-heated palate. **Cards:** AE, DS, MC, VI. ✕

CAPE HAZE pop. 500

——— **WHERE TO STAY** ———

COLONY DON PEDRO
AAA SAVE ▼▼▼

Condominium

Phone: (941)697-2192

12/1-5/1 Wkly	2P: $850-$1850	
5/2-11/30 Wkly	2P: $750-$1750	

Location: I-75, exit 34, on Don Pedro Island, access by car ferry from Island Transit Ferry terminal, just w of CR 775. 40 S Gulf Blvd 34224 (7025 Placida Rd, ENGLEWOOD). Fax: 941/697-8441. **Facility:** Remote island location. Villas with balcony or patio. Most gulf front. Tranquil atmosphere. Weekly ferry pass $100. 30 units with kitchen. 25 two-bedroom units and 4 three-bedroom units. 2 stories, exterior corridors. **Terms:** cancellation fee imposed, daily & monthly rates available. **Amenities:** extended cable TV. Some: CD players. **Leisure Activities:** 2 heated pools, boat dock, fishing, 2 lighted tennis courts. Fee: golf carts, bicycles. **Guest Services:** complimentary laundry. **Special Amenities:** free local telephone calls and preferred room (subject to availability with advanced reservations). SOME UNITS

🛶 ✕ 🎦 🖥 💻 🖨 🛏 DATA PORT / ✕ VCR /
FEE

PALM ISLAND RESORT
AAA SAVE ▼▼▼

Resort

Phone: (941)697-4800

1/6-4/22	1P: $275-$310	2P: $310-$400	XP: $30 F6
12/17-1/5	1P: $265-$290	2P: $265-$380	XP: $25 F6
4/23-11/30	1P: $190-$205	2P: $190-$280	XP: $20 F6
12/1-12/16	1P: $180-$195	2P: $180-$270	XP: $20 F6

Location: I-75, exit 34, jct CR 771/775/776, 5 mi s to Panama Blvd, just w to Ferry Landing; Gulf Blvd, 1.1 mi w. 7092 Placida Rd 33946. Fax: 941/697-0696. **Facility:** Spacious, gulf front one- to three-bedroom condo villas on Palm Island, reached by car ferry from 7 am-10 pm. Also offers 24 one-bedroom condos on mainland with fine marina views. Guest register at reception area once they arrive on island. 130 units with kitchen. 50 two-bedroom units and 28 three-bedroom units. Some suites. 2-3 stories. **Terms:** 21 day cancellation notice-fee imposed, monthly rates available, package plans. **Amenities:** irons. **Dining:** restaurant, noon-9 pm, Fri & Sat-9:30 pm convenience store, $9-$17, cocktails. **Leisure Activities:** 5 heated pools, whirlpools, fishing, charter fishing, golf carts for rent on island, 11 tennis courts, children's program, nature program, playground. Fee: boats, canoeing, paddleboats, sailboating, boat dock, marina, snorkeling & equipment, tennis instruction, tennis pro shop, bicycles. **Guest Services:** gift shop, complimentary laundry. **Cards:** AE, DS, MC, VI. **Special Amenities:** free local telephone calls. (See ad below) SOME UNITS

🍽 🍸 🛶 ✕ 🖥 💻 🖨 🛏 DATA PORT / VCR /
FEE

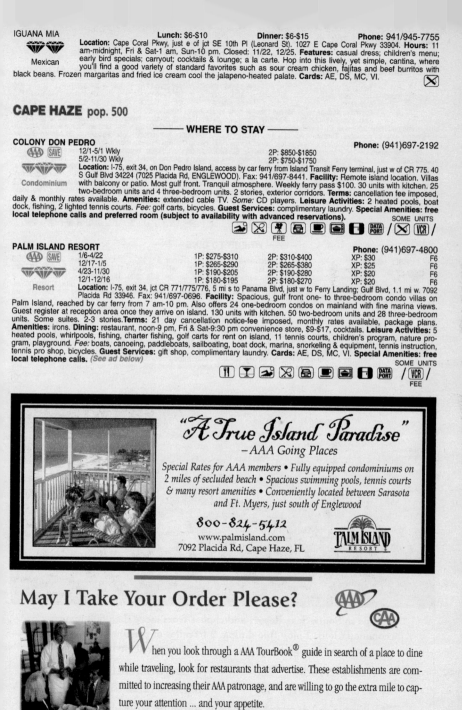
May I Take Your Order Please?

AAA   CAA

When you look through a AAA TourBook® guide in search of a place to dine while traveling, look for restaurants that advertise. These establishments are committed to increasing their AAA patronage, and are willing to go the extra mile to capture your attention ... and your appetite.

So, the next time you're using a TourBook to make dining reservations, be sure to look at the advertisements first ... for a dining experience you won't soon forget!

CAPTIVA pop. 1,300

——— WHERE TO STAY ———

SOUTH SEAS RESORT & YACHT HARBOR
    AAA SAVE
    ▽▽▽▽
    Resort

Phone: (941)472-5111

2/16-4/21	1P: $355-$900	2P: $355-$900	XP: $20	F16
12/1-2/15	1P: $335-$710	2P: $335-$710	XP: $20	F16
4/22-5/28	1P: $290-$590	2P: $290-$590	XP: $20	F16
5/29-11/30	1P: $215-$505	2P: $215-$505	XP: $20	F16

Location: 15.8 mi nw of Sanibel Cswy at north tip of Captiva Island. 5400 South Seas Plantation Rd 33924 (PO Box 194). Fax: 941/472-7541. **Facility:** Extensive facility, variety of room types. Secluded site, some units bayside; some gulf front. 550 units. 201 two-bedroom units, 75 three-bedroom units and 450 units with kitchen. Some whirlpool units. 1-3 stories, exterior corridors. **Terms:** check-in 4 pm, 14 day cancellation notice-fee imposed, package plans, $8 service charge. **Amenities:** extended cable TV, voice mail, safes, irons. *Some:* hair dryers. **Dining:** 2 dining rooms, 3 restaurants, deli, 7:30 am-midnight; ice cream parlor, grocery; 18% service charge, $9-$30, cocktails, nightclub, entertainment. **Leisure Activities:** 18 heated pools, saunas, whirlpools, beach, swimming, fishing, charter fishing, putting green, children's program, nature program, recreation program, social program, playground, game room, aerobic & aqua exercise instruction, store, salon, clothing store, specialty shops. *Fee:* boats, canoeing, sailboating, windsurfing, boat dock, marina, waterskiing, scuba diving/snorkeling & equipment, aqua bikes, fishing guides, parasailing, sailing & instruction, shelling charters, sightseeing cruises, waverunners, golf-9 holes, 18 tennis courts (5 lighted), bicycles. **Guest Services:** gift shop, area transportation-within resort, valet laundry. *Fee:* massage. **Business Services:** meeting rooms, administrative services, PC, fax. **Cards:** AE, DI, DS, MC, VI. *(See color ad below)*

SOME UNITS

🍴 🍸 FEE 🛗 🌀 🏖 👥 ✕ 🎥 VCR 📠 🛏 / 💻 🖨 /

——— WHERE TO DINE ———

THE BUBBLE ROOM
▽▽ ▽▽▽
American

Lunch: $7-$14   **Dinner:** $14-$27   **Phone:** 941/472-5558
Location: At jct Andy Rosse Ln. 15001 Captiva Rd 33924. **Hours:** 11:30 am-2:30 & 5:30-10 pm. **Features:** casual dress; children's menu; cocktails & lounge; a la carte. The decor is a whimsical mix of Christmas, nostalgia, 30s & 40s memorabilia & Hollywood. Friendly servers efficiently manage their tables. The menu features steak, fresh fish and thick cut prime rib. Portions are generous and the desserts are not to be ignored. **Cards:** AE, DI, DS, MC, VI.
✕

CHADWICK'S RESTAURANT
AAA
▽▽ ▽▽
Seafood

Dinner: $19-$25   **Phone:** 941/472-7575
Location: At north tip of Captiva Island; at entrance to South Seas Resort and Yacht Harbor. Captiva Dr 33924. **Hours:** 5:30 pm-9:30 pm, Sun from 9 am. **Reservations:** suggested; 2/1-4/30. **Features:** casual dress; children's menu; cocktails & lounge; entertainment. Located at the entrance to the South Seas Resort, it features an extensive themed dinner buffet Monday through Sunday, and a lovely brunch on Sundays. A limited standard menu is also available. Please note the 18% service charge added to each bill. **Cards:** AE, CB, DI, DS, MC, VI.
✕

CARRABELLE pop. 1,200

──────── WHERE TO STAY ────────

THE MOORINGS AT CARRABELLE
Motel

5/1-7/31	2P: $75-$90	XP: $5	F12
2/1-4/30 & 8/1-11/30	2P: $55-$75	XP: $5	F12
12/1-1/31	2P: $48-$55	XP: $5	F12

Phone: 850/697-2800

Location: US 98, just e of bridge. 1000 US 98 32322. Fax: 850/697-3950. **Facility:** On the Carrabelle River. 22 units with kitchen. 2 stories, exterior corridors. **Terms:** weekly & monthly rates available, pets ($10 extra charge, $50 deposit). **Leisure Activities:** boat ramp, marina, fishing, charter fishing. **Guest Services:** coin laundry. **Business Services:** meeting rooms. **Cards:** AE, CB, DI, DS, MC, VI.

SOME UNITS

ASK ⬛ 🛏 🍽 🏊 ✖ 📠 💻 📧 📱 / VCR /

CASSELBERRY —*See Orlando p. 628.*

CEDAR KEY pop. 700

──────── WHERE TO STAY ────────

DOCKSIDE MOTEL
Motel

All Year	1P: $49-$77	2P: $49-$77	XP: $5	F12

Phone: 352/543-5432

Location: SR 24, just w on Front St to Dock St, then just w. 491 Dock St 32625 (PO Box 55). Fax: 352/543-9955. **Facility:** The only motel on the dock, with rooms above quaint gift shops. Overlooks a fishing pier on the Gulf of Mexico. Good sized rooms with cheerful decor. Gulf or harbor views. 10 units. 2 stories, interior corridors. **Parking:** street only. **Terms:** weekly rates available. **Leisure Activities:** adjacent to public marina & fishing pier. **Business Services:** fax. **Cards:** DS, MC, VI. **Special Amenities:** free local telephone calls.

🍽 📱

PARK PLACE MOTEL & CONDOMINIUMS
Cottage

All Year	1P: $65-$80	2P: $65-$80	XP: $5	F13

Phone: 352/543-5737

Location: At A St. 211 2nd St 32625 (PO Box 613). Fax: 352/543-8011. **Facility:** 12 third floor bi-level units with sleeping loft. Private balcony with view of gulf. Mostly singles with extra sleeper sofa. 30 efficiencies. 3 stories (no elevator), exterior corridors. **Terms:** weekly & monthly rates available, small pets only ($5 extra charge). **Leisure Activities:** gazebo with grill. **Business Services:** fax. **Cards:** AE, DS, MC, VI. **Special Amenities:** free local telephone calls.

SOME UNITS

🛏 🍽 💻 📧 📱 / ✖ VCR 📠 /
FEE

──────── WHERE TO DINE ────────

ISLAND HOTEL
American

Dinner: $18-$26   **Phone: 352/543-5111**

Location: Center. 373 2nd St, PO Box 460 32625. **Hours:** 6 pm-9 pm, Sat & Sun 8 am-10 & 6-9 pm. Closed: Tues. **Features:** No A/C; casual dress; cocktails & lounge. On the National Register of Historic Places, the hotel has a quaint, full-service lounge featuring beers from around the world and a "special occasion" dining room. Fresh seafood, including Florida Rock Lobster, Cedar Key oysters and stone crab (in season); shrimp and grouper are specialties. Lamb, pork, chicken, Angus beef and a few vegetable dishes round out the menu. Try the Baked Whole Garlic or Lobster Bisque for starters. Service is as expected on the island, folksy and laid back. Smoke free premises. **Cards:** DS, MC, VI.

✖

THE ISLAND ROOM AT CEDAR COVE
Seafood

Lunch: $8-$9   **Dinner:** $11-$28   **Phone: 352/543-6520**

Location: At the Cedar Cove Beach and Yacht Club. 10 E 2nd St 32625. **Hours:** 11:30 am-2:30 & 5-10 pm, Sat 9 am-10 pm, Sun 9 am-9 pm. **Reservations:** suggested. **Features:** casual dress; children's menu; carryout; cocktails & lounge; a la carte. Hearty food at reasonable prices is the focus, featuring certified Angus beef, pasta and local seafood. A fabulous view of the Gulf of Mexico adds to your experience as you savor flavorful dishes like blackened grouper. A children's menu is available. **Cards:** AE, DS, MC, VI.

✖

CELEBRATION —*See Orlando p. 629.*

CHARLOTTE HARBOR pop. 3,300

──────── WHERE TO STAY ────────

BANANA BAY WATERFRONT MOTEL
Motel

1/1-4/30	1P: $49-$72	2P: $49-$72	XP: $6	F12
12/1-12/31 & 5/1-11/30	1P: $39-$54	2P: $39-$54	XP: $6	F12

Phone: (941)743-4441

Location: At jct US 41. 23285 Bayshore Rd 33980. Fax: 941/743-4172. **Facility:** Waterfront locale at mouth of the Peace River. 14 units, 10 with efficiency. *Bath:* shower only. 1 story, exterior corridors. **Terms:** age restrictions may apply, 3 day cancellation notice-fee imposed, weekly & monthly rates available, pets ($15 deposit). **Amenities:** extended cable TV. **Leisure Activities:** fishing, kayaks, bicycles, shuffleboard. **Guest Services:** coin laundry. **Cards:** AE, DI, DS, MC, VI.

SOME UNITS

⬛ 🛏 🍽 ✖ / ✖ VCR 📧 📱 /
FEE

CHIEFLAND pop. 1,900

──────── WHERE TO STAY ────────

BEST WESTERN SUWANNEE VALLEY INN
(AAA) [SAVE] ▼▼ ▼▼
Motel
All Year   1P: $60-$75   2P: $70-$85   XP: $10   F16
Phone: (352)493-0663
Location: On US 19/98, just n of jct US 129. 1125 N Young Blvd 32626. Fax: 352/493-0663. **Facility:** 60 units, 1 with kitchen. 2 stories, exterior corridors. **Terms:** cancellation fee imposed, small pets only ($6 extra charge). **Amenities:** extended cable TV. **Guest Services:** coin laundry. **Business Services:** meeting rooms, fax. **Cards:** AE, DI, DS, MC, VI. **Special Amenities:** free continental breakfast and free room upgrade (subject to availability with advanced reservations).
SOME UNITS
[icons] FEE FEE

HOLIDAY INN EXPRESS
▼▼ ▼▼
Motel
All Year   1P: $65-$120   2P: $70-$125   XP: $7   F14
Phone: (352)493-9400
Location: US 19/98, 1.5 mi n of jct US 129. 809 NW 21st Ave 32626. Fax: 352/493-4050. **Facility:** 65 units. 2 stories, exterior corridors. **Terms:** 7 day cancellation notice. **Amenities:** extended cable TV, voice mail, irons, hair dryers. **Leisure Activities:** whirlpool. **Guest Services:** [ECP] meal plan available, coin laundry. **Business Services:** meeting rooms, fax. **Cards:** AE, DI, DS, JC, MC, VI.
SOME UNITS
[icons]

──────── WHERE TO DINE ────────

BAR-B-Q BILL'S
▼▼
American
Lunch: $5-$10   Dinner: $5-$10   Phone: 352/493-4444
Location: On US 19 at jct NW 19th Ave. 1901 N Young Blvd 32626. **Hours:** 7 am-9 pm, Wed from 11 am, Fri & Sat-10 pm. Closed: 11/22, 12/25; also 12/24 for dinner. **Features:** casual dress; children's menu; carryout; salad bar; beer only; a la carte. Barbecue items are the specialty here with traditional preparations of ribs, pork, chicken and steak. Topped with a zesty sauce, the barbecue beef sandwich comes with coleslaw and savory baked beans. Professional service and attentiveness are key. **Cards:** MC, VI.
[icon]

CHIPLEY pop. 3,900

──────── WHERE TO STAY ────────

SUPER 8 MOTEL
▼▼
Motel
5/1-8/31   1P: $45-$50   2P: $50-$55   XP: $5   F12
All Year & 9/1-11/30   1P: $40-$45   2P: $45-$48   XP: $5   F12
Phone: (850)638-8530
Location: I-10, exit 18, just n. 1700 Main St 32428. Fax: 850/638-9895. **Facility:** 40 units. 1 story, exterior corridors. **Terms:** small pets only ($5 extra charge). **Amenities:** extended cable TV. **Guest Services:** [CP] meal plan available. **Cards:** AE, CB, DI, DS, MC, VI.
SOME UNITS
[icons]

CLEARWATER —See Tampa Bay p. 843.

CLEARWATER BEACH —See Tampa Bay p. 851.

CLERMONT —See Orlando p. 629.

CLEWISTON pop. 6,100

──────── WHERE TO STAY ────────

BEST WESTERN OF CLEWISTON
(AAA) [SAVE] ▼▼ ▼▼
Motel
12/1-3/31   1P: $79-$119   2P: $89-$129   XP: $10   D12
4/1-11/30   1P: $69-$89   2P: $79-$89   XP: $10   D12
Phone: (863)983-3400
Location: On US 27/SR 80. 1021 W Sugarland Hwy 33440. Fax: 863/983-3441. **Facility:** A quiet location. Spacious lobby and units with a contemporary flair. 48 units, 3 with efficiency. Some whirlpool units ($89-$129). *Bath:* combo or shower only. 2 stories, exterior corridors. **Amenities:** extended cable TV, voice mail, irons, hair dryers. **Leisure Activities:** small heated indoor pool. **Guest Services:** [ECP] meal plan available. **Business Services:** meeting rooms. **Cards:** AE, CB, DI, DS, MC, VI. **Special Amenities:** free continental breakfast and free newspaper.
SOME UNITS
[icons]

COCOA pop. 17,700

──────── WHERE TO STAY ────────

BEST WESTERN COCOA INN
(AAA) [SAVE] ▼▼ ▼▼
Motel
2/1-4/30   2P: $69-$79
12/1-1/31 & 5/1-11/30   2P: $59-$79
Phone: (321)632-1065
Location: I-95, exit 75, (SR 520), 0.3 mi e. 4225 W King St 32926. Fax: 321/631-3302. **Facility:** Fenced and secured parking. Paved truck parking. 120 units. *Bath:* combo or shower only. 2 stories, exterior corridors. **Terms:** 10 day cancellation notice, weekly & monthly rates available, pets ($6 extra charge). **Amenities:** extended cable TV, voice mail. **Dining:** cocktails. **Leisure Activities:** heated pool, game room, barbecue grills, covered wood deck, picnic tables, darts, pool table, large screen TV. **Guest Services:** valet and coin laundry. **Business Services:** meeting rooms. **Cards:** AE, DI, DS, MC, VI.
SOME UNITS
[icons] FEE

CAMPBELL MOTEL

Phone: 321/636-6111

AAA SAVE

Motel

| All Year | 1P: $45-$55 | 2P: $55-$65 | XP: $5 |

Location: 1.5 mi s of jct SR 528. 1084 N Cocoa Blvd 32922. Fax: 321/636-6111. **Facility:** 19 units. *Bath:* combo or shower only. 1 story, exterior corridors. **Terms:** 7 day cancellation notice, weekly rates available. **Amenities:** extended cable TV. **Cards:** AE, DS, MC, VI. **Special Amenities: early check-in/late check-out and free local telephone calls.**

SOME UNITS

ECONO LODGE-SPACE CENTER

Phone: 321/632-4561

AAA SAVE

Motor Inn

| All Year | 1P: $54-$125 | 2P: $59-$125 | F17 |

Location: US 1, just n of jct SR 528. 3220 N Cocoa Blvd 32926. Fax: 321/631-3756. **Facility:** Elevated location. Designated smoking area. 142 units. 3 stories, exterior corridors. **Terms:** 7 day cancellation notice, weekly rates available, small pets only. **Dining:** restaurant, 6:30 am-11:30 & 5-9:30 pm, Fri & Sat-10 pm, $6-$16, cocktails, name entertainment. **Leisure Activities:** shuffleboard. **Guest Services:** coin laundry. **Business Services:** meeting rooms. **Cards:** AE, CB, DI, DS, JC, MC, VI. **Special Amenities: free room upgrade and preferred room (each subject to availability with advanced reservations).**

SOME UNITS

FEE   FEE   FEE

RAMADA INN COCOA-KENNEDY SPACE CENTER

Phone: (321)631-1210

AAA SAVE

Motor Inn

2/10-4/21	1P: $89-$99	2P: $89-$99	XP: $10	F18
12/1-2/9	1P: $69-$89	2P: $69-$89	XP: $10	F18
4/22-11/30	1P: $69-$79	2P: $69-$79	XP: $10	F18

Location: I-95, exit 76 (SR 524), just w. 900 Friday Rd 32926. Fax: 321/636-8661. **Facility:** 98 units. 2 stories, exterior corridors. **Terms:** weekly & monthly rates available, package plans, small pets only ($25 deposit). **Amenities:** extended cable TV, voice mail. **Dining:** restaurant, 6 am-10 pm, Sat & Sun from 7 am, $6-$12, cocktails. **Leisure Activities:** heated pool, boat dock, fishing, putting green, jogging, shuffleboard. **Guest Services:** coin laundry. **Business Services:** meeting rooms. **Cards:** AE, CB, DI, DS, JC, MC, VI. **Special Amenities: early check-in/late check-out and free local telephone calls.** *(See color ad below)*

SOME UNITS

SUPER 8 MOTEL

Phone: (321)631-1212

AAA SAVE

Motel

2/10-4/21	1P: $79-$89	2P: $79-$89	XP: $10	F18
12/1-2/9	1P: $59-$79	2P: $59-$79	XP: $10	F18
4/22-11/30	1P: $59-$69	2P: $59-$69	XP: $10	F18

Location: I-95, exit 76, 0.5 mi sw. 900A Friday Rd 32926. Fax: 321/636-8661. **Facility:** 53 units. 2 stories, exterior corridors. **Terms:** small pets only ($20 deposit). **Amenities:** extended cable TV, voice mail. **Leisure Activities:** heated pool, fishing, putting green, jogging, shuffleboard. **Guest Services:** coin laundry. **Cards:** AE, CB, DI, DS, JC, MC, VI. **Special Amenities: early check-in/late check-out and free local telephone calls.**

SOME UNITS

WHERE TO DINE

THE BLACK TULIP

| Lunch: $4-$9 | Dinner: $14-$20 | Phone: 321/631-1133 |

Continental

Location: In Historic Cocoa Village; on SR 520, just e of jct US 1. 207 Brevard Ave 32922. **Hours:** 11:30 am-2 & 5:30-10 pm. Closed major holidays; also Sun. **Reservations:** suggested. **Features:** casual dress; early bird specials; carryout; beer & wine only; entertainment. Charming and comfortable, this cafe features classic dishes with innovative touches and creative presentations. For a flavorful lunch, try one of the fresh salads or the sandwiches. Subdued lighting sets a romantic mood for a special getaway. Smoke free premises. **Cards:** AE, DS, MC, VI.

CAFE MARGAUX

| Lunch: $5-$11 | Dinner: $16-$26 | Phone: 321/639-8343 |

French

Location: In Historic Cocoa Village off SR 520, just e of US 1. 220 Brevard Ave 32922. **Hours:** 11 am-3 & 5-9:30 pm. Closed: Tues & Sun. **Reservations:** accepted. **Features:** casual dress; carryout; cocktails. Bright during the day and romantic at night, the cozy dining areas and outside courtyard terrace are reminiscent of New Orleans. An extensive wine list includes selections to complement a nice variety of seafood, lamb, beef, pasta and mixed grill dishes. **Cards:** AE, DI, DS, MC, VI.

COCOA BEACH pop. 12,100

BEST WESTERN OCEAN INN
Phone: (321)784-2550

(AAA) [SAVE]

▽▽▽▽▽ Motel

2/9-4/21	1P: $99-$189	2P: $109-$199	XP: $10 F19
4/22-6/14 & 6/15-11/30	1P: $79-$189	2P: $89-$199	XP: $10 F19
12/1-2/8	1P: $79-$169	2P: $89-$199	XP: $10 F19

Location: SR A1A, 0.8 mi n of jct SR 520. 5500 N Atlantic Ave 32931. Fax: 321/868-7124. **Facility:** Three buildings, one block from beach. 103 units, 14 with efficiency. Some suites ($139-$169). 2 stories, exterior corridors. **Terms:** small pets only. **Amenities:** extended cable TV, video games, voice mail, hair dryers. *Some:* safes, irons. **Leisure Activities:** heated pool, exercise room, barbecue grills, picnic area & sun deck. **Guest Services:** coin laundry. **Cards:** AE, CB, DI, DS, JC, MC, VI. **Special Amenities:** free newspaper.

SOME UNITS

COCOA BEACH OCEANSIDE INN
Phone: (321)784-3126

(AAA) [SAVE]

▽▽▽▽▽ Motor Inn

All Year	1P: $69-$179	2P: $69-$179	XP: $10 F17

Location: Just e of SR A1A; 0.8 mi n of jct SR 520. 1 Hendry Ave 32931. Fax: 321/799-0883. **Facility:** Tropical public areas. Units with oceanfront or ocean view balcony. Designated smoking area. 76 units. Some suites ($175-$200) and whirlpool units ($250-$300). 5-6 stories, exterior corridors. **Terms:** package plans. **Amenities:** extended cable TV, safes, hair dryers. **Dining:** restaurant, coffee shop, 7 am-11 & 4-10 pm, $5-$7, cocktails. **Leisure Activities:** heated pool, beach, swimming, rooftop observation deck for shuttle launches. **Guest Services:** valet laundry. **Business Services:** meeting rooms. **Cards:** AE, CB, DI, DS, MC, VI.
(See color ad below)

SOME UNITS

COMFORT INN & SUITE RESORT
Phone: (321)783-2221

(AAA) [SAVE]

▽▽▽▽▽ Motel

2/9-4/22	1P: $85-$190	2P: $85-$200	XP: $10 F12
4/23-9/2	1P: $75-$190	2P: $75-$200	XP: $10 F12
12/1-2/8	1P: $65-$190	2P: $65-$200	XP: $10 F12
9/3-11/30	1P: $60-$190	2P: $60-$200	XP: $10 F12

Location: SR A1A, 0.3 mi s of jct SR 520. 3901 N Atlantic Ave 32931. Fax: 321/783-0461. **Facility:** 144 units, 40 with efficiency. Some suites. 6 stories, exterior corridors. **Terms:** 14 day cancellation notice-fee imposed. **Amenities:** extended cable TV, safes (fee), hair dryers. *Some:* irons. **Dining:** tiki bar, cocktails. **Leisure Activities:** heated pool, whirlpool, poolside grills, playground, shuffleboard, volleyball, game room, pool tables, table tennis. **Guest Services:** coin laundry. **Business Services:** meeting rooms, fax. **Cards:** AE, CB, DI, DS, JC, MC, VI. **Special Amenities:** early check-in/late check-out and free newspaper. *(See ad p 263)*

SOME UNITS

DAYS INN OCEANFRONT RESORT

Phone: (321)783-7621

2/9-4/21	1P: $119-$219	2P: $129-$229	XP: $10 F19
6/15-11/30	1P: $99-$219	2P: $109-$229	XP: $10 F19
12/1-2/8 & 4/22-6/14	1P: $99-$199	2P: $109-$209	XP: $10 F19

AAA SAVE

Motel

Location: SR A1A, 0.8 mi n of jct SR 520. 5600 N Atlantic Ave 32931. Fax: 321/799-4576. **Facility:** Tower rooms with balcony have ocean views; rooms more modest in the two story buildings. 180 units, 41 with efficiency. *Bath:* combo or shower only. 2-7 stories, interior/exterior corridors. **Terms:** small pets only (in designated rooms). **Amenities:** extended cable TV, video games, voice mail, hair dryers. *Some:* irons. **Leisure Activities:** heated pool, beach, swimming, sun deck, playground, exercise room, shuffleboard, barbecue grills. **Guest Services:** gift shop, coin laundry. **Business Services:** meeting rooms. **Cards:** AE, CB, DI, DS, JC, MC, VI. **Special Amenities:** free newspaper.

SOME UNITS

DISCOVERY BEACH RESORT & TENNIS CLUB

Phone: (321)868-7777

12/16-9/15 & 11/16-11/30	2P: $180-$250
12/1-12/15 & 9/16-11/15	2P: $110-$145

AAA SAVE

Condominium

Location: Just e of SR A1A, 0.8 mi n of jct SR 520. 300 Barlow Ave 32931. Fax: 321/868-0086. **Facility:** Upscale condo with spacious units featuring full kitchen, including dishwasher and washer/dryer. All rooms with 2 or more bathrooms and private ocean view balcony; most with king size bed. 66 units with kitchen. 56 two-bedroom units and 4 three-bedroom units. 8 stories, exterior corridors. **Terms:** check-in 4 pm, 3 day cancellation notice, weekly rates available. **Amenities:** extended cable TV, voice mail, irons. **Dining:** restaurant, 11 am-midnight, $6-$14, cocktails. **Leisure Activities:** heated pool, sauna, whirlpool, beach, swimming, 2 lighted tennis courts, exercise room, basketball, game room, rental videos. **Guest Services:** complimentary laundry. **Cards:** CB, DI, MC, VI.

DOUBLETREE HOTEL OF COCOA BEACH

Phone: (321)783-9222

2/11-4/30	1P: $110-$135	2P: $119-$145	XP: $15 F18
12/1-2/10 & 5/1-11/30	1P: $99-$125	2P: $109-$135	XP: $15 F18

Hotel

Location: SR A1A, 1 mi s of jct SR 520. 2080 N Atlantic Ave 32931. Fax: 321/799-3234. **Facility:** High-rise oceanfront with balcony. Attractive public areas and guest rooms. 148 units. Some suites. 2-6 stories, interior corridors. **Terms:** 14 day cancellation notice-fee imposed, package plans. **Amenities:** extended cable TV, video games, voice mail, irons, hair dryers. **Leisure Activities:** heated pool, wading pool, beach, swimming, large brick sun deck, exercise room, game room. **Guest Services:** gift shop, coin laundry. **Business Services:** conference facilities. **Cards:** AE, CB, DI, DS, JC, MC, VI.

SOME UNITS

HAMPTON INN COCOA BEACH　　　　　　　　　　　　　　　　　　　　**Phone:** (321)799-4099

(AAA) (SAVE) ▼▼▼▼　All Year　　　　　　　1P: $89-$129　　　　　2P: $89-$129

Motel

Location: 0.5 mi s of jct SR 520. 3425 N Atlantic Ave 32931. Fax: 321/799-4991. **Facility:** 150 units. *Bath:* combo or shower only. 8 stories, exterior corridors. **Terms:** 7 day cancellation notice-fee imposed, monthly rates available. **Amenities:** video games, voice mail, irons, hair dryers. **Leisure Activities:** heated pool, beach, swimming, private walkway to beach, exercise room. **Guest Services:** [ECP] meal plan available, gift shop, coin laundry. **Business Services:** meeting rooms, fax. **Cards:** AE, CB, DI, DS, MC, VI. **Special Amenities: free continental breakfast and free local telephone calls.** *(See color ad below)*　　SOME UNITS

[icons] FEE /⊗/

HILTON COCOA BEACH OCEANFRONT　　　　　　　　　　　　　　**Phone:** (321)799-0003

(AAA) (SAVE) ▼▼▼▼　2/9-4/21　　　　　　　1P: $129-$179　　　2P: $139-$199
12/1-2/8 & 4/22-11/30　　1P: $119-$149　　　2P: $129-$169

Hotel

Location: SR A1A, 1.5 mi s of jct SR 520. 1550 N Atlantic Ave 32931. Fax: 321/799-0344. **Facility:** Some rooms overlook beach and ocean. Very good guest room lighting. 296 units. Some suites ($139-$219). *Bath:* combo or shower only. 7 stories, interior corridors. *Some:* check-in 4 pm, cancellation fee imposed, package plans. **Amenities:** voice mail, irons, hair dryers. **Dining:** 2 restaurants, 6:30 am-10:30 pm, $10-$20, cocktails. **Leisure Activities:** heated pool, beach, swimming, boogie boards, surfboards,, exercise room, volleyball, game room. *Fee:* beach set-up. **Guest Services:** gift shop, coin laundry. *Fee:* massage. **Business Services:** conference facilities, fax. **Cards:** AE, CB, DI, DS, MC, VI. **Special Amenities: free newspaper.** *(See ad p 44 & color ad p 265)*　　SOME UNITS

[icons] FEE /⊗[icons]/ FEE

HOLIDAY INN/COCOA BEACH RESORT　　　　　　　　　　　　　**Phone:** (321)783-2271

(AAA) (SAVE) ▼▼▼▼　12/25-4/28　　　　　　1P: $109-$159　　　2P: $109-$159
6/30-11/30　　　　　　1P: $99-$159　　　　2P: $99-$159
4/29-6/29　　　　　　 1P: $89-$149　　　　2P: $89-$149
12/1-12/24　　　　　　1P: $79-$129　　　　2P: $79-$129

Motor Inn

Location: SR A1A, 1.8 mi s of jct SR 520. 1300 N Atlantic Ave 32931. Fax: 321/784-8878. **Facility:** Extensive complex on 27 acres offering a wide variety of unit types, some with ocean view. 500 units, 33 with kitchen. Some suites. *Bath:* combo or shower only. 2-3 stories, exterior corridors. **Terms:** check-in 4 pm, package plans, small pets only. **Amenities:** video games, voice mail, irons, hair dryers. *Some:* CD players, safes. **Dining:** 2 restaurants, 6:30 am-10 pm; live entertainment in season, $8-$19, cocktails. **Leisure Activities:** heated pool, wading pool, whirlpool, beach, swimming, 2 lighted tennis courts, children's program, recreation program, playground, exercise room, shuffleboard, game room, beach volleyball. *Fee:* waverunners, boogie boards, cabanas, umbrellas, beach chairs. **Guest Services:** [BP] meal plan available, gift shop, coin laundry. **Business Services:** conference facilities. **Cards:** AE, CB, DI, DS, JC, MC, VI. **Special Amenities: early check-in/late check-out and free room upgrade (subject to availability with advanced reservations).** *(See color ad p 265)*　　SOME UNITS

[icons] FEE /⊗ [VCR icons]/

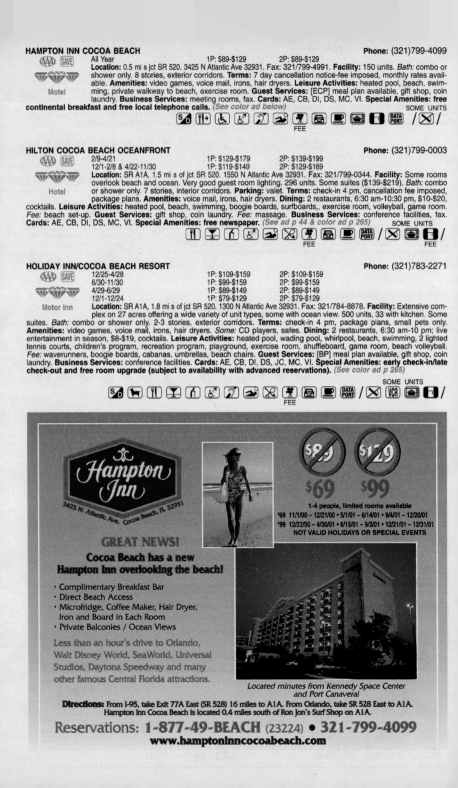

THE INN AT COCOA BEACH-BED & BREAKFAST

Motel

All Year   1P: $125-$300   2P: $125-$300   XP: $10   **Phone:** (321)799-3460

Location: Just s of SR 520 Extension; just e of SR A1A. 4300 Ocean Beach Blvd 32931. Fax: 321/784-8632. **Facility:** Charming bed and breakfast style operation with compact to spacious individually furnished rooms, most with patio or balcony. Ocean view from higher floors. One building with three stories and no elevator, four story building with elevator. Designated smoking area. 50 units. Some whirlpool units ($250-$300). 2-4 stories, interior/exterior corridors. **Terms:** 7 day cancellation notice. **Amenities:** extended cable TV, safes. *Some:* hair dryers. **Leisure Activities:** steamroom, beach, swimming, sundeck, bicycles, shuffleboard. **Guest Services:** [ECP] meal plan available, gift shop, complimentary evening beverages, valet laundry. *Fee:* massage. **Business Services:** meeting rooms. **Cards:** AE, DS, MC, VI.

SOME UNITS

(ASK) (S☎) (✉) (¶↑) (⇌) (✕) (🖨) / (VCR) /
FEE

LUNA SEA BED & BREAKFAST

(AAA) (SAVE)

Motel

12/1-4/30   1P: $68   2P: $99   XP: $6   F12   **Phone:** (321)783-0500
5/1-11/30   1P: $58   2P: $80   XP: $6   F12

Location: 0.7 mi s of SR 520 on A1A. 3185 N Atlantic Ave 32931. Fax: 321/784-6515. **Facility:** 44 units, 5 with kitchen. 2 stories, exterior corridors. **Terms:** 7 day cancellation notice, weekly & monthly rates available. **Amenities:** extended cable TV, hair dryers. **Leisure Activities:** heated pool, picnic area. **Guest Services:** coin laundry. **Cards:** AE, CB, DI, DS, JC, MC, VI. **Special Amenities:** free continental breakfast and preferred room (subject to availability with advanced reservations).** (See color ad p 266)*

SOME UNITS

(S☎) (¶↑) (⇌) (DATA PORT) / (✕) (🖨) (🖨) (🗋) /

THE RESORT ON COCOA BEACH

Phone: (321)783-4000

AAA SAVE

▽▽▽▽

Condominium

12/1-5/31 & 6/17-9/5	2P: $210-$225	
6/1-6/16	2P: $165-$180	
9/6-11/30	2P: $130-$180	

Location: SR A1A, 2 mi s of jct SR 520. 1600 N Atlantic Ave 32931. Fax: 321/799-0272. **Facility:** 124 two-bedroom units with kitchen. Some whirlpool units. 8 stories, exterior corridors. **Terms:** check-in 4 pm, 3 day cancellation notice. **Amenities:** voice mail, irons, hair dryers. **Dining:** restaurant, 11 am-10 pm, $5-$10. **Leisure Activities:** heated pool, sauna, whirlpool, water sprite for kids, 2 lighted tennis courts, children's program, recreation program, exercise room, basketball, large kids area, movie theater, sand volleyball, rental videos. *Fee:* beach furniture. **Guest Services:** gift shop, complimentary laundry. **Cards:** AE, DI, DS, MC, VI.

🍴 🍸 🏋 ♿ ⚷ ✍ 🏊 ✕ 📹 VCR 🖨 💻 🖥 📞 DATA PORT

SOUTH BEACH INN

Phone: (321)784-3333

AAA SAVE

▽▽ ▽▽

Motel

1/21-4/21	1P: $85-$130	2P: $85-$130	XP: $10	F10
4/22-9/10	1P: $75-$120	2P: $75-$120		
12/1-1/20	1P: $75-$120	2P: $75-$120	XP: $10	F10
9/11-11/30	1P: $65-$110	2P: $65-$110		

Location: SR A1A northbound, 5 mi s of jct SR 520 at Indian Village Tr, 1.5 mi n of Patrick AFB. 1701 S Atlantic Ave 32931. Fax: 321/784-9486. **Facility:** Set on the beach. 16 units with kitchen. 3 two-bedroom units. Some suites. 2 stories, exterior corridors. **Terms:** 10 day cancellation notice, weekly rates available, small pets only ($10 extra charge, $50 deposit). **Amenities:** extended cable TV. **Leisure Activities:** beach, swimming, grills & tables. **Guest Services:** coin laundry. **Cards:** MC, VI. **Special Amenities:** early check-in/late check-out and free local telephone calls.

🐕 🍴 🏊 💻 🖥 📞

SURF STUDIO BEACH RESORT

Phone: 321/783-7100

▽▽▽ ▽▽

Suite Motel

1/16-4/30	2P: $85-$150	XP: $15	F10
5/1-10/15	2P: $80-$140	XP: $15	F10
12/1-1/15 & 10/16-11/30	2P: $60-$105	XP: $15	F10

Location: SR A1A northbound, 5 mi s of jct SR 520 at Francis St, 1.3 mi n of Patrick AFB. 1801 S Atlantic Ave 32931. Fax: 321/783-2695. **Facility:** On oceanfront grounds. Nicely kept units. Family owned and operated since 1947. 11 units. 2 efficiencies and 7 units with kitchen. Some suites ($95-$150). *Bath:* combo or shower only. 1 story, exterior corridors. **Terms:** 7 day cancellation notice-fee imposed, weekly rates available, pets ($20 extra charge). **Amenities:** extended cable TV, voice mail. **Leisure Activities:** heated pool, beach, swimming, bicycles. **Guest Services:** coin laundry. **Cards:** AE, CB, DI, DS, MC, VI.

🐕 🍴 🏊 💻 🖥 📞

WAKULLA MOTEL

AAA (SAVE)
♦♦♦ ♦♦♦
Apartment

2/1-4/30   2P: $102-$112   XP: $6   F4
12/1-1/31 & 5/1-11/30   2P: $92-$102   XP: $6   F4
Phone: (321)783-2230

Location: SR A1A, 0.5 mi s of jct SR 520. 3550 N Atlantic Ave 32931. **Fax:** 321/783-0980. **Facility:** 2-bedroom housekeeping apartments, a few oceanfront. Outstanding tropical courtyard brimming with exotic fruit trees and rare flowers. Small lobby with an autographed collection of NASA memorabilia. 116 two-bedroom units with kitchen. 2 stories, exterior corridors. **Terms:** 7 day cancellation notice-fee imposed, weekly & monthly rates available. **Amenities:** extended cable TV, voice mail. *Some:* irons. **Leisure Activities:** heated pool, wading pool, beach, swimming, shuffleboard, barbecue grills, beach volleyball, oceanside deck. **Guest Services:** coin laundry. **Cards:** AE, DI, DS, MC, VI. **Special Amenities:** free newspaper.

─────── *The following lodging was either not evaluated or did not* ───────
meet AAA rating requirements but is listed for your information only.

COURTYARD BY MARRIOTT COCOA BEACH

(fyi)
Motel

Under construction, scheduled to open January 2001. **Location:** I-95, exit 77A, e on SR 528. 3345 N Atlantic Ave 32931. **Planned Amenities:** 131 units, radios, coffeemakers, pool. *(See color ad below)*

─────── **WHERE TO DINE** ───────

ALMA'S SEAFOOD & ITALIAN RESTAURANT   **Dinner:** $7-$15   **Phone:** 321/783-1981

AAA
♦♦♦ ♦♦♦
Italian

Location: On SR A1A southbound; 2.5 mi s of jct SR 520. 306 N Orlando Ave 32931. **Hours:** 5 pm-10 pm. Closed major holidays; also Super Bowl Sun. **Reservations:** suggested. **Features:** casual dress; children's menu; early bird specials; carryout; cocktails & lounge. Family owned since 1963, this bistro emphasizes seafood and Italian cuisine. An ample selection of appetizers and salads provide a good start to any meal. The wine list offers international selections. Enjoy live entertainment on Thursdays and Saturdays. **Cards:** AE, CB, DI, DS, MC, VI.

BERNARD'S SURF   **Dinner:** $18-$25   **Phone:** 321/783-2401

♦♦♦ ♦♦♦
American

Location: SR A1A northbound, 2.3 mi s of jct SR 520 at Minutemen Cswy. 2 S Atlantic Ave 32931. **Hours:** 4 pm-11 pm. Closed: 12/25. **Reservations:** suggested. **Features:** casual dress; children's menu; early bird specials; carryout; cocktails & lounge. This family owned restaurant has been a Cocoa Beach favorite since 1948. Excellent steak and market-fresh seafood is served in a relaxed, fine-dining atmosphere. A lengthy wine list and a very nice variety of appetizers makes happy hour a celebration. **Cards:** AE, CB, DI, DS, MC, VI.

HEIDELBERG RESTAURANT   **Lunch:** $5-$10   **Dinner:** $13-$19   **Phone:** 321/783-6806

♦♦♦ ♦♦♦
German

Location: SR A1A, 3 mi s of jct SR 520. 7 N Orlando Ave 32931. **Hours:** 10 am-10 pm, Sun from 5 pm. Closed: 7/4, 11/22, 12/25; also Mon. **Reservations:** suggested; weekends. **Features:** casual dress; carryout; cocktails & lounge; entertainment; minimum charge-$10; street parking. Such specialties as goulash, stroganoff and luscious Viennese pastries make up the decidedly German and Austrian menu in the romantic restaurant. European decor enhances the cozy, classical feel. A pianist performs on Friday and Saturday evenings. **Cards:** AE, MC, VI.

THE MANGO TREE RESTAURANT   **Dinner:** $13-$39   **Phone:** 321/799-0513

♦♦♦ ♦♦♦
Continental

Location: SR A1A northbound, 2.5 mi s of jct SR 520. 118 N Atlantic Ave 32931. **Hours:** 6 pm-9:30 pm, Fri & Sat-10 pm. Closed: 1/1, 12/25; also Mon. **Reservations:** suggested. **Features:** semi-formal attire; children's menu; carryout; cocktails & lounge; entertainment. Several cozy areas—from an elegantly formal dining room to the tropically decorated garden terrace, complete with graceful swans all lend to the intimate plantation-home ambience of the restaurant. Attractive presentation is a trademark of every dish. **Cards:** AE, MC, VI.

PUNJAB INDIAN CUISINE   **Lunch:** $5-$14   **Dinner:** $8-$14   **Phone:** 321/799-4696

♦♦♦ ♦♦♦
Indian

Location: Just e of SR 520 and A1A; in White Rose Shopping Center. 285 W Cocoa Beach Cswy 32931. **Hours:** 11:30 am-2:30 & 5-10 pm, Fri & Sat-10:30 pm, Sun from 5 pm. Closed major holidays. **Reservations:** accepted. **Features:** casual dress; carryout; beer & wine only. A Northern influence is evident in the excellent menu variety, which includes breads, lassi and kulfi. Favorites include shrimp curry and tandoori chicken and lamb as well as seafood and vegetarian dishes. Textured walls and subdued lighting set the mood. **Cards:** AE, DS, MC, VI.

ROBERTO'S LITTLE HAVANA RESTAURANT   **Lunch:** $7-$11   **Dinner:** $7-$11   **Phone:** 321/784-1868

Cuban

Location: SR A1A southbound, 2.7 mi s of jct SR 520. 26 N Orlando Ave 32931. **Hours:** 6 am-3 & 5-9 pm, Fri & Sat-10 pm. Closed: Mon nights & 2 weeks in July. **Reservations:** accepted. **Features:** casual dress; early bird specials; carryout; beer & wine only. The unpretentious downtown eatery serves up a delicious variety of Cuban dishes, such as yucca, plantain, French-bread Cuban sandwiches and beans with rice, as well as beef, chicken and pork entrees. Locals often drop by for breakfast. **Cards:** AE, DS, MC, VI. ⊠

YEN YEN CHINESE RESTAURANT   **Lunch:** $5-$9   **Dinner:** $8-$16   **Phone:** 321/783-9512

Chinese

Location: On A1A. 2 N Atlantic Ave 32931. **Hours:** 11:30 am-10 pm, Fri & Sat-11 pm; 4:30 pm-10 pm, Fri & Sat-11 pm, 6/1-11/30. Closed: one week in summer (call ahead 7/1-8/31). **Reservations:** accepted. **Features:** casual dress; children's menu; early bird specials; carryout; cocktails & lounge. Delicate sauces and exotic seasonings flavor such entrees as Shelly's chicken and the signature snow white prawn. Comfortable and quiet, the atmosphere borrows from the discrete cultures of Europe and Asia to create an distinct and elegant feel. **Cards:** AE, DI, MC, VI. ⊠

COCONUT GROVE —See Miami-Miami Beach p. 512.

CORAL GABLES —See Miami-Miami Beach p. 514.

CORAL SPRINGS —See Fort Lauderdale p. 374.

CRESCENT BEACH

——— WHERE TO STAY ———

BEACHER'S LODGE   **Phone:** (904)471-8849

Suite Motel

2/9-10/1	2P: $99-$189
12/1-2/8 & 10/2-11/30	2P: $79-$125

Location: Just s of jct SR 206. 6970 A1A S 32086. Fax: 904/471-3002. **Facility:** 110 units. 4 stories, exterior corridors. **Terms:** cancellation fee imposed. **Leisure Activities:** beach, swimming. **Guest Services:** [CP] meal plan available, coin laundry. *Fee:* area transportation. **Business Services:** meeting rooms. **Cards:** DS, MC, VI. SOME UNITS

ASK [S/D] [📞] [🛏] [💻] [🔌] / [VCR] [🖼] /

CRESCENT CITY pop. 1,900

——— WHERE TO STAY ———

LAKE VIEW MOTEL   **Phone:** 904/698-1090

Motel

12/1-2/8	1P: $43-$65	2P: $50-$65	XP: $5	F13
3/11-11/30	1P: $65	2P: $65	XP: $5	F13
2/9-3/10	1P: $43	2P: $50	XP: $5	F13

Location: 1 mi n on US 17. 1004 N Summit St 32112. Fax: 904/698-4616. **Facility:** Designated smoking area. 19 units. *Bath:* combo or shower only. 1 story, exterior corridors. **Terms:** weekly & monthly rates available, pets (small house pets only). **Amenities:** extended cable TV. **Cards:** AE, DI, DS, MC, VI. SOME UNITS

[🐕] [📞] [🛏] / [⊠] [💻] [🖼] [🔌] /

CRESTVIEW pop. 9,900

——— WHERE TO STAY ———

ECONO LODGE   **Phone:** (850)682-6255

SAVE

Motel

All Year	1P: $40-$45	2P: $45-$50	XP: $5	D12

Location: SR 85, 0.3 mi n of I-10, exit 12. 3101 S Ferdon Blvd 32536 (PO Box 1466). Fax: 850/682-7500. **Facility:** Hilltop with vista. 84 units. 2 stories, exterior corridors. **Terms:** 10 day cancellation notice. **Amenities:** extended cable TV. **Cards:** AE, CB, DI, DS, JC, MC, VI. SOME UNITS

[S/D] [📞] / [⊠] [💻] /

HOLIDAY INN   **Phone:** (850)682-6111

Motor Inn

All Year	1P: $52	2P: $89	XP: $6	F18

Location: SR 85, 0.5 mi s of I-10, exit 12. 4050 S Ferdon Blvd 32536 (PO Box 1358). Fax: 850/689-1189. **Facility:** 119 units. *Bath:* some combo or shower only. 2 stories, exterior corridors. **Terms:** small pets only. **Amenities:** extended cable TV, voice mail, irons, hair dryers. **Leisure Activities:** exercise room. **Guest Services:** [BP] meal plan available, valet and coin laundry. **Business Services:** meeting rooms. **Cards:** AE, CB, DI, DS, JC, MC, VI. SOME UNITS

ASK [S/D] [🐕] [🍴] [🍸] [🔥] [🛏] [📠] [💻] [DATA PORT] / [⊠] [🔌] /
FEE

SUPER 8 MOTEL   **Phone:** (850)682-9649

SAVE

Motel

All Year	1P: $38-$58		XP: $5 F12

Location: I-10, exit 12, 0.3 mi se. 3925 S Ferdon Blvd 32539. Fax: 850/682-9649. **Facility:** 63 units, 9 with efficiency. 2 stories, exterior corridors. **Terms:** pets ($5 extra charge). **Amenities:** extended cable TV. **Cards:** AE, DI, DS, MC, VI. SOME UNITS

[S/D] [🐕] [📞] / [⊠] [🖼] [🔌] /

CROSS CITY pop. 2,000

―――― **WHERE TO STAY** ――――

CARRIAGE INN
AAA SAVE
Motor Inn

All Year   1P: $29-$39   2P: $36-$45   XP: $5   F12   **Phone:** (352)498-0001
Location: 0.5 mi s on US 19, 27A and 98. 280 E Main (US 19/98/27A) 32628 (PO Box 1360). Fax: 352/498-5054.
Facility: 25 units. *Bath:* combo or shower only. 2 stories, exterior corridors. **Amenities:** extended cable TV.
Dining: restaurant, 6 am-10 pm; buffet Sat & Sun, $5-$11, beer only. **Guest Services:** airport transportation-
Cross City Airport. **Business Services:** meeting rooms, fax. **Cards:** AE, DI, DS, MC, VI. **Special Amenities:**
free local telephone calls and preferred room (subject to availability with advanced reservations).

SOME UNITS

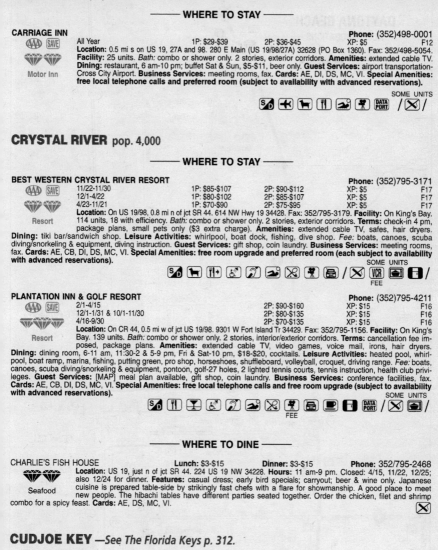

CRYSTAL RIVER pop. 4,000

―――― **WHERE TO STAY** ――――

BEST WESTERN CRYSTAL RIVER RESORT   **Phone:** (352)795-3171
AAA SAVE
Resort

11/22-11/30	1P: $85-$107	2P: $90-$112	XP: $5 F17
12/1-4/22	1P: $80-$102	2P: $85-$107	XP: $5 F17
4/23-11/21	1P: $70-$90	2P: $75-$95	XP: $5 F17

Location: On US 19/98, 0.8 mi n of jct SR 44. 614 NW Hwy 19 34428. Fax: 352/795-3179. **Facility:** On King's Bay.
114 units, 18 with efficiency. *Bath:* combo or shower only. 2 stories, exterior corridors. **Terms:** check-in 4 pm,
package plans, small pets only ($3 extra charge). **Amenities:** extended cable TV, safes, hair dryers.
Dining: tiki bar/sandwich shop. **Leisure Activities:** whirlpool, boat dock, fishing, dive shop. *Fee:* boats, canoes, scuba
diving/snorkeling & equipment, diving instruction. **Guest Services:** gift shop, coin laundry. **Business Services:** meeting rooms,
fax. **Cards:** AE, CB, DI, DS, MC, VI. **Special Amenities:** free room upgrade and preferred room (each subject to availability
with advanced reservations).

SOME UNITS

VCR FEE

PLANTATION INN & GOLF RESORT   **Phone:** (352)795-4211
AAA SAVE
Resort

2/1-4/15	2P: $90-$160	XP: $15 F16
12/1-1/31 & 10/1-11/30	2P: $80-$135	XP: $15 F16
4/16-9/30	2P: $70-$135	XP: $15 F16

Location: On CR 44, 0.5 mi w of jct US 19/98. 9301 W Fort Island Tr 34429. Fax: 352/795-1156. **Facility:** On King's
Bay. 139 units. *Bath:* combo or shower only. 2 stories, interior/exterior corridors. **Terms:** cancellation fee imposed, package plans. **Amenities:** extended cable TV, video games, voice mail, irons, hair dryers.
Dining: dining room, 6-11 am, 11:30-2 & 5-9 pm, Fri & Sat-10 pm, $18-$20, cocktails. **Leisure Activities:** heated pool, whirlpool, boat ramp, marina, fishing, putting green, pro shop, horseshoes, shuffleboard, volleyball, croquet, driving range. *Fee:* boats,
canoes, scuba diving/snorkeling & equipment, pontoon, golf-27 holes, 2 lighted tennis courts, tennis instruction, health club privileges. **Guest Services:** [MAP] meal plan available, gift shop, coin laundry. **Business Services:** conference facilities, fax.
Cards: AE, CB, DI, DS, MC, VI. **Special Amenities:** free local telephone calls and free room upgrade (subject to availability
with advanced reservations).

SOME UNITS

FEE

―――― **WHERE TO DINE** ――――

CHARLIE'S FISH HOUSE   **Lunch:** $3-$15   **Dinner:** $3-$15   **Phone:** 352/795-2468
Seafood
Location: US 19, just n of jct SR 44. 224 US 19 NW 34228. **Hours:** 11 am-9 pm. Closed: 4/15, 11/22, 12/25;
also 12/24 for dinner. **Features:** casual dress; early bird specials; carryout; beer & wine only. Japanese
cuisine is prepared table-side by strikingly fast chefs with a flare for showmanship. A good place to meet
new people. The hibachi tables have different parties seated together. Order the chicken, filet and shrimp
combo for a spicy feast. **Cards:** AE, DS, MC, VI.

CUDJOE KEY —*See The Florida Keys p. 312.*

CUTLER RIDGE —*See Miami-Miami Beach p. 517.*

DADE CITY —*See Tampa Bay p. 861.*

DANIA BEACH —*See Fort Lauderdale p. 374.*

DAVENPORT —*See Orlando p. 629.*

DAVIE —*See Fort Lauderdale p. 376.*

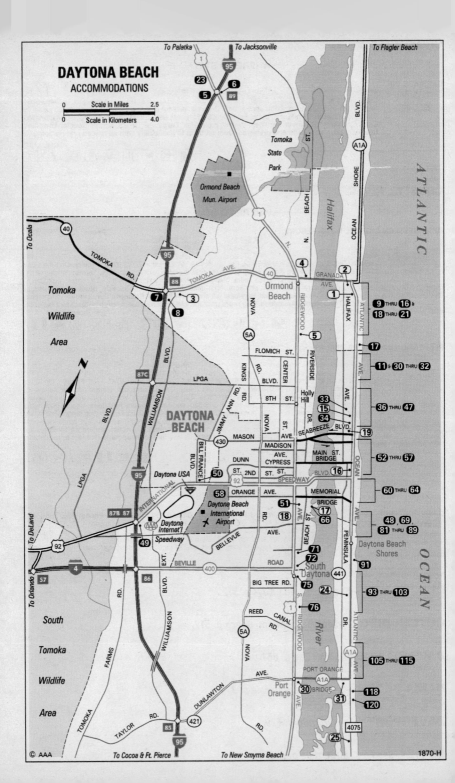

✈ Airport Accommodations

Spotter/Map Page Number	OA	DAYTONA BEACH REGIONAL	Diamond Rating	Rate Range High Season	Listing Page
58 / p. 270		Hampton Inn-Airport, 1 mi n of airport terminal	▽▽▽	$89-$94	281
60 / p. 270	AAA	Ramada Inn Speedway, 1 mi nw of airport terminal	▽▽▽	$79-$279 SAVE	285

Daytona Beach and Vicinity

This index helps you "spot" where approved accommodations are located on the corresponding detailed maps. Rate ranges are for comparison only and show the property's high season. Turn to the listing page for more detailed rate information and consult display ads for special promotions. Restaurant rate range is for dinner, unless only lunch (L) is served.

Spotter/Map Page Number	OA	DAYTONA BEACH - Lodgings	Diamond Rating	Rate Range High Season	Listing Page
30 / p. 270	AAA	Howard Johnson Ocean Front Hotel	▽▽▽	$94-$210 SAVE	281
31 / p. 270	AAA	Best Western La Playa Resort - see color ad p 275	▽▽▽	$119-$139 SAVE	274
32 / p. 270	AAA	Beachcomer Daytona Beach Resort - see color ad p 275	▽▽▽	$89-$139 SAVE	274
33 / p. 270		The Villa Bed & Breakfast	▽▽▽	$125-$250	286
34 / p. 270	AAA	Travelers Inn - see color ad p 281	▽▽	$29-$79 SAVE	286
36 / p. 270	AAA	Aruba Inn - see ad p 278	▽▽	$35-$75 SAVE	274
38 / p. 270	AAA	Tropical Winds Oceanfront Resort	▽▽	$49-$119 SAVE	286
40 / p. 270	AAA	Ocean Villa Motel - see color ad starting on p 276	▽▽	$49-$149 SAVE	283
41 / p. 270	AAA	Del Aire Motel	▽▽	$69-$97 SAVE	280
44 / p. 270	AAA	Capri Motel - see color ad starting on p 276	▽	$49-$149 SAVE	279
46 / p. 270	AAA	Casa Marina Motel - see color ad starting on p 276	▽▽	$39-$99 SAVE	279
47 / p. 270	AAA	The Plaza Resort & Spa - see color ad p 275	▽▽▽	$149-$169 SAVE	285
48 / p. 270	AAA	Royal Beach Motel	▽	$46-$255 SAVE	285
49 / p. 270		La Quinta Inn	▽▽▽	$59-$75	281
50 / p. 270	AAA	Ramada Inn Speedway	▽▽▽	$79-$279 SAVE	285
51 / p. 270		The Coquina Inn Bed & Breakfast	▽▽▽	$80-$110	280
52 / p. 270	AAA	Saxony Motel	▽	$35-$99 SAVE	285
53 / p. 270	AAA	Breakers Beach Oceanfront Motel - see color ad p 278	▽▽	$67-$117 SAVE	274
54 / p. 270	AAA	Radisson Resort - see color ad p 285	▽▽▽	$109-$169 SAVE	285
55 / p. 270	AAA	Adam's Mark Resort - see color ad p 278	▽▽▽	$95-$200 SAVE	274
56 / p. 270	AAA	Esquire Beach Motel	▽	$70-$165 SAVE	280
57 / p. 270	AAA	Best Western Mayan Inn Beachfront - see color ad p 279	▽▽	$85-$185 SAVE	274
58 / p. 270		Hampton Inn-Airport	▽▽▽	$89-$94	281
60 / p. 270		Howard Johnson Plaza	▽▽	Failed to provide	281
63 / p. 270	AAA	Travelodge Ocean Jewels Resort - see color ad p 278	▽▽▽	$79-$119 SAVE	286
64 / p. 270	AAA	Inn on the Beach - see color ad p 284	▽▽▽	$63-$97 SAVE	281
66 / p. 270		Live Oak Inn Bed & Breakfast & Restaurant	▽▽▽	Failed to provide	283
69 / p. 270	AAA	Nautilus Inn	▽▽▽	$99-$139 SAVE	283

Spotter/Map Page Number	OA	DAYTONA BEACH - Lodgings (continued)	Diamond Rating	Rate Range High Season	Listing Page
71 / p. 270	AAA	Budget Host Inn, The Candlelight - see color ad p 240	◇	$34-$44 SAVE	279
72 / p. 270	AAA	Scottish Inns	◇	$35-$140 SAVE	286
		DAYTONA BEACH - Restaurants			
15 / p. 270	AAA	Riccardo's Italian Restaurant	◇◇	$9-$17	286
16 / p. 270		Starlite Diner	◇	$4-$8	287
17 / p. 270		Rosario's Italian Restaurant	◇◇	$11-$17	287
18 / p. 270	AAA	Hungarian Village Restaurant	◇◇	$10-$16	286
19 / p. 270		The St. Regis Restaurant & Patio Garden	◇◇◇	$15-$28	287
		ORMOND BEACH - Lodgings			
5 / p. 270	AAA	Days Inn Ormond Beach I-95	◇◇	$40-$199 SAVE	707
6 / p. 270		Comfort Inn Interstate	◇◇◇	$75-$160	706
7 / p. 270		Hampton Inn Ormond Beach	◇◇◇	$79-$89	707
8 / p. 270	AAA	Sleep Inn	◇◇◇	$65-$70 SAVE	708
9 / p. 270	AAA	Coral Beach Motel - see color ad p 280	◇◇◇	$55-$155 SAVE	706
10 / p. 270	AAA	Driftwood Beach Motel - see ad p 280	◇◇	$53-$71 SAVE	707
11 / p. 270	AAA	Ron Jon Resort-Ormond Beach - see color ad p 635	◇◇◇	$49-$269 SAVE	708
14 / p. 270	AAA	Comfort Inn On The Beach - see color ad p 282	◇◇	$85-$165 SAVE	706
15 / p. 270	AAA	Jamaican Beach Motel - see color ad p 282	◇	$45-$170 SAVE	707
16 / p. 270	AAA	Symphony Beach Club	◇◇	$54-$95 SAVE	708
17 / p. 270		Days Inn Daytona Oceanfront North	◇◇	$55-$150	706
18 / p. 270		Econo Lodge on the Beach - see color ad p 282	◇◇	Failed to provide	707
19 / p. 270	AAA	Best Western Mainsail Inn and Suites - see color ad p 282	◇◇	$75-$180 SAVE	706
20 / p. 270		Quality Inn and Suites Oceanside Resort	◇◇◇	$89-$220	708
21 / p. 270	AAA	Ivanhoe Beach Resort - see color ad p 707	◇◇	$75-$150 SAVE	707
23 / p. 270	AAA	Super 8	◇◇	$70 SAVE	708
		ORMOND BEACH - Restaurants			
1 / p. 270	AAA	Julian's	◇◇	$8-$17	708
2 / p. 270	AAA	La Crepe En Haut	◇◇◇	$23-$40	708
3 / p. 270		Royal Dynasty Restaurant & Lounge	◇◇	$8-$17	709
4 / p. 270		English Rose Tea Room	◇◇	$5-$7(L)	708
5 / p. 270		Mario's	◇◇	$9-$17	708
		SOUTH DAYTONA - Lodgings			
75 / p. 270	AAA	Red Carpet Inn	◇	$35-$45 SAVE	784
76 / p. 270	AAA	Sun Ranch Motor Lodge	◇◇	$39-$55 SAVE	784
		DAYTONA BEACH SHORES - Lodgings			
81 / p. 270	AAA	Bahama House - see color ad p 288	◇◇◇	$155-$267 SAVE	289
82 / p. 270	AAA	Grand Prix	◇	$50-$70 SAVE	292
83 / p. 270	AAA	Old Salty's Inn - see color ad p 281	◇◇◇	$51-$98 SAVE	293
84 / p. 270	AAA	Flamingo Inn	◇◇◇	$119-$299 SAVE	292

Spotter/Map Page Number	OA	DAYTONA BEACH SHORES - Lodgings (continued)	Diamond Rating	Rate Range High Season	Listing Page
86 / p. 270	AAA	Atlantic Waves Motel	◇◇	$40-$150 SAVE	289
87 / p. 270	AAA	Treasure Island Resort - see color ad p 275	◇◇◇	$129-$169 SAVE	298
88 / p. 270		Sunny Shore Motel	◇◇	Failed to provide	297
89 / p. 270		Anchorage Beach Suites - see color ad p 279	◇◇	$60-$169	287
91 / p. 270	AAA	Perry's Ocean-Edge - see color ad p 294	◇◇◇	$84-$140 SAVE	293
93 / p. 270	AAA	Pelican Shoals Motel & Cottages	◇◇	$65 SAVE	293
94 / p. 270	AAA	Hawaiian Inn - see color ad p 292	◇◇	$49-$229 SAVE	292
95 / p. 270	AAA	Sun Viking Lodge - see color ad starting on p 276	◇◇◇	$69-$199 SAVE	297
96 / p. 270	AAA	Shoreline All Suites Inn - see color ad p 297	◇◇	$79-$149 SAVE	296
97 / p. 270	AAA	Acapulco Resort - see color ad p 275	◇◇◇	$79-$149 SAVE	287
98 / p. 270		Super 8 Daytona Sands	◇	$35-$99 SAVE	297
99 / p. 270	AAA	Hilton Daytona Beach Oceanfront Resort - see ad p 44 & color ad p 293	◇◇◇	$149-$359 SAVE	292
100 / p. 270	AAA	Quality Inn Ocean Palms - see color ad p 295	◇◇	$85-$195 SAVE	294
102 / p. 270	AAA	Best Western-Aku Tiki Inn - see color ad p 289	◇◇	$65-$178 SAVE	291
103 / p. 270	AAA	Tropical Manor Motel - see color ad p 298	◇◇	$61-$107 SAVE	298
105 / p. 270	AAA	Atlantic Ocean Palm Inn - see color ad p 287	◇◇	$39-$149 SAVE	287
106 / p. 270	AAA	Ramada Inn-Surfside - see color ad p 296	◇◇	$99-$139 SAVE	294
107 / p. 270	AAA	Seagarden Inn - see color ad p 297	◇◇	$75-$85 SAVE	295
109 / p. 270		Holiday Inn Daytona Beach Shores	◇◇	$79-$260	293
110 / p. 270	AAA	Beachside Motel - see color ad p 290	◇◇	$89-$129 SAVE	291
111 / p. 270	AAA	Palm Plaza Oceanfront Resort - see color ad p 290	◇◇◇	$119-$149 SAVE	293
112 / p. 270	AAA	Beach House Oceanfront Motel	◇◇	$62-$99 SAVE	289
114 / p. 270	AAA	Dream Inn Motel - see color ad p 291	◇◇	$49-$129 SAVE	292
115 / p. 270	AAA	Days Inn Oceanfront South Tropical Seas	◇◇	$49-$119 SAVE	291
118 / p. 270	AAA	Pier Side Inn - see color ad p 295	◇◇◇	$73-$225 SAVE	294
120 / p. 270	AAA	Colonial Palms Inn Oceanfront	◇◇	$64-$91 SAVE	291
		DAYTONA BEACH SHORES - Restaurants			
24 / p. 270	AAA	China-American Garden	◇◇	$7-$12	298
25 / p. 270		Boondocks	◇	$5-$15	298
		PORT ORANGE - Restaurants			
30 / p. 270		Aunt Catfish's On The River	◇◇	$9-$29	734
31 / p. 270		Sindbad's Restaurant	◇◇	$7-$18	734

DAYTONA BEACH pop. 61,900 (See map p. 270; index p. 271)

──────── WHERE TO STAY ────────

ADAM'S MARK RESORT
Phone: (904)254-8200 **55**

(AAA) (SAVE)

Hotel

1/1-11/30	1P: $95-$200	2P: $95-$200	XP: $25	F17
12/1-12/31	1P: $95-$195	2P: $95-$195	XP: $25	F17

Location: SR A1A, 0.5 mi n of US 92; opposite convention center. 100 N Atlantic Ave 32118. Fax: 904/253-8841. **Facility:** Beautiful beachfront location. Upscale guest room appointments. Many units with ocean view. Many luxury services available. Lovely public areas. 437 units. Some suites ($165-$1600) and whirlpool units ($165-$260). 16 stories, interior corridors. **Parking:** valet. **Terms:** check-in 4 pm, cancellation fee imposed, package plans. **Amenities:** voice mail, irons, hair dryers. *Some:* honor bars. **Dining:** restaurant, 7 am-11 pm, food court, beach bar, $16-$28, cocktails. **Leisure Activities:** heated pool, wading pool, sauna, whirlpools, steamroom, beach, playground, game room, beach volleyball, tanning. **Guest Services:** gift shop, valet laundry. *Fee:* massage. **Business Services:** conference facilities, PC, fax. **Cards:** AE, CB, DI, DS, MC, VI. **Special Amenities:** early check-in/late check-out and preferred room (subject to availability with advanced reservations).** *(See color ad p 278)*

SOME UNITS

ARUBA INN
Phone: (904)253-5643 **36**

(AAA) (SAVE)

Motel

All Year	2P: $35-$75	XP: $5	F15

Location: SR A1A, 1.5 mi n of jct US 92. 1254 N Atlantic Ave 32118. Fax: 904/248-1279. **Facility:** 32 units, 12 with efficiency. 2 stories, exterior corridors. **Terms:** weekly & monthly rates available. **Leisure Activities:** beach, shuffleboard. **Guest Services:** coin laundry. **Cards:** AE, DS, MC, VI. *(See ad p 278)*

BEACHCOMER DAYTONA BEACH RESORT
Phone: (904)252-8513 **32**

(AAA) (SAVE)

Motor Inn

2/1-4/21 & 8/19-11/30	1P: $89-$139	2P: $89-$139	XP: $8	F18
12/1-1/31 & 4/22-8/18	1P: $59-$99	2P: $59-$99	XP: $8	F18

Location: On SR A1A; 2.8 mi n of jct US 92. 2000 N Atlantic Ave 32118. Fax: 904/252-7400. **Facility:** Most rooms with balcony or patio and overlook or view the ocean; but a few are compact, street-side units. Pool area overlooks ocean. Designated smoking area. 174 units, 128 with efficiency. *Bath:* combo or shower only. 7 stories, interior/exterior corridors. **Terms:** 7 day cancellation notice, weekly & monthly rates available, package plans. **Amenities:** extended cable TV, voice mail, safes (fee). **Dining:** dining room, 7 am-1 pm; 5 pm-10 pm 12/1-3/31, $5-$13, cocktails. **Leisure Activities:** heated pool, wading pool, whirlpool, beach, social program. **Guest Services:** gift shop, area transportation, coin laundry. **Cards:** AE, DI, DS, MC, VI. **Special Amenities:** free continental breakfast. *(See color ad p 275)*

SOME UNITS

BEST WESTERN LA PLAYA RESORT
Phone: (904)672-0990 **31**

(AAA) (SAVE)

Motor Inn

6/1-8/16	1P: $119-$139	2P: $119-$139	XP: $6	F18
3/2-5/31	1P: $99-$139	2P: $99-$139	XP: $6	F18
12/1-3/1 & 8/17-11/30	1P: $79-$109	2P: $79-$109	XP: $6	F18

Location: SR A1A, 3.3 mi n of jct US 92. 2500 N Atlantic Ave 32118. Fax: 904/677-0982. **Facility:** Many oceanfront or view rooms with balcony. Designated smoking area. 239 units. 126 efficiencies and 106 units with kitchen. *Bath:* combo or shower only. 10 stories, exterior corridors. **Terms:** 5 day cancellation notice-fee imposed, weekly & monthly rates available, package plans. **Amenities:** extended cable TV, voice mail, safes (fee). **Dining:** coffee shop, 7 am-1:30 pm; breakfast buffet (in season) and Sunday champagne brunch. Seasonal pool bar. **Leisure Activities:** 2 pools (1 heated, 1 indoor), wading pool, saunas, whirlpools, steamrooms, beach, exercise room, shuffleboard, volleyball. **Guest Services:** coin laundry. **Business Services:** meeting rooms. **Cards:** AE, CB, DI, DS, MC, VI. **Special Amenities:** free newspaper. *(See color ad p 275)*

SOME UNITS

BEST WESTERN MAYAN INN BEACHFRONT
Phone: 904/252-2378 **57**

(AAA) (SAVE)

Motel

2/2-4/20	1P: $85-$185	2P: $85-$185	XP: $5	F15
4/21-8/31	1P: $81-$99	2P: $81-$99	XP: $5	F15
9/1-11/30	1P: $71-$95	2P: $71-$95		
12/1-2/1	1P: $71-$95	2P: $71-$95	XP: $5	F15

Location: From jct US 92 and SR A1A; n, just e, then n. 103 S Ocean Ave 32118. Fax: 904/252-8670. **Facility:** Contemporary guest unit decor. Many units with balcony and ocean view. 112 units, 49 with efficiency. Some whirlpool units. 8 stories, interior/exterior corridors. **Terms:** 7 day cancellation notice, weekly & monthly rates available, package plans. **Amenities:** extended cable TV, safes (fee). **Leisure Activities:** heated pool, wading pool, beach, swimming, game room. **Guest Services:** coin laundry. **Cards:** AE, CB, DI, DS, MC, VI. **Special Amenities:** free continental breakfast. *(See color ad p 279)*

SOME UNITS

BREAKERS BEACH OCEANFRONT MOTEL
Phone: (904)252-0863 **53**

(AAA) (SAVE)

Motel

2/1-4/24	2P: $67-$117	XP: $10	F15
4/25-9/6	2P: $52-$102	XP: $10	F15
12/1-1/31 & 9/7-11/30	2P: $47-$97	XP: $10	F15

Location: 27 S Ocean Ave 32118-4363. Fax: 904/238-1247. **Facility:** Nice location, just s of pier and boardwalk. Older well-maintained motel. Office hours 8 am-10 pm. 23 units. 13 efficiencies and 1 unit with kitchen. Some suites ($97-$124). *Bath:* combo or shower only. 2 stories, exterior corridors. **Terms:** 21 day cancellation notice-fee imposed, weekly & monthly rates available, small pets only ($10 extra charge). **Amenities:** extended cable TV. **Leisure Activities:** heated pool, beach, picnic area with gas grills. **Guest Services:** coin laundry. **Cards:** AE, CB, DI, DS, MC, VI. **Special Amenities:** free newspaper and preferred room (subject to availability with advanced reservations). *(See color ad p 278)*

SOME UNITS

There's so much to do at
Oceans Resorts, it's easy to
lose sight of your family.

10%-40% off published rates.
Free continental breakfast.

With oceanfront rooms close to some of
Central Florida's best attractions, your
family can have a great time while you relax
in our world-class Ocean Waters Spa.
To make reservations, call **1-800-874-7420**
or visit www.daytonahotels.com.

Oceans Resorts

A Family of Fine Hotels
Daytona Beach

Plaza Resort & Spa - Acapulco Hotel & Resort - Beachcomer Resort
Treasure Island Resort - Best Western La Playa Resort

2025 South Atlantic Avenue, Daytona Beach, FL • www.daytonahotels.com

Based on availability. Tax not included. Not available during special events and/or holidays.

Old Florida Charm ...

Recapture an old fashioned excursion to the beach. Our oceanfront setting, along a picturesque turquoise surf, offers a vacation filled with sunshine, smiles and warm memories. Affordable, comfortable accommodations and a genuinely friendly staff provide relaxed Florida charm.

Stroll our sugar white sandy beach, put in a few laps in one of our heated pools, and enjoy poolside fun with our complimentary guest recreation program designed for all ages. Kids will love "slip-sliding away" on our 60-foot waterslide, splashing in our kiddie pool, testing their skill in our game room and watching the latest in-room movies.

Great golf packages are available year round and moments from our door you will find local restaurants, shopping and night clubs. A day-trip offers you all of central Florida's attractions including the Walt Disney World® Resort, just an hour's drive away. Come and enjoy our genuine southern hospitality.

... the way vacations were meant to be.

Ocean Villa Motel

Oceanfront Rooms, Efficiencies and Suites

Capri Motel

Oceanfront Rooms and Efficiencies

Casa Marina Motel

Oceanfront access just steps away. Spacious Apartments

Imagine ...

A tranquil seaside
where gentle waves caress
silky white sands. Coastal
pleasures are always in
season including sunning,
surfing, sailing, sports fishing and golfing. Explore our
beautiful beach. Swim in our sparkling oceanside pools.
Ride our 60 foot waterslide. Exercise in our Nautilus
equipped fitness room. Entertain your family with
our year round guest recreation program,
and relax in our hot tub and sauna.

*... a place where
you are always
welcome.*

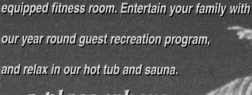
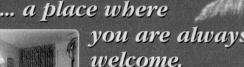

Sun Viking Lodge

"A Unique Family Resort"

800-815-2508

www.sunviking.com

904-252-6252 · FAX 904-252-5463

2411 South Atlantic Avenue · Daytona Beach Shores, Florida 32118

(See map p. 270)

BUDGET HOST INN, THE CANDLELIGHT

AAA SAVE
◇◇◇
Motel

| | | | Phone: (904)252-1142 | **71** |
12/1-4/30 & 7/1-9/4   1P: $34-$38   2P: $40-$44   XP: $5   F12
5/1-6/30 & 9/5-11/30   1P: $32-$36   2P: $38-$42   XP: $5   F12

Location: I-95, exit 86A, 2.5 mi e on SR 400, 0.4 mi n on US 1 (Ridgwood Ave). 1305 S Ridgewood Ave 32114. Fax: 904/252-1142. **Facility:** Pleasant residential location. Spacious guest rooms with contemporary furnishings. Office hours 7 am-11 pm. Designated smoking area. 25 units, 4 with efficiency. 1 story, exterior corridors. **Terms:** weekly & monthly rates available, small pets only ($5 extra charge). **Amenities:** extended cable TV. **Leisure Activities:** shuffleboard, grill at umbrellas & tables. **Guest Services:** coin laundry. **Cards:** AE, MC, VI.
(See color ad p 240)

SOME UNITS

⎙ 🛏 📷 / ✕ 🖥 📞 /

CAPRI MOTEL

AAA SAVE
◇◇◇
Motel

| | | | Phone: (904)252-2555 | **44** |
2/9-8/18   1P: $49-$149   2P: $49-$149   XP: $10   F17
12/1-2/8 & 8/19-11/30   1P: $45-$89   2P: $45-$89   XP: $6   F17

Location: SR A1A, 1.5 mi n of jct US 92. Registration next door at Ocean Villa Motel. Office hours 8 am-10:30 pm. 24 units. 12 efficiencies and 6 units with kitchen. *Bath:* combo or shower only. 1-2 stories, exterior corridors. **Terms:** 7 day cancellation notice, weekly & monthly rates available. **Amenities:** extended cable TV, safes (fee). **Leisure Activities:** 2 pools (1 heated), waterslide, beach, game room, video movie rentals. **Guest Services:** coin laundry. **Cards:** AE, CB, DI, DS, MC, VI. **Special Amenities:** free newspaper. *(See color ad starting on p 276)*

SOME UNITS

⎙ 🍴 ♨ DATA PORT / VCR 🖥 📺 📞 /
FEE

CASA MARINA MOTEL

AAA SAVE
◇◇◇ ◇◇
Suite Apartment

| | | | Phone: (904)252-4644 | **46** |
2/9-8/18   2P: $39-$99   XP: $10   F17
12/1-2/8 & 8/19-11/30   2P: $29-$79   XP: $6   F17

Location: SR A1A, 1.5 mi n of jct US 92. 837 N Atlantic Ave 32118. Fax: 904/788-4065. **Facility:** Registration across street at Ocean Villa Motel. Office hours 8 am-10:30 pm. All units have good room space and ceiling fans in addition to A/C units. 13 units. 3 efficiencies and 10 units with kitchen. *Bath:* combo or shower only. 1-2 stories, exterior corridors. **Terms:** check-in 4 pm, 7 day cancellation notice, weekly & monthly rates available. **Amenities:** extended cable TV, safes (fee). **Leisure Activities:** off-site recreational facility privileges and beach access. **Cards:** AE, CB, DI, DS, MC, VI. **Special Amenities:** free newspaper. *(See color ad starting on p 276)*

SOME UNITS

⎙ 🚭 🖥 📺 📞 / VCR /
FEE

(See map p. 270)

THE COQUINA INN BED & BREAKFAST
Phone: (904)254-4969   **51**
▼▼▼▼

| | 12/1-4/30 & 9/1-11/30 | 1P: $80-$110 | 2P: $80-$110 | XP: $20 | F |
| | 5/1-8/31 | 1P: $60-$90 | 2P: $60-$90 | XP: $20 | F |

Historic Bed & Breakfast

Location: 0.5 mi s on US 1 (S Ridgewood Ave) from jct of US 92, just e on Cedar St. 544 S Palmetto Ave 32114. **Fax:** 904/254-4969. **Facility:** This 1912 bed & breakfast is listed on the National Register of Historic Places and located in the heart of Daytona's historic district. Located 1 1/2 blocks from the Daytona and Halifax Harbor Marinas, the inn is named after the abundant local quarry, coquina rock, found in the Tomoka River basin. The thick walls and archways are examples of Florida architecture. A spa in gazebo with large deck in landscaped outdoor setting. Designated smoking area. 4 units. 3 stories (no elevator), interior corridors. **Terms:** age restrictions may apply, 14 day cancellation notice, weekly rates available. **Amenities:** extended cable TV. **Leisure Activities:** whirlpool. **Guest Services:** [BP] meal plan available, complimentary evening beverages. **Cards:** AE, DS, MC, VI.

ASK ✕ ☎ ⬚ 🖨

DEL AIRE MOTEL
Phone: (904)252-2563   **41**
AAA SAVE

| | 3/2-9/3 | | 2P: $69-$97 | XP: $8 | F16 |
| | 2/1-3/1 | | 2P: $59-$79 | XP: $8 | F16 |
▼▼▼ ▼▼ | | 12/1-1/31 & 9/4-11/30 | | 2P: $45-$65 | XP: $8 | F16 |

Motel

Location: SR A1A, 1.3 mi n of jct US 92. 744 N Atlantic Ave 32118. Fax: 904/252-4866. **Facility:** Landscaped beachfront property with pool overlooking ocean. Office hours 8:30 am-10 pm. Designated smoking area. 20 units. 9 efficiencies and 5 units with kitchen. Some suites ($70-$110). 2 stories, exterior corridors. **Terms:** 7 day cancellation notice, weekly & monthly rates available. **Amenities:** extended cable TV, safes (fee). **Leisure Activities:** heated pool, beach, playground. **Cards:** AE, MC, VI. **Special Amenities:** early check-in/late check-out and free local telephone calls.

SOME UNITS
🏊 🖥 / ✕ 💻 📺 /

ESQUIRE BEACH MOTEL
Phone: 904/255-3601   **56**
AAA SAVE

| | 2/14-4/23 | 1P: $70-$105 | 2P: $95-$165 | XP: $10 | F12 |
| | 4/24-8/25 | 1P: $45-$70 | 2P: $55-$85 | XP: $10 | F12 |
▼▼▼ | | 12/1-2/13 | 1P: $35-$45 | 2P: $50-$60 | XP: $10 | F12 |
| | 8/26-11/30 | 1P: $35-$45 | 2P: $40-$50 | XP: $10 | F12 |

Motel

Location: SR A1A, 0.8 mi n of US 92. 422 N Atlantic Ave 32118. Fax: 904/255-2166. **Facility:** Units range in size and style, some with ocean view. 68 units, 29 with kitchen. *Bath:* combo or shower only. 2-3 stories, exterior corridors. **Terms:** 10 day cancellation notice, weekly & monthly rates available. **Amenities:** extended cable TV, safes (fee). **Leisure Activities:** heated pool, beach. **Guest Services:** coin laundry. **Cards:** AE, DS, MC, VI.

SOME UNITS
📶 🏊 🐕 🖥 / 💻 /

(See map p. 270)

HAMPTON INN-AIRPORT

SAVE
▼▼▼
Motel

Phone: 904/257-4030 **58**

All Year   1P: $89   2P: $94

Location: I-95, northbound exit 87; southbound exit 87B, 2.3 mi e on US 92. 1715 W International Speedway Blvd 32114. Fax: 904/257-5721. **Facility:** Just e of Daytona International Speedway and in a landscaped setting off main road. Designated smoking area. 121 units. 4 stories, interior corridors. **Amenities:** extended cable TV, voice mail, irons, hair dryers. **Leisure Activities:** whirlpool. **Guest Services:** [CP] meal plan available, area transportation, valet laundry. **Business Services:** meeting rooms. **Cards:** AE, CB, DI, DS, JC, MC, VI.

SOME UNITS

HOWARD JOHNSON OCEAN FRONT HOTEL

(AAA) **SAVE**
▼▼▼
Motel

Phone: (904)672-1440 **30**

2/3-4/30	1P: $94-$210	2P: $94-$210	XP: $8 F17
5/1-9/3	1P: $79-$142	2P: $79-$142	XP: $8 F17
12/1-2/2	1P: $59-$79	2P: $59-$79	XP: $8 F17
9/4-11/30	1P: $55-$79	2P: $55-$79	XP: $8 F17

Location: SR A1A, 3.3 mi n of jct US 92. 2560 N Atlantic Ave 32118. Fax: 904/677-8811. **Facility:** Many rooms oceanfront or ocean views with private balcony. Designated smoking area. 143 units. 88 efficiencies and 30 units with kitchen. *Bath:* combo or shower only. 8 stories, interior/exterior corridors. **Terms:** 5 day cancellation notice, weekly & monthly rates available, package plans. **Amenities:** extended cable TV, safes (fee), irons, hair dryers. **Leisure Activities:** heated pool, wading pool, whirlpool, beach. **Guest Services:** coin laundry. **Business Services:** meeting rooms. **Cards:** AE, CB, DI, DS, JC, MC, VI. **Special Amenities:** free newspaper.

SOME UNITS

HOWARD JOHNSON PLAZA

▼▼▼
Motel

Phone: (904)258-8522 **60**

Property failed to provide current rates

Location: 0.4 mi s of US 92 on A1A. 701 S Atlantic Ave 32118. Fax: 904/257-9122. **Facility:** 125 units with kitchen. 8 stories, exterior corridors. **Terms:** 30 day cancellation notice, weekly & monthly rates available, package plans. **Leisure Activities:** heated pool, whirlpool, beach, swimming. **Guest Services:** coin laundry. **Business Services:** meeting rooms. **Cards:** AE, DI, DS, MC, VI.

SOME UNITS

INN ON THE BEACH

(AAA) **SAVE**
▼▼▼
Motel

Phone: (904)255-0921 **64**

2/5-4/29	1P: $63-$97	2P: $63-$97	XP: $8 F18
4/30-8/13	1P: $52-$74	2P: $52-$74	XP: $8 F18
12/1-2/4 & 8/14-11/30	1P: $52-$59	2P: $52-$59	XP: $6 F18

Location: SR A1A, 1.3 mi s of jct US 92. 1615 S Atlantic Ave 32118. Fax: 904/255-3849. **Facility:** Most rooms offer a fine ocean view. Basic continental plan. 195 units, 101 with kitchen. Some whirlpool units. *Bath:* combo or shower only. 7 stories, interior/exterior corridors. **Terms:** check-in 4 pm, 3 day cancellation notice-fee imposed, weekly & monthly rates available, package plans. **Amenities:** extended cable TV. **Dining:** cocktails. **Leisure Activities:** heated pool, wading pool, sauna, whirlpool, beach, swimming, putting green, social program, playground, exercise room, shuffleboard, volleyball, game room. **Guest Services:** coin laundry. *Fee:* massage. **Business Services:** meeting rooms. **Cards:** AE, CB, DI, DS, MC, VI. **Special Amenities:** free continental breakfast and free newspaper. (See color ad p 284)

SOME UNITS

LA QUINTA INN

SAVE
▼▼▼
Motel

Phone: (904)255-7412 **49**

All Year   1P: $59-$75   2P: $59-$75

Location: I-95, exit 87 northbound; exit 87B southbound, just e. 2725 W International Speedway Blvd 32114. Fax: 904/255-5350. **Facility:** Busy commercial location. Very comfortable, large guest rooms. 143 units. Some suites. *Bath:* combo or shower only. 2 stories, interior corridors. **Terms:** small pets only. **Amenities:** video games, voice mail. **Leisure Activities:** wading pool. **Guest Services:** [CP] meal plan available, coin laundry. **Business Services:** meeting rooms. **Cards:** AE, CB, DI, DS, MC, VI.

SOME UNITS

FEE

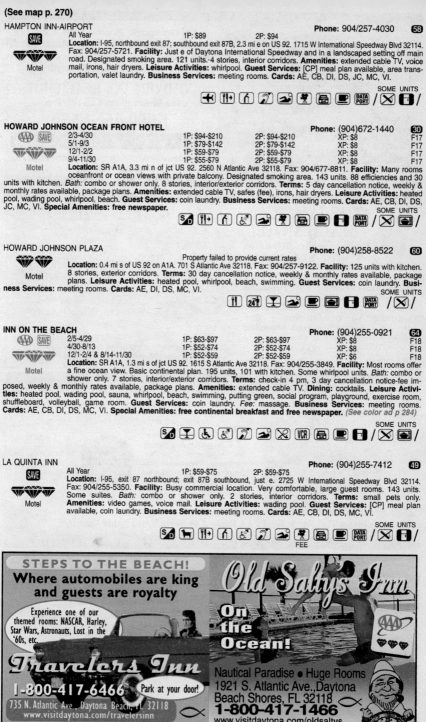

(See map p. 270)

LIVE OAK INN BED & BREAKFAST & RESTAURANT Phone: (904)252-4667 66
▼▼▼▼
Property failed to provide current rates
Historic Country Inn
Location: Just e on US 92 from jct of US 1, 0.5 mi s. 444-448 S Beach St 32114. Fax: 904/239-0068. **Facility:** Historic inn with comfortable units, each having a private bath. Each unit represents people or events which took part in Florida's history. Designated smoking area. 12 units. Some whirlpool units. 2 stories, interior/exterior corridors. **Terms:** age restrictions may apply, 7 day cancellation notice. **Dining:** Rosario's Italian Restaurant, see separate listing. **Guest Services:** [CP] meal plan available. **Business Services:** meeting rooms. **Cards:** MC, VI.

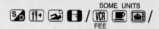

NAUTILUS INN Phone: (904)254-8600 69

6/1-9/3	1P: $99-$139	2P: $99-$139	XP: $10	F17
2/2-5/31	1P: $99-$129	2P: $99-$129	XP: $10	F17
9/4-11/30	1P: $80-$109	2P: $80-$109	XP: $10	F17
12/1-2/1	1P: $75-$102	2P: $75-$102	XP: $10	F17

Suite Motel
Location: SR A1A, 1.5 mi s of jct US 92. 1515 S Atlantic Ave 32118. Fax: 904/254-8627. **Facility:** Tends to be group or tour oriented in winter. Well maintained, nice pool area. Smoke free premises. 99 units, 63 with efficiency. 10 stories, interior corridors. **Terms:** 10 day cancellation notice, weekly & monthly rates available. **Amenities:** extended cable TV, safes. **Leisure Activities:** heated pool, whirlpool, beach, recreation program, social program. **Guest Services:** [ECP] meal plan available, complimentary evening beverages, coin laundry. **Cards:** AE, DS, MC, VI. **Special Amenities: free continental breakfast.**

OCEAN VILLA MOTEL Phone: (904)252-4644 40

2/9-8/18	1P: $49-$149	2P: $49-$149	XP: $10	F17
12/1-2/8 & 8/19-11/30	1P: $45-$89	2P: $45-$89	XP: $6	F17

Motel
Location: SR A1A, 1.5 mi n of jct US 92. 828 N Atlantic Ave 32118. Fax: 904/255-7378. **Facility:** Units range in size from compact to more spacious two-room suites. Contemporary room appeal. Office hours 8 am-10:30 pm. 38 units. 12 efficiencies and 8 units with kitchen. *Bath:* combo or shower only. 2 stories, exterior corridors. **Terms:** 7 day cancellation notice, weekly & monthly rates available. **Amenities:** extended cable TV, safes (fee). **Leisure Activities:** 2 pools (1 heated), wading pool, waterslide, beach, game room, video movie rentals. **Guest Services:** coin laundry. **Cards:** AE, CB, DI, DS, MC, VI. **Special Amenities: free newspaper.** *(See color ad starting on p 276)*

(See map p. 270)

THE PLAZA RESORT & SPA

AAA SAVE

Hotel

		Phone: (904)255-4471	47
2/1-8/18	1P: $149-$169	XP: $15	F12
12/1-1/31 & 8/19-11/30	1P: $119-$139	XP: $15	F12

Location: SR A1A, 1 mi n of US 92. 600 N Atlantic Ave 32118. Fax: 904/253-7672. **Facility:** 322 units. Some suites and whirlpool units. 9-13 stories, interior corridors. **Parking:** valet. **Terms:** check-in 4 pm, 10 day cancellation notice-fee imposed, weekly & monthly rates available, package plans, $2 service charge, pets ($100 deposit). **Amenities:** voice mail, safes, irons, hair dryers. **Dining:** restaurant, deli, 6 am-10 pm seasonal bar & grill, $10-$17, cocktails, nightclub. **Leisure Activities:** heated pool, wading pool, beach, children's program in summer, social program in summer, exercise room, sports court, game room. **Guest Services:** gift shop, coin laundry. **Business Services:** conference facilities, fax. *Fee:* PC. **Cards:** AE, CB, DI, DS, JC, MC, VI. **Special Amenities: free continental breakfast.**
(See color ad p 275)

SOME UNITS
🆂🅳 🛏 🍴 🍸 🎱 🏊 ✕ 🎮 🖨 💻 🖥 🔌 🖥 /✕/

RADISSON RESORT

AAA SAVE

Hotel

			Phone: (904)239-9800	54
12/1-4/15	1P: $109-$169	2P: $109-$169	XP: $10	
10/1-11/30	1P: $99-$139	2P: $99-$139	XP: $10	
4/16-9/30	1P: $89-$129	2P: $89-$129	XP: $10	

Location: SR A1A, 1 mi n of jct SR 90. 640 N Atlantic Ave 32118. Fax: 904/253-0735. **Facility:** 206 units. *Bath:* combo or shower only. 11 stories, interior corridors. **Parking:** extra charge. **Terms:** check-in 4 pm, package plans, small pets only ($50 extra charge). **Amenities:** extended cable TV, video games, voice mail, safes, irons. **Dining:** 6:30 am-10 pm, $7-$15, cocktails. **Leisure Activities:** heated pool, wading pool, beach, swimming, exercise room. **Guest Services:** gift shop, coin laundry. **Business Services:** meeting rooms. **Cards:** AE, CB, DI, DS, MC, VI.
(See color ad below)

SOME UNITS
🆂🅳 🛏 24🍴 🍸 ♿ 👤 🎱 🏊 🎮 🖨 💻 🔌 /✕ 🖥 🛗 /
FEE

RAMADA INN SPEEDWAY

AAA SAVE

Motor Inn

			Phone: (904)255-2422	50
All Year	1P: $79-$279	2P: $79-$279		

Location: I-95, exit 87 B, southbound; exit 87 northbound, 2 mi e on US 92. 1798 W International Speedway Blvd 32114. Fax: 904/253-1749. **Facility:** Many units overlook large outdoor pool courtyard area with covered seating area. Across the street from Daytona International Speedway and adjacent to Volusia Mall. Designated smoking area. 127 units. 2 stories, interior corridors. **Terms:** pets ($25 extra charge). **Amenities:** extended cable TV, voice mail, safes. **Dining:** restaurant, 6:30 am-1 am, $7-$14, cocktails. **Guest Services:** area transportation-within 3 mi, valet laundry. **Business Services:** meeting rooms. **Cards:** AE, CB, DI, DS, JC, MC, VI. **Special Amenities: free local telephone calls.**

SOME UNITS
🆂🅳 ✈ 🛏 🍴 🍸 🎱 🏊 🎮 🖨 💻 🔌 /✕ 🛗 /

ROYAL BEACH MOTEL

AAA SAVE

Motel

		Phone: 904/255-8341	48
2/1-9/7	2P: $46-$255	XP: $10	F10
9/8-11/30	2P: $32-$109	XP: $10	F10
12/1-1/31	2P: $35-$99	XP: $10	F10

Location: SR A1A, 2 mi s of jct SR 92. 1601 S Atlantic Ave 32118. Fax: 904/258-0135. **Facility:** 49 units, 23 with efficiency. *Bath:* combo or shower only. 2 stories, exterior corridors. **Terms:** 14 day cancellation notice-fee imposed. **Leisure Activities:** heated pool, beach, swimming, game room. **Guest Services:** coin laundry. **Cards:** AE, DS, MC, VI. **Special Amenities: free room upgrade and preferred room (each subject to availability with advanced reservations).**

SOME UNITS
🆂🅳 🍴 🍸 🏊 /💻 🖥 🛗 /

SAXONY MOTEL

AAA SAVE

Motel

			Phone: (904)252-4703	52
All Year	1P: $35-$85	2P: $45-$99	XP: $10	F13

Location: From jct US 92 and SR A1A, just n and e. 35 S Ocean Ave 32118. **Facility:** Large units with contemporary decor. Designated smoking area. 27 units. Some whirlpool units ($129-$275). *Bath:* combo or shower only. 3 stories (no elevator), exterior corridors. **Terms:** 14 day cancellation notice-fee imposed. **Amenities:** safes. **Leisure Activities:** beach, swimming. **Cards:** AE, DS, MC, VI.

SOME UNITS
🆂🅳 🍴 🏊 /✕ 💻 🖥 🛗 /

SCOTTISH INNS

AAA SAVE · ◆◆◆ (Diamond rating)

Motel

Phone: 904/258-5742 72

2/1-4/30	1P: $35-$129	2P: $48-$140	XP: $5	F8
7/1-11/30	1P: $35-$99	2P: $45-$110	XP: $5	F8
5/1-6/30	1P: $35-$89	2P: $39-$99	XP: $5	F8
12/1-1/31	1P: $28-$39	2P: $45-$59	XP: $5	F8

Location: I-95, exit 86A, 2.5 mi e on SR 400, just n on US 1. 1515 S Ridgewood Ave 32114. Fax: 904/253-7635. **Facility:** Pool with patio furniture is centered in front of property and has all day sun exposure. Designated smoking area. 20 units. 1 story, exterior corridors. **Terms:** 10 day cancellation notice-fee imposed, weekly rates available, small pets only ($5 extra charge). **Amenities:** extended cable TV, safes (fee). **Cards:** AE, CB, DI, DS, MC, VI. **Special Amenities: free newspaper and free room upgrade (subject to availability with advanced reservations).**

SOME UNITS — FEE

TRAVELERS INN

AAA SAVE · ◆◆◆◆

Motel

Phone: (904)253-3501 34

All Year	1P: $29-$59	2P: $39-$79	XP: $10	F12

Location: SR A1A, 1 mi n of US 92. 735 N Atlantic Ave 32118. Fax: 904/441-5977. **Facility:** Boutique style motel with parking at-door and creative styling to develop themed rooms complete with local artist murals. 3-D shark is incorporated into the setting at the landscaped pool area. Designated smoking area. 21 units, 4 with kitchen. *Bath:* combo or shower only. 1 story, exterior corridors. **Terms:** 30 day cancellation notice-fee imposed, weekly & monthly rates available. **Amenities:** extended cable TV. *Some:* hair dryers. **Leisure Activities:** heated pool, beach bikes. **Guest Services:** [CP] meal plan available, coin laundry. **Cards:** AE, DS, MC, VI. **Special Amenities: free newspaper and preferred room (subject to availability with advanced reservations).**
(See color ad p 281)

SOME UNITS

TRAVELODGE OCEAN JEWELS RESORT

AAA SAVE · ◆◆◆

Motor Inn

Phone: (904)252-2581 63

2/1-3/31	1P: $79-$119	2P: $79-$119	XP: $10	F18
4/1-9/3	1P: $69-$109	2P: $69-$109	XP: $10	F18
12/1-1/31 & 9/4-11/30	1P: $59-$79	2P: $59-$79	XP: $10	F18

Location: 0.6 mi s of US 92 on A1A. 935 S Atlantic Ave 32118. Fax: 904/257-3608. **Facility:** Decor of island colors. Rooms range from small to spacious; all are well equipped. 198 units. 1 two-bedroom unit, 40 efficiencies and 158 units with kitchen. Some suites ($149-$189). *Bath:* combo or shower only. 6 stories, exterior corridors. **Terms:** weekly & monthly rates available. **Amenities:** extended cable TV. **Dining:** restaurant, 7 am-10 pm, $6-$11. **Leisure Activities:** 2 pools (1 heated), wading pool, beach, swimming, exercise room. **Guest Services:** coin laundry. **Cards:** AE, DI, DS, MC, VI. **Special Amenities: early check-in/late check-out and free room upgrade (subject to availability with advanced reservations).** *(See color ad p 278)*

SOME UNITS

TROPICAL WINDS OCEANFRONT RESORT

AAA SAVE · ◆◆◆

Apartment

Phone: (904)258-1016 38

12/1-4/21	1P: $49-$119	2P: $49-$119	XP: $10	F17
6/8-8/19	1P: $72-$114	2P: $72-$114	XP: $10	F17
4/22-6/7	1P: $54-$94	2P: $54-$94	XP: $10	F17
8/20-11/30	1P: $42-$79	2P: $42-$79	XP: $10	F17

Location: SR A1A, 2 mi n of jct US 92. 1398 N Atlantic Ave 32118. Fax: 904/255-6462. **Facility:** 94 units. 7 two-bedroom units, 64 efficiencies and 7 units with kitchen. Some suites. 8 stories, interior corridors. **Terms:** weekly & monthly rates available. **Amenities:** hair dryers. **Dining:** coffee shop, 7 am-2 pm. **Leisure Activities:** 2 pools (1 heated, 1 indoor), beach, shuffleboard, game room. **Guest Services:** coin laundry. **Cards:** AE, DI, DS, MC, VI.

SOME UNITS

THE VILLA BED & BREAKFAST

◆◆◆◆

Classic Bed & Breakfast

Phone: (904)248-2020 33

2/3-4/15	2P: $125-$250
12/1-2/2	2P: $100-$250
4/16-11/30	2P: $125-$190

Location: N of A1A from jct of US 92, just w on Seabreeze Blvd, 0.4 mi n. 801 N Peninsula Dr 32118. Fax: 904/248-2020. **Facility:** 1920s Florida Spanish mansion with gated entry to two acres of landscaped grounds complete with flowering gardens surrounding the tiled patio with spa and seating areas. Guest unit are theme designed. Smoke free premises. 4 units. 2 stories, interior corridors. **Terms:** age restrictions may apply, 15 day cancellation notice-fee imposed. **Amenities:** extended cable TV, hair dryers. **Leisure Activities:** whirlpool. **Guest Services:** [CP] meal plan available, complimentary evening beverages. **Cards:** AE, MC, VI.

------ **WHERE TO DINE** ------

HUNGARIAN VILLAGE RESTAURANT

AAA · ◆◆◆

Hungarian

Dinner: $10-$16 **Phone: 904/226-0115** 18

Location: On US 1, 0.5 mi s of jct US 92. 424 S Ridgewood Ave 32114. **Hours:** 4:30 pm-9:30 pm. Closed major holidays; also Sun & Mon. **Reservations:** accepted. **Features:** casual dress; early bird specials; cocktails. Authentic Hungarian specialties include stuffed cabbage, goulash, Wiener schnitzel and pork with potatoes served hot on "the Wooden Plate." The cozy atmosphere gives this restaurant a homey touch. **Cards:** DS, MC, VI.

RICCARDO'S ITALIAN RESTAURANT

AAA · ◆◆◆

Italian

Dinner: $9-$17 **Phone: 904/253-3035** 15

Location: SR A1A, 1 mi n of jct US 92, just w. 610 Glenview Blvd 32118. **Hours:** 5 pm-10 pm, closing hours may vary. **Closed:** 11/22, 12/24, 12/25. **Reservations:** suggested. **Features:** casual dress; children's menu; cocktails. The casual, contemporary setting caters to families and candlelight diners alike. Homemade offerings include not only the pasta, but also the yummy bread and ice cream. The kitchen does a great job of preparing delicious entrees of fresh seafood. **Cards:** AE, MC, VI.

(See map p. 270)

ROSARIO'S ITALIAN RESTAURANT Country Inn   **Lunch:** $4-$7   **Dinner:** $11-$17   **Phone:** 904/258-6066   ⑰

American

Location: Just e on US 92 from jct of US 1, 0.5 mi s; in Live Oak Inn Bed & Breakfast & Restaurant. 448 S Beach St 32114. **Hours:** 5 pm-10 pm. Closed: Sun & Mon. **Reservations:** suggested. **Features:** cocktails. Smoke free premises. **Cards:** AE, MC, VI.   ⊠

STARLITE DINER   **Lunch:** $4-$6   **Dinner:** $4-$8   **Phone:** 904/255-9555   ⑯

American

Location: SR A1A, 0.8 mi n of US 92. 401 N Atlantic Ave 32118. **Hours:** 7 am-11 pm. **Features:** casual dress; children's menu; carryout. This '60s-era jukebox joint is the place to go for comfort food and lots of it. Mom's meatloaf, juicy burgers, homemade cakes and pies, and decadent fountain creations might not do much for your waistline, but they'll work wonders for your state of mind. **Cards:** MC, VI. ⌂ ⊠

THE ST. REGIS RESTAURANT & PATIO GARDEN   **Lunch:** $6-$13   **Dinner:** $15-$28   **Phone:** 904/252-8743   ⑲

Continental

Location: 509 Seabreeze Blvd. **Hours:** 6 pm-11 pm; Wed-Fri also noon-3 pm. Closed: 1/1, 12/25; also Sun & Mon. **Reservations:** suggested. **Features:** dressy casual; children's menu; cocktails & lounge; street parking & fee for valet parking. Enjoy the covered, outdoor environment of the garden patio while partaking of classic dishes from continental and American cuisine. Or, dine in the ambience of a vintage home, circa 1886. Converted to a restaurant, the house is furnished with some antiques, but the atmosphere is still casual. Smoke free premises. **Cards:** AE, DS, MC, VI.   ⊠

DAYTONA BEACH SHORES pop. 2,300   (See map p. 270; index p. 272)

—— WHERE TO STAY ——

ACAPULCO RESORT   **Phone:** (904)761-2210   97

ⒶⒶⒶ ⟨SAVE⟩	2/1-6/7 & 6/8-8/18	1P: $79-$149	2P: $79-$149	XP: $10	F17
▽▽▽▽	12/1-1/31 & 8/19-11/30	1P: $59-$99	2P: $59-$99	XP: $10	F17

Motor Inn

Location: SR A1A, 2.8 mi s of jct US 92. 2505 S Atlantic Ave 32118. Fax: 904/761-2216. **Facility:** Standard type guest rooms. All rooms with balcony, most have cooking facilities but there are some standard rooms also. Located right along beach. 133 units, 91 with efficiency. 8 stories, interior corridors. **Terms:** 7 day cancellation notice-fee imposed, weekly & monthly rates available, package plans. **Amenities:** extended cable TV, voice mail, safes (fee). **Dining:** coffee shop, 7 am-1:30 pm, cocktails. **Leisure Activities:** heated pool, wading pool, whirlpools, beach, recreation program. **Guest Services:** gift shop, coin laundry. **Business Services:** meeting rooms. **Cards:** AE, DI, DS, MC, VI. **Special Amenities: free continental breakfast.** *(See color ad p 275)*   SOME UNITS

⟨S🅿⟩ ⟨🍴⟩ ⟨📺⟩ ⟨🏊⟩ ⟨🎥⟩ ⟨🔒⟩ ⟨DATA PORT⟩ / ⊠ ⟨🖨⟩ /

ANCHORAGE BEACH SUITES   **Phone:** (904)255-5394   89

▽▽▽▽ ▽▽▽▽	2/4-6/2	1P: $60-$169	2P: $60-$169	XP: $10	F12
	6/3-9/5	1P: $60-$139	2P: $60-$139	XP: $10	F12
Suite Motel	12/1-2/3	1P: $45-$98	2P: $45-$98	XP: $10	F12
	9/6-11/30	1P: $40-$89	2P: $40-$89	XP: $10	F12

Location: 1 mi s on SR A1A from jct, w on US 92. 1901 S Atlantic Ave 32118. Fax: 904/258-7327. **Facility:** 22 units. 4 two-bedroom units and 18 units with kitchen. 2 stories, exterior corridors. **Terms:** 30 day cancellation notice-fee imposed, monthly rates available. **Leisure Activities:** heated pool, beach, swimming. **Guest Services:** coin laundry. **Cards:** DS, MC, VI. *(See color ad p 279)*   SOME UNITS

⟨🏊⟩ / ⟨🖨⟩ ⟨🔒⟩ /

ATLANTIC OCEAN PALM INN   **Phone:** 904/761-8450   105

ⒶⒶⒶ ⟨SAVE⟩	All Year		2P: $39-$149	XP: $7	F12

▽▽▽▽

Motel

Location: SR A1A, 5 mi s of jct US 92. 3247 S Atlantic Ave 32118. Fax: 904/304-3079. **Facility:** Large units with contemporary decor, some at-door parking. 50 units. 1 two-bedroom unit and 28 efficiencies. Some whirlpool units ($99-$149). 3 stories, exterior corridors. **Terms:** 30 day cancellation notice-fee imposed, weekly rates available, small pets only ($5 extra charge). **Amenities:** extended cable TV, hair dryers. **Leisure Activities:** heated pool, beach, sun deck, shuffleboard. **Guest Services:** coin laundry. **Cards:** AE, DS, MC, VI. **Special Amenities: early check-in/late check-out and free room upgrade (subject to availability with advanced reservations).** *(See color ad below)*   SOME UNITS

⟨🐑⟩ ⟨📶⟩ ⟨🏊⟩ ⟨DATA PORT⟩ / ⊠ ⟨📺⟩ ⟨🖨⟩ ⟨🔒⟩ /

Savings at Your Fingertips

(SAVE)

Travel With Someone You Trust

When you have a AAA TourBook® guide in your hand, you have a world of savings right at your fingertips. Official Appointment lodgings that display the bright-red AAA logo, (SAVE) icon and Diamond rating in their listing want AAA member business, and offer discounts and special amenities to members.

So, when planning your next vacation, be sure to consult your AAA TourBook for the familiar red (SAVE) icon. This symbol represents a minimum 10 percent discount off published TourBook standard room rates to AAA members!

(See map p. 270)

ATLANTIC WAVES MOTEL

Phone: (904)253-7186   86

2/1-5/31	1P: $40-$145	2P: $45-$150	XP: $5	F12
6/1-8/31	1P: $50-$125	2P: $55-$135	XP: $5	F12
9/1-11/30	1P: $30-$90	2P: $35-$95	XP: $5	F12
12/1-1/31	1P: $30-$65	2P: $35-$70	XP: $5	F12

Suite Motel

Location: SR A1A, 1.5 mi s of jct US 92. 1925 S Atlantic Ave 32118. Fax: 904/252-3779. **Facility:** Attractive, family run motel on "The World's Most Famous Beach". Accessible to local attractions, dining and shopping. 22 units. 4 efficiencies and 18 units with kitchen. 2 stories, exterior corridors. **Terms:** 14 day cancellation notice-fee imposed, weekly & monthly rates available. **Amenities:** extended cable TV, safes (fee). **Leisure Activities:** heated pool, beach. **Guest Services:** coin laundry. **Cards:** AE, MC, VI.

BAHAMA HOUSE

Phone: (904)248-2001   81

2/2-4/21	1P: $155-$267	2P: $155-$267	XP: $10 F18
12/1-2/1 & 4/22-11/30	1P: $121	2P: $121	XP: $10 F18

Suite Motel

Location: SR A1A, 1.5 mi s of jct US 92. 2001 S Atlantic Ave 32118. Fax: 904/248-0991. **Facility:** Striking building with large to very large, finely appointed units. All units with balcony. Underground parking garage. 87 efficiencies. Some suites ($229-$385) and whirlpool units. 10 stories, interior corridors. **Terms:** 10 day cancellation notice, weekly & monthly rates available, package plans. **Amenities:** extended cable TV, voice mail, safes (fee), irons, hair dryers. **Leisure Activities:** heated pool, whirlpool, beach, social program. **Guest Services:** [ECP] meal plan available, complimentary evening beverages, coin laundry. **Cards:** AE, DI, DS, MC, VI. **Special Amenities:** free continental breakfast and free newspaper. (See color ad p 288)

SOME UNITS

BEACH HOUSE OCEANFRONT MOTEL

Phone: (904)788-7107   112

2/3-4/25 & 6/22-11/30	2P: $62-$99	XP: $10 F12
12/1-2/2 & 4/26-6/21	2P: $49-$76	XP: $10 F12

Motel

Location: SR A1A, 0.5 mi n of Port Orange Bridge. 3221 S Atlantic Ave 32118. Fax: 904/760-3672. **Facility:** 10 units. 1 three-bedroom unit and 9 efficiencies. *Bath:* combo or shower only. 1 story, exterior corridors. **Terms:** 30 day cancellation notice-fee imposed, weekly & monthly rates available. **Amenities:** extended cable TV, safes. **Leisure Activities:** heated pool, whirlpool, beach. **Cards:** AE, DS, MC, VI. **Special Amenities:** free local telephone calls and free newspaper.

SOME UNITS

(See map p. 270)

BEACHSIDE MOTEL

Phone: (904)788-5569 **110**

(AAA) SAVE

♦♦♦

Motel

2/2-9/3   1P: $89-$129   2P: $89-$129
12/1-2/1 & 9/4-11/30   1P: $69-$99   2P: $69-$99

Location: SR A1A, 5.3 mi s of US 92, 0.3 mi n of Port Orange Bridge. 3309 S Atlantic Ave 32118 (3301 S Atlantic Ave). Fax: 904/756-8394. **Facility:** Comfortable, well appointed guest units. Most with ocean view. Some very large suites with inland view. Smoke free premises. 31 efficiencies. 3 two-bedroom units. 5 stories, interior corridors. **Terms:** 10 day cancellation notice. **Amenities:** extended cable TV. **Leisure Activities:** heated pool. **Guest Services:** coin laundry. **Cards:** AE, CB, DI, DS, JC, MC, VI. **Special Amenities:** early check-in/late check-out and free continental breakfast. *(See color ad p 290)*

BEST WESTERN-AKU TIKI INN

Phone: (904)252-9631 **102**

(AAA) SAVE

♦♦♦

Motor Inn

3/13-8/15   1P: $65-$178   2P: $65-$178   XP: $10   F12
12/1-3/12   1P: $55-$178   2P: $55-$178   XP: $10   F12
8/16-10/22   1P: $55-$135   2P: $55-$135   XP: $10   F12
10/23-11/30   1P: $55-$100   2P: $55-$100   XP: $10   F12

Location: SR A1A, 2.2 mi s of jct US 92. 2225 S Atlantic Ave 32118. Fax: 904/252-1198. **Facility:** A nicely maintained older property featuring some of the largest guest units along the beach. All units with private balcony and most units have some view of the ocean. 132 units, 62 with efficiency. 5 stories, interior corridors. **Terms:** 30 day cancellation notice, monthly rates available. **Amenities:** extended cable TV. **Dining:** restaurant, 7 am-10 pm, $9-$15, cocktails. **Leisure Activities:** heated pool, wading pool, beach. **Guest Services:** gift shop, coin laundry. **Cards:** AE, CB, DI, DS, MC, VI. *(See color ad p 289)*

COLONIAL PALMS INN OCEANFRONT

Phone: (904)767-9261 **120**

(AAA) SAVE

♦♦

Motel

12/17-4/21 & 5/25-8/11   2P: $64-$91   XP: $10   F16
4/22-5/24 & 8/12-11/26   2P: $51-$73   XP: $10   F16

Location: I-95, Port Orange exit, approx 6 mi e to Atlantic Ave, 0.8 mi s. 3801 S Atlantic Ave 32127. Fax: 904/767-0390. **Facility:** This older, family owned property offers something different from larger property's, a quiet stay. The rooms are smaller but all are nicely maintained and decorated with a pleasant, at-home type feel. Located on the beach. 13 units, 10 with efficiency. *Bath:* shower only. 1 story, exterior corridors. **Terms:** open 12/17-11/26, 14 day cancellation notice-fee imposed, weekly & monthly rates available. **Amenities:** extended cable TV. **Leisure Activities:** heated pool, whirlpool, beach. **Guest Services:** coin laundry. **Cards:** DS, MC, VI. **Special Amenities:** free newspaper and preferred room (subject to availability with advanced reservations).

DAYS INN OCEANFRONT SOUTH TROPICAL SEAS

Phone: (904)767-8737 **115**

(AAA) SAVE

♦♦

Motel

12/1-4/21   1P: $49-$119   2P: $49-$119   XP: $10   F17
6/8-8/19   1P: $72-$114   2P: $72-$114   XP: $10   F17
4/22-6/7   1P: $54-$94   2P: $54-$94   XP: $10   F17
8/20-11/30   1P: $42-$79   2P: $42-$79   XP: $10   F17

Location: SR A1A, just n of Port Orange Bridge, 5.8 mi s of US 92. 3357 S Atlantic Ave 32118. Fax: 904/756-9612. **Facility:** Some covered parking in 2-level ramp. Many rooms face the ocean and have a balcony. 75 units, 36 with efficiency. 7 stories, interior corridors. **Terms:** weekly & monthly rates available. **Amenities:** extended cable TV. **Leisure Activities:** heated pool, whirlpool, beach. **Guest Services:** coin laundry. **Cards:** AE, CB, DI, DS, MC, VI. **Special Amenities:** free local telephone calls and free newspaper.

SOME UNITS / FEE

(See map p. 270)

DREAM INN MOTEL

Phone: (904)767-2821 **114**

(AAA) (SAVE)

♦♦♦♦ ♦♦♦♦

Motel

2/1-8/31	1P: $49-$129	2P: $49-$129	XP: $10
12/1-1/31 & 9/1-11/30	1P: $39-$99	2P: $39-$99	XP: $5

Location: On SR A1A, 0.5 mi n of Port Orange Bridge. 3217 S Atlantic Ave 32118. Fax: 904/767-7778. **Facility:** This family operated property offers well-maintained guest units. Some units offer ocean view, others nicely landscaped grounds. Office closes at 10 pm. 26 units. 16 efficiencies and 1 unit with kitchen. *Bath:* combo or shower only. 2 stories, exterior corridors. **Terms:** 30 day cancellation notice-fee imposed, weekly rates available. **Amenities:** extended cable TV, hair dryers. **Leisure Activities:** heated pool, beach. **Guest Services:** coin laundry. **Cards:** DS, MC, VI. **Special Amenities:** free newspaper and preferred room (subject to availability with advanced reservations). *(See color ad p 291)*

SOME UNITS

(S) (D) (¶+) (⊷) (⌕) (▭) (▭) (🔒) / (⊠) /

FLAMINGO INN

Phone: (904)252-1412 **84**

(AAA) (SAVE)

♦♦♦♦ ♦♦♦♦

Motel

2/1-4/30	2P: $119-$299	XP: $20
10/2-11/30	2P: $49-$199	XP: $20
5/1-8/30	2P: $79-$179	XP: $20
12/1-1/31	2P: $69-$139	XP: $20

Location: SR A1A, 1.8 mi s of jct US 92. 2011 S Atlantic Ave 32118. Fax: 904/252-1412. **Facility:** Spacious guest rooms. Varied office hours. 27 units, 20 with efficiency. Some suites. 3 stories (no elevator), exterior corridors. **Terms:** open 12/1-8/30 & 10/2-11/30, 30 day cancellation notice-fee imposed, weekly & monthly rates available. **Amenities:** extended cable TV, safes (fee). **Leisure Activities:** heated pool, beach, volleyball. **Guest Services:** coin laundry. **Cards:** DS, MC, VI.

SOME UNITS

(S) (D) (¶+) (⊷) (🔒) / (▭) /

GRAND PRIX

Phone: 904/255-2446 **82**

(AAA) (SAVE)

♦♦♦♦

Suite Motel

2/1-8/31	1P: $50-$70	2P: $50-$70	XP: $5	F16
9/1-11/30	1P: $45-$60	2P: $45-$60	XP: $5	F16
12/1-1/31	1P: $37-$50	2P: $37-$50	XP: $5	F16

Location: SR A1A, 1.8 mi s of jct US 92. 2015 S Atlantic Ave 32118. Fax: 904/258-9084. **Facility:** An older basic motel. 41 units. 13 efficiencies and 20 units with kitchen. 2 stories, exterior corridors. **Terms:** 7 day cancellation notice-fee imposed, weekly & monthly rates available. **Amenities:** extended cable TV, safes (fee). **Leisure Activities:** heated pool, beach. **Guest Services:** coin laundry. **Cards:** AE, CB, DI, DS, MC, VI. **Special Amenities:** free newspaper and free room upgrade (subject to availability with advanced reservations).

SOME UNITS

(⊷) / (⊠) (▭) (▭) (🔒) /

HAWAIIAN INN

Phone: (904)255-5411 **94**

(AAA) (SAVE)

♦♦♦

Condominium

All Year	1P: $49-$229	2P: $49-$229	XP: $15	F16

Location: SR A1A, 2.3 mi s of jct US 92. 2301 S Atlantic Ave 32118. Fax: 904/253-1209. **Facility:** Located directly on the beach, this older property offers large guest units with balcony and view of the ocean. For those on a budget and want to be near the beach, give this a try. 208 units. 4 two-bedroom units, 42 efficiencies and 96 units with kitchen. 5 stories, interior/exterior corridors. **Terms:** cancellation fee imposed, monthly rates available. **Amenities:** extended cable TV. **Dining:** coffee shop, 7 am-2 & 5-9 pm, $7-$19, cocktails, entertainment. **Leisure Activities:** 2 pools (1 heated, 1 indoor), wading pool, beach. **Guest Services:** gift shop, coin laundry. **Business Services:** meeting rooms. **Cards:** AE, CB, DI, DS, MC, VI. **Special Amenities:** free room upgrade and preferred room (each subject to availability with advanced reservations). *(See color ad below)*

SOME UNITS

(S) (D) (¶+) (Y) (⊷) (⊷) (⌕) (🔒) / (⊠) /

HILTON DAYTONA BEACH OCEANFRONT RESORT

Phone: (904)767-7350 **99**

(AAA) (SAVE)

♦♦♦

Hotel

2/1-3/11	1P: $149-$359	2P: $149-$359	XP: $15	F18
3/12-9/3	1P: $129-$189	2P: $129-$189	XP: $15	F18
12/1-1/31 & 9/4-11/30	1P: $89-$149	2P: $89-$149	XP: $15	F18

Location: SR A1A, 3.2 mi s of jct US 92. 2637 S Atlantic Ave 32118. Fax: 904/760-3651. **Facility:** A wonderful property featuring lovely public areas and large, colorful guest units with balcony and view of the ocean. 214 units, 5 with efficiency. Some whirlpool units ($350-$400). 11 stories, interior corridors. **Terms:** 5 day cancellation notice-fee imposed, package plans. **Amenities:** voice mail, safes (fee), irons, hair dryers. **Dining:** restaurant, coffee shop, 7 am-10 pm, Fri & Sat-11 pm, $9-$17, cocktails. **Leisure Activities:** heated pool, wading pool, whirlpool, beach, tennis privileges available, exercise room, game room. **Guest Services:** gift shop, coin laundry. *Fee:* massage. **Business Services:** meeting rooms, fax. **Cards:** AE, CB, DI, DS, MC, VI. **Special Amenities:** free local telephone calls and free newspaper. *(See ad p 44 & color ad p 293)*

SOME UNITS

(S) (D) (¶+) (Y) (♿) (&) (⊷) (⌕) (▭) (🔒) (DATA PORT) / (⊠) (▭) /
FEE

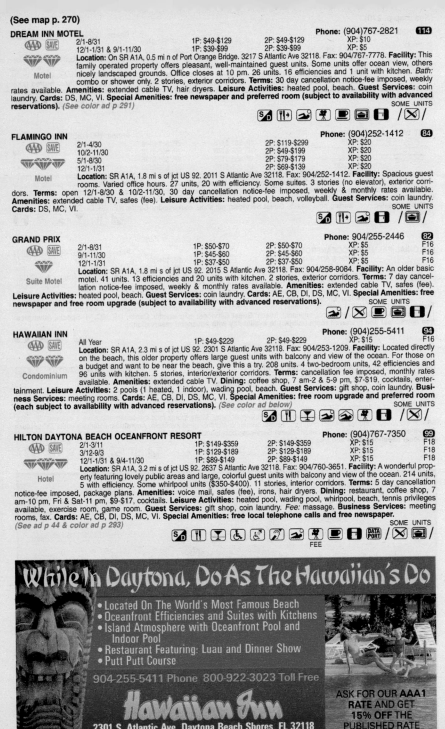

(See map p. 270)

HOLIDAY INN DAYTONA BEACH SHORES

Phone: (904)761-2050   [109]

| | 12/1-4/30 | 1P: $79-$260 | 2P: $79-$260 | XP: $10 | F16 |
| | 5/1-11/30 | 1P: $89-$245 | 2P: $89-$245 | XP: $10 | F16 |

Motor Inn   **Location:** SR A1A, 5 mi s of jct US 92. 3209 S Atlantic Ave 32118. Fax: 904/761-3922. **Facility:** Located right at the beach. This property offers good, standard style guest units with some efficiency units available for those who need cooking facilities. 193 units, 49 with efficiency. Some suites. 8 stories, interior corridors. **Terms:** 3 day cancellation notice. **Amenities:** extended cable TV, safes (fee), irons, hair dryers. **Leisure Activities:** heated pool, wading pool, beach, exercise room, game room. **Guest Services:** gift shop, coin laundry. **Business Services:** meeting rooms. **Cards:** AE, DI, DS, MC, VI.

SOME UNITS

(ASK) (S/D) (YI) (⊇) (🖥) (▣) (DATA PORT) / (✕) (▤) (♨) /

OLD SALTY'S INN

Phone: (904)252-8090   [83]

(AAA) (SAVE)

| | 12/1-12/31 | | 2P: $51-$98 | XP: $10 | F12 |
| | 1/1-11/30 | | 2P: $49-$79 | XP: $10 | F12 |

Motel   **Location:** SR A1A, 1.4 mi s of US 92. 1921 S Atlantic Ave 32118. Fax: 904/441-5977. **Facility:** Attractive grounds with nautical theme. Cheerful, pleasant and modern guest units ranging from average sized to spacious. 19 units. 9 efficiencies and 2 units with kitchen. *Bath:* combo or shower only. 2 stories, exterior corridors. **Terms:** 30 day cancellation notice-fee imposed, weekly & monthly rates available. **Amenities:** extended cable TV, hair dryers. **Leisure Activities:** heated pool, beach, beach bikes. **Guest Services:** coin laundry. **Cards:** AE, DS, MC, VI. **Special Amenities:** free newspaper and preferred room (subject to availability with advanced reservations).
(See color ad p 281)

SOME UNITS

(YI+) (⊇) (🎞) (▤) (♨) / (✕) /

PALM PLAZA OCEANFRONT RESORT

Phone: (904)767-1711   [111]

(AAA) (SAVE)

| | 2/2-9/3 | 1P: $119-$149 | 2P: $119-$149 | | |
| | 12/1-2/1 & 9/4-11/30 | 1P: $79-$109 | 2P: $79-$109 | | |

Motel   **Location:** SR A1A, 5.3 mi s of US 92, 0.3 mi n of Port Orange Bridge. 3301 S Atlantic Ave 32118-6308. Fax: 904/756-8394. **Facility:** A nicely maintained property. All units with wonderful views of the ocean, located right on the beach. 98 efficiencies. 4 two-bedroom units. 12 stories, exterior corridors. **Terms:** 10 day cancellation notice, weekly & monthly rates available, package plans. **Amenities:** extended cable TV, safes (fee). **Dining:** poolside snack bar. **Leisure Activities:** heated pool, wading pool, whirlpool, beach, game room. **Guest Services:** coin laundry. **Cards:** AE, CB, DI, DS, MC, VI. **Special Amenities:** early check-in/late check-out and free continental breakfast. *(See color ad p 290)*

SOME UNITS

(S/D) (YI+) (⊇) (🎞) (▤) (♨) / (✕) /

PELICAN SHOALS MOTEL & COTTAGES

Phone: (904)253-7962   [93]

(AAA) (SAVE)

	2/5-8/13		2P: $65	XP: $10	F16
	8/14-11/30		2P: $50	XP: $10	F16
	12/1-2/4		2P: $44	XP: $10	F16

Motel   **Location:** SR A1A, 2.5 mi s of US 92. 2407 S Atlantic Ave 32118. Fax: 904/258-0973. **Facility:** Office hours 8 am-10 pm. 24 units. 2 two-bedroom units, 23 efficiencies and 9 units with kitchen. *Bath:* combo or shower only. 2 stories, exterior corridors. **Terms:** weekly & monthly rates available. **Leisure Activities:** heated pool, beach, horseshoes, shuffleboard. **Guest Services:** coin laundry. **Cards:** AE, MC, VI. **Special Amenities:** early check-in/late check-out and free newspaper.

SOME UNITS

(⊇) (🎞) (♨) / (▤) (♨) /

PERRY'S OCEAN-EDGE

Phone: (904)255-0581   [91]

(AAA) (SAVE)

	2/13-8/11		2P: $84-$140		
	12/1-2/12		2P: $70-$110		
	8/12-11/30		2P: $73-$104		

Suite Motel   **Location:** SR A1A, 2 mi s of jct US 92. 2209 S Atlantic Ave 32118. Fax: 904/255-0540. **Facility:** A long time family owned property since 1940. This older property offers standard type guest units in various sizes as there are three different sections to this property. Most have view of ocean. Right on the beach. 204 units, 140 with kitchen. 2-6 stories, interior/exterior corridors. **Terms:** check-in 4 pm, 3 day cancellation notice, weekly & monthly rates available, package plans. **Amenities:** extended cable TV, voice mail, safes (fee), hair dryers. **Dining:** coffee shop, 7 am-2 pm; poolside tiki bar. **Leisure Activities:** 3 pools (1 heated, 1 indoor), wading pool, whirlpool, beach, putting green, children's program, nature program, recreation program, social program, "Parent's Night Out", playground, basketball, horseshoes, shuffleboard, bocci, lawn games, tetherball. **Guest Services:** gift shop, coin laundry. **Business Services:** meeting rooms. **Cards:** AE, CB, DI, DS, MC, VI. **Special Amenities:** free continental breakfast. Affiliated with Best Value Inn Brand Membership.
(See color ad p 294)

SOME UNITS

(S/D) (YI) (YI) (⊇) (🖥) (✕) (DATA PORT) / (▤) (♨) /

(See map p. 270)

PIER SIDE INN

AAA SAVE

Motel

	2/1-4/30	2P: $73-$225	XP: $10	F12
	5/1-8/31	2P: $59-$225	XP: $10	F12
	12/1-1/31 & 9/1-11/30	2P: $51-$134	XP: $10	F12

Phone: (904)767-4650 — 118

Location: Off SR A1A on CR 4075, 6.3 mi s of jct US 92, 0.3 mi s of Port Orange Bridge. 3703 S Atlantic Ave 32127. Fax: 904/788-0592. **Facility:** Large comfortable guest rooms. 35 units. 31 efficiencies and 2 units with kitchen. **Bath:** combo or shower only. 2 stories, exterior corridors. **Terms:** 7 day cancellation notice, weekly & monthly rates available, package plans. **Amenities:** extended cable TV, voice mail. **Leisure Activities:** heated pool, wading pool, beach, putting green, shuffleboard, game room, grills, pool table. **Guest Services:** coin laundry. **Cards:** DS, MC, VI. **Special Amenities:** free newspaper. *(See color ad p 295)*

QUALITY INN OCEAN PALMS

AAA SAVE

Motel

2/1-9/4	1P: $85-$195	2P: $85-$195	XP: $10	F18
9/5-11/30	1P: $65-$139	2P: $65-$139	XP: $10	F18
12/1-1/31	1P: $55-$129	2P: $55-$129	XP: $10	F18

Phone: (904)255-0476 — 100

Location: SR A1A, 2.5 mi s of jct US 92. 2323 S Atlantic Ave 32118. Fax: 904/255-3376. **Facility:** Some compact units, large rooms poolside with patio. 110 units. 20 efficiencies and 60 units with kitchen. **Bath:** combo or shower only. 6 stories, exterior corridors. **Terms:** weekly & monthly rates available, small pets only ($50 deposit). **Amenities:** extended cable TV, voice mail, hair dryers. **Dining:** coffee shop. **Leisure Activities:** heated pool, wading pool, beach, swimming, children's program, game room, sand volleyball. **Guest Services:** [ECP] meal plan available, coin laundry. **Business Services:** meeting rooms. **Cards:** AE, CB, DI, DS, MC, VI. **Special Amenities:** free continental breakfast and free local telephone calls. *(See color ad p 295)*

SOME UNITS

RAMADA INN-SURFSIDE

AAA SAVE

Motor Inn

4/21-8/11	1P: $99-$139	2P: $99-$139	XP: $12	F18
3/3-4/20	1P: $109-$129	2P: $109-$129	XP: $12	F18
8/12-11/30	1P: $79-$99	2P: $79-$99	XP: $12	F18
12/1-3/2	1P: $69-$89	2P: $69-$89	XP: $12	F18

Phone: (904)788-1000 — 106

Location: On SR A1A, 4.5 mi s of jct US 92. 3125 S Atlantic Ave 32118. Fax: 904/756-9906. **Facility:** A wonderfully solid listing featuring very well maintained guest units with private balcony and wonderful view of the ocean. Choose between standard rooms or rooms with some cooking facilities. 119 units. 12 two-bedroom units, 68 efficiencies and 12 units with kitchen. **Bath:** combo or shower only. 7 stories, exterior corridors. **Terms:** 5 day cancellation notice, weekly & monthly rates available, package plans. **Amenities:** extended cable TV, voice mail, safes (fee). *Some:* hair dryers. **Dining:** restaurant, 7 am-1 & 5-9 pm, $8-$15, cocktails. **Leisure Activities:** heated pool, wading pool, whirlpool, beach. **Guest Services:** gift shop, coin laundry. **Business Services:** meeting rooms. **Cards:** AE, CB, DI, DS, MC, VI. **Special Amenities:** free local telephone calls and free newspaper. *(See color ad p 296)*

SOME UNITS

(See map p. 270)

SEAGARDEN INN

AAA SAVE

Motel

All Year   1P: $75   2P: $85   Phone: (904)761-2335   **107**

Location: SR A1A, 5 mi s of jct US 92. 3161 S Atlantic Ave 32118. Fax: 904/756-6676. **Facility:** Offering large, comfortable guest units; some with an additional ceiling fan. All units with balcony overlooking the ocean. Located right at the beach. 144 units. 55 efficiencies and 36 units with kitchen. 10 stories, interior/exterior corridors. **Terms:** weekly & monthly rates available, package plans. **Amenities:** extended cable TV, safes (fee). **Dining:** snack bar open seasonally. **Leisure Activities:** heated pool, wading pool, whirlpool, beach. **Guest Services:** coin laundry. **Business Services:** meeting rooms. **Cards:** AE, DI, DS, MC, VI. *(See color ad p 297)*

SOME UNITS

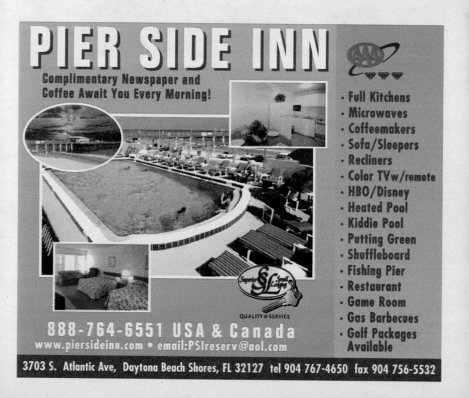

(See map p. 270)

SHORELINE ALL SUITES INN

AAA SAVE

WWWW

Suite Motel

2/1-9/4	2P: $79-$149	XP: $10	F12	
12/1-1/31	2P: $59-$119	XP: $10	F12	
9/5-11/30	2P: $119	XP: $10	F12	

Phone: (904)252-1692   96

Location: SR A1A, 2.8 mi s of jct 92. 2435 S Atlantic Ave 32118. Fax: 904/239-7068. **Facility:** Beautiful location on the beach with spacious lawns and decks. Office hours 7 am-10 pm. 17 units with kitchen. 5 two-bedroom units. *Bath:* combo or shower only. 2 stories, exterior corridors. **Terms:** 30 day cancellation notice-fee imposed, weekly & monthly rates available, package plans. **Amenities:** extended cable TV. **Leisure Activities:** heated pool, beach, sun deck, shuffleboard, barbecue grills, beach volleyball. *Fee:* movies. **Guest Services:** coin laundry. **Cards:** AE, DS, MC, VI. **Special Amenities:** free continental breakfast and free room upgrade (subject to availability with advanced reservations). *(See color ad p 297)*

SOME UNITS

(See map p. 270)

SUNNY SHORE MOTEL

Suite Motel

Phone: 904/252-4569   88

Property failed to provide current rates

Location: SR A1A, 1.8 mi s of jct US 92. 2037 S Atlantic Ave 32118. **Fax:** 904/255-4991. **Facility:** A few oceanfront rooms. Pleasant comfortable guest rooms. 34 units. 3 two-bedroom units and 28 efficiencies. 2 stories, exterior corridors. **Terms:** weekly & monthly rates available. **Amenities:** extended cable TV. **Leisure Activities:** beach. **Guest Services:** coin laundry. **Cards:** DS, MC, VI.

SOME UNITS

SUN VIKING LODGE

Motel

Phone: (904)252-6252   95

2/9-8/18	1P: $69-$199	2P: $69-$199	XP: $15	F17
12/1-2/8 & 8/19-11/30	1P: $65-$159	2P: $65-$159	XP: $10	F17

Location: SR A1A, 2.5 mi s of jct US 92. 2411 S Atlantic Ave 32118. **Fax:** 904/252-5463. **Facility:** A truly unique property. Long time family owned offering two different sections, from spacious motel style units, most with full kitchens, to spacious rooms in high-rise building with view of ocean. A real gem. 91 units. 1 two-bedroom unit and 70 units with kitchen. Some suites ($95-$369) and whirlpool units. 2-8 stories, interior/exterior corridors. **Terms:** 7 day cancellation notice, weekly & monthly rates available, package plans. **Amenities:** extended cable TV, safes (fee). **Dining:** coffee shop, 7:30 am-2:30 pm. **Leisure Activities:** 2 heated pools, wading pool, sauna, whirlpool, waterslide, beach, beach volleyball, social program, playground, exercise room, basketball, shuffleboard, game room, video movie rentals. **Guest Services:** coin laundry. **Business Services:** meeting rooms. **Cards:** AE, CB, DI, DS, MC, VI. **Special Amenities:** free newspaper. *(See color ad starting on p 276)*

SOME UNITS

SUPER 8 DAYTONA SANDS

Motel

Phone: (904)767-2551   98

All Year	1P: $35-$85	2P: $45-$99	XP: $10	F13

Location: SR A1A, 2.8 mi s of jct US 92. 2523 S Atlantic Ave 32118. **Fax:** 904/322-4847. **Facility:** Modest property with good sized units and contemporary decors. Designated smoking area. 40 units, 12 with efficiency. 3 stories, exterior corridors. **Terms:** 14 day cancellation notice-fee imposed. **Amenities:** safes (fee). **Leisure Activities:** beach, swimming. **Cards:** AE, DS, MC, VI.

SOME UNITS

(See map p. 270)

TREASURE ISLAND RESORT

Phone: (904)255-8371   87

AAA SAVE

WWWW

Motor Inn

	2/1-4/21	1P: $129-$169	2P: $129-$169	XP: $10	F17
	4/22-8/18	1P: $99-$169	2P: $99-$169	XP: $10	F17
	12/1-1/31 & 8/19-11/30	1P: $99-$134	2P: $99-$134	XP: $10	F17

Location: SR A1A, 1.8 mi s of jct US 92. 2025 S Atlantic Ave 32118. Fax: 904/255-4984. **Facility:** 232 units, 145 with efficiency. 11 stories, interior corridors. **Parking:** valet. **Terms:** check-in 4 pm, 10 day cancellation notice-fee imposed, weekly & monthly rates available. **Amenities:** extended cable TV, voice mail, safes (fee), irons. **Dining:** dining room, 7 am-2 & 5-9:30 pm seasonal poolside cafe, $7-$15, cocktails, entertainment. **Leisure Activities:** 2 pools (1 heated), wading pool, whirlpools, beach, children's program. **Guest Services:** gift shop, coin laundry. **Business Services:** meeting rooms, fax. **Cards:** AE, DS, MC, VI. **Special Amenities:** free continental breakfast. *(See color ad p 275)*

SOME UNITS

[amenity icons] / [icons] / [icon]

TROPICAL MANOR MOTEL

Phone: 904/252-4920   103

AAA SAVE

WWWW

Apartment

| | 12/1-9/4 | | 2P: $61-$107 | XP: $5 |
| | 9/5-11/30 | | 2P: $46-$90 | XP: $5 |

Location: SR A1A, 2.2 mi s of jct US 92. 2237 S Atlantic Ave 32118. Fax: 904/258-9415. **Facility:** An absolute gem! A truly magnificent property, very well maintained units, lovely landscaped grounds and pool area. Families most welcome. Look for the floral painted murals and tropical pink colored motel. 36 units. 2 two-bedroom units, 4 efficiencies and 28 units with kitchen. *Bath:* combo or shower only. 1-3 stories, exterior corridors. **Terms:** 14 day cancellation notice, weekly & monthly rates available. **Amenities:** extended cable TV. **Leisure Activities:** heated pool, wading pool, beach. **Guest Services:** coin laundry. **Cards:** AE, DI, DS, MC, VI. *(See color ad below)*

[icons]

WHERE TO DINE

BOONDOCKS

Phone: 904/760-9001   25

WW

Seafood

Lunch: $5-$15   **Dinner:** $5-$15

Location: 1.3 mi s of Dunlawton Ave. 3948 S Peninsula Dr 32127. **Hours:** 11 am-10 pm. **Features:** No A/C; casual dress; cocktails; a la carte. Located by a local marina, that offers casual outdoor dining overlooking the Halifax River. Menu offers fresh seafood, terrific burgers, chowders, salads and dinner size entrees as well. A favorite local spot for locals and tourists. **Cards:** DS, MC, VI.

CHINA-AMERICAN GARDEN

Phone: 904/788-6269   24

AAA

WWW

Chinese

Lunch: $4-$5   **Dinner:** $7-$12

Location: On SR A1A, 2.8 mi s of jct US 92; in Pappas Plaza Shopping Center. 2516 S Atlantic Ave 32118. **Hours:** 11:30 am-2 & 5-10 pm, Fri 5 pm-11 pm, Sat 4 pm-11 pm. Closed: 12/1-12/25. **Reservations:** accepted. **Features:** casual dress; children's menu; carryout; cocktails & lounge. The hot and sour soup rates high on the list of favorites. This is casual family dining specializing in Cantonese with some Szechuan and Mandarin dishes. Also, now serving Thai cuisine. **Cards:** AE, MC, VI.

[icon]

DEBARY pop. 7,200

——— WHERE TO STAY ———

HAMPTON INN
Phone: (407)668-5758

AAA SAVE

▼▼▼ Motel

| | 1/1-4/30 | 1P: $69 | 2P: $79 |
| | 12/1-12/31 & 5/1-11/30 | 1P: $64 | 2P: $74 |

Location: I-4, exit 53, just nw. 308 Sunrise Blvd 32713. Fax: 407/668-1284. **Facility:** 77 units. Some whirlpool units ($129-$149). *Bath:* combo or shower only. 3 stories, interior corridors. **Amenities:** extended cable TV, irons. **Leisure Activities:** whirlpool. **Guest Services:** [ECP] meal plan available, coin laundry. **Cards:** AE, CB, DI, DS, JC, MC, VI. **Special Amenities: free continental breakfast and free newspaper** SOME UNITS

⬛⬛ ⬛ ⬛ ⬛ ⬛ ⬛ ⬛ ⬛ ⬛ ⬛ ⬛ / ⨉ /

DEERFIELD BEACH —See Fort Lauderdale p. 376.

DE FUNIAK SPRINGS pop. 5,100

——— WHERE TO STAY ———

BEST WESTERN CROSSROADS INN
Phone: (850)892-5111

▼▼▼ Motor Inn

All Year   1P: $60-$70   2P: $60-$70   XP: $5   F18

Location: I-10, exit 14, just s. 2343 Freeport Rd 32433 (PO Box 852). Fax: 850/892-2439. **Facility:** Rural, quiet setting back from interstate. 100 units. 2 stories, interior/exterior corridors. **Terms:** 7 day cancellation notice, weekly & monthly rates available. **Amenities:** extended cable TV. **Business Services:** meeting rooms. **Cards:** AE, CB, DI, DS, JC, MC, VI.

SOME UNITS

ASK ⬛ ⬛ ⬛ ⬛ ⬛ ⬛ ⬛ / ⨉ /

DAYS INN
Phone: 850/892-6115

AAA SAVE

▼▼▼ Motel

	3/1-8/31	1P: $60-$65	2P: $70-$95	XP: $5
	1/1-2/28	1P: $55-$65	2P: $60-$90	XP: $5
	12/1-12/31	1P: $50-$60	2P: $55-$60	XP: $5
	9/1-11/30	1P: $55	2P: $60	XP: $5

Location: I-10, exit 14, just n. 472 Hugh Adams Rd 32433. Fax: 850/892-0707. **Facility:** Basic accommodations. 58 units. 1 story, exterior corridors. **Terms:** weekly rates available, pets ($10 extra charge). **Amenities:** extended cable TV. **Cards:** AE, DI, DS, MC, VI. **Special Amenities: free continental breakfast and free local telephone calls.**

SOME UNITS

⬛ ⬛ ⬛ / ⨉ ⬛ ⬛ /

HOTEL DE FUNIAK-CHAUTAUQUA DINING ROOM
Phone: (850)892-4383

▼▼▼ Classic Hotel

All Year   1P: $70-$90   2P: $80-$100

Location: Center; on US 90. 400 E Nelson 32433. Fax: 850/892-5346. **Facility:** Historic. Smoke free premises. 12 units. *Bath:* combo or shower only. 2 stories, interior/exterior corridors. **Parking:** street only. **Terms:** weekly rates available, package plans. **Guest Services:** [BP] meal plan available, complimentary laundry. **Business Services:** meeting rooms. **Cards:** AE, DS, MC, VI.

ASK ⬛ ⬛ ⬛ ⨉

RAMADA LIMITED
Phone: (850)892-3125

▼▼▼ Motel

All Year   1P: $45-$65   2P: $55-$75   XP: $8

Location: I-10, exit 14, just n. 90 Business Park Rd 32433. Fax: 850/892-5072. **Facility:** 55 units. *Bath:* combo or shower only. 1 story, exterior corridors. **Terms:** 5 day cancellation notice. **Amenities:** extended cable TV, voice mail. **Guest Services:** [CP] meal plan available. **Cards:** AE, CB, DI, DS, MC, VI.

SOME UNITS

ASK ⬛ ⬛ ⬛ ⬛ ⬛ ⬛ / ⨉ ⬛ ⬛ /

DELAND pop. 16,500

——— WHERE TO STAY ———

COMFORT INN
Phone: (904)736-3100

SAVE

▼▼▼ Motel

	2/1-4/30	1P: $85-$175	2P: $85-$175	XP: $10	F12
	5/1-7/31	1P: $65-$135	2P: $65-$135	XP: $10	F12
	8/1-11/30	1P: $65-$95	2P: $65-$95	XP: $10	F12
	12/1-1/31	1P: $65-$75	2P: $65-$75	XP: $5	F12

Location: 0.5 mi ne on US 92 at jct US 17. 400 E International Speedway Blvd 32724. Fax: 904/740-0570. **Facility:** Large comfortable rooms of contemporary decors. 68 units. Some whirlpool units ($95-$200). *Bath:* combo or shower only. 3 stories, interior corridors. **Terms:** 15 day cancellation notice. **Leisure Activities:** whirlpool. **Guest Services:** [CP] meal plan available, coin laundry. **Cards:** AE, DI, DS, MC, VI.

⬛ ⬛ ⬛ ⬛ ⬛ ⬛ ⬛ / ⨉ ⬛ ⬛ /

HOLIDAY INN
Phone: (904)738-5200

▼▼▼ Motor Inn

| | 1/23-3/31 | 1P: $89-$119 | 2P: $89-$119 | XP: $10 | F |
| | 12/1-1/22 & 4/1-11/30 | 1P: $69-$99 | 2P: $69-$99 | XP: $10 | F |

Location: 0.3 mi ne on US 92 from jct US 17. 350 E International Speedway Blvd 32724. Fax: 904/734-7552. **Facility:** 148 units. Some suites. 6 stories, interior corridors. **Terms:** package plans, pets ($10 extra charge). **Amenities:** extended cable TV, voice mail, irons, hair dryers. **Leisure Activities:** heated pool, whirlpool, exercise room. **Guest Services:** valet laundry. **Business Services:** conference facilities, fax. **Cards:** AE, CB, DI, DS, MC, VI.   SOME UNITS

ASK ⬛ ⬛ ⬛ ⬛ ⬛ ⬛ ⬛ ⬛ ⬛ / ⨉ ⬛ /

HONTOON LANDING RESORT & MARINA

Phone: (904)734-2474

All Year | 1P: $70-$195 | 2P: $70-$195 | XP: $10

Complex

Location: 2.1 mi w on SR 44 from US 17/92, then 1.9 mi sw on CR 4110 (Old New York), then 3.4 mi s on CR 4125 (Hontoon Rd). 2317 River Ridge Rd 32720. **Fax:** 904/738-9743. **Facility:** Quiet location on the St Johns River. Attractive landscaping touches abound. Range from compact motel units to spacious multi-room suites, with bright cheerful decors. 18 units. 1 two-bedroom unit and 11 units with kitchen. Some suites ($130-$195) and whirlpool units ($195). *Bath:* combo or shower only. 2 stories, exterior corridors. **Terms:** 30 day cancellation notice-fee imposed. **Amenities:** extended cable TV. *Some:* irons. **Dining:** deli, convenience store. **Leisure Activities:** boat dock, fishing. *Fee:* boats, marina, fishing boats, houseboats, pontoon boats. **Guest Services:** gift shop. **Business Services:** meeting rooms. **Cards:** DS, MC, VI. **Special Amenities:** free local telephone calls and preferred room (subject to availability with advanced reservations).

SOME UNITS

WHERE TO DINE

CHRISTO'S & ELENI'S

Italian

Lunch: $5-$7 | **Dinner:** $7-$11 | **Phone:** 904-734-5705

Location: 0.3 mi w of jct SR 5A and New York Ave. 803 W New York Ave 32720. **Hours:** 11 am-9 pm, Fri & Sat-10 pm. Closed major holidays; also Sun. **Features:** casual dress; children's menu; carryout; beer & wine only. This relaxed family restaurant features homemade pasta, sauces and desserts. Menu choices include veal and seafood dishes. Both the shrimp Rafaelo and the seafood plate give a rich taste of butter and herbs. On Monday nights the owner's wife sings, accompanied by a keyboardist. **Cards:** DS, MC, VI.

THE ORIGINAL HOLIDAY HOUSE

American

Lunch: $9 | **Dinner:** $10 | **Phone:** 904-734-6319

Location: US 17, 0.8 mi n of jct SR 44. 704 N Woodland Blvd 32720. **Hours:** 11 am-9 pm. Closed: 12/24 for dinner. **Features:** casual dress; Sunday brunch; children's menu; salad bar; buffet. Informal dining in a homey setting features signature items like carved lamb, turkey, roast beef and ham. An excellent selection of homemade desserts like the triple-layer chocolate cake and peach cobbler round out this comfort-food buffet. **Cards:** DS, MC, VI.

PONDO'S

American

Dinner: $9-$19 | **Phone:** 904-734-1995

Location: 3 mi w on SR 44, just s. 1915 Old New York Ave 32720. **Hours:** 5 pm-9 pm, Fri & Sat-10 pm. **Reservations:** suggested. **Features:** casual dress; children's menu; early bird specials; carryout; cocktails & lounge. This secluded two-story house exudes a country inn ambience. Homemade dressings and herbs plucked from the on-site garden provide for delicious salads. Attentive servers bring well-prepared entrees of seafood, beef, veal, lamb and duck. **Cards:** AE, MC, VI.

DE LEON SPRINGS pop. 1,500

WHERE TO DINE

KARLING'S INN

American

Cards: MC, VI.

Dinner: $12-$20 | **Phone:** 904-985-5535

Location: On US 17, 5 mi n of jct US 92. 4640 N US 17 32130. **Hours:** 5 pm-9 pm. Closed: Sun & Mon. **Reservations:** suggested. **Features:** casual dress; beer & wine only. The simple Tudor-style building, in an out-of-the-way location, is well worth visiting for its attentive service, European country setting and pleasingly presented Continental dishes. The house specialty is duck in a dark bing cherry sauce.

DELRAY BEACH pop. 47,200

WHERE TO STAY

BUDGET INN

Motel

Phone: 561-276-8961

12/15-4/15	1P: $79	2P: $89	XP: $10 F12
12/1-12/14 & 4/16-11/30	1P: $49	2P: $59	XP: $10 F12

Location: US 1, 1.8 mi n of jct SR 806, Atlantic Ave. 2500 N Federal Hwy 33483. **Fax:** 561/276-1455. **Facility:** Quiet location. 17 units, 1 with efficiency (no utensils). *Bath:* shower only. 1 story, exterior corridors. **Terms:** 3 day cancellation notice-fee imposed, weekly rates available. **Amenities:** extended cable TV. **Cards:** AE, DS, MC, VI.

SOME UNITS

THE COLONY HOTEL & CABANA CLUB

Historic Hotel

Phone: (561)276-4123

12/22-3/17	1P: $165-$205	2P: $165-$205	XP: $20
3/18-4/30	1P: $95-$135	2P: $95-$135	XP: $20
11/1-11/30	1P: $79-$99	2P: $79-$99	XP: $20
12/1-12/21	1P: $75-$95	2P: $75-$95	XP: $20

Location: Center; on SR 806 at jct US 1 northbound. 525 E Atlantic Ave 33483 (PO Box 970, 33447). **Fax:** 561/276-0123. **Facility:** Charming, intimate 1926 hotel on turn-of-the-century main street. Smoke free premises. 66 units. 20 two-bedroom units. *Bath:* combo or shower only. 3 stories, interior corridors. **Terms:** open 12/1-5/1 & 11/1-11/30, 3 day cancellation notice, $3 service charge, pets ($20 extra charge). **Amenities:** extended cable TV, voice mail, irons, hair dryers. **Dining:** restaurant, 7:30 am-9:30 & 6:30-8:30 pm; entertainment in season, 1/16-4/4 18% service charge, $11-$18, cocktails, entertainment. **Leisure Activities:** transportation provided to private beach club with heated saltwater pool & restaurant, social program in season, exercise room with limited equipment. **Guest Services:** [BP] meal plan available, gift shop, valet laundry. **Business Services:** meeting rooms. *Fee:* fax. **Cards:** AE, DI, MC, VI. **Special Amenities:** free continental breakfast and free newspaper.

MARRIOTT DELRAY BEACH
Hotel

		Phone: (561)274-3200
12/22-4/22	1P: $249-$299	XP: $10	F18
4/23-9/30	1P: $149-$189	XP: $10	F18
12/1-12/21	1P: $143-$183	XP: $10	F18
10/1-11/30	1P: $125-$165	XP: $10	F18

Location: SR A1A at jct Atlantic Ave. 10 N Ocean Blvd 33483. Fax: 561/274-3202. **Facility:** Across from the ocean. Very nice public and pool area. Rooms nicely furnished and decorated. All units with personal computer. 268 units. 1 two-bedroom unit. Some suites. *Bath:* combo or shower only. 6 stories, interior/exterior corridors. **Parking:** extra charge or valet. **Terms:** check-in 4 pm, cancellation fee imposed, package plans. **Amenities:** voice mail, safes, honor bars, irons, hair dryers. **Leisure Activities:** heated pool, whirlpool, exercise room. *Fee:* massage. **Business Services:** meeting rooms, administrative services. *Fee:* PC, fax. **Cards:** AE, CB, DI, DS, MC, VI.

SOME UNITS

PARLIAMENT INN
Motel

			Phone: (561)276-6245
12/16-4/1	1P: $70-$180	2P: $70-$180	XP: $10	D12
4/2-5/1	1P: $70-$145	2P: $70-$145	XP: $10	D12
12/1-12/15	1P: $55-$117	2P: $55-$117	XP: $10	D12
5/2-11/30	1P: $50-$101	2P: $50-$101	XP: $10	D12

Location: I-95, exit 42A, Atlantic Ave, SR 806 E, 1.9 mi to US A1A, n on A1A 0.9 mi, then just left. 1236 George Bush Blvd 33483. Fax: 561/274-3939. **Facility:** Phone hookups availble. Quiet place, very nice grounds. 7 units. 3 efficiencies and 4 units with kitchen. *Bath:* combo or shower only. 1 story, exterior corridors. **Terms:** 3 night minimum stay, age restrictions may apply, weekly rates available. **Amenities:** extended cable TV. *Some:* irons. **Leisure Activities:** heated pool. **Guest Services:** coin laundry.

SOME UNITS

SEAGATE HOTEL & BEACH CLUB
Motor Inn

			Phone: (561)276-2421
12/1-4/22 & 11/17-11/30	1P: $185-$756	2P: $185-$756	XP: $15	F18
4/23-5/6	1P: $139-$509	2P: $139-$509	XP: $15	F18
5/7-11/16	1P: $92-$341	2P: $92-$341	XP: $15	F18

Location: SR A1A, 0.5 mi s of jct SR 806, Atlantic Ave. 400 S Ocean Blvd 33483. Fax: 561/243-4714. **Facility:** Opposite ocean and beach club. Inviting property on landscaped grounds. Studios, one- and two-bedroom apartments. 70 units. 8 two-bedroom units, 1 three-bedroom unit, 9 efficiencies and 61 units with kitchen. Some suites and whirlpool units. *Bath:* combo or shower only. 2-3 stories, exterior corridors. **Terms:** check-in 4 pm, 7 day cancellation notice, in-season-fee imposed, package plans. **Dining:** restaurant, guests only 11:30 am-2:30 & 6-9:30 pm, $7-$24, cocktails. **Leisure Activities:** 2 heated pools, beach, swimming, guided kayak tours. *Fee:* paddleboats, sailboating, windsurfing, snorkeling equipment, water sports. **Guest Services:** coin laundry. **Business Services:** meeting rooms. **Cards:** AE, DI, DS, MC, VI. **Special Amenities:** free continental breakfast and free newspaper.

SOME UNITS

WRIGHT BY THE SEA
Motel

		Phone: 561/278-3355
12/21-1/31	2P: $165-$328	XP: $20
2/1-4/30	2P: $158-$312	XP: $20
12/1-12/20	2P: $132-$266	XP: $20
5/1-11/30	2P: $87-$203	XP: $20

Location: SR A1A, just s of jct Linton Blvd. 1901 S Ocean Blvd 33483. Fax: 561/278-2871. **Facility:** Oceanfront location, many units with ocean and pool view. Large grassy landscaped grounds. Designated smoking area. 28 units. 2 two-bedroom units, 4 efficiencies and 24 units with kitchen. 2 stories, exterior corridors. **Terms:** 14 day cancellation notice-fee imposed, weekly & monthly rates available. **Amenities:** extended cable TV, voice mail, irons. *Some:* CD players. **Leisure Activities:** heated pool, beach, swimming. **Guest Services:** coin laundry. **Cards:** AE, CB, DI, DS, MC, VI. **Special Amenities:** free newspaper and preferred room (subject to availability with advanced reservations).
(See ad below)

------- WHERE TO DINE -------

32 EAST
American

	Dinner: $18-$26	Phone: 561/276-7868

Location: I-95, exit 42A, 1 mi e, just e of Swinton Ave. 32 E Atlantic Ave 33444. **Hours:** 5:30 pm-10 pm, Fri & Sat-11 pm. Closed: 12/25; also 1/2 & Super Bowl Sun. **Reservations:** required. **Features:** dressy casual; children's menu; carryout; cocktails & lounge; street parking & fee for valet parking; a la carte. Contemporary American cuisine using fresh local and regional seafood and produce. A fantastic wine list available. The atmosphere is upbeat. The dining room is comfortable, a fun place to eat. **Cards:** AE, DS, MC, VI.

ANTONIO'S MAMA ROSA ITALIAN RESTAURANT　　　　　　**Dinner:** $9-$16　　　　　　**Phone:** 561/276-2569

▼▼▼ ▼▼▼

Italian

Location: On US 1, 1.5 mi n of jct SR 806, (Atlantic Ave). 1645 N Federal Hwy 33444. **Hours:** 5 pm-10 pm, Sun 4:30 pm-9:30 pm. Closed: 11/22; also Mon 4/17-12/18. **Reservations:** accepted. **Features:** casual dress; children's menu; beer & wine only. The owner, who is also the chef, mingles with his guests at this local favorite. Homemade Italian meals are served in a relaxed, friendly atmosphere. Dinners start with an antipasto plate, followed by a house salad. **Cards:** AE, MC, VI.　　　　　　　　　　　　　　　　　　　⊠

EAST CITY BISTRO　　　　　　**Lunch:** $8-$25　　　　　　**Dinner:** $10-$25　　　　　　**Phone:** 561/266-0744

▼▼▼ ▼▼▼

American

Location: At corner of NE 7th St & Atlantic Ave; in Atlantic Plaza, just w of the bridge & A1A. 777 E Atlantic Ave 33483. **Hours:** 11 am-10 pm, Fri & Sat-11 pm, Sun 5:30 pm-10:30 pm. Closed: Super Bowl Sun. **Reservations:** suggested. **Features:** dressy casual; cocktails & lounge; a la carte. A bright dining room with colorful booths and tables. The food is the freshest available with local seafood items. A variety of meat and poultry is available. All courses arrive with an artistic presentation. A nice wine list compliments the menu. **Cards:** AE, MC, VI.　　　　　　　　　　　　　　　　　　　⊠

MASQUERADE CAFE　　　　　　**Dinner:** $14-$25　　　　　　**Phone:** 561/279-0229

▼▼▼ ▼▼▼

Continental

Location: Center; jct Atlantic and SE 7th aves; in shopping gallery. 640 E Atlantic Ave 33483. **Hours:** 5 pm-11 pm. Closed: Mon & Tues. **Reservations:** suggested. **Features:** dressy casual; cocktails; a la carte. Fresh seafood, rack of lamb and crispy Asian duck are the specialties in this intimate, whimsical escape from the ordinary. The sesame crusted tuna prepared rare is awesome. Wonderful breads made in-house. Smoke free premises. **Cards:** MC, VI.　　　　　　　　　　　　　　　　　　　⊠

DELTONA pop. 40,500

─────── **WHERE TO STAY** ───────

BEST WESTERN DELTONA INN　　　　　　　　　　　　　　　　　　　**Phone:** (407)574-6693

ⒶⒶⒶ (SAVE)

▼▼▼ ▼▼▼

Motor Inn

All Year　　　　　　1P: $50-$210　　　　　　2P: $50-$210
Location: I-4, exit 53. 481 Deltona Blvd 32725. Fax: 407/860-2687. **Facility:** Contemporary units range from king to two-room suites. Some units overlook a lake that attracts native birds of Florida. 130 units. 2 stories, exterior corridors. **Terms:** 7 day cancellation notice. **Dining:** dining room, 7 am-2 & 5:30-10 pm, $7-$12, cocktails. **Business Services:** meeting rooms. **Cards:** AE, CB, DI, DS, MC, VI.　　　SOME UNITS

[icons] 🆂 🍴 🛎 ⚊ 🛥 ⚡ 🖨 / ⊠ 📶 🛗 /

DESTIN pop. 8,100

─────── **WHERE TO STAY** ───────

BAY CLUB OF SANDESTIN　　　　　　　　　　　　　　　　　　　**Phone:** (850)837-8866

ⒶⒶⒶ (SAVE)

▼▼ ▼▼

Condominium

3/1-10/31　　　　　　1P: $125-$190
11/1-11/30　　　　　1P: $90-$190
12/1-2/28　　　　　　1P: $80-$175
Location: Next to Conference Centre Bayside. 120 N Sandestin Blvd 32541. Fax: 850/654-9188. **Facility:** 45 units. 13 two-bedroom units and 44 units with kitchen. Some suites and whirlpool units. 6 stories, interior corridors. **Terms:** age restrictions may apply, 3 day cancellation notice. **Amenities:** extended cable TV. Some: voice mail, irons, hair dryers. **Dining:** 2 restaurants, deli, 7 am-9 pm, $7-$25, cocktails, also, Elephant Walk, see separate listing. **Leisure Activities:** 4 pools, wading pools, saunas, whirlpools, beach, swimming, fishing, charter fishing, children's program in summer, recreation program, social program in season, bicycles, jogging. Fee: boats, sailboating, marina, waterskiing, jet skis, golf-63 holes, 20 tennis courts (2 lighted). **Guest Services:** complimentary laundry. Fee: area transportation, massage. **Business Services:** meeting rooms. **Cards:** AE, DS, MC, VI.　　　SOME UNITS

[icons] 🆂 🍴 🛎 🛥 ✙ ⊠ 📶 / 🅺 🛥 📼 🖨 🖵 📶 🛗 /

BEST WESTERN SUMMERPLACE INN　　　　　　　　　　　　　　　**Phone:** (850)650-8003

ⒶⒶⒶ (SAVE)

▼▼▼ ▼▼▼

Motel

5/31-9/5	1P: $99-$124	2P: $99-$124	XP: $10	F17
3/1-5/30	1P: $79-$109	2P: $79-$109	XP: $10	F17
9/6-11/30	1P: $59-$79	2P: $59-$79	XP: $10	F17
12/1-2/28	1P: $59-$69	2P: $59-$69	XP: $10	F17

Location: US 98, 2.2 mi e. 14047 Emerald Coast Pkwy 32541. Fax: 850/650-8004. **Facility:** Valet laundry avail. 72 units. 2 two-bedroom units. Some whirlpool units ($89-$189). *Bath:* combo or shower only. 4 stories, interior corridors. **Terms:** 3 day cancellation notice, weekly rates available, package plans. **Amenities:** extended cable TV. **Leisure Activities:** heated pool, whirlpool, small outdoor pool, exercise equipment. **Guest Services:** [ECP] meal plan available, valet and coin laundry. **Business Services:** meeting rooms, administrative services. **Cards:** AE, CB, DI, DS, JC, MC, VI. **Special Amenities:** free continental breakfast and free local telephone calls.　　　SOME UNITS

[icons] 🆂 🍴✙ 🐾 🏠 🖨 🖵 🛗 📶 / ⊠ 📶 /

COMFORT INN　　　　　　　　　　　　　　　　　　　**Phone:** (850)654-8611

(SAVE)

▼▼▼ ▼▼▼

Motel

5/12-9/4	1P: $136-$151	2P: $136-$151	XP: $10	F18
3/2-5/11	1P: $91-$106	2P: $91-$106	XP: $10	F18
9/5-11/30	1P: $81-$96	2P: $81-$96	XP: $10	F18
12/1-3/1	1P: $69-$84	2P: $69-$84	XP: $10	F18

Location: US 98, 1.9 mi e. 19001 Emerald Coast Pkwy 32541. Fax: 850/654-8815. **Facility:** Completed in the spring of 2000, this chain property is decorated in a tropical theme with custom made furniture. 100 units. Some suites ($79-$190) and whirlpool units ($79-$190). *Bath:* combo or shower only. 4 stories, interior corridors. Check-in 4 pm. **Amenities:** extended cable TV, dual phone lines, voice mail, irons, hair dryers. **Leisure Activities:** 2 pools (1 heated, 1 indoor), exercise room. **Guest Services:** [ECP] meal plan available, gift shop, valet and coin laundry. **Business Services:** meeting rooms. **Cards:** AE, DI, DS, MC, VI.　　　SOME UNITS

[icons] 🆂 🛥 🏠 ⚡ 🖨 🖵 🖵 🛗 📶 / ⊠ /

COUNTRY INN & SUITES BY CARLSON

Suite Motel

Phone: (850)650-9191

	2P:	XP:	
6/1-9/15	$105-$185	$10	F17
3/1-5/31	$99-$165	$10	F17
9/16-11/30	$75-$115		
12/1-2/28	$68-$112	$10	F17

Location: US 98, behind TGIF. 4415 Commons Dr E 32541. Fax: 850/654-1802. **Facility:** Set back from US 98 near beaches. 83 units. Some suites. *Bath:* combo or shower only. 3 stories, interior corridors. **Terms:** package plans. **Amenities:** extended cable TV, voice mail, irons, hair dryers. **Leisure Activities:** heated pool, whirlpool, exercise room. **Guest Services:** [CP] & [ECP] meal plans available, coin laundry. **Business Services:** meeting rooms. **Cards:** AE, CB, DI, DS, MC, VI. *(See color ad p 572)*

SOME UNITS

(ASK) (SO) (☰↑) (&) (✏) (➚) (▤) (▣) (DATA PORT) / (✕) (VCR) (▤) (🔒) /

HAMPTON INN

SAVE

Motel

Phone: 850/654-2677

	1P:	2P:
5/26-9/3	$129-$139	$129-$139
3/10-5/25	$109-$139	$109-$139
9/4-11/30	$69-$99	$79-$109
12/1-3/9	$69-$79	$79-$89

Location: US 98, 1 mi e. 1625 Hwy 98 E 32541. Fax: 850/654-0745. **Facility:** Near beach. 104 units. Some suites ($139-$169). *Bath:* combo or shower only. 2 stories, exterior corridors. **Terms:** check-in 4 pm. **Amenities:** extended cable TV, voice mail, irons, hair dryers. **Leisure Activities:** heated pool, whirlpool. **Guest Services:** [CP] & [ECP] meal plans available, valet and coin laundry. **Business Services:** meeting rooms. **Cards:** AE, DI, DS, MC, VI.

SOME UNITS

(☰↑) (&) (➚) (♣) (▣) (▣) (▣) (🔒) (DATA PORT) / (✕) /

HILTON SANDESTIN BEACH, GOLF RESORT

(AAA) SAVE

Resort

Phone: (850)267-9500

	2P:	XP:	
5/10-9/3	$240-$365	$20	F16
3/15-5/9	$200-$325	$20	F16
9/4-11/30	$185-$320	$20	F16
12/1-3/14	$130-$230	$20	F16

Location: 10 mi e at Sandestin. 4000 Sandestin Blvd S 32541. Fax: 850/267-3076. **Facility:** Gulf view. 598 units. Some suites ($230-$365) and whirlpool units ($230-$365). *Bath:* combo or shower only. 15 stories, interior corridors. **Parking:** valet. **Terms:** check-in 4 pm, 3 day cancellation notice, package plans, $8 service charge. **Amenities:** extended cable TV, dual phone lines, voice mail, safes, honor bars, irons, hair dryers. **Dining:** restaurant, deli, 7 am-2 & 6-10 pm, $16-$23, cocktails, also, Seagar's Prime Steaks and Seafood, see separate listing, entertainment. **Leisure Activities:** 3 pools (1 heated, 1 indoor), saunas, whirlpools, beach, charter fishing, children's program 3/15-9/6, exercise room, volleyball. *Fee:* sailboating, kayak, golf-72 holes, 16 tennis courts (2 lighted), bicycles. **Guest Services:** gift shop, area transportation, valet and coin laundry. **Business Services:** conference facilities, administrative services, fax. **Cards:** AE, CB, DI, DS, MC, VI. **Special Amenities:** free newspaper and preferred room (subject to availability with advanced reservations). *(See ad p 44)*

SOME UNITS

(SO) (☰↑) (24↑) (Y) (🔥) (➚) (✕) (♣) (VCR) (▣) (▣) (▣) (🔒) (DATA PORT) / (✕) /
FEE

HOLIDAY INN OF DESTIN

				Phone: (850)837-6181
	3/10-9/3	1P: $150-$200	2P: $150-$200	XP: $10	F18
	9/4-10/13	1P: $100-$150	2P: $100-$150		F18
Motor Inn	10/14-11/30	1P: $80-$125	2P: $80-$125	XP: $10	F18
	12/1-3/9	1P: $78-$125	2P: $78-$125	XP: $10	F18

Location: 2.2 mi e of bridge on US 98. 1020 Hwy 98 E 32541 (PO Box 577). Fax: 850/837-1523. **Facility:** Gulf front circular high-rise. 233 units. *Bath:* combo or shower only. 9 stories, interior corridors. **Terms:** 3 day cancellation notice-fee imposed. **Amenities:** extended cable TV, voice mail, safes, irons, hair dryers. **Leisure Activities:** 2 pools (1 heated, 1 indoor), wading pool, sauna, whirlpool, beach, recreation program in season, exercise room. **Guest Services:** gift shop, valet laundry. **Business Services:** meeting rooms. **Cards:** AE, CB, DI, DS, MC, VI. SOME UNITS

SANDESTIN GOLF AND BEACH RESORT

				Phone: (850)267-8000
	3/29-8/11	1P: $155-$685	2P: $155-$685	
	3/1-3/28	1P: $135-$540	2P: $135-$540	
Resort	8/12-11/30	1P: $125-$465	2P: $125-$465	
	12/1-2/28	1P: $75-$315	2P: $75-$315	

Location: 10 mi e on US 98. 9300 Hwy 98 West 32541. Fax: 850/267-6332. **Facility:** Two- and three-bedroom housekeeping villas on spacious bayside, gulfside grounds and bordering golf courses. Also conventional hotel units. 755 units. 289 two-bedroom units, 191 three-bedroom units, 175 efficiencies and 580 units with kitchen. Some suites. 22 stories, interior/exterior corridors. **Terms:** check-in 4 pm, 14 day cancellation notice-fee imposed, weekly & monthly rates available, package plans. **Amenities:** extended cable TV, dual phone lines, voice mail, irons. *Some:* hair dryers. **Dining:** Elephant Walk, see separate listing. **Leisure Activities:** 12 pools (3 heated), wading pools, saunas, whirlpools, beach, swimming, fishing, charter fishing, children's program in summer, recreation program, social program in season, bicycles, jogging. *Fee:* boats, sailboating, marina, waterskiing, golf-72 holes, 20 tennis courts (2 lighted). **Guest Services:** gift shop, valet and coin laundry. *Fee:* massage. **Business Services:** conference facilities, fax. **Cards:** AE, DI, DS, MC, VI. *(See color ad p 303)* SOME UNITS

SLEEP INN

SAVE

				Phone: 850/654-7022
	5/2-9/9	1P: $92-$122	2P: $97-$127	XP: $5	F18
	3/1-5/1	1P: $82-$85	2P: $87-$90	XP: $5	F18
Motel	12/1-2/28 & 9/10-11/30	1P: $64-$80	2P: $69-$85	XP: $5	F18

Location: US 98, 8 mi e of bridge. 10775 W Emerald Coast Pkwy 32541. Fax: 850/654-7022. **Facility:** 77 units. Some suites ($125-$200). *Bath:* combo or shower only. 2 stories, interior corridors. **Terms:** 7 day cancellation notice. **Amenities:** extended cable TV, safes (fee). *Some:* irons, hair dryers. **Guest Services:** [CP] meal plan available, coin laundry. **Business Services:** meeting rooms. **Cards:** AE, DI, DS, MC, VI. SOME UNITS

——— WHERE TO DINE ———

CHAN'S MARKET CAFE

Lunch: $5-$13 **Dinner:** $6-$16 **Phone:** 850/837-1334

Specialty

Location: 10 mi e of Destin at the Market at Sandestin. 9375 Hwy 98 W #22 32541. **Hours:** 8 am-9 pm 2/1-11/30; 8 am-6 pm 12/1-1/31. Closed: 11/22, 12/25. **Features:** casual dress; children's menu; carryout; cocktails; a la carte. Hard to believe this pondside setting is just off the main highway. It offers both inside and outside dining with a very good selection of deli items as well as signature sandwiches. The gourmet deli and bakery are part of this establishment and entice one to try not only the fresh local seafoods but their selection of meat and freshly baked bread. Don't forget breakfast - linger over freshly brewed coffee, pancakes, biscuits, eggs and sausage while overlooking the duck pond. **Cards:** DS, MC, VI.

ELEPHANT WALK

Dinner: $27-$32 **Phone:** 850/267-4800

Seafood

Location: Next to Conference Centre Bayside; in Bay Club of Sandestin. 9300 Hwy 98 W 32541. **Hours:** 6 pm-10 pm, lounge from 5 pm. Closed: New Year's Eve. **Reservations:** suggested. **Features:** casual dress; cocktails & lounge; a la carte. Experience the Asian exotica of Sri Lanka on the Gulf of Mexico in this restaurant based on the film "Elephant Walk." Among the more unusual fare featured on an ever-changing menu are the macadamia fried shrimp, Key lime cannoli and grouper Elizabeth. **Cards:** AE, DI, DS, MC, VI.

THE LIGHTHOUSE

Dinner: $10-$21 **Phone:** 850/654-2828

Seafood

Location: 2 mi e on US 98; in Shoreline Village Plaza. 878 Hwy 98 32541. **Hours:** 4:30 pm-8:30 pm. Closed major holidays. **Features:** casual dress; children's menu; early bird specials; cocktails & lounge. Bring your whole family and enjoy the relaxed atmosphere. An extensive menu offers a wide selection with an emphasis seafood. An authentic Key lime pie has a taste of the tropics. **Cards:** AE, DI, DS, MC, VI.

MCGUIRE'S IRISH PUB & BREWERY

Lunch: $8-$12 **Dinner:** $12-$22 **Phone:** 850/650-0000

Steak House

Location: On US 98 at e end of Destin Pass Bridge. 33 US 98 E 32541. **Hours:** 11 am-2 am. Closed: 11/22, 12/25. **Features:** casual dress; children's menu; cocktails & lounge; entertainment. A pleasant experience, this restaurant features steaks, seafood and tasty, oversized burgers. Sing along to nostalgic music or watch the action on the gulf and bay from an open upper deck. Homemade bread and butter pudding makes a delicious treat. **Cards:** AE, DI, DS, MC, VI.

SAKURA ORIENTAL CUISINE AND SUSHI BAR

Lunch: $4-$15 **Dinner:** $9-$15 **Phone:** 850/654-5818

Chinese

Location: In downtown Destin K-Mart Shopping Center. 763 Hwy 98 E 32541. **Hours:** 11 am-2:30 & 5-9:30 pm, Fri-10 pm, Sat 5 pm-10 pm. Closed major holidays; also 12/24 & Sun. **Features:** casual dress; children's menu; carryout; beer & wine only. A limited menu enables the casual and intimate restaurant to focus on a small assortment of tasty dishes, including sushi. Especially good are the piquant sweet and sour soup and a shrimp and beef dish served in a spicy brown sauce. **Cards:** AE, CB, DI, MC, VI.

SEAGAR'S PRIME STEAKS AND SEAFOOD   Dinner: $21-$34   Phone: 850/267-9500

△△△

▽▽▽▽ ▽▽▽▽

Steak House

Location: 10 mi e at Sandestin; in Hilton Sandestin Beach, Golf Resort. 4000 Sandestin Blvd S 32541. **Hours:** 6 pm-10 pm, Fri & Sat-11 pm. **Reservations:** suggested. **Features:** cocktail lounge; entertainment; valet parking; a la carte. A sophisticated setting features lavish appointments and an upscale dress code. An open kitchen offers prime steaks and seafood with an innovative use of fresh ingredients. A separate lounge with a cigar steward is perfect for after-dinner relaxation. **Cards:** AE, CB, DI, DS, MC, VI.   ✗

THE VERANDA RESTAURANT AT HENDER PARK INN   Lunch: $5-$9   Dinner: $18-$23   Phone: 850/654-0404

▽▽▽▽

American

Location: Dead end at e end of state park. 2700 Scenic Hwy 98 E 32541. **Hours:** 7 am-10 & 11:30-2 pm, Tues-Sat also 6 pm-9 pm. **Reservations:** suggested. **Features:** dressy casual; Sunday brunch; cocktails. A beachfront view completes the lovely setting of porch swings and rocking chairs. Skillful use of local seafood and vegetables displays a Louisiana influence. Breakfast is by reservation only, with a daily lunch buffet and Sunday brunch also featured. Smoke free premises. **Cards:** AE, DS, MC, VI.   ✗

────── *The following restaurant has not been evaluated by AAA* ──────
but is listed for your information only.

THE CRAB TRAP   Phone: 904/654-2722

fyi

Not evaluated. **Location:** Beach Rd 98 at James Lee Park. Beach Rd 98. **Features:** Located at the beach, with some tables and booths having good views. Seafood specialties; also sandwiches. Inexpensive.

DUNDEE pop. 2,300

────── **WHERE TO STAY** ──────

DAYS INN CYPRESS GARDENS/DUNDEE   Phone: (863)439-1591

△△△ SAVE

▽▽▽▽

Motor Inn

2/1-3/31	1P: $99-$129	2P: $99-$129
4/1-4/30	1P: $79-$109	2P: $79-$109
12/1-1/31	1P: $69-$99	2P: $69-$99
5/1-11/30	1P: $59-$89	2P: $59-$89

Location: On US 27; just n of jct SR 542. 339 Hwy 27 N 33838. Fax: 863/439-5297. **Facility:** 100 units. 2 stories, exterior corridors. **Terms:** package plans. **Amenities:** irons, hair dryers. **Dining:** restaurant, 6:30 am-2 & 5-9 pm, $7-$20, entertainment. **Leisure Activities:** heated pool, wading pool. **Guest Services:** coin laundry. **Business Services:** meeting rooms. **Cards:** AE, CB, DI, DS, MC, VI. **Special Amenities:** free local telephone calls and free newspaper.

SOME UNITS

🅂🄳 🍴 ⛾ 🎣 📷 🏊 🎥 🖨 💻 [DATA PORT] / ✗ /

DUNEDIN —See Tampa Bay p. 862.

EAST PALATKA —See also PALATKA.

——— WHERE TO STAY ———

BEST WESTERN INN OF PALATKA

Phone: (904)325-7800

| | All Year | 1P: $60-$95 | 2P: $65-$105 | XP: $5 | F12 |

Motel

Location: On US 17, just s of St John's River Bridge. 119 Hwy 17 S 32131. Fax: 904/328-4008. **Facility:** Modern contemporary rooms. 56 units. *Bath:* combo or shower only. 2 stories, exterior corridors. **Amenities:** extended cable TV. **Leisure Activities:** whirlpool. **Guest Services:** [CP] meal plan available, coin laundry. **Business Services:** meeting rooms. **Cards:** AE, DI, DS, MC, VI.

SOME UNITS

ASK S/D ⑪ ⬛ ⬛ ⬛ ⬛ ⬛ DATA PORT / ✕ ⬛ ⬛ /

ELKTON pop. 200 (See map p. 739; index p. 741)

——— WHERE TO STAY ———

COMFORT INN ST. AUGUSTINE

Phone: (904)829-3435 ⑥⑤

SAVE	1/31-4/15	1P: $54-$184	2P: $59-$189	XP: $5	F18
	4/16-9/3	1P: $54-$164	2P: $59-$169	XP: $5	F18
	9/4-11/30	1P: $54-$94	2P: $59-$99	XP: $5	F18
Motel	12/1-1/30	1P: $54-$84	2P: $59-$89	XP: $5	F18

Location: I-95, exit 94, just w. 2625 SR 207 32033. Fax: 904/824-1558. **Facility:** 62 units. 2 stories, exterior corridors. **Terms:** pets ($10 extra charge). **Amenities:** *Some:* irons, hair dryers. **Guest Services:** [CP] meal plan available. **Cards:** AE, CB, DI, DS, JC, MC, VI.

SOME UNITS

S/D ⬛ ⬛ ⬛ ⬛ DATA PORT / ✕ ⬛ /

——— WHERE TO DINE ———

BUNKERS ON THE ST. JOHNS
COUNTY GOLF COURSE **Lunch:** $3-$6 **Dinner:** $3-$6 **Phone:** 904/829-6930 ⑤⓪

American

Location: I-95, exit 94, 0.3 mi w on SR 207, then 2 mi s to golf course. 4900 Cypress Lakes Blvd 32033. **Hours:** 6:30 am-6:30 pm. **Features:** casual dress; a la carte. A delightful spot to have a leisurely meal while looking out over golf course. Even non-golfers will feel at home in the casual atmosphere with friendly service. Hearty sandwiches, burgers, hot dogs and salads. The Reuben is a favorite with home-made cookies for dessert. **Cards:** DS, MC, VI.

ELLENTON pop. 2,600 (See map p. 764; index p. 767)

——— WHERE TO STAY ———

BEST WESTERN INN

Phone: (941)729-8505 ⑨⑥

	2/1-4/15	1P: $80-$110	2P: $80-$110	XP: $5	F
	12/1-1/31	1P: $70-$85	2P: $70-$85	XP: $5	F
Motel	4/16-11/30	1P: $65-$85	2P: $65-$85		

Location: I-75, exit 43, 0.3 mi w on US 301, just n on 51st Ave E, just w. 5218 17th St E 34222. Fax: 941/729-1110. **Facility:** 73 units, 11 with kitchen. Some suites and whirlpool units. 2 stories, exterior corridors. **Terms:** cancellation fee imposed, weekly & monthly rates available, small pets only ($10 extra charge). **Amenities:** extended cable TV. *Some:* irons, hair dryers. **Leisure Activities:** heated pool, whirlpool. **Guest Services:** [ECP] meal plan available, coin laundry. **Business Services:** meeting rooms, fax. **Cards:** AE, CB, DI, DS, MC, VI.

SOME UNITS

ASK S/D ⬛ ⑪ ⬛ ⬛ ⬛ DATA PORT / ✕ ⬛ ⬛ /

——— *The following lodging was either not evaluated or did not* ———
meet AAA rating requirements but is listed for your information only.

SHONEY'S INN LAKESIDE

Phone: 941/729-0600

[fyi]

Motel

Does not meet all AAA rating requirements for property operations; previously evaluated on 02/08/2000. **Location:** I-75, exit 43, 0.3 mi w on US 301, just n on 51st Ave E, just w. 4915 17th St E 34222. Facilities, services, and decor characterize a mid-range property.

——— WHERE TO DINE ———

CRAB TRAP II **Lunch:** $5-$13 **Dinner:** $9-$38 **Phone:** 941/729-7777 ⑷⑹

Seafood

Location: I-75, exit 43, 0.4 mi s on US 301; just w on 51st Ave, then s. 4815 Memphis Rd 34222. **Hours:** 11:30 am-9 pm, Fri & Sat-10 pm. Closed: 11/22, 12/25. **Features:** casual dress; children's menu; early bird specials; cocktails & lounge. The bustling and rustic shanty overlooking a small pond and bird refuge is noted for quality seafood as well as such exotic temptations as kangaroo, buffalo, alligator, ostrich and barbecued wild pig. Wood carvings, mounted wildlife and pictures add effect to the rustic spot. **Cards:** DS, MC, VI. ✕

ENGLEWOOD pop. 7,200

———— WHERE TO STAY ————

PALM MANOR CONDOMINIUMS   **Phone:** 941/474-3700

▼▼▼ ▼▼▼
Cottage

12/16-4/15 Wkly	2P: $675	
4/16-11/30 Dly	2P: $415	
12/1-12/15 Wkly	2P: $415	

Location: I-75, exit 35, CR 775 just w of jct SR 776. 1531 Placida Rd 34223. Fax: 941/475-5366. **Facility:** Residential complex near commercial area. All units with screened porch. 45 two-bedroom units with kitchen. Some suites. 2 stories, exterior corridors. **Terms:** 30 day cancellation notice-fee imposed, monthly rates available, package plans - off season. **Amenities:** extended cable TV, irons. **Leisure Activities:** heated pool, tennis court, shuffleboard. **Guest Services:** complimentary laundry. **Cards:** DS, MC, VI.

SEAFARER BEACH MOTEL   **Phone:** (941)474-4388

AAA SAVE
▼▼▼ ▼▼▼
Apartment

2/1-4/30 Wkly	2P: $750-$956	XP: $82
12/1-1/2 Wkly	2P: $678-$823	XP: $82
1/3-1/31 Wkly	2P: $598-$678	XP: $82
5/1-11/30 Wkly	2P: $484-$666	XP: $82

Location: I-75, exit 35, on Manasota Key; 7 mi n on SR 776, 1.7 mi w on Manasota Beach Rd, then just s. 8520 Manasota Key Rd 34223. Fax: 941/474-4388. **Facility:** Modest property with contemporary room package, remote location on the Gulf of Mexico. 9 units with kitchen. *Bath:* combo or shower only. 1 story, exterior corridors. **Terms:** 30 day cancellation notice-fee imposed, daily rates available. **Amenities:** extended cable TV. **Leisure Activities:** heated pool, beach, swimming, fishing, table tennis. **Guest Services:** coin laundry. **Cards:** DS, MC, VI. **Special Amenities: early check-in/late check-out and preferred room (subject to availability with advanced reservations).**   SOME UNITS

———— WHERE TO DINE ————

FLYING BRIDGE II RESTAURANT   **Lunch:** $4-$6   **Dinner:** $7-$12   **Phone:** 941/474-2206

▼▼▼
American

Location: On SR 776, 0.5 mi e of CR 775 (Merchants Crossing). 2080 S McCall Rd 34224. **Hours:** 11 am-9 pm. **Features:** casual dress; children's menu; early bird specials; carryout; beer & wine only. This casual waterfront restaurant is popular with the locals for its nautically-themed outdoor patio, bustling atmosphere and quick and friendly service. The Florida grouper sandwich with a cup of clam chowder is your best bet at this seafood spot. **Cards:** DS, MC, VI.

PRIME TIME STEAK & SPIRITS   **Dinner:** $6-$20   **Phone:** 941/697-7799

▼▼▼ ▼▼▼
American

Location: From jct SR 776, 4.1 mi w on CR 775; in Rotonda Plaza. 5855 Placida Rd 34224. **Hours:** 4 pm-10:30 pm, Fri & Sat-11:30 pm. **Features:** casual dress; children's menu; early bird specials; carryout; cocktails & lounge. A Southwestern aura punctuates this restaurant, where the menu dabbles in seafood, Mexican dishes, pasta, steak and poultry, all prepared from scratch. Watch romantic sunsets over Lemon Bay, or slip into the sports-themed bar for a livelier experience. **Cards:** AE, DS, MC, VI.

EVERGLADES CITY pop. 300

———— WHERE TO DINE ————

THE OYSTER HOUSE RESTAURANT   **Lunch:** $5-$20   **Dinner:** $5-$20   **Phone:** 941/695-2073

AAA
▼▼▼ ▼▼
Seafood

Location: 3 mi s on SR 29 (Chokoloskee Cswy). 905 Copeland Ave 34139. **Hours:** 11 am-10 pm. Closed: 11/22, 12/25. **Reservations:** suggested; 1/1-4/30. **Features:** casual dress; children's menu; carryout; cocktails & lounge; entertainment. Serving seasonal offerings of fresh local seafood, alligator, frog legs and stone crab claws. This rustic restaurant feels like old Florida, with stuffed wildlife and maritime decor. The bright and airy dining room looks out over the Gulf of Mexico. **Cards:** MC, VI.

Take a Trip

AAA

*B*efore you head out on the open road for your next vacation, make sure you visit your local AAA Travel Office. From TripTik® routings and TourBook® guides to cruise bookings and international tour packages, AAA's staff of knowledgeable professionals can make your next trip a dream vacation. To find out more ways AAA can help you "get away from it all," call your local AAA Travel Office.

Travel With Someone You Trust

FERNANDINA BEACH —See Jacksonville p. 443.

FERN PARK —See Orlando p. 631.

FLAGLER BEACH pop. 3,800

———— WHERE TO STAY ————

BEACH FRONT MOTEL
[AAA] [SAVE]
◈◈◈ ◈◈
Motel

2/1-8/31 & 9/1-11/30	1P: $49-$54	2P: $49-$54	XP: $5 F18
12/1-1/31	1P: $45-$49	2P: $45-$49	XP: $5 F18

Phone: (904)439-0089

Location: On SR A1A, 1 mi s of SR 100. 1544 S A1A 32136. Fax: 904/439-0083. **Facility:** Quaint oceanfront accommodations with most units offering great ocean view. 20 units, 7 with efficiency. 2 stories, exterior corridors. **Terms:** weekly & monthly rates available, pets ($20 extra charge, small dogs only). **Amenities:** extended cable TV. **Leisure Activities:** beach, swimming, jogging. **Cards:** AE, DS, MC, VI.
Special Amenities: early check-in/late check-out and free local telephone calls.
SOME UNITS
[S/D] [🛏] [🍴] [📠] / [✕] [📺] /

FLAGLER BEACH MOTEL & RENTALS
◈◈◈
◈
Motel

2/1-10/1	2P: $50	XP: $10 F12
12/1-1/31 & 10/2-11/30	2P: $45	XP: $10 F12

Phone: 904/439-7717

Location: On SR A1A, 1.5 mi s of SR 100. 1820 S Ocean Shore Blvd 32136. Fax: 904/439-7717. **Facility:** Lovely 2 room suite with full kitchen, balcony facing ocean. Designated smoking area. 24 units, 1 with kitchen. Some suites ($95). *Bath:* combo or shower only. 1 story, exterior corridors. **Amenities:** extended cable TV. **Cards:** DS, MC, VI.
[🛏] [☎] [📷]

SHIRE HOUSE BED AND BREAKFAST
◈◈◈
Bed & Breakfast

All Year 2P: $95-$160 XP: $15

Phone: (904)445-8877

Location: On SR A1A, 4.6 mi n of SR 100. 3398 N Oceanshore Blvd 32136. Fax: 904/446-5585. **Facility:** Across the street from the ocean. Modern building with the convenience of double whirlpool tubs and wet bar in every units. Many Old World furnishings. Smoke free premises. 5 units. Some suites ($110-$170) and whirlpool units ($85-$170). 2 stories, interior corridors. **Terms:** 7 day cancellation notice. **Amenities:** extended cable TV. **Leisure Activities:** heated pool, beach access. **Guest Services:** [BP] meal plan available, complimentary evening beverages, complimentary laundry. **Cards:** AE, DI, MC, VI.
[ASK] [🏊] [✕] [📷] [💻] [📠]

TOPAZ MOTEL
[AAA] [SAVE]
◈◈◈ ◈◈
Motel

All Year 1P: $48-$141 2P: $48-$141 XP: $5 F12

Phone: (904)439-3301

Location: 0.5 mi s of SR 100, on SR A1A. 1224 S Oceanshore Blvd 32136. Fax: 904/439-3942. **Facility:** 58 units, 15 with efficiency. Some whirlpool units ($111-$175). *Bath:* combo or shower only. 2 stories, interior/exterior corridors. **Parking:** valet, winter plug-ins. **Terms:** 14 day cancellation notice, weekly & monthly rates available, pets ($11 fee, deposit, dogs only). **Amenities:** extended cable TV, voice mail. **Dining:** restaurant, 5:30 pm-9:30 pm; closed Sun & Mon, $14-$22. **Leisure Activities:** beach, swimming. **Guest Services:** coin laundry. **Business Services:** meeting rooms. **Cards:** AE, DS, MC, VI.
SOME UNITS
[🛏] [🍴] [🏊] / [✕] [VCR] [📠] /

THE WHITE ORCHID OCEANFRONT INN
◈◈◈
Bed & Breakfast

All Year 1P: $119-$179 2P: $119-$179 XP: $45

Phone: (904)439-4944

Location: On A1A, 0.5 mi s of SR 100. 1104 S Oceanshore Blvd 32136. Fax: 904/439-4946. **Facility:** Across the street from ocean. Lovely home and carriage house with art-deco decor. Smoke free premises. 8 units. Some whirlpool units ($139-$179). *Bath:* combo or shower only. 2 stories, interior/exterior corridors. **Terms:** age restrictions may apply, 7 day cancellation notice-fee imposed, weekly rates available, package plans. **Amenities:** extended cable TV. **Leisure Activities:** heated pool, whirlpool, beach, swimming, bicycles. **Guest Services:** [BP] meal plan available, gift shop, complimentary evening beverages, complimentary laundry. **Cards:** AE, DS, MC, VI.
[🍴] [🏊] [✕] [📷] [📠]

———— WHERE TO DINE ————

TOPAZ CAFE
◈◈◈
American

Dinner: $15-$25

Phone: 904/439-3275

Location: 0.5 mi s of SR 100, on SR A1A; in Topaz Motel. 1224 S Oceanshore Blvd 32136. **Hours:** 5:30 pm-10 pm; Fri & Sat-10:30 pm. Closed: 12/25; also Mon & Sun except some major holidays. **Reservations:** suggested. **Features:** casual dress; beer & wine only. A nostalgic feeling washes over the restaurant, located in one of the city's oldest buildings. A fireplace and antiques add to the cozy ambiance of the parlor, while the covered porch offers beautiful views of the ocean. Gourmet menu items vary weekly. **Cards:** AE, MC, VI.

FLORAL CITY

———— WHERE TO STAY ————

MOONRISE RESORT
◈◈◈
Cottage

All Year 1P: $50-$85 2P: $50-$85 XP: $5

Phone: 352/726-2553

Location: Just e on CR 48, 1.5 mi n on Old Floral City Rd. 8801 E Moonrise Ln 34436. Fax: 352/726-2904. **Facility:** On Lake Tsala Apopka. 10 units with kitchen. 1 two-bedroom unit. *Bath:* combo or shower only. 1 story, exterior corridors. **Terms:** 14 day cancellation notice, pets ($20 extra charge). **Amenities:** extended cable TV. **Leisure Activities:** beach, boat dock, fishing, shuffleboard. *Fee:* boating, canoeing, paddleboats. **Guest Services:** coin laundry.
[🛏] [✕] [☎] [📺] [💻] [📷] [📠]

FLORIDA CITY —See Miami-Miami Beach p. 517.

Well Read

When you pick up a AAA TourBook® guide, look for establishments that display a bright red AAA logo, SAVE icon, and Diamond rating in their listing. These Official Appointment establishments place a high value on the patronage they receive from AAA members. And, by offering members a minimum 10% discount off published TourBook standard room rates, they are willing to go the extra mile to get your business.

So, when you turn to the AAA TourBook guide to make your travel plans, look for the establishments that will give you the special treatment you deserve.

Travel With Someone You Trust®

Destination Florida Keys

T hey've been called a string of pearls, draped across a sweep of turquoise water.

T hat's only half the truth. Fact is, these Keys are many things to many people. From sport-fishers' gold mine to scuba divers' sunken treasure, they offer a pirate's chest full of activities for all.

The Road That Went to Sea. With a seascape this stunning, who needs a big-city skyline?

An underwater wonderland. For snorkelers and scuba divers alike, the Keys can't be beat.

See Vicinity map page 320

P *laces included in this AAA Destination Area:*

Duval Street, Key West.
Laid-back, loose and proud to
be loud, this main-drag mecca
amuses by day and mesmerizes
by night. (See mention page 66)

Key
Largo

Islamorada

Long Key

Marathon Key Colony
Beach

Florida Keys

Sport fishing central.
From tourist charters
to tournament
challenges, on this
chain of islands, sport
fishing stands out.

*Sunset at Mallory Square,
Key West.*
It remains one of the
most entertaining shows
to be had for only the cost
of a few folded favors.
(See mention page 60)

The Florida Keys

CUDJOE KEY pop. 1,700

──────── WHERE TO DINE ────────

RAIMONDO'S RISTORANTE ITALIANO   **Dinner:** $11-$21   Phone: 305/745-9999
♦♦♦ ♦♦♦   **Location:** From US 1 MM 21, 0.5 mi s; in Cudjoe Gardens. 457 Drost Dr 33042. **Hours:** 5:30 pm-10 pm. Closed:
9/15-9/30 & Tues 6/1-10/31. **Reservations:** accepted. **Features:** casual dress; cocktail lounge; beer &
Italian   wine only; a la carte. Settle down in the relaxed tropical setting with an outdoor patio overlooking the
          waterway. Two fireplaces and fresh flowers convey a cozy, warm mood. Old World style entrees of seafood
and pasta are prepared from the freshest ingredients. **Cards:** AE, CB, DI, DS, MC, VI.

ISLAMORADA pop. 1,200

──────── WHERE TO STAY ────────

CHEECA LODGE   Phone: (305)664-4651
(AAA) (SAVE)   12/1-4/30   2P: $295-$650   XP: $25   F16
          5/1-11/30   2P: $215-$450   XP: $25   F16
♦♦♦ ♦♦♦   **Location:** US 1 at MM 82, oceanside. 81801 Overseas Hwy 33036 (PO Box 527). Fax: 305/664-2893.
Resort   **Facility:** Beachfront or golf course villas, lodge rooms. 203 units, 63 with kitchen. Some suites ($335-$1500)
          and whirlpool units. *Bath:* combo or shower only. 2-4 stories, interior/exterior corridors. **Parking:** valet.
Terms: check-in 4 pm, 14 day cancellation notice-fee imposed, package plans. **Amenities:** extended cable
TV, CD players, voice mail, honor bars, irons, hair dryers. **Dining:** dining room, restaurant, 7 am-10 pm, Fri & Sat-11 pm, $13-
$37, cocktails, also, Atlantic's Edge, see separate listing. **Leisure Activities:** 2 heated pools, wading pool, whirlpools, beach,
swimming, boat dock, snorkeling, fishing, 525 ft fishing pier, putting green, 9-hole, par 3 golf course, children's program, playground. *Fee:* boating, paddleboats, sailboating, windsurfing, scuba diving, scuba & snorkeling equipment, charter fishing, dive
trips, sunset cruises, parasailing, 6 lighted tennis courts, bicycles. **Guest Services:** [AP], [BP] & [MAP] meal plans available, gift
shop, area transportation, valet laundry. *Fee:* airport transportation-Miami Airport, massage. **Business Services:** meeting rooms.
Fee: fax. **Cards:** AE, CB, DI, DS, MC, VI. *(See color ad p 313)*
                                                                                SOME UNITS
          [icons] FEE ... FEE ... FEE

EL CAPITAN AT HOLIDAY ISLE   Phone: (305)664-2711
♦♦♦ ♦♦♦   12/25-4/22   1P: $160-$285   2P: $160-$285   XP: $15   F17
          12/1-12/24 & 4/23-11/30   1P: $130-$250   2P: $130-$250   XP: $15   F17
Motel   **Location:** US 1, MM 84.5. 84001 Overseas Hwy 33036. Fax: 305/664-2703. **Facility:** Secluded comfort by private
          lagoon. Registration at Howard Johnson's. 14 units. 2 two-bedroom units and 12 efficiencies. Some suites.
Bath: combo or shower only. 1 story, exterior corridors. **Terms:** check-in 3:30 pm, 3 day cancellation notice. **Amenities:** extended
cable TV, voice mail, safes (fee). **Leisure Activities:** beach, swimming, fishing, charter fishing. **Guest Services:** gift shop. **Business Services:** meeting rooms. *Fee:* fax. **Cards:** AE, CB, DI, DS, MC, VI.
                                                                                SOME UNITS
          [icons]

HAMPTON INN & SUITES   Phone: (305)664-0073
(SAVE)   2/9-4/16   1P: $209-$309   2P: $219-$329
          1/1-2/8   1P: $140-$235   2P: $155-$255
♦♦♦ ♦♦♦   4/17-11/30   1P: $99-$190   2P: $109-$235
Resort   12/1-12/31   1P: $99-$209   2P: $109-$219
          Location: US 1, MM80. 80001 Overseas Hwy 33036. Fax: 305/664-0807. **Facility:** Oceanfront resort. Contempo-
rary rooms, most with ocean views and full kitchens. All rooms with balcony. Designated smoking area. 79
units. 23 two-bedroom units and 66 efficiencies. Some suites. *Bath:* combo or shower only. 5 stories, interior corridors. **Terms:** 3
day cancellation notice-fee imposed, weekly rates available. **Amenities:** extended cable TV, voice mail, safes, irons, hair dryers.
Leisure Activities: heated pool, whirlpool, beach, swimming, fishing, charter fishing, exercise room. *Fee:* boating, canoeing,
paddleboats, sailboating, windsurfing, boat dock, scuba diving/snorkeling & equipment, bicycles. **Guest Services:** [ECP] meal
plan available, gift shop, coin laundry. *Fee:* massage. **Business Services:** meeting rooms, fax. **Cards:** AE, CB, DI, DS, JC,
MC, VI.
                                                                                SOME UNITS
          [icons]

HOWARD JOHNSON LODGE AT HOLIDAY ISLE   Phone: (305)664-2711

CAAD SAVE

VVVV VV

Motor Inn

| | 12/25-4/22 | 1P: $160-$185 | 2P: $160-$185 |
| | 12/1-12/24 & 4/23-11/30 | 1P: $130-$150 | 2P: $130-$150 |

Location: US 1 at MM84.5. 84001 Overseas Hwy 33036. Fax: 305/664-2703. **Facility:** 56 units. *Bath:* combo or shower only. 2 stories, interior/exterior corridors. **Terms:** check-in 3:30 pm, 3 day cancellation notice. **Amenities:** voice mail, safes (fee). *Some:* irons, hair dryers. **Dining:** 2 restaurants, 7 am-11 pm, $6-$15, cocktails, entertainment. **Leisure Activities:** 2 pools (1 heated), beach, swimming, fishing, charter fishing, jet ski, kayak rentals. *Fee:* boats. **Guest Services:** gift shop, coin laundry. **Business Services:** meeting rooms. *Fee:* fax. **Cards:** AE, CB, DI, DS, MC, VI.

SOME UNITS

⬛🍽🍸🎿📷🏊🏐 /✕/

PELICAN COVE RESORT   Phone: (305)664-4435

CAAD SAVE

VVVV VV

Motel

	12/1-12/31	1P: $115-$695	2P: $115-$695	XP: $20	F16
	1/1-4/22	1P: $185-$225	2P: $185-$225	XP: $20	F16
	4/23-9/3	1P: $135-$155	2P: $135-$155	XP: $20	F16
	9/4-11/30	1P: $115-$135	2P: $115-$135	XP: $20	F16

Location: US 1 at MM84.5; behind Theater of the Sea. 84457 Old Overseas Hwy 33036 (PO Box 633). Fax: 305/664-5134. **Facility:** All rooms with balcony and some with view of ocean. 63 units, 27 with kitchen. Some suites ($365-$585) and whirlpool units ($195-$325). 3 stories, exterior corridors. **Terms:** check-in 4 pm, 5 day cancellation notice-fee imposed, weekly & monthly rates available. **Amenities:** extended cable TV, hair dryers. **Dining:** poolside cafe for lunch only. **Leisure Activities:** heated pool, whirlpool, beach, swimming, snorkeling, fishing, tennis court. *Fee:* boating, boat dock, marina, snorkeling equipment, snorkel trips, wave runners. **Guest Services:** [ECP] meal plan available, valet laundry. **Business Services:** meeting rooms. *Fee:* fax. **Cards:** AE, CB, DI, DS, JC, MC, VI. **Special Amenities:** free continental breakfast and free newspaper. *(See color ad below)*

SOME UNITS

⬛🍸📷🏊🏐📺📶 /📷/

SANDS OF ISLAMORADA   Phone: 305/664-2791

CAAD SAVE

VV VV

Motel

	12/21-9/4	1P: $120-$195	2P: $120-$195	XP: $15
	9/5-11/30	1P: $95-$170	2P: $95-$170	XP: $15
	12/1-12/20	1P: $90-$160	2P: $90-$160	XP: $15

Location: US 1, MM80. 80051 Overseas Hwy 33036. Fax: 305/664-2886. **Facility:** Oceanfront quiet, cozy rooms. Various styles of rooms and decor. Resident tropical birds. 9 units, 4 with efficiency. *Bath:* combo or shower only. 1-2 stories, exterior corridors. **Terms:** 3 day cancellation notice, pets ($10 extra charge). **Amenities:** extended cable TV, voice mail. **Leisure Activities:** whirlpool, boat dock, barbecue grill. *Fee:* fax. **Cards:** MC, VI.   SOME UNITS

🐾📷🏐📺📶📶 /VCR/

——————— *The following lodging was either not evaluated or did not* ———————
meet AAA rating requirements but is listed for your information only.

WHITE GATE COURT   Phone: 305/664-4136

fyi

Not evaluated. **Location:** On US 1, just s of MM77, s side of the road. 76010 Overseas Hwy 33036. Facilities, services, and decor characterize a basic property.

——————— **WHERE TO DINE** ———————

ATLANTIC'S EDGE   **Dinner:** $16-$39   Phone: 305/664-4651

VVVV VVVV

Regional American

Location: US 1 at MM82, oceanside; in Cheeca Lodge. 81801 Overseas Hwy 33036. **Hours:** 5:30 pm-10 pm, Fri & Sat-11 pm, Sun 6 pm-10 pm. **Reservations:** suggested. **Features:** dressy casual; children's menu; cocktails & lounge; valet parking; area transportation; a la carte. Find an excellent meal in this elegant, candlelit dining room overlooking the ocean. The innovative menu features local seafood specialties along with some California items. Pan-seared scallops are a treat to share. Sunday brunch is offered in season. **Cards:** AE, CB, DI, DS, MC, VI.

✕

CORAL GRILL RESTAURANT   **Dinner:** $9-$20   Phone: 305/664-4803

CAAD

VV VV

American

Location: US 1 at MM83.5. 83532 Overseas Hwy 33036. **Hours:** 4:30 pm-9:30 pm, Sun noon-9 pm. Closed: 12/25; also Mon & 9/1-10/31. **Features:** casual dress; Sunday brunch; children's menu; early bird specials; carryout; salad bar; cocktails; buffet. The upstairs of the casual, two-level restaurant is noted for its extensive buffet of soups, salads and desserts. The downstairs has the feel of a diner. Ample portions of such tasty fare as barbecue ribs lend to the eatery's popularity with locals. **Cards:** AE, DI, DS, MC, VI.

♿✕

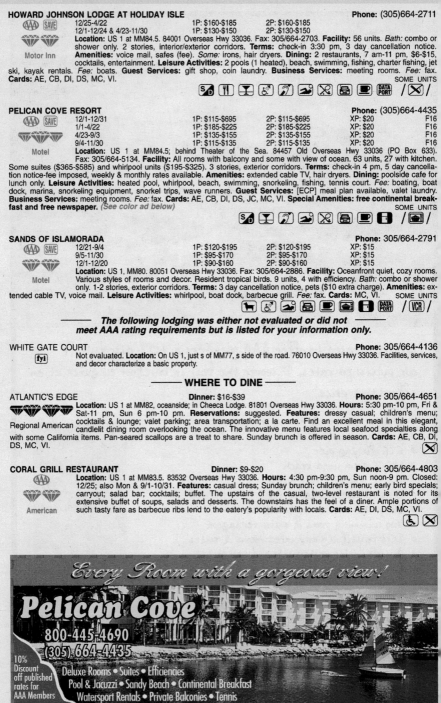

MARKER 88 RESTAURANT **Dinner:** $17-$30 **Phone:** 305/852-9315
AAA
Location: US Hwy 1, MM 88 33036. **Hours:** 5 pm-11 pm. Closed: 11/22, 12/25; also Mon.
Reservations: suggested. **Features:** casual dress; children's menu; cocktails; a la carte. An elaborate
menu offers local seafood specials. The dining room overlooks Florida Bay. Both the soup and salad are
very good. Try the yellowtail rangoon for a tropical twist. The service is pleasant and very professional.
Seafood   **Cards:** AE, DI, DS, MC, VI.   ✕

SQUID ROW RESTAURANT **Lunch:** $4-$7 **Dinner:** $9-$19 **Phone:** 305/664-9865
AAA
Location: On US 1 and MM81.9. 89901 Overseas Hwy 33070. **Hours:** 11:30 am-9:30 pm, Fri & Sat-10 pm.
Closed: 11/22, 12/25. **Reservations:** suggested; for dinner. **Features:** casual dress; children's menu;
cocktails & lounge. A wide range of fresh seafood, steak, chicken and pasta is prepared to order.
Bouillabaisse is house specialty; dessert, bread and dressing made on premises. A tasty grilled fish
Steak & Seafood   sandwich with french fries provides a satisfying lunch for those on the go. Inside or covered, screened
patio dining. **Cards:** AE, CB, DI, DS, MC, VI.   ✕

KEY COLONY BEACH pop. 1,000

——— WHERE TO STAY ———

CONTINENTAL INN **Phone:** 305/289-0101
AAA SAVE
| 12/1-4/30 | 1P: $125 | 2P: $125-$165 | XP: $10 |
| 5/1-11/30 | 1P: $100 | 2P: $100-$140 | XP: $10 |

Location: 1.2 mi sw from jct US 1 and Sadowski Cswy (MM53.8). 1121 W Ocean Dr 33051 (P O Box 510201).
Fax: 305/743-8150. **Facility:** All units individually decorated with small porches. 40 units with kitchen. 2 two-
Condominium   bedroom units. 2 stories, exterior corridors. **Terms:** 3 day cancellation notice-fee imposed. **Amenities:** ex-
tended cable TV. *Some:* irons. **Leisure Activities:** heated pool, beach, swimming, barbecue area, tiki huts.
Guest Services: coin laundry. *Fee:* fax. **Cards:** AE, DS, MC, VI. **Special Amenities:** free local telephone calls.

SOME UNITS
🏊 💻 📠 🛏 / ✕ VCR 📠 /

KEY LARGO pop. 11,300

——— WHERE TO STAY ———

BAY BREEZE MOTEL **Phone:** (305)852-5248
AAA SAVE
| 12/1-4/15 | 2P: $79-$199 | XP: $20 |
| 4/16-11/30 | 2P: $89-$179 | XP: $20 |

Location: 7.5 mi s from center of town, at MM 92.5. 160 Sterling Rd 33070. Fax: 305/852-5758. **Facility:** A quiet location, most units with view of the gulf. Motel units also available. 15 efficiencies. *Bath:* combo or shower
Cottage   only. 2 stories, exterior corridors. **Terms:** 30 day cancellation notice-fee imposed, weekly & monthly rates
available. **Leisure Activities:** heated pool, beach, swimming, boating, paddleboats, boat dock.
Cards: MC, VI. **Special Amenities:** free local telephone calls and free room upgrade (subject to availability with advanced
reservations).

SOME UNITS
🍴 🏊 ✕ 🎦 📠 💻 🛏 DATA PORT / ✕ VCR 📠 /
FEE

BEST WESTERN THE SUITES AT KEY LARGO **Phone:** (305)451-5081
AAA SAVE
12/1-1/31	1P: $150-$400	2P: $160-$400	XP: $10	F18
2/1-4/30	1P: $135-$175	2P: $145-$175	XP: $10	F18
9/1-11/30	1P: $79-$175	2P: $79-$175	XP: $10	F18
5/1-8/31	1P: $89-$150	2P: $99-$160	XP: $10	F18

Suite Motel   **Location:** 0.3 mi e of US 1 at MM 100. 201 Ocean Dr 33037. Fax: 305/451-4173. **Facility:** All units are bi-level with
screen porch overlooking the marina off living area. All rooms entered from 2nd floor. 40 units with kitchen.
2 stories, exterior corridors. **Terms:** 7 day cancellation notice-fee imposed, weekly & monthly rates available, package plans.
Amenities: extended cable TV. **Leisure Activities:** fishing, charter fishing. *Fee:* scuba diving/snorkeling & equipment. **Guest
Services:** [ECP] meal plan available, coin laundry. *Fee:* fax. **Cards:** AE, CB, DI, DS, JC, MC, VI. **Special Amenities:** free continental breakfast and free local telephone calls.

SOME UNITS
SD 🍴 🏊 ✕ 🎦 📠 💻 🛏 / ✕ VCR /
FEE

HOLIDAY INN RESORT & MARINA
Phone: (305)451-2121

	1P: $149-$209	2P: $149-$209	XP: $10	F1
1/1-4/14				
12/1-12/31 & 9/3-11/30	1P: $109-$199	2P: $109-$199	XP: $10	F1
4/15-9/2	1P: $109-$169	2P: $109-$169	XP: $10	F1

Motor Inn **Location:** US 1, at MM100. 99701 Overseas Hwy 33037. Fax: 305/451-5592. **Facility:** Some units overlook the tropical pool courtyard or the canal. Home of the "African Queen". 132 units. 2 stories, interior/exterior corridors. **Terms:** 3 day cancellation notice, package plans. **Amenities:** extended cable TV, voice mail, irons, hair dryers. **Leisure Activities:** 2 pools (heated), whirlpool, fishing, playground, exercise room. *Fee:* marina, scuba diving/snorkeling & equipment, charter fishing. **Guest Services:** [AP] & [CP] meal plans available, gift shop, coin laundry. **Business Services:** meeting rooms. *Fee:* fax. **Cards:** AE CB, DI, DS, JC, MC, VI. *(See color ad p 315)*

SOME UNITS

HOWARD JOHNSON RESORT KEY LARGO
Phone: (305)451-1400

	12/22-4/28	1P: $155-$215	2P: $155-$215	XP: $10	F1
	4/29-11/30	1P: $125-$165	2P: $125-$165	XP: $10	F1
	12/1-12/21	1P: $115-$165	2P: $115-$165	XP: $10	F1

Motor Inn **Location:** US 1, at MM 102. 10245 Overseas Hwy 33037 (PO Box 1024). Fax: 305/451-3953. **Facility:** Bayside Large units with balcony or patio. 100 units. 2 stories, interior corridors. **Terms:** weekly rates available package plans, pets ($10 extra charge). **Amenities:** extended cable TV, safes (fee). **Dining:** restaurant, am-3 pm; tiki bar, $7-$13, cocktails. **Leisure Activities:** beach, swimming, boat dock. *Fee:* boating, canoes, scuba diving/snorkeling & equipment. **Guest Services:** coin laundry. **Business Services:** meeting rooms. *Fee:* fax. **Cards:** AE, DI, DS MC, VI. *(See color ad below)*

SOME UNITS

MARINA DEL MAR BAYSIDE   Phone: (305)451-4450

(AAA) [SAVE]   12/23-4/21   1P: $99-$189
               9/1-11/30   1P: $89-$189
▼▽▼▽▼▽   4/22-8/31   1P: $89-$149
               12/1-12/22   1P: $79-$99

Motel   **Location:** US 1 at MM99.5. 99470 Overseas Hwy 33037 (PO Box 1050). Fax: 305/451-9650. **Facility:** Set back from highway on grounds along Florida Bay. 56 units, 2 with efficiency. Some suites ($169-$299). 1-3 stories, exterior corridors. **Terms:** 3 day cancellation notice, package plans. **Amenities:** extended cable TV. *Some:* safes, hair dryers. **Leisure Activities:** small heated pool, beach, swimming, fishing, volleyball, facilities of Marina del Mar Resort & Marina avail to guests. **Guest Services:** gift shop. *Fee:* fax. **Cards:** AE, DI, DS, MC, VI. **Special Amenities: free continental breakfast and free local telephone calls.** *(See color ad p 316 & below)*

SOME UNITS

[S/D] [↾↿+] [🍽] [⟳] [⟲] [✕] / [✕] [▣] [🖨] [🔋] /
                                                          FEE

MARINA DEL MAR RESORT & MARINA   Phone: (305)451-4107

(AAA) [SAVE]   12/22-4/23   1P: $119-$189   2P: $119-$189
               4/24-9/3   1P: $109-$189   2P: $109-$189
▼▽▼▽▼▽   9/4-11/30   1P: $99-$169   2P: $99-$169
               12/1-12/21   1P: $99-$129   2P: $99-$129

Motor Inn   **Location:** Off US 1 at MM 100; adjacent to Holiday Inn via Laguna Ave. 527 Caribbean Dr 33037-1050 (PO Box 1050). Fax: 305/451-1891. **Facility:** On canal, overlooking marina. Rooms, studio and one-bedroom units, many with marina view. 76 units. 3 two-bedroom units, 1 three-bedroom unit and 20 units with kitchen. Some suites ($149-$349) and whirlpool units. 2-4 stories, exterior corridors. **Terms:** 3 day cancellation notice, package plans. **Amenities:** extended cable TV, irons, hair dryers. **Dining:** restaurant, 11 am-10 pm, $9-$15, cocktails, also, Coconuts Restaurant & Lounge, see separate listing, entertainment. **Leisure Activities:** heated pool, whirlpool, boat ramp, 2 lighted tennis courts, exercise room. *Fee:* marina, scuba diving/snorkeling & equipment, fishing, charter fishing, diving trips. **Guest Services:** [CP] meal plan available, gift shop, coin laundry. **Business Services:** meeting rooms. *Fee:* fax. **Cards:** AE, DI, DS, MC, VI. **Special Amenities: early check-in/late check-out and free room upgrade (subject to availability with advanced reservations).** *(See color ad p 316 & below)*

SOME UNITS

[S/D] [↾↿] [Y] [⟳] [⟲] [✕] [▣] [🔋] / [✕] [▣] [🖨] /

MARRIOTT'S KEY LARGO BAY BEACH RESORT   Phone: (305)453-0000

▼▽▼▽▼▽   12/1-12/31 & 9/3-11/30   1P: $165-$295   2P: $165-$295   XP: $10   F18
               1/1-4/14   1P: $225-$285   2P: $225-$285   XP: $10   F18
Resort   4/15-9/2   1P: $199-$219   2P: $199-$219   XP: $10   F18

Location: US 1 at MM103.8. 103800 Overseas Hwy 33037. Fax: 305/453-0093. **Facility:** On extensive grounds overlooking Florida Bay. Inviting multi-faceted resort. Well-appointed rooms and suites decorated with tropical flair, many with balcony. 153 units. 20 two-bedroom units and 24 units with kitchen. Some suites ($365-$1500). 4 stories, exterior corridors. **Terms:** 3 day cancellation notice, package plans. **Amenities:** extended cable TV, voice mail, safes, honor bars, irons, hair dryers. **Leisure Activities:** heated pool, whirlpool, beach, swimming, boat dock, fishing, tennis court, children's program, jogging, exercise room. *Fee:* boats, canoes, paddleboats, marina, scuba diving/snorkeling & equipment, charter fishing, miniature golf, bicycles. **Guest Services:** gift shop, valet laundry. **Business Services:** conference facilities. *Fee:* fax. **Cards:** AE, DI, MC, VI. *(See color ad p 315)*

SOME UNITS

[ASK] [S/D] [✈] [↾↿] [Y] [⟳] [⟲] [✕] [📷] [▣] [▣] [DATA PORT] / [✕] [VCR] [🖨] [🔋] /
          FEE   FEE   FEE

RAMADA LIMITED RESORT AND MARINA   Phone: (305)451-3939

▼▽▼▽▼▽   All Year   1P: $149-$189   2P: $149-$189

Motel   **Location:** US 1, at MM100. 99751 Overseas Hwy 33037. Fax: 305/453-0222. **Facility:** Many units overlooking waterway. 90 units. Some whirlpool units. 4 stories, interior corridors. **Amenities:** extended cable TV, voice mail, hair dryers. *Some:* irons. **Leisure Activities:** heated pool, whirlpool, charter fishing. *Fee:* boats, marina, scuba diving/snorkeling & equipment, fishing. **Guest Services:** [CP] meal plan available, coin laundry. **Business Services:** meeting rooms. *Fee:* fax. **Cards:** AE, CB, DI, MC, VI.

SOME UNITS

[ASK] [S/D] [↾↿+] [⟲] [♨+] [✕] [📷] [▣] [▣] [🔋] [DATA PORT] / [✕] /

ROCK REEF RESORT

Phone: 305/852-2401

(AAA) (SAVE)

◇◇◇

Motel

12/16-4/25		2P: $109-$220	XP: $15
4/26-9/15		2P: $94-$193	XP: $15
12/1-12/15 & 9/16-11/30		2P: $88-$165	XP: $15

Location: On US 1 (southbound) at MM98. 97850 Overseas Hwy 33037 (PO Box 73). Fax: 305/852-5355. **Facility:** Bayside on spacious tropically landscaped grounds. Mostly large units, some with ceiling fan. 21 units. 4 two-bedroom units and 9 units with kitchen. Some suites. *Bath:* combo or shower only. 1-2 stories, exterior corridors. **Terms:** cancellation fee imposed, package plans. **Amenities:** extended cable TV. **Leisure Activities:** whirlpool, beach, swimming, paddleboats, boat dock, fishing, fishing pier, shuffleboard, barbecue area, tetherball. **Guest Services:** coin laundry. *Fee:* fax. **Cards:** AE, DS, MC, VI. **Special Amenities:** free local telephone calls and free room upgrade (subject to availability with advanced reservations).

SOME UNITS

⟨icons⟩

THE WESTIN BEACH RESORT, KEY LARGO

Phone: (305)852-5553

(AAA) (SAVE)

◇◇◇

Hotel

12/22-4/28	1P: $259-$359	2P: $259-$359	XP: $15	F18
4/29-11/30	1P: $199-$289	2P: $199-$289	XP: $15	F18
12/1-12/21	1P: $179-$249	2P: $179-$249	XP: $15	F18

Location: US 1 southbound Carriageway at MM 97, overlooking Florida Bay. 97000 S Overseas Hwy 33037. Fax: 305/852-8669. **Facility:** In heart of Hardwood Hammock along the gulf shore. Some rooms with balcony and waterview. 200 units. Some whirlpool units ($389-$509). *Bath:* combo or shower only. 4 stories, exterior corridors. **Parking:** valet. **Terms:** package plans, $5 service charge. **Amenities:** video games, voice mail, safes, honor bars, irons, hair dryers. **Dining:** dining room, restaurant, 2 delis, 6:30 am-11 pm, $8-$25, cocktails. **Leisure Activities:** 2 heated pools, sauna, whirlpool, beach, swimming, boat dock, fishing, jet skis, kayaks, parasailing, 2 lighted tennis courts, children's program, nature program, jogging, exercise room, game room, beauty salon. *Fee:* paddleboats, sailboats, windsurfing, charter fishing. **Guest Services:** gift shop, valet laundry. *Fee:* massage. **Business Services:** conference facilities. *Fee:* fax. **Cards:** AE, CB, DI, DS, MC, VI. **Special Amenities:** free newspaper. *(See color ad below)*

SOME UNITS

⟨icons⟩ FEE ⟨icons⟩ FEE ⟨icons⟩

———— **WHERE TO DINE** ————

BAYSIDE GRILL

◇◇◇

American

Lunch: $6-$10   **Dinner:** $8-$23   Phone: 305/451-3380

Location: US 1, MM99.5. 99530 Overseas Hwy 33037. **Hours:** 11:30 am-10 pm. Closed: 11/22, 12/25. **Features:** casual dress; children's menu; carryout; cocktails & lounge; a la carte. Offering Caribbean-style dishes with local seafood and steaks, this popular spot also features a lovely sunset view of Florida Bay. A very good wine list and a wide selection of imported beers will help you choose just the right beverage for your meal. **Cards:** AE, MC, VI.

⟨icon⟩

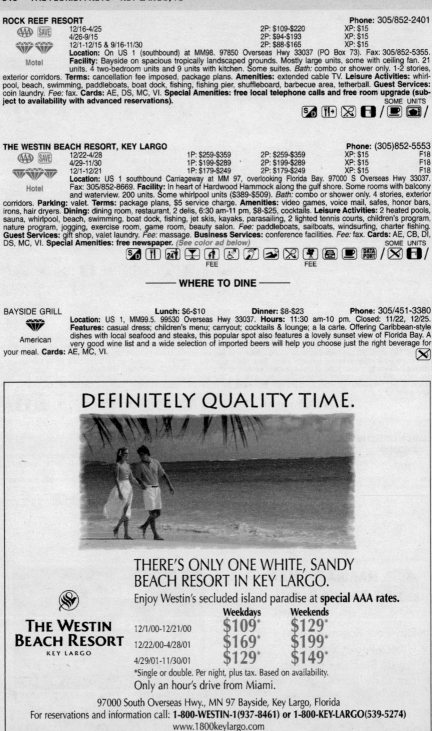

BJ'S BAR-B-Q

American

Lunch: $4-$14   **Dinner:** $4-$14   **Phone:** 305/451-0900
Location: On US 1 at MM102.5. 102570 Overseas Hwy 33037. **Hours:** 11 am-9 pm. Closed: 11/22, 12/25; also Wed. **Features:** casual dress; children's menu; early bird specials; carryout; beer & wine only. This family-oriented spot is decked out with a rustic western motif. Efficient servers bring you traditional barbecue favorites like charbroiled steak, chicken, seafood, ribs and homemade baked beans. Try the onion rings for a delicious treat. **Cards:** AE, DS, MC, VI.

CAFE LARGO

Italian

Dinner: $8-$23   **Phone:** 305/451-4885
Location: US 1, MM99.5. 99530 Overseas Hwy 33037. **Hours:** 4:30 pm-11 pm. Closed: 11/22, 12/25. **Features:** casual dress; children's menu; carryout; cocktails & lounge; a la carte. Dine on fresh local seafood, certified steak, pasta dishes and other Italian specialties. Consult a very good wine list or choose from an extensive selection of imported beers. Soups are homemade and change daily at this perfect spot for a quick meal. **Cards:** AE, MC, VI.

COCONUTS RESTAURANT & LOUNGE

Steak & Seafood

Lunch: $5-$7   **Dinner:** $9-$15   **Phone:** 305/453-9794
Location: Off US 1 at MM 100; adjacent to Holiday Inn via Laguna Ave; in Marina Del Mar Resort & Marina. 528 Caribbean Dr 33037-1050. **Hours:** 11 am-10 pm. **Features:** casual dress; children's menu; carryout; cocktails & lounge; entertainment; a la carte. No need to dress up for this casual restaurant with a wooden deck overlooking the marina. Watch the yachts dock for lunch and enjoy a delicious meal with consistent service. The stuffed shrimp with crab meat is accompanied by summer squash and zucchini. **Cards:** AE, DI, MC, VI.

THE FISH HOUSE RESTAURANT & SEAFOOD MARKET

Seafood

Lunch: $4-$10   **Dinner:** $9-$25   **Phone:** 305/451-4665
Location: US 1 at MM102.4. 102401 Overseas Hwy 33037. **Hours:** 11:30 am-10 pm. Closed: 11/22; also 12/25 for lunch. **Features:** casual dress; children's menu; carryout; beer & wine only. Small but always bustling, the restaurant boasts ample portions of seafood, such as pan-sauteed fish, as well as shrimp and lobster specials that change daily. The wait staff is energetic, and the meringue-topped key lime pie is a tempting treat. **Cards:** AE, DI, DS, MC, VI.

FRANK KEYS CAFE

Regional American

Dinner: $12-$28   **Phone:** 305/453-0310
Location: US 1 at MM 100.2. 100211 Overseas Hwy 33037. **Hours:** 5 pm-10 pm. Closed: Tues. **Reservations:** accepted. **Features:** dressy casual; beer & wine only. Look beyond the trees to find this Victorian-style, Caribbean home. The wrap-around porch invites alfresco dining in casual attire. Imaginatively prepared cuisine with continental touches features fresh seafood, pasta and daily chefs specials. **Cards:** MC, VI.

ITALIAN FISHERMAN RESTAURANT

Italian

Lunch: $5-$15   **Dinner:** $7-$15   **Phone:** 305/451-4471
Location: US 1 at MM104. 104000 Overseas Hwy 33037. **Hours:** 11:30 am-10 pm. Closed: 12/25; also Mon off season. **Reservations:** suggested. **Features:** No A/C; casual dress; children's menu; early bird specials; carryout; cocktails & lounge. Relaxed dining on a large, waterfront terrace is the trademark of this family-oriented restaurant. A good menu selection includes many local seafood dishes, specialized frozen drinks, and a dessert menu featuring homemade tiramisu and tangy key lime pie. **Cards:** AE, MC, VI.

SNOOKS BAYSIDE

American

Lunch: $5-$8   **Dinner:** $15-$22   **Phone:** 305/453-3799
Location: Just off US 1 at MM99.9, between Marina del Mar Bayside and Largo Honda. 99470 Overseas Hwy 33037. **Hours:** 11:30 am-10:30 pm, Sun 10 am-10 pm. **Reservations:** accepted. **Features:** casual dress; Sunday brunch; children's menu; carryout; cocktails & lounge; entertainment. Choose either the terrace or an attractive dining room overlooking Florida Bay. Featuring seafood, steak, veal and chicken; the cuisine is fresh and served by a capable staff. Select tastefully arranged dessert choices brought to you on a silver tray. Extensive wine list. **Cards:** AE, DI, DS, MC, VI.

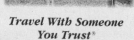

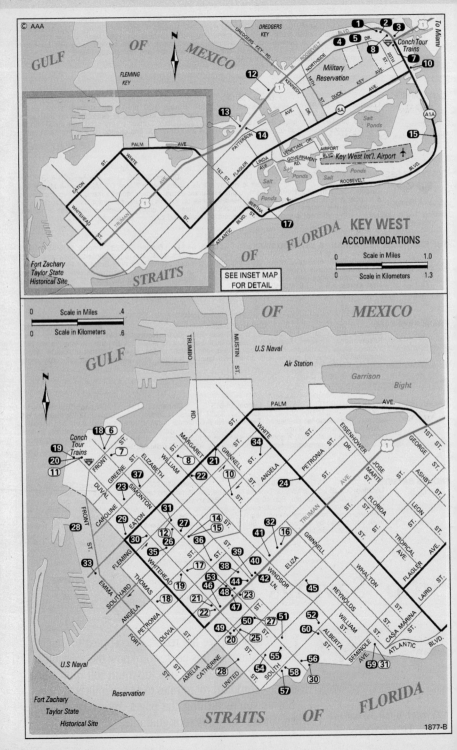

© AAA

GULF OF MEXICO

KEY WEST
ACCOMMODATIONS

SEE INSET MAP
FOR DETAIL

| Scale in Miles | 0 | 1.0 |
| Scale in Kilometers | 0 | 1.3 |

Fort Zachary
Taylor State
Historical Site

STRAITS

OF FLORIDA

Fleming Key

Dredgers Key

To Miami

Conch Tour Trains

Military Reservation

Key West Int'l. Airport

Salt Ponds

GULF OF MEXICO

Scale in Miles   .4
Scale in Kilometers   .6

U.S Naval Air Station

Garrison Bight

Conch Tour Trains

Fort Zachary
Taylor State
Historical Site

U.S Naval Reservation

STRAITS OF FLORIDA

1877-B

Key West

This index helps you "spot" where approved accommodations are located on the corresponding detailed maps. Rate ranges are for comparison only and show the property's high season. Turn to the listing page for more detailed rate information and consult display ads for special promotions. Restaurant rate range is for dinner, unless only lunch (L) is served.

Spotter/Map Page Number	OA	KEY WEST - Lodgings	Diamond Rating	Rate Range High Season	Listing Page
1 / p. 320	AAA	Radisson Hotel Key West - see color ad p 336	▽▽▽	$169-$399 SAVE	337
2 / p. 320	AAA	Comfort Inn - see color ad p 328	▽▽▽	$119-$359 SAVE	328
3 / p. 320		Holiday Inn-Beachside Key West - see color ad p 332	▽▽▽	$149-$255	333
4 / p. 320	AAA	Courtyard by Marriott - see color ad p 329	▽▽▽	$189-$229	329
5 / p. 320	AAA	Travelodge & Suites - see color ad p 337	▽▽▽	$129-$189 SAVE	338
7 / p. 320		Days Inn-Key West	▽▽▽	$69-$150	330
8 / p. 320	AAA	Quality Inn Resort - see color ad p 328	▽▽▽	$119-$359 SAVE	336
10 / p. 320		Coconut Mallory Resort & Marina	▽▽▽	$250-$300	327
12 / p. 320	AAA	Hampton Inn - see color ad p 332	▽▽▽	$159-$214 SAVE	331
13 / p. 320		Banana Bay Resort-Key West - see color ad p 331	▽▽▽	$150-$250	324
14 / p. 320		Fairfield Inn by Marriott - see color ad p 330	▽▽	$90-$120	331
15 / p. 320	AAA	Best Western Key Ambassador Resort Inn - see color ad p 326	▽▽▽	$139-$229 SAVE	325
17 / p. 320		Sheraton Suites-Key West - see color ad p 337	▽▽▽	$229-$359	337
18 / p. 320	AAA	Hyatt Key West - see ad p 333	▽▽▽	$355-$400 SAVE	333
19 / p. 320		Ocean Key, A Noble House Resort	▽▽▽	$199-$449	335
20 / p. 320	AAA	Pier House Resort & Caribbean Spa - see color ad p 336	▽▽▽	$290 SAVE	336
21 / p. 320	AAA	Westwinds	▽▽	$90-$250 SAVE	338
22 / p. 320		Island City House Hotel	▽▽▽	$175-$240	333
23 / p. 320		Curry Mansion Inn	▽▽▽	$180-$325	330
24 / p. 320	AAA	The Palms Hotel	▽▽	$160-$185 SAVE	335
26 / p. 320	AAA	Heron House	▽▽▽▽	$189-$209 SAVE	331
27 / p. 320	AAA	Watson House	▽▽▽	$105-$500 SAVE	338
28 / p. 320	AAA	Hilton Key West Resort & Marina - see ad p 44	▽▽▽▽	$295-$495 SAVE	332
29 / p. 320	AAA	The Banyan Resort - see color ad p 324	▽▽▽	$200-$350 SAVE	324
30 / p. 320		Holiday Inn La Concha Hotel	▽▽▽	$189-$600	333
31 / p. 320		The Marquesa Hotel	▽▽▽▽	$265-$405	335
32 / p. 320	AAA	Lightbourn Inn - see color ad p 335	▽▽▽	$128-$258 SAVE	335
33 / p. 320		The Weatherstation Inn	▽▽▽	$195-$315	338
34 / p. 320	AAA	Frances St Bottle Inn	▽▽▽	$135-$165 SAVE	331
35 / p. 320	AAA	Pegasus International Hotel	▽▽	$129-$499 SAVE	336
36 / p. 320	AAA	Courtney's Place Historic Guest Cottages and Inn	▽▽	$119-$199 SAVE	329
37 / p. 320	AAA	Cypress House Bed & Breakfast	▽▽▽	$140-$350 SAVE	330

Spotter/Map Page Number	OA	KEY WEST - Lodgings (continued)	Diamond Rating	Rate Range High Season	Listing Page
38 / p. 320		Blue Parrot Inn	◆◆	Failed to provide	326
39 / p. 320	AAA	Chelsea House - see color ad p 327	◆◆◆	$135-$225 [SAVE]	327
40 / p. 320	AAA	The Colony Exclusive Cottages - see ad p 327	◆◆◆◆	$1555 [SAVE]	328
41 / p. 320	AAA	La Pensione	◆◆◆	$168-$178 [SAVE]	334
42 / p. 320	AAA	Key Lime Inn - see color ad p 334	◆◆◆	$149-$235 [SAVE]	334
44 / p. 320		The Conch House Heritage Inn	◆◆◆	$148-$228	328
45 / p. 320	AAA	Andrews Inn	◆◆◆	$165-$185 [SAVE]	324
46 / p. 320		Duval House - see color ad p 331	◆◆◆	$180-$335	330
47 / p. 320	AAA	Center Court Historic Inn & Cottages	◆◆◆	$88-$388 [SAVE]	327
48 / p. 320		Key West Villas Resort	◆◆◆	$150-$175	334
49 / p. 320	AAA	La Casa de Luces	◆◆	$149-$279 [SAVE]	334
50 / p. 320	AAA	The Cuban Club Suites	◆◆◆	$249-$599 [SAVE]	330
51 / p. 320	AAA	Best Western Hibiscus Motel - see color ad p 325	◆◆◆	$149-$279 [SAVE]	324
52 / p. 320	AAA	Alexander Palms Court	◆◆	$150-$265 [SAVE]	324
53 / p. 320		The Courtyard	◆◆	$99-$355	329
54 / p. 320	AAA	Southernmost Motel in the U.S.A. - see color ad p 323	◆◆◆	$165-$240 [SAVE]	338
55 / p. 320	AAA	Blue Marlin Resort Motel - see color ad p 325	◆◆◆	$159-$299 [SAVE]	326
56 / p. 320		Wyndham's Reach Resort	◆◆◆	$139-$599	339
57 / p. 320		La Mer Hotel & Dewey House - see color ad p 323	◆◆◆	$220-$330	334
58 / p. 320		South Beach Oceanfront Motel - see color ad p 323	◆◆◆	$99-$300	337
59 / p. 320	AAA	Wyndham Casa Marina Resort & Beach House	◆◆◆	$164-$399 [SAVE]	339
60 / p. 320	AAA	Blue Skies Inn	◆◆◆	$155-$195 [SAVE]	326
		KEY WEST - Restaurants			
6 / p. 320		Nicola Seafood	◆◆◆	$13-$25	341
7 / p. 320		Bagatelle Restaurant	◆◆	$15-$24	340
8 / p. 320		Pepe's Cafe	◆	$10-$20	341
10 / p. 320		Mangia Mangia	◆◆	$9-$15	341
11 / p. 320	AAA	Pier House Restaurant	◆◆◆◆	$18-$30	341
12 / p. 320		Cafe Marquesa	◆◆◆◆	$17-$30	340
14 / p. 320		Dim Sum Far East Restaurant	◆◆	$12-$20	340
15 / p. 320		Antonia's Restaurant	◆◆◆	$12-$23	340
16 / p. 320		Kyushu	◆◆	$12-$18	341
17 / p. 320		Camille's	◆◆	$11-$22	340
18 / p. 320		Blue Heaven	◆	$10-$24	340
19 / p. 320		Mangoes	◆◆	$11-$22	341
20 / p. 320		Alice's at La Te Da	◆◆◆	$13-$28	339

Spotter/Map Page Number	OA	KEY WEST - Restaurants (continued)	Diamond Rating	Rate Range High Season	Listing Page
㉑ / p. 320		El Siboney	◈◈	$6-$14	340
㉒ / p. 320		Croissants de France	◈	$5-$9(L)	340
㉓ / p. 320		Cafe des Artistes	◈◈◈◈	$23-$39	340
㉕ / p. 320		Square One Restaurant	◈◈◈	$15-$30	341
㉗ / p. 320		Abbondanza Italian Restaurant	◈◈	$9-$17	339
㉘ / p. 320		Banana Cafe	◈◈	$8-$22	340
㉚ / p. 320		Louie's Backyard	◈◈◈	$24-$32	341
㉛ / p. 320		Flagler's Steak House & Lounge	◈◈◈	$17-$38	340

Travel Back to Yesterday

Let AAA help you visit a bygone era of romance and elegance with the *AAA Guide to North American Bed & Breakfasts, Country Inns and Historical Lodgings*. This fascinating guide includes diamond ratings of more than 2,500 lodgings, with more than 1,500 illustrations and 100 full-color photos focusing on these tranquil accommodations. The guide also features maps illustrating scenic byways and listings of historical sites.

Bring a little of the past into the present. Purchase a copy of the *AAA Guide to North American Bed & Breakfasts, Country Inns and Historical Lodgings* at your local AAA office today.

KEY WEST pop. 24,800 (See map p. 320; index p. 321)

———— WHERE TO STAY ————

ALEXANDER PALMS COURT
Phone: 305/296-6413 52

(AAA) (SAVE)
(diamonds)

Motel

12/18-1/2	1P: $150-$265	2P: $150-$265	XP: $10	F12
1/3-4/30	1P: $110-$210	2P: $110-$210	XP: $10	F12
5/1-11/30	1P: $90-$160	2P: $90-$160	XP: $10	F12
12/1-12/17	1P: $80-$145	2P: $80-$145	XP: $10	F12

Location: Just 2 n of Duval St. 715 South St 33040. Fax: 305/292-3975. **Facility:** Variety of accommodations in tropical courtyard setting. Standard, studio and full 1- and 2-bedroom apartments available. 11 units. 3 efficiencies and 6 units with kitchen. *Bath:* combo or shower only. 1 story, exterior corridors. **Terms:** 14 day cancellation notice, pets ($25 extra charge). **Amenities:** extended cable TV, safes. **Leisure Activities:** heated pool, whirlpool. **Cards:** MC, VI.
Special Amenities: free continental breakfast and free local telephone calls.
SOME UNITS
(icons) / (icons) /

ANDREWS INN
Phone: (305)294-7730 45

(AAA) (SAVE)
(diamonds)

Bed & Breakfast

12/21-4/30	1P: $165-$185	2P: $165-$185
5/1-11/30	1P: $115-$135	2P: $115-$135
12/1-12/20	1P: $115-$125	2P: $115-$125

Location: Just s of Duval St between US 1 and Olivia St. 0 Whalton Lane 33040. Fax: 305/294-0021. **Facility:** Quiet location, tranquil pool setting. 6 units. 1-2 stories, exterior corridors. **Terms:** 14 day cancellation notice-fee imposed. **Amenities:** extended cable TV. **Leisure Activities:** small pool. *Fee:* bicycles. **Guest Services:**
[ECP] meal plan available. **Cards:** AE, DS, MC, VI. **Special Amenities: free continental breakfast and free local telephone calls.**
SOME UNITS
(icons) / (icons) /

BANANA BAY RESORT-KEY WEST
Phone: (305)296-6925 13

(diamonds)

Motel

12/22-4/28	1P: $150-$250	2P: $150-$250	XP: $15
4/29-11/30	1P: $95-$210	2P: $95-$210	XP: $15
12/1-12/21	1P: $95-$150	2P: $95-$150	XP: $15

Location: On US 1, 1 mi s of entrance to island. 2319 N Roosevelt Blvd 33040. Fax: 305/296-2004. **Facility:** Spacious rooms, all with ceiling fans. 48 units, 8 with efficiency. Some suites. 2 stories, interior corridors. **Terms:** age restrictions may apply, 7 day cancellation notice, weekly rates available, package plans. **Amenities:** extended cable TV, voice mail, irons, hair dryers. **Leisure Activities:** whirlpools, scuba diving, snorkeling, fishing, charter fishing, exercise room. *Fee:* boats, boat dock, scuba & snorkeling equipment. **Guest Services:** [ECP] meal plan available, gift shop, coin laundry. **Business Services:** meeting rooms. *Fee:* fax. **Cards:** AE, CB, DI, DS, MC, VI. *(See color ad p 331)*
SOME UNITS
(icons) / (icons) /

THE BANYAN RESORT
Phone: (305)296-7786 29

(AAA) (SAVE)
(diamonds)

Motel

12/21-4/30	1P: $200-$250	2P: $200-$350	XP: $20
12/1-12/20 & 5/1-11/30	1P: $150-$175	2P: $150-$275	XP: $20

Location: In Old Town; just s of Duval St. 323 Whitehead St 33040. Fax: 305/294-1107. **Facility:** Studios, lofts or suites all with contemporary decor in tranquil tropical garden featuring two banyan trees centuries old. 38 units with kitchen. 5 two-bedroom units. Some suites. *Bath:* combo or shower only. 2-3 stories (no elevator), interior/exterior corridors. **Parking:** extra charge. **Terms:** check-in 4 pm, 3 night minimum stay - weekends, age restrictions may apply, 14 day cancellation notice, weekly rates available. **Amenities:** extended cable TV, voice mail, safes, irons. **Dining:** tiki bar, barbecue areas. **Leisure Activities:** 2 pools (1 heated), whirlpool. *Fee:* bicycles. **Guest Services:** coin laundry. *Fee:* fax. **Cards:** AE, CB, DI, DS, MC. *(See color ad below)*
SOME UNITS
(icons) / (VCR) /

BEST WESTERN HIBISCUS MOTEL
Phone: (305)294-3763 51

(AAA) (SAVE)
(diamonds)

Motel

12/22-4/15	1P: $149-$279	2P: $149-$279
4/16-5/31	1P: $119-$169	2P: $119-$169
12/1-12/21 & 6/1-11/30	1P: $99-$159	2P: $99-$159

Location: In Old Town; corner United and Simonton sts. 1313 Simonton St 33040-0552. Fax: 305/293-9243. **Facility:** Large units with light wood tones. Relaxing pool area. Close to the beach. 61 units, 5 with efficiency. *Bath:* combo or shower only. 2 stories, exterior corridors. **Terms:** 3 day cancellation notice. **Amenities:** extended cable TV, safes. **Leisure Activities:** heated pool, whirlpool. **Guest Services:** coin laundry. **Cards:** AE, CB, DI, JC, VI.
Special Amenities: free continental breakfast. *(See color ad p 325)*
(icons)

(See map p. 320)

BEST WESTERN KEY AMBASSADOR RESORT INN

				Phone: (305)296-3500	**15**
	12/22-3/31	1P: $139-$229	2P: $139-$229	XP: $15	F12
	4/1-11/30	1P: $89-$229	2P: $89-$229	XP: $10	F12
	12/1-12/21	1P: $89-$139	2P: $89-$139	XP: $10	F12

Motel

Location: In New Town; on SR A1A, 1 mi s of jct US 1. 3755 S Roosevelt Blvd 33040. **Fax:** 305/296-9961. **Facility:** Spacious units with contemporary decor. All with private screened porch or balcony. 100 units. 2 stories, exterior corridors. **Terms:** 3 day cancellation notice. **Amenities:** extended cable TV, hair dryers. **Dining:** tiki bar. **Leisure Activities:** heated pool, shuffleboard, barbecue/picnic area, outdoor fitness center. **Guest Services:** [ECP] meal plan available, coin laundry. **Cards:** AE, CB, DI, DS, MC, VI. **Special Amenities:** free continental breakfast and free newspaper. *(See color ad p 326)*

(See map p. 320)

BLUE MARLIN RESORT MOTEL

AAA **SAVE**

Phone: (305)294-2585 55

12/22-4/15	1P: $159-$299	2P: $159-$299
4/16-5/31	1P: $119-$159	2P: $119-$159
12/1-12/21 & 6/1-11/30	1P: $99-$159	2P: $99-$159

Motel

Location: In Old Town; just s of US 1 (Truman Ave). 1320 Simonton St 33040. **Fax:** 305/296-1209. **Facility:** Large rooms with light wood tones. Soft color decor. Close to the beach. 53 units, 10 with efficiency. 2 stories, exterior corridors. **Amenities:** extended cable TV. **Leisure Activities:** heated pool. **Guest Services:** coin laundry. **Cards:** AE, DI, DS, MC, VI. **Special Amenities: free continental breakfast.** *(See color ad p 325)*

BLUE PARROT INN

Phone: (305)296-0033 38

Property failed to provide current rates

Bed & Breakfast

Location: In Old Town; just nw of jct Elizabeth St and US 1, Truman Ave. 916 Elizabeth St 33040. **Fax:** 305/296-5697. **Facility:** Bahamian style residence built in 1884, offers a variety of room decor and sizes in the main house and garden cottage building. Relaxed easy going ambience centered around the tropically landscaped pool. 10 units. *Bath:* combo or shower only. 1-2 stories, interior/exterior corridors. **Parking:** street only. **Terms:** age restrictions may apply, 14 day cancellation notice-fee imposed. **Amenities:** extended cable TV. **Leisure Activities:** heated pool. *Fee:* bicycles. **Guest Services:** [ECP] meal plan available. **Cards:** AE, CB, DI, DS, MC, VI.

SOME UNITS

BLUE SKIES INN

AAA **SAVE**

Phone: (305)295-9464 60

12/1-3/31	1P: $155-$195	2P: $155-$195	XP: $20	F5
4/1-4/30	1P: $135-$175	2P: $135-$175	XP: $20	F5
5/1-5/31	1P: $105-$145	2P: $105-$145	XP: $20	F5
6/1-11/30	1P: $75-$125	2P: $75-$125	XP: $20	F5

Historic Bed & Breakfast

Location: From Truman Ave e on Duval St, turn left onto South St, just a few blks. 630 South St 33040. **Fax:** 305/294-9110. **Facility:** Spacious rooms decorated with primarily soft color tones with accented bright colors. A wood deck area around the whirlpool, surrounded by tropical trees. 5 units. *Bath:* combo or shower only. 2 stories, exterior corridors. **Parking:** street only. **Terms:** cancellation fee imposed. **Amenities:** extended cable TV. **Dining:** 2 restaurants. **Leisure Activities:** whirlpool. **Guest Services:** [CP] meal plan available. **Cards:** AE, DS, MC, VI. **Special Amenities: early check-in/late check-out and free local telephone calls.**

SOME UNITS

(See map p. 320)

CENTER COURT HISTORIC INN & COTTAGES

Phone: 305/296-9292 47

(AAA) (SAVE)

12/1-4/30　　　　　　　　　　2P: $88-$388　　　　XP: $15
5/1-11/30　　　　　　　　　　2P: $88-$288　　　　XP: $15

Bed & Breakfast

Location: In Old Town; 0.5 mi n of jct US 1, between Duval and Simonton sts. 915 Center St 33040. Fax: 305/294-4104. **Facility:** Quietly located in private compound around a lovely pool courtyard. Individually furnished rooms in historic home and large cottages. Designated smoking area. 6 units. 2 two-bedroom units, 1 efficiency and 2 units with kitchen. *Bath:* combo or shower only. 1-2 stories, interior/exterior corridors. **Parking:** street only. **Terms:** age restrictions may apply, 14 day cancellation notice-fee imposed, weekly rates available, pets ($10 extra charge). **Amenities:** extended cable TV, safes, irons, hair dryers. **Leisure Activities:** small heated pool, whirlpool, sun deck, exercise equipment. **Guest Services:** [ECP] meal plan available, valet laundry. **Cards:** AE, DS, MC, VI. **Special Amenities: free local telephone calls and free room upgrade (subject to availability with advanced reservations).**

SOME UNITS

🅂🄳 🐕 🍽 🏊 ✕ 🖨 / 📼 📷 🛄 /

CHELSEA HOUSE

Phone: (305)296-2211 39

(AAA) (SAVE)

12/20-4/15　　　　　　　　　　2P: $135-$225　　　　XP: $20
12/1-12/19 & 4/16-5/31　　　　2P: $109-$189　　　　XP: $20
6/1-11/30　　　　　　　　　　2P: $79-$135　　　　XP: $15

Historic Bed & Breakfast

Location: At the corner of Elizabeth St and Truman Ave. 707 Truman Ave 33040. Fax: 305/296-4822. **Facility:** Two Victorian style homes built in 1870. Attractive grounds. Smoke free premises. 21 units, 2 with kitchen. *Bath:* combo or shower only. 2 stories. **Terms:** age restrictions may apply, 14 day cancellation notice-fee imposed, weekly rates available, package plans, small pets only ($10 extra charge). **Amenities:** extended cable TV, safes. **Leisure Activities:** heated pool. **Guest Services:** [ECP] meal plan available. **Cards:** AE, CB, DI, DS, MC, VI.

(See color ad below)

SOME UNITS

➕ 🐕 🍽 🏊 ✕ 🖨 🛄 / 💻 📷 /
FEE

COCONUT MALLORY RESORT & MARINA

Phone: (305)292-0017 10

♦♦♦

12/16-4/15　　　1P: $250　　　2P: $300
4/16-5/31　　　 1P: $200　　　2P: $250
6/1-11/30　　　 1P: $150　　　2P: $200
12/1-12/15　　　1P: $150　　　2P: $175

Apartment

Location: On A1A, 0.3 mi s at Flagler and Roosevelt Blvd. 1445 S Roosevelt Blvd 33040. Fax: 305/292-5698. **Facility:** Spacious 1- and 2-bedroom apartment-type units overlooking the mangroves or the water. Decorated with light-wood tones. 34 units with kitchen. 4 two-bedroom units. 3 stories, exterior corridors. **Terms:** check-in 4 pm, 3 day cancellation notice-fee imposed. **Amenities:** extended cable TV, voice mail, safes. **Leisure Activities:** 2 pools, whirlpool, fishing. **Guest Services:** coin laundry. **Cards:** AE, DS, MC, VI.

SOME UNITS

🏊 📷 🛄 / ✕ /

(See map p. 320)

THE COLONY EXCLUSIVE COTTAGES

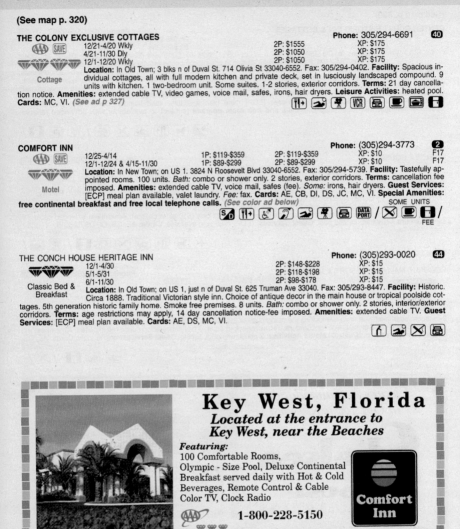

Phone: 305/294-6691 **40**

12/21-4/20 Wkly	2P: $1555	XP: $175
4/21-11/30 Dly	2P: $1050	XP: $175
12/1-12/20 Wkly	2P: $1050	XP: $175

Cottage

Location: In Old Town; 3 blks n of Duval St. 714 Olivia St 33040-6552. Fax: 305/294-0402. **Facility:** Spacious individual cottages, all with full modern kitchen and private deck, set in lusciously landscaped compound. 9 units with kitchen. 1 two-bedroom unit. Some suites. 1-2 stories, exterior corridors. **Terms:** 21 day cancellation notice. **Amenities:** extended cable TV, video games, voice mail, safes, irons, hair dryers. **Leisure Activities:** heated pool. **Cards:** MC, VI. *(See ad p 327)*

COMFORT INN

Phone: (305)294-3773 **2**

12/25-4/14	1P: $119-$359	2P: $119-$359	XP: $10 F17
12/1-12/24 & 4/15-11/30	1P: $89-$299	2P: $89-$299	XP: $10 F17

Motel

Location: In New Town; on US 1. 3824 N Roosevelt Blvd 33040-6552. Fax: 305/294-5739. **Facility:** Tastefully appointed rooms. 100 units. *Bath:* combo or shower only. 2 stories, exterior corridors. **Terms:** cancellation fee imposed. **Amenities:** extended cable TV, voice mail, safes (fee). *Some:* irons, hair dryers. **Guest Services:** [ECP] meal plan available, valet laundry. **Fee:** fax. **Cards:** AE, CB, DI, DS, JC, MC, VI. **Special Amenities:** free continental breakfast and free local telephone calls. *(See color ad below)*

SOME UNITS / FEE

THE CONCH HOUSE HERITAGE INN

Phone: (305)293-0020 **44**

12/1-4/30	2P: $148-$228	XP: $15
5/1-5/31	2P: $118-$198	XP: $15
6/1-11/30	2P: $98-$178	XP: $15

Classic Bed & Breakfast

Location: In Old Town; on US 1, just n of Duval St. 625 Truman Ave 33040. Fax: 305/293-8447. **Facility:** Historic. Circa 1888. Traditional Victorian style inn. Choice of antique decor in the main house or tropical poolside cottages. 5th generation historic family home. Smoke free premises. 8 units. *Bath:* combo or shower only. 2 stories, interior/exterior corridors. **Terms:** age restrictions may apply, 14 day cancellation notice-fee imposed. **Amenities:** extended cable TV. **Guest Services:** [ECP] meal plan available. **Cards:** AE, DS, MC, VI.

(See map p. 320)

COURTNEY'S PLACE HISTORIC GUEST COTTAGES AND INN   Phone: (305)294-3480   [36]

| | 12/21-4/30 | 1P: $119-$199 | 2P: $119-$199 | XP: $20 | F12 |
| | 12/1-12/20 & 5/1-11/30 | 1P: $79-$149 | 2P: $79-$149 | XP: $20 | F12 |

Historic Cottage

Location: In Old Town; just e from jct Petronia and Simonton sts. 720 Whitmarsh Ln 33040-6552. Fax: 305/294-7019. **Facility:** Located in the historic district. Office closed from 6 pm; units vary from compact to spacious. Many units with walls of Dade County Pine. Rooms with a contemporary style decor. All are surrounded by lush tropical vegatation. 16 units. 5 two-bedroom units, 1 three-bedroom unit, 2 efficiencies and 6 units with kitchen. Some suites. *Bath:* combo or shower only. 2 stories, exterior corridors. **Terms:** 21 day cancellation notice-fee imposed, weekly rates available, 4% service charge, pets (pets on premises). **Amenities:** extended cable TV. **Leisure Activities:** small pool. **Guest Services:** valet laundry. **Cards:** AE, DS, MC, VI. **Special Amenities: free continental breakfast and free local telephone calls.**

SOME UNITS

THE COURTYARD   Phone: (305)296-1148   [53]

	12/1-4/18	2P: $99-$355	XP: $20
	4/19-5/31 & 10/18-11/30	2P: $99-$225	XP: $20
Historic Cottage	6/1-10/17	2P: $79-$190	XP: $20

Location: Just w of US 1 (Truman Blvd). 910 Simonton St 33040. Fax: 305/292-7924. **Facility:** Charming ambience, a small attractive courtyard that gives you a secluded feeling. 6 units. 1 two-bedroom unit, 1 three-bedroom unit, 1 efficiency and 4 units with kitchen. *Bath:* combo or shower only. 1 story, exterior corridors. **Parking:** street only. **Terms:** 2 night minimum stay - weekends, 10 day cancellation notice. **Amenities:** extended cable TV. **Cards:** AE, CB, DI, DS, MC, VI.

SOME UNITS

COURTYARD BY MARRIOTT   Phone: 305/294-5541   [4]

	3/11-4/22	1P: $189-$229	2P: $189-$229	XP: $10	F14
	12/1-3/10	1P: $169-$199	2P: $169-$199	XP: $10	F14
	4/23-7/4	1P: $139-$169	2P: $139-$169	XP: $10	F14
Motel	7/5-11/30	1P: $129-$169	2P: $129-$169	XP: $10	F14

Location: In New Town; on US 1. 3420 N Roosevelt Blvd 33040. Fax: 305/294-7932. **Facility:** Located across from the gulf. Enter the large lobby to a Southern staircase, a large sitting area, area rugs and wood floors. Behind the lobby is a one acre pool with tropical plants and fountains. The rooms are decorated with warm colors and very good furniture. 104 units. Some suites ($179-$299). *Bath:* combo or shower only. 2 stories, interior/exterior corridors. **Dining:** tiki bar, cocktails. **Leisure Activities:** heated pool, whirlpool, exercise equipment. **Guest Services:** valet and coin laundry. **Cards:** AE, CB, DI, DS, MC, VI. **Special Amenities: free newspaper.** (See color ad below)

SOME UNITS
FEE

(See map p. 320)

THE CUBAN CLUB SUITES
Phone: (305)296-0465 [50]

AAA SAVE	12/21-4/15 & 10/22-11/30	2P: $249-$599 XP: $25 F16
▼▼▼	4/16-10/21	2P: $199-$499 XP: $25 F16
Apartment	12/1-12/20	2P: $149-$249 XP: $25 F16

Location: In Old Town; corner of Duval and Amelia sts; registration at La Casa de Luces on Amelia St. 1108 Duval St 33040. Fax: 305/293-7669. **Facility:** Spacious individually decorated suites, some with loft bedrooms, few have wraparound porches with rocking chairs. Bright and airy, each unit is finely equipped and on the 2nd floor of a restored 1900s building. 8 units with kitchen. 4 two-bedroom units. 2 stories, interior corridors. **Terms:** 21 day cancellation notice-fee imposed, small pets only ($200 cash deposit). **Amenities:** extended cable TV. **Leisure Activities:** Fee: beach & pool privileges. **Guest Services:** complimentary laundry. **Cards:** AE, MC, VI. SOME UNITS

CURRY MANSION INN
Phone: (305)294-5349 [23]

▼▼▼	1/16-4/15	2P: $180-$325 XP: $50 F21
	12/1-1/15 & 4/16-6/15	2P: $150-$250 XP: $50 F21
Historic Bed & Breakfast	6/16-11/30	2P: $130-$220 XP: $50 F21

Location: In Old Town; just n of jct Duval St. 511 Caroline St 33040-6552. Fax: 305/294-4093. **Facility:** Tall trees surround this historic mansion, built in the late 1800s with a relaxing pool area behind the main house. Many of the rooms have period antiques; others have wicker and tropical colors. Smoke free premises. 28 units. Some whirlpool units ($200-$220). **Bath:** combo or shower only. 2 stories, interior/exterior corridors. **Terms:** 15 day cancellation notice-fee imposed, weekly rates available, small pets only. **Amenities:** extended cable TV. **Leisure Activities:** heated pool, whirlpools. **Guest Services:** [BP] meal plan available, complimentary evening beverages, valet laundry. **Business Services:** meeting rooms. **Cards:** AE, CB, DI, DS, MC, VI.

CYPRESS HOUSE BED & BREAKFAST
Phone: (305)294-6969 [37]

AAA SAVE	12/21-4/30	1P: $140-$350	2P: $140-$350 XP: $20
	5/1-11/30	1P: $109-$248	2P: $109-$248 XP: $20
▼▼▼	12/1-12/20	1P: $99-$228	2P: $99-$228 XP: $20
Historic Bed & Breakfast			

Location: At corner of Caroline and Simonton sts. 601 Caroline St 33040. Fax: 305/296-1174. **Facility:** A Bahamian style house circa 1888. Spacious rooms decorated with some period antiques. A soothing pool area. 15 units. 1 two-bedroom unit and 1 efficiency. Some suites. **Bath:** some shower only. 3 stories (no elevator), interior/exterior corridors. **Terms:** 14 day cancellation notice-fee imposed. **Amenities:** extended cable TV, voice mail. **Leisure Activities:** small heated pool, bicycles. **Guest Services:** [ECP] meal plan available, complimentary evening beverages. **Cards:** AE, DS, MC, VI. **Special Amenities:** free continental breakfast and free newspaper. SOME UNITS

DAYS INN-KEY WEST
Phone: (305)294-3742 [7]

SAVE	All Year	1P: $69-$150	2P: $69-$150
▼▼▼ Motel			

Location: Just e of jct US 1 and SR A1A. 3852 N Roosevelt Blvd 33040. Fax: 305/296-7260. **Facility:** Newly renovated. Nicely landscaped grounds with tropical foliage. A relaxing pool area. Rooms are brightly decorated with light wood tone furniture. 133 units, 18 with kitchen. Some suites ($125-$195). **Bath:** combo or shower only. 2 stories, exterior corridors. **Terms:** cancellation fee imposed. **Amenities:** extended cable TV, dual phone lines, voice mail, safes, hair dryers. **Leisure Activities:** heated pool. **Guest Services:** [CP] meal plan available, coin laundry. **Cards:** AE, CB, DI, DS, MC, VI. SOME UNITS FEE

DUVAL HOUSE
Phone: (305)294-1666 [46]

▼▼▼	12/25-4/30	1P: $180-$335	2P: $180-$335
	5/1-11/30	1P: $140-$250	2P: $140-$250
Historic Bed & Breakfast	12/1-12/24	1P: $120-$235	2P: $120-$235

Location: In Center of Old Town; just n of jct Truman and Duval sts. 815 Duval St 33040. Fax: 305/292-1701. **Facility:** Compact to more spacious rooms all elegantly appointed in a restored 1885 Conch house compound. 28 units. 1 two-bedroom unit and 3 efficiencies. **Bath:** combo or shower only. 2 stories, exterior corridors. **Terms:** age restrictions may apply, 7 day cancellation notice, weekly rates available. **Amenities:** extended cable TV, voice mail, hair dryers. **Cards:** AE, DI, DS, JC, MC, VI. *(See color ad p 331)* SOME UNITS

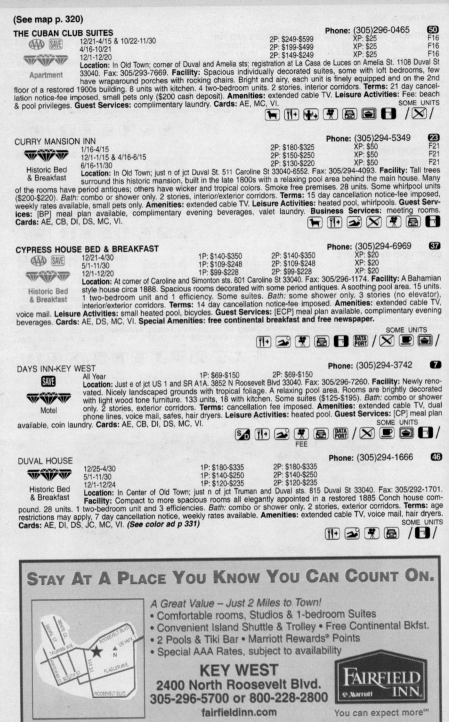

(See map p. 320)

FAIRFIELD INN BY MARRIOTT
Phone: (305)296-5700 **14**

12/1-4/30	1P: $90-$120
5/1-11/30	1P: $70-$100

Motel
Location: On US 1, 1 mi s of entrance to island. 2400 N Roosevelt Blvd 33040. Fax: 305/292-9840. **Facility:** Modern furnishings. 132 units. 2 two-bedroom units. Some suites. *Bath:* combo or shower only. 2 stories, exterior corridors. **Amenities:** extended cable TV, video games, irons. **Leisure Activities:** 2 heated pools. **Guest Services:** [ECP] meal plan available, coin laundry. *Fee:* fax. **Cards:** AE, DI, DS, MC, VI. *(See color ad p 330)*

SOME UNITS
[icons] FEE

FRANCES ST BOTTLE INN
Phone: (305)294-8530 **34**

12/16-4/30	1P: $135-$165	2P: $135-$165	XP: $15 F12
12/1-12/15 & 5/1-11/30	1P: $80-$135	2P: $80-$135	XP: $15 F12

Historic Bed & Breakfast
Location: From US 1/Roosevelt Blvd, right onto White St, then left onto Southard St at corner of Frances and Southard sts. 535 Frances St 33040. Fax: 305/294-1628. **Facility:** A Conch style house built in 1875. Relaxing and tastefully decorated rooms. Quiet location. A tropical canopy over the courtyard of palms and the sky. A relaxing hot tub in the middle. A soothing setting. Designated smoking area. 8 units. *Bath:* combo or shower only. 2 stories, interior corridors. **Parking:** street only. **Terms:** 14 day cancellation notice-fee imposed, weekly rates available, small pets only. **Amenities:** extended cable TV. **Leisure Activities:** hot tub. **Cards:** AE, MC, VI. **Special Amenities: free continental breakfast and free local telephone calls.**

SOME UNITS
[icons]

HAMPTON INN
Phone: (305)294-2917 **12**

2/16-4/14	1P: $159-$204	2P: $169-$214
12/24-2/15	1P: $129-$209	2P: $139-$209
4/15-11/30	1P: $89-$149	2P: $94-$159
12/1-12/23	1P: $84-$114	2P: $89-$119

Motel
Location: In New Town; on US 1, 1.5 mi w of jct SR A1A on the gulf side. 2801 N Roosevelt Blvd 33040. Fax: 305/296-0221. **Facility:** Back from highway on spacious grounds. 159 units. Some whirlpool units. *Bath:* combo or shower only. 2 stories, exterior corridors. **Terms:** cancellation fee imposed. **Amenities:** voice mail, safes, irons, hair dryers. **Dining:** tiki bar, noon-11 pm. **Leisure Activities:** heated pool, whirlpool. *Fee:* jet skiing, parasailing, bicycles. **Guest Services:** [ECP] meal plan available, gift shop, coin laundry. **Business Services:** meeting rooms, fax. **Cards:** AE, CB, DI, DS, MC, VI. **Special Amenities: early check-in/late check-out and free continental breakfast.** *(See color ad p 332)*

SOME UNITS
[icons]

HERON HOUSE
Phone: (305)294-9227 **26**

12/20-4/30	1P: $189-$209	2P: $189-$209
12/1-12/19 & 5/1-5/31	1P: $139-$149	2P: $139-$149
6/1-11/30	1P: $129-$149	2P: $129-$149

Classic Bed & Breakfast
Location: From Truman Ave, w on Simonton, near corner of Fleming St. 512 Simonton St 33040. Fax: 305/294-5692. **Facility:** Historic. 4 renovated conch houses dating from 1856 to 1993 surrounding a tropical setting with many varieties of on-site grown orchids and plants. Rooms furnished and decorated with luxurious, tropical, contemporary decor. 23 units. Some whirlpool units. *Bath:* combo or shower only. 2 stories, exterior corridors. **Parking:** street only. **Terms:** age restrictions may apply. **Amenities:** extended cable TV, voice mail, safes, irons, hair dryers. **Leisure Activities:** heated pool, sun deck. **Guest Services:** [ECP] meal plan available, complimentary evening beverages. **Cards:** AE, CB, DI, MC, VI. **Special Amenities: free continental breakfast and free newspaper.**

SOME UNITS
[icons]

(See map p. 320)

HILTON KEY WEST RESORT & MARINA　　　　　　　　　　　　　　　　　　　　**Phone:** (305)294-4000　〔28〕

AAA SAVE	12/19-4/28	1P: $295-$495	2P: $295-$495	XP: $20	F18
	4/29-5/28	1P: $225-$375	2P: $225-$375	XP: $20	F18
	5/29-11/30	1P: $199-$329	2P: $199-$329	XP: $20	F18
Resort	12/1-12/18	1P: $185-$325	2P: $185-$325	XP: $20	F18

Location: In Old Town; adjacent to Mallory Square. 245 Front St 33040. Fax: 305/294-4086. **Facility:** Very attractive; built in Key West/Caribbean style. Large, very comfortable rooms, many with balcony. Sunset key cottages on an island. A walk over bridge connects to Mallory Square. 215 units. 43 two-bedroom units, 10 three-bedroom units and 37 units with kitchen. Some suites ($295-$895) and whirlpool units ($345-$895). *Bath:* combo or shower only. 3-4 stories, interior/exterior corridors. **Parking:** extra charge or valet. **Terms:** check-in 4 pm, 3 day cancellation notice-fee imposed, package plans. **Amenities:** extended cable TV, dual phone lines, voice mail, safes, honor bars, irons, hair dryers. *Some:* CD players. **Dining:** 2 restaurants, 7 am-11 pm, $6-$26, cocktails, entertainment. **Leisure Activities:** 2 heated pools, whirlpools, beach, swimming, scuba & snorkeling equipment, charter fishing, launch shuttle to island beach, children's program, exercise room, casino cruises. *Fee:* boating, marina, scuba diving, snorkeling, jet ski, parasailing, waverunners. **Guest Services:** gift shop, valet laundry. *Fee:* massage. **Business Services:** conference facilities, administrative services, PC, fax. **Cards:** AE, CB, DI, DS, JC, MC, VI. **Special Amenities:** free newspaper. *(See ad p 44)*

SOME UNITS

🍴 🍷 ⓩ 🐕 🏊 ✕ 📹 🖨 💻 📠 / ✕ VCR 📶 🔒

FEE

(See map p. 320)

HOLIDAY INN-BEACHSIDE KEY WEST

	Phone: (305)294-2571		3
1/3-4/22	2P: $149-$255	XP: $10	F19
12/1-1/2	2P: $99-$255	XP: $10	F19
Motor Inn 4/23-11/30	2P: $99-$175	XP: $10	F19

Location: On entering island, jct US 1 and SR A1A. 3841 N Roosevelt Blvd 33040-6552. Fax: 305/292-7252. **Facility:** Gulf side. Sandy sunbathing beach. Some waterfront rooms or suites with balcony. An attractive pool area. 222 units. Some suites ($145-$255). *Bath:* combo or shower only. 2-4 stories, exterior corridors. **Terms:** 3 day cancellation notice, package plans. **Amenities:** voice mail, irons, hair dryers. *Some:* safes (fee). **Leisure Activities:** whirlpool, 2 lighted tennis courts. *Fee:* paddleboats, scuba diving/snorkeling & equipment. **Guest Services:** [BP] meal plan available, gift shop, valet and coin laundry. **Business Services:** meeting rooms. **Cards:** AE, CB, DI, DS, JC, MC, VI. *(See color ad p 332)*

SOME UNITS
(ASK) (S/D) (YI) (Y) (⟨) (⌂) (♒) (✕) (📷) (🖥) (💻) (DATA PORT) / (✕) (♨) /
                         FEE   FEE

HOLIDAY INN LA CONCHA HOTEL

| | Phone: (305)296-2991 | | 30 |
| All Year | 1P: $189-$600   2P: $189-$600 | XP: $15 | F17 |

Location: In Center Old Town; corner Duval and Fleming sts. 430 Duval St 33040. Fax: 305/294-3283. **Facility:** Restored Old Town Key West Landmark. Some compact rooms, 1920s decor. Impressive view from The Top Lounge. 160 units. Some suites. 4-7 stories, interior corridors. **Parking:** extra charge. **Terms:** check-in 4 pm, 3 day cancellation notice, package plans. **Amenities:** extended cable TV, video games, irons, hair dryers. **Leisure Activities:** spa pool. *Fee:* bicycles. **Guest Services:** [AP] meal plan available, gift shop, valet laundry. **Business Services:** meeting rooms. *Fee:* fax. **Cards:** AE, CB, DI, DS, JC, MC, VI.

SOME UNITS
(ASK) (S/D) (YI) (Y) (⌂) (♒) (📷) (🖥) (💻) (DATA PORT) / (✕) (💻) (♨) /
                    FEE

HYATT KEY WEST

	Phone: (305)296-9900		18
12/1-4/15	1P: $355 2P: $400	XP: $45	F18
4/16-8/31	1P: $270 2P: $315	XP: $45	F18
9/1-11/30	1P: $230 2P: $275	XP: $45	F18

Location: In Old Town; Simonton and Front sts, just n of Mallory Square. 601 Front St 33040. Fax: 305/292-1038. **Facility:** Located on the waterfront. The pool in the middle, the gulf in back and the city all around. Spacious rooms with a tropical flair. All rooms with a balcony. 120 units. Some whirlpool units. *Bath:* combo or shower only. 5 stories, exterior corridors. **Parking:** extra charge or valet. **Terms:** check-in 4 pm, 14 day cancellation notice-fee imposed, package plans. **Amenities:** voice mail, safes, honor bars, irons, hair dryers. *Some:* CD players. **Dining:** poolside bar & grill, cocktails, also, Nicola Seafood, see separate listing. **Leisure Activities:** heated pool, whirlpool, beach, swimming, exercise room. *Fee:* boating, boat dock, scuba diving/snorkeling & equipment, scuba & sunset cruises, snorkeling & scuba instruction, waverunners; parasailing; charter sailing, bicycles. **Guest Services:** gift shop, valet laundry. *Fee:* massage. **Business Services:** meeting rooms. **Cards:** AE, CB, DI, DS, JC, MC, VI. *(See ad below)*

SOME UNITS
(YI) (Y) (⌂) (⟨) (♒) (✕) (📷) (💻) (DATA PORT) / (✕) (VCR) /
     FEE   FEE   FEE

ISLAND CITY HOUSE HOTEL

	Phone: (305)294-5702		22
12/21-5/31	2P: $175-$240	XP: $20	F12
12/1-12/20	2P: $115-$175		
Historic Bed 6/1-11/30	2P: $115-$175	XP: $20	F12

& Breakfast **Location:** In Old Town; just e of Duval St. 411 William St 33040. Fax: 305/294-1289. **Facility:** 2 Victorian homes built circa 1880. The third building is a replica of the Alfonso Cigar Factory. Spacious, colorful rooms decorated with some period antiques. There is a large tropical courtyard with a pool. A very peaceful setting. Designated smoking area. 24 units with kitchen. 4 two-bedroom units. Some suites. 2-3 stories (no elevator), interior/exterior corridors. **Parking:** street only. **Terms:** 14 day cancellation notice-fee imposed, weekly & monthly rates available. **Amenities:** extended cable TV, voice mail, hair dryers. *Some:* irons. **Leisure Activities:** heated pool, whirlpool. *Fee:* bicycles. **Guest Services:** [CP] meal plan available. **Cards:** AE, CB, DI, DS, MC, VI.

SOME UNITS
(♒) (✕) (📷) (♨) / (VCR) (💻) /

(See map p. 320)

KEY LIME INN   Phone: (305)294-5229 **42**

AAA SAVE
▽▽▽
Historic Bed
& Breakfast

12/22-4/23   1P: $149-$235   2P: $149-$235
12/1-12/21 & 4/24-11/30 1P: $98-$159   2P: $98-$159
Location: On US 1, just n of Duval St. 725 Truman Ave 33040. Fax: 305/294-9623. **Facility:** A Bahamain style home and cottage like rooms, some pool side, with private outside sitting areas. Soothing colors both inside and outside. Designated smoking area. 37 units. *Bath:* shower only. 1-2 stories, exterior corridors. **Terms:** 7 day cancellation notice, package plans. **Amenities:** extended cable TV, safes. *Some:* irons, hair dryers. **Leisure Activities:** Fee: bicycles. **Guest Services:** [CP] meal plan available. **Cards:** AE, DS, MC, VI.
Special Amenities: free newspaper and free room upgrade (subject to availability with advanced reservations).
(See color ad below)

SOME UNITS
[🍽] [🏊] [✕] [🖨] [DATA PORT] / [VCR] [📺] [📶] /

KEY WEST VILLAS RESORT   Phone: (305)294-4427 **48**
                                                                   XP: $15   F8
▽▽▽
Motel

All Year   1P: $150-$175   2P: $150-$175
Location: Just w of Duval St, off Truman Ave. 921 Center St 33040. Fax: 305/292-9044. **Facility:** Attractive courtyard with local foliage. Large whirlpool in center of courtyard. Spacious units. 12 units with kitchen. 2 stories, exterior corridors. **Parking:** street only. **Terms:** 14 day cancellation notice-fee imposed, weekly & monthly rates available, package plans. **Amenities:** extended cable TV. **Leisure Activities:** whirlpool. Fee: bicycles. **Guest Services:** complimentary laundry. **Cards:** AE, DS, MC, VI.

[ASK] [S▽] [🍽] [📺] [VCR] [📺] [📶] [📶]

LA CASA DE LUCES   Phone: (305)296-3993 **49**

AAA SAVE
▽▽▽
Historic Bed
& Breakfast

12/21-4/15 & 10/22-11/30   2P: $149-$279   XP: $15   F16
4/16-10/21   2P: $99-$199   XP: $15   F16
12/1-12/20   2P: $89-$199   XP: $15   F16
Location: Truman Ave e on Duval St, then just s. 422 Amelia St 33040. Fax: 305/293-7669. **Facility:** Some small rooms. Attractive room decor. 8 units, 4 with efficiency. *Bath:* some shared or private, combo or shower only. 2 stories, exterior corridors. **Terms:** 21 day cancellation notice-fee imposed. **Amenities:** extended cable TV. **Leisure Activities:** whirlpool. **Guest Services:** [CP] meal plan available. **Cards:** AE, MC, VI.

SOME UNITS
[🍽] [📺] [🖨] / [📺] [📶] /

LA MER HOTEL & DEWEY HOUSE   Phone: (305)296-5611 **57**

▽▽▽
Classic Bed &
Breakfast

12/25-4/21   1P: $220-$330   2P: $220-$330   XP: $25
4/22-5/27   1P: $155-$240   2P: $155-$240   XP: $20
5/28-11/30   1P: $135-$205   2P: $135-$205   XP: $15
12/1-12/24   1P: $129-$200   2P: $129-$200   XP: $15
Location: In Old Town; South St below Simonton St. 504-506 South St 33040. Fax: 305/294-8272. **Facility:** Historic. Overlooking South Beach. Restored Conch clapboard house. Facilities and parking lot of adjacent South Beach. Spacious and attractively appointed rooms with balcony. 19 units, 6 with efficiency. Some whirlpool units. 2 stories, interior/exterior corridors. **Terms:** age restrictions may apply, weekly rates available. **Amenities:** extended cable TV, voice mail, safes, honor bars. **Leisure Activities:** whirlpool, beach, swimming, off-site pool privileges. **Guest Services:** [ECP] meal plan available, afternoon tea, valet laundry. **Cards:** AE, MC, VI. *(See color ad p 323)*

SOME UNITS
[🍽] [🖨] [📺] [DATA PORT] / [✕] [📶] [📶] /

LA PENSIONE   Phone: 305/292-9923 **41**

AAA SAVE
▽▽▽
Historic Bed
& Breakfast

12/22-3/31   1P: $168-$178   XP: $25
4/1-4/30   1P: $128   XP: $15
12/1-12/21   1P: $88-$98   XP: $15
5/1-11/30   1P: $88   XP: $15
Location: In Old Town; on US 1, just n of Duval St. 809 Truman Ave 33040. Fax: 305/296-6509. **Facility:** A classic revival circa 1891 home. Spacious and tastefully appointed rooms. 9 units. *Bath:* combo or shower only. 2 stories, interior/exterior corridors. **Terms:** age restrictions may apply, 7 day cancellation notice-fee imposed. **Amenities:** no TVs. **Guest Services:** [ECP] meal plan available. **Cards:** AE, CB, DI, DS, JC, MC, VI. **Special Amenities:** free continental breakfast and free local telephone calls.

[S▽] [🏊] [🖨]

(See map p. 320)

LIGHTBOURN INN

AAA SAVE

Historic Bed
& Breakfast

12/1-1/1		2P: $128-$258	XP: $25
1/2-4/15		2P: $158-$178	XP: $25
4/16-5/31		2P: $128-$148	XP: $25
6/1-11/30		2P: $98-$148	XP: $25

Phone: (305)296-5152 [32]

Location: US 1, just n of Duval St. 907 Truman Ave 33040. Fax: 305/294-9490. **Facility:** 1903 Victorian home built in Queen Anne style. Extensive public areas are furnished with antiques and artifacts of the owners extensive travels. Individually decorated rooms in the main home and poolside buildings. 10 units. *Bath:* shower only. 2 stories, interior/exterior corridors. **Terms:** age restrictions may apply, 14 day cancellation notice-fee imposed. **Amenities:** extended cable TV. **Leisure Activities:** heated pool. **Guest Services:** [BP] meal plan available. **Cards:** AE, CB, DI, DS, MC, VI. *(See color ad below)*

[icons]

THE MARQUESA HOTEL

Classic Hotel

12/20-4/15	1P: $265		2P: $405	XP: $25
5/29-11/30	1P: $260		2P: $345	XP: $25
4/16-5/28	1P: $240		2P: $345	XP: $25
12/1-12/19	1P: $220		2P: $320	XP: $25

Phone: (305)292-1919 [31]

Location: In Old Town; jct Simonton and Fleming sts. 600 Fleming St 33040. Fax: 305/294-2121. **Facility:** Historic. Restored 1884 historic house with elegant rooms and personalized service. Tropical pools set in a garden of abundant tropical plants and several varieties of orchids. 27 units. 1-3 stories (no elevator), interior/exterior corridors. **Parking:** valet. **Terms:** age restrictions may apply, 10 day cancellation notice. **Amenities:** extended cable TV, voice mail, safes, irons, hair dryers. **Dining:** Cafe Marquesa, see separate listing. **Leisure Activities:** 2 pools (1 heated). *Fee:* bicycles. **Guest Services:** valet laundry. **Cards:** AE, DI, MC, VI.

SOME UNITS

[icons] / [icon] /

OCEAN KEY, A NOBLE HOUSE RESORT

Hotel

All Year	1P: $199-$449	2P: $199-$449	XP: $25

Phone: (305)296-7701 [19]
F16

Location: In Old Town at Mallory Square. Zero Duval St 33040. Fax: 305/292-7685. **Facility:** Many with a balcony, some over look the Gulf and/or Mallory Square. Spacious suites, comfortable rooms, all decorated with a Key West and Caribbean flair. 100 units. 15 two-bedroom units and 40 units with kitchen. Some whirlpool units ($239-$539). *Bath:* combo or shower only. 4 stories, exterior corridors. **Parking:** extra charge. **Terms:** check-in 4 pm, 2 night minimum stay, 13 day cancellation notice. **Amenities:** voice mail, irons, hair dryers. **Leisure Activities:** heated pool, snorkeling equipment, fishing, charter fishing. **Guest Services:** gift shop, valet laundry. **Business Services:** meeting rooms. **Cards:** AE, CB, DI, DS, MC, VI.

SOME UNITS

[icons] / [icons] /

THE PALMS HOTEL

AAA SAVE

Historic Bed
& Breakfast

12/21-4/15	1P: $160-$185	2P: $160-$185	XP: $10
12/1-12/20 & 4/16-11/30	1P: $95-$105	2P: $95-$105	XP: $10

Phone: 305/294-3146 [24]
F18
F18

Location: Just w of Truman. 820 White St 33040. Fax: 305/294-8463. **Facility:** Variety of accommodations in the 1889 main house or around the tropical courtyard area. The room furnishings are white wicker. A relaxing pool area is surrounded by tropical plants, tiki bar is at the pool and deck area. 21 units. *Bath:* shower only. 2 stories, exterior corridors. **Parking:** street only. **Terms:** 7 day cancellation notice. **Amenities:** extended cable TV. **Dining:** tiki bar, wine/beer only. **Leisure Activities:** heated pool, exercise room, sun deck, pool table. *Fee:* bicycles. **Cards:** AE, DS, MC, VI. **Special Amenities:** free continental breakfast and preferred room (subject to availability with advanced reservations).

[icons]

(See map p. 320)

PEGASUS INTERNATIONAL HOTEL

Ⓐ SAVE
▽▽▽
Motel

Phone: (305)294-9323 35

12/24-3/31	2P: $129-$499	XP: $20	F10
4/1-11/30	2P: $139-$299	XP: $20	F10
12/1-12/23	2P: $109-$229	XP: $20	F10

Location: Corner of Duval and Southard sts. 501 Southard St 33040. Fax: 305/294-4741. **Facility:** Rooms with contemporary appeal; in busy town center. Some rooms compact. 25 units. *Bath:* shower only. 3 stories, interior/exterior corridors. **Terms:** 14 day cancellation notice-fee imposed, weekly & monthly rates available. **Amenities:** extended cable TV, irons, hair dryers. **Leisure Activities:** heated pool, whirlpool, sun deck. **Cards:** AE, CB, DI, DS, MC, VI. **Special Amenities:** early check-in/late check-out and free room upgrade (subject to availability with advanced reservations).

SOME UNITS

🅂🄳 📶⁺ 🏊 🐕 🗔 / 📼 📺 🛗

PIER HOUSE RESORT & CARIBBEAN SPA

Ⓐ SAVE
▽▽▽
Hotel

Phone: (305)296-4600 20

12/1-12/31 & 1/1-4/15	2P: $290	XP: $35	F17
4/16-11/30	2P: $200	XP: $35	F17

Location: In Old Town; on the gulf, at Mallory Square. One Duval St 33040. Fax: 305/296-7568. **Facility:** Located at the edge of the Gulf of Mexico. The courtyard has lush tropical foliage. The rooms have a Caribbean flair with soft wood tones, decorated with warm colors and accented bright colors. Many rooms with Gulf view. 142 units. 2 two-bedroom units. 2-4 stories, interior/exterior corridors. **Terms:** check-in 4 pm, 7 day cancellation notice-fee imposed, package plans. **Amenities:** extended cable TV, voice mail, honor bars, hair dryers. *Some:* CD players. **Dining:** dining room, 2 restaurants, 7:30 am-11 pm, $8-$30, cocktails, restaurant, see separate listing, entertainment. **Leisure Activities:** heated pool, whirlpools, beach, swimming. *Fee:* bicycles, motor scooters & full service spa and hair salon. **Guest Services:** valet laundry. *Fee:* massage. **Business Services:** meeting rooms. **Cards:** AE, CB, DI, DS, MC, VI. *(See color ad below)*

SOME UNITS

✈ 📶 📺 🐕 🗭 🏊 📼 📺 🛗 / ❌ 🛗

QUALITY INN RESORT

Ⓐ SAVE
▽▽▽
Motor Inn

Phone: 305/294-6681 8

12/1-1/1	2P: $119-$359		
1/2-3/31	2P: $139-$259		
4/1-4/27	2P: $139-$199	XP: $20	F18
4/28-11/30	2P: $109-$169	XP: $10	F18

Location: On entering island, jct US 1 and SR A1A. 3850 N Roosevelt Blvd 33040. Fax: 305/292-4190. **Facility:** Large rooms with attractive decor. 148 units, 10 with efficiency. *Bath:* combo or shower only. 2-3 stories, exterior corridors. **Terms:** cancellation fee imposed, package plans. **Amenities:** extended cable TV, video games, hair dryers. *Some:* irons. **Dining:** restaurant, 6 am-11 pm, Fri & Sat-midnight, $6-$20. **Leisure Activities:** Fee: bicycles. **Guest Services:** gift shop, coin laundry. **Business Services:** meeting rooms. **Cards:** AE, CB, DI, DS, JC, MC, VI. **Special Amenities:** free local telephone calls and free newspaper. *(See color ad p 328)*

SOME UNITS

📶 📺 🗭 🏊 🐕 🗗 📺 / ❌ 🛗 /
FEE

(See map p. 320)

RADISSON HOTEL KEY WEST   **Phone: (305)294-5511** ❶
(AAA) [SAVE]   12/25-4/14   1P: $169-$399   2P: $169-$399   XP: $10
▼▼▼▼   12/1-12/24 & 4/15-11/30   1P: $109-$399   2P: $109-$399   XP: $10
Motor Inn   **Location:** In New Town; on US 1. 3820 N Roosevelt Blvd 33040-6552. Fax: 305/296-1939. **Facility:** Well kept, modern rooms, some facing the gulf. 145 units. Some suites ($199-$500). *Bath:* combo or shower only. 6 stories, exterior corridors. Cancellation fee imposed. **Amenities:** extended cable TV, voice mail, safes (fee), irons, hair dryers. **Dining:** restaurant, 24 hours, pool bar, $6-$13. **Leisure Activities:** sun deck. **Guest Services:** coin laundry. **Cards:** AE, CB, DI, DS, JC, MC, VI. **Special Amenities:** early check-in/late check-out and free room upgrade (subject to availability with advanced reservations). *(See color ad p 336)*   SOME UNITS

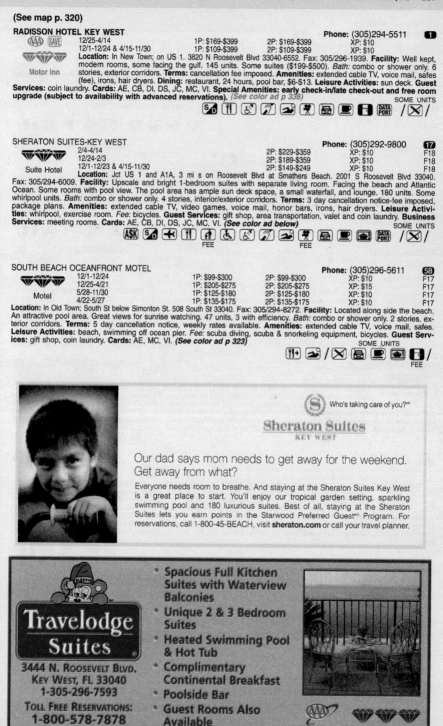

SHERATON SUITES-KEY WEST   **Phone: (305)292-9800** ⓱
▼▼▼   2/4-4/14   2P: $229-$359   XP: $10   F18
Suite Hotel   12/24-2/3   2P: $189-$359   XP: $10   F18
             12/1-12/23 & 4/15-11/30   2P: $149-$249   XP: $10   F18
Location: Jct US 1 and A1A, 3 mi s on Roosevelt Blvd at Smathers Beach. 2001 S Roosevelt Blvd 33040. Fax: 305/294-6009. **Facility:** Upscale and bright 1-bedroom suites with separate living room. Facing the beach and Atlantic Ocean. Some rooms with pool view. The pool area has ample sun deck space, a small waterfall, and lounge. 180 units. Some whirlpool units. *Bath:* combo or shower only. 4 stories, interior/exterior corridors. **Terms:** 3 day cancellation notice-fee imposed, package plans. **Amenities:** extended cable TV, video games, voice mail, honor bars, irons, hair dryers. **Leisure Activities:** whirlpool, exercise room. **Fee:** bicycles. **Guest Services:** gift shop, area transportation, valet and coin laundry. **Business Services:** meeting rooms. **Cards:** AE, CB, DI, DS, JC, MC, VI. *(See color ad below)*   SOME UNITS

SOUTH BEACH OCEANFRONT MOTEL   **Phone: (305)296-5611** ㊹
▼▼▼   12/1-12/24   1P: $99-$300   2P: $99-$300   XP: $10   F17
Motel   12/25-4/21   1P: $205-$275   2P: $205-$275   XP: $15   F17
             5/28-11/30   1P: $125-$180   2P: $125-$180   XP: $10   F17
             4/22-5/27   1P: $135-$175   2P: $135-$175   XP: $10   F17
Location: In Old Town; South St below Simonton St. 508 South St 33040. Fax: 305/294-8272. **Facility:** Located along side the beach. An attractive pool area. Great views for sunrise watching. 47 units, 3 with efficiency. *Bath:* combo or shower only. 2 stories, exterior corridors. **Terms:** 5 day cancellation notice, weekly rates available. **Amenities:** extended cable TV, voice mail, safes. **Leisure Activities:** beach, swimming off ocean pier. **Fee:** scuba diving, scuba & snorkeling equipment, bicycles. **Guest Services:** gift shop, coin laundry. **Cards:** AE, MC, VI. *(See color ad p 323)*   SOME UNITS

(See map p. 320)

SOUTHERNMOST MOTEL IN THE U.S.A.　　　　　　　　　　　　　**Phone: (305)296-6577**　54

(AAA) (SAVE)

▽▽▽▽

Motel

12/25-4/21	1P: $165-$240	2P: $165-$240	XP: $15　F17
4/22-5/27	1P: $115-$180	2P: $115-$180	XP: $10　F17
5/28-11/30	1P: $105-$160	2P: $105-$160	XP: $10　F17
12/1-12/24	1P: $95-$160	2P: $95-$160	XP: $10　F17

Location: In Old Town; jct Duval and United sts. 1319 Duval St 33040. Fax: 305/294-8272. **Facility:** Attractive pool areas, one with the tiki bar and a good sized tanning deck. Contemporary room decor with light color tones. 127 units, 1 with efficiency. 2-3 stories, exterior corridors. **Terms:** 5 day cancellation notice, weekly rates available, package plans. **Amenities:** extended cable TV, voice mail, safes. **Dining:** tiki bars. **Leisure Activities:** 2 heated pools, whirlpool. *Fee:* bicycles. **Guest Services:** gift shop, coin laundry. **Business Services:** meeting rooms. **Cards:** AE, MC, VI.
(See color ad p 323)

SOME UNITS

🆂🄳 🍴📶 🏊 📷 🖥️ / ✕ 🏧 💷 🖥️ 🛢️ /
FEE

TRAVELODGE & SUITES　　　　　　　　　　　　　　　　　　**Phone: (305)296-7593**　5

(AAA) (SAVE)

▽▽▽▽

Apartment

12/24-4/28	1P: $129-$189	2P: $129-$189
4/29-11/30	1P: $89-$169	2P: $89-$169
12/1-12/23	1P: $79-$129	2P: $79-$129

Location: On US 1 (New Town). 3444 N Roosevelt Blvd 33040. Fax: 305/294-5246. **Facility:** Some covered parking. Some rooms with balcony and view of the gulf. Suites with washer/dryer. 64 units. 3 two-bedroom units, 5 three-bedroom units and 32 units with kitchen. Some suites ($149-$529). 4 stories, exterior corridors. **Terms:** cancellation fee imposed, package plans. **Amenities:** extended cable TV, voice mail, irons. *Some:* safes. **Dining:** tiki pool bar. **Leisure Activities:** heated pool. **Guest Services:** [CP] meal plan available. **Business Services:** meeting rooms. *Fee:* fax. **Cards:** AE, DI, DS, JC, MC, VI. *(See color ad p 337)*

SOME UNITS

🆂🄳 🍴📶 🏊 📷 🖨️ 💷 🗃️ / ✕ 🏧 🛢️ /

WATSON HOUSE　　　　　　　　　　　　　　　　　　　　**Phone: (305)294-6712**　27

(AAA) (SAVE)

▽▽▽▽

Historic Bed & Breakfast

12/1-4/30	2P: $105-$500
10/23-11/1	2P: $160-$350
5/1-10/22	2P: $125-$290
11/2-11/30	2P: $105-$250

Location: In Old Town; just s of Mallory Square. 525 Simonton St 33040. Fax: 305/294-7501. **Facility:** In the historic district, Cabana style and 2nd floor suites. A soothing pool area. Designated smoking area. 3 units, 2 with kitchen. *Bath:* combo or shower only. 1-2 stories, exterior corridors. **Terms:** 2 night minimum stay, age restrictions may apply, 14 day cancellation notice-fee imposed. **Amenities:** extended cable TV, irons, hair dryers. **Leisure Activities:** heated pool, whirlpool. **Cards:** AE, MC, VI. **Special Amenities:** free continental breakfast and free local telephone calls.

SOME UNITS

🍴📶 🏊 📷 🖨️ 💷 🛢️ / ✕ 📼 🖥️ /

THE **WEATHERSTATION INN**　　　　　　　　　　　　　　　**Phone: (305)294-7277**　33

▽▽▽

Classic Bed & Breakfast

12/20-4/30	2P: $195-$315	XP: $15
12/1-12/19 & 5/1-11/30	2P: $150-$215	XP: $15

Location: From US 1/Truman Ave to Whitehead St turn right, then left onto Southard St into Truman Annex Complex. 57 Front St 33040. Fax: 305/294-0544. **Facility:** Historic. A large white two story structure with a stately look. The grounds have a variety of tropical trees and flowering plants. A secluded pool in back, a white picket fence surrounds the property. The 3rd floor offers great views. Smoke free premises. 8 units. *Bath:* shower only. 2 stories, interior corridors. **Terms:** age restrictions may apply, 15 day cancellation notice-fee imposed. **Amenities:** extended cable TV, voice mail. **Leisure Activities:** heated pool. **Guest Services:** [CP] meal plan available, valet laundry. **Cards:** AE, MC, VI.

🍴📶 🛗 🏊 ✕ 📼 🖨️ 📶

WESTWINDS　　　　　　　　　　　　　　　　　　　　　　**Phone: 305/296-4440**　21

(AAA) (SAVE)

▽▽▽▽▽

Bed & Breakfast

12/21-4/30	1P: $90-$250	2P: $90-$250	XP: $20
12/1-12/20 & 5/1-11/30	1P: $70-$200	2P: $70-$200	XP: $20

Location: In Old Town; just n of Duval St; near historic seaport. 914 Eaton St 33040. Fax: 305/293-0931. **Facility:** Units in cottage cluster. The pool area has a small, soothing waterfall. All this is surrounded with many tropical plants and trees. The rooms are furnished with white wicker accented with a soft tropical color scheme. 22 units. 1 efficiency and 1 unit with kitchen. Some suites ($200-$250). *Bath:* some combo or shower only. 1-2 stories, interior/exterior corridors. **Parking:** street only. **Terms:** age restrictions may apply, 14 day cancellation notice-fee imposed, weekly rates available. **Amenities:** *Some:* hair dryers. **Leisure Activities:** 2 pools (1 heated). **Guest Services:** coin laundry. **Business Services:** meeting rooms. **Cards:** AE, DS, MC, VI. **Special Amenities:** free continental breakfast.

SOME UNITS

🏊 🖨️ / 💷 🗃️ 🛢️ /

(See map p. 320)

WYNDHAM CASA MARINA RESORT & BEACH HOUSE Phone: (305)296-3535 [59]

AAA [SAVE]
▼▼▼ ◇◇

Historic Resort

12/1-4/29	1P: $164-$399
11/1-11/30	1P: $164-$299
4/30-7/4	1P: $159-$299
7/5-10/31	1P: $139-$299

Location: 4 mi s on Flagler (CR-5A) from jct SR A1A. 1500 Reynolds St 33040-6552. Fax: 305/296-4633. **Facility:** Historic hotel built in 1921 by Henry Flagler. Many rooms and suites with ocean view. Some with balcony or patio, some with attractive color schemes. 311 units. 5 two-bedroom units. Some suites. *Bath:* some combo or shower only. 3-4 stories, interior/exterior corridors. **Parking:** valet. **Terms:** check-in 4 pm, 3 day cancellation notice-fee imposed, 10% service charge. **Amenities:** extended cable TV, video games, voice mail, safes, honor bars, irons, hair dryers. **Dining:** Flagler's Steak House & Lounge, see separate listing, entertainment. **Leisure Activities:** 2 heated pools, sauna, whirlpool, beach, swimming, pier, wave runners, scuba lessons, 3 lighted tennis courts, children's program, exercise room. *Fee:* windsurfing, waterskiing, scuba diving/snorkeling & equipment, charter fishing, golf privileges, bicycles, catamaran, mopeds, parasailing. **Guest Services:** [MAP] meal plan available, gift shop, valet laundry. *Fee:* massage. **Business Services:** conference facilities, administrative services, fax. **Cards:** AE, CB, DI, DS, JC, MC, VI.

SOME UNITS

[icons: S/D ✈ ⊣⏐ ☂ ⚐ FEE ⊘ ⊘ ⊘ ⊘ ⊘ FEE ⊟ ▭ DATA PORT / ⊠ ▯ /]

WYNDHAM'S REACH RESORT Phone: (305)296-5000 [56]

▼▼▼ ◇

Hotel

12/1-12/31	1P: $139-$599	XP: $20	F18
1/1-4/29	1P: $239-$399	XP: $20	F18
4/30-11/30	1P: $139-$299	XP: $20	F18

Location: Just s of jct Truman Ave and Simonton St. 1435 Simonton St 33040. Fax: 305/296-2830. **Facility:** Stylish hotel with resort atmosphere. Sandy beach pier. Many rooms with ocean view. 150 units. Some suites. *Bath:* combo or shower only. 4-5 stories, exterior corridors. **Parking:** valet. **Terms:** check-in 4 pm, 3 day cancellation notice-fee imposed, package plans. **Amenities:** extended cable TV, video games, voice mail, safes, honor bars, irons, hair dryers. **Leisure Activities:** heated pool, sauna, whirlpool, beach, swimming, snorkeling, charter fishing, recreation program, exercise room. *Fee:* canoeing, paddleboats, sailboats, windsurfing, scuba diving, scuba & snorkeling equipment. **Guest Services:** [MAP] meal plan available, gift shop, valet laundry. *Fee:* massage. **Business Services:** meeting rooms. **Cards:** AE, CB, DI, DS, JC, MC, VI.

SOME UNITS

[icons: ASK S/D ✈ ⊣⏐ ☂ ⚐ FEE ⊘ ⊘ ⊘ ⊘ FEE ⊟ ▭ DATA PORT / ⊠ /]

──── *The following lodging was either not evaluated or did not* ────
meet AAA rating requirements but is listed for your information only.

GRAND KEY RESORT Phone: 305/293-1818

[fyi]

Resort

Location: Under construction, scheduled to open February 2000. **Location:** US 1 from Florida Tpke end in Florida City (Overseas Hwy). 3980 S Roosevelt Blvd 33040. Fax: 305/296-6962. **Planned Amenities:** 216 units, restaurant. *(See color ad below)*

──── **WHERE TO DINE** ────

ABBONDANZA ITALIAN RESTAURANT Dinner: $9-$17 Phone: 305/292-1199 [27]

▼▼▼ ◇

Italian

Location: At corner of Louise and Simonton sts. 1208 Simonton St 33040. **Hours:** 5 pm-11 pm. **Features:** casual dress; cocktails & lounge; street parking; a la carte. The name (Abbondanza) means lots of food—and that's what you get! A fresh and inviting ambience and decor. Well prepared entrees using local seafood. Also a variety of pasta and sauces. **Cards:** AE, MC, VI.

[⊠]

ALICE'S AT LA TE DA Dinner: $13-$28 Phone: 305/296-6706 [20]

▼▼▼▼

Regional American

Location: In the historic La Te Da Guest House, at the corner of Duval and Catherine sts. 1125 Duval St 33040. **Hours:** 8:30 am-2:30 & 6-11 pm, Sun from 10:30 am. Closed: Mon. **Reservations:** suggested. **Features:** dressy casual; carryout; cocktails & lounge; entertainment; street parking; a la carte. New World fusion cuisine captures the flavors of the Caribbean, Asia and the American Southwest, with a great use of fresh local seafood, meat and tropical fruits. Dine outdoors under the stars or inside with the signed Picasso lithographs. Live entertainment nightly. **Cards:** AE, DS, MC, VI.

[⊠]

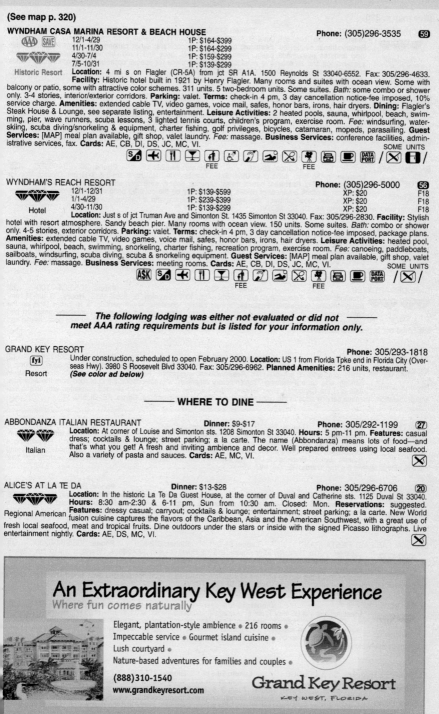

(See map p. 320)

ANTONIA'S RESTAURANT   Dinner: $12-$23   Phone: 305/294-6565   ⑮
Regional Italian
Location: In Old Town. 615 Duval St 33040. **Hours:** 6 pm-11 pm; from 6:30 pm in summer. Closed: 11/22. **Reservations:** suggested. **Features:** dressy casual; cocktails; street parking; a la carte. Regional Italian food features homemade pasta, fresh seafood, veal, beef and lamb. Innovative presentations, warm surroundings and an extensive wine list make this a place for special occasions. A complimentary cookie plate will satisfy your sweet tooth. **Cards:** AE, DI, MC, VI.

BAGATELLE RESTAURANT   Lunch: $7-$13   Dinner: $15-$24   Phone: 305/296-6609   ⑦
Regional American
Location: Downtown. 115 Duval St 33040. **Hours:** 11:30 am-3 & 6-10 pm, Fri & Sat-11 pm; from 5:30 pm 10/15-4/1. Closed: 4/7, 11/22, 12/25. **Reservations:** suggested. **Features:** casual dress; children's menu; carryout; cocktails & lounge; street parking; a la carte. An inviting wrap-around porch makes this 1884 sea captain's revival home a great location for leisurely dining. Seafood specialties are featured with other traditional entrees. Sample the grilled grouper for a light, mouth-watering taste of Florida. **Cards:** AE, DI, DS, MC, VI.

BANANA CAFE   Lunch: $6-$10   Dinner: $8-$22   Phone: 305/294-7227   ㉘
French
Location: In Old Town; just s of jct US 1. 1211 Duval St 33040. **Hours:** 8 am-3 & 7-11 pm. Closed: Mon for dinner & 9/1-9/30. **Features:** casual dress; carryout; beer & wine only; street parking. A charming, casual restaurant, it offers a variety of dishes you may enjoy on the covered patio or in the outdoor dining area. The shredded tuna sandwich with spinach leaves, capers and a hard-boiled egg is a fresh twist on the traditional lunch entree. **Cards:** AE, DI, DS, MC, VI.

BLUE HEAVEN   Lunch: $5-$12   Dinner: $10-$24   Phone: 305/296-8666   ⑱
American
Location: Just s of Duval, corner of Petronia and Thomas sts. 729 Thomas St 33040. **Hours:** 8 am-11:30, noon-3 & 6-10:30 pm. Closed: 9/9-10/15. **Features:** No A/C; casual dress; Sunday brunch; children's menu; carryout; cocktails; street parking. The Caribbean-influenced menu features seafood and a popular Sunday brunch with lobster Benedict and shrimp in grits. Roosters run around the converted barn house; a rooster graveyard is the resting place of prize cockfighters from the early 1900s. **Cards:** DS, MC, VI.

CAFE DES ARTISTES   Dinner: $23-$39   Phone: 305/294-7100   ㉓
French
Location: Corner Truman Ave and Simonton St. 1007 Simonton St 33040-6552. **Hours:** 6 pm-11 pm. **Reservations:** suggested. **Features:** dressy casual; cocktails; street parking; a la carte. Dine on the cafe-terrasse or in the intimate indoor dining room. Local seafood entrees are creatively prepared and presented with a tropical French flair, like the snail appetizer served in a puff pastry with goat cheese and bits of red bell pepper. **Cards:** AE, MC, VI.

CAFE MARQUESA   Dinner: $17-$30   Phone: 305/292-1244   ⑫
Regional American
Location: In Old Town; jct Simonton and Fleming sts; in The Marquesa Hotel. 600 Fleming St 33040. **Hours:** 6 pm-11 pm; from 7 pm 6/1-11/1. **Reservations:** suggested. **Features:** dressy casual; cocktails; street parking; a la carte. Featuring "Contemporary American" a cross-cultural blend of food from the Americas, Asia and the Caribbean, the changing menu includes meat and fresh seafood presented with artistic skill and preparation. Attentive service adds to the cozy atmosphere. Smoke free premises. **Cards:** AE, DI, MC, VI.

CAMILLE'S   Lunch: $6-$13   Dinner: $11-$22   Phone: 305/296-4811   ⑰
American
Location: In Old Town; on Duval St at corner of Angela St. 703 1/2 Duval St 33040. **Hours:** 8 am-3 & 6-10 pm; Sun & Mon-3 pm. **Features:** casual dress; Sunday brunch; carryout; beer & wine only. Resembling a roadside diner, this funky, Key West-style eatery projects a casual atmosphere with modest tables and counter seating. Breakfast is the most popular meal, with an assortment of sandwiches, seafood and beef entrees served later in the day. **Cards:** AE, DS, MC, VI.

CROISSANTS DE FRANCE   Lunch: $5-$9   Phone: 305/294-2624   ㉒
French
Location: In Old Town. 816 Duval St 33040. **Hours:** 7:30 am-2 pm. Closed: Wed. **Features:** No A/C; casual dress; carryout; beer & wine only; street parking. Gazpacho, brioche, quiche and assorted croissants are among the popular, light offerings of the tropical, outdoor cafe. Fountains and plants add to the European character. An adjacent bakery stays open in the evenings for take-out customers. **Cards:** AE, DI, MC, VI.

DIM SUM FAR EAST RESTAURANT   Lunch: $4-$20   Dinner: $12-$20   Phone: 305/294-6230   ⑭
Asian
Location: In Old Town; Key Lime Square. 613 1/2 Duval St (rear) 33040-6552. **Hours:** 5 pm-10 pm. Closed: 9/1-9/30. **Reservations:** suggested. **Features:** casual dress; carryout; beer & wine only; a la carte. Exuding the ambiance of an Asian teahouse, the intimate restaurant serves Thai, Burmese and Chinese cuisine. You'll get sizable portions of such specialties as dragon noodles and duck in red Thai curry. Check out the seafood specials and vegetarian fare. **Cards:** AE, DI, DS, MC, VI.

EL SIBONEY   Dinner: $6-$14   Phone: 305/296-4184   ㉑
Cuban
Location: Just s of US Hwy 1, corner of Margaret and Catherine sts. 900 Catherine St 33040. **Hours:** 11 am-9:30 pm. Closed major holidays; also Sun. **Features:** children's menu; carryout; beer & wine only. Casual and family-oriented, the energetic restaurant is decorated with original Cuban paintings. The roast pork, shrimp paella, grilled chicken breast and the signature Siboney steak are menu favorites. Large windows make for excellent people-watching.

FLAGLER'S STEAK HOUSE & LOUNGE   Lunch: $8-$12   Dinner: $17-$38   Phone: 305/296-3535   ㉛
Steak House
Location: 4 mi s on Flagler (CR-5A) from jct SR A1A; in Wyndham's Casa Marina Resort & Beach House. 1500 Reynolds St 33040-6552. **Hours:** 7 am-2 & 6-10:30 pm; Fri & Sat-11 pm. **Reservations:** suggested. **Features:** dressy casual; Sunday brunch; children's menu; cocktails & lounge; entertainment; fee for valet parking; a la carte. A pleasant, comfortable setting overlooks a pool and the beach. This place is known for its aged steak and fresh seafood. The cooked-to-order steak is smothered in a delicious onion butter, and the Cuban creme brulee perfectly ends a great meal. **Cards:** AE, CB, DI, DS, JC, MC, VI.

(See map p. 320)

KYUSHU　　　　　　　Lunch: $7-$12　　　　Dinner: $12-$18　　　　Phone: 305/294-2995　　⑯
Ethnic
Location: In Old Town; on US 1. 921 Truman Ave 33040. **Hours:** noon-2:30 & 5:30-10:30 pm, Sat & Sun from 5:30 pm. **Reservations:** suggested. **Features:** casual dress; children's menu; carryout; cocktails & lounge; a la carte. Attentive and friendly service at the sushi bar and in the tatami rooms make for a pleasant visit. The sushi is fresh and presented with a touch of class. Order the fried pork loin cooked with an egg splash and served on a bed of rice with sauteed onions. **Cards:** AE, CB, DI, DS, MC, VI.

LOUIE'S BACKYARD　　　Lunch: $10-$15　　　Dinner: $24-$32　　　Phone: 305/294-1061　　㉚
Regional American
Location: Just s of Truman Ave via Simonton to South St, just e to Vernon, then s. 700 Waddell Ave 33040. **Hours:** 11:30 am-3 & 6:30-10:30 pm. Closed: 9/1-9/30. **Reservations:** suggested. **Features:** dressy casual; Sunday brunch; cocktails & lounge; street parking; a la carte. The charming 1908 Victorian house features hardwood floors and a facade with many windows. Outdoor decks on both floors offer great views of the ocean. Beautifully prepared fish and steaks and an excellent wine list make the restaurant notable. **Cards:** AE, DI, MC, VI.

MANGIA MANGIA　　　　　　　　　Dinner: $9-$15　　　　Phone: 305/294-2469　　⑩
Italian
Location: Just n of US 1, corner of Margaret and Southard sts. 900 Southard St 33040. **Hours:** 5:30 pm-10 pm. Closed major holidays; also Super Bowl Sun. **Features:** casual dress; children's menu; carryout; beer & wine only; street parking. Rigatoni with jumbo shrimp, fresh pasta and homemade tiramisu encourage you to "eat eat" at the casual, small restaurant. Palms, plants and herbs envelop the outdoor garden. Caribbean decor is the theme inside. Award winning wine list. **Cards:** AE, MC, VI.

MANGOES　　　　　　　Lunch: $5-$12　　　　Dinner: $11-$22　　　Phone: 305/292-4606　　⑲
Ethnic
Location: In Old Town; on Duval at Angela St. 700 Duval St 33040. **Hours:** 11 am-1 am. **Features:** casual dress; carryout; cocktails. This restaurant serves an unusual mix of well-prepared Cuban, French and Italian dishes, such as bouillabaisse, jerk chicken and pork loin mojo Creole. Savor the white conch chowder while dining under the shelter of market umbrellas on the patio. **Cards:** AE, DI, DS, MC, VI.

NICOLA SEAFOOD　　　Lunch: $8-$14　　　Dinner: $13-$25　　　Phone: 305/296-9900　　⑥
Seafood
Location: In Old Town; Simonton and Front sts, just n of Mallory Square; in Hyatt Key West. 601 Front St 33040. **Hours:** 7 am-3 & 6-10 pm. **Reservations:** suggested. **Features:** children's menu; cocktails & lounge; valet parking; a la carte. Have a drink and enjoy an excellent sunset view on the gulf with indoor or terrace dining. Seafood is the house specialty with local fresh fish, lobster and crab cakes. **Cards:** AE, CB, DI, DS, JC, MC, VI.

PEPE'S CAFE　　　　　　Lunch: $5-$9　　　　Dinner: $10-$20　　　Phone: 305/294-7192　　⑧
American
Location: Just e of Duval St. 806 Caroline St 33040. **Hours:** 6:30 am-4 & 5:30-10:30 pm. **Features:** casual dress; children's menu; carryout; cocktails; street parking. The oldest restaurant in Key West, it features pleasant service and picnic-style seating on a patio shaded by blooming bougainvillea. Feast on homemade meals like meatloaf with mashed potatoes and an authentic, onion-and-sausage-filled black bean soup. **Cards:** DS, MC, VI.

PIER HOUSE RESTAURANT　　　　Dinner: $18-$30　　　　Phone: 305/296-4600　　⑪
(AAA)
Regional American
Location: In Old Town; on the gulf, at Mallory Square; in Pier House Resort and Caribbean Spa. One Duval St 33040. **Hours:** 6 pm-10:30 pm. **Reservations:** suggested. **Features:** dressy casual; cocktails & lounge; entertainment; a la carte. A stylish waterfront dining room also features a patio for viewing the activity in Mallory Square. Market-fresh seafood and a conch chowder that will give you a taste of the Keys are offered with other excellent choices like spinach salad and veal. **Cards:** AE, CB, DI, DS, JC, MC, VI.

SQUARE ONE RESTAURANT　　　　Dinner: $15-$30　　　　Phone: 305/296-4300　　㉕
American
Location: At Duval Square. 1075 Duval St 33040. **Hours:** 6 pm-10:30 pm. **Reservations:** suggested. **Features:** dressy casual; cocktails; entertainment; a la carte. Expect creative steak and seafood entrees-such as grilled filet mignon, New Zealand rack of lamb and sauteed sea scallops-in this intimate restaurant. The tropical courtyard is illuminated at night. For dessert, try key lime pie or creme brulee. **Cards:** AE, DS, MC, VI.

LITTLE TORCH KEY pop. 700

——— WHERE TO STAY ———

LITTLE PALM ISLAND　　　　　　　　　　　　　　　　　　　　Phone: (305)872-2524
(AAA) (SAVE)
Resort
All Year　　　　　　1P: $599-$1699　　　2P: $599-$1699　　　XP: $100
Location: Shore Station on US 1 at MM28.5, jct Pirate Rd, 15 minute launch ride to island leaving hourly on the half hour. 28500 Overseas Hwy 33042. Fax: 305/872-2524. **Facility:** A 10 minute boat ride to a tropical island hideaway. A 5.5 acre island with manicured grounds with lush tropical vegetation. Palm thatched cottages with a lavish decor and furnishings, six cottages with outside hot tubs. Designated smoking area. 30 units. Some suites and whirlpool units. 1 story, exterior corridors. **Terms:** age restrictions may apply, 14 day cancellation notice-fee imposed, package plans. **Amenities:** safes, honor bars, irons, hair dryers. **Dining:** dining room, see separate listing. **Leisure Activities:** heated pool, beach, swimming, canoeing, paddleboats, sailboating, windsurfing, boat dock, marina, snorkeling & equipment, fishing, water bikes, kayaks, jogging, exercise room. *Fee:* boats, scuba diving & equipment, charter fishing, fishing guides, seaplane tours, kee cats (electric power boats), back country exploring, sunset trips. **Guest Services:** gift shop, valet laundry. *Fee:* airport transportation-by seaplane & limo, area transportation, massage. **Cards:** AE, DI, DS, MC, VI. **Special Amenities:** free newspaper.

SOME UNITS

——— **WHERE TO DINE** ———

THE DINING ROOM AT LITTLE PALM ISLAND   **Lunch:** $14-$24   **Dinner:** $26-$41   **Phone:** 305/872-2551
▼▼▼ ▼▼▼ **Location:** Shore Station on US 1 at MM28.5, jct Pirate Rd, 15 minute launch ride to island leaving hourly on the half hour; on Little Palm Island. 28500 Overseas Hwy 33042. **Hours:** 7:30-10 am, 11:30-2:30 & 6:30-10 pm.
Reservations: required. **Features:** dressy casual; Sunday brunch; cocktails & lounge; a la carte, also prix
French   fixe. Florida and French regional dishes are featured with a nouvelle presentation. Outdoor tables and a
lengthy wine list are available. Dining is by reservation only and you must be at least 16 years old. **Cards:** AE, CB, DI, DS, MC, VI.

LONG KEY pop. 200

——— **WHERE TO STAY** ———

LIME TREE BAY RESORT MOTEL   **Phone:** (305)664-4740
(AAA) [SAVE] 12/21-4/30   1P: $102-$235   2P: $102-$235   XP: $7   F8
            12/1-12/20 & 5/1-11/30 1P: $80-$180   2P: $80-$180   XP: $7   F8
▼▼ ▼▼ **Location:** US 1, at MM68.5. 68500 Overseas Hwy 33001 (PO Box 839). Fax: 305/664-0750. **Facility:** On palm
Motor Inn   fringed bay-side grounds. Variety of accommodations. Great location for a view of the sunset. 29 units. 2
two-bedroom units, 10 efficiencies and 6 units with kitchen. *Bath:* combo or shower only. 1-2 stories, exterior
corridors. **Terms:** 15 day cancellation notice-fee imposed, weekly & monthly rates available. **Amenities:** extended cable TV, voice mail. **Dining:** restaurant, 7 am-10 pm, $11-$16, wine/beer only. **Leisure Activities:** whirlpool, beach, swimming, fishing, tennis court. *Fee:* boats, sailboating, wave runners. **Cards:** AE, DI, DS, MC, VI. *(See color ad p 312)*

SOME UNITS

MARATHON pop. 8,900

——— **WHERE TO STAY** ———

BANANA BAY RESORT-MARATHON KEY   **Phone:** (305)743-3500
▼▼▼ 12/22-4/28   1P: $115-$210   2P: $115-$210   XP: $15   F5
     4/29-11/30   1P: $85-$160   2P: $85-$160   XP: $15   F5
Motor Inn 12/1-12/21   1P: $85-$125   2P: $85-$125   XP: $15   F5
Location: On US 1; gulfside at MM49.5. 4590 Overseas Hwy 33050. Fax: 305/743-2670. **Facility:** Attractive rooms
between highway and gulf; most with small balcony. 61 units. 2 stories, interior corridors. **Terms:** 7 day cancellation notice-fee imposed, package plans. **Amenities:** extended cable TV, voice mail, irons, hair dryers. **Leisure Activities:** whirlpool, beach, swimming, fishing, 2 tennis courts, exercise room, horseshoes, volleyball. *Fee:* boating, sailboats, windsurfing, boat dock, marina, scuba diving/snorkeling & equipment, charter fishing. **Guest Services:** [ECP] meal plan available, gift shop, coin laundry.
Business Services: meeting rooms. *Fee:* fax. **Cards:** AE, CB, DI, DS, MC, VI. *(See color ad p 331)*   SOME UNITS

COCO PLUM BEACH & TENNIS CLUB   **Phone:** (305)743-0240
(AAA) [SAVE] 12/1-4/21   2P: $150-$400
            4/22-9/2   2P: $185-$310
▼▼ ▼▼   9/3-11/30   2P: $150-$260
Location: Off US 1 at MM 54.5, then 1.5 mi. 109 Coco Plum Dr 33050. Fax: 305/743-9351. **Facility:** 20 two-
Condominium bedroom units with kitchen. 2 stories, exterior corridors. **Terms:** 3 night minimum stay, 15 day cancellation
notice-fee imposed, weekly rates available. **Amenities:** extended cable TV, voice mail, hair dryers. **Leisure
Activities:** heated pool, whirlpool, beach, tennis court, barbecue and picnic area, hammocks. **Guest Services:** complimentary laundry. *Fee:* fax. **Cards:** AE, MC, VI. **Special Amenities: free local telephone calls and free room upgrade (subject to availability with advanced reservations).**

CORAL LAGOON RESORT & MARINA   **Phone:** 305/289-0121
(AAA) [SAVE] 12/21-4/20   1P: $110-$150   2P: $110-$150   XP: $10   F3
            4/21-9/6   1P: $85-$125   2P: $85-$125   XP: $10   F3
▼▼ ▼▼   12/1-12/20 & 9/7-11/30 1P: $60-$100   2P: $60-$100   XP: $10   F3
Cottage   **Location:** On US 1, MM53.5. 12399 Overseas Hwy 33050. Fax: 305/289-0195. **Facility:** All units with wood deck,
hammock and at-door boat docking, located along canal. Office hours 8 am-6 pm. 18 units with kitchen. 1
two-bedroom unit. *Bath:* combo or shower only. 1 story, exterior corridors. **Terms:** 14 day cancellation notice, monthly rates available. **Amenities:** extended cable TV, safes, hair dryers. **Leisure Activities:** boat dock, fishing, tennis court. *Fee:* charter fishing, diving tours & instruction, snorkeling trips, beach club privileges. **Guest Services:** coin laundry. *Fee:* fax.
Cards: AE, DS, MC, VI.
FEE   FEE

FLAMINGO INN   **Phone:** 305/289-1478
(AAA) [SAVE] 12/21-4/20   2P: $70-$80   XP: $5   F6
            4/21-9/5   2P: $69   XP: $7   F6
▼▼ ▼▼   12/1-12/20   2P: $50-$62   XP: $5   F6
Motel   9/6-11/30   2P: $62   XP: $5   F6
Location: On Grassy Key, on US 1, MM59.5. 59299 Overseas Hwy 33050. Fax: 305/743-4399. **Facility:** Very clean, modern rooms. 10 units. 1 two-bedroom unit and 4 efficiencies. Some suites ($74-$123). *Bath:* combo or shower only. 1-2 stories, exterior corridors. **Terms:** 3 day cancellation notice, weekly rates available. **Amenities:** extended cable
TV. **Cards:** DS, MC, VI.
SOME UNITS

HAMPTON INN & SUITES

[SAVE]

Motel

12/22-4/15	1P: $209-$299	2P: $219-$315
4/16-11/30	1P: $119-$175	2P: $129-$190
12/1-12/21	1P: $109-$155	2P: $119-$170

Phone: (305)743-9009

Location: US 1 at MM 48. 1688 Overseas Hwy 33050. Fax: 305/743-3835. **Facility:** Located on the Gulfside. The pool, with a tiki bar and grill, is a great place to view the sunsets of the Keys. A spacious lobby and breakfast area. Spacious rooms and suites with tropical decor. 79 units, 24 with efficiency. Some suites. *Bath:* combo or shower only. 3 stories, interior corridors. **Terms:** package plans. **Amenities:** extended cable TV, voice mail, irons, hair dryers. **Leisure Activities:** heated pool, whirlpool, fishing, charter fishing, exercise room. *Fee:* boating, canoeing, boat dock, scuba diving/snorkeling & equipment, bicycles. **Guest Services:** [ECP] meal plan available, coin laundry. **Business Services:** meeting rooms. **Cards:** AE, CB, DI, DS, MC, VI.

SOME UNITS

HAWK'S CAY RESORT

[AAA] [SAVE]

Resort

4/23-11/30	2P: $195-$485	XP: $25 F16
12/1-4/22	2P: $190-$435	XP: $25 F16

Phone: (305)743-7000

Location: On Duck Key, 0.5 mi s of US 1. 6100 Hawk's Cay Blvd 33050. Fax: 305/743-2805. **Facility:** West Indies-style resort on small island with beach and salt water lagoon. Large rooms with balcony. Dolphin training center and interactive programs. 387 units. 211 two-bedroom units and 181 units with kitchen. Some suites. 2-5 stories, interior/exterior corridors. **Terms:** check-in 4 pm, 7 day cancellation notice-fee imposed, package plans, $10 service charge, small pets only ($25 extra charge). **Amenities:** extended cable TV, voice mail, irons, hair dryers. **Dining:** dining room, 3 restaurants, 7 am-11 pm, $10-$30, cocktails, nightclub. **Leisure Activities:** 4 pools (3 heated), wading pool, sauna, whirlpools, steamroom, fishing, charter fishing, putting green, 8 tennis courts (2 lighted), children's program in summer, recreation program, playground, sports court, ecology tours, kayak trips, sunset cruise. *Fee:* boating, waterskiing, scuba diving/snorkeling & equipment, diving trip & scuba instruction, glass-bottom boat tours, parasailing. **Guest Services:** gift shop, airport transportation-marathon, area transportation-golf courses, valet laundry. *Fee:* massage. **Business Services:** conference facilities, administrative services. *Fee:* PC, fax. **Cards:** AE, DI, DS, MC, VI. **Special Amenities:** free newspaper and free room upgrade (subject to availability with advanced reservations). *(See color ad below)*

SOME UNITS

FEE   FEE

ROYAL HAWAIIAN MOTEL/BOTEL

[AAA] [SAVE]

Motel

2/1-4/15	1P: $105-$115	2P: $105-$115	XP: $10 F10
12/1-1/31	1P: $79-$115	2P: $79-$115	XP: $10 F10
4/16-11/30	1P: $69-$115	2P: $69-$115	XP: $10 F10

Phone: (305)743-7500

Location: US 1 at MM53. 12020 Overseas Hwy 33050. **Facility:** All units have dock space and view of the canal. Barbecue and picnic area avail for guests use. 8 units, 5 with kitchen. *Bath:* shower only. 1 story, exterior corridors. **Terms:** 7 day cancellation notice-fee imposed. **Amenities:** extended cable TV. **Leisure Activities:** small pool, boat dock, fishing. **Cards:** AE, DS, MC, VI.

WELLESLEY INN & SUITES　　　　　　　　　　　　　　　　　　　**Phone:** 305/743-8550

Motel

12/1-1/31	2P: $109-$119
2/1-5/1	2P: $80-$90
5/2-11/30	2P: $70-$80

Location: On US 1, MM54. 13351 Overseas Hwy 33050. Fax: 305/743-8832. **Facility:** Modern rooms. 80 units. *Bath:* combo or shower only. 2 stories, interior corridors. **Terms:** 3 day cancellation notice, weekly & monthly rates available, small pets only ($20 fee). **Amenities:** extended cable TV, voice mail. **Dining:** restaurant, 6 am-10 pm, $6-$11, wine/beer only. **Leisure Activities:** scuba diving, snorkeling, fishing, charter fishing. *Fee:* boating, canoeing, paddleboats, sailboating, windsurfing, scuba & snorkeling equipment, jet ski, waverunner. **Guest Services:** coin laundry. **Business Services:** fax. **Cards:** AE, CB, DI, DS, JC, MC, VI. **Special Amenities: free continental breakfast and free local telephone calls.** *(See color ad opposite title page)*

SOME UNITS

🆂 🐾 🖥 🍴 ☕ 🛶 ✕ 🎿 📠 💻 〔DATA PORT〕 / ✕ 📺 🛄 /

─────── **WHERE TO DINE** ───────

THE QUAY MARATHON　　　　　**Lunch:** $4-$15　　　　**Dinner:** $12-$35　　　　**Phone:** 305/289-1810

Steak & Seafood

Location: US 1 at MM54. 12650 Overseas Hwy 33050. **Hours:** 11 am-10 pm, Fri & Sat-11 pm. **Reservations:** suggested; in season. **Features:** casual dress; children's menu; early bird specials; carryout; cocktails. Gulf views enhance the mellow experience, whether you dine in a cozy dining room or on the crisp, fresh patio. Woodwork and artifacts suggest a nautical theme. Prime rib, dolphin, alligator, swordfish and homemade cheesecake are among tasty offerings. **Cards:** AE, CB, DI, DS, MC, VI.　✕

SUMMERLAND KEY pop. 900

─────── **WHERE TO DINE** ───────

MONTE'S RESTAURANT & FISH MARKET　　　**Lunch:** $4-$8　　　**Dinner:** $12-$14　　　**Phone:** 305/745-3731

Seafood

Location: At MM 25, just off US 1. MM 25, US 1 33042. **Hours:** 9:30 am-10 pm, Sun 11 am-9 pm. **Features:** No A/C; beer & wine only; a la carte. Market-fresh fish is served with distinction in a no-frills patio dining area with raw bar and seafood market. Try the super seafood basket and the soft-shell crab sandwich for good and filling selections. Lots of cars mean plenty of satisfied customers.　✕

This ends listings for The Florida Keys.
The following page resumes the alphabetical listings of
cities in Florida.

Destination Ft. Lauderdale
pop. 149,400

C anals, lagoons, rivers, the
Atlantic Ocean and the
Intracoastal Waterway-Fort
Lauderdale is literally shaped
by various bodies of H_2O.

C ruise ships depart its port for
Caribbean destinations, divers
snorkel in crystal blue waters, waterfront cafes prepare feasts of locally
caught seafood, sailboats and yachts
mingle in marinas and a floating taxi
takes you from here to there.

Convention Center, Fort Lauderdale.
A sculpture of a soaring sailfish
leaps from the fountain plaza of
Greater Fort Lauderdale/Broward
County's exhibit hall.

Water taxi, Fort Lauderdale.
These floating cabs provide sightseeing
as well as transportation along the
Intracoastal Waterway and New River.

*Fort Lauderdale
skyline.*
Legions of high-rise
lodgings seem to
parade down
Fort Lauderdale's
beachfront.

**See Vicinity
map page 346**

*Scuba diving in
Fort Lauderdale's waters.*
Encounter underwater
creatures up-close-and-
personal in nearby
offshore reefs.

P laces included in this AAA Destination City:

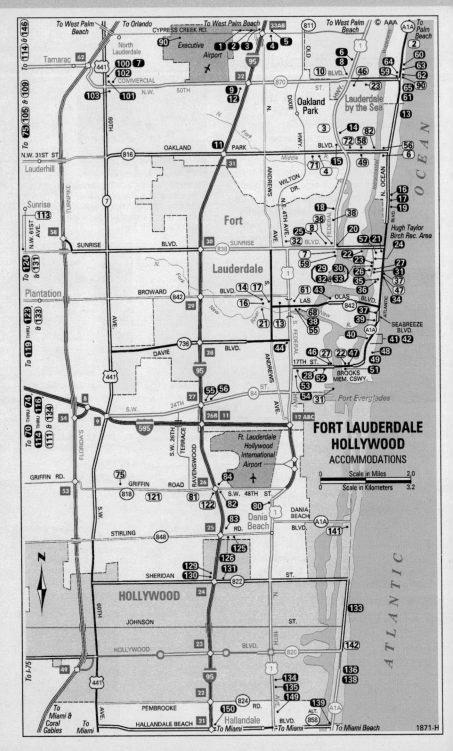

FORT LAUDERDALE
HOLLYWOOD
ACCOMMODATIONS

✈ Airport Accommodations

Spotter/Map Page Number	OA	FORT LAUDERDALE-HOLLYWOOD	Diamond Rating	Rate Range High Season	Listing Page
84 / p. 346		Fort Lauderdale Airport Hilton, 2 mi sw of airport entrance at I-95 exit 26	◈◈	$149-$239	374
82 / p. 346		Sheraton Fort Lauderdale Airport Hotel, 2 mi sw of airport entrance at I-95 exit 26	◈◈	$129-$349	375
83 / p. 346	ⒶⒶ	**SpringHill Suites by Marriott Fort Lauderdale Airp, 3 mi s of entrance**	◈◈	$119-$147 (SAVE)	375
52 / p. 346	ⒶⒶ	**AmeriSuites Fort Lauderdale/17th Street, 2.6 mi n of entrance**	◈◈	$152-$179 (SAVE)	352
51 / p. 346	ⒶⒶ	**Best Western Marina Inn & Yacht Harbor, 3.2 mi n of entrance**	◈◈	$119-$149 (SAVE)	353
42 / p. 346	ⒶⒶ	**Best Western-Oceanside Inn, 4 mi n of entrance**	◈◈	$119-$199 (SAVE)	354
54 / p. 346		Comfort Suites-Convention Center, 1.8 mi n of entrance	◈◈◈	$99-$199	355
53 / p. 346		Embassy Suites-Fort Lauderdale, 2.3 mi n of entrance	◈◈◈	$219-$229	358
46 / p. 346		Fort Lauderdale Marina Marriott, 2.9 mi n of entrance	◈◈◈	$129-$239	359
28 / p. 346		Holiday Inn Express Port Everglades Cruise & Conve, 2.5 mi n of entrance	◈◈◈	$89-$179	361
47 / p. 346	ⒶⒶ	**Hyatt Regency Pier Sixty Six, 3.2 mi n of entrance**	◈◈◈◈	$239-$264 (SAVE)	362
48 / p. 346	ⒶⒶ	**Marriott's Harbor Beach Resort, 4 mi n of entrance**	◈◈◈◈	$339-$419 (SAVE)	364
41 / p. 346	ⒶⒶ	**Sheraton-Yankee Clipper Beach Hotel, 4 mi n of entrance**	◈◈◈	$239-$289 (SAVE)	369
126 / p. 346	ⒶⒶ	**Comfort Inn-Ft. Lauderdale/Hollywood Airport, 3 mi s of entrance**	◈◈◈	$61-$133 (SAVE)	381
129 / p. 346		Days Inn Fort Lauderdale/Hollywood Airport South, 4 mi n of entrance	◈◈◈	$79-$179	381
125 / p. 346	ⒶⒶ	**Hampton Inn & Suites-Ft Lauderdale/Hollywood Airpo, 3 mi s of entrance**	◈◈◈	$99-$169 (SAVE)	382
130 / p. 346		Holiday Inn Fort Lauderdale/Airport, 4 mi s of entrance	◈◈◈	$169-$189	382
131 / p. 346		La Quinta Inn & Suites, 4 mi s of entrance	◈◈◈	$89-$129	382

Fort Lauderdale/Hollywood and Vicinity

This index helps you "spot" where approved accommodations are located on the corresponding detailed maps. Rate ranges are for comparison only and show the property's high season. Turn to the listing page for more detailed rate information and consult display ads for special promotions. Restaurant rate range is for dinner, unless only lunch (L) is served.

Spotter/Map Page Number	OA	FORT LAUDERDALE - Lodgings	Diamond Rating	Rate Range High Season	Listing Page
1 / p. 346		La Quinta Inn-Cypress Creek - see color ad p 363	◈◈◈	$65-$99	363
2 / p. 346		Sheraton Suites Cypress Creek	◈◈◈	$134-$250	369
3 / p. 346		Fort Lauderdale Marriott North	◈◈◈	$149-$199	359
4 / p. 346	ⒶⒶ	**Hampton Inn-Cypress Creek** - see color ad p 360	◈◈◈	$119-$129 (SAVE)	360
5 / p. 346		The Westin, Fort Lauderdale	◈◈◈	$139	370
6 / p. 346	ⒶⒶ	**Fairfield Inn by Marriott-Ft Lauderdale North**	◈◈◈	$64-$103 (SAVE)	358
7 / p. 346		TownePlace Suites by Marriott - see color ad p 357	◈◈◈	$99-$119	369
8 / p. 346		Fort Lauderdale Courtyard by Marriott East - see color ad p 359	◈◈◈	$169-$189	358

Spotter/Map Page Number	OA	FORT LAUDERDALE - Lodgings (continued)	Diamond Rating	Rate Range High Season	Listing Page
9 / p. 346	◈◈◈	**Red Roof Inn**	◈◈	$50-$90 [SAVE]	366
11 / p. 346		Days Inn-Fort Lauderdale	◈◈	$65-$80	357
12 / p. 346		Holiday Inn Fort Lauderdale I-95	◈◈◈	$85-$110	362
13 / p. 346		Ramada Plaza Beach Resort	◈◈	$139-$300	366
14 / p. 346		Holiday Inn Express - see color ad p 360	◈◈◈	$69-$189	360
15 / p. 346	◈◈◈	**Oakland Park Inn**	◈◈	$85-$150 [SAVE]	364
16 / p. 346	◈◈◈	**Ireland's Inn Beach Resort** - see color ad p 362	◈◈◈	$166-$299 [SAVE]	363
17 / p. 346	◈◈◈	**Best Western Pelican Beach Resort** - see color ad p 356	◈◈◈	$130-$210 [SAVE]	355
18 / p. 346		Presidio Motel	◈	Failed to provide	364
19 / p. 346	◈◈◈	**Ocean Hacienda Inn** - see color ad p 365	◈◈	$99-$195 [SAVE]	364
20 / p. 346	◈◈◈	**The River Inn On The Water**	◈◈◈	$110-$145 [SAVE]	366
21 / p. 346	◈◈◈	**Holiday Inn Ft. Lauderdale Beach** - see color ad p 361	◈◈◈	$139-$169 [SAVE]	361
22 / p. 346		The Doubletree Guest Suites/Galleria/Intracoastal Waterway - see color ad p 357	◈◈◈	$189-$259	357
23 / p. 346		Birch Patio Motel	◈◈	$50-$95	355
24 / p. 346		Sans Souci at the Beach	◈◈	Failed to provide	368
25 / p. 346	◈◈◈	**By-Eddy Apartment Motel**	◈◈	$50-$60 [SAVE]	355
26 / p. 346		Florida Beach Resort Motel	◈	Failed to provide	358
27 / p. 346		Three Suns Inn	◈◈	$75-$108	369
28 / p. 346		Holiday Inn Express Port Everglades Cruise & Convention Center - see color ad p 361	◈◈◈	$89-$179	361
29 / p. 346	◈◈◈	**Sea Chateau Resort Motel**	◈	$70-$80 [SAVE]	368
30 / p. 346	◈◈◈	**Sea View Resort Motel** - see color ad p 368	◈◈◈	$75-$135 [SAVE]	368
31 / p. 346	◈◈◈	**The Royal Pavilion**	◈◈	$75-$105 [SAVE]	367
32 / p. 346	◈◈◈	**Royal Saxon Apartments**	◈◈	$75-$125 [SAVE]	367
34 / p. 346		Waterfront Inns Beach Retreat	◈◈	$99-$249	370
35 / p. 346	◈◈◈	**Sheraton Yankee Trader Beach Hotel**	◈◈◈	$239-$289 [SAVE]	369
36 / p. 346	◈◈◈	**Caribbean Quarters, A Bed & Breakfast**	◈◈◈	$95-$225 [SAVE]	355
37 / p. 346		DoubleTree Oceanfront Hotel	◈◈◈	$199-$319	357
38 / p. 346	◈◈◈	**Riverside Hotel** - see color ad p 366	◈◈◈	$169-$219 [SAVE]	367
39 / p. 346	◈◈◈	**Radisson Bahia Mar Beach Resort** - see color ad p 365	◈◈◈	$134-$198 [SAVE]	365
40 / p. 346	◈◈◈	**Nina Lee/Imperial House Motel**	◈	$49-$135 [SAVE]	364
41 / p. 346	◈◈◈	**Sheraton-Yankee Clipper Beach Hotel**	◈◈◈	$239-$289 [SAVE]	369
42 / p. 346	◈◈◈	**Best Western-Oceanside Inn** - see color ad p 354	◈◈◈	$119-$199 [SAVE]	354
43 / p. 346	◈◈◈	**Fort Lauderdale Waterfront Inns Island Resort**	◈◈	$99-$179 [SAVE]	360
44 / p. 346	◈◈◈	**Royal Travel Inn**	◈	$59-$119 [SAVE]	368
46 / p. 346		Fort Lauderdale Marina Marriott	◈◈◈	$129-$239	359
47 / p. 346	◈◈◈	**Hyatt Regency Pier Sixty Six**	◈◈◈◈	$239-$264 [SAVE]	362

Spotter/Map Page Number	OA	FORT LAUDERDALE - Lodgings (continued)	Diamond Rating	Rate Range High Season	Listing Page
48 / p. 346	AAA	**Marriott's Harbor Beach Resort**	◆◆◆◆	$339-$419 SAVE	364
49 / p. 346		Lago Mar Resort Hotel & Club	◆◆◆	$195-$685	363
50 / p. 346	AAA	**Flying Cloud Motel**	◆◆	$59-$109 SAVE	358
51 / p. 346	AAA	**Best Western Marina Inn & Yacht Harbor -** see color ad p 353	◆◆◆	$119-$149 SAVE	353
52 / p. 346	AAA	**AmeriSuites Fort Lauderdale/17th Street -** see color ad p 5	◆◆◆	$152-$179 SAVE	352
53 / p. 346		Embassy Suites-Fort Lauderdale	◆◆◆	$219-$229	358
54 / p. 346		Comfort Suites-Convention Center - see ad p 355	◆◆◆	$99-$199	355
55 / p. 346	AAA	**Best Western Fort Lauderdale Inn**	◆◆◆	$89-$159 SAVE	352
56 / p. 346		Motel 6 - 55	◆	$58-$74	364
57 / p. 346	AAA	**Tropi Rock Resort**	◆◆◆	$65-$98 SAVE	369
		FORT LAUDERDALE - Restaurants			
2 / p. 346		Sea Watch Restaurant	◆◆	$15-$31	373
3 / p. 346		Mai-Kai Restaurant	◆◆◆	$16-$30	372
4 / p. 346		Gibby's	◆◆	$14-$28	371
6 / p. 346		Charley's Crab	◆◆◆	$12-$34	371
7 / p. 346		Big Louie's Italian Restaurant	◆	$5-$13	370
8 / p. 346		La Ferme	◆◆◆	$20-$35	372
10 / p. 346		Big Louie's Italian Restaurant	◆	$4-$14	370
13 / p. 346		Jackson's 450	◆◆◆	$16-$36	372
14 / p. 346		Himmarshee Bar & Grille	◆◆◆	$13-$25	371
16 / p. 346		The River House	◆◆◆	$12-$28	373
17 / p. 346		TarponBend Food & Tackle	◆◆	$6-$18	373
21 / p. 346	AAA	**Shirttail Charlie's Restaurant**	◆◆	$10-$20	373
22 / p. 346		California Cafe	◆◆◆	$10-$28	370
23 / p. 346		The Ambry	◆◆	$11-$26	370
27 / p. 346		Bimini Boatyard	◆◆	$6-$22	370
31 / p. 346		Burt & Jack's	◆◆◆	$15-$35	370
32 / p. 346		By Word of Mouth	◆◆◆	$20-$30	370
36 / p. 346		Canyon	◆◆◆	$13-$25	371
37 / p. 346		Casablanca Cafe	◆◆	$11-$17	371
38 / p. 346		The Caves	◆◆	$11-$24	371
46 / p. 346		Eduardo de San Angel	◆◆◆	$15-$22	371
47 / p. 346		Evangeline Restaurant	◆◆◆	$12-$19	371
49 / p. 346		Food Lovers American Cafe	◆◆	$11-$18	371
55 / p. 346	AAA	**The Grill Room on Las Olas** - see color ad p 366	◆◆◆◆	$20-$40	371
56 / p. 346		La Reserve	◆◆◆	$16-$30	372
58 / p. 346		Las Vegas	◆◆	$7-$20	372
59 / p. 346	AAA	**La Tavernetta-The Italian Bistro by the Water**	◆◆◆	$16-$24	372
61 / p. 346		The Left Bank	◆◆◆	$18-$26	372

Spotter/Map Page Number	OA	FORT LAUDERDALE - Restaurants (continued)	Diamond Rating	Rate Range High Season	Listing Page
68 / p. 346		Mark's Las Olas	◆◆◆	$17-$36	372
71 / p. 346		Primavera Restaurant	◆◆◆	$20-$35	372
72 / p. 346	AAA	**Rainbow Palace**	◆◆◆◆	$19-$40	372
75 / p. 346		Royal India	◆◆	$9-$16	373
81 / p. 346		Tropical Acres	◆◆	$11-$16	373
82 / p. 346		Yesterday's	◆◆◆	$12-$29	373
		LAUDERDALE-BY-THE-SEA - Lodgings			
59 / p. 346		Blue Seas Courtyard	◆◆	$94-$105	384
60 / p. 346	AAA	**Tropic Seas Resort** - see color ad p 367	◆◆	$140-$205 SAVE	385
61 / p. 346	AAA	**Holiday Inn-Lauderdale-By-The-Sea North Beach**	◆◆	$89-$149 SAVE	385
62 / p. 346	AAA	**A Little Inn By The Sea** - see color ad p 363	◆◆	$109-$189 SAVE	384
63 / p. 346	AAA	**Clarion Lauderdale Beach Resort** - see color ad p 358	◆◆	$135-$375 SAVE	384
64 / p. 346	AAA	**Seascape Resort Motel**	◆	$59-$89 SAVE	385
65 / p. 346	AAA	**Courtyard Villa On The Ocean** - see color ad p 384	◆◆◆	$150-$190 SAVE	385
		LAUDERDALE-BY-THE-SEA - Restaurant			
90 / p. 346		Aruba Beach Cafe	◆◆	$5-$11	385
		SUNRISE - Lodgings			
70 / p. 346	AAA	**Wellesley Inn & Suites** - see color ad opposite title page	◆◆◆	$99-$119 SAVE	392
74 / p. 346		Baymont Inn & Suites-Sunrise Sawgrass - see color ad p 391	◆◆◆	$109-$114	391
75 / p. 346	AAA	**Hilton Fort Lauderdale Sunrise** - see ad p 44	◆◆◆	$119-$149 SAVE	392
		SUNRISE - Restaurants			
105 / p. 346		La Stella South	◆◆	$13-$25	392
109 / p. 346		Rio Vista Isle Cafe	◆◆	$11-$22	392
111 / p. 346		La Cucina Toscana	◆◆◆	$16-$25	392
113 / p. 346		Legal Sea Foods	◆◆	$14-$30	392
114 / p. 346		Emerald Coast	◆◆	$17	392
		DANIA BEACH - Lodgings			
80 / p. 346	AAA	**Luckey's Motel**	◆◆	$59-$119 SAVE	375
82 / p. 346		Sheraton Fort Lauderdale Airport Hotel	◆◆◆	$129-$349	375
83 / p. 346	AAA	**SpringHill Suites by Marriott Fort Lauderdale Airport** - see color ad p 368	◆◆◆	$119-$147 SAVE	375
84 / p. 346		Fort Lauderdale Airport Hilton - see ad p 44, p 375	◆◆◆	$149-$239	374
		DANIA BEACH - Restaurants			
121 / p. 346		Le Petit Cafe	◆◆	$14-$17	375
122 / p. 346		Islamorada Fish Company	◆◆	$5-$20	375
		NORTH LAUDERDALE - Lodgings			
90 / p. 346		Courtyard by Marriott Fort Lauderdale North	◆◆◆	$129-$159	386

Spotter/Map Page Number	OA	TAMARAC - Lodgings	Diamond Rating	Rate Range High Season	Listing Page
100 / p. 346		Ramada Plaza Resort	◆◆◆	Failed to provide	393
101 / p. 346	AAA	**Wellesley Inn & Suites** - see color ad opposite title page	◆◆	$70-$80 SAVE	393
102 / p. 346		Homestead Village Guest Studios-Fort Lauderdale	◆◆	$59-$69	393
103 / p. 346		Baymont Inn & Suites-Fort Lauderdale NW (Tamarac) - see color ad p 391	◆◆	$89-$94	392
		PLANTATION - Lodgings			
114 / p. 346		Residence Inn by Marriott-Plantation	◆◆◆	$134-$144	388
115 / p. 346		La Quinta Inn & Suites - see color ad p 363	◆◆◆	$89-$109	388
116 / p. 346	AAA	**Wellesley Inn & Suites** - see color ad opposite title page	◆◆◆	$99-$119 SAVE	388
119 / p. 346		Hampton Inn Plantation	◆◆◆	$69-$159	387
120 / p. 346	AAA	**Sheraton Suites-Plantation**	◆◆◆	$279-$349 SAVE	388
122 / p. 346		Courtyard by Marriott-Plantation - see color ad p 359	◆◆◆	$139-$149	387
123 / p. 346	AAA	**AmeriSuites Plantation** - see color ad p 5	◆◆◆	$89-$149 SAVE	387
124 / p. 346	AAA	**Holiday Inn Plantation** - see ad p 387	◆◆◆	$129 SAVE	387
		PLANTATION - Restaurants			
131 / p. 346		Brasserie Max	◆◆	$8-$17	388
133 / p. 346		Takeyama	◆◆	$10-$30	389
134 / p. 346		Pebbles	◆◆	$8-$15	388
		HOLLYWOOD - Lodgings			
125 / p. 346	AAA	**Hampton Inn & Suites-Ft Lauderdale/Hollywood Airport** - see color ad p 381	◆◆◆	$99-$169 SAVE	382
126 / p. 346	AAA	**Comfort Inn-Ft. Lauderdale/Hollywood Airport** - see color ad p 381	◆◆◆	$61-$133 SAVE	381
129 / p. 346		Days Inn Fort Lauderdale/Hollywood Airport South	◆◆◆	$79-$179	381
130 / p. 346		Holiday Inn Fort Lauderdale/Airport	◆◆◆	$169-$189	382
131 / p. 346		La Quinta Inn & Suites - see color ad p 363	◆◆◆	$89-$129	382
133 / p. 346		Howard Johnson Plaza Resort Hollywood Beach	◆◆	$141-$214	382
134 / p. 346	AAA	**Shell Motel** - see ad p 383	◆◆	$45-$74 SAVE	383
135 / p. 346	AAA	**Richards Motel** - see ad p 383	◆◆	$49-$74 SAVE	383
136 / p. 346	AAA	**Greenbriar Beach Club**	◆◆	$95-$175 SAVE	381
138 / p. 346	AAA	**Holiday Inn** - see ad p 382	◆◆◆	$109-$209 SAVE	382
139 / p. 346	AAA	**Clarion Hotel Hollywood Beach** - see color ad p 380	◆◆◆	$129-$229 SAVE	380
		HOLLYWOOD - Restaurants			
141 / p. 346		Martha's on the Intracoastal	◆◆◆	$15-$29	384
142 / p. 346		Giorgio's Grill	◆◆◆	$10-$28	383
		HALLANDALE - Lodgings			
149 / p. 346		Hallandale Resort Motel	◆	$55-$70	379
150 / p. 346		Best Western Hallandale	◆◆	$95-$125	379
		LAUDERHILL - Restaurant			
146 / p. 346		Crab House Seafood Restaurant	◆◆	$12-$21	385

FORT LAUDERDALE (See map p. 346; index p. 347)

———— WHERE TO STAY ————

AMERISUITES FORT LAUDERDALE/17TH STREET　　　　　　　　**Phone:** (954)763-7670　〔52〕

(AAA) [SAVE]

▽▽▽▽

Suite Motel

	12/1-12/31	1P: $152-$179	2P: $152-$179	XP: $10	F17
	1/1-4/15	1P: $143-$170	2P: $143-$170	XP: $10	F17
	10/1-11/30	1P: $116-$143	2P: $116-$143	XP: $10	F17
	4/16-9/30	1P: $80-$107	2P: $80-$107	XP: $10	F17

Location: From A1A/17th St Cswy, just s. 1851 SE Tenth Ave 33316. Fax: 954/763-6269. **Facility:** Stylish lobby area. Rooms spacious and nicely appointed. Many rooms are business person friendly. 128 units. *Bath:* combo or shower only. 6 stories, interior corridors. **Terms:** check-in 4 pm, weekly rates available. **Amenities:** extended cable TV, voice mail, irons, hair dryers. **Leisure Activities:** heated pool, exercise room. **Guest Services:** [ECP] meal plan available, area transportation-Port Everglades, valet and coin laundry. **Business Services:** meeting rooms, administrative services. **Cards:** AE, CB, DI, DS, JC, MC, VI. **Special Amenities: free continental breakfast and free newspaper.**
(See color ad p 5)　　　　　　　　　　　　　　　　　　　　　　　　　　　　　　SOME UNITS

[icons]

BEST WESTERN FORT LAUDERDALE INN　　　　　　　　**Phone:** (954)462-7005　〔55〕

(AAA) [SAVE]

▽▽▽▽

Motel

| | 12/1-4/15 | 1P: $89-$159 | 2P: $89-$159 |
| | 4/16-11/30 | 1P: $69-$109 | 2P: $69-$109 |

Location: I-95, exit 27 (SR 84), then 0.7 mi e. 1221 SR 84 33315. Fax: 954/462-5949. **Facility:** Large rooms, tastefully furnished and decorated. 50 units. *Bath:* combo or shower only. 2 stories, interior corridors. **Amenities:** extended cable TV, voice mail, irons, hair dryers. **Leisure Activities:** heated pool. **Guest Services:** [ECP] meal plan available, area transportation-Port Everglades & Convention Center. **Business Services:** meeting rooms. **Cards:** AE, CB, DI, DS, JC, MC, VI. **Special Amenities: free continental breakfast and free local telephone calls.**
　　　　　　　　　　　　　　　　　　　　　　　　　　　　　　SOME UNITS

[icons]

(See map p. 346)

BEST WESTERN MARINA INN & YACHT HARBOR Phone: (954)525-3484 **51**

AAA SAVE	12/27-4/20	1P: $119-$149	2P: $119-$149	XP: $10	F12
	10/16-11/30	1P: $99-$129	2P: $99-$129	XP: $10	F12
	12/1-12/26	1P: $89-$119	2P: $89-$119	XP: $10	F12
	4/21-10/15	1P: $89-$109	2P: $89-$109	XP: $10	F12

Motor Inn   **Location:** SR A1A, 1.2 mi e of US 1. 2150 SE 17th St Cswy 33316. Fax: 954/764-2915. **Facility:** On Intracoastal Waterway. Some rooms overlook the pool area with its tropical foliage all around. A few with a view of the waterway. Rooms with soft tropical colors. 165 units. Some suites. *Bath:* combo or shower only. 4 stories, exterior corridors. **Terms:** 3 day cancellation notice-fee imposed, weekly rates available, $2 service charge. **Amenities:** extended cable TV, voice mail, safes, irons, hair dryers. **Dining:** restaurant, 7 am-10 pm, $9-$20, cocktails, entertainment. **Leisure Activities:** heated pool, whirlpool, putting green. *Fee:* marina. **Guest Services:** [CP] meal plan available, gift shop, airport transportation-FTL, area transportation-convention center, Port Everglades, coin laundry. **Business Services:** meeting rooms. **Cards:** AE, DS, JC, MC, VI. *(See color ad below)*

SOME UNITS

(See map p. 346)

BEST WESTERN-OCEANSIDE INN

					Phone: (954)525-8115	42
	12/1-4/30	1P: $119-$199	2P: $119-$199	XP: $10		F12
	10/1-11/30	1P: $99-$179	2P: $99-$179	XP: $10		F12
	5/1-5/31	1P: $99-$159	2P: $99-$159	XP: $10		F12
	6/1-9/30	1P: $85-$125	2P: $85-$125	XP: $10		F12

Motel   **Location:** SR A1A, just s of Bahia Mar Marina. 1180 Seabreeze Blvd 33316. Fax: 954/527-0957. **Facility:** Attractive pool area. 101 units. Some suites. 5 stories, interior/exterior corridors. **Terms:** 3 day cancellation notice-fee imposed, package plans. **Amenities:** extended cable TV, voice mail, safes (fee), irons, hair dryers. **Dining:** coffee shop, 7 am-3 pm. **Leisure Activities:** heated pool, beach access, sun deck. **Guest Services:** [BP] meal plan available, valet and coin laundry. **Business Services:** meeting rooms. **Cards:** AE, CB, DI, DS, JC, MC, VI. **Special Amenities:** free continental breakfast and free newspaper. *(See color ad below)*

SOME UNITS
FEE   FEE

(See map p. 346)

BEST WESTERN PELICAN BEACH RESORT
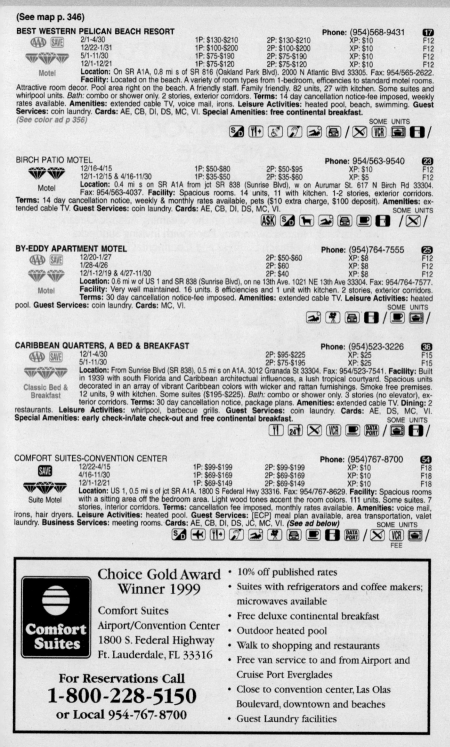

Phone: (954)568-9431 **17**

	2/1-4/30	1P: $130-$210	2P: $130-$210	XP: $10	F12
AAA SAVE	12/22-1/31	1P: $100-$200	2P: $100-$200	XP: $10	F12
	5/1-11/30	1P: $75-$190	2P: $75-$190	XP: $10	F12
Motel	12/1-12/21	1P: $75-$120	2P: $75-$120	XP: $10	F12

Location: On SR A1A, 0.8 mi s of SR 816 (Oakland Park Blvd). 2000 N Atlantic Blvd 33305. Fax: 954/565-2622. **Facility:** Located on the beach. A variety of room types from 1-bedroom, efficiencies to standard motel rooms. Attractive room decor. Pool area right on the beach. A friendly staff. Family friendly. 82 units, 27 with kitchen. Some suites and whirlpool units. *Bath:* combo or shower only. 2 stories, exterior corridors. **Terms:** 14 day cancellation notice-fee imposed, weekly rates available. **Amenities:** extended cable TV, voice mail, irons. **Leisure Activities:** heated pool, beach, swimming. **Guest Services:** coin laundry. **Cards:** AE, CB, DI, DS, MC, VI. **Special Amenities: free continental breakfast.**
(See color ad p 356)

SOME UNITS

BIRCH PATIO MOTEL

Phone: 954/563-9540 **23**

	12/16-4/15	1P: $50-$80	2P: $50-$95	XP: $10	F12
	12/1-12/15 & 4/16-11/30	1P: $35-$50	2P: $35-$60	XP: $5	F12
Motel					

Location: 0.4 mi s on SR A1A from jct SR 838 (Sunrise Blvd), w on Aurumar St. 617 N Birch Rd 33304. Fax: 954/563-4037. **Facility:** Spacious rooms. 14 units, 11 with kitchen. 1-2 stories, exterior corridors. **Terms:** 14 day cancellation notice, weekly & monthly rates available, pets ($10 extra charge, $100 deposit). **Amenities:** extended cable TV. **Guest Services:** coin laundry. **Cards:** AE, CB, DI, DS, MC, VI.

SOME UNITS

BY-EDDY APARTMENT MOTEL

Phone: (954)764-7555 **25**

	12/20-1/27		2P: $50-$60	XP: $8	F12
AAA SAVE	1/28-4/26		2P: $60	XP: $8	F12
	12/1-12/19 & 4/27-11/30		2P: $40	XP: $8	F12
Motel					

Location: 0.6 mi w of US 1 and SR 838 (Sunrise Blvd), on ne 13th Ave. 1021 NE 13th Ave 33304. Fax: 954/764-7577. **Facility:** Very well maintained. 16 units. 8 efficiencies and 1 unit with kitchen. 2 stories, exterior corridors. **Terms:** 30 day cancellation notice-fee imposed. **Amenities:** extended cable TV. **Leisure Activities:** heated pool. **Guest Services:** coin laundry. **Cards:** MC, VI.

SOME UNITS

CARIBBEAN QUARTERS, A BED & BREAKFAST

Phone: (954)523-3226 **36**

| | 12/1-4/30 | | 2P: $95-$225 | XP: $25 | F15 |
| AAA SAVE | 5/1-11/30 | | 2P: $75-$195 | XP: $25 | F15 |

Location: From Sunrise Blvd (SR 838), 0.5 mi s on A1A. 3012 Granada St 33304. Fax: 954/523-7541. **Facility:** Built in 1939 with south Florida and Caribbean architectual influences, a lush tropical courtyard. Spacious units decorated in an array of vibrant Caribbean colors with wicker and rattan furnishings. Smoke free premises. 12 units, 9 with kitchen. Some suites ($195-$225). *Bath:* combo or shower only. 3 stories (no elevator), exterior corridors. **Terms:** 30 day cancellation notice, package plans. **Amenities:** extended cable TV. **Dining:** 2 restaurants. **Leisure Activities:** whirlpool, barbecue grills. **Guest Services:** coin laundry. **Cards:** AE, DS, MC, VI. **Special Amenities: early check-in/late check-out and free continental breakfast.**

Classic Bed & Breakfast

SOME UNITS

COMFORT SUITES-CONVENTION CENTER

Phone: (954)767-8700 **54**

	12/22-4/15	1P: $99-$199	2P: $99-$199	XP: $10	F18
SAVE	4/16-11/30	1P: $69-$169	2P: $69-$169	XP: $10	F18
	12/1-12/21	1P: $69-$149	2P: $69-$149	XP: $10	F18
Suite Motel					

Location: US 1, 0.5 mi s of jct SR A1A. 1800 S Federal Hwy 33316. Fax: 954/767-8629. **Facility:** Spacious rooms with a sitting area off the bedroom area. Light wood tones accent the room colors. 111 units. Some suites. 3 stories, interior corridors. **Terms:** cancellation fee imposed, monthly rates available. **Amenities:** voice mail, irons, hair dryers. **Leisure Activities:** heated pool. **Guest Services:** [ECP] meal plan available, area transportation, valet laundry. **Business Services:** meeting rooms. **Cards:** AE, CB, DI, DS, JC, MC, VI. **(See ad below)**

SOME UNITS
FEE

(See map p. 346)

DAYS INN-FORT LAUDERDALE

				Phone: (954)484-9290	11
	12/1-4/30	1P: $65-$80	2P: $65-$80	XP: $10	F18
	5/1-11/30	1P: $50-$65	2P: $50-$65	XP: $10	F18

Motel

Location: On SR 816 (Oakland Park Blvd), just w of jct I-95 exit 31. 1595 W Oakland Park Blvd 33311. Fax: 954/485-9025. **Facility:** Located off the interstate. Some rooms with at-door parking. 144 units. 5 stories, exterior corridors. **Terms:** 7 day cancellation notice. **Amenities:** safes (fee). **Guest Services:** [CP] meal plan available, coin laundry. **Cards:** AE, CB, DI, DS, MC, VI.

SOME UNITS

THE DOUBLETREE GUEST SUITES/GALLERIA/
INTRACOASTAL WATERWAY

				Phone: (954)565-3800	22
	1/1-4/30	1P: $189-$259	2P: $189-$259	XP: $10	F18
	10/1-11/30	1P: $149-$259	2P: $149-$259	XP: $10	F18
	12/1-12/31	1P: $139-$259	2P: $139-$259	XP: $10	F18
	5/1-9/30	1P: $99-$159	2P: $99-$159	XP: $10	F18

Suite Hotel

Location: Intracoastal Bridge on Sunrise Blvd (SR 838); 3 blks w of jct A1A. 2670 E Sunrise Blvd 33304. Fax: 954/561-0387. **Facility:** Adjacent to the Galleria Mall. Suites with kitchen and balcony. Many overlooking Intracoastal Waterway. An attractive lobby with marble floors. Comfortable sitting areas. The restaurant has outdoor seating overlooking the waterway. 230 units with kitchen. 22 two-bedroom units. 14 stories, interior corridors. **Parking:** extra charge or valet. **Terms:** cancellation fee imposed, monthly rates available, package plans, pets ($15 extra charge). **Amenities:** dual phone lines, voice mail, honor bars, irons, hair dryers. **Leisure Activities:** heated pool, saunas, whirlpool, boat dock, exercise room. **Guest Services:** valet and coin laundry. **Business Services:** meeting rooms, administrative services. **Cards:** AE, DI, DS, MC, VI. *(See color ad below)*

SOME UNITS

FEE

DOUBLETREE OCEANFRONT HOTEL

				Phone: 954/524-8733	37
	1/1-4/30	1P: $199-$299	2P: $219-$319	XP: $20	F17
	10/1-11/30	1P: $179-$289	2P: $199-$309	XP: $20	F17
	12/1-12/31 & 5/1-9/30	1P: $159-$199	2P: $179-$219	XP: $20	F17

Motor Inn

Location: Just s of Las Olas Blvd, on SR A1A. 440 Seabreeze Blvd 33316. Fax: 954/467-7489. **Facility:** Attractive pool area with poolside bar. All rooms with view of ocean or city skyline and river. The beach is across the street. Beach nearby. 230 units. *Bath:* combo or shower only. 12 stories, interior corridors. **Parking:** valet. **Terms:** 3 day cancellation notice-fee imposed, small pets only ($50 deposit). **Amenities:** dual phone lines, voice mail, irons, hair dryers. **Leisure Activities:** heated pool, whirlpool, beach access, exercise room. **Guest Services:** area transportation, valet laundry. **Business Services:** meeting rooms. **Cards:** AE, CB, DI, DS, MC, VI.

SOME UNITS

(See map p. 346)

EMBASSY SUITES-FORT LAUDERDALE Phone: (954)527-2700 53

▽▽▽▽	12/25-4/30	1P: $219-$229	2P: $219-$229	XP: $10	F17
	5/1-9/30	1P: $134-$209	2P: $134-$209	XP: $10	F17
	10/1-11/30	1P: $194-$204	2P: $194-$204	XP: $10	F17
Suite Hotel	12/1-12/24	1P: $189-$199	2P: $189-$199	XP: $10	F17

Location: On SR A1A, just e of jct US 1. 1100 SE 17th St Cswy 33316. Fax: 954/760-7202. **Facility:** A large Spanish style structure with a tiled roof. Tropical trees and flowering plants surround this property. A soothing pool area. The lobby has large murals of tropical Florida. The atrium has waterfalls, tropical trees and orchids. Spacious colorful suites to relax in. 358 units. *Bath:* combo or shower only. 12 stories, interior corridors. **Parking:** extra charge or valet. **Terms:** monthly rates available. **Amenities:** video games, dual phone lines, voice mail, irons, hair dryers. **Leisure Activities:** heated pool, sauna, whirlpool, steamroom, exercise room. **Guest Services:** [BP] meal plan available, gift shop, complimentary evening beverages, airport transportation, valet and coin laundry. **Business Services:** conference facilities, administrative services. **Cards:** AE, DI, DS, MC, VI.   SOME UNITS

ASK Sℹ ✈ ❙❙ ▼ 🔊 ⚿ ➔ 🏊 🎥 🖥 ▭ ▭ 🅗 DATA PORT / ✕ /
                                                      FEE

FAIRFIELD INN BY MARRIOTT-FT LAUDERDALE NORTH Phone: (954)491-2500 6

AAA SAVE	12/1-4/15	1P: $64-$98	2P: $69-$103
▽▽▽	4/16-11/30	1P: $54-$74	2P: $59-$79

Location: 0.5 mi n on Federal Hwy (US 1) from Commercial Blvd (SR 870). 5727 N Federal Hwy 33308. Fax: 954/491-7945. **Facility:** Spacious rooms with a colorful decor. Attractive pool area. 162 units. *Bath:* shower or tub only. 2 stories, exterior corridors. **Terms:** weekly rates available. **Amenities:** extended cable TV, video games, voice mail, irons, hair dryers. **Leisure Activities:** heated pool, whirlpool, exercise room. **Guest Services:** [ECP] meal plan available, valet and coin laundry. **Business Services:** meeting rooms. **Cards:** AE, DI, DS, MC, VI. **Special Amenities:** early check-in/late check-out and free continental breakfast.   SOME UNITS

❙❙ ♿ 🔊 ⚿ ➔ 🎥 🖥 DATA PORT / ✕ /

FLORIDA BEACH RESORT MOTEL Phone: (954)563-5872 26

                    Property failed to provide current rates

♦ Motel

Location: Just w of SR A1A, between Terramar and Rio Mar sts. 505 Orton Ave 33304. Fax: 954/565-5165. **Facility:** Spacious rooms. Attractive pool area. 18 units. 6 efficiencies and 6 units with kitchen. 3 stories, exterior corridors. **Terms:** 30 day cancellation notice. **Amenities:** extended cable TV. *Some:* safes (fee). **Leisure Activities:** pool heated, in winter. **Guest Services:** coin laundry. **Cards:** MC, VI.

➔ 🅗

FLYING CLOUD MOTEL Phone: (954)563-7062 50

AAA SAVE	12/18-4/15	1P: $59-$109	2P: $59-$109	XP: $10	F12
▽▽▽ ▽▽	4/16-11/30	1P: $50-$65	2P: $50-$65	XP: $10	F12
Motel	12/1-12/17	1P: $45-$60	2P: $45-$60	XP: $10	F12

Location: Just w of SR A1A; between Terramar and Rio Mar sts, 0.5 mi s of Sunrise Blvd. 533 Orton Ave 33304. Fax: 954/561-2767. **Facility:** Inviting pool patio, spacious rooms. 10 units, 6 with efficiency. *Bath:* combo or shower only. 2 stories, exterior corridors. **Terms:** 7 day cancellation notice-fee imposed. **Amenities:** extended cable TV. **Leisure Activities:** heated pool. **Guest Services:** coin laundry. **Cards:** AE, DI, DS, MC, VI.   SOME UNITS

Sℹ ➔ 🅗 / ▭ /

FORT LAUDERDALE COURTYARD BY MARRIOTT EAST Phone: (954)771-8100 8

▽▽▽	12/1-5/1	1P: $169-$189	2P: $169-$189
	10/2-11/30	1P: $129-$169	2P: $129-$169
Motor Inn	5/2-10/1	1P: $99-$139	2P: $99-$139

Location: On US 1, at jct SR 870, Commercial Blvd. 5001 N Federal Hwy 33308. Fax: 954/776-7980. **Facility:** Attractive public areas. A relaxing pool area. Spacious rooms with an attractive room package. 104 units. *Bath:* combo or shower only. 5 stories, interior corridors. **Terms:** cancellation fee imposed, weekly rates available. **Amenities:** extended cable TV, voice mail, irons, hair dryers. **Leisure Activities:** heated pool, whirlpool, exercise room. **Guest Services:** valet and coin laundry. **Business Services:** meeting rooms. **Cards:** AE, DI, DS, MC, VI. *(See color ad p 359)*   SOME UNITS

ASK Sℹ ❙❙ ▼ ⚿ ➔ 🎥 🖥 ▭ DATA PORT / ✕ ▭ 🅗 /

(See map p. 346)

FORT LAUDERDALE MARINA MARRIOTT   Phone: (954)463-4000   46

◆◆◆◆	12/1-4/1	1P: $129-$239	2P: $129-$239	XP: $10	F
	4/2-6/1	1P: $99-$199	2P: $99-$199	XP: $10	F
Hotel	10/1-11/30	1P: $99-$189	2P: $99-$189	XP: $10	F
	6/2-9/30	1P: $89-$139	2P: $89-$139	XP: $10	F

Location: SR A1A, 1 mi e of jct US 1. 1881 SE 17th St Cswy 33316. Fax: 954/527-6705. **Facility:** On Intracoastal Waterway. A large pool area surrounded by tropical trees and flowering plants. The marina is just steps away. Rooms with light wood tones and a light tropical decor package. All rooms with a balcony. 580 units. Some suites ($350-$600). *Bath:* combo or shower only. 3-14 stories, interior corridors. **Parking:** extra charge or valet. **Terms:** check-in 4 pm, cancellation fee imposed, package plans. **Amenities:** voice mail, safes, honor bars, irons, hair dryers. **Leisure Activities:** heated pool, saunas, whirlpool, charter fishing, exercise room. *Fee:* marina. **Guest Services:** [BP] meal plan available, gift shop, area transportation, valet and coin laundry. *Fee:* massage. **Business Services:** conference facilities, fax. **Cards:** AE, CB, DI, DS, JC, MC, VI.

SOME UNITS

⟨symbols⟩

FORT LAUDERDALE MARRIOTT NORTH   Phone: (954)771-0440   3

◆◆◆◆	12/1-4/12	1P: $149-$199	2P: $149-$199
	4/13-5/24	1P: $119-$159	2P: $119-$159
Hotel	9/30-11/30	1P: $109-$159	2P: $109-$159
	5/25-9/29	1P: $99-$119	2P: $99-$119

Location: Nw of I-95, exit 33B, 0.5 mi n of jct Cypress Creek Rd. 6650 N Andrews Ave 33309. Fax: 954/772-9834. **Facility:** A striking building located in a small wooded area. A contemporary lobby with comfortable sitting areas. Spacious rooms with attractive room decor and furniture package. 321 units. Some suites. 16 stories, interior corridors. **Parking:** valet. **Amenities:** extended cable TV, dual phone lines, voice mail, honor bars, irons, hair dryers. **Leisure Activities:** heated pool, whirlpool, exercise room. **Guest Services:** gift shop, valet and coin laundry. **Business Services:** conference facilities, fax. *Fee:* PC. **Cards:** AE, CB, DI, DS, JC, MC, VI.

SOME UNITS

⟨symbols⟩

(See map p. 346)

FORT LAUDERDALE WATERFRONT INNS ISLAND RESORT   Phase: (954)527-0026   **43**

Ⓐ SAVE   12/1-5/14 & 10/15-11/30   1P: $99-$179   2P: $99-$179   XP: $10   F14
   5/15-10/14   1P: $69-$109   2P: $69-$109   XP: $10   F14
◇◇   **Location:** 1 mi e of US 1 on Las Olas Blvd to Isle of Venice, then just n. 91 Isle of Venice 33301. Fax: 954/527-1732.
Motel   **Facility:** In a quiet location on one of many canals. Nicely landscaped grounds with many fruit trees. The dock is just steps away. Rooms are spacious with light wood tones. 48 units. 27 two-bedroom units and 21 efficiencies. Some suites. *Bath:* combo or shower only. 2-7 stories, exterior corridors. **Terms:** 3 day cancellation notice, weekly & monthly rates available. **Amenities:** extended cable TV, voice mail. *Some:* safes. **Leisure Activities:** 2 heated pools. *Fee:* boat dock. **Guest Services:** coin laundry. **Cards:** AE, CB, DI, DS, MC, VI. **Special Amenities:** early check-in/late check-out and free continental breakfast.

SOME UNITS

Ⓢ▾ 🏊 🖨 ▣ 🖥 🛏 / ✕ VCR /
                                         FEE

HAMPTON INN-CYPRESS CREEK   Phone: (954)776-7677   **4**

Ⓐ SAVE   1/1-3/31   1P: $119   2P: $129   XP: $5   F19
   12/1-12/31 & 4/1-4/30   1P: $75   2P: $85   XP: $5   F19
◇◇◇   5/1-11/30   1P: $59   2P: $69   XP: $5   F19
Motel   **Location:** 0.5 mi e of jct I-95, exit 33. 720 E Cypress Creek Rd 33334. Fax: 954/776-0805. **Facility:** The pool is surrounded by tropical trees and flowering plants. A comfortable lobby and breakfast area. Rooms with light wood tones and contemporary decor. 123 units. 4 stories, interior corridors. **Terms:** cancellation fee imposed.
Amenities: extended cable TV, voice mail, irons, hair dryers. **Leisure Activities:** whirlpool, exercise room. **Guest Services:** [ECP] meal plan available, valet laundry. **Business Services:** meeting rooms. **Cards:** AE, CB, DI, DS, MC, VI.
Special Amenities: free continental breakfast and free local telephone calls. *(See color ad below)*   SOME UNITS

Ⓢ▾ 🍴 🏋 🐕 🏊 📹 🖨 ▣ DATA/PORT / ✕ 🖥 🛏 /
                       FEE   FEE FEE

HOLIDAY INN EXPRESS   Phone: (954)566-4301   **14**

◇◇◇   All Year   1P: $69-$189   2P: $69-$189   XP: $10   F19
Motel   **Location:** US 1; just n of jct SR 816 (Oakland Park Blvd). 3355 N Federal Hwy 33306. Fax: 954/565-1472.
Facility: Bright colors with contemporary furnishings. 144 units. *Bath:* combo or shower only. 2 stories, exterior corridors. **Terms:** cancellation fee imposed. **Amenities:** extended cable TV, hair dryers. *Some:* irons.
Leisure Activities: heated pool. **Guest Services:** [ECP] meal plan available, valet and coin laundry. **Business Services:** meeting rooms. **Cards:** AE, CB, DI, DS, MC, VI. *(See color ad below)*   SOME UNITS

ASK Ⓢ▾ 🍴 🎣 🐕 🏊 📹 🖨 ▣ DATA/PORT / ✕ 🛏 /
                                        FEE

(See map p. 346)

HOLIDAY INN EXPRESS PORT EVERGLADES
CRUISE & CONVENTION CENTER   **Phone:** (954)728-2577 [28]

	6/1-11/30	1P: $89-$179	2P: $89-$179
Motel	12/21-4/15	1P: $139-$159	2P: $139-$159
	12/1-12/20	1P: $99-$109	2P: $99-$109
	4/16-5/31	1P: $89-$99	2P: $89-$99

Location: SR A1A, 1 mi e of US 1. 1500 SE 17th St Cswy 33316. Fax: 954/728-2591. **Facility:** A comfortable lobby and breakfast area. Spacious rooms with light wood tones and colorful room decor. 78 units. *Bath:* combo or shower only. 5 stories, interior corridors. **Terms:** 30 day cancellation notice. **Amenities:** extended cable TV, dual phone lines, voice mail, irons, hair dryers. **Guest Services:** [ECP] meal plan available, area transportation, valet laundry. **Business Services:** meeting rooms. **Cards:** AE, DI, DS, JC, MC, VI. *(See color ad below)*

SOME UNITS

(ASK) (S▽D) (🔌) (📶) (🚹) (🍽) (✆) (🖨) (DATA PORT) / (❌) (📱) /
FEE

HOLIDAY INN FT. LAUDERDALE BEACH   **Phone:** (954)563-5961 [21]

(AAA) (SAVE)	12/25-4/17	1P: $139-$169	XP: $10	F17
	4/18-11/30	1P: $89-$119	XP: $10	F17
Hotel	12/1-12/24	1P: $89-$109	XP: $10	F17

Location: SR A1A, jct SR 838, (E Sunrise Blvd). 999 Ft. Lauderdale Beach Blvd 33304. Fax: 954/564-5261. **Facility:** Large rooms with view of the beach. The wood tones compliment the colors of the decor. The restaurant and lounge area with some art-deco feel to it. New sidewalk cafe opposite the beach. 240 units. Some suites. *Bath:* combo or shower only. 12 stories, interior corridors. **Parking:** extra charge. **Terms:** monthly rates available, package plans. **Amenities:** voice mail, safes, irons, hair dryers. **Dining:** restaurant, 7 am-10 pm, beachfront cafe, $8-$15, cocktails. **Leisure Activities:** heated pool, exercise room. **Guest Services:** [BP] meal plan available, valet laundry. **Business Services:** meeting rooms, administrative services. **Cards:** AE, CB, DI, DS, MC, VI. **Special Amenities:** free newspaper. *(See color ad below)*

SOME UNITS

(S▽D) (🍽) (🍸) (✆) (🏊) (🐟) (✆) (🖨) (💻) (📱) (DATA PORT) / (❌) /
FEE

(See map p. 346)

HOLIDAY INN FORT LAUDERDALE I-95　　　　　　　　　　　**Phone:** (954)776-4880 　⑫

| | 12/1-4/15 | 1P: $85-$110 | 2P: $85-$110 | XP: $10 | F17 |
| Motor Inn | 4/16-11/30 | 1P: $55-$65 | 2P: $55-$65 | XP: $10 | F17 |

Location: I-95, exit 32, just sw of jct Commercial Blvd. 4900 9th Ave (Powerline Rd) 33309. **Fax:** 954/776-1261. **Facility:** A pool area with off-setting colored pavers. Tropical trees and flowing shrubbery. The rooms with classic style Queen Anne furniture. The room decor compliments the furniture. 193 units. Some suites ($85-$120). *Bath:* combo or shower only. 5 stories, exterior corridors. **Terms:** weekly & monthly rates available, package plans. **Amenities:** voice mail, safes, irons, hair dryers. **Leisure Activities:** heated pool, exercise room. **Guest Services:** area transportation, valet and coin laundry. **Business Services:** meeting rooms. **Cards:** AE, CB, DI, DS, MC, VI.　　　　　SOME UNITS

HYATT REGENCY PIER SIXTY SIX　　　　　　　　　　　　**Phone:** (954)525-6666 　㊼

| | All Year | 1P: $239 | 2P: $264 | XP: $25 | F18 |

Location: SR A1A, 1.3 mi e of jct US 1. 2301 SE 17th St Cswy 33316. **Fax:** 954/728-3541. **Facility:** Along the Intracoastal Waterway. Rooms with balcony or patio in garden and tower building. A very relaxing pool area with waterfalls and large deck area. Tropical foliage surrounds all of the property. Just steps away is a very well equipped marina. Rooms are large and have a tropical luxury feel to them. 388 units. Some suites and whirlpool units. *Bath:* combo or shower only. 2-17 stories, interior/exterior corridors. **Parking:** extra charge or valet. **Terms:** check-in 4 pm, 3 day cancellation notice-fee imposed, package plans. **Amenities:** dual phone lines, voice mail, safes, honor bars, irons, hair dryers. *Some:* CD players, fax. **Dining:** 4 restaurants, 6:30 am-11 pm; revolving rooftop lounge, poolside bar & grill, $9-$28, cocktails, also, California Cafe, see separate listing, nightclub, entertainment. **Leisure Activities:** 2 heated pools, whirlpool, fishing, charter fishing, golf privileges, children's program in summer, health spa & salon. *Fee:* sauna, boats, boat dock, marina, scuba diving/snorkeling & equipment, scuba instructions, 2 lighted tennis courts. **Guest Services:** gift shop, area transportation-beach, valet laundry. *Fee:* massage. **Business Services:** conference facilities, administrative services, PC, fax. **Cards:** AE, CB, DI, DS, JC, MC, VI. Affiliated with Hyatt Hotels & Lodges.　　　SOME UNITS

(See map p. 346)

IRELAND'S INN BEACH RESORT

AAA SAVE ◈◈◈
◈◈◈
Motor Inn

			Phone: (954)565-6661	16
12/1-4/30	1P: $166-$299	2P: $166-$299	XP: $10	F16
10/24-11/30	1P: $109-$229	2P: $109-$229	XP: $10	F16
5/1-10/23	1P: $95-$209	2P: $95-$209	XP: $10	F16

Location: 0.8 mi s of Oakland Park Blvd/SR 816, then just e of A1A. 2220 N Atlantic Blvd 33305. Fax: 954/565-8893. **Facility:** Located on the oceanfront. Many rooms with oceanfront views. Many rooms with a washed oak finish and tropical color accents. 74 units. 1 two-bedroom unit, 4 efficiencies and 27 units with kitchen. Some suites ($209-$269) and whirlpool units ($239-$299). 7 stories, exterior corridors. **Parking:** valet. **Terms:** 7 day cancellation notice-fee imposed, weekly rates available, package plans. **Amenities:** extended cable TV, voice mail, safes. *Some:* irons, hair dryers. **Dining:** restaurant, 7:30 am-3 & 5:30-10 pm; beachfront grill 11:30 am-6 pm, $15-$28, entertainment. **Leisure Activities:** 2 heated pools, beach, swimming. **Guest Services:** gift shop, valet laundry. **Business Services:** meeting rooms. **Cards:** AE, MC, VI. **Special Amenities:** free newspaper. *(See color ad p 362)*

SOME UNITS

⟨🅢🄳⟩ ⟨🍴⟩ ⟨🍽⟩ ⟨🏊⟩ ⟨🚗⟩ ⟨💻⟩ ⟨🖥⟩ ⟨🛗⟩ ⟨DATA PORT⟩ / ⟨✕⟩ /

LAGO MAR RESORT HOTEL & CLUB

◈◈◈
Hotel

		Phone: (954)523-6511	49
12/17-4/30	1P: $195-$685	XP: $10	
5/1-11/30	1P: $125-$685	XP: $10	
12/1-12/16	1P: $115-$480	XP: $10	

Location: Just e of SR A1A; 0.5 mi ne of 17th St Cswy Bridge. 1700 S Ocean Ln 33316. Fax: 954/524-6627. **Facility:** Between the ocean and lake on landscaped beachfront grounds. Manicured grounds with tropical trees and flowering plants. Two pools with ample deck space. Elegant public areas. Lobby with a mosaic tile mural. Rooms are spacious with soft tropical colors. 212 units. 17 two-bedroom units. Some suites ($150-$685). *Bath:* combo or shower only. 3-5 stories, interior/exterior corridors. **Parking:** valet. **Terms:** 14 day cancellation notice, in winter, 7 day in summer-fee imposed. **Amenities:** extended cable TV, voice mail, safes, irons, hair dryers. **Leisure Activities:** 2 heated pools, beach, swimming, miniature golf, playground. *Fee:* 4 tennis courts. **Guest Services:** gift shop, complimentary laundry. **Business Services:** conference facilities, fax. **Cards:** AE, CB, DI, MC, VI.

SOME UNITS

⟨🍴⟩ ⟨🍽⟩ ⟨🛗⟩ ⟨🔑⟩ ⟨📷⟩ ⟨🏊⟩ ⟨✕⟩ ⟨📹⟩ ⟨🚗⟩ ⟨DATA PORT⟩ / ⟨VCR⟩ ⟨💻⟩ ⟨🖥⟩ ⟨🛗⟩
FEE

LA QUINTA INN-CYPRESS CREEK

SAVE ◈◈◈
Motel

			Phone: (954)491-7666	1
All Year	1P: $65-$99	2P: $65-$99		

Location: 0.8 mi w of jct I-95, exit 33; 33B northbound at Powerline Rd. 999 W Cypress Creek Rd 33309. Fax: 954/491-7669. **Facility:** Very attractive rooms. Nicely landscaped pool area. 145 units. Some suites and whirlpool units. 4 stories, interior corridors. **Terms:** package plans, small pets only. **Amenities:** video games, dual phone lines, voice mail. **Leisure Activities:** whirlpool, exercise room. **Guest Services:** [ECP] meal plan available, valet and coin laundry. **Business Services:** meeting rooms. **Cards:** AE, CB, DI, DS, MC, VI.

(See color ad below)

SOME UNITS

⟨🅢🄳⟩ ⟨🐾⟩ ⟨🍴⟩ ⟨🏋⟩ ⟨🏊⟩ ⟨💻⟩ ⟨🚗⟩ ⟨💻⟩ ⟨DATA PORT⟩ / ⟨✕⟩ ⟨🖥⟩ ⟨🛗⟩ /
FEE   FEE FEE

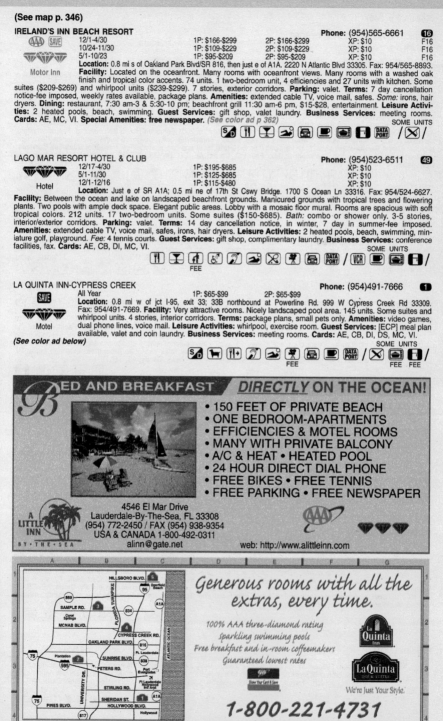

(See map p. 346)

MARRIOTT'S HARBOR BEACH RESORT
Phone: (954)525-4000 📍48

🔶🔶 SAVE

🔻🔻🔻 🔻🔻🔻

Resort

12/1-4/18		2P: $339-$419
9/30-11/30		2P: $249-$399
4/19-6/16		2P: $249-$319
6/17-9/29		2P: $159-$239

Location: E of SR A1A and s of Bahia Mar Marina. 3030 Holiday Dr 33316. Fax: 954/766-6152. **Facility:** Located on the oceanfront. A large beautiful pool area surrounded by tropical foliage and a huge beach. An attractive sitting area in the center lobby. The rooms recently renovated. Warm tropical colors decorate the rooms. 624 units. Some suites ($399-$2500) and whirlpool units. *Bath:* combo or shower only. 15 stories, interior corridors. **Parking:** extra charge or valet. **Terms:** check-in 4 pm, 10 day cancellation notice-fee imposed, package plans. **Amenities:** video games, voice mail, safes, honor bars, irons, hair dryers. *Some:* CD players, fax. **Dining:** dining room, restaurant, 6 am-midnight, pool grill, $12-$30, cocktails, entertainment. **Leisure Activities:** heated pool, saunas, whirlpools, beach, swimming, private beach, fishing, charter sailing, children's program, recreation program, social program, May 15, 2001 European Health Spa opening. *Fee:* windsurfing, waterskiing, scuba diving/snorkeling & equipment, jet skis, sunfish, parasailing, golf privileges, 5 tennis courts, tennis instruction, bicycles. **Guest Services:** gift shop, area transportation-5-10 mile, valet and coin laundry. *Fee:* massage. **Business Services:** conference facilities, administrative services, fax. *Fee:* PC. **Cards:** AE, CB, DI, DS, JC, MC, VI. **Special Amenities: free newspaper.**

SOME UNITS

🔳 FEE 🔳 🔳 🔳 FEE 🔳 🔳 🔳 FEE 🔳 🔳 🔳 DATA PORT / 🔳 VCR 🔳

MOTEL 6 - 55
Phone: 954/760-7999 📍56

🔻

Motel

1/18-4/15	1P: $58-$68		2P: $64-$74	XP: $3	F17
12/1-1/17	1P: $52-$62		2P: $58-$68	XP: $3	F17
4/16-11/30	1P: $45-$55		2P: $51-$61	XP: $3	F17

Location: I-95, exit 27 (SR 84E), just e, then U-turn at light. 1801 SR 84 33315. Fax: 954/832-0653. **Facility:** For the budget traveler. Rooms are small, with contemporary decor. Just off the interstate. 106 units. *Bath:* shower only. 2 stories. **Leisure Activities:** heated pool. **Guest Services:** coin laundry. **Cards:** AE, CB, DI, DS, MC, VI.

SOME UNITS

🔳 🔳 🔳 🔳 🔳 🔳 / 🔳 /

NINA LEE/IMPERIAL HOUSE MOTEL
Phone: (954)524-1568 📍40

🔶🔶 SAVE

🔻

Motel

12/1-12/23 & 4/16-11/30	1P: $49-$135	2P: $49-$135	XP: $9	F18
12/24-4/15	1P: $79	2P: $135	XP: $12	F18

Location: 0.3 mi s of Bahia Mar; just w of SR A1A. 3048 Harbor Dr 33316. Fax: 954/763-2931. **Facility:** Small and cozy property. Nice sitting area around pool; one- and two- bedroom units with sitting room. Beach is just a block away. A gem of a place to stay. 25 units. 4 two-bedroom units, 6 efficiencies and 12 units with kitchen. 2 stories, exterior corridors. **Terms:** weekly & monthly rates available. **Amenities:** extended cable TV. **Leisure Activities:** heated pool, recreation privileges at Sheraton Yankee Trader. **Cards:** AE, CB, DI, MC, VI.

🔳 🔳 🔳 🔳 🔳

OAKLAND PARK INN
Phone: (954)565-4601 📍15

🔶🔶 SAVE

🔻🔻🔻 🔻🔻🔻

Motel

2/9-4/15	1P: $85-$150	2P: $85-$150	XP: $10	F16
12/23-2/8	1P: $55-$119	2P: $55-$119	XP: $10	F16
4/16-11/30	1P: $55-$95	2P: $55-$95	XP: $10	F16
12/1-12/22	1P: $48-$85	2P: $48-$85	XP: $10	F16

Location: US 1, just s of jct SR 816, Oakland Park Blvd. 3001 N Federal Hwy 33306. Fax: 954/565-0384. **Facility:** All rooms overlook central pool patio. Some themed rooms with exotic decor. 108 units, 19 with efficiency. Some whirlpool units ($75-$150). 3 stories, exterior corridors. **Terms:** cancellation fee imposed, weekly rates available. **Amenities:** *Some:* safes. **Leisure Activities:** heated pool. **Guest Services:** coin laundry. **Cards:** AE, CB, DI, DS, MC, VI. **Special Amenities: free continental breakfast and free room upgrade (subject to availability with advanced reservations).**

SOME UNITS

🔳 🔳 / 🔳 VCR 🔳 FEE

OCEAN HACIENDA INN
Phone: (954)564-7800 📍19

🔶🔶 SAVE

🔻🔻 🔻🔻

Motel

12/1-5/31	1P: $99-$195	2P: $99-$195	XP: $10	F12
6/1-11/30	1P: $65-$129	2P: $65-$129	XP: $10	F12

Location: On SR A1A, 1 mi n of SR 816. 1924 N Atlantic Blvd 33305. Fax: 954/396-9971. **Facility:** Located on the ocean. Most rooms with pool view. Some with ocean view. 39 units. 4 two-bedroom units and 20 efficiencies. Some whirlpool units. *Bath:* combo or shower only. 3 stories, exterior corridors. **Terms:** 14 day cancellation notice, 3 day off season, weekly & monthly rates available. **Amenities:** extended cable TV, voice mail. **Leisure Activities:** heated pool, beach, swimming. **Guest Services:** [CP] meal plan available, coin laundry. **Cards:** AE, CB, DI, DS, MC, VI. **Special Amenities: early check-in/late check-out and free room upgrade (subject to availability with advanced reservations).** *(See color ad p 365)*

SOME UNITS

🔳 🔳 🔳 / 🔳 VCR 🔳 🔳 🔳 /

PRESIDIO MOTEL
Phone: (954)564-6548 📍18

🔻🔻

Motel

MC, VI.

Property failed to provide current rates

Location: I-95, exit 31, 3.4 mi e to US 1 (Federal Hwy), then 1.3 mi s. 1601 N Federal Hwy 33305. **Facility:** Small rooms. Nice pool area. 22 units, 1 with efficiency. Some whirlpool units. *Bath:* combo or shower only. 1 story, exterior corridors. **Terms:** weekly rates available. **Leisure Activities:** pool heated in winter. **Cards:** AE, DI,

SOME UNITS

🔳 🔳 🔳 🔳 / 🔳 🔳 /

(See map p. 346)

RADISSON BAHIA MAR BEACH RESORT

AAA SAVE
▽▽▽▽

Hotel

			Phone: (954)764-2233	**39**
12/1-5/31	1P: $134-$188	2P: $144-$198	XP: $10	F12
10/1-11/30	1P: $116-$152	2P: $126-$162	XP: $10	F12
6/1-9/30	1P: $89-$125	2P: $99-$135	XP: $10	F12

Location: SR A1A, 0.5 mi s of Las Olas Blvd. 801 Seabreeze Blvd 33316. Fax: 954/523-5424. **Facility:** Opposite ocean and beach. Private sky bridge to beach. Some rooms with ocean, city or harbor view. Pool area overlooks the Intracoastal Waterway and harbor. 298 units. Some suites ($450-$1000). **Bath:** combo or shower only. 4-16 stories, interior corridors. **Parking:** extra charge or valet. **Terms:** 3 day cancellation notice-fee imposed, package plans. **Amenities:** voice mail, safes, honor bars, irons, hair dryers. **Dining:** restaurant, deli, 6:30 am-10:30 pm, $7-$15, cocktails. **Leisure Activities:** heated pool, charter fishing, 4 lighted tennis courts, exercise room. *Fee:* marina, scuba diving/snorkeling & equipment, fishing, PADI dive school, water taxi stop. **Guest Services:** [BP] meal plan available, gift shop, valet and coin laundry. **Business Services:** meeting rooms, fax. **Cards:** AE, CB, DI, DS, JC, MC, VI. **Special Amenities:** free room upgrade (subject to availability with advanced reservations). *(See color ad below)* SOME UNITS

⑤Ⓓ ⑪ 🍴 Ⓣ 🅰️ 🅴 📶 🛟 ✖️ 🏋️ 🖨️ 💻 DATA PORT / ✖️ 🛗 /
　　　　FEE　　　　　　　　　　FEE　　　　　　　　　　　　　FEE

(See map p. 346)

RAMADA PLAZA BEACH RESORT — Phone: (954)565-6611   **13**

Hotel

12/16-4/15	1P: $139-$300	2P: $139-$300	XP: $10	F17
4/16-11/30	1P: $129-$299	2P: $129-$299	XP: $10	F17
12/1-12/15	1P: $109-$199	2P: $109-$209	XP: $10	F17

Location: Just e of SR A1A, 0.5 mi n of jct SR 816 (Oakland Park Blvd). 4060 Galt Ocean Dr 33308-6597. Fax: 954/564-7730. **Facility:** Attractive public areas and inviting pool deck overlooking the ocean. Most rooms with balcony, some with ocean view. 225 units, 15 with efficiency. Some suites. 9 stories, interior corridors. **Parking:** extra charge or valet. **Terms:** check-in 4 pm, cancellation fee imposed, package plans. **Amenities:** extended cable TV, voice mail, safes (fee), irons, hair dryers. **Leisure Activities:** heated pool, whirlpool, beach, swimming, scuba diving, snorkeling, exercise room. *Fee:* sailboats, scuba & snorkeling equipment. **Guest Services:** gift shop, valet laundry. **Business Services:** meeting rooms, fax. **Cards:** AE, CB, DI, DS, MC, VI.

SOME UNITS

RED ROOF INN — Phone: (954)776-6333   **9**

Motel

12/1-4/15	1P: $50-$80	2P: $70-$90	XP: $6	F18
4/16-11/30	1P: $45-$55	2P: $50-$80	XP: $6	F18

Location: On Powerline Rd; just sw of jct Commercial Blvd and I-95, exit 32. 4800 Powerline Rd 33309. Fax: 954/776-3648. **Facility:** Comfortable, modern, contemporary room furnishings and decor. 104 units. *Bath:* combo or shower only. 4 stories, interior corridors. **Terms:** small pets only. **Amenities:** video games, voice mail. **Leisure Activities:** heated pool. **Guest Services:** [CP] meal plan available. **Cards:** AE, CB, DI, DS, MC, VI. **Special Amenities:** free local telephone calls and free newspaper.

SOME UNITS

THE RIVER INN ON THE WATER — Phone: (954)564-6411   **20**

Motel

12/23-4/12	1P: $110-$145	2P: $110-$145	XP: $10	F12
12/1-12/22 & 4/13-11/30	1P: $66-$87	2P: $66-$87	XP: $10	F12

Location: 0.3 mi n of jct US 1 and 838 (Sunrise Blvd). 1180 N Federal Hwy 33304. Fax: 954/566-6477. **Facility:** Oversized rooms, some with river view. Close to Galleria Mall. 58 units, 18 with efficiency. *Bath:* combo or shower only. 2 stories, exterior corridors. **Amenities:** extended cable TV, safes (fee). **Leisure Activities:** boat dock, picnic tables with grills along the riverside. **Guest Services:** coin laundry. **Business Services:** meeting rooms. **Cards:** AE, CB, DI, DS, MC. **Special Amenities:** free continental breakfast.

SOME UNITS

(See map p. 346)

RIVERSIDE HOTEL

Phone: (954)467-0671 **38**

(AAA) [SAVE]

Classic Hotel

12/18-4/15	2P: $169-$219	XP: $15	F16
12/1-12/17 & 10/1-11/30	2P: $139-$169	XP: $10	F16
4/16-9/30	2P: $124-$144	XP: $10	F16

Location: 2 mi w of SR A1A, on Las Olas Blvd; at jct US 1 underpass, main entrance on SE 4th St. 620 E Las Olas Blvd 33301. Fax: 954/462-2148. **Facility:** Historic. In fashionable historic district with lush gardens along The New River. Old World charm, some rooms with canopy beds. 109 units. Some suites ($199-$389). *Bath:* combo or shower only. 3-6 stories, interior corridors. **Parking:** extra charge or valet. **Terms:** package plans. **Amenities:** extended cable TV, video games, voice mail, irons, hair dryers. **Dining:** dining room, restaurant, 6:30 am-midnight, $10-$40, cocktails, also, The Grill Room on Las Olas, see separate listing. **Leisure Activities:** heated pool. **Guest Services:** gift shop, afternoon tea, valet laundry. **Business Services:** meeting rooms. **Cards:** AE, CB, DI, MC, VI. **Special Amenities:** free newspaper and free room upgrade (subject to availability with advanced reservations). *(See color ad p 366)*

SOME UNITS

FEE

THE ROYAL PAVILION

Phone: (954)564-8556 **31**

(AAA) [SAVE]

Motel

12/1-5/15	2P: $75-$105	XP: $10	F5
5/16-11/30	2P: $45-$90	XP: $10	F5

Location: Just w of SR A1A; 0.5 mi s of SR 838 (Sunrise Blvd); at Viramar St and Breakers Ave. 3003 Viramar St 33304. Fax: 954/566-5159. **Facility:** European touches. Very well maintained grounds. 19 units, 15 with kitchen. *Bath:* combo or shower only. 2 stories, exterior corridors. **Terms:** 14 day cancellation notice-fee imposed, weekly & monthly rates available. **Amenities:** extended cable TV. **Guest Services:** coin laundry. **Cards:** MC, VI. **Special Amenities:** free room upgrade and preferred room (each subject to availability with advanced reservations).

SOME UNITS

ROYAL SAXON APARTMENTS

Phone: 954/566-7424 **32**

(AAA) [SAVE]

Motel

All Year 1P: $75-$125 2P: $75-$125

Location: Just w of SR A1A; 0.5 mi s of SR 838 (Sunrise Blvd) at corner of Breakers Ave and Terranar St. 551 Breakers Ave 33304. Fax: 954/566-8305. **Facility:** Attractive pool courtyard. 15 units with kitchen. 2 stories, exterior corridors. **Terms:** age restrictions may apply. **Amenities:** extended cable TV. **Leisure Activities:** heated pool. **Guest Services:** [CP] meal plan available, coin laundry. **Cards:** MC, VI. **Special Amenities:** early check-in/late check-out and free newspaper.

(See map p. 346)

ROYAL TRAVEL INN
(AAA) (SAVE)

Motel

12/15-4/15	1P: $59-$119	2P: $59-$119
12/1-12/14 & 4/16-11/30	1P: $49-$59	2P: $49-$59

Phone: (954)525-1436　
XP: $10　F12
XP: $10　F12

Location: On US 1, just s of jct Davie Blvd. 1215 S Federal Hwy 33316. Fax: 954/424-9825. **Facility:** Smaller rooms located on busy highway. 15 units. **Bath:** shower only. 1 story, exterior corridors. **Terms:** weekly rates available. **Amenities:** extended cable TV, hair dryers. **Cards:** AE, DI, MC, VI.　SOME UNITS

SANS SOUCI AT THE BEACH

Motel

Property failed to provide current rates　**Phone:** 954/564-4311　②④

Location: 0.4 mi s on SR A1A from jct SR 838 (Sunrise Blvd), w on Aurumar St on corner. 618 N Birch Rd 33304. Fax: 954/564-4472. **Facility:** A comfortable courtyard with pool and plant life. Many of the rooms overlook this area. The rooms are spacious and attractively decorated. 20 units, 4 with efficiency. 3 stories (no elevator), exterior corridors. **Amenities:** extended cable TV, safes (fee). **Leisure Activities:** heated pool. **Guest Services:** coin laundry. **Cards:** AE, DS, MC, VI.

SEA CHATEAU RESORT MOTEL
(AAA) (SAVE)

Motel

2/1-4/30	1P: $70-$80	2P: $70-$80
12/1-1/31	1P: $55-$65	2P: $55-$65
5/1-11/30	1P: $45-$55	2P: $45-$55

Phone: (954)566-8331　②⑨
XP: $15
XP: $15
XP: $10

Location: 2 blks w of SR A1A, 0.5 mi s of SR 838, (Sunrise Blvd). 555 N Birch Rd & Terramar St 33304. Fax: 954/564-2411. **Facility;** Individually decorated rooms. Landscaped pool courtyard area. 19 units, 5 with efficiency. 2 stories, exterior corridors. **Terms:** age restrictions may apply, 7 day cancellation notice, monthly rates available. **Special Amenities:** free room upgrade and preferred room (each subject to availability with advanced reservations).　SOME UNITS

FEE

SEA VIEW RESORT MOTEL
(AAA) (SAVE)

Motel

12/14-4/20	1P: $75-$135	2P: $75-$135
12/1-12/13 & 4/21-11/30	1P: $45-$85	2P: $45-$85

Phone: (954)564-3151　③⓪
XP: $10　F12
XP: $10　F12

Location: 2 blks w of SR A1A; 0.5 mi s of Sunrise Blvd. 550 N Birch Rd 33304. Fax: 954/561-9147. **Facility:** Inviting pool terrace. 21 units. 10 efficiencies and 7 units with kitchen. 2 stories, exterior corridors. **Terms:** 3 day cancellation notice-fee imposed, weekly & monthly rates available. **Amenities:** extended cable TV, safes (fee). **Leisure Activities:** heated pool. **Guest Services:** coin laundry. **Cards:** AE, MC, VI. *(See color ad below)*　SOME UNITS

(See map p. 346)

SHERATON SUITES CYPRESS CREEK

Suite Hotel

Phone: (954)772-5400 [2]

	1P	2P	XP	
1/1-5/18	1P: $134-$250	2P: $134-$250	XP: $10	F17
10/1-11/30	1P: $123-$199	2P: $123-$199	XP: $10	F17
12/1-12/31	1P: $123-$189	2P: $123-$189	XP: $10	F17
5/19-9/30	1P: $95-$179	2P: $95-$179	XP: $10	F17

Location: I-95, exit 33B (Cypress Creek Rd), just w. 555 NW 62nd St 33309. Fax: 954/772-5490. **Facility:** A Spanish style structure surrounded by trees and flowers. The pool area is relaxing with lots of tropical plants. A marble tile lobby with very comfortable sitting areas. A large atrium area with soothing surroundings. Large rooms with a tropical Florida look. 253 units. Some suites. 8 stories, exterior corridors. **Parking:** valet. **Amenities:** extended cable TV, dual phone lines, voice mail, irons, hair dryers. *Some:* fax. **Leisure Activities:** heated pool, sauna, whirlpool. **Guest Services:** gift shop, area transportation, valet and coin laundry. **Business Services:** meeting rooms, fax. **Cards:** AE, CB, DI, DS, MC, VI.

SOME UNITS

ASK Sᴅ ⑂ ⓨ ⊘ ⟰ ⊠ 🖭 🗁 ⊟ DATA PORT /⊠/
FEE

SHERATON-YANKEE CLIPPER BEACH HOTEL

Hotel

Phone: (954)524-5551 [41]

	1P	2P	XP	
12/1-4/14	1P: $239-$289	2P: $239-$289	XP: $20	F17
4/15-6/2 & 10/12-11/30	1P: $209-$269	2P: $209-$269	XP: $20	F17
6/3-10/11	1P: $169-$199	2P: $169-$199	XP: $20	F17

Location: SR A1A, just s of Bahia Mar Marina. 1140 Seabreeze Blvd (A1A) 33316. Fax: 954/523-5376. **Facility:** In 4 inter-connected buildings on and across from beach. Spacious rooms furnished with light wood-tone furniture. Decor is bright to soft Island color scheme. 502 units. Some suites. *Bath:* combo or shower only. 5-11 stories, interior/exterior corridors. **Parking:** extra charge or valet. **Terms:** cancellation fee imposed, package plans. **Amenities:** dual phone lines, voice mail, safes, irons, hair dryers. **Dining:** restaurant, deli, 24 hours, $10-$20, cocktails, entertainment. **Leisure Activities:** 3 heated pools, beach, swimming, beach volleyball, children's program, exercise room. **Guest Services:** gift shop, valet and coin laundry. **Business Services:** meeting rooms, fax. **Cards:** AE, CB, DI, DS, MC, VI. **Special Amenities:** free newspaper.

SOME UNITS

Sᴅ ⑂ ⓨ ⓣ ⚿ ⊘ ⟰ ⊠ 🖭 🗁 DATA PORT /⊠ ⊟/
FEE FEE

SHERATON YANKEE TRADER BEACH HOTEL

Hotel

Phone: (954)467-1111 [35]

	1P	2P	XP	
12/1-4/14	1P: $239-$289	2P: $239-$289	XP: $20	F17
4/15-6/2 & 10/12-11/30	1P: $209-$269	2P: $209-$269	XP: $20	F17
6/3-10/11	1P: $169-$199	2P: $169-$199	XP: $20	F17

Location: SR A1A, 0.75 mi s of Sunrise Blvd. 321 N Fort Lauderdale Beach Blvd 33304. Fax: 954/462-2342. **Facility:** Two adjoining towers, walking bridge to beach. Attractive public areas. Rooms furnished in light wood tones. Color scheme is bright to soft Island colors. 460 units. *Bath:* combo or shower only. 14-15 stories, interior corridors. **Parking:** extra charge or valet. **Terms:** cancellation fee imposed, package plans. **Amenities:** dual phone lines, voice mail, safes, irons, hair dryers. **Dining:** restaurant, deli, 24 hour sidewalk cafe, $9-$34, cocktails, entertainment. **Leisure Activities:** 2 heated pools, beach access, 3 tennis courts, exercise room. **Guest Services:** gift shop, valet and coin laundry. **Business Services:** conference facilities, fax. **Cards:** AE, CB, DI, DS, MC, VI. **Special Amenities:** free newspaper.

SOME UNITS

Sᴅ ⑂ ⓨ ⓣ ⚿ ⊘ ⟰ ⊠ 🖭 🗁 DATA PORT /⊠ ⊟/
FEE FEE

THREE SUNS INN

Motel

Phone: (954)563-7926 [27]

	2P	XP	
12/1-4/14	2P: $75-$108	XP: $5	F12
4/15-11/30	2P: $45-$75	XP: $5	F12

Location: 6 blks s of Sunrise Blvd on SR A1A, w corner of Breakers and Windamar St. 3016 Windamar St 33304. Fax: 954/563-7988. **Facility:** Some large rooms. Well kept property. 19 units. 5 efficiencies and 6 units with kitchen. 3 stories (no elevator), exterior corridors. **Terms:** 5 day cancellation notice, weekly & monthly rates available. **Amenities:** extended cable TV. *Some:* safes (fee). **Leisure Activities:** heated pool. *Fee:* bicycles. **Guest Services:** coin laundry. **Cards:** AE, DI, MC, VI.

SOME UNITS

ASK ⟰ 🖭 ⊟ /⊠ 🗁/

TOWNEPLACE SUITES BY MARRIOTT

Extended Stay
Motel

Phone: (954)484-2214 [7]

12/21-3/31	1P: $99-$119	
12/1-12/20 & 4/1-11/30	1P: $65-$85	

Location: I-95, exit 33, Cypress Creek Rd/SR 811, 2.7 mi w, then 0.5 mi s on NW 31st St. 3100 Prospect Rd 33309. Fax: 954/484-4533. **Facility:** Spacious and well equipped units. 95 efficiencies. 22 two-bedroom units. Some suites ($65-$119). *Bath:* combo or shower only. 3 stories, interior corridors. **Terms:** cancellation fee imposed, small pets only (fee). **Amenities:** extended cable TV, video games, dual phone lines, voice mail, irons. **Leisure Activities:** small heated pool, exercise room. **Cards:** AE, DI, DS, JC, MC, VI. *(See color ad p 357)*

ASK Sᴅ 🐾 ⚿ ⊘ ⟰ ⊠ 🖭 🗁 ⊟ DATA PORT

TROPI ROCK RESORT

Motel

Phone: (954)564-0523 [57]

	2P	XP	
All Year	2P: $65-$98	XP: $5	F12

Location: 0.3 mi s of jct SR 838 (Sunrise Blvd) on SR A1A, then just right. 2900 Belmar St 33304. Fax: 954/564-1313. **Facility:** Rooms are decorated to a theme decor. An attractive pool area. 32 units. 3 efficiencies and 17 units with kitchen. 3 stories, exterior corridors. **Terms:** 14 day cancellation notice-fee imposed, weekly & monthly rates available. **Amenities:** extended cable TV, voice mail, hair dryers. *Some:* CD players. **Leisure Activities:** heated pool, rooftop sun deck, 2 lighted tennis courts, exercise room. **Guest Services:** coin laundry. **Cards:** AE, CB, DI, DS, MC, VI.

SOME UNITS

Sᴅ ⑂ ⟰ 🗁 ⊟ DATA PORT /⊠ VCR 🗁/
FEE

(See map p. 346)

WATERFRONT INNS BEACH RETREAT   Phone: (954)564-4341   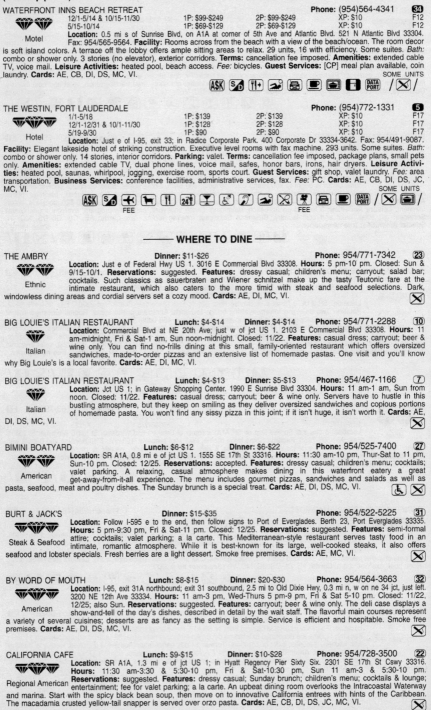 34
♥♥ ♥♥

12/1-5/14 & 10/15-11/30	1P: $99-$249	2P: $99-$249	XP: $10 F12
5/15-10/14	1P: $69-$129	2P: $69-$129	XP: $10 F12

Motel   **Location:** 0.5 mi s of Sunrise Blvd, on A1A at corner of 5th Ave and Atlantic Blvd. 521 N Atlantic Blvd 33304. Fax: 954/565-9564. **Facility:** Rooms across from the beach with a view of the beach/ocean. The room decor is soft island colors. A terrace off the lobby offers ample sitting areas to relax. 29 units, 16 with efficiency. Some suites. *Bath:* combo or shower only. 3 stories (no elevator), exterior corridors. **Terms:** cancellation fee imposed. **Amenities:** extended cable TV, voice mail. **Leisure Activities:** heated pool, beach access. *Fee:* bicycles. **Guest Services:** [CP] meal plan available, coin laundry. **Cards:** AE, CB, DI, DS, MC, VI.

SOME UNITS

THE WESTIN, FORT LAUDERDALE   Phone: (954)772-1331   5
♥♥♥

1/1-5/18	1P: $139	2P: $139	XP: $10 F17
12/1-12/31 & 10/1-11/30	1P: $128	2P: $128	XP: $10 F17
5/19-9/30	1P: $90	2P: $90	XP: $10 F17

Hotel   **Location:** Just e of I-95, exit 33; in Radice Corporate Park. 400 Corporate Dr 33334-3642. Fax: 954/491-9087. **Facility:** Elegant lakeside hotel of striking construction. Executive level rooms with fax machine. 293 units. Some suites. *Bath:* combo or shower only. 14 stories, interior corridors. **Parking:** valet. **Terms:** cancellation fee imposed, package plans, small pets only. **Amenities:** extended cable TV, dual phone lines, voice mail, safes, honor bars, irons, hair dryers. **Leisure Activities:** heated pool, saunas, whirlpool, jogging, exercise room, sports court. **Guest Services:** gift shop, valet laundry. *Fee:* area transportation. **Business Services:** conference facilities, administrative services, fax. *Fee:* PC. **Cards:** AE, CB, DI, DS, JC, MC, VI.

SOME UNITS

─── **WHERE TO DINE** ───

THE AMBRY   Dinner: $11-$26   Phone: 954/771-7342   23
♥♥   **Location:** Just e of Federal Hwy US 1. 3016 E Commercial Blvd 33308. **Hours:** 5 pm-10 pm. Closed: Sun & 9/15-10/1. **Reservations:** suggested. **Features:** dressy casual; children's menu; carryout; salad bar; cocktails. Such classics as sauerbraten and Wiener schnitzel make up the tasty Teutonic fare at the
Ethnic   intimate restaurant, which also caters to the more timid with steak and seafood selections. Dark, windowless dining areas and cordial servers set a cozy mood. **Cards:** AE, DI, MC, VI.

BIG LOUIE'S ITALIAN RESTAURANT   Lunch: $4-$14   Dinner: $4-$14   Phone: 954/771-2288   10
♥   **Location:** Commercial Blvd at NE 20th Ave; just w of jct US 1. 2103 E Commercial Blvd 33308. **Hours:** 11 am-midnight, Fri & Sat-1 am, Sun noon-midnight. Closed: 11/22. **Features:** casual dress; carryout; beer & wine only. You can find no-frills dining at this small, family-oriented restaurant which offers oversized
Italian   sandwiches, made-to-order pizzas and an extensive list of homemade pastas. One visit and you'll know why Big Louie's is a local favorite. **Cards:** AE, DI, MC, VI.

BIG LOUIE'S ITALIAN RESTAURANT   Lunch: $4-$13   Dinner: $5-$13   Phone: 954/467-1166   7
♥   **Location:** Jct US 1; in Gateway Shopping Center. 1990 E Sunrise Blvd 33304. **Hours:** 11 am-1 am, Sun from noon. Closed: 11/22. **Features:** casual dress; carryout; beer & wine only. Servers have to hustle in this
Italian   bustling atmosphere, but they keep on smiling as they deliver oversized sandwiches and copious portions
DI, DS, MC, VI.   of homemade pasta. You won't find any sissy pizza in this joint; if it isn't huge, it isn't worth it. **Cards:** AE,

BIMINI BOATYARD   Lunch: $6-$12   Dinner: $6-$22   Phone: 954/525-7400   27
♥♥ ♥♥   **Location:** SR A1A, 0.8 mi e of jct US 1. 1555 SE 17th St 33316. **Hours:** 11:30 am-11 pm, Thur-Sat to 11 pm, Sun-10 pm. Closed: 12/25. **Reservations:** accepted. **Features:** dressy casual; children's menu; cocktails; valet parking. A relaxing, casual atmosphere makes dining in this waterfront eatery a great
American   get-away-from-it-all experience. The menu includes gourmet pizzas, sandwiches and salads as well as pasta, seafood, meat and poultry dishes. The Sunday brunch is a special treat. **Cards:** AE, DI, DS, MC, VI.

BURT & JACK'S   Dinner: $15-$35   Phone: 954/522-5225   31
♥♥♥♥   **Location:** Follow I-595 e to the end, then follow signs to Port of Everglades. Berth 23, Port Everglades 33335. **Hours:** 5 pm-9:30 pm, Fri & Sat-11 pm. Closed: 12/25. **Reservations:** suggested. **Features:** semi-formal attire; cocktails; valet parking; a la carte. This Mediterranean-style restaurant serves tasty food in an
Steak & Seafood   intimate, romantic atmosphere. While it is best-known for its large, well-cooked steaks, it also offers seafood and lobster specials. Fresh berries are a light dessert. Smoke free premises. **Cards:** AE, MC, VI.

BY WORD OF MOUTH   Lunch: $8-$15   Dinner: $20-$30   Phone: 954/564-3663   32
♥♥♥   **Location:** I-95, exit 31A northbound; exit 31 southbound, 2.5 mi to Old Dixie Hwy, 0.3 mi n, w on ne 34 jct, just left. 3200 NE 12th Ave 33334. **Hours:** 11 am-3 pm, Wed-Thurs 5 pm-9 pm, Fri & Sat 5-10 pm. Closed: 11/22, 12/25; also Sun. **Reservations:** suggested. **Features:** carryout; beer & wine only. The deli case displays a
American   show-and-tell of the day's dishes, described in detail by the wait staff. The flavorful main courses represent a variety of several cuisines; desserts are as fancy as the setting is simple. Service is efficient and hospitable. Smoke free premises. **Cards:** AE, DI, DS, MC, VI.

CALIFORNIA CAFE   Lunch: $9-$15   Dinner: $10-$28   Phone: 954/728-3500   22
♥♥♥♥   **Location:** SR A1A, 1.3 mi e of jct US 1; in Hyatt Regency Pier Sixty Six. 2301 SE 17th St Cswy 33316. **Hours:** 11:30 am-3:30 & 5:30-10 pm, Fri & Sat-10:30 pm, Sun 11 am-3 & 5:30-10 pm.
Regional American   **Reservations:** suggested. **Features:** dressy casual; Sunday brunch; children's menu; cocktails & lounge; entertainment; fee for valet parking; a la carte. An upbeat dining room overlooks the Intracoastal Waterway and marina. Start with the spicy black bean soup, then move on to innovative California entrees with hints of the Caribbean. The macadamia crusted yellow-tail snapper is served over orzo pasta. **Cards:** AE, CB, DI, DS, JC, MC, VI.

(See map p. 346)

CANYON
▼▼▼
Southwest
American

Dinner: $13-$25 **Phone:** 954/765-1950 36
Location: Just w of jct US 1 (Federal Hwy) and 19th Ave. 1818 E Sunrise Blvd 33304. **Hours:** 5 pm-11 pm; Fri & Sat-midnight. **Closed:** 11/22, 12/25. **Reservations:** suggested. **Features:** dressy casual; cocktails & lounge; street parking; a la carte. Fabulous green chilies are used in many dishes on this eclectic menu. You'll also find an unusual group of Southwestern dishes with some Asian touches. The decor is very warm and Southwestern, and the service will fulfill your every need. **Cards:** AE, DI, DS, MC, VI. ✕

CASABLANCA CAFE
▼▼ ▼▼
American

Lunch: $7-$13 **Dinner:** $11-$17 **Phone:** 954/764-3500 37
Location: At Alhambra St and Atlantic Blvd. 3049 Alhambra St 33305. **Hours:** 11:30 am-11 pm, Fri & Sat-11:30 pm. **Features:** carryout; cocktails; entertainment; fee for parking; a la carte. An extraordinary menu combines influences from the cuisines of Morocco, Mexico, Japan, Italy, Spain, Cuba, the Caribbean and even Louisiana Cajun country. Fresh, authentic ingredients and a chic Moroccan setting make this a truly exotic experience. **Cards:** AE, CB, DI, DS, MC, VI.

THE CAVES
▼▼ ▼▼
American

Dinner: $11-$24 **Phone:** 954/561-4622 38
Location: 1 mi n of jct SR 838 (Sunrise Blvd). 2205 N Federal Hwy 33305. **Reservations:** suggested; weekends. **Features:** casual dress; children's menu; salad bar; cocktails. The kids will love the sculpted caves and the sight of servers dressed in leopard-print prehistoric garb. You'll enjoy good, hearty fare with classic meat and seafood dishes, as well as children's selections like "fried pterodactyl" (chicken nuggets). **Cards:** AE, CB, DI, DS, MC, VI. ✕

CHARLEY'S CRAB
▼▼▼
Seafood

Lunch: $6-$17 **Dinner:** $12-$34 **Phone:** 954/561-4800 6
Location: Off SR A1A, just s of jct Oakland Park Blvd via NE 30th St. 3000 NE 32nd Ave 33308. **Hours:** 11:30 am-10 pm, Fri & Sat-11 pm, Sun from 11 am. **Reservations:** suggested. **Features:** dressy casual; Sunday brunch; children's menu; early bird specials; carryout; cocktails & lounge; valet parking; a la carte. A knowledgeable wait staff can reel off the characteristics of the tantalizing array of dishes on the restaurant's menu. On the Intracoastal Waterway, the eatery features cozy, indoor dining as well as a comfortable, breezy terrace. **Cards:** AE, DI, DS, MC, VI. ✕

EDUARDO DE SAN ANGEL
▼▼▼
Ethnic

Dinner: $15-$22 **Phone:** 954/772-4731 46
Location: Just e of US Federal Hwy. 2822 E Commercial Blvd 33308. **Hours:** 5:30 pm-10:30 pm. **Closed:** Sun & 6/1-6/13. **Reservations:** required. **Features:** cocktails; a la carte. Not your typical Mexican cuisine, this menu lists gourmet specialties masterfully presented in sophisticated surroundings. Mexican crepes overflow with asadero cheese in a squash-blossom sauce, and a wonderful goat cheese laces the black bean soup. **Cards:** AE, DI, MC, VI. ✕

EVANGELINE RESTAURANT
▼▼▼
Ethnic

Lunch: $7-$16 **Dinner:** $12-$19 **Phone:** 954/522-7001 47
Location: 211 S Atlantic Blvd 33316. **Hours:** 10:30 am-1 am, Fri & Sat-2 am, Sun from 10:30 am. **Reservations:** suggested. **Features:** dressy casual; Sunday brunch; cocktails; street parking; a la carte. Elegant and romantic, it offers sophisticated dishes highlighted by Cajun ingredients. "Swamp spawns"—alligator, crawfish and catfish—create an unusual balance with traditional meat and poultry entrees. Enjoy performances by a Dixieland band. **Cards:** AE, DI, MC, VI.

FOOD LOVERS AMERICAN CAFE
▼▼ ▼▼
American

Dinner: $11-$18 **Phone:** 954/566-9606 49
Location: 1576 E Oakland Park Blvd 33334. **Hours:** 5:30 pm-9:30 pm, Fri & Sat-10:30 pm, Sun-9:30 pm. **Closed:** Mon. **Reservations:** suggested. **Features:** dressy casual; beer & wine only. Excellent fare with a French flair is the norm in this polished, yet homey, atmosphere. Although the menu comprises primarily seafood, meat and poultry dishes, it also boasts a multicultural flavor, with such entrees as Hungarian goulash over linguine. **Cards:** DS, MC, VI. ✕

GIBBY'S
▼▼▼
Steak & Seafood

Lunch: $13 **Dinner:** $14-$28 **Phone:** 954/565-2929 4
Location: Just s of Oakland Park Blvd (SR 816); 1.5 mi e of I-95 exit 31A northbound, exit 31 southbound. 2900 NE 12 Terr 33334. **Hours:** 5 pm-10 pm, Sat noon-2:30 & 4:30-11 pm, Sun noon-2:30 & 4:30-10 pm. **Reservations:** suggested. **Features:** dressy casual; early bird specials; cocktails & lounge; valet parking. A mouth-watering menu features such entrees as prime-aged steak, rack of lamb, stone crab and live Maine lobster as well as homemade pastries and straight-from-the-oven cracked wheat bread. The country-club-style dining rooms offer relaxed comfort. **Cards:** AE, DI, DS, MC, VI. ✕

THE GRILL ROOM ON LAS OLAS
AAA
▼▼▼▼
Continental

Dinner: $20-$40 **Phone:** 954/467-2555 55
Location: 2 mi w of SR A1A, on Las Olas Blvd; at jct US 1 underpass, main entrance on SE 4th St; in Riverside Hotel. 620 E Las Olas Blvd 33301. **Hours:** 6 pm-11 pm. **Closed:** Sun. **Reservations:** required. **Features:** dressy casual; cocktails & lounge; entertainment; fee for parking & valet parking; a la carte. Excellent preparations feature aged meat and fresh fish and are served in a contemporary dining room. Cordial servers bring such exquisitely presented dishes as shrimp Wellington. Consult an extensive wine list to find the right complement for your meal. **Cards:** AE, CB, DI, MC, VI. *(See color ad p 366)* ✕

HIMMARSHEE BAR & GRILLE
▼▼▼
American

Lunch: $5-$10 **Dinner:** $13-$25 **Phone:** 959/764-5154 14
Location: From W Broward Blvd, s on Nugent Ave/SW 3rd Ave, then just e. 210 SW 2nd St 33301. **Hours:** 11:30 am-2:30 & 6-10:30 pm, Fri & Sat-11:30 pm, Sun 6 pm-10 pm. **Closed:** 12/25; also 5/24. **Reservations:** suggested. **Features:** dressy casual; cocktails & lounge; street parking & fee for valet parking; a la carte. The chef calls it "eclectic american cuisine" with influences of Mediterranean, Asian, Italian, and European flares. Using only the freshest of seafood, meat and poultry for his creations. You have to save room for dessert. The dining room has great color with changing local art. Tables available on the sidewalk too. A great bar on the second floor and a table on the balcony, entertainment on the weekends. **Cards:** AE, MC, VI. ✕

(See map p. 346)

JACKSON'S 450 **Dinner:** $16-$36 **Phone:** 954/527-4450 (13)

Steak House

Location: Just w of S Federal Hwy/US 1. 450 E Las Olas Blvd. **Hours:** 5 pm-10:30 pm. **Reservations:** suggested. **Features:** dressy casual; cocktails & lounge; entertainment; street parking & fee for valet parking; a la carte. Located in the heart of Fort Lauderdale and on the trendy Los Olas Blvd. When you step into the place you will get the impression you are in a private club. Wood paneled walls and beamed ceiling, lots of art work and the right brightness to the dining room. Serving the finest meat and freshest seafood. An extensive wine list to choose from to accompany your food selection. **Cards:** AE, CB, DI, DS, MC, VI.

LA FERME **Dinner:** $20-$35 **Phone:** 954/764-0987 (8)

French

Location: US 1, just w of jct Sunrise Blvd and Federal Hwy at NE 16th Ave. 1601 E Sunrise Blvd 33304. **Hours:** 5:30 pm-10 pm. Closed: Mon & 9/1-9/30. **Reservations:** suggested. **Features:** early bird specials; cocktails; minimum charge-$10; a la carte. Intricate and flavorful dishes are served in a charming, elegant atmosphere characterized by dim lighting, fresh flowers and candles. The restaurant is popular with the theater-going crowd. **Cards:** AE, MC, VI.

LA RESERVE **Dinner:** $16-$30 **Phone:** 954/563-6644 (56)

French

Location: At the base of the bridge, just n of bridge at jct of NE 32nd Ave and N Ocean. 3115 NE 32nd Ave 33308. **Hours:** 5:45 pm-11 pm. **Reservations:** suggested. **Features:** early bird specials; cocktails & lounge; a la carte. Try the unusual chicken dishes including one sprinkled with pink peppercorns and another topped with shrimp and cognac. Sweetbreads and chateaubriand are served in a refined ambiance with views of passing yachts. **Cards:** AE, DI, DS, MC, VI.

LAS VEGAS **Lunch:** $5-$6 **Dinner:** $7-$20 **Phone:** 954/564-1370 (58)

Cuban

Location: I-95, exit 31A northbound, exit 31, then 3.2 mi e, just w of SR A1A and intercoastal bridge. 2807 E Oakland Park Blvd 33306. **Hours:** 11 am-10 pm; Fri-Sun to 11 pm. **Reservations:** accepted. **Features:** wine only; street parking. Authentic Cuban food, music and decor contribute to the restaurant's atmosphere. Safe standbys grilled chicken and roast pork co-exist with more sophisticated dishes, such as Argentine-style grilled flank steak, to create a tasty and diverse menu. **Cards:** AE, DI, DS, VI.

LA TAVERNETTA-THE ITALIAN BISTRO BY THE WATER **Dinner:** $16-$24 **Phone:** 954/463-2566 (59)

AAA

Northern Italian

Location: Just s of Sunrise Blvd, between the Galleria and jct US 1 (Federal Hwy). 926 NE 20th Ave 33304. **Hours:** 5 pm-10:30 pm; Sun 5pm-10 pm, in season. Closed: 11/22, 12/25; also Mon & 9/1-9/30. **Reservations:** suggested. **Features:** casual dress; beer & wine only; street parking. A water taxi stop on the Middle River, this restaurant offers an intimate, bistro-style dining room as well as a large, open-air terrace that gives breathtaking views. The owner/chef uses the freshest ingredients to prepare fine, classic cuisine. **Cards:** AE, CB, DI, DS, MC, VI.

THE LEFT BANK **Dinner:** $18-$26 **Phone:** 954/462-5376 (61)

Regional American

Location: N end of the New River Tunnel. 214 SE 6th Ave 33301. **Hours:** 6 pm-11 pm. **Reservations:** suggested. **Features:** wine only. A new world cuisine with French influences consists only of fresh, local ingredients. Mango puree drips down the sides of a Key lime mousse topped with fresh berries. Knowledgeable and attentive, the polished wait staff makes certain you dine at ease. **Cards:** AE, DI, DS, MC, VI.

MAI-KAI RESTAURANT **Dinner:** $16-$30 **Phone:** 954/563-3272 (3)

Chinese

Location: On US 1, 0.3 mi n of jct SR 816 (Oakland Park Blvd). 3599 N Federal Hwy 33308. **Hours:** 5 pm-10:30 pm, Fri & Sat-midnight. **Reservations:** required. **Features:** children's menu; early bird specials; carryout; cocktails & lounge; valet parking; a la carte. A bright, exotic atmosphere spices up the restaurant, noted for its lobster Bora Bora, filet mignon and Mandarin pressed duck. Pay a cover charge to enjoy the Polynesian revue, or instead opt to sit in a secluded, romantic dining room or on the patio. **Cards:** AE, DI, DS, MC, VI.

MARK'S LAS OLAS **Lunch:** $7-$18 **Dinner:** $17-$36 **Phone:** 954/463-1000 (68)

American

Location: E of US 1; on s side of street. 1032 E Las Olas Blvd 33301. **Hours:** 11:30 am-2:30 & 6:30-10 pm, Fri 11:30 am-2:30 & 6-11 pm, Sat 6 pm-11 pm, Sun 6 pm-10 pm. Dinner hours vary in winter. Closed: 11/22, 12/25. **Reservations:** suggested. **Features:** dressy casual; cocktails & lounge; valet parking; a la carte. Located in the heart of shopping and dining district, New Florida fusion cuisine is showcased by a South Florida celebrity chef. Open kitchen design sets off the dining room's art deco accents. Extensive wine list and bustling ambience at this popular spot. **Cards:** AE, DI, MC, VI.

PRIMAVERA RESTAURANT **Dinner:** $20-$35 **Phone:** 954/564-6363 (71)

Northern Italian

Location: I-95, exit 31A northbuond, exit 31 southbound, then 1.5 mi e. 830 E Oakland Park Blvd 33334. **Hours:** 5:30 pm-10:30 pm. Closed: Mon. **Reservations:** suggested. **Features:** dressy casual; carryout; cocktails & lounge; a la carte. In addition to homemade pasta and dessert, there is a wide variety of seafood and meat that makes for difficult decisions. The owner visits each table keeping diners happy. **Cards:** AE, DI, DS, MC, VI.

RAINBOW PALACE **Lunch:** $8-$14 **Dinner:** $19-$40 **Phone:** 954/565-5652 (72)

AAA

Chinese

Location: 0.5 mi s of US 1. 2787 E Oakland Park Blvd 33306. **Hours:** 5 pm-10 pm, Fri & Sat-11 pm, Thurs & Fri also noon-3 pm. Closed: 7/4, 11/22. **Reservations:** suggested. **Features:** dressy casual; carryout; cocktails & lounge; a la carte. Gourmet selections in a plush setting include nine vegetarian offerings. Start with an exquisite mushroom appetizer with portobellos, shiitakes and buttons in a light scallion sauce. An extensive wine list is available. Gentlemen's jackets are suggested. **Cards:** AE, CB, DI, DS, MC, VI.

(See map p. 346)

THE RIVER HOUSE   **Dinner:** $12-$28   **Phone: 954/525-7661** ⑯
▼△▽△▼

American   **Location:** From W Broward Blvd, 0.3 mi s on Nugent Ave/SW 3rd Ave. 301 SW 3rd Ave 33301. **Hours:** 5:30 pm-11 pm, Sun 11:30 am-3 & 5:30-10 pm. **Closed:** 5/28, 12/25. **Reservations:** suggested. **Features:** dressy casual; Sunday brunch; cocktails & lounge; street parking & fee for valet parking; a la carte. Located on the riverfront, you can sit under the canopy of trees and the stars to eat and watch the passing boats. Other areas to eat in are the separate rooms or the porch area. A menu with fresh seafood, meat and poultry done American style. **Cards:** AE, MC, VI. ✕

ROYAL INDIA   **Dinner:** $9-$16   **Phone: 954/964-0071** ⑦⑤
▽△▽△ ▽△▽△

Indian   **Location:** I-95, exit 26 (Griffin Rd); then 2 mi w. 3801 Griffin Rd 32746. **Hours:** 5 pm-10:30 pm, Sat & Sun noon-3 pm. **Reservations:** suggested; on weekends. **Features:** dressy casual; children's menu; carryout; beer & wine only; a la carte. The user-friendly menu adeptly describes the savory dishes on this varied menu. If the tangy and heady roasting don't add enough flavor to your entree, you can sample from a sizable assortment of chutneys and other relishes to achieve the taste you favor. **Cards:** AE, DI, DS, MC, VI. ✕

SEA WATCH RESTAURANT   **Lunch:** $6-$18   **Dinner:** $15-$31   **Phone: 954/781-2200** ②
▽△▽△ ▽△▽△

Steak House   **Location:** SR A1A, 1 mi n of jct SR 870 (Commercial Blvd). 6002 N Ocean Blvd 33308. **Hours:** 11:30 am-3:30 & 5-10 pm. **Closed:** 12/25. **Reservations:** accepted. **Features:** dressy casual; children's menu; early bird specials; carryout; cocktails & lounge; valet parking. Several dining rooms in this nautically decorated restaurant give diners beautiful views of the beach and ocean. You'll find a wide variety of entrees, including a tasty grilled dolphin over a black bean puree, served by a friendly, attentive wait staff. **Cards:** AE, CB, DS, MC, VI. ✕

SHIRTTAIL CHARLIE'S RESTAURANT   **Lunch:** $4-$10   **Dinner:** $10-$20   **Phone: 954/463-3474** ㉑
ⒶⒶⒶ
▽△▽△ ▽△▽△

Seafood   **Location:** Downtown; on s bank of the New River, just sw of Andrews Ave, via sw 5th St. 400 SW 3rd Ave 33315. **Hours:** 11:30 am-10 pm. **Closed:** 11/22, 12/25; also Mon 9/1-11/23. **Reservations:** accepted. **Features:** casual dress; children's menu; carryout; cocktails & lounge. Overlooking the scenic New River, the restaurant lets you unwind while enjoying fried alligator and stuffed yellowtail snapper. Indoor and outdoor dining both lend the same tropical experience. After eating, take advantage of a complimentary boat ride. **Cards:** AE, DI, DS, MC, VI. ✕

TARPONBEND FOOD & TACKLE   **Lunch:** $6-$9   **Dinner:** $6-$18   **Phone: 954/523-3233** ⑰
▽△▽△ ▽△▽△

Seafood   **Location:** From W Broward Blvd, s on Nugent Ave/SW 3rd Ave, then just e. 200 SW 2nd St 33301. **Hours:** 11:30 am-12:30 am. **Closed:** 5/28, 11/22, 12/25. **Features:** casual dress; children's menu; early bird specials; carryout; cocktails & lounge; street parking & fee for valet parking; a la carte. Located on the corner of the street. Tables available on the sidewalk. The dining room has a fishing decor theme with tackle and fish pictures all around. The menu features fish, burgers, chicken and pasta. A fun place to eat. Entertainment Thursday-Sunday. **Cards:** AE, MC, VI. ✕

TROPICAL ACRES   **Dinner:** $11-$16   **Phone: 954/989-2500** ㉛
▽△▽△ ▽△▽△

Steak & Seafood   **Location:** I-95, exit 26 (Griffin Rd); 0.3 mi w. 2500 Griffin Rd 33312. **Hours:** 4:30 pm-10 pm, Sun 3 pm-9 pm. **Closed:** 12/24, 12/25. **Reservations:** accepted. **Features:** dressy casual; children's menu; carryout; cocktails & lounge; valet parking. Family-owned since 1949, the popular restaurant serves cuts of meat on sizzling skillets plucked straight out of the fireplace grill. The menu also lists 40 other tempting entrees. Cozy banquet facilities make the place a top choice for private parties. **Cards:** AE, DS, MC, VI. ✕

YESTERDAY'S   **Dinner:** $12-$29   **Phone: 954/561-4400** ㉜
▽△▽△ ▽△▽△

Regional American   **Location:** By the Intracoastal Waterway. 3001 E Oakland Park Blvd. **Hours:** 4:30 pm 11 pm, Fri & Sat-midnight. **Features:** dressy casual; children's menu; cocktails & lounge; entertainment; valet parking; a la carte. Consistently good food mixes classics with Caribbean, Cajun and Latin favorites. An art deco design enhances the vast, multi-level dining room. The lighting is done with moon shapes. The menu is very diverse. **Cards:** AE, DI, MC, VI. ✕

———— *The following restaurants have not been evaluated by AAA* ————
but are listed for your information only.

DAN MARINO'S TOWN TAVERN   **Phone: 954/522-1313**
[fyi]   **Not evaluated. Location:** 300 SW 1st Ave 33301. **Features:** Dine inside or out. Most tables overlook the riverwalk area. Featuring pasta, burgers, sandwiches, salad, seafood and ribs. Lots of Dan's football memorobilia and photo's.

FLANIGAN'S SEAFOOD BAR & GRILL   **Phone: 954/493-5329**
[fyi]   **Not evaluated. Location:** 1479 E Commercial Blvd 33334. **Features:** Casual atmosphere that is inexpensive and family friendly. Known for their baby back ribs, large burgers and fresh seafood.

FLANIGAN'S SEAFOOD BAR & GRILL   **Phone: 954/267-4877**
[fyi]   **Not evaluated. Location:** 1721 N Andrews Blvd. **Features:** Casual atmosphere that is inexpensive and family friendly. Known for their baby back ribs, large burgers and fresh local seafood.

HOT CHOCOLATES RESTAURANT & NITE CLUB   **Phone: 954/564-5552**
[fyi]   **Not evaluated. Location:** At corner of Oakland Blvd (SR 816) and Federal Hwy; in the round building. 3101 Federal Hwy 33306. **Features:** New World cuisine with eclectic combinations with seafood, meat and fowl. Outlandish desserts. An elegant room to go along with great foods. Night club next door.

The Fort Lauderdale Vicinity

CORAL SPRINGS pop. 79,400

——— WHERE TO STAY ———

LA QUINTA INN

SAVE

▼▼▼

Motel

Phone: (954)753-9000

All Year   1P: $65-$95   2P: $65-$95

Location: SR 817, just n of jct Sample Rd (SR 834). 3701 University Dr 33065. Fax: 954/755-4012. **Facility:** Some rooms overlooking golf course. Some with balcony. 122 units. *Bath:* combo or shower only. 5 stories, interior corridors. **Terms:** small pets only. **Amenities:** video games, voice mail, irons, hair dryers. **Leisure Activities:** heated pool. **Guest Services:** [ECP] meal plan available, coin laundry. **Business Services:** meeting rooms. **Cards:** AE, CB, DI, DS, MC, VI. *(See color ad p 363)*

SOME UNITS

RADISSON RESORT CORAL SPRINGS

ⓐⓐⓐ **SAVE**

▼▼▼

Motor Inn

Phone: (954)753-5598

12/21-4/15	1P: $169-$249	2P: $169-$249	XP: $20	F18
12/1-12/20	1P: $129-$179	2P: $129-$179	XP: $20	F18
10/1-11/30	1P: $119-$159	2P: $119-$159		
4/16-9/30	1P: $109-$149	2P: $109-$149	XP: $20	F18

Location: From Sawgrass Expwy/SR 869, exit Coral Ridge Dr N for 0.3 mi, then left onto Heron Bay Blvd, then first right. 11775 Heron Bay Blvd 33076. Fax: 954/753-2888. **Facility:** Large atrium lobby. Contemporary room decor. Some rooms with golf course view. Few with small balcony. 224 units. Some suites ($169-$249) and whirlpool units ($499-$899). *Bath:* combo or shower only. 7 stories, interior corridors. **Terms:** 3 day cancellation notice, small pets only ($100 fee). **Amenities:** extended cable TV, video games, voice mail, irons, hair dryers. **Dining:** restaurant, 7 am-10 pm, $12-$30, cocktails. **Leisure Activities:** heated pool, sauna, whirlpool, putting green, exercise room. *Fee:* golf-18 holes, golf instruction. **Guest Services:** gift shop, area transportation-within 5 mi, valet and coin laundry. **Business Services:** meeting rooms. **Cards:** AE, DI, DS, MC, VI. **Special Amenities:** free newspaper and free room upgrade (subject to availability with advanced reservations).

SOME UNITS

WELLESLEY INN & SUITES

ⓐⓐⓐ **SAVE**

▼▼▼

Motel

Phone: (954)344-2200

12/1-4/14	1P: $89-$109	2P: $89-$109
4/15-11/30	1P: $59-$79	2P: $59-$79

Location: SR 817; just s of jct Sample Rd (SR 834). 3100 N University Dr 33065. Fax: 954/344-7885. **Facility:** Attractive public areas. 106 units. *Bath:* combo or shower only. 4 stories, interior corridors. **Terms:** small pets only ($10 extra charge). **Amenities:** extended cable TV, video games. **Leisure Activities:** heated pool. **Guest Services:** [ECP] meal plan available, valet laundry. *Fee:* fax. **Cards:** AE, CB, DI, DS, JC, MC, VI. **Special Amenities:** free continental breakfast and free local telephone calls. *(See color ad opposite title page)*

SOME UNITS

——— WHERE TO DINE ———

CHOWDER'S

▼▼▼

Continental

Dinner: $17-$29   Phone: 954/753-7374

Location: SR 817 (University Dr); 0.5 mi n of jct SR 814 (Atlantic Blvd). 1460 N University Dr 33065. **Hours:** 5 pm-10:30 pm, Fri & Sat-11:30 pm. **Reservations:** suggested. **Features:** dressy casual; children's menu; carryout; cocktails & lounge; entertainment; valet parking. Attractive modern dining rooms offer inviting meals with hearty portions. Fresh seafood and homemade chowder are featured in addition to beef, veal and poultry prepared with a continental touch. End the night with fresh strawberries in a chocolate cup. **Cards:** AE, CB, DI, DS, MC, VI.

RUNYON'S

▼▼

American

Lunch: $5-$15   Dinner: $15-$25   Phone: (954)752-2333

Location: On SR 834 (Sample Rd); 0.5 mi w of jct SR 817 (University Dr). 9810 W Sample Rd 33065. **Hours:** 11:30 am-2:30 & 4-10:30 pm, Fri-11 pm, Sat 4 pm-11 pm, Sun 4 pm-10 pm. Closed major holidays. **Reservations:** suggested. **Features:** casual dress; children's menu; carryout; cocktails & lounge. Unusual dining rooms are decorated with autographs of scores of local celebrities who have dined here. Steak and seafood are featured with fish cooked in a variety of ways. Try the snapper in white cream sauce with capers over a bed of angel hair pasta or savor the snapper filets. **Cards:** AE, DI, DS, MC, VI.

DANIA BEACH (See map p. 346; index p. 350)

——— WHERE TO STAY ———

FORT LAUDERDALE AIRPORT HILTON

SAVE

▼▼▼

Hotel

Phone: 954/920-3300   **84**

All Year   1P: $149-$229   2P: $159-$239   XP: $10   F18

Location: I-95, exit 26. 1870 Griffin Rd 33004. Fax: 954/920-3348. **Facility:** Attractive landscaped grounds. The pool has a tropical setting. Elegant public areas. Rooms are large with medium wood tones and warm colors. 388 units. Some suites. *Bath:* combo or shower only. 2-8 stories, interior/exterior corridors. **Parking:** valet. **Terms:** package plans. **Amenities:** extended cable TV, voice mail, irons, hair dryers. **Leisure Activities:** heated pool, whirlpool, 2 lighted tennis courts, exercise room. **Guest Services:** gift shop, valet laundry. *Fee:* massage. **Business Services:** conference facilities, fax. **Cards:** AE, CB, DI, DS, JC, MC, VI. *(See ad p 44 & p 375)*

SOME UNITS

(See map p. 346)

LUCKEY'S MOTEL

AAA [SAVE]

♦♦♦

Motel

Phone: (954)925-5500   [80]

12/15-4/15	1P: $59-$119	2P: $59-$119	XP: $10	F12
12/1-12/14 & 4/16-11/30	1P: $49-$59	2P: $49-$59	XP: $10	F12

Location: US 1, 0.5 mi n of jct Sterling Rd, 0.5 mi s of jct Griffin Rd. 205 N Federal Hwy 33004. Fax: 954/424-9825. **Facility:** Very large, modern furnished rooms. 10 units, 2 with efficiency. *Bath:* shower only. 1 story, exterior corridors. **Terms:** weekly rates available. **Amenities:** extended cable TV, irons, hair dryers. **Guest Services:** coin laundry. **Cards:** AE, DS, MC, VI.

SOME UNITS

[S] [📶] [🍴] [♦] [📷] [🔲] / [✕] /

SHERATON FORT LAUDERDALE AIRPORT HOTEL

♦♦♦♦

Hotel

Phone: (954)920-3500   [82]

1/1-4/30	1P: $129-$349	2P: $129-$349	XP: $10	F17
5/1-5/31	1P: $99-$349	2P: $99-$349	XP: $10	F17
12/1-12/31 & 6/1-11/30	1P: $89-$349	2P: $89-$349	XP: $10	F17

Location: I-95, exit 26, adjoining Design Center of the Americas. 1825 Griffin Rd 33004. Fax: 954/920-3571. **Facility:** Spacious public areas, sitting areas with attractive, comfortable furniture. A relaxing pool area. 250 units. Some suites ($349). *Bath:* combo or shower only. 12 stories, interior corridors. **Amenities:** dual phone lines, voice mail, irons, hair dryers. *Some:* fax. **Leisure Activities:** heated pool, saunas, whirlpool, 2 lighted tennis courts, exercise room. **Guest Services:** gift shop, area transportation, valet laundry. **Business Services:** meeting rooms, administrative services. **Cards:** AE, CB, DI, DS, MC, VI.

SOME UNITS

[ASK] [✈] [🐾] [🍴] [Y] [👤] [⌖] [📄] [🏊] [♦] [🖨] [🔲] [DATA PORT] / [✕] [VCR] [🔲] /
　　　　　　　　　　　　　　　　　FEE　　　　　　　　　　　　　　　　　　　　　　　　　FEE FEE

SPRINGHILL SUITES BY MARRIOTT FORT LAUDERDALE AIRPORT

AAA [SAVE]

♦♦♦♦

Motel

Phone: 954/920-9696   [83]

12/31-4/15	1P: $119-$147	2P: $119-$147	
12/1-12/30	1P: $94-$119	2P: $94-$119	
4/16-11/30	1P: $89-$119	2P: $89-$119	

Location: I-95, exit 25 (Stirling Rd), just e. 151 SW 18th Ct 33004. Fax: 954/929-3577. **Facility:** Spacious suite like rooms. Contemporary decor. 168 units. *Bath:* combo or shower only. 7 stories, interior corridors. **Amenities:** extended cable TV, dual phone lines, voice mail, irons, hair dryers. **Leisure Activities:** heated pool, whirlpool, exercise room. **Guest Services:** [ECP] meal plan available, area transportation-Port Everglades, valet and coin laundry. **Business Services:** meeting rooms, administrative services, PC. **Cards:** AE, DI, DS, MC, VI. **Special Amenities:** free continental breakfast and free newspaper. *(See color ad p 368)*

SOME UNITS

[✈] [📶] [📄] [🏊] [♦] [🖨] [🔲] [🔲] [🔲] [DATA PORT] / [✕] /
　　　　　　　FEE

------ **WHERE TO DINE** ------

ISLAMORADA FISH COMPANY

♦♦

Seafood

Lunch: $5-$20　　Dinner: $5-$20　　Phone: 954/927-7737   [122]

Location: I-95, exit 26, w on Griffin Rd (SR 818) to Anglers Ave, then s; in the Bass Pro Shop Outdoor World. 220 Gulfstream Way 33004. **Hours:** 11 am-10 pm; light menu 10 pm-midnight. Closed: 12/25. **Features:** casual dress; children's menu; carryout; cocktails & lounge. Selections of local seafood. A casual atmosphere with an aquatic tank in the middle of the dining room or eat outside overlooking the man-made lake. Family friendly. **Cards:** AE, DS, VI.

[♿] [✕]

LE PETIT CAFE

♦♦

French

Lunch: $6-$8　　Dinner: $14-$17　　Phone: 954/967-9912   [121]

Location: 1.4 mi w of I-95, exit 26. 3308 Griffin Rd 33004. **Hours:** 11:30 am-2:30 & 4:30-10 pm, Sat & Sun from 4:30 pm. Closed: Mon. **Features:** dressy casual; wine only. Familiar classics dominate the menu in this spiffy creperie. Hearts-of-palm salad, frog legs, beef bourguignonne and, of course, many crepe choices are served in a quietly charming atmosphere featuring the music of Edith Paif. Don't leave without dessert. **Cards:** AE, MC, VI.

DAVIE pop. 47,210

———— WHERE TO STAY ————

HOMESTEAD VILLAGE GUEST STUDIOS DAVIE/PLANTATION   **Phone: (954)476-1211**

▼▼▼ ▼▼▼   12/1-2/28 & 9/1-11/30   1P: $65-$85   2P: $65-$85
       3/1-8/31   1P: $55-$75   2P: $55-$75
Motel   **Location:** I-595, exit University Dr/SR 817, to SR 84 E, then 0.3 mi. 7550 SR 84 E 33317. Fax: 954/476-0026.
Facility: Spacious rooms with contemporary decor. Limited office hours and housekeeping. 125 efficiencies.
Bath: combo or shower only. 2 stories, exterior corridors. **Terms:** weekly & monthly rates available, small pets only ($85 fee).
Amenities: voice mail, irons. **Guest Services:** coin laundry. **Business Services:** meeting rooms. **Cards:** AE, DI, DS, MC, VI.

SOME UNITS

🐾 🍴 ♿ 🛄 📷 🎥 🖨 💻 📧 🔒 DATA PORT / ✕ /

———— WHERE TO DINE ————

ARMADILLO CAFE   **Dinner:** $15-$30   **Phone: 954/791-4866**

▼▼▼ ▼▼▼   **Location:** Florida Tpke exit 53 (Griffin Rd/SR 818), 1 mi e, corner of Griffin Rd & SW 64th Ave. 4630 SW 64th Ave
Southwest   33314. **Hours:** 5 pm-10 pm, Fri & Sat-11 pm. Closed major holidays. **Reservations:** suggested.
American   **Features:** dressy casual; children's menu; carryout; cocktails & lounge; a la carte. Entrees include a
variety with meat and seafood items prepared with the Southwestern flair. The chilis are used to enhance
free premises. **Cards:** AE, DI, MC, VI.   the flavor of the foods not to be over domineering. The wine list compliments the menu very nicely. Smoke

✕

DAVIE ALE HOUSE   **Lunch:** $5-$11   **Dinner:** $6-$11   **Phone: 954/236-0062**

▼▼▼   **Location:** I-95, exit at I-595, then w. 2080 University Dr 33324. **Hours:** 11 am-2 am, Thurs-Sat to 3 am. Closed:
American   11/22. **Features:** casual dress; children's menu; cocktail lounge. Munch on huge onion rings or cheese
fries and revel in the lively sports bar atmosphere. A menu of fun favorites includes burgers, steaks,
chicken, pasta and a nice raw bar. Wash it all down with one of an extensive list of draft and bottled beers.
Cards: AE, DI, DS, MC, VI.

✕

GERONIMOS' CASUAL GOURMET GRILL & BAR   **Lunch:** $5-$9   **Dinner:** $8-$15   **Phone: 954/474-9992**

▼▼▼ ▼▼▼   **Location:** In University Park Plaza; on SR 817 (University Dr), 1.5 mi s of jct SR 84. 3528 S University Dr 33328.
American   **Hours:** 11:30 am-4 am. Closed major holidays. **Features:** casual dress; children's menu; early bird
specials; cocktails. A creative menu featuring California and international dishes with fresh ingredients
brings repeat business to this eatery. The atmosphere is simple and casual. Sample the black bean soup
or order the grilled swordfish topped with sun-dried tomato salsa. **Cards:** AE, MC, VI.

✕

DEERFIELD BEACH pop. 46,300

———— WHERE TO STAY ————

CARRIAGE HOUSE RESORT MOTEL   **Phone: (954)427-7670**

ⒶⒶⒶ [SAVE]	2/1-3/14	2P: $105-$195	XP: $10	F6
	3/15-4/5	2P: $88-$140	XP: $10	F6
▼▼▼ ▼▼▼	12/1-1/31	2P: $54-$140	XP: $10	F6
Motel	4/6-11/30	2P: $54-$95	XP: $10	F6

Location: SR A1A, just s of jct SR 810 (Hillsboro Blvd). 250 S Ocean Blvd 33441. Fax: 954/428-4790. **Facility:** Age
restrictions may apply 1/15-3/15. Attractively landscaped pool area. Very well kept. 30 units, 24 with kitchen.
Bath: combo or shower only. 2 stories, exterior corridors. **Terms:** 40 day cancellation notice, weekly & monthly rates available.
Amenities: voice mail, safes (fee). **Leisure Activities:** heated pool. **Guest Services:** coin laundry. **Cards:** AE, DS, JC, MC, VI.
Special Amenities: early check-in/late check-out and preferred room (subject to availability with advanced reserva-
tions).

SOME UNITS

🅂🄳 🏊 📧 🔒 / 💻 /

COMFORT INN-OCEANSIDE   **Phone: (954)428-0650**

ⒶⒶⒶ [SAVE]	12/1-4/21	1P: $129-$189	2P: $139-$199	XP: $10	F18
	4/22-11/30	1P: $69-$89	2P: $79-$99	XP: $10	F18

▼▼▼ ▼▼▼   **Location:** SR A1A, at jct SR 810 (Hillsboro Blvd). 50 SE 20th Ave 33441. Fax: 954/427-2666. **Facility:** Half block
Motel   from ocean. Contemporary room decor package. 69 units. 6 stories, interior corridors. **Terms:** 24 day can-
cellation notice, package plans, small pets only ($25 fee). **Amenities:** video games. *Some:* irons, hair dryers.
Dining: deli, 7:30 am-11 pm, Sun 8 am-10 pm, $3-$7. **Leisure Activities:** wading pool. **Guest Services:**
[ECP] meal plan available, coin laundry. **Business Services:** meeting rooms. **Cards:** AE, CB, DI, DS, JC, MC, VI.
Special Amenities: early check-in/late check-out. *(See color ad p 352)*   SOME UNITS

🅂🄳 🐾 🍴 📷 🎥 💻 DATA PORT / ✕ 🔒 /
                 FEE FEE

COMFORT SUITES   **Phone: (954)570-8887**

ⒶⒶⒶ [SAVE]	1/14-3/31	1P: $119-$189	2P: $129-$199		
	12/17-1/13	1P: $79-$139	2P: $89-$149	XP: $10	F18
▼▼▼ ▼▼▼	12/1-12/16	1P: $69-$129	2P: $79-$139	XP: $10	F18
Motel	4/1-11/30	1P: $59-$119	2P: $69-$129	XP: $10	F18

Location: I-95, exit 36C, jct SW 10th St to SW 12th Ave, then s. 1040 E Newport Center Dr 33442. Fax: 954/428-7638.
Facility: Well-equipped rooms with separate sitting area. 101 units. 4 stories, exterior corridors. **Terms:** cancellation fee imposed, monthly rates available, pets ($25 fee). **Amenities:** video games, voice mail, safes (fee). **Leisure Activi-
ties:** heated pool, whirlpool. **Guest Services:** [ECP] meal plan available, valet and coin laundry. **Cards:** AE, DI, DS, MC, VI.
Special Amenities: early check-in/late check-out and free room upgrade (subject to availability with advanced reservations). *(See color ad p 352)*   SOME UNITS

🅂🄳 🐾 🍴 📷 🎥 🖨 🔒 DATA PORT / ✕ 📧 /
            FEE

CRYSTAL CAY MOTEL

Phone: (954)428-5122

Property failed to provide current rates

Motel

Location: SR A1A, 0.6 mi s of jct SR 810 (Hillsboro Blvd). 925 SE 20th Ave 33441. Fax: 954/481-8696. **Facility:** 20 units, 19 with kitchen. 2 stories, exterior corridors. **Terms:** weekly rates available. **Amenities:** extended cable TV, voice mail. **Leisure Activities:** heated pool. **Guest Services:** coin laundry. **Cards:** AE, CB, DI, DS, MC, VI.

DEERFIELD BEACH/BOCA RATON HILTON

Phone: (954)427-7700

12/1-4/8	1P: $129-$189	2P: $129-$189	XP: $10	F13
4/9-5/23 & 9/28-11/30	1P: $99-$149	2P: $99-$149	XP: $10	F13
5/24-9/27	1P: $79-$139	2P: $79-$139	XP: $10	F13

Hotel

Location: Hillsboro Blvd, just e of jct I-95, exit 37 southbound; exit 37A, northbound. 100 Fairway Dr 33441. Fax: 954/427-2308. **Facility:** Striking pyramid architecture. Tastefully decorated public rooms and large guest rooms. 221 units. Some suites. *Bath:* combo or shower only. 8 stories, interior corridors. **Parking:** valet. **Terms:** cancellation fee imposed, package plans. **Amenities:** dual phone lines, voice mail, safes, irons, hair dryers. **Dining:** restaurant, 6:30 am-10 pm, $8-$22, cocktails. **Leisure Activities:** heated pool, whirlpool, exercise room. **Guest Services:** [BP] & [CP] meal plans available, gift shop, area transportation-within 5 mi, valet laundry. **Business Services:** conference facilities, fax. **Cards:** AE, CB, DI, DS, MC, VI. **Special Amenities: free newspaper.** *(See ad p 44)*

SOME UNITS

EMBASSY SUITES-DEERFIELD BEACH RESORT

Phone: (954)426-0478

12/1-1/6	1P: $285-$425	2P: $285-$425	XP: $20	F18
1/7-4/21	1P: $280-$420	2P: $280-$420	XP: $20	F18
10/1-11/30	1P: $170-$260	2P: $170-$260	XP: $20	F18
4/22-9/30	1P: $155-$230	2P: $155-$230	XP: $20	F18

Suite Motor Inn

Location: SR A1A, 0.5 mi s of jct SR 810 (Hillsboro Blvd). 950 SE 20th Ave 33441. Fax: 954/360-0539. **Facility:** A seven story Spanish style structure. Extensive tropical trees and flowers surrounding the grounds. The pool is behind the building with the ocean just steps away. The lobby has many comfortable sitting areas. Spacious rooms with a contemporary decor, some with small balcony and some with ocean view. 244 units. *Bath:* combo or shower only. 7 stories, interior corridors. **Parking:** extra charge or valet. **Terms:** 3 day cancellation notice-fee imposed, monthly rates available, package plans. **Amenities:** extended cable TV, video games, voice mail, irons, hair dryers. **Dining:** restaurant, 11 am-11 pm, $8-$18, cocktails, entertainment. **Leisure Activities:** heated pool, whirlpool, beach, swimming, snorkeling, children's program, exercise room. *Fee:* snorkeling equipment. **Guest Services:** [BP] meal plan available, gift shop, complimentary evening beverages, valet and coin laundry. **Business Services:** meeting rooms, PC, fax. **Cards:** AE, DI, JC, MC, VI. **Special Amenities: free continental breakfast and free newspaper.**

SOME UNITS

HOWARD JOHNSON PLAZA RESORT HOTEL

Phone: (954)428-2850

12/23-4/21	1P: $165-$185	2P: $175-$195	XP: $10	F18
4/22-11/30	1P: $105-$125	2P: $115-$135	XP: $10	F18
12/1-12/22	1P: $99-$119	2P: $109-$129	XP: $10	F18

Motor Inn

Location: SR A1A, just n of jct SR 810 (Hillsboro Blvd). 2096 NE 2nd St 33441. Fax: 954/480-9639. **Facility:** Facing ocean and beach, attractive rooms with small balcony. 177 units. Some suites ($195-$335). 8 stories, interior corridors. **Terms:** cancellation fee imposed, weekly & monthly rates available, package plans. **Amenities:** safes (fee), irons, hair dryers. **Leisure Activities:** heated pool, beach, swimming, game room. **Guest Services:** gift shop, valet laundry. **Business Services:** meeting rooms. **Cards:** AE, CB, DI, DS, JC, MC, VI.

SOME UNITS

LA QUINTA INN

Phone: (954)421-1004

All Year 1P: $55-$95 2P: $55-$95

Motel

Location: I-95, exit 37, SR 810, 0.3 mi s. 351 W Hillsboro Blvd 33441-1801. Fax: 954/427-8069. **Facility:** Southwestern architecture and decor, set back from hwy. 130 units. 3 stories, exterior corridors. **Terms:** small pets only. **Amenities:** video games, voice mail. **Leisure Activities:** heated pool. **Guest Services:** [CP] meal plan available, valet and coin laundry. **Business Services:** meeting rooms. **Cards:** AE, CB, DI, DS, MC, VI. *(See color ad p 363)*

SOME UNITS

OCEAN TERRACE SUITES

Phone: (954)427-8400

1/3-4/15	2P: $163-$482	XP: $10
12/1-1/2	2P: $119-$438	XP: $10
10/15-11/30	2P: $119-$284	XP: $10
4/16-10/14	2P: $101-$250	XP: $10

Apartment

Location: Just e of jct SR A1A and 810 (Hillsboro Blvd). 2080 E Hillsboro Blvd 33441. Fax: 954/427-0555. **Facility:** All rooms with balcony or patio. 27 units. 2 three-bedroom units, 1 efficiency and 26 units with kitchen. 4 stories, exterior corridors. **Terms:** 30 day cancellation notice, weekly & monthly rates available, package plans. **Amenities:** extended cable TV, irons, hair dryers. **Leisure Activities:** heated pool, beach access. **Guest Services:** coin laundry. **Cards:** AE, DS, MC, VI.

PANTHER MOTEL & APARTMENTS

Phone: (954)427-0700

1/8-4/15 Wkly	1P: $407-$627	2P: $407-$627	XP: $70
4/1-1/7 Wkly	1P: $234-$508	2P: $234-$508	XP: $70
4/16-5/1 Wkly	1P: $314-$446	2P: $314-$446	XP: $70
5/2-11/30 Wkly	1P: $240-$340	2P: $240-$340	XP: $70

Motel

Location: SR A1A, 0.5 mi s of jct SR 810 (Hillsboro Blvd). 715 S A1A 33441. Fax: 954/481-2389. **Facility:** Studio and 1-bedroom apartments. Exceptionally well kept. 20 units, 18 with kitchen. 2 stories, exterior corridors. **Terms:** age restrictions may apply, 45 day cancellation notice. **Amenities:** extended cable TV, safes. **Leisure Activities:** heated pool, shuffleboard. **Guest Services:** coin laundry.

QUALITY SUITES

Phone: (954)570-8888

AAA SAVE

1/14-3/31	1P: $139-$199	2P: $149-$209	XP: $10	F18
12/17-1/13	1P: $89-$149	2P: $99-$159	XP: $10	F18
12/1-12/16	1P: $79-$139	2P: $89-$149	XP: $10	F18
4/1-11/30	1P: $69-$129	2P: $79-$139	XP: $10	F18

Suite Motor Inn   **Location:** I-95, exit 36C, SW 10th St, to SW 12th Ave, then s. 1050 E Newport Center Dr 33442. Fax: 954/570-5346. **Facility:** Large units with separate sitting room. Very attractive pool courtyard overlooking lake. 107 units. 5 stories, exterior corridors. **Terms:** cancellation fee imposed, monthly rates available, package plans. **Amenities:** video games, voice mail, safes (fee), irons, hair dryers. **Dining:** restaurant, 6:30-9:30 am, 11-2 & 5-9 pm, Sat & Sun 7-10 am, $3-S9. **Leisure Activities:** heated pool, whirlpool, jogging. **Guest Services:** [BP] meal plan available, gift shop, complimentary evening beverages, valet and coin laundry. **Business Services:** meeting rooms. **Cards:** AE, DI, DS, MC, VI. **Special Amenities:** early check-in/late check-out and free room upgrade (subject to availability with advanced reservations).** *(See color ad p 352)*

SOME UNITS

(icons) / [X] / FEE

RAMADA DEERFIELD BEACH/BOCA RATON

Phone: (954)481-2094

AAA SAVE

1/1-3/31	1P: $89-$99	2P: $99-$109	XP: $10	F16
4/1-11/30	1P: $65	2P: $65-$75	XP: $10	F16
12/1-12/31	1P: $65	2P: $65	XP: $10	F16

Motor Inn   **Location:** I-95, exit 37, SR 810, just w. 1250 W Hillsboro Blvd 33442. Fax: 954/481-1619. **Facility:** Well maintained rooms with a contemporary decor. Inviting pool and courtyard. 157 units, 6 with kitchen. 2 stories, exterior corridors. **Terms:** weekly & monthly rates available, package plans. **Amenities:** voice mail, safes (fee). **Dining:** restaurant, 24 hours, pool bar, $4-$12. **Leisure Activities:** heated pool, exercise room. **Guest Services:** valet and coin laundry. **Business Services:** meeting rooms. **Cards:** AE, CB, DI, DS, MC, VI. **Special Amenities:** early check-in/late check-out and free continental breakfast.

SOME UNITS

(icons) FEE / [X] (icons) /

RAMADA INN DEERFIELD BEACH EAST

Phone: (954)421-5000

AAA SAVE

2/21-4/14	1P: $69-$99	2P: $79-$109	XP: $10	F16
12/20-2/10	1P: $59-$89	2P: $69-$99	XP: $10	F16
12/1-12/19 & 4/15-11/30	1P: $49-$69	2P: $59-$79	XP: $10	F16

Motor Inn   **Location:** On US 1, 1.3 mi s of jct SR 810 (Hillsboro Blvd). 1401 S Federal Hwy 33441. Fax: 954/426-2811. **Facility:** 107 units, 8 with efficiency. 2 stories, interior/exterior corridors. **Terms:** weekly rates available, pets ($10 extra charge, in limited rooms). **Amenities:** extended cable TV. **Dining:** restaurant, 7 am-10 pm, $8-$15, cocktails. **Leisure Activities:** heated pool. **Guest Services:** coin laundry. **Business Services:** meeting rooms. **Cards:** AE, DI, DS, JC, MC, VI. **Special Amenities:** free room upgrade and preferred room (each subject to availability with advanced reservations).

SOME UNITS

(icons) / [X] (icons) /

RETTGER RESORTS BEACH CLUB

Phone: (954)427-7900

12/17-4/15		2P: $109-$249	XP: $10
12/1-12/16 & 4/16-11/30		2P: $59-$169	XP: $10

Motel   **Location:** Just n on SR A1A from SR 810 (Hillsboro Blvd) to 20th Tr. 100 NE 20th Tr 33441. Fax: 954/427-7978. **Facility:** Across from ocean. All rooms with view of ocean. Very nicely furnished and decorated rooms. Smoke free premises. 18 units. 6 efficiencies and 2 units with kitchen. Some suites ($129-$249) and whirlpool units ($169-$249). 2 stories, exterior corridors. **Terms:** cancellation fee imposed, weekly & monthly rates available. **Amenities:** extended cable TV, dual phone lines, voice mail. **Leisure Activities:** heated pool, beach access. **Cards:** AE, CB, DI, DS, MC, VI.

SOME UNITS

[ASK] (icons) [X] (icons) / (icons) /

SHORE ROAD INN

Phone: (954)427-8820

AAA SAVE

1/21-4/1		2P: $107-$140	XP: $12
12/1-1/20		2P: $96-$121	XP: $12
4/2-5/1		2P: $70-$98	XP: $12
5/2-11/30		2P: $50-$85	XP: $12

Motel   **Location:** SR A1A, just s of jct SR 810 (Hillsboro Blvd). 460 S A1A 33441. Fax: 954/427-4881. **Facility:** Exceptionally well kept. Attractive pool patio. 18 units, 16 with kitchen. *Bath:* combo or shower only. 2 stories, exterior corridors. **Terms:** age restrictions may apply, 40 day cancellation notice-fee imposed. **Amenities:** extended cable TV, voice mail. *Some:* irons. **Leisure Activities:** heated pool. **Guest Services:** coin laundry. **Cards:** AE, CB, DI, DS, MC, VI.

SOME UNITS

(icons) / [X] [VCR] (icons) /

TROPIC ISLE BEACH RESORT

Phone: (954)427-1000

AAA SAVE

1/16-4/6 Wkly		2P: $524-$708	XP: $56	F12
12/1-1/15 Wkly		2P: $280-$585	XP: $56	F12
4/7-4/21 Wkly		2P: $381-$518	XP: $56	F12
4/22-11/30 Wkly		2P: $280-$393	XP: $56	F12

Motel   **Location:** SR A1A, 0.3 mi s of jct SR 810 (Hillsboro Blvd). 370 S A1A 33441. Fax: 954/429-9754. **Facility:** Bright and open, well-kept studio, efficiencies and one bedroom apartments. All rooms with two beds. 15 units with kitchen. *Bath:* combo or shower only. 2 stories, exterior corridors. **Terms:** 30 day cancellation notice, daily rates available. **Amenities:** extended cable TV, voice mail, safes. **Leisure Activities:** heated pool. **Guest Services:** coin laundry. **Cards:** DS, MC, VI. **Special Amenities:** early check-in/late check-out and preferred room (subject to availability with advanced reservations). *(See ad p 353)*

(icons)

WELLESLEY INN & SUITES

Phone: (954)428-0661

1/1-4/14	1P: $79-$119	2P: $79-$119	XP: $10 F18
12/1-12/31 & 4/15-11/30	1P: $59-$79	2P: $59-$79	XP: $10 F18

(AAA) (SAVE)

Motel

Location: I-95, exit 37, just w on SR 810 (Hillsboro Blvd), just s. 100 12th Ave SW 33442. Fax: 954/427-6701. **Facility:** Very nicely landscaped grounds. Attractive public areas and rooms. 79 units. Some suites. *Bath:* combo or shower only. 4 stories, interior corridors. **Terms:** 3 day cancellation notice, small pets only ($10 extra charge). **Amenities:** video games, voice mail. *Some:* irons, hair dryers. **Leisure Activities:** heated pool. **Guest Services:** [ECP] meal plan available, coin laundry. **Cards:** AE, CB, DI, DS, JC, MC, VI. **Special Amenities:** free continental breakfast and free local telephone calls. *(See color ad opposite title page)* SOME UNITS

WHERE TO DINE

BROOKS RESTAURANT

Dinner: $20-$27　　　**Phone: 954/427-9302**

Continental

Location: US 1, 0.5 mi s of jct SR 810 (Hillsboro Blvd). 500 S Federal Hwy 33441. **Hours:** 6 pm-10 pm. Closed: 12/25; also Mon & Tues 5/8-11/25. **Reservations:** suggested. **Features:** semi-formal attire; children's menu; cocktails & lounge; valet parking; a la carte, also prix fixe. Dress up yet feel comfortable amid the subdued, attractive decor. Generous portions of well-prepared entrees are presented in an inviting manner. Start with the spinach and goat cheese salad topped with toasted walnuts, and move on to first-rate lobster. Smoke free premises. **Cards:** AE, CB, DI, MC, VI.

CAFE CLAUDE

Lunch: $8-$14　　　**Dinner:** $15-$25　　　**Phone: 954/421-7337**

French

Location: 0.5 mi e of US 1; in Cove Plaza off Hillsboro Blvd. 1544 SE 3rd Ct 33441. **Hours:** 11:30 am-2 & 5:15-10 pm, Sat & Sun from 5:15 pm. Closed: Mon. **Reservations:** suggested. **Features:** semi-formal attire; early bird specials; carryout; cocktails & lounge. Claude Pottier, the French owner and chef, prepares authentic French cuisine in a nice, casual atmosphere. Each entree has visual appeal with decoratively carved vegetables accented with sauce. The homemade desserts top off the superb presentation. **Cards:** AE, MC, VI.

CARAFIELLO'S

Dinner: $11-$24　　　**Phone: 954/421-2481**

Italian

Location: US 1, 1 mi s of jct SR 810, (Hillsboro Blvd); at SE 10th St. 949 S Federal Hwy 33441. **Hours:** 5 pm-11 pm. Closed: Tues 8/1-9/30. **Reservations:** suggested. **Features:** casual dress; children's menu; carryout; beer & wine only. The owner/chef of this cozy mom-and-pop operation prepares tasty dishes such as gnocchi, spinach-stuffed breast of chicken, seafood and a delectable assortment of homemade desserts. You can get Continental cuisine here, too. **Cards:** AE, DS, MC, VI.

PAL'S CHARLEY'S CRAB

Lunch: $6-$14　　　**Dinner:** $12-$26　　　**Phone: 954/427-4000**

Seafood

Location: On Intracoastal Waterway; just off Hillsboro Blvd; 0.5 mi e of jct US 1, in the Cove Plaza. 1755 SE 3rd Ct 33441. **Hours:** 11:30 am-3:30 & 4-10 pm. **Reservations:** suggested. **Features:** Sunday brunch; children's menu; early bird specials; carryout; cocktails; entertainment; valet parking. A well-established restaurant, it overlooks the scenic Intracoastal Waterway. A wide variety of delicious seafood dishes are served along with featured pasta specials. Start with the spicy black bean soup and order a fresh catch from Florida waters. **Cards:** AE, DI, DS, MC, VI.

The following restaurant has not been evaluated by AAA but is listed for your information only.

FLANIGAN'S SEAFOOD BAR & GRILL

Phone: 954/427-9304

[fyi]

Not evaluated. **Location:** 2041 NE 2nd St. **Features:** A casual atmosphere that is inexpensive and family friendly. Known for their barbecue baby back ribs, large burgers and fresh local seafood.

HALLANDALE pop. 31,000 (See map p. 346; index p. 351)

WHERE TO STAY

BEST WESTERN HALLANDALE

Phone: (954)456-8333　150

12/15-1/2	1P: $95-$125	2P: $95-$125	XP: $6 F17
1/3-4/15	1P: $85-$109	2P: $85-$109	XP: $6 F17
12/1-12/14 & 4/16-11/30	1P: $69-$79	2P: $69-$79	XP: $6 F17

Motel

Location: On Hallandale Beach Blvd at jct I-95, exit 21. 101 Ansin Blvd 33009. Fax: 954/456-8333. **Facility:** Older contemporary surroundings located close to restaurants with shopping within a short drive Older contemporary surroundings located close to restaurants with shopping within a short drive Older contemporary surroundings located close to restaurants with shopping within a short drive. 98 units. 5 stories, interior corridors. **Terms:** package plans. **Amenities:** extended cable TV. **Leisure Activities:** exercise room. **Guest Services:** [CP] meal plan available, coin laundry. **Business Services:** meeting rooms. **Cards:** AE, DI, DS, MC, VI. SOME UNITS

HALLANDALE RESORT MOTEL

Phone: (954)456-3024　149

2/1-3/31	1P: $55-$70	2P: $55-$70	XP: $7 F12
12/1-1/31	1P: $40-$60	2P: $40-$60	XP: $7 F12
10/16-11/30	1P: $40-$45	2P: $40-$45	XP: $7 F12
4/1-10/15	1P: $35-$40	2P: $35-$40	XP: $7 F12

Motel

Location: I-95, exit 22 Pembroke Rd (SR 824), 1.5 mi e to US 1, 0.3 mi s to NE 7th St, then just left. 703 NE 7th St 33009. Fax: 954/457-3843. **Facility:** Very well kept rooms. Attractive pool area. 23 units. 6 efficiencies and 17 units with kitchen. *Bath:* combo or shower only. 1 story, exterior corridors. **Terms:** 30 day cancellation notice-fee imposed, weekly & monthly rates available. **Amenities:** voice mail. **Leisure Activities:** heated pool, whirlpool, horseshoes, shuffleboard. **Guest Services:** coin laundry. *Fee:* fax. **Cards:** AE, MC, VI.

WHERE TO DINE

The following restaurant has not been evaluated by AAA but is listed for your information only.

FLANIGAN'S SEAFOOD BAR & GRILL **Phone:** 954/458-2566

fyi

Not evaluated. **Location:** 4 N Federal Hwy 33009. **Features:** Casual atmosphere that is inexpensive and family friendly. Known for their baby back ribs, large burgers and fresh local seafood.

HILLSBORO BEACH pop. 1,700

WHERE TO STAY

ROYAL FLAMINGO VILLAS **Phone:** (954)427-0660

Cottage

12/1-4/30	1P: $124-$180	2P: $161-$229	XP: $10	F12
5/1-11/30	1P: $72-$125	2P: $89-$144	XP: $10	F12

Location: SR A1A, 0.8 mi s of jct SR 810 (Hillsboro Blvd). 1225 Hillsboro Mile 33062. Fax: 954/427-6110. **Facility:** Extensive landscaped grounds extending from ocean across SR A1A to the Intracoastal Waterway. 38 units with kitchen. 26 two-bedroom units. 1 story, exterior corridors. **Terms:** 45 day cancellation notice. **Amenities:** extended cable TV, voice mail, irons. **Leisure Activities:** heated pool, beach, swimming, putting green. **Guest Services:** coin laundry. **Cards:** DS, MC, VI.

ASK VCR

SEABONAY BEACH RESORT **Phone:** (954)427-2525

SAVE

Apartment

12/16-4/15	1P: $159-$399	2P: $159-$399
12/1-12/15	1P: $69-$199	2P: $69-$199
4/16-11/30	1P: $79-$109	2P: $79-$109

Location: SR A1A, 1.2 mi s of jct SR 810 (Hillsboro Blvd). 1159 Hillsboro Mile 33062. Fax: 954/427-3228. **Facility:** Modern efficiency and 1-bedroom apartments, some with ocean view and balcony. 65 units with kitchen. *Bath:* combo or shower only. 6 stories, interior/exterior corridors. **Terms:** 3 day cancellation notice, weekly & monthly rates available, package plans. **Amenities:** extended cable TV, voice mail. **Leisure Activities:** heated pool, beach, swimming, boat dock, exercise room. **Guest Services:** coin laundry. **Cards:** AE, DS, MC, VI.

SOME UNITS

FEE / VCR / FEE

HOLLYWOOD pop. 121,700 (See map p. 346; index p. 351)

WHERE TO STAY

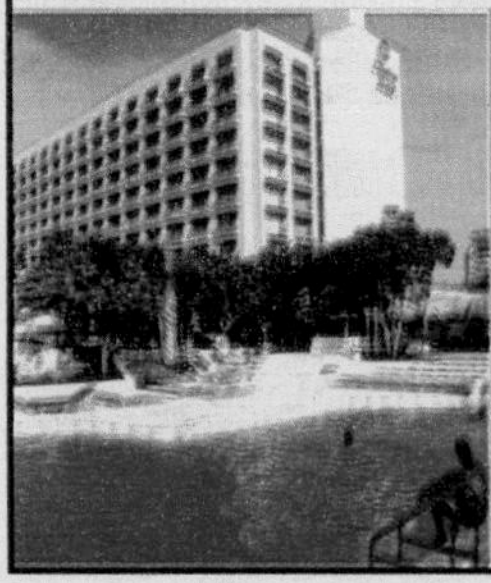

CLARION HOTEL HOLLYWOOD BEACH **Phone:** (954)458-1900 139

SAVE

Hotel

12/16-4/30	1P: $129	2P: $229	XP: $10
5/1-11/30	1P: $109	2P: $179	XP: $10
12/1-12/15	1P: $89	2P: $149	

Location: SR A1A, at jct SR 858 (Hallandale Beach Blvd). 4000 S Ocean Dr 33019. Fax: 954/458-7222. **Facility:** On the Intracoastal Waterway, all units with balcony. 309 units. *Bath:* combo or shower only. 10 stories, interior corridors. **Parking:** extra charge or valet. **Terms:** monthly rates available. **Amenities:** video games, voice mail, safes (fee). *Some:* irons, hair dryers. **Dining:** restaurant, 6:30 am-11 pm; also food court, $8-$20. **Leisure Activities:** heated pool, wading pool, sauna, whirlpool, 2 tennis courts, exercise room. **Guest Services:** gift shop, coin laundry. *Fee:* massage. **Business Services:** conference facilities, administrative services. *Fee:* PC, fax. **Cards:** AE, CB, DI, DS, JC, MC, VI. **Special Amenities: early check-in/late check-out and free room upgrade (subject to availability with advanced reservations).** *(See color ad below)*

SOME UNITS

FEE DATA PORT / /

(See map p. 346)

COMFORT INN-FT. LAUDERDALE/HOLLYWOOD AIRPORT   Phone: 954/922-1600   126

(AAA) (SAVE)   All Year   1P: $61-$133   2P: $61-$133   XP: $10   F18

▼▼▼   **Location:** Just e of jct I-95, exit 25, 2 mi s of airport, 4 mi sw of airport entrance. 2520 Stirling Rd 33020.

Motel   Fax: 954/923-5363. **Facility:** Oakwood Shopping Center within walking distance. 190 units. *Bath:* combo or shower only. 4 stories, exterior corridors. **Terms:** weekly & monthly rates available, pets ($25 extra charge). **Amenities:** extended cable TV, voice mail, hair dryers. **Leisure Activities:** heated pool. **Guest Services:** area transportation-within 5 mi Point Everglades, valet and coin laundry. **Business Services:** meeting rooms. *Fee:* PC. **Cards:** AE, CB, DI, DS, JC, MC, VI. **Special Amenities: free continental breakfast and free newspaper.**
(See color ad below)

DAYS INN FORT LAUDERDALE/HOLLYWOOD AIRPORT SOUTH   Phone: (954)923-7300   129

(SAVE)   12/1-4/30   2P: $79-$179   XP: $10   F17

   5/1-11/30   2P: $69-$129   XP: $10   F17

▼▼▼   **Location:** SR 822 (Sheridan St), just nw of I-95, exit 24. 2601 N 29th Ave 33020. Fax: 954/921-6706. **Facility:** In-

Motel   viting public areas with a few sitting areas. Units newly renovated with light wood tones and a tropical color scheme. 114 units. 7 stories, interior corridors. **Terms:** small pets only ($10 extra charge). **Amenities:** extended cable TV, voice mail, irons, hair dryers. **Leisure Activities:** whirlpool, exercise room. **Guest Services:** [ECP] meal plan available, valet and coin laundry. **Business Services:** meeting rooms. **Cards:** AE, CB, DI, DS, JC, MC, VI.

GREENBRIAR BEACH CLUB   Phone: (954)922-2606   136

(AAA) (SAVE)   12/1-4/15   1P: $95-$175   2P: $95-$175   XP: $15   F12

   4/16-11/30   1P: $65-$149   2P: $65-$149   XP: $15   F12

▼▼   **Location:** Hollywood Blvd 0.8 mi s on A1A/Ocean Blvd to Iris Terrace, turn left to S-Surf, then just n. 1900 S Surf Rd

Apartment   33019. Fax: 954/923-0897. **Facility:** Tastefully decorated units, some with oceanfront view. 47 units with kitchen. Some suites ($99-$175). 3 stories (no elevator), exterior corridors. **Terms:** 30 day cancellation notice, weekly & monthly rates available. **Amenities:** extended cable TV, voice mail. **Leisure Activities:** heated pool, beach, swimming. **Guest Services:** coin laundry. **Cards:** AE, DI, DS, MC, VI. **Special Amenities: free continental breakfast.**

(See map p. 346)

HAMPTON INN & SUITES-FT LAUDERDALE/HOLLYWOOD AIRPORT

Phone: 954/922-0011 [125]

All Year   1P: $99-$169   2P: $99-$169   XP: $10   F18

Location: Just e of jct I-95, exit 25, 2 mi s of airport, 4 mi sw of airport entrance. 2500 Stirling Rd 33020. Fax: 954/929-7118. **Facility:** Standard units and one-bedroom suites with living room and kitchen. 104 units, 51 with efficiency. Some suites ($109-$169). *Bath:* combo or shower only. 5 stories, interior corridors. **Terms:** weekly & monthly rates available. **Amenities:** extended cable TV, voice mail, irons, hair dryers. **Leisure Activities:** small heated pool, exercise room. **Guest Services:** complimentary evening beverages; Mon-Thurs, area transportation-within 5 mi Pt Everglades, valet and coin laundry. **Business Services:** meeting rooms, administrative services. *Fee:* PC. **Cards:** AE, CB, DI, DS, JC, MC, VI. **Special Amenities: free continental breakfast and free local telephone calls.** *(See color ad p 381)*

SOME UNITS

HOLIDAY INN FORT LAUDERDALE/AIRPORT

Phone: (954)925-9100 [130]

12/31-4/15   1P: $169-$189   2P: $169-$189

12/16-12/30 & 4/16-11/30   1P: $129-$169   2P: $129-$169

Motor Inn   **Location:** SR 822 (Sheridan St); just w of jct I-95, exit 24. 2905 Sheridan St 33020. Fax: 954/925-5512. **Facility:** Very attractively furnished units and public areas. A soothing and relaxing pool area. A regional award winner from Holiday Inn. 150 units. *Bath:* combo or shower only. 6 stories, interior corridors. **Terms:** package plans. **Amenities:** extended cable TV, dual phone lines, voice mail, irons, hair dryers. **Leisure Activities:** heated pool, whirlpool, exercise room. **Guest Services:** [BP] meal plan available, valet and coin laundry. *Fee:* area transportation. **Business Services:** meeting rooms, administrative services, fax. **Cards:** AE, DI, DS, MC, VI.

SOME UNITS

HOLIDAY INN

Phone: (954)923-8700 [138]

All Year   1P: $109-$209   2P: $109-$209   XP: $10   F19

Motor Inn   **Location:** SR A1A, 0.5 mi n of jct SR 858 (Hallandale Beach Blvd). 2711 S Ocean Dr 33019. Fax: 954/923-7059. **Facility:** Most units with balcony, few oceanfront or overlooking landscaped pool patio. 201 units. Some suites. *Bath:* some combo or shower only. 2-4 stories, interior corridors. **Parking:** extra charge. **Terms:** check-in 4 pm, 3 day cancellation notice. **Amenities:** voice mail, safes, irons, hair dryers. **Dining:** restaurant, 6:30 am-2:30 & 4-11 pm patio dining, $10-$25, cocktails, entertainment. **Leisure Activities:** heated pool, beach, swimming, children's program, shuffleboard, convenience store. *Fee:* bicycles. **Guest Services:** gift shop, coin laundry. **Business Services:** meeting rooms. *Fee:* fax. **Cards:** AE, CB, DI, DS, MC, VI. **Special Amenities: free local telephone calls.** *(See ad below)*

SOME UNITS

HOWARD JOHNSON PLAZA RESORT HOLLYWOOD BEACH

Phone: (954)925-1411 [133]

1/2-4/22   1P: $141-$214   2P: $141-$214   XP: $10   F18

12/1-1/1   1P: $136-$209   2P: $136-$209   XP: $10   F18

4/23-11/30   1P: $83-$141   2P: $83-$141   XP: $10   F18

Motor Inn   **Location:** SR A1A, 1 mi n of jct SR 820 (Hollywood Blvd). 2501 N Ocean Dr 33019. Fax: 954/921-5565. **Facility:** Pool deck overlooks beach. Units with balcony. 242 units, 20 with efficiency. 11 stories, interior corridors. **Amenities:** voice mail, safes (fee). *Some:* irons, hair dryers. **Leisure Activities:** heated pool, wading pool, beach, swimming. **Guest Services:** gift shop, coin laundry. **Business Services:** meeting rooms. *Fee:* fax. **Cards:** AE, CB, DS, MC, VI.

SOME UNITS

LA QUINTA INN & SUITES

Phone: (954)922-2295 [131]

All Year   1P: $89-$129   2P: $89-$129

Location: I-95, exit 24 (Sheridan St/SR 822), just e to Oakwood, then just left. 2620 N 26th Ave 33020. Fax: 954/922-2995. **Facility:** Large rooms. contemporary decor. 131 units. Some suites ($119-$159). *Bath:* combo or shower only. 6 stories, interior corridors. **Terms:** small pets only. **Amenities:** video games, dual phone lines, voice mail, irons, hair dryers. **Leisure Activities:** heated pool, whirlpool, fishing, exercise room. **Guest Services:** [ECP] meal plan available, area transportation, valet and coin laundry. **Business Services:** meeting rooms. **Cards:** AE, CB, DI, DS, JC, MC, VI. *(See color ad p 363)*

SOME UNITS

(See map p. 346)

RICHARDS MOTEL

AAA SAVE
◈◈◈◈
Motel

Phone: 954/921-6418 `135`

1/26-3/31	1P: $49-$74	2P: $59-$74	XP: $10	D10
12/1-1/9	1P: $34-$74	2P: $39-$74	XP: $10	D10
1/10-1/25	1P: $59-$64	2P: $49-$64	XP: $10	D10
4/1-11/30	1P: $34-$64	2P: $39-$64	XP: $10	D10

Location: US 1, 0.7 mi s of Hollywood Circle, 0.3 mi n of jct Pembroke Rd. 1219 S Federal Hwy 33020. Fax: 954/925-1797. **Facility:** Variety of units and one-bedroom housekeeping units. 24 units, 11 with efficiency. Some suites. *Bath:* combo or shower only. 1-2 stories, exterior corridors. **Terms:** 30 day cancellation notice-fee imposed, weekly & monthly rates available. **Amenities:** extended cable TV. **Leisure Activities:** heated pool. **Guest Services:** coin laundry. *Fee:* fax. **Cards:** AE, CB, DI, DS, MC, VI. *(See ad below)*　　　SOME UNITS

🛗 🏊 🎥 🛄 / 💻 📠 /

SHELL MOTEL

AAA SAVE
◈◈◈◈
Motel

Phone: (954)923-8085 `134`

12/1-4/30	1P: $45-$70	2P: $49-$74	XP: $10	F7
10/1-11/30	1P: $40-$65	2P: $40-$65	XP: $10	F7
5/1-9/30	1P: $35-$45	2P: $39-$49	XP: $10	F7

Location: US 1, 0.7 mi s of Hollywood Circle, 0.3 mi n of jct Pembroke Rd. 1201 S Federal Hwy 33020. Fax: 954/925-8750. **Facility:** A variety accommodations with contemporary appointments. 35 units. 2 two-bedroom units, 11 efficiencies and 11 units with kitchen. *Bath:* combo or shower only. 1 story, exterior corridors. **Terms:** 30 day cancellation notice-fee imposed, weekly & monthly rates available. **Leisure Activities:** heated pool, shuffleboard. **Guest Services:** coin laundry. *Fee:* fax. **Cards:** AE, MC, VI. *(See ad below)*　　　SOME UNITS

🅂🄳 🏊 🎥 🛄 / 📠 📠 /

––––––– **WHERE TO DINE** –––––––

GIORGIO'S GRILL

◈◈◈
Italian

MC, VI.

Dinner: $10-$28　　　Phone: 954/929-7030 `142`

Location: On SR A1A, just n of Hollywood Blvd (SR 820). 606 N Ocean Dr 33019. **Hours:** 4 pm-11 pm. **Reservations:** accepted. **Features:** dressy casual; early bird specials; cocktails & lounge; fee for parking; valet parking; a la carte, also prix fixe. Located on the Intracoastal Waterway. Dine indoors or outdoors. Seafood a specialty, but also Mediterranean entrees of pasta, pizza, beef and chicken. **Cards:** AE, DI, DS,

❌

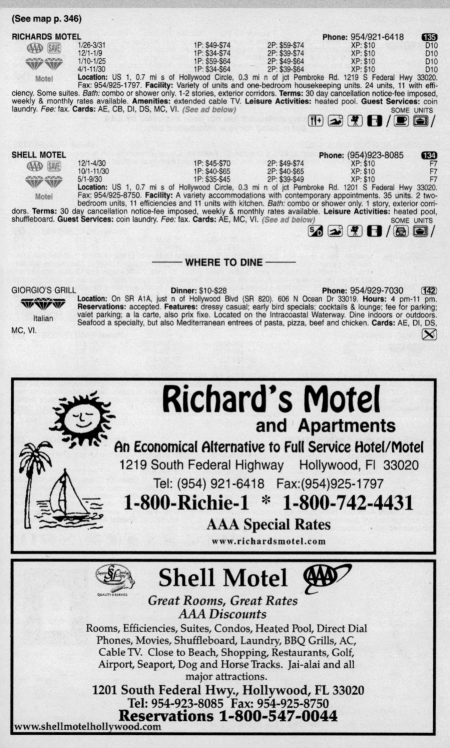

(See map p. 346)

MARTHA'S ON THE INTRACOASTAL   **Lunch:** $6-$12   **Dinner:** $15-$29   **Phone:** 954/923-5444   `141`
▼▼◇◇▼▼   **Location:** Between Dania Beach Blvd Bridge and Sheridan St. 6024 N Ocean Dr 33019. **Hours:** 11:30 am-11 pm,
              Fri & Sat-midnight. **Reservations:** suggested. **Features:** dressy casual; Sunday brunch; children's menu;
American   early bird specials; carryout; cocktails; entertainment; valet parking. An island feel tinges the cuisine and
              decor of this waterfront eatery. The views are outstanding. Seafood dazzlers dominate the first plates, and
the main plates are equally enticing and innovative. Fresh seafood is always available. **Cards:** AE, DI, DS, MC, VI.   ⊠

The following restaurant has not been evaluated by AAA
but is listed for your information only.

FLANIGAN'S SEAFOOD BAR & GRILL   **Phone:** 954/964-3793
`fyi`   Not evaluated. **Location:** 2505 N University Dr. **Features:** Casual atmosphere that is inexpensive and family
              friendly. Known for their baby back ribs, large burgers and fresh local seafood.

LAUDERDALE-BY-THE-SEA pop. 3,000   (See map p. 346; index p. 350)

-------- WHERE TO STAY --------

A LITTLE INN BY THE SEA   **Phone:** (954)772-2450   `62`
ⒶⒶⒶ [SAVE]   12/16-4/30   1P: $109-$189   2P: $109-$189   XP: $10   F12
              12/1-12/15 & 5/1-11/30   1P: $79-$139   2P: $79-$139   XP: $10   F12
▼▼◇◇▼▼   **Location:** Just e of SR A1A, 0.4 mi n of SR 870 (Commercial Blvd). 4546 El Mar Dr 33308. **Fax:** 954/938-9354.
Motel   **Facility:** Extremely charming 1940s deco style building and 2-story modern addition. Most rooms with bal-
              cony, some with beach/ocean view. 3-story lobby atrium. 29 units. 7 efficiencies and 12 units with kitchen.
              2-3 stories (no elevator), interior/exterior corridors. **Terms:** 30 day cancellation notice-fee imposed, package
plans. **Amenities:** extended cable TV, voice mail. **Leisure Activities:** heated pool, beach, swimming, bicycles, rooftop sun deck.
Guest Services: [CP] meal plan available. **Cards:** AE, DI, DS, MC, VI. **Special Amenities:** free newspaper and preferred
room (subject to availability with advanced reservations). *(See color ad p 363)*   SOME UNITS

🛉 🏊 🛗 [DATA PORT] / ⊠ 🖨 /

BLUE SEAS COURTYARD   **Phone:** 954/772-3336   `59`
▼▼◇◇▼▼   1/21-4/30   1P: $94-$105   2P: $94-$105   XP: $10
              12/1-1/20   1P: $64-$100   2P: $64-$100   XP: $10
Motel   11/2-11/30   1P: $64-$75   2P: $64-$75   XP: $10
              5/1-11/1   1P: $58-$70   2P: $58-$70   XP: $10
Location: 0.5 mi n of Commercial Blvd/SR 810. 4525 El Mar Dr 33308. **Fax:** 954/772-6337. **Facility:** A small property with lots of charm.
Attractive pool area with a small fountain beside it. Rooms with a Southwestern decor with hand-painted accents. Across from
the ocean. 12 units, 10 with efficiency. *Bath:* combo or shower only. 2 stories, exterior corridors. **Terms:** age restrictions may
apply, 30 day cancellation notice-fee imposed, monthly rates available. **Amenities:** extended cable TV. **Leisure Activities:** heated pool. **Cards:** MC, VI.   SOME UNITS

🛉 🏊 🛗 [DATA PORT] / 🖼 /

CLARION LAUDERDALE BEACH RESORT   **Phone:** (954)776-5660   `63`
ⒶⒶⒶ [SAVE]   12/25-2/8   1P: $135-$375   2P: $145-$375   XP: $10   F17
              2/9-4/15   1P: $135-$210   2P: $145-$210   XP: $10   F17
▼▼◇◇▼▼   12/1-12/24   1P: $79-$180   2P: $89-$180   XP: $10   F17
Motor Inn   4/16-11/30   1P: $79-$155   2P: $89-$155   XP: $10   F17
              Location: SR A1A, 0.5 mi n of SR 870 (Commercial Blvd). 4660 N Ocean Dr 33308. **Fax:** 954/776-4689.
              Facility: Spacious rooms with contemporary decor. A few rooms with oceanfront view, many with ocean view.
149 units. *Bath:* combo or shower only. 2-5 stories, interior corridors. **Terms:** 3 day cancellation notice, weekly & monthly rates
available, package plans. **Amenities:** extended cable TV, irons, hair dryers. **Dining:** restaurant, patio bar 7 am-9:30 pm, $8-$14,
cocktails. **Leisure Activities:** heated pool, wading pool, beach, swimming, children's program, exercise room. **Guest Services:**
valet and coin laundry. **Business Services:** meeting rooms. **Cards:** AE, DI, DS, MC, VI. **Special Amenities:** free newspaper
and preferred room (subject to availability with advanced reservations). *(See color ad p 358)*   SOME UNITS

[S/D] 🛉 📺 🏊 ⊠ 🖨 🗔 [DATA PORT] / ⊠ 🖼 🛗 /

(See map p. 346)

COURTYARD VILLA ON THE OCEAN
Phone: (954)776-1164 [65]

(AAA) (SAVE)

12/19-4/25	1P: $150-$190	2P: $150-$190	XP: $10	F17
12/1-12/18	1P: $105-$135	2P: $105-$135	XP: $10	F17
4/26-11/30	1P: $105-$130	2P: $105-$130	XP: $10	F17

Historic Motel

Location: From Commerical Blvd (SR 870) just s. 4312 El Mar Dr 33308. Fax: 954/491-0768. **Facility:** All rooms furnished with 19th century antique reproductions. Small tropical courtyard leading to the beach. 8 efficiencies. *Bath:* shower only. 2 stories, exterior corridors. **Terms:** age restrictions may apply, 30 day cancellation notice, weekly & monthly rates available, package plans. **Amenities:** extended cable TV, voice mail, irons, hair dryers. **Leisure Activities:** heated pool, beach, swimming, beach towels, sun deck, scuba diving, snorkeling, tennis court, bicycles, grill, padi dive resort. **Guest Services:** valet laundry. **Cards:** AE, DI, MC, VI. **Special Amenities:** early check-in/late check-out and free continental breakfast. *(See color ad p 384)*

SOME UNITS

HOLIDAY INN-LAUDERDALE-BY-THE-SEA NORTH BEACH
Phone: (954)776-1212 [61]

(AAA) (SAVE)

4/21-11/30	1P: $89-$149	2P: $89-$149	
12/1-12/20	1P: $89-$149	2P: $89-$149	XP: $10
12/21-4/20	1P: $149	2P: $149	F18

Motor Inn

Facility: Across from beach, some rooms with private balcony. 186 units. 5 stories, exterior corridors. **Location:** SR A1A, just s of jct SR 870, Commercial Blvd. 4116 N Ocean Dr 33308. Fax: 954/776-1411. **Terms:** 3 day cancellation notice-fee imposed, package plans. **Amenities:** extended cable TV, voice mail, irons, hair dryers. *Some:* safes. **Dining:** restaurant, 6 am-10 pm; patio bar, $6-$11, cocktails. **Leisure Activities:** heated pool, beach access, scuba diving, snorkeling, exercise room. *Fee:* scuba & snorkeling equipment. **Guest Services:** gift shop, valet and coin laundry. **Business Services:** meeting rooms. **Cards:** AE, DI, DS, MC, VI.

SOME UNITS

SEASCAPE RESORT MOTEL
Phone: (954)776-0767 [64]

(AAA) (SAVE)

12/18-4/15	1P: $59-$69	2P: $69-$89
12/1-12/17 & 4/16-11/30	1P: $35-$45	2P: $45-$55

Motel

Location: SR A1A, just n of SR 870 (Commercial Blvd). 4425 N Ocean Dr 33308. Fax: 954/351-6986. **Facility:** Spacious rooms, tastefully decorated and furnished. Attractive pool area. 22 units, 10 with efficiency. Some suites ($89-$120). 2 stories, exterior corridors. **Terms:** 3 day cancellation notice, weekly rates available. **Amenities:** extended cable TV. **Leisure Activities:** heated pool. **Guest Services:** coin laundry. **Cards:** AE, MC, VI. **Special Amenities:** early check-in/late check-out and free continental breakfast.

TROPIC SEAS RESORT
Phone: (954)772-2555 [60]

(AAA) (SAVE)

2/1-4/22	2P: $140-$205	XP: $10 F12
12/1-1/31	2P: $90-$185	XP: $10 F12
10/1-11/30	2P: $95-$160	XP: $10 F12
4/23-9/30	2P: $85-$150	XP: $10 F12

Motel

Location: Just e of SR A1A; 0.5 mi n of jct SR 870 (Commercial Blvd). 4616 El Mar Dr 33308. Fax: 954/771-5711. **Facility:** Landscaped pool patio, all units with beach view. 16 units. 6 efficiencies and 7 units with kitchen. 2 stories, exterior corridors. **Terms:** 15 day cancellation notice, written notice req-fee imposed, monthly rates available. **Amenities:** extended cable TV, voice mail. **Leisure Activities:** heated pool, beach, swimming. **Guest Services:** coin laundry. **Cards:** AE, DI, DS, MC, VI. **Special Amenities:** early check-in/late check-out and free continental breakfast. *(See color ad p 367)*

SOME UNITS

WHERE TO DINE

ARUBA BEACH CAFE   Lunch: $3-$13   Dinner: $5-$11   Phone: 954/776-0001 [90]

Caribbean

Location: Just e of SR A1A. 1 E Commercial Blvd 33308. **Hours:** 11 am-11 pm. **Reservations:** accepted. **Features:** casual dress; Sunday brunch; carryout; cocktails & lounge; fee for valet parking. A casual, fun place to eat, it affords a panoramic view of the beach and offers fresh seafood items, pasta and meat entrees. Crusted with white sesame seeds, the tasty salmon comes with white rice and steamed vegetables for a nice, light meal. **Cards:** AE, DI, DS, MC, VI.

LAUDERHILL pop. 49,700   (See map p. 346; index p. 351)

WHERE TO DINE

CRAB HOUSE SEAFOOD RESTAURANT   Lunch: $5-$10   Dinner: $12-$21   Phone: 954/749-2722 [146]

Seafood

Location: SR 817 (University Dr); 1 mi s of Commercial Blvd at NW 44th St. 4402 N University Dr 33351. **Hours:** 11:30 am-10:15 pm, Fri & Sat-11:15 pm. Closed: 11/22. **Reservations:** accepted. **Features:** casual dress; children's menu; early bird specials; carryout; cocktails & lounge. This popular, casual restaurant in a warehouse-style building is decorated in a nautical theme. Fresh seafood and several varieties of crab are menu staples. If you're hungry, head for the all-you-can-eat shellfish and salad bar. **Cards:** AE, CB, DI, DS, MC, VI.

LIGHTHOUSE POINT pop. 10,400

WHERE TO DINE

CAP'S PLACE-ISLAND RESTAURANT & BAR   Historical   Dinner: $13-$25   Phone: 954/941-0418

Seafood

Location: Just n on US 1 from jct Copans Rd, 1.1 mi e and n via NE 24th St following signs to Cap's Dock for short boat ride to the island. 2765 NE 28thle #2 Ct 33064. **Hours:** 5:30 pm-10 pm, Fri & Sat-11 pm. Closed: 11/22, 12/24, 12/25; also Super Bowl Sun. **Reservations:** suggested. **Features:** casual dress; children's menu; carryout; cocktails & lounge. Operating out of a building that once was a gambling casino, the restaurant sits on an island in the Intracoastal Waterway and has been a source of rich history since 1929. Grouper chowder, hearts of palm salad and fresh broiled fish are menu favorites. **Cards:** AE, MC, VI.

FIFTH AVENUE GRILL   **Lunch:** $6-$15   **Dinner:** $18-$40   **Phone:** 954/782-4433

Steak House

Location: On US 1 (Federal Hwy), 1.1 mi n of Sample Rd. 4650 N Federal Hwy 33064. **Hours:** 11:30 am-4 & 5-10 pm, Fri & Sat-11 pm. Closed: Superbowl Sun. **Reservations:** accepted. **Features:** dressy casual; children's menu; early bird specials; carryout; cocktails & lounge; entertainment; valet parking. Open flamed broiled steak and chops. Fresh seafood items also available. An award winning wine list compliments the menu. A cozy room. **Cards:** AE, DI, MC, VI.

LE BISTRO   **Dinner:** $15-$28   **Phone:** 954/946-9240

French

Location: From Sample Rd, just n; in Main St Plaza. 4626 N Federal Hwy 33064. **Hours:** 5 pm-9:30 pm. Closed: 1/1, 12/25; also Mon in summer. **Reservations:** suggested. **Features:** early bird specials; beer & wine only. Classic cuisine is served in generous portions at this small, quaint eatery. Great attention is given to every detail from preparation to presentation, from service to atmosphere. Recommended is the delicious swordfish in a lemon and wine sauce. **Cards:** MC, VI.

MAUI GRILLE   **Dinner:** $13-$25   **Phone:** 954/571-7788

Polynesian

Location: From Sample Rd, SR 834 1.1 mi n; in the Georgetown Plaza. 5000 N Federal Hwy 33064. **Hours:** 5 pm-10 pm; Fri & Sat-11 pm. Closed: Mon. **Reservations:** suggested. **Features:** dressy casual; beer & wine only; a la carte. Very well prepared and presented entrees with authentic Hawaiian cuisine. With the use of fresh seafood and the creativeness of the chef, it's like eating and being in Hawaii. There are other meat items such as pork, lamb, and poultry. A small dining room with painted murals of the island. This is gourmet food in a casual atmosphere. Smoke free premises. **Cards:** AE, MC, VI.

MARGATE pop. 43,000

——— **WHERE TO DINE** ———

JASMINE THAI   **Lunch:** $6-$13   **Dinner:** $10-$19   **Phone:** 954/979-5530

Thai

Location: Atlantic Blvd (SR 814), 0.7 mi n on SR 7 and US 441, then just e on Coconut Creek Pkwy; in the Cocogate Plaza. 5103 Coconut Creek Pkwy 33063. **Hours:** 4:30 pm-10 pm, also Mon-Fri 11 am-3 pm. Closed: 4/15, 7/4, 11/22; also Super Bowl Sun. **Reservations:** accepted. **Features:** casual dress; early bird specials; carryout; beer & wine only. Fresh, carefully prepared cuisine such as snapper with chili garlic sauce, roast duckling, panang curry and tornado chicken is served by a friendly wait staff. A quaint bridge and large pictures in the small, comfortable setting convey an Oriental feel. **Cards:** AE, CB, DI, DS, MC, VI.

NORTH LAUDERDALE pop. 26,500   (See map p. 346; index p. 350)

——— **WHERE TO STAY** ———

COURTYARD BY MARRIOTT FORT LAUDERDALE NORTH   **Phone:** (954)772-7770

1/1-4/18	1P: $129-$149	2P: $139-$159
12/1-12/31 & 4/19-11/30	1P: $59-$89	2P: $69-$99

Motor Inn

Location: I-95, exit 33B, 2.3 mi w; Cypress Creek Rd, at Ft Lauderdale Executive Airport. 2440 W Cypress Creek Rd 33309. **Fax:** 954/772-4780. **Facility:** Very inviting public areas and pool courtyard. Some rooms with small balcony. 136 units. Some suites ($169-$269). *Bath:* combo or shower only. 4 stories, interior corridors. **Amenities:** extended cable TV, dual phone lines, voice mail, irons, hair dryers. **Leisure Activities:** heated pool, whirlpool, exercise room. **Guest Services:** area transportation, coin laundry. **Business Services:** meeting rooms. **Cards:** AE, CB, DI, DS, MC, VI.

SOME UNITS

PEMBROKE PINES pop. 68,700

——— **WHERE TO STAY** ———

GRAND PALMS GOLF & COUNTRY CLUB RESORT   **Phone:** (954)431-8800

12/21-4/15	2P: $148-$158	XP: $10	F16
12/1-12/20	2P: $92-$130	XP: $10	F16
4/16-11/30	2P: $115-$125	XP: $10	F16

Resort

Location: SR 820, 0.4 mi w of jct I-75, exit 5B (Pines Blvd). 110 Grand Palms Dr 33027. **Fax:** 954/435-5988. **Facility:** On landscaped grounds, with tropical trees and flowering plants. A large pool area surrounded by small fountains. Nicely furnished rooms with a view of the golf course or pool area. 137 units. Some suites ($133-$228). 2 stories, exterior corridors. **Parking:** valet. **Terms:** 3 day cancellation notice-fee imposed, package plans. **Amenities:** extended cable TV. **Leisure Activities:** saunas, putting green, jogging. *Fee:* golf-27 holes, 6 tennis courts (4 lighted), exercise room. **Guest Services:** coin laundry. *Fee:* area transportation. **Business Services:** meeting rooms. **Cards:** AE, CB, DI, DS, MC, VI.

SOME UNITS

HAMPTON INN PEMBROKE PINES   **Phone:** 954/441-4242

Property failed to provide current rates

Motel

Location: I-75, exit 6A, 0.4 mi e on Sheridan St (SR 522) to NW 146th Ave, then 0.4 mi s. 1900 NW 150 Ave 33028. **Fax:** 954/441-1118. **Facility:** Just off the interstate, a relaxing pool area. The lobby is comfortable with a large breakfast area. Spacious rooms with light wood tones and warm accent colors. 107 units. Some whirlpool units. *Bath:* combo or shower only. 5 stories, interior corridors. **Amenities:** voice mail, irons, hair dryers. **Leisure Activities:** whirlpool, exercise room. **Guest Services:** [ECP] meal plan available, valet and coin laundry. **Cards:** AE, DI, DS, JC, MC, VI.

SOME UNITS

------- WHERE TO DINE -------

THE ROASTED PEPPER ITALIAN SEAFOOD & GRILL   **Lunch:** $5-$9   **Dinner:** $10-$20   **Phone:** 954/450-8800
♦♦♦ ♦♦♦   **Location:** 4.4 mi e of I-75, exit 5A E; in The Roasted Pepper Pine Plaza Center. 9893 Pines Blvd 33024.
     Hours: 11:30 am-9:30 pm, Fri-11 pm, Sat 3 pm-11 pm, Sun 4 pm-9:30 pm. Closed major holidays.
Italian   **Features:** casual dress; children's menu; carryout; cocktails & lounge; entertainment; minimum charge-10.
     This busy family restaurant serves traditional favorites like brick-oven pizza. When the singer takes a
break, the servers dance and sing to keep the beat going. A neat, entertaining place to go for generous portions of authentic
Italian food. **Cards:** AE, DS, MC, VI.
☒

PLANTATION pop. 66,700   (See map p. 346; index p. 351)

------- WHERE TO STAY -------

AMERISUITES PLANTATION   **Phone:** (954)370-2220   123
Ⓐ SAVE | 1/1-4/14   1P: $89-$149   2P: $89-$149   XP: $10   F18
        | 12/1-12/31 & 4/15-11/30 1P: $79-$129   2P: $79-$129   XP: $10   F18
♦♦♦♦♦ **Location:** I-595, exit 5 and Pine Island Rd, 1.3 mi n; behind the Westside Corporate Center. 8530 W Broward Blvd
Suite Motel 33324. Fax: 954/370-2272. **Facility:** A stylish lobby. Spacious and nicely furnished units. Many units are work
friendly. 128 units. *Bath:* combo or shower only. 7 stories, interior corridors. **Terms:** cancellation fee imposed,
small pets only ($10 extra charge). **Amenities:** video games, voice mail, irons, hair dryers. **Leisure Activi-**
ties: heated pool, exercise room. **Guest Services:** [ECP] meal plan available, valet and coin laundry. **Business Services:**
meeting rooms, administrative services. **Cards:** AE, CB, DI, DS, JC, MC, VI. **Special Amenities:** free continental breakfast
and free newspaper. *(See color ad p 5)*
SOME UNITS
[icons] /☒/

COURTYARD BY MARRIOTT-PLANTATION   **Phone:** (954)475-1100   122
♦♦♦♦ | 12/1-4/30   1P: $139   2P: $149   XP: $10   F18
      | 5/1-11/30   1P: $99   2P: $109   XP: $10   F18
Motel **Location:** Just w of University Dr (SR 817) at s edge of Broward Mall; 0.5 mi sw of Broward Blvd (SR 842). 7780 SW
6th St 33324. Fax: 954/424-8402. **Facility:** Built around attractively landscaped courtyard. 149 units. Some
suites. *Bath:* combo or shower only. 3 stories, interior corridors. **Amenities:** voice mail, irons, hair dryers. **Leisure Activi-**
ties: heated pool, whirlpool, exercise room. **Guest Services:** valet and coin laundry. **Cards:** AE, DI, DS, MC, VI.
(See color ad p 359)
SOME UNITS
ASK [icons] /☒ 🖼 ⦿/

HAMPTON INN PLANTATION   **Phone:** (954)382-4500   119
SAVE | All Year   1P: $69-$159   2P: $69-$159
♦♦♦♦ **Location:** Just w of University Dr (SR 817) at the edge of Broward Blvd, 0.5 mi sw of Broward Blvd. 7801 SW 6th St
Motel 33321. Fax: 854/382-4510. **Facility:** Nestled between a major mall and an office park area. A fenced pool
area with some tropical foliage. A large lobby area with comfortable sitting areas and breakfast area. Com-
fortable units with light wood tones with colorful decor accents. 128 units. *Bath:* combo or shower only. 5 sto-
ries, interior corridors. **Amenities:** extended cable TV, dual phone lines, voice mail, irons, hair dryers.
Leisure Activities: heated pool, whirlpool, exercise room. **Guest Services:** [ECP] meal plan available, valet and coin laundry.
Business Services: meeting rooms. **Cards:** AE, CB, DI, DS, JC, MC, VI.
SOME UNITS
[icons] /☒ 🖼 ⦿/

HOLIDAY INN PLANTATION   **Phone:** (954)472-5600   124
Ⓐ SAVE | 12/1-12/26 & 12/27-4/30   1P: $129
       | 10/1-11/30   1P: $119
♦♦♦♦ | 5/1-9/30   1P: $89
Motor Inn **Location:** SR 817, just s of jct SR 838, Sunrise Blvd. 1711 N University Dr 33322. Fax: 954/370-3201. **Facility:** Close
to multiple mall outlets and many dining possibilities. 335 units. Some suites. *Bath:* combo or shower only.
2-5 stories, interior/exterior corridors. **Terms:** small pets only. **Amenities:** voice mail, irons, hair dryers.
Dining: restaurant, 6:30 am-2 & 5-10 pm, $9-$14, cocktails. **Leisure Activities:** heated pool, exercise room. **Guest Services:**
coin laundry. **Business Services:** meeting rooms. **Cards:** AE, CB, DI, DS, JC, MC, VI. **Special Amenities:** free newspaper and
free room upgrade (subject to availability with advanced reservations). *(See ad below)*
SOME UNITS
[icons] /☒ 🖼 ⦿/

(See map p. 346)

LA QUINTA INN & SUITES   Phone: (954)476-6047 [115]

[SAVE]

[▽▽▽]
Motel

All Year   1P: $89-$109   2P: $89-$109
Location: I-595, exit 6, University Dr (SR 817 N), just w of University (SR 817); in the Crossroad Office Park. 8101 Pe-
ters Rd 33324. Fax: 954-476-6547. **Facility:** Large units, contemporary decor. 131 units. Some suites ($119-
$139). *Bath:* combo or shower only. 4 stories, interior corridors. **Terms:** small pets only. **Amenities:** video
games, voice mail, irons, hair dryers. **Leisure Activities:** heated pool, whirlpool, exercise room. **Guest Services:** [ECP] meal plan available, valet and coin laundry. **Business Services:** meeting rooms. **Cards:** AE, CB,
DI, DS, MC, VI. *(See color ad p 363)*

SOME UNITS

[icons] / FEE

RESIDENCE INN BY MARRIOTT-PLANTATION   Phone: (954)723-0300 [114]

[▽▽▽]
Extended Stay
Apartment

12/1-5/11   1P: $134-$144   2P: $134-$144
5/12-11/30   1P: $116-$126   2P: $116-$126
Location: University Dr (SR 817), just n of jct Broward Blvd (SR 842). 130 N University Dr 33324. Fax: 954/474-7385.
Facility: Very well equipped studios and 1- and 2-bedroom suites, few with fireplace. A warm and inviting
lobby area. 138 units with kitchen. 30 two-bedroom units. *Bath:* combo or shower only. 1-4 stories, interior
corridors. **Terms:** weekly & monthly rates available, small pets only ($150-$200 extra charge). **Amenities:** video games, dual
phone lines, voice mail. **Leisure Activities:** heated pool, whirlpool, exercise room, sports court. **Guest Services:** [BP] meal plan
available, complimentary evening beverages: Mon-Thurs, valet and coin laundry. **Business Services:** meeting rooms.
Cards: AE, CB, DI, DS, MC, VI.

SOME UNITS

[ASK] [icons] / FEE

SHERATON SUITES-PLANTATION   Phone: (954)424-3300 [120]

[AAA] [SAVE]

[▽▽▽]
Suite Hotel

1/1-4/30   1P: $279-$349   2P: $279-$349   XP: $20   F17
12/1-12/31   1P: $225-$349   2P: $225-$349   XP: $20   F17
10/1-11/30   1P: $259   2P: $259   XP: $20   F17
5/1-9/30   1P: $229   2P: $229   XP: $20   F17
Location: On University Dr (SR 817), 0.3 mi n of jct Broward Blvd (SR 842); at the Fashion Mall. 311 N University Dr
33324. Fax: 954/452-8887. **Facility:** Impressive, modern facility with direct access to mall. Large, tastefully
furnished suites with separate living room. 263 units. 1 two-bedroom unit. Some whirlpool units ($269-$349). *Bath:* combo or
shower only. 9 stories, interior corridors. **Terms:** cancellation fee imposed, monthly rates available, package plans.
Amenities: video games, dual phone lines, voice mail, honor bars, irons, hair dryers. *Some:* fax. **Dining:** restaurant, 6:30 am-
2:30 & 5:30-10:30 pm, Sun from 7 am, $8-$24, cocktails. **Leisure Activities:** sauna, heated rooftop pool & whirlpool, exercise
room. **Guest Services:** valet laundry. **Business Services:** meeting rooms, fax. *Fee:* PC. **Cards:** AE, CB, DI, DS, JC, MC, VI.
Special Amenities: free newspaper and preferred room (subject to availability with advanced reservations).** SOME UNITS

[icons] / FEE

WELLESLEY INN & SUITES   Phone: (954)473-8257 [116]

[AAA] [SAVE]

[▽▽▽]
Motel

12/18-4/15   1P: $99-$119   2P: $99-$119   XP: $10   F17
12/1-12/17 & 4/16-11/30   1P: $69-$79   2P: $69-$79   XP: $10   F17
Location: 0.3 mi w of University Dr (SR 817), at s edge of Broward Mall; 0.5 mi sw of jct Broward Blvd (SR 842). 7901
SW 6th St 33324. Fax: 954/473-9804. **Facility:** At the edge of Broward Mall. 105 units. Some suites ($89-
$139). *Bath:* combo or shower only. 4 stories, interior corridors. **Terms:** small pets only ($10 extra charge).
Amenities: extended cable TV, video games, voice mail. **Leisure Activities:** heated pool. **Guest Services:**
[ECP] meal plan available, valet laundry. **Business Services:** meeting rooms. **Cards:** AE, CB, DI, DS, MC, VI.
Special Amenities: free continental breakfast and free local telephone calls. *(See color ad opposite title page)*

SOME UNITS

[icons] / FEE

The following lodging was either not evaluated or did not
meet AAA rating requirements but is listed for your information only.

STAYBRIDGE SUITES FT-LAUDERDALE-PLANTATION   Phone: 770/604-5777

[fyi]
Extended Stay
Motel

Property failed to provide current rates
Too new to rate, opening scheduled for November 2000. **Location:** I-595, exit 5, 2 mi n on Pine Island Rd.
American Express Way 33324. **Amenities:** 141 units, pets, radios, coffeemakers, microwaves, refrigerators,
pool. **Cards:** AE, CB, DI, DS, JC, MC, VI.

——— WHERE TO DINE ———

BRASSERIE MAX   Lunch: $5-$13   Dinner: $8-$17   Phone: 954/424-8000 [131]

[▽▽▽]
American

Location: I-95, exit Broward Blvd; in Fashion Mall. 321 N University Dr 33324. **Hours:** 11:30 am-10 pm, Fri &
Sat-11 pm, Sun-9 pm. Closed: 11/22, 12/25. **Features:** casual dress; children's menu; cocktails. This
fashionable bistro sets the mood with soft lighting, a grand piano and cozy wooden booths. Entrees include
nut-crusted dolphin with spicy sweet potato sauce, and an almond basket makes a unique dessert. Build
your own omelet until 2 pm on Sundays. **Cards:** AE, DI, DS, MC, VI.

[X]

PEBBLES   Lunch: $5-$12   Dinner: $8-$15   Phone: 954/424-0330 [134]

[▽▽▽]
American

Location: Cornerstore Office Park; at the corner of Peter's Pond and S Pine Island Rd. 1280 S Pine Island Rd 33324.
Hours: 11:30 am-10 pm; Fri & Sat-11 pm. **Features:** dressy casual; children's menu; early bird specials;
carryout; cocktails; a la carte. The striking Caribbean atmosphere - which is light, open and airy - caters to
young and old alike. Exotic and visually appealing entrees, such as grilled tuna with pasta and half-roasted
duck with sweet triple glaze, make up an enticing menu. **Cards:** AE, DI, DS, MC, VI.

[X]

(See map p. 346)

TAKEYAMA

Ethnic

Lunch: $7-$12   Dinner: $10-$30   Phone: 954/792-0350 (133)
Location: Just n of Broward Blvd at NW 69th Ave and Cypress Rd; in the Cypress Square Center. 6920 Cypress Rd 33317. **Hours:** 11:30 am-2 & 5:30-9:30 pm, Fri & Sat-10 pm. Closed: Mon. **Reservations:** suggested; on weekends. **Features:** dressy casual; beer & wine only. This sushi bar presents a variety of dishes that could be considered edible works of art. The Takeyama inside-out roll has a unique stone crab filling. Vegetarian sushi is offered with sukiyaki, teriyaki and tempura dishes. Try the unusual pizza sushi. **Cards:** AE, MC, VI.

POMPANO BEACH pop. 72,400

──────── WHERE TO STAY ────────

BEST WESTERN BEACHCOMBER HOTEL & VILLAS   Phone: (954)941-7830

(AAA) (SAVE)

12/26-4/30	1P: $115-$295	2P: $115-$295	XP: $15	F17
12/1-12/25 & 5/1-11/30	1P: $59-$231	2P: $59-$231	XP: $15	F17

Motor Inn

Location: SR A1A, 0.5 mi s of jct SR 814 (Atlantic Blvd). 1200 S Ocean Blvd 33062. Fax: 954/942-7680. **Facility:** On tropical, oceanfront grounds. Some units with balcony. 147 units. 8 two-bedroom units and 86 efficiencies. Some suites ($178-$275). *Bath:* combo or shower only. 1-8 stories, interior/exterior corridors. **Terms:** 3 day cancellation notice, package plans. **Amenities:** video games, voice mail, safes, irons, hair dryers. **Dining:** restaurant, entertainment Fri & Sat 7 am-3 & 5-9 pm, $10-$19, cocktails. **Leisure Activities:** 2 pools (1 heated), beach, swimming, beach volleyball, putting green, playground, shuffleboard. **Guest Services:** gift shop, coin laundry. **Business Services:** meeting rooms. **Cards:** AE, DI, DS, MC, VI. *(See color ad p 359)*

SOME UNITS

[icons] FEE ... FEE

CROTON ARMS APARTMENTS/MOTEL   Phone: (954)941-1766

1/26-3/31	2P: $70-$98	XP: $10
12/1-1/25	2P: $40-$88	XP: $10
4/1-4/16	2P: $48-$73	XP: $10
4/17-11/30	2P: $39-$65	XP: $10

Motel

Location: Just w of SR A1A; 1.3 mi n of jct SR 814 (Atlantic Blvd). 3237 NE 11th St 33062. Fax: 954/941-1775. **Facility:** 2 buildings facing over quiet street. Inviting landscaped pool area. 20 units with kitchen. *Bath:* combo or shower only. 1-2 stories, exterior corridors. **Terms:** 30 day cancellation notice, weekly rates available. **Amenities:** extended cable TV. **Leisure Activities:** heated pool, whirlpool. **Guest Services:** coin laundry.

SOME UNITS

[icons]

DOLPHIN APARTMENT MOTEL   Phone: (954)941-7373

(AAA) (SAVE)

2/1-3/31	2P: $65-$98	XP: $8	F10
12/1-1/31	2P: $37-$88	XP: $8	F10
4/1-4/30	2P: $42-$70	XP: $8	F10
5/1-11/30	2P: $35-$60	XP: $8	F10

Motel

Location: 0.8 mi n on SR A1A from jct SR 814 (Atlantic Blvd), just w. 3215 NE 7th St 33062. Fax: 954/941-7388. **Facility:** Exceptionally well-kept property. 20 units. 6 efficiencies and 10 units with kitchen. 2 stories, exterior corridors. **Terms:** 30 day cancellation notice, weekly rates available. **Amenities:** extended cable TV. **Leisure Activities:** heated pool, shuffleboard. **Guest Services:** coin laundry. **Cards:** MC, VI.

[icons]

FOUR POINTS HOTEL BY SERATON   Phone: (954)782-5300

12/16-4/1	1P: $89-$99	2P: $89-$99	XP: $10	F12
12/1-12/15 & 4/2-11/30	1P: $69-$89	2P: $69-$89	XP: $10	F12

Motor Inn

Location: On SR A1A; 1.3 mi n of jct SR 814 (Atlantic Blvd). 1208 N Ocean Blvd 33062. Fax: 954/946-1853. **Facility:** Large rooms all with balcony with oceanfront or ocean view. Attractive public areas. Very nice rooms. 94 units. Some suites ($89-$99). 6-9 stories, interior/exterior corridors. **Terms:** 7 day cancellation notice, weekly & monthly rates available, package plans. **Amenities:** extended cable TV, voice mail, irons. **Leisure Activities:** heated pool, beach, swimming, exercise room. **Guest Services:** gift shop, valet and coin laundry. *Fee:* massage. **Business Services:** meeting rooms. **Cards:** AE, DI, DS, JC, MC, VI.

SOME UNITS

[icons]

HOLIDAY INN ON THE OCEAN

Phone: (954)941-7300

(AAA) SAVE	12/1-4/21	2P: $99-$190	XP: $10	F19
▽▽▽▽	4/22-5/31 & 10/1-11/30	2P: $69-$175	XP: $10	F19
	6/1-9/30	2P: $82-$150	XP: $10	F19

Motor Inn   **Location:** SR A1A, 0.8 mi s of jct SR 814, Atlantic Blvd. 1350 S Ocean Blvd 33062. Fax: 954/941-7300. **Facility:** Some rooms on oceanfront grounds others along the Spanish River over A1A. Some with balcony or patio. 133 units, 89 with kitchen. Some suites ($100-$275). *Bath:* combo or shower only. 1-3 stories, exterior corridors. **Terms:** monthly rates available, package plans. **Amenities:** irons, hair dryers. **Dining:** restaurant, 7 am-10 pm; tiki bar, $8-$13, cocktails. **Leisure Activities:** 2 heated pools, beach, swimming, putting green, 3 tennis courts. *Fee:* boat dock, dock on Spanish River, jet ski, catamarans. **Guest Services:** [BP] meal plan available, valet and coin laundry. **Business Services:** meeting rooms. **Cards:** AE, CB, DI, DS, JC, MC, VI.

SOME UNITS

HOWARD JOHNSON PLAZA RESORT

Phone: (954)781-1300

▽▽▽▽	12/25-4/14	2P: $115-$189	XP: $10	F17
	12/1-12/24	2P: $85-$129	XP: $10	F17
	4/15-11/30	2P: $90-$110	XP: $10	F17

Motor Inn   **Location:** Just e of SR A1A at Atlantic Blvd. 9 N Pompano Beach Blvd 33062. Fax: 954/782-5585. **Facility:** Located across from the beach. All rooms with a balcony. 104 units, 8 with efficiency. 8 stories, interior corridors. **Terms:** cancellation fee imposed, weekly & monthly rates available, package plans. **Amenities:** video games, safes (fee), irons, hair dryers. **Leisure Activities:** heated pool, beach access, exercise room, game room. **Guest Services:** gift shop, valet and coin laundry. **Business Services:** meeting rooms. **Cards:** AE, CB, DI, DS, JC, MC, VI. *(See color ad p 389)*

SOME UNITS

PALM OCEAN VILLAS OCEANFRONT RESORT

Phone: (954)941-7330

▽▽	12/18-4/15	1P: $109-$159	2P: $109-$159	F10
	12/1-12/17 & 4/16-11/30	1P: $69-$109	2P: $69-$109	F10

Motel   **Location:** On SR A1A; 1.3 mi s of jct SR 814 (Atlantic Blvd). 1430 S Ocean Blvd 33062. Fax: 954/941-7331. **Facility:** Quiet location, spacious rooms. 24 units, 19 with kitchen. *Bath:* combo or shower only. 1-2 stories, exterior corridors. **Terms:** 30 day cancellation notice. **Amenities:** extended cable TV. **Leisure Activities:** heated pool, beach, swimming. **Guest Services:** coin laundry. **Cards:** AE, DS, MC, VI.

SOME UNITS

RONNY DEE MOTEL

Phone: 954/943-3020

▽▽	12/21-3/24	2P: $49-$80	XP: $7	D12
	3/25-4/16	2P: $49-$65	XP: $7	D12
	12/1-12/20 & 4/17-11/30	2P: $35-$45	XP: $5	D12

Motel   **Location:** SR A1A, just s of jct SR 814 (Atlantic Blvd). 717 S Ocean Blvd 33062. Fax: 954/783-5112. **Facility:** Attractive pool area. Well kept property. 31 units. 8 efficiencies and 12 units with kitchen. *Bath:* combo or shower only. 1-2 stories, exterior corridors. **Terms:** 21 day cancellation notice-fee imposed, weekly & monthly rates available. **Amenities:** extended cable TV. **Leisure Activities:** heated pool, shuffleboard. **Guest Services:** coin laundry. **Business Services:** meeting rooms. **Cards:** AE, MC, VI.

SOME UNITS

SEA CASTLE RESORT INN

Phone: (954)941-2570

(AAA) SAVE	12/1-4/30	1P: $89-$149	2P: $89-$149	XP: $12	F12
▽▽▽▽	5/1-11/30	1P: $44-$88	2P: $44-$88	XP: $10	F12

Motel   **Location:** On SR A1A; 1 mi n of jct SR 814 (Atlantic Blvd). 730 N Ocean Blvd 33062. Fax: 954/941-3150. **Facility:** A few rooms with ocean view. Nicely furnished and decorated rooms. 40 units, 14 with efficiency. 2 stories, exterior corridors. **Terms:** 4 day cancellation notice, weekly & monthly rates available, pets ($10 extra charge, in limited rooms). **Amenities:** extended cable TV. **Leisure Activities:** heated pool, beach, swimming, complimentary green fees at local club 4/15-12/15. **Guest Services:** [CP] meal plan available, coin laundry. **Cards:** AE, CB, DI, DS, MC, VI.

SOME UNITS

TRADERS OCEAN RESORT

Phone: (954)941-8400

(AAA) SAVE	12/20-4/16	1P: $115-$239	2P: $115-$239	XP: $10	F12
▽▽▽▽	12/1-12/19 & 4/17-11/30	1P: $79-$139	2P: $79-$139	XP: $10	F12

Motor Inn   **Location:** SR A1A, 1.5 mi s of jct SR 814 (Atlantic Blvd). 1600 S Ocean Blvd 33062. Fax: 954/941-1024. **Facility:** Located on the oceanfront. Some rooms with view of the pool and the ocean. 93 units. 42 efficiencies and 9 units with kitchen. Some suites ($139-$239). 3 stories, exterior corridors. **Terms:** 3 day cancellation notice-fee imposed, package plans. **Amenities:** extended cable TV, safes (fee). **Dining:** restaurant, 7 am-11 & noon-3 & 5-9 pm, Thurs-Sun to 11 pm, $12-$18, cocktails. **Leisure Activities:** heated pool, beach, swimming, golf privileges 4/15-12/15. *Fee:* aqua bikes, boogie boards, cabanas, catamarans, waverunners. **Guest Services:** coin laundry. **Cards:** AE, CB, DI, MC, VI.

SOME UNITS

VILLAMAR INN

Phone: (954)941-3530

(AAA) SAVE	12/1-4/9	2P: $74-$149	XP: $10	D7
▽▽▽▽	4/10-11/30	2P: $45-$118	XP: $10	D7

Motel   **Location:** SR A1A, 1 mi n of jct SR 814 (Atlantic Blvd). 740 N Ocean Blvd 33062. Fax: 954/782-2778. **Facility:** Some rooms with balcony and ocean view. Peaceful setting. 18 units, 13 with kitchen. 1-2 stories, exterior corridors. **Terms:** 30 day cancellation notice. **Amenities:** extended cable TV, safes (fee). **Leisure Activities:** heated pool, beach, swimming, putting green, shuffleboard. **Guest Services:** coin laundry. **Cards:** MC, VI.

SOME UNITS

WELLESLEY INN & SUITES

AAA **SAVE**

Extended Stay Motel

| | 1/1-4/14 | 1P: $79-$119 | 2P: $79-$119 | XP: $10 | F18 |
| | 12/1-12/31 & 4/15-11/30 | 1P: $59-$79 | 2P: $59-$79 | XP: $10 | F18 |

Phone: (954)783-1050

Location: I-95, exit 33B, Cypress Creek Rd to Andrews Ave, just s, then turn left onto McNab St. 1401 SW 15th St 33069. Fax: 954/783-1610. **Facility:** Spacious rooms, attractive room decor. 130 efficiencies. Some suites. **Bath:** combo or shower only. 3 stories, interior corridors. **Terms:** 3 day cancellation notice, weekly & monthly rates available, pets ($100 fee). **Amenities:** extended cable TV, video games, dual phone lines, voice mail, irons. **Leisure Activities:** heated pool. **Guest Services:** [BP] meal plan available, coin laundry. **Cards:** AE, CB, DI, DS, MC, VI. **Special Amenities:** free continental breakfast and free local telephone calls.

(See color ad opposite title page)

SOME UNITS

WHERE TO DINE

CHEZ PORKY'S

American

Lunch: $5-$16   Dinner: $7-$19   Phone: 954/946-5590

Location: From Atlantic Blvd (SR 820) 0.6 mi s on Old Dixie Hwy; 0.3 mi e; in the Robert Thomas Plaza. 105 SW Sixth St 33060. **Hours:** 11 am-9:30 pm, Sat & Sun 4:30 pm-10 pm. Closed major holidays. **Reservations:** suggested; weekends. **Features:** casual dress; children's menu; carryout; beer & wine only. Hard to find friendlier folks than at this Louisiana kitchen and barbecue. Baby back ribs, chicken and Cajun seafood dishes are served with your choice of two delicious side dishes. This restaurant is worth any wait, so sit back and relax for a spell. **Cards:** AE, MC, VI.

DARREL & OLIVER'S CAFE MAXX

AAA

Regional American

Dinner: $16-$32   Phone: 954/782-0606

Location: SR 814, Atlantic Blvd; 0.3 mi e of jct US 1. 2601 E Atlantic Blvd at NE 26th St 33062. **Hours:** 5:30 pm-11 pm, Sun-10 pm. Closed: 7/4; also Super Bowl Sun. **Reservations:** suggested. **Features:** dressy casual; beer & wine only; valet parking; a la carte. A casually elegant affair with a cafe ambience features innovative preparation and presentation with some dishes suggesting an Oriental influence. Try the savory Bahamian conch and yucca soup. Chop sticks are available for the more experienced dinner. **Cards:** AE, DI, DS, MC, VI.

NICKEL'S

American

Lunch: $7-$13   Dinner: $7-$13   Phone: 954/942-7030

Location: I-95, exit 35A southbound; exit 35 northbound (Copans Rd), 2.1 mi then just n. 2341 N Federal Hwy 33060. **Hours:** 7 am-11 pm, Fri & Sat-1 am. **Features:** casual dress; children's menu; carryout; cocktails & lounge; a la carte. A diner with 1950s decor. Lots of pictures of the stars and entertainers of that era. Diner type food with meatloaf, big sandwiches, lots of different types of burgers, small pizza, and tall desserts. Very family oriented—a fun place to eat. **Cards:** AE, CB, DI, DS, MC, VI.

VESUVIO'S RESTAURANT

Italian

Dinner: $12-$28   Phone: 954/941-1594

Location: 2715 E Atlantic Blvd 33062. **Hours:** 5:30 pm-11 pm. Closed: 7/1-7/31, Mon 5/1-12/25. **Reservations:** suggested. **Features:** cocktails & lounge. You'll have to wait for the made-to-order entrees, but every second will be worth it. The many offerings of veal, chicken, beef, vegetables and seafood are just delicious. Cozy and crowded at the same time, the restaurant boasts a friendly wait staff. **Cards:** AE, CB, DI, DS, MC, VI.

SUNRISE pop. 64,400   (See map p. 346; index p. 350)

WHERE TO STAY

BAYMONT INN & SUITES-SUNRISE SAWGRASS

Motel

	1/26-4/14	1P: $109-$114	2P: $109-$114
	12/1-1/25	1P: $89-$99	2P: $89-$99
	4/15-11/30	1P: $89-$94	2P: $89-$94

Phone: (954)846-1200   **74**

Location: SW 136th Ave, 0.3 mi n of jct I-595, exit 1 and SR 84; 0.5 mi e of jct I-75 and Sawgrass Expwy; adjoining the Blockbuster Family Entertainment Park. 13651 NW 2nd St 33325. Fax: 954/845-0100. **Facility:** Inviting, with modern functional rooms. Pool deck overlooks small pond. 1 mile south of Sawgrass Mills Mall. 102 units. Some suites ($104-$179). **Bath:** combo or shower only. 4 stories, interior corridors. **Terms:** monthly rates available, small pets only. **Amenities:** video games, voice mail, irons, hair dryers. **Leisure Activities:** heated pool. **Guest Services:** [CP] meal plan available, valet and coin laundry. **Business Services:** meeting rooms. **Cards:** AE, CB, DI, DS, MC, VI. *(See color ad below)*

SOME UNITS

FEE

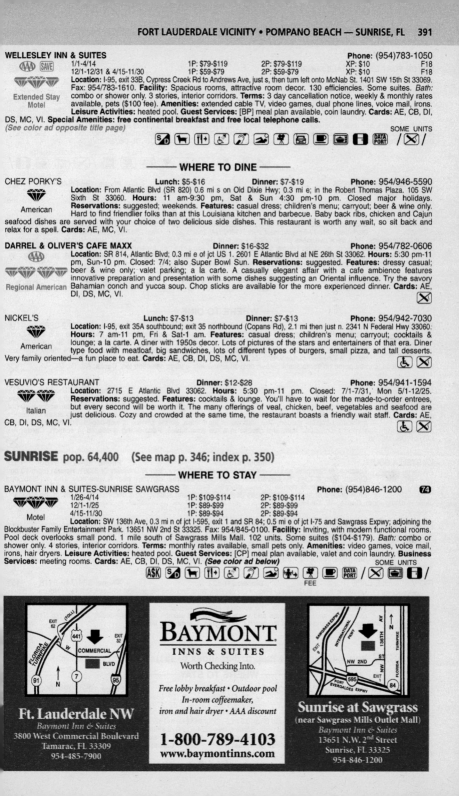

(See map p. 346)

HILTON FORT LAUDERDALE SUNRISE

Phone: (954)748-7000   **75**

(AAA) (SAVE)

12/1-3/31	1P: $119-$149	2P: $119-$149	
4/1-11/30	1P: $99-$119	2P: $99-$119	

Motor Inn

Location: University Dr (SR 817), just s of jct Oakland Park Blvd. 3003 N University Dr 33322. Fax: 954/572-0799. **Facility:** Exterior of modernistic design. Very impressive lobby. Large rooms with soft tones. 297 units, 6 with efficiency (no utensils). Some suites ($109-$159) and whirlpool units. 5-6 stories, interior corridors. **Terms:** monthly rates available, package plans. **Amenities:** extended cable TV, dual phone lines, voice mail, honor bars, irons, hair dryers. **Dining:** restaurant, 7 am-10 pm, $10-$25, cocktails. **Leisure Activities:** heated pool, sauna, whirlpool, exercise room. **Guest Services:** [BP] meal plan available, gift shop, area transportation-local shopping malls, valet laundry. **Business Services:** conference facilities, administrative services, fax. **Cards:** AE, CB, DI, DS, MC, VI. *(See ad p 44)*

SOME UNITS

(icons)

WELLESLEY INN & SUITES

Phone: (954)845-9929   **70**

(AAA) (SAVE)

12/22-12/31	1P: $99-$119	2P: $99-$119	XP: $10	F18
1/1-4/30	1P: $99-$119	2P: $99-$114	XP: $10	F18
5/1-11/30	1P: $69-$99	2P: $99-$109		F18
12/1-12/21	1P: $69-$99	2P: $69-$99	XP: $10	F18

Motel

Location: SW 136th Ave, 0.3 mi n of int I-595, exit 1 and SR 84; 0.5 mi e of jct I-75 and Sawgrass Expwy; adjoining Blockbuster Family Entertainment Park. 13600 NW 2nd St 33325. Fax: 954/845-9996. **Facility:** Inviting, with elegant public rooms. Pool deck overlooks small pond. 1 mi s of Sawgrass Mills Mall. 104 units. Some suites. *Bath:* combo or shower only. 4 stories, interior corridors. **Terms:** small pets only ($10 extra charge). **Amenities:** video games, voice mail. **Leisure Activities:** heated pool. **Guest Services:** valet laundry. **Business Services:** meeting rooms. **Cards:** AE, CB, DI, DS, MC, VI. **Special Amenities:** free continental breakfast and free local telephone calls. *(See color ad opposite title page)*

SOME UNITS

(icons)

WHERE TO DINE

EMERALD COAST

Lunch: $8   **Dinner:** $17   **Phone:** 954/572-3822   **114**

Chinese

Location: From the Sawgrass Expwy (SR 869), 1.8 mi e on Commercial Blvd (SR 870), then 0.9 mi s; in the Gold's Plaza. 4519 N Pine Island Rd 33351. **Hours:** 11:30 am-2:30 & 4-9 pm, Fri-10:30 pm, Sat 4:30 pm-10:30 pm, Sun noon-2:30 & 4-9:30 pm. **Reservations:** accepted. **Features:** casual dress; children's menu; cocktails; buffet. A Chinese buffet with over 100 items. Different islands of food, with many favorites as well as at times crab legs, carved prime rib some sushi rolls. A dessert island with a large selection too. **Cards:** AE, DI, MC, VI.

LA CUCINA TOSCANA

Dinner: $16-$25   **Phone:** 954/349-5712   **111**

Italian

Location: SR 84 and I-595; 11 mi w of turnpike, exit 54 at Bonaventure; westbound use I-595, exit 1 (SW 136th Ave) to Bonaventure Blvd; in Wyndham Resort & Spa, Ft. Lauderdale. 250 Racquet Club Rd 33326. **Hours:** 6 pm-10 pm. **Reservations:** suggested. **Features:** cocktails; valet parking; a la carte. Intimate dining areas overlook a manicured tropical garden. The staff works as a team, so the service is well-paced. Try the delicious veal scaloppine with mushrooms, prosciutto ham and cheese in a red wine sauce. Patio dining is offered in season. **Cards:** AE, CB, DI, DS, MC, VI.

LA STELLA SOUTH

Dinner: $13-$25   **Phone:** 954/748-4788   **105**

Italian

Location: At Springtree and University Dr; in Country Club Plaza. 3801 N University Dr 33351. **Hours:** 5 pm-10 pm. Closed: Mon & Tues. **Reservations:** suggested. **Features:** carryout; beer & wine only. This old-fashioned restaurant presents dishes of veal, chicken, seafood and fish, including the distinctive fish marechiara. Photographs of such celebrities as Jackie Gleason and Natalie Cole decorate the walls of the pleasant, dimly lit dining room. **Cards:** AE, DI, MC, VI.

LEGAL SEA FOODS

Lunch: $5-$13   **Dinner:** $14-$30   **Phone:** 954/846-9011   **113**

Seafood

Location: From Sawgrass Expwy/SR 869, exit 1 (Sunrise Blvd and SR 838), 1 mi e to Sawgrass Mills Mall. 2602 Sawgrass Mills Center 33323. **Hours:** 11:30 am-10 pm, Fri & Sat-11 pm, Sun noon-10 pm. Closed: 11/22, 12/25. **Features:** dressy casual; children's menu; carryout; cocktails & lounge; a la carte. In the Oasis at Sawgrass, featuring fresh seafood with an emphasis on New England. Unique dining room. A very good wine list. **Cards:** AE, MC, VI.

RIO VISTA ISLE CAFE

Dinner: $11-$22   **Phone:** 954/749-8118   **109**

American

Location: Just w of University Blvd; in Lincoln Park West Shopping Plaza. 7836 NW 44th St 33351. **Hours:** 5-10 pm, Sat & Sun 4:30 pm-10 pm. Closed: Mon; in summer, Mon & Tues. **Reservations:** suggested. **Features:** beer & wine only. The upscale, intimate restaurant's menu includes such well-prepared entrees as rack of lamb, crab cakes and vermouth-steamed salmon with julienne leeks and carrots. The Belgian chocolate torte with rum raisins and nuts is a top-notch chocolate fix. **Cards:** DS, MC, VI.

TAMARAC pop. 44,800   (See map p. 346; index p. 351)

WHERE TO STAY

BAYMONT INN & SUITES-FORT LAUDERDALE NW (TAMARAC)

Phone: (954)485-7900   **103**

1/26-4/14	1P: $89-$94	2P: $89-$94	
12/1-1/25	1P: $79-$84	2P: $79-$84	
4/15-11/30	1P: $59-$64	2P: $59-$64	

Motel

Location: SR 870 (Commercial Blvd); 0.8 mi e of Florida Tpke, exit 62, just e of jct SR 7 and US 441. 3800 W Commercial Blvd 33309. Fax: 954/733-5469. **Facility:** 98 units. Some suites ($74-$134). 3 stories, interior corridors. **Terms:** small pets only ($50 deposit). **Amenities:** extended cable TV, video games, irons, hair dryers. **Leisure Activities:** small pool. **Guest Services:** [CP] meal plan available, coin laundry. **Business Services:** meeting rooms. **Cards:** AE, CB, DI, DS, MC, VI. *(See color ad p 391)*

SOME UNITS

(icons)

(See map p. 346)

HOMESTEAD VILLAGE GUEST STUDIOS-FORT LAUDERDALE   **Phone: (954)733-6644**   102
▼▼ ▼▼   12/1-3/31   1P: $59-$64   2P: $64-$69   XP: $5   F
                4/1-11/30   1P: $55-$59   2P: $59-$65   XP: $5   F
Extended Stay   **Location:** SR 870 (Commercial Blvd), 0.7 mi e of Florida Tpke, exit 62, then just e of jct SR 7 and US 441. 3873 W
Motel   Commercial Blvd 33309. Fax: 954/733-9301. **Facility:** Spacious rooms. Office hours 7 am-11 pm. 145 efficiencies. *Bath:* combo or shower only. 2 stories, exterior corridors. **Terms:** cancellation fee imposed, weekly rates
available, pets ($75 fee). **Amenities:** voice mail, irons. **Guest Services:** coin laundry. **Cards:** AE, CB, DI, DS, MC, VI.

SOME UNITS

🐕 🍴 📶 🍽 🐾 🎥 📺 📷 🖥 📠 / ✕ 📠 /

RAMADA PLAZA RESORT   **Phone: (954)739-4000**   100
▼▼▼ ▼▼   Property failed to provide current rates
Motor Inn   **Location:** SR 7 and US 441, just n of jct SR 870 (Commercial Blvd); 0.5 mi e of Florida Tpke, exit 62. 5100 N SR 7
33309. Fax: 954/733-9301. **Facility:** Attractive pool area and rooms. 260 units, 6 with efficiency. Some suites.
5 stories, interior corridors. **Amenities:** video games, voice mail, irons. **Leisure Activities:** heated pool,
whirlpool, 2 lighted tennis courts, exercise room. **Guest Services:** gift shop, valet and coin laundry. **Business Services:** meeting
rooms. **Cards:** AE, CB, DI, DS, MC, VI.

SOME UNITS

🍴 🍽 📷 🏊 🎥 📷 🖥 📠 / ✕ 📷 📠 /
        FEE   FEE

WELLESLEY INN & SUITES   **Phone: (954)484-6909**   101
AAA SAVE   12/18-4/15   1P: $70-$80   2P: $70-$80   XP: $10   F18
                12/1-12/17 & 4/16-11/30   1P: $50-$60   2P: $50-$60   XP: $10   F18
▼▼▼ ▼▼   **Location:** SR 7 and US 441; just n of jct SR 870 (Commercial Blvd); 0.5 mi e of Florida Tpke exit 62. 5070 N SR 7 33319.
Motel   Fax: 954/731-2374. **Facility:** Attractive public areas. Comfortable rooms. 100 units. Some suites ($80-$90).
Bath: combo or shower only. 4 stories, interior corridors. **Terms:** small pets only ($10 fee). **Amenities:** video
games, voice mail, irons. *Some:* hair dryers. **Leisure Activities:** heated pool. **Guest Services:** coin laundry.
Business Services: meeting rooms. **Cards:** AE, CB, DI, DS, JC, MC, VI. **Special Amenities: free continental breakfast and
free local telephone calls.** *(See color ad opposite title page)*

SOME UNITS

Ⓢ🄳 🐕 🍴 📶 📷 🏊 🎥 📷 🖥 📠 / ✕ 📷 📠 /
                                                        FEE   FEE

———— **WHERE TO DINE** ————

———— *The following restaurant has not been evaluated by AAA* ————
but is listed for your information only.

FLANIGAN'S SEAFOOD BAR & GRILL   **Phone: 954/733-0514**
[fyi]   Not evaluated. **Location:** 5450 N SR 7 33319. **Features:** Casual atmosphere that is inexpensive and family
friendly. Known for their baby back ribs, large burgers and fresh local seafood.

WESTON

———— **WHERE TO STAY** ————

WYNDHAM RESORT & SPA, FT. LAUDERDALE   **Phone: (954)389-3300**
AAA SAVE   12/1-4/9   1P: $189-$270
                4/10-5/26 & 9/9-11/30   1P: $144-$225
▼▼▼ ▼▼▼   5/27-9/8   1P: $89-$165
Resort   **Location:** SR 84 and I-595; 11 mi w of turnpike, exit 54 at Bonaventure; westbound use I-595, exit 1 (SW 136th Ave) to
Bonaventure Blvd. 250 Racquet Club Rd 33326. Fax: 954/384-1416. **Facility:** In exclusive country club community, rooms and suites in cluster buildings. Full service European style spa facilities. A large pool area surrounded by tropical trees and plants. A waterfall at the pool accents the pool's soothing effect. 496 units. Some suites. *Bath:*
combo or shower only. 4 stories, exterior corridors. **Parking:** valet. **Terms:** check-in 4 pm, 3 day cancellation notice-fee imposed,
package plans, $8 service charge. **Amenities:** voice mail, honor bars, irons, hair dryers. **Dining:** 3 restaurants, 7 am-11 pm,
$11-$35, cocktails, also, La Cucina Toscana, see separate listing, entertainment. **Leisure Activities:** 5 heated pools, saunas,
whirlpools, children's program, recreation program, jogging, playground. *Fee:* golf-36 holes, golf instruction, 6 tennis courts (5
lighted), racquetball courts, tennis instructions, squash court. **Guest Services:** [AP], [BP], [CP] & [MAP] meal plans available,
gift shop, valet laundry. *Fee:* massage. **Business Services:** conference facilities, fax. *Fee:* PC. **Cards:** AE, CB, DI, DS, JC,
MC, VI.

SOME UNITS

Ⓢ🄳 🄳 🍴 🍽 🏋 📷 🏊 🐾 ✕ 🎥 🖥 📠 / ✕ 📼 📠 /
        FEE   FEE   FEE   FEE

This ends listings for the Fort Lauderdale Vicinity.
The following page resumes the alphabetical listings of
cities in Florida.

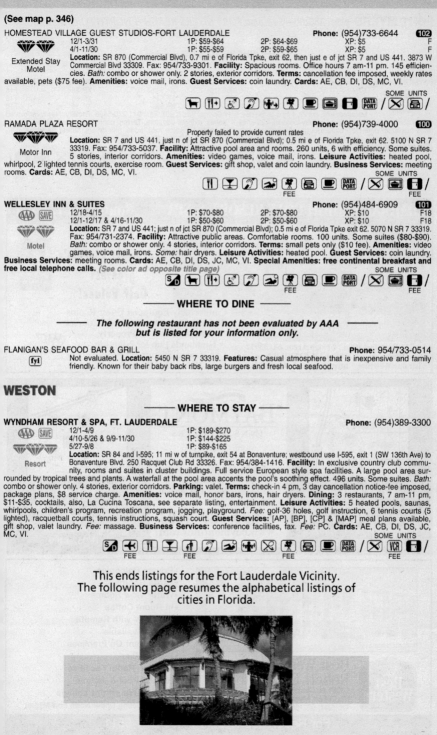

FORT MYERS pop. 45,200—*See also FORT MYERS BEACH & NORTH FORT MYERS.*

—— WHERE TO STAY ——

BAYMONT INN-FORT MYERS
♦♦♦♦   1/7-4/15   1P: $90-$110   2P: $96-$116   XP: $6   F18
           12/1-1/6   1P: $80   2P: $86   XP: $6   F18
Motel   4/16-11/30   1P: $60   2P: $66   XP: $6   F18

Phone: (941)275-3500

Location: I-75, exit 22, 4 mi w on SR 884. 2717 Colonial Blvd 33907. Fax: 941/275-5426. **Facility:** Newly renovated stylish guest units. Convenient highway location. 123 units. 4 stories, exterior corridors. **Terms:** cancellation fee imposed, weekly rates available, pets ($25 extra charge). **Amenities:** extended cable TV, voice mail, irons, hair dryers. **Guest Services:** [CP] meal plan available, valet laundry. **Business Services:** meeting rooms, PC, fax. **Cards:** AE, DI, DS, MC, VI.
(See color ad below)

SOME UNITS

(ASK) (SD) (🛑) (🐾) (📶) (🅟) (🛒) (🎿) (📠) (💻) (DATA PORT) / (⊠) (📺) (🔒) /
FEE

BEST WESTERN AIRPORT INN
Phone: (941)561-7000

Motel

3/1-4/15	1P: $140-$150	2P: $150-$160	XP: $5	F12
1/1-2/28	1P: $120-$130	2P: $130-$140	XP: $5	F12
12/1-12/31	1P: $70-$80	2P: $80-$90	XP: $5	F12
4/16-11/30	1P: $60-$70	2P: $70-$80	XP: $5	F12

Location: I-75, exit 21, 0.6 mi w. 8955 Daniels Pkwy 33912. Fax: 941/561-5963. **Facility:** Good sized, bright rooms with contemporary furnishings. 106 units. Some whirlpool units ($100-$200). *Bath:* combo or shower only. 4 stories, interior corridors. **Terms:** 7 day cancellation notice-fee imposed, package plans. **Amenities:** voice mail, hair dryers. **Leisure Activities:** whirlpool. **Guest Services:** [CP] meal plan available, coin laundry. **Business Services:** meeting rooms. **Cards:** AE, DS, MC, VI. SOME UNITS

BEST WESTERN SPRINGS RESORT
Phone: (941)267-7900

Motor Inn

1/16-4/30	1P: $109-$119	2P: $119-$139	XP: $10	F12
12/1-1/15	1P: $70-$80	2P: $70-$80	XP: $10	F12
5/1-11/30	1P: $60-$70	2P: $60-$70	XP: $5	F12

Location: I-75, exit 21, on US 41 at jct Constitution Blvd. 18051 S Tamiami Tr 33908. Fax: 941/267-9763. **Facility:** Good sized rooms with decent furnishings. 2 units. 2 stories, exterior corridors. **Terms:** 7 day cancellation notice, weekly rates available, pets ($10 extra charge). **Amenities:** extended cable TV, voice mail. **Dining:** restaurant, 6 am-9 pm; tiki bar, $6-$8. **Leisure Activities:** sauna, warm mineral springs bathing pool, exercise room. **Guest Services:** coin laundry. *Fee:* massage. **Cards:** AE, DS, MC, VI. **Special Amenities:** free local telephone calls and free newspaper. SOME UNITS

FEE FEE

COMFORT INN
Phone: (941)936-3993

Motel

2/11-4/15	1P: $99-$155	2P: $99-$155	XP: $10	F12
12/1-2/10	1P: $69-$119	2P: $69-$119	XP: $10	F12
10/1-11/30	1P: $69-$89	2P: $69-$89	XP: $10	F12
4/16-9/30	1P: $59-$79	2P: $59-$79	XP: $10	F12

Location: I-75, exit 21, On US 41, 1.5 mi n of jct Daniels Pkwy. 11501 S Cleveland Ave 33907. Fax: 941/936-7234. **Facility:** Good sized guest rooms with contemporary decor. 80 units. 2 stories, interior corridors. **Amenities:** extended cable TV. **Guest Services:** [CP] meal plan available. **Business Services:** meeting rooms. **Cards:** AE, DI, DS, JC, MC, VI. SOME UNITS

COMFORT INN OF FORT MYERS
Phone: (941)694-9200

Motel

12/16-4/15	1P: $90-$130	2P: $90-$130	XP: $10	F18
12/1-12/15 & 4/16-11/30	1P: $64-$84	2P: $71-$91	XP: $10	F18

Location: I-75, exit 25, just se; behind gas station and restaurant. 4171 Boatways Rd 33905. Fax: 941/690-0180. **Facility:** 61 units. *Bath:* combo or shower only. 3 stories, interior corridors. **Terms:** pets ($10 extra charge). **Amenities:** extended cable TV. *Some:* irons, hair dryers. **Leisure Activities:** heated pool, whirlpool. **Guest Services:** [CP] & [ECP] meal plans available, valet and coin laundry. **Business Services:** meeting rooms. **Cards:** AE, CB, DI, DS, MC, VI. SOME UNITS

COMFORT SUITES AIRPORT
Phone: (941)768-0005

Motel

All Year	1P: $69-$149	2P: $69-$149	XP: $6	F18

Location: I-75, exit 21, just w. 13651A Indian Paint Ln 33912. Fax: 941/768-5458. **Facility:** Good sized guest rooms with many amenities. 65 units. Some whirlpool units ($69-$149). 2 stories, interior corridors. **Terms:** pets ($10 extra charge). **Amenities:** extended cable TV, voice mail, irons, hair dryers. **Leisure Activities:** heated pool, whirlpool, exercise room. **Guest Services:** complimentary evening beverages, coin laundry. **Business Services:** meeting rooms. **Cards:** AE, DI, DS, MC, VI. **Special Amenities:** free continental breakfast and free local telephone calls. SOME UNITS

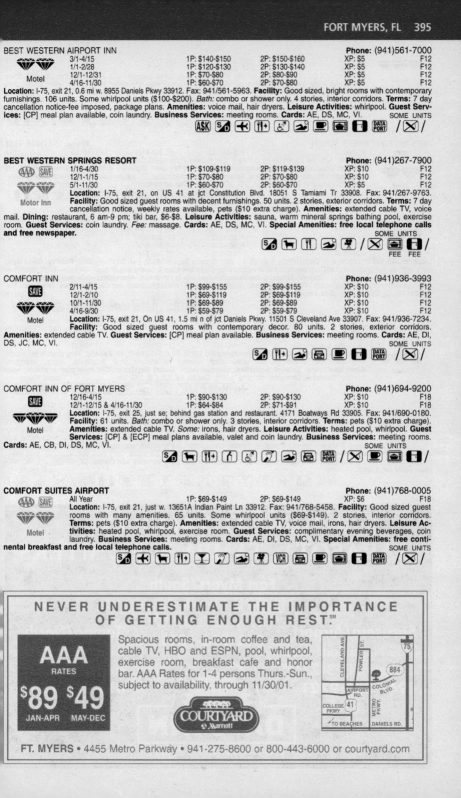

COURTYARD BY MARRIOTT

Motel

			Phone: (941)275-8600
12/1-4/30	1P: $139	2P: $149	XP: $10 F18
5/1-11/30	1P: $99	2P: $109	XP: $10 F18

Location: I-75, exit 22, 3.5 mi w on SR 884. 4455 Metro Pkwy 33916. Fax: 941/275-7087. **Facility:** Standard guest rooms and some 1-bedroom suites, all with attractive furnishings and decor. Most rooms with balcony. 149 units. Some suites. *Bath:* combo or shower only. 3 stories, interior corridors. **Amenities:** extended cable TV, voice mail, irons, hair dryers. **Leisure Activities:** heated pool, whirlpool, exercise room. **Guest Services:** coin laundry. **Business Services:** meeting rooms. **Cards:** AE, DI, DS, MC, VI. *(See color ad p 395)*   SOME UNITS

DAYS INN FORT MYERS SOUTH

SAVE

Motel

			Phone: (941)936-1311
All Year	1P: $45-$115	2P: $51-$121	XP: $6 F17

Location: I-75, exit 21, on US 41, 1.6 mi n of jct Daniels Pkwy. 11435 Cleveland Ave S 33907. Fax: 941/936-7076. **Facility:** Good sized rooms with contemporary decor. 121 units. 3 stories, exterior corridors. **Terms:** 7 day cancellation notice, package plans. **Amenities:** extended cable TV, safes. *Some:* hair dryers. **Guest Services:** coin laundry. **Cards:** AE, DI, DS, JC, MC, VI. *(See ad below)*   SOME UNITS

FAIRFIELD INN BY MARRIOTT

Motel

			Phone: (941)437-5600
12/17-4/16	1P: $79-$119	2P: $79-$119	
4/17-5/25	1P: $59-$99	2P: $59-$99	
12/1-12/16	1P: $64-$79	2P: $64-$79	
5/26-11/30	1P: $49-$79	2P: $49-$79	

Location: I-75, exit 21, 4.5 mi w on Daniels Pkwy, s on US 41. 7090 Cypress Terrace 33907. Fax: 941/437-5616. **Facility:** Good sized units with contemporary decor. Convenient to highway location. Close to movie theaters and shops. 104 units. *Bath:* combo or shower only. 3 stories, interior corridors. **Terms:** 3 day cancellation notice-fee imposed. **Amenities:** voice mail. **Leisure Activities:** heated pool, exercise room. **Guest Services:** [ECP] meal plan available, valet laundry. **Business Services:** fax. **Cards:** AE, DI, DS, MC, VI. *(See color ad p 397)*   SOME UNITS

HAMPTON INN AIRPORT

SAVE

Motel

			Phone: (941)768-2525
12/25-4/15	1P: $109-$119	2P: $115-$125	XP: $7 F18
12/1-12/24 & 4/16-11/30	1P: $65-$75	2P: $71-$81	XP: $7 F18

Location: I-75, exit 21, just w. 9241 Marketplace Rd 33912. Fax: 941/768-6049. **Facility:** Very good sized rooms with attractive furnishings. 87 units. *Bath:* combo or shower only. 3 stories, interior corridors. **Amenities:** irons. **Leisure Activities:** exercise room. **Guest Services:** [CP] meal plan available, valet laundry. **Business Services:** meeting rooms. **Cards:** AE, DI, DS, MC, VI.   SOME UNITS

HOLIDAY INN SELECT FT. MYERS AIRPORT AREA

Hotel

			Phone: (941)482-2900
All Year	1P: $69-$179	2P: $79-$189	XP: $10 F18

Location: I-75, exit 21, US 41 in Bell Tower Mall at jct Daniels Pkwy. 13051 Bell Tower Dr 33907. Fax: 941/482-2900. **Facility:** Standard and executive level rooms, adjacent to shopping mall, movie theater and restaurants. 227 units. 5 stories, interior corridors. **Terms:** cancellation fee imposed, package plans. **Amenities:** voice mail, irons, hair dryers. **Leisure Activities:** heated pool, jogging, exercise room. **Guest Services:** [BP] meal plan available, area transportation, coin laundry. **Business Services:** conference facilities, administrative services, fax. **Cards:** AE, DI, DS, JC, MC, VI. *(See color ad p 397)*   SOME UNITS

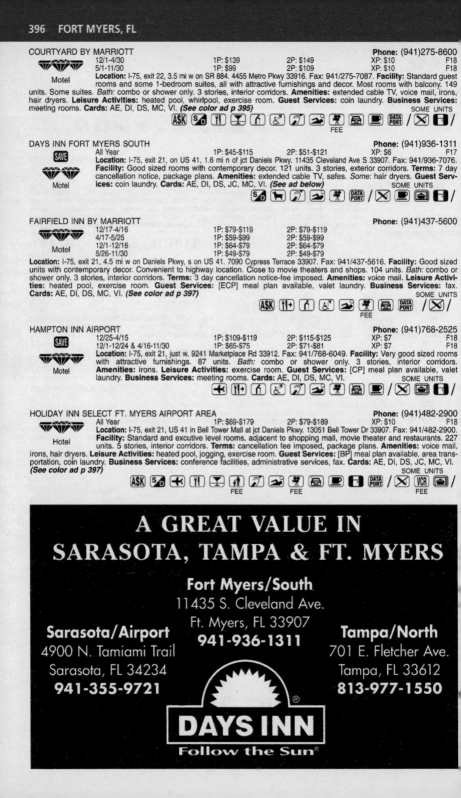

HOLIDAY INN SUNSPREE RESORT
Phone: (941)334-3434

	1P: $139-$149	2P: $139-$149	XP: $10	F16
1/1-4/15				
12/1-12/31 & 4/16-11/30	1P: $89	2P: $89	XP: $10	F16

Motor Inn

Location: 1 mi w of Caloosahatchee River Bridge (US 41), on the riverfront. 2220 W 1st St 33901. Fax: 941/334-3844. **Facility:** 146 units. Some suites ($139-$189) and whirlpool units ($109-$139). *Bath:* combo or shower only. 2-3 stories, interior/exterior corridors. **Terms:** package plans. **Amenities:** extended cable TV, voice mail, safes, irons, hair dryers. **Dining:** restaurant, deli, 7 am-10 pm, Fri & Sat-11 pm; tiki bar, convenience court, $6-$24, cocktails. **Leisure Activities:** heated pool, wading pool, boat dock, charter fishing, slips for guest use, children's program, children's center, lending library, playground, exercise room, game room. **Guest Services:** gift shop, coin laundry. *Fee:* massage. **Business Services:** meeting rooms, administrative services, PC, fax. **Cards:** AE, CB, DI, DS, MC, VI. **Special Amenities: free local telephone calls and free newspaper.** *(See color ad p 397)*   SOME UNITS

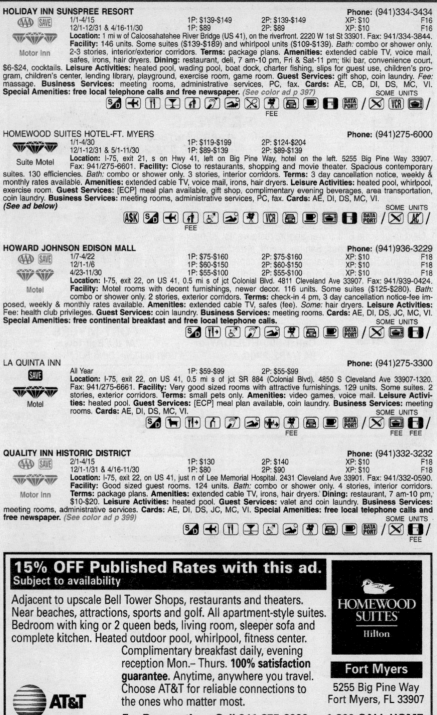

HOMEWOOD SUITES HOTEL-FT. MYERS
Phone: (941)275-6000

| 1/1-4/30 | 1P: $119-$199 | 2P: $124-$204 |
| 12/1-12/31 & 5/1-11/30 | 1P: $89-$139 | 2P: $89-$139 |

Suite Motel

Location: I-75, exit 21, s on Hwy 41, left on Big Pine Way, hotel on the left. 5255 Big Pine Way 33907. Fax: 941/275-6601. **Facility:** Close to restaurants, shopping and movie theater. Spacious contemporary suites. 130 efficiencies. *Bath:* combo or shower only. 3 stories, interior corridors. **Terms:** 3 day cancellation notice, weekly & monthly rates available. **Amenities:** extended cable TV, voice mail, irons, hair dryers. **Leisure Activities:** heated pool, whirlpool, exercise room. **Guest Services:** [ECP] meal plan available, gift shop, complimentary evening beverages, area transportation, coin laundry. **Business Services:** meeting rooms, administrative services, PC, fax. **Cards:** AE, DI, DS, MC, VI. *(See ad below)*   SOME UNITS

HOWARD JOHNSON EDISON MALL
Phone: (941)936-3229

1/7-4/22	1P: $75-$160	2P: $75-$160	XP: $10	F18
12/1-1/6	1P: $60-$150	2P: $60-$150	XP: $10	F18
4/23-11/30	1P: $55-$100	2P: $55-$100	XP: $10	F18

Motel

Location: I-75, exit 22, on US 41, 0.5 mi s of jct Colonial Blvd. 4811 Cleveland Ave 33907. Fax: 941/939-0424. **Facility:** Motel rooms with decent furnishings, newer decor. 116 units. Some suites ($125-$280). *Bath:* combo or shower only. 2 stories, exterior corridors. **Terms:** check-in 4 pm, 3 day cancellation notice-fee imposed, weekly & monthly rates available. **Amenities:** extended cable TV, safes (fee). *Some:* hair dryers. **Leisure Activities:** Fee: health club privileges. **Guest Services:** coin laundry. **Business Services:** meeting rooms. **Cards:** AE, DI, DS, JC, MC, VI. **Special Amenities: free continental breakfast and free local telephone calls.**   SOME UNITS

LA QUINTA INN
Phone: (941)275-3300

| All Year | 1P: $59-$99 | 2P: $55-$99 |

Motel

Location: I-75, exit 22, on US 41, 0.5 mi s of jct SR 884 (Colonial Blvd). 4850 S Cleveland Ave 33907-1320. Fax: 941/275-6661. **Facility:** Very good sized rooms with attractive furnishings. 129 units. Some suites. 2 stories, exterior corridors. **Terms:** small pets only. **Amenities:** video games, voice mail. **Leisure Activities:** heated pool. **Guest Services:** [ECP] meal plan available, coin laundry. **Business Services:** meeting rooms. **Cards:** AE, DI, DS, MC, VI.   SOME UNITS

QUALITY INN HISTORIC DISTRICT
Phone: (941)332-3232

| 2/1-4/15 | 1P: $130 | 2P: $140 | XP: $10 | F18 |
| 12/1-1/31 & 4/16-11/30 | 1P: $80 | 2P: $90 | XP: $10 | F18 |

Motor Inn

Location: I-75, exit 22, on US 41, just n of Lee Memorial Hospital. 2431 Cleveland Ave 33901. Fax: 941/332-0590. **Facility:** Good sized guest rooms. 124 units. *Bath:* combo or shower only. 4 stories, interior corridors. **Terms:** package plans. **Amenities:** extended cable TV, irons, hair dryers. **Dining:** restaurant, 7 am-10 pm, $10-$20. **Leisure Activities:** heated pool. **Guest Services:** valet and coin laundry. **Business Services:** meeting rooms, administrative services. **Cards:** AE, DI, DS, JC, MC, VI. **Special Amenities: free local telephone calls and free newspaper.** *(See color ad p 399)*   SOME UNITS

Ride our waters free.

Redeem your $50 voucher* (reverse side) and enjoy a free ride on Greater Fort Lauderdale's Water Taxi, Jungle Queen, Billie Swamp Airboat Tour, Sawgrass Recreation Park Airboat Ride, SeaEscape Cruise or Glass Bottom Boat Tour. With special hotel rates, plus exclusive offers at restaurants and shops, there's never been a better time to climb aboard.

Immerse yourself.

CALL: 800-22-SUNNY OR VISIT US AT WWW.SUNNY.ORG

Yes! Please send me Free Greater Fort Lauderdale information:

☐ **Free list of participating "Ride Our Waters Free" hotels** (available May 2001).

☐ **Free Vacation Planner**

☐ **Free Superior Small Lodgings Guide**

Name_____

Address _____

City/State/Zip _____

Phone _____ Fax _____ E-mail_____

Voucher valid June – September 2001.

$50

Upon your 2-night minimum hotel check-in, June-September 2001, present this $50 free ride voucher for validation.*

One voucher per room. Valid with original voucher only, at participating hotels. (Hotel list available May 2001.)

LAS

From a reader of AAA TourBook 2000/2001 (105)

Name _____

Address _____

City/State/Zip _____

Place
Stamp
Here

GREATER FORT LAUDERDALE
CONVENTION & VISITORS BUREAU
P. O. Box 1
Hollywood, Florida 33022

RADISSON INN FORT MYERS

AAA SAVE

WWWW

Motor Inn

2/1-4/29	1P: $119-$179	2P: $119-$179	XP: $10	F17
12/21-1/31	1P: $109-$149	2P: $109-$149	XP: $10	F17
4/30-11/30	1P: $79-$139	2P: $79-$139	XP: $10	F17
12/1-12/20	1P: $69-$129	2P: $69-$129	XP: $10	F17

Phone: (941)936-4300

Location: I-75, exit 21, US 41, 0.8 mi n of Daniels Pkwy/Cypress. 12635 Cleveland Ave 33907. Fax: 941/936-2058. **Facility:** Well-appointed poolside motel rooms with adjoining conference center tower with spacious executive rooms. 192 units. Some suites ($139-$199). 2-5 stories, interior/exterior corridors. **Terms:** check-in 4 pm, package plans. **Amenities:** voice mail, irons, hair dryers. **Dining:** restaurant, 6:30 am-11 pm; seasonal entertainment Rum Runner Tiki Bar & Beach Club, $9-$21, cocktails, entertainment. **Leisure Activities:** heated pool, volleyball. **Guest Services:** gift shop, coin laundry. **Business Services:** meeting rooms, PC, fax. **Cards:** AE, DI, DS, JC, MC, VI. **Special Amenities:** free newspaper and preferred room (subject to availability with advanced reservations). (See color ad below)

SOME UNITS

FEE   FEE

RADISSON INN SANIBAL GATEWAY

Phone: (941)466-1200

AAA SAVE Motor Inn

2/11-4/21	2P: $124	
12/1-2/10 & 4/22-11/30	2P: $74	

Location: I-75, exit 21, 3 mi e of Sanibel Cswy on SR 869. 20091 Summerlin Rd SW 33908. Fax: 941/466-3797. **Facility:** Spacious rooms many with courtyard view, lovely Southwestern appeal. 158 units. Some whirlpool units. *Bath:* combo or shower only. 3 stories, exterior corridors. **Terms:** 3 day cancellation notice-fee imposed, pets ($50 extra charge). **Amenities:** video games, voice mail, irons, hair dryers. **Leisure Activities:** heated pool, whirlpool, ping pong. **Guest Services:** restaurant, 6:30 am-10 pm, $10-$20, cocktails. **Business Services:** [BP] meal plan available, coin laundry. **Business Services:** meeting rooms, PC, fax. **Cards:** AE, DI, DS, MC, VI. *(See ad p 399)* SOME UNITS

RESIDENCE INN BY MARRIOTT

Phone: (941)936-0110

Apartment

1/21-11/30	1P: $130-$166	2P: $130-$166
12/17-1/20	1P: $98-$125	2P: $98-$125
12/1-12/16	1P: $80-$98	2P: $80-$98

Location: I-75, exit 22, 3.5 mi w on SR 884. 2960 Colonial Blvd 33912. Fax: 941/936-4144. **Facility:** Studio, 1- and 2-bedroom suites, some with fireplace. 78 units. 12 two-bedroom units, 63 efficiencies and 15 units with kitchen. Some suites. 3 stories, interior corridors. **Terms:** weekly & monthly rates available, pets ($100 extra charge). **Amenities:** extended cable TV, voice mail, irons, hair dryers. **Leisure Activities:** heated pool, whirlpool, exercise room, sports court. **Guest Services:** [ECP] meal plan available, coin laundry. **Business Services:** meeting rooms. **Cards:** AE, DI, DS, MC, VI. SOME UNITS

SANIBEL HARBOUR RESORT & SPA

Phone: (941)466-4000

AAA SAVE Resort

12/23-4/30	1P: $251-$648	XP: $20	F18
12/1-12/22 & 11/1-11/30	1P: $170-$459	XP: $20	F18
5/1-10/31	1P: $134-$414	XP: $20	F18

Location: I-75, exit 21, at Sanibel Island Cswy entrance overlooking San Carlos Bay enter at Punta Rassa Rd. 17260 Harbour Pointe Dr 33908. Fax: 941/466-6050. **Facility:** Informal elegance on 80 unspoiled acres on Intracoastal Waterway. Upscale hotel and condo units, all with balcony and water view. 412 units. 65 two-bedroom units and 65 units with kitchen. Some suites ($179-$377) and whirlpool units ($500-$1300). 3-12 stories, interior/exterior corridors. **Parking:** valet. **Terms:** 7 day cancellation notice-fee imposed, weekly rates available, package plans. **Amenities:** extended cable TV, video games, voice mail, irons, hair dryers. *Some:* CD players, honor bars. **Dining:** 4 restaurants, 6:30 am-midnight, $9-$30, cocktails, also, Chez Le Bear, see separate listing, entertainment. **Leisure Activities:** 6 heated pools, whirlpools, beach, swimming, boat dock, fishing, charter fishing, racquetball courts, children's program, recreation program, jogging. *Fee:* boats, canoes, sailboating, marina, waverunners, kayaks, fishing pier, golf privileges, 13 lighted tennis courts, tennis instruction, body & skin treatments, beauty salon, spa & fitness center, dinner cruises on 100 ft yacht. **Guest Services:** gift shop, afternoon tea, area transportation-Sanibel Island, valet laundry. *Fee:* massage. **Business Services:** conference facilities, administrative services, fax. *Fee:* PC. **Cards:** AE, DI, DS, MC, VI. **Special Amenities:** free local telephone calls and free newspaper. *(See color ad p 758)* SOME UNITS

SHELL POINT GUEST HOUSE

Phone: (941)466-1111

AAA SAVE Motor Inn

12/1-4/30	1P: $91	2P: $101	XP: $6	F18
5/1-11/30	1P: $47	2P: $47	XP: $6	F18

Location: 1.3 mi ne of Sanibel Cswy; 2 mi nw on Shell Point Blvd from jct McGregor Blvd. 15000 Shell Point Blvd 33908. Fax: 941/466-2266. **Facility:** Located in Christian retirement community complex. 37 units. 2 stories, exterior corridors. **Terms:** monthly rates available. **Amenities:** extended cable TV. **Dining:** 7-10 am, 11:30-2 & 4-6:30 pm, Sun 7-10 am, 11:15-2 & 4-6 pm, $5-$12. **Leisure Activities:** heated pool, putting green, 2 lighted tennis courts, exercise room. **Guest Services:** gift shop, coin laundry. **Business Services:** meeting rooms. **Cards:** MC, VI. SOME UNITS

SLEEP INN AIRPORT

Phone: (941)561-1117

Motel

Property failed to provide current rates

Location: I-75, exit 21, just w on Daniels Pkwy. 13651 Indian Paint Ln 33912. Fax: 941/768-0377. **Facility:** Good sized rooms. 50 units. *Bath:* shower only. 2 stories, interior corridors. **Amenities:** voice mail. *Some:* irons, hair dryers. **Leisure Activities:** heated pool, whirlpool. **Guest Services:** [CP] meal plan available, complimentary evening beverages. **Cards:** AE, DI, DS, MC, VI. SOME UNITS

TA KI-KI MOTEL

Phone: (941)334-2135

AAA SAVE Motel

12/16-4/15	1P: $70-$80	2P: $70-$80	XP: $5
4/16-11/30	1P: $42-$54	2P: $44-$54	XP: $5
12/1-12/15	1P: $38-$52	2P: $42-$52	XP: $5

Location: I-75, exit 25, 4.5 mi w on SR 80. 2631 First St 33916. Fax: 941/332-1879. **Facility:** Riverfront traditional rooms. 23 units. 3 efficiencies and 2 units with kitchen. 1 story, exterior corridors. **Terms:** 4 night minimum stay - kitchen and efficiency units, 7 day cancellation notice, weekly rates available. **Leisure Activities:** heated pool, boat dock, fishing. **Cards:** AE, DI, DS, MC, VI. **Special Amenities:** early check-in/late check-out and free local telephone calls. SOME UNITS

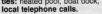

WELLESLEY INN & SUITES

AAA [SAVE]

🔷🔷🔷

Motel

12/18-4/14		1P: $89-$129	2P: $89-$129	XP: $10	F18
12/1-12/17 & 4/15-11/30		1P: $49-$79	2P: $49-$79	XP: $10	F18

Location: I-75, exit 22, 3.7 mi w on SR 884. 4400 Ford St Extension 33916. Fax: 941/278-3670. **Facility:** Very good sized bright rooms with newer furnishings and many amenities. 106 units. *Bath:* combo or shower only. 4 stories, interior corridors. **Terms:** small pets only ($10 extra charge). **Amenities:** video games, voice mail. *Some:* irons, hair dryers. **Leisure Activities:** heated pool. **Guest Services:** [ECP] meal plan available, coin laundry. **Cards:** AE, DI, DS, MC, VI. **Special Amenities: free continental breakfast and free local telephone calls.**
(See color ad opposite title page)

SOME UNITS

[icons]

─────── **WHERE TO DINE** ───────

CHEZ LE BEAR

AAA

🔷🔷🔷

American

Dinner: $23-$36   **Phone:** 941/466-2136

Location: I-75, exit 21, At Sanibel Island Cswy entrance overlooking San Carlos Bay enter at Punta Rassa Rd; in Sanibel Harbour Resort & Spa. 17260 S Harbour Pointe Dr 33908. **Hours:** 6 pm-10 pm. Closed: Sun & Mon. **Features:** dressy casual; children's menu; carryout; cocktails & lounge; entertainment; valet parking; a la carte. A professional wait staff provides imaginative dishes and excellent service. The menu includes a varied selection of local seafood, rack of lamb and beef. A basket of five different breads accompanies the meal. The blue shrimp and lobster are superb. Smoke free premises. **Cards:** AE, DI, DS, MC, VI. [icon]

PRAWNBROKER

🔷🔷

Seafood

Dinner: $14-$20   **Phone:** 941/489-2226

Location: US 41, 2.6 mi w on Cypress Lake Dr at jct McGregor Blvd. 13451-16 McGregor Blvd 33919. **Hours:** 4 pm-10 pm, Sun-9 pm. Closed: 11/22; also Super Bowl Sun. **Reservations:** suggested. **Features:** casual dress; children's menu; carryout; cocktails & lounge. The intimate restaurant is a prime spot for slightly upscale dining. Although there are numerous steak and pasta selections, seafood is the specialty, and such dishes as crunchy grouper don't disappoint. Two dining rooms overlook lush tropical gardens. Fresh fish market adjacent to restaurant. **Cards:** AE, MC, VI. [icon]

THE VERANDA

🔷🔷🔷

American

Lunch: $6-$10   **Dinner:** $20-$28   **Phone:** 941/332-2065

Location: Center; corner Second at Broadway, across from City Hall. 2122 Second St 33901. **Hours:** 11 am-2:30 & 5:30-10 pm, Sat from 5:30. Closed: 1/1, 12/25; also Sun. **Reservations:** suggested. **Features:** casual dress; children's menu; cocktails & lounge; entertainment; a la carte. A restored house built circa 1900 boasts a brick courtyard and koi pond. Choose from an interesting selection of local seafood, beef, lamb, veal, pasta and chicken. Finish your meal with an outstanding key lime pie. Valet parking is provided. **Cards:** AE, MC, VI. [icon]

FORT MYERS BEACH pop. 9,300—*See also FORT MYERS.*

─────── **WHERE TO STAY** ───────

BAY TO BEACH RESORTS

🔷🔷🔷

Apartment

Phone: (941)463-5846

12/1-12/29 Wkly		2P: $850-$2180
12/30-6/1 Wkly		2P: $1050-$1450
6/2-11/30 Wkly		2P: $850-$1300

Location: I-75, exit 21, 0.5 mi nw. 740 Estero Blvd 33931. Fax: 941/463-5846. **Facility:** On the gulf. 12 two-bedroom apartments with private balcony, washer/dryer. Covered parking. 14 units with kitchen. 12 two-bedroom units. Some suites and whirlpool units. 5 stories, exterior corridors. **Terms:** 30 day cancellation notice, daily & monthly rates available. **Amenities:** extended cable TV, irons. **Leisure Activities:** heated pool, beach, swimming. **Guest Services:** gift shop, complimentary laundry. **Cards:** MC, VI.

SOME UNITS

[icons] VCR FEE

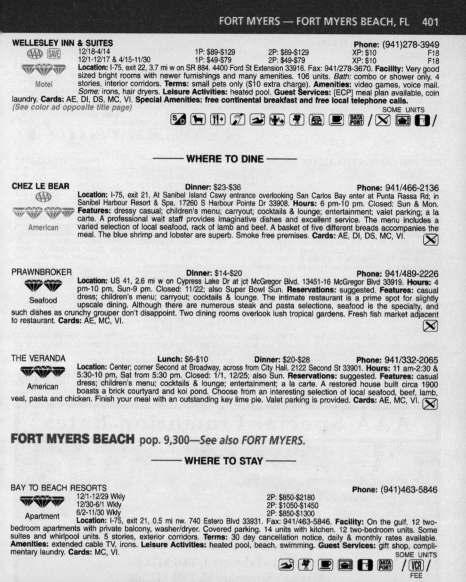

BEST WESTERN BEACH RESORT

Phone: (941)463-6000

2/4-4/15	1P: $209-$229	2P: $209-$229	XP: $10	F17
4/16-5/31	1P: $129-$159	2P: $129-$159	XP: $10	F17
12/1-2/3	1P: $109-$159	2P: $109-$159	XP: $10	F17
6/1-11/30	1P: $109-$139	2P: $109-$139	XP: $10	F17

Motel   **Location:** I-75, exit 21, 0.5 mi nw. 684 Estero Blvd 33931. Fax: 941/463-3013. **Facility:** Gulf front motel with traditional motel rooms and 1-bedroom suites. 75 efficiencies. 4 two-bedroom units. Some suites ($189-$349). *Bath:* combo or shower only. 5 stories, exterior corridors. **Terms:** 7 day cancellation notice, weekly rates available, package plans, small pets only ($10 extra charge). **Amenities:** *Some:* irons, hair dryers. **Leisure Activities:** heated pool, beach, swimming, playground, shuffleboard, volleyball. *Fee:* sailboats, jet skis, parasailing, cabanas. **Guest Services:** coin laundry. **Cards:** AE, DI, DS, MC, VI. **Special Amenities: free continental breakfast and free newspaper.**   SOME UNITS

BEST WESTERN PINK SHELL BEACH RESORT

Phone: (941)463-6181

12/1-12/31	1P: $239-$325	2P: $239-$325	XP: $20	F16
2/5-5/12	1P: $205-$325	2P: $205-$325	XP: $20	F16
1/1-2/1	1P: $149-$219	2P: $149-$219	XP: $20	F16
5/13-11/30	1P: $135-$219	2P: $135-$219	XP: $20	F16

Complex   **Location:** I-75, exit 21, at n end of Estero Island. 275 Estero Blvd 33931. Fax: 941/463-1229. **Facility:** Stilt cottages, efficiencies, apartments and motel rooms. Multi-lingual staff, currency exchange. 208 units. 72 two-bedroom units, 6 three-bedroom units, 149 efficiencies and 99 units with kitchen. Some suites ($155-$449). 2-5 stories, exterior corridors. **Terms:** check-in 4 pm, 14 day cancellation notice-fee imposed, package plans. **Amenities:** safes. **Dining:** restaurant, 7:30 am-9 pm; beach grill, convenience store, $8-$20, wine/beer only. **Leisure Activities:** 3 heated pools, wading pool, beach, swimming, fishing, 2 tennis courts, children's program, recreation program, social program, playground, shuffleboard, volleyball. *Fee:* boats, paddleboats, sailboats, windsurfing, boat dock, excursion boats, parasailing, waverunners, bicycles. **Guest Services:** gift shop, coin laundry. *Fee:* massage. **Business Services:** meeting rooms, fax. **Cards:** AE, DI, DS, MC, VI. **Special Amenities: free newspaper and preferred room (subject to availability with advanced reservations).** *(See color ad below)*   SOME UNITS

FEE

CASA PLAYA HOTEL

Phone: (941)765-0510

1/16-4/30	1P: $149-$249	2P: $149-$249
12/1-1/15	1P: $79-$199	2P: $79-$199
5/1-11/30	1P: $59-$169	2P: $59-$169

Suite Motel   **Location:** I-75, exit 21, 0.5 mi n of Matanzas Pass Bridge via 5th St. 510 Estero Blvd 33931. Fax: 941/765-0514. **Facility:** Gulf front motel with very good sized rooms with contemporary decor. Designated smoking area. 28 units. 7 two-bedroom units and 21 units with kitchen. Some suites. 8 stories, exterior corridors. **Terms:** 30 day cancellation notice, weekly rates available, pets ($20 extra charge). **Amenities:** extended cable TV. **Leisure Activities:** heated pool, beach, gas grill. **Guest Services:** coin laundry. **Cards:** AE, DS, MC, VI. *(See color ad p 403)*

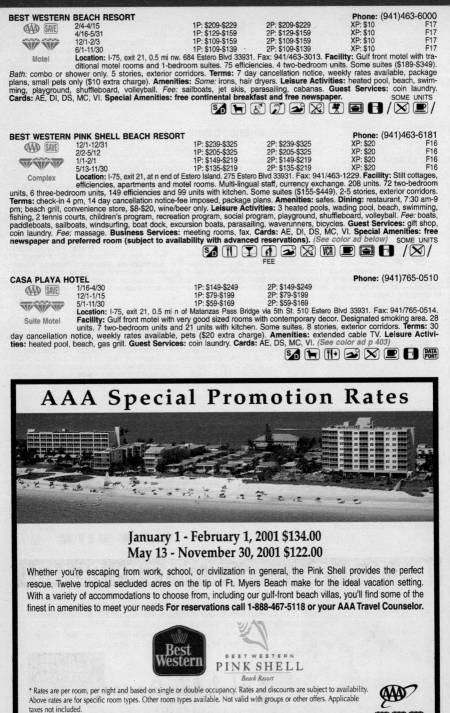

DIAMOND HEAD ALL SUITE BEACH RESORT
Phone: (941)765-7654

AAA SAVE

Suite Hotel

2/2-4/21	1P: $245-$275	2P: $245-$275	XP: $10 F17
12/1-1/2	1P: $145-$265	2P: $145-$265	XP: $10 F17
1/3-2/1	1P: $195-$215	2P: $195-$215	XP: $10 F17
4/22-11/30	1P: $155-$175	2P: $155-$175	XP: $10 F17

Location: I-75, exit 21, 2.9 mi s of Matanzas Pass Bridge. 2000 Estero Blvd 33931. Fax: 941/765-1694. **Facility:** Newer construction with contemporary spacious suites and superior sized balcony, many with gulf views. 124 units. *Bath:* combo or shower only. 12 stories, interior corridors. **Terms:** 7 day cancellation notice, package plans. **Amenities:** extended cable TV, voice mail, irons, hair dryers. **Dining:** restaurant, 7:30 am-10 pm, $12-$25, cocktails. **Leisure Activities:** heated pool, whirlpools, swimming, children's program, recreation program, exercise room. *Fee:* parasailing. **Guest Services:** gift shop, coin laundry. *Fee:* massage. **Business Services:** meeting rooms. **Cards:** AE, DS, MC, VI. **Special Amenities:** free newspaper and preferred room (subject to availability with advanced reservations).
(See color ad p 405)

SOME UNITS

THE GRANDVIEW
Phone: 941/765-4422

AAA SAVE

Condominium

2/2-4/21	2P: $160-$230	XP: $10 F18
12/23-2/1	2P: $112-$225	XP: $10 F18
12/1-12/22 & 4/22-11/30	2P: $89-$129	XP: $10 F18

Location: I-75, exit 18, 11 mi nw via Bonita Beach Rd and Estero Blvd. 8701 Estero Blvd 33931. Fax: 941/765-4499. **Facility:** Condominium units located at the edge of nature preserve. 75 units with kitchen. Some suites. *Bath:* combo or shower only. 14 stories, interior corridors. **Terms:** 7 day cancellation notice. **Amenities:** voice mail, irons. **Leisure Activities:** heated pool, beach, swimming, fishing. *Fee:* boats, canoes, sailboats, jet boats, nature cruises, shelling trips, kayaks. **Guest Services:** coin laundry. **Business Services:** meeting rooms. **Cards:** AE, DS, MC, VI.
(See color ad p 405)

GUESTHOUSE INN MARINER'S LODGE AND MARINA
Phone: (941)466-9700

AAA SAVE

Motel

12/18-4/14	1P: $85-$135	2P: $85-$135	XP: $10 F16
12/1-12/17 & 4/15-11/30	1P: $60-$70	2P: $60-$70	XP: $5 F16

Location: I-75, exit 21, 1.5 mi n of Matanzas Pass Bridge, on SR 865. 17990 San Carlos Blvd 33931. Fax: 941/466-6116. **Facility:** Within a marina, spacious rooms, gas barbecue grill and picnic table. 34 units, 18 with efficiency. *Bath:* combo or shower only. 1-2 stories, exterior corridors. **Terms:** weekly & monthly rates available. **Amenities:** extended cable TV. **Leisure Activities:** heated pool, whirlpool, fishing, playground. *Fee:* boat dock, bicycles. **Guest Services:** coin laundry. **Cards:** AE, DS, MC, VI. **Special Amenities:** free local telephone calls and preferred room (subject to availability with advanced reservations). *(See color ad below)*

SOME UNITS

GULFVIEW MANOR

Phone: (941)463-4446

(AAA) [SAVE]
▽▽▽▽

Apartment

12/1-4/20	1P: $149-$269	2P: $149-$269	XP: $10	
4/21-6/1	1P: $119-$179	2P: $119-$179	XP: $10	
10/6-11/30	1P: $109-$169	2P: $109-$169	XP: $10	
6/2-10/5	1P: $99-$159	2P: $99-$159	XP: $10	

Location: I-75, exit 21, 4.2 mi se of the Matanzas Pass Bridge. 6530 Estero Blvd 33931. Fax: 941/463-7634. **Facility:** Gulf front apartments with screened balcony. 33 units with kitchen. 5 two-bedroom units. Some suites. 6 stories, exterior corridors. **Terms:** 30 day cancellation notice-fee imposed, daily rates available. **Leisure Activities:** heated pool, beach, swimming, diving, fishing, cabanas, golf nearby, barbecue grills. **Fee:** boats, parasailing. **Guest Services:** coin laundry. **Cards:** DS, MC, VI. *(See color ad below)*

SOME UNITS
(S/D) (⫴◆) (≋) (✕) (📠) (▣) (▱) (🖨) (☎) (DATA PORT) / (VCR) FEE

GULLWING BEACH RESORT

Phone: (941)765-4300

(AAA) [SAVE]
▽▽▽▽

Condominium

2/2-4/21	2P: $310-$430	
12/1-1/2	2P: $160-$420	
1/3-2/1	2P: $230-$350	
4/22-11/30	2P: $170-$260	

Location: 4.5 mi se of Matanza Pass Bridge. 6620 Estero Rd 33931. Fax: 941/765-4646. **Facility:** Luxury accommodations tastefully furnished, all with large screened lanai; overlooking the gulf. One-bedroom can be created by locking connecting room doors. 66 units with kitchen. 22 two-bedroom units and 22 three-bedroom units. Some whirlpool units. 12 stories, interior corridors. **Terms:** 7 day cancellation notice, Maid service, $40 extra charge. **Amenities:** extended cable TV, voice mail, irons. **Leisure Activities:** heated pool, whirlpool, beach, swimming, tennis court, social program, exercise room, barbecue area. **Guest Services:** complimentary laundry. **Business Services:** meeting rooms, PC. **Cards:** AE, DS, MC, VI. **Special Amenities:** free newspaper. *(See color ad p 405)*

(S/D) (⫴◆) (≋) (✕) (⚡) (📠) (▣) (▱) (🖨) (☎) (DATA PORT) FEE

HOLIDAY INN

Phone: (941)463-5711

▽▽▽▽

Motor Inn

12/1-4/21	1P: $185-$230	
4/22-11/30	1P: $95-$145	

Location: I-75, exit 21, 4.3 mi se on SR 865. 6890 Estero Blvd 33931. Fax: 941/463-7038. **Facility:** 103 units. 2 two-bedroom units and 2 units with kitchen. Some suites ($270-$400). 2 stories, exterior corridors. **Terms:** 7 day cancellation notice-fee imposed. **Amenities:** voice mail, safes (fee), irons, hair dryers. **Leisure Activities:** heated pool, beach, swimming, exercise room, shuffleboard, volleyball. **Guest Services:** [MAP] meal plan available, coin laundry. **Business Services:** meeting rooms. **Cards:** AE, DI, DS, JC, MC, VI. *(See ad p 401)*

SOME UNITS
(ASK) (S/D) (⫴) (▢) (𝄞) (🏊) (≋) (⚡) (📠) (▣) (DATA PORT) / (✕) (VCR) (🖨) (☎) /

ISLAND HOUSE MOTEL

Phone: (941)463-9282

▽

Motel

12/1-4/30	2P: $99-$115	XP: $10
5/1-11/30	2P: $59-$79	XP: $10

Location: I-75, exit 21, 0.5 mi n on Estero Blvd from Matanzas Pass Bridge. 701 Estero Blvd 33931. Fax: 941/463-9283. **Facility:** Family owned and operated units in residential type setting near resorts and beach attraction. 5 units with kitchen. 1 story. **Terms:** 30 day cancellation notice, weekly & monthly rates available. **Amenities:** extended cable TV, irons. **Leisure Activities:** heated pool, boat dock, bicycles. **Guest Services:** coin laundry. **Cards:** MC, VI.

(≋) (✕) (📠) (▣) (▱) (🖨) (☎)

LIGHTHOUSE ISLAND RESORT

Phone: (941)463-9392

(AAA) [SAVE]
▽▽ ▽▽

Motel

1/21-4/21	1P: $95-$140	2P: $95-$155	XP: $10	F6
12/21-1/20	1P: $64-$85	2P: $64-$90	XP: $10	F6
12/1-12/20 & 4/22-11/30	1P: $49-$69	2P: $49-$79	XP: $10	F6

Location: I-75, exit 21, jct of SR 865 and 5th St, at s end of Matanzas Pass Bridge. 1051 5th St 33931. Fax: 941/765-5297. **Facility:** Busy central location. Housekeeping provided daily upon request only. 66 units. 2 two-bedroom units and 34 units with kitchen. Some suites ($69-$235). *Bath:* combo or shower only. 2-3 stories, exterior corridors. **Terms:** 21 day cancellation notice-fee imposed, weekly & monthly rates available. **Amenities:** extended cable TV. **Dining:** tiki bar, wine/beer only. **Leisure Activities:** 2 heated pools, public pier fishing, playground, basketball, shuffleboard, tennis privileges. **Guest Services:** coin laundry. **Cards:** AE, DI, DS, MC, VI. *(See color ad p 406)*

SOME UNITS
(🍸) (≋) (✕) (⚡) (☎) / (✕) (VCR) (▱) (🖨) (☎) /

OUTRIGGER BEACH RESORT

Phone: (941)463-3131

	12/1-1/1	1P: $85-$225	2P: $85-$225	XP: $10	F3
	2/4-4/21	1P: $115-$215	2P: $115-$215	XP: $10	F3
Motor Inn	1/2-2/3	1P: $100-$185	2P: $100-$185	XP: $10	F3
	4/22-11/30	1P: $85-$150	2P: $85-$150	XP: $10	F3

Location: I-75, exit 21, 4 mi se on SR 865. 6200 Estero Blvd 33931-1281. Fax: 941/463-6577. **Facility:** Good-sized to spacious rooms, some newly renovated rooms with gulf view. 144 units, 68 with efficiency. Some suites. *Bath:* combo or shower only. 2-4 stories (no elevator), exterior corridors. **Terms:** check-in 4 pm, 3 day cancellation notice. **Amenities:** extended cable TV, safes. *Some:* hair dryers. **Leisure Activities:** heated pool, beach, swimming. *Fee:* bicycles. **Guest Services:** gift shop, coin laundry. **Business Services:** meeting rooms. **Cards:** AE, DS, MC, VI. *(See color ad p 406)*

SOME UNITS

PALM TERRACE APTS. RESORT

Phone: 941/765-5783

| | 12/20-4/20 | 1P: $85-$130 | 2P: $85-$130 | XP: $10 | F8 |
| Apartment | 12/1-12/19 & 4/21-11/30 | 1P: $49-$81 | 2P: $49-$81 | XP: $10 | F8 |

Location: I-75, exit 21, 1.7 mi s of the Matanza Pass Bridge. 3333 Estero Blvd 33931. Fax: 941/765-5783. **Facility:** Spacious 1- and 2-bedroom apartments with contemporary decor. Located in close proximity to public beach. 9 units. 4 two-bedroom units, 4 efficiencies and 5 units with kitchen. Some suites. 2 stories, exterior corridors. **Terms:** 21 day cancellation notice-fee imposed, weekly rates available. **Amenities:** extended cable TV, irons. **Leisure Activities:** heated pool, shuffleboard. **Guest Services:** coin laundry. **Cards:** AE, DS, MC, VI.

SOME UNITS

POINTE ESTERO RESORT HOTEL

Phone: (941)765-1155

	2/2-4/21	1P: $245-$425	2P: $245-$425
	12/1-1/2	1P: $135-$420	2P: $135-$420
	1/3-2/1	1P: $185-$320	2P: $185-$320
Condominium	4/22-11/30	1P: $140-$275	2P: $140-$275

Location: I-75, exit 21, 4.5 mi se of the Matanzas Pass Bridge. 6640 Estero Blvd 33931. Fax: 941/765-0657. **Facility:** Luxury apartments overlooking the gulf. 1-bedroom can be created by locking connecting room door. 60 two-bedroom units with kitchen. Some whirlpool units ($135-$425). 16 stories, interior corridors. **Terms:** 7 day cancellation notice-fee imposed, package plans. **Amenities:** voice mail, irons. **Leisure Activities:** heated pool, whirlpool, beach, swimming, lighted tennis court, recreation program, volleyball, barbecue grills, rental videos. **Guest Services:** gift shop, complimentary laundry. **Cards:** AE, DS, MC, VI. *(See color ad p 405)*

SANDPIPER GULF RESORT

Phone: 941/463-5721

	2/1-4/22		2P: $139-$189	XP: $8	F6
	12/23-1/31		2P: $130-$189	XP: $8	F6
	4/23-11/30		2P: $84-$110	XP: $8	F6
Motel	12/1-12/22		2P: $75-$102	XP: $8	F6

Location: I-75, exit 21, 3.1 mi s of Matanzas Pass Bridge. 5550 Estero Blvd 33931. Fax: 941/765-0039. **Facility:** Remodeled units, some with private balcony. 63 efficiencies. 2-5 stories, interior/exterior corridors. **Terms:** 14 day cancellation notice, weekly & monthly rates available. **Amenities:** hair dryers. **Leisure Activities:** 2 pools (1 heated), whirlpool, beach, swimming, shuffleboard. *Fee:* jet skis, parasailing, bicycles. **Guest Services:** gift shop, coin laundry. **Cards:** DS, JC, MC, VI.

SANTA MARIA RESORT

Phone: (941)765-6700

	12/1-1/2	1P: $169-$279
	2/2-4/21	1P: $165-$275
	1/3-2/1	1P: $119-$199
Condominium	4/22-11/30	1P: $99-$180

Location: I-75, exit 21, 5 mi s of Matanzas Pass Bridge. 7317 Estero Blvd 33931. Fax: 941/765-6909. **Facility:** Set back from road among water canals. Large apartments with modern furnishing. 54 units with kitchen. 47 two-bedroom units and 4 three-bedroom units. Some suites. 4 stories, exterior corridors. **Terms:** age restrictions may apply, 8 day cancellation notice, monthly rates available. **Amenities:** extended cable TV, voice mail, irons. **Leisure Activities:** heated pool, sauna, whirlpools, fishing. *Fee:* boat dock, children's program, bicycles. **Guest Services:** gift shop, complimentary laundry. **Cards:** AE, DS, MC, VI. **Special Amenities:** free room upgrade (subject to availability with advanced reservations).
(See color ad p 405)

SOME UNITS
FEE FEE

SILVER SANDS VILLAS

Phone: (941)463-6554

| | 12/1-4/30 | | 2P: $90-$170 | XP: $15 | D5 |
| Apartment | 5/1-11/30 | | 2P: $75-$150 | XP: $15 | D5 |

Location: I-75, exit 21, just s of Matanzas Pass Bridge. 1207 Estero Blvd 33931. Fax: 941/463-2260. **Facility:** Set on Estero Bay. Just across street from Fort Myers Beach. Designated smoking area. 20 units. 4 two-bedroom units, 2 efficiencies and 18 units with kitchen. Some suites ($100-$300). *Bath:* combo or shower only. 2 stories, exterior corridors. **Terms:** age restrictions may apply, 21 day cancellation notice, weekly rates available, small pets only ($95 fee). **Amenities:** extended cable TV. *Some:* irons, hair dryers. **Leisure Activities:** heated pool. *Fee:* boats. **Guest Services:** coin laundry. **Business Services:** PC. **Cards:** AE, DS, MC, VI.

SOME UNITS

SUN DECK RESORT

Phone: (941)463-1842

	12/18-4/10		2P: $99-$179	XP: $10	F12
	12/1-12/17		2P: $69-$129	XP: $10	F12
Motel	4/11-11/30		2P: $49-$129	XP: $10	F12

Location: Just off and under the Matanza Pass Bridge. 1051 Third St 33931. Fax: 941/463-1970. **Facility:** 7 units. 1 two-bedroom unit, 1 efficiency and 3 units with kitchen. Some suites ($179-$225). 3 stories, exterior corridors. **Terms:** 90 day cancellation notice, weekly & monthly rates available, small pets only ($60 extra charge). **Amenities:** extended cable TV. **Guest Services:** complimentary laundry. **Cards:** MC, VI.

TROPICAL INN RESORT MOTEL   **Phone:** 941/463-3124

(AAA) [SAVE]   12/23-4/22   2P: $133-$159   XP: $10
              12/1-12/22 & 4/23-11/30   2P: $69-$89   XP: $10
▼▼▼▼ ▼▼▼▼
Apartment   **Location:** I-75, exit 21, 3 mi s of Matanzas Pass Bridge. 5210 Estero Blvd 33931. Fax: 941/463-0417. **Facility:** On gulf. Studio apartments with full kitchen and balcony. 28 units. 1 two-bedroom unit and 27 units with kitchen. Some suites. *Bath:* combo or shower only. 3 stories (no elevator), exterior corridors. **Terms:** 30 day cancellation notice-fee imposed, weekly rates available. **Amenities:** extended cable TV. **Leisure Activities:** heated
pool, beach, swimming. **Guest Services:** coin laundry. **Cards:** AE, DS, MC, VI. *(See color ad p 406)*   SOME UNITS

🏊 💻 🍴 / 🖨 /

─────── **WHERE TO DINE** ───────

ANTHONY'S ON THE GULF   **Lunch:** $9-$21   **Dinner:** $11-$21   **Phone:** 941/463-2600

▼▼▼▼ ▼▼▼▼   **Location:** On SR 865 2 mi s of Matanzas Pass Bridge. 3040 Estero Blvd 33931. **Hours:** 11:30 am-10 pm, Fri &
Italian   Sat-11 pm. **Features:** casual dress; children's menu; carryout; cocktails & lounge. Picturesque beach views and a tropical decor await diners at this casual gulf-shore restaurant. The menu dips into both American and Italian cuisine to assemble enticing dishes such as baked stuffed mushrooms, manicotti with sausage,
and buffalo shrimp. **Cards:** AE, DS, MC, VI.   ✕

BALLENGER'S   **Dinner:** $10-$21   **Phone:** 941/466-2626

(AAA)   **Location:** 2.5 mi n of Matanzas Pass Bridge, at jct San Carlos Blvd and Summerlin Rd. 11390 Summerlin Square Dr
▼▼▼▼ ▼▼▼▼   33931-5300. **Hours:** 4 pm-10 pm, Sun 10 am-9 pm. **Features:** casual dress; Sunday brunch; children's
Seafood   menu; carryout; salad bar; cocktails & lounge. Casually dressed, yet knowledgeable servers offer suggestions from a menu composed of seafood, steak and chicken dishes. Value-priced entrees, including Black Angus steak and grouper, include freshly baked bread and a trip to the salad bar. **Cards:** AE, CB, DS, MC, VI.   🍴 ✕

CHARLEY BROWN'S RESTAURANT   **Dinner:** $12-$26   **Phone:** 941/463-6660

▼▼▼▼ ▼▼▼▼   **Location:** On SR 865, 4 mi s of Matanzes Pass Bridge. 6225 Estero Blvd 33931. **Hours:** 5 pm-10 pm. Closed:
Steak & Seafood 11/22; also Super Bowl Sun. **Features:** casual dress; children's menu; early bird specials; carryout; salad bar; cocktails & lounge. Fresh seafood specials and beef cut on the premises are the highlights of this beach area restaurant. Savor slow-cooked, all-you-can-eat prime rib, and a fresh, 50-item salad bar while
taking in a lovely view of the backwater and its resident birds. **Cards:** AE, CB, DI, DS, MC, VI.   ✕

THE FISH MONGER   **Dinner:** $10-$18   **Phone:** 941/765-5544

▼▼▼▼ ▼▼▼▼   **Location:** I-75, exit 21, just n of Matanzas Pass Bridge. 19030 San Carlos Blvd 33931. **Hours:** 4 pm-10 pm.
Seafood   Closed major holidays. **Reservations:** suggested. **Features:** casual dress; children's menu; cocktails & lounge; a la carte. Casual family-friendly seafood restaurant specializing in fresh fish directly from local fishing fleet. Menu includes grouper, snapper, mahi mahi, tuna, tilefish, Cobia, Amberjack, salmon,
swordfish, Pompano catfish. New York steak, ribs and chicken. They'll also cook your fresh catch. **Cards:** MC, VI.

THE MUCKY DUCK   **Dinner:** $10-$30   **Phone:** 941/463-5519

▼▼▼▼ ▼▼▼▼   **Location:** SR 865 1 mi s of Matanzas Bridge. 2500 Estero Blvd 33931. **Hours:** 5 pm-10 pm. Closed: 11/22,
American   12/25; also Super Bowl Sun. **Features:** casual dress; children's menu; early bird specials; carryout; cocktails & lounge; a la carte. Although parking is hard to come by in this popular restaurant, the flavorful cuisine makes trolling the lot worthwhile. Such specialties as grouper cafe de Paris, duck a l'orange and
barbecue shrimp are among the tasty seafood, pasta and steak offerings. **Cards:** AE, DI, DS, MC, VI.   🧡 ✕

MUNCH BOX   **Lunch:** $4-$8   **Dinner:** $10-$13   **Phone:** 941/463-1889

▼▼▼▼   **Location:** On SR 865, 3.8 mi s of Matanzas Pass Bridge. 6101 Estero Blvd 33931. **Hours:** 8 am-7 pm, Sun-1 pm.
American   Closed major holidays; also Mon. **Features:** casual dress; children's menu; carryout; beer & wine only; a la carte. The family on a budget will favor the meat-and-potatoes fare and child-friendly atmosphere of this comfortable mom-and-pop restaurant, which serves up such home-style staples as omelets, hash browns,
sandwiches, meatloaf and pot roast.   ✕

FORT PIERCE pop. 36,800

─────── **WHERE TO STAY** ───────

COMFORT INN   **Phone:** (561)461-2323

(AAA) [SAVE]   1/1-3/31   1P: $79-$89   2P: $89-$99   XP: $5   F18
              12/1-12/31   1P: $69-$79   2P: $79-$89   XP: $5   F18
▼▼▼▼ ▼▼▼▼   4/1-11/30   1P: $59-$69   2P: $69-$79   XP: $5   F18
Motel   **Location:** US 1, 1.3 mi s of jct SR 70. 3236 US 1 S 34982. Fax: 561/464-5151. **Facility:** 60 units, 14 with kitchen. Some whirlpool units ($100-$175). 2 stories, exterior corridors. **Terms:** small pets only ($10 extra charge, $50 deposit). **Amenities:** *Some:* irons, hair dryers. **Leisure Activities:** heated pool, whirlpool. **Guest Services:**
valet and coin laundry. **Cards:** AE, CB, DI, DS, MC, VI. **Special Amenities:** free continental breakfast and free local telephone calls.   SOME UNITS

🛏 🏊 📺 💻 📠 / ✕ 🖨 /

DAYS INN   **Phone:** (561)466-4066

[SAVE]   12/1-4/30   1P: $59-$89   2P: $59-$89   XP: $5   F17
               5/1-11/30   1P: $39-$59   2P: $39-$59   XP: $5   F17
▼▼▼▼ ▼▼▼▼   **Location:** I-95, exit 65. 6651 Darter Ct 34945. Fax: 561/468-3260. **Facility:** Designated smoking area. 125 units.
Motel   2 stories, exterior corridors. **Terms:** small pets only ($10 extra charge). **Amenities:** irons, hair dryers. **Leisure Activities:** heated pool. **Guest Services:** coin laundry. **Business Services:** meeting rooms. **Cards:** AE, CB, DI, DS, JC, MC.   SOME UNITS

🆂 🐾 🍴 🏊 📺 📠 💻 📠 / ✕ 🍴 /

DAYS INN HUTCHINSON ISLAND

Phone: (561)461-8737

AAA SAVE

12/15-4/15	1P: $95-$135	2P: $95-$135	XP: $10	F18
12/1-12/14 & 4/16-11/30	1P: $70-$95	2P: $70-$95	XP: $10	F18

Motel

Location: SR A1A southbound, Hutchinson Island. 2.5 mi e of jct US 1. 1920 Seaway Dr 34949. Fax: 561/460-2218. **Facility:** On grounds along inlet to Intracoastal Waterway. Very well maintained. 36 units, 10 with kitchen. 1 story, interior/exterior corridors. **Terms:** 3 night minimum stay. **Amenities:** extended cable TV. **Leisure Activities:** heated pool, fishing, private fishing pier. **Guest Services:** coin laundry. **Cards:** AE, CB, DI, DS, MC, VI. **Special Amenities:** free continental breakfast.

SOME UNITS

DOCKSIDE HARBORLIGHT

Phone: (561)468-3555

AAA SAVE

12/15-4/14	1P: $89-$115	2P: $89-$115	XP: $10	F16
12/1-12/14 & 4/15-11/30	1P: $69-$89	2P: $69-$89	XP: $10	F16

Motel

Location: SR A1A southbound, 2 mi e of jct US 1. 1160 Seaway Dr 34949. Fax: 561/489-9848. **Facility:** 10 rooms with patio or balcony overlooking inlet and Intracoastal Waterway. 20 units, 5 with kitchen. 2 stories, exterior corridors. **Terms:** 3 day cancellation notice, weekly & monthly rates available. **Amenities:** extended cable TV, voice mail. **Leisure Activities:** heated pool, whirlpool, fishing, fishing piers. *Fee:* boats, boat dock. **Guest Services:** coin laundry. **Business Services:** meeting rooms. **Cards:** AE, CB, DI, DS, MC, VI. **Special Amenities:** free continental breakfast and preferred room (subject to availability with advanced reservations).

SOME UNITS

HAMPTON INN

Phone: (561)460-9855

Property failed to provide current rates

Motel

Location: SR 70, 0.3 mi e of Florida Tpke, exit 152; 0.4 mi w of jct I-95, exit 65. 2831 Reynolds Dr 34945. Fax: 561/465-7117. **Facility:** Elegantly furnished rooms. Designated smoking area. 72 units. *Bath:* combo or shower only. 2 stories, exterior corridors. **Amenities:** voice mail, irons. **Guest Services:** [CP] meal plan available, valet laundry. **Cards:** AE, CB, DI, DS, MC, VI.

SOME UNITS

HOLIDAY INN EXPRESS

Phone: (561)464-5000

AAA SAVE

12/1-5/31 & 11/1-11/30	1P: $80
6/1-10/31	1P: $70

Motel

Location: I-95, exit 65, 0.7 mi w on SR 70; at Florida Tpke, exit 152. 7151 Okeechobee Rd 34945. Fax: 561/461-9573. **Facility:** Very inviting landscaped courtyard; modern rooms. 100 units. *Bath:* combo or shower only. 2 stories, exterior corridors. **Terms:** cancellation fee imposed, package plans, small pets only ($15 deposit). **Amenities:** extended cable TV, voice mail, irons, hair dryers. **Leisure Activities:** wading pool. **Guest Services:** [CP] meal plan available, valet and coin laundry. **Business Services:** meeting rooms. **Cards:** AE, CB, DI, DS, JC, MC, VI.

SOME UNITS

HOLIDAY INN EXPRESS HOTEL & SUITES

Phone: (561)595-0711

12/1-4/30	1P: $89-$99	2P: $89-$99	XP: $10	F18
5/1-11/30	1P: $65-$75	2P: $65-$75	XP: $10	F18

Motel

Location: SR A1A southbound, Hutchinson Island, 2 mi e of jct US 1. 1230 Seaway Dr 34949. Fax: 561/595-0712. **Facility:** Along inlet to Intracoastal Waterway. Many rooms with balcony. 70 units. *Bath:* combo or shower only. 4 stories, interior corridors. **Amenities:** extended cable TV, dual phone lines, voice mail, safes, irons, hair dryers. **Leisure Activities:** heated pool, whirlpool, boat dock, fishing. **Guest Services:** [ECP] meal plan available, gift shop, valet and coin laundry. **Cards:** AE, DI, DS, JC, MC.

SOME UNITS

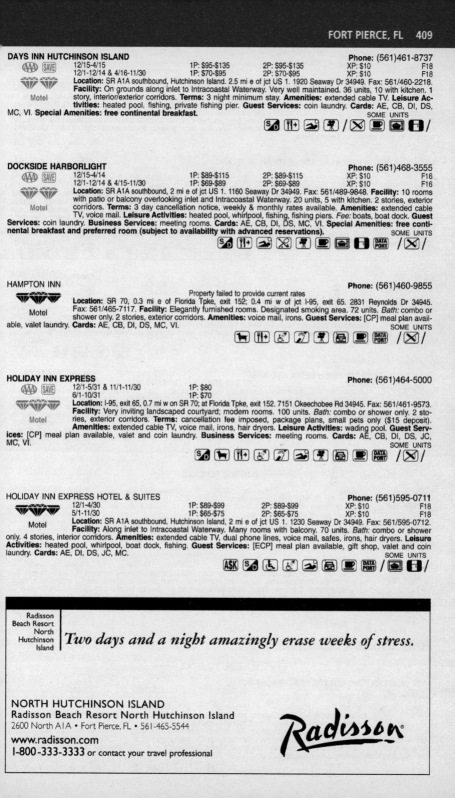

THE MELLON PATCH INN

Phone: (561)461-5231

AAA SAVE

12/16-4/30	1P: $140-$165	2P: $140-$165	XP: $20	D
5/1-11/30	1P: $100-$135	2P: $100-$135		
12/1-12/15	1P: $95-$130	2P: $95-$130	XP: $15	D

Bed & Breakfast

Location: SR A1A, (N Hutchinson Island) 3.5 mi ne of jct US 1. 3601 N A1A 34949. Fax: 561/464-6463. **Facility:** Modern bright and airy inn, across highway from the ocean and with grounds reaching down to the lagoon. Individually decorated rooms also reflect the location. Smoke free premises. 4 units. 2 stories, interior corridors. **Terms:** age restrictions may apply, 7 day cancellation notice-fee imposed. **Amenities:** extended cable TV. **Leisure Activities:** whirlpool, canoeing, fishing, lagoon with dock, bicycles, public tennis courts across the street. **Guest Services:** [BP] meal plan available. **Cards:** AE, DS, MC, VI. **Special Amenities:** free local telephone calls and preferred room (subject to availability with advanced reservations).

RADISSON BEACH RESORT NORTH HUTCHINSON ISLAND

Phone: (561)465-5544

AAA SAVE

2/1-4/15	1P: $129-$189	2P: $129-$189	XP: $10	F18
12/24-1/31	1P: $109-$169	2P: $109-$169	XP: $10	F18
12/1-12/23 & 4/16-11/30	1P: $99-$149	2P: $99-$149	XP: $10	F18

Hotel

Location: SR A1A northbound, 2.3 mi e of US 1. 2600 North A1A 34949. Fax: 561/465-5540. **Facility:** 150 units. Some suites ($159-$329) and whirlpool units. *Bath:* combo or shower only. 4 stories, interior corridors. **Terms:** cancellation fee imposed, package plans. **Amenities:** extended cable TV, video games, irons, hair dryers. **Dining:** dining room, restaurant, 7 am-11 pm, $12-$21, cocktails. **Leisure Activities:** heated pool, beach, swimming, snorkeling, fishing, tennis court, exercise room, boogie boards, sand volleyball. *Fee:* bicycles. **Guest Services:** gift shop, valet and coin laundry. *Fee:* massage. **Business Services:** conference facilities, fax. **Cards:** AE, CB, DI, DS, JC, MC, VI. **Special Amenities:** free newspaper. *(See ad p 409)*

SOME UNITS

ROYAL INN

Phone: (561)464-0405

AAA SAVE

1/15-4/15	1P: $59-$69	2P: $69-$89	XP: $10	F12
12/1-1/14 & 4/16-11/30	1P: $39-$49	2P: $49-$59	XP: $10	F12

Motel

Location: 2.5 mi e on SR A1A, southbound to Hernando St, just s. 222 Hernando St 34949. Fax: 561/464-0405. **Facility:** All rooms with balcony, some rooms with water view, sun deck. Designated smoking area. 18 units. 3 stories, exterior corridors. **Terms:** weekly rates available, pets ($15 extra charge, $25 deposit). **Amenities:** extended cable TV. **Guest Services:** [CP] meal plan available, coin laundry. **Cards:** AE, DS, DS, JC, MC, VI. **Special Amenities:** free local telephone calls and free room upgrade (subject to availability with advanced reservations).

SOME UNITS

VILLA NINA ISLAND INN BEACH BED & BREAKFAST

Phone: 561/467-8673

All Year	1P: $125-$195	2P: $125-$195

Bed & Breakfast

Location: SR A1A, (North Hutchinson Island), 4 mi ne of jct US 1. 3851 N A1A 34949. **Facility:** Lovely home. All rooms with private entrance. Smoke free premises. 4 units. *Bath:* combo or shower only. 1 story, exterior corridors. **Terms:** check-in 4 pm, age restrictions may apply, 21 day cancellation notice, written cancellation-fee imposed. **Leisure Activities:** heated pool, canoeing, paddleboats, bicycles. **Guest Services:** complimentary laundry. **Cards:** DS, MC, VI.

SOME UNITS

——— WHERE TO DINE ———

KRISTI'S ON THE OCEAN

Lunch: $7-$18   **Dinner:** $10-$29   **Phone:** 561/465-4200

American

Location: On SR A1A, S Hutchinson Island; 4.7 mi se of jct US 1; in Ocean Village residential complex. 2400 S Ocean Dr 34949. **Hours:** 11:30 am-2:30 pm, Sun 11 am-2 & 5-9 pm. **Reservations:** suggested. **Features:** casual dress; Sunday brunch; children's menu; carryout; cocktails & lounge; entertainment; a la carte. The songs of Nat King Cole combined with lovely ocean views set the mood for a romantic evening out. Share the chateaubriand for two, delicious roasted tenderloin with grilled vegetables; or keep the coco shrimp in calypso sauce all to yourself. **Cards:** AE, MC, VI.

MANGROVE MATTIES

Lunch: $7-$15   **Dinner:** $12-$19   **Phone:** 561/466-1044

Seafood

Location: SR A1A southbound; 2.3 mi e of jct US 1. 1640 Seaway Dr 34949. **Hours:** 11:30 am-10 pm, Sun noon-9:30 pm. **Reservations:** suggested. **Features:** casual dress; children's menu; early bird specials; carryout; cocktails & lounge. Feast on fresh seafood on an open air terrace only 20 feet from the inlet. To continuously offer a good variety, the menu changes daily and features such dishes as crab and shrimp Alfredo and coco shrimp. Be sure to save room for homemade key lime pie. **Cards:** AE, DI, DS, MC, VI.

FORT WALTON BEACH pop. 21,500

——— WHERE TO STAY ———

BEST WESTERN FORT WALTON BEACHFRONT HOTEL

Phone: (850)243-9444

AAA SAVE

3/1-9/3	1P: $99-$169	2P: $99-$169	XP: $10	F12
9/4-10/31	1P: $99-$129	2P: $99-$129	XP: $10	F12
12/1-2/28 & 11/1-11/30	1P: $69-$99	2P: $69-$99	XP: $10	F12

Motel

Location: US 98, just sw on Okaloosa Island. 380 Santa Rosa Blvd 32548. Fax: 850/243-5445. **Facility:** Bright attractive art-deco/retro interior decor. 100 units. Some whirlpool units ($99-$169). *Bath:* combo or shower only. 6 stories, interior corridors. **Terms:** age restrictions may apply, cancellation fee imposed, weekly & monthly rates available, package plans. **Amenities:** extended cable TV, voice mail, hair dryers. **Leisure Activities:** heated pool, beach, swimming, children's program in summer. *Fee:* kayak. **Guest Services:** [CP] & [ECP] meal plans available, coin laundry. **Business Services:** meeting rooms. **Cards:** AE, DI, DS, JC, MC, VI.

SOME UNITS

CAYO GRANDE SUITES

Phone: 850/862-9888

▼▼▼

Suite Motel

4/1-11/30	1P: $99-$175	
12/1-3/31	1P: $85-$149	

Location: US 98, n on SR 393 to SR 189, w and n on SR 189 1.6 mi to Racetrack Rd, then 0.9 mi e. 214 Racetrack Rd 32547. Fax: 850/862-7467. **Facility:** 103 units. 14 two-bedroom units and 58 units with kitchen. Some suites and whirlpool units. 6 stories, interior/exterior corridors. **Terms:** cancellation fee imposed, weekly & monthly rates available, package plans. **Amenities:** extended cable TV, voice mail, irons. *Some:* honor bars, hair dryers. **Leisure Activities:** 3 pools, saunas, putting green, tennis court, exercise room. **Guest Services:** [CP] meal plan available, gift shop, valet and coin laundry. **Business Services:** meeting rooms. **Cards:** AE, DI, DS, MC, VI.

SOME UNITS

DAYS INN

Phone: 850/244-6184

AAA SAVE

▼▼ ▼▼

Motel

3/14-9/4	1P: $67-$72	2P: $77	XP: $5	F17
9/5-11/30	1P: $46-$50	2P: $55	XP: $5	F17
12/1-3/13	1P: $41-$46	2P: $51	XP: $5	F17

Location: 1.3 mi w on US 98. 135 Miracle Strip Pkwy 32548. Fax: 850/243-5764. **Facility:** Across from Intracoastal Waterway. 62 units. 2 stories, exterior corridors. **Terms:** 21 day cancellation notice. **Amenities:** extended cable TV, irons, hair dryers. **Business Services:** meeting rooms. **Cards:** AE, DI, DS, JC, MC, VI.
Special Amenities: free continental breakfast and free local telephone calls.

SOME UNITS

ECONO LODGE

Phone: (850)243-7123

SAVE

▼▼ ▼▼

Motel

5/16-9/15	1P: $65	2P: $65	XP: $10	F18
3/2-5/15	1P: $55	2P: $55	XP: $10	F18
12/1-3/1 & 9/16-11/30	1P: $45	2P: $45	XP: $10	F18

Location: US 98, at ne end of bridge; eastbound take south service road under bridge. 1284 Marler Ave 32548. Fax: 850/243-7109. **Facility:** On Intracoastal Waterway. 59 units. *Bath:* combo or shower only. 2 stories, interior/exterior corridors. **Terms:** cancellation fee imposed. **Amenities:** extended cable TV. **Leisure Activities:** fishing. **Guest Services:** [CP] meal plan available, coin laundry. **Cards:** AE, DI, DS, JC, MC, VI.

SOME UNITS

FOUR POINTS HOTEL SHERATON

Phone: (850)243-8116

▼▼ ▼▼

Hotel

5/25-9/2	1P: $140-$185	2P: $140-$185	XP: $10	F18
3/16-5/24 & 9/3-11/30	1P: $110-$135	2P: $110-$135	XP: $10	F18
12/1-3/15	1P: $95-$115	2P: $95-$115	XP: $10	F18

Location: US 98, 0.7 mi e. 1325 Miracle Strip Pkwy 32548. Fax: 850/243-3064. **Facility:** 217 units. Some whirlpool units ($150-$275). *Bath:* combo or shower only. 7 stories, interior/exterior corridors. **Terms:** age restrictions may apply, 3 day cancellation notice-fee imposed, package plans. **Amenities:** extended cable TV, video games, voice mail, irons, hair dryers. **Leisure Activities:** 2 pools (1 heated), whirlpools, beach, swimming, exercise room. **Guest Services:** [BP] meal plan available, gift shop, valet and coin laundry. **Business Services:** meeting rooms, fax. **Cards:** AE, CB, DI, DS, JC, MC, VI.   SOME UNITS

FEE

MARINA MOTEL & EFFICIENCIES

Phone: (850)244-1129

AAA SAVE

▼▼ ▼▼

Motel

5/1-9/6	1P: $75-$85	2P: $75-$85	XP: $10	F16
3/1-4/30 & 9/7-11/30	1P: $60-$68	2P: $60-$68	XP: $10	F16
12/1-2/28	1P: $44	2P: $44	XP: $10	F16

Location: 1 mi e on US 98. 1345 Miracle Strip Pkwy E 32548. Fax: 850/243-6063. **Facility:** Bayside. Across from gulf beach. 38 units. 16 efficiencies and 2 units with kitchen. Some suites ($80-$125). *Bath:* combo or shower only. 1-2 stories, interior/exterior corridors. **Terms:** weekly & monthly rates available, pets ($10 extra charge, $50 deposit). **Amenities:** extended cable TV, irons. **Leisure Activities:** charter fishing. *Fee:* boat dock, fishing. **Guest Services:** coin laundry. **Cards:** AE, CB, DI, DS, MC, VI. **Special Amenities: free continental breakfast.**

SOME UNITS

RADISSON BEACH RESORT FT. WALTON BEACH

Phone: (850)243-9181

AAA SAVE

▼▼ ▼▼

Hotel

5/21-9/5	1P: $149-$189	2P: $154-$194	XP: $6	F18
9/6-11/30	1P: $89-$129	2P: $94-$134		
12/1-5/20	1P: $89-$129	2P: $94-$134	XP: $6	F18

Location: US 98, just s. 1110 Santa Rosa Blvd 32548. Fax: 850/664-7652. **Facility:** 287 units. Some suites. 7 stories, interior/exterior corridors. **Terms:** check-in 4 pm, 3 day cancellation notice, package plans. **Amenities:** extended cable TV, video games, voice mail, irons, hair dryers. **Dining:** 2 restaurants, 6 am-11 pm, $8-$20, cocktails. **Leisure Activities:** 2 pools (1 heated), wading pool, beach, swimming, 2 lighted tennis courts, exercise room. **Guest Services:** gift shop, valet and coin laundry. **Business Services:** conference facilities, administrative services. **Cards:** AE, DI, DS, JC, MC, VI. **Special Amenities: free room upgrade and preferred room (each subject to availability with advanced reservations).**

SOME UNITS

FEE   FEE   FEE

RAMADA PLAZA BEACH RESORT

Phone: (850)243-9161

▼▼▼

Hotel

4/27-9/2		2P: $120-$185	XP: $10	F18
12/1-4/26 & 9/3-11/30		2P: $95-$140	XP: $10	F18

Location: US 98, 1 mi e. 1500 Miracle Strip Pkwy SE 32548. Fax: 850/243-2391. **Facility:** 335 units. Some suites ($150-$350). 6 stories, interior/exterior corridors. **Terms:** 3 day cancellation notice imposed. **Amenities:** extended cable TV, video games, voice mail, safes, irons, hair dryers. **Leisure Activities:** 2 pools (1 heated), wading pool, whirlpool, beach, swimming, exercise room. **Guest Services:** gift shop, valet and coin laundry. **Business Services:** conference facilities. **Cards:** AE, DI, DS, MC, VI.

SOME UNITS

FEE

SEA ISLE MOTEL   Phone: (850)243-5563

AAA SAVE

5/1-9/15	1P: $60-$85	2P: $70-$85	XP: $8	F16
3/1-4/30	1P: $49-$65	2P: $55-$70	XP: $8	F16
9/16-11/30	1P: $45-$60	2P: $50-$65	XP: $8	F16
12/1-2/28	1P: $37-$50	2P: $47-$55	XP: $8	F16

Motel

Location: US 98, just e of bridge. 1214 Hwy 98 E 32548. **Fax:** 850/243-0166. **Facility:** Near gulf beaches. 60 units, 10 with efficiency. 6 stories, interior corridors. **Terms:** 10 day cancellation notice-fee imposed, weekly & monthly rates available. **Amenities:** extended cable TV. **Leisure Activities:** small pool, whirlpool, steamroom, exercise room. **Guest Services:** coin laundry. **Cards:** AE, CB, DI, DS, MC, VI. **Special Amenities:** free continental breakfast and free local telephone calls.

SOME UNITS

SUPER 8 MOTEL   Phone: 850/244-4999

Motel

Property failed to provide current rates

Location: 1.5 mi w on US 98. 333 Miracle Strip Pkwy 32548. **Fax:** 850/243-1928. **Facility:** 34 units. 2 stories, exterior corridors. **Amenities:** extended cable TV. **Leisure Activities:** small pool. **Cards:** AE, CB, DI, DS, MC, VI.

SOME UNITS

———— **WHERE TO DINE** ————

———— *The following restaurant has not been evaluated by AAA but is listed for your information only.* ————

PANDORA'S STEAK HOUSE   Phone: 850/244-8669

[fyi]   Not evaluated. **Location:** 1120B Santa Rosa Blvd. **Features:** On Okaloosa Island, specializing in seafood and steaks. Moderate prices.

GAINESVILLE pop. 84,800

———— **WHERE TO STAY** ————

BAYMONT INN & SUITES-GAINESVILLE   Phone: (352)376-0004

All Year   1P: $61   2P: $66

Motel

Location: I-75, exit 75, just w. 3905 SW 43rd St 32608. **Fax:** 352/376-1979. **Facility:** 115 units, 4 with kitchen. Some suites ($129-$134) and whirlpool units ($79-$84). *Bath:* combo or shower only. 4 stories, interior corridors. **Terms:** small pets only (in designated rooms). **Amenities:** extended cable TV, video games, voice mail, irons, hair dryers. **Leisure Activities:** heated pool, exercise room. **Guest Services:** [ECP] meal plan available, coin laundry. **Business Services:** meeting rooms, fax. **Cards:** AE, DI, DS, MC, VI. *(See color ad below)*

SOME UNITS
FEE

BEST INN-GAINESVILLE   Phone: (352)378-2405

| 12/1-12/31 & 9/1-11/30 | 1P: $125 | 2P: $150 | XP: $10 | F18 |
| 1/1-8/31 | 1P: $58 | 2P: $68 | XP: $10 | F18 |

Motel

Location: I-75, exit 74, just w. 3455 SW Williston Rd 32618. **Fax:** 352/381-8742. **Facility:** 88 units. Some suites ($75-$150). *Bath:* combo or shower only. 2 stories, interior/exterior corridors. **Terms:** 14 day cancellation notice, pets ($50 deposit, in exterior bldg). **Amenities:** extended cable TV, voice mail, irons, hair dryers. **Leisure Activities:** exercise room. **Guest Services:** [ECP] meal plan available, valet laundry. **Business Services:** meeting rooms, fax. **Cards:** AE, DI, DS, MC, VI.

SOME UNITS

BEST WESTERN GATEWAY GRAND   Phone: (352)331-3336

AAA SAVE

All Year   1P: $64-$99   2P: $64-$99

Motel

Location: I-75, exit 77, just n of SR 222, just w. 4200 NW 97th Blvd 32606. **Fax:** 352/331-3337. **Facility:** Upscale public areas, plesant view from pool deck. 152 units. *Bath:* combo or shower only. 3 stories, interior corridors. **Terms:** check-in 4 pm, small pets only ($15 extra charge). **Amenities:** video games, voice mail. *Some:* irons, hair dryers. **Leisure Activities:** whirlpool, exercise room. **Guest Services:** [ECP] meal plan available, coin laundry. **Business Services:** conference facilities, fax. **Cards:** AE, CB, DI, DS, MC, VI. **Special Amenities:** free continental breakfast and free local telephone calls.

SOME UNITS
FEE

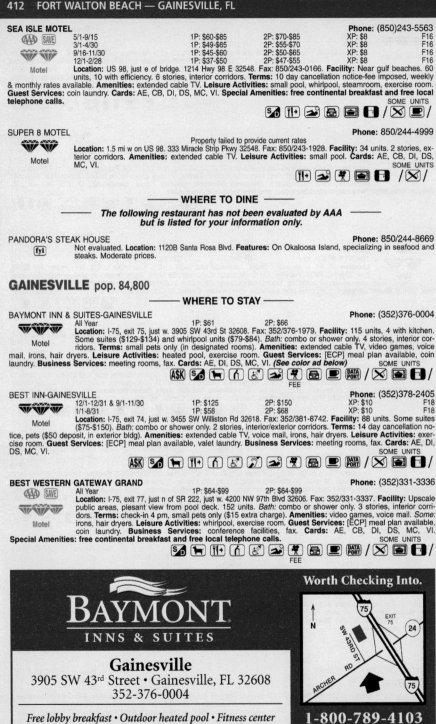

CABOT LODGE

▼▼▼
Motel

All Year | 1P: $80-$105 | 2P: $87-$112 | XP: $7
Phone: (352)375-2400 / F18

Location: I-75, exit 75, just ne on SR 24. 3726 SW 40th Blvd 32608. Fax: 352/335-2321. **Facility:** 208 units. 3 stories, interior corridors. **Terms:** package plans. **Amenities:** voice mail, irons. *Some:* hair dryers. **Guest Services:** [CP] meal plan available, complimentary evening beverages, valet laundry. **Business Services:** meeting rooms, administrative services, PC, fax. **Cards:** AE, CB, DI, DS, MC, VI.

SOME UNITS
(ASK) (S) (🛏) (🎫) (�"🚪) (📶) (🖨) (DATA PORT) / (✕) (💻)
FEE

COMFORT INN

(AAA) (SAVE)
▼▼ ▼▼
Motel

All Year | 1P: $48-$58 | 2P: $54-$64 | XP: $6
Phone: (352)373-6500 / F18

Location: I-75, exit 74, 2 mi ne on SR 331, then 1 mi n on US 441. 2435 SW 13th St 32608. Fax: 352/373-6500. **Facility:** 59 units, 6 with kitchen. Some whirlpool units ($85-$105). *Bath:* combo or shower only. 2 stories, exterior corridors. **Amenities:** extended cable TV. *Some:* irons, hair dryers. **Leisure Activities:** whirlpool. **Guest Services:** [ECP] meal plan available, coin laundry. **Business Services:** fax. **Cards:** AE, DI, DS, JC, MC, VI. **Special Amenities:** early check-in/late check-out and free continental breakfast.

SOME UNITS
(S) (🛏) (🚙) (🚪) (🖨) / (✕) (💻) (🖥) (🛢) /

COURTYARD BY MARRIOTT

▼▼ ▼▼
Motel

All Year | 1P: $66-$81 | 2P: $66-$81
Phone: (352)335-9100

Location: I-75, exit 75, just e on SR 24. 3700 SW 42nd St 32608. Fax: 352/335-1502. **Facility:** 81 units. Some suites and whirlpool units. *Bath:* combo or shower only. 3 stories, interior corridors. **Amenities:** extended cable TV, voice mail, irons, hair dryers. **Leisure Activities:** heated pool, whirlpool, exercise room. **Guest Services:** coin laundry. **Business Services:** meeting rooms, fax. **Cards:** AE, DI, DS, MC, VI.

SOME UNITS
(🛏) (🚶) (🚙) (🚪) (🖨) (💻) (DATA PORT) / (✕) (🛢) (🛢) /

EXTENDED STAY AMERICA

▼▼ ▼▼
Apartment

All Year | 1P: $49-$54 | 2P: $59-$64 | XP: $5
Phone: (352)375-0073 / F4

Location: I-75, exit 75, just ne. 3600 SW 42nd St 32608. Fax: 352/375-0960. **Facility:** 120 efficiencies. *Bath:* combo or shower only. 3 stories, exterior corridors. **Terms:** weekly rates available. **Amenities:** extended cable TV, voice mail. **Guest Services:** coin laundry. **Cards:** AE, DI, DS, MC, VI.

SOME UNITS
(♿) (🚪) (💻) (🖥) (🛢) (DATA PORT) / (✕) /

FAIRFIELD INN

▼▼ ▼▼
Motel

All Year | 1P: $52-$57
Phone: (352)332-8292

Location: I-75, exit 76, just w on SR 26 to 75th St, just s to NW 4th Blvd, then e. 6901 NW 4th Blvd 32607. Fax: 352/332-8292. **Facility:** 135 units. 3 stories, interior/exterior corridors. **Terms:** 3 day cancellation notice. **Leisure Activities:** heated pool. **Guest Services:** [ECP] meal plan available, valet laundry. **Business Services:** fax. **Cards:** AE, DI, DS, MC, VI.

SOME UNITS
(🎫) (🚙) (🚶🚪) (🚪) (🖨) (DATA PORT) / (✕) (🛢) /
FEE

HAMPTON INN

(SAVE)
▼▼ ▼▼
Motel

5/1-5/17 & 8/16-11/30 | 2P: $76-$169
12/1-4/30 & 5/18-8/15 | 2P: $76-$97
Phone: (352)371-4171

Location: I-75, exit 75, just se. 4225 SW 40th Blvd 32608. Fax: 352/371-4234. **Facility:** 106 units. Some suites and whirlpool units. *Bath:* combo or shower only. 4 stories, interior corridors. **Amenities:** extended cable TV, irons. **Leisure Activities:** heated pool. **Guest Services:** [ECP] meal plan available. **Business Services:** meeting rooms, fax. **Cards:** AE, DI, DS, MC, VI.

SOME UNITS
(🛏) (🚙) (🚶🚪) (🚪) (🖨) (💻) (DATA PORT) / (✕) (🛢) (🛢) /

HOLIDAY INN UNIVERSITY CENTER

(AAA) (SAVE)
▼▼ ▼▼
Motor Inn

All Year | 1P: $89-$130 | 2P: $89-$130
Phone: (352)376-1661

Location: Downtown at jct US 441/SR 24; adjacent to the University of Florida. 1250 W University Ave 32601. Fax: 352/336-8717. **Facility:** 166 units. *Bath:* some combo or shower only. 6 stories, interior corridors. **Terms:** 14 day cancellation notice, weekly & monthly rates available. **Amenities:** voice mail, irons, hair dryers. **Dining:** restaurant, 24 hours, $5-$9. **Leisure Activities:** exercise room. **Guest Services:** area transportation-hospital, valet laundry. **Business Services:** meeting rooms. **Cards:** AE, DI, DS, JC, MC, VI. **Special Amenities:** early check-in/late check-out and free newspaper.

SOME UNITS
(S) (➕) (🛏) (♿) (🚙) (🚪) (🖨) (💻) (DATA PORT) / (✕) (VCR) (🛢) /
FEE   FEE

HOLIDAY INN-WEST

AAA **SAVE**

♦♦♦ ♦♦♦ ♦♦♦

Motor Inn

Phone: 352/332-7500

All Year   1P: $95-$350   2P: $95-$350
Location: I-75, exit 76, just w. 7417 NW 8th Ave 32605. Fax: 352/332-0487. **Facility:** 276 units. Some suites. 2 stories, exterior corridors. **Terms:** package plans. **Amenities:** voice mail, irons, hair dryers. *Some:* fax. **Dining:** restaurant, 6 am-2 & 5-10 pm; Comedy Club, $7-$16, cocktails. **Leisure Activities:** 2 pools (1 heated), wading pool, exercise room. **Guest Services:** area transportation-hospital, valet and coin laundry. **Business Services:** conference facilities, fax. **Cards:** AE, CB, DI, MC, VI. **Special Amenities:** free room upgrade and preferred room **(each subject to availability with advanced reservations).** *(See color ad below)*

SOME UNITS
✈ ⏹ 𝐘 ⬒ ⬛ 🖨 ▯ DATA PORT / ✕ 🖼 ❚ /
FEE

LA QUINTA INN

SAVE

♦♦♦ ♦♦♦ ♦♦♦

Motel

Phone: (352)332-6466

All Year   1P: $65-$69   2P: $65-$69
Location: SR 26, ne of jct I-75, exit 76; behind Red Lobster. 920 NW 69th Terrace 32605. Fax: 352/332-7074. **Facility:** 134 units. 3-4 stories, exterior corridors. **Terms:** small pets only. **Amenities:** video games, voice mail. **Leisure Activities:** heated pool. **Guest Services:** [ECP] meal plan available, valet laundry. **Business Services:** meeting rooms, fax. **Cards:** AE, CB, DI, DS, MC, VI.

SOME UNITS
S▯ 🐾 ⏹ ⏹▯ ⬒ 🛠 ⬛ 🖨 ▯ DATA PORT / ✕ 🖼 ❚ /
FEE

RED ROOF INN-GAINESVILLE

AAA **SAVE**

♦♦♦ ♦♦♦

Motel

Phone: (352)336-3311

All Year   1P: $41-$53   2P: $47-$58   XP: $6   F17
Location: I-75, exit 75, just ne. 3500 SW 42nd St 32608. Fax: 352/336-7855. **Facility:** 129 units. *Bath:* combo or shower only. 4 stories, interior corridors. **Terms:** weekly rates available. **Amenities:** voice mail. **Leisure Activities:** heated pool. **Guest Services:** coin laundry. **Business Services:** fax. **Cards:** AE, CB, DI, DS, MC, VI. **Special Amenities:** free local telephone calls and free newspaper.

SOME UNITS
S▯ 🐾 🏠 🗑 ⬒ 🛠 ⬛ 🖨 DATA PORT / ✕ 🖼 ❚ /
FEE

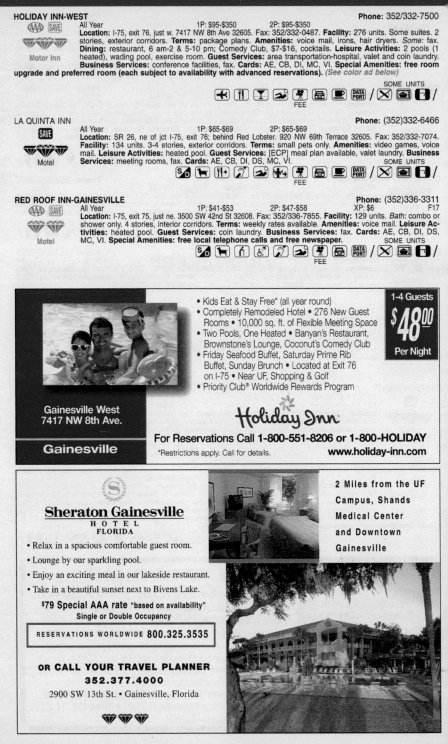

SHERATON GAINESVILLE
Phone: (352)377-4000
All Year   1P: $79   2P: $79   XP: $10   F18
▼▼▼▼
Motor Inn
Location: I-75, exit 74, 2 mi ne on SR 331, 0.8 mi n on US 441. 2900 SW 13th St 32608. Fax: 352/377-7766. **Facility:** Beside lake and nature refuge. 197 units. Some suites ($105). 4 stories, interior corridors. **Terms:** cancellation fee imposed, weekly & monthly rates available, package plans. **Amenities:** video games, voice mail, irons, hair dryers. Some: fax. **Leisure Activities:** nature trails. **Guest Services:** [BP] meal plan available, area transportation, coin laundry. **Business Services:** conference facilities, fax. **Cards:** AE, CB, DI, DS, JC, MC, VI. *(See color ad p 414)*

SOME UNITS

⊞ ⦵ 🍸 🛅 🏊 🚣 🐾 🍴 🖨 💻 📠 / ⊠ VCR 🖨 🔔 /
   FEE   FEE   FEE   FEE

SUPER 8 OF GAINESVILLE
Phone: (352)372-3654

2/16-3/31	1P: $42	2P: $45	XP: $5 F13
4/1-10/31	1P: $42	2P: $44	XP: $5 F13
12/1-2/15	1P: $40	2P: $43	XP: $4 F13
11/1-11/30	1P: $40	2P: $43	XP: $5 F13

Motel
Location: I-75, exit 74E, 441 N. 2000 SW 13th St 32608. Fax: 352/335-7936. **Facility:** Close to Shands Hospital. 40 units. 2 stories, exterior corridors. **Terms:** 7 day cancellation notice. **Amenities:** extended cable TV. **Business Services:** fax. **Cards:** AE, DI, DS, MC, VI. **Special Amenities:** free continental breakfast and free local telephone calls.

SOME UNITS

SÐ ⦵ 🐾 📠 / ⊠ 🖨 🔔 /

SWEETWATER BRANCH INN BED & BREAKFAST
Phone: 352/373-6760
All Year   1P: $85-$150   2P: $85-$150   XP: $20   D14
▼▼▼
Bed & Breakfast
Location: SR 26; 1.3 mi e of the University (US 441); 7.3 mi e of I-75, exit 76. 625 E University Ave 32601. Fax: 352/371-3771. **Facility:** A restored 1885 Victorian home with antique furnished rooms. Three with working fireplace. Designated smoking area. 13 units. Some suites ($125-$150) and whirlpool units ($125-$150). 2 stories, interior corridors. **Terms:** 7 day cancellation notice-fee imposed, weekly & monthly rates available. **Amenities:** extended cable TV, voice mail, irons, hair dryers. **Guest Services:** [BP] meal plan available, complimentary evening beverages. **Business Services:** meeting rooms, fax. **Cards:** AE, MC, VI.

🐾 / ⊠ 🖨 📠
FEE

---

*The following lodging was either not evaluated or did not
meet AAA rating requirements but is listed for your information only.*

UNIVERSITY OF FLORIDA HOTEL & CONFERENCE CENTER
Phone: 352/371-3600

[fyi]	8/31-11/30	1P: $129-$199	2P: $129-$199	XP: $10 F17
Motel	2/1-6/30	1P: $109-$199	2P: $109-$199	XP: $10 F17
	12/1-1/31 & 7/1-8/30	1P: $99-$129	2P: $99-$129	XP: $10 F17

Too new to rate. **Location:** I-75, exit 75, e to SW 34th St, then left. 1714 SW 34th St 32607. Fax: 352/371-0306. **Amenities:** 248 units, radios, coffeemakers, pool. **Cards:** AE, DI, DS, MC, VI. *(See color ad below)*

--- **WHERE TO DINE** ---

AMELIA'S
Lunch: $7-$9   **Dinner:** $9-$19   **Phone:** 352/373-1919
▼▼▼
Italian
Location: Just s on SR 329, just e behind Hippodrome Theatre; in Sun Centre Mall; entrance thru courtyard. 235 S Main St 32601. **Hours:** 11:30 am-2:30 & 5-10 pm, Fri-11 pm, Sat 5 pm-11 pm, Sun 5 pm-9 pm. Closed major holidays; also Mon. **Reservations:** suggested; weekends. **Features:** casual dress; cocktails; street parking. A charming, cozy atmosphere and a courtyard setting can be found in the historic district. Olive oil complements the warm loaf of Italian bread and crisp, green salad. A chicken liver, onion and mushroom dish is a tasty departure from traditional entrees. **Cards:** AE, DI, MC, VI.

⊠

THE SOVEREIGN RESTAURANT **Dinner:** $18-$27 **Phone:** 352/378-6307

Continental

Location: Just e of SR 329. 12 SE 2nd Ave 32601. **Hours:** 5:30 pm-10 pm, Fri & Sat-11 pm. Closed major holidays; also Sun & middle 2 weeks of Aug. **Reservations:** suggested. **Features:** casual dress; cocktails; street parking. Located in the historic district in a rustic converted carriage house, this local favorite features specialties like sweetbread and a decent wine selection. The margarita pie is prepared in-house and will bring a rich ending to a wonderful dinner. **Cards:** AE, CB, DI, DS, MC, VI.

STEVE'S CAFE AMERICAIN **Dinner:** $15-$26 **Phone:** 352/377-9337

American

Location: Just w of Main St (SR 329). 12 W University Ave 32601. **Hours:** 5 pm-10 pm. Closed major holidays. **Reservations:** accepted. **Features:** casual dress; cocktail lounge. This restaurant is located in a storefront in the older section of downtown. The service is attentive and friendly. The menu offers a variety of well-prepared dishes with a wide selection of homemade desserts to tempt any sweet tooth. Smoke free premises. **Cards:** AE, MC, VI.

GOLDEN GATE pop. 14,100

——— WHERE TO STAY ———

QUALITY INN & SUITES GOLF RESORT **Phone:** (941)455-1010

SAVE

Motor Inn

12/1-1/3	1P: $65-$119	2P: $65-$119
2/1-4/15	1P: $119	2P: $119
1/4-1/31	1P: $95	2P: $95
4/16-11/30	1P: $65	2P: $65

Location: I-75, exit 15, 1.6 mi n via SR 951 (Isle of Capri Rd). 4100 Golden Gate Pkwy 34116. Fax: 941/455-4038. **Facility:** On golf course. 153 units. 10 two-bedroom units and 31 efficiencies. Some suites ($109-$288). 2-4 stories, interior/exterior corridors. **Terms:** cancellation fee imposed, weekly rates available, package plans. **Leisure Activities:** heated pool, whirlpool, 2 lighted tennis courts. **Fee:** golf-18 holes. **Guest Services:** valet laundry. **Business Services:** meeting rooms. **Cards:** AE, CB, DI, DS, MC, VI.

SOME UNITS

GREEN COVE SPRINGS —See Jacksonville p. 443.

GULF BREEZE pop. 5,500

——— WHERE TO DINE ———

THE CREAMERY CAFE **Lunch:** $5-$7 **Dinner:** $6-$11 **Phone:** 850/932-1525

Regional German

Location: US 98; at Gulf Breeze Shopping Ctr. 348 Gulf Breeze Pkwy 32561. **Hours:** 8 am-9 pm. Closed: 11/22, 12/25. **Features:** casual dress; children's menu; carryout; beer only. Stop on the way to or from the coast at this family run cafe. As the name so aptly describes, creamy delicious ice cream is a must at this delightful eatery. This is not their only feature, lunch and dinner selections include German and Gulf Coast style soup, sandwiches and entrees. Complimentary glass of wine served with a dinner entree. Smoke free premises. **Cards:** AE, DS, MC, VI.

GULFPORT —See Tampa Bay p. 862.

HAINES CITY pop. 11,700

——— WHERE TO STAY ———

BEST WESTERN LAKE HAMILTON **Phone:** (863)421-6929

AAA SAVE

Motel

2/10-4/20	1P: $71-$91	2P: $71-$91
12/1-2/9	1P: $64-$84	2P: $64-$84
4/21-8/16	1P: $49-$74	2P: $49-$74
8/17-11/30	1P: $49-$69	2P: $49-$69

Location: On US 27, just s of jct SR 544, 2 mi s of jct US 17/92. 605 B Moore Rd 33844. Fax: 863/422-0409. **Facility:** In rural area. Large, contemporary rooms and 1-bedroom suites. Lovely grounds with covered picnic tables and inviting pool. Set back off highway. Discounted privileges at nearby golf club. 50 units. Some suites. 1 story, exterior corridors. **Terms:** package plans. **Amenities:** extended cable TV. **Leisure Activities:** heated pool, putting green, lighted tennis court, shuffleboard. **Guest Services:** coin laundry. **Business Services:** meeting rooms. **Cards:** AE, CB, DI, DS, JC, MC, VI. **Special Amenities:** early check-in/late check-out and free continental breakfast.

SOME UNITS

HOWARD JOHNSON INN **Phone:** 863/422-8621

AAA SAVE

Motor Inn

			F18
All Year	2P: $49-$89	XP: $5	

Location: US 27, 1.8 mi s of jct US 17/92. 1504 US 27S 33844. Fax: 863/421-4745. **Facility:** 120 units. 2 stories, exterior corridors. **Terms:** cancellation fee imposed, weekly & monthly rates available, package plans, pets ($10 extra charge). **Dining:** restaurant, 6:30 am-9 pm, $5-$14, cocktails. **Leisure Activities:** heated pool. **Guest Services:** coin laundry. **Business Services:** meeting rooms. **Cards:** AE, CB, DI, DS, MC, VI. **Special Amenities:** early check-in/late check-out and preferred room (subject to availability with advanced reservations).

SOME UNITS

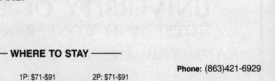

FEE FEE

HALLANDALE —See Fort Lauderdale p. 379.

HAVANA pop. 1,700

——— WHERE TO DINE ———

NICHOLSON FARMHOUSE   Historical   **Dinner:** $10-$26   **Phone:** 850/539-5931
▼▼▼ ▼▼▼   **Location:** SR 12, 3.5 mi w of US 27. SR 12 32333. **Hours:** 4 pm-10 pm. Closed major holidays; also Sun &
            Mon. **Reservations:** suggested. **Features:** casual dress; children's menu; carryout. This complex of five
Steak House historic houses on 40 rustic acres is an unusual location in which to enjoy monstrous portions of quality
            beef, well-aged and cooked to order. Down-to-earth servers are attentive and friendly. Save room for
strawberry shortcake. **Cards:** AE, DS, MC, VI.   ☒

HEATHROW —See Orlando p. 631.

HERNANDO pop. 2,100

——— WHERE TO STAY ———

BEST WESTERN CITRUS HILLS LODGE   **Phone:** (352)527-0015
▼▼▼▼ ▼▼▼▼   12/1-4/30 & 11/1-11/30   1P: $85-$95   2P: $85-$95   XP: $7   F18
            5/1-10/31   1P: $75-$85   2P: $75-$85   XP: $7   F18
Motor Inn   **Location:** On CR 486 at jct Citrus Hills Blvd, 3.3 mi w of US 41. 350 E Norvell Bryant Hwy 34442. Fax: 352/527-2360.
            Facility: 50 units. Some whirlpool units ($85-$95). *Bath:* combo or shower only. 2 stories, exterior corridors.
Terms: 14 day cancellation notice, weekly rates available, package plans, small pets only ($10 fee). **Amenities:** extended cable
TV, voice mail. **Leisure Activities:** heated pool. **Guest Services:** [CP] meal plan available, gift shop, coin laundry. *Fee:* mas-
sage. **Business Services:** meeting rooms, fax. **Cards:** AE, CB, DI, DS, JC, MC, VI.   SOME UNITS

(ASK) (S🐾) (🐾) (🍴) (🏠) (🎧) (🏊) (🎦) (💻) (DATA PORT) / (☒) (🖼) (🔌) /

——— WHERE TO DINE ———

ANDRE'S OF CITRUS HILLS   **Lunch:** $6-$10   **Dinner:** $13-$20   **Phone:** 352/746-6855
▼▼▼ ▼▼▼   **Location:** 1 mi s of CR 486 on Citrus Hills Blvd; 3.3 mi w of US 441; at Citrus Hills Country Club. 505 E Hartford St
            34442. **Hours:** 11:30 am-9 pm, Fri-9:30 pm, Sat & Sun noon-9:30 pm. Closed: 12/25; also 12/24.
American   **Features:** dressy casual; children's menu; salad bar; cocktails & lounge; buffet. Voted Best Atmosphere in
            Citrus County, 1999, this country club restaurant offers informal dining overlooking a golf course. House
specialties include baked prime rib, ostrich and seafood FraDiablo. Peruse the "Wall of Fame" featuring George Bush.
Cards: AE, DI, DS, MC, VI.   ☒

HIALEAH —See Miami-Miami Beach p. 518.

HIGHLAND BEACH pop. 3,200

——— WHERE TO STAY ———

HOLIDAY INN-HIGHLAND BEACH   **Phone:** (561)278-6241
▼▼▼ ▼▼▼   12/22-1/6 & 1/7-4/30   1P: $199
            12/1-12/21 & 5/1-11/30   1P: $109
Motor Inn   **Location:** SR A1A, 1 mi s of Linton Blvd. 2809 S Ocean Blvd 33487. Fax: 561/278-7133. **Facility:** Some rooms with
            balcony; few oceanfront. Nicely appointed rooms. 114 units. Some suites. *Bath:* combo or shower only. 3-6
stories, interior/exterior corridors. **Terms:** package plans. **Amenities:** extended cable TV, dual phone lines, voice mail, safes,
irons, hair dryers. **Leisure Activities:** heated pool, wading pool, beach, swimming, exercise room. *Fee:* beach cabanas. **Guest
Services:** gift shop, coin laundry. **Business Services:** meeting rooms. *Fee:* fax. **Cards:** AE, CB, DI, DS, JC, MC, VI.
                                                                                                        SOME UNITS

(ASK) (S🐾) (🍴) (🍸) (🏊) (🎧) (🏊) (🖼) (💻) (DATA PORT) / (☒) (🖼) (🔌) /

HIGH SPRINGS pop. 3,100

——— WHERE TO STAY ———

GRADY HOUSE INN   **Phone:** (904)454-2206
▼▼▼ ▼▼▼   All Year   1P: $89-$119   2P: $89-$119   XP: $15
            Location: 0.5 mi n on US 27. 420 NW 1st Ave 32643 (PO Box 205, 32655). Fax: 904/454-3486. **Facility:** 1917 home
Historic Bed with extensive collection of reproduction and original artwork. On National Register of Historic Places. Des-
& Breakfast   ignated smoking area. 5 units. *Bath:* combo or shower only. 2 stories, interior corridors. **Terms:** age restric-
            tions may apply, 7 day cancellation notice-fee imposed, package plans. **Amenities:** no TVs. **Guest Services:**
[BP] meal plan available. **Cards:** AE, DI, DS, MC, VI.

                                                                          (🍴) (☒) (📞)

THE RUSTIC INN BED & BREAKFAST   **Phone:** 904/454-1223
▼▼▼ ▼▼▼   All Year   1P: $79-$89   2P: $79-$89   XP: $10
            Location: 2.2 mi s on US 27/41. 3105 S Main St 32643. Fax: 904/454-1225. **Facility:** Spacious, modern rooms
Motel   detached from owner's residence. Each room uniquely themed to animals of endangered species, with
            many whimsical touches. TV's upon request. Breakfast served in the rooms. Smoke free premises. 6 units. 1 story,
exterior corridors. **Terms:** 7 day cancellation notice-fee imposed, weekly rates available. **Amenities:** no TVs. **Leisure Activities:** hiking trails. **Guest Services:** [CP] meal plan available. **Cards:** AE, MC, VI.

                                                                (🏊) (☒) (🖼) (💻) (🔌) (🔌)

——— WHERE TO DINE ———

THE GREAT OUTDOORS TRADING
COMPANY & CAFE　Historical　　　　　**Lunch:** $6-$13　　　　**Dinner:** $6-$15　　　　**Phone:** 904/454-2900
　　　　　　Location: Center; on US 27/41. 65 N Main St 32643. **Hours:** 10 am-9 pm, Fri-10 pm, Sat 9 am-10 pm, Sun 9
　　　　　　am-9 pm; hours may vary in winter. Closed: 11/22, 12/25; also Sun, in season. **Features:** casual dress;
　American　　Sunday brunch; carryout; beer & wine only; a la carte. Set in a refurbished early 1900s barber shop, the
　　　　　　cozy restaurant is noted for down-home food such as corn bread and chicken with stuffing. If you need a
jolt, peruse the wide selection of espresso drinks or shoot for sugar shock with a homemade dessert. Smoke free premises.
Cards: AE, DI, DS, MC, VI.

HILLSBORO BEACH —*See Fort Lauderdale p. 380.*

HOLIDAY —*See Tampa Bay p. 863.*

HOLLYWOOD —*See Fort Lauderdale p. 380.*

HOLMES BEACH pop. 4,800 　(See map p. 764; index p. 767)

——— WHERE TO STAY ———

THE BEACH INN　　　　　　　　　　　　　　　　　　**Phone:** (941)778-9597　　84
　(AAA) (SAVE)　　5/1-11/30　　　　　　　　　　　2P: $129-$209　　　XP: $25
　　　　　　12/1-4/30　　　　　　　　　　　　2P: $99-$199　　　　XP: $25
　　　　　　Location: On CR 789, 1.5 mi n of jct SR 64. 101 66th St 34217. Fax: 941/778-8303. **Facility:** Gulf front. Four
　Motel　　　rooms with gas burning remote control fireplace. Designated smoking area. 18 units, 4 with kitchen. Some
　　　　　　suites and whirlpool units ($209-$239). 2 stories, exterior corridors. **Terms:** 14 day cancellation notice,
　　　　　　weekly & monthly rates available. **Amenities:** voice mail, irons, hair dryers. **Leisure Activities:** heated pool,
beach. **Guest Services:** [ECP] meal plan available, coin laundry. **Business Services:** fax. **Cards:** MC, VI. **Special Amenities:**
free local telephone calls.

SOME UNITS

HARRINGTON HOUSE BEACHFRONT BED & BREAKFAST　　　**Phone:** (941)778-5444　　85
　(AAA) (SAVE)　　12/17-4/30　　　　　　　　　　　2P: $179-$249　　　XP: $25
　　　　　　12/1-12/16 & 5/1-11/30　　　　　　　2P: $129-$249　　　XP: $25
　　　　　　Location: 1.2 mi n of jct SR 64, on CR 789. 5626 Gulf Dr 34217. Fax: 941/778-0527. **Facility:** Coquina block struc-
　　　　　　ture built in 1925. Beautifully decorated public areas. Nicely landscaped grounds with gazebo. Small groups
　Bed & Breakfast　only for meetings in dining room or in beach house. Available for small weddings. Fireplace in some units.
　　　　　　Smoke free premises. 16 units. Some suites and whirlpool units. *Bath:* combo or shower only. 3 stories,
interior/exterior corridors. **Terms:** age restrictions may apply, 14 day cancellation notice-fee imposed, weekly & monthly rates
available. **Amenities:** voice mail, irons, hair dryers. **Dining:** popcorn & cookie time. **Leisure Activities:** heated pool, beach, sea
kayaks, bicycles. **Guest Services:** [BP] meal plan available, gift shop. **Business Services:** meeting rooms, PC, fax.
Cards: MC, VI. **Special Amenities: free local telephone calls and preferred room (subject to availability with advanced
reservations).**

SOME UNITS

——— WHERE TO DINE ———

OOH LA LA!　　　　　　　　**Lunch:** $5-$15　　　　**Dinner:** $18-$27　　　　**Phone:** 941/778-5320　　44
　　　　　　Location: Just off Gulf Dr; in Island Shopping Center. 5406 Marina Dr 34217. **Hours:** 8 am-2:30 & 5:30-9:30 pm,
　French　　Sun 8 am-1:30 & 5:30-9 pm. Closed: Mon. **Features:** casual dress; carryout; beer & wine only. Located in
　　　　　　an older strip mall setting, this small but quaint bistro type setting with it's French flair for decor; offers a
friendly, welcoming staff ready to serve such items as veal, salmon, lamb, duck, venison, omelettes and
croissants all freshly prepared by the owner/chef. Try the potato-crusted grouper with it's rich variety of spices and a wonderful
gravy blend. Wine available with top California selections. Smoke free premises. **Cards:** MC, VI.

HOMESTEAD —*See Miami-Miami Beach p. 519.*

HOMOSASSA pop. 2,100

——— WHERE TO STAY ———

THE LAST RESORT　　　　　　　　　　　　　　　　**Phone:** 352/628-7117
　　　　　　All Year　　　　　1P: $90　　　　2P: $90　　　　XP: $10　　　F10
　　　　　　Location: 2.5 mi w of US 19/98. 10738 W Halls River Rd 34448. Fax: 352/628-0036. **Facility:** Set on the Homo-
　Apartment　sassa River. Stilt cottages. 6 units with kitchen. 1 story, exterior corridors. **Terms:** daily & monthly rates avail-
　　　　　　able. **Amenities:** extended cable TV. **Leisure Activities:** boat dock, fishing. **Guest Services:** coin laundry.
Cards: AE, DS, MC, VI.

——— WHERE TO DINE ———

K C CRUMP RESTAURANT　　　　　　**Dinner:** $11-$22　　　　　　　**Phone:** 352/628-1500
　　　　　　Location: 3.5 mi w of US 19 via CR 490A. 11210 W Halls River Rd 34448. **Hours:** noon-2:30 & 4-9 pm, Fri &
　　　　　　Sat-10 pm, Sun noon-9 pm. Closed: 12/25. **Reservations:** suggested. **Features:** casual dress; children's
　Seafood　　menu; carryout; cocktails & lounge. A converted 19th-century fishing lodge set on the scenic Homosassa
　　　　　　River, this popular lunch and dinner spot features fresh local shrimp, seafood and steak choices. Savor the
tender filet served with a baked potato and fresh vegetables. **Cards:** MC, VI.

HOWEY-IN-THE-HILLS —*See Orlando p. 631.*

INDIALANTIC pop. 2,800

—— WHERE TO STAY ——

BUDGET LODGE
Phone: (321)779-9994

Motor Inn

12/1-4/30	1P: $42-$99	2P: $52-$150	XP: $10
5/1-11/30	1P: $39-$89	2P: $49-$110	XP: $10

Location: 0.4 mi s of SR 518 (Eau Gallie Cswy). 2900 N A1A Hwy 32903. Fax: 321/779-3933. **Facility:** 2 blocks to beach access. Designated smoking area. 26 units, 6 with kitchen. 2 stories, exterior corridors. **Terms:** 5 day cancellation notice, weekly & monthly rates available, small pets only ($10 extra charge). **Amenities:** extended cable TV. **Dining:** restaurant, 11 am-9 pm, Fri & Sat-11 pm, $9-$10. **Leisure Activities:** small pool, whirlpool. **Guest Services:** coin laundry. **Cards:** AE, CB, DI, DS, MC, VI.

CASABLANCA INN
Phone: (321)728-7188

Motel

1/1-4/30		2P: $65-$85	XP: $5	F18
5/1-8/31		2P: $55-$75	XP: $5	F18
12/1-12/31 & 9/1-11/30		2P: $45-$65	XP: $5	F18

Location: SR A1A, 1.8 mi s of SR 518 (Eau Gallie Cswy). 1805 N Hwy A1A 32903. Fax: 321/728-1462. **Facility:** Lovely older property with large rooms. 34 units, 26 with kitchen. *Bath:* combo or shower only. 2 stories, exterior corridors. **Terms:** 3 day cancellation notice, weekly & monthly rates available, pets ($5 extra charge, small house pets only). **Guest Services:** coin laundry. **Cards:** AE, DS, MC, VI.

HOLIDAY INN MELBOURNE OCEANFRONT
Phone: (321)777-4100

Motor Inn

2/1-4/15	1P: $99-$129	2P: $99-$129	
4/16-8/15	1P: $89-$109	2P: $89-$109	
12/1-1/31 & 8/16-11/30	1P: $79-$99	2P: $79-$99	

Location: SR A1A, 2.3 mi n of jct US 192. 2605 N SR A1A 32903. Fax: 321/773-6132. **Facility:** Wood deck overlooks beach and ocean. Some rooms with ocean view. 295 units. 1 two-bedroom unit. Some suites ($129-$199). 5-8 stories, interior/exterior corridors. **Parking:** on-site. **Terms:** check-in 4 pm, weekly & monthly rates available, package plans. **Amenities:** extended cable TV, voice mail, irons, hair dryers. **Dining:** restaurant, 6:30 am-2 & 5-10 pm, $10-$20, cocktails. **Leisure Activities:** heated pool, whirlpool, beach, swimming, charter fishing, 2 tennis courts, playground, exercise room, volleyball, game room. **Guest Services:** [BP] & [CP] meal plans available, gift shop, valet and coin laundry. **Business Services:** conference facilities. **Cards:** AE, CB, DI, DS, JC, MC, VI. *(See color ad p 470)*

MELBOURNE BEACH HILTON OCEANFRONT
Phone: (321)777-5000

Motor Inn

1/2-5/31	1P: $129-$229	XP: $10	F18
12/1-1/1 & 6/1-11/30	1P: $99-$139	XP: $10	F18

Location: N SR A1A, 3 mi n of jct US 192. 3003 N SR A1A 32903. Fax: 321/777-3713. **Facility:** Sunken heated pool overlooks beach and ocean. Sunken lounge area in lobby overlooks pool and ocean. 118 units. 11 stories, interior corridors. **Terms:** cancellation fee imposed, package plans, pets ($25 deposit). **Amenities:** voice mail, irons, hair dryers. **Dining:** restaurant, 7 am-2 & 5-10 pm, $15-$25, cocktails. **Leisure Activities:** heated pool, whirlpool, beach, swimming, exercise room. *Fee:* beach items. **Guest Services:** gift shop, valet laundry. **Business Services:** conference facilities, PC, fax. **Cards:** AE, CB, DI, DS, JC, MC, VI. *(See color ad p 469 & ad p 44)*

MELBOURNE OCEANFRONT QUALITY SUITES HOTEL
Phone: (321)723-4222

Suite Motor Inn

12/17-1/1	1P: $159-$199	2P: $159-$199	XP: $10	F18
1/2-4/30	1P: $109-$169	2P: $119-$189	XP: $10	F18
12/1-12/16 & 5/1-11/30	1P: $109-$139	2P: $109-$139	XP: $10	F18

Location: SR A1A, 1.5 mi n of jct US 192. 1665 N SR A1A 32903. Fax: 321/768-2438. **Facility:** Ocean and river views from 2nd floor balconies up. Rooms with contemporary decor and cassette am/fm stereo system. 208 units. Some suites. 9 stories, exterior corridors. **Terms:** weekly & monthly rates available, pets ($10 extra charge, $25 deposit). **Amenities:** video games, voice mail, safes, honor bars, irons, hair dryers. **Dining:** restaurant, 6:30-10 am, 11:30-9 pm, Fri & Sat 7 am-10 & noon-10 pm, Sun 7 am-10, noon-9 pm, $8-$16, cocktails. **Leisure Activities:** whirlpool, beach, swimming, heated pool with underwater sound system, game room. *Fee:* fishing equipment. **Guest Services:** [ECP] meal plan available, gift shop, coin laundry. **Business Services:** meeting rooms. **Cards:** AE, CB, DI, DS, JC, MC, VI. *(See color ad p 469)*

OCEANFRONT COTTAGES
Phone: 321/725-8474

Cottage

All Year	1P: $99-$135	2P: $99-$135	XP: $15

Location: Just s of e end of US 192. 612 Wavecrest Ave 32903. Fax: 208/723-2067. **Facility:** Cottages with 1-bedroom suites, all with balcony or patio. Quaint poolside courtyard. 2 suites with fireplace. Smoke free premises. 4 units with kitchen. *Bath:* combo or shower only. 2 stories, exterior corridors. **Terms:** age restrictions may apply, 60 day cancellation notice-fee imposed, weekly rates available, small pets only ($15 extra charge). **Amenities:** extended cable TV, irons, hair dryers. **Leisure Activities:** small pool, bicycles. **Guest Services:** coin laundry. **Cards:** MC, VI.

RADISSON SUITE HOTEL OCEANFRONT
Phone: (321)773-9260

Motor Inn

1/29-4/30	1P: $130	2P: $130	XP: $10	F10
12/1-1/28 & 5/1-11/30	1P: $120	2P: $120	XP: $10	F10

Location: 3.2 mi n of jct US 192. 3101 N Hwy A1A 32903. Fax: 321/777-3190. **Facility:** All rooms with balcony overlooking ocean and beach. Wood sun deck overlooks beach. Designated smoking area. 168 units, 6 with efficiency. Some whirlpool units. 16 stories, exterior corridors. **Terms:** check-in 4 pm, cancellation fee imposed, package plans. **Amenities:** extended cable TV, video games, safes, irons, hair dryers. **Leisure Activities:** heated pool, whirlpools, beach, swimming. **Guest Services:** valet and coin laundry. **Business Services:** conference facilities. **Cards:** AE, DI, DS, MC, VI.

THE TUCKAWAY SHORES RESORT

AAA [SAVE]

Motel

				Phone: (321)723-3355
2/1-4/30	1P: $90-$110	2P: $90-$110	XP: $9	F
12/16-1/31	1P: $75-$90	2P: $75-$90	XP: $9	F
5/1-11/30	1P: $70-$80	2P: $70-$80	XP: $9	F
12/1-12/15	1P: $65-$75	2P: $65-$75	XP: $9	F

Location: SR A1A, 0.8 mi s of jct US 192. 1441 S Miramar Ave 32903. **Fax:** 321/727-1441. **Facility:** Rooms with mix of furnishing types, some with patio or balcony. Nicely landscaped pool area with small clubhouse. Designated smoking area. 31 efficiencies. 3 stories (no elevator), exterior corridors. **Terms:** 3 day cancellation notice-fee imposed, weekly rates available. **Amenities:** extended cable TV. **Leisure Activities:** beach, swimming. **Guest Services:** coin laundry. **Business Services:** meeting rooms. **Cards:** AE, DI, DS, MC, VI.
SOME UNITS

⟨S⟩ ⟨D⟩ ⟨swim⟩ ⟨film⟩ ⟨TV⟩ / ⟨box⟩ /

--------- WHERE TO DINE ---------

ELENA'S GREEK AMERICAN RESTAURANT

Greek

Lunch: $4-$13 **Dinner:** $4-$13 **Phone:** 321/779-8050
Location: SR A1A, 2 mi n of jct US 192. 2324 N A1A 32903. **Hours:** 11 am-10 pm, Sat-11 pm, Sun 8 am-2 pm. Closed: 11/22, 12/25; also Mon. **Features:** casual dress; children's menu; carryout; beer & wine only; a la carte. The piquant flavors of Cajun, Creole and Greek dishes spice up the menu at this quaint cafe, which caters to meat lovers and vegetarians alike. The patio captures the classic New Orleans feel. Save some room to indulge in a slice of Jack Daniels pie. **Cards:** DS, MC, VI.
⊠

LEBANESE GOURMET RESTAURANT

Lebanese

DS, MC, VI.

Lunch: $4-$8 **Dinner:** $8-$17 **Phone:** 321/727-8944
Location: Center; on SR 192, just w of A1A. 144 Fifth Ave. **Hours:** 11 am-9:30 pm. Closed: 1/1, 11/22, 12/25; also Sun. **Features:** casual dress; children's menu; carryout; beer & wine only. Authentic Middle Eastern atmosphere with belly dancing nightly via satellite from Lebanon. A delicious taste of classic Middle East and Lebanese cuisine with some Continental items. Be sure to try the Knafeh for dessert. **Cards:** AE, DI,

VILLA PALMA RISTORANTE

Italian

Lunch: $2-$7 **Dinner:** $11-$19 **Phone:** 321/951-0051
Location: US 192, just w of jct SR A1A. 110 Wavecrest Ave 32903. **Hours:** 11:30 am-10 pm, Fri & Sat-10:30 pm. Closed: 11/22, 12/25. **Reservations:** suggested. **Features:** casual dress; children's menu; carryout; beer & wine only. In an authentic Italian atmosphere, the owner/chef makes pasta from scratch. For a nice treat, try the shrimp parni with ziti. Other entrees include beef, chicken, veal and seafood. Parking and entrance on Sixth Ave. Lunch is served upstairs on the deck. **Cards:** AE, DI, DS, MC, VI.
⊠

INDIAN ROCKS BEACH —See Tampa Bay p. 863.

INDIAN SHORES —See Tampa Bay p. 864.

INDIANTOWN pop. 4,800

--------- WHERE TO STAY ---------

SEMINOLE INN

Country Inn

			Phone: 561/597-3777
12/1-5/31	1P: $75-$95	2P: $75-$95	XP: $10 F12
6/1-11/30	1P: $65-$85	2P: $65-$85	

Location: On SR 710. 15885 SW Warfield 34956 (PO Box 1818). **Fax:** 561/597-2883. **Facility:** Renovated Inn built in 1926. Variety of rooms and sizes. Dicken's Christmas with tree lighting. 23 units. 2 stories, interior corridors. **Terms:** 7 day cancellation notice-fee imposed. **Amenities:** extended cable TV, hair dryers. **Guest Services:** [CP] meal plan available. **Business Services:** meeting rooms. **Cards:** AE, DS, MC, VI.
SOME UNITS

⟨ASK⟩ ⟨S⟩ ⟨D⟩ ⟨TI⟩ ⟨swim⟩ ⟨TV⟩ ⟨DATA PORT⟩ / ⟨X⟩ /

INVERNESS pop. 5,800

--------- WHERE TO STAY ---------

THE CROWN HOTEL

Historic Country Inn

			Phone: (352)344-5555
All Year	1P: $40-$70	2P: $60-$80	

Location: Center; just n of jct US 41/SR 44. 109 N Seminole Ave 34450. **Fax:** 352/726-4040. **Facility:** Structure circa 1890s, transformed into English style inn. Small to very small rooms, mostly singles. Victorian decor. 34 units. *Bath:* combo or shower only. 3 stories, interior corridors. **Parking:** limited. **Terms:** weekly & monthly rates available, package plans, small pets only ($10 extra charge). **Guest Services:** [AP] & [ECP] meal plans available, gift shop. **Business Services:** meeting rooms, fax. **Cards:** AE, DI, MC, VI.
SOME UNITS

⟨ASK⟩ ⟨S⟩ ⟨D⟩ ⟨pet⟩ ⟨TI⟩ ⟨Y⟩ ⟨swim⟩ ⟨DATA PORT⟩ / ⟨X⟩ /

--------- WHERE TO DINE ---------

COACH'S PUB & EATERY

American

Lunch: $10-$18 **Dinner:** $10-$18 **Phone:** 352/344-3333
Location: Downtown; adjacent to courthouse. 114 W Main St 34450. **Hours:** 10 am-11:30 pm, Fri & Sat-midnight, Sun noon-11:30 pm. **Features:** No A/C; casual dress; carryout; cocktails; a la carte. Racing car hoods, college and professional sports banners highlight an entire wall in this sports bar themed restaurant. Try the Pub fare featuring sandwiches, salads and chili. Extensive selection of 40 drafts and 70 bottled beers. Pool tables. **Cards:** MC, VI.

ISLAMORADA —See The Florida Keys p. 312.

Destination Jacksonville
pop. 635,200

*T*he principal city of Florida's First Coast, Jacksonville is no longer known just as a banking and insurance center.

*I*ts nearby beaches are meccas for sun worshipers. The PGA thought so much of the area it established its tour headquarters here. And architecture buffs revel in the Victorian atmosphere of Amelia Island.

Jacksonville skyline.
A skyline enhanced by contemporary sky-scrapers and riverfront marketplaces defines northeast Florida's hub city.

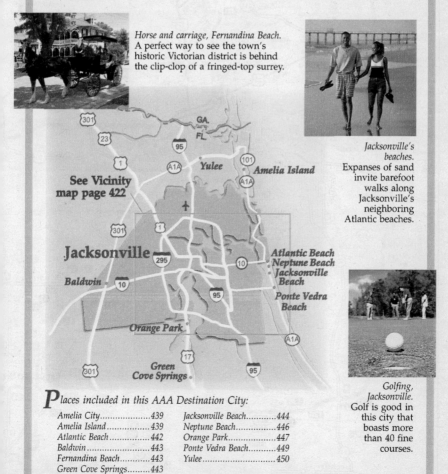

Horse and carriage, Fernandina Beach.
A perfect way to see the town's historic Victorian district is behind the clip-clop of a fringed-top surrey.

Jacksonville's beaches.
Expanses of sand invite barefoot walks along Jacksonville's neighboring Atlantic beaches.

See Vicinity map page 422

Jacksonville

Baldwin

Atlantic Beach
Neptune Beach
Jacksonville Beach
Ponte Vedra Beach

Orange Park

Green Cove Springs

Golfing, Jacksonville.
Golf is good in this city that boasts more than 40 fine courses.

*P*laces included in this AAA Destination City:

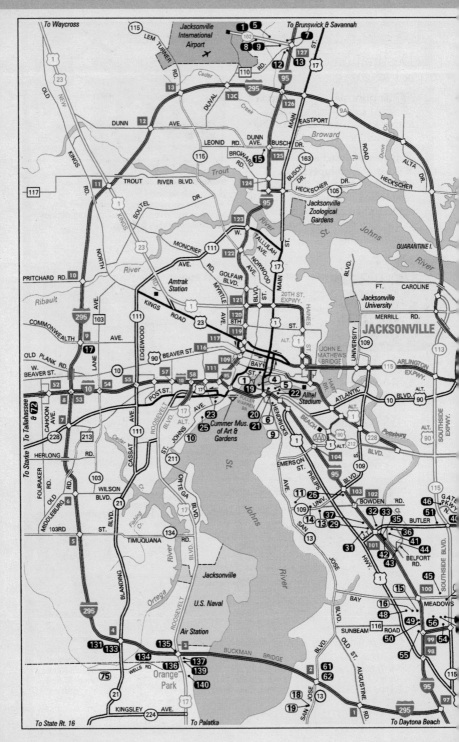

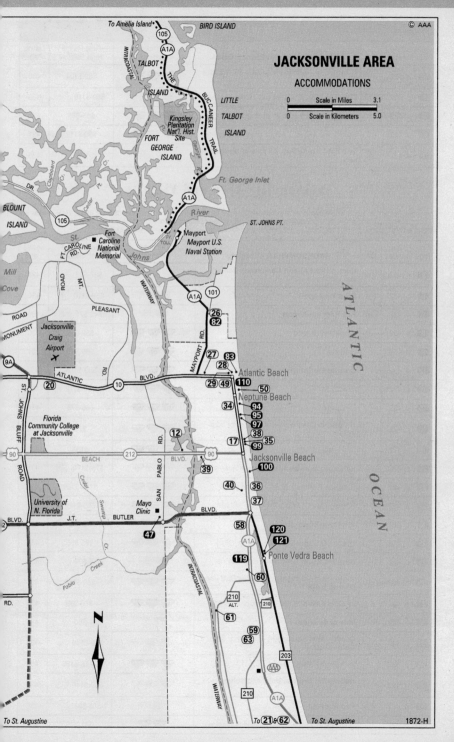

© AAA

JACKSONVILLE AREA

ACCOMMODATIONS

Scale in Miles		
0		3.1
Scale in Kilometers		
0		5.0

1872-H

✈ Airport Accommodations

Spotter/Map Page Number	OA	JACKSONVILLE INTERNATIONAL	Diamond Rating	Rate Range High Season	Listing Page
12 / p. 422		Courtyard by Marriott Jax Airport I-95, 2.5 mi e of terminal	◇◇◇	$89-$104	430
5 / p. 422	ⒶⒶⒶ	**Days Inn Airport, 2.3 mi e of terminal at I-95**	◇◇◇	$59-$110 SAVE	430
9 / p. 422		Hampton Inn, 2.3 mi e of terminal at I-95	◇◇◇	$65-$85	431
13 / p. 422		Holiday Inn Airport, 2.5 mi e of terminal at I-95	◇◇◇	$80-$112	431
7 / p. 422	ⒶⒶⒶ	**Red Roof Inn-Airport, 2.5 mi e of terminal at I-95**	◇◇	$45-$71 SAVE	436

Jacksonville Area and Vicinity

This index helps you "spot" where approved accommodations are located on the corresponding detailed maps. Rate ranges are for comparison only and show the property's high season. Turn to the listing page for more detailed rate information and consult display ads for special promotions. Restaurant rate range is for dinner, unless only lunch (L) is served.

Spotter/Map Page Number	OA	JACKSONVILLE - Lodgings	Diamond Rating	Rate Range High Season	Listing Page
1 / p. 422	ⒶⒶⒶ	**Clarion Hotel Airport Conference Center -** see color ad p 429	◇◇◇	$87-$95 SAVE	428
5 / p. 422	ⒶⒶⒶ	**Days Inn Airport**	◇◇◇	$59-$110 SAVE	430
7 / p. 422	ⒶⒶⒶ	**Red Roof Inn-Airport**	◇◇	$45-$71 SAVE	436
8 / p. 422		Fairfield Inn Airport	◇◇◇	$59-$65	430
9 / p. 422		Hampton Inn	◇◇◇	$65-$85	431
12 / p. 422		Courtyard by Marriott Jax Airport I-95	◇◇◇	$89-$104	430
13 / p. 422		Holiday Inn Airport	◇◇◇	$80-$112	431
15 / p. 422		La Quinta Inn-North - see color ad p 434	◇◇◇	$65-$75	434
17 / p. 422		Holiday Inn-Commonwealth - see color ad p 432	◇◇◇	$79	432
19 / p. 422		Omni Jacksonville Hotel - see color ad p 434	◇◇◇	$134	435
20 / p. 422	ⒶⒶⒶ	**Hilton Jacksonville Riverfront - see ad p 44**	◇◇◇	$75-$179 SAVE	431
21 / p. 422		Radisson Riverwalk Hotel - see ad p 435	◇◇◇	$119-$189	436
22 / p. 422		Hampton Inn Central	◇◇◇	$69-$115	431
23 / p. 422	ⒶⒶⒶ	**Plantation Manor Inn**	◇◇◇◇	$135-$175 SAVE	435
25 / p. 422		House On Cherry Street	◇◇◇	$85-$95	433
26 / p. 422	ⒶⒶⒶ	**Days Inn South - see color ad p 430**	◇◇	$55-$99 SAVE	430
29 / p. 422		Jacksonville Courtyard at J T Butler Blvd - see color ad p 429	◇◇◇	$69-$149	433
31 / p. 422		La Quinta Inn & Suites - see color ad p 434	◇◇◇	$79-$99	433
32 / p. 422	ⒶⒶⒶ	**Inns of America**	◇◇	$54-$60 SAVE	433
33 / p. 422	ⒶⒶⒶ	**Quality Hotel Southpoint - see color ad p 427**	◇◇◇	$59-$149 SAVE	435
35 / p. 422		Jacksonville Marriott Hotel	◇◇◇	$178-$188	433
36 / p. 422	ⒶⒶⒶ	**Holiday Inn Express Hotel and Suites - see color ad p 432**	◇◇◇	$59-$140 SAVE	432
37 / p. 422	ⒶⒶⒶ	**Red Roof Inn**	◇◇	$65-$87 SAVE	436
40 / p. 422		Homestead Village Guest Studios Southside	◇◇	$41-$49	433

Spotter/Map Page Number	OA	JACKSONVILLE - Lodgings (continued)	Diamond Rating	Rate Range High Season	Listing Page
41 / p. 422	AAA	MainStay Suites-Jacksonville - see color ad p 427	◆◆◆	$80-$90 [SAVE]	434
42 / p. 422	AAA	Hampton Inn Jacksonville I-95 South - see ad p 431	◆◆◆	$79 [SAVE]	431
43 / p. 422	AAA	Club Hotel by Doubletree	◆◆◆	$79-$119 [SAVE]	429
44 / p. 422		Candlewood Suites	◆◆◆	$69-$119	428
45 / p. 422	AAA	Fairfield Inn by Marriott	◆◆	$72-$159 [SAVE]	430
46 / p. 422		Hilton Garden Inn Deerwood Park-Jacksonville, Fl - see ad p 44	◆◆◆	$124	431
47 / p. 422		Courtyard by Marriott - see color ad p 429	◆◆◆	$119-$129	429
48 / p. 422		Homewood Suites	◆◆◆	$149-$189	433
49 / p. 422	AAA	Best Inns of America	◆◆	$45-$48 [SAVE]	428
50 / p. 422		La Quinta Inn-Baymeadows - see color ad p 434	◆◆◆	$69-$75	434
51 / p. 422	AAA	Wellesley Inn & Suites - see color ad opposite title page	◆◆◆	$69-$89 [SAVE]	437
54 / p. 422	AAA	AmeriSuites/BayMeadows - see color ad p 5	◆◆◆	$79-$139 [SAVE]	428
55 / p. 422		Residence Inn by Marriott	◆◆◆	$119-$130	436
56 / p. 422		Holiday Inn Baymeadows	◆◆◆	$59-$79	432
57 / p. 422		Homestead Village Guest Studios-Baymeadows	◆◆◆	$49-$69	432
58 / p. 422	AAA	Embassy Suites Hotel	◆◆◆	$99-$169 [SAVE]	430
61 / p. 422		Baymont Inn & Suites-Jacksonville - see color ad p 428	◆◆	$69-$74	428
62 / p. 422		Ramada Inn Conference Center - see color ad p 435	◆◆◆	$73-$83	436
63 / p. 422		Country Inn & Suites - see color ad p 572	◆◆◆	$75-$100	429
		JACKSONVILLE - Restaurants			
1 / p. 422		Juliette's	◆◆◆	$17-$25	437
4 / p. 422		River City Brewing Company	◆◆	$12-$20	438
5 / p. 422		Crawdaddy's	◆◆	$15-$22	437
6 / p. 422	AAA	Matthew's	◆◆◆◆	$20-$60	438
9 / p. 422		Wilfried's 24 Miramar	◆◆◆	$23-$28	439
10 / p. 422		Biscotti's Espresso Cafe	◆◆	$7-$17	437
11 / p. 422		Worman's Deli & Bakery	◆	$7-$13	439
12 / p. 422		Marker 32	◆◆◆	$13-$23	438
13 / p. 422		La Cena Ristorante	◆◆	$9-$20	438
14 / p. 422		Siboney Cafe	◆◆	$3-$17	438
15 / p. 422		Bombay Bicycle Club	◆◆	$7-$13	437
16 / p. 422	AAA	Pagoda Chinese Restaurant	◆◆	$8-$19	438
17 / p. 422		Thai Room	◆◆	$4-$14	438
18 / p. 422		Mandarin Dragon	◆◆	$6-$12	438
19 / p. 422		The Tree Steak House	◆◆	$12-$20	438

Spotter/Map Page Number	OA	**JACKSONVILLE - Restaurants (continued)**	Diamond Rating	Rate Range High Season	Listing Page
② / p. 422		Pattaya Thai Restaurant	▽▽	$6-$18	438
㉑ / p. 422		Clark's Fish Camp	▽	$5-$14	437
㉒ / p. 422		Joseph's Italian Restaurant	▽	$7-$15	437
		BALDWIN - Lodgings			
⑫ / p. 422	AAA	**Best Western Inn Baldwin**	▽▽	$45-$95 SAVE	443
		ATLANTIC BEACH - Lodgings			
⑫ / p. 422	AAA	**Comfort Inn Mayport**	▽▽▽	$59-$89 SAVE	442
⑬ / p. 422	AAA	**Sea Turtle Inn - see color ad p 442**	▽▽▽	$109-$189 SAVE	442
		ATLANTIC BEACH - Restaurants			
㉖ / p. 422		Mayport Gardens Chinese Restaurant	▽	$4-$7	442
㉗ / p. 422		Sergio's Northern Italian & Continental Cuisine	▽▽	$13-$22	443
㉘ / p. 422		Ragtime Tavern & Seafood Grill	▽▽	$10-$20	442
㉙ / p. 422		Sticky Fingers Restaurant & Bar	▽	$5-$15	443
		JACKSONVILLE BEACH - Lodgings			
⑭ / p. 422		Pelican Path B & B by the Sea	▽▽	$95-$165	445
⑮ / p. 422	AAA	**Holiday Inn Sunspree Resort - see color ad p 445**	▽▽▽	$99-$179 SAVE	444
⑰ / p. 422		Comfort Inn Oceanfront - see color ad p 444	▽▽	$99-$159	444
⑲ / p. 422	AAA	**Best Western Inn & Suites Oceanfront**	▽▽▽	$99-$189 SAVE	444
⑩⓪ / p. 422	AAA	**Days Inn Oceanfront Resort**	▽▽	$105-$155 SAVE	444
		JACKSONVILLE BEACH - Restaurants			
㉞ / p. 422		Billy's	▽▽	$8-$18	445
㉟ / p. 422		Ichiban Japanese Steak House	▽▽	$8-$15	446
㊱ / p. 422		Pagoda Chinese	▽▽	$4-$12	446
㊲ / p. 422		Uli's European Restaurant	▽▽	$9-$20	446
㊳ / p. 422	AAA	**First Street Grille**	▽▽	$14-$19	446
㊴ / p. 422		The Homestead	▽	$7-$14	446
㊵ / p. 422		Ellen's Kitchen	▽	$3-$9(L)	445
		NEPTUNE BEACH - Lodgings			
⑪⓪ / p. 422		Sea Horse Oceanfront Inn	▽▽	$79-$139	446
		NEPTUNE BEACH - Restaurants			
㊾ / p. 422		Sun Dog Diner	▽▽	$5-$10	446
㊿ / p. 422		Mezza Luna Vagabondo Ristorante	▽▽	$10-$19	446
		PONTE VEDRA BEACH - Lodgings			
⑪⑲ / p. 422		Country Inn & Suites By Carlson - see color ad p 572	▽▽▽	$99-$249	449
⑫⓪ / p. 422	AAA	**Ponte Vedra Inn and Club**	▽▽▽▽	$310 SAVE	449
⑫① / p. 422	AAA	**Ponte Vedra Lodge and Club**	▽▽▽▽	$310 SAVE	449
		PONTE VEDRA BEACH - Restaurants			
㊽ / p. 422		J J's Cuisine & Wine	▽▽	$14-$25	450

Spotter/Map Page Number	OA	PONTE VEDRA BEACH - Restaurants (continued)	Diamond Rating	Rate Range High Season	Listing Page
⑤⑨ / p. 422		The Tavern at Sawgrass	♦♦	varies	450
⑥⓪ / p. 422		Gio's Cafe	♦♦♦	$15-$40	450
⑥① / p. 422		Lulu's Waterfront Grill	♦	$12-$18	450
⑥② / p. 422		Eddie's Palm Valley Crossing	♦	$8-$16	449
⑥③ / p. 422		Santioni's of Sawgrass	♦♦	$9-$17	450
		ORANGE PARK - Lodgings			
131 / p. 422		Hampton Inn-Orange Park	♦♦♦	$71-$78	448
133 / p. 422	AAA	**Red Roof Inn-South**	♦♦	$41-$61 SAVE	448
134 / p. 422		La Quinta Inn-Jacksonville/Orange Park - see color ad p 434	♦♦♦	$59-$69	448
136 / p. 422	AAA	**Holiday Inn-Orange Park - see color ad p 447**	♦♦♦	$69-$89 SAVE	448
137 / p. 422	AAA	**Days Inn**	♦♦	$59-$79 SAVE	447
139 / p. 422		Fairfield Inn by Marriott	♦♦♦	$89-$109	447
140 / p. 422	AAA	**Comfort Inn - see color ad p 447**	♦♦♦	$69-$89 SAVE	447
		ORANGE PARK - Restaurant			
⑦⑤ / p. 422		The Hilltop	♦♦	$7-$18	448

JACKSONVILLE (See map p. 422; index p. 424)

──── WHERE TO STAY ────

AMERISUITES/BAYMEADOWS

Phone: (904)737-4477 **54** F18

(AAA) [SAVE]
▼▼▼▼
Suite Motel

All Year   1P: $79-$139   2P: $79-$139   XP: $10

Location: I-95, exit 100, just e off Baymeadows Rd. 8277 Western Way Cir 32256. Fax: 904/739-1649. **Facility:** Business units available with extra large desks with added amenities. 112 efficiencies. Some whirlpool units ($119-$159). 6 stories, interior corridors. **Terms:** small pets only. **Amenities:** voice mail, irons, hair dryers. **Leisure Activities:** heated pool, exercise room. **Guest Services:** [ECP] meal plan available, area transportation-hospitals & Mayo Clinic, coin laundry. **Business Services:** meeting rooms, administrative services. **Cards:** AE, CB, DI, DS, MC, VI. **Special Amenities: free continental breakfast and free newspaper.**
(See color ad p 5)

SOME UNITS

BAYMONT INN & SUITES-JACKSONVILLE

Phone: (904)268-9999 **61**

▼▼▼
Motel

5/25-11/30   1P: $69-$74   2P: $69-$74
12/1-5/24   1P: $64-$69   2P: $64-$69

Location: I-295, exit 2A, northbound; exit 2 southbound, at SR 13. 3199 Hartley Rd 32257. Fax: 904/268-9611. **Facility:** 101 units. 3 stories, interior corridors. **Terms:** small pets only. **Amenities:** video games, voice mail, irons, hair dryers. **Guest Services:** [ECP] meal plan available, coin laundry. **Business Services:** fax. **Cards:** AE, CB, DI, DS, MC, VI. *(See color ad below)*

SOME UNITS

BEST INNS OF AMERICA

Phone: (904)739-3323 **49**

(AAA) [SAVE]
▼▼ ▼▼
Motel

All Year   1P: $45   2P: $48

Location: I-95, exit 101, Baymeadows Rd, just sw. 8220 Dix Ellis Tr 32256. Fax: 904/739-3323. **Facility:** Comfortable unit set-up. Accommodating staff. 109 units. 2 stories, exterior corridors. **Terms:** small pets only. **Amenities:** extended cable TV. **Guest Services:** [BP] meal plan available. **Cards:** AE, CB, DI, DS, MC, VI. **Special Amenities: free continental breakfast and free local telephone calls.**

SOME UNITS

CANDLEWOOD SUITES

Phone: (904)296-7785 **44**

▼▼▼
Extended Stay Motel

All Year   1P: $69-$119

Location: I-95, exit 101, e to Belfort Rd, just s on sw corner. 4990 Belfort Rd 32256. Fax: 904/296-9281. **Facility:** Limited office hours. Well equipped units. 111 efficiencies. Some suites ($99-$119). *Bath:* combo or shower only. 3 stories, interior corridors. **Amenities:** CD players, dual phone lines, voice mail, irons, hair dryers. **Leisure Activities:** exercise room. **Guest Services:** complimentary laundry. **Business Services:** fax. **Cards:** AE, DI, DS, JC, MC, VI.

SOME UNITS

CLARION HOTEL AIRPORT CONFERENCE CENTER

Phone: (904)741-1997 **1**

(AAA) [SAVE]
▼▼▼▼
Hotel

12/1-8/31   1P: $87-$95   2P: $87-$95
9/1-11/30   1P: $79-$87   2P: $79-$87

Location: I-95, exit 127; at the airport terminal. 2101 Dixie Clipper Rd 32218. Fax: 904/741-5520. **Facility:** Attractive pool area by duck pond. 200 units. Some suites ($139-$149) and whirlpool units ($189-$299). *Bath:* combo or shower only. 6 stories, interior/exterior corridors. **Amenities:** video games, dual phone lines, voice mail, irons, hair dryers. **Dining:** restaurant, deli, 6:30 am-11 pm, $14-$20. **Leisure Activities:** whirlpool, exercise room. **Guest Services:** [BP] meal plan available, airport transportation-Jacksonville International, area transportation-within 15 mi, valet laundry. **Business Services:** conference facilities, administrative services, PC, fax. **Cards:** AE, DI, DS, MC, VI. **Special Amenities: free continental breakfast and free local telephone calls.** *(See color ad p 429)*

SOME UNITS

(See map p. 422)

CLUB HOTEL BY DOUBLETREE

					Phone: (904)281-9700	⁴³
(AAA) (SAVE)	12/1-4/1	1P: $79-$119	2P: $89-$119	XP: $10		F18
	4/2-11/30	1P: $79-$99	2P: $79-$99	XP: $10		F18

Motor Inn

Location: I-95, exit 101, just e, then s. 4700 Salisbury Rd 32256. **Fax:** 904/281-1957. **Facility:** Spacious units with added amenities. Close to St Lukes Hospital. 167 units. Some suites ($119-$129). 6 stories, interior corridors. **Terms:** weekly & monthly rates available, package plans. **Amenities:** extended cable TV, irons, hair dryers. **Dining:** coffee shop, 6 am-11 pm. **Leisure Activities:** whirlpool, exercise room. **Guest Services:** area transportation-within 8 mi & Mayo Clinic, valet laundry. **Business Services:** meeting rooms, administrative services. *Fee:* fax. **Cards:** AE, DI, DS, JC, MC, VI. **Special Amenities:** free local telephone calls and free newspaper. SOME UNITS

COUNTRY INN & SUITES

					Phone: (904)772-7771	⁶³
	2/1-3/31	1P: $75-$90	2P: $85-$100	XP: $10		F18
	6/1-11/30	1P: $70-$90	2P: $80-$100	XP: $10		F18
	12/1-1/31 & 4/1-5/31	1P: $70-$85	2P: $80-$95	XP: $10		F18

Motel

Location: I-295, exit 4, se corner. 5945 Youngerman Circle E 32244. **Fax:** 904/772-7071. **Facility:** Comfortably designed units. King units well equipped with desk and ergonomic chair. Short drive to mall and walking distance to movie theatres. 61 units. Some suites ($85-$100) and whirlpool units ($90-$120). *Bath:* combo or shower only. 3 stories, interior corridors. **Terms:** check-in 4 pm. **Amenities:** extended cable TV, voice mail, irons, hair dryers. **Leisure Activities:** exercise room. **Guest Services:** [ECP] meal plan available, coin laundry. **Business Services:** administrative services. *Fee:* PC, fax. **Cards:** AE, DS, MC, VI. *(See color ad p 572)* SOME UNITS

COURTYARD BY MARRIOTT

					Phone: (904)223-1700	⁴⁷
	12/1-4/30	1P: $119	2P: $129	XP: $10		F18
	5/1-11/30	1P: $109	2P: $119	XP: $10		F18

Motor Inn

Location: Just n of J T Butler Blvd; across from Mayo Clinic. 4600 San Pablo Rd 32224. **Fax:** 904/223-1026. **Facility:** Offers mix of standard accommodations, as well as, two-room suites, charming landscape courtyard area with gazebo. 146 units. Some suites. *Bath:* combo or shower only. 3 stories, interior corridors. **Amenities:** voice mail, irons, hair dryers. **Leisure Activities:** whirlpool, exercise room. **Guest Services:** area transportation, coin laundry. **Business Services:** meeting rooms. **Cards:** AE, DI, DS, MC, VI. *(See color ad below)* SOME UNITS
FEE

(See map p. 422)

COURTYARD BY MARRIOTT JAX AIRPORT I-95   Phone: (904)741-1122 `12`
All Year   1P: $89-$104   2P: $89-$104   XP: $15   F18
Location: I-95, exit 127, sw of Airport Blvd. 14668 Duval Road 32218 (PO Box 18369, 32229). Fax: 904/741-0929.
Motel **Facility:** Large, nicely decorated units. 81 units. Some whirlpool units ($99-$114). *Bath:* combo or shower
only. 3 stories, interior corridors. **Amenities:** extended cable TV, voice mail, irons, hair dryers. **Leisure Ac-**
tivities: whirlpool, exercise room. **Guest Services:** coin laundry. **Business Services:** meeting rooms, fax. Cards: AE, DI, DS,
MC, VI.

SOME UNITS

DAYS INN AIRPORT   Phone: (904)741-4000 `5`
All Year   1P: $59-$99   2P: $71-$110   XP: $10   F6
Location: I-95, exit 127, just w. 1181 Airport Rd 32218. Fax: 904/741-0609. **Facility:** Some units with pull-out
sofas. 64 units. 2 stories, exterior corridors. **Terms:** 10 day cancellation notice. **Amenities:** extended cable
Motel TV. **Guest Services:** coin laundry. **Cards:** AE, CB, DI, DS, MC, VI. **Special Amenities:** free continental
breakfast and free newspaper.

SOME UNITS

DAYS INN SOUTH   Phone: (904)733-3890 `26`
All Year   1P: $55-$99   2P: $65-$99   XP: $6   F10
Location: I-95, southbound exit 103B; northbound exit 102. 5649 Cagle Rd 32216. Fax: 904/636-9841. **Facility:** 120
units. *Bath:* combo or shower only. 2 stories, exterior corridors. **Amenities:** extended cable TV. **Leisure Ac-**
Motel **tivities:** exercise room. **Guest Services:** [ECP] meal plan available. **Business Services:** meeting rooms,
fax. **Cards:** AE, CB, DI, DS, JC, MC, VI. **Special Amenities:** free continental breakfast and preferred
room (subject to availability with advanced reservations). *(See color ad below)*   SOME UNITS

EMBASSY SUITES HOTEL   Phone: (904)731-3555 `58`
12/30-3/31   1P: $99-$169   2P: $99-$169   XP: $10   F18
4/1-11/30   1P: $94-$154   2P: $94-$154   XP: $10   F18
12/1-12/29   1P: $99-$139   2P: $99-$139   XP: $10   F18
Suite Hotel **Location:** I-95, exit 100, 0.5 mi e. 9300 Baymeadows Rd 32256. Fax: 904/731-4972. **Facility:** Units are spacious
two-room suites. Interior of building is an impressive open atrium with seven-story ceiling. 277 units. *Bath:*
combo or shower only. 7 stories, interior corridors. **Terms:** cancellation fee imposed, package plans.
Amenities: voice mail, irons, hair dryers. **Dining:** 11 am-10 pm, $10-$16, cocktails, entertainment. **Leisure Activities:** heated
pool, sauna, whirlpool, golf privileges, exercise room. **Guest Services:** [BP] meal plan available, gift shop, complimentary
evening beverages, area transportation-within 7 mi, coin laundry. **Business Services:** conference facilities, administrative services. **Cards:** AE, CB, DI, DS, JC, MC, VI. **Special Amenities:** free continental breakfast and free newspaper. SOME UNITS

FEE

FAIRFIELD INN AIRPORT   Phone: (904)741-3500 `8`
All Year   1P: $59-$65
Location: I-95, exit 127B, 0.3 mi w at airport. 1300 Airport Rd 32218. Fax: 904/741-3600. **Facility:** New property
with spacious public areas and comfortable rooms with added amenities. 107 units. Some whirlpool units. *Bath:*
Motel combo or shower only. 2 stories, exterior corridors. **Amenities:** extended cable TV, voice mail. **Leisure**
Activities: heated pool, whirlpool, exercise room. **Guest Services:** [ECP] meal plan available, valet laundry. **Business Serv-**
ices: meeting rooms, fax. **Cards:** AE, CB, DI, DS, JC, MC, VI.

SOME UNITS

FAIRFIELD INN BY MARRIOTT   Phone: (904)739-0739 `45`
1/16-6/1   1P: $72-$159   2P: $72-$159
12/1-1/15 & 6/2-11/30   1P: $69-$159   2P: $69-$159
Location: I-95, exit 100, ne corner. 8050 Baymeadows Cir W 32256. Fax: 904/739-3080. **Facility:** 102 units. Some
whirlpool units ($109-$159). *Bath:* combo or shower only. 2 stories, exterior corridors. **Terms:** package plans.
Motel **Amenities:** extended cable TV, irons. **Guest Services:** [ECP] meal plan available, coin laundry. **Business**
Services: meeting rooms, fax. **Cards:** AE, DI, DS, MC, VI. **Special Amenities:** free continental breakfast
and free local telephone calls.

SOME UNITS

(See map p. 422)

HAMPTON INN

SAVE

Motel

Phone: 904/741-4980 **⑨**

All Year 1P: $65-$85
Location: I-95, exit 127, jct Airport Rd. 1170 Airport Entrance Rd 32218. Fax: 904/741-4186. **Facility:** Spacious units in a "gated community", card entry security. 113 units. 2 stories, exterior corridors. **Amenities:** extended cable TV, video games, irons, hair dryers. **Guest Services:** [ECP] meal plan available, coin laundry. **Business Services:** meeting rooms, fax. **Cards:** AE, CB, DI, DS, JC, MC, VI.
SOME UNITS

HAMPTON INN CENTRAL

SAVE

Motel

Phone: (904)396-7770 **㉒**
XP: $5 F18

All Year 1P: $69-$100 2P: $69-$115
Location: Southside of Main St Bridge. 1331 Prudential Dr 32207. Fax: 904/396-8044. **Facility:** 118 units. Some whirlpool units ($79-$120). *Bath:* combo or shower only. 5 stories, interior corridors. **Amenities:** extended cable TV, video games, voice mail, irons. **Guest Services:** [ECP] meal plan available, valet laundry. **Business Services:** meeting rooms, fax. **Cards:** AE, CB, DI, DS, MC, VI.
SOME UNITS

HAMPTON INN JACKSONVILLE I-95 SOUTH

(AAA) (SAVE)

Motel

(See ad below)

Phone: (904)281-0443 **㊷**

All Year 1P: $79 2P: $79
Location: I-95, exit 100 (Butler Blvd), just e, then just s. 4690 Salisbury Rd 32256. Fax: 904/281-0144. **Facility:** Large sunken lobby area. 129 units. 4 stories, interior corridors. **Terms:** weekly & monthly rates available. **Amenities:** irons, hair dryers. **Leisure Activities:** exercise room. **Guest Services:** [ECP] meal plan available, valet laundry. *Fee:* area transportation. **Business Services:** meeting rooms. **Cards:** AE, CB, DI, DS, MC, VI. **Special Amenities:** early check-in/late check-out and free continental breakfast.
SOME UNITS

HILTON GARDEN INN DEERWOOD PARK-JACKSONVILLE, FL

SAVE

Motor Inn

Phone: (904)997-6600 **㊻**

All Year 1P: $124 2P: $124
Location: I-95, exit 101, e on JT Butler, 2.4 mi to SR 115 (Southside Blvd N), 0.8 mi n to Gate Pkwy, just e. 9745 Gate Pkwy N 32246. Fax: 904/997-6601. **Facility:** Gracious public areas and spacious guest units. Mid way between downtown and beaches. 119 units. *Bath:* combo or shower only. 5 stories, interior corridors. **Terms:** cancellation fee imposed, package plans. **Amenities:** extended cable TV, video games, voice mail, irons, hair dryers. **Leisure Activities:** whirlpool, exercise room. **Guest Services:** area transportation, coin laundry. **Business Services:** meeting rooms, administrative services. **Cards:** AE, DI, DS, JC, MC, VI. *(See ad p 44)*
SOME UNITS

HILTON JACKSONVILLE RIVERFRONT

(AAA) (SAVE)

Hotel

Phone: 904/396-8871 **⑳**
XP: $10 F18

All Year 1P: $75-$179 2P: $75-$179
Location: Center; on southbank of river. 1201 Riverplace Blvd 32207. Fax: 904/396-8844. **Facility:** Many units with river and city views. 292 units. Some suites ($175-$400) and whirlpool units. *Bath:* some combo or shower only. 8 stories, interior corridors. **Parking:** valet. **Terms:** check-in 4 pm, cancellation fee imposed, package plans. **Amenities:** video games, voice mail, irons, hair dryers. **Dining:** dining room, restaurant, 6 am-11 pm, $8-$30, cocktails. **Leisure Activities:** heated pool, whirlpool, charter fishing. **Guest Services:** gift shop, area transportation-within 1 mi, valet laundry. **Business Services:** conference facilities, administrative services. **Cards:** AE, DI, DS, MC, VI. **Special Amenities:** free local telephone calls. *(See ad p 44)*
SOME UNITS

HOLIDAY INN AIRPORT

Motor Inn

Phone: (904)741-4404 **⑬**
XP: $6 F16

All Year 1P: $80-$108 2P: $84-$112
Location: Jct Airport Rd and I-95, exit 127. 14670 Duval Rd 32229 (PO Drawer 18409, 32229-0409). Fax: 904/741-4907. **Facility:** 489 units. *Bath:* combo or shower only. 2-6 stories, interior/exterior corridors. **Terms:** package plans, pets (not permitted on concierge floors). **Amenities:** extended cable TV, voice mail, safes, irons, hair dryers. **Leisure Activities:** 2 pools (1 heated indoor/outdoor), wading pool, 2 lighted tennis courts, exercise room. **Guest Services:** gift shop, coin laundry. **Business Services:** conference facilities, fax. **Cards:** AE, CB, DI, DS, JC, MC, VI.
SOME UNITS

(See map p. 422)

HOLIDAY INN BAYMEADOWS
Motor Inn

Phone: (904)737-1700 **56**

All Year 1P: $59-$79 2P: $59-$79

Location: I-95, exit 100, 0.3 mi e. 9150 Baymeadows Rd 32256. Fax: 904/737-0207. **Facility:** Recently renovated rooms have upscale features. 248 units. Some suites. 2-4 stories, interior/exterior corridors. **Terms:** package plans, small pets only ($35 fee). **Amenities:** voice mail, irons, hair dryers. **Guest Services:** coin laundry. **Business Services:** meeting rooms. **Cards:** AE, CB, DI, DS, JC, MC, VI.

SOME UNITS

HOLIDAY INN-COMMONWEALTH
Motor Inn

Phone: (904)781-6000 **17**

All Year 1P: $79

Location: Jct Commonwealth Ave and I-295, exit 9. 6802 Commonwealth Ave 32254. Fax: 904/781-2784. **Facility:** 178 units. 2 stories, interior/exterior corridors. **Amenities:** extended cable TV, irons, hair dryers. **Leisure Activities:** heated pool, saunas, whirlpool, exercise room. **Guest Services:** coin laundry. **Business Services:** meeting rooms, fax. **Cards:** AE, DI, DS, MC, VI. *(See color ad below)*

SOME UNITS

HOLIDAY INN EXPRESS HOTEL AND SUITES
Motel

Phone: (904)332-9500 **36**
F15

All Year 1P: $59-$99 2P: $69-$140 XP: $10

Location: I-95, exit 101, just e, then s. 4675 Salisbury Rd 32256. **Facility:** Some units with two-line phones. 88 units. *Bath:* combo or shower only. 4 stories, interior corridors. **Terms:** package plans, small pets only ($25 deposit). **Amenities:** extended cable TV, voice mail, irons, hair dryers. **Leisure Activities:** heated pool, exercise room. **Guest Services:** coin laundry. **Business Services:** meeting rooms, administrative services. **Cards:** AE, CB, DI, DS, JC, MC, VI. **Special Amenities:** free newspaper and free room upgrade (subject to availability with advanced reservations).** *(See color ad below)*

SOME UNITS

HOMESTEAD VILLAGE GUEST STUDIOS-BAYMEADOWS
Extended Stay Motel
MC, VI.

Phone: 904/739-1881 **57**

All Year 1P: $49-$69

Location: I-95, exit 100, just e to Western Way, just s. 8300 Western Way 32256. Fax: 904/739-0557. **Facility:** Limited office hours 6:30 am-9 pm, Sat 9 am-5 pm, Sun noon-8 pm. Spacious units with easy to live in set up. 134 units. *Bath:* combo or shower only. 3 stories, interior corridors. **Terms:** pets ($75 fee). **Amenities:** voice mail, irons. **Guest Services:** valet and coin laundry. **Business Services:** fax. **Cards:** AE, DI, DS, JC,

SOME UNITS

(See map p. 422)

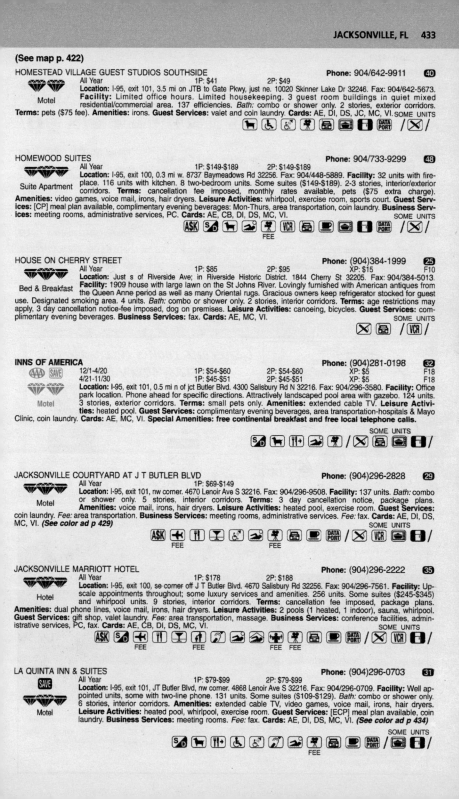

HOMESTEAD VILLAGE GUEST STUDIOS SOUTHSIDE
Phone: 904/642-9911 40
Motel
All Year   1P: $41   2P: $49
Location: I-95, exit 101, 3.5 mi on JTB to Gate Pkwy, just ne. 10020 Skinner Lake Dr 32246. Fax: 904/642-5673. **Facility:** Limited office hours. Limited housekeeping. 3 guest room buildings in quiet mixed residential/commercial area. 137 efficiencies. *Bath:* combo or shower only. 2 stories, exterior corridors. **Terms:** pets ($75 fee). **Amenities:** irons. **Guest Services:** valet and coin laundry. **Cards:** AE, DI, DS, JC, MC, VI. SOME UNITS

HOMEWOOD SUITES
Phone: 904/733-9299 48
Suite Apartment
All Year   1P: $149-$189   2P: $149-$189
Location: I-95, exit 100, 0.3 mi w. 8737 Baymeadows Rd 32256. Fax: 904/448-5889. **Facility:** 32 units with fireplace. 116 units with kitchen. 8 two-bedroom units. Some suites ($149-$189). 2-3 stories, interior/exterior corridors. **Terms:** cancellation fee imposed, monthly rates available, pets ($75 extra charge). **Amenities:** video games, voice mail, irons, hair dryers. **Leisure Activities:** whirlpool, exercise room, sports court. **Guest Services:** [CP] meal plan available, complimentary evening beverages: Mon-Thurs, area transportation, coin laundry. **Business Services:** meeting rooms, administrative services, PC. **Cards:** AE, CB, DI, DS, MC, VI. SOME UNITS

HOUSE ON CHERRY STREET
Phone: (904)384-1999 25
Bed & Breakfast
All Year   1P: $85   2P: $95   XP: $15   F10
Location: Just s of Riverside Ave; in Riverside Historic District. 1844 Cherry St 32205. Fax: 904/384-5013. **Facility:** 1909 house with large lawn on the St Johns River. Lovingly furnished with American antiques from the Queen Anne period as well as many Oriental rugs. Gracious owners keep refrigerator stocked for guest use. Designated smoking area. 4 units. *Bath:* combo or shower only. 2 stories, interior corridors. **Terms:** age restrictions may apply, 3 day cancellation notice-fee imposed, dog on premises. **Leisure Activities:** canoeing, bicycles. **Guest Services:** complimentary evening beverages. **Business Services:** fax. **Cards:** AE, MC, VI. SOME UNITS

INNS OF AMERICA
Phone: (904)281-0198 32
Motel
12/1-4/20   1P: $54-$60   2P: $54-$60   XP: $5   F18
4/21-11/30   1P: $45-$51   2P: $45-$51   XP: $5   F18
Location: I-95, exit 101, 0.5 mi n of jct Butler Blvd. 4300 Salisbury Rd N 32216. Fax: 904/296-3580. **Facility:** Office park location. Phone ahead for specific directions. Attractively landscaped pool area with gazebo. 124 units. 3 stories, exterior corridors. **Terms:** small pets only. **Amenities:** extended cable TV. **Leisure Activities:** heated pool. **Guest Services:** complimentary evening beverages, area transportation-hospitals & Mayo Clinic, coin laundry. **Cards:** AE, MC, VI. **Special Amenities:** free continental breakfast and free local telephone calls.
SOME UNITS

JACKSONVILLE COURTYARD AT J T BUTLER BLVD
Phone: (904)296-2828 29
Motel
All Year   1P: $69-$149
Location: I-95, exit 101, nw corner. 4670 Lenoir Ave S 32216. Fax: 904/296-9508. **Facility:** 137 units. *Bath:* combo or shower only. 5 stories, interior corridors. **Terms:** 3 day cancellation notice, package plans. **Amenities:** voice mail, irons, hair dryers. **Leisure Activities:** heated pool, exercise room. **Guest Services:** coin laundry. *Fee:* area transportation. **Business Services:** meeting rooms, administrative services. *Fee:* fax. **Cards:** AE, DI, DS, MC, VI. *(See color ad p 429)*
SOME UNITS

JACKSONVILLE MARRIOTT HOTEL
Phone: (904)296-2222 35
Hotel
All Year   1P: $178   2P: $188
Location: I-95, exit 100, se corner off J T Butler Blvd. 4670 Salisbury Rd 32256. Fax: 904/296-7561. **Facility:** Upscale appointments throughout; some luxury services and amenities. 256 units. Some suites ($245-$345) and whirlpool units. 9 stories, interior corridors. **Terms:** cancellation fee imposed, package plans. **Amenities:** dual phone lines, voice mail, irons, hair dryers. **Leisure Activities:** 2 pools (1 heated, 1 indoor), sauna, whirlpool. **Guest Services:** gift shop, valet laundry. *Fee:* area transportation, massage. **Business Services:** conference facilities, administrative services, PC, fax. **Cards:** AE, CB, DI, DS, MC, VI.
SOME UNITS

LA QUINTA INN & SUITES
Phone: (904)296-0703 31
Motel
All Year   1P: $79-$99   2P: $79-$99
Location: I-95, exit 101, JT Butler Blvd, nw corner. 4868 Lenoir Ave S 32216. Fax: 904/296-0709. **Facility:** Well appointed units, some with two-line phone. 131 units. Some suites ($109-$129). *Bath:* combo or shower only. 6 stories, interior corridors. **Amenities:** extended cable TV, video games, voice mail, irons, hair dryers. **Leisure Activities:** heated pool, whirlpool, exercise room. **Guest Services:** [ECP] meal plan available, coin laundry. **Business Services:** meeting rooms. *Fee:* fax. **Cards:** AE, DI, DS, MC, VI. *(See color ad p 434)*
SOME UNITS

(See map p. 422)

LA QUINTA INN-BAYMEADOWS

[SAVE]

Motel

All Year   1P: $69-$75   2P: $69-$75   **Phone: (904)731-9940**   **50**
Location: I-95, exit 101, (Baymeadows Rd), sw corner. 8255 Dix Ellis Tr 32256. **Fax:** 904/731-3854. **Facility:** Buildings look out to attractive courtyard with picnic tables. 106 units. 2 stories, exterior corridors. **Terms:** small pets only. **Leisure Activities:** basketball. **Guest Services:** [CP] meal plan available, coin laundry. **Fee:** fax. **Cards:** AE, CB, DI, DS, MC, VI. *(See color ad below)*

SOME UNITS

LA QUINTA INN-NORTH

[SAVE]

Motel

All Year   1P: $65-$75   2P: $65-$75   **Phone: (904)751-6960**   **15**
Location: I-95, exit 25, sw corner. 812 Dunn Ave 32218. **Fax:** 904/751-9769. **Facility:** "King-Plus" units available with added amenities. 129 units. 3 stories, exterior corridors. **Terms:** small pets only. **Amenities:** voice mail. **Leisure Activities:** meeting rooms. **Cards:** AE, CB, DI, DS, MC, VI. *(See color ad below)*

SOME UNITS

MAINSTAY SUITES-JACKSONVILLE

[AAA] [SAVE]

Extended Stay Motel

All Year   1P: $80-$90   2P: $80-$90   **Phone: (904)296-0661**   **41**
Location: I-95, exit 101, J Turner Butler Blvd, e on Butler, then s. 4693 Salisbury Rd S 32256. **Fax:** 904/296-3965. **Facility:** Office hours 6 am-9 pm; Sat and Sun 8 am-6 pm. During non-office hours check-ins require use of credit card and automated self-serve system. 100 efficiencies. Some suites. **Bath:** combo or shower only. 3 stories, interior corridors. **Terms:** pets ($10 deposit). **Amenities:** extended cable TV, video games, dual phone lines, voice mail, irons, hair dryers. **Leisure Activities:** exercise room, grill at pool area for guest use. **Guest Services:** [ECP] meal plan available, valet and coin laundry. **Business Services:** PC, fax. **Cards:** AE, CB, DI, DS, JC, MC, VI. **Special Amenities:** early check-in/late check-out. *(See color ad p 427)*

SOME UNITS

(See map p. 422)

OMNI JACKSONVILLE HOTEL Phone: (904)355-6664 **19**
All Year 1P: $134 2P: $134
Location: Downtown; corner of Pearl and Water sts; adjacent to The Landing. 245 Water St 32202.
Hotel Fax: 904/791-4812. **Facility:** Spacious units. Service-oriented staff. Conveniently located to Civic Auditorium and short drive to Alltel Stadium. 354 units. 15 stories, interior corridors. **Parking:** extra charge or valet.
Terms: 3 day cancellation notice, package plans. **Amenities:** video games, dual phone lines, voice mail, honor bars, irons, hair dryers. *Some:* CD players. **Dining:** Juliette's, see separate listing. **Leisure Activities:** heated pool. **Guest Services:** gift shop, valet laundry. **Business Services:** conference facilities, administrative services, PC. *Fee:* fax. **Cards:** AE, CB, DI, DS, MC, VI.
(See color ad p 434)

PLANTATION MANOR INN Phone: 904/384-4630 **23**
All Year 1P: $135-$160 2P: $150-$175 XP: $20
Location: Corner of Copeland and Oak sts, in Riverside Historic District. 1630 Copeland St 32204. Fax: 904/387-0960.
Historic Bed & Breakfast **Facility:** A gracious 1905 plantation home. Some units with fireplace. Wrap around porch supported by Greek Revival Doric columns. Smoke free premises. 9 units. Some suites. *Bath:* combo or shower only. 3 stories (no elevator), interior corridors. **Terms:** 7 day cancellation notice-fee imposed. **Leisure Activities:** whirlpool. **Guest Services:** [BP] meal plan available. **Cards:** AE, DI, MC, VI. **Special Amenities:** free continental breakfast and free local telephone calls.

QUALITY HOTEL SOUTHPOINT Phone: (904)281-0900 **33**
All Year 1P: $59-$129 2P: $59-$149 XP: $10 F17
Location: I-95, exit 101 (J T Butler Blvd), just e. 4660 Salisbury Rd 32256. Fax: 904/281-0417. **Facility:** Spacious units, well equipped business rooms cater to the corporate traveler. 184 units. 6 stories, interior corridors. **Terms:** 7 day cancellation notice, package plans, small pets only ($25 extra charge). **Amenities:** extended cable TV, video games, voice mail, irons, hair dryers. **Dining:** restaurant, coffee shop, 11 am-2 & 5-10 pm, Sun from 5 pm, $8-$19, cocktails. **Leisure Activities:** sauna, exercise room. **Guest Services:** [ECP] meal plan available, valet laundry. **Business Services:** meeting rooms. **Cards:** AE, CB, DI, DS, JC, MC, VI. **Special Amenities:** early check-in/late check-out and free room upgrade (subject to availability with advanced reservations).
(See color ad p 427)

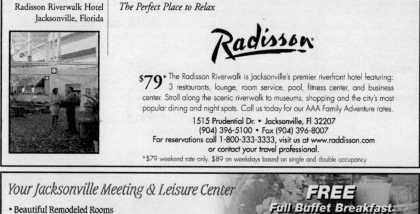

(See map p. 422)

RADISSON RIVERWALK HOTEL
All Year | 1P: $119-$178 | 2P: $129-$189 | XP: $10 | **21**
Phone: (904)396-5100 | F12

Hotel

Location: South side of the St Johns River; at St Johns Place. 1515 Prudential Dr 32207. Fax: 904/396-8007. **Facility:** Many units with view of downtown and activity on the St Johns River. 322 units. Some whirlpool units. 5 stories, interior corridors. **Terms:** package plans. **Amenities:** video games, voice mail, irons, hair dryers. **Leisure Activities:** 2 lighted tennis courts, exercise room. **Guest Services:** gift shop, valet laundry. **Business Services:** conference facilities, administrative services, fax. **Cards:** AE, CB, DI, DS, JC, MC, VI. *(See ad p 435)* SOME UNITS

RAMADA INN CONFERENCE CENTER
1/1-11/30 | 1P: $73-$78 | 2P: $78-$83 | XP: $5 | **62**
Phone: (904)268-8080 | F18

Motor Inn

Location: I-295, exit 2A northbound; exit 2 southbound, just n on SR 13. 3130 Hartley Rd 32257. Fax: 904/262-8718. **Facility:** 152 units. 2 stories, exterior corridors. **Terms:** 7 day cancellation notice, weekly & monthly rates available, small pets only ($10 extra charge, $25 deposit). **Amenities:** *Some:* irons, hair dryers. **Leisure Activities:** wading pool. **Guest Services:** [CP] meal plan available, coin laundry. **Business Services:** meeting rooms, fax. **Cards:** AE, CB, DI, DS, JC, MC, VI. *(See color ad p 435)* SOME UNITS

RED ROOF INN
2/1-2/28	1P: $65-$80	2P: $72-$87	XP: $7	F19
3/1-4/30	1P: $60-$80	2P: $67-$87	XP: $7	F19
12/1-1/31	1P: $55-$75	2P: $62-$82	XP: $7	F19
5/1-11/30	1P: $50-$70	2P: $57-$77	XP: $7	F19

Phone: 904/296-1006 | **37**

Motel

Location: I-95, exit 101, (JT Butler Blvd), nw corner. 6969 Lenoir Ave E 32216. Fax: 904/296-1007. **Facility:** 128 units. *Bath:* combo or shower only. 5 stories, interior corridors. **Terms:** weekly rates available. **Amenities:** voice mail. **Cards:** AE, CB, DI, DS, MC, VI. **Special Amenities:** free local telephone calls and free newspaper. SOME UNITS

RED ROOF INN-AIRPORT
10/1-11/30	1P: $45-$65	2P: $61-$71	XP: $6	F18
1/27-4/30	1P: $45-$65	2P: $51-$71	XP: $6	F18
12/1-1/26	1P: $40-$65	2P: $46-$71	XP: $6	F18
5/1-9/30	1P: $35-$60	2P: $41-$66	XP: $6	F18

Phone: (904)741-4488 | **7**

Motel

Location: Jct Airport Rd and I-95, exit 127. 14701 Airport Entrance Rd 32218. Fax: 904/741-4493. **Facility:** Comfortably furnished units. Convenient to restaurant and interstate. 108 units. 2 stories, exterior corridors. **Terms:** small pets only. **Amenities:** voice mail. **Leisure Activities:** heated pool. **Business Services:** fax. **Cards:** AE, CB, DI, DS, MC, VI. **Special Amenities:** free local telephone calls and free newspaper. SOME UNITS

RESIDENCE INN BY MARRIOTT
All Year | 1P: $119-$130 | 2P: $119-$130 | **55**
Phone: (904)733-8088

Apartment

Location: I-95, exit 100, sw off Baymeadows Rd. 8365 Dix Ellis Tr 32256. Fax: 904/731-8354. **Facility:** 28 bi-level loft units with fireplace and 2 baths. 112 units with kitchen. 28 two-bedroom units. 2 stories, exterior corridors. **Terms:** pets ($75 cleaning fee). **Amenities:** extended cable TV, voice mail, irons, hair dryers. **Leisure Activities:** heated pool, whirlpools, sports court. **Guest Services:** [ECP] meal plan available, complimentary evening beverages: Mon-Thurs, coin laundry. **Business Services:** meeting rooms. **Cards:** AE, DI, DS, JC, MC, VI. SOME UNITS

(See map p. 422)

WELLESLEY INN & SUITES
AAA SAVE
▼▼▼▼
Motel

Phone: (904)620-9008 [51]
All Year   1P: $69-$89   2P: $69-$89   XP: $10   F15
Location: I-95, exit 101, 2.5 mi e on JT Butler Blvd to Southside Blvd, just n on west side of road. 8801 Perimeter Park Blvd 32216. Fax: 904/620-9068. **Facility:** Spacious units with stovetop and full size refrigerator. 127 efficiencies. *Bath:* combo or shower only. 3 stories, interior corridors. **Terms:** check-in 4 pm, pets ($25 extra charge). **Dining:** sundries shop, weekly manager reception. **Leisure Activities:** exercise room, game room. **Guest Services:** coin laundry. **Business Services:** meeting rooms. **Special Amenities:** free continental breakfast and free local telephone calls. *(See color ad opposite title page)*   SOME UNITS

🆂 🐾 🔲 ⬜ 💺 🖨 🖼 📶 DATA PORT /✖/
FEE

───────── *The following lodgings were either not evaluated or did not* ─────────
meet AAA rating requirements but are listed for your information only.

RESIDENCE INN-AIRPORT
fyi
Motel

Phone: 904/741-6550
All Year   1P: $109   2P: $109
Too new to rate. **Location:** I-95, exit 127B, 0.3 mi w at airport. 1310 Airport Rd 32218. **Amenities:** 78 units, pets, coffeemakers, microwaves, refrigerators. **Cards:** AE, CB, DI, DS, MC, VI.

SPRINGHILL SUITES BY MARRIOTT JACKSONVILLE DEERWOOD PARK
fyi
Motel

Phone: 904/997-6650
All Year   1P: $79-$129
Too new to rate. **Location:** I-95, exit 101 (Butler) just e, then 1 mi n. 4385 Southside Blvd 32246. Fax: 904/997-6610. **Amenities:** 102 units, radios, coffeemakers, microwaves, refrigerators, pool. **Cards:** AE, CB, DI, DS, JC, MC, VI.

WINGATE INN/SOUTHSIDE
fyi
Motel

Phone: 904/281-2600
All Year   1P: $59-$109   2P: $59-$109
Too new to rate. **Location:** I-95, exit 101 (Butler Blvd), left, right on Bonneval. 4681 Lenor Ave 32216. Fax: 904/281-1166. **Amenities:** 102 units, radios, coffeemakers, microwaves, refrigerators, pool. **Cards:** AE, CB, DI, DS, JC, MC, VI. *(See color ad p 436)*

───────── **WHERE TO DINE** ─────────

BISCOTTI'S ESPRESSO CAFE
▼▼▼ ▼▼▼
American

Lunch: $6-$10   **Dinner:** $7-$17   **Phone:** 904/387-2060 [10]
Location: I-10, exit 57, 2 mi s on McDuff Ave, 1 mi w. 3556 St. Johns Ave 32204. **Hours:** 7 am-10 pm, Mon 11 am-3 pm, Fri 7 am-midnight, Sat 8 am-midnight, Sun 8 am-3 pm. **Features:** casual dress; Sunday brunch; beer & wine only; street parking; a la carte. Indoor-outdoor dining in relaxed neighborhood gathering spot, overlooking Avondale shopping district. Eclectic menu offering pizza, salad and hearty sandwiches. Fresh ground coffee, espresso and cappucino to accompany decadent desserts. Recognized as one of Jacksonville's top 25 restaurants. Smoke free premises. **Cards:** AE, DS, MC, VI.   ✖

BOMBAY BICYCLE CLUB
▼▼ ▼▼
American

Lunch: $5-$10   **Dinner:** $7-$13   **Phone:** 904/737-9555 [15]
Location: I-95, exit 100, nw corner. 8909 Baymeadows Rd 32256. **Hours:** 11:30 am-1 am. **Reservations:** suggested. **Features:** casual dress; children's menu; cocktails & lounge; a la carte. The busy, casual eatery is decorated with bicycle memorabilia. The freshly brewed beer brings out the younger crowd for happy hour. Order the Chinese grilled salad filled with sweet and sour chicken. Many traditional favorites like big burgers are served. **Cards:** AE, CB, DI, DS, MC, VI.   ✖

CLARK'S FISH CAMP
▼▼▼
Seafood

Dinner: $5-$14   **Phone:** 904/268-3474 [21]
Location: I-295, exit 1, 1 mi s, then 3 mi e. 12903 Hood Landing Rd 32217. **Hours:** 4:30 pm-9:30 pm. **Features:** casual dress; cocktails; a la carte. Old Florida charm at its best! Enjoy all the Southern favorites including fried fish with hushpuppies and cole slaw while dining indoors or out overlooking waterway. Most meals come with choices of vegetables and salad. **Cards:** AE, DI, DS, MC, VI.   ✖

CRAWDADDY'S
▼▼▼ ▼▼
Seafood

Lunch: $5-$10   **Dinner:** $15-$22   **Phone:** 904/396-3546 [5]
Location: On the south side of the St John's River at St John's Place. 1643 Prudential Dr 32207. **Hours:** 11 am-10 pm, Fri-11 pm, Sat 5 pm-11 pm, Sun 9 am-2:30 & 5-10 pm. **Reservations:** suggested; for dinner. **Features:** dressy casual; Sunday brunch; children's menu; early bird specials; carryout; cocktails & lounge. Offerings range from finger foods to heavy entrees at the waterfront restaurant, which replicates the rustic feel of a 1920s fish camp. Listen to New Orleans jazz and take in the spectacular sights of the skyline and the mighty St. Johns River. **Cards:** AE, DI, DS, MC, VI.   ✖

JOSEPH'S ITALIAN RESTAURANT
▼▼▼
Italian

Lunch: $6-$10   **Dinner:** $7-$15   **Phone:** 904/642-3444 [22]
Location: I-95, exit 101, 1.5 mi e; in Baymeadows Village shopping center. 9802 Baymeadows Rd 32216. **Hours:** 11 am-10 pm, Sun-9 pm. Closed major holidays. **Features:** casual dress; beer & wine only; a la carte. Enjoy all your Italian favorites from pizza to calzone to lasagne! All entrees cooked fresh and made to the guest's liking. Daily soup and salad specials. Joseph's is conveniently located only minutes from I-95 making it an easy and nice respite while traveling. **Cards:** AE, MC, VI.   ✖

JULIETTE'S
▼▼▼▼
American

Lunch: $7-$12   **Dinner:** $17-$25   **Phone:** 904/355-7118 [1]
Location: Downtown; corner of Pearl and Water sts; adjacent to The Landing; in Omni Jacksonville Hotel. 245 Water St 32202. **Hours:** 6:30 am-10:30 pm, Fri & Sat-11 pm. **Reservations:** suggested. **Features:** dressy casual; Sunday brunch; children's menu; cocktails & lounge; fee for parking & valet parking. The upscale bistro offers dining in an open-ceiling, high-rise atrium. The seasonally changing menu combines the flavors of America and Italy in its pasta, seafood, steak and chicken dishes. The wine list shows breadth, and the servers are knowledgeable. **Cards:** AE, CB, DI, DS, JC, MC, VI.   ✖

(See map p. 422)

LA CENA RISTORANTE
     Dinner: $9-$20
     Phone: 904/737-5350   ⑬
Italian
Location: 0.3 mi s of jct University Blvd W and St Augustine Rd; in the Dupont Station Shopping Center. 6271-7 St. Augustine Rd 32217. **Hours:** 6 pm-11 pm. Closed major holidays; also Sun & Mon. **Reservations:** suggested. **Features:** casual dress; beer & wine only. Excellent award winning Italian wine list. Classic entrees prepared with the finest ingredients by chef-owner. **Cards:** AE, MC, VI.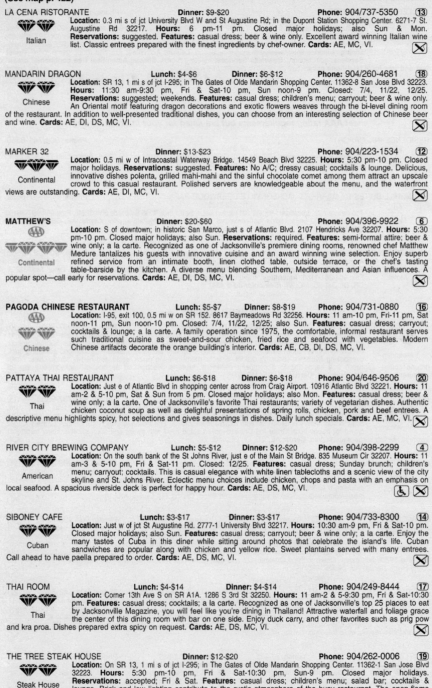

MANDARIN DRAGON
     Lunch: $4-$6
     Dinner: $6-$12
     Phone: 904/260-4681   ⑱
Chinese
Location: SR 13, 1 mi s of jct I-295; in The Gates of Olde Mandarin Shopping Center. 11362-8 San Jose Blvd 32223. **Hours:** 11:30 am-9:30 pm, Fri & Sat-10 pm, Sun noon-9 pm. Closed: 7/4, 11/22, 12/25. **Reservations:** suggested; weekends. **Features:** casual dress; children's menu; carryout; beer & wine only. An Oriental motif featuring dragon decorations and exotic flowers weaves through the bi-level dining room of the restaurant. In addition to well-presented traditional dishes, you can choose from an interesting selection of Chinese beer and wine. **Cards:** AE, DI, DS, MC, VI.

MARKER 32
     Dinner: $13-$23
     Phone: 904/223-1534   ⑫
Continental
Location: 0.5 mi w of Intracoastal Waterway Bridge. 14549 Beach Blvd 32225. **Hours:** 5:30 pm-10 pm. Closed major holidays. **Reservations:** suggested. **Features:** No A/C; dressy casual; cocktails & lounge. Delicious, innovative dishes polenta, grilled mahi-mahi and the sinful chocolate comet among them attract an upscale crowd to this casual restaurant. Polished servers are knowledgeable about the menu, and the waterfront views are outstanding. **Cards:** AE, DI, MC, VI.

MATTHEW'S
     Dinner: $20-$60
     Phone: 904/396-9922   ⑥
Continental
Location: S of downtown; in historic San Marco, just s of Atlantic Blvd. 2107 Hendricks Ave 32207. **Hours:** 5:30 pm-10 pm. Closed major holidays; also Sun. **Reservations:** required. **Features:** semi-formal attire; beer & wine only; a la carte. Recognized as one of Jacksonville's premiere dining rooms, renowned chef Matthew Medure tantalizes his guests with innovative cuisine and an award winning wine selection. Enjoy superb refined service from an intimate booth, linen clothed table, outside terrace, or the chef's tasting table-barside by the kitchen. A diverse menu blending Southern, Mediterranean and Asian influences. A popular spot—call early for reservations. **Cards:** AE, DI, DS, MC, VI.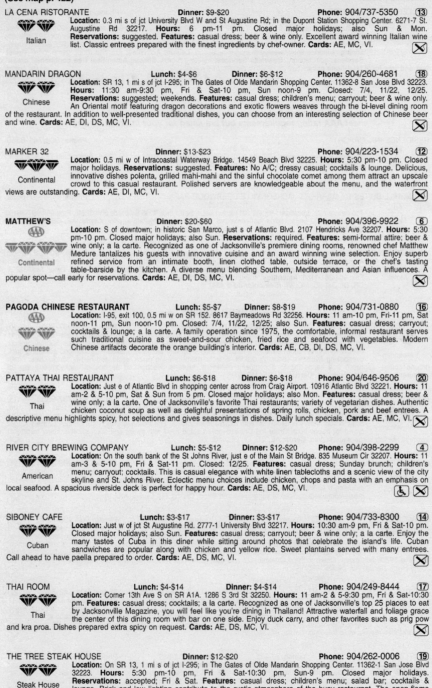

PAGODA CHINESE RESTAURANT
     Lunch: $5-$7
     Dinner: $8-$19
     Phone: 904/731-0880   ⑯
Chinese
Location: I-95, exit 100, 0.5 mi w on SR 152. 8617 Baymeadows Rd 32256. **Hours:** 11 am-10 pm, Fri-11 pm, Sat noon-11 pm, Sun noon-10 pm. Closed: 7/4, 11/22, 12/25; also Sun. **Features:** casual dress; carryout; cocktails & lounge; a la carte. A family operation since 1975, the comfortable, informal restaurant serves such traditional cuisine as sweet-and-sour chicken, fried rice and seafood with vegetables. Modern Chinese artifacts decorate the orange building's interior. **Cards:** AE, CB, DI, DS, MC, VI.

PATTAYA THAI RESTAURANT
     Lunch: $6-$18
     Dinner: $6-$18
     Phone: 904/646-9506   ⑳
Thai
Location: Just e of Atlantic Blvd in shopping center across from Craig Airport. 10916 Atlantic Blvd 32221. **Hours:** 11 am-2 & 5-10 pm, Sat & Sun from 5 pm. Closed major holidays; also Mon. **Features:** casual dress; beer & wine only; a la carte. One of Jacksonville's favorite Thai restaurants; variety of vegetarian dishes. Authentic chicken coconut soup as well as delightful presentations of spring rolls, chicken, pork and beef entrees. A descriptive menu highlights spicy, hot selections and gives seasonings in dishes. Daily lunch specials. **Cards:** AE, MC, VI.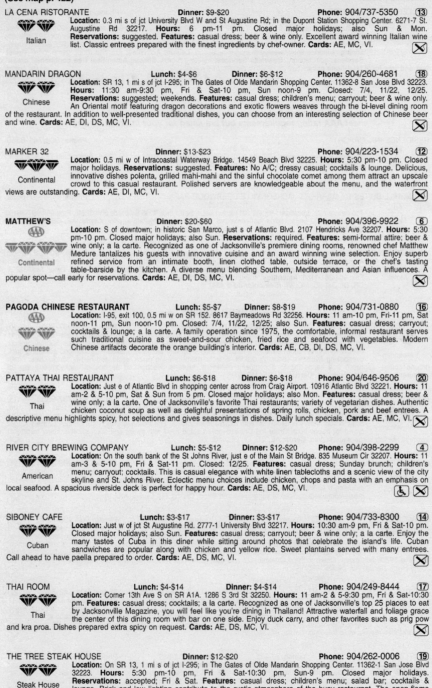

RIVER CITY BREWING COMPANY
     Lunch: $5-$12
     Dinner: $12-$20
     Phone: 904/398-2299   ④
American
Location: On the south bank of the St Johns River, just e of the Main St Bridge. 835 Museum Cir 32207. **Hours:** 11 am-3 & 5-10 pm, Fri & Sat-11 pm. Closed: 12/25. **Features:** casual dress; Sunday brunch; children's menu; carryout; cocktails. This is casual elegance with white linen tablecloths and a scenic view of the city skyline and St. Johns River. Eclectic menu choices include chicken, chops and pasta with an emphasis on local seafood. A spacious riverside deck is perfect for happy hour. **Cards:** AE, DS, MC, VI.

SIBONEY CAFE
     Lunch: $3-$17
     Dinner: $3-$17
     Phone: 904/733-8300   ⑭
Cuban
Location: Just w of jct St Augustine Rd. 2777-1 University Blvd 32217. **Hours:** 10:30 am-9 pm, Fri & Sat-10 pm. Closed major holidays; also Sun. **Features:** casual dress; carryout; beer & wine only; a la carte. Enjoy the many tastes of Cuba in this diner while sitting around photos that celebrate the island's life. Cuban sandwiches are popular along with chicken and yellow rice. Sweet plantains served with many entrees. Call ahead to have paella prepared to order. **Cards:** AE, DS, MC, VI.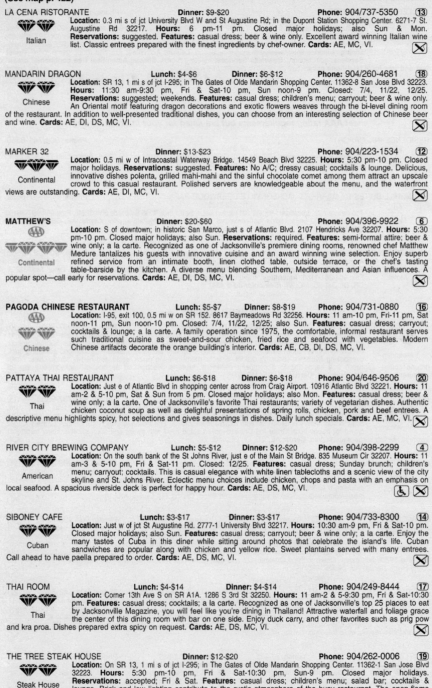

THAI ROOM
     Lunch: $4-$14
     Dinner: $4-$14
     Phone: 904/249-8444   ⑰
Thai
Location: Corner 13th Ave S on SR A1A. 1286 S 3rd St 32250. **Hours:** 11 am-2 & 5-9:30 pm, Fri & Sat-10:30 pm. **Features:** casual dress; cocktails; a la carte. Recognized as one of Jacksonville's top 25 places to eat by Jacksonville Magazine, you will feel like you're dining in Thailand! Attractive waterfall and foliage grace the center of this dining room with bar on one side. Enjoy duck carry, and other favorites such as prig pow and kra proa. Dishes prepared extra spicy on request. **Cards:** AE, DS, MC, VI.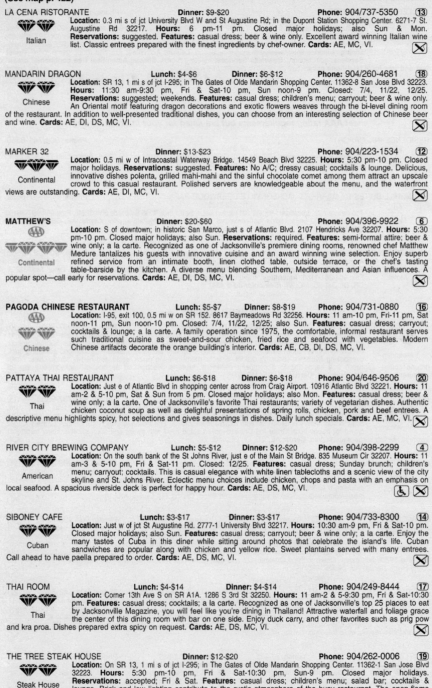

THE TREE STEAK HOUSE
     Dinner: $12-$20
     Phone: 904/262-0006   ⑲
Steak House
Location: On SR 13, 1 mi s of jct I-295; in The Gates of Olde Mandarin Shopping Center. 11362-1 San Jose Blvd 32223. **Hours:** 5:30 pm-10 pm, Fri & Sat-10:30 pm, Sun-9 pm. Closed major holidays. **Reservations:** accepted; Fri & Sat. **Features:** casual dress; children's menu; salad bar; cocktails & lounge. Brick and low lighting contribute to the rustic atmosphere of the busy restaurant. The open-flame grill faces the dining room, and steaks are cut to order at the table. An extensive wine list and a varied salad bar complement the entrees. **Cards:** AE, CB, DI, DS, MC, VI.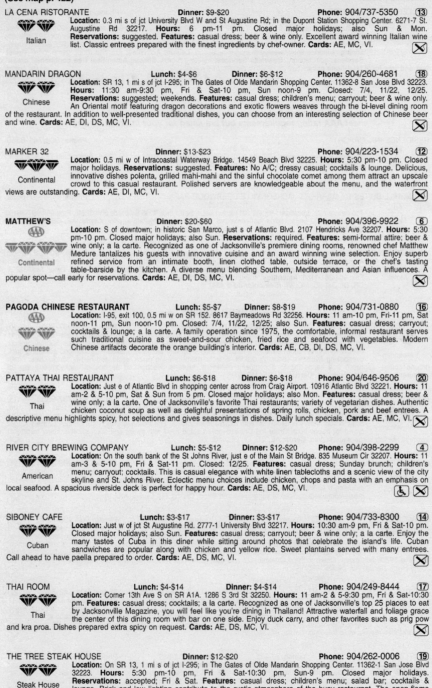

(See map p. 422)

WILFRIED'S 24 MIRAMAR
▼▼▼
American

Dinner: $23-$28   **Phone:** 904/448-2424   ⑨
Location: 3 mi s on SR 13, just n of jct San Jose Blvd. 4446 Hendricks Ave 32207. **Hours:** 5:30 pm-10 pm, Fri & Sat-11 pm. Closed: 7/4, 12/25; also Sun. **Reservations:** suggested. **Features:** semi-formal attire; beer & wine only; a la carte. The chef's innovation shines through in imaginatively prepared and presented dishes and enticing puff pastry desserts. The influences of California, Asia and the Caribbean intermingle in many dishes. Art deco designs bring the small restaurant to life. **Cards:** AE, DI, DS, MC, VI.   ✕

WORMAN'S DELI & BAKERY
▼
American

Lunch: $5-$10   **Dinner:** $7-$13   **Phone:** 904/739-9911   ⑪
Location: Corner of University Blvd W and San Jose Blvd. 5613 San Jose Blvd 32207. **Hours:** 7 am-9 pm, Sun-4:30 pm. Closed major holidays. **Features:** No A/C; casual dress; children's menu; beer & wine only; a la carte. An area tradition since the 1920s, the bright and airy bakery is well-known for scrumptious sandwiches, such as chicken salad with almonds, and homemade desserts, most notably the double-fudge suicide cheesecake and assorted danishes and eclairs. **Cards:** AE, CB, DI, DS, MC, VI.   ✕

――――― *The following restaurant has not been evaluated by AAA* ―――――
but is listed for your information only.

PARTNERS
fyi

Phone: 904/387-3585
Not evaluated. **Location:** 3 mi w of downtown; in historic Avondale, on corner of Ingleside Ave. 3585 St Johns Ave 32205. **Features:** Neighborhood gathering spot featuring creative dishes. Indoor/outdoor dining.

The Jacksonville Vicinity

AMELIA CITY

――――― WHERE TO DINE ―――――

CENTRE STREET CAFE
▼▼▼
Danish

Lunch: $8-$20   **Dinner:** $12-$25   **Phone:** 904/277-6600
Location: Downtown; in historic district on west side of street. 316-D Centre St 32097. **Hours:** 11:30 am-2 & 6-9 pm, Sun brunch first week of each month. Closed major holidays. **Features:** casual dress; beer & wine only; street parking; a la carte. Creative dishes, prepared by Danish chef-owner, are full of robust tast with a mixture of flavors. The Danish meatballs are a fun entree to enjoy. The house salad is enhanced with asparagus and delightful homemade dressings. For dessert try the Coconut Creme Brule'. Only the freshest and finest ingredients are used. A superb wine list is enlighting offering lesser known high quality vineyards. Enjoy. **Cards:** MC, VI.   ✕

AMELIA ISLAND

――――― WHERE TO STAY ―――――

ADDISON HOUSE
▼▼▼
Bed & Breakfast

Phone: (904)277-1604
All Year   1P: $99-$225   2P: $99-$225   XP: $20
Location: In Fernandina Beach Historic District; just s of Center St, corner Ash and S 7th St. 614 Ash St 32034. Fax: 904/277-8124. **Facility:** The main house is an 1876 restored Victorian home and contains five tastefully decorated guest units with fireplaces, premium bedding and highly decorative window treatments. Remaining units are in the Garden House and Coulter Cottage that overlook an attractive, well manicured courtyard. Enjoy cookies and lemonade every afternoon in this memorable, relaxed environment. Smoke free premises. 13 units. Some whirlpool units ($125-$225). **Bath:** combo or shower only. 2 stories, interior/exterior corridors. **Parking:** street only. **Terms:** age restrictions may apply, 7 day cancellation notice-fee imposed, package plans. **Amenities:** extended cable TV, hair dryers. *Some:* irons. **Guest Services:** [BP] meal plan available. **Business Services:** meeting rooms. **Cards:** AE, MC, VI.   SOME UNITS
🍽 ✕ 🖨 / VCR /

AMELIA ISLAND PLANTATION
AAA SAVE
▼▼▼ ▼▼▼
Resort

Phone: (904)261-6161
All Year   1P: $150-$337   2P: $165-$352   XP: $15   F16
Location: In Amelia City; SR A1A, 6.5 mi s of the bridge. 3000 First Coast Hwy 32034 (PO Box 3000, AMELIA CITY, 32035-1307). Fax: 904/277-5159. **Facility:** Secluded, wooded grounds along ocean. Hotel-like rooms, apartments and one- to four-bedroom villas, four with private pool. Varied unit styles and appointments throughout. Many units have washer/dryer. On property shuttle service. 660 units. 206 two-bedroom units, 73 three-bedroom units and 350 units with kitchen. **Bath:** some combo or shower only. 1-8 stories, interior/exterior corridors. **Terms:** check-in 4 pm, 14 day cancellation notice, weekly & monthly rates available, package plans. **Amenities:** extended cable TV, dual phone lines, voice mail, safes, honor bars, irons, hair dryers. **Dining:** dining room, 7 restaurants, 7 ammidnight 20% service charge, $7-$35, cocktails, entertainment. **Leisure Activities:** 19 pools (1 indoor, 2 heated), wading pool, saunas, whirlpools, steamrooms, beach, swimming, boat dock, fishing, charter fishing, children's program, nature program, recreation program, social program, hiking trails, jogging, playground, sports court. *Fee:* canoes, paddleboats, kayaks, golf-45 holes, golf carts, 25 tennis courts (3 lighted), racquetball courts, bicycles, horseback riding. **Guest Services:** [AP], [CP] & [MAP] meal plans available, gift shop, complimentary laundry. *Fee:* area transportation-Amelia Island, massage. **Business Services:** conference facilities, administrative services, fax. *Fee:* PC. **Cards:** AE, DI, DS, MC, VI. *(See color ad p 440)*   SOME UNITS
✈ 🍽 🍸 🛏 📶 📷 🛥 ⛱ ✚ ✕ 🎿 🖨 💳 DATA PORT / VCR 🔌 /
FEE   FEE

BAILEY HOUSE

AAA SAVE

▽▽▽▽

Historic Bed
& Breakfast

Phone: (904)261-5390

All Year   1P: $125-$185   2P: $125-$185   XP: $25
Location: In Fernandina Historic District, just s of Center St. 28 S 7th St 32034. Fax: 904/321-0103. **Facility:** Victorian home with authentic Queen Anne furnishings. On the National Register of Historic Places. The home has been meticulously restored with original heart of pine floors, ornate fireplace mantels and stained glass. All guest units are furnished with 19th century antiques including hand carved beds, claw foot bathtubs, and oriental carpets. One fully equipped carriage house efficiency unit is available. Designated smoking area. 10 units. Some whirlpool units ($165-$185). *Bath:* combo or shower only. 3 stories, interior corridors. **Terms:** age restrictions may apply, 5 day cancellation notice, weekly rates available. **Amenities:** extended cable TV. **Leisure Activities:** bicycles. **Guest Services:** [BP] meal plan available. **Cards:** AE, DS, MC, VI. **Special Amenities: free continental breakfast and free local telephone calls.**

 🛜➕ 📶 ✕

ELIZABETH POINTE LODGE

AAA SAVE

▽▽▽▽

Bed & Breakfast

Phone: (904)277-4851

All Year   1P: $155-$280   2P: $170-$280   XP: $20
Location: In Amelia City, SR A1A, just s on the ocean. 98 S Fletcher Ave 32034. Fax: 904/277-6500. **Facility:** New England style house with comfortable rooms reminiscent of Nantucket with nautical motif and Roman tubs. Cozy lobby area with fireplace, perfect for relaxing with the numerous books on hand. The wraparound piazza is ideal for gazing at the lulling surf. Professional, accommodating staff always available. Designated smoking area. 25 units. 1 two-bedroom unit, 2 efficiencies and 1 unit with kitchen. Some whirlpool units ($185-$220). 4 stories, interior/exterior corridors. **Terms:** 7 day cancellation notice, package plans. **Amenities:** extended cable TV, irons, hair dryers. **Dining:** wine/beer only. **Leisure Activities:** beach, swimming. *Fee:* bicycles. **Guest Services:** [BP] meal plan available, complimentary evening beverages, valet laundry. **Business Services:** meeting rooms. **Cards:** AE, DS, MC, VI. **Special Amenities: free local telephone calls and free newspaper.**

SOME UNITS

📶 🆓 24📶 ✕ 📺 🖨 / 📠 📞 /

THE FAIRBANKS HOUSE

▽▽▽▽

Historic Bed
& Breakfast

Phone: (904)277-0500

All Year   1P: $150-$250   2P: $150-$250   XP: $50
Location: In Fernandina Beach Historic District; just s of Center St. 227 S 7th St 32034. Fax: 904/277-3103. **Facility:** An 1885 Italianate villa and cottages on a one acre landscaped lot with garden pool area. The oldest cottage dates from 1880 and was a schoolhouse. Exuberant owners lavish attention on guests in this peaceful environment. Guest units are well appointed with antiques and oriental rugs. Fireplaces and carved moldings are striking works of craftsmanship. Attractive garden courtyard invites relaxation. Smoke free premises. 12 units. 2 two-bedroom units. Some suites ($225-$250) and whirlpool units ($195-$250). *Bath:* combo or shower only. 3 stories, interior/exterior corridors. **Terms:** age restrictions may apply, 14 day cancellation notice, package plans. **Amenities:** extended cable TV, irons, hair dryers. **Leisure Activities:** bicycles. **Guest Services:** [BP] meal plan available, complimentary evening beverages. **Business Services:** meeting rooms. **Cards:** AE, DS, MC, VI.

SOME UNITS

🛜➕ 🏊 ✕ 📺 🖨 📶 / 📞 /

FLORIDA HOUSE INN

(AAA) SAVE

Historic Country Inn

Phone: (904)261-3300

| All Year | 1P: $79-$179 | 2P: $79-$179 | XP: $10 | F10 |

Location: In Fernandina Beach Historic District, just s of Centre St. 22 S 3rd St 32034 (PO Box 688, FERNANDINA BEACH, 32035). Fax: 904/277-3831. **Facility:** Reported to be the oldest continuously operating hotel in the state. Some rooms are small and sparse. 4 new units along treehouse row with pioneer country theme decor. 9 guest units have working fireplace. Through the years, several historical figures have frequented this inn, known for its reputation of genteel hospitality. Designated smoking area. 15 units. Some whirlpool units ($159-$179). *Bath:* combo or shower only. 2 stories, interior/exterior corridors. **Terms:** 7 day cancellation notice, weekly rates available, pets ($10 extra charge, with prior approval). **Amenities:** extended cable TV. *Some:* irons. **Dining:** dining room, see separate listing. **Leisure Activities:** bicycles. **Guest Services:** [AP], [BP] & [MAP] meal plans available, complimentary evening beverages, complimentary laundry. **Business Services:** meeting rooms. **Cards:** AE, CB, DI, DS, MC, VI. **Special Amenities:** free local telephone calls and free newspaper.

HAMPTON INN/AMELIA ISLAND-FERNANDINA BEACH

SAVE

Motel

Phone: (904)321-1111

3/1-8/31	1P: $109-$129
9/1-11/30	1P: $89-$119
12/1-2/28	1P: $89-$109

Location: In Amelia City, just w jct A1A and Sadler Rd. 2549 Sadler Rd 32034. Fax: 904/321-0115. **Facility:** Modern, contemporary accommodations with very good sized guest units. Short walk to public beach. 82 units. Some suites and whirlpool units. *Bath:* combo or shower only. 3 stories, interior corridors. **Terms:** cancellation fee imposed. **Amenities:** video games, dual phone lines, voice mail, irons, hair dryers. **Leisure Activities:** small pool. **Guest Services:** [ECP] meal plan available. **Cards:** AE, CB, DI, DS, JC, MC, VI.

SOME UNITS

HOYT HOUSE B&B

(AAA) SAVE

Historic Bed & Breakfast

Phone: (904)277-4300

| 1/1-11/30 | 1P: $119-$164 | 2P: $119-$164 | XP: $15 | F12 |
| 12/1-12/31 | 1P: $114-$159 | 2P: $114-$159 | XP: $15 | F12 |

Location: In Fernandina Beach Historic District; on Atlantic Ave/SR 200 at Center & S 8th sts. 804 Atlantic Ave 32034. Fax: 904/277-9626. **Facility:** A 1905 Victorian home in the Queen Anne style full of charm. The guest rooms are all tastefully decorated with antiques and period reproductions. Property is conveniently located to many dining options. Enjoy the gourmet breakfast served in the fine dining room with all the accouterments. Designated smoking area. 10 units. Some whirlpool units ($114-$119). *Bath:* combo or shower only. 2 stories, interior corridors. **Terms:** 7 day cancellation notice-fee imposed, package plans. **Amenities:** extended cable TV. **Leisure Activities:** whirlpool. **Guest Services:** [BP] meal plan available. **Business Services:** meeting rooms. **Cards:** AE, DS, MC, VI.

THE RITZ-CARLTON, AMELIA ISLAND

(AAA) SAVE

Resort

Phone: (904)277-1100

2/15-8/11	1P: $309-$625	2P: $309-$625
8/12-11/30	1P: $299-$419	2P: $299-$419
12/1-2/14	1P: $239-$419	2P: $239-$419

Location: On SR A1A; in Summer Beach. 4750 Amelia Island Pkwy 32034. Fax: 904/261-9063. **Facility:** All rooms with comfortable, private balcony with view of the Atlantic Ocean. Extensive antique and art collection. 449 units. 14 two-bedroom units. Some whirlpool units ($359-$625). 8 stories, interior corridors. **Parking:** valet. **Terms:** 7 day cancellation notice-fee imposed, package plans. **Amenities:** extended cable TV, video games, dual phone lines, voice mail, safes, honor bars, irons, hair dryers. **Dining:** 2 restaurants, 6:30 am-10 pm, poolside restaurant open seasonally, $12-$25, cocktails, also, The Grill Room, see separate listing, entertainment. **Leisure Activities:** 2 heated pools, saunas, whirlpools, steamrooms, beach, swimming, wave runners, children's program, nature program, playground, volleyball. *Fee:* golf-18 holes, 9 tennis courts (6 lighted), bicycles. **Guest Services:** gift shop, valet laundry. *Fee:* area transportation-Fernandina Beach shuttle, massage. **Business Services:** conference facilities, administrative services, PC, fax. **Cards:** AE, CB, DI, DS, JC, MC, VI. **Special Amenities:** free newspaper.

SOME UNITS

WHERE TO DINE

BEECH STREET GRILL

American

Dinner: $18-$26   **Phone:** 904/277-3662

Location: In Fernandina Beach Historic District, corner of 8th and Beech sts. 801 Beech St 32034. **Hours:** 6 pm-10 pm. Closed: 11/22, 12/25; also Super Bowl Sun. **Features:** dressy casual; children's menu; cocktails. In a 1889 Victorian house that exudes a contemporary feel inside. Progressive, imaginative treatments of such specialties as fresh local seafood, such as Grouper with macadamia nut crust topped with curried citrus cream and mango chili salsa. Savory dishes are winners, as well as the roasted venison loin with black currant sauce or the apple chipolte glazed pork with roasted garlic. **Cards:** AE, DI, DS, MC, VI.

BRETT'S WATERWAY CAFE

American

Lunch: $8-$13   **Dinner:** $16-$26   **Phone:** 904/261-2660

Location: In Fernandina Beach, on the Amelia River (Intracoastal Waterway) at the end of Centre St. 1 S Front St 32034. **Hours:** 11:30 am-2:30 & 5:30-9:30 pm, Sun from 5:30 pm. Closed major holidays. **Features:** casual dress; cocktails & lounge. Popular for its Southern hospitality, the restaurant is noted for its excellent seafood and beef selections, a small but impressive wine list and homemade desserts. The dining rooms face the Fernandina Harbor and a marina on the Amelia River. **Cards:** AE, MC, VI.

FLORIDA HOUSE INN DINING ROOM   Historical

Regional American

Lunch: $8   **Dinner:** $13   **Phone:** 904/261-3300

Location: In Fernandina Beach Historic District; just s of Centre St; in Florida House Inn. 22 S 3rd St 32034. **Hours:** 11:30 am-2:30 & 5:30-9 pm; Sun 10:30 am-2 pm. Closed: Sun & Mon for dinner. **Reservations:** accepted. **Features:** casual dress; Sunday brunch; carryout; cocktails & lounge; street parking. Traditional Southern cooking is served boarding-house style all-you-care-to-eat. International beer selections from over 100 countries. Smoke free premises. **Cards:** AE, CB, DI, DS, MC, VI.

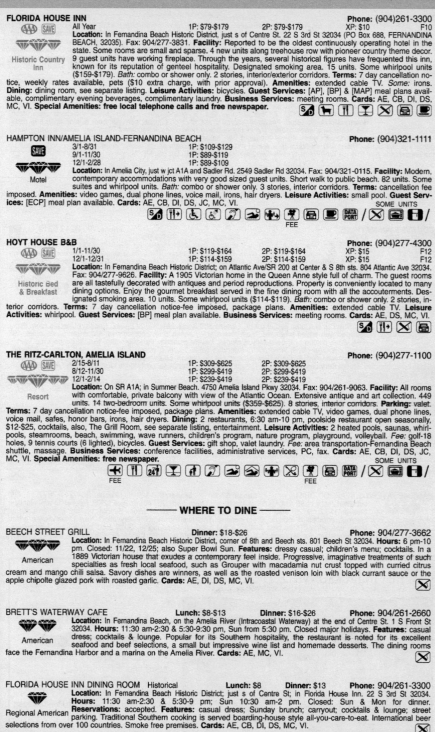

THE GRILL ROOM **Dinner:** $65-$95 **Phone:** 904/277-1100
  (AAA) **Location:** On SR A1A; in Summer Beach; in The Ritz-Carlton, Amelia Island. 4750 Amelia Island Pkwy 32034.
  ▼▼▼▼▼ **Hours:** 6 pm-10 pm, Fri & Sat-11 pm, Sun 10:30 am-2:00 pm. **Reservations:** suggested.
  Features: semi-formal attire; Sunday brunch; children's menu; cocktails & lounge; entertainment; fee for
  American valet parking; a la carte, also prix fixe. An airy, club-like dining room overlooks the Atlantic Ocean. Although
  the setting is formal, the service is friendly and unpretentious. Creative, international influences abound in
  Florida seafood, grilled meat and wild game dishes. Smoke free premises. **Cards:** AE, CB, DI, DS, JC,
MC, VI.
  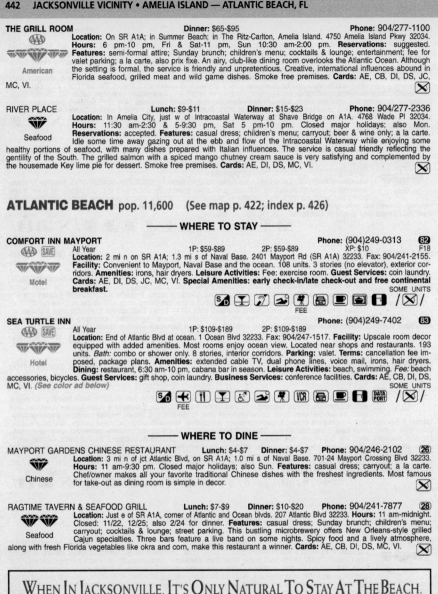

RIVER PLACE **Lunch:** $9-$11 **Dinner:** $15-$23 **Phone:** 904/277-2336
  ▼ **Location:** In Amelia City, just w of Intracoastal Waterway at Shave Bridge on A1A. 4768 Wade Pl 32034.
  Hours: 11:30 am-2:30 & 5-9:30 pm, Sat 5 pm-10 pm. Closed major holidays; also Mon.
  Seafood **Reservations:** accepted. **Features:** casual dress; children's menu; carryout; beer & wine only; a la carte.
  Idle some time away gazing out at the ebb and flow of the Intracoastal Waterway while enjoying some
healthy portions of seafood, with many dishes prepared with Italian influences. The service is casual friendly reflecting the
gentility of the South. The grilled salmon with a spiced mango chutney cream sauce is very satisfying and complemented by
the housemade Key lime pie for dessert. Smoke free premises. **Cards:** AE, DI, DS, MC, VI.

ATLANTIC BEACH pop. 11,600   (See map p. 422; index p. 426)

─── WHERE TO STAY ───

COMFORT INN MAYPORT **Phone:** (904)249-0313 82
  (AAA) (SAVE) All Year 1P: $59-$89 2P: $59-$89 XP: $10 F18
  ▼▼▼ **Location:** 2 mi n on SR A1A; 1.3 mi s of Naval Base. 2401 Mayport Rd (SR A1A) 32233. Fax: 904/241-2155.
  Facility: Convenient to Mayport, Naval Base and the ocean. 108 units. 3 stories (no elevator), exterior cor-
  Motel ridors. **Amenities:** irons, hair dryers. **Leisure Activities:** Fee: exercise room. **Guest Services:** coin laundry.
  Cards: AE, DI, DS, JC, MC, VI. **Special Amenities:** early check-in/late check-out and free continental
  breakfast.
  SOME UNITS
  [S/D] [🛁] [📺] [↻] [🛋] [🏃] [🖥] [💻] [🖼] [🔌] / [⊠] /
  FEE

SEA TURTLE INN **Phone:** (904)249-7402 83
  (AAA) (SAVE) All Year 1P: $109-$189 2P: $109-$189
  ▼▼▼ **Location:** End of Atlantic Blvd at ocean. 1 Ocean Blvd 32233. Fax: 904/247-1517. **Facility:** Upscale room decor
  equipped with added amenities. Most rooms enjoy ocean view. Located near shops and restaurants. 193
  Hotel units. *Bath:* combo or shower only. 8 stories, interior corridors. **Parking:** valet. **Terms:** cancellation fee im-
  posed, package plans. **Amenities:** extended cable TV, dual phone lines, voice mail, irons, hair dryers.
  Dining: restaurant, 6:30 am-10 pm, cabana bar in season. **Leisure Activities:** beach, swimming. *Fee:* beach
accessories, bicycles. **Guest Services:** gift shop, coin laundry. **Business Services:** conference facilities. **Cards:** AE, CB, DI, DS,
MC, VI. *(See color ad below)*
  SOME UNITS
  [S/D] [♿] [🍴] [📺] [🔊] [🛋] [🏃] [VCR] [🖥] [💻] [🔌] [DATA PORT] / [⊠] /
  FEE

─── WHERE TO DINE ───

MAYPORT GARDENS CHINESE RESTAURANT **Lunch:** $4-$7 **Dinner:** $4-$7 **Phone:** 904/246-2102 26
  ▼ **Location:** 3 mi n of jct Atlantic Blvd, on SR A1A; 1.0 mi s of Naval Base. 701-24 Mayport Crossing Blvd 32233.
  Hours: 11 am-9:30 pm. Closed major holidays; also Sun. **Features:** casual dress; carryout; a la carte.
  Chinese Chef/owner makes all your favorite traditional Chinese dishes with the freshest ingredients. Most famous
  for take-out as dining room is simple in decor.
  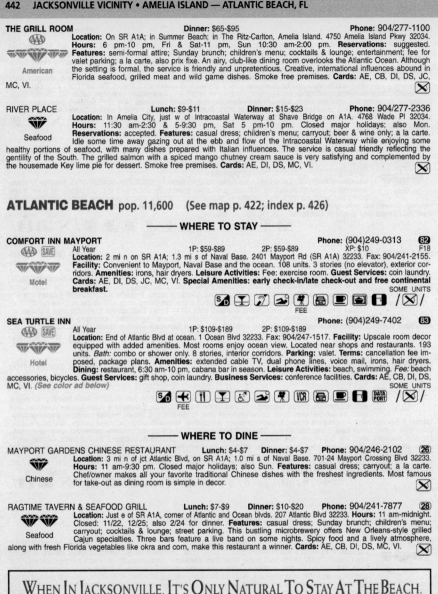

RAGTIME TAVERN & SEAFOOD GRILL **Lunch:** $7-$9 **Dinner:** $10-$20 **Phone:** 904/241-7877 28
  ▼▼ **Location:** Just e of SR A1A, corner of Atlantic and Ocean blvds. 207 Atlantic Blvd 32233. **Hours:** 11 am-midnight.
  Closed: 11/22, 12/25; also 2/24 for dinner. **Features:** casual dress; Sunday brunch; children's menu;
  Seafood carryout; cocktails & lounge; street parking. This bustling microbrewery offers New Orleans-style grilled
  Cajun specialties. Three bars feature a live band on some nights. Spicy food and a lively atmosphere,
along with fresh Florida vegetables like okra and corn, make this restaurant a winner. **Cards:** AE, CB, DI, DS, MC, VI.

(See map p. 422)

SERGIO'S NORTHERN ITALIAN & CONTINENTAL CUISINE   **Dinner:** $13-$22   **Phone:** 904/249-0101   ㉗
Italian
Location: Located in Atlantic Village Shopping Center, 1 mi e Intracoastal Waterway Bridge. 1021 Atlantic Blvd 32233. **Hours:** 5:30 pm-10:30 pm. Closed: 12/25; also Mon. **Features:** casual dress; cocktails & lounge; a la carte. It was voted Best Italian Restaurant for three of its four years of operation by readers of Jacksonville Magazine. Sergio's offers a broad selection of seafood, steak and chicken entrees, emphasizing presentation and moving away from traditional dishes. **Cards:** AE, CB, DI, DS, MC, VI.   ☒

STICKY FINGERS RESTAURANT & BAR   **Lunch:** $5-$15   **Dinner:** $5-$15   **Phone:** 904/241-7427   ㉙
American
Location: In Shoppes of North Shore at jct A1A. 363-1 Atlantic Blvd 32233. **Hours:** 11 am-10 pm, Fri & Sat-11 pm. Closed: 11/22, 12/25. **Features:** casual dress; carryout; cocktails; a la carte. Food and Wine Magazine calls this rib place "delicious!" Yet there is a lot more than just the ribs. Enjoy the barbecue beef, chicken or pork with a selection of sauce. Leave room for the homemade dessert. Covered outdoor dining and weekend entertainment on weekends. **Cards:** AE, DI, DS, MC, VI.   ☒

BALDWIN pop. 1,500   (See map p. 422; index p. 426)

———— WHERE TO STAY ————

BEST WESTERN INN BALDWIN   **Phone:** (904)266-9759   ㉘
AAA SAVE   All Year   1P: $45-$90   2P: $50-$95   XP: $5   F12
Motel
Location: I-10, exit 50, just s. 1088 US 301 & I-10 32234. Fax: 904/266-9759. **Facility:** 44 units. 1 story, exterior corridors. **Terms:** cancellation fee imposed, pets ($8 extra charge). **Amenities:** extended cable TV. **Guest Services:** [CP] meal plan available. **Cards:** AE, DI, DS, MC, VI. **Special Amenities:** early check-in/late check-out.
SOME UNITS
☒

FERNANDINA BEACH pop. 8,760

———— WHERE TO STAY ————

———— *The following lodging was either not evaluated or did not* ————
meet AAA rating requirements but is listed for your information only.

HAMPTON INN & SUITES-AMELIA ISLAND   **Phone:** 904/491-4911
[fyi]   All Year   1P: $124-$144   2P: $134-$154
Motel   Too new to rate. **Location:** I-95, exit 129 (Hwy A1A), 16 mi then left on Ash St. 19 S 2nd St 32034. Fax: 904/491-4910. **Amenities:** 122 units, radios, coffeemakers, microwaves, refrigerators, pool. **Cards:** AE, CB, DI, DS, JC, MC, VI.

GREEN COVE SPRINGS pop. 4,500

———— WHERE TO STAY ————

RIVER PARK INN, THE 1887 HOUSE   **Phone:** 904/284-2994
All Year   1P: $65-$100
Historic Bed & Breakfast
Location: Historic business district; corner of Spring; across from park. 103 S Magnolia Ave 32043. **Facility:** Spring fed mineral water pool in park across street. Close to public pier on river with boat slips and on city walking tour. Designated smoking area. 5 units. Some whirlpool units ($95-$100). *Bath:* combo, shower or tub only. 2 stories, interior corridors. **Amenities:** voice mail, irons, hair dryers. *Some:* CD players. **Leisure Activities:** whirlpool, bicycles. **Guest Services:** [BP] meal plan available, complimentary laundry. *Fee:* area transportation. **Cards:** AE, DS, MC, VI.
SOME UNITS
(ASK) ⊕ FEE

———— WHERE TO DINE ————

RONNIE'S WINGS, OYSTERS & MORE   **Lunch:** $5-$15   **Dinner:** $5-$15   **Phone:** 904/284-4728
American
Location: Corner of Magnolia; across from park. 232 Walnut St 32043. **Hours:** 11 am-11 pm. **Features:** No A/C; casual dress; cocktails; a la carte. You'll be amazed at the many selections on this menu. Choose a lighter fare from a wide selection of appetizers including calamari, or chow down on one of the house specials of shrimp, fish or chicken. Friendly servers are eager to please. **Cards:** AE, DS, MC, VI.

RUMOR'S CAFE & GIFTS   **Lunch:** $3   **Dinner:** $15   **Phone:** 904/284-3717
American
Location: Downtown, just n of park, just e of SR 17. 116 N Magnolia Ave 32042. **Hours:** 11 am-9 pm, Fri-10 pm. Closed major holidays; also Sat & Sun. **Features:** casual dress; a la carte. Cozy wooden tables and regional crafts create a nice setting for this counter service cafe. A wide selection of soups and sandwiches with homemade desserts such as pies, cakes, tortes and ice cream are offered. A gift shop sells hand-crafted delights. **Cards:** AE, MC, VI.

JACKSONVILLE BEACH pop. 17,800 (See map p. 422; index p. 426)

———— WHERE TO STAY ————

BEST WESTERN INN & SUITES OCEANFRONT

Phone: (904)249-4949   99

	3/1-9/4	1P: $99-$189	2P: $99-$189	XP: $10	F16
	12/1-2/28 & 9/5-11/30	1P: $89-$139	2P: $89-$139	XP: $10	F16

Motel

Location: 0.4 mi n of Beach Blvd (US 90). 305 N First St 32250. Fax: 904/249-6040. **Facility:** Spacious rooms most with balcony affording ocean view. 51 units. Some whirlpool units ($139-$189). 3 stories, interior corridors. **Terms:** 7 day cancellation notice, package plans. **Amenities:** extended cable TV, voice mail. **Leisure Activities:** beach, swimming. **Guest Services:** valet laundry. *Fee:* area transportation. **Cards:** AE, DI, DS, JC, MC, VI. **Special Amenities: free continental breakfast and free local telephone calls.**

SOME UNITS

🆘 ✈ 🏊 🐾 🖨 💻 📠 🛗 DATA PORT / ✖ /
      FEE

COMFORT INN OCEANFRONT

Phone: (904)241-2311   97

	5/25-9/3	1P: $99-$159	2P: $99-$159	XP: $10	F18
	3/1-5/24	1P: $89-$149	2P: $89-$149	XP: $10	F18
	12/1-2/28 & 9/4-11/30	1P: $79-$139	2P: $79-$139	XP: $10	F18

Motel

Location: Just e of SR A1A, on 1st St at 14th Ave N. 1515 N 1st St 32250. Fax: 904/249-3830. **Facility:** Attractive pool with waterfalls. 177 units. Some whirlpool units. *Bath:* combo or shower only. 7 stories, interior corridors. **Terms:** weekly & monthly rates available, package plans. **Amenities:** video games, safes (fee), irons. *Some:* hair dryers. **Leisure Activities:** heated pool, whirlpool, beach, swimming, exercise room. **Guest Services:** [ECP] meal plan available, gift shop, valet laundry. **Business Services:** meeting rooms. **Cards:** AE, CB, DI, DS, JC, MC, VI. *(See color ad below)*

SOME UNITS

🆘 🍽 🍸 🐾 🏊 🐾 💻 DATA PORT / ✖ 📠 🛗
      FEE

DAYS INN OCEANFRONT RESORT

Phone: (904)249-7231   100

	6/1-9/3	1P: $105-$155	2P: $105-$155	
	3/1-5/31	1P: $95-$135	2P: $95-$135	
	9/4-11/30	1P: $85-$135	2P: $85-$135	
	12/1-2/28	1P: $85-$119	2P: $85-$119	

Motor Inn

Location: At 11th Ave S. 1031 S 1st St 32250. Fax: 904/249-7924. **Facility:** All rooms have balcony. 154 units. 1-8 stories, exterior corridors. **Terms:** package plans, small pets only ($25 extra charge). **Amenities:** extended cable TV, safes (fee). **Dining:** dining room, 6 am-11 & 5-9 pm, $6-$13, cocktails. **Leisure Activities:** beach, swimming. **Guest Services:** area transportation-Mayo Clinic, coin laundry. **Business Services:** meeting rooms. **Cards:** AE, CB, DI, DS, JC, MC, VI. **Special Amenities: free newspaper.**

SOME UNITS

🆘 🐾 🍽 🍸 🏊 🐾 / ✖ 📠 🛗
    FEE FEE

HOLIDAY INN SUNSPREE RESORT

Phone: (904)249-9071   95

	5/26-9/5	1P: $99-$159	2P: $99-$179	XP: $10	F19
	3/1-5/25	1P: $89-$139	2P: $89-$159	XP: $10	F19
	9/6-11/30	1P: $85-$109	2P: $85-$119	XP: $10	F19
	12/1-2/28	1P: $75-$99	2P: $75-$109	XP: $10	F19

Motor Inn

Location: Just e of SR A1A, at 16th Ave N. 1617 N 1st St 32250. Fax: 904/241-4321. **Facility:** Accommodating staff. 143 units. Some suites ($199-$299). 4-7 stories, interior/exterior corridors. **Terms:** check-in 4 pm, cancellation fee imposed, package plans. **Amenities:** extended cable TV, video games, voice mail. **Dining:** dining room, 6:30 am-11 & 5-10 pm; snack shop 9 am-9 pm, $7-$16, cocktails. **Leisure Activities:** beach, swimming, beach activities, children's program, exercise room. *Fee:* beach supplies & games, kayaks, bicycles. **Guest Services:** [BP] meal plan available, gift shop, area transportation-Mayo Clinic, coin laundry. **Business Services:** meeting rooms. **Cards:** AE, DI, DS, MC, VI. **Special Amenities: free local telephone calls and free newspaper.** *(See color ad p 445)*

SOME UNITS

🆘 🍽 🍸 🏋 🏊 🐾 ✖ 🐾 💻 📠 🛗 DATA PORT / ✖ /
      FEE

(See map p. 422)

PELICAN PATH B & B BY THE SEA

▼ ▼ ▼

Bed & Breakfast

2/1-10/31   1P: $95-$165   2P: $95-$165   XP: $20
12/1-1/31 & 11/1-11/30   1P: $80-$140   2P: $80-$140   XP: $20

Phone: (904)249-1177   94

Location: Oceanfront at 1st St. 11 N 19th Ave 32250. Fax: 904/346-5412. **Facility:** A friendly welcome from gracious owners awaits you in this home by the sea with two spacious rooms overlooking the ocean. Enjoy hearty breakfast with fruit, Pan Dowdy being a specialty. Golf and tennis facilities nearby. 4 units. Some whirlpool units ($120-$165). 3 stories (no elevator), interior corridors. **Terms:** age restrictions may apply, 7 day cancellation notice. **Amenities:** extended cable TV, hair dryers. **Leisure Activities:** beach, swimming, bicycles. **Guest Services:** [BP] meal plan available, complimentary evening beverages. **Cards:** AE, DS, MC, VI.

(ASK) (S/D) (✕) (VCR) (🖨) (💻) (📶) (DATA PORT)

──────── *The following lodging was either not evaluated or did not* ────────
meet AAA rating requirements but is listed for your information only.

HAMPTON INN PONTE VEDRA AT JACKSONVILLE BEACH

(fyi)

Motel

Phone: 904/280-9101

Under construction, scheduled to open January 2001. **Location:** I-95N, exit 99(Southside Blvd/SR 115), merge onto FL-115N; SR 202 E Butler toward University of Florida, merge onto J Turner Blvd, exit Marsh Landing. 1220 Marsh Landing 32250. Fax: 904/280-9101. **Planned Amenities:** 118 units, radios, coffeemakers, pool.
(See color ad p 449)

──────── **WHERE TO DINE** ────────

BILLY'S

▼ ▼ ▼

American

Lunch: $5-$12   Dinner: $8-$18   Phone: 904/246-8099   34

Location: Corner of SR A1A and 17th Ave N. 1728 N 3rd St 32234. **Hours:** 11 am-11 pm, Sun from noon. Closed major holidays. **Features:** casual dress; cocktails; a la carte. Come casual and ready for a lively time! Billy's is a hopping place for food, fun and spirits, churning out gourmet food. Enjoy conch fritters, mushroom caps, local fresh seafood and big burgers. Great selection of domestic and imported brews.

Cards: AE, MC, VI.   (✕)

ELLEN'S KITCHEN

▼

American

Lunch: $3-$9   Phone: 904/246-1572   40

Location: Pablo Plaza Shopping Center, n end. 1824 S 3rd St 32250. **Hours:** 7 am-2 pm. Closed: 11/22, 12/25. **Features:** The locals line up at this cheery diner for breakfast every day of the week. Make your own omelette with home-made biscuits. Eat breakfast and other fine Southern cooking all day long. The crab cake benedict is an unusual offering. Servers are informed and pleasant. **Cards:** MC, VI.   (✕)

(See map p. 422)

FIRST STREET GRILLE Lunch: $6-$9 Dinner: $14-$19 Phone: 904/246-6555 (38)
AAA
WWW **Location:** Just e of SR A1A, corner N First St and 7th Ave. 807 N First St 32250. **Hours:** 11:30 am-10 pm, Fri &
Sat 11 pm. Closed: 1/1, 11/22, 12/25. **Features:** casual dress; Sunday brunch; children's menu; carryout;
American cocktails & lounge. A comfortable beach setting, it features selections from around the world. Grilled steak
and seafood are offered at value prices. A salad of spinach, nuts and fruits topped with a raspberry
vinaigrette offers a unique flavor. Outdoor dining is available. **Cards:** AE, CB, DI, DS, MC, VI. (X)

THE HOMESTEAD Lunch: $7-$14 Dinner: $7-$14 Phone: 904/249-5240 (39)
WWW **Location:** Just e of Intracoastal Waterway Bridge. 1712 Beach Blvd 32250. **Hours:** 5 pm-11 pm, Sun noon-11 pm.
Reservations: suggested. **Features:** casual dress; children's menu; cocktails & lounge. prix fixe.
American Family-oriented home-style dining is what you'll get in this bustling environment. The 1920s log cabin
teems with personality, helped in part by interesting, yesteryear photographs of the community and simple,
camp-style place settings. **Cards:** AE, DI, DS, MC, VI. (X)

ICHIBAN JAPANESE STEAK HOUSE Dinner: $8-$15 Phone: 904/247-8228 (35)
WWW WWW **Location:** From jct US 90 (Beach Blvd) and A1A (3rd St), 0.4 mi n. 675 N 3rd St 32250. **Hours:** 5 pm-9:45 pm, Fri
& Sat-10:45 pm. **Features:** casual dress; early bird specials; carryout; wine only; a la carte. Sushi, Teriyaki,
Japanese Tempura or steak table delicacies may all be found at Ichiban. Casual atmosphere with attentive service
and hearty portions serve up an oriental feast for the senses. Choose Sushi made to order as you watch
or steak, seafood and beef combinations offered by a smiling chef at spotless steak table grills. Japanese cookery with an
American accent is found in entrees such as hibachi shrimp, scallops, chicken, steak and lobster. **Cards:** AE, DI, MC, VI. (X)

PAGODA CHINESE Lunch: $4-$12 Dinner: $4-$12 Phone: 904/241-0414 (36)
WWW WWW **Location:** Corner of 3rd St (SR A1A), south of Beach Blvd. 223 S 9th St 32250. **Hours:** 11:30 am-10 pm, Sat 5
pm-11 pm, Sun noon-10 pm. Closed: 7/4, 11/22, 12/25. **Features:** casual dress; carryout; cocktails; a la
Chinese carte. Friendly attentive service awaits you in this family owned restaurant. Lots of traditional dishes to
choose including Szechuan delights, sesame chicken, almond pressed duck, as well as vegetarian entrees.
Cards: AE, DS, MC, VI. (X)

ULI'S EUROPEAN RESTAURANT Lunch: $5-$12 Dinner: $9-$20 Phone: 904/241-4969 (37)
WW WW **Location:** Just e of 3rd St (SR A1A). 216 S 11th Ave 32224. **Hours:** 11 am-2:30 & 5-9:30 pm, Fri & Sat 5 pm-10
pm, Sun noon-9 pm. Closed: Mon. **Features:** casual dress; carryout; beer & wine only; a la carte. You'll
German feel like you're in Germany at Uli's! Vivacious owner greets guests at door with friendly welcome. Enjoy
light lunches of crab cakes, reuben sandwich or heartier dinner meals with all the German favorites -
rouladen and sauerbraten. Don't leave without trying the homemade desserts. **Cards:** AE, MC, VI. (X)

---

*The following restaurant has not been evaluated by AAA
but is listed for your information only.*

DOLPHIN DEPOT Phone: 904/270-1424
[fyi] Not evaluated. **Location:** Corner of 6th Ave N and 1st St. 704 N 1st St 32221. **Features:** Eclectic Carolina
coastal cuisine including lobster and variety of fish.

NEPTUNE BEACH pop. 6,800 (See map p. 422; index p. 426)

——— WHERE TO STAY ———

SEA HORSE OCEANFRONT INN Phone: 904/246-2175 (110)
WWW WWW All Year 1P: $79-$139 2P: $79-$139 XP: $10 F18
Location: Jct of Atlantic Blvd and 1st St. 120 Atlantic Blvd 32266. Fax: 904/246-4256. **Facility:** Enjoy ocean views
Motel from all rooms. Picturesque lawn area with pool. Convenient to quaint shopping area. 38 units, 1 with kitchen.
Bath: combo or shower only. 3 stories, exterior corridors. **Leisure Activities:** beach, swimming, shuffleboard.
Cards: AE, DI, DS, MC, VI. SOME UNITS
(S/D) (H+) (ra) (Z) / (X) (D) (m) (D) /

——— WHERE TO DINE ———

MEZZA LUNA VAGABONDO RISTORANTE Dinner: $10-$19 Phone: 904/246-5100 (50)
WWW WWW **Location:** Corner shopping area of Atlantic Blvd and 1st St; adjacent to court house. 110 1st Ave 32266. **Hours:** 4
pm-11 pm, Fri & Sat-midnight, Sun 3 pm-11 pm. Closed major holidays; also Mon.
Italian **Reservations:** suggested. **Features:** casual dress; cocktail lounge; street parking; a la carte. Enjoy special
seafood and veal entrees and pizza made in a wood-burning oven. A trained and knowledgeable staff
make this restaurant seem like home. A scrumptious dessert menu includes a thin, caramelized layer of creme brulee in a
thick raspberry sauce. **Cards:** AE, DS, MC, VI. (X)

SUN DOG DINER Lunch: $5-$10 Dinner: $5-$10 Phone: 904/241-8221 (49)
WW WW **Location:** Just e of 3rd St (A1A). 207 Atlantic Blvd 32233. **Hours:** 7 am-11 pm. Closed: 12/25; also 12/24 for
dinner. **Features:** No A/C; casual dress; cocktails; street parking; a la carte. Voted one of the top
American restaurants in Jacksonville. This "diner" has it all. A popular spot frequented by locals offering hamburgers,
hot dogs, as well as seared tuna and filet mignon. Half of the restaurant is a lively night spot with
entertainment. For the cigar connoisseur, try the smoker's room with comfy chairs and a TV. A great place to stop in and sit at
the counter with one of their ever popular thick and rich milkshakes. **Cards:** AE, DI, DS, MC, VI. (X)

ORANGE PARK pop. 9,500 (See map p. 422; index p. 427)

——— WHERE TO STAY ———

COMFORT INN
AAA SAVE
Motel
All Year   1P: $69-$89   2P: $69-$89   **Phone:** (904)264-3297   140
Location: I-295, exit 3, just s on US 17. 341 Park Ave 32073. Fax: 904/215-9585. **Facility:** Large pool area, property is adjacent to kennel club. 119 units. 2 stories, exterior corridors. **Terms:** package plans, pets ($25 fee). **Amenities:** irons, hair dryers. **Leisure Activities:** tennis court. **Guest Services:** coin laundry. **Business Services:** meeting rooms. **Cards:** AE, CB, DI, DS, MC, VI. **Special Amenities:** free continental breakfast and free room upgrade (subject to availability with advanced reservations). *(See color ad below)*
SOME UNITS

DAYS INN
AAA SAVE
Motel
All Year   1P: $59-$79   2P: $59-$79   **Phone:** (904)269-8887   137
Location: I-295, exit 3, just s on US 17. 4280 Eldridge Loop 32073. Fax: 904/215-9294. **Facility:** Some double rooms tend to be crowded. 62 units. 3 stories (no elevator), interior corridors. **Terms:** pets ($25 extra charge). **Leisure Activities:** pool & tennis privileges at nearby property. **Guest Services:** valet laundry. **Cards:** AE, CB, DI, DS, MC, VI. **Special Amenities:** free continental breakfast and free room upgrade (subject to availability with advanced reservations).
SOME UNITS

FAIRFIELD INN BY MARRIOTT
Motel
				Phone: (904)278-7442 139
12/31-1/1	1P: $89-$99	2P: $99-$109	XP: $10	F
1/2-11/30	1P: $70-$75	2P: $75-$80	XP: $5	F
12/1-12/30	1P: $65-$75	2P: $70-$80	XP: $5	F

Location: I-295, exit 3, 0.3 mi s to Wells Rd, then w. 450 Eldridge Ave 32073. Fax: 904/278-5022. **Facility:** Convenient to large mall. 83 units. *Bath:* combo or shower only. 3 stories, interior corridors. **Amenities:** extended cable TV. **Leisure Activities:** whirlpool, exercise room. **Guest Services:** [ECP] meal plan available, valet laundry. **Cards:** AE, DI, DS, JC, MC, VI.
SOME UNITS

(See map p. 422)

HAMPTON INN-ORANGE PARK
Phone: (904)777-5313   **131**

SAVE
▼▼▼
Motel

All Year   1P: $71   2P: $78
Location: I-295, exit 4, sw corner off of SR 21. 6135 Youngerman Cir 32244. **Fax:** 904/778-1545. **Facility:** Adjacent to shopping center. Short drive to large mall. 121 units. 2 stories, exterior corridors. **Terms:** cancellation fee imposed. **Amenities:** voice mail, safes, irons. *Some:* hair dryers. **Leisure Activities:** heated pool. **Guest Services:** [ECP] meal plan available, valet laundry. **Business Services:** meeting rooms, fax. *Fee:* PC. **Cards:** AE, CB, DI, DS, MC, VI.

SOME UNITS

HOLIDAY INN-ORANGE PARK
Phone: (904)264-9513   **136**

(AAA) **SAVE**
▼▼▼
Motor Inn

All Year   1P: $69-$89   2P: $69-$89
Location: I-295, exit 3, just sw on US 17. 150 Park Ave 32073. **Fax:** 904/278-1575. **Facility:** 299 units. Some suites ($99-$199). 2 stories, exterior corridors. **Amenities:** extended cable TV, video games, voice mail, irons, hair dryers. **Dining:** dining room, 6 am-10 & 11-11 pm, $7-$14, cocktails. **Leisure Activities:** wading pool. **Guest Services:** coin laundry. **Business Services:** meeting rooms. **Cards:** AE, CB, DI, DS, JC, MC, VI. *(See color ad p 447)*

SOME UNITS

LA QUINTA INN-JACKSONVILLE/ORANGE PARK
Phone: (904)778-9539   **134**

SAVE
▼▼▼
Motel

All Year   1P: $59-$69   2P: $59-$69
Location: I-295, exit 4, just se on SR 21. 8555 Blanding Blvd 32244-5797. **Fax:** 904/779-5214. **Facility:** Large king rooms with two phones, recliner and padded desk chair. 122 units. 2 stories, exterior corridors. **Terms:** small pets only. **Guest Services:** coin laundry. **Business Services:** meeting rooms. **Cards:** AE, CB, DI, DS, MC, VI. *(See color ad p 434)*

SOME UNITS

RED ROOF INN-SOUTH
Phone: (904)777-1000   **133**

(AAA) **SAVE**
▼▼ ▼▼
Motel

12/1-12/31	1P: $41-$54	2P: $48-$61	XP: $7 F18
1/1-11/30	1P: $44-$50	2P: $51-$57	XP: $7 F18

Location: I-295, exit 4, jct SR 21. 6099 Youngerman Cir 32244. **Fax:** 904/777-1005. **Facility:** 108 units. 2 stories, exterior corridors. **Terms:** small pets only. **Cards:** AE, CB, DI, DS, MC, VI. **Special Amenities:** free local telephone calls and free newspaper.

SOME UNITS

——— **WHERE TO DINE** ———

THE HILLTOP
▼▼ ▼▼
Chinese

Lunch: $7-$18   Dinner: $7-$18   Phone: 904-272-5959   **75**
Location: I-295, exit 4, s on Blanding Blvd, then 0.3 mi. 2030 Wells Rd. **Hours:** 11:30 am-2 & 5-9:30 pm, Sat 5-9:30 pm. Closed: Sun & Mon. **Features:** No A/C; semi-formal attire; cocktail lounge; a la carte. A prominent Orange Park landmark. The Hilltop offers gracious Southern hospitality in the charming environment of the Old South. Enjoy lunch on the sunny porch overlooking the old oak trees and pool or enjoy dinner in the stately formal dining room. Extensive wine list. **Cards:** AE, DI, DS, MC, VI.

——— *The following restaurant has not been evaluated by AAA* ———
but is listed for your information only.

SARNELLI'S RISTORANTE
[fyi]

Phone: 904-269-1331
Not evaluated. Location: Corner of Kingsley and US 17. 2023 Park Ave 32073. **Features:** Classic Italian dishes.

PONTE VEDRA BEACH pop. 2,900   (See map p. 422; index p. 426)

─── WHERE TO STAY ───

COUNTRY INN & SUITES BY CARLSON   Phone: (904)280-1661   **119**

12/1-4/30   1P: $99-$249
5/1-11/30   1P: $99-$159

Motel   **Location:** 5 mi s of jct J Turner Butler Blvd on US A1A, just e; in Sawgrass Village Shopping Center. 1300 Saw Grass Village Dr 32082. Fax: 904/280-1544. **Facility:** Plush room decor. Suites offer additional room and amenities. Adjacent to trendy shopping center. 128 units. Some suites and whirlpool units. 6 stories, interior corridors. **Terms:** cancellation fee imposed. **Amenities:** extended cable TV, dual phone lines, voice mail, irons, hair dryers. **Leisure Activities:** whirlpool. **Guest Services:** [ECP] meal plan available, coin laundry. **Cards:** AE, DI, DS, MC, VI. *(See color ad p 572)*   SOME UNITS

PONTE VEDRA INN AND CLUB   Phone: (904)285-1111   **120**

(AAA) (SAVE)

3/1-5/31   1P: $310   2P: $310
9/1-11/30   1P: $250   2P: $250
12/1-2/28   1P: $175-$235   2P: $175-$235
6/1-8/31   1P: $225   2P: $225

Resort   **Location:** I-95, exit 101, Turner-Butler Expwy (SR 202) to A1A, 0.5 mi n to 36th Ave s, s via CR 203 and Ponte Vedra Blvd. 200 Ponte Vedra Blvd 32082-9305. Fax: 904/285-2111. **Facility:** Renowned beach club resort founded in 1927. A charming blend of the traditional with bright, contemporary, oceanfront guestrooms with balcony or patio. Skilled, experienced service staff. 200 units. 38 efficiencies and 4 units with kitchen. Some suites ($275-$410) and whirlpool units ($215-$350). 2 stories, exterior corridors. **Parking:** valet. **Terms:** 3 day cancellation notice-fee imposed, package plans. **Amenities:** extended cable TV, dual phone lines, voice mail, safes, honor bars, irons, hair dryers. **Dining:** 4 dining rooms, guests only, cocktails, entertainment. **Leisure Activities:** 4 pools (2 heated), wading pool, saunas, whirlpool, steamrooms, beach, swimming, fishing, putting green, children's program, recreation program, jogging, playground, aerobics room. *Fee:* boating, paddleboats, sailboating, windsurfing, golf-36 holes, 15 tennis courts (7 lighted), bicycles, full service health & beauty spa. **Guest Services:** gift shop, area transportation-Ponte Vedra, coin laundry. *Fee:* massage. **Business Services:** conference facilities, administrative services, fax. **Cards:** AE, CB, DI, DS, MC, VI. **Special Amenities:** free local telephone calls and free newspaper.   SOME UNITS

PONTE VEDRA LODGE AND CLUB   Phone: (904)273-9500   **121**

(AAA) (SAVE)

3/1-5/31   1P: $310   2P: $310
9/1-11/30   1P: $250   2P: $250
12/1-2/28   1P: $175-$235   2P: $175-$235
6/1-8/31   1P: $225   2P: $225

Resort   **Location:** I-95, exit 101, Butler Crossway (SR 202) to A1A, 0.5 mi n to 36th Ave, 2 mi s. 607 Ponte Vedra Blvd 32082. Fax: 904/273-0210. **Facility:** Spacious, well appointed rooms in a sophisticated, Mediterranean-flavored, oceanside resort. Warm and energetic staff offer personalized services. Many seaside activities or enjoy guest rooms with fireplace and balcony over looking the ocean. 66 units. Some whirlpool units ($215-$350). *Bath:* some combo or tub only. 2 stories (no elevator), exterior corridors. **Parking:** valet. **Terms:** check-in 4 pm, 3 day cancellation notice-fee imposed, package plans. **Amenities:** extended cable TV, dual phone lines, voice mail, safes, honor bars, irons. *Some:* hair dryers. **Dining:** dining room, guests only; seasonal outdoor dining 3/1-12/31; 18% service charge, $11-$25, cocktails, entertainment. **Leisure Activities:** 3 heated pools, wading pool, saunas, whirlpools, steamrooms, beach, swimming, social program, seasonal bar & grill poolside. *Fee:* sailboating, kayaks, bicycles. **Guest Services:** gift shop, afternoon tea, area transportation-Ponte Vedra, valet laundry. *Fee:* massage. **Business Services:** meeting rooms. **Cards:** AE, DI, DS, MC, VI. **Special Amenities:** free local telephone calls and free newspaper. Affiliated with A Preferred Hotel.   SOME UNITS

─── WHERE TO DINE ───

EDDIE'S PALM VALLEY CROSSING   **Lunch:** $3-$10   **Dinner:** $8-$16   Phone: 904/285-5028   **62**

Location: Ne side of Palm Valley Bridge, CR 210. 3020 Palm Valley Rd 32082. **Hours:** 11 am-9 pm, Fri & Sat-10 pm. Closed: Mon. **Features:** casual dress; children's menu; cocktails. Sea critters decorate the walls of this wonderful seafood find. Exceptional Florida-style country cooking is featured in a nautical dining room overlooking the Intracoastal Waterway. This is simply good home cooking without the fuss. **Cards:** AE, MC, VI.

American

(See map p. 422)

GIO'S CAFE
Continental
Dinner: $15-$40
Phone: 904/273-0101   60
Location: Center, Sawgrass Village Shopping Center. 900 Sawgrass Village 32082. **Hours:** 5:30 pm-11 pm, Fri & Sat-midnight. Closed major holidays. **Features:** No A/C; casual dress; cocktails & lounge; street parking & fee for valet parking; a la carte. Much thought clearly goes into the preparation and presentation of such entrees as garlic-stuffed fillet and signature veal. An impressive wine list includes selections to complement any meal. The art deco atmosphere is energetic; the service impeccable. **Cards:** AE, DI, MC, VI.

J J'S CUISINE & WINE
French
Lunch: $6-$15   **Dinner:** $14-$25
Phone: 904/273-7980   58
Location: 2 mi s of jct JTB Blvd; in Shoppes at Ponte Vedra. 330 A1A N Ste 209 32082. **Hours:** 11:30 am-9:30 pm, Fri & Sat-10:30 pm. Closed major holidays. **Features:** casual dress; beer & wine only; a la carte. When you enter JJ's, you enter the streets of Paris! Enjoy browsing the gourmet groceries and bakery, then dine in the cafe. Choose from quiche, soup and sandwiches for lunch or enjoy a heartier dinner of roast loin, salmon or seared tuna. **Cards:** AE, DI, DS, MC, VI.

LULU'S WATERFRONT GRILL
Seafood
Lunch: $4-$8   **Dinner:** $12-$18
Phone: 904/285-0139   61
Location: 1 mi s on Roscoe Blvd. 301 N Roscoe Blvd 32082. **Hours:** 11 am-9:30 pm, Fri & Sat-10 pm. Closed major holidays. **Features:** casual dress; cocktails. Dining on the screened porch of this restaurant, which resembles a clapboard house, is darned close to what old Florida is all about. Feast on shrimp jambalaya, caper-coated catch of the day and the native dessert, key lime pie. **Cards:** AE, MC, VI.

SANTIONI'S OF SAWGRASS
Italian
Dinner: $9-$17
Phone: 904/273-7272   63
Location: 1 mi n of jct A1A and CR 210; in Tournament Plaza Shopping Center. 832-1 A1A N 32082. **Hours:** 5 pm-10 pm, Fri & Sat-11 pm. Closed: 4/15, 11/22, 12/25. **Reservations:** suggested. **Features:** casual dress; cocktails; a la carte. Classic Italian fare prepared by chef-owner for over 28 years. Feature shrimp fra diavalo, linguine with clam sauce, and gnoochi. Wide selection of California wines. All dishes are made to order, pizza avail as carry-out. **Cards:** AE, DS, MC, VI.

THE TAVERN AT SAWGRASS
American
Phone: 904/285-3133   59
Location: Just off SR A1A; in Sawgrass Village Shopping Center. 500 Sawgrass Village 32082. **Hours:** 11 am-1 am, Sat from 4 pm, Sun 4 pm-11:30 pm. **Features:** casual dress; cocktails & lounge; a la carte. A relaxed and friendly atmosphere awaits you at this popular neighborhood eatery. Enjoy large selection of finger foods or such delicacies as salmon, one of the chef's specialties. Take time to look over framed pictures taken at local golfing events. **Cards:** AE, DI, DS, MC, VI.

YULEE pop. 2,750

——— WHERE TO STAY ———

COMFORT INN
SAVE
Motel
Phone: (904)225-2600
All Year   1P: $50-$99   2P: $50-$109   XP: $10   F14
Location: I-95, exit 129, just e on SR 200/US A1A. 126 Sidney Pl 32097. Fax: 904/225-1966. **Facility:** King rooms available with desk and recliner or sofa. Must drive to nearest town. 59 units. Interior corridors. **Terms:** check-in 4 pm. **Amenities:** irons, hair dryers. **Guest Services:** [CP] meal plan available. **Cards:** AE, DS, MC, VI.

HOLIDAY INN EXPRESS
Motel
Phone: (904)225-5114
All Year   1P: $65-$95   2P: $65-$95   XP: $6   F18
Location: I-95, exit 130, just w. 3276 US 17N 32097. Fax: 904/225-5274. **Facility:** 52 units. *Bath:* combo or shower only. 2 stories, exterior corridors. **Terms:** weekly & monthly rates available. **Amenities:** irons, hair dryers. **Guest Services:** [CP] meal plan available, coin laundry. **Business Services:** meeting rooms.
Cards: AE, CB, DI, DS, JC, MC, VI.
SOME UNITS

**This ends listings for the Jacksonville Vicinity.
The following page resumes the alphabetical listings of
cities in Florida.**

JACKSONVILLE BEACH —See Jacksonville p. 444.

JENSEN BEACH pop. 9,900

------ WHERE TO STAY ------

COURTYARD BY MARRIOTT OCEANSIDE

Phone: (561)229-1000

12/1-4/30	1P: $80-$180	2P: $80-$180	XP: $10	F
11/1-11/30	1P: $70-$150	2P: $70-$150	XP: $10	F
5/1-10/31	1P: $70-$140	2P: $70-$140	XP: $10	F

Motor Inn   **Location:** SR A1A, Hutchinson Island, 0.7 mi n of jct SR 732. 10978 S Ocean Dr 34957. Fax: 561/229-0253.
Facility: Some units with balcony. 110 units. 8 stories, interior corridors. **Terms:** cancellation fee imposed, monthly rates available, package plans. **Amenities:** voice mail, irons, hair dryers. **Leisure Activities:** heated pool, beach, swimming, exercise room. **Guest Services:** valet and coin laundry. **Business Services:** meeting rooms, fax. **Cards:** AE, DI, DS, MC, VI.

SOME UNITS

HOLIDAY INN OCEANSIDE-HUTCHINSON ISLAND

Phone: (561)225-3000

1/28-4/21	1P: $169-$199	2P: $169-$199	XP: $10	F19
12/1-1/27	1P: $89-$169	2P: $89-$169	XP: $10	F19
4/22-5/27	1P: $129-$159	2P: $129-$159	XP: $10	F19
5/28-11/30	1P: $89-$129	2P: $89-$129	XP: $10	F19

Motor Inn   **Location:** SR A1A; Hutchinson Island, 0.3 mi s of jct SR 732. 3793 NE Ocean Blvd 34957. Fax: 561/225-1956.
Facility: All rooms with balcony, some overlook the beach or the Indian River. 179 units. Some suites ($205-$525). **Bath:** combo or shower only. 5 stories, interior corridors. **Terms:** check-in 4 pm, cancellation fee imposed, package plans. **Amenities:** extended cable TV, video games, voice mail, safes, irons, hair dryers. **Dining:** restaurant, 6 am-2 & 5-10 pm, $13-$17, cocktails, entertainment. **Leisure Activities:** heated pool, beach, swimming, 3 tennis courts (1 lighted), exercise room. **Fee:** boogie boards. **Guest Services:** gift shop, coin laundry. **Fee:** massage. **Business Services:** meeting rooms, fax. **Cards:** AE, CB, DI, DS, JC, MC, VI. **Special Amenities:** early check-in/late check-out.

SOME UNITS

HUTCHINSON INN

Phone: (561)229-2000

	2P	XP	
All Year	2P: $80-$225	XP: $20	

Motel   **Location:** SR A1A, Hutchinson Island, 2.5 mi n of jct SR 732; I-95, exit 61, e to SR 76, following signs to beach. 9750 S Ocean Dr 34957. Fax: 561/229-8875. **Facility:** Charming establishment with touches of a B and B. Designated smoking area. 21 units. 5 two-bedroom units and 17 efficiencies. 2 stories, exterior corridors. **Terms:** 30 day cancellation notice, 14 day off season-fee imposed, monthly rates available, pet bulldogs add character to the inn. **Amenities:** extended cable TV, irons, hair dryers. **Leisure Activities:** heated pool, beach, swimming, tennis court. **Guest Services:** [ECP] meal plan available, gift shop, complimentary laundry. **Fee:** massage. **Cards:** MC, VI.

SOME UNITS

RIVER PALM COTTAGES

Phone: (561)334-0401

	2P	XP	
12/16-1/5	2P: $125-$398	XP: $15	F17
1/6-4/22	2P: $89-$398	XP: $15	F17
12/11-12/15 & 4/23-11/30	2P: $55-$250	XP: $15	F17

Cottage   **Location:** On SR 707 (NE Indian River Dr) 1.4 mi s of jct 732 (Jensen Cswy). 2325 NE Indian River Dr 34957.
Fax: 561/334-0527. **Facility:** Eight acres of waterfront property with brightly painted cottages and some with porches; pre-arrange in-room phones. 24 units. 8 two-bedroom units, 4 efficiencies and 20 units with kitchen. 1 story, exterior corridors. **Terms:** 7 day cancellation notice-fee imposed, small pets only ($50 deposit). **Leisure Activities:** heated pool, boat dock, marina. **Guest Services:** coin laundry. **Cards:** AE, CB, DI, DC, MC, VI.

SOME UNITS

------ WHERE TO DINE ------

CONCHY JOE'S SEAFOOD RESTAURANT

Lunch: $5-$12   Dinner: $10-$23   Phone: 561/334-1130

Seafood   **Location:** On CR 707, just n of jct SR 732 (Jensen Cswy). 3945 NE Indian River Dr 34957. **Hours:** 11:30 am-2:30 & 5-10 pm. Closed: 11/22, 12/25; also for dinner 12/24. **Features:** casual dress; children's menu; carryout; cocktails & lounge; entertainment. Enjoy waterfront dining in rustic, tropical ambience. Native Florida and Bahamian seafood dishes are the specialties. Start with the raw bar and a luscious lobster dip. Conch chowder recipe has been requested by some magazines. **Cards:** AE, DS, MC, VI.

LOBSTER SHANTY

Lunch: $6-$11   Dinner: $14-$18   Phone: 561/334-6400

Seafood   **Location:** CR 707, 3 mi sw of Jensen Cswy (SR 732), 1.8 mi e of jct US 1. 999 N East Anchorage Dr 33497.
Hours: 11:30 am-9 pm, Fri & Sat-10 pm. Closed: 11/22. **Features:** casual dress; children's menu; early bird specials; carryout; salad bar; cocktails & lounge. You will find a great view from an expansive porch overlooking the St Lucie River. Wonderful lobster soup and salmon in lemon sauce are specialties of this clean, comfortable eatery. Finish your meal with the Key lime pie and a robust blend of coffee. **Cards:** AE, DI, MC, VI.

JUNO BEACH pop. 2,100   (See map p. 710; index p. 713)

—— WHERE TO STAY ——

HAMPTON INN-JUNO BEACH   **Phone:** (561)626-9090   **74**

[SAVE]

| | 12/1-4/22 | 1P: $119-$199 | 2P: $129-$199 |
| | 4/23-11/30 | 1P: $65-$199 | 2P: $75-$139 |

Motel

Location: US 1, just s of jct Donald Ross Rd. 13801 US Hwy 1 33408. Fax: 561/624-9936. **Facility:** Very attractive rooms and public areas with traditional decor and furnishings. 88 units. Some whirlpool units. *Bath:* combo or shower only. 2 stories, interior corridors. **Terms:** cancellation fee imposed. **Amenities:** extended cable TV, voice mail, irons, hair dryers. **Leisure Activities:** heated pool, whirlpool, exercise room. **Guest Services:** [ECP] meal plan available, valet laundry. **Business Services:** meeting rooms. **Cards:** AE, CB, DI, DS, MC, VI.

SOME UNITS

🅂🄳 🛉🄼 🕭 🄴 🕩 🏊 🎥 🖭 🖵 🕰 / ✕ 🖥 🛄 /

HOLIDAY INN EXPRESS-NORTH PALM BEACH   **Phone:** (561)622-4366   **72**

	12/21-4/30	1P: $139-$199	2P: $139-$199
	12/1-12/20	1P: $89-$149	2P: $89-$149
	10/1-11/30	1P: $79-$129	2P: $79-$129
	5/1-9/30	1P: $59-$99	2P: $59-$99

Motel

Location: US 1, at jct Donald Ross Rd. 13950 US Hwy 1 33408. Fax: 561/625-5245. **Facility:** Spacious rooms with patio or balcony. 106 units. Some suites ($99-$199). 3 stories, interior/exterior corridors. **Terms:** 10 day cancellation notice, weekly & monthly rates available, package plans, pets ($25 extra charge). **Amenities:** extended cable TV, voice mail, irons, hair dryers. **Guest Services:** [ECP] meal plan available, valet laundry. **Business Services:** meeting rooms. **Cards:** AE, CB, DI, DS, JC, MC, VI.

SOME UNITS

[ASK] 🅂🄳 🐾 🛉🄼 🕩 🏊 🎥 🖭 🖵 / ✕ 🖥 🛄 /

—— WHERE TO DINE ——

CLASSICO'S ITALIAN RESTAURANT   **Dinner:** $8-$20   **Phone:** 561/622-9772   **40**

Italian

Location: US 1, just n of jct Donald Ross Rd; in Loggerhead Plaza. 14131 US Hwy 1 33408. **Hours:** 4:30 pm-10 pm, Sun 5 pm-9 pm. **Closed:** 11/22, 12/25. **Reservations:** suggested. **Features:** casual dress; early bird specials; carryout; cocktails & lounge. Candlelight dinners feature creative dishes of veal, chicken, pasta and seafood, all cooked to order with only fresh ingredients. The eatery is noted for its displays of movie memorabilia from the '20s through the '50s and its sinful homemade desserts. **Cards:** AE, MC, VI.

✕

JUPITER pop. 24,900

—— WHERE TO STAY ——

BEST WESTERN INTRACOASTAL INN   **Phone:** (561)575-2936

[AAA] [SAVE]

| | 2/5-4/15 | 1P: $129-$139 | 2P: $139-$149 | XP: $10 | F17 |
| | 12/1-2/4 & 4/16-11/30 | 1P: $59-$99 | 2P: $79-$99 | XP: $10 | F17 |

Motel

Location: On US 1, 0.5 mi s of jct SR 706 (Indiantown Rd). 810 S US Hwy 1 33477. Fax: 561/575-9346. **Facility:** Pool and deck overlooks the Intracoastal Waterway and mangroves. 53 units. Some whirlpool units. *Bath:* combo or shower only. 2 stories, interior corridors. **Terms:** weekly rates available. **Amenities:** extended cable TV, hair dryers. **Leisure Activities:** heated pool. **Guest Services:** [ECP] meal plan available, coin laundry. **Cards:** AE, CB, DI, DS, MC, VI. **Special Amenities:** free continental breakfast.

SOME UNITS

🅂🄳 🏊 / ✕ 🛄 /

FAIRFIELD INN & SUITES BY MARRIOTT   **Phone:** (561)748-5252

	12/22-4/15	1P: $99-$139	2P: $99-$139
	10/1-11/30	1P: $89-$119	2P: $89-$119
	12/1-12/21 & 4/16-9/30	1P: $69-$99	2P: $69-$99

Motel

Location: I-95, exit 59A, 0.8 mi e on SR 706 (Indiantown Rd). 6748 W Indiantown Rd 33458. Fax: 561/748-5251. **Facility:** An attractive property. Rooms with light wood tone furniture and bright decor colors. 110 units, 6 with efficiency. Some suites. *Bath:* combo or shower only. 4 stories, interior corridors. **Terms:** 3 day cancellation notice, in season 12/22-4/15 1 day notice; by 4:00 day of arrival-fee imposed. **Amenities:** extended cable TV, dual phone lines, voice mail, irons, hair dryers. **Leisure Activities:** heated pool, whirlpool, exercise room. **Guest Services:** [ECP] meal plan available, valet laundry. **Cards:** AE, CB, DI, DS, JC, MC, VI.

SOME UNITS

🛉🄼 🏊 🎥 🖭 🖵 🕰 / ✕ 🖥 🛄 /

THE JUPITER BEACH RESORT   **Phone:** (561)746-2511

[AAA] [SAVE]

	12/16-4/30	1P: $200-$450	2P: $200-$450	XP: $25	F17
	12/1-12/15 & 10/1-11/30	1P: $140-$240	2P: $140-$240	XP: $25	F17
	5/1-9/30	1P: $125-$205	2P: $125-$205	XP: $25	F17

Hotel

Location: SR A1A, 1 mi se of jct US 1; at jct SR 706, Indiantown Rd. 5 North A1A 33477-5190. Fax: 561/744-1741. **Facility:** Located on oceanfront. An attractive pool area with the beach just steps away. A large lobby with several sitting areas. Rooms are spacious with a tropical feel with light wood tones and complementing accent colors. 152 units. Some suites ($500-$1000). 9 stories, interior corridors. **Parking:** valet. **Terms:** check-in 4 pm, 7 day cancellation notice-fee imposed, weekly & monthly rates available, package plans. **Amenities:** voice mail, honor bars, irons, hair dryers. **Dining:** restaurant, 6:30 am-10 pm, $10-$28, cocktails, entertainment. **Leisure Activities:** heated pool, beach, swimming, lighted tennis court, exercise room. **Fee:** scuba diving/snorkeling & equipment, boogie boards, catamarans, kayaks, seadoos. **Guest Services:** gift shop, valet and coin laundry. **Business Services:** meeting rooms, fax. **Cards:** AE, CB, DI, DS, MC, VI. **Special Amenities:** free newspaper.

SOME UNITS

🅂🄳 🛉 🍽 🛗 🄴 🏊 🎾 🎥 🖭 🖵 🕰 / ✕ [VCR] 🖥 🛄 /
FEE   FEE   FEE

WELLESLEY INN & SUITES

Phone: (561)575-7201

	12/18-4/15	1P: $99-$139	2P: $99-$139	XP: $10	F17
	12/1-12/17 & 4/16-11/30	1P: $59-$79	2P: $59-$79	XP: $10	F17

Motel

Location: SR 706 (Indiantown Rd); 0.3 mi w of jct US 1; in Fisherman's Wharf Plaza. 34 Fishermans Wharf 33477. Fax: 561/575-1169. **Facility:** Rooms with a bright color scheme. Light wood tone furniture. Attractive lobby area. 105 units. Some suites ($129-$179). *Bath:* combo or shower only. 3 stories, interior corridors. **Terms:** small pets only. **Amenities:** video games, voice mail, hair dryers. *Some:* safes. **Leisure Activities:** heated pool. **Guest Services:** [ECP] meal plan available, coin laundry. **Business Services:** meeting rooms. **Cards:** AE, DI, DS, MC, VI. **Special Amenities:** free continental breakfast and free local telephone calls.
(See color ad opposite title page)

SOME UNITS

———— WHERE TO DINE ————

CHARLEY'S CRAB   **Lunch:** $6-$16   **Dinner:** $15-$30   **Phone:** 561/744-4710

Seafood

Location: At jct SR A1A on sw side of bridge; in Jupiter Harbor Complex. 1000 Hwy US 1 N 33477. **Hours:** 11:30 am-10 pm, Sun from 10:30 am. **Reservations:** suggested. **Features:** casual dress; Sunday brunch; children's menu; early bird specials; carryout; cocktails & lounge; valet parking; a la carte. Atrium-style dining is the mode at the busy, waterfront restaurant, which offers views of the Jupiter lighthouse. The strains of jazz and calypso fill the air on weekends. Sample the crab cakes and homemade pasta, or enjoy the Sunday champagne brunch. Outdoor tables available. **Cards:** AE, CB, DI, DS, MC, VI.

———— The following restaurant has not been evaluated by AAA but is listed for your information only. ————

BOGART'S HIDEAWAY CAFE   **Phone:** 561/575-2100

[fyi]   Not evaluated. **Location:** 725 N A1A. **Features:** Continental type menu. Decorated with autographed pictures of movie stars. Inexpensive to moderate prices. In Alhamba Shopping Center.

KENDALL —See Miami-Miami Beach p. 520.

KEY BISCAYNE —See Miami-Miami Beach p. 521.

KEY COLONY BEACH —See The Florida Keys p. 315.

KEY LARGO —See The Florida Keys p. 315.

KEY WEST —See The Florida Keys p. 324.

KISSIMMEE —See Orlando p. 632.

LADY LAKE —See Orlando p. 673.

LAKE BUENA VISTA —See Orlando p. 673.

LAKE CITY pop. 10,000

———— WHERE TO STAY ————

BEST WESTERN INN

Phone: (904)752-3801

	All Year	1P: $40-$70	2P: $50-$80	XP: $5	F11

Motel

Location: I-75, exit 82, just w. 4720 US 90 W 32055. Fax: 904/755-4846. **Facility:** 80 units. 2 stories, exterior corridors. **Terms:** small pets only ($5 extra charge). **Amenities:** voice mail, hair dryers. **Leisure Activities:** sauna, whirlpool, playground, game room. **Guest Services:** [ECP] meal plan available, coin laundry. **Business Services:** meeting rooms. **Cards:** AE, DI, DS, JC, MC, VI. **Special Amenities:** free continental breakfast and free local telephone calls.

SOME UNITS

COMFORT INN

Phone: (904)755-1344

	All Year	1P: $64-$78	2P: $69-$83	XP: $5	F18

Motel

Location: I-75, exit 82, just w. 4515 US 90 W 32055 (PO Box 1985, 32056). Fax: 904/752-8957. **Facility:** Sunny rooms with floor-to-ceiling windows, some with pleasant courtyard view. 100 units. Some whirlpool units ($85-$95). *Bath:* combo or shower only. 2 stories, exterior corridors. **Terms:** package plans. **Amenities:** extended cable TV. **Leisure Activities:** 2 lighted tennis courts, playground, basketball, shuffleboard. **Guest Services:** [ECP] meal plan available, valet laundry. **Cards:** AE, CB, DI, DS, JC, MC, VI.

SOME UNITS

DAYS INN

Phone: (904)752-9350

	All Year	1P: $45-$60	2P: $49-$65	XP: $5	F12

Motel

Location: I-75, exit 82, 0.3 mi e. 4510 US 90 W 32055. Fax: 904/752-9350. **Facility:** Short distance to shopping center. 120 units. 2 stories, exterior corridors. **Cards:** AE, CB, DI, DS, MC, VI. **Special Amenities:** free continental breakfast and free newspaper.

SOME UNITS

DAYS INN I-10

[SAVE]

◆◆ ◆◆
Motel

Phone: (904)758-4224

All Year   1P: $45-$55   2P: $48-$65   XP: $4   F18
Location: I-10, exit 44, just s. US 441 32055 (Rt 16, Box 38310). Fax: 904/758-7612. **Facility:** 46 units. 2 stories, exterior corridors. **Terms:** pets ($5 fee). **Amenities:** extended cable TV, hair dryers. **Guest Services:** [CP] meal plan available, coin laundry. **Cards:** AE, DI, DS, MC, VI.

SOME UNITS

DRIFTWOOD MOTEL

(AAA) [SAVE]

◆◆ ◆◆
Motel

Phone: (904)755-3545

All Year   1P: $27-$32   2P: $29-$34   XP: $5
Location: I-75, exit 82, 0.7 mi e. 4380 US Hwy 90 W 32055. Fax: 904/961-8798. **Facility:** An older style motor inn with contemporary furnishings. Closest motel to downtown; across highway from shopping center. 59 units. 1 story, exterior corridors. **Terms:** small pets only ($5 extra charge). **Cards:** AE, DI, DS, MC, VI. **Special Amenities: free continental breakfast.**

SOME UNITS

ECONO LODGE SOUTH

(AAA) [SAVE]

◆◆ ◆◆
Motel

Phone: 904/755-9311

3/8-11/30   1P: $38-$100   2P: $50-$100   XP: $4   F16
12/1-3/7   1P: $38-$43   2P: $50-$70   XP: $4   F16
Location: I-75, exit 80, at US 441. Rt 2, Box 6008 32024. Fax: 904/755-8864. **Facility:** Modern property offers ten units catering to seniors with safety bars in the baths and outside amenities. Adjacent truck parking. 1 story, exterior corridors. **Terms:** small pets only. **Cards:** AE, DI, DS, MC, VI. **Special Amenities: free continental breakfast and free newspaper.**

SOME UNITS
FEE

HOLIDAY INN

◆◆ ◆◆ ◆◆
Motor Inn

Phone: (904)752-3901

All Year   1P: $63-$73   2P: $63-$73
Location: I-75, exit 82, just w on US 90. (PO Box 1239, 32056). Fax: 904/752-3901. **Facility:** Tasteful, contemporary rooms. 27 executive king rooms with print calculator and speaker phone. Buildings surround courtyard lawn with large oak trees. 227 units. Some suites ($150-$200). *Bath:* combo or shower only. 2 stories, exterior corridors. **Terms:** cancellation fee imposed, package plans. **Amenities:** voice mail, irons, hair dryers. **Leisure Activities:** 2 pools, wading pool, 2 lighted tennis courts, playground, exercise room, basketball. **Guest Services:** coin laundry. **Business Services:** meeting rooms. **Cards:** AE, CB, DI, DS, JC, MC, VI.

SOME UNITS

JAMESON INN

◆◆ ◆◆ ◆◆
Motel

Phone: (904)758-8440

All Year   1P: $61-$66   2P: $66-$71   XP: $5   F18
Location: I-75, exit 82, just e, then s. 1393 Commerce Blvd 32055. Fax: 904/758-8166. **Facility:** Enjoy cookies and milk every evening! You'll sink into these spacious rooms with attractive functional furnishings. 55 units. Some suites. *Bath:* combo or shower only. 3 stories, interior corridors. **Terms:** small pets only ($10 fee). **Amenities:** extended cable TV, dual phone lines, voice mail, irons. *Some:* hair dryers. **Leisure Activities:** exercise room. **Guest Services:** [ECP] meal plan available. **Business Services:** meeting rooms. *Fee:* fax. **Cards:** AE, DI, DS, MC, VI.

SOME UNITS

SCOTTISH INNS

(AAA) [SAVE]

◆◆
Motel

Phone: (904)755-0230

All Year   1P: $29-$34   2P: $35-$39   XP: $5
Location: I-75, exit 82, 0.6 mi e. 4450 US 90 W 32055 (Rt 13, Box 1150). Fax: 904/755-5277. **Facility:** Basic accommodations for the budget-minded. 34 units. 1 story, exterior corridors. **Terms:** pets ($5 extra charge). **Cards:** AE, DS, MC, VI. **Special Amenities: free continental breakfast and preferred room (subject to availability with advanced reservations).**

SOME UNITS

SUPER 8 MOTEL

◆◆ ◆◆
Motel
DS, MC, VI.

Phone: 904/752-6450

Property failed to provide current rates
Location: I-75, exit 81, 0.3 mi w on SR 47. Rt 14, Box 1002 32024 (PO Box 7094, 32055). Fax: 904/752-6450. **Facility:** Set away from road in quiet, rural area. Attractive courtyard with picturesque gardens. 87 units. 2 stories, exterior corridors. **Terms:** 10 day cancellation notice. **Amenities:** extended cable TV. **Cards:** AE, DI,

SOME UNITS

——— WHERE TO DINE ———

DESOTO DRUG STORE

◆◆
American

Lunch: $4-$8   **Phone: 904/752-9958**

Location: Downtown, just n of US 90. 405 N Marion St 32055. **Hours:** 8 am-4:30 pm. Closed major holidays; also Sat & Sun. **Features:** casual dress; street parking. An authentic soda fountain in the heart of downtown's antique shopping district. Come by and sit at the counter with a shake or better yet, enjoy a scrumptious lunch featuring one of the chefs specialties including Bordeaux chicken or steak Diane. Make a special trip to enjoy the hearty breakfasts which include pecan Belgium waffles, omeletes, or French toast. Smoke free premises. **Cards:** MC, VI.

EL POTRO

◆◆ ◆◆
Mexican

Lunch: $4-$6   **Dinner: $5-$10**   **Phone: 904/758-3100**

Location: I-75, exit 82, 1 mi e on US 90; opposite Gleason Mall. Hwy 90 32055. **Hours:** 11 am-10 pm. Closed major holidays. **Features:** casual dress; children's menu; carryout; cocktails; a la carte. Authentic Mexican cuisine is served in semi-private booths around an open fireplace. Authentic recipes are used for true south-of-the-border taste. Attention to detail and professionalism go a long way here. A weekday buffet tempts hungry travelers. **Cards:** AE, MC, VI.

KEN'S BBQ

American

Lunch: $4-$8   **Dinner:** $4-$8   **Phone:** 904/752-5919
Location: 4 mi e of jct I-95. US Hwy 90 W 32056. **Hours:** 11 am-9 pm. Closed: Sun. **Features:** casual dress; children's menu; a la carte. Locally owned and operated for many years, Ken's is a popular Lake City institution. One visit and ya'll have to come back! Friendly efficient service is a characteristic enjoyed at all locations. The BBQ sauces go well with the pork, ribs, chicken, or beef. Most plates or dinners include a choice of the famous baked beans and a side of cole slaw! Enjoy fresh Texas style garlic bread with your dinner. If your in a hurry order at the take-out menu. **Cards:** AE, DS, MC, VI.

LAKE HELEN pop. 2,300

-------- WHERE TO STAY --------

CLAUSER'S BED & BREAKFAST

Historic Bed & Breakfast

Phone: (904)228-0310
All Year   1P: $85-$130   2P: $95-$140   XP: $20
Location: I-4, exit 55, 1 mi e on Main St, 0.5 mi s on CR 4139, turn left on Ohio St, right on Pleasant Rd, then right. 201 E Kicklighter Rd 32744. Fax: 904/228-2337. **Facility:** On National Register of Historic Places. Built circa early 1890s. Two-story carriage house has six modern units, each decorated in a unique theme, one with fireplace. Small pub on lower level. Walking path to lake. Antique shopping. Smoke free premises. 8 units. Some whirlpool units ($130-$140). **Bath:** combo or shower only. 2 stories, interior/exterior corridors. **Terms:** age restrictions may apply, 7 day cancellation notice-fee imposed, weekly rates available, package plans. **Activities:** whirlpool, bicycles, croquet, electronic darts, lending library, video games, walking trails. **Guest Services:** [BP] meal plan available, gift shop. **Business Services:** meeting rooms. **Cards:** AE, DS, MC, VI. **Special Amenities: free local telephone calls.**

LAKELAND pop. 70,600

-------- WHERE TO STAY --------

AMERISUITES LAKELAND CENTER

Motel

Phone: (863)413-1122
All Year   1P: $79-$129   2P: $79-$129   XP: $10   F17
Location: I-4, exit 18, 3.2 mi s on US 98, just w; at the Lakeland Center. 525 W Orange St 33815. Fax: 863/413-1133. **Facility:** Lovely spacious rooms, very nice public areas. 128 units. **Bath:** combo or shower only. 6 stories, interior corridors. **Terms:** small pets only. **Amenities:** video games, voice mail, irons, hair dryers. **Leisure Activities:** heated pool, exercise room. **Guest Services:** [ECP] meal plan available, complimentary evening beverages: Wed, coin laundry. **Business Services:** meeting rooms, administrative services. **Cards:** AE, CB, DI, DS, JC, MC, VI. **Special Amenities: free continental breakfast and free newspaper.** *(See color ad p 5)*   SOME UNITS

FEE

BAYMONT INN & SUITES-LAKELAND

Motel

Phone: (863)815-0606
1/26-4/14   1P: $89-$94   2P: $89-$94
12/1-1/25 & 4/15-11/30   1P: $74-$79   2P: $74-$79
Location: Just nw of jct SR 33 and I-4, exit 19. 4315 Lakeland Park Dr 33809. Fax: 863/815-9711. **Facility:** 103 units. **Bath:** combo or shower only. 4 stories, interior corridors. **Terms:** pets ($10 deposit). **Amenities:** video games, voice mail, irons, hair dryers. **Guest Services:** [ECP] meal plan available, coin laundry. **Business Services:** meeting rooms. **Cards:** AE, CB, DI, DS, MC, VI. *(See color ad p 428)*   SOME UNITS

FEE

BEST WESTERN DIPLOMAT INN

Motel

Phone: (863)688-7972
2/1-4/30   1P: $79-$99   2P: $79-$99   XP: $10   F16
12/21-1/31   1P: $69-$89   2P: $69-$89   XP: $10   F16
12/1-12/20 & 5/1-11/30   1P: $59-$79   2P: $59-$79   XP: $10   F16
Location: I-4, exit 18, just s. 3311 US 98 N 33805. Fax: 863/688-8377. **Facility:** 120 units. 2 stories, exterior corridors. **Terms:** 3 day cancellation notice-fee imposed, weekly rates available, package plans. **Amenities:** Some: irons, hair dryers. **Leisure Activities:** wading pool. **Guest Services:** [BP] meal plan available, valet laundry. **Business Services:** meeting rooms. **Cards:** AE, DI, DS, JC, MC, VI. *(See ad below)*   SOME UNITS

COMFORT INN
(AAA) (SAVE)
Motel

Phone: (863)688-9221

All Year   1P: $60-$75   2P: $75-$85   XP: $10   F17
Location: 2 mi e of jct US 98 and 92. 1817 E Memorial Blvd 33801. Fax: 863/687-4797. **Facility:** Across from Lake Parker. 64 units, 4 with efficiency. 2 stories, exterior corridors. **Terms:** pets ($5 extra charge). **Amenities:** extended cable TV. *Some:* voice mail, irons, hair dryers. **Cards:** AE, DI, DS, MC, VI. **Special Amenities:** free continental breakfast and free newspaper.

SOME UNITS

HAMPTON INN
(SAVE)
Motel

Phone: (863)816-2525

12/29-4/30   1P: $99-$115   2P: $99-$115
5/1-11/30   1P: $79-$115   2P: $79-$115
12/1-12/28   1P: $77-$86   2P: $77-$86
Location: I-4, exit 19, just nw. 4420 N Socrum Loop Rd 33809. Fax: 863/816-2727. **Facility:** 70 units. *Bath:* combo or shower only. 3 stories, interior corridors. **Terms:** 7 day cancellation notice. **Amenities:** voice mail, irons, hair dryers. **Leisure Activities:** heated pool, exercise room. **Guest Services:** [ECP] meal plan available, coin laundry. **Business Services:** meeting rooms. **Cards:** AE, CB, DI, DS, JC, MC, VI.

SOME UNITS

FEE   FEE

HOLIDAY INN LAKELAND SOUTH
Motor Inn

Phone: (863)646-5731

12/1-4/15   1P: $90   2P: $90
4/16-11/30   1P: $86   2P: $86
Location: 3 mi s on SR 37. 3405 S Florida Ave 33803. Fax: 863/646-5215. **Facility:** Four units with wet bar. 172 units. *Bath:* combo or shower only. 2 stories, exterior corridors. **Terms:** package plans. **Amenities:** voice mail, irons, hair dryers. **Leisure Activities:** whirlpool, exercise room. **Guest Services:** [CP] meal plan available, complimentary evening beverages: Mon-Fri, valet laundry. **Business Services:** meeting rooms. **Cards:** AE, DI, DS, MC, VI.

SOME UNITS

ASK   FEE   FEE FEE FEE

HOWARD JOHNSON LAKESIDE HOTEL
Motor Inn

Phone: 863/682-0101

2/1-4/30   1P: $49-$64   2P: $49-$64   XP: $5
12/1-1/31   1P: $49-$54   2P: $49-$54   XP: $5
5/1-11/30   1P: $45-$49   2P: $45-$49   XP: $5
Location: I-4, exit 18, 2.8 mi s on US 98, 0.3 mi e. 910 E Memorial Blvd 33801. Fax: 863/683-0815. **Facility:** On Lake Parker. 130 units. 2 stories, exterior corridors. **Amenities:** irons. **Leisure Activities:** wading pool, boat dock, fishing, exercise room. **Guest Services:** coin laundry. **Business Services:** meeting rooms. **Cards:** AE, CB, DI, DS, JC, MC, VI.

SOME UNITS

FEE   FEE FEE

LA QUINTA INN & SUITES
(SAVE)
Motel

Phone: (863)859-2866

All Year   1P: $79-$109   2P: $79-$109
Location: I-4, exit 18, just n on US 98. 1024 Crevasse St 33809. Fax: 863/859-2956. **Facility:** 119 units. Some suites ($109-$139). *Bath:* combo or shower only. 6 stories, interior corridors. **Terms:** small pets only. **Amenities:** video games, voice mail, irons, hair dryers. **Leisure Activities:** heated pool, whirlpool, exercise room. **Guest Services:** [CP] meal plan available, coin laundry. **Business Services:** meeting rooms. **Cards:** AE, DI, DS, MC, VI.

SOME UNITS

FEE

ROYALTY INN
(AAA) (SAVE)
Motel

Phone: (863)858-4481

1/20-4/30   1P: $55-$85   2P: $65-$95   XP: $10   F12
12/20-1/19   1P: $49-$69   2P: $59-$79   XP: $10   F12
12/1-12/19 & 5/1-11/30   1P: $39-$59   2P: $49-$69   XP: $10   F12
Location: I-4, exit 18, just ne. 3425 Hwy 98 N 33809. Fax: 863/853-2514. **Facility:** 64 units. 2 stories, interior corridors. **Terms:** weekly rates available, small pets only ($10 extra charge). **Amenities:** safes (fee). *Some:* hair dryers. **Leisure Activities:** wading pool. **Guest Services:** coin laundry. **Cards:** AE, DS, MC, VI. **Special Amenities:** free continental breakfast. *(See color ad below)*

SOME UNITS

SCOTTISH INNS

AAA [SAVE]

Phone: 863/687-2530

2/1-4/15	1P: $45-$55	2P: $59-$80	XP: $5	F12
1/1-1/31 & 4/16-11/30	1P: $42-$47	2P: $47-$65	XP: $5	F12
12/1-12/31	1P: $39-$44	2P: $45-$62	XP: $5	F12

Motel

Location: On US 98 business route, 0.6 mi s of jct US 92 and 98. 244 N Florida Ave 33801. Fax: 863/688-1961. **Facility:** A few units with balcony overlooking Lake Wire. An older, solid motel that has been well kept. 46 units. *Bath:* combo or shower only. 2 stories, exterior corridors. **Terms:** 3 day cancellation notice, weekly rates available. **Guest Services:** coin laundry. **Cards:** AE, CB, DI, DS, MC, VI.   SOME UNITS

SHERATON FOUR POINTS HOTEL

Phone: (863)647-3000

1/1-5/15	1P: $139-$159	2P: $149-$169	XP: $10	F16
12/1-12/31 & 5/16-11/30	1P: $125-$145	2P: $135-$155	XP: $10	F16

Hotel

Location: SR 37, 3.5 mi s of US 98 business route. 4141 S Florida Ave 33813. Fax: 863/644-0467. **Facility:** 168 units. Some suites ($125-$200) and whirlpool units ($125-$190). 7 stories, interior corridors. **Terms:** cancellation fee imposed, monthly rates available, package plans. **Amenities:** video games, voice mail, irons, hair dryers. **Leisure Activities:** sauna, whirlpool, exercise room. **Guest Services:** valet laundry. **Business Services:** meeting rooms. **Cards:** AE, CB, DI, DS, MC, VI.   SOME UNITS

SUPER 8 MOTEL

AAA [SAVE]

Phone: (863)683-5961

1/21-4/20	1P: $50-$65	2P: $55-$75	XP: $5	F12
4/21-11/30	1P: $39-$55	2P: $45-$65	XP: $5	F12
12/1-1/20	1P: $39-$50	2P: $45-$60	XP: $5	F12

Motel

Location: Just e of jct SR 33. 601 E Memorial Blvd 33801. Fax: 863/683-7723. **Facility:** Designated smoking area. 83 units. 2 stories, interior/exterior corridors. **Terms:** 3 day cancellation notice, weekly rates available, small pets only ($10 extra charge). **Amenities:** extended cable TV. **Leisure Activities:** heated pool. **Guest Services:** coin laundry. **Cards:** AE, CB, DI, MC, VI. **Special Amenities:** free local telephone calls and preferred room (subject to availability with advanced reservations).   SOME UNITS

WELLESLEY INN & SUITES

AAA [SAVE]

Phone: (863)859-3399

1/1-5/15	1P: $80-$98	2P: $80-$98	XP: $10	F17
12/1-12/31 & 5/16-11/30	1P: $71-$89	2P: $71-$89	XP: $10	F17

Motel

Location: I-4, exit 18, just nw on US 98; at Lakeland Square Mall. 3520 Hwy US 98 N 33809. Fax: 863/859-3483. **Facility:** 106 units. *Bath:* combo or shower only. 6 stories, interior corridors. **Terms:** small pets only. **Amenities:** video games, voice mail, hair dryers. *Some:* irons. **Leisure Activities:** heated pool. **Guest Services:** coin laundry. **Business Services:** meeting rooms. **Cards:** AE, DI, DS, MC, VI. **Special Amenities:** free continental breakfast and free local telephone calls. *(See color ad opposite title page)*   SOME UNITS

─────── WHERE TO DINE ───────

PAN YE'S CHINESE RESTAURANT

Lunch: $4-$10   **Dinner:** $4-$10   **Phone:** 863/686-2052

Chinese

Location: I-4, exit 18, 2.8 mi s to jct US 92, then 0.4 mi e. 743 E Memorial Blvd 33801. **Hours:** 11 am-9 pm. Closed: 7/4, 11/22, 12/25; also Mon. **Features:** casual dress; carryout; beer & wine only; a la carte. Reliable, Americanized Chinese fare is served by a friendly family. The house specials include pork, poultry, beef and seafood combinations. Egg rolls, fried rice and many other tasty entrees can be sampled at the buffet from 11 am-2:30 pm. **Cards:** AE, DS, MC, VI.

LAKE MARY —*See Orlando p. 696.*

LAKE PARK pop. 6,700   (See map p. 710; index p. 713)

─────── WHERE TO DINE ───────

CAFE DU PARK

Dinner: $16-$26   **Phone:** 561/845-0529   58

French

Location: US 1, 1.3 mi n of jct SR A1A (Blue Heron Blvd). 612 N Federal Hwy 33403. **Hours:** Open 12/1-8/31 & 10/15-11/30; 5:30 pm-10 pm. Closed: Sun. **Reservations:** suggested. **Features:** semi-formal attire; beer & wine only; also prix fixe. Several cozy dining rooms in a former private home offer an intimate experience. The owner-chef prepares the cuisine with a continental touch, and the severs are attentive and friendly. Try the snails wrapped in phyllo pastry with a white wine sauce. **Cards:** AE, MC, VI.

HOLIDAY HOUSE

Lunch: $6   **Dinner:** $4-$7   **Phone:** 561/842-7791   56

American

Location: On US 1, 1.3 mi n of jct SR A1A (Blue Heron Blvd). 720 N Federal Hwy 33403. **Hours:** 11 am-3 & 4-8:30 pm, Sun 11 am-8:30 pm. Closed: 12/24 for dinner. **Features:** casual dress; children's menu; carryout; salad bar; buffet. An appealing buffet-style restaurant, especially popular with seniors, Holiday House in historic Kelsey Park serves delicious, "Sunday-dinner-style" meals. Hand-carved roast beef, leg of lamb and baked turkey with stuffing are the main attractions. Smoke free premises. **Cards:** AE, DS, MC, VI.

LAKE PLACID pop. 1,200

──────── WHERE TO STAY ────────

LAKE BLUE RESORT
Phone: 863/465-3371
▼▼▼ ▼▼▼   1/1-3/31   2P: $62-$68   XP: $5   F10
         12/1-12/31 & 4/1-11/30   2P: $53-$62   XP: $5   F10
Cottage   **Location:** 1.5 mi n on US 27, 0.3 mi e following signs. 735 S Lakeview Rd 33852. Fax: 863/465-3371. **Facility:** Quiet
lakefront location. Duplex housekeeping units with screened porch. 20 units with kitchen. *Bath:* shower only.
1 story, exterior corridors. **Terms:** 14 day cancellation notice-fee imposed, weekly & monthly rates available. **Leisure Activities:** heated pool, beach, swimming, boat dock, fishing, shuffleboard, volleyball. **Guest Services:**

LAKE WALES pop. 9,700

──────── WHERE TO STAY ────────

CHALET SUZANNE COUNTRY INN & RESTAURANT
Phone: (863)676-6011
(AAA) (SAVE)   1P: $139-$189   2P: $169-$189   XP: $12
▼▼▼ ▼▼▼   **Location:** CR 17A, 1.5 mi e of jct US 27, at US 27 Alt. 3800 Chalet Suzanne Dr 33853. Fax: 863/676-1814.
         Facility: Nestled on 70 acres with private lake. A combination of architectural styles give a "fairy tale" look
Country Inn   to the inn. Rooms are individually furnished each with its own character, few are compact; gardens with gazebo. 30 units. Some suites ($189-$239) and whirlpool units ($189-$239). *Bath:* combo or shower only. 1-2
stories, exterior corridors. **Terms:** 3 day cancellation notice-fee imposed, package plans. **Amenities:** *Some:*
hair dryers. **Dining:** restaurant, see separate listing. **Leisure Activities:** ceramic studio, 2500 ft private lighted airstrip. **Guest
Services:** [BP] & [MAP] meal plans available, gift shop, valet laundry. **Business Services:** meeting rooms. **Cards:** AE, CB, DI,
DS, JC, MC, VI. **Special Amenities:** free local telephone calls and free newspaper.
SOME UNITS

GREEN GABLES INN
Phone: (863)676-2511
(AAA) (SAVE)   2/11-4/21   1P: $68-$82   2P: $68-$82   XP: $3   F15
▼▼▼ ▼▼▼   12/1-12/31   1P: $48-$68   2P: $48-$68   XP: $3   F15
         1/1-2/10   1P: $52-$62   2P: $52-$62   XP: $3   F15
Motel   4/22-11/30   1P: $48-$58   2P: $48-$58   XP: $3   F15
Location: 2 mi n jct US 60. 1747 US Hwy 27 N 33853. Fax: 863/676-3140. **Facility:** 56 units. 1 story, exterior corridors. **Terms:** package plans. **Amenities:** extended cable TV, hair dryers. *Some:* CD players. **Leisure Activities:** heated pool, boat dock, fishing, 2 lighted tennis courts, exercise room, picnic area with grill & sun deck. **Guest Services:**
coin laundry. **Business Services:** meeting rooms. **Cards:** AE, DI, DS, MC, VI. **Special Amenities:** free local telephone calls
and free newspaper. *(See color ad below)*
SOME UNITS
FEE

THE GV TILLMAN HOUSE BED & BREAKFAST
Phone: (863)676-5499
▼▼▼ ▼▼▼   12/1-5/31   1P: $95   2P: $95   XP: $15
         6/1-11/30   1P: $90   2P: $90   XP: $15
Bed & Breakfast   **Location:** Just e of US 27 Alt, just n of Central Ave. 301 E Sessoms Ave 33853. Fax: 863/676-5499. **Facility:** Designated smoking area. 5 units. *Bath:* some shared or private, combo or shower only. 2 stories, interior corridors. **Terms:** age restrictions may apply, 3 day cancellation notice. **Amenities:** *Some:* video games. **Guest Services:** [CP] meal
plan available, complimentary laundry. **Cards:** AE, MC, VI.

──────── WHERE TO DINE ────────

CHALET SUZANNE RESTAURANT   Country Inn   **Lunch:** $19-$46   **Dinner:** $59-$79   **Phone:** 863/676-6011
▼▼▼ ▼▼▼   **Location:** CR 17A, 1.5 mi e of jct US 27, at US 27 Alt; in Chalet Suzanne Country Inn & Restaurant. 3800 Chalet
         Suzanne Dr 33853. **Reservations:** suggested. **Features:** dressy casual;
American   children's menu; cocktails & lounge; prix fixe. Quaint ambience is the overwhelming appeal of this
multilevel, lakefront restaurant. Decorated with antiques and memorabilia, each dining room has its own
individual charm. Six-course inclusive dinners feature cuisine with a Continental flair. **Cards:** AE, CB, DI, DS, MC, VI.

THE FOREST BUFFET RESTAURANT   **Lunch:** $6   **Dinner:** $8   **Phone:** 863/638-3036
American

Location: 4 mi s of jct SR 60. 4441 US 27 S 33853. **Hours:** 6 am-8 pm, Fri & Sat-8:30 pm; summer hrs may vary. **Reservations:** suggested; in season. **Features:** casual dress; cocktails; buffet. Friendly, casual dining that features food just like Mom always made. A variety of hand-carved, roasted meats and a wide assortment of vegetables are what makes this pleasant eatery so popular. The buffet line eliminates waiting at lunch and dinner. **Cards:** AE, DS, MC, VI.

LEKARICA RESTAURANT   **Lunch:** $6-$9   **Dinner:** $13-$25   **Phone:** 863/676-8281
American

Location: 2.8 mi s of jct SR 60, off Rt 27; in Highland Park Hills Golf Course. 1650 S Highland Park Dr 33853. **Hours:** 11 am-2 & 6-9 pm, Sun-2 pm. Closed: 1/1; also Mon. **Reservations:** accepted. **Features:** casual dress; Sunday brunch; children's menu; carryout; cocktails & lounge. This charming Old Florida restaurant resides in a refurbished lakeside house. Imaginative food is served in a casual setting for lunch, and in a more formal ambience for dinner. Entrees include veal, chicken, New Zealand lamb, steak, pasta and seafood. Smoke free premises. **Cards:** AE, DS, MC, VI.

VINTON'S RESTAURANT   **Dinner:** $24-$39   **Phone:** 863/676-8242
French

Location: Just w of US 27 Alt; in historic downtown district. 229 E Stuart Ave 33853. **Hours:** 6 pm-10 pm. Closed major holidays; also Sun & Mon. **Reservations:** suggested. **Features:** semi-formal attire; cocktails & lounge. Submerge yourself in New Orleans ambience with lavish French antiques and jazz music. There are several inviting dining rooms in which to savor delicious Louisiana cooking, and a new wine cellar with an extensive collection for the discriminating palate. **Cards:** AE, MC, VI.

LAKE WORTH pop. 28,600   (See map p. 710; index p. 713)

———— WHERE TO STAY ————

GULFSTREAM HOTEL HOLIDAY INN HOTEL & SUITES   **Phone:** (561)540-6000   80
Historic Hotel

	1P: $119-$129	2P: $129-$139	XP: $10	F18
12/1-4/30				
5/1-11/30	1P: $109-$129	2P: $119-$129	XP: $10	F18

Location: On eastern edge of downtown, overlooking Lake Worth. 1 Lake Ave 33460. Fax: 561/582-6904. **Facility:** 1925 hotel on the National Register of Historic Places. Some rooms with view of Intracoastal Waterway. Attractive rooms and public areas. 106 units. Some suites ($269-$309). **Bath:** combo or shower only. 6 stories, interior corridors. **Terms:** 3 day cancellation notice, for long stays, weekly & monthly rates available. **Amenities:** extended cable TV, voice mail, irons, hair dryers. *Some:* video games. **Leisure Activities:** heated pool. **Guest Services:** area transportation, coin laundry. **Business Services:** meeting rooms. **Cards:** AE, DS, MC, VI.   SOME UNITS

HOLIDAY INN WEST PALM BEACH-TURNPIKE   **Phone:** (561)968-5000   79
Motor Inn

1/16-3/25	2P: $110-$115	XP: $6	F19
12/1-1/15 & 3/26-4/23	2P: $99-$104	XP: $6	F19
4/24-11/30	2P: $79-$88	XP: $6	F19

Location: SR 802, just e of Florida Tpke, exit 93. 7859 Lake Worth Rd 33467. Fax: 561/968-2451. **Facility:** Attractively landscaped courtyard. Large rooms with a new contemporary room package, offering medium wood tones and a classic decor. Business person friendly. Pool area features a large assortment of flowers. 114 units. 2 stories, interior/exterior corridors. **Terms:** 3 day cancellation notice, monthly rates available. **Amenities:** extended cable TV, dual phone lines, voice mail, irons, hair dryers. **Leisure Activities:** heated pool, tennis court. **Guest Services:** coin laundry. **Business Services:** meeting rooms. **Cards:** AE, CB, DI, DS, JC, MC, VI.   SOME UNITS   FEE

LAGO-MAR MOTEL & APARTMENTS   **Phone:** 561/585-4243   78
Motel

| 12/1-4/30 | 1P: $66 | 2P: $66 | XP: $10 |
| 5/1-11/30 | 1P: $46 | 2P: $46 | XP: $10 |

Location: I-95, exit 48N (10 Ave), 1 mi e, then just s. 317 N Federal Hwy 33460. Fax: 561/585-4243. **Facility:** Large rooms well kept. 16 efficiencies. 2 stories, exterior corridors. **Terms:** 14 day cancellation notice, weekly & monthly rates available. **Amenities:** extended cable TV. **Cards:** MC, VI.   SOME UNITS

LAGO MOTOR INN   **Phone:** 561/585-5246   83
Motel

| 12/1-5/1 | 1P: $62-$72 | 2P: $62-$72 | XP: $10 | F10 |
| 5/2-11/30 | 1P: $45-$50 | 2P: $45-$50 | XP: $10 | F10 |

Location: US 1, just s of jct 6th Ave S; from jct I-95, exit 47, 0.7 mi e, just s on US 1. 714 S Dixie Hwy 33460. Fax: 561/547-2001. **Facility:** Very well maintained, good sized rooms. Garden-like setting. 24 units. 1 villa, 5 with efficiency. 2 stories, exterior corridors. **Terms:** weekly rates available, pets ($9 extra charge). **Amenities:** extended cable TV. **Guest Services:** coin laundry. **Cards:** AE, MC, VI.   SOME UNITS

MARTINIQUE MOTOR LODGE   **Phone:** 561/585-2502   82
Motel

| 12/1-4/30 | 1P: $50-$58 | 2P: $55-$75 |
| 5/1-11/30 | 1P: $40-$48 | 2P: $50-$60 |

Location: US 1, just s of jct 6th Ave S, 0.5 mi e of jct I-95, exit 47. 801 S Dixie Hwy 33460. Fax: 561/585-2503. **Facility:** Modest to large rooms, pleasant garden patio. 24 units. 1 efficiency and 2 units with kitchen. **Bath:** combo or shower only. 1-2 stories, exterior corridors. **Terms:** 7 day cancellation notice-fee imposed, weekly rates available, small pets only ($7 extra charge, $20 deposit). **Amenities:** extended cable TV. **Cards:** AE, MC, VI. **Special Amenities:** free newspaper.   SOME UNITS

(See map p. 710)

NEW SUN GATE MOTEL
Phone: (561)588-8110   **84**

AAA [SAVE]

12/1-4/15	1P: $54-$74	2P: $59-$79	XP: $5 F14
4/16-5/31 & 10/1-11/30	1P: $36-$56	2P: $41-$61	XP: $5 F14
6/1-9/30	1P: $34-$56	2P: $39-$61	XP: $5 F14

Motel

Location: 1 mi e on 6th Ave S from jct I-95 exit 47, just s on SR 5 (Federal Hwy). 901 S Federal Hwy 33460. Fax: 561/588-8041. **Facility:** All rooms dedicated to famous movie stars and furnished in art deco style. Very well maintained. 31 units. *Bath:* shower only. 2 stories, exterior corridors. **Terms:** 14 day cancellation notice, 7 day off season, weekly & monthly rates available. **Dining:** coffee shop, 8 am-8 pm; Mon-2 pm 10/1-5/31, $5-$10. **Leisure Activities:** Fee: sauna. **Guest Services:** [AP] & [BP] meal plans available, coin laundry. **Cards:** DI, DS, MC, VI. **Special Amenities:** free room upgrade and preferred room (each subject to availability with advanced reservations).

SOME UNITS

[icons]

SABAL PALM HOUSE B & B INN
Phone: (561)582-1090   **81**

12/1-4/30 & 11/15-11/30	2P: $100-$180
5/1-11/14	2P: $75-$150

Historic Bed & Breakfast

Location: Just n of SR 820 at e end of Intracoastal Bridge. 109 N Golfview Rd 33460. Fax: 561/582-0933. **Facility:** Located along side of the Intracoastal Waterway and golf course. All rooms named after a famous artist and decorated with their work. Furnished with antiques and lavish decor. Smoke free premises. 7 units. Some suites ($150-$180) and whirlpool units ($115-$180). *Bath:* combo or shower only. 2 stories, interior/exterior corridors. **Terms:** age restrictions may apply. **Amenities:** no TVs, hair dryers. **Guest Services:** [BP] meal plan available, complimentary evening beverages. **Business Services:** fax. **Cards:** AE, DS, MC, VI.

[ASK] [icons]

WHITE MANOR MOTEL
Phone: (561)582-7437   **85**

AAA [SAVE]

12/1-4/30	1P: $50-$56	2P: $54-$64	XP: $7
5/1-11/30	1P: $36-$40	2P: $38-$46	XP: $7

Motel

Location: 1 mi e of I-95, exit 47, 0.8 mi s on SR 5 (Federal Hwy). 1618 S Federal Hwy 33460. **Facility:** Quiet location. 15 units, 9 with kitchen. *Bath:* combo or shower only. 1-2 stories, exterior corridors. **Terms:** 14 day cancellation notice, weekly rates available, pets ($10-$25 extra charge, $50 deposit). **Amenities:** extended cable TV. **Guest Services:** coin laundry. **Cards:** AE, DS, MC, VI.

[icons]

—— **WHERE TO DINE** ——

BOHEMIAN GARDEN RESTAURANT
Dinner: $8-$21   Phone: 561/968-4111   **44**

AAA

Location: SR 802, 1 mi w of jct Military Tr. 5450 Lake Worth Rd 33463. **Hours:** 4:30 pm-10 pm, Sun 4 pm-9 pm. **Reservations:** suggested; in season. **Features:** casual dress; children's menu; early bird specials; cocktails & lounge. Old World charm can be found in this 53-year-old restaurant with paneled walls and oil paintings of Bohemia. An extensive menu offers chicken, beef and local seafood. The warm spinach salad will help nourish you as well as satisfy your taste buds. **Cards:** AE, CB, DI, DS, MC, VI.

Steak & Seafood

[icon]

—— *The following restaurants have not been evaluated by AAA* ——
but are listed for your information only.

FLANIGAN'S SEAFOOD BAR & GRILL
Phone: 561/964-4666

[fyi]

Not evaluated. **Location:** 2401 10th Ave N. **Features:** A casual atmosphere that is inexpensive and family friendly. Known for their barbecue baby back ribs, large and fresh local seafood.

JOHN G'S
Phone: 561/585-9860

[fyi]

Not evaluated. **Location:** 10 S Ocean Blvd. **Features:** Open for breakfast and lunch. Casual dining with ocean view. Inexpensive.

LANTANA pop. 8,400   (See map p. 710; index p. 713)

—— **WHERE TO STAY** ——

BEST WESTERN/INN OF AMERICA
Phone: (561)588-0456   **111**

AAA [SAVE]

12/16-4/15	1P: $89-$99	2P: $89-$99
12/1-12/15 & 4/16-11/30	1P: $69-$99	2P: $69-$99

Motel

Location: Just e of jct I-95, exit 45 (Hypoluxo Rd), then s. 7051 Seacrest Blvd 33462. Fax: 561/585-0607. **Facility:** Inviting rooms. 92 units. *Bath:* combo or shower only. 4 stories, interior corridors. **Terms:** weekly rates available, small pets only. **Amenities:** extended cable TV. **Guest Services:** coin laundry. **Cards:** AE, MC, VI. **Special Amenities:** free continental breakfast and free local telephone calls.

SOME UNITS

[icons]

COMFORT INN-LANTANA/BOYNTON BEACH
Phone: (561)582-7878   **110**

AAA [SAVE]

12/1-2/28	1P: $75-$119	2P: $75-$119
3/1-4/1	1P: $99	2P: $99
10/1-11/30	1P: $75	2P: $75
4/2-9/30	1P: $69	2P: $69

Motel

Location: I-95, exit 45, 0.3 mi e. 1221 Hypoluxo Rd 33462. Fax: 561/582-8878. **Facility:** Attractive, spacious rooms. 60 units. Some whirlpool units ($79-$149). *Bath:* combo or shower only. 3 stories, interior corridors. **Amenities:** extended cable TV, voice mail, hair dryers. **Leisure Activities:** small heated pool, exercise room. **Guest Services:** [ECP] meal plan available, coin laundry. **Business Services:** meeting rooms. **Cards:** AE, CB, DI, DS, MC, VI. **Special Amenities:** free continental breakfast and free local telephone calls. *(See ad p 249)*

SOME UNITS

[icons]

(See map p. 710)

——— WHERE TO DINE ———

ANCHOR INN RESTAURANT   **Dinner:** $14-$26   **Phone:** 561/965-4794   **55**
Location: I-95, exit 45, 0.5 mi w. 2810 Hypoluxo Rd 33462. **Hours:** 5 pm-9:30 pm. Closed: 11/22, 12/25.
Steak House   **Reservations:** accepted. **Features:** casual dress; children's menu; carryout; cocktails & lounge. A comfortable, Key West-style decor contributes to the casual, happy aura of the lakefront restaurant, long established in the area. A menu featuring such seafood dishes as shrimp scampi and broiled salmon is bolstered by steak, chicken and chops. **Cards:** AE, MC, VI.   ⊠

LARGO —See Tampa Bay p. 865.

LAUDERDALE-BY-THE-SEA —See Fort Lauderdale p. 384.

LAUDERHILL —See Fort Lauderdale p. 385.

LEESBURG —See Orlando p. 697.

LEHIGH ACRES pop. 13,600

——— WHERE TO STAY ———

ADMIRAL LEHIGH GOLF RESORT & SPA   **Phone:** (941)369-2121

1/14-3/31	2P: $96-$103	XP: $6	F17
9/23-11/30	2P: $73-$83	XP: $6	F17
12/1-1/13	2P: $69-$83	XP: $6	F17
4/1-9/22	2P: $67-$83	XP: $6	F17

Motor Inn   **Location:** 2.5 mi n on CR 884. 225 E Joel Blvd 33972. Fax: 941/368-1660. **Facility:** Traditional motel rooms, mostly doubles, on 400 acres of country club grounds. Two championship golf courses. Juice bar, gourmet grocery. 131 units. Some suites and whirlpool units. *Bath:* combo or shower only. 1-2 stories, exterior corridors. **Terms:** 7 day cancellation notice, package plans. **Amenities:** extended cable TV, voice mail, hair dryers. **Dining:** 3 restaurants, deli, 6:30 am-9 pm, $9-$18, cocktails, entertainment. **Leisure Activities:** heated pool, saunas, putting green, lighted driving range, 2 pro shops, jogging, sports court, basketball, shuffleboard, aerobics, beauty salon. *Fee:* golf-36 holes, bicycles. **Guest Services:** coin laundry. *Fee:* massage. **Business Services:** conference facilities, PC, fax. **Cards:** AE, DI, DS, MC, VI. *(See color ad p 394)*

SOME UNITS

FEE   FEE FEE

LEHIGH RESORT CLUB   **Phone:** (941)368-2022

12/16-4/15 Wkly	1P: $575-$700	2P: $575-$700	
12/1-12/15 & 4/16-11/30 Wkly	1P: $395-$525	2P: $395-$525	

Condominium   **Location:** 2.5 mi n on CR 884. 231 Joel Blvd 33972. Fax: 941/368-5088. **Facility:** 20 units with kitchen. Some suites. 2 stories, exterior corridors. **Terms:** 3 day cancellation notice-fee imposed, weekly rates available. **Amenities:** extended cable TV, voice mail, irons. **Leisure Activities:** heated pool, wading pool, whirlpool, golf cage, racquetball courts, children's program, recreation program, social program, playground, exercise room, basketball, horseshoes, shuffleboard, game room, gazebo picnic area, ping pong. *Fee:* fishing & Everglades trips, golf priviliges. **Guest Services:** complimentary laundry. **Cards:** MC, VI.

LIGHTHOUSE POINT —See Fort Lauderdale p. 385.

LITTLE TORCH KEY —See The Florida Keys p. 341.

LIVE OAK pop. 6,300

——— WHERE TO STAY ———

ECONO LODGE   **Phone:** (904)362-7459

All Year	1P: $49-$69	2P: $54-$74	XP: $5 F18

Motel   **Location:** I-10, exit 40, just s on US 129. 6811 N US 129 & I-10 32064 (PO Box 820). Fax: 904/364-6598. **Facility:** Six rooms for senior guests, with bathroom grab bars, outsized phones and TV remotes. 52 units. Some whirlpool units ($75-$95). 2 stories, exterior corridors. **Terms:** pets ($10 extra charge). **Amenities:** extended cable TV. **Leisure Activities:** whirlpool. **Guest Services:** coin laundry. **Business Services:** meeting rooms. **Cards:** AE, CB, DI, DS, JC, MC, VI. **Special Amenities:** free continental breakfast and preferred room (subject to availability with advanced reservations).

SOME UNITS
FEE

SUWANNEE RIVER BEST WESTERN INN   **Phone:** (904)362-6000

All Year	1P: $53	2P: $56	XP: $5 F12

Motel   **Location:** I-10, exit 40, 0.3 mi s. 6819 US 129 32060. Fax: 904/364-1308. **Facility:** Lobby features a collection of photos of country music stars. 64 units, 1 with efficiency (no utensils). 2 stories, exterior corridors. **Terms:** 3 day cancellation notice, small pets only ($5 fee). **Guest Services:** coin laundry. **Cards:** AE, CB, DI, DS, JC, MC, VI.

SOME UNITS

———— **WHERE TO DINE** ————

LACY J'S FAMILY STEAKHOUSE **Lunch:** $4-$13 **Dinner:** $8-$20 **Phone:** 904/362-2121

American

Location: I-10, exit 40, 1 mi s. 1018 N Ohio Ave 32064. **Hours:** 6 am-10 pm, Sun from 11 am. Closed: 12/25. **Features:** casual dress; children's menu; salad bar; beer only; a la carte. A warm and personable staff welcomes you to this country kitchen. Fried green tomatoes and Southern fried chicken are the house specialties. Steaks, seafood and a huge selection of appetizers complete the menu, with fresh fruit served at the salad bar. **Cards:** AE, MC, VI. ⊗

LONGBOAT KEY pop. 5,900   (See map p. 764; index p. 767)

———— **WHERE TO STAY** ————

THE COLONY BEACH & TENNIS RESORT **Phone:** (941)383-6464 **67**

	12/1-4/28	1P: $270-$540	2P: $330-$695	XP: $20	F
	9/28-11/30	1P: $275-$395	2P: $335-$455	XP: $20	F
Condominium	4/29-9/27	1P: $195-$395	2P: $255-$455	XP: $20	F

Location: SR 789, 2 mi n of New Pass Bridge. 1620 Gulf of Mexico Dr 34228. **Fax:** 941/383-7549. **Facility:** Gulf front. 234 units with kitchen. 109 two-bedroom units. Some whirlpool units. *Bath:* combo or shower only. 6 stories, interior/exterior corridors. **Parking:** valet. **Terms:** check-in 4 pm, 15 day cancellation notice-fee imposed, monthly rates available, package plans. **Amenities:** extended cable TV, voice mail, safes, irons, hair dryers. **Dining:** The Colony Restaurant, see separate listing. **Leisure Activities:** heated pool, saunas, whirlpools, steamrooms, beach, fishing, 21 tennis courts (2 lighted), children's program, recreation program, social program, playground. *Fee:* sailboating, snorkeling & equipment, bicycles. **Guest Services:** gift shop, valet and coin laundry. *Fee:* area transportation, massage. **Business Services:** conference facilities, administrative services, fax. *Fee:* PC. **Cards:** AE, DI, DS, MC, VI.

SOME UNITS

(ASK) ⊷ ⅋⅋ ▽ ⅋⅋ ⓖ ⅋⅋ ⅋⅋ ⊗ ⅋⅋ 🖨 💻 ⅋⅋ 🔌 DATA PORT / VCR /
FEE   FEE   FEE

DIPLOMAT RESORT **Phone:** (941)383-3791 **66**

	2/1-4/16	1P: $133-$212	2P: $133-$212	XP: $10	F12
	12/1-1/31	1P: $102-$175	2P: $102-$175	XP: $10	F12
Condominium	4/17-11/30	1P: $86-$160	2P: $86-$160	XP: $10	F12

Location: On SR 789, 3.7 mi n of New Pass Bridge. 3155 Gulf of Mexico Dr 34228. **Fax:** 941/383-0983. **Facility:** Gulf front. 50 units. 2 two-bedroom units, 20 efficiencies and 30 units with kitchen. 2 stories, exterior corridors. **Terms:** 21 day cancellation notice, weekly & monthly rates available. **Amenities:** extended cable TV, voice mail. **Leisure Activities:** heated pool, beach, sun deck, boating, fishing. **Guest Services:** coin laundry. **Business Services:** fax. **Cards:** DS, MC, VI.

SOME UNITS

⅋⅋ ⊷ 🖨 💻 ⅋⅋ 🔌 DATA PORT / VCR /

HARBOUR VILLA CLUB **Phone:** (941)383-9544 **60**

(AAA) (SAVE)	1/1-4/30 Wkly	1P: $1895-$1995	2P: $1895-$1995	XP: $20	F12
	12/1-12/31 & 11/1-11/30 Wkly	1P: $1335-$1435	2P: $1335-$1435	XP: $20	F12
Condominium	5/1-10/31 Wkly	1P: $975-$1050	2P: $975-$1050	XP: $20	F12

Location: 4 mi s of jct SR 684, just e of SR 789. 615 Dream Island Rd 34228. **Fax:** 941/383-8028. **Facility:** Spacious, fully equipped units with large patio or balcony overlooking the Intracoastal Waterway. 15 two-bedroom units with kitchen. Some whirlpool units. 3 stories, exterior corridors. **Terms:** check-in 4 pm, 21 day cancellation notice-fee imposed, monthly rates available. **Amenities:** extended cable TV, voice mail, irons. *Some:* CD players. **Leisure Activities:** heated pool, whirlpool, boat ramp, fishing, 4 tennis courts (2 lighted), barbecue grills. *Fee:* marina. **Guest Services:** complimentary laundry. **Business Services:** fax. **Cards:** AE, MC, VI.

SOME UNITS

⅋⅋ ⊷ ⊗ VCR 🖨 💻 ⅋⅋ 🔌 / ⊗ /

HILTON LONGBOAT KEY BEACHFRONT RESORT **Phone:** (941)383-2451 **64**

(SAVE)	12/1-1/2 & 1/26-4/28	1P: $199-$329	2P: $199-$329
	1/3-1/25	1P: $179-$329	2P: $179-$329
Hotel	4/29-11/30	1P: $149-$249	2P: $149-$249

Location: On SR 789, 6.2 mi n of New Pass Bridge. 4711 Gulf of Mexico Dr 34228. **Fax:** 941/383-7979. **Facility:** Gulf front. 102 units, 2 with kitchen. Some suites ($159-$359). *Bath:* combo or shower only. 5 stories, interior/exterior corridors. **Terms:** 14 day cancellation notice, 7 day off season-fee imposed, package plans - in summer. **Amenities:** extended cable TV, dual phone lines, voice mail, safes, honor bars, irons, hair dryers. **Leisure Activities:** heated pool, beach, volleyball. *Fee:* boats, sailboats, windsurfing, bicycles. **Guest Services:** [MAP] meal plan available, gift shop, area transportation, valet laundry. **Business Services:** conference facilities, fax. **Cards:** AE, CB, DI, DS, MC, VI.
(See ad p 44 & color ad below)

SOME UNITS

S/D ⅋⅋ ▽ ⅋⅋ ⓖ ⅋⅋ ⅋⅋ ⊗ ⅋⅋ 🖨 💻 🔌 DATA PORT / ⊗ 🖨 🔌 /
FEE   FEE

SHOW YOUR CARD & SAVE
10% AAA DISCOUNT
3,000 US LOCATIONS
KIDS STAY FREE
RESERVE A ROOM
ANYTIME, ANYWHERE
3,000 US LOCATIONS
SHOW YOUR CARD & SAVE
20% DISCOUNT AT MOST CLARIONS
10% AAA DISCOUNT
RESERVE A ROOM!
ANYTIME! ANYWHERE!
KIDS STAY FREE
WWW.CHOICEHOTELS.COM
3,000 US LOCATIONS
10% AAA DISCOUNT
100% SATISFACTION GUARANTEE
1-800-228-1AAA

**For reservations,
call 1-800-228-1AAA,
visit www.choicehotels.com,
pull in off the road or contact
your local AAA office.**

AAA TourBookMark
Lodging Listing Symbols

Member Values

(AAA)	Official Appointment
SAVE	Offers minimum 10% discount
SAVE	SYC&S chain partners
ASK	May offer discount
S/D	Offers senior discount
fyi	Informational listing only

Member Services

✈	Airport transportation
🐾	Pets allowed
¶¶	Restaurant on premises
¶¶→	Restaurant off premises (walking distance)
24¶¶	24-hour room service
Y	Cocktail lounge
🎎	Child care

Accessibility Features

♿	Fully accessible
🛗	Semi-accessible
🚿	Roll-in showers
👂	Hearing impaired

Leisure Activities

🏊	Outdoor pool
🏊	Indoor Pool
🏊	Indoor/outdoor pool
💪	Health Club on premises
💪	Health Club off premises
⊠	Recreational activities

In-Room Amenities

✕	Non-smoking rooms
ℳ	No air conditioning
☎	No telephones
📺	No cable TV
🎬	Movies
VCR	VCR
📻	Radio
▣	Coffee maker
▣	Microwave
▤	Refrigerator
DATA PORT	Data port/modem line

Call property for detailed information about fees & restrictions relating to the lodging listing symbols.

CHOICE HOTELS
INTERNATIONAL

(See map p. 764)

HOLIDAY INN HOTEL & SUITES

AAA SAVE ▼▼▼▼▼ Resort

				Phone: (941)383-3771	62
2/1-4/30	1P: $229-$399	2P: $229-$399	XP: $15		F18
12/21-1/31	1P: $219-$369	2P: $219-$369	XP: $15		F18
12/1-12/20 & 5/1-11/30	1P: $159-$259	2P: $159-$259	XP: $15		F18

Location: SR 789, 6.5 mi n of New Pass Bridge. 4949 Gulf of Mexico Dr 34228. Fax: 941/383-7871. **Facility:** Gulf front locale enhances this large property with the well known "Holidome" which is tropically decorated and nautical touches. The public areas are very nice with lots of marble, sandstone and pickled wood touches; a fresh inviting lobby area. The grounds are very appealing with a wonderful beach just steps away and tropical landscaping throughout. Many recreational facilities are on-site with something for everyone. 146 units, 25 with kitchen. Some suites ($259-$399). *Bath:* combo or shower only. 2-3 stories, interior/exterior corridors. **Terms:** check-in 3:30 pm, 3 day cancellation notice-fee imposed, weekly & monthly rates available, package plans. **Amenities:** extended cable TV, video games, dual phone lines, voice mail, safes, irons, hair dryers. *Some:* CD players. **Dining:** 2 restaurants, 6:30 am-10 pm weekend entertainment in lounge, food court, beach bar, $8-$16, cocktails. **Leisure Activities:** 2 heated pools, wading pool, saunas, whirlpool, beach, fishing, putting green, 4 lighted tennis courts, children's program, recreation program, jogging, exercise room, shuffleboard, volleyball, shuffleboard, billiards, ping pong, video game room, kid suites available. *Fee:* cabanas, paddleboats, sailboating, windsurfing, aqua cycles, boogie boards, hobie cats, kayaks, rafts, bicycles. **Guest Services:** [BP] meal plan available, gift shop, valet and coin laundry. *Fee:* massage. **Business Services:** conference facilities, fax. **Cards:** AE, CB, DI, DS, JC, MC, VI.

SOME UNITS

⟨icons⟩ FEE ... FEE ... DATA PORT / ⊗ VCR ▦ /

HOLIDAY LODGE

▼▼▼ Apartment

			Phone: 941/383-3788	65
12/1-4/30 Wkly	2P: $910-$2660	XP: $10		F5
5/1-11/30 Wkly	2P: $860-$2135	XP: $10		F5

Location: On SR 789; 5.5 mi n of New Pass Bridge. 4235 Gulf of Mexico Dr 34228. Fax: 941/387-7966. **Facility:** Gulf front property with beach house available. 30 units. 3 two-bedroom units, 1 efficiency and 28 units with kitchen. *Bath:* combo or shower only. 5 stories, exterior corridors. **Terms:** cancellation fee imposed. **Amenities:** extended cable TV, irons. **Leisure Activities:** heated pool, whirlpool, beach, cabanas, putting green, recreation program in winter, shuffleboard. **Guest Services:** coin laundry. **Cards:** AE, DS, MC, VI. *(See color ad below)*

⟨icons⟩ VCR

(See map p. 764)

THE RESORT AT LONGBOAT KEY CLUB

Phone: (941)383-8821 69

AAA SAVE

12/20-4/21	1P: $325-$625	2P: $400-$1075	XP: $15	F17
4/22-5/31	1P: $230-$380	2P: $280-$515	XP: $15	F17
6/1-11/30	1P: $175-$380	2P: $195-$515	XP: $15	F17
12/1-12/19	1P: $200-$355	2P: $200-$505	XP: $15	F17

Condominium

Location: SR 789, 0.5 mi n of New Pass Bridge. 301 Gulf of Mexico Dr 34228. Fax: 941/383-0359. **Facility:** Gulf front. All units with private balcony, most with washer/dryer. Harborside complex with complimentary transportation is north of main property. 232 units. 53 two-bedroom units, 131 efficiencies and 77 units with kitchen. Some suites. 4-10 stories, exterior corridors. **Terms:** 14 day cancellation notice-fee imposed, package plans. **Amenities:** extended cable TV, video games, CD players, dual phone lines, voice mail, safes, honor bars, irons, hair dryers. **Dining:** 3 dining rooms, 2 restaurants, 7 am-midnight, $12-$35, cocktails, entertainment. **Leisure Activities:** heated pool, whirlpool, steamrooms, beach, charter fishing putting green, children's program in summer, recreation program, social program, seasonal kids club, jogging, playground, basketball, aerobics class, beach volleyball, fitness trail, library. *Fee:* canoeing, paddleboats, windsurfing, aqua cycles, golf-45 holes golf lessons, golf & tennis pro shops, 38 tennis courts (6 lighted), adult tennis clinic, bicycles. **Guest Services:** gift shop, area transportation-within 5 mi, valet laundry. *Fee:* massage. **Business Services:** conference facilities, fax. *Fee:* PC. **Cards:** AE, DI, MC, VI. **Special Amenities: free newspaper.** *(See ad p 463)* SOME UNITS

RIVIERA BEACH RESORT

Phone: 941/383-2552 61

Apartment

2/1-4/30 Wkly		2P: $820-$1150	XP: $10
12/18-1/31 Wkly		2P: $700-$935	XP: $10
12/1-12/17 & 5/1-11/30 Wkly		2P: $600-$850	XP: $10

Location: On SR 789, 5 mi s of jct SR 684 (Cortez Rd). 5451 Gulf of Mexico Dr 34228. Fax: 941/383-2245. **Facility:** Gulf front. Lushly landscaped walkways. 9 units. 2 two-bedroom units, 2 efficiencies and 7 units with kitchen. 1 story exterior corridors. **Terms:** 30 day cancellation notice, 60 day off season, daily & monthly rates available, small pets only ($10 extra charge, $100 deposit). **Amenities:** extended cable TV. *Some:* irons, hair dryers. **Leisure Activities:** heated pool, whirlpool, beach, shuffleboard. **Guest Services:** coin laundry. **Cards:** AE, MC, VI. SOME UNITS

────── WHERE TO DINE ──────

THE COLONY RESTAURANT

Lunch: $9-$14 **Dinner:** $20-$36 **Phone:** 941/383-5558 40

American

Location: SR 789, 2 mi n of New Pass Bridge; in The Colony Beach & Tennis Resort. 1620 Gulf of Mexico Dr 34228 **Hours:** 7 am-9:30 pm, Fri & Sat-10 pm. **Reservations:** suggested. **Features:** dressy casual; Sunday brunch; children's menu; carryout; cocktails & lounge; valet parking; a la carte. Adjacent to the sparkling gulf, the restaurant boasts an original, lavish menu of contemporary Continental dishes and an extensive wine list. Fresh seafood is always popular. Live entertainment contributes to the dining experience. **Cards:** AE, DI, DS, MC, VI

EUPHEMIA HAYE

Dinner: $18-$34 **Phone:** 941/383-3633 36

Continental

Location: On SR 789, 7.8 mi n of New Pass Bridge. 5540 Gulf of Mexico Dr 34228. **Hours:** 5 pm-10 pm, Fri & Sat-10:30 pm; hours vary in season. Haye Loft dessert lounge 6 pm-midnight. **Closed:** 9/5-9/26 **Reservations:** suggested. **Features:** casual dress; cocktails & lounge; entertainment; a la carte. An eclectic and creative menu features roast duckling served over stuffing with a seasonal fruit sauce. A comfortable, very clean restaurant where the service and food make you want to mark your map for the next trip to town Smoke free premises. **Cards:** CB, DI, DS, MC, VI.

HARRY'S CONTINENTAL KITCHENS

Lunch: $7-$19 **Dinner:** $19-$32 **Phone:** 941/383-0777 37

Continental

Location: Just e of SR 789; 4.7 mi s of jct SR 684 (Cortez Rd). 525 St Judes Dr 34228. **Hours:** 11 am-2:30 & 5-9:30 pm, Sun 10 am-3 & 5-9:30 pm; call for off season hours. **Closed:** 12/25. **Reservations:** suggested **Features:** casual dress; Sunday brunch; carryout; cocktails; a la carte. Pleasant, professional service and an innovative menu with fresh herbs, homemade soup and delectable desserts make this quaint, tropical eatery perfect for a gourmet seafood meal. 80% of the dining area is designated as non-smoking during the off season Smoke free premises. **Cards:** AE, MC, VI.

LYNCHES LANDING BAR & GRILL

Lunch: $5-$17 **Dinner:** $5-$17 **Phone:** 941/383-0791 38

Irish

Location: On SR 789, 5 mi n of New Pass Bridge. 4000 Gulf of Mexico Dr 34228. **Hours:** 11:30 am-midnight Closed: 11/22, 12/25; also 6/1-6/14, 9/6-10/1 & Sun (off season). **Reservations:** suggested; in season **Features:** casual dress; children's menu; carryout; cocktails & lounge. An Irish theme carries through the energetic restaurant, which offers open-air dining overlooking the Gulf of Mexico. Although Irish food is the primary draw, the key lime pie is outstanding. After eating, walk off a few calories on the beach just across the road and enjoy a beautiful sunset. **Cards:** AE, CB, DI, DS, MC, VI.

MAUREEN RESTAURANT & MARTINI BAR

Dinner: $17-$25 **Phone:** 941/383-7774 35

Continental

Location: On SR 789, 7 mi n of New Pass Bridge; in Centre Shops. 5350 Gulf of Mexico Dr 34228. **Hours:** Open 12/1-7/31 & 10/1-11/30; 5:30 pm-10 pm. **Closed:** Sun & Mon. **Features:** dressy casual; cocktails & lounge a la carte. A trendy decor incorporates melon-colored walls with interesting artwork, and sets the right mood for adult fine dining. Creatively prepared and displayed entrees including seafood, lamb, and steak feature carpaccio and a fabulous bouillabaisse. **Cards:** AE, DI, DS, MC, VI.

POSEIDON OCEAN HARVEST RESTAURANT

Dinner: $18-$31 **Phone:** 941/383-2500 39

Seafood

Location: On SR 789, 4 mi n of New Pass Bridge. 3454 Gulf of Mexico Dr 34228. **Hours:** 5:30 pm-10 pm. **Closed:** 1/1. **Reservations:** suggested. **Features:** casual dress; children's menu; cocktails & lounge; valet parking a la carte. You will find fine dining in a scenic locale on Sarasota Bay. Order the shrimp cocktail as an appetizer and try the colorfully presented swordfish as an entree. Attentive servers make you feel immediately welcome and comfortable. **Cards:** AE, CB, DI, DS, MC, VI.

LONG KEY —See The Florida Keys p. 342.

LONGWOOD —See Orlando p. 697.

LOXAHATCHEE pop. 300

—————— WHERE TO STAY ——————

SOUTHERN PALM BED & BREAKFAST   **Phone:** (561)790-1413
12/1-5/1   2P: $125   XP: $10
5/2-11/30   2P: $79   XP: $10
Bed & Breakfast   **Location:** From SR 7, 4.4 mi w on Southern Blvd, SR 90/S US 441 to D Rd, then left on Collection Canal Rd, just right on C Rd. 15130 Southern Palm Way 33470. Fax: 561/791-3035. **Facility:** A quite location in the country. Ample trees, noises of nature. A small pond can be seen from all rooms and balconies. Spacious rooms with a variety of antique funiture. Soft colors accent the room's package. Smoke free premises. 5 units. 2 stories, interior/exterior corridors. **Terms:** age restrictions may apply, 7 day cancellation notice-fee imposed, weekly rates available. **Amenities:** extended cable TV, hair dryers. **Guest Services:** [CP] meal plan available. **Cards:** AE, MC, VI.   (ASK) ⊠ ▤

MACCLENNY pop. 4,000

—————— WHERE TO STAY ——————

ECONO LODGE   **Phone:** (904)259-3000
AAA SAVE   All Year   1P: $52-$62   2P: $57-$67   XP: $5   F18
Location: I-10, exit 48, just s of jct SR 121. I-10 & SR 121 32063 (PO Box 425). Fax: 904/259-4418. **Facility:** Basic accommodations. 53 units. Some whirlpool units ($65-$80). 2 stories, exterior corridors. **Terms:** small pets only. **Leisure Activities:** whirlpool. **Business Services:** meeting rooms. **Cards:** AE, CB, DI, DS, JC, MC, VI.
Motel   **Special Amenities:** free continental breakfast and preferred room (subject to availability with advanced reservations).
                         SOME UNITS
(S▤) 🐾 ▦ 🏊 🎥 / ⊠ (VCR) ▣ ▤ ▤ /
                         FEE

MADEIRA BEACH —See Tampa Bay p. 865.

MADISON pop. 3,300

—————— WHERE TO STAY ——————

HOLIDAY INN EXPRESS-I-10 MADISON   **Phone:** 850/973-2020
All Year   2P: $65   XP: $5
Motel   **Location:** I-10, exit 37, just ne. Rt 1 Box 3200 32340. Fax: 850/973-3366. **Facility:** Well-furnished rooms, accommodating staff. In quiet location within short drive of town center. 60 units. Bath: combo or shower only. 3 stories, interior corridors. **Amenities:** irons, hair dryers. **Guest Services:** [ECP] meal plan available, coin laundry. **Business Services:** meeting rooms. **Cards:** AE, CB, DI, DS, JC, MC, VI.
                         SOME UNITS
▦ 🔥 🔥 🏊 👟 🍴 🖼 / ⊠ (VCR) ▣ ▤ ▤ /
                    FEE

MAITLAND —See Orlando p. 698.

MANALAPAN pop. 310   (See map p. 710; index p. 713)

—————— WHERE TO STAY ——————

THE RITZ-CARLTON, PALM BEACH   **Phone:** (561)533-6000   94
AAA SAVE   12/1-5/1   2P: $450-$850
9/19-11/30   2P: $295-$575
5/2-5/30   2P: $265-$545
5/31-9/18   2P: $185-$365
Hotel   **Location:** On SR A1A, 9 mi s of Palm Beach. 100 S Ocean Blvd 33462. Fax: 561/588-4202. **Facility:** Elegant ocean or garden view rooms with balcony or patio. 270 units. Some suites ($485-$1490) and whirlpool units. 5-6 stories, interior corridors. **Parking:** valet. **Terms:** 14 day cancellation notice, 14 day 1/3-4/30, weekly & monthly rates available, package plans. **Amenities:** extended cable TV, video games, dual phone lines, voice mail, safes, honor bars, irons, hair dryers. Some: CD players. **Dining:** 2 dining rooms, restaurant, luncheon cafe terrace, weather permitting 6:30 am-11 pm; to midnight, in season, $16-$38, cocktails, also, The Grill, 100 South Ocean, see separate listing, entertainment. **Leisure Activities:** heated pool, sauna, whirlpool, steamroom, beach, swimming, snorkeling, charter fishing, children's program, recreation program, social program, exercise room, beauty salon, sightseeing trips arranged. Fee: spa treatments, snorkeling equipment, seasonal jet skis, golf privilges, 7 tennis courts (3 lighted), tennis instruction, bicycles. **Guest Services:** [CP] meal plan available, gift shop, afternoon tea, area transportation-within 9 mi, valet laundry. Fee: massage. **Business Services:** conference facilities, administrative services, fax. Fee: PC. **Cards:** AE, CB, DI, DS, JC, MC, VI.
                         SOME UNITS
🍴 24 🍷 🏋 🏊 ⊠ 🍴 🖼 (DATA PORT) / ⊠ (VCR) ▤ ▤ /
FEE   FEE   FEE   FEE FEE

—————— WHERE TO DINE ——————

100 SOUTH OCEAN   **Dinner:** $25-$48   **Phone:** 561/533-6000   52
Location: On SR A1A, 9 mi s of Palm Beach; in The Ritz-Carlton, Palm Beach. 100 S Ocean Blvd 33462. **Hours:** 6 pm-10:30 pm. Closed: Sun. **Reservations:** suggested; jackets for men. **Features:** semi-formal attire; cocktails; valet parking; a la carte, also prix fixe. An intimate and refined dining room affords lovely views of the ocean. Innovative dishes from classical European cuisine incorporate the flavors and ingredients indigenous to South Florida. The menu changes seasonally to offer many fresh choices. Smoke free premises. **Cards:** AE, CB, DI, DS, JC, MC, VI.
                                                                    ⊠

(See map p. 710)

THE GRILL   **Dinner:** $20-$38   **Phone:** 561/533-6000   51
▼▼▼ ▼▼▼
        Location: On SR A1A, 9 mi s of Palm Beach; in The Ritz-Carlton, Palm Beach. 100 S Ocean Blvd 33462. **Hours:** 6
Continental   pm-10 pm. Closed: Mon. **Reservations:** suggested. **Features:** semi-formal attire; children's menu;
       cocktails; entertainment; valet parking; a la carte, also prix fixe. An elegant club-like setting with warm
wood tones and original oil paintings features professional service, fresh seafood and aged beef. A nice
tureen presentation of the vichyssoise and a wonderful roasted rack of lamb are menu signatures. **Cards:** AE, CB, DI, DS, JC,
MC, VI.   ✕

MARATHON —See The Florida Keys p. 342.

MARCO ISLAND pop. 9,400

——— **WHERE TO STAY** ———

HILTON MARCO ISLAND BEACH RESORT   **Phone:** (941)394-5000

◉◉◉ SAVE	12/1-4/28	1P: $289	2P: $289	XP: $25	F18
	10/29-11/30	1P: $179-$249	2P: $179-$249	XP: $25	F18
▼▼▼ ▼▼▼	4/29-5/27	1P: $169-$239	2P: $169-$239	XP: $25	F18
Resort	5/28-10/28	1P: $119-$219	2P: $119-$219	XP: $25	F18

Location: I-75, exit 15, 1 mi s of SR 92. 560 S Collier Blvd (SR 951) 34145. Fax: 941/394-5251. **Facility:** Large
rooms with balcony. Elegant public areas. 297 units. Some suites ($169-$479). **Bath:** combo or shower only.
11 stories, interior corridors. **Parking:** valet. **Terms:** 7 day cancellation notice, 3 day off season-fee imposed, weekly & monthly
rates available, package plans, $8 service charge. **Amenities:** video games, voice mail, safes, honor bars, irons, hair dryers.
Dining: dining room, restaurant, 11 am-5 pm, pool side snack bar, $13-$26, cocktails, also, Sandcastles, see separate listing,
entertainment. **Leisure Activities:** heated pool, sauna, whirlpool, beach, swimming, children's program, recreation program, social program, video game room. *Fee:* sailboating, windsurfing, waterskiing, parasailing, sea kayaks, waverunners, charter fishing,
3 lighted tennis courts. **Guest Services:** [CP] meal plan available, gift shop, complimentary evening beverages: Mon, valet
laundry. *Fee:* massage. **Business Services:** conference facilities, administrative services, PC, fax. **Cards:** AE, DI, DS, JC,
MC, VI. **Special Amenities:** free room upgrade (subject to availability with advanced reservations).
(See ad p 44 & color ad below)   SOME UNITS

〔S⃣D⃣〕 ⏹ ⎟⍓ ⏹ ⎾⎿ 🏊 🛶 ⚓ 🎾 ✕ 🎥 🖨 💳 🛎 DATA PORT / ✕ /
       FEE   FEE   FEE

MARCO ISLAND MARRIOTT RESORT & GOLF CLUB   **Phone:** 941/394-2511

▼▼▼ ▼▼▼	12/1-4/28	1P: $325-$464	2P: $325-$464
	4/29-5/28 & 9/17-11/30	1P: $230-$365	2P: $230-$365
Resort	5/29-9/16	1P: $149-$269	2P: $149-$269

Location: I-75, exit 15, 0.5 mi s of SR 92. 400 S Collier Blvd (SR 951) 34145. Fax: 941/642-2672. **Facility:** Extensive gulf front facility. Large rooms with balcony. 735 units. 12 two-bedroom units. Some suites ($399-$1500). **Bath:** combo or
shower only. 11 stories, interior corridors. **Parking:** valet. **Terms:** 7 day cancellation notice-fee imposed, package plans.
Amenities: extended cable TV, voice mail, safes, honor bars, irons, hair dryers. **Leisure Activities:** 3 pools (2 heated), wading
pool, whirlpool, beach, swimming, charter fishing, children's program, recreation program, social program, playground, exercise
room. *Fee:* sailboats, golf-18 holes, miniature golf, 16 tennis courts (4 lighted), bicycles. **Guest Services:** [BP] meal plan available, gift shop, valet laundry. *Fee:* area transportation, massage. **Business Services:** conference facilities, administrative services, PC, fax. **Cards:** AE, DI, DS, JC, MC, VI.   SOME UNITS

🏖 ⏹ ⎟⍓ ⎾⎿ 🏊 🛶 ⚓ ✕ 🎾 🖨 💳 🛎 DATA PORT / ✕ VCR 📷
   FEE   FEE   FEE   FEE

RADISSON SUITE BEACH RESORT ON MARCO ISLAND   Phone: (941)394-4100

(AAA) (SAVE)

	12/1-1/1	1P: $149-$549	2P: $149-$549	XP: $10	F17
	1/2-4/21	1P: $269-$519	2P: $269-$519	XP: $10	F17
	4/22-5/27	1P: $169-$309	2P: $169-$309	XP: $10	F17
Suite Hotel | 5/28-11/30 | 1P: $149-$289 | 2P: $149-$289 | XP: $10 | F17 |

Location: I-75, exit 15, from causeway, SR 951 (Collier Blvd), 3.1 mi sw. 600 S Collier Blvd (SR 951) 34145. Fax: 941/394-0419. **Facility:** Extensive public areas. High-rise with semi-enclosed corridors. 268 units. 46 two-bedroom units and 209 units with kitchen. Some suites. *Bath:* combo or shower only. 14 stories, exterior corridors. **Parking:** valet. **Terms:** check-in 4 pm, 14 day cancellation notice, varies by season, weekly & monthly rates available, package plans. **Amenities:** extended cable TV, voice mail, safes, irons, hair dryers. **Dining:** dining room, restaurant, 7 am-11 pm, $7-$16, cocktails. **Leisure Activities:** heated pool, whirlpool, beach, swimming, lighted tennis court, children's program, recreation program, exercise room, basketball, volleyball. *Fee:* sailboating, windsurfing, waterskiing, parasailing, waverunners, bicycles. **Guest Services:** gift shop, coin laundry. **Business Services:** conference facilities, administrative services, PC, fax. **Cards:** AE, DI, DS, MC, VI. *(See color ad below)*

SOME UNITS

[icons] FEE   FEE   / [X] [VCR] / FEE

THE SURF CLUB OF MARCO   Phone: (941)642-5800

	12/1-1/5 Wkly	1P: $1050-$2100
	2/17-4/20 Wkly	1P: $1855-$2030
Condominium	1/6-2/16 Wkly	1P: $1295-$1540
	4/21-11/30 Wkly	1P: $1120-$1295

Location: I-75, exit 15, 0.9 mi s of SR 92. 540 S Collier Blvd (SR 951) 34145. Fax: 941/642-7245. **Facility:** Large two-bedroom apartments with extra queen-size sleeper sofa. Private balcony, some with full gulf view; others partial view. 44 two-bedroom units with kitchen. Some suites. 8 stories, exterior corridors. **Terms:** 7 day cancellation notice, in season, weekly rates available, 2% service charge. **Amenities:** extended cable TV, irons, hair dryers. **Leisure Activities:** heated pool, whirlpool, beach, swimming, tennis courts. **Guest Services:** gift shop, coin laundry. **Cards:** AE, DI, DS, MC, VI. *(See color ad p 757)*

[ASK] [icons] [VCR] [icons] [DATA PORT]

———— **WHERE TO DINE** ————

ARTURO'S ITALIAN RESTAURANT   **Dinner:** $10-$23   **Phone:** 941/642-0550

Italian

Location: Just n of SR 951. 844 Bald Eagle Dr 34145. **Hours:** 5 pm-9:30 pm. Closed: 11/22, 12/25; also 6/1-6/28. **Reservations:** suggested. **Features:** casual dress; children's menu; carryout; cocktail lounge; beer & wine only. Casual, comfortable dining is what to expect at this noisy, bustling restaurant. Such well-prepared traditional dishes as bruscetta and the signature mozzarella and prosciutto-stuffed pork chop roast a flavorful taste and colorful presentation. Smoke free premises. **Cards:** MC, VI.   [X]

BAVARIAN INN   **Dinner:** $9-$17   **Phone:** 941/394-7233

German

Location: 1.1 mi se of SR 92; just off Collier Blvd. 960 Winterberry Dr 34145. **Hours:** 4:30 pm-10 pm. Closed: 12/24 & Mon 5/1-10/30. **Reservations:** suggested; 11/1-4/30. **Features:** casual dress; children's menu; early bird specials; carryout; cocktails & lounge; a la carte. Large portions of wholesome food are offered at reasonable prices in a casual Bavarian-style setting. The German-American cuisine includes prime rib, steak and seafood selections, as well as unique appetizers like hot, delicious pretzel bread. **Cards:** AE, CB, DI, DS, MC, VI.   [X]

KONRAD'S SEAFOOD & GRILLE ROOM   Lunch: $8-$11   Dinner: $13-$35   Phone: 941/642-3332
Steak & Seafood

Location: 1 mi s of SR 92; in Mission Plaza. 599 S Collier Blvd 34145. Hours: 11:30 am-2:30 & 5-10 pm, Sun from 5 pm; Mon-Sat from 5 pm in summer. Closed: 12/24, 12/25; also Super Bowl Sun. Reservations: suggested. Features: dressy casual; children's menu; early bird specials; salad bar; cocktails & lounge. A slightly upscale ambience hangs in the air at this neoclassically decorated restaurant. The flavorful oak-grilled salmon is popular, as is the marinated flank steak with stuffed shrimp, plum tomatoes and cilantro. Live jazz musicians perform seasonally. Cards: AE, DI, DS, MC, VI.

MAREKS COLLIER HOUSE RESTAURANT   Historical   Dinner: $17-$26   Phone: 941/642-9948
AAA
Continental

Location: 1.2 mi n of SR 951. 1121 Bald Eagle Dr 34145. Hours: Open 12/1-7/31 & 9/25-11/30; 5:30 pm-9:30 pm. Closed: Sun 9/25-12/30. Reservations: suggested. Features: dressy casual; beer & wine only; a la carte. In restored historic home of Capt. Bill Collier, this intimate restaurant has three dining areas: a main room, cozy library and quaint veranda. Award-winning chef prepares imaginative gourmet fare, such as Maine lobster, Thermidor, lamb and duckling. Cards: AE, DS, MC, VI.

SANDCASTLES   Dinner: $18-$26   Phone: 941/394-5000
American

Location: I-75, exit 15, 1 mi s of SR 92; in Marco Island Hilton Beach Resort. 560 S Collier Blvd 33415. Hours: 6 pm-10 pm. Closed: Sun-Thurs 5/1-12/22. Reservations: suggested. Features: dressy casual; early bird specials; cocktails & lounge; entertainment; valet parking; a la carte. This intimate and classy restaurant is known for fine dining with many upscale specialties, including entrees of beef, veal, lamb and seafood. A good selection of decadent desserts; creme brulee, strawberry shortcake or Milky Way pie tame the sweet tooth. Cards: AE, DI, DS, JC, MC, VI.

THE SNOOK INN   Lunch: $8-$10   Dinner: $8-$20   Phone: 941/394-3313
Seafood

Location: SR 951, 2.5 mi n. 1215 Bald Eagle Dr 34145. Hours: 11 am-10 pm. Closed major holidays. Features: casual dress; children's menu; carryout; salad bar; cocktails & lounge; entertainment; area transportation. Enjoy a drink at the bar while you take in a view of the Marco River. A casual nautical theme includes a large aquarium and tabletops inset with sand, shells and faux pieces of eight. The menu offers an abundance of fresh seafood, steak, sandwiches and appetizers. Cards: AE, DI, DS, MC, VI.

MARGATE —See Fort Lauderdale p. 386.

MARIANNA pop. 6,300

———— WHERE TO STAY ————

BEST WESTERN MARIANNA INN   Phone: (850)526-5666
AAA [SAVE]
Motel

All Year   1P: $47   2P: $52   XP: $5   F12
Location: I-10, exit 21, 0.3 mi s. 2086 Hwy 71 32448 (PO Box 980, 32447). Fax: 850/482-2287. Facility: 80 units. 2 stories, exterior corridors. Terms: small pets only ($5 extra charge, in smoking rooms). Amenities: extended cable TV. Guest Services: coin laundry. Cards: AE, CB, DI, DS, MC, VI. Special Amenities: free continental breakfast and free local telephone calls.

SOME UNITS

COMFORT INN   Phone: 850/526-5600
AAA [SAVE]
Motel

All Year   1P: $48-$66   2P: $54-$71   XP: $5   F18
Location: I-10, exit 21, just nw. 2175 Hwy 71 32448 (PO Box 1507, 32447). Fax: 850/482-7899. Facility: 80 units. 2 stories, exterior corridors. Terms: 10 day cancellation notice, pets (in smoking rooms). Amenities: extended cable TV. Some: irons, hair dryers. Guest Services: coin laundry. Cards: AE, CB, DI, DS, JC, MC, VI. Special Amenities: free continental breakfast and free local telephone calls.

SOME UNITS

HAMPTON INN   Phone: (850)526-1006
[SAVE]
Motel

All Year   1P: $58   2P: $58-$62
Location: I-10, exit 21, just nw. 2185 Hwy 71 S 32448 (PO Box 698, 32447). Fax: 850/526-1824. Facility: 70 units. 2 stories, exterior corridors. Amenities: extended cable TV, irons. Guest Services: [ECP] meal plan available, coin laundry. Cards: AE, CB, DI, DS, MC, VI.

SOME UNITS
FEE

HINSON HOUSE BED & BREAKFAST   Phone: (850)526-1500
Bed & Breakfast

All Year   1P: $65-$95   2P: $65-$95   XP: $7   F5
Location: Just w of downtown center. 4338 Lafayette St 32446. Fax: 850/482-4449. Facility: Christmas decorated house year round, accommodating gracious hosts. Stocked refrigerator privileges. Designated smoking area 5 units. Some suites ($80-$95). 2 stories, interior/exterior corridors. Terms: check-in 4 pm, 10 day cancellation notice, weekly rates available. Amenities: extended cable TV. Guest Services: [BP] meal plan available. Cards: AE, DI, DS, MC, VI.

———— WHERE TO DINE ————

RED CANYON GRILL   Dinner: $8-$15   Phone: 850/482-4256
Southwestern

Location: 2.5 mi n of jct SR 90 on SR 166 N; across from Florida Caverns. 3297 Caverns Rd 32446. Hours: 5 pm-9 pm, Fri & Sat-9:30 pm. Closed major holidays; also Sun & Mon. Features: casual dress; children's menu; carryout; cocktail lounge; beer only; a la carte. The restaurant carries off its Southwestern theme with a large antler chandelier and assorted artifacts hanging on the walls. Such dishes as fajitas, mesquite grilled shrimp, pasta with grilled vegetables, and corn soup are well-presented and flavorful. Cards: AE, MC, VI.

ONY'S RESTAURANT
Lunch: $3-$15   Dinner: $3-$16   Phone: 850/482-2232
Location: I-10, exit 20, just w on Hwy 90. 4133 Lafayette St 32448. Hours: 11 am-9 pm, Sat 4-10 pm. Closed
major holidays; also Sun. Features: casual dress; children's menu; carryout; beer only. Expect long lines
at this popular family-owned and family-friendly eatery. The atmosphere, red booths and soft rock music
piped through speakers, is as comfortable and familiar as the basic, tasty fare of such dishes as chicken
armesan and spaghetti. Cards: AE, CB, DI, MC, VI.

Italian

MELBOURNE pop. 59,600—
ee also INDIALANTIC, MELBOURNE BEACH & WEST MELBOURNE.

✈ **Airport Accommodations**

MELBOURNE REGIONAL	Diamond Rating	Rate Range High Season	Listing Page
Hilton Melbourne Airport, 0.5 mi se of airport	◈◈◈	$99	471

———— WHERE TO STAY ————

AYMONT INN & SUITES-MELBOURNE
Phone: (321)242-9400
1/26-4/14   1P: $84-$89   2P: $89-$94
12/1-1/25 & 4/15-11/30   1P: $69-$74   2P: $74-$79
Motel   Location: SR 509, just w of I-95, exit 73. 7200 George T Edwards Dr 32940. Fax: 321/242-9440. Facility: All rooms
with ceiling fan. 103 units. Bath: combo or shower only. 4 stories, interior corridors. Terms: weekly rates
available. Amenities: video games, voice mail, irons, hair dryers. Leisure Activities: heated pool. Guest Services: [CP] meal
an available, valet and coin laundry. Business Services: meeting rooms. Cards: AE, CB, DI, DS, MC, VI.
See color ad p 585)

EST WESTERN HARBORVIEW
Phone: (321)724-4422
All Year   1P: $59-$129   2P: $59-$129
Location: 2 mi n of SR 192 on US 1 at jct Nasa Blvd. 964 S Harbor City Blvd 32901. Fax: 321/951-9974.
Facility: Some rooms with river view. Designated smoking area. 122 units. Some suites ($109-$129). 6 sto-
ries, interior corridors. Terms: small pets only ($10 extra charge). Amenities: extended cable TV.
Motor Inn   Dining: dining room, 7 am-2:30 & 5-2 am, $8-$16, cocktails. Leisure Activities: game room. Guest Serv-
ices: area transportation-limited, coin laundry. Business Services: meeting rooms. Cards: AE, CB, DI, DS,
C, VI. Special Amenities: free room upgrade and preferred room (each subject to availability with advanced reserva-
ns).

COMFORT HOTEL & CONFERENCE CENTER
Phone: (321)255-0077

(AAA) (SAVE)

Motor Inn

2/2-4/28	1P: $89-$129	2P: $89-$129	XP: $10	F18
12/1-2/1 & 4/29-11/30	1P: $70-$89	2P: $70-$89	XP: $10	F18

Location: I-95, exit 73 (SR 509). 8298 N Wickham Rd 32940. **Fax:** 321/259-9633. **Facility:** Beautifully decorated public areas and large, well-furnished rooms. 127 units. Some suites ($90-$149). 5 stories, interior corridors. **Terms:** weekly & monthly rates available, package plans. **Amenities:** video games, voice mail, irons. Some fax. **Dining:** dining room, 11 am-10 pm, $8-$15, cocktails. **Guest Services:** valet and coin laundry. **Business Services:** conference facilities, fax. **Cards:** AE, CB, DI, DS, MC, VI. **Special Amenities:** free continental breakfast and free newspaper.

SOME UNITS

COURTYARD BY MARRIOTT
Phone: (321)724-6400

Motel

12/1-4/30	1P: $109	2P: $119	XP: $10	F18
5/1-11/30	1P: $94	2P: $104	XP: $10	F18

Location: US 192, 3.3 mi e of jct I-95, exit 71. 2101 W New Haven Ave 32904. **Fax:** 321/984-4006. **Facility:** Very attractive with landscaped pool courtyard. Patio or balcony. 146 units. Some suites. *Bath:* combo or shower only. 3 stories, interior corridors. **Terms:** package plans. **Amenities:** voice mail, irons, hair dryers. **Leisure Activities:** heated pool, whirlpool, exercise room. **Guest Services:** valet and coin laundry. **Business Services:** meeting rooms. **Cards:** AE, DI, MC, VI. *(See color ad below)*

SOME UNITS

CRANE CREEK INN WATERFRONT BED & BREAKFAST

All Year   1P: $75-$110   2P: $75-$110   XP: $15   **Phone:** 321/768-6416

Bed & Breakfast   **Location:** From jct US 192, just s on Babcock, then 0.9 mi e. 907 E Melbourne Ave 32901. **Fax:** 321/726-1645. **Facility:** Charming Floridian decor in 1924 home overlooking Crane Creek. Smoke free premises. 5 units. **Bath:** combo or shower only. 2 stories, interior/exterior corridors. **Terms:** age restrictions may apply, 7 day cancellation notice. **Amenities:** extended cable TV, hair dryers. **Leisure Activities:** heated pool, whirlpool, canoeing, paddleboats, fishing, bicycles. **Guest Services:** [BP] meal plan available. **Cards:** AE, DI, MC, VI.

SOME UNITS

HILTON MELBOURNE AIRPORT

SAVE

1/15-4/30	1P: $99	2P: $99	XP: $15	F18
10/1-11/30	1P: $89	2P: $89	XP: $15	F18
5/1-9/30	1P: $84	2P: $84	XP: $15	F18
12/1-1/14	1P: $79	2P: $79	XP: $15	F18

Hotel   **Location:** 1 mi w of US 1, 0.8 mi n of US 192. 200 Rialto Pl 32901. **Fax:** 321/984-2528. **Facility:** Attractive, modern glass/block building with nicely appointed public areas with use of marble in lobby area, waterfall and tiered lounge area. Car rental facilities on site. 240 units. Some suites ($108-$157) and whirlpool units. **Bath:** combo or shower only. 8 stories, interior corridors. **Terms:** pets ($20 extra charge). **Amenities:** dual phone lines, voice mail, irons, hair dryers. **Leisure Activities:** heated pool, whirlpool, lighted tennis court, exercise room. **Guest Services:** gift shop, area transportation, valet and coin laundry. **Fee:** massage. **Business Services:** conference facilities, fax. **Cards:** AE, DI, DS, JC, MC, VI. **(See ad p 44 & p 470)**

SOME UNITS

FEE   FEE FEE

HOLIDAY INN-MELBOURNE RIVERFRONT

12/1-5/1	1P: $69-$83	2P: $74-$88	XP: $5	F12
5/2-11/30	1P: $50-$73	2P: $55-$78	XP: $5	F12

Motor Inn   **Location:** US 1, 1.7 mi n of US 192. 420 S Harbor City Blvd 32901. **Fax:** 321/724-0581. **Facility:** Designated smoking area. 100 units. 2 stories, exterior corridors. **Terms:** package plans, pets ($25 extra charge). **Amenities:** dual phone lines, irons, hair dryers. **Guest Services:** valet and coin laundry. **Business Services:** meeting rooms. **Cards:** AE, CB, DI, DS, JC, MC, VI.

SOME UNITS

FEE FEE

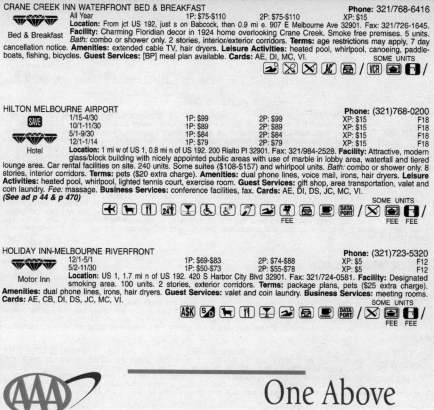

SUPER 8

(AAA) [SAVE]

◇◇◇ ◇◇◇
Motel

	1/1-3/31	1P: $52	2P: $52	XP: $6 F12
	12/1-12/31 & 4/1-11/30	1P: $46	2P: $46	XP: $6 F12

Phone: (321)723-4430

Location: I-95, exit 71, 7 mi e to US 1 on SR 192, then 0.5 mi n. 1515 S Harbor City Blvd 32901. Fax: 321/723-4312. **Facility:** Rooms vary in size; some large, second floor rooms. Contemporary furnishings. Designated smoking area. 56 units. 2 stories, interior corridors. **Terms:** small pets only ($20 deposit). **Amenities:** extended cable TV. **Cards:** AE, DI, DS, MC, VI. **Special Amenities:** early check-in/late check-out and free continental breakfast.

SOME UNITS

[S/D] [🛏] [⊞] [⛱] [&] [🎥] [DATA PORT] / [✕] [📷] [🔲] /

──────── **WHERE TO DINE** ────────

BANANA BAY WATERFRONT RESTAURANT

◇◇◇ ◇◇◇
American

Lunch: $5-$10   **Dinner:** $10-$16   **Phone:** 321/242-2401

Location: On US 1, 5 mi n of jct US 192; behind Orlando Junior College. 2425 Pineapple Ave 32935. **Hours:** 11 am-9 pm, Fri & Sat-10 pm, Sun noon-9 pm. **Reservations:** suggested. **Features:** casual dress; children's menu; early bird specials; senior's menu; carryout; cocktails & lounge. Creative preparations of Floridian and trendy American cuisine are served in a clean and pleasant environment. Casual dining available indoors and outdoors with a nice view of the Indian River. The coconut shrimp appetizer is a sweet, crunchy concoction. **Cards:** AE, DS, MC, VI.

[♿] [✕]

CONCHY JOE'S SEAFOOD RESTAURANT

◇◇◇ ◇◇◇
Seafood

Lunch: $5-$12   **Dinner:** $10-$25   **Phone:** 321/253-3131

Location: 0.3 mi e of US 1 via Eau Gallie Blvd, north side of the causeway. 1477 Pineapple Ave 32935. **Hours:** 11:30 am-2:30 & 5-10 pm. Closed: 11/22, 12/25; also 12/24 for dinner. **Features:** casual dress; children's menu; early bird specials; carryout; salad bar; cocktails & lounge; entertainment. Deep-fried alligator, conch salad and grouper marsala are specialties in the nautically themed restaurant, on the site of the 1925 Oleander's Hotel. Photographs and memorabilia are displayed throughout the casual, riverfront establishment. **Cards:** AE, DS, MC, VI.

[♿] [✕]

MELBOURNE BEACH pop. 3,000

──────── **WHERE TO DINE** ────────

CAFE COCONUT COVE

◇◇◇ ◇◇◇
Continental

are featured.

Dinner: $12-$20   **Phone:** 321/727-3133

Location: On SR A1A, 6.8 mi s of jct US 192. 4210 S SR A1A 32951. **Hours:** 5 pm-9 pm. Closed: 12/25; also Sun, Mon & 9/1-9/30. **Features:** casual dress; carryout; beer & wine only. Enjoy beautiful sunsets from a cozy dining room that overlooks the Indian River. Hearty North German cuisine is prepared by the chef/owner who extends a warm welcome to his guests. Favorites like spaetzle, bratwurst and schnitzel

DJON'S RESTAURANT

◇◇◇ ◇◇◇
French

Dinner: $20-$40   **Phone:** 321/722-2737

Location: 2.5 mi s of jct US 192 & A1A, 0.5 mi w. 522 Ocean Ave 32951. **Hours:** 5 pm-11 pm. **Reservations:** suggested. **Features:** casual dress; cocktails & lounge; entertainment; street parking. This inn was started under the 1842 Homestead Act and used by steamboat crews. The unique tile stove came from Europe. Nice variety on the menu from escargot to salad to crab cakes, chicken, veal, filet, rack of lamb to desserts flambeed table side. Temperature controlled wine cellar. **Cards:** AE, CB, DI, DS, MC, VI.

[✕]

MERRITT ISLAND pop. 35,400

──────── **WHERE TO STAY** ────────

CLARION HOTEL

[SAVE]

◇◇◇ ◇◇◇
Motor Inn

	2/15-4/15		2P: $69-$130	XP: $10 F18
	12/1-2/14		2P: $69-$95	XP: $10 F18
	4/16-11/30		2P: $69-$90	XP: $10 F18

Phone: (321)452-7711

Location: On SR 520, 0.3 mi e of SR 3. 260 E Merritt Island Cswy 32952. Fax: 321/452-9462. **Facility:** Contemporary decor. 128 units. 2 stories, exterior corridors. **Terms:** monthly rates available. **Amenities:** extended cable TV, voice mail, safes, irons, hair dryers. **Leisure Activities:** tennis court, exercise room. **Guest Services:** valet laundry. **Business Services:** meeting rooms, administrative services. **Cards:** AE, CB, DI, DS, JC, MC, VI. *(See color ad below)*

SOME UNITS

[S/D] [⊞] [🍽] [📺] [🏊] [🎥] [📠] [🖥] [DATA PORT] / [✕] [📷] [🔲] /

Look for a SAVE Place to Stay!

When selecting a AAA Approved lodging, look for properties that participate in our SAVE programs. These properties understand the value of AAA business and offer discounts to AAA members.

- A red **SAVE** icon in their TourBook® guide listing indicates an **Official Appointment** property that offers a minimum 10% discount off published TourBook standard room rates to AAA members.

- A black **SAVE** icon indicates a chain hotel that participates in the **Show Your Card & Save**® program. SYC&S partners offer a satisfaction guarantee and the lowest available rate for your dates of stay.* Reservations must be made by calling their exclusive AAA member toll-free numbers:

Days Inn 800-432-9755 ■ **La Quinta Inns** 800-221-4731
Hampton Inns 800-456-7793 ■ **Hilton Hotels** 800-916-2221
Hyatt Hotels 800-532-1496
Sleep, Comfort, Quality, Clarion, Econo Lodge, Rodeway
800-228-1222

*Sleep, Comfort, Quality, Clarion, Econo Lodge, Rodeway offer a 10-20% discount.

Destination Miami
pop. 358,500

Pioneering Julia Tuttle convinced millionaire Henry Flagler to extend his railroad farther south, and the rest has been history.

Miami skyline.
International business is at the forefront of Miami's bustling downtown.

Now a cosmopolitan metropolis and a leader in the world of global commerce, Miami and the Beaches also are internationally known as a vacation paradise where cultures, both pop and ethnic, blend under a bright, tropical sun.

See Vicinity maps pages 475 and 478

Outdoor dining, Coconut Grove.
Serious shoppers flock to this trendy area for its eclectic boutiques and sidewalk cafes.

Boating, Miami.
With a bay, a river and an ocean nearby, it's no wonder water sports of all sorts are enjoyed here. (See mention page 120)

Places included in this AAA Destination City:

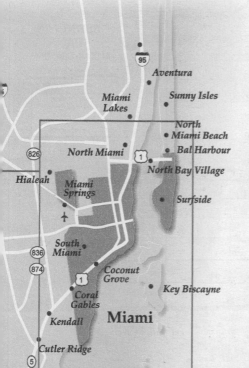

Aventura

Sunny Isles

Miami
Lakes

North
Miami Beach

North Miami

Bal Harbour

North Bay Village

Hialeah

Miami
Springs

Surfside

South
Miami

Coconut
Grove

Key Biscayne

Coral
Gables

Miami

Kendall

Cutler Ridge

nestead

*Aerial view,
Miami Beach.*
Long known as a
resort destination,
Miami Beach's
swank oceanfront
hotels draw
vacationers eager
to escape colder
climates.

*South Beach,
Miami Beach.*
Funky art deco
design, neon
accents and
tropical colors
characterize
ultra-hip SoBe's
revitalized hotels.
(See mention
page 31)

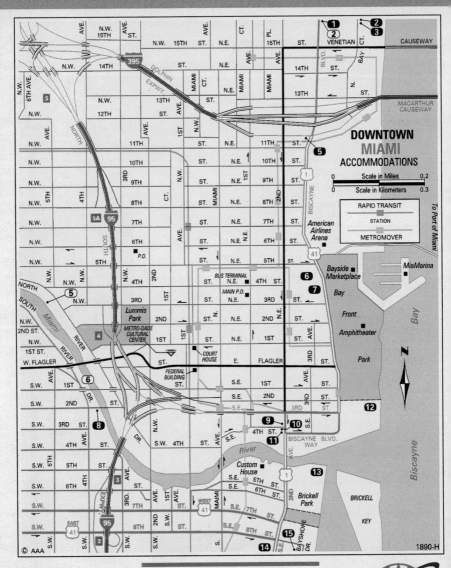

DOWNTOWN
MIAMI
ACCOMMODATIONS

Scale in Miles　0　0.2
Scale in Kilometers　0　0.3

RAPID TRANSIT
STATION
METROMOVER

Downtown Miami

This index helps you "spot" where approved accommodations are located on the corresponding detailed maps. Rate ranges are for comparison only and show the property's high season. Turn to the listing page for more detailed rate information and consult display ads for special promotions. Restaurant rate range is for dinner, unless only lunch (L) is served.

Spotter/Map Page Number	OA	**DOWNTOWN MIAMI - Lodgings**	Diamond Rating	Rate Range High Season	Listing Page
1 / p. 476		Wyndham Hotel Miami-Biscayne Bay	🔹🔹🔹	$164-$399	489
2 / p. 476		Doubletree Grand Hotel	🔹🔹🔹	$189-$209	488
3 / p. 476		Biscayne Bay Marriott Hotel	🔹🔹🔹	Failed to provide	487
5 / p. 476	AAA	**Howard Johnson Hotel-Downtown/Port of Miami**	🔹🔹🔹	$89-$119 SAVE	489
6 / p. 476	AAA	**Best Western-Marina Park Hotel** - see color ad p 487	🔹🔹	$129-$169 SAVE	487
7 / p. 476		Everglades Hotel	🔹🔹	$95	488
8 / p. 476		Miami River Inn	🔹🔹	$99-$199	489
9 / p. 476		Holiday Inn-Downtown	🔹🔹	$109-$149	488
10 / p. 476		Clarion Hotel & Suites	🔹🔹🔹	$109-$179	488
11 / p. 476	AAA	**Hyatt Regency Miami** - see ad p 489	🔹🔹🔹🔹	$209-$234 SAVE	489
12 / p. 476		Hotel Inter-Continental Miami	🔹🔹🔹🔹	$229-$450	488
13 / p. 476		Sheraton Biscayne Bay Hotel	🔹🔹🔹	$209-$339	489
14 / p. 476		Hampton Inn-Downtown	🔹🔹	$110-$120	488
15 / p. 476		Fortune House All Suite Hotel	🔹🔹🔹	$210-$250	488
		DOWNTOWN MIAMI - Restaurants			
② / p. 476		The Fish Market	🔹🔹🔹	$20-$35	490
⑤ / p. 476		Joe's Seafood Restaurant	🔹🔹	$12-$20	490
⑥ / p. 476		East Coast Fisheries	🔹🔹	$10-$29	490

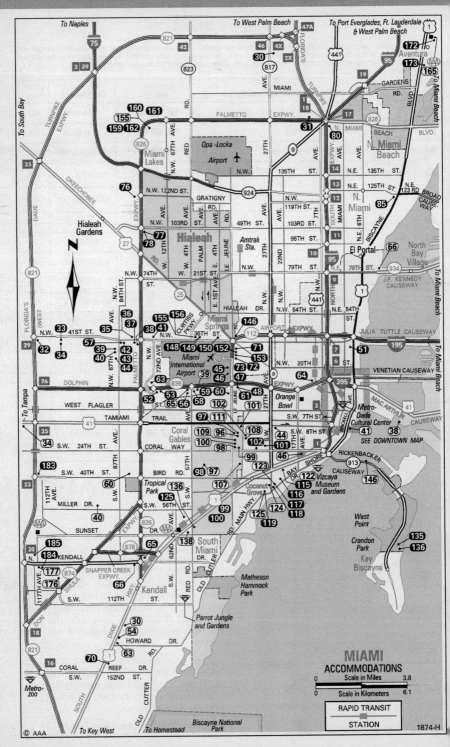

✈ Airport Accommodations

Spotter/Map Page Number	OA	MIAMI INTERNATIONAL	Diamond Rating	Rate Range High Season	Listing Page
37 / p. 478	AAA	**Amerisuites Airport West, 4.9 mi nw of entrance**	◈◈◈	$159 [SAVE]	490
46 / p. 478	AAA	**Best Western-Miami Airport Inn, 0.5 mi s of entrance**	◈◈◈	$89-$129 [SAVE]	490
39 / p. 478		Candlewood Suites Miami Airport West, 4.5 mi nw of entrance	◈◈◈	$169	491
36 / p. 478		Courtyard by Marriott-Miami West/Doral Area, 4.8 mi nw of entrance	◈◈◈	$139-$149	491
47 / p. 478		Courtyard Miami Airport South, 0.8 mi s of entrance	◈◈◈	$99	491
60 / p. 478	AAA	**Crowne Plaza Miami International Airport, 1 mi s of entrance**	◈◈◈	$179 [SAVE]	491
63 / p. 478	AAA	**Days Inn Miami International Airport Hotel, 4.3 mi sw of terminal**	◈◈◈	$89-$119 [SAVE]	492
58 / p. 478		DoubleTree Club Miami Airport Hotel, 2.5 mi sw of entrance	◈◈◈	$109	492
71 / p. 478		Embassy Suites Miami International Airport, 0.8 mi n of airport entrance	◈◈◈	$169-$239	492
35 / p. 478		Fairfield Inn by Marriott-Miami West/Doral Area, 4.8 mi nw of entrance	◈◈◈	$80-$84	492
48 / p. 478		Fairfield Inn Miami Airport South, 0.8 mi s of entrance	◈◈◈	$89	493
38 / p. 478	AAA	**Hampton Inn-Miami Airport West, 4.8 mi nw of entrance**	◈◈◈	$110-$150 [SAVE]	493
59 / p. 478		Hilton Miami Airport & Towers, 2.5 mi sw of airport entrance	◈◈◈◈	$119-$249	493
43 / p. 478	AAA	**Holiday Inn-Miami Airport West, 5.1 mi nw of entrance**	◈◈◈	$139-$189 [SAVE]	494
53 / p. 478		Homestead Village Guest Studios-Blue Lagoon, 2 mi s of entrance	◈◈	Failed to provide	494
40 / p. 478		Homestead Village Guest Studios Miami Airport/Dora, 5.1 mi nw	◈◈	$79-$109	494
45 / p. 478	AAA	**Howard Johnson Hotel Miami International Airport, 0.3 mi s**	◈◈◈	$90-$135 [SAVE]	494
44 / p. 478		La Quinta Inn & Suites, 5.1 mi nw	◈◈◈	$89-$109	494
41 / p. 478		La Quinta Inn Miami Airport North, 4.5 mi nw of entrance	◈◈◈	$65-$95	494
61 / p. 478		Miami Airport Marriott, 0.8 mi s of entrance	◈◈◈	$170	494
72 / p. 478	AAA	**Quality Inn & Suites, at entrance**	◈◈	$90-$100 [SAVE]	495
52 / p. 478	AAA	**Radisson Mart Plaza Hotel, 4 mi sw of terminal**	◈◈◈	$159 [SAVE]	495
57 / p. 478		Staybridge Suites Miami-Airport West, 5.1 mi sw of entrance	◈◈◈	$119	496
56 / p. 478		Summerfield Suites by Wyndham-Miami Airport, 2.5 mi sw of entrance	◈◈◈	$109	496
42 / p. 478	AAA	**Wellesley Inn & Suites, 4.9 mi nw of entrance**	◈◈◈	$90-$110 [SAVE]	496
73 / p. 478		Wyndham Miami Airport Hotel, 0.3 mi e of entrance	◈◈◈	$139-$249	497
152 / p. 478		Baymont Inn & Suites-Miami/Airport, 0.8 mi n of entrance	◈◈◈	$99-$104	523
148 / p. 478	AAA	**Clarion Hotel-Miami International Airport, 2 mi nw of entrance**	◈◈◈	$126-$186 [SAVE]	523
149 / p. 478	AAA	**Comfort Inn & Suites-Miami International Airport, 2 mi nw of entrance**	◈◈◈	$116-$176 [SAVE]	523
146 / p. 478		Holiday Inn-Airport North Miami Springs, 1 mi n of entrance	◈◈◈	$104-$114	523

Spotter/Map Page Number	OA	MIAMI INTERNATIONAL (continued)	Diamond Rating	Rate Range High Season	Listing Page
150 / p. 478	AAA	Holiday Inn Express Miami International Airport, 2 mi nw of entrance	▽▽ ▽▽ ▽▽	$116-$176 SAVE	524
155 / p. 478	AAA	Sleep Inn-Miami Airport, 2 mi nw of entrance	▽▽ ▽▽	SAVE	524

Miami and Vicinity

This index helps you "spot" where approved accommodations are located on the corresponding detailed maps. Rate ranges are for comparison only and show the property's high season. Turn to the listing page for more detailed rate information and consult display ads for special promotions. Restaurant rate range is for dinner, unless only lunch (L) is served.

Spotter/Map Page Number	OA	MIAMI - Lodgings	Diamond Rating	Rate Range High Season	Listing Page
30 / p. 478		Holiday Inn-Calder/Pro Player Stadium - see ad p 493	▽▽ ▽▽ ▽▽	$89-$1000	493
31 / p. 478	AAA	El Palacio Resort Hotel & Suites	▽▽ ▽▽ ▽▽	$98-$170 SAVE	492
32 / p. 478		Hampton Inn & Suites	▽▽ ▽▽ ▽▽	$84-$159	493
33 / p. 478		Baymont Inn & Suites Miami West - see color ad p 523	▽▽ ▽▽ ▽▽	$89-$109	490
34 / p. 478		TownePlace Suites by Marriott	▽▽ ▽▽ ▽▽	$89-$139	496
35 / p. 478		Fairfield Inn by Marriott-Miami West/Doral Area - see color ad p 492, p 491	▽▽ ▽▽ ▽▽	$80-$84	492
36 / p. 478		Courtyard by Marriott-Miami West/Doral Area - see color ad p 491	▽▽ ▽▽ ▽▽	$139-$149	491
37 / p. 478	AAA	Amerisuites Airport West - see color ad p 5	▽▽ ▽▽ ▽▽	$159 SAVE	490
38 / p. 478	AAA	Hampton Inn-Miami Airport West	▽▽ ▽▽ ▽▽	$110-$150 SAVE	493
39 / p. 478		Candlewood Suites Miami Airport West	▽▽ ▽▽ ▽▽	$169	491
40 / p. 478		Homestead Village Guest Studios Miami Airport/Doral	▽▽ ▽▽	$79-$109	494
41 / p. 478		La Quinta Inn Miami Airport North	▽▽ ▽▽ ▽▽	$65-$95	494
42 / p. 478	AAA	Wellesley Inn & Suites - see color ad opposite title page	▽▽ ▽▽ ▽▽	$90-$110 SAVE	496
43 / p. 478	AAA	Holiday Inn-Miami Airport West	▽▽ ▽▽ ▽▽	$139-$189 SAVE	494
44 / p. 478		La Quinta Inn & Suites	▽▽ ▽▽ ▽▽	$89-$109	494
45 / p. 478	AAA	Howard Johnson Hotel Miami International Airport	▽▽ ▽▽ ▽▽	$90-$135 SAVE	494
46 / p. 478	AAA	Best Western-Miami Airport Inn	▽▽ ▽▽ ▽▽	$89-$129 SAVE	490
47 / p. 478		Courtyard Miami Airport South	▽▽ ▽▽ ▽▽	$99	491
48 / p. 478		Fairfield Inn Miami Airport South - see color ad p 492	▽▽ ▽▽ ▽▽	$89	493
51 / p. 478		Super 8 Motel	▽▽ ▽▽	$60-$120	496
52 / p. 478	AAA	Radisson Mart Plaza Hotel	▽▽ ▽▽ ▽▽	$159 SAVE	495
53 / p. 478		Homestead Village Guest Studios-Blue Lagoon	▽▽ ▽▽	Failed to provide	494
56 / p. 478		Summerfield Suites by Wyndham-Miami Airport	▽▽ ▽▽ ▽▽	$109	496
57 / p. 478		Staybridge Suites Miami-Airport West	▽▽ ▽▽ ▽▽	$119	496
58 / p. 478		DoubleTree Club Miami Airport Hotel	▽▽ ▽▽ ▽▽	$109	492
59 / p. 478		Hilton Miami Airport & Towers - see ad p 44	▽▽ ▽▽ ▽▽ ▽▽	$119-$249	493
60 / p. 478	AAA	Crowne Plaza Miami International Airport	▽▽ ▽▽ ▽▽	$179 SAVE	491
61 / p. 478		Miami Airport Marriott	▽▽ ▽▽ ▽▽	$170	494
63 / p. 478	AAA	Days Inn Miami International Airport Hotel	▽▽ ▽▽ ▽▽	$89-$119 SAVE	492
64 / p. 478		Days Inn Medical Center/Civic Center	▽▽ ▽▽	$69-$79	491

Spotter/Map Page Number	OA	MIAMI - Lodgings (continued)	Diamond Rating	Rate Range High Season	Listing Page
65 / p. 478		Miami Marriott-Dadeland	◊◊◊	$164-$219	495
66 / p. 478		Ramada Limited South Miami Dadeland	◊◊◊	$89-$109	495
70 / p. 478	AAA	**Quality Inn-South** - see color ad p 495	◊◊◊	$81-$135 [SAVE]	495
71 / p. 478		Embassy Suites Miami International Airport	◊◊◊	$169-$239	492
72 / p. 478	AAA	**Quality Inn & Suites**	◊◊	$90-$100 [SAVE]	495
73 / p. 478		Wyndham Miami Airport Hotel	◊◊◊	$139-$249	497
		MIAMI - Restaurants			
30 / p. 478		Anacapri	◊◊	$10-$18	497
34 / p. 478		Cami's Seafood & Pasta	◊	$5-$15	497
38 / p. 478		Islas Canarias Restaurant	◊	$4-$18	498
39 / p. 478		94th Aero Squadron	◊◊	$15-$24	497
40 / p. 478		The Fish House	◊	$10-$20	497
41 / p. 478		Giacomo Restaurant	◊◊	$7-$19	498
44 / p. 478		Casa Juancho Restaurant	◊◊	$14-$29	497
46 / p. 478		Old Lisbon Restaurant	◊◊	$14-$47	498
54 / p. 478		Tani Thai Restaurant	◊◊	$9-$20	498
60 / p. 478		Tropical Chinese Restaurant	◊◊	$10-$30	498
63 / p. 478		Fleming: A Taste of Denmark	◊◊◊	$11-$23	497
65 / p. 478		Le Cafe Royal	◊◊◊	$17-$24	498
66 / p. 478		Mike Gordon Seafood Restaurant	◊◊	$12-$25	498
		HIALEAH - Lodgings			
76 / p. 478		Holiday Inn Hialeah/Miami Lakes	◊◊	Failed to provide	519
77 / p. 478	AAA	**Days Inn Miami Airport/Miami Lakes** - see ad p 519	◊◊	$69-$109 [SAVE]	518
78 / p. 478	AAA	**Ramada Inn-Miami Airport North** - see ad p 519	◊◊	$69-$109 [SAVE]	519
		NORTH MIAMI - Lodgings			
80 / p. 478		Howard Johnson North Miami	◊◊◊	$67-$89	525
85 / p. 478	AAA	**Holiday Inn North Miami (Bal Harbor Area)**	◊◊◊	$99-$200 [SAVE]	525
		CORAL GABLES - Lodgings			
97 / p. 478		Holiday Inn Coral Gables Business District	◊◊◊	$129-$159	514
98 / p. 478		The Biltmore Hotel Coral Gables	◊◊◊◊	$319-$489	514
99 / p. 478	AAA	**Riviera Court Motel** - see color ad p 515	◊◊	$75-$87 [SAVE]	515
100 / p. 478	AAA	**Holiday Inn University of Miami**	◊◊	$149-$189 [SAVE]	514
101 / p. 478	AAA	**Hyatt Regency Coral Gables**	◊◊◊	$274-$299 [SAVE]	515
102 / p. 478		Omni Colonnade Hotel - see color ad p 514	◊◊◊◊	$285-$325	515
		CORAL GABLES - Restaurants			
96 / p. 478		Botticelli Trattoria	◊◊	$10-$20	515
97 / p. 478		Le Palme D'or	◊◊◊◊	$20-$40	516
98 / p. 478		Giacosa	◊◊◊	$14-$30	516
99 / p. 478		Ortanique on the Mile	◊◊◊	$15-$30	516
100 / p. 478		Mozart Stube Restaurant	◊◊	$18-$30	516

Spotter/Map Page Number	OA	CORAL GABLES - Restaurants (continued)	Diamond Rating	Rate Range High Season	Listing Page
101 / p. 478		Mylos Restaurant & Bar	◆◆	$10-$25	516
102 / p. 478		NORMAN'S	◆◆◆◆	$26-$39	516
107 / p. 478		Christy's	◆◆◆	$17-$32	516
108 / p. 478		Restaurant St. Michel	◆◆◆	$15-$33	516
109 / p. 478		Caffe Abbracci	◆◆◆	$14-$28	515
111 / p. 478		Le Festival	◆◆◆	$16-$27	516
		COCONUT GROVE - Lodgings			
115 / p. 478		Hampton Inn-Coconut Grove/Coral Gables	◆◆◆	$129-$149	512
116 / p. 478		The Doubletree Hotel at Coconut Grove	◆◆◆	$209-$319	512
117 / p. 478		Wyndham Grand Bay Hotel	◆◆◆	$233-$293	513
118 / p. 478		The Mutiny Hotel	◆◆◆	$375	513
119 / p. 478	▲▲▲	**Mayfair House Hotel**	◆◆◆◆	$269-$800 SAVE	512
		COCONUT GROVE - Restaurants			
122 / p. 478		Baleen	◆◆◆	$19-$40	513
123 / p. 478		Bici Ristorante	◆◆◆	$14-$36	513
124 / p. 478		Mezzanotte In The Grove	◆◆	$12-$21	513
125 / p. 478		Mayfair Grill	◆◆◆	$20-$40	513
		SOUTH MIAMI - Lodgings			
125 / p. 478		Hotel Vila-Miami University	◆◆	$139-$159	525
		SOUTH MIAMI - Restaurants			
136 / p. 478		El Manara	◆◆	$10-$16	525
138 / p. 478		Khoury's	◆◆	$11-$23	525
		KEY BISCAYNE - Lodgings			
135 / p. 478		Silver Sands Beach Resort	◆◆	$169-$349	521
136 / p. 478	▲▲▲	**Sonesta Beach Resort Key Biscayne** - see color ad p 521	◆◆◆◆	$295-$380 SAVE	521
		KEY BISCAYNE - Restaurant			
146 / p. 478	▲▲▲	**Rusty Pelican**	◆◆	$16-$30	522
		MIAMI SPRINGS - Lodgings			
146 / p. 478		Holiday Inn-Airport North Miami Springs	◆◆◆	$104-$114	523
148 / p. 478	▲▲▲	**Clarion Hotel-Miami International Airport**	◆◆◆	$126-$186 SAVE	523
149 / p. 478	▲▲▲	**Comfort Inn & Suites-Miami International Airport** - see color ad p 483	◆◆◆	$116-$176 SAVE	523
150 / p. 478	▲▲▲	**Holiday Inn Express Miami International Airport** - see color ad p 487	◆◆◆	$116-$176 SAVE	524
152 / p. 478		Baymont Inn & Suites-Miami/Airport - see color ad p 523	◆◆◆	$99-$104	523
153 / p. 478	▲▲▲	**Red Roof Inn Miami Airport**	◆◆◆	$95-$102 SAVE	524
155 / p. 478	▲▲▲	**Sleep Inn-Miami Airport** - see color ad p 483	◆◆	SAVE	524
156 / p. 478	▲▲▲	**MainStay Suites-Miami Springs**	◆◆◆	$116-$176 SAVE	524
		MIAMI LAKES - Lodgings			
159 / p. 478		Towne Place Suites by Marriott	◆◆◆	$69-$149	522
160 / p. 478		Don Shula's Hotel & Golf Club	◆◆◆	$109-$129	522

Spotter/Map Page Number	OA	MIAMI LAKES - Lodgings (continued)	Diamond Rating	Rate Range High Season	Listing Page
161 / p. 478		Courtyard by Marriott-Miami Lakes Area - see color ad p 491	▽▽▽	$129-$139	522
162 / p. 478	AAA	**Wellesley Inn & Suites** - see color ad opposite title page	▽▽	$89-$109 [SAVE]	522
		MIAMI LAKES - Restaurant			
155 / p. 478		Shula's Steakhouse	▽▽▽	$18-$33	522
		AVENTURA - Lodgings			
172 / p. 478		Turnberry Isle Resort & Club	▽▽▽▽	$265-$485	511
173 / p. 478		Courtyard by Marriott Aventura Mall	▽▽▽	$139-$159	511
		AVENTURA - Restaurant			
165 / p. 478		Chef Allen's	▽▽▽▽	$26-$38	512
		KENDALL - Lodgings			
183 / p. 478	AAA	**Comfort Suites** - see color ad p 520	▽▽▽	$109-$129 [SAVE]	520
184 / p. 478	AAA	**AmeriSuites** - see color ad p 5	▽▽▽	$129-$179 [SAVE]	520
185 / p. 478	AAA	**Wellesley Inn & Suites** - see color ad opposite title page	▽▽▽	$99-$119 [SAVE]	520
		KENDALL - Restaurants			
176 / p. 478		Gil Capa's Bistro	▽▽	$7-$14	521
177 / p. 478		PastaBilities	▽▽	$10-$15	521

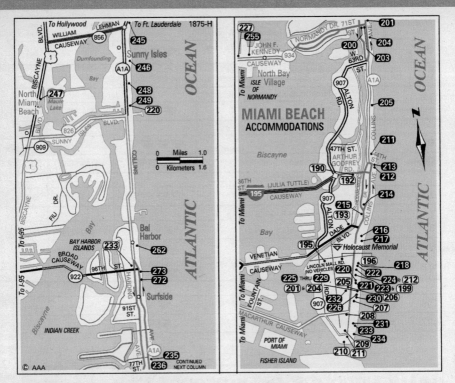

Miami Beach and Vicinity

This index helps you "spot" where approved accommodations are located on the corresponding detailed maps. Rate ranges are for comparison only and show the property's high season. Turn to the listing page for more detailed rate information and consult display ads for special promotions. Restaurant rate range is for dinner, unless only lunch (L) is served.

Spotter/Map Page Number	OA	**MIAMI BEACH - Lodgings**	Diamond Rating	Rate Range High Season	Listing Page
200 / above	AAA	**Holiday Inn Indian Creek -** see color ad p 503	▽▽▽	$129-$189 SAVE	502
201 / above	AAA	**Clarion Suites Crystal Beach & Health Club** - see color ad p 499	▽▽▽	$144-$245 SAVE	501
203 / above	AAA	**Comfort Inn On the Beach -** see color ad p 501	▽▽▽	$125-$165 SAVE	501
204 / above	AAA	**Radisson Deauville Resort Miami Beach -** see ad p 506	▽▽▽	$239 SAVE	505
205 / above	AAA	**Wyndham Miami Beach Resort**	▽▽▽	$159-$395 SAVE	509
211 / above		Fontainebleau Hilton Resort & Towers - see ad p 44	▼▼▼	$209-$399	502
212 / above		Ramada Inn Miami Beach	▼▼	$125-$150	505
213 / above	AAA	**Sovereign Hotel -** see color ad p 507	▽▽▽	$149 SAVE	508
214 / above	AAA	**The Indian Creek Hotel -** see color ad p 503	▽▽▽	$140-$260 SAVE	504
215 / above		The Abbey Hotel	▼▼▼	$179-$199	499
216 / above	AAA	**Holiday Inn South Beach Resort**	▽▽▽	$189-$229 SAVE	503
217 / above	AAA	**Days Inn Art Deco/Convention Center**	▽▽	$149-$169 SAVE	501
218 / above		Riande Continental Hotel	▼▼	$175	506
220 / above		Surfcomber-Hampton Inn - see color ad p 508	▼▼▼	$139-$309	508

Spotter/Map Page Number	OA	**MIAMI BEACH** - Lodgings (continued)	Diamond Rating	Rate Range High Season	Listing Page
221 / p. 484		Tudor Travelodge Hotel & Suites	◈◈	$149	508
222 / p. 484	AAA	**Shelborne Beach Resort-South Beach -** see color ad p 507	◈◈◈	$185-$2500 SAVE	507
223 / p. 484		Loews Miami Beach Hotel - see color ad p 504	◈◈◈◈	$349-$499	504
224 / p. 484		The Hotel	◈◈◈	$295-$425	503
225 / p. 484		Casa Grande Hotel	◈◈◈	$310-$1500	500
226 / p. 484	AAA	**Hotel Edison-South Beach**	◈◈	$165-$325 SAVE	503
227 / p. 484		Cavalier	◈◈◈	$185-$395	501
228 / p. 484		Leslie Hotel	◈◈◈	$195-$395	504
229 / p. 484	AAA	**The Tides Hotel**	◈◈◈◈	$475-$575 SAVE	508
230 / p. 484		Breakwater Hotel - see color ad p 500	◈◈	$149-$239	500
231 / p. 484		The Rose	◈◈	$125	506
232 / p. 484		The Blue Moon, A Merv Griffin Hotel	◈◈◈◈	$215-$345	500
233 / p. 484		The Savoy on South Beach	◈◈◈	Failed to provide	507
234 / p. 484		Century Hotel	◈◈◈	Failed to provide	501
235 / p. 484	AAA	**Days Inn North Beach -** see color ad p 502	◈◈	$89-$159 SAVE	502
236 / p. 484	AAA	**Ocean Surf Hotel -** see color ad p 505	◈◈	$99-$139 SAVE	505
		MIAMI BEACH - Restaurants			
190 / p. 484	AAA	**Crystal Cafe**	◈◈◈	$13-$25	510
192 / p. 484	AAA	**The Forge**	◈◈◈	$20-$37	510
193 / p. 484		Mama Vieja Restaurant	◈	$7-$18	510
195 / p. 484		Pacific Time	◈◈◈	$17-$32	510
196 / p. 484		Yuca Restaurant	◈◈◈	$6-$40	511
199 / p. 484		Gaucho Room	◈◈◈◈	$18-$40	510
201 / p. 484		Cardoza Cafe	◈◈	$6-$25	509
204 / p. 484		Mezzaluna, South Beach	◈◈◈	$10-$24	510
205 / p. 484		Mark's South Beach	◈◈◈	$18-$45	510
206 / p. 484		Astor Place Bar & Grill	◈◈◈	$7-$30	509
207 / p. 484		Boulevard Bistro	◈◈	$8-$45	509
208 / p. 484		China Grill	◈◈◈	$21-$35	510
209 / p. 484		Nemo Restaurant	◈◈◈	$18-$28	510
210 / p. 484		Smith & Wollensky	◈◈◈	$22-$38	511
211 / p. 484		Joe's Stone Crab Restaurant	◈◈	$5-$60	510
212 / p. 484		Wish	◈◈◈	$12-$25	511
		SUNNY ISLES - Lodgings			
245 / p. 484	AAA	**Ramada Plaza Marco Polo Beach Resort -** see color ad p 506	◈◈◈	$155-$195 SAVE	526
246 / p. 484	AAA	**Suez Ocean Front Resort -** see color ad p 526	◈◈	$95-$135 SAVE	527
248 / p. 484	AAA	**Monaco Oceanfront Resort**	◈◈	$70-$109 SAVE	526

Spotter/Map Page Number	OA	**SUNNY ISLES** - Lodgings (continued)	Diamond Rating	Rate Range High Season	Listing Page
249 / p. 484	AAA	**Newport Beachside Hotel & Resort**	▽▽▽	$99-$289 SAVE	526
		SUNNY ISLES - Restaurant			
220 / p. 484		The World Famous Newport Pub	▽▽	$9-$20	527
		NORTH BAY VILLAGE - Lodgings			
255 / p. 484	AAA	**Best Western on the Bay Inn & Marina** - see color ad p 499	▽▽	$74-$114 SAVE	524
		NORTH BAY VILLAGE - Restaurant			
227 / p. 484		The Crab House Seafood Restaurant	▽▽	$11-$39	524
		BAL HARBOUR - Lodgings			
262 / p. 484		Sheraton Bal Harbour Beach Resort	▽▽▽	$305-$445	512
		BAL HARBOUR - Restaurant			
233 / p. 484		Carpaccio	▽▽	$14-$21	512
		SURFSIDE - Lodgings			
272 / p. 484	AAA	**Beekman Hotel Suites** - see ad p 527	▽▽	$165-$315 SAVE	527
273 / p. 484	AAA	**Best Western Oceanfront Resort** - see color ad p 500 & ad p 527	▽▽▽	$99-$149 SAVE	527
		NORTH MIAMI BEACH - Restaurant			
247 / p. 484		Tuna's Waterfront Grille	▽▽	$10-$25	525

DOWNTOWN MIAMI (See map p. 476; index p. 477)

──── WHERE TO STAY ────

BEST WESTERN-MARINA PARK HOTEL

Phone: (305)371-4400   **6**

2/15-2/28	1P: $129-$159	2P: $139-$169	XP: $10	F17
1/1-2/14	1P: $109-$139	2P: $119-$149	XP: $10	F17
3/1-11/30	1P: $99-$139	2P: $109-$149	XP: $10	F17
12/1-12/31	1P: $99-$129	2P: $109-$139	XP: $10	F17

Hotel

Location: On US 1, facing Port of Miami and Bayside Marketplace. 340 Biscayne Blvd 33132. Fax: 305/372-2862. **Facility:** Across the street from Bayside Market Place Village of shops. Spacious rooms. 200 units. *Bath:* combo or shower only. 10 stories, interior corridors. **Parking:** extra charge. **Terms:** 3 day cancellation notice-fee imposed, monthly rates available, package plans. **Amenities:** voice mail, safes (fee). **Dining:** restaurant, 6:30 am-10:30 pm, $12-$27, cocktails. **Leisure Activities:** video arcade. **Guest Services:** gift shop, valet laundry. **Business Services:** meeting rooms, administrative services, fax. *Fee:* PC. **Cards:** AE, DI, DS, MC, VI. **Special Amenities:** early check-in/late check-out and free newspaper. *(See color ad below)*

BISCAYNE BAY MARRIOTT HOTEL

Phone: (305)374-3900   **3**

Property failed to provide current rates

Hotel

Location: Just e of US 1 (Biscayne Blvd) at 15th St. 1633 N Bayshore Dr 33132. Fax: 305/375-0597. **Facility:** Striking modern hotel on Biscayne Bay. All units with balcony. 601 units. Some suites. *Bath:* combo or shower only. 31 stories, interior corridors. **Parking:** extra charge or valet. **Terms:** check-in 4 pm, 3 day cancellation notice-fee imposed, package plans. **Amenities:** dual phone lines, honor bars, irons, hair dryers. *Some:* voice mail. **Leisure Activities:** heated pool, whirlpool, exercise room. *Fee:* boats, marina, charter fishing. **Guest Services:** gift shop, coin laundry. **Business Services:** conference facilities, administrative services. *Fee:* PC. **Cards:** AE, CB, DI, DS, MC, VI.

(See map p. 476)

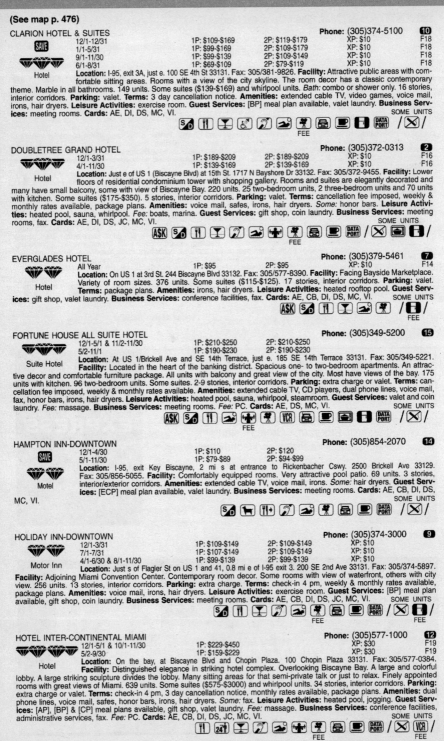

CLARION HOTEL & SUITES
Phone: (305)374-5100 10

[SAVE]

Hotel

12/1-12/31	1P: $109-$169	2P: $119-$179	XP: $10	F18
1/1-5/31	1P: $99-$169	2P: $109-$179	XP: $10	F18
9/1-11/30	1P: $99-$139	2P: $109-$149	XP: $10	F18
6/1-8/31	1P: $69-$109	2P: $79-$119	XP: $10	F18

Location: I-95, exit 3A, just e. 100 SE 4th St 33131. Fax: 305/381-9826. **Facility:** Attractive public areas with comfortable sitting areas. Rooms with a view of the city skyline. The room decor has a classic contemporary theme. Marble in all bathrooms. 149 units. Some suites ($139-$169) and whirlpool units. *Bath:* combo or shower only. 16 stories, interior corridors. **Parking:** valet. **Terms:** 3 day cancellation notice. **Amenities:** extended cable TV, video games, voice mail, irons, hair dryers. **Leisure Activities:** exercise room. **Guest Services:** [BP] meal plan available, valet laundry. **Business Services:** meeting rooms. **Cards:** AE, DI, DS, MC, VI.
SOME UNITS

DOUBLETREE GRAND HOTEL
Phone: (305)372-0313 2

Hotel

12/1-3/31	1P: $189-$209	2P: $189-$209	XP: $10	F16
4/1-11/30	1P: $139-$169	2P: $139-$169	XP: $10	F16

Location: Just e of US 1 (Biscayne Blvd) at 15th St. 1717 N Bayshore Dr 33132. Fax: 305/372-9455. **Facility:** Lower floors of residential condominium tower with shopping gallery. Rooms and suites are elegantly decorated and many have small balcony, some with view of Biscayne Bay. 220 units. 25 two-bedroom units, 2 three-bedroom units and 70 units with kitchen. Some suites ($175-$350). 5 stories, interior corridors. **Parking:** valet. **Terms:** cancellation fee imposed, weekly & monthly rates available, package plans. **Amenities:** voice mail, safes, irons, hair dryers. *Some:* honor bars. **Leisure Activities:** heated pool, sauna, whirlpool. *Fee:* boats, marina. **Guest Services:** gift shop, coin laundry. **Business Services:** meeting rooms, fax. **Cards:** AE, DI, DS, JC, MC, VI.
SOME UNITS

EVERGLADES HOTEL
Phone: (305)379-5461 7

Hotel

All Year	1P: $95	2P: $95	XP: $10	F14

Location: On US 1 at 3rd St. 244 Biscayne Blvd 33132. Fax: 305/577-8390. **Facility:** Facing Bayside Marketplace. Variety of room sizes. Some suites ($115-$125). 17 stories, interior corridors. **Parking:** valet. **Terms:** package plans. **Amenities:** irons, hair dryers. **Leisure Activities:** heated rooftop pool. **Guest Services:** gift shop, valet laundry. **Business Services:** conference facilities, fax. **Cards:** AE, CB, DI, DS, MC, VI.
SOME UNITS

FORTUNE HOUSE ALL SUITE HOTEL
Phone: (305)349-5200 15

Suite Hotel

12/1-5/1 & 11/2-11/30	1P: $210-$250	2P: $210-$250
5/2-11/1	1P: $190-$230	2P: $190-$230

Location: At US 1/Brickell Ave and SE 14th Terrace, just e. 185 SE 14th Terrace 33131. Fax: 305/349-5221. **Facility:** Located in the heart of the banking district. Spacious one- to two-bedroom apartments. An attractive decor and comfortable furniture package. All units with balcony and great view of the city. Most have views of the bay. 175 units with kitchen. 96 two-bedroom units. Some suites. 2-9 stories, interior corridors. **Parking:** extra charge or valet. **Terms:** cancellation fee imposed, weekly & monthly rates available. **Amenities:** extended cable TV, CD players, dual phone lines, voice mail, fax, honor bars, irons, hair dryers. **Leisure Activities:** heated pool, sauna, whirlpool, steamroom. **Guest Services:** valet and coin laundry. *Fee:* massage. **Business Services:** meeting rooms. *Fee:* PC. **Cards:** AE, DS, MC, VI.
SOME UNITS

HAMPTON INN-DOWNTOWN
Phone: (305)854-2070 14

[SAVE]

Motel

12/1-4/30	1P: $110	2P: $120
5/1-11/30	1P: $79-$89	2P: $94-$99

Location: I-95, exit Key Biscayne, 2 mi s at entrance to Rickenbacher Cswy. 2500 Brickell Ave 33129. Fax: 305/856-5055. **Facility:** Comfortably equipped rooms. Very attractive pool patio. 69 units. 3 stories, interior/exterior corridors. **Amenities:** extended cable TV, voice mail, irons. *Some:* hair dryers. **Business Services:** meeting rooms. **Cards:** AE, CB, DI, DS, MC, VI.
SOME UNITS

HOLIDAY INN-DOWNTOWN
Phone: (305)374-3000 9

Motor Inn

12/1-3/31	1P: $109-$149	2P: $109-$149	XP: $10
7/1-7/31	1P: $107-$149	2P: $109-$149	XP: $10
4/1-6/30 & 8/1-11/30	1P: $99-$139	2P: $99-$139	XP: $10

Location: Just s of Flagler St on US 1 and 41, 0.8 mi e of I-95 exit 3. 200 SE 2nd Ave 33131. Fax: 305/374-5897. **Facility:** Adjoining Miami Convention Center. Contemporary room decor. Some rooms with view of waterfront, others with city view. 256 units. 13 stories, interior corridors. **Parking:** extra charge. **Terms:** check-in 4 pm, weekly & monthly rates available, package plans. **Amenities:** voice mail, irons, hair dryers. **Leisure Activities:** exercise room. **Guest Services:** [BP] meal plan available, gift shop, coin laundry. **Business Services:** meeting rooms. **Cards:** AE, CB, DI, DS, JC, MC, VI.
SOME UNITS

HOTEL INTER-CONTINENTAL MIAMI
Phone: (305)577-1000 12

Hotel

12/1-5/1 & 10/1-11/30	1P: $229-$450	XP: $30	F19
5/2-9/30	1P: $159-$229	XP: $30	F19

Location: On the bay, at Biscayne Blvd and Chopin Plaza. 100 Chopin Plaza 33131. Fax: 305/577-0384. **Facility:** Distinguished elegance in striking hotel complex. Overlooking Biscayne Bay. A large and colorful lobby. A large striking sculpture divides the lobby. Many sitting areas for that semi-private talk or just to relax. Finely appointed rooms with great views of Miami. 639 units. Some suites ($575-$3000) and whirlpool units. 34 stories, interior corridors. **Parking:** extra charge or valet. **Terms:** check-in 4 pm, 3 day cancellation notice, monthly rates available, package plans. **Amenities:** dual phone lines, voice mail, safes, honor bars, irons, hair dryers. *Some:* fax. **Leisure Activities:** heated pool, jogging. **Guest Services:** [AP], [BP] & [CP] meal plans available, gift shop, valet laundry. *Fee:* massage. **Business Services:** conference facilities, administrative services, fax. *Fee:* PC. **Cards:** AE, CB, DI, DS, JC, MC, VI.
SOME UNITS

(See map p. 476)

HOWARD JOHNSON HOTEL-DOWNTOWN/PORT OF MIAMI

Phone: (305)358-3080 **5**

AAA SAVE	12/1-3/31	1P: $89-$99	2P: $99-$119	XP: $10	F18
	4/1-11/30	1P: $65-$99	2P: $69-$89	XP: $10	F18

Motor Inn **Location:** On US 1; at jct I-395. 1100 Biscayne Blvd 33132. Fax: 305/358-8631. **Facility:** Across from entrance of Port of Miami. 115 units. *Bath:* some combo or shower only. 7 stories, interior corridors. **Parking:** extra charge. **Terms:** cancellation fee imposed. **Amenities:** video games, voice mail. *Some:* irons, hair dryers. **Dining:** restaurant, 7 am-10 pm, $9-$16, cocktails. **Guest Services:** [CP] meal plan available, area transportation-Port of Miami, coin laundry. **Business Services:** meeting rooms. **Cards:** AE, CB, DI, DS, JC, MC, VI. **Special Amenities:** free local telephone calls and free newspaper.

SOME UNITS

HYATT REGENCY MIAMI

Phone: (305)358-1234 **11**

AAA SAVE	12/1-5/15 & 9/16-11/30	1P: $209	2P: $234	XP: $25	F18
	5/16-9/15	1P: $169	2P: $194	XP: $25	F18

Hotel **Location:** Corner of SE 4th St and SE Second Ave. 400 SE Second Ave 33131-2107. Fax: 305/358-0529. **Facility:** Located next to convention center. All rooms have contemporary decor, balcony and great view of city. 587 units. 38 two-bedroom units. Some suites. *Bath:* combo or shower only. 24 stories, interior corridors. **Parking:** valet. **Terms:** cancellation fee imposed, package plans. **Amenities:** voice mail, safes (fee), irons, hair dryers. *Some:* CD players, fax. **Dining:** 2 restaurants, 7 am-10 pm, $8-$29, entertainment. **Leisure Activities:** heated pool, exercise room. **Guest Services:** gift shop, valet laundry. *Fee:* airport transportation-shuttle, massage. **Business Services:** conference facilities, administrative services, PC, fax. **Cards:** AE, CB, DI, DS, MC, VI. *(See ad below)*

SOME UNITS

MIAMI RIVER INN

Phone: (305)325-0045 **8**

	12/1-4/30	1P: $99-$199	2P: $99-$199	XP: $15	F12
	10/1-11/30	1P: $89-$169	2P: $89-$169	XP: $15	F12
Historic Bed & Breakfast	5/1-9/30	1P: $69-$169	2P: $69-$169	XP: $15	F12

Location: I-95, exit 2 (SW 7th St), just w to SW 5th Ave, just n to SW 2nd St, then e. 118 SW South River Dr 33130. Fax: 305/325-9227. **Facility:** Several historical buildings. Rooms vary in size and are individually decorated in period styles from 1906-1914. The pool area with a large grassy area with lots of tropical foliage. Smoke free premises. 40 units. *Bath:* some shared or private, combo, shower or tub only. 2-3 stories, interior/exterior corridors. **Terms:** 3 day cancellation notice, small pets only ($25 extra charge, with reservation). **Leisure Activities:** whirlpool. **Guest Services:** [CP] meal plan available, coin laundry. **Business Services:** meeting rooms. **Cards:** AE, CB, DI, DS, MC, VI.

SHERATON BISCAYNE BAY HOTEL

Phone: (305)373-6000 **13**

	12/1-3/31	1P: $209-$329	2P: $219-$339	XP: $10	F17
	4/1-5/19 & 9/16-11/30	1P: $159-$279	2P: $169-$289	XP: $10	F17
Hotel	5/20-9/15	1P: $119-$159	2P: $129-$179	XP: $10	F17

Location: 0.5 mi s on US 1. 495 Brickell Ave 33131. Fax: 305/374-2279. **Facility:** Overlooking Biscayne Bay. Some rooms with balcony. A relaxing pool area surrounded by tropical palms. Biscayne Bay and the Miami River surrounding three sides of the hotel. Large rooms with great views of the city and the waters. 598 units. Some suites. *Bath:* combo or shower only. 17 stories, interior corridors. **Parking:** extra charge or valet. **Terms:** cancellation fee imposed, package plans. **Amenities:** extended cable TV, dual phone lines, voice mail, irons, hair dryers. *Some:* fax. **Leisure Activities:** heated pool, boat dock, exercise room. **Guest Services:** gift shop, valet laundry. **Business Services:** conference facilities, PC, fax. **Cards:** AE, CB, DI, DS, JC, MC, VI.

SOME UNITS

WYNDHAM HOTEL MIAMI-BISCAYNE BAY

Phone: (305)374-0000 **1**

	12/1-4/29	1P: $164-$399	XP: $20	F18
	4/30-11/30	1P: $139-$299	XP: $20	F18

Hotel **Location:** US 1, 1 mi n of Flagler St. 1601 Biscayne Blvd 33132. Fax: 305/374-0020. **Facility:** Higher floors have extensive views of Miami and Biscayne Bay. Large rooms with light wood tones and complimenting colors. 528 units. Some suites. *Bath:* combo or shower only. 20 stories, interior corridors. **Parking:** extra charge or valet. **Terms:** 3 day cancellation notice-fee imposed, weekly & monthly rates available, package plans. **Amenities:** video games, dual phone lines, voice mail, safes (fee), irons, hair dryers. **Dining:** The Fish Market, see separate listing. **Leisure Activities:** heated pool, sauna, exercise room. **Guest Services:** [AP], [BP], [CP] & [MAP] meal plans available, gift shop, valet laundry. **Business Services:** conference facilities, administrative services, fax. *Fee:* PC. **Cards:** AE, CB, DI, DS, JC, MC, VI.

SOME UNITS

(See map p. 476)

——— WHERE TO DINE ———

EAST COAST FISHERIES   Lunch: $6-$10   Dinner: $10-$29   Phone: 305/577-3000   ⑥
▼▼▼   **Location:** Downtown side of Miami River, at foot of River Dr and Flagler St Bridge. 360 W Flagler St 33130.
               Hours: 11 am-midnight, Fri & Sat 24 hours. Closed major holidays. **Reservations:** suggested.
Seafood   **Features:** casual dress; Sunday brunch; carryout; cocktails; street parking & valet parking. Fresh fish is
the key to success of the riverfront restaurant, in business since 1925. The banana red snapper, broiled
with white bananas, lemon juice and paprika, is a house specialty. Take in live jazz and salsa music on Friday and Saturday
nights. **Cards:** AE, MC, VI.   ☒

THE FISH MARKET   Dinner: $20-$35   Phone: 305/374-4399   ②
▼▼▼   **Location:** US 1, 1 mi n of Flagler St; in Omni Shopping and Entertainment Complex; in Wyndham Hotel
Miami-Biscayne Bay. 1601 Biscayne Blvd 33132. **Hours:** 6 pm-11 pm. Closed: 12/25.
Seafood   **Reservations:** suggested. **Features:** dressy casual; children's menu; cocktails; fee for parking & valet
parking; a la carte. Smart, contemporary decor sets off a market-style setting. Sample innovative
presentations of fresh seafood, meat and poultry. The tuna filet with peppercorn topping is garnished with star fruits and
mango. A tropical theme is seen throughout the meal. **Cards:** AE, CB, DI, DS, MC, VI.   ☒

JOE'S SEAFOOD RESTAURANT   Lunch: $7-$14   Dinner: $12-$20   Phone: 305/381-9329   ⑤
▼▼▼   **Location:** 0.8 mi w of I-95 on Miami River; corner NW 4th St and North River Dr. 400 NW North River Dr 33128.
               Hours: 11 am-9 pm, Fri & Sat-10 pm. Closed: 12/24 for dinner. **Reservations:** accepted. **Features:** casual
Seafood   dress; children's menu; carryout; cocktails. The casual, bustling restaurant serves fish caught from its own
fleet as well as appetizing preparations of stone crab, shrimp, scallops and lobster. An open-air terrace
offers sunny, yet breezy, dining and the occasional glimpse of a celebrity yacht. Smoke free premises. **Cards:** AE, CB, DI,
MC, VI.   ☒

——— *The following restaurants have not been evaluated by AAA* ———
but are listed for your information only.

CAPITAL GRILLE   Phone: 305/374-4500
[fyi]   Not evaluated. **Location:** 444 Brickell Ave. **Features:** Popular steakhouse; rich and scrumptious desserts.
Expensive.

FIREHOUSE FOUR OF MIAMI   Phone: 305/379-1923
[fyi]   Not evaluated. **Location:** S of Miami River, 2 blks w of US 1 (Brickell Ave), at S Miami Ave. 1000 S Miami Ave
33130. **Features:** Large menu; gourmet lunch items. American cuisine, with dinner including some steak
and seafood items. Moderately priced.

MIAMI pop. 358,500   (See map p. 478; index p. 480)

——— WHERE TO STAY ———

AMERISUITES AIRPORT WEST   Phone: (305)718-8292   ㊲
(AAA) [SAVE]   1/1-3/31   1P: $159   2P: $159   XP: $10   F18
                4/1-11/30   1P: $129   2P: $129   XP: $10   F18
▼▼▼   12/1-12/31   1P: $119   2P: $119   XP: $10   F18
Suite Motel   **Location:** 0.4 mi w on NW 36th St from jct SR 826 (Palmetto Expwy). 3655 NW 82nd Ave 33166. **Fax:** 305/718-8295.
               Facility: Property has a large breakfast and lobby area. Spacious rooms with contemporary decor and com-
plimenting colors. 126 units. *Bath:* combo or shower only. 6 stories, interior corridors. **Terms:** cancellation fee
imposed. **Amenities:** voice mail, irons, hair dryers. **Leisure Activities:** heated pool, exercise room. **Guest Services:** [ECP] meal
plan available, valet and coin laundry. **Business Services:** meeting rooms, administrative services. *Fee:* PC. **Cards:** AE, CB, DI,
DS, MC, VI. **Special Amenities: free continental breakfast and free newspaper.** *(See color ad p 5)*   SOME UNITS
⬛ ⬛ ⬛ ⬛ ⬛ ⬛ ⬛ ⬛ ⬛ ⬛ ⬛ ⬛ ⬛ / ☒ ⬛
                                      FEE

BAYMONT INN & SUITES MIAMI WEST   Phone: (305)640-9896   ㉝
▼▼▼   12/1-4/15 & 10/16-11/30   1P: $89-$109   2P: $89-$109   XP: $10   F18
                4/16-10/15   1P: $79-$99   2P: $79-$99   XP: $10   F18
Motel   **Location:** Florida Tpke, exit 29, 1.2 mi e to 107th Ave, then right. 3805 NW 107th Ave 33178. **Fax:** 305/640-0608.
               Facility: An attractive lobby with comfortable sitting and breakfast areas. Spacious rooms with rich colors and
a contemporary style furniture package. 92 units. Some suites ($109-$139). *Bath:* combo or shower only. 4 stories, interior corridors. **Amenities:** extended cable TV, video games, voice mail, irons, hair dryers. *Some:* safes. **Leisure Activities:** exercise
room. **Guest Services:** [ECP] meal plan available, valet and coin laundry. **Business Services:** meeting rooms. **Cards:** AE, CB,
DI, DS, MC, VI. *(See color ad p 523)*   SOME UNITS
[ASK] ⬛ ⬛ ⬛ ⬛ ⬛ ⬛ ⬛ ⬛ / ☒ ⬛ ⬛
                                      FEE

BEST WESTERN-MIAMI AIRPORT INN   Phone: (305)871-2345   ㊻
(AAA) [SAVE]   All Year   1P: $89-$119   2P: $99-$129   XP: $10   F13
▼▼▼   **Location:** On SR 953 (Le Jeune Rd), just n of jct SR 836 (Dolphin Expwy). 1550 NW Le Jeune Rd 33126 (PO Box
               996638, 33299-6638). **Fax:** 305/871-2811. **Facility:** Rooms recently renovated. Subtle colors; warm and in-
Motor Inn   viting. 208 units. *Bath:* combo or shower only. 6 stories, interior corridors. **Terms:** cancellation fee imposed,
               package plans. **Amenities:** extended cable TV, video games, voice mail, safes, irons, hair dryers.
               Dining: restaurant, 6 am-2 am, $7-$17, cocktails. **Leisure Activities:** exercise room. *Fee:* tennis privileges.
Guest Services: gift shop, valet and coin laundry. **Business Services:** meeting rooms. **Cards:** AE, DI, DS, MC, VI.
Special Amenities: free newspaper and free room upgrade (subject to availability with advanced reservations).
                                                                                                            SOME UNITS
⬛ ⬛ ⬛ ⬛ ⬛ ⬛ ⬛ ⬛ ⬛ ⬛ ⬛ / ☒ ⬛ ⬛ /
                                      FEE   FEE

(See map p. 478)

CANDLEWOOD SUITES MIAMI AIRPORT WEST

Phone: (305)591-9099   [39]

1/1-4/15	1P: $169	2P: $169	XP: $10 F18
12/1-12/31	1P: $139	2P: $159	XP: $10 F18
4/16-11/30	1P: $139	2P: $139	XP: $10 F18

Extended Stay Motel

Location: From SR 826 (Dolphin Expwy), exit NW 87th Ave N, just n on NW 87th Ave. 8855 NW 27th St 33172. Fax: 305/591-4117. **Facility:** Limited office hours. Large, spacious rooms with contemporary room decor. 128 efficiencies. *Bath:* combo or shower only. 3 stories, interior corridors. **Terms:** small pets only ($100 fee). **Amenities:** extended cable TV, CD players, dual phone lines, voice mail, irons, hair dryers. **Leisure Activities:** exercise room. **Guest Services:** valet and coin laundry. **Cards:** AE, DI, DS, MC, VI.

SOME UNITS

COURTYARD BY MARRIOTT-MIAMI WEST/DORAL AREA

Phone: (305)477-8118   [36]

12/1-4/30	1P: $139	2P: $149	XP: $10 F18
5/1-11/30	1P: $89	2P: $99	XP: $10 F18

Motor Inn

Location: NW 36th St, jct SR 826 (Palmetto Expwy). 3929 NW 79th Ave 33166. Fax: 305/599-9363. **Facility:** Inviting landscaped pool courtyard. Rooms with a rich cherry finish wood tones and soft pastel color scheme. 145 units. Some suites. *Bath:* combo or shower only. 4 stories, interior corridors. **Terms:** check-in 4 pm. **Amenities:** extended cable TV, dual phone lines, voice mail, safes, irons, hair dryers. **Leisure Activities:** heated pool, whirlpool, exercise room. **Guest Services:** valet and coin laundry. **Business Services:** meeting rooms. **Cards:** AE, CB, DI, DS, MC, VI. *(See color ad below)*

SOME UNITS   FEE

COURTYARD MIAMI AIRPORT SOUTH

Phone: (305)642-8200   [47]

12/1-4/30	1P: $99
5/1-11/30	1P: $59

Motel

Location: Se of jct Rt 836. 1201 NW LeJeune Rd 33126. Fax: 305/644-1168. **Facility:** Airport transportation fully equipped for accessibility needs. Shared recreational facilities with two adjoining Marriott properties. Spacious rooms nicely appointed. 125 units. Some suites. *Bath:* combo or shower only. 5 stories, interior corridors. **Terms:** check-in 4 pm, package plans. **Amenities:** voice mail, irons, hair dryers. **Leisure Activities:** heated pool, whirlpools, 8 tennis courts (6 lighted), jogging, exercise room, basketball, volleyball, game room. **Guest Services:** valet and coin laundry. **Cards:** AE, CB, DI, DS, MC, VI.

SOME UNITS   FEE

CROWNE PLAZA MIAMI INTERNATIONAL AIRPORT

Phone: (305)446-9000   [60]

1/1-3/31	1P: $179	2P: $179	XP: $10 F18
10/1-11/30	1P: $149	2P: $149	XP: $10 F18
12/1-12/31	1P: $139	2P: $139	XP: $10 F18
4/1-9/30	1P: $129	2P: $129	XP: $10 F18

Hotel

Location: 1 mi s of terminal entrance, just s of jct SR 836, Dolphin Expwy. 950 NW Le Jeune Rd 33126. Fax: 954/441-0725. **Facility:** Controlled access facility. Very nice rooms and public areas. Rooms feature a contemporary decor. Good working space. 304 units. Some suites. 6 stories, interior corridors. **Terms:** small pets only. **Amenities:** voice mail, irons, hair dryers. **Dining:** restaurant, 6:30 am-2 & 5:30-11 pm, $9-$18, cocktails. **Leisure Activities:** saunas, whirlpool, exercise room. **Guest Services:** gift shop, valet and coin laundry. **Business Services:** meeting rooms, administrative services, fax. **Fee:** PC. **Cards:** AE, CB, DI, DS, JC, MC, VI. **Special Amenities:** early check-in/late check-out and free local telephone calls.

SOME UNITS   FEE   FEE

DAYS INN MEDICAL CENTER/CIVIC CENTER

Phone: (305)324-0200   [64]

12/1-3/31	1P: $69-$79	2P: $69-$79	XP: $10 F12
4/1-11/30	1P: $59-$69	2P: $59-$69	XP: $10 F12

Motor Inn

Location: Just ne of jct NW 12th Ave and SR 836, Dolphin Expwy; westbound use NW 14th St exit. 1050 NW 14th St 33136. Fax: 305/545-8482. **Facility:** Adjacent to hospital district. Fenced pool area. 209 units. *Bath:* combo or shower only. 5 stories, exterior corridors. **Terms:** cancellation fee imposed, weekly & monthly rates available. **Amenities:** voice mail, safes (fee). **Leisure Activities:** exercise room. **Guest Services:** gift shop, area transportation, coin laundry. **Cards:** AE, CB, DI, DS, MC, VI.

SOME UNITS

(See map p. 478)

DAYS INN MIAMI INTERNATIONAL AIRPORT HOTEL　　　　　Phone: (305)261-4230　63

12/1-3/31	1P: $89-$119	2P: $89-$119	XP: $10　F12
4/1-11/30	1P: $59-$75	2P: $59-$75	XP: $10　F12

Location: Just n of Milam Dairy Rd and NW 11th St off SR 836. 7250 NW 11th St 33126. Fax: 305/264-9685. **Facility:** Large rooms with light contemporary wood tones. The surrounding colors are tropical. 103 units. 4 stories, interior corridors. **Terms:** 3 day cancellation notice-fee imposed. **Amenities:** extended cable TV, safes (fee), irons, hair dryers. **Dining:** restaurant, 7:30 am-10 & 11-10 pm, Fri & Sat-3 am, $6-$16, cocktails.
Leisure Activities: exercise room. **Guest Services:** coin laundry. **Cards:** AE, CB, DI, DS, MC, VI.　　SOME UNITS

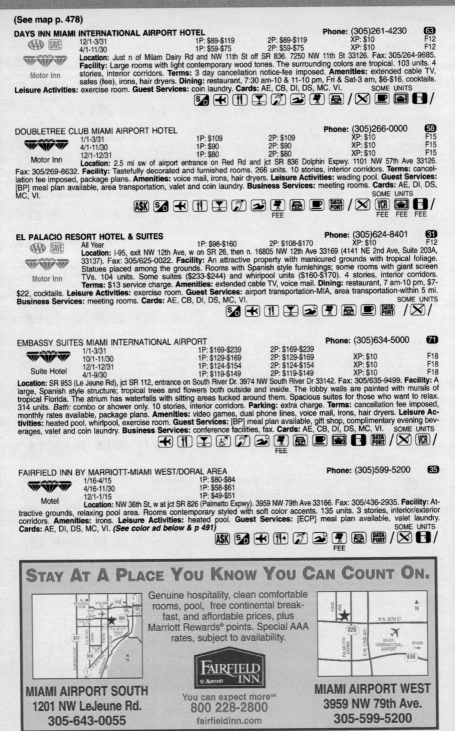

DOUBLETREE CLUB MIAMI AIRPORT HOTEL　　　　　Phone: (305)266-0000　58

1/1-3/31	1P: $109	2P: $109	XP: $10　F15
4/1-11/30	1P: $90	2P: $90	XP: $10　F15
12/1-12/31	1P: $80	2P: $80	XP: $10　F15

Location: 2.5 mi sw of airport entrance on Red Rd and jct SR 836 Dolphin Expwy. 1101 NW 57th Ave 33126. Fax: 305/269-8632. **Facility:** Tastefully decorated and furnished rooms. 266 units. 10 stories, interior corridors. **Terms:** cancellation fee imposed, package plans. **Amenities:** voice mail, irons, hair dryers. **Leisure Activities:** wading pool. **Guest Services:** [BP] meal plan available, area transportation, valet and coin laundry. **Business Services:** meeting rooms. **Cards:** AE, DI, DS, MC, VI.　SOME UNITS

EL PALACIO RESORT HOTEL & SUITES　　　　　Phone: (305)624-8401　31

All Year	1P: $96-$160	2P: $108-$170　XP: $10　F12

Location: I-95, exit NW 12th Ave, w on SR 26, then n. 16805 NW 12th Ave 33169 (4141 NE 2nd Ave, Suite 203A, 33137). Fax: 305/625-0022. **Facility:** An attractive property with manicured grounds with tropical foliage. Statues placed among the grounds. Rooms with Spanish style furnishings; some rooms with giant screen TVs. 104 units. Some suites ($233-$244) and whirlpool units ($160-$170). 4 stories, interior corridors. **Terms:** $13 service charge. **Amenities:** extended cable TV, voice mail. **Dining:** restaurant, 7 am-10 pm, $7-$22, cocktails. **Leisure Activities:** exercise room. **Guest Services:** airport transportation-MIA, area transportation-within 5 mi. **Business Services:** meeting rooms. **Cards:** AE, CB, DI, DS, MC, VI.　　SOME UNITS

EMBASSY SUITES MIAMI INTERNATIONAL AIRPORT　　　　　Phone: (305)634-5000　71

1/1-3/31	1P: $169-$239	2P: $169-$239	
10/1-11/30	1P: $129-$169	2P: $129-$169	XP: $10　F18
12/1-12/31	1P: $124-$154	2P: $124-$154	XP: $10　F18
4/1-9/30	1P: $119-$149	2P: $119-$149	XP: $10　F18

Location: SR 953 (Le Jeune Rd), jct SR 112, entrance on South River Dr. 3974 NW South River Dr 33142. Fax: 305/635-9499. **Facility:** A large, Spanish style structure; tropical trees and flowers both outside and inside. The lobby walls are painted with murals of tropical Florida. The atrium has waterfalls with sitting areas tucked around them. Spacious suites for those who want to relax. 314 units. *Bath:* combo or shower only. 10 stories, interior corridors. **Parking:** extra charge. **Terms:** cancellation fee imposed, monthly rates available, package plans. **Amenities:** video games, dual phone lines, voice mail, irons, hair dryers. **Leisure Activities:** heated pool, whirlpool, exercise room. **Guest Services:** [BP] meal plan available, gift shop, complimentary evening beverages, valet and coin laundry. **Business Services:** conference facilities, fax. **Cards:** AE, CB, DI, DS, MC, VI.　SOME UNITS

FAIRFIELD INN BY MARRIOTT-MIAMI WEST/DORAL AREA　　　　　Phone: (305)599-5200　35

1/16-4/15	1P: $80-$84
4/16-11/30	1P: $58-$61
12/1-1/15	1P: $49-$51

Location: NW 36th St, w at jct SR 826 (Palmetto Expwy). 3959 NW 79th Ave 33166. Fax: 305/436-2935. **Facility:** Attractive grounds, relaxing pool area. Rooms contemporary styled with soft color accents. 135 units. 3 stories, interior/exterior corridors. **Amenities:** irons. **Leisure Activities:** heated pool. **Guest Services:** [ECP] meal plan available, valet laundry. **Cards:** AE, DI, DS, MC, VI. (*See color ad below & p 491*)　SOME UNITS

(See map p. 478)

FAIRFIELD INN MIAMI AIRPORT SOUTH
Phone: (305)643-0055 48

12/1-4/30	1P: $89
5/1-11/30	1P: $49

Motel
Location: Se of jct Rt 836 and NW LeJune Rd. 1201 NW LeJune Rd 33126. Fax: 305/649-3997. **Facility:** Shared recreational facilities with two adjoining Marriott properties. Airport transportation fully-equipped for accessibility needs. Rooms with a contemporary decor. 281 units. *Bath:* combo or shower only. 3 stories, exterior corridors. **Amenities:** voice mail, irons, hair dryers. **Leisure Activities:** heated pool, whirlpool, 8 tennis courts (6 lighted), exercise room, basketball, volleyball, game room. **Guest Services:** [ECP] meal plan available, valet laundry. **Cards:** AE, DI, DS, JC, MC, VI. *(See color ad p 492)*

HAMPTON INN & SUITES
Phone: (305)500-9300 32

All Year	1P: $84-$139	2P: $94-$159	XP: $10	F18

Motel
Location: Florida Tpke, exit 29 (NW 41st St). 11600 NW 41st St 33178. Fax: 305/500-9400. **Facility:** Located just off the turnpike and near the Dolphin Mall. A relaxing pool with a large deck. The lobby has a large saltwater fish tank. Large breakfast area. Spacious rooms with a contemporary decor. 121 units, 44 with kitchen. Some suites ($104-$199). *Bath:* combo or shower only. 6 stories, interior corridors. **Amenities:** extended cable TV, video games, dual phone lines, voice mail, safes, irons, hair dryers. **Leisure Activities:** heated pool, exercise room. **Guest Services:** [ECP] meal plan available, area transportation, valet and coin laundry. **Business Services:** meeting rooms, administrative services. **Cards:** AE, CB, DI, DS, MC, VI.

HAMPTON INN-MIAMI AIRPORT WEST
Phone: (305)513-0777 38

1/1-3/31	1P: $110-$140	2P: $120-$150
12/1-12/31 & 4/1-11/30	1P: $80-$120	2P: $90-$120

Motel
Location: From Palmetto Expwy (SR 826), exit NW 36th St, just s of jct NW 58th St, exit to 79th Ave; in the Boykin Center. 3620 NW 79th Ave 33166. Fax: 305/513-9019. **Facility:** A spacious lobby and breakfast area. A fenced pool with tropical foliage. Room furnishings with light wood tones and warm color scheme. 127 units. *Bath:* combo or shower only. 6 stories, interior corridors. **Terms:** 3 day cancellation notice, pets ($25 extra charge). **Leisure Activities:** heated pool, exercise room. **Guest Services:** [ECP] meal plan available, area transportation-within 3 mi, valet and coin laundry. **Business Services:** meeting rooms, administrative services. **Cards:** AE, CB, DI, DS, MC, VI.

HILTON MIAMI AIRPORT & TOWERS
Phone: (305)262-1000 59

1/1-4/6	1P: $119-$249	2P: $119-$249	XP: $25	F18
12/1-12/31 & 10/1-11/30	1P: $99-$199	2P: $99-$199	XP: $25	F18
4/7-9/30	1P: $89-$179	2P: $89-$179	XP: $25	F18

Hotel
Location: Se of jct SR 836, Dolphin Expwy exit Red Rd. 0.7 mi e. 5101 Blue Lagoon Dr 33126. Fax: 305/267-0038. **Facility:** On peninsula overlooking lagoon. Many units with water view, some with view of airport. Units large with a comfortable color scheme. All units work friendly. 500 units. Some suites ($144-$298). *Bath:* combo or shower only. 14 stories, interior corridors. **Parking:** extra charge or valet. **Terms:** cancellation fee imposed, package plans. **Amenities:** dual phone lines, honor bars, irons, hair dryers. *Some:* fax. **Leisure Activities:** heated pool, saunas, whirlpool, boat dock, fishing, 2 tennis courts (1 lighted), children's program, jogging, exercise room, basketball. **Guest Services:** gift shop, valet laundry. **Fee:** area transportation. **Business Services:** conference facilities, administrative services, fax. **Fee:** PC. **Cards:** AE, CB, DI, DS, JC, MC, VI. *(See ad p 44)*

HOLIDAY INN-CALDER/PRO PLAYER STADIUM
Phone: 305/621-5801 30

10/2-11/30	1P: $89-$1000	2P: $1000	XP: $10	F12
12/1-12/31	1P: $149	2P: $1000	XP: $10	F12
1/1-10/1	1P: $82	2P: $1000	XP: $10	F12

Motor Inn
Location: SR 852 at jct SR 817 and Florida Tpke, exit 47. 21485 NW 27th Ave 33056. Fax: 305/624-8202. **Facility:** Some rooms overlook the racetrack. All rooms with a step out balcony. Rooms with a contempory room decor. Designated smoking area. 214 units. 9 stories, interior corridors. **Terms:** cancellation fee imposed, weekly rates available, package plans. **Amenities:** extended cable TV, voice mail, irons, hair dryers. **Leisure Activities:** heated pool, exercise room. **Guest Services:** gift shop, coin laundry. **Business Services:** meeting rooms, fax. **Cards:** AE, CB, DI, DS, MC, VI. *(See ad below)*

(See map p. 478)

HOLIDAY INN-MIAMI AIRPORT WEST

AAA **SAVE**

Motor Inn

12/1-4/15	1P: $139-$189
4/16-11/30	1P: $109-$139

Phone: (305)500-9000 43

Location: From SR 826 (Palmetto Expwy), exit NW 58th and NW 36th sts, then 0.6 mi s. 3255 NW 87th Ave 33172. **Fax:** 305/500-9500. **Facility:** Spacious rooms, contemporary decor. 120 units. Some suites ($159-$199). **Bath:** combo or shower only. 6 stories, interior corridors. **Terms:** cancellation fee imposed, package plans. **Amenities:** extended cable TV, video games, dual phone lines, voice mail, safes, honor bars, irons, hair dryers. **Dining:** restaurant, 6 am-3 & 5-11 pm, $8-$15, cocktails. **Leisure Activities:** heated pool, exercise room. **Guest Services:** area transportation-within 5 mi, valet and coin laundry. **Business Services:** meeting rooms, administrative services, fax. **Cards:** AE, CB, DI, DS, MC, VI.

SOME UNITS

HOMESTEAD VILLAGE GUEST STUDIOS-BLUE LAGOON

Extended Stay Motel

Property failed to provide current rates

Phone: 305/260-0085 53

Location: From Dolphin Expwy (SR 836), exit Milam Dairy Rd S, 0.3 mi e. 6605 NW 7th St 33126. **Fax:** 305/260-0042. **Facility:** Spacious rooms. 149 efficiencies. **Bath:** combo or shower only. 2-3 stories, exterior corridors. **Amenities:** extended cable TV, voice mail, irons. **Guest Services:** valet and coin laundry. **Cards:** AE, DI, DS, JC, MC, VI.

SOME UNITS

HOMESTEAD VILLAGE GUEST STUDIOS MIAMI AIRPORT/DORAL

Extended Stay Motel

12/1-4/30	1P: $79-$109
5/1-11/30	1P: $59-$84

Phone: 305/436-1811 40

Location: SR 826 (Palmetto Expwy), 0.8 mi w on NW 36th St, then s on 87th St, 0.6 mi on right; in Westpoint Office Park. 8720 NW 33rd St 33172. **Fax:** 305/436-1864. **Facility:** Office hours 6:30 am-11 pm. Spacious rooms. 149 efficiencies. **Bath:** combo or shower only. 2 stories, exterior corridors. **Terms:** cancellation fee imposed, weekly rates available, pets ($75). **Amenities:** extended cable TV, voice mail, irons. **Guest Services:** coin laundry. **Cards:** AE, DI, DS, MC, VI.

SOME UNITS

HOWARD JOHNSON HOTEL MIAMI INTERNATIONAL AIRPORT

AAA **SAVE**

Hotel

All Year   1P: $90-$135   2P: $90-$135   XP: $10   F12

Phone: (305)871-4350 45

Location: 0.3 mi s of Miami Airport entrance. 1850 NW Le Jeune Rd 33126. **Fax:** 305/871-6810. **Facility:** Striking exterior and plush public areas. Rooms with a contemporary decor. 255 units. Some whirlpool units ($125-$160). **Bath:** combo or shower only. 2-4 stories, interior corridors. **Terms:** package plans. **Amenities:** voice mail. **Dining:** restaurant, 6 am-1 am, $15-$22, cocktails. **Leisure Activities:** whirlpool. **Guest Services:** gift shop, valet laundry. **Fee:** area transportation-Port of Miami. **Business Services:** meeting rooms. **Cards:** AE, CB, DI, DS, MC, VI.

SOME UNITS

LA QUINTA INN & SUITES

SAVE

Motel

All Year   1P: $89-$109   2P: $89-$109

Phone: (305)436-0830 44

Location: From SR 836 (Dolphin Expwy), just n on 87th NW Ave. 8730 NW 27th St 33172. **Fax:** 305/436-0840. **Facility:** Large rooms. Contemporary decor. 143 units. Some suites ($119-$139). **Bath:** combo or shower only. 6 stories, interior corridors. **Terms:** small pets only. **Amenities:** video games, voice mail, irons, hair dryers. **Leisure Activities:** heated pool, whirlpool, exercise room. **Business Services:** meeting rooms. **Cards:** AE, CB, DI, DS, MC, VI.

SOME UNITS

LA QUINTA INN MIAMI AIRPORT NORTH

SAVE

Motel

All Year   1P: $65-$95   2P: $65-$95

Phone: (305)599-9902 41

Location: NW 36th St, just e of jct SR 826, Palmetto Expwy. 7401 NW 36th St 33166. **Fax:** 305/594-0552. **Facility:** An inviting lobby. Rooms with contemporary decor and furnishings. 165 units. 3 stories, exterior corridors. **Terms:** small pets only. **Amenities:** video games, voice mail. **Guest Services:** [ECP] meal plan available, valet and coin laundry. **Business Services:** meeting rooms. **Cards:** AE, CB, DI, DS, MC, VI.

SOME UNITS

MIAMI AIRPORT MARRIOTT

Hotel

12/1-4/13	1P: $170
9/30-11/30	1P: $138
4/14-9/29	1P: $116

Phone: (305)649-5000 61

Location: Se of jct Rt 836 and NW Le Jeune Rd. 1201 NW Le Jeune Rd 33126. **Fax:** 305/642-3369. **Facility:** Lovely public areas with a business center in the gift shop. Airport transportation fully equipped for accessibility needs. Rooms tastefully decorated and furnished. 366 units. Some suites. **Bath:** combo or shower only. 10 stories, interior corridors. **Terms:** check-in 4 pm, package plans. **Amenities:** voice mail, irons, hair dryers. **Leisure Activities:** heated pool, whirlpools, 8 tennis courts (6 lighted), jogging, exercise room, basketball, volleyball, game room. **Guest Services:** gift shop, valet and coin laundry. **Business Services:** conference facilities, administrative services. **Cards:** AE, CB, DI, DS, JC, MC, VI.

SOME UNITS

(See map p. 478)

MIAMI MARRIOTT-DADELAND

			Phone: (305)670-1035	65
	12/1-4/14	1P: $164-$219		
	9/30-11/30	1P: $69-$199		
Hotel	4/15-5/26	1P: $159-$189		
	5/27-9/29	1P: $134-$164		

Location: SR 826 (Palmetto Expwy), exit Kendall Dr E, then 2 blks. 9090 S Dadeland Blvd 33156. Fax: 305/670-5721. **Facility:** Attractive public areas. Spacious rooms with contemporary decor. 302 units. Some suites. 24 stories, interior corridors. **Parking:** extra charge or valet. **Terms:** check-in 4 pm, cancellation fee imposed, package plans. **Amenities:** voice mail, safes, honor bars, irons, hair dryers. **Leisure Activities:** heated pool, whirlpool, exercise room. **Guest Services:** [CP] meal plan available, gift shop, valet laundry. **Business Services:** conference facilities, administrative services, PC, fax. **Cards:** AE, CB, DI, DS, MC, VI.

SOME UNITS

(ASK) (SD) 🚼 🍴 (24) ▾ ⬭ ⛱ 📷 🖨 📠 (DATA PORT) /✕/
FEE

QUALITY INN & SUITES

				Phone: (305)871-3230	72
AAA (SAVE)	12/1-3/31	1P: $90	2P: $100	XP: $10	F18
	4/1-11/30	1P: $80	2P: $90	XP: $10	F18

Motor Inn

Location: Just n of SR 836 (Dolphin Expwy) from LeJeune Rd. 2373 NW 42nd Ave 33142. Fax: 305/871-1006. **Facility:** Some large rooms, all with contemporary decor. 180 units. 3 stories, interior corridors. **Terms:** 3 day cancellation notice-fee imposed. **Amenities:** voice mail, irons. *Some:* hair dryers. **Dining:** 6 am-midnight food court, wine/beer only. **Leisure Activities:** exercise room. **Guest Services:** valet laundry. **Business Services:** meeting rooms. **Cards:** AE, DI, DS, MC, VI. **Special Amenities:** early check-in/late check-out and free local telephone calls.

SOME UNITS

(SD) 🚼 ⬭ ⛱ 📷 🖨 📠 /✕/

QUALITY INN-SOUTH

			Phone: (305)251-2000	70
AAA (SAVE)	12/22-4/28	2P: $81-$135	XP: $5	F18
	4/29-11/30	2P: $73-$135	XP: $5	F18
Motor Inn	12/1-12/21	2P: $77-$92	XP: $5	F18

Location: US 1 at SW 145th St. 14501 S Dixie Hwy (US 1) 33176. Fax: 305/235-2225. **Facility:** Variety of room decors with light wood tones. Nice pool area. Designated smoking area. 100 units. 2 stories, exterior corridors. **Terms:** 2 night minimum stay, weekly & monthly rates available, small pets only. **Amenities:** extended cable TV, dual phone lines. **Dining:** restaurant, 6:30 am-10 pm, Fri & Sat-11 pm, $6-$13, cocktails. **Leisure Activities:** heated pool, game room. **Guest Services:** coin laundry. **Business Services:** meeting rooms. **Cards:** AE, CB, DI, DS, MC, VI. **Special Amenities:** early check-in/late check-out and free newspaper. *(See color ad below)*

SOME UNITS

(SD) 🐾 🍴 ▾ ⬭ ⛱ 📷 🖨 📠 /✕ 📠 🔌/

RADISSON MART PLAZA HOTEL

				Phone: (305)261-3800	52
AAA (SAVE)	12/1-3/31	1P: $159	2P: $159	XP: $20	F12
	9/17-11/30	1P: $139	2P: $139	XP: $20	F12
	4/1-6/15	1P: $129	2P: $129	XP: $20	F12
Hotel	6/16-9/16	1P: $99	2P: $99	XP: $20	F12

Location: At Milam Dairy Rd off SR 836, Dolphin Expwy; adjoining Merchandise Mart Complex. 711 NW 72nd Ave 33126. Fax: 305/261-7665. **Facility:** Direct access to Merchandise Mart. All rooms are large with a contemporary room decor. 334 units. Some suites ($149-$209) and whirlpool units ($149-$209). 12 stories, interior corridors. **Parking:** valet. **Terms:** package plans. **Amenities:** dual phone lines, voice mail, irons, hair dryers. *Some:* honor bars. **Dining:** dining room, restaurant, 6 am-11 pm, $10-$22, cocktails, entertainment. **Leisure Activities:** heated pool, saunas, whirlpools, 2 lighted tennis courts, racquetball courts, exercise room. **Guest Services:** [BP] & [CP] meal plans available, gift shop, valet laundry. **Business Services:** conference facilities, administrative services, fax. **Fee:** PC. **Cards:** AE, CB, DI, DS, MC, VI. **Special Amenities:** free newspaper and preferred room (subject to availability with advanced reservations).

SOME UNITS

(SD) 🚼 🍴 ▾ ⬭ ⛱ ✕ 📷 🖨 📠 (DATA PORT) /✕ 🔌/
FEE

RAMADA LIMITED SOUTH MIAMI DADELAND

				Phone: (305)595-6000	66
	12/1-4/30	1P: $89-$109	2P: $89-$109	XP: $10	F18
Motel	5/1-11/30	1P: $89-$99	2P: $59-$99	XP: $10	F18

Location: From SR 826 (Palmetto Expwy), exit Kendall Dr, just w. 7600 N Kendall Dr 33156. Fax: 305/279-6988. **Facility:** An attractive lobby with cozy sitting areas. Large rooms with a contemporary room decor package. Close to shopping centers. 122 units. 6 stories, interior corridors. **Amenities:** voice mail, irons. **Guest Services:** [ECP] meal plan available. **Business Services:** meeting rooms. **Cards:** AE, CB, DI, DS, JC, MC, VI.

SOME UNITS

(ASK) (SD) 🍴 ⬭ ⛱ 📷 🖨 📠 (DATA PORT) /✕ 🔌/
FEE

(See map p. 478)

STAYBRIDGE SUITES MIAMI-AIRPORT WEST   **Phone: (305)500-9100**   57

All Year   1P: $119   2P: $119   XP: $10   F18

Extended Stay Motel   **Location:** From SR 826 (Palmetto Expwy), exit NW 58th and 36th sts, then 0.6 mi s. 3265 NW 87th Ave 33172. Fax: 305/500-9200. **Facility:** A spacious and comfortable lobby. The property offers a library for guests to relax. The rooms are spacious and furnished for that long stay. 96 efficiencies. Some suites ($119). **Bath:** combo or shower only. 8 stories, interior corridors. **Terms:** 72 day cancellation notice, small pets only ($75 extra charge). **Amenities:** dual phone lines, voice mail, irons, hair dryers. **Leisure Activities:** exercise room, basketball. **Guest Services:** [BP] meal plan available, area transportation, valet and coin laundry. **Business Services:** meeting rooms, administrative services. **Cards:** AE, CB, DI, DS, JC, MC, VI.

SOME UNITS

(ASK) (SD) (🛫) (🐾) (🍴) (🕐) (🏊) (VCR FEE) (📠) (💻) (📺) (🖥) (DATA PORT) / (✕) /

SUMMERFIELD SUITES BY WYNDHAM-MIAMI AIRPORT   **Phone: (305)269-1922**   56

12/1-4/15 & 10/2-11/30   1P: $109
4/16-10/1   1P: $99

Suite Motel   **Location:** 2.5 mi sw of airport entrance, se of jct SR 836 (Dolphin Expwy), exit Red Rd, just w. 5710 Blue Lagoon Dr 33126. Fax: 305/269-1925. **Facility:** Great location for business or pleasure. A nicely appointed lobby with a large breakfast area. An attractive pool area with barbecue grills. Spacious units with a very nice room decor package. 156 units with kitchen. 57 two-bedroom units. **Bath:** combo or shower only. 3 stories, interior corridors. **Terms:** 3 day cancellation notice-fee imposed, pets ($200 fee). **Amenities:** extended cable TV, dual phone lines, voice mail, safes, irons, hair dryers. **Leisure Activities:** heated pool, whirlpool. **Guest Services:** [BP] meal plan available, complimentary evening beverages: Mon-Thurs, area transportation, valet and coin laundry. **Business Services:** meeting rooms. **Cards:** AE, CB, DI, DS, MC, VI.

SOME UNITS

(ASK) (SD) (🛫) (🐾) (🍴) (🕐) (🏊) (🕐) (VCR) (📠) (💻) (🖥) (DATA PORT) / (✕) /

SUPER 8 MOTEL   **Phone: 305/573-7700**   51

12/1-4/30 & 10/1-11/30   1P: $60-$100   2P: $65-$120   XP: $5   F5
5/1-9/30   1P: $50-$100   2P: $55-$110   XP: $5   F5

Motel   **Location:** From I-195, exit US 1/Biscayne Blvd, just s. 3400 Biscayne Blvd 33137. Fax: 305/573-7706. **Facility:** Spacious rooms. 49 units. 2 stories, exterior corridors. **Amenities:** extended cable TV. **Guest Services:** coin laundry. **Cards:** AE, DI, DS, MC, VI.

SOME UNITS

(ASK) (SD) (🍴) (🏊) (🕐) (DATA PORT) / (✕) /

TOWNEPLACE SUITES BY MARRIOTT   **Phone: (305)718-4144**   34

1/1-3/31   1P: $89-$139   2P: $89-$139
4/1-11/30   1P: $79-$119   2P: $79-$119
12/1-12/31   1P: $69-$109   2P: $69-$109

Extended Stay Motel   **Location:** Florida Tpke, exit 29, 1.2 mi e to 107th Ave, just s on 107th Ave. 10505 NW 36th St 33178. Fax: 305/718-4480. **Facility:** Located in an office park area and close to the Dolphin Mall. Spacious and well equipped rooms with a colorful contemporary decor. Limited housekeeping. 95 efficiencies. 30 two-bedroom units. Some suites. **Bath:** combo or shower only. 2-4 stories, interior corridors. **Terms:** cancellation fee imposed, pets ($60 extra charge). **Amenities:** extended cable TV, dual phone lines, voice mail, irons. **Leisure Activities:** small pool. **Guest Services:** valet and coin laundry. **Cards:** AE, CB, DI, DS, JC, MC, VI.

SOME UNITS

(ASK) (SD) (🐾) (🍴) (🕐) (🏊) (🕐) (📠) (💻) (🖥) (DATA PORT) / (✕) /

WELLESLEY INN & SUITES   **Phone: (305)592-4799**   42

(AAA) (SAVE)

2/15-3/7   1P: $90-$100   2P: $100-$110   XP: $10   F18
12/1-2/14 & 3/8-4/15   1P: $80-$90   2P: $90-$100   XP: $10   F18
4/16-11/30   1P: $65-$75   2P: $75-$80   XP: $10   F18

Motel   **Location:** 0.8 mi w of jct SR 826 (Palmetto Expwy). 8436 NW 36th St 33166. Fax: 305/471-8461. **Facility:** Very attractive public areas. Light wood tone furniture with colorful decor package. 106 units. Some suites ($79-$120). 4 stories, interior corridors. **Amenities:** video games, voice mail. **Dining:** 7:30 am-8 pm, poolside eatery. **Leisure Activities:** heated pool. **Guest Services:** [ECP] meal plan available, valet and coin laundry. **Business Services:** meeting rooms. **Cards:** AE, CB, DI, DS, MC, VI. **Special Amenities:** free continental breakfast and free local telephone calls. (See color ad opposite title page)

SOME UNITS

(SD) (🕐) (🏊) (🕐) (📠) (💻) (DATA PORT) / (✕ FEE) (📺 FEE) (🖥 FEE) /

 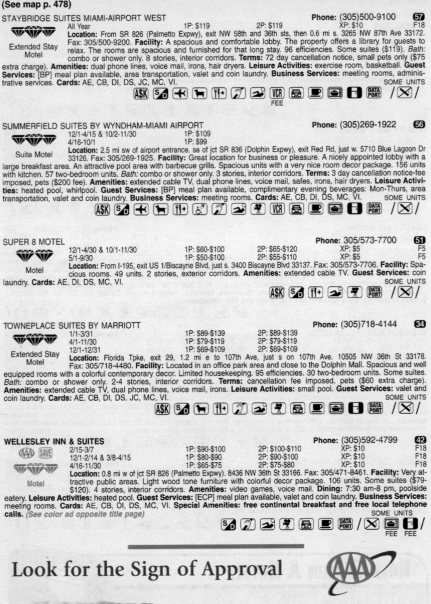

(See map p. 478)

WYNDHAM MIAMI AIRPORT HOTEL Phone: (305)871-3800 73
Hotel
	12/1-3/31	1P: $139-$249	XP: $20	F18
	9/30-11/30	1P: $139-$229	XP: $20	F18
	4/1-9/29	1P: $104-$165	XP: $20	F18

Location: From LeJeune Rd, 0.3 mi e on NW 25th St, then s on NW 39th Ave, to end of street. 3900 NW 21st St 33142. Fax: 305/871-0447. **Facility:** Overlooking waterway and golf course. 408 units. 10 stories, interior corridors. **Parking:** valet. **Terms:** 3 day cancellation notice-fee imposed, package plans. **Amenities:** voice mail, irons, hair dryers. *Some:* fax. **Leisure Activities:** heated pool, saunas, whirlpool, 3 lighted tennis courts, exercise room. *Fee:* golf-18 holes. **Guest Services:** gift shop, valet laundry. **Business Services:** meeting rooms, administrative services. *Fee:* PC, fax. **Cards:** AE, DI, DS, MC, VI.

SOME UNITS
ASK SD 🛬 🐾 🍴 24 Y 🕶 🦢 ✕ 📷 🖨 💻 📠 / ✕ 📞 /
FEE

───── *The following lodgings were either not evaluated or did not* ─────
meet AAA rating requirements but are listed for your information only.

DORAL GOLF RESORT AND SPA Phone: 305/592-2000
fyi Not evaluated. **Location:** 1 mi w of jct SR 826 (Palmetto Expwy) at jct NW 36th St and NW 87th Ave; entrance on NW 87th Ave. 4400 NW 87th Ave 33178. Facilities, services, and decor characterize an upscale property.

HAMPTON INN & SUITES-MIAMI AIRPORT Phone: 305/262-5400
Motel
| | 12/25-4/14 | 1P: $119-$129 | 2P: $129-$139 |
| | 12/1-12/24 & 4/15-11/30 | 1P: $89-$99 | 2P: $99-$109 |

Too new to rate. **Location:** From SR 836 (Dolphin Expwy), exit Rael Rd/57th Ave S, just s of NW 7th St. 777 NW 57th Ave 33126. Fax: 305/262-5400. **Amenities:** 147 units. **Terms:** 14 day cancellation notice. **Cards:** AE, DI, DS, MC, VI.

───── **WHERE TO DINE** ─────

94TH AERO SQUADRON Lunch: $6-$11 Dinner: $15-$24 Phone: 305/261-4220 39
American **Location:** E from SR 836, exit Red Rd; NW 57th Ave then u-turn at light from SR 836 W exit Red Rd. 1395 NW 57th Ave 33126. **Hours:** 11 am-11 pm, Fri & Sat-midnight, Sun 10 am-10:30 pm. **Reservations:** accepted. **Features:** Sunday brunch; children's menu; early bird specials; carryout; cocktails & lounge; a la carte. Fans of flying appreciate this replica of a World War II French farmhouse for its runway views and for the headsets that let users get an earful of talk from the tower. The prime rib of beef, filet mignon and upside-down apple walnut cake are favorites. **Cards:** AE, DI, DS, MC, VI.
🔥 ✕

ANACAPRI Lunch: $6-$9 Dinner: $10-$18 Phone: 305/232-8001 30
Italian **Location:** Just n of SW 128th and (US 1) S Dixie Hwy; in Southpark Centre. 12669 S Dixie Hwy 33156. **Hours:** 11:30 am-2:30 & 5-10:30 pm, Sat 5 pm-11:30 pm. Closed major holidays. **Reservations:** suggested; after 6:30 pm. **Features:** semi-formal attire; beer & wine only. This clean, friendly neighborhood restaurant combines salmon with tomato, onion and balsamic oil, and wraps it in foil for an aromatic entree. For dessert, indulge in Grandma's cake or the custard tart made with orange rind and pine nuts. Smoke free premises.
✕

CAMI'S SEAFOOD & PASTA Lunch: $4-$10 Dinner: $5-$15 Phone: 305/223-2911 34
Seafood **Location:** Just e of SW 122nd Ave. 12170 SW 8th St 33184. **Hours:** 11:30 am-10:30 pm, Fri & Sat-11:30 pm. Closed: 11/22. **Features:** casual dress; children's menu; carryout; beer & wine only. Here you will find fresh seafood served fast. Menu highlights include a shrimp pasta in cream sauce and stone crabs when in season. If you have a taste for garlic, choose penne pasta with spinach and shrimp. For dessert, try the local favorite, Key lime pie. **Cards:** AE, DI, DS, MC, VI.
✕

CASA JUANCHO RESTAURANT Lunch: $10-$29 Dinner: $14-$29 Phone: 305/642-2452 44
Ethnic **Location:** Just e of jct SW 8th St and SW 25th Ave. 2436 SW 8th St 33135. **Hours:** noon-midnight, Fri & Sat-1 am. Closed: 12/24. **Reservations:** suggested. **Features:** dressy casual; carryout; cocktails & lounge; street parking & fee for valet parking. Freshly prepared dishes of authentic Spanish cuisine are served in a tranquil garden setting with lush plants and the rush of a waterfall. Choose from a display case of live lobsters and iced red snapper, or try the shrimp sauteed in olive oil and garlic. **Cards:** AE, DI, DS, MC, VI.
✕

THE FISH HOUSE Lunch: $6-$8 Dinner: $10-$20 Phone: 305/595-8453 40
Seafood **Location:** 2.3 mi w of 56th St exit Palmetto Expwy (SR 826); in the Miller Rd Plaza. 10000 SW 56th St 33165. **Hours:** noon-10 pm, Sat-11 pm. **Features:** casual dress; children's menu; beer & wine only. This family-oriented restaurant features an adjacent seafood market. Wonderfully fresh and flavorful snapper, mahi mahi and salmon are the best entrees. Try a fried blue crab sandwich with coleslaw and perhaps the savory fish soup on the side. **Cards:** AE, DI, DS, MC, VI.
✕

FLEMING: A TASTE OF DENMARK Dinner: $11-$23 Phone: 305/232-6444 63
Danish **Location:** Jct US 1, just e on 136th St. 8511 SW 136th St 33156. **Hours:** 5:30 pm-10:30 pm. Closed: Mon & 8/1-8/31. **Reservations:** suggested. **Features:** dressy casual; carryout; cocktails & lounge. Salmon, duck and pan-seared sea bass over couscous are among the extensive menu offerings of this intimate, family-owned restaurant. Artifacts, copper pots and displays of antiques add authenticity to the Scandinavian aura. Smoke free premises. **Cards:** AE, MC, VI.
♿ ✕

(See map p. 478)

GIACOMO RESTAURANT   **Lunch:** $6-$10   **Dinner:** $7-$19   **Phone:** 305/379-1525   ㊶
Location: Just w of S Miami Ave; across from Capital Bank. 1060 Brickell Ave 33131. **Hours:** 8 am-11 pm. Closed: 1/1, 12/25. **Reservations:** accepted. **Features:** dressy casual; cocktails. This innovative eatery is the marriage a sushi bar and an Italian ristorante. The entrees include warm panini sandwiches, sublime crepes with ricotta and pink sauce, and skewered shrimp with garlic. Please note, there is a fee for parking at lunch. **Cards:** AE, MC, VI.
Italian

ISLAS CANARIAS RESTAURANT   **Lunch:** $4-$16   **Dinner:** $4-$18   **Phone:** 305/649-0440   ㊳
Location: 2 blks n of Flagler St. 285 NW 27th Ave 33125. **Hours:** 7 am-11 pm, Sun from 8 am. **Features:** casual dress; beer & wine only; a la carte. A casual deli and diner located in Miami's "Little Havana" features authentic Cuban dishes. Decorated with an abundance of locally painted pictures of Cuba, the dining room is the perfect backdrop for well-prepared food and efficient service. **Cards:** AE, MC, VI.
English

LE CAFE ROYAL   **Lunch:** $17-$19   **Dinner:** $17-$24   **Phone:** 305/264-4888   ㊻
Location: Just sw of jct SR 836 (Dolphin Expwy), exit Red Rd; in Hotel Sofitel Miami. 5800 Blue Lagoon Dr 33126. **Hours:** 11:30 am-2 & 6:30-10 pm. Closed: Sat for lunch & Sun. **Reservations:** suggested; weekends. **Features:** semi-formal attire; cocktails; valet parking; a la carte. An elegant Belle Epoque dining room features a cozy French atmosphere. The entree of Chilean sea bass is topped with a champagne beurre blanc sauce and sauteed with julienne vegetables and parsnips. Dine at ease with exquisite, professional service. **Cards:** AE, DI, DS, MC, VI.
French

MIKE GORDON SEAFOOD RESTAURANT   **Lunch:** $6-$14   **Dinner:** $12-$25   **Phone:** 305/751-4429   ㊻
Location: At west end of 79th St Cswy; 1 mi e of jct US 1. 1201 NE 79th St 33138. **Hours:** noon-10 pm. Closed: 11/22. **Reservations:** accepted. **Features:** children's menu; early bird specials; carryout; cocktails & lounge; valet parking. Gaze out over the water and watch the pelicans at this established restaurant on the shore of Biscayne Bay. Sumptuous seafood, such as pan-fried grouper and Caribbean grilled dolphin, is the centerpiece of the menu. Expect a rustic, casual atmosphere. **Cards:** AE, DI, DS, MC, VI.
Seafood

OLD LISBON RESTAURANT   **Lunch:** $9-$16   **Dinner:** $14-$47   **Phone:** 305/854-0039   ㊻
Location: Jct SW 17th Ave and 24th St. 1698 SW 22 St 33145. **Hours:** noon-11 pm. **Reservations:** suggested; weekends. **Features:** dressy casual; cocktails & lounge; valet parking. Take a joyous journey to Portugal without a passport! This quaint neighborhood eatery serves appetizers like fresh octopus salad; entrees like codfish served five ways, Alentejana-style clams and grilled sardines; and, of course, decadent desserts. **Cards:** AE, DI, DS, MC, VI.
Ethnic

TANI THAI RESTAURANT   **Lunch:** $6-$10   **Dinner:** $9-$20   **Phone:** 305/253-3583   ㊾
Location: US 1 (S Dixie Hwy). 12269 S Dixie Hwy 33156. **Hours:** 11:30 am-3 & 5-10:30 pm, Fri & Sat-11 pm, Sun 5 pm-10 pm. Closed: 11/22. **Reservations:** accepted. **Features:** early bird specials; carryout; beer & wine only. Peculiarly named dishes, such as Gang Dang and Cocky Bob, belie the sophisticated dishes for which the restaurant is known. Check out the pad ha pow with pork, a savory brown sauce with basil and pepper flavored juicy white meat pork. **Cards:** AE, MC, VI.
Thai

TROPICAL CHINESE RESTAURANT   **Lunch:** $7-$15   **Dinner:** $10-$30   **Phone:** 305/262-7576   ㊿
Location: From SR 826, just w. 7991 Bird Rd 33155. **Hours:** 11:30 am-10:30 pm, Fri-11:30 pm, Sat 11 am-11:30 pm, Sun 10:30 am-10 pm. **Reservations:** accepted. **Features:** casual dress; carryout; cocktails & lounge. Exuding an air of sophistication normally not reserved for businesses of its type, the restaurant dishes up a wide variety of well-prepared entrees. Regulars are fond of the emperor's shrimp, which is fried and sauteed with white sweet and sour sauce. **Cards:** AE, DI, DS, MC, VI.
Chinese

MIAMI BEACH pop. 92,600   (See map p. 484; index p. 484)

──── WHERE TO STAY ────

THE ABBEY HOTEL
Phone: (305)531-0031 215

	12/27-4/2	1P: $179-$199	2P: $179-$199	XP: $25
	4/3-5/30	1P: $149-$179	2P: $149-$179	XP: $25
Classic Motel	12/1-12/26 & 5/31-11/30	1P: $129-$149	2P: $129-$149	XP: $25

Location: Collins Ave, just w. 300 21st St 33139. Fax: 305/672-1663. **Facility:** Historic. Attractive public areas. Rooms furnished and decorated with the art deco period. 50 units. *Bath:* shower only. 3 stories, interior corridors. **Parking:** extra charge. **Terms:** cancellation fee imposed. **Amenities:** extended cable TV, dual phone lines, voice mail, honor bars, irons, hair dryers. **Leisure Activities:** exercise room. **Guest Services:** [ECP] meal plan available, valet laundry. **Cards:** AE, CB, DI, DS, MC, VI.

SOME UNITS

(ASK) (Y+) (Y) (≡) (DATA PORT) / (X) /

On The Bay Inn & Marina
Home of Shuckers' Dockside Restaurant

- Heated Pool
- 310' Marina
- Guest Laundry
- Breakfast Bar
- In-room Safes
- Free Self Parking

- 26' T.V.'s
- Mini-Suites Available
- Non-smoking rooms available
- In room hair dryers & irons

AAA

$49.⁰⁰ plus tax

1 or 2 persons (with AAA Tour Book ad).
Must book direct with hotel. 12/25/00 - 4/15/01 add $20.
Special events & holidays excluded. Subject to availability.
Weekends add $10.

FOR RESERVATIONS CALL:
1-800-624-3961

(See map p. 484)

THE BLUE MOON, A MERV GRIFFIN HOTEL
Phone: (305)673-2262 [232]

12/16-4/15	1P: $215-$345	2P: $215-$345
12/1-12/15 & 4/16-11/30	1P: $149-$345	2P: $149-$345

Classic Hotel
Location: On SR A1A; at 10th St. 944 Collins Ave 33139. Fax: 305/534-5399. **Facility:** Located in the heart of the "Deco area". Warm public areas, small pool deck in back. Rooms with soft and vivid colors. 75 units. Some suites ($325-$495). *Bath:* combo or shower only. 2-3 stories, interior corridors. **Parking:** extra charge or valet. **Terms:** 3 day cancellation notice-fee imposed. **Amenities:** extended cable TV, CD players, dual phone lines, voice mail, honor bars, irons, hair dryers. *Some:* safes. **Leisure Activities:** whirlpool. **Guest Services:** valet laundry. **Business Services:** conference facilities. **Cards:** AE, CB, DI, DS, MC, VI.

SOME UNITS

BREAKWATER HOTEL
Phone: (305)532-1220 [230]

12/1-4/14	1P: $149-$239	2P: $149-$239	XP: $10	F12
4/15-11/30	1P: $139-$229	2P: $139-$229		F12

Historic Hotel
Location: E of SR A1A, between 9th and 10th sts. 940 Ocean Dr 33139. Fax: 305/532-4451. **Facility:** Restored art deco hotel facing the beach in heart of the vibrant South Beach. 59 units. Some whirlpool units. 4 stories, interior corridors. **Parking:** extra charge or valet. **Terms:** 3 day cancellation notice, small pets only. **Amenities:** extended cable TV, voice mail. **Guest Services:** valet laundry. **Business Services:** meeting rooms. **Cards:** AE, CB, DI, DS, MC, VI. *(See color ad below)*

SOME UNITS

CASA GRANDE HOTEL
Phone: (305)672-7003 [225]

12/26-5/31 & 10/1-11/30	2P: $310-$1500	XP: $15	F12
12/1-12/25	2P: $295-$1500	XP: $15	F12
6/1-9/30	2P: $195-$750	XP: $15	F12

Classic Hotel
Location: E of SR A1A (Collins Ave) and 8th Ave. 834 Ocean Dr 33139. Fax: 305/673-3669. **Facility:** A European boutique suite style hotel. Large rooms with furniture from Indonesia with some tapestries from Eastern Asia. 34 units with kitchen. 2 two-bedroom units and 1 three-bedroom unit. *Bath:* combo or shower only. 5 stories, interior corridors. **Parking:** valet. **Terms:** 5 day cancellation notice, package plans. **Amenities:** extended cable TV, CD players, voice mail, safes, honor bars, irons, hair dryers. **Leisure Activities:** pool privileges at the Tides Hotel. **Guest Services:** valet laundry. **Business Services:** meeting rooms. **Cards:** AE, DI, DS, MC, VI.

FEE   FEE

(See map p. 484)

CAVALIER

◈◈◈

Classic Motel

12/26-5/31	2P: $185-$395	XP: $15	F
12/1-12/25 & 10/1-11/30	2P: $170-$375	XP: $15	F
6/1-9/30	2P: $130-$275	XP: $15	F

Phone: (305)604-5000   **227**

Location: E of SR A1A (Collins Ave) and 13th Ave. 1320 Ocean Dr 33139. Fax: 305/531-5543. **Facility:** A renovated art deco property. Room size of the 30s, decorated and furnished to a degree of the era. Oceanfront location. 43 units. Some suites. *Bath:* combo or shower only. 3 stories, interior corridors. **Parking:** valet. **Terms:** 5 day cancellation notice, package plans. **Amenities:** extended cable TV, CD players, voice mail, safes, honor bars. **Leisure Activities:** off-site pool privileges. **Guest Services:** valet laundry. **Business Services:** meeting rooms. **Cards:** AE, DI, DS, MC, VI.

SOME UNITS

🛎️📶 📠 🎥 VCR 🖨️ DATA PORT 📺 🛏️
FEE   FEE

CENTURY HOTEL

◈◈◈

Classic Hotel

Property failed to provide current rates

Phone: 305/674-8855   **234**

Location: Just e of Collins Ave (A1A), just s of 2nd St. 140 Ocean Dr 33139. Fax: 305/538-5733. **Facility:** Built in 1939. Rooms with an eclectic decor and charm. 31 units. Some suites. 2 stories, interior corridors. **Parking:** valet. **Amenities:** CD players, dual phone lines, voice mail, safes, honor bars, irons, hair dryers. **Leisure Activities:** beach access. **Guest Services:** [CP] meal plan available, valet laundry. **Business Services:** meeting rooms. **Cards:** AE, CB, DI, MC, VI.

🛎️ 🍴 📶 VCR 🖨️ DATA PORT

CLARION SUITES CRYSTAL BEACH & HEALTH CLUB

AAA SAVE

◈◈◈

Suite Motel

All Year	1P: $144-$245	2P: $144-$245

Phone: (305)865-9555   **201**

Location: SR A1A at 71st St E. 6985 Collins Ave 33141-3205. Fax: 305/866-3514. **Facility:** One-bedroom suites with living room. A large lobby with comfortable sitting area. A fenced pool area surrounded by tropical trees and sea grape plants. The beach just steps away. Rooms with contemporary decor, a few with ocean view. 84 efficiencies. *Bath:* combo or shower only. 4 stories, interior corridors. **Parking:** check-in 4 pm, 3 day cancellation notice-fee imposed, package plans. **Amenities:** extended cable TV, voice mail, irons, hair dryers. **Leisure Activities:** sauna, whirlpool, steamroom, beach, swimming. **Guest Services:** coin laundry. *Fee:* massage. **Business Services:** meeting rooms. **Cards:** AE, CB, DI, DS, JC, MC, VI. **Special Amenities: free continental breakfast and free local telephone calls.** *(See color ad p 499)*

SOME UNITS

SD 🍴 🏊 ♿ VCR 🖨️ 📺 🖥️ 🛏️ DATA PORT ⊠
FEE

COMFORT INN ON THE BEACH

AAA SAVE

◈◈◈

Motel

12/16-4/30	1P: $125-$155	2P: $135-$165	XP: $10	F21
5/1-11/30	1P: $95-$130	2P: $100-$135	XP: $10	F21
12/1-12/15	1P: $90-$125	2P: $95-$130	XP: $10	F21

Phone: (305)868-1200   **203**

Location: A1A/Collins Ave at 63rd St. 6261 Collins Ave 33140. Fax: 305/868-3003. **Facility:** Art deco influences in the lobby areas. A large, attractive pool area surrounded by tropical foliage. The ocean is just steps away. The room decor is soft pastels and light wood tones. 153 units. *Bath:* combo or shower only. 9 stories, interior corridors. **Parking:** extra charge or valet. **Terms:** package plans, small pets only (deposit). **Amenities:** extended cable TV, video games, voice mail, safes (fee). **Leisure Activities:** beach, swimming, exercise room. **Guest Services:** [ECP] meal plan available, coin laundry. **Business Services:** meeting rooms. **Cards:** AE, DI, DS, MC, VI. **Special Amenities: early check-in/late check-out.** *(See color ad below)*

SOME UNITS

SD 🐕 📶 🍴 📠 🏊 🎥 🖨️ DATA PORT ⊠ 📺 🖥️ 🛏️
FEE

DAYS INN ART DECO/CONVENTION CENTER

AAA SAVE

◈◈

Motor Inn

2/15-2/25	1P: $149-$169	2P: $149-$169	XP: $10	F17
12/1-2/14 & 2/26-4/30	1P: $119-$149	2P: $119-$149	XP: $10	F17
5/1-11/30	1P: $89-$109	2P: $89-$109	XP: $10	F17

Phone: (305)538-6631   **217**

Location: SR A1A (Collins Ave) at 21st St. 100 21st St 33139. Fax: 305/674-0954. **Facility:** Restored property. Some rooms with balcony and few with direct beach access. 172 units. *Bath:* combo or shower only. 7 stories, interior/exterior corridors. **Parking:** extra charge or valet. **Terms:** 7 day cancellation notice, small pets only ($50 deposit). **Amenities:** safes (fee), irons, hair dryers. **Dining:** coffee shop, 7-11 am, Sat & Sun-noon. **Leisure Activities:** beach, swimming. **Guest Services:** gift shop, valet and coin laundry. **Cards:** AE, DI, DS, JC, MC, VI.

SOME UNITS

SD 🐕 🍴 🍽️ ♿ 📠 🏊 🎥 🖨️ DATA PORT ⊠ 📺 🛏️
FEE

(See map p. 484)

DAYS INN NORTH BEACH   **Phone:** (305)866-1631   235
| | 12/22-4/15 | 1P: $89-$159 | 2P: $89-$159 | XP: $5 | F17 |
| | 12/1-12/21 & 4/16-11/30 | 1P: $69-$109 | 2P: $69-$109 | XP: $5 | F17 |

Motel **Location:** From A1A/Collins Ave and 75th St, just e on 75th St, then a right turn. 7450 Ocean Terrace 33141. Fax: 305/868-4617. **Facility:** Exterior and lobby with art deco influences. Some rooms with ocean view, a few oceanfront. Room furnishings with light wood tones and soft tropical color scheme. 93 units. Some suites ($99-$169). *Bath:* combo or shower only. 7 stories, interior corridors. **Parking:** extra charge. **Terms:** 14 day cancellation notice, package plans. **Amenities:** extended cable TV, voice mail, irons, hair dryers. **Leisure Activities:** beach, swimming. **Guest Services:** coin laundry. **Business Services:** meeting rooms. **Cards:** AE, CB, DI, DS, MC, VI. **Special Amenities: free newspaper and free room upgrade (subject to availability with advanced reservations).**
(See color ad below)   SOME UNITS

FONTAINEBLEAU HILTON RESORT & TOWERS   **Phone:** (305)538-2000   211
| | 12/1-4/30 | 1P: $209-$369 | 2P: $239-$399 | XP: $30 | F18 |
| | 5/1-11/30 | 1P: $159-$259 | 2P: $189-$289 | XP: $30 | F18 |

Hotel **Location:** On SR A1A. 4441 Collins Ave 33140. Fax: 305/531-9274. **Facility:** Extensive facilities with spacious public areas. Variety of rooms, some compact in spa building. Some with balcony. Beautifully landscaped grounds and pool areas. 1206 units. Some suites ($525-$1240) and whirlpool units. *Bath:* combo or shower only. 8-17 stories, interior corridors. **Parking:** valet only. **Terms:** 5 day cancellation notice, package plans, small pets only. **Amenities:** dual phone lines, voice mail, safes (fee), honor bars, irons, hair dryers. *Some:* fax. **Leisure Activities:** 2 pools, saunas, whirlpools, steamrooms, beach, swimming, 2 pools (1 heated, 1 saltwater) octopus kiddy pool and water slide, children's program, recreation program, social program. *Fee:* boats, paddleboats, sailboating, windsurfing, charter fishing, 7 lighted tennis courts. **Guest Services:** gift shop, valet laundry. *Fee:* massage. **Business Services:** conference facilities, administrative services, fax. *Fee:* PC. **Cards:** AE, CB, DI, DS, JC, MC, VI. *(See ad p 44)*   SOME UNITS

HOLIDAY INN INDIAN CREEK   **Phone:** (305)865-2565   200
| | 12/1-4/30 | | 2P: $129-$189 | XP: $10 | F |
| | 5/1-11/30 | | 2P: $109-$119 | XP: $10 | F |

Motor Inn **Location:** 2 mi n of Julia Tuttle Cswy, I-195 on A1A southbound. 6060 Indian Creek Dr 33140. Fax: 305/865-2506. **Facility:** All rooms with balcony and a view of the ocean area or city. Large rooms with light wood tones and contemporary decor. 78 units, 2 with efficiency. Some suites ($250-$350). *Bath:* combo or shower only. 15 stories, interior corridors. **Parking:** valet. **Terms:** 14 day cancellation notice. **Amenities:** extended cable TV, video games, voice mail, irons, hair dryers. **Dining:** restaurant, 6:30 am-10:30 & 6-10:30 pm, $10-$20, cocktails. **Leisure Activities:** small pool, whirlpool, exercise room. **Guest Services:** coin laundry. **Business Services:** meeting rooms, fax. **Cards:** AE, CB, DI, DS, JC, MC, VI. **Special Amenities: free newspaper and preferred room (subject to availability with advanced reservations).** *(See color ad p 503)*   SOME UNITS

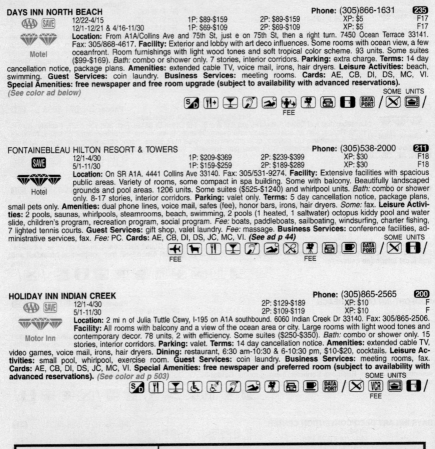

(See map p. 484)

HOLIDAY INN SOUTH BEACH RESORT   Phone: (305)534-1511   216

AAA SAVE	12/28-4/15	1P: $189-$229	2P: $189-$229	XP: $15	F12
	4/16-11/30	1P: $159-$179	2P: $159-$179	XP: $15	F12
Motor Inn	12/1-12/27	1P: $149-$169	2P: $149-$169	XP: $15	F12

Location: SR A1A, at 22nd St. 2201 Collins Ave 33139. Fax: 305/532-1403. **Facility:** Tropical atmosphere. Family oriented with a unique thatched poolside coffee shop and easy access to shops and the ocean. Public areas have a deco theme with neutral colors; while rooms have bright colors. 355 units. *Bath:* combo or shower only. 3-12 stories, interior/exterior corridors. **Parking:** extra charge. **Terms:** cancellation fee imposed, package plans. **Amenities:** dual phone lines, voice mail, irons, hair dryers. **Dining:** restaurant, coffee shop, 7 am-2 & 5-10 pm, $15-$25, cocktails. **Leisure Activities:** whirlpool, beach, swimming, 2 lighted tennis courts, exercise room, game room, beach volleyball. *Fee:* jet skis, catamarans, parasailing. **Guest Services:** [AP], [BP] & [MAP] meal plans available, gift shop, valet and coin laundry. **Cards:** AE, CB, DI, DS, JC, MC, VI. **Special Amenities: early check-in/late check-out and free newspaper.** SOME UNITS

THE HOTEL   Phone: (305)531-2222   224

	11/1-11/30	1P: $295-$425
	12/1-5/31	1P: $275-$425
Classic Hotel	6/1-10/31	1P: $215-$365

Location: On SR A1A (Collins Ave) and 8th St. 801 Collins Ave 33139. Fax: 305/531-3222. **Facility:** Located in the art deco area. Rooms and lobby designed by fashion designer Todd Oldham. Light wood tones, soft bright colors used. 54 units. Some suites ($365-$425) and whirlpool units. *Bath:* combo or shower only. 4 stories, interior corridors. **Parking:** valet. **Terms:** 3 day cancellation notice-fee imposed, package plans. **Amenities:** extended cable TV, CD players, dual phone lines, voice mail, safes, honor bars. **Dining:** Wish, see separate listing. **Leisure Activities:** small rooftop pool, exercise room. **Guest Services:** gift shop, valet laundry. *Fee:* massage. **Business Services:** meeting rooms. **Cards:** AE, CB, DI, DS, MC, VI.

HOTEL EDISON-SOUTH BEACH   Phone: (305)531-2744   226

AAA SAVE	11/1-11/30	1P: $165-$325	2P: $165-$325	XP: $25	F12
	12/1-5/31	1P: $155-$300	2P: $155-$300	XP: $20	F12
Classic Hotel	6/1-10/31	1P: $145-$285	2P: $145-$285	XP: $25	F12

Location: At corner of 10th St and Ocean Dr. 960 Ocean Dr 33139. Fax: 305/622-4153. **Facility:** A six story structure in the heart of the art deco area and facing the ocean. The rooms are decorated in the colors of the art deco era. The pool and courtyard are right next to the All Star Cafe. 58 units. *Bath:* combo or shower only. 6 stories, interior corridors. **Parking:** extra charge. **Dining:** restaurant, 9 am-3:30 am, $6-$12. **Leisure Activities:** beach access. **Guest Services:** valet laundry. **Cards:** AE, DI, DS, JC, MC, VI. **Special Amenities: free continental breakfast and free newspaper.**

(See map p. 484)

THE INDIAN CREEK HOTEL

AAA **SAVE**
▽▼▽▼▽▼
Classic Hotel

12/1-4/30 & 11/1-11/30	2P: $140-$260	XP: $10	F10
5/1-10/31	2P: $90-$150	XP: $10	F10

Phone: (305)531-2727 **214**

Location: A1A southbound, at 28th St, just w of Collins Ave. 2727 Indian Creek Dr 33140. Fax: 305/531-5651. **Facility:** 1936 art deco hotel of national fame and recognition. Rooms furnished and decorated from this era. It's like stepping back in time once you enter. A lovely tropical garden for relaxing. 61 units. 3 stories, interior corridors. **Parking:** street only. **Terms:** cancellation fee imposed. **Amenities:** voice mail, irons. *Some:* CD players. **Dining:** restaurant, 7 am-11 & 6-11 pm, Sun 6 pm-10 pm; closed for dinner Tues, $5-$20, wine/beer only. **Guest Services:** valet laundry. **Business Services:** meeting rooms. **Cards:** AE, CB, DI, DS, JC, MC, VI. *(See color ad p 503)*

SOME UNITS

⊖⊖ ⊠ ⊕ ⊠ ⊟ DATA PORT / ⊠ VCR ⊟ /
FEE

LESLIE HOTEL

▽▼▽▼▽
Classic Hotel

12/26-5/31 & 10/1-11/30	2P: $195-$395	XP: $15	
12/1-12/25	2P: $170-$375	XP: $15	
6/1-9/30	2P: $145-$295	XP: $15	

Phone: (305)604-5000 **228**

Location: E of SR A1A (Collins Ave) and 12th Ave. 1244 Ocean Dr 33139. Fax: 305/672-5611. **Facility:** An art deco boutique hotel. Room size reflects the 30s. Decorated in bright colors. Oceanfront location. 45 units. Some suites. *Bath:* combo or shower only. 3 stories, interior corridors. **Parking:** valet. **Terms:** 5 day cancellation notice, package plans. **Amenities:** extended cable TV, CD players, voice mail, safes, honor bars. **Leisure Activities:** off-site pool privileges. **Guest Services:** [CP] meal plan available, valet laundry. **Cards:** AE, DI, DS, MC, VI.

⊖⊖ ⊠ ⊘ ⊕ VCR ⊟ DATA PORT
FEE

LOEWS MIAMI BEACH HOTEL

▽▼▽▼ ▽▼▽▼
Hotel

12/24-5/31	1P: $349-$499	2P: $349-$499	XP: $30	F18
12/1-12/23	1P: $339-$439	2P: $339-$439	XP: $30	F18
9/16-11/30	1P: $269-$439	2P: $269-$439	XP: $30	F18
6/1-9/15	1P: $229-$399	2P: $229-$399	XP: $30	F18

Phone: (305)604-1601 **223**

Location: On SR A1A, at Collins and 16th aves. 1601 Collins Ave 33139. Fax: 305/604-3999. **Facility:** Sitting on the oceanfront and in the middle of the "Art Deco" area. Two buildings surrounded by tropical trees, plants and fountains throughout. Two lobbies, one with the traditional "Art Deco" style; the other very large lobby with shops and eateries. Rooms decorated in a stylish "Deco" theme. 790 units. Some suites ($650-$5000). *Bath:* combo or shower only. 9-18 stories, interior corridors. **Parking:** valet. **Terms:** check-in 4 pm, 3 day cancellation notice, package plans, small pets only. **Amenities:** extended cable TV, dual phone lines, voice mail, safes, honor bars, irons, hair dryers. *Some:* CD players, fax. **Leisure Activities:** heated pool, wading pool, saunas, whirlpools, beach, swimming. **Guest Services:** gift shop, valet laundry. *Fee:* massage. **Business Services:** conference facilities, administrative services, PC, fax. **Cards:** AE, CB, DI, DS, JC, MC, VI. *(See color ad below)*

SOME UNITS

ASK $⊟ ⊕ ⊠ ⊖⊖ 24 ⊘ ⊘ ⊠ ⊕ ⊠ ⊟ ⊟ DATA PORT / ⊠ VCR ⊟ /
FEE   FEE   FEE

(See map p. 484)

OCEAN SURF HOTEL   Phone: (305)866-1648   236

(AAA) (SAVE)
▼▼ ▼▼
Classic Motel

| | 12/1-4/14 | 1P: $99-$139 | 2P: $99-$139 | XP: $6 | F12 |
| | 4/15-11/30 | 1P: $74-$114 | 2P: $74-$114 | XP: $6 | F12 |

Location: Collins Ave and 75th St, just e on 75th St, then a right turn. 7436 Ocean Terrace 33141. Fax: 305/866-1649. **Facility:** Historic. Just across from ocean. A multi-colored building with art deco colors and furnishings. 49 units. *Bath:* combo or shower only. 4 stories, interior corridors. **Parking:** extra charge. **Terms:** weekly rates available. **Amenities:** safes (fee), hair dryers. **Leisure Activities:** beach access. **Guest Services:** valet laundry. **Cards:** AE, DI, DS, MC, VI. **Special Amenities:** early check-in/late check-out and free continental breakfast.
(See color ad below)   SOME UNITS

[icons] /[X]/

RADISSON DEAUVILLE RESORT MIAMI BEACH   Phone: (305)865-8511   204

(AAA) (SAVE)
▼▼▼▼
Hotel

| | 12/1-4/15 | 1P: $239 | XP: $15 | F18 |
| | 4/16-11/30 | 1P: $189 | XP: $15 | F18 |

Location: SR A1A at 67th St. 6701 Collins Ave 33141. Fax: 305/861-0590. **Facility:** Extensive public areas, some shops and beauty salon. Very nicely furnished and decorated rooms. Some rooms with a balcony. 474 units. Some suites. *Bath:* combo or shower only. 17 stories, interior corridors. **Parking:** valet. **Terms:** package plans. **Amenities:** video games, voice mail, safes (fee), irons, hair dryers. **Dining:** dining room, deli, 6:30 am-10 pm; pool grill & bar, $9-$16, cocktails. **Leisure Activities:** heated pool, whirlpool, beach, swimming, charter fishing, parasailing, waverunners, 3 tennis courts, exercise room, game room. *Fee:* scuba diving/snorkeling & equipment. **Guest Services:** gift shop, coin laundry. **Business Services:** meeting rooms, administrative services. *Fee:* PC, fax. **Cards:** AE, CB, DI, DS, JC, MC, VI. **Special Amenities:** free continental breakfast and free room upgrade (subject to availability with advanced reservations). *(See ad p 506)*   SOME UNITS

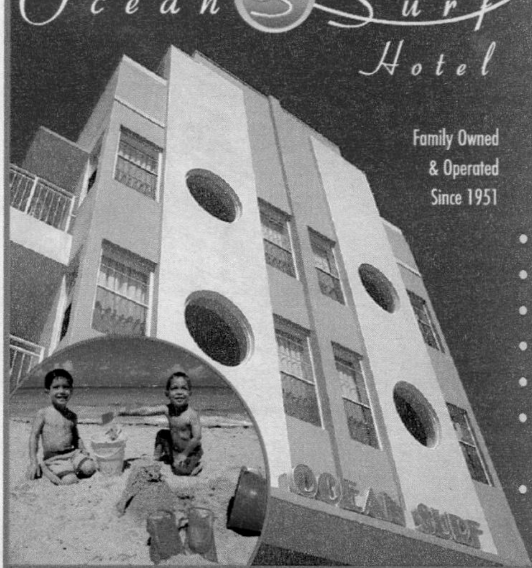

[icons] /[X]/

RAMADA INN MIAMI BEACH   Phone: (305)531-5771   212

▼▼ ▼▼
Motor Inn

	12/20-4/30	2P: $125-$150	XP: $10
	5/1-11/30	2P: $89-$99	XP: $10
	12/1-12/19	2P: $85-$95	XP: $10

Location: On SR A1A (Collins Ave), at Collins Ave and 40th St. 4041 Collins Ave 33140. Fax: 305/538-3568. **Facility:** Contemporary room decor. Many rooms with view of ocean. A large lobby with many sitting areas. 251 units. 16 stories, interior corridors. **Parking:** valet. **Amenities:** voice mail, safes (fee). **Leisure Activities:** heated pool, beach, swimming, heated saltwater pool, playground. **Guest Services:** gift shop, valet laundry. **Business Services:** meeting rooms. **Cards:** AE, CB, DI, DS, MC, VI.   SOME UNITS

[icons] /[X]/

(See map p. 484)

RIANDE CONTINENTAL HOTEL
♦♦♦♦ Phone: (305)531-3503 **218**

12/15-4/15	1P: $175	2P: $175	XP: $10 F12
4/16-11/30	1P: $155	2P: $155	XP: $10 F12
12/1-12/14	1P: $150	2P: $150	XP: $10 F12

Hotel **Location:** On SR A1A (Collins Ave), just n of 18th St. 1825 Collins Ave 33139. Fax: 305/531-5602. **Facility:** Contemporary appointments wrapped in an art deco package. A large lobby with bar area. Pool in back, with just a short walk to the beach. 251 units. 8 stories, interior corridors. **Parking:** valet. **Terms:** package plans. **Amenities:** voice mail, safes (fee), hair dryers. *Some:* honor bars. **Leisure Activities:** beach, swimming. **Guest Services:** gift shop, valet laundry. **Business Services:** meeting rooms. **Cards:** AE, DI, MC, VI.

SOME UNITS

(ASK) [S] [↑↑] [Y] [≈] [✦] [🖨] [DATA PORT] / [X] /

THE ROSE
♦♦♦ Phone: (305)532-7093 **231**

4/16-11/30	1P: $125	2P: $125	XP: $10 F12
12/1-4/15	1P: $105	2P: $105	XP: $10 F12

Classic Motel **Location:** Just e of Collins Ave (A1A) between 4th and 5th sts. 436 Ocean Dr 33139. Fax: 305/534-7353. **Facility:** Boutique-style motel across street from the ocean. Rooms decorated with Spanish-style furniture and bright, modern color schemes. 61 units. *Bath:* combo or shower only. 2-3 stories, interior corridors. **Parking:** valet. **Terms:** 3 day cancellation notice-fee imposed, package plans. **Amenities:** voice mail. **Leisure Activities:** jogging. *Fee:* bicycles. **Guest Services:** valet laundry. **Cards:** AE, MC, VI.

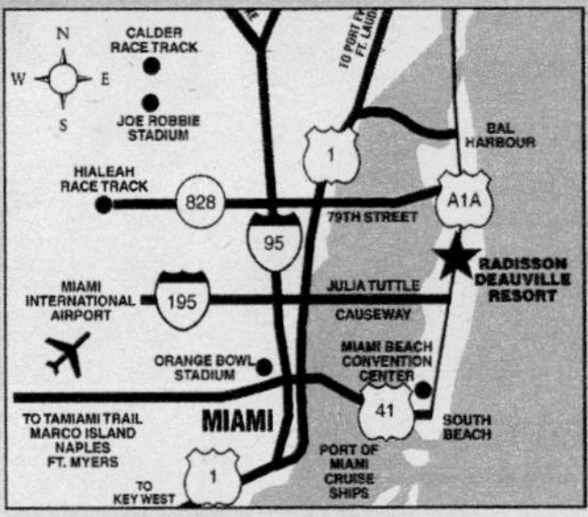

SOME UNITS

(ASK) [S] [↔] [↑↑] [Y] [📷] [🖨] [DATA PORT] / [X] /
FEE

(See map p. 484)

THE SAVOY ON SOUTH BEACH   Phone: (305)532-0200   233

Property failed to provide current rates

Suite Motor Inn

Location: E of SR A1A. 455 Ocean Dr 33139. Fax: 305/534-7436. **Facility:** Large, spacious suites with a tranquil decor and unique art; some with view of ocean. Attractive pool area. 38 units. 5 two-bedroom units. 3 stories, interior corridors. **Parking:** extra charge. **Terms:** check-in 4 pm, cancellation fee imposed. **Amenities:** extended cable TV, dual phone lines, voice mail, safes, irons, hair dryers. *Some:* CD players. **Leisure Activities:** 2 pools, whirlpool, beach, swimming, exercise room. **Guest Services:** valet laundry. **Cards:** AE, DI, DS, MC, VI.

SOME UNITS

SHELBORNE BEACH RESORT-SOUTH BEACH   Phone: (305)531-1271   222

12/1-5/31 & 9/15-11/30	1P: $185-$2500	2P: $185-$2500	XP: $10	F16
6/1-9/14	1P: $145-$2000	2P: $145-$2000	XP: $10	F16

Hotel

Location: SR A1A at 18th St. 1801 Collins Ave 33139. Fax: 305/531-2206. **Facility:** Individually decorated rooms, few with balcony. Very relaxing pool area with beach right behind it. Some suites with pool view or at pool level. 185 units. 10 two-bedroom units and 11 units with kitchen. Some suites ($500-$1500). *Bath:* combo or shower only. 2-16 stories, interior corridors. **Parking:** valet. **Terms:** 7 day cancellation notice, package plans. **Amenities:** extended cable TV, voice mail, safes (fee), hair dryers. *Some:* CD players. **Dining:** restaurant, 7 am-11 pm, $12-$20, cocktails, nightclub. **Leisure Activities:** sauna, whirlpools, beach, swimming, exercise room. **Guest Services:** valet and coin laundry. **Business Services:** conference facilities, fax. **Cards:** AE, DS, MC, VI. **Special Amenities:** free room upgrade and preferred room (each subject to availability with advanced reservations). *(See color ad below)*

SOME UNITS
FEE

(See map p. 484)

SOVEREIGN HOTEL
Phone: (305)531-3232 **213**

[AAA] [SAVE] 12/22-4/16   1P: $149   2P: $149   XP: $25   F17
12/1-12/21 & 4/17-11/30   1P: $99   2P: $99   XP: $25   F17

▽▽▽ **Location:** On SR A1A, jct of Collins Ave and 43rd St. 4385 Collins Ave 33140. Fax: 305/531-1077. **Facility:** Located
Classic Hotel   on the oceanfront. The pool is just behind the hotel with a nice deck and grassy area. The beach is just steps
away. Lobby has comfortable sitting areas. Rooms have a contemporary decor package. 107 units. Some
suites ($189-$299). *Bath:* combo or shower only. 7 stories, interior corridors. **Parking:** valet. **Terms:** 3 day
cancellation notice-fee imposed. **Amenities:** voice mail, irons, hair dryers. **Dining:** restaurant, 6:30 am-12:30 am, $8-$16, cocktails. **Leisure Activities:** heated pool, whirlpool. **Guest Services:** valet laundry. **Business Services:** meeting rooms. **Cards:** AE,
CB, DI, DS, JC, MC, VI. **Special Amenities:** free newspaper and free room upgrade (subject to availability with advanced
reservations).** *(See color ad p 507)*

SOME UNITS
[S/D] [⊤⊤] [24] [⊤] [⊴] [⊶⊷] [♦] [☎] [▭] [DATA PORT] / [✕] [VCR] [◨] /
                                                       FEE   FEE

SURFCOMBER-HAMPTON INN
Phone: (305)532-7715 **220**

[SAVE] 4/1-4/30 & 10/1-11/30   1P: $139-$299   2P: $149-$309
12/1-3/31   1P: $129-$289   2P: $139-$299
5/1-9/30   1P: $119-$279   2P: $129-$289

▽▽▽ **Location:** On SR A1A (Collins Ave) at Collins and 17th aves. 1717 Collins Ave 33139. Fax: 305/532-7280.
Classic Motor Inn   **Facility:** Located in the heart of the "Deco area". Some rooms with oceanfront view. Some with city view.
Property decorated and furnished with the "Deco Look". 185 units. Some suites ($189-$309). *Bath:* some
combo or shower only. 3 stories, interior corridors. **Parking:** valet. **Terms:** 3 day cancellation notice-fee imposed. **Amenities:** extended cable TV, video games, dual phone lines, voice mail, safes (fee), irons. *Some:* CD players. **Leisure Activities:** beach,
swimming. **Guest Services:** [ECP] meal plan available, gift shop, valet laundry. **Business Services:** meeting rooms. **Cards:** AE,
CB, DI, DS, MC, VI. *(See color ad below)*

SOME UNITS
[S/D] [⊤] [&] [⊘] [⊴] [♦] [☎] [▭] [DATA PORT] / [✕] [◨] /
                                        FEE   FEE

THE TIDES HOTEL
Phone: (305)604-5070 **229**

[AAA] [SAVE] 12/26-5/31   2P: $475-$575
12/1-12/25 & 10/1-11/30   2P: $450-$525
▽▽▽▽ 6/1-9/30   2P: $350-$450
Hotel   **Location:** E of jct SR A1A (Collins Ave) and 12th Ave. 1220 Ocean Dr 33139. Fax: 305/604-5182. **Facility:** A fully
restored art deco hotel. A large lobby reminiscent of the 30s. Large rooms all facing the ocean. Lavishly furnished and decorated. 45 units. Some whirlpool units. *Bath:* combo or shower only. 10 stories, interior corridors. **Parking:** valet. **Terms:** cancellation fee imposed, package plans. **Amenities:** extended cable TV, CD players, dual phone
lines, voice mail, safes, honor bars, irons, hair dryers. *Some:* fax. **Dining:** dining room, restaurant, pool bar & grill, $8-$35, cocktails. **Leisure Activities:** heated pool, beach access, limited exercise equipment. **Guest Services:** gift shop, valet laundry. **Business Services:** meeting rooms, fax. *Fee:* PC. **Cards:** AE, DI, MC, VI.

SOME UNITS
[⊤⊤] [24] [⊤] [&] [⊘] [⊴] [♦] [VCR] [☎] [DATA PORT] / [✕] /
                                         FEE   FEE

TUDOR TRAVELODGE HOTEL & SUITES
Phone: (305)534-2934 **221**

▽▽▽ 12/16-4/15   1P: $149   2P: $149   XP: $20   F12
12/1-12/15 & 4/16-11/30   1P: $119   2P: $119   XP: $20   F12
Hotel   **Location:** On A1A (Collins Ave) at 11th Ave. 1111 Collins Ave 33139. Fax: 305/531-1874. **Facility:** In the heart of
the Deco area. Contemporary room decor with some deco influences. One block from the beach. 94 units.
2 two-bedroom units. Some whirlpool units. 4 stories, interior corridors. **Parking:** valet. **Terms:** 3 day cancellation notice-fee imposed. **Amenities:** extended cable TV, voice mail, hair dryers. **Dining:** [ECP] meal plan available, valet and coin
laundry. **Cards:** AE, DS, MC, VI.

SOME UNITS
[ASK] [S/D] [⊤⊤] [⊤] [♦] [▭] [DATA PORT] / [✕] [▤] [◨] /

(See map p. 484)

WYNDHAM MIAMI BEACH RESORT   Phone: (305)532-3600   [205]

(AAA) [SAVE]   12/1-4/15   1P: $159-$395
                10/1-11/30   1P: $159-$274
▼▼▼▼▼   4/16-5/31   1P: $149-$255
                6/1-9/30   1P: $124-$225
Hotel   **Location:** On SR A1A; 0.5 mi n of jct Arthur Godfrey Rd. 4833 Collins Ave 33140. Fax: 305/534-7409. **Facility:** Elegant traditional oceanfront hotel with a grand lobby and public areas. A large pool area surrounded by
tropical trees and flowering plants. Large rooms with light wood tone, contemporary decor. 424 units. Some suites and whirlpool
units. *Bath:* combo or shower only. 18 stories, interior corridors. **Parking:** valet. **Terms:** 3 day cancellation notice-fee imposed,
package plans. **Amenities:** extended cable TV, video games, dual phone lines, voice mail, honor bars, irons, hair dryers.
Dining: dining room, restaurant, 6:30 am-1:30 am; pool terrace dining; 19%, $15-$30, cocktails. **Leisure Activities:** heated pool,
saunas, steamrooms, beach, swimming, paddleboats, sailboating, windsurfing, charter fishing, lighted tennis court, children's program, recreation program, social program, jogging, exercise room. *Fee:* boat dock, waterskiing, scuba diving/snorkeling & equipment, catamarans, jet skis, scuba instruction. **Guest Services:** gift shop, valet laundry. *Fee:* massage. **Business Services:**
conference facilities, administrative services, fax. *Fee:* PC. **Cards:** AE, CB, DI, DS, JC, MC, VI.   SOME UNITS

[S][Ⓓ] [❙|] [⊥] [📶] [&] [📡] [🏊] [✖] [FEE] [🚗] [💻] [DATA PORT] / [✖] [VCR FEE] [🔒] /
FEE   FEE

───── *The following lodgings were either not evaluated or did not* ─────
meet AAA rating requirements but are listed for your information only.

CARDOZO HOTEL SOUTH BEACH   Phone: 305/535-6500
[fyi]   Not evaluated; management refused inspection. **Location:** From SR A1A (Collins Ave), e on 13th st. 1300 Ocean
Blvd 33139. Facilities, services, and decor characterize an upscale property.

DELANO HOTEL   Phone: 305/672-2000
[fyi]   Not evaluated; management refused inspection. **Location:** on SR A1A (Collins Ave) at 16th st. 1685 Collins Ave
33139. Facilities, services, and decor characterize an upscale property.

HOTEL ASTOR   Phone: 305/531-8081
[fyi]   Not evaluated. **Location:** From Mac Arthur Causeway/US 41 to 5th St, then n. 956 Washington Ave 33139. Facilities,
services, and decor characterize an upscale property.

THE KENT   Phone: 305/604-5000
[fyi]   Not evaluated. **Location:** On SR A1A at Collins Ave and 11th St. 1131 Collins Ave 33139. Facilities, services, and decor
characterize a mid-range property.

THE MARLIN   Phone: 305/604-5063
[fyi]   Not evaluated. **Location:** On SR A1A at Collins Ave and 12th St. 1200 Collins Ave 33139. Facilities, services, and decor
characterize an upscale property.

THE NATIONAL HOTEL   Phone: 305/532-2311
[fyi]   Does not meet all AAA rating requirements; lacks locking devices in some guest rooms; previously evaluated
Hotel   on. **Location:** On SR A1A/Collins Ave and 16th St. 1677 Collins Ave 33139. Facilities, services, and decor characterize
an upscale property.

PRESIDENT HOTEL   Phone: 305/538-2882
[fyi]   Does not meet all AAA rating requirements for room decor/ambiance; previously evaluated on 05/21/1999.
Motel   **Location:** On A1A/Collins Ave, just s of Espanola Way. 1423 Collins Ave 33139. Facilities, services, and decor characterize a mid-range property.

───── **WHERE TO DINE** ─────

ASTOR PLACE BAR & GRILL   **Lunch:** $7-$20   **Dinner:** $7-$30   Phone: 305/672-7217   [206]
▼▼▼   **Location:** 956 Washington Ave 33139. **Hours:** 11:30 am-2:30 & 7-11 pm, Fri-midnight, Sat 6 pm-midnight, Sun
noon-2:30 & 6-11 pm. **Reservations:** suggested. **Features:** dressy casual; Sunday brunch; cocktails;
American   street parking; a la carte. Featuring new Florida cuisine with fresh seafood, meat and poultry, all dishes are
flavorful and excellently presented in a bustling modern dining room. Savor barbecued wasabi tuna fillet
served on a bed of rice with cashews and shrimp. **Cards:** AE, DI, DS, MC, VI.   [✖]

BOULEVARD BISTRO   **Lunch:** $6-$19   **Dinner:** $8-$45   Phone: 305/532-9069   [207]
▼▼▼   **Location:** 740 Ocean Dr 33139. **Hours:** 11 am-midnight, Sat & Sun 9 am-1 am. **Reservations:** accepted.
Features: casual dress; early bird specials; cocktails & lounge; fee for parking & valet parking. Expect a
American   concise menu and no-frills cooking. Grilled seafood dishes with snapper, tuna and sea bass are flavorful
and satisfying. Tasty side dishes include couscous, acorn squash and fried green tomatoes. Impeccable
service heightens the experience. **Cards:** AE, DI, MC, VI.   [✖]

CARDOZA CAFE   **Lunch:** $6-$25   **Dinner:** $6-$25   Phone: 305/538-0553   [201]
▼▼▼▼   **Location:** E of SR A1A (Collins Ave) and 13th Ave. 1300 Ocean Dr 33139. **Hours:** 8 am-11 pm, Fri &
Sat-midnight. **Reservations:** accepted. **Features:** dressy casual; cocktails & lounge;
English   entertainment; fee for parking & valet parking; a la carte. Mostly outdoor porch dining, it has a relaxed and
romantic style with live acoustical music and late night salsa dancing in the lounge. Authentic and tasty, the
Cuban dishes are well-prepared and served by an extremely hospitable staff. **Cards:** AE, DI, DS, MC, VI.

(See map p. 484)

CHINA GRILL   **Lunch: $21-$35**   **Dinner: $21-$35**   **Phone: 305/534-2211**   ⟨208⟩
▽▽▽▽
Asian
Location: Corner of 5th St and Washington Ave. 404 Washington Ave 33139. **Hours:** 11:45 am-midnight, Fri & Sat 6 pm-1 am, Sun 6 pm-midnight. **Reservations:** accepted. **Features:** dressy casual; cocktails & lounge; street parking & fee for valet parking. Noisy, bustling and never boring, this clublike spot is the "see-and-be-seen" place for sake, vodka and ample portions of dramatically prepared delights such as porterhouse lobster. Just eyeing the sinful desserts is likely to stretch your waistband. **Cards:** AE, DI, DS, MC, VI.   ✕

CRYSTAL CAFE   **Dinner: $13-$25**   **Phone: 305/673-8266**   ⟨190⟩
◈◈◈
▽▽▽◈
Continental
Location: Just e of Chase Ave. 726 Arthur Godfrey Rd 33140. **Hours:** 5 pm-10 pm, Fri & Sat-11 pm. Closed: Mon. **Reservations:** suggested. **Features:** dressy casual; beer & wine only; also prix fixe. Voted one of Florida's top 20 restaurants year after year. Its a cozy romantic dining room with soft indirect lighting and a good use of mirrors. One of the specialties is the Osso Bucco that is done with a French flair. A large menu with a variety of meat, seafood and pasta entrees. You have to go back several times to find your favorite as there are many. A nice wine list compliments this menu. Several half bottles available too.
Cards: AE, DS, MC, VI.

THE FORGE   **Dinner: $20-$37**   **Phone: 305/538-8533**   ⟨192⟩
◈◈◈
▽▽▽▽
Nouvelle American
Location: Arthur Godfrey Rd; 0.5 mi w of jct Collins Ave, SR A1A. 432 41st St 33140. **Hours:** 6 pm-midnight, Fri & Sat-1 am. **Reservations:** accepted. **Features:** semi-formal attire; Sunday brunch; cocktails & lounge; entertainment; fee for valet parking; a la carte; also prix fixe. This tastefully appointed restaurant always draws a crowd. The steak is cooked to perfection and served with sauteed green beans. An extensive wine list and spa menu items are featured. Go for the berries and cream for dessert after this sumptuous dinner. **Cards:** AE, DI, MC, VI.   ✕

GAUCHO ROOM   **Dinner: $18-$40**   **Phone: 305/604-1601**   ⟨199⟩
▽▽▽▽
Steak House
Location: On SR A1A, at Collins and 16th aves; in Loews Miami Beach Hotel. 1601 Collins Ave 33139. **Hours:** 7 pm-midnight. Closed: Mon. **Reservations:** suggested. **Features:** dressy casual; children's menu; carryout; cocktails & lounge; entertainment; fee for valet parking; a la carte. The room is large and warm, you are surrounded by pictures with scenes of Argentina and its Gauchos. Booths with pony style fabric patterns, saddles of the Gauchos. Both Argentinean and American meats featured, seafood and pasta items available. A wine list with many south of the equator selections as well as north of the equator favorites. **Cards:** AE, CB, DI, DS, MC, VI.   ⟨♿⟩ ✕

JOE'S STONE CRAB RESTAURANT   **Lunch: $5-$60**   **Dinner: $5-$60**   **Phone: 305/673-0365**   ⟨211⟩
▽▽▽
Seafood
Location: 6 blks s of SR A1A. 11 Washington Ave 33139. **Hours:** Open 12/1-5/15 & 10/15-11/30; 11:30 am-2:30 & 5-10 pm, Fri & Sat-11 pm. Closed: 11/22. **Features:** carryout; cocktails & lounge; fee for valet parking; a la carte. As the restaurant's name implies, the stone crab is mighty popular here. But then again, so is the homemade key lime pie. Owned by the same family since the early 1900s, the popular eatery offers generous portions of delectable food. **Cards:** AE, DI, DS, MC, VI.   ✕

MAMA VIEJA RESTAURANT   **Lunch: $5-$9**   **Dinner: $7-$18**   **Phone: 305/538-2400**   ⟨193⟩
▽▽▽
Colombian
Location: Just w of Collins Ave, SR A1A. 235 23rd St 33139. **Hours:** noon-midnight. Closed: 12/25. **Reservations:** accepted. **Features:** casual dress; carryout; cocktails & lounge; entertainment; street parking. A warm, family atmosphere embraces diners in this little slice of Colombia. The architecture and decor combine to reflect the roots of South America, as do the well-prepared dishes of seafood, pasta and steaks, such as the bandeja paisa. **Cards:** AE, CB, DI, DS, MC, VI.   ✕

MARK'S SOUTH BEACH   **Dinner: $18-$45**   **Phone: 305/604-9050**   ⟨205⟩
▽▽▽▽▽
Northern American
Location: On SR A1A, at corner of 11th St and Collins Ave; in the Nash Hotel. 1120 Collins Ave 33136. **Hours:** 7 pm-11 pm, Fri & Sat-midnight. **Reservations:** suggested. **Features:** dressy casual; cocktails & lounge; fee for valet parking; a la carte. New American cuisine with worldly influences and techniques as well as ingredients. Excellent preparation and presentation of meat, seafood, and pasta in a stylish atmosphere. Eat in the dining room or in the terrace area near the pools. **Cards:** AE, DI, MC, VI.   ⟨♿⟩ ✕

MEZZALUNA, SOUTH BEACH   **Lunch: $15-$16**   **Dinner: $10-$24**   **Phone: 305/674-1330**   ⟨204⟩
▽▽▽
Italian
Location: E of SR A1A (Collins Ave) and 8th Ave. 834 Ocean Dr 33139. **Hours:** 8 am-midnight, Fri & Sat-1 am. **Reservations:** suggested. **Features:** dressy casual; early bird specials; carryout; cocktails & lounge; fee for parking & valet parking; a la carte. Authentic Italian cuisine served in a setting replete with Italian tiles and hand-painted pottery give this bustling bistro a Mediterranean flair. Fresh tomatoes top the complimentary bruscetta appetizer, which is almost a meal by itself. **Cards:** AE, DI, MC, VI.   ⟨♿⟩ ✕

NEMO RESTAURANT   **Lunch: $8-$14**   **Dinner: $18-$28**   **Phone: 305/532-4550**   ⟨209⟩
▽▽▽▽
English
Location: I-95 S to 395 E to MacArthur Cswy; (5th St) s on Collins, w onto 1st St; jct 1st and Collins. 100 Collins Ave 33139. **Hours:** noon-3 & 7-midnight, Sun 11 am-3 & 6-11 pm. Closed: 8/1-8/31. **Reservations:** suggested. **Features:** Sunday brunch; cocktails & lounge; street parking & fee for valet parking; a la carte. Trendy and unique, this eatery features Asian-influenced dishes prepared with the utmost care and expertise. A nice wine list is offered for your perusal. Coconut creme brulee served in a semi-soft shell brings your meal to a sweet close. **Cards:** AE, MC, VI.

PACIFIC TIME   **Dinner: $17-$32**   **Phone: 305/534-5979**   ⟨195⟩
▽▽▽▽
Asian
Location: Between Jefferson and Michigan aves; in Lincoln Rd Pedestrain Mall. 915 Lincoln Rd 33139. **Hours:** 6 pm-11 pm, Fri & Sat-midnight. Closed: 11/22, 12/25. **Reservations:** suggested. **Features:** casual dress; early bird specials; cocktails & lounge; street parking; a la carte. California Pacific Rim cuisine is served in a bustling environment. Superb entrees are presented in an attractive, artful and innovative way by a chef who is a master of seafood preparation. Order the Key lime baked Alaska for an unusual treat. **Cards:** AE, MC, VI.   ✕

(See map p. 484)

SMITH & WOLLENSKY   Lunch: $19-$23   Dinner: $22-$38   Phone: 305/673-2800   (210)
▼▼▼▼
Traditional Steak House
Location: At Washington Ave and Biscayne St behind tall condo bldg in South Pointe Park. 1 Washington Ave 33139. **Hours:** noon-1:30 am. **Reservations:** suggested. **Features:** dressy casual; cocktails & lounge; fee for valet parking; a la carte. At the tip of "South Beach" and the entrance to Port Miami. Serving large aged prime beef, cooked as you like it. Large sides with the steak, prime rib, chops and fresh fish. A friendly and comfortable place with a very large and award winning wine list. **Cards:** AE, DI, DS, MC, VI.

WISH   Dinner: $12-$25   Phone: 305/674-9474   (212)
▼▼▼▼
Northern American
Location: On SR A1A (Collins Ave) and 8th St; in The Hotel. 801 Collins Ave 33139. **Hours:** 8 am-noon & 6-midnight. **Reservations:** suggested. **Features:** dressy casual; carryout; cocktails & lounge; fee for valet parking; a la carte. Featuring "American Fusion" with influences of Asian, Southwestern, Italian and French. All done with beef, poultry, fresh fish and some vegetarian appetizers and entrees. Beautiful desserts. The dining room and bar decor with an art deco flair. **Cards:** AE, CB, DI, DS, MC, VI.

YUCA RESTAURANT   Lunch: $5-$14   Dinner: $6-$40   Phone: 305/532-9822   (196)
▼▼▼▼
Ethnic
Location: In the Lincoln Rd Pedestrian Mall. 501 Lincoln Rd 33139. **Hours:** noon-3 & 6-11 pm, Fri & Sat midnight, Sun-10 pm. Closed: 1/1, 11/22, 12/25. **Reservations:** accepted. **Features:** dressy casual; cocktails. Expect cutting-edge Cuban entrees with a more global appeal. Gourmet items such as plantain-coated dolphin, black bean soup, and yuca filled with a wild mushroom picadillo will stir the palate. Try the dessert of coconut custard served in the shell. **Cards:** AE, DI, MC, VI.

The following restaurants have not been evaluated by AAA but are listed for your information only.

RED SQUARE   Phone: 305/672-0200
[fyi]
Not evaluated. **Location:** 411 Washington Ave. **Features:** Traditional favorites with exciting twists. Over 100 varieties of vodka. Dinner only; moderately priced.

TUSCAN STEAK   Phone: 305/534-2233
[fyi]
Not evaluated. **Location:** 431 Washington Ave. **Features:** Creative, upscale Italian cuisine. Casual, yet upscale ambience. Expensive.

TWELVE TWENTY   Phone: 305/604-5000
[fyi]
Not evaluated. **Location:** On Ocean Dr, just s of 13th St. 1220 Ocean Dr 33139. **Features:** Light French cuisine with a Mediterranean flair. Unique presentations using fresh seafood as well as meat. A neat bar area.

The Miami-Miami Beach Vicinity

AVENTURA pop. 14,900   (See map p. 478; index p. 483)

--- WHERE TO STAY ---

COURTYARD BY MARRIOTT AVENTURA MALL   Phone: (305)937-0805   (173)
▼▼▼▼
	1P: $139-$159	2P: $139-$159
12/1-12/25, 1/2-3/31 & 10/1-11/30		
4/1-9/30	1P: $139-$159	2P: $139-$159
Motel
Location: Just e of US 1 (Biscayne Blvd) at NE 191st and 28th Ave, just se of SR 856. 2825 NE 191 St 33180. Fax: 305/937-0806. **Facility:** Just a short hop from everything in Aventura. A quiet courtyard area with a relaxing pool. Many comfortable sitting areas in the lobby. Spacious rooms with light wood tones accented with soft, bright colors. 161 units. Some suites ($199-$259) and whirlpool units ($109-$209). *Bath:* combo or shower only. 5 stories, interior corridors. **Terms:** open 12/1-12/25 & 1/2-11/30, cancellation fee imposed. **Amenities:** dual phone lines, voice mail, irons, hair dryers. **Leisure Activities:** heated pool, whirlpool, exercise room. **Guest Services:** valet and coin laundry. **Business Services:** meeting rooms. **Cards:** AE, CB, DI, DS, MC, VI.

SOME UNITS
(ASK) (S₀) (†↓↑) (⟨⟩) (🖉) (🛏) (🎦) (🖨) (🖥) (DATA PORT) / (✕) (📺) (🛗) /
FEE   FEE

TURNBERRY ISLE RESORT & CLUB   Phone: (305)932-6200   (172)
▼▼▼ ▼▼▼
	1P: $265-$485	2P: $265-$485	XP: $50	F12
12/1-1/3				
1/4-4/30	1P: $375-$465	2P: $375-$465	XP: $50	F12
9/7-11/30	1P: $275-$385	2P: $275-$405	XP: $50	F12
5/1-9/6	1P: $275-$365	2P: $275-$365	XP: $50	F12
Resort
Location: 0.5 mi w of SR A1A via SR 856; or from US 1 via 199th St and Biscayne Blvd. 19999 W Country Club Dr 33180. Fax: 305/933-6554. **Facility:** In exclusive residential setting. Large well-appointed rooms. Very elegant public areas at country club. 392 units, 8 with kitchen. Some suites ($375-$3500) and whirlpool units. 5-7 stories, interior/exterior corridors. **Parking:** valet. **Terms:** check-in 4 pm, 3 day cancellation notice-fee imposed, package plans, $5 service charge. **Amenities:** extended cable TV, video games, voice mail, fax, safes, honor bars, irons, hair dryers. **Leisure Activities:** 3 heated pools, saunas, whirlpools, steamrooms, beach, swimming, charter fishing, children's program in season, jogging. *Fee:* sailboats, windsurfing, boat dock, marina, golf-36 holes, 20 tennis courts (18 lighted), bicycles. **Guest Services:** [MAP] meal plan available, gift shop, area transportation, valet laundry. *Fee:* massage. **Business Services:** conference facilities, administrative services, fax. *Fee:* PC. **Cards:** AE, CB, DI, DS, JC, MC, VI.

SOME UNITS
(¶↓) (24↑) (▼) (⟨⟩) (🖉) (🛏) (👥) (✕) (🎦) (🖨) (DATA PORT) / (✕) (VCR) (🛗) /
FEE   FEE   FEE

(See map p. 478)

─────── WHERE TO DINE ───────

CHEF ALLEN'S
▼▼▼▼ ▼▼▼▼
American

Dinner: $26-$38 **Phone:** 305/935-2900 (165)
Location: Just e of US 1 (Biscayne Blvd) at NE 191st St and NE 28th Ave, just se of jct SR 856. 19088 NE 29th Ave 33180. **Hours:** 6 pm-10:30 pm, Fri & Sat-11 pm. Closed: 7/4; also Super Bowl Sun. **Reservations:** suggested. **Features:** dressy casual; cocktails; valet parking; a la carte. Innovative New World cuisine is excellently presented in an art deco dining room. Watch the cook whip up your meal through the glass-enclosed "al vista" kitchen. A very extensive wine list and professional service add the finishing touch to a great meal. **Cards:** AE, DI, MC, VI.

BAL HARBOUR pop. 3,000   (See map p. 484; index p. 486)

─────── WHERE TO STAY ───────

SHERATON BAL HARBOUR BEACH RESORT
▼▼▼ ▼▼▼
Hotel

12/1-4/14	2P: $305-$445	XP: $25	F
10/1-11/30	2P: $245-$385	XP: $25	F
4/15-5/27	2P: $245-$285	XP: $25	F
5/28-9/30	2P: $155-$285	XP: $25	F

Phone: (305)865-7511 (262)

Location: On SR A1A, just n on SR 922. 9701 Collins Ave 33154. Fax: 305/868-2571. **Facility:** Located on the ocean. The pool area has a waterfall. The landscaped grounds consist of tropical trees and flowering plants. A large round lobby; shops on the lower level. Rooms have ocean or city views, some with balcony. 642 units. Some suites ($750-$1500) and whirlpool units. *Bath:* combo or shower only. 8-16 stories, interior corridors. **Parking:** valet. **Terms:** 3 day cancellation notice, package plans. **Amenities:** extended cable TV, video games, voice mail, safes, honor bars, irons, hair dryers. *Some:* CD players, fax. **Leisure Activities:** 2 pools, wading pool, sauna, whirlpools, waterslide, beach, swimming, landscaped heated river swimming pool with lagoons & cave, 2 lighted tennis courts, jogging. *Fee:* paddleboats, sailboating, windsurfing, scuba diving/snorkeling & equipment, charter fishing. **Guest Services:** gift shop, valet laundry. *Fee:* massage. **Business Services:** conference facilities, administrative services, fax. *Fee:* PC. **Cards:** AE, CB, DI, DS, JC, MC, VI.   SOME UNITS

─────── WHERE TO DINE ───────

CARPACCIO
▼▼▼ ▼▼
Italian

Lunch: $8-$15 **Dinner:** $14-$21 **Phone:** 305/867-7777 (233)
Location: In Bal Harbour Shops. 9700 Collins Ave 33154. **Hours:** 11:30 am-11 pm. Closed: 11/22, 12/25. **Reservations:** suggested; dinner. **Features:** casual dress; children's menu; cocktails & lounge; fee for parking. Filet mignon is used in the meat carpaccio, thin cuts of cured beef cooked and served with tangy accompaniments. Also try the swordfish carpaccio, a nice variation on the original. Salad, crusty bread, pasta and oven-baked pizza round out the menu. **Cards:** AE, DI, MC, VI.

COCONUT GROVE   (See map p. 478; index p. 482)

─────── WHERE TO STAY ───────

THE DOUBLETREE HOTEL AT COCONUT GROVE
▼▼▼ ▼▼▼
Hotel

12/29-4/15	1P: $209-$319	2P: $209-$319	XP: $10	F12
4/16-11/30	1P: $169-$209	2P: $169-$209	XP: $10	F12
12/1-12/28	1P: $149-$209	2P: $149-$209	XP: $10	F12

Phone: (305)858-2500 (116)

Location: Facing the marina. 2649 S Bayshore Dr 33133. Fax: 305/858-5776. **Facility:** Variety of rooms, some with balcony. Some facing Dinner Key Marina. 192 units. Some suites ($219-$329). *Bath:* combo or shower only. 20 stories, interior corridors. **Parking:** valet. **Terms:** cancellation fee imposed, package plans. **Amenities:** dual phone lines, voice mail, irons, hair dryers. **Leisure Activities:** heated pool, 2 lighted tennis courts, exercise room. **Business Services:** area transportation, valet laundry. *Fee:* massage. **Business Services:** meeting rooms, fax. **Cards:** AE, CB, DI, DS, JC, MC, VI.   SOME UNITS

HAMPTON INN-COCONUT GROVE/CORAL GABLES
[SAVE]
▼▼▼
Motel

12/21-4/7	1P: $129-$139	2P: $139-$149
12/1-12/20 & 4/8-11/30	1P: $94	2P: $104

Phone: (305)448-2800 (115)

Location: Just e of US 1. 2800 SW 28th Ter 33133. Fax: 305/442-8655. **Facility:** Spacious lobby. Rooms with light colors. Two level gated parking. Designated smoking area. 135 units. *Bath:* combo or shower only. 6 stories, interior corridors. **Terms:** 14 day cancellation notice. **Amenities:** extended cable TV, voice mail, irons, hair dryers. **Leisure Activities:** whirlpool, exercise room. **Guest Services:** [ECP] meal plan available, valet and coin laundry. **Business Services:** meeting rooms. **Cards:** AE, CB, DI, DS, MC, VI.   SOME UNITS

MAYFAIR HOUSE HOTEL
(AAA) [SAVE]
▼▼▼ ▼▼▼
Hotel

12/1-4/30	1P: $269-$800	2P: $269-$800	XP: $35	F14
10/1-11/30	1P: $239-$800	2P: $239-$800	XP: $35	F14
5/1-6/30	1P: $229-$800	2P: $229-$800	XP: $35	F14
7/1-9/30	1P: $189-$800	2P: $189-$800	XP: $35	F14

Phone: (305)441-0000 (119)

Location: Center; adjoining Mayfair shops at Florida Ave and Virginia St. 3000 Florida Ave 33133. Fax: 305/447-9173. **Facility:** Exotic architecture and decorations, built around tiled fountains and ground floor shopping mall. Individually designed suites. 179 units. 3 two-bedroom units. Some suites ($189-$800) and whirlpool units ($189-$800). *Bath:* combo or shower only. 5 stories, interior/exterior corridors. **Parking:** extra charge or valet. **Terms:** check-in 4 pm, cancellation fee imposed, package plans, small pets only ($200 deposit). **Amenities:** extended cable TV, video games, CD players, dual phone lines, voice mail, honor bars, irons, hair dryers. **Dining:** Mayfair Grill, see separate listing, entertainment. **Leisure Activities:** sauna, whirlpool, large rooftop bi-level whirlpool, Jamaican wading pool. *Fee:* exercise room. **Guest Services:** valet laundry. *Fee:* massage. **Business Services:** conference facilities, administrative services, fax. *Fee:* PC. **Cards:** AE, CB, DI, DS, MC, VI.   SOME UNITS

(See map p. 478)

THE MUTINY HOTEL

Phone: (305)441-2100 [118]

	12/1-3/31	1P: $375	2P: $375	XP: $25	F17
	4/1-6/15 & 10/1-11/30	1P: $275	2P: $275	XP: $25	F17
Suite Hotel	6/16-9/30	1P: $200	2P: $200	XP: $25	F17

Location: 2951 S Bayshore Dr 33133. Fax: 305/441-2822. **Facility:** The grounds are surrounded by tropical foliage. The pool also has tropical foliage and a waterfall. The lobby is decorated with soothing colors. All rooms with soft colors, light wood tones and balcony. Smoke free premises. 120 units with kitchen. 14 two-bedroom units. Some whirlpool units. 12 stories, interior corridors. **Parking:** valet. **Terms:** monthly rates available, package plans. **Amenities:** CD players, voice mail, fax, safes, irons, hair dryers. **Leisure Activities:** heated pool, sauna, whirlpool, steamroom, exercise room. *Fee:* bicycles. **Guest Services:** valet laundry. **Business Services:** meeting rooms. **Cards:** AE, CB, DI, DS, MC, VI.

SOME UNITS

WYNDHAM GRAND BAY HOTEL

Phone: (305)858-9600 [117]

	12/1-4/15	1P: $233-$293	2P: $233-$293
	10/1-11/30	1P: $245	2P: $245
Hotel	4/16-6/11	1P: $229	2P: $229
	6/12-9/30	1P: $172	2P: $172

Location: On Water Front Dr; facing Dinner Key Marinas. 2669 S Bayshore Dr 33133. Fax: 305/858-7998. **Facility:** Strikingly designed with flowering plants on each balcony. All rooms with balcony, many with view of the bay. The rooms furnished and decorated with a classic touch. 178 units. Some suites ($221-$1225). *Bath:* combo or shower only. 12 stories, interior corridors. **Parking:** valet. **Terms:** cancellation fee imposed, package plans. **Amenities:** extended cable TV, video games, CD players, dual phone lines, voice mail, fax, safes, honor bars, irons, hair dryers. **Leisure Activities:** heated pool, saunas, whirlpool, exercise room. **Guest Services:** gift shop, afternoon tea, area transportation, valet laundry. *Fee:* massage. **Business Services:** conference facilities, administrative services, fax. *Fee:* PC. **Cards:** AE, DI, MC, VI.

SOME UNITS

--------- **WHERE TO DINE** ---------

BALEEN

Lunch: $9-$18   Dinner: $19-$40   Phone: 305/857-5007 [122]

Seafood

Location: From Bayshore Dr, e on Fair Isle across bridge to Grove Isle; in the Grove Isle Resort. 4 Grove Isle 33133. **Hours:** 7 am-3 & 6-11 pm. **Reservations:** suggested. **Features:** dressy casual; Sunday brunch; cocktails & lounge; entertainment; fee for valet parking; a la carte. Two places to sit, outside and it has to be one of the most romantic in this area. All tables have view of the bay and the stars. Inside a classic room that has a golden glow. The foods will not let you down, excellent preparation and presentation. A diverse menu with plenty of seafood choices and landfood. **Cards:** AE, DI, MC, VI.

BICI RISTORANTE

Lunch: $9-$16   Dinner: $14-$36   Phone: 305/860-0960 [123]

Italian

Location: 2669 S Bayshore Dr 33133. **Hours:** 7-11 am, 11:30-3 & 6-10:30 pm, Fri & Sat-11:30 pm. **Reservations:** suggested. **Features:** dressy casual; cocktails & lounge; entertainment; fee for valet parking; a la carte. Traditional Italian cuisine served in a romantic setting, whether it's on the terrace overlooking the courtyard or in the dining room. The dining room has soft, indirect lighting. Soft jazz from the lounge flows into the room to set the mood. An assortment of fresh pasta with a variety of preparations, fresh seafood and various meat selections to choose from. An excellent wine list to compliment the courses chosen. **Cards:** AE, DI, MC, VI.

MAYFAIR GRILL

Lunch: $10-$25   Dinner: $20-$40   Phone: 305/441-0000 [125]

American

Location: Center; adjoining Mayfair shops at Florida Ave and Virginia St; in Mayfair House Hotel. 3000 Florida Ave 33133. **Hours:** 7 am-11 pm. **Reservations:** suggested. **Features:** dressy casual; Sunday brunch; cocktails & lounge; fee for valet parking; a la carte. The wait staff does a superb job of making you feel comfortable in the elegant restaurant. International flavors punctuate such artfully prepared dishes as yellowtail snapper with citrus sauce. Pureed raspberries over sponge cake make a tasty dessert. **Cards:** AE, CB, DI, DS, MC, VI.

MEZZANOTTE IN THE GROVE

Lunch: $9-$15   Dinner: $12-$21   Phone: 305/448-7677 [124]

Italian

Location: Center; adjacent Mayfair Shops at Mary and Florida sts. 3390 Mary St 33133. **Hours:** noon-3 & 6 pm-midnight, Sat & Sun 6 pm-midnight. **Reservations:** suggested. **Features:** dressy casual; cocktails & fee for valet parking. A popular, upscale bistro, it serves pizza, pasta, grilled meat and fish all cooked to perfection. An impressive seafood salad comes with shrimp and squid on a bed of arugula. Veal-stuffed tortellini smothered in cheese sauce makes a delightful entree. **Cards:** AE, DI, DS, MC, VI.

CORAL GABLES pop. 40,100   (See map p. 478; index p. 481)

—————— WHERE TO STAY ——————

THE BILTMORE HOTEL CORAL GABLES   **Phone:** (305)913-3139   98

12/1-3/31 & 10/1-11/30	1P: $319-$489	2P: $339-$489	XP: $20 F
4/1-6/30	1P: $289-$309	2P: $459	XP: $20 F
7/1-9/30	1P: $239-$409	2P: $259-$409	

Classic Hotel   **Location:** 1 mi w of Le Jeune Rd; in residential area. 1200 Anastasia Ave 33134. Fax: 305/913-3152. **Facility:** Historic. A grand hotel circa 1920s with architetural style of Mediterranean-revival with Spanish style with Moorish and Italian accents. The lobby area is most impressive with the hand painted fresco ceilings. One of America's largest and famous pools is surrounded with flowering plants and tropical trees. Some rooms overlook the Donald Ross golf course. 278 units. Some suites ($409-$489) and whirlpool units. 5-15 stories, interior corridors. **Parking:** valet. **Terms:** weekly & monthly rates available, package plans, $5 service charge. **Amenities:** extended cable TV, video games, dual phone lines, voice mail, safes, honor bars, irons, hair dryers. **Leisure Activities:** heated pool, saunas, steamrooms, jogging. *Fee:* golf-18 holes, 10 lighted tennis courts, bicycles. **Guest Services:** gift shop, afternoon tea, area transportation, valet laundry. *Fee:* massage. **Business Services:** conference facilities, administrative services, fax. *Fee:* PC. **Cards:** AE, CB, DI, DS, JC, MC, VI.   SOME UNITS

(ASK) (SD) (⊀) (📶) (24) (❗) (👁) (🏊) (🐾) (✕) (📷) (🖨) (DATA PORT) / (✕) (🛗) /
FEE   FEE

HOLIDAY INN CORAL GABLES BUSINESS DISTRICT   **Phone:** (305)443-2301   97

1/15-4/30	1P: $129-$159	2P: $129-$159	XP: $10 F18
9/16-11/30	1P: $109-$139	2P: $109-$134	XP: $10 F18
12/1-1/14	1P: $109-$129	2P: $109-$129	XP: $10 F18
5/1-9/15	1P: $99-$129	2P: $99-$129	XP: $10 F18

Motor Inn   **Location:** On SR 953 (Le Jeune Rd), 0.8 mi s of jct US 41. 2051 Le Jeune Rd 33134. Fax: 305/446-6827. **Facility:** Contemporary room appointments with light tropical wood tones with soft accent decor package. 168 units. *Bath:* combo or shower only. 6 stories, interior corridors. **Terms:** package plans. **Amenities:** irons, hair dryers. **Leisure Activities:** exercise room. **Guest Services:** [BP] meal plan available, coin laundry. **Business Services:** meeting rooms. **Cards:** AE, CB, DI, DS, JC, MC, VI.   SOME UNITS

(ASK) (SD) (⊀) (❗) (❗) (👁) (🏊) (📷) (🖥) (DATA PORT) / (✕) (🛗)
FEE

HOLIDAY INN UNIVERSITY OF MIAMI   **Phone:** (305)667-5611   100

1/1-4/15	2P: $149-$189	
12/17-12/31	2P: $129-$169	
4/16-11/30	2P: $119-$159	
12/1-12/16	2P: $119-$139	

(AAA) (SAVE)

Motor Inn   **Location:** US 1; facing University of Miami campus. 1350 S Dixie Hwy 33146. Fax: 305/669-3153. **Facility:** An inviting lobby with comfortable sitting areas. Attractive pool area with large deck and a tropical feel. Rooms with a contemporary flair. 155 units. *Bath:* combo or shower only. 3 stories, interior corridors. **Terms:** weekly & monthly rates available. **Amenities:** video games, irons, hair dryers. **Dining:** restaurant, 6:30 am-2 & 5-10 pm patio dining, $9-$15, cocktails. **Leisure Activities:** exercise room. **Guest Services:** [CP] & [MAP] meal plans available, valet and coin laundry. **Business Services:** meeting rooms. **Cards:** AE, CB, DI, DS, JC, MC, VI. **Special Amenities:** preferred room (subject to availability with advanced reservations).   SOME UNITS

(SD) (❗) (❗) (👶) (👁) (🏊) (📷) (🖨) (🖥) (DATA PORT) / (✕) (🖥) (🛗) /
FEE   FEE

(See map p. 478)

HYATT REGENCY CORAL GABLES

AAA SAVE

Hotel

Phone: (305)441-1234   101

12/1-6/15 & 9/16-11/30	1P: $274	2P: $299	XP: $25 F18
6/16-9/15	1P: $199	2P: $224	XP: $25 F18

Location: Downtown at Alhambra Plaza and Douglas Rd. 50 Alhambra Plaza 33134. Fax: 305/441-0520. **Facility:** Elegantly decorated with Spanish theme. Large rooms with decor and furniture affording light airy relaxed living style. Few rooms with balcony. Foreign exchange. 242 units, 2 with efficiency. Some suites and whirlpool units. *Bath:* combo or shower only. 14 stories, interior corridors. **Parking:** extra charge or valet. **Terms:** cancellation fee imposed, package plans. **Amenities:** dual phone lines, voice mail, safes, honor bars, irons, hair dryers. *Some:* CD players. **Dining:** restaurant, 7 am-3 & 6-11 pm, $18-$25, cocktails, nightclub. **Leisure Activities:** heated pool, saunas, whirlpool, steamrooms, exercise room. *Fee:* children's program. **Guest Services:** [BP] meal plan available, gift shop, valet laundry. **Business Services:** conference facilities, administrative services, fax. *Fee:* PC. **Cards:** AE, CB, DI, DS, JC, MC, VI.

SOME UNITS

🍴 🍸 ♿ 🛁 📡 🏞 🎦 🖥 💻 📊PORT / ✕ VCR 🖥 📱 /
FEE   FEE

OMNI COLONNADE HOTEL

Hotel

Phone: (305)441-2600   102

1/7-5/5	1P: $285-$325	2P: $285-$325	XP: $20 F18
7/1-11/30	1P: $195-$325	2P: $195-$325	XP: $20 F18
12/1-1/6	1P: $269-$309	2P: $269-$309	XP: $20 F18
5/6-6/30	1P: $239-$279	2P: $239-$279	XP: $20 F18

Location: Downtown at Aragon Ave and Ponce de Leon Ave. 180 Aragon Ave 33134. Fax: 305/445-3929. **Facility:** Elegant luxury hotel, built around restored 1926 Rotunda building. The floors with pink and green marble, hand blown chandeliers and mahogany trim accent the public areas. The rooms are oversized with handcrafted mahogany furniture. The restaurant is a theme of the 1920s. 157 units. Some suites. 7 stories, interior corridors. **Parking:** extra charge or valet. **Terms:** cancellation fee imposed, package plans. **Amenities:** dual phone lines, voice mail, fax, honor bars, irons, hair dryers. *Some:* CD players, safes. **Leisure Activities:** heated pool, saunas, whirlpool, exercise room. **Guest Services:** gift shop, valet laundry. **Business Services:** conference facilities. **Cards:** AE, CB, DI, DS, JC, MC, VI. *(See color ad p 514)*

SOME UNITS

A$K S📊D 🍴 24🍴 🍸 🛁 🏞 🎦 🖥 💻 📊PORT / ✕ /
FEE

RIVIERA COURT MOTEL

AAA SAVE

Motel

Phone: (305)665-3528   99

12/20-4/15	1P: $75-$87	2P: $75-$87	XP: $5 F12
4/16-11/30	1P: $68-$80	2P: $68-$80	XP: $5 F12
12/1-12/19	1P: $63-$75	2P: $63-$75	XP: $5 F12

Location: US 1, just s of jct SR 953 (LeJeune Rd). 5100 Riviera Dr 33146. Fax: 305/667-8993. **Facility:** A motel built in the 50s located along the waterway. Most rooms overlook the waterway and the pool. The rooms are very well maintained. 31 units, 14 with efficiency. *Bath:* combo or shower only. 2 stories, exterior corridors. **Terms:** 7 day cancellation notice-fee imposed. **Amenities:** extended cable TV, voice mail. **Leisure Activities:** heated pool. **Cards:** AE, CB, DI, DS, MC, VI. **Special Amenities:** free room upgrade and preferred room (each subject to availability with advanced reservations). *(See color ad below)*

SOME UNITS

S📊D 🏞 🖥 📊PORT / 💻 🖥 📱 /

------ **WHERE TO DINE** ------

BOTTICELLI TRATTORIA

Italian

Lunch: $10-$15   **Dinner:** $10-$20   **Phone:** 305/444-3357   96

Location: Just n of Alhambra Plaza, just n of Coral Gables Elementary School. 1915 Ponce de Leon Blvd 33134. **Hours:** noon-2:30 & 6-10:30 pm, Fri-11 pm, Sat 6 pm-11 pm. Closed: Sun. **Reservations:** accepted. **Features:** dressy casual; children's menu; carryout; beer & wine only; street parking. Simple dishes like veal scaloppini and chicken thighs with sausage and peppers are served in an Italian village setting. Seafood specials like grouper with spinach, tomato, radicchio and garlic are not to be missed. Fresh pasta makes a tasty side dish. Smoke free premises. **Cards:** AE, DI, MC, VI.

✕

CAFFE ABBRACCI

Northern Italian

Lunch: $9-$15   **Dinner:** $14-$28   **Phone:** 305/441-0700   109

Location: Downtown; at Aragon Ave and Salzedo, just e of Le Jeune Rd. 318 Aragon Ave 33134. **Hours:** 11:30 am-3 & 6-11:30 pm, Fri-midnight, Sat 6 pm-midnight, Sun 6 pm-11:30 pm. **Reservations:** suggested. **Features:** dressy casual; cocktails & lounge; street parking & fee for valet parking; a la carte. Exquisitely prepared Venetian specialties are served in an elegant yet casually decorated dining room with a wonderful, fun ambience. The owner supervises the entire operation so rest assured you will enjoy a well-prepared, delicious dinner. **Cards:** AE, CB, DI, MC, VI.

✕

(See map p. 478)

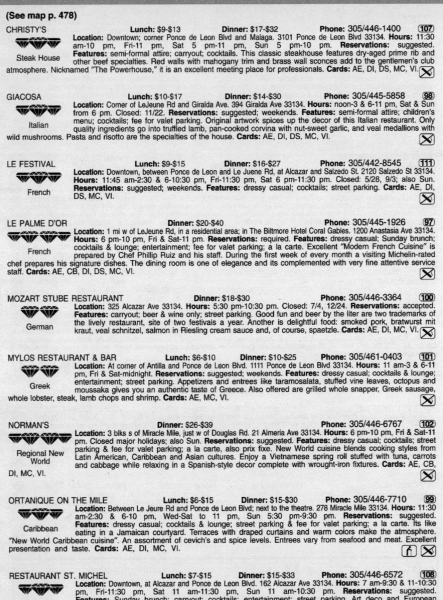

CHRISTY'S
▼▼▼▼
Steak House
Lunch: $9-$13   **Dinner:** $17-$32   **Phone:** 305/446-1400   (107)
Location: Downtown; corner Ponce de Leon Blvd and Malaga. 3101 Ponce de Leon Blvd 33134. **Hours:** 11:30 am-10 pm, Fri-11 pm, Sat 5 pm-11 pm, Sun 5 pm-10 pm. **Reservations:** suggested. **Features:** semi-formal attire; carryout; cocktails. This classic steakhouse features dry-aged prime rib and other beef specialties. Red walls with mahogany trim and brass wall sconces add to the gentlemen's club atmosphere. Nicknamed "The Powerhouse," it is an excellent meeting place for professionals. **Cards:** AE, DI, DS, MC, VI.

GIACOSA
▼▼▼▼
Italian
Lunch: $10-$17   **Dinner:** $14-$30   **Phone:** 305/445-5858   (98)
Location: Corner of LeJeune Rd and Giralda Ave. 394 Giralda Ave 33134. **Hours:** noon-3 & 6-11 pm, Sat & Sun from 6 pm. **Closed:** 11/22. **Reservations:** suggested; weekends. **Features:** semi-formal attire; children's menu; cocktails; fee for valet parking. Original artwork spices up the decor of this Italian restaurant. Only quality ingredients go into truffled lamb, pan-cooked corvina with nut-sweet garlic, and veal medallions with wild mushrooms. Pasta and risotto are the specialties of the house. **Cards:** AE, DI, DS, MC, VI.

LE FESTIVAL
▼▼▼▼
French
Lunch: $9-$15   **Dinner:** $16-$27   **Phone:** 305/442-8545   (111)
Location: Downtown, between Ponce de Leon and Le Juene Rd, at Alcazar and Salzedo St. 2120 Salzedo St 33134. **Hours:** 11:45 am-2:30 & 6-10:30 pm, Fri-11:30 pm, Sat 6 pm-11:30 pm. **Closed:** 5/28, 9/3; also Sun. **Reservations:** suggested; weekends. **Features:** dressy casual; cocktails; street parking. **Cards:** AE, DI, DS, MC, VI.

LE PALME D'OR
▼▼▼▼▼
French
Dinner: $20-$40   **Phone:** 305/445-1926   (97)
Location: 1 mi w of LeJeune Rd, in a residential area; in The Biltmore Hotel Coral Gables. 1200 Anastasia Ave 33134. **Hours:** 6 pm-10 pm, Fri & Sat-11 pm. **Reservations:** required. **Features:** dressy casual; Sunday brunch; cocktails & lounge; entertainment; fee for valet parking; a la carte. Excellent "Modern French Cuisine" is prepared by Chef Phillip Ruiz and his staff. During the first week of every month a visiting Michelin-rated chef prepares his signature dishes. The dining room is one of elegance and its complemented with very fine attentive service staff. **Cards:** AE, CB, DI, DS, MC, VI.

MOZART STUBE RESTAURANT
▼▼▼▼
German
Dinner: $18-$30   **Phone:** 305/446-3364   (100)
Location: 325 Alcazar Ave 33134. **Hours:** 5:30 pm-10:30 pm. **Closed:** 7/4, 12/24. **Reservations:** accepted. **Features:** carryout; beer & wine only; street parking. Good fun and beer by the liter are two trademarks of the lively restaurant, site of two festivals a year. Another is delightful food: smoked pork, bratwurst mit kraut, veal schnitzel, salmon in Riesling cream sauce and, of course, spaetzle. **Cards:** AE, DI, MC, VI.

MYLOS RESTAURANT & BAR
▼▼▼
Greek
Lunch: $6-$10   **Dinner:** $10-$25   **Phone:** 305/461-0403   (101)
Location: At corner of Antilla and Ponce de Leon Blvd 33134. 1111 Ponce de Leon Blvd 33134. **Hours:** 11 am-3 & 6-11 pm, Fri & Sat-midnight. **Reservations:** suggested; weekends. **Features:** dressy casual; cocktails & lounge; entertainment; street parking. Appetizers and entrees like taramosalata, stuffed vine leaves, octopus and moussaka gives you an authentic taste of Greece. Also offered are grilled whole snapper, Greek sausage, whole lobster, steak, lamb chops and shrimp. **Cards:** AE, MC, VI.

NORMAN'S
▼▼▼▼ ▼▼▼▼
Regional New
World
Dinner: $26-$39   **Phone:** 305/446-6767   (102)
Location: 3 blks s of Miracle Mile, just w of Douglas Rd. 21 Almeria Ave 33134. **Hours:** 6 pm-10 pm, Fri & Sat-11 pm. Closed major holidays; also Sun. **Reservations:** suggested. **Features:** dressy casual; cocktails; street parking & fee for valet parking; a la carte, also prix fixe. New World cuisine blends cooking styles from Latin American, Caribbean and Asian cultures. Enjoy a Vietnamese spring roll stuffed with tuna, carrots and cabbage while relaxing in a Spanish-style decor complete with wrought-iron fixtures. **Cards:** AE, CB, DI, MC, VI.

ORTANIQUE ON THE MILE
▼▼▼
Caribbean
Lunch: $6-$15   **Dinner:** $15-$30   **Phone:** 305/446-7710   (99)
Location: Between Le Jeure Rd and Ponce de Leon Blvd; next to the theatre. 278 Miracle Mile 33134. **Hours:** 11:30 am-2:30 & 6-10 pm, Wed-Sat to 11 pm, Sun 5:30 pm-9:30 pm. **Reservations:** suggested. **Features:** dressy casual; cocktails & lounge; street parking & fee for valet parking; a la carte. Its like eating in a Jamaican courtyard. Terraces with draped curtains and warm colors make the atmosphere. "New World Caribbean cuisine". An assortment of cevich's and spice levels. Entrees vary from seafood and meat. Excellent presentation and taste. **Cards:** AE, DI, MC, VI.

RESTAURANT ST. MICHEL
▼▼▼
American
Lunch: $7-$15   **Dinner:** $15-$33   **Phone:** 305/446-6572   (108)
Location: Downtown, at Alcazar and Ponce de Leon Blvd. 162 Alcazar Ave 33134. **Hours:** 7 am-9:30 & 11-10:30 pm, Fri-11:30 pm, Sat 11 am-11:30 pm, Sun 11 am-10:30 pm. **Reservations:** suggested. **Features:** Sunday brunch; carryout; cocktails; entertainment; street parking. Art deco and European influences intermingle in the intimate dining room of the 1926 hotel. Glowing pink lights and fancy chandeliers contribute to an air of romance. Savor the Maryland crabcakes and the yellowtail snapper with tropical fruit salsa. **Cards:** AE, DI, MC, VI.

———— *The following restaurant has not been evaluated by AAA* ————
but is listed for your information only.

THE HEIGHTS
[fyi]
Phone: 305/461-1774
Not evaluated. **Location:** 2530 Ponce de Leon Blvd. **Features:** Creative blending of Southwest and Asian cuisine. Excellent combinations of flavors and ingredients; expensive.

CUTLER RIDGE pop. 21,200

———— WHERE TO STAY ————

BAYMONT INN & SUITES-MIAMI (CUTLER RIDGE)   Phone: (305)278-0001

1/26-4/14	1P: $84-$89	2P: $84-$89
12/1-1/25	1P: $74-$79	2P: $74-$79
4/15-11/30	1P: $69-$74	2P: $69-$74

Motel
Location: Florida Tpke, exit 12 (US 1), nw corner. 10821 Caribbean Blvd 33189. Fax: 305/278-0222. **Facility:** A contemporary structure with nearby shopping and eating choices. Designated smoking area. 105 units. Some suites ($89-$134). *Bath:* combo or shower only. 4 stories, interior corridors. **Terms:** small pets only ($50 deposit). **Amenities:** video games, voice mail, irons, hair dryers. **Guest Services:** [CP] meal plan available, valet and coin laundry. **Business Services:** meeting rooms. **Cards:** AE, CB, DI, DS, MC, VI. *(See color ad p 523)*

SOME UNITS

FLORIDA CITY pop. 5,600

———— WHERE TO STAY ————

BEST WESTERN GATEWAY TO THE KEYS   Phone: (305)246-5100

12/23-4/30	1P: $89-$179	2P: $89-$179	XP: $10	F18
5/1-11/30	1P: $69-$179	2P: $79-$179	XP: $10	F18
12/1-12/22	1P: $69-$89	2P: $69-$99	XP: $10	F18

Motel
Location: On US 1, 0.8 mi s of Florida Tpke terminus. 411 S Krome Ave 33034. Fax: 305/242-0056. **Facility:** Very attractive, built in Key West style with tropical courtyard. Smoke free premises. 114 units. *Bath:* combo or shower only. 2 stories, exterior corridors. **Terms:** 5 day cancellation notice. **Amenities:** extended cable TV. **Leisure Activities:** whirlpool. **Guest Services:** coin laundry. **Business Services:** meeting rooms. **Cards:** AE, CB, DI, DS, MC, VI. **Special Amenities:** free continental breakfast and free local telephone calls.

SOME UNITS

COMFORT INN   Phone: (305)248-4009

12/25-3/25		2P: $36-$199	XP: $10	F18
3/26-11/30		2P: $32-$199	XP: $5	F18
12/1-12/24		2P: $32-$79	XP: $5	F18

Motel
Location: On US 1, 0.8 mi s of Florida Tpke terminus. 333 SE 1st Ave 33034. Fax: 305/248-7935. **Facility:** Large rooms, contemporary decor. 83 units. 2 stories, interior corridors. **Terms:** weekly rates available. **Amenities:** extended cable TV, voice mail, safes. *Some:* irons, hair dryers. **Guest Services:** [ECP] meal plan available, coin laundry. **Cards:** AE, CB, DI, DS, JC, MC, VI.

SOME UNITS

CORAL ROC MOTEL   Phone: (305)246-2888

12/24-3/31	1P: $45-$68	2P: $48-$78	XP: $5	F12
4/1-11/30	1P: $30-$34	2P: $32-$36		
12/1-12/23	1P: $30-$34	2P: $32-$36	XP: $5	F12

Motel
Location: On SR 997; just w of US 1, 0.5 mi s of Homestead. 1100 N Krome Ave 33034. Fax: 305/242-1580. **Facility:** Bright contemporary appeal. All rooms with two double beds and at-door parking. 17 units. 2 efficiencies and 2 units with kitchen (no utensils). 1 story, exterior corridors. **Terms:** pets ($50 deposit). **Leisure Activities:** small pool. **Guest Services:** coin laundry. **Cards:** AE, CB, DI, DS, MC, VI. **Special Amenities:** free local telephone calls and preferred room (subject to availability with advanced reservations).

ECONO LODGE   Phone: (305)248-9300

1/1-3/31	1P: $65-$145	2P: $70-$150	XP: $7	F10
12/1-12/31	1P: $65-$137	2P: $70-$137	XP: $7	F10
4/16-11/30	1P: $45-$75	2P: $50-$80	XP: $7	F10

Motel
Location: US 1 at Florida Tpke, exit 1. 553 NE 1st Ave 33034. Fax: 305/245-2753. **Facility:** Large rooms, contemporary decor. 42 units. *Bath:* combo or shower only. 2 stories, interior corridors. **Terms:** 7 day cancellation notice-fee imposed. **Amenities:** extended cable TV. **Leisure Activities:** small pool. **Guest Services:** valet laundry. **Business Services:** meeting rooms. **Cards:** AE, CB, DI, DS, MC, VI. **Special Amenities:** free continental breakfast and preferred room (subject to availability with advanced reservations).

SOME UNITS

HAMPTON INN   Phone: (305)247-8833

12/1-4/15	1P: $80-$100	XP: $10	F19
4/16-11/30	1P: $55-$70	XP: $10	F19

Motel
Location: On US 1, 0.3 mi s of Florida Tpke terminus. 124 E Palm Dr 33034. Fax: 305/247-6456. **Facility:** Contemporary appointed rooms. 123 units. 2 stories, exterior corridors. **Terms:** small pets only. **Amenities:** extended cable TV, voice mail, irons, hair dryers. **Guest Services:** [ECP] meal plan available, valet laundry. **Cards:** AE, CB, DI, DS, MC, VI.

SOME UNITS

KNIGHTS INN

◆◆◆ ◆◆◆

Motel

	1P: $39-$99	2P: $39-$99	XP: $5	F16
12/22-3/31	1P: $30-$36	2P: $30-$36	XP: $5	F16
12/1-12/21 & 4/1-11/30				

Phone: (305)247-6633

Location: On US 1, just n of Florida Tpke terminus/exit 1. 1223 NE 1st Ave (US Hwy 1) 33034. Fax: 305/247-7515. **Facility:** Contemporary decor. Many rooms with ground floor entry. 48 units, 5 with kitchen. 1-2 stories, exterior corridors. **Terms:** 14 day cancellation notice, weekly rates available. **Amenities:** extended cable TV. **Guest Services:** [CP] meal plan available, coin laundry. **Cards:** AE, DI, DS, MC, VI.

SOME UNITS

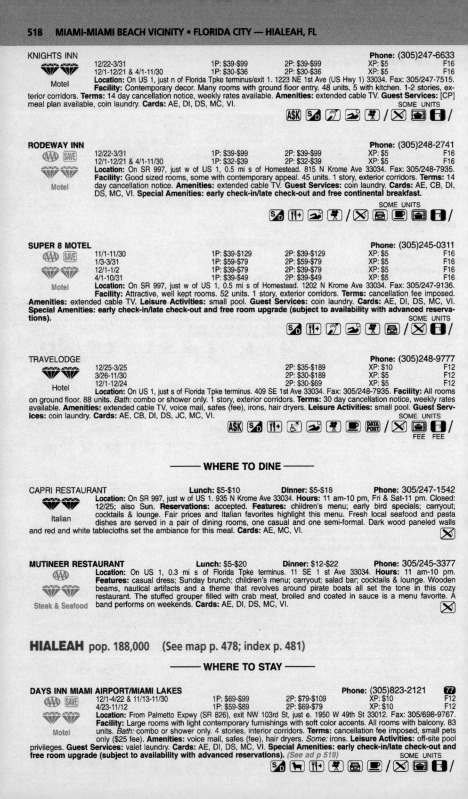

RODEWAY INN

◆◆◆ [SAVE]

◆◆ ◆◆

Motel

	1P: $39-$99	2P: $39-$99	XP: $5	F16
12/22-3/31	1P: $32-$39	2P: $32-$39	XP: $5	F16
12/1-12/21 & 4/1-11/30				

Phone: (305)248-2741

Location: On SR 997, just w of US 1, 0.5 mi s of Homestead. 815 N Krome Ave 33034. Fax: 305/248-7935. **Facility:** Good sized rooms, some with contemporary appeal. 45 units. 1 story, exterior corridors. **Terms:** 14 day cancellation notice. **Amenities:** extended cable TV. **Guest Services:** coin laundry. **Cards:** AE, CB, DI, DS, MC, VI. **Special Amenities:** early check-in/late check-out and free continental breakfast.

SOME UNITS

SUPER 8 MOTEL

◆◆◆ [SAVE]

◆◆ ◆◆

Motel

	1P: $39-$129	2P: $39-$129	XP: $5	F16
11/1-11/30	1P: $59-$79	2P: $59-$79	XP: $5	F16
1/3-3/31	1P: $39-$79	2P: $39-$79	XP: $5	F16
12/1-1/2	1P: $39-$49	2P: $39-$49	XP: $5	F16
4/1-10/31				

Phone: (305)245-0311

Location: On SR 997, just w of US 1, 0.5 mi s of Homestead. 1202 N Krome Ave 33034. Fax: 305/247-9136. **Facility:** Attractive, well kept rooms. 52 units. 1 story, exterior corridors. **Terms:** cancellation fee imposed. **Amenities:** extended cable TV. **Leisure Activities:** small pool. **Guest Services:** coin laundry. **Cards:** AE, DI, DS, MC, VI. **Special Amenities:** early check-in/late check-out and free room upgrade (subject to availability with advanced reservations).

SOME UNITS

TRAVELODGE

◆◆ ◆◆

Hotel

		2P: $35-$189	XP: $10	F12
12/25-3/25		2P: $30-$189	XP: $5	F12
3/26-11/30		2P: $30-$69	XP: $5	F12
12/1-12/24				

Phone: (305)248-9777

Location: On US 1, just s of Florida Tpke terminus. 409 SE 1st Ave 33034. Fax: 305/248-7935. **Facility:** All rooms on ground floor. 88 units. *Bath:* combo or shower only. 1 story, exterior corridors. **Terms:** 30 day cancellation notice, weekly rates available. **Amenities:** extended cable TV, voice mail, safes (fee), irons, hair dryers. **Leisure Activities:** small pool. **Guest Services:** coin laundry. **Cards:** AE, CB, DI, DS, JC, MC, VI.

SOME UNITS

FEE   FEE

───── **WHERE TO DINE** ─────

CAPRI RESTAURANT

◆◆◆ ◆◆◆

Italian

Lunch: $5-$10   **Dinner:** $5-$18   **Phone:** 305/247-1542

Location: On SR 997, just w of US 1. 935 N Krome Ave 33034. **Hours:** 11 am-10 pm, Fri & Sat-11 pm. Closed: 12/25; also Sun. **Reservations:** accepted. **Features:** children's menu; early bird specials; carryout; cocktails & lounge. Fair prices and Italian favorites highlight this menu. Fresh local seafood and pasta dishes are served in a pair of dining rooms, one casual and one semi-formal. Dark wood paneled walls and red and white tablecloths set the ambiance for this meal. **Cards:** AE, MC, VI.

MUTINEER RESTAURANT

◆◆◆

◆◆ ◆◆

Steak & Seafood

Lunch: $5-$20   **Dinner:** $12-$22   **Phone:** 305/245-3377

Location: On US 1, 0.3 mi s of Florida Tpke terminus. 11 SE 1 st Ave 33034. **Hours:** 11 am-10 pm. **Features:** casual dress; Sunday brunch; children's menu; carryout; salad bar; cocktails & lounge. Wooden beams, nautical artifacts and a theme that revolves around pirate boats all set the tone in this cozy restaurant. The stuffed grouper filled with crab meat, broiled and coated in sauce is a menu favorite. A band performs on weekends. **Cards:** AE, DI, DS, MC, VI.

HIALEAH pop. 188,000   (See map p. 478; index p. 481)

───── **WHERE TO STAY** ─────

DAYS INN MIAMI AIRPORT/MIAMI LAKES

◆◆◆ [SAVE]

◆◆ ◆◆

Motel

	1P: $69-$99	2P: $79-$109	XP: $10	F12
12/1-4/22 & 11/13-11/30	1P: $59-$89	2P: $69-$79	XP: $10	F12
4/23-11/12				

Phone: (305)823-2121   [77]

Location: From Palmetto Expwy (SR 826), exit NW 103rd St, just e. 1950 W 49th St 33012. Fax: 305/698-9767. **Facility:** Large rooms with light contemporary furnishings with soft color accents. All rooms with balcony. 83 units. *Bath:* combo or shower only. 4 stories, interior corridors. **Terms:** cancellation fee imposed, small pets only ($25 fee). **Amenities:** voice mail, safes (fee), hair dryers. *Some:* irons. **Leisure Activities:** off-site pool privileges. **Guest Services:** valet laundry. **Cards:** AE, DI, DS, MC, VI. **Special Amenities:** early check-in/late check-out and free room upgrade (subject to availability with advanced reservations). *(See ad p 519)*

SOME UNITS

(See map p. 478)

HOLIDAY INN HIALEAH/MIAMI LAKES

Phone: (305)362-7777   **76**

Property failed to provide current rates

Motor Inn

Location: At jct of SR 826 (Palmetto Expwy) and NW 122nd St, NW 138th St and W 68th St exit, then w on NW 122nd St. 6650 W 20th Ave 33016. Fax: 305/826-8107. **Facility:** Located just off the freeway. A fenced pool area. Contemporary room decor. 144 units. Some suites and whirlpool units. 5 stories, interior corridors. **Terms:** 3 day cancellation notice-fee imposed, weekly & monthly rates available. **Amenities:** video games, irons, hair dryers. **Leisure Activities:** heated pool. **Guest Services:** valet and coin laundry. **Business Services:** meeting rooms. **Cards:** AE, CB, DI, DS, MC, VI.

SOME UNITS

RAMADA INN-MIAMI AIRPORT NORTH

Phone: (305)823-2000   **78**

12/1-4/22	1P: $69-$99	2P: $79-$109	XP: $10 F17
4/23-11/30	1P: $59-$89	2P: $69-$99	XP: $10 F17

Motor Inn

Location: From Palmetto Expwy (SR 826), exit NW 103rd St, just e. 1950 W 49th St 33012. Fax: 305/362-4562. **Facility:** Large rooms with contemporary decor. All rooms with balcony, some with pool view. 171 units. 4 stories, interior corridors. **Terms:** 3 day cancellation notice, weekly & monthly rates available, small pets only ($25 extra charge). **Amenities:** voice mail, safes (fee). *Some:* irons, hair dryers. **Dining:** restaurant, 6 am-2 & 5-10 pm, $7-$18, cocktails. **Leisure Activities:** wading pool. **Guest Services:** gift shop, airport transportation-MIA, area transportation-Port of Miami, valet and coin laundry. **Business Services:** meeting rooms. **Cards:** AE, CB, DI, DS, MC, VI. **Special Amenities:** early check-in/late check-out and free newspaper. *(See ad below)*

SOME UNITS

WHERE TO DINE

The following restaurant has not been evaluated by AAA but is listed for your information only.

FLANIGAN'S SEAFOOD BAR & GRILL

Phone: 305/821-0993

[fyi] Not evaluated. **Location:** 1550 W 84th St. **Features:** Casual atmosphere that is inexpensive and family friendly. Known for their baby back ribs, large burgers and fresh local seafood.

HOMESTEAD pop. 26,900

WHERE TO STAY

EVERGLADES MOTEL

Phone: (305)247-4117

12/24-3/31	1P: $39-$58	2P: $44-$68	XP: $5 F12
12/1-12/23 & 4/1-11/30	1P: $27-$32	2P: $29-$34	XP: $5 F12

Motel

Location: Just w of US 1 between Lucy and 6th sts; on SR 997, 0.5 mi s of center of town. 605 S Krome Ave 33030. **Facility:** Rooms with bright contemporary appeal. Located at the edge of the downtown area. All rooms with at-door parking. 14 units. *Bath:* combo or shower only. 1 story, exterior corridors. **Terms:** weekly rates available, small pets only. **Amenities:** extended cable TV. **Leisure Activities:** small pool. **Guest Services:** coin laundry. **Cards:** AE, DI, DS, MC, VI. **Special Amenities:** free local telephone calls and preferred room (subject to availability with advanced reservations).

SOME UNITS

HOMESTEAD DAYS INN

Phone: (305)245-1260

12/24-4/15	1P: $78	2P: $99-$109	XP: $10 F
4/16-11/30	1P: $52-$59	2P: $55-$65	XP: $10 F
12/1-12/23	1P: $52	2P: $65	XP: $10 F

Motel

Location: On US 1; 1.2 mi n of Florida Tpke. 320 St SW and US 1. 51 S Homestead Blvd 33030. Fax: 305/247-0939. **Facility:** Attractively furnished rooms in several buildings. Located at the edge of the business district. 109 units. 2 stories, exterior corridors. **Terms:** 3 day cancellation notice, pets ($7 extra charge). **Guest Services:** [CP] meal plan available, coin laundry. **Cards:** AE, CB, DI, DS, JC, MC, VI. **Amenities:** extended cable TV, safes (fee).

SOME UNITS

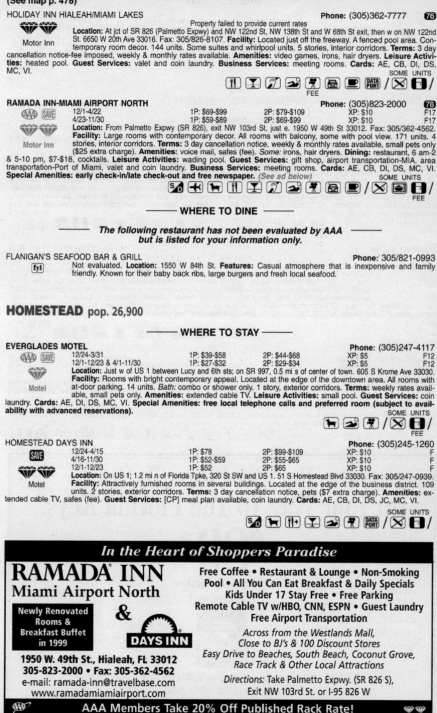

--------- WHERE TO DINE ---------

EL TORO TACO

♦

Mexican

Lunch: $4-$9   **Dinner:** $7-$11   **Phone:** 305/245-8182
Location: Corner of Mowry Dr and SW 177 Ave. 1 S Krome Ave 33030. **Hours:** 10 am-9 pm, Fri-10 pm.
Features: casual dress; carryout; street parking. Enchiladas, burritos and fajitas are served up mild style in this warm and cozy family-owned restaurant, where everything is made from scratch. Take in the fresh air in the outdoor courtyard or dine inside. You're welcome to brown bag your own beer. **Cards:** DS, MC, VI.

KENDALL pop. 17,900   (See map p. 478; index p. 483)

--------- WHERE TO STAY ---------

AMERISUITES

Ⓐ ⓢⒶⓋⒺ

▽▽▽▽

Suite Motel

Phone: (305)279-8688   184

1/1-4/15	1P: $129-$169	2P: $139-$179	XP: $10 F18
12/1-12/31 & 4/16-11/30	1P: $119-$149	2P: $129-$159	XP: $10 F18

Location: Florida Tpke, exit 20 (SW 88th [Kendall Dr], just e on SR 94; behind McDonalds, 0.3 mi s. 11520 SW 88th St 33176. Fax: 305/279-7907. **Facility:** Across from Town and Country Mall. Stylish lobby area, spacious rooms tastefully furnished. 67 units. *Bath:* combo or shower only. 5 stories, interior corridors. **Terms:** small pets only. **Amenities:** video games, voice mail, irons, hair dryers. **Leisure Activities:** heated pool. **Guest Services:** [ECP] meal plan available, complimentary evening beverages: midweek, valet and coin laundry. **Business Services:** meeting rooms, administrative services, PC. **Cards:** AE, DI, DS, MC, VI. **Special Amenities:** free continental breakfast and free newspaper. *(See color ad p 5)*   SOME UNITS

COMFORT SUITES

Ⓐ ⓢⒶⓋⒺ

▽▽▽▽

Motel

Phone: (305)220-3901   183

12/1-4/30	1P: $109-$119	2P: $119-$129	XP: $10 F18
5/1-11/30	1P: $99-$109	2P: $109-$119	XP: $10 F18

Location: From Florida Tpke, s to SW 40th St, exit 23, e to SW 117th Ave, n to entrance. 3901 SW 117th Ave 33175. Fax: 305/221-1348. **Facility:** Large, colorful rooms with bright accents and sitting area. 132 units. Some suites ($99-$129) and whirlpool units ($159-$199). *Bath:* combo or shower only. 5 stories, interior corridors. **Amenities:** dual phone lines, voice mail, irons, hair dryers. **Leisure Activities:** heated pool, whirlpool, exercise room. **Guest Services:** [ECP] meal plan available, valet and coin laundry. **Business Services:** meeting rooms, administrative services, PC, fax. **Cards:** AE, CB, DI, JC, MC, VI. **Special Amenities:** free continental breakfast and free local telephone calls. *(See color ad below)*   SOME UNITS

WELLESLEY INN & SUITES

Ⓐ ⓢⒶⓋⒺ

▽▽▽▽

Motel

Phone: (305)270-0359   185

12/1-3/31	1P: $99-$109	2P: $109-$119	XP: $10 F16
4/1-11/30	1P: $79-$89	2P: $89-$99	XP: $10 F16

Location: Florida Tpke, SW 88th exit (Kendall Dr), 0.3 mi w on SR 94, 0.3 mi n on SW 117 Ave; adjoining Town and Country Mall. 11750 Mills Dr 33183. Fax: 305/270-1334. **Facility:** Overlooking small ornamental lake. Tastefully furnished and decorated rooms. 106 units. Some suites. *Bath:* combo or shower only. 4 stories, interior corridors. **Amenities:** extended cable TV, video games, voice mail, hair dryers. **Leisure Activities:** heated pool. **Guest Services:** [ECP] meal plan available, valet laundry. **Cards:** AE, CB, DI, DS, MC, VI. **Special Amenities:** free continental breakfast and free local telephone calls. *(See color ad opposite title page)*   SOME UNITS

(See map p. 478)

——— **WHERE TO DINE** ———

GIL CAPA'S BISTRO   **Lunch:** $5-$6   **Dinner:** $7-$14   **Phone:** 305/273-1102   `176`
▼▼▼ ▼▼▼   **Location:** Jct SW 113th Pl and SW 107th St. 10712 SW 113th Pl 33176. **Hours:** 11:30 am-2 & 5:30-10 pm, Sat
          from 5:30 pm, Sun 5 pm-8:30 pm. Closed major holidays; also Mon. **Reservations:** suggested.
Italian   **Features:** dressy casual; beer & wine only. Health-conscious diners take note: You can enjoy low-fat
          adaptations of old-style, Southern Italian dishes like sausage with peppers, eggplant parmigiana, steak
pizzaiola, veal marsala and lasagna in this small, cozy neighborhood eatery. **Cards:** AE, DI, DS, MC, VI.   ⊠

PASTABILITIES   **Lunch:** $6-$8   **Dinner:** $10-$15   **Phone:** 305/598-9868   `177`
▼▼▼ ▼▼▼   **Location:** Jct of 117th Ave and Kendall Dr; in the "Crossroads" Shopping Center, just e of Florida Tpke SR 821, exit
          20. 11652 N Kendall Dr 33176. **Hours:** 11:30 am-2:30 & 5:30-10 pm, Sun from 5:30 pm, Fri-11 pm, Sat 5:30
Italian   pm-11 pm. Closed major holidays; also Mon. **Reservations:** accepted. **Features:** casual dress; carryout;
          beer & wine only. The small, family-run restaurant is noted for delicious food prepared with twists of
creative inspiration. Among the many house specialties made with fresh ingredients are a spinach linguine with mint sauce and
salads with homemade dressings. **Cards:** AE, DI, DS, MC, VI.   ⊠

KEY BISCAYNE pop. 8,800   (See map p. 478; index p. 482)

——— **WHERE TO STAY** ———

SILVER SANDS BEACH RESORT   **Phone:** (305)361-5441   `135`
▼▼▼ ▼▼▼   12/19-4/24   1P: $169-$349   2P: $169-$349   XP: $30   F14
          12/1-12/18 & 4/25-11/30   1P: $129-$309   2P: $129-$309   XP: $30   F14
Motel   **Location:** 0.3 mi e of Crandon Blvd via East Dr. 301 Ocean Dr 33149. Fax: 305/361-5477. **Facility:** Oceanfront lo-
          cation. A large courtyard in the middle with numerous tropical trees and flowering plants. There are many
umbrella covered tables in the courtyard. The ocean is behind the pool and courtyard. Large rooms with a bright look. 56 units,
7 with efficiency. Bath: combo or shower only. 1 story, exterior corridors. **Terms:** 10 day cancellation notice, weekly rates available. **Amenities:** extended cable TV, voice mail, hair dryers. **Leisure Activities:** heated pool, beach, swimming. **Guest Services:** coin laundry. **Cards:** AE, DI, MC, VI.   SOME UNITS

⊞ ♿ 🏊 📷 💻 🖥 🛄 / VCR /

SONESTA BEACH RESORT KEY BISCAYNE   **Phone:** (305)361-2021   `136`
Ⓐ SAVE   12/1-4/30   1P: $295-$380   2P: $295-$380   XP: $35   F17
          5/1-6/9 & 9/16-11/30   1P: $245-$295   2P: $245-$295   XP: $35   F17
▼▼▼ ▼▼▼   6/10-9/15   1P: $195-$260   2P: $195-$260   XP: $35   F17
Resort   **Location:** 0.3 mi e of Crandon Blvd via East Dr. 350 Ocean Dr 33149. Fax: 305/361-3096. **Facility:** In Caribbean-
          like setting with lush tropical trees and flowering plants. A large pool and deck located just off the beach. Ac-
          tivities to please everyone. The rooms have a luxurious decor. Most rooms with balcony. Rooms with views
of the Atlantic Ocean or the bay. 292 units. Some suites ($875-$1425). Bath: combo or shower only. 8 stories, interior corridors.
Parking: valet. **Terms:** 3 day cancellation notice-fee imposed, package plans. **Amenities:** extended cable TV, dual phone lines,
voice mail, safes, honor bars, irons, hair dryers. **Dining:** 3 restaurants, 7 am-midnight; terrace dining; 15% service charge, $12-
$24, cocktails, entertainment. **Leisure Activities:** heated pool, saunas, whirlpools, steamroom, beach, swimming, 9 tennis courts
(3 lighted), children's program, social program, playground, sports court. Fee: sailboating, windsurfing, charter fishing, aquacycles, tour boat, windsurfing instruction, tennis instruction, bicycles. **Guest Services:** [MAP] meal plan available, gift shop, area
transportation-Key Biscayne, valet laundry. Fee: massage. **Business Services:** conference facilities, administrative services,
fax. Fee: PC. **Cards:** AE, CB, DI, DS, JC, MC, VI. **Special Amenities:** free newspaper. (See color ad below)   SOME UNITS

$▫ ⊞ 🍸 ♿ ♿ ☎ 🏊 🛁 ⊠ 📷 VCR 🖥 DATA PORT / ⊠ /
        FEE   FEE

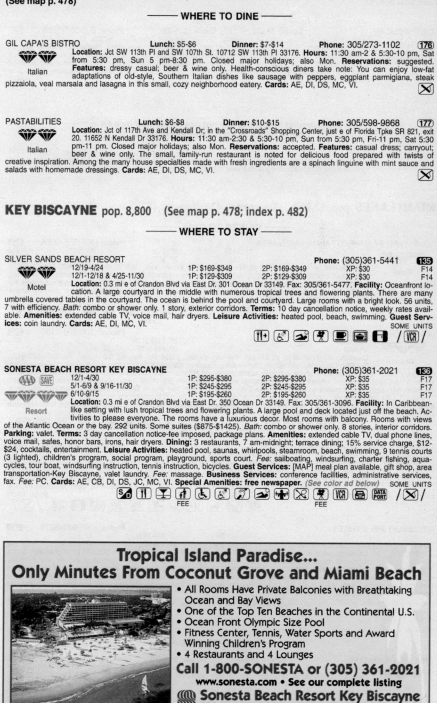

(See map p. 478)

———— WHERE TO DINE ————

RUSTY PELICAN   **Lunch:** $5-$12   **Dinner:** $16-$30   **Phone:** 305/361-3818   146

Seafood

Location: At end of bridge, entrance via marina. 3201 Rickenbacker Cswy 33149. **Hours:** 11:30 am-4 & 5-11 pm, Fri & Sat-midnight, Sun 10:30 am-3 & 5-11 pm. **Reservations:** suggested. **Features:** Sunday brunch; children's menu; carryout; cocktails & lounge; valet parking. A family restaurant with a nautical decor, it offers a view of the bay and the downtown area. Attractive dining rooms, gracious service and a varied menu are highlights. Try the grilled salmon in beurre blanc sauce. Valet parking is available after 5 p.m. **Cards:** AE, CB, DI, DS, MC, VI.

———— *The following restaurant has not been evaluated by AAA* ————
but is listed for your information only.

LINDA B STEAK HOUSE   **Phone:** 305/361-1111

[fyi]   Not evaluated. **Location:** On SR 913, about middle of the island. 320 Crandon Blvd 33149. **Features:** Angus beef, fresh seafood and pasta. A wonderful wine list; all in an elegant dining room.

MIAMI LAKES pop. 12,800   (See map p. 478; index p. 482)

———— WHERE TO STAY ————

COURTYARD BY MARRIOTT-MIAMI LAKES AREA   **Phone:** (305)556-6665   161

| | 12/1-4/30 | 1P: $129 | 2P: $139 | XP: $10 | F18 |
| | 5/1-11/30 | 1P: $99 | 2P: $109 | XP: $10 | F18 |

Motel
Location: Nw on service road at jct SR 826 (Palmetto Expwy) and 154th St exit. 15700 NW 77th Ct 33016. **Fax:** 305/556-0282. **Facility:** Inviting comfortable rooms most with balcony or patio. 151 units. Some suites. *Bath:* combo or shower only. 4 stories, interior corridors. **Amenities:** dual phone lines, voice mail, irons, hair dryers. **Leisure Activities:** heated pool, whirlpool, exercise room. **Guest Services:** valet and coin laundry. **Business Services:** meeting rooms. **Cards:** AE, DI, DS, MC, VI. *(See color ad p 491)*

SOME UNITS

DON SHULA'S HOTEL & GOLF CLUB   **Phone:** (305)821-1150   160

| | 10/1-11/30 | | 2P: $109-$129 |
| | 5/1-9/30 | | 2P: $99-$119 |

Resort
Location: NW 154th St at jct SR 826 (Palmetto Expwy). 15255 Bull Run Rd 33014-2097. **Fax:** 305/820-8190. **Facility:** Decorated with sports memorabilia. Features cozy, country club rooms at the golf course and contemporary rooms at the modern inn facility with main street shops and entertainment. Inn 0.5 mi e of golf resort. 282 units. Some suites ($119-$169). 2-3 stories, interior corridors. **Parking:** valet. **Terms:** open 5/1-11/30, 3 day cancellation notice, monthly rates available, package plans. **Amenities:** extended cable TV, voice mail, irons, hair dryers. **Dining:** Shula's Steakhouse, see separate listing. **Leisure Activities:** 2 pools, sauna, whirlpool, jogging. *Fee:* 9 lighted tennis courts, racquetball courts. **Guest Services:** gift shop, area transportation, valet laundry. *Fee:* massage. **Business Services:** conference facilities, administrative services. *Fee:* PC. **Cards:** AE, CB, DI, MC, VI.

SOME UNITS

TOWNE PLACE SUITES BY MARRIOTT   **Phone:** (305)512-9191   159

All Year   1P: $69-$149
Location: From SR 836 (Palmetto Expwy), exit 154th St, then 0.4 mi w. 8079 NW 154th St 33016. **Fax:** 305/512-1284. **Facility:** Spacious and well equipped rooms with a colorful, contemporary decor. Limited housekeeping. 85 units. 22 two-bedroom units and 95 efficiencies. Some suites. *Bath:* combo or shower only. 2-3 stories, interior corridors. **Terms:** cancellation fee imposed, pets ($60 extra charge). **Amenities:** extended cable TV, dual phone lines. **Guest Services:** valet and coin laundry. **Cards:** AE, DI, DS, JC, MC, VI.

Extended Stay Motel

SOME UNITS

WELLESLEY INN & SUITES   **Phone:** (305)821-8274   162

| | 1/1-3/31 | 1P: $89-$109 | 2P: $89-$109 | XP: $10 | F18 |
| | 12/1-12/31 & 4/1-11/30 | 1P: $69-$89 | 2P: $69-$89 | XP: $10 | F18 |

Motel
Location: Just w of jct SR 826 (Palmetto Expwy). 7925 NW 154th St 33016. **Fax:** 305/828-2257. **Facility:** Bright, functional rooms and attractive public areas. 100 units. Some suites. *Bath:* combo or shower only. 4 stories, interior corridors. **Terms:** small pets only ($10 extra charge). **Amenities:** video games, voice mail. **Leisure Activities:** heated pool. **Guest Services:** [ECP] meal plan available, valet and coin laundry. **Business Services:** meeting rooms. **Cards:** AE, CB, DI, DS, MC, VI. **Special Amenities:** free continental breakfast and free local telephone calls. *(See color ad opposite title page)*

SOME UNITS

———— WHERE TO DINE ————

SHULA'S STEAKHOUSE   **Lunch:** $8-$24   **Dinner:** $18-$33   **Phone:** 305/820-8102   155

Steak House
Location: NW 154th St at jct SR 826 (Palmetto Expwy); in Don Shula's Hotel & Golf Club. 7601 NW 154th St 33014. **Hours:** 11:30-2:30 & 6-11 pm, Sat & Sun breakfast & dinner 5/1-11/30. **Reservations:** suggested. **Features:** dressy casual; carryout; cocktails & lounge; valet parking; a la carte. Comfortable and clublike, the dining room is decorated with Dolphins football memorabilia. Finish off the 48-ounce porterhouse steak and be recognized on a plaque. The lamb chops and seafood are good, too, as is the to-die-for seven-layer chocolate cake. The dinner menu is also available at lunch. **Cards:** AE, CB, DI, MC, VI.

MIAMI SPRINGS pop. 13,300 (See map p. 478; index p. 482)

──────── WHERE TO STAY ────────

BAYMONT INN & SUITES-MIAMI/AIRPORT   Phone: (305)871-1777 **152**

1/26-4/14	1P: $99-$104	2P: $99-$104
12/1-1/25	1P: $79-$84	2P: $79-$84
4/15-11/30	1P: $74-$79	2P: $74-$79

Motel **Location:** SR 953 (Le Jeune Rd) at jct SR 112. 3501 NW Le Jeune Rd 33142. Fax: 305/871-8080. **Facility:** Lobby with a comfortable sitting area. Large breakfast area. Contemporary room decor. 145 units. Some suites ($87-$154). *Bath:* combo or shower only. 4 stories, interior corridors. **Terms:** small pets only. **Amenities:** video games, dual phone lines, voice mail, irons, hair dryers. **Guest Services:** [CP] meal plan available, valet and coin laundry. **Business Services:** meeting rooms. **Cards:** AE, CB, DI, DS, MC, VI. *(See color ad below)*

SOME UNITS

🔒 🖥️ ✈️ 🛏️ 🍴 📶 🤿 🏊 🎥 🖨️ 💻 📠 / ✖️ 🧺 📱 /
FEE

CLARION HOTEL-MIAMI INTERNATIONAL AIRPORT   Phone: (305)871-1000 **148**

2/1-3/31	1P: $126-$176	2P: $136-$186	XP: $10	F18
12/1-1/31	1P: $110-$160	2P: $120-$170	XP: $10	F18
11/1-11/30	1P: $106-$156	2P: $106-$156	XP: $10	F18
4/1-10/31	1P: $86-$136	2P: $96-$146	XP: $10	F18

Motor Inn **Location:** Between Le Jeune Rd and SR 826 (Palmetto Expwy). 5301 NW 36th St 33166. Fax: 305/871-4971. **Facility:** Multiple outlet food court with a business center for the corporate traveler. In house hair salon and rental car agency. Light color package with wood tone finish and room colors. 110 units. *Bath:* combo or shower only. 7 stories, interior corridors. **Terms:** cancellation fee imposed, package plans, small pets only ($25 fee). **Amenities:** video games, voice mail, safes (fee), irons, hair dryers. **Dining:** Food court; 6 am-10 pm, Fri & Sat-11 pm, $5-$12, cocktails. **Leisure Activities:** tennis court, racquetball court, exercise room. *Fee:* golf privileges. **Guest Services:** [ECP] meal plan available, gift shop, valet and coin laundry. **Business Services:** meeting rooms, administrative services. **Cards:** AE, CB, DI, DS, JC, MC, VI. **Special Amenities: early check-in/late check-out and free room upgrade (subject to availability with advanced reservations).**

SOME UNITS

🖥️ ✈️ 🛏️ 🍴 📶 🤿 🏊 ✖️ 🎥 🖨️ 💻 📠 / ✖️ 📼 🧺 📱 /
FEE   FEE   FEE

COMFORT INN & SUITES-MIAMI INTERNATIONAL AIRPORT   Phone: (305)871-6000 **149**

2/1-3/31	1P: $116-$166	2P: $126-$176	XP: $10	F18
12/1-1/31	1P: $100-$150	2P: $110-$160	XP: $10	F18
11/1-11/30	1P: $86-$136	2P: $96-$146	XP: $10	F18
4/1-10/31	1P: $76-$126	2P: $86-$136	XP: $10	F18

Motel **Location:** Between Le Jeune Rd and SR 826 (Palmetto Expwy). 5301 NW 36th St 33166. Fax: 305/871-4971. **Facility:** Shared recreational facilities with Clarion Hotel. Hair salon. Rental car agency. Rooms with light wood finish. Soft color package for in room colors. 165 units. Some suites ($119-$179). 7-11 stories, interior corridors. **Terms:** cancellation fee imposed, package plans, small pets only ($25 fee). **Amenities:** video games, voice mail, safes (fee), irons, hair dryers. **Leisure Activities:** tennis court, racquetball court, exercise room. *Fee:* golf privileges. **Guest Services:** [ECP] meal plan available, gift shop, valet and coin laundry. **Business Services:** meeting rooms, administrative services. **Cards:** AE, CB, DI, DS, JC, MC, VI. **Special Amenities: early check-in/late check-out and free room upgrade (subject to availability with advanced reservations).** *(See color ad on p 483)*

SOME UNITS

🖥️ ✈️ 🛏️ 🍴 📶 🤿 🏊 ✖️ 🎥 🖨️ 💻 📠 / ✖️ 📱 /
FEE   FEE

HOLIDAY INN-AIRPORT NORTH MIAMI SPRINGS   Phone: (305)885-1941 **146**

12/1-4/15	1P: $104-$114	2P: $104-$114	XP: $10	F19
4/16-11/30	1P: $71-$81	2P: $71-$81	XP: $10	F19

Motor Inn **Location:** Le Jeune Rd, at jct NW 36th St and SR 112. 1111 S Royal Poinciana Blvd 33166. Fax: 305/884-1881. **Facility:** Public areas with a south-of-the-border flavor. Rooms have light wood tones and take on a Florida look with the use of teals in the decor package. 220 units. 9 stories, interior corridors. **Terms:** cancellation fee imposed, package plans. **Amenities:** voice mail, irons, hair dryers. **Leisure Activities:** heated pool, exercise room. **Guest Services:** gift shop, valet and coin laundry. *Fee:* area transportation. **Business Services:** meeting rooms, fax. **Cards:** AE, DI, DS, JC, MC, VI.

SOME UNITS

🔒 🖥️ ✈️ 🍴 📶 🤿 🏊 🎥 🖨️ 💻 📠 / ✖️ 📼 📱 /
FEE FEE

(See map p. 478)

HOLIDAY INN EXPRESS MIAMI INTERNATIONAL AIRPORT

Phone: (305)887-2153 [150]

2/1-3/31	1P: $116-$166	2P: $126-$176	XP: $10	F18
12/1-1/31	1P: $100-$150	2P: $110-$160	XP: $10	F18
11/1-11/30	1P: $86-$136	2P: $96-$146	XP: $10	F18
4/1-10/31	1P: $76-$126	2P: $86-$136	XP: $10	F18

Motel

Location: Between Le Jeune Rd and SR 826 (Palmetto Expwy). 5125 NW 36th St 33166. Fax: 305/887-3559. **Facility:** Spacious rooms with light wood tones and soft pastel room decor. 110 units. 6 stories, interior corridors. **Terms:** cancellation fee imposed, package plans, small pets only ($25 fee). **Amenities:** video games, safes (fee). **Guest Services:** [ECP] meal plan available, valet and coin laundry. *Fee:* area transportation-Port of Miami. **Cards:** AE, CB, DI, DS, JC, MC, VI. **Special Amenities: early check-in/late check-out and free room upgrade (subject to availability with advanced reservations).** *(See color ad p 487)*

MAINSTAY SUITES-MIAMI SPRINGS

Phone: (305)870-0448 [156]

2/1-3/31	1P: $116-$166	2P: $126-$176	XP: $10	F18
12/1-1/31	1P: $100-$150	2P: $110-$160	XP: $10	F18
11/1-11/30	1P: $86-$136	2P: $96-$146	XP: $10	F18
4/1-10/31	1P: $76-$126	2P: $86-$136	XP: $10	F18

Extended Stay Motel

Location: I-95 to SR 112 W, exit NW 36th St, then w, right on Palmetto Dr, then w; behind the Clarion Hotel. Between LeJeune Rd and SR 826 (Palmetto Expwy). 101 Fairway Dr 33166. Fax: 305/871-5044. **Facility:** Office hours 6:30 am-11 pm and 8 am-9 pm weekends. During non-office hours, check-in requires use of credit card and automated self-serve system. A good sized pool area with a fenced area. 102 efficiencies. Some suites. *Bath:* combo or shower only. 3 stories, interior corridors. **Terms:** cancellation fee imposed, small pets only ($100 deposit). **Amenities:** video games, dual phone lines, voice mail, irons, hair dryers. **Leisure Activities:** heated pool. **Guest Services:** valet and coin laundry. *Fee:* area transportation-Port of Miami. **Cards:** AE, CB, DI, DS, JC, MC, VI. **Special Amenities: early check-in/late check-out.**

RED ROOF INN MIAMI AIRPORT

Phone: (305)871-4221 [153]

2/1-3/15	1P: $95	2P: $102	XP: $7	F
12/1-1/31	1P: $75	2P: $82	XP: $7	F
3/16-6/7	1P: $65	2P: $72	XP: $7	F
6/8-11/30	1P: $60	2P: $67	XP: $7	F

Motel

Location: 0.5 mi n of airport entrance; on SR 953 at jct SR 112. 3401 NW LeJeune Rd 33142. Fax: 305/871-3933. **Facility:** Attractive landscaping with tropical trees and flowering plants surrounding the building. A nice pool between the building with table and chairs. A warm lobby with comfortable sitting areas. Contemporary decor with light wood tone furnishings. 201 units. *Bath:* some combo or shower only. 4-5 stories, interior corridors. **Terms:** small pets only. **Guest Services:** [CP] meal plan available, area transportation-Port of Miami, valet and coin laundry. **Business Services:** meeting rooms. **Cards:** AE, CB, DI, DS, MC, VI. **Special Amenities: free local telephone calls and free newspaper.**

SLEEP INN-MIAMI AIRPORT

Phone: (305)871-7553 [155]

2/1-3/31	1P: $106-$156	2P: $116-$166	XP: $10	F18
12/1-1/31	1P: $90-$140	2P: $100-$150	XP: $10	F18
11/1-11/30	1P: $80-$130	2P: $90-$140	XP: $10	F18
4/1-10/31	1P: $70-$120	2P: $80-$130	XP: $10	F18

Motel

Location: I-95 to SR 112 W, exit NW 36th St, then w, right on Palmetto Dr, then w; behind the Clarion Hotel, between LeJeune Rd and SR 826 (Palmetto Expwy). 105 Fairway Dr 33166. Fax: 305/871-5441. **Facility:** Lobby with large sitting area. A good sized fenced pool area. Rooms with a contemporary decor. 119 units. *Bath:* shower only. 3 stories, interior corridors. **Terms:** cancellation fee imposed, pets ($25 fee). **Amenities:** extended cable TV, video games, voice mail, irons. **Leisure Activities:** heated pool. **Guest Services:** [CP] meal plan available, valet laundry. **Cards:** AE, CB, DI, DS, JC, MC, VI. **Special Amenities: early check-in/late check-out.** *(See color ad p 483)*

NORTH BAY VILLAGE pop. 5,400   (See map p. 484; index p. 486)

——— WHERE TO STAY ———

BEST WESTERN ON THE BAY INN & MARINA

Phone: (305)865-7100 [255]

12/23-4/15	1P: $74-$114	2P: $79-$109	XP: $5	F12
12/1-12/22 & 4/16-11/30	1P: $64-$104	2P: $69-$109	XP: $5	F12

Motor Inn

Location: 2 mi w of A1A (Collins Ave). 1819 79th St Cswy 33141. Fax: 305/868-3483. **Facility:** Most rooms with view of the bay. 97 units. 5 stories, exterior corridors. **Terms:** 3 day cancellation notice, weekly rates available. **Amenities:** extended cable TV, voice mail, irons, hair dryers. **Dining:** restaurant, 11 am-1 am, $6-$16, cocktails. **Leisure Activities:** heated pool, sauna. *Fee:* boat dock. **Guest Services:** coin laundry. **Business Services:** meeting rooms. *Fee:* fax. **Cards:** AE, CB, DI, DS, JC, MC, VI. **Special Amenities: free continental breakfast.** *(See color ad p 499)*

——— WHERE TO DINE ———

THE CRAB HOUSE SEAFOOD RESTAURANT

Lunch: $7-$11   Dinner: $11-$39   Phone: 305/868-7085 [227]

Seafood

Location: 2.1 mi w of SR A1A (Collins Ave). 1551 79th St Cswy 33141. **Hours:** 11:30 am-11:15 pm, Fri & Sat-midnight. Closed: 11/22. **Features:** casual dress; children's menu; early bird specials; carryout; salad bar; cocktails & lounge; valet parking. The atmosphere is boisterous and fun amid the hanging fish, crabs and plants that contribute to an unmistakable nautical feel. The all-you-can-eat seafood bar is always a popular choice, but don't rule out the Alaskan trio and several varieties of shrimp. **Cards:** AE, CB, DI, DS, MC, VI.

NORTH MIAMI pop. 49,990 (See map p. 478; index p. 481)

──────── WHERE TO STAY ────────

HOLIDAY INN NORTH MIAMI (BAL HARBOR AREA)   Phone: (305)891-7350   85

AAA SAVE   12/1-4/22   1P: $99-$200   2P: $99-$200   XP: $10   F
     4/23-11/30   1P: $80-$99   2P: $85-$99   XP: $10   F

Motor Inn   **Location:** On US 1 at NE 125th St and jct Broad Cswy. 12210 Biscayne Blvd 33181. Fax: 305/891-6322. **Facility:** Contemporary room decor. Lobby with a small sitting area, a casual eatery. Fenced pool area. Rooms with a modern contemporary decor, good use of colors. 98 units. *Bath:* combo or shower only. 5 stories, interior corridors. **Terms:** 3 night minimum stay. **Amenities:** extended cable TV, video games, voice mail, irons, hair dryers. **Dining:** restaurant, 7 am-10 pm, $5-$15, cocktails. **Leisure Activities:** wading pool. **Guest Services:** valet laundry. **Business Services:** meeting rooms. **Cards:** AE, CB, DI, DS, JC, MC, VI.

SOME UNITS

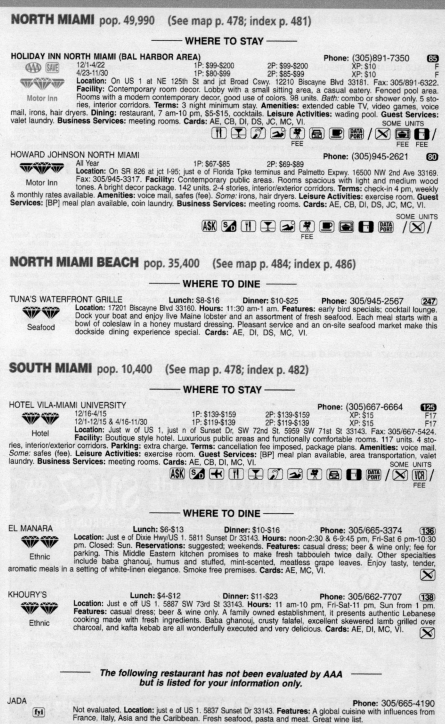

FEE   FEE   FEE

HOWARD JOHNSON NORTH MIAMI   Phone: (305)945-2621   80

     All Year   1P: $67-$85   2P: $69-$89

Motor Inn   **Location:** On SR 826 at jct I-95; just e of Florida Tpke terminus and Palmetto Expwy. 16500 NW 2nd Ave 33169. Fax: 305/945-3317. **Facility:** Contemporary public areas. Rooms spacious with light and medium wood tones. A bright decor package. 142 units. 2-4 stories, interior/exterior corridors. **Terms:** check-in 4 pm, weekly & monthly rates available. **Amenities:** voice mail, safes (fee). *Some:* irons, hair dryers. **Leisure Activities:** exercise room. **Guest Services:** [BP] meal plan available, coin laundry. **Business Services:** meeting rooms. **Cards:** AE, CB, DI, DS, JC, MC, VI.

SOME UNITS

FEE

NORTH MIAMI BEACH pop. 35,400 (See map p. 484; index p. 486)

──────── WHERE TO DINE ────────

TUNA'S WATERFRONT GRILLE   Lunch: $8-$16   Dinner: $10-$25   Phone: 305/945-2567   247

Seafood   **Location:** 17201 Biscayne Blvd 33160. **Hours:** 11:30 am-1 am. **Features:** early bird specials; cocktail lounge. Dock your boat and enjoy live Maine lobster and an assortment of fresh seafood. Each meal starts with a bowl of coleslaw in a honey mustard dressing. Pleasant service and an on-site seafood market make this dockside dining experience special. **Cards:** AE, DI, DS, MC, VI.

SOUTH MIAMI pop. 10,400 (See map p. 478; index p. 482)

──────── WHERE TO STAY ────────

HOTEL VILA-MIAMI UNIVERSITY   Phone: (305)667-6664   125

     12/16-4/15   1P: $139-$159   2P: $139-$159   XP: $15   F17
     12/1-12/15 & 4/16-11/30   1P: $119-$139   2P: $119-$139   XP: $15   F17

Hotel   **Location:** Just w of US 1, just n of Sunset Dr, SW 72nd St. 5959 SW 71st St 33143. Fax: 305/667-5424. **Facility:** Boutique style hotel. Luxurious public areas and functionally comfortable rooms. 117 units. 4 stories, interior/exterior corridors. **Parking:** extra charge. **Terms:** cancellation fee imposed, package plans. **Amenities:** voice mail. *Some:* safes (fee). **Leisure Activities:** exercise room. **Guest Services:** [BP] meal plan available, area transportation, valet laundry. **Business Services:** meeting rooms. **Cards:** AE, CB, DI, MC, VI.

SOME UNITS

FEE

──────── WHERE TO DINE ────────

EL MANARA   Lunch: $6-$13   Dinner: $10-$16   Phone: 305/665-3374   136

Ethnic   **Location:** Just e of Dixie Hwy/US 1. 5811 Sunset Dr 33143. **Hours:** noon-2:30 & 6-9:45 pm, Fri-Sat 6 pm-10:30 pm. Closed: Sun. **Reservations:** suggested; weekends. **Features:** casual dress; beer & wine only; fee for parking. This Middle Eastern kitchen promises to make fresh tabbouleh twice daily. Other specialties include baba ghanouj, humus and stuffed, mint-scented, meatless grape leaves. Enjoy tasty, tender, aromatic meals in a setting of white-linen elegance. Smoke free premises. **Cards:** AE, MC, VI.

KHOURY'S   Lunch: $4-$12   Dinner: $11-$23   Phone: 305/662-7707   138

Ethnic   **Location:** Just e off US 1. 5887 SW 73rd St 33143. **Hours:** 11 am-10 pm, Fri-Sat-11 pm, Sun from 1 pm. **Features:** casual dress; beer & wine only. A family owned establishment, it presents authentic Lebanese cooking made with fresh ingredients. Baba ghanouj, crusty falafel, excellent skewered lamb grilled over charcoal, and kafta kebab are all wonderfully executed and very delicious. **Cards:** AE, DI, MC, VI.

──────── **The following restaurant has not been evaluated by AAA** ────────
but is listed for your information only.

JADA   Phone: 305/665-4190

fyi   Not evaluated. **Location:** just e of US 1. 5837 Sunset Dr 33143. **Features:** A global cuisine with influences from France, Italy, Asia and the Caribbean. Fresh seafood, pasta and meat. Great wine list.

SUNNY ISLES pop. 11,800   (See map p. 484; index p. 485)

——— WHERE TO STAY ———

MONACO OCEANFRONT RESORT   **Phone:** (305)932-2100   248

(AAA) (SAVE)

▼▼▼ ▼▼▼

Motor Inn

12/1-3/15	1P: $70-$109	2P: $70-$109	XP: $10	F16
3/16-4/30	1P: $80-$100	2P: $80-$100	XP: $10	F16
7/2-11/30	1P: $70-$90	2P: $70-$90	XP: $10	F16
5/1-7/1	1P: $65-$85	2P: $65-$85	XP: $10	F16

Location: SR A1A at 175th St. 17501 Collins Ave 33160. Fax: 305/931-5519. **Facility:** Decor of an era gone by of older contemporary surroundings and small bathing areas. 113 units. 30 efficiencies and 9 units with kitchen. 2 stories, interior/exterior corridors. **Terms:** 3 day cancellation notice-fee imposed. **Amenities:** extended cable TV, hair dryers. **Dining:** restaurant, 7 am-2 & 5-10 pm, cocktails, entertainment. **Leisure Activities:** heated pool, wading pool, sauna, beach, swimming, social program, exercise room. **Guest Services:** coin laundry. **Cards:** AE, CB, DI, DS, JC, MC, VI. **Special Amenities: free room upgrade and preferred room (each subject to availability with advanced reservations).**

SOME UNITS

🍽 🍸 🏊 ✕ 🎥 🎬 / 🖨 📺

NEWPORT BEACHSIDE HOTEL & RESORT   **Phone:** (305)949-1300   249

(AAA) (SAVE)

▼▼▼ ▼▼▼

Hotel

12/1-1/2	1P: $99-$279	2P: $109-$289	XP: $10	F18
1/3-3/15	1P: $129-$199	2P: $139-$199	XP: $10	F18
3/16-11/30	1P: $89-$159	2P: $99-$169	XP: $10	F18

Location: SR A1A, at jct SR 826, Sunny Isles Blvd. 16701 Collins Ave 33160. Fax: 305/956-2733. **Facility:** Many rooms with balcony, a very attractive lobby with a tropical flavor with live birds in cages filling the air with melody. 300 units. Some suites ($179-$289). *Bath:* combo or shower only. 12 stories, interior corridors. **Parking:** valet. **Terms:** package plans, small pets only. **Amenities:** voice mail, safes, irons, hair dryers. **Dining:** 2 restaurants, deli, 7 am-1 am, $10-$30, cocktails, also, The World Famous Newport Pub, see separate listing, nightclub. **Leisure Activities:** heated pool, wading pool, whirlpool, beach, swimming, fishing, fishing pier, children's program, social program, exercise room. *Fee:* sailboats, windsurfing, scuba diving/snorkeling & equipment, charter fishing, banana boat rides, jet boat, wave runners. **Guest Services:** gift shop, coin laundry. *Fee:* massage. **Business Services:** meeting rooms. *Fee:* fax. **Cards:** AE, CB, DI, DS, JC, MC, VI. **Special Amenities: free newspaper and free room upgrade (subject to availability with advanced reservations).**

SOME UNITS

🆂🅳 🐕 🍽 🍸 🏋 📷 🏊 ✕ 🎥 🖨 📺 🎬 DATA PORT / ✕ VCR 📺 /
       FEE   FEE   FEE

RAMADA PLAZA MARCO POLO BEACH RESORT   **Phone:** (305)932-2233   245

(AAA) (SAVE)

▼▼▼ ▼▼▼

Hotel

12/21-3/31	1P: $155-$195	2P: $155-$195	XP: $10	F18
12/1-12/20 & 4/1-11/30	1P: $89-$129	2P: $89-$129	XP: $10	F18

Location: SR A1A at 192nd St. 19201 Collins Ave 33160. Fax: 305/935-5009. **Facility:** Spectacular panoramic views from any side and built-in shops on the lower level. 350 units, 200 with efficiency. Some suites ($139-$245). 12 stories, interior corridors. **Parking:** valet. **Terms:** 3 day cancellation notice, 7 days in season, monthly rates available. **Amenities:** extended cable TV, voice mail, safes (fee), hair dryers. **Dining:** dining room, 7 am-10:30 pm, $8-$25, cocktails. **Leisure Activities:** heated pool, wading pool, beach, swimming, basketball, shuffleboard, volleyball, pool table, table tennis. **Guest Services:** gift shop, coin laundry. **Business Services:** meeting rooms, administrative services. *Fee:* PC, fax. **Cards:** AE, CB, DI, DS, JC, MC, VI. **Special Amenities: free continental breakfast and free newspaper.** *(See color ad p 506)*

SOME UNITS

🆂🅳 🍽 🍸 📷 🏊 🚲 ✕ 🎥 🖨 📺 🎬 DATA PORT / ✕

(See map p. 484)

SUEZ OCEAN FRONT RESORT   Phone: (305)932-0661   246

AAA SAVE

12/21-4/15	1P: $95-$135	2P: $95-$135
12/1-12/20 & 4/16-11/30	1P: $70-$125	2P: $70-$125

Motor Inn

Location: SR A1A at 182nd St. 18215 Collins Ave 33160. Fax: 305/937-0058. **Facility:** Very attractive facilities with landscaped courtyards. Older style annex section. 196 units, 45 with efficiency. *Bath:* combo or shower only. 2 stories, exterior corridors. **Amenities:** hair dryers. **Dining:** restaurant, 7:30 am-9 pm, $13-$22, cocktails, entertainment. **Leisure Activities:** 2 pools (1 heated), wading pool, saunas, beach, swimming, lighted tennis court, playground, volleyball, limited exercise equipment. **Guest Services:** [BP] meal plan available, coin laundry. *Fee:* fax. **Cards:** AE, DI, MC, VI. *(See color ad p 526)*

------ **WHERE TO DINE** ------

THE WORLD FAMOUS NEWPORT PUB   **Dinner:** $9-$20   Phone: 305/949-1300   220

Steak House

Location: SR A1A, at jct SR 826, Sunny Isles Blvd; in Newport Beachside Hotel & Resort. 16701 Collins Ave 33160. **Hours:** 6 pm-10:30 pm. Closed: Mon. **Reservations:** suggested; weekends. **Features:** casual dress; children's menu; early bird specials; carryout; cocktails; valet parking. Here you will find aged beef and fresh fish cooked slowly on an open hearth over hard woods and charcoal. French onion soup would be a nice start to a satisfying meal. Good, attentive service and hearty portions make this a worthwhile experience. **Cards:** AE, CB, DI, DS, JC, MC, VI.

SURFSIDE pop. 4,100   (See map p. 484; index p. 486)

------ **WHERE TO STAY** ------

BEEKMAN HOTEL SUITES   Phone: (305)861-4801   272

AAA SAVE

12/1-4/30	2P: $165-$315
5/1-11/30	2P: $160-$295

Motel

Location: On SR A1A (Collins Ave), just s of SR 922. 9499 Collins Ave 33154. Fax: 305/865-5971. **Facility:** Some rooms with oceanfront view. Spacious rooms decorated with white pine wood tones. 125 units with kitchen. 16 two-bedroom units. Some suites ($185-$205). 12 stories. **Parking:** extra charge. **Terms:** 3 day cancellation notice-fee imposed, weekly & monthly rates available. **Amenities:** voice mail, safes (fee), hair dryers. **Dining:** coffee shop, 8:30 am-1 pm. **Leisure Activities:** heated pool, whirlpool, beach, swimming. **Guest Services:** coin laundry. **Cards:** AE, MC, VI. **Special Amenities:** free newspaper and preferred room (subject to availability with advanced reservations). *(See ad below)*

SOME UNITS

BEST WESTERN OCEANFRONT RESORT   Phone: (305)864-2232   273

AAA SAVE

12/1-4/16	1P: $99-$149	2P: $99-$149	XP: $10	F
6/15-9/4	1P: $99	2P: $149		F
4/17-6/14 & 9/5-11/30	1P: $79-$119	2P: $79-$119	XP: $10	F

Motel

Location: On SR A1A (Collins Ave) just s of SR 922. 9365 Collins Ave 33154. Fax: 305/864-3045. **Facility:** Located on the oceanfront and a quiet part of town. Walking distance to many small shops and eateries. A large white sand beach behind with emerald green water. Large rooms with a contemporary decor package. 100 units with kitchen. Some suites ($79-$149). *Bath:* combo or shower only. 3 stories, exterior corridors. **Terms:** weekly & monthly rates available. **Amenities:** extended cable TV. **Leisure Activities:** 2 pools (1 heated), beach, swimming. **Guest Services:** valet laundry. **Cards:** AE, CB, DI, DS, MC, VI. **Special Amenities:** free continental breakfast. *(See color ad p 500 & ad below)*

SOME UNITS

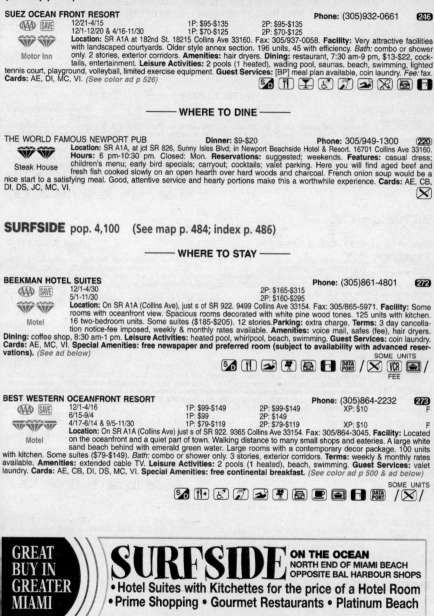

The previous listings were for the Miami-Miami Beach Vicinity.
This page resumes the alphabetical listings of cities in Florida.

MIAMI LAKES —See Miami-Miami Beach p. 522.

MIAMI SPRINGS —See Miami-Miami Beach p. 523.

MICANOPY pop. 610

——— WHERE TO STAY ———

HERLONG MANSION

Phone: (352)466-3322

All Year   1P: $70-$179   2P: $70-$179   XP: $20

Location: Downtown; just n on US 441. 402 NE Cholokka Blvd 32667 (PO Box 667). Fax: 352/466-3322.

Historic Bed & Breakfast

Facility: Circa 1840 manor and built originally as a cracker style house. The now Greek revival style home offers high ceilings, mahogany in-laid floors, oak woodwork, elegantly decorated rooms, some with fireplace. Decorated with a variety of antiques and nicknacks. Designated smoking area. 11 units. 1 two-bedroom unit. Some suites ($169-$179) and whirlpool units ($140-$179). **Bath:** combo or shower only. 3 stories (no elevator), interior/exterior corridors. **Terms:** 7 day cancellation notice-fee imposed, weekly rates available, pets (cottages only). **Amenities:** Some: CD players, irons, hair dryers. **Leisure Activities:** bicycles. **Guest Services:** [BP] meal plan available. **Business Services:** meeting rooms, fax. **Cards:** MC, VI.

SOME UNITS

MILTON pop. 7,200

——— WHERE TO STAY ———

HOLIDAY INN EXPRESS HOTEL & SUITES

Phone: 850/626-9060

All Year   1P: $72-$80   2P: $72-$80   F18

Motel

Location: I-10, exit 10, just nw. 8510 Keshav Taylor Dr 32583. Fax: 850/626-8989. **Facility:** 64 units. Some suites ($85-$200) and whirlpool units ($90-$95). **Bath:** combo or shower only. 3 stories, interior corridors. **Terms:** pets ($50 extra charge). **Amenities:** extended cable TV, voice mail, irons, hair dryers. **Leisure Activities:** exercise room. **Guest Services:** [CP] & [ECP] meal plans available, valet and coin laundry. **Business Services:** meeting rooms. **Cards:** AE, CB, DI, DS, JC, MC, VI.

SOME UNITS

MONTICELLO pop. 2,600

——— WHERE TO STAY ———

PALMER PLACE B&B

Phone: 850/997-5519

All Year   1P: $70-$90   2P: $75-$95   XP: $10   F5

Location: Jct US 90 and 19, 0.4 mi w of downtown, just s on Hickory St. 625 W Palmer Mill Rd 32344 (PO Box 507,

Historic Bed & Breakfast

32345). **Facility:** Antebellum home circa 1836. Good sized rooms appointed with mahogany antiques, many with two beds. On National Register of Historic Places. Smoke free premises. 5 units. 1 two-bedroom unit. 2 stories (no elevator), interior corridors. **Terms:** check-in 4 pm, cancellation fee imposed. **Guest Services:** complimentary evening beverages. **Cards:** AE, MC, VI.

SOME UNITS

SUPER 8

Phone: (850)997-8888

All Year   1P: $50   2P: $55   XP: $5   F

Motel

Location: I-10, exit 33. just s on US 19. Rt 1, Box 164-E 32336. Fax: 850/997-9614. **Facility:** Adjacent to antique mall. 52 units. 2 stories, exterior corridors. **Terms:** 15 day cancellation notice. **Guest Services:** coin laundry. **Cards:** AE, DS, MC, VI.

SOME UNITS

——— WHERE TO DINE ———

THE COURTYARD CAFE

Lunch: $2-$6   Phone: 850/997-1990

Location: Center, corner of US 19, just n of US 90. 110 E Dogwood 32345. **Hours:** 6 am-2 pm, Fri also 5 pm-8:30 pm. Closed major holidays. **Features:** casual dress; carryout. Located in historic downtown

American

Monticello close to antique shops, you'll enjoy the friendly atmosphere and efficient service. Try the famous buttermilk biscuits with an omelette for breakfast or enjoy a variety of entrees including shepherd's pie and fried chicken on the lunch buffet with salad bar, fruit, and dessert.

MOUNT DORA —See Orlando p. 699.

NAPLES pop. 19,500

——— WHERE TO STAY ———

BAYMONT INN & SUITES NAPLES

Phone: (941)352-8400

1/26-4/14   1P: $105-$109   2P: $105-$109

12/1-1/25   1P: $89-$94   2P: $89-$94

4/15-11/30   1P: $59-$64   2P: $59-$64

Motel

Location: I-75, exit 15, just w. 185 Bedzel Circle 34104. Fax: 941/352-8401. **Facility:** Close to multiple shopping malls. Good sized rooms with contemporary decor. 103 units. Some suites ($69-$159). **Bath:** combo or shower only. 4 stories, interior corridors. **Terms:** small pets only (in smoking rooms). **Amenities:** video games, voice mail, irons, hair dryers. **Leisure Activities:** heated pool. **Guest Services:** [ECP] meal plan available, coin laundry. **Cards:** AE, DI, DS, MC, VI.

(See color ad p 394)

SOME UNITS

FEE   FEE FEE

BEST WESTERN NAPLES INN & SUITES

AAA (SAVE)

WWW

Motel

2/1-3/31	2P: $129-$219
12/20-1/31	2P: $99-$189
12/1-12/19 & 4/1-11/30	2P: $59-$119

Phone: (941)261-1148

Location: I-75, exit 15, 2.3 mi n on US 41 at Mooringline Dr. 2329 9th St N (US 41) 34103. Fax: 941/262-4684. **Facility:** Standard contemporary rooms, and one- and two-bedroom suites. Multi-lingual staff. Appealing courtyard with waterfall and ponds stocked with Japanese Koi fish. Abundant tropical landscaping. Suites have full kitchens. 110 units. 6 two-bedroom units and 30 units with kitchen. Some suites ($89-$219). 2-4 stories, exterior corridors. **Terms:** 3 day cancellation notice-fee imposed, weekly rates available. **Amenities:** extended cable TV, voice mail, safes, irons, hair dryers. **Dining:** dining room, also, Chardonnay, see separate listing. **Leisure Activities:** 2 heated pools, whirlpools. **Guest Services:** [ECP] meal plan available, coin laundry. **Cards:** AE, DI, DS, MC, VI. **Special Amenities:** free continental breakfast. *(See color ad below)*

SOME UNITS

CHARTER CLUB RESORT ON NAPLES BAY
Phone: (941)261-5559

▼▼▼
Condominium

1/27-4/20	2P: $259-$299
12/23-1/26	2P: $209-$239
4/21-11/30	2P: $139-$149
12/1-12/22	2P: $139

Location: I-75, exit 15, at 10th St, on the bay. 1000 10th Ave S 34102. Fax: 941/261-6782. **Facility:** Large units, each with private screened lanai overlooking the bay. 33 two-bedroom units with kitchen. Some suites. 3 stories (no elevator), exterior corridors. **Terms:** check-in 4 pm, 30 day cancellation notice-fee imposed, weekly rates available. **Amenities:** voice mail, irons, hair dryers. **Leisure Activities:** heated pool, wading pool, whirlpool, boat dock, fishing, recreation program, bicycles. **Fee:** boating, sailboating. **Guest Services:** complimentary laundry. **Cards:** AE, DS, MC, VI.

ASK ⓢ🔃 📶 🏊 ⊠ VCR 🖥 💻 🖨 📠 🛗
FEE

CLARION INN
Phone: 941/649-5500

AAA SAVE
▼▼▼▼
Hotel

1/4-4/21	1P: $130-$285	2P: $130-$285
11/1-11/30	1P: $108-$285	2P: $108-$285
12/1-1/3	1P: $105-$285	2P: $105-$285
4/22-10/31	1P: $82-$135	2P: $82-$135

Location: I-75, exit 16, 3.5 mi n on US 41, just n of Park Shore Dr. 4055 Tamiami Tr N 34103. Fax: 941/430-0422. **Facility:** Mediterranean-style architecture. Attractive, spacious rooms with private balcony. All rooms with white terry cloth bathrobes. 100 units. Some suites. *Bath:* combo or shower only. 5 stories, interior corridors. **Terms:** 3 day cancellation notice. **Amenities:** extended cable TV, voice mail, safes (fee), honor bars, irons. *Some:* hair dryers. **Dining:** restaurant, 11:30 am-2:30 & 5-10 pm, lunch Mon-Fri in summer, $16-$23, cocktails. **Leisure Activities:** heated pool, whirlpool, exercise room, video rentals. **Guest Services:** [ECP] meal plan available, valet laundry. **Business Services:** meeting rooms, fax. **Cards:** AE, DI, DS, MC, VI. **Special Amenities:** free local telephone calls and free newspaper. *(See color ad p 535)*

SOME UNITS
ⓢ 🔃 📶 🎦 🍴 ᕕ 🏊 🎦 VCR 🖥 💻 🖨 DATA PORT / ⊠ 🖨 /

COMFORT INN & MARINA-DOWNTOWN ON THE BAY
Phone: (941)649-5800

AAA SAVE
▼▼▼
Motel

2/1-4/16	1P: $140-$250	2P: $140-$250
12/21-1/31	1P: $100-$250	2P: $100-$250
12/1-12/20 & 4/17-11/30	1P: $66-$100	2P: $66-$100

Location: I-75, exit 15, jct US 41 and Goodlette Frank Rd (SR 864). 1221 5th Ave S 34102. Fax: 941/649-0523. **Facility:** Average sized rooms with contemporary appointments and small bathrooms. Close to Tin City and Bayfront marketplace. 101 units. 4 stories, interior corridors. **Terms:** 10 day cancellation notice, weekly rates available, package plans - summer. **Amenities:** extended cable TV, voice mail, hair dryers. *Some:* irons. **Leisure Activities:** heated pool, whirlpool. **Guest Services:** coin laundry. **Business Services:** meeting rooms. **Cards:** AE, DI, DS, JC, MC, VI. **Special Amenities:** free continental breakfast. *(See color ad below)*

SOME UNITS
ⓢ 🔃 🏊 🛗 🎦 🖥 💻 DATA PORT / ⊠ 🖨 🛗 /
FEE

COMFORT INN & SUITES
Phone: (941)353-9500

SAVE
▼▼▼
Motel

1/22-4/15	1P: $99-$185	2P: $99-$185	XP: $10	F18
12/1-1/21	1P: $79-$99	2P: $79-$99	XP: $10	F18
4/16-11/30	1P: $54-$89	2P: $54-$89	XP: $10	F18

Location: I-75, exit 15. 3860 Tollgate Blvd 34114. Fax: 941/353-0035. **Facility:** Modern spacious rooms, many with balcony. Spacious bathrooms. 198 units. 45 efficiencies and 12 units with kitchen. Some whirlpool units ($85-$170). *Bath:* combo or shower only. 4 stories, interior/exterior corridors. **Terms:** check-in 4 pm, cancellation fee imposed, weekly & monthly rates available, package plans. **Amenities:** *Some:* irons, hair dryers. **Leisure Activities:** heated pool, whirlpool, game room. **Guest Services:** [CP] meal plan available, gift shop, valet laundry. **Business Services:** meeting rooms. **Cards:** AE, DI, DS, MC, VI.

SOME UNITS
ⓢ 🔃 📶 🎦 🐾 🏊 🖨 DATA PORT / ⊠ 🖨 💻 /

COURTYARD BY MARRIOTT

Motel

	12/1-4/15	1P: $155-$185	2P: $155-$185	Phone: (941)434-8700
	4/16-11/30	1P: $74-$104	2P: $74-$104	XP: $10 F18
				XP: $10 F18

Location: I-75, exit 15, 3 mi n on US 41. 3250 Tamiami Tr N (US 41) 34103. **Fax:** 941/434-7787. **Facility:** Located in a quiet area close to shopping and other restaurants. 102 units. Some suites. *Bath:* combo or shower only. 4 stories, interior corridors. **Amenities:** extended cable TV, voice mail, irons, hair dryers. **Leisure Activities:** heated pool, whirlpool, exercise room. **Guest Services:** coin laundry. **Business Services:** meeting rooms. **Cards:** AE, DI, DS, MC, VI.

SOME UNITS

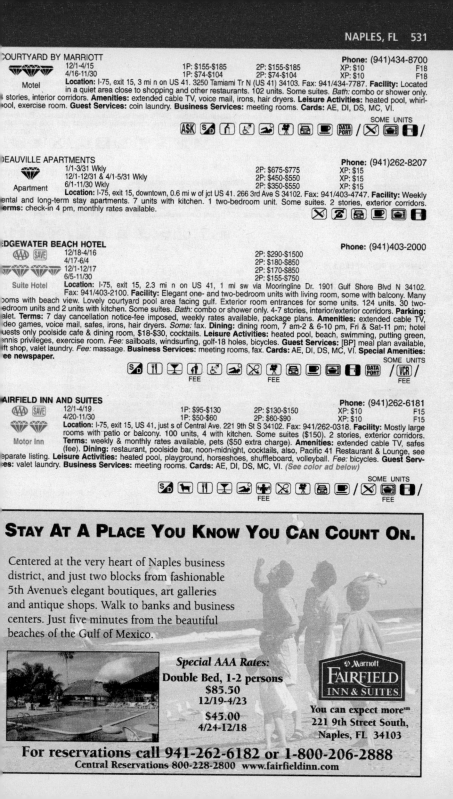

DEAUVILLE APARTMENTS

Apartment

	1/1-3/31 Wkly		2P: $675-$775	Phone: (941)262-8207
	12/1-12/31 & 4/1-5/31 Wkly		2P: $450-$550	XP: $15
	6/1-11/30 Wkly		2P: $350-$550	XP: $15
				XP: $15

Location: I-75, exit 15, downtown, 0.6 mi w of jct US 41. 266 3rd Ave S 34102. **Fax:** 941/403-4747. **Facility:** Weekly rental and long-term stay apartments. 7 units with kitchen. 1 two-bedroom unit. Some suites. 2 stories, exterior corridors. **Terms:** check-in 4 pm, monthly rates available.

EDGEWATER BEACH HOTEL

Suite Hotel

	12/18-4/16		2P: $290-$1500	Phone: (941)403-2000
	4/17-6/4		2P: $180-$850	
	12/1-12/17		2P: $170-$850	
	6/5-11/30		2P: $155-$750	

Location: I-75, exit 15, 2.3 mi n on US 41, 1 mi sw via Mooringline Dr. 1901 Gulf Shore Blvd N 34102. **Fax:** 941/403-2100. **Facility:** Elegant one- and two-bedroom units with living room, some with balcony. Many rooms with beach view. Lovely courtyard pool area facing gulf. Exterior room entrances for some units. 124 units. 30 two-bedroom units and 2 units with kitchen. Some suites. *Bath:* combo or shower only. 4-7 stories, interior/exterior corridors. **Parking:** valet. **Terms:** 7 day cancellation notice-fee imposed, weekly rates available, package plans. **Amenities:** extended cable TV, video games, voice mail, safes, irons, hair dryers. *Some:* fax. **Dining:** dining room, 7 am-2 & 6-10 pm, Fri & Sat-11 pm; hotel guests only poolside cafe & dining room, $18-$30, cocktails. **Leisure Activities:** heated pool, beach, swimming, putting green, tennis privileges, exercise room. *Fee:* sailboats, windsurfing, golf-18 holes, bicycles. **Guest Services:** [BP] meal plan available, gift shop, valet laundry. *Fee:* massage. **Business Services:** meeting rooms, fax. **Cards:** AE, DI, DS, MC, VI. **Special Amenities:** free newspaper.

SOME UNITS

FAIRFIELD INN AND SUITES

Motor Inn

	12/1-4/19	1P: $95-$130	2P: $130-$150	Phone: (941)262-6181
	4/20-11/30	1P: $50-$60	2P: $60-$90	XP: $10 F15
				XP: $10 F15

Location: I-75, exit 15, US 41, just s of Central Ave. 221 9th St S 34102. **Fax:** 941/262-0318. **Facility:** Mostly large rooms with patio or balcony. 100 units, 4 with kitchen. Some suites ($150). 2 stories, exterior corridors. **Terms:** weekly & monthly rates available, pets ($50 extra charge). **Amenities:** extended cable TV, safes (fee). **Dining:** restaurant, poolside bar, noon-midnight; cocktails, also, Pacific 41 Restaurant & Lounge, see separate listing. **Leisure Activities:** heated pool, playground, horseshoes, shuffleboard, volleyball. *Fee:* bicycles. **Guest Services:** valet laundry. **Business Services:** meeting rooms. **Cards:** AE, DI, DS, MC, VI. *(See color ad below)*

SOME UNITS

THE FAIRWAYS RESORT
AAA [SAVE]
▼▼ ▼▼
Motel

Phone: (941)597-8181
XP: $10   F18

| 12/21-4/15 | 1P: $95-$125 |
| 12/1-12/20 & 4/16-11/30 | 1P: $50-$70 |

Location: I-75, exit 17, 2.2 mi w on CR 846. 103 Palm River Blvd 34110. Fax: 941/597-5413. **Facility:** Air conditioned garden pavilion with terrace. Attractive setting with heavy tropical landscaping; bordering residential area. 45 units, 20 with efficiency. 2 stories, exterior corridors. **Terms:** 3 day cancellation notice-fee imposed weekly rates available. **Amenities:** extended cable TV. *Some:* irons, hair dryers. **Leisure Activities:** heated pool, whirlpool, shuffleboard, barbecue gas grills, pavilion. **Guest Services:** [ECP] meal plan available, coin laundry. **Business Services:** meeting rooms, fax. **Cards:** AE, DI, MC, VI. **Special Amenities: free continental breakfast and free local telephone calls.**

SOME UNITS

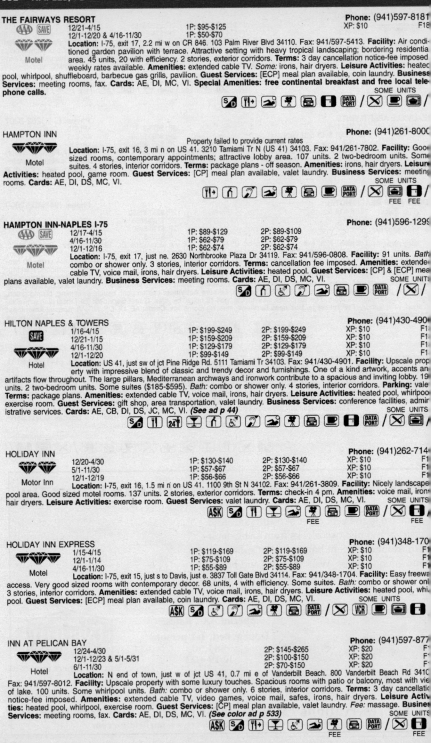

HAMPTON INN
▼▼▼
Motel

Phone: (941)261-8000

Property failed to provide current rates

Location: I-75, exit 16, 3 mi n on US 41. 3210 Tamiami Tr N (US 41) 34103. Fax: 941/261-7802. **Facility:** Good sized rooms, contemporary appointments; attractive lobby area. 107 units. 2 two-bedroom units. Some suites. 4 stories, interior corridors. **Terms:** package plans - off season. **Amenities:** irons, hair dryers. **Leisure Activities:** heated pool, game room. **Guest Services:** [CP] meal plan available, valet laundry. **Business Services:** meeting rooms. **Cards:** AE, DI, DS, MC, VI.

SOME UNITS

FEE FEE

HAMPTON INN-NAPLES I-75
AAA [SAVE]
▼▼▼▼
Motel

Phone: (941)596-1299

12/17-4/15	1P: $89-$129	2P: $89-$109
4/16-11/30	1P: $62-$79	2P: $62-$79
12/1-12/16	1P: $62-$74	2P: $62-$74

Location: I-75, exit 17, just ne. 2630 Northbrooke Plaza Dr 34119. Fax: 941/596-0808. **Facility:** 91 units. *Bath:* combo or shower only. 3 stories, interior corridors. **Terms:** cancellation fee imposed. **Amenities:** extended cable TV, voice mail, irons, hair dryers. **Leisure Activities:** heated pool. **Guest Services:** [CP] & [ECP] meal plans available, valet laundry. **Business Services:** meeting rooms. **Cards:** AE, DI, DS, MC, VI.

SOME UNITS

/×/

HILTON NAPLES & TOWERS
[SAVE]
▼▼▼▼
Hotel

Phone: (941)430-4900

1/16-4/15	1P: $199-$249	2P: $199-$249	XP: $10	F1
12/21-1/15	1P: $159-$209	2P: $159-$209	XP: $10	F1
4/16-11/30	1P: $129-$179	2P: $129-$179	XP: $10	F1
12/1-12/20	1P: $99-$149	2P: $99-$149	XP: $10	F1

Location: US 41, just sw of jct Pine Ridge Rd. 5111 Tamiami Tr 34103. Fax: 941/430-4901. **Facility:** Upscale property with impressive blend of classic and trendy decor and furnishings. One of a kind artwork, accents and artifacts flow throughout. The large pillars, Mediterranean archways and ironwork contribute to a spacious and inviting lobby. 19 units. 2 two-bedroom units. Some suites ($185-$595). *Bath:* combo or shower only. 4 stories, interior corridors. **Parking:** vale **Terms:** package plans. **Amenities:** extended cable TV, voice mail, irons, hair dryers. **Leisure Activities:** heated pool, whirlpool exercise room. **Guest Services:** gift shop, area transportation, valet laundry. **Business Services:** conference facilities, administrative services. **Cards:** AE, CB, DI, DS, JC, MC, VI. *(See ad p 44)*

SOME UNITS

HOLIDAY INN
▼▼ ▼▼
Motor Inn

Phone: (941)262-7146

12/20-4/30	1P: $130-$140	2P: $130-$140	XP: $10	F1
5/1-11/30	1P: $57-$67	2P: $57-$67	XP: $10	F1
12/1-12/19	1P: $56-$66	2P: $56-$66	XP: $10	F1

Location: I-75, exit 16, 1.5 mi n on US 41. 1100 9th St N 34102. Fax: 941/261-3809. **Facility:** Nicely landscaped pool area. Good sized motel rooms. 137 units. 2 stories, exterior corridors. **Terms:** check-in 4 pm. **Amenities:** voice mail, irons hair dryers. **Leisure Activities:** exercise room. **Guest Services:** valet laundry. **Cards:** AE, DI, DS, MC, VI.

SOME UNITS

FEE   FEE

HOLIDAY INN EXPRESS
▼▼▼
Motel

Phone: (941)348-1700

1/15-4/15	1P: $119-$169	2P: $119-$169	XP: $10	F1
12/1-1/14	1P: $75-$109	2P: $75-$109	XP: $10	F1
4/16-11/30	1P: $55-$89	2P: $55-$89	XP: $10	F1

Location: I-75, exit 15, just s to Davis, just e. 3837 Toll Gate Blvd 34114. Fax: 941/348-1704. **Facility:** Easy freeway access. Very good sized rooms with contemporary decor. 68 units, 4 with efficiency. Some suites. *Bath:* combo or shower only 3 stories, interior corridors. **Amenities:** extended cable TV, voice mail, irons, hair dryers. **Leisure Activities:** heated pool, whi pool. **Guest Services:** [ECP] meal plan available, coin laundry. **Cards:** AE, DI, DS, MC, VI.

INN AT PELICAN BAY
▼▼▼
Hotel

Phone: (941)597-8771

12/24-4/30		2P: $145-$265	XP: $20	F
12/1-12/23 & 5/1-5/31		2P: $100-$150	XP: $20	F
6/1-11/30		2P: $70-$150	XP: $20	F

Location: N end of town, just w of jct US 41, 0.7 mi e of Vanderbilt Beach. 800 Vanderbilt Beach Rd 3410 Fax: 941/597-8012. **Facility:** Upscale property with some luxury touches. Spacious rooms with patio or balcony, most with vie of lake. 100 units. Some whirlpool units. *Bath:* combo or shower only. 6 stories, interior corridors. **Terms:** 3 day cancellatio notice-fee imposed. **Amenities:** extended cable TV, video games, voice mail, safes, irons, hair dryers. **Leisure Activities:** heated pool, whirlpool, exercise room. **Guest Services:** [CP] meal plan available, valet laundry. *Fee:* massage. **Business Services:** meeting rooms, fax. **Cards:** AE, DI, DS, MC, VI. *(See color ad p 533)*

SOME UNITS

FEE

INN BY THE SEA

Phone: (941)649-4124

Bed & Breakfast

| | 12/14-4/18 | 1P: $149-$169 | 2P: $149-$169 |
| | 12/1-12/13 & 4/19-11/30 | 1P: $94-$104 | 2P: $94-$104 |

Location: I-75, exit 15, between 2nd and 3rd sts S, at jct 3rd St. 287 Eleventh Ave S 34102-7022. Fax: 941/434-2842. **Facility:** 1937 guest house with rooms themed to area islands. Cozy quarters with polished pine floors and plenty of sunlight; two blocks to beach or Third St shopping. Hosts live next door and speak several languages; English, Italian, Dutch, French and Russian. Smoke free premises. 5 units. Some suites ($114-$189). **Bath:** combo or shower only. 2 stories, interior corridors. **Terms:** age restrictions may apply, 7 day cancellation notice. **Amenities:** no TVs. **Leisure Activities:** bicycles. **Guest Services:** [CP] meal plan available. **Cards:** AE, DS, MC, VI.

THE INN ON FIFTH

Phone: (941)403-8777

Hotel

	12/1-4/16	1P: $189-$359	2P: $189-$359	XP: $20	F15
	4/17-5/31 & 10/1-11/30	1P: $119-$269	2P: $119-$269	XP: $20	F15
	6/1-9/30	1P: $99-$239	2P: $99-$239	XP: $20	F15

Location: Downtown; just w of jct US 41. 699 5th Ave S 34102. Fax: 941/403-8778. **Facility:** Elegant European style and luxuriously decorated public areas and rooms. 87 units. Some suites and whirlpool units. **Bath:** some combo or shower only. 3 stories, interior corridors. **Parking:** valet. **Terms:** 3 day cancellation notice-fee imposed, package plans. **Amenities:** extended cable TV, voice mail, safes, irons, hair dryers. **Leisure Activities:** heated pool, whirlpool, spa, exercise room. **Guest Services:** valet laundry. **Business Services:** meeting rooms. **Cards:** AE, CB, DI, DS, MC, VI. *(See color ad below)*

SOME UNITS

LAPLAYA BEACH RESORT

Phone: (941)597-3123

Resort

	12/1-4/16	1P: $225-$550	2P: $225-$550	XP: $30	F16
	4/17-5/24 & 10/1-11/30	1P: $190-$350	2P: $190-$350	XP: $30	F16
	5/25-9/30	1P: $130-$260	2P: $130-$260	XP: $30	F16

Location: N end of town; from US 41, 1.3 mi w on Vanderbilt Beach Rd (SR 862), 0.5 mi n. 9891 Gulf Shore Dr 34108. Fax: 941/597-1672. **Facility:** High-rise rooms with gulf view or older-style low-rise section. All rooms with upscale decor package. 191 units. 4 two-bedroom units and 38 efficiencies. Some suites ($355-$1405). **Bath:** combo or shower only. 4-15 stories, interior/exterior corridors. **Parking:** extra charge or valet. **Terms:** check-in 4 pm, 7 day cancellation notice-fee imposed, package plans. **Amenities:** voice mail, honor bars, irons, hair dryers. **Dining:** dining room, 7 am-10 pm, $14-$25, cocktails. **Leisure Activities:** 2 heated pools, beach, swimming, boat dock, catamaran, kayaks, parasailing, waverunners, recreation program, exercise room, fitness center, spa services. **Fee:** paddleboats, sailboating, bicycles. **Guest Services:** gift shop, valet and coin laundry. **Business Services:** conference facilities. **Cards:** AE, CB, DI, DS, MC, VI. *(See color ad p 534)*

SOME UNITS

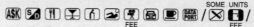

LEMON TREE INN

AAA SAVE

	12/24-4/23	1P: $125-$149	2P: $125-$149	XP: $10	F13
	12/1-12/23	1P: $99-$129	2P: $99-$129	XP: $10	F13
	4/24-11/30	1P: $59-$79	2P: $59-$79	XP: $10	F13

Motel

Location: I-75, exit 15 (US 41), just s of Central Ave. 250 9th St S 34102. Fax: 941/262-2638. **Facility:** Attractive, cute rooms and public areas. Well landscaped and impeccably kept courtyard, gazebo and pool. Located in "Old Naples", near downtown and great shopping. 35 units, 8 with efficiency. 1 story, exterior corridors. **Terms:** 3 day cancellation notice. **Amenities:** voice mail. **Leisure Activities:** heated pool. **Cards:** AE, DS, MC, VI. **Special Amenities: early check-in/late check-out and free continental breakfast.**

SOME UNITS

$\boxed{\text{S}_\text{D}}$ $\boxed{\text{T}}$ $\boxed{\text{🏊}}$ $\boxed{\text{🖨}}$ $\boxed{\text{🖳}}$ $\boxed{\text{🛏}}$ $\boxed{\text{DATA PORT}}$ / $\boxed{\text{✕}}$ $\boxed{\text{VCR}}$

THE NAPLES BEACH HOTEL & GOLF CLUB

AAA SAVE

	12/21-5/31	1P: $190-$495	2P: $190-$495	XP: $15	F18
	9/27-11/30	1P: $190-$340	2P: $190-$340	XP: $15	F18
	12/1-12/20	1P: $115-$330	2P: $115-$330	XP: $15	F18
	6/1-9/26	1P: $100-$280	2P: $100-$280	XP: $15	F18

Resort

Location: I-75, exit 15, 1 mi n via US 41, 0.7 mi w on 7th Ave N. 851 Gulf Shore Blvd N 34102. Fax: 941/261-7380. **Facility:** Traditional destination resort, family-owned since 1946. Rooms decorated in vivid Florida hues and accented by art and photographs produced by regional artists. 5,000 plant private orchid collection. 318 units. 12 two-bedroom units. Some suites. 2-9 stories, interior/exterior corridors. **Parking:** valet. **Terms:** check-in 4 pm, 7 day cancellation notice-fee imposed, package plans. **Amenities:** extended cable TV, voice mail, safes, honor bars, irons, hair dryers. **Dining:** 2 dining rooms, 2 restaurants, deli, 7 am-10:30 pm, $13-$25, cocktails, entertainment. **Leisure Activities:** beach, swimming, children's program, recreation program. *Fee:* paddleboats, sailboating, windsurfing, golf-18 holes, putting green, 6 tennis courts, bicycles. **Guest Services:** [BP] meal plan available, gift shop, afternoon tea, valet laundry. *Fee:* massage. **Business Services:** conference facilities, fax. **Cards:** AE, DI, DS, MC, VI. **Special Amenities: free newspaper and preferred room (subject to availability with advanced reservations).** *(See color ad below)*

SOME UNITS

$\boxed{\text{T}}$ $\boxed{\text{Y}}$ $\boxed{\text{🏌}}$ $\boxed{\text{🏊}}$ $\boxed{\text{👪}}$ $\boxed{\text{✕}}$ $\boxed{\text{📷}}$ $\boxed{\text{🖨}}$ $\boxed{\text{DATA PORT}}$ / $\boxed{\text{✕}}$ $\boxed{\text{🖳}}$ $\boxed{\text{🖳}}$ $\boxed{\text{🛏}}$
FEE   FEE

OLD NAPLES INN & SUITES

AAA SAVE

	12/1-12/21 & 10/29-11/30	1P: $75-$128	2P: $75-$128	XP: $6	F18
	5/1-10/28	1P: $59-$110	2P: $59-$110	XP: $6	F18
	12/22-4/30	1P: $99	2P: $99	XP: $6	F18

Motel

Location: I-75, exit 15, at 8th Ave S. 801 Third St S 34102. Fax: 941/262-4876. **Facility:** Older style property with contemporary room furnishings. Some small rooms. 2 blocks from gulf; convenient to shopping. Office hours 7 am-11 pm. Night phone. 60 units. 2 two-bedroom units and 45 units with kitchen. Some suites. *Bath:* combo or shower only. 1-2 stories, exterior corridors. **Terms:** 14 day cancellation notice, package plans - in summer. **Amenities:** voice mail. **Leisure Activities:** 2 heated pools, shuffleboard. *Fee:* bicycles. **Guest Services:** coin laundry. **Cards:** AE, DS, MC, VI. **Special Amenities: free continental breakfast.**

SOME UNITS

$\boxed{\text{🏊}}$ $\boxed{\text{🛏}}$ / $\boxed{\text{✕}}$ $\boxed{\text{🖨}}$ $\boxed{\text{🖳}}$ $\boxed{\text{🖳}}$

PARK SHORE RESORT

			Phone: (941)263-2222
12/1-1/2	1P: $145-$250	2P: $145-$250	XP: $10	F18
1/3-4/21	1P: $149-$235	2P: $149-$235	XP: $10	F18
11/1-11/30	1P: $119-$145	2P: $119-$145	XP: $10	F18
4/22-10/31	1P: $99-$125	2P: $99-$125	XP: $10	F18

Condominium **Location:** I-75, exit 16, just w of jct US 41 via Island Club Loop. 600 Neapolitan Way 34103. Fax: 941/263-0946. **Facility:** Tropically landscaped ground surrounded by private waterway. All units with patio or balcony. Adjacent to shopping mall and grocery stores. 103 units with kitchen. 64 two-bedroom units. Some suites. 2-4 stories, exterior corridors. **Terms:** 3 day cancellation notice, monthly rates available. **Amenities:** extended cable TV, voice mail, irons. **Dining:** restaurant, 11:30 am-9 pm, $9-$20, cocktails. **Leisure Activities:** heated pool, whirlpool, sun deck, 4 tennis courts, racquetball courts, children's program, recreation program, basketball, shuffleboard, volleyball, gas barbecue grills, picnic table & gazebo area. **Guest Services:** area transportation-beach, coin laundry. **Business Services:** meeting rooms. **Cards:** AE, DI, DS, MC, VI. *(See color ad below)*

QUALITY INN-GULFCOAST

			Phone: (941)261-6046
1/16-4/20	1P: $110-$120	2P: $120-$130	XP: $10	F18
12/21-1/15	1P: $100-$110	2P: $110-$120	XP: $10	F18
4/21-11/30	1P: $55-$85	2P: $60-$70	XP: $10	F18
12/1-12/20	1P: $55-$65	2P: $60-$70	XP: $10	F18

Motor Inn **Location:** I-75, exit 16, 2.5 mi n on US 41, between 26th Ave N and Harbour Dr. 2555 Tamiami Tr N (US 41) 34103. Fax: 941/261-5742. **Facility:** Courtyard style structure, many rooms facing pool area. Traditional motel rooms. 105 units. 2 stories, exterior corridors. **Terms:** package plans - in summer. **Amenities:** extended cable TV, voice mail, safes (fee), irons, hair dryers. **Dining:** 3 restaurants, 11:30 am-3 & 5-10 pm, $9-$20, cocktails. **Leisure Activities:** heated pool, shuffleboard, pool table, video games. **Guest Services:** [CP] meal plan available, valet laundry. **Business Services:** meeting rooms. **Cards:** AE, DI, DS, JC, MC, VI. **Special Amenities:** free local telephone calls and free newspaper. *(See ad below)*

RAMADA PLAZA HOTEL
Motor Inn
▼▼▼
12/23-4/30   1P: $109-$133   2P: $109-$133   XP: $10
12/1-12/22 & 5/1-11/30   1P: $79-$109   2P: $79-$109   XP: $10
Phone: (941)430-3500
Location: I-75, exit 16, 2.5 mi w. 1100 Pine Ridge Rd 34108. Fax: 944/430-3501. **Facility:** 104 units. Some suites ($189-$235). *Bath:* combo or shower only. 4 stories, interior corridors. **Terms:** package plans, pets ($25 extra charge, 1st floor only). **Amenities:** extended cable TV, video games, voice mail, safes, irons, hair dryers. **Leisure Activities:** heated pool, exercise room. **Guest Services:** valet laundry. **Business Services:** meeting rooms, administrative services, PC, fax. **Cards:** AE, CB, DI, DS, JC, MC, VI. *(See color ad below)*   SOME UNITS

RED ROOF INN
Motel
ⓐⓐⓐ SAVE
▼▼ ▼▼
2/1-3/31   1P: $90-$120   2P: $90-$120
12/22-1/31   1P: $85-$109   2P: $85-$109
12/1-12/21 & 4/1-11/30   1P: $45-$70   2P: $45-$70
Phone: (941)774-3117
Location: I-75, exit 15 (SR 84), just e of jct US 41. 1925 Davis Blvd 34104. Fax: 941/775-5333. **Facility:** Contemporary rooms with some tropical touches. 157 units, 30 with kitchen. Some suites ($70-$150). *Bath:* combo or shower only. 3 stories, exterior corridors. **Terms:** small pets only. **Amenities:** extended cable TV, video games, voice mail. **Leisure Activities:** heated pool, whirlpool, barbecue grills, picnic tables. **Guest Services:** coin laundry. **Cards:** AE, DI, DS, MC, VI. **Special Amenities:** free local telephone calls and free newspaper.   SOME UNITS

THE REGISTRY RESORT
Resort
ⓐⓐⓐ SAVE
▼▼▼ ▼▼
5/1-5/31   1P: $355-$490   2P: $355-$490   XP: $25   F18
10/1-11/30   1P: $285-$440   2P: $285-$440   XP: $25   F18
12/1-4/30   1P: $295-$395   2P: $295-$395   XP: $25   F18
6/1-9/30   1P: $180-$315   2P: $180-$315   XP: $25   F18
Phone: (941)597-3232
Location: I-75, exit 16, north end of town; 0.5 mi w of US 41 via CR 896 (Pine Ridge/Seagate Blvd). 475 Seagate Dr 34103. Fax: 941/597-3147. **Facility:** Luxurious, contemporary high-rise with public areas finished in Italian marble. 1/2 mile to beach across protected mangrove lagoon by hotel trolley. Luxurious guest rooms with balcony or ground floor terrace. 474 units. Some suites ($290-$715) and whirlpool units. *Bath:* combo or shower only. 1-18 stories, interior/exterior corridors. **Parking:** valet. **Terms:** 7 day cancellation notice-fee imposed, package plans. **Amenities:** voice mail, safes, honor bars, irons, hair dryers. **Dining:** 2 dining rooms, restaurant, coffee shop, 7 am-11 pm Sun brunch, customized picnic lunch to go, $13-$34, cocktails, also, Lafite, see separate listing, nightclub, entertainment. **Leisure Activities:** 3 heated pools, whirlpools, beach access, fishing, golf clinic, golf concierge/master & golf privileges, children's program, recreation program, social program, basketball, access to nature preserve. *Fee:* canoeing, sailboats, windsurfing, aqua bikes, catamarans, sea kayaks, golf-18 holes, 15 tennis courts (5 lighted), bicycles. **Guest Services:** [BP] meal plan available, gift shop, afternoon tea, valet laundry. *Fee:* area transportation, massage. **Business Services:** conference facilities, administrative services, fax. *Fee:* PC. **Cards:** AE, CB, DI, DS, JC, MC, VI.   SOME UNITS

RESIDENCE INN BY MARRIOTT, NAPLES
Motel
▼▼▼
12/22-3/31   1P: $169-$249
4/1-4/30   1P: $149-$219
12/1-12/21   1P: $109-$129
5/1-11/30   1P: $89-$119
Phone: (941)659-1300
Location: I-75, exit 16, on US 41. 4075 Tamiami Tr N 34103. Fax: 941/659-2300. **Facility:** Studios, one- and two-bedroom suites. Some units with fireplace. Centrally located one mile from gulf beaches. 120 units. 29 two-bedroom units, 77 efficiencies and 53 units with kitchen. Some suites. *Bath:* combo or shower only. 3 stories, interior corridors. **Parking:** valet. **Terms:** cancellation fee imposed, pets ($85 fee, $3.50 extra charge). **Amenities:** extended cable TV, voice mail, irons, hair dryers. **Leisure Activities:** heated pool, whirlpool, exercise room, sports court. **Guest Services:** [ECP] meal plan available, complimentary evening beverages: Mon-Thurs, area transportation, valet and coin laundry. **Business Services:** meeting rooms, fax. **Cards:** AE, DI, DS, JC, MC, VI. *(See color ad p 537)*   SOME UNITS

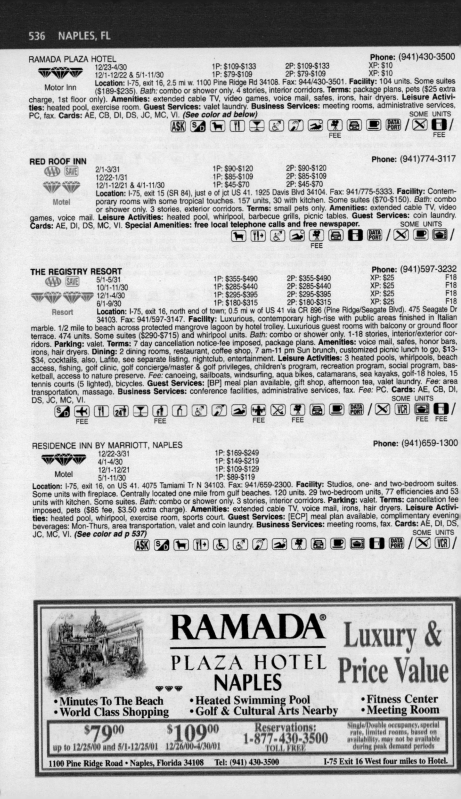

THE RITZ-CARLTON, NAPLES

▼▼▼▼▼
Hotel

	1P: $449-$569	2P: $449-$569	XP: $25	F18
12/1-5/8				
5/9-5/25 & 9/30-11/30	1P: $255-$355	2P: $255-$355	XP: $25	F18
5/26-9/29	1P: $215-$275	2P: $215-$275	XP: $25	F18

Phone: (941)598-3300

Location: From US 41, 1.3 mi w on Vanderbilt Beach Rd (CR 846). 280 Vanderbilt Beach Rd 34108. Fax: 941/598-6690. **Facility:** Gulf front. Skillful blend of Old World elegance and lush tropical setting. Public area accented with fine antiques and art work. Many rooms with coastal view, some with balcony. 463 units. Some suites ($495-$4000). *Bath:* combo or shower only. 13 stories, interior corridors. **Parking:** valet. **Terms:** 14 day cancellation notice, 7 day off season-fee imposed, package plans. **Amenities:** extended cable TV, video games, dual phone lines, voice mail, safes, honor bars, irons, hair dryers. **Dining:** 6 restaurants, 6:30 am-10 pm; beach pavilion (seasonal), $13-$37, cocktails, also, The Grill, The Dining Room, see separate listing, entertainment. **Leisure Activities:** heated pool, saunas, whirlpool, steamrooms, beach, charter fishing, pro shop, children's program, social program, jogging, exercise room, aerobics daily, billiards, barber & beauty salon, spa services, jewelry store, car rental agency. *Fee:* sailboating, boogie boards, catamarans, kayaks, jet skis, suncats, golf-27 holes, putting green, golf instruction, 6 lighted tennis courts, tennis instruction, bicycles. **Guest Services:** gift shop, valet laundry. *Fee:* area transportation, massage. **Business Services:** conference facilities, administrative services, fax. *Fee:* PC. **Cards:** AE, CB, DI, DS, JC, MC, VI.

SOME UNITS
[✈ FEE] [▐¶] [24] [▼] [♿] [⅄] [◈] [⇆] [✕] [♥ FEE] [VCR] [🖨] [DATA PORT] / [✕] /

STAYBRIDGE SUITES HOTEL BY HOLIDAY INN

▼▼▼
Extended Stay Motel

	1P: $87-$142	2P: $87-$142	
12/22-4/14			
12/1-12/21 & 10/28-11/30	1P: $80-$116	2P: $80-$116	
4/15-10/27	1P: $67-$116	2P: $67-$116	

Phone: (941)643-8002

Location: I-75, exit 15, w on Pine Ridge Rd to US 41 (Tamiami Tr), turn left. 4805 Tamiami Tr N 34103. Fax: 941/643-8069. **Facility:** Spacious upscale studios and one- or two-bedroom suites. 122 efficiencies. 8 two-bedroom units. Some suites ($67-$142). *Bath:* combo or shower only. 4 stories, interior corridors. **Terms:** cancellation fee imposed, weekly & monthly rates available, package plans, pets ($25 fee, $10 extra charge). **Amenities:** extended cable TV, voice mail, irons, hair dryers. **Leisure Activities:** whirlpool, exercise room. **Guest Services:** [ECP] meal plan available, complimentary evening beverages: Mon-Thurs, complimentary laundry. **Business Services:** meeting rooms, administrative services, PC, fax. **Cards:** AE, DI, DS, MC, VI. *(See color ad below)*

SOME UNITS
[ASK] [🐂] [♿] [⅄] [◈] [⇆] [✕] [VCR] [🖨] [▣] [🖥] [🛏] [🔋] [DATA PORT] / [✕] /

STONEY'S COURTYARD INN

(AAA) [SAVE]
▼▼▼
Motel

	1P: $95-$105	2P: $95-$105	XP: $10	F16
1/26-4/15				
12/1-1/25 & 4/16-11/30	1P: $50	2P: $50	XP: $10	F16

Phone: (941)261-3870

Location: I-75, exit 16, US 41, just s of Harbor Dr. 2630 N Tamiami Tr 34103. Fax: 941/261-4932. **Facility:** Good sized guest rooms. 76 units. Some suites ($70-$130). 2 stories, exterior corridors. **Amenities:** voice mail. *Some:* safes. **Leisure Activities:** heated pool, shuffleboard. **Guest Services:** coin laundry. **Cards:** AE, DS, MC, VI. **Special Amenities:** free continental breakfast and free room upgrade (subject to availability with advanced reservations).

SOME UNITS
[▐¶+] [⇆] [🖨] / [✕] [VCR FEE] [🖥] [🛏] [🔋 FEE] /

TIDES INN OF NAPLES

	12/18-4/14	1P: $159-$369	2P: $129-$345	XP: $10	F12
	12/1-12/17 & 11/15-11/30	1P: $79-$225	2P: $79-$225	XP: $10	F12
Motel	4/15-11/14	1P: $65-$165	2P: $65-$165	XP: $10	F12

Phone: (941)262-6196

Location: I-76, exit 16, 1.1 mi s of jct Mooringline Dr. 1801 Gulf Shore Blvd N 34102. Fax: 941/262-3055. **Facility:** Gulf front property; some rooms with balcony and gulf view. 36 units. 1 two-bedroom unit, 2 efficiencies and 25 units with kitchen. Some suites ($124-$355). 2 stories, interior/exterior corridors. **Terms:** 30 day cancellation notice, 90 days 12/1-4/30. **Amenities:** extended cable TV, voice mail, hair dryers. **Leisure Activities:** heated pool, beach, shuffleboard. **Guest Services:** [CP] meal plan available, complimentary laundry. **Cards:** AE, DS, MC, VI.

SOME UNITS

TRIANON OLD NAPLES

	12/1-3/31	1P: $165-$400	2P: $165-$400	XP: $10	F18
	10/1-11/30	1P: $115-$300	2P: $115-$300	XP: $10	F18
Motel	4/1-4/30	1P: $95-$300	2P: $95-$300	XP: $10	F18
	5/1-9/30	1P: $75-$175	2P: $75-$175	XP: $10	F18

Phone: (941)435-9600

Location: Downtown; just s of jct US 41. 955 7th Ave S 34102. Fax: 941/261-0025. **Facility:** Elegantly decorated public areas. Luxurious and spacious guest rooms. 58 units. Some suites ($350). **Bath:** combo or shower only. 3 stories, interior corridors. **Terms:** cancellation fee imposed, package plans. **Amenities:** extended cable TV, voice mail, safes, irons, hair dryers. **Leisure Activities:** heated pool. **Guest Services:** [ECP] meal plan available, area transportation, valet laundry. **Business Services:** meeting rooms, fax. **Cards:** AE, DI, DS, MC, VI.

SOME UNITS

VANDERBILT BEACH RESORT

	2/1-4/30		2P: $140-$280	XP: $6	F3
	12/1-1/31		2P: $74-$280	XP: $6	F3
Motel	5/1-11/30		2P: $78-$145	XP: $6	F3

Phone: 941/597-3144

Location: I-75, exit 17, north end of town; 1.5 mi w of US 41 via Vanderbilt Beach Rd (SR 862), just n. 9225 Gulfshore Dr N 34108. Fax: 941/597-2199. **Facility:** Traditional rooms with entrance from gulf front courtyard; up-to-date room package. Some condo units opposite street on Vanderbilt Lagoon. 66 units. 16 two-bedroom units, 20 efficiencies and 36 units with kitchen. Some suites. 1-4 stories, exterior corridors. **Terms:** 10 day cancellation notice, weekly rates available, package plans. **Amenities:** extended cable TV. **Leisure Activities:** heated pool, beach, swimming, beach chairs, cabanas, boat dock, tennis court. *Fee:* sailboating. **Guest Services:** coin laundry. **Cards:** AE, MC, VI.

SOME UNITS

VANDERBILT INN ON THE GULF

	2/1-4/15		2P: $195-$320	XP: $10	F18
	12/1-1/31		2P: $140-$320	XP: $10	F18
Motor Inn	4/16-9/30		2P: $110-$290	XP: $10	F18
	10/1-11/30		2P: $140-$210	XP: $10	F18

Phone: (941)597-3151

Location: I-75, exit 17, north end of town; 1.5 mi w of US 41 via SR 846 (111th Ave). 11000 Gulfshore Dr N 34108. Fax: 941/597-3099. **Facility:** Adjacent to Delnor Wiggins state recreation area. Family oriented resort. Live music weekends. Some smaller rooms. 147 units, 16 with efficiency. 2 stories, exterior corridors. **Terms:** 3 day cancellation notice-fee imposed, weekly rates available, package plans - 5/1-12/24. **Amenities:** extended cable TV, voice mail, safes, hair dryers. **Leisure Activities:** heated pool, whirlpool, beach, swimming. *Fee:* boats, sailboats, windsurfing. **Guest Services:** gift shop, coin laundry. **Business Services:** meeting rooms. **Cards:** AE, DI, DS, MC, VI. *(See color ad below)*

SOME UNITS

WELLESLEY INN & SUITES

Phone: (941)793-4646

AAA [SAVE]

Motel

| | 12/18-4/14 | 1P: $89-$129 | 2P: $89-$129 | |
| | 12/1-12/17 & 4/15-11/30 | 1P: $49-$79 | 2P: $49-$79 | XP: $10 | F18 |

Location: I-75, exit 15, 1 mi s on US 41, at jct SR 84. 1555 5th Ave S 34102. Fax: 941/793-5248. **Facility:** Up-to-date property, traditional motel rooms. Some smaller rooms. 105 units. *Bath:* combo or shower only. 3 stories, interior corridors. **Terms:** weekly & monthly rates available, pets ($10 extra charge). **Amenities:** video games, voice mail. **Leisure Activities:** heated pool. **Guest Services:** valet laundry. **Cards:** AE, DI, DS, MC, VI. **Special Amenities:** free continental breakfast and free local telephone calls. *(See color ad opposite title page)*

The following lodgings were either not evaluated or did not meet AAA rating requirements but are listed for your information only.

DOUBLETREE GUEST SUITES

Phone: 941/593-8733

[fyi]

Suite Hotel

	12/15-4/30	1P: $145-$210	2P: $145-$210	XP: $10	F17
	12/1-12/14 & 10/1-11/30	1P: $140-$200	2P: $140-$200	XP: $10	F17
	5/1-9/30	1P: $89-$110	2P: $89-$110	XP: $10	F17

Too new to rate. **Location:** I-75, exit 17, 3.3 mi w on Naples-Immokalee Rd to US 41, just sw. 12200 Tamiami Tr N 34110. Fax: 941/593-8734. **Amenities:** 101 units, restaurant, radios, coffeemakers, refrigerators, pool. **Terms:** cancellation fee imposed. **Cards:** AE, DI, DS, MC, VI. *(See color ad p 127)*

HAWTHORN SUITES

Phone: 941/593-1300

[fyi]

Suite Motel

	1/15-4/30	1P: $104-$204	2P: $104-$204	
	10/1-11/30	1P: $84-$164	2P: $84-$164	
	12/1-1/14	1P: $79-$159	2P: $79-$159	
	5/1-9/30	1P: $54-$115	2P: $54-$115	

Too new to rate, opening scheduled for September 2000. **Location:** I-75, exit 16, 0.5 mi w. 3557 Pine Ridge Rd 34109. Fax: 941/593-1301. **Amenities:** 82 units, radios, coffeemakers, microwaves, refrigerators, pool. **Cards:** AE, CB, DI, DS, MC. *(See color ad below)*

WHERE TO DINE

BANGKOK CUISINE

Lunch: $7-$10   **Dinner:** $11-$22   **Phone:** 941/261-5900

Thai

Location: On US 41 N, just n of Naples Community Hospital, between 5th and 6th aves. 572 9th St N 34102. **Hours:** 11:30 am-2 & 4:30-10 pm. Closed major holidays. **Reservations:** suggested. **Features:** casual dress; early bird specials; carryout; beer & wine only; a la carte. On a scale of 1 to 5, how spicy do you like your curried beef and chicken stir-fry? You control how hot or how mild your entree tastes at this conveniently located restaurant. A good selection of seafood and flavorful Thai vegetarian dishes. Sushi bar. Smoke free premises. **Cards:** AE, MC, VI.

BAYSIDE-A SEAFOOD GRILL & BAR

Lunch: $7-$12   **Dinner:** $16-$25   **Phone:** 941/649-5552

AAA

Seafood

Location: 1 mi w of US 41 via Park Shore Dr; in the Village on Venetian Bay, sw corner. 4270 Gulfshore Blvd N 34103. **Hours:** 11:30 am-11 pm. **Reservations:** suggested. **Features:** casual dress; Sunday brunch; children's menu; carryout; cocktails & lounge; entertainment; a la carte. Beautiful watercolors by artist Tracy Taylor, live piano music by Chuck Jobes, and a fine view of the bay, all enhance the Mediterranean decor. An international cuisine features seafood and pasta selections. Valet parking for dinner is offered in winter. **Cards:** AE, DI, DS, MC, VI.

BILL'S PIER ON FIFTH

Lunch: $5-$27   **Dinner:** $12-$27   **Phone:** 941/261-1811

Steak & Seafood

Location: At Tin City, jct US 41 and Goodlette-Frank Rd. 1200 5th Ave S 34102. **Hours:** 11 am-10 pm. Closed: 11/22, 12/25. **Reservations:** accepted. **Features:** casual dress; children's menu; carryout; cocktails & lounge. Enjoy indoor and outdoor dining on the Gordon River. The natural wood interior is inviting, and the staff is warm and friendly. The restaurant serves meat, chicken, fish and a good selection of salad and sandwiches. **Cards:** AE, DI, DS, MC, VI.

CAFE MERAN
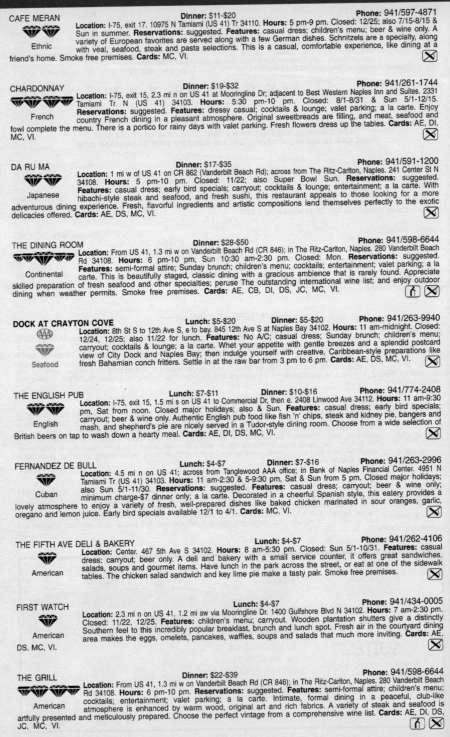
Ethnic

Dinner: $11-$20   **Phone:** 941/597-4871
Location: I-75, exit 17. 10975 N Tamiami (US 41) Tr 34110. **Hours:** 5 pm-9 pm. Closed: 12/25; also 7/15-8/15 & Sun in summer. **Reservations:** suggested. **Features:** casual dress; children's menu; beer & wine only. A variety of European favorites are served along with a few German dishes. Schnitzels are a specialty, along with veal, seafood, steak and pasta selections. This is a casual, comfortable experience, like dining at a friend's home. Smoke free premises. **Cards:** MC, VI.

CHARDONNAY
French

Dinner: $19-$32   **Phone:** 941/261-1744
Location: I-75, exit 15, 2.3 mi n on US 41 at Mooringline Dr; adjacent to Best Western Naples Inn and Suites. 2331 Tamiami Tr N (US 41) 34103. **Hours:** 5:30 pm-10 pm. Closed: 8/1-8/31 & Sun 5/1-12/15. **Reservations:** suggested. **Features:** dressy casual; cocktails & lounge; valet parking; a la carte. Enjoy country French dining in a pleasant atmosphere. Original sweetbreads are filling, and meat, seafood and fowl complete the menu. There is a portico for rainy days with valet parking. Fresh flowers dress up the tables. **Cards:** AE, DI, MC, VI.

DA RU MA
Japanese

Dinner: $17-$35   **Phone:** 941/591-1200
Location: 1 mi w of US 41 on CR 862 (Vanderbilt Beach Rd); across from The Ritz-Carlton, Naples. 241 Center St N 34108. **Hours:** 5 pm-10 pm. Closed: 11/22; also Super Bowl Sun. **Reservations:** suggested. **Features:** casual dress; early bird specials; carryout; cocktails & lounge; entertainment; a la carte. With hibachi-style steak and seafood, and fresh sushi, this restaurant appeals to those looking for a more adventurous dining experience. Fresh, flavorful ingredients and artistic compositions lend themselves to the exotic delicacies offered. **Cards:** AE, DS, MC, VI.

THE DINING ROOM
Continental

Dinner: $28-$50   **Phone:** 941/598-6644
Location: From US 41, 1.3 mi w on Vanderbilt Beach Rd (CR 846); in The Ritz-Carlton, Naples. 280 Vanderbilt Beach Rd 34108. **Hours:** 6 pm-10 pm, Sun 10:30 am-2:30 pm. Closed: Mon. **Reservations:** suggested. **Features:** semi-formal attire; Sunday brunch; children's menu; cocktails; entertainment; valet parking; a la carte. This is beautifully staged, classic dining with a gracious ambience that is rarely found. Appreciate skilled preparation of fresh seafood and other specialties; peruse The outstanding international wine list; and enjoy outdoor dining when weather permits. Smoke free premises. **Cards:** AE, CB, DI, DS, JC, MC, VI.

DOCK AT CRAYTON COVE
AAA
Seafood

Lunch: $5-$20   **Dinner:** $5-$20   **Phone:** 941/263-9940
Location: 8th St S to 12th Ave S, e to bay. 845 12th Ave S at Naples Bay 34102. **Hours:** 11 am-midnight. Closed: 12/24, 12/25; also 11/22 for lunch. **Features:** No A/C; casual dress; Sunday brunch; children's menu; carryout; cocktails & lounge; a la carte. Whet your appetite with gentle breezes and a splendid postcard view of City Dock and Naples Bay; then indulge yourself with creative, Caribbean-style preparations like fresh Bahamian conch fritters. Settle in at the raw bar from 3 pm to 6 pm. **Cards:** AE, DS, MC, VI.

THE ENGLISH PUB
English

Lunch: $7-$11   **Dinner:** $10-$16   **Phone:** 941/774-2408
Location: I-75, exit 15, 1.5 mi s on US 41 to Commercial Dr, then e. 2408 Linwood Ave 34112. **Hours:** 11 am-9:30 pm, Sat from noon. Closed major holidays; also & Sun. **Features:** casual dress; early bird specials; carryout; beer & wine only. Authentic English pub food have fish 'n' chips, steak and kidney pie, bangers and mash, and shepherd's pie are nicely served in a Tudor-style dining room. Choose from a wide selection of British beers on tap to wash down a hearty meal. **Cards:** AE, DI, DS, MC, VI.

FERNANDEZ DE BULL
Cuban

Lunch: $4-$7   **Dinner:** $7-$16   **Phone:** 941/263-2996
Location: 4.5 mi n on US 41; across from Tanglewood AAA office; in Bank of Naples Financial Center. 4951 N Tamiami Tr (US 41) 34103. **Hours:** 11 am-2:30 & 5-9:30 pm, Sat & Sun from 5 pm. Closed major holidays; also Sun 5/1-11/30. **Reservations:** suggested. **Features:** casual dress; carryout; beer & wine only; minimum charge-$7 dinner only; a la carte. Decorated in a cheerful Spanish style, this eatery provides a lovely atmosphere to enjoy a variety of fresh, well-prepared dishes like baked chicken marinated in sour oranges, garlic, oregano and lemon juice. Early bird specials available 12/1 to 4/1. **Cards:** MC, VI.

THE FIFTH AVE DELI & BAKERY
American

Lunch: $4-$7   **Phone:** 941/262-4106
Location: Center. 467 5th Ave S 34102. **Hours:** 8 am-5:30 pm. Closed: Sun 5/1-10/31. **Features:** casual dress; carryout; beer only. A deli and bakery with a small service counter, it offers great sandwiches, salads, soups and gourmet items. Have lunch in the park across the street, or eat at one of the sidewalk tables. The chicken salad sandwich and key lime pie make a tasty pair. Smoke free premises.

FIRST WATCH
American

Lunch: $4-$7   **Phone:** 941/434-0005
Location: 2.3 mi n on US 41, 1.2 mi sw via Mooringline Dr. 1400 Gulfshore Blvd N 34102. **Hours:** 7 am-2:30 pm. Closed: 11/22, 12/25. **Features:** children's menu; carryout. Wooden plantation shutters give a distinctly Southern feel to this incredibly popular breakfast, brunch and lunch spot. Fresh air in the courtyard dining area makes the eggs, omelets, pancakes, waffles, soups and salads that much more inviting. **Cards:** AE, DS, MC, VI.

THE GRILL
American

Dinner: $22-$39   **Phone:** 941/598-6644
Location: From US 41, 1.3 mi w on Vanderbilt Beach Rd (CR 846); in The Ritz-Carlton, Naples. 280 Vanderbilt Beach Rd 34108. **Hours:** 6 pm-10 pm. **Reservations:** suggested. **Features:** semi-formal attire; children's menu; cocktails; entertainment; valet parking; a la carte. Intimate, formal dining in a peaceful, club-like atmosphere is enhanced by warm wood, original art and rich fabrics. A variety of steak and seafood is artfully presented and meticulously prepared. Choose the perfect vintage from a comprehensive wine list. **Cards:** AE, DI, DS, JC, MC, VI.

GROUPER HOUSE

Dinner: $10-$25   **Phone:** 941/263-4900

Steak & Seafood

Location: Just n of jct US 41 and Goodlette-Frank Rd S. 396 Goodlette 34102. **Hours:** 5 pm-9 pm, Fri & Sat-10 pm. **Features:** casual dress; children's menu; early bird specials; cocktails & lounge; buffet. A captain's buffet includes seafood, beef, pork, lamb, and chicken, plus salads and desserts with a build-your-own sundae area. This is a popular, busy restaurant so be prepared for a wait; but homey service and a rustic decor make any wait worthwhile. **Cards:** DS, MC, VI.

LAFITE

Dinner: $27-$39   **Phone:** 941/597-3232

Continental

Location: I-75, exit 16, north end of town; 0.5 mi w of US 41 via CR 896 (Pine Ridge/Seagate Blvd); in The Registry Resort. 475 Seagate Dr 34102. **Hours:** 6 pm-10 pm, Fri & Sat-11 pm; 7/1-9/1 Thurs-Sat only. **Reservations:** suggested. **Features:** formal attire; cocktails & lounge; valet parking; a la carte, also prix fixe. Look for formal dining in a vintage setting. Dinner features steak and seafood, but also offers varied game dishes with an international flavor. Sorbet is served between courses to cleanse the palate. A harpist plays Thursday through Saturday, 7/1-9/1. Smoke free premises. **Cards:** AE, DI, DS, JC, MC, VI.

MICHELBOB'S

Lunch: $5-$13   **Dinner:** $8-$16   **Phone:** 941/643-2877

American

Location: I-75, exit 16, 2 mi w on Pine Ridge Rd (SR 896), 4 mi s on Airport-Pulling Rd (CR 31). 371 Airport Rd N 34104. **Hours:** 11 am-9 pm, Sat from 4 pm, Sun 9 am-8:30 pm. Closed: 11/22; also Mon 6/1-10/31. **Features:** casual dress; Sunday brunch; children's menu; early bird specials; carryout; cocktails. Return to the 50s in this comfortable family dining room decorated with period memorabilia. The menu offers basic ribs and chicken selections with fries, coleslaw and homemade baked beans. Friendly and attentive service makes this a popular stop. Smoke free premises. **Cards:** AE, DI, DS, MC, VI.

PACIFIC 41 RESTAURANT & LOUNGE

Lunch: $6-$8   **Dinner:** $10-$20   **Phone:** 941/649-5858

American

Location: I-75, exit 15, US 41, just s of Central Ave; in Fairfield Inn and Suites. 173 9th St S (US 41) 34102. **Hours:** 8 am-10 pm. Closed: 5/29. **Reservations:** accepted. **Features:** casual dress; children's menu; early bird specials; carryout; cocktails & lounge; a la carte. A casual eatery located just minutes from the Gulf of Mexico, features a varied menu selection including prime rib, filet mignon, turkey breast and fresh seafood. The colorful nautical theme and cheerful atmosphere make this a pleasant, family-oriented experience. **Cards:** AE, DI, DS, MC, VI.

PIPPIN'S

Dinner: $10-$20   **Phone:** 941/262-2880

Steak & Seafood

Location: 1.5 mi n on US 41 (Tamiami Tr). 1390 9th St N 34102. **Hours:** 4:30 pm-10 pm, Fri & Sat-10:30 pm. Closed: 6/8, 11/22. **Reservations:** suggested. **Features:** casual dress; children's menu; early bird specials; carryout; salad bar; cocktails & lounge. A casual interior design features a huge saltwater aquarium as the centerpiece. A friendly and efficient staff serves up tasty meals like a generously portioned yellow-fin tuna cooked to taste. A modest dessert selection is offered for meal's end. **Cards:** AE, CB, DI, DS, MC, VI.

RISTORANTE CIAO

Dinner: $18-$30   **Phone:** 941/263-3889

Northern Italian

Location: Just w of US 41. 835 4th Ave S 34102. **Hours:** Open 12/1-6/10 & 9/1-11/30; 5:30 pm-10 pm. Closed: 4/15, 11/22; also 7/1-8/31 & Super Bowl Sun. **Reservations:** suggested. **Features:** dressy casual; beer & wine only; a la carte. European elegance is in the details, from Italian music to fresh roses on the tables. The owner/chef creates lush preparations like fettuccine Ciao with lobster and mushrooms in a rich cream sauce over pasta. Look for the chef's evening specials. Smoke free premises. **Cards:** AE, DI, DS, MC, VI.

RIVERWALK FISH & ALE HOUSE

Lunch: $8-$22   **Dinner:** $8-$22   **Phone:** 941/263-2734

Seafood

Location: At Tin City, jct US 41 and Goodlett Rd. 1200 5th Ave S 34102. **Hours:** 11 am-11 pm. Closed: 11/22, 12/25. **Features:** No A/C; casual dress; children's menu; carryout; cocktails & lounge; a la carte. Located in historic Tin City, this bustling open-air restaurant offers waterfront dining with a nautical theme. Casual attire is the order of the day. Well-prepared seafood is their specialty, such as the flavorful and filling grouper and chips. **Cards:** AE, DS, MC, VI.

SAVANNAH RESTAURANT

Dinner: $16-$24   **Phone:** 941/261-2555

Regional American

Location: Just s of SR 896 (Pine Ridge Rd). 5200 Tamiami Tr N, Ste 103 34103. **Hours:** 5 pm-10 pm. Closed: Mon. **Reservations:** suggested. **Features:** dressy casual; cocktails; a la carte. Decorated with antiques and Oriental rugs, the Williamsburg-style dining rooms are cozy settings in which to savor a relaxed meal of fresh fish, seafood, meat or poultry, as well as stir-fried vegetables. Creme brulee is a dessert favorite. **Cards:** AE, MC, VI.

SEAWITCH FISHMARKET & RESTAURANT

Lunch: $6-$10   **Dinner:** $14-$22   **Phone:** 941/566-1514

Seafood

Location: N end of town, 1.5 mi w of US 41 via Vanderbilt Beach Dr (SR 862), just n on Gulfshore Dr, just e. 179 Southbay Dr 34108. **Hours:** 11:30 am-4:30 & 5-9:30 pm, Sat & Sun from 5 pm. Closed major holidays; also Super Bowl Sun. **Features:** casual dress; children's menu; carryout; cocktails & lounge. Laid-back waterfront dining is what you'll get at this nautically themed restaurant. Whether you grill it, bake it, fry it or blacken it, the yellowtail snapper rarely misses the mark. Same goes for the landlubber steak and chicken and the yummy mud pie. **Cards:** AE, DS, MC, VI.

SIGN OF THE VINE

Dinner: $28-$39   **Phone:** 941/261-6745

American

Location: 3.5 mi n on US 41, just e. 980 Solana Rd 34102. **Hours:** 6 pm-10 pm, Fri & Sat only 8/1-9/30. Closed: Sun. **Reservations:** suggested. **Features:** dressy casual; beer & wine only. Unique semi-formal dining in a former private home, meals are a multi-course affair featuring a lengthy menu of creations, including game and specialty items. Sorbets are served between courses, and a relish tray with homemade pickles gives a nice start. **Cards:** AE.

ST. GEORGE & THE DRAGON **Lunch:** $6-$17 **Dinner:** $15-$30 **Phone:** 941/262-6546
▼▼▼▼ **Location:** Downtown; on US 41. 936 5th Ave S 34102. **Hours:** 11 am-10 pm, Sun 5 pm-9 pm. Closed: 12/25;
Steak & Seafood also Sun 4/1-12/31. **Reservations:** accepted. **Features:** semi-formal attire; cocktails & lounge. A local
favorite for 30 years, the menu features seafood, prime steak, fresh salad and homemade desserts served
in a warm setting of brass, hand-carved beams and an outstanding collection of nautical antiques. Valet
parking is offered at dinner. **Cards:** AE, DI, MC, VI. ⊠

TERRA THIRD STREET GRILL **Lunch:** $8-$14 **Dinner:** $14-$28 **Phone:** 941/262-5500
ⒶⒶⒶ **Location:** On 13th Ave, between 2nd and 3rd sts s. 1300 3rd St S 34102. **Hours:** 11:30 am-3 & 5-10 pm, Fri &
▼▼▼ Sat-11 pm. **Reservations:** suggested. **Features:** casual dress; carryout; cocktails & lounge; entertainment;
Continental a la carte. Casual, yet sophisticated, the restaurant blends Italian, Mediterranean, American and Asian
cuisine. The landscaped garden is a lovely dining setting. The lump crab cakes and fresh peach-berry
cobbler shouldn't be missed. **Cards:** AE, DI, DS, MC, VI. ⋔ ⊠

TOMMY BAHAMA'S **Lunch:** $8-$9 **Dinner:** $14-$21 **Phone:** 941/643-6889
▼▼ ▼▼ **Location:** In historic district at jct 12th Ave S. 1220 3rd St S 34102. **Hours:** 11 am-midnight. **Features:** No A/C;
Caribbean casual dress; street parking; a la carte. Tropical Bahamian setting with a variety of artfully displayed and
creative menu choices with Caribbean flair. **Cards:** MC, VI.

——— *The following restaurant has not been evaluated by AAA* ———
but is listed for your information only.

BHA! BHA! A PERSIAN BISTRO **Phone:** 941/594-5557
[fyi] Not evaluated. **Location:** 847 Vanderbilt Beach Rd. **Features:** Enjoy couscous, lamb and duck in desert oasis
ambience. Moderately priced.

NAVARRE pop. 1,000

——— **WHERE TO STAY** ———

BEST WESTERN NAVARRE **Phone:** (850)939-9400
ⒶⒶⒶ [SAVE] 5/1-9/7 1P: $79-$99 2P: $85-$105 XP: $6 F18
3/1-4/30 & 9/8-11/30 1P: $59-$79 2P: $65-$85 XP: $6 F18
▼▼▼▼ 12/1-2/28 1P: $49-$69 2P: $55-$75 XP: $6 F18
Motel **Location:** US 98, just e on bridge. 8697 Navarre Pkwy 32566. Fax: 850/939-4040. **Facility:** On Santa Rosa Sound.
69 units. 3 stories, exterior corridors. **Terms:** package plans. **Amenities:** extended cable TV. **Leisure Activi-**
ties: heated pool, fishing. **Guest Services:** [ECP] meal plan available, coin laundry. **Business Services:**
meeting rooms. **Cards:** AE, CB, DI, DS, JC, MC, VI. SOME UNITS

⑤🅓 🍴 🏊 🎥 📠 🖥 🧳 📵 [DATA PORT] / ⊠

COMFORT INN & CONFERENCE CENTER **Phone:** (850)939-1761
[SAVE] 5/26-9/4 1P: $89-$113 2P: $89-$113 XP: $8 F18
3/1-5/25 1P: $69-$83 2P: $69-$83 XP: $8 F18
▼▼▼ 12/1-2/28 & 9/5-11/30 1P: $59-$73 2P: $59-$73 XP: $8 F18
Motel **Location:** US 98, 0.3 mi n of Navarre Beach Bridge. 8700 Navarre Pkwy 32566. Fax: 850/939-2084. **Facility:** On
Santa Rosa Sound. 63 units. 2 stories, exterior corridors. **Terms:** package plans, pets ($10 extra charge).
Amenities: extended cable TV. *Some:* irons, hair dryers. **Guest Services:** [CP] meal plan available, coin
laundry. **Business Services:** conference facilities. **Cards:** AE, CB, DI, DS, JC, MC, VI. SOME UNITS

⑤🅓 🐾 🍴 🏊 🎥 📠 🖥 / ⊠ 📵 /

———— WHERE TO DINE ————

———— *The following restaurant has not been evaluated by AAA* ————
but is listed for your information only.

COWBOY'S
[fyi]
Not evaluated. **Location:** Hwy 98, e of Navarre Bridge. 8673 Navarre Pkwy. **Features:** Steakhouse at water's edge on the sound. Western decor. Very popular family restaurant. Also barbecue. Moderate prices.
Phone: 904/939-0502

NAVARRE BEACH

———— WHERE TO STAY ————

HOLIDAY INN
Motor Inn

5/25-9/30	1P: $120-$160	2P: $120-$160	XP: $10 F18
3/1-5/24	1P: $95-$125	2P: $95-$125	XP: $10 F18
12/1-2/28	1P: $80-$100	2P: $80-$100	XP: $10 F18
10/1-11/30	1P: $75-$100	2P: $75-$100	XP: $10 F18

Phone: (850)939-2321

Location: On SR 399, 0.6 mi s of bridge. 8375 Gulf Blvd 32566. Fax: 850/939-4768. **Facility:** 254 units. 2-3 stories, interior/exterior corridors. **Terms:** 3 day cancellation notice, package plans. **Amenities:** extended cable TV, voice mail, safes, irons, hair dryers. **Leisure Activities:** 2 pools (1 heated, 1 indoor), whirlpools, children's program in summer, exercise room. **Guest Services:** gift shop, valet and coin laundry. **Business Services:** meeting rooms. **Cards:** AE, CB, DI, DS, JC, MC, VI.

SOME UNITS

FEE

NEPTUNE BEACH —*See Jacksonville p. 446.*

NEW PORT RICHEY —*See Tampa Bay p. 868.*

NEW SMYRNA BEACH pop. 16,500

———— WHERE TO STAY ————

BUENA VISTA MOTEL AND APARTMENTS
Motel

All Year   1P: $60-$75   XP: $8   F12
Phone: 904/428-5565

Location: 2 mi e on Business 44, at w end of North Cswy Bridge. 500 N Causeway 32169. Fax: 904/428-5565. **Facility:** Rooms and one-bedroom apartments on the Indian River. 1/2 mile from ocean. A clean well-kept property. 8 units, 5 with kitchen. *Bath:* combo or shower only. 1 story, exterior corridors. **Terms:** 14 day cancellation notice-fee imposed, weekly rates available, small pets only ($5). **Amenities:** extended cable TV, irons. **Leisure Activities:** boat dock. **Guest Services:** coin laundry. **Cards:** MC, VI.

SOME UNITS

COASTAL WATERS INN
[AAA] [SAVE]
Motel

All Year   1P: $69-$199   2P: $69-$199   XP: $9   F12
Phone: (904)428-3800

Location: SR A1A; 3.4 mi s of SR 44. 3509 S Atlantic Ave 32169. Fax: 904/423-5002. **Facility:** Peaceful location on oceanfront. Variety of motel and multi-room units. 40 units, 32 with kitchen. *Bath:* combo or shower only. 2-3 stories (no elevator), exterior corridors. **Terms:** 3 day cancellation notice, weekly & monthly rates available. **Amenities:** extended cable TV. **Leisure Activities:** heated pool, wading pool. **Cards:** MC, VI. **Special Amenities:** free newspaper and preferred room (subject to availability with advanced reservations).

SOME UNITS

HOLIDAY INN HOTEL & SUITES
[AAA] [SAVE]
Motor Inn

2/6-4/24	1P: $120-$245	2P: $120-$245	XP: $10 F18
4/25-9/4	1P: $120-$185	2P: $120-$185	XP: $10 F18
9/5-11/30	1P: $120-$145	2P: $120-$145	XP: $10 F18
12/1-2/5	1P: $89-$135	2P: $89-$135	XP: $10 F18

Phone: (904)426-0020

Location: SR A1A, s of SR 44. 1401 S Atlantic Ave 32169. Fax: 904/423-3977. **Facility:** Comfortable studio and two-room suites. Designated smoking area. 102 units. 6 two-bedroom units and 101 units with kitchen. 8 stories, interior corridors. **Terms:** cancellation fee imposed, package plans. **Amenities:** extended cable TV, irons, hair dryers. **Dining:** restaurant, 7 am-11 & 5-9 pm, $6-$12, wine/beer only. **Leisure Activities:** beach. **Guest Services:** coin laundry. **Business Services:** fax. **Cards:** AE, CB, DI, DS, JC, MC, VI.

SOME UNITS

FEE

LITTLE RIVER INN B & B
Bed & Breakfast

All Year   1P: $80-$160   2P: $80-$160   XP: $15
Phone: (904)424-0100

Location: 1.3 mi e on Business Rt 44, then 0.5 mi n. 532 N Riverside Dr 32168. Fax: 904/424-5732. **Facility:** Located 1 mi e on the Indian River. This 1883 estate home provides a wonderful view of a nature preserve. Smoke free premises. 6 units. Some whirlpool units ($100-$160). *Bath:* some combo or shower only. 3 stories (no elevator), interior corridors. **Terms:** age restrictions may apply, 14 day cancellation notice-fee imposed, weekly rates available. **Amenities:** no TVs. **Leisure Activities:** whirlpool, tennis court, bicycles. **Guest Services:** [BP] meal plan available. **Cards:** AE, CB, DI, DS, MC, VI.

NIGHT SWAN INTRACOASTAL BED & BREAKFAST

Phone: (904)423-4940

AAA SAVE

Historic Bed & Breakfast

All Year   1P: $85-$160   2P: $85-$160   XP: $20   F12
Location: West side of Intracoastal Waterway; just s of SR 44 bridge. 512 S Riverside Dr 32168. Fax: 904/427-2814. **Facility:** Two homes overlook the Indian River, circa 1900s. Three units with private, enclosed sitting rooms. Smoke free premises. 15 units. Some whirlpool units ($120-$160). *Bath:* combo or shower only. 2-3 stories (no elevator), interior/exterior corridors. **Terms:** 3 day cancellation notice-fee imposed, weekly rates available. **Amenities:** extended cable TV, irons, hair dryers. **Leisure Activities:** boat dock. **Guest Services:** [BP] meal plan available, area transportation-marinas, complimentary laundry. **Business Services:** meeting rooms. **Cards:** AE, DI, DS, MC, VI. **Special Amenities:** early check-in/late check-out and free local telephone calls.

SOME UNITS

RIVERVIEW HOTEL

Phone: (904)428-5858

AAA SAVE

Historic Country Inn

All Year   1P: $80-$200   2P: $80-$200   XP: $10   D
Location: East end of North Cswy Bridge. 103 Flagler Ave 32169. Fax: 904/423-8927. **Facility:** 1930s hotel on Intracoastal Waterway. 2 rooms date to 1886. 19 units. 1 two-bedroom unit and 1 efficiency. *Bath:* combo or shower only. 3 stories (no elevator), interior/exterior corridors. **Terms:** weekly rates available. **Amenities:** extended cable TV, safes, irons. **Dining:** Riverview Charlies, see separate listing. **Leisure Activities:** heated pool, boat dock, bicycles. **Guest Services:** gift shop. **Cards:** AE, CB, DI, DS, MC, VI. **Special Amenities:** free continental breakfast and free newspaper.

SOME UNITS

SMYRNA MOTEL

Phone: 904/428-2495

AAA SAVE

Motel

12/1-4/30   1P: $45-$55   2P: $55-$75   XP: $10   F10
5/1-11/30   1P: $40-$50   2P: $45-$55   XP: $10   F10
Location: 1.2 mi n on US 1. 1050 N Dixie Frwy 32168. **Facility:** Modestly furnished guest rooms. Bald eagle nest at the rear of the motel. 10 units. *Bath:* shower only. 1 story, exterior corridors. **Terms:** 14 day cancellation notice, weekly rates available. **Amenities:** extended cable TV. **Cards:** DS, MC, VI.

SOME UNITS

—— WHERE TO DINE ——

CHASES

Steak & Seafood

Lunch: $6-$9   Dinner: $10-$18   Phone: 904/423-8787
Location: SR A1A, 3.3 mi s of SR 44. 3401 S Atlantic Blvd 32169. **Hours:** 11 am-10 pm. Closed: 12/25. **Features:** casual dress; children's menu; early bird specials; cocktails & lounge; entertainment. A scenic oceanfront location offering both indoor and outdoor dining. The menu is traditional fare which includes tasty burgers, homemade soup, creative salads and seafood or landlubber entrees. **Cards:** AE, DS, MC, VI.

JB'S FISH CAMP

Seafood

Lunch: $8-$17   Dinner: $8-$17   Phone: 904/427-5747
Location: SR A1A, 8.5 mi s of SR 44 on the Indian River. 859 Pompano Ave 32169. **Hours:** 11:30 am-9:30 pm, Fri & Sat-10:30 pm. Closed: 11/22, 12/25. **Features:** casual dress; children's menu; carryout; cocktails. A docking place for hopeful fishermen, this rustic, Florida-style structure resembles an old shack but offers delicious local oysters and fresh river clams right off the boat. A popular local spot, it is perfect for a good meal after a day at the beach. **Cards:** AE, MC, VI.

NORWOOD'S SEAFOOD RESTAURANT

Seafood

Lunch: $6-$9   Dinner: $6-$29   Phone: 904/428-4621
Location: SR 44, 1 mi e of Intracoastal Waterway Bridge. 400 E 2nd Ave 32169. **Hours:** 11:30 am-9:30 pm. Closed: 12/25. **Reservations:** accepted. **Features:** casual dress; children's menu; early bird specials; carryout; cocktails. Ease into this very popular, very comfortable restaurant. Early bird specials offer the best bargain, with a variety of fresh seafood and beef dishes and an extensive wine list. Try the coconut shrimp served with a tangy, sweet-and-sour sauce. **Cards:** AE, DI, DS, MC, VI.

PATIO RESTAURANT

American

Lunch: $4-$6   Dinner: $7-$16   Phone: 904/423-8355
Location: Downtown on US 1. 626 N Dixie Frwy 32168. **Hours:** 11 am-2:30 & 4:30-9 pm. Closed: 12/25; also Sun. **Reservations:** suggested. **Features:** casual dress; early bird specials; carryout; beer & wine only. Step into a quaint, romantic world of classical music, wrought iron gates and gardens of night-blooming jasmine. Gourmet dining in an intimate setting showcases an award-winning menu with seafood, a lovely vegetarian entree and a portobello-stuffed filet. Smoke free premises. **Cards:** AE, CB, DI, DS, MC, VI.

RIVERVIEW CHARLIES

Seafood

Lunch: $5-$7   Dinner: $14-$23   Phone: 904/428-1865
Location: East end of North Cswy Bridge; at Riverview Hotel. 101 Flagler Ave 32169. **Hours:** 11 am-2:30 & 4:30-10 pm, Sun 11 am-3 & 5-10 pm. Closed: 12/25. **Reservations:** required. **Features:** semi-formal attire; Sunday brunch; cocktails; valet parking. Located in a restored brick building, guests receive riverview dining from an inside window or the under cover deck dining. Creative menu offers fresh fish and shellfish, pasta and chicken. A pastry chef prepares sinful desserts. **Cards:** AE, DI, DS, MC, VI.

NICEVILLE pop. 10,500

—— WHERE TO STAY ——

HOLIDAY INN EXPRESS

Phone: (850)678-9131

Motel

12/1-12/31 & 7/4-11/30   1P: $82-$95   2P: $82-$95   XP: $10
6/1-7/3   1P: $95   2P: $95   XP: $10
1/1-5/31   1P: $82   2P: $82   XP: $10
Location: Hwy 85, just se on jct Hwy 20. 106 Bayshore Dr 32578. Fax: 850/678-9272. **Facility:** 67 units. *Bath:* combo or shower only. 2 stories, interior corridors. **Terms:** cancellation fee imposed, monthly rates available. **Amenities:** extended cable TV, irons, hair dryers. **Leisure Activities:** heated pool. **Guest Services:** [CP] & [ECP] meal plans available, valet laundry. **Business Services:** meeting rooms. **Cards:** AE, CB, DI, DS, JC, MC, VI.

SOME UNITS

WHERE TO DINE

GIUSEPPI'S WHARF RESTAURANT & MARINA   **Lunch:** $7-$10   **Dinner:** $10-$15   **Phone:** 850/678-4229

▽▽
Seafood

Location: US 85, just se on jct US 20, then 0.8 mi se. 821 Bayshore Dr 32578. **Hours:** 11 am-9 pm; to 10 pm in summer. Closed: 11/22, 12/25. **Features:** children's menu; early bird specials; carryout; salad bar; cocktails & lounge. Hard to believe this attractive wharfside setting was once known as "Boggy Bayou," an early fishing village! The name was changed to Niceville and a 'nicer' friendlier bunch you couldn't hope to meet. The fishing is appropriate with a predominance of seafood and once a week, fresh live Maine lobster are a steamin' - but landlubbers are also well served. Ramp access available to the lounge, restaurant smoking area, outdoor tiki bar and upper floor deck. Enjoy view of boats and bay. **Cards:** AE, CB, DI, DS, MC, VI. ✕

NOKOMIS pop. 3,400

WHERE TO STAY

LAUREL VILLA MOTEL   **Phone:** 941/484-3656

▽▽▽ ◆◆

Apartment

12/20-4/30	1P: $45-$60	2P: $50-$65	XP: $8	F11
12/1-12/19 & 5/1-11/30	1P: $38-$45	2P: $42-$48	XP: $4	F11

Location: I-75, exit 36, 2.8 mi w on SR 681, just s on US 41. 1409 N Tamiami Tr 34275. **Fax:** 941/488-7444. **Facility:** 11 efficiencies. *Bath:* shower only. 1 story, exterior corridors. **Terms:** 30 day cancellation notice, weekly & monthly rates available. **Amenities:** *Some:* irons, hair dryers. **Leisure Activities:** putting green, bicycles. **Guest Services:** coin laundry. **Cards:** DS, MC, VI.

SOME UNITS

🍴 🏊 ☕ 📷 📞 / ✕ 📠 /

WHERE TO DINE

PELICAN ALLEY   **Lunch:** $8-$10   **Dinner:** $8-$20   **Phone:** 941/485-1893

▽▽▽
Seafood

Location: US 41, 1 mi w on Albee Rd at the s bridge to Casey Key. 1009 W Albee Rd 34275. **Hours:** 11:30 am-10 pm. Closed: 4/15, 11/22, 12/25; also Tues 5/15-11/2 & 9/8-9/20. **Features:** casual dress; children's menu; carryout; cocktails. Warm, cozy and casual, this restaurant is a popular place to watch traffic on the Intracoastal Waterway. Fresh seafood is a big draw, but the place is known for its chowder, delectably flavored with substantial chunks of seafood. **Cards:** AE, CB, DI, DS, MC, VI. ✕

NORTH BAY VILLAGE —*See Miami-Miami Beach p. 524.*

NORTH FORT MYERS pop. 16,900—*See also FORT MYERS.*

WHERE TO STAY

BEST WESTERN ROBERT E. LEE HOTEL   **Phone:** (941)997-5511

AAA SAVE
▽▽▽ ◆◆◆
Motel

1/1-4/30	1P: $79-$225	2P: $79-$225	XP: $5	F16
12/1-12/31	1P: $59-$225	2P: $59-$225	XP: $5	F16
5/1-11/30	1P: $59-$159	2P: $59-$159	XP: $5	F16

Location: US 41, just n of Caloosahatchee Bridge. 13021 N Cleveland Ave 33903. **Fax:** 941/656-6962. **Facility:** Riverfront with balcony or patio. 108 units. Some suites ($79-$225). 6 stories, exterior corridors. **Terms:** cancellation fee imposed. **Amenities:** extended cable TV, safes (fee). *Some:* hair dryers. **Dining:** entertainment. **Leisure Activities:** heated pool, whirlpool, fishing pier. **Guest Services:** coin laundry. **Business Services:** meeting rooms. **Cards:** AE, DI, DS, MC, VI. *(See ad p 394)*

SOME UNITS

S/D 🍴 🍸 🔈 🏊 ☕ DATA PORT / ✕ 📷 📞 /

CACTUS MOTEL   **Phone:** (941)995-2456

AAA SAVE
▽
Motel

12/1-4/30	2P: $65-$89	XP: $10	F12
5/1-11/30	2P: $50-$60	XP: $8	F12

Location: On US business 41, just s of jct Bayshore Rd. 1677 N Tamiami Tr 33903. **Facility:** 12 units, 7 with efficiency. 1 story, exterior corridors. **Terms:** 30 day cancellation notice-fee imposed. **Amenities:** extended cable TV, voice mail. *Some:* irons, hair dryers. **Leisure Activities:** shuffleboard, gas barbecue grill area with covered seating. **Cards:** DI, DS, MC, VI. **Special Amenities:** early check-in/late check-out and free local telephone calls.

SOME UNITS

S/D 🍴 / ✕ 📷 📞 /

ECONO LODGE   **Phone:** (941)995-0571

AAA SAVE
▽▽ ◆▽
Motel

2/2-4/1	1P: $89-$99	2P: $99	XP: $5	F18
12/1-2/1	1P: $59-$69	2P: $64-$74	XP: $5	F18
4/2-11/30	1P: $59-$69	2P: $59-$69	XP: $5	F18

Location: US 41, 1.1 mi n of Caloosahatchee Bridge. 13301 N Cleveland Ave 33903. **Fax:** 941/995-0571. **Facility:** 48 units. 2 stories, exterior corridors. **Terms:** 14 day cancellation notice, small pets only. **Leisure Activities:** heated pool. **Guest Services:** coin laundry. **Cards:** AE, CB, DI, DS, JC, MC, VI. **Special Amenities:** free continental breakfast and preferred room (subject to availability with advanced reservations).

SOME UNITS

S/D 🐾 🍴 🏊 📷 / ✕ VCR 📞 📷 📞 /
      FEE   FEE   FEE FEE

HOWARD JOHNSON EXPRESS INN   **Phone:** (941)656-4000

AAA SAVE
▽▽▽
Motel

2/16-4/30	1P: $82-$109	2P: $87-$114	XP: $5	F18
12/1-2/15 & 5/1-11/30	1P: $63-$89	2P: $72-$102	XP: $5	F18

Location: US 41, 1 mi n of Caloosahatchee Bridge. 13000 N Cleveland Ave 33903. **Fax:** 941/656-1612. **Facility:** Some rooms are riverfront. 121 units. 2 stories, exterior corridors. **Amenities:** irons. **Guest Services:** coin laundry. **Business Services:** meeting rooms. **Cards:** AE, CB, DI, DS, MC, VI. **Special Amenities:** free continental breakfast and free local telephone calls.

SOME UNITS

S/D 🍴 🔈 🏊 🛁 📷 📠 ☕ DATA PORT / ✕ 📷 📞 /
          FEE   FEE FEE

––––––– WHERE TO DINE –––––––

LAND & SEA FAMILY RESTAURANT **Lunch:** $4-$12 **Dinner:** $4-$12 **Phone:** 941-656-3030

American
Location: US 41, just n of Caloosahatchee River Bridge. 13121 Cleveland Ave 33903. **Hours:** 6 am-10 pm. **Features:** casual dress; children's menu; carryout; cocktails. This large family diner, a big favorite with the over-age-55 crowd, serves up a great selection of comfort foods, such as fried catfish, chicken fingers, mashed potatoes and country-fried steak. Expect good value: ample portions at reasonable prices.
Cards: AE, DS, MC, VI.

MARINERS INN **Dinner:** $8-$19 **Phone:** 941-997-8300

American
Location: Just w on Hancock Bridge Pkwy from jct US 41. 3448 Marinatown Ln 33903. **Hours:** 4 pm-10 pm; Fri & Sat-midnight. **Reservations:** suggested; window tables. **Features:** casual dress; early bird specials; carryout; cocktails & lounge. A maritime feel envelops the restaurant, which overlooks the marina. The grouper mariner is popular, but if you're feeling more turf than surf, lean toward the prime rib. One bite of the cognac chocolate sour cake should quiet your sweet tooth for hours. **Cards:** AE, MC, VI.

NORTH LAUDERDALE —*See Fort Lauderdale p. 386.*

NORTH MIAMI —*See Miami-Miami Beach p. 525.*

NORTH MIAMI BEACH —*See Miami-Miami Beach p. 525.*

NORTH PALM BEACH pop. 11,300 (See map p. 710; index p. 712)—

––––––– WHERE TO STAY –––––––

THE WATERFORD HOTEL & CONFERENCE CENTER **Phone:** (561)624-7186 **43**

1/1-4/30	1P: $139-$209	2P: $149-$209	XP: $10	F18
12/1-12/31 & 10/1-11/30	1P: $89-$149	2P: $99-$149	XP: $10	F18
5/1-9/30	1P: $79-$149	2P: $89-$149	XP: $10	F18

Motel
Location: US 1, just s of jct PGA Blvd (SR 786) and SR A1A. 11360 US Hwy 1 33408. **Fax:** 561/622-4258. **Facility:** Attractive Spanish Mediterranean style with very comfortable rooms. 90 units. Some suites ($99-$149) and whirlpool units ($149-$209). 4 stories, interior corridors. **Terms:** cancellation fee imposed, package plans. **Amenities:** extended cable TV, dual phone lines, voice mail, irons, hair dryers. *Some:* safes. **Dining:** coffee shop, 6:30 am-10:30 & 11:30-2:30 pm, cocktails. **Leisure Activities:** heated pool, exercise room. **Guest Services:** [ECP] meal plan available, valet laundry. **Business Services:** meeting rooms, administrative services. **Cards:** AE, CB, DI, DS, JC, MC, VI. **Special Amenities: free continental breakfast and free local telephone calls.**
SOME UNITS

––––––– WHERE TO DINE –––––––

EDDIE D'S **Lunch:** $5-$12 **Dinner:** $13-$27 **Phone:** 561/626-7373 **23**

Regional American
Location: US 1, 0.5 mi s of jct PGA Blvd; in Crystal Tree Plaza. 1201 US Hwy 1 33408. **Hours:** 11:30 am-2:30 & 4-10 pm, Sat 4 pm-10:30 pm; Sun 4 pm-9 pm. Closed: 12/25. **Reservations:** suggested. **Features:** casual dress; early bird specials; cocktails & lounge; entertainment. A comfortable, elegant dining room boasts a lively ambiance. The chef creates innovative entrees like the superb veal Oscar. Add to that a bowl of clam chowder and an exotic mixed-greens salad for a delicious meal. Valet parking is available at dinner. **Cards:** AE, DS, MC, VI.

NORTH PORT pop. 1,200

––––––– WHERE TO DINE –––––––

OLDE WORLD RESTAURANT & LOUNGE **Lunch:** $5-$18 **Dinner:** $5-$18 **Phone:** 941/426-1155

American
Location: Center, on US 41, just s of North Port Blvd. 14415 S Tamiami Tr 34287. **Hours:** 7 am-10 pm. Closed: 1/1, 12/25. **Reservations:** suggested. **Features:** casual dress; children's menu; early bird specials; carryout; cocktails & lounge. Friendly, open and casual, this relaxed restaurant boasts a bubbly service staff and all-day breakfast. Browse the varied menu for burgers, filet mignon, stuffed flounder and the three-layer chocolate fantasy, which incorporates seven types of chocolate. **Cards:** AE, DS, MC, VI.

NORTH REDINGTON BEACH —*See Tampa Bay p. 868.*

OCALA pop. 42,000

––––––– WHERE TO STAY –––––––

7 SISTERS INN **Phone:** (352)867-1170

Historic Bed & Breakfast
		2P	XP	
All Year		2P: $95-$185	XP: $25	

Location: 1 blk s of SR 40; 3.5 mi e of I-75, exit 69. 820 SE Fort King St 34471. **Fax:** 352/867-5266. **Facility:** Two restored 1880s Queen Anne style Victorian houses. Individually decorated rooms range in size from compact to more spacious. Designated smoking area. 15 units. Some suites and whirlpool units ($165-$185). **Bath:** combo or shower only. 3 stories (no elevator), interior corridors. **Terms:** age restrictions may apply, 7 day cancellation notice-fee imposed, package plans - weekends. **Amenities:** extended cable TV, hair dryers. **Leisure Activities:** bicycles. **Guest Services:** [BP] meal plan available, afternoon tea. **Business Services:** meeting rooms, fax. **Cards:** AE, DS, MC, VI.

BEST WESTERN OCALA PARK CENTRE

AAA **SAVE**

Motel

12/1-4/12	1P: $68-$86	2P: $68-$86	XP: $7	F17
4/13-11/30	1P: $58-$86	2P: $58-$86	XP: $7	F17

Phone: (352)237-4848

Location: I-75, exit 68, on SR 200. 3701 SW 38th Ave 34474. Fax: 352/237-2281. **Facility:** Close to Paddock Shopping Mall. 139 units, 1 with kitchen. Some suites. 4 stories, interior corridors. **Terms:** weekly rates available. **Leisure Activities:** heated pool, whirlpool. **Guest Services:** [ECP] meal plan available, coin laundry. **Business Services:** meeting rooms, fax. **Cards:** AE, CB, DI, DS, MC, VI. **Special Amenities:** free continental breakfast and free local telephone calls.

BUDGET HOST INN

AAA **SAVE**

Motel

12/1-4/14	1P: $36-$46	2P: $42-$62	XP: $10	F12
4/15-11/30	1P: $28-$38	2P: $32-$52	XP: $6	F12

Phone: (352)732-6940

Location: I-75, exit 70, 0.3 mi w on US 27. 4013 NW Blitchton Rd 34482. Fax: 352/629-8048. **Facility:** Modern, bright rooms with at-door parking. 21 units. *Bath:* combo or shower only. 1 story, exterior corridors. **Terms:** weekly rates available, pets ($4 extra charge). **Amenities:** extended cable TV. **Business Services:** fax. **Cards:** AE, DS, MC, VI. **Special Amenities:** early check-in/late check-out and free continental breakfast. *(See color ad p 240)*

COMFORT INN

AAA **SAVE**

Motel

All Year	1P: $45-$65	2P: $55-$75	XP: $5	F18

Phone: (352)629-8850

Location: I-75, exit 69, just w on SR 40. 4040 W Silver Springs Blvd 34482. Fax: 352/732-0831. **Facility:** 130 units. Some whirlpool units ($95-$125). 2 stories, exterior corridors. **Terms:** small pets only ($5 extra charge). **Amenities:** extended cable TV. *Some:* irons, hair dryers. **Guest Services:** [ECP] meal plan available, coin laundry. **Business Services:** meeting rooms, fax. **Cards:** AE, CB, DI, DS, JC, MC, VI. **Special Amenities:** free continental breakfast and free local telephone calls.

COURTYARD BY MARRIOTT

Motor Inn

2/1-4/30	1P: $79-$99	2P: $79-$99	
12/1-1/31 & 5/1-11/30	1P: $69-$99	2P: $69-$99	

Phone: (352)237-8000

Location: On SR 200 at jct I-75, exit 68. 3712 SW 38th Ave 34474. Fax: 352/237-0580. **Facility:** Close to Paddock Shopping Mall. Public areas and guest rooms offer upscale appointments. 175 units. Some whirlpool units. 3 stories, interior corridors. **Terms:** cancellation fee imposed, package plans. **Amenities:** extended cable TV, voice mail, irons, hair dryers. **Leisure Activities:** heated pool, whirlpool, exercise room. **Guest Services:** coin laundry. **Business Services:** meeting rooms, fax. **Cards:** AE, CB, DI, DS, MC, VI. *(See color ad p 549)*

DAYS INN

AAA **SAVE**

Motel

All Year	1P: $40-$65	2P: $45-$75	XP: $5	F17

Phone: (352)629-7041

Location: I-75, exit 70, just w on US 27. 3811 NW Blitchton Rd 34482. Fax: 352/629-1026. **Facility:** 65 units. Some whirlpool units ($75-$125). 2 stories, interior/exterior corridors. **Terms:** pets ($5 extra charge). **Amenities:** extended cable TV. **Leisure Activities:** playground. **Guest Services:** coin laundry. **Business Services:** fax. **Cards:** AE, CB, DI, DS, JC, MC, VI. **Special Amenities:** free continental breakfast and free local telephone calls.

FAIRFIELD INN BY MARRIOTT

Motel

1/16-4/30	1P: $69-$95	2P: $69-$95	
12/1-1/15 & 5/1-11/30	1P: $56-$82	2P: $56-$82	

Phone: 352/861-8400

Location: I-75, exit 68, just w on SR 200. 4101 SW 38th Ct 34474. Fax: 352/861-8401. **Facility:** 97 units. *Bath:* combo or shower only. 3 stories, interior corridors. **Amenities:** extended cable TV, voice mail, irons. **Leisure Activities:** heated pool, whirlpool, exercise room. **Guest Services:** [ECP] meal plan available, valet and coin laundry. **Business Services:** fax. **Cards:** AE, CB, DI, DS, MC, VI.

HAMPTON INN OCALA

SAVE

Motel

12/25-4/30	1P: $80-$92	2P: $86-$99	
5/1-11/30	1P: $72-$92	2P: $80-$89	
12/1-12/24	1P: $64-$68	2P: $80-$83	

Phone: (352)854-3200

Location: SR 200, 0.4 mi e of I-75, exit 68. 3434 SW College Rd 34474. Fax: 352/854-5633. **Facility:** Located close to Paddock Mall. 152 units. Some suites ($139-$169) and whirlpool units ($92-$169). 3 stories, exterior corridors. **Amenities:** irons. **Leisure Activities:** heated pool. **Guest Services:** [ECP] meal plan available, coin laundry. **Business Services:** meeting rooms, fax. **Cards:** AE, CB, DI, DS, MC, VI.

HERITAGE COUNTRY INN

Bed & Breakfast

All Year	1P: $59-$69	2P: $89-$104	XP: $15	F7

Phone: (352)489-0023

Location: I-75, exit 69, 11 mi w. 14343 W SR 40 34481. **Facility:** Rural setting. Spacious, finely furnished, ground level units with private entrances off courtyard. All units have wood-burning fireplace. Designated smoking area. 6 units. Some whirlpool units. 1 story, exterior corridors. **Terms:** check-in 4 pm, 7 day cancellation notice-fee imposed, weekly rates available. **Guest Services:** [BP] meal plan available. **Cards:** AE, DS, MC, VI.

HILTON OCALA

Phone: (352)854-1400

Hotel

1/1-5/14 & 9/1-11/30	1P: $89-$139	2P: $89-$139	XP: $10	F18
5/15-8/31	1P: $79-$139	2P: $79-$139	XP: $10	F18
12/1-12/31	1P: $89-$129	2P: $89-$129	XP: $10	F18

Location: I-75, exit 68, 0.3 mi e on SR 200. 3600 SW 36th Ave 34474. Fax: 352/854-4010. **Facility:** 197 units. Some suites ($195-$250) and whirlpool units ($295-$350). 9 stories, interior corridors. **Terms:** package plans. **Amenities:** voice mail, irons, hair dryers. **Dining:** Arthur's, see separate listing. **Leisure Activities:** heated pool, whirlpool, 2 lighted tennis courts, exercise room. **Guest Services:** valet laundry. **Business Services:** meeting rooms, fax. **Cards:** AE, CB, DI, DS, MC, VI. *(See ad p 44 & color ad below)*

SOME UNITS

HOLIDAY INN EXPRESS

Phone: (352)629-7300

Motel

1/15-4/15	1P: $67-$75
12/1-1/14 & 4/16-11/30	1P: $64-$72

Location: 0.8 mi s on US 27, 301 and 441, just s of SR 200. 1212 S Pine Ave 34474. Fax: 352/629-3331. **Facility:** Close to the regional medical centers. 55 units. Some whirlpool units. *Bath:* combo or shower only. 3 stories, interior corridors. **Terms:** weekly & monthly rates available. **Amenities:** extended cable TV, irons, hair dryers. **Guest Services:** [ECP] meal plan available, coin laundry. **Business Services:** meeting rooms, fax. **Cards:** AE, CB, DI, DS, JC, MC, VI.

SOME UNITS

HOLIDAY INN OCALA

Phone: (352)629-0381

Motor Inn

3/1-3/31	1P: $99-$119
2/1-2/28	1P: $89-$99
12/1-1/31 & 4/1-11/30	1P: $79-$89

Location: I-75, exit 69, just e. 3621 W Silver Springs Blvd 34475. Fax: 352/629-8813. **Facility:** 270 units. 2 stories, exterior corridors. **Terms:** weekly & monthly rates available, package plans, small pets only. **Amenities:** extended cable TV, irons, hair dryers. **Leisure Activities:** heated pool, wading pool, exercise room. **Guest Services:** coin laundry. **Business Services:** meeting rooms, fax. **Cards:** AE, CB, DI, DS, JC, MC, VI. *(See color ad below)*

SOME UNITS

HOWARD JOHNSON INN

Phone: (352)629-7021

Motor Inn

2/1-3/31	1P: $44-$99	2P: $50-$125	XP: $10	F12
12/1-1/31 & 4/1-11/30	1P: $40-$80	2P: $50-$99	XP: $10	F12

Location: I-75, exit 70, just w. 3951 NW Blitchton Rd 34482. Fax: 352/629-0510. **Facility:** Contemporary rooms. 125 units. Some whirlpool units ($50-$125). 3 stories (no elevator), exterior corridors. **Amenities:** extended cable TV. **Dining:** restaurant, 6:30 am-noon & 5:30-10 pm, $7-$13, wine/beer only. **Leisure Activities:** miniature golf. **Guest Services:** coin laundry. **Business Services:** meeting rooms, fax. **Cards:** AE, DI, DS, MC, VI. **Special Amenities:** early check-in/late check-out and free newspaper. *(See color ad p 549)*

SOME UNITS

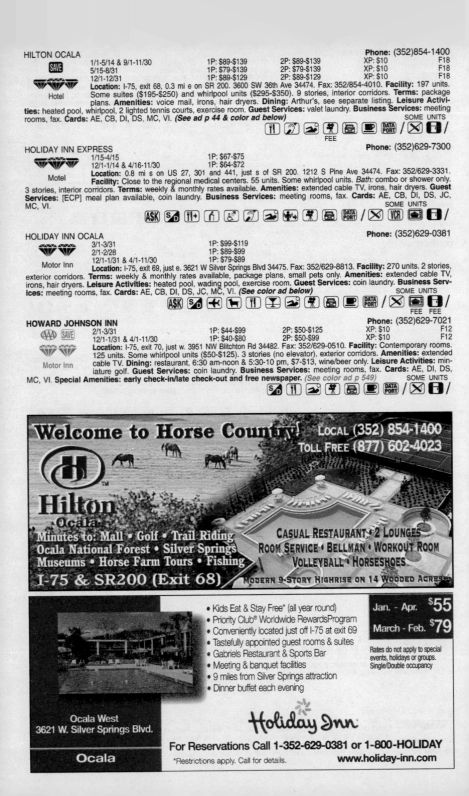

LA QUINTA INN & SUITES
Phone: (352)861-1137

All Year | 1P: $89-$99 | 2P: $89-$99

Motel

Location: I-75, exit 68, just e. 3530 SW 36th Ave 34474. Fax: 352/861-1157. **Facility:** 117 units. Some suites ($119-$129). *Bath:* combo or shower only. 6 stories, interior corridors. **Terms:** small pets only. **Amenities:** extended cable TV, video games, voice mail, irons, hair dryers. **Leisure Activities:** heated pool, whirlpool, exercise room. **Guest Services:** [ECP] meal plan available, coin laundry. **Business Services:** meeting rooms, fax. **Cards:** AE, CB, DI, DS, MC, VI.

SOME UNITS

STEINBRENNER'S RAMADA INN & CONFERENCE CENTER
Phone: (352)732-3131

2/1-4/30 | 2P: $61-$101 | XP: $10 | F17
12/1-1/31 & 5/1-11/30 | 2P: $57-$87 | XP: $10 | F17

Motor Inn

Location: US 27, just w of jct I-75, exit 70. 3810 NW Blitchton Rd 34482. Fax: 352/732-3821. **Facility:** 124 units. *Bath:* some combo or shower only. 2 stories, exterior corridors. **Terms:** cancellation fee imposed, weekly & monthly rates available, package plans, pets ($5 extra charge, $50 deposit). **Amenities:** extended cable TV, voice mail, hair dryers. **Leisure Activities:** heated pool, whirlpool, playground, exercise room. **Guest Services:** coin laundry. **Business Services:** meeting rooms, fax. **Cards:** AE, DI, DS, JC, MC, VI. *(See color ad below)*

SOME UNITS

TRAVELODGE OCALA NORTH

Motor Inn

12/1-4/18	1P: $36-$85	2P: $46-$95	XP: $10 F18
4/19-11/30	1P: $29-$65	2P: $39-$75	XP: $10 F18

Location: I-75, exit 70, just w. 4020 NW Blitchton Rd 34482. Fax: 352/629-9890. **Facility:** 141 units. 1 two-bedroom unit and 3 units with kitchen. Some suites ($65-$195). 2 stories, exterior corridors. **Amenities:** extended cable TV. *Some:* irons, hair dryers. **Guest Services:** [CP] meal plan available, coin laundry. **Cards:** AE, DS, MC, VI.

SOME UNITS

TRAVELODGE-OCALA SOUTH

Motel

12/1-4/15	1P: $55-$65	2P: $60-$70	XP: $5 F16
4/16-11/30	1P: $50-$60	2P: $55-$65	XP: $5 F16

Location: 1 mi s on US 27, 301 and 441. 2635 SW Pine Ave 34474. Fax: 352/732-6324. **Facility:** Close to the regional medical centers. Older, well maintained property. 68 units. 1 two-bedroom unit. *Bath:* combo or shower only. 2 stories, exterior corridors. **Amenities:** extended cable TV. **Guest Services:** [CP] meal plan available, coin laundry. **Business Services:** fax. **Cards:** AE, CB, DI, DS, JC, MC, VI. **Special Amenities:** free local telephone calls and free newspaper.

SOME UNITS
FEE FEE

--------- **WHERE TO DINE** ---------

AMRIT PALACE INDIAN RESTAURANT

Indian

Dinner: $11-$16 **Phone:** 352/873-8500

Location: I-75, exit 68, on SR 200, 1.6 mi ne. 2635 SW College Rd 34474. **Hours:** 11:30 am-9:30 pm, Fri & Sat-10:30 pm, Sun & Mon 5 pm-9:30 pm. **Features:** casual dress; carryout; beer & wine only; minimum charge-$5; a la carte. Cheery decor, laid-back service. Wide range of traditional Indian preparations - chutney, achar, curry, lamb, chicken, seafood, Biryani rice and vegetarian specialties. Specialty breads. Many items cooked in tandoor oven. Multi-course dinners available. Lunch buffet. **Cards:** AE, MC, VI.

ARTHUR'S

Regional Steak & Seafood

Lunch: $6-$8 **Dinner:** $14-$27 **Phone:** 352/854-1400

Location: I-75, exit 68, 0.3 mi e on SR 200; in Hilton Ocala. 3600 SW 36th Ave 34474. **Hours:** 6:30 am-10 pm. **Reservations:** suggested; in winter. **Features:** casual dress; Sunday brunch; children's menu; early bird specials; cocktails & lounge. Noted for lobster bisque, the menu also offers tempting steak dishes. the grouper, covered in an herbed nut crust, gives new a twist to an old theme. Large windows overlook a courtyard, and fine linen tablecloths and napkins add an air of sophistication. **Cards:** AE, CB, DI, DS, MC, VI.

BELLA LUNA CAFE

Italian

Lunch: $5-$9 **Dinner:** $9-$20 **Phone:** 352/237-9155

Location: I-75, exit 68, 0.4 mi e on SR 200. 3425 SW College Rd 34474. **Hours:** 11 am-10 pm, Fri & Sat-11 pm. **Closed:** 11/22, 12/25. **Reservations:** suggested; weekends. **Features:** dressy casual; children's menu; cocktails & lounge; valet parking. Fine dining in an elegant, romantic setting boasts an excellent variety of entrees with unique combinations certain to inspire a return visit. The chicken and spinach served on a bed of pasta is generously portioned as well as flavorful. **Cards:** AE, DI, DS, MC, VI.

CARMICHAEL'S RESTAURANT

American

Lunch: $4-$7 **Dinner:** $7-$15 **Phone:** 352/622-3636

Location: I-75, on SR 40, 7 mi e. 3105 NE Silver Springs Blvd 34470. **Hours:** 6:30 am-9 pm, Sun noon-8 pm. **Reservations:** suggested; holidays. **Features:** casual dress; children's menu; early bird specials; carryout; cocktails & lounge. An array of made-from-scratch specialties are the attraction in this dining room. Friendly and attentive servers welcome you to a warm, wood-accented interior. Choose from a good selection of well-prepared fish, meat, chicken and pasta dishes. Smoke free premises. **Cards:** AE, MC, VI.

HARRY'S SEAFOOD BAR & GRILLE

American

Lunch: $5-$7 **Dinner:** $5-$18 **Phone:** 352/840-0900

Location: Just e on SR 40 from jct US 27/301/441. 24 SE First Ave 34471. **Hours:** 11 am-10 pm, Wed-Fri to 11 pm, Sat 4 pm-midnight, Sun noon-9 pm. **Closed:** 1/1, 12/25. **Features:** casual dress; children's menu; carryout; cocktails & lounge. Expect tasty, well-presented food in a bustling, laid-back atmosphere. the menu features great variety highlighted with a few Cajun choices. Peruse the ample appetizer section or order a meal of steak, chicken or seafood. **Cards:** AE, DI, DS, MC, VI.

HOLIDAY HOUSE RESTAURANT

American

Lunch: $6 **Dinner:** $7 **Phone:** 352/236-3014

Location: 4.3 mi e on SR 40. 4011 E Silver Springs Blvd 34470. **Hours:** 11 am-8:30 pm. **Closed:** 12/24 from 3:30 pm. **Reservations:** accepted. **Features:** casual dress; children's menu; salad bar; buffet. Veer off the highway for a casual buffet dining experience with carved meats and a host of fresh vegetables and salads. A friendly, uniformed staff serves you at the buffet table and delivers beverages with a warm basket of buttered bread sticks. Smoke free premises. **Cards:** AE, DS, MC, VI.

R.J. GATORS

American

Lunch: $7-$18 **Dinner:** $7-$18 **Phone:** 352/873-8088

Location: I-75, exit 68, just e in Park Centre. 3510 SW 36th Ave 34474. **Hours:** 11 am-10 pm. **Closed:** 11/22, 12/25. **Features:** casual dress; carryout; cocktails & lounge; a la carte. Very ecclectic and festive mix of colors with all kinds of recreational equipment hanging about. Menu has very good variety of choices such as-wings, gator, fish platters, fajitas, ribs, steak, poultry dishes, appetizers, salad and dessert. **Cards:** AE, DS, MC, VI.

OCOEE —*See Orlando p. 700.*

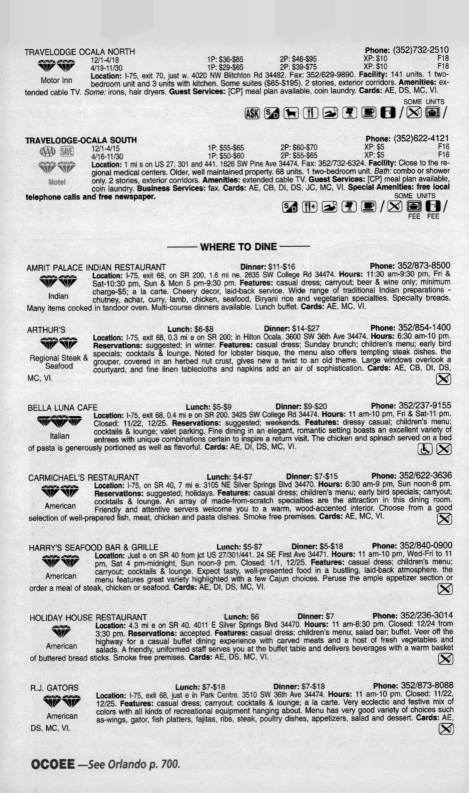

OKEECHOBEE pop. 4,900

——— WHERE TO STAY ———

BUDGET INN
AAA SAVE
Motel

1/1-4/14	1P: $59-$69	2P: $59-$89	XP: $10 F12
12/1-12/31	1P: $49-$59	2P: $49-$65	XP: $10 F12
4/15-11/30	1P: $39-$59	2P: $49-$59	XP: $10 F12

Phone: (863)763-3185

Location: US 98 and 441, just s of jct SR 70. 201 S Parrott Ave 34974. Fax: 863/763-3185. **Facility:** 24 units. *Bath:* combo or shower only. 1 story, exterior corridors. **Terms:** weekly rates available, small pets only ($10 extra charge). **Amenities:** extended cable TV. **Cards:** AE, DS, MC, VI. **Special Amenities:** free local telephone calls and preferred room (subject to availability with advanced reservations). SOME UNITS

ECONOMY INN
AAA SAVE
Motel

12/16-4/15	1P: $45-$65	2P: $59-$79	XP: $10 F12
12/1-12/15 & 4/16-11/30	1P: $30-$40	2P: $35-$45	XP: $5 F12

Phone: 863/763-1148

Location: US 441, 0.3 mi n of jct SR 70. 507 N Parrott Ave 34972. Fax: 863/763-1149. **Facility:** Some compact rooms. 24 units. *Bath:* shower only. 1 story, exterior corridors. **Terms:** 3 day cancellation notice, weekly rates available, small pets only ($5 extra charge). **Cards:** AE, DS, MC, VI. **Special Amenities:** free local telephone calls and preferred room (subject to availability with advanced reservations). SOME UNITS

HOLIDAY INN EXPRESS
Motel

1/1-4/30	1P: $79-$150	2P: $89-$150	XP: $10
12/1-12/31		2P: $79-$89	XP: $10
5/1-11/30		2P: $69-$89	

Phone: 863/357-3529

Location: US 98 and 441, 3 mi s of jct SR 70, 0.3 mi n of Lake Okeechobee and jct SR 78. 3975 Hwy 441 S 34974. Fax: 863/357-3529. **Facility:** Modern well-equipped inviting units. 43 units. Some whirlpool units ($100-$200). 2 stories, exterior corridors. **Terms:** cancellation fee imposed, small pets only ($10 extra charge). **Amenities:** irons, hair dryers. **Guest Services:** [CP] meal plan available, valet and coin laundry. **Business Services:** meeting rooms. **Cards:** AE, CB, DI, DS, JC, MC, VI. SOME UNITS

——— WHERE TO DINE ———

LIGHTSEY'S RESTAURANT
Seafood

Lunch: $5-$7   **Dinner:** $8-$17   **Phone:** 863/763-4276

Location: SR 78, 4.5 mi sw of jct US 98 and 441; in Okeetanti Recreational Area. 10430 Hwy 78 W 34974. **Hours:** 11 am-9 pm, Fri & Sat-10 pm, Sun-8 pm. Closed: 4/15, 11/22, 12/24, 12/25. **Features:** casual dress; cocktails. Within Okeetanti Park, the restaurant gleans its character from the many fish tanks, animal mounts and huge bay windows that overlook the marina. Cooter fritters (turtle), catnips (catfish), alligator and frog legs are among the down-to-earth selections. **Cards:** DS, MC, VI.

OLD TOWN pop. 300

——— WHERE TO STAY ———

SUWANNEE GABLES MOTEL
AAA SAVE
Motel

All Year	1P: $52-$68	2P: $62-$120	XP: $7 D10

Phone: 352/542-7752

Location: US 19, 98 and 27A; 2 mi s of jct SR 349. HC 3 Box 208 32680. Fax: 352/542-9212. **Facility:** On the Suwanee River. Motel rooms and duplex cottages, older property with some updates. 22 units, 8 with efficiency. 1 story, exterior corridors. **Terms:** cancellation fee imposed, small pets only ($8 extra charge). **Amenities:** extended cable TV. **Leisure Activities:** Fee: boat dock. **Guest Services:** coin laundry. **Cards:** AE, DS, MC, VI. SOME UNITS
FEE FEE

ORANGE CITY pop. 5,300

——— WHERE TO STAY ———

COMFORT INN
AAA SAVE
Motel

All Year	1P: $54-$200	2P: $54-$200	XP: $7 F

Phone: (904)775-7444

Location: I-4, exit 54, 2.8 mi w on SR 472, 2 mi s on US 17-92. 445 S Volusia Ave 32763. Fax: 904/775-9887. **Facility:** Commercial area, comfortable motel units set back from highway. 60 units. 2 stories, exterior corridors. **Terms:** 30 day cancellation notice-fee imposed, weekly rates available. **Amenities:** extended cable TV. *Some:* irons. **Cards:** AE, CB, DI, DS, JC, MC, VI. **Special Amenities:** free continental breakfast. SOME UNITS
FEE FEE

DAYS INN
AAA SAVE
Motel

12/1-7/5	1P: $54-$95	2P: $54-$95	XP: $5
7/6-11/30	1P: $50-$95	2P: $50-$95	XP: $5

Phone: 904/775-4522

Location: I-4, exit 54, 2.8 mi w on SR 472, 0.3 mi s on US 17-92. 2501 N Volusia Ave 32763. Fax: 904/775-0919. **Facility:** Pleasant older property has a one-story drive-up building and new two-story section. Large guest rooms. Designated smoking area. 37 units. 17 efficiencies and 2 units with kitchen. 1-2 stories, exterior corridors. **Terms:** 14 day cancellation notice-fee imposed, weekly rates available. **Amenities:** extended cable TV. *Some:* irons, hair dryers. **Cards:** AE, CB, DI, DS, JC, MC, VI. **Special Amenities:** free continental breakfast and free newspaper. SOME UNITS

ORANGE PARK —See Jacksonville p. 447.

Destination Orlando
pop. 173,900

Park Avenue, Winter Park. Tree-shaded and trendy, the avenue is a popular shopping and dining thoroughfare near downtown Orlando.

*T*here's much more to Orlando than theme parks. Mother Nature has blessed central Florida with an abundance of sunshine—and locals love to take advantage of it.

*R*ecreational opportunities abound—frolicking in the waters of a nearby lake or river, hiking or bicycling along plentiful trails, golfing at one of the area's plush resorts. Still, others maintain that sufficient exercise can be obtained by walking from store to store.

Lake Eola Park, Orlando. This popular landmark, with the Clinton Allen Fountain as its centerpiece and Orlando's skyline as a backdrop, is a peaceful downtown haven. (See listing page 142)

See Downtown map page 560

*P*laces included in this AAA Destination City:

On map (right side): Lady Lake, Mount Dora, 441, Leesburg, Tavares, Howey-In-The-Hills, Clermont, Winter Garden, 27, Walt Disney World Resort, 4

Canoeing, Orlando.
Row, row, row your boat along
your choice of central Florida's
many lakes and rivers.

See Vicinity map page 554

Water skiing, Orlando.
With more than 1,200
lakes in the vicinity, it's
no problem finding
just the right one for
the water sport of
your choice.

A golfing vacation.
Many of Orlando's luxurious
resorts come equipped with golf
courses; just drive up, check in
and head for the first hole.

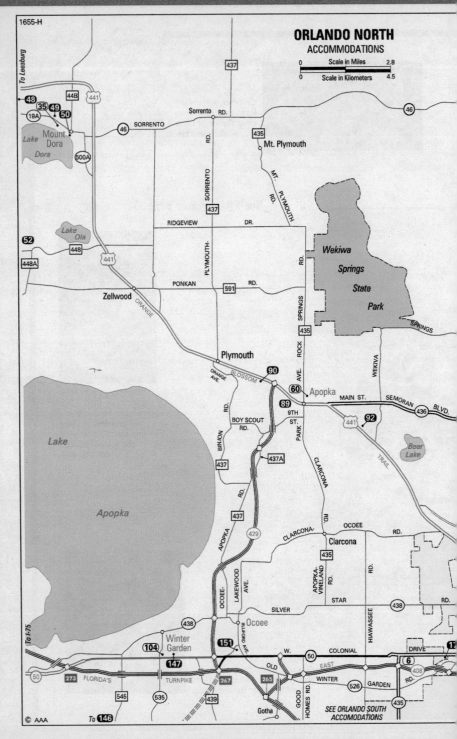

ORLANDO NORTH
ACCOMMODATIONS

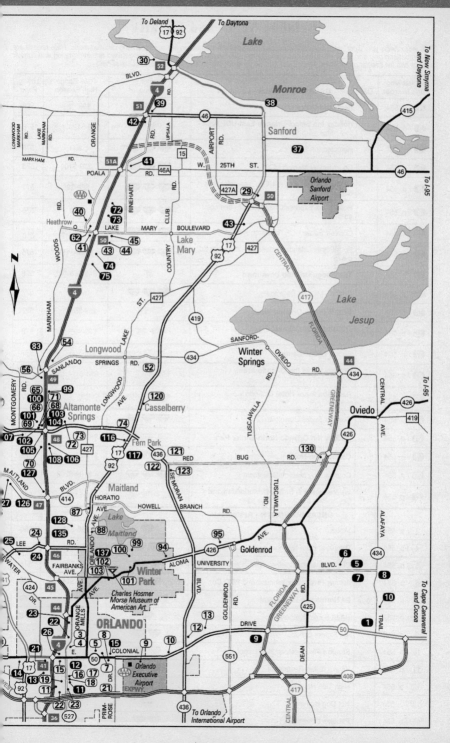

Orlando North and Vicinity

This index helps you "spot" where approved accommodations are located on the corresponding detailed maps. Rate ranges are for comparison only and show the property's high season. Turn to the listing page for more detailed rate information and consult display ads for special promotions. Restaurant rate range is for dinner, unless only lunch (L) is served.

Spotter/Map Page Number	OA	ORLANDO NORTH - Lodgings	Diamond Rating	Rate Range High Season	Listing Page
1 / p. 554	AAA	Radisson University Hotel	◇◇◇	$99 SAVE	578
5 / p. 554	AAA	Holiday Inn Select-Orlando East-UCF Area - see color ad p 576	◇◇◇	$99-$129 SAVE	576
6 / p. 554		Hampton Inn & Suites	◇◇◇	$99	575
7 / p. 554		Courtyard by Marriott UCF	◇◇◇	$79-$109	573
8 / p. 554		La Quinta Inn & Suites UCF - see color ad p 604	◇◇◇	$89-$99	577
9 / p. 554		Holiday Inn Express Orlando East - see color ad p 576	◇◇◇	$79	576
10 / p. 554		Comfort Suites UCF-Research Park	◇◇◇	$97-$139	573
11 / p. 554		Four Points Orlando Downtown - see color ad p 575	◇◇◇	$129-$159	575
12 / p. 554	AAA	Travelodge Orlando Downtown	◇	$45-$85 SAVE	578
13 / p. 554		Orlando Marriott Downtown	◇◇◇	$85	577
14 / p. 554	AAA	Best Western Orlando West	◇◇	$69-$99 SAVE	572
15 / p. 554	AAA	Travelodge at Colonial Plaza - see color ad p 577	◇◇	$79-$99 SAVE	578
17 / p. 554	AAA	Econo Lodge-Central	◇	$36-$85 SAVE	573
21 / p. 554	AAA	Holiday Inn at the Orlando Arena - see ad p 575	◇◇◇	$84-$114 SAVE	575
22 / p. 554	AAA	Radisson Plaza Hotel Orlando - see color ad p 577	◇◇◇	$82 SAVE	577
23 / p. 554		Comfort Suites Downtown	◇◇◇	$99-$119	572
24 / p. 554	AAA	Holiday Inn Orlando North-Winter Park	◇◇◇	$89-$119 SAVE	576
25 / p. 554	AAA	Comfort Inn-North - see color ad p 573	◇◇◇	$79-$125 SAVE	572
26 / p. 554		Courtyard by Marriott Downtown	◇◇◇	$109-$209	573
27 / p. 554	AAA	Wellesley Inn & Suites-Orlando/Maitland - see color ad opposite title page	◇◇◇	$59-$119 SAVE	578
		ORLANDO NORTH - Restaurants			
3 / p. 554		Misuzu	◇	$6-$24	580
4 / p. 554		Gargi's at Lake Ivanhoe	◇◇	$9-$15	579
5 / p. 554		Chan's Chinese Cuisine	◇◇	$7-$28	578
6 / p. 554		Johnny Rivers Smokehouse and BBQ Co	◇◇	$9-$14	579
7 / p. 554	AAA	La Normandie Restaurant	◇◇◇	$12-$26	579
8 / p. 554		BAJA Burrito Kitchen	◇	$4-$9	578
9 / p. 554		4th Fighter Group	◇◇	$12-$25	578
10 / p. 554		Straub's Fine Seafood Restaurant	◇◇	$12-$25	580
11 / p. 554		Vivaldi Italian Restaurant	◇◇	$12-$24	580
12 / p. 554		High Tide Harry's	◇	$4-$30	579
13 / p. 554		Hot Dog Heaven	◇	$2-$6	579
15 / p. 554		Pebbles Downtown	◇◇	$6-$19	580

Spotter/Map Page Number	OA	**ORLANDO NORTH - Restaurants (continued)**	Diamond Rating	Rate Range High Season	Listing Page
⑯ / p. 554		Sushi Hatsu	♦	$9-$19	580
⑰ / p. 554		Dexter's of Thornton Park	♦♦	$5-$16	579
⑱ / p. 554		First Watch	♦	$5-$7(L)	579
⑲ / p. 554	AAA	**Manuel's on the 28th**	♦♦♦♦	$27-$39	579
㉑ / p. 554	AAA	**Lee's Lakeside Restaurant & Lounge**	♦♦	$19-$29	579
㉓ / p. 554		Le Provence	♦♦♦	$15-$33	579
㉔ / p. 554		Straub's Boatyard	♦♦	$12-$27	580
		SANFORD - Lodgings			
(37) / p. 554	AAA	**The Higgins House Bed & Breakfast**	♦♦♦	$80-$120 SAVE	701
(38) / p. 554		Best Western Marina Hotel & Conference Center	♦♦	$79-$89	701
(39) / p. 554		Super 8 Motel	♦	$55-$75	702
(41) / p. 554		Cherry Laurel Inn	♦♦♦	$130-$170	701
(42) / p. 554		SpringHill Suites by Marriott	♦♦♦	$99	702
(43) / p. 554	AAA	**Holiday Inn Express-Sanford**	♦♦♦	$80-$175 SAVE	701
		SANFORD - Restaurants			
㉙ / p. 554		Sergio's Italian Restaurant	♦♦	$5-$15	702
㉚ / p. 554		Otter's Riverside Restaurant	♦♦	$9-$25	702
		MOUNT DORA - Lodgings			
(48) / p. 554	AAA	**Comfort Inn**	♦♦♦	$68-$94 SAVE	699
(49) / p. 554		Darst Victorian Manor	♦♦♦♦	$125-$220	700
(50) / p. 554	AAA	**The Lakeside Inn** - see ad p 700	♦♦	$110-$180 SAVE	700
(52) / p. 554	AAA	**The Emerald Hill Inn**	♦♦♦	$99-$149 SAVE	700
		MOUNT DORA - Restaurant			
㉟ / p. 554	AAA	**The Gables Restaurant**	♦♦	$10-$25	700
		HEATHROW - Lodgings			
(62) / p. 554	AAA	**Courtyard by Marriott**	♦♦♦	$115-$135 SAVE	631
		HEATHROW - Restaurants			
㊵ / p. 554	AAA	**Luigino's Pasta & Steak House**	♦♦	$11-$30	631
㊶ / p. 554		Stonewood Tavern & Grill	♦♦♦	$10-$20	631
		LAKE MARY - Lodgings			
(72) / p. 554	AAA	**Hilton Garden Inn Lake Mary** - see ad p 44	♦♦♦	$79-$129 SAVE	696
(73) / p. 554	AAA	**Homewood Suites by Hilton** - see color ad p 696	♦♦♦	$89-$199 SAVE	696
(74) / p. 554	AAA	**MainStay Suites Hotel** - see color ad p 573	♦♦♦	$79-$125 SAVE	696
(75) / p. 554		La Quinta Inn & Suites - see color ad p 604	♦♦♦	$89-$109	696
		LAKE MARY - Restaurants			
㊸ / p. 554		Bistro Cappuccino	♦♦♦	$12-$22	696
㊹ / p. 554		Kumquat Tree	♦♦	$6-$25	697
㊺ / p. 554		Galleria	♦♦	$12-$19	697

Spotter/Map Page Number	OA		Diamond Rating	Rate Range High Season	Listing Page
83 / p. 554		**LONGWOOD - Lodgings**			
83 / p. 554		Ramada Inn North-Orlando	♦♦	$82-$102	697
		LONGWOOD - Restaurants			
51 / p. 554		First Watch	♦	$6-$8(L)	698
52 / p. 554	AAA	**Enzo's Restaurant On The Lake**	♦♦♦	$20-$38	698
54 / p. 554	AAA	**Peter Scott's**	♦♦♦♦	$20-$32	698
56 / p. 554		Pebbles Restaurant	♦♦	$8-$20	698
		APOPKA - Lodgings			
89 / p. 554		Days Inn	♦♦	$45-$99	628
90 / p. 554		Crosby's Motor Inn	♦♦	$59-$79	628
92 / p. 554	AAA	**Howard Johnson Express Inn**	♦♦	$69-$104 SAVE	628
		APOPKA - Restaurant			
60 / p. 554		Catfish Place of Apopka	♦♦	$7-$16	628
		ALTAMONTE SPRINGS - Lodgings			
99 / p. 554		Candlewood Suites	♦♦♦	$69-$109	625
100 / p. 554		Residence Inn by Marriott	♦♦♦	$94-$139	626
101 / p. 554	AAA	**Hampton Inn**	♦♦♦	$88-$139 SAVE	626
102 / p. 554		SpringHill Suites by Marriott Orlando/Altamonte Springs	♦♦♦	$99	627
103 / p. 554	AAA	**Best Western Altamonte Springs**	♦♦♦	$85-$99 SAVE	625
104 / p. 554		Embassy Suites Orlando North - see color ad starting on p 592	♦♦♦	$99-$153	626
105 / p. 554	AAA	**Holiday Inn of Altamonte Springs**	♦♦♦	$99-$119 SAVE	626
106 / p. 554		Homestead Village Guest Studios	♦♦♦	$69	626
107 / p. 554		La Quinta Inn-Orlando North - see color ad p 604	♦♦♦	$65-$89	626
108 / p. 554		Hilton Orlando/Altamonte Springs - see ad p 44	♦♦♦	$130-$180	626
		ALTAMONTE SPRINGS - Restaurants			
65 / p. 554	AAA	**La Scala Ristorante**	♦♦♦	$16-$35	627
66 / p. 554	AAA	**Bangkok Restaurant**	♦♦	$7-$12	627
67 / p. 554		Baja Burrito Kitchen	♦	$4-$8	627
68 / p. 554		Kohinoor Indian Restaurant	♦♦	$8-$15	627
69 / p. 554		Amigos	♦♦	$6-$12	627
70 / p. 554	AAA	**Maison & Jardin**	♦♦♦♦	$20-$35	627
71 / p. 554		First Watch	♦	$5-$7(L)	627
72 / p. 554		Bahama Breeze	♦♦	$7-$18	627
73 / p. 554		Straub's Fine Seafood Restaurant	♦♦	$12-$22	628
74 / p. 554		Amira's	♦	$5-$13	627
		FERN PARK - Lodgings			
116 / p. 554		Days Inn	♦♦	$54-$69	631
117 / p. 554	AAA	**Comfort Inn-Fern Park**	♦♦♦	$66 SAVE	631
		MAITLAND - Lodgings			
126 / p. 554		Courtyard by Marriott Orlando/Maitland	♦♦♦	$69-$129	698

Spotter/Map Page Number	OA	MAITLAND - Lodgings (continued)	Diamond Rating	Rate Range High Season	Listing Page
127 / p. 554		Sheraton Orlando North Hotel	◆◆◆	$89-$159	698
128 / p. 554		Thurston House	◆◆◆	$130-$160	699
		MAITLAND - Restaurants			
87 / p. 554	AAA	**Antonio's La Fiamma Ristorante**	◆◆◆	$13-$30	699
88 / p. 554	AAA	**Nicole St Pierre Restaurant**	◆◆◆	$16-$27	699
		WINTER PARK - Lodgings			
135 / p. 554		Fairfield Inn-Winter Park	◆◆◆	$69	704
137 / p. 554	AAA	**Best Western Mt. Vernon Inn** - see ad p 704	◆◆◆	$85-$125 SAVE	704
		WINTER PARK - Restaurants			
94 / p. 554		Brian's Bar-B-Que	◆◆	$5-$12	704
95 / p. 554		Stefano's Trattoria	◆◆	$8-$19	705
99 / p. 554		The Park Avenue Grill	◆◆	$10-$20	704
100 / p. 554		Park Plaza Gardens	◆◆◆	$19-$30	705
101 / p. 554		Brazilian Pavilion	◆◆	$11-$25	704
103 / p. 554		Trastevere Ristorante	◆◆	$7-$22	705
		WINTER GARDEN - Lodgings			
146 / p. 554		Orange County National Golf Center and Lodge	◆◆◆	$95-$110	703
147 / p. 554	AAA	**Best Value Inn West Orlando** - see color ad p 703	◆◆◆	$69-$79 SAVE	703
		WINTER GARDEN - Restaurant			
104 / p. 554		Taquitos Jalisco	◆	$3-$12	704
		OCOEE - Lodgings			
151 / p. 554		Holiday Inn Orlando West	◆◆◆	$79-$87	700
		CASSELBERRY - Restaurants			
120 / p. 554		Whiskey Creek Steakhouse	◆	$8-$18	629
121 / p. 554		Rolando's Cuban Restaurant	◆◆	$7-$18	628
122 / p. 554		Aladdin's Cafe	◆	$13	628
123 / p. 554		Colorado Fondue Company	◆◆	$10-$25	628
		OVIEDO - Restaurant			
130 / p. 554		Oldenberg Brewering Company	◆◆	$9-$19	701

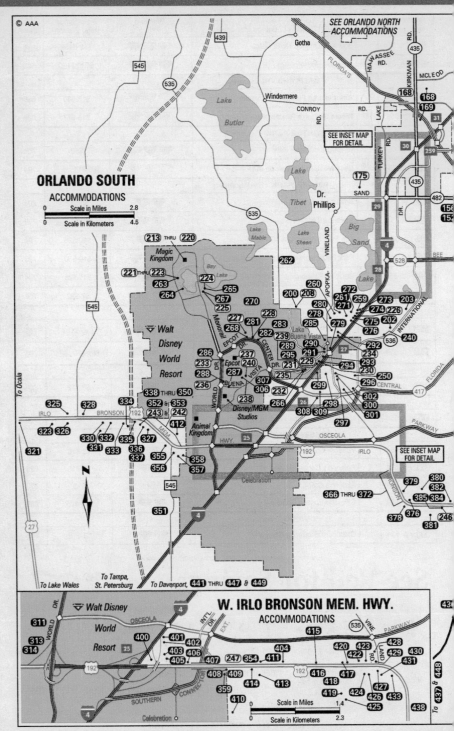

© AAA

SEE ORLANDO NORTH
ACCOMMODATIONS

Gotha

Windermere

Lake
Butler

CONROY   RD.

SEE INSET MAP
FOR DETAIL

ORLANDO SOUTH
ACCOMMODATIONS

Scale in Miles   2.8
Scale in Kilometers   4.5

Lake
Tibet

Dr.
Phillips

Big
Sand
Lake

175
SAND

Lake
Mable

Lake
Sheen

262

213 THRU 220

221 THRU 223

Magic
Kingdom

263
264

224

265

267
225

270

260

200 208

APOPKA.

272
259

261
271

273

274 226 203
275 202
276

240

265

270

260

VINELAND

Walt
Disney
World
Resort

227
268

281

223

283

282

239

Lake
Buena Vista

280

278

285

289
295

290

234

292

293
230

250

296 CENTRAL

286
233
288
236

237

240
287

307
306
238

231
229

235

232

299

294

To Ocala

338 THRU 350

352 & 353

243 & 242

412

266

308 309

298

297

302
300
301

SEE INSET MAP
FOR DETAIL

325

328

334

BRONSON 192

355
356

358
357

Disney/MGM
Studios

Animal
Kingdom

HWY. 25

Celebration

OSCEOLA

192   IRLO

379   380
382

385 384
246

323 326

330 332
331 333

335
327
336
337

321

545

351

366 THRU 372

378 376
381

To Lake Wales

To Tampa,
St. Petersburg

To Davenport, 441 THRU 447 & 449

4

W. IRLO BRONSON MEM. HWY.
ACCOMMODATIONS

Walt Disney

311

World

OSCEOLA

400

401 402

403 406
405

407

247 354

408 409

359

414   413

410

415

535 VINE LAND PARKWAY

420 423
422

404
411

416 417

418
419

428
429 430
431

424

427

426 433
425

438

313
314

Celebration

Scale in Miles   1.4
Scale in Kilometers   2.3

To 437 & 448

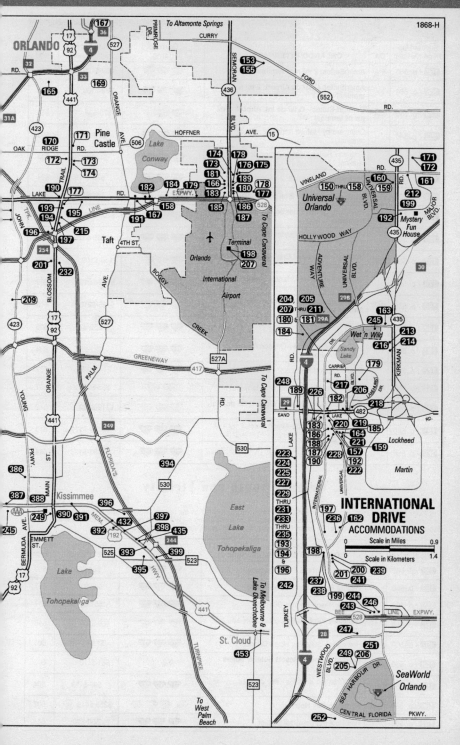

1868-H

✈ Airport Accommodations

Spotter/Map Page Number	OA	ORLANDO INTERNATIONAL	Diamond Rating	Rate Range High Season	Listing Page
166 / p. 560	AAA	AmeriSuites, 2 mi n of terminal	◈◈◈	$89-$129 SAVE	581
186 / p. 560	AAA	AmeriSuites Orlando Airport, 2 mi n of terminal	◈◈◈	$79-$109 SAVE	585
179 / p. 560	AAA	Comfort Suites - Orlando Int. Airport, 2 mi nw of terminal	◈◈◈	$75-$99 SAVE	589
185 / p. 560		Courtyard by Marriott Airport, 2 mi n of terminal	◈◈◈	$79-$139	591
176 / p. 560		Embassy Suites Orlando Airport, 2 mi n of terminal	◈◈◈	$149-$179	594
175 / p. 560		Fairfield Inn by Marriott, 2 mi n of terminal	◈◈◈	$79-$119	594
174 / p. 560		Hampton Inn Airport, 2 mi n of terminal	◈◈◈	$84-$114	596
189 / p. 560	AAA	Hawthorn Suites Orlando Airport, 2 mi n of terminal	◈◈◈	$109-$129 SAVE	597
180 / p. 560		Hilton Garden Inn Orlando International Airport, 2 mi n of terminal	◈◈◈	$89-$129	597
191 / p. 560	AAA	Holiday Inn Express Orlando Airport West, 4 mi nw of terminal	◈◈◈	$69-$109 SAVE	598
178 / p. 560	AAA	Holiday Inn Select Orlando International Airport, 2 mi n of terminal	◈◈◈	$149-$219 SAVE	599
198 / p. 560	AAA	Hyatt Regency Orlando International Airport, at the terminal	◈◈◈	$185-$210 SAVE	603
184 / p. 560		La Quinta Inn Airport West, 4.5 mi w of terminal	◈◈◈	$55-$79	603
183 / p. 560		La Quinta Inn & Suites Orlando Airport North, 2 mi n of terminal	◈◈◈	$82-$96	604
177 / p. 560		Orlando Airport Marriott, 2 mi n of terminal	◈◈◈	$169	607
182 / p. 560	AAA	Quality Inn Airport, 5 mi w of terminal	◈◈	$55-$99 SAVE	607
173 / p. 560	AAA	Radisson Hotel Orlando Airport, 2.5 mi n of terminal	◈◈◈	$119-$169 SAVE	610
181 / p. 560		Renaissance Orlando-Airport Hotel, 2 mi n of terminal	◈◈◈	$119-$179	613
187 / p. 560		Sheraton Suites Orlando Airport, 2 mi ne of terminal	◈◈◈	$105-$139	614

Orlando South and Vicinity

This index helps you "spot" where approved accommodations are located on the corresponding detailed maps. Rate ranges are for comparison only and show the property's high season. Turn to the listing page for more detailed rate information and consult display ads for special promotions. Restaurant rate range is for dinner, unless only lunch (L) is served.

Spotter/Map Page Number	OA	ORLANDO SOUTH - Lodgings	Diamond Rating	Rate Range High Season	Listing Page
152 / p. 560		Homestead Village Guest Studios	◈◈◈	$64-$69	599
153 / p. 560		Ventura Resort Rentals-Kissimmee	◈◈◈	$83-$175	617
155 / p. 560		Ventura Resort Rentals Orlando	◈◈◈	$51-$145	617
156 / p. 560	AAA	Wellesley Inn & Suites - see color ad opposite title page	◈◈◈	$69-$119 SAVE	618
157 / p. 560		Homewood Suites by Hilton-Orlando	◈◈◈	$169-$179	601
158 / p. 560	AAA	Howard Johnson Resort Hotel & Suites - see color ad p 602	◈◈	$81-$110 SAVE	603
159 / p. 560		La Quinta Inn & Suites - see color ad p 604	◈◈◈	$99-$119	604
160 / p. 560	AAA	Portofino Bay Hotel	◈◈◈◈	$255-$445 SAVE	607
161 / p. 560		Red Roof Inn Universal Studios	◈◈◈	$60-$90	611

Spotter/Map Page Number	OA	ORLANDO SOUTH - Lodgings (continued)	Diamond Rating	Rate Range High Season	Listing Page
162 / p. 560		Residence Inn by Marriott Orlando Convention Center - see color ad p 582	♦♦♦	$149-$179	613
163 / p. 560	AAA	Sheraton Studio City Hotel - see ad p 615	♦♦♦	$130-$170 SAVE	614
164 / p. 560		Spring Hill Suites by Marriott Orlando Convention Center/Int'l Drive Area - see color ad p 582	♦♦♦	$89-$129	616
165 / p. 560		Club Orlando	♦♦	Failed to provide	587
166 / p. 560	AAA	AmeriSuites - see color ad p 581	♦♦♦	$89-$129 SAVE	581
167 / p. 560		Best Western Airport Inn & Suites	♦♦♦	$86-$115	586
168 / p. 560		Studio Inn		$79-$139	620
169 / p. 560	AAA	Wingate Inn/Universal Studios	♦♦♦	$89-$99 SAVE	618
170 / p. 560		The Seasons Resort	♦♦♦	Failed to provide	614
171 / p. 560	AAA	Hampton Inn at Universal Studios - see color ad p 634	♦♦♦	$74-$82 SAVE	596
172 / p. 560	AAA	Wellesley Inn & Suites - see color ad opposite title page	♦♦♦	$107 SAVE	618
173 / p. 560	AAA	Radisson Hotel Orlando Airport	♦♦♦	$119-$169 SAVE	610
174 / p. 560		Hampton Inn Airport - see color ad p 582	♦♦♦	$84-$114	596
175 / p. 560		Fairfield Inn by Marriott	♦♦♦	$79-$119	594
176 / p. 560		Embassy Suites Orlando Airport - see color ad starting on p 592	♦♦♦	$149-$179	594
177 / p. 560		Orlando Airport Marriott	♦♦♦	$169	607
178 / p. 560	AAA	Holiday Inn Select Orlando International Airport	♦♦♦	$149-$219 SAVE	599
179 / p. 560	AAA	Comfort Suites - Orlando Int. Airport - see color ad p 633	♦♦♦	$75-$99 SAVE	589
180 / p. 560		Hilton Garden Inn Orlando International Airport - see color ad p 582 & ad p 44	♦♦♦	$89-$129	597
181 / p. 560		Renaissance Orlando-Airport Hotel - see color ad p 612	♦♦♦	$119-$179	613
182 / p. 560	AAA	Quality Inn Airport	♦♦	$55-$99 SAVE	607
183 / p. 560		La Quinta Inn & Suites Orlando Airport North - see color ad p 604	♦♦♦	$82-$96	604
184 / p. 560		La Quinta Inn Airport West - see color ad p 604	♦♦♦	$55-$79	603
185 / p. 560		Courtyard by Marriott Airport - see color ad p 589	♦♦♦	$79-$139	591
186 / p. 560	AAA	AmeriSuites Orlando Airport - see color ad p 5	♦♦♦	$79-$109 SAVE	585
187 / p. 560		Sheraton Suites Orlando Airport - see color ad p 615	♦♦♦	$105-$139	614
189 / p. 560	AAA	Hawthorn Suites Orlando Airport - see color ad starting on p 608	♦♦♦	$109-$129 SAVE	597
190 / p. 560	AAA	GuestHouse Hotel-Orlando - see color ad p 619	♦♦♦	$93 SAVE	619
191 / p. 560	AAA	Holiday Inn Express Orlando Airport West - see color ad starting on p 608	♦♦♦	$69-$109 SAVE	598
192 / p. 560		Holiday Inn Hotel & Suites At Main Entrance to Universal Studios - see color ad p 600	♦♦♦	$79-$149	599
193 / p. 560	AAA	Best Western-Florida Mall - see color ad p 587	♦♦	$52-$122 SAVE	586
194 / p. 560		Howard Johnson Hotel-Florida Mall	♦♦	$29-$45	601
195 / p. 560	AAA	Adam's Mark Orlando	♦♦♦	$84-$152 SAVE	581

Spotter/Map Page Number	OA	ORLANDO SOUTH - Lodgings (continued)	Diamond Rating	Rate Range High Season	Listing Page
196 / p. 560	AAA	Shoney's Inn & Suites	♦♦	$50-$85 SAVE	616
197 / p. 560		Fairfield Inn by Marriott-Orlando South - see color ad p 594	♦♦	$61-$69	594
198 / p. 560	AAA	Hyatt Regency Orlando International Airport - see color ad p 603	♦♦♦	$185-$210 SAVE	603
199 / p. 560	AAA	Radisson Hotel Universal Orlando - see color ad p 611	♦♦♦	$169-$209 SAVE	611
200 / p. 560		The Villas of Grand Cypress	♦♦♦♦	$340-$1800	617
201 / p. 560		Baymont Inn & Suites-Orlando South - see color ad p 585	♦♦♦	$74-$79	585
202 / p. 560	AAA	Parc Corniche Resort - see color ad p 606	♦♦♦	$75-$185 SAVE	607
203 / p. 560	AAA	Ramada Inn All Suites at International Drive Center - see color ad p 612	♦♦♦	$170-$190 SAVE	611
204 / p. 560	AAA	Holiday Inn-International Drive Resort	♦♦♦	$89-$139 SAVE	599
205 / p. 560		Rodeway Inn International - see color ad p 606	♦♦	$35-$95	613
206 / p. 560	AAA	Hawthorn Suites Universal - see color ad starting on p 608	♦♦♦	$99-$139 SAVE	597
207 / p. 560		Quality Inn International - see color ad p 606	♦♦	$39-$99	607
208 / p. 560	AAA	Howard Johnson Inn-International Drive	♦♦	$49-$99 SAVE	601
209 / p. 560		Best Western Movieland	♦♦	$65-$105	586
210 / p. 560	AAA	Holiday Inn Express - see color ad p 644	♦♦♦	$79-$129 SAVE	598
211 / p. 560		Travelodge International Drive - see color ad p 617	♦♦	$59-$79	617
212 / p. 560	AAA	Best Western Universal Inn	♦♦♦	$89-$109 SAVE	587
213 / p. 560	AAA	Clarion Hotel Universal - see color ad p 590	♦♦♦	$89-$109 SAVE	587
214 / p. 560		Hampton Inn-South of Universal Studios - see color ad p 582	♦♦♦	$69-$139	596
215 / p. 560	AAA	Hampton Inn-Florida Mall - see color ad p 633	♦♦♦	$79-$109 SAVE	596
216 / p. 560		Howard Johnson Plaza Resort Universal Gateway - see color ad p 602	♦♦	$72-$108	602
217 / p. 560	AAA	Quality Suites International Drive Area - see color ad starting on p 608	♦♦♦	$89-$119 SAVE	610
218 / p. 560		Hampton Inn Sand Lake - see color ad p 582	♦♦♦	$69-$139	596
219 / p. 560		Residence Inn by Marriott-Orlando International Dr	♦♦♦	$129-$184	613
220 / p. 560	AAA	Wyndham Orlando Resort - see color ad p 581	♦♦♦	$99-$219 SAVE	618
221 / p. 560	AAA	DoubleTree Castle Hotel - see color ad starting on p 592	♦♦♦	$169-$229 SAVE	591
222 / p. 560		Sierra Suites Hotel-Pointe Orlando - see ad p 690	♦♦♦	$69-$159	616
223 / p. 560	AAA	Comfort Suites Orlando - see color ad p 590	♦♦	$69-$109 SAVE	589
224 / p. 560	AAA	Summerfield Suites by Wyndham - see color ad p 616	♦♦♦	$159-$229 SAVE	617
225 / p. 560		Courtyard by Marriott - see color ad p 589	♦♦♦	$119-$149	589
226 / p. 560		Comfort Inn	♦♦♦	$79-$89	589
227 / p. 560	AAA	Embassy Suites International Drive/Jamaican Ct	♦♦♦	$129-$229 SAVE	594
228 / p. 560	AAA	AmeriSuites (Orlando/Convention Center) - see color ad p 5, p 585	♦♦♦	$89-$129 SAVE	585

Spotter/Map Page Number	OA	**ORLANDO SOUTH** - Lodgings (continued)	Diamond Rating	Rate Range High Season	Listing Page
229 / p. 560		La Quinta Inn-Orlando International Drive - see color ad p 604	◈◈◈	$75-$95	604
230 / p. 560	AAA	**Radisson Barcelo Hotel** - see color ad p 610	◈◈◈	$105-$145 [SAVE]	610
231 / p. 560	AAA	**Best Western Plaza International** - see color ad p 588	◈◈◈	$85-$115 [SAVE]	587
232 / p. 560	AAA	**Holiday Homes of Orlando** - see color ad p 584, p 598	◈◈◈	$169-$269 [SAVE]	598
233 / p. 560		Embassy Suites Orlando International Dr /Convention Center - see color ad starting on p 592	◈◈◈	$169-$299	594
234 / p. 560		Quality Inn-Plaza - see color ad p 606	◈◈	$39-$99	610
235 / p. 560		Fairfield Inn by Marriott-International Drive - see color ad p 594	◈◈◈	$59-$89	594
236 / p. 560		Hampton Inn-Convention Center	◈◈◈	$69-$139	596
237 / p. 560		Clarion Plaza	◈◈◈	Failed to provide	587
238 / p. 560		Rosen Centre Hotel	◈◈◈	$99	613
239 / p. 560	AAA	The Peabody Orlando	◈◈◈◈	$360-$1600 [SAVE]	607
240 / p. 560		Crowne Plaza Resort Orlando - see color ad p 591	◈◈◈	$199-$239	591
241 / p. 560		Country Hearth Inn	◈◈	Failed to provide	589
242 / p. 560	AAA	**Westgate Lakes Resort** - see color ad p 614	◈◈◈	$275-$650 [SAVE]	618
243 / p. 560	AAA	**Red Roof Inn Convention Center**	◈◈	$57-$116 [SAVE]	611
244 / p. 560	AAA	**Howard Johnson Plaza Hotel & Suites/International Dr South** - see color ad p 601	◈◈◈	$69-$129 [SAVE]	601
245 / p. 560		Best Inn & Suites International Drive	◈◈◈	$69-$109	586
246 / p. 560	AAA	**Days Inn-Convention Center/Sea World**	◈◈	$98-$108 [SAVE]	591
247 / p. 560		Hawthorn Suites Orlando - see color ad p 597	◈◈◈	$95-$189	596
248 / p. 560	AAA	**Days Inn Orlando Lakeside**	◈◈	$34-$99 [SAVE]	591
249 / p. 560	AAA	**Renaissance Orlando Resort at SeaWorld**	◈◈◈◈	$179 [SAVE]	613
250 / p. 560		Oasis Lakes Resort	◈◈◈	$175-$215	604
251 / p. 560		Sheraton World Resort - see color ad p 615	◈◈◈	$249-$299	615
252 / p. 560		Hilton Grand Vacations Club - see color ad p 597	◈◈◈	$119-$349	598
		ORLANDO SOUTH - Restaurants			
(150) / p. 560		Emeril's Restaurant Orlando	◈◈◈	$20-$34	622
(151) / p. 560		Jimmy Buffett's Margaritaville	◈◈	$8-$20	623
(152) / p. 560		Latin Quarter	◈◈◈	$7-$25	623
(153) / p. 560		NASCAR Cafe	◈◈	$7-$18	624
(155) / p. 560		Motown Cafe	◈◈	$6-$15	624
(156) / p. 560		Pastamore'	◈◈	$9-$22	624
(158) / p. 560		Pat O'Brien's	◈◈	$8-$12	624
(159) / p. 560		Delfino Riviera	◈◈◈◈	$24-$32	622
(167) / p. 560		RNO Seafood	◈	$3-$6	624
(168) / p. 560		BAJA Burrito Kitchen	◈	$4-$9	621
(169) / p. 560	AAA	**Le Coq au Vin**	◈◈◈	$13-$20	624

Spotter/Map Page Number	OA	ORLANDO SOUTH - Restaurants (continued)	Diamond Rating	Rate Range High Season	Listing Page
171 / p. 560		Gain's German Restaurant	◆◆	$10-$16	623
172 / p. 560		Amigos	◆◆	$8-$15	621
173 / p. 560		Charley's Steak House	◆◆◆	$12-$26	622
174 / p. 560		Larry's Cedar River Seafood	◆◆	$9-$16	623
175 / p. 560		Chatham's Place	◆◆◆	$20-$38	622
177 / p. 560		Boston Lobster Feast	◆	$10-$27	621
178 / p. 560		Murphy's Chop House	◆◆◆	$19-$29	624
179 / p. 560	AAA	**Siam Orchid**	◆◆◆	$10-$18	625
180 / p. 560		Wild Jack's Steaks & BBQ	◆◆	$10-$22	625
181 / p. 560		Shamiana	◆	$9-$15	625
182 / p. 560		Fishbones	◆◆	$13-$40	623
183 / p. 560		Italianni's Restaurant	◆◆	$9-$20	623
184 / p. 560		A Taste of Japan	◆◆	$11-$24	621
185 / p. 560		Charley's Steak House	◆◆	$13-$35	622
186 / p. 560		Bergamo's Italian Restaurant	◆◆◆	$15-$39	621
187 / p. 560		Vito's Chop House	◆◆◆	$14-$33	625
188 / p. 560		Cafe Tu Tu Tango	◆◆	$4-$9	622
189 / p. 560		1-6-8 Restaurant	◆◆	$6-$22	621
190 / p. 560		Charlie's Lobster House	◆◆	$16-$36	622
192 / p. 560		The Butcher Shop Steak House	◆◆	$16-$31	621
193 / p. 560		Race Rock Restaurant	◆◆	$6-$17	624
194 / p. 560		Ran-Getsu of Tokyo	◆◆	$14-$34	624
196 / p. 560		Ming Court	◆◆◆	$12-$33	624
197 / p. 560		Bahama Breeze	◆◆	$7-$15	621
198 / p. 560		Everglades	◆◆◆	$17-$30	622
199 / p. 560	AAA	**Jack's Place**	◆◆◆	$16-$28	623
200 / p. 560		Capriccio	◆◆◆	$12-$25	622
201 / p. 560		Dux	◆◆◆◆	$19-$35	622
205 / p. 560		Haifeng	◆◆◆	$17-$25	623
206 / p. 560		Atlantis	◆◆◆◆	$27-$35	621
207 / p. 560		Hemisphere	◆◆◆	$12-$21	623
208 / p. 560		The Black Swan	◆◆◆◆	$25-$40	621
209 / p. 560		La Piaza	◆◆	$7-$16	623
		LAKE BUENA VISTA - Lodgings			
259 / p. 560		Sierra Suites Hotel-Lake Buena Vista - see ad p 690	◆◆◆	$69-$159	691
260 / p. 560	AAA	**Hampton Inn Lake Buena Vista -** see color ad p 634	◆◆◆	$75-$139 SAVE	686
261 / p. 560	AAA	**Homewood Suites Hotel-Lake Buena Vista -** see color ad p 675	◆◆◆	$99-$159 SAVE	686
262 / p. 560		Perri House Bed & Breakfast Inn	◆◆◆	$90-$140	687
263 / p. 560	AAA	**Disney's Grand Floridian Resort & Spa**	◆◆◆◆	$359-$710	683

Spotter/Map Page Number	OA	LAKE BUENA VISTA - Lodgings (continued)	Diamond Rating	Rate Range High Season	Listing Page
264 / p. 560	AAA	Disney's Polynesian Resort	◈◈◈◈	$324-$560	683
265 / p. 560	AAA	Disney's Contemporary Resort	◈◈◈	$244-$630	682
266 / p. 560	AAA	Wyndham Palace Resort & Spa	◈◈◈	$209-$355 [SAVE]	691
267 / p. 560	AAA	Disney's Wilderness Lodge	◈◈◈	$219-$430	684
268 / p. 560	AAA	Disney's Dixie Landings Resort	◈◈◈	$149-$199	682
270 / p. 560	AAA	Disney's Fort Wilderness Cabins & Homes	◈◈	$184-$289	682
271 / p. 560	AAA	Blue Tree Resort at Lake Buena Vista - see color ad p 675	◈◈◈	$119-$239 [SAVE]	673
272 / p. 560	AAA	Courtyard by Marriott Vista Centre - see color ad p 678	◈◈◈	$159-$199 [SAVE]	677
273 / p. 560		Embassy Suites Resort-Lake Buena Vista - see color ad starting on p 592	◈◈◈	$129-$299	685
274 / p. 560	AAA	Comfort Inn Lake Buena Vista - see color ad p 606	◈◈	$39-$99 [SAVE]	676
275 / p. 560	AAA	Radisson Inn Lake Buena Vista - see ad p 688	◈◈◈	$89-$159 [SAVE]	688
276 / p. 560	AAA	RIU Orlando Hotel - see color ad p 674	◈◈◈	$99-$125 [SAVE]	689
278 / p. 560	AAA	Sheraton Safari Hotel - see color ad p 689	◈◈◈	$105-$165 [SAVE]	689
279 / p. 560	AAA	Days Inn Lake Buena Vista Hotel - see color ad p 678	◈◈	$110-$215 [SAVE]	677
280 / p. 560	AAA	Summerfield Suites by Wyndham - see color ad p 616	◈◈◈	$159-$229 [SAVE]	691
281 / p. 560	AAA	Disney's Port Orleans Resort	◈◈◈	$149-$199	683
282 / p. 560	AAA	Disney's Old Key West Resort	◈◈◈	$269-$1170	683
283 / p. 560	AAA	Villas at the Disney Institute	◈◈◈	$204-$1700	691
285 / p. 560	AAA	DoubleTree Club Hotel Lake Buena Vista - see color ad p 684	◈◈◈	$79-$159 [SAVE]	684
286 / p. 560	AAA	Disney's Yacht & Beach Club Resorts	◈◈◈◈	$309-$605	684
287 / p. 560	AAA	Disney's Coronado Springs Resort	◈◈◈	$149-$199	682
288 / p. 560	AAA	Walt Disney World Swan and Dolphin	◈◈◈◈	$310-$490 [SAVE]	691
289 / p. 560	AAA	Courtyard by Marriott-In the Walt Disney World Resort - see color ad p 678	◈◈◈	$129-$219 [SAVE]	677
290 / p. 560		Country Inn & Suites By Carlson - see color ad p 582, p 572	◈◈◈	$79-$149	677
291 / p. 560	AAA	Best Western Lake Buena Vista Resort Hotel in the Walt Disney World Resorts - see color ad p 675	◈◈◈	$99-$169 [SAVE]	673
292 / p. 560		Doubletree Guest Suites in the Walt Disney World Resort - see color ad starting on p 592	◈◈◈	$159-$249	684
293 / p. 560	AAA	Orlando Royal Plaza - see color ad p 688	◈◈◈	$139-$229 [SAVE]	687
294 / p. 560	AAA	Hilton in the WALT DISNEY WORLD Resort - see ad p 44	◈◈◈◈	$175-$370 [SAVE]	686
295 / p. 560	AAA	Grosvenor Resort at Walt Disney World Resort - see color ad p 685	◈◈◈	$115-$155 [SAVE]	685
296 / p. 560	AAA	Holiday Inn-SunSpree Resort-Lake Buena Vista - see color ad p 687	◈◈◈	$129-$169 [SAVE]	686
297 / p. 560	AAA	Bryan's Spanish Cove - see color ad p 584, p 635	◈◈◈	$114-$177 [SAVE]	673
298 / p. 560		Sheraton's Vistana Resort - see color ad p 690	◈◈◈	$129-$269	689
299 / p. 560		Residence Inn by Marriott, Lake Buena Vista - see color ad p 582	◈◈◈	Failed to provide	688
300 / p. 560		Embassy Vacation Resort Grand Beach	◈◈◈	$149-$369	685

Spotter/Map Page Number	OA	LAKE BUENA VISTA - Lodgings (continued)	Diamond Rating	Rate Range High Season	Listing Page
301 / p. 560	◈	Buena Vista Suites - see color ad p 677	◈◈◈	$149-$169 SAVE	676
302 / p. 560	◈	Caribe Royale Resort Suites & Villas - see color ad p 676	◈◈◈	$149-$229 SAVE	676
306 / p. 560	◈	Disney's BoardWalk Resort	◈◈◈◈	$269-$1695	679
307 / p. 560	◈	Disney's Caribbean Beach Resort	◈◈◈	$149-$199	679
308 / p. 560		Holiday Inn Family Suites Resort Lake Buena Vista - see color ad p 686	◈◈◈	$125-$170	686
309 / p. 560		Orlando World Center Marriott	◈◈◈◈	$249-$289	687
311 / p. 560	◈	Disney's All Star Sports	◈◈◈	$99-$104	679
313 / p. 560	◈	Disney's All Star Music	◈◈◈	$99-$104	679
314 / p. 560	◈	Disney's All Star Movies	◈◈◈	$99-$104	679
		LAKE BUENA VISTA - Restaurants			
213 / p. 560		Cinderella's Royal Table	◈◈	$20-$30	692
216 / p. 560		The Crystal Palace	◈	$10-$20	693
217 / p. 560		Liberty Tree Tavern	◈◈	$10-$20	693
219 / p. 560		The Plaza Restaurant	◈	$8-$10	694
220 / p. 560		Tony's Town Square Restaurant	◈◈	$10-$23	694
221 / p. 560		Citricos	◈◈◈	$25-$40	693
222 / p. 560		Narcoosee's	◈◈	$21-$32	693
223 / p. 560		Victoria & Albert's	◈◈◈◈◈	$80-$100	694
224 / p. 560		California Grill	◈◈◈	$19-$30	692
225 / p. 560		Artist Point	◈◈◈	$17-$28	692
226 / p. 560		Crab House Seafood Restaurant	◈◈	$14-$25	693
227 / p. 560		Boatwright's Dining Hall	◈◈	$11-$18	692
228 / p. 560		Bonfamille's Cafe	◈◈	$10-$24	692
229 / p. 560		Arthur's 27	◈◈◈◈	$24-$28	692
230 / p. 560		Finn's Grill	◈◈	$19-$26	693
231 / p. 560		Fulton's Crab House	◈◈◈	$15-$42	693
232 / p. 560		Bongos Cuban Cafe	◈◈	$12-$24	692
233 / p. 560		Yachtsman's Steak House	◈◈◈	$22-$31	694
234 / p. 560		Pebbles/Lake Buena Vista	◈◈	$11-$26	693
235 / p. 560		Portobello Yacht Club	◈◈	$15-$30	694
236 / p. 560		Palio	◈◈◈	$17-$30	693
237 / p. 560		Restaurant Marrakesh	◈◈	$19-$25	694
238 / p. 560		Flying Fish Cafe	◈◈◈	$18-$26	693
239 / p. 560		Rain Forest Cafe	◈◈	$14-$23	694
240 / p. 560		Spoodles	◈◈	$18-$29	694
		KISSIMMEE - Lodgings			
321 / p. 560	◈	Comfort Inn-Maingate West - see color ad p 637	◈◈◈	$30-$140 SAVE	637
323 / p. 560		Destiny Secret Lake Resort	◈◈	$79-$89	641
325 / p. 560	◈	Ron Jon Resort-Orlando - see color ad p 584, p 635	◈◈◈	$99-$369 SAVE	662

Spotter/Map Page Number	OA	**KISSIMMEE** - Lodgings (continued)	Diamond Rating	Rate Range High Season	Listing Page
326 / p. 560	AAA	Sleep Inn Maingate - see color ad p 664	◇◇	$49-$99 SAVE	662
327 / p. 560	AAA	Westgate Towers/Westgate Vacation Villas - see color ad p 614	◇◇◇	$200-$675 SAVE	671
328 / p. 560		Orange Lake Resort & Country Club	◇◇◇	$120-$275	655
330 / p. 560	AAA	Travelodge Hotel Maingate - see color ad p 667	◇◇	$49-$105 SAVE	666
331 / p. 560	AAA	Lindfields Reserve	◇◇◇	$235-$343 SAVE	653
332 / p. 560	AAA	The Villages at Mango Key	◇◇◇	$900-$1100 SAVE	670
333 / p. 560	AAA	Days Inn Maingate West Of Walt Disney World Resort - see color ad p 640	◇◇	$49-$99 SAVE	640
334 / p. 560	AAA	Orbit One Vacation Villas - see color ad p 635	◇◇	$119-$189 SAVE	655
335 / p. 560	AAA	Comfort Suites Main Gate Resort - see ad p 638	◇◇	$59-$150 SAVE	638
337 / p. 560		Orlando's Key Vacation Homes	◇◇◇	$115-$225	655
338 / p. 560	AAA	Holiday Inn Maingate West - see color ad p 644	◇◇	$79-$129 SAVE	648
339 / p. 560	AAA	Ramada Inn Resort Maingate - see color ad p 644	◇◇	$69-$129 SAVE	660
340 / p. 560	AAA	Knights Inn-Maingate - see color ad p 636	◇	$42-$94 SAVE	652
344 / p. 560	AAA	Diplomat Resort at Maingate - see color ad p 671		$79-$99 SAVE	672
345 / p. 560	AAA	Doubletree Orlando Resort and Conference Center - see color ad p 643	◇◇◇	$119-$289 SAVE	643
347 / p. 560		Clarion Maingate - see color ad p 637	◇◇◇	$79-$109	635
350 / p. 560	AAA	Hampton Inn Main Gate West - see color ad p 633	◇◇	$84-$119 SAVE	647
351 / p. 560		The Palms - see color ad p 656	◇◇◇	$180-$319	656
352 / p. 560	AAA	Sheraton Four Points Lakeside - see color ad p 663	◇◇◇	$79-$109 SAVE	662
353 / p. 560	AAA	Quality Inn Maingate West - see color ad p 659	◇◇◇	$50-$90 SAVE	657
354 / p. 560		Motel 6 - 464	◇◇	$39-$55	655
355 / p. 560	AAA	Masters Inn-Main Gate	◇◇	$49-$99 SAVE	655
356 / p. 560	AAA	Econo Lodge Maingate-Resort - see color ad p 644	◇◇	$49-$89 SAVE	643
357 / p. 560	AAA	Ramada Plaza Hotel and Inns-Gateway - see color ad p 661	◇◇◇	$69-$129 SAVE	661
358 / p. 560	AAA	Holiday Inn-Nikki Bird Resort-Maingate	◇◇◇	$59-$109 SAVE	648
359 / p. 560	AAA	Quality Suites Maingate East - see color ad p 659	◇◇◇	$119-$229 SAVE	659
366 / p. 560	AAA	Sevilla Inn	◇◇	$40-$65 SAVE	662
367 / p. 560	AAA	Best Western Suite & Resort Hotel - see color ad p 636	◇◇◇	$64-$127 SAVE	635
368 / p. 560	AAA	Super 8 Motel	◇◇	$39-$69 SAVE	666
371 / p. 560	AAA	Central Motel	◇	$35-$90 SAVE	635
372 / p. 560	AAA	Four Winds Motel	◇◇	$30-$75 SAVE	646
376 / p. 560	AAA	Magic Castle Inn & Suites Eastgate - see color ad p 654, p 605	◇◇	$45-$65 SAVE	653
378 / p. 560		Quality Inn Main Gate - see color ad p 658	◇◇	$35-$70	657
379 / p. 560		Orlando Sun Village	◇◇◇	$95-$210	656

Spotter/Map Page Number	OA	KISSIMMEE - Lodgings (continued)	Diamond Rating	Rate Range High Season	Listing Page
380 / p. 560	AAA	Hampton Vacation Resort/Oak Plantation - see color ad p 647	◇◇◇	$79-$199 SAVE	647
381 / p. 560	AAA	Days Inn-Hwy 192 - see color ad p 639	◇◇	$50-$100 SAVE	640
382 / p. 560	AAA	Super 8 Motel - see ad p 665	◇◇	$39-$69 SAVE	665
384 / p. 560	AAA	Holiday Inn Kissimmee Downtown - see color ad p 653	◇◇	$69-$99 SAVE	648
385 / p. 560		Four Points Hotel Sheraton Orlando/Kissimmee - see color ad p 645	◆◆◆	$74-$114	646
386 / p. 560	AAA	Summerfield Resort	◇◇◇	$99-$159 SAVE	664
387 / p. 560		Days Inn 192-North	◆◆	$50-$100	638
388 / p. 560	AAA	Florida Palms Resort	◇◇	$119 SAVE	645
390 / p. 560	AAA	Apollo Inn - see color ad p 632	◇◇	$33-$70 SAVE	632
391 / p. 560	AAA	Flamingo Inn - see color ad p 632	◇◇	$29-$39 SAVE	645
392 / p. 560	AAA	Stadium Inn & Suites	◇◇	$65-$125 SAVE	662
393 / p. 560	AAA	Best Western-Kissimmee - see color ad p 636	◇◇	$42-$99 SAVE	635
394 / p. 560		Lago Vista Resort	◆◆	$89-$129	652
395 / p. 560	AAA	Riviera Motel	◇	$26-$46 SAVE	662
396 / p. 560		Villas at Fortune Place	◆◆◆	$119-$159	671
397 / p. 560	AAA	Travelodge Hotel/Airport South - see ad p 666	◇◇	$42-$55 SAVE	666
398 / p. 560	AAA	Holiday Inn Express	◇◇	$69-$89 SAVE	648
399 / p. 560	AAA	Howard Johnson Hotel - see color ad p 650	◇◇	$35-$75 SAVE	652
400 / p. 560	AAA	Hyatt Orlando - see color ad p 603	◇◇◇	$119-$144 SAVE	652
401 / p. 560		Hampton Inn-Maingate East - see color ad p 600	◆◆◆	$69-$99	647
402 / p. 560		Homewood Suites by Hilton - see color ad p 600	◆◆◆	$89-$109	649
403 / p. 560	AAA	Radisson Resort Parkway - see color ad p 660	◇◇◇	$89-$129 SAVE	660
404 / p. 560	AAA	Best Western-Eastgate - see color ad p 634	◇◇	$49-$159 SAVE	634
405 / p. 560	AAA	Parkway International - see color ad p 635	◇◇◇	$129-$199 SAVE	656
406 / p. 560	AAA	Larson's Inn & Family Suites - see color ad p 653	◇◇	$79-$99 SAVE	653
407 / p. 560	AAA	Howard Johnson Maingate East	◇◇	$99-$109 SAVE	652
408 / p. 560	AAA	Days Inn Maingate East	◇	$79-$169 SAVE	640
409 / p. 560	AAA	Days Suites/Main Gate East of Walt Disney World Resort - see color ad p 642	◇◇	$109-$269 SAVE	641
410 / p. 560	AAA	Tropical Palms Resort - see color ad starting on p 668	◇◇	$59-$99 SAVE	667
411 / p. 560	AAA	Travelodge Hotel Main Gate East - see color ad p 666	◇◇	$59 SAVE	667
412 / p. 560		Motel 6 - 436	◆◆	$33-$56	655
413 / p. 560	AAA	Holiday Inn Hotel & Suites Main Gate East	◇◇◇	$59-$135 SAVE	648
414 / p. 560	AAA	Comfort Suites Maingate East - see color ad p 638	◇◇◇	$95-$250 SAVE	637
415 / p. 560	AAA	Masters Inn-Kissimmee	◇◇	$45-$89 SAVE	655
416 / p. 560	AAA	Travelodge Suites Kissimmee East Gate Orange - see ad p 599 & color ad p 670	◇◇	$69-$129 SAVE	667

Spotter/Map Page Number	OA	KISSIMMEE - Lodgings (continued)	Diamond Rating	Rate Range High Season	Listing Page
417 / p. 560	AAA	Royal Oaks of Kissimmee	◊◊◊	$99-$199 SAVE	662
418 / p. 560	AAA	Star Island Resort & Club	◊◊◊	$127-$285 SAVE	663
419 / p. 560	AAA	Clarion Suites Resort World - see color ad p 632	◊◊◊	$89-$225 SAVE	637
420 / p. 560	AAA	Magic Castle Inn & Suites Maingate - see color ad p 654, p 605	◊◊	$48-$68 SAVE	653
422 / p. 560	AAA	Fantasy World Club Villas - see color ad p 645	◊◊◊	$165-$195 SAVE	645
423 / p. 560	AAA	Howard Johnson Enchanted Land Resort Hotel - see color ad p 650	◊◊◊	$75-$109 SAVE	649
424 / p. 560	AAA	Sun Motel - see color ad p 665	◊	$80-$95 SAVE	665
425 / p. 560	AAA	Deluxe Florida Villas	◊◊◊	$140-$150 SAVE	641
426 / p. 560		Quality Inn Lake Cecile - see color ad p 658	◊◊◊	$39-$70	657
427 / p. 560	AAA	Ramada Disney Area Eastgate/Fountain Park - see color ad p 661	◊◊	$69-$129 SAVE	660
428 / p. 560	AAA	Red Roof Inn	◊◊	$50-$60 SAVE	661
429 / p. 560	AAA	Holiday Villas - see color ad p 649	◊◊◊	$155-$339 SAVE	648
430 / p. 560		DoubleTree Guest Suites-Orlando Maingate - see color ad starting on p 592	◊◊◊	$166-$206	643
431 / p. 560	AAA	Golden Link Motel	◊◊	$36-$59 SAVE	646
432 / p. 560		Quality Inn Kissimmee	◊◊	$69-$89	657
433 / p. 560	AAA	Howard Johnson Express Inn & Suites Lakefront Park - see color ad p 651	◊◊	$59-$119 SAVE	649
435 / p. 560		Days Inn	◊◊	Failed to provide	638
436 / p. 560	AAA	Wonderland Inn	◊◊◊	$79-$139 SAVE	671
437 / p. 560		Poinciana Golf & Racquet Resort	◊◊◊	$80-$160	657
438 / p. 560	AAA	Parkside Record Inn & Suites - see color ad p 657	◊◊	$39-$69 SAVE	656
		KISSIMMEE - Restaurants			
242 / p. 560		Key W. Kool's Open Pit Grill	◊◊	$10-$24	673
243 / p. 560		Giordano's	◊◊	$7-$11	673
245 / p. 560	AAA	Twin Dragons Restaurant	◊◊	$8-$22	673
246 / p. 560		Fusions	◊◊	$9-$17	672
247 / p. 560		Pacino's Italian Ristorante	◊◊	$10-$23	673
249 / p. 560		Gianni's Restaurant	◊◊	$8-$16	672
		DAVENPORT - Lodgings			
441 / p. 560	AAA	Days Inn-South of Disney - see color ad p 630	◊◊◊	$46-$115 SAVE	629
442 / p. 560	AAA	Tropicana Resort Hotel	◊◊◊	$59-$89 SAVE	630
445 / p. 560	AAA	Comfort Inn Main Gate South	◊◊◊	$39-$129 SAVE	629
446 / p. 560		Hampton Inn Orlando-S of Walt Disney Resort	◊◊◊	$59-$129	630
447 / p. 560	AAA	Global Vacation Rentals at Westridge - see color ad p 586	◊◊◊	$159-$289 SAVE	630
448 / p. 560	AAA	Prestige Vacation Homes - see color ad p 595	◊◊◊	$139-$219 SAVE	630
449 / p. 560	AAA	Super 8 Motel Maingate South	◊◊◊	$39-$79 SAVE	630
		ST. CLOUD - Lodgings			
453 / p. 560	AAA	Budget Inn of St Cloud	◊◊	$35-$45 SAVE	701

ORLANDO NORTH   (See map p. 554; index p. 556)

———— WHERE TO STAY ————

BEST WESTERN ORLANDO WEST   **Phone:** (407)841-8600   **14**
AAA SAVE   12/24-4/29   2P: $69-$99   XP: $10   F12
            4/30-10/31   2P: $55-$99   XP: $10   F12
            12/1-12/23 & 11/1-11/30   2P: $49-$79   XP: $10   F12
            Location: I-4, exit 41, 1.5 mi w on SR 50, 0.4 mi e of SR 423. 2014 W Colonial Dr 32804. Fax: 407/843-7080.
Motel   **Facility:** Located on busy highway. 110 units. 2 stories, interior corridors. **Terms:** 3 day cancellation
notice-fee imposed, small pets only ($5 extra charge, $25 deposit). **Amenities:** extended cable TV, voice
mail, safes (fee). **Dining:** coffee shop, 6:30 am-2:30 pm, Sat-1:30 pm, Sun-11 am, cocktails. **Guest Services:** coin laundry.
Cards: AE, DI, DS, MC, VI. **Special Amenities:** free newspaper.

SOME UNITS

[icons] / [icons]   FEE   FEE

COMFORT INN-NORTH   **Phone:** 407/629-4000   **25**
AAA SAVE   12/24-4/22   1P: $79-$125   2P: $79-$125
            4/23-11/30   1P: $59-$69   2P: $59-$79
            12/1-12/23   1P: $59-$69   2P: $59-$75
            Location: I-4, exit 46, 0.4 mi w on SR 423. 830 Lee Rd 32810. Fax: 407/645-2809. **Facility:** A solid property of-
Motel   fering modern guest rooms, all nicely maintained. 145 units. 5 stories, interior corridors. **Terms:** monthly rates
available, package plans, small pets only ($10 extra charge, $25 fee). **Amenities:** video games, voice mail,
safes (fee), irons. *Some:* hair dryers. **Leisure Activities:** heated pool, sauna, whirlpool, game room. **Guest Services:** [ECP]
meal plan available, coin laundry. **Business Services:** meeting rooms. **Cards:** AE, CB, DI, DS, JC, MC, VI. **Special Amenities:**
early check-in/late check-out and free room upgrade (subject to availability with advanced reservations).
(See color ad p 573)

SOME UNITS

[icons]   FEE   [icons] / [icons]   FEE   FEE

COMFORT SUITES DOWNTOWN   **Phone:** (407)228-4007   **23**
SAVE   1/16-4/25   1P: $99-$119   2P: $99-$119   XP: $10   F
            12/1-1/15   1P: $89-$109   2P: $89-$109   XP: $10   F
            4/26-11/30   1P: $79-$109   2P: $79-$109   XP: $10   F
Motel   **Location:** I-4, exit 43, just e on Princeton, then just n. 2416 N Orange Ave 32804. Fax: 407/228-3820. **Facility:** 78
units, 9 with efficiency. Some whirlpool units. *Bath:* combo or shower only. 3 stories, interior corridors.
Terms: check-in 4 pm, 10 day cancellation notice. **Amenities:** extended cable TV, voice mail, hair dryers.
Some: irons. **Leisure Activities:** heated pool, whirlpool. **Guest Services:** [CP] meal plan available, area transportation, coin
laundry. **Business Services:** meeting rooms. **Cards:** AE, CB, DI, DS, MC, VI.

SOME UNITS

[icons] / [icons] /

(See map p. 554)

COMFORT SUITES UCF-RESEARCH PARK

[SAVE] Motel

All Year   1P: $97-$139   2P: $97-$139
Phone: (407)737-7303   [10]   F12
XP: $10
Location: On SR 434 (Alafaya Tr); 1.6 mi n of SR 408, exit 21; 0.4 mi n of SR 50. 12101 Challenger Pkwy 32826. **Fax:** 407/737-7304. **Facility:** 70 units. Some whirlpool units ($119-$159). **Bath:** combo or shower only. 3 stories, interior corridors. **Terms:** 3 day cancellation notice-fee imposed. **Amenities:** extended cable TV, voice mail, irons, hair dryers. **Leisure Activities:** exercise room. **Guest Services:** [ECP] meal plan available, valet laundry. **Business Services:** meeting rooms. **Cards:** AE, DI, DS, MC, VI.
SOME UNITS

COURTYARD BY MARRIOTT DOWNTOWN

Motel

12/1-12/31   2P: $109-$209
1/1-4/9   2P: $129
9/20-11/30   2P: $109
4/10-9/19   2P: $99
Phone: (407) 996-1000   [26]
Location: Just n of SR 50 (Colonial Dr); just e of I-4, exit 41. 730 N Magnolia Ave 32803. **Fax:** 407/996-1001. **Facility:** 200 units. Some suites ($139) and whirlpool units ($129). **Bath:** combo or shower only. 6 stories, interior corridors. **Amenities:** dual phone lines, voice mail, irons, hair dryers. **Leisure Activities:** whirlpool, exercise room. **Guest Services:** complimentary laundry. **Business Services:** meeting rooms. **Cards:** AE, DI, DS, MC, VI.
SOME UNITS

COURTYARD BY MARRIOTT UCF

Motel

All Year   1P: $79-$109   2P: $79-$109
Phone: (407)277-7676   [7]
Location: On University Blvd, 2.2 mi e of SR 417, exit 32A, just w of SR 434 (Alafaya Tr); at Collegiate Square. 12000 Collegiate Way 32817. **Fax:** 407/277-5710. **Facility:** 123 units. Some suites ($109-$139). **Bath:** combo or shower only. 4 stories, interior corridors. **Amenities:** voice mail, irons, hair dryers. **Leisure Activities:** heated pool, whirlpool, exercise room. **Guest Services:** coin laundry. **Business Services:** meeting rooms. **Cards:** AE, CB, DI, DS, MC, VI.
SOME UNITS

ECONO LODGE-CENTRAL

Motel

All Year   1P: $36-$85   2P: $36-$85
Phone: (407)293-7221   [17]   F18
XP: $6
Location: I-4, exit 41, 2 mi w on SR 50. 3300 W Colonial Dr 32808. **Fax:** 407/293-1166. **Facility:** 102 units, 9 with efficiency. **Bath:** combo or shower only. 2 stories, exterior corridors. **Terms:** 3 day cancellation notice-fee imposed, weekly rates available, pets ($6 extra charge). **Amenities:** extended cable TV. Some: safes (fee). **Leisure Activities:** shuffleboard. **Guest Services:** coin laundry. **Business Services:** meeting rooms. **Cards:** AE, CB, DI, DS, MC, VI. **Special Amenities:** free room upgrade (subject to availability with advanced reservations).
SOME UNITS

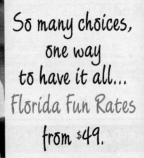

(See map p. 554)

FOUR POINTS ORLANDO DOWNTOWN   Phone: (407)841-3220   ⑪
All Year   1P: $129-$159   2P: $129-$159   XP: $10   F18
Hotel   **Location:** I-4, eastbound exit 40 (Robinson St); westbound exit US 17-92 and SR 50, s on Orange Ave to Washington St, then just e. 151 E Washington St Ave 32801. Fax: 407/648-4758. **Facility:** Facing Lake Eola and park. 250 units. 2 two-bedroom units. Some suites and whirlpool units. *Bath:* combo or shower only. 5 stories, interior/exterior corridors. **Parking:** valet. **Terms:** package plans. **Amenities:** voice mail, irons, hair dryers. **Leisure Activities:** heated pool, exercise room. **Guest Services:** gift shop, valet laundry. **Business Services:** conference facilities, administrative services. **Cards:** AE, CB, DI, DS, JC, MC, VI. *(See color ad below)*

SOME UNITS

HAMPTON INN & SUITES   Phone: 407/282-0029   ⑥
All Year   1P: $99   2P: $99   XP: $10   F12
Motel   **Location:** 2.2 mi e of SR 417 on University Blvd; then just n in Quadrangle Office Park. 3450 Quadrangle Blvd 32817. Fax: 407/206-3001. **Facility:** 110 units, 34 with efficiency. Some suites ($129). *Bath:* combo or shower only. 3 stories, interior corridors. **Terms:** cancellation fee imposed. **Amenities:** extended cable TV, irons, hair dryers. **Leisure Activities:** heated pool, whirlpool, exercise room. **Guest Services:** [ECP] meal plan available, complimentary evening beverages: Mon-Thurs, coin laundry. **Business Services:** meeting rooms. **Cards:** AE, CB, DI, DS, JC, MC, VI.

SOME UNITS

HOLIDAY INN AT THE ORLANDO ARENA   Phone: (407)996-0100   ㉑
All Year   1P: $84-$114   2P: $84-$114
Hotel   **Location:** I-4, exit 41, just w on SR 50. 304 W Colonial Dr 32801. Fax: 407/996-0103. **Facility:** Half the rooms have lake view. 276 units. 1 two-bedroom unit. Some suites and whirlpool units. *Bath:* combo or shower only. 14 stories, interior corridors. **Terms:** cancellation fee imposed. **Amenities:** extended cable TV, video games, voice mail, safes, irons, hair dryers. *Some:* CD players. **Dining:** restaurant, 6 am-midnight, $6-$11, cocktails. **Leisure Activities:** heated pool, exercise room. **Guest Services:** gift shop, coin laundry. *Fee:* area transportation. **Business Services:** meeting rooms. **Cards:** AE, CB, DI, DS, JC, MC, VI. **Special Amenities:** early check-in/late check-out and free room upgrade (subject to availability with advanced reservations).** *(See ad below)*

SOME UNITS

(See map p. 554)

HOLIDAY INN EXPRESS ORLANDO EAST   **Phone:** (407)282-3900   **9**
　　　2/1-8/18   1P: $79   2P: $79
▽▽▽   12/1-1/31 & 8/19-11/30   1P: $69   2P: $69
Motel   **Location:** SR 417, exit Colonial Dr (SR 50), just w. 8750 E Colonial Dr 32817. Fax: 407/282-0416. **Facility:** 118 units. 2 stories, exterior corridors. **Terms:** weekly rates available. **Amenities:** irons, hair dryers. **Leisure Activities:** whirlpool. **Guest Services:** [ECP] meal plan available, coin laundry. **Business Services:** meeting rooms. **Cards:** AE, CB, DI, DS, JC, MC, VI. *(See color ad below)*

SOME UNITS
(ASK) (S🄳) 🖥️ 📶 🎬 🖨️ 🖵 / ✕ 🖵 🔧 /

HOLIDAY INN ORLANDO NORTH-WINTER PARK   **Phone:** (407)645-5600   **24**
(AAA) (SAVE)   All Year   1P: $89-$119   2P: $89-$119
▽▽▽   **Location:** I-4, exit 46 (Lee Rd), just w on SR 438. 626 Lee Rd 32810. Fax: 407/740-7912. **Facility:** Comfortable guest rooms. 200 units. Some suites and whirlpool units ($169-$199). *Bath:* combo or shower only. 5 stories, Motor Inn   interior corridors. **Amenities:** voice mail, irons, hair dryers. **Dining:** restaurant, 6:30 am-11 & 4-10 pm, $7-$15, cocktails, nightclub. **Leisure Activities:** exercise room, game room. **Guest Services:** coin laundry. **Business Services:** meeting rooms, administrative services. **Cards:** AE, CB, DI, DS, JC, MC, VI.
Special Amenities: early check-in/late check-out and free newspaper.

SOME UNITS
(S🄳) 🍴 🍸 🛝 📷 🏊 🎬 🖨️ 🖵 DATA PORT / ✕ 🖵 🔧 /
　　　　　　　FEE　　　　　　　　　　　　　　　　　　FEE FEE

HOLIDAY INN SELECT-ORLANDO EAST-UCF AREA   **Phone:** (407)275-9000   **5**
(AAA) (SAVE)   2/1-4/30   1P: $99-$129   XP: $10   F18
▽▽▽   12/1-1/31 & 5/1-11/30   1P: $79-$129   XP: $10   F18
Motor Inn   **Location:** 2.4 mi e of SR 417 on University Blvd, then just n. 12125 High Tech Ave 32817. Fax: 407/381-0019. **Facility:** Adjacent to 41 acre lake. 250 units. Some suites. 6 stories, interior corridors. **Amenities:** voice mail, irons, hair dryers. *Some:* CD players, fax. **Dining:** restaurant, 6:30 am-11 pm, $8-$16, cocktails. **Leisure Activities:** sauna, whirlpool, jogging, exercise room, volleyball. **Guest Services:** area transportation-within 5 mi, valet laundry. **Business Services:** meeting rooms, administrative services. **Fee:** PC, fax. **Cards:** AE, CB, DI, DS, JC, MC, VI. *(See color ad below)*

SOME UNITS
(S🄳) 🛬 🍴 🍸 📷 🏊 ✕ 🎬 🖨️ 🖵 DATA PORT / ✕ (VCR) 🔧 /
　　　FEE　　　　　　　　　　　　　　　FEE　　　　　　　　　　FEE

(See map p. 554)

LA QUINTA INN & SUITES UCF — Phone: (407)737-6075 **8**

Motel
All Year — 1P: $89-$99 — 2P: $89-$99
Location: Just se of jct University Blvd and SR 434 (Alafaya Tr). 11805 Research Pkwy 32826. Fax: 407/737-7562. **Facility:** 130 units. Some suites ($119-$129). *Bath:* combo or shower only. 6 stories, interior corridors. **Terms:** check-in 4 pm, small pets only. **Amenities:** video games, voice mail, irons, hair dryers. **Leisure Activities:** heated pool, whirlpool, exercise room. **Guest Services:** [ECP] meal plan available, coin laundry. **Business Services:** meeting rooms. **Cards:** AE, CB, DI, DS, MC, VI. *(See color ad p 604)*

ORLANDO MARRIOTT DOWNTOWN — Phone: (407)843-6664 **13**

Hotel
All Year — 1P: $85 — 2P: $85 — XP: $15 — F17
Location: I-4, exit 41, (Colonial Dr) westbound; exit 40 (Robinson St) eastbound, just w at jct Livingston and Hughey sts. 400 W Livingston St 32801. Fax: 407/648-5414. **Facility:** Connected to Centroplex, opposite TD Waterhouse Centre and Bob Carr Performing Arts Center. 290 units. Some suites and whirlpool units. 15 stories, interior corridors. **Parking:** valet. **Terms:** cancellation fee imposed. **Amenities:** extended cable TV, voice mail, irons, hair dryers. **Leisure Activities:** heated pool, whirlpool, exercise room. **Guest Services:** gift shop, valet laundry. **Business Services:** conference facilities, administrative services. **Cards:** AE, CB, DI, DS, MC, VI.

RADISSON PLAZA HOTEL ORLANDO — Phone: (407)425-4455 **22**

Hotel
All Year — 1P: $82 — 2P: $82
Location: I-4, Ivanhoe Blvd exit. 60 S Ivanhoe Blvd 32804. Fax: 407/843-0262. **Facility:** Stylish rooms, many overlooking Lake Ivanhoe. 337 units. Some whirlpool units. 15 stories, interior corridors. **Parking:** extra charge or valet. **Terms:** cancellation fee imposed, package plans. **Amenities:** dual phone lines, voice mail, honor bars, irons, hair dryers. **Dining:** restaurant, 6:30 am-10 pm, $8-$20, cocktails. **Leisure Activities:** heated pool, whirlpool, 2 lighted tennis courts, exercise room, basketball. **Guest Services:** gift shop, area transportation-downtown, valet laundry. *Fee:* massage. **Business Services:** meeting rooms, administrative services, fax. **Cards:** AE, CB, DI, DS, MC, VI. *(See color ad below)*

(See map p. 554)

RADISSON UNIVERSITY HOTEL
Phone: (407)658-9008   **1**

AAA SAVE

Motor Inn

12/1-4/30	1P: $99	2P: $99	
5/1-11/30	1P: $84	2P: $84	

Location: 1 mi n of East-West Expwy (SR 408) on Alafaya Tr, 0.3 mi n of SR 50, 3.8 mi e of jct SR 50 and Central Florida Greenway (SR 417). 1724 Alafaya Tr 32826. Fax: 407/381-5456. **Facility:** Elegant lobby and warmly decorated dining room. 149 units. 7 stories, interior corridors. **Terms:** cancellation fee imposed. **Amenities:** extended cable TV, video games, voice mail, irons, hair dryers. *Some:* honor bars. **Dining:** dining room, 6:30 am-1:30 & 5-10 pm, $8-$21, cocktails. **Leisure Activities:** exercise room. **Guest Services:** valet laundry. **Business Services:** meeting rooms. **Cards:** AE, CB, DI, DS, JC, MC, VI. **Special Amenities:** early check-in/late check-out and free local telephone calls.

SOME UNITS

TRAVELODGE AT COLONIAL PLAZA
Phone: (407)894-2741   **15**

AAA SAVE

Motel

12/26-4/21	1P: $79-$99	2P: $79-$99	XP: $10 F18
10/2-11/30	1P: $69-$89	2P: $69-$89	XP: $10 F18
12/1-12/25 & 4/22-10/1	1P: $59-$79	2P: $59-$79	XP: $10 F18

Location: I-4, exit 41, 2 mi e on SR 50. 2801 E Colonial Dr 32803. Fax: 407/896-7913. **Facility:** 227 units. *Bath:* combo or shower only. 2 stories, exterior corridors. **Terms:** 60 day cancellation notice. **Amenities:** fax, safes (fee), irons, hair dryers. **Leisure Activities:** heated pool, whirlpool. **Guest Services:** coin laundry. **Business Services:** meeting rooms. **Cards:** AE, CB, DI, DS, MC, VI. **Special Amenities:** early check-in/late check-out and free continental breakfast. *(See color ad p 577)*

SOME UNITS

TRAVELODGE ORLANDO DOWNTOWN
Phone: (407)423-1671   **12**

AAA SAVE

Motel

All Year	1P: $45-$85	2P: $45-$85	XP: $5 F18

Location: Corner of Magnolia Ave, Rosalind Ave and Livingston St. 409 N Magnolia Ave 32801. Fax: 407/423-1523. **Facility:** 76 units. *Bath:* shower only. 2 stories, interior/exterior corridors. **Terms:** weekly rates available, pets ($10 extra charge). **Guest Services:** coin laundry. **Cards:** AE, DI, DS, JC, MC, VI. **Special Amenities:** free local telephone calls and free newspaper.

SOME UNITS

WELLESLEY INN & SUITES-ORLANDO/MAITLAND
Phone: 407/659-0066   **27**

AAA SAVE

Extended Stay Motel

All Year	1P: $59-$119	2P: $59-$119	XP: $10 F17

Location: I-4, exit 47, 1 mi w. 1951 Summit Tower Blvd 32810. Fax: 407/659-0067. **Facility:** 135 efficiencies. Some suites. *Bath:* combo or shower only. 3 stories, interior corridors. **Terms:** weekly & monthly rates available, small pets only. **Amenities:** extended cable TV, voice mail, irons, hair dryers. **Leisure Activities:** exercise room. **Guest Services:** coin laundry. **Business Services:** meeting rooms. **Cards:** AE, CB, DI, DS, MC, VI. **Special Amenities:** free continental breakfast and free local telephone calls. *(See color ad opposite title page)*

SOME UNITS

The following lodging was either not evaluated or did not meet AAA rating requirements but is listed for your information only.

EMBASSY SUITES ORLANDO DOWNTOWN
Phone: 407/841-1000

fyi

Suite Hotel

All Year	1P: $109-$189	2P: $109-$189	XP: $15 F18

Too new to rate, opening scheduled for October 2000. **Location:** I-4, exit 38 (Anderson), just e, left on Rosalind. 191 E Pine St 32801. Fax: 407/841-0010. **Amenities:** 167 units, restaurant, radios, coffeemakers, microwaves, refrigerators, pool. **Cards:** AE, CB, DI, DS, MC, VI. *(See color ad p 595)*

WHERE TO DINE

4TH FIGHTER GROUP
Lunch: $6-$10   Dinner: $12-$25   Phone: 407/898-4251   **9**

Steak & Seafood

Location: I-4, exit 41, 2.6 mi e on E Colonial Dr, then just s; at Orlando Executive Airport. 494 Rickenbacker Dr 32803. **Hours:** 11 am-2 & 4:30-10 pm, Fri & Sat-11 pm, Sun from 9 am. **Reservations:** suggested. **Features:** casual dress; Sunday brunch; children's menu; early bird specials; cocktails & lounge; a la carte. World War II memorabilia and a location at the side of the runway of Orlando Executive Airport give the casual, intimate restaurant its personality. While watching planes take off and land, savor entrees of prime rib, steaks and veal. **Cards:** AE, CB, DI, DS, MC, VI.

BAJA BURRITO KITCHEN
Lunch: $4-$9   Dinner: $4-$9   Phone: 407/895-6112   **8**

American

Location: Just s of SR 50; 2 mi e of I-4 exit 41; in Colonial Market Center. 2716 E Colonial Dr 32803. **Hours:** 11 am-10 pm, Sun 11:30 am-9 pm. Closed: 4/15, 11/22, 12/25. **Features:** casual dress; children's menu; carryout; beer & wine only. This fast-food shop located in a shopping complex serves good, freshly prepared Tex-Mex dishes. A salsa bar offers a variety of tasty toppings from fresh tomatoes to hot havanero salsa and chopped cilantro. Enjoy a nice made-to-order meal served up fast. Smoke free premises.

CHAN'S CHINESE CUISINE
Lunch: $4-$6   Dinner: $7-$28   Phone: 407/896-0093   **5**

Ethnic

Location: On SR 50 (Colonial Dr), 1.5 mi e of I-4. 1901 E Colonial Dr 32803. **Hours:** 10 am-11 pm. **Features:** casual dress; carryout; cocktails. Feast on a far-ranging menu of dim sum and Hong Kong-style dinners. Delectable dishes include fried chicken with ginger sauce and stir-fried jumbo shrimp with honey walnut sauce. Traditional Chinese paintings and curios create a serene setting. **Cards:** AE, MC, VI.

(See map p. 554)

DEXTER'S OF THORNTON PARK **Lunch:** $4-$9 **Dinner:** $5-$16 **Phone:** 407/648-2777 17
Nouvelle American
Location: From I-4, 0.7 mi e on Robinson, just s on Eola, then just e, 0.3 mi e of Lake Eola Park. 808 E Washington St 32801. **Hours:** 11 am-midnight, Sun-10 pm. Closed major holidays. **Features:** casual dress; carryout; beer & wine only. This eclectic neighborhood meeting place serves a variety of creative soups, pastas, salads and entrees. Some may be content to have a glass of wine and a platter of gourmet cheese with fresh bread and fruit, but don't stop there. The food is wonderful. **Cards:** AE, DI, DS, MC, VI.

FIRST WATCH **Lunch:** $5-$7 **Phone:** 407/841-5544 18
American
Location: Downtown; between Orange Ave and Magnolia St. 63 E Pine St 32801. **Hours:** 7 am-2:30 pm. Closed: 11/22, 12/25. **Features:** casual dress; children's menu; carryout; street parking. A popular breakfast and lunch spot, it serves omelets, pancakes, waffles and crepes. A nice assortment of salad, sandwiches and fresh soup changes daily to provide a variety of choices. An efficient staff will have you savoring every bite in no time. Smoke free premises. **Cards:** AE, DS, MC, VI.

GARGI'S AT LAKE IVANHOE **Lunch:** $5-$9 **Dinner:** $9-$15 **Phone:** 407/894-7907 4
Italian
Location: I-4, exit 43 (Princeton St), 0.8 mi se. 1421 Orange Ave 32804. **Hours:** 11:30 am-2 & 6-10 pm, Fri & Sat-11 pm. Closed: 11/22, 12/25; also Sun. **Reservations:** accepted. **Features:** semi-formal attire; carryout; beer & wine only; street parking. Good cuisine is served in a small, intimate restaurant that maintains the feel of a New York-style neighborhood eatery. A busy lunch crowd from nearby downtown keeps this place hopping. Wonderful eggplant and a rich cheesecake are menu highlights. Smoke free premises. **Cards:** AE, CB, DI, MC, VI.

HIGH TIDE HARRY'S **Lunch:** $5-$10 **Dinner:** $4-$30 **Phone:** 407/273-4422 12
Seafood
Location: Just n on SR 436 from jct SR 50. 925 N Semoran Blvd 32807. **Hours:** 11 am-10 pm, Fri & Sat-11 pm. Closed: 11/22, 12/25. **Features:** casual dress; children's menu; early bird specials; cocktails. This laid-back eatery features a fishing motif. Quality seafood includes all-you-can-eat dinner specials Sun-Thurs. Expect simple presentation at affordable prices. An excellent selection of microbrewed beer is offered with two-for-one specials on Wednesday nights. **Cards:** AE, CB, DI, DS, JC, MC, VI.

HOT DOG HEAVEN **Lunch:** $2-$6 **Dinner:** $2-$6 **Phone:** 407/282-5746 13
American
Location: SR 50, just w of jct SR 436. 5355 E Colonial Dr 32807. **Hours:** 11 am-6 pm. Closed major holidays; also Sun. **Features:** casual dress; carryout; cafeteria. Authentic Chicago hot dogs and hand-dipped ice cream are served in a pristine '50s-style cafeteria. Pile on the sauerkraut or choose a chili-cheese combo. A lunch-time favorite, it offers outside seating when crowded. Look for the landmark hot dog sign. Smoke free premises.

JOHNNY RIVERS SMOKEHOUSE AND BBQ CO **Lunch:** $6-$8 **Dinner:** $9-$14 **Phone:** 407/293-5803 6
Steak House
Location: I-4, exit 41, 4.4 mi w on SR 50; just e of SR 435. 5370 W Colonial Dr 32808. **Hours:** 11 am-10 pm, Fri-11 pm, Sat & Sun noon-11:30 pm. Closed: 11/22, 12/25. **Features:** casual dress; children's menu; carryout; cocktails & lounge. Not the average smokehouse. There are etched glass dividers and booths with denim covered backs. The food is creative and down-home with specialties like smoked pork, baby back ribs and bourbon oysters. Don't miss the Hershey Bar bread pudding. **Cards:** AE, DI, DS, MC, VI.

LA NORMANDIE RESTAURANT **Lunch:** $8-$14 **Dinner:** $12-$26 **Phone:** 407/896-9976 7
French
Location: I-4, exit 41, 1.5 mi e on SR 50. 2021 E Colonial Dr 32803. **Hours:** 11:30 am-2 & 5-10 pm, Sat from 5 pm. Closed: 1/1, 7/4, 12/25; also Sun. **Reservations:** suggested. **Features:** dressy casual; early bird specials; cocktails & lounge; a la carte. This outstanding French restaurant offers a wide selection of seafood, beef, fowl, pasta, and veal. Choose from two excellent four-course dinners — salmon or beef Wellington. Luscious pastries and a signature souffle truly enhance the experience. **Cards:** AE, DI, DS, MC, VI.

LEE'S LAKESIDE RESTAURANT & LOUNGE **Lunch:** $9-$14 **Dinner:** $19-$29 **Phone:** 407/841-1565 21
American
Location: On Lake Eola at Central Blvd and Osceola Ave. 431 E Central Blvd 32801. **Hours:** 11 am-10 pm, Fri-11 pm, Sat 5 pm-11 pm, Sun 11 am-9 pm. **Reservations:** suggested. **Features:** casual dress; Sunday brunch; children's menu; early bird specials; carryout; cocktails & lounge; entertainment; minimum charge-$8. From large bay windows, look out at the Lake Eola fountain and the downtown skyline. Tasty and well-presented dishes, such as tenderloin stuffed with crabmeat and pina colada muffins, and attentive service are trademarks of the elegant restaurant. Patio dining available. **Cards:** AE, CB, DI, DS, MC, VI.

LE PROVENCE **Dinner:** $15-$33 **Phone:** 407/843-1320 23
French
Location: Center; between Orange and Magnolia aves at corner of Court Ave. 50 E Pine St 32801. **Hours:** 5:30 pm-9:30 pm, Fri & Sat-10:30 pm. Closed major holidays; also Sun. **Features:** semi-formal attire; carryout; cocktails; a la carte. The upscale French bistro includes such mouth-watering dishes as roasted rack of lamb, grilled lobster in a saffron cream sauce and creme caramel. Highlights of the decor are an impressive mahogany bar, French antiques and Impressionist paintings. **Cards:** AE, DI, MC, VI.

MANUEL'S ON THE 28TH **Dinner:** $27-$39 **Phone:** 407/246-6580 19
International
Location: Orange Ave and E Livingston, on the 28th floor of the Bank of America Bldg. 390 N Orange Ave 32801. **Hours:** 6 pm-10 pm. Closed: 1/1, 11/22, 12/25; also Sun & Mon. **Reservations:** suggested. **Features:** semi-formal attire; cocktails; fee for parking; a la carte; prix fixe. A candlelit setting on the 28th floor offers unparalleled views of the downtown area. Changing seasonally, the menu features unique dishes with an international flair. The blue lump crab bisque is wonderful, as is the signature pan seared chilean sea bass with sea scallops. Smoke free premises. **Cards:** AE, CB, DI, DS, MC, VI.

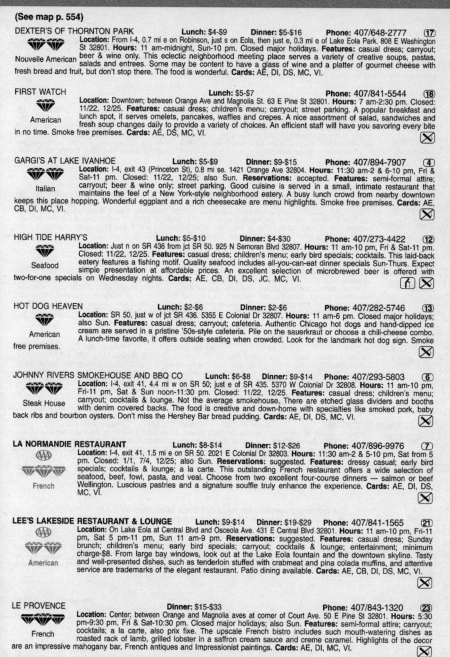

(See map p. 554)

MISUZU
Ethnic
Lunch: $6-$8   **Dinner:** $6-$24   **Phone:** 407/895-8396   ③
Location: I-4, exit 43 (Princeton St), 0.5 mi se. 1905 N Orange Ave 32804. **Hours:** 11:30 am-2:30 & 5:30-9 pm, Fri-10 pm, Sat 5:30 pm-10 pm. Closed major holidays; also Sun & Mon. **Features:** casual dress; beer & wine only; street parking. A storefront eatery tucked among antique shops, its menu offers everything from finger foods to full meals, including tepan-yaki. Also try an excellent variety of sushi and sashimi. You may ask for samples if you're unsure of what to order. **Cards:** AE, CB, DI, DS, MC, VI.

PEBBLES DOWNTOWN
American
Lunch: $6-$9   **Dinner:** $6-$19   **Phone:** 407/839-0892   ⑮
Location: Center; just w of Orange Ave. 17 W Church St 32801. **Hours:** 11 am-11 pm, Mon-10 pm, Fri-1 am, Sat 5 pm-1 am, Sun 5 pm-10 pm. Closed: 5/28, 11/22, 12/25. **Reservations:** accepted. **Features:** casual dress; children's menu; carryout; cocktails; fee for parking; a la carte. The distinctive decor of this informal, upbeat restaurant is highlighted by a ceiling covered with carved ship figureheads. A broad menu includes herb-crusted chicken, grilled pork tenderloin with citrus sauce, scallops in puff pastry and grilled mahi tuna. **Cards:** AE, DI, DS, MC, VI.

STRAUB'S BOATYARD
Steak & Seafood
Lunch: $5-$9   **Dinner:** $12-$27   **Phone:** 407/628-0067   ㉔
Location: I-4, exit 46, 0.3 mi w. 743 Lee Rd 32810. **Hours:** 11 am-10 pm, Fri-11 pm, Sat 4:30-11 pm. Closed: 11/22, 12/25; also Sun. **Reservations:** suggested; dinner. **Features:** casual dress; early bird specials; cocktails & lounge. Nautical touches add warmth to this seafood specialty house. Ample portions of fresh, flavorful fish at reasonable prices is the main draw, with warm bread and spicy soup rounding out the meal. An impeccable staff extends a sincere invitation to return. **Cards:** AE, DI, DS, MC, VI.

STRAUB'S FINE SEAFOOD RESTAURANT
Seafood
Dinner: $12-$25   **Phone:** 407/273-9330   ⑩
Location: I-4, exit 41, 3.8 mi e on SR 50. 5101 E Colonial Dr 32803. **Hours:** 4:30 pm-10 pm. Closed: 11/22, 12/25. **Reservations:** suggested. **Features:** casual dress; children's menu; early bird specials; carryout; cocktails & lounge. Here you will find seafood prepared in a wide range of styles: traditional, blackened, broiled, baked or mesquite-grilled. The salmon is marinated in Straub's own special sauce. You may also choose pasta dishes and a limited selection of beef and chicken. Smoke free premises. **Cards:** AE, CB, DI, DS, MC, VI.

SUSHI HATSU
Ethnic
Lunch: $6-$9   **Dinner:** $9-$19   **Phone:** 407/422-1551   ⑯
Location: Between Magnolia and Orange aves. 24 E Washington St 32801. **Hours:** 11 am-2:30 & 5-10 pm; Fri & Sat-11 pm. Closed: Sun. **Reservations:** accepted; Mon-Fri. **Features:** casual dress; carryout; beer & wine only. A few Korean dishes are found among sushi and other Japanese items on the menu. Try the bibimbap — small chunks of beef, shredded vegetables and a fried egg, drizzled with a spicy sauce and served over rice. Quick and helpful service makes dinner easy. **Cards:** AE, DI, MC, VI.

VIVALDI ITALIAN RESTAURANT
Italian
Lunch: $7-$13   **Dinner:** $12-$24   **Phone:** 407/423-2335   ⑪
Location: I-4, exit 38, just ne. 107 W Pine St 32801. **Hours:** 11:30 am-3 & 4-11 pm, Fri-1 am, Sat 4 pm-1 am. Closed: 12/25. **Reservations:** suggested. **Features:** casual dress; children's menu; carryout; cocktails & lounge. Relax and enjoy traditional Italian hospitality and cuisine in this convenient family dining environment. Try the Mare e Monte, a dish combining jumbo shrimp flamed in cognac and veal pizzaiola, for an interesting presentation. **Cards:** AE, MC, VI.

───── *The following restaurants have not been evaluated by AAA* ─────
but are listed for your information only.

ATHENINAN GARDEN CAFE
[fyi]
Phone: 407/898-2151
Not evaluated. **Location:** 2918 N Orange Ave 32804. **Features:** A diamond in the rough. Owners warmly welcome you with service and very tasty well prepared food, including stuffed grape leaves and appetizers of lamb; combo is great value.

LITTLE SAIGON
[fyi]
Phone: 407/423-8539
Not evaluated. **Location:** 1106 E Colonial Dr 32801. **Features:** Vietnamese cuisine. Large menu selection of traditional items and other interesting offerings. Inexpensive.

MICHAEL'S
[fyi]
Phone: 407/273-3631
Not evaluated. **Location:** 13 mi e on SR 50 from I-4; 4 mi e of Eastern Beltway. 12309 E Colonial Dr 32803. **Features:** A long time eating establishment with comfy ambience and items from wonderful veal a la Romana to pizza. At each visit the family makes you feel right at home. Ample size dishes and don't forget the cheesecake.

WHITE WOLF CAFE
[fyi]
Phone: 407/895-5590
Not evaluated. **Location:** 1829 N Orange Ave. **Features:** American cuisine, plus a few international specialties. Eclectic, casual surroundings; furnished with many antiques.

ORLANDO SOUTH   (See map p. 560; index p. 562)

———— WHERE TO STAY ————

ADAM'S MARK ORLANDO
Phone: (407)859-1500   195
(AAA) (SAVE)   All Year   1P: $84-$152   2P: $84-$152   XP: $25   F17
▽▽▽▽   **Location:** Just s of jct Sand Lake Rd and S Orange Blossom Tr, at south end of Florida Mall. 1500 Sand Lake Rd 32809.
Hotel   Fax: 407/855-1585. **Facility:** Right next door to the Florida Mall, this full service listing caters to the business traveller weekdays and families on the weekends. 510 units. Some suites ($350-$1000) and whirlpool units. *Bath:* combo or shower only. 11 stories, interior corridors. **Parking:** valet. **Terms:** package plans. **Amenities:** voice mail, irons, hair dryers. **Dining:** restaurant, 6 am-11 pm, $12-$22, cocktails. **Leisure Activities:** heated pool, sauna, whirlpool, exercise room. **Guest Services:** gift shop, valet laundry. **Business Services:** conference facilities. **Cards:** AE, CB, DI, DS, JC, MC, VI. **Special Amenities:** early check-in/late check-out and preferred room (subject to availability with advanced reservations).

SOME UNITS
[icons]

AMERISUITES
Phone: (407)816-7800   166
(AAA) (SAVE)   2/1-5/31   1P: $89-$129   2P: $89-$129   XP: $10   F17
▽▽▽▽   12/1-1/31 & 6/1-11/30   1P: $79-$129   2P: $79-$129   XP: $10   F17
Suite Motel   **Location:** SR 528 (Bee Line Expwy), exit 11, 0.5 mi n on SR 436, just w. 5435 Forbes Place 32812. Fax: 407/816-0050. **Facility:** 135 units. *Bath:* combo or shower only. 6 stories, interior corridors. **Terms:** 3 day cancellation notice. **Amenities:** extended cable TV, dual phone lines, voice mail, irons, hair dryers. **Leisure Activities:** heated pool, exercise room. **Guest Services:** [ECP] meal plan available, complimentary evening beverages, area transportation-within 5 mi, coin laundry. **Business Services:** meeting rooms. **Cards:** AE, DI, DS, MC, VI. *(See color ad below)*

SOME UNITS
[icons]

(See map p. 560)

AMERISUITES ORLANDO AIRPORT

AAA SAVE

WWW

Suite Motel

12/1-4/14	1P: $79-$109	2P: $79-$109	**Phone: (407)240-3939**
4/15-11/30	1P: $69-$99	2P: $69-$99	XP: $10

186
F18

Location: SR 528 (BeeLine Expwy), exit 11, 0.5 mi n on SR 436, just e on TG Lee Blvd, then just s. 7500 Augusta National Dr 32822. Fax: 407/240-3920. **Facility:** 128 efficiencies. Some suites. *Bath:* combo or shower only. 4 stories, interior corridors. **Terms:** small pets only. **Amenities:** video games, voice mail, irons, hair dryers. **Leisure Activities:** heated pool, exercise room. **Guest Services:** [ECP] meal plan available, coin laundry. **Business Services:** meeting rooms, administrative services. **Cards:** AE, CB, DI, DS, JC, MC, VI. **Special Amenities:** free continental breakfast and free newspaper. *(See color ad p 5)*

SOME UNITS

AMERISUITES (ORLANDO/CONVENTION CENTER)

AAA SAVE

WWW

Motel

12/1-4/30 & 6/16-8/15	1P: $89-$129	2P: $89-$129	**Phone: (407)370-4720**
5/1-6/15 & 8/16-11/30	1P: $79-$119	2P: $79-$119	XP: $10
			XP: $10

228
F18
F18

Location: 0.7 mi s of SR 482 (Sandlake Rd), just e of I-4, exit 29A. 8741 International Dr 32819. Fax: 407/370-4721. **Facility:** 152 units. *Bath:* combo or shower only. 7 stories, interior corridors. **Terms:** cancellation fee imposed, small pets only ($50 fee). **Amenities:** video games, voice mail, irons, hair dryers. **Leisure Activities:** heated pool, exercise room. **Guest Services:** [ECP] meal plan available, area transportation-within 5 mi, coin laundry. **Business Services:** meeting rooms, administrative services. **Cards:** AE, CB, DI, DS, JC, MC, VI. **Special Amenities:** free continental breakfast and free newspaper. *(See color ad p 5 & below)*

SOME UNITS

BAYMONT INN & SUITES-ORLANDO SOUTH

WWW

Motel

2/2-4/14	1P: $74-$79	2P: $74-$79	**Phone: (407)240-0500**
4/15-11/30	1P: $64-$69	2P: $64-$69	
12/1-2/1	1P: $59-$64	2P: $59-$64	

201

Location: US 17-92 and 441, just s of SR 528 (Beeline Expwy), off Florida Tpke, exit 254. 2051 Consulate Dr 32837. Fax: 407/240-5194. **Facility:** Comfortably modern rooms. 125 units. Some whirlpool units. 3 stories, interior corridors. **Terms:** small pets only. **Amenities:** video games, voice mail, irons, hair dryers. **Guest Services:** [CP] meal plan available, coin laundry. **Business Services:** meeting rooms. **Cards:** AE, CB, DI, DS, MC, VI. *(See color ad below)*

SOME UNITS

(See map p. 560)

BEST INN & SUITES INTERNATIONAL DRIVE　　　　　　　　　Phone: (407)351-4410　245
▼▼▼　All Year　　　　　　　1P: $69-$109　　　　2P: $69-$109
　　　　　Location: I-4, exit 30A, just s on Kirkland Rd, then just w. 5858 International Dr 32819. Fax: 407/351-2481.
Motel　Facility: 265 units. Some suites ($129-$159). Bath: combo or shower only. 4 stories, exterior corridors.
Terms: 3 day cancellation notice-fee imposed, weekly rates available. Amenities: voice mail, safes (fee).
Leisure Activities: game room. Guest Services: [ECP] meal plan available, gift shop, coin laundry. Fee: area transportation.
Cards: AE, DI, DS, MC, VI.
SOME UNITS
ASK ⓢ🇩 🍴 ⓨ ⊘ ⓗ 🏊 📹 🖨 /✕ 💻 📷 🛏 /

BEST WESTERN AIRPORT INN & SUITES　　　　　　　　　Phone: (407)581-2800　167
▼▼▼　2/1-3/31　　　　1P: $86-$106　　2P: $95-$115　　XP: $5　　F17
　　　4/1-11/30　　　1P: $70-$85　　2P: $80-$95　　XP: $5　　F17
Motel　12/1-1/31　　　1P: $50-$80　　2P: $60-$90　　XP: $5　　F17
Location: SR 528 (Bee Line Expwy), exit 8, just w on McCoy Rd. 8101 Aircenter Ct 32809. Fax: 407/581-2810.
Facility: 95 units. Some suites. Bath: combo or shower only. 5 stories, interior corridors. Amenities: extended cable TV, irons,
hair dryers. Leisure Activities: exercise room. Guest Services: [ECP] meal plan available, coin laundry. Fee: area transporta-
tion. Cards: AE, CB, DI, DS, MC, VI.
SOME UNITS
ASK ⓢ🇩 🔌 🍴 🏋 ⓗ 🏊 📹 🖨 💻 🇩🇦🇹🇦 /✕ 📷 🛏 /

BEST WESTERN-FLORIDA MALL　　　　　　　　　　　Phone: (407)855-6060　193
ⒶⒶⒶ SAVE　All Year　　　1P: $52-$122　　2P: $52-$122　　XP: $7　　F18
　　　Location: US 17-92 and 441, 0.5 mi s of jct SR 482 (Sand Lake Rd), 0.8 mi n of Tpke, exit 254. 8421 S Orange Blossom
▼▼▼◇◇◇　Tr 32809. Fax: 407/859-5132. Facility: Adjacent to the Florida Mall. Large rooms and baths. 204 units. 2 sto-
Motor Inn　ries, exterior corridors. Terms: check-in 4 pm, cancellation fee imposed, package plans. Amenities: ex-
tended cable TV, safes (fee). Some: hair dryers. Dining: restaurant, 7 am-11 & 5-10 pm, $7-$9, cocktails.
Leisure Activities: heated pool, playground, game room. Guest Services: gift shop, area transportation-
major attractions, coin laundry. Business Services: meeting rooms. Cards: AE, CB, DI, DS, JC, MC, VI. Special Amenities:
free local telephone calls and free newspaper. (See color ad p 587)
SOME UNITS
ⓢ🇩 🍴 🏋 🎵 🏊 🖨 /✕ 📷 🛏 /
FEE　FEE

BEST WESTERN MOVIELAND　　　　　　　　　　　Phone: (407)351-3900　209
▼▼▼◇◇◇　All Year　　1P: $65-$105　　2P: $65-$105
　　Location: I-4, exit 29, 1.5 mi n of SR 482 (Sand Lake Rd). 6233 International Dr 32819. Fax: 407/363-5119.
Motel　Facility: Near attractions, across from Wet-N-Wild. 262 units. Some whirlpool units. 4 stories, interior corri-
dors. Terms: cancellation fee imposed, $2 service charge. Amenities: safes (fee). Leisure Activi-
ties: heated pool. Guest Services: gift shop, area transportation, coin laundry. Business Services: meeting rooms. Cards: AE,
CB, DI, DS, JC, MC, VI.
SOME UNITS
ASK ⓢ🇩 🍴 🏋 🏊 VCR 🖨 /✕ 🛏 /
FEE

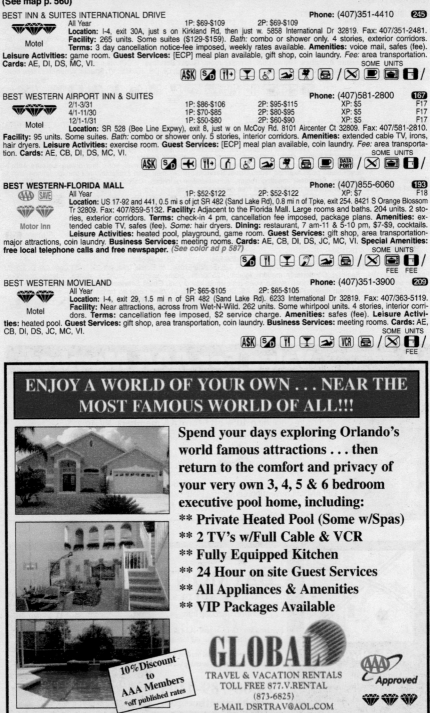

(See map p. 560)

BEST WESTERN PLAZA INTERNATIONAL
Phone: (407)345-8195 231

AAA SAVE
Motel
Location: I-4, exit 29, just e on SR 482 (Sand Lake Rd), then 0.8 mi s. 8738 International Dr 32819. **Fax:** 407/363-5979. **Facility:** 672 units. 105 two-bedroom units. Some suites ($105-$129) and whirlpool units ($105-$129). *Bath:* combo or shower only. 4 stories, exterior corridors. **Terms:** check-in 4 pm, package plans. **Amenities:** video games, safes (fee), irons, hair dryers. **Dining:** pool bar. **Leisure Activities:** heated pool, wading pool, whirlpool. **Guest Services:** gift shop, area transportation-major attractions, coin laundry. **Cards:** AE, CB, DI, DS, MC, VI. **Special Amenities:** early check-in/late check-out and free room upgrade (subject to availability with advanced reservations). *(See color ad p 588)*

1P: $85-$115   2P: $85-$115

BEST WESTERN UNIVERSAL INN
Phone: (407)226-9119 212

AAA SAVE
Motel
12/16-1/1	1P: $89-$109	2P: $89-$109	XP: $10	F15
12/1-12/15	1P: $69-$89	2P: $69-$89	XP: $10	F15
1/2-11/30	1P: $59-$89	2P: $59-$89	XP: $10	F15

Location: I-4, exit 30B, 0.5 mi n, then just e. 5618 Vineland Rd 32819. **Fax:** 407/370-2448. **Facility:** 70 units. *Bath:* combo or shower only. 3 stories, interior corridors. **Terms:** 7 day cancellation notice, $2 service charge. **Amenities:** extended cable TV, safes, hair dryers. **Guest Services:** [ECP] meal plan available, coin laundry. **Cards:** AE, CB, DI, DS, JC, MC, VI. **Special Amenities:** free continental breakfast.

CLARION HOTEL UNIVERSAL
Phone: (407)351-5009 213

AAA SAVE
Hotel
Location: I-4, exit 30A, just e of International Dr; adjacent to Wet'n Wild. 7299 Universal Blvd 32819. **Fax:** 407/363-7807. **Facility:** Designated smoking area. 303 units. 7-8 stories, interior corridors. **Terms:** check-in 4 pm, cancellation fee imposed. **Amenities:** extended cable TV, video games, voice mail, safes (fee), irons, hair dryers. **Dining:** restaurant, deli, 7 am-11 & 5-10 pm, $8-$15, cocktails. **Leisure Activities:** heated pool, whirlpools, lighted tennis court, basketball, game room. **Guest Services:** area transportation-major attraction, coin laundry. **Business Services:** meeting rooms, fax. **Cards:** AE, CB, DI, DS, MC, VI. **Special Amenities:** free local telephone calls. *(See color ad p 590)*

All Year   1P: $89-$109   2P: $89-$109   XP: $10   F18

CLARION PLAZA
Phone: (407)996-9700 237

Hotel
Property failed to provide current rates
Location: I-4, exit 28, just n; from Bee Line Expwy (SR 528), exit 1, then just n. 9700 International Dr 32819. **Fax:** 407/354-5774. **Facility:** A modern property catering to business travellers or convention groups, but families are also most welcome. Spacious and attractive public areas. 810 units. Some suites. *Bath:* combo, shower or tub only. 14 stories, interior corridors. **Parking:** valet. **Terms:** cancellation fee imposed. **Amenities:** video games, voice mail, safes, irons, hair dryers. **Dining:** Jack's Place, see separate listing. **Leisure Activities:** heated pool, whirlpool, game room. **Guest Services:** gift shop, coin laundry. *Fee:* area transportation. **Business Services:** conference facilities, administrative services, PC, fax. **Cards:** AE, DI, DS, JC, MC, VI.

CLUB ORLANDO
Phone: (407)855-9551 165

Condominium
Property failed to provide current rates
Location: I-4, exit 32, 1.6 mi s on SR 423, 0.7 mi e on Americana Blvd, then 0.3 mi n. 5305 San Antonio St 32839. **Fax:** 407/240-3837. **Facility:** Full housekeeping units. Located in residential area. 28 units with kitchen. 2 stories, exterior corridors. **Terms:** check-in 4 pm, 14 day cancellation notice-fee imposed. **Amenities:** safes, irons, hair dryers. **Leisure Activities:** heated pool, tennis court, playground. **Guest Services:** coin laundry. **Cards:** AE, DI, DS, MC, VI.

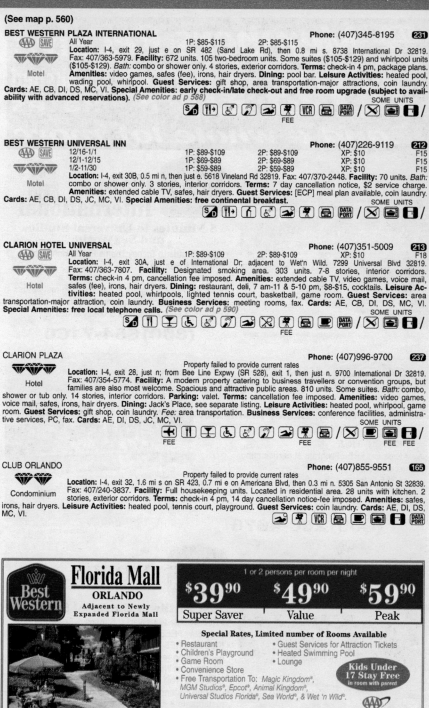

(See map p. 560)

COMFORT INN

[SAVE]

Motel

Phone: (407)313-4000   226   F18

All Year   1P: $79-$89   2P: $79-$89   XP: $5
Location: I-4, exit 29, just e on Sand Lake Rd, then just s. 8134 International Dr 32819. Fax: 407/313-4001. **Facility:** 112 units. *Bath:* combo or shower only. 6 stories, interior corridors. **Terms:** 3 day cancellation notice, $3 service charge. **Amenities:** extended cable TV, voice mail, safes, irons, hair dryers. **Guest Services:** [ECP] meal plan available, gift shop, coin laundry. **Cards:** AE, CB, DI, DS, JC, MC, VI.
SOME UNITS

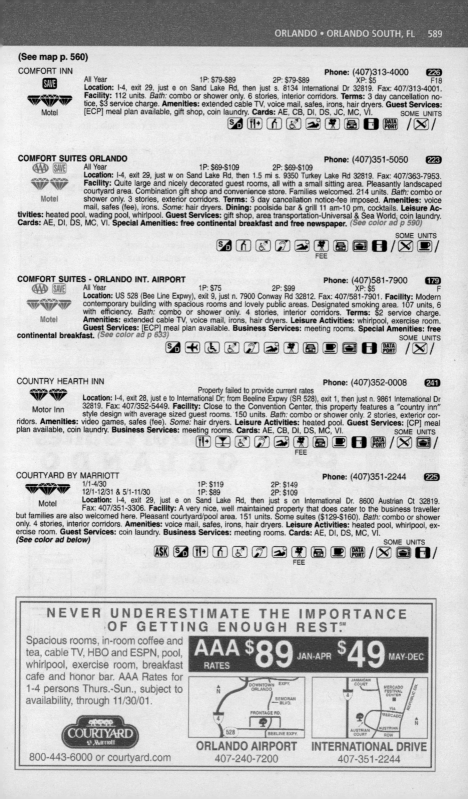

COMFORT SUITES ORLANDO

(AAA) [SAVE]

Motel

Phone: (407)351-5050   223

All Year   1P: $69-$109   2P: $69-$109
Location: I-4, exit 29, just w on Sand Lake Rd, then 1.5 mi s. 9350 Turkey Lake Rd 32819. Fax: 407/363-7953. **Facility:** Quite large and nicely decorated guest rooms, all with a small sitting area. Pleasantly landscaped courtyard area. Combination gift shop and convenience store. Families welcomed. 214 units. *Bath:* combo or shower only. 3 stories, exterior corridors. **Terms:** 3 day cancellation notice-fee imposed. **Amenities:** voice mail, safes (fee), irons. *Some:* hair dryers. **Dining:** poolside bar & grill 11 am-10 pm, cocktails. **Leisure Activities:** heated pool, wading pool, whirlpool. **Guest Services:** gift shop, area transportation-Universal & Sea World, coin laundry. **Cards:** AE, DI, DS, MC, VI. **Special Amenities:** free continental breakfast and free newspaper. *(See color ad p 590)*
SOME UNITS

FEE

COMFORT SUITES - ORLANDO INT. AIRPORT

(AAA) [SAVE]

Motel

Phone: (407)581-7900   179   F

All Year   1P: $75   2P: $99   XP: $5
Location: US 528 (Bee Line Expwy), exit 9, just n. 7900 Conway Rd 32812. Fax: 407/581-7901. **Facility:** Modern contemporary building with spacious rooms and lovely public areas. Designated smoking area. 107 units, 6 with efficiency. *Bath:* combo or shower only. 4 stories, interior corridors. **Terms:** $2 service charge. **Amenities:** extended cable TV, voice mail, irons, hair dryers. **Leisure Activities:** whirlpool, exercise room. **Guest Services:** [ECP] meal plan available. **Business Services:** meeting rooms. **Special Amenities:** free continental breakfast. *(See color ad p 633)*
SOME UNITS

COUNTRY HEARTH INN

Motor Inn

Phone: (407)352-0008   241

Property failed to provide current rates
Location: I-4, exit 28, just e to International Dr; from Beeline Expwy (SR 528), exit 1, then just n. 9861 International Dr 32819. Fax: 407/352-5449. **Facility:** Close to the Convention Center, this property features a "country inn" style design with average sized guest rooms. 150 units. *Bath:* combo or shower only. 2 stories, exterior corridors. **Amenities:** video games, safes (fee). *Some:* hair dryers. **Leisure Activities:** heated pool. **Guest Services:** [CP] meal plan available, coin laundry. **Business Services:** meeting rooms. **Cards:** AE, CB, DI, DS, MC, VI.
SOME UNITS

FEE

COURTYARD BY MARRIOTT

Motel

Phone: (407)351-2244   225

1/1-4/30   1P: $119   2P: $149
12/1-12/31 & 5/1-11/30   1P: $89   2P: $109
Location: I-4, exit 29, just e on Sand Lake Rd, then just s on International Dr. 8600 Austrian Ct 32819. Fax: 407/351-3306. **Facility:** A very nice, well maintained property that does cater to the business traveller but families are also welcomed here. Pleasant courtyard/pool area. 151 units. Some suites ($129-$160). *Bath:* combo or shower only. 4 stories, interior corridors. **Amenities:** voice mail, safes, irons, hair dryers. **Leisure Activities:** heated pool, whirlpool, exercise room. **Guest Services:** coin laundry. **Business Services:** meeting rooms. **Cards:** AE, DI, DS, MC, VI.
(See color ad below)
SOME UNITS

FEE

(See map p. 560)

COURTYARD BY MARRIOTT AIRPORT
Motel

Phone: (407)240-7200 `185`

All Year — 1P: $79-$129 — 2P: $89-$139
Location: SR 436, 0.3 mi n of SR 528 (Bee Line Expwy). 7155 N Frontage Rd 32812. Fax: 407/240-8962. **Facility:** 149 units. Some suites ($99-$159). *Bath:* combo or shower only. 3 stories, interior corridors. **Terms:** weekly rates available. **Amenities:** voice mail, irons, hair dryers. **Leisure Activities:** heated pool, whirlpool, exercise room. **Guest Services:** coin laundry. **Business Services:** meeting rooms. **Cards:** AE, DI, DS, MC, VI.
(See color ad p 589)

SOME UNITS

CROWNE PLAZA RESORT ORLANDO
Hotel

Phone: (407)239-1222 `240`

All Year — 1P: $199-$239 — 2P: $199-$239 — XP: $10 — F
Location: I-4, exit 28, just e on SR 528 (Beeline Expwy) to exit 1, then 2.7 mi s. 12000 International Dr 32821. Fax: 407/239-1190. **Facility:** 140 units, 76 with efficiency. Some suites ($199-$239). *Bath:* combo or shower only. 5 stories, exterior corridors. **Terms:** 3 day cancellation notice-fee imposed. **Amenities:** video games, voice mail, safes, irons, hair dryers. **Leisure Activities:** 2 heated pools, wading pool, whirlpools, 2 lighted tennis courts, exercise room, game room. **Guest Services:** [BP] meal plan available, gift shop, area transportation, coin laundry. *Fee:* massage. **Business Services:** meeting rooms. **Cards:** AE, CB, DI, DS, JC, MC, VI. *(See color ad below)*

SOME UNITS

DAYS INN-CONVENTION CENTER/SEA WORLD
Motor Inn

Phone: (407)352-8700 `246`

All Year — 1P: $98 — 2P: $108 — XP: $10 — F12
Location: I-4, exit 28, just e to International Dr; Bee Line Expwy (SR 528), exit 1, then just n. 9990 International Dr 32819. Fax: 407/363-3965. **Facility:** An older, mature type property offering decent rooms for those on a bit of a budget. Pleasant courtyard area with pool. 221 units. 4 stories, exterior corridors. **Terms:** check-in 4 pm. **Amenities:** voice mail, safes (fee), hair dryers. **Dining:** restaurant, 6 am-11 pm, $7-$11, wine/beer only. **Leisure Activities:** playground. **Guest Services:** coin laundry. **Cards:** AE, CB, DI, DS, JC, MC, VI. **Special Amenities:** early check-in/late check-out and preferred room (subject to availability with advanced reservations).

SOME UNITS

DAYS INN ORLANDO LAKESIDE
Motor Inn

Phone: (407)351-1900 `248`

All Year — 1P: $34-$89 — 2P: $99 — XP: $6 — F17
Location: I-4, exit 29, just w. 7335 Sand Lake Rd 32819. Fax: 407/352-2690. **Facility:** Modest accommodations, some rooms with lake view. 695 units. Some suites ($55-$110). *Bath:* combo or shower only. 2-3 stories, exterior corridors. **Terms:** check-in 4 pm, 3 day cancellation notice-fee imposed, weekly & monthly rates available. **Amenities:** video games, voice mail, safes (fee). **Dining:** deli, 7 am-11:30 & 4:30-9:30 pm; lakeside tiki bar, $2-$5. **Leisure Activities:** 3 pools (1 heated), beach, picnic area with grills, playground, volleyball, game room. **Guest Services:** gift shop, coin laundry. **Cards:** AE, DI, DS, JC, MC, VI. **Special Amenities:** free room upgrade (subject to availability with advanced reservations).

SOME UNITS

DOUBLETREE CASTLE HOTEL
Hotel

Phone: (407)345-1511 `221`

12/23-1/2 — 1P: $169-$229 — 2P: $169-$229
12/1-12/22 & 1/3-11/30 — 1P: $149-$169 — 2P: $149-$169
Location: Just e of International Dr; 0.5 mi s of SR 482 (Sand Lake Rd); 1 mi se of I-4, exit 29. 8629 International Dr 32819. Fax: 407/248-8181. **Facility:** Theme hotel replicating a storybook castle. Unique public areas decorated with a fanciful touch; atmosphere continued in guest rooms with whimsical decor in rich shades of purple and gold. 216 units. *Bath:* combo or shower only. 9 stories, interior corridors. **Terms:** check-in 4 pm, 3 day cancellation notice-fee imposed, package plans, $2 service charge. **Amenities:** video games, voice mail, safes, irons, hair dryers. **Dining:** restaurant, coffee shop, 6:30 am-10:30 & 11-11 pm; Fri & Sat-2 am, $7-$24, also, Cafe Tu Tu Tango, Vito's Chop House, see separate listing. **Leisure Activities:** heated pool, whirlpool, exercise room, game room. **Guest Services:** gift shop, area transportation-major attractions, coin laundry. **Business Services:** meeting rooms. **Cards:** AE, CB, DI, DS, MC, VI. **Special Amenities:** free local telephone calls and free newspaper. *(See color ad starting on p 592)*

SOME UNITS

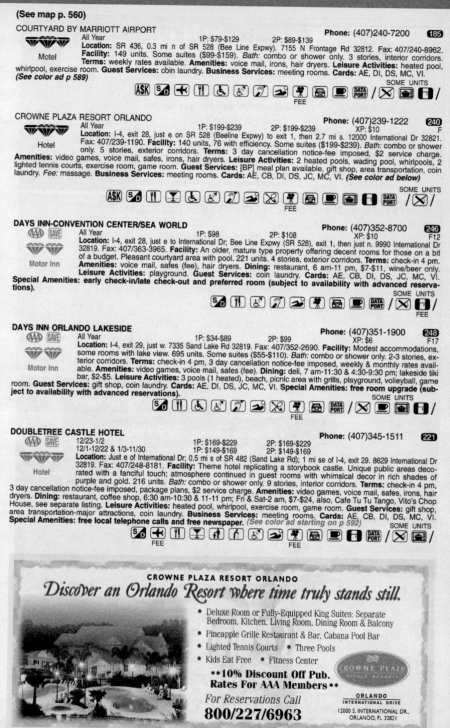

(See map p. 560)

EMBASSY SUITES INTERNATIONAL DRIVE/JAMAICAN CT
Phone: (407)345-8250 [227]

Ⓐ SAVE | All Year | 1P: $129-$229 | 2P: $139-$229 | XP: $10 | F18
♦♦♦♦ | **Location:** I-4, exit 29, just e on Sand Lake Rd, then just s on International Dr. 8250 Jamaican Ct 32819.
Suite Hotel | Fax: 407/352-1463. **Facility:** An all-suite style property with separate bedroom area. Very nice atrium area.
Located just off busy International Dr. 246 units. 8 stories, interior corridors. **Terms:** 3 day cancellation notice-fee imposed. **Amenities:** voice mail, safes, irons, hair dryers. **Leisure Activities:** sauna, whirlpool, steamroom, exercise room. **Guest Services:** [BP] meal plan available, gift shop, complimentary evening beverages, area transportation-major attractions, coin laundry. **Business Services:** meeting rooms. **Cards:** AE, CB, DI, DS, JC, MC, VI. **Special Amenities: free continental breakfast and free newspaper.** SOME UNITS

EMBASSY SUITES ORLANDO AIRPORT
Phone: (407)888-9339 [176]

♦♦♦ | 1/1-3/31 | 1P: $149-$179 | 2P: $149-$179 | XP: $15 | F18
Hotel | 12/1-12/31 & 4/1-11/30 | 1P: $119-$139 | 2P: $119-$139 | XP: $15 | F18
Location: SR 528 (BeeLine Expwy), exit 11, 0.5 mi n on SR 436, just e. 5835 TG Lee Blvd 32822. Fax: 407/856-5956.
Facility: Designated smoking area. 174 efficiencies. Some suites ($119-$179). *Bath:* combo or shower only.
7 stories, interior corridors. **Terms:** check-in 4 pm, cancellation fee imposed. **Amenities:** video games, voice mail, irons, hair dryers. **Leisure Activities:** heated pool, whirlpool, exercise room. **Guest Services:** gift shop, coin laundry. **Business Services:** meeting rooms, fax. **Cards:** AE, CB, DI, DS, JC, MC, VI. *(See color ad starting on p 592)* SOME UNITS

EMBASSY SUITES ORLANDO INTERNATIONAL DR /CONVENTION CENTER
Phone: (407)352-1400 [233]

♦♦♦ | All Year | 1P: $169-$299 | 2P: $169-$299 | XP: $10 | F18
Suite Hotel | **Location:** I-4, exit 29, just e on Sand Lake Rd, then just s. 8978 International Dr 32819. Fax: 407/363-1120.
Facility: All guest rooms are quite large with a separate bedroom and sitting room. Attractively decorated atrium area with lush plants and waterfall. Perfect for families or business travellers. 244 units. 1 two-bedroom unit. Some suites ($299-$499). *Bath:* combo or shower only. 8 stories, interior corridors. **Parking:** valet. **Terms:** check-in 4 pm, 3 day cancellation notice. **Amenities:** voice mail, irons, hair dryers. *Some:* CD players. **Leisure Activities:** 2 heated pools, wading pool, sauna, whirlpools, steamroom, exercise room, game room. **Guest Services:** [BP] meal plan available, gift shop, complimentary evening beverages, area transportation, coin laundry. **Business Services:** meeting rooms. **Cards:** AE, CB, DI, DS, MC, VI. *(See color ad starting on p 592)* SOME UNITS

FAIRFIELD INN BY MARRIOTT
Phone: (407)888-2666 [175]

♦♦♦ | 12/1-4/30 | 1P: $79-$119 | 2P: $79-$119
Motel | 5/1-11/30 | 1P: $59-$99 | 2P: $59-$99
Location: SR 528 (BeeLine Expwy), exit 11, 0.5 mi n on SR 436, just e. 7100 Augusta National Dr 32822.
Fax: 407/888-8464. **Facility:** 139 units. Some whirlpool units ($99-$129). *Bath:* combo or shower only. Interior corridors. **Amenities:** irons. **Leisure Activities:** heated pool, whirlpool. **Guest Services:** [ECP] meal plan available, coin laundry. **Business Services:** meeting rooms. **Cards:** AE, CB, DI, DS, MC, VI. SOME UNITS

FAIRFIELD INN BY MARRIOTT-INTERNATIONAL DRIVE
Phone: (407)363-1944 [235]

♦♦♦ | All Year | 1P: $59-$89 | 2P: $59-$89
Motel | **Location:** I-4, exit 29, then just e on Sand Lake Rd, then just s on International Dr. 8342 Jamaican Ct 32819.
Fax: 407/363-1944. **Facility:** A well maintained property featuring very comfortable, standard motel style guest rooms. Third floor guest rooms are larger and feature interior hallway. 135 units. 3 stories, interior/exterior corridors. **Terms:** 3 day cancellation notice-fee imposed. **Amenities:** safes. **Leisure Activities:** heated pool. **Guest Services:** [CP] meal plan available, valet laundry. **Cards:** AE, CB, DI, DS, MC, VI. *(See color ad below)* SOME UNITS

FAIRFIELD INN BY MARRIOTT-ORLANDO SOUTH
Phone: 407/240-8400 [197]

♦♦ | All Year | 1P: $61-$65 | 2P: $65-$69
Motel | **Location:** Just e of Landstreet Rd and S Orange Blossom Tr; from Florida Tpke exit 254, then just n. 1850 Landstreet Rd 32809. Fax: 407/240-8400. **Facility:** 132 units. 3 stories, interior/exterior corridors. **Leisure Activities:** heated pool. **Guest Services:** [CP] meal plan available, valet laundry. **Cards:** AE, DI, DS, MC, VI.
(See color ad below) SOME UNITS

Prestige Vacation Pool Homes!
Like having a hotel to yourself. Only Better!

* Actual Vacation Home Pictured Above

All Homes Company Owned and are located in just one new subdivision completely surrounded by a Lush Conservation Site only *8½ miles from Walt Disney World® Resort*

All our 2, 3, 4, 5 & 6 Bedroom Homes are completely furnished and include...

- 2 Color Cable TV's/1 Large Screen and Video Player
- All Kitchens Equipped with all Appliances and Cookware
- Washer and Dryer
- Towels and Linens
- Private, Screened in Pool (Heated Pool Available)
- 24 Hour Onsite Assistance
- And much more!

Prestige Vacation Homes, Inc.
(Formerly known as Affordable Florida Vacation Rentals)
Toll Free US & Canada

1-800-999-0188
1-863-424-7400 • Fax: 1-863-424-7500
www.prestigevacationhomes.com

(See map p. 560)

HAMPTON INN AIRPORT
Phone: (407)888-2995   **174**

SAVE

Motel

| | 12/1-4/30 | 1P: $84-$114 | 2P: $84-$114 |
| | 5/1-11/30 | 1P: $64-$94 | 2P: $64-$94 |

Location: SR 528 (BeeLine Expwy), exit 11, 0.5 mi n on SR 436, just e. 5767 T G Lee Blvd 32822. Fax: 407/888-2418. **Facility:** Modern, well-lighted rooms with tasteful decor. Designated smoking area. 124 units. *Bath:* combo or shower only. 7 stories, interior corridors. **Amenities:** voice mail, irons, hair dryers. **Leisure Activities:** exercise room. **Guest Services:** [CP] meal plan available, coin laundry. **Business Services:** meeting rooms, fax. **Cards:** AE, CB, DI, DS, MC, VI. *(See color ad p 582)*   SOME UNITS

HAMPTON INN AT UNIVERSAL STUDIOS
Phone: (407)351-6716   **171**

AAA SAVE

Motel

	5/23-8/19	1P: $74-$79	2P: $79-$82
	8/20-11/30	1P: $69-$74	2P: $74-$82
	12/1-5/22	1P: $69-$74	2P: $74-$79

Location: I-4, exit 30B, 1 mi n on SR 435 (Kirkman Rd), just e. 5621 Windhover Dr 32819. Fax: 407/363-1711. **Facility:** 120 units. *Bath:* combo or shower only. 5 stories, interior corridors. **Terms:** cancellation fee imposed. **Amenities:** safes, irons. **Leisure Activities:** heated pool, game room. **Guest Services:** [ECP] meal plan available, valet laundry. **Business Services:** meeting rooms. **Cards:** AE, CB, DI, DS, MC, VI. **Special Amenities:** free continental breakfast and free newspaper. *(See color ad p 634)*   SOME UNITS

HAMPTON INN-CONVENTION CENTER
Phone: (407)354-4447   **236**

SAVE

Motel

| | 12/1-2/15 | 1P: $69-$139 | 2P: $69-$139 |
| | 2/16-11/30 | 1P: $69-$129 | 2P: $69-$129 |

Location: I-4, exit 29, 0.5 mi e on SR 482 (Sand Lake Rd), then 0.9 mi s. 8900 Universal Blvd 32819. Fax: 407/354-3031. **Facility:** Designated smoking area. 170 units. *Bath:* combo or shower only. 7 stories, interior corridors. **Terms:** 3 day cancellation notice. **Amenities:** extended cable TV, video games, voice mail, irons. **Leisure Activities:** heated pool, exercise room, game room. **Guest Services:** [ECP] meal plan available, valet laundry. **Business Services:** meeting rooms, fax. **Cards:** AE, CB, DI, DS, MC, VI.   SOME UNITS

HAMPTON INN-FLORIDA MALL
Phone: (407)859-4100   **215**

AAA SAVE

Motel

| | All Year | 1P: $79-$89 | 2P: $89-$109 |

Location: On US 17-92 and 441, 0.5 mi n of Florida Tpke, exit 254. 8601 S Orange Blossom Tr 32809. Fax: 407/240-4736. **Facility:** 128 units. Some suites ($109). *Bath:* combo or shower only. 2 stories, interior corridors. **Terms:** 10 day cancellation notice-fee imposed. **Amenities:** extended cable TV, voice mail, irons. *Some:* hair dryers. **Leisure Activities:** exercise room. **Guest Services:** [ECP] meal plan available, coin laundry. **Business Services:** meeting rooms. **Cards:** AE, CB, DI, DS, MC, VI. **Special Amenities:** free continental breakfast and free newspaper. *(See color ad p 633)*   SOME UNITS

HAMPTON INN SAND LAKE
Phone: (407)363-7886   **218**

SAVE

Motel

	12/1-1/2	1P: $69-$139	2P: $69-$139
	1/3-4/22	1P: $72-$99	2P: $72-$99
	6/14-11/30	1P: $69-$94	2P: $69-$94
	4/23-6/13	1P: $69-$89	2P: $69-$89

Location: I-4, exit 29, 0.3 mi e on SR 482, at Universal Blvd 32819. Fax: 407/345-0670. **Facility:** Comfortable guest rooms, pleasant courtyard and pool area. 336 units. *Bath:* combo or shower only. 4 stories, exterior corridors. **Amenities:** voice mail, irons, hair dryers. **Leisure Activities:** wading pool, exercise room, game room. **Guest Services:** [ECP] meal plan available, gift shop, area transportation, coin laundry. **Business Services:** meeting rooms. **Cards:** AE, CB, DI, DS, JC, MC, VI. *(See color ad p 582)*   SOME UNITS

HAMPTON INN-SOUTH OF UNIVERSAL STUDIOS
Phone: (407)345-1112   **214**

SAVE

Motel

	12/1-1/2	1P: $69-$139	2P: $69-$139
	1/3-4/22	1P: $72-$99	2P: $72-$99
	6/14-11/30	1P: $69-$94	2P: $69-$94
	4/23-6/13	1P: $69-$89	2P: $69-$89

Location: I-4, exit 30, 0.8 mi s on SR 435. 7110 S Kirkman Rd 32819. Fax: 407/352-6591. **Facility:** A very strong property featuring nicely maintained guest rooms and public areas. A real gem. 170 units. Some suites and whirlpool units. *Bath:* combo or shower only. 8 stories, interior corridors. **Amenities:** extended cable TV, voice mail, irons, hair dryers. **Leisure Activities:** wading pool, exercise room, game room. **Guest Services:** [ECP] meal plan available, gift shop, area transportation, coin laundry. **Business Services:** meeting rooms. **Cards:** AE, CB, DI, DS, MC, VI. *(See color ad p 582)*   SOME UNITS

HAWTHORN SUITES ORLANDO
Phone: (407)351-6600   **247**

Suite Motel

| | All Year | 1P: $95-$189 | 2P: $95-$189 |

Location: I-4, exit 28, just e on SR 52B (Beeline Expwy) to exit 1, then just s. 6435 Westwood Blvd 32821. Fax: 407/351-1977. **Facility:** Very large, comfortable suites with separate bedrooms; many feature cooking facilities. Close to Sea World. 150 units, 120 with efficiency. Some suites. 5 stories, interior corridors. **Terms:** check-in 4 pm, cancellation fee imposed, package plans. **Amenities:** extended cable TV, video games, voice mail, irons, hair dryers. **Leisure Activities:** heated pool, wading pool, whirlpool, playground, exercise room. **Guest Services:** [BP] meal plan available, area transportation, coin laundry. **Business Services:** meeting rooms. **Cards:** AE, CB, DI, DS, JC, MC, VI. *(See color ad p 597)*   SOME UNITS

(See map p. 560)

HAWTHORN SUITES ORLANDO AIRPORT   Phone: (407)438-2121   `189`

1/26-4/14	1P: $109-$129	2P: $109-$129
12/25-1/25	1P: $99-$119	2P: $99-$119
12/1-12/24 & 4/15-11/30	1P: $89-$99	2P: $89-$99

Suite Motel   **Location:** SR 528 (Bee Line Expwy), exit 11, 0.5 mi on SR 436, just e, then just s. 7450 Augusta National Dr 32822. **Fax:** 407/438-2275. **Facility:** 135 units. 6 two-bedroom units, 129 efficiencies and 6 units with kitchen. *Bath:* combo or shower only. 3 stories, interior corridors. **Amenities:** extended cable TV, CD players, dual phone lines, voice mail, fax, safes, irons, hair dryers. **Leisure Activities:** heated pool, whirlpool, lighted tennis court, exercise room, basketball, volleyball, game room. **Guest Services:** [BP] meal plan available, complimentary evening beverages: Mon-Fri, coin laundry. **Business Services:** meeting rooms, administrative services. **Cards:** AE, CB, DI, DS, JC, MC, VI. **Special Amenities:** free continental breakfast and free local telephone calls. *(See color ad starting on p 608)*   SOME UNITS

HAWTHORN SUITES UNIVERSAL   Phone: (407)581-2151   `206`

12/25-1/25	1P: $99-$139	2P: $99-$139
1/26-8/18	1P: $99-$129	2P: $99-$129
12/1-12/24 & 8/19-11/30	1P: $89-$109	2P: $89-$109

Suite Motel   **Location:** Just e of jct Sand Lake Rd and International Dr. 7601 Canada Dr 32819. **Fax:** 407/581-2152. **Facility:** 143 units with kitchen. 10 two-bedroom units. 6 stories, interior corridors. **Amenities:** extended cable TV, safes. **Leisure Activities:** heated pool, whirlpool, sports court. **Guest Services:** complimentary evening beverages: Mon-Thurs, area transportation-major attractions, coin laundry. **Business Services:** meeting rooms. **Cards:** AE, MC, VI. **Special Amenities:** free continental breakfast and free newspaper. *(See color ad starting on p 608)*   SOME UNITS

HILTON GARDEN INN ORLANDO INTERNATIONAL AIRPORT   Phone: (407)240-3725   `180`

12/1-4/30	1P: $89-$129	2P: $89-$129
5/1-11/30	1P: $79-$119	2P: $79-$119

Motor Inn   **Location:** SR 528, exit 11, 0.5 mi on SR 436, just e, then just s (Bee Line Expwy). 7300 Augusta National Dr 32822. **Fax:** 407/240-3825. **Facility:** 132 units. Some suites and whirlpool units. *Bath:* combo or shower only. 4 stories, interior corridors. **Amenities:** video games, voice mail, irons, hair dryers. **Leisure Activities:** heated pool, exercise room. **Guest Services:** coin laundry. **Business Services:** meeting rooms, administrative services. **Cards:** AE, CB, DI, DS, JC, MC, VI. *(See color ad p 582 & ad p 44)*   SOME UNITS

FEE

(See map p. 560)

HILTON GRAND VACATIONS CLUB　　　　　　　　　　　　　　**Phone:** (407)239-0100　☐252

[SAVE]　12/1-1/4 & 2/16-4/20　　　1P: $119-$349
　　　　4/21-11/30　　　　　　　　1P: $109-$329
▼▼◇▽▽▽　1/5-2/15　　　　　　　　　1P: $99-$299

Apartment　**Location:** I-4, exit 28, just s on International Dr, 1 mi w on Sea Harbour Dr; Bee Line Expwy (SR 528), exit 1, s to Sea Harbour Dr. 6924 Grand Vacations Way 32821. Fax: 407/239-0200. **Facility:** A mix of studio, 1-, 2- or 3-bedroom units; many with full cooking facilities. All rooms are colorfully decorated. The grounds are truly beautiful, especially around the pool areas. 414 units. 162 two-bedroom units, 48 three-bedroom units and 256 units with kitchen. Some whirlpool units. *Bath:* combo or shower only. 1-6 stories, exterior corridors. **Terms:** check-in 4 pm, 14 day cancellation notice-fee imposed. **Amenities:** extended cable TV, voice mail, irons, hair dryers. *Some:* CD players. **Leisure Activities:** 3 pools (2 heated), wading pools, whirlpools, putting green, children's program, recreation program, playground, exercise room, shuffleboard. **Guest Services:** gift shop, area transportation, complimentary laundry. *Fee:* massage. **Cards:** AE, DI, DS, MC, VI.
(See color ad p 597)　　　　　　　　　　　　　　　　　　　　　　　SOME UNITS

[icons] /⊠/

HOLIDAY HOMES OF ORLANDO　　　　　　　　　　　　　　**Phone:** (407)240-5527　☐232

(AAA) [SAVE]　12/1-1/3　　　　　1P: $169-$269
　　　　　　　　1/4-8/31　　　　　1P: $149-$269
▼▼◇▽▽▽　9/1-11/30　　　　　1P: $129-$229

Condominium　**Location:** 0.5 mi s of jct Florida Tpke, exit 254. 9521 S Orange Blossom Tr-118A 32837. Fax: 407/240-5530. **Facility:** Has off-site registration. State-of-the-art homes with full kitchen, professionally decorated. Shopping and attractions nearby. 130 units with kitchen. 9 two-bedroom units and 121 three-bedroom units. Some whirlpool units. 2 stories, exterior corridors. **Terms:** check-in 4 pm, 30 day cancellation notice-fee imposed, monthly rates available, package plans. **Amenities:** extended cable TV, irons. **Leisure Activities:** each home has own screened pool, condos have community pool, golf nearby. *Fee:* golf-18 holes. **Guest Services:** complimentary laundry. **Cards:** MC, VI. **Special Amenities:** free local telephone calls. *(See color ad p 584 & below)*　　　　　　　　　　　　SOME UNITS

[icons] /⊠/ [VCR]/

HOLIDAY INN EXPRESS　　　　　　　　　　　　　　　　**Phone:** (407)351-4430　☐210

(AAA) [SAVE]　12/20-8/17　　　　1P: $79-$129　　2P: $79-$129　　XP: $10　　F18
　　　　　　　　12/1-12/19 & 8/18-11/30　1P: $69-$109　2P: $69-$109　XP: $10　F18
▼▼◇▽▽▽　**Location:** I-4, exit 29, just e on Sand Lake Rd, then 0.7 mi n. 6323 International Dr 32819. Fax: 407/345-0742.

Motel　**Facility:** Well-kept, fresh and modern guest rooms. Ground floor rooms feature balcony doors that lead to landscaped grounds and pool area. 218 units. *Bath:* combo or shower only. 2 stories, interior corridors. **Terms:** check-in 4 pm, 3 day cancellation notice-fee imposed, small pets only ($75 deposit). **Amenities:** voice mail, safes (fee), irons, hair dryers. **Leisure Activities:** heated pool, game room. **Guest Services:** [ECP] meal plan available, area transportation-Disney, coin laundry. **Cards:** AE, CB, DI, DS, JC, MC, VI. **Special Amenities:** free local telephone calls. *(See color ad p 644)*　　　　　　　　　　　　　SOME UNITS

[icons] /⊠/

HOLIDAY INN EXPRESS ORLANDO AIRPORT WEST　　　　**Phone:** (407)851-1113　☐191

(AAA) [SAVE]　12/26-1/15　　　　1P: $69-$109　　2P: $69-$109
　　　　　　　　1/16-4/21　　　　　1P: $89-$99　　　2P: $89-$99
▼▼◇▽▽▽　12/1-12/25 & 4/22-11/30　1P: $69-$79　　2P: $69-$79

Suite Motel　**Location:** SR 482, just w of jct SR 528 (Bee Line Expwy). 1853 McCoy Rd 32809. Fax: 407/438-5883. **Facility:** Attractive contemporary decors, some units with efficiency. 168 units, 54 with efficiency. Some suites ($79-$119). *Bath:* combo or shower only. 3 stories, interior/exterior corridors. **Amenities:** extended cable TV, voice mail, irons, hair dryers. *Some:* CD players, safes. **Leisure Activities:** whirlpool. **Guest Services:** [ECP] meal plan available, complimentary evening beverages, coin laundry. **Business Services:** meeting rooms, administrative services. **Cards:** AE, CB, DI, DS, JC, MC, VI. **Special Amenities:** free newspaper and free room upgrade (subject to availability with advanced reservations). *(See color ad starting on p 608)*　　　　　　　　　　　SOME UNITS

[icons] /⊠/ [VCR] [icons]/

(See map p. 560)

HOLIDAY INN HOTEL & SUITES AT MAIN ENTRANCE TO UNIVERSAL STUDIOS   **Phone:** (407)351-3333   [192]
▼▼▼▼   All Year   1P: $79-$149
Motor Inn   **Location:** I-4, exit 30B, 0.5 mi n on SR 435 (Kirkman Rd). 5905 S Kirkman Rd 32819. Fax: 407/351-3577. **Facility:** A nicely renovated property featuring over 100 one-bedroom suites with sitting room, two-bedroom suites with sitting room and large, standard-style guest rooms. Located close to Universal Studios. 390 units. 44 two-bedroom units. Some suites ($99-$169). *Bath:* combo or shower only. 10 stories, interior corridors. **Terms:** check-in 4 pm, package plans, pets ($50 extra charge). **Amenities:** extended cable TV, video games, voice mail, irons. *Some:* safes (fee). **Leisure Activities:** heated pool, wading pool, exercise room. **Guest Services:** gift shop, area transportation, coin laundry. **Business Services:** conference facilities, administrative services. **Cards:** AE, CB, DI, DS, JC, MC, VI. *(See color ad p 600)*

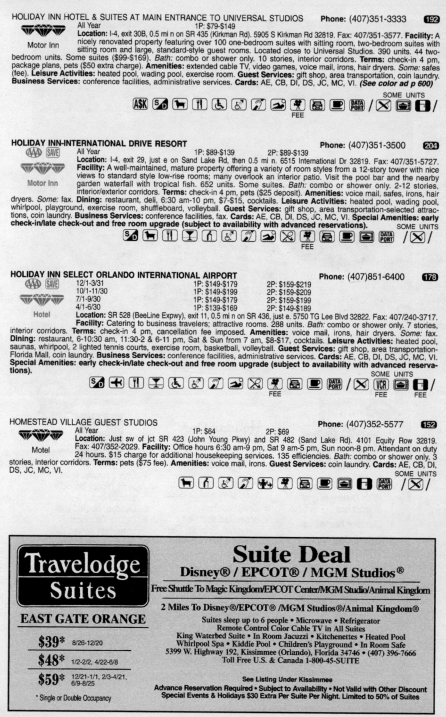

SOME UNITS

HOLIDAY INN-INTERNATIONAL DRIVE RESORT   **Phone:** (407)351-3500   [204]
ⒶⒶⒶ ⟨SAVE⟩   All Year   1P: $89-$139   2P: $89-$139
▼▼▼   **Location:** I-4, exit 29, just e on Sand Lake Rd, then 0.5 mi n. 6515 International Dr 32819. Fax: 407/351-5727.
Motor Inn   **Facility:** A well-maintained, mature property offering a variety of room styles from a 12-story tower with nice views to standard style low-rise rooms; many overlook an interior patio. Visit the pool bar and the nearby garden waterfall with tropical fish. 652 units. Some suites. *Bath:* combo or shower only. 2-12 stories, interior/exterior corridors. **Amenities:** voice mail, safes, irons, hair dryers. *Some:* fax. **Dining:** restaurant, deli, 6:30 am-10 pm, $7-$15, cocktails. **Leisure Activities:** heated pool, wading pool, whirlpool, playground, exercise room, shuffleboard, volleyball. **Guest Services:** gift shop, area transportation-selected attractions, coin laundry. **Business Services:** conference facilities, fax. **Cards:** AE, CB, DI, DS, JC, MC, VI. **Special Amenities:** early check-in/late check-out and free room upgrade (subject to availability with advanced reservations).

SOME UNITS

FEE

HOLIDAY INN SELECT ORLANDO INTERNATIONAL AIRPORT   **Phone:** (407)851-6400   [178]
ⒶⒶⒶ ⟨SAVE⟩   12/1-3/31   1P: $149-$179   2P: $159-$219
▼▼▼   10/1-11/30   1P: $149-$199   2P: $159-$209
Hotel   7/1-9/30   1P: $149-$179   2P: $159-$199
   4/1-6/30   1P: $139-$169   2P: $149-$189
Location: SR 528 (BeeLine Expwy), exit 11, 0.5 mi n on SR 436, just e. 5750 TG Lee Blvd 32822. Fax: 407/240-3717. **Facility:** Catering to business travelers; attractive rooms. 288 units. *Bath:* combo or shower only. 7 stories, interior corridors. **Terms:** check-in 4 pm, cancellation fee imposed. **Amenities:** voice mail, irons, hair dryers. *Some:* fax. **Dining:** restaurant, 6-10:30 am, 11:30-2 & 6-11 pm, Sat & Sun from 7 am, $8-$17, cocktails. **Leisure Activities:** heated pool, saunas, whirlpool, 2 lighted tennis courts, exercise room, basketball, volleyball. **Guest Services:** gift shop, area transportation-Florida Mall, coin laundry. **Business Services:** conference facilities, administrative services. **Cards:** AE, CB, DI, DS, JC, MC, VI. **Special Amenities:** early check-in/late check-out and free room upgrade (subject to availability with advanced reservations).

SOME UNITS

FEE   VCR FEE   FEE

HOMESTEAD VILLAGE GUEST STUDIOS   **Phone:** (407)352-5577   [152]
▼▼▼▼   All Year   1P: $64   2P: $69
Motel   **Location:** Just sw of jct SR 423 (John Young Pkwy) and SR 482 (Sand Lake Rd). 4101 Equity Row 32819. Fax: 407/352-2029. **Facility:** Office hours 6:30 am-9 pm, Sat 9 am-5 pm, Sun noon-8 pm. Attendant on duty 24 hours. $15 charge for additional housekeeping services. 135 efficiencies. *Bath:* combo or shower only. 3 stories, interior corridors. **Terms:** pets ($75 fee). **Amenities:** voice mail, irons. **Guest Services:** coin laundry. **Cards:** AE, CB, DI, DS, JC, MC, VI.

SOME UNITS

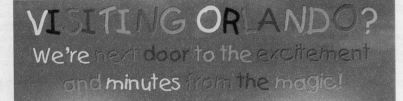

(See map p. 560)

HOMEWOOD SUITES BY HILTON-ORLANDO

Phone: (407)248-2232 157

Suite Motel

1/3-4/22	1P: $169-$179	2P: $169-$179	
4/23-8/31	1P: $139-$149	2P: $139-$149	
12/1-1/2 & 9/1-11/30	1P: $129-$139	2P: $129-$139	

Location: I-4, exit 29, just e on SR 482 (Sand Lake Rd), then 0.5 mi s. 8745 International Dr 32819 (8403 South Park Circle, ORLANDO). Fax: 407/248-6552. **Facility:** 252 units. 20 two-bedroom units. *Bath:* combo or shower only. 6 stories, interior corridors. **Terms:** check-in 4 pm, cancellation fee imposed, $1 service charge. **Amenities:** video games, voice mail, safes (fee), irons. **Leisure Activities:** heated pool, whirlpool, exercise room. **Guest Services:** [ECP] meal plan available, complimentary evening beverages: Mon-Thurs, area transportation, coin laundry. **Business Services:** meeting rooms, administrative services. **Cards:** AE, CB, DI, DS, MC, VI.

SOME UNITS

HOWARD JOHNSON HOTEL-FLORIDA MALL

Phone: (407)851-2330 194

Motor Inn

12/1-1/1	1P: $29-$45	2P: $29-$45	
1/2-6/26	1P: $29-$39	2P: $29-$39	
6/27-11/30	1P: $39	2P: $39	

Location: On US 17-92 and 441, 0.5 mi n of Florida Tpke, exit 254. 8700 S Orange Blossom Trail 32809. Fax: 407/857-6747. **Facility:** 194 units. 2 stories, exterior corridors. **Terms:** 48 day cancellation notice. **Amenities:** safes (fee). *Some:* irons, hair dryers. **Guest Services:** gift shop, coin laundry. **Business Services:** meeting rooms. **Cards:** AE, CB, DI, DS, JC, MC, VI.

SOME UNITS

HOWARD JOHNSON INN-INTERNATIONAL DRIVE

Phone: (407)351-2900 208

Motel

All Year   2P: $49-$99

Location: I-4, exit 29, just e on Sand Lake Rd, then 0.4 mi n. 6603 International Dr 32819. Fax: 407/352-2738. **Facility:** 173 units. 3 stories, exterior corridors. **Terms:** cancellation fee imposed. **Amenities:** extended cable TV, safes, hair dryers. **Leisure Activities:** wading pool, exercise room. **Guest Services:** area transportation-selected attractions, coin laundry. **Cards:** AE, DI, DS, MC, VI. **Special Amenities:** free newspaper.

SOME UNITS

HOWARD JOHNSON PLAZA HOTEL & SUITES/ INTERNATIONAL DR SOUTH

Phone: (407)351-5100 244

Motel

6/1-8/31	1P: $69-$129	2P: $69-$129	
12/1-5/31	1P: $59-$109	2P: $59-$109	
9/1-11/30	1P: $49-$99	2P: $49-$99	

Location: I-4, exit 28, just e to International Dr; from Bee Line Expwy (SR 528) exit 1, then just n. 9956 Hawaiian Ct 32819. Fax: 407/352-7188. **Facility:** Very pleasant guest rooms all nicely decorated with a colorful, modern decor. Choose between large suites with a separate living room area or standard style guest rooms. 223 units. Some suites ($89-$159) and whirlpool units. 2 stories, interior corridors. **Terms:** check-in 4 pm. **Amenities:** extended cable TV, video games, voice mail, safes (fee). *Some:* irons, hair dryers. **Leisure Activities:** whirlpool, exercise room. **Guest Services:** [ECP] meal plan available, area transportation-selected attractions, coin laundry. **Business Services:** meeting rooms. **Cards:** AE, CB, DI, DS, JC, MC, VI. **Special Amenities:** free continental breakfast and free newspaper.
(See color ad below)

SOME UNITS

(See map p. 560)

HOWARD JOHNSON PLAZA RESORT UNIVERSAL GATEWAY Phone: (407)351-2000 **216**

♦♦♦ ♦♦	4/22-8/18	1P: $72-$108	2P: $72-$108	XP: $6	F18
	1/3-4/21	1P: $62-$108	2P: $62-$108	XP: $6	F18
Motor Inn	12/1-1/2	1P: $59-$105	2P: $59-$105	XP: $6	F18
	8/19-11/30	1P: $62-$92	2P: $62-$92	XP: $6	F18

Location: I-4, exit 30, 0.8 mi s on SR 435. 7050 S Kirkman Rd 32819-8284. Fax: 407/363-1835. **Facility:** Most rooms with two double beds. Ample public areas. Resident toucan in the lobby; a starring attraction. 356 units. 2 stories, interior corridors. **Terms:** cancellation fee imposed, package plans, pets ($50 deposit). **Amenities:** voice mail, safes (fee). **Leisure Activities:** 2 pools (1 heated), wading pool, playground, shuffleboard, game room. *Fee:* miniature golf. **Guest Services:** gift shop, area transportation, coin laundry. **Business Services:** meeting rooms. **Cards:** AE, DI, DS, MC, VI. *(See color ad below)* SOME UNITS

(See map p. 560)

HOWARD JOHNSON RESORT HOTEL & SUITES

Motel

AAA SAVE

3/1-4/15	1P: $81-$110	2P: $81-$110	XP: $10	F18
12/1-2/28 & 4/16-11/30	1P: $72-$100	2P: $72-$100	XP: $10	F18

Phone: (407)581-5000 [158]

Location: SR 528 (Bee Line Expwy), exit 8, just nw. 2323 McCoy Rd 32809. Fax: 407/581-5001. **Facility:** 269 units. *Bath:* combo or shower only. 3 stories, exterior corridors. **Terms:** check-in 4 pm, cancellation fee imposed. **Amenities:** extended cable TV, voice mail, safes (fee), hair dryers. *Some:* irons. **Leisure Activities:** heated pool, putting green, exercise room. **Guest Services:** valet laundry. **Cards:** AE, CB, DI, DS, MC, VI.

(See color ad p 602)

SOME UNITS

HYATT REGENCY ORLANDO INTERNATIONAL AIRPORT

Hotel

AAA SAVE

All Year	1P: $185	2P: $210	XP: $25	F18

Phone: (407)825-1234 [198]

Location: At the Orlando International Airport. 9300 Airport Blvd 32827. Fax: 407/856-1672. **Facility:** Attractively decorated rooms with excellent work space. Some rooms have furnished balcony. 446 units. *Bath:* combo or shower only. 10 stories, interior corridors. **Parking:** extra charge or valet. **Terms:** check-in 4 pm, cancellation fee imposed, package plans. **Amenities:** voice mail, irons, hair dryers. **Dining:** 2 restaurants, 6:30 am-11 pm, $7-$16, cocktails, also, Hemisphere, see separate listing. **Leisure Activities:** whirlpool, swimming pool size spa, exercise room. **Guest Services:** gift shop, valet laundry. **Business Services:** conference facilities, administrative services, PC, fax. **Cards:** AE, CB, DI, DS, JC, MC, VI. *(See color ad below)*

SOME UNITS

FEE

LA QUINTA INN AIRPORT WEST

Motel

SAVE

All Year	1P: $55-$79	2P: $55-$79

Phone: (407)857-9215 [184]

Location: Bee Line Expwy (SR 528); at Trade Port exit 9, via McCoy Rd. 7931 Daetwyler Dr 32812-4809. Fax: 407/857-0877. **Facility:** Modern rooms attractively decorated. 128 units. *Bath:* combo or shower only. 3 stories, exterior corridors. **Terms:** small pets only. **Amenities:** video games, voice mail. **Leisure Activities:** heated pool. **Guest Services:** [CP] meal plan available, coin laundry. **Business Services:** meeting rooms. **Cards:** AE, CB, DI, DS, MC, VI. *(See color ad p 604)*

SOME UNITS

FEE   FEE FEE

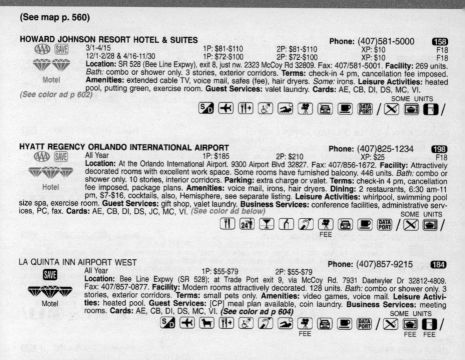
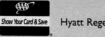

(See map p. 560)

LA QUINTA INN & SUITES Phone: (407)345-1365 **159**

All Year 1P: $99-$119 2P: $99-$119

SAVE

Motel

Location: I-4, exit 29, 0.5 mi e on SR 482 (Sand Lake Rd), then 0.5 mi s. 8504 Universal Blvd 32819. Fax: 407/345-5586. **Facility:** 184 units. Some suites ($129-$149). *Bath:* combo or shower only. 7 stories, interior corridors. **Terms:** check-in 4 pm, small pets only. **Amenities:** video games, voice mail, irons, hair dryers. **Leisure Activities:** heated pool, whirlpool, exercise room. **Guest Services:** [CP] meal plan available, area transportation, coin laundry. **Business Services:** meeting rooms. **Cards:** AE, CB, DI, DS, MC, VI.

(See color ad below)

SOME UNITS

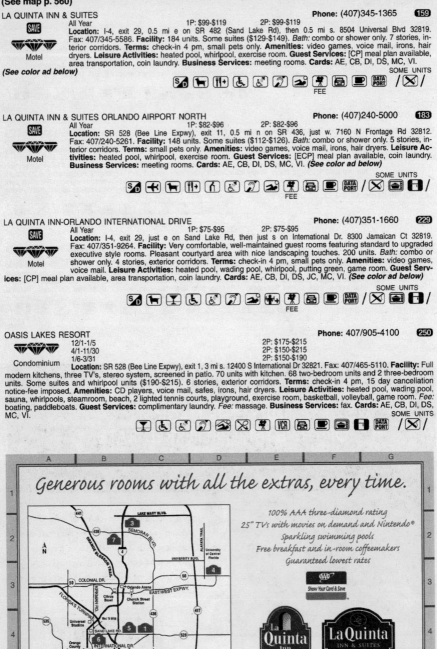

FEE

LA QUINTA INN & SUITES ORLANDO AIRPORT NORTH Phone: (407)240-5000 **183**

All Year 1P: $82-$96 2P: $82-$96

SAVE

Motel

Location: SR 528 (Bee Line Expwy), exit 11, 0.5 mi n on SR 436, just w. 7160 N Frontage Rd 32812. Fax: 407/240-5261. **Facility:** 148 units. Some suites ($112-$126). *Bath:* combo or shower only. 5 stories, interior corridors. **Terms:** small pets only. **Amenities:** video games, voice mail, irons, hair dryers. **Leisure Activities:** heated pool, whirlpool, exercise room. **Guest Services:** [ECP] meal plan available, coin laundry. **Business Services:** meeting rooms. **Cards:** AE, CB, DI, DS, MC, VI. *(See color ad below)*

SOME UNITS

FEE

LA QUINTA INN-ORLANDO INTERNATIONAL DRIVE Phone: (407)351-1660 **229**

All Year 1P: $75-$95 2P: $75-$95

SAVE

Motel

Location: I-4, exit 29, just e on Sand Lake Rd, then just s on International Dr. 8300 Jamaican Ct 32819. Fax: 407/351-9264. **Facility:** Very comfortable, well-maintained guest rooms featuring standard to upgraded executive style rooms. Pleasant courtyard area with nice landscaping touches. 200 units. *Bath:* combo or shower only. 4 stories, exterior corridors. **Terms:** check-in 4 pm, small pets only. **Amenities:** video games, voice mail. **Leisure Activities:** heated pool, wading pool, whirlpool, putting green, game room. **Guest Services:** [CP] meal plan available, area transportation, coin laundry. **Cards:** AE, CB, DI, DS, JC, MC, VI. *(See color ad below)*

SOME UNITS

FEE

OASIS LAKES RESORT Phone: 407/905-4100 **250**

12/1-1/5 2P: $175-$215
4/1-11/30 2P: $150-$215
1/6-3/31 2P: $150-$190

Condominium

Location: SR 528 (Bee Line Expwy), exit 1, 3 mi s. 12400 S International Dr 32821. Fax: 407/465-5110. **Facility:** Full modern kitchens, three TV's, stereo system, screened in patio. 70 units with kitchen. 68 two-bedroom units and 2 three-bedroom units. Some suites and whirlpool units ($190-$215). 6 stories, exterior corridors. **Terms:** check-in 4 pm, 15 day cancellation notice-fee imposed. **Amenities:** CD players, voice mail, safes, irons, hair dryers. **Leisure Activities:** heated pool, wading pool, sauna, whirlpools, steamroom, beach, 2 lighted tennis courts, playground, exercise room, basketball, volleyball, game room. *Fee:* boating, paddleboats. **Guest Services:** complimentary laundry. *Fee:* massage. **Business Services:** fax. **Cards:** AE, CB, DI, DS, MC, VI.

SOME UNITS

(See map p. 560)

ORLANDO AIRPORT MARRIOTT   Phone: (407)851-9000   [177]

▽▽▽   12/1-4/6   1P: $169   2P: $169
      4/7-6/2 & 9/9-11/30   1P: $149   2P: $149
Hotel 6/3-9/8   1P: $129   2P: $129

Location: SR 528 (BeeLine Expwy), exit 11, 0.5 mi n on SR 436, just e and s. 7499 Augusta National Dr 32822. Fax: 407/857-6211. **Facility:** Extensive conference facilities. 484 units. Some whirlpool units. *Bath:* combo or shower only. 9 stories, interior corridors. **Parking:** valet. **Amenities:** voice mail, irons, hair dryers. **Dining:** Murphy's Chop House, see separate listing. **Leisure Activities:** heated pool, wading pool, saunas, whirlpool, 2 lighted tennis courts, jogging, basketball. **Guest Services:** [BP] meal plan available, gift shop, valet laundry. *Fee:* massage. **Business Services:** conference facilities, administrative services, PC. *Fee:* fax. **Cards:** AE, CB, DI, DS, JC, MC, VI.

SOME UNITS

(ASK) (SD) (✈) (ﮒ) (Y) (&) (ⅉ) (☆) (♣) (✕) (🎥) (🖨) (💻) (PORT) / (✕) (🍴) /
                                    FEE

PARC CORNICHE RESORT   Phone: (407)239-7100   [202]

(AAA) (SAVE)   12/1-1/3   1P: $75-$115   2P: $105-$185   XP: $20   F
               1/4-11/30   1P: $75-$85   2P: $105-$135   XP: $20   F
▽▽▽▽
Condominium   **Location:** I-4, exit 28, just e on Bee Line Expwy (SR 528) to exit 1, then 1.7 mi s on International Dr. 6300 Parc Corniche Dr 32821-7306. Fax: 407/239-4003. **Facility:** Large condo units with cooking facilities, located in quiet area off busy International Drive and surrounded by golf course. 210 units. 120 two-bedroom units, 208 efficiencies and 2 units with kitchen. 3 stories, exterior corridors. **Terms:** 3 day cancellation notice-fee imposed, weekly & monthly rates available, package plans. **Amenities:** voice mail, safes, irons. *Some:* hair dryers. **Dining:** restaurant, noon-11 pm; convenience store, $8-$13, cocktails. **Leisure Activities:** heated pool, wading pool, whirlpool, playground, game room. *Fee:* golf privileges. **Guest Services:** gift shop, area transportation-some attractions, coin laundry. **Business Services:** meeting rooms. **Cards:** AE, DI, DS, MC, VI. **Special Amenities:** free continental breakfast and free local telephone calls.
(See color ad p 606)

SOME UNITS

(SD) (ﮒ) (Y) (↾↿) (☆) (🎥) (🖨) (💻) (📠) (🍴) / (✕) /
         FEE   FEE

THE PEABODY ORLANDO   Phone: (407)352-4000   [239]

(AAA) (SAVE)   1/1-11/30   1P: $360-$1600   XP: $15   F17
               12/1-12/31 1P: $330-$1500   XP: $15   F17
▽▽▽▽ ▽▽▽▽
Hotel   **Location:** 0.5 mi n of SR 528 (Bee Line Expwy) opposite Orange County Convention Center. 9801 International Dr 32819. Fax: 407/351-0073. **Facility:** Particularly well-trained staff at this elegant luxury hotel. Marbled public areas trimmed with orchids and objects d'art. Known for a team of resident ducks who reside in the lobby fountain and parade twice daily. 891 units. Some suites ($520-$1600) and whirlpool units. *Bath:* combo or shower only. 27 stories, interior corridors. **Parking:** valet. **Terms:** 3 day cancellation notice-fee imposed, package plans. **Amenities:** video games, voice mail, honor bars, irons, hair dryers. *Some:* CD players. **Dining:** 2 restaurants, 24 hours, $11-$34, cocktails, also, Capriccio, see separate listing, entertainment. **Leisure Activities:** heated pool, wading pool, saunas, whirlpools, steamrooms, 4 lighted tennis courts, pro shop, game room, beauty salon. *Fee:* swim shop, tennis instruction, aerobics, personal trainer, tanning bed. **Guest Services:** gift shop, afternoon tea, valet laundry. *Fee:* area transportation-Disney, massage. **Business Services:** conference facilities, administrative services, PC, fax. **Cards:** AE, CB, DI, DS, JC, MC, VI. **Special Amenities:** free newspaper and preferred room (subject to availability with advanced reservations). Affiliated with A Preferred Hotel.

SOME UNITS

(SD) (✈) (ﮒ) (24) (Y) (↾↿) (&) (ⅉ) (🎥) (♣) (🖨) (PORT) / (✕) (💻) (🍴) /
      FEE   FEE   FEE FEE   FEE FEE

PORTOFINO BAY HOTEL   Phone: (407)503-1000   [160]

(AAA) (SAVE)   2/16-7/4   1P: $255-$445   2P: $255-$445   XP: $25   F18
               10/1-11/30   1P: $255-$415   2P: $255-$415   XP: $25   F18
▽▽▽▽ ▽▽▽▽   12/1-2/15   1P: $240-$395   2P: $240-$395   XP: $25   F18
Hotel   7/5-9/30   1P: $235-$395   2P: $235-$395   XP: $25   F18

Location: I-4, exit 30, just n on SR 435 (Kirkman Rd), then just w via Major Blvd or Vineland Rd at Universal Studios. 5601 Universal Blvd 32819. Fax: 407/503-1010. **Facility:** Journey to a unique lodging of Old World charm in the middle of the high tech adventure of Universal attractions. Sheltered by creative landscaping, the replica of a small town in the Italian Riviera is built around its miniature bay, garden areas and piazzas. It offers a range of diversions: dining from very casual to elegant; several pools, one with its own sandy beach; shopping for vacation momentos or fine art. Designated smoking area. 750 units. Some suites ($340-$2020) and whirlpool units. *Bath:* combo or shower only. 6 stories, interior corridors. **Parking:** valet. **Terms:** 5 day cancellation notice-fee imposed, package plans. **Amenities:** extended cable TV, video games, voice mail, safes, honor bars, irons, hair dryers. *Some:* fax. **Dining:** dining room, 2 restaurants, coffee shop, deli, $9-$20, also, Delfino Riviera, see separate listing, entertainment. **Leisure Activities:** 3 heated pools, wading pool, whirlpools, waterslide, social program, playground, bocci ball, full service spa. **Guest Services:** gift shop, complimentary evening beverages: in villas, area transportation-Universal attractions, valet laundry. **Business Services:** conference facilities, administrative services, PC, fax. **Cards:** AE, CB, DI, DS, JC, MC, VI.

SOME UNITS

(✈) (ﮒ) (24) (Y) (↾↿) (&) (ⅉ) (🎥) (♣) (💻) (PORT) / (✕) (VCR) (🖨) (🍴) /
      FEE   FEE   FEE

QUALITY INN AIRPORT   Phone: (407)856-4663   [182]

(AAA) (SAVE)   2/1-4/15   1P: $55-$99   2P: $59-$99
               12/1-1/31 & 4/16-11/30 1P: $49-$99   2P: $55-$99
▽▽ ▽▽
Motel   **Location:** SR 482, at jct SR 528 (Bee Line Expwy). 2601 McCoy Rd 32809. Fax: 407/856-4663. **Facility:** 10 business rooms with king beds featuring oversized desk and extra phone. Designated smoking area. 98 units. 2 stories, exterior corridors. **Terms:** cancellation fee imposed. **Amenities:** extended cable TV, safes (fee), irons, hair dryers. **Guest Services:** complimentary evening beverages, coin laundry. **Cards:** AE, CB, DI, DS, JC, MC, VI. **Special Amenities:** free continental breakfast and free local telephone calls.

SOME UNITS

(SD) (✈) (ⅉ) (🎥) (♣) (💻) (PORT) / (✕) (🖨) (🍴) /

QUALITY INN INTERNATIONAL   Phone: 407/996-1600   [207]

(SAVE)   All Year   1P: $39-$99
▽▽ ▽▽   **Location:** I-4, exit 29, just e on Sand Lake Rd, then just n. 7600 International Dr 32819. Fax: 407/996-5328. **Facility:** A really nice, budget-oriented property offering very well-maintained guest rooms. Lush landscaped courtyard and pool area. Geared for families. 728 units. *Bath:* combo or shower only. 2-6 stories, exterior corridors. **Terms:** $2 service charge, pets ($6 extra charge). **Amenities:** voice mail, safes. **Leisure Activities:** 2 heated pools, wading pool, game room. **Guest Services:** gift shop, coin laundry. *Fee:* area transportation. **Cards:** AE, CB, DI, DS, JC, MC, VI. *(See color ad p 606)*

SOME UNITS

(SD) (🛏) (ﮒ) (Y) (↾↿) (&) (🎥) / (✕) (💻) (🖨) (🍴) /
                    FEE

608 ORLANDO • ORLANDO SOUTH, FL

(See map p. 560)

QUALITY INN-PLAZA   Phone: (407)996-8585 234

SAVE

Motor Inn

All Year   1P: $39-$99   2P: $39-$99
Location: I-4, exit 29, just e on SR 482 (Sand Lake Rd), then 1 mi s. 9000 International Dr 32819. Fax: 407/996-6839. **Facility:** A well maintained property featuring average sized guest rooms with a pleasant decor. The real highlight here is the landscaped grounds around the three swimming pools. Geared for families. 1020 units. **Bath:** combo or shower only. 4-10 stories, exterior corridors. **Terms:** pets ($6 extra charge). **Amenities:** voice mail, safes. *Some:* irons, hair dryers. **Leisure Activities:** 3 pools (2 heated), game room. **Guest Services:** gift shop, coin laundry. *Fee:* area transportation. **Cards:** AE, CB, DI, DS, JC, MC, VI. *(See color ad p 606)*

SOME UNITS

QUALITY SUITES INTERNATIONAL DRIVE AREA   Phone: (407)363-0332 217

AAA SAVE

Suite Motel

12/25-1/25   1P: $89-$119   2P: $89-$119
1/26-8/18   1P: $79-$109   2P: $79-$109
12/1-12/24 & 8/19-11/30   1P: $79-$99   2P: $79-$99
Location: I-4, exit 29, just e on Sand Lake Rd, then just n. 7400 Canada Ave 32819. Fax: 407/352-2598. **Facility:** Quiet location just off International Dr. High-rise style property with extra large guest rooms, all have a separate sitting/living room area. Lush landscaping around pool area. Better view from top floors. 154 units. 7 stories, exterior corridors. **Amenities:** extended cable TV, CD players, safes, irons, hair dryers. **Leisure Activities:** heated pool, whirlpool, playground, exercise room, arcade room. **Guest Services:** [BP] meal plan available, gift shop, complimentary evening beverages, area transportation-major attractions, coin laundry. **Business Services:** meeting rooms. **Cards:** AE, DI, DS, JC, MC, VI. **Special Amenities:** free continental breakfast and free local telephone calls. *(See color ad starting on p 608)*

SOME UNITS

RADISSON BARCELO HOTEL   Phone: (407)345-0505 230
                                                                                                F

AAA SAVE

Motor Inn

All Year   1P: $105-$145   2P: $105-$145   XP: $10
Location: I-4, exit 29, just e on Sand Lake Rd, then just s. 8444 International Dr 32819. Fax: 407/352-5894. **Facility:** Nicely appointed guest rooms, several overlook nicely landscaped pool area. 520 units. *Bath:* combo or shower only. 7 stories, interior/exterior corridors. **Terms:** check-in 4 pm, 3 day cancellation notice-fee imposed. **Amenities:** video games, voice mail, safes, irons, hair dryers. **Dining:** restaurant, 6:30 am-11 pm; poolside bar, seasonal, $10-$20, cocktails. **Leisure Activities:** heated pool, whirlpool, lighted tennis court, playground, sand volleyball. **Guest Services:** gift shop, area transportation-Universal, coin laundry. **Business Services:** meeting rooms. **Cards:** AE, CB, DI, DS, JC, MC, VI. **Special Amenities:** free local telephone calls and free newspaper.** *(See color ad below)*

SOME UNITS

RADISSON HOTEL ORLANDO AIRPORT   Phone: (407)856-0100 173
                                                                                                F12

AAA SAVE

Hotel

All Year   1P: $119-$169   2P: $119-$169   XP: $10
Location: SR 528 (Bee Line Expwy), exit 11, 0.8 mi n on SR 436, just w. 5555 Hazeltine National Dr 32812. Fax: 407/855-7991. **Facility:** Business-oriented hotel. 347 units. Some suites ($269). *Bath:* combo or shower only. 10 stories, interior corridors. **Amenities:** extended cable TV, voice mail, irons, hair dryers. **Dining:** restaurant, 6 am-11 pm, $10-$18, cocktails. **Leisure Activities:** heated pool, whirlpool, exercise room, game room. **Guest Services:** gift shop, valet laundry. **Business Services:** conference facilities, fax. **Cards:** AE, CB, DI, DS, JC, MC, VI.

SOME UNITS

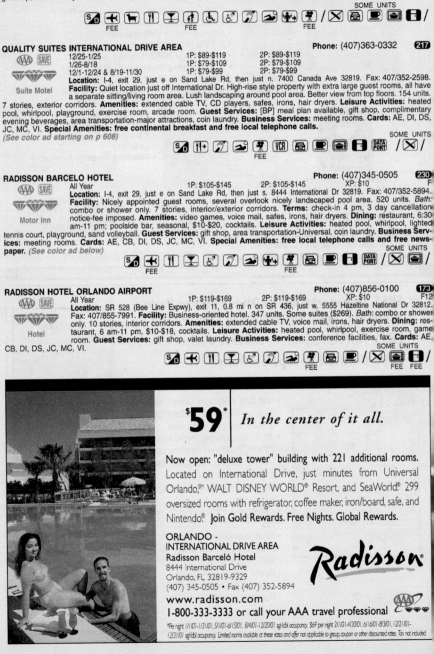

(See map p. 560)

RADISSON HOTEL UNIVERSAL ORLANDO

Phone: (407)351-1000   199

AAA SAVE
Hotel

All Year   1P: $169-$209   2P: $169-$209   XP: $10   F17
Location: I-4, exit 30B, 0.7 mi n on SR 435 (Kirkman Rd). 5780 Major Blvd 32819. Fax: 407/363-0106. **Facility:** Located opposite Universal Studios main entrance. High-rise with attractive public area, including pleasant outdoor courtyard. 742 units. Some suites. *Bath:* combo or shower only. 18 stories, interior corridors. **Parking:** valet. **Terms:** check-in 4 pm, cancellation fee imposed, weekly rates available, package plans. **Amenities:** voice mail, safes (fee), irons, hair dryers. *Some:* CD players. **Dining:** restaurant, deli, 24 hours, $9-$20, cocktails. **Leisure Activities:** heated pool, wading pool, whirlpool, children's program, playground, exercise room. **Guest Services:** gift shop, area transportation-Universal Studios, coin laundry. **Business Services:** conference facilities, administrative services, fax. *Fee:* PC. **Cards:** AE, CB, DI, DS, JC, MC, VI. **Special Amenities: early check-in/late check-out and preferred room (subject to availability with advanced reservations).** *(See color ad below)*

SOME UNITS

RAMADA INN ALL SUITES AT INTERNATIONAL DRIVE CENTER

Phone: (407)239-0707   203

AAA SAVE
Apartment

All Year   1P: $170-$190   2P: $170-$190   XP: $10   F18
Location: I-4, exit 28, just e on SR 528 (Bee Line Expwy) to exit 1 (International Dr), then just s to Westwood Blvd, then 2.5 mi sw. 6800 Villa de Costa Dr 32821. Fax: 407/239-8243. **Facility:** A cluster of three story buildings situated on lovely landscaped grounds. All units are large two separate bedroom apartments with two full baths and screened in balcony. Perfect for large families. 145 two-bedroom units with kitchen. 2-3 stories (no elevator), exterior corridors. **Terms:** check-in 4 pm, 3 day cancellation notice-fee imposed, package plans, $2 service charge. **Amenities:** extended cable TV, safes, irons, hair dryers. **Dining:** deli, 11 am-10 pm, $6-$15, wine/beer only. **Leisure Activities:** 2 pools, whirlpools, paddleboats, children's program, playground, exercise room, basketball, sand volleyball, outside exercise course. **Guest Services:** gift shop, area transportation-selected attractions, coin laundry. **Business Services:** meeting rooms. **Cards:** AE, DI, DS, JC, MC, VI. **Special Amenities: early check-in/late check-out and free continental breakfast.** *(See color ad p 612)*

SOME UNITS

RED ROOF INN CONVENTION CENTER

Phone: (407)352-1507   243

AAA SAVE
Motel

1/1-11/30   1P: $57-$106   2P: $67-$116   XP: $10   F18
12/1-12/31   1P: $52-$100   2P: $62-$110   XP: $10   F18
Location: I-4, exit 28, just e on Bee Line Expwy (SR 528), to exit 1, then just n. 9922 Hawaiian Ct 32819. Fax: 407/352-5550. **Facility:** A very well maintained, budget oriented property offering nice, comfortable guest rooms. 134 units. 2 stories, exterior corridors. **Amenities:** video games, voice mail. **Leisure Activities:** whirlpool. **Guest Services:** coin laundry. **Cards:** AE, CB, DI, DS, MC, VI. **Special Amenities: free local telephone calls and free newspaper.**

SOME UNITS

RED ROOF INN UNIVERSAL STUDIOS

Phone: 407/313-3100   161

Motel

6/1-8/15   1P: $60-$90   2P: $60-$90
8/16-11/30   1P: $50-$70   2P: $50-$70
12/1-5/31   1P: $50-$70   2P: $50-$70   XP: $4   F18
Location: I-4, exit 30B, just n, then just e. 5621 Major Blvd 32819. Fax: 407/313-3131. **Facility:** 80 units. *Bath:* combo or shower only. 3 stories, interior corridors. **Terms:** cancellation fee imposed. **Amenities:** extended cable TV. **Guest Services:** [CP] meal plan available, coin laundry. **Cards:** AE, CB, DI, DS, MC, VI.

SOME UNITS

(See map p. 560)

RENAISSANCE ORLANDO-AIRPORT HOTEL
Phone: (407)240-1000 **181**

Hotel

12/1-3/31	1P: $119-$179
9/14-11/30	1P: $109-$169
4/1-9/13	1P: $89-$149

Location: SR 436; just n of SR 528 (Bee Line Expwy). 5445 Forbes Pl 32812. Fax: 407/240-1005. **Facility:** Large, attractively furnished rooms and baths. 298 units. *Bath:* combo or shower only. 9 stories, interior corridors. **Parking:** valet. **Terms:** cancellation fee imposed. **Amenities:** video games, voice mail, honor bars, irons, hair dryers. **Leisure Activities:** heated pool, sauna, whirlpool, exercise room. **Guest Services:** gift shop, valet laundry. *Fee:* massage. **Business Services:** conference facilities, administrative services, PC, fax. **Cards:** AE, CB, DI, DS, JC, MC, VI. *(See color ad p 612)*

SOME UNITS

RENAISSANCE ORLANDO RESORT AT SEAWORLD
Phone: (407)351-5555 **249**

Hotel

12/29-5/6 & 9/10-11/30	1P: $179	2P: $179	XP: $10	F18
12/1-12/28 & 5/7-9/9	1P: $119	2P: $119	XP: $10	F18

Location: I-4, exit 28, just e on Central Florida Pkwy, 0.3 mi n of International Dr; facing Sea World. 6677 Sea Harbor Dr 32821-8092. Fax: 407/351-9991. **Facility:** Champagne at arrival and morning coffee with wake up calls. Stylish convention hotel with impressive atrium lobby featuring an aviary and waterfall pond stocked with Koi fish. Spacious rooms. 778 units. 10 stories, interior corridors. **Parking:** valet. **Terms:** 3 day cancellation notice-fee imposed, package plans. **Amenities:** video games, dual phone lines, voice mail, safes, honor bars, irons, hair dryers. **Dining:** dining room, restaurant, deli, poolside bar & grill, cocktails, also, Haifeng, see separate listing, entertainment. **Leisure Activities:** heated pool, wading pool, sauna, whirlpools, steamroom, golf privileges, 3 lighted tennis courts, jogging, playground, basketball, beauty salon, sand volleyball. *Fee:* tennis instruction & equipment. **Guest Services:** [BP] meal plan available, gift shop, valet laundry. *Fee:* area transportation-major attractions, massage. **Business Services:** conference facilities, administrative services, PC, fax. **Cards:** AE, CB, DI, DS, JC, MC, VI. **Special Amenities:** free newspaper.

SOME UNITS

RESIDENCE INN BY MARRIOTT ORLANDO CONVENTION CENTER
Phone: (407)226-0288 **162**

Extended Stay Motel

12/1-1/2	1P: $149-$179	2P: $149-$179
1/3-4/22	1P: $129-$179	2P: $129-$179
6/14-11/30	1P: $99-$159	2P: $99-$159
4/23-6/13	1P: $92-$149	2P: $92-$149

Location: I-4, exit 29A, 0.5 mi e on SR 482 (Sand Lake Rd), then 0.8 mi s. 8800 Universal Blvd 32819. Fax: 407/226-9979. **Facility:** 124 units. 23 two-bedroom units, 67 efficiencies and 57 units with kitchen. Some suites and whirlpool units. *Bath:* combo or shower only. 5 stories, interior corridors. **Terms:** check-in 4 pm, weekly & monthly rates available. **Amenities:** extended cable TV, voice mail, irons, hair dryers. **Leisure Activities:** heated pool, whirlpool, exercise room, sports court. **Guest Services:** [ECP] meal plan available, area transportation, coin laundry. **Business Services:** meeting rooms. **Cards:** AE, CB, DI, DS, JC, MC, VI. *(See color ad p 582)*

SOME UNITS

RESIDENCE INN BY MARRIOTT-ORLANDO INTERNATIONAL DR
Phone: (407)345-0117 **219**

Apartment

12/1-1/5	1P: $129-$179	2P: $139-$184
1/6-4/18	1P: $119-$169	2P: $129-$179
4/19-8/31	1P: $119-$169	2P: $129-$169
9/1-11/30	1P: $109-$149	2P: $119-$159

Location: I-4, exit 29, just e on Sand Lake Rd (SR 482). 7975 Canada Ave 32819. Fax: 407/352-2689. **Facility:** A very well maintained property offering a choice between studio, 1- and 2-bedroom units, all with small living room and full kitchens. Extended stays and families are most welcome. 176 units with kitchen. 44 two-bedroom units. 2 stories, exterior corridors. **Terms:** check-in 4 pm, cancellation fee imposed, weekly & monthly rates available, $1 service charge, small pets only ($50 fee, $10 extra charge). **Amenities:** extended cable TV, voice mail, safes, irons, hair dryers. *Some:* video games. **Leisure Activities:** heated pool, whirlpool, poolside gas grills, sports court, volleyball. **Guest Services:** [CP] meal plan available, complimentary evening beverages: Mon-Thurs, area transportation, coin laundry. **Business Services:** meeting rooms. **Cards:** AE, DI, DS, JC, MC, VI.

SOME UNITS

RODEWAY INN INTERNATIONAL
Phone: (407)996-4444 **205**

Motel

All Year   1P: $35-$95   2P: $35-$95

Location: I-4, exit 29, just e on Sand Lake Rd, then 0.7 mi n. 6327 International Dr 32819. Fax: 407/996-5806. **Facility:** 315 units. *Bath:* combo or shower only. 4-9 stories, interior/exterior corridors. **Terms:** $2 service charge, pets ($5 extra charge). **Amenities:** voice mail, safes. **Leisure Activities:** heated pool, game room. **Guest Services:** gift shop, coin laundry. *Fee:* area transportation. **Cards:** AE, CB, DI, DS, JC, MC, VI. *(See color ad p 606)*

SOME UNITS

ROSEN CENTRE HOTEL
Phone: (407)996-9840 **238**

Hotel

All Year   1P: $99   2P: $99   XP: $20   F17

Location: I-4, exit 28, just e on SR 528 (Bee Line Expwy) to exit 1 (International Dr), then just n. 9840 International Dr 32819. Fax: 407/996-0865. **Facility:** Adjacent to the Convention Center. Beautifully appointed public areas, this convention oriented hotel offers well maintained and very comfortable guest rooms. 1334 units. Some whirlpool units. *Bath:* some combo or shower only. 24 stories, interior corridors. **Parking:** valet. **Amenities:** voice mail, safes, irons, hair dryers. **Dining:** Everglades, see separate listing. **Leisure Activities:** heated pool, wading pool, whirlpools. *Fee:* 2 lighted tennis courts. **Guest Services:** gift shop, coin laundry. *Fee:* area transportation, massage. **Business Services:** conference facilities, administrative services. **Cards:** AE, DI, DS, JC, MC, VI.

SOME UNITS

(See map p. 560)

THE SEASONS RESORT
▼▼▼▼
Apartment
Phone: (407)851-2278 **170**
Property failed to provide current rates
Location: I-4, exit 32, 2.6 mi s on SR 423 (John Young Pkwy), 0.3 mi e on Oak Ridge Rd, just n. 5736 S Texas Ave 32839. Fax: 407/438-1362. **Facility:** Spacious 2-bedroom, 2-bath apartments with full kitchens, including dishwasher and washer/dryer. All units with king master bedrooms and screened patio or balcony. 44 two-bedroom units with kitchen. Some whirlpool units. 2 stories, exterior corridors. **Terms:** check-in 4 pm, 14 day cancellation notice, weekly & monthly rates available. **Amenities:** extended cable TV, safes, irons, hair dryers. **Leisure Activities:** heated pool, wading pool, sauna, whirlpool, 2 lighted tennis courts, racquetball court, playground, exercise room, game room. **Cards:** AE, DI, DS, MC, VI.

SHERATON STUDIO CITY HOTEL
(AAA) (SAVE)
▼▼▼▼
Hotel
Phone: (407)351-2100 **163**
All Year   1P: $130-$170   2P: $130-$170   XP: $10   F18
Location: I-4, exit 30, just w of SR 435. 5905 International Dr 32819. Fax: 407/352-2991. **Facility:** 302 units. *Bath:* combo or shower only. 21 stories, interior corridors. **Terms:** 3 day cancellation notice-fee imposed, package plans, $2 service charge. **Amenities:** extended cable TV, video games, voice mail, safes, irons, hair dryers. *Some:* fax. **Dining:** restaurant, 6:30-10:30 am, 11:30-1:30 & 6-10 pm, $13-$19, cocktails. **Leisure Activities:** heated pool, wading pool, whirlpool, exercise room, game room. **Guest Services:** gift shop, area transportation-major attractions, coin laundry. **Business Services:** conference facilities, administrative services. **Cards:** AE, CB, DI, DS, JC, MC, VI. **Special Amenities:** free newspaper. *(See ad p 615)*
SOME UNITS

SHERATON SUITES ORLANDO AIRPORT
▼▼▼▼
Suite Hotel
Phone: (407)240-5555 **187**
1/1-4/30   1P: $105-$139   2P: $105-$139   XP: $10   F18
12/1-12/31 & 5/1-11/30 1P: $89-$125   2P: $89-$125   XP: $10   F18
Location: 2 mi n of airport terminal; via SR 436 and TG Lee Blvd. 7550 Augusta National Dr 32822. Fax: 407/240-1300. **Facility:** Business hotel featuring elegant public areas and spacious suites. Designated smoking area. 150 units. 3 stories, interior corridors. **Terms:** cancellation fee imposed, package plans. **Amenities:** irons, hair dryers. **Leisure Activities:** heated pool, whirlpool, exercise room. **Guest Services:** [BP] meal plan available, gift shop, area transportation, coin laundry. **Business Services:** meeting rooms. *Fee:* fax. **Cards:** AE, CB, DI, DS, JC, MC, VI.
(See color ad p 615)
SOME UNITS

(See map p. 560)

SHERATON WORLD RESORT — Phone: (407)352-1100 **251**

▼▼▼▼▼	12/29-4/29	1P: $249-$299	2P: $249-$299	XP: $20	F12
	4/30-9/30	1P: $209-$259	2P: $209-$299	XP: $20	F12
Cottage	10/1-11/30	1P: $229-$279	2P: $229-$279	XP: $20	F12
	12/1-12/28	1P: $209-$259	2P: $209-$259	XP: $20	F12

Location: I-4, exit 28, just s on International Dr; Bee Line Expwy (SR 528), exit 1, just e. 10100 International Dr 32821. Fax: 407/352-3679. **Facility:** Several separate two-story buildings and a 16-story tower situated on 30 landscaped acres offering a tranquil setting within the hectic International Drive area. Convenient to Sea World and the Convention Center. 1102 units. *Bath:* combo or shower only. 3-16 stories, interior/exterior corridors. **Parking:** valet. **Terms:** 3 day cancellation notice-fee imposed, weekly rates available, package plans. **Amenities:** video games, dual phone lines, voice mail, safes, irons, hair dryers. **Leisure Activities:** 3 heated pools, wading pools, whirlpool, miniature golf, playground, exercise room, game room. **Guest Services:** gift shop, area transportation, coin laundry. *Fee:* massage. **Business Services:** conference facilities, administrative services, PC, fax. **Cards:** AE, CB, DI, DS, JC, MC, VI. *(See color ad below)*   SOME UNITS

(See map p. 560)

SHONEY'S INN & SUITES   Phone: (407)851-8200 **196**

AAA SAVE   All Year   1P: $50-$85   2P: $50-$85

Location: Florida Tpke, exit 254, then just n. 8820 S Orange Blossom Tr 32809. Fax: 407/855-7153. **Facility:** Property features a mixture of large suites with a separate sitting area and two full baths or standard style guest rooms. Many of the ground floor units feature patio doors leading to pool. 156 units. Some suites ($79-$109). *Bath:* combo or shower only. 2 stories, interior corridors. **Terms:** 14 day cancellation notice-fee imposed. **Leisure Activities:** wading pool. **Guest Services:** [CP] meal plan available, coin laundry. **Business Services:** meeting rooms. **Cards:** AE, CB, DI, DS, MC, VI.

Motel

SOME UNITS

SIERRA SUITES HOTEL-POINTE ORLANDO   Phone: (407)903-1500 **222**

All Year   1P: $69-$159   2P: $69-$159

Location: I-4, exit 29A, 0.5 mi e on SR 482 (Sand Lake Rd), then 0.7 mi s. 8750 Universal Blvd 32819. Fax: 407/903-1555. **Facility:** 137 efficiencies. *Bath:* combo or shower only. 3 stories, interior corridors. **Terms:** check-in 4 pm, 3 day cancellation notice-fee imposed. **Amenities:** extended cable TV, voice mail, safes (fee), irons, hair dryers. **Leisure Activities:** heated pool, whirlpool, exercise room. **Guest Services:** coin laundry. **Cards:** AE, CB, DI, DS, JC, MC, VI. *(See ad p 690)*

Motel

SOME UNITS

SPRING HILL SUITES BY MARRIOTT ORLANDO CONVENTION CENTER/INT'L DRIVE AREA   Phone: (407)345-9073 **164**

1/3-6/13   1P: $89-$129   2P: $89-$129
12/1-1/2 & 6/14-11/30   1P: $79-$119   2P: $79-$119

Location: I-4, exit 29, 0.5 mi e on SR 482 (Sand Lake Rd), then 0.8 mi s. 8840 Universal Blvd 32819. Fax: 407/345-9075. **Facility:** 167 units. *Bath:* combo or shower only. 7 stories, interior corridors. **Terms:** check-in 4 pm. **Amenities:** voice mail, irons, hair dryers. **Leisure Activities:** heated pool, wading pool, exercise room, game room. **Guest Services:** [ECP] meal plan available, gift shop, area transportation, coin laundry. **Business Services:** administrative services. **Cards:** AE, CB, DI, DS, MC, VI. *(See color ad p 582)*

Suite Motel

SOME UNITS

(See map p. 560)

SUMMERFIELD SUITES BY WYNDHAM

AAA [SAVE] ◆◆◆◆

Apartment

All Year   1P: $159-$229   2P: $159-$229   **Phone: (407)352-2400** [224]

Location: I-4, exit 29, just e on Sand Lake Rd, then just s. 8480 International Dr 32819. **Fax:** 407/352-4631. **Facility:** Very large apartment type units geared for larger families who like to stay in one unit. 146 units with kitchen. 104 two-bedroom units. Some suites. 5 stories, exterior corridors. **Terms:** check-in 4 pm, 3 day cancellation notice-fee imposed, package plans, 2% service charge. **Amenities:** voice mail, safes (fee), irons. **Leisure Activities:** heated pool, wading pool, whirlpool, exercise room, game room, rental videos. **Guest Services:** [ECP] meal plan available, gift shop, coin laundry. *Fee:* area transportation-attractions. **Business Services:** meeting rooms. **Cards:** AE, CB, DI, DS, JC, MC, VI. **Special Amenities:** free continental breakfast and free newspaper. *(See color ad p 616)*

SOME UNITS

[S/D] [✈ FEE] [♦♦] [▼] [⊘] [🏊 FEE] [VCR] [🖨] [▣] [🖳] [🛄] [DATA PORT] / [✕] /

TRAVELODGE INTERNATIONAL DRIVE

◆◆

Motel

2/1-11/30   2P: $59-$79
12/1-12/31   2P: $59-$69   **Phone: (407)345-8880** [211]
1/1-1/31   2P: $40-$54

Location: I-4, exit 29, e on Sand Lake Rd to International Dr, 2 mi n, then just w. 5859 American Way 32819. **Fax:** 407/363-9366. **Facility:** 192 units. 4 stories, exterior corridors. **Amenities:** extended cable TV, voice mail, safes (fee). **Leisure Activities:** heated pool, game room. **Guest Services:** area transportation, coin laundry. **Cards:** AE, CB, DI, DS, MC, VI. *(See color ad below)*

SOME UNITS

[ASK] [S/D] [♦♦+] [🅰] [🖨] [▣] [DATA PORT] / [✕] [🛄] /
                                                           FEE FEE

VENTURA RESORT RENTALS-KISSIMMEE

◆◆◆

Condominium

12/1-1/1 & 6/1-8/31   1P: $83-$175   2P: $83-$175   **Phone: (407)273-8770** [153]
1/2-5/31 & 9/1-11/30   1P: $72-$154   2P: $72-$154

Location: 0.6 mi e of SR 436. 5946 Curry Ford Rd 32822. **Fax:** 407/658-6530. **Facility:** From two-bedroom condos to multi-bedroom houses, these units are located in residential communities 10 to 15 miles south of the management offices, on either side of SR 417, near Landstar Blvd. While a few houses have a small pool, each community offers use of pool and discounted green fees at nearby golf course. 59 units with kitchen. 8 two-bedroom units and 51 three-bedroom units. 2 stories, exterior corridors. **Terms:** 15 day cancellation notice-fee imposed. **Amenities:** extended cable TV, irons. **Guest Services:** complimentary laundry. **Cards:** AE, DS, MC, VI.

SOME UNITS

[ASK] [S/D] [🖨] [🖳] [🛄] / [VCR]

VENTURA RESORT RENTALS ORLANDO

◆◆◆

Condominium

All Year   1P: $51-$145   2P: $145   **Phone: (407)273-8770** [155]

Location: 0.6 mi e of SR 436. 5946 Curry Ford Rd 32822. **Fax:** 407/658-6530. **Facility:** Ranging from one-bedroom condos to multi-bedroom houses, all are located just east of the registration office in a gated community featuring an 18-hole golf course and a clubhouse with olympic pool. Housekeeping available for a fee. 127 units with kitchen. 78 two-bedroom units and 30 three-bedroom units. 2 stories, exterior corridors. **Terms:** 15 day cancellation notice-fee imposed, pets ($100 extra charge, $200 deposit). **Amenities:** extended cable TV, irons. **Leisure Activities:** 6 pools, 4 lighted tennis courts, playground, basketball, shuffleboard. **Guest Services:** complimentary laundry. **Cards:** AE, DS, MC, VI.

SOME UNITS

[ASK] [S/D] [🐾] [♦♦+] [🅰] [✕] [🖨] [🖳] [🛄] / [VCR]

THE VILLAS OF GRAND CYPRESS

◆◆◆◆ ◆◆◆◆

Apartment

1/1-4/30   2P: $340-$1800
12/1-12/31   2P: $325-$1600   **Phone: (407)239-4700** [200]
10/1-11/30   2P: $340-$1360
5/1-9/30   2P: $245-$1360

Location: I-4, exit 27, 2.3 mi nw on SR 535. 1 N Jacaranda 32836. **Fax:** 407/239-7219. **Facility:** Extensive recreational facilities, surrounded by beautiful golf course. Guests also have access to all facilities at Hyatt Grand Cypress. Most units have patio or balcony, some with fireplace. 121 units. 25 two-bedroom units and 48 units with kitchen. Some whirlpool units. 2 stories, exterior corridors. **Terms:** check-in 4 pm, 3 day cancellation notice, $10 service charge. **Amenities:** extended cable TV, voice mail, safes, honor bars, irons, hair dryers. **Dining:** The Black Swan, see separate listing. **Leisure Activities:** heated pool, whirlpools, 12 tennis courts (3 lighted), children's program in summer, nature trails, bicycles, jogging, playground, exercise room. *Fee:* paddleboats, golf-45 holes, horseback riding. **Guest Services:** gift shop, valet laundry. *Fee:* massage. **Business Services:** meeting rooms, administrative services. **Cards:** AE, CB, DI, DS, JC, MC, VI.

SOME UNITS

[♦♦] [24] [▼] [🅰] [🏊] [✕] [🐾] [VCR] [🖨] [▣] [DATA PORT] / [✕] [🛄] /

(See map p. 560)

WELLESLEY INN & SUITES

Phone: (407)345-0026 172

AAA SAVE

▽▽▽▽

Motel

| 12/22-8/15 | 1P: $107 | 2P: $107 |
| 12/1-12/21 & 8/16-11/30 | 1P: $71 | 2P: $71 |

Location: I-4, exit 30B, 1 mi n on SR 435 (Kirkman Rd), just e. 5635 Windhover Dr 32819. Fax: 407/345-8809. **Facility:** 105 units. **Bath:** some combo or shower only. 4 stories, interior corridors. **Terms:** small pets only ($10 extra charge). **Amenities:** video games, voice mail. *Some:* irons, hair dryers. **Leisure Activities:** heated pool. **Guest Services:** area transportation-Universal, coin laundry. **Cards:** AE, CB, DI, DS, MC, VI. **Special Amenities:** free continental breakfast and free local telephone calls. *(See color ad opposite title page)*

SOME UNITS

[icons] FEE

WELLESLEY INN & SUITES

Phone: (407)248-8010 156

AAA SAVE

▽▽▽▽

Extended Stay
Motel

All Year 1P: $69 2P: $119 XP: $10 F18

Location: Just sw of jct of SR 423 (John Young Pkwy) and 482 (Sand Lake Rd). 8687 Commodity Cir 32819. Fax: 407/248-9940. **Facility:** Very good public areas and landscaping. Studio rooms tend to be small. 138 efficiencies. Some suites. **Bath:** combo or shower only. 3 stories, interior corridors. **Terms:** weekly & monthly rates available, pets ($100 fee, $150 deposit). **Amenities:** video games, voice mail, irons, hair dryers. **Leisure Activities:** exercise room. **Guest Services:** [ECP] meal plan available, coin laundry. **Cards:** AE, CB, DI, DS, JC, MC, VI. **Special Amenities:** free continental breakfast and free local telephone calls.

(See color ad opposite title page)

SOME UNITS

[icons] FEE FEE

WESTGATE LAKES RESORT

Phone: (407)345-0000 242

AAA SAVE

▽▽▽▽

Condominium

12/15-1/2	1P: $275-$650
1/3-11/30	1P: $68-$325
12/1-12/14	1P: $68-$225

Location: I-4, exit 29, 0.3 mi w on Sand Lake Rd (SR 482), 2.5 mi s. 10000 Turkey Lake Rd 32819. Fax: 407/345-5384. **Facility:** One and two bedroom villas with living room and kitchen, some with lake view. 1540 units. 796 two-bedroom units and 796 units with kitchen. Some suites and whirlpool units. 6 stories, exterior corridors. **Terms:** check-in 4 pm, 14 day cancellation notice-fee imposed, package plans. **Amenities:** voice mail, safes. *Some:* irons, hair dryers. **Dining:** dining room, deli, 6:30 am-11 pm, Sun-Thurs to 10 pm, $6-$20, cocktails. **Leisure Activities:** 6 heated pools, wading pools, whirlpools, beach, boat dock, fishing, parasailing, lighted tennis court, children's program, recreation program, jogging, playground, basketball. *Fee:* paddleboats, waterskiing, jet ski, bicycles, full service spa. **Guest Services:** gift shop, coin laundry. **Business Services:** meeting rooms. **Cards:** AE, CB, DI, DS, JC, MC, VI. *(See color ad p 614)*

[icons] FEE

WINGATE INN/UNIVERSAL STUDIOS

Phone: (407)226-0900 169

AAA SAVE

▽▽▽▽

Motel

| 12/1-1/31 & 4/22-11/30 | 1P: $89-$99 | 2P: $89-$99 |
| 2/1-4/21 | 1P: $99 | 2P: $99 |

Location: From jct SR 435 (Kirkman Rd) and I-4 exit, 1 mi n, then just e. 5661 Windhover Rd 32819. Fax: 407/226-0920. **Facility:** 100 units. Some suites ($120-$130). **Bath:** combo or shower only. 4 stories, interior corridors. **Terms:** cancellation fee imposed. **Amenities:** extended cable TV, video games, voice mail, safes, irons, hair dryers. **Leisure Activities:** whirlpool, exercise room. **Guest Services:** [ECP] meal plan available, area transportation-Universal, coin laundry. **Business Services:** meeting rooms, administrative services. **Cards:** AE, CB, DI, DS, JC, MC, VI. **Special Amenities:** free continental breakfast and free local telephone calls.

SOME UNITS

[icons] FEE

WYNDHAM ORLANDO RESORT

Phone: (407)351-2420 220

AAA SAVE

▽▽▽▽

Complex

All Year 1P: $99-$219

Location: I-4, exit 29, just e at Sand Lake Rd (SR 482). 8001 International Dr 32819. Fax: 407/345-5611. **Facility:** A truly unique property featuring several separate buildings scattered about on 48 acres of nicely landscaped grounds. Guest rooms are all very nicely maintained, some feature patio or balcony doors overlooking lagoon. 1052 units. Some suites and whirlpool units. **Bath:** combo or shower only. 2 stories, interior/exterior corridors. **Terms:** check-in 4 pm, 3 day cancellation notice-fee imposed, small pets only ($50 extra charge). **Amenities:** voice mail, safes (fee), irons, hair dryers. **Dining:** 2 restaurants, 6:30 am-midnight, $9-$20, cocktails. **Leisure Activities:** 3 heated pools, wading pools, saunas, whirlpool, steamrooms, 4 lighted tennis courts, children's program, playground, basketball, game room, sand volleyball. **Guest Services:** gift shop, area transportation-Universal, coin laundry. **Business Services:** conference facilities, administrative services, fax. **Cards:** AE, DI, DS, JC, MC, VI. *(See color ad p 581)*

SOME UNITS

[icons] FEE FEE

──────── The following lodgings were either not evaluated or did not ────────
meet AAA rating requirements but are listed for your information only.

AMERISUITES ORLANDO/UNIVERSAL

Phone: 407/351-0627

fyi

Suite Motel

| 12/1-4/21 & 6/8-8/16 | 1P: $89-$129 | 2P: $89-$129 | XP: $10 | F18 |
| 4/22-6/7 & 8/17-11/30 | 1P: $79-$119 | 2P: $79-$119 | XP: $10 | F18 |

Too new to rate, opening scheduled for September 2000. **Location:** I-4, exit 30B, 0.6 mi ne. 5901 Caravan Ct 32819. Fax: 407/351-3317. **Amenities:** 151 units, pets, radios, coffeemakers, microwaves, refrigerators, pool. **Terms:** 3 day cancellation notice-fee imposed, **Cards:** AE, CB, DI, DS, JC, MC, VI.

COUNTRY INN & SUITES

Phone: 407/313-4200

fyi

Motel

| 12/23-8/17 | 1P: $89-$99 | 2P: $89-$99 | XP: $5 | F18 |
| 12/1-12/22 & 8/18-11/30 | 1P: $79-$89 | 2P: $79-$89 | XP: $5 | F18 |

Too new to rate, opening scheduled for July 2000. **Location:** I-4, exit 29/29A (Sand Lake Rd). 7701 Universal Blvd 32819. Fax: 407/313-4201. **Amenities:** 170 units, radios, coffeemakers, microwaves, refrigerators, pool. **Cards:** AE, CB, DI, DS, JC, MC, VI. *(See color ad p 572)*

(See map p. 560)

COURTYARD BY MARRIOTT IN THE MARRIOTT VILLAGE AT LITTLE LAKE BRYAN **Phone: 407/938-9001**

(fyi) All Year   1P: $119-$145   2P: $119-$145

Motel Too new to rate, opening scheduled for September 2000. **Location:** I-4, exit 27, e on 535 to Vineland Ave. 8623 Vineland Ave 32821. Fax: 407/938-9002. **Amenities:** 312 units, restaurant, radios, coffeemakers, refrigerators, pool. **Terms:** cancellation fee imposed. **Cards:** AE, CB, DI, DS, MC, VI. *(See ad below)*

FAIRFIELD INN & SUITES BY MARRIOTT-
INTERNATIONAL COVE   **Phone: 407/351-7000**

(fyi) Under construction, scheduled to open January 2001. **Location:** I-4, exit 29 (Sand Lake Rd), just e, then left. 7495 Canada Ave 32819. Fax: 407/351-0052. **Planned Amenities:** 200 units, radios, coffeemakers, microwaves, re-

Motor Inn frigerators, pool. *(See color ad p 594)*

FAIRFIELD INN BY MARRIOTT IN THE MARRIOTT VILLAGE
AT LITTLE LAKE BRYAN   **Phone: 407/938-9004**

(fyi) All Year   1P: $99-$125   2P: $99-$125

Motel Too new to rate, opening scheduled for September 2000. **Location:** I-4, exit 27, e on 535 to Vineland Ave. 8615 Vineland Ave 32821. Fax: 407/938-9005. **Amenities:** 388 units, restaurant, radios, coffeemakers, refrigerators, pool. **Terms:** cancellation fee imposed. **Cards:** AE, CB, DI, DS, MC, VI.

GUESTHOUSE HOTEL-ORLANDO   **Phone: (407)859-7900**   190

(AAA) (SAVE) 12/21-1/8   1P: $93   2P: $93   XP: $15   F

7/1-11/30   1P: $67   2P: $67   XP: $15   F

(fyi) 12/1-12/20 & 1/9-6/30   1P: $63   2P: $63   XP: $15   F

Motor Inn Under major renovation, scheduled to be completed March 2000. **Last rated:** ♥♥♥ **Location:** Corner of Sand Lake Rd and S Orange Blossom Tr. 7900 S Orange Blossom Tr 32809. Fax: 407/859-7442. **Facility:** 266 units. 2 stories, exterior corridors. **Terms:** 3 day cancellation notice. **Amenities:** irons, hair dryers. **Leisure Activities:** wading pool, exercise room. **Guest Services:** coin laundry. **Business Services:** meeting rooms. **Cards:** AE, CB, DI, DS, MC, VI. **Special Amenities:** free newspaper and preferred room (subject to availability with advanced reservations). *(See color ad below)*

SOME UNITS

(See map p. 560)

SHERATON'S VISTANA VILLAGES
Phone: 407/238-5000

[fyi]
Resort

All Year   1P: $99-$269   2P: $99-$269
Too new to rate, opening scheduled for August 2000. **Location:** Between SR 535 and Central Florida Parkway.
12401 International Dr 32821. **Amenities:** 200 units, restaurant, radios, coffeemakers, microwaves, refrigerators, pool. **Terms:** 3 day cancellation notice. **Cards:** AE, DI, DS, MC, VI. *(See color ad below)*

SLEEP INN AND SUITES
Phone: 407/363-1333
XP: $10   F17

[fyi]
Motel

All Year   1P: $59   2P: $139
Too new to rate, opening scheduled for July 2000. **Location:** I-4, exit 30B, to Major Blvd, then right. 5605 Major
Blvd 32819. Fax: 407/363-4510. **Amenities:** 196 units, radios, coffeemakers, microwaves, refrigerators, pool.
Terms: 3 day cancellation notice-fee imposed. **Cards:** AE, CB, DI, DS, JC, MC, VI.

SPRINGHILL SUITES BY MARRIOTT IN THE MARRIOTT VILLAGE
AT LITTLE LAKE BRYAN
Phone: 407/938-9007

[fyi]
Motel

All Year   1P: $109-$135   2P: $109-$135
Too new to rate, opening scheduled for October 2000. **Location:** I-4, exit 27, s on 535 to Vineland Ave. 8601 Vineland Ave 32821. Fax: 407/938-9008. **Amenities:** 400 units, restaurant, radios, coffeemakers, microwaves, refrigerators, pool. **Terms:** cancellation fee imposed. **Cards:** AE, CB, DI, DS, MC, VI.

STUDIO INN
Phone: (407)313-1000   [168]
XP: $10

[fyi]
Suite Motel

All Year   1P: $79-$129   2P: $89-$139
Under major renovation, scheduled to be completed December 2000. **Last rated:** ◆◆ **Location:** I-4, exit 30B,
1.7 mi n. 4601 S Kirkman Rd 32811. Fax: 407/295-6585. **Facility:** One bedroom apartments. 225 units. 1 two-
bedroom unit and 128 efficiencies. Some suites. 2 stories, exterior corridors. **Terms:** check-in 4 pm, weekly
& monthly rates available, $1 service charge, pets ($50 extra charge). **Amenities:** extended cable TV, voice mail, safes (fee).
Leisure Activities: lighted tennis court, playground, exercise room, shuffleboard, volleyball. **Guest Services:** coin laundry. **Business Services:** meeting rooms. **Cards:** AE, DS, MC, VI.

[ASK] [icons] / [X] [VCR] /   SOME UNITS

(See map p. 560)

———— WHERE TO DINE ————

1-6-8 RESTAURANT
Lunch: $5-$8   **Dinner:** $6-$22   **Phone:** 407/363-1688   189

Chinese

Location: From I-4, just w on Sand Lake Rd (SR 482), just n on Turkey Lake Rd; in Bay Hill Plaza Shopping Center. 7721 Turkey Lake Rd 32819. **Hours:** 11:30 am-10 pm, Fri & Sat-10:30 pm. Closed: 11/22, 12/25. **Features:** casual dress; carryout; beer & wine only; a la carte. More than 40 daily lunch specials featuring Mandarin and Szechuan cuisine attract the local business crowd. Spotless and clean with pleasant, congenial service, this dining room, located in a small shopping mall, displays lovely decorator touches. **Cards:** AE, MC, VI.

AMIGOS
Lunch: $6-$12   **Dinner:** $8-$15   **Phone:** 407/857-3144   172

Mexican

Location: I-4, exit 33, 2 mi s. 6036 S Orange Blossom Trail 32809. **Hours:** 11 am-9:30 pm, Fri & Sat-10 pm, Sun-9 pm. Closed major holidays. **Features:** casual dress; children's menu; carryout; cocktails & lounge; a la carte. A lively crowd keeps the staff moving at a bustling pace to deliver oversized burritos and platefuls of tacos. Casual surroundings and popular Tex-Mex dishes are sure to please the whole family. Order the fajitas for a sizzling, hot sensation. **Cards:** AE, MC, VI.

A TASTE OF JAPAN
Dinner: $11-$24   **Phone:** 407/363-0360   184

Japanese

Location: I-4, exit 29, 0.5 mi nw; in the Bayhill Plaza. 7637 Turkey Lake Rd 32819. **Hours:** 11:30 am-2:30 & 5-10 pm, Sat from 5 pm. Closed: Sun. **Features:** casual dress; children's menu; beer & wine only. Nightly karaoke performances set the mood in this cozy restaurant, where the menu includes sushi, sashimi, noodles, rice, meat and seafood. If you're in the mood to walk a little on the wild side, ask for the separate Japanese menu. **Cards:** AE, MC, VI.

ATLANTIS
Dinner: $27-$35   **Phone:** 407/351-5555   206

Seafood

Location: I-4, exit 28, just e on Central Florida Pkwy, 0.3 mi n or 0.7 mi w of International Dr facing Sea World; in Renaissance Orlando Resort. 6677 Sea Harbor Dr 32821-8092. **Hours:** 6 pm-10 pm. Closed: Sun. **Reservations:** suggested. **Features:** casual dress; cocktails & lounge; fee for valet parking; a la carte. Relax in a lovely formal setting complete with crystal chandeliers and hand-painted murals. Fresh, expertly prepared seafood is offered along with lamb and filet mignon. Savor a glass of wine from a very select list. Resort-casual attire is accepted. **Cards:** AE, CB, DI, DS, JC, MC, VI.

BAHAMA BREEZE
Dinner: $7-$15   **Phone:** 407/248-2499   197

Caribbean

Location: From I-4 exit 29, Sand Lake Rd, 1 mi s. 8849 International Dr 32817. **Hours:** 4 pm-1:30 am, Sun-Tues to midnight. Closed: 11/22, 12/25. **Features:** casual dress; children's menu; cocktails & lounge; entertainment; valet parking; a la carte. Move to an island beat at this popular restaurant featuring Caribbean fare in a tropical decor. Many favorites are offered, including a jerk chicken that gives you a spicy taste of Jamaica. Visit the on-site gift shop for a little after-dinner browsing. **Cards:** AE, DI, DS, MC, VI.

BAJA BURRITO KITCHEN
Lunch: $4-$9   **Dinner:** $4-$9   **Phone:** 407/299-5001   168

Mexican

Location: On w side of SR 435, 1.3 mi n of I-4 exit 30, 2.1 mi n of International Dr; in Kirkman Oaks Center. 4642 Kirkman Rd 32811. **Hours:** 11 am-10 pm, Sun 11:30 am-9 pm. Closed: 4/15, 11/22, 12/25. **Features:** casual dress; children's menu; carryout; beer & wine only; a la carte. Fresh Tex-Mex favorites are prepared hot and fast. Sample a host of toppings at the salsa bar, from fresh tomatoes to very hot habanero salsa and chopped cilantro. Enjoy casual, no-fuss, paper plate dining and savor a nice made-to-order meal. Smoke free premises.

BERGAMO'S ITALIAN RESTAURANT
Dinner: $15-$39   **Phone:** 407/352-3805   186

Italian

Location: I-4, exit 29, just e on Sand Lake Rd, then 0.5 mi s; on west side of Mercado Shopping Village. 8445 International Dr 32819. **Hours:** 5 pm-10 pm, Fri & Sat-11 pm. Closed: 12/25. **Reservations:** suggested. **Features:** casual dress; children's menu; cocktails; entertainment; a la carte. Although the elegant decor might lead you to believe this place is haughty and stiff, you'll quickly notice a more casual and noisy atmosphere pervades. Accomplished vocalists, the servers take turns belting out opera and Broadway tunes at the mic. **Cards:** AE, DI, DS, MC, VI.

THE BLACK SWAN
Dinner: $25-$40   **Phone:** 407/239-1999   208

Continental

Location: I-4, exit 27, 2.3 mi nw on SR 535; in The Villas of Grand Cypress. 1 North Jacaranda 32819. **Hours:** 6 pm-10 pm. **Reservations:** suggested. **Features:** semi-formal attire; cocktails & lounge; entertainment; valet parking; a la carte. Piano music plays while an extensive menu is served in multi-level dining room that overlooks an emerald green golf course. The seared tuna is peppered, sliced thin and tied with orange rind to a tower of scallions. A 16% service charge will be assessed. Smoke free premises. **Cards:** AE, CB, DI, DS, JC, MC, VI.

BOSTON LOBSTER FEAST
Dinner: $10-$27   **Phone:** 407/438-0607   177

Seafood

Location: Se of jct SR 482 (Sand Lake Rd) and US 17-92/441. 8204 Crystal Clear Ln 32809. **Hours:** 4 pm-10 pm, Sat & Sun from 2 pm. **Features:** casual dress; children's menu; early bird specials; buffet; a la carte. Famished after a day of shopping at the Florida Mall? This casual, all-you-can-eat Maine lobster buffet may be just what you need. Lobster, crab, beef, salad and soup are among the many selections served in an inventive, nautical atmosphere. **Cards:** AE, CB, DI, DS, MC, VI.

THE BUTCHER SHOP STEAK HOUSE
Dinner: $16-$31   **Phone:** 407/363-9727   192

Steak & Seafood

Location: I-4, exit 29, just e on Sand Lake Rd, then 0.5 mi s; in Mercado Shopping Village. 8445 International Dr, S-140 32819. **Hours:** 5 pm-10 pm, Fri & Sat-11 pm. Closed: 11/22, 12/25. **Reservations:** suggested. **Features:** casual dress; children's menu; cocktails & lounge. Richly appointed dining rooms decked out in mahogany are the setting for surprisingly informal dining. The menu is primarily charcoal-broiled steak and prime rib ranging in size from an 8-oz filet to a 32-oz bone-in rib. Features a cook-your-own option. **Cards:** AE, CB, DI, DS, JC, MC, VI.

(See map p. 560)

CAFE TU TU TANGO
ⵠⵠⵠ
Ethnic
Lunch: $4-$9 **Dinner:** $4-$9 **Phone:** 407/248-2222 (188)
Location: I-4, exit 29, 1 mi se, just e of International Dr; 0.5 mi s of SR 482 (Sand Lake Rd). 8625 International Dr 32819. **Hours:** 11:30 am-11 pm, Fri & Sat-midnight. Closed: 11/22, 12/25. **Features:** casual dress; children's menu; carryout; cocktails & lounge; entertainment; a la carte. A multiethnic menu that reaches into different parts of the world offers a broad variety of exclusively appetizer-sized dishes. Creativity and flair shows in such specialties as Cajun chicken egg rolls, Barcelona stir-fry and tenderloin skewers. View the works of local artists on display throughout the restaurant. **Cards:** AE, DI, DS, MC, VI. ☒

CAPRICCIO
◈◈
Northern
Italian
Dinner: $12-$25 **Phone:** 407/345-4540 (200)
Location: 0.5 mi n of SR 528 (Bee Line Expwy) opposite Orange County Convention Center; in The Peabody Orlando. 9801 International Dr 32819. **Hours:** 6 pm-11 pm, Sun 11 am-2 & 6-11 pm. **Closed:** Mon. **Reservations:** suggested. **Features:** cocktails & lounge; valet parking; a la carte. Buzzing with a bustling atmosphere, this upscale, casual eatery features an exhibition kitchen with a wood-burning pizza oven. Sunday champagne brunch is popular and offers an abundance of hearty, delicious choices. Choose from a well-rounded wine list. Smoke free premises. **Cards:** AE, DI, DS, JC, MC, VI. ☒

CHARLEY'S STEAK HOUSE
ⵠⵠⵠ
Steak House
Dinner: $12-$26 **Phone:** 407/851-7130 (173)
Location: US 17-92 and 441, 3.8 mi s of jct I-4 exit 33. 6107 S Orange Blossom Tr 32809. **Hours:** 4:30 pm-10 pm, Fri & Sat-11 pm, Sun-10 pm. Closed: 11/22, 12/25. **Reservations:** suggested. **Features:** casual dress; children's menu; salad bar; cocktails & lounge. Specializing in aged steak, chops and chicken grilled over an open flame of oak and orange woods, the casually elegant restaurant offers ample portions and an impressive wine list. Desserts are huge in taste and size, a great value, enough to share for two. **Cards:** AE, MC, VI. ☒

CHARLEY'S STEAK HOUSE
ⵠⵠ
Steak House
Dinner: $13-$35 **Phone:** 407/363-0228 (185)
Location: I-4, exit 29, just e on SR 482 (Sand Lake Rd), then 0.3 mi s. 8255 International Dr 32819. **Hours:** 5 pm-10:30 pm, Fri & Sat-11 pm. Closed: 11/22, 12/25. **Reservations:** suggested. **Features:** casual dress; children's menu; cocktails & lounge; a la carte. Charlie's specializes in steak, chicken and seafood grilled over an open-flame. Five dining rooms with an antique look are available. Peruse the extensive wine list to find the perfect compliment to the 20 ounce filet mignon or the 52 ounce porterhouse steak. **Cards:** AE, MC, VI.

CHARLIE'S LOBSTER HOUSE
ⵠⵠ
Seafood
Dinner: $16-$36 **Phone:** 407/352-6929 (190)
Location: I-4, exit 29, just e on Sand Lake Rd, then just s on International Dr; in the Mercado Shopping Village. 8445 International Dr 32819. **Hours:** 5 pm-10 pm. Closed: 11/22, 12/25. **Reservations:** suggested. **Features:** casual dress; children's menu; carryout; cocktails. New England and fresh Florida seafood are featured along with black Angus beef in this bustling, lively restaurant. This is the place for smothering fresh lobster in melted butter and feasting on delicious side dishes like mashed potatoes and vegetables. **Cards:** AE, DI, DS, MC, VI. ☒

CHATHAM'S PLACE
ⵠⵠⵠ
Continental
Lunch: $7-$17 **Dinner:** $20-$38 **Phone:** 407/345-2992 (175)
Location: I-4, exit 29, 0.5 mi w; opposite Market Place Shopping Ctr. 7575 Dr Phillips Blvd 32819. **Hours:** 11:30 am-2 & 5:30-10 pm. Closed major holidays. **Reservations:** suggested. **Features:** dressy casual; cocktails; entertainment. Relaxed elegance is evoked in the small, intimate dining room where live music is performed nightly and the refined menu boasts a selection of entrees ranging from rack of lamb to fresh black grouper with a pecan butter crust. Smoke free premises. **Cards:** AE, DI, DS, MC, VI. ☒

DELFINO RIVIERA
ⵠⵠⵠⵠ
Northern
Italian
Dinner: $24-$32 **Phone:** 407/503-1000 (159)
Location: I-4, exit 30, just n on SR 435 (Kirkman Rd), then just w via Major Blvd or Vineland Rd at Universal Studios; in Portofino Bay Hotel. 5601 Universal Blvd 32819. **Hours:** 6 pm-10 pm. Closed: Sun & Mon. **Reservations:** suggested. **Features:** dressy casual; children's menu; cocktails & lounge; entertainment; valet parking. Wonderful food in a romantic, quiet, upscale setting. In its menu, service and decor, this restaurant successfully captures the concept of the Portofino Bay Hotel as a credible representation of life on the Italian Riviera. Delightful appetizers and the menu of main items is inviting and excellent. Desserts are truly artful presentations to enjoy. All this, and a roving guitarist/vocalist to create a dining experience to remember. Suggest reservations well in advance. Smoke free premises. **Cards:** AE, CB, DI, DS, JC, MC, VI. ⛨ ☒

DUX
ⵠⵠ ⵠⵠ
Continental
Dinner: $19-$35 **Phone:** 407/352-4000 (201)
Location: 0.5 mi n of SR 528 (Bee Line Expwy) opposite Orange County Convention Center; in The Peabody Orlando. 9801 International Dr 32819. **Hours:** 6 pm-10 pm, Fri & Sat-11 pm. Closed: Sun & 8/1-8/31. **Reservations:** suggested. **Features:** semi-formal attire; cocktails & lounge; valet parking; a la carte. An intimate, elegant dining room and refined service set the scene for traditional cuisine with a creative, international spin. The menu changes seasonally and features dishes like skewered beef in a spicy, tangy sauce. Gentlemen's jackets are suggested. Smoke free premises. **Cards:** AE, CB, DI, DS, JC, MC, VI. ♿ ☒

EMERIL'S RESTAURANT ORLANDO
ⵠⵠⵠ
Creole
Lunch: $18-$22 **Dinner:** $20-$34 **Phone:** 407/224-2424 (150)
Location: In Universal Studios CityWalk. 6000 Universal Blvd, S-702 32819. **Hours:** 11:30 am-2:30 & 5:30-10 pm, Fri & Sat-11 pm. **Reservations:** suggested. **Features:** casual dress; cocktails; fee for parking. You will find a wonderful mix of Old World, Louisiana cooking with the style of today's modern kitchen. From oven-baked pizza to rack of lamb to ham crusted snapper, all dishes are fabulously well-prepared and graciously served in a New Vogue setting. **Cards:** AE, DS, MC, VI. ♿ ☒

EVERGLADES
ⵠⵠⵠ
Regional American
Dinner: $17-$30 **Phone:** 407/996-9840 (198)
Location: I-4, exit 28, just e on SR 528 (Bee Line Expwy) to exit 1 (International Dr), then just n; in Rosen Centre Hotel. 9840 International Dr 32819. **Hours:** 5:30 pm-11 pm. **Reservations:** suggested. **Features:** casual dress; children's menu; cocktails; valet parking; a la carte. A satisfying soup of cherrystone clams with roasted garlic, plum tomatoes and linguica sausage tops the menu. Venison pepper steak, blackened crab cakes with citrus sour cream and gator chowder are also delicious. Please note the 18% gratuity. **Cards:** AE, DI, DS, JC, MC, VI. ☒

(See map p. 560)

FISHBONES
▼▼ ▼▼
Seafood

Dinner: $13-$40   **Phone:** 407/352-0135   [182]
Location: I-4, exit 29, 0.3 mi s; on SR 482. 6707 Sand Lake Rd 32819. **Hours:** 5 pm-10:30 pm, Fri & Sat-11 pm. Closed: 11/22, 12/25. **Reservations:** suggested. **Features:** casual dress; children's menu; cocktails & lounge. Nine dining rooms cast off a nautical personality, with plenty of wood, fishing poles and a big saltwater fish tank. Fresh fish cooked over an open citrus and oak flame, pan-seared sesame tuna and crab-stuffed filet mignon are all good choices. **Cards:** AE, MC, VI.
☒

GAIN'S GERMAN RESTAURANT
▼▼ ▼▼
German

Lunch: $7-$8   **Dinner:** $10-$16   **Phone:** 407/438-8997   [171]
Location: I-4, exit 33, 1.8 mi s; on US 17-92 and 441. 5731 S Orange Blossom Tr 32819. **Hours:** 11:30 am-2:30 & 4:30-10 pm, Fri-11 pm, Sun 4:30-10 pm. Closed: 11/22, 12/25; also 12/24 & Mon. **Reservations:** suggested; Fri & Sat. **Features:** casual dress; early bird specials; carryout; beer & wine only; a la carte. Featuring authentic German cuisine and a homey decor, this pleasant little restaurant also serves a good selection of German draft and bottled beer. **Cards:** AE, DI, DS, MC, VI.
☒

HAIFENG
▼▼▼▼
Chinese

Dinner: $17-$25   **Phone:** 407/351-5555   [205]
Location: I-4, exit 28, just e on Central Florida Pkwy, 0.3 mi n or 0.7 mi w of International Dr facing Sea World; in Renaissance Orlando Resort. 6677 Sea Harbor Dr 32821. **Hours:** 6 pm-10 pm. Closed: Mon. **Reservations:** suggested. **Features:** casual dress; cocktails; a la carte, also prix fixe. Elegant presentation elevates the gourmet Szechwan, Hunan and Mandarin cuisine. Peking duck for two is a crunchy, spicy house specialty. Tableside dessert preparation and unique chocolate-dipped fortune cookies make this a memorable treat. **Cards:** AE, CB, DI, DS, JC, MC, VI.
☒

HEMISPHERE
▼▼ ▼▼
Italian

Dinner: $12-$21   **Phone:** 407/825-1234   [207]
Location: At the Orlando International Airport; in Hyatt Regency Orlando International Airport. 9300 Airport Blvd 32827. **Hours:** 6:30 am-11 & 5:30 pm, Sat 6:30 am-noon & 5:30-10 pm, Sun 6:30 am-noon. **Reservations:** suggested. **Features:** casual dress; children's menu; cocktails & lounge; valet parking; a la carte. Watch planes depart while enjoying a delightful meal in this rich, airy 9th floor dining room overlooking a terminal and runway. A tasteful decor and delicious food are the strong points. Be sure to make a reservation as this restaurant is quite popular. **Cards:** AE, CB, DI, DS, JC, MC, VI.
♿ ☒

ITALIANNI'S RESTAURANT
▼▼ ▼▼
Italian

Lunch: $7-$14   **Dinner:** $9-$20   **Phone:** 407/345-8884   [183]
Location: I-4, exit 29, just e on Sand Lake Rd, then 0.3 mi s. 8148 International Dr 32819. **Hours:** 11:30 am-11 pm. Closed: 11/22. **Reservations:** accepted. **Features:** casual dress; children's menu; carryout; cocktails & lounge. An imaginative chef prepares a good variety of dishes with distinctive flavor. Pizza, pasta, chicken and seafood, such as shrimp fried diablo, are served along with daily specials and wonderful desserts, most notably a chocolate black raspberry cake. **Cards:** AE, CB, DI, DS, MC, VI.
♿ ☒

JACK'S PLACE
🔶 AAA
▼▼ ▼▼
Steak & Seafood

Dinner: $16-$28   **Phone:** 407/996-9700   [199]
Location: I-4, exit 28, just n; from Bee Line Expwy (SR 528), exit 1, then just n; in Clarion Plaza. 9700 International Dr 32819. **Hours:** 5:30 pm-11 pm. **Reservations:** suggested. **Features:** casual dress; cocktails & lounge; valet parking; a la carte. A casually elegant decor features a collection of autographed celebrity caricatures. Excellent cuisine is skillfully prepared, and offered along with list of daily specials. Please note, a service charge of 18% is automatically added to the check. **Cards:** AE, DI, DS, JC, MC, VI.
☒

JIMMY BUFFETT'S MARGARITAVILLE
▼▼ ▼▼
American

Lunch: $5-$10   **Dinner:** $8-$20   **Phone:** 407/224-2155   [151]
Location: In Universal Studios CityWalk. 6000 Universal Blvd, S-704 32819. **Hours:** 11 am-2 am. **Reservations:** required. **Features:** casual dress; children's menu; carryout; cocktails & lounge; entertainment; fee for parking; valet parking. Kick back with a margarita and feast on cheeseburgers in paradise. Island trinkets and twinkling lights decorate a two-story dining room where favorite Buffett tunes are played to set the perfect lazy-day-at-the-beach mood. A must for devoted parrotheads. **Cards:** AE, DS, MC, VI.
♿ ☒

LA PIAZA
▼▼ ▼▼
Italian

Lunch: $5-$7   **Dinner:** $7-$16   **Phone:** 407/855-1170   [209]
Location: From Central Florida Greenway (SR 417) exit 10, 1 mi s on John Young Pkwy; in Colonial Hunter Creek Promenade shopping mall. 4060 Town Center 32837. **Hours:** 11:30 am-9:30 pm; Fri & Sat-10:30 pm. Closed major holidays. **Reservations:** accepted. **Features:** children's menu; cocktails; a la carte. Decorated to resemble the patio of an Italian villa, this restaurant offers delicious food and gracious service. The menu features reliable Italian fare such as pizza, pasta and sandwiches. Simple food preparations make this a pleasant place for lunch. **Cards:** AE, DS, MC, VI.
☒

LARRY'S CEDAR RIVER SEAFOOD
▼▼▼ ▼▼
Seafood

Lunch: $6-$11   **Dinner:** $9-$16   **Phone:** 407/858-0525   [174]
Location: US 17-92 and 441, 2 mi n of Florida Tpke, exit 254; 3 mi s of I-4. 7101 S Orange Blossom Tr 32809. **Hours:** 11 am-9:30 pm, Fri-10:30 pm, Sat 4 pm-10:30 pm. Closed major holidays. **Reservations:** suggested. **Features:** casual dress; children's menu; early bird specials; senior's menu; carryout; cocktails & lounge. Combining the styles of New England and the South, the restaurant is notable for nicely prepared fresh seafood served grilled, fried, broiled, sauteed or blackened. A raw bar entices adventurous palates. If it's not too hot, pay a visit to the patio. **Cards:** AE, DI, DS, MC, VI.
♿ ☒

LATIN QUARTER
▼▼▼ ▼▼
Latino

Lunch: $7-$25   **Dinner:** $7-$25   **Phone:** 407/363-5922   [152]
Location: I-4 exit 29B; in Universal Studios CityWalk. Universal/City Walk S-606 32835. **Hours:** 11 am-2 am. **Features:** fee for parking. Elegant, lively and earthy decor features colorful mosaic tile, strobe lighting and fine table settings. Menu items are light, creative and artistic combining distinct ingredients to pork, lamb, chicken and beef. Get your "mojo" going and dance all night. **Cards:** AE, DI, MC, VI.

(See map p. 560)

LE COQ AU VIN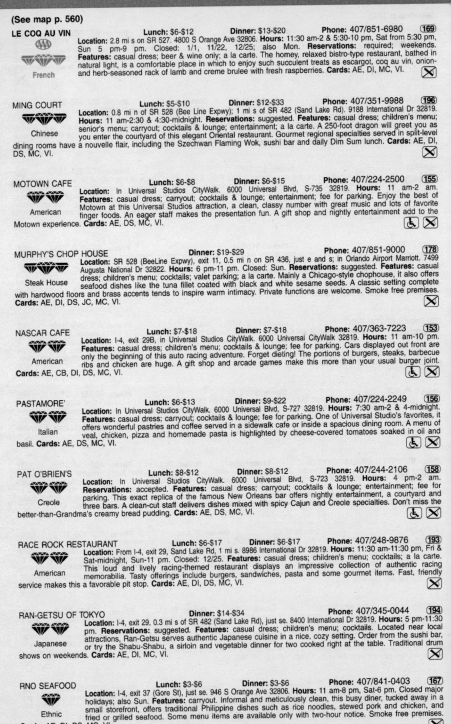
AAA
French
Lunch: $6-$12　**Dinner:** $13-$20　**Phone:** 407/851-6980　169
Location: 2.8 mi s on SR 527. 4800 S Orange Ave 32806. **Hours:** 11:30 am-2 & 5:30-10 pm, Sat from 5:30 pm, Sun 5 pm-9 pm. Closed: 1/1, 11/22, 12/25; also Mon. **Reservations:** required; weekends. **Features:** casual dress; beer & wine only; a la carte. The homey, relaxed bistro-type restaurant, bathed in natural light, is a comfortable place in which to enjoy such succulent treats as escargot, coq au vin, onion- and herb-seasoned rack of lamb and creme brulee with fresh raspberries. **Cards:** AE, DI, MC, VI.

MING COURT
Chinese
Lunch: $5-$10　**Dinner:** $12-$33　**Phone:** 407/351-9988　196
Location: 0.8 mi n of SR 528 (Bee Line Expwy); 1 mi s of SR 482 (Sand Lake Rd). 9188 International Dr 32819. **Hours:** 11 am-2:30 & 4:30-midnight. **Reservations:** suggested. **Features:** casual dress; children's menu; senior's menu; carryout; cocktails & lounge; entertainment; a la carte. A 250-foot dragon will greet you as you enter the courtyard of this elegant Oriental restaurant. Gourmet regional specialties served in split-level dining rooms have a nouvelle flair, including the Szechwan Flaming Wok, sushi bar and daily Dim Sum lunch. **Cards:** AE, DI, DS, MC, VI.

MOTOWN CAFE
American
Lunch: $6-$8　**Dinner:** $6-$15　**Phone:** 407/224-2500　155
Location: In Universal Studios CityWalk. 6000 Universal Blvd, S-735 32819. **Hours:** 11 am-2 am. **Features:** casual dress; carryout; cocktails & lounge; entertainment; fee for parking. Enjoy the best of Motown at this Universal Studios attraction, a clean, classy number with great music and lots of favorite finger foods. An eager staff makes the presentation fun. A gift shop and nightly entertainment add to the Motown experience. **Cards:** AE, DS, MC, VI.

MURPHY'S CHOP HOUSE
Steak House
Dinner: $19-$29　**Phone:** 407/851-9000　178
Location: SR 528 (BeeLine Expwy), exit 11, 0.5 mi n on SR 436, just e and s; in Orlando Airport Marriott. 7499 Augusta National Dr 32822. **Hours:** 6 pm-11 pm. Closed: Sun. **Reservations:** suggested. **Features:** casual dress; children's menu; cocktails; valet parking; a la carte. Mainly a Chicago-style chophouse, it also offers seafood dishes like the tuna fillet coated with black and white sesame seeds. A classic setting complete with hardwood floors and brass accents tends to inspire warm intimacy. Private functions are welcome. Smoke free premises. **Cards:** AE, DI, DS, JC, MC, VI.

NASCAR CAFE
American
Lunch: $7-$18　**Dinner:** $7-$18　**Phone:** 407/363-7223　153
Location: I-4, exit 29B, in Universal Studios CityWalk. 6000 Universal CityWalk 32819. **Hours:** 11 am-10 pm. **Features:** casual dress; children's menu; cocktails & lounge; fee for parking. Cars displayed out front are only the beginning of this auto racing adventure. Forget dieting! The portions of burgers, steaks, barbecue ribs and chicken are huge. A gift shop and arcade games make this more than your usual burger joint. **Cards:** AE, CB, DI, DS, MC, VI.

PASTAMORE'
Italian
Lunch: $6-$13　**Dinner:** $9-$22　**Phone:** 407/224-2249　156
Location: In Universal Studios CityWalk. 6000 Universal Blvd, S-727 32819. **Hours:** 7:30 am-2 & 4-midnight. **Features:** casual dress; carryout; cocktails & lounge; fee for parking. One of Universal Studio's favorites, it offers wonderful pastries and coffee served in a sidewalk cafe or inside a spacious dining room. A menu of veal, chicken, pizza and homemade pasta is highlighted by cheese-covered tomatoes soaked in oil and basil. **Cards:** AE, DS, MC, VI.

PAT O'BRIEN'S
Creole
Lunch: $8-$12　**Dinner:** $8-$12　**Phone:** 407/244-2106　158
Location: In Universal Studios CityWalk. 6000 Universal Blvd, S-723 32819. **Hours:** 4 pm-2 am. **Reservations:** accepted. **Features:** casual dress; carryout; cocktails & lounge; entertainment; fee for parking. This exact replica of the famous New Orleans bar offers nightly entertainment, a courtyard and three bars. A clean-cut staff delivers dishes mixed with spicy Cajun and Creole specialties. Don't miss the better-than-Grandma's creamy bread pudding. **Cards:** AE, DS, MC, VI.

RACE ROCK RESTAURANT
American
Lunch: $6-$17　**Dinner:** $6-$17　**Phone:** 407/248-9876　193
Location: From I-4, exit 29, Sand Lake Rd, 1 mi s. 8986 International Dr 32819. **Hours:** 11:30 am-11:30 pm, Fri & Sat-midnight, Sun-11 pm. Closed: 12/25. **Features:** casual dress; children's menu; cocktails; a la carte. This loud and lively racing-themed restaurant displays an impressive collection of authentic racing memorabilia. Tasty offerings include burgers, sandwiches, pasta and some gourmet items. Fast, friendly service makes this a favorable pit stop. **Cards:** AE, DI, DS, MC, VI.

RAN-GETSU OF TOKYO
Japanese
Dinner: $14-$34　**Phone:** 407/345-0044　194
Location: I-4, exit 29, 0.3 mi s of SR 482 (Sand Lake Rd), just se. 8400 International Dr 32819. **Hours:** 5 pm-11:30 pm. **Reservations:** suggested. **Features:** casual dress; children's menu; cocktails. Located near local attractions, Ran-Getsu serves authentic Japanese cuisine in a nice, cozy setting. Order from the sushi bar, or try the Shabu-Shabu, a sirloin and vegetable dinner for two cooked right at the table. Traditional drum shows on weekends. **Cards:** AE, DI, MC, VI.

RNO SEAFOOD
Ethnic
Lunch: $3-$6　**Dinner:** $3-$6　**Phone:** 407/841-0403　167
Location: I-4, exit 37 (Gore St), just se. 946 S Orange Ave 32806. **Hours:** 11 am-8 pm, Sat-6 pm. Closed major holidays; also Sun. **Features:** carryout. Informal and meticulously clean, this busy diner, tucked away in a small storefront, offers traditional Philippine dishes such as rice noodles, stewed pork and chicken, and fried or grilled seafood. Some menu items are available only with two-hour notice. Smoke free premises. **Cards:** AE, DI, DS, MC, VI.

(See map p. 560)

SHAMIANA
◆
East Indian

Lunch: $4-$9   **Dinner:** $9-$15   **Phone:** 407/354-1160   [181]
Location: I-4, exit 29E (Sand Lake Rd), just n on International Dr; in small shopping plaza. 7040 International Dr 32819. **Hours:** noon-3 & 5-11 pm, Sat from 5 pm. Closed: 7/4, 11/22, 12/24; also Tues. **Reservations:** suggested. **Features:** beer & wine only; a la carte. A far-ranging menu offers popular East Indian fare as well as Tandoori selections. Spicy flavors can be adjusted to suit the tastes of the uninitiated. Vegetarian dishes are available, and a wonderful flat bread is served with the meal. **Cards:** AE, DI, DS, MC, VI.
[X]

SIAM ORCHID
AAA
▼▼▼
Thai

Dinner: $10-$18   **Phone:** 407/351-0821   [179]
Location: I-4, exit 29, 0.5 mi e on SR 482 (Sand Lake Rd), 0.3 mi n. 7575 Universal Blvd 32819. **Hours:** 5 pm-11 pm. Closed major holidays. **Reservations:** suggested; weekends. **Features:** casual dress; carryout; cocktails & lounge; a la carte. Fine khundoke, or "sit-on-the-floor" style dining in a subdued, relaxing atmosphere. Thai and other Oriental specialties are the focus, including Baddthai pot pie filled with rice, noodles, vegetables, shrimp and crabmeat. Also whole, deep-fried snapper. **Cards:** AE, CB, DS, MC, VI.
[X]

VITO'S CHOP HOUSE
▼▼▼
Steak House

Dinner: $14-$33   **Phone:** 407/354-2467   [187]
Location: I-4, exit 29, just e, then 1 mi s. 8633 International Dr 32821. **Hours:** 5 pm-10:30 pm, Fri & Sat-11 pm. Closed: 11/22, 12/25. **Reservations:** accepted. **Features:** dressy casual; children's menu; cocktails & lounge. Wonderful class operation with touches of Tuscany. Comfortable masculine decor, ample portions of double thick veal chops that are tender all the way through, expansive wine list and don't forget the key lime pie. **Cards:** AE, MC, VI.
[f] [X]

WILD JACK'S STEAKS & BBQ
▼▼▼
American

Dinner: $10-$22   **Phone:** 407/352-4407   [180]
Location: On International Dr; 0.3 mi n of Sandlake Rd (SR 482); 0.5 mi ne of I-4, exit 29. 7364 International Dr 32819. **Hours:** 4 pm-10 pm, Fri & Sat-10:30 pm. **Reservations:** accepted. **Features:** casual dress; children's menu; carryout; cocktails & lounge. Antler-rack chandeliers, exposed beam ceilings and simulated animal hide seats evoke the rustic air of the Old West. Servers in jeans and plaid shirts or deputy uniforms and badges serve such dishes as a well-seasoned chili-crusted New York strip. **Cards:** AE, CB, DI, DS, MC, VI.
[&] [X]

———— *The following restaurants have not been evaluated by AAA* ————
but are listed for your information only.

BOB MARLEY-A TRIBUTE TO FREEDOM
[fyi]

Phone: 407/224-2262
Not evaluated. **Location:** I-4, exit 29B; in Universal Studios CityWalk. Universal Studios. **Features:** Popular, lively reggae dance club set in replica of Bob Marley's home. Light Jamaican influenced menu available.

CHRISTINI'S
[fyi]

Phone: 407/345-8770
Not evaluated. **Location:** I-4, exit 29, 0.5 mi w; in Marketplace Shopping Center. 7600 Dr Phillips Blvd 32819. **Features:** Famous for their 26 ounce veal chop, Christini's also makes their own fresh pasta. Menu selections include shrimp diablo, veal with four cheeses and calamari. Italian art and a strolling accordionist add charm to a friendly, though bustling atmosphere.

CITYJAZZ
[fyi]

Phone: 407/224-2189
Not evaluated. **Location:** I-4, exit 29B; in Universal Studios CityWalk. Universal Studios. **Features:** Best jazz Orlando has to offer! Light menu offers appetizers, drinks, coffees and cigars. Open nightly.

The Orlando Vicinity

ALTAMONTE SPRINGS pop. 34,900   (See map p. 554; index p. 558)

———— **WHERE TO STAY** ————

BEST WESTERN ALTAMONTE SPRINGS
AAA [SAVE]
▼▼▼
Motel

2/1-3/31	1P: $85-$99	**Phone:** (407)862-8200 [103]
12/1-1/31 & 4/1-11/30	1P: $75	

Location: I-4, exit 4B, just nw. 150 Douglas Ave 32714. Fax: 07/862-5750. **Facility:** Pleasant accommodations featuring modern style decor with a lush courtyard setting. 144 units. *Bath:* combo or shower only. 3 stories, exterior corridors. **Amenities:** extended cable TV, voice mail, irons, hair dryers. **Leisure Activities:** exercise room. **Guest Services:** [ECP] meal plan available, complimentary evening beverages: Mon, coin laundry. **Business Services:** meeting rooms. **Cards:** AE, CB, DI, DS, JC, MC, VI.
SOME UNITS
[SD] [▯] [&] [⟲] [⟳] [☀] [📷] [⊟] [▣] [⊞] [🖥] [🅗] [DATA PORT] /[X]/

CANDLEWOOD SUITES
▼▼▼
Extended Stay Motel

All Year	1P: $69-$89 2P: $89-$109	**Phone:** (407)767-5757 [99]

Location: I-4, exit 48, just w to Douglas Ave, 0.8 mi n to Central Pkwy, just e. 644 Raymond Ave 32701. Fax: 407/767-0097. **Facility:** Office hours 7 am-8 pm; 10 am-6 pm weekends. No after hours walk-ins. 122 efficiencies. Some suites. *Bath:* combo or shower only. 3 stories, interior corridors. **Terms:** weekly & monthly rates available. **Amenities:** CD players, voice mail, irons, hair dryers. **Leisure Activities:** exercise room. **Guest Services:** complimentary laundry. **Business Services:** administrative services. **Cards:** AE, CB, DI, DS, JC, MC, VI.
SOME UNITS
[ASK] [SD] [&] [⟲] [⟳] [☀] [VCR] [⊟] [▣] [⊞] [🖥] [DATA PORT] /[X]/

(See map p. 554)

EMBASSY SUITES ORLANDO NORTH
Phone: (407)834-2400 **104**

▽▼▽▼▽▼ Suite Hotel

All Year   1P: $99-$153   2P: $99-$153
Location: I-4, exit 48, 0.3 mi e on SR 436, just n on North Lake Blvd. 225 E Altamonte Dr 32701. Fax: 407/834-2117. **Facility:** Landscaped atrium with waterfall. 1-bedroom suites with separate living room and 2 TV's; some with walkout balcony. 277 units. Some suites. *Bath:* combo or shower only. 4-7 stories, interior corridors. **Terms:** package plans, pets ($15 fee). **Amenities:** voice mail, irons, hair dryers. **Leisure Activities:** heated pool, sauna, whirlpool, steamroom, exercise room. **Guest Services:** [BP] meal plan available, gift shop, complimentary evening beverages, area transportation, coin laundry. **Business Services:** conference facilities, fax. **Cards:** AE, CB, DI, DS, JC, MC, VI.
(See color ad starting on p 592)

SOME UNITS

ASK 🛏 🍴 🍽 🕎 🏃 🚭 🌀 🚤 🎥 🖨 💻 📷 📶 DATA PORT /✕/
FEE

HAMPTON INN
Phone: (407)869-9000 **101**

AAA SAVE
▽▼▽▼▽▼ Motel

2/11-3/11   1P: $88-$139
3/12-7/7   1P: $88-$129
7/8-11/30   1P: $89-$99
12/1-2/10   1P: $85-$95
Location: I-4, exit 48, just nw. 151 N Douglas Ave 32714. Fax: 407/869-9870. **Facility:** Attractively landscaped courtyard. Social activities each evening. 210 units. *Bath:* combo or shower only. 2 stories, exterior corridors. **Terms:** pets ($60 extra charge). **Amenities:** video games, voice mail, irons, hair dryers. **Leisure Activities:** heated pool, whirlpool, exercise room. **Guest Services:** [ECP] meal plan available, coin laundry. **Business Services:** meeting rooms, administrative services. **Cards:** AE, CB, DI, DS, MC, VI. **Special Amenities:** free continental breakfast and free local telephone calls.

SOME UNITS

SD 🛏 🍴 🏃 🚭 🌀 🚤 🎥 🖨 💻 📷 DATA PORT /✕/
FEE

HILTON ORLANDO/ALTAMONTE SPRINGS
Phone: (407)830-1985 **108**

SAVE
▽▼▽▼▽▼ Hotel

1/1-4/30   1P: $130-$170   2P: $140-$180   XP: $10   F18
5/1-11/30   1P: $120-$160   2P: $130-$170   XP: $10   F18
12/1-12/31   1P: $125-$150   2P: $135-$160   XP: $10   F18
Location: I-4, exit 48, just e on SR 436, then 0.5 mi s. 350 S North Lake Blvd 32715. Fax: 407/331-2911. **Facility:** Convenient to large regional mall. 322 units. Some suites ($295-$500). *Bath:* combo or shower only. 8 stories, interior corridors. **Terms:** package plans. **Amenities:** voice mail, irons, hair dryers. **Leisure Activities:** heated pool, whirlpool, exercise room. **Guest Services:** [CP] meal plan available, gift shop, valet laundry. *Fee:* area transportation. **Business Services:** conference facilities, fax. **Cards:** AE, CB, DI, DS, JC, MC, VI. *(See ad p 44)*

SOME UNITS

SD ✈ 🍴 🍽 🕎 🏃 🚭 🌀 🚤 🎥 🖨 💻 📷 DATA PORT /✕/
FEE   FEE

HOLIDAY INN OF ALTAMONTE SPRINGS
Phone: (407)862-4455 **105**

AAA SAVE
▽▼▽▼▽▼ Motor Inn

All Year   1P: $99-$119   2P: $99-$119
Location: I-4, exit 48, just sw. 230 W Hwy 436 32714. Fax: 407/682-5982. **Facility:** Attractive pool courtyard and very inviting rooms. 263 units. Some suites ($109-$119) and whirlpool units ($149-$169). *Bath:* combo or shower only. 4 stories, interior/exterior corridors. **Terms:** check-in 4 pm, package plans. **Amenities:** extended cable TV, video games, voice mail, irons, hair dryers. **Dining:** restaurant, 6 am-2 & 5-10 pm, poolside dining terrace, $7-$20, cocktails, entertainment. **Leisure Activities:** exercise room. **Guest Services:** area transportation-within 5 mi, coin laundry. **Business Services:** conference facilities. **Cards:** AE, CB, DI, DS, JC, MC, VI. **Special Amenities:** free newspaper and free room upgrade (subject to availability with advanced reservations).

SOME UNITS

SD 🍴 🍽 🏃 🚭 🌀 🚤 🎥 🖨 💻 📷 DATA PORT /✕/
FEE

HOMESTEAD VILLAGE GUEST STUDIOS
Phone: 407/332-9300 **106**

▽▼▽▼▽▼ Extended Stay Motel

All Year   1P: $69
Location: I-4, exit 48, just e, then 0.3 mi s. 302 S Northlake Blvd 32701 (571 Kings Castle Dr, ORANGE CITY, 32763). Fax: 407/332-9330. **Facility:** Office hours 7 am-9 pm, Saturday 9 am-5 pm, Sunday noon-8 pm. Attendant on duty 24 hours. 135 efficiencies. *Bath:* combo or shower only. 3 stories, interior corridors. **Terms:** cancellation fee imposed. Additional housekeeping services, $15 extra charge, pets ($75 extra charge). **Amenities:** voice mail, irons. **Guest Services:** coin laundry. **Cards:** AE, CB, DI, DS, MC, VI.

SOME UNITS

🛏 🏃 🚭 🌀 🚤 📶 🎥 🖨 💻 📷 DATA PORT /✕/

LA QUINTA INN-ORLANDO NORTH
Phone: (407)788-1411 **107**

SAVE
▽▼▽▼▽▼ Motel

All Year   1P: $65-$89   2P: $65-$89
Location: I-4, exit 48, 0.3 mi w, just s of SR 436. 150 S Westmonte Dr 32714. Fax: 407/788-6472. **Facility:** Hacienda style architecture. Very attractive patio/courtyard with fountain, pool and lush landscaping. Some rooms are modest in size. 115 units. *Bath:* combo or shower only. 2 stories, exterior corridors. **Terms:** check-in 4 pm, small pets only. **Amenities:** video games, voice mail. **Leisure Activities:** heated pool. **Guest Services:** [CP] meal plan available, valet laundry. **Business Services:** meeting rooms. **Cards:** AE, CB, DI, DS, MC, VI. *(See color ad p 604)*

SOME UNITS

SD 🛏 🍴 🏃 🚭 🌀 🚤 🎥 💻 DATA PORT /✕/ 🍽 🖨
FEE

RESIDENCE INN BY MARRIOTT
Phone: (407)788-7991 **100**

▽▼▽▼▽▼ Apartment

All Year   1P: $94-$139   2P: $94-$139
Location: I-4, exit 48, just w on SR 436, just n. 270 Douglas Ave 32714. Fax: 407/869-5468. **Facility:** One- and two-bedroom suites with living room and kitchen, some with fireplace, in cluster buildings on landscaped grounds. 128 units with kitchen. 32 two-bedroom units. Some suites. *Bath:* combo or shower only. 2 stories, exterior corridors. **Terms:** pets ($150 fee, $5 extra charge). **Amenities:** extended cable TV, voice mail, irons, hair dryers. **Leisure Activities:** heated pool, whirlpools, sports court. **Guest Services:** [ECP] meal plan available, complimentary evening beverages Mon-Thurs, coin laundry. **Business Services:** meeting rooms. **Cards:** AE, CB, DI, DS, JC, MC, VI.

SOME UNITS

ASK SD 🛏 🍴 🍽 🏃 🚭 🌀 🚤 📶 🎥 🖨 💻 📷 DATA PORT /✕/

(See map p. 554)

SPRINGHILL SUITES BY MARRIOTT ORLANDO/ALTAMONTE SPRINGS   Phone: (407)865-6400   [102]

▼▼▼▼ 2/1-3/31   1P: $99
       12/1-1/31 & 4/1-11/30   1P: $89
Suite Motel   **Location:** I-4, exit 48, just w. 205 W Hwy 436 32714. **Fax:** 407/865-6773. **Facility:** 91 units. *Bath:* combo or shower only. 4 stories, interior corridors. **Amenities:** dual phone lines, voice mail, irons, hair dryers. **Leisure Activities:** small heated indoor pool, whirlpool, exercise room. **Guest Services:** [ECP] meal plan available, coin laundry. **Business Services:** meeting rooms. **Cards:** AE, CB, DI, DS, MC, VI.

SOME UNITS

---------- **WHERE TO DINE** ----------

AMIGOS   **Lunch:** $6-$7   **Dinner:** $6-$12   Phone: 407/774-4334   [69]
▼▼ ▼▼   **Location:** Just n of SR 436, 0.5 mi w of jct I-4 exit 48. 120 N Westmonte Dr 32714. **Hours:** 11 am-9:30 pm, Fri & Sat-10 pm, Sun-9 pm. Closed major holidays. **Features:** casual dress; children's menu; carryout; cocktails; a la carte. Very popular on weekends, this Tex-Mex style of dining is enjoyed in an establishment decorated with license-plates and Mexican curios. Your favorite Tex-Mex entrees overflow the plates, so grab a pitcher of margaritas, and settle down to a hearty meal. **Cards:** AE, MC, VI.
Mexican

AMIRA'S   **Lunch:** $5-$8   **Dinner:** $5-$13   Phone: 407/831-0999   [74]
▼▼   **Location:** Between CR 427 and US 17-92 on SR 436. 1349 E Altamonte Dr 32701. **Closed:** All Jewish holidays, Passover week & Sat. **Features:** casual dress; Sunday brunch; children's menu; carryout. A kosher deli with an adjoining market, it serves a wide range of deli sandwiches, plus specialties like falafel, humus, chopped liver and stuffed cabbage rolls. Prompt, friendly service and homemade soups make this a takeout lover's paradise. Smoke free premises. **Cards:** AE, DS, MC, VI.
Ethnic

BAHAMA BREEZE   **Dinner:** $7-$18   Phone: 407/831-2929   [72]
▼▼ ▼▼   **Location:** I-4, exit 48, 1.5 mi e. 499 E Altamonte Dr 32701. **Hours:** 4 pm-1:30 am, Sun-Tues to midnight. **Features:** casual dress; children's menu; carryout; cocktails & lounge; entertainment. Capturing the sights, sounds and sensations of the Caribbean, Bahama Breeze caters to those seeking an exciting evening out. In addition to delicious food such as fresh mahi-mahi and Key Lime pie, there is a full bar, retail shop and live entertainment. **Cards:** AE, CB, DI, DS, MC, VI.
Caribbean

BAJA BURRITO KITCHEN   **Lunch:** $4-$8   **Dinner:** $4-$8   Phone: 407/788-2252   [67]
▼▼   **Location:** 1 mi n of jct SR 434 and 436; Jamestown Place. 931 N SR 434 32714. **Hours:** 11 am-10 pm, Sun 11:30 am-9 pm. **Closed:** 11/22, 12/25. **Features:** casual dress; carryout; beer & wine only. A salsa bar offers an impressive array of fresh choices, from basic chopped tomatoes to very hot habanero salsa. Fast, walk-up counter service provides good food made to order at this friendly shop tucked into a strip mall.
Mexican

BANGKOK RESTAURANT   **Lunch:** $4-$7   **Dinner:** $7-$12   Phone: 407/788-2685   [66]
AAA   **Location:** Just n of jct SR 436 and Douglas Ave, just w and n of jct I-4 exit 48. 260 Douglas Ave 32714. **Hours:** 11:30 am-3 & 5-11 pm. **Closed:** Sun. **Features:** casual dress; carryout; beer & wine only; a la carte, also prix fixe. Reasonably priced Thai cuisine is colorfully presented and offered with hot, spicy or mild options. Smooth, consistent service and a convenient location are highlights. Order beef and vegetables with won-ton soup for an authentic Thai meal. **Cards:** AE, DI, DS, MC, VI.
▼▼ ▼▼
Ethnic

FIRST WATCH   **Lunch:** $5-$7   Phone: 407/682-2315   [71]
▼▼   **Location:** I-4, exit 48, nw; in Ethan Allen Plaza. 249 W SR 436 32714. **Hours:** 7 am-2:30 pm. **Closed:** 11/22, 12/25. **Features:** casual dress; children's menu; carryout. This eatery serves breakfast and lunch, from traditional eggs and omelets to waffles and crepes. Pancakes fill the entire plate and are topped with fresh fruits and syrup. Great salad, soups and sandwiches are featured to satisfy the busy lunch crowd. Smoke free premises. **Cards:** AE, DS, MC, VI.
American

KOHINOOR INDIAN RESTAURANT   **Lunch:** $7   **Dinner:** $8-$15   Phone: 407/788-6004   [68]
▼▼ ▼▼   **Location:** 0.3 mi w of jct I-4 and SR 436; in Ethan Allen Plaza. 249 W SR 436 32714. **Hours:** 11:30 am-2:30 & 5-10 pm, Fri & Sat-10 pm, Sun 5 pm-10 pm. **Closed:** Mon. **Reservations:** accepted. **Features:** semi-formal attire; beer & wine only; a la carte. Partake of expertly prepared Indian cuisine made with fine ingredients and fresh spices. The mixed tandoori platter offers a chance to sample all the meats cooked in the tandor oven. Freshly made mango ice cream for dessert makes this a worthy venture. Korma dishes are the specialty. **Cards:** AE, DS, MC, VI.
Ethnic

LA SCALA RISTORANTE   **Lunch:** $10-$15   **Dinner:** $16-$35   Phone: 407/862-3257   [65]
AAA   **Location:** I-4, exit 48, just w on SR 436, 0.3 mi n on Douglas Ave. 205 Loraine Dr 32714. **Hours:** 11:30 am-2 & 5:30-10:30 pm. Closed major holidays; also Sun except 4/23 & 5/14. **Features:** semi-formal attire; cocktails; a la carte. Expect Old World congeniality in an elegant, upscale, European setting. You can look forward to something new and intriguing on each visit. Among the very nicely presented dishes are melon and prosciutto ham, and salmon in a tomato, onion and caper sauce. **Cards:** AE, DI, MC, VI.
▼▼ ▼▼
Italian

MAISON & JARDIN   **Dinner:** $20-$35   Phone: 407/862-4410   [70]
AAA   **Location:** I-4, exit 48, just w on SR 436, then 0.5 mi s. 430 S Wymore Rd 32714. **Hours:** 6 pm-10 pm, Sun 11 am-2 & 6-9 pm. Closed major holidays; also Sun 6/28-9/27. **Reservations:** suggested. **Features:** semi-formal attire; Sunday brunch; children's menu; cocktails & lounge; a la carte. Expect an elegant, candlelit meal in a secluded Mediterranean villa and service that caters to your every whim. A variety of fresh seafood, prime beef, veal, lamb and wild game is prepared with a French-continental flair. The wine list is extensive. **Cards:** AE, CB, DI, DS, MC, VI.
▼▼ ▼▼
Continental

(See map p. 554)

STRAUB'S FINE SEAFOOD RESTAURANT   Dinner: $12-$22   Phone: 407/831-2250   [73]

♦♦♦   **Location:** SR 436; 0.8 mi e of jct I-4 exit 48. 512 E Altamonte Dr 32701. **Hours:** 4:30 pm-10 pm, Fri & Sat-11 pm.
Seafood   **Closed:** 7/4, 11/22, 12/25. **Reservations:** suggested. **Features:** casual dress; children's menu; early bird
specials; carryout; cocktails. Cajun and mesquite-grilled seafood entrees are the main attraction here, with
beef, chicken and pasta dishes also offered. Friendly, efficient service and delicious food make this a
winning experience that brings guests back time and time again. **Cards:** AE, DI, DS, MC, VI.   [X]

APOPKA pop. 13,500   (See map p. 554; index p. 558)

──────── **WHERE TO STAY** ────────

CROSBY'S MOTOR INN   Phone: (407)886-3220   [90]

♦♦♦♦   12/1-5/1 & 9/29-11/30   1P: $59-$69   2P: $69-$79   XP: $10   F
5/2-9/28   1P: $49   2P: $59   XP: $10   F
Motel   **Location:** 1.8 mi nw on US 441. 1440 W Orange Blossom Tr Hwy 441 32712. Fax: 407/886-7458. **Facility:**
location. 61 units, 14 with kitchen. Some whirlpool units ($100-$125). *Bath:* combo, shower or tub only. 2 stories, exterior corridors. **Terms:** 7 day cancellation notice, weekly rates available, small pets only ($10 extra charge). **Guest Serv-
ices:** coin laundry. **Cards:** AE, MC, VI.

SOME UNITS
[🐄] [⚓] [📷] / [X] [📠] [📶] /

DAYS INN   Phone: (407)880-3800   [89]

[SAVE]   2/1-4/15   1P: $45-$99   2P: $49-$99
4/16-11/30   1P: $39-$89   2P: $39-$89
♦♦♦   12/1-1/31   1P: $35-$85   2P: $39-$89
Motel   **Location:** On US 441, 0.5 mi w of Park Ave. 228 W Main St 32703. Fax: 407/884-0690. **Facility:** 59 units. 2 stories, exterior corridors. **Terms:** cancellation fee imposed, weekly rates available. **Amenities:** extended cable
TV. **Leisure Activities:** heated pool. **Cards:** AE, DI, DS, MC, VI.

SOME UNITS
[S/D] [⚓] [📷] / [X] [📶] [📠] /

HOWARD JOHNSON EXPRESS INN   Phone: (407)886-1010   [92]

(AAA) [SAVE]   All Year   1P: $69-$99   2P: $74-$104   XP: $5   F12
♦♦♦ ♦♦   **Location:** On US 441; 1.5 mi s of jct SR 436. 1317 S Orange Blossom Tr 32703. Fax: 407/886-1010. **Facility:** 32
Motel   units. *Bath:* combo or shower only. 2 stories, exterior corridors. **Terms:** 3 day cancellation notice-fee imposed. **Cards:** AE, CB, DI, DS, MC, VI. **Special Amenities:** early check-in/late check-out and free room
upgrade (subject to availability with advanced reservations).

SOME UNITS
[S/D] [♿] [⚓] [📷] [📠] [💻] [DATA PORT] / [X] [📶] [📠] /

──────── **WHERE TO DINE** ────────

CATFISH PLACE OF APOPKA   Lunch: $5-$8   Dinner: $7-$16   Phone: 407/889-7980   [60]

♦♦♦ ♦♦   **Location:** Hwy 441 and Forest Ave; across from Chamber of Commerce. 311 S Forest Ave 32703. **Hours:** 11 am-9
pm, Fri & Sat-10 pm. **Features:** casual dress; children's menu; early bird specials; carryout; beer & wine
Steak & Seafood   only. Sample crispy fried catfish at this aptly named, fish camp-style favorite. A simple menu features
well-seasoned, boneless or fingerling catfish, chunky clam chowder, creamy coleslaw and crunchy hush
puppies. Take out dinners are available. **Cards:** DS, MC, VI.   [X]

CASSELBERRY pop. 18,800   (See map p. 554; index p. 559)

──────── **WHERE TO DINE** ────────

ALADDIN'S CAFE   Lunch: $8   Dinner: $13   Phone: 407/331-0488   [122]

♦♦♦   **Location:** On SR 436, 1 mi se of US 17-92. 1015 E Semoran Blvd 32707. **Hours:** 11:30 am-10 pm, Fri-11 pm,
Sat 4 pm-11 pm. Closed major holidays; also Sun. **Reservations:** suggested. **Features:** casual dress;
Ethnic   carryout; beer & wine only; buffet. Freshly made kabobs with rice, tabbouleh, falafel and baklava are
among the samplings of traditional Middle Eastern cuisine, primarily of the Lebanese persuasion, served at
this small and cozy restaurant. The dinner buffet is especially popular. **Cards:** AE, DI, DS, MC, VI.   [X]

COLORADO FONDUE COMPANY   Dinner: $10-$25   Phone: 407/767-8232   [123]

♦♦♦ ♦♦   **Location:** SR 436 and Red Bug Lake Rd; in Goodings Plaza. 1016 E Semoran Blvd 32707. **Hours:** 5:30 pm-9 pm,
Sat & Sun 5 pm-10 pm. Closed: 11/22, 12/25. **Reservations:** suggested. **Features:** casual dress;
American   children's menu; cocktail lounge; beer & wine only. Elegant touches like grapevine-shaped wine bottle
holders set a romantic tone. A menu of mixed fondue and hot-rock table cooking, its taste comes from an
array of dipping sauces. Meals with fresh ingredients and a warm welcome make this a good night out. **Cards:** AE, DI, DS,
MC, VI.   [X]

ROLANDO'S CUBAN RESTAURANT   Lunch: $4-$6   Dinner: $7-$18   Phone: 407/767-9677   [121]

♦♦♦   **Location:** SR 436, 1.3 mi se of US 17-92. 870 E Semoran Blvd 32707. **Hours:** 11 am- 8:45 pm, Fri & Sat-9:45
pm, Sun 1 pm-7:45 pm. Closed: 1/1, 12/24, 12/25; also Mon. **Features:** casual dress; carryout; beer &
Cuban   wine only. Simple textured walls and basic decor belie the sumptuous offerings of this casual
establishment. Try the Cuban sandwich or picadillo for lunch, or take advantage of an extensive dinner
menu that tempts with tamales, fried eggplant and sweet plantains. **Cards:** AE, DI, MC, VI.   [X]

(See map p. 554)

WHISKEY CREEK STEAKHOUSE   **Lunch:** $5-$10   **Dinner:** $8-$18   **Phone:** 407/834-3385   120

Steak House

Location: US 17-92, 1.5 mi n of SR 436. 3385 US 17-92 (Orlando Ave) 32707. **Hours:** 11 am-10 pm, Fri & Sat-11 pm, Sun noon-9 pm. Closed: 11/22, 12/25. **Features:** casual dress; children's menu; carryout; cocktails & lounge. Quality and a bit of creativity can be found in the preparation of oak-fired prime rib, smoked "loaded" chicken, and a colossal onion bloom served with a spicy horseradish sauce. A friendly, pleasant atmosphere and good service make this a popular spot. **Cards:** AE, DI, DS, MC, VI.

***The following restaurant has not been evaluated by AAA
but is listed for your information only.***

CYPRIANA   **Phone:** 407/834-8088

fyi

Not evaluated. Location: SR 436, just n of Red Bug Lake Rd. 505 Semoran Blvd. **Features:** Very good food in a bustling atmosphere is enhanced by a strolling guitarist. Traditional Moussaka of potatoes and eggplant layered with meat sauce is wonderful, combination dinners with gyros too.

CELEBRATION

——— WHERE TO STAY ———

CELEBRATION HOTEL   **Phone:** (407)566-6000

Hotel

| All Year | 1P: $165-$295 | 2P: $165-$295 | XP: $20 | F17 |

Location: I-4, exit 25, just w to Celebration Ave, then s. 700 Bloom St 34747. **Fax:** 407/566-6001. **Facility:** Designated smoking area. 115 units. Some suites ($340-$470). **Bath:** combo or shower only. 3 stories, interior corridors. **Parking:** valet. **Terms:** check-in 4 pm, 3 day cancellation notice, package plans. **Amenities:** extended cable TV, video games, dual phone lines, voice mail, safes, irons, hair dryers. **Leisure Activities:** heated pool, whirlpool, exercise room. **Guest Services:** [BP] meal plan available, area transportation, valet laundry. **Fee:** massage. **Business Services:** meeting rooms, fax. **Cards:** AE, CB, DI, DS, JC, MC, VI. **(See color ad p 633)**

SOME UNITS

(ASK) (SD/FEE) (TI) (X) (T) (&) (&) (D) (S) (%) (DATA PORT/FEE) / (X) (C) (C) (H) /

CLERMONT pop. 6,900

——— WHERE TO STAY ———

HOLIDAY INN EXPRESS   **Phone:** (352)243-7878

Motel

| All Year | 1P: $79-$109 | 2P: $79-$109 |

Location: Just s of SR 50. 1810 S US Hwy 27 34711. **Fax:** 352/243-7882. **Facility:** 69 units. Some whirlpool units ($109). **Bath:** combo or shower only. 3 stories, interior corridors. **Terms:** cancellation fee imposed. **Amenities:** extended cable TV, dual phone lines, voice mail, irons, hair dryers. **Guest Services:** [ECP] meal plan available, coin laundry. **Business Services:** meeting rooms. **Cards:** AE, CB, DI, DS, JC, MC, VI.

SOME UNITS

(ASK) (SD) (TI) (&) (&) (D) (S) (%) (DATA PORT) / (X) (C) (C) (H) /

MULBERRY INN B&B   **Phone:** (352)242-0670

Country Inn

| All Year | 1P: $70-$100 | 2P: $75-$105 |

Location: 1.6 mi w of US 27 on SR 50, 0.3 mi n on 8th St, just w. 915 W Montrose St 34711. **Fax:** 352/242-9898. **Facility:** A white picket fence surrounds this home built in 1890. In back is the carriage house accommodations. Weekend entertainment. Designated smoking area. 5 units, 1 with kitchen. **Bath:** combo or shower only. 2 stories, interior/exterior corridors. **Terms:** check-in 4 pm, 14 day cancellation notice-fee imposed, weekly & monthly rates available. **Amenities:** Some: irons. **Leisure Activities:** bicycles. **Guest Services:** gift shop. **Business Services:** meeting rooms. **Cards:** AE, DS, MC, VI.

SOME UNITS

(TI) (X) (DATA PORT) / (C) (C) (C) (C) (H) /

DAVENPORT pop. 1,500   (See map p. 560; index p. 571)

——— WHERE TO STAY ———

COMFORT INN MAIN GATE SOUTH   **Phone:** (863)424-2811   445

Motel

| All Year | 1P: $39-$129 | 2P: $39-$129 | XP: $6 | F18 |

Location: I-4, exit 23. 5510 US 27 N 33837. **Fax:** 863/424-1723. **Facility:** 150 units. Some whirlpool units. 3 stories, exterior corridors. **Terms:** pets ($25 extra charge). **Amenities:** Some: hair dryers. **Guest Services:** coin laundry. **Business Services:** meeting rooms. **Cards:** AE, CB, DI, DS, JC, MC, VI. **Special Amenities:** free local telephone calls and free newspaper.

SOME UNITS

(SD) (I) (TI) (&) (D) (S) (%) / (X) (C) (H) /

DAYS INN-SOUTH OF DISNEY   **Phone:** (863)424-2596   441

Motel

2/1-6/16	1P: $46-$109	2P: $55-$115	XP: $6	F17
12/1-12/31	1P: $49-$74	2P: $55-$74	XP: $6	F17
6/17-11/30	1P: $49-$63	2P: $55-$69	XP: $6	F17
1/1-1/31	1P: $48	2P: $54	XP: $6	F17

Location: I-4, exit 23, just s on US 27. 2425 Frontage Rd 33837. **Fax:** 863/420-8717. **Facility:** 122 units. 2 stories, exterior corridors. **Terms:** weekly & monthly rates available, small pets only ($10 extra charge). **Amenities:** extended cable TV, hair dryers. **Leisure Activities:** heated pool, whirlpool, game room. **Guest Services:** gift shop, coin laundry. **Cards:** AE, CB, DI, DS, MC, VI. **(See color ad p 630)**

SOME UNITS

(SD) (I) (TI) (A) (S) (%) (D) (S) / (X) (C) (H) /
FEE FEE

(See map p. 560)

GLOBAL VACATION RENTALS AT WESTRIDGE Phone: (352)394-1232 447
All Year 1P: $159-$289 2P: $159-$289
Location: On US 27, 4 mi n of jct I-4, exit 23. 256 New Mexico Ln 33837 (11228 Country Hill Rd, CLERMONT, 34711). Fax: 352/394-1232. Facility: Lovely 3-6 bedroom houses with fully enclosed patio and pool, full housekeeping amenities and garage. Smoke free premises. 60 three-bedroom units with kitchen. 1 story, exterior corridors. Terms: 60 day cancellation notice-fee imposed, package plans, Maid service, extra charge. Amenities: extended cable TV, irons, hair dryers. Some: CD players, fax. Leisure Activities: 60 heated pools, whirlpool, 2 lighted tennis courts, exercise room, basketball, volleyball. Fee: golf equipment, golfing nearby, tennis equipment, bicycles. Guest Services: complimentary laundry. Cards: DS, MC, VI. Special Amenities: free local telephone calls and preferred room (subject to availability with advanced reservations). (See color ad p 586)

Condominium

HAMPTON INN ORLANDO-S OF WALT DISNEY RESORT Phone: (863)420-9898 446
All Year 1P: $59-$119 2P: $69-$129 XP: $10
Location: I-4, exit 23, just nw. 5530 US Hwy 27 N 33837. Fax: 863/420-9797. Facility: 83 units. Bath: combo or shower only. 5 stories, interior corridors. Amenities: extended cable TV, voice mail, irons, hair dryers. Leisure Activities: heated pool, whirlpool, exercise room. Guest Services: [ECP] meal plan available, coin laundry. Cards: AE, CB, DI, DS, JC, MC, VI.

Motel

PRESTIGE VACATION HOMES Phone: (863)424-7400 448
All Year 1P: $139-$219 2P: $139-$219
Location: I-4, exit 24, 1 mi e on CR 532, then 1 mi s on CR 545 and 1 mi e on CR 54. 101 Thousand Oaks Blvd 33837. Fax: 863/424-7500. Facility: Subdivision of 3-5 bedroom rental houses, each equipped with washer/dryer, outdoor pool, grill, some with whirlpool. Quiet, tranquil location away from mainstream, yet close to major attractions. 65 units with kitchen. 36 two-bedroom units and 29 three-bedroom units. 1 story, exterior corridors. Terms: check-in 4 pm, cancellation fee imposed, weekly rates available. Amenities: extended cable TV, irons, hair dryers. Guest Services: complimentary laundry. Cards: AE, DS, MC, VI. Special Amenities: free local telephone calls and preferred room (subject to availability with advanced reservations). (See color ad p 595)

Condominium

SUPER 8 MOTEL MAINGATE SOUTH Phone: (863)420-8888 449 F
All Year 1P: $39-$79 2P: $39-$79 XP: $6
Location: I-4, exit 23, 0.5 mi n. 5620 US Hwy 27 N 33837. Fax: 863/424-6602. Facility: 149 units. Bath: combo or shower only. 2 stories, exterior corridors. Terms: cancellation fee imposed, pets ($10 extra charge). Amenities: hair dryers. Leisure Activities: heated pool. Guest Services: coin laundry. Cards: AE, CB, DI, DS, JC, MC, VI. Special Amenities: free continental breakfast and free local telephone calls.

Motel

TROPICANA RESORT HOTEL Phone: (863)424-2211 442
4/1-11/30 2P: $59-$89
12/1-1/1 2P: $49-$89
1/2-3/31 2P: $49-$79
Location: I-4, exit 23, 0.5 mi s on US 27. 4825 Hwy 27 33837. Fax: 863/424-6714. Facility: 157 efficiencies. 2 stories, exterior corridors. Terms: 3 day cancellation notice. Amenities: Some: safes (fee). Leisure Activities: 2 pools (1 heated), wading pool, whirlpool, miniature golf, lighted tennis court, basketball, horseshoes, volleyball, picnic area with grills. Guest Services: gift shop, coin laundry. Business Services: meeting rooms. Cards: AE, DS, MC, VI. Special Amenities: early check-in/late check-out and free room upgrade (subject to availability with advanced reservations).

Condominium

FERN PARK pop. 8,300   (See map p. 554; index p. 558)

———— WHERE TO STAY ————

COMFORT INN-FERN PARK   Phone: (407)339-3333   **117**
AAA SAVE   All Year   1P: $66   2P: $66   XP: $6   F18
Location: I-4, exit 48, 3 mi e on SR 436, then 0.8 mi e. 8245 S Hwy 17-92 32730. **Fax:** 407/332-6659. **Facility:** 75
VVVV   units. Some whirlpool units ($100-$130). 1-4 stories, exterior corridors. **Terms:** 5 day cancellation notice.
Motel   **Amenities:** *Some:* irons, hair dryers. **Leisure Activities:** whirlpool. **Guest Services:** valet laundry.
Cards: AE, CB, DI, DS, MC, VI. **Special Amenities:** free continental breakfast and free newspaper.

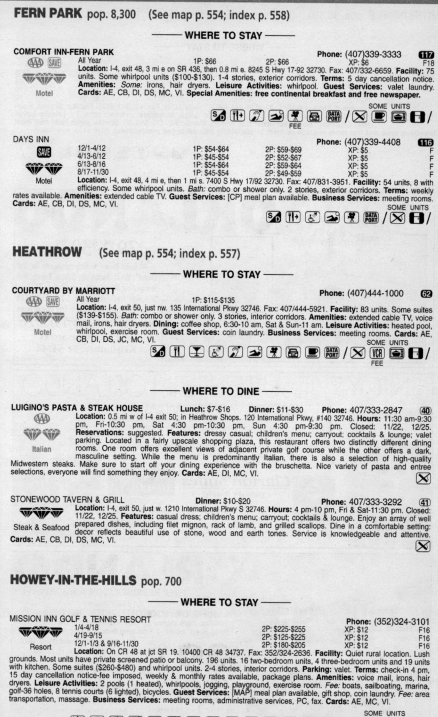

DAYS INN   Phone: (407)339-4408   **116**
SAVE   12/1-4/12   1P: $54-$64   2P: $59-$69   XP: $5   F
         4/13-6/12   1P: $45-$54   2P: $52-$67   XP: $5   F
VVVV   6/13-8/16   1P: $54-$64   2P: $59-$64   XP: $5   F
         8/17-11/30   1P: $45-$54   2P: $49-$59   XP: $5   F
Motel   **Location:** I-4, exit 48, 4 mi e, then 1 mi s. 7400 S Hwy 17/92 32730. **Fax:** 407/831-3951. **Facility:** 54 units, 8 with
efficiency. Some whirlpool units. *Bath:* combo or shower only. 3 stories, interior corridors. **Terms:** weekly
rates available. **Amenities:** extended cable TV. **Guest Services:** [CP] meal plan available. **Business Services:** meeting rooms.
Cards: AE, CB, DI, DS, MC, VI.

HEATHROW   (See map p. 554; index p. 557)

———— WHERE TO STAY ————

COURTYARD BY MARRIOTT   Phone: (407)444-1000   **62**
AAA SAVE   All Year   1P: $115-$135
Location: I-4, exit 50, just nw. 135 International Pkwy 32746. **Fax:** 407/444-5921. **Facility:** 83 units. Some suites
VVVV   ($139-$155). *Bath:* combo or shower only. 3 stories, interior corridors. **Amenities:** extended cable TV, voice
Motel   mail, irons, hair dryers. **Dining:** coffee shop, 6:30-10 am, Sat & Sun-11 am. **Leisure Activities:** heated pool,
whirlpool, exercise room. **Guest Services:** coin laundry. **Business Services:** meeting rooms. **Cards:** AE,
CB, DI, DS, JC, MC, VI.

———— WHERE TO DINE ————

LUIGINO'S PASTA & STEAK HOUSE   Lunch: $7-$16   Dinner: $11-$30   Phone: 407/333-2847   **40**
AAA   **Location:** 0.5 mi w of I-4 exit 50; in Heathrow Shops. 120 International Pkwy, #140 32746. **Hours:** 11:30 am-9:30
pm, Fri-10:30 pm, Sat 4:30 pm-10:30 pm, Sun 4:30 pm-9:30 pm. Closed: 11/22, 12/25.
VVVV   **Reservations:** suggested. **Features:** dressy casual; children's menu; carryout; cocktails & lounge; valet
Italian   parking. Located in a fairly upscale shopping plaza, this restaurant offers two distinctly different dining
rooms. One room offers excellent views of adjacent private golf course while the other offers a dark,
masculine setting. While the menu is predominantly Italian, there is also a selection of high-quality
Midwestern steaks. Make sure to start off your dining experience with the bruschetta. Nice variety of pasta and entree
selections, everyone will find something they enjoy. **Cards:** AE, DI, MC, VI.

STONEWOOD TAVERN & GRILL   Dinner: $10-$20   Phone: 407/333-3292   **41**
VVV   **Location:** I-4, exit 50, just w. 1210 International Pkwy S 32746. **Hours:** 4 pm-10 pm, Fri & Sat-11:30 pm. Closed:
11/22, 12/25. **Features:** casual dress; children's menu; carryout; cocktails & lounge. Enjoy an array of well
Steak & Seafood   prepared dishes, including filet mignon, rack of lamb, and grilled scallops. Dine in a comfortable setting;
decor reflects beautiful use of stone, wood and earth tones. Service is knowledgeable and attentive.
Cards: AE, CB, DI, DS, MC, VI.

HOWEY-IN-THE-HILLS pop. 700

———— WHERE TO STAY ————

MISSION INN GOLF & TENNIS RESORT   Phone: (352)324-3101
VVVV   1/4-4/18   2P: $225-$255   XP: $12   F16
         4/19-9/15   2P: $125-$225   XP: $12   F16
Resort   12/1-1/3 & 9/16-11/30   2P: $180-$205   XP: $12   F16
Location: On CR 48 at jct SR 19. 10400 CR 48 34737. **Fax:** 352/324-2636. **Facility:** Quiet rural location. Lush
grounds. Most units have private screened patio or balcony. 196 units. 16 two-bedroom units, 4 three-bedroom units and 19 units
with kitchen. Some suites ($260-$480) and whirlpool units. 2-4 stories, interior corridors. **Parking:** valet. **Terms:** check-in 4 pm,
15 day cancellation notice-fee imposed, weekly & monthly rates available, package plans. **Amenities:** voice mail, irons, hair
dryers. **Leisure Activities:** 2 pools (1 heated), whirlpools, jogging, playground, exercise room. *Fee:* boats, sailboating, marina,
golf-36 holes, 8 tennis courts (6 lighted), bicycles. **Guest Services:** [MAP] meal plan available, gift shop, coin laundry. *Fee:* area
transportation, massage. **Business Services:** meeting rooms, administrative services, PC, fax. **Cards:** AE, MC, VI.

KISSIMMEE pop. 30,100 (See map p. 560; index p. 568)

―――― WHERE TO STAY ――――

APOLLO INN ▲▲▲ SAVE ◆◆◆◆ Motel

Phone: (407)933-7237 390

12/1-1/2	1P: $33-$70	2P: $35-$70	XP: $10	F9
1/3-9/8	1P: $43	2P: $45	XP: $5	F9
9/9-11/30	1P: $33	2P: $35	XP: $5	F9

Location: 0.3 mi e of jct US 17-92 on SR 192. 670 E Vine St 34744. **Fax:** 407/846-0675. **Facility:** 39 units. 2 stories, exterior corridors. **Terms:** 3 day cancellation notice. **Amenities:** extended cable TV. **Leisure Activities:** basketball. **Guest Services:** coin laundry. **Cards:** AE, DS, MC, VI. **Special Amenities:** free local telephone calls and free room upgrade (subject to availability with advanced reservations). *(See color ad below)*

SOME UNITS

APOLLO INN

ORLANDO

$29.95-$39.95 sgl./dbl.

◆ 40 Guest Rooms ◆ Only minutes to The Walt Disney® World Resort ◆ Deluxe Rooms With Refrigerator/ Microwave ◆ Large Pool ◆ 27" Color TV's with Free Cable, HBO 1-2-3, ESPN, CNN ◆ Laundry ◆ Free Local Calls ◆ Free Internet Access

800-999-2765/(407) 933-7237
670 East Vine Street
Kissimmee, FL 34744
Visit our website: www.apolloinn.net

ENJOY THE SUITE LIFE IN ORLANDO

SPACIOUS VACATION VILLAS

All suite resorts are conveniently located near the I-4/Disney exchange or adjacent to DOWNTOWN DISNEY Lake Buena Vista. Offering: one, two and three bedroom villas with as much as 1340 square feet with fully equipped kitchens. Some with washer/dryer, video player, HBO, stereo system. ■ Outdoor heated pool ■ Whirlpool ■ Tennis courts ■ Game room ■ Children's playground

Clarion Suites
Resort World
2800 North Poinciana Blvd.
Kissimmee, FL 34746

20% AAA DISCOUNT
ASK FOR FL071
FAX 407.997.5222
www.clarionflorida.com

For reservations call 800.CLARION (252.7466)

ORLANDO

FREE REFRIGERATOR & MICROWAVE
AAA Discounted Rate
"A SUPERIOR ECONOMY HOTEL IN ORLANDO"
• Minutes. from Disney by New Expressway • Swimming Pool
• Discounted Tickets • 2 Extra long Beds or a King Bed

$29.95 To **$39.95**
(all year, 1 - 4 persons)

801 E. Vine Street (Hwy. 192)
Kissimmee, FL 34744
I-4 Exit 25A
Turnpike Exit 244 Southbound
Exit 242 Northbound
US & Canada Reservations Only:
1-800-780-7617
Office: 407-846-1935 / Fax: 407-846-7225

www.flamingoinn.com (Rates not valid during holiday weekends and /special events.)

(See map p. 560)

BEST WESTERN-EASTGATE Phone: (407)396-0707 **404**

Motor Inn

12/1-1/2	1P: $49-$159	2P: $49-$159
4/23-8/23	1P: $49-$99	2P: $49-$99
1/3-4/22 & 8/24-11/30	1P: $49-$89	2P: $49-$89

Location: I-4, exit 25A, on US 192, 2 mi e. 5565 W Irlo Bronson Memorial Hwy 34746. Fax: 407/396-6644. **Facility:** 403 units. 5 stories, exterior corridors. **Terms:** check-in 4 pm, $1 service charge, pets ($10 extra charge, in specific rooms). **Amenities:** safes (fee). **Dining:** restaurant, 7 am-11 & 5:30-10 pm, $5-$12, wine/beer only. **Leisure Activities:** heated pool, whirlpool, 2 lighted tennis courts, playground, game room. **Guest Services:** gift shop, area transportation-Disney. **Cards:** AE, DI, DS, JC, MC, VI. *(See color ad below)* SOME UNITS

REQUEST THE BEST FOR YOUR FAMILY.

Located only 3 miles from WALT DISNEY WORLD® Resort with FREE scheduled shuttle service to the Theme Parks. 403 clean and comfortable rooms with electronic locks and TV's with remotes. Enjoy our 60 ft. heated pool, whirlpool, 2 lighted tennis courts, a video game room, children's playground, gift shop and our restaurant has great prices for the family including an all you can eat breakfast buffet in a casual dining atmosphere. AAA Family Gateway. Pets welcome, $15 per night.

10-25% OFF 1/2/2001-12/20/2001 published rates Limited rooms available. Doesn't apply to groups or other discount offers.

Best Western Eastgate 5565 West Irlo Bronson Hwy. (U.S. 192) Kissimmee, FL 34746

FOR RESERVATIONS CALL 1-800-223-5361 OR 1-800-528-1234 • FAX 407-396-6644

CLOSEST HAMPTON INN TO UNIVERSAL STUDIOS

Hampton Inn *at Universal Studios*

TOLL FREE: 1.800.HAMPTON "Ask for MCOWH"
5621 Windhover Drive • Orlando, FL 32819
Direct: 1.800.231.8395 • 407.351.6716
Fax 407.363.1711
www.avistahotels.com/aaa
email: mcowh01@hi-hotel.com

SPECIAL RATES FROM
$69.00 - $109.00 Dbl. Occ.

• 120 Spacious Guest Rooms with Interior Corridors • In-Room Coffeemakers • Full size Iron and Ironing Board • 25" Cable TV, HBO, CNN, ESPN • Data Ports/Free Local Calls • Outdoor Heated Pool • Complimentary Deluxe Breakfast Bar • Complimentary Newspaper (Mon.-Fri.) • Accessible Rooms Available • Meeting Room • 100% Satisfaction Guaranteed

UNIVERSAL STUDIOS Escape

Hilton HHonors

CLOSEST HAMPTON INN TO DISNEY

Hampton Inn *Lake Buena Vista*

TOLL FREE: 1.800.HAMPTON "Ask for MCOLV"
8150 Palm Parkway • Orlando, FL 32836
Direct: 1.800.370.9259 • 407.465.8150 • Fax 407.465.0150
www.avistahotels.com/aaa
email: mcolv01@hi-hotel.com

RATES
$79.00-$119.00 Dbl. Occ.

• 147 Spacious Guest Rooms with Interior Corridors • In-Room Coffeemakers • Cable TV, HBO, CNN, ESPN • Data Ports • Outdoor Pool & Spa • Complimentary Deluxe Continental Breakfast • Free Local Calls • Exercise Facility • Hair Dryers in Every Room • Iron and Ironing Board • Rooms with Microwaves, Refrigerators available upon request • 100% Satisfaction Guaranteed • Scheduled Shuttle to Walt Disney World Resort®

Hilton HHonors

(See map p. 560)

BEST WESTERN-KISSIMMEE

AAA SAVE

Motor Inn

Phone: (407)846-2221 393

All Year   2P: $42-$99

Location: US 192 and 441 at Florida Tpke, exit 244. 2261 E Irlo Bronson Memorial Hwy 34744. Fax: 407/846-1095. **Facility:** Evergreen rooms available. 282 units, 10 with efficiency. 3 stories, exterior corridors. **Terms:** 3 night minimum stay, cancellation fee imposed. **Amenities:** safes (fee). *Some:* irons. **Dining:** dining room, 7 am-11 & 6-10 pm. **Leisure Activities:** 2 pools (1 heated), playground, basketball, volleyball. **Guest Services:** gift shop, area transportation-Disney, coin laundry. **Business Services:** meeting rooms. **Cards:** AE, CB, DI, DS, MC, VI. **Special Amenities:** free room upgrade and preferred room (each subject to availability with advanced reservations).** (See color ad p 636)

SOME UNITS

BEST WESTERN SUITE & RESORT HOTEL

AAA SAVE

Apartment

Phone: (407)396-2056 367

All Year   1P: $64-$72   2P: $127

Location: On US 192, 4.8 mi w of jct US 17-92 and 441; 4 mi e of I-4 on US 192. 4786 W Irlo Bronson Memorial Hwy 34746. Fax: 407/396-2909. **Facility:** 160 units with kitchen. 40 two-bedroom units. 2 stories, exterior corridors. **Terms:** check-in 4 pm, 3 day cancellation notice, weekly & monthly rates available. **Amenities:** safes (fee), irons, hair dryers. **Leisure Activities:** heated pool, whirlpool, beach, swimming, boat dock, fishing, recreational dock, playground, sports court, small picnic area with grills. *Fee:* waterskiing. **Guest Services:** [BP] meal plan available, area transportation-Disney, coin laundry. **Business Services:** conference facilities. **Cards:** AE, CB, DI, DS, JC, MC, VI. **Special Amenities:** free continental breakfast and free local telephone calls. *(See color ad p 636)*

SOME UNITS

CENTRAL MOTEL

AAA SAVE

Motel

Phone: (407)396-2333 371

12/1-1/5	1P: $35-$90	2P: $40-$90	XP: $5	F5
4/16-9/15	1P: $35-$65	2P: $40-$85	XP: $5	F5
1/6-4/15	1P: $30-$80	2P: $35-$85	XP: $5	F5
9/16-11/30	1P: $30-$60	2P: $35-$80	XP: $5	F5

Location: US 192, 4.8 mi e of I-4, exit 25A; 1.3 mi e of SR 535. 4698 W Irlo Bronson Hwy 34746-7812. Fax: 407/396-0739. **Facility:** 50 units. 2 stories, exterior corridors. **Terms:** 3 day cancellation notice-fee imposed, weekly rates available. **Amenities:** extended cable TV. **Cards:** AE, DS, MC, VI. **Special Amenities:** early check-in/late check-out and free room upgrade (subject to availability with advanced reservations).

SOME UNITS

CLARION MAINGATE

SAVE

Motor Inn

Phone: (407)396-4000 347

All Year   1P: $79-$109   2P: $79-$109

Location: US 192, 2.7 mi w of I-4, exit 25B; 1 mi w of Disney main gate. 7675 W Irlo Bronson Memorial Hwy 34747. Fax: 407/396-0714. **Facility:** 198 units. *Bath:* combo or shower only. 5 stories, interior corridors. **Terms:** cancellation fee imposed. **Amenities:** voice mail, safes (fee), irons, hair dryers. **Leisure Activities:** heated pool, wading pool, whirlpool, exercise room, game room. **Guest Services:** gift shop, area transportation, coin laundry. **Business Services:** meeting rooms. **Cards:** AE, DI, DS, JC, MC, VI. *(See color ad p 637)*

SOME UNITS

(See map p. 560)

CLARION SUITES RESORT WORLD

Extended Stay
Apartment

Phone: (407)997-5000   419

All Year   1P: $89-$225   2P: $89-$225

Location: I-4, exit 25A, 2.8 mi e on US 192, then just s; between MM 10 and 11. 2800 N Poinciana Blvd 34746-5258. Fax: 407/997-5225. **Facility:** Gated entry to spacious property. 1- to 3-bedroom, 2-bath apartments with laundry facilities. 311 units with kitchen. 151 two-bedroom units and 156 three-bedroom units. Some suites ($89-$225) and whirlpool units ($89-$225). 2-3 stories, exterior corridors. **Terms:** check-in 4 pm, 3 day cancellation notice-fee imposed. **Amenities:** extended cable TV, voice mail, safes (fee), irons, hair dryers. **Dining:** restaurant, $4-$8. **Leisure Activities:** 4 pools (3 heated), wading pool, saunas, whirlpools, 6 tennis courts (4 lighted), racquetball courts, recreation program, bicycles, exercise room, game room, recreation area in spa section. **Guest Services:** complimentary laundry. *Fee:* area transportation-attractions. **Business Services:** meeting rooms. **Cards:** AE, CB, DI, DS, JC, MC, VI. *(See color ad p 632)*

COMFORT INN-MAINGATE WEST

Motel

Phone: (863)424-8420   321

All Year   1P: $30-$140   2P: $30-$140   XP: $5   F18

Location: 7.2 mi w of jct I-4; 0.7 mi e of jct US 27. (9330 W Hwy 192, CLERMONT, 34711). Fax: 863/424-9670. **Facility:** 73 units. *Bath:* combo or shower only. 2 stories, exterior corridors. **Terms:** check-in 4 pm, 7 day cancellation notice. **Amenities:** extended cable TV, voice mail. *Some:* hair dryers. **Cards:** AE, DI, DS, JC, MC, VI. **Special Amenities:** free continental breakfast and free local telephone calls. *(See color ad below)*

SOME UNITS

COMFORT SUITES MAINGATE EAST

Motel

Phone: (407)397-7848   414

2/12-8/19   1P: $95-$250   2P: $95-$250   XP: $15   F18
12/1-2/11 & 8/20-11/30   1P: $75-$250   2P: $75-$250   XP: $15   F18

Location: I-4, exit 25A, 1.7 mi e on US Hwy 192, then just s. 2775 Florida Plaza Blvd 34746. Fax: 407/396-7045. **Facility:** 198 units. Some suites and whirlpool units. *Bath:* combo or shower only. 7 stories, interior corridors. **Terms:** package plans, $2 service charge. **Amenities:** voice mail, safes, irons, hair dryers. **Leisure Activities:** heated pool, wading pool, whirlpool, exercise room, game room. **Guest Services:** [ECP] meal plan available, gift shop, area transportation-major attractions, coin laundry. **Business Services:** meeting rooms, administrative services. **Cards:** AE, CB, DI, DS, JC, MC, VI. **Special Amenities:** free continental breakfast and free newspaper. *(See color ad p 638)*

SOME UNITS

(See map p. 560)

COMFORT SUITES MAIN GATE RESORT   Phone: (407)390-9888   335

   (AAA) [SAVE]   12/22-11/30   1P: $59-$150   2P: $59-$150
                12/1-12/21   1P: $59-$99   2P: $59-$99

▼▼ ▼▼   **Location:** I-4, exit 25, 3.5 mi w, on US 192. 7888 W Irlo Bronson Hwy 34747. Fax: 407/390-0981. **Facility:** Adjacent
Motel   to Splendid China. Modern rooms with contemporary decor. 150 units, 1 with kitchen. *Bath:* combo or shower
only. 3 stories, exterior corridors. **Terms:** check-in 4 pm, cancellation fee imposed. **Amenities:** voice mail,
safes (fee), hair dryers. *Some:* irons. **Leisure Activities:** heated pool, wading pool, whirlpool, game room,
poolside cabana. **Guest Services:** gift shop, area transportation-major attractions, coin laundry. **Business Services:** meeting
rooms. **Cards:** AE, CB, DI, DS, MC, VI. **Special Amenities: free continental breakfast and preferred room (subject to availability with advanced reservations).** *(See ad below)*   SOME UNITS

                [S/D] [📶] [♿] [⚙] [🎾] [⛱] [📹] [🖨] [💻] [📠] [🔌] [DATA PORT] / [✕] /

DAYS INN   Phone: 407/846-7136   435

▼▼ ▼▼   Property failed to provide current rates
       Location: Florida Tpke, exit 244, 1 mi w. 2095 E Irlo Bronson Memorial Hwy 34744. Fax: 407/846-8423.
Motel   **Facility:** Designated smoking area. 122 units. 2 stories, exterior corridors. **Terms:** pets ($50 deposit).
Amenities: extended cable TV, safes (fee). **Guest Services:** coin laundry. *Fee:* area transportation.
Cards: AE, CB, DI, DS, JC, MC, VI.   SOME UNITS

                      [✈] [🐾] [📶] [🎾] [📹] / [✕] [📠] [🔌] /
                     FEE

DAYS INN 192-NORTH   Phone: (407)933-5732   387

  [SAVE]   12/22-4/21   1P: $50-$100   2P: $50-$100
          4/22-8/25   1P: $50-$85   2P: $50-$85

▼▼ ▼▼   12/1-12/21 & 8/26-11/30   1P: $45-$70   2P: $45-$70
Motel   **Location:** US 192, 2.8 mi w of jct US 17-92 and 441. 4125 W Irlo Bronson Memorial Hwy 192 34741.
Fax: 407/932-2699. **Facility:** 52 units, 1 with kitchen. Some whirlpool units ($75-$130). 2 stories, exterior
corridors. **Terms:** cancellation fee imposed. **Amenities:** safes (fee). **Leisure Activities:** heated pool. **Guest
Services:** [CP] meal plan available, area transportation. **Cards:** AE, DI, DS, MC, VI.   SOME UNITS

                    [S/D] [✈] [📶] [🎾] [📹] [DATA PORT] / [✕] [📠] [🔌] /
                     FEE

(See map p. 560)

DAYS INN-HWY 192

AAA **SAVE**

◆◆ ◆◆

Motor Inn

Phone: (407)846-4714 381

12/22-4/21	1P: $50-$100	2P: $50-$100	
4/22-8/25	1P: $50-$85	2P: $50-$85	
12/1-12/21 & 8/26-11/30	1P: $45-$70	2P: $45-$70	

Location: US 192, 3 mi w of jct US 17-92 and 441. 4104 W Irlo Bronson Memorial Hwy 34741. **Fax:** 407/932-2699. **Facility:** Units in two buildings on each side of street. Designated smoking area. 174 units, 25 with efficiency (no utensils). *Bath:* combo or shower only. 3 stories, exterior corridors. **Terms:** cancellation fee imposed. **Amenities:** safes (fee). **Leisure Activities:** heated pool, game room. **Guest Services:** area transportation-major attractions, coin laundry. **Cards:** AE, DI, DS, MC, VI. *(See color ad p 639)*

SOME UNITS

[S D] [↔] [¶¶] [≫] [▣] / [✕] [▣] [📞] /
FEE

DAYS INN MAINGATE EAST

AAA **SAVE**

◆◆◆

Motor Inn

Phone: (407)396-7969 408

12/22-1/6	1P: $79-$169	2P: $79-$169	
1/7-8/18	1P: $69-$169	2P: $69-$169	
8/19-11/30	1P: $49-$89	2P: $49-$89	
12/1-12/21	1P: $42-$89	2P: $42-$89	

Location: I-4, exit 25A, 1 mi e, on US 192. 5840 W Irlo Bronson Memorial Hwy 34746. **Fax:** 407/396-8103. **Facility:** 404 units. *Bath:* combo or shower only. 3 stories, exterior corridors. **Terms:** check-in 4 pm, 3 day cancellation notice-fee imposed. **Amenities:** safes (fee). **Dining:** 2 restaurants, 6:30 am-1 & 5-10 pm; pool bar, $6-$10, cocktails. **Leisure Activities:** heated pool, playground, game room. **Guest Services:** area transportation-Disney, coin laundry. **Cards:** AE, DI, DS, JC, MC, VI. **Special Amenities:** preferred room (subject to availability with advanced reservations).

SOME UNITS

[S D] [↔] [¶¶] [✦] [⊘] [≫] [▣] [DATA PORT] / [✕] /
FEE   FEE

DAYS INN MAINGATE WEST OF WALT DISNEY WORLD RESORT

AAA **SAVE**

◆◆ ◆◆

Motor Inn

Phone: (407)997-1000 333

All Year	1P: $49-$99	2P: $49-$99

Location: 4 mi w of jct I-4, exit 25B; 4 mi e of jct US 27. 7980 W US 192 34747. **Fax:** 407/997-6542. **Facility:** 333 units. Some whirlpool units. *Bath:* combo or shower only. 3 stories, exterior corridors. **Amenities:** voice mail, safes (fee). **Dining:** restaurant, 7 am-11 & 5:30-10 pm, $5-$15, cocktails. **Leisure Activities:** exercise room, basketball, game room, picnic area with barbecue grill. **Guest Services:** gift shop, area transportation-Disney, coin laundry. **Business Services:** meeting rooms. **Cards:** AE, CB, DI, DS, MC, VI.

(See color ad below)

SOME UNITS

[S D] [↔] [¶¶] [✦] [≫] [✕] [▣] [DATA PORT] / [✕] [💻] [▣] /
FEE   FEE   FEE

(See map p. 560)

DAYS SUITES/MAIN GATE EAST OF WALT DISNEY WORLD RESORT
Phone: (407)396-7900 409

AAA [SAVE]
Suite Motel

12/22-1/7	1P: $109-$269	2P: $109-$269
1/8-8/18	1P: $79-$189	2P: $79-$189
12/1-12/21 & 8/19-11/30	1P: $69-$99	2P: $69-$99

Location: US 192, 1.5 mi e of I-4, exit 25A. 5820 W Irlo Bronson Memorial Hwy 34746. Fax: 407/396-0940. **Facility:** 603 units with kitchen. 12 two-bedroom units. 2 stories, exterior corridors. **Terms:** check-in 4 pm, 3 day cancellation notice-fee imposed, utensil extra charge. **Amenities:** extended cable TV, video games, voice mail, safes (fee). **Leisure Activities:** 3 pools (2 heated). **Guest Services:** [BP] meal plan available, area transportation-Disney, coin laundry. **Cards:** AE, CB, DI, DS, MC, VI. **Special Amenities:** preferred room (subject to availability with advanced reservations). *(See color ad p 642)*

SOME UNITS

DELUXE FLORIDA VILLAS
Phone: (407)396-2744 425

AAA [SAVE]
Extended Stay Apartment

12/1-5/1 & 6/16-8/15	2P: $140-$150
8/16-11/30	2P: $100-$110
5/2-6/15	2P: $90-$100

Location: I-4, exit 25A, 2.8 mi e on US 192 (between MM 11 and 12), 0.3 mi s. 2777 Poinciana Blvd 34746. Fax: 407/396-8447. **Facility:** Washer/dryer in large housekeeping units. Villas scattered throughout 4 complexes which are separate from listed registration address. 128 units with kitchen. 12 two-bedroom units and 116 three-bedroom units. 2 stories, exterior corridors. **Terms:** check-in 4 pm, 14 day cancellation notice-fee imposed. **Leisure Activities:** heated pool, sauna, whirlpool, lighted tennis court, playground, exercise room, game room, club house with pool tables. *Fee:* videos. **Business Services:** meeting rooms. **Cards:** AE, DS, MC, VI. **Special Amenities:** free local telephone calls and free newspaper.

SOME UNITS

DESTINY SECRET LAKE RESORT
Phone: 407/396-6101 323

Cottage

12/1-4/30	1P: $79-$89	2P: $79-$89
5/1-11/30	1P: $59	2P: $59

Location: I-4, exit 25, 5.5 mi w, on US 192. 8550 W Irlo Bronson Hwy 34747. Fax: 407/396-2958. **Facility:** Units in RV park have wood deck, open grassy sites. Designated smoking area. 20 units with kitchen. 1 story, exterior corridors. **Terms:** check-in 4 pm. **Leisure Activities:** 2 heated pools, wading pool, whirlpools, jogging, playground, shuffleboard. **Guest Services:** gift shop, coin laundry. **Cards:** AE, DS, MC, VI.

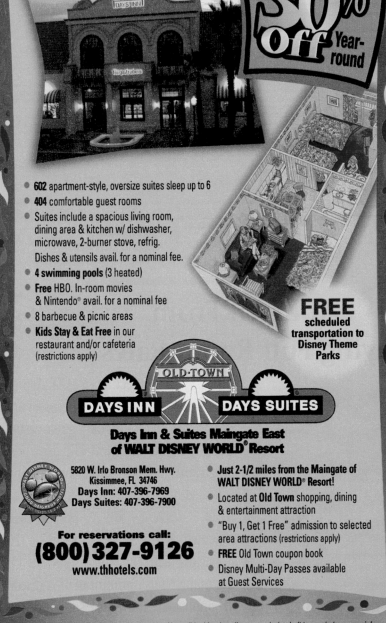

(See map p. 560)

DOUBLETREE GUEST SUITES-ORLANDO MAINGATE

Phone: (407)397-0555 **430**

Suite Motor Inn

1/7-4/30	1P: $166-$206	2P: $166-$206
6/4-11/30	1P: $134-$206	2P: $134-$206
12/1-1/6 & 5/1-6/3	1P: $134-$170	2P: $134-$170

Location: On US 192 at MM 12, 4.8 mi w of jct US 17-92 and 441; 0.5 mi e of jct SR 535. 4787 W Irlo Bronson Memorial Hwy 34746. Fax: 407/397-0553. **Facility:** Gated entry to landscaped grounds. 2- and 3-bedroom units with patios. Designated smoking area. 150 units with kitchen. 100 two-bedroom units and 50 three-bedroom units. 2 stories, exterior corridors. **Amenities:** extended cable TV, voice mail, safes (fee), irons, hair dryers. **Leisure Activities:** heated pool, wading pool, whirlpool, lighted tennis court, playground, exercise room, basketball. **Guest Services:** [BP] meal plan available, area transportation, coin laundry. **Business Services:** meeting rooms. **Cards:** AE, CB, DI, DS, MC, VI. *(See color ad starting on p 592)*

SOME UNITS

(ASK) (SD) [+] [FEE] [YI] [swim] [X] [FEE] [fax] [TV] [micro] [fridge] [DATA PORT] / [X] /

DOUBLETREE ORLANDO RESORT AND CONFERENCE CENTER

Phone: (407)396-1400 **345**

Motor Inn

12/1-1/3		2P: $119-$289	XP: $10	F17
1/4-8/25		2P: $139-$179	XP: $10	F17
8/26-11/30		2P: $139	XP: $10	F17

Location: US 192, 2.8 mi w of I-4, 1 mi w of Disney World main gate access road. 3011 Maingate Ln 34747. Fax: 407/396-0660. **Facility:** 577 units. 7 stories, interior corridors. **Terms:** check-in 4 pm, 3 day cancellation notice-fee imposed, package plans. **Amenities:** video games, voice mail, safes, irons, hair dryers. **Dining:** dining room, 7 am-10:30 pm, food court evening, entertainment for children, $6-$15, cocktails. **Leisure Activities:** 2 heated pools, wading pool, whirlpool, 2 lighted tennis courts, social program, playground, exercise room, game room, sand volleyball, pool tables. **Guest Services:** gift shop, area transportation-Disney, coin laundry. **Fee:** massage. **Business Services:** conference facilities, administrative services, fax. **Cards:** AE, CB, DI, DS, MC, VI. *(See color ad below)*

SOME UNITS

[YI] [24] [cocktails] [swim] [X] [FEE] [fax] [TV] [micro] [DATA PORT] / [X] /

ECONO LODGE MAINGATE-RESORT

Phone: (407)396-2000 **356**

Motel

12/20-8/17	1P: $49-$89	2P: $49-$89
12/1-12/19 & 8/18-11/30	1P: $39-$59	2P: $39-$59

Location: I-4, exit 25, 2.4 mi w, 1 mi w of Disney main gate. 7514 W Hwy 192 34747. Fax: 407/396-2832. **Facility:** Designated smoking area. 445 units, 1 with efficiency. 2 stories, exterior corridors. **Terms:** check-in 4 pm, 3 day cancellation notice-fee imposed, $2 service charge. **Amenities:** safes. **Dining:** restaurant, deli, 7 am-midnight, pool bar & snack bar. **Leisure Activities:** heated pool, wading pool, whirlpool, game room. **Business Services:** meeting rooms. **Guest Services:** gift shop, area transportation-attractions, coin laundry. **Cards:** AE, CB, DI, DS, JC, MC, VI. *(See color ad p 644)*

SOME UNITS

[SD] [YI] [cocktails] [gym] [access] [phone] [swim] [photo] [DATA PORT] / [X] [fax] [TV] [micro] [H] /
FEE FEE

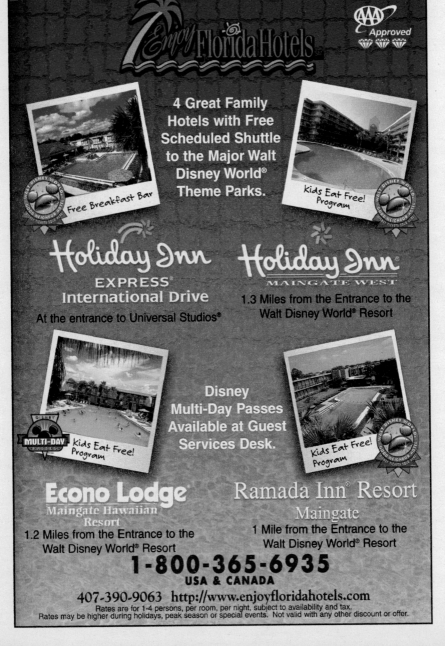

(See map p. 560)

FANTASY WORLD CLUB VILLAS

AAA **SAVE**
▽▽▽ ▽▽

Extended Stay Apartment

Phone: (407)396-1808 **422**

12/1-2/16 & 4/22-8/8	1P: $165-$195	2P: $165-$195
2/17-4/21	1P: $195	2P: $195
8/19-11/30	1P: $165	2P: $165

Location: I-4, exit 25A, 3.5 mi e on US 192 and just n; at MM 1. 5005 Kyngs Heath Rd 34746. Fax: 407/396-6737. **Facility:** Landscaped grounds with most units grouped on cul-de-sacs. Townhouses with 2-bedroom, 2-bath, screened patio with patio furniture, and laundry facilities. Main building has a 24-hour front desk and convenience store. Designated smoking area. 334 two-bedroom units with kitchen. Some whirlpool units. 2-4 stories, exterior corridors. **Terms:** check-in 4 pm, cancellation fee imposed. **Amenities:** voice mail, hair dryers. *Some:* safes. **Dining:** poolside bar. **Leisure Activities:** 3 pools (1 heated), whirlpool, 6 lighted tennis courts, playground, volleyball, game room. *Fee:* tennis equipment. **Guest Services:** area transportation-major attractions, coin laundry. **Cards:** AE, CB, DI, DS, MC, VI. *(See color ad below)*

SOME UNITS

(icons) FEE

FLAMINGO INN

AAA **SAVE**
▽▽▽ ▽▽

Motel

Phone: (407)846-1935 **391**

All Year	1P: $29-$39	2P: $29-$39

Location: US 192, 0.3 mi e of jct 441 and 192. 801 E Vine St 34744. Fax: 407/846-7225. **Facility:** 40 units. 2 stories, exterior corridors. **Terms:** 3 day cancellation notice, weekly rates available, small pets only ($8 extra charge). **Amenities:** extended cable TV. **Cards:** AE, DS, MC, VI. *(See color ad p 632)*

SOME UNITS

(icons)

FLORIDA PALMS RESORT

AAA **SAVE**
▽▽▽ ▽▽

Condominium

Phone: (407)944-9418 **388**

12/20-1/7 & 6/1-11/30	2P: $119
12/1-12/19 & 1/8-5/31	2P: $99

Location: 0.5 mi w of jct US 441 and 192 at Bassinger Rd. 1600 Sanibel Dr 34741. Fax: 407/944-9419. **Facility:** 2-story units with full kitchen and washer/dryer. Designated smoking area. 35 units with kitchen. 17 two-bedroom units and 18 three-bedroom units. 2 stories, exterior corridors. **Terms:** check-in 4 pm, 3 day cancellation notice-fee imposed, small pets only. **Amenities:** irons. **Leisure Activities:** whirlpool, lighted tennis court. **Guest Services:** complimentary laundry. **Cards:** AE, DS, MC, VI. **Special Amenities:** early check-in/late check-out and free local telephone calls.

(icons)

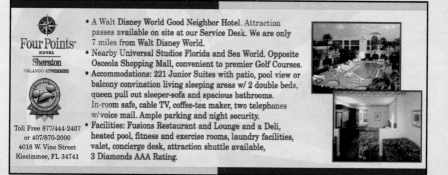

(See map p. 560)

FOUR POINTS HOTEL SHERATON ORLANDO/KISSIMMEE   Phone: (407)870-2000   385

Motor Inn

12/1-4/24 & 6/25-8/28	1P: $74-$114	2P: $74-$114	XP: $10	F17
4/25-6/24 & 8/29-11/30	1P: $64-$104	2P: $64-$104	XP: $10	F17

Location: I-4, exit 25, 7 mi e on US 192. 4018 W Vine St 34741. Fax: 407/870-2010. **Facility:** 1 room suites with small parlor area. 14 units with private patio. Some rooms with balcony. 222 units. 5 stories, exterior corridors. **Terms:** cancellation fee imposed, package plans, $4 service charge. **Amenities:** extended cable TV, voice mail, safes, irons, hair dryers. **Dining:** Fusions, see separate listing. **Leisure Activities:** heated pool, wading pool, whirlpool, exercise room, game room. **Guest Services:** coin laundry. **Business Services:** meeting rooms. **Cards:** AE, CB, DI, DS, MC, VI.
(See color ad p 645)

SOME UNITS

(ASK) 🚭 🍴 📺 🏊 ⊠ 🎦 🖥 💻 📠 / 🖨 🔌 / FEE

FOUR WINDS MOTEL   Phone: (407)396-4011   372

(AAA) (SAVE)

Motel

12/1-1/3	1P: $30-$49	2P: $35-$75	XP: $10	F18
2/9-4/30	1P: $39-$45	2P: $45-$55	XP: $10	F18
5/1-11/30	1P: $30-$45	2P: $35-$55	XP: $10	F18
1/4-2/8	1P: $30-$35	2P: $35-$45	XP: $10	F18

Location: US 192, 3.8 mi w of jct US 17-92 and 441, 1.3 mi e of SR 535. 4596 W Irlo Bronson Memorial Hwy 34746. Fax: 407/396-6531. **Facility:** 48 units. 1 two-bedroom unit. 2 stories, exterior corridors. **Terms:** 3 day cancellation notice. **Amenities:** safes (fee). **Cards:** AE, DI, DS, MC, VI. **Special Amenities:** early check-in/late check-out and preferred room (subject to availability with advanced reservations).

SOME UNITS

🚭 🍴 🏊 🎦 / ⊠ 🖨 🔌 / FEE FEE

GOLDEN LINK MOTEL   Phone: (407)396-0555   431

(AAA) (SAVE)

Motel

6/17-8/21	1P: $36-$59	2P: $36-$59	XP: $2
12/1-5/6	1P: $32-$59	2P: $32-$59	XP: $2
5/7-6/16	1P: $29-$49	2P: $29-$49	XP: $2
8/22-11/30	1P: $29-$39	2P: $29-$39	XP: $2

Location: I-4, exit 25A, 3.8 mi e on US 192 (between MM 11 and 12); jct SR 535/192. 4914 W Irlo Bronson Memorial Hwy 34746. Fax: 407/396-6531. **Facility:** Property sits adjacent to Lake Cecile, with access to lake and barbeque area. 84 units. **Bath:** combo or shower only. 2 stories, exterior corridors. **Amenities:** extended cable TV, safes (fee). **Leisure Activities:** heated pool, beach, swimming. **Guest Services:** coin laundry. **Cards:** AE, DS, MC, VI.

SOME UNITS

🍴 🏊 🎦 / ⊠ 🖨 🔌 / FEE FEE

(See map p. 560)

HAMPTON INN-MAINGATE EAST

[SAVE]

Motel

6/22-8/11   1P: $69-$99
12/1-2/8   1P: $59-$89
2/9-6/21 & 8/12-11/30   1P: $59-$79

Phone: 407/396-8484   [401]

Location: I-4, exit 25A, 0.3 mi e on US 192, 0.5 mi n. 3104 Parkway Blvd 34747. Fax: 407/396-7344. **Facility:** 164 units. 4 stories, interior corridors. **Terms:** 3 day cancellation notice-fee imposed. **Amenities:** extended cable TV, safes (fee), irons. **Leisure Activities:** heated pool, sports court. **Guest Services:** [ECP] meal plan available, coin laundry. *Fee:* area transportation. **Cards:** AE, CB, DI, DS, MC, VI. *(See color ad p 600)*

SOME UNITS

[SD] [🅗] [🍴] [🏋] [🏊] [📷] [📠] [📺] [DATA PORT] / [⊠] [🖥] [🛏] /
      FEE   FEE FEE

HAMPTON INN MAIN GATE WEST

[AAA] [SAVE]

Motel

2/15-5/5   1P: $84-$119   2P: $94-$119   XP: $10   F17
12/1-12/31   1P: $79-$119   2P: $79-$119   XP: $10   F17
1/1-2/14 & 5/6-11/30   1P: $74-$84   2P: $79-$94   XP: $10   F17

Phone: (407)396-6300   [350]

Location: US 192, 2.8 mi w of I-4, exit 25. 3000 Main Gate Ln 34747. Fax: 407/396-8989. **Facility:** 118 units. *Bath:* combo or shower only. 5 stories, interior corridors. **Terms:** cancellation fee imposed. **Amenities:** extended cable TV, voice mail, irons, hair dryers. **Guest Services:** [ECP] meal plan available, area transportation-Disney, valet laundry. **Cards:** AE, CB, DI, DS, MC, VI. **Special Amenities:** free continental breakfast and free newspaper. *(See color ad p 633)*

SOME UNITS

[SD] [♿] [🍴] [🖊] [🏊] [🏋] [📷] [📠] [📺] [DATA PORT] / [⊠] [🖥] [🛏] /

HAMPTON VACATION RESORT/OAK PLANTATION

[AAA] [SAVE]

Apartment

All Year   1P: $79-$199   2P: $79-$199

Phone: (407)847-8200   [380]

Location: Just n of jct SR 192 and Hoagland Blvd. 4090 Enchanted Oaks Cir 34741. Fax: 407/847-7948. **Facility:** Lovely setting in wooded area; gated property. 242 units with kitchen. 75 two-bedroom units. 3 stories, exterior corridors. **Terms:** check-in 4 pm, 3 day cancellation notice. **Amenities:** voice mail, safes, irons, hair dryers. **Leisure Activities:** 2 heated pools, wading pool, whirlpool, lighted tennis court, jogging, playground, exercise room, basketball, game room, car wash station, grills, movie rentals. **Guest Services:** complimentary laundry. *Fee:* area transportation-major attractions. **Business Services:** meeting rooms. **Cards:** AE, DS, MC, VI. **Special Amenities:** free local telephone calls and preferred room (subject to availability with advanced reservations). *(See color ad below)*

SOME UNITS

[SD] [🅗] [🏊] [✂] [VCR] [📠] [📺] [📷] [🛏] / [⊠] /
      FEE

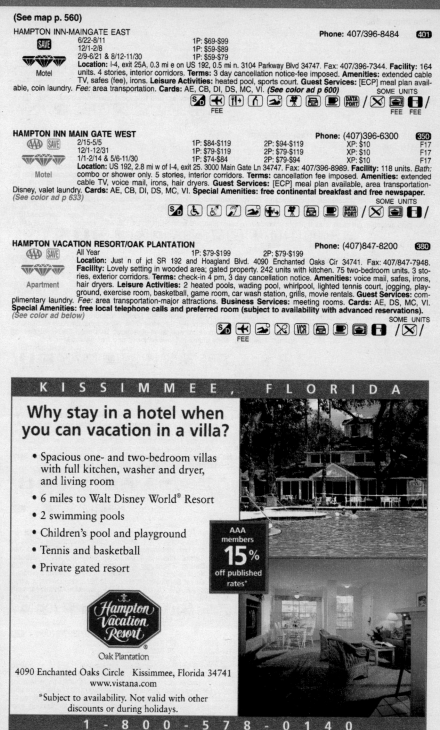

(See map p. 560)

HOLIDAY INN EXPRESS
Phone: (407)846-4646   **398**

AAA SAVE

Motor Inn

4/16-11/30	1P: $69-$89	
12/1-1/3 & 2/9-4/15	1P: $89	
1/4-2/8	1P: $69	

Location: US 192 and 441, 0.5 mi w of Florida Tpke, exit 244. 2145 E Irlo Bronson Memorial Hwy 34744. Fax: 407/932-2467. **Facility:** Designated smoking area. 146 units. 2 stories, exterior corridors. **Amenities:** voice mail, safes, irons, hair dryers. **Leisure Activities:** wading pool, game room. **Guest Services:** [ECP] meal plan available, gift shop, area transportation-Disney, coin laundry. **Business Services:** meeting rooms. **Cards:** AE, DI, DS, JC, MC, VI. **Special Amenities: free continental breakfast and free local telephone calls.** SOME UNITS

HOLIDAY INN HOTEL & SUITES MAIN GATE EAST
Phone: (407)396-4488   **413**

AAA SAVE

Motor Inn

12/1-1/2	1P: $59-$135	
1/3-8/15	1P: $69-$109	
8/16-11/30	1P: $59-$79	

Location: I-4, exit 25A, on US 192; between MM 9 and 10. 5678 W Irlo Bronson Memorial Hwy 34746. Fax: 407/396-1296. **Facility:** Extensively oriented towards children, including separate registration, dining facilities, activity building, and some children themed rooms with bunk beds. Designated smoking area. 614 units. Some suites ($99-$169) and whirlpool units ($99-$169). *Bath:* combo or shower only. 2 stories, exterior corridors. **Terms:** check-in 4 pm. **Amenities:** extended cable TV, voice mail, safes (fee), irons, hair dryers. *Some:* CD players. **Dining:** restaurant, 6:30 am-11 & 6-midnight, food court, $6-$14, cocktails. **Leisure Activities:** 2 heated pools, wading pool, whirlpools, 2 lighted tennis courts, children's program, playground, exercise room, basketball, volleyball, game room. **Guest Services:** [BP] meal plan available, gift shop, area transportation-Disney, coin laundry. **Cards:** AE, CB, DI, DS, MC, VI. SOME UNITS

HOLIDAY INN KISSIMMEE DOWNTOWN
Phone: (407)846-2713   **384**

AAA SAVE

Motor Inn

12/21-2/7	2P: $69-$99	
2/8-4/19	2P: $79-$89	
12/1-12/20 & 4/20-11/30	2P: $69-$89	

Location: I-4, exit 25A, 8 mi e; on US 192 1.3 mi w of jct US 17-92 and 441. 2009 W Vine St 34741. Fax: 407/846-8695. **Facility:** Designated smoking area. 200 units, 12 with efficiency. 3-4 stories, exterior corridors. **Terms:** check-in 4 pm, 7 day cancellation notice, monthly rates available, package plans, pets ($8 extra charge). **Amenities:** extended cable TV, voice mail, safes (fee), irons, hair dryers. **Dining:** restaurant, 7 am-11 pm, $7-$12, cocktails. **Leisure Activities:** 2 pools (1 heated), wading pool, whirlpool, lighted tennis court, playground, exercise room, game room, sun deck. **Guest Services:** gift shop, coin laundry. *Fee:* area transportation-attractions. **Business Services:** meeting rooms. **Cards:** AE, DI, DS, JC, MC, VI. **Special Amenities: early check-in/late check-out and free newspaper.**
(See color ad p 653)   SOME UNITS

HOLIDAY INN MAINGATE WEST
Phone: (407)396-1100   **338**

AAA SAVE

Motor Inn

12/20-8/17	1P: $79-$129	2P: $79-$129	XP: $10 F18
12/1-12/19	1P: $69-$99	2P: $69-$99	XP: $10 F18
8/18-11/30	1P: $59-$99	2P: $59-$99	XP: $10 F18

Location: Just n of US 192, 2.8 mi w of I-4, exit 25B; 1 mi w of Disney main gate access road. 7601 Black Lake Rd 34747. Fax: 407/396-0689. **Facility:** Child oriented with their own check-in and dining area. 30 kid suites available. 295 units. 6 stories, exterior corridors. **Terms:** check-in 4 pm, 3 day cancellation notice-fee imposed, small pets only ($50 fee, $50 deposit). **Amenities:** extended cable TV, safes (fee), irons, hair dryers. *Some:* CD players. **Dining:** restaurant, deli, 7 am-11 & 5-10 pm; pool bar 3/1-9/30, $7-$15, cocktails. **Leisure Activities:** heated pool, wading pool, playground, game room, sand volleyball. **Guest Services:** gift shop, area transportation-Disney, coin laundry. **Business Services:** meeting rooms. **Cards:** AE, CB, DI, DS, JC, MC, VI. **Special Amenities: free local telephone calls.**
(See color ad p 644)   SOME UNITS

HOLIDAY INN-NIKKI BIRD RESORT-MAINGATE
Phone: (407)396-7300   **358**

AAA SAVE

Motor Inn

12/24-11/30	1P: $59-$109	2P: $59-$109
12/1-12/23	1P: $59-$99	2P: $59-$99

Location: US 192, 2.3 mi w of jct I-4 exit 25B; 1 mi w of Disney World main gate. 7300 W Irlo Bronson Memorial Hwy 34747. Fax: 407/396-7555. **Facility:** A family-oriented property with modern, contemporary-style rooms, 75 kid suites, kid-themed scheduled entertainment and lush landscaping. 530 units. Some suites. *Bath:* combo or shower only. 2 stories, exterior corridors. **Terms:** check-in 4 pm, small pets only ($250 deposit). **Amenities:** voice mail, safes, irons, hair dryers. *Some:* CD players. **Dining:** 2 restaurants, coffee shop, 6:30 am-11 pm, $8-$25, cocktails, entertainment. **Leisure Activities:** 3 heated pools, wading pools, whirlpools, 3 lighted tennis courts, children's program, playground, exercise room, basketball, horseshoes, sand volleyball. **Guest Services:** gift shop, area transportation-major attractions, coin laundry. **Business Services:** meeting rooms, fax. **Cards:** AE, CB, DI, DS, JC, MC, VI. **Special Amenities: early check-in/late check-out and free room upgrade (subject to availability with advanced reservations).** SOME UNITS

HOLIDAY VILLAS
Phone: (407)397-0700   **429**

AAA SAVE

Extended Stay Apartment

12/1-1/1	1P: $155-$339	2P: $155-$339
1/2-8/23	1P: $155-$219	2P: $155-$219
8/24-11/30	1P: $155-$169	2P: $155-$169

Location: I-4, exit 25A, 2.8 mi e on US 192; nw corner of jct US 192 and SR 535; between MM 11 and 12; International Promenade Shopping Plaza. 2928 Vineland Rd 34746. Fax: 407/397-0566. **Facility:** Large housekeeping units with washer/dryer in three different landscaped complex locations. Each complex complete with recreational facilities. On-site 24 hour management office for registration. 255 units with kitchen. 100 two-bedroom units and 155 three-bedroom units. Some suites. 2 stories, exterior corridors. **Terms:** check-in 4 pm, 3 day cancellation notice-fee imposed. **Amenities:** extended cable TV, safes (fee). **Leisure Activities:** heated pool, sauna, lighted tennis court, exercise room, clubhouse at poolside with billiards & games. *Fee:* videos. **Cards:** AE, DS, MC, VI. *(See color ad p 649)*

(See map p. 560)

HOMEWOOD SUITES BY HILTON

Phone: 407/396-2229   402

	6/22-8/11	1P: $89-$109
	12/1-2/8	1P: $79-$109
Apartment	2/9-6/21 & 8/12-11/30	1P: $79-$99

Location: I-4, exit 25A, 0.3 mi e on US 192, 0.5 mi n. 3100 Parkway Blvd 34747. Fax: 407/396-4833. **Facility:** Spacious 1- and 2-bedroom suites in clusters of buildings on landscaped grounds. 156 units with kitchen. 9 two-bedroom units. Some suites. *Bath:* combo or shower only. 2-3 stories, interior/exterior corridors. **Terms:** 3 day cancellation notice-fee imposed, pets ($75 extra charge, $250 deposit). **Amenities:** extended cable TV, video games, voice mail, safes (fee), irons, hair dryers. **Leisure Activities:** heated pool, wading pool, whirlpool, playground, exercise room, sports court. **Guest Services:** [ECP] meal plan available, gift shop, complimentary evening beverages: Mon-Thurs, coin laundry. *Fee:* area transportation. **Business Services:** meeting rooms. **Cards:** AE, CB, DI, DS, MC, VI. *(See color ad p 600)*

SOME UNITS

HOWARD JOHNSON ENCHANTED LAND RESORT HOTEL

Phone: (407)396-4343   423

	All Year	1P: $75-$109	2P: $75-$109	XP: $7	F18

Motor Inn

Location: I-4, exit 25A, 3.2 mi e on US 192; between MM 11 and 12. 4985 W Irlo Bronson Memorial Hwy 34746. Fax: 407/396-8998. **Facility:** Children check-in at Tyler's Tree House while parents register in the traditional manner. Some children themed rooms. 160 units. Some whirlpool units ($99-$129). 2 stories, exterior corridors. **Terms:** cancellation fee imposed. **Amenities:** extended cable TV, voice mail, safes (fee). *Some:* irons, hair dryers. **Dining:** restaurant, 7 am-11:30 & 5-11 pm; poolside bar & grill, snack shop, $8-$10, cocktails. **Leisure Activities:** heated pool, whirlpool, game room. *Fee:* Children's Adventure Club. **Guest Services:** gift shop, area transportation-major attractions, coin laundry. **Cards:** AE, DI, DS, JC, MC, VI. **Special Amenities:** early check-in/late check-out and free newspaper. *(See color ad p 650)*

SOME UNITS

HOWARD JOHNSON EXPRESS INN & SUITES LAKEFRONT PARK

Phone: (407)396-4762   433

	12/21-8/25	1P: $59-$119	2P: $59-$119	XP: $5	F12
	12/1-12/20 & 8/26-11/30	1P: $39-$79	2P: $39-$79	XP: $5	F12

Motel

Location: US 192, 6 mi w of jct US 17-92 and 441; between MM 11 and 12. 4836 W Irlo Bronson Memorial Hwy 34746. Fax: 407/396-4866. **Facility:** Rooms range in size from king to 3 room suites. Close to area attractions. Designated smoking area. 131 units, 42 with kitchen. Some suites ($69-$129) and whirlpool units ($69-$129). 2 stories, exterior corridors. **Amenities:** extended cable TV, safes (fee). **Leisure Activities:** heated pool, wading pool, whirlpool, boat dock, fishing, playground, covered picnic pavilion. **Guest Services:** area transportation-Disney, coin laundry. **Cards:** AE, DS, MC, VI. **Special Amenities:** free continental breakfast. *(See color ad p 651)*

SOME UNITS

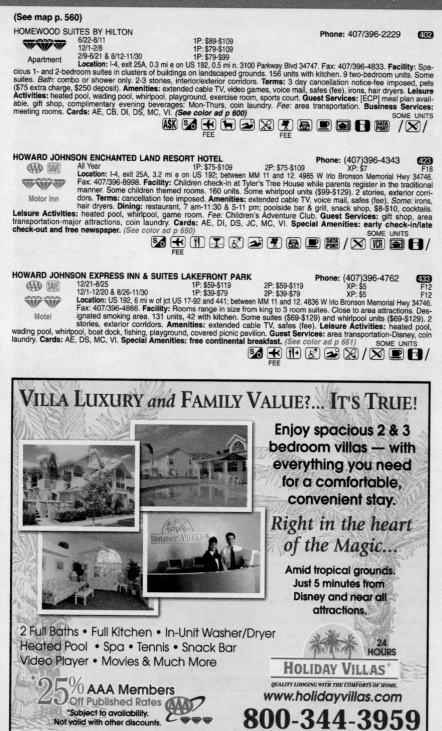

(See map p. 560)

HOWARD JOHNSON HOTEL
Phone: (407)846-4900 **399**

AAA (SAVE)
▼▼▼ ▼▼▼

Motor Inn

12/1-8/25		2P: $35-$75
8/26-11/30		2P: $35-$45

Location: On US 192 and 441; 0.3 mi e of Florida Tpke. 2323 E Irlo Bronson Memorial Hwy 34744. **Fax:** 407/994-0188. **Facility:** 198 units. 2 stories, interior corridors. **Terms:** check-in 4 pm, cancellation fee imposed, pets ($10 extra charge). **Amenities:** safes (fee). *Some:* irons, hair dryers. **Dining:** restaurant, 7 am-2 & 6-10 pm, $6-$10, cocktails. **Leisure Activities:** game room. **Guest Services:** gift shop, area transportation-Disney, coin laundry. **Special Amenities:** free newspaper and free room upgrade **(subject to availability with advanced reservations).** *(See color ad p 650)*

SOME UNITS

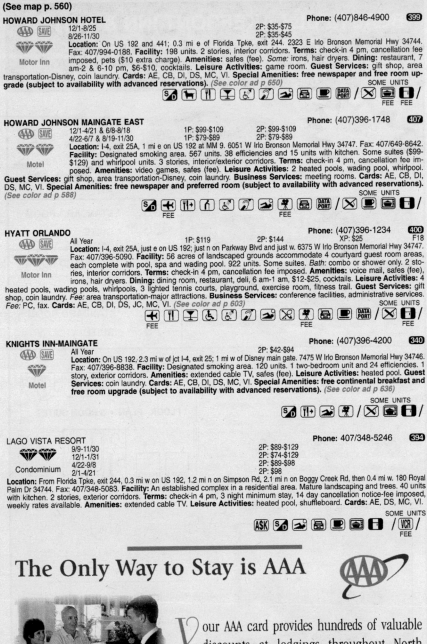

HOWARD JOHNSON MAINGATE EAST
Phone: (407)396-1748 **407**

AAA (SAVE)
▼▼▼ ▼▼▼

Motor

12/1-4/21 & 6/8-8/18	1P: $99-$109	2P: $99-$109
4/22-6/7 & 8/19-11/30	1P: $79-$89	2P: $79-$89

Location: I-4, exit 25A, 1 mi e on US 192 at MM 9. 6051 W Irlo Bronson Memorial Hwy 34747. **Fax:** 407/649-8642. **Facility:** Designated smoking area. 567 units. 38 efficiencies and 15 units with kitchen. Some suites ($99-$129) and whirlpool units. 3 stories, interior/exterior corridors. **Terms:** check-in 4 pm, cancellation fee imposed. **Amenities:** video games, safes (fee). **Leisure Activities:** 2 heated pools, wading pool, whirlpool. **Guest Services:** gift shop, area transportation-Disney, coin laundry. **Business Services:** meeting rooms. **Cards:** AE, CB, DI, DS, MC, VI. **Special Amenities:** free newspaper and preferred room **(subject to availability with advanced reservations).** *(See color ad p 588)*

SOME UNITS

HYATT ORLANDO
Phone: (407)396-1234 **400**

AAA (SAVE)
▼▼▼ ▼▼▼

Motor Inn

All Year	1P: $119	2P: $144	XP: $25	F18

Location: I-4, exit 25A, just e on US 192; just n on Parkway Blvd and just w. 6375 W Irlo Bronson Memorial Hwy 34747. **Fax:** 407/396-5090. **Facility:** 56 acres of landscaped grounds accommodate 4 courtyard guest room areas, each complete with pool, spa and wading pool. 922 units. Some suites. *Bath:* combo or shower only. 2 stories, interior corridors. **Terms:** check-in 4 pm, cancellation fee imposed. **Amenities:** voice mail, safes (fee), irons, hair dryers. **Dining:** dining room, restaurant, deli, 6 am-1 am, $12-$25, cocktails. **Leisure Activities:** 4 heated pools, wading pools, whirlpools, 3 lighted tennis courts, playground, exercise room, fitness trail. **Guest Services:** gift shop, coin laundry. *Fee:* area transportation-major attractions. **Business Services:** conference facilities, administrative services. *Fee:* PC, fax. **Cards:** AE, CB, DI, DS, JC, MC, VI. *(See color ad p 603)*

SOME UNITS

KNIGHTS INN-MAINGATE
Phone: (407)396-4200 **340**

AAA (SAVE)
▼▼▼

Motel

All Year		2P: $42-$94

Location: On US 192, 2.3 mi w of jct I-4, exit 25; 1 mi w of Disney main gate. 7475 W Irlo Bronson Memorial Hwy 34746. **Fax:** 407/396-8838. **Facility:** Designated smoking area. 120 units. 1 two-bedroom unit and 24 efficiencies. 1 story, exterior corridors. **Amenities:** extended cable TV, safes (fee). **Leisure Activities:** heated pool. **Guest Services:** coin laundry. **Cards:** AE, CB, DI, DS, MC, VI. **Special Amenities:** free continental breakfast and free room upgrade **(subject to availability with advanced reservations).** *(See color ad p 636)*

SOME UNITS

LAGO VISTA RESORT
Phone: 407/348-5246 **394**

▼▼▼ ▼▼▼

Condominium

9/9-11/30		2P: $89-$129
12/1-1/31		2P: $74-$129
4/22-9/8		2P: $89-$98
2/1-4/21		2P: $98

Location: From Florida Tpke, exit 244, 0.3 mi w on US 192, 1.2 mi n on Simpson Rd, 2.1 mi n on Boggy Creek Rd, then 0.4 mi w. 180 Royal Palm Dr 34744. **Fax:** 407/348-5083. **Facility:** An established complex in a residential area. Mature landscaping and trees. 40 units with kitchen. 2 stories, exterior corridors. **Terms:** check-in 4 pm, 3 night minimum stay, 14 day cancellation notice-fee imposed, weekly rates available. **Amenities:** extended cable TV. **Leisure Activities:** heated pool, shuffleboard. **Cards:** AE, DS, MC, VI.

SOME UNITS

(See map p. 560)

LARSON'S INN & FAMILY SUITES

AAA SAVE

Motor Inn

				Phone: (407)396-6100	406
12/22-1/2	1P: $79-$89	2P: $89-$99		XP: $10	F18
4/1-11/30	1P: $69-$79	2P: $79-$89		XP: $10	F18
1/3-3/31	1P: $59-$69	2P: $59-$69		XP: $10	F18
12/1-12/21	1P: $49-$59	2P: $59-$69		XP: $10	F18

Location: I-4, exit 25A, 1 mi e on US 192; between MM 8 and 9. 6075 W Irlo Bronson Memorial Hwy 34747. **Fax:** 407/396-6965. **Facility:** Adjacent to Water Mania. 176 units. 16 two-bedroom units and 16 efficiencies. 4 stories, exterior corridors. **Terms:** check-in 4 pm, 3 day cancellation notice-fee imposed, pets ($10 extra charge). **Amenities:** extended cable TV, voice mail, safes (fee), irons, hair dryers. **Dining:** restaurant, 6 am-midnight, $5-$9. **Leisure Activities:** heated pool, whirlpool, playground, game room. **Guest Services:** gift shop, coin laundry. **Fee:** area transportation-attractions. **Cards:** AE, DI, DS, MC, VI. **Special Amenities:** early check-in/late check-out and free newspaper. Affiliated with Best Value Inn Brand Membership. *(See color ad below)*

SOME UNITS

LINDFIELDS RESERVE

AAA SAVE

Condominium

		Phone: (407)396-2262	331
All Year	1P: $235-$343		

Location: 1 mi e of US 27 and 6 mi w of I-4, exit 25A. 7799 Styles Blvd 34747. **Fax:** 407/396-1588. **Facility:** Full kitchen, washer/dryer, entertainment center, intercom system and use of club house. 2 five-bedrooms and 4 four-bedrooms available. Smoke free premises. 16 three-bedroom units with kitchen. 2 stories, exterior corridors. **Terms:** check-in 4 pm, 31 day cancellation notice-fee imposed. **Amenities:** CD players, voice mail, irons, hair dryers. **Leisure Activities:** each home has enclosed pool, lighted tennis court, exercise room. **Guest Services:** complimentary laundry. **Cards:** AE, DS, MC, VI. **Special Amenities:** free local telephone calls.

MAGIC CASTLE INN & SUITES EASTGATE

AAA SAVE

Motel

				Phone: (407)396-1212	376
6/10-8/23	1P: $45-$59	2P: $49-$65		XP: $6	F17
12/20-6/9	1P: $30-$59	2P: $36-$65		XP: $6	F17
12/1-12/19 & 8/24-11/30	1P: $30-$39	2P: $36-$45		XP: $6	F17

Location: 4.5 mi w of US 17-92 and 441; 6.5 mi e of Disney/Epcot entrance. 4559 W Hwy 192 34746. **Fax:** 407/396-7926. **Facility:** 114 units. Some suites ($50-$100). 2 stories, exterior corridors. **Terms:** small pets only ($6 extra charge, $25 deposit). **Amenities:** safes (fee). **Leisure Activities:** playground. **Guest Services:** area transportation-Disney, coin laundry. **Cards:** AE, CB, DI, DS, MC, VI. **Special Amenities:** free continental breakfast. *(See color ad p 654 & p 605)*

SOME UNITS

MAGIC CASTLE INN & SUITES MAINGATE

AAA SAVE

Motel

				Phone: (407)396-2212	420
6/10-8/23	1P: $48-$62	2P: $52-$68		XP: $6	F17
12/20-6/9	1P: $33-$62	2P: $39-$68		XP: $6	F17
12/1-12/19 & 8/24-11/30	1P: $33-$42	2P: $39-$48		XP: $6	F17

Location: I-4, exit 25A, 3.2 mi e on US 192; between MM 10 and 11. 5055 W Irlo Bronson Memorial Hwy 34746. **Fax:** 407/396-0253. **Facility:** 107 units. 3 stories, exterior corridors. **Terms:** pets ($6 extra charge, $25 deposit). **Amenities:** safes (fee). **Leisure Activities:** playground, picnic tables & grills. **Guest Services:** coin laundry. **Cards:** AE, DI, DS, MC, VI. **Special Amenities:** free continental breakfast. *(See color ad p 654 & p 605)*

SOME UNITS
FEE

(See map p. 560)

MASTERS INN-KISSIMMEE

AAA SAVE   Phone: (407)396-4020   415

Motel

All Year   1P: $45-$79   2P: $55-$89

Location: US 192, 2.5 mi e of jct I-4, exit 25. 5367 W Irlo Bronson Hwy 34746. Fax: 407/396-5450. **Facility:** 188 units. Some suites ($69-$99). 2 stories, exterior corridors. **Terms:** 3 day cancellation notice-fee imposed, small pets only ($5-$10 extra charge). **Amenities:** safes (fee). **Leisure Activities:** heated pool. **Guest Services:** coin laundry. **Cards:** AE, CB, DI, DS, MC, VI. **Special Amenities: free continental breakfast and free local telephone calls.**

SOME UNITS

MASTERS INN-MAIN GATE

AAA SAVE   Phone: (407)396-7743   355

Motel

All Year   1P: $49-$85   2P: $59-$99

Location: On US 192; 2.5 mi w of jct I-4, exit 25; 1 mi w of Disney World main gate. 2945 Entry Point Blvd 34747. Fax: 407/396-6307. **Facility:** Designated smoking area. 117 units. 3 stories, exterior corridors. **Terms:** check-in 4 pm, small pets only ($10 fee). **Amenities:** extended cable TV, safes (fee). **Leisure Activities:** heated pool. **Guest Services:** coin laundry. **Cards:** AE, DI, DS, MC, VI. **Special Amenities: free continental breakfast and free local telephone calls.**

SOME UNITS

FEE

MOTEL 6 - 436

Phone: 407/396-6422   412

Motel

12/1-12/31	1P: $33-$50	2P: $39-$56	XP: $3	F17
4/16-11/30	1P: $36-$46	2P: $42-$52	XP: $3	F17
1/1-4/15	1P: $34-$44	2P: $40-$52	XP: $3	F17

Location: I-4, exit 25B, 1.3 mi w on US 192. 7455 W Irlo Bronson Hwy 34747. Fax: 407/396-0720. **Facility:** 148 units. *Bath:* combo or shower only. 2 stories, exterior corridors. **Terms:** check-in 4 pm, small pets only. **Leisure Activities:** heated pool. **Guest Services:** coin laundry. *Fee:* area transportation. **Cards:** AE, CB, DI, DS, MC, VI.

SOME UNITS

MOTEL 6 - 464

Phone: 407/396-6333   354

Motel

12/1-4/15	1P: $39-$49	2P: $45-$55	XP: $3	F17
4/16-11/30	1P: $36-$46	2P: $42-$52	XP: $3	F17

Location: I-4, exit 25, 2 mi e. 5731 W Irlo Bronson Hwy 34746. Fax: 407/396-7715. **Facility:** 347 units. 2 stories, exterior corridors. **Terms:** small pets only. **Leisure Activities:** 2 heated pools. **Guest Services:** coin laundry. **Cards:** AE, CB, DI, DS, MC, VI.

SOME UNITS

ORANGE LAKE RESORT & COUNTRY CLUB

Phone: (407)239-0000   328

Resort

6/15-8/26	1P: $120-$275
12/1-6/14	1P: $99-$275
8/27-11/30	1P: $99-$225

Location: US 192, 3.5 mi e of US 27 and 5 mi w of I-4, exit 25. 8505 W Irlo Bronson Memorial Hwy 34747. Fax: 407/239-5119. **Facility:** Single room efficiencies in main building. 2-bedroom villas, all surrounded by 2- and 3-bedroom units in mid-rise buildings. Lush landscaped grounds. Extensive facilities. A 1200 unit timeshare. 105 units. 65 two-bedroom units, 15 three-bedroom units and 80 units with kitchen. 2 stories, interior corridors. **Terms:** check-in 4 pm, 2 night minimum stay, 3 day cancellation notice-fee imposed, package plans. **Leisure Activities:** 5 heated pools, wading pools, whirlpools, beach, swimming, 1 olympic sized pool, 12 lighted tennis courts, racquetball courts, children's program, recreation program, playground, exercise room, basketball, game room. *Fee:* boats, canoes, paddleboats, waterskiing, fishing, golf-90 holes. **Guest Services:** [MAP] meal plan available, gift shop, complimentary laundry. *Fee:* area transportation. **Business Services:** meeting rooms. **Cards:** AE, DI, MC, VI.

SOME UNITS

FEE   FEE

ORBIT ONE VACATION VILLAS

AAA SAVE   Phone: (407)396-1300   334

Condominium

All Year   1P: $119-$189   2P: $119-$189

Location: US 192, 2.5 mi w of I-4, exit 25. 2950 Entry Point Blvd 34747. Fax: 407/396-0814. **Facility:** 2-bedroom housekeeping units with large modern kitchens, washer/dryer, 2-bathrooms and screened patio or balcony. 116 two-bedroom units with kitchen. Some whirlpool units ($119-$189). 2-3 stories (no elevator), exterior corridors. **Terms:** check-in 4 pm, 15 day cancellation notice-fee imposed, weekly rates available. **Amenities:** extended cable TV, irons, hair dryers. **Leisure Activities:** 2 heated pools, wading pool, sauna, whirlpool, putting green, 2 lighted tennis courts, racquetball court, playground, exercise room, volleyball. **Guest Services:** [CP] meal plan available, complimentary laundry. **Cards:** AE, CB, DI, DS, MC, VI. **Special Amenities: free local telephone calls and preferred room (subject to availability with advanced reservations).** *(See color ad p 635)*

ORLANDO'S KEY VACATION HOMES

Phone: (407)933-7789   337

Condominium

12/1-1/3 & 6/11-8/31	1P: $115-$225	2P: $115-$225
1/4-6/10 & 9/1-11/30	1P: $90-$199	2P: $90-$199

Location: I-4, exit 25B, 3 mi w to Formosa Gardens Blvd, 0.8 mi s. 102 Park Place Blvd, Bldg D, Ste 2 34741. Fax: 407/932-2742. **Facility:** Three-, four-, five- and six-bedroom houses available. Address above is the rental agency location. The spotting map number shows location of the houses. Designated smoking area. 40 three-bedroom units with kitchen. Some whirlpool units ($150-$192). 2 stories, exterior corridors. **Terms:** 8 day cancellation notice-fee imposed, housekeeping, extra charge. **Amenities:** extended cable TV, irons. *Some:* CD players, safes. **Leisure Activities:** 40 pools (35 heated), whirlpools. **Guest Services:** complimentary laundry. **Cards:** AE, MC, VI.

(See map p. 560)

ORLANDO SUN VILLAGE   Phone: (407)390-4000   379

Extended Stay Apartment

All Year   2P: $95-$210
Location: On Old Vineland Rd, 6 mi e of I-4, exit 25. 4403 Sun Village Blvd 34746. Fax: 407/390-9335. **Facility:** Some units can be as three-bedroom units. 70 units with kitchen. 24 two-bedroom units. 2 stories, exterior corridors. **Terms:** check-in 4 pm, 3 day cancellation notice, weekly & monthly rates available, package plans. **Amenities:** extended cable TV, voice mail, irons, hair dryers. **Leisure Activities:** 2 heated pools, whirlpool, playground, game room. **Guest Services:** area transportation, complimentary laundry. **Cards:** AE, DI, MC, VI.

THE PALMS   Phone: (407)396-1311   351

Condominium

5/25-8/9   1P: $180-$214   2P: $274-$319
12/1-5/24 & 8/10-11/30   1P: $119-$149   2P: $180-$229
Location: I-4, exit 25B, 2.5 mi w on US 192, then 1.2 mi s on Old Lake Wilson Rd. 7900 Palms Pkwy 34747. Fax: 407/390-1765. **Facility:** Peaceful, relaxing setting. All rooms with washer/dryer. 36 one-bedroom units have tub with hand held shower fixtures. Three-bedroom units available. 264 units with kitchen. 150 two-bedroom units. Some whirlpool units. **Bath:** combo, shower or tub only. 3 stories, exterior corridors. **Terms:** check-in 4 pm, 3 day cancellation notice, weekly rates available. **Amenities:** extended cable TV, safes, irons. **Leisure Activities:** 2 heated pools, wading pool, miniature golf, 2 lighted tennis courts, children's program, recreation program, social program, bicycles, playground, basketball. **Guest Services:** [CP] meal plan available, gift shop. **Cards:** AE, DS, MC, VI. *(See color ad below)*

PARKSIDE RECORD INN & SUITES   Phone: (407)396-8400   438

Motel

AAA [SAVE]

6/29-8/18   1P: $39-$69   2P: $49-$69   XP: $15   F10
12/1-4/14   1P: $35-$69   2P: $39-$69   XP: $15   F10
4/15-6/28   1P: $35-$59   2P: $39-$59
8/19-11/30   1P: $35-$59   2P: $39-$59   XP: $10   F10
Location: US 192; 5 mi w of jct US 17-92 and 441; between MM 13 and 14. 4651 W Irlo Bronson Memorial Hwy 34746. Fax: 407/396-8415. **Facility:** Office hours 7 am-midnight. Designated smoking area. 57 units, 1 with efficiency. 1-2 stories, exterior corridors. **Terms:** 5 day cancellation notice. **Leisure Activities:** heated pool. **Guest Services:** coin laundry. **Cards:** AE, DI, DS, JC, MC, VI. **Special Amenities:** early check-in/late check-out and free continental breakfast. *(See color ad p 657)*

SOME UNITS

FEE

PARKWAY INTERNATIONAL   Phone: (407)396-6600   405

Suite Condominium

AAA [SAVE]

All Year   2P: $129-$199
Location: I-4, exit 25A, 0.3 mi e on US 192, just n. 6200 Safari Tr 34746. Fax: 407/396-6165. **Facility:** Safari themed condominiums fully equipped for housekeeping including washer/dryer, screened patio or balcony with patio furniture, paddle fans and whirlpool. Recreation facilities in developed landscaped setting. 144 two-bedroom units with kitchen. Some suites ($129-$199) and whirlpool units. 3 stories (no elevator), exterior corridors. **Terms:** check-in 4 pm, 15 day cancellation notice-fee imposed, weekly rates available. **Amenities:** extended cable TV, CD players, voice mail, safes, irons, hair dryers. **Dining:** pool snack bar 11 am-5:30 pm, Fri-Sun 9 pm. **Leisure Activities:** heated pool, wading pool, whirlpool, lighted tennis court, social program, playground. **Guest Services:** complimentary laundry. **Fee:** area transportation. **Cards:** AE, CB, DI, DS, MC, VI. **Special Amenities:** free local telephone calls and preferred room (subject to availability with advanced reservations). *(See color ad p 635)*

FEE

(See map p. 560)

POINCIANA GOLF & RACQUET RESORT

▼▼▼ All Year   1P: $80-$160   Phone: (407)933-0700   437

Extended Stay Apartment
Location: 4 mi sw on US 17/92 from jct of US 192, 8 mi s on Pleasant Hill Rd, 2 mi w. 500 E Cypress Pkwy 34759. Fax: 407/870-5412. **Facility:** All suites with washer/dryer, screened patio or balcony; few single stand rooms on property; oversized tubs. Office hours 8 am-8 pm; Sat 7 am-11 pm; security staffed off hours. 112 units, 56 with kitchen. Some whirlpool units. 2 stories, exterior corridors. **Terms:** check-in 4 pm, 14 day cancellation notice-fee imposed, weekly & monthly rates available, package plans. **Leisure Activities:** heated pool, wading pool, putting green, 4 lighted tennis courts, jogging, playground, shuffleboard. *Fee:* golf-18 holes. **Guest Services:** complimentary laundry. **Business Services:** meeting rooms. **Cards:** AE, MC, VI.

SOME UNITS

(ASK) ⊤ 🚫 🏊 ⊠ 📹 ▣ 📠 🔒 / ⊠ /

QUALITY INN KISSIMMEE

SAVE   12/1-4/30   2P: $69-$89   XP: $5   Phone: (407)846-4545   432
       5/1-11/30   2P: $49-$69   XP: $5   F18
▼▼▼   F18
Motel
Location: Florida Tpke, exit 244, 1 mi w on US 192. 2050 E Irlo Bronson Memorial Hwy 34744. Fax: 407/932-2268. **Facility:** 152 units. *Bath:* combo or shower only. 2 stories, exterior corridors. **Terms:** check-in 4 pm, cancellation fee imposed. **Amenities:** extended cable TV, voice mail. *Some:* safes, irons, hair dryers. **Leisure Activities:** 2 lighted tennis courts, playground, exercise room, game room. **Guest Services:** [ECP] meal plan available, coin laundry. **Business Services:** meeting rooms. **Cards:** AE, CB, DI, DS, MC, VI.

SOME UNITS

(S/D) ⊤⏐⊤ ⓧ 🏊 ⊠ 📹 ▣ 📠 / ⊠ 📠 🔒 /

QUALITY INN LAKE CECILE

SAVE   All Year   1P: $39-$70   2P: $39-$70   Phone: (407)396-4455   426
▼▼▼
Motel
Location: On US 192, 3.2 mi e of I-4, exit 25A; at jct SR 535. 4944 W Irlo Bronson Memorial Hwy 34746. Fax: 407/396-4182. **Facility:** On Lake Cecile. 222 units. 5 stories, interior corridors. **Terms:** cancellation fee imposed. **Amenities:** video games, safes (fee). *Some:* irons, hair dryers. **Leisure Activities:** game room. *Fee:* boat dock, waterskiing. **Guest Services:** area transportation, coin laundry. **Cards:** AE, DI, DS, MC, VI. *(See color ad p 658)*

SOME UNITS

(S/D) ⊕ ⏐⊤⏐ 🏊 ⊠ 📹 ▣ 📠 / ⊠ 📠 🔒 /
     FEE   FEE   FEE

QUALITY INN MAIN GATE

SAVE   All Year   1P: $35-$70   2P: $35-$70   Phone: (407)870-7374   378
▼▼▼
Motel
Location: US 192, 2.8 mi w of jct US 17-92 and 441. 4156 W Vine St 34741. Fax: 407/870-2154. **Facility:** 130 units. 3 stories, exterior corridors. **Terms:** cancellation fee imposed. **Amenities:** extended cable TV, safes (fee). *Some:* irons, hair dryers. **Guest Services:** gift shop, coin laundry. *Fee:* area transportation. **Cards:** AE, DI, DS, MC, VI. *(See color ad p 658)*

SOME UNITS

(S/D) ⊕ ⏐⊤⏐ 🏊 📹 ▣ 📠 / ⊠ 🔒 /
     FEE

QUALITY INN MAINGATE WEST

▲▲▲ SAVE   2/16-8/18   1P: $50-$90   2P: $50-$90   XP: $5   Phone: (407)396-1828   353
▼▼▼   12/1-2/15 & 8/19-11/30   1P: $40-$70   2P: $40-$70   XP: $5   F17
Motel   F17
Location: On US 192; 3 mi w of I-4, exit 25B; 2 mi w of Disney World main gate. 7785 W Irlo Bronson Memorial Hwy 34747. Fax: 407/396-1305. **Facility:** Opposite Splendid China Theme Park and shopping. 200 units, 20 with efficiency. 3 stories, exterior corridors. **Terms:** cancellation fee imposed. **Amenities:** extended cable TV. *Some:* irons, hair dryers. **Dining:** poolside tiki bar. **Leisure Activities:** heated pool, playground, game room. **Guest Services:** gift shop, area transportation-Disney, coin laundry. **Cards:** AE, DI, DS, MC, VI. **Special Amenities:** free continental breakfast. *(See color ad p 659)*

SOME UNITS

(S/D) ⊕ ⏐⊤⏐ ♿ 🚫 🚫 🏊 📹 📠 ▣ 📠 / ⊠ 📠 🔒 /
     FEE   FEE FEE

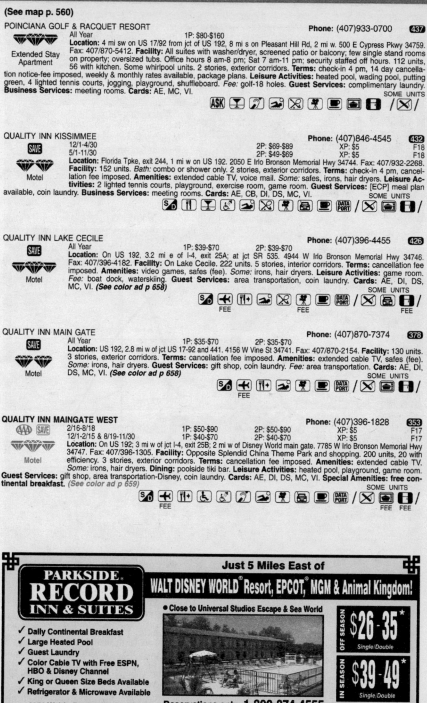

(See map p. 560)

QUALITY SUITES MAINGATE EAST

Phone: (407)396-8040   **359**

12/1-4/30 & 6/15-9/1	1P: $119-$229	2P: $119-$229
5/1-6/14 & 9/2-11/30	1P: $109-$209	2P: $109-$209

Location: I-4, exit 25A, 1 mi e on US 192. 5876 W Irlo Bronson Memorial Hwy 34746. Fax: 407/396-6766. **Facility:** 225 efficiencies. 113 two-bedroom units. *Bath:* combo or shower only. 5 stories, exterior corridors. **Terms:** check-in 4 pm, 3 day cancellation notice-fee imposed. **Amenities:** video games, voice mail, safes (fee), irons. **Dining:** restaurant, 7 am-11 & 6-9 pm, $6-$12. **Leisure Activities:** heated pool, wading pool, whirlpool, playground, game room. **Guest Services:** [ECP] meal plan available, gift shop, complimentary evening beverages, area transportation-Disney, coin laundry. **Cards:** AE, CB, DI, DS, MC, VI. **Special Amenities: free continental breakfast and free newspaper.** *(See color ad below)*

Suite Motel

SOME UNITS

(See map p. 560)

RADISSON RESORT PARKWAY

Phone: (407)396-7000 **403**

AAA SAVE
◇◇◇◇
Hotel

All Year   1P: $89-$129   2P: $89-$129
Location: I-4, exit 25A, just e on US 192, then just n. 2900 Parkway Blvd 34747. **Fax:** 407/396-6792. **Facility:** 27 acres of landscaped grounds with covered, lighted walkways connecting all facilities. Designated smoking area. 718 units. 8 stories, interior corridors. **Terms:** check-in 4 pm, cancellation fee imposed. **Amenities:** voice mail, safes, honor bars, irons, hair dryers. *Some:* CD players, fax. **Dining:** 2 restaurants, deli, 6:30 am-11 & 5-1 am; seasonal pool bar, $6-$15, cocktails. **Leisure Activities:** 2 pools (1 heated), wading pool, saunas, steamroom, waterslide, 2 lighted tennis courts, playground, exercise room, volleyball, game room. **Guest Services:** [BP], [CP] & [MAP] meal plans available, gift shop, area transportation-major attractions, coin laundry. **Business Services:** meeting rooms, administrative services, PC, fax. **Cards:** AE, CB, DI, DS, JC, MC, VI. *(See color ad below)*

SOME UNITS

RAMADA DISNEY AREA EASTGATE/FOUNTAIN PARK

Phone: (407)396-1111 **427**

AAA SAVE
◇◇◇◇
Motor Inn

All Year   1P: $69-$129   2P: $69-$129
Location: On US 192, 2.8 mi e of I-4, exit 25A. 5150 W Irlo Bronson Memorial Hwy 34746. **Fax:** 407/396-1607. **Facility:** 402 units. *Bath:* combo or shower only. 10 stories, interior corridors. **Terms:** check-in 4 pm. **Amenities:** voice mail, safes (fee), irons, hair dryers. **Dining:** restaurant, 6 am-11 & 5-10 pm, $6-$13, cocktails. **Leisure Activities:** heated pool, wading pool, whirlpool, playground. **Guest Services:** area transportation-major attractions, coin laundry. **Business Services:** meeting rooms. **Cards:** AE, CB, DI, DS, MC, VI. *(See color ad p 661)*

SOME UNITS

RAMADA INN RESORT MAINGATE

Phone: (407)396-4466 **339**

AAA SAVE
◇◇◇◇
Motor Inn

12/20-8/17	1P: $69-$129	2P: $69-$129	XP: $10	F18
8/18-11/30	1P: $49-$79	2P: $49-$79	XP: $10	F18
12/1-12/19	1P: $49-$69	2P: $49-$69	XP: $10	F18

Location: On US 192; 2 mi w of jct I-4, 1 mi w of Disney World access road. 2950 Reedy Creek Blvd 34747. **Fax:** 407/396-6418. **Facility:** 391 units. *Bath:* combo or shower only. 2 stories, exterior corridors. **Terms:** check-in 4 pm, 3 day cancellation notice-fee imposed, pets ($75 fee). **Amenities:** voice mail, safes (fee). **Dining:** restaurant, deli, 7 am-2 & 4-11 pm, $6-$15, cocktails. **Leisure Activities:** 2 heated pools, wading pool, lighted tennis court, exercise room, basketball, game room. **Guest Services:** [BP] meal plan available, gift shop, area transportation-Disney, coin laundry. **Business Services:** meeting rooms. **Cards:** AE, CB, DI, DS, JC, MC, VI. *(See color ad p 644)*

SOME UNITS

(See map p. 560)

RAMADA PLAZA HOTEL AND INNS-GATEWAY   Phone: (407)396-4400   357
AAA SAVE
Motor Inn
1/2-8/18	1P: $69-$129	2P: $69-$129
12/1-1/1	1P: $59-$129	2P: $59-$129
8/19-11/30	1P: $59-$99	2P: $59-$99

Location: US 192, 2.3 mi w of jct I-4, exit 25; 1 mi w of Disney World maingate. 7470 W Irlo Bronson Memorial Hwy 34747. Fax: 407/397-4481. **Facility:** 2 buildings, exterior corridor low-rise and interior corridor high-rise plaza. 500 units. Some suites ($149-$189). *Bath:* combo or shower only. 2-8 stories, interior/exterior corridors. **Terms:** check-in 4 pm, cancellation fee imposed. **Amenities:** extended cable TV, voice mail. *Some:* irons, hair dryers. **Dining:** dining room, deli, 7 am-midnight, $8-$20, cocktails. **Leisure Activities:** 2 pools (1 heated), putting green, exercise room, basketball, shuffleboard. **Guest Services:** gift shop, area transportation-major attractions, coin laundry. **Business Services:** meeting rooms. **Cards:** AE, CB, DI, DS, MC, VI. *(See color ad below)*

RED ROOF INN   Phone: (407)396-0065   428
AAA SAVE
Motel
All Year   1P: $50   2P: $60

Location: I-4, exit 25A, 3.7 mi e, jct of SR 192 and 535, between MM 11 and 12. 4970 Kyngs Heath Rd 34746. Fax: 407/396-0245. **Facility:** Guest rooms with comtemporary appointments range in size from compact singles to more spacious king-bedded rooms. 102 units. 3 stories, exterior corridors. **Terms:** 15 day cancellation notice. **Amenities:** extended cable TV, video games, voice mail. **Leisure Activities:** heated pool, whirlpool. **Guest Services:** coin laundry. *Fee:* area transportation-major attractions. **Cards:** AE, CB, DI, DS, MC, VI. **Special Amenities:** early check-in/late check-out and free continental breakfast.

(See map p. 560)

RIVIERA MOTEL
Phone: 407/847-9494 395

AAA SAVE

Motel

12/1-1/2	1P: $26-$36	2P: $36-$46	XP: $5
2/11-4/20	1P: $26-$36	2P: $36-$42	XP: $5
1/3-2/10 & 4/21-11/30	1P: $26-$32	2P: $32-$37	XP: $5

Location: US 192 and 441, at Florida Tpke, exit 244. 2248 E Irlo Bronson Memorial Hwy 34744. **Facility:** 28 units. *Bath:* combo or shower only. 2 stories, exterior corridors. **Terms:** 3 day cancellation notice, weekly rates available. **Cards:** AE, DS, MC, VI.

SOME UNITS

RON JON RESORT-ORLANDO
Phone: (407)239-5000 325

AAA SAVE

Condominium

All Year   1P: $99-$369   2P: $99-$369

Location: 7 mi w of jct I-4, exit 25B, 1.5 mi of jct US 27. 17777 Bali Blvd 34787 (17777 Bali Blvd, WINTER GARDEN). Fax: 407/239-5092. **Facility:** Units available in 5-story building and 2-story townhouses in 4-plex buildings. Washer/dryer and screened patio or open balcony in every unit. 408 units with kitchen. 235 two-bedroom units and 30 three-bedroom units. Some whirlpool units ($99-$369). *Bath:* some shared or private. 2-5 stories, exterior corridors. **Terms:** check-in 4 pm, 15 day cancellation notice-fee imposed, weekly rates available. **Amenities:** voice mail, safes, irons, hair dryers. *Some:* CD players. **Dining:** poolside snack bar. **Leisure Activities:** 2 heated pools, saunas, whirlpools, waterslide, liki tiki lagoon water island, wave pool, water volleyball, paddleboats, fishing, putting green, 2 lighted tennis courts, bicycles, playground, basketball, volleyball, game room, fitness trail. **Guest Services:** [CP] meal plan available, gift shop, complimentary laundry. *Fee:* area transportation-major attractions. **Business Services:** meeting rooms. **Cards:** AE, CB, DI, DS, MC, VI. **Special Amenities:** free local telephone calls and preferred room (subject to availability with advanced reservations). *(See color ad p 584 & p 635)*

FEE

ROYAL OAKS OF KISSIMMEE
Phone: (407)390-8200 417

AAA SAVE

Condominium

All Year   1P: $99-$199   2P: $99-$199

Location: I-4, exit 25A, 6 mi e. 5075 W Irlo Bronson Hwy 34746. Fax: 407/390-0718. **Facility:** Designated smoking area. 55 units with kitchen. *Bath:* combo or shower only. 2 stories, exterior corridors. **Terms:** check-in 4 pm, 31 day cancellation notice-fee imposed, small pets only ($50 extra charge). **Amenities:** extended cable TV, irons. **Leisure Activities:** heated pool, whirlpool, playground, barbecue grills, picnic tables. **Guest Services:** complimentary laundry. **Cards:** DS, MC, VI. **Special Amenities:** free local telephone calls and preferred room (subject to availability with advanced reservations).

SEVILLA INN
Phone: (407)396-4135 366

AAA SAVE

Motel

6/21-9/6	1P: $40-$50	2P: $45-$65	XP: $10 D9
12/1-5/1	1P: $30-$50	2P: $35-$65	XP: $10 D9
5/2-6/20 & 9/7-11/30	1P: $30-$35	2P: $35-$45	XP: $10 D9

Location: On US 192, 4.2 mi w of jct US 17/92/441. 4640 W Irlo Bronson Memorial Hwy 34746. Fax: 407/396-4942. **Facility:** 47 units. 3 stories (no elevator), exterior corridors. **Amenities:** *Some:* safes (fee). **Leisure Activities:** heated pool. **Guest Services:** coin laundry. **Cards:** AE, DS, MC, VI. **Special Amenities:** free local telephone calls.

SOME UNITS

SHERATON FOUR POINTS LAKESIDE
Phone: (407)396-2222 352

AAA SAVE

Motor Inn

2/9-8/11	1P: $79-$109	2P: $79-$109	XP: $10 F17
12/1-2/8 & 8/12-11/30	1P: $69-$99	2P: $69-$99	XP: $10 F17

Location: US 192; 3 mi w of I-4 exit 25; 1.8 mi w of Disney main gate. 7769 W Irlo Bronson Memorial Hwy 34747-1750. Fax: 407/239-2650. **Facility:** Opposite "Splendid China" theme park. 651 units. *Bath:* combo or shower only. 2 stories, exterior corridors. **Terms:** check-in 4 pm, cancellation fee imposed, $4 service charge. **Amenities:** extended cable TV, voice mail, safes (fee), irons, hair dryers. **Dining:** 2 restaurants, 6 am-11:30 & 5-11 pm, 2 pool bars, $6-$15, cocktails. **Leisure Activities:** 3 heated pools, wading pools, paddleboats, 4 lighted tennis courts, children's program, playground, exercise room, game room. *Fee:* miniature golf. **Guest Services:** gift shop, area transportation-Disney, coin laundry. **Business Services:** meeting rooms. **Cards:** AE, CB, DI, DS, JC, MC, VI. **Special Amenities:** free local telephone calls and free newspaper. *(See color ad p 663)*

FEE   FEE   SOME UNITS

SLEEP INN MAINGATE
Phone: (407)396-1600 326

AAA SAVE

Motel

All Year   1P: $49-$79   2P: $59-$99   XP: $10   F16

Location: On US 192, 2.8 mi e of jct US 27; 5.5 mi w of I-4, exit 25B. 8536 W Irlo Bronson Memorial Hwy 34747. Fax: 407/396-1971. **Facility:** 104 units. *Bath:* combo or shower only. 3 stories, interior corridors. **Amenities:** safes, hair dryers. **Guest Services:** area transportation-Disney, coin laundry. **Cards:** AE, CB, DI, DS, JC, MC, VI. **Special Amenities:** free continental breakfast and free local telephone calls. *(See color ad p 664)*

SOME UNITS

STADIUM INN & SUITES
Phone: (407)846-7814 392

AAA SAVE

Suite Motor Inn

12/21-1/5	1P: $65-$125	2P: $65-$125
1/6-8/31	1P: $56-$80	2P: $56-$80
9/1-11/30	1P: $50-$60	2P: $50-$60
12/1-12/20	1P: $49-$60	2P: $49-$60

Location: 1 mi w of Florida Tpke, exit 244; on SR 192. 2039 E Irlo Bronson Memorial Hwy 34744. Fax: 407/846-1863. **Facility:** 112 units, 56 with efficiency. 2 stories, interior corridors. **Terms:** 30 day cancellation notice, weekly & monthly rates available. **Amenities:** extended cable TV. **Leisure Activities:** heated pool, whirlpool, game room. **Guest Services:** coin laundry. **Business Services:** meeting rooms. **Cards:** AE, CB, DI, DS, JC, MC, VI.

SOME UNITS

(See map p. 560)

STAR ISLAND RESORT & CLUB   **Phone:** (407)997-8000 `418`

All Year   1P: $127-$285   2P: $127-$285

Suite Resort

Location: I-4, exit 25A, 3.5 mi e on US 192, 0.5 mi s; between MM 10 and 11. 5000 Avenue of the Stars 34746. **Fax:** 407/997-5252. **Facility:** Gated entry to a large, landscaped, Mediterranean-style golf and tennis resort and spa. Features one- and two-bedroom condo style units with patio or balcony. 316 units. 158 two-bedroom units, 158 efficiencies and 158 units with kitchen. Some whirlpool units ($127-$285). **Bath:** combo or shower only. 6 stories, exterior corridors. **Terms:** check-in 4 pm, 3 day cancellation notice-fee imposed. **Amenities:** extended cable TV, voice mail, hair dryers. *Some:* CD players, safes (fee), irons. **Dining:** poolside bar. **Leisure Activities:** heated pool, saunas, whirlpools, steamrooms, beach, driving range, golf pro, 10 lighted tennis courts, children's program, recreation program, bicycles, playground, sports court. *Fee:* paddleboats, jet ski, putting green, stadium tennis courts with instruction & equipment. **Guest Services:** gift shop, complimentary laundry. *Fee:* massage. **Business Services:** meeting rooms. **Cards:** AE, CB, DI, DS, JC, MC, VI.

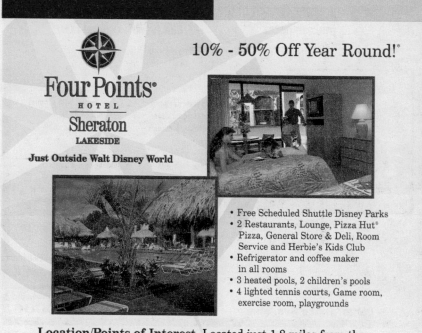

(See map p. 560)

SUMMERFIELD RESORT   **Phone:** (407)847-7222   386
AAA SAVE   All Year   2P: $99-$159   XP: $15
▼▼▼▼   **Location:** SR 423 (Bermuda Ave), 1 mi n of US 192; Florida Tpke, exit 249, 2.5 mi w, 2.5 mi s. 2422 Summerfield Pl
Apartment   34741. Fax: 407/847-6774. **Facility:** 2-bedroom, 2 1/2 bath townhouses with fully equipped kitchen and
washer/dryer. 37 two-bedroom units with kitchen. 2 stories, exterior corridors. **Terms:** 15 day cancellation
notice, monthly rates available, package plans, pets ($25-$75 extra charge). **Amenities:** extended cable TV,
irons. **Leisure Activities:** heated pool, whirlpool, playground, gazebo with grill. **Guest Services:** area
transportation-Disney, complimentary laundry. **Cards:** AE, DS, MC, VI. **Special Amenities: free continental breakfast and free
local telephone calls.**
                                                                              SOME UNITS

(See map p. 560)

SUN MOTEL   Phone: (407)396-2673   **424**

AAA [SAVE]

12/20-1/4	1P: $80-$90	2P: $90-$95	XP: $10	D3
1/5-9/3	1P: $55-$65	2P: $65-$80	XP: $10	D3
12/1-12/19 & 9/4-11/30	1P: $27-$38	2P: $38-$42	XP: $10	D3

Motel   **Location:** US 192, 3.3 mi e of I-4, exit 25A; at jct SR 535. 5020 W Hwy 192 34746. **Facility:** Older style property; office hours 6:30 am-1 am. 106 units. 2 stories, exterior corridors. **Terms:** 3 day cancellation notice-fee imposed. **Amenities:** extended cable TV. **Guest Services:** coin laundry.
Cards: AE, DI, DS, JC, MC, VI. *(See color ad below)*

SOME UNITS

SUPER 8 MOTEL   Phone: (407)847-6121   **382**

AAA [SAVE]

12/1-1/3	2P: $39-$69	XP: $5	F12
6/5-11/30	2P: $36-$69	XP: $5	F12
2/9-6/4	2P: $29-$69	XP: $5	F12
1/4-2/8	2P: $29-$39	XP: $5	F12

Motel   **Location:** I-4, 8 mi e at exit 25A; on US 193, 1.3 mi w of jct US 17-92 and 441. 1815 W Vine St 34746. Fax: 407/847-0728. **Facility:** 123 units, 28 with kitchen. Some suites ($59-$99). 2 stories, exterior corridors.
Amenities: extended cable TV. **Guest Services:** coin laundry. **Cards:** AE, CB, DI, DS, MC, VI. **Special Amenities:** free continental breakfast and preferred room (subject to availability with advanced reservations). *(See ad below)*

SOME UNITS

(See map p. 560)

SUPER 8 MOTEL

AAA SAVE

♦♦♦ ♦♦

Motel

12/1-1/3	2P: $39-$69	XP: $5	F12
6/5-11/30	2P: $36-$69	XP: $5	F12
2/9-6/4	2P: $29-$69	XP: $5	F12
1/4-2/8	2P: $29-$39	XP: $5	F12

Phone: (407)396-1144 **368**

Location: On US 192, 3.8 mi e of jct I-4, exit 25A; just e of jct SR 535. 4880 W Irlo Bronson Memorial Hwy 34746. Fax: 407/396-4389. **Facility:** Few rooms face lake. Some with private patio or balcony. 126 units, 10 with efficiency. 2 stories, exterior corridors. **Amenities:** safes (fee). **Guest Services:** coin laundry. **Cards:** AE, CB, DI, DS, JC, MC, VI. **Special Amenities: free continental breakfast and preferred room (subject to availability with advanced reservations).**

SOME UNITS

[icons] FEE / [icons] FEE FEE /

TRAVELODGE HOTEL/AIRPORT SOUTH

AAA SAVE

♦♦♦ ♦♦

Hotel

All Year   1P: $42-$55   2P: $42-$55   XP: $9   F18

Phone: (407)846-1530 **397**

Location: Florida Tpke exit 244; 0.3 mi w on US 192, just n. 201 Simpson Rd 34744. Fax: 407/846-2162. **Facility:** 198 units. 4 stories, exterior corridors. **Terms:** cancellation fee imposed, small pets only ($5 extra charge, $50 deposit). **Amenities:** safes (fee). **Dining:** dining room, 7 am-11 & 6-11 pm, $7-$11. **Leisure Activities:** game room. **Guest Services:** gift shop, area transportation-Disney, coin laundry. **Cards:** AE, CB, DI, DS, MC, VI. *(See ad below)*

SOME UNITS

[icons] DATA PORT / [icons] FEE FEE

TRAVELODGE HOTEL MAINGATE

AAA SAVE

♦♦♦ ♦♦

Motel

12/21-4/30	1P: $49-$105	2P: $49-$105
5/1-8/21	1P: $45-$95	2P: $45-$95
12/1-12/20	1P: $45-$85	2P: $45-$85
8/22-11/30	1P: $42-$85	2P: $42-$85

Phone: (407)396-0100 **330**

Location: US 192, 5.3 mi w of jct I-4, 2.8 mi e of US 27. 8600 W Irlo Bronson Memorial Hwy 34747. Fax: 407/396-6718. **Facility:** 299 units. 2 stories, exterior corridors. **Terms:** cancellation fee imposed. **Amenities:** extended cable TV, safes (fee). *Some:* hair dryers. **Dining:** restaurant, 7 am-10:30 & 7-10 pm; breakfast & dinner buffet, $9-$20. **Leisure Activities:** wading pool. **Guest Services:** gift shop, area transportation-Disney, coin laundry. **Cards:** AE, CB, DI, DS, MC, VI. **Special Amenities: early check-in/late check-out and free newspaper.** *(See color ad p 667)*

SOME UNITS

[icons] / [icons] FEE /

(See map p. 560)

TRAVELODGE HOTEL MAIN GATE EAST   Phone: (407)396-4222   **411**

AAA SAVE
◆◆ ◆◆
Motor Inn

2/9-11/30	1P: $59	2P: $59	
12/1-12/31	1P: $49	2P: $49	
1/1-2/8	1P: $44	2P: $44	

Location: US 192, 2 mi e of I-4, exit 25. 5711 W Irlo Bronson Hwy 34746. Fax: 407/396-1834. **Facility:** 2 mid-rise towers connected by restaurant, lounge and shops. Some rooms with balcony. 446 units, 29 with efficiency. 8 stories, interior corridors. **Terms:** check-in 4 pm, cancellation fee imposed. **Amenities:** voice mail, safes (fee), irons, hair dryers. **Dining:** 7 am-10:30 pm, food court. **Leisure Activities:** heated pool, wading pool, saunas, whirlpool, sand volleyball. **Guest Services:** gift shop, area transportation-Disney, coin laundry. **Business Services:** meeting rooms. **Cards:** AE, CB, DI, DS, MC, VI. **Special Amenities:** free newspaper and free room upgrade (subject to availability with advanced reservations).** (See color ad p 666)

SOME UNITS

🅂ⓓ FEE ✦ 🍽 🏊 FEE 🎥 🖨 💻 DATAPORT / ✕ 📱 FEE

TRAVELODGE SUITES KISSIMMEE EAST GATE ORANGE   Phone: (407)396-7666   **416**

AAA SAVE
◆◆ ◆◆
Motel

12/21-8/25	1P: $69-$129	2P: $69-$129	XP: $5 F12
12/1-12/20 & 8/26-11/30	1P: $49-$89	2P: $49-$89	XP: $5 F12

Location: I-4, exit 25A, 2.5 mi e on US 192; between MM 10 and 11. 5399 W Irlo Bronson Memorial Hwy 34746. Fax: 407/396-0696. **Facility:** Single, large room with sofa. Some rooms overlook pool courtyard area. Designated smoking area. 156 units. 3 two-bedroom units and 15 units with kitchen. Some whirlpool units ($69-$129). 2 stories, exterior corridors. **Amenities:** extended cable TV, safes (fee). **Leisure Activities:** heated pool, wading pool, whirlpool, playground. **Guest Services:** [CP] meal plan available, area transportation-Disney, coin laundry. **Business Services:** meeting rooms. **Cards:** AE, CB, DI, DS, MC, VI. (See ad p 599 & color ad p 670)

SOME UNITS

🅂ⓓ FEE ✦ 🛗 🖥 🏊 FEE 🎥 💻 📱 / ✕ VCR

TROPICAL PALMS RESORT   Phone: (407)396-4595   **410**

AAA SAVE
◆◆ ◆◆
Cottage

All Year   2P: $59-$99

Location: I-4, exit 25A, 1.2 mi e on US 192, 0.5 mi s; at MM 9. 2650 Holiday Tr 34746. Fax: 407/396-8938. **Facility:** 60 acres of landscaped grounds for individual guest units in small cul-de-sac groupings. Each unit has living area, kitchen with eating area, large deck with patio furniture, and bedrooms that are 2 separate rooms or studio style. Designated smoking area. 144 units with kitchen. 92 two-bedroom units. 1 story, exterior corridors. **Terms:** check-in 4 pm, 7 day cancellation notice. **Dining:** poolside cafe. **Leisure Activities:** heated pool, wading pool, fishing, playground, basketball, horseshoes, shuffleboard, volleyball. **Guest Services:** coin laundry. **Fee:** area transportation. **Cards:** AE, DS, MC, VI. (See color ad starting on p 668)

✦ 🏊 FEE ✕ 💻 🖥 📱

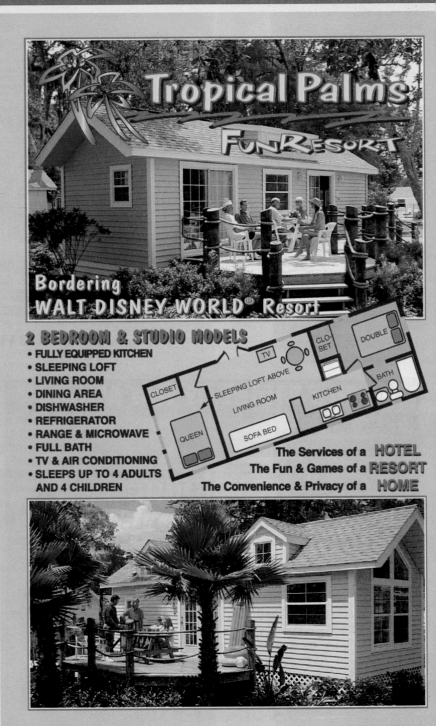

POOL-SIDE CAFÉ

SPECIAL AAA RATES $69 - $99*

KIDDIE POOL

HEATED POOL OPEN 24 HOURS

DIRECTIONS:
FROM I-4 EXIT 25-A, GO EAST ON 192
ONE MILE. TURN RIGHT ON HOLIDAY
TRAIL. THE RESORT IS LOCATED
BEHIND OLD TOWN.

Tropical Palms
2650 Holiday Trail
Kissimmee, Florida 34746
Ph:(407) 396-4595
Fax:(407) 396-8938
E-MAIL: stay@tropicalpalms.com
Internet: funsuites.com

*Rate is for Studio Model 1-6 people, based on season and availability.

(See map p. 560)

THE VILLAGES AT MANGO KEY
Phone: (407)397-2211   332

AAA SAVE
Apartment

12/17-1/2 Wkly   2P: $900-$1100
4/9-11/30 Wkly   2P: $700-$1100
12/1-12/16 & 1/3-4/8 Wkly   2P: $700-$900

Location: Just s of US 192; 1 mi e of US 27 and 5.7 mi w of I-4 exit 25A; 4.5 mi w of Disney main gate access road. 3201 Lindfields Blvd 34747. Fax: 407/397-2789. **Facility:** Two to three bedroom townhouse units with screened patio and full sized washer/dryer. Quiet location. 33 units with kitchen. 28 two-bedroom units and 5 three-bedroom units. 2 stories, exterior corridors. **Terms:** check-in 4 pm, 30 day cancellation notice-fee imposed. **Amenities:** extended cable TV, safes, irons, hair dryers. *Some:* CD players. **Dining:** small snack bar. **Leisure Activities:** heated pool, whirlpool, golf privileges, playground, volleyball. **Guest Services:** complimentary laundry. **Cards:** AE, DS, MC, VI. **Special Amenities:** free local telephone calls.

(See map p. 560)

VILLAS AT FORTUNE PLACE
All Year — 2P: $119-$159 — **Phone:** (407)348-0330   396
▼▼▼▼
Apartment
Location: 0.3 mi w of Florida Tpke, exit 244 on US 192, 1.2 mi n. 1201 Simpson Rd 34744. Fax: 407/348-0232. **Facility:** 2- and 3-bedroom housekeeping units. 100 units with kitchen. 78 two-bedroom units and 22 three-bedroom units. 2 stories, exterior corridors. **Terms:** check-in 4 pm, 14 day cancellation notice. **Amenities:** irons. **Leisure Activities:** heated pool, whirlpool, fishing, tennis court, playground, basketball. **Guest Services:** complimentary laundry. **Cards:** AE, MC, VI.

SOME UNITS
[ASK] [SD] [≈] [X] [▶] [VCR] [🖨] [📶] [🍳] [❚] / [X] /
FEE

WESTGATE TOWERS/WESTGATE VACATION VILLAS
[AAA] [SAVE]
12/15-1/2 — 1P: $200-$675 — **Phone:** (407)396-2500   327
1/3-11/30 — 1P: $120-$575
▼▼▼▼
12/1-12/14 — 1P: $120-$475
Condominium
Location: Jct SR 545 on US 192, 2.5 mi w of jct I-4, exit 25A, 1 mi w of Disney World main gate. 7600 W Irlo Bronson Memorial Hwy 34747. Fax: 407/396-2096. **Facility:** Very comfortable units, including 900 villa units. 1000 units with kitchen. 882 two-bedroom units. Some whirlpool units. 3-5 stories, interior corridors. **Terms:** check-in 4 pm, 14 day cancellation notice-fee imposed. **Amenities:** extended cable TV, safes. **Dining:** 2 coffee shops, 7 am-11 pm, $7-$20, entertainment. **Leisure Activities:** 11 heated pools, wading pool, whirlpool, paddleboats, 4 lighted tennis courts, bicycles, exercise room, basketball, volleyball. **Guest Services:** gift shop, complimentary laundry. *Fee:* area transportation-attractions. **Cards:** AE, DI, DS, MC, VI. *(See color ad p 614)*

[SD] [➦] [♨] [≈] [X] [▶] [VCR] [📶] [🍳] [❚]
FEE

WONDERLAND INN
[AAA] [SAVE]
8/27-11/30 — 1P: $79 — 2P: $139 — **Phone:** (407)847-2477   436
4/30-6/15 — 1P: $79 — 2P: $129
▼▼▼▼
6/16-8/26 — 1P: $59 — 2P: $99
12/1-4/29 — 1P: $59 — 2P: $89
Bed & Breakfast
Location: From US 192, 3 mi s on John Young Pkwy/Bermuda Ave. 3601 S Orange Blossom Tr 34741. Fax: 407/847-4099. **Facility:** Charming motel with a French country decor, attractive gardens and breakfast room. Guest rooms are well appointed though some are compact. Very well maintained property. Smoke free premises. 11 units, 5 with efficiency. Some whirlpool units ($129-$169). *Bath:* combo or shower only. 1 story, exterior corridors. **Terms:** 7 day cancellation notice. **Amenities:** extended cable TV, voice mail, hair dryers. **Leisure Activities:** lawn games. **Guest Services:** [ECP] meal plan available, complimentary evening beverages. *Fee:* massage. **Cards:** AE, DI, DS, MC, VI. **Special Amenities: preferred room (subject to availability with advanced reservations).**

SOME UNITS
[SD] [X] [▶] [🖨] [📶] [❚] / [🍳] /

(See map p. 560)

———— *The following lodgings were either not evaluated or did not* ————
meet AAA rating requirements but are listed for your information only.

AMERISUITES AT CALYPSO CAY   **Phone: 407/997-1500**
[fyi]   12/1-4/30 & 6/15-9/4   1P: $159   2P: $159
              5/1-6/14 & 9/5-11/30   1P: $99   2P: $99
Suite Motel   Too new to rate, opening scheduled for November 2000. **Location:** I-4, exit 27, s towards Hwy 192. 5000 Thatcher
Dr 34746. Fax: 407/997-1550. **Amenities:** 151 units, radios, coffeemakers, microwaves, refrigerators, pool.
Terms: 3 day cancellation notice. **Cards:** AE, CB, DI, DS, JC, MC, VI.

COUNTRY INN & SUITES   **Phone: 407/644-9055**
[fyi]   Under construction, scheduled to open April 2001. **Location:** I-4, exit 27, s towards Hwy 192. Calypso Cay Way
Motel   34746. Fax: 407/644-9845. **Planned Amenities:** 162 units, radios, coffeemakers, microwaves, refrigerators,
pool.

DIPLOMAT RESORT AT MAINGATE   **Phone: (407)396-6000** [344]
(AAA) [SAVE]   All Year   1P: $79-$99   2P: $79-$99   XP: $10   F17
[fyi]   Under major renovation, scheduled to be completed March 2000. **Last rated:** ♛♛♛ **Location:** On US 192;
Motor Inn   2.1 mi w of jct I-4, exit 25; 1 mi w of Disney World main gate. 7491 W Irlo Bronson Memorial Hwy 34747.
Fax: 407/396-2895. **Facility:** Family-oriented with registration and dining areas for children. 442 units. 4 stories, interior corridors. **Terms:** 3 day cancellation notice-fee imposed, package plans, $2 service charge.
Amenities: voice mail, safes (fee), irons. **Dining:** dining room, 7 am-11 & 5-10 pm food court & ice cream parlor, $9-$14, cocktails, entertainment. **Leisure Activities:** 2 heated pools, whirlpool, children's program, indoor recreation area. **Guest Services:**
gift shop, area transportation-Disney, coin laundry. **Cards:** AE, DS, JC, MC, VI. *(See color ad p 671)*   SOME UNITS

[icons] FEE

———— **WHERE TO DINE** ————

FUSIONS   **Lunch: $4-$13**   **Dinner: $9-$17**   **Phone: 407/994-2046** [246]
♛♛ ♛♛   **Location:** I-4, exit 25, 7 mi e on US 192; in Four Points Hotel Sheraton Orlando/Kissimmee. 4018 W Vine St 34741.
American   **Hours:** 6:30 am-11 & 5-10 pm. **Reservations:** accepted. **Features:** casual dress; children's menu;
carryout; salad bar; cocktails & lounge. Comfortable seating, some with pool-side view. Pleasant decor.
Menu has limited variety, but items are well prepared. Seafood, beef, chicken and pasta are represented.
Limited wine selection. Dining on covered patio in-season. **Cards:** AE, CB, DI, DS, MC, VI.   [icons]

GIANNI'S RESTAURANT   **Lunch: $6-$8**   **Dinner: $8-$16**   **Phone: 407/846-4331** [249]
♛♛ ♛♛   **Location:** 0.3 mi e of jct US 17 and US 92 on SR 192. 610 E Vine St 34744. **Hours:** 11 am-10 pm. Closed major
Italian   holidays; also Sun. **Features:** casual dress; carryout; beer & wine only. This family-run eatery offers a wide
selection of lasagna, stuffed shells, ravioli, chicken, veal and eggplant dishes. For a nice, casual meal, try
the grilled scallops on angel hair pasta, served in a deep bowl with a chilled plate of mixed greens.
Cards: AE, CB, DI, DS, MC, VI.   [icon]

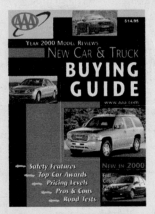

(See map p. 560)

GIORDANO'S
▼▼ ▼▼
Italian
Lunch: $6-$8   **Dinner: $7-$11**   **Phone: 407/397-0044** 243
Location: 3.5 mi w of jct I-4 exit 25, on US 192; in Formosa Garden Shopping Center. 7866 W Irlo Bronson Hwy 34747. **Hours:** 11 am-midnight. **Features:** casual dress; children's menu; senior's menu; carryout; cocktails & lounge. Chicago-style stuffed pizza is the specialty of the house with home delivery an option. A friendly, casual atmosphere with traditional Italian dishes is offered here. Feast on the pizza, but don't skip dessert at this family-oriented restaurant. **Cards:** AE, CB, DI, MC, VI.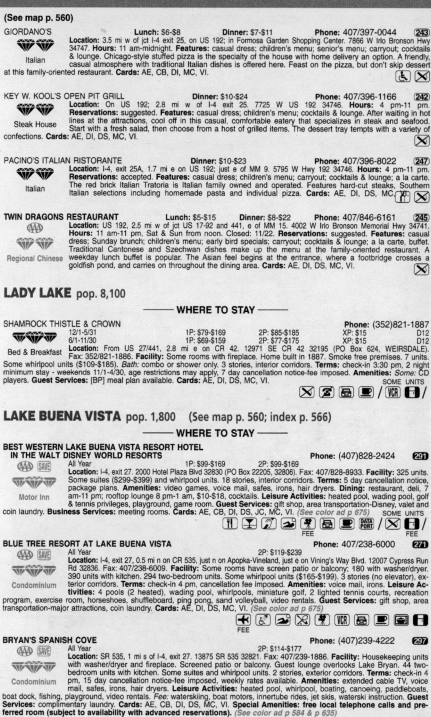

KEY W. KOOL'S OPEN PIT GRILL
▼▼ ▼▼
Steak House
Dinner: $10-$24   **Phone: 407-396-1166** 242
Location: On US 192; 2.8 mi w of I-4 exit 25. 7725 W US 192 34746. **Hours:** 4 pm-11 pm. **Reservations:** suggested. **Features:** casual dress; children's menu; cocktails & lounge. After waiting in hot lines at the attractions, cool off in this casual, comfortable eatery that specializes in steak and seafood. Start with a fresh salad, then choose from a host of grilled items. The dessert tray tempts with a variety of confections. **Cards:** AE, DI, DS, MC, VI.

PACINO'S ITALIAN RISTORANTE
▼▼ ▼▼
Italian
Dinner: $10-$23   **Phone: 407/396-8022** 247
Location: I-4, exit 25A, 1.7 mi e on US 192; just e of MM 9. 5795 W Hwy 192 34746. **Reservations:** accepted. **Features:** casual dress; children's menu; carryout; cocktails & lounge; a la carte. The red brick Italian Tratoria is Italian family owned and operated. Features hard-cut steaks, Southern Italian selections including homemade pasta and individual pizza. **Cards:** AE, DI, DS, MC,

TWIN DRAGONS RESTAURANT
AAA
▼▼ ▼▼
Regional Chinese
Lunch: $5-$15   **Dinner: $8-$22**   **Phone: 407/846-6161** 245
Location: US 192, 2.5 mi w of jct 17-92 and 441, e of MM 15. 4002 W Irlo Bronson Memorial Hwy 34741. **Hours:** 11 am-11 pm, Sat & Sun from noon. **Closed:** 11/22. **Reservations:** suggested. **Features:** casual dress; Sunday brunch; children's menu; early bird specials; carryout; cocktails & lounge; a la carte, buffet. Traditional Cantonese and Szechwan dishes make up the menu at the family-oriented restaurant. A weekday lunch buffet is popular. The Asian feel begins at the entrance, where a footbridge crosses a goldfish pond, and carries on throughout the dining area. **Cards:** AE, DI, DS, MC, VI.

LADY LAKE pop. 8,100

——— **WHERE TO STAY** ———

SHAMROCK THISTLE & CROWN   **Phone: (352)821-1887**
▼▼ ▼▼
12/1-5/31   1P: $79-$169   2P: $85-$185   XP: $15   D12
6/1-11/30   1P: $69-$159   2P: $77-$175   XP: $15   D12
Bed & Breakfast
Location: From US 27/441, 2.8 mi e on CR 42. 12971 SE CR 42 32195 (PO Box 624, WEIRSDALE). **Fax:** 352/821-1886. **Facility:** Some rooms with fireplace. Home built in 1887. Smoke free premises. 7 units. Some whirlpool units ($109-$185). *Bath:* combo or shower only. 3 stories, interior corridors. **Terms:** check-in 3:30 pm, 2 night minimum stay - weekends 11/1-4/30, age restrictions may apply, 7 day cancellation notice-fee imposed. **Amenities:** *Some:* CD players. **Guest Services:** [BP] meal plan available. **Cards:** AE, DI, DS, MC, VI.   SOME UNITS

LAKE BUENA VISTA pop. 1,800   (See map p. 560; index p. 566)

——— **WHERE TO STAY** ———

BEST WESTERN LAKE BUENA VISTA RESORT HOTEL
IN THE WALT DISNEY WORLD RESORTS   **Phone: (407)828-2424** 291
AAA SAVE
▼▼ ▼▼
Motor Inn
All Year   1P: $99-$169   2P: $99-$169
Location: I-4, exit 27. 2000 Hotel Plaza Blvd 32830 (PO Box 22205, 32806). **Fax:** 407/828-8933. **Facility:** 325 units. Some suites ($299-$399) and whirlpool units. 18 stories, interior corridors. **Terms:** 5 day cancellation notice, package plans. **Amenities:** video games, voice mail, safes, irons, hair dryers. **Dining:** restaurant, deli, 7 am-11 pm; rooftop lounge 8 pm-1 am, $10-$18, cocktails. **Leisure Activities:** heated pool, wading pool, golf & tennis privileges, playground, game room. **Guest Services:** gift shop, area transportation-Disney, valet and coin laundry. **Business Services:** meeting rooms. **Cards:** AE, CB, DI, DS, JC, MC, VI. *(See color ad p 675)*   SOME UNITS

BLUE TREE RESORT AT LAKE BUENA VISTA   **Phone: 407/238-6000** 271
AAA SAVE
▼▼ ▼▼
Condominium
All Year   2P: $119-$239
Location: I-4, exit 27, 0.5 mi n on CR 535, just n on Apopka-Vineland; just e on Vining's Way Blvd. 12007 Cypress Run Rd 32836. **Fax:** 407/238-6009. **Facility:** Some rooms have screen patio or balcony; 180 with washer/dryer. 390 units with kitchen. 294 two-bedroom units. Some whirlpool units ($165-$199). 3 stories (no elevator), exterior corridors. **Terms:** check-in 4 pm, cancellation fee imposed. **Amenities:** voice mail, irons. **Leisure Activities:** 4 pools (2 heated), wading pool, whirlpools, miniature golf, 2 lighted tennis courts, recreation program, exercise room, horseshoes, shuffleboard, ping pong, sand volleyball, video rentals. **Guest Services:** gift shop, area transportation-major attractions, coin laundry. **Cards:** AE, DI, DS, MC, VI. *(See color ad p 675)*

BRYAN'S SPANISH COVE   **Phone: (407)239-4222** 297
AAA SAVE
▼▼ ▼▼
Condominium
All Year   2P: $114-$177
Location: SR 535, 1 mi s of I-4, exit 27. 13875 SR 535 32821. **Fax:** 407/239-1886. **Facility:** Housekeeping units with washer/dryer and fireplace. Screened patio or balcony. Guest lounge overlooks Lake Bryan. 44 two-bedroom units with kitchen. Some suites and whirlpool units. 2 stories, exterior corridors. **Terms:** check-in 4 pm, 15 day cancellation notice-fee imposed, weekly rates available. **Amenities:** extended cable TV, voice mail, safes, irons, hair dryers. **Leisure Activities:** heated pool, whirlpool, boating, canoeing, paddleboats, boat dock, fishing, playground, video rentals. *Fee:* waterskiing, boat motors, innertube rides, jet skis, waterski instruction. **Guest Services:** complimentary laundry. **Cards:** AE, CB, DI, DS, MC, VI. **Special Amenities:** free local telephone calls and preferred room (subject to availability with advanced reservations).** *(See color ad p 584 & p 635)*

(See map p. 560)

BUENA VISTA SUITES
Phone: (407)239-8588   **301**

AAA SAVE

Suite Hotel

12/24-1/3	1P: $149-$169	2P: $149-$169
1/4-9/1	1P: $139-$159	2P: $139-$159
12/1-12/23 & 9/2-11/30	1P: $129-$149	2P: $129-$149

Location: At jct SR 535 and 536, 1.3 mi e of I-4, exit 26A. 8203 World Center Dr 32830 (PO Box 22826). **Fax:** 407/239-1401. **Facility:** Tastefully decorated 1-bedroom spacious suites. 280 units. Some suites and whirlpool units ($149-$189). *Bath:* combo or shower only. 7 stories, interior corridors. **Terms:** package plans. **Amenities:** voice mail, safes (fee). *Some:* irons, hair dryers. **Dining:** coffee shop, 6:30 am-9:30 pm, $4-$8, cocktails. **Leisure Activities:** heated pool, whirlpool, 2 lighted tennis courts, exercise room. **Guest Services:** [BP] meal plan available, gift shop, coin laundry. *Fee:* area transportation-major attractions. **Business Services:** meeting rooms. *Fee:* PC. **Cards:** AE, CB, DI, JC, MC, VI. *(See color ad p 677)*

SOME UNITS

⬛ ✈ 🍽 🍸 👤 ♿ 🛎 📷 🛥 📹 VCR 🖨 📺 🖥 🔌 DATA PORT / ✗ /
FEE

CARIBE ROYALE RESORT SUITES & VILLAS
Phone: (407)238-8000   **302**

AAA SAVE

Suite Hotel

All Year   2P: $149-$229

Location: I-4, exit 27, 1.2 mi s on SR 535, 0.3 mi e. 8101 World Center Dr 32821 (PO Box 22847, 32830). **Fax:** 407/238-8050. **Facility:** 1338 units. 120 two-bedroom units and 120 units with kitchen. Some suites and whirlpool units ($169-$249). *Bath:* combo or shower only. 4-10 stories, interior/exterior corridors. **Terms:** 3 day cancellation notice-fee imposed, package plans. **Amenities:** extended cable TV, video games, voice mail, safes (fee), irons, hair dryers. *Some:* CD players, honor bars. **Dining:** dining room, deli, 24 hours, $14-$25, cocktails. **Leisure Activities:** 2 heated pools, wading pool, whirlpools, waterslide, 2 lighted tennis courts, playground, exercise room. **Guest Services:** [BP] meal plan available, gift shop, area transportation-Disney, valet and coin laundry. **Business Services:** conference facilities, administrative services, PC, fax. **Cards:** AE, CB, DI, DS, JC, MC, VI. **Special Amenities:** free continental breakfast. *(See color ad below)*

SOME UNITS

🍽 📶 🍸 👤 ♿ 🛎 📷 🛥 ✗ 📹 🖨 📺 🖥 🔌 DATA PORT / ✗ /
FEE

COMFORT INN LAKE BUENA VISTA
Phone: (407)996-7300   **274**

AAA SAVE

Motor Inn

All Year   1P: $39-$99

Location: 0.5 mi n on CR 535 from jct I-4, exit 27, 0.5 mi e. 8442 Palm Pkwy 32836 (PO Box 22776, 32830). **Fax:** 407/996-7301. **Facility:** 640 units. *Bath:* combo or shower only. 5 stories, exterior corridors. **Terms:** small pets only ($6 fee). **Amenities:** safes. *Some:* irons, hair dryers. **Dining:** restaurant, 6:30 am-10:30 & 5:30-9 pm, $6-$10, cocktails. **Leisure Activities:** 2 pools (1 heated). **Guest Services:** gift shop, area transportation-Disney, coin laundry. **Cards:** AE, CB, DI, DS, JC, MC, VI. **Special Amenities:** free newspaper. *(See color ad p 606)*

SOME UNITS

⬛ 🐾 🍽 🍸 👤 ♿ 🛎 📷 🛥 / ✗ VCR 🖨 📺 🖥 🔌 /
FEE

(See map p. 560)

COUNTRY INN & SUITES BY CARLSON

Phone: (407)239-1115 `290`

Motel

1/3-4/22	1P: $79-$149	2P: $79-$149
12/1-1/2	1P: $69-$149	2P: $69-$149
6/14-11/30	1P: $79-$109	2P: $79-$109
4/23-6/13	1P: $69-$99	2P: $69-$99

Location: I-4, exit 27, 0.5 mi n on SR 535. 12191 S Apopka-Vineland Rd 32830. Fax: 407/239-8882. **Facility:** Well appointed guest rooms with some rooms designed for young families. 170 units. Some whirlpool ($99-$169). **Bath:** combo or shower only. 5 stories, interior corridors. **Amenities:** extended cable TV, voice mail, irons, hair dryers. **Leisure Activities:** heated pool, exercise room, game room. **Guest Services:** [CP] meal plan available, gift shop, area transportation, coin laundry. **Business Services:** meeting rooms. **Cards:** AE, CB, DI, DS, MC, VI. *(See color ad p 582 & p 572)*

SOME UNITS

ASK SD ⊞ & ⟨⟩ ⓘ ⊘ ⛵ 🎥 🚗 💻 📷 🍴 DATA PORT / ✕ /
FEE

COURTYARD BY MARRIOTT-IN THE WALT DISNEY WORLD RESORT

Phone: (407)828-8888 `289`

Motor Inn

12/27-8/18			
8/19-11/30	2P: $129-$219	XP: $15	F17
12/1-12/26	2P: $119-$199	XP: $15	F17
	2P: $119-$139	XP: $15	F17

Location: I-4, exit 27. 1805 Hotel Plaza Blvd 32830 (PO Box 22204). Fax: 407/394-5270. **Facility:** 323 units. **Bath:** combo or shower only. 6-14 stories, interior corridors. **Terms:** check-in 4 pm, cancellation fee imposed, package plans. **Amenities:** video games, voice mail, safes, irons, hair dryers. **Dining:** restaurant, deli, 6:30 am-midnight; pool bar in season, $15-$24, cocktails. **Leisure Activities:** 2 heated pools, wading pool, whirlpool, playground, exercise room. **Guest Services:** gift shop, area transportation-Disney, valet and coin laundry. **Business Services:** meeting rooms. **Cards:** AE, CB, DI, DS, MC, VI. **Special Amenities:** free newspaper. *(See color ad p 678)*

SOME UNITS

SD ✈ ⊞ ⟨⟩ ⓘ & ⊘ ⛵ 🚗 💻 DATA PORT ✕ 🍴
FEE   FEE   FEE

COURTYARD BY MARRIOTT VISTA CENTRE

Phone: (407)239-6900 `272`

Motor Inn

2/1-4/30 & 10/1-11/30	1P: $159-$199	2P: $159-$199
5/1-9/30	1P: $139-$179	2P: $139-$179
12/1-1/31	1P: $139-$179	2P: $179

Location: I-4, exit 27, 0.5 mi n on SR 535, 0.3 mi e. 8501 Palm Pkwy 32836 (PO Box 22818, 32830). Fax: 407/239-1287. **Facility:** 308 units. Some suites ($159-$189). **Bath:** combo or shower only. 3 stories, interior/exterior corridors. **Terms:** check-in 4 pm, cancellation fee imposed. **Amenities:** extended cable TV, voice mail, safes, irons, hair dryers. **Dining:** restaurant, deli, 6:30-11 am, cocktails. **Leisure Activities:** 2 heated pools, wading pool, whirlpool, playground, exercise room, game room. **Guest Services:** gift shop, area transportation-major attractions, coin laundry. **Business Services:** meeting rooms, administrative services. **Cards:** AE, CB, DI, DS, JC, MC, VI. **Special Amenities:** free newspaper. *(See color ad p 678)*

SOME UNITS

SD ⊞ ⟨⟩ ⓘ ⊘ ⛵ 🎥 🚗 💻 DATA PORT / ✕ 🍴 📷 /

DAYS INN LAKE BUENA VISTA HOTEL

Phone: (407)239-4441 `279`

Motor Inn

2/9-4/21	1P: $110-$205	2P: $120-$215	XP: $10	F17
1/1-2/8	1P: $89-$195	2P: $99-$205	XP: $10	F17
12/1-12/31	1P: $99-$185	2P: $99-$185	XP: $10	F17
4/22-11/30	1P: $79-$109	2P: $89-$119	XP: $10	F17

Location: CR 535 at jct I-4, exit 27. 12799 Apopka Vineland Rd 32836. Fax: 407/239-0325. **Facility:** 203 units. 8 stories, interior corridors. **Terms:** cancellation fee imposed, small pets only ($10 extra charge). **Amenities:** hair dryers. **Dining:** dining room, 6:30 am-11 & 5-10 pm, $6-$12, cocktails. **Leisure Activities:** playground. **Guest Services:** gift shop, area transportation-Disney, coin laundry. **Cards:** AE, CB, DI, DS, JC, MC, VI. **Special Amenities:** early check-in/late check-out and free room upgrade (subject to availability with advanced reservations). *(See color ad p 678)*

SOME UNITS

SD 🐕 ⊞ ⟨⟩ ⊘ ⛵ 🎥 🚗 💻 DATA PORT / ✕ VCR /

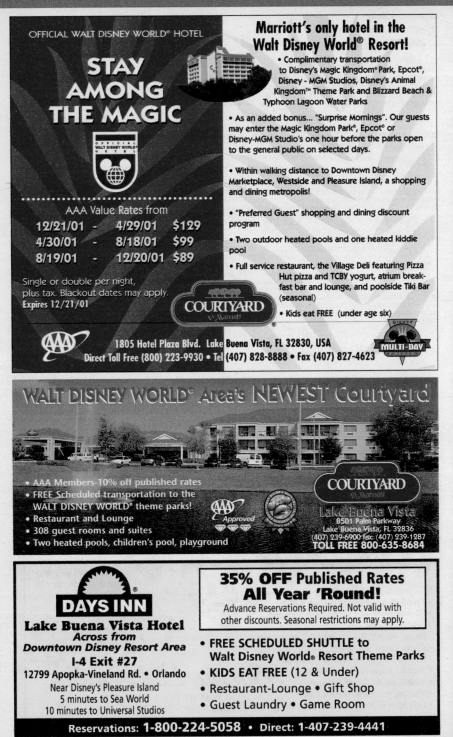

(See map p. 560)

DISNEY'S ALL STAR MOVIES

Phone: (407)939-7000 · 314

2/15-8/25	1P: $99-$104	2P: $99-$104	XP: $10	F17
12/1-12/31	1P: $74-$104	2P: $74-$104	XP: $10	F17
8/26-11/30	1P: $77-$99	2P: $77-$99	XP: $10	F17
1/1-2/14	1P: $77	2P: $77	XP: $10	F17

Resort

Location: I-4, exit 25B, 1.3 mi w on US 192, 1 min on World Dr, just w of Disney main gate access road. 1991 W Buena Vista Dr 32830-1000 (PO Box 10,000). Fax: 407/939-7111. **Facility:** This resort is the only Disney resort with a specifically Disney theme. Each building is named for a Disney movie and decorated accordingly. The Toy Story building, for example, has giant figures of toy soldiers standing guard on the roof. Other building themes include 101 Dalmatians, Mighty Ducks, Herbie the Love Bug, Fantasia and Fantasia 2000. Designated smoking area. 1920 units. *Bath:* combo or shower only. 3 stories, exterior corridors. **Terms:** check-in 4 pm, 5 day cancellation notice-fee imposed, package plans. **Amenities:** voice mail, safes. **Dining:** multi outlet food court, 6:30 am-midnight; pool bar, $5-$10. **Leisure Activities:** 2 heated pools, wading pool, playground, wet decks, arcade. **Guest Services:** gift shop, area transportation-within Disney complex, coin laundry. *Fee:* fax. **Cards:** AE, DI, DS, JC, MC, VI.

SOME UNITS

DISNEY'S ALL STAR MUSIC

Phone: (407)939-6000 · 313

2/15-8/25	1P: $99-$104	2P: $99-$104	XP: $10	F17
12/1-12/31	1P: $74-$104	2P: $74-$104	XP: $10	F17
8/26-11/30	1P: $77-$99	2P: $77-$99	XP: $10	F17
1/1-2/14	1P: $77	2P: $77	XP: $10	F17

Resort

Location: Just w of Disney main gate access road (World Dr); 1 min of US 192. 1801 W Buena Vista Dr 32830-1000 (PO Box 10,000). Fax: 407/939-7222. **Facility:** Unique music theme features larger-than-life icons at stairways, vending areas and in courtyards. 1920 units. *Bath:* combo or shower only. 3 stories, exterior corridors. **Terms:** check-in 4 pm, 5 day cancellation notice-fee imposed, package plans. **Amenities:** voice mail, safes. **Dining:** food court 6 am-midnight; pool bar, $5-$16. **Leisure Activities:** 2 heated pools, wading pool, playground, arcade room. **Guest Services:** gift shop, area transportation-Disney, valet and coin laundry. **Business Services:** fax. **Cards:** AE, DI, DS, JC, MC, VI.

SOME UNITS

DISNEY'S ALL STAR SPORTS

Phone: (407)939-5000 · 311

2/15-8/25	1P: $99-$104	2P: $99-$104	XP: $10	F17
12/1-12/31	1P: $74-$104	2P: $74-$104	XP: $10	F17
8/26-11/30	1P: $77-$99	2P: $77-$99	XP: $10	F17
1/1-2/14	1P: $77	2P: $77	XP: $10	F17

Resort

Location: Just w of Disney main gate access road (World Dr); 1 min of US 192. 1701 W Buena Vista Dr 32830-1000 (PO Box 10,000). Fax: 407/939-7333. **Facility:** Unique sports theme features larger-than-life icons at stairways, vending areas and in courtyards. 1920 units. *Bath:* combo or shower only. 3 stories, exterior corridors. **Terms:** check-in 4 pm, 5 day cancellation notice-fee imposed, package plans. **Amenities:** voice mail, safes. **Dining:** food court 6 am-midnight; pool bar. **Leisure Activities:** 2 heated pools, wading pool, playground, arcade room. **Guest Services:** gift shop, area transportation-Disney, valet and coin laundry. **Cards:** AE, DI, DS, JC, MC, VI.

SOME UNITS

DISNEY'S BOARDWALK RESORT

Phone: (407)939-5100 · 306

12/1-12/31	1P: $269-$1695	2P: $269-$1695	XP: $25	F17
2/15-7/3	1P: $309-$1595	2P: $309-$1595	XP: $25	F17
7/4-11/30	1P: $279-$1440	2P: $279-$1440	XP: $25	F17
1/1-2/14	1P: $279-$1275	2P: $279-$1275	XP: $25	F17

Hotel

Location: 0.5 mi e of Disney main gate access road, 2 min of US 192. 2101 N Epcot Resorts Blvd 32830 (PO Box 10,000). Fax: 407/939-5150. **Facility:** A Boardwalk resort of the 1920s and 1930s era. Excellent decor in public areas and rooms. Inn or villa rooms. 893 units. 143 two-bedroom units, 7 three-bedroom units, 134 efficiencies and 383 units with kitchen. Some whirlpool units ($365-$1960). *Bath:* combo or shower only. 5 stories, interior/exterior corridors. **Parking:** valet. **Terms:** check-in 4 pm, 5 day cancellation notice-fee imposed, package plans. **Amenities:** voice mail, safes, irons, hair dryers. **Dining:** 2 restaurants, coffee shop, 7 am-midnight, $7-$34; cocktails, also, Flying Fish Cafe, see separate listing. **Leisure Activities:** 3 heated pools, wading pool, sauna, whirlpools, 2 lighted tennis courts, jogging, playground. *Fee:* bicycles. **Guest Services:** gift shop, area transportation-Disney, coin laundry. *Fee:* massage. **Business Services:** conference facilities, administrative services, PC, fax. **Cards:** AE, DI, DS, JC, MC, VI.

SOME UNITS

DISNEY'S CARIBBEAN BEACH RESORT

Phone: (407)934-3400 · 307

2/15-8/25	1P: $149-$199	2P: $149-$199	XP: $15	F17
12/1-12/31	1P: $124-$189	2P: $124-$189	XP: $15	F17
8/26-11/30	1P: $124-$164	2P: $124-$164	XP: $15	F17
1/1-2/14	1P: $129-$144	2P: $129-$144	XP: $15	F17

Resort

Location: 1.5 mi e of Disney main gate access rd, 2 min of US 192; off Buena Vista Dr, 1 mi w of Typhoon Lagoon. 900 Cayman Way 32830 (PO Box 10,000). Fax: 407/934-3288. **Facility:** Complex of five villages, each modeling it's namesake Caribbean Island. Extensive landscaped grounds. Designated smoking area. 2112 units. *Bath:* combo or shower only. 2 stories, exterior corridors. **Terms:** 5 day cancellation notice-fee imposed, package plans. **Amenities:** extended cable TV, safes, honor bars, hair dryers. **Dining:** restaurant, pool bar 6 am-midnight food court & pizza delivery, $10-$17, cocktails. **Leisure Activities:** 7 heated pools, wading pool, whirlpool, beach, boating, boat dock, marina, jogging, playground, children's recreation island. *Fee:* paddleboats, sailboats, pontoon boats, bicycles. **Guest Services:** gift shop, area transportation-Disney, coin laundry. **Cards:** AE, DI, DS, JC, MC, VI.

SOME UNITS

You've decided to make the dream come true — the *Walt Disney World*® Resort is the vacation for you. But where are you going to stay? We have exactly what you're looking for. One of the *Walt*

Stay in a room with a magical view.

Disney World® Resort Hotels. Each has a wonderfully different theme, but all feature benefits that are uniquely Disney. Magical location inside the *Walt Disney World*® Resort, so your hotel becomes a seamless part of your Disney vacation. Renowned Disney service and hospitality. Special passes which slip you into Disney Theme Parks before they open to the public. And easy access to complimentary Disney transportation. Besides that, you can take advantage of special AAA member packages featuring *Walt Disney World*® Resort Hotels. Along with special savings on rooms, based on availability. To make the dream come true, call or visit your AAA Travel office today.

Disney's Animal Kingdom Lodge opening Spring 2001.

© Disney

Walt Disney World® Resort
FLORIDA

See our ad in the Attractions section of this TourBook for more information about making the dream come true at the *Walt Disney World® Resort.*

(See map p. 560)

DISNEY'S CONTEMPORARY RESORT

Phone: (407)824-1000 265

	2/15-7/3	1P: $244-$630	2P: $244-$630	XP: $25	F17
	12/1-12/31	1P: $219-$615	2P: $219-$615	XP: $25	F17
	7/4-11/30	1P: $224-$570	2P: $224-$570	XP: $25	F17
	1/1-2/14	1P: $224-$520	2P: $224-$520	XP: $25	F17

Resort **Location:** Adjacent to Magic Kingdom; in Walt Disney World. 4600 N World Dr 32830 (PO Box 10,000). Fax: 407/824-3539. **Facility:** This resort caters to both conventions and families. One of the three original lodging properties of the Magic Kingdom, it is a soaring A-shape structure of concrete and glass with a mono-rail line running right through the building. Public areas and rooms are decorated with a "busy" contemporary decor including lavish use of bright colors and contrasting patterns. Designated smoking area. 1030 units. Some suites ($945-$1460). *Bath:* combo or shower only. 3-15 stories, interior corridors. **Parking:** valet. **Terms:** 5 day cancellation notice-fee imposed, package plans, kennel avail. **Amenities:** voice mail, safes, irons, hair dryers. *Some:* fax. **Dining:** 3 restaurants, coffee shop, deli, 7 am-midnight, $8-$16, cocktails, also, California Grill, see separate listing. **Leisure Activities:** 3 heated pools, wading pool, sauna, whirlpool, waterslide, beach, swimming, fishing, charter fishing, golf-99 holes, recreation program, social program, hiking trails, jogging, playground, game room, arcade. *Fee:* boats, waterskiing, 6 lighted tennis courts, tennis instruction, hair salon, tanning booth. **Guest Services:** gift shop, area transportation-Disney, valet and coin laundry. *Fee:* massage. **Business Services:** conference facilities, administrative services. *Fee:* PC, fax. **Cards:** AE, DI, DS, JC, MC, VI.

SOME UNITS

DISNEY'S CORONADO SPRINGS RESORT

Phone: (407)939-1000 287

	2/15-8/25	1P: $149-$199	2P: $149-$199	XP: $15	F17
	12/1-12/31	1P: $124-$189	2P: $124-$189	XP: $15	F17
	8/26-11/30	1P: $129-$164	2P: $129-$164	XP: $15	F17
	1/1-2/14	1P: $129-$144	2P: $129-$144	XP: $15	F17

Resort **Location:** I-4, exit 26B, nw and follow signs to Disney's Animal Kingdom Park. 1000 W Buena Vista Blvd 32830 (PO Box 10,000). Fax: 407/939-1001. **Facility:** Experience Mexican and American Southwest flavors in this unique setting of expansive landscaped resort grounds, complete with El Centro. An array of dining and shopping activities. Stay in the Cabana, Casita or Rancho guest rooms. Designated smoking area. 1967 units. Some suites ($258-$1010) and whirlpool units ($810-$1010). *Bath:* combo or shower only. 4 stories, exterior corridors. **Terms:** 5 day cancellation notice-fee imposed. **Amenities:** voice mail, safes, irons, hair dryers. **Dining:** restaurant, 7 am-11 & 5-10 pm, pool bar. 7 am-11 pm, food court, $10-$28, cocktails. **Leisure Activities:** 4 heated pools, wading pool, sauna, whirlpool, waterslide, playground, volleyball, game room, paved walkway around lake. *Fee:* paddleboats, pontoon boats, surrey bikes, water mice, bicycles. **Guest Services:** gift shop, area transportation-Disney, coin laundry. *Fee:* massage. **Business Services:** conference facilities, administrative services. *Fee:* PC, fax. **Cards:** AE, DI, DS, JC, MC, VI.

SOME UNITS

DISNEY'S DIXIE LANDINGS RESORT

Phone: (407)934-6000 268

	2/15-8/25	1P: $149-$199	2P: $149-$199	XP: $15	F17
	12/1-12/31	1P: $124-$189	2P: $124-$189	XP: $15	F17
	8/26-11/30	1P: $129-$164	2P: $129-$164	XP: $15	F17
	1/1-2/14	1P: $129-$144	2P: $129-$144	XP: $15	F17

Resort **Location:** I-4, exit 26B, nw and follow signs to Disney's Downtown Disney. 1251 Dixie Dr 32830 (PO Box 10,000). Fax: 407/934-5777. **Facility:** Gated entry with 350 acres of landscaped grounds designed to coordinate with the Magnolia Antebellum style section and the Alligator Bayou area. On Disney canal system with boat transportation to Downtown Disney and Pleasure Island. Designated smoking area. 2048 units. *Bath:* combo or shower only. 2-3 stories, exterior corridors. **Terms:** 5 day cancellation notice-fee imposed, package plans. **Amenities:** voice mail, safes. **Dining:** restaurant, 6 am-midnight; food court, $10-$17, cocktails, also, Boatwright's Dining Hall, see separate listing, entertainment. **Leisure Activities:** 7 heated pools, wading pool, whirlpool, waterslide, playground. *Fee:* paddleboats, bicycles. **Guest Services:** gift shop, area transportation-Disney, coin laundry. **Cards:** AE, DI, DS, JC, MC, VI.

SOME UNITS

DISNEY'S FORT WILDERNESS CABINS & HOMES

Phone: (407)824-2900 270

	12/1-12/31	1P: $184-$289	2P: $184-$289	XP: $5	F17
	2/15-8/25	1P: $224-$279	2P: $224-$279	XP: $5	F17
	8/26-11/30	1P: $184-$254	2P: $184-$254	XP: $5	F17
	1/1-2/14	1P: $184-$219	2P: $184-$219	XP: $5	F17

Cottage **Location:** Off US 192; in Walt Disney World. 4510 N Fort Wilderness Tr 32830-1000. Fax: 407/824-3508. **Facility:** Manufactured cabins and houses in a campground-like setting. Nestled in a wooded area, setting is quiet and secluded yet with easy access to all areas of Walt Disney World. Each unit has grill, picnic table, patio or deck. 408 units with kitchen. *Bath:* combo or shower only. 1 story, exterior corridors. **Terms:** 5 day cancellation notice-fee imposed, package plans. **Amenities:** extended cable TV, voice mail. *Some:* safes, irons, hair dryers. **Dining:** restaurant, 7:30-11 am, 11:30-3:30 & 4-10 pm, $15. **Leisure Activities:** 2 heated pools, wading pool, fishing, 2 lighted tennis courts, children's program in summer, jogging, playground, hay rides, nightly campfire & Disney movie, petting farm, game rooms, tetherball, horseshoes, sand volleyball, basketball. *Fee:* canoes, paddleboats, fishing equipment, tennis, bicycles, horseback riding. **Guest Services:** area transportation-within Disney World, coin laundry. **Cards:** AE, DI, DS, JC, MC, VI.

SOME UNITS

(See map p. 560)

DISNEY'S GRAND FLORIDIAN RESORT & SPA

Phone: (407)824-3000 263

2/15-7/3	1P: $359-$710	2P: $359-$710	XP: $25	F17
12/1-12/31	1P: $304-$670	2P: $304-$670	XP: $25	F17
7/4-11/30	1P: $314-$630	2P: $341-$630	XP: $25	F17
1/1-2/14	1P: $314-$565	2P: $314-$565	XP: $25	F17

Resort

Location: 8 mi nw of jct I-4 and US 192. 4401 Grand Floridian Way 32830 (PO Box 10,000). Fax: 407/824-3186. **Facility:** Located in Disney's Magic Kingdom, this elegant lakefront resort holds court amidst manicured lawns, verdant shrubbery and lush magnolias and cypress trees. Traditional white frame buildings are accent by terra cotta-color roofs. The spacious lobby with its chandeliers, grand piano, upscale shops and restaurants has the refined air of a Victorian spa but with a Florida touch, including potted palms and a huge hardwood birdcage inhabited by Australian songbirds. 900 units. 15 two-bedroom units. Some suites ($690-$1960) and whirlpool units ($555-$710). *Bath:* some combo or shower only. 5 stories, interior corridors. **Parking:** valet. **Terms:** 5 day cancellation notice-fee imposed, package plans, kennel on property. **Amenities:** voice mail, safes, honor bars, irons, hair dryers. *Some:* CD players. **Dining:** 3 dining rooms, 2 restaurants, $8-$42, cocktails, also, Victoria & Albert's, see separate listing, entertainment. **Leisure Activities:** heated pool, saunas, whirlpools, beach, swimming, charter fishing, pontoon boats,, children's program, recreation program in summer, jogging, playground, sand volleyball, croquet, pool bar, spa. *Fee:* boats, sailboats, waterskiing, yacht, golf-99 holes, 2 lighted tennis courts, tennis instruction. **Guest Services:** gift shop, afternoon tea, area transportation-Disney, valet and coin laundry. *Fee:* massage. **Business Services:** conference facilities, administrative services, PC. *Fee:* fax. **Cards:** AE, DI, DS, JC, MC, VI.

DISNEY'S OLD KEY WEST RESORT

Phone: (407)827-7700 282

2/15-7/3	1P: $269-$1170	2P: $269-$1170
12/1-12/31	1P: $234-$1155	2P: $234-$1155
7/4-11/30	1P: $244-$1050	2P: $244-$1050
1/1-2/14	1P: $244-$955	2P: $244-$955

Complex

Location: I-4, exit 26B, 2 mi nw on SR 536 and Bennet Creek Pkwy. 1510 N Cove Rd 32830 (PO Box 10,000). Fax: 407/827-1192. **Facility:** One- to two-bedroom apartments with patio or balcony. Extensively landscaped Key West theme. Bright airy, pastel gingerbread buildings with high quality furnishings. All units with golf course or water view. 761 units. 274 two-bedroom units, 27 three-bedroom units and 531 units with kitchen. Some whirlpool units ($315-$1170). *Bath:* combo or shower only. 2-3 stories (no elevator), exterior corridors. **Terms:** check-in 4 pm, 5 day cancellation notice-fee imposed, package plans. **Amenities:** extended cable TV, voice mail, irons, hair dryers. *Some:* safes. **Dining:** restaurant, 7:30 am-10 pm; 7 am-11 pm convenience store; 2 poolside snack bars, $6-$16, cocktails. **Leisure Activities:** 4 heated pools, wading pool, sauna, whirlpools, 3 tennis courts (2 lighted), children's program, recreation program, social program, jogging, playground, exercise room, basketball, shuffleboard, volleyball. *Fee:* paddleboats, canopy boats, pontoon boats, tennis equipment & instruction, bicycles. **Guest Services:** gift shop, area transportation-Disney, complimentary laundry. *Fee:* massage. *Fee:* fax. **Cards:** AE, DI, DS, JC, MC, VI.

DISNEY'S POLYNESIAN RESORT

Phone: (407)824-2000 264

2/15-7/3	1P: $324-$560	2P: $324-$560	XP: $25	F17
12/1-12/31	1P: $279-$550	2P: $279-$550	XP: $25	F17
7/4-11/30	1P: $289-$490	2P: $289-$490	XP: $25	F17
1/1-2/14	1P: $289-$445		XP: $25	F17

Resort

Location: I-4, exit 26B, nw and follow route to Disney's Magic Kingdom Park. 1600 Seven Seas Dr 32830 (PO Box 10,000). Fax: 407/824-3174. **Facility:** Located on Seven Seas Lagoon in Disney's Magic Kingdom Park. Guests can take the convenient monorail to Magic Kingdom and Epcot. Designated smoking area. 853 units, 4 with efficiency. Some suites ($435-$2015) and whirlpool units ($1665-$2015). *Bath:* combo or shower only. 2-3 stories, interior corridors. **Parking:** valet. **Terms:** 5 day cancellation notice-fee imposed, package plans. **Amenities:** extended cable TV, voice mail, safes, irons, hair dryers. *Some:* CD players. **Dining:** dining room, restaurant, coffee shop, deli, attraction dinner shows Polynesian revue, extra charge, $7-$28, cocktails. **Leisure Activities:** 3 pools (2 heated), wading pool, waterslide, beach, swimming, charter fishing, 2 tennis courts (1 lighted), racquetball court, children's program, playground, game room. *Fee:* boats, sailboats, waterskiing, fishing, pontoon boats; specialty cruises; water mice; 1.5 mi paved walking trail, golf-99 holes, recreation & social programs, bicycles. **Guest Services:** gift shop, area transportation-Disney, coin laundry. *Fee:* massage. **Business Services:** meeting rooms, fax. **Cards:** AE, DI, DS, JC, MC, VI.

DISNEY'S PORT ORLEANS RESORT

Phone: (407)934-5000 281

2/15-8/25	1P: $149-$199	2P: $149-$199	XP: $15	F17
12/1-12/31	1P: $124-$189	2P: $124-$189	XP: $15	F17
8/26-11/30	1P: $129-$164	2P: $129-$164	XP: $15	F17
1/1-2/14	1P: $129-$144	2P: $129-$144	XP: $15	F17

Resort

Location: I-4, exit 26B, 2.3 mi nw on SR 536 and Bennet Creek Pkwy. 2201 Orleans Dr 32830 (PO Box 10,000). Fax: 407/934-5353. **Facility:** As redolent of New Orleans as beignets and chicory coffee, this resort offers some rooms with a view of landscaped courtyards, the pool area, or the river (albeit not the Mississippi). Take a stroll through the French Quarter and admire the manicured grounds which complement the pastel stucco buildings with their black wrought iron railings. Relax by a quiet fountain in the lobby. 1008 units. *Bath:* combo or shower only. 3 stories, exterior corridors. **Terms:** 5 day cancellation notice-fee imposed, package plans. **Amenities:** voice mail, safes, hair dryers. **Dining:** restaurant, 6 am-midnight food court, pool bar, $7-$12, cocktails, also, Bonfamille's Cafe, see separate listing, entertainment. **Leisure Activities:** heated pool, wading pool, whirlpool, waterslide, boat transportation to Marketplace & Pleasure Island, playground. *Fee:* boating, canoeing, paddleboats, canopy boats, float boats, bicycles. **Guest Services:** gift shop, area transportation-Disney, coin laundry. *Fee:* fax. **Cards:** AE, DI, DS, JC, MC, VI.

(See map p. 560)

DISNEY'S WILDERNESS LODGE
Phone: (407)824-3200 [267]

Lodge

2/15-8/25	1P: $219-$430	2P: $219-$430	XP: $25 — F17
12/1-12/31	1P: $185-$410	2P: $185-$410	XP: $25 — F17
8/26-11/30	1P: $189-$385	2P: $199-$385	XP: $25 — F17
1/1-2/14	1P: $189-$335	2P: $189-$335	XP: $25 — F17

Location: In Walt Disney World. 901 W Timberline Dr 32830 (PO Box 10,000). Fax: 407/824-3232. **Facility:** This rustic lodge is fashioned after Old Faithful Inn in Yellowstone National Park. Set on the edge of a forest of cypress and slash pine, the lodge's most impressive feature is a soaring lobby with walls and pillars hewn out of logs, some from Mt. St. Helens. The public areas include numerous reproductions of American Indian art including totem poles and animal hide drawings. There is a hot spring located in the lobby. 728 units. Some suites ($250-$870). *Bath:* combo or shower only. 7 stories, interior corridors. **Parking:** valet. **Terms:** 5 day cancellation notice-fee imposed, package plans. **Amenities:** voice mail, safes, hair dryers. *Some:* CD players. **Dining:** dining room, restaurant, 7 am-midnight snack bar, pool bar, $15-$30, cocktails, also, Artist Point, see separate listing. **Leisure Activities:** heated pool, wading pool, whirlpools, waterslide, beach, children's program, nature trails, jogging, playground. *Fee:* sailboating, float boats, water sprites, bicycles. **Guest Services:** gift shop, area transportation-Disney, coin laundry. **Business Services:** meeting rooms, fax. **Cards:** AE, DI, DS, JC, MC, VI.

SOME UNITS

DISNEY'S YACHT & BEACH CLUB RESORTS
Phone: (407)934-7000 [286]

Resort

2/15-7/3	1P: $309-$605	2P: $309-$605	XP: $25 — F17
12/1-12/31	1P: $269-$580	2P: $269-$580	XP: $25 — F17
7/4-11/30	1P: $279-$545	2P: $279-$545	XP: $25 — F17
1/1-2/14	1P: $279-$490	2P: $279-$490	XP: $25 — F17

Location: I-4, exit 26B nw and follow signage to Disney's Epcot Park. 1700 Epcot Resorts Blvd 32830 (PO Box 10,000). Fax: 407/934-3450. **Facility:** Turn-of-the century yachting resort themed property with guest rooms and registration areas in each of the Yacht Club and Beach Club sections. Themed, large pool area complete with sand bottom and beach. Designated smoking area. 1213 units. Some suites ($430-$1895) and whirlpool units ($670-$1895). *Bath:* combo or shower only. 5 stories, interior corridors. **Parking:** valet. **Terms:** 5 day cancellation notice-fee imposed, package plans. **Amenities:** voice mail, safes, honor bars, irons, hair dryers. *Some:* CD players. **Dining:** 2 restaurants, 7-11 am, 11:30-2:30 & 4:30-10 pm; pool bar, $6-$22, cocktails, also, Yachtsman's Steak House, see separate listing. **Leisure Activities:** 3 heated pools, wading pool, sauna, whirlpools, waterslide, beach, 2 lighted tennis courts, tennis equipment, children's program, playground, hair salon, paved walking trail around lake. *Fee:* fishing, "breathless" boat rides, floaters for pool, pontoon boats, water mice. **Guest Services:** gift shop, area transportation-Disney, coin laundry. *Fee:* massage. **Business Services:** conference facilities, administrative services, PC, fax. **Cards:** AE, DI, DS, JC, MC, VI.

SOME UNITS

DOUBLETREE CLUB HOTEL LAKE BUENA VISTA
Phone: (407)239-4646 [285]

Motor Inn

All Year	1P: $79-$159	2P: $79-$159

Location: I-4, exit 27, 0.5 mi n; on SR 535. 12490 Apopka-Vineland Rd 32836. Fax: 407/239-8469. **Facility:** Comfortable, well appointed guest rooms. 13 kid club units. 246 units. 7 stories, interior corridors. **Terms:** check-in 4 pm, cancellation fee imposed. **Amenities:** voice mail, safes (fee), irons, hair dryers. **Dining:** dining room, 6 am-11 pm, $7-$18, cocktails. **Leisure Activities:** heated pool, wading pool, whirlpool, exercise room. **Guest Services:** gift shop, area transportation-major attractions, coin laundry. **Business Services:** meeting rooms, administrative services. **Cards:** AE, CB, DI, DS, JC, MC, VI. **Special Amenities:** free local telephone calls and free newspaper. *(See color ad below)*

SOME UNITS

DOUBLETREE GUEST SUITES IN THE WALT DISNEY WORLD RESORT
Phone: (407)934-1000 [292]

Suite Hotel

12/1-5/6	1P: $159-$249	2P: $159-$249	XP: $20 — F17
5/7-8/26 & 10/3-11/30	1P: $149-$199	2P: $149-$199	XP: $20 — F17
8/27-10/2	1P: $129-$169	2P: $129-$169	XP: $20 — F17

Location: I-4, exit 27 (SR 535); in Walt Disney World Village. 2305 Hotel Plaza Blvd 32830. Fax: 407/934-1015. **Facility:** Suites with living room/dining room area and bedroom. Some first floor rooms have furnished patio, kids check-in. 229 units. 5 stories, 7 stories, interior corridors. **Terms:** check-in 4 pm, 5 day cancellation notice-fee imposed, package plans. **Amenities:** voice mail, safes (fee), irons, hair dryers. **Leisure Activities:** heated pool, wading pool, whirlpool, 2 lighted tennis courts, playground, exercise room, volleyball. **Guest Services:** [BP] meal plan available, gift shop, area transportation, coin laundry. **Business Services:** meeting rooms. **Cards:** AE, CB, DI, DS, MC, VI. *(See color ad starting on p 592)*

SOME UNITS

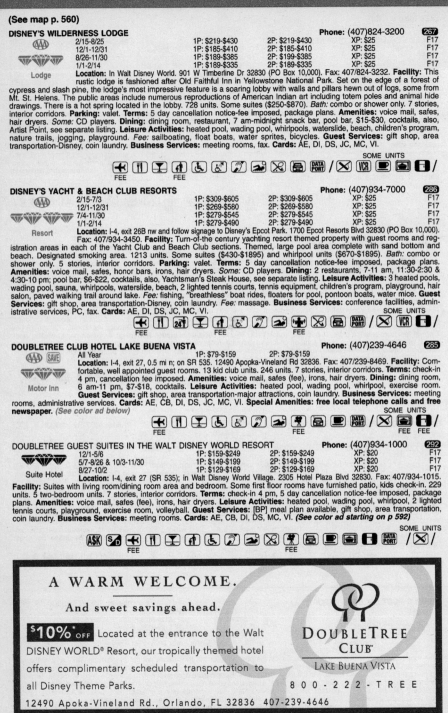

(See map p. 560)

EMBASSY SUITES RESORT-LAKE BUENA VISTA   Phone: (407)239-1144   273

All Year   1P: $129-$299   2P: $129-$299   XP: $15   F17

Suite Hotel   **Location:** I-4, exit 27, 1 mi n on SR 535, then 0.5 mi e. 8100 Lake Ave 32836. Fax: 407/239-1718. **Facility:** Cheery, fun atmosphere. Some family friendly suites with protective locks on refrigerators and microwave ovens. 333 units. Some suites. *Bath:* combo or shower only. 5-6 stories, interior/exterior corridors. **Parking:** valet. **Terms:** check-in 4 pm, 3 day cancellation notice, package plans. **Amenities:** voice mail, safes, irons, hair dryers. **Leisure Activities:** heated pool, wading pool, sauna, whirlpool, 2 lighted tennis courts, children's program, jogging, playground, exercise room, basketball, shuffleboard, volleyball. **Guest Services:** [BP] meal plan available, gift shop, complimentary evening beverages, area transportation, coin laundry. **Business Services:** meeting rooms. *Fee:* PC, fax. **Cards:** AE, CB, DI, DS, JC, MC, VI. *(See color ad starting on p 592)*   SOME UNITS

ASK SD ⊤⊤ ⊤ 🛗 & 🎣 🌊 ✕ 🎥 VCR 🖨 💻 🖥 🖪 DATA PORT / ✕ /
FEE   FEE

EMBASSY VACATION RESORT GRAND BEACH   Phone: (407)238-2500   300

12/23-2/24   1P: $149   2P: $369
2/25-11/30   1P: $99   2P: $299

Apartment   **Location:** I-4, exit 27, 1.1 mi s. 8317 Lake Bryan Beach Blvd 32821. Fax: 407/238-1825. **Facility:** Pleasant location bordering small lake. Well appointed, tastefully decorated guest rooms. All very large units. 210 three-bedroom units with kitchen. Some whirlpool units. 5 stories, interior corridors. **Terms:** check-in 4 pm, 3 day cancellation notice-fee imposed. **Amenities:** voice mail, irons, hair dryers. **Leisure Activities:** wading pool, whirlpool, boating, canoeing, paddleboats, exercise room, game room. **Guest Services:** gift shop, complimentary laundry. **Cards:** AE, DI, DS, MC, VI.

ASK SD ✈ 🛗 & 🎣 🌊 ✕ 🎥 VCR 🖨 💻 🖥 🖪 DATA PORT
FEE   FEE

GROSVENOR RESORT AT WALT DISNEY WORLD RESORT   Phone: (407)828-4444   295

2/11-4/20   1P: $115-$155   2P: $115-$155   XP: $15   F18
12/24-2/10   1P: $99-$155   2P: $99-$155   XP: $15   F18
4/21-11/30   1P: $105-$125   2P: $105-$125   XP: $15   F18
12/1-12/23   1P: $89-$115   2P: $89-$115   XP: $15   F18

Hotel   **Location:** I-4, exit 27, ; opposite the Disney Marketplace. 1850 Hotel Plaza Blvd 32830. Fax: 407/827-6703. **Facility:** Exceptional view of the area from the tower rooms. 626 units. Some *Bath:* combo or shower only. 5-19 stories, interior/exterior corridors. **Parking:** valet. **Terms:** 5 day cancellation notice-fee imposed, package plans. **Amenities:** voice mail, safes (fee), irons, hair dryers. **Dining:** dining room, deli, 24 hours; pool bar & grill, $9-$20, cocktails. **Leisure Activities:** 2 heated pools, wading pool, whirlpool, 2 lighted tennis courts, tennis equipment, playground, exercise room, sports court, shuffleboard, sand volleyball. **Guest Services:** [BP] meal plan available, gift shop, area transportation-Disney, valet and coin laundry. **Business Services:** conference facilities, administrative services. *Fee:* PC. **Cards:** AE, CB, DI, DS, JC, MC, VI. **Special Amenities:** free newspaper. *(See color ad below)*   SOME UNITS

SD ⊤⊤ ⊤ 🛗 & 🎣 🌊 ✕ 🎥 VCR 🖨 💻 🖪 DATA PORT / ✕ 🖥 /

(See map p. 560)

HAMPTON INN LAKE BUENA VISTA
Phone: (407)465-8150 260

(AAA) (SAVE)

12/1-1/1	1P: $75-$139	2P: $85-$139
1/2-11/30	1P: $75-$119	2P: $85-$129

Motel

Location: I-4, exit 27, 0.6 mi n on SR 535, 0.6 mi e. 8150 Palm Pkwy 32836. Fax: 407/465-0150. **Facility:** 147 units. *Bath:* combo or shower only. 5 stories, interior corridors. **Terms:** cancellation fee imposed. **Amenities:** extended cable TV, voice mail, irons, hair dryers. **Leisure Activities:** whirlpool, jogging, exercise room. **Guest Services:** [ECP] meal plan available, area transportation-major attractions, valet laundry. **Cards:** AE, CB, DI, DS, MC, VI. **Special Amenities: free continental breakfast and free newspaper.** *(See color ad p 634)* SOME UNITS

HILTON IN THE WALT DISNEY WORLD RESORT
Phone: (407)827-4000 294

(AAA) (SAVE)

1/3-4/11	1P: $175-$350	2P: $195-$370	XP: $20	F18
4/12-11/30	1P: $155-$340	2P: $175-$360	XP: $20	F18
12/1-11/30	1P: $145-$340	2P: $165-$360	XP: $20	F18

Hotel

Location: I-4 and SR 535 exit; in Walt Disney World Resort. 1751 Hotel Plaza Blvd 32830 (PO Box 22781). Fax: 407/827-6369. **Facility:** Extensive facilites. 814 units. *Bath:* combo or shower only. 10 stories, interior corridors. **Parking:** valet. **Terms:** 5 day cancellation notice-fee imposed. **Amenities:** voice mail, honor bars, irons, hair dryers. **Dining:** 2 restaurants, coffee shop, poolside terrace 7:30 am-2 am; sundries store and deli, $6-$19, cocktails, also, Finn's Grill, see separate listing, entertainment. **Leisure Activities:** 2 heated pools, wading pool, sauna, whirlpools. *Fee:* children's program. **Guest Services:** [CP] meal plan available, gift shop, area transportation-Disney, coin laundry. **Business Services:** conference facilities, administrative services, PC, fax. **Cards:** AE, CB, DI, DS, JC, MC, VI. **Special Amenities: free local telephone calls and free newspaper.** *(See ad p 44)* SOME UNITS

HOLIDAY INN FAMILY SUITES RESORT LAKE BUENA VISTA
Phone: (407)387-5437 308

4/30-8/19	1P: $125-$170	2P: $125-$170
12/26-4/29	1P: $130-$160	2P: $130-$160
12/1-12/25 & 8/20-11/30	1P: $89-$115	2P: $89-$115

Suite Hotel

Location: I-4, exit 26A, 0.5 mi e on SR 536. 14500 Continental Gateway 32821. Fax: 407/387-1488. **Facility:** Train theme in public areas. Seven distinct suite types. 800 units. 686 two-bedroom units and 74 efficiencies. Some whirlpool units ($125-$170). *Bath:* combo or shower only. 6 stories, exterior corridors. **Terms:** check in 4 pm, cancellation fee imposed. **Amenities:** extended cable TV, dual phone lines, voice mail, safes, irons, hair dryers. *Some:* video games, fax. **Leisure Activities:** 2 heated pools, wading pool, whirlpools, social program, playground, exercise room, game room. **Guest Services:** [BP] meal plan available, gift shop, area transportation, valet and coin laundry. **Business Services:** administrative services, PC, fax. **Cards:** AE, CB, DI, DS, JC, MC, VI. **(See color ad below)** SOME UNITS

HOLIDAY INN-SUNSPREE RESORT-LAKE BUENA VISTA
Phone: (407)239-4500 296

(AAA) (SAVE)

12/1-12/31 & 2/11-8/27	1P: $129-$169	2P: $129-$169
1/1-2/10 & 8/28-11/30	1P: $99-$139	2P: $99-$139

Hotel

Location: I-4, exit 27, 0.3 mi se on SR 535. 13351 SR 535 32821. Fax: 407/239-7713. **Facility:** Family friendly. Especially cater to children. 507 units. Some whirlpool units. 6 stories, exterior corridors. **Terms:** cancellation fee imposed, package plans, small pets only ($25 fee). **Amenities:** extended cable TV, safes, irons, hair dryers. *Some:* video games. **Dining:** deli, 7 am-10 pm; buffet breakfast; convenience store; pool snack bar; food court, cocktails. **Leisure Activities:** heated pool, wading pool, whirlpools, children's program, playground, exercise room, basketball, game room, family movie theater. **Guest Services:** gift shop, area transportation-Disney, valet and coin laundry. **Cards:** AE, CB, DI, DS, JC, MC, VI. **(See color ad p 687)** SOME UNITS

HOMEWOOD SUITES HOTEL-LAKE BUENA VISTA
Phone: (407)465-8200 261

(AAA) (SAVE)

All Year	1P: $99-$159	2P: $99-$159

Suite Motel

Location: I-4, exit 27, 0.6 mi n on SR 535, 0.5 mi e. 8200 Palm Pkwy 32836. Fax: 407/465-0200. **Facility:** 123 efficiencies. 3 two-bedroom units. 4 stories, interior corridors. *Bath:* combo or shower only. **Terms:** cancellation fee imposed. **Amenities:** extended cable TV, voice mail, irons, hair dryers. **Dining:** Suite shop, 24 hrs. **Leisure Activities:** whirlpool, swimming, jogging, exercise room, basketball, game room. **Guest Services:** [ECP] meal plan available, gift shop, complimentary evening beverages: Mon-Thurs, area transportation-major attractions, coin laundry. **Business Services:** meeting rooms. **Cards:** AE, CB, DI, DS, MC, VI. **Special Amenities: free continental breakfast and free newspaper.** *(See color ad p 675)* SOME UNITS

(See map p. 560)

ORLANDO ROYAL PLAZA

2/16-4/21 & 10/1-11/30   2P: $139-$229   **Phone:** (407)828-2828   293
12/1-2/15 & 4/22-9/30   2P: $109-$169

Hotel

Location: Sw jct I-4 and SR 535; in Walt Disney World Village. 1905 Hotel Plaza Blvd 32830. Fax: 407/827-6338. **Facility:** Two-story and tower sections. Large guest rooms, many with whirlpool or soaker tub. Some units in two-story section border the freeway. 394 units. Some suites and whirlpool units. *Bath:* combo or shower only. 2-16 stories, interior corridors. **Parking:** valet. **Terms:** check-in 4 pm, 5 day cancellation notice-fee imposed, package plans. **Amenities:** extended cable TV, voice mail, safes (fee), honor bars, irons, hair dryers. **Dining:** restaurant, 6:30 am-midnight, $6-$18, cocktails. **Leisure Activities:** heated pool, whirlpool, 4 lighted tennis courts, exercise room. **Guest Services:** gift shop, area transportation-major attractions, coin laundry. **Business Services:** meeting rooms. **Cards:** AE, CB, DI, DS, MC, VI. **Special Amenities:** free newspaper. *(See color ad p 688).*

SOME UNITS

ORLANDO WORLD CENTER MARRIOTT

1/1-4/30   1P: $249-$289   2P: $249-289   **Phone:** (407)239-4200   309
12/1-12/31 & 5/1-11/30   1P: $189-$289   2P: $189-$289

Resort

Location: I-4, exit 26, 0.5 mi e on SR 536. 8701 World Center Dr 32821. Fax: 407/238-8777. **Facility:** Expansive property with rooms in several sections. Excellent recreational facilities. 2000 units. *Bath:* combo or shower only. 27 stories, interior corridors. **Parking:** valet. **Terms:** check-in 4 pm, cancellation fee imposed, package plans. **Amenities:** voice mail, safes (fee), honor bars, irons, hair dryers. **Leisure Activities:** 5 heated pools, wading pools, saunas, whirlpools, children's program, playground, exercise room, sports court. *Fee:* golf-18 holes, 4 lighted tennis courts. **Guest Services:** gift shop, coin laundry. *Fee:* area transportation, massage. **Business Services:** conference facilities, administrative services, PC, fax. **Cards:** AE, CB, DI, DS, JC, MC, VI.

SOME UNITS

PERRI HOUSE BED & BREAKFAST INN

All Year   1P: $90-$120   2P: $100-$140   **Phone:** (407)876-4830   262
                                                    XP: $10   F16

Bed & Breakfast

Location: I-4, exit 27, 3.4 mi n on SR 535; adjacent to Grand Cypress Equestrian Center. 10417 Centurion Ct 32836. Fax: 407/876-0241. **Facility:** Modern home in natural rural setting. Each unit has an entrance to common areas, as well as its own private exterior entrance. Property is a developing bird sanctuary. Smoke free premises. 8 units. 1 story, interior/exterior corridors. **Terms:** 3 day cancellation notice-fee imposed. **Amenities:** CD players. **Leisure Activities:** whirlpool. **Guest Services:** coin laundry. **Cards:** AE, DI, DS, MC, VI.

(See map p. 560)

RADISSON INN LAKE BUENA VISTA   **Phone:** (407)239-8400

Motor Inn

12/22-11/30   2P: $89-$159
12/1-12/21   2P: $89-$139
Location: I-4, exit 27, 0.5 mi n on CR 535, 0.3 mi e. 8686 Palm Pkwy 32836. Fax: 407/239-8025. **Facility:** 200 units. 7 stories, interior corridors. **Terms:** 3 day cancellation notice-fee imposed. **Amenities:** irons, hair dryers. **Dining:** coffee shop, 6:30-11 am, $5-$10, cocktails. **Leisure Activities:** heated pool, whirlpool, waterslide, playground, game room. **Guest Services:** [BP] meal plan available, gift shop, area transportation-major attractions, valet laundry. **Cards:** AE, DI, DS, JC, MC, VI. **Special Amenities: free room upgrade (subject to availability with advanced reservations).** *(See ad below)*

SOME UNITS

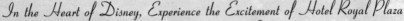
FEE

RESIDENCE INN BY MARRIOTT, LAKE BUENA VISTA   **Phone:** (407)239-7700   299
Property failed to provide current rates

Apartment

Location: I-4, exit 27, 0.5 mi se on SR 535, 0.5 mi s at sign. 8800 Meadow Creek Dr 32821. Fax: 407/239-7605. **Facility:** One- and two-bedroom apartments in two story eight-plex buildings. Some ground floor rooms with washer/dryer. Dine at Marriott World Center and charge to room. 688 units with kitchen. 411 two-bedroom units. *Bath:* combo or shower only. 2 stories, exterior corridors. **Terms:** check-in 4 pm, cancellation fee imposed, pets ($150 deposit). **Amenities:** voice mail, safes (fee), irons, hair dryers. **Leisure Activities:** 3 heated pools, whirlpools, lighted tennis court, playground, sports court. **Guest Services:** [ECP] meal plan available, gift shop, valet and coin laundry. *Fee:* area transportation. **Business Services:** meeting rooms. **Cards:** AE, DI, DS, MC, VI. *(See color ad p 582)*

SOME UNITS

FEE   FEE

(See map p. 560)

RIU ORLANDO HOTEL

Phone: (407)239-8500   276

(AAA) (SAVE)

Hotel

All Year   1P: $99-$125   2P: $99-$125

Location: I-4, exit 27, 0.5 mi n on CR 535, then just e. 8688 Palm Pkwy 32836. Fax: 407/239-8591. **Facility:** Foreign currency exhange available at front desk. 167 units. Some suites. 6 stories, interior corridors. **Terms:** cancellation fee imposed. **Amenities:** extended cable TV, video games, safes (fee), honor bars, irons, hair dryers. **Dining:** dining room, 7 am-10, noon-2 & 6:30-midnight, $10-$15, cocktails. **Leisure Activities:** heated pool, whirlpool. **Guest Services:** [BP] meal plan available, area transportation-major attractions, coin laundry. **Business Services:** meeting rooms. Fee: fax. **Cards:** AE, CB, DI, DS, JC, MC, VI. **Special Amenities: free continental breakfast.** (See color ad p 674)

SHERATON SAFARI HOTEL

Phone: (407)239-0444   278

(AAA) (SAVE)

Hotel

2/15-4/28	1P: $105-$165	2P: $105-$165
12/1-2/14	1P: $89-$155	2P: $89-$155
9/30-11/30	1P: $89-$149	2P: $89-$149
4/29-9/29	1P: $89-$145	2P: $89-$145

Location: On SR 535, 0.5 mi n of I-4, exit 27. 12205 Apopka-Vineland Rd 32836. Fax: 407/239-1778. **Facility:** 489 units. 90 efficiencies and 6 units with kitchen. Some suites ($119-$195). Bath: combo or shower only. 6 stories, interior/exterior corridors. **Terms:** check-in 4 pm, cancellation fee imposed. **Amenities:** extended cable TV, video games, voice mail, safes (fee), irons, hair dryers. **Dining:** dining room, deli, 6:30 am-10 pm, $9-$24, cocktails. **Leisure Activities:** heated pool, wading pool, whirlpool, waterslide, playground, exercise room, game room. **Guest Services:** gift shop, area transportation-Disney, coin laundry. **Business Services:** conference facilities, administrative services. **Cards:** AE, DI, DS, MC, VI. **Special Amenities: free newspaper and preferred room (subject to availability with advanced reservations).** (See color ad below)

SHERATON'S VISTANA RESORT

Phone: (407)239-3100   298

Condominium

All Year   1P: $129-$269   2P: $129-$269

Location: Jct I-4 and SR 535, exit 27, 0.6 mi s. 8800 Vistana Center Dr 32821. Fax: 407/239-3541. **Facility:** Extensive complex near major attractions. All rooms with washer/dryer and screened patio or balcony. Designated smoking area. 200 units with kitchen. 170 two-bedroom units. Some whirlpool units. 3-5 stories, exterior corridors. **Terms:** check-in 4 pm, 3 day cancellation notice, package plans. **Amenities:** extended cable TV, voice mail, safes, irons. **Leisure Activities:** 7 heated pools, wading pools, saunas, whirlpools, steamrooms, 13 lighted tennis courts, children's program, recreation program, social program, jogging, playground, shuffleboard. Fee: scuba equipment, miniature golf, bicycles. **Guest Services:** gift shop, complimentary laundry. Fee: area transportation, massage. **Business Services:** meeting rooms. **Cards:** AE, DI, DS, MC, VI. **(See color ad p 690)**

(See map p. 560)

SIERRA SUITES HOTEL-LAKE BUENA VISTA
▽▽▽▽
Motel

Phone: (407)239-4300 259

All Year 1P: $69-$159 2P: $69-$159
Location: I-4, exit 27, 0.5 mi n on SR 535, then 0.7 mi e. 8100 Palm Pkwy 32836. Fax: 407/239-4446. **Facility:** 125 efficiencies. *Bath:* combo or shower only. 3 stories, interior corridors. **Terms:** check-in 4 pm, 3 day cancellation notice-fee imposed. **Amenities:** extended cable TV, voice mail, safes, irons, hair dryers. **Leisure Activities:** heated pool, whirlpool, exercise room. **Guest Services:** coin laundry. *Fee:* fax. **Cards:** AE, DI, DS, JC, MC, VI.
(See ad p 690)

SOME UNITS

SUMMERFIELD SUITES BY WYNDHAM
(AAA) [SAVE]
▽▽▽▽
Suite Motor Inn

Phone: (407)238-0777 280

All Year 1P: $159-$229 2P: $159-$229
Location: I-4, exit 27, 0.8 mi n. 8751 Suiteside Dr 32836. Fax: 407/238-2640. **Facility:** 150 units with kitchen. 103 two-bedroom units. *Bath:* combo or shower only. 3 stories (no elevator), interior/exterior corridors. **Terms:** check-in 4 pm, 3 day cancellation notice-fee imposed, monthly rates available, package plans, $3 service charge. **Amenities:** extended cable TV, voice mail, safes (fee), irons. **Dining:** deli, 7 am-10:30 pm, $4-$6, wine/beer only. **Leisure Activities:** heated pool, wading pool, whirlpool, game room. *Fee:* video rental. **Guest Services:** [ECP] meal plan available, gift shop, area transportation-Disney, valet and coin laundry. **Business Services:** meeting rooms. **Cards:** AE, CB, DI, DS, JC, MC, VI. **Special Amenities:** free continental breakfast and free newspaper. *(See color ad p 616)*

SOME UNITS

VILLAS AT THE DISNEY INSTITUTE
(AAA)
▽▽▽▽
Resort

Phone: (407)827-1100 283

12/1-12/31 1P: $204-$1700 2P: $204-$1700
2/15-7/3 1P: $239-$1550 2P: $239-$1550
7/4-11/30 1P: $209-$1450 2P: $209-$1450
1/1-2/14 1P: $209-$1350 2P: $209-$1350
Location: Adjacent to Downtown Disney. 1960 N Magnolia Way 32830 (PO Box 10,000). Fax: 407/827-4101. **Facility:** Varied room types include fairway villas, treehouse, townhouse and bungalows. Well appointed guest rooms on spacious grounds. All units with crib, some with washer and dryer. 585 units. 94 two-bedroom units, 118 three-bedroom units, 316 efficiencies and 269 units with kitchen. Some whirlpool units. *Bath:* combo or shower only. 2 stories, exterior corridors. **Terms:** check-in 4 pm, 5 day cancellation notice-fee imposed, package plans. **Amenities:** extended cable TV, voice mail, irons, hair dryers. **Dining:** restaurant, 7 am-2:30 & 5:30-10 pm, $20-$30, cocktails. **Leisure Activities:** 6 heated pools, whirlpools, aerobics pool, canoeing, golf-18 holes, golf equipment & instruction, 4 lighted tennis courts, tennis equipment & instruction, children's program, nature program, recreation program, social program, jogging, playground, basketball, rock climbing, culinary arts program, animation arts, photography. *Fee:* bicycles. **Guest Services:** gift shop, area transportation-Disney, complimentary laundry. *Fee:* massage. **Business Services:** meeting rooms. **Cards:** AE, DI, DS, JC, MC, VI.

SOME UNITS
FEE

WALT DISNEY WORLD SWAN AND DOLPHIN
(AAA) [SAVE]
▽▽▽▽
Hotel

Phone: (407)934-3000 288

All Year 1P: $310-$490 2P: $310-$490 XP: $25 F17
Location: 0.3 mi e of Disney main gate access road, 2 mi n of US 192; from I-4 exit 26B, follow Epcot Resort area signs. 1200 Epcot Resorts Blvd 32830-2786 (PO Box 22786). Fax: 407/934-4710. **Facility:** This full service hotel primarily serves conventions but also offers many features that will appeal to couples and families. Graced on the exterior with outsize statues of the swan and dolphin, the hotel complex consists of a glass pyramid surrounded by an honor guard of pastel masonry buildings. Extensive public areas include tile-flagged lobbies, numerous restaurants and meeting facilities. 2267 units. 6 two-bedroom units, 2 three-bedroom units and 8 efficiencies. Some suites ($595-$3100) and whirlpool units. 12-23 stories, interior corridors. **Parking:** valet. **Terms:** 5 day cancellation notice-fee imposed, package plans, $5 service charge. **Amenities:** dual phone lines, voice mail, safes, honor bars, irons, hair dryers. *Some:* CD players, fax. **Dining:** 2 dining rooms, 7 restaurants, coffee shop, deli, 6:30 am-11 pm; coffee bar 6-11 am; 24 hour convenience store, $10-$35, cocktails, also, Palio, see separate listing. **Leisure Activities:** 4 heated pools, wading pools, saunas, whirlpools, waterslide, beach, fishing, 4 lighted tennis courts, children's program, jogging, playground, exercise room, volleyball. *Fee:* boating, miniature golf, tennis instruction. **Guest Services:** gift shop, area transportation-Disney, valet laundry. *Fee:* massage. **Business Services:** conference facilities, administrative services, PC. *Fee:* fax. **Cards:** AE, CB, DI, DS, JC, MC, VI.

SOME UNITS
FEE FEE FEE

WYNDHAM PALACE RESORT & SPA
(AAA) [SAVE]
▽▽▽▽
Hotel

Phone: (407)827-2727 266

12/1-4/30 1P: $209-$355
5/1-5/31 & 10/1-11/30 1P: $169-$280
6/1-9/30 1P: $149-$239
Location: I-4, exit 27, 0.3 mi n on SR 535 to Hotel Plaza Blvd (Walt Disney World Resort), then 0.7 mi. 1900 Buena Vista Dr 32830. Fax: 407/827-6034. **Facility:** 1013 units. Some whirlpool units. 27 stories, interior/exterior corridors. **Parking:** valet. **Terms:** 3 day cancellation notice-fee imposed, package plans. **Amenities:** extended cable TV, safes, honor bars. **Dining:** dining room, 2 restaurants, 6 am-11 pm; snack bar available at pool, $8-$30, also, Arthur's 27, see separate listing, nightclub, entertainment. **Leisure Activities:** 3 pools, wading pool, saunas, whirlpools, 3 lighted tennis courts, children's program, arcade, sand volleyball. **Guest Services:** gift shop, area transportation-within Disney complex, valet laundry. *Fee:* airport transportation-shuttle, massage. **Business Services:** conference facilities, administrative services, PC, fax. **Cards:** AE, CB, DI, DS, MC, VI.

SOME UNITS
FEE FEE FEE FEE

(See map p. 560)

The following lodgings were either not evaluated or did not meet AAA rating requirements but are listed for your information only.

DISNEY'S ANIMAL KINGDOM LODGE
[fyi]
Resort
Phone: 407/938-3000
Under construction, scheduled to open March 2001. **Location:** N of US 192 on World Dr, follow signs on Osceola Pkwy. 2901 Osceola Pkwy 32830. **Planned Amenities:** 1293 units, radios, refrigerators, pool.

HYATT REGENCY GRAND CYPRESS
[fyi]
Phone: 407/239-1234
Not evaluated; management refused inspection. **Location:** I-4, exit 27, just w on CR 535, near entrance to Walt Disney World Village. 1 Grand Cypress Blvd 32836. Facilities, services, and decor characterize an upscale property.

THE VILLAS AT WILDERNESS LODGE
[fyi]
Hotel
Phone: 407/938-4300
Under construction, scheduled to open January 2001. **Location:** 801 Timberline Dr 32830 (PO Box 10,000). Fax: 407/938-3232. **Planned Amenities:** 181 units, radios, coffeemakers, microwaves, refrigerators.

——— **WHERE TO DINE** ———

ARTHUR'S 27
▼▼ ▼▼ ▼▼ ▼▼
Continental
Dinner: $24-$28   **Phone: 407/827-3450** [229]
Location: I-4, exit 27, 0.3 mi n on SR 535 to Hotel Plaza Blvd (Walt Disney World Resort), then 0.7 mi; in Wyndham Palace Resort & Spa. 1900 Buena Vista Dr 32830. **Hours:** 6 pm-10:30 pm. **Reservations:** required. **Features:** semi-formal attire; cocktails & lounge; entertainment; valet parking; a la carte, also prix fixe. A unique culinary experience on the hotel's 27th floor, this sophisticated dining room affords a dramatic panoramic view of Walt Disney World. Expect creative, attractive presentation and exceptional service at one of Orlando's best restaurants. **Cards:** AE, DI, DS, MC, VI. ✕

ARTIST POINT
▼▼ ▼▼ ▼▼
Regional American
Dinner: $17-$28   **Phone: 407/824-3200** [225]
Location: In Walt Disney World; in Disney's Wilderness Lodge. 901 W Timberline Dr 32830. **Hours:** 7:30 am-11:30 & 5:30-10 pm. **Reservations:** suggested. **Features:** casual dress; children's menu; cocktails & lounge; valet parking. Bring the kids to the character breakfast and enjoy folksy service in a lodge setting. A selection of Northwestern steak and seafood favorites, vegetarian dishes as well, are cooked over an open hardwood fire. Fresh ingredients and homemade desserts make this a delicious find. Smoke free premises. **Cards:** AE, MC, VI. ♿ ✕

BOATWRIGHT'S DINING HALL
▼▼ ▼▼
South American
Dinner: $11-$18   **Phone: 407/934-5422** [227]
Location: I-4, exit 26B, nw and follow signs to Disney's Downtown Disney; in Disney's Dixie Landings Resort. 1251 Dixie Dr 32830. **Hours:** 7 am-11:30 & 5-10 pm. **Reservations:** suggested. **Features:** casual dress; children's menu; cocktails & lounge; entertainment; area transportation. Traditional and unique American, Southern and Cajun specialties are offered in Dixie Landing's restored boat building warehouse along the Sassagoula River. On the Disney canal system with boat transportation to and from Downtown Disney and Pleasure Island. Smoke free premises. **Cards:** AE, MC, VI. ♿ ✕

BONFAMILLE'S CAFE
▼▼ ▼▼
American
Dinner: $10-$24   **Phone: 407/934-5391** [228]
Location: I-4, exit 26B, 2.3 mi nw on SR 536 and Bennet Creek Pkwy; in Disney's Port Orleans Resort. 2201 Orleans Dr 32830. **Hours:** 7 am-11:30 & 5-10 pm. **Reservations:** suggested. **Features:** casual dress; children's menu; cocktails & lounge; entertainment. Bonfamille's Cafe represents American cuisine with a Louisiana flair. Look for all your favorites plus a few traditional Louisiana favorites. Smoke free premises. **Cards:** AE, MC, VI. ✕

BONGOS CUBAN CAFE
▼▼ ▼▼
Cuban
Lunch: $9-$18   **Dinner: $12-$24**   **Phone: 407/828-0999** [232]
Location: In downtown Disney. Buena Vista Dr 32830. **Hours:** 11 am-1 am. **Reservations:** suggested. **Features:** casual dress; children's menu; cocktails & lounge; entertainment. Choose from an enticing mix of soup, sandwiches, chicken, pork and beef. Set in an old Havana setting with the flair of a traditional Cuban South Beach. A favorite is the churrasco, a skirt steak marinated in a typically Cuban sauce. **Cards:** AE, DS, MC, VI. ♿ ✕

CALIFORNIA GRILL
▼▼ ▼▼ ▼▼
Regional American
Dinner: $19-$30   **Phone: 407/824-1576** [224]
Location: In Walt Disney World, adjacent to Magic Kingdom; in Disney's Contemporary Resort. 4600 W World Dr 32830. **Hours:** 5:30 pm-10 pm. **Reservations:** suggested; Priority Seat. **Features:** casual dress; children's menu; cocktails & lounge; valet parking; a la carte. This is a full service, fine dining restaurant appealing to adults, particularly those with an appetite for innovative concepts in food. The menu is revised weekly but it consistently offers sophisticated, cutting edge California dishes with Pacific Rim influences throughout. House specialties include flatbread appetizers baked in a brick oven, sushi, sashimi and some vegetarian dishes. The wine list is primarily California vintages. Laidback service from staff clad entirely in black. Smoke free premises. **Cards:** AE, DI, DS, JC, MC, VI. ♿ ✕

CINDERELLA'S ROYAL TABLE
▼▼ ▼▼
American
Lunch: $10-$20   **Dinner: $20-$30**   **Phone: 407/939-3463** [213]
Location: In Walt Disney World's Magic Kingdom. **Hours:** 8-10 am, 11:30-2:45 & 4-9 pm. **Reservations:** required. **Features:** casual dress; children's menu; fee for parking. Experience all the grandeur of royalty set in legendary Cinderella's castle. Popular Disney character breakfast. Menu features prime rib, beef pie, roast chicken, barbecue and other comfort foods. Most popular eatery in the Magic Kingdom. Smoke free premises. **Cards:** AE, MC, VI. ✕

(See map p. 560)

CITRICOS
Dinner: $25-$40   Phone: 407/824-3000   221

Nouvelle French

Location: 8 mi nw of jct I-4 and US 192; at Disney's Grand Floridian Resort & Spa. 4401 Grand Floridian Way 32830. **Hours:** 5:30 pm-10 pm. **Reservations:** accepted. **Features:** dressy casual; carryout; cocktails & lounge; valet parking. Wonderful open kitchen with fusion of French and Mediterranean styles of cooking and decor, soft lighting and warm service top off the evening. Entrees range from seafood to roast leg of lamb and duck. A chef's vegetarian special and wine pairing is available. Smoke free premises. **Cards:** AE, MC, VI.

CRAB HOUSE SEAFOOD RESTAURANT
Lunch: $9-$22   Dinner: $14-$25   Phone: 407/239-1888   226

Seafood

Location: In Vista Center off SR 535, 0.5 mi n of jct I-4 exit 27. 8496 Palm Pkwy 32836. **Hours:** 11:30 am-11 pm, Sun from 1 pm. **Features:** casual dress; children's menu; salad bar; cocktails & lounge; a la carte. Featuring casual family dining amid a nautical decor, this is the place for an abundance of crab and other seafood choices. For a fresh taste of the ocean, try the shrimp scampi with rice pilaf. A self-serve salad bar completes a delicious meal. **Cards:** AE, CB, DI, DS, JC, MC, VI.

THE CRYSTAL PALACE
Lunch: $10-$16   Dinner: $10-$20   Phone: 407/939-3463   216

American

Location: In Walt Disney World's Magic Kingdom. **Hours:** 8:05-10:30 am, 11:30-2:45 & 4-9 pm; closing hours may vary. **Features:** casual dress; children's menu; fee for parking; buffet. Left of Main Street USA, this stunning, beautifully designed glass palace features a family oriented all you can eat buffet. Salad, pasta and dessert bars compliment entree selections of freshly roasted and carved meat. Disney characters appear. Smoke free premises. **Cards:** AE, DI, DS, JC, MC, VI.

FINN'S GRILL
Dinner: $19-$26   Phone: 407/827-3838   230

American

Location: I-4 and SR 535 exit; in Walt Disney World Resort; in Hilton in the WALT DISNEY WORLD Resort. 1751 Hotel Plaza Blvd 32830. **Hours:** 5:30 pm-11 pm. **Features:** casual dress; children's menu; carryout; cocktails & lounge; valet parking. Kick back in an upbeat Key West atmosphere where a variety of seafood, Black Angus steak, pasta and salads are served by a professional staff. Do not miss the hearty, spicy Cajun gumbo. Come in on a Saturday for the excellent seafood buffet. **Cards:** AE, CB, DI, DS, JC, MC, VI.

FLYING FISH CAFE
Dinner: $18-$26   Phone: 407/939-2359   238

Seafood

Location: 0.5 mi e of Disney main gate access road, 2 mi n of US 192; in Disney's BoardWalk Inn. 2101 N Epcot Resorts Blvd 32830. **Hours:** 5:30 pm-10 pm, Fri & Sat-10:30 pm. **Reservations:** suggested. **Features:** casual dress; children's menu; cocktails & lounge; valet parking. Casual dining in an eclectic decor offers fresh, seasonal specialties served from a cutting-edge open kitchen. The lobster appetizer is creatively produced. Stroll around the boardwalk after dinner to walk off those extra calories from dessert. Smoke free premises. **Cards:** AE, MC, VI.

FULTON'S CRAB HOUSE
Lunch: $11-$17   Dinner: $15-$42   Phone: 407/934-2628   231

Seafood

Location: Downtown Disney; between Pleasure Island and Disney Village Marketplace. 1670 Buena Vista Dr 32830. **Hours:** 11:30 am-11 pm. **Reservations:** accepted; priority seat. **Features:** casual dress; children's menu; cocktails & lounge; fee for valet parking. Exceptionally fresh and expertly prepared seafood is the highlight of a menu that changes daily. Alaskan king crab is a house specialty. If you experience a wait, you can enjoy a drink and savor the appetizers outside on the patio deck. Smoke free premises. **Cards:** AE, DI, DS, MC, VI.

LIBERTY TREE TAVERN
Lunch: $10-$20   Dinner: $10-$20   Phone: 407/939-3463   217

American

Location: In Walt Disney World's Magic Kingdom. **Hours:** 11 am-3 & 4-9 pm. **Reservations:** suggested. **Features:** casual dress; children's menu; fee for parking. This colonial style eatery, located in Liberty Square features nightly Disney character dinners. Menu is fixed price offering a hearty selection of regal foods including salad, entree and beverage. Fresh baked desserts are extra. Smoke free premises. **Cards:** AE, DS, MC, VI.

NARCOOSEE'S
Dinner: $21-$32   Phone: 407/824-2442   222

Spanish

Location: 8 mi nw of jct I-4 and US 192; at Disney's Grand Floridian Resort & Spa. 4401 Grand Floridian Way 32830. **Hours:** 5 pm-10 pm. **Reservations:** accepted; groups of 12. **Features:** casual dress; children's menu; carryout; cocktails & lounge; valet parking. Lovely location on the water, octagon building with a rotunda depicting a sea mural and the same innovative samplings of grilled salmon, tuna, chops, and filets. The wine list is matched daily and the dessert should never be missed. Smoke free premises.

PALIO
Dinner: $17-$30   Phone: 407/934-1610   236

Northern Italian

Location: 0.3 mi e of Disney main gate access road, 2 mi n of US 192; from I-4 exit 26B, follow Epcot Resort area signs; in Walt Disney World Swan and Dolphin. 1200 Epcot Resorts Blvd 32830-2786. **Hours:** 6 pm-11 pm. **Reservations:** suggested. **Features:** casual dress; children's menu; cocktails & lounge; entertainment; fee for valet parking; a la carte. Dinner at this full service, fine dining restaurant starts with tempting antipasto including carpaccio, bruschetta, and porcini risotto. The restaurant also serves a variety of seafood, veal and pasta entrees. Hearty Northern Italian dishes are the backbone of the menu: oso buco with saffron risotto, piccata alla Milanese and a beef filet with polenta and shallots. The decor theme is taken from the Palio Horse Race in Siena and includes colorful flags from the city. **Cards:** AE, DI, DS, JC, MC, VI.

PEBBLES/LAKE BUENA VISTA
Lunch: $8-$22   Dinner: $11-$26   Phone: 407/827-1111   234

American

Location: I-4, exit 27, and SR 535, 0.3 mi n ; in Crossroads Shopping Center. 12551 SR 535 32836. **Hours:** 11 am-11 pm, Fri-midnight, Sat noon-midnight, Sun noon-11 pm. **Closed:** 11/22, 12/25. **Features:** casual dress; children's menu; carryout; cocktails; a la carte. This is a casual gourmet dining adventure. The homemade soups and salads are fresh and spicy. Well-seasoned seafood, duck, lamb, beef and pasta specialties round out this menu. A Tiki bar and patio provide a nice setting for outdoor dining. **Cards:** AE, CB, DI, DS, MC, VI.

(See map p. 560)

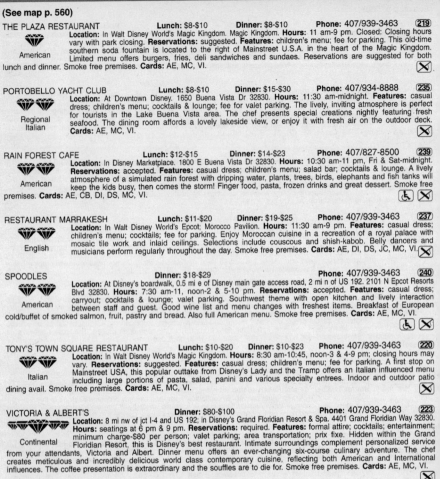

THE PLAZA RESTAURANT
American
Lunch: $8-$10 **Dinner:** $8-$10 **Phone:** 407/939-3463 ⌑219⌑
Location: In Walt Disney World's Magic Kingdom. Magic Kingdom. **Hours:** 11 am-9 pm. Closed: Closing hours vary with park closing. **Reservations:** suggested. **Features:** children's menu; fee for parking. This old-time southern soda fountain is located to the right of Mainstreet U.S.A. in the heart of the Magic Kingdom. Limited menu offers burgers, fries, deli sandwiches and sundaes. Reservations are suggested for both lunch and dinner. Smoke free premises. **Cards:** AE, MC, VI.

PORTOBELLO YACHT CLUB
Regional Italian
Lunch: $8-$10 **Dinner:** $15-$30 **Phone:** 407/934-8888 ⌑235⌑
Location: At Downtown Disney. 1650 Buena Vista Dr 32830. **Hours:** 11:30 am-midnight. **Features:** casual dress; children's menu; cocktails & lounge; fee for valet parking. The lively, inviting atmosphere is perfect for tourists in the Lake Buena Vista area. The chef presents special creations nightly featuring fresh seafood. The dining room affords a lovely lakeside view, or enjoy it with fresh air on the outdoor deck. **Cards:** AE, MC, VI.

RAIN FOREST CAFE
American
Lunch: $12-$15 **Dinner:** $14-$23 **Phone:** 407/827-8500 ⌑239⌑
Location: In Disney Marketplace. 1800 E Buena Vista Dr 32830. **Hours:** 10:30 am-11 pm, Fri & Sat-midnight. **Reservations:** accepted. **Features:** casual dress; children's menu; salad bar; cocktails & lounge. A lively atmosphere of a simulated rain forest with dripping water, plants, trees, birds, elephants and fish tanks will keep the kids busy, then comes the storm! Finger food, pasta, frozen drinks and great dessert. Smoke free premises. **Cards:** AE, CB, DI, DS, MC, VI.

RESTAURANT MARRAKESH
English
Lunch: $11-$20 **Dinner:** $19-$25 **Phone:** 407/939-3463 ⌑237⌑
Location: In Walt Disney World's Epcot; Morocco Pavilion. **Hours:** 11:30 am-9 pm. **Features:** casual dress; children's menu; cocktails; fee for parking. Enjoy Moroccan cuisine in a recreation of a royal palace with mosaic tile work and inlaid ceilings. Selections include couscous and shish-kabob. Belly dancers and musicians perform regularly throughout the day. Smoke free premises. **Cards:** AE, DI, DS, JC, MC, VI.

SPOODLES
American
Dinner: $18-$29 **Phone:** 407/939-3463 ⌑240⌑
Location: At Disney's boardwalk, 0.5 mi e of Disney main gate access road, 2 mi n of US 192. 2101 N Epcot Resorts Blvd 32830. **Hours:** 7:30 am-11, noon-2 & 5-10 pm. **Reservations:** accepted. **Features:** casual dress; carryout; cocktails & lounge; valet parking. Southwest theme with open kitchen and lively interaction between staff and guest. Good wine list and menu changes with freshest items. Breakfast of European cold/buffet of smoked salmon, fruit, pastry and bread. Also full American menu. Smoke free premises. **Cards:** AE, MC, VI.

TONY'S TOWN SQUARE RESTAURANT
Italian
Lunch: $10-$20 **Dinner:** $10-$23 **Phone:** 407/939-3463 ⌑220⌑
Location: In Walt Disney World's Magic Kingdom. **Hours:** 8:30 am-10:45, noon-3 & 4-9 pm; closing hours may vary. **Reservations:** suggested. **Features:** casual dress; children's menu; fee for parking. A first stop on Mainstreet USA, this popular outtake from Disney's Lady and the Tramp offers an Italian influenced menu including large portions of pasta, salad, panini and various specialty entrees. Indoor and outdoor patio dining avail. Smoke free premises. **Cards:** AE, MC, VI.

VICTORIA & ALBERT'S
Continental
Dinner: $80-$100 **Phone:** 407/939-3463 ⌑223⌑
Location: 8 mi nw of jct I-4 and US 192; in Disney's Grand Floridian Resort & Spa. 4401 Grand Floridian Way 32830. **Hours:** seatings at 6 pm & 9 pm. **Reservations:** required. **Features:** formal attire; cocktails; entertainment; minimum charge-$80 per person; valet parking; area transportation; prix fixe. Hidden within the Grand Floridian Resort, this is Disney's best restaurant. Intimate surroundings complement personalized service from your attendants, Victoria and Albert. Dinner menu offers an ever-changing six-course culinary adventure. The chef creates meticulous and incredibly delicious world class contemporary cuisine, reflecting both American and International influences. The coffee presentation is extraordinary and the souffles are to die for. Smoke free premises. **Cards:** AE, MC, VI.

YACHTSMAN'S STEAK HOUSE
Steak House
Dinner: $22-$31 **Phone:** 407/934-1270 ⌑233⌑
Location: I-4, exit 26B, 2.5 mi nw, near Epcot Center and MGM Studios; in Disney's Yacht & Beach Club Resorts. 1700 Epcot Resorts Blvd 32830. **Hours:** 5:30 pm-10 pm. **Reservations:** suggested. **Features:** casual dress; children's menu; cocktails & lounge; valet parking; a la carte. Spacious wood beamed dining room is setting for guests to enjoy choice, dry-aged steaks cut daily and cooked over wood-burning grill with oak wood. Various fresh seafood selections, lighter creative vegetarian menu offerings and creative assortment of unique dessert creations. Smoke free premises. **Cards:** AE, MC, VI.

**The following restaurants have not been evaluated by AAA
but are listed for your information only.**

AKERSHUS
[fyi]
Phone: 407/939-3463
Not evaluated. **Location:** In Walt Disney World's Epcot Center. Norway, World Showcase. **Features:** 40 plus item selection of Scandinavian cuisine, including seafood and smoked meat. The restaurant is modeled after a medieval Norwegian castle.

ALFREDO'S
[fyi]
Phone: 407/939-3463
Not evaluated. **Location:** in Walt Disney World's Epcot Center. Italy, World Showcase. **Features:** Dark and rich decor accents the Italian piazza murals. Traditional Italian cuisine; selection of Italian wines.

BIERGARTEN
[fyi]
Phone: 407/939-3463
Not evaluated. **Location:** In Walt Disney World's Epcot Center. Germany, World Showcase. **Features:** All-you-can-eat buffet featuring assorted sausage, cabbage, spaetzle, strudel, etc.

(See map p. 560)

BOULANGERIE PATISSERIE
Phone: 407/939-3463

fyi Not evaluated. **Location:** In Walt Disney World's Epcot Center. France, World Showcase. **Features:** Counter service. Specialties include French pastry, quiche and coffee.

CHEFS DE FRANCE
Phone: 407/939-3463

fyi Not evaluated. **Location:** In Walt Disney World's Epcot Center. France, World Showcase. **Features:** Creative menu of French cuisine, served in a more formal surrounding. Varied wine selections; exceptional pastries and desserts.

THE CORAL REEF
Phone: 407/939-3463

fyi Not evaluated. **Location:** In Walt Disney World's Epcot Center. Living Seas, Future World. **Features:** Seafood offerings; menu varies seasonally. Tiered dining room offers view of the marine life tank.

THE GARDEN GRILL
Phone: 407/939-3463

fyi Not evaluated. **Location:** In Walt Disney World's Epcot Center. The Land, Future World. **Features:** Character meals at breakfast and lunch. Dining room revolves through scenes in nature. Meals served family style, with some vegetables grown on-site.

HOLLYWOOD AND VINE CAFE OF STARS
Phone: 407/939-3463

fyi Not evaluated. **Location:** In Walt Disney World, MGM. **Features:** Recreates a 40's-50's diner, with stainless steel and deco touches. Serve yourself buffet offering traditional American fare. Moderately priced.

THE HOLLYWOOD BROWN DERBY
Phone: 407/939-3463

fyi Not evaluated. **Location:** In Walt Disney World, MGM. Hollywood Blvd. **Features:** Recreation of the original Brown Derby, including caricatures of stars. American cuisine. Moderately priced.

LE CELLIER STEAK HOUSE
Phone: 407/939-3463

fyi Not evaluated. **Location:** In Walt Disney World's Epcot Center. Canada, World Showcase. **Features:** "Canadian" foods served in the wine cellar (lower level) of a replica of a Canadian national historic hotel.

MAMA MELROSE'S
Phone: 407/939-3463

fyi Not evaluated. **Location:** In Walt Disney World, MGM. **Features:** Recreating the look of a neighborhood restaurant. Traditional pasta selections and seafood specialties. Moderately priced.

MITSUKOSHI TEPPANYAKI
Phone: 407/939-3463

fyi Not evaluated. **Location:** In Walt Disney World's Epcot Center. Japan, World Showcase. **Features:** Grilled meat, seafood and chicken prepared at your teppanyaki table. Be entertained as you watch your chef prepare your meal. Touches of traditional Japanese decor. Sushi available.

NINE DRAGONS
Phone: 407/939-3463

fyi Not evaluated. **Location:** In Walt Disney World's Epcot Center. China, World Showcase. **Features:** Menu selections include Mandarin, Cantonese and Szechuan items. Dining room rich in Oriental decor.

PRIME TIME CAFE
Phone: 407/939-3463

fyi Not evaluated. **Location:** In Walt Disney World, MGM. **Features:** Fun atmosphere. Decor reminiscent of a 50's TV sitcom kitchen. Home-type specialties and soda fountain drinks. Moderately priced.

ROSE AND CROWN
Phone: 407/939-3463

fyi Not evaluated. **Location:** In Walt Disney World's Epcot Center. UK, World Showcase. **Features:** Limited menu selection of traditional English pub fare. Selections of British beer and ale. Rustic dining room and outdoor patio seating.

SAN ANGEL INN
Phone: 407/939-3463

fyi Not evaluated. **Location:** In Walt Disney World's Epcot Center. Mexico, World Showcase. **Features:** Selection of traditional Mexican offerings with some creative combinations. Standard, commercial type Mexican decor; dim lighting.

SCI-FI DINE-IN THEATRE
Phone: 407/939-3463

fyi Not evaluated. **Location:** In Walt Disney World, MGM. Backlot. **Features:** Dine in a 50's style replica car at the drive-in theater while watching clips of sci-fi films. Traditional American menu selections. Moderate prices.

WILDHORSE SALOON
Phone: 407/827-4947

fyi Not evaluated. **Location:** In Downtown Disney. Pleasure Island 32830. **Features:** Saloon with country dancing and old American features of barbecue, steak, chops and lots of finger food.

LAKE MARY pop. 5,900   (See map p. 554; index p. 557)

———— WHERE TO STAY ————

HILTON GARDEN INN LAKE MARY
Phone: (407)531-9900   **72**

(AAA) (SAVE)

▼▼▼▼

Motel

1/1-11/30	1P: $79-$129	2P: $79-$129
12/1-12/31	1P: $69-$119	2P: $69-$119

Location: I-4, exit 50, just ne via Lake Mary Blvd and Primera. 705 Currency Cir 32746. Fax: 407/531-1144. **Facility:** 123 units. Some suites and whirlpool units. *Bath:* combo or shower only. 3 stories, interior corridors. **Amenities:** extended cable TV, video games, voice mail, irons, hair dryers. **Dining:** restaurant, 6:30-10:30 am; breakfast buffet; evening honor bar. **Leisure Activities:** heated pool, whirlpool, exercise room. **Guest Services:** coin laundry. **Business Services:** meeting rooms, administrative services, PC. **Cards:** AE, DI, DS, JC, MC, VI. **Special Amenities:** free newspaper and preferred room (subject to availability with advanced reservations). *(See ad p 44)*

SOME UNITS

[icons] FEE /⊠/

HOMEWOOD SUITES BY HILTON
Phone: 407/805-9111   **73**

(AAA) (SAVE)

▼▼▼▼

Suite Motel

All Year   1P: $89-$199

Location: I-4, exit 50, just ne via Lake Mary Blvd and Primera. 755 Currency Cir 32746. Fax: 407/805-0236. **Facility:** 112 efficiencies. *Bath:* combo or shower only. 5 stories, interior corridors. **Terms:** cancellation fee imposed. **Amenities:** extended cable TV, video games, voice mail, irons, hair dryers. **Dining:** small convenience store. **Leisure Activities:** exercise room. **Guest Services:** [BP] meal plan available, complimentary evening beverages: Mon-Thurs, coin laundry. **Business Services:** meeting rooms, administrative services, PC. **Cards:** AE, DI, DS, MC, VI. **Special Amenities:** free continental breakfast and free newspaper. *(See color ad below)*

SOME UNITS

[icons] FEE /⊠/ VCR FEE

LA QUINTA INN & SUITES
Phone: (407)805-9901   **75**

(SAVE)

▼▼▼▼

Motel

All Year   1P: $89-$109   2P: $89-$109

Location: I-4, exit 50, Just se, via Lake Mary Blvd. 1060 Greenwood Blvd 32746. Fax: 407/805-9968. **Facility:** Designated smoking area. 128 units. Some suites ($119-$139). *Bath:* combo or shower only. 5 stories, interior corridors. **Terms:** small pets only. **Amenities:** video games, voice mail, irons, hair dryers. **Leisure Activities:** heated pool, whirlpool, exercise room. **Guest Services:** [ECP] meal plan available, area transportation, coin laundry. **Business Services:** meeting rooms. **Cards:** AE, CB, DI, DS, MC, VI. *(See color ad p 604)*

SOME UNITS

[icons] FEE /⊠/

MAINSTAY SUITES HOTEL
Phone: 407/829-2332   **74**

(AAA) (SAVE)

▼▼▼▼

Extended Stay Motel

All Year   1P: $79-$125   2P: $79-$125

Location: I-4, exit 50, 0.5 mi s on Lake Emma Rd; in Commerce Park. 1040 Greenwood Blvd 32746. Fax: 407/829-4436. **Facility:** Office hours 7 am-10 pm. During non-office hours check-in requires use of credit card and automated self-serve system. 100 units with kitchen. 3 stories, interior corridors. **Terms:** 7 day cancellation notice-fee imposed, weekly & monthly rates available, package plans, small pets only ($5-$10 extra charge). **Leisure Activities:** exercise room, gas grill. **Guest Services:** [CP] meal plan available, complimentary evening beverages: Mon-Wed, coin laundry. **Business Services:** fax. **Cards:** AE, CB, DI, DS, JC, MC, VI. **Special Amenities:** early check-in/late check-out. *(See color ad p 573)*

SOME UNITS

[icons] /⊠/

———— WHERE TO DINE ————

BISTRO CAPPUCCINO
Lunch: $7-$12   **Dinner:** $12-$22   Phone: 407/321-3333   **43**

▼▼▼▼

Continental

Location: I-4, exit 50, 0.3 mi s, then 0.5 mi s on Lake Emma Rd, just e. 951 Greenwood Blvd 32746. **Hours:** 11 am-2 & 5-11 pm. Closed: Mon. **Reservations:** accepted. **Features:** dressy casual; children's menu; carryout; cocktails & lounge; entertainment. A tantalizing array of bistro dishes are prepared with high quality ingredients and skill that demonstrates years of training. Bread, salad, soup, entrees and desserts all rate high on taste and flavor, and exceptional service makes for a leisurely meal. **Cards:** AE, DI, DS, MC, VI.

⊠

(See map p. 554)

GALLERIA ▼▼▼ ▼▼▼
Italian

Lunch: $6-$9   **Dinner:** $12-$19   **Phone:** 407/333-0872 45
Location: I-4, exit 50, 0.5 mi e side of Lake Mary Centre. 3837 Lake Emma Rd 32746. **Hours:** 11:30 am-9:30 pm, Fri-10:30 pm, Sat 4 pm-10:30 pm, Sun 4 pm-9:30 pm. Closed: 12/25. **Features:** casual dress; children's menu; carryout; cocktails & lounge. This bright, contemporary setting is perfect for sampling the very good selection of home-style Italian favorites. Attentive servers bring such delicious offerings as fried calamari, Caesar salad and veal. Don't miss the fresh house-made soups and pasta. Pizza from a wood-burning oven a specialty. **Cards:** AE, MC, VI.
🅧

KUMQUAT TREE ◈◈ ◈◈
Chinese

Lunch: $5-$7   **Dinner:** $6-$25   **Phone:** 407/333-0099 44
Location: I-4, exit 50, 0.5 mi e; in Lake Mary Centre. 3705 Lake Emma Rd 32746. **Hours:** 11 am-9 pm, Fri-10 pm, Sat noon-10 pm, Sun 4 pm-9 pm. Closed major holidays. **Features:** casual dress; carryout; beer & wine only; minimum charge-$5; a la carte. Cantonese, Mandarin, Szechwan and Hunan are all offered at this modest, informal restaurant. You will find many delicious selections at the popular lunch buffet served every weekday, or taste such specialties as Rainbow Delight or General Teau chicken. **Cards:** AE, DI, MC, VI.
🅧

LEESBURG pop. 14,900

--------- WHERE TO STAY ---------

DAYS INN LEESBURG
AAA SAVE
▼▼▼ ▼▼▼
Motel

	1/1-3/31	1P: $39-$59	2P: $54-$79	XP: $5	F14
	12/1-12/31	1P: $39-$59	2P: $49-$65	XP: $5	F14
	4/1-11/30	1P: $39-$49	2P: $44-$59	XP: $5	F14

Phone: (352)787-3131
Location: On US 441, 0.5 mi s of jct US 27. 1115 W North Blvd 34748. Fax: 352/365-1497. **Facility:** Adjacent to small shopping center. 61 units, 5 with efficiency (no utensils). Some whirlpool units ($99-$125). 2 stories, exterior corridors. **Amenities:** extended cable TV, hair dryers. **Leisure Activities:** heated pool. **Guest Services:** coin laundry. **Cards:** AE, DS, MC, VI. **Special Amenities:** free continental breakfast and free local telephone calls.

SHONEY'S INN MEETING & CONFERENCE CENTER
AAA SAVE
▼▼▼ ▼▼▼
Motel

	12/1-5/1 & 9/2-11/30	1P: $55-$65	XP: $5	F
	5/2-9/1	1P: $50-$60	XP: $5	F

Phone: (352)787-1210
Location: At jct US 27 and 441. 1308 N 14th St 34748. Fax: 352/365-0163. **Facility:** Lounge closed Sun. 116 units. 2 stories, exterior corridors. **Terms:** 7 day cancellation notice, small pets only ($5-$10 fee). **Amenities:** extended cable TV. **Guest Services:** [ECP] meal plan available, coin laundry. **Business Services:** meeting rooms. **Cards:** AE, CB, DI, DS, MC, VI. **Special Amenities:** free continental breakfast and free newspaper.

SUPER 8 MOTEL
▼▼▼ ▼▼▼
Motel

	12/28-4/16	1P: $65-$75	2P: $65-$75	XP: $6	F12
	12/1-12/27 & 4/17-11/30	1P: $50-$65	2P: $50-$65	XP: $6	F12

Phone: (352)787-6363
Location: At jct US 27 and 441. 1392 North Blvd W 34748. Fax: 352/787-6363. **Facility:** Attractive tree lined lot. 52 units. 3 stories, interior corridors. **Terms:** 3 day cancellation notice, small pets only. **Amenities:** extended cable TV, safes (fee). **Leisure Activities:** heated pool. **Cards:** AE, DI, DS, MC, VI.

--------- WHERE TO DINE ---------

VIC'S EMBERS ▼▼▼ ▼▼▼
American

Dinner: $12-$22   **Phone:** 352-728-8989
Location: On US 441, 4.4 mi se of jct US 27. 7940 US 441 34788. **Hours:** 4:30 pm-10 pm, Fri & Sat-11 pm, Sun 11:30 am-2:30 & 4-9:30 pm. Closed major holidays. **Features:** casual dress; Sunday brunch; children's menu; early bird specials; cocktails & lounge; entertainment; valet parking. This casual, somewhat elegant diner boasts a pleasant atmosphere and some tableside preparations. Watch the planes fly into Leesburg Airport and order the Polynesian salmon heaped with vegetables and garlic mashed potatoes. **Cards:** MC, VI.
🅧

LONGWOOD pop. 13,300   (See map p. 554; index p. 558)

--------- WHERE TO STAY ---------

RAMADA INN NORTH-ORLANDO
▼▼▼ ▼▼▼
Motor Inn

	2/12-2/28	1P: $82	2P: $102	XP: $6	F18
	1/1-2/11 & 3/1-11/30	1P: $66	2P: $78	XP: $6	F18
	12/1-12/31	1P: $66	2P: $76	XP: $6	F18

Phone: (407)862-4000 83
Location: I-4, exit 49. 2025 W SR 434 32779 (PO Box 520312, 32750-0312). Fax: 407/862-3530. **Facility:** Lush outdoor garden area. Some rooms with large desk; a few with recliners. 192 units. 2 stories, exterior corridors. **Terms:** small pets only. **Amenities:** extended cable TV, voice mail, hair dryers. Some: irons. **Guest Services:** coin laundry. **Business Services:** meeting rooms, administrative services. **Cards:** AE, CB, DI, DS, MC, VI.

(See map p. 554)

—— WHERE TO DINE ——

ENZO'S RESTAURANT ON THE LAKE
Dinner: $20-$38
Phone: 407/834-9872   52
AAA
Location: 0.5 mi s of SR 434. 1130 S Hwy 17-92 32750. **Hours:** 6 pm-10:30 pm. Closed: 1/1, 12/25; also Sun.
Reservations: suggested. **Features:** dressy casual; cocktails & lounge; a la carte. Elegant trattoria ambience is found in a converted house on Lake Fairy. Go early for the sunsets since dinner is a very busy time. Excellent house pastas, fresh veal and fish specialties are served with finesse. The tiramisu is rich with flavor. **Cards:** AE, DI, DS, MC, VI.
Italian

FIRST WATCH
Lunch: $6-$8
Phone: 407/774-1830   51
Location: I-4 exit 49, 2 mi w; in Albertsons Shopping Plaza. 2425 W SR 434 32750. **Hours:** 7 am-2:30 pm.
American   Closed: 11/22, 12/25. **Features:** casual dress; children's menu; cocktails. One of a dozen like it in Florida, it serves breakfast, brunch and lunch with traditional omelets, pancakes, waffles and crepes. Great salads and sandwiches are accompanied by fresh fruits and muffins. Attentive and accurate service brings patrons back. Smoke free premises. **Cards:** AE, DS, MC, VI.

PEBBLES RESTAURANT
Lunch: $7-$15
Dinner: $8-$20
Phone: 407/774-7111   56
Location: On SR 434, 0.3 mi w of I-4 exit 49. 2110 W SR 434 32779. **Hours:** 11 am-11 pm, Fri & Sat-midnight.
American   Closed: 11/22, 12/25. **Features:** casual dress; children's menu; carryout; cocktails & lounge; a la carte. This informal, tropical restaurant features fresh fish, lamb and duck. The black-pepper-crusted filet is flavorful and well-presented. Unique salads can be accompanied by tapas for a complete meal. Fresh, homemade soups and desserts make this a favorite. **Cards:** AE, DI, DS, MC, VI.

PETER SCOTT'S
Dinner: $20-$32
Phone: 407/834-4477   54
AAA
Location: SR 434, 0.3 mi ne of I-4 exit 49; in the Longwood Village Shoppes. 1811 W SR 434 32750. **Hours:** 6 pm-1 am. Closed: 7/4, 11/22, 12/25; also Sun & Mon. **Reservations:** suggested. **Features:** semi-formal attire; cocktails & lounge; entertainment; a la carte. Dance to jazz and swing, and delight in fine, candlelit dining in a formal setting. The menu offers a nice variety of poultry, fish, veal and beef. Private rooms and a lengthy wine list create a special mood. Smoking permitted in the lounge only. **Cards:** AE, CB, DI, DS, MC, VI.
Continental

MAITLAND pop. 9,100   (See map p. 554; index p. 558)

—— WHERE TO STAY ——

COURTYARD BY MARRIOTT ORLANDO/MAITLAND
Phone: (407)659-9100   126

1/7-4/14	1P: $69-$129	2P: $69-$129
9/30-11/30	1P: $69-$119	2P: $69-$119
4/15-9/29	1P: $59-$109	2P: $59-$109
12/1-1/6	1P: $59-$99	2P: $59-$99

Motel
Location: I-4, exit 47B, 0.5 mi w, just s on Keller Rd, then just w. 1750 Pembrook Dr 32810. Fax: 407/659-9101. **Facility:** Lovely outdoor courtyard with beautiful gardens. 112 units. Some suites ($89-$149) and whirlpool units ($79-$139). *Bath:* combo or shower only. 4 stories, interior corridors. **Terms:** cancellation fee imposed. **Amenities:** extended cable TV, voice mail, irons, hair dryers. **Leisure Activities:** heated pool, whirlpool, exercise room. **Guest Services:** coin laundry. **Business Services:** meeting rooms, PC, fax. **Cards:** AE, CB, DI, DS, MC, VI.   SOME UNITS

[ASK] [S] [D] [⫢] [⊡] [⛾] [✇] [🐾] [⊿] [☆] [⛴] [▣] [DATA PORT] / [✕] [VCR] [▤] [🛏] /

SHERATON ORLANDO NORTH HOTEL
Phone: (407)660-9000   127

1/1-5/1	1P: $89-$159	2P: $89-$159	XP: $10 F17
12/1-12/31 & 10/1-11/30	1P: $99-$139	2P: $99-$139	XP: $10 F17
5/2-9/30	1P: $89-$139	2P: $89-$139	XP: $10 F17

Hotel
Location: I-4, exit 47, just w on SR 414 (Maitland Blvd). 600 N Lake Destiny Dr 32751 (PO Box 538300, ORLANDO, 32853-8300). Fax: 407/660-9008. **Facility:** Excellent public facilities. Few rooms with balcony. 394 units. Some suites ($450-$600) and whirlpool units. 6 stories, interior corridors. **Parking:** valet. **Terms:** 24 day cancellation notice-fee imposed, package plans. **Amenities:** video games, voice mail, irons, hair dryers. *Some:* fax. **Leisure Activities:** lighted tennis court. **Guest Services:** gift shop, valet laundry. **Business Services:** conference facilities, administrative services, PC, fax. **Cards:** AE, CB, DI, DS, JC, MC, VI.   SOME UNITS

[ASK] [⫢] [⊡] [🐾] [⊿] [☆] [▣] [DATA PORT] / [✕] /
                              FEE

Look for the Sign Along the Way   *AAA*

When selecting a place to dine while traveling, look for Official Appointment restaurants that display the AAA Approved sign. It's the only sign you need to be assured of an enjoyable dining experience.

As a AAA member, you already know the AAA sign indicates quality establishments.

So, when you don't have advance dining reservations, look for the AAA Approved sign along the way, for a meal you'll long remember!

(See map p. 554)

THURSTON HOUSE
▼▼▼▼
Historic Bed
& Breakfast

All Year   1P: $130-$160   2P: $130-$160   **Phone:** (407)539-1911   [128]
Location: 0.5 mi w of US 17/92. 851 Lake Ave 32751. Fax: 407/539-0365. **Facility:** 1885 Queen Anne and Victorian architecture, with country eclectic decor. Screened porch with swing and rocking chairs, parlor with cable TV and fireplace. Designated smoking area. 4 units. *Bath:* combo or shower only. 2 stories, interior corridors. **Terms:** age restrictions may apply, 5 day cancellation notice, weekly & monthly rates available.
Amenities: hair dryers. **Guest Services:** [ECP] meal plan available. **Cards:** AE, MC, VI.   SOME UNITS

[ASK] [S/D] [X] [📠] [DATA PORT] / [VCR]

--------- *The following lodging was either not evaluated or did not* ---------
meet AAA rating requirements but is listed for your information only.

HOMEWOOD SUITES BY HILTON
[fyi]
Apartment

1/16-4/30   1P: $109-$149   2P: $109-$149   XP: $5   F17
12/1-1/15 & 5/1-11/30   1P: $105-$149   2P: $105-$149   XP: $5   F17   **Phone:** 407/875-8777
Too new to rate, opening scheduled for October 2000. **Location:** I-4, exit 47 (Maitland Ave), then w, 0.3 mi on Lake Destiny. 290 Southhall Lane 32751. Fax: 407/875-8812. **Amenities:** 143 units, pets, radios, coffeemakers, microwaves, refrigerators, pool. **Terms:** cancellation fee imposed, **Cards:** AE, CB, DI, DS, MC, VI. *(See color ad below)*

--------- **WHERE TO DINE** ---------

ANTONIO'S LA FIAMMA RISTORANTE   **Lunch:** $6-$13   **Dinner:** $13-$30   **Phone:** 407/645-5523   [87]
(AAA)
▼▼▼▼
Italian

Location: On US 17-92, 1.3 mi n of jct SR 423 (Lee Rd). 611 S Orlando Ave 32751. **Hours:** 11:30 am-2:30 & 5-10 pm, Fri-11 pm, Sat 5 pm-11 pm. Closed major holidays; also Sun. **Reservations:** suggested. **Features:** dressy casual; carryout; cocktails & lounge; a la carte. The second floor dining room of the energetic and elegant restaurant overlooks Lake Lily. Wood-fired ovens contribute to the rich flavors of gourmet creations of chicken, fish and beef. Be sure to try their version of that classic dessert, tiramisu. The first-floor delicatessen has a feel all its own. **Cards:** AE, CB, DS, MC, VI.   [X]

NICOLE ST PIERRE RESTAURANT   **Lunch:** $8-$17   **Dinner:** $16-$27   **Phone:** 407/647-7575   [88]
(AAA)
▼▼▼▼
Continental

Location: US 17-92, 0.5 mi n of jct SR 423 (Lee Rd). 1300 S Orlando Ave 32751. **Hours:** 11:30 am-2:30 & 5:30-10 pm. Closed: Sun. **Reservations:** suggested. **Features:** dressy casual; children's menu; carryout; cocktails & lounge. The elegant bistro is set in a private park with well-aged oak trees, brilliant flowers and ponds. Imaginative dishes, such as grilled lamb chops and key lime strawberry tarts, show the innovation of the chef. The wine list is extensive. Smoke free premises. **Cards:** AE, CB, DI, DS, MC, VI.   [X]

MOUNT DORA pop. 7,200   (See map p. 554; index p. 557)

--------- **WHERE TO STAY** ---------

COMFORT INN
(AAA) [SAVE]
▼▼▼▼
Motel

12/20-4/20   1P: $68-$83   2P: $78-$94   XP: $5   F18
12/1-12/19 & 4/21-11/30   1P: $60-$74   2P: $64-$85   XP: $5   F18   **Phone:** (352)383-3400   [48]
Location: Just s of southern jct SR 19. 16630 Hwy 441 W 32757. Fax: 352/383-8499. **Facility:** 89 units, 3 with efficiency. Some suites ($92-$110) and whirlpool units ($95-$110). *Bath:* combo or shower only. 2 stories, exterior corridors. **Terms:** 14 day cancellation notice. **Amenities:** extended cable TV. *Some:* irons, hair dryers. **Leisure Activities:** whirlpool. **Guest Services:** coin laundry. **Business Services:** meeting rooms. **Cards:** AE, DI, DS, MC, VI. **Special Amenities:** free continental breakfast and free local telephone calls.
                                                                                          SOME UNITS

[S/D] [🍴] [♿] [🏊] [📹] [📠] [DATA PORT] / [X] [🖥] [🧺] /

(See map p. 554)

DARST VICTORIAN MANOR
Phone: (352)383-4050 **49**

▼▼▼▼ ▼▼▼▼
12/1-5/31 & 10/16-11/30   1P: $125-$210   2P: $135-$220   XP: $25
6/1-10/15   1P: $115-$190   2P: $125-$200   XP: $25

Bed & Breakfast   **Location:** 0.3 mi w on CR 441 (old US 441). 495 Old Hwy 441 32757. Fax: 352/383-7653. **Facility:** An elegant, nicely landscaped reproduction of a Queen Anne style Victorian house from the late 1800s overlooking Lake Dora. Smoke free premises. 5 units. *Bath:* combo or shower only. 3 stories (no elevator), interior corridors. **Terms:** 2 night minimum stay - weekends, age restrictions may apply, 7 day cancellation notice-fee imposed, weekly rates available. **Amenities:** no TVs, irons, hair dryers. **Leisure Activities:** whirlpool. **Guest Services:** [BP] meal plan available, afternoon tea. *Fee:* massage. **Cards:** AE, DS, MC, VI.

THE EMERALD HILL INN
Phone: 352/383-2777 **52**

ⒶⒶⒶ SAVE
All Year   1P: $99-$149   2P: $99-$149   XP: $25
▼▼▼ ▼▼▼
Location: From jct US 441 and CR 448 (Sadler Ave), 2.5 mi w on CR 448, 0.5 mi n on East Jem Rd, then n. 27751 Lake Jem Rd 32757. **Facility:** Light, airy rooms in a 1941 limestone block on a 2 acre estate. On Lake Victoria. Smoke free premises. 4 units. *Bath:* combo or shower only. 1 story, interior corridors. **Parking:** valet.

Bed & Breakfast   **Terms:** age restrictions may apply, 7 day cancellation notice, weekly & monthly rates available. **Guest Services:** [BP] meal plan available. **Cards:** DS, MC, VI.

SOME UNITS

THE LAKESIDE INN
Phone: (352)383-4101 **50**

ⒶⒶⒶ SAVE
12/1-4/30   1P: $110-$180   2P: $110-$180   XP: $15   F20
5/1-6/15 & 9/16-11/30   1P: $100-$180   2P: $100-$180   XP: $15   F20
▼▼▼ ▼▼▼
6/16-9/15   1P: $92-$180   2P: $92-$180   XP: $15   F20

Historic Motor Inn   **Location:** Just s from downtown. 100 N Alexander St 32757. Fax: 352/735-2642. **Facility:** Listed on the National Register of Historic Places, this turn-of-the-century resort offers a feeling of tranquility with sunsets across Lake Dora. 88 units. *Bath:* combo or shower only. 2-3 stories (no elevator), interior corridors. **Terms:** 3 day cancellation notice, package plans. **Dining:** dining room, 7 am-2:30 & 5-9 pm, Fri & Sat-9:30 pm entertainment-Sun brunch, $13-$22, cocktails. **Leisure Activities:** whirlpool, boat dock, fishing, 2 lighted tennis courts. *Fee:* canoeing, bicycles. **Business Services:** meeting rooms. **Cards:** AE, DI, DS, MC, VI. **Special Amenities:** free continental breakfast and free newspaper. *(See ad below)*

SOME UNITS

———— **WHERE TO DINE** ————

THE GABLES RESTAURANT
Lunch: $6-$12   Dinner: $10-$25   Phone: 352/383-8993 **35**

ⒶⒶⒶ
Location: Just s of old US 441, opposite Chamber of Commerce. 322 Alexander St 32757. **Hours:** 11 am-2:30 & 5-9 pm. Closed: 1/1, 12/25. **Reservations:** suggested. **Features:** casual dress; cocktails & lounge. A country garden setting includes limited dining on the front porch. International offerings feature beef, poultry and seafood selections. Consistent servers bring dishes like turkey chili made with fresh vegetables and a rich peanut butter pie. **Cards:** AE, DS, JC, MC, VI.

American

OCOEE pop. 12,800   (See map p. 554; index p. 559)

———— **WHERE TO STAY** ————

HOLIDAY INN ORLANDO WEST
Phone: (407)656-5050 **151**

▼▼▼▼
12/1-1/5   1P: $79   2P: $87
1/6-11/30   1P: $69-$77   2P: $69-$77

Motor Inn   **Location:** I-4, exit 41, 10 mi w on SR 50, 0.5 mi e of Florida Tpke, exit 267. 10945 W Colonial Dr 34761. Fax: 407/877-9346. **Facility:** Designated smoking area. 169 units. 3 stories, exterior corridors. **Terms:** 7 day cancellation notice, weekly rates available. **Amenities:** extended cable TV, voice mail, safes (fee), irons, hair dryers. **Leisure Activities:** whirlpool, exercise room. **Guest Services:** coin laundry. **Business Services:** meeting rooms. **Cards:** AE, CB, DI, DS, JC, MC, VI.

SOME UNITS
FEE

OVIEDO pop. 11,100   (See map p. 554; index p. 559)

──────── WHERE TO DINE ────────

OLDENBERG BREWERING COMPANY ▼▼▼ ▼▼▼ American
Lunch: $6-$8   **Dinner:** $9-$19   **Phone:** 407/359-6567   130
Location: Just e of SR 417; in Oviedo Market Place Mall. 1280 Oviedo Marketplace Blvd 32765. **Hours:** 11 am-10 pm, Fri & Sat-midnight, Sun-9:30 pm. **Features:** casual dress; carryout; cocktails. Microbrewery serving prime rib, meat loaf, tuna, pork chops and nice mix of appetizers. Specialty beers at the lounge while you wait for a table. Come early to avoid the line at this busy shopping mall location. Friendly, somewhat noisey atmosphere. **Cards:** AE, MC, VI.

RIVER RANCH pop. 100

──────── WHERE TO STAY ────────

RIVER RANCH RESORT ▼▼ ▼▼ Condominium
Property failed to provide current rates   **Phone:** 863/692-1321
Location: On SR 60. 3200 River Ranch Rd 33867 (PO Box 30030). Fax: 863/692-1303. **Facility:** 175 units. 13 two-bedroom units, 82 efficiencies and 13 units with kitchen. Some suites. 2 stories, exterior corridors. **Terms:** 3 day cancellation notice, weekly rates available, package plans. **Amenities:** extended cable TV. **Leisure Activities:** 2 pools (1 heated), whirlpool, boat dock, marina, fishing, charter fishing, golf-9 holes, putting green, miniature golf, 2 tennis courts, children's program, hiking trails, jogging, horseback riding, playground. *Fee:* boats, canoeing, bicycles. **Guest Services:** gift shop, coin laundry. **Business Services:** meeting rooms. **Cards:** AE, DS, MC, VI.

ST. CLOUD pop. 12,500   (See map p. 560; index p. 571)

──────── WHERE TO STAY ────────

BUDGET INN OF ST CLOUD AAA SAVE ▼▼ ▼▼ Motel
All Year   1P: $35-$45   2P: $35-$45   XP: $5   453
F9
Location: On US 192, 0.5 mi e of The Water Tower. 602 13th St 34769. Fax: 407/892-8063. **Facility:** Compact modern contemporary rooms. 17 units, 1 with efficiency. *Bath:* combo or shower only. 1 story, exterior corridors. **Terms:** 3 day cancellation notice. **Amenities:** extended cable TV, hair dryers. **Cards:** AE, DS, MC, VI.
Phone: (407)892-2858
SOME UNITS

SANFORD pop. 32,400   (See map p. 554; index p. 557)

──────── WHERE TO STAY ────────

BEST WESTERN MARINA HOTEL & CONFERENCE CENTER ▼▼ ▼▼ Motor Inn
2/1-3/31   1P: $79   2P: $89   XP: $10   38
12/1-1/31 & 4/1-11/30   1P: $69   2P: $79   XP: $10   F10
Phone: (407)323-1910
F10
Location: I-4, exit 51C, 4.8 mi e. 530 N Palmetto Ave 32771. Fax: 407/322-7076. **Facility:** Located on an island with adjacent cruise and plane tours, fishing trips, jet ski rentals, parasailing and house boat. 96 units. 1-2 stories, exterior corridors. **Terms:** check-in 4 pm, small pets only ($20 extra charge). **Amenities:** honor bars. *Some:* irons, hair dryers. **Leisure Activities:** boat dock, marina. **Guest Services:** [CP] meal plan available, coin laundry. **Business Services:** meeting rooms. **Cards:** AE, CB, DI, DS, MC, VI.
SOME UNITS

CHERRY LAUREL INN ▼▼▼ ▼▼ Bed & Breakfast
All Year   1P: $130-$150   2P: $150-$170   XP: $25   41
F5
Phone: (407)323-5515
Location: I-4, exit 51 (CR 46A), just e. 2461 Cherry Laurel Dr 32771 (PO Box 952458, LAKE MARY, 32795). Fax: 407/320-9964. **Facility:** Beautifully appointed rooms and public area. Designated smoking area. 5 units. Some whirlpool units ($200-$250). 2 stories, interior corridors. **Terms:** 7 day cancellation notice. **Amenities:** extended cable TV, irons. *Some:* CD players, hair dryers. **Leisure Activities:** game room. **Guest Services:** [ECP] meal plan available. **Cards:** AE, DI, MC, VI.

THE HIGGINS HOUSE BED & BREAKFAST AAA SAVE ▼▼ ▼▼ Historic Bed & Breakfast
All Year   1P: $80-$90   2P: $95-$120   XP: $15   37
Phone: (407)324-9238
Location: Just s of 1st St; in historic district. 420 S Oak Ave 32771. Fax: 407/324-5060. **Facility:** Circa 1894; offers Victorian ambience from days gone by. Smoke free premises. 4 units. 1 two-bedroom unit and 1 unit with kitchen. *Bath:* combo or tub only. 2 stories, interior corridors. **Parking:** street only. **Terms:** age restrictions may apply. **Dining:** small intimate pub room. **Leisure Activities:** whirlpool, bicycles. **Guest Services:** [BP] meal plan available, complimentary evening beverages. **Cards:** AE, DS, MC, VI. **Special Amenities:** free continental breakfast and free local telephone calls.
SOME UNITS

HOLIDAY INN EXPRESS-SANFORD AAA SAVE ▼▼ ▼▼ Motel
2/15-7/8   2P: $80-$175   43
12/1-2/14 & 7/9-11/30   2P: $80-$110
Phone: (407)320-0845
Location: I-4, exit 50, e on Lake Mary Blvd, then 0.5 mi n on US 17-92. 3401 S Orlando Dr 32773 (3320 Shalimar Cir, DELTONA, 32738). Fax: 407/328-6306. **Facility:** 72 units. Some suites ($110-$179) and whirlpool units. *Bath:* combo or shower only. 4 stories, interior corridors. **Amenities:** voice mail, irons, hair dryers. **Guest Services:** valet laundry. *Fee:* airport transportation-Sanford. **Business Services:** meeting rooms. **Cards:** AE, CB, DI, DS, JC, MC, VI. **Special Amenities:** free continental breakfast and free local telephone calls.
SOME UNITS
FEE

(See map p. 554)

SPRINGHILL SUITES BY MARRIOTT **Phone:** (407)995-1000 **42**

| | 1/1-11/30 | 1P: $99 | 2P: $99 |
| | 12/1-12/31 | 1P: $89 | 2P: $89 |

Motel **Location:** I-4, exit 51, just se. 201 N Towne Rd 32771. Fax: 407/995-5921. **Facility:** Located near the interstate exit, this newly opened property is in a commercial area and near Seminole Towne Center Mall. Upscale appointments and decor give the lobby a rich and inviting look. Very good sized rooms have a wall partition, partially divides the sleeping and living areas. The attractively decorated guestrooms are very comfortable and well equipped for the business traveler or a family, whether staying one or several nights. 105 units. Some whirlpool units ($109-$129). *Bath:* combo or shower only. 5 stories, interior corridors. **Amenities:** extended cable TV, dual phone lines, voice mail, irons, hair dryers. **Leisure Activities:** heated pool, whirlpool, exercise room. **Guest Services:** valet and coin laundry. **Business Services:** meeting rooms, administrative services. **Cards:** AE, CB, DI, DS, MC, VI.

SOME UNITS

(ASK) (S⊘) (¶†) (&) (➷) (🎥) (🖨) (💻) (📷) (🔒) (DATA PORT) / (⊠) /

SUPER 8 MOTEL **Phone:** (407)323-3445 **39**

| | 12/1-4/15 | 1P: $55-$65 | 2P: $65-$75 | XP: $7 | F16 |
| | 4/16-11/30 | 1P: $50-$65 | 2P: $55-$75 | XP: $7 | F16 |

Motel **Location:** I-4, exit 51. 4750 SR 46 W 32771. Fax: 407/323-3445. **Facility:** Across from shopping mall. Modest units. Designated smoking area. 104 units, 7 with efficiency. 1 story, exterior corridors. **Business Services:** meeting rooms. **Cards:** AE, CB, DI, DS, MC, VI.

SOME UNITS

(ASK) (S⊘) (🐾) (¶†) (➷) (🎥) / (⊠) (📷) (🔒) /

────── WHERE TO DINE ──────

OTTER'S RIVERSIDE RESTAURANT **Lunch:** $6-$9 **Dinner:** $9-$25 **Phone:** 407/323-3991 **30**

Steak & Seafood **Location:** I-4, exit 52, , in the "Port of Sanford". 4380 Carraway Pl 32773. **Hours:** 11 am-10 pm, Sun 10 am-1 pm. **Closed:** 11/22, 12/25. **Features:** casual dress; cocktails & lounge. At this very popular spot, you may dine on an enclosed patio while the kids splash and play in the swimming pool. A view of the marina sets the mood for feasting on all-you-can-eat crab legs, or partake of the champagne brunch buffet on Sundays. **Cards:** AE, CB, DI, DS, MC, VI.

(⊠)

SERGIO'S ITALIAN RESTAURANT **Lunch:** $5-$8 **Dinner:** $5-$15 **Phone:** 407/323-4040 **29**

Italian **Location:** On US 17/92, 0.5 mi n of Airport Blvd. 2895 Orlando Dr 32773. **Hours:** 11 am-10 pm, Sun noon-9 pm. **Closed:** 11/22, 12/25. **Reservations:** accepted. **Features:** casual dress; children's menu; carryout; cocktails & lounge. Traditional selection of well prepared items. Moderate prices. Straight forward Italian dining in a family environment. Tables are well spaced, with non-smoking area well removed and partitioned from the lounge area. **Cards:** AE, CB, DI, DS, MC, VI.

(🛗) (⊠)

TAVARES pop. 7,400

——— WHERE TO STAY ———

BUDGET INN
(AAA) (SAVE)
◆◆◆
Motel

1/1-4/14	1P: $54-$62	2P: $62-$74	XP: $6 F12
12/1-12/31 & 4/15-11/30	1P: $36-$40	2P: $45-$52	XP: $6 F12

Phone: (352)343-4666

Location: On US 441, 0.3 mi e of jct SR 19 S. 101 W Burleigh Blvd 32778-2498. Fax: 352/742-2717. **Facility:** 40 units, 6 with efficiency. 2 stories, exterior corridors. **Terms:** 14 day cancellation notice, weekly rates available, utensil deposit required, small pets only ($5 fee). **Amenities:** extended cable TV. **Cards:** AE, DS, MC, VI.

SOME UNITS

[icons] / [icons]

INN ON THE GREEN
(AAA) (SAVE)
◆◆◆◆
Motel

12/18-4/14	1P: $69-$200
12/1-12/17 & 4/15-11/30	1P: $48-$200

Phone: (352)343-6373
XP: $6   F12
XP: $6   F12

Location: On US 441, 1 mi e of jct SR 19. 700 E Burleigh Blvd 32778. Fax: 352/343-7216. **Facility:** On small lake. 77 units. 1 two-bedroom unit, 14 efficiencies and 1 unit with kitchen. Some suites ($99-$135). 2 stories, exterior corridors. **Terms:** weekly & monthly rates available, package plans, utensil deposit required, small pets only ($55 deposit). **Amenities:** extended cable TV. *Some:* irons, hair dryers. **Leisure Activities:** putting green, shuffleboard. **Guest Services:** [CP] meal plan available, coin laundry. **Cards:** AE, DI, MC, VI. **Special Amenities:** free local telephone calls and free newspaper.

SOME UNITS

[icons] / [icons]

——— WHERE TO DINE ———

DEAD RIVER VIC'S
◆◆ ◆◆
Steak & Seafood
DS, MC, VI.

Lunch: $7-$10   **Dinner:** $7-$20   **Phone:** 352/742-5000

Location: On US 441, 2 mi w of SR 19. 3351 W Burleigh Blvd 32778. **Hours:** 11 am-11 pm. **Features:** casual dress; children's menu; carryout; cocktails & lounge. Golf carts will ferry you from the parking lot to this lovely, waterfront restaurant with outdoor seating, a gift shop and boat slips. Fresh seafood, chicken and ribs are featured, and the banana muffin with caramel ice cream will make your mouth water. **Cards:** AE,

WINTER GARDEN pop. 9,700   (See map p. 554; index p. 559)

——— WHERE TO STAY ———

BEST VALUE INN WEST ORLANDO
(AAA) (SAVE)
◆◆◆◆
Motel

All Year	1P: $69	2P: $79	XP: $5 F17

Phone: (407)654-1188   [147]

Location: SR 50, just e of jct CR 535. 13603 W Colonial Ave. Fax: 407/654-0140. **Facility:** 102 units. 8 efficiencies and 2 units with kitchen. Some suites ($95-$119). 2 stories, exterior corridors. **Terms:** check-in 4 pm, cancellation fee imposed. **Amenities:** *Some:* hair dryers. **Dining:** restaurant, 6 am-11 pm, $2-$6. **Leisure Activities:** heated pool, volleyball. **Fee:** exercise room. **Guest Services:** coin laundry. **Business Services:** meeting rooms. **Cards:** AE, CB, DI, DS, MC, VI. *(See color ad below)*

SOME UNITS

[icons] / [icons]   FEE FEE

ORANGE COUNTY NATIONAL GOLF CENTER AND LODGE
◆◆◆
Motor Inn

12/1-4/1	1P: $95	2P: $110	XP: $15 F17
4/2-11/30	1P: $75	2P: $90	XP: $15 F17

Phone: (407)905-2300   [146]

Location: From US 192, 6.8 mi n on CR 545. 16301 Phil Ritson Way 34787. Fax: 407/905-2299. **Facility:** Property geared more for golfers. 50 units. *Bath:* combo or shower only. 1 story, exterior corridors. **Terms:** 14 day cancellation notice-fee imposed, package plans. **Amenities:** extended cable TV, voice mail, irons, hair dryers. **Leisure Activities:** Fee: golf-45 holes. **Guest Services:** [CP] meal plan available, gift shop. **Business Services:** meeting rooms. **Cards:** AE, DI, MC, VI.

SOME UNITS

[ASK] [icons] / [icons]

(See map p. 554)

——— WHERE TO DINE ———

TAQUITOS JALISCO
Lunch: $3-$9   Dinner: $3-$12   Phone: 407/654-0363   104
Location: In Tri-City Shopping Center. 1041 S Dillard St 34787. Hours: 11 am-9 pm; Sat & Sun 9:30 am-10:30 pm. Closed: Mon. Features: casual dress; carryout; beer & wine only. A friendly staff serves up cuisine with fresh ingredients, lots of heat and lots of flavor. Entrees are presented with a colorful flair and prepared from authentic recipes. A modest place with only a few tables and chairs, it is important to arrive early. Cards: AE, CB, DI, DS, JC, MC, VI.
Mexican

WINTER PARK pop. 22,600 (See map p. 554; index p. 559)

——— WHERE TO STAY ———

BEST WESTERN MT. VERNON INN
Phone: (407)647-1166   137
AAA [SAVE]   All Year   1P: $85-$119   2P: $91-$125   XP: $6   F17
Location: I-4, exit 45 (Fairbanks Ave), 1 mi e, then 0.3 mi n on US 17/92; opposite Winter Park Civic Center. 110 S Orlando Ave 32789-3698. Fax: 407/647-8011. Facility: Rooms have homey decor and furnishings. 47 rooms with air filter machines. Large park and Winter Park Civic Center are adjacent to back side of lodging. 144 units. Some suites. Bath: some combo or shower only. 2 stories, interior/exterior corridors. Terms: monthly rates available. Amenities: extended cable TV, voice mail. Some: irons, hair dryers. Dining: restaurant, 7 am-2 pm, cocktails, entertainment. Leisure Activities: jogging. Fee: tennis privileges. Guest Services: valet laundry. Business Services: conference facilities, fax. Cards: AE, CB, DI, DS, MC, VI. Special Amenities: free newspaper. (See ad below)
Motel

SOME UNITS

FAIRFIELD INN-WINTER PARK
Phone: (407)539-1955   135
12/1-11/1   1P: $69   2P: $69
11/2-11/30   1P: $59   2P: $59
Location: I-4, exit 46, just ne. 951 Wymore Rd 32789. Fax: 407/539-1955. Facility: 135 units. 3 stories, interior/exterior corridors. Terms: 7 day cancellation notice. Amenities: irons. Leisure Activities: heated pool. Guest Services: [ECP] meal plan available, valet laundry. Cards: AE, CB, DI, DS, MC, VI.
Motel

SOME UNITS

FEE

——— WHERE TO DINE ———

BRAZILIAN PAVILION
Lunch: $8-$11   Dinner: $11-$25   Phone: 407/740-7440   101
Location: Just w of Rollins College and jct of Park and Fairbanks aves. 140 W Fairbanks Ave 32789. Hours: 11:30 am-3 & 5:30-11 pm. Closed: Sun. Reservations: accepted. Features: casual dress; carryout; beer & wine only. Authentic, gourmet Brazilian cuisine includes Feijoada, Churrasco steak and fresh fish dishes, all generously seasoned and served in simple elegance. Arrive early for lunch to beat the crowd. Proper attire for dinner is suggested. Cards: AE, CB, DI, MC, VI.
Brazilian

BRIAN'S BAR-B-QUE
Lunch: $4-$7   Dinner: $5-$12   Phone: 407/671-2222   94
Location: 1 mi w of jct SR 436. 2415 Aloma Ave 32792. Hours: 11 am-9 pm. Closed major holidays. Reservations: accepted. Features: casual dress; children's menu; carryout; salad bar; beer & wine only. Enjoy ribs and barbecue chicken in a family dining environment. Super friendly staff makes sure you have a pleasant experience with these expertly done barbecue standards. Cards: AE, DI, DS, MC, VI.
American

THE PARK AVENUE GRILL
Lunch: $6-$13   Dinner: $10-$20   Phone: 407/647-4556   99
Location: At corner of Park and Canton aves. 358 N Park Ave 32789. Hours: 11 am-9 pm, Fri & Sat-11:30 pm, Sun 10 am-10 pm. Closed: 11/22, 12/25. Reservations: suggested; weekends. Features: casual dress; Sunday brunch; children's menu; carryout; cocktails & lounge; street parking. The upscale, yet informal, cafe gives off the feel of a bright French bistro. Choose from selections of salads, sandwiches, pastries and full entrees, such as the chicken portobello, or opt for fresh fish, which can be blackened, chargrilled or broiled. Cards: AE, CB, DI, DS, MC, VI.
American

(See map p. 554)

PARK PLAZA GARDENS   **Lunch:** $6-$12   **Dinner:** $19-$30   **Phone:** 407/645-2475   ⑩
▼▼▼▼
Continental
Location: Center; at jct Park Ave S and New England Ave. 319 Park Ave S 32789. **Hours:** 11:30 am-2 & 6-10 pm, Fri & Sat-11 pm, Sun 11 am-9 pm. Closed major holidays. **Reservations:** suggested. **Features:** semi-formal attire; Sunday brunch; children's menu; carryout; cocktails & lounge; street parking; a la carte. A glass-enclosed garden filled with lush plants brings the outdoors indoors. You will find impeccable service with great attention to detail. Beef, seafood and pork are featured with lighter fair available in the lounge between lunch and dinner. **Cards:** AE, CB, DI, DS, MC, VI.
❌

STEFANO'S TRATTORIA   **Lunch:** $6-$7   **Dinner:** $8-$19   **Phone:** 407/657-0101   ⑨⑤
▼▼▼▼
Italian
Location: 7325 Aloma Ave 32792. **Hours:** 11 am-9:15 pm, Sat from noon, Sun 4 pm-9 pm. Closed major holidays; also Mon. **Reservations:** accepted. **Features:** casual dress; carryout; beer & wine only. A popular weekend spot for locals, it serves authentic food in a small, unpretentious setting. Chicken parmigiana and sauteed snapper with capers and pepperoncini over linguini are two of the best entrees; and if you're craving pizza, look no further. **Cards:** AE, DI, DS, MC, VI.

TRASTEVERE RISTORANTE   **Lunch:** $7-$11   **Dinner:** $7-$22   **Phone:** 407/628-1277   ⑩③
▼▼▼
Italian
Location: US 17-92, just n of SR 426 (Fairbanks Ave); 0.5 mi s of SR 423 (Lee Rd). 400 S Orlando Ave 32789. **Hours:** 11:30 am-2:30 & 5:30-10 pm; Sat, Sun & Mon from 5:30 pm. Closed: 5/28, 12/25. **Reservations:** suggested. **Features:** casual dress; carryout; beer & wine only. Charm and character bathe this quiet, romantic restaurant, which in some areas has the unmistakable feel of a wine cellar. Veal and seafood specialties are prepared with a touch of richness; pasta dishes can be ordered in half or full portions. Smoke free premises. **Cards:** AE, DS, MC, VI.
❌

────── *The following restaurants have not been evaluated by AAA* ──────
but are listed for your information only.

BUBBALOU'S BODACIOUS BAR-B-QUE   **Phone:** 407/628-1212
[fyi]   Not evaluated. **Location:** 1471 Lee Rd. **Features:** Barbecue sandwiches and meats. Limited inside dining. Counter service. Inexpensive.

FUJI SUSHI   **Phone:** 407/645-1299
[fyi]   Not evaluated. **Location:** 1449 Lee Rd 32789. **Features:** Strictly Japanese, no blending of Chinese influences, very large extensive menu. Sashimi and sushi are expertly done by chefs in main dining room. Combination dinners are a good choice here.

P. F. CHANG'S   **Phone:** 407/622-0188
[fyi]   Not evaluated. **Location:** 436 N Orlando Ave 32789. **Features:** Good "Americanized" Chinese with some close to genuine preparations.

SIAM GARDEN   **Phone:** 407/599-7443
[fyi]   Not evaluated. **Location:** Just e of US 17-92, across from Winter Park mall. 111 Webster Ave 32789. **Features:** Wonderful soup, full bodied and flavorful. Try the pad thai of flat noodles stir-fried with shrimp, scallions, egg and paprika; it is very good.

This ends listings for the Orlando Vicinity.
The following page resumes the alphabetical listings of cities in Florida.

ORMOND BEACH pop. 29,700 (See map p. 270; index p. 272)

──────── WHERE TO STAY ────────

BEST WESTERN MAINSAIL INN AND SUITES
Phone: (904)677-2131 **19**

2/12-4/22	1P: $75-$180	2P: $75-$180	XP: $5 F17
4/23-8/19	1P: $70-$125	2P: $70-$125	XP: $5 F17
8/20-11/30	1P: $65-$100	2P: $65-$100	XP: $5 F17
12/1-2/11	1P: $75-$90	2P: $75-$90	XP: $5 F17

AAA [SAVE] ▽▽ ▽▽ Motel

Location: SR A1A, 0.5 mi s of SR 40. 281 S Atlantic Ave 32176. Fax: 904/676-0323. **Facility:** 44 units. 2 two-bedroom units, 17 efficiencies and 14 units with kitchen. Some suites ($150-$350) and whirlpool units ($100-$250). *Bath:* combo or shower only. 4 stories, interior/exterior corridors. **Terms:** check-in 4 pm, 3 day cancellation notice. **Amenities:** voice mail, safes (fee). **Leisure Activities:** heated pool, wading pool, beach. **Guest Services:** [CP] meal plan available, coin laundry. **Cards:** AE, CB, DI, DS, MC, VI. *(See color ad p 282)*
SOME UNITS

COMFORT INN INTERSTATE
Phone: (904)677-9107 **6**

2/1-4/30	1P: $75-$160	2P: $75-$160	XP: $6 F18
7/1-11/30	1P: $53-$160	2P: $53-$160	XP: $6 F18
12/1-1/31 & 5/1-6/30	1P: $53-$70	2P: $53-$70	XP: $6 F18

[SAVE] ▽▽ ▽▽ Motel

Location: At jct I-95, exit 89. 1567 N US 1 & I-95 32174. Fax: 904/677-9107. **Facility:** 75 units. 2 stories, exterior corridors. **Terms:** 30 day cancellation notice-fee imposed. **Amenities:** extended cable TV. *Some:* irons. **Guest Services:** [CP] meal plan available, coin laundry. **Cards:** AE, CB, DI, DS, JC, MC, VI.
SOME UNITS

COMFORT INN ON THE BEACH
Phone: (904)677-8550 **14**

7/1-8/31	2P: $85-$165	XP: $10 F18
12/1-3/11	2P: $75-$165	XP: $10 F18
9/1-11/30	2P: $70-$165	XP: $10 F18
3/12-6/30	2P: $85-$98	XP: $10 F18

AAA [SAVE] ▽▽ ▽▽ Motel

Location: SR A1A, 1 mi s of jct SR 40. 507 S Atlantic Ave 32176. Fax: 904/673-6260. **Facility:** Few units on the beach; street side units face the ocean directly. 47 units, 23 with efficiency. 4 stories, exterior corridors. **Terms:** 10 day cancellation notice, weekly & monthly rates available, small pets only ($5 extra charge). **Amenities:** safes (fee), irons, hair dryers. **Leisure Activities:** heated pool, wading pool, beach. **Cards:** AE, CB, DI, DS, JC, MC, VI. **Special Amenities:** free continental breakfast and free newspaper. *(See color ad p 282)*
SOME UNITS

CORAL BEACH MOTEL
Phone: 904/677-4712 **9**

All Year	1P: $55-$155	2P: $55-$155	XP: $10 F17

AAA [SAVE] ▽▽ ▽▽ Apartment

Location: On SR A1A, 1.5 mi s of SR 40. 711 S Atlantic Ave 32176. Fax: 904/677-4712. **Facility:** Family oriented. Some rooms with furnished balcony. 97 units. 20 two-bedroom units and 65 efficiencies. 7 stories, interior/exterior corridors. **Amenities:** extended cable TV, safes (fee). **Leisure Activities:** 2 pools (1 heated, 1 indoor), beach. **Guest Services:** [CP] meal plan available, coin laundry. **Cards:** AE, MC, VI. **Special Amenities:** free local telephone calls. *(See color ad p 280)*
SOME UNITS

DAYS INN DAYTONA OCEANFRONT NORTH
Phone: (904)677-6600 **17**

2/1-4/30	1P: $55-$150	2P: $55-$150	XP: $10 F18
5/1-9/2	1P: $49-$150	2P: $49-$150	XP: $10 F18
9/3-11/30	1P: $45-$110	2P: $45-$110	XP: $10 F18
12/1-1/31	1P: $45-$55	2P: $45-$55	XP: $10 F18

[SAVE] ▽▽ ▽▽ Motel

Location: On SR A1A, 1.7 mi s of SR 40. 839 S Atlantic Ave 32176. Fax: 904/677-0438. **Facility:** Standard and efficiency guest rooms with some offering ocean or pool courtyard view. 128 units, 46 with efficiency. 2-3 stories, exterior corridors. **Terms:** check-in 4 pm, 7 day cancellation notice-fee imposed, weekly & monthly rates available, small pets only ($15 extra charge). **Leisure Activities:** beach, swimming. **Cards:** AE, CB, DI, DS, JC, MC, VI.
SOME UNITS

(See map p. 270)

DAYS INN ORMOND BEACH I-95
AAA SAVE
♦♦♦ ♦♦♦
Motel

All Year   1P: $40-$189   2P: $40-$199
Phone: (904)672-7341   **5**
XP: $5   F12
Location: I-95, exit 89, just nw on US 1. 1608 N US 1 & I-95 32174. Fax: 904/672-3717. **Facility:** Attractive motel with very nice guest rooms just off the interstate. 72 units. 2 stories, exterior corridors. **Terms:** 15 day cancellation notice, small pets only ($5 extra charge). **Guest Services:** coin laundry. **Cards:** AE, DI, DS, MC, VI. **Special Amenities: free continental breakfast and free newspaper.**

SOME UNITS

DRIFTWOOD BEACH MOTEL
AAA SAVE
♦♦♦ ♦♦♦
Motel

2/9-4/19   1P: $53-$71   2P: $53-$71   XP: $5   F15
4/20-8/12   1P: $47-$65   2P: $47-$65   XP: $5   F15
12/1-2/8 & 8/13-11/30   1P: $40-$53   2P: $40-$53   XP: $5   F15
Phone: (904) 677-1331   **10**
Location: On SR A1A, 1.5 mi s of jct SR 40. 657 S Atlantic Ave 32176. Fax: 904/677-0625. **Facility:** Some rooms tend to be small, but are nicely furnished. 44 units. 2 two-bedroom units, 17 efficiencies and 10 units with kitchen. *Bath:* combo or shower only. 2-3 stories (no elevator), exterior corridors. **Terms:** 3 night minimum stay - efficiencies & kitchens, 15 day cancellation notice-fee imposed, weekly & monthly rates available, small pets only ($10 extra charge). **Leisure Activities:** beach. **Guest Services:** coin laundry. **Cards:** DS, MC, VI. **Special Amenities: free newspaper.** *(See ad p 280)*

SOME UNITS

ECONO LODGE ON THE BEACH
♦♦♦ ♦♦♦
Motel

Property failed to provide current rates
Phone: (904)672-2651   **18**
Location: SR A1A, 0.5 mi s of jct SR 40. 295 S Atlantic Ave 32176. Fax: 904/672-2651. **Facility:** 58 units, 31 with efficiency. 4 stories, exterior corridors. **Terms:** 5 day cancellation notice, weekly & monthly rates available. **Amenities:** extended cable TV, safes (fee). **Leisure Activities:** heated pool, wading pool, beach, swimming. **Guest Services:** coin laundry. **Cards:** AE, CB, DI, DS, MC, VI. *(See color ad p 282)*

SOME UNITS

HAMPTON INN ORMOND BEACH
SAVE
♦♦♦ ♦♦♦
Motel

1/2-3/31 & 7/1-11/30   1P: $79-$89   2P: $79-$89   XP: $10   F18
12/1-1/1 & 4/1-6/30   1P: $59-$65   2P: $59-$65   XP: $10   F18
Phone: (904)677-9999   **7**
Location: I-95, exit 88, sw corner. 155 Interchange Blvd 32174. Fax: 904/677-0663. **Facility:** Designated smoking area. 84 units. Some whirlpool units ($79-$89). *Bath:* combo or shower only. 4 stories, interior corridors. **Terms:** check-in 4 pm, 3 day cancellation notice-fee imposed, package plans. **Amenities:** extended cable TV, voice mail, irons. **Leisure Activities:** exercise room. **Guest Services:** [ECP] meal plan available, coin laundry. **Business Services:** meeting rooms. **Cards:** AE, CB, DI, DS, MC, VI.

SOME UNITS

IVANHOE BEACH RESORT
AAA SAVE
♦♦♦ ♦♦♦
Motor Inn

2/1-8/21   1P: $75-$150   2P: $75-$150   XP: $5   F12
12/1-1/31 & 8/22-11/30   1P: $50-$80   2P: $50-$80   XP: $5   F12
Phone: (904)672-6711   **21**
Location: On SR A1A; 0.5 mi s of jct SR 40. 205 S Atlantic Ave 32176. Fax: 904/676-9494. **Facility:** Large, well-furnished rooms with balcony. 147 units. 98 efficiencies and 6 units with kitchen. 7 stories, exterior corridors. **Terms:** weekly & monthly rates available. **Amenities:** extended cable TV, safes. **Dining:** restaurant, 7 am-1 pm. **Leisure Activities:** heated pool, wading pool, beach, swimming. **Guest Services:** coin laundry. **Business Services:** meeting rooms. **Cards:** AE, MC, VI. *(See color ad below)*

SOME UNITS

JAMAICAN BEACH MOTEL
AAA SAVE
♦♦♦
Motel

2/1-4/30   1P: $45-$170   2P: $45-$170   XP: $10   F15
5/1-9/5   1P: $45-$160   2P: $45-$160   XP: $5   F15
12/1-1/31   1P: $65-$75   2P: $65-$75   XP: $5   F15
9/6-11/30   1P: $35-$70   2P: $35-$70   XP: $5   F15
Phone: (904)677-3353   **15**
Location: SR A1A, 1 mi s of SR 40. 505 S Atlantic Ave 32176. Fax: 904/672-3190. **Facility:** Motel rooms, efficiencies and 1-bedroom apartments. 42 units. 15 efficiencies and 15 units with kitchen. 3 stories (no elevator), exterior corridors. **Terms:** 10 day cancellation notice, weekly & monthly rates available, small pets only ($3 extra charge). **Amenities:** extended cable TV, safes (fee). **Leisure Activities:** wading pool, beach. **Guest Services:** coin laundry. **Cards:** AE, DS, MC, VI. *(See color ad p 282)*

SOME UNITS

(See map p. 270)

QUALITY INN AND SUITES OCEANSIDE RESORT　　　　　　Phone: (904)672-8510　🔟

[SAVE]

▽▽▽
Motor Inn

2/2-5/1	1P: $89-$220　　2P: $89-$220
6/16-11/30	1P: $79-$165　　2P: $79-$165
5/2-6/15	1P: $79-$119　　2P: $79-$119
12/1-2/1	1P: $69-$89　　2P: $69-$89

Location: SR A1A, 0.5 mi s of jct SR 40. 251 S Atlantic Ave 32176. Fax: 904/672-7221. **Facility:** All units with balcony, many with ocean view. 146 units. 7 stories, exterior corridors. **Terms:** check-in 4 pm, cancellation fee imposed, weekly & monthly rates available. **Amenities:** voice mail, safes (fee). **Leisure Activities:** 2 pools (1 heated, 1 indoor), wading pool, whirlpool, beach, swimming, exercise room, volleyball. *Fee:* bicycles. **Guest Services:** coin laundry. **Cards:** AE, CB, DI, DS, MC, VI.

SOME UNITS

🆂🅳 🍽 🍸 🏊 🏊 ⊠ 📹 💳 🖥 / ⊠ 🛗 /
　　　　　　　　　FEE

RON JON RESORT-ORMOND BEACH　　　　　　Phone: (904)677-1446　🕚

(AAA) [SAVE]

▽▽▽ ▽▽▽
Condominium

All Year　　1P: $49-$269　　2P: $49-$269

Location: Just s of jct SR 40. 145 S Atlantic 32176. Fax: 904/677-2834. **Facility:** 54 efficiencies. 18 two-bedroom units. *Bath:* combo or shower only. 7 stories, interior corridors. **Terms:** check-in 4 pm, 15 day cancellation notice-fee imposed, weekly rates available, package plans. **Amenities:** extended cable TV, voice mail, irons, hair dryers. **Leisure Activities:** heated pool, beach, playground, exercise room. **Guest Services:** coin laundry. **Business Services:** meeting rooms. **Cards:** AE, MC, VI. **Special Amenities:** free local telephone calls and preferred room (subject to availability with advanced reservations). *(See color ad p 635)*

SOME UNITS

🆂🅳 🍽 🏊 🖥 🖥 🖥 🖥 / ⊠ /

SLEEP INN　　　　　　Phone: (904)673-6030　🎱

(AAA) [SAVE]

▽▽▽
Motel

12/1-1/2	2P: $65-$70	XP: $5　F18
1/3-11/30	2P: $64-$70	XP: $5　F18

Location: I-4, exit 88. 170 Williamson Blvd 32174. Fax: 904/673-7017. **Facility:** 83 units. *Bath:* shower only. 3 stories, interior corridors. **Amenities:** extended cable TV. **Guest Services:** coin laundry. **Cards:** AE, CB, DI, DS, JC, MC, VI. **Special Amenities:** free continental breakfast and free local telephone calls.

SOME UNITS

🆂🅳 🍽 ♿ 🖥 🏊 🏊 📹 🖨 🖥 / ⊠ /
　　　　　　　　　FEE

SUPER 8　　　　　　Phone: 904/672-6222　㉓

(AAA) [SAVE]

▽▽▽ ▽▽▽
Motel

12/1-3/31 & 10/18-11/30	1P: $70　　2P: $70
4/1-10/17	1P: $45　　2P: $45

Location: I-95, exit 89, just nw on US 1. 1634 N US 1 32174. Fax: 904/677-2401. **Facility:** 48 units. 2 stories, exterior corridors. **Amenities:** extended cable TV. **Cards:** AE, DS, MC, VI. **Special Amenities:** early check-in/late check-out and free local telephone calls.

SOME UNITS

🆂🅳 🍽 📹 / ⊠ /

SYMPHONY BEACH CLUB　　　　　　Phone: (904)672-7373　🔟

(AAA) [SAVE]

▽▽▽ ▽▽▽
Condominium

2/1-8/31	1P: $54-$95　　2P: $54-$95
12/1-1/31	1P: $49-$85　　2P: $49-$85
9/1-11/30	1P: $45-$85　　2P: $45-$85

Location: SR A1A, 0.8 mi s of jct SR 40. 453 S Atlantic Ave 32176. Fax: 904/673-1174. **Facility:** Some oceanfront rooms, the rest ocean view. All with balcony. 32 efficiencies. 4 stories, exterior corridors. **Terms:** 14 day cancellation notice-fee imposed, weekly & monthly rates available. **Amenities:** extended cable TV. **Leisure Activities:** heated pool, beach. **Guest Services:** coin laundry. **Cards:** DS, MC, VI.

SOME UNITS

🆂🅳 🍽 🏊 🖥 / ⊠ 🖥 /

────── WHERE TO DINE ──────

ENGLISH ROSE TEA ROOM　　Lunch: $5-$7　　Phone: 904/672-7673　④

▽▽ ▽▽
English

Location: A1A, Rt 40, 1.3 mi n. 49 W Granada Blvd (Rt 40) 32174. **Hours:** 9 am-3 pm, Tues-Fri to 4 pm. Closed: Sun. **Features:** casual dress. Serving breakfast, lunch and afternoon tea. British and vegetarian foods. British groceries. Smoke free premises.　　　　　　⊠

JULIAN'S　　　　　　Dinner: $8-$17　　Phone: 904/677-6767　①

(AAA)

▽▽ ▽▽
American

Location: On SR A1A, just s of SR 40. 88 S Atlantic Ave 32176. **Hours:** 4 pm-11 pm. **Features:** casual dress; children's menu; carryout; entertainment. Vintage decor in a Polynesian motif sets a tropical feel in the casual restaurant. A wall mural of a Hawaiian village brightens the sunken bar. The cordial and knowledgeable wait staff adeptly describe the menu offerings, such as grilled salmon. **Cards:** AE, CB, DI, DS, MC, VI.　　⊠

LA CREPE EN HAUT　　Lunch: $8-$12　　Dinner: $23-$40　　Phone: 904/673-1999　②

(AAA)

▽▽ ▽▽
French

Location: SR 40, just w of se A1A. 142 E Granada Blvd 32176. **Hours:** 11:30 am-2:30 & 5:30-10 pm, Sat & Sun from 5:30 pm. Closed major holidays; also Mon. **Reservations:** suggested. **Features:** semi-formal attire; cocktails; a la carte. Expect fine French cuisine offered in a charming dining room. A polished wait staff gives personalized service and extends a warm invitation for a return visit. Excellent veal smothered in a fabulous sauce is colorfully presented with crisp vegetables. **Cards:** AE, MC, VI.　　⊠

MARIO'S　　　　　　Dinner: $9-$17　　Phone: 904/677-2711　⑤

▽▽ ▽▽
Traditional Italian

Location: US 1. 521 S Yonge St 32176. **Hours:** 4:30 pm-10 pm. Closed: 11/22, 12/25. **Features:** casual dress; children's menu; early bird specials; carryout; cocktails & lounge; a la carte. Family owned Italian restaurant serving lunch and dinner with tasty traditional entrees at moderate prices. Atmosphere is casual and comfortable. Menu includes a nice selection of pasta, salad, pizza, lasagna and seafood. **Cards:** AE, MC, VI.　　⊠

(See map p. 270)

ROYAL DYNASTY RESTAURANT & LOUNGE   **Lunch:** $5-$8   **Dinner:** $8-$17   **Phone:** 904/676-2266   ③

Chinese
Location: 1482 W Granada Blvd 32174. **Hours:** 11 am-9:30 pm, Fri & Sat 3 pm-10:30 pm, Sun 3 pm-9:30 pm. **Features:** casual dress; carryout; cocktails & lounge. Delectable moo shu chicken is prepared right at your table. Lunch combination plates as well as an a la carte menu feature a very good variety of traditional Chinese entrees. Clean and neat service with quality table settings are nice touches. **Cards:** AE, MC, VI.

OSPREY pop. 2,600   (See map p. 764; index p. 768)

—————— WHERE TO STAY ——————

RAMADA INN-SARASOTA SOUTH   **Phone:** (941)966-2121   [132]
AAA [SAVE]

2/7-4/21	1P: $97-$106	2P: $97-$106	XP: $10	F18
12/1-12/31	1P: $59-$79	2P: $59-$79	XP: $10	F18
1/1-2/6	1P: $70	2P: $70	XP: $10	F18
4/22-11/30	1P: $54-$62	2P: $54-$62	XP: $10	F18

Motor Inn
Location: US 41, 1.8 mi n of jct SR 681. 1660 S Tamiami Tr 34229. **Fax:** 941/966-1124. **Facility:** 139 units. 12 efficiencies and 7 units with kitchen. 2 stories, interior/exterior corridors. **Terms:** 3 day cancellation notice-fee imposed, package plans. **Amenities:** voice mail. **Dining:** restaurant, 6:30 am-1 & 5-8 pm; tiki bar, $7-$14. **Leisure Activities:** heated pool, sauna. **Guest Services:** coin laundry. **Business Services:** meeting rooms. **Cards:** AE, DI, DS, MC, VI.
(See color ad p 776)

SOME UNITS
[icons] 🆂🅳 🍴 🅿 🏊 🎥 🖨 💻 DATA PORT / ⊠ 🛗 /

OVIEDO —See Orlando p. 701.

PALATKA pop. 10,200—See also EAST PALATKA.

—————— WHERE TO STAY ——————

HOLIDAY INN   **Phone:** (904)328-3481
All Year   2P: $64-$95   XP: $5   F18
Motor Inn
Location: At foot of St. John's River Bridge on US 17. 201 N First St 32177. **Fax:** 904/329-9907. **Facility:** Riverfront rooms. Dining and lounge on waterfront. 130 units. 2 stories, exterior corridors. **Amenities:** voice mail, irons, hair dryers. **Leisure Activities:** boat dock, marina, fishing, exercise room. **Guest Services:** coin laundry. **Business Services:** meeting rooms. **Cards:** AE, CB, DI, DS, MC, VI.

SOME UNITS
[ASK] 🍴 🏊 ⊠ 🎥 🖨 💻 DATA PORT / ⊠ 🛗 /
FEE

PALM BAY pop. 62,600

—————— WHERE TO STAY ——————

DAYS INN   **Phone:** (321)951-0350
AAA [SAVE]
All Year   1P: $40-$80   2P: $46-$85   XP: $6   F17
Motel
Location: 4.8 mi s of US 192 on US 1. 4700 Dixie Hwy NE 32905. **Fax:** 321/728-5632. **Facility:** 122 units. 2 stories, exterior corridors. **Terms:** weekly & monthly rates available. **Guest Services:** [CP] meal plan available, coin laundry. **Cards:** AE, DI, DS, JC, MC, VI.

SOME UNITS
🍴 🅿 🏊 🎥 / ⊠ 🖨 🛗 /

—————— WHERE TO DINE ——————

THE CROW'S NEST   **Lunch:** $5-$10   **Dinner:** $8-$26   **Phone:** 321/725-4020
Seafood
Location: Just e off US 1, 1.3 mi n of jct SR 514 on the river. 3450 Gran Ave 32905. **Hours:** 11 am-9 pm, Fri & Sat-10 pm, Sun noon-9 pm. **Reservations:** suggested. **Features:** casual dress; children's menu; early bird specials; senior's menu; carryout; cocktails & lounge. Look out over the Indian River marina, where you may catch an occasional glimpse of a dolphin or manatee. Steaks, shrimp New Orleans and herb-crusted salmon are tasty entrees; the hot fudge brownie sundae is a tempting topper. **Cards:** AE, DS, MC, VI.   ⊠

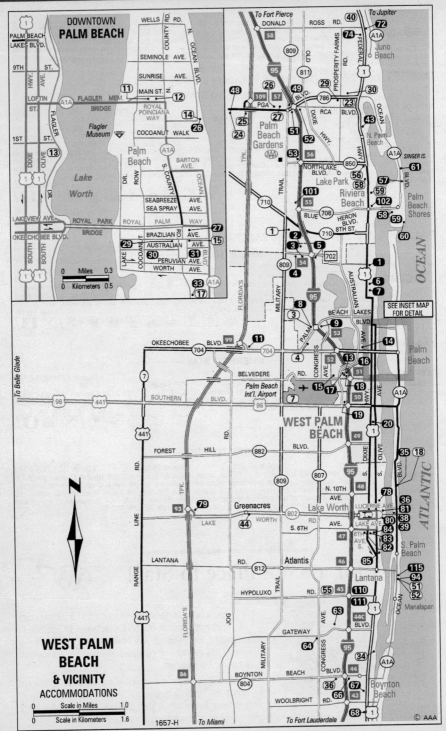

✈ Airport Accommodations

Spotter/Map Page Number	OA	PALM BEACH INTERNATIONAL	Diamond Rating	Rate Range High Season	Listing Page
15 / p. 710	AAA	Crowne Plaza West Palm Beach, 0.3 mi n of airport entrance	◆◆◆	$144-$174 SAVE	898
16 / p. 710		Hampton Inn Palm Beach/International Airport, 0.5 mi ne of airport entrance	◆◆◆	$71	899
19 / p. 710		Hilton Palm Beach Airport, 0.8 mi s of airport entrance	◆◆◆	$157-$166	899
18 / p. 710	AAA	Holiday Inn Palm Beach Airport, 0.8 mi ne of airport entrance	◆◆◆	$89-$119 SAVE	900
17 / p. 710	AAA	Radisson Suite Inn Palm Beach Airport, 0.8 mi n of airport entrance	◆◆◆	$119-$139 SAVE	901

West Palm Beach and Vicinity

This index helps you "spot" where approved accommodations are located on the corresponding detailed maps. Rate ranges are for comparison only and show the property's high season. Turn to the listing page for more detailed rate information and consult display ads for special promotions. Restaurant rate range is for dinner, unless only lunch (L) is served.

Spotter/Map Page Number	OA	PALM BEACH - Lodgings	Diamond Rating	Rate Range High Season	Listing Page
26 / p. 710	AAA	The Breakers	◆◆◆◆◆	$465-$740	714
27 / p. 710		Heart of Palm Beach Hotel	◆◆◆	$159-$259	715
29 / p. 710		Plaza Inn	◆◆◆	$205-$275	716
30 / p. 710	AAA	The Chesterfield Hotel - see color ad p 714	◆◆◆	$239-$459 SAVE	714
31 / p. 710	AAA	Palm Beach Historic Inn	◆◆◆	$150-$325 SAVE	716
33 / p. 710	AAA	The Colony	◆◆◆	$285-$305 SAVE	714
35 / p. 710	AAA	The Four Seasons Resort, Palm Beach	◆◆◆◆	$395-$695	715
36 / p. 710	AAA	Palm Beach Hilton Oceanfront Resort - see ad p 44, p 715	◆◆◆	$229-$389 SAVE	715
38 / p. 710		Howard Johnson Palm Beach	◆	$109-$139	715
39 / p. 710	AAA	Beachcomber Apartment Motel	◆◆	$95-$250 SAVE	714
		PALM BEACH - Restaurants			
11 / p. 710	AAA	Testa's Restaurant	◆◆	$12-$25	717
12 / p. 710		Chuck & Harold's	◆◆	$14-$34	716
13 / p. 710		My Martini Grille	◆◆◆	$13-$26	716
14 / p. 710		The Florentine	◆◆◆◆	$32-$40	716
15 / p. 710	AAA	Cafe L'Europe	◆◆◆	$18-$35	716
17 / p. 710		Charley's Crab	◆◆	$12-$28	716
18 / p. 710	AAA	The Restaurant at The Four Seasons	◆◆◆◆◆	$29-$36	717
		WEST PALM BEACH - Lodgings			
1 / p. 710		Royal Palm House B & B	◆◆◆	$75-$125	901
2 / p. 710		Courtyard by Marriott-West Palm Beach - see color ad p 242	◆◆◆	$139-$149	898
3 / p. 710	AAA	Red Roof Inn-West Palm Beach	◆◆	$40-$90 SAVE	901
4 / p. 710		Residence Inn by Marriott West Palm Beach	◆◆◆	$120-$199	901
5 / p. 710		Days Inn Airport North	◆◆	$69-$110	899
6 / p. 710		Tropical Gardens Bed & Breakfast	◆◆◆	$75-$125	901
7 / p. 710		Hibiscus House Bed & Breakfast	◆◆◆	$95-$180	899
8 / p. 710	AAA	Comfort Inn-on Palm Beach Lakes - see color ad p 898	◆◆◆	$99-$119 SAVE	898

Spotter/Map Page Number	OA	WEST PALM BEACH - Lodgings (continued)	Diamond Rating	Rate Range High Season	Listing Page
9 / p. 710	AAA	Best Western Palm Beach Lakes Inn	◈◈	$89-$94 SAVE	898
11 / p. 710		Fairfield Inn by Marriott	◈◈◈	Failed to provide	899
13 / p. 710		Hampton Inn Palm Beach/International Airport	◈◈◈	$71	899
14 / p. 710		Sheraton Hotel	◈◈◈	$169	901
15 / p. 710	AAA	Crowne Plaza West Palm Beach	◈◈◈	$144-$174 SAVE	898
16 / p. 710		Homestead Village Guest Studios	◈◈	$90-$110	900
17 / p. 710	AAA	Radisson Suite Inn Palm Beach Airport - see color ad p 900	◈◈◈	$119-$139 SAVE	901
18 / p. 710	AAA	Holiday Inn Palm Beach Airport - see color ad p 899	◈◈◈	$89-$119 SAVE	900
19 / p. 710		Hilton Palm Beach Airport - see ad p 44	◈◈◈	$157-$166	899
20 / p. 710	AAA	Parkview Motor Lodge - see color ad p 900	◈◈	$70-$88 SAVE	900
		WEST PALM BEACH - Restaurants			
1 / p. 710		Great Texas Land & Cattle Co.	◈◈	$9-$23	902
3 / p. 710		No Anchovies! Neighborhood Pastaria	◈◈	$9-$17	902
4 / p. 710		Rain Dancer Steak House	◈◈◈	$15-$30	902
7 / p. 710		391st Bomb Group	◈◈	$12-$29	901
		NORTH PALM BEACH - Lodgings			
43 / p. 710	AAA	The Waterford Hotel & Conference Center	◈◈◈	$139-$209 SAVE	546
		NORTH PALM BEACH - Restaurant			
23 / p. 710		Eddie D's	◈◈◈	$13-$27	546
		PALM BEACH GARDENS - Lodgings			
48 / p. 710	AAA	PGA National Resort & Spa	◈◈◈◈	$249-$289 SAVE	718
49 / p. 710	AAA	DoubleTree Hotel In The Gardens - see color ad p 717	◈◈◈	$179 SAVE	717
51 / p. 710		Embassy Suites Hotel	◈◈◈	$159-$249	717
52 / p. 710		Palm Beach Gardens Marriott	◈◈◈	$179-$249	718
53 / p. 710	AAA	Inns of America	◈◈	$85 SAVE	718
		PALM BEACH GARDENS - Restaurants			
24 / p. 710		Shula's Steak House	◈◈◈	$30-$50	719
25 / p. 710		Ebisu Japanese Restaurant	◈◈	$12-$20	718
26 / p. 710		Cafe Chardonnay	◈◈◈	$17-$32	718
27 / p. 710		Paddy Mac's	◈◈	$9-$19	718
29 / p. 710		No Anchovies! Neighborhood Pastaria	◈◈	$9-$17	718
30 / p. 710		The River House	◈◈◈	$17-$40	719
		PALM BEACH SHORES - Lodgings			
57 / p. 710		Sheraton Oceanfront North Palm Beach Hotel - see color ad p 719	◈◈◈	$250-$320	720
58 / p. 710		Sailfish Marina & Resort	◈◈	$99-$139	720
59 / p. 710		Radisson Palm Beach Shores Resort and Vacation Villas	◈◈◈	$259-$319	720
60 / p. 710	AAA	Best Western Seaspray Inn - see ad p 719	◈◈	$109-$179 SAVE	719
61 / p. 710		Hilton Singer Island Oceanfront Resort - see ad p 44	◈◈◈	$179-$249	720
		BOYNTON BEACH - Lodgings			
63 / p. 710		Hampton Inn Boynton Beach	◈◈◈	$169-$219	249

Spotter/Map Page Number	OA	BOYNTON BEACH - Lodgings (continued)	Diamond Rating	Rate Range High Season	Listing Page
64 / p. 710		Holiday Inn-Catalina	◆◆◆	$169-$199	249
66 / p. 710	AAA	Holiday Inn Express I-95 - see color ad p 249	◆◆	$66-$127 [SAVE]	249
67 / p. 710		Boynton Motel	◆	$65-$70	248
68 / p. 710	AAA	Atlantic Lodge	◆◆	$66-$77 [SAVE]	248
		BOYNTON BEACH - Restaurants			
34 / p. 710		Holiday House	◆	$4-$7	250
36 / p. 710	AAA	Mama Jennie's Italian Restaurant	◆	$8-$15	250
		JUNO BEACH - Lodgings			
72 / p. 710		Holiday Inn Express-North Palm Beach	◆◆	$139-$199	452
74 / p. 710		Hampton Inn-Juno Beach	◆◆◆	$119-$199	452
		JUNO BEACH - Restaurant			
40 / p. 710		Classico's Italian Restaurant	◆◆	$8-$20	452
		LAKE WORTH - Lodgings			
78 / p. 710		Lago-Mar Motel & Apartments	◆	$66	459
79 / p. 710		Holiday Inn West Palm Beach-Turnpike	◆◆◆	$110-$115	459
80 / p. 710		Gulfstream Hotel Holiday Inn Hotel & Suites	◆◆◆	$119-$139	459
81 / p. 710		Sabal Palm House B & B Inn	◆◆◆	$100-$180	460
82 / p. 710	AAA	Martinique Motor Lodge	◆	$50-$75 [SAVE]	459
83 / p. 710	AAA	Lago Motor Inn	◆◆	$62-$72 [SAVE]	459
84 / p. 710	AAA	New Sun Gate Motel	◆◆	$54-$79 [SAVE]	460
85 / p. 710	AAA	White Manor Motel	◆	$50-$64 [SAVE]	460
		LAKE WORTH - Restaurant			
44 / p. 710	AAA	Bohemian Garden Restaurant	◆◆	$8-$21	460
		MANALAPAN - Lodgings			
94 / p. 710	AAA	The Ritz-Carlton, Palm Beach	◆◆◆◆◆	$450-$850 [SAVE]	465
		MANALAPAN - Restaurants			
51 / p. 710		The Grill	◆◆◆	$20-$38	466
52 / p. 710		100 South Ocean	◆◆◆	$25-$48	465
		RIVIERA BEACH - Lodgings			
101 / p. 710		Super 8 Motel West Palm Beach/Riviera Beach	◆◆	$89	738
102 / p. 710		Riviera Beach Motel	◆	Failed to provide	738
		LANTANA - Lodgings			
110 / p. 710	AAA	Comfort Inn-Lantana/Boynton Beach - see ad p 249	◆◆◆	$75-$119 [SAVE]	460
111 / p. 710	AAA	Best Western/Inn of America	◆◆◆	$89-$99 [SAVE]	460
		LANTANA - Restaurant			
55 / p. 710		Anchor Inn Restaurant	◆◆	$14-$26	461
		SOUTH PALM BEACH - Lodgings			
115 / p. 710		Palm Beach Hawaiian Ocean Inn	◆◆	$150-$320	784
		LAKE PARK - Restaurants			
56 / p. 710		Holiday House	◆	$4-$7	457
58 / p. 710		Cafe du Park	◆◆◆	$16-$26	457

PALM BEACH pop. 9,800 (See map p. 710; index p. 711)

—— WHERE TO STAY ——

BEACHCOMBER APARTMENT MOTEL
Phone: (561)585-4646 ⓿39

(AAA) (SAVE) 1/15-11/30 1P: $95-$250 2P: $95-$250 XP: $10 F14
1/15-11/30 1P: $95-$250 2P: $95-$250 XP: $10 F14
12/1-1/14 1P: $85-$180 2P: $85-$180 XP: $10 F14
Apartment **Location:** SR A1A, 0.3 mi s of jct SR 802. 3024 S Ocean Blvd 33480. Fax: 561/547-9438. **Facility:** 50 units, 45 with kitchen. *Bath:* combo or shower only. 1-2 stories, exterior corridors. **Terms:** 4 day cancellation notice. **Leisure Activities:** beach, saltwater pool, shuffleboard, gas grills. **Guest Services:** coin laundry. **Cards:** AE, DS, MC, VI.

SOME UNITS

THE BREAKERS
Phone: (561)655-6611 ⓿26

(AAA) 12/20-1/6 1P: $465-$740 2P: $465-$740 XP: $50 F16
12/1-12/19 & 1/7-5/20 1P: $405-$630 2P: $405-$630 XP: $50 F16
5/21-11/30 1P: $260-$460 2P: $260-$460 XP: $50 F16
Classic Resort **Location:** On SR A1A, 0.3 mi s of jct Royal Poinciana Way. One South County Rd 33480. Fax: 561/659-8403. **Facility:** This Italian villa style grand hotel built by Henry Flagler in 1896 sets on expansive, beutifully landscaped grounds next to the beach and ocean. Distinctive public areas offer intricate and detailed craftsmanship. Guest rooms are luxuriously decorated with the finest hardwoods, artwork and linens. Many rooms have splendid ocean views. Spacious bathrooms feature exquisite amenities. From the moment you arrive, well-trained staff provide impeccable service. 569 units. Some suites ($695-$3500) and whirlpool units. *Bath:* combo or shower only. 5-9 stories, interior corridors. **Parking:** valet. **Terms:** check-in 4 pm, cancellation fee imposed, package plans. **Amenities:** extended cable TV, video games, CD players, voice mail, safes, honor bars, irons, hair dryers. **Dining:** 5 restaurants, terrace dining 7 am-10 pm; Sunday Brunch 19% service charge; afternoon tea 12/15-4/15, $16-$55, cocktails, also, The Florentine, see separate listing, entertainment. **Leisure Activities:** 3 heated pools, wading pool, beach, swimming, charter fishing, putting green, children's program, recreation program, social program, playground, barber shop, beauty salon. *Fee:* scuba diving/snorkeling & equipment, golf-36 holes, golf instruction, 14 tennis courts (5 lighted), tennis instruction, bicycles, full luxury spa, pool & beach cabana. **Guest Services:** [AP], [BP] & [MAP] meal plans available, gift shop, valet laundry. *Fee:* massage. **Business Services:** conference facilities, administrative services, fax. *Fee:* PC. **Cards:** AE, CB, DI, DS, MC, VI. Affiliated with A Preferred Hotel.

SOME UNITS

THE CHESTERFIELD HOTEL
Phone: (561)659-5800 ⓿30

(AAA) (SAVE) 12/22-4/30 1P: $239-$459 2P: $239-$459 XP: $15 F17
12/1-12/21 & 5/1-5/31 1P: $139-$259 2P: $139-$259 XP: $15 F17
6/1-11/30 1P: $99-$259 2P: $99-$259 XP: $15 F17
Historic Hotel **Location:** Just w of SR A1A at Australian Ave and Cocoanut Row. 363 Cocoanut Row 33480. Fax: 561/659-6707. **Facility:** Attractively restored 1926 hotel; some compact rooms. Large private landscaped pool patio. Street parking after 6 pm. Library and cigar room. 55 units. Some suites ($239-$1099). 4 stories, interior corridors. **Parking:** valet. **Terms:** 7 day cancellation notice-fee imposed, weekly & monthly rates available, package plans, pets ($150 deposit). **Amenities:** extended cable TV, voice mail, safes, irons, hair dryers. *Some:* CD players, honor bars. **Dining:** restaurant, 7-10:30 am, 11:30-2:30 & 6-1 am; courtyard dining, $19-$40, cocktails, entertainment. **Leisure Activities:** heated pool, whirlpool, golf, tennis nearby, video & CD library. *Fee:* health club privileges. **Guest Services:** afternoon tea, valet laundry. *Fee:* massage. **Business Services:** meeting rooms, PC. **Cards:** AE, CB, DI, DS, MC, VI. **Special Amenities:** free newspaper and preferred room (subject to availability with advanced reservations).** *(See color ad below)*

SOME UNITS

THE COLONY
Phone: (561)655-5430 ⓿33

(AAA) (SAVE) 12/23-4/15 1P: $285-$305 2P: $285-$305 XP: $25 F16
4/16-5/31 1P: $159-$199 2P: $159-$199 XP: $25 F16
12/1-12/22 1P: $149-$199 2P: $149-$199 XP: $25 F16
6/1-11/30 1P: $119-$199 2P: $119-$199 XP: $25 F16
Hotel **Location:** SR A1A, just s of Worth Ave. 155 Hammon Ave 33480. Fax: 561/659-8104. **Facility:** 90 units. 7 two-bedroom units. Some suites ($199-$695). 6 stories, interior corridors. **Parking:** extra charge or valet. **Terms:** check-in 4 pm, weekly & monthly rates available, package plans. **Amenities:** extended cable TV, voice mail, irons, hair dryers. *Some:* safes. **Dining:** restaurant, 7 am-10 pm; luncheon dining terrace, $13-$30, cocktails, entertainment. **Leisure Activities:** heated pool. *Fee:* bicycles, health club privileges, beach chairs. **Guest Services:** valet laundry. *Fee:* massage. **Business Services:** meeting rooms, fax. **Cards:** AE, DI, DS, MC, VI. **Special Amenities:** free room upgrade (subject to availability with advanced reservations).

SOME UNITS

(See map p. 710)

THE FOUR SEASONS RESORT, PALM BEACH

	10/1-11/30	1P: $395-$695	2P: $395-$695	Phone: (561)582-2800	⭐35
Hotel	12/1-9/30	1P: $375-$675	2P: $375-$675	XP: $30	F12
				XP: $30	F12

Location: SR A1A, 0.3 mi n of jct SR 802. 2800 S Ocean Blvd 33480. Fax: 561/547-1374. **Facility:** This distinguished hotel offers a casual elegance, a tranquil oceanfront setting and beautifully landscaped grounds. Inviting public areas, outstanding dining and the spa combine with other amenities and facilities to provide a very pleasurable experience. In many units, you can relax on your balcony, either overlooking the enticing pool and enjoy splendid ocean views. The staff pamper their guests and will make every effort to accommodate your whims. 210 units. 4 two-bedroom units. Some suites ($1200-$2500). **Bath:** combo or shower only. 4 stories, interior corridors. **Parking:** extra charge or valet. **Terms:** check-in 4 pm, 7 day cancellation notice-fee imposed, monthly rates available, package plans, small pets only. **Amenities:** extended cable TV, video games, dual phone lines, voice mail, safes, honor bars, irons, hair dryers. *Some:* CD players, fax. **Dining:** The Restaurant at The Four Seasons, see separate listing. **Leisure Activities:** heated pool, saunas, whirlpools, steamrooms, beach, children's program in season, jogging. *Fee:* sailboating, windsurfing, 3 tennis courts, bicycles. **Guest Services:** [BP] meal plan available, gift shop, area transportation, valet laundry. *Fee:* massage. **Business Services:** conference facilities, administrative services, PC, fax. **Cards:** AE, CB, DI, DS, JC, MC, VI.

SOME UNITS

HEART OF PALM BEACH HOTEL

	12/15-4/30	1P: $159-$259	2P: $159-$259	Phone: (561)655-5600	⭐27
	5/1-11/30	1P: $69-$159	2P: $69-$159	XP: $15	F18
Motor Inn	12/1-12/14	1P: $69-$149	2P: $69-$149	XP: $15	F18
				XP: $15	F18

Location: Center; just e of SR A1A. 160 Royal Palm Way 33480. Fax: 561/832-1201. **Facility:** Half block from the ocean. Designated smoking area. 88 units. Some suites ($175-$275). 3 stories, interior corridors. **Terms:** weekly & monthly rates available, package plans, small pets only. **Amenities:** extended cable TV, voice mail, irons, hair dryers. **Leisure Activities:** heated pool. *Fee:* bicycles. **Guest Services:** [AP], [BP], [CP] & [MAP] meal plans available, valet laundry. **Business Services:** meeting rooms, fax. **Cards:** AE, CB, DI, MC, VI.

SOME UNITS

HOWARD JOHNSON PALM BEACH

	12/20-4/15	1P: $109-$139	2P: $109-$139	Phone: (561)582-2581	⭐38
Motel	12/1-12/19 & 4/16-11/30	1P: $59-$79	2P: $59-$79	XP: $10	F18
				XP: $10	F18

Location: On SR A1A; at jct SR 802. 2870 S Ocean Blvd 33480. Fax: 561/582-7189. **Facility:** On Intracoastal Waterway, most units with balcony or patio. 98 units. 3 stories, interior corridors. **Terms:** cancellation fee imposed, package plans - in summer. **Amenities:** *Some:* irons, hair dryers. **Leisure Activities:** heated pool. **Guest Services:** coin laundry. **Business Services:** meeting rooms. **Cards:** AE, DI, DS, MC, VI.

SOME UNITS

PALM BEACH HILTON OCEANFRONT RESORT

	12/16-4/30	1P: $229-$389	2P: $229-$389	Phone: (561)586-6542	⭐36
Hotel	12/1-12/15 & 5/1-11/30	1P: $139-$259	2P: $139-$259	XP: $15	F18
				XP: $15	F18

Location: SR A1A; just n of jct SR 802. 2842 S Ocean Blvd 33480. Fax: 561/585-0188. **Facility:** Oceanfront. 134 units. Some suites ($369-$750) and whirlpool units. 5 stories, interior corridors. **Parking:** extra charge or valet. **Terms:** 14 day cancellation notice-fee imposed, package plans. **Amenities:** voice mail, honor bars, irons, hair dryers. **Dining:** 2 restaurants, 7 am-10 pm, $13-$25, cocktails. **Leisure Activities:** heated pool, sauna, whirlpool, beach, 2 tennis courts. *Fee:* sailboating, snorkeling equipment, jet skis & kayak. **Guest Services:** [AP] meal plan available, gift shop, valet laundry. *Fee:* massage. **Business Services:** meeting rooms, PC, fax. **Cards:** AE, DI, DS, MC, VI. **Special Amenities:** early check-in/late check-out and free newspaper. *(See ad p 44 & below)*

SOME UNITS

(See map p. 710)

PALM BEACH HISTORIC INN
Phone: (561)832-4009 **31**

12/15-5/1	2P: $150-$325	XP: $25	F13
5/2-11/30	2P: $75-$200	XP: $25	F13
12/1-12/14	2P: $75-$150	XP: $25	F13

Historic Bed & Breakfast

Location: Center; on SR A1A at Chilian Ave just n of Worth Ave. 365 S County Rd 33480. Fax: 561/832-6255. **Facility:** Tastefully, individually decorated and furnished rooms in 1921 building. Smoke free public areas. All bedrooms second floor. Four dedicated parking spots on site. Small sitting area with library. 13 units. 4 two-bedroom units. Some suites. 2 stories, interior corridors. **Parking:** street only. **Terms:** package plans. **Amenities:** extended cable TV, irons, hair dryers. **Guest Services:** [ECP] meal plan available. **Business Services:** fax. **Cards:** AE, CB, DI, DS, MC, VI. **Special Amenities:** free continental breakfast and free newspaper.

SOME UNITS
🅢🄳 🍴 🖨 🔲 / ✕ / VCR /

PLAZA INN
Phone: (561)832-8666 **29**

12/16-4/30	1P: $205-$275	2P: $225-$275	XP: $15 F12
5/1-5/31	1P: $125-$175	2P: $135-$185	XP: $15 F12
12/1-12/15	1P: $115-$165	2P: $125-$175	XP: $15 F12
6/1-11/30	1P: $115-$165	2P: $115-$165	XP: $15 F12

Historic Motel

Location: Center; at Brazilian Ave and SR A1A (S County Rd). 215 Brazilian Ave 33480. Fax: 561/835-8776. **Facility:** Restored art deco building. Some compact rooms. 47 units. Some suites ($225-$350). *Bath:* combo or shower only. 3 stories, interior corridors. **Terms:** 7 day cancellation notice, weekly & monthly rates available, package plans, small pets only. **Amenities:** extended cable TV. **Leisure Activities:** heated pool, whirlpool. **Guest Services:** [BP] meal plan available, valet laundry. **Cards:** AE, MC, VI.

SOME UNITS
ASK 🅢🄳 🐾 🍴 🍽 🕉 🛄 🔲 / ✕ / VCR /

The following lodging was either not evaluated or did not meet AAA rating requirements but is listed for your information only.

BRAZILIAN COURT HOTEL
Phone: 561/655-7740

[fyi] Not evaluated. **Location:** From Royal Palm Way (SR 204) s on Cocoanut Row, 2 blks to Australian Ave, then just e at corner of Hibiscus and Australian aves. 301 Australian Ave 33480. Facilities, services, and decor characterize an upscale property.

--- **WHERE TO DINE** ---

CAFE L'EUROPE
Lunch: $10-$15   Dinner: $18-$35   Phone: 561/655-4020 **15**

Continental

Location: Center; on SR A1A at S County Rd and Brazilian Ave. 331 S County Rd 33480. **Hours:** noon-3 & 6-10:30 pm, Sun & Mon from 6 pm. Closed: Sun & Mon for lunch. **Reservations:** required; for dinner. **Features:** dressy casual; cocktails & lounge; entertainment; street parking & valet parking; a la carte. Servers deliver excellent, innovative entrees in either a formal dining room or a casual bistro. Jackets are required in the formal area, while casual attire is fine for the bistro. Take advantage of an extensive wine list and valet parking at dinner. **Cards:** AE, DI, MC, VI. ✕

CHARLEY'S CRAB
Lunch: $7-$19   Dinner: $12-$28   Phone: 561/659-1500 **17**

Seafood

Location: Across from ocean; 0.4 mi s of Royal Palm Way. 456 S Ocean Blvd 33480. **Hours:** 11:30 am-10 pm, Fri & Sat-11 pm, Sun 10:30 am-2:30 & 4:30-10 pm. A complimentary wine list. **Reservations:** suggested; for dinner. **Features:** dressy casual; Sunday brunch; children's menu; early bird specials; carryout; cocktails & lounge; valet parking; a la carte. A snappy chipotle pepper sauce adds intrigue to the spring roll stuffed with crab, alfalfa sprouts and bamboo shoots. A knowledgeable staff helps you select from an extensive menu of fresh seafood. Enjoy cozy ambience with an ocean view from the bar. **Cards:** AE, CB, DI, DS, MC, VI. ✕

CHUCK & HAROLD'S
Lunch: $5-$16   Dinner: $14-$34   Phone: 561/659-1440 **12**

American

Location: 0.3 mi e of Flager Memorial Bridge on SR A1A. 207 Royal Poinciana Way 33480. **Hours:** 7:30 am-1 am. **Reservations:** suggested. **Features:** Sunday brunch; children's menu; carryout; cocktails & lounge; entertainment; street parking; a la carte. An astounding dinner menu features meat and fresh seafood dishes like grilled swordfish Tuscany over chopped cannellini beans with a side of haverts. The casual, upbeat atmosphere and clean, well-kept environment is also found on the patio area. **Cards:** AE, DI, DS, MC, VI. ✕

THE FLORENTINE
Dinner: $32-$40   Phone: 561/655-6611 **14**

Continental

Location: On SR A1A, 0.3 mi s of jct Royal Poinciana Way; in The Breakers. 1 S County Rd 33480. **Hours:** 6 pm-10 pm. **Reservations:** suggested; jackets for men. **Features:** dressy casual; children's menu; cocktails & lounge; entertainment; valet parking; a la carte. Located in the "grand dame," The Breakers Resort, this decor-rich dining room displays detailed workmanship, including the handcrafted fresco on the 30 foot high ceilings. Through "the renaissance of classic European cuisine" and French and Mediterranean influences, the chef transforms local ingredients into a sumptuous dining occasion. Enjoy the delectable roast duck appetizer, lobster salad and venison. Be sure to try the wonderful cheese offerings and sensational desserts. Smoke free premises. **Cards:** AE, CB, DI, DS, MC, VI. ✕

MY MARTINI GRILLE
Lunch: $7-$13   Dinner: $13-$26   Phone: 561/832-8333 **13**

American

Location: Downtown; at jct Olive Ave. 225 Clematis St 33401. **Hours:** 11:30 am-3 & 5-10 pm, Sat 5 pm-11 pm. Closed major holidays; also Sun. **Reservations:** accepted. **Features:** dressy casual; carryout; cocktails & lounge; street parking; a la carte. A bistro type restaurant serving a variety of meat and fresh local seafood. Entrees include crispy crusted snapper, seasame seared tuna and prime rib. Located in a trendy area popular for its nightlife. Over 70 types of martinis. Cafe outdoor seating available. **Cards:** AE, MC, VI. ✕

(See map p. 710)

THE RESTAURANT AT THE FOUR SEASONS

(AAA)
◆◆◆◆◆
Regional American

Dinner: $29-$36   **Phone:** 561/533-3750   ⑱

Location: SR A1A, 0.3 mi n of jct SR 802; in The Four Seasons Resort, Palm Beach. 2800 S Ocean Blvd 33480. **Hours:** 6 pm-10 pm. Closed: Mon; Tues 5/1-11/15. **Reservations:** suggested; jackets req. **Features:** semi-formal attire; children's menu; cocktails & lounge; entertainment; valet parking; a la carte. Dining here is a very pleasurable experience with a casual elegance in the wait staff's service approach; one is in for a treat. A tranquil, oceanfront setting in the cozy dining area offering pleasant views of the grounds. The chef transforms a variety of local ingredients into a sumptuous, mouthwatering meal. The Key West gold prawns are a must; the duck is transformed into a tasty, beautifully presented creation. Finish your meal with a delightful Creme Brulee Trio. Smoke free premises. **Cards:** AE, CB, DI, DS, MC, VI.   ♿ ✖

TESTA'S RESTAURANT

(AAA)
◆◆◆
Steak & Seafood

Lunch: $7-$12   **Dinner:** $12-$25   **Phone:** 561/832-0992   ⑪

Location: 0.3 mi e of Flagler Memorial Bridge on SR A1A. 221 Royal Poinciana Way 33480. **Hours:** 7 am-10 pm. Closed: 11/22. **Reservations:** accepted. **Features:** dressy casual; children's menu; early bird specials; carryout; cocktails & lounge. This eatery promises consistency with the same family ownership for more than 80 years. Seafood, steak and Italian dishes are offered in the dining room, sidewalk terrace or open-air patio. Sample the delicious she-crab soup. Valet parking is available. **Cards:** AE, CB, DI, DS, MC, VI.   ✖

PALM BEACH GARDENS pop. 23,000   (See map p. 710; index p. 712)—

———— WHERE TO STAY ————

DOUBLETREE HOTEL IN THE GARDENS

(AAA) (SAVE)
◆◆◆◆
Hotel

Phone: (561)622-2260   ㊾

1/7-4/15	1P: $179	2P: $179	XP: $15 F16
10/1-11/30	1P: $99-$149	2P: $99-$149	XP: $15 F16
4/16-9/30	1P: $89-$139	2P: $89-$139	XP: $15 F16
12/1-1/6	1P: $84-$114	2P: $84-$114	XP: $15 F16

Location: Jct I-95, exit 57, 1.8 mi e of Florida Tpke exit 109. 4431 PGA Blvd 33410. Fax: 561/624-1043. **Facility:** Landscaped grounds with the pool area surrounded by tropical trees and shrubbery. The lobby is furnished with an art deco look. Rooms have a modern, contemporary look with medium wood tones. Brightly colored accents. 280 units. *Bath:* combo or shower only. 6 stories, interior corridors. **Terms:** package plans. **Amenities:** video games, dual phone lines, voice mail, irons, hair dryers. **Dining:** restaurant, 6:30 am-11 pm, $10-$24, cocktails. **Leisure Activities:** heated pool, whirlpool, exercise room. **Guest Services:** gift shop, area transportation-Gardens Mall, valet laundry. **Business Services:** meeting rooms, administrative services. **Cards:** AE, CB, DI, DS, MC, VI. **Special Amenities:** early check-in/late check-out and free newspaper. *(See color ad below)*

SOME UNITS

ⓈⒹ 🍽🍷 ♿ 🐕 📶 🤿 📷 🖨 🖥 DATA PORT / ✖ 📞 /

FEE

EMBASSY SUITES HOTEL

◆◆◆◆
Suite Hotel

Phone: (561)622-1000   �51

12/1-4/15	1P: $159-$249	2P: $159-$249	XP: $10 F17
4/16-5/31 & 10/1-11/30	1P: $109-$159	2P: $109-$159	XP: $10 F17
6/1-9/30	1P: $89-$139	2P: $89-$139	XP: $10 F17

Location: Jct I-95, exit 57, 1.8 mi e of Florida Tpke, exit 109. 4350 PGA Blvd 33410. Fax: 561/626-6254. **Facility:** Landscaped atrium has small lake with swans. Well furnished one and two-bedroom suites with separate living room. 160 units. 5 two-bedroom units. Some whirlpool units. *Bath:* combo or shower only. 10 stories, interior corridors. **Terms:** 3 day cancellation notice, in season-fee imposed, monthly rates available, package plans. **Amenities:** extended cable TV, voice mail, irons, hair dryers. **Leisure Activities:** heated pool, sauna, whirlpool, tennis court, jogging, exercise room. **Guest Services:** [BP] meal plan available, gift shop, complimentary evening beverages, area transportation, valet and coin laundry. **Business Services:** meeting rooms. **Cards:** AE, CB, DI, DS, JC, MC, VI.

SOME UNITS

ⒶⓈⓀ ⓈⒹ 🍽🍷 🐕 📶 🤿 🏊 ✖ 📷 🖨 🖥 🧳 📞 DATA PORT / ✖ /

(See map p. 710)

INNS OF AMERICA

AAA [SAVE]

◇◇ ◇◇

Motel

Phone: (561)626-4918 **53**

1/16-4/30	1P: $85	XP: $10	F12
12/1-1/15	1P: $72	XP: $10	F12
5/1-11/30	1P: $59	XP: $10	F12

Location: I-95, exit 56. 4123 Northlake Blvd 33410. Fax: 561/626-8790. **Facility:** Comfortable rooms and appointments. 95 units. 3 stories, exterior corridors. **Terms:** weekly rates available. **Amenities:** extended cable TV. **Leisure Activities:** heated pool. **Guest Services:** coin laundry. **Cards:** AE, DS, MC, VI. **Special Amenities:** free continental breakfast and free local telephone calls.

SOME UNITS

[S/D] [dog] [TV+] [phone] [spa] [camera] [fridge] [iron] [B] [DATA PORT] / [X] /

PALM BEACH GARDENS MARRIOTT

◇◇◇◇ ◇◇◇◇

Hotel

Phone: (561)622-8888 **52**

12/1-3/31	1P: $179-$249	2P: $179-$249
4/1-5/25	1P: $159-$219	2P: $159-$219
9/30-11/30	1P: $119-$189	2P: $119-$189
5/26-9/29	1P: $99-$169	2P: $99-$169

Location: I-95, exit 57, just se of PGA Blvd, 2 mi e of Florida Tpke. 4000 RCA Blvd 33410. Fax: 561/622-0052. **Facility:** Attractive public areas, well-appointed units. 279 units. *Bath:* combo or shower only. 11 stories, interior corridors. **Parking:** valet. **Terms:** check-in 4 pm, cancellation fee imposed, package plans. **Amenities:** voice mail, irons, hair dryers. **Leisure Activities:** heated pool, sauna, whirlpool, steamroom, exercise room. **Guest Services:** gift shop, area transportation, valet laundry. **Business Services:** conference facilities, administrative services, PC, fax. **Cards:** AE, DI, DS, MC, VI.

SOME UNITS

[S/D] [tray] [Y] [wheelchair] [ear] [spa] [camera] [B] [coffee] [DATA PORT] / [X] [VCR] [B]
FEE   FEE

PGA NATIONAL RESORT & SPA

AAA [SAVE]

◇◇◇◇ ◇◇◇◇

Resort

Phone: (561)627-2000 **48**

1/1-5/24	1P: $249-$289	2P: $249-$289	XP: $18	F18
9/16-11/30	1P: $189-$229	2P: $189-$229	XP: $18	F18
12/1-12/31	1P: $179-$229	2P: $179-$229	XP: $18	F18
5/25-9/15	1P: $99-$119	2P: $99-$119	XP: $18	F18

Location: Just w of Florida Tpke, exit 109; 2 mi w of I-95, exit 57 at PGA National. 400 Ave of the Champions 33418. Fax: 561/622-0261. **Facility:** In exclusive community on lake. Extensive supervised European style spa and salon facilities including two mineral pools. A large lobby with many sitting areas and a balcony sitting area overlooks a pool area and golf course. Large units with medium wood tones. Attractive unit decor. All with balcony or patio. 339 units. Some suites. *Bath:* combo or shower only. 3-4 stories, interior corridors. **Parking:** valet. **Terms:** cancellation fee imposed, package plans. **Amenities:** dual phone lines, voice mail, safes, honor bars, irons, hair dryers. **Dining:** dining room, 2 restaurants, 6:30 am-midnight; 18% service charge, $6-$40, cocktails, also, Shula's Steak House, see separate listing, entertainment. **Leisure Activities:** 3 pools (1 heated), wading pool, saunas, whirlpools, beach, fishing, jogging. *Fee:* lap-pool, golf-90 holes & instruction, tennis-19 courts, 10 lighted & instruction, bicycles, croquet & instruction. **Guest Services:** gift shop, valet laundry. *Fee:* area transportation-within 8 mi, massage. **Business Services:** conference facilities, administrative services, fax. *Fee:* PC. **Cards:** AE, DI, DS, JC, MC, VI. **Special Amenities:** free newspaper and preferred room (subject to availability with advanced reservations).

SOME UNITS

[S/D] [key] [tray] [Y] [gym] [ear] [spa] [hiker] [X] [B] [coffee] [DATA PORT] / [X] [VCR] [B]
FEE   FEE   FEE   FEE

——— WHERE TO DINE ———

CAFE CHARDONNAY

◇◇◇

American

Lunch: $6-$12   Dinner: $17-$32   Phone: 561/627-2662 **26**

Location: Jct PGA Blvd and Military Tr; in Garden Square Shoppes, 0.3 mi w of I-95, exit 57. 4533 PGA Blvd 33418. **Hours:** 11:30 am-2:30 & 5:30-10 pm, Sat & Sun from 5:30 pm. Closed: 11/22, 12/25. **Reservations:** suggested. **Features:** dressy casual; children's menu; carryout; beer & wine only; a la carte. For an inventive meal, step into this bright, colorful, bi-level dining room. The house speciality is macadamia nut crusted yellowtail snapper. An efficient team provides good service and sets the tone for an enjoyable evening out. **Cards:** AE, CB, MC, VI. [X]

EBISU JAPANESE RESTAURANT

◇◇◇

Japanese

Lunch: $7-$10   Dinner: $12-$20   Phone: 561/622-4495 **25**

Location: PGA Blvd; in Shoppes on the Green Shopping Center, just w of jct Florida Tpke, exit 102; 1.7 mi w of jct I-95, exit 57. 7100 Fairway Dr 33418. **Hours:** 11:30 am-2 & 5:30-10 pm, Fri-10:30 pm, Sat 5:30 pm-10:30 pm, Sun 5:30 pm-9:30 pm. Closed: 7/4, 11/22, 12/25; also Sun. **Reservations:** accepted. **Features:** casual dress; carryout; beer & wine only. Beautifully presented, authentic Japanese cuisine features several styles of preparation, including sushi and sashimi. A traditional dining room offers both Western and Japanese seating. The owner/chef sends out pickled bean sprouts as an appetizer. **Cards:** AE, MC, VI. [X]

NO ANCHOVIES! NEIGHBORHOOD PASTARIA

◇◇◇

Italian

Lunch: $5-$8   Dinner: $9-$17   Phone: 561/622-7855 **29**

Location: 0.5 mi w of jct US 1, on PGA Blvd at Prosperity Farms Rd; in PGA Plaza. 2650 PGA Blvd 33410. **Hours:** 11:30 am-2:30 & 5-10:30 pm, Fri & Sat-11 pm, Sun 5 pm-10 pm. Closed: 11/22, 12/25; also 1/1 for lunch. **Features:** casual dress; children's menu; carryout; cocktails & lounge. The name is a solemn promise. An open kitchen adds to the lively ambience of this modern pastaria. Some of the specialty pasta dishes are prepared in a wood-burning oven along with tasty pizzas. This is a great value on family favorites. **Cards:** AE, DI, MC, VI. [X]

PADDY MAC'S

◇◇◇

Irish

Lunch: $6-$9   Dinner: $9-$19   Phone: 561/691-4366 **27**

Location: Jct Military Tr and PGA Blvd; at north end of Garden Square Shoppes; 0.3 mi w of jct I-95, exit 57. 10971 N Military Tr 33418. **Hours:** 11:30 am-3 & 4:30-10 pm, Sun from 4:30 pm. Closed: 5/28, 11/22, 12/25. **Reservations:** accepted; 5/1-12/1. **Features:** casual dress; children's menu; carryout; cocktails & lounge; a la carte. Log fireplaces, Irish paintings and a wood bar evoke the aura of a Dublin pub. Casual and noisy, the restaurant serves up such entrees as salmon with citrus butter and chicken with apple-honey stuffing. Entertainers perform on Friday and Saturday nights. **Cards:** AE, DI, DS, MC, VI. [X]

(See map p. 710)

THE RIVER HOUSE
▼▼▼▼
Steak & Seafood
Dinner: $17-$40   **Phone:** 561/694-1188   ⊞30
Location: On PGA Blvd, 0.5 mi w of jct US 1; at Soverel Harbour. 2373 PGA Blvd 33410. **Hours:** 5 pm-10 pm, Fri & Sat-10:30 pm. Closed: 11/22, 12/25. **Reservations:** required; Fri & Sat. **Features:** dressy casual; children's menu; carryout; salad bar; cocktails & lounge; valet parking. Bustling and warm, the atmosphere of the restaurant lends itself to a pleasant dining experience. Lots of windows offer views of the Intracoastal Waterway. A sweet fresh fruit chutney accompanies the grilled mahi-mahi, which is topped with macadamia nuts. Another favorite is the 25 ounce prime rib on the bone. **Cards:** AE, DI, DS, MC, VI.   ☒

SHULA'S STEAK HOUSE
▼▼▼▼
Steak House
Dinner: $30-$50   **Phone:** 561/627-4852   ⊞24
Location: Just w of Florida Tpke, exit 109; 2 mi w of I-95, exit 57, at PGA National; in PGA National Resort & Spa. 400 Ave of the Champions 33418. **Hours:** 6 pm-10:30 pm. **Features:** cocktails; valet parking; a la carte. Miami's honored football coach filled his dining room with rich wood and Dolphin memorabilia. Extra-large lobsters and Angus beef will please the heartiest of appetites. Menu options are listed on a football along with a fine selection of delicious wines. **Cards:** AE, CB, DI, DS, JC, MC, VI.   ☒

PALM BEACH SHORES pop. 1,000   (See map p. 710; index p. 712)—

—— WHERE TO STAY ——

BEST WESTERN SEASPRAY INN
ⒶⒶⒶ ⟨SAVE⟩
▼▼ ▼▼
Motor Inn

			Phone: (561)844-0233	⊞60
2/10-3/31	1P: $109-$179	2P: $119-$179	XP: $10	F18
12/1-2/9	1P: $69-$149	2P: $104-$149	XP: $10	F18
4/1-4/29	1P: $89-$139	2P: $99-$139	XP: $10	F18
4/30-11/30	1P: $59-$115	2P: $69-$115	XP: $10	F18

Location: On Singer Island; 0.5 mi s of SR A1A. 123 S Ocean Ave 33404. Fax: 561/844-9885. **Facility:** Comfortable units, most with balcony, many with beach view. 50 units, 10 with efficiency. 4 stories, interior corridors. **Terms:** weekly rates available, package plans - off season, pets ($15 extra charge). **Amenities:** extended cable TV, safes (fee). *Some:* hair dryers. **Dining:** Rooftop dining room 8 am-2:30 & 5:30-9:30 pm, $7-$21, cocktails, entertainment. **Leisure Activities:** heated pool, beach, swimming. **Guest Services:** [AP] meal plan available, valet laundry. **Cards:** AE, CB, DI, DS, MC, VI. **Special Amenities:** free local telephone calls and free room upgrade (subject to availability with advanced reservations). (See ad below)

SOME UNITS
🐕 🍸 🏊 💻 ᴅᴀᴛᴀ ᴘᴏʀᴛ / ☒ 🖥 🛗 /
                                        FEE FEE

(See map p. 710)

HILTON SINGER ISLAND OCEANFRONT RESORT
Phone: (561)848-3888 **61**

12/15-4/30	1P: $179-$249	2P: $179-$249	XP: $15	F18
12/1-12/14 & 5/1-11/30	1P: $99-$149	2P: $99-$149	XP: $15	F18

SAVE

▽▼▽▼
Hotel

Location: On Singer Island; 1.8 mi n and e on SR A1A from jct US 1. 3700 N Ocean Dr 33404. Fax: 561/848-4299. **Facility:** All units with walk out balcony. 222 units. 8 stories, interior corridors. **Terms:** check-in 4 pm, 3 day cancellation notice, package plans. **Amenities:** extended cable TV, video games, voice mail, irons, hair dryers. **Leisure Activities:** heated pool, wading pool, beach, swimming, snorkeling & equipment, children's program, exercise room. *Fee:* bicycles. **Guest Services:** gift shop, valet and coin laundry. *Fee:* massage. **Business Services:** meeting rooms, fax. **Cards:** AE, CB, DI, DS, MC, VI. *(See ad p 44)*

SOME UNITS

🍴 ▬ 🛋 🏊 🐕 ✎ 📹 🖥 💻 📶 DATA PORT /✕/
FEE

RADISSON PALM BEACH SHORES RESORT AND VACATION VILLAS
Phone: (561)863-4000 **59**

12/27-5/1	1P: $259-$319	2P: $259-$319	XP: $15	F
12/1-12/26 & 5/2-11/30	1P: $159-$219	2P: $159-$219	XP: $15	F

▽▼▽▼
Suite Hotel

Location: On Singer Island; 0.3 mi s of SR A1A. 181 Ocean Ave 33404. Fax: 561/845-3245. **Facility:** One-bedroom suites with balcony, some with ocean view. 240 units. 10 two-bedroom units. 6 stories, interior corridors. **Parking:** extra charge or valet. **Terms:** check-in 4 pm, 3 day cancellation notice-fee imposed, package plans. **Amenities:** video games, voice mail, irons, hair dryers. **Leisure Activities:** heated pool, whirlpool, beach, swimming, snorkeling, children's program, exercise room. *Fee:* windsurfing, snorkeling equipment. **Guest Services:** gift shop, valet and coin laundry. *Fee:* massage. **Business Services:** conference facilities, fax. **Cards:** AE, DI, DS, MC, VI.

SOME UNITS

ASK 🅢🅓 🍴 ▬ 🛋 🐕 🏊 ✕ 📹 🖥 💻 📶 📶 DATA PORT /✕/
FEE   FEE

SAILFISH MARINA & RESORT
Phone: (561)844-1724 **58**

12/1-5/15	2P: $99-$139	XP: $15	F12
5/16-11/30	2P: $79-$109	XP: $15	F12

▽▼▽▼
Motor Inn

Location: From US 1, 1 mi e, then 0.4 mi s. 98 Lake Dr 33404 (PO Box 10848, 33419). Fax: 561/848-9684. **Facility:** Cute units, located in a quiet and tranquil setting. Behind the room area is a marina that has a paved walk-way area. Ample shade on the shore to relax and just watch the boats. The restaurant, with large windows, offers great views of the water. 23 units. 10 efficiencies and 6 units with kitchen. Some suites ($109-$139). 1 story, exterior corridors. **Terms:** 7 day cancellation notice, weekly & monthly rates available, package plans. **Leisure Activities:** fishing, charter fishing. *Fee:* boats, sailboating, boat dock, marina, scuba diving, snorkeling, bicycles. **Guest Services:** gift shop, coin laundry. **Business Services:** meeting rooms. **Cards:** AE, MC, VI.

SOME UNITS

ASK 🅢🅓 🍴 ▬ 🏊 ♿ ✕ 🐕 🖥 💻 /✕/ 🖨 📶

SHERATON OCEANFRONT NORTH PALM BEACH HOTEL
Phone: (561)842-6171 **57**

12/18-5/5	1P: $250-$320	2P: $250-$320	XP: $15	F18
5/6-11/30	1P: $170-$230	2P: $170-$230	XP: $15	F18
12/1-12/17	1P: $160-$220	2P: $160-$220	XP: $15	F18

▽▼▽▼
Motor Inn

Location: 1.8 mi e, n on SR A1A from jct US 1. 3200 N Ocean Dr 33404. Fax: 561/848-6842. **Facility:** A few units oceanfront. Most with view of the ocean. Nicely furnished and decorated rooms. 193 units. Some suites. *Bath:* combo or shower only. 9 stories, interior corridors. **Parking:** extra charge or valet. **Terms:** check-in 4 pm, 3 day cancellation notice-fee imposed, weekly & monthly rates available, package plans. **Amenities:** video games, dual phone lines, voice mail, safes (fee), irons, hair dryers. *Some:* fax. **Leisure Activities:** heated pool, whirlpool, beach, swimming, children's program, exercise room. *Fee:* scuba diving/snorkeling & equipment, bicycles. **Guest Services:** [MAP] meal plan available, gift shop, valet and coin laundry. *Fee:* massage. **Business Services:** meeting rooms, administrative services, fax. *Fee:* PC. **Cards:** AE, CB, DI, DS, JC, MC, VI.
(See color ad p 719)

SOME UNITS

ASK 🅢🅓 🍴 ▬ ♿ 🛋 🐕 🏊 ✕ 📹 🖥 💻 DATA PORT /✕/ 🖨 📶/
FEE   FEE

PALM COAST pop. 14,300

——— WHERE TO STAY ———

HAMPTON INN
AAA [SAVE]
♦♦♦
Motel

Phone: (904)446-4457

1/1-4/30	1P: $69-$225	2P: $79-$225
5/1-9/30	1P: $64-$189	2P: $74-$189
10/1-11/30	1P: $69-$129	2P: $74-$129
12/1-12/31	1P: $69-$99	2P: $74-$99

Location: I-95, exit 91C, 0.5 mi se via Old Kings Rd; in Kingswood Center. 5 Kingswood Dr 32137. Fax: 904/445-1438. **Facility:** 50 units. 2 stories, exterior corridors. **Amenities:** extended cable TV, irons. **Leisure Activities:** heated pool, whirlpool. **Guest Services:** [ECP] meal plan available. **Cards:** AE, CB, DI, DS, MC, VI. **Special Amenities:** free continental breakfast.

SOME UNITS
[S/D] [▯↕] [🏊] [📹] [DATA PORT] / [⊗] /

PALM COAST RESORT
♦♦♦
Motor Inn

Phone: (904)445-3000
XP: $25   F18

All Year   1P: $89-$249   2P: $89-$249

Location: I-95, exit 91C, 2 mi e. 300 Clubhouse Dr 32137-9985. Fax: 904/445-2947. **Facility:** Resort community along the Intracoastal Waterway. Walkways by the water. 154 units. 3 stories (no elevator), exterior corridors. **Terms:** 30 day cancellation notice-fee imposed, package plans. **Amenities:** extended cable TV, voice mail, safes, irons, hair dryers. *Some:* honor bars. **Leisure Activities:** 3 pools, whirlpool, boat dock, fishing, 19 tennis courts (17 lighted), children's program, hiking trails, jogging, playground, exercise room. *Fee:* boats, marina, golf-90 holes, racquetball courts, bicycles. **Guest Services:** gift shop, coin laundry. **Business Services:** conference facilities, fax. **Cards:** AE, DI, DS, MC, VI. **(See color ad below)**

SOME UNITS
[ASK] [S/D] [▯↕] [🍽] [🏊] [⊗] [📹] [🖨] [▭] [DATA PORT] / [⊗] /
FEE

PALM COAST VILLAS
AAA [SAVE]
♦♦ ♦♦
Motel

Phone: 904/445-3525

All Year   1P: $59   2P: $59

Location: I-95, exit 91C, 2.8 mi e to SR A1A, 1.8 mi n. 5454 N Oceanshore Blvd 32137. **Facility:** Originally constructed in 1930s of native coquina stone with attractive appearance and well maintained grounds; smaller and modestly furnished units. 22 units. 2 two-bedroom units and 18 efficiencies. *Bath:* some combo or shower only. 2 stories, exterior corridors. **Terms:** 30 day cancellation notice, weekly rates available, small pets only. **Amenities:** extended cable TV. **Guest Services:** coin laundry. **Cards:** DS, MC, VI.

[🐕] [🏊]

SLEEP INN

SAVE

◆◆ ◆◆
Motel

2/1-3/31	1P: $75-$154	2P: $75-$154	XP: $10	F16
6/30-11/30	1P: $65-$119	2P: $65-$119	XP: $10	F16
12/1-1/31 & 4/1-6/29	1P: $65-$75	2P: $65-$75	XP: $10	F16

Phone: (904)446-8180

Location: I-95, exit 91C, 0.5 mi se via Old Kings Rd; in Kingswood Center. 10 Kingswood Dr 32137. **Fax:** 904/446-4004. **Facility:** 78 units. *Bath:* shower only. 3 stories, interior corridors. **Amenities:** extended cable TV. *Some:* irons, hair dryers. **Leisure Activities:** whirlpool. **Guest Services:** coin laundry. **Cards:** AE, CB, DI, DS, JC, MC, VI.

SOME UNITS

----- **WHERE TO DINE** -----

THE MEETING PLACE

◆◆ ◆◆
American

Lunch: $6-$8   **Dinner:** $9-$15   **Phone:** 904/445-1310

Location: In Palm Harbor Shopping Village; 0.5 mi ne of I-95 exit 91C; towards south end of complex. 278 Palm Coast Pkwy 32137. **Hours:** 11 am-3 & 4-9 pm; Thurs-Sat to 10 pm. Closed major holidays. **Reservations:** suggested. **Features:** casual dress; children's menu; early bird specials; carryout; cocktails & lounge. A relaxed, casual atmosphere, popular with the local business crowd, offers the chance to enjoy flavorful entrees like the traditional Reuben sandwich served with a New York deli-style pickle. An organized staff expertly attends to your needs. **Cards:** CB, DI, DS, MC, VI.

PALMETTO pop. 9,300   (See map p. 764; index p. 768)

----- **WHERE TO STAY** -----

SEA INN HOTEL

◆◆ ◆◆
Motel

Phone: 941/721-0365   **124**

Property failed to provide current rates

Location: I-75, exit 43, 3.3 mi w on US 301, 2.2 mi n on US 19. 5515 Hwy 19 N 34221. **Fax:** 941/723-1105. **Facility:** Near Terra Cela Bay, some units with limited water view. 8 units. Some suites. *Bath:* shower only. 2 stories, exterior corridors. **Terms:** weekly & monthly rates available. **Amenities:** *Some:* irons, hair dryers. **Guest Services:** [CP] meal plan available. **Cards:** AE, DS, MC, VI.

SOME UNITS

----- **WHERE TO DINE** -----

CRAB TRAP 1

◆◆ ◆◆
Seafood

Lunch: $5-$14   **Dinner:** $10-$40   **Phone:** 941/722-6255   **62**

Location: I-275, exit 2, just s on US 19; I-75 exit 43, 3.3 mi sw on US 301, 2.3 mi n. 5611 US 19 34221. **Hours:** 11:30 am-9 pm, Fri & Sat-10 pm. Closed: 11/22, 12/25. **Features:** casual dress; early bird specials; cocktails & lounge. Stone crabs, three-crab soup and other rural Florida dishes are served in a very rustic setting. Among the more daring selections are the gator and wild boar. Frog legs, scalloped bananas, conch fritters and fresh lobster are all prepared from scratch. **Cards:** DS, MC, VI.

PALM HARBOR —*See Tampa Bay p. 870.*

PANAMA CITY pop. 34,400

----- **WHERE TO STAY** -----

BAYSIDE INN

AAA **SAVE**

◆◆ ◆◆
Motor Inn

12/1-7/5	1P: $74-$265	2P: $79-$265	XP: $5	F12
7/6-11/30	1P: $74-$165	2P: $79-$170	XP: $5	F12

Phone: (850)763-4622

Location: Business Rt US 98, 0.5 mi w of jct US 231. 711 W Beach Dr 32401. **Fax:** 850/747-9522. **Facility:** 8 mi from gulf beaches, on the bay. Small beach. 100 units. 2 stories, exterior corridors. **Terms:** 7 day cancellation notice, small pets only ($10 extra charge). **Amenities:** extended cable TV. **Dining:** restaurant, 6 am-2 & 5-10 pm, Sat & Sun 7 am; Sun 7 am-noon off season, $7-$16, cocktails. **Leisure Activities:** playground. **Guest Services:** coin laundry. **Business Services:** meeting rooms. **Cards:** AE, CB, DI, DS, MC, VI. **Special Amenities:** free local telephone calls and free room upgrade (subject to availability with advanced reservations).

SOME UNITS

BEST WESTERN SUITES

◆◆ ◆◆
Motel

Phone: (850)784-7700

Property failed to provide current rates

Location: From US 98, 1.5 mi ne on US 231, just w on SR 368. 1035 E 23rd St 32405. **Fax:** 850/763-9095. **Facility:** 50 units. Some whirlpool units. *Bath:* combo or shower only. 2 stories, interior corridors. **Terms:** 7 day cancellation notice. **Amenities:** extended cable TV, hair dryers. **Leisure Activities:** exercise room. **Guest Services:** [CP] meal plan available, valet laundry. **Business Services:** meeting rooms. **Cards:** AE, DI, DS, MC, VI.

SOME UNITS

COMFORT INN & CONFERENCE CENTER

AAA **SAVE**

◆◆ ◆◆
Motel

3/1-9/3	1P: $82-$110	2P: $82-$110	XP: $6	F18
12/1-2/28 & 9/4-11/30	1P: $52-$65	2P: $52-$65	XP: $6	F18

Phone: (850)769-6969

Location: SR 368, just w of jct US 231. 1013 E 23rd St 32405. **Fax:** 850/763-4353. **Facility:** Near Panama City Mall. 105 units. 2 stories, exterior corridors. **Terms:** 7 day cancellation notice. **Amenities:** extended cable TV, voice mail, irons, hair dryers. **Leisure Activities:** exercise room. **Guest Services:** [ECP] meal plan available, complimentary evening beverages: Mon-Thurs, coin laundry. **Business Services:** conference facilities. **Cards:** AE, CB, DI, DS, JC, MC, VI. **Special Amenities:** free continental breakfast and free local telephone calls.

SOME UNITS

FEE

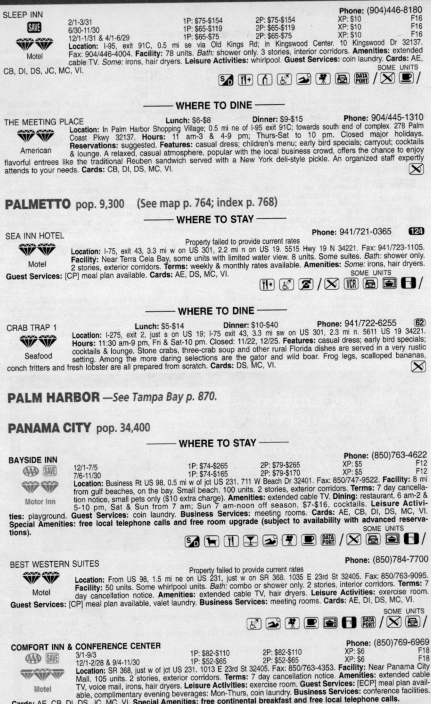

COMFORT INN AND SUITES

SAVE

Motel

2/21-4/9 & 4/10-9/10   1P: $95-$105   2P: $95-$105   XP: $10   F14
12/1-2/20 & 9/11-11/30   1P: $45-$55   2P: $55-$65   XP: $10   F14
Location: 4 mi w of jct SR 231. 4128 W US 98 32401. Fax: 850/763-4234. **Facility:** 40 units. Some whirlpool units ($125-$145). 2 stories, exterior corridors. **Terms:** 7 day cancellation notice. **Guest Services:** [CP] meal plan available. **Cards:** AE, DI, DS, MC, VI.

SOME UNITS

Phone: (850)763-0101

COUNTRY INN & SUITES BY CARLSON PANAMA CITY

Motel

Property failed to provide current rates

Phone: (850)913-0074

Location: 0.5 mi w of US 231, just s of 23rd St. 2203 Harrison Ave 32405. Fax: 850/913-9970. **Facility:** 53 units. Some suites and whirlpool units. *Bath:* combo or shower only. 2 stories, interior corridors. **Terms:** 7 day cancellation notice. **Amenities:** extended cable TV, irons, hair dryers. **Leisure Activities:** exercise room. **Guest Services:** [ECP] meal plan available, valet laundry. **Business Services:** meeting rooms. **Cards:** AE, CB, DI, DS, MC, VI.
(See color ad p 572)

SOME UNITS

DAYS INN & SUITES

SAVE

Motel

2/24-9/3   1P: $77-$130   2P: $87-$140   XP: $10   F12
12/1-2/23   1P: $50-$110   2P: $60-$110   XP: $10   F12
9/4-11/30   1P: $50-$100   2P: $60-$110   XP: $10   F12
Location: On US 98 E, 2 mi e of jct US 98 E and Transmitter Rd. 435 N Tyndall Pkwy 32404. Fax: 850/769-9558. **Facility:** 52 units. Some whirlpool units ($105-$155). *Bath:* combo or shower only. 2 stories, interior corridors. **Amenities:** extended cable TV, hair dryers. *Some:* irons. **Guest Services:** [ECP] meal plan available. **Cards:** AE, DI, DS, MC, VI.

SOME UNITS

Phone: (850)769-7400

HOLIDAY INN SELECT

Motor Inn

All Year   1P: $89-$129   XP: $10   F19
Location: SR 77, just n of jct US 231. 2001 N Cove Blvd 32405. Fax: 850/763-3828. **Facility:** 173 units. Some whirlpool units. 6 stories, interior corridors. **Terms:** package plans. **Amenities:** extended cable TV, voice mail, irons, hair dryers. **Leisure Activities:** heated pool, saunas, whirlpool, jogging, exercise room. **Guest Services:** valet laundry. **Business Services:** meeting rooms. **Cards:** AE, CB, DI, DS, JC, MC, VI.

SOME UNITS

Phone: (850)769-0000

HOWARD JOHNSON INN

Motel

3/1-3/31   1P: $85   2P: $110   XP: $10   F12
4/1-9/4   1P: $56-$66   2P: $70-$80   XP: $10   F12
12/1-2/28 & 9/5-11/30   1P: $50-$60   2P: $60-$70   XP: $10   F12
Location: On US 98, 0.8 mi e of Hathaway Bridge. 4601 W Hwy 98 32401. Fax: 850/769-3472. **Facility:** On the bay. 80 units. 1-3 stories (no elevator), exterior corridors. **Amenities:** extended cable TV. **Leisure Activities:** boat dock. **Business Services:** meeting rooms. **Cards:** AE, DI, DS, MC, VI.

SOME UNITS

Phone: (850)785-0222

LA QUINTA INN & SUITES

SAVE

Motel

All Year   1P: $49-$69   2P: $49-$69
Location: Jct US 231 and CR 390A. 1030 E 23rd St 32405. Fax: 850/914-0027. **Facility:** 119 units. Some suites. *Bath:* combo or shower only. 6 stories, interior corridors. **Terms:** small pets only. **Amenities:** extended cable TV, video games, voice mail, irons, hair dryers. **Leisure Activities:** heated pool, whirlpool, exercise room. **Guest Services:** [ECP] meal plan available, coin laundry. **Business Services:** meeting rooms. **Cards:** AE, DI, DS, MC, VI.

SOME UNITS

Phone: (850)914-0022

SLEEP INN

SAVE

Motel

4/1-9/4   1P: $79-$125   2P: $89-$150   XP: $10   F12
12/1-2/28 & 9/5-11/30   1P: $59-$79   2P: $69-$89   XP: $10   F12
Location: On US 98, 0.5 mi e of Hathaway Bridge. 5126 W Hwy 98 32401. Fax: 850/785-9545. **Facility:** 82 units. *Bath:* shower only. 2 stories, interior corridors. **Terms:** open 12/1-2/28 & 4/1-11/30, cancellation fee imposed. **Amenities:** *Some:* irons, hair dryers. **Guest Services:** [ECP] meal plan available. **Business Services:** meeting rooms. **Cards:** AE, CB, DI, DS, JC, MC, VI.

SOME UNITS

FEE

Phone: (850)763-7777

SUPER 8 MOTEL

Motel

3/1-9/30   1P: $50-$80   2P: $55-$85
10/1-11/30   1P: $35-$50   2P: $38-$53
12/1-2/28   1P: $35-$50   2P: $38-$53   XP: $5   F17
Location: Just n of jct US 98. 207 Hwy 231 N 32405. Fax: 850/763-9154. **Facility:** Near Panama City Mall. 63 units. 2 stories, interior/exterior corridors. **Terms:** small pets only ($10 extra charge). **Amenities:** extended cable TV, safes. **Cards:** AE, CB, DI, DS, MC, VI.

SOME UNITS

FEE

Phone: (850)784-1988

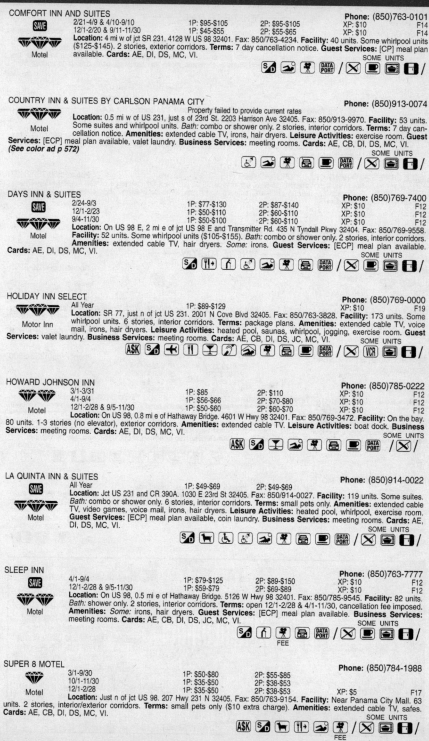

——— **WHERE TO DINE** ———

HOUSE OF CHAN
Chinese
Dinner: $6-$16   **Phone:** 850/769-9404
Location: 1 mi e of bridge on US 98. 4425 W Hwy 98 32401. **Hours:** 4 pm-11 pm, Fri & Sat-midnight. Closed: 11/22. **Features:** casual dress; carryout; cocktails & lounge. Chinese entrees are the focus with a few American offerings. Enjoy the bay view and order from the cart rolled out of an immaculate kitchen by the friendly wait staff. Five soups and numerous entrees make this tempting menu difficult to choose from.
Cards: AE, DS, MC, VI.

——— *The following restaurants have not been evaluated by AAA but are listed for your information only.* ———

JP'S FOOD & BREW
[fyi]   **Phone:** 850/769-3711
Not evaluated. **Location:** 4701 US 98W. **Features:** Specializing in steaks, seafood and homemade pasta. Moderate prices.

UNCLE ERNIE'S BAYFRONT GRILL & BREWHOUSE
[fyi]   **Phone:** 850/763-8427
Not evaluated. **Location:** US 98 S, 0.5 mi w on US 98 Bus (Beck St), then just e on 12th Ave. 1151 Bayview Ave. **Features:** Specializing in steaks, seafood and pasta. In-house brewery. View of the bay; patio seating. Inexpensive to moderate prices.

PANAMA CITY BEACH pop. 4,100

——— **WHERE TO STAY** ———

ANDY'S MOTEL
Motel
                 Phone: 850/230-8999

6/1-9/15	2P: $115	XP: $5	F17
3/1-5/31	2P: $88	XP: $5	F17
9/16-11/30	2P: $85	XP: $5	F17
12/1-2/28	2P: $75	XP: $5	F17

Location: US 98 A, 1.5 mi s on Joan Ave, then 0.5 mi e. 8101 W Surf Dr 32408. Fax: 850/230-3723. **Facility:** Comfortable suites, many with oceanfront views. 25 units with kitchen. *Bath:* combo or shower only. 3 stories, exterior corridors. **Terms:** 7 day cancellation notice. **Leisure Activities:** heated pool, beach, swimming. **Guest Services:** coin laundry. **Cards:** AE, MC, VI.

BEACHCOMBER BY THE SEA
[AAA] [SAVE]
Suite Motel
               Phone: (850)233-3600

5/25-8/11	1P: $129-$179	2P: $129-$179	XP: $10	F17
3/2-5/24	1P: $99-$129	2P: $99-$129	XP: $10	F17
8/12-11/30	1P: $49-$99	2P: $49-$99	XP: $10	F17
12/1-3/1	1P: $49-$79	2P: $49-$79	XP: $10	F17

Location: Jct SR 79 and US 98, beachside. 17101 Front Beach Rd 32413. Fax: 850/233-3622. **Facility:** Located on the oceanfront. Fenced pool located just steps away from the beach. Spacious units. All units oceanfront with balcony. 96 units. Some whirlpool units ($99-$199). *Bath:* combo or shower only. 8 stories, exterior corridors. **Terms:** check-in 4 pm, package plans. **Amenities:** extended cable TV, irons, hair dryers. **Leisure Activities:** heated pool, whirlpool, beach, swimming, fee for water sports and lounge chairs, game room. **Guest Services:** [ECP] meal plan available, coin laundry. **Business Services:** meeting rooms. **Cards:** AE, DS, MC, VI. **Special Amenities: free continental breakfast and free newspaper.**
(See color ad below)

BEACH TOWER RESORT MOTEL
Motel
     Property failed to provide current rates   **Phone:** 850/235-0089
Location: US 98, exit D, just e. 12001 Front Beach Rd 32407 (PO Box 9227, 32417). Fax: 850/235-2025. **Facility:** Located on the ocean. Spacious units. All units with balcony and oceanview. 48 units, 36 with kitchen. 7 stories, exterior corridors. **Terms:** check-in 4 pm, 10 day cancellation notice-fee imposed, weekly & monthly rates available. **Amenities:** extended cable TV. **Leisure Activities:** heated pool, beach, swimming, beach accessory rentals in season. **Cards:** AE, DS, MC, VI.

BEST WESTERN CASA LOMA

Motel

2/25-9/10 Wkly   1P: $119-$169   2P: $119-$169
12/1-2/24 & 9/11-11/30 Wkly   1P: $69-$89   2P: $69-$89

Phone: (850)234-1100

Location: US 98A, 3.2 mi sw of jct CR 392. 13615 Front Beach Rd 32413 (PO Box 18049, 32407). Fax: 850/234-0864. **Facility:** Located on the ocean front. A large pool deck with the ocean just behind. Spacious units. All units oceanfront balcony. 101 units, 47 with kitchen. *Bath:* combo or shower only. 3 stories (no elevator), exterior corridors. **Terms:** check-in 4 pm, weekly & monthly rates available. **Amenities:** extended cable TV. **Leisure Activities:** heated pool, beach, swimming, exercise room. **Cards:** AE, CB, DI, DS, MC, VI.

SOME UNITS

ASK ⊞ 🏊 🎦 🖨 / ✖ ▭ ▭ 🛠 /
         FEE

DAYS INN

Motel

2/24-9/9   1P: $129-$169   2P: $129-$169
9/10-10/31   1P: $89-$109   2P: $89-$109
12/1-2/23 & 11/1-11/30   1P: $79-$89   2P: $79-$89

Phone: (850)233-3333

Location: US 98A, 2.5 mi sw of jct CR 392. 12818 Front Beach Rd 32407. Fax: 850/233-9568. **Facility:** 188 units, 28 with kitchen. 7 stories, exterior corridors. **Terms:** check-in 4 pm, 3 day cancellation notice, weekly & monthly rates available. **Amenities:** extended cable TV, voice mail. **Dining:** Spacious oceanfront units with balcony. **Leisure Activities:** whirlpool, beach, swimming. **Cards:** AE, DI, DS, MC, VI. **Special Amenities: free continental breakfast and free room upgrade (subject to availability with advanced reservations).**

SOME UNITS

🆂 🅳 ⊞ 🏊 🎦 🖨 / ✖ ▭ 🛠 /
         FEE

EDGEWATER BEACH RESORT

Condominium

5/24-8/30   1P: $164-$295   2P: $194-$348
3/1-5/23   1P: $147-$260   2P: $165-$301
8/31-11/30   1P: $140-$251   2P: $165-$296
12/1-2/28   1P: $89-$142   2P: $102-$161

Phone: (850)235-4044

Location: US 98A, 1.3 mi sw of jct CR 392. 11212 Front Beach Rd 32407. Fax: 850/233-7591. **Facility:** Spacious one-, two- and three-bedroom apartments. Some with ocean view, some with golf course view. All with balcony or patio. A large pool area with view of the ocean. 510 units with kitchen. 252 two-bedroom units and 63 three-bedroom units. Some suites. 2-12 stories, exterior corridors. **Terms:** check-in 4 pm, 3 day cancellation notice-fee imposed, monthly rates available, $3 service charge, pets on premises. **Amenities:** extended cable TV, voice mail, irons, hair dryers. **Leisure Activities:** 11 pools (10 heated), whirlpools, beach, swimming, children's program, exercise room, shuffleboard. *Fee:* sailboats, golf-9 holes, 11 tennis courts (6 lighted). **Guest Services:** [AP], [BP] & [CP] meal plans available, gift shop, complimentary laundry. **Business Services:** conference facilities. **Cards:** AE, DI, DS, MC, VI.

⊞ ⊞ 🍴 🍸 🏊 🎣 🎦 🖨 ▭ 🛠
FEE

HOLIDAY INN SUNSPREE RESORT

Phone: (850)234-1111

(AAA) [SAVE]

Hotel

2/24-4/21	1P: $252	2P: $252	XP: $15	F19
4/22-9/2	1P: $197	2P: $197	XP: $15	F19
12/1-2/23 & 9/3-11/30	1P: $83	2P: $83	XP: $15	F19

Location: US 98A, 1.1 mi sw of jct CR 392. 11127 Front Beach Rd 32407. Fax: 850/235-1907. **Facility:** Located on the oceanfront. All units with balcony have pool and beach view. 340 units. Some whirlpool units. 15 stories, exterior corridors. **Terms:** check-in 4 pm, 3 day cancellation notice-fee imposed. **Amenities:** extended cable TV, safes, irons, hair dryers. **Dining:** restaurant, 6:30 am-11 & 5-10 pm; grill service for lunch, in season; seasonal entertainment, $7-$17, cocktails. **Leisure Activities:** heated pool, sauna, whirlpools, steamroom, beach, swimming, sailboating, children's program, social program, exercise room. *Fee:* paddleboats, scuba diving/snorkeling & equipment, beach watersports, golf-8 holes, 9 hole par 3, lighted driving range. **Guest Services:** gift shop, coin laundry. **Business Services:** meeting rooms. **Cards:** AE, CB, DI, DS, JC, MC, VI. **Special Amenities:** free local telephone calls and free newspaper.
(See color ad p 725)

SOME UNITS

MARRIOTT'S BAY POINT RESORT VILLAGE

Phone: (850)236-6000

Resort

2/12-7/31	1P: $189-$219	2P: $189-$219	XP: $20	F17
1/1-2/11 & 8/1-11/30	1P: $139-$169	2P: $139-$169	XP: $20	F17
12/1-12/31	1P: $129-$159	2P: $129-$159	XP: $20	F17

Location: 0.5 mi w of bridge on US 98, 2 mi s on CR 3031, 1.8 mi e on Magnolia Beach Rd following signs. 4200 Marriott Dr 32408. Fax: 850/233-1308. **Facility:** Located on 1,100 acres. Every unit has a scenic view from the patio or balcony of the bay or the wildlife sanctuary. The units offer a soft color scheme for a soothing feel. 350 units. Some suites. 5 stories, interior/exterior corridors. **Parking:** valet. **Terms:** check-in 4 pm, 10 day cancellation notice-fee imposed, package plans. **Amenities:** dual phone lines, voice mail. **Leisure Activities:** 4 pools (1 indoor, 3 heated), wading pool, whirlpools, beach, swimming, fishing, charter fishing, children's program in season, exercise room. *Fee:* boats, sailboats, windsurfing, marina, waterskiing, scuba diving & equipment, snorkeling, golf-36 holes, 4 lighted tennis courts, bicycles. **Guest Services:** [BP] meal plan available, gift shop, area transportation, valet laundry. *Fee:* massage. **Business Services:** conference facilities, administrative services, fax. **Cards:** AE, CB, DI, DS, JC, MC, VI.

SOME UNITS

MOONSPINNER CONDOMINIUM

Phone: 850/234-8900

Condominium

5/27-8/17 Wkly	2P: $1140-$1550
3/1-5/26 Wkly	2P: $940-$1200
8/18-11/30 Wkly	2P: $70-$950
12/1-2/28 Wkly	2P: $700-$940

Location: Jct US 98, 3.5 mi s on CR 3031, then e. 4425 Thomas Dr 32408. Fax: 850/233-0719. **Facility:** Two- and three-bedroom individually decorated units located on the beach. All with balcony and ocean view. 120 units with kitchen. 89 two-bedroom units and 31 three-bedroom units. Some suites. 8 stories, exterior corridors. **Terms:** age restrictions may apply, 3 day cancellation notice-fee imposed, daily & monthly rates available, pets on premises. **Amenities:** extended cable TV, irons. *Some:* CD players. **Leisure Activities:** wading pool, whirlpool, beach, swimming, 2 lighted tennis courts, exercise room, shuffleboard, game room. **Guest Services:** complimentary laundry. **Cards:** MC, VI.

SOME UNITS

RAMADA LIMITED

Phone: (850)234-1700

(AAA) [SAVE]

Motel

2/24-9/9	1P: $129-$169	2P: $129-$169
9/10-10/31	1P: $89-$99	2P: $89-$99
12/1-2/23 & 11/1-11/30	1P: $79-$89	2P: $79-$89

Location: US 98, 2.7 mi sw of jct CR 392. 12907 Front Beach Rd 32407. Fax: 850/235-2700. **Facility:** Located on the ocean. A large pool area surrounded by tropical foilage. One pool with manmade cliffs and waterfall. All units with a balcony area and view of the ocean. Spacious units. 147 units. *Bath:* combo or shower only. 4 stories, exterior corridors. **Terms:** check-in 4 pm, 3 day cancellation notice. **Amenities:** extended cable TV, voice mail. **Dining:** poolside bar & grill, cocktails. **Leisure Activities:** 2 pools (1 heated), whirlpool, beach, swimming. **Guest Services:** [ECP] meal plan available, coin laundry. **Business Services:** meeting rooms. **Cards:** AE, CB, DI, DS, MC, VI. **Special Amenities:** free continental breakfast and free newspaper.

SOME UNITS

SUNSET INN

Motel

Phone: 850/234-7370

5/24-9/3	1P: $65-$120	2P: $65-$120	XP: $5	F
3/1-5/23	1P: $60-$95	2P: $60-$95	XP: $5	F
12/1-2/28 & 9/4-11/30	1P: $55-$85	2P: $55-$85	XP: $5	F

Location: US 98A, 1.5 mi s on Joan Ave, then 0.5 mi e. 8109 Surf Dr 32408. Fax: 850/234-7370. **Facility:** Located on the ocean. Some units with ocean front view. Comfortable units. 62 units. 18 two-bedroom units, 44 efficiencies and 8 units with kitchen. *Bath:* combo or shower only. 2 stories, exterior corridors. **Terms:** 7 day cancellation notice-fee imposed, weekly rates available. **Amenities:** extended cable TV. **Leisure Activities:** heated pool, beach, swimming. **Guest Services:** coin laundry. **Cards:** AE, DS, JC, MC, VI. *(See color ad p 726)*

SUPER 8 MOTEL

Motel

Phone: (850)234-7334

3/2-5/1	1P: $109-$129	2P: $109-$129
5/2-9/15	1P: $79-$89	2P: $79-$89
12/1-3/1 & 9/16-11/30	1P: $29-$39	2P: $29-$39

Location: 1 mi sw of jct CR 392. 11004 Front Beach Rd 32407. Fax: 850/233-5508. **Facility:** Across highway from Gulf Beach. 96 units. 5 stories, exterior corridors. **Terms:** check-in 4 pm, 3 day cancellation notice. **Amenities:** extended cable TV. **Guest Services:** [CP] meal plan available. **Cards:** AE, CB, CB, DI, DS, MC, VI.

SOME UNITS

WHERE TO DINE

ANGELO'S STEAK PIT

Steak & Seafood

Dinner: $12-$23

Phone: 850/234-2531

Location: 3 mi w of bridge on US 98A. 9527 W Hwy 98A (Front Beach Rd) 32407. **Hours:** Open 3/12-9/30; 4:30 pm-10 pm. Closed: 10/1-3/11 & Sun. **Features:** casual dress; children's menu; carryout; cocktails & lounge. "Big Gus," the restaurant's 20-foot, 10-ton resident steer, welcomes diners to come on in, where they'll find a casual, family atmosphere. Flavorful hickory-broiled steaks, chicken, seafood and homemade key lime pie make for an enticing menu. **Cards:** AE, DS, MC, VI.

BOAR'S HEAD RESTAURANT

Seafood

Dinner: $14-$26

Phone: 850/234-6628

Location: 0.3 mi w of jct SR 78, on US 98. 17290 Front Beach Rd 32413. **Hours:** 4:30 pm-9 pm, Fri & Sat-10 pm. Closed: 11/22, 12/20-12/27. **Features:** casual dress; children's menu; carryout; cocktails & lounge; a la carte. This quiet, rustic spot offers many seafood and steak entrees, and appeals to those who recognize good value. The eager-to-please staff aims for professional service. Try fried shrimp served with sweet potatoes, green beans, and a scrumptious dessert. **Cards:** AE, DI, DS, MC, VI.

HAMILTON'S RESTAURANT

Seafood

Dinner: $11-$19

Phone: 850/234-1255

Location: Jct Thomas Dr. 5711 N Lagoon Dr 32408. **Hours:** 5 pm-10 pm. **Features:** casual dress; children's menu; carryout; cocktails & lounge. Taste the zesty flavor of feta cheese in the shrimp Christo entree or the decadent chocolate sweetness of mud pie while you gaze out over the scenic lagoon. Hardwood floors and stained glass windows help to give the restaurant a romantic feel. **Cards:** AE, DS, MC, VI.

The following restaurant has not been evaluated by AAA but is listed for your information only.

ALL AMERICAN DINER

[fyi]

Phone: 850/235-2443

Not evaluated. **Location:** 10590 W US 98. **Features:** '50s style diner. Inexpensive.

PEMBROKE PINES — *See Fort Lauderdale p. 386.*

PENSACOLA pop. 58,200

WHERE TO STAY

BEST WESTERN VILLAGE INN

Motel

Phone: (850)479-1099

5/27-9/3	1P: $61-$80	2P: $61-$80	XP: $5	F12
3/2-5/26	1P: $54-$72	2P: $54-$72	XP: $5	F12
12/1-3/1 & 9/4-11/30	1P: $54-$63	2P: $54-$63	XP: $5	F12

Location: I-10, exit 5, 0.8 mi n. 8240 N Davis Hwy 32514. Fax: 850/479-9320. **Facility:** Opposite West Florida Hospital. 142 units, 46 with kitchen. Some suites ($63-$80). *Bath:* combo or shower only. 3 stories, interior/exterior corridors. **Guest Services:** valet laundry. **Business Services:** meeting rooms. **Cards:** AE, CB, DI, DS, JC, MC, VI. **Special Amenities:** free continental breakfast and free local telephone calls.

SOME UNITS

COMFORT INN-NAS CORRY

Motel

Phone: (850)455-3233

3/1-9/30	1P: $59-$70	2P: $59-$70	XP: $6	F18
12/1-2/28 & 10/1-11/30	1P: $55-$70	2P: $55-$70	XP: $6	F18

Location: Just n of jct US 98 and SR 292. 3 New Warrington Rd 32506. Fax: 850/453-3445. **Facility:** At entrance to Corry Field. 101 units. 2-3 stories (no elevator), exterior corridors. **Terms:** check-in 4 pm, cancellation fee imposed, pets ($25 extra charge). **Amenities:** extended cable TV, voice mail. *Some:* irons, hair dryers. **Dining:** entertainment. **Guest Services:** coin laundry. **Business Services:** meeting rooms. **Cards:** AE, CB, DI, DS, MC, VI. **Special Amenities:** free continental breakfast and free local telephone calls.

SOME UNITS

FEE

DAYS INN NORTH

Phone: 850/476-9090

AAA SAVE

Motel

5/1-7/31	1P: $49-$69	2P: $54-$74	XP: $10 F15
12/1-4/30 & 8/1-11/30	1P: $49	2P: $49-$59	XP: $7 F15

Location: I-10, exit 3A, 0.3 mi s on US 29. 7051 Pensacola Blvd 32505. Fax: 850/476-9090. **Facility:** 80 units. 2 stories, interior corridors. **Terms:** 7 day cancellation notice, pets ($9 extra charge). **Amenities:** extended cable TV, safes. **Leisure Activities:** exercise room. **Guest Services:** coin laundry. **Cards:** AE, CB, DI, DS, JC, MC, VI. **Special Amenities:** free local telephone calls and free room upgrade (subject to availability with advanced reservations).

SOME UNITS

FAIRFIELD INN BY MARRIOTT

Phone: 850/484-8001

Motel

All Year   1P: $60-$66

Location: I-10, exit 5, just sw. 7325 N Davis Hwy 32514. Fax: 850/484-6008. **Facility:** Near University Mall. 63 units. *Bath:* combo or shower only. 3 stories, interior corridors. **Amenities:** extended cable TV. **Leisure Activities:** heated pool. **Guest Services:** [CP] & [ECP] meal plans available, valet laundry. **Cards:** AE, CB, DI, DS, JC, MC, VI.

SOME UNITS

HAMPTON INN UNIVERSITY

Phone: (850)477-3333

AAA SAVE

Motel

6/2-8/12	1P: $69-$83	2P: $79-$89
3/2-6/1	1P: $65	2P: $75
12/1-3/1 & 8/13-11/30	1P: $65	2P: $69

Location: I-10, exit 5, just sw; at University Mall entrance. 7330 Plantation Rd 32504. Fax: 850/477-8163. **Facility:** Shady grounds at University Mall. 124 units. 3 stories, interior corridors. **Amenities:** extended cable TV, voice mail, irons, hair dryers. **Leisure Activities:** pool privileges. **Guest Services:** [CP] & [ECP] meal plans available, valet laundry. **Business Services:** meeting rooms. **Cards:** AE, CB, DI, DS, JC, MC, VI.

SOME UNITS

HOLIDAY INN EXPRESS

Phone: (850)476-7200

AAA SAVE

Motel

All Year   1P: $62   2P: $62

Location: I-10, exit 3, 1.3 mi s on US 29. 6501 Pensacola Blvd 32505. Fax: 850/476-1277. **Facility:** At Car City. 214 units. *Bath:* combo or shower only. 2 stories, exterior corridors. **Amenities:** extended cable TV, voice mail, irons, hair dryers. **Leisure Activities:** exercise room. **Guest Services:** [ECP] meal plan available, airport transportation-Pensacola, coin laundry. **Business Services:** meeting rooms. **Cards:** AE, CB, DI, DS, MC, VI.

SOME UNITS

HOLIDAY INN-UNIVERSITY MALL

Phone: 850/474-0100

AAA SAVE

Motor Inn

6/1-8/31	1P: $79-$94	XP: $10 F18
4/1-5/31	1P: $74-$79	XP: $10 F18
12/1-3/31 & 9/1-11/30	1P: $69-$74	XP: $10 F18

Location: I-10, exit 5, just s University Mall entrance. 7200 Plantation Rd 32504. Fax: 850/477-9821. **Facility:** Shaded grounds with large courtyard area. 152 units. *Bath:* combo or shower only. 2 stories, exterior corridors. **Terms:** cancellation fee imposed. **Amenities:** extended cable TV, voice mail, irons, hair dryers. **Dining:** restaurant, 6 am-2 & 5-10 pm, Sun-9 pm, $9-$18, cocktails, entertainment. **Guest Services:** valet and coin laundry. **Business Services:** meeting rooms. **Cards:** AE, CB, DI, DS, JC, MC, VI.

SOME UNITS

HOSPITALITY INN

Phone: (850)477-2333

Motel

All Year   1P: $55-$75

Location: I-10, exit 3A, 0.5 mi s on US 29. 6900 Pensacola Blvd 32505. Fax: 850/479-3575. **Facility:** 124 units. Some suites. 1 story, interior/exterior corridors. **Terms:** 3 day cancellation notice, weekly & monthly rates available, pets ($25 extra charge, in limited rooms). **Amenities:** extended cable TV. *Some:* hair dryers. **Leisure Activities:** exercise room. **Guest Services:** [CP] & [ECP] meal plans available, valet and coin laundry. **Business Services:** meeting rooms. **Cards:** AE, CB, DI, DS, MC, VI.

SOME UNITS

HOSPITALITY INN

Phone: (850)453-3333

Motel

All Year   1P: $72-$90   2P: $95

Location: 4 mi w on US 90. 4910 Mobile Hwy 32506. Fax: 850/455-6008. **Facility:** 80 units. 1 story, interior/exterior corridors. **Terms:** cancellation fee imposed, weekly & monthly rates available. **Amenities:** extended cable TV. **Guest Services:** [CP] & [ECP] meal plans available, coin laundry. **Cards:** AE, CB, DI, DS, MC, VI.

SOME UNITS

LA QUINTA INN

Phone: (850)474-0411

SAVE

Motel

All Year   1P: $55-$75   2P: $55-$75

Location: I-10, exit 5, just n on SR 291. 7750 N Davis Hwy 32514-7557. Fax: 850/474-1521. **Facility:** Near University Mall. 130 units. Some suites. *Bath:* combo or shower only. 3 stories, exterior corridors. **Terms:** small pets only. **Amenities:** video games, voice mail. *Some:* hair dryers. **Guest Services:** [CP] meal plan available, coin laundry. **Cards:** AE, CB, DI, DS, MC, VI.

SOME UNITS

THE PENSACOLA GRAND HOTEL
▼▼▼▼   All Year   1P: $95   2P: $105
Hotel
Phone: (850)433-3336
XP: $10   F18
Location: Jct I-110 and US 98. 200 E Gregory St 32501. Fax: 850/432-7572. **Facility:** In restored 1912 train station. Units and suites in attached modern structure. Across from Civic Center. 212 units. Some suites ($250-$408) and whirlpool units. 15 stories, interior corridors. **Terms:** small pets only ($50 extra charge). **Amenities:** extended cable TV, voice mail, irons, hair dryers. **Dining:** 1912 The Restaurant, see separate listing. **Leisure Activities:** heated pool, exercise room. **Guest Services:** gift shop, valet laundry. **Business Services:** conference facilities, administrative services, PC, fax. **Cards:** AE, CB, DI, DS, MC, VI.
SOME UNITS
ASK ⑤Ⓓ ➕ 🐾 ⑪ ⛾ 🛥 🎥 🖨 💻 🔌 / ✕ VCR 📶 🛗 /

RAMADA INN BAYVIEW
ⒶⒶⒶ SAVE
▼▼▼▼
Motor Inn
5/15-8/31   1P: $72   2P: $78
12/1-5/14   1P: $64-$70   2P: $70
9/1-11/30   1P: $64   2P: $70
Phone: (850)477-7155
XP: $6   F18
XP: $6   F18
XP: $6   F18
Location: I-10, exit 6, just sw on US 90. 7601 Scenic Hwy 32504. Fax: 850/477-7155. **Facility:** 150 units. Some suites ($94-$100). 2 stories, interior corridors. **Terms:** package plans, small pets only. **Amenities:** extended cable TV, video games, voice mail, irons, hair dryers. **Dining:** restaurant, 6 am-1 & 6-10 pm, $8-$15, cocktails, entertainment. **Leisure Activities:** whirlpool, exercise room. **Guest Services:** [BP] meal plan available, valet laundry. **Business Services:** meeting rooms. **Cards:** AE, CB, DI, DS, JC, MC, VI. **Special Amenities:** free continental breakfast and free newspaper. *(See color ad below)*
SOME UNITS
⑤Ⓓ ➕ 🐾 ⑪ ⛾ 🛥 🎥 🖨 💻 🔌 / ✕ 📶 🛗 /
FEE

RAMADA INN NORTH
ⒶⒶⒶ SAVE
▼▼▼▼
Motor Inn
5/16-9/10   1P: $56   2P: $68
12/1-5/15 & 9/11-11/30   1P: $52   2P: $64
Phone: (850)477-0711
XP: $8   F18
XP: $8   F18
Location: I-10, exit 3, 1.2 mi s on US 29. 6550 N Pensacola Blvd 32505. Fax: 850/479-1977. **Facility:** At Car City. 106 units. Some whirlpool units ($113). 2 stories, exterior corridors. **Terms:** 3 day cancellation notice-fee imposed, pets ($25-$50 extra charge). **Amenities:** extended cable TV, voice mail. *Some:* irons, hair dryers. **Dining:** restaurant, 11 am-10 pm, $10-$15, cocktails. **Leisure Activities:** wading pool. **Guest Services:** [ECP] meal plan available, coin laundry. **Business Services:** meeting rooms. **Cards:** AE, CB, DI, DS, JC, MC, VI. **Special Amenities:** free continental breakfast and free local telephone calls.
SOME UNITS
⑤Ⓓ ➕ 🐾 ⑪ ⛾ 🛥 🖨 🔌 / ✕ 📶 🛗 /

RAMADA LIMITED
▼▼▼
Motel
5/26-8/20   1P: $74   2P: $79
4/1-5/25   1P: $64   2P: $69
12/1-3/31 & 8/21-11/30   1P: $54   2P: $59
Phone: (850)944-0333
XP: $6   F17
XP: $6   F17
XP: $6   F17
Location: I-10, exit 2A, just sw. 8060 Lavalle Way 32526. Fax: 850/941-1961. **Facility:** 93 units. 2 stories, exterior corridors. **Terms:** weekly & monthly rates available, package plans, small pets only ($50 deposit). **Amenities:** extended cable TV. **Guest Services:** [CP] & [ECP] meal plans available, coin laundry. **Business Services:** meeting rooms. **Cards:** AE, CB, DI, DS, MC, VI.
SOME UNITS
ASK ⑤Ⓓ 🐾 ⑪➕ 🛥 🖨 🔌 / ✕ 📶 🛗 /
FEE

RED ROOF INN
▼▼ ▼▼
Motel
5/25-11/30   1P: $44-$89   2P: $48-$93
12/1-5/24   1P: $44-$79   2P: $48-$83
Phone: (850)478-4499
XP: $4   F18
XP: $4   F18
Location: I-10, exit 3A, 0.5 mi s. 6919 Pensacola Blvd 32505. Fax: 850/857-1250. **Facility:** 120 units. 2 stories, interior corridors. **Terms:** 14 day cancellation notice. **Amenities:** extended cable TV. **Guest Services:** [CP] meal plan available, coin laundry. **Cards:** AE, CB, DI, DS, MC, VI.
SOME UNITS
ASK ⑤Ⓓ 🐾 ⑪➕ 🛥 🖨 🔌 / ✕ 📶 🛗 /

RED ROOF INN
ⒶⒶⒶ SAVE
▼▼▼▼
Motel
3/1-9/7   1P: $39-$49   2P: $47-$57
12/1-2/28 & 9/8-11/30   1P: $39-$45   2P: $45-$53
Phone: (850)476-7960
XP: $8   F18
XP: $6   F18
Location: I-110, exit 5, just s at University Mall entrance. 7340 Plantation Rd 32504. Fax: 850/479-4706. **Facility:** At University Mall. 108 units. 2 stories, exterior corridors. **Terms:** small pets only. **Amenities:** video games. **Cards:** AE, CB, DI, DS, MC, VI. **Special Amenities:** free local telephone calls and free newspaper.
SOME UNITS
🐾 ⑪➕ 🎥 🖨 🔌 / ✕ 📶 🛗 /
FEE

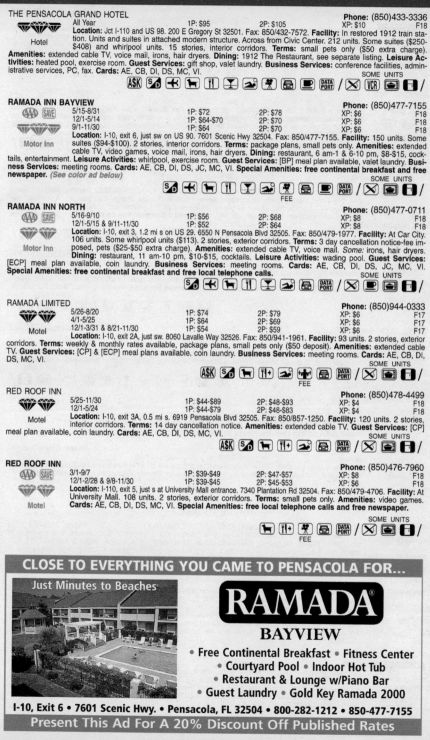

RESIDENCE INN BY MARRIOTT
Apartment

Phone: (850)479-1000

All Year 1P: $95-$140 2P: $95-$140
Location: I-10, exit 5, just sw at University Mall entrance. 7230 Plantation Rd 32504. **Fax:** 850/477-3399. **Facility:** Very well appointed suites with fireplace. 64 units with kitchen. 2 stories, exterior corridors. **Terms:** weekly & monthly rates available. **Amenities:** extended cable TV, voice mail, irons, hair dryers. **Leisure Activities:** whirlpool, sports court. **Guest Services:** [CP] & [ECP] meal plans available, valet and coin laundry. **Business Services:** meeting rooms. **Cards:** AE, CB, DI, DS, MC, VI.

SOME UNITS

RODEWAY INN
SAVE
Motel

Phone: (850)477-9150

All Year 1P: $40 2P: $50 XP: $5 F12
Location: I-10, exit 2, just ne. 8500 Pine Forest Rd 32534. **Fax:** 850/477-9150. **Facility:** 100 units. 2 stories, exterior corridors. **Terms:** 7 day cancellation notice, weekly & monthly rates available. **Amenities:** extended cable TV. *Some:* irons, hair dryers. **Guest Services:** [CP] meal plan available, coin laundry. **Cards:** AE, CB, DI, DS, MC, VI.

SOME UNITS

SHONEY'S INN & SUITES
AAA SAVE
Motel

Phone: (850)484-8070

5/25-9/6 1P: $56-$62 2P: $56-$62 XP: $5 F18
12/1-5/24 & 9/7-11/30 1P: $49-$54 2P: $49-$54 XP: $5 F18
Location: I-10, exit 5, just n on SR 291. 8080 N Davis Hwy 32514. **Fax:** 850/484-3853. **Facility:** Near University Mall. 115 units. 5 stories, interior corridors. **Terms:** pets ($17 extra charge, $50 deposit). **Amenities:** extended cable TV, voice mail. **Guest Services:** [ECP] meal plan available, coin laundry. **Business Services:** meeting rooms. **Cards:** AE, CB, DI, DS, MC, VI. **Special Amenities:** free continental breakfast and free local telephone calls.

SOME UNITS

SLEEP INN
SAVE
Motel

Phone: (850)941-0908

All Year 1P: $56-$70 2P: $56-$70 XP: $5 F18
Location: I-10, exit 2A, just sw. 2591 Wilde Lake Blvd 32526. **Fax:** 850/941-0760. **Facility:** 77 units. *Bath:* combo or shower only. 3 stories, interior corridors. **Amenities:** extended cable TV. *Some:* irons, hair dryers. **Guest Services:** [CP] meal plan available, coin laundry. **Business Services:** meeting rooms. **Cards:** AE, CB, DI, DS, JC, MC, VI.

SOME UNITS

TRAVELODGE INN & SUITES
Motel

Phone: (850)473-0222

5/1-9/5 1P: $43-$89 2P: $89 XP: $4 F18
12/1-4/30 & 9/6-11/30 1P: $39-$54 2P: $43-$59 XP: $5 F18
Location: I-10, exit 3A, just se on US 29. 6950 Pensacola Blvd 32505. **Fax:** 850/475-9358. **Facility:** 60 units. Some whirlpool units. 2 stories, interior corridors. **Terms:** 14 day cancellation notice. **Amenities:** extended cable TV. **Guest Services:** coin laundry. **Cards:** AE, CB, DI, DS, MC, VI.

SOME UNITS

The following lodging was either not evaluated or did not meet AAA rating requirements but is listed for your information only.

COMFORT INN
(fyi)
Motel

Phone: 850/476-8989

All Year 1P: $65-$120 2P: $70-$120 XP: $5 F16
Too new to rate. **Location:** I-10, westbound exit 2; eastbound exit 2B. 8714 Pine Forest Rd 32534. **Amenities:** 62 units, radios, coffeemakers, microwaves, refrigerators, pool. **Terms:** 10 day cancellation notice. **Cards:** AE, DI, DS, MC, VI.

WHERE TO DINE

1912 THE RESTAURANT
Regional American

Lunch: $6-$7 Dinner: $11-$19 Phone: 850/433-3336

Location: Jct I-110 and US 98; in The Pensacola Grand Hotel. 200 E Gregory St 32501. **Hours:** 6:30 am-2 & 5-10 pm. **Reservations:** suggested. **Features:** casual dress; cocktails & lounge. Inside a historic 1912 train depot, this casual restaurant is decorated throughout with period antiques. Although most people visit to sample from a good variety of fresh seafood specialties, you'll find other tasty entrees, such as seared chicken. **Cards:** AE, DI, DS, MC, VI.

GROUPER SEAFOOD & STEAK RESTAURANT
AAA
Seafood

Lunch: $5-$8 Dinner: $10-$18 Phone: 850/438-3141

Location: On US 98 at west end of Bay Bridge. 830 E Gregory St 32501. **Hours:** 11 am-11 pm, Sun from 10 am. **Closed:** 1/1, 12/25. **Features:** casual dress; Sunday brunch; children's menu; early bird specials; senior's menu; carryout; cocktails & lounge. Stuffed flounder is the house specialty, with Italian and Greek dishes, steaks and sandwiches also served. The dinner menu is available at lunch, and a location convenient to the business section of town makes this the perfect spot for business travelers. **Cards:** AE, DI, DS, MC, VI.

MCGUIRE'S IRISH PUB
AAA
Steak House

Lunch: $7-$11 Dinner: $9-$25 Phone: 850/433-6789

Location: Downtown; 0.3 mi e of civic center. 600 E Gregory St 32501. **Hours:** 11 am-2 am. **Closed:** 12/25. **Features:** casual dress; children's menu; cocktails & lounge; entertainment. Here is a pleasant surprise in a unique wine cellar atmosphere. After a hearty welcome from the staff, start with a chicken, bean and corn eggroll in a delicious avocado sauce; then feast on steak, seafood and an exceptional variety of large hamburgers. **Cards:** AE, DI, DS, MC, VI.

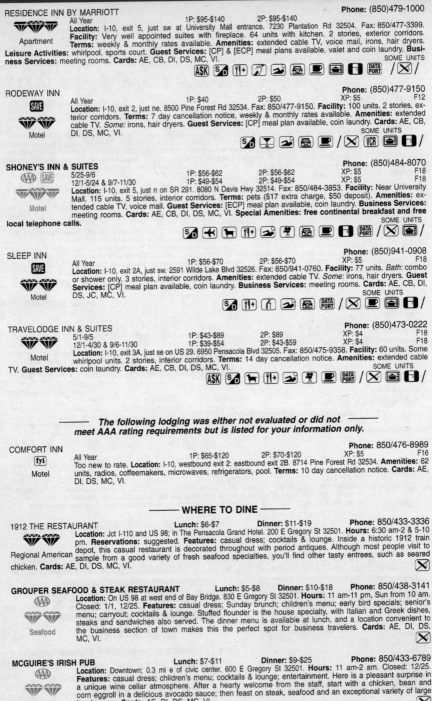

MESQUITE CHARLIE'S STEAKS & SEAFOOD **Lunch:** $4-$6 **Dinner:** $8-$16 **Phone:** 850/434-0498
Location: I-110, exit 5, 1.5 mi w on Brent Ln, 0.8 mi n. 5901 North W St 32505. **Hours:** 11 am-10 pm, Fri & Sat-11 pm. Closed: 12/25. **Features:** casual dress; children's menu; carryout; cocktails. Round up the family and head to this casual restaurant, where the flavor of the West is evident in everything from the charcoal-grilled steaks to the late 1900s decor. Seafood is also a must. Cattle and deer heads, antiques and bronze sculptures convey the mood. **Cards:** AE, DS, MC, VI.

Steak & Seafood

THE OYSTER BAR **Lunch:** $5-$23 **Dinner:** $6-$23 **Phone:** 850/455-3925
Location: 3.5 mi w on US 98. 709 N Navy Blvd 32507. **Hours:** 11 am-10 pm, Fri & Sat-11 pm. Closed major holidays; also Tues. **Features:** casual dress; children's menu; carryout; cocktail lounge; beer & wine only. The attractive, well-coordinated decor, which revolves around the sea, enhances your experience in this large and busy restaurant. Seasonal ingredients give the New Orleans-style seafood gumbo a snappy kick. The extensive menu also features steaks. **Cards:** AE, DI, DS, MC, VI.

Seafood

PEG LEG PETE'S OYSTER BAR **Lunch:** $10-$14 **Dinner:** $10-$14 **Phone:** 850/932-4139
Location: US 98, 1.5 mi w. 1010 Fort Pickens Rd 32561. **Hours:** 11 am-1 am. Closed: 11/22, 12/24, 12/25. **Features:** casual dress; children's menu; carryout; cocktails. Plastic serving baskets do not detract from the enjoyment of this tasty cuisine. Cajun influences can be found in the seafood, steak and pasta entrees. A shrimp po'boy overflows with an ample portion of shrimp on a big, fresh bun. **Cards:** AE, DS, MC, VI.

Seafood

THE SCREAMING COYOTE **Lunch:** $5-$10 **Dinner:** $5-$10 **Phone:** 850/435-9002
Location: Downtown; corner of Gregory. 196 N Palafox 32501. **Hours:** 11 am-9:30 pm, Fri & Sat-11 pm. Closed: 11/22, 12/25; also Sun. **Features:** casual dress; beer & wine only; street parking. For a touch of the hot stuff that will keep you 'screaming' try this popular local Mexican style eatery. From mild to hot with a range of 8 toppings the salsa bar certainly adds spice to life and never mind the twist of lime in the beer. Spicy cajun crawfish or crabmeat gives a new twist to a Latino menu. Made from scratch, local produce is part of the act and vegetarians are certainly not left out in the cold. Friendly and fun, modest setting with modest prices to match. Smoke free premises. **Cards:** AE, DS, MC, VI.

Mexican

SKOPELOS ON THE BAY **Lunch:** $6-$12 **Dinner:** $14-$23 **Phone:** 850/432-6565
Location: US 90/Scenic Hwy, e, continuation of Cervantes. 670 Scenic Hwy 32503. **Hours:** 5 pm-10:30 pm, Fri also 11:30 am. Closed: 12/25; also Sun, Mon & 1/1-1/2. **Reservations:** suggested. **Features:** casual dress; children's menu; cocktails & lounge. Fresh vegetables and seafood are well-prepared and served to you in this bayfront dining room. Local patrons rave about the seafood, lamb, steak and veal choices including the tender roasted lamb accompanied by a traditional green jelly. **Cards:** AE, DS, MC, VI.

Seafood

The following restaurants have not been evaluated by AAA but are listed for your information only.

ANNIE'S ON THE LAKE **Phone:** 904/458-2550
[fyi] Not evaluated. **Location:** 9722 Hwy 98w 32506. **Features:** Dockside. Friendly service. Mostly seafood.

COFFEE CUP **Phone:** 850/432-7060
[fyi] Not evaluated. **Location:** 520 E Cervantes St. **Features:** Breakfast diner; old fashioned style establishment. Inexpensive.

JAMIE'S FRENCH RESTAURANT **Phone:** 850/434-2911
[fyi] Not evaluated. **Location:** 424 E Zarragossa 32501. **Features:** Located in a cottage built circa 1884. Award winning restaurant and wine list. Provencial style French cuisine.

PENSACOLA BEACH pop. 3,900

--- WHERE TO STAY ---

BEACHSIDE RESORT & CONFERENCE CENTER **Phone:** (850)932-5331

5/16-8/31	1P: $109-$169	2P: $109-$169
3/1-5/15	1P: $89-$139	2P: $89-$139
9/1-11/30	1P: $69-$99	2P: $69-$99
12/1-2/28	1P: $59-$89	2P: $59-$89

Motor Inn
Location: SR 399, just e of traffic light. 14 Via De Luna Dr 32561. Fax: 850/932-3011. **Facility:** 100 units. *Bath:* combo or shower only. 4 stories, interior corridors. **Terms:** check-in 4 pm, 3 day cancellation notice. **Amenities:** extended cable TV, irons, hair dryers. **Dining:** restaurant, 6:30 am-10 pm, $9-$16, cocktails. **Leisure Activities:** heated pool, wading pool, beach, swimming. **Guest Services:** valet and coin laundry. **Business Services:** conference facilities. **Cards:** AE, CB, DI, DS, MC, VI. **Special Amenities:** free local telephone calls. *(See color ad p 732)* SOME UNITS

BEST WESTERN PENSACOLA BEACH **Phone:** (850)934-3300

	1P	2P	XP
5/2-9/5	1P: $131-$158	2P: $134-$161	XP: $10	F18
2/14-5/1 & 9/6-11/30	1P: $104-$113	2P: $107-$116	XP: $10	F18
12/1-2/13	1P: $65-$74	2P: $68-$77	XP: $10	F18

Motel
Location: 0.5 mi e on SR 399. 16 Via De Luna 32561. Fax: 850/934-4366. **Facility:** Large, well-equipped units on Gulf Beach. 123 units. 3 stories, exterior corridors. **Terms:** package plans. **Amenities:** voice mail, irons, hair dryers. **Leisure Activities:** 2 pools, beach, swimming, playground. **Guest Services:** [CP] meal plan available, valet and coin laundry. **Business Services:** meeting rooms. **Cards:** AE, DI, DS, JC, MC, VI. **Special Amenities:** free room upgrade and preferred room (each subject to availability with advanced reservations). SOME UNITS

CLARION SUITES RESORT & CONVENTION CENTER

Phone: (850)932-4300

(AAA) (SAVE)

WWWW

Suite Motel

5/1-9/3	1P: $127-$178	2P: $127-$178	XP: $10 F17
9/4-11/30	1P: $84-$140	2P: $84-$140	XP: $10 F17
3/1-4/30	1P: $94-$134	2P: $94-$134	XP: $10 F17
12/1-2/28	1P: $84-$114	2P: $84-$114	XP: $10 F17

Location: On SR 399, just e. 20 Via DeLuna 32561. Fax: 850/934-9112. **Facility:** On Gulf Beach. 86 units. Some suites. *Bath:* combo or shower only. 2 stories, exterior corridors. **Terms:** 3 day cancellation notice-fee imposed, package plans. **Amenities:** extended cable TV, irons, hair dryers. **Leisure Activities:** beach, swimming. **Guest Services:** [ECP] meal plan available, valet and coin laundry. **Business Services:** meeting rooms. **Cards:** AE, CB, DI, DS, JC, MC, VI. **Special Amenities:** free continental breakfast.

SOME UNITS

(icons) FEE

COMFORT INN PENSACOLA BEACH

Phone: (850)934-5400

(SAVE)

WWWW

Motel

5/16-9/10	1P: $109-$179	2P: $109-$179	XP: $10 F18
3/1-5/15	1P: $89-$139	2P: $89-$139	XP: $10 F18
9/11-11/30	1P: $69-$119	2P: $69-$119	XP: $10 F18
12/1-2/28	1P: $69-$109	2P: $69-$109	XP: $10 F18

Location: Just off SR 399. 40 Fort Pickens Rd 32561. Fax: 850/932-7210. **Facility:** On Santa Rosa Sound, across from Gulf Beach. Most units have a gulf or sound view. Comfortable units. 100 units. *Bath:* combo or shower only. 4 stories, exterior corridors. **Terms:** 3 day cancellation notice, package plans. **Amenities:** extended cable TV, voice mail, hair dryers. *Some:* irons. **Leisure Activities:** heated pool. **Guest Services:** [CP] & [ECP] meal plans available, valet and coin laundry. **Business Services:** meeting rooms. **Cards:** AE, CB, DI, DS, MC, VI.

SOME UNITS

(icons) FEE

HAMPTON INN PENSACOLA BEACH

Phone: (850)932-6800

(SAVE)

WWWW

Motel

5/18-9/2	1P: $129-$169	2P: $135-$175	XP: $6 F18
3/1-5/17	1P: $89-$139	2P: $95-$145	XP: $6 F18
9/3-11/30	1P: $89-$129	2P: $95-$135	XP: $6 F18
12/1-2/28	1P: $79-$99	2P: $85-$105	XP: $6 F18

Location: Center; SR 399. Two Via DeLuna 32561. Fax: 850/932-6833. **Facility:** All units have gulf or sound view, and are large and airy. Attractively furnished with tasteful decor. Designated smoking area. 181 units. Some suites ($199-$299). *Bath:* combo or shower only. 4 stories, interior corridors. **Terms:** 3 day cancellation notice, weekly & monthly rates available, package plans. **Amenities:** voice mail, irons, hair dryers. **Leisure Activities:** 2 heated pools, beach, children's program in summer, exercise room. *Fee:* paddleboats. **Guest Services:** [ECP] meal plan available, valet and coin laundry. **Business Services:** meeting rooms. **Cards:** AE, CB, DI, DS, JC, MC, VI.

SOME UNITS

(icons)

——— WHERE TO DINE ———

FLOUNDERS CHOWDER & ALE HOUSE   **Lunch:** $6-$14   **Dinner:** $6-$19   **Phone:** 850/932-2003

Steak & Seafood

Location: Just e of Quietwater Beach Boardwalk. 800 Quietwater Beach 32561. **Hours:** 11 am-midnight, Fri & Sat-2 am. Closed: 11/22, 12/25. **Features:** children's menu; carryout; cocktails & lounge. On Santa Rosa Sound, the restaurant is known for its friendly service and generous portions of such dishes as blackened tuna, stuffed flounder and eye-watering barbecue shrimp. The three-layer key lime pie will leave you with serious pucker power. **Cards:** AE, CB, DI, DS, MC, VI.

JUBILEE RESTAURANT   **Dinner:** $15-$23   **Phone:** 850/934-3108

Seafood

Location: On Quietwater Beach Boardwalk. 400 Quietwater Beach Rd 32561. **Hours:** 6 pm-10 pm, Sun 9 am-2 & 6-10 pm. **Reservations:** suggested; Sun-Thurs. **Features:** casual dress; children's menu; carryout; cocktails & lounge. View the stunning sunset on Santa Rosa Sound as you dine on absolutely delicious entrees like New York strip poivre crusted with black peppercorns, red wine and brandy in a creamy mushroom sauce. A superb chocolate creme caramel brings a sweet ending. **Cards:** AE, DI, DS, MC, VI.

PERRY pop. 7,200

——— WHERE TO STAY ———

BEST BUDGET INN   **Phone:** (850)584-6231

Motel

All Year   1P: $39   2P: $44   XP: $5   F13
Location: US 19 and 98, 0.4 mi s of jct US 221. 2220 US 19 S 32347. Fax: 850/584-3700. **Facility:** 61 units. 2 stories, exterior corridors. **Terms:** 14 day cancellation notice, pets ($3 extra charge). **Amenities:** extended cable TV. **Cards:** AE, CB, DI, DS, MC, VI. **Special Amenities: free continental breakfast and free local telephone calls.**

SOME UNITS

THE CHAPARRAL INN   **Phone:** (850)584-2441

Motel

All Year   1P: $38   2P: $42   XP: $4   F12
Location: US 19 and 98, 0.3 mi s of jct US 221. 2159 S Byron Butler Pkwy 32347. **Facility:** Good sized rooms with nice decor. 24 units. 1 story, exterior corridors. **Guest Services:** coin laundry. **Cards:** AE, DS, MC, VI. **Special Amenities: free local telephone calls and preferred room (subject to availability with advanced reservations).**

SOME UNITS

——— *The following lodging was either not evaluated or did not meet AAA rating requirements but is listed for your information only.* ———

HAMPTON INN   **Phone:** 850/223-3000

[fyi]

Motel

All Year   1P: $64-$70   2P: $72-$76
Too new to rate, opening scheduled for August 2000. **Location:** 1 mi s of jct US 221 and 19 (Byron Butler Pkwy). 2399 S Byron Butler Pkwy 32348 (PO Box 111). Fax: 850/838-2969. **Amenities:** 60 units, radios, coffeemakers, refrigerators, pool. **Terms:** check-in 4 pm, 3 day cancellation notice. **Cards:** AE, DS.

——— WHERE TO DINE ———

POUNCEY'S RESTAURANT   **Lunch:** $4-$6   **Dinner:** $8-$12   **Phone:** 850/584-9942

American

Location: US 19 and 98, 0.3 mi s of jct US 221. 2186 S Byron Butler Pkwy 32347. **Hours:** 6 am-10 pm. Closed: 11/22, 12/25. **Features:** casual dress; a la carte. Simple but scrumptious describes the menu offerings at this family-style diner. Walk in, seat yourself and enjoy from BLT sandwiches, seafood specials to fresh vegetables and chocolate meringue pie. The dishes leave your taste buds satisfied.

PINELLAS PARK —*See Tampa Bay p. 871.*

PLANTATION —*See Fort Lauderdale p. 387.*

PLANT CITY —*See Tampa Bay p. 871.*

POMPANO BEACH —*See Fort Lauderdale p. 389.*

PONCE INLET pop. 1,700

——— WHERE TO DINE ———

INLET HARBOR MARINA & RESTAURANT   **Lunch:** $6-$9   **Dinner:** $9-$23   **Phone:** 904/767-3266

American

Location: 0.5 mi w of S Atlantic Ave, 4.8 mi s of jct Dunlawton. 133 Inlet Harbor Rd 32127. **Hours:** 11 am-3:30 & 4-10 pm. Closed: 11/22, 12/25. **Features:** casual dress; early bird specials; cocktails & lounge; entertainment. It's hard to say what's most notable at this waterfront restaurant; the scenic views of birds, boats and the nearby sandbar or the savory flavors that go into the many steak, chicken and seafood dishes. Dine on the deck for maximum ambience. **Cards:** AE, DS, MC, VI.

PONTE VEDRA BEACH —*See Jacksonville p. 449.*

PORT CHARLOTTE pop. 46,200

—— WHERE TO STAY ——

DAYS INN OF PORT CHARLOTTE
Phone: 941/627-8900

[SAVE]

Motel

2/11-4/1	1P: $89-$99	2P: $94-$104	XP: $5 F17
12/25-2/10	1P: $47-$79	2P: $57-$89	XP: $5 F17
12/1-12/24 & 4/2-11/30	1P: $42-$54	2P: $47-$64	XP: $5 F17

Location: On US 41. 1941 Tamiami Tr 33948. Fax: 941/743-8503. **Facility:** 126 units. 3 stories, exterior corridors. **Terms:** small pets only. **Amenities:** extended cable TV. **Leisure Activities:** heated pool, exercise room. **Guest Services:** coin laundry. **Business Services:** meeting rooms. **Cards:** AE, CB, DI, DS, MC, VI.

SOME UNITS

HAMPTON INN
Phone: (941)627-5600

[SAVE]

Motel

2/2-4/1	1P: $89-$109	2P: $99-$119	XP: $10 F18
12/24-2/1	1P: $69-$84	2P: $74-$94	XP: $10 F18
12/1-12/23 & 4/2-11/30	1P: $59-$69	2P: $69-$79	XP: $10 F18

Location: I-75, exit 31, just e on Kings Hwy, just s. 24480 Sand Hill Blvd 33983. Fax: 941/627-6883. **Facility:** Property overlooks a small lake teeming with fish and wildlife. Nicely appointed units. 73 units. 3 stories, interior corridors. **Amenities:** extended cable TV, voice mail, irons. **Leisure Activities:** heated pool. **Guest Services:** [ECP] meal plan available, coin laundry. **Business Services:** administrative services. *Fee:* PC. **Cards:** AE, CB, DI, DS, MC, VI.

SOME UNITS

THE LITCHFIELD INN
Phone: (941)625-4181

(AAA) [SAVE]

Motel

1/16-4/30	2P: $89-$149	XP: $5 F18
12/1-1/15 & 10/16-11/30	2P: $69-$99	XP: $5 F18
5/1-10/15	2P: $59-$89	XP: $5 F18

Location: Center on US 41, just s of jct Harbor Blvd. 3400 Tamiami Tr 33952. Fax: 941/629-1740. **Facility:** 105 units. *Bath:* combo or shower only. 2 stories, interior/exterior corridors. **Terms:** check-in 4 pm, weekly & monthly rates available, package plans, small pets only ($6 extra charge). **Amenities:** extended cable TV. *Some:* irons. **Leisure Activities:** heated pool, travel agency. **Guest Services:** [ECP] meal plan available, coin laundry. **Business Services:** meeting rooms. **Cards:** AE, DI, DS, JC, MC, VI. **Special Amenities:** free local telephone calls and free room upgrade (subject to availability with advanced reservations).

SOME UNITS

FEE FEE

PORT CHARLOTTE MOTEL
Phone: (941)625-4177

Motel

1/1-3/31	1P: $80-$100	2P: $80-$100	XP: $10 F13
4/1-4/30	1P: $60-$70	2P: $60-$70	XP: $10 F13
12/1-12/31	1P: $55-$65	2P: $55-$65	XP: $10 F13
5/1-11/30	1P: $39-$60	2P: $39-$60	XP: $10 F13

Location: Center; on US 41, just s of jct Harbor Blvd. 3491 Tamiami Tr 33952. Fax: 941/624-5591. **Facility:** 53 units, 6 with efficiency. 2 stories, exterior corridors. **Terms:** 7 day cancellation notice, weekly & monthly rates available. **Amenities:** extended cable TV. **Leisure Activities:** heated pool, wading pool, whirlpool, boat dock, fishing, shuffleboard. **Guest Services:** coin laundry. **Cards:** DI, DS, JC, MC, VI.

SOME UNITS

—— WHERE TO DINE ——

CAP'N & THE COWBOY
Lunch: $6-$11 **Dinner:** $11-$22 **Phone:** 941/743-3969

Steak & Seafood

Location: I-75 S, exit 31, 1.6 mi w on Kings Hwy; in the Maple Leaf Plaza. 2200 Kings Hwy 33980. **Hours:** 11 am-9 pm, Fri & Sat-10 pm. Closed major holidays; also Mon. **Features:** casual dress; children's menu; carryout; cocktails. A favorite spot of the locals, this laid-back restaurant has a menu of such tasty dishes as coconut fried shrimp, fresh grouper, yellowfin tuna and a signature filet topped with Jack Daniels, mushrooms, onions and Monterey Jack cheese. **Cards:** AE, DI, DS, MC, VI.

PORT ORANGE pop. 35,300 (See map p. 270; index p. 273)

—— WHERE TO DINE ——

AUNT CATFISH'S ON THE RIVER
Lunch: $7-$15 **Dinner:** $9-$29 **Phone:** 904/767-4768 (30)

American

Location: On SR A1A, just e of US 1; on the Intracoastal Waterway at west end of Port Orange Bridge Cswy (Dunlawton Ave). 4009 Halifax DR 32127. **Hours:** 11:30 am-9:30 pm, Fri & Sat-10 pm, Sun 9 am-9 pm. Closed: 12/25. **Reservations:** suggested. **Features:** Sunday brunch; children's menu; early bird specials; senior's menu; salad bar; cocktails. Southern hospitality, a waterfront view and a down-home menu complete with grits and catfish can be found at this bustling, casual eatery. Fresh local seafood, chicken, steak, ribs and an extensive salad bar make any wait during peak hours worthwhile. **Cards:** AE, DS, MC, VI.

SINDBAD'S RESTAURANT
Lunch: $5-$9 **Dinner:** $7-$18 **Phone:** 904/756-2921 (31)

Seafood

Location: Just w of A1A; "Down Under" Port Orange Bridge. 78 Dunlawton Ave 32127. **Hours:** 11:30 am-9 pm, Fri & Sat 11:30 am-10 pm, Sun 8 am-9 pm. Closed: Mon 9/7-1/1. **Reservations:** accepted. **Features:** children's menu; early bird specials; cocktails & lounge. Overlooking the Intercoastal Waterway, you will find pleasant casual dining in a contemporary setting. A khaki-clad staff serves an excellent variety of sandwiches, seafood, chicken, steak and ribs. For a light alternative, order the chicken Caesar salad. **Cards:** AE, CB, DI, MC, VI.

PORT RICHEY —See Tampa Bay p. 873.

PORT ST. LUCIE pop. 55,900

WHERE TO STAY

BEST WESTERN PORT ST. LUCIE SUITES **Phone:** (561)878-7600

AAA SAVE — Suite Motel

2/1-3/31	1P: $89-$129	2P: $89-$129	XP: $5	F17
12/1-1/31	1P: $59-$89	2P: $59-$89	XP: $5	F17
4/1-11/30	1P: $59-$79	2P: $59-$79	XP: $5	F17

Location: 0.5 mi s of Prima Vista Blvd, at Spanish Lakes Blvd. 7900 S US 1 34952. Fax: 561/340-0422. **Facility:** All units with separate living room. 98 units. 2 stories, exterior corridors. **Terms:** weekly & monthly rates available, package plans. **Amenities:** video games. **Leisure Activities:** heated pool, whirlpool. **Guest Services:** [CP] meal plan available, coin laundry. **Business Services:** meeting rooms. **Cards:** AE, CB, DI, DS, JC, MC, VI. **Special Amenities: early check-in/late check-out and free local telephone calls.**

SOME UNITS / FEE / FEE

HOLIDAY INN-PORT ST LUCIE **Phone:** (561)337-2200

Motor Inn

12/31-4/5	1P: $149-$169	2P: $149-$169	XP: $10	F18
12/1-12/30 & 4/6-11/30	1P: $69-$89	2P: $69-$89	XP: $10	F18

Location: US 1, 0.5 mi n of jct SR 716, Port St Lucie Blvd. 10120 S Federal Hwy, Rt 1 34952. Fax: 561/335-7872. **Facility:** All units with wet bar. Many with separate living room. 142 units. Some suites ($89-$169) and whirlpool units ($129-$200). 5 stories, interior corridors. **Terms:** weekly rates available, package plans. **Amenities:** extended cable TV, voice mail, irons, hair dryers. **Leisure Activities:** heated pool, whirlpool, lagoon style pool with rock waterfall. **Guest Services:** [AP], [BP] & [MAP] meal plans available, valet and coin laundry. **Business Services:** meeting rooms, fax. **Cards:** AE, CB, DI, DS, MC, VI.

A$K DATA PORT / SOME UNITS / FEE / FEE

SHERATON'S PGA VACATION RESORT **Phone:** (561)460-5700

Condominium

All Year 2P: $89-$209

Location: 8702 Champions Way 34986. Fax: 561/460-5705. **Facility:** 42 units. 18 two-bedroom units, 12 efficiencies and 30 units with kitchen. Some whirlpool units. 3 stories, exterior corridors. **Terms:** check-in 4 pm, 3 day cancellation notice, package plans. **Amenities:** extended cable TV, voice mail, safes, irons, hair dryers. *Some:* CD players. **Leisure Activities:** heated pool, wading pool, whirlpool, golf-72 holes, playground. **Guest Services:** complimentary laundry. **Cards:** AE, CB, DI, DS, MC, VI. ***(See color ad below)***

A$K VCR DATA PORT

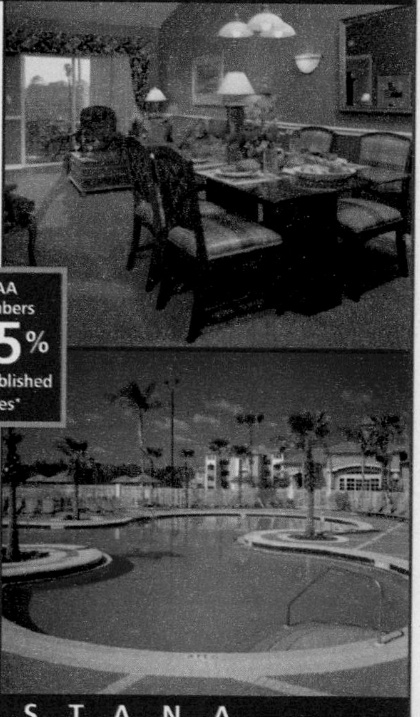

SPRINGHILL SUITES

▼▼▼▼

Suite Motel

1/1-3/31	1P: $129
12/1-12/31 & 4/1-11/30	1P: $79

Phone: (561)871-2929

Location: I-95, exit 63C. 2000 NW Courtyard Cir 34986. Fax: 561/871-0016. **Facility:** 105 units. *Bath:* combo or shower only. 4 stories, interior corridors. **Amenities:** dual phone lines, voice mail, irons, hair dryers. **Leisure Activities:** heated pool, whirlpool, exercise room. **Guest Services:** [ECP] meal plan available, valet and coin laundry. **Business Services:** meeting rooms. **Cards:** AE, CB, DI, DS, MC, VI.

SOME UNITS

(ASK) 🛡️ 👤 📶 📶 📶 📶 📹 📠 💻 📶 🛗 DATA PORT / ✗ /

───── WHERE TO DINE ─────

LE BRITTANY

▼▼▼ ▼▼▼

Continental

Dinner: $12-$25

Phone: 561-871-2231

Location: At jct US 1 and Prima Vista Blvd; in St. Lucie Shopping Center. 899A Prima Vista Blvd 34952. **Hours:** 4:30 pm-9 pm. Closed: Mon & 9/1-9/30. **Reservations:** suggested. **Features:** casual dress; early bird specials; beer & wine only. Fine home-style cooking with a French flair is what you'll get in this cozy restaurant. The chef/owner whips up tasty offerings, such as beef and vegetable soup and the scrumptious duck, served with chutney and a carrot-broccoli medley. **Cards:** MC, VI.

PUNTA GORDA pop. 10,700

───── WHERE TO STAY ─────

BEST WESTERN WATERFRONT INN

(AAA) [SAVE]

▼▼▼▼

Motor Inn

2/1-4/10	1P: $89-$104	2P: $99-$114	XP: $10	F18
1/1-1/31	1P: $82-$97	2P: $92-$107	XP: $10	F18
12/1-12/31 & 4/11-11/30	1P: $69-$84	2P: $79-$94	XP: $10	F18

Phone: (941)639-1165

Location: US 41 southbound, just s of Peace River Bridge. 300 Retta Esplanade 33950. Fax: 941/639-4752. **Facility:** On Peace River. Spacious units in tower. Some units with balcony or patio. 183 units. Some whirlpool units. 2-5 stories, interior corridors. **Terms:** check-in 4 pm, cancellation fee imposed, weekly & monthly rates available, package plans, pets ($25 extra charge). **Amenities:** voice mail, irons, hair dryers. **Dining:** restaurant, 6:30 am-9 pm, $9-$18. **Leisure Activities:** heated pool, whirlpool, boat dock, fishing. **Guest Services:** gift shop, coin laundry. **Business Services:** meeting rooms. **Cards:** AE, DI, DS, JC, MC, VI. **Special Amenities:** free local telephone calls. *(See color ad below)*

SOME UNITS

🛡️ 🐾 🍴 📶 📶 📶 📹 📠 💻 DATA PORT / ✗ 🛗 VCR 📶 🛗 /
　　　　　FEE　　　　　　　　　　　　　　FEE　FEE　FEE

DAYS INN PUNTA GORDA

[SAVE]

▼▼▼ ▼▼▼

Motel

2/15-4/14	1P: $83-$99	2P: $88-$104	XP: $5	F17
1/15-2/14	1P: $73-$94	2P: $78-$99	XP: $5	F17
4/15-11/30	1P: $51-$94	2P: $56-$99	XP: $5	F17
12/1-1/14	1P: $49-$94	2P: $54-$99	XP: $5	F17

Phone: (941)637-7200

Location: I-75, exit 28, just w. 26560 N Jones Loop Rd 33950. Fax: 941/639-0848. **Facility:** 74 units, 12 with kitchen. Some suites ($85-$150). 2 stories, exterior corridors. **Terms:** 3 day cancellation notice, weekly & monthly rates available. **Amenities:** extended cable TV. **Leisure Activities:** heated pool, whirlpool, playground. **Guest Services:** [CP] meal plan available, coin laundry. **Cards:** AE, CB, DI, DS, MC, VI.

SOME UNITS

🛡️ 🍴 📶 📶 📹 / ✗ 🛗 /

GILCHRIST BED & BREAKFAST INN

| | 1P: $95 | 2P: $95 | Phone: 941/575-4129 |

Historic Bed & Breakfast

1/1-4/30   1P: $95   2P: $95   XP: $10   F14
12/1-12/31 & 5/1-11/30   1P: $65-$75   2P: $65-$75   XP: $10   F14

Location: 0.5 mi w on Marion Ave, just n. 115 Gilchrist St 33950. **Fax:** 941/575-9666. **Facility:** Cozy turn-of-the-century home circa 1914; convenient location in downtown historic district, one block from Peace River. Carriage house or two rooms sharing a common area. 3 units, 1 with kitchen. *Bath:* combo or shower only. 1 story, interior/exterior corridors. **Terms:** 5 day cancellation notice-fee imposed, weekly & monthly rates available. **Amenities:** *Some:* voice mail, irons. **Leisure Activities:** whirlpool, bicycles. **Guest Services:** [CP] meal plan available. **Business Services:** meeting rooms. **Cards:** DS, MC, VI.

SOME UNITS

HOLIDAY INN HARBORSIDE

Motor Inn

4/16-11/30   1P: $79-$169   2P: $79-$169   XP: $10   F
12/21-4/15   1P: $99-$139   2P: $99-$139   XP: $10   F
12/1-12/20   1P: $89-$119   2P: $89-$119   XP: $10   F

Phone: (941)639-2167

Location: US 41, northbound lane; at Peace River Bridge. 33 Tamiami Tr 33950. **Fax:** 941/639-1707. **Facility:** On Peace River. Some units with balcony or patio, many riverfront. 100 units, 3 with kitchen. *Bath:* combo or shower only. 2 stories, interior corridors. **Terms:** cancellation fee imposed, weekly & monthly rates available. **Amenities:** extended cable TV, voice mail, irons, hair dryers. **Dining:** restaurant, 7 am-9:30 pm; live music Fri & Sat in lounge, $4-$15. **Leisure Activities:** heated pool, boat ramp, marina, fishing. **Guest Services:** coin laundry. **Business Services:** meeting rooms. **Cards:** AE, CB, DI, DS, MC, VI. **Special Amenities:** early check-in/late check-out and free local telephone calls.
(See color ad below)

SOME UNITS
FEE   FEE

MARINA INN

Condominium

12/18-4/30   2P: $150-$195   XP: $10   F12
12/1-12/17 & 5/1-11/30   2P: $89-$99   XP: $10   F12

Phone: 941/575-4488

Location: I-75, exit 28, 11.2 mi w on CR 765 (Burnt Store Rd); in Burnt Store Marina and Country Club. 3160 Matecumbe Key Rd 33955. **Fax:** 941/575-2363. **Facility:** All suites with king bed and sleeper sofa; tranquil location on gated resort complex with extensive grounds. Screened porches; some with balcony for marina or pool view. 5 units with washer/dryer. 40 units with kitchen. 5 two-bedroom units. 3 stories, interior corridors. **Terms:** 3 day cancellation notice-fee imposed, weekly & monthly rates available, package plans. **Amenities:** extended cable TV, irons. **Leisure Activities:** heated pool, sauna, marina, fishing, charter fishing. *Fee:* boats, boat dock, golf-27 holes, 4 lighted tennis courts, bicycles. **Guest Services:** gift shop, coin laundry. **Business Services:** meeting rooms. **Cards:** AE, DS, MC, VI.

SOME UNITS
FEE   FEE

──────── **WHERE TO DINE** ────────

CAPTAIN'S TABLE Lunch: $7-$11 Dinner: $17-$30 Phone: 941/637-1177
▼▼▼ **Location:** In Fisherman's Village; 1.5 mi w off Marion Ave. 1200 W Retta Esplanade 33951-1289. **Hours:** 11 am-9 pm, Fri & Sat-10 pm. Closed: 1/1. **Features:** casual dress; Sunday brunch; children's menu; carryout; Seafood salad bar; cocktails & lounge; a la carte, buffet. A lovely, scenic view of Charlotte Harbor and plenty of fresh seafood bring in the locals. The fisherman's platter spills over with whitefish, shrimp, mussels, scallops and fried rice. A lunch and dinner buffet offers seafood with nice crisp salads. **Cards:** AE, DS, MC, VI. ☒

SALTY'S HARBORSIDE RESTAURANT Lunch: $14-$37 Dinner: $14-$37 Phone: 941/639-3650
▼▼▼ **Location:** I-75, exit 28, 11.2 mi w on CR 765; in Burnt Store Marina and Country Club. 5000 Burnt Store Rd 33955. **Hours:** 11:30 am-3 & 5-9 pm, Sun 11:30 am-3 pm. Closed: Mon. **Features:** casual dress; Sunday brunch; Continental children's menu; cocktails & lounge. Beautiful harbor view of many luxurious boats and yachts. Cozy surroundings and nicely decorated restaurant with a welcoming atmosphere. Though service is casual, well prepared menu offerings are chef prepared and beautifully presented. The chicken marsala is a delight. Limited menu in lounge 3 pm-5 pm. **Cards:** AE, DS, MC, VI. ☒

QUINCY pop. 7,400

──────── **WHERE TO STAY** ────────

ALLISON HOUSE INN Phone: (850)875-2511
▼▼ All Year 1P: $70-$85 2P: $80-$95 XP: $10 F12
Location: Just e of town center; in historic district. 215 N Madison St 32351. Fax: 850/875-2511. **Facility:** 1843
Historic Bed Greek Revival home built by former Florida governor in historic neighborhood. Large, sunny units. Gracious
& Breakfast owners are well known for their homemade goodies, especially granola and biscotti. Smoke free premises. 5 units. *Bath:* combo or shower only. 2 stories, interior corridors. **Terms:** 14 day cancellation notice-fee imposed, small pets only (pet on premises). **Amenities:** extended cable TV, hair dryers. **Leisure Activities:** bicycles. **Guest Services:** [ECP] meal plan available. **Cards:** AE, DS, MC, VI. A$K S/D 🐾 ☒ 🖨

MCFARLIN HOUSE BED & BREAKFAST INN Phone: (850)875-2526
▼▼▼ All Year 2P: $85-$175 XP: $20
Location: Historic district, corner King and Love sts. 305 E King St 32351. Fax: 850/627-4703. **Facility:** 1895 Queen
Historic Bed Ann Victorian. Designated smoking area. 9 units. Some whirlpool units ($150-$175). *Bath:* combo, shower or
& Breakfast tub only. 4 stories (no elevator), interior corridors. **Terms:** check-in 4 pm, 14 day cancellation notice-fee imposed, package plans. **Guest Services:** [BP] meal plan available, area transportation. **Cards:** AE, DI, DS,
MC, VI. SOME UNITS
A$K S/D ✈ ☒ DATA PORT / VCR /

REDINGTON BEACH —See Tampa Bay p. 873.

REDINGTON SHORES —See Tampa Bay p. 874.

RIVER RANCH —See Orlando p. 701.

RIVERVIEW (HILLSBOROUGH COUNTY) —See Tampa Bay p. 874.

RIVIERA BEACH pop. 27,600 (See map p. 710; index p. 713)

──────── **WHERE TO STAY** ────────

RIVIERA BEACH MOTEL Phone: (561)844-1857 102
◆ Property failed to provide current rates
Location: On US 1; 0.3 mi n of jct SR A1A (Blue Heron Blvd). 3124 Broadway 33404-2324. Fax: 561/863-8877.
Motel **Facility:** Older exceptionally well-kept property. Some compact units. 18 units, 10 with kitchen. *Bath:* shower only. 1 story, exterior corridors. **Terms:** 14 day cancellation notice-fee imposed. **Amenities:** *Some:* safes
(fee). **Leisure Activities:** heated pool. **Guest Services:** coin laundry. **Cards:** AE, CB, DI, JC, MC, VI. SOME UNITS
🍴 🏊 🎞 💻 / ☒ VCR 🛗
FEE

SUPER 8 MOTEL WEST PALM BEACH/RIVIERA BEACH Phone: 561/848-1188 101
▼▼ ▼▼ 2/1-4/15 1P: $89 2P: $89 XP: $5 F16
12/1-1/31 & 11/16-11/30 1P: $69 2P: $69 XP: $5 F16
Motel 4/16-11/15 1P: $59 2P: $59 XP: $5 F16
Location: I-95, exit 55, just w. 4112 W Blue Heron Blvd 33404. Fax: 561/848-4583. **Facility:** 100 units. 2 stories, exterior corridors. **Terms:** 3 day cancellation notice. **Amenities:** extended cable TV. *Some:* hair dryers. **Leisure Activities:** heated pool. **Guest Services:** coin laundry. **Cards:** AE, DI, DS, MC, VI. SOME UNITS
A$K S/D 🍴 🏊 🎞 / ☒ 💻 📠 🛗

RUSKIN —See Tampa Bay p. 874.

SAFETY HARBOR —See Tampa Bay p. 875.

ST. AUGUSTINE &
ST. AUGUSTINE BEACH
ACCOMMODATIONS

1873-H

St. Augustine & St. Augustine Beach and Vicinity

This index helps you "spot" where approved accommodations are located on the corresponding detailed maps. Rate ranges are for comparison only and show the property's high season. Turn to the listing page for more detailed rate information and consult display ads for special promotions. Restaurant rate range is for dinner, unless only lunch (L) is served.

Spotter/Map Page Number	OA	ST. AUGUSTINE - Lodgings	Diamond Rating	Rate Range High Season	Listing Page
1 / above		Days Inn-West	▽▽	$49-$104	746
2 / above	AAA	Hampton Inn St. Augustine Outlet Center	▽▽▽	$69-$225 SAVE	746
3 / above	AAA	Ramada Limited St Augustine - see color ad p 742	▽▽	$69-$149 SAVE	750
4 / above	AAA	Best Western Inn - see color ad p 743	▽▽	$42-$125 SAVE	743
5 / above	AAA	Holiday Inn Express	▽▽▽	$60-$150 SAVE	748
6 / above	AAA	Radisson Ponce de Leon Golf & Conference Center Resort - see color ad p 750	▽▽▽	$89 SAVE	749
7 / above	AAA	Days Inn Historic	▽▽	$51-$115 SAVE	746
8 / above	AAA	Quality Inn Alhambra	▽▽▽	$69-$175 SAVE	749
10 / above	AAA	Hampton Inn Historic - see color ad p 747	▽▽▽	$65-$175 SAVE	746

Spotter/Map Page Number	OA	ST. AUGUSTINE - Lodgings (continued)	Diamond Rating	Rate Range High Season	Listing Page
11 / p. 739	AAA	**Best Western Historical Inn** - see color ad p 747	▽▽▽	$59-$150 [SAVE]	743
12 / p. 739	AAA	**Travelodge & Suites**	▽▽▽	$49-$54 [SAVE]	751
13 / p. 739		Clarion Inn Historic Downtown - see color ad p 745	▽▽	$59-$169	745
15 / p. 739	AAA	**Best Western Spanish Quarters Inn** - see color ad p 747	▽▽	$49-$150 [SAVE]	744
16 / p. 739		Casablanca Inn on the Bay	▽▽▽	Failed to provide	744
17 / p. 739	AAA	**Lion Inn**	▽▽	$50-$175 [SAVE]	748
18 / p. 739		Conch House Marina Resort	▽▽	$85-$110	746
19 / p. 739	AAA	**Scottish Inns**	▽	$37-$75 [SAVE]	750
20 / p. 739	AAA	**Casa de Suenos Bed & Breakfast**	▽▽▽	$120-$190 [SAVE]	744
22 / p. 739	AAA	**Alexander Homestead Bed & Breakfast**	▽▽▽	$125-$175 [SAVE]	743
23 / p. 739	AAA	**The Inn At Camachee Harbor**	▽▽▽	$69-$129 [SAVE]	748
24 / p. 739	AAA	**Casa de la Paz Bayfront Bed & Breakfast**	▽▽▽	$120-$250 [SAVE]	744
25 / p. 739	AAA	**Edgewater Inn** - see color ad p 746	▽▽	$42-$105 [SAVE]	746
26 / p. 739	AAA	**Monterey Inn** - see color ad p 748	▽	$45-$150 [SAVE]	749
27 / p. 739	AAA	**Centennial House Bed & Breakfast**	▽▽▽	$115-$225 [SAVE]	745
28 / p. 739		Cedar House Inn Victorian B & B	▽▽▽	$99-$129	745
29 / p. 739		Old City House Inn	▽▽▽	$79-$179	749
30 / p. 739		Casa De Solana Bed & Breakfast Inn	▽▽▽	$95-$229	744
31 / p. 739	AAA	**Anastasia Inn**	▽▽▽	$50-$110 [SAVE]	743
32 / p. 739		St Francis Inn	▽▽▽	$89-$195	751
33 / p. 739	AAA	**Bayfront Inn** - see color ad p 742	▽▽▽	$59-$135 [SAVE]	743
34 / p. 739		Bayfront Westcott House	▽▽▽	$135-$195	743
35 / p. 739	AAA	**Comfort Suites**	▽▽▽	$67-$97 [SAVE]	745
36 / p. 739		Sheraton's Vistana Resort at World Golf Village - see color ad p 750	▽▽▽	$79-$199	751
37 / p. 739		World Golf Village Renaissance Resort - see color ad p 751	▽▽▽	$109-$189	752
39 / p. 739		Hilton Garden Inn-St. Augustine Beach - see ad p 44	▽▽▽	$69-$199	748
40 / p. 739		Castle Garden Bed & Breakfast	▽▽	$65-$165	745
41 / p. 739		Casa Monica Hotel - see color ad p 744	▽▽▽	$149-$209	744
		ST. AUGUSTINE - Restaurants			
1 / p. 739		King's Head British Pub	▽	$4-$10	753
2 / p. 739		Jeff's Place	▽	$3-$8	753
3 / p. 739		Marty's Seafood & Steak House	▽	$6-$15	753
4 / p. 739		Harborside Cafe	▽	$4-$16	753
5 / p. 739	AAA	**Raintree Restaurant**	▽▽▽	$15-$29	753
6 / p. 739	AAA	**Barnacle Bill's Seafood House**	▽	$8-$16	752
7 / p. 739		Columbia Restaurant	▽▽	$10-$18	752
8 / p. 739		Tavern on the Bay	▽	$8-$17	753

Spotter/Map Page Number	OA	ST. AUGUSTINE - Restaurants (continued)	Diamond Rating	Rate Range High Season	Listing Page
⑨ / p. 739		Le Pavillon	◆◆◆	$14-$22	753
⑩ / p. 739		Gypsy Cab Co	◆◆	$9-$17	753
⑪ / p. 739		Cafe Alcazar	◆◆	$3-$9(L)	752
⑫ / p. 739	AAA	**Theos' Restaurant**	◆	$4-$6(L)	754
⑬ / p. 739		Cortesse's Bistro & Flamingo Room	◆◆	$11-$20	753
⑭ / p. 739		Denoel French Pastry Shop	◆	$5-$7(L)	753
⑮ / p. 739		Azalea's Cafe	◆	$4-$10(L)	752
⑯ / p. 739	AAA	**Creekside Dinery**	◆	$6-$14	753
⑰ / p. 739		The Conch House Restaurant and Lounge	◆◆	$12-$17	752
⑱ / p. 739		White Lion Restaurant	◆◆	$6-$18	754
⑲ / p. 739		95 Cordova	◆◆◆	$14-$25	752
⑳ / p. 739		A1A Ale Works Brewery and Restaurant	◆◆	$5-$10	752
		ST. AUGUSTINE BEACH - Lodgings			
㊻ / p. 739	AAA	**Econo Lodge** - see color ad p 742	◆◆	$54-$189 SAVE	754
㊼ / p. 739	AAA	**Days Inn-St. Augustine Beach** - see color ad p 747	◆◆◆	$69-$150 SAVE	754
㊾ / p. 739	AAA	**La Fiesta Oceanside Inn** - see color ad p 755	◆◆	$69-$259 SAVE	755
㊿ / p. 739	AAA	**Holiday Inn-St Augustine Beach**	◆◆◆	$110-$155 SAVE	755
(51) / p. 739		Ramada Limited, at the Beach	◆◆	$80-$140	755
(52) / p. 739	AAA	**Comfort Inn at St. Augustine Beach**	◆◆	$49-$139 SAVE	754
(53) / p. 739	AAA	**Best Western Ocean Inn**	◆◆	$59-$149 SAVE	754
(54) / p. 739		Hampton Inn-St. Augustine Beach	◆◆◆	$89-$199	754
		ST. AUGUSTINE BEACH - Restaurants			
㉚ / p. 739		Aruanno's Italian Restaurant	◆◆	$10-$18	756
㉜ / p. 739		Greenstreet's	◆	$2-$7(L)	756
㉝ / p. 739		The Oasis	◆	$4-$14	756
㉞ / p. 739	AAA	**Saltwater Cowboys**	◆◆	$5-$14	756
		VILANO BEACH - Lodgings			
(60) / p. 739	AAA	**Ocean Sands Motor Inn** - see color ad p 749	◆◆	$69-$99 SAVE	896
		VILANO BEACH - Restaurant			
㊵ / p. 739	AAA	**Fiddler's Green**	◆◆	$9-$18	896
		ELKTON - Lodgings			
(65) / p. 739		Comfort Inn St. Augustine	◆◆	$54-$189	306
		ELKTON - Restaurant			
㊿ / p. 739		Bunkers on the St. Johns County Golf Course	◆	$3-$6	306

ST. AUGUSTINE pop. 11,700 (See map p. 739; index p. 739)

------ WHERE TO STAY ------

ALEXANDER HOMESTEAD BED & BREAKFAST
Phone: (904)826-4147   22

AAA SAVE   All Year   1P: $125-$175   2P: $125-$175   XP: $15   F
▽▽▽▽▽   **Location:** Center; just s of Orange St. 14 Sevilla St 32084. Fax: 904/823-9503. **Facility:** Authentic Victorian home
Historic Bed   built in 1888 with many beautiful antiques and artwork. Two units with wood burning fireplace. Smoke free
& Breakfast   premises. 4 units. Some whirlpool units ($175). 2 stories, interior corridors. **Terms:** 7 day cancellation
notice-fee imposed, weekly rates available, pets on premises. **Amenities:** extended cable TV, hair dryers.
Leisure Activities: bicycles. **Guest Services:** [BP] meal plan available. **Cards:** AE, DI, DS, MC, VI.
Special Amenities: free local telephone calls and free newspaper.

SOME UNITS   ✈ ✕ 🖨 / VCR

ANASTASIA INN
Phone: (904)825-2879   31

AAA SAVE   All Year   1P: $50-$110   2P: $50-$110   XP: $4   D16
▽▽▽▽▽   **Location:** 0.3 mi s of Bridge of Lions on A1A. 218 Anastasia Blvd 32084. Fax: 904/825-2724. **Facility:** Very small
Motel   pool area. 23 units. **Bath:** combo or shower only. 2 stories, exterior corridors. **Terms:** cancellation fee im-
posed. **Amenities:** extended cable TV. **Guest Services:** [CP] meal plan available. **Business Services:** fax.
Cards: AE, DS, MC, VI.

SOME UNITS   S🅳 📶➕ ♿ 🏊 ⛵ ⊗ 🖨 💳 🖥 🛏 DATA PORT / ✕

BAYFRONT INN
Phone: (904)824-1681   33

AAA SAVE   All Year   2P: $59-$135   XP: $6
▽▽▽▽▽   **Location:** Center; just s of SR A1A and Bridge of Lions. 138 Avenida Menendez 32084. Fax: 904/829-8721.
Motel   **Facility:** Quiet location in the heart of historical area; overlooking bay. Units range from compact to spacious.
Designated smoking area. 39 units. **Bath:** combo or shower only. 1-2 stories, exterior corridors. **Terms:** 3 day
cancellation notice-fee imposed. **Amenities:** extended cable TV, hair dryers. **Leisure Activities:** small pool,
whirlpool. **Guest Services:** [CP] meal plan available. **Business Services:** fax. **Cards:** AE, DS, MC, VI.
Special Amenities: free local telephone calls and free newspaper. *(See color ad p 742)*

📶➕ ⛵ ✕ 🖨

BAYFRONT WESTCOTT HOUSE
Phone: (904)824-4301   34

▽▽▽▽▽   All Year   1P: $135-$195   2P: $135-$195   XP: $10
Historic Bed   **Location:** 1 blk s of The Bridge of Lions. 146 Avenida Menendez 32084-5049. Fax: 904/824-1502. **Facility:** Over-
& Breakfast   looking Matanzas Bay across street. Built circa 1890. Elegant Victorian furnishings. Designated smoking
area. 9 units. **Bath:** combo or shower only. 2 stories, interior/exterior corridors. **Parking:** street only.
Terms: age restrictions may apply, 7 day cancellation notice-fee imposed. **Amenities:** hair dryers. **Leisure**
Activities: bicycles. **Guest Services:** [BP] meal plan available. **Business Services:** fax. **Cards:** AE, DS, MC, VI.

ASK S🅳 📶➕ ✕ DATA PORT

BEST WESTERN HISTORICAL INN
Phone: (904)829-9088   11

AAA SAVE   2/2-9/1   1P: $59-$150   2P: $59-$150   XP: $6   F16
  12/1-2/1 & 9/2-11/30   1P: $49-$99   2P: $49-$99   XP: $6   F16
▽▽▽▽▽   **Location:** 0.5 mi s of jct SR 16 and US 1, n 6 blks from historic district. 2010 N Ponce de Leon Blvd 32084.
Motel   Fax: 904/829-6629. **Facility:** 39 units. 1 two-bedroom unit and 1 unit with kitchen. 2 stories, exterior corridors. **Terms:** 4 day cancellation notice. **Amenities:** hair dryers. **Leisure Activities:** whirlpool. **Guest Serv-**
ices: [BP] meal plan available, coin laundry. **Cards:** AE, CB, DI, DS, JC, MC, VI. **Special Amenities: free**
continental breakfast. *(See color ad p 747)*

SOME UNITS   S🅳 ⛵ 🖨 💳 / ✕ 🖥 🛏 /

BEST WESTERN INN
Phone: (904)829-1999   4

AAA SAVE   All Year   1P: $42-$110   2P: $49-$125   XP: $6   F12
▽▽▽▽▽   **Location:** I-95, exit 95, sw corner. 2445 SR 16 32092. Fax: 904/829-1999. **Facility:** 120 units. **Bath:** combo or
Motel   shower only. 2 stories, exterior corridors. **Terms:** pets ($6 extra charge). **Amenities:** safes. **Guest Services:**
[CP] meal plan available, coin laundry. **Business Services:** fax. **Cards:** AE, CB, DI, DS, JC, MC, VI.
Special Amenities: early check-in/late check-out and free room upgrade (subject to availability with
advanced reservations). *(See color ad below)*

SOME UNITS   S🅳 🐾 📶➕ ⛵ / ✕ /

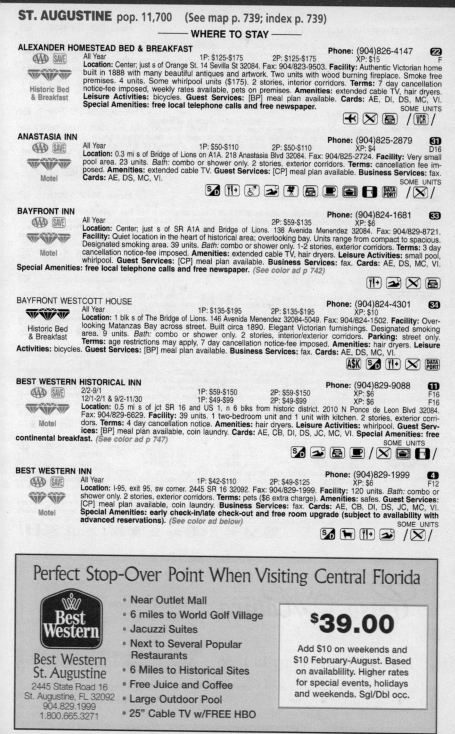

(See map p. 739)

BEST WESTERN SPANISH QUARTERS INN
Phone: (904)824-4457 🔟5️⃣
AAA SAVE · All Year · 1P: $49 · 2P: $150 · XP: $5 · F12
◆◆◆ · **Location:** Just w of San Marcos Ave, across from visitor's center. 6 Castillo Dr 32084. Fax: 904/829-8330.
Motel · **Facility:** Contemporary unit appointments. 40 units. 2 stories, exterior corridors. **Terms:** 30 day cancellation notice. **Amenities:** extended cable TV, irons, hair dryers. **Leisure Activities:** whirlpool. **Guest Services:** [ECP] meal plan available. **Business Services:** fax. **Cards:** AE, CB, DI, DS, JC, MC, VI. **Special Amenities:** free continental breakfast. *(See color ad p 747)* SOME UNITS

CASABLANCA INN ON THE BAY
Phone: (904)829-0928 🔟6️⃣
Property failed to provide current rates
◆◆◆◆ · **Location:** just n of Bridge of Lions; in historic district. 24 Avenida Menendez 32084. Fax: 904/829-1414. **Facility:** Verandas viewing river and historic district in a relaxed setting. Cottage house available. Designated smoking area. 20 units. Some whirlpool units. *Bath:* combo or shower only. 2 stories, interior/exterior corridors.
Bed & Breakfast
Terms: age restrictions may apply, 7 day cancellation notice-fee imposed. **Amenities:** extended cable TV. **Leisure Activities:** bicycles. **Guest Services:** [BP] meal plan available. **Business Services:** fax. **Cards:** AE, DS, MC, VI. SOME UNITS

CASA DE LA PAZ BAYFRONT BED & BREAKFAST
Phone: (904)829-2915 2️⃣4️⃣
AAA SAVE · All Year · 2P: $120-$250
◆◆◆ · **Location:** 0.3 mi n of Bridge of Lions on SR A1A. 22 Avenida Menendez 32084. Fax: 904/824-6269. **Facility:** Overlooking Matanzas Bay. Mediterranean revival home. One unit has a working fireplace. Smoke free premises.
Historic Bed & Breakfast · 6 units. *Bath:* combo or shower only. 3 stories (no elevator), interior/exterior corridors. **Terms:** age restrictions may apply, 7 day cancellation notice-fee imposed. **Amenities:** extended cable TV, hair dryers. **Guest Services:** [BP] meal plan available, complimentary evening beverages. **Business Services:** fax. **Cards:** DS, MC, VI. **Special Amenities:** free local telephone calls.

CASA DE SOLANA BED & BREAKFAST INN
Phone: (904)824-3555 3️⃣0️⃣
All Year · 2P: $95-$229
◆◆◆◆ · **Location:** In historic district; Aviles St at Cadiz St. 21 Aviles St 32084. Fax: 904/824-3316. **Facility:** Spanish Colonial house overlooking a courtyard. Most units with separate sleeping and parlor area. Loading and unloading zone on Aviles St. Smoke free premises. 4 units. 3 stories (no elevator), interior corridors. **Parking:** street only. **Terms:** age restrictions may apply, 7 day cancellation notice-fee imposed. **Amenities:** extended cable TV. **Guest Services:** [BP] meal plan available. **Business Services:** fax. **Cards:** AE, DS, MC, VI.
Historic Bed & Breakfast

CASA DE SUENOS BED & BREAKFAST
Phone: (904)824-0887 2️⃣0️⃣
All Year · 1P: $120-$190 · 2P: $120-$190 · XP: $15
◆◆◆ · **Location:** Center; corner of Saragossa St. 20 Cordova St 32084. Fax: 904/825-0074. **Facility:** Tastefully decorated units; some with fireplace. Designated smoking area. 6 units. Some whirlpool units ($160-$190). *Bath:* combo or shower only. 2 stories, interior/exterior corridors. **Terms:** age restrictions may apply, 14 day cancellation notice, weekly rates available, pets on premises. **Leisure Activities:** bicycles. **Guest Services:** [BP] meal plan available, complimentary evening beverages. **Business Services:** meeting rooms. **Cards:** DI, DS, MC, VI. **Special Amenities:** free local telephone calls and free newspaper. SOME UNITS
Bed & Breakfast

CASA MONICA HOTEL
Phone: (904)827-1888 4️⃣1️⃣
◆◆◆ · 2/1-5/31 & 9/1-11/30 · 1P: $149-$209 · 2P: $149-$209 · XP: $20 · F16
Historic Hotel · 12/1-1/31 & 6/1-8/31 · 1P: $139-$199 · 2P: $139-$199 · XP: $20 · F16
Location: Downtown; across from Lightner Musuem and Flagler College. 95 Cordova St 32084. Fax: 904/827-0426.
Facility: The grandeur of days gone by can once again be seen in this historic hotel originally built in 1888. Quaint cozy units have Spanish style furnishings adding to the ambience. 137 units. Some suites ($249-$599) and whirlpool units ($399). *Bath:* combo, shower or tub only. 5 stories, interior corridors. **Parking:** valet. **Terms:** check-in 4 pm, 3 day cancellation notice-fee imposed. **Amenities:** video games, voice mail, irons, hair dryers. **Dining:** 95 Cordova, see separate listing. **Leisure Activities:** heated pool, whirlpool, exercise room. *Fee:* bicycles. **Guest Services:** area transportation, valet laundry. **Business Services:** administrative services, PC, fax. **Cards:** AE, DI, DS, JC, MC, VI. *(See color ad below)* SOME UNITS

(See map p. 739)

CASTLE GARDEN BED & BREAKFAST
Phone: (904)829-3839 **40** D18
Historic Bed & Breakfast
All Year — 1P: $65-$165 — 2P: $65-$165 — XP: $20
Location: Downtown center; opposite Ripley's Believe It or Not Museum. 15 Shenandoah St 32084. Fax: 904/829-9049. **Facility:** Built in late 1800s as a carriage house for the mansion which now houses the museum across the street. Cozy units with period antiques. Smoke free premises. 6 units. Some whirlpool units ($115-$165). *Bath:* combo or shower only. 2 stories, interior corridors. **Terms:** age restrictions may apply, 7 day cancellation notice-fee imposed, weekly & monthly rates available, package plans. **Guest Services:** [BP] meal plan available. **Business Services:** fax. **Cards:** AE, DS, MC, VI.

CEDAR HOUSE INN VICTORIAN B & B
Phone: (904)829-0079 **28**
Historic Bed & Breakfast
All Year — 1P: $99-$129 — 2P: $99-$129 — XP: $35
Location: Just w of Lightner Museum, just s of King St via Granada. 79 Cedar St 32084-4311. Fax: 904/825-0916. **Facility:** 1893 Victorian home in historic district. Smoke free premises. 6 units. Some whirlpool units ($124-$169). 2 stories (no elevator), interior/exterior corridors. **Terms:** age restrictions may apply, 14 day cancellation notice-fee imposed, weekly & monthly rates available, package plans. **Amenities:** voice mail, irons, hair dryers. **Leisure Activities:** whirlpool, bicycles. **Guest Services:** [BP] meal plan available. **Business Services:** administrative services, fax. **Cards:** AE, DS, MC, VI.

CENTENNIAL HOUSE BED & BREAKFAST
Phone: 904/810-2218 **27**
Bed & Breakfast
All Year — 1P: $115-$225 — 2P: $115-$225
Location: Historic district; corner of Saragossa and Cordova. 26 Cordova St 32084. Fax: 904/810-1930. **Facility:** Comfortable and upscale units, some with fireplace. Smoke free premises. 7 units. Some whirlpool units ($140-$225). *Bath:* combo or shower only. 2 stories, interior/exterior corridors. **Terms:** age restrictions may apply, 7 day cancellation notice-fee imposed, package plans. **Amenities:** extended cable TV, hair dryers. **Guest Services:** [BP] meal plan available, complimentary evening beverages. **Business Services:** fax. **Cards:** AE, DI, MC, VI. **Special Amenities:** early check-in/late check-out and free local telephone calls.

CLARION INN HISTORIC DOWNTOWN
Phone: (904)824-3383 **13**
Motor Inn
2/9-9/5 — 1P: $59-$149 — 2P: $69-$169 — XP: $10 — F18
12/1-2/8 & 9/6-11/30 — 1P: $49-$89 — 2P: $59-$99 — XP: $10 — F18
Location: US 1, 1 mi n. 1300 Ponce de Leon Blvd 32084. Fax: 904/829-0668. **Facility:** Spanish style exterior. Guest units have been recently renovated in a contemporary style and are well equipped. Professional staff able to assist with guest needs. 102 units. 2 stories, exterior corridors. **Terms:** package plans, pets ($25 extra charge, small dogs only). **Amenities:** extended cable TV, voice mail, safes (fee), irons, hair dryers. **Leisure Activities:** game room. **Guest Services:** coin laundry. **Business Services:** meeting rooms. **Cards:** AE, CB, DI, DS, JC, MC, VI. *(See color ad below)*

COMFORT SUITES
Phone: (904)940-9500 **35**
Motel
2/1-3/31 — 1P: $67-$97 — 2P: $67-$97 — XP: $10 — F18
12/1-1/31 & 4/1-11/30 — 1P: $57-$87 — 2P: $57-$87 — XP: $10 — F18
Location: I-95, exit 95A, just e, then just s. 475 Commerce Lake Dr 32095. Fax: 904/940-9600. **Facility:** Short drive to World Golf Village. 162 units. 2 two-bedroom units. Some whirlpool units ($79-$99). *Bath:* combo or shower only. 6 stories, interior corridors. **Terms:** package plans. **Amenities:** extended cable TV, video games, hair dryers. **Leisure Activities:** 2 pools (1 heated, 1 indoor), whirlpool, exercise room, off-site golf privileges. **Guest Services:** [ECP] meal plan available, coin laundry. **Business Services:** meeting rooms, administrative services. **Cards:** AE, DI, DS, MC, VI. **Special Amenities:** free continental breakfast.

(See map p. 739)

CONCH HOUSE MARINA RESORT
Motor Inn

Phone: (904)829-8646 **18**

All Year 1P: $85-$110 2P: $85-$110 XP: $10 F12
Location: 1 m s of Bridge of Lions on A1A, then 0.3 mi n. 57 Comares Ave 32084. Fax: 904/829-5414. **Facility:** A unique motel located in quiet riverfront neighborhood. Enjoy spacious well-equipped units on the Intracoastal Waterway. Convenient to historic district, lighthouse and beaches. 24 units. 4 two-bedroom units and 16 units with kitchen. Some suites ($105-$185). Exterior corridors. **Terms:** 7 day cancellation notice-fee imposed, weekly rates available, package plans, pets ($50 fee). **Amenities:** extended cable TV, hair dryers. **Dining:** The Conch House Restaurant and Lounge, see separate listing. **Leisure Activities:** charter fishing. *Fee:* boating, sailboating, windsurfing, boat dock, marina, scuba diving & equipment, fishing. **Guest Services:** gift shop, coin laundry. **Cards:** AE, MC, VI.

SOME UNITS

ASK ⓢ🐾 ❝❞ 🛗 ➰ ⊠ ✆ 🖨 / ▭ 🖵 📶

DAYS INN HISTORIC
AAA SAVE
Motel

Phone: (904)829-6581 **7**

All Year 1P: $51-$110 2P: $56-$115 XP: $5 F13
Location: US 1 at SR 16. 2800 N Ponce de Leon Blvd 32084. Fax: 904/824-0135. **Facility:** Located in historic district, next to sightseeing tour trams. 124 units. 2 stories, exterior corridors. **Terms:** 14 day cancellation notice, small pets only ($10 extra charge, designated rooms). **Dining:** coffee shop, 6-11:30 am. **Leisure Activities:** gazebo & picnic tables in large, shaded lawn area. **Guest Services:** gift shop, airport transportation-St. Augustine Airport, coin laundry. **Business Services:** fax. **Cards:** AE, CB, DI, DS, JC, MC, VI.

SOME UNITS

ⓢ ✈ 🐾 ❝❞ 🛗 ➰ ➰ 📶 🎥 🖨 DATA PORT / ⊠ 🖵 📶
FEE

DAYS INN-WEST
SAVE
Motor Inn

Phone: (904)824-4341 **1**

All Year 1P: $49-$99 2P: $54-$104 XP: $5 F18
Location: I-95, exit 95, nw corner. 2560 SR 16 32092. Fax: 904/824-1158. **Facility:** Adjacent to outlet mall, pleasant courtyard and pool area. 120 units. 2 stories, exterior corridors. **Terms:** small pets only ($10 extra charge). **Amenities:** extended cable TV. *Some:* hair dryers. **Guest Services:** coin laundry. *Fee:* fax. **Cards:** AE, DI, DS, MC, VI.

SOME UNITS

ⓢ 🐾 ❝❞ 🛗 ➰ 🎥 🖨 ▭ / ⊠ 🖵 📶 /

EDGEWATER INN
AAA SAVE
Motel

Phone: (904)825-2697 **25**

All Year 1P: $42-$105 2P: $42-$105 XP: $6
Location: SR A1A, s of Bridge of Lions. 2 St. Augustine Blvd 32080. Fax: 904/824-0436. **Facility:** Bayfront with view of city. Veranda with rocking chairs and benches. 18 units. 1 story, exterior corridors. **Terms:** cancellation fee imposed. **Amenities:** extended cable TV, voice mail, hair dryers. **Business Services:** fax. **Cards:** AE, DS, MC, VI. **Special Amenities:** free continental breakfast and free local telephone calls. *(See color ad below)*

➰ ⊠ 🎥 🖨 DATA PORT /

HAMPTON INN HISTORIC
AAA SAVE
Motel

Phone: (904)829-1996 **10**

2/2-9/1 1P: $65-$175 2P: $75-$175 XP: $10 F18
12/1-2/1 & 9/2-11/30 1P: $55-$145 2P: $65-$165 XP: $10 F18
Location: I-95, exit 95, 7 mi e on SR 16, just s on US 1, n of downtown. 2050 N Ponce de Leon Blvd 32084. Fax: 904/829-1988. **Facility:** Six blocks north of historic district. Sightseeing trolleys make stop. 52 units. Some whirlpool units ($95-$255). *Bath:* combo or shower only. 3 stories, interior corridors. **Terms:** 4 day cancellation notice, package plans. **Amenities:** extended cable TV, irons, hair dryers. **Leisure Activities:** whirlpool. **Guest Services:** [ECP] meal plan available. **Business Services:** fax. **Cards:** AE, CB, DI, DS, MC, VI.

(See color ad p 747)

SOME UNITS

ⓢ 🐾 📠 ➰ ➰ 🎥 🖨 ▭ DATA PORT / ⊠ 🖵 📶 /

HAMPTON INN ST. AUGUSTINE OUTLET CENTER
AAA SAVE
Motel

Phone: (904)824-4422 **2**

12/1-1/30 1P: $69-$225 2P: $79-$225
1/31-4/30 1P: $74-$199 2P: $79-$199
5/1-9/30 1P: $64-$159 2P: $69-$159
10/1-11/30 1P: $64-$99 2P: $69-$99
Location: I-95, exit 95, just w to CR 208, then s. 2525 CR 208 32092. Fax: 904/824-4400. **Facility:** 67 units. *Bath:* combo or shower only. 4 stories, interior corridors. **Terms:** 3 day cancellation notice, package plans. **Amenities:** irons. **Leisure Activities:** whirlpool. **Guest Services:** [ECP] meal plan available, coin laundry. **Business Services:** fax. **Cards:** AE, CB, DI, DS, JC, MC, VI. **Special Amenities:** free continental breakfast.

SOME UNITS

ⓢ ➰ 🎥 ▭ DATA PORT / ⊠ 🖵

Historic St. Augustine, FL

(See map p. 739)

HILTON GARDEN INN-ST. AUGUSTINE BEACH

Motel

Phone: 904/471-5559 **39**

All Year 1P: $69-$199
Location: From jct CR 312 and A1A, 1.2 mi e. 401 A1A Beach Blvd 32084. Fax: 904/471-7146. **Facility:** Spacious guest units. Across from beach with in-house food pavilion. 83 units. Some whirlpool units. *Bath:* combo or shower only. 3 stories, interior corridors. **Terms:** package plans. **Amenities:** extended cable TV, video games, irons, hair dryers. **Leisure Activities:** exercise room. **Guest Services:** coin laundry. **Business Services:** meeting rooms, administrative services. Cards: AE, CB, DI, DS, JC, MC, VI. *(See ad p 44)*

SOME UNITS

HOLIDAY INN EXPRESS
Motel

Phone: (904)823-8636 **5**
XP: $6 F15

All Year 1P: $60-$150
Location: I-95, exit 95, just e. 2310 SR 16 32095. Fax: 904/823-8728. **Facility:** 51 units. Some whirlpool units ($90-$150). 2 stories, exterior corridors. **Terms:** 3 day cancellation notice. **Amenities:** extended cable TV, irons, hair dryers. **Guest Services:** [ECP] meal plan available, coin laundry. *Fee:* area transportation-historic tour pickup. **Business Services:** meeting rooms, fax. Cards: AE, DI, DS, JC, MC, VI. **Special Amenities:** free continental breakfast and free local telephone calls.

SOME UNITS

THE INN AT CAMACHEE HARBOR
Motel

Phone: (904)825-0003 **23**
XP: $15 D12

All Year 1P: $69-$129 2P: $69-$129
Location: On the Intracoastal Waterway at w side of Usine Bridge, 1 mi e of jct N A1A and San Marco Blvd. 201 Yacht Club Dr 32095. Fax: 904/825-0048. **Facility:** Spacious units with view of water and marina. 19 units, 5 with kitchen. Some suites ($99-$119) and whirlpool units ($109-$129). 2 stories, interior/exterior corridors. **Terms:** 3 day cancellation notice. **Amenities:** extended cable TV. **Leisure Activities:** charter fishing, adjacent to full service marina. *Fee:* sailboating, boat dock, fishing. **Guest Services:** *Fee:* area transportation-historic tour pick-up. **Business Services:** meeting rooms. Cards: AE, MC, VI. **Special Amenities:** free continental breakfast and free local telephone calls.

SOME UNITS

LION INN
Motel

Phone: (904)824-2831 **17**
XP: $5 F

All Year 1P: $50-$175 2P: $50-$175
Location: 1 mi s of Bridge of Lions. 420 Anastasia Blvd 32084. Fax: 904/824-2831. **Facility:** Some spacious units. 36 units. *Bath:* combo or shower only. 1 story, exterior corridors. **Terms:** cancellation fee imposed. Cards: AE, DS, MC, VI. **Special Amenities:** early check-in/late check-out and free continental breakfast.

SOME UNITS

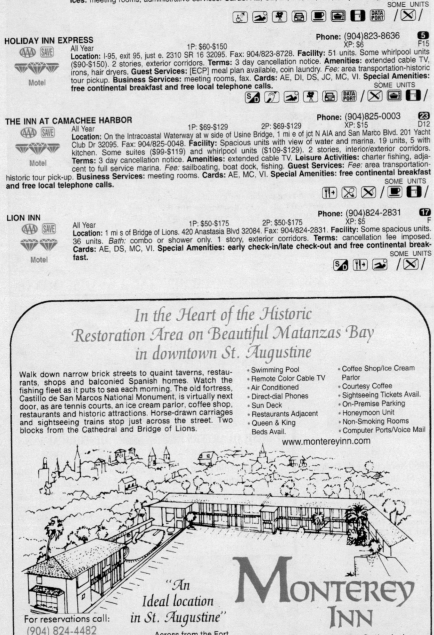

(See map p. 739)

MONTEREY INN

(AAA) (SAVE)

Motel

All Year   1P: $45-$150   2P: $49-$150   **Phone:** 904/824-4482   [26]
XP: $7

Location: Center; US 1 business route and SR A1A. 16 Avenida Menendez 32084. **Fax:** 904/829-8854. **Facility:** Opposite Matanzas Bay, in the historic restoration area. 59 units, 2 with efficiency. *Bath:* combo or shower only. 2 stories, exterior corridors. **Terms:** cancellation fee imposed. **Amenities:** voice mail. **Dining:** coffee shop, 7 am-9 pm. **Business Services:** fax. **Cards:** AE, CB, DI, DS, MC, VI. *(See color ad p 748)*

SOME UNITS

[icons] / FEE

OLD CITY HOUSE INN

Bed & Breakfast

All Year   1P: $79-$179   2P: $79-$179   **Phone:** 904/826-0113   [29]
XP: $20

Location: Center; across from Lightner Museum. 115 Cordova St 32084. **Fax:** 904/823-8960. **Facility:** In Spanish historical district, charming 19th-century building with a feel of the old world. Comfortably decorated units. Designated smoking area. 7 units. Some whirlpool units ($129-$179). *Bath:* combo or shower only. 2 stories (no elevator), exterior corridors. **Terms:** age restrictions may apply, 7 day cancellation notice-fee imposed. **Amenities:** extended cable TV. **Dining:** restaurant, see separate listing. **Leisure Activities:** bicycles. **Guest Services:** [BP] meal plan available. **Cards:** AE, CB, DI, MC, VI.

[ASK] [icons]

QUALITY INN ALHAMBRA

(AAA) (SAVE)

Motor Inn

			Phone: (904)824-2883	[8]
2/1-4/30	1P: $69-$175	2P: $69-$175	XP: $6	F18
5/1-9/2	1P: $59-$149	2P: $59-$149	XP: $6	F18
12/1-1/31 & 9/3-11/30	1P: $49-$99	2P: $49-$99	XP: $6	F18

Location: Jct US 1 and SR 16. 2700 N Ponce de Leon Blvd 32084. **Facility:** Variety of unit decors. 77 units. Some whirlpool units ($135-$300). *Bath:* combo or shower only. 2 stories, exterior corridors. **Terms:** check-in 4 pm. **Amenities:** extended cable TV. **Dining:** restaurant, 6 am-10 pm, $6-$10. **Leisure Activities:** whirlpool. **Guest Services:** gift shop. **Business Services:** fax. **Cards:** AE, CB, DI, DS, JC, MC, VI. **Special Amenities:** free local telephone calls and free room upgrade (subject to availability with advanced reservations).

SOME UNITS

[icons] / [VCR] [icon] / FEE

RADISSON PONCE DE LEON GOLF & CONFERENCE CENTER RESORT

(AAA) (SAVE)

Motor Inn

All Year   1P: $89   2P: $89   **Phone:** (904)824-2821   [6]
XP: $10   F18

Location: 3 mi n on US 1. 4000 Hwy 1 N 32095. **Fax:** 904/824-8254. **Facility:** Sprawling, well manicured grounds. Sightseeing tours make pickup stop at property. 193 units. *Bath:* combo or shower only. 1-4 stories, interior/exterior corridors. **Terms:** cancellation fee imposed, package plans. **Amenities:** extended cable TV, voice mail, irons, hair dryers. **Dining:** dining room, 6:30 am-2:30 & 5-9 pm, Fri & Sat-10 pm, $11-$25, cocktails. **Leisure Activities:** whirlpool, putting green, golf pro shop, 6 tennis courts, jogging. *Fee:* golf-18 holes. **Guest Services:** [BP] & [MAP] meal plans available, coin laundry. **Business Services:** conference facilities. **Cards:** AE, CB, DI, DS, JC, MC, VI. *(See color ad p 750)*

SOME UNITS

[icons] / FEE

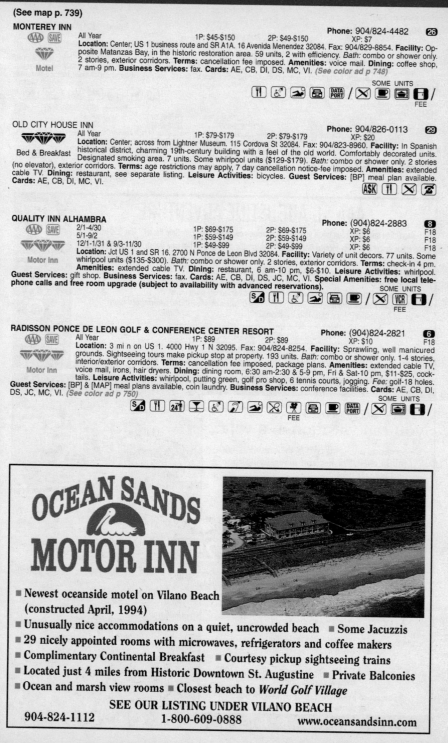

(See map p. 739)

RAMADA LIMITED ST AUGUSTINE   **Phone:** (904)829-5643 **3**

AAA SAVE

	1/31-4/30	1P: $69-$149	2P: $69-$149
	5/1-9/30	1P: $59-$129	2P: $59-$129
	12/1-1/30 & 10/1-11/30	1P: $59-$109	2P: $59-$109

Motel

Location: I-95, exit 95, just w. 2535 SR 16 32092. Fax: 904/829-0804. **Facility:** Basic accommodations. 140 units. 2 stories, exterior corridors. **Terms:** 14 day cancellation notice, small pets only ($15 extra charge). **Leisure Activities:** wading pool. **Cards:** AE, CB, DI, DS, JC, MC, VI. **Special Amenities:** free continental breakfast and free local telephone calls. *(See color ad p 742)*

SOME UNITS

SCOTTISH INNS   **Phone:** (904)824-2871 **19**

AAA SAVE

| | 2/1-8/31 | 1P: $37-$65 | 2P: $45-$75 | XP: $5 | F17 |
| | 12/1-1/31 & 9/1-11/30 | 1P: $32-$55 | 2P: $40-$65 | XP: $5 | F17 |

Motel

Location: Center; Old Mission and San Marco aves, across from Mission of Nombre de Dios. 110 San Marco Ave 32084. Fax: 904/826-4149. **Facility:** Sightseeing train stops for pickup. Motor-in style accommodation with historic 400 year old oak tree in center of complex. 27 units. 1-2 stories, exterior corridors. **Terms:** pets ($5 extra charge). **Amenities:** extended cable TV. **Business Services:** fax. **Cards:** AE, DS, MC, VI. **Special Amenities:** free local telephone calls and free newspaper.

SOME UNITS

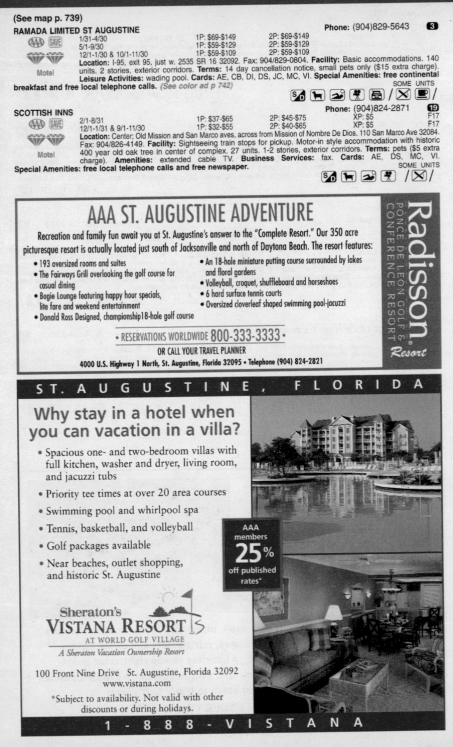

(See map p. 739)

SHERATON'S VISTANA RESORT AT WORLD GOLF VILLAGE
▽▽▽▽ All Year   1P: $79-$199   2P: $79-$199   **Phone: (904)940-2000** [36]
Cottage   **Location:** I-95, exit 95A, just w to WGV Blvd, n 1.3 mi, just s. 200 S Legacy Tr 32092. Fax: 904/940-0741.
Facility: 102 units with kitchen. 30 two-bedroom units. Some whirlpool units. 5 stories, exterior corridors.
Terms: check-in 4 pm, 3 day cancellation notice, weekly & monthly rates available, package plans.
Amenities: extended cable TV, voice mail, safes, irons, hair dryers. **Leisure Activities:** heated pool, whirlpool, charter fishing,
putting green, 2 lighted tennis courts, social program, exercise room. *Fee:* golf-18 holes. **Guest Services:** complimentary
laundry. *Fee:* area transportation. **Business Services:** fax. **Cards:** AE, DS, MC, VI. *(See color ad p 750)*

ST FRANCIS INN
▽▽▽▽ All Year   1P: $89-$195   2P: $89-$195   **Phone: (904)824-6068** [32]
Historic Bed   **Location:** Just s; in historic district. 279 St George St 32084. Fax: 904/810-5525. **Facility:** In the heart of the his-   D21
& Breakfast   toric district, this inn dates back to the late 1700s. Varied unit styles, courtyard with tropical plants. Sunday
night live entertainment. Smoke free premises. 11 units. 1 two-bedroom unit, 2 efficiencies and 1 unit with
kitchen. Some whirlpool units ($145-$195). *Bath:* combo or shower only. 3 stories (no elevator),
interior/exterior corridors. **Terms:** age restrictions may apply, 7 day cancellation notice-fee imposed, package plans.
Amenities: extended cable TV, hair dryers. **Leisure Activities:** small pool, bicycles. **Guest Services:** [BP] meal plan available,
complimentary evening beverages. **Cards:** AE, DI, DS, MC, VI.

TRAVELODGE & SUITES
[AAA] [SAVE]   All Year   1P: $49   2P: $54   **Phone: (904)829-3850** [12]
▽▽▽   **Location:** 2 mi n of city center, just off US 1. 290 San Marco Ave 32084. Fax: 904/829-0313. **Facility:** Attractive pool   F17
Motel   area. 30 units. Some whirlpool units ($120-$160). 2 stories, exterior corridors. **Amenities:** hair dryers. **Guest**
Services: airport transportation-St. Augustine, area transportation, coin laundry. **Business Services:** fax.
Cards: AE, DS, MC, VI. **Special Amenities:** early check-in/late check-out and free newspaper.

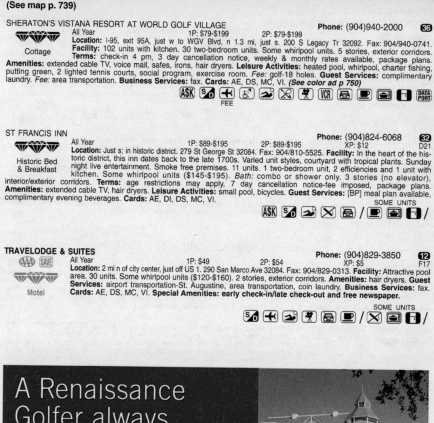

(See map p. 739)

WORLD GOLF VILLAGE RENAISSANCE RESORT

Phone: (904)940-8000   **37**

♦♦♦♦♦	1/11-4/15 & 10/1-11/30	1P: $109-$189	2P: $109-$189	XP: $20 F16
	12/1-1/10 & 4/16-9/30	1P: $79-$139	2P: $79-$139	XP: $20 F16

Resort   **Location:** I-95, exit 95A, just w, then 2.0 mi follow signs. 500 S Legacy Trail 32092. Fax: 904/940-8008. **Facility:** Cozy to spacious units with many overlooking golf course, some with balcony. All units are upscale in decor with additional amenities, including wet bar. Next door to Golf Hall of Fame, as well as specialty shopping. 300 units. Some suites ($179-$289). *Bath:* combo or shower only. 9 stories, interior corridors. **Terms:** check-in 4 pm, 3 day cancellation notice-fee imposed, package plans. **Amenities:** extended cable TV, video games, dual phone lines, voice mail, irons, hair dryers. **Leisure Activities:** heated pool, sauna, whirlpool, putting green, 2 lighted tennis courts, exercise room. *Fee:* golf-18 holes, bicycles. **Guest Services:** gift shop. **Business Services:** conference facilities, administrative services. **Cards:** AE, DI, DS, JC, MC, VI. *(See color ad p 751)*

SOME UNITS

(ASK) S/D ᵀ¶ ᵀ ⚊ ✕ ⚒ 🖨 ▭ 🅗 DATA PORT /✕ VCR / FEE

The following lodging was either not evaluated or did not meet AAA rating requirements but is listed for your information only.

SLEEP INN

Phone: 904/825-4535

fyi	6/1-9/4	1P: $75-$150	2P: $75-$150	XP: $7 F16
	2/10-5/31	1P: $55-$150	2P: $65-$150	XP: $7 F16
Motel	12/1-2/9 & 9/5-11/30	1P: $45-$95	2P: $45-$95	XP: $7 F16

Too new to rate. **Location:** 601 Anastasia Blvd 32084. Fax: 904/829-8963. **Amenities:** 50 units, radios, microwaves, refrigerators, pool. **Terms:** check-in 4 pm, 7 day cancellation notice. **Cards:** AE, DS, MC, VI.

WHERE TO DINE
---

95 CORDOVA   Historical   **Lunch:** $5-$12   **Dinner:** $14-$25   **Phone:** 904-827-1887   **19**
♦♦♦♦   **Location:** Downtown; across from Lightner Museum and Flagler College; in Casa Monica Hotel. 95 Cordova St 32084. **Hours:** 6:45-10 am, 11-2:30 & 5-10 pm. **Reservations:** suggested. **Features:** dressy casual; cocktails; fee for valet parking; a la carte. Enjoy a special experience in the newly renovated Casa Monica Hotel, dating American   to 1888. An intriguing wine list with many selections by the glass accompanies an enticing menu of steak, seafood and chicken entrees. Salmon is popular and also the Key lime pie. **Cards:** AE, DI, DS, JC, MC, VI.

A1A ALE WORKS BREWERY AND RESTAURANT   **Lunch:** $5-$10   **Dinner:** $5-$10   **Phone:** 904/829-2977   **20**
♦♦♦   **Location:** Downtown; corner of Avenida Menendez. 1 King St 32084. **Hours:** 11 am-10:30 pm, Fri & Sat-11:30 pm. Closed: 11/22, 12/25; also 12/24 for dinner. **Features:** casual dress; cocktails; street parking; a la Caribbean   carte. Indoor-outdoor dining on second floor overlooking bay and Bridge of Lions. Featuring new world cuisine of seafood paella, island cavatappi pasta. Their brews are renowned. If you're coming in for a quick bite enjoy selecting calamari, boniachos or "hommus" from a long appetizer list. **Cards:** AE, DI, DS, MC, VI. ✕

AZALEA'S CAFE   **Lunch:** $4-$10   **Phone:** 904/824-6465   **15**
♦   **Location:** Historic district, s of King St. 4 Aviles St 32084. **Hours:** 10 am-4 pm. Closed: 12/25. **Features:** casual dress; beer & wine only; street parking. Watch the horses trot by and enjoy a cozy, friendly cafe with indoor and outdoor seating. The owner/chef has drawn up a health-conscious menu with a host of Continental   vegetable selections. Breakfast is served all day, and the desserts are made right in the kitchen. **Cards:** MC, VI. ✕

BARNACLE BILL'S SEAFOOD HOUSE   **Lunch:** $5-$10   **Dinner:** $8-$16   **Phone:** 904/824-3663   **6**
(AAA)   **Location:** Across from visitor's information center. 14 Castillo Dr 32084. **Hours:** 11 am-9 pm, Sun from 4:30 pm. ♦   Closed: 11/22, 12/24, 12/25. **Features:** casual dress; children's menu; carryout; cocktails; a la carte. A St. Augustine tradition since 1981. Lines can be long at this popular laid back restaurant. Enjoy Minorcan clam Seafood   chowder, Florida gator tail, catfish and grits, or the ever popular shrimp dinner. A good selection of steak and chicken for the landlubber. **Cards:** AE, CB, DI, DS, MC, VI. ✕

CAFE ALCAZAR   Historical   **Lunch:** $3-$9   **Phone:** 904/824-7813   **11**
♦♦   **Location:** In Lightner Museum Complex. 25 Granada St 32084. **Hours:** 11 am-3 pm. Closed: 1/1, 11/22, 12/25; also Sun & Mon. **Features:** casual dress; beer & wine only; street parking. In the deep end of what was once a huge swimming pool, the elegant cafe exudes a quaint ambience that makes it an ideal place to Continental   take your mom. Creativity characterizes the entrees. Top one off with warm oatmeal cookies coated with ice cream. Smoke free premises. **Cards:** MC, VI. 🅛 ✕

COLUMBIA RESTAURANT   **Lunch:** $5-$17   **Dinner:** $10-$18   **Phone:** 904/824-3341   **7**
♦♦♦   **Location:** Center; St George St at Hypolita St. 98 St. George St 32084. **Hours:** 11 am-4 & 4:30-10 pm, Fri & Sat-10 pm, Sun 11 am-3 & 3:30-9 pm. **Reservations:** suggested; for dinner. **Features:** Sunday brunch; children's menu; carryout; cocktails & lounge. Hearty portions of Cuban and Mexican specialties can be Ethnic   found in this bustling tourist destination in the Old Quarter. An informal atmosphere includes a violin trio to set the mood, and the outdoor lounge is a popular gathering spot. Parking is limited. **Cards:** AE, CB, DI, DS, MC, VI. ✕

THE CONCH HOUSE RESTAURANT AND LOUNGE   **Lunch:** $4-$9   **Dinner:** $12-$17   **Phone:** 904/829-8646   **17**
♦♦♦   **Location:** 1 m s of Bridge of Lions on A1A, then 0.3 mi n; in Conch House Marina Resort. 57 Comares Ave 32092. **Hours:** 8 am-9 pm. Closed: 12/25. **Features:** casual dress; children's menu; cocktails & lounge. Spanish   Palm-thatched dining huts give diners unusual vantage points from which to gaze out over the Intracoastal Waterway. A Caribbean influence is evident in many dishes, which are presented with colorful garnishes. The tangy key lime pie is homemade. **Cards:** AE, MC, VI. ✕

(See map p. 739)

CORTESSE'S BISTRO & FLAMINGO ROOM Historical **Lunch:** $5-$10 **Dinner:** $11-$20 **Phone:** 904/825-6775 ⑬

Continental

Location: Historic district; corner of San Marco and San Carlos. 172 San Marco 32084. **Hours:** 11 am-9:30 pm. Closed: 12/25. **Reservations:** suggested; weekends. **Features:** casual dress; Sunday brunch; children's menu; cocktails. Such culinary treats as sauteed veal with crabmeat are dished up in the late-19th-century house. Sounds from the jazz bar fill the dining room and drift into the casual courtyard. Works by local artists enliven the walls of the restaurant. Smoke free premises. **Cards:** AE, DS, MC, VI. ✕

CREEKSIDE DINERY **Dinner:** $6-$14 **Phone:** 904/829-6113 ⑯

Seafood

Location: Just e of US 1, just n of jct SR 312. 160 Nix Boatyard Rd 32084. **Hours:** 5 pm-10 pm, 11/1-2/28 to 9 pm, Fri & Sat-10 pm. Closed: 11/22, 12/24, 12/25. **Features:** casual dress; children's menu; carryout; cocktails. Settle into a rocking chair and relax in this quaint, Southern-style atmosphere complete with a jasmine-entwined, columned porch under sheltering oaks and magnolias. Well-chosen spices enliven entrees served with sweet potato compote and Indian corn. **Cards:** AE, DI, DS, MC, VI. ✕

DENOEL FRENCH PASTRY SHOP **Lunch:** $5-$7 **Phone:** 904/829-3974 ⑭

French

Location: In historic district; just s of the plaza. 212 Charlotte St 32084. **Hours:** 10 am-5 pm. Closed major holidays; also Mon & Tues. **Features:** casual dress; carryout; street parking; a la carte. A local favorite since 1966, this nifty, out-of-the-way place features a bakery that's the real reason to visit. Scrumptious croissants and wonderful pastries are all baked right on the premises. Sandwiches, soups, and salads are also a lunch-time treat.

GYPSY CAB CO **Lunch:** $6-$9 **Dinner:** $9-$17 **Phone:** 904/824-8244 ⑩

Ethnic

Location: SR A1A, 1 mi s of the Bridge of Lions. 828 Anastasia Blvd 32084. **Hours:** 11 am-3 & 4:30-10 pm, Fri-11pm, Sat 11 am-11 pm, Sun 10:30 am-10 pm. Closed: 7/4, 12/25. **Features:** casual dress; Sunday brunch; children's menu; cocktails. A casual atmosphere with an eclectic decor. The "surprise" menu changes daily, reflecting cuisine from around the world served up in hearty portions. Mainstays include black bean soup, key lime and peanut butter pies. Come early for specials. **Cards:** AE, DI, DS, MC, VI. ✕

HARBORSIDE CAFE **Lunch:** $4-$6 **Dinner:** $4-$16 **Phone:** 904/826-1667 ④

American

Location: 1 mi e of jct A1A and US 1 business route. 252 Yacht Club Dr 32084. **Hours:** 11 am-10 pm, Sat & Sun from 7:30 am. Closed: 12/25. **Features:** casual dress; cocktails. A "come as you are" kind of seafood place, they offer casual, relaxed indoor and outdoor dining overlooking the Intracoastal Waterway. Fresh local catches such as grouper, flounder and oysters are featured, with Snapper Almondine as the house specialty. **Cards:** AE, DS, MC, VI. ✕

JEFF'S PLACE **Lunch:** $3-$8 **Dinner:** $3-$8 **Phone:** 904/829-6726 ②

Mexican

Location: 2 mi n of jct A1A, just s of airport. 4660 US 1 N 32084. **Hours:** 10 am-8 pm. **Features:** casual dress; carryout; a la carte. Don't let the austere exterior/interior cause you to hesitate or bypass this place. Jeff's is a great place for good food and great service without the hassle of trying to find a parking place! Located on the outskirts of town, Jeff serves up Mexican favorites such as taco salad as well as a variety of traditional sandwiches and salad. **Cards:** AE, MC, VI.

KING'S HEAD BRITISH PUB **Lunch:** $4-$10 **Dinner:** $4-$10 **Phone:** 904/823-9787 ①

English

Location: 6 mi n. 6460 Hwy 1 N 32084. **Hours:** 11:30 am-9 pm, Fri & Sat-10 pm. Closed: 11/22, 12/25; also Mon. **Features:** casual dress; children's menu; cocktails; a la carte. An authentic British Pub owned and operated by English chef. Wide selection of European beer. Enjoy scotch eff, bangers and mash, cornish pastry, or fish and chips. Friendly atmosphere with walls lined with British keepsakes. **Cards:** AE, MC, VI. ✕

LE PAVILLON **Lunch:** $5-$10 **Dinner:** $14-$22 **Phone:** 904/824-6202 ⑨

Continental

MC, VI.

Location: 0.8 mi n on SR A1A, just n of Mulbery St. 45 San Marco Ave 32084. **Hours:** 11:30 am-2:30 & 5-10 pm. **Reservations:** suggested; weekends. **Features:** cocktails. Antiques and fresh flowers set the stage for quiet, intimate dining in an old-style house. A varied menu offers selections ranging from light dining, to more robust entrees like the marinated rack of lamb. Tiramisu is a house specialty. **Cards:** AE, CB, DI, DS, ✕

MARTY'S SEAFOOD & STEAK HOUSE **Lunch:** $4-$10 **Dinner:** $6-$15 **Phone:** 904/829-8679 ③

American

Location: Sw corner US1 N and SR 16. 2703 Ponce De Leon Blvd 32095. **Hours:** 11:30 am-9:30 pm, Fri-Sun to 3:30 pm. Closed: 12/25; also 12/7-12/13. **Features:** casual dress; children's menu; cocktails; a la carte. A different fresh-baked bread is offered each day, and seafood selections like the half lobster stuffed with crab meat are enjoyed in a nautical antique decor. If you can save room, indulge in the Key lime pie. A well-trained staff keeps the pace smooth. **Cards:** MC, VI. ✕

RAINTREE RESTAURANT **Dinner:** $15-$29 **Phone:** 904/824-7211 ⑤

Continental

Location: 1 mi n of Bridge of Lions on San Marco Ave. 102 San Marco Ave 32084. **Hours:** 5 pm-9:30 pm, Sat-10 pm; from 6 pm in summer. Closed: 12/25. **Reservations:** suggested. **Features:** casual dress; children's menu; early bird specials; cocktails & lounge; a la carte. A rambling Victorian home with brick courtyards, an aviary and antiques provides the setting for outstanding, creative selections like the lamb chop in a potato basket accompanied by mini zucchini and yellow squash. Be sure to save room for dessert. **Cards:** AE, MC, VI. ✕

TAVERN ON THE BAY **Lunch:** $5-$17 **Dinner:** $8-$17 **Phone:** 904/810-1919 ⑧

American

Cards: MC, VI.

Location: On bayfront in historic downtown area. 20 Avenida Menendez 32221. **Hours:** 11:30 am-9 pm, Sat-10 pm. **Features:** casual dress; street parking; a la carte. Bayfront indoor/outdoor dining. Enjoy people or whale watching! Variety of menu offerings from gourmet burgers to seafood dishes all with creative names of jolly old England. Large selection of appetizers and the house is famous for their spicey chicken wings. ✕

(See map p. 739)

THEOS' RESTAURANT 　　　　Lunch: $4-$6 　　　Phone: 904/824-5022 　⑫
American
Location: From jct US 1 and King St, just e. 169 King St 32084. **Hours:** 6:45 am-3 pm, Sun 7:45 am-2 pm.
Closed: 11/22, 12/24, 12/25. **Features:** casual dress; carryout; beer & wine only; a la carte. A small,
attractive spot that is popular with locals, the decor reflects St. Augustine's rich history, with vintage photos
and paintings by local artists. Generous portions of pastitso (Greek lasagna) and homemade bread are
highlights of a varied menu. Smoke free premises. **Cards:** AE, DS, MC, VI.

WHITE LION RESTAURANT 　　Lunch: $4-$8 　　Dinner: $6-$18 　　Phone: 904/829-2388 　⑱
American
Location: Center; historic district across street from fort. 20 Cuna St 32084. **Hours:** 11:30 am-11 pm. Closed:
11/22, 12/25. **Features:** casual dress; cocktails; street parking; a la carte. Located in the historic district,
White Lion offers indoor and outdoor dining in the tradition of old English taverns. The menu spotlights
grilled, blackened and fried seafood, and desserts like Key Lime pie. Florida folk music is featured on
weekends. **Cards:** MC, VI.

ST. AUGUSTINE BEACH pop. 3,700 (See map p. 739; index p. 741)

——— WHERE TO STAY ———

BEST WESTERN OCEAN INN 　　　　　　　　　　Phone: (904)471-8010 　53
Motel
			XP: $10	F17
2/2-9/6	1P: $59-$149	2P: $59-$149	XP: $10	F17
9/7-11/30	1P: $89-$109	2P: $89-$109	XP: $10	F17
12/1-2/1	1P: $39-$109	2P: $39-$109	XP: $10	F17

Location: 2 mi s of jct SR 312. 3955 A1A S 32084-6933. Fax: 904/460-9124. **Facility:** 34 units. 2 stories. Interior
corridors. **Terms:** 3 day cancellation notice-fee imposed, pets ($10 extra charge). **Cards:** AE, CB, DI, DS,
JC, MC, VI. **Special Amenities: free continental breakfast and free local telephone calls.** SOME UNITS

COMFORT INN AT ST. AUGUSTINE BEACH 　　　　　Phone: (904)471-1474 　52
Motel
1/26-9/5	1P: $49-$119	2P: $55-$139		F16
12/1-1/25	1P: $39-$69	2P: $45-$99	XP: $10	
9/6-11/30	1P: $42-$69	2P: $45-$79		

Location: 1.6 mi s of jct SR 312 and A1A, on business A1A. 901 A1A Beach Blvd 32084. Fax: 904/461-9659.
Facility: Attractively landscaped with pool area in back of building. 70 units. 3 stories, exterior corridors.
Terms: 24 day cancellation notice. **Leisure Activities:** heated pool, whirlpool. **Guest Services:** coin laundry.
Cards: AE, CB, DI, DS, MC, VI. **Special Amenities: free continental breakfast and free local telephone calls.**
SOME UNITS

DAYS INN-ST. AUGUSTINE BEACH 　　　　　　　Phone: (904)461-9990 　47
Motel
2/1-3/31	1P: $69-$150	2P: $69-$150	XP: $5	F12
4/1-9/3	1P: $49-$150	2P: $49-$150	XP: $5	F12
9/4-11/30	1P: $49-$130	2P: $49-$130	XP: $5	F12
12/1-1/31	1P: $49-$99	2P: $49-$99	XP: $5	F12

Location: 1.3 mi s of jct SR 312 and A1A, on business A1A. 541 A1A Beach Blvd 32084. Fax: 904/471-4774.
Facility: Short walk to public beach. 50 units. 1 two-bedroom unit. Some whirlpool units. 2 stories, exterior
corridors. **Terms:** 30 day cancellation notice. **Amenities:** extended cable TV, whirlpool. **Leisure Activities:** whirlpool. **Guest
Services:** coin laundry. **Cards:** AE, CB, DI, DS, MC, VI. **Special Amenities: free continental breakfast.**
(See color ad p 747) 　　　　　　　　　　　　　　　　SOME UNITS

ECONO LODGE 　　　　　　　　　　　　　Phone: (904)471-2330 　46
Motel
2/9-4/30	1P: $54-$184	2P: $59-$189	XP: $10	F18
5/1-9/3	1P: $44-$164	2P: $49-$169	XP: $10	F18
12/1-2/8	1P: $44-$84	2P: $49-$89	XP: $10	F18
9/4-11/30	1P: $44-$79	2P: $49-$89	XP: $10	F18

Location: 1 mi s of jct SR 312 & A1A; on business route A1A. 311 A1A Beach Blvd 32084. Fax: 904/471-1018.
Facility: Short walk to public beach. 50 units. 2 stories (no elevator), exterior corridors. **Amenities:** extended
cable TV. **Leisure Activities:** whirlpool. **Guest Services:** coin laundry. **Cards:** AE, DI, DS, JC, MC, VI. **Special Amenities: free
continental breakfast and free local telephone calls.** (See color ad p 742) 　　SOME UNITS

HAMPTON INN-ST. AUGUSTINE BEACH 　　　　　Phone: (904)471-4000 　54
Motel
5/28-9/2	1P: $89-$189	2P: $99-$199	XP: $10	F18
2/4-5/27	1P: $79-$189	2P: $89-$199	XP: $10	F18
9/3-11/30	1P: $74-$149	2P: $84-$159	XP: $10	F18
12/1-2/3	1P: $65-$139	2P: $75-$149	XP: $10	F18

Location: 1.3 mi s of jct SR 312 and A1A on Business Rt A1A. 430 A1A Beach Blvd 32084. Fax: 904/471-4888.
Facility: 100 units. Some suites ($139-$199) and whirlpool units ($139-$199). **Bath:** combo or shower only.
4 stories, interior/exterior corridors. **Terms:** 7 day cancellation notice. **Amenities:** video games, dual phone lines, irons, hair
dryers. **Leisure Activities:** whirlpool, beach, swimming, exercise room. **Guest Services:** [CP] meal plan available, coin laundry.
Business Services: meeting rooms, administrative services. **Cards:** AE, CB, DI, DS, JC, MC, VI. 　　SOME UNITS

(See map p. 739)

HOLIDAY INN-ST AUGUSTINE BEACH

Phone: (904)471-2555 [50]

3/30-9/3	2P: $110-$155
2/14-3/29	2P: $99-$155
9/4-11/30	2P: $89-$109
12/1-2/13	2P: $79-$99

Motor Inn

Location: 1.8 mi s of jct SR 312 and A1A, on Business Rt A1A. 860 A1A Beach Blvd 32084. Fax: 904/461-8450. **Facility:** Balconies. Some oceanfront units; many units with partial ocean views. 151 units. *Bath:* combo or shower only. 5 stories, interior/exterior corridors. **Terms:** small pets only ($10 extra charge). **Amenities:** irons, hair dryers. **Dining:** restaurant, 7 am-11:30 & 5-10 pm, Sun 7 am-noon; tiki bar in season, $7-$14, cocktails. **Leisure Activities:** beach, swimming. **Guest Services:** valet laundry. **Business Services:** meeting rooms. **Cards:** AE, DI, DS, JC, MC, VI. **Special Amenities:** free newspaper.

SOME UNITS

LA FIESTA OCEANSIDE INN

Phone: (904)471-2220 [49]

2/15-9/3	1P: $69-$259	2P: $69-$259
		XP: $10
12/1-2/14 & 9/4-11/30	1P: $59-$199	2P: $59-$199
		XP: $10

Motel

Location: 1.7 mi s of jct SR 312 and A1A, on Business Rt A1A. 810 A1A Beach Blvd 32084. Fax: 904/471-0186. **Facility:** Walkway over the dunes to the beach. 44 units. Some suites ($139-$259). *Bath:* combo or shower only. 2 stories (no elevator), exterior corridors. **Terms:** 7 day cancellation notice. **Dining:** coffee shop, 7 am-noon. **Leisure Activities:** beach. *Fee:* miniature golf. **Guest Services:** coin laundry. **Cards:** CB, DI, DS, MC, VI. *(See color ad below)*

SOME UNITS

RAMADA LIMITED, AT THE BEACH

Phone: (904)471-1440 [51]

2/11-9/2	1P: $80-$140	2P: $80-$140	XP: $10
			F18
12/1-2/10 & 9/3-11/30	1P: $50-$100	2P: $50-$100	XP: $10
			F18

Motel

Location: 2 mi s of jct SR 312 and A1A, on Business Rt A1A. 894 A1A Beach Blvd 32084. Fax: 904/471-2922. **Facility:** On east side of street. Some units have limited view of ocean. 38 units. Some whirlpool units ($130-$250). *Bath:* combo or shower only. 3 stories, interior corridors. **Amenities:** extended cable TV. **Guest Services:** [ECP] meal plan available, coin laundry. **Cards:** AE, CB, DI, DS, MC, VI.

SOME UNITS
FEE

(See map p. 739)

—————— *The following lodging was either not evaluated or did not* ——————
meet AAA rating requirements but is listed for your information only.

WELLESLEY INN & SUITES
[fyl]
Motel
All Year   1P: $55-$69   2P: $70-$109   XP: $10   F18
Too new to rate, opening scheduled for July 2001. **Location:** I-95, exit 94, e on SR 207, then e on 312 to A1A. 331 A1A (Beach Blvd) 32084. **Amenities:** 65 units, coffeemakers, microwaves, refrigerators, pool. **Terms:** 7 day cancellation notice. **Cards:** AE, CB, DI, DS, MC, VI.
Phone: 904/471-7700

—————— **WHERE TO DINE** ——————

ARUANNO'S ITALIAN RESTAURANT
💎💎
Italian
MC, VI.
Dinner: $10-$18   **Phone: 904/471-9373**   (30)
Location: S of jct of SR 312 & A1A, on A1A business route at "D" St. 105 D St 32084. **Hours:** 5 pm-10 pm. Closed major holidays; also Sun. **Reservations:** suggested. **Features:** casual dress; carryout; beer & wine only; a la carte. Aruanno's is a family operation that aims to please. Enjoy all the Italian classics, as well as steak, rack of lamb and nightly pasta specials. Don't leave without trying the homemade dessert. **Cards:** AE, DI,

GREENSTREET'S
💎
American
Lunch: $2-$7   **Phone: 904/471-5573**   (32)
Location: Just n of SR 206. 4320 A1A S 32084. **Hours:** 7:30 am-3:30 pm. Closed: 12/25. **Features:** No A/C. Join the local crowd as they flock here for hearty breakfasts and linger in the friendly atmosphere over lunch. Large selection of omelets and pancakes. Enjoy the famous homemade pies for dessert.

THE OASIS
💎
Seafood
the beach. **Cards:** AE, DI, DS, MC, VI.
Lunch: $4-$14   Dinner: $4-$14   **Phone: 904/471-3424**   (33)
Location: 0.3 mi s of jct A1A at Ocean Trace Rd. 4000 A1A S 32095. **Hours:** 6:30 am-midnight. Closed: 11/22, 12/25; also 11/30-12/16. **Features:** No A/C; casual dress; children's menu; cocktails; entertainment; a la carte. Bustling, friendly neighborhood spot. Join the locals for a breakfast of omelettes or a salad for lunch. Dinner specials daily featuring steak, chicken or fish. Open air deck is great place to unwind after a day on
❌

SALTWATER COWBOYS
AAA
💎💎
Regional American
Dinner: $5-$14   **Phone: 904/471-2332**   (34)
Location: At the western end of Dondanville Rd; off SR A1A, 0.8 mi s of southern jct SR 3. 299 Dondanville Rd 32084. **Hours:** 5 pm-9 pm; 3/2-9/30 to 10 pm. Closed major holidays. **Features:** casual dress; children's menu; carryout; cocktails; a la carte. Travel down a dirt road to a saltwater marsh to find this quaint, waterfront restaurant. A casual atmosphere recaptures the charm of Old Florida, with a menu offering seafood, rib and chicken dishes. The authentic derby pie is a chocolate lover's dream. **Cards:** AE, DS, MC, VI.
❌

ST. CLOUD —*See Orlando p. 701.*

ST. MARKS pop. 300

—————— **WHERE TO STAY** ——————

SWEET MAGNOLIA INN
💎💎💎💎
Bed & Breakfast
area transportation, complimentary laundry. **Cards:** AE, DI, DS, MC, VI.
All Year   2P: $85-$115   XP: $10
Location: Center on CR 363. 803 Port Leon Dr 32355. Fax: 850/925-0117. **Facility:** 7 units. Some whirlpool units ($105-$115). *Bath:* combo or shower only. 2 stories, interior corridors. **Terms:** age restrictions may apply, 7 day cancellation notice. **Leisure Activities:** boat dock, bicycles. **Guest Services:** [BP] meal plan available,
Phone: 850/925-7670
SOME UNITS
[ASK] [SD] [📶] [❌] [☎] [📽] / [VCR] /

ST. PETERSBURG —*See Tampa Bay p. 811.*

ST. PETE BEACH —*See Tampa Bay p. 876.*

SANFORD —*See Orlando p. 701.*

SANIBEL pop. 5,500

—————— **WHERE TO STAY** ——————

BEST WESTERN SANIBEL ISLAND BEACH RESORT
AAA [SAVE]
💎💎💎
Motel

2/9-4/21	1P: $239-$415	2P: $239-$415	XP: $20	F16
12/1-2/8	1P: $125-$405	2P: $125-$405	XP: $20	F16
4/22-5/28	1P: $169-$285	2P: $169-$285	XP: $20	F16
5/29-11/30	1P: $129-$269	2P: $129-$269	XP: $20	F16

Phone: (941)472-1700

Location: Causeway, 3 mi w on Periwinkle Way, 1 mi s on Tarpon Bay Rd, 1.3 mi w. 3287 W Gulf Dr 33957. Fax: 941/472-5032. **Facility:** Gulf front contemporary units. 45 units. 3 two-bedroom units, 28 efficiencies and 4 units with kitchen. 2 stories, exterior corridors. **Terms:** check-in 4 pm, 14 day cancellation notice-fee imposed, package plans. **Amenities:** extended cable TV, safes. **Leisure Activities:** heated pool, beach, swimming, fishing, tennis court, bicycles, shuffleboard, badminton, barbecue grills, croquet, picnic area. **Guest Services:** [CP] meal plan available, coin laundry. **Cards:** AE, DI, DS, MC, VI. *(See color ad p 762)*
[SD] [🚲] [🏊] [❌] [📽] [🍴] [💻] [🧺] [🛗] [DATA PORT]

BRENNEN'S TARPON TALE INN

AAA SAVE
▼▼▼

Apartment

Phone: (941)472-0939

12/22-5/15 — 2P: $149-$229
12/1-12/21 & 5/16-11/30 — 2P: $99-$189

Location: From causeway, just e on Periwinkle Way, just s. 367 Periwinkle Way 33957. Fax: 941/472-6202. **Facility:** Eclectic comtemporary appointments within walking distance of shops. Smoke free premises. 5 units with kitchen. *Bath:* shower only. 1 story, exterior corridors. **Terms:** 30 day cancellation notice-fee imposed, weekly & monthly rates available. **Amenities:** extended cable TV. **Leisure Activities:** whirlpool, bicycles, grill, beach chairs, small library. **Guest Services:** coin laundry. **Cards:** DS, MC, VI. **Special Amenities:** early check-in/late check-out and free continental breakfast.

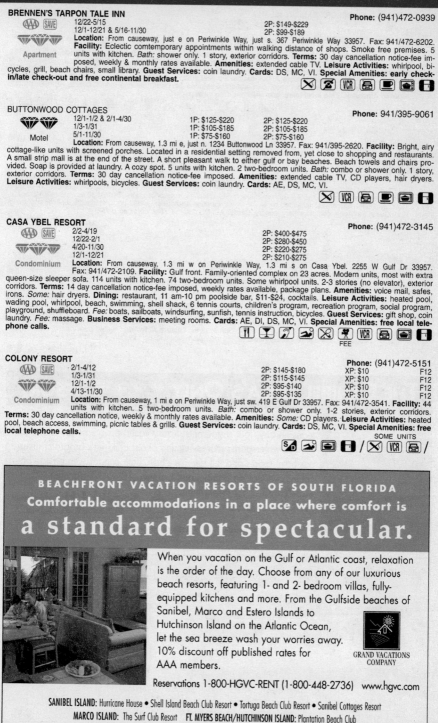

BUTTONWOOD COTTAGES

▼▼ ▼▼

Motel

Phone: 941/395-9061

12/1-1/2 & 2/1-4/30 — 1P: $125-$220 — 2P: $125-$220
1/3-1/31 — 1P: $105-$185 — 2P: $105-$185
5/1-11/30 — 1P: $75-$160 — 2P: $75-$160

Location: From causeway, 1.3 mi e, just n. 1234 Buttonwood Ln 33957. Fax: 941/395-2620. **Facility:** Bright, airy cottage-like units with screened porches. Located in a residential setting removed from, yet close to shopping and restaurants. A small strip mall is at the end of the street. A short pleasant walk to either gulf or bay beaches. Beach towels and chairs provided. Soap is provided at laundry. A cozy spot. 5 units with kitchen. 2 two-bedroom units. *Bath:* combo or shower only. 1 story, exterior corridors. **Terms:** 30 day cancellation notice-fee imposed. **Amenities:** extended cable TV, CD players, hair dryers. **Leisure Activities:** whirlpools, bicycles. **Guest Services:** coin laundry. **Cards:** AE, DS, MC, VI.

CASA YBEL RESORT

AAA SAVE
▼▼▼

Condominium

Phone: (941)472-3145

2/2-4/19 — 2P: $400-$475
12/22-2/1 — 2P: $280-$450
4/20-11/30 — 2P: $220-$275
12/1-12/21 — 2P: $210-$275

Location: From causeway, 1.3 mi w on Periwinkle Way, 1.3 mi s on Casa Ybel. 2255 W Gulf Dr 33957. Fax: 941/472-2109. **Facility:** Gulf front. Family-oriented complex on 23 acres. Modern units, most with extra queen-size sleeper sofa. 114 units with kitchen. 74 two-bedroom units. Some whirlpool units. 2-3 stories (no elevator), exterior corridors. **Terms:** 14 day cancellation notice-fee imposed, weekly rates available, package plans. **Amenities:** voice mail, safes, irons. *Some:* hair dryers. **Dining:** restaurant, 11 am-10 pm poolside bar, $11-$24, cocktails. **Leisure Activities:** heated pool, wading pool, whirlpool, beach, swimming, shell shack, 6 tennis courts, children's program, recreation program, social program, playground, shuffleboard. *Fee:* boats, sailboats, windsurfing, sunfish, tennis instruction, bicycles. **Guest Services:** gift shop, coin laundry. *Fee:* massage. **Business Services:** meeting rooms. **Cards:** AE, DI, DS, MC, VI. **Special Amenities:** free local telephone calls.

COLONY RESORT

AAA SAVE
▼▼▼

Condominium

Phone: (941)472-5151

2/1-4/12 — 2P: $145-$180 — XP: $10 — F12
1/3-1/31 — 2P: $115-$145 — XP: $10 — F12
12/1-1/2 — 2P: $95-$140 — XP: $10 — F12
4/13-11/30 — 2P: $95-$135 — XP: $10 — F12

Location: From causeway, 1 mi e on Periwinkle Way, just sw. 419 E Gulf Dr 33957. Fax: 941/472-3541. **Facility:** 44 units with kitchen. 5 two-bedroom units. *Bath:* combo or shower only. 1-2 stories, exterior corridors. **Terms:** 30 day cancellation notice, weekly & monthly rates available. **Amenities:** *Some:* CD players. **Leisure Activities:** heated pool, beach access, swimming, picnic tables & grills. **Guest Services:** coin laundry. **Cards:** DS, MC, VI. **Special Amenities:** free local telephone calls.

SOME UNITS

HOLIDAY INN BEACH RESORT SANIBEL ISLAND

Phone: (941)472-4123

AAA SAVE ▽▽▽

Motor Inn

	2/4-4/28	1P: $229-$269	2P: $229-$269
	12/18-2/3	1P: $179-$259	2P: $179-$259
	4/29-11/30	1P: $169-$199	2P: $169-$199
	12/1-12/17	1P: $149-$179	2P: $149-$179

Location: From causeway, 0.7 mi w on Periwinkle Way, 0.5 mi s on Donax St. 1231 Middle Gulf Dr 33957. Fax: 941/472-0930. **Facility:** Gulf front. Contemporary decor. 98 units, 2 with efficiency. 2 stories, exterior corridors. **Terms:** 3 day cancellation notice, package plans. **Amenities:** safes, irons, hair dryers. **Dining:** restaurant, 7 am-11 & 5-10 pm, tiki bar, $15-$24, cocktails. **Leisure Activities:** heated pool, beach, swimming, beach cabanas, 2 tennis courts, ping pong. *Fee:* bicycles. **Guest Services:** gift shop, coin laundry. **Business Services:** meeting rooms. **Cards:** AE, CB, DI, DS, MC, VI. **Special Amenities:** free local telephone calls and free newspaper. SOME UNITS

HURRICANE HOUSE

Phone: (941)472-1696

SAVE ▽▽▽

Motel

	2/16-4/19	2P: $335-$355
	12/1-1/4	2P: $335-$345
	1/5-2/15	2P: $185-$210
	4/20-11/30	2P: $220-$235

Location: From causeway, 2.8 mi w on Periwinkle Way to Tarpon Bay Rd, then s; 0.7 mi w of jct Tarpon Bay Rd. 2939 W Gulf Dr 33957. Fax: 941/472-1718. **Facility:** Gulf front two-bath townhouses, fully equipped with dishwasher. 15 two-bedroom units with kitchen. Some whirlpool units. 3 stories, exterior corridors. **Terms:** 30 day cancellation notice, weekly rates available. **Amenities:** extended cable TV, irons. **Leisure Activities:** heated pool, whirlpools, beach, swimming, tennis court. **Guest Services:** complimentary laundry. **Cards:** AE, DS, MC, VI. *(See color ad p 757)*

ISLAND INN

Phone: (941)472-1561

▽▽

Historic Complex

	1/20-4/30	1P: $150-$405	2P: $200-$405	XP: $50	D10
	12/20-1/19	1P: $135-$390	2P: $175-$390	XP: $50	D10
	5/1-11/30	1P: $90-$340	2P: $105-$340	XP: $50	D10
	12/1-12/19	1P: $125-$330	2P: $165-$330	XP: $50	D10

Location: From causeway, 2.8 mi w to Tarpon Bay Rd, then s; 1 mi w of jct Tarpon Bay Rd. 3111 W Gulf Dr 33957 (PO Box 659). Fax: 941/472-0051. **Facility:** Gulf front. Circa 1894. Modest decor; mostly standard motel units, some duplexes and cottages. Historic office building. Most guest rooms of more recent construction. 57 units. 2 two-bedroom units, 1 three-bedroom unit, 22 efficiencies and 5 units with kitchen. *Bath:* combo or shower only. 1-2 stories, interior/exterior corridors. **Terms:** 30 day cancellation notice-fee imposed. **Amenities:** extended cable TV. *Some:* safes. **Leisure Activities:** heated pool, beach, swimming, 2 tennis courts, shuffleboard, volleyball. **Guest Services:** [MAP] meal plan available, coin laundry. **Cards:** AE, DS, MC, VI.

PELICANS ROOST

Phone: (941)472-2996

Condominium

2/1-4/28 Wkly	2P: $2200-$2300
12/1-12/31 Wkly	2P: $975-$2300
1/1-1/31 Wkly	2P: $1650
4/29-11/30 Wkly	2P: $1050

Location: From causeway, 0.6 mi w on Periwinkle Way, 0.6 mi s. 605 Donax St 33957. **Fax:** 941/472-0317. **Facility:** Gulf front, family oriented property offering two-bathroom guest units. Grocery/luggage carts are provided at parking area. Short drive to shops and restaurants, yet off the beaten track. Bicycles can be arranged. Many repeat guests and booking early is advised. 20 two-bedroom units with kitchen. 4 stories, exterior corridors. **Terms:** 60 day cancellation notice, monthly rates available. **Amenities:** extended cable TV, irons. **Leisure Activities:** heated pool, beach, swimming, fishing, 2 lighted tennis courts, horseshoes, shuffleboard. **Guest Services:** complimentary laundry. *(See color ad p 758)*

SANDALFOOT CONDOMINIUMS

Phone: (941)472-2275

Property failed to provide current rates

Condominium

Location: From causeway, 0.6 mi e. 671 E Gulf Dr 33957. **Fax:** 941/472-5135. **Facility:** Gulf front. 60 units with kitchen. 45 two-bedroom units. 3 stories, exterior corridors. **Terms:** 60 day cancellation notice. **Amenities:** extended cable TV, irons. **Leisure Activities:** heated pool, beach, swimming, tennis court, shuffleboard. **Guest Services:** coin laundry. **Cards:** MC, VI.

SOME UNITS

SANIBEL ARMS WEST

Phone: (941)472-1138

Condominium

12/1-4/30 Wkly	2P: $1375-$1725
5/1-11/30 Wkly	2P: $695-$975

Location: From causeway, 0.6 mi e. 827 E Gulf Dr 33957. **Fax:** 941/472-9688. **Facility:** Two-bedroom units with good sized screened porch, some with gulf view. Family oriented. Bike path at front door. Close to shopping and restaurants. Office and reception area is located in a little building across the road next to the tennis court. 87 two-bedroom units with kitchen. *Bath:* combo or shower only. 2 stories, exterior corridors. **Terms:** 30 day cancellation notice, daily rates available. **Amenities:** extended cable TV, irons. **Leisure Activities:** heated pool, beach, swimming, boat dock, 2 tennis courts. **Guest Services:** coin laundry. **Business Services:** meeting rooms. **Cards:** MC, VI. **Special Amenities:** early check-in/late check-out and free local telephone calls.

SOME UNITS

SANIBEL BEACH CLUB II

Phone: 941/472-5772

Condominium

2/5-4/30 Wkly	2P: $2050
12/1-2/4 Wkly	2P: $1825
5/1-11/30 Wkly	2P: $1250

Location: From causeway, 1.5 mi e. 205 Periwinkle Way 33957. **Fax:** 941/472-3790. **Facility:** Gulf front. Screened terraces. 29 two-bedroom units with kitchen. 3 stories (no elevator), exterior corridors. **Terms:** 30 day cancellation notice-fee imposed, daily rates available. **Amenities:** extended cable TV, CD players, irons. **Leisure Activities:** heated pool, beach, swimming, tennis court, bicycles, playground, shuffleboard. **Guest Services:** complimentary laundry. **Cards:** DS, MC, VI.

SANIBEL COTTAGES

Phone: (941)472-1868

Cottage

2/16-4/19	2P: $375-$395
12/1-1/4	2P: $365-$385
1/5-2/15	2P: $250-$275
4/20-11/30	2P: $225-$250

Location: From causeway, 2.8 mi w to Tarpon Bay Rd, then s; 0.3 mi e of jct Tarpon Bay. 2341 W Gulf Dr 33957. **Fax:** 941/472-8711. **Facility:** Gulf front. All corner units with upscale decor and private screened terrace. Beautifully landscaped grounds with waterfall and gazebo in center courtyard. 28 two-bedroom units with kitchen. Some whirl-pool units. 2 stories, exterior corridors. **Terms:** 30 day cancellation notice, daily rates available, package plans. **Amenities:** extended cable TV, safes, irons. **Leisure Activities:** heated pool, whirlpool, beach, swimming, fishing, 2 tennis courts, shuffleboard. **Guest Services:** complimentary laundry. **Cards:** AE, DS, MC, VI. *(See color ad p 757)*

THE SANIBEL INN

Phone: (941)472-3181

Motor Inn

2/9-4/21	2P: $299-$489	XP: $20 F16
12/1-2/8	2P: $205-$299	XP: $20 F16
4/22-5/28	2P: $229-$269	XP: $20 F16
5/29-11/30	2P: $165-$239	XP: $20 F16

Location: Straight ahead after causeway to E Gulf Dr. 937 E Gulf Dr 33957. **Fax:** 941/472-5234. **Facility:** Gulf front. Standard rooms, efficiencies and one- to two-bedroom apartments with screened balcony. Elevators at two-bedroom apartments only. 96 units. 28 two-bedroom units and 28 units with kitchen. 2-3 stories (no elevator), exterior corridors. **Terms:** check-in 4 pm, 14 day cancellation notice-fee imposed, weekly rates available, package plans. **Amenities:** extended cable TV, voice mail, safes, irons, hair dryers. **Dining:** restaurant, 7:30 am-11 & 5-10 pm, $12-$21, cocktails. **Leisure Activities:** heated pool, beach, swimming, 2 tennis courts, children's program, nature program, recreation program, exercise room privileges. *Fee:* kayaks, bicycles, beach cabanas, umbrellas, barbecue grills, environmental lectures. **Guest Services:** gift shop, valet laundry. **Business Services:** meeting rooms. **Cards:** AE, DI, DS, MC, VI. *(See color ad p 762)*

SOME UNITS

SANIBEL MOORINGS

Phone: (941)472-4119

Condominium

2/3-4/23 Wkly	1P: $1330-$2233	2P: $1330-$2233	XP: $15
12/1-1/5 Dly		2P: $110-$319	XP: $15
1/6-2/2 Dly		2P: $150-$255	XP: $15
4/24-11/30 Dly		2P: $137-$235	XP: $15

Location: Straight after causeway to E Gulf Dr, then just e. 845 E Gulf Dr 33957 (PO Box 899). **Fax:** 941/472-8148. **Facility:** Located in a quiet area convenient to shopping, restaurants and theaters. All guest units are large, nicely decorated and have a screened porch. Many units are gulf front, however, some units are across a road. 110 units with kitchen. 82 two-bedroom units and 11 three-bedroom units. 2 stories, exterior corridors. **Terms:** check-in 4:30 pm, 7 night minimum stay, 30 day cancellation notice-fee imposed, monthly rates available. **Amenities:** extended cable TV, voice mail, irons. **Leisure Activities:** 2 heated pools, wading pool, beach, swimming, boat dock, fishing, horticultural tours, barbecue grill area, video rentals. *Fee:* 2 tennis courts. **Guest Services:** coin laundry. **Business Services:** meeting rooms, administrative services, PC. **Cards:** MC, VI. *(See color ad p 760)*

SANIBEL'S SEASIDE INN

Phone: (941)472-1400

AAA (SAVE)
Apartment

2/9-4/21	1P: $295-$385	2P: $295-$385	XP: $20	F16
12/1-2/8 & 4/22-5/28	1P: $205-$275	2P: $205-$275	XP: $20	F16
5/29-11/30	1P: $169-$219	2P: $169-$219	XP: $20	F16

Location: From causeway, 0.8 mi e. 541 E Gulf Dr 33957. Fax: 941/395-0833. **Facility:** Nestled in the palms on the Gulf of Mexico. Rooms with shared, open air balcony or wraparound screened porches. Quiet, family oriented property. The landscaping and pool area are pleasant. Some sundries are offered at the reception area. Short drive to shopping and restaurants. Smoke free premises. 32 units. 1 two-bedroom unit, 1 three-bedroom unit, 22 efficiencies and 10 units with kitchen. *Bath:* combo or shower only. 1-2 stories, exterior corridors. **Terms:** 14 day cancellation notice-fee imposed, weekly rates available. **Amenities:** extended cable TV, safes, hair dryers. **Leisure Activities:** heated pool, beach, swimming, fishing, bicycles, shuffleboard, complimentary videos. **Guest Services:** [CP] meal plan available, gift shop, coin laundry. **Cards:** AE, DI, DS, MC, VI. *(See color ad p 762)*

SANIBEL'S SONG OF THE SEA, A EUROPEAN-STYLE SEASIDE INN

Phone: (941)472-2220

AAA (SAVE)
Apartment

2/9-4/21	2P: $315-$419	XP: $20	F16
12/1-2/8	2P: $219-$370	XP: $20	F16
4/22-5/28	2P: $219-$295	XP: $20	F16
5/29-11/30	2P: $155-$235	XP: $20	F16

Location: From causeway, just e. 863 E Gulf Dr 33957. Fax: 941/472-8569. **Facility:** This, quiet gulf front property is couple (of all ages) oriented. Rooms are cozy and private screened porches are a pleasant place to catch gulf breezes. Shopping, restaurants, art galleries and theaters are only a short drive away. The small number of guest units lends itself well to an intimate atmosphere, yet privileges at related larger properties provide bigger resort opportunities. 30 efficiencies. Some suites. 2 stories, exterior corridors. **Terms:** check-in 4 pm, 14 day cancellation notice-fee imposed, package plans. **Amenities:** extended cable TV, voice mail, safes, irons, hair dryers. **Leisure Activities:** heated pool, whirlpool, beach, swimming, tennis courts, bicycles, shuffleboard, gas grill. *Fee:* golf privileges, exercise room. **Guest Services:** [CP] meal plan available, gift shop, coin laundry. **Cards:** AE, DI, DS, MC, VI. *(See color ad p 762)*

SHALIMAR MOTEL

Phone: 941/931-4702

AAA (SAVE)
Apartment

2/1-4/30 Wkly	2P: $1635-$2160	XP: $85	
12/20-1/31 Wkly	2P: $1341-$2160	XP: $85	
5/1-11/30 Wkly	2P: $843-$1560	XP: $70	
12/1-12/19 Wkly	2P: $843-$1507	XP: $70	

Location: From causeway, 3 mi w on Periwinkle Way, 1.5 mi s on Tarpon Bay Rd, 0.5 mi w. 2823 W Gulf Dr 33957 (PO Box 389). Fax: 941/931-4704. **Facility:** Gulf front housekeeping cottages and efficiencies. 33 units with kitchen. 2 two-bedroom units. 1-2 stories, exterior corridors. **Terms:** 30 day cancellation notice, daily & monthly rates available. **Amenities:** extended cable TV, voice mail. **Leisure Activities:** heated pool, beach, swimming, fishing, basketball, shuffleboard, gas barbecues. *Fee:* bicycles. **Guest Services:** [CP] meal plan available, coin laundry. **Cards:** DS, MC, VI. **Special Amenities:** free local telephone calls. *(See color ad p 761)*

SHELL ISLAND BEACH CLUB

Phone: 941/472-4497

(SAVE)
Condominium

2/17-4/20 Wkly	1P: $2100-$2240
12/1-1/5 Wkly	1P: $1190-$2170
1/6-2/16 Wkly	1P: $1330-$1540
4/21-11/30 Wkly	1P: $1260-$1400

Location: From causeway, 1.2 mi e on Periwinkle Way, just s. 255 Periwinkle Way 33957. Fax: 941/472-4218. **Facility:** Nestled in a quiet residential area, this gulf front property offers screened terraces and covered parking. Beach chairs are provided with each unit. Gas barbecues are available. By beach front, it is a short walk to the historic Sanibel lighthouse. It is a short drive to shops and restaurants. This property is family oriented. 44 two-bedroom units with kitchen. 3 stories (no elevator), exterior corridors. **Terms:** 2 night minimum stay, 30 day cancellation notice, 14 day off season, daily rates available. **Amenities:** irons. *Some:* CD players. **Leisure Activities:** 2 heated pools, sauna, whirlpool, beach, swimming, tennis court, bicycles, shuffleboard. **Guest Services:** complimentary laundry. **Business Services:** meeting rooms. **Cards:** AE, DS, MC, VI. *(See color ad p 757)*

SUNDIAL BEACH RESORT

AAA SAVE
WWW ◇◇◇
Condominium

Phone: (941)472-4151

2/9-4/21	1P: $325-$669	2P: $325-$669	XP: $20	F16
12/1-2/8	1P: $209-$405	2P: $209-$405	XP: $20	F16
5/29-11/30	1P: $159-$365	2P: $159-$365	XP: $20	F16
4/22-5/28	1P: $229-$269	2P: $229-$269	XP: $20	F16

Location: From causeway, 0.7 mi w on Periwinkle Way, s on Donax St to Gulf Dr, 1 mi nw. 1451 Middle Gulf Dr 33957. Fax: 941/472-8892. **Facility:** Spacious one- and two-bedroom apartments; extensive grounds fronting one mile of gulf beach. 271 units with kitchen. 151 two-bedroom units. 4 stories, exterior corridors. **Terms:** check-in 4 pm, 14 day cancellation notice-fee imposed, weekly & monthly rates available, package plans. **Amenities:** extended cable TV, voice mail, safes, irons, hair dryers. **Dining:** 2 dining rooms, restaurant, deli, 7 am-midnight, $8-$25, cocktails, also, Windows on the Water, see separate listing, entertainment. **Leisure Activities:** 5 heated pools, whirlpool, beach, swimming, charter fishing, 12 tennis courts (2 lighted), children's program, nature program, recreation program, jogging, playground, exercise room, shuffleboard, volleyball, ecological center. *Fee:* sailboats, windsurfing, scuba diving & equipment, catamaran, golf privileges, tennis instruction, bicycles. **Guest Services:** [BP] meal plan available, gift shop, coin laundry. *Fee:* massage. **Business Services:** conference facilities, administrative services, PC, fax. **Cards:** AE, DI, DS, MC, VI. **Special Amenities:** free newspaper.
(See color ad p 762)

SOME UNITS

🍽 🍸 📶 FEE 🔧 🏊 ✂ VCR 📠 💻 📷 🔒 DATA PORT / ✖ /

TORTUGA BEACH CLUB

SAVE
WWW ◇◇◇
Condominium

Phone: (941)472-0400

2/16-4/19	1P: $350-$370	2P: $350-$370
12/1-1/4	1P: $365	2P: $365
1/5-2/15	1P: $245-$265	2P: $245-$265
4/20-11/30	1P: $215-$235	2P: $215-$235

Location: From causeway, 0.6 mi w on Periwinkle Way, 0.5 mi s on Donax St just e on Middle Gulf, then just e. 959 E Gulf Dr 33957. Fax: 941/472-6540. **Facility:** Conveniently located to shops and restaurants yet in a residential area, this gulf front, family-oriented property offers spacious bi-level townhouses. All master bedrooms feature king beds and kitchens have diswashers. Covered gas barbecue cooking area is surrounded by pleasant landscaping. One building has an elevator. 54 two-bedroom units with kitchen. Some whirlpool units. 3 stories (no elevator), exterior corridors. **Terms:** 30 day cancellation notice, daily rates available. **Amenities:** irons. **Leisure Activities:** heated pool, whirlpool, beach, swimming, 4 tennis courts, children's program, recreation program, social program, shuffleboard. **Guest Services:** complimentary laundry. **Cards:** AE, DI, DS, MC, VI. *(See color ad p 757)*

🍽 🏊 ✂ VCR 📠 📷 🔒

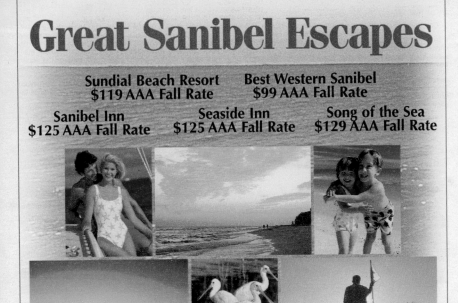
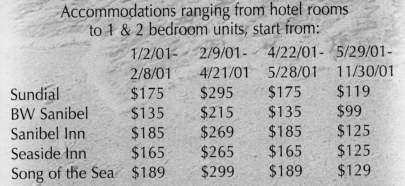

WATERSIDE INN ON THE BEACH

Phone: (941)472-1345

AAA (SAVE)

Motel

1/4-4/23	1P: $160-$230	2P: $160-$230	XP: $20	F16
12/1-1/3	1P: $133-$208	2P: $133-$208	XP: $20	F16
4/24-5/29	1P: $160-$199	2P: $160-$199	XP: $20	F16
5/30-11/30	1P: $138-$171	2P: $138-$171	XP: $20	F16

Location: From causeway, Periwinkle Way 4 mi w to Tarpon Bay Rd, 1 mi s, then 1 mi w. 3033 W Gulf Dr 33957. Fax: 941/472-2148. **Facility:** Gulf front with self-contained cottages or professionally decorated motel rooms with balconies and kitchens. Pleasant public areas. Landscaping creates a lush private pool area. Gas barbecue available. 41 units, 37 with kitchen. Some whirlpool units ($177-$295). *Bath:* combo or shower only. 2 stories, exterior corridors. **Terms:** 14 day cancellation notice, 60 day 12/16-5/25, weekly & monthly rates available, package plans, small pets only (in limited rooms). **Amenities:** extended cable TV, hair dryers. **Leisure Activities:** 2 heated pools, beach, swimming, shuffleboard, "sunset celebration" with snacks & beverages on the beach in season. *Fee:* bicycles. **Guest Services:** coin laundry. **Business Services:** meeting rooms. **Cards:** AE, DS, MC, VI.

SOME UNITS

WEST WIND INN

Phone: (941)472-1541

AAA (SAVE)

Motor Inn

12/21-4/30	1P: $228-$288	2P: $228-$288	XP: $21	F14
5/1-11/30	1P: $140-$195	2P: $140-$195	XP: $21	F14
12/1-12/20	1P: $136-$190	2P: $136-$190	XP: $21	F14

Location: From causeway, 3 mi w on Periwinkle Way, 1.5 mi s on Tarpon Bay Rd, 1.5 mi w. 3345 W Gulf Dr 33957. Fax: 941/472-8134. **Facility:** Gulf front. All rooms with screened balcony or terrace. 104 units, 55 with efficiency. 2 stories, exterior corridors. **Terms:** 7 day cancellation notice, weekly rates available, package plans. **Dining:** restaurant, 8 am-2 pm, Fri & Sat 5 pm-9 pm pool bar; guests only, $11-$17, cocktails. **Leisure Activities:** heated pool, wading pool, beach, swimming, golf privileges, 2 tennis courts, tennis clinics, shuffleboard, croquet, sand volleyball. *Fee:* boats, windsurfing, sunfish, floats, catamarans, kayaks, bicycles. **Guest Services:** gift shop, coin laundry. **Business Services:** meeting rooms. **Cards:** AE, DS, MC, VI. **Special Amenities:** free local telephone calls and free newspaper.

SOME UNITS

——— WHERE TO DINE ———

JEAN-PAUL'S FRENCH CORNER

French

Dinner: $20-$28   **Phone:** 941/472-1493

Location: From causeway, 2.8 mi w on Periwinkle Way, just n. 708 Tarpon Bay Rd 33957. **Hours:** Open 12/15-5/1; 6 pm-10 pm. Closed: Sun. **Reservations:** suggested. **Features:** casual dress; beer & wine only; minimum charge-$20 per adult. Popular with islanders, this dressy-casual restaurant tempts patrons with French favorites from escargot to chocolate mousse. The dining room is located on the first floor of a residential building. Tables are intimately spaced, so whisper your secrets. **Cards:** MC, VI.

MAD HATTER

American

Dinner: $20-$31   **Phone:** 941/472-0033

Location: 7.5 mi n from jct Periwinkle Way and Sanibel-Captiva Rd. 6460 Sanibel-Captiva Rd 33957. **Hours:** 5 pm-9:30 pm; noon-9:30 pm 12/15-7/4. **Reservations:** suggested. **Features:** casual dress; carryout; beer & wine only; valet parking; a la carte. A charming, small dining room with a superior vantage point to view sunsets. Service is friendly, unpretentious and informative. The menu features market fresh fish and veal. Dishes prepared with care and artistic food preparation. A delightful find. Smoke free premises. **Cards:** AE, MC, VI.

PIPPIN'S BAR & GRILL

Steak & Seafood

Dinner: $10-$25   **Phone:** 941/395-2255

Location: From causeway, 1.8 mi w on Periwinkle Way; in Tahitian Gardens Shopping Center. 1975 Periwinkle Way 33957. **Hours:** 4:30 pm-9:30 pm. Closed: 11/22; also Super Bowl Sun. **Features:** casual dress; children's menu; early bird specials; carryout; salad bar; cocktails & lounge. This restaurant ages its own beef for six to eight weeks, which along with thoughtful grilling and seasoning, makes up the rich flavor of the sirloin and other steaks. Ribs, chicken and fish also are popular in this intimate, tropical-themed eatery. **Cards:** AE, CB, DI, DS, MC, VI.

TARWINKLE'S SEAFOOD EMPORIUM

Seafood

Lunch: $5-$9   **Dinner:** $14-$19   **Phone:** 941/472-1366

Location: At corner of Periwinkle Way and Tarpon Bay. 2499 Periwinkle Way 33957. **Hours:** 11:30 am-10 pm. **Reservations:** suggested. **Features:** casual dress; children's menu; early bird specials; carryout; cocktails & lounge; entertainment; a la carte. The emphasis is on island seafood with a few chicken, pasta, steak and pork entrees also served. Try shrimp stuffed with crab meat and salad with an interesting honey-mustard dressing. An attractive salt-water aquarium will entertain the kids. **Cards:** AE, DI, DS, MC, VI.

WINDOWS ON THE WATER

Regional American

Lunch: $7-$13   **Dinner:** $17-$25   **Phone:** 941/395-6014

Location: Causeway, 0.7 mi w on Periwinkle Way, s on Donax St to Gulf Dr, 1 mi nw; in Sundial Beach Resort. 1451 Middle Gulf Dr 33957. **Hours:** 7:30-10:30 am, 11:30-2 & 5:30-9:30 pm, Sun 7:30-10 am, 11-2 & 5:30-9:30 pm. **Reservations:** suggested. **Features:** casual dress; Sunday brunch; children's menu; carryout; cocktails & lounge; entertainment. Bright, airy dining room with view of the Gulf of Mexico. Floridian dishes, fresh local seafood seasoned with spices used from Mexico to the Caribbean. Smoke free premises. **Cards:** AE, CB, DI, DS, MC, VI.

SANTA ROSA BEACH pop. 250

——— WHERE TO STAY ———

A HIGHLANDS HOUSE BED & BREAKFAST

Bed & Breakfast

Phone: (850)267-0110

12/26-11/30	1P: $90-$200	2P: $90-$200	XP: $20	F10

Location: US 98, 2 mi s to CR 393, just e on SR 30A. 4193 W Scenic SR 30A 32459 (PO Box 1189). Fax: 850/267-3602. **Facility:** Located on the beach. A large porch on the second floor to view the ocean and sunsets. Rooms nicely appointed. A short walk on the boardwalk puts you on the beach. Smoke free premises. 8 units. Some whirlpool units ($160). *Bath:* combo or shower only. 2 stories, interior corridors. **Terms:** open 12/26-11/30, 3 day cancellation notice, pet on premises. **Amenities:** no TVs. **Leisure Activities:** beach access. **Guest Services:** [BP] meal plan available. **Cards:** DS, MC, VI.

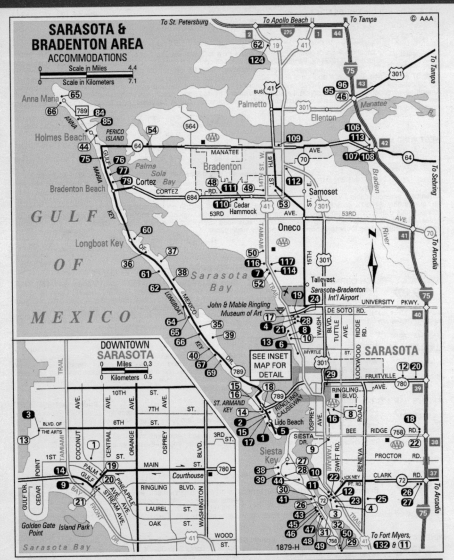

SARASOTA & BRADENTON AREA ACCOMMODATIONS

Scale in Miles 0 — 4.4
Scale in Kilometers 0 — 7.1

© AAA

DOWNTOWN SARASOTA
Miles 0 — 0.3
Kilometers 0 — 0.5

SEE INSET MAP FOR DETAIL

1879-H

✈ Airport Accommodations					
Spotter/Map Page Number	OA	SARASOTA-BRADENTON	Diamond Rating	Rate Range High Season	Listing Page
8 / above	AAA	Best Western Golden Host Resort, 1.5 mi s of airport	◆◆	$95-$120 SAVE	769
28 / below		Days Inn-Airport, 0.5 mi s of airport	◆◆	$50-$101	771
4 / above	AAA	Hampton Inn-Sarasota/Bradenton, 0.5 mi s of terminal	◆◆	$104-$124 SAVE	772
7 / above		Holiday Inn-Airport Marina, 3.7 mi n of terminal	◆◆◆	$109-$149	772
21 / above	AAA	Knights Inn, 0.5 mi s of airport	◆	$72-$95 SAVE	774
24 / above		Sarasota/Bradenton Courtyard By Marriott, At entrance	◆◆◆	$140-$150	775
19 / above		Sleep Inn, at entrance	◆◆	$99-$110	777

Sarasota & Bradenton Area and Vicinity

This index helps you "spot" where approved accommodations are located on the corresponding detailed maps. Rate ranges are for comparison only and show the property's high season. Turn to the listing page for more detailed rate information and consult display ads for special promotions. Restaurant rate range is for dinner, unless only lunch (L) is served.

Spotter/Map Page Number	OA	SARASOTA - Lodgings	Diamond Rating	Rate Range High Season	Listing Page
1 / p. 764	AAA	The Helmsley Sandcastle Hotel - see color ad p 772	◈◈◈	$159-$299 [SAVE]	772
2 / p. 764	AAA	Holiday Inn-Lido Beach - see color ad p 773	◈◈◈	$169-$259 [SAVE]	773
3 / p. 764	AAA	Hyatt Sarasota	◈◈◈	$175-$200	774
4 / p. 764	AAA	Hampton Inn-Sarasota/Bradenton	◈◈◈	$104-$124 [SAVE]	772
5 / p. 764	AAA	Half Moon Beach Club - see color ad p 771	◈◈◈	$139-$269 [SAVE]	772
6 / p. 764	AAA	Best Western Royal Palms	◈◈	$75-$110 [SAVE]	770
7 / p. 764		Holiday Inn-Airport Marina - see color ad p 773	◈◈◈	$109-$149	772
8 / p. 764	AAA	Best Western Golden Host Resort	◈◈	$95-$120 [SAVE]	769
9 / p. 764		The Cypress, A Bed & Breakfast Inn	◈◈◈	$150-$210	771
10 / p. 764	AAA	The Calais Motel-Apartments	◈◈	$75-$99 [SAVE]	770
11 / p. 764	AAA	The Tides Inn	◈◈	$96-$107 [SAVE]	777
12 / p. 764	AAA	La Rue Motel Apartments	◈	$84-$105 [SAVE]	774
13 / p. 764	AAA	Wellesley Inn & Suites - see color ad opposite title page	◈◈◈	$89-$129 [SAVE]	777
14 / p. 764		Holiday Inn-Downtown By The Bay	◈◈◈	$114-$129	773
15 / p. 764	AAA	Radisson Lido Beach Resort - see color ad p 776	◈◈◈	$219-$365 [SAVE]	775
16 / p. 764	AAA	Best Western Midtown - see color ad p 769	◈◈	$99-$119 [SAVE]	770
17 / p. 764	AAA	Coquina on the Beach Resort - see color ad p 771	◈◈◈	$169-$199 [SAVE]	770
18 / p. 764		Hampton Inn I-75/Bee Ridge	◈◈◈	$129	772
19 / p. 764		Sleep Inn	◈◈	$99-$110	777
20 / p. 764		AmericInn Hotel & Suites - see color ad p 818	◈◈◈	$129-$189	769
21 / p. 764	AAA	Knights Inn	◈◈	$72-$95 [SAVE]	774
22 / p. 764		Holiday Inn Express Sarasota Siesta Key	◈◈◈	$119-$139	773
23 / p. 764		The Sunset Lodge Motel	◈◈	$90-$98	777
24 / p. 764		Sarasota/Bradenton Courtyard By Marriott	◈◈◈	$140-$150	775
25 / p. 764	AAA	Timberwoods Vacation Villas Resort - see color ad p 776	◈◈	$84-$142 [SAVE]	777
26 / p. 764		Ramada Limited	◈◈◈	$110-$130	775
27 / p. 764	AAA	Comfort Inn	◈◈◈	$79-$129 [SAVE]	770
28 / p. 764		Days Inn-Airport - see ad p 396	◈◈	$50-$101	771
29 / p. 764		Quayside Inn	◈◈	$60-$86	774

Spotter/Map Page Number	OA	SARASOTA - Restaurants	Diamond Rating	Rate Range High Season	Listing Page
① / p. 764	AAA	**The Bijou Cafe**	◆◆◆	$15-$24	777
③ / p. 764		Coasters Seafood Co at the Southbridge	◆◆	$14-$22	778
④ / p. 764		Le Champagne Restaurant	◆◆◆	$20-$31	778
⑧ / p. 764	AAA	**Michael's on East**	◆◆◆◆	$17-$32	778
⑨ / p. 764		Cafe Baci	◆◆◆	$11-$23	777
⑩ / p. 764		Cuoco Matto Ristorante	◆◆	$7-$17	778
⑪ / p. 764		Roessler's Restaurant	◆◆◆	$15-$31	779
⑫ / p. 764		Johnny Leverock's Seafood House	◆◆	$6-$19	778
⑭ / p. 764		Osteria Northern Italian Restaurant	◆◆◆	$12-$26	778
⑮ / p. 764		Columbia Restaurant	◆◆◆	$15-$22	778
⑯ / p. 764		Charley's Crab	◆◆◆	$12-$26	778
⑰ / p. 764		Cafe of the Arts	◆◆◆	$12-$36	777
⑱ / p. 764		Tommy Bahama's Tropical Cafe	◆◆	$15-$23	779
⑲ / p. 764		First Watch Restaurant	◆◆	$3-$8(L)	778
⑳ / p. 764		Tropical Thai Restaurant and Sushi Bar	◆◆	$6-$20	779
㉑ / p. 764		Patrick's Restaurant & Tavern	◆◆	$6-$19	778
㉒ / p. 764		Sugar & Spice	◆◆	$4-$14	779
		SIESTA KEY - Lodgings			
㊳ / p. 764	·	Miramar Beach Apartments of Siesta Key	◆◆	$120-$200	781
㊴ / p. 764	AAA	**Tropical Breeze Inn**	◆◆	$139-$295 SAVE	782
㊶ / p. 764	AAA	**Palm Bay Club - see color ad p 775**	◆◆◆	$250-$625 SAVE	782
㊸ / p. 764		Crescent View Beach Club - see color ad p 770	◆◆◆	$149-$439	781
㊹ / p. 764	AAA	**Sunsets on the Key**	◆◆◆	$129-$199 SAVE	782
㊺ / p. 764	AAA	**Sara Sea Inn at the Beach - see color ad p 774**	◆◆◆	$159-$369 SAVE	782
㊻ / p. 764	AAA	**Tropical Shores Beach Resort - see color ad p 768**	◆◆◆	$189-$395 SAVE	782
㊼ / p. 764	AAA	**Captiva Beach Resort - see color ad p 769**	◆◆◆	$650-$1450 SAVE	781
㊽ / p. 764	AAA	**Conclare Motel & Apartments**	◆◆	$135-$275 SAVE	781
㊾ / p. 764		Gulf Terrace Vacation Apartments	◆◆	$640-$775	781
㊿ / p. 764	AAA	**Turtle Beach Resort**	◆◆◆	$250-$370 SAVE	782
		SIESTA KEY - Restaurants			
㉖ / p. 764		Chez Daniel	◆◆	$16-$24	783
㉗ / p. 764		Village Cafe	◆	$4-$8(L)	783
㉘ / p. 764		Beach Cafe & Sports Bar	◆	$7-$21	783
㉙ / p. 764	AAA	**Ophelia's on the Bay**	◆◆◆	$15-$27	783

Spotter/Map Page Number	OA	SIESTA KEY - Restaurants (continued)	Diamond Rating	Rate Range High Season	Listing Page
㉚ / p. 764		The Summerhouse Restaurant	◆◆◆	$10-$25	783
㉛ / p. 764		Bob's Boathouse Restaurant	◆◆	$5-$16	783
㉜ / p. 764	AAA	**Turtles on Little Sarasota Bay**	◆◆	$7-$19	783
		LONGBOAT KEY - Lodgings			
(60) / p. 764	AAA	**Harbour Villa Club**	◆◆◆	$1895-$1995 SAVE	462
(61) / p. 764		Riviera Beach Resort	◆◆	$820-$1150	464
(62) / p. 764	AAA	**Holiday Inn Hotel & Suites**	◆◆◆	$229-$399 SAVE	463
(64) / p. 764		Hilton Longboat Key Beachfront Resort - see ad p 44 & color ad p 462	◆◆◆	$199-$329	462
(65) / p. 764		Holiday Lodge - see color ad p 463	◆◆	$910-$2660	463
(66) / p. 764		Diplomat Resort	◆◆	$133-$212	462
(67) / p. 764		The Colony Beach & Tennis Resort	◆◆◆	$270-$695	462
(69) / p. 764	AAA	**The Resort at Longboat Key Club - see ad p 463**	◆◆◆◆	$325-$1075 SAVE	464
		LONGBOAT KEY - Restaurants			
㉟ / p. 764		Maureen Restaurant & Martini Bar	◆◆◆	$17-$25	464
㊱ / p. 764		Euphemia Haye	◆◆◆	$18-$34	464
㊲ / p. 764		Harry's Continental Kitchens	◆◆	$19-$32	464
㊳ / p. 764	AAA	**Lynches Landing Bar & Grill**	◆◆	$5-$17	464
㊴ / p. 764		Poseidon Ocean Harvest Restaurant	◆◆◆	$18-$31	464
㊵ / p. 764		The Colony Restaurant	◆◆◆	$20-$36	464
		BRADENTON BEACH - Lodgings			
(75) / p. 764		Econo Lodge Surfside - see color ad p 250	◆◆	$119-$170	253
(76) / p. 764	AAA	**Sunset Beach Motel**	◆◆	$110-$129 SAVE	253
(77) / p. 764	AAA	**Tradewinds Resort**	◆◆◆	$125-$263 SAVE	253
(79) / p. 764		Tortuga Inn	◆◆◆	$99-$229	253
		HOLMES BEACH - Lodgings			
(84) / p. 764	AAA	**The Beach Inn**	◆◆◆	$129-$209 SAVE	418
(85) / p. 764	AAA	**Harrington House Beachfront Bed & Breakfast**	◆◆◆	$179-$249 SAVE	418
		HOLMES BEACH - Restaurant			
㊹ / p. 764		OOH LA LA!	◆◆	$18-$27	418
		ELLENTON - Lodgings			
(96) / p. 764		Best Western Inn	◆◆◆	$80-$110	306
		ELLENTON - Restaurant			
㊻ / p. 764		Crab Trap II	◆◆	$9-$38	306

Spotter/Map Page Number	OA	BRADENTON - Lodgings	Diamond Rating	Rate Range High Season	Listing Page
106 / p. 764	AAA	**Comfort Inn-Bradenton**	▽▽▽	$89-$109 SAVE	250
107 / p. 764		Holiday Inn Express	▽▽▽	$65-$170	251
108 / p. 764		Days Inn I-75	▽▽	$77	250
109 / p. 764		Holiday Inn-Riverfront	▽▽▽	$129	251
110 / p. 764	AAA	**Park Inn & Suites** - see color ad p 251	▽▽▽	$74-$124 SAVE	251
111 / p. 764		Shorewalk Vacation Villas Resort	▽▽	$129	252
112 / p. 764		Quality Inn & Suites	▽▽▽	$70-$95	252
113 / p. 764	AAA	**Econo Lodge I-75** - see color ad p 250	▽▽	$69-$99 SAVE	251
114 / p. 764	AAA	**Econo Lodge**	▽▽	$69-$109 SAVE	250
116 / p. 764	AAA	**Super 8 Motel**	▽▽	$69-$99 SAVE	252
117 / p. 764	AAA	**Howard Johnson Express Inn**	▽▽	$56-$90 SAVE	251
		BRADENTON - Restaurants			
49 / p. 764		Tropical Thai Restaurant	▽▽	$8-$20	252
50 / p. 764		Cattle Company Cafe	▽	$5-$11	252
52 / p. 764	AAA	**Anna Maria Oyster Bar**	▽▽	$5-$25	252
53 / p. 764		Miller's Dutch Kitch'n	▽▽	$4-$14	252
54 / p. 764		Leverock's of Perico Harbor	▽▽	$9-$21	252
		PALMETTO - Lodgings			
124 / p. 764		Sea Inn Hotel	▽▽	Failed to provide	722
		PALMETTO - Restaurant			
62 / p. 764		Crab Trap 1	▽▽	$10-$40	722
		OSPREY - Lodgings			
132 / p. 764	AAA	**Ramada Inn-Sarasota South** - see color ad p 776	▽▽	$97-$106 SAVE	709
		ANNA MARIA - Restaurants			
65 / p. 764		Bistro at Island's End	▽▽▽	$8-$27	240
66 / p. 764		Sandbar	▽▽	$11-$18	240

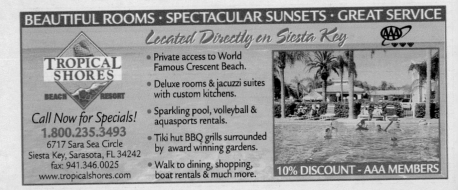

SARASOTA pop. 51,000   (See map p. 764; index p. 765)

───── WHERE TO STAY ─────

AMERICINN HOTEL & SUITES   Phone: (941)342-8778 ㉕

2/1-4/16	1P: $129-$189	2P: $129-$189
12/24-1/31	1P: $103-$139	2P: $103-$179
12/1-12/23	1P: $89-$129	2P: $89-$169
4/17-11/30	1P: $94-$135	2P: $94-$135

Motel

Location: I-75, exit 39, 0.4 mi w, just n on N Cattleman, just e on Commercial Way. 5931 Fruitville Rd 34232. Fax: 941/342-8668. **Facility:** 111 units. Some suites ($129-$189) and whirlpool units ($129-$189). *Bath:* combo or shower only. 4 stories, interior corridors. **Amenities:** extended cable TV, dual phone lines, voice mail, irons, hair dryers. **Leisure Activities:** heated pool, whirlpool, exercise room. **Guest Services:** [ECP] meal plan available, coin laundry. **Business Services:** meeting rooms, fax. **Cards:** AE, DI, DS, MC, VI. *(See color ad p 818)* SOME UNITS

⟨ASK⟩ ⟨SD⟩ ⟨†┿⟩ ⟨&⟩ ⟨&⟩ ⟨∅⟩ ⟨⤢⟩ ⟨📺⟩ ⟨🖨⟩ ⟨▦⟩ ⟨▭⟩ ⟨⊟⟩ ⟨DATA PORT⟩ / ⟨✕⟩ /

BEST WESTERN GOLDEN HOST RESORT   Phone: (941)355-5141 ⑧

2/1-4/21	1P: $95-$120	2P: $95-$120
12/1-1/31 & 4/22-5/12	1P: $65-$90	2P: $65-$90
5/13-11/30	1P: $55-$80	2P: $55-$80

Motel

Location: On US 41, 0.6 mi s of jct University. 4675 N Tamiami Tr 34234. Fax: 941/355-9286. **Facility:** 80 units, 3 with efficiency. 2 stories, exterior corridors. **Terms:** weekly rates available, package plans. **Amenities:** safes. *Some:* irons, hair dryers. **Dining:** cocktails. **Leisure Activities:** heated pool, shuffleboard. **Guest Services:** coin laundry. **Business Services:** meeting rooms, fax. **Cards:** AE, DI, DS, MC, VI. **Special Amenities:** free continental breakfast.

SOME UNITS

⟨SD⟩ ⟨Y⟩ ⟨⤢⟩ ⟨📺⟩ ⟨🖨⟩ ⟨DATA PORT⟩ / ⟨✕⟩ / ⟨▭⟩ ⟨⊟⟩ ⟨⊟⟩ /
FEE

(See map p. 764)

BEST WESTERN MIDTOWN

Phone: (941)955-9841 16

AAA SAVE
♦♦ ♦♦
Motel

2/1-4/14	1P: $99-$119	2P: $99-$119	XP: $6	F18
12/1-1/31	1P: $69-$99	2P: $69-$99	XP: $6	F18
4/15-11/30	1P: $59-$79	2P: $59-$79	XP: $6	F18

Location: On US 41, just n of Sarasota Memorial Hospital. 1425 S Tamiami Tr 34239. **Facility:** 100 units. 3 stories, exterior corridors. **Terms:** weekly & monthly rates available, package plans. **Amenities:** extended cable TV, voice mail, irons, hair dryers. **Leisure Activities:** heated pool, barbecue area. **Guest Services:** [ECP] meal plan available, coin laundry. **Business Services:** meeting rooms, fax. **Cards:** AE, CB, DI, DS, JC, MC, VI. **Special Amenities:** free continental breakfast and free newspaper. *(See color ad p 769)*

SOME UNITS

[icons] FEE

BEST WESTERN ROYAL PALMS

Phone: (941)365-1342 6

AAA SAVE
♦♦ ♦♦
Motel

2/1-4/22	1P: $75-$110	2P: $75-$110	XP: $10	F12
12/24-1/31	1P: $59-$79	2P: $59-$79	XP: $10	F12
12/1-12/23 & 4/23-11/30	1P: $49-$69	2P: $49-$69	XP: $5	F12

Location: 0.9 mi n jct SR 780. 1701 N Tamiami Tr 34234. Fax: 941/955-8066. **Facility:** 37 units, 10 with kitchen. *Bath:* combo or shower only. 1 story, exterior corridors. **Terms:** 3 day cancellation notice-fee imposed, package plans. **Amenities:** extended cable TV. **Leisure Activities:** small heated pool, shuffleboard. **Cards:** AE, CB, DI, DS, MC, VI. **Special Amenities:** free continental breakfast and free local telephone calls. SOME UNITS

[icons] FEE

THE CALAIS MOTEL-APARTMENTS

Phone: (941)921-5797 10

AAA SAVE
♦♦ ♦♦
Apartment

1/20-4/20	1P: $75-$89	2P: $85-$99	XP: $10
12/20-1/19	1P: $60-$70	2P: $65-$75	XP: $8
12/1-12/19 & 4/21-11/30	1P: $44-$50	2P: $49-$55	XP: $6

Location: On SR 72, 0.3 mi sw of jct US 41. 1735 Stickney Point Rd 34231. Fax: 941/922-1284. **Facility:** 26 units. 1 two-bedroom unit and 25 units with kitchen. Some suites ($75-$125). 2 stories, exterior corridors. **Terms:** 3 day cancellation notice, 30 day in season (12/00-4/01)-fee imposed, weekly & monthly rates available, pets ($5-$8 extra charge). **Amenities:** *Some:* irons, hair dryers. **Leisure Activities:** heated pool, barbecue grill. **Guest Services:** coin laundry. **Cards:** AE, DS, MC, VI.

SOME UNITS

[icons] FEE

COMFORT INN

Phone: (941)921-7750 27

AAA SAVE
♦♦ ♦♦
Motel

2/1-4/20	1P: $79-$129	2P: $89-$129	XP: $10	F18
12/1-1/31	1P: $69-$109	2P: $69-$109	XP: $10	F18
4/21-11/30	1P: $59-$89	2P: $59-$99	XP: $10	F18

Location: I-75, exit 37, just w on SR 72. 5778 Clark Rd 34233. Fax: 941/925-2474. **Facility:** 63 units. *Bath:* combo or shower only. 3 stories, interior corridors. **Terms:** 7 day cancellation notice, weekly & monthly rates available, pets ($10 extra charge). **Amenities:** extended cable TV. *Some:* irons, hair dryers. **Leisure Activities:** heated pool, whirlpool. **Guest Services:** [ECP] meal plan available, coin laundry. **Business Services:** meeting rooms, fax. **Cards:** AE, DI, DS, MC, VI. **Special Amenities:** free continental breakfast and free newspaper. SOME UNITS

[icons] FEE FEE

COQUINA ON THE BEACH RESORT

Phone: (941)388-2141 17

AAA SAVE
♦♦ ♦♦
Motel

2/1-4/30	1P: $169-$199	2P: $169-$199	XP: $8	F18
12/23-1/31	1P: $109-$179	2P: $109-$179	XP: $8	F18
5/1-11/30	1P: $89-$139	2P: $89-$139	XP: $8	F18
12/1-12/22	1P: $89-$119	2P: $89-$119	XP: $8	F18

Location: St Armands Key, on Lido Beach, 0.9 mi s of St Armands Cir. 1008 Ben Franklin Dr 34236. Fax: 941/388-3017. **Facility:** Gulf front. Large units, all with balcony or patio. 34 units. 1 two-bedroom unit, 26 efficiencies and 8 units with kitchen. Some suites ($149-$319). *Bath:* combo or shower only. 2 stories, exterior corridors. **Terms:** 14 day cancellation notice-fee imposed, pets ($25 extra charge). **Amenities:** extended cable TV. *Some:* irons, hair dryers. **Leisure Activities:** heated pool, beach, barbecues, beach loungers. **Guest Services:** coin laundry. **Business Services:** fax. **Cards:** AE, DI, DS, MC, VI. **Special Amenities:** free newspaper. *(See color ad p 771)*

SOME UNITS

[icons]

(See map p. 764)

THE CYPRESS, A BED & BREAKFAST INN
Phone: 941/955-4683 9

▼▼▼
12/1-4/30   2P: $150-$210   XP: $20
5/1-11/30   2P: $150-$170   XP: $20

Bed & Breakfast   **Location:** Just n on Palm Ave from jct US 41; or just n on Ringling Blvd, just s on Palm Ave. 621 Gulfstream Ave S 34236. Fax: 941/906-8952. **Facility:** Adjacent to marina and Bayfront Park. Beautiful gardens are relaxing. It's a pleasure to choose from various room themes such as Victorian, Key West, Floral and French elegance. Designated smoking area. 4 units. 1 two-bedroom unit. Some suites and whirlpool units. *Bath:* combo or shower only. 2 stories, interior corridors. **Terms:** age restrictions may apply, 14 day cancellation notice-fee imposed. **Amenities:** extended cable TV. **Leisure Activities:** bicycles. **Guest Services:** [BP] meal plan available, complimentary evening beverages. **Cards:** AE, DS, MC, VI.

SOME UNITS

[🍽️+] [✕] / [VCR] /

DAYS INN-AIRPORT
Phone: (941)355-9721 28

SAVE

▼▼▼

Motel

All Year   1P: $50-$95   2P: $56-$101   XP: $6   F13

Location: US 41, just s of jct University Pkwy. 4900 N Tamiami Tr 34234. Fax: 941/351-7316. **Facility:** 121 units. 2 stories, exterior corridors. **Terms:** check-in 4 pm, weekly & monthly rates available, pets ($6 extra charge). **Amenities:** extended cable TV. *Some:* safes (fee), irons, hair dryers. **Leisure Activities:** playground, shuffleboard. **Guest Services:** [BP] meal plan available, coin laundry. **Cards:** AE, CB, DI, DS, JC, MC, VI.
(See ad p 396)

SOME UNITS

[S🄳] [✈] [🐕] [🍽️] [🚫] [🏊] [📷] / [✕] [🐾] [▭] [📺] [🔌] /
                        FEE   FEE   FEE

(See map p. 764)

HALF MOON BEACH CLUB

AAA SAVE
▽▽▽▽
Motor Inn

Phone: (941)388-3694   **5**

12/20-4/30	2P: $139-$269	XP: $15 F17
12/1-12/19 & 5/1-11/30	2P: $119-$189	XP: $15 F17

Location: On St Armands Key of Lido Beach, 1.6 mi s of St Armands Cir. 2050 Ben Franklin Dr 34236. **Fax:** 941/388-1938. **Facility:** Gulf front. Spacious units with balcony or patio. 85 units. 27 efficiencies and 12 units with kitchen. Some suites. *Bath:* combo or shower only. 2 stories, interior/exterior corridors. **Terms:** 3 day cancellation notice, in season, package plans - off season. **Amenities:** extended cable TV, voice mail, irons, hair dryers. **Dining:** restaurant, 7 am-11 pm, $12-$18, cocktails. **Leisure Activities:** heated pool, beach, shuffleboard, volleyball. *Fee:* bicycles, video library. **Guest Services:** coin laundry. **Business Services:** meeting rooms, PC, fax. **Cards:** AE, CB, DI, DS, MC, VI. **Special Amenities:** free newspaper. *(See color ad p 771)*

SOME UNITS

HAMPTON INN I-75/BEE RIDGE

SAVE
▽▽▽▽
Motel

Phone: (941)371-1900   **18**

1/21-4/15	1P: $129
12/24-1/20	1P: $104
4/16-11/30	1P: $99
12/1-12/23	1P: $84-$94

Location: I-75, exit 38, just w on Bee Ridge, then just n. 5995 Cattleridge Rd 34232. **Fax:** 941/371-0241. **Facility:** 121 units. *Bath:* combo or shower only. 5 stories, interior corridors. **Terms:** check-in 4 pm, package plans. **Amenities:** extended cable TV, video games, dual phone lines, voice mail, irons, hair dryers. **Leisure Activities:** heated pool, whirlpool, exercise room. **Guest Services:** [ECP] meal plan available, valet and coin laundry. **Business Services:** meeting rooms, fax. **Cards:** AE, DI, DS, JC, MC, VI.

SOME UNITS

FEE

HAMPTON INN-SARASOTA/BRADENTON

AAA SAVE
▽▽▽▽
Motel

Phone: (941)351-7734   **4**

12/1-4/30	1P: $104-$114	2P: $114-$124
5/1-11/30	1P: $62-$72	2P: $72-$82

Location: US 41, just s of jct University Pkwy. 5000 N Tamiami Tr 34234. **Fax:** 941/351-8820. **Facility:** 97 units. 3 stories, exterior corridors. **Amenities:** video games, irons. *Some:* hair dryers. **Leisure Activities:** heated pool, exercise room. **Guest Services:** [ECP] meal plan available, valet and coin laundry. **Business Services:** meeting rooms. **Cards:** AE, CB, DI, DS, MC, VI. **Special Amenities:** free continental breakfast and free local telephone calls.

SOME UNITS

FEE   FEE   FEE   FEE

THE HELMSLEY SANDCASTLE HOTEL

AAA SAVE
▽▽▽▽
Motor Inn

Phone: (941)388-2181   **1**

2/3-4/22	1P: $159-$299	2P: $159-$299 XP: $10 F18
4/23-11/30	1P: $99-$199	2P: $99-$199 XP: $10 F18
12/1-2/2	1P: $95-$195	2P: $95-$195 XP: $10 F18

Location: On St Armands Key, at Lido Beach, 1.3 mi s of St Armands Cir. 1540 Ben Franklin Dr 34236. **Fax:** 941/388-2655. **Facility:** Gulf front. 179 units. Some whirlpool units. *Bath:* combo or shower only. 4 stories, exterior corridors. **Terms:** package plans. **Amenities:** extended cable TV, safes, hair dryers. *Some:* irons. **Dining:** 2 restaurants, 7 am-10 pm, pool bar, $7-$26, cocktails, entertainment. **Leisure Activities:** 2 pools (1 heated), beach, recreation program, childrens programs weekends only, shuffleboard, game room, table tennis. *Fee:* boats, sailboating, aqua cycles, cabanas, bicycles. **Guest Services:** gift shop, valet and coin laundry. **Business Services:** meeting rooms, fax. **Cards:** AE, CB, DI, DS, MC, VI. **Special Amenities:** free newspaper. *(See color ad below)*

HOLIDAY INN-AIRPORT MARINA

▽▽▽
Motor Inn

Phone: (941)355-2781   **7**

1/15-5/31	1P: $109-$149
12/1-1/14 & 6/1-11/30	1P: $79-$99

Location: On US 41, 2.4 mi n of jct University Pkwy. 7150 N Tamiami Tr 34243. **Fax:** 941/355-1605. **Facility:** 179 units. 1 two-bedroom unit. Some suites ($119-$189). 2 stories, interior/exterior corridors. **Terms:** package plans. **Amenities:** extended cable TV, dual phone lines, voice mail, irons, hair dryers. **Leisure Activities:** heated pool, charter fishing, exercise room. *Fee:* marina. **Guest Services:** gift shop, area transportation, valet and coin laundry. **Business Services:** meeting rooms, administrative services, PC, fax. **Cards:** AE, CB, DI, DS, JC, MC, VI. *(See color ad p 773)*

SOME UNITS

(See map p. 764)

HOLIDAY INN-DOWNTOWN BY THE BAY

WWW   Motor Inn

			Phone: (941)365-1900	**14**
1/29-4/14	1P: $114-$129	2P: $114-$129	XP: $10	F12
12/1-1/28	1P: $99-$114	2P: $99-$114	XP: $10	F12
4/15-11/30	1P: $74-$89	2P: $74-$89	XP: $10	F12

Location: Jct US 41 and SR 789. 1 N Tamiami Tr 34236. Fax: 941/365-1900. **Facility:** Opposite the Sarasota Bay. 100 units. *Bath:* combo or shower only. 6 stories, interior/exterior corridors. **Amenities:** extended cable TV, voice mail, irons, hair dryers. **Leisure Activities:** exercise room. **Guest Services:** coin laundry. **Business Services:** meeting rooms, fax. **Cards:** AE, CB, DI, DS, JC, MC, VI.

SOME UNITS
(ASK) (S/D) (Y1) (⌂) (&) (⟋) (⟋) (≋) (⎘) (▭) (DATA PORT) / (✕) (⊟) (🔒) / FEE FEE

HOLIDAY INN EXPRESS SARASOTA SIESTA KEY

WWW   Motel

		Phone: (941)924-4900	**22**
12/1-1/1 & 2/9-4/21	1P: $119-$139		
1/2-2/8	1P: $89-$109		
4/22-11/30	1P: $69-$89		

Location: On US 41, just s of jct SR 72. 6600 S Tamiami Tr 34231. Fax: 941/923-7774. **Facility:** 130 units. *Bath:* combo or shower only. 4 stories, exterior corridors. **Terms:** check-in 4 pm, package plans, small pets only ($30 extra charge). **Amenities:** extended cable TV, video games, dual phone lines, voice mail, safes, irons, hair dryers. **Leisure Activities:** heated pool, whirlpool, exercise room. **Guest Services:** [ECP] meal plan available, valet and coin laundry. **Business Services:** meeting rooms, fax. **Cards:** AE, CB, DI, DS, JC, MC, VI.

SOME UNITS
(ASK) (S/D) (🐾) (⫙) (⌂) (&) (⟋) (⟋) (≋) FEE (⎘) (▭) (DATA PORT) / (✕) (🔒) / FEE

HOLIDAY INN-LIDO BEACH

(AAA) (SAVE)
WWW   Hotel

		Phone: (941)388-5555	**2**
1/26-4/28	1P: $169-$259	XP: $15	F18
12/1-1/2 & 4/29-11/30	1P: $125-$239	XP: $15	F18
1/3-1/25	1P: $149-$219	XP: $15	F18

Location: St Armands Key, at Lido Beach, 0.4 mi s of St Armands Cir. 233 Ben Franklin Dr 34236. Fax: 941/388-4321. **Facility:** Across the street from the gulf, many units have balcony and gulf views. 135 units. Some suites ($180-$375) and whirlpool units. *Bath:* combo or shower only. 7 stories, interior corridors. **Terms:** check-in 4 pm, cancellation fee imposed, package plans. **Amenities:** extended cable TV, video games, voice mail, irons, hair dryers. **Dining:** dining room, rooftop dining, entertainment (seasonal Fri-Sat); 6:30 am-2 & 5-10 pm; pool bar, lobby lounge, $10-$25. **Leisure Activities:** heated pool, beach access, exercise room. Fee: bicycles, beach chairs & umbrellas. **Guest Services:** gift shop, valet and coin laundry. **Business Services:** meeting rooms, fax. Fee: PC. **Cards:** AE, DI, DS, MC, VI. **Special Amenities:** free newspaper. *(See color ad below)*

SOME UNITS
(✈) FEE (Y1) (⫏) (&) (⟋) (≋) (⎘) (▭) (DATA PORT) / (✕) (VCR) FEE (⊞) (🔒) /

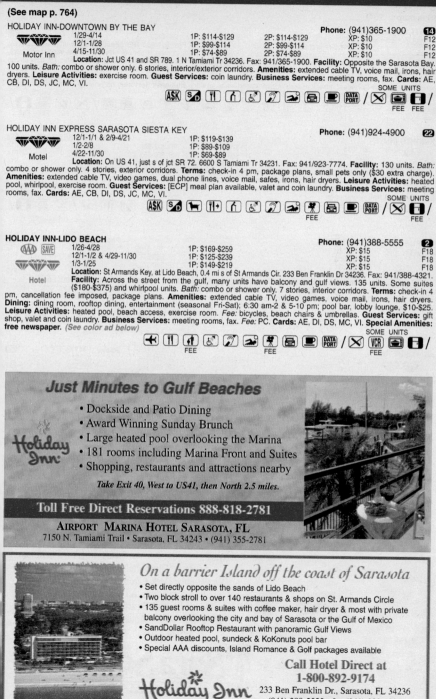

(See map p. 764)

HYATT SARASOTA

AAA [SAVE]

Hotel

Phone: (941)953-1234 **3**
XP: $25 F18

All Year 1P: $175 2P: $200

Location: Just w of jct US 41. 1000 Blvd of the Arts 34236. Fax: 941/952-1987. **Facility:** Many units with balcony, overlooking Sarasota Bay. 297 units. Some suites. *Bath:* combo or shower only. 10 stories, interior corridors. **Parking:** valet. **Terms:** cancellation fee imposed, package plans. **Amenities:** extended cable TV, dual phone lines, voice mail, irons, hair dryers. *Some:* CD players, fax. **Dining:** restaurant, 6 am-midnight, pool grill, $7-$35, cocktails. **Leisure Activities:** heated pool, charter fishing, pool tables. *Fee:* boat dock, cruising boats, scuba boat. **Guest Services:** gift shop, area transportation, valet laundry. **Business Services:** conference facilities, administrative services, PC, fax. **Cards:** AE, CB, DI, DS, JC, MC, VI.

SOME UNITS

[icons] FEE ... FEE ... FEE ... FEE FEE FEE

KNIGHTS INN

AAA [SAVE]

Motel

Phone: (941)355-8867 **21**

2/1-4/15	1P: $72-$95	2P: $72-$95	XP: $10	F14
12/1-1/31	1P: $50-$65	2P: $50-$65	XP: $10	F14
4/16-11/30	1P: $45-$55	2P: $45-$55	XP: $10	F14

Location: On US 41, just s of jct University Pkwy. 5340 N Tamiami Tr 34234. Fax: 941/925-1718. **Facility:** 48 units. 2 stories, exterior corridors. **Terms:** 4 day cancellation notice. **Amenities:** extended cable TV. *Some:* irons, hair dryers. **Guest Services:** coin laundry. **Cards:** AE, DS, MC, VI. **Special Amenities:** free continental breakfast and free newspaper.

SOME UNITS

[icons]

LA RUE MOTEL APARTMENTS

AAA [SAVE]

Apartment

Phone: (941)921-7957 **12**

1/21-4/18	2P: $84-$105	XP: $10	F12
1/1-1/20	2P: $59-$77	XP: $10	F12
12/1-12/31	2P: $49-$77	XP: $10	F12
4/19-11/30	2P: $44-$69	XP: $6	F12

Location: On SR 72, 0.3 mi sw of jct US 41. 1710 Stickney Point Rd 34231. Fax: 941/925-3580. **Facility:** Some motel units available. 19 units. 3 efficiencies and 8 units with kitchen. *Bath:* combo or shower only. 2 stories, exterior corridors. **Terms:** weekly & monthly rates available. **Amenities:** extended cable TV. **Leisure Activities:** heated pool, basketball. **Guest Services:** coin laundry. **Cards:** AE, MC, VI.

SOME UNITS

[icons]

QUAYSIDE INN

[diamonds]

Motel

Phone: (941)366-0414 **29**

12/1-4/30	1P: $60-$76	2P: $65-$86	XP: $10	F12
5/1-11/30	1P: $50-$65	2P: $60-$80	XP: $10	F12

Location: On US 41 at jct Fruitville Rd. 270 N Tamiami Tr 34236. Fax: 941/954-3379. **Facility:** Designated smoking area. 27 units. *Bath:* combo or shower only. 2 stories, exterior corridors. **Terms:** 3 day cancellation notice-fee imposed, weekly & monthly rates available, package plans, pets ($25 extra charge). **Amenities:** extended cable TV. *Some:* irons. **Leisure Activities:** sun deck. **Cards:** AE, DS, MC, VI.

SOME UNITS

[icons]

(See map p. 764)

RADISSON LIDO BEACH RESORT

AAA [SAVE]
◆◆◆
Motor Inn

			Phone: (941)388-2161	**15**
2/9-4/21	1P: $219-$365	2P: $219-$365	XP: $15	F16
4/22-11/30	1P: $105-$365	2P: $105-$365	XP: $15	F16
1/2-2/8	1P: $105-$295	2P: $105-$295	XP: $15	F16
12/1-1/1	1P: $95-$279	2P: $95-$279	XP: $13	F16

Location: St Armands Key on Lido Beach, 0.8 mi s of St Armands Cir. 700 Ben Franklin Dr 34236. Fax: 941/388-3175. **Facility:** Contemporary and nicely appointed units. Most units with gulf view and balcony or patio. 116 units, 85 with efficiency. Some suites. **Bath:** combo or shower only. 4 stories, exterior corridors. **Terms:** check-in 4 pm, package plans. **Amenities:** video games, voice mail, safes, irons, hair dryers. **Dining:** restaurant, 6:30 am-10 pm; tiki bar, $7-$16, cocktails. **Leisure Activities:** heated pool, beach, fishing. **Fee:** sailboating, windsurfing, cabanas, jet skis, kayaks, waverunners. **Guest Services:** [BP] meal plan available, area transportation, coin laundry. **Business Services:** meeting rooms, fax. **Fee:** PC. **Cards:** AE, CB, DI, DS, JC, MC, VI. **Special Amenities:** free newspaper. *(See color ad p 776)*

SOME UNITS

[icons]

RAMADA LIMITED

◆◆
Motel

			Phone: (941)921-7812	**26**
1/16-4/20	1P: $110-$120	2P: $120-$130	XP: $10	F18
1/1-1/15	1P: $80-$90	2P: $90-$100	XP: $10	F18
12/1-12/31 & 4/21-11/30	1P: $70-$80	2P: $80-$90	XP: $10	F18

Location: I-75, exit 37, just w on SR 76. 5774 Clark Rd 34233. Fax: 941/921-1982. **Facility:** 63 units. *Bath:* combo or shower only. 3 stories, interior corridors. **Terms:** 7 day cancellation notice, weekly rates available, pets ($10 extra charge). **Amenities:** extended cable TV, voice mail. *Some:* irons, hair dryers. **Leisure Activities:** heated pool. **Guest Services:** [ECP] meal plan available, coin laundry. **Business Services:** meeting rooms. **Cards:** AE, DI, DS, MC, VI.

SOME UNITS

[icons] FEE FEE

SARASOTA/BRADENTON COURTYARD BY MARRIOTT

◆◆◆
Motel

			Phone: (941)355-3337	**24**
12/1-4/15	1P: $140	2P: $150	
10/1-11/30	1P: $94	2P: $104	
4/16-9/30	1P: $89	2P: $99	

Location: Just e of jct US 41. 850 University Pkwy 34234. Fax: 941/355-5518. **Facility:** 81 units, 3 with kitchen. Some suites ($130-$150) and whirlpool units ($104-$150). *Bath:* combo or shower only. 3 stories, interior corridors. **Terms:** cancellation fee imposed. **Amenities:** extended cable TV, dual phone lines, voice mail, irons, hair dryers. **Leisure Activities:** heated pool, whirlpool, exercise room. **Guest Services:** valet and coin laundry. **Business Services:** meeting rooms, fax. **Cards:** AE, CB, DI, DS, MC, VI.

SOME UNITS

[icons] FEE

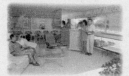

Beach and Bay We Have Got It All!

The Palm Bay Club is a luxury condominium resort located *directly* on world famous Crescent Beach. The Club requires a three night minimum stay. Enjoy the beach, the pools, the spa, the bay, and nearby shopping. This is a perfect vacation spot offering something for everyone.

Guests may choose from the 11-story Grand Tower directly on the beach, Gulfside family suites or Bayside apartments adjacent to the Intercoastal. Each suite is fully equipped, featuring cable television, and a convenient kitchen.

- two heated pools/spa
- free health spa
- lighted tennis courts
- boat docks
- barbecue grills
- fishing pier
- private beach

The Palm Bay Club

THE PALM BAY CLUB
1·800·725·6229

5960 Midnight Pass Road • Siesta Key, Sarasota, Florida 34242
(941) 349-1911 • www.palmbayclub.com

Special 10% discount to AAA Members off published rates. We require Visa or Mastercard

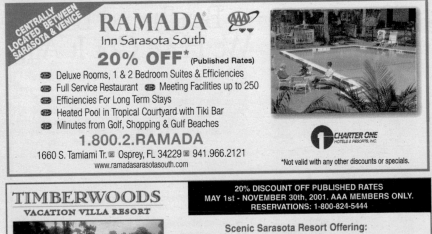

(See map p. 764)

SLEEP INN — **SAVE** — Motel — **Phone: (941)359-8558** — [19]

12/31-4/30	1P: $99-$110	2P: $99-$110
12/1-12/30 & 9/1-11/30	1P: $89-$110	2P: $89-$110
5/1-8/31	1P: $69-$89	2P: $69-$89

Location: Just e of jct US 41. 900 University Pkwy 34234. Fax: 941/359-8558. **Facility:** 80 units. Some suites ($150). *Bath:* combo or shower only. 3 stories, interior corridors. **Terms:** package plans. **Amenities:** safes (fee). *Some:* irons, hair dryers. **Guest Services:** [CP] meal plan available, valet and coin laundry. **Business Services:** meeting rooms, fax. **Cards:** AE, DI, DS, MC, VI.

SOME UNITS

THE SUNSET LODGE MOTEL — Apartment — **Phone: 941/925-1151** — [23]

1/12-4/16		2P: $90-$98	XP: $10	F16
12/1-1/11		2P: $68-$75	XP: $10	F16
4/17-11/30		2P: $58-$65	XP: $10	F16

Location: Jct Stickney Point Rd, just s on Ave C, just w. 1765 Dawn St 34231. Fax: 941/925-8168. **Facility:** Designated smoking area. 6 efficiencies. *Bath:* shower only. 1 story, exterior corridors. **Terms:** 14 day cancellation notice-fee imposed, weekly & monthly rates available, small pets only (in designated units). **Amenities:** extended cable TV, hair dryers. *Some:* irons. **Leisure Activities:** bicycles, shuffleboard. **Guest Services:** complimentary laundry. **Business Services:** fax. **Cards:** AE, DS, MC, VI.

THE TIDES INN — **SAVE** — Apartment — **Phone: 941/924-7541** — [11]

1/21-4/15	1P: $96-$107	2P: $96-$107	XP: $10	D12
12/17-1/20	1P: $65-$77	2P: $65-$77	XP: $7	D12
12/1-12/16 & 4/16-11/30	1P: $52-$66	2P: $52-$66	XP: $7	D12

Location: On SR 72, 0.3 mi sw of jct US 41. 1800 Stickney Point Rd 34231. Fax: 941/923-6445. **Facility:** 12 efficiencies. *Bath:* combo or shower only. 1 story, exterior corridors. **Terms:** 21 day cancellation notice, in season-fee imposed. **Amenities:** *Some:* irons. **Leisure Activities:** heated pool, shuffleboard, barbecue grills. **Cards:** AE, MC, VI. **Special Amenities:** free room upgrade and preferred room (each subject to availability with advanced reservations).

SOME UNITS

TIMBERWOODS VACATION VILLAS RESORT — **SAVE** — Condominium — **Phone: (941)923-4966** — [25]

12/1-4/22	1P: $84-$142	2P: $84-$142	XP: $5	F17
6/18-8/19	1P: $94-$104	2P: $84-$104	XP: $5	F17
4/23-6/17 & 8/20-11/30	1P: $84-$104	2P: $84-$104	XP: $5	F17

Location: I-75, exit 37, 2.9 mi w on SR 72 (Clark Rd), 2.2 mi s on Beneva Rd. 7964 Timberwood Cir 34238. Fax: 941/924-3109. **Facility:** Duplex or four-plex unit on tree-shaded grounds. Units with garage and screened patio. Office hours 9 am-10 pm. 110 two-bedroom units with kitchen. 1 story, exterior corridors. **Terms:** 31 day cancellation notice-fee imposed, monthly rates available, package plans. **Amenities:** extended cable TV, voice mail, irons, hair dryers. **Dining:** wine & cheese reception, Fri. **Leisure Activities:** heated pool, whirlpool, putting green, 2 tennis courts (1 lighted), basketball, shuffleboard, volleyball, barbecue & picnic area, billiard room & library, ping pong. **Guest Services:** complimentary laundry. **Business Services:** fax. **Cards:** AE, DI, DS, MC, VI. **Special Amenities:** free local telephone calls and preferred room (subject to availability with advanced reservations). *(See color ad p 776)*

SOME UNITS

WELLESLEY INN & SUITES — **SAVE** — Motel — **Phone: (941)366-5128** — [13]

12/18-4/14	1P: $89-$129	2P: $89-$129	XP: $10	F
12/1-12/17 & 4/15-11/30	1P: $49-$79	2P: $49-$79	XP: $10	F

Location: US 41, 1 mi n of jct SR 780. 1803 N Tamiami Tr 34234. Fax: 941/953-4322. **Facility:** Some rooms with marina view. 105 units. *Bath:* combo or shower only. 4 stories, interior corridors. **Terms:** small pets only ($10 extra charge). **Amenities:** video games, dual phone lines, voice mail, irons, hair dryers. **Leisure Activities:** heated pool. **Guest Services:** [ECP] meal plan available, valet laundry. **Business Services:** meeting rooms. **Cards:** AE, DI, DS, MC, VI. **Special Amenities:** free continental breakfast and free local telephone calls. *(See color ad opposite title page)*

SOME UNITS

——— WHERE TO DINE ———

THE BIJOU CAFE — Continental — **Lunch: $8-$16** — **Dinner: $15-$24** — **Phone: 941/366-8111** — [1]

Location: Downtown; between Coconut and Pineapple. 1287 1st St 34236. **Hours:** 11:30 am-2 & 5-9:30 pm, Fri & Sat-10 pm. Closed major holidays; also 12/24, & Sun 5/14-12/25. **Reservations:** suggested. **Features:** dressy casual; carryout; cocktails; a la carte. A stylish bistro in the heart of the theater and arts district, this upscale restaurant draws diners in search of romance. The Bijou pepper steak, pan-sizzled in a spicy hot sauce, and the rack of lamb are examples of the award-winning cuisine. **Cards:** AE, CB, DI, MC, VI.

CAFE BACI — Northern Italian — **Lunch: $7-$10** — **Dinner: $11-$23** — **Phone: 941/924-0963** — [9]

Location: On US 41, just s of jct Bee Ridge Rd. 4001 S Tamiami Trail 34231. **Hours:** 11:30 am-2:30 & 4:30-10 pm, Fri-11 pm, Sat 4:30 pm-11 pm, Sun 4:30 pm-10 pm. Closed: 12/25. **Features:** dressy casual; children's menu; early bird specials; carryout; cocktails & lounge. Settle into a comfortable chair and relish the lovely upscale setting. Authentic Italian dishes are tastefully presented, including the excellent shrimp cocktail loaded with huge, fresh shrimp. Also, for a hearty taste of the ocean, try the seafood pasta. **Cards:** AE, DI, DS, MC, VI.

CAFE OF THE ARTS — French — **Lunch: $7-$15** — **Dinner: $12-$36** — **Phone: 941/351-4304** — [17]

Location: On US 41 just s of jct University. 5230 N Tamiami Tr 34234. **Hours:** 11 am-3 & 5-9 pm. Closed: 1/1, 12/25; also Mon after 4 pm & 5/26-10/1. **Reservations:** suggested. **Features:** casual dress; Sunday brunch; carryout; cocktails & lounge; a la carte. Varied courses are offered in intimate, sociable surroundings with a French theme. A wonderful concoction is a French loaf filled with seafood, ratatouille and rice in a flavorful cream sauce. Kudos to the staff for outstanding, attentive service. **Cards:** AE, DS, MC, VI.

(See map p. 764)

CHARLEY'S CRAB — Lunch: $6-$14 — Dinner: $12-$26 — Phone: 941-388-3964 ⑯
▼▽▼▽ ▼▽▼▽
Seafood
Location: On St Armands Key at The Circle at St Armands. 420 St. Armands Cir 34236. **Hours:** 11:30 am-10 pm, Fri & Sat-10:30 pm, Sun noon-10 pm. Closed: 11/22, 12/25. **Reservations:** suggested; for dinner. **Features:** casual dress; children's menu; early bird specials; carryout; cocktails & lounge; entertainment; street parking. A pianist often plays in the background of the light and airy upscale dining room. Extensive menu offerings of homemade pasta, rack of veal, domestic lamb shank and many varieties of fresh fish, flown in daily, make it difficult to narrow down a choice. **Cards:** AE, CB, DI, MC, VI. ✖

COASTERS SEAFOOD CO AT THE SOUTHBRIDGE — Lunch: $9-$17 — Dinner: $14-$22 — Phone: 941-925-0300 ③
▼▽▼▽
Seafood
Location: SR 72, 0.6 mi sw of jct US 41; in Boatyard Village. 1500 Stickney Pt Rd 34231. **Hours:** 11:30 am-10 pm, Sun-9 pm. **Reservations:** suggested. **Features:** casual dress; children's menu; carryout; cocktails & lounge; entertainment; valet parking; a la carte. Relax and enjoy either waterfront or patio dining. You'll find an array of health-conscious items as well as an extensive menu of pork, poultry and steak choices. The delicious grilled salmon tastes like they just plucked it from the water. **Cards:** CB, DI, DS, MC, VI. ✖

COLUMBIA RESTAURANT — Lunch: $8-$14 — Dinner: $15-$22 — Phone: 941-388-3987 ⑮
▼▽▼▽ ▼▽▼▽
Spanish
Location: On St Armands Key at The Circle at St Armands. 411 St Armands Cir 34236. **Hours:** 11 am-10 pm, Sun from noon. **Reservations:** suggested; in season. **Features:** casual dress; children's menu; early bird specials; carryout; cocktails & lounge; street parking; a la carte. A Mediterranean motif, with colorful handpainted tiles, weaves through the cozy restaurant. Such dishes as the 1905 Salad in garlic dressing and the Red Snapper Alicante brim with flavor, whether you eat them in an indoor dining room or on the airy porch. **Cards:** AE, DI, DS, MC, VI.

CUOCO MATTO RISTORANTE — Lunch: $5-$9 — Dinner: $7-$17 — Phone: 941-365-0000 ⑩
▼▽ ▼▽
Italian
Location: On US 41, 2.1 mi s of jct University. 1603 N Tamiami Tr 34236. **Hours:** 11:30 am-11 pm. **Features:** casual dress; children's menu; carryout; cocktails; a la carte. Italian Bistro type setting with various Italian scenes making for a cozy dining experience. Menu has varied selections such as pasta, pizza, fish and meat dishes. Try the tuttu mare which is excellent! The bread served is delicious dipped in the herbal olive oil. **Cards:** AE, DI, DS, MC, VI. ✖

FIRST WATCH RESTAURANT — Lunch: $3-$8 — Phone: 941-954-1395 ⑲
▼▽ ▼▽
American
Location: Downtown; corner of Main and Pineapple. 1395 Main St 34236. **Hours:** 7 am-2:30 pm. Closed: 11/22, 12/25. **Features:** casual dress; children's menu; carryout; street parking. "Eggsellent" culinary experimentation results in such light specialties as crepes, pancakes, omelets, sandwiches and salads. The classic Reuben is served with fried potatoes, salad and a small bowl of fresh fruit wedges. Service is friendly and attentive. Smoke free premises. **Cards:** AE, DS, MC, VI. ✖

JOHNNY LEVEROCK'S SEAFOOD HOUSE — Lunch: $6-$19 — Dinner: $6-$19 — Phone: 941-342-8865 ⑫
▼▽ ▼▽
Seafood
Location: I-275, exit 39, 0.4 mi w on Fruitville, just n on North Cattlemen, just e on Commercial Way. 5981 Fruitville Rd 34234. **Hours:** 11 am-10 pm, Fri & Sat-11 pm. Closed: 11/22, 12/25. **Features:** casual dress; children's menu; early bird specials; carryout; cocktails & lounge. A nautical and friendly atmosphere abounds at this popular destination teeming with fishing memorablilia of the restaurant's name sake, Johnny Leverocke. The menu offers so many palatable treats, such as the onion-roasted salmon or the seafood platter with it's fresh caught bounty. **Cards:** AE, DI, DS, MC, VI. ✖

LE CHAMPAGNE RESTAURANT — Dinner: $20-$31 — Phone: 941-926-8000 ④
▼▽▼▽ ▼▽▼▽
French
Location: On Us 41, 1.3 mi s of jct SR 72. 7500 S Tamiami Tr 34231. **Hours:** 6 pm-9:30 pm. **Features:** cocktail lounge; a la carte. Professional chef/owner with 35 years experience and some 25 plus as owners of two Paris, France located restaurants. This establishment offers an exceptional dining experience. The menu offers numerous choices such as rabbit stew provencale, veal, kidney, scallops and shrimp, red snapper, cheese tray of French varieties and dessert, hors d'oeuvres. On-site boutique. **Cards:** AE, DS, MC, VI. ✖

MICHAEL'S ON EAST — Lunch: $8-$18 — Dinner: $17-$32 — Phone: 941-366-0007 ⑧
AAA
▼▽▼▽ ▼▽▼▽
Continental
Location: On US 41; in Midtown Plaza, e entrance at jct Bahia Vista Dr. 1212 East Ave S 34239. **Hours:** 11:30 am-2 & 6-10 pm, Sat from 5:30, Sun from 6 pm. Closed: 1/1. **Reservations:** suggested. **Features:** dressy casual; children's menu; carryout; cocktails & lounge; valet parking; a la carte. Creative dishes awaken your taste buds in this very upscale restaurant. Spicy seafood gumbo will whet your appetite for larger catches like grilled salmon, attractively presented with a colorful vegetable medley. A prix-fixe theater menu is available until 6:30 pm, $50 per couple. **Cards:** AE, DI, MC, VI. ✖

OSTERIA NORTHERN ITALIAN RESTAURANT — Dinner: $12-$26 — Phone: 941-388-3671 ⑭
▼▽▼▽ ▼▽▼▽
Northern Italian
Location: Just n of jct St. Armands Circle. 29 1/2 N Blvd of Presidents 34236. **Hours:** 4 pm-10 pm. **Reservations:** suggested. **Features:** casual dress; children's menu; carryout; salad bar; cocktails & lounge; street parking; a la carte. Photographs of northern Italy help to set the tone in the friendly restaurant, on the building's second floor. A full bar and extensive wine list complement such entrees as veal over homemade linguine and lobster with mussels, clams, shrimp and scallops. **Cards:** AE, DI, DS, MC, VI. ✖

PATRICK'S RESTAURANT & TAVERN — Lunch: $6-$19 — Dinner: $6-$19 — Phone: 941-952-1170 ㉑
▼▽▼▽ ▼▽▼▽
American
Location: Downtown; in Kress International Plaza. 1400 Main St 34236. **Hours:** 11 am-midnight. Closed: 12/25. **Features:** casual dress; Sunday brunch; carryout; cocktails & lounge; street parking; a la carte. A chicken Vesuvio that erupts with flavor is the highlight of this upscale sports bar with a nice roadside appeal. Pull in for a variety of entree choices such as steak, pasta, pizza and burgers. Fresh flowers and cloth napkins add a nice touch. **Cards:** AE, MC, VI. ✖

(See map p. 764)

ROESSLER'S RESTAURANT
Continental

Dinner: $15-$31   Phone: 941/966-5688   ⑪

Location: 0.8 mi s of Sarasota Square Mall, just e of jct US 41. 2033 Vamo Way 34238. **Hours:** 5 pm-10 pm. **Reservations:** suggested. **Features:** dressy casual; carryout; cocktails & lounge; valet parking. In an elegant estate setting beside an ornamental pond, this romantic restaurant cooks at tableside splendid entrees of duck, veal, lamb and seafood. A raspberry mango glaze coats the delicious almond pecan crusted grouper. The service is exemplary. **Cards:** AE, DI, DS, MC, VI.

✕

SUGAR & SPICE
American

Lunch: $4-$14   Dinner: $4-$14   Phone: 941/342-1649   ㉒

Location: I-75, exit 38, just w on Bee Ridge, just s. 4000 Cattleman Rd 34233. **Hours:** 11 am-10 pm. Closed major holidays; also Sun. **Features:** casual dress; children's menu; carryout. Experience Amish-style cooking in a homey setting. The staff is dressed in conservative attire and dish up such good, hearty meals as fried chicken with mashed potatoes, green beans and a basket of bread. This enormously popular eatery is well worth any wait. Smoke free premises. **Cards:** DS, MC, VI.

🏠 ✕

TOMMY BAHAMA'S TROPICAL CAFE
Caribbean

Lunch: $8-$10   Dinner: $15-$23   Phone: 941/388-2888   ⑱

Location: On St. Armands Key; at The Circle of St. Armands. 300 John Ringling Blvd 34236. **Hours:** 11 am-midnight. **Features:** casual dress; carryout; cocktails & lounge; street parking; a la carte. Extremely popular spot so expect a wait but well worth it. A tropical paradise influenced decor with Caribbean flair. The food is wonderful with such choices as island pasta, boca chica chicken, Trinidad tuna, Martinique mahi, quiche, salmon, ribs; many salads, sandwiches, and appetizers as well. **Cards:** MC, VI.

TROPICAL THAI RESTAURANT AND SUSHI BAR
Thai

Lunch: $6-$7   Dinner: $6-$20   Phone: 941/364-5775   ⑳

Location: Downtown; 0.5 mi e of jct US 41. 1420 Main St 34236. **Hours:** 11:30 am-3 & 4-10 pm, Fri & Sat-11 pm. Closed: 11/22; also Superbowl Sun. **Features:** casual dress; carryout; beer & wine only; street parking. Authentic Thai cuisine is served in an intimate, nicely decorated dining room. Vegetable lovers will enjoy the sweet and sour shrimp, which is loaded with fresh vegetables and comes with a perfectly cooked bowl of rice. The service is outstanding. **Cards:** AE, DS, MC, VI.

✕

SATELLITE BEACH pop. 9,900

—— WHERE TO STAY ——

DAYS INN
Motel

Phone: (321)777-3552

	1P: $59-$69	2P: $65-$75	XP: $6	F17
12/24-4/15				
4/16-11/30	1P: $59-$69	2P: $64-$74	XP: $6	F17
12/1-12/23	1P: $57-$67	2P: $63-$73	XP: $6	F17

Location: 0.3 mi s of jct SR 404. 180 SR A1A 32937. Fax: 321/777-1090. **Facility:** Adjacent to Patrick Air Force Base, across the street from ocean with whirlpool corner units. 104 units. Some whirlpool units ($75-$125). *Bath:* combo or shower only. 2 stories, exterior corridors. **Terms:** small pets only. **Amenities:** extended cable TV. **Leisure Activities:** whirlpool, exercise room, shuffleboard, volleyball. **Guest Services:** coin laundry. **Cards:** AE, CB, DI, DS, JC, MC, VI. **Special Amenities:** free continental breakfast and free local telephone calls.

RAMADA INN OCEANFRONT RESORT HOTEL
Motor Inn

Phone: (321)777-7200

	1P: $99-$119	2P: $99-$119
2/1-4/30		
12/1-1/31 & 5/1-11/30	1P: $79-$99	2P: $79-$99

Location: SR A1A, 2 mi s of jct SR 404. 1035 Hwy A1A 32937. Fax: 321/773-4608. **Facility:** Deck area overlooks ocean; some units with ocean view. Designated smoking area. 108 units, 2 with kitchen. 7 stories, interior corridors. **Terms:** 30 day cancellation notice, weekly & monthly rates available, package plans. **Amenities:** extended cable TV, voice mail. *Some:* irons, hair dryers. **Dining:** dining room, 6:30-10:30 am, 11-2 & 5-9 pm; to 10 pm in summer, Sun 10 am-2 & 5-8 pm, $9-$15, cocktails. **Leisure Activities:** heated pool, beach, swimming, tennis court. **Guest Services:** valet laundry. **Business Services:** meeting rooms. **Cards:** AE, CB, DI, DS, JC, MC, VI. **Special Amenities:** free room upgrade (subject to availability with advanced reservations).

—— WHERE TO DINE ——

DOVE RESTAURANT
Italian

Lunch: $6-$8   Dinner: $10-$15   Phone: 321/777-5817

Location: 4 mi s of jct SR 404. 1790 SR A1A 32937. **Hours:** 11:30 am-2:30 & 5-9 pm, Fri & Sat 5 pm-10 pm. Closed: Sun & 3 weeks 9/1-9/30. **Reservations:** suggested. **Features:** semi-formal attire; children's menu; carryout; cocktails & lounge. A tangy, pepper sauce is the draw at this delightful Italian spot. Doggy bags may be necessary as these traditional pasta specialties are heaped on an oversized dish. The tuxedo-clad wait staff bring an air of formality to this extraordinarily good meal. **Cards:** AE, CB, DI, MC, VI.

✕

THE PHOENIX
Continental

Dinner: $17-$24   Phone: 321/777-8414

Location: SR A1A, 3.3 mi s of jct SR 404. 1550 Hwy A1A 32937. **Hours:** 6 pm-10 pm. Closed: 12/25. **Reservations:** suggested. **Features:** semi-formal attire; cocktails & lounge. Elegant without being stuffy, the neoclassic restaurant exudes intimacy, with dim lighting and cozy seating. Among the traditional entrees are rack of lamb with a rosemary honey mustard crust, shrimp madras and calf liver with onions and apples. **Cards:** AE, CB, DI, DS, MC, VI.

✕

SEASIDE

—— WHERE TO STAY ——

JOSEPHINE'S FRENCH COUNTRY INN   **Phone:** (850)231-1940
▼▼▼▼   All Year   2P: $165-$240
           Location: Jct SR 395, 0.5 mi w on SR 30A, just n on Quincy Cir. 38 Seaside Ave 32459 (PO Box 4767).
Country Inn   **Fax:** 850/231-2446. **Facility:** In unique beach cottage area, with cottages and replica homes from the Victorian Era. Close to the ocean and boutique shops. Smoke free premises. 9 units. Some suites. *Bath:* combo or shower only. 2 stories, interior corridors. **Terms:** check-in 4 pm, 2 night minimum stay - weekends, age restrictions may apply, 14 day cancellation notice-fee imposed, weekly & monthly rates available, package plans. **Amenities:** extended cable TV, irons. **Guest Services:** [BP] meal plan available. **Business Services:** meeting rooms. **Cards:** AE, MC, VI.

[ASK] [SD] [♦] [✕] [📷] [VCR] [🖨] [💻] [🖼] [🛏] [DATA PORT]

SEBASTIAN pop. 10,200

—— WHERE TO STAY ——

THE DAVIS HOUSE INN   **Phone:** 561/589-4114
▼▼▼ ▼▼▼   12/1-5/1   1P: $80   2P: $80   XP: $10
           5/2-11/30   1P: $60-$70   2P: $60-$70   XP: $10
Bed & Breakfast   **Location:** I-95, exit 69, 7.5 mi e, n on Indian River, 1.3 mi to Davis St. 607 Davis St 32958. Fax: 561/589-1722. **Facility:** Spacious efficiency suites with comfy decors. 12 efficiencies. *Bath:* combo or shower only. 2 stories, exterior corridors. **Terms:** 3 day cancellation notice-fee imposed, weekly rates available. **Amenities:** extended cable TV. **Guest Services:** coin laundry. **Cards:** AE, DS, MC, VI.

[ASK] [SD] [♦] [⚙] [🖨] [🖼] [🛏]

KEY WEST INN AT CAPT HIRAM'S   **Phone:** (561)388-8588
(AAA) [SAVE]   2/9-6/1   1P: $94-$164   2P: $94-$164   XP: $10   F17
           6/2-8/5   1P: $89-$159   2P: $89-$159   XP: $10   F17
▼▼▼ ▼▼▼   12/1-2/8 & 8/6-11/30   1P: $79-$159   2P: $79-$159   XP: $10   F17
Motor Inn   **Location:** I-95, exit 69, 7.5 mi e, then 0.5 mi n. 1580 US 1 32958. Fax: 561/388-3118. **Facility:** 56 units, 5 with efficiency. Some suites and whirlpool units. *Bath:* some combo or shower only. 3 stories, interior corridors. **Amenities:** extended cable TV, voice mail. *Some:* irons, hair dryers. **Dining:** restaurant, 11:30 am-10 pm, $11-$17, cocktails. **Leisure Activities:** heated pool, beach, marina. **Guest Services:** [ECP] meal plan available, coin laundry. **Business Services:** meeting rooms. **Cards:** AE, CB, DI, DS, MC, VI. **Special Amenities:** free continental breakfast and free local telephone calls. *(See color ad below)*

                                                 SOME UNITS

[SD] [♦] [Y] [⚙] [♦] [🖨] [🖼] [📷] [🖨] [💻] [DATA PORT] / [✕] [VCR] [🖼] [🛏] /

SEBRING pop. 8,900

—— WHERE TO STAY ——

INN ON THE LAKES   **Phone:** (863)471-9400
(AAA) [SAVE]   1/1-4/30   1P: $65-$89   2P: $65-$89
           12/1-12/31 & 5/1-11/30   1P: $65-$82   2P: $65-$82
▼▼▼ ▼▼▼   **Location:** US 27, 1.5 mi n of jct SR 17. 3100 Golfview Rd 33870. Fax: 863/471-9400. **Facility:** Pleasant Mediterranean style building with some units offering pool and lake views. Some with balcony. Attractive public
Motor Inn   areas. 161 units, 1 with kitchen. Some suites ($88-$150). 2-3 stories, interior/exterior corridors. **Terms:** 3 day cancellation notice, package plans, pets ($40 extra charge). **Amenities:** extended cable TV, voice mail, hair dryers. *Some:* irons. **Dining:** restaurant, 6:30 am-11 pm, $5-$17, cocktails. **Leisure Activities:** golf privileges, exercise room. *Fee:* jet skis. **Guest Services:** coin laundry. *Fee:* massage. **Business Services:** meeting rooms, fax. **Cards:** AE, CB, DI, DS, MC, VI. **Special Amenities:** free room upgrade and preferred room (each subject to availability with advanced reservations).

                                                 SOME UNITS

[SD] [🐾] [Y] [⚙] [🖨] [🖨] [🖼] [💻] [DATA PORT] / [✕] [🖼] [🛏] /
                FEE   FEE   FEE

QUALITY INN & SUITES CONFERENCE CENTER

Phone: (863)385-4500

(AAA) (SAVE)

Motor Inn

12/27-4/15	1P: $129-$249	2P: $129-$249	XP: $10	F18
12/1-12/26 & 10/1-11/30	1P: $129-$169	2P: $129-$169	XP: $5	F18
4/16-9/30	1P: $110-$149	2P: $110-$149	XP: $5	F18

Location: On US 27, 7 mi n of jct SR 17. 6525 US 27 N 33870. **Fax:** 863/382-4793. **Facility:** 148 units. 2 stories, exterior corridors. **Terms:** check-in 4 pm, cancellation fee imposed, weekly & monthly rates available, package plans, pets ($50 deposit). **Amenities:** extended cable TV, irons. *Some:* hair dryers. **Dining:** restaurant, 6:30 am-2 & 4:30-9 pm, $7-$18, cocktails. **Leisure Activities:** wading pool, volleyball. **Guest Services:** [BP] meal plan available, coin laundry. *Fee:* massage. **Business Services:** conference facilities, fax. **Cards:** AE, CB, DI, DS, JC, MC, VI. **Special Amenities:** free local telephone calls and preferred room (subject to availability with advanced reservations).

SOME UNITS / FEE VCR FEE FEE

SIESTA KEY pop. 7,800   (See map p. 764; index p. 766)

——— WHERE TO STAY ———

CAPTIVA BEACH RESORT

Phone: 941-349-4131   **47**

(AAA) (SAVE)

Apartment

1/2-3/31 Wkly		2P: $650-$1450	XP: $56
12/1-1/1 Wkly		2P: $400-$1450	XP: $56
4/1-4/30 Wkly		2P: $650-$1150	XP: $56
5/1-11/30 Wkly		2P: $400-$795	XP: $56

Location: Just w of jct Midnight Pass Rd. 6772 Sara Sea Cir 34242. **Fax:** 941/349-8141. **Facility:** Tropical setting. Designated smoking area. 20 units. 2 two-bedroom units, 2 efficiencies and 18 units with kitchen. *Bath:* combo or shower only. 1 story, exterior corridors. **Terms:** check-out 9:30 am, 60 day cancellation notice-fee imposed, daily & monthly rates available. **Amenities:** voice mail, hair dryers. *Some:* irons. **Leisure Activities:** heated pool, beach access, shuffleboard, outdoor gas grills. **Guest Services:** coin laundry. **Cards:** AE, DS, MC, VI. *(See color ad p 769)*

SOME UNITS / VCR /

CONCLARE MOTEL & APARTMENTS

Phone: (941)349-2322   **48**

(AAA) (SAVE)

Apartment

2/1-4/30	1P: $135-$275	2P: $135-$275	XP: $8	F12
12/16-1/31	1P: $109-$240	2P: $109-$246	XP: $8	F12
12/1-12/15 & 5/1-11/30	1P: $89-$195	2P: $89-$195	XP: $8	F12

Location: Just w of jct Midnight Pass Rd. 6738 Sara Sea Cir 34242. **Fax:** 941/349-6572. **Facility:** 18 units. 1 two-bedroom unit, 5 efficiencies and 12 units with kitchen. Some suites. *Bath:* combo or shower only. 1 story, exterior corridors. **Terms:** 30 day cancellation notice, weekly rates available. **Amenities:** *Some:* irons. **Leisure Activities:** heated pool, beach access, shuffleboard, gas grills. **Cards:** AE, DS, MC, VI. **Special Amenities:** free local telephone calls and free room upgrade (subject to availability with advanced reservations).

CRESCENT VIEW BEACH CLUB

Phone: (941)349-2000   **43**

Apartment

12/15-5/15		2P: $149-$439	XP: $12	F12
5/16-11/30		2P: $120-$379	XP: $12	F12
12/1-12/14		2P: $100-$379	XP: $12	F12

Location: Just s of jct SR 72 (Stickney Point Rd). 6512 Midnight Pass Rd 34242. **Fax:** 941/349-9748. **Facility:** Gulf front. 27 units. 15 two-bedroom units and 26 units with kitchen. 2-4 stories, exterior corridors. **Terms:** 21 day cancellation notice-fee imposed, package plans. **Amenities:** *Some:* irons, hair dryers. **Leisure Activities:** heated pool, whirlpool, beach. **Guest Services:** complimentary laundry. **Business Services:** fax. **Cards:** AE, DI, DS, MC, VI. *(See color ad p 770)*

SOME UNITS /

GULF TERRACE VACATION APARTMENTS

Phone: (941)349-4444   **49**

Apartment

2/1-4/30 Wkly	1P: $640-$775	2P: $640-$775	XP: $70	F15
12/18-1/31 Dly	1P: $82-$98	2P: $82-$98	XP: $10	F15
12/1-12/17 & 5/1-11/30 Dly	1P: $62-$75	2P: $62-$75	XP: $10	F15

Location: 0.5 mi s of jct SR 72 (Stickney Point Rd) on Midnight Pass Rd, just w. 1105 Point of Rocks Rd 34242. **Fax:** 941/349-4444. **Facility:** 1/2 blk from Crescent Beach. Designated smoking area. 12 units with kitchen. 2 stories, exterior corridors. **Terms:** 30 day cancellation notice, weekly & monthly rates available, pets ($10 extra charge, dogs only). **Amenities:** extended cable TV. **Leisure Activities:** heated pool, whirlpool, shuffleboard. **Guest Services:** coin laundry. **Cards:** MC, VI.

MIRAMAR BEACH APARTMENTS OF SIESTA KEY

Phone: (941)349-6800   **38**

Apartment

2/1-4/30	1P: $120-$200	2P: $120-$200	XP: $10	F
12/1-1/31	1P: $100-$200	2P: $100-$200	XP: $10	F
5/1-11/30	1P: $60-$160	2P: $60-$160	XP: $10	F

Location: In Siesta Village; just w of Ocean Blvd. 92 Avenida Messina 34242. **Fax:** 941/349-6800. **Facility:** Designated smoking area. 12 units with kitchen. 2 two-bedroom units. *Bath:* combo or shower only. 2 stories, exterior corridors. **Terms:** 60 day cancellation notice-fee imposed, weekly rates available. **Amenities:** extended cable TV. **Leisure Activities:** heated pool. **Guest Services:** coin laundry. **Cards:** MC, VI.

(See map p. 764)

PALM BAY CLUB

Phone: (941)349-1911 **41**

AAA SAVE

3/23-4/30	2P: $250-$625	XP: $25	F
2/1-3/22	2P: $210-$500	XP: $25	F
12/1-1/31	2P: $125-$425	XP: $25	F
5/1-11/30	2P: $120-$400	XP: $25	F

Condominium

Location: On SR 758, 0.8 mi n of jct SR 72 (Stickney Pt Rd). 5960 Midnight Pass Rd 34242. Fax: 941/349-1034. **Facility:** Buildings are set on gulf or bayside; all units with private screened patio. Office hours 9 am-5 pm. 145 units with kitchen. 105 two-bedroom units and 1 three-bedroom unit. 3-11 stories, interior/exterior corridors. **Terms:** 60 day cancellation notice-fee imposed, weekly & monthly rates available. **Amenities:** extended cable TV, voice mail, irons. *Some:* CD players, hair dryers. **Leisure Activities:** 2 heated pools, saunas, whirlpool, beach, marina, cabanas, fishing pier, 2 lighted tennis courts, exercise room, recreation room, barbecue grills. **Guest Services:** coin laundry. **Business Services:** fax. **Cards:** MC, VI. *(See color ad p 775)*

SOME UNITS

SARA SEA INN AT THE BEACH

Phone: (941)349-3244 **45**

AAA SAVE

2/1-4/30	1P: $159-$369	2P: $159-$369	XP: $15	F12
5/1-11/30	1P: $99-$299	2P: $99-$299	XP: $15	F12
12/1-1/31	1P: $89-$289	2P: $89-$289	XP: $15	F12

Apartment

Location: Just w of jct Midnight Pass Rd. 6760 Sara Sea Cir 34242. Fax: 941/349-4999. **Facility:** Contemporary decor and tropical landscaping with koi pond. One unit with fireplace. 30 units. 2 two-bedroom units, 1 three-bedroom unit, 17 efficiencies and 11 units with kitchen. Some suites ($149-$369). 1 story, exterior corridors. **Terms:** 3 night minimum stay - 2 and 3 bedroom suites; 2 night min 1 bedroom suit, 30 day cancellation notice-fee imposed, weekly rates available. **Amenities:** extended cable TV, voice mail. *Some:* irons, hair dryers. **Leisure Activities:** 2 heated pools, whirlpool, beach access, beach chairs, umbrellas, fishing, shuffleboard, tour assistance, gas barbecue, picnic area. *Fee:* sailboating, windsurfing, catamaran, waterbikes, kayaks, bicycles, rollerblades. **Guest Services:** coin laundry. **Business Services:** meeting rooms, fax. **Cards:** AE, DS, MC, VI. **Special Amenities:** free room upgrade and preferred room (each subject to availability with advanced reservations). *(See color ad p 774)*

SOME UNITS

SUNSETS ON THE KEY

Phone: 941/312-9797 **44**

AAA SAVE

12/19-4/30	2P: $129-$199
12/1-12/18 & 5/1-11/30	2P: $79-$119

Apartment

Location: In Siesta Village; just w on Ocean Blvd via Avenida Messina. 5203 Avenida Navarre 34242. Fax: 941/312-9105. **Facility:** Designated smoking area. 8 units. 4 two-bedroom units, 2 efficiencies and 6 units with kitchen. *Bath:* combo or shower only. 2 stories, exterior corridors. **Terms:** 30 day cancellation notice, weekly rates available. **Amenities:** extended cable TV, CD players, voice mail, irons, hair dryers. **Leisure Activities:** bicycles, barbecue grill & deck/patio area. **Guest Services:** coin laundry. **Cards:** MC, VI. **Special Amenities:** early check-in/late check-out.

TROPICAL BREEZE INN

Phone: (941)349-1125 **39**

AAA SAVE

2/1-5/15	2P: $139-$295	XP: $15	F14
12/18-1/31	2P: $109-$225	XP: $15	F14
12/1-12/17 & 5/16-11/30	2P: $79-$185	XP: $15	F14

Apartment

Location: In Siesta Village; just w of Ocean Blvd via Avenida Messina. 140 Columbus Blvd 34242. Fax: 941/349-0057. **Facility:** Some units are across the street from beach. Designated smoking area. 22 units with kitchen. 3 two-bedroom units. *Bath:* combo or shower only. 1 story, exterior corridors. **Terms:** 14 day cancellation notice-fee imposed, weekly rates available, pets (10% surcharge, $40 min deposit). **Amenities:** extended cable TV. *Some:* irons, hair dryers. **Leisure Activities:** heated pool, whirlpool, beach access, sun deck, shuffleboard, barbecue grills. **Guest Services:** coin laundry. **Cards:** AE, DS, MC, VI. **Special Amenities:** early check-in/late check-out and free room upgrade (subject to availability with advanced reservations).

TROPICAL SHORES BEACH RESORT

Phone: (941)349-3330 **46**

AAA SAVE

12/16-4/28	1P: $189-$395	2P: $189-$395	XP: $25	F18
12/1-12/15 & 4/29-11/30	1P: $99-$325	2P: $99-$325	XP: $25	F18

Apartment

Location: S of jct SR 72, on Midnight Pass Rd, just w. 6717 Sara Sea Cir 34242. Fax: 941/346-0025. **Facility:** Set amid tropical gardens, just a short walk. 30 units. 1 two-bedroom unit, 24 efficiencies and 6 units with kitchen. Some whirlpool units ($175-$395). *Bath:* combo or shower only. 2 stories, exterior corridors. **Terms:** 3 night minimum stay, 21 day cancellation notice-fee imposed, weekly rates available. **Amenities:** extended cable TV, voice mail. *Some:* irons, hair dryers. **Leisure Activities:** heated pool, beach access, shuffleboard, volleyball, barbecue grills. **Guest Services:** coin laundry. **Cards:** AE, MC, VI. **Special Amenities:** early check-in/late check-out. *(See color ad p 768)*

SOME UNITS

TURTLE BEACH RESORT

Phone: (941)349-4554 **50**

AAA SAVE

12/15-4/30	2P: $250-$370	XP: $15	F18
5/1-11/30	2P: $170-$275	XP: $15	F18
12/1-12/14	2P: $165-$265	XP: $15	F18

Apartment

Location: 2.8 mi s of jct SR 72 (Stickney Pt). 9049 Midnight Pass Rd 34242. Fax: 941/312-9034. **Facility:** On Little Sarasota Bay. All units are individually themed and decorated, each with private hot tub and patio. Designated smoking area. 10 units with kitchen. 6 two-bedroom units. Some whirlpool units ($155-$350). *Bath:* combo or shower only. 1 story, exterior corridors. **Terms:** 60 day cancellation notice-fee imposed, package plans, pets (10% surcharge). **Amenities:** extended cable TV, hair dryers. *Some:* CD players, irons. **Leisure Activities:** heated pool, boating, canoeing, paddleboats, boat dock, fishing, docking fee, fishing equipment, kayak, bicycles, barbecue grills, gazebo, 10 slips. **Guest Services:** complimentary laundry. **Cards:** AE, DS, MC, VI. **Special Amenities:** free local telephone calls.

FEE

(See map p. 764)

—— WHERE TO DINE ——

BEACH CAFE & SPORTS BAR   **Lunch:** $7-$9   **Dinner:** $7-$21   **Phone:** 941/349-7117   (28)
American
Location: Just s on SR 758; in Siesta Village. 431 Beach Rd 34242. **Hours:** 11 am-10 pm. **Features:** casual dress; cocktails & lounge; a la carte. Lunch is served in very casual Floridian style patio type dining with loud music and casual service style while dinner is in a more cozy, elegant area to the rear of the restaurant. The menu has a variety of offerings prepared fresh and very tasty. **Cards:** MC, VI.

BOB'S BOATHOUSE RESTAURANT   **Lunch:** $5-$16   **Dinner:** $5-$16   **Phone:** 941/312-9111   (31)
American
Location: Just e of jct Midnight Pass Rd. 1310 Old Stickney Point Rd 34242. **Hours:** 11 am-2 am, Sun-midnight. Closed: 12/25. **Features:** casual dress; children's menu; early bird specials; carryout; cocktails & lounge; entertainment. Enter through the side of a wrecked ship to discover an interesting boat repair house. Boat sails serve as section dividers in this quaint nautical atmosphere. Choose from a variety of seafood, steak, pasta and chicken, or select a chalkboard special. **Cards:** AE, DS, MC, VI.   ⊠

CHEZ DANIEL   **Lunch:** $6-$14   **Dinner:** $16-$24   **Phone:** 941/346-9228   (26)
French
Location: On SR 758 just s of jct SR 72, (Stickney Point Rd); in Crest Plaza. 6621 Midnight Pass Rd 34242. **Hours:** 11:30 am-2 & 5-9 pm, Sat & Sun from 5. Closed: Sun (off season). **Features:** casual dress; beer & wine only; a la carte. Quaint and cozy little French restaurant with a chef/owner preparing authentic cuisine such as Canard a l'Orange, steak au poivre, filet mignon bordelaise, salmon grille au beurre blanc. Desserts are a treat. Staff welcoming and very French, giving pleasant service and gracious feel. Smoke free premises. **Cards:** AE, DI, MC, VI.   ⊠

OPHELIA'S ON THE BAY   **Dinner:** $15-$27   **Phone:** 941/349-2212   (29)
AAA
American
Location: 2.8 mi s of jct SR 72 (Stickney Point Rd). 9105 Midnight Pass Rd 34242. **Hours:** 5 pm-10 pm. Closed: 12/25. **Reservations:** suggested. **Features:** casual dress; children's menu; carryout; cocktails & lounge; valet parking; a la carte. Set on Little Sarasota Bay, the intimate restaurant creates varied dishes of duckling, veal, lamb, pasta and seafood, most notably the house specialty - pompano wrapped in parchment paper. The atmosphere is gracious, as are the attentive servers. **Cards:** AE, DI, DS, MC, VI.   ⊠

THE SUMMERHOUSE RESTAURANT   **Dinner:** $10-$25   **Phone:** 941/349-1100   (30)
American
Location: 0.6 mi n of jct SR 72 (Stickney Pt.). 6101 Midnight Pass Rd 34242. **Hours:** 5 pm-11 pm, Sun 10:30 am-2 & 5-10 pm. **Reservations:** suggested. **Features:** dressy casual; Sunday brunch; children's menu; early bird specials; carryout; cocktails & lounge; entertainment; valet parking; a la carte. A lush tropical landscape serves as the backdrop for this continental cuisine. Enjoy the manicured lawn from the outdoor dining deck. The abundant seasoning on the roast duck entree is spectacular. A light fare menu is available in the lounge. **Cards:** AE, CB, DI, DS, MC, VI.   ⊠

TURTLES ON LITTLE SARASOTA BAY   **Lunch:** $6-$9   **Dinner:** $7-$19   **Phone:** 941/346-2207   (32)
AAA
American
Location: 2.7 mi s of jct Stickney Point Rd; opposite Turtle Beach. 8875 Midnight Pass Rd 34242. **Hours:** 11:30 am-10 pm. **Features:** casual dress; Sunday brunch; children's menu; early bird specials; carryout; cocktails & lounge; a la carte. Potato-crusted mahi-mahi and snapper New Orleans are among the exquisite seafood entrees of the tropical restaurant, which also serves up chicken, pork and steak. Lots of windows overlook the bay. Enjoy the crisp air on the outdoor deck. Nightly entertainment in season. Dancing Mon-Thurs. **Cards:** AE, DS, MC, VI.   ⊠

VILLAGE CAFE   **Lunch:** $4-$8   **Phone:** 941/349-2822   (27)
American
Location: Center, in Siesta Village. 5133 Ocean Blvd 34242. **Hours:** 7 am-2:30 pm. Closed: 12/25. **Features:** casual dress; children's menu; carryout; beer & wine only. Popular cafe setting centrally located in "the village area" in a small strip mall of variety stores. This local favorite though basically decorated has a friendly waitstaff and the menu offers many breakfast items, salads and sandwiches. Try the turkey club with its fresh crisp ingredients. Smoke free premises. **Cards:** MC, VI.   ⊠

SILVER SPRINGS pop. 1,000

———— WHERE TO STAY ————

DAYS INN

Phone: (352)236-2891

AAA SAVE

	1/1-4/30	1P: $60-$75	2P: $65-$85	XP: $5	F16
	5/1-7/31	1P: $55-$75	2P: $60-$75	XP: $5	F16
	12/1-12/31	1P: $45-$75	2P: $50-$75	XP: $5	F16
Motel	8/1-11/30	1P: $45-$75	2P: $50-$75	XP: $50	F16

Location: SR 40, 0.5 mi w of jct CR 35. 5001 E Silver Springs Blvd 34488. Fax: 352/236-3546. **Facility:** 56 units. 2 stories, exterior corridors. **Terms:** 3 day cancellation notice, pets ($5 extra charge). **Amenities:** extended cable TV. **Leisure Activities:** playground. **Guest Services:** coin laundry. **Business Services:** fax. **Cards:** AE, CB, DI, DS, JC, MC, VI. **Special Amenities:** free continental breakfast.

SOME UNITS

HOLIDAY INN-SILVER SPRINGS

Phone: (352)236-2575

	2/2-4/7	1P: $69-$89	2P: $69-$89	XP: $8	F19
	4/8-11/30	1P: $59-$79	2P: $59-$79	XP: $8	F19
Motor Inn	12/1-2/1	1P: $59-$69	2P: $59-$69	XP: $8	F19

Location: SR 40 across from Silver Springs entrance. 5751 E Silver Springs Blvd 34488 (PO Box 156, 34489). Fax: 352/236-2575. **Facility:** 103 units. Some suites ($150-$225). 2 stories, exterior corridors. **Terms:** small pets only ($25 deposit). **Amenities:** extended cable TV, safes, irons, hair dryers. **Guest Services:** wading pool, exercise room. **Guest Services:** valet laundry. **Business Services:** meeting rooms, fax. **Cards:** AE, CB, DI, DS, JC, MC, VI.

SOME UNITS

SUN PLAZA MOTEL

Phone: 352/236-2343

AAA SAVE

| | All Year | 1P: $40-$65 | 2P: $40-$65 | | F12 |

Location: SR 40 at jct CR 35. 5461 E Silver Springs Blvd 34488 (PO Box 216, 34489-0216). Fax: 352/236-1214. **Facility:** Different sized units. 47 units. 9 with efficiency. *Bath:* combo or shower only. 1 story, exterior corridors. **Terms:** cancellation fee imposed, weekly & monthly rates available, pets ($10 extra charge). **Leisure Activities:** playground. **Business Services:** fax. **Cards:** AE, CB, DI, DS, MC, VI.

SOME UNITS

SOUTH DAYTONA pop. 12,500 (See map p. 270; index p. 272)

———— WHERE TO STAY ————

RED CARPET INN

Phone: 904/767-6681 **75**

AAA SAVE

| | All Year | 1P: $35-$45 | | XP: $10 | F10 |

Location: US 1, 0.5 mi s of SR 400. 1855 S Ridgewood Ave 32119. Fax: 904/767-6681. **Facility:** 30 units, 19 with kitchen. *Bath:* combo or shower only. 2 stories, exterior corridors. **Terms:** 14 day cancellation notice-fee imposed, weekly & monthly rates available. **Amenities:** extended cable TV. **Cards:** AE, DS, MC, VI.

SOME UNITS

SUN RANCH MOTOR LODGE

Phone: (904)767-0661 **76**

AAA SAVE

| | All Year | 1P: $39-$45 | 2P: $40-$55 | XP: $5 | F10 |

Location: US 1, 1 mi s of SR 400. 2425 S Ridgewood Ave 32119. Fax: 904/761-9766. **Facility:** 22 units, 9 with efficiency. *Bath:* combo or shower only. 1 story, exterior corridors. **Terms:** 14 day cancellation notice-fee imposed, weekly & monthly rates available. **Amenities:** extended cable TV. **Leisure Activities:** shuffleboard. **Guest Services:** coin laundry. **Cards:** AE, DS, MC, VI. **Special Amenities:** early check-in/late check-out and free continental breakfast.

SOME UNITS

SOUTH MIAMI —See Miami-Miami Beach p. 525.

SOUTH PALM BEACH pop. 1,500 (See map p. 710; index p. 713)—

———— WHERE TO STAY ————

PALM BEACH HAWAIIAN OCEAN INN

Phone: (561)582-5631 **115**

| | 12/1-4/30 | | 2P: $150-$320 | XP: $10 | F18 |
| Motor Inn | 5/1-11/30 | | 2P: $90-$220 | XP: $10 | F18 |

Location: On SR A1A, 1.5 mi s of jct SR 802. 3550 S Ocean Blvd 33480. Fax: 561/582-5631. **Facility:** Large units. 58 units. 2 two-bedroom units and 12 efficiencies. *Bath:* combo or shower only. 2 stories, exterior corridors. **Terms:** 3 day cancellation notice-fee imposed, weekly rates available, package plans - in summer. **Amenities:** extended cable TV, safes (fee), hair dryers. **Leisure Activities:** heated pool, beach, swimming. **Guest Services:** coin laundry. **Fee:** fax. **Cards:** AE, CB, DI, DS, MC, VI.

SOME UNITS

SOUTH PASADENA —See Tampa Bay p. 876.

SPRING HILL pop. 34,900

―――――― WHERE TO STAY ――――――

HAMPTON INN

SAVE

▼▼▼

Motel

				Phone: (352)684-5000
1/16-4/30	1P: $75-$80	2P: $80-$85	XP: $5	F18
12/1-1/15 & 5/1-11/30	1P: $70-$80	2P: $75-$85	XP: $5	F18

Location: On US 19, 1.4 mi n of SR 578 (County Line Rd) and 0.4 mi s of SR 574 (Spring Hill Rd). 1344 Commercial Way 34606. Fax: 352/684-5075. **Facility:** 72 units. Some whirlpool units ($109-$115). **Bath:** combo or shower only. 3 stories, interior corridors. **Terms:** cancellation fee imposed. **Amenities:** voice mail, irons, hair dryers. **Leisure Activities:** exercise room. **Guest Services:** [ECP] meal plan available. **Business Services:** meeting rooms, fax. **Cards:** AE, DI, DS, MC, VI.

SOME UNITS

⬛ 🏠 🐕 🏊 📷 🖨 💻 [DATA PORT] / ✕ 🖼 📱 /

FEE FEE

―――――― WHERE TO DINE ――――――

MICHAEL'S BISTRO

▼▼ ▼▼

Italian

| **Lunch:** $5-$8 | **Dinner:** $6-$19 | **Phone:** 352/683-8420 |

Location: On US 19, 0.8 mi n of jct Spring Hill Rd (CR 574); in the Village at Timber Pines Shopping Center. 2410 Commercial Way 34608. **Hours:** 11 am-10 pm, Sat & Sun from noon. Closed: Mon 6/1-8/31. **Reservations:** suggested; for dinner. **Features:** dressy casual; children's menu; early bird specials; carryout; beer & wine only. Lovely touches like chandeliers, crystal candlesticks, and linen napkins and tablecloths, add romantic elegance to the small, single dining room. Or you can enjoy meals like the chicken Cordon Bleu with roasted potatoes in the outdoor dining cafe. **Cards:** DS, MC, VI.

✕

STARKE pop. 5,200

―――――― WHERE TO STAY ――――――

BEST WESTERN MOTOR INN

(AAA) **SAVE**

▼▼ ▼▼

Motel

				Phone: (904)964-6744
3/16-3/18	1P: $95-$125	2P: $95-$125	XP: $10	F12
12/1-3/15 & 3/19-11/30	1P: $42-$65	2P: $54-$95	XP: $5	F12

Location: 1 mi n on US 301 from jct SR 100. 1290 N Temple Ave 32091. Fax: 904/964-3355. **Facility:** Compact to spacious guest units with bright cheerful decor throughout. 51 units. 2 stories, exterior corridors. **Terms:** 30 day cancellation notice, pets ($25 deposit). **Amenities:** extended cable TV. **Guest Services:** [CP] meal plan available. **Cards:** AE, CB, DI, DS, MC, VI. **Special Amenities:** free local telephone calls and free news-paper.

SOME UNITS

⬛ 🛏 🍴 🏊 📷 [DATA PORT] / ✕ 📱 /

―――――― WHERE TO DINE ――――――

LAREDO MEXICAN RESTAURANT

▼▼ ▼▼

Southwest
Mexican

| **Lunch:** $4-$8 | **Dinner:** $5-$10 | **Phone:** 904/966-2323 |

Location: 0.5 mi n on Hwy 301. 800 N Temple Ave 32091. **Hours:** 11 am-10 pm. Closed major holidays; also Sun. **Reservations:** suggested. **Features:** casual dress; children's menu; cocktails; a la carte. A must for the best food and service south of the border. Colorful flower beds and a bright, attractive decor create an inviting setting. Try the chalupa, a thick, toasty tortilla topped with hot beans, lettuce, tomato and a generous scoop of guacamole. **Cards:** AE, DS, MC, VI.

✕

STEINHATCHEE pop. 750

—— WHERE TO STAY ——

STEINHATCHEE LANDING RESORT

Phone: (352)498-3513

▽▽▽ 5/21-9/11   2P: $205-$440
12/1-5/20 & 9/12-11/30   2P: $120-$300

Cottage   **Location:** SR 51, 8 mi w of jct US 19/98. SR 51 N 32359 (PO Box 789). Fax: 352/498-2346. **Facility:** Southern-style cottages in secluded compound beside river. Attractive decor. Oak-shaded grounds. 21 units with kitchen. 11 two-bedroom units and 4 three-bedroom units. Some whirlpool units ($210-$430). 2 stories, exterior corridors. **Terms:** 14 day cancellation notice-fee imposed, weekly & monthly rates available, pets ($250 deposit). **Leisure Activities:** 2 pools (1 heated), whirlpool, canoeing, boat dock, fishing, lighted tennis court, nature trails, playground, exercise room. **Guest Services:** [CP] meal plan available. **Cards:** DS, MC, VI.

[ASK] [✈] [🛏] [🍴] [🏊] [✕] [VCR] [▭] [▬] [🔌] / [✕] /

STEINHATCHEE RIVER INN

Phone: (352)498-4049

▽▽▽ 5/21-9/11   2P: $60-$70   XP: $10   F3
12/1-5/20 & 9/12-11/30   2P: $50-$60   XP: $10   F3

Motel   **Location:** Center of town. 1111 Riverside Dr 32359 (PO Box 828). **Facility:** Peaceful setting with view of river. 17 units, 8 with kitchen. 2 stories, exterior corridors. **Terms:** 14 day cancellation notice-fee imposed, pets (dogs only extra charge). **Amenities:** extended cable TV. **Leisure Activities:** across from marina.

[🛏] [🏊] [▭] [🔌] / [✕] [Z] /

THE SUNSET PLACE RESORT MOTEL

Phone: 352/498-0860

(AAA) (SAVE)   All Year   2P: $85-$115   XP: $7   F11

▽▽▽   **Location:** SR 51, 12 mi w of jct US 98. 115 1st St SW 32359 (PO Box 975). Fax: 352/498-0840. **Facility:** Rooms overlook gulf. 19 units with kitchen. 3 stories (no elevator), exterior corridors. **Terms:** 14 day cancellation notice-fee imposed, pets ($5 extra charge). **Leisure Activities:** boat dock, boat tie-up at dock for fee, exercise room. **Cards:** AE, CB, DS, JC, MC, VI.

Motel

[🛏] [🏊] [✕] [🎥] [▭] [▬] [🔌] / [VCR] /

—— WHERE TO DINE ——

ROY'S   **Lunch:** $6-$14   **Dinner:** $10-$18   Phone: 352/498-5000

▽▽   **Location:** Just w of town center on gulf. Hwy 51 Jct 361 32359. **Hours:** 11 am-9 pm. Closed major holidays. **Features:** casual dress; children's menu; a la carte. A lovely gulf view and superbly prepared food explain

Spanish   why this restaurant has been serving for 30 years. Here you will find the tastiest shrimp in the region along with other ocean fare that is fried, broiled or steamed, and served with great hushpuppies. **Cards:** AE,

MC, VI.

[♿] [✕]

STUART pop. 11,900

—— WHERE TO STAY ——

HOLIDAY INN-DOWNTOWN

Phone: (561)287-6200

▽▽▽ 2/1-3/31   2P: $139-$144   XP: $8   F19
1/1-1/31   2P: $95-$100   XP: $8   F19
4/1-11/30   2P: $79-$100   XP: $8   F19

Motor Inn   12/1-12/31   2P: $79-$89   XP: $8   F19

Location: On US 1, 0.5 mi s of jct SR 76. 1209 S Federal Hwy 34994 (PO Box 566-34997). Fax: 561/287-6200. **Facility:** Designated smoking area. 119 units. Some suites ($179-$229). 2 stories, exterior corridors. **Amenities:** extended cable TV, video games, voice mail, irons, hair dryers. **Leisure Activities:** heated pool, sauna, exercise room. **Guest Services:** valet and coin laundry. **Business Services:** meeting rooms. **Cards:** AE, CB, DI, DS, JC, MC, VI.

[ASK] [SD] [🍴] [Y] [🏊] [🚶] [🎥] [📠] [▭] [DATA PORT] / [✕] [▬] [🔌] /
     FEE   FEE

HOWARD JOHNSON HOTEL

Phone: (561)287-3171

▽▽▽ 2/1-3/31   1P: $99   2P: $99   XP: $8   F18
12/1-1/31   1P: $70-$85   2P: $70-$85   XP: $8   F18
4/4-4/12   1P: $85   2P: $85   XP: $8   F18

Motor Inn   4/13-11/30   1P: $70   2P: $70   XP: $8   F18

Location: On US 1, just s of jct SR 76. 950 S Federal Hwy 34994. Fax: 561/220-3594. **Facility:** Lush landscaped pool courtyard. Designated smoking area. 81 units. 2 stories, interior corridors. **Terms:** 7 day cancellation notice. **Amenities:** extended cable TV. **Guest Services:** [CP] meal plan available, valet and coin laundry. **Business Services:** meeting rooms. **Cards:** AE, CB, DI, DS, JC, MC, VI.

[ASK] [SD] [✈] [🍴] [Y] [🏊] [♿] [🎥] [📠] [▭] [DATA PORT] / [✕] [🔌] /
                       FEE

HUTCHINSON ISLAND MARRIOTT BEACH RESORT & MARINA

Phone: (561)225-3700

▽▽▽ 12/1-4/30   2P: $209-$259
5/1-5/31 & 9/17-11/30   2P: $159-$209
6/1-9/16   2P: $89-$139

Resort   **Location:** 4 mi ne on SR A1A, on south end of Hutchinson Island at east end of causeway. 555 NE Ocean Blvd 34996. Fax: 561/225-7131. **Facility:** Florida plantation style hotel on extensive river to ocean grounds. Large hotel units and oceanfront housekeeping apartments with balcony. 299 units. 16 two-bedroom units, 70 efficiencies and 29 units with kitchen. Some suites ($179-$279) and whirlpool units. *Bath:* combo or shower only. 4 stories, interior/exterior corridors. **Amenities:** extended cable TV, voice mail, irons, hair dryers. **Dining:** Scalawags Restaurant, see separate listing. **Terms:** 3 day cancellation notice-fee imposed, package plans, pets ($75 extra charge). **Parking:** valet. **Leisure Activities:** 3 heated pools, whirlpools, beach, swimming, fishing, children's program, social program, playground, exercise room. *Fee:* boat dock, marina, waterskiing, snorkeling equipment, charter fishing, golf-18 holes, 13 tennis courts (5 lighted), bicycles. **Guest Services:** gift shop, area transportation, valet and coin laundry. **Business Services:** conference facilities, administrative services, fax. **Cards:** AE, CB, DI, DS, JC, MC, VI.

[✈] [🛏] [🍴] [Y] [🏌] [♿] [🚣] [🏊] [✕] [🎥] [📠] [▭] [🔌] [DATA PORT] / [✕] [VCR] [▬]
FEE   FEE   FEE   FEE

PIRATES COVE RESORT & MARINA

Phone: (561)287-2500

(AAA) [SAVE] ♦♦♦♦

Motor Inn

12/1-5/31		2P: $120-$175	XP: $15	F18
11/1-11/30		2P: $120-$140	XP: $15	F18
6/1-10/31		2P: $90-$110	XP: $15	F18

Location: 0.3 mi e of CR A1A. 4307 SE Bayview St 34997. **Fax:** 561/220-2704. **Facility:** Waterfront; overlooking Manatee pocket and marina. Units with balcony, all with water views. Arts and craft show on the water, 6 pm-9 pm Tuesday. Designated smoking area. 50 units. *Bath:* combo or shower only. 3-4 stories, exterior corridors. **Terms:** check-in 4 pm, pets ($100 extra charge). **Amenities:** extended cable TV. **Dining:** cocktails, also, Pirate's Loft Restaurant, see separate listing, entertainment. **Leisure Activities:** heated pool, rack storage. *Fee:* marina, fishing, charter fishing. **Guest Services:** gift shop, coin laundry. **Business Services:** meeting rooms. **Cards:** AE, CB, DI, DS, MC, VI.

SOME UNITS
FEE

PLANTATION BEACH CLUB AT INDIAN RIVER PLANTATION

Phone: (561)225-0074

♦♦♦♦

Condominium

2/17-4/20	1P: $240-$260	2P: $270-$290
12/23-2/16	1P: $199-$250	2P: $235-$280
4/21-11/30	1P: $185-$210	2P: $225-$250
12/1-12/22		2P: $220-$235

Location: Within Indian River Plantation Resort. 0.5 mi se of SR A1A, via McArthur Blvd, just ne on NE Plantation Rd to NE Tradewind Lane and follow signs. 329 NE Tradewind Lane 34996. **Fax:** 561/225-6318. **Facility:** Large fully equipped units, many bi-level, all with water and screened porch and water views. 30 units with kitchen. 20 two-bedroom units. Some whirlpool units. 1-4 stories, exterior corridors. **Terms:** 30 day cancellation notice, daily rates available. **Amenities:** extended cable TV, irons. **Leisure Activities:** heated pool, sauna, whirlpool, beach, swimming, exercise room. **Guest Services:** area transportation, complimentary laundry. **Cards:** AE, DS, MC, VI. *(See color ad p 757)*

RAMADA INN

Phone: (561)287-6900

♦♦♦

Motel

2/1-4/30	1P: $92-$119	2P: $92-$119	XP: $5	F17
1/1-1/31	1P: $82-$119	2P: $82-$119	XP: $5	F17
12/1-12/31 & 5/1-11/30	1P: $62-$119	2P: $62-$119	XP: $5	F17

Location: US 1, 0.5 mi s of jct SR 76. 1200 S Federal Hwy 34994. **Fax:** 561/286-8188. **Facility:** 120 units. Some whirlpool units ($99-$119). *Bath:* combo or shower only. 2 stories, exterior corridors. **Terms:** check-in 4 pm, cancellation fee imposed. **Amenities:** extended cable TV, voice mail, safes (fee). *Some:* hair dryers. **Leisure Activities:** heated pool, game room. **Guest Services:** [CP] meal plan available, valet and coin laundry. **Business Services:** meeting rooms. **Cards:** AE, CB, DI, DS, JC, MC, VI.

SOME UNITS

—— WHERE TO DINE ——

DON RAMON RESTAURANT

Lunch: $4-$7   **Dinner:** $6-$19   **Phone: 561/221-7711**

♦♦

Cuban

Location: Jct of SR 76 and Monterey Rd. 100 SW Monterey Rd 34994. **Hours:** 11 am-10 pm, Fri & Sat-10:30 pm, Sun 4 pm-9:30 pm. **Features:** casual dress; children's menu; carryout; cocktails & lounge; a la carte. Warm ambience fills the dining room and the airy patio of the comfortable restaurant, a favorite with the locals. On the enticing menu are chicken, fish and shredded pork dishes, as well as sweet fried plantains and black beans with rice. **Cards:** AE, DI, DS, MC, VI.

THE FLAGLER GRILL

Dinner: $14-$22   **Phone: 561/221-9517**

♦♦♦

Regional American

Location: Just e of US 1; in historic downtown area. 47 SW Flagler Ave 34994. **Hours:** Open 12/1-8/30 & 10/1-11/30; 5:30 pm-9:30 pm. Closed major holidays; also Sun 7/1-12/31. **Reservations:** suggested. **Features:** casual dress; cocktails & lounge; street parking; a la carte. In a turn-of-the-20th-century building, the cozy, friendly restaurant is noted for excellent service and innovative cuisine. Fresh ingredients and international seasonings contribute to the food's great taste; a well-balanced wine list enhances it. Smoke free premises. **Cards:** AE, DS, MC, VI.

MARIO'S ITALIAN RESTAURANT

Dinner: $6-$15   **Phone: 561/283-6660**

♦♦

Italian

Location: On US 1, 1 mi s of jct SR 76; in Federal Plaza Shops. 1924 S Federal Hwy 34994. **Hours:** 3 pm-10 pm. Closed major holidays; also Mon & 6/26-7/9. **Features:** casual dress; children's menu; carryout; beer & wine only. Although the decor is plain and simple, the food is far from it. The owner/chef shares time-tested family recipes and freshly baked desserts, such as cheesecake, tiramisu and cannoli. Generous portions and a friendly staff add to the experience. **Cards:** AE, MC, VI.

PIRATE'S LOFT RESTAURANT

Lunch: $5-$12   **Dinner:** $7-$20   **Phone: 561/223-5048**

♦♦♦

Seafood

Location: 0.3 mi e of CR A1A; in Pirates Cove Resort & Marina. 4307 SE Bayview St 34997. **Hours:** 7 am-10 pm, Fri & Sat-11 pm. **Reservations:** suggested. **Features:** casual dress; children's menu; early bird specials; carryout; cocktails & lounge; entertainment. Fish nets and nautical decorations set the mood in the restaurant, which overlooks the marina. The menu features surf and turf specials and such specialties as the seafood sampler, which includes crab cake, scallops, shrimp and the fresh catch. **Cards:** AE, CB, DI, DS, MC, VI.

RIVERWALK CAFE

Lunch: $5-$9   **Dinner:** $11-$20   **Phone: 561/221-1511**

♦♦♦

Regional American

Location: Just e of US 1; in historic downtown area, close to the river. 201 SW St Lucie Ave 34994. **Hours:** 11:30 am-2:30 pm, Mon-2:30 pm, Fri & Sat-10 pm. Closed: Sun. **Reservations:** accepted. **Features:** casual dress; beer & wine only; street parking; a la carte. Although the menu changes regularly at the small, gourmet cafe, diners can always count on innovative, well-presented cuisine that samples intricate flavors from around the world. Created in the bistro style, the restaurant bustles with activity. Smoke free premises. **Cards:** AE, DI, MC, VI.

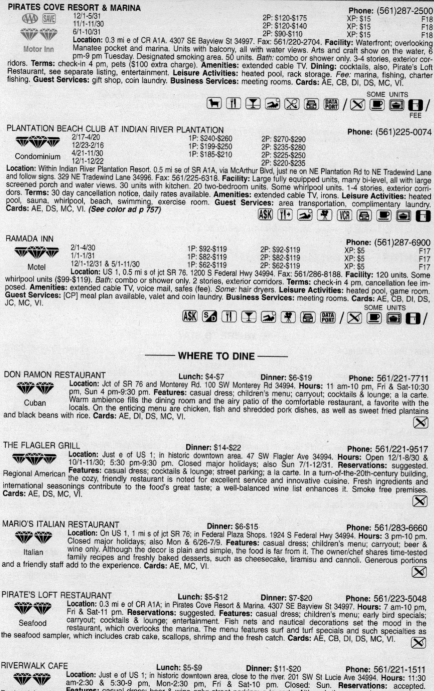

SCALAWAGS RESTAURANT

▽▽▽▽

American

Dinner: $19-$29   **Phone:** 561/225-6818

Location: 4 mi ne on SR A1A, on south end of Hutchinson Island at east end of causeway; in Hutchinson Island Marriott Beach Resort & Marina. 555 NE Ocean Blvd 34996. **Hours:** 7 am-10 pm. **Reservations:** suggested. **Features:** casual dress; Sunday brunch; children's menu; early bird specials; cocktails & lounge; fee for valet parking. Overlooking a marina on the Intracoastal Waterway, the breezy restaurant exudes an island feel, with many tropical plants, brass lanterns and paddle fans. Specialties include the Mediterranean crusted rack of lamb and the decadent chocolate cake. **Cards:** AE, CB, DI, DS, MC, VI.   ⊠

The following restaurant has not been evaluated by AAA but is listed for your information only.

THE ASHLEY
[fyi]

Phone: 561/221-9476

Not evaluated. **Location:** 61 SW Oceola St. **Features:** Eclectic menu and decor. In historic building, circa 1900's. Moderate prices.

SUMMERLAND KEY —See The Florida Keys p. 344.

SUN CITY CENTER —See Tampa Bay p. 881.

SUNNY ISLES —See Miami-Miami Beach p. 526.

SUNRISE —See Fort Lauderdale p. 391.

SURFSIDE —See Miami-Miami Beach p. 527.

TALLAHASSEE pop. 124,800

——— WHERE TO STAY ———

BEST INNS OF AMERICA

🔺🔺🔺 [SAVE]
▽▽▽▽ ▽▽

Motel

9/1-11/30	1P: $66-$79	2P: $69-$76	XP: $7 F
12/1-8/31	1P: $41-$55	2P: $45-$66	XP: $7 F

Phone: (850)562-2378

Location: I-10; exit 29, just nw on US 27. 2738 Graves Rd 32303. Fax: 850/562-2378. **Facility:** Traditional motel units for budget-minded travelers. 75 units. 2 stories, exterior corridors. **Terms:** 7 day cancellation notice, small pets only. **Guest Services:** [BP] meal plan available. **Cards:** AE, CB, DI, DS, MC, VI.

Special Amenities: free continental breakfast and free local telephone calls.   SOME UNITS

🆂🅳 🛏 🍽⁺ 🏊 📺 📠 / ⊠ 🛗 /

BEST WESTERN PRIDE INN

🔺🔺🔺 [SAVE]
▽▽▽▽

Motel

All Year	1P: $49-$85	2P: $53-$95	XP: $5 F12

Phone: (850)656-6312

Location: 2.1 mi s on US 27. 2016 Apalachee Pkwy 32301. Fax: 850/942-4312. **Facility:** Quiet location set back off highway. 78 units. 2 stories, exterior corridors. **Amenities:** extended cable TV. **Guest Services:** [ECP] meal plan available, coin laundry. **Business Services:** meeting rooms. **Cards:** AE, DI, DS, MC, VI.

Special Amenities: free continental breakfast and free local telephone calls.   SOME UNITS

🆂🅳 🏊 📺 🖨 / ⊠ 🛗 /

BEST WESTERN SEMINOLE INN

🔺🔺🔺 [SAVE]
▽▽▽▽ ▽▽

Motel

All Year	1P: $49-$80	2P: $52-$95	XP: $5 F12

Phone: 850/656-2938

Location: I-10, exit 31A, just w on US 90. 6737 Mahan Dr 32308. Fax: 850/656-6380. **Facility:** Rural surroundings. Quiet atmosphere. 60 units. 2 stories, exterior corridors. **Terms:** cancellation fee imposed. **Amenities:** extended cable TV. **Guest Services:** [ECP] meal plan available, coin laundry. **Cards:** AE, CB, DI, DS, MC, VI.

Special Amenities: free continental breakfast and free local telephone calls.   SOME UNITS

🆂🅳 🏊 📺 / ⊠ /

CABOT LODGE-NORTH

▽▽▽▽

Motel

All Year	1P: $65-$70	2P: $70-$76	XP: $6 F18

Phone: (850)386-8880

Location: I-10, exit 29, 0.3 mi s on US 27. 2735 N Monroe St 32303. Fax: 850/386-4254. **Facility:** Quiet, peaceful location on six nicely landscaped acres, with a distinctive country inn flair. Large screened veranda off lobby overlooks pool area and grounds. Contemporary units. 160 units. 2 stories, exterior corridors. **Terms:** 3 day cancellation notice. **Amenities:** extended cable TV, irons, hair dryers. **Guest Services:** [CP] meal plan available, complimentary evening beverages, valet laundry. **Cards:** AE, DI, DS, MC, VI.   SOME UNITS

[ASK] 🆂🅳 🍽⁺ 🚫 🏊 🛗⁺ 📺 🖨 📠 / ⊠ /

CABOT LODGE-THOMASVILLE RD

▽▽▽▽

Motel

All Year	1P: $72-$82	2P: $82-$92

Phone: (850)386-7500

Location: I-10, exit 30, 0.4 mi se. 1653 Raymond Diehl Rd 32308. Fax: 850/386-1136. **Facility:** Executive-level rooms with robes, two-line speaker phones, and an office area with copier and fax machine. 135 units. Some suites ($125). **Bath:** combo or shower only. 5 stories, interior corridors. **Amenities:** voice mail, irons, hair dryers. **Guest Services:** [CP] meal plan available, coin laundry. **Business Services:** meeting rooms. **Cards:** AE, CB, DI, DS, JC, MC, VI.   SOME UNITS

🏠 🚫 🏊 🛗⁺ 📺 🖨 📠 / ⊠ 📼 🛗 /

CALHOUN STREET INN BED AND BREAKFAST

▼▼▼

Historic Bed & Breakfast

12/1-5/1 & 6/1-11/30 — 1P: $65-$95 — 2P: $65-$95 — **Phone:** 850/425-5095 — XP: $25

Location: Downtown historic district; corner Calhoun and E Georgia, parking off Georgia St. 525 N Calhoun St 32301. Fax: 207/863-4866. **Facility:** Large comfortable units in historic Colonial Revival home built in 1907. Located in tree lined neighborhood within walking distance to park with recreational facilities. Designated smoking area. 4 units. *Bath:* combo or shower only. 2 stories, interior corridors. **Terms:** open 12/1-5/1 & 6/1-11/30, age restrictions may apply. **Amenities:** extended cable TV. **Guest Services:** [BP] meal plan available. **Cards:** AE, DS, MC, VI.

⊠ ☎ 🖨

COMFORT INN

SAVE

▼▼▼

Motel

All Year — 1P: $79 — 2P: $79 — **Phone:** 850/562-7200

Location: I-10, exit 29, nw corner, just off US 27. 2727 Graves Rd 32303. Fax: 850/562-6335. **Facility:** Generally good sized guest units. 100 units. Some whirlpool units. *Bath:* combo or shower only. 3 stories, interior corridors. **Terms:** 7 day cancellation notice. **Amenities:** extended cable TV, voice mail, irons, hair dryers. **Guest Services:** [CP] meal plan available, coin laundry. **Cards:** AE, CB, DI, DS, MC, VI. *(See color ad p 790)*

SOME UNITS
S🄳 🍴 ⟲ ⟲ FEE 🖨 📠 DATA PORT ⊠ 🖥 🛗 /

COURTYARD BY MARRIOTT

▼▼▼

Motor Inn

1/1-5/11 — 1P: $89 — 2P: $89 — **Phone:** (850)222-8822
12/1-12/31 & 5/12-11/30 — 1P: $49 — 2P: $49

Location: 1 mi se on US 27. 1018 Apalachee Pkwy 32301. Fax: 850/561-0354. **Facility:** Some units with balcony over courtyard. Upscale lobby. 154 units. 2-4 stories, interior corridors. **Terms:** 3 day cancellation notice. **Amenities:** dual phone lines, voice mail, irons, hair dryers. **Leisure Activities:** whirlpool, exercise room. **Guest Services:** coin laundry. **Business Services:** meeting rooms. **Cards:** AE, CB, DI, DS, JC, MC, VI. *(See color ad below)*

SOME UNITS
ASK S🄳 🍴 ⟲ ⟲ FEE 🖥 📠 DATA PORT ⊠ 🛗 /

DOUBLETREE HOTEL TALLAHASSEE

▼▼▼

Hotel

All Year — 1P: $79-$149 — 2P: $89-$159 — **Phone:** (850)224-5000 — XP: $10 — F18

Location: Downtown; jct Adams St and Park Ave; opposite the courthouse. 101 S Adams St 32301. Fax: 850/513-9516. **Facility:** In walking distance to capital and other government entities. Spacious rooms. Well trained, accommodating staff. 242 units. *Bath:* combo or shower only. 16 stories, interior corridors. **Terms:** check-in 3:30 pm. **Amenities:** voice mail, irons, hair dryers. **Guest Services:** gift shop, valet laundry. **Business Services:** meeting rooms, fax. **Cards:** AE, CB, DI, DS, MC, VI. *(See color ad below)*

SOME UNITS
ASK S🄳 🍴 🍷 ⟲ 🖥 ⟲ 👤 📹 FEE FEE 🖨 🖥 DATA PORT ⊠ 🖥 🛗 /

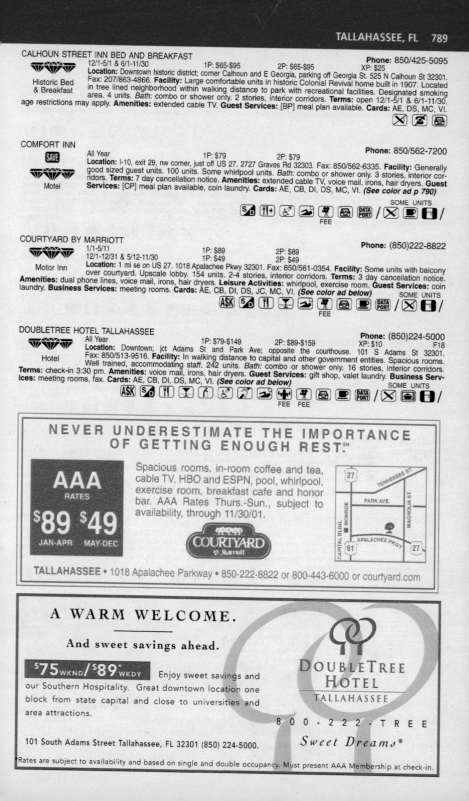

ECONO LODGE
(AAA) (SAVE)
▼▼ ▼▼
Motel

Phone: (850)385-6155

2/1-4/30	1P: $50-$65	2P: $55-$65
5/1-11/30	1P: $45-$60	2P: $50-$65
12/1-1/31	1P: $45-$60	2P: $50-$65
		XP: $7 F16

Location: I-10, exit 29, 0.5 mi s. 2681 N Monroe St 32303. Fax: 850/385-6155. **Facility:** A few units catering to the senior market with safety bars in showers. 82 units. 2 stories, exterior corridors. **Terms:** 7 day cancellation notice, small pets only. **Amenities:** extended cable TV. **Cards:** AE, CB, DI, DS, JC, MC, VI.
Special Amenities: free continental breakfast and preferred room (subject to availability with advanced reservations).

SOME UNITS
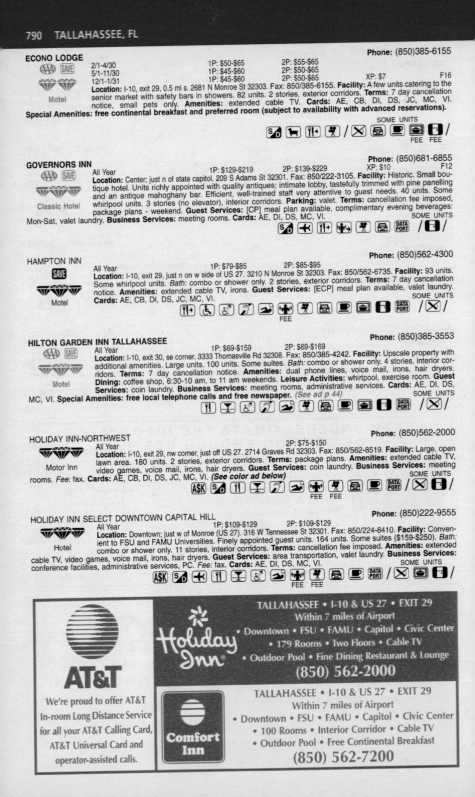

GOVERNORS INN
(AAA) (SAVE)
▼▼ ▼▼
Classic Hotel

Phone: (850)681-6855

All Year   1P: $129-$219   2P: $139-$229   XP: $10   F12
Location: Center; just n of state capitol. 209 S Adams St 32301. Fax: 850/222-3105. **Facility:** Historic. Small boutique hotel. Units richly appointed with quality antiques; intimate lobby, tastefully trimmed with pine panelling and an antique mahogany bar. Efficient, well-trained staff very attentive to guest needs. 40 units. Some whirlpool units. 3 stories (no elevator), interior corridors. **Parking:** valet. **Terms:** cancellation fee imposed, package plans - weekend. **Guest Services:** [CP] meal plan available, complimentary evening beverages: Mon-Sat, valet laundry. **Business Services:** meeting rooms. **Cards:** AE, DI, DS, MC, VI.

SOME UNITS

HAMPTON INN
(SAVE)
▼▼▼
Motel

Phone: (850)562-4300

All Year   1P: $79-$85   2P: $85-$95
Location: I-10, exit 29, just n on w side of US 27. 3210 N Monroe St 32303. Fax: 850/562-6735. **Facility:** 93 units. Some whirlpool units. **Bath:** combo or shower only. 2 stories, exterior corridors. **Terms:** 7 day cancellation notice. **Amenities:** extended cable TV, irons. **Guest Services:** [ECP] meal plan available, valet laundry. **Cards:** AE, CB, DI, DS, JC, MC, VI.

SOME UNITS

HILTON GARDEN INN TALLAHASSEE
(AAA) (SAVE)
▼▼▼▼
Motel

Phone: (850)385-3553

All Year   1P: $69-$159   2P: $69-$169
Location: I-10, exit 30, se corner. 3333 Thomasville Rd 32308. Fax: 850/385-4242. **Facility:** Upscale property with additional amenities. Large units. 100 units. Some suites. **Bath:** combo or shower only. 4 stories, interior corridors. **Terms:** 7 day cancellation notice. **Amenities:** dual phone lines, voice mail, irons, hair dryers. **Dining:** coffee shop, 6:30-10 am, to 11 am weekends. **Leisure Activities:** whirlpool, exercise room. **Guest Services:** coin laundry. **Business Services:** meeting rooms, administrative services. **Cards:** AE, DI, DS, MC, VI. **Special Amenities:** free local telephone calls and free newspaper. (See ad p 44)

SOME UNITS

HOLIDAY INN-NORTHWEST
▼▼▼▼
Motor Inn

Phone: (850)562-2000

All Year   2P: $75-$150
Location: I-10, exit 29, nw corner, just off US 27. 2714 Graves Rd 32303. Fax: 850/562-8519. **Facility:** Large, open lawn area. 180 units. 2 stories, exterior corridors. **Terms:** package plans. **Amenities:** extended cable TV, video games, voice mail, irons, hair dryers. **Guest Services:** coin laundry. **Business Services:** meeting rooms. Fee: fax. **Cards:** AE, CB, DI, DS, JC, MC, VI. (See color ad below)

SOME UNITS

HOLIDAY INN SELECT DOWNTOWN CAPITAL HILL
▼▼▼▼
Hotel

Phone: (850)222-9555

All Year   1P: $109-$129   2P: $109-$129
Location: Downtown; just w of Monroe (US 27). 316 W Tennessee St 32301. Fax: 850/224-8410. **Facility:** Convenient to FSU and FAMU Universities. Finely appointed guest units. 164 units. Some suites ($159-$250). **Bath:** combo or shower only. 11 stories, interior corridors. **Terms:** cancellation fee imposed. **Amenities:** extended cable TV, video games, voice mail, irons, hair dryers. **Guest Services:** area transportation, valet laundry. **Business Services:** conference facilities, administrative services, PC. Fee: fax. **Cards:** AE, DI, DS, MC, VI.

SOME UNITS

LA QUINTA INN-NORTH

SAVE

Motel

All Year   1P: $65-$79   2P: $65-$79   **Phone: (850)385-7172**
Location: I-10, exit 29, just s on US 27, east side. 2905 N Monroe St (US 27) 32303-3636. Fax: 850/422-2463. **Facility:** Up-to-date property with a Southwestern motif. Limited number of first floor units; many face courtyard. 154 units. 2-3 stories, exterior corridors. **Terms:** small pets only. **Guest Services:** [CP] meal plan available, valet laundry. **Business Services:** meeting rooms. **Cards:** AE, CB, DI, DS, MC, VI.

LA QUINTA INN-TALLAHASSEE SOUTH

SAVE

Motel

All Year   1P: $65-$75   2P: $65-$75   **Phone: (850)878-5099**
Location: 3 mi se on US 27. 2850 Apalachee Pkwy 32301-3608. Fax: 850/878-6665. **Facility:** Bright contemporary rooms with a Southwestern flair. 134 units. 3-4 stories, exterior corridors. **Terms:** package plans, small pets only. **Amenities:** video games. **Guest Services:** [CP] meal plan available, valet laundry. **Business Services:** meeting rooms. **Cards:** AE, CB, DI, DS, MC, VI.

MICROTEL INN & SUITES

Motel

All Year   1P: $45   2P: $55   **Phone: (850)562-3800**
Location: I-10, exit 29, upper nw corner. (3216 N Monroe St, 32303). Fax: 850/562-8611. **Facility:** Compact to spacious rooms. 91 units. *Bath:* combo or shower only. 3 stories, interior corridors. **Amenities:** voice mail. **Guest Services:** [CP] meal plan available, valet laundry. **Cards:** AE, DI, DS, MC, VI.

MOTEL 6 - 420

Motel

5/25-11/30   1P: $37-$47   2P: $43-$53   XP: $3   F17
12/1-5/24   1P: $35-$45   2P: $41-$51   XP: $3   F17   **Phone: 850/668-2600**
Location: I-10, exit 30, just n, w on Timberlane, next to Market Square Shopping Center. 1481 Timberlane Dr 32308. Fax: 850/894-3104. **Facility:** Simply attired units for the budget-minded traveler. 131 units. 2 stories, exterior corridors. **Cards:** AE, DI, DS, MC, VI.

QUALITY INN & SUITES

AAA **SAVE**

Motel

1/1-4/30   2P: $61-$69   XP: $10   F18
9/1-11/30   2P: $61-$64   XP: $10   F18   **Phone: (850)877-4437**
5/1-8/31   2P: $59-$64   XP: $10   F18
12/1-12/31   2P: $59-$61   XP: $10   F18
Location: 2.2 mi s on US 27. 2020 Apalachee Pkwy 32301. **Facility:** Short distance to large shopping mall. 89 units. 3 stories, interior corridors. **Terms:** weekly & monthly rates available. **Amenities:** extended cable TV, video games, voice mail, irons, hair dryers. **Guest Services:** valet laundry. **Business Services:** meeting rooms, administrative services, PC, fax. **Cards:** AE, DI, DS, MC, VI. **Special Amenities:** free continental breakfast and free room upgrade (subject to availability with advanced reservations).

RADISSON HOTEL TALLAHASSEE

Hotel

Property failed to provide current rates   **Phone: (850)224-6000**
Location: 0.5 mi n of Capitol. 415 N Monroe St 32301. Fax: 850/222-0335. **Facility:** Upscale units within walking distance to downtown capitol area. 119 units. Some suites and whirlpool units. 7 stories, interior corridors. **Parking:** valet. **Terms:** 7 day cancellation notice, package plans. **Amenities:** voice mail, irons, hair dryers. **Leisure Activities:** sauna, exercise room. **Guest Services:** area transportation, valet laundry. **Business Services:** meeting rooms. **Cards:** AE, CB, DI, DS, JC, MC, VI.

RED ROOF INN

AAA **SAVE**

Motel

All Year   1P: $45-$90   2P: $50-$95   XP: $5   F18   **Phone: (850)385-7884**
Location: I-10, exit 29, sw side, just off US 27. 2930 Hospitality St 32303. Fax: 850/386-8896. **Facility:** Modern units with basic amenities in quiet, wooded setting; next to a Cracker Barrel. 108 units. 2 stories, exterior corridors. **Terms:** small pets only. **Amenities:** voice mail. **Cards:** AE, CB, DI, DS, MC, VI. **Special Amenities:** free local telephone calls and free newspaper.

SHONEY'S INN & SUITES

AAA **SAVE**

Motel

All Year   1P: $65-$95   **Phone: (850)386-8286**
Location: I-10, exit 29, se side. 2801 N Monroe St 32303. Fax: 850/422-1074. **Facility:** Appealing Spanish-style decor, featuring a pleasant courtyard. "Economy" units very compact, with basic unit package; other units more spacious. 112 units. Some whirlpool units ($150-$200). *Bath:* combo or shower only. 2 stories, exterior corridors. **Terms:** monthly rates available, pets ($10 extra charge). **Guest Services:** coin laundry. **Business Services:** meeting rooms. **Cards:** AE, DI, DS, MC, VI. **Special Amenities:** free continental breakfast and free local telephone calls.

SUPER 8 MOTEL
Motel

Phone: (850)386-8818
F17
All Year   1P: $44-$65   2P: $44-$65   XP: $5
Location: I-10, exit 29, 0.4 mi s on US 27. 2702 N Monroe St 32303. Fax: 850/386-8818. **Facility:** Simply attired units for budget minded travelers. 61 units. 3 stories, interior corridors. **Terms:** pets ($10 fee). **Amenities:** extended cable TV. **Business Services:** fax. **Cards:** AE, DI, DS, JC, MC, VI.   SOME UNITS

The following lodging was either not evaluated or did not meet AAA rating requirements but is listed for your information only.

FAIRFIELD INN BY MARRIOTT
[fyi]
Motel

Phone: 850-562-8766
XP: $10
F17
All Year
Too new to rate. **Location:** I-10, exit 29, then just n. 3211 N Monroe St 32303. Fax: 850/562-2194. **Amenities:** 79 units, radios, microwaves, refrigerators, pool. **Terms:** 3 day cancellation notice-fee imposed. **Cards:** AE, DI, DS, MC, VI.

——— WHERE TO DINE ———

ALBERT'S PROVENCE
French

Lunch: $5-$8   Dinner: $8-$20   Phone: 850/850-9003
Location: I-10, exit 30, 0.3 mi n, then e; in Market Square. 1415 Timberlane Rd 32312. **Hours:** 11:30 am-2 & 6-9:30 pm, Fri & Sat-10 pm. Closed major holidays; also Sun. **Reservations:** suggested. **Features:** casual dress; cocktails; a la carte. Enjoy classic French Mediterranean cuisine in an intimate dining room with well trained service. Hailing from France, Albert delights diners with his fabulous lobster bisque and locals rave over his crab cakes a l'aubergine. Choose from a wide variety of wine, many available by the glass. The homemade plate changes daily. Always leave room to make a selection from the dessert tray. For those wishing a more casual experience, sit at the de artiste to the rear of the dining room. **Cards:** AE, DS, MC, VI.

BARNACLE BILL'S
American

Lunch: $4-$8   Dinner: $8-$12   Phone: 850/385-8734
Location: I-10, exit 29, 2 mi s. 1830 N Monroe St 32303. **Hours:** 11 am-11 pm, Fri & Sat-midnight. Closed: 11/22, 12/25; also 12/24. **Features:** casual dress; children's menu; senior's menu; carryout; cocktails. A popular local gathering spot, it features Florida seafood, pasta and an oyster bar with seasonal outdoor seating. The efficient wait staff excels at keeping guests happy. A close cousin of jambalaya, the shrimp skillet is a nice mix of rice and sausage. **Cards:** AE, DI, DS, MC, VI.

CAFE DI LORENZO
Italian

Dinner: $13-$19   Phone: 850/681-3622
Location: 0.5 mi n of jct US 90 and 27. 1002 N Monroe St 32303. **Hours:** 5 pm-11 pm. Closed: 11/22, 12/25. **Features:** casual dress; children's menu; carryout; beer & wine only; a la carte. House specialties feature large portions of hearty, delicious American-Italian favorites. A laid-back ambience and an opportunity for outdoor dining make this place special. The dessert list includes creme brulee, chocolate mousse and rich Key lime pie. **Cards:** AE, MC, VI.

CHEZ PIERRE
French

Lunch: $6-$10   Dinner: $10-$20   Phone: 850/222-0936
Location: Center; corner of Thomasville Rd and 6th Ave, just e of Monroe. 1215 Thomasville Rd 32303. **Hours:** 11 am-10 pm. Closed major holidays; also Sun. **Reservations:** suggested. **Features:** casual dress; carryout; cocktails; a la carte. A romantic atmosphere popular with couples, the restaurant features such intimate touches as fresh flowers, French artwork and a deck bedecked with tiny white lights. Sample from creatively presented specials or from a sinful selection of pastries. **Cards:** AE, DI, DS, MC, VI.

LUCY HO'S ORIENTAL BISTRO
Chinese

Lunch: $6-$9   Dinner: $6-$20   Phone: 850/893-4112
Location: I-10 exit 30, 0.3 mi n on SR 61, just e on Capitol Circle Rd; in Oak Lake Village. 1700-5 Halstead Blvd 32308. **Hours:** 11 am-10 pm. Closed major holidays. **Features:** casual dress; Sunday brunch; early bird specials; carryout; cocktails; buffet. A professional staff will gladly help you select from the many entrees featured on this Chinese-Japanese menu. Crab ragoons are delicious with huge pieces of crab prepared with a light peanut oil. Large portions and a sushi bar will please every appetite. **Cards:** AE, DI, DS, MC, VI.

NINO - A RESTAURANT
Italian

Dinner: $8-$18   Phone: 850/878-8141
Location: 7 mi e of the Capitol Building on US 27. 6497 Apalachee Pkwy 32311. **Hours:** 5 pm-10 pm; hours vary on holidays. Closed major holidays; also Sun, Mon & week of July 4th. **Reservations:** suggested; weekends. **Features:** casual dress; children's menu; carryout; cocktails & lounge; a la carte. An intimate, cozy atmosphere derives from candlelit tables, lace-curtained windows and charming, old farmhouse decor. Enjoy an excellent variety of veal and seafood entrees, as well as tasty Bavarian favorites such as wiener schnitzel. **Cards:** AE, DI, DS, MC, VI.

SILVER SLIPPER
Steak & Seafood

Dinner: $14-$25   Phone: 850/386-9366
Location: I-10, exit 29, 1.3 mi s, on US 27, 0.3 mi e on John Knox, just s. 531 Scotty's Ln 32303. **Hours:** 5 pm-11 pm. Closed: 12/25; also Sun. **Reservations:** suggested. **Features:** casual dress; children's menu; early bird specials; carryout; cocktails & lounge; entertainment; a la carte. The restaurant has lots of history and greenery once was a hot spot for an impressive list of celebrity and political guests. It's still a good place to enjoy steaks and seafood and delicious baklava. Low lighting and greenery sets the table for romance. **Cards:** AE, CB, DI, DS, MC, VI.

TAMARAC —*See Fort Lauderdale p. 392.*

TAMPA —*See Tampa Bay p. 818.*

Special People Get Special Treatment

Want to be sure you'll be treated right on your next travel adventure?

*L*ook for establishments that advertise in the AAA TourBook® guides. These are the businesses that cater to AAA members. They value the business they receive from AAA members, and are willing to go the extra mile to get it. And in turn, they pass value on to you.

So, when you're using the TourBook to make your travel plans, be sure to look at the advertisements first.

Travel With Someone You Trust®

Destination Tampa-St. Petersburg

Tampa pop. 280,000
St. Petersburg pop. 238,600

Although often considered as one, Tampa, St. Petersburg and their neighboring beach communities are distinct entities. Taken collectively or individually, though, these cities by the bay are liberally sprinkled with enticements.

While Tampa is more oriented toward business and industry, St. Petersburg and its sister sun-dappled beaches appeal to those seeking a resort atmosphere. The best of both worlds come together here, and the combination is hard to beat.

Tampa skyline.
Anchored by the bay, Tampa's modern skyline is testament to the city's bustling business environment.

See Vicinity map page 796 —

*Sunshine Skyway,
St. Petersburg.*
Fifteen miles long, the expansive bridge connects St. Petersburg with Manatee County across Tampa Bay.
(See listing page 213)

*P*laces included in this AAA Destination City:

St. Pete Beach.
Warm Gulf of Mexico waters draw
vacationers to this suburban resort
community. (See listing page 228)

University of Tampa.
Instantly recognizable by
its Moorish architecture,
the university occupies
a former hotel built by
magnate Henry Plant.
(See listing page 217)

See Vicinity
map page 805

Local cuisine, Tampa Bay.
Freshly caught and freshly
grown—there's lots to tempt
the most discriminating palate.

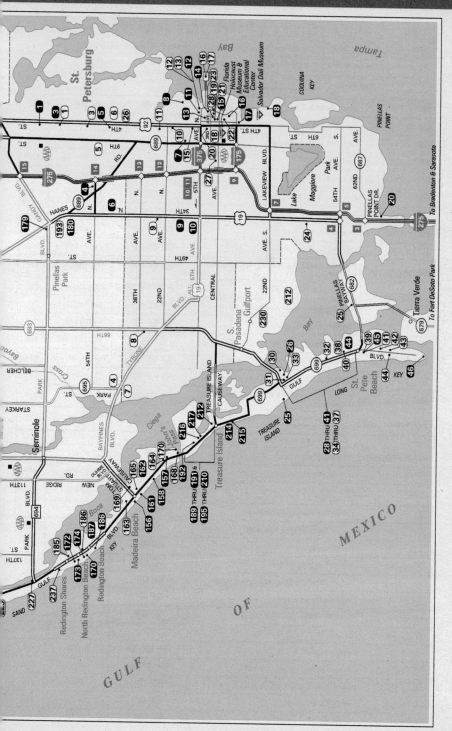

St. Petersburg & Beach Area and Vicinity

This index helps you "spot" where approved accommodations are located on the corresponding detailed maps. Rate ranges are for comparison only and show the property's high season. Turn to the listing page for more detailed rate information and consult display ads for special promotions. Restaurant rate range is for dinner, unless only lunch (L) is served.

Spotter/Map Page Number	OA	ST. PETERSBURG - Lodgings	Diamond Rating	Rate Range High Season	Listing Page
1 / p. 796	AAA	Grant Motel & Apts	◇◇	$38-$50 SAVE	812
3 / p. 796	AAA	Tops Motel & Apartments	◇◇	$40-$50 SAVE	814
4 / p. 796	AAA	Days Inn of St. Petersburg	◇◇	$59-$74 SAVE	812
5 / p. 796	AAA	Kentucky Motel	◇	$36-$48 SAVE	813
6 / p. 796	AAA	La Quinta Inn - see color ad p 829	◇◇	$59-$89 SAVE	814
7 / p. 796	AAA	Empress Motel Apartments	◇	$45-$55 SAVE	812
8 / p. 796	AAA	Sunset Bay Inn	◇◇◇	$170-$250 SAVE	814
9 / p. 796		Comfort Inn & Suites	◇◇◇	$69-$89	812
10 / p. 796		Days Inn St. Pete Central	◇◇◇	$60-$66	812
11 / p. 796	AAA	Mansion House B & B and The Courtyard on Fifth	◇◇◇	$115-$165 SAVE	814
12 / p. 796	AAA	Renaissance Vinoy Resort	◇◇◇◇	$250-$300 SAVE	814
13 / p. 796	AAA	The Claiborne House at Bay Gables	◇◇◇	$95-$115 SAVE	811
14 / p. 796		The Heritage-A Holiday Inn Hotel	◇◇◇	$120-$150	813
15 / p. 796	AAA	Colonial Bayfront Hotel	◇◇	$85-$150 SAVE	811
16 / p. 796		St. Petersburg Bayfront Hilton - see ad p 44	◇◇◇	Failed to provide	814
17 / p. 796	AAA	Bayboro Inn & Hunt Room Bed & Breakfast	◇◇◇	$75-$110 SAVE	811
18 / p. 796	AAA	Bayboro House Bed & Breakfast On Old Tampa Bay	◇◇◇	$155-$195 SAVE	811
20 / p. 796	AAA	Holiday Inn Sunspree Resort Marina Cove - see color ad p 813	◇◇◇	$107-$170 SAVE	813
		ST. PETERSBURG - Restaurants			
1 / p. 796		Paisano's Pizza & Pasta	◇	$7-$18	817
2 / p. 796		Crab Shack	◇	$5-$14	815
3 / p. 796		Red Mesa Regional Mexican & Southwest Cuisine	◇◇	$7-$18	817
4 / p. 796		Carmelita's Mexican Restaurant	◇◇	$8-$11	815
5 / p. 796		Casual Clam Seafood Restaurant	◇◇	$5-$11	815
6 / p. 796		Pepin Restaurant	◇◇	$14-$30	817
7 / p. 796		Saffron's at Jungle Prada	◇◇	$9-$22	817
8 / p. 796		Arigato Japanese Steak House Restaurant	◇◇	$11-$21	815
9 / p. 796		Texas Cattle Company	◇◇	$10-$30	817
10 / p. 796		Cockney Rebel	◇◇	$9-$18	815
11 / p. 796		El Cap	◇	$3-$6	815
12 / p. 796		Marchand's Bar & Grill	◇◇◇	$11-$25	816
13 / p. 796		Terrace Room	◇◇◇	$11-$29	817
14 / p. 796		Ollie's Cork & Bottle	◇◇	$5-$13	816
15 / p. 796		4th Street Shrimp Store	◇◇	$4-$21	815
16 / p. 796		Cafe Lido	◇◇	$9-$18	815

Spotter/Map Page Number	OA	ST. PETERSBURG - Restaurants (continued)	Diamond Rating	Rate Range High Season	Listing Page
(17) / p. 796		Columbia Restaurant	◆◆	$14-$22	815
(18) / p. 796		Ovo Cafe	◆◆◆	$9-$16	817
(19) / p. 796		Moon Under Water	◆◆	$7-$17	816
(20) / p. 796		The Keystone Club	◆◆	$12-$21	816
(21) / p. 796		The Firehouse Bar & Grille	◆◆	$4-$13	816
(22) / p. 796		Jo Jo's in Citta Restaurant, Piano Bar & Lounge	◆◆	$8-$17	816
(23) / p. 796		Apropos Bistro & Bar	◆	$13-$21	815
(24) / p. 796		Leverocks at Maximo	◆◆	$9-$21	816
(25) / p. 796		Native Seafood & Trading Company	◆◆	$10-$18	816
(26) / p. 796		Fred's Famous Bar-B-Que and Brewery	◆◆	$5-$17	816
(27) / p. 796		Grand Finale	◆◆◆	$10-$25	816
(28) / p. 796		The Garden-A Mediterranean Bistro	◆◆	$7-$18	816
		ST. PETE BEACH - Lodgings			
(25) / p. 796	AAA	**Lamara Motel Apartments**	◆◆	$65-$75 SAVE	878
(26) / p. 796	AAA	**Pasa Tiempa Bed & Breakfast**	◆◆◆	$100-$150 SAVE	878
(28) / p. 796	AAA	**Beach Haven**	◆◆	$88-$144 SAVE	876
(29) / p. 796	AAA	**Alden Beach Resort** - see color ad p 876	◆◆	$164-$249 SAVE	876
(30) / p. 796	AAA	**Beach House Suites By The Don Cesar**	◆◆◆	$325-$393 SAVE	876
(31) / p. 796	AAA	**Travelodge St. Pete Beach** - see color ad p 877	◆◆	$80-$135 SAVE	880
(34) / p. 796	AAA	**Best Western Beachfront Resort**	◆◆	$108-$268 SAVE	877
(35) / p. 796		Howard Johnson Lodge St Pete Beach Resort Inn	◆◆	$115	878
(36) / p. 796	AAA	**TradeWinds Sandpiper Hotel & Suites** - see color ad p 879	◆◆	$149-$245 SAVE	879
(37) / p. 796	AAA	**TradeWinds Island Grand Beach Resort** - see color ad p 879	◆◆◆	$199-$349 SAVE	878
(39) / p. 796		Holiday Inn Hotel & Suites Beachfront Resort & Conference Center	◆◆◆	$268-$498	877
(40) / p. 796	AAA	**Palm Crest Resort Motel**	◆◆	$85-$103 SAVE	878
(41) / p. 796	AAA	**TradeWinds Sirata Beach Resort** - see color ad p 879	◆◆◆	$175-$317 SAVE	880
(44) / p. 796		Ritz Motel	◆◆	$66-$85	878
(45) / p. 796	AAA	**The Don CeSar Beach Resort & Spa**	◆◆◆◆	$329-$363 SAVE	877
(46) / p. 796	AAA	**Island's End Resort**	◆◆	$116-$195 SAVE	878
		ST. PETE BEACH - Restaurants			
(30) / p. 796		Johnny Leverock's on the Beach	◆◆	$7-$19	880
(31) / p. 796		La Croisette Family Restaurant	◆	$10-$19	880
(32) / p. 796		Skidder's Restaurant	◆◆	$6-$24	881
(33) / p. 796		Der Eisenhut	◆◆	$9-$15	880
(34) / p. 796		Aunt Heidi's Italian Restaurant	◆	$6-$12	880
(35) / p. 796		Starlite Diner	◆◆	$4-$12	881
(36) / p. 796		Palm Court Restaurant	◆◆◆	$16-$25	881
(37) / p. 796		The Sloppy Pelican	◆	$5-$12	881

Spotter/Map Page Number	OA	ST. PETE BEACH - Restaurants (continued)	Diamond Rating	Rate Range High Season	Listing Page
38 / p. 796		Brunello	♦♦♦	$18-$22	880
39 / p. 796		Sea Porch Cafe	♦♦♦	$9-$21	881
40 / p. 796		Silas Dent's Steakhouse	♦♦	$8-$21	881
41 / p. 796		Maritana Grille	♦♦♦	$20-$30	880
42 / p. 796	⬥⬥⬥	**Sea Critters Cafe**	♦♦	$6-$17	881
43 / p. 796		The Wharf Seafood Restaurant	♦	$5-$16	881
44 / p. 796		The Seahorse Tavern & Restaurant	♦♦	$5-$11(L)	881
		CLEARWATER - Lodgings			
53 / p. 796		Ramada Inn Countryside	♦♦♦	$89-$99	848
54 / p. 796	⬥⬥⬥	**Bay Queen Motel - see ad p 853**	♦♦	$68-$78 SAVE	843
55 / p. 796	⬥⬥⬥	**Econo Lodge Clearwater**	♦♦	$72-$75 SAVE	846
56 / p. 796	⬥⬥⬥	**Clearwater Central-Best Western**	♦♦	$79-$89 SAVE	844
57 / p. 796		Super 8 of Clearwater	♦♦	$69	848
59 / p. 796		Holiday Inn Hotel & Suites Bayside City Centre	♦♦♦	$95-$255	847
60 / p. 796		Hampton Inn Clearwater Central	♦♦♦	$89-$105	846
61 / p. 796		Days Inn-Clearwater Central	♦♦	$74-$86	845
62 / p. 796		Quality Inn Clearwater Central	♦♦♦	$79-$120	848
63 / p. 796		Days Inn Clearwater North	♦♦	Failed to provide	845
64 / p. 796	⬥⬥⬥	**Belleview Biltmore Resort & Spa - see color ad p 843**	♦♦	$139-$169 SAVE	844
65 / p. 796		Candlewood Suites Clearwater-St Petersburg - see ad p 844	♦♦♦	$99-$119	844
66 / p. 796	⬥⬥⬥	**Holiday Inn Express - see color ad p 845**	♦♦♦	$99-$134 SAVE	847
67 / p. 796		Hampton Inn-Clearwater/St. Petersburg Airport	♦♦♦	$85	847
69 / p. 796		Holiday Inn Select-St. Pete/Clearwater Int'l Airport	♦♦♦	$119-$139	847
70 / p. 796		La Quinta Inn Clearwater-Airport - see color ad p 829	♦♦♦	$55-$85	848
71 / p. 796		Courtyard by Marriott - see color ad p 812	♦♦♦	$129-$139	845
72 / p. 796		Residence Inn by Marriott	♦♦♦	$145-$175	848
74 / p. 796	⬥⬥⬥	**Days Inn-St.Pete/Clearwater Airport - see color ad p 846**	♦♦♦	$79-$104 SAVE	846
75 / p. 796	⬥⬥⬥	**Comfort Inn/Clearwater - see color ad p 845**	♦♦♦	$85-$104 SAVE	844
76 / p. 796		Super 8 Motel-St. Petersburg	♦♦	$49-$74	848
77 / p. 796		St. Petersburg/Clearwater Fairfield Inn by Marriott	♦♦♦	$89-$109	848
78 / p. 796		Homestead Village Guest Studios	♦♦♦	$69-$89	847
79 / p. 796		Homewood Suites by Hilton	♦♦♦	$109-$199	847
80 / p. 796		Wingate Inn	♦♦♦	$89-$99	849
		CLEARWATER - Restaurants			
48 / p. 796		Sam Seltzer's Steakhouse	♦♦	$10-$19	851
49 / p. 796		Harrison's Grill & Bar	♦♦	$7-$19	850
50 / p. 796		Durango Steakhouse	♦♦	$7-$18	850
51 / p. 796		Schmooze Inc of Clearwater	♦♦	$7-$17	851

Spotter/Map Page Number	OA	CLEARWATER - Restaurants (continued)	Diamond Rating	Rate Range High Season	Listing Page
52 / p. 796		First Watch	◆◆	$5-$7(L)	850
54 / p. 796		Arigato Japanese Steak House	◆◆	$11-$21	849
56 / p. 796		Marco Polo	◆◆◆	$13-$29	850
57 / p. 796		Lenny's	◆◆	$4-$8(L)	850
58 / p. 796		Key West Grill	◆◆	$10-$30	850
59 / p. 796		Tio Pepe Restaurante	◆◆◆	$11-$25	851
60 / p. 796		Alfanso's Restaurant	◆◆	$12-$25	849
61 / p. 796		Tucson's	◆◆	$7-$23	851
62 / p. 796		Pepe's Fine Dining & Tapas Cafe	◆◆	$14-$23	851
63 / p. 796		Joe's Crab Shack	◆◆	$5-$18	850
64 / p. 796		Peking Palace	◆	$5-$20	851
65 / p. 796		Jillian's Bistro & Piano Bar	◆◆	$16-$26	850
66 / p. 796		Sweetwater's Restaurant	◆◆	$6-$20	851
67 / p. 796		Johnny's Italian Grille	◆◆	$6-$15	850
68 / p. 796		Primo's Pasta-Ribs	◆◆	$6-$16	851
69 / p. 796		G. Bellini's Ristorante & Bar	◆◆	$11-$27	850
70 / p. 796		Carmelita's Mexican Restaurant	◆◆	$5-$11	849
71 / p. 796		The Grill at Feather Sound	◆◆◆	$17-$26	850
		CLEARWATER BEACH - Lodgings			
85 / p. 796	AAA	**The Palm Pavilion Inn -** see color ad p 857	◆◆	$87-$125 SAVE	857
86 / p. 796	AAA	**East Shore Resort Apartment Motel**	◆◆◆	$615-$680 SAVE	854
88 / p. 796	AAA	**Koli-Bree Motel/Apt**	◆	$82 SAVE	856
89 / p. 796	AAA	**Pelican Cove Motel**	◆◆	$52-$82 SAVE	857
90 / p. 796	AAA	**Blue Jay Motel**	◆◆	$63-$98 SAVE	854
91 / p. 796	AAA	**Island Queen Resort Motel**	◆◆	$72-$98 SAVE	856
92 / p. 796	AAA	**Casa Rosa Apartment Motel**	◆◆	$65-$130 SAVE	854
93 / p. 796	AAA	**New Yorker Motel**	◆	$75-$98 SAVE	857
94 / p. 796	AAA	**Echo Sails Motel & Apts**	◆◆	$55-$80 SAVE	854
95 / p. 796	AAA	**Tropical Breeze Motel**	◆◆	$80-$95 SAVE	860
96 / p. 796	AAA	**Chart House Suites on Clearwater Bay**	◆◆◆	$129-$199 SAVE	854
97 / p. 796	AAA	**Leisure Inn & Suites**	◆◆	$85-$105 SAVE	857
98 / p. 796	AAA	**Howard Johnson Express Inn**	◆◆	$99-$149 SAVE	856
99 / p. 796	AAA	**Sea Captain Resort On the Bay**	◆◆◆	$80-$100 SAVE	859
100 / p. 796	AAA	**Bel Crest Beach Resort**	◆	$99-$171 SAVE	853
101 / p. 796	AAA	**Ramada Limited**	◆◆	$74-$149 SAVE	859
104 / p. 796	AAA	**Mannings On The Bay**	◆◆	$85-$149 SAVE	857
105 / p. 796	AAA	**The Dunes Motel**	◆◆	$75-$174 SAVE	854
106 / p. 796	AAA	**Hilton Clearwater Beach Resort -** see ad p 44 & color ad p 852	◆◆◆	$189-$299 SAVE	855
109 / p. 796	AAA	**Falcon Motel**	◆◆	$36-$82 SAVE	855

Spotter/Map Page Number	OA	CLEARWATER BEACH - Lodgings (continued)	Diamond Rating	Rate Range High Season	Listing Page
110 / p. 796	AAA	Shephard's Beach Resort - see color ad p 859	◇◇◇	$129-$159 SAVE	859
111 / p. 796		Beachouse	◇◇	$95-$185	853
112 / p. 796	AAA	Holiday Inn Sunspree Resort & Conference Center - see color ad p 856	◇◇◇	$149-$199 SAVE	855
115 / p. 796	AAA	Best Western Sea Stone Resort & Suites - see ad p 853	◇◇◇	$99-$190 SAVE	853
116 / p. 796	AAA	Ramada Inn Gulfview - see color ad p 852	◇◇◇	$144-$184 SAVE	859
117 / p. 796	AAA	Adam's Mark Clearwater Beach Resort - see color ad p 852	◇◇◇	$89-$229 SAVE	851
118 / p. 796	AAA	Econo Lodge - see ad p 855	◇◇	$100-$200 SAVE	855
119 / p. 796	AAA	Quality Inn Beach Resort - see color ad p 858	◇◇◇	$159-$199 SAVE	858
120 / p. 796	AAA	Best Western Sea Wake Inn - see ad p 853	◇◇◇	$155-$196 SAVE	854
122 / p. 796	AAA	Travelodge Beachview Resort	◇◇	$99-$158 SAVE	860
123 / p. 796	AAA	Americana Gulf Resort	◇◇	$95-$150 SAVE	852
125 / p. 796		Sheraton Sand Key Resort	◇◇◇	$160-$270	860
126 / p. 796	AAA	Radisson Suite Resort on Sand Key - see ad p 858	◇◇◇	$269-$310 SAVE	858
		CLEARWATER BEACH - Restaurants			
95 / p. 796		Waterfront Restaurant	◇	$7-$24	861
96 / p. 796		Cooters Raw Bar & Restaurant	◇	$6-$14	860
97 / p. 796		Frenchy's Cafe	◇	$5-$8	861
98 / p. 796		Frenchy's Rockaway Grill & Beach Club	◇◇	$6-$13	861
99 / p. 796		Bob Heilman's Beachcomber	◇◇◇	$13-$30	860
102 / p. 796		Big Ben British Restaurant & Pub	◇	$7-$16(L)	860
104 / p. 796		Gondolier Pizza and Italian Restaurant	◇	$6-$19	861
109 / p. 796		Legends Steakhouse	◇◇	$8-$16	861
110 / p. 796		Post Corner Pizza	◇	$5-$15	861
111 / p. 796		Bonsai Japanese Cuisine-Sushi Bar	◇	$11-$18	860
112 / p. 796		Seafood & Sunsets at Julie's Cafe	◇◇	$6-$17	861
113 / p. 796		Frenchy's Saltwater Cafe	◇	$6-$10	861
114 / p. 796	AAA	Shephard's Waterfront Restaurant	◇◇	$18	861
115 / p. 796		Leverock's of Clearwater Beach	◇◇	$9-$21	861
116 / p. 796		Columbia Restaurant	◇◇	$13-$20	860
		DUNEDIN - Lodgings			
130 / p. 796		Inn on the Bay	◇◇	$74	862
131 / p. 796	AAA	Best Western Yacht Harbor Inn & Suites	◇◇◇	$119-$139 SAVE	862
		DUNEDIN - Restaurants			
130 / p. 796		Jesse's Dockside	◇◇	$9-$21	862
131 / p. 796		"Kelly's For Just About...Anything!"	◇◇	$10-$18	862
133 / p. 796		Bon Appetit Restaurant	◇◇◇	$12-$15	862
136 / p. 796		Sea Sea Riders	◇◇	$6-$16	862
		INDIAN ROCKS BEACH - Lodgings			
137 / p. 796	AAA	Holiday Isle Apartments	◇◇	$89-$110 SAVE	864

Spotter/Map Page Number	OA	INDIAN ROCKS BEACH - Lodgings (continued)	Diamond Rating	Rate Range High Season	Listing Page
138 / p. 796	AAA	Anchor Court Apartments	◈◈	$85-$111 SAVE	863
140 / p. 796		810 Gulfside	◈◈◈	$695	863
141 / p. 796		Gulf Towers Resort Motel	◈◈	$476-$630	863
142 / p. 796	AAA	Holiday Inn Harbourside	◈◈◈	$119-$600 SAVE	864
143 / p. 796		Sea Resort Motel	◈◈	$60-$100	864
		INDIAN ROCKS BEACH - Restaurants			
146 / p. 796		Thai Pan Alley & Bamboo Beach Bar	◈◈	$7-$9	864
147 / p. 796		Guppy's on the Beach	◈◈	$6-$28	864
		LARGO - Lodgings			
150 / p. 796		Le Versailles Courts	◈	$75-$289	865
		LARGO - Restaurant			
155 / p. 796		The Gathering Restaurant	◈	$4-$8(L)	865
		MADEIRA BEACH - Lodgings			
156 / p. 796	AAA	Holiday Inn Madeira Beach - see color ad p 865	◈◈◈	$124-$164 SAVE	865
157 / p. 796		The Lighthouse Bed & Breakfast Motel	◈◈	$80-$95	866
158 / p. 796	AAA	Wits End Motel - see color ad p 866	◈◈	$79-$130 SAVE	867
161 / p. 796	AAA	Shoreline Island Resort Motel - see color ad p 866	◈◈◈	$92-$233 SAVE	867
162 / p. 796	AAA	Sea Dawn Motel	◈	$50-$60 SAVE	867
		MADEIRA BEACH - Restaurants			
163 / p. 796		The Apple of Madeira Beach Family Restaurant & Lounge	◈◈	$7-$18	867
164 / p. 796		Village Landing	◈◈	$5-$14	867
168 / p. 796		Scully's Boardwalk Grille	◈◈	$8-$21	867
169 / p. 796		Johnny Leverock's Seafood House	◈◈	$9-$23	867
170 / p. 796		Friendly Fisherman Seafood Restaurant	◈◈	$6-$16	867
		NORTH REDINGTON BEACH - Lodgings			
170 / p. 796		Sails Resort Motel	◈◈	$75-$105	869
172 / p. 796		Far Horizons Motel	◈◈	$588-$637	868
173 / p. 796	AAA	RamSea - see color ad p 869	◈◈	$1020 SAVE	869
174 / p. 796		Hilton Tampa Bay/North Redington Beach Resort - see ad p 44	◈◈◈	$160-$260	869
		NORTH REDINGTON BEACH - Restaurants			
185 / p. 796	AAA	Wine Cellar Restaurant & Catering Service	◈◈◈	$10-$30	869
186 / p. 796		The Frog Pond	◈◈	$6-$11(L)	869
		PINELLAS PARK - Lodgings			
179 / p. 796		La Quinta Inn-Pinellas Park - see color ad p 829	◈◈◈	$69-$95	871
180 / p. 796	AAA	La Mark Charles Motel - see color ad p 871	◈◈	$75-$120 SAVE	871
		PINELLAS PARK - Restaurant			
193 / p. 796		Johnny Leverock's Seafood House	◈◈	$9-$23	871
		SAFETY HARBOR - Lodgings			
184 / p. 796	AAA	Safety Harbor Resort and Spa on Tampa Bay - see ad p 875	◈◈◈	$149-$209 SAVE	875

Spotter/Map Page Number	OA		Diamond Rating	Rate Range High Season	Listing Page
(199) / p. 796		**SAFETY HARBOR** - Restaurant	◆	$4-$9	875
(199) / p. 796		Enver's Paradise Restaurant	◆	$4-$9	875
		REDINGTON BEACH - Lodgings			
(186) / p. 796	AAA	La Playa Beach Resort	◆◆	$75-$105 SAVE	873
(187) / p. 796	AAA	El Morocco Resort Motel	◆	$375-$425 SAVE	873
		TREASURE ISLAND - Lodgings			
(189) / p. 796	AAA	Algiers Gulf Resort	◆◆	$70-$100 SAVE	883
(190) / p. 796	AAA	Fargo Motel	◆◆	$60-$90 SAVE	884
(191) / p. 796	AAA	Gulf Sounds Beach Rentals	◆◆◆	$74-$99 SAVE	884
(192) / p. 796		Jolly Roger Motel	◆◆	$45-$100	885
(195) / p. 796	AAA	Best Western Sea Castle Suites	◆◆	$95-$142 SAVE	884
(196) / p. 796	AAA	Bilmar Beach Resort	◆◆◆	$130-$150 SAVE	884
(197) / p. 796	AAA	Best Western Treasure Island - see color ad p 877	◆◆◆	$74-$129 SAVE	884
(198) / p. 796		The Twins Apartments	◆◆	$270-$370	887
(199) / p. 796	AAA	Ramada Inn Treasure Island	◆◆	$120-$150 SAVE	886
(200) / p. 796		Holiday Inn-Treasure Island Beach	◆◆◆	$110-$149	884
(205) / p. 796	AAA	The Sea Chest	◆◆	$82-$119 SAVE	886
(207) / p. 796	AAA	Trails End Resort Motel - see color ad p 885	◆◆	$75-$103 SAVE	886
(209) / p. 796	AAA	Thunderbird Beach Resort - see color ad p 886	◆◆	$125-$159 SAVE	886
(210) / p. 796	AAA	Arvilla Resort Motel	◆◆	$61-$98 SAVE	883
(212) / p. 796		Mardi Gras Motel	◆	Failed to provide	885
(214) / p. 796	AAA	Page Terrace Motel - see color ad p 885	◆◆	$66-$98 SAVE	885
(215) / p. 796	AAA	The Jefferson Motel Apts.	◆◆	$679 SAVE	885
(216) / p. 796	AAA	Roadside Inn	◆◆	$55-$106 SAVE	886
(217) / p. 796		The Bayside Inn	◆◆	$59-$540	884
		BELLEAIR BLUFFS - Restaurant			
(205) / p. 796		E & E Stakeout Grill	◆◆	$6-$19	840
		GULFPORT - Restaurant			
(212) / p. 796		Casa Cortes	◆	$3-$11	862
		INDIAN SHORES - Restaurants			
(222) / p. 796		The Pub Restaurant & Lounge	◆◆	$7-$17	864
(224) / p. 796		The Hungry Fisherman	◆◆	$6-$23	864
(225) / p. 796		Chateau Madrid	◆◆◆	$10-$23	864
(227) / p. 796		Salt Rock Grill	◆◆◆	$11-$31	865
		SOUTH PASADENA - Restaurant			
(230) / p. 796		Horse & Jockey British Restaurant & Bar	◆◆	$7-$11	876
		REDINGTON SHORES - Restaurant			
(237) / p. 796	AAA	The Lobster Pot	◆◆◆	$16-$46	874

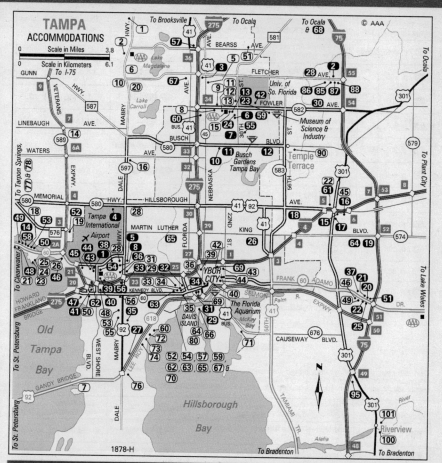

TAMPA
ACCOMMODATIONS

1878-H

✈ Airport Accommodations

Spotter/Map Page Number	OA	**TAMPA INTERNATIONAL**	Diamond Rating	Rate Range High Season	Listing Page
1 / above	AAA	**Amerisuites-Tampa Airport, 2.5 mi se of terminal**	◆◆◆	$149-$169 SAVE	818
50 / above		Chase Suite Hotel by Woodfin, 4.5 mi sw of airport terminal	◆◆◆	$125-$195	819
33 / above		Courtyard By Marriott, 3.5 mi se of the terminal	◆◆◆	$164-$185	820
43 / above		Crowne Plaza Tampa-Westshore, 3 mi se of terminal	◆◆◆	$129-$159	820
8 / above	AAA	**Days Inn Airport Stadium, 4 mi n of terminal**	◆◆	$85-$105 SAVE	820
14 / above		Days Inn Rocky Point Island, 4 mi sw of airport terminal	◆◆	$89-$109	821
49 / above		DoubleTree Guest Suites Tampa Bay, 4.3 mi sw of terminal	◆◆◆	$139-$229	821
40 /·above		Embassy Suites Hotel-Tampa/Airport/Westshore, 3.5 mi s of terminal	◆◆◆	$149-$209	824
44 / above	AAA	**Hampton Inn Tampa Int'l Airport, 2.5 mi se of terminal**	◆◆◆	$109-$129 SAVE	825

Spotter/Map Page Number	OA	TAMPA INTERNATIONAL (continued)	Diamond Rating	Rate Range High Season	Listing Page
38 / p. 805	AAA	Hilton Tampa Airport Westshore, 2 mi e of airport terminal	◇◇◇	$100-$210 [SAVE]	826
53 / p. 805		Holiday Inn Express Hotel & Suites, 4 mi sw of terminal	◇◇◇	$109-$129	826
4 / p. 805		Holiday Inn Express Hotel & Suites Stadium/Airport, 5.3 mi ne of terminal	◇◇◇	$85-$95	826
5 / p. 805	AAA	Howard Johnson Airport-Stadium, 4.5 mi se of terminal	◇	$64-$84 [SAVE]	827
46 / p. 805	AAA	Hyatt Regency Westshore, 3 mi w of terminal	◇◇◇◇	$234-$259 [SAVE]	828
45 / p. 805		La Quinta Inn Tampa Airport, 2.5 mi e of terminal	◇◇◇	$75-$99	828
48 / p. 805	AAA	Radisson Bay Harbor Hotel, 4.3 mi w of airport terminal	◇◇◇	$133-$143 [SAVE]	830
47 / p. 805	AAA	Ramada Airport Inn & Conference Center, 3 mi s of terminal	◇◇	$129-$139 [SAVE]	831
36 / p. 805		Sheraton Suites Tampa Airport, 3.5 mi se of terminal	◇◇◇	$199-$210	832
52 / p. 805		Tampa Airport Marriott, in terminal	◇◇◇	Failed to provide	832
54 / p. 805	AAA	Wellesley Inn & Suites, 3.5 mi w of terminal	◇◇◇	$99-$199 [SAVE]	832
41 / p. 805	AAA	Wyndham Westshore, 3 mi s of airport terminal	◇◇◇	$111-$118 [SAVE]	833

Tampa and Vicinity

This index helps you "spot" where approved accommodations are located on the corresponding detailed maps. Rate ranges are for comparison only and show the property's high season. Turn to the listing page for more detailed rate information and consult display ads for special promotions. Restaurant rate range is for dinner, unless only lunch (L) is served.

Spotter/Map Page Number	OA	TAMPA - Lodgings	Diamond Rating	Rate Range High Season	Listing Page
1 / p. 805	AAA	Amerisuites-Tampa Airport - see color ad p 5	◇◇◇	$149-$169 [SAVE]	818
2 / p. 805		Courtyard by Marriott Tampa North	◇◇◇	$98	820
3 / p. 805		Days Inn-Tampa North - see ad p 396	◇◇	$60-$99	821
4 / p. 805		Holiday Inn Express Hotel & Suites Stadium/Airport	◇◇◇	$85-$95	826
5 / p. 805	AAA	Howard Johnson Airport-Stadium	◇	$64-$84 [SAVE]	827
6 / p. 805		DoubleTree Guest Suites Tampa/Busch Gardens - see color ad p 823	◇◇◇	$94	823
7 / p. 805		Baymont Inn & Suites-Tampa near Busch Gardens - see color ad p 819	◇◇◇	$94-$104	818
8 / p. 805	AAA	Days Inn Airport Stadium - see color ad p 821	◇◇◇	$85-$105 [SAVE]	820
10 / p. 805	AAA	Value Inn	◇	$59-$75 [SAVE]	832
11 / p. 805	AAA	Red Roof Inn	◇◇	$50-$85 [SAVE]	831
12 / p. 805		Howard Johnson Near Busch Gardens MainGate	◇◇◇	$79-$99	827
13 / p. 805		Holiday Inn Tampa - see color ad p 827	◇◇◇	$89-$99	826
14 / p. 805		Days Inn Rocky Point Island - see color ad p 822	◇◇	$89-$109	821
15 / p. 805	AAA	Red Roof Inn-Fairgrounds	◇◇	$49-$69 [SAVE]	832
16 / p. 805		Four Points Hotel by Sheraton Tampa East	◇◇◇	$105-$115	824

Spotter/Map Page Number	OA	**TAMPA - Lodgings (continued)**	Diamond Rating	Rate Range High Season	Listing Page
17 / p. 805		Baymont Inn-Tampa Fairgrounds - see color ad p 819	◈◈	$84-$94	818
18 / p. 805	AAA	**East Lake Inn**	◈	$45-$55 [SAVE]	823
19 / p. 805	AAA	**Radisson Hotel at Sabal Park -** see ad p 831	◈◈◈	$89-$189 [SAVE]	831
20 / p. 805		Baymont Inn-Tampa Southeast (Brandon) - see color ad p 819	◈◈	$89-$94	819
21 / p. 805	AAA	**Days Inn/State Fairgrounds -** see color ad p 822	◈◈	$69-$79 [SAVE]	821
22 / p. 805		Fairfield Inn by Marriott	◈◈◈	$90-$120	824
23 / p. 805		Wingate Inn-USF Near Busch Gardens	◈◈◈	$80-$115	833
24 / p. 805	AAA	**AmeriSuites Tampa Busch Gardens -** see color ad p 5	◈◈◈	$79-$209 [SAVE]	818
25 / p. 805		Courtyard by Marriott	◈◈◈	$119-$275	820
26 / p. 805		La Quinta Inn State Fair - see color ad p 829	◈◈◈	$65-$75	828
27 / p. 805	AAA	**Howard Johnson Express Inn & Suites -** see color ad p 828	◈◈◈	$55-$75 [SAVE]	827
28 / p. 805		Hampton Inn & Suites - see color ad p 825	◈◈◈	$85-$95	825
29 / p. 805		The Wyndham Harbour Island Hotel - see color ad p 833	◈◈◈	$139	833
30 / p. 805		Shoney's Inn	◈◈◈	$60-$125	832
31 / p. 805	AAA	**Hyatt Regency Tampa**	◈◈◈	$219-$244 [SAVE]	828
32 / p. 805		Holiday Inn City Centre	◈◈◈	$153	826
33 / p. 805		Courtyard By Marriott - see color ad p 812	◈◈◈	$164-$185	820
34 / p. 805		Courtyard by Marriott-Downtown Tampa	◈◈◈	$149	820
35 / p. 805	AAA	**Econo Lodge Midtown -** see color ad p 824	◈◈	$55-$80 [SAVE]	824
36 / p. 805		Sheraton Suites Tampa Airport	◈◈◈	$199-$210	832
37 / p. 805	AAA	**Comfort Suites**	◈◈◈	$79-$169 [SAVE]	820
38 / p. 805	AAA	**Hilton Tampa Airport Westshore -** see ad p 826, p 44	◈◈◈	$100-$210 [SAVE]	826
40 / p. 805		Embassy Suites Hotel-Tampa/Airport/Westshore	◈◈◈	$149-$209	824
41 / p. 805	AAA	**Wyndham Westshore -** see color ad p 833	◈◈◈	$111-$118 [SAVE]	833
42 / p. 805		Embassy Suites USF Campus	◈◈◈	$149-$199	824
43 / p. 805		Crowne Plaza Tampa-Westshore	◈◈◈	$129-$159	820
44 / p. 805	AAA	**Hampton Inn Tampa Int'l Airport**	◈◈◈	$109-$129 [SAVE]	825
45 / p. 805		La Quinta Inn Tampa Airport - see color ad p 829	◈◈◈	$75-$99	828
46 / p. 805	AAA	**Hyatt Regency Westshore**	◈◈◈◈	$234-$259 [SAVE]	828
47 / p. 805	AAA	**Ramada Airport Inn & Conference Center**	◈◈	$129-$139 [SAVE]	831
48 / p. 805	AAA	**Radisson Bay Harbor Hotel -** see ad p 830	◈◈◈	$133-$143 [SAVE]	830
49 / p. 805		DoubleTree Guest Suites Tampa Bay	◈◈◈	$139-$229	821
50 / p. 805		Chase Suite Hotel by Woodfin	◈◈◈	$125-$195	819
51 / p. 805	AAA	**Red Roof Inn-Brandon**	◈◈	$79-$99 [SAVE]	831
52 / p. 805		Tampa Airport Marriott	◈◈◈	Failed to provide	832

Spotter/Map Page Number	OA	TAMPA - Lodgings (continued)	Diamond Rating	Rate Range High Season	Listing Page
53 / p. 805		Hampton Inn - see color ad p 822	◆◆◆	$99-$106	825
54 / p. 805	AAA	**Wellesley Inn & Suites -** see color ad opposite title page	◆◆◆	$99-$199 SAVE	832
55 / p. 805	AAA	**Best Western All Suites Hotel Behind Busch Gardens -** see color ad p 811	◆◆◆	$109-$139 SAVE	819
56 / p. 805	AAA	**Double Tree Hotel Tampa Airport-Westshore** - see color ad p 823	◆◆◆	$134 SAVE	823
57 / p. 805	AAA	**Quality Inn-Busch Gardens -** see color ad p 830	◆◆◆	$89 SAVE	829
58 / p. 805		Holiday Inn Express Hotel & Suites - see color ad p 822	◆◆◆	$109-$129	826
59 / p. 805		La Quinta Inn & Suites USF - see color ad p 829	◆◆◆	$89-$109	828
60 / p. 805		Motel 6 - 483	◆◆	$40-$56	829
61 / p. 805		Motel 6 Tampa East - 1192	◆◆	$40-$56	829
62 / p. 805		Quality Hotel Westshore - see color ad p 830	◆◆	$89-$109	829
63 / p. 805	AAA	**Radisson Riverwalk Hotel Tampa**	◆◆◆	$189-$239 SAVE	831
64 / p. 805	AAA	**AmeriSuites -** see color ad p 817	◆◆◆	$95 SAVE	818
65 / p. 805		Gram's Place Bed, Breakfast & Music	◆◆	$85-$100	825
67 / p. 805	AAA	**Super 8 Motel-Tampa**	◆◆	$43-$56 SAVE	832
68 / p. 805		Wingate Inn-Tampa North	◆◆◆	$89-$119	833
69 / p. 805		Hilton Garden Inn/Tampa Ybor Historic District - see ad p 44 & color ad p 822	◆◆◆	$159	825
		TAMPA - Restaurants			
1 / p. 805		Jasmine Thai Restaurant	◆◆	$6-$19	837
2 / p. 805		Crabby Tom's Old Time Oyster Bar & Seafood Restaurant	◆◆	$4-$18	835
5 / p. 805		Skipper's Smokehouse Restaurant & Oyster Bar	◆	$7-$16	838
6 / p. 805		Arigato Japanese Steak House	◆◆	$10-$22	834
7 / p. 805		Jimmy Mac's Marina Restaurant	◆◆	$6-$21	837
8 / p. 805		Hops Restaurant Bar & Brewery	◆◆	$7-$17	837
9 / p. 805		Woody's Bar-B-Que	◆	$6-$12	840
10 / p. 805		Windy City Pizza	◆	$6-$19	839
11 / p. 805		First Watch	◆◆	$5-$7(L)	836
12 / p. 805		Lemongrass Restaurant	◆◆	$6-$15	837
13 / p. 805		Taj Indian Cuisine	◆◆	$9-$17	839
14 / p. 805		Logan's Roadhouse	◆◆	$6-$23	837
15 / p. 805		Tia's Tex Mex	◆◆	$7-$15	839
16 / p. 805		Sukhothai Restaurant	◆◆	$6-$20	839
17 / p. 805		Crabby Tom's Old Time Oyster Bar & Seafood Restaurant	◆◆	$4-$18	835
19 / p. 805		CK's Restaurant	◆◆	$14-$26	835
20 / p. 805		Vallarto's Restaurante Mexicano	◆◆	$6-$11	839
21 / p. 805		The Castaway	◆◆	$11-$20	835

Spotter/Map Page Number	OA	**TAMPA - Restaurants (continued)**	Diamond Rating	Rate Range High Season	Listing Page
㉒ / p. 805		Frontier Steak House	◆◆	$9-$31	836
㉓ / p. 805		The Rusty Pelican	◆◆◆	$18-$23	838
㉔ / p. 805		Crawdaddy's	◆◆	$16-$36	836
㉕ / p. 805		Armani's	◆◆◆◆	$23-$35	834
㉖ / p. 805		Oystercatchers	◆◆◆	$12-$30	838
㉘ / p. 805		Sam Seltzer's Steakhouse	◆◆	$10-$19	838
㉙ / p. 805		First Watch	◆◆	$5-$7(L)	836
㉛ / p. 805		Tia's Tex-Mex	◆◆	$8-$15	839
㉝ / p. 805		Valencia Garden	◆◆	$10-$17	839
㉞ / p. 805		Cafe European	◆	$8-$17	835
㉟ / p. 805		Mise en Place	◆◆◆	$13-$23	837
㊱ / p. 805		Boca	◆◆◆	$14-$26	834
㊴ / p. 805		Cafe Creole	◆◆	$12-$17	834
㊵ / p. 805		Tampa Bay Brewing Company	◆◆	$8-$20	839
㊷ / p. 805		Don Quixote Cafeteria	◆	$6-$9	836
㊸ / p. 805		Columbia Restaurant	◆◆	$14-$22	835
㊹ / p. 805		Ovo Cafe	◆◆	$10-$16	838
㊺ / p. 805		V.P.'s Country BBQ & Catering	◆	$5-$16	839
㊻ / p. 805		First Choice Bar-B-Que	◆	$4-$8	836
㊽ / p. 805	AAA	**Bay Cafe**	◆◆	$8-$20	834
㊾ / p. 805		Sweet Tomatoes	◆	$7	839
㊿ / p. 805		Shula's Steakhouse	◆◆◆	$17-$33	838
(51) / p. 805		Remington's Steakhouse	◆◆	$9-$21	838
(52) / p. 805		The Wine Exchange	◆◆	$6-$13	840
(53) / p. 805		Lauro Ristorante Italiano	◆◆◆	$12-$23	837
(54) / p. 805		Cafe Winberie	◆◆	$6-$14	835
(55) / p. 805		Durango Steakhouse	◆◆	$7-$18	836
(56) / p. 805		Donatello	◆◆	$16-$29	836
(57) / p. 805		Royal Palace Thai Restaurant	◆◆	$9-$16	838
(59) / p. 805		The Cactus Club Southwestern Grill & Bar	◆◆	$7-$16	834
(60) / p. 805		The Old Meeting House	◆	$4-$8	838
(62) / p. 805		Tuscan Oven	◆◆	$11-$18	839
(63) / p. 805		Ho Ho Windows	◆◆	$6-$13	836
(64) / p. 805		Jackson's Bistro-Bar & Sushi	◆◆◆	$13-$21	837
(65) / p. 805		42nd Street The Bistro	◆◆	$7-$18	834
(66) / p. 805		Harbour View Room	◆◆◆	$15-$25	836
(67) / p. 805		Hugo's Spanish Restaurant	◆◆	$4-$10	837

Spotter/Map Page Number	OA	TAMPA - Restaurants (continued)	Diamond Rating	Rate Range High Season	Listing Page
⑥⑨ / p. 805		Lonni's Sandwiches, Etc	◆	$3-$7(L)	837
⑦⓪ / p. 805		Ragin' Ribs	◆	$6-$15	838
⑦① / p. 805		Seabreeze Restaurant By the Bay	◆◆	$7-$19	838
⑦② / p. 805		Bern's Steak House	◆◆◆	$23-$35	834
⑦③ / p. 805		The Colonnade	◆◆	$6-$21	835
⑦④ / p. 805		Le Bordeaux	◆◆◆	$17-$33	837
⑦⑥ / p. 805		Caffe Paradiso	◆◆	$8-$24	835
⑦⑦ / p. 805		A J Catfish	◆◆	$5-$15	834
⑦⑧ / p. 805		Cody's Original Roadhouse	◆◆	$6-$16	835
⑧⓪ / p. 805		Estela's Mexican Restaurant	◆◆	$4-$12	836
TEMPLE TERRACE - Lodgings					
⑧⑤ / p. 805		Sleep Inn	◆◆	Failed to provide	883
⑧⑥ / p. 805		Residence Inn by Marriott Tampa North	◆◆◆	Failed to provide	883
⑧⑦ / p. 805		Fairfield Inn Tampa North	◆◆◆	$80-$90	883
⑧⑧ / p. 805		Extended Stay of America	◆◆	$54-$69	883
TEMPLE TERRACE - Restaurant					
⑨⓪ / p. 805		Vallarto's Restaurante Mexicano	◆◆	$6-$11	883
RIVERVIEW (HILLSBOROUGH COUNTY) - Lodgings					
⑨⑤ / p. 805	AAA	**Bianchi Motel**	◆	$45-$65 [SAVE]	874
RIVERVIEW (HILLSBOROUGH COUNTY) - Restaurants					
⑩⓪ / p. 805		ABC Pizza	◆	$7-$18	874
⑩① / p. 805		Beef 'O' Brady's	◆◆	$5-$7	874

ST. PETERSBURG pop. 238,600   (See map p. 796; index p. 798)

———— WHERE TO STAY ————

BAYBORO HOUSE BED & BREAKFAST ON OLD TAMPA BAY
Phone: (727)823-4955   **18**

(AAA) [SAVE]
12/1-4/30	1P: $155-$195	2P: $155-$195	XP: $30	F12
10/1-11/30	1P: $145-$175	2P: $145-$175	XP: $30	F12
5/1-9/30	1P: $135-$155	2P: $135-$155	XP: $30	F12

Historic Bed & Breakfast

Location: I-275, exit 9, e to 4th St S, 0.5 mi s to 22nd Ave S, 0.4 mi e to Tampa Bay, 0.3 mi n. 1719 Beach Dr SE 33701. **Fax:** 727/823-4955. **Facility:** Set on Tampa Bay. 1907 Victorian home offers beautifully decorated theme units, each with view of the bay. On the historic register. Age restrictions in main house. Designated smoking area. 6 units. 1 two-bedroom unit and 1 unit with kitchen. Some suites ($155-$195). *Bath:* combo or shower only. 2 stories, interior corridors. **Terms:** 10 day cancellation notice, weekly rates available, package plans. **Amenities:** extended cable TV, hair dryers. *Some:* irons. **Leisure Activities:** heated pool, whirlpool. **Guest Services:** [ECP] meal plan available, complimentary evening beverages, complimentary laundry. **Business Services:** fax. **Cards:** AE, DI, MC, VI. **Special Amenities:** free newspaper and preferred room (subject to availability with advanced reservations).

SOME UNITS

[S/D] [🏊] [✕] [🎦] [VCR] [DATA PORT] / [☎] [💷] [🍽] [📖] /

BAYBORO INN & HUNT ROOM BED & BREAKFAST
Phone: 727/823-0498   **17**

(AAA) [SAVE]
12/1-5/31	1P: $75	2P: $110	XP: $25
6/1-11/30	1P: $60	2P: $85	XP: $25

Historic Bed & Breakfast

Location: I-275, exit 9, e to 3rd St S, 1 blk n to 4 Ave S. 357 3rd St S 33701. **Fax:** 727/821-0088. **Facility:** Built in 1914 with variety of unit themes from Art Deco and Renaissance to Victorian. Designated smoking area. 6 units. *Bath:* shower only. 2 stories, interior corridors. **Parking:** street only. **Terms:** age restrictions may apply, 7 day cancellation notice-fee imposed, weekly rates available, package plans. **Amenities:** no TVs. **Leisure Activities:** bicycles. **Guest Services:** [BP] meal plan available, complimentary evening beverages, valet laundry. **Business Services:** PC. **Cards:** MC, VI. **Special Amenities:** early check-in/late check-out and free continental breakfast.

SOME UNITS

[S/D] [✕] [💷] / [☎] [🍽] /

THE CLAIBORNE HOUSE AT BAY GABLES
Phone: (813)822-8855   **13**

(AAA) [SAVE]
All Year	2P: $95-$115
	XP: $12

Historic Bed & Breakfast

Location: Downtown; 0.3 mi n at jct 4th Ave NE and 1st St N. 340 Rowland Ct NE 33701. **Fax:** 813/824-7223. **Facility:** Designated a local landmark, restored Victorian with lovely garden and gazebo area. Designated smoking area. 9 units. 4 two-bedroom units and 4 efficiencies. Some suites ($100-$115) and whirlpool units ($115). 3 stories (no elevator), exterior corridors. **Terms:** 7 day cancellation notice-fee imposed, weekly rates available, package plans. **Amenities:** extended cable TV, hair dryers. *Some:* irons. **Guest Services:** [BP] meal plan available. **Business Services:** fax. **Cards:** AE, DS, MC, VI. **Special Amenities:** free continental breakfast and free newspaper.

[S/D] [🍴+] [✕] [🎦] [💷] [📖] [🍽] [🍽] [DATA PORT]

COLONIAL BAYFRONT HOTEL
Phone: (727)896-6400   **15**

(AAA) [SAVE]
11/1-11/30	1P: $85-$150		XP: $10	F10
12/1-4/30	1P: $85-$150		XP: $20	F10
5/1-10/31	1P: $55-$95		XP: $10	F10

Historic Motel

Location: Downtown; just e of jct 1st St NE. 126 2nd Ave NE 33701. **Fax:** 727/896-0505. **Facility:** Designated smoking area. 64 units. Some suites ($85-$150). *Bath:* combo or shower only. 4 stories, interior corridors. **Parking:** street only. **Amenities:** extended cable TV. *Some:* irons. **Dining:** dining room, 7 am-2 pm. **Leisure Activities:** exercise room, reading room. **Guest Services:** [BP] meal plan available, coin laundry. **Business Services:** meeting rooms, fax. **Cards:** AE, DI, DS, MC, VI. **Special Amenities:** early check-in/late check-out and free continental breakfast.

SOME UNITS

[S/D] [🍴] [✕] [💷] / [VCR] [🍽] /

(See map p. 796)

COMFORT INN & SUITES

SAVE | Motel

▼▼▼▼

Phone: (727)323-3100 **9**

	1P: $69-$89	2P: $69-$89	XP: $7	F18
1/1-4/30				
12/1-12/31 & 5/1-11/30	1P: $59-$79	2P: $59-$79	XP: $7	F18

Location: I-275, exit 12, 1.2 mi w on 22nd Ave N, 0.5 mi s. 1400 34th St N 33713. Fax: 727/327-5792. **Facility:** 75 units, 34 with efficiency. Some suites. 3 stories, exterior corridors. **Terms:** 14 day cancellation notice. **Amenities:** extended cable TV. *Some:* irons, hair dryers. **Leisure Activities:** heated pool, whirlpool, sun deck. **Guest Services:** [ECP] meal plan available, coin laundry. **Business Services:** meeting rooms.
Cards: AE, CB, DI, DS, MC, VI.

SOME UNITS

⬛ 🏋 📺 📶 🏊 🍽 🖨 💻 [DATA PORT] / ✕ 🗄 🛄 /
FEE

DAYS INN OF ST. PETERSBURG

AAA SAVE | Motor Inn

▼▼▼ ▼▼▼

Phone: (727)522-3191 **4**

2/2-4/15	1P: $59-$64	2P: $69-$74	XP: $5	F12
4/16-11/30	1P: $49-$59	2P: $54-$64	XP: $5	F12
12/1-2/1	1P: $49-$54	2P: $54-$64	XP: $5	F12

Location: I-275, exit 14B, 0.3 mi w. 2595 54th Ave N 33714. Fax: 727/527-6120. **Facility:** 158 units. *Bath:* combo or shower only. 2 stories, exterior corridors. **Terms:** 14 day cancellation notice-fee imposed, weekly rates available, pets ($10 extra charge). **Amenities:** extended cable TV, safes (fee), hair dryers. *Some:* irons. **Dining:** restaurant, 6 am-10 pm, $5-$9, cocktails. **Leisure Activities:** wading pool, playground. **Guest Services:** coin laundry. **Business Services:** meeting rooms, fax. **Cards:** AE, DI, DS, JC, MC, VI.

SOME UNITS

⬛ 🐕 🍽 📺 📶 🏊 🍽 🖨 [DATA PORT] / ✕ 🗄 🛄 /
FEE FEE

DAYS INN ST. PETE CENTRAL

SAVE | Motel

▼▼▼▼

Phone: (727)321-2958 **10**

| All Year | | 2P: $60-$66 | XP: $7 | F12 |

Location: I-275, exit 12, 1.2 mi w on 22nd Ave N, 1 mi s. 650 34th St N 33713. Fax: 727/327-1625. **Facility:** 28 units, 8 with efficiency. 2 stories, exterior corridors. **Terms:** cancellation fee imposed, weekly rates available. **Amenities:** hair dryers. *Some:* irons. **Leisure Activities:** heated pool, whirlpool. **Guest Services:** [CP] meal plan available, coin laundry. **Cards:** AE, CB, DI, DS, JC, MC, VI.

SOME UNITS

⬛ 🍽 🏊 📺 [DATA PORT] / ✕ 🗄 🛄 /

EMPRESS MOTEL APARTMENTS

AAA SAVE | Motel

▼▼ ▼▼

Phone: (727)894-0635 **7**

| 12/15-4/15 | 1P: $45-$50 | 2P: $45-$55 | XP: $5 | |
| 12/1-12/14 & 4/16-11/30 | 1P: $35-$40 | 2P: $40-$45 | XP: $5 | |

Location: I-275, exit 12 (22nd Ave N), 1 mi e to 9th St, 0.3 mi s. 1503 9th St N 33704. Fax: 727/823-1446. **Facility:** 34 units. 4 two-bedroom units, 14 efficiencies and 6 units with kitchen. 2 stories, exterior corridors. **Terms:** weekly & monthly rates available. **Amenities:** extended cable TV. **Guest Services:** coin laundry. **Cards:** AE, DS, MC, VI. **Special Amenities:** early check-in/late check-out and free room upgrade (subject to availability with advanced reservations).

SOME UNITS

⬛ 🏊 📺 / ✕ 🗄 🛄 /

GRANT MOTEL & APTS

AAA SAVE | Motel

▼▼ ▼▼

Phone: (727)576-1369 **1**

2/1-4/15	1P: $38-$50	2P: $50	XP: $5	F3
12/20-1/31	1P: $38-$45	2P: $38-$45	XP: $5	F3
12/1-12/19 & 4/16-11/30	1P: $35-$40	2P: $35-$40	XP: $5	F3

Location: I-275, exit 15, southbound, 4th St exit 19, 0.8 mi s on US 92. 9046 4th St N 33702. Fax: 727/579-0148. **Facility:** Office hours 8:30 am-9 pm. 31 units. 2 two-bedroom units, 6 efficiencies and 8 units with kitchen. *Bath:* combo or shower only. 1 story, exterior corridors. **Terms:** 3 day cancellation notice, in season, weekly & monthly rates available. **Amenities:** extended cable TV. **Leisure Activities:** shuffleboard. **Guest Services:** coin laundry. **Cards:** AE, DS, MC, VI. **Special Amenities:** early check-in/late check-out and preferred room (subject to availability with advanced reservations).

SOME UNITS

⬛ 🍽 📺 🛄 / ✕ 📷 🗄 /

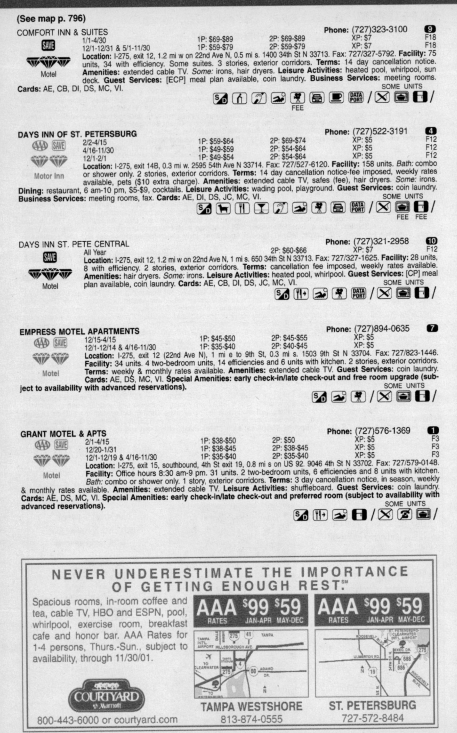

(See map p. 796)

THE HERITAGE-A HOLIDAY INN HOTEL   Phone: (727)822-4814 **14**

Historic Motor Inn

| 12/1-4/30 & 10/1-11/30 | 1P: $120-$150 | 2P: $120-$150 |
| 5/1-9/30 | 1P: $80-$110 | 2P: $80-$110 |

Location: Downtown; jct 2nd St and 3rd Ave N. 234 3rd Ave N 33701. Fax: 727/823-1644. **Facility:** Located in a residential area, this restored 1920s property offers modern amenities with a touch of the historic elegance of yesteryear. 71 units. Some suites ($119-$139). *Bath:* combo or shower only. 3 stories, interior corridors. **Terms:** package plans. **Amenities:** irons, hair dryers. **Leisure Activities:** heated pool, whirlpool. **Guest Services:** complimentary evening beverages: Wed, valet laundry. **Business Services:** meeting rooms, fax. **Cards:** AE, DI, DS, JC, MC, VI.

SOME UNITS

ASK ⓢ ¶ ▦ ⊒ ⊿ (•) 🖨 DATA PORT / ✕ ⊒ 🖶 /
FEE

HOLIDAY INN SUNSPREE RESORT MARINA COVE   Phone: (727)867-1151 **20**

AAA SAVE

Resort

3/1-4/30	1P: $107-$170	2P: $107-$170	XP: $10	F19
2/1-2/28	1P: $98-$152	2P: $98-$152	XP: $10	F19
12/1-1/31 & 5/1-11/30	1P: $71-$134	2P: $71-$134	XP: $10	F19

Location: I-275, exit 3, just n of Sunshine Skyway Bridge, 1st frontage road exit. 6800 Sunshine Skyway Ln 33711. Fax: 727/864-4494. **Facility:** Located on Old Tampa Bay, this eighteen acre resort hosts an abundance of recreational activities. Dock your boat and enjoy the poolside deli or dine in the main restaurant which has an interesting nautical decor. 156 units. 12 efficiencies and 11 units with kitchen. Some suites ($170). *Bath:* combo or shower only. 2 stories, interior/exterior corridors. **Terms:** 3 day cancellation notice, weekly rates available, package plans. **Amenities:** extended cable TV, dual phone lines, voice mail, safes (fee), irons, hair dryers. *Some:* video games. **Dining:** restaurant, deli, 7 am-10 pm, $6-$19, cocktails. **Leisure Activities:** 2 pools (1 heated), whirlpool, beach, fishing, charter fishing, 5 lighted tennis courts, children's program, nature program, recreation program, social program, playground, exercise room, shuffleboard, volleyball, game room. *Fee:* sailboating, boat dock, marina, sailing school, water bike, waverunners, tennis instruction, fishing equipment. **Guest Services:** gift shop, coin laundry. *Fee:* massage. **Business Services:** meeting rooms, fax. **Cards:** AE, CB, DI, DS, JC, MC, VI. **Special Amenities:** free room upgrade and preferred room (each subject to availability with advanced reservations).** *(See color ad below)*

SOME UNITS

¶ ▦ ♦ ⧓ ⊿ ⊒ ✕ 🎥 🖨 ⊒ 🖶 DATA PORT / ✕ VCR 🖵 /

KENTUCKY MOTEL   Phone: (727)526-7373 **5**

AAA SAVE

Motel

12/1-4/20 & 11/1-11/30	1P: $36-$39	2P: $44-$48	XP: $5	F5
9/1-10/31	1P: $34-$36	2P: $38-$40	XP: $5	F5
4/21-8/31	1P: $32	2P: $35	XP: $5	F5

Location: I-275, southbound exit 14B; northbound exit 14, 1.4 mi e on 54th Ave N, 0.7 mi s on US 92. 4246 4th St N 33703. Fax: 727/526-7373. **Facility:** 10 units. *Bath:* combo or shower only. 1 story, exterior corridors. **Terms:** 5 day cancellation notice, weekly rates available. **Amenities:** extended cable TV. *Some:* irons, hair dryers. **Business Services:** fax. **Cards:** AE, DS, MC, VI. **Special Amenities:** early check-in/late check-out and preferred room (subject to availability with advanced reservations).

SOME UNITS

ⓢ ¶ 🖶 / ✕ /

(See map p. 796)

LA QUINTA INN

(AAA) (SAVE)

▽▽▽▽

Motel

Phone: (727)527-8421 **6**

All Year   1P: $59-$89   2P: $59-$89

Location: I-275, exit 14, just w on 54th Ave N, just s on US 19 (34th St). 4999 34th St N 33714. Fax: 727/527-8851. **Facility:** Beautifully landscaped courtyard area with fountain. 120 units. *Bath:* combo or shower only. 2 stories, exterior corridors. **Terms:** small pets only. **Amenities:** video games. **Leisure Activities:** heated pool, exercise room. **Guest Services:** [ECP] meal plan available, coin laundry. **Business Services:** meeting rooms. **Cards:** AE, CB, DI, DS, MC, VI. **Special Amenities:** free continental breakfast and free local telephone calls. *(See color ad p 829)*

SOME UNITS

[icons]

MANSION HOUSE B & B AND THE COURTYARD ON FIFTH

(AAA) (SAVE)

▽▽▽▽

Historic Bed & Breakfast

Phone: (800)274-7520 **11**

All Year   1P: $115-$165   2P: $115-$165   XP: $25   D18

Location: Downtown; 0.5 mi n at jct 5th Ave NE and 1st St N. 105 5th Ave NE 33701. Fax: 727/821-6906. **Facility:** Refurbished turn-of-the-century home. Designated smoking area. 12 units. Some whirlpool units ($150-$165). *Bath:* combo or shower only. 2 stories, interior corridors. **Terms:** cancellation fee imposed, weekly & monthly rates available, package plans. **Amenities:** extended cable TV, hair dryers. *Some:* irons. **Dining:** baked goods, snacks, wine & complimentary beverages. **Leisure Activities:** heated pool, whirlpool, bicycles, 2 TV/library rooms with VCR & refrigerator. *Fee:* boat cruises (shelling, moonlight cruise). **Guest Services:** [BP] meal plan available, valet laundry. **Business Services:** meeting rooms, PC, fax. **Cards:** AE, CB, DI, MC, VI. **Special Amenities:** early check-in/late check-out and free continental breakfast.

SOME UNITS

[icons]

RENAISSANCE VINOY RESORT

(AAA) (SAVE)

▽▽▽▽

Classic Resort

Phone: (727)894-1000 **12**

12/1-4/29	1P: $250-$300	2P: $250-$300
4/30-5/27 & 10/1-11/30	1P: $220-$270	2P: $220-$270
5/28-9/30	1P: $120-$170	2P: $120-$170

Location: Downtown; 1.8 mi e on 4th Ave, just n on Beach Dr. 501 Fifth Ave NE 33701. Fax: 727/894-2067. **Facility:** Stately hotel, originally opened in 1925 as a haven for the rich and famous. While a lavish restoration has modernized the Grande Dame, great care has been taken to maintain its historical grandeur. 360 units. Some suites and whirlpool units. *Bath:* combo or shower only. 7 stories, interior corridors. **Parking:** extra charge or valet. **Terms:** check-in 4 pm, 3 day cancellation notice-fee imposed, package plans. **Amenities:** video games, voice mail, honor bars, irons, hair dryers. **Dining:** 5 restaurants, 6 am-11 pm, $10-$30, cocktails, also, Marchand's Bar & Grill, Terrace Room, see separate listing, entertainment. **Leisure Activities:** 2 heated pools, saunas, whirlpools, steamrooms, fishing, charter fishing, putting green, golf & tennis pro shop, children's program, recreation program, aerobics, hair salon, spa. *Fee:* sailboating, marina, sailing lessons, golf-18 holes, 12 lighted tennis courts, bicycles. **Guest Services:** [BP] meal plan available, gift shop, area transportation-within 5 mi, valet laundry. *Fee:* massage. **Business Services:** conference facilities, administrative services, fax. *Fee:* PC. **Cards:** AE, CB, DI, DS, JC, MC, VI.

SOME UNITS

[icons]

ST. PETERSBURG BAYFRONT HILTON

▽▽▽▽

Hotel

Phone: (727)894-5000 **16**

Property failed to provide current rates

Location: Downtown; across from Al Lang Stadium. 333 1st St S 33701. Fax: 727/894-7655. **Facility:** Spacious units, many with view of the bay. Elegantly decorated public areas. 333 units. Some suites. *Bath:* some combo or shower only. 15 stories, interior corridors. **Parking:** extra charge or valet. **Terms:** 3 day cancellation notice-fee imposed, package plans, pets ($100 extra charge). **Amenities:** extended cable TV, dual phone lines, voice mail, irons, hair dryers. *Some:* CD players. **Leisure Activities:** heated pool, whirlpool, water aerobics, aerobics with professional trainers. **Guest Services:** gift shop, area transportation, valet laundry. **Business Services:** conference facilities, fax. **Cards:** AE, CB, DI, DS, MC, VI. *(See ad p 44)*

SOME UNITS

[icons]

SUNSET BAY INN

(AAA) (SAVE)

▽▽▽▽

Bed & Breakfast

Phone: (727)896-6701 **8**

12/1-4/30	1P: $170-$250	2P: $170-$250	XP: $30	D
10/1-11/30	1P: $160-$240	2P: $160-$240	XP: $30	D
5/1-9/30	1P: $150-$230	2P: $150-$230	XP: $30	D

Location: Downtown; just w of Beach Dr via 6th Ave NE. 635 Bay St NE 33701. Fax: 727/898-5311. **Facility:** Circa 1910 and designated a historic landmark; beautifully restored home and guest units very tastefully decorated. Designated smoking area. 6 units. Some suites ($250-$270) and whirlpool units ($150-$250). 3 stories (no elevator), interior corridors. **Parking:** street only. **Terms:** 14 day cancellation notice-fee imposed, weekly & monthly rates available, package plans. **Amenities:** extended cable TV, voice mail, irons, hair dryers. **Leisure Activities:** bicycles. **Guest Services:** [BP] meal plan available, complimentary evening beverages, afternoon tea, valet laundry. **Business Services:** meeting rooms, fax. **Cards:** AE, DS, MC, VI. **Special Amenities:** early check-in/late check-out and free local telephone calls.

SOME UNITS

[icons]

TOPS MOTEL & APARTMENTS

(AAA) (SAVE)

▽▽▽▽

Motel

Phone: (727)526-9071 **3**

| 12/18-4/16 | | 2P: $40-$50 | XP: $5 |
| 12/1-12/17 & 4/17-11/30 | | 2P: $35-$40 | XP: $5 |

Location: I-275, exit 14 (54th Ave) southbound; exit 14B northbound, 1.4 mi e on 54th Ave, 1.5 mi n on 4th St, n on US 92. 7141 4th St N 33702. Fax: 727/525-4295. **Facility:** 16 units. 7 efficiencies and 3 units with kitchen. *Bath:* combo or shower only. 2 stories, interior corridors. **Terms:** 5 day cancellation notice, weekly rates available. **Amenities:** extended cable TV. *Some:* irons. **Business Services:** fax. **Cards:** AE, DS, MC, VI. **Special Amenities:** early check-in/late check-out and free room upgrade (subject to availability with advanced reservations).

SOME UNITS

[icons]

(See map p. 796)

──────── WHERE TO DINE ────────

4TH STREET SHRIMP STORE   **Lunch:** $4-$21   **Dinner:** $4-$21   **Phone:** 727/822-0325   ⑮
Location: 0.7 mi n at jct 10th Ave N. 1006 4th St N 33701. **Hours:** 11 am-9 pm, Fri & Sat-10 pm. Closed: 11/22, 12/25. **Features:** casual dress; carryout; cocktails & lounge. A bright, nautical decor with colorful
Seafood   knickknacks will put you in the mood for fresh, delicious seafood. An extensive menu of sandwiches, chowder, fish and shrimp is served on throwaway plates and paper place mats for a no-fuss, no-muss
meal. **Cards:** MC, VI.

APROPOS BISTRO & BAR   **Lunch:** $6-$10   **Dinner:** $13-$21   **Phone:** 727/823-8934   ㉓
Location: Downtown; at corner of 2nd Ave NE and Bayshore Dr. 300 2nd Ave NE 33701. **Hours:** 7:30 am-midnight, Tues-2 pm, Sun 8:30 am-2 pm. Closed: 11/22, 12/25; also Mon & Super Bowl Sun. **Features:** casual
American   dress; Sunday brunch; carryout; cocktails & lounge. Lunch features a variety of sandwiches, salads, filets and pork served in a lively waterfront setting. The turkey club, with potato salad and a side of fresh fruit, is
a sure favorite. Enjoy live entertainment on the weekends with available boat docking. **Cards:** AE, DS, MC, VI.

ARIGATO JAPANESE STEAK HOUSE RESTAURANT   **Dinner:** $11-$21   **Phone:** 727/343-5200   ⑧
Location: Just s of jct 38th Ave N. 3600 66th St N 33710. **Hours:** 5 pm-10 pm, Sun 4 pm-9 pm. Closed: 1/1, 7/4, 11/22, 12/24. **Reservations:** suggested. **Features:** casual dress; children's menu; early bird specials;
Ethnic   cocktails & lounge. Come for the show as the entertaining chef prepares Japanese specialties right at your table. The ichiban lets you sample shrimp, chicken and filet with piquant oils and spices. This is a popular
place so expect to wait on groupings at the hibachi table. **Cards:** AE, CB, DI, DS, MC, VI.

CAFE LIDO   **Lunch:** $6-$11   **Dinner:** $9-$18   **Phone:** 727/898-5800   ⑯
Location: Downtown; 1st floor of The Pier. 800 2nd Ave NE 33701. **Hours:** 11:30 am-10 pm, Fri & Sat-11 pm. **Features:** casual dress; children's menu; carryout; cocktails & lounge; valet parking; a la carte.
Italian   Handpainted murals by an Italian artist add to the romantic appeal of this bayfront locale. A tempting array of main dishes, such as rigatoni a la vodka and chicken parmesan, makes up a well-varied menu. Service
is pleasant and prompt. **Cards:** AE, DS, MC, VI.

CARMELITA'S MEXICAN RESTAURANT   **Lunch:** $6-$10   **Dinner:** $8-$11   **Phone:** 727/545-2956   ④
Location: On Park St at jct 54th Ave N, 0.6 mi n of jct Tyrone Blvd. 5211 Park St N 33709. **Hours:** 11 am-9:30 pm, Fri & Sat-10:30 pm. Closed major holidays; also Super Bowl Sun. **Features:** casual dress; children's
Mexican   menu; carryout; beer & wine only; a la carte. Some of the best Mexican food east of the Mississippi! A wide variety of entrees are featured like the Del Ray burrito, a good mixture of seasoned ground beef,
tomatoes, onion and cheese. A live mariachi band performs on Tuesday nights. **Cards:** AE, DS, MC, VI.

CASUAL CLAM SEAFOOD RESTAURANT   **Lunch:** $5-$11   **Dinner:** $5-$11   **Phone:** 727/895-2526   ⑤
Location: I-275, exit 13, 38th Ave, 0.9 mi e, 0.3 mi s on M L King St (9th St N). 3336 9th St N 33704. **Hours:** 11 am-10 pm, Sun-9 pm. Closed: 11/22, 12/25. **Features:** casual dress; children's menu; early bird specials;
Seafood   carryout; beer & wine only; a la carte. A popular neighborhood hangout, this light and airy eatery has the feel of rustic New England. Steamed clams, fish and chips, snow crab and shrimp scampi are among
menu specialties. Pleasant servers in T-shirts and shorts add to the casual mood. **Cards:** MC, VI.

COCKNEY REBEL   **Lunch:** $6-$7   **Dinner:** $9-$18   **Phone:** 727/895-2049   ⑩
Location: I-275, exit 12, 1.4 mi e on 22nd Ave N, just s. 1492 4th St N 33704. **Hours:** 11 am-2 am, Sun noon-midnight. Closed: 11/22, 12/25. **Features:** casual dress; children's menu; carryout; cocktails &
English   lounge; entertainment; a la carte. The ambience of an English pub is pervasive in these down-to-earth surroundings. Fresh air makes the deck a comfy place to dine. The beef in Guinness pie-steak marinated
in hearty beer and baked with chunks of pastry-satisfies the hungries. Cozy deck dining and kiddie playland on-site.
Cards: AE, CB, DI, MC, VI.

COLUMBIA RESTAURANT   **Lunch:** $7-$10   **Dinner:** $14-$22   **Phone:** 727/822-8000   ⑰
Location: Downtown; 4th floor of The Pier. 800 2nd Ave NE 33701. **Hours:** 11 am-10 pm, Fri & Sat-11 pm. **Reservations:** suggested. **Features:** casual dress; children's menu; carryout; cocktails & lounge; valet
Spanish   parking. Many of the tables afford a spectacular view of Tampa Bay and the St. Petersburg skyline. Traditional Spanish and Cuban cuisine is prepared with chicken, beef and Florida seafood. Try the pollo de
arroz, baked chicken with yellow rice and pepper strips. **Cards:** AE, DI, DS, MC, VI.

CRAB SHACK   **Lunch:** $5-$14   **Dinner:** $5-$14   **Phone:** 727/576-7813   ②
Location: 0.6 mi e of jct 4th St n. 11400 Gandy Blvd 33702. **Hours:** 11 am-10 pm. **Features:** casual dress; carryout; cocktails. Just as the name suggests, a rustic crab shack setting awaits you with picnic table
Seafood   style seating in the main dining room area or small tables in the bar area. The menu has numerous items to choose from, some 26 appetizers to at least 37 entrees and sandwich choices—gator, frog legs, shrimp,
crab, even steak and chicken for the land lovers. **Cards:** DS, MC, VI.

EL CAP   **Lunch:** $3-$6   **Dinner:** $3-$6   **Phone:** 727/521-1314   ⑪
Location: At jct 35th Ave N. 3500 4th St N 33704. **Hours:** 11 am-11 pm. Closed: 11/22, 12/25. **Features:** casual dress; carryout; beer & wine only; a la carte. Munch on the best burgers around at this
American   basic sports bar where you'll also find subs, sandwiches, chili fries and jalapeno poppers. Expect good stick-to-your-ribs food served in a no-frills atmosphere. Patio dining and a carry-out window are available.
Cards: MC, VI.

(See map p. 796)

THE FIREHOUSE BAR & GRILLE   Lunch: $4-$8   Dinner: $4-$13   Phone: 727/895-4716   21
American
Location: Downtown; at jct 1st Ave S and 3rd St S; in AmSouth Bank Building (lower level). 260 1st Ave S 33701. **Hours:** 11 am-8:30 pm, Fri-10:30 pm, Sat 4:30 pm-10:30 pm. Closed major holidays; also Sun. **Features:** casual dress; carryout; cocktails & lounge; street parking. True to its name, this restaurant is in a historic, old firehouse with antique artifacts throughout. The comfortable atmosphere makes it the perfect place in which to chew on a half-pound burger, devour some wings or savor a juicy rack of ribs. **Cards:** DI, MC, VI.

FRED'S FAMOUS BAR-B-QUE AND BREWERY   Lunch: $5-$17   Dinner: $5-$17   Phone: 727/822-3733   26
American
Location: I-275, exit 14B southbound; 1.8 mi e on 54th Ave N, 1 mi s on US 92. 4351 4th St N 33703. **Hours:** 11 am-10 pm. Closed: 4/15, 11/22, 12/25. **Features:** casual dress; children's menu; carryout; beer & wine only. Contemporary setting with Southern barbecue theme present. Menu has excellent variety of entrees, including beef and pork dinners, smoked chicken, hickory grilled filet mignon or porterhouse. Also sandwiches, salad, appetizers and desserts. **Cards:** AE, MC, VI.

THE GARDEN-A MEDITERRANEAN BISTRO   Lunch: $6-$8   Dinner: $7-$18   Phone: 727/896-3800   28
Mediterranean
Location: Downtown; just e of jct 2nd St S. 217 Central Ave 33701. **Hours:** 11:30 am-10:30 pm, Fri & Sat-12:30 am. **Features:** casual dress; cocktails & lounge; street parking; a la carte. Bistro type setting with indoor or the very popular garden dining. Decorated in a Mediterranean style with bright colors and lots of plants. A wonderful meal awaits prepared by on site chef de cuisine - entrees such as fennel crusted tuna or grilled lamb steak are a tasty delight. Live jazz Thursday-Saturday evenings. **Cards:** MC, VI.

GRAND FINALE   Dinner: $10-$25   Phone: 727/823-9921   27
Continental
Location: Just e of jct Central Ave at jct 11th St N. 1101 1st Ave N 33701. **Hours:** 5 pm-1 am. Closed: Sun & Mon. **Features:** dressy casual; cocktails & lounge; a la carte. "New American Cuisine" is the bill of fare at this trendy establishment with a menu that will make your mouth water. From the Sashimi Tuna to the chilled Duck Salad to the seared Duck Confit for an entree; a wonderful dinner awaits! Interesting "Andy Warhol" style of artwork on display for comfortable eye appealing surroundings. **Cards:** MC, VI.

JO JO'S IN CITTA RESTAURANT,
PIANO BAR & LOUNGE   Lunch: $7-$12   Dinner: $8-$17   Phone: 727/894-0075   22
Italian
Location: Downtown at jct 3rd St S; in Nations Bank Tower. 200 Central Ave 33701. **Hours:** 11 am-9 pm, Fri & Sat-10 pm, Sun noon-9 pm. Closed major holidays. **Features:** casual dress; children's menu; carryout; cocktails & lounge; street parking; a la carte. Live entertainment adds pizzazz to your Friday and Saturday evenings at this casual restaurant. Pasta, pizza and calzones are some of the dishes served in a fresh, modern, cafe-style dining room. Bring a healthy appetite to handle the hearty portions. **Cards:** AE, DI, MC, VI.

THE KEYSTONE CLUB   Dinner: $12-$21   Phone: 727/822-6600   20
Steak & Seafood
Location: Center; just n of jct 4th St N and 3rd Ave N. 320 4th St N 33701. **Hours:** 4:30 pm-9 pm, Fri & Sat-10 pm. Closed major holidays; also Super Bowl Sun. **Reservations:** suggested. **Features:** dressy casual; children's menu; cocktails & lounge; a la carte. This New York-style chop house offers a wide selection of salad, steak and fish. Try one of the specials or order the filet mignon with mashed potatoes. House specialty is prime rib. The decor is pleasant, and prompt service will get you back on the road in no time. **Cards:** AE, DI, DS, MC, VI.

LEVEROCKS AT MAXIMO   Lunch: $9-$21   Dinner: $9-$21   Phone: 727/864-3883   24
Steak & Seafood
Location: I-275, exit 4, just w on 54th Ave S, just n on US 19. 4801 37th St S 33712. **Hours:** 11:30 am-10 pm. Closed: 11/22, 12/25. **Features:** casual dress; children's menu; early bird specials; carryout; cocktails & lounge. This popular marina restaurant offers free boat docking, so after an active day on the water, bring the family in for prompt, pleasant service and a tasty meal. Mainly a seafood menu, it features fresh catches cooked with a variety of favorite recipes. **Cards:** AE, CB, DI, DS, MC, VI.

MARCHAND'S BAR & GRILL   Lunch: $8-$15   Dinner: $11-$25   Phone: 727/894-1000   12
Continental
Location: Downtown; 1.8 mi e on 4th Ave, just n on Beach Dr; in Renaissance Vinoy Resort. 501 Fifth Ave NE 33701. **Hours:** 11 am-3 & 5:30-10 pm. **Reservations:** suggested. **Features:** semi-formal attire; Sunday brunch; children's menu; cocktails & lounge; entertainment; fee for parking & valet parking; a la carte. Dine in Mediterranean elegance on meat and seafood with a hint of international flavoring. Two types of warm bread are brought with each meal. Savor grilled sea bass with a colorful collection of vegetables and mashed potatoes as your catch of the day. **Cards:** AE, CB, DI, DS, JC, MC, VI.

MOON UNDER WATER   Lunch: $7-$9   Dinner: $7-$17   Phone: 727/896-6160   19
British
Location: I-275, exit 10, downtown; just s of jct 4th Ave NE. 332 Beach Dr NE 33701. **Hours:** 11:30 am-11 pm, Fri & Sat-12:30 am. Closed: 11/22, 12/25. **Features:** casual dress; cocktails & lounge; street parking; a la carte. This restaurant has the look and feel of a British pub. Lunch features sandwiches and salads, with the Philly cheese steak as the standout. Tiered patio dining and excellent service make for a pleasant meal. **Cards:** AE, DI, MC, VI.

NATIVE SEAFOOD & TRADING COMPANY   Dinner: $10-$18   Phone: 727/866-8772   25
Seafood
Location: I-275, exit 4 (Pinellas Bayway), 2.3 mi w; in Shoppers Village at jct SR 679. 5901 Sun Blvd, Suite 100 C 33715. **Hours:** 5 pm-10 pm, Fri & Sat-11 pm. Closed: 12/25. **Features:** casual dress; carryout; cocktails & lounge. A rainforest motif comes complete with cleverly contrived Caribbean accents. Edible flowers garnish tropical dishes, making this a colorful dining experience. Local seafood, fresh herbs and an Aztec wood-burning grill combine to create delicious exotic cuisine. **Cards:** AE, DS, MC, VI.

OLLIE'S CORK & BOTTLE   Lunch: $5-$13   Dinner: $5-$13   Phone: 727/895-2200   14
American
Location: Downtown; at jct 1st St N and 2nd Ave N; in Plaza Tower Courtyard Shops. 111 2nd Ave NE 33701. **Hours:** 11 am-8 pm. Closed: Sun. **Features:** casual dress; carryout; cocktails & lounge; street parking. Sandwiches too fat to fit in the average mouth are the claim to fame of this light and airy restaurant. If you're (unjustly) skeptical about whether a sandwich can fill you, browse the other entrees, which come mostly from the steak and seafood families. **Cards:** AE, MC, VI.

(See map p. 796)

OVO CAFE **Lunch:** $7-$14 **Dinner:** $9-$16 **Phone:** 727/895-5515 ⓲
▼▼▼▼
American
Location: Downtown; just w of jct 5th St N. 515 Central Ave 33701. **Hours:** 11 am-10 pm, Mon-3 pm, Fri & Sat-midnight, Sun-9 pm. Closed major holidays. **Features:** dressy casual; cocktails & lounge; street parking; a la carte. This very trendy, upscale cafe gives the feeling of a night out in New York. The chicken mushroom pirogue is marvelously tasty and artfully presented. A polished espresso machine brews up the perfect accompaniment to a fine selection of desserts. **Cards:** AE, DI, DS, MC, VI. ✕

PAISANO'S PIZZA & PASTA **Lunch:** $5-$18 **Dinner:** $7-$18 **Phone:** 727/521-2656 ①
▼▼▼
Italian
Location: I-275, exit 14 southbound; exit 14B northbound, 1.4 mi e on 54th Ave N, 1 mi n on US 92. 6000 4th St N 33703. **Hours:** 11 am-10 pm, Fri & Sat-midnight. Closed: 11/22, 12/25. **Features:** casual dress; early bird specials; carryout; cocktails & lounge; a la carte, buffet. A true local favorite having been in business since 1974. This popular eatery is known for it's gourmet pizzas, calzones, stromboli, pasta dishes and lunch buffet. **Cards:** AE, CB, DI, DS, MC, VI.

PEPIN RESTAURANT **Lunch:** $8-$12 **Dinner:** $14-$30 **Phone:** 727/821-3773 ⑥
▼▼▼
Spanish
Location: I-275, exit 14B southbound; exit 14 northbound, 1.8 mi e on 54th Ave N, 7 mi s on US 92. 4125 4th St N 33703. **Hours:** 11 am-10 pm, Fri-11 pm, Sat 5 pm-11 pm, Sun 5 pm-10 pm. Closed major holidays; also Mon. **Reservations:** suggested. **Features:** casual dress; children's menu; carryout; cocktails & lounge; entertainment. Dali and Picasso prints appeal to an artistic eye, while a concert pianist fascinates a musical ear. The friendly restaurant serves up a splendid salad as well as steak, seafood and dishes with a delightfully piquant Spanish influence. **Cards:** AE, CB, DI, DS, MC, VI.

**RED MESA REGIONAL MEXICAN &
SOUTHWEST CUISINE** **Lunch:** $5-$9 **Dinner:** $7-$18 **Phone:** 727/527-8728 ③
▼▼▼
Mexican
Location: I-275, exit 14, 1.4 mi e on 54th Ave N, just s. 4912 4th St N 33703. **Hours:** 11:30 am-9:30 pm, Fri-10:30 pm, Sat 5 pm-10:30 pm, Sun 5 pm-9 pm. Closed major holidays; also Super Bowl Sun. **Features:** casual dress; children's menu; carryout; cocktail lounge; beer & wine only. Latin flavors spice up such intricate dishes as honey-marinated tuna, which is cured with sugar cane, oven roasted and served with black bean puree and roasted potatoes. Theme carries over into the colorful dining room as well as in the music. Smoke free premises. **Cards:** AE, CB, DI, DS, MC, VI. ✕

SAFFRON'S AT JUNGLE PRADA **Dinner:** $9-$22 **Phone:** 727/345-6400 ⑦
▼▼▼
Caribbean
MC, VI.
Location: From jct Tyrone Blvd, 1.5 mi s. 1700 Park St N 33710. **Hours:** 3 pm-10 pm. Closed: 5/28. **Features:** casual dress; children's menu; carryout; cocktails & lounge; entertainment; a la carte. Ample portions of Caribbean cuisine are served in a comfortable setting on the Intercoastal Waterway. Jamaican jerk chicken is colorfully displayed with plantains, cabbage and yellow rice. **Cards:** AE, CB, DI, DS, ✕

TERRACE ROOM **Lunch:** $7-$16 **Dinner:** $11-$29 **Phone:** 727/894-1000 ⓭
▼▼▼▼
American
Location: Downtown; 1.8 mi e on 4th Ave, just n on Beach Dr; in Renaissance Vinoy Resort. 501 Fifth Ave NE 33701. **Hours:** 6 am-3 & 5:30-10 pm. **Reservations:** suggested. **Features:** semi-formal attire; Sunday brunch; children's menu; early bird specials; cocktails & lounge; entertainment; fee for parking & valet parking. Relish formal dining in vintage elegance. A lightly breaded and fried calamari is an excellent start. Dinner features steak, seafood, pasta and meat dishes with an international flair. Lunch is the popular medley of salad, sandwiches and burgers. **Cards:** AE, CB, DI, DS, JC, MC, VI. ✕

TEXAS CATTLE COMPANY **Dinner:** $10-$30 **Phone:** 727/527-3335 ⑨
▼▼▼
Steak House
Location: I-275, exit 12, 1.2 mi w on 22nd Ave N, just n on US 19. 2600 34th St N 33713. **Hours:** 5 pm-10 pm, Fri & Sat-11 pm, Sun-9:30 pm. Closed: 11/22, 12/25. **Features:** casual dress; children's menu; carryout; cocktails & lounge. Wood accents convey a decidedly Western aura in this rustic steakhouse. Sure, you'll find a juicy filet mignon, but the menu also includes fresh fish, chicken and tasty rock lobster. Try not to giggle when ordering the Charlie Brownie ice cream pie. **Cards:** AE, MC, VI. ✕

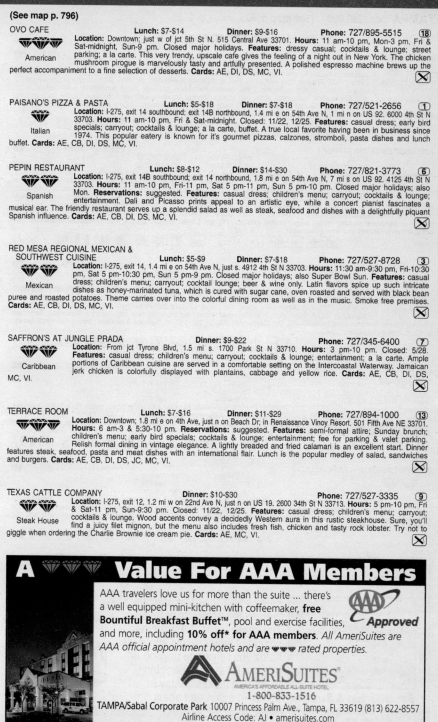

TAMPA pop. 280,000   (See map p. 805; index p. 806)

———— WHERE TO STAY ————

AMERISUITES

AAA SAVE
WWWW
Suite Motel

Phone: 813/622-8557   **64**

All Year   1P: $95   2P: $95   XP: $10

Location: I-75, exit 52 southbound; exit 52B northbound, 0.5 mi w, just s on Falkenburg Rd, just w; in Sabal Corporate Center. 10007 Princess Palm Ave 33619. Fax: 813/620-4866. **Facility:** 59 units. *Bath:* combo or shower only. 2 stories, interior corridors. **Terms:** 7 day cancellation notice, package plans. **Amenities:** extended cable TV, dual phone lines, voice mail, irons, hair dryers. **Dining:** cocktails. **Leisure Activities:** heated pool, jogging, exercise room. **Guest Services:** [ECP] meal plan available, complimentary evening beverages, valet and coin laundry. **Business Services:** meeting rooms, fax. **Cards:** AE, CB, DI, DS, MC, VI. *(See color ad p 817)*   SOME UNITS

AMERISUITES-TAMPA AIRPORT

AAA SAVE
WWWW
Suite Motel

Phone: (813)282-1037   **1**

1/1-4/8   1P: $149-$159   2P: $159-$169   XP: $10   F18
12/1-12/31 & 4/9-11/30   1P: $129-$139   2P: $139-$149   XP: $10   F18

Location: I-275, exit 21, 0.5 mi w on Westshore; exit 20A northbound, 1 mi n on Kennedy Blvd, 1 mi w on Westshore. 4811 W Main St 33607. Fax: 813/282-1148. **Facility:** Inviting architectural design with welcoming fountain at portico and tropical landscaping abounds. Public area is rich in marble and dark woods, classy looking. Units are very nice with dark oaks and separate living room with wet bar area. 126 units. *Bath:* combo or shower only. 6 stories, interior corridors. **Terms:** weekly rates available, package plans, small pets only. **Amenities:** voice mail, irons, hair dryers. **Leisure Activities:** heated pool, exercise room. **Guest Services:** [ECP] meal plan available, valet and coin laundry. **Business Services:** meeting rooms, administrative services, PC, fax. **Cards:** AE, CB, DI, DS, MC, VI. **Special Amenities:** free continental breakfast and free newspaper. *(See color ad p 5)*   SOME UNITS

AMERISUITES TAMPA BUSCH GARDENS

AAA SAVE
WWWW
Suite Motel

Phone: (813)979-1922   **24**

12/1-1/28   1P: $79-$209   2P: $99-$209   XP: $10   F17
1/29-11/30   1P: $89-$119   2P: $99-$119   XP: $10   F17

Location: I-275, exit 34, 1.8 mi e, then just s. 11408 N 30th St 33612-6446. Fax: 813/979-1926. **Facility:** 128 units. *Bath:* combo or shower only. 6 stories, interior corridors. **Terms:** weekly rates available, package plans, small pets only ($25 fee). **Amenities:** voice mail, irons. **Leisure Activities:** heated pool, exercise room. **Guest Services:** [ECP] meal plan available, area transportation, valet and coin laundry. **Business Services:** meeting rooms, administrative services, PC, fax. **Cards:** AE, CB, DI, DS, MC, VI. **Special Amenities:** free continental breakfast and free newspaper. *(See color ad p 5)*   SOME UNITS

BAYMONT INN & SUITES-TAMPA NEAR BUSCH GARDENS

WWW
Motel

Phone: (813)930-6900   **7**

2/9-4/23   1P: $94-$104   2P: $94-$104
6/8-11/30   1P: $84-$94   2P: $84-$94
12/1-2/8   1P: $74-$84   2P: $74-$84
4/24-6/7   1P: $64-$74   2P: $64-$74

Location: I-275, exit 33, 2 mi w. 9202 N 30th St 33612. Fax: 813/930-0563. **Facility:** 143 units. Some suites ($84-$149). 3 stories, exterior corridors. **Terms:** small pets only ($10 extra charge). **Amenities:** extended cable TV, video games, irons, hair dryers. **Leisure Activities:** game room. **Guest Services:** [ECP] meal plan available, coin laundry. **Business Services:** meeting rooms. **Cards:** AE, CB, DI, DS, MC, VI. *(See color ad p 819)*   SOME UNITS

BAYMONT INN-TAMPA FAIRGROUNDS

WWW
Motel

Phone: (813)626-0885   **17**

1/5-4/14   1P: $84-$89   2P: $89-$94
4/15-11/30   1P: $69-$74   2P: $69-$74
12/1-1/4   1P: $65-$70   2P: $65-$70

Location: I-4, westbound exit 6; eastbound exit 6A, just se. 4811 US 301 N 33610. Fax: 813/623-3321. **Facility:** 101 units. 3 stories, interior corridors. **Terms:** weekly rates available, small pets only ($10 extra charge). **Amenities:** video games, voice mail, irons, hair dryers. **Guest Services:** [ECP] meal plan available, coin laundry. **Business Services:** meeting rooms, fax. **Cards:** AE, CB, DI, DS, MC, VI. *(See color ad p 819)*   SOME UNITS

(See map p. 805)

BAYMONT INN-TAMPA SOUTHEAST (BRANDON)　　　　　　　　　　**Phone: (813)684-4007**　[20]

♦♦♦　1/12-4/14　　　　　1P: $89-$94　　　2P: $89-$94
　　　12/1-1/11　　　　1P: $65-$84　　　2P: $65-$84
Motel　4/15-11/30　　　1P: $69-$79　　　2P: $69-$79
Facility: 99 units. Some suites ($84-$129). 3 stories, interior corridors. **Terms:** small pets only. **Amenities:** video games, voice mail, irons, hair dryers. **Guest Services:** [ECP] meal plan available, coin laundry. **Business Services:** meeting rooms, fax. **Cards:** AE, CB, DI, DS, MC, VI. *(See color ad below)*

SOME UNITS

BEST WESTERN ALL SUITES HOTEL BEHIND BUSCH GARDENS　　　　**Phone: (813)971-8930**　[55]

♦♦♦ SAVE　2/2-4/26　　　　1P: $109-$139　　2P: $109-$139　　　XP: $10　　F17
　　　　　12/1-2/1 & 4/27-11/30　1P: $89-$119　　2P: $89-$119　　　XP: $10　　F17
♦♦♦　**Location:** I-75, exit 54, 4.5 mi w, 0.5 mi s of Fowler Ave on 30th St. 3001 University Center Dr 33612.
Suite Motor Inn　Fax: 813/971-8935. **Facility:** 150 units. 3 stories, exterior corridors. **Terms:** package plans, pets ($10 extra charge). **Amenities:** extended cable TV, voice mail, irons, hair dryers. **Dining:** restaurant, 6 am-10 & 4:30-10 pm; tiki bar, $5-$10, cocktails. **Leisure Activities:** heated pool, whirlpool, sun deck, billiards, ping pong. *Fee:* health club privileges, video movie rentals. **Guest Services:** [BP] meal plan available, gift shop, valet and coin laundry. **Business Services:** meeting rooms, fax. **Cards:** AE, CB, DI, DS, JC, MC, VI. **Special Amenities:** free continental breakfast and free local telephone calls. *(See color ad p 811)*

SOME UNITS

CHASE SUITE HOTEL BY WOODFIN　　　　　　　　　　　　　　　　**Phone: (813)281-5677**　[50]

♦♦♦♦　12/1-12/31 & 1/1-4/30　　1P: $125-$185　　2P: $135-$195　　　XP: $10　　F17
　　　　5/1-11/30　　　　　　1P: $99-$145　　2P: $109-$155　　　XP: $10　　F17
Apartment　**Location:** I-275, exit 20, exit 20B northbound; 3 mi w on SR 60 just n; in Rocky Point Harbor. 3075 N Rocky Point Dr 33607. Fax: 813/289-0266. **Facility:** Set on Old Tampa Bay; studios and bi-level units with loft; many with fireplace. 176 units with kitchen. 2 stories, exterior corridors. **Terms:** weekly & monthly rates available, pets ($50 fee, $5 extra charge). **Amenities:** extended cable TV, CD players, voice mail, irons, hair dryers. **Leisure Activities:** heated pool, whirlpool, boat dock, fishing, sports court. **Guest Services:** [ECP] meal plan available, complimentary evening beverages, area transportation, valet and coin laundry. **Business Services:** meeting rooms, fax. **Cards:** AE, DI, DS, MC, VI.

SOME UNITS

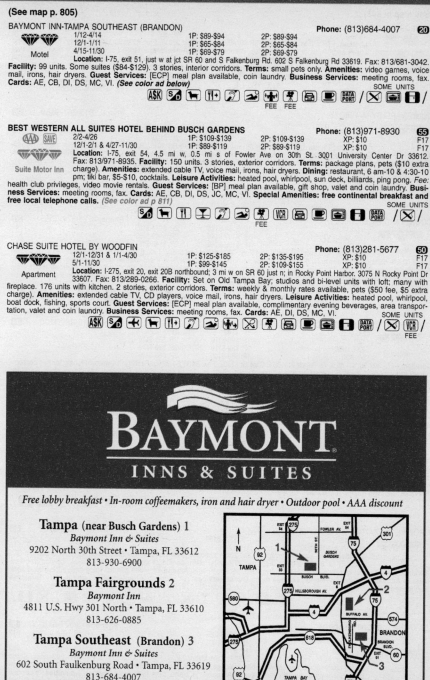

(See map p. 805)

COMFORT SUITES

(AAA) [SAVE]
▼▼▼
Suite Motel

Phone: (813)630-4444 **37** F18

All Year   1P: $79-$159   2P: $89-$169   XP: $5

Location: I-75, exit 51, 0.5 mi w on SR 60. 9932 E Adamo Dr 33619. Fax: 813/630-2093. **Facility:** 67 units. Some suites and whirlpool units. 4 stories, interior corridors. **Amenities:** extended cable TV, voice mail, irons, hair dryers. **Leisure Activities:** heated pool, exercise room. **Guest Services:** [ECP] meal plan available, gift shop, coin laundry. **Business Services:** meeting rooms, fax. **Cards:** AE, CB, DI, DS, MC, VI.
Special Amenities: free continental breakfast and free newspaper.

SOME UNITS

COURTYARD BY MARRIOTT

▼▼▼
Motel

Phone: (813)661-9559 **25**

1/25-4/30   2P: $119-$275
12/1-1/24   2P: $99-$159
5/1-11/30   2P: $109-$139

Location: I-75, exit 51, just w on SR 60, just s on Falkenburg Rd. 10152 Palm River Rd 33619. Fax: 813/661-4583. **Facility:** 90 units. Some suites ($129-$149) and whirlpool units ($109-$129). *Bath:* combo or shower only. 3 stories, interior corridors. **Amenities:** video games, dual phone lines, voice mail, irons, hair dryers. **Leisure Activities:** heated pool, whirlpool, exercise room. **Guest Services:** coin laundry. **Business Services:** meeting rooms, fax. **Cards:** AE, DI, DS, MC, VI.

SOME UNITS

FEE

COURTYARD BY MARRIOTT

▼▼▼
Motel

Phone: (813)874-0555 **33**

1/1-4/30   1P: $164-$175   2P: $174-$185   XP: $10   F17
12/1-12/31   1P: $139-$149   2P: $149-$159   XP: $10   F17
5/1-11/30   1P: $132-$149   2P: $142-$159   XP: $10   F17

Location: I-275, exit 23B, just s on SR 92. 3805 W Cypress 33607. Fax: 813/870-0685. **Facility:** 145 units. Some suites. *Bath:* combo or shower only. 4 stories, interior corridors. **Terms:** check-in 4 pm, weekly rates available, package plans. **Amenities:** extended cable TV, voice mail, irons, hair dryers. **Leisure Activities:** heated pool, whirlpool, exercise room. *Fee:* downhill skiing. **Guest Services:** area transportation, valet and coin laundry. **Business Services:** meeting rooms, administrative services, fax. **Cards:** AE, DI, DS, MC, VI. *(See color ad p 812)*

SOME UNITS

FEE   FEE

COURTYARD BY MARRIOTT-DOWNTOWN TAMPA

▼▼▼
Hotel

Phone: (813)229-1100 **34**

1/8-4/30   1P: $149   2P: $149
12/1-1/7   1P: $99-$119   2P: $99-$119
10/1-11/30   1P: $89-$129   2P: $89-$129
5/1-9/30   1P: $89-$109   2P: $89-$109

Location: I-275, exit 25, 0.4 mi w via Tampa St. 102 E Cass St 33602. Fax: 813/224-9200. **Facility:** Downtown locale for this contemporary property. 141 units. Some suites and whirlpool units. *Bath:* combo or shower only. 6 stories, interior corridors. **Parking:** extra charge or valet. **Terms:** check-in 4 pm. **Amenities:** extended cable TV, dual phone lines, voice mail, irons, hair dryers. **Leisure Activities:** heated pool, whirlpool, exercise room. **Guest Services:** valet and coin laundry. **Business Services:** meeting rooms, administrative services, fax. **Cards:** AE, CB, DI, DS, MC, VI.

SOME UNITS

COURTYARD BY MARRIOTT TAMPA NORTH

▼▼▼
Motel

Phone: (813)978-9898 **2**

1/16-4/1   1P: $98   2P: $98
12/1-1/15 & 4/2-11/30   1P: $62   2P: $62

Location: I-75, exit 55, 0.5 mi w on Fletcher Ave; at Hidden River Corporate Park. 13575 Cypress Glen Ln 33637. Fax: 813/978-1835. **Facility:** 81 units, 3 with kitchen. Some suites and whirlpool units. *Bath:* combo or shower only. 3 stories, interior corridors. **Terms:** package plans. **Amenities:** extended cable TV, dual phone lines, voice mail, irons, hair dryers. **Leisure Activities:** heated pool, whirlpool, exercise room. **Guest Services:** valet and coin laundry. **Business Services:** meeting rooms, fax. **Cards:** AE, CB, DI, DS, MC, VI.

SOME UNITS

CROWNE PLAZA TAMPA-WESTSHORE

▼▼▼
Hotel

Phone: (813)289-8200 **43**

1/2-4/15   1P: $129-$159   XP: $10   F18
12/1-1/1 & 4/16-11/30   1P: $99-$129   XP: $10   F18

Location: I-275, exit 21 southbound; exit 20A northbound, 1 mi n on Kennedy Blvd, 0.9 mi w. 700 N Westshore Blvd 33609. Fax: 813/289-9166. **Facility:** 272 units. *Bath:* combo or shower only. 11 stories, interior corridors. **Parking:** valet. **Terms:** weekly & monthly rates available, package plans. **Amenities:** video games, voice mail, irons, hair dryers. **Leisure Activities:** saunas, whirlpool, exercise room. **Guest Services:** gift shop, area transportation, valet laundry. **Business Services:** meeting rooms, administrative services, PC, fax. **Cards:** AE, CB, DI, DS, MC, VI.

SOME UNITS

FEE   FEE

DAYS INN AIRPORT STADIUM

(AAA) [SAVE]
▼▼▼
Motel

Phone: 813/877-6181 **8**

12/27-4/15   1P: $85-$105   2P: $85-$105   XP: $6   F12
4/16-11/30   1P: $70-$80   2P: $70-$80
12/1-12/26   1P: $70-$80   2P: $70-$80   XP: $6   F12

Location: I-275, exit 23A, 0.6 mi n. 2522 N Dale Mabry 33607. Fax: 813/875-6171. **Facility:** 293 units. Some suites. *Bath:* combo or shower only. 2 stories, exterior corridors. **Terms:** 14 day cancellation notice-fee imposed, weekly & monthly rates available, package plans, pets ($25 extra charge). **Amenities:** extended cable TV, voice mail, safes (fee), irons, hair dryers. **Leisure Activities:** 2 pools (1 heated). *Fee:* health club privileges. **Guest Services:** [ECP] meal plan available, area transportation, valet and coin laundry. **Business Services:** meeting rooms, administrative services, PC, fax. **Cards:** AE, CB, DI, DS, MC, VI. **Special Amenities: free continental breakfast and free newspaper.** *(See color ad p 821)*

SOME UNITS

(See map p. 805)

DAYS INN ROCKY POINT ISLAND

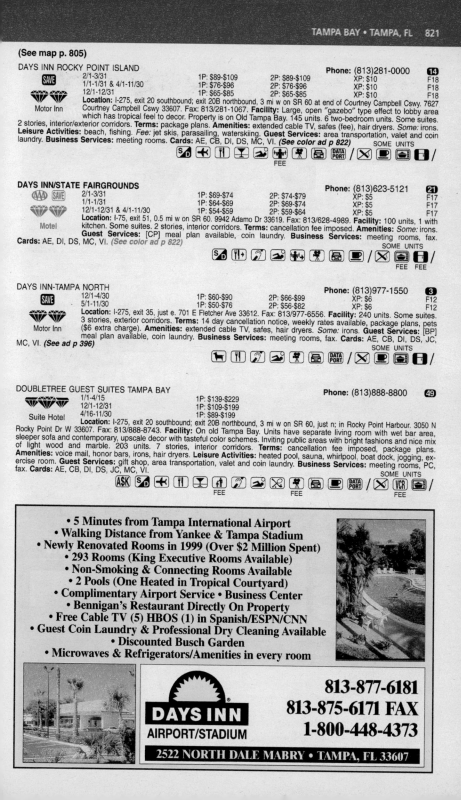

			Phone: (813)281-0000	14
SAVE	2/1-3/31	1P: $89-$109	2P: $89-$109	XP: $10	F18
	1/1-1/31 & 4/1-11/30	1P: $76-$96	2P: $76-$96	XP: $10	F18
Motor Inn	12/1-12/31	1P: $65-$85	2P: $65-$85	XP: $10	F18

Location: I-275, exit 20 southbound; exit 20B northbound, 3 mi w on SR 60 at end of Courtney Campbell Cswy. 7627 Courtney Campbell Cswy 33607. Fax: 813/281-1067. **Facility:** Large, open "gazebo" type effect to lobby area which has tropical feel to decor. Property is on Old Tampa Bay. 145 units. 6 two-bedroom units. Some suites. 2 stories, interior/exterior corridors. **Terms:** package plans. **Amenities:** extended cable TV, safes (fee), hair dryers. *Some:* irons. **Leisure Activities:** beach, fishing. *Fee:* jet skis, parasailing, waterskiing. **Guest Services:** area transportation, valet and coin laundry. **Business Services:** meeting rooms. **Cards:** AE, CB, DI, DS, MC, VI. *(See color ad p 822)* SOME UNITS

DAYS INN/STATE FAIRGROUNDS

			Phone: (813)623-5121	21
AAA SAVE	2/1-3/31	1P: $69-$74	2P: $74-$79	XP: $5	F17
	1/1-1/31	1P: $64-$69	2P: $69-$74	XP: $5	F17
Motel	12/1-12/31 & 4/1-11/30	1P: $54-$59	2P: $59-$64	XP: $5	F17

Location: I-75, exit 51, 0.5 mi w on SR 60. 9942 Adamo Dr 33619. Fax: 813/628-4989. **Facility:** 100 units, 1 with kitchen. Some suites. 2 stories, interior corridors. **Terms:** cancellation fee imposed. **Amenities:** *Some:* irons. **Guest Services:** [CP] meal plan available, coin laundry. **Business Services:** meeting rooms, fax. **Cards:** AE, DI, DS, MC, VI. *(See color ad p 822)* SOME UNITS FEE FEE

DAYS INN-TAMPA NORTH

			Phone: (813)977-1550	3
SAVE	12/1-4/30	1P: $60-$90	2P: $66-$99	XP: $6	F12
Motor Inn	5/1-11/30	1P: $50-$76	2P: $56-$82	XP: $6	F12

Location: I-275, exit 35, just e. 701 E Fletcher Ave 33612. Fax: 813/977-6556. **Facility:** 240 units. Some suites. 3 stories, exterior corridors. **Terms:** 14 day cancellation notice, weekly rates available, package plans, pets ($6 extra charge). **Amenities:** extended cable TV, safes, hair dryers. *Some:* irons. **Guest Services:** [BP] meal plan available, coin laundry. **Business Services:** meeting rooms, fax. **Cards:** AE, CB, DI, DS, JC, MC, VI. *(See ad p 396)* SOME UNITS

DOUBLETREE GUEST SUITES TAMPA BAY

		Phone: (813)888-8800	49
	1/1-4/15	1P: $139-$229	
	12/1-12/31	1P: $109-$199	
Suite Hotel	4/16-11/30	1P: $89-$199	

Location: I-275, exit 20 southbound; exit 20B northbound, 3 mi w on SR 60, just n; in Rocky Point Harbour. 3050 N Rocky Point Dr W 33607. Fax: 813/888-8743. **Facility:** On old Tampa Bay. Units have separate living room with wet bar area, sleeper sofa and contemporary, upscale decor with tasteful color schemes. Inviting public areas with bright fashions and nice mix of light wood and marble. 203 units. 7 stories, interior corridors. **Terms:** cancellation fee imposed, package plans. **Amenities:** voice mail, honor bars, irons, hair dryers. **Leisure Activities:** heated pool, sauna, whirlpool, boat dock, jogging, exercise room. **Guest Services:** gift shop, area transportation, valet and coin laundry. **Business Services:** meeting rooms, PC, fax. **Cards:** AE, CB, DI, DS, JC, MC, VI. SOME UNITS FEE FEE FEE

(See map p. 805)

DOUBLETREE GUEST SUITES TAMPA/BUSCH GARDENS

◆◆◆◆

Suite Motel

	1/1-4/15	1P: $94	2P: $94	XP: $10	F18
	12/1-12/31 & 9/6-11/30	1P: $89	2P: $89	XP: $10	F18
	4/16-9/5	1P: $79	2P: $79	XP: $10	F18

Phone: (813)971-7690   6

Location: I-275, exit 34, 1.8 mi e, just s. 11310 N 30th St 33612. **Fax:** 813/972-5525. **Facility:** Two units with separate living and bedroom. Luscious landscaping in tiered courtyard with waterfall. 129 units. 3 stories, exterior corridors. **Terms:** cancellation fee imposed, package plans. **Amenities:** video games, irons, hair dryers. **Leisure Activities:** heated pool, whirlpool. **Guest Services:** [BP] meal plan available, area transportation, coin laundry. **Business Services:** meeting rooms, fax. **Cards:** AE, CB, DI, DS, MC, VI. **(See color ad below)**

SOME UNITS

ASK FEE ⊞ ⊘ ⌨ 🌊 📹 FEE 📠 ▣ 🍽 ▮ DATA PORT / ⊗ VCR FEE /

DOUBLE TREE HOTEL TAMPA AIRPORT-WESTSHORE

AAA SAVE

◆◆◆◆

Hotel

| | 12/1-4/30 & 10/1-11/30 | 1P: $134 | | | |
| | 5/1-9/30 | 1P: $116 | | | |

Phone: (813)879-4800   56

Location: I-275, exit 21, northbound exit 20B, just w on Westshore, then just n. 4500 W Cypress St 33607. **Fax:** 813/873-2401. **Facility:** 493 units. Some suites. *Bath:* combo or shower only. 10 stories, interior corridors. **Terms:** package plans. **Amenities:** dual phone lines, irons, hair dryers. *Some:* voice mail. **Dining:** 2 restaurants, 6:30 am-1 am, $6-$20, cocktails. **Leisure Activities:** heated pool, whirlpool, exercise room, rental car. **Guest Services:** gift shop, area transportation-within 2 mi, valet and coin laundry. **Business Services:** conference facilities. **Cards:** AE, CB, DI, DS, MC, VI. **Special Amenities:** early check-in/late check-out and free newspaper. *(See color ad below)*

SOME UNITS

SD ✈ 🍴 🍸 🌊 FEE 📠 ▣ DATA PORT / ⊗ ▮ /

EAST LAKE INN

AAA SAVE

◆

Motel

| | 12/1-4/15 | 1P: $45-$50 | 2P: $50-$55 | XP: $5 | F6 |
| | 4/16-11/30 | 1P: $35-$40 | 2P: $40-$45 | XP: $5 | F6 |

Phone: 813/622-8339   18

Location: I-4, exit 6, westbound; exit 6B eastbound, 1 mi w on US 92. 6529 E Hillsborough Ave 33610. **Fax:** 813/622-8339. **Facility:** 25 units, 6 with efficiency (no utensils). 2 stories, exterior corridors. **Terms:** 3 day cancellation notice, weekly rates available. **Guest Services:** coin laundry. **Cards:** AE, DS, MC, VI.

SOME UNITS

SD 📹 / ▮ /

(See map p. 805)

ECONO LODGE MIDTOWN

AAA SAVE

◆◆◆◆ Motel

1/16-4/15	1P: $55-$70	2P: $60-$80	XP: $5	F
12/1-1/15	1P: $50-$65	2P: $55-$70	XP: $5	F
4/16-11/30	1P: $45-$65	2P: $50-$70	XP: $5	F

Phone: (813)254-3005 35

Location: I-275, exit 23B, northbound; exit 23 southbound, 1.5 mi s. 1020 S Dale Mabry Hwy 33629. Fax: 813/253-2909. **Facility:** 74 units. *Bath:* combo or shower only. 2 stories, exterior corridors. **Terms:** weekly rates available. **Amenities:** extended cable TV, voice mail. *Some:* irons, hair dryers. **Leisure Activities:** heated pool. **Guest Services:** coin laundry. **Business Services:** fax. **Cards:** AE, CB, DI, DS, JC, MC, VI. **Special Amenities:** free continental breakfast and free local telephone calls. *(See color ad below)*

SOME UNITS

EMBASSY SUITES HOTEL-TAMPA/AIRPORT/WESTSHORE

◆◆◆◆ Suite Hotel

12/31-4/8	1P: $149-$209	2P: $149-$209	XP: $10	F18
10/1-11/30	1P: $139-$209	2P: $139-$209	XP: $10	F18
12/1-12/30 & 4/9-9/30	1P: $129-$209	2P: $129-$209	XP: $10	F18

Phone: (813)875-1555 40

Location: I-275, exit 21 southbound; exit 20A northbound, 1 mi on Kennedy Blvd, 0.5 mi w. 555 N Westshore Blvd 33609. Fax: 813/287-3664. **Facility:** Large units most with balcony. 221 units. 26 two-bedroom units and 43 units with kitchen. Some suites. *Bath:* combo or shower only. 16 stories, interior corridors. **Parking:** valet. **Terms:** cancellation fee imposed, package plans. **Amenities:** voice mail, honor bars, irons, hair dryers. **Dining:** Bay Cafe, see separate listing. **Leisure Activities:** heated pool, saunas, whirlpool, exercise room. **Guest Services:** [BP] meal plan available, gift shop, complimentary evening beverages, area transportation, valet laundry. **Business Services:** conference facilities. **Cards:** AE, CB, DI, DS, MC, VI.

SOME UNITS

EMBASSY SUITES USF CAMPUS

◆◆◆◆ Suite Hotel

1/1-4/30	1P: $149-$179	2P: $159-$199	XP: $15	F18
5/1-11/30	1P: $129-$149	2P: $144-$164	XP: $15	F18
12/1-12/31	1P: $119-$139	2P: $134-$154	XP: $15	F18

Phone: (813)977-7066 42

Location: I-75, exit 34, 4.7 mi w on Fowler Ave at USF Campus. 3705 Spectrum Blvd 33612. Fax: 813/977-7933. **Facility:** Upscale public areas with atrium, lush interior landscaping and waterfall. 247 units. Some whirlpool units. *Bath:* combo or shower only. 8 stories, interior corridors. **Terms:** cancellation fee imposed, monthly rates available, package plans. **Amenities:** video games, dual phone lines, voice mail, irons, hair dryers. **Leisure Activities:** heated pool, sauna, whirlpool, exercise room, game room. **Guest Services:** [BP] meal plan available, gift shop, complimentary evening beverages, area transportation, valet and coin laundry. **Business Services:** conference facilities, administrative services, PC, fax. **Cards:** AE, DI, DS, MC, VI.

SOME UNITS

FAIRFIELD INN BY MARRIOTT

◆◆◆ Motel

12/1-4/30	1P: $90-$120
5/1-11/30	1P: $70-$100

Phone: (813)661-9719 22

Location: I-75, exit 51, just w on SR 60, just s on Falkenburg Rd. 10150 Palm River Rd 33619. Fax: 813/661-0416. **Facility:** 107 units. Some suites and whirlpool units ($100-$230). *Bath:* combo or shower only. 3 stories, interior corridors. **Amenities:** video games, irons. *Some:* hair dryers. **Leisure Activities:** heated pool, exercise room. **Guest Services:** [CP] meal plan available, valet and coin laundry. **Business Services:** fax. **Cards:** AE, DS, MC, VI.

SOME UNITS

FOUR POINTS HOTEL BY SHERATON TAMPA EAST

◆◆◆ Hotel

3/16-4/30	1P: $105-$110	2P: $110-$115	XP: $5	F18
1/1-3/15	1P: $90-$95	2P: $95-$100	XP: $5	F18
5/1-11/30	1P: $79-$84	2P: $85-$90	XP: $5	F18
12/1-12/31	1P: $65-$70	2P: $70-$75	XP: $5	F18

Phone: (813)626-0999 16

Location: I-4, exit 6 westbound; exit 5 eastbound, 0.6 mi w on SR 92. 7401 E Hillsborough Ave 33610. Fax: 813/622-7893. **Facility:** Set on Seminole Indian Reservation. 275 units. Some suites. *Bath:* combo or shower only. 6 stories, interior/exterior corridors. **Terms:** package plans, pets ($45 extra charge). **Amenities:** video games, dual phone lines, voice mail, irons, hair dryers. **Leisure Activities:** whirlpool, exercise room. **Guest Services:** gift shop, valet laundry. **Business Services:** conference facilities, administrative services, PC, fax. **Cards:** AE, CB, DI, DS, MC, VI.

SOME UNITS

(See map p. 805)

GRAM'S PLACE BED, BREAKFAST & MUSIC
Phone: (813)221-0596 65

▼▼▼ 12/1-5/31   1P: $85-$100
     6/1-11/30   1P: $70-$85

Bed & Breakfast **Location:** I-275, exit 29, 0.6 mi w on E Dr Martin Luther King Jr Blvd, 0.6 mi s on N Ola Ave at jct Plymouth St. 3109 N Ola Ave 33603. Fax: 813/221-0596. **Facility:** This is a very different B&B; made for the laid back relaxed music lover in you. Pick up a guitar and strum away. Jam in the 16 track recording studio on site. Enjoy the relaxing courtyard with a tile bar setting and Key West style. Each room is themed to blues, rock, jazz, folk, reggae and big band. Designated smoking area. 6 units. *Bath:* some combo or shower only. 1 story, interior/exterior corridors. **Terms:** 7 day cancellation notice-fee imposed. **Leisure Activities:** whirlpool. **Guest Services:** [CP] meal plan available, complimentary laundry. **Cards:** AE, MC, VI.

[ASK] [S/D] [X]

HAMPTON INN
Phone: (813)289-6262 53

[SAVE] 1/16-4/30   1P: $99-$106
     12/1-1/15 & 5/1-11/30   1P: $78-$85

▼▼▼ **Location:** I-275, exit 20, exit 20B northbound, 3 mi w on SR 60; in Rocky Point Harbor. 3035 N Rocky Point Dr 33607.
Motel   Fax: 813/287-9363. **Facility:** Inviting lobby and breakfast area overlooking landscaped waterfall area; nice cherry finish furniture throughout. 70 units. *Bath:* combo or shower only. 5 stories, interior corridors. **Amenities:** extended cable TV, video games, voice mail, irons, hair dryers. **Guest Services:** [ECP] meal plan available, valet and coin laundry. **Business Services:** fax. **Cards:** AE, CB, DI, JC, MC, VI. *(See color ad p 822)*

SOME UNITS
[S/D] [+] [†|†] [♿] [⌕] [♿] [⌒] [⇆] [▦] [▤] [▥] [DATA PORT] / [X] [▦] [♨] /
FEE

HAMPTON INN & SUITES
Phone: (813)903-6000 28

[SAVE] All Year   1P: $85-$95   2P: $85-$95

▼▼▼ **Location:** I-75, exit 55, 0.8 mi w on Fletcher Ave; at Hidden River Corporate Park. 8210 Hidden River Pkwy 33637.
Motel   Fax: 813/977-3343. **Facility:** 127 units, 38 with kitchen. Some suites ($110-$125). *Bath:* combo or shower only. 4 stories, interior corridors. **Terms:** package plans. **Amenities:** extended cable TV, video games, voice mail, irons, hair dryers. **Leisure Activities:** heated pool, exercise room. **Guest Services:** [ECP] meal plan available, complimentary evening beverages, coin laundry. **Business Services:** meeting rooms, fax. **Cards:** AE, CB, DI, DS, JC, MC, VI. *(See color ad below)*

SOME UNITS
[S/D] [♿] [⌕] [⌒] [⇆] [▦] [▤] [▥] [DATA PORT] / [X] [VCR] [▦] [♨] /
FEE

HAMPTON INN TAMPA INT'L AIRPORT
Phone: (813)287-0778 44

[AAA] [SAVE] 1/1-4/15 & 9/16-11/30   1P: $109-$119   2P: $119-$129   XP: $10   F18
▼▼▼ 4/16-9/15   1P: $105-$115   2P: $115-$125   XP: $10   F18
Motel   12/1-12/31   1P: $99-$109   2P: $109-$119   XP: $10   F18
Location: I-275, exit 21 southbound; exit 20A northbound (Kennedy Blvd), 1 mi w on Westshore, 0.3 mi s. 4817 W Laurel St 33607. Fax: 813/287-0882. **Facility:** 134 units. 6 stories, interior corridors. **Terms:** package plans - off season. **Amenities:** irons, hair dryers. **Guest Services:** [ECP] meal plan available, complimentary evening beverages, area transportation-within 2 mi, valet laundry. **Business Services:** meeting rooms, fax. **Cards:** AE, CB, DI, DS, MC, VI. **Special Amenities:** early check-in/late check-out and free continental breakfast.

SOME UNITS
[S/D] [+] [†|†] [♿] [⌒] [⇆] [♿|♿] [▦] [▤] [▥] [DATA PORT] / [X] [▦] [♨] /
FEE

HILTON GARDEN INN/TAMPA YBOR HISTORIC DISTRICT
Phone: (813)769-9267 69

[SAVE] 2/1-3/31   1P: $159   2P: $159   XP: $10   F18
▼▼▼ 1/1-1/31   1P: $129   2P: $129   XP: $10   F18
Hotel   12/1-12/31 & 4/1-11/30   1P: $99   2P: $99   XP: $10   F18
Location: I-4, exit 1, just e on 21st St, then just s. 1700 E 9th Ave 33605. Fax: 813/769-3299. **Facility:** 95 units. 4 stories, interior corridors. **Amenities:** extended cable TV, voice mail, irons, hair dryers. **Leisure Activities:** whirlpool, exercise room. **Guest Services:** coin laundry. **Business Services:** meeting rooms, administrative services. **Cards:** AE, CB, DI, DS, JC, MC, VI. *(See ad p 44 & color ad p 822)*

SOME UNITS
[S/D] [+] [⇆] [▦] [▤] [▥] [♨] [DATA PORT] / [X] /
FEE

(See map p. 805)

HILTON TAMPA AIRPORT WESTSHORE

AAA SAVE

Hotel

Phone: (813)877-6688   **38** F18

All Year   1P: $100-$200   2P: $110-$210   XP: $10
($250-$350). **Location:** I-275, exit 22, 0.8 mi n. 2225 N Lois Ave 33607. **Fax:** 813/879-3264. **Facility:** 238 units. Some suites ($250-$350). *Bath:* combo or shower only. 12 stories, interior corridors. **Terms:** cancellation fee imposed, weekly & monthly rates available, package plans. **Amenities:** voice mail, irons, hair dryers. **Dining:** restaurant, 6:30 am-10:30 pm, $12-$19, cocktails. **Leisure Activities:** heated pool, whirlpool, lighted tennis court, exercise room. **Guest Services:** [BP] meal plan available, gift shop, area transportation-within 3 mi, valet laundry. **Business Services:** conference facilities, fax. **Special Amenities:** early check-in/late check-out and free continental breakfast. *(See ad below & p 44)*

SOME UNITS

[icons] FEE

HOLIDAY INN CITY CENTRE

Hotel

Phone: (813)223-1351   **32**

	1P: $153	2P: $153	XP: $10	F18
1/7-4/14	1P: $153	2P: $153	XP: $10	F18
4/15-11/30	1P: $129	2P: $129	XP: $10	F18
12/1-12/16	1P: $119	2P: $119	XP: $10	F18
12/17-1/6	1P: $99	2P: $99	XP: $10	F18

Location: I-275, exit 25, 0.3 mi sw via Ashley St. 111 W Fortune St 33602. **Fax:** 813/221-2000. **Facility:** Downtown locale adjacent to the performing arts center. 312 units. 13 stories, interior corridors. **Terms:** 14 day cancellation notice-fee imposed, weekly & monthly rates available, package plans. **Amenities:** dual phone lines, voice mail, irons, hair dryers. **Leisure Activities:** whirlpool, exercise room. **Guest Services:** gift shop, area transportation, valet and coin laundry. **Business Services:** conference facilities, administrative services, fax. *Fee:* PC. **Cards:** AE, CB, DI, DS, JC, MC, VI.

SOME UNITS

[icons] ASK FEE   FEE FEE

HOLIDAY INN EXPRESS HOTEL & SUITES

Motel

Phone: 813/287-8585   **58** F18

	1P: $109-$129	XP: $8	F18
1/1-4/30	1P: $109-$129	XP: $8	F18
12/1-12/31 & 5/1-11/30	1P: $89-$109	XP: $8	F18

Location: I-275, exit 20 southbound; exit 20B northbound, 3 mi w on SR 60, just n; in Rocky Point Harbour. 3025 N Rocky Point Dr 33607. **Fax:** 813/287-8484. **Facility:** On Old Tampa Bay. Inviting lobby area with breakfast area overlooking pool and bay. Contemporary decor to units with cherry finish furnishings. 88 units. Some suites ($109-$159). *Bath:* combo or shower only. 4 stories, interior corridors. **Terms:** 14 day cancellation notice. **Amenities:** extended cable TV, irons, hair dryers. **Leisure Activities:** exercise room. **Guest Services:** [CP] meal plan available, area transportation, coin laundry. **Business Services:** meeting rooms, administrative services. *Fee:* PC. **Cards:** AE, DI, DS, JC, MC, VI. *(See color ad p 822)*

SOME UNITS

[icons] ASK

HOLIDAY INN EXPRESS HOTEL & SUITES STADIUM/AIRPORT

Motel

Phone: (813)877-6061   **4**

12/25-4/15	1P: $85	2P: $95	XP: $10	F18
12/1-12/24 & 4/16-11/30	1P: $75	2P: $85	XP: $10	F18

Location: I-275, northbound exit 23A; southbound exit 23, 2 mi n. 4732 N Dale Mabry 33614. **Fax:** 813/876-1531. **Facility:** 235 units. 37 efficiencies and 2 units with kitchen. Some suites ($99-$135). 2 stories, exterior corridors. **Terms:** cancellation fee imposed, weekly rates available, package plans, pets ($25 extra charge). **Amenities:** extended cable TV, irons, hair dryers. **Leisure Activities:** exercise room, game room. **Guest Services:** [ECP] meal plan available, area transportation, coin laundry. **Business Services:** conference facilities, administrative services, PC, fax. **Cards:** AE, CB, DI, DS, JC, MC, VI.

SOME UNITS

[icons] ASK FEE

HOLIDAY INN TAMPA

Motor Inn

Phone: (813)971-4710   **13**

1/16-4/15	1P: $89-$99
12/1-1/15 & 4/16-11/30	1P: $79-$89

Location: I-275, exit 34, 1.5 mi e on SR 582. 2701 E Fowler Ave 33612. **Fax:** 813/910-8038. **Facility:** 408 units. Some suites and whirlpool units. *Bath:* combo or shower only. 2 stories, interior/exterior corridors. **Terms:** cancellation fee imposed, monthly rates available, package plans, pets ($25 deposit). **Amenities:** video games, voice mail, irons, hair dryers. *Some:* CD players. **Leisure Activities:** heated pool, exercise room, game room. **Guest Services:** [BP] meal plan available, gift shop, area transportation, coin laundry. **Business Services:** conference facilities, fax. **Cards:** AE, CB, DI, DS, JC, MC, VI. *(See color ad p 827)*

SOME UNITS

[icons] ASK FEE FEE FEE FEE

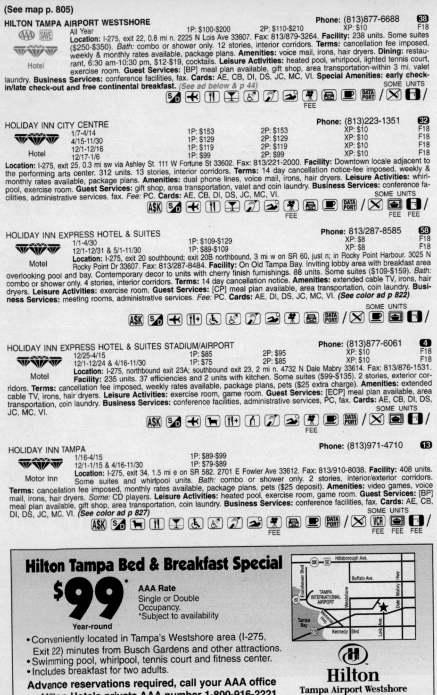

(See map p. 805)

HOWARD JOHNSON AIRPORT-STADIUM

Phone: (813)875-8818 **⑤**

12/1-4/30	1P: $64-$79	2P: $69-$84	XP: $5	F
5/1-11/30	1P: $64	2P: $69	XP: $5	F

Location: I-275, exit 23A, 0.5 mi n. 2055 N Dale Mabry 33607. Fax: 813/876-4964. **Facility:** 137 units. Some suites ($109-$120). 2 stories, exterior corridors. **Terms:** weekly & monthly rates available, package plans, pets ($25 deposit). **Amenities:** extended cable TV, voice mail, safes (fee), irons, hair dryers. **Dining:** 3 restaurants, 11:15 am-10:30 pm, Sat & Sun 2:15 pm-10 pm; donut & sandwich shop, $6-$14, cocktails. **Leisure Activities:** heated pool, exercise room. **Fee:** health club privileges. **Guest Services:** area transportation-within 6 mi, coin laundry. **Business Services:** meeting rooms, fax. **Cards:** AE, CB, DI, DS, JC, MC, VI. **Special Amenities: free continental breakfast and free local telephone calls.**

SOME UNITS

HOWARD JOHNSON EXPRESS INN & SUITES

Phone: (813)832-4656 **㉗**

12/1-4/15	1P: $55-$70	2P: $60-$75	XP: $5
4/16-11/30	1P: $45-$65	2P: $50-$70	XP: $5

Location: I-275, northbound exit 23B; southbound exit 23, 2.5 mi s. 3314 S Dale Mabry Hwy 33629. Fax: 813/832-5454. **Facility:** 80 units, 28 with efficiency. Some suites ($60-$90). 2 stories, exterior corridors. **Terms:** weekly & monthly rates available. **Amenities:** extended cable TV. Some; irons, hair dryers. **Leisure Activities:** heated pool, whirlpool. **Guest Services:** coin laundry. **Business Services:** meeting rooms. **Cards:** AE, CB, DI, DS, JC, MC, VI. **Special Amenities: early check-in/late check-out and free continental breakfast.**
(See color ad p 828)

SOME UNITS

HOWARD JOHNSON NEAR BUSCH GARDENS MAINGATE

Phone: (813)988-9191 **⑫**

7/1-9/15	1P: $79-$89	2P: $89-$99	XP: $10	F17
2/1-6/30	1P: $69-$79	2P: $79-$89	XP: $10	F17
12/1-1/31 & 9/16-11/30	1P: $59-$69	2P: $69-$79	XP: $10	F17

Location: I-275, exit 33, 3 mi e on SR 580 (Busch Blvd). 4139 E Busch Blvd 33617. Fax: 813/988-9195. **Facility:** 99 units. *Bath:* combo or shower only. 2 stories, interior corridors. **Terms:** 3 day cancellation notice, weekly & monthly rates available, package plans, pets ($25 fee). **Amenities:** extended cable TV, safes (fee). Some; irons, hair dryers. **Leisure Activities:** heated pool, saunas, whirlpool, game room. **Guest Services:** [BP] meal plan available, coin laundry. **Business Services:** meeting rooms, fax. **Cards:** AE, DI, DS, MC, VI.

SOME UNITS

(See map p. 805)

HYATT REGENCY TAMPA

AAA SAVE

▽▽▽

Hotel

Phone: (813)225-1234 **31**

All Year   1P: $219   2P: $244   XP: $25   F18

Location: Downtown; I-275, exit 25, 0.8 mi s on Ashley St to Jackson, just e on Tampa St S. 2 Tampa City Center 33602-5187. Fax: 813/273-0234. **Facility:** Connects to office and shopping complex. 521 units. Some whirlpool units. *Bath:* combo or shower only. 17 stories, interior corridors. **Parking:** extra charge or valet. **Terms:** cancellation fee imposed, weekly & monthly rates available, package plans. **Amenities:** voice mail, irons, hair dryers. *Some:* fax. **Dining:** 2 dining rooms, deli, 6:30 am-11 pm, $10-$20, cocktails. **Leisure Activities:** heated pool, whirlpool, exercise room. **Guest Services:** gift shop, area transportation-Harbour Island, valet laundry. **Business Services:** conference facilities, administrative services, fax. *Fee:* PC. **Cards:** AE, CB, DI, DS, JC, MC, VI.

SOME UNITS

[✈] [🍽] [24🛎] [⊡] [⌂] [♿] [👂] [🏊] [👕] [🖥] [💻] [DATA PORT] / [✕] [VCR] [🛢]
                                    FEE   FEE FEE

HYATT REGENCY WESTSHORE

AAA SAVE

▽▽▽

Hotel

Phone: (813)874-1234 **46**

All Year   1P: $234   2P: $259   XP: $25   F18

Location: SR 60 at east end of Courtney Campbell Cswy. 6200 Courtney Campbell Cswy 33607. Fax: 813/281-9168. **Facility:** Located on ecologically-protected salt marsh overlooking Old Tampa Bay. City and bay views. 445 units. Some suites and whirlpool units. *Bath:* combo or shower only. 13 stories, interior/exterior corridors. **Parking:** valet. **Terms:** cancellation fee imposed, package plans. **Amenities:** voice mail, honor bars, irons, hair dryers. *Some:* fax. **Dining:** 3 restaurants, 6:30 am-10 pm, $12-$25, cocktails, also, Oystercatchers, see separate listing, entertainment. **Leisure Activities:** 2 heated pools, saunas, whirlpools, 2 lighted tennis courts, nature preserve, nature walk & observation deck. **Guest Services:** gift shop, valet laundry. **Business Services:** conference facilities, administrative services, fax. *Fee:* PC. **Cards:** AE, CB, DI, DS, JC, MC, VI.

SOME UNITS

[✈] [🍽] [⊡] [👂] [🏊] [👕🔧] [💻] [💻] [DATA PORT] / [✕] [🛢] [🛢] /
           FEE   FEE

LA QUINTA INN & SUITES USF

SAVE

▽▽▽

Motel

Phone: (813)910-7500 **59**

All Year   1P: $89-$109   2P: $89-$109

Location: I-275, exit 34, 2.2 mi e. 3701 E Fowler 33612. Fax: 813/910-7600. **Facility:** 109 units. Some suites ($119-$139). *Bath:* combo or shower only. 4 stories, interior corridors. **Terms:** small pets only. **Amenities:** video games, voice mail, irons, hair dryers. **Leisure Activities:** heated pool, whirlpool, exercise room. **Guest Services:** [ECP] meal plan available, valet and coin laundry. **Business Services:** meeting rooms, fax. **Cards:** AE, CB, DI, DS, MC, VI. *(See color ad p 829)*

SOME UNITS

[S/D] [🐾] [🍽] [♿] [👂] [🏊] [👕] [💻] [💻] [DATA PORT] / [✕] [🛢] [🛢] /
                                            FEE

LA QUINTA INN STATE FAIR

SAVE

▽▽▽

Motel

Phone: (813)623-3591 **26**

All Year   1P: $65-$75   2P: $65-$75

Location: I-4, exit 3, just n. 2904 Melbourne Blvd 33605-2457. Fax: 813/620-1375. **Facility:** 128 units. 3 stories, interior/exterior corridors. **Terms:** small pets only. **Amenities:** video games, voice mail. **Leisure Activities:** heated pool. **Business Services:** meeting rooms. **Cards:** AE, CB, DI, DS, MC, VI. *(See color ad p 829)*

SOME UNITS

[S/D] [🐾] [⌂] [👂] [🏊] [👕] [💻] [💻] [DATA PORT] / [✕] [🛢] /
                                    FEE

LA QUINTA INN TAMPA AIRPORT

SAVE

▽▽▽

Motel

Phone: (813)287-0440 **45**

All Year   1P: $75-$99   2P: $75-$99

Location: I-275, exit 21, southbound; exit 20A northbound Westshore Dr, exit 0.8 mi w, then just w. 4730 Spruce St 33607-1497. Fax: 813/286-7399. **Facility:** Inviting lobby with a Mediterranean feel, faux fireplace, fountain and lots of knick-knacks decorating the seating and breakfast area. Furnishings are of contemporary design with a blond oak finish. 122 units. 2 stories, exterior corridors. **Terms:** small pets only. **Amenities:** extended cable TV, video games. **Leisure Activities:** heated pool. **Guest Services:** [ECP] meal plan available, valet laundry. **Business Services:** meeting rooms, fax. **Cards:** AE, CB, DI, DS, MC, VI. *(See color ad p 829)*

SOME UNITS

[S/D] [✈] [🐾] [🍽🔧] [👂] [🏊] [👕🔧] [💻] [💻] [DATA PORT] / [✕] [🛢] [🛢] /
                                        FEE   FEE FEE

(See map p. 805)

MOTEL 6 - 483

▼▼ ▼▼
Motel

				Phone: 813/932-4948	60
1/18-4/15	1P: $40-$50	2P: $46-$56		XP: $3	F17
12/1-1/17 & 4/16-11/30	1P: $36-$46	2P: $42-$52		XP: $3	F17

Location: I-275, exit 34, just w. 333 E Fowler Ave 33612. **Fax:** 813/931-4577. **Facility:** 150 units. 2 stories, exterior corridors. **Leisure Activities:** heated pool. **Guest Services:** coin laundry. **Cards:** AE, DI, DS, MC, VI.

SOME UNITS

[S/D] [🛏] [📶] [🐾] [📺] [DATA PORT] / [✕] /

MOTEL 6 TAMPA EAST - 1192

▼▼ ▼▼
Motel

| | | | Phone: 813/628-0888 | 61 |
| All Year | 1P: $40-$50 | 2P: $46-$56 | XP: $3 | F17 |

Location: I-4, exit 6 westbound; exit 6A eastbound, 0.7 mi n. 6510 N US 301 33610. **Fax:** 813/620-4899. **Facility:** 108 units. **Bath:** combo or shower only. 3 stories, exterior corridors. **Terms:** small pets only. **Leisure Activities:** heated pool. **Guest Services:** coin laundry. **Cards:** AE, CB, DI, DS, MC, VI. SOME UNITS

[S/D] [🛏] [📶] [🐾] [📺] [DATA PORT] / [✕] /

QUALITY HOTEL WESTSHORE

[SAVE]

▼▼ ▼▼
Motor Inn

				Phone: (813)282-3636	62
1/1-4/30	1P: $89-$99	2P: $99-$109		XP: $5	F12
12/1-12/31	1P: $89-$99	2P: $99		XP: $5	F12
5/1-10/1 & 10/2-11/30	1P: $69-$99	2P: $79-$89		XP: $5	F12

Location: I-275, exit 21, northbound exit 20A (Kennedy Blvd), 0.8 mi w. 1200 N Westshore Blvd 33607. **Fax:** 813/282-0055. **Facility:** 238 units. Some suites ($99-$129). 5 stories, exterior corridors. **Terms:** cancellation fee imposed, monthly rates available, package plans. **Amenities:** Some: irons, hair dryers. **Leisure Activities:** game room. **Guest Services:** gift shop, valet and coin laundry. **Business Services:** conference facilities. **Cards:** AE, CB, DI, DS, JC, MC, VI. **(See color ad p 830)**

SOME UNITS

[S/D] [✈] [🍴] [🍷] [🐾] [📷] [☕] [DATA PORT] / [✕] [📺] [🔌] /

QUALITY INN-BUSCH GARDENS

(AAA) [SAVE]

▼▼ ▼▼
Motel

			Phone: (813)961-1000	57
1/1-4/30	1P: $89	2P: $89	XP: $5
12/1-12/31	1P: $69-$79	2P: $69-$79	
5/1-11/30	1P: $69-$79	2P: $69-$79	XP: $5

Location: I-275, exit 36, just w. 400 E Bearss Ave 33613. **Fax:** 813/961-5704. **Facility:** 154 units. Some suites ($115-$125). **Bath:** combo or shower only. 2 stories, exterior corridors. **Terms:** 10 day cancellation notice, weekly rates available, package plans, pets ($10 extra charge). **Amenities:** irons, hair dryers. **Leisure Activities:** wading pool. **Guest Services:** valet and coin laundry. **Business Services:** meeting rooms, fax. **Cards:** AE, CB, DI, DS, MC, VI. **Special Amenities:** free continental breakfast and free local telephone calls. *(See color ad p 830)*

SOME UNITS

[S/D] [🛏] [📶] [🐾] [🐾] [📷] [☕] [DATA PORT] / [✕] [📺] [🔌] /
FEE FEE

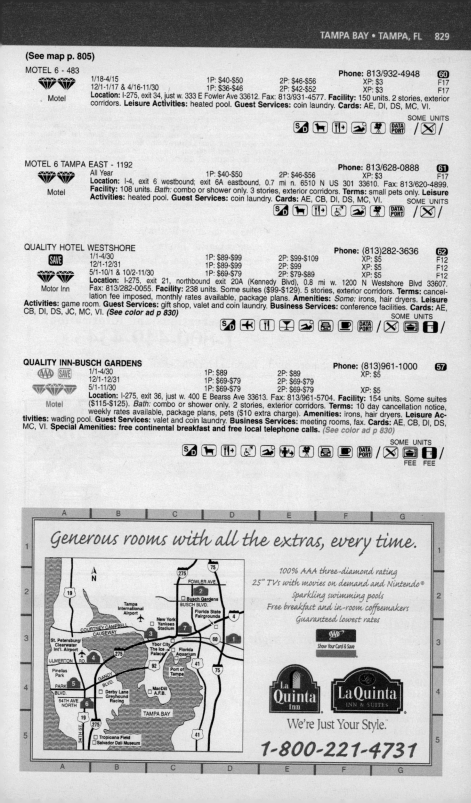

(See map p. 805)

RADISSON BAY HARBOR HOTEL

(AAA) (SAVE)

▽▽▽▽

Hotel

1/1-4/30	2P: $133-$143	XP: $10	F16
10/1-11/30	2P: $126-$136	XP: $10	F16
5/1-9/30	2P: $119-$129	XP: $10	F16
12/1-12/31	2P: $112-$120	XP: $10	F16

Phone: (813)281-8900 [48]

Location: I-275, exit 20 southbound; exit 20B norhtbound, 3 mi w on SR 60. 7700 Courtney Campbell Cswy 33607. **Fax:** 813/281-0927. **Facility:** Overlooking Old Tampa Bay. Rooms have balcony with bay or city view. 257 units. Some suites. *Bath:* combo or shower only. 6 stories, interior corridors. **Parking:** valet. **Terms:** 3 day cancellation notice-fee imposed, package plans. **Amenities:** extended cable TV, dual phone lines, voice mail, irons, hair dryers. *Some:* fax. **Dining:** restaurant, 6:30 am-11 pm, Fri & Sat 7 am-midnight; tiki bar, $6-$16, cocktails. **Leisure Activities:** heated pool, boat dock, fishing, 2 lighted tennis courts, exercise room, basketball, game room. **Guest Services:** gift shop, area transportation-within 3 mi, valet and coin laundry. **Business Services:** conference facilities, fax. **Cards:** AE, CB, DI, DS, MC, VI. **Special Amenities:** free continental breakfast and free newspaper. *(See ad below)*

SOME UNITS

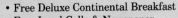

(See map p. 805)

RADISSON HOTEL AT SABAL PARK

Phone: (813)623-6363 [19]

	12/1-4/12	1P: $89-$189	2P: $89-$189	XP: $10	F18
	9/9-11/30	1P: $89-$169	2P: $89-$169	XP: $10	F18
	4/13-9/8	1P: $79-$155	2P: $79-$155	XP: $10	F18

Hotel

Location: I-75, exit 52 southbound; exit 52B northbound, just w; in Sabal Center. 10221 Princess Palm Ave 33610. Fax: 813/621-7224. **Facility:** 265 units. 5 two-bedroom units and 1 unit with kitchen. Some suites ($104-$204) and whirlpool units. 5 stories, interior corridors. **Parking:** valet. **Terms:** package plans. **Amenities:** video games, dual phone lines, voice mail, irons, hair dryers. **Dining:** restaurant, 6 am-11 pm, $8-$26, cocktails, entertainment. **Leisure Activities:** heated pool, whirlpool, heated lap pool, lighted tennis court, jogging, exercise room, basketball. **Guest Services:** gift shop, area transportation-within 3 mi, valet and coin laundry. **Business Services:** conference facilities, administrative services, PC, fax. **Cards:** AE, CB, DI, DS, MC, VI. **Special Amenities:** early check-in/late check-out and free newspaper. *(See ad below)*

SOME UNITS

RADISSON RIVERWALK HOTEL TAMPA

Phone: (813)223-2222 [63]

	1/1-4/5	1P: $189-$229	2P: $199-$239	XP: $10	F18
	9/17-11/30	1P: $179-$219	2P: $189-$229	XP: $10	F18
	4/6-9/16	1P: $169-$209	2P: $179-$219	XP: $10	F18
	12/1-12/31	1P: $169-$179	2P: $179-$189	XP: $10	F18

Hotel

Location: I-275, exit 25. 200 N Ashley Dr 33602. Fax: 813/273-0839. **Facility:** Downtown hotel. Lovely spacious decor. Elegant restaurant serves creative dishes to both hotel guests and outside diners. 284 units. 6 stories, interior corridors. **Parking:** valet. **Terms:** weekly & monthly rates available, package plans. **Amenities:** voice mail, irons, hair dryers. **Dining:** restaurant, 5 am-1 am, $9-$25, cocktails. **Leisure Activities:** sauna, exercise room. **Guest Services:** gift shop, area transportation. **Business Services:** conference facilities. **Cards:** AE, MC, VI. **Special Amenities:** early check-in/late check-out and free newspaper.

SOME UNITS

RAMADA AIRPORT INN & CONFERENCE CENTER

Phone: (813)289-1950 [47]

	2/1-4/30	1P: $129	2P: $139	XP: $10	F18
	12/1-1/31 & 5/1-11/30	1P: $99	2P: $109	XP: $10	F18

Hotel

Location: I-275, exit 21 southbound, 0.4 mi e on Westshore, 0.5 mi s; exit 20B northbound, just e. 5303 W Kennedy Blvd 33609. Fax: 813/282-8964. **Facility:** 248 units. **Bath:** combo or shower only. 11 stories, interior/exterior corridors. **Terms:** weekly rates available, package plans, pets (in outside access rooms, $20 deposit). **Amenities:** extended cable TV, voice mail, hair dryers. *Some:* irons. **Dining:** restaurant, 6 am-10 pm, $6-$16, cocktails. **Leisure Activities:** exercise room. **Guest Services:** area transportation-within 10-15 mi, coin laundry. **Business Services:** conference facilities, administrative services. *Fee:* PC. **Cards:** AE, CB, DI, DS, JC, MC, VI.

SOME UNITS

RED ROOF INN

Phone: (813)932-0073 [11]

	1/15-11/30	1P: $50-$75	2P: $60-$85	XP: $10	F18
	12/1-1/14	1P: $42-$66	2P: $52-$76	XP: $10	F18

Motel

Location: I-275, exit 33, 1.7 mi w. 2307 E Busch Blvd 33612. Fax: 813/933-5689. **Facility:** 108 units. 2 stories, exterior corridors. **Terms:** weekly rates available, small pets only. **Amenities:** video games. **Cards:** AE, DI, DS, MC, VI. **Special Amenities:** free local telephone calls and free newspaper.

SOME UNITS

RED ROOF INN-BRANDON

Phone: (813)681-8484 [51]

	1/16-4/30	1P: $79-$99	2P: $79-$99	XP: $5	F18
	12/1-1/15 & 5/1-11/30	1P: $48-$68	2P: $48-$68	XP: $5	F18

Motel

Location: I-75, exit 51, just w to S Falkenberg Rd, just n. 10121 Horace Ave 33619. Fax: 813/681-8892. **Facility:** 120 units. 3 stories, exterior corridors. **Terms:** cancellation fee imposed, small pets only. **Amenities:** video games, voice mail. *Some:* irons, hair dryers. **Guest Services:** coin laundry. **Business Services:** fax. **Cards:** AE, CB, DI, DS, MC, VI. **Special Amenities:** free local telephone calls and free newspaper.

SOME UNITS

(See map p. 805)

RED ROOF INN-FAIRGROUNDS

Phone: (813)623-5245 — **15**

AAA SAVE

♦♦ ♦♦

Motel

	1P: $49-$64	2P: $54-$69	XP: $5	F17
1/16-4/30				
12/1-1/15 & 5/1-11/30	1P: $39-$54	2P: $44-$59	XP: $5	F17

Location: I-4, exit 6 westbound; exit 6A eastbound, just se. 5001 N US 301 33610. Fax: 813/623-5240. **Facility:** 108 units. 2 stories, exterior corridors. **Terms:** cancellation fee imposed, small pets only. **Amenities:** video games, voice mail. *Some:* irons, hair dryers. **Business Services:** fax. **Cards:** AE, CB, DI, DS, MC, VI. **Special Amenities:** free local telephone calls and free newspaper.

SOME UNITS

SHERATON SUITES TAMPA AIRPORT

Phone: 813/873-8675 — **36**

♦♦ ♦♦ ♦

Suite Hotel

| 12/1-4/15 & 9/6-11/30 | 1P: $199 | 2P: $210 | XP: $20 | F17 |
| 4/16-9/5 | 1P: $179 | 2P: $199 | XP: $20 | F17 |

Location: I-275, exit 22, n to Cypress, 0.3 mi w; northbound exit 20B. 4400 W Cypress St 33607. Fax: 813/877-6766. **Facility:** Units with living room and kitchen area. 260 units. *Bath:* combo or shower only. 8 stories, interior corridors. **Terms:** cancellation fee imposed, package plans. **Amenities:** voice mail, irons, hair dryers. **Leisure Activities:** heated pool, sauna, whirlpool, steamroom, exercise room. **Guest Services:** area transportation, coin laundry. **Business Services:** conference facilities, fax. **Cards:** AE, CB, DI, DS, MC, VI.

SOME UNITS

FEE

SHONEY'S INN

Phone: (813)985-8525 — **30**

♦♦ ♦♦ ♦

Motor Inn

1/16-1/30	1P: $60	2P: $125	XP: $6	F17
1/31-4/15	1P: $60-$90	2P: $60-$90	XP: $6	F17
12/1-1/15 & 4/16-11/30	1P: $50	2P: $70	XP: $6	F17

Location: I-75, exit 54, 0.5 mi w on SR 582. 8602 Morris Bridge Rd 33617. Fax: 813/988-3552. **Facility:** 122 units. 2 stories, exterior corridors. **Terms:** cancellation fee imposed, package plans. **Amenities:** extended cable TV. *Some:* hair dryers. **Guest Services:** [CP] meal plan available, valet laundry. **Business Services:** meeting rooms, fax. **Cards:** AE, CB, DI, DS, MC, VI.

SOME UNITS

FEE FEE

SUPER 8 MOTEL-TAMPA

Phone: (813)933-4545 — **67**

AAA SAVE

♦♦ ♦♦

Motel

| All Year | 1P: $43-$56 | | XP: $5 | F10 |

Location: I-275, exit 35, just w. 321 E Fletcher Ave 33612. Fax: 813/935-4118. **Facility:** 100 units, 20 with efficiency. Some suites ($57-$85). 2 stories, exterior corridors. **Terms:** weekly rates available. **Amenities:** extended cable TV. *Some:* irons, hair dryers. **Guest Services:** coin laundry. **Cards:** AE, CB, DI, DS, MC, VI. **Special Amenities:** free continental breakfast and free room upgrade (subject to availability with advanced reservations).

SOME UNITS

TAMPA AIRPORT MARRIOTT

Phone: (813)879-5151 — **52**

♦♦ ♦♦ ♦

Hotel

Property failed to provide current rates

Location: I-275, exit 20 southbound; exit 20B northbound, 2 mi w on SR 60 to Tampa International Airport. Tampa International Airport 33607. Fax: 813/873-0945. **Facility:** Lobby access to airport and boutiques. 296 units. Some suites. *Bath:* combo or shower only. 8 stories, interior corridors. **Parking:** valet. **Terms:** package plans. **Amenities:** voice mail, irons, hair dryers. **Dining:** CK's Restaurant, see separate listing. **Leisure Activities:** heated pool, exercise room. **Guest Services:** [BP] meal plan available, gift shop, valet laundry. **Business Services:** conference facilities, administrative services, fax. *Fee:* PC. **Cards:** AE, CB, DI, DS, JC, MC, VI.

SOME UNITS

FEE FEE

VALUE INN

Phone: (813)933-6760 — **10**

AAA SAVE

♦♦ ♦♦

Motel

1/31-4/30	1P: $59-$65	2P: $69-$75	XP: $5	F10
5/1-9/30	1P: $49-$55	2P: $59-$65	XP: $5	F10
10/1-11/30	1P: $45-$55	2P: $55-$65	XP: $5	F10
12/1-1/30		2P: $45-$55	XP: $5	F10

Location: I-275, exit 33, 1.5 mi e on SR 580. 2523 E Busch Blvd 33612. Fax: 813/933-2372. **Facility:** 40 units. 2 stories, exterior corridors. **Terms:** 3 day cancellation notice, $4 service charge. **Cards:** AE, CB, DI, DS, MC, VI.

SOME UNITS

WELLESLEY INN & SUITES

Phone: (813)637-8990 — **54**

AAA SAVE

♦♦ ♦♦

Suite Motel

| All Year | 1P: $99-$199 | 2P: $99-$199 | XP: $10 | F18 |

Location: I-275, exit 21 southbound; exit 20A northbound, 1 mi n on Kennedy Blvd, 1.3 mi w. 1805 N Westshore Blvd 33607. Fax: 813/637-8991. **Facility:** Inviting exterior architectural design with pillared entry. Very classy, elegant lobby area with beautiful use of dark woods and marble. Rooms are inviting, contemporary design with separate living room area. 133 efficiencies. Some whirlpool units. *Bath:* combo or shower only. 3 stories, interior corridors. **Terms:** weekly rates available, package plans, pets ($15 extra charge). **Amenities:** video games, dual phone lines, voice mail, irons, hair dryers. **Leisure Activities:** heated pool, exercise room, barbeque grill, picnic area. **Guest Services:** [ECP] meal plan available, valet and coin laundry. **Business Services:** meeting rooms, fax. **Cards:** AE, CB, DI, DS, JC, MC, VI. **Special Amenities:** free continental breakfast and free local telephone calls.

(See color ad opposite title page)

SOME UNITS

(See map p. 805)

WINGATE INN-TAMPA NORTH

♦♦♦ 1/1-11/30   1P: $89-$109   2P: $89-$119   XP: $10   **68**
         12/1-12/31   1P: $79-$99   2P: $79-$99   XP: $5   F16
Motor Inn   **Location:** I-75, exit 56, just n on Bruce B Downs Blvd. 17301 Dona Michelle Dr 33647. **Fax:** 813/910-0950. **Facility:** 85 units. Some suites ($119-$189) and whirlpool units ($149-$189). *Bath:* combo or shower only. 4 stories, interior corridors. **Terms:** cancellation fee imposed, package plans. **Amenities:** web TV, video games, dual phone lines, voice mail, safes, irons, hair dryers. **Leisure Activities:** whirlpool, exercise room. **Guest Services:** [ECP] meal plan available, complimentary evening beverages: Mon-Thurs, area transportation. **Business Services:** meeting rooms, administrative services, PC, fax. **Cards:** AE, DI, DS, JC, MC, VI.

SOME UNITS

🅰🆂🅺 🆂🅳 🍴 ♿ 🅸 🕮 🏊 🎥 🖨 💻 🔌 DATA PORT / ✖ 📠 /
                         FEE

WINGATE INN-USF NEAR BUSCH GARDENS

♦♦♦ 1/24-4/10   1P: $80-$110   2P: $85-$115   XP: $10   **23**
       12/1-1/23 & 4/11-11/30   1P: $70-$90   2P: $75-$95   XP: $10   F17
Motel   **Location:** I-275, exit 34, 2.2 mi e. 3751 E Fowler Ave 33612. **Fax:** 813/977-1818. **Facility:** 84 units. Some suites ($100-$160) and whirlpool units ($100-$160). 4 stories, interior corridors. **Terms:** 3 day cancellation notice, monthly rates available, package plans. **Amenities:** extended cable TV, video games, voice mail, safes, irons, hair dryers. **Leisure Activities:** whirlpool, exercise room. **Guest Services:** [ECP] meal plan available, area transportation, valet and coin laundry. **Business Services:** meeting rooms, administrative services, PC, fax. **Cards:** AE, DI, DS, JC, MC, VI.

SOME UNITS

🅰🆂🅺 🆂🅳 🍴 ♿ 🅸 🕮 🏊 🎥 🖨 💻 🔌 DATA PORT / ✖ 📼 📠 🔓 /
                         FEE

THE WYNDHAM HARBOUR ISLAND HOTEL

♦♦♦♦ 1/1-4/29   2P: $139   XP: $20   **29**
       12/1-12/31 & 10/1-11/30   2P: $99-$129   XP: $20   F18
Hotel   4/30-9/30   2P: $99-$119   XP: $20   F18
      Location: I-275, exit 25 (Tampa St), 2 mi e, follow signs to Harbour Island; opposite Convention Center. 725 S Harbour Island Blvd 33602. **Fax:** 813/229-5322. **Facility:** In up-scale office/commercial development. 300 units. Some suites. 12 stories, interior corridors. **Parking:** extra charge or valet. **Terms:** 3 day cancellation notice-fee imposed, package plans. **Amenities:** voice mail, honor bars, irons, hair dryers. **Dining:** Harbour View Room, see separate listing. **Leisure Activities:** heated pool, charter fishing, exercise room. *Fee:* boat dock. **Business Services:** conference facilities, PC, fax. **Cards:** AE, CB, DI, DS, JC, MC, VI. *(See color ad below)*

SOME UNITS

🅰🆂🅺 🆂🅳 ✈ 🍴 🍸 🛗 🏊 ✖ 🎥 🖨 💻 🔌 DATA PORT / ✖ 📼 📠 🔓 /
            FEE   FEE   FEE

WYNDHAM WESTSHORE

AAA [SAVE] 1/1-4/29   1P: $111-$118   XP: $20   **41**
             12/1-12/31   1P: $94-$108   F18
♦♦♦ 10/1-11/30   1P: $94-$108   XP: $20   F18
          4/30-9/30   1P: $83-$100   XP: $20   F18
Hotel   **Location:** I-275, exit 21, 0.5 mi s; at jct SR 60 and Westshore Blvd. 4860 W Kennedy Blvd 33609-2591. **Fax:** 813/286-4053. **Facility:** 324 units. Some suites. 11 stories, interior corridors. **Parking:** valet. **Terms:** 3 day cancellation notice-fee imposed, package plans. **Amenities:** voice mail, irons, hair dryers. **Dining:** 3 restaurants, 6 am-2 am, sports bar, deli, $9-$15, cocktails, also, Shula's Steakhouse, see separate listing, entertainment. **Leisure Activities:** heated pool, jogging, exercise room, salon, florist, cigar shop. *Fee:* health club privileges, shoe shine. **Guest Services:** gift shop, area transportation, valet laundry. *Fee:* massage. **Business Services:** conference facilities, administrative services, fax. *Fee:* PC. **Cards:** AE, CB, DI, DS, JC, MC, VI. **Special Amenities:** early check-in/late check-out and preferred room (subject to availability with advanced reservations).** *(See color ad below)*

SOME UNITS

🆂🅳 ✈ 🍴 🍸 🛗 🏊 ✖ 🎥 🖨 💻 🔌 DATA PORT / ✖ 📼 🔓 /
                  FEE   FEE

(See map p. 805)

———— *The following lodging was either not evaluated or did not* ————
meet AAA rating requirements but is listed for your information only.

MARRIOTT-TAMPA WESTSHORE
[fyi]   Does not meet all AAA rating requirements for property operations; previously evaluated on 12/03/1999.
                         Location: I-275, exit 21 southbound; exit 20A northbound, 1 mi n on Kennedy Blvd, 0.9 mi w. 1001 N Westshore Blvd
Hotel   33607. Facilities, services, and decor characterize a mid-range property.

———— **WHERE TO DINE** ————

42ND STREET THE BISTRO   **Lunch:** $7-$18   **Dinner:** $7-$18   **Phone:** 813/253-0042   65
▼▼▼   **Location:** I-275, exit 24, 1 mi s on Armenia Ave, just e on Azeele, 0.6 mi s on Howard Ave at jct W De Leon St. 516 S
                   Howard Ave 33606. **Hours:** 11:30 am-11 pm, Tues & Wed-midnight, Thurs & Fri-1 am, Sat noon-1 am, Sun 4
American   pm-10 pm. **Features:** casual dress; cocktails & lounge; a la carte. Very trendy and upscale establishment
                   with New York Broadway type theme and city library look to setting. Very well thought out menu offers
"show stoppers", gourmet pizza, salad, variety of entrees. **Cards:** AE, DI, DS, MC, VI.

A J CATFISH   **Lunch:** $5-$15   **Dinner:** $5-$15   **Phone:** 813/932-3474   77
▼▼▼   **Location:** 1.7 mi w of jct Waters Ave. 8751 N Hines Ave 33614. **Hours:** 11:30 am-10 pm, Fri-11 pm, Sat 5 pm-11
                   pm, Sun 5 pm-10 pm. Closed: 4/15, 12/25; also Mon. **Features:** casual dress; children's menu; cocktails; a
Seafood   la carte. This rustic fish shanty offers catfish favorites along with a host of other seafood choices. Start with
                   the gator bites topped with a rich barbecue sauce for a tangy, deep-fried taste of Florida. Efficient,
thorough service makes sure you dine at ease. **Cards:** AE, DI, DS, MC, VI.   ✕

ARIGATO JAPANESE STEAK HOUSE   **Dinner:** $10-$22   **Phone:** 813/960-5050   6
▼▼▼   **Location:** US 92, just w of jct Fletcher Ave. 13755 N Dale Mabry Hwy 33618. **Hours:** 5 pm-10 pm, Fri & Sat-10:30
                   pm. Closed major holidays; also Christmas Eve. **Features:** casual dress; children's menu; early bird
Japanese   specials; cocktails & lounge. Traditional floor seating lends an air of authenticity as you enjoy the
                   showmanship of professional table-side chefs. You may need to wait for group seatings, but Japanese
entrees like ichiban, a spicy mix of shrimp, chicken and beef, are well worth it. **Cards:** AE, DI, DS, MC, VI.

ARMANI'S   **Dinner:** $23-$35   **Phone:** 813/281-9165   25
▼▼▼ ▼▼▼   **Location:** SR 60 at east end of Courtney Campbell Cswy; in Hyatt Regency Westshore. 6200 Courtney Campbell
                   Cswy 33607. **Hours:** 6 pm-10 pm, Fri & Sat-11 pm. Closed: Sun. **Reservations:** required. **Features:** formal
Northern   attire; cocktails & lounge; valet parking; a la carte. Choose your own salad or ask the waiter to bring
Italian   selections from the elegant antipasto bar. Enjoy view from top floor of the hotel overlooking Old Tampa
                   Bay. A well-mannered staff caters to your every whim. The seafood medley is artfully done. Smoke free
premises. **Cards:** AE, CB, DI, DS, JC, MC, VI.   🔥 ✕

BAY CAFE   **Lunch:** $9   **Dinner:** $8-$20   **Phone:** 813/875-1555   48
AAA   **Location:** I-275, exit 21 southbound; exit 20A northbound, 1 mi n on Kennedy Blvd, 0.5 mi w; in Embassy Suites
▼▼-2   Hotel-Tampa/Airport/Westshore. 555 N Westshore Blvd 33609. **Hours:** 11:30 am-2 & 5-10 pm.
                   Reservations: suggested; weekends. **Features:** casual dress; children's menu; early bird specials;
American   cocktails & lounge. An extensive menu offers many choices from such favorites as surf and turf to chicken
                   and shrimp with pasta. Fresh flowers on every table and contemporary paintings contribute to the tropical
                   theme, with mohogany wood. The atrium is a delightful dining getaway. **Cards:** AE, CB, DI, DS, MC, VI.
                                                                                                            ✕

BERN'S STEAK HOUSE   **Dinner:** $23-$35   **Phone:** 813/251-2421   72
▼▼▼▼   **Location:** I-275, exit 24, 1 mi s on Armenia Ave, just e on Azeele, 0.8 mi s, under overpass. 1208 S Howard Ave
                   33606. **Hours:** 5 pm-1 pm. Closed: 12/25. **Reservations:** suggested. **Features:** dressy casual; cocktails &
Steak House   lounge; fee for valet parking. A local landmark, it is renowned for its beef entrees. Guests are invited to
                   tour the kitchen and wine cellar before dinner. A comprehensive wine list and a separate dessert lounge
make the visit enjoyable. A 12% gratuity is added in the dining room. **Cards:** AE, CB, DI, DS, MC, VI.   ✕

BOCA   **Lunch:** $14-$26   **Dinner:** $14-$26   **Phone:** 813/241-2622   36
▼▼▼▼   **Location:** I-4, exit 1, 0.5 mi e on 22nd Ave, just s on 7th Ave; in Ybor City. 1930 E 7th Ave 33605. **Hours:** 11:30
                   am-2:30 & 6-10:30 pm, Sat from 6 pm. Closed: 4/15, 11/22, 12/25; also Sun & Mon. **Features:** dressy
Continental   casual; cocktails; a la carte. Upscale, trendy atmosphere with an art deco feel. Creative dishes with
                   decorative presentation include seafood, cisotto, wildgame and duckling. Smoke free premises. **Cards:** AE,
DI, DS, MC, VI.   ✕

THE CACTUS CLUB SOUTHWESTERN GRILL & BAR   **Lunch:** $7-$16 **Dinner:** $7-$16 **Phone:** 813/251-4089 59
▼▼ ▼▼   **Location:** In Old Hyde Park; at jct Dakota. 1601 Snow Ave 33606. **Hours:** 11 am-10:30 pm, Fri & Sat-11:30 pm,
                   Sun-10 pm. Closed: 11/22, 12/25. **Features:** casual dress; children's menu; carryout; cocktails & lounge;
Southwestern   street parking; a la carte. Munch on sizzling fajitas at this casual eatery. Outdoor cafe-style seating is
                   available to enjoy a wide choice of border favorites in the fresh air. At this attractive spot, service is first
rate and will keep you coming back for more. **Cards:** AE, CB, DI, MC, VI.   ✕

CAFE CREOLE   **Lunch:** $6-$9   **Dinner:** $12-$17   **Phone:** 813/247-6283   39
▼▼▼   **Location:** I-4, exit 1, just s to 8th Ave, 0.5 mi w to 13th St, just n. 1330 9th Ave 33605. **Hours:** 11:30 am-10 pm,
                   Fri-11:30 pm, Sat 5 pm-11:30 pm. Closed major holidays; also Sun. **Features:** casual dress; children's
Cajun   menu; carryout; cocktails & lounge; street parking; a la carte. Why go to New Orleans when you can taste
                   authentic Cajun and Creole cuisine in the lively historic setting of Ybor City? Feast on oysters Bienville,
jambalaya and crawfish etouffe in the courtyard dining area. Wonderful service will enhance your meal. **Cards:** AE, DI, DS,
MC, VI.   ✕

(See map p. 805)

CAFE EUROPEAN

Continental

Lunch: $5-$8   **Dinner:** $8-$17   **Phone:** 813/254-9458   [34]

Location: Opposite entrance to University of Tampa; just s of jct Kennedy Blvd. 113 Hyde Park Ave 33606. **Hours:** 11 am-2:30 & 5:30-9 pm, Fri-11 pm, Sat 5:30 pm-11 pm. Closed: 4/15, 12/25; also Sun. **Reservations:** suggested. **Features:** casual dress; carryout; beer & wine only; street parking; a la carte. This family-operated restaurant dedicates itself to preparing traditional foods with a European flair. Good, basic meals in a pleasant cafe setting include delicious fish and chips served hot and fast. Kids may choose from an available children's menu. **Cards:** AE, MC, VI.

CAFE WINBERIE

American

Lunch: $6-$12   **Dinner:** $6-$14   **Phone:** 813/253-6500   [54]

Location: In Old Hyde Park; at jct Snow Ave. 1610 W Swann Ave 33606. **Hours:** 11 am-11 pm, Fri & Sat-midnight, Sun-10:30 pm. **Features:** casual dress; children's menu; cocktails & lounge; a la carte. Offered in a cafe-style setting, an eclectic menu displays a distinctly European influence. Start with fried pita chips covered with feta cheese and an avocado-scallion dip; then for a moist, tender entree, select the salmon prepared in parchment paper. **Cards:** AE, CB, DI, DS, MC, VI.

CAFFE PARADISO

Northern
Italian

Dinner: $8-$24   **Phone:** 813/835-6622   [76]

Location: In St Croix's Plaza; 0.5 mi w of jct W Gandy Blvd. 4205 S MacDill 33611. **Hours:** 5:30 pm-10:30 pm. Closed: Sun. **Features:** casual dress; cocktails & lounge; a la carte. Elegant, chic and intimate, this ristorante is the place to go on special occasions. You will find traditional appetizers, whole or half orders of pasta, red snapper and veal piccata, all nicely done and expertly served by a trained and cordial staff. Smoke free premises. **Cards:** AE, CB, DI, DS, MC, VI.

THE CASTAWAY

Seafood

Lunch: $6-$12   **Dinner:** $11-$20   **Phone:** 813/281-0770   [21]

Location: I-275, exit 20A northbound; exit 21 southbound, 3.3 mi w on SR 60. 7720 Courtney Campbell Cswy 33607. **Hours:** 11 am-10:30 pm, Sun 9:30 am-2:30 & 5-10 pm. **Features:** casual dress; Sunday brunch; children's menu; early bird specials; cocktails & lounge; a la carte. Bright Caribbean decor enlivens the breezy, bayfront setting. The Thai-style whole snapper, drenched in a spicy yet sweet chili sauce and served with a head and tail, gets your taste buds jumping. The rich tiramisu settles them back down. **Cards:** AE, CB, DI, DS, MC, VI.

CK'S RESTAURANT

Continental

Dinner: $14-$26   **Phone:** 813/878-6500   [19]

Location: I-275, exit 20 southbound; exit 20B northbound, 2 mi w on SR 60 to Tampa International Airport; in Tampa Airport Marriott. **Hours:** 5 pm-10 pm, Fri & Sat-11 pm, Sun 10:30 am-2:30 & 5-10 pm. **Reservations:** suggested; weekends. **Features:** casual dress; Sunday brunch; children's menu; early bird specials; cocktails & lounge; fee for parking; valet parking; a la carte. A revolving, rooftop restaurant, it affords panoramic views of Tampa Bay, the airport and the downtown skyline. Try a nice presentation of the grilled pork chop with new potatoes and a vegetable medley, topped off with a moist carrot cake and an espresso. **Cards:** AE, CB, DI, DS, JC, MC, VI.

CODY'S ORIGINAL ROADHOUSE

Steak House

Dinner: $6-$16   **Phone:** 813/855-2787   [78]

Location: 1.9 mi w on SR 580, from jct Memorial Hwy; in Silver Mill Plaza. 11202 W Hillsborough Ave 33635. **Hours:** 3:30 pm-11 pm. **Features:** casual dress; children's menu; early bird specials; carryout; cocktails & lounge; a la carte. Rustic decor with lots of use of hardwoods and old nostalgic type of signs give this a "road house" feel. Welcoming and efficient staff assist in a nice dining experience. Menu offers many things such as ribs steaks, chicken, chops, burgers, and sandwiches. The fajitas are an experience. **Cards:** MC, VI.

THE COLONNADE

Seafood

Lunch: $6-$21   **Dinner:** $6-$21   **Phone:** 813/839-7558   [73]

Location: I-275, exit 23B, 4.2 mi s, 1.2 mi e on W Gandy, 1.3 mi n. 3401 Bayshore Blvd 33629. **Hours:** 11 am-10 pm, Fri & Sat-11 pm. Closed: 11/22, 12/25. **Features:** casual dress; children's menu; early bird specials; carryout; cocktails & lounge. Established in 1935, the warm and friendly atmosphere makes this a comfy place to savor a meal while enjoying panoramas of downtown Tampa from across the bay. The shrimp sampler platter is a favorite, as is the delectable chocolate bourbon pecan pie. **Cards:** AE, DI, DS, MC, VI.

COLUMBIA RESTAURANT   Historical

Spanish

Lunch: $6-$15   **Dinner:** $14-$22   **Phone:** 813/248-4961   [43]

Location: I-4, exit 1, in Ybor City; on 7th Ave at 22nd St. 2117 E 7th Ave 33605. **Hours:** 11 am-10 pm, Fri & Sat-11 pm, Sun noon-9 pm. **Features:** casual dress; children's menu; carryout; cocktails & lounge; entertainment; valet parking; a la carte. This is the original Columbia restaurant established in 1905. Situated in Ybor City, it is a popular tourist destination surrounded by clubs and shops. Flamenco dancing and Spanish cuisine are enjoyed in a spacious dining area that seats 1,600. **Cards:** AE, DI, DS, MC, VI.

CRABBY TOM'S OLD TIME OYSTER BAR & SEAFOOD RESTAURANT

Seafood

Lunch: $4-$18   **Dinner:** $4-$18   **Phone:** 813/961-3499   [2]

Location: I-275, exit 23A, 8.4 mi n. 14404 N Dale Mabry 33618. **Hours:** 11 am-10 pm, Fri & Sat-11 pm, Sun noon-9 pm. Closed: 4/15, 11/22, 12/25. **Features:** casual dress; children's menu; early bird specials; carryout; cocktails & lounge; a la carte. Hardwood tables and floors give this nautical sports bar a comfortably worn air. Seafood is the favorite, and the chef will prepare your fish any way you like. The blackened seafood pasta is a marvel, with plenty to share or to take home. **Cards:** AE, DI, DS, MC, VI.

CRABBY TOM'S OLD TIME OYSTER BAR & SEAFOOD RESTAURANT

Seafood

Lunch: $4-$18   **Dinner:** $4-$18   **Phone:** 813/870-1652   [17]

Location: I-275, exit 30, 2.3 mi w on US 92. 3120 W Hillsborough Ave 33614. **Hours:** 11 am-10 pm, Fri & Sat-11 pm, Sun noon-9 pm. Closed: 4/15, 11/22, 12/25. **Features:** casual dress; children's menu; early bird specials; carryout; beer & wine only; a la carte. Come with an appetite and feast on all-you-can-eat snow crabs for a delicious treat. This sports bar with a nautical flair has plenty of TVs for catching the big game. Broiled or fried seafood are the best choices after a long, hard day at the beach. **Cards:** AE, DI, DS, MC, VI.

(See map p. 805)

CRAWDADDY'S

American

Dinner: $16-$36   **Phone:** 813/281-0407   **24**
Location: From east end of Courtney Campbell Cswy (SR 60); just s. 2500 Rocky Point Dr 33607. **Hours:** 5 pm-10 pm, Fri & Sat-11 pm. **Reservations:** suggested. **Features:** casual dress; children's menu; early bird specials; carryout; cocktails & lounge. In the spirit of the roaring '20s, this feisty fish camp dishes up spicy jambalaya and smashed bourbon sweet potatoes, both of which boast a decidedly New Orleans flavor. Menu features steak, poultry and seafood. Great views of Old Tampa Bay. **Cards:** AE, DI, DS, MC, VI.   ✖

DONATELLO
Northern Italian

Lunch: $9-$18   **Dinner:** $16-$29   **Phone:** 813/875-6660   **56**
Location: I-275, exit 23 northbound; exit 23B southbound, 0.5 mi s on SR 92 (N Dale Mabry). 232 N Dale Mabry Hwy 33609. **Hours:** Noon-3 & 6-11 pm, Sat & Sun from 6 pm. Closed major holidays. **Reservations:** suggested. **Features:** dressy casual; cocktails & lounge; entertainment; a la carte. Homemade pasta and veal specialties are the highlights on a menu of regional Italian dishes. A nicely seasoned chicken and yellow rice is a tasty choice, followed by a wonderful chocolate mousse cake. After dinner, retire to the cigar and piano bar. **Cards:** AE, DI, DS, MC, VI.   ✖

DON QUIXOTE CAFETERIA
English

Dinner: $6-$9   **Phone:** 813/248-3080   **42**
Location: I-4, exit 1, just e on 22nd Ave, 0.6 mi s on E Palm Ave, just e of 13th St; in Ybor Square. 1901 13th St 33605. **Hours:** 10:30 am-3 pm. Closed: 11/22, 12/25; also Sat & Sun. **Features:** casual dress; street parking; a la carte. Cuban cuisine served in hearty portions. Eclectic decor with variety of items. This rustic locale with wood beam ceilings and brick walls and floors, was once a cigar factory. **Cards:** AE, DI, DS, MC, VI.   ✖

DURANGO STEAKHOUSE
Steak House

Lunch: $6-$10   **Dinner:** $7-$18   **Phone:** 813/354-8413   **55**
Location: I-275, exit 23B, 0.8 mi s. 217 Dale Mabry Hwy S 33619. **Hours:** 11 am-10 pm, Fri & Sat-11 pm, Sun 11:30 am-9 pm. Closed: 11/22, 12/25. **Features:** casual dress; children's menu; carryout; cocktails & lounge; a la carte. Settle down to oak-grilled favorites at this Southwestern eatery. Start with a basket of tortilla chips and salsa to whet your appetite for a spicy meal. The combo fajita plate makes a grand entrance, sizzling with flavor and loaded with fresh toppings. **Cards:** AE, DI, DS, MC, VI.   ✖

ESTELA'S MEXICAN RESTAURANT
Mexican

Lunch: $4-$12   **Dinner:** $4-$12   **Phone:** 813/251-0558   **80**
Location: Center; on Davis Island. 209 E Davis Blvd 33606. **Hours:** 11 am-10 pm, Fri & Sat-11 pm. **Features:** casual dress; carryout; beer & wine only; a la carte. Quaint little Mexican cantina type setting reminiscent of a true Mexican eatery, set among the many eclectic shops of the area. The menu has many choices such as chimichanga, nachos, fajitas, huevos ranchero, chapala, quesadilla, poblano, burritos, soup, salads and chicken dishes. **Cards:** MC, VI.

FIRST CHOICE BAR-B-QUE
American

Lunch: $4-$8   **Dinner:** $4-$8   **Phone:** 813/621-7434   **46**
Location: I-75, exit 51, 0.5 mi w on SR 60. 10113 Adamo Dr 33619. **Hours:** 11 am-9 pm, Fri & Sat-10 pm, Sun noon-6 pm. Closed major holidays; also 5/14. **Features:** casual dress; carryout; a la carte. Listen as the meat sizzles on an open-pit grill for a traditional Southern barbecue. Locals flock here for the marvelous food and a staff that tends to your every need. Barbecue beef, pork, chicken, turkey, ham and sausage are all featured. **Cards:** AE, CB, DI, DS, MC, VI.

FIRST WATCH
American

Lunch: $5-$7   **Phone:** 813/975-1718   **11**
Location: I-75, exit 54, 6 mi w on Fowler Ave (SR 582); in University Collection. 2726 E Fowler Ave. **Hours:** 7 am-2:30 pm. Closed: 11/22, 12/25. **Features:** casual dress; children's menu; carryout. Smooth service and an excellent breakfast menu make this a family favorite. Hefty portions of waffles, eggs, crepes and omelets are served during the morning hours, and salad, soups and sandwiches round out the lunch menu. Healthy options are listed, too.

FIRST WATCH
American

Lunch: $5-$7   **Phone:** 813/307-9006   **29**
Location: Downtown; at jct Twiggs St. 520 Tampa St 33602. **Hours:** 7 am-2:30 pm. Closed: 11/22, 12/25. **Features:** No A/C; children's menu; carryout; street parking. Pancakes and crepes fill the plates and are only two types of varied breakfast entrees that make regulars out of first-time guests. Fruit and salad options for the health-conscious and sandwiches you need both hands to hold please the lunch crowd. Smoke free premises. **Cards:** AE, DS, MC, VI.   ✖

FRONTIER STEAK HOUSE
Steak House

Dinner: $9-$31   **Phone:** 813/621-3050   **22**
Location: I-4, exit 6, westbound; exit 6A eastbound, 0.9 mi n on US 301, just w. 8602 E Sligh Ave 33610. **Hours:** 3 pm-10 pm, Fri & Sat-11 pm. **Features:** casual dress; early bird specials; cocktails; entertainment; a la carte. A local favorite. Don't expect quick service here, but the steaks are wonderful. The "six pound challenge" is what they're famous for. Other items available are chicken, chops, ribs, lobster tail, and a variety of salads, appetizers and desserts. **Cards:** AE, DI, DS, MC, VI.

HARBOUR VIEW ROOM
American

Lunch: $9-$14   **Dinner:** $15-$25   **Phone:** 813/229-5001   **66**
Location: I-275, exit 25 (Tampa St), 2 mi e following signs to Harbour Island; opposite Convention Center; in The Wyndham Harbour Island Hotel. 725 S Harbour Island Blvd 33602. **Hours:** 6:30-11 am, 11:30-2 & 6-11 pm. **Reservations:** suggested. **Features:** casual dress; Sunday brunch; children's menu; cocktails & lounge; fee for parking & valet parking; a la carte. This popular pasta bar keeps the working crowd well-fed at lunch. An attractive dining room overlooks Hillsborough Bay. A colorful mixed green salad accompanies the meal. Order the grilled sirloin steak sandwich, which is topped with a zesty sauce. **Cards:** AE, CB, DI, DS, JC, MC, VI.   ✖

HO HO WINDOWS
Chinese

Lunch: $6-$13   **Dinner:** $6-$13   **Phone:** 813/254-9557   **63**
Location: I-275, exit 24, 1 mi s on Armenia Ave just e on Azeele, 0.4 mi s; in Whaley's Market Place. 533 S Howard Ave 33606. **Hours:** 11:30 am-9:45 pm, Fri-10:45 pm, Sat 4 pm-10:45 pm, Sun from 4 pm. Closed: 7/4, 11/22, 12/25. **Features:** casual dress; children's menu; carryout; beer & wine only; a la carte, buffet. Contemporary and inviting decor welcomes you to this oriental restaurant. Very expansive menu with at least seventy five items to choose such as - mandarin beef, General Tzo chicken, spicy vegetable, dragon in the nest, honey chicken, mo pu tofu Peking beef to name a few of the chef's suggestions. Smoke free premises. **Cards:** AE, DI, DS, MC, VI.   ✖

(See map p. 805)

HOPS RESTAURANT BAR & BREWERY
Lunch: $7-$17   **Dinner:** $7-$17   **Phone:** 813/632-0717   8

▼▼▼
American
Location: I-275, exit 34, 0.5 mi e on SR 582. 1241 E Fowler Ave 33612. **Hours:** 11 am-11 pm, Fri & Sat-midnight, Sun-10 pm. Closed: Sun. **Features:** casual dress; children's menu; cocktails & lounge. Famous for their on-site microbrewery - fresh from scratch menu items include steak, filet mignon, rib-eye, pork chops, prime rib and top sirloin. Try the baby back ribs, grilled chichen, pasta dishes, burger or sandwich.
Cards: AE, DI, DS, MC, VI.

HUGO'S SPANISH RESTAURANT
Lunch: $4-$10   **Dinner:** $4-$10   **Phone:** 813/251-2842   67

▼▼
Spanish
Location: I-275, exit 24, 1 mi s on Armenia Ave, just e on Azeele, 0.6 mi s at jct W Morrison Ave. 931 S Howard Ave 33606. **Hours:** 11 am-9 pm, Sat from 7:30 am. Closed: Sun. **Features:** casual dress; carryout; beer only; a la carte. In Hyde Park area since 1975, known for it's Cubans and black beans and rice. Menu also has steak and chicken choices, Italian and sandwiches. **Cards:** MC, VI.

JACKSON'S BISTRO-BAR & SUSHI
Lunch: $7-$12   **Dinner:** $13-$21   **Phone:** 813/277-0339   64

▼▼▼
American
Location: I-275, exit 25, 2 mi e on Tampa St to Harbour Island; in Knights Point. 601 S Harbor Island Blvd 33602. **Hours:** 11:30 am-2:30 & 5-11 pm, Sat noon-2:30 & 5-11 pm, Sun from 10:30 am. **Features:** dressy casual; Sunday brunch; cocktails & lounge; entertainment; fee for parking & valet parking; a la carte. On the waterfront in trendy complex of shops and businesses. This very upscale appearing restaurant is beautifully decorated. Many choices of expertly prepared items by trained chefs. Dessert is a must! Try the scrumptious raspberry macadamia nut pie! **Cards:** AE, DS, MC, VI.

JASMINE THAI RESTAURANT
Lunch: $6-$9   **Dinner:** $6-$19   **Phone:** 813/968-1501   1

▼▼
Thai
Location: I-275, exit 23A northbound; 8 mi e; in the Village Center. 13248 N Dale Mabry Hwy 33618. **Hours:** 11:30 am-10:30 pm, Fri & Sat-11 pm, Sun-10 pm. Closed: 11/22; also Super Bowl Sun. **Features:** casual dress; carryout; beer & wine only; a la carte. Thai cuisine is served in very attractive surroundings by a pleasant wait staff. Try the duck mixed with mushroom caps, corn and broccoli and garnished with a butterfly-shaped carrot. You will find several nice touches during this excellent meal. **Cards:** AE, DS, MC, VI.

JIMMY MAC'S MARINA RESTAURANT
Lunch: $6-$21   **Dinner:** $6-$21   **Phone:** 813/839-3449   7

▼▼
Seafood
Location: At the e end of the Gandy Bridge, 0.5 mi w of jct W Shore Blvd. 5000 W Gandy Blvd 33611. **Hours:** 11 am-10 pm, Thurs-Sat to midnight, Sun noon-midnight. **Features:** casual dress; children's menu; early bird specials; carryout; cocktails & lounge. Beautiful marina setting with great views of boats and sunsets. A nautical decor with lots of wood enhancements. Menu is extensive with many appetizers, rawbar items, steamers, salads, soups, sandwiches, burgers, fresh fish, steak and chicken - something for everyone. **Cards:** MC, VI.

LAURO RISTORANTE ITALIANO
Lunch: $7-$10   **Dinner:** $12-$23   **Phone:** 813/281-2100   53

▼▼▼
Northern
Italian
Location: I-275, exit 23B southbound, 1.5 mi w to Henderson Blvd, just s. 3915 Henderson Blvd 33629. **Hours:** 11:30 am-2 & 5:30-close. Closed: 1/1; also Sun. **Features:** dressy casual; cocktails & lounge; entertainment. Private parties are welcome in this quaint eatery. A wide selection of pasta, fish and meat dishes is served by a staff that is well-trained to meet guests' needs. Fresh, crisp salads served with sliced bread will really whet your appetite. **Cards:** AE, CB, DI, DS, MC, VI.

LE BORDEAUX
Dinner: $17-$33   **Phone:** 813/254-4387   74

▼▼▼
French
MC, VI.
Location: I-275, exit 24, 1 mi s on Armenia Ave, just e on Azeele, 1 mi s. 1502 S Howard Ave 33606. **Hours:** 5 pm-11 pm. Closed: 1/1, 12/25. **Features:** dressy casual; cocktails & lounge; entertainment; street parking & valet parking; a la carte. Bistro setting with cozy romantic decor and seating. Variety of freshly prepared and artfully displayed entrees such as roast duckling, baby lamb, veal chops and salmon. **Cards:** AE, DI,

LEMONGRASS RESTAURANT
Lunch: $5-$15   **Dinner:** $6-$15   **Phone:** 813/971-0854   12

▼▼▼
Vietnamese
Location: I-275, exit 34, 1.5 mi e; in Fowler Plaza South. 2373 E Fowler Ave 33612. **Hours:** 11:30 am-2:30 & 4:30-10 pm. Closed: 11/22, 12/25; also Sun. **Features:** casual dress; senior's menu; carryout; beer & wine only; a la carte, buffet. Traditional artwork and decor characterizes this intimate Vietnamese restaurant. A lunch buffet features such tasty favorites as chicken wings, white rice, pork, fried squash and puffed sugar pastry. Or make a selection from the full menu. **Cards:** AE, DS, MC, VI.

LOGAN'S ROADHOUSE
Dinner: $6-$23   **Phone:** 813/884-5229   14

▼▼ ▼▼
Steak House
Location: Just s of jct Linebaugh. 9218 Anderson 33612. **Hours:** 11 am-10 pm, Fri & Sat-11 pm. **Features:** casual dress; children's menu; cocktails & lounge. Rustic effects enhance this replica of an old "road house" with a relaxed atmosphere. Friendly wait staff ready to assist you. The menu has many offerings such as appetizers, salad, sandwiches, burgers, chicken, ribs, steak and dessert. The porterhouse is quite good. **Cards:** MC, VI.

LONNI'S SANDWICHES, ETC
Lunch: $3-$7   **Phone:** 813/223-2333   69

▼▼
American
Location: Downtown; just n of jct Tampa St. 513 E Jackson St 33602. **Hours:** 9 am-4 pm. Closed major holidays; also Sat & Sun. **Features:** street parking. Sandwich shop setting with variety of sandwiches, salads and soups. A local favorite. Smoke free premises. **Cards:** AE.

MISE EN PLACE
Lunch: $6-$10   **Dinner:** $13-$23   **Phone:** 813/254-5373   35

▼▼▼
American
Location: I-275, exit 25, 0.4 mi s on Ashley, 0.3 mi w on Kennedy; in Grand Central Place; opposite University of Tampa. 442 W Kennedy Blvd 33606. **Hours:** 11 am-3 & 5:30-10 pm, Mon-3 pm, Fri-11 pm, Sat 5:30 pm-11 pm. Closed major holidays; also Sun. **Reservations:** accepted; dinner. **Features:** dressy casual; carryout; cocktails & lounge; street parking; a la carte. This trendy bistro features expertly created dishes with a Mediterranean flair. An interesting grilled grouper chili with a cheese-filled pasta base is wonderfully presented. An appealing lunch menu is also offered. This is a smoke-free dining area. **Cards:** AE, CB, DI, DS, MC, VI.

(See map p. 805)

THE OLD MEETING HOUSE
Dinner: $4-$8 **Phone:** 813/251-1754 ⑥⓪

American

Location: I-275, exit 24, 1 mi s on Armenia Ave, just e on Azeele, 0.6 mi s. 901 S Howard Ave 33606. **Hours:** 7 am-10:30 pm, Fri & Sat-11:30 pm. Closed: 12/25. **Features:** casual dress. Established in 1947, a local-favorite for its '40-'50s look, ice cream, home cooked entrees and daily blue plate specials.

OVO CAFE
Lunch: $10-$16 **Dinner:** $10-$16 **Phone:** 813/248-6979 ④④

American

Location: I-4, exit 1, just e on 21st St, just s; in Ybor City. 1907 E 7th Ave 33607. **Hours:** 11 am-3 pm, Tues-Thurs & Sun-9 pm, Fri & Sat-midnight. Closed major holidays. **Features:** casual dress; cocktails & lounge; street parking; a la carte. This trendy place in Ybor City attracts the younger party crowd. Appetizing menu choices and many low-cal delights keep you light on your feet for dancing all night. Opt for the white-wine barbecue pizza for a twist on traditional late-night pig-out food. **Cards:** AE, DI, DS, MC, VI.

OYSTERCATCHERS
Lunch: $8-$12 **Dinner:** $12-$30 **Phone:** 813/281-9116 ②⑥

Seafood

Location: SR 60 at east end of Courtney Campbell Cswy; in Hyatt Regency Westshore. 6200 Courtney Campbell Cswy 33607. **Hours:** 11:30 am-2:30 & 6-10 pm, Sun 10:30 am-2:45 pm. **Reservations:** suggested. **Features:** casual dress; Sunday brunch; children's menu; cocktails & lounge; entertainment; valet parking; a la carte. This dramatic location overlooks the salt marshes of Old Tampa Bay. Market-fresh seafood and Cajun dishes will spice up any evening. The fried calamari appetizer is excellently breaded and lightly fried. Enjoy the view and the prompt, attentive service. **Cards:** AE, CB, DI, DS, JC, MC, VI.

RAGIN' RIBS
Lunch: $6-$15 **Dinner:** $6-$15 **Phone:** 813/259-1501 ⑦⓪

American

Location: I-275, exit 24, 1 mi s on Armenia Ave, just e. 2307 Azeele St 33606. **Hours:** 11 am-10 pm, Fri & Sat-11 pm, Sun noon-10 pm. Closed: 1/1, 12/25. **Features:** casual dress; carryout. Very simple decor but out of this world ribs! Fabulous sauce used to enhance specialties such as pork and baby back beef ribs, wings, barbecue sandwiches, roasted chicken. Salad and dessert also are available. **Cards:** AE, DI, DS, MC, VI.

REMINGTON'S STEAKHOUSE
Dinner: $9-$21 **Phone:** 813/972-1646 ⑤①

Steak House

Location: I-75, exit 55, 3.8 mi w on Fletcher, 0.5 mi n on Bruce B Downs, just w on Bearss Ave. 2836 E Bearss Ave 33613. **Hours:** 4 pm-10 pm, Fri & Sat-11 pm. **Features:** casual dress. Rustic Western decor with setting of Western town as interior design. Exterior looks like a rustic barn and the landscaping is very nice for good roadside appeal. A varied menu with choices like steak, ribs, chicken, pork chops and fajitas. Also an array of appetizers, salads and desserts. **Cards:** MC, VI.

ROYAL PALACE THAI RESTAURANT
Lunch: $9-$16 **Dinner:** $9-$16 **Phone:** 813/258-5893 ⑤⑦

Thai

Location: I-275, exit 24, 1 mi s on Armenia Ave, just e on Azeele, 0.7 mi s. 811 S Howard Ave 33606. **Hours:** 11:30 am-2:30 & 4:30-10:30 pm, Sun from 11 am. **Features:** casual dress; Sunday brunch; carryout; beer & wine only; a la carte. Beautifully decorated restaurant surroundings with Thai themed setting welcomes one to this establishment. Authentic Thai cuisine and charming staff makes for a delightful meal. Menu is quite extensive with numerous chef specialties. **Cards:** MC, VI.

THE RUSTY PELICAN
Dinner: $18-$23 **Phone:** 813/281-1943 ②③

Seafood

Location: 0.5 mi s of east end of Courtney Campbell Cswy (SR 60). 2425 Rocky Point Dr 33607. **Hours:** 5 pm-10 pm, Fri & Sat-11 pm. **Reservations:** suggested; weekends. **Features:** semi-formal attire; children's menu; early bird specials; cocktails & lounge; valet parking; a la carte. Tableside cooking is just one enticement at this intimate restaurant. Fireplace parlors offer Tampa Bay panoramas. Holiday brunches are special treats and beautifully prepared dessert, such as bananas foster and cherries jubilee, is a fitting final touch. Banquet facilities from 20 to 460 may be accommodated. **Cards:** AE, DI, DS, MC, VI.

SAM SELTZER'S STEAKHOUSE
Lunch: $8-$19 **Dinner:** $10-$19 **Phone:** 813/873-7267 ②⑧

Steak & Seafood

Location: I-275, exit 23A, 2.1 mi n. 4744 N Dale Mabry Hwy 33614. **Hours:** 11:30 am-10:30 pm, Fri-11 pm, Sat noon-11:30 pm, Sun noon-10 pm. Closed: 11/22, 12/25. **Reservations:** suggested. **Features:** casual dress; children's menu; carryout; cocktails & lounge. Old family portraits and Western knick knacks adorn the wood walls of the rustic restaurant. Hearty portions of mostly steak and chicken entrees satisfy the biggest of appetites. Sam's Napoleon custard cream in a graham-cracker crust is a sweet treat. **Cards:** AE, DI, DS, MC, VI.

SEABREEZE RESTAURANT BY THE BAY
Lunch: $5-$9 **Dinner:** $7-$19 **Phone:** 813/247-2103 ⑦①

Seafood

Location: On SR 676, 1.2 mi e of jct Maritime Blvd at Port of Tampa. 3409 Causeway Blvd 33619. **Hours:** 11 am-10 pm, Fri & Sat-11 pm. Closed: 11/22, 12/25. **Features:** casual dress; children's menu; carryout; cocktails & lounge. A good mix of seafood and Cuban favorites served here since 1929 includes large portions of rock shrimp and snow crabs in season. You can watch the catch of the day come off the boats at the nearby dock while sampling beef, pasta, chicken or frog legs. **Cards:** AE, DI, DS, MC, VI.

SHULA'S STEAKHOUSE
Lunch: $17-$33 **Dinner:** $17-$33 **Phone:** 813/286-4366 ⑤⓪

Steak House

Location: I-275, exit 21, 0.5 mi s at jct SR 60 and Westshore Blvd; in Wyndham Westshore. 4860 W Kennedy Blvd 33609. **Hours:** 11:30 am-2:30 & 5:30-10 pm, Fri & Sat-10:30 pm, Sun-9:30 pm. **Reservations:** suggested. **Features:** casual dress; children's menu; carryout; cocktails & lounge; entertainment; fee for valet parking; a la carte. A classy decor is intermingled with football memorabilia. The emphasis is on steaks but there are also a few poultry and seafood choices. A wonderful seven-layer chocolate mousse cake tastes like the chef had nothing better to do than bake all day. **Cards:** AE, CB, DI, DS, JC, MC, VI.

SKIPPER'S SMOKEHOUSE RESTAURANT & OYSTER BAR
Lunch: $4-$15 **Dinner:** $7-$16 **Phone:** 813/971-0666 ⑤

Seafood

Location: I-275, exit 34, 1.6 mi n on Nebraska, just e. 910 Skipper Rd 33612. **Hours:** 11 am-11 pm. Closed: Mon. **Features:** casual dress; carryout; cocktails & lounge; entertainment; a la carte. Casual Key West style restaurant and oyster bar. Florida fare with Caribbean and Louisiana accents. Menu selections include alligator, crab, shrimp, wings, ribs and conch chowder. Live entertainment outdoors. **Cards:** MC, VI.

(See map p. 805)

SUKHOTHAI RESTAURANT
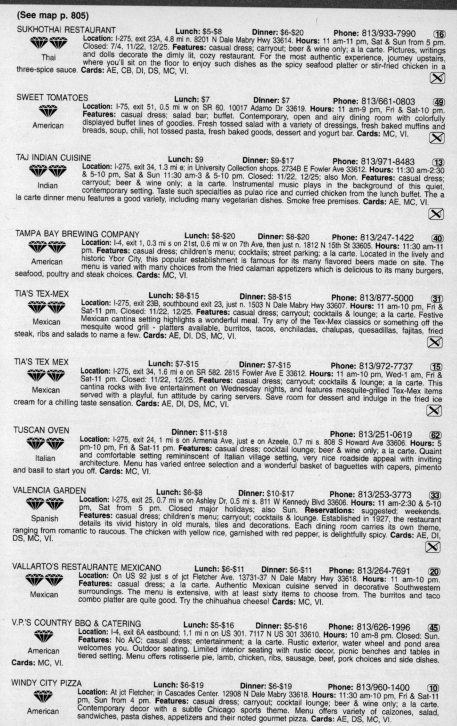
Thai

Lunch: $5-$8   **Dinner:** $6-$20   **Phone:** 813/933-7990   16
Location: I-275, exit 23A, 4.8 mi n. 8201 N Dale Mabry Hwy 33614. **Hours:** 11 am-11 pm, Sat & Sun from 5 pm. Closed: 7/4, 11/22, 12/25. **Features:** casual dress; carryout; beer & wine only; a la carte. Pictures, writings and dolls decorate the dimly lit, cozy restaurant. For the most authentic experience, journey upstairs, where you'll sit on the floor to enjoy such dishes as the spicy seafood platter or stir-fried chicken in a three-spice sauce. **Cards:** AE, CB, DI, DS, MC, VI.

SWEET TOMATOES
American

Lunch: $7   **Dinner:** $7   **Phone:** 813/661-0803   49
Location: I-75, exit 51, 0.5 mi w on SR 60. 10017 Adamo Dr 33619. **Hours:** 11 am-9 pm, Fri & Sat-10 pm. **Features:** casual dress; salad bar; buffet. Contemporary, open and airy dining room with colorfully displayed buffet lines of goodies. Fresh tossed salad with a variety of dressings, fresh baked muffins and breads, soup, chili, hot tossed pasta, fresh baked goods, dessert and yogurt bar. **Cards:** MC, VI.

TAJ INDIAN CUISINE
Indian

Lunch: $9   **Dinner:** $9-$17   **Phone:** 813/971-8483   13
Location: I-275, exit 34, 1.3 mi e; in University Collection shops. 2734B E Fowler Ave 33612. **Hours:** 11:30 am-2:30 & 5-10 pm, Sat & Sun 11:30 am-3 & 5-10 pm. Closed: 11/22, 12/25; also Mon. **Features:** casual dress; carryout; beer & wine only; a la carte. Instrumental music plays in the background of this quiet, contemporary setting. Taste such specialties as pulao rice and curried chicken from the lunch buffet. The a la carte dinner menu features a good variety, including many vegetarian dishes. Smoke free premises. **Cards:** AE, MC, VI.

TAMPA BAY BREWING COMPANY
American

Lunch: $8-$20   **Dinner:** $8-$20   **Phone:** 813/247-1422   40
Location: I-4, exit 1, 0.3 mi s on 21st, 0.6 mi w on 7th Ave, then just n. 1812 N 15th St 33605. **Hours:** 11:30 am-11 pm. **Features:** casual dress; children's menu; cocktails; street parking; a la carte. Located in the lively and historic Ybor City, this popular establishment is famous for its many flavored beers made on site. The menu is varied with many choices from the fried calamari appetizers which is delicious to its many burgers, seafood, poultry and steak choices. **Cards:** MC, VI.

TIA'S TEX-MEX
Mexican

Lunch: $8-$15   **Dinner:** $8-$15   **Phone:** 813/877-5000   31
Location: I-275, exit 23B, southbound exit 23, just n. 1503 N Dale Mabry Hwy 33607. **Hours:** 11 am-10 pm, Fri & Sat-11 pm. Closed: 11/22, 12/25. **Features:** casual dress; carryout; cocktails & lounge; a la carte. Festive Mexican cantina setting highlights a wonderful meal. Try any of the Tex-Mex classics or something off the mesquite wood grill - platters available, burritos, tacos, enchiladas, chalupas, quesadillas, fajitas, fried steak, ribs and salads to name a few. **Cards:** AE, DI, DS, MC, VI.

TIA'S TEX MEX
Mexican

Lunch: $7-$15   **Dinner:** $7-$15   **Phone:** 813/972-7737   15
Location: I-275, exit 34, 1.6 mi w on SR 582. 2815 Fowler Ave E 33612. **Hours:** 11 am-10 pm, Wed-1 am, Fri & Sat-11 pm. Closed: 11/22, 12/25. **Features:** casual dress; carryout; cocktails & lounge; a la carte. This cantina rocks with live entertainment on Wednesday nights, and features mesquite-grilled Tex-Mex items served with a playful, fun attitude by caring servers. Save room for dessert and indulge in the fried ice cream for a chilling taste sensation. **Cards:** AE, DI, DS, MC, VI.

TUSCAN OVEN
Italian

Dinner: $11-$18   **Phone:** 813/251-0619   62
Location: I-275, exit 24, 1 mi s on Armenia Ave, just e on Azeele, 0.7 mi s. 808 S Howard Ave 33606. **Hours:** 5 pm-10 pm, Fri & Sat-11 pm. **Features:** casual dress; cocktail lounge; beer & wine only; a la carte. Quaint and comfortable setting reminiscent of Italian village setting, very nice roadside appeal with inviting architecture. Menu has varied entree selection and a wonderful basket of baguettes with capers, pimento and basil to start you off. **Cards:** MC, VI.

VALENCIA GARDEN
Spanish

Lunch: $6-$8   **Dinner:** $10-$17   **Phone:** 813/253-3773   33
Location: I-275, exit 25, 0.7 mi w on Ashley Dr, 0.5 mi s. 811 W Kennedy Blvd 33606. **Hours:** 11 am-2:30 & 5-10 pm, Sat from 5 pm. Closed major holidays; also Sun. **Reservations:** suggested; weekends. **Features:** casual dress; children's menu; carryout; cocktails & lounge. Established in 1927, the restaurant details its vivid history in old murals, tiles and decorations. Each dining room carries its own theme, ranging from romantic to raucous. The chicken with yellow rice, garnished with red pepper, is delightfully spicy. **Cards:** AE, DI, DS, MC, VI.

VALLARTO'S RESTAURANTE MEXICANO
Mexican

Lunch: $6-$11   **Dinner:** $6-$11   **Phone:** 813/264-7691   20
Location: On US 92 just s of jct Fletcher Ave. 13731-37 N Dale Mabry Hwy 33618. **Hours:** 11 am-10 pm. **Features:** casual dress; a la carte. Authentic Mexican cuisine served in decorative Southwestern surroundings. The menu is extensive, with at least sixty items to choose from. The burritos and taco combo platter are quite good. Try the chihuahua cheese! **Cards:** MC, VI.

V.P.'S COUNTRY BBQ & CATERING
American
Cards: MC, VI.

Lunch: $5-$16   **Dinner:** $5-$16   **Phone:** 813/626-1996   45
Location: I-4, exit 6A eastbound; 1.1 mi n on US 301. 7117 N US 301 33610. **Hours:** 10 am-8 pm. Closed: Sun. **Features:** No A/C; casual dress; entertainment; a la carte. Rustic exterior, water wheel and pond area welcomes you. Outdoor seating. Limited interior seating with rustic decor, picnic benches and tables in tiered setting. Menu offers rotisserie pie, lamb, chicken, ribs, sausage, beef, pork choices and side dishes.

WINDY CITY PIZZA
American

Lunch: $6-$19   **Dinner:** $6-$19   **Phone:** 813/960-1400   10
Location: At jct Fletcher; in Cascades Center. 12908 N Dale Mabry 33618. **Hours:** 11:30 am-10 pm, Fri & Sat-11 pm, Sun from 4 pm. **Features:** casual dress; carryout; cocktail lounge; beer & wine only; a la carte. Contemporary decor with a subtle Chicago sports theme. Menu offers variety of calzones, salad, sandwiches, pasta dishes, appetizers and their noted gourmet pizza. **Cards:** AE, DS, MC, VI.

(See map p. 805)

THE WINE EXCHANGE   **Lunch:** $6-$9   **Dinner:** $6-$13   **Phone:** 813/254-9463   52

🔱🔱🔱   **Location:** In Old Hyde Park at jct Snow Ave. 1611 W Swann Ave 33606. **Hours:** 11:30 am-10:15 pm, Fri &
American   Sat-11:15 pm. Closed major holidays. **Features:** casual dress; beer & wine only; street parking; a la carte.
Dine among Greek ruins at this upscale, cafe-style restaurant. An Italian influenced menu features many
different dishes ranging from filet mignon served with mushrooms to traditional pasta and pizza. Smoking is
allowed on the patio area only. Smoke free premises. **Cards:** AE, MC, VI.   ✕

WOODY'S BAR-B-QUE   **Lunch:** $4-$6   **Dinner:** $6-$12   **Phone:** 813/978-9132   9

🔱🔱   **Location:** I-275, exit 34, just w. 1120 E Fowler Ave 33612. **Hours:** 11 am-10 pm. Closed major holidays; also
American   12/24 for dinner. **Features:** casual dress; children's menu; cocktail lounge; beer & wine only; a la carte.
Vintage movie posters, '50s music and bright colors pique your senses in this rustic diner. Wood-smoked
pork, beef, ribs and chicken are topped with a distinctive hickory barbecue sauce and served in record
time with baked beans by a khaki-clad staff. **Cards:** AE, DI, DS, MC, VI.   ✕

The Tampa Vicinity

APOLLO BEACH pop. 6,000

——— WHERE TO STAY ———

RAMADA BAYSIDE INN & RESORT   **Phone:** (813)641-2700

AAA SAVE   1/26-4/30   2P: $85-$105
🔱🔱   12/1-1/25   2P: $55-$105
Motor Inn   5/1-11/30   2P: $55-$85
Location: I-75, exit 47, 1.8 mi w on CR 672; US 41, 1.8 mi s to Apollo Beach Blvd, 2.4 mi w to Surfside Blvd. 6414 Surfside Blvd 33572. **Fax:** 813/645-9294. **Facility:** Bayfront. 102 units. 2 stories, exterior corridors.
Terms: check-in 4 pm, 3 day cancellation notice-fee imposed, weekly & monthly rates available, package
plans, pets ($15 extra charge). **Amenities:** voice mail, safes (fee). *Some:* irons, hair dryers. **Dining:** restaurant, 7:30 am-10 pm,
Fri & Sat-11 pm; tiki bar (seasonal hours), $9-$15, cocktails. **Leisure Activities:** heated pool, beach, fishing, bicycles, sand volleyball. *Fee:* aqua trikes, jet skis, pontoon boat rides (seasonal). **Guest Services:** [BP] meal plan available, valet and coin
laundry. **Business Services:** meeting rooms. *Fee:* fax. **Cards:** AE, CB, DI, DS, MC, VI. **Special Amenities:** early check-in/late
check-out and free newspaper.   SOME UNITS

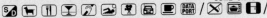

——— WHERE TO DINE ———

BEEF O'BRADY'S   **Lunch:** $5-$7   **Dinner:** $5-$7   **Phone:** 813/641-1989

🔱🔱🔱   **Location:** I-75, exit 47, 1.8 mi w on CR 672, 1.8 mi s on US 41. 205 Apolly Beach Blvd 33572. **Hours:** 11 am-11
American   pm, Sun 1 pm-10 pm. Closed: 11/22, 12/25. **Features:** casual dress; children's menu; carryout; cocktail
lounge; beer & wine only. Big screen TVs keep this spot hopping on game days. A bustling family sports
pub that cooks up a variety of traditional burgers, sandwiches, salads and wings, it features a terrific Philly
cheese steak served with french fries and a pickle spear. **Cards:** AE, DI, DS, MC, VI.   ✕

BELLEAIR BLUFFS pop. 2,100   (See map p. 796; index p. 804)

——— WHERE TO DINE ———

E & E STAKEOUT GRILL   **Lunch:** $6-$19   **Dinner:** $6-$19   **Phone:** 727/585-6399   205

🔱🔱   **Location:** At jct Indian Rocks Rd and West Bay; in The Plaza. 100 N Indian Rocks Rd 33770. **Hours:** 11:30 am-10
American   pm, Fri-10:30 pm, Sat 4 pm-10:30 pm, Sun 4 pm-10 pm. Closed: 7/4, 9/3, 12/25; also Super Bowl Sunday.
Features: casual dress; children's menu; carryout; cocktails & lounge; a la carte. Located in strip mall of
galleries and upscale boutiques, this Southwestern themed restaurant gives you the feel of New Mexico
with kokopelli, the mischievious spirit, the mascot. Choices include steak, seafood, poultry and appetizers. Dessert is a must.
Cards: AE, DI, DS, MC, VI.   ✕

BRANDON pop. 60,400

——— WHERE TO STAY ———

BEHIND THE FENCE BED & BREAKFAST   **Phone:** (813)685-8201

🔱🔱🔱   All Year   1P: $69-$79   2P: $79-$89   XP: $10   F10
Location: I-75, exit 49, just s on US 301 (northbound), 1.5 mi s on US 301 (southbound); 2.5 mi e on Bloomingdale Ave,
Bed & Breakfast   just n on Countryside St at jct Viola Dr. 1400 Viola Dr 33511. **Facility:** Rustic decor with public areas and rooms
authentically decorated with 18th-century antiques and artifacts replicating an 1800s Salt Box. Smoke free
premises. 5 units. 1 two-bedroom unit. 2 stories, interior/exterior corridors. **Terms:** check-in 4 pm, 10 day cancellation notice-fee
imposed, weekly & monthly rates available, small pets only ($10 deposit). **Guest Services:** [CP] meal plan available, afternoon
tea. **Business Services:** meeting rooms.   SOME UNITS

BRANDON MOTOR LODGE

Phone: (813)689-1261

AAA SAVE
Motel

2/1-4/25	1P: $59-$69	2P: $69-$79
12/1-1/31	1P: $49-$59	2P: $59-$69
4/26-11/30	1P: $39-$49	2P: $49-$59

Location: I-75, exit 51, 4.1 mi e on SR 60. 906 E Brandon Blvd 33511. **Fax:** 813/685-0975. **Facility:** 35 units. *Bath:* combo or shower only. 2 stories, exterior corridors. **Terms:** 7 day cancellation notice, weekly rates available. **Amenities:** *Some:* irons. **Guest Services:** coin laundry. **Cards:** AE, CB, DI, DS, MC, VI. **Special Amenities:** early check-in/late check-out and free room upgrade (subject to availability with advanced reservations).

SOME UNITS

HOLIDAY INN EXPRESS-BRANDON

Phone: (813)643-3800

Motel

12/26-4/14	1P: $99-$155	2P: $105-$161
4/15-11/30	1P: $89-$149	2P: $95-$155
12/1-12/25	1P: $79-$145	2P: $85-$151

Location: I-75, exit 51, just e to Grand Regency Blvd, just n; in Regency Office Park. 510 Grand Regency Blvd 33510. **Fax:** 813/643-5888. **Facility:** 119 units. Some suites and whirlpool units. *Bath:* combo or shower only. 4 stories, interior corridors. **Terms:** package plans. **Amenities:** extended cable TV, voice mail, irons. *Some:* hair dryers. **Leisure Activities:** heated pool, exercise room. **Guest Services:** [ECP] meal plan available, complimentary laundry. **Business Services:** meeting rooms, fax. **Cards:** AE, CB, DI, DS, MC, VI.

SOME UNITS

HOMESTEAD VILLAGE BRANDON

Phone: (813)643-5900

Motel

1/24-4/30	1P: $79	2P: $85
12/1-1/23 & 5/1-11/30	1P: $69	2P: $75

Location: I-75, exit 51, just e on SR 60, 0.4 mi n; in Regency Park. 330 Grand Regency Blvd 33510. **Fax:** 813/643-4343. **Facility:** 141 efficiencies. *Bath:* combo or shower only. 2 stories, exterior corridors. **Terms:** cancellation fee imposed, daily rates available. **Amenities:** voice mail, irons. *Some:* hair dryers. **Guest Services:** coin laundry. **Business Services:** fax. **Cards:** AE, CB, DI, DS, MC, VI.

SOME UNITS

LA QUINTA INN & SUITES

Phone: (813)643-0574

SAVE
Motel

All Year	1P: $89-$109	2P: $89-$109

Location: I-75, exit 51, just e on SR 60, 0.4 mi n; in Regency Park. 310 Grand Regency Blvd 33510. **Fax:** 813/643-5408. **Facility:** 128 units. Some suites ($119-$139). *Bath:* combo or shower only. 5 stories, interior corridors. **Terms:** small pets only ($35 deposit). **Amenities:** extended cable TV, video games, voice mail, irons, hair dryers. **Leisure Activities:** heated pool, whirlpool, exercise room. **Guest Services:** [ECP] meal plan available, coin laundry. **Business Services:** meeting rooms, fax. **Cards:** AE, CB, DI, DS, JC, MC, VI. *(See color ad p 829)*

SOME UNITS
FEE

──────── **WHERE TO DINE** ────────

A1A CAFE

Lunch: $5-$6   **Dinner:** $10-$15   **Phone:** 813/685-5257

Seafood

Location: I-75, exit 51, 3.1 mi e on SR 60, just s. 108 S Lithia-Pinecrest Rd 33511. **Hours:** 11 am-10 pm, Fri & Sat-1 am. Closed: 11/22, 12/25. **Features:** casual dress; children's menu; carryout; cocktails & lounge. Touches of Key West accent the decor, and live entertainment on Fridays and Saturdays keeps the mood jovial. Enjoy fresh seafood, sandwiches and steaks, including a savory seafood gumbo with a generous helping of fish in a seasoned tomato broth. **Cards:** AE, DS, MC, VI.

ARMEL'S GRILL

Dinner: $7-$16   **Phone:** 813/653-9876

American

Location: Jct Kings Ave, 1 mi s of SR 60. 701 W Lumsden Rd 33511. **Hours:** 11:30 am-10 pm, Fri-11 pm, Sat 4 pm-11 pm. Closed: 7/4, 12/25; also Sun. **Features:** casual dress; children's menu; carryout; cocktails & lounge; entertainment. Serving dishes ranging from steak, seafood and pasta, this eatery's eclectic menu includes a delicious prime rib, Flambeed Steak Diane or famous grouper Benton. Live entertainment nightly. **Cards:** AE, DI, DS, MC, VI.

BEN'S FAMILY RESTAURANT

Lunch: $6-$14   **Dinner:** $6-$14   **Phone:** 813/685-5501

American

Location: I-75, exit 51, 3.3 mi e on SR 60 at jct Ridgewood Ave. 704 E Brandon Ave 33511. **Hours:** 7:30 am-9 pm. **Features:** casual dress; a la carte. Relax in this comfortable, family style restaurant with country decor and a nautical touch. Variety of home cooking type entrees such as steak, chicken, pork and sandwiches. Try one of their many homemade desserts. **Cards:** MC, VI.

BRANDON ALE HOUSE & RAW BAR

Lunch: $6-$13   **Dinner:** $6-$13   **Phone:** 813/643-0511

Seafood

Location: I-75, exit 51, 2.4 mi e on SR 60. 1817 W Brandon Blvd 33511. **Hours:** 11 am-2 am. **Features:** casual dress; children's menu; carryout; cocktails & lounge. This sports-themed restaurant will impress many fans with 40 TV monitors and four satellite dishes. Catch the big game and enjoy a variety of sandwiches, pasta and seafood. All-you-can-eat crab legs come with clam chowder, salad, rice pilaf and coleslaw. **Cards:** AE, DI, DS, MC, VI.

BUDDY FREDDY'S

Lunch: $6-$8   **Dinner:** $8-$11   **Phone:** 813/661-6005

American

Location: I-75, exit 51, 0.7 mi e on SR 60, just s. 134 S Gornto Lake Rd 33511. **Hours:** 7 am-9 pm, Fri & Sat-10 pm. Closed: 4/15, 7/4, 12/25. **Features:** casual dress; children's menu; early bird specials; senior's menu; carryout; salad bar; a la carte; buffet. This is good, old-fashioned home cooking dished up in a country decor. An excellent lunch and dinner buffet is offered with an a la carte menu for added variety. Bring the whole family, and take advantage of early bird specials and senior discounts. Smoke free premises. **Cards:** AE, DS, MC, VI.

CRABBY TOM'S OYSTER BAR & SEAFOOD RESTAURANT Lunch: $4-$18 Dinner: $4-$18 Phone: 813/651-3499
Location: I-75, exit 51, 2.6 mi e on SR 60. 1414 W Brandon Blvd 33511. **Hours:** 11 am-10 pm, Fri & Sat-11 pm, Sun noon-9 pm. **Closed:** 4/15, 11/22, 12/25. **Features:** casual dress; children's menu; early bird specials; carryout; cocktails; a la carte. An eclectic sports bar with nautical touches provides an appealing menu of
Seafood sandwiches, salads and seafood platters. For instance, the seafood sampler offers shrimp, scallops, oysters and clams with fries, coleslaw and homemade hushpuppies. **Cards:** AE, DI, DS, MC, VI.

DURANGO STEAKHOUSE Lunch: $6-$10 Dinner: $7-$18 Phone: 813/681-3999
Location: At jct Providence Rd in Brandon Town Centre South. 1995 W Lumsden Rd 33511. **Hours:** 11:30 am-10 pm, Fri & Sat from noon. **Closed:** 11/22, 12/25. **Features:** casual dress; children's menu; carryout; cocktails & lounge. Ample servings of tasty food abound in this Southwestern eatery that serves a variety
Steak House of oak-grilled entrees such as ribs, steak and chicken. Murals and knotty-pine hardwood floors lend a warm and distinctive ambience to the dining area. **Cards:** AE, DI, DS, MC, VI.

EL ZARAPE RESTAURANT Lunch: $4-$13 Dinner: $4-$13 Phone: 813/651-9659
Location: I-75, exit 51, 2.2 mi e on SR 60, just s. 104 S Kings Ave 33511. **Hours:** 11 am-10 pm. **Features:** casual dress; children's menu; cocktails & lounge; a la carte, buffet. Sombreros and Mexican blankets provide the backdrop for this clean and friendly cantina. From burritos to tacos, the menu offers
Mexican an extensive variety of traditional Mexican dishes. Live entertainers perform on Friday and Saturday nights.
Cards: AE, DI, DS, MC, VI.

ESTELA'S MEXICAN RESTAURANT Lunch: $3-$6 Dinner: $5-$10 Phone: 813/657-1421
Location: I-275, exit 51, SR 60 just w of jct Kings Ave. 312 E Brandon Blvd 33511. **Hours:** 11 am-10 pm, Fri & Sat-11 pm. **Features:** casual dress; beer & wine only. **Cards:** MC, VI.
Mexican

GATORZ SOUTHERN ROCK CAFE Lunch: $6-$10 Dinner: $6-$10 Phone: 813/662-1557
Location: On SR 60, just w of jct Bryan. 509 E Brandon Blvd 33511. **Hours:** 11 am-3 am, Sun from noon. **Closed:** 12/25. **Features:** casual dress; carryout; cocktails & lounge; entertainment. Rock 'n' roll memorabilia and nostalgic knickknacks create an eye-catching decor. Sandwiches, ribs, pizza and
American market-fresh crab fill out a fun-food menu. Start with the fried wing appetizers with celery and dressing, and you can't go wrong. **Cards:** AE, DI, DS, MC, VI.

HAO ONE CHINESE RESTAURANT Lunch: $4-$11 Dinner: $4-$11 Phone: 813/685-6381
Location: I-75, exit 51, 0.6 mi e on SR 60. 2020 W Brandon Blvd Suite 145 33511. **Hours:** 11 am-10 pm. **Closed:** 11/22, 12/25. **Features:** casual dress; children's menu; carryout; beer & wine only; a la carte, buffet. Chinese food in all its variety is the focus at this relaxing, Asian-themed restaurant. The lomein, beef and
Chinese broccoli, and General Tso's chicken are particularly tasty, and an extensive buffet is available. **Cards:** AE, DS, MC, VI.

JO-TO JAPANESE STEAK HOUSE Dinner: $12-$25 Phone: 813/684-0221
Location: 1.1 mi s of jct SR 60; in Lithia Square. 905 Lithia Pinecrest Rd 33511. **Hours:** 5 pm-10 pm, Fri & Sat-11 pm. **Closed:** 7/4, 11/22; also Super Bowl Sun. **Features:** casual dress; cocktails & lounge. Appreciate traditional Japanese cuisine prepared with the Teppan-yaki method of cooking. Choose from seafood,
Japanese steak and chicken teriyaki or tempura dishes. Watch the cooks practice their craft table-side, or sample delicacies from the sushi bar. **Cards:** AE, CB, DI, MC, VI.

LATIN CAFE 2000 Lunch: $4-$8 Dinner: $4-$8 Phone: 813/643-9475
Location: At jct Bell Shoals Rd; in Bloomingdale Square. 829 E Bloomingdale Ave 33594. **Hours:** 7 am-10 pm. **Features:** casual dress; children's menu; carryout; beer & wine only; a la carte. Very trendy decor, upscale setting. Several breakfast items to choose and main menu offers numerous sandwiches, several meat
Spanish dishes, soup, chicken, seafood, salad and dessert all with a latin flair. **Cards:** MC, VI.

LENNY & VINNY'S NEW YORK PIZZERIA AND BAKERY Lunch: $6-$18 Dinner: $6-$18 Phone: 813/661-3636
Location: At jct Bell Shoals Rd; in Bloomingdale Square. 887 E Bloomingdale Ave 33511. **Hours:** 11 am-10 pm, Fri & Sat-11 pm. **Features:** casual dress; children's menu; carryout; a la carte. Colorful and unique setting gives one the feel of being in a New York subway car. Menu has variety of pastas, subs, calzones,
American stromboli, and desserts. Try a famous gourmet pizza. Smoke free premises. **Cards:** AE, DS, MC, VI.

PAT'S PLACE RESTAURANT Lunch: $5-$7 Dinner: $6-$10 Phone: 813/685-7259
Location: At jct Bloomingdale and John Moore Rd; in Bloomingdale Plaza. 147 E Bloomingdale Ave 33511. **Hours:** 7 am-8:30 pm, Fri-8:30 pm, Mon & Sat-2 pm, Sun 8 am-2 pm. **Features:** No A/C; casual dress; a la carte. Country decor and homestyle cooking. Fresh-baked desserts made on-site are a must. Menu has many
American homemade items with a variety of dinner baskets, sandwiches, country dinners, steak, seafood and even Italian items to choose from.

RIO BRAVO CANTINA Lunch: $6-$14 Dinner: $8-$14 Phone: 813/655-1495
Location: At jct Providence Rd; in Lake Brandon Village. 11395 Causeway Blvd 33511. **Hours:** 11 am-10 pm, Fri & Sat-11 pm. **Closed:** 11/22, 12/25. **Features:** casual dress; cocktails; a la carte. Step into a Mexican cantina setting and enjoy made from scratch entrees. Selections include the usual favorites of baby back ribs and
Mexican tacos al carbon or create your own combo. **Cards:** AE, DI, DS, MC, VI.

ROADHOUSE GRILL Lunch: $7-$18 Dinner: $7-$18 Phone: 813/657-9892
Location: I-75, exit 51, on SR 60 2.8 mi e. 775 W Brandon Blvd 33511. **Hours:** 11 am-10 pm, Fri & Sat-11 pm. **Closed:** 11/22, 12/25. **Features:** casual dress; children's menu; carryout; cocktails & lounge. As the name says; gives you the feel of stepping into an old Texas roadhouse. Peanuts in a pail; eat, relax and toss the
Steak House shells on the floor; a mess no problem, just have fun. Great steaks, ribs, chicken, mesquite grilled pork chops to name a few choices. **Cards:** AE, DI, DS, MC, VI.

SIMPLY THAI

Thai

Lunch: $7-$14   **Dinner:** $7-$14   **Phone:** 813/681-4470
Location: At jct Bell Shoals Rd; in Bloomingdale Square. 875 E Bloomingdale Ave 33511. **Hours:** 11:30 am-3 & 5-9 pm, Fri-9:30 pm, Sat 5 pm-9:30 pm, Sun 5 pm-9 pm. Closed: Mon. **Features:** casual dress; beer & wine only; a la carte. Oriental surroundings highlight this Tai establishment. Many entre items to choose from. **Cards:** MC, VI.

TIA'S TEX MEX

Mexican

Lunch: $7-$15   **Dinner:** $7-$15   **Phone:** 813/681-7716
Location: I-75, exit 51, just e on SR 60 in Brandon Town Center. 144 Brandon Town Center 33511. **Hours:** 11 am-10 pm, Fri & Sat-11 pm. Closed: 11/22, 12/25. **Features:** casual dress; carryout; cocktails & lounge; a la carte. Tex-Mex and mesquite-grilled dishes are served in a Mexican-style cantina setting complete with a torch-lit courtyard dining area. Fresh, hearty portions mean flavorful choices with burritos, tacos, fajitas and the chalupa tortilla. **Cards:** AE, DI, DS, MC, VI.

WIZEGUYZ PIZZERIA

Italian

Lunch: $5-$14   **Dinner:** $5-$14   **Phone:** 813/643-1200
Location: I-75, exit 51, just w; in Regency Square. 2498 W Brandon Blvd 33511. **Hours:** 11 am-10 pm, Fri & Sat-midnight. **Features:** casual dress; carryout; beer only; a la carte. Some of the best Italian food this side of the border with a casual New York pizzeria setting. Basic window type service but you'll enjoy the food which is freshly prepared once you order. Menu has a variety of items from pizza by the slice to pizza pies, hoagies, sandwiches, dinners such as lasagna, spaghetti, baked ziti and parmesian dishes. **Cards:** MC, VI.

YOKOHAMA JAPANESE RESTAURANT SUSHI BAR

Japanese

Cards: MC, VI.

Lunch: $11-$21   **Dinner:** $11-$21   **Phone:** 813/684-3485
Location: At jct King St; in La Viva Plaza. 760 W Lumsden 33511. **Hours:** 11:30 am-2 & 5-10 pm, Fri & Sat-10:30 pm, Sun 5 pm-10 pm. **Features:** dressy casual. Cozy, intimate restaurant with varied menu of freshly prepared, artistically decorated entrees. Try the tempura, sashimi, eel, beef, poultry, lobster, soup and various appetizers. There is also a wide variety of sushi choices. Very gracious service.

The following restaurant has not been evaluated by AAA but is listed for your information only.

CHOP STIX CHINESE RESTAURANT

[fyi]

Chinese around.

Phone: 813/654-5195
Not evaluated. **Location:** On SR 60, just w of jct Mt Carmel. 801 E Brandon Blvd 33511. **Features:** Very basic decor in this small restaurant; drive thru service also available. Extensive menu offering some of the best Chinese around.

CLEARWATER pop. 98,800   (See map p. 796; index p. 800)

——— WHERE TO STAY ———

BAY QUEEN MOTEL

AAA [SAVE]

Apartment

Phone: (727)441-3295 [54]

2/1-3/31	1P: $68-$78	2P: $68-$78	XP: $10	F18
4/1-4/30	1P: $52-$59	2P: $52-$59	XP: $10	F18
12/1-1/31	1P: $44-$59	2P: $44-$59	XP: $10	F18
5/1-11/30	1P: $44-$52	2P: $44-$52	XP: $10	F18

Location: US 19 Alt; just n of jct Sunset Point Rd (CR 576). 1925 Edgewater Dr 33755. Fax: 727/466-6186. **Facility:** Extensively landscaped and well manicured grounds. Setting with view of Clearwater Harbor. 18 units, 17 with efficiency. *Bath:* combo or shower only. 2 stories, exterior corridors. **Terms:** 14 day cancellation notice, weekly rates available. **Amenities:** extended cable TV, irons. *Some:* hair dryers. **Leisure Activities:** shuffleboard, barbecue grill. **Guest Services:** coin laundry. **Cards:** AE, MC, VI. **Special Amenities:** early check-in/late check-out and free local telephone calls.
(See ad p 853)

SOME UNITS

(See map p. 796)

BELLEVIEW BILTMORE RESORT & SPA

Phone: (727)442-6171 64

(AAA) (SAVE)

◆◆ ◆◆
Classic Hotel

1/19-4/21	1P: $139-$169	2P: $139-$169	XP: $10	F18
12/1-1/18 & 9/28-11/30	1P: $109-$139	2P: $109-$139	XP: $10	F18
4/22-9/27	1P: $89-$119	2P: $89-$119	XP: $10	F18

Location: 1.5 mi s of US 60 on Alt 19 (Fort Harrison), 0.5 mi w. 25 Belleview Blvd 33756 (PO Box 2317, 33757). Fax: 727/441-4173. **Facility:** Historic. Historic resort built in 1897 on Old Clearwater Bay. Old World atmosphere units. Variety of boutiques and specialty shops on premises. On National Register of Historic Places. 47 different room types offered here from smaller compact rooms to larger more spacious units. 244 units. *Bath:* combo or shower only. 4 stories, interior corridors. **Parking:** valet. **Terms:** package plans. **Amenities:** extended cable TV, voice mail, irons, hair dryers. **Dining:** dining room, 7 am-10:30 pm; pool bar, golf club with bar and grill with multiscreen TVs, $10-$32, cocktails. **Leisure Activities:** 2 pools (1 heated, 1 indoor), saunas, whirlpools, boat dock, water aerobics, putting green, playground, exercise room, basketball, volleyball, game room, aerobics, tai chi, spa services, yoga. *Fee:* golf-18 holes, 4 tennis courts, bicycles. **Guest Services:** [AP], [BP] & [MAP] meal plans available, gift shop, area transportation-beach and golf club, valet laundry. *Fee:* massage. **Business Services:** conference facilities, administrative services, PC, fax. **Cards:** AE, DS, MC, VI.
(See color ad p 843)

SOME UNITS

[icons]

CANDLEWOOD SUITES CLEARWATER-ST PETERSBURG

Phone: (727)573-3344 65

◆◆◆
Extended Stay
Motel

1/22-4/30	2P: $99-$119
1/1-1/21	2P: $109
5/1-11/30	2P: $104
12/1-12/31	2P: $99

Location: I-275, exit 18, northbound exit 16, just s of jct Ulmerton Blvd (SR 688). 13231 49th St N 33762. Fax: 727/573-3074. **Facility:** Front desk hours 7 am-11 pm, Fri-8 pm, Sat & Sun 10 am-6 pm. 104 efficiencies. *Bath:* combo or shower only. 3 stories, interior corridors. **Amenities:** extended cable TV, CD players, dual phone lines, voice mail, irons, hair dryers. **Leisure Activities:** exercise room. **Guest Services:** valet and coin laundry. **Cards:** AE, CB, DI, DS, MC, VI.
(See ad below)

SOME UNITS

[icons]

CLEARWATER CENTRAL-BEST WESTERN

Phone: (727)799-1565 56

(AAA) (SAVE)

◆◆◆
Motel

2/1-4/15	1P: $79-$89	2P: $79-$89	
1/1-1/31 & 4/16-11/30	1P: $59-$69	2P: $59-$69	
12/1-12/31	1P: $55-$65	2P: $55-$65	XP: $5	F18

Location: On US 19, just n of jct SR 60. 21338 US 19 N 33765. Fax: 727/797-6801. **Facility:** 150 units. Some suites. 2 stories, interior corridors. **Terms:** 3 day cancellation notice, in season. **Amenities:** extended cable TV. *Some:* irons, hair dryers. **Leisure Activities:** heated pool, whirlpool, 2 tennis courts, basketball, horseshoes, shuffleboard, volleyball, picnic area with grill. **Guest Services:** coin laundry. **Business Services:** meeting rooms. **Cards:** AE, CB, DI, DS, MC, VI. **Special Amenities:** free local telephone calls.

SOME UNITS

[icons]

COMFORT INN/CLEARWATER

Phone: (727)573-1171 75

(AAA) (SAVE)

◆◆◆
Motel

1/16-4/20	1P: $85-$99	2P: $90-$104	XP: $5	F18
4/21-11/30	1P: $69-$85	2P: $74-$90	XP: $5	F18
12/1-1/15	1P: $69-$79	2P: $74-$84	XP: $5	F18

Location: I-275, southbound exit 18; northbound exit 16, 1.8 mi w on SR 688. 3580 Ulmerton Rd 33762. Fax: 727/572-8736. **Facility:** Inviting public areas with very nicely landscaped pool area in center courtyard. The rooms have a bright, contemporary decor with oriental influences. 119 units. Some suites. 3 stories, interior corridors. **Terms:** cancellation fee imposed, weekly & monthly rates available. **Amenities:** extended cable TV, voice mail. *Some:* irons, hair dryers. **Leisure Activities:** heated pool, whirlpool. **Guest Services:** [ECP] meal plan available, complimentary evening beverages, airport transportation-Tampa & Clearwater, valet and coin laundry. **Business Services:** meeting rooms, administrative services. **Cards:** AE, DI, DS, MC, VI. **Special Amenities:** free continental breakfast and free local telephone calls. *(See color ad p 845)*

SOME UNITS

[icons] FEE FEE

(See map p. 796)

COURTYARD BY MARRIOTT

				Phone: (727)572-8484	71
	12/1-4/30	1P: $129	2P: $139	XP: $10	F18
	5/1-11/30	1P: $99	2P: $109	XP: $10	F18

Motel
Location: I-275, southbound exit 18; northbound exit 16, 1.6 mi w on SR 688. 3131 Executive Dr 33762. Fax: 727/572-6991. **Facility:** Inviting public areas with nicely decorated tiered lobby seating and dining area. Rooms have rich cherry finish to contemporary furnishings. Grounds are beautifully landscaped and courtyard area houses pool and gazebo. 149 units. Some suites. *Bath:* combo or shower only. 3 stories, interior corridors. **Terms:** weekly rates available. **Amenities:** extended cable TV, voice mail, irons, hair dryers. **Leisure Activities:** heated pool, whirlpool, exercise room. **Guest Services:** valet and coin laundry. **Business Services:** meeting rooms, fax. **Cards:** AE, DI, DS, MC, VI. **(See color ad p 812)**

SOME UNITS

DAYS INN-CLEARWATER CENTRAL

				Phone: (727)799-0100	61
	1/25-4/16	1P: $74-$86	2P: $74-$86	XP: $6	F12
	12/16-1/24	1P: $59-$71	2P: $59-$71	XP: $6	F12
	4/17-11/30	1P: $54-$71	2P: $54-$71	XP: $6	F12
	12/1-12/15	1P: $54-$66	2P: $54-$66	XP: $6	F12

Motel
Location: On SR 60, 0.8 mi e of jct US 19. 2940 Gulf-to-Bay Blvd 33759. Fax: 727/726-6569. **Facility:** 90 units, 38 with efficiency. Some suites. 2 stories, exterior corridors. **Terms:** weekly & monthly rates available. **Amenities:** extended cable TV, hair dryers. **Leisure Activities:** heated pool, whirlpool, 2 sun decks, playground, shuffleboard. **Guest Services:** [CP] meal plan available, coin laundry. **Business Services:** meeting rooms, fax. **Cards:** AE, CB, DI, DS, JC, MC, VI.

SOME UNITS

DAYS INN CLEARWATER NORTH

	Phone: (727)797-3000	63

Property failed to provide current rates

Motel
Location: US 19, 1 mi n of jct SR 580. 28596 US 19N 33761. Fax: 727/796-7402. **Facility:** 57 units, 25 with efficiency. 2 stories, exterior corridors. **Terms:** cancellation fee imposed, weekly rates available. **Amenities:** hair dryers. *Some:* irons. **Leisure Activities:** heated pool. **Guest Services:** [CP] meal plan available, coin laundry. **Cards:** AE, CB, DI, DS, MC, VI.

SOME UNITS

(See map p. 796)

DAYS INN-ST.PETE/CLEARWATER AIRPORT   Phone: (727)573-3334 🄴

| (AAA) (SAVE) | 12/26-4/30 | 1P: $79-$99 | 2P: $84-$104 | XP: $5 | F18 |
| | 12/1-12/25 & 5/1-11/30 | 1P: $49-$69 | 2P: $54-$74 | XP: $5 | F18 |

Location: I-275, exit 18, southbound; exit 16 northbound, 2 mi w on SR 688. 3910 Ulmerton Rd 33762. Fax: 727/572-4845. **Facility:** Sunken lobby seating area is inviting and with contemporary furnishings. Comfortable rooms with oak finish furnishings. Large pool and deck area. 117 units. 4 stories, interior corridors.
Motel   **Terms:** 3 day cancellation notice-fee imposed. **Amenities:** extended cable TV, video games, safes (fee).
Some: irons, hair dryers. **Leisure Activities:** heated pool. **Guest Services:** [ECP] meal plan available, airport transportation-Tampa International and St. Pete/Clearwater, area transportation, valet and coin laundry. **Business Services:** meeting rooms.
Cards: AE, CB, DI, DS, MC, VI. **Special Amenities:** early check-in/late check-out and free continental breakfast.
(See color ad below)

SOME UNITS

🅢🄳 ✈ 🍴 🎬 📺 📠 💻 DATA PORT / ☒ 📠 🛏 /
FEE   FEE FEE

ECONO LODGE CLEARWATER   Phone: (727)799-1569 🄵

(AAA) (SAVE)	2/1-4/15	1P: $72-$75	2P: $72-$75		
	1/1-1/31 & 4/16-11/30	1P: $52-$55	2P: $52-$55		
	12/1-12/31	1P: $50-$53	2P: $50-$53	XP: $5	F18

Location: US 19, just n of jct SR 60. 21252 US 19 N 33765. Fax: 727/796-3165. **Facility:** Comfortable lobby and pool area are the strong points here. A peaceful setting giving a relaxed feel with large, nicely landscaped deck area. Rooms have contemporary decor. 120 units. 2 stories, exterior corridors. **Leisure Activities:** heated pool, 2 tennis courts,
Motel
tion notice, in season. **Amenities:** extended cable TV. *Some:* irons, hair dryers. **Leisure Activities:** heated pool, 2 tennis courts, horseshoes, shuffleboard, barbecue area. **Guest Services:** valet and coin laundry. **Business Services:** meeting rooms, fax.
Cards: AE, CB, DI, DS, JC, MC, VI. **Special Amenities:** free local telephone calls.

SOME UNITS

🅢🄳 🍴 🎬 🏊 ☒ 📺 📠 💻 / ☒ 📠 🛏 /

HAMPTON INN CLEARWATER CENTRAL   Phone: (727)797-8173 🄶

(SAVE)	1/26-4/30	1P: $89-$96	2P: $95-$105	XP: $6	F18
	5/1-11/30	1P: $79-$86	2P: $95-$105	XP: $6	F18
	1/1-1/25	1P: $85-$91	2P: $91-$98	XP: $6	F18
	12/1-12/31	1P: $77-$83	2P: $83-$89	XP: $6	F18

Location: Just n of jct SR 60. 21030 US 19 N 33765. Fax: 727/791-7759. **Facility:** 158 units, 39 with efficiency.
Motel   *Bath:* combo or shower only. 2 stories, exterior corridors. **Terms:** check-in 4 pm, cancellation fee imposed, package plans. **Amenities:** extended cable TV, video games, voice mail, irons, hair dryers. **Leisure Activities:** heated pool, wading pool, sauna, whirlpool, waterfall, gazebo area, putting green, playground, exercise room. **Guest Services:** [ECP] meal plan available, gift shop, coin laundry. **Business Services:** meeting rooms, administrative services, fax. *Fee:* PC. **Cards:** AE, CB, DI, DS, JC, MC, VI.

SOME UNITS

🍴 ♿ 🎬 📺 🏊 ☒ 📠 💻 DATA PORT / ☒ 📠 🛏 /
FEE

(See map p. 796)

HAMPTON INN-CLEARWATER/ST. PETERSBURG AIRPORT

Phone: (727)577-9200   67

1/3-4/15	1P: $85	2P: $85
4/16-11/30	1P: $76	2P: $76
12/1-1/2	1P: $71	2P: $71

SAVE
Motel

Location: I-275, southbound exit 18; northbound exit 16, 1.8 mi w on SR 688. 3655 Hospitality at Ulmerton Rd 33762. **Fax:** 727/572-8931. **Facility:** Brightly decorated lobby and breakfast area with contemporary design. Comfortable, modern furnishings and decorative colors to fabrics. Exterior is inviting with contemporary architecture and nice landscaping. 118 units. 2 stories, exterior corridors. **Terms:** 7 day cancellation notice. **Amenities:** extended cable TV, voice mail, irons, hair dryers. **Leisure Activities:** sauna, whirlpool, exercise room. **Guest Services:** [ECP] meal plan available, complimentary evening beverages: Mon-Thurs, valet and coin laundry. **Business Services:** meeting rooms, fax. **Cards:** AE, DI, DS, MC, VI.

SOME UNITS

HOLIDAY INN EXPRESS

Phone: (727)536-7275   66

1/8-4/30	1P: $99-$129	2P: $104-$134	XP: $5	F18
5/1-11/30	1P: $95-$114	2P: $100-$119	XP: $5	F18
12/1-1/7	1P: $95-$104	2P: $100-$109	XP: $5	F18

AAA SAVE
Motel

Location: 0.5 mi e of jct US 19; in Icot Center, just off Ulmerton Rd (SR 688). 13625 Icot Blvd 33760. **Fax:** 727/530-3053. **Facility:** Large, open lobby area nicely decorated with contemporary look and nicely tiled floors, overlooks the pool area which has lovely landscaping and is in private courtyard area. Contemporary furnishings in units with colonial touch and mahogany grains for rich look, some have separate living room area with sleeper sofa. 127 units. Some suites and whirlpool units. *Bath:* combo or shower only. 3 stories, interior corridors. **Terms:** cancellation fee imposed. **Amenities:** extended cable TV, voice mail, irons, hair dryers. **Leisure Activities:** heated pool, whirlpool. **Guest Services:** [ECP] meal plan available, valet laundry. **Business Services:** meeting rooms. **Cards:** AE, CB, DI, DS, MC, VI. **Special Amenities:** free continental breakfast and free local telephone calls. *(See color ad p 845)*

SOME UNITS

HOLIDAY INN HOTEL & SUITES BAYSIDE CITY CENTRE

Phone: (727)799-1181   59

All Year	1P: $95-$255	2P: $95-$255	XP: $6	F18

Motor Inn

Location: On US 19, just n of jct SR 60. 20967 US 19N 33765. **Fax:** 727/712-8404. **Facility:** 148 units. Some suites and whirlpool units. 3 stories, exterior corridors. **Amenities:** extended cable TV, video games, voice mail, irons, hair dryers. **Leisure Activities:** heated pool, wading pool, sauna, whirlpool, playground, exercise room, game room. **Guest Services:** gift shop, valet and coin laundry. **Business Services:** meeting rooms, fax. **Cards:** AE, CB, DI, DS, JC, MC, VI.

SOME UNITS

FEE   FEE

HOLIDAY INN SELECT-ST. PETE/CLEARWATER INT'L AIRPORT

Phone: (727)577-9100   69

All Year	1P: $119-$139

Hotel

Location: I-275, southbound exit 18; northbound exit 16, 1.8 mi w on SR 688. 3535 Ulmerton Rd 33762. **Fax:** 727/573-5022. **Facility:** Inviting lobby with tiered restaurant area with nice use of marble and mahogany finish furnishings. Very pretty slate stone waterfall area off restaurant. Units are very nice with comfortable, contemporary furnishings. 173 units. Some suites. 5 stories, interior corridors. **Terms:** package plans. **Amenities:** extended cable TV, voice mail, irons, hair dryers. **Leisure Activities:** whirlpool, 2 lighted tennis courts, exercise room. *Fee:* golf-18 holes. **Guest Services:** gift shop, valet and coin laundry. **Business Services:** conference facilities, administrative services, PC, fax. **Cards:** AE, CB, DI, MC, VI.

SOME UNITS

FEE   FEE FEE

HOMESTEAD VILLAGE GUEST STUDIOS

Phone: (727)572-4800   78

1/1-5/1	1P: $69-$79	2P: $78-$89
5/2-11/30	1P: $49-$69	2P: $59-$79
12/1-12/31	1P: $54	2P: $54

Extended Stay
Apartment

Location: I-275, southbound exit 18; northbound exit 16, 1.5 mi w on SR 688. 2311 Ulmerton Rd 33762. **Fax:** 727/572-1200. **Facility:** Office hours 7 am-10 pm, Sat 9 am-5 pm, Sun noon-8 pm. All rooms have combination sleeping/kitchen area with eat-in counter top. Contemporary furnishings with knotty pine look, to sleeper sofa in some. Grounds are nicely kept with nice roadside appeal. 113 efficiencies. *Bath:* combo or shower only. 2 stories, exterior corridors. **Terms:** daily rates available, pets ($75 non-refundable deposit). **Amenities:** voice mail, irons. *Some:* hair dryers. **Guest Services:** valet and coin laundry. **Cards:** AE, CB, DI, DS, MC, VI.

SOME UNITS

HOMEWOOD SUITES BY HILTON

Phone: (727)573-1500   79

1/1-4/30	1P: $109-$199	2P: $109-$199
12/1-12/31 & 5/1-11/30	1P: $89-$129	2P: $89-$129

Suite Motel

Location: I-275, exit 18 (southbound); northbound exit 16, 1.3 mi w on SR 688. 2233 Ulmerton Rd 33762. **Fax:** 727/573-5950. **Facility:** Welcoming roadside appeal to this property with nicely landscaped grounds. Beautifully decorated public areas with comfortable seating; eye appealing hardwoods and large breakfast area set up similar to lodge. All rooms very nicely decorated with separate living room and kitchen area, 2 televisions (one is console), sleeper sofa, and many extras. 112 units with kitchen. 8 two-bedroom units. *Bath:* combo or shower only. 2 stories, interior corridors. **Terms:** 7 day cancellation notice, monthly rates available, package plans, pets ($150 fee). **Amenities:** extended cable TV, video games, voice mail, irons, hair dryers. **Leisure Activities:** exercise room. **Guest Services:** [ECP] meal plan available, valet and coin laundry. **Business Services:** meeting rooms, administrative services, PC, fax. **Cards:** AE, CB, DI, DS, MC, VI.

SOME UNITS

FEE

(See map p. 796)

LA QUINTA INN CLEARWATER-AIRPORT

Phone: (727)572-7222 70

[SAVE] | Motel

All Year — 1P: $55-$85 — 2P: $55-$85

Location: I-275, exit 18 southbound; northbound exit 16, 1.7 mi w on SR 688. 3301 Ulmerton Rd 33762. Fax: 727/572-0076. **Facility:** Spanish style exterior architecture. Inviting rooms with mahogany finish furnishings and contemporary look. Sun deck/patio overlooks courtyard pool area. 115 units. Some suites and whirlpool units. *Bath:* combo or shower only. 3 stories, interior corridors. **Terms:** weekly rates available, package plans, small pets only. **Amenities:** video games, voice mail. *Some:* irons, hair dryers. **Leisure Activities:** heated pool, sauna, whirlpool, exercise room. **Guest Services:** [ECP] meal plan available, valet and coin laundry. **Business Services:** meeting rooms, fax. **Cards:** AE, CB, DI, DS, MC, VI. *(See color ad p 829)*

SOME UNITS

QUALITY INN CLEARWATER CENTRAL

Phone: (727)799-6133 62

[SAVE] | Motel

2/4-4/22	1P: $79-$120	2P: $79-$120	XP: $20	F18
12/18-2/3	1P: $62-$109	2P: $62-$109	XP: $20	F18
12/1-12/17 & 4/23-11/30	1P: $52-$89	2P: $52-$89	XP: $20	F18

Location: On US 19, just s of jct SR 60, at jct Druid. 20162 US Hwy 19 N 33764. Fax: 727/726-6564. **Facility:** Inviting architectural design and very attractive pool with fountained water activity area. Attractive lobby with bright tiled floor and Queen Anne style to furnishings. Contemporary furnishings in rooms with light oak finish, spacious rooms. 76 units, 31 with efficiency. *Bath:* combo or shower only. 3 stories, interior/exterior corridors. **Terms:** weekly rates available. **Amenities:** extended cable TV, voice mail, irons, hair dryers. **Leisure Activities:** heated pool, whirlpool, sun deck, exercise room. **Guest Services:** [ECP] meal plan available, coin laundry. **Business Services:** meeting rooms, fax. **Cards:** AE, DI, DS, MC, VI.

SOME UNITS

RAMADA INN COUNTRYSIDE

Phone: (727)796-1234 53

Motor Inn

All Year — 1P: $89 — 2P: $99 — XP: $10 — F18

Location: US 19; just s of jct SR 580, adjacent to Countryside Mall. 26508 US 19N 33761. Fax: 727/796-0452. **Facility:** Contemporary inviting exterior appeal. Comfortable lobby and breakfast area with modern touches. Large rooms with pickled oak finish to modern furnishings. 125 units, 9 with efficiency. Some suites and whirlpool units. 5 stories, interior corridors. **Terms:** 30 day cancellation notice, package plans. **Amenities:** extended cable TV, voice mail. *Some:* irons, hair dryers. **Dining:** Arigato Japanese Steak House, see separate listing. **Leisure Activities:** whirlpool, lighted tennis court. **Guest Services:** [ECP] meal plan available, valet and coin laundry. **Business Services:** meeting rooms. **Cards:** AE, CB, DI, DS, JC, MC, VI.

SOME UNITS

RESIDENCE INN BY MARRIOTT

Phone: (727)573-4444 72

Apartment

All Year — 1P: $145-$175 — 2P: $145-$175

Location: 1 mi e of jct US 19; on SR 688. 5050 Ulmerton Rd 33760. Fax: 727/572-4446. **Facility:** 4 room types availabe from 1-bedroom suites to 2-bedroom loft units. All with working gas fireplace. the grounds are nicely maintained with a variety of tropical plantings. Quiet and makes for a homey feel. 88 units with kitchen. 22 two-bedroom units. *Bath:* combo or shower only. 2 stories, exterior corridors. **Terms:** weekly & monthly rates available, pets ($150 fee). **Amenities:** extended cable TV, irons, hair dryers. **Leisure Activities:** heated pool, whirlpool, sports court. **Guest Services:** [BP] meal plan available, valet and coin laundry. **Business Services:** meeting rooms. **Cards:** AE, CB, DI, DS, MC, VI.

SOME UNITS

ST. PETERSBURG/CLEARWATER FAIRFIELD INN BY MARRIOTT

Phone: (727)572-4400 77

Motel

2/5-4/30	1P: $89-$109	2P: $89-$109
12/1-2/4 & 5/1-11/30	1P: $79-$84	2P: $79-$84

Location: I-275, exit 18 southbound; exit 16 northbound, 1.6 mi w on SR 688; in The Centres Office Park. 3211 Executive Dr 34615. Fax: 727/572-8500. **Facility:** Inviting lobby and breakfast room with bright floral accents and contemporary furnishings. Spacious rooms have contemporary whitewash finish (pickled) furnishings. 83 units. *Bath:* combo or shower only. 3 stories, interior corridors. **Terms:** package plans. **Amenities:** extended cable TV, irons. *Some:* hair dryers. **Leisure Activities:** sauna, exercise room. **Guest Services:** [ECP] meal plan available, valet laundry. **Business Services:** fax. **Cards:** AE, CB, DI, DS, JC, MC, VI.

SOME UNITS

SUPER 8 MOTEL-ST. PETERSBURG

Phone: (727)572-8881 76

Motel

All Year — 1P: $49-$65 — 2P: $55-$74 — XP: $6 — F12

Location: I-275 southbound exit 18; northbound exit 16, 1 mi w on SR 688, just s. 13260 34th St N 33762. Fax: 727/572-8881. **Facility:** Exterior has chalet look appeal with pool area in front landscaped courtyard area. The rooms are comfortable with average quality but well maintained faux oak finish furnishings. 80 units. Some suites. 3 stories, interior corridors. **Terms:** weekly rates available. **Amenities:** extended cable TV, safes (fee). *Some:* irons, hair dryers. **Leisure Activities:** heated pool. **Guest Services:** [CP] meal plan available, valet and coin laundry. **Business Services:** meeting rooms. **Cards:** AE, CB, DI, DS, JC, MC, VI.

SOME UNITS

SUPER 8 OF CLEARWATER

Phone: (727)799-2678 57

Motel

2/16-4/15	1P: $69	2P: $69	XP: $6	F17
12/1-1/28	1P: $49-$60	2P: $49-$60	XP: $6	F17
1/29-2/15 & 4/16-11/30	1P: $49	2P: $49	XP: $6	F17

Location: US 19, 1.5 mi n of jct SR 60. 22950 US 19N 33765. Fax: 727/726-7263. **Facility:** Set back from busy highway with nice road side appeal. Variety of rooms with comfortable furnishings and oak finish modern rooms. Nice pool area set in rear courtyard area is relaxing. 100 units. 2-3 stories (no elevator), exterior corridors. **Terms:** check-in 4 pm, weekly & monthly rates available. **Amenities:** safes (fee). *Some:* irons, hair dryers. **Guest Services:** complimentary evening beverages, coin laundry. **Business Services:** meeting rooms, fax. **Cards:** AE, CB, DI, DS, JC, MC, VI.

SOME UNITS

(See map p. 796)

WINGATE INN
Motel
▼▼▼

2/1-4/30   2P: $89-$99
12/1-1/31 & 5/1-11/30   2P: $79-$89

Phone: (727)299-9800   [80]

Location: On US 19, 2.3 mi s of jct Ulmerton Rd (SR 688). 5000 Lake Blvd 33760. **Fax:** 727/299-0088. **Facility:** 84 units. Some suites ($119-$130). *Bath:* combo or shower only. 4 stories, interior corridors. **Terms:** package plans. **Amenities:** extended cable TV, video games, dual phone lines, voice mail, safes, irons, hair dryers. **Leisure Activities:** heated pool, whirlpool, exercise room. **Guest Services:** [ECP] meal plan available, valet and coin laundry. **Business Services:** meeting rooms, administrative services, PC, fax. **Cards:** AE, CB, DI, DS, MC, VI.

SOME UNITS

ASK S⊘ ♿ 🛁 🅿 ➰ 📹 📠 📇 DATA PORT / ✕ 🔲 🔋 /
FEE

─────── **WHERE TO DINE** ───────

ALFANSO'S RESTAURANT
Italian
◈◈◈ ◈◈◈

Lunch: $6-$10   Dinner: $12-$25   Phone: 727/584-2125   [60]

Location: On Alt US 19, 0.5 mi n of jct East Bay; in Belleair Place. 1702 Clearwater-Largo Rd 33756. **Hours:** 11:30 am-2:30 & 5-10 pm, Fri & Sat-11 pm. Closed: 11/22, 12/25. **Features:** dressy casual; children's menu; early bird specials; carryout; cocktails; entertainment; a la carte. Striking interior design with gorgeous use of fabric and elements giving feel of an Italian villa. Wall tapestries and various artifacts are unique. The menu is well-rounded with pasta and unique dishes prepared by trained chef. **Cards:** AE, DS, MC, VI.

✕

ARIGATO JAPANESE STEAK HOUSE
Japanese
▼▼ ▼▼

Dinner: $11-$21   Phone: 727/799-0202   [54]

Location: US 19; just s of jct SR 580; in Ramada Inn Countryside. 26508 US 19 N 34621. **Hours:** 5 pm-10 pm, Fri & Sat-10:30 pm, Sun 4 pm-9 pm. Closed: 1/1, 7/4, 11/22, 12/24. **Reservations:** suggested. **Features:** casual dress; children's menu; early bird specials; cocktails & lounge. Japanese cuisine is prepared table-side by strikingly fast chefs with a flare for showmanship. A good place to meet new people, the hibachi tables have different parties seated together. Order the chicken, filet and shrimp combo for a spicy feast. **Cards:** AE, DI, DS, MC, VI.

✕

CARMELITA'S MEXICAN RESTAURANT
Mexican
◈◈◈ ◈◈◈

Lunch: $5-$8   Dinner: $5-$11   Phone: 727/524-8226   [70]

Location: At jct US 19 and SR 686; in TriCity Plaza. 5042 E Bay Dr 33764. **Hours:** 11 am-9:30 pm, Fri & Sat-10:30 pm. Closed major holidays. **Features:** casual dress; children's menu; carryout; cocktails & lounge; a la carte. The large, friendly restaurant serves a wide variety of authentic, made-to-order choices, ranging from grilled chicken quesadillas to a hearty taco salad. Colorful wall decorations and servers in Mexican dress contribute to the south-of-the-border feel. **Cards:** AE, DS, MC, VI.

✕

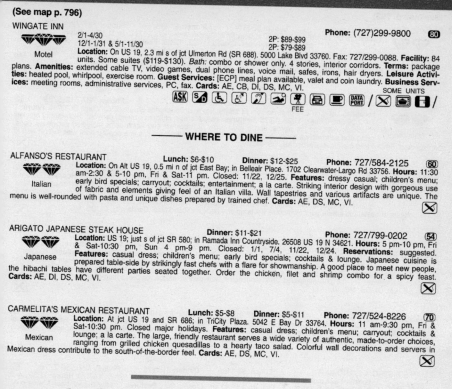

(See map p. 796)

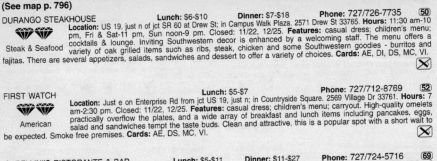

DURANGO STEAKHOUSE
♦♦♦♦ / ♦♦♦♦
Steak & Seafood
Lunch: $6-$10 **Dinner:** $7-$18 **Phone:** 727/726-7735 ⑤⓪
Location: US 19, just n of jct SR 60 at Drew St; in Campus Walk Plaza. 2571 Drew St 33765. **Hours:** 11:30 am-10 pm, Fri & Sat-11 pm, Sun noon-9 pm. Closed: 11/22, 12/25. **Features:** casual dress; children's menu; cocktails & lounge. Inviting Southwestern decor is enhanced by a welcoming staff. The menu offers a variety of oak grilled items such as ribs, steak, chicken and some Southwestern goodies - burritos and fajitas. There are several appetizers, salads, sandwiches and dessert to offer a variety of choices. **Cards:** AE, DI, DS, MC, VI.

FIRST WATCH
♦♦♦♦ / ♦♦♦♦
American
Lunch: $5-$7 **Phone:** 727/712-8769 ⑤②
Location: Just e on Enterprise Rd from jct US 19, just n; in Countryside Square. 2569 Village Dr 33761. **Hours:** 7 am-2:30 pm. Closed: 11/22, 12/25. **Features:** casual dress; children's menu; carryout. High-quality omelets practically overflow the plates, and a wide array of breakfast and lunch items including pancakes, eggs, salad and sandwiches tempt the taste buds. Clean and attractive, this is a popular spot with a short wait to be expected. Smoke free premises. **Cards:** AE, DS, MC, VI.

G. BELLINI'S RISTORANTE & BAR
♦♦♦♦ / ♦♦♦♦
Italian
Lunch: $5-$11 **Dinner:** $11-$27 **Phone:** 727/724-5716 ⑥⑨
Location: On CR 611 at jct Enterprise Rd; in Northwood Plaza. 2544 McMullen Booth Rd 33761. **Hours:** 11:30 am & 4:30-9:30 pm, Fri & Sat-10:30 pm, Sun 4:30 pm-9 pm. Closed major holidays. **Features:** casual dress; children's menu; early bird specials; carryout; cocktails & lounge. An authentic Italian eatery specializing in quality ingredients. The setting is trendy and cosmopolitan. Innovative offerings of antipasto, fresh seafood, ample portions of pasta and create your own pizza will bring you back a second time. **Cards:** AE, DI, DS, MC, VI.

THE GRILL AT FEATHER SOUND
♦♦♦♦ / ♦♦♦♦
American
Lunch: $7-$15 **Dinner:** $17-$26 **Phone:** 727/571-3400 ⑦①
Location: I-275, exit 18, 1.5 mi w; in Feather Sound Square. 2325 Ulmerton Rd 33762. **Hours:** 11:30 am-3 & 5:30-10 pm, Fri-11 pm, Sat 5:30 pm-11 pm. Closed major holidays; also Sun. **Reservations:** suggested. **Features:** dressy casual; children's menu; carryout; cocktails & lounge; a la carte. Here you will find creative dishes served in a sleek, stylish setting. Extraordinary entrees feature quality ingredients used to their best advantage. Try the chili-marinated pork tenderloins with peanut sauce, or the potato-crusted fresh salmon filet. **Cards:** AE, CB, DI, DS, MC, VI.

HARRISON'S GRILL & BAR
♦♦♦♦
American
Lunch: $7-$19 **Dinner:** $7-$19 **Phone:** 727/449-2942 ④⑨
Location: Downtown, just s of jct SR 60. 401 S Ft Harrison Ave 33756. **Hours:** 11 am-11 pm. **Features:** casual dress. Diner style setting with interesting train section that now has a second life as a bar area. The menu features a wide variety of sandwiches, steak, ribs and poultry dishes. **Cards:** MC, VI.

JILLIAN'S BISTRO & PIANO BAR
♦♦♦♦ / ♦♦♦♦
Continental
Lunch: $6-$10 **Dinner:** $16-$26 **Phone:** 727/538-7776 ⑥⑤
Location: Just n of jct SR 688; in Summit Office Building at Icot Center. 13575 58th St N 33760. **Hours:** 11:30 am-2 & 4-9 pm, Fri & Sat-11 pm; Mon from 11:30 am. Closed: Sun. **Features:** dressy casual; beer & wine only; entertainment; buffet. Located in lower level of office complex building, this trendy bistro is casual with a touch of sophistication. Patio dining and catering available. **Cards:** MC, VI.

JOE'S CRAB SHACK
♦♦♦♦ / ♦♦♦♦
Seafood
Lunch: $5-$18 **Dinner:** $5-$18 **Phone:** 727/799-8530 ⑥③
Location: On SR 60 just e of jct US 19. 2730 Gulf to Bay Blvd 33767. **Hours:** 11 am-10 pm. **Features:** casual dress. Eclectic and festive atmosphere with bright lights and multiple colors to enhance this fish camp/shanty themed restaurant. Many items to choose on the menu with appetizers, salad, sandwiches, pasta, seafood and grilled items. The fisherman's platter is superb with the stuffed crab a plus. **Cards:** MC, VI.

JOHNNY'S ITALIAN GRILLE
♦♦♦♦ / ♦♦♦♦
Italian
Lunch: $6-$15 **Dinner:** $6-$15 **Phone:** 727/524-6867 ⑥⑦
Location: 0.5 mi e of jct US 19; in Icot Center, just off Ulmerton Rd. 13505 Icot Blvd 33760. **Hours:** 11 am-9:30 pm. **Features:** casual dress; carryout; cocktails & lounge. Located in upscale shopping and restaurant area. This trendy looking restaurant offers a variety of pasta dishes, pizza, calzones and their famous "Johnny bread." Outdoor patio dining is also available. **Cards:** DS, MC, VI.

KEY WEST GRILL
♦♦♦♦ / ♦♦♦♦
Seafood
Lunch: $6-$12 **Dinner:** $10-$30 **Phone:** 727/797-1988 ⑤⑧
Location: On US 60, just e of jct US 19. 2660 Gulf to Bay Blvd 33759. **Hours:** 11:30 am-10 pm, Fri & Sat-11 pm. Closed: 11/22, 12/25. **Features:** casual dress; children's menu; carryout; cocktails & lounge. Partake of a variety of fresh seafood entrees served in a Key West-style setting. Start with the seafood chowder, a creamy broth with tasty chunks of seafood. The fried shrimp are large and cooked to a golden brown with beans and rice as a side dish. **Cards:** AE, CB, DI, DS, MC, VI.

LENNY'S
♦♦♦♦ / ♦♦♦♦
American
Lunch: $4-$8 **Phone:** 727/799-0402 ⑤⑦
Location: On US 19, 0.3 mi n of SR 60. 21220 US 19N 34625. **Hours:** 6 am-3 pm. Closed: 2 weeks in Sept. **Features:** casual dress; children's menu; carryout. Sensory overload is what you get in this eclectic sports diner. Memorabilia competes for your eyes; a noisy atmosphere conveys an energetic personality; and unusual specialties, such as alligator omelet, pique the attention of your nose and taste buds. **Cards:** DS, MC, VI.

MARCO POLO
♦♦♦♦ / ♦♦♦♦
Continental
Lunch: $4-$12 **Dinner:** $13-$29 **Phone:** 727/791-7979 ⑤⑥
Location: 3.5 mi n of jct US 60; in Northwood Plaza. 2516 McMullen Booth Rd 33761. **Hours:** 11 am-10 pm, Fri & Sat-11:30 am-midnight, Sun noon-9 pm. Closed: Mon. **Reservations:** suggested. **Features:** dressy casual; cocktails & lounge. Elegant surroundings and a broad spectrum of menu choices enhance this dining experience. Servers tend to your every need, allowing you to dine at ease. Try the nicely presented sea trout smothered in a medley of tomatoes, mushrooms and peppers. **Cards:** AE, DI, DS, MC, VI.

(See map p. 796)

PEKING PALACE
Chinese
Lunch: $5-$20   **Dinner:** $5-$20   **Phone:** 727/461-4414 ⑥④
Location: SR 60, 2.5 mi w of jct US 19. 1608 Gulf-to-Bay Blvd 33755. **Hours:** 11:30 am-10 pm, Fri-11 pm, Sat 4:30 pm-11 pm, Sun noon-10 pm. Closed: 11/22. **Reservations:** suggested. **Features:** casual dress; children's menu; early bird specials; carryout; cocktails & lounge; a la carte. A calm, quiet and easy atmosphere pervades the modest dining room, decorated in a simple, Oriental style with paintings and calligraphy. Mandarin, Szechwan, Hunan and Cantonese dishes are cooked fresh and readily modified to suit your taste. **Cards:** AE, DI, DS, MC, VI.

PEPE'S FINE DINING & TAPAS CAFE
Spanish
Lunch: $10-$19   **Dinner:** $14-$23   **Phone:** 727/573-3363 ⑥②
Location: I-275, exit 18, northbound exit 16, 1.9 mi on SR 688. 3665 Ulmerton Rd 33762. **Hours:** 11 am-4 pm, 5-11:30 pm. **Features:** dressy casual; cocktails; a la carte. Intimate surroundings and fine dining with Spanish flair. Classy decor throughout with use of dark woods and multi-color tiles with brass accents. The menu has a variety of salad, sandwiches and appetizers. The Trout LaRussa is quite good and worth trying. **Cards:** MC, VI.

PRIMO'S PASTA-RIBS
Italian
Lunch: $6-$11   **Dinner:** $6-$16   **Phone:** 727/573-7656 ⑥⑧
Location: I-275, exit 18, northbound exit 16, 1.8 mi w on SR 688. 3580 Ulnerto Rd 33762. **Hours:** 11 am-1:30 am. **Features:** casual dress; early bird specials; carryout; cocktails & lounge. Commercially located near many of our listed lodgings and the local airport. Contemporarily decorated with Italian touches, offering a varied menu of pasta dishes, steak, seafood and sandwiches. **Cards:** AE, MC, VI.

SAM SELTZER'S STEAKHOUSE
Steak House
Dinner: $10-$19   **Phone:** 727/519-7267 ④⑧
Location: On US 19, 1.5 mi s of SR 60. 18409 US Hwy 19 N 33764. **Hours:** 4 pm-10 pm, Fri-11 pm, Sat 3:30 pm-11:30 pm, Sun 1 pm-10 pm. Closed: 11/22, 12/25. **Features:** casual dress; children's menu; carryout; cocktails & lounge. Ample portions of chicken, pork and various steak choices are what make this busy chain so popular. Any wait is worthwhile for a good steak, cooked to order. Meals are accompanied by hot rolls, choice of side items and salad. **Cards:** AE, DI, DS, MC, VI.

SCHMOOZE INC OF CLEARWATER
American
Lunch: $7-$17   **Dinner:** $7-$17   **Phone:** 727/449-9777 ⑤①
Location: On SR 60 just e of jct Keene. 1849 Gulf to Bay Blvd 33767. **Hours:** 11 am-midnight, Sat-1 am. Closed: 11/22, 12/25. **Features:** casual dress; children's menu; early bird specials; carryout; beer & wine only. Sit back and enjoy the jazz music in this contemporary setting with record studio theme, including rock group pictures, ticket stubs and albums. Menu includes salad, soup, sandwiches and various entrees. Try the Drunk Monkey Cheesecake! **Cards:** AE, DI, DS, MC, VI.

SWEETWATER'S RESTAURANT
Steak & Seafood
Lunch: $6-$20   **Dinner:** $6-$20   **Phone:** 727/799-0818 ⑥⑥
Location: On SR 60, 0.5 mi w of jct US 19. 2400 Gulf-to-Bay Blvd 33765. **Hours:** 11:30 am-10 pm. Closed: 12/25. **Reservations:** required. **Features:** casual dress; children's menu; early bird specials; carryout; cocktails & lounge. Very popular, local restaurant for tour groups and buses. Varied menu offers steak, poultry, seafood, salad, appetizers and dessert. **Cards:** AE, DI, DS, MC, VI.

TIO PEPE RESTAURANTE
Spanish
Lunch: $6-$11   **Dinner:** $11-$25   **Phone:** 727/799-3082 ⑤⑨
Location: SR 60, 0.8 mi e of jct US 19. 2930 Gulf-to-Bay Blvd 33759. **Hours:** 11 am-2:30 & 5-11 pm, Fri-11:30 pm, Sat 5 pm-11:30 pm, Sun 4 pm-10 pm. Closed: 1/1, 11/22, 12/25; also Mon. **Reservations:** suggested. **Features:** casual dress; children's menu; carryout; cocktails & lounge. Servers crush fruit and blend in brown sugar to make a one-of-a-kind table-side sangria. Ample portions of Spanish cuisine make for a satisfying meal. For something unique, try the pork in an apple-prune sauce; then indulge in rich chocolate mousse cake. **Cards:** AE, MC, VI.

TUCSON'S
American
Lunch: $7-$23   **Dinner:** $7-$23   **Phone:** 727/530-0637 ⑥①
Location: On SR 688, just e of jct US 19; in Icot Center. 13563 Icot Blvd 34620. **Hours:** 11 am-midnight, Sun 4 pm-10 pm. Closed: 11/22, 12/25. **Features:** casual dress; children's menu; early bird specials; carryout; cocktails & lounge; a la carte; buffet. Oak grilled steak and seafood; featuring Southwest themed menu-enchiladas, burritos, tacos, chimichungas, pasta dishes and fajitas. Outside patio bar and dining. Three private rooms and banquet facilities. **Cards:** AE, DI, DS, MC, VI.

CLEARWATER BEACH   (See map p. 796; index p. 801)

—— WHERE TO STAY ——

ADAM'S MARK CLEARWATER BEACH RESORT
Hotel
Phone: (727)443-5714 ①①⑦

	1P: $89-$219	2P: $99-$229	XP: $10	F18
12/1-1/24				
1/25-11/30	1P: $99-$219	2P: $99-$219	XP: $10	F18

Location: 0.5 mi s of roundabout. 430 S Gulfview Blvd 33767. Fax: 727/442-8389. **Facility:** Gulf front. 217 units. Some suites ($250-$550). **Bath:** combo or shower only. 14 stories, interior corridors. **Parking:** extra charge or valet. **Terms:** check-in 4 pm, 3 day cancellation notice-fee imposed, package plans. **Amenities:** voice mail, irons, hair dryers. **Dining:** 2 restaurants, 6:30 am-11 pm; outdoor tiki lounge, $13-$26, cocktails, entertainment. **Leisure Activities:** heated pool, wading pool, whirlpool, beach access, fishing, recreation program, social program, volleyball. *Fee:* parasailing, waverunners. **Guest Services:** [BP] meal plan available, gift shop, valet and coin laundry. *Fee:* area transportation-trolley. **Business Services:** conference facilities, fax. **Cards:** AE, CB, DI, DS, MC, VI. **Special Amenities:** early check-in/late check-out and preferred room (subject to availability with advanced reservations). *(See color ad p 852)*

SOME UNITS

(See map p. 796)

AMERICANA GULF RESORT

Apartment

2/2-4/15
4/16-9/6
12/1-2/1
9/7-11/30

1P: $95-$150
1P: $69-$135
1P: $69-$109
1P: $62-$99

2P: $95-$150
2P: $69-$135
2P: $69-$109
2P: $62-$99

Phone: (727)461-7695

XP: $8
XP: $5
XP: $5
XP: $5

F15
F15
F15
F15

Location: 0.5 mi s of jct SR 60 (causeway). 325 S Gulfview Blvd 33767. Fax: 727/447-5293. **Facility:** Some motel units available. 60 units, 48 with efficiency. 5 stories, exterior corridors. **Terms:** 3 day cancellation notice, weekly & monthly rates available. **Amenities:** extended cable TV, safes (fee). *Some:* irons. **Leisure Activities:** heated pool, beach access. **Guest Services:** gift shop. **Cards:** AE, DS, MC, VI. **Special Amenities:** free newspaper and preferred room (subject to availability with advanced reservations).

(See map p. 796)

BEACHOUSE

Apartment

2/1-4/29	1P: $95-$185	2P: $95-$185
12/1-1/31 & 4/30-11/30	1P: $55-$150	2P: $55-$150

Phone: 727/461-4862   **111**

Location: 0.5 mi s of jct SR 60 (causeway) via Coronado just n. 421 Hamden Dr 33767. **Facility:** Very nice courtyard area with property overlooking Intracoastal Waterway. Smoke free premises. 6 units. 2 efficiencies and 4 units with kitchen. Some suites. *Bath:* combo or shower only. 1 story, exterior corridors. **Terms:** age restrictions may apply, 30 day cancellation notice-fee imposed, weekly rates available. **Leisure Activities:** heated pool, sun deck. **Cards:** MC, VI.

BEL CREST BEACH RESORT

Condominium

2/7-4/30		
12/22-2/6	2P: $99-$171	XP: $8
12/1-12/21 & 5/1-11/30	2P: $76-$128	XP: $6
	2P: $59-$112	XP: $6

Phone: (727)442-4923   **100**

Location: 1 mi s of jct 60 (causeway) via Gulfview Blvd. 706 Bayway Blvd 33767. Fax: 727/442-7455. **Facility:** On Intracoastal Waterway. 19 units. 3 two-bedroom units, 2 efficiencies and 17 units with kitchen. 2 stories, exterior corridors. **Terms:** age restrictions may apply, 10 day cancellation notice-fee imposed, weekly & monthly rates available. **Amenities:** extended cable TV, safes, irons. *Some:* hair dryers. **Leisure Activities:** heated pool, boat dock, fishing. **Guest Services:** coin laundry. **Business Services:** fax. **Cards:** AE, DS, MC, VI. **Special Amenities:** early check-in/late check-out and preferred room (subject to availability with advanced reservations).

SOME UNITS

BEST WESTERN SEA STONE RESORT & SUITES

Motel

2/12-4/21	1P: $99-$190	2P: $109-$190	XP: $10	F18
12/1-12/31	1P: $59-$179	2P: $69-$174	XP: $10	F18
1/1-2/11 & 4/22-11/30	1P: $69-$159	2P: $79-$159	XP: $10	F18

Phone: (727)441-1722   **115**

Location: 0.8 mi s of jct roundabout. 445 Hamden Dr 33767. Fax: 727/461-1680. **Facility:** On Intracoastal Waterway, with private marina. Nicely appointed units with contemporary design. 106 units, 44 with efficiency. Some suites ($149-$190). 6 stories, exterior corridors. **Terms:** check-in 4 pm, 3 day cancellation notice, package plans, small pets only ($50 extra charge). **Amenities:** extended cable TV, voice mail, safes, irons, hair dryers. **Dining:** dining room, 7-11 am, Sat & Sun-noon; lobby bar 3 pm-11 pm, bar menu available, cocktails. **Leisure Activities:** heated pool, whirlpool, fishing, children's program in summer, hair salon, rental car. *Fee:* boat dock, charter fishing, boat tours, jet ski, parasailing, sailing lessons. **Guest Services:** [BP] meal plan available, valet and coin laundry. **Business Services:** meeting rooms. **Cards:** AE, CB, DI, DS, JC, MC, VI. **Special Amenities:** free newspaper and free room upgrade (subject to availability with advanced reservations). *(See ad below)*

SOME UNITS

(See map p. 796)

BEST WESTERN SEA WAKE INN
AAA SAVE
WWW
Motel

Phone: (727)443-7652 120

	1P: $155-$186	2P: $165-$196	XP: $10	F18
2/12-4/21	1P: $148-$178	2P: $158-$188	XP: $10	F18
12/1-12/31	1P: $111-$143	2P: $121-$153	XP: $10	F18
1/1-2/11 & 4/22-11/30				

Location: 0.9 mi s of jct SR 60 (causeway). 691 S Gulfview Blvd 33767. Fax: 727/461-2836. **Facility:** Gulf front. 110 units. 6 stories, interior corridors. **Terms:** check-in 4 pm, 3 day cancellation notice, package plans. **Amenities:** extended cable TV, safes, irons, hair dryers. **Dining:** restaurant, 7 am-2 pm, cocktails. **Leisure Activities:** heated pool, beach, sun deck, fishing, children's program in summer, playground, volleyball. **Guest Services:** gift shop, valet and coin laundry. **Business Services:** meeting rooms, fax. **Cards:** AE, CB, DI, DS, MC, VI. **Special Amenities:** free newspaper and free room upgrade (subject to availability with advanced reservations). *(See ad p 853)* SOME UNITS

[icons] FEE

BLUE JAY MOTEL
AAA SAVE
WWW
Apartment

Phone: (727)446-0356 90

2/2-4/21	1P: $63-$98	2P: $63-$98	XP: $10	F4
12/16-2/1	1P: $45-$80	2P: $45-$80	XP: $10	F4
4/22-11/30	1P: $42-$75	2P: $42-$75	XP: $6	F4
12/1-12/15	1P: $38-$72	2P: $38-$72		

Location: 0.5 mi s on Coronado Dr, 0.4 mi e. 150 Brightwater Dr 33767. Fax: 727/446-0356. **Facility:** On Intracoastal Waterway. 18 units, 17 with kitchen. 1-2 stories, exterior corridors. **Terms:** 30 day cancellation notice-fee imposed, weekly rates available. **Amenities:** extended cable TV. **Leisure Activities:** heated pool, fishing, dock for small boats, shuffleboard. **Guest Services:** coin laundry. **Cards:** AE, DS, MC, VI. **Special Amenities:** free local telephone calls and free newspaper. SOME UNITS

[icons]

CASA ROSA APARTMENT MOTEL
AAA SAVE
WWW
Apartment

Phone: (727)446-9775 92

2/1-4/20	1P: $65-$130	2P: $65-$130		
12/21-1/31	1P: $50-$100	2P: $50-$100		
4/21-11/30	1P: $39-$79	2P: $39-$79		
12/1-12/20	1P: $39-$79	2P: $39-$79	XP: $5	

Location: 0.5 mi s on Coronado Dr; 0.5 mi e. 200 Brightwater Dr 34630. Fax: 727/443-1798. **Facility:** On Intracoastal Waterway. 18 units. 8 efficiencies and 10 units with kitchen. *Bath:* combo or shower only. 2 stories, exterior corridors. **Terms:** 28 day cancellation notice, daily & monthly rates available. **Amenities:** extended cable TV. *Some:* irons. **Leisure Activities:** 2 pools (1 heated), boat dock, fishing, small library. **Guest Services:** coin laundry. **Business Services:** fax. **Cards:** MC, VI. **Special Amenities:** early check-in/late check-out and preferred room (subject to availability with advanced reservations). SOME UNITS

[icons]

CHART HOUSE SUITES ON CLEARWATER BAY
AAA SAVE
WWW
Suite Motel

Phone: (727)449-8007 96

| 12/16-4/30 | 1P: $129-$199 | 2P: $129-$199 | XP: $10 | F18 |
| 12/1-12/15 & 5/1-11/30 | 1P: $89-$159 | 2P: $89-$159 | XP: $10 | F18 |

Location: 1.3 mi s of jct SR 60 (causeway) via Gulf View Blvd. 850 Bayway Blvd 33767. Fax: 727/443-6081. **Facility:** On Intracoastal Waterway, all units with private balcony or patio. Office hours 8 am-9 pm. 25 units. 3 three-bedroom units, 16 efficiencies and 9 units with kitchen. Some whirlpool units. 4 stories, interior corridors. **Terms:** check-in 4 pm, 3 day cancellation notice, weekly & monthly rates available. **Amenities:** extended cable TV, voice mail, irons, hair dryers. **Leisure Activities:** heated pool, marina, fishing. *Fee:* boat slips. **Guest Services:** valet and coin laundry. **Business Services:** fax. **Cards:** AE, DI, DS, MC, VI. SOME UNITS

[icons] DATA PORT

THE DUNES MOTEL
AAA SAVE
WWW
Motel

Phone: (727)441-4939 105

2/16-4/19	1P: $75-$174		XP: $5	F12
12/1-2/15	1P: $54-$150		XP: $5	F12
4/20-8/31	1P: $53-$112		XP: $5	F12
9/1-11/30	1P: $48-$112		XP: $5	F12

Location: 0.5 mi s of jct SR 60 (causeway). 514 S Gulfview Blvd 33767. Fax: 727/441-0490. **Facility:** On Intracoastal Waterway. Private balcony or patio in all units; nicely landscaped grounds. 36 units. 5 two-bedroom units, 1 three-bedroom unit and 26 efficiencies. *Bath:* combo or shower only. 2 stories, interior/exterior corridors. **Terms:** 10 day cancellation notice, weekly & monthly rates available. **Amenities:** extended cable TV. *Some:* irons, hair dryers. **Leisure Activities:** heated pool, fishing, gas barbecue grill, fishing pier, sun deck. **Guest Services:** coin laundry. **Business Services:** fax. **Cards:** AE, DS, MC, VI. SOME UNITS

[icons]

EAST SHORE RESORT APARTMENT MOTEL
AAA SAVE
WWWW
Apartment

Phone: 727/442-3636 86

| 12/1-4/30 Wkly | | 2P: $615-$680 | XP: $70 | |
| 5/1-11/30 Wkly | | 2P: $440-$515 | XP: $43 | |

Location: Just n on East Shore Dr from jct SR 60 (causeway). 473 E Shore Dr 33767. Fax: 978/957-6390. **Facility:** On Intracoastal Waterway. 10 units. 1 efficiency and 9 units with kitchen. 2 stories, exterior corridors. **Terms:** 30 day cancellation notice, daily & monthly rates available. **Amenities:** extended cable TV, irons. *Some:* safes. **Leisure Activities:** heated pool, cabana, boat dock, fishing, bicycles, barbecue grill & patio area. **Guest Services:** complimentary laundry. **Business Services:** meeting rooms. **Special Amenities:** free local telephone calls. SOME UNITS

[icons] DATA PORT VCR

ECHO SAILS MOTEL & APTS
AAA SAVE
WWW
Apartment

Phone: (727)442-6962 94

2/1-4/21		2P: $55-$80	XP: $10	F3
12/20-1/31		2P: $40-$60	XP: $10	F3
12/1-12/19 & 4/22-11/30		2P: $35-$55	XP: $8	F3

Location: 0.3 mi s of jct SR 60 (causeway). 216 Hamden Dr 33767. Fax: 727/442-6962. **Facility:** 16 units. 1 two-bedroom unit, 4 efficiencies and 12 units with kitchen. 2 stories, exterior corridors. **Terms:** 30 day cancellation notice-fee imposed, weekly rates available. **Leisure Activities:** heated pool, shuffleboard. **Guest Services:** coin laundry. **Cards:** MC, VI. **Special Amenities:** free local telephone calls. SOME UNITS

[icons]

(See map p. 796)

ECONO LODGE

AAA [SAVE]
♦♦♦ Motel

			Phone: (727)446-3400	118
2/12-4/30	1P: $100-$200	2P: $100-$200	XP: $10	F18
5/1-11/30	1P: $64-$200	2P: $64-$200	XP: $10	F18
12/18-2/11	1P: $74-$150	2P: $74-$150	XP: $10	F18
12/1-12/17	1P: $64-$150	2P: $64-$150	XP: $10	F18

Location: 0.8 mi s of jct SR 60 (causeway). 625 S Gulfview Blvd 33767. Fax: 727/446-4615. **Facility:** Gulf front. 64 units. 63 efficiencies and 1 unit with kitchen. *Bath:* combo or shower only. 5 stories, interior corridors. **Amenities:** safes. **Leisure Activities:** heated pool, whirlpool, beach, fishing. **Guest Services:** coin laundry. **Cards:** AE, CB, DI, DS, JC, MC, VI. *(See ad below)*

SOME UNITS
[S/D] [♦] [FEE] [symbols] / [X] /

FALCON MOTEL

AAA [SAVE]
♦♦♦ Apartment

			Phone: 727/447-8714	109
12/16-3/31	1P: $36-$82	2P: $38-$82	XP: $8	
4/1-8/31	1P: $36-$65	2P: $38-$65	XP: $8	
12/1-12/15 & 9/1-11/30	1P: $30-$45	2P: $33-$45	XP: $8	

Location: 0.7 mi s of jct SR 60 (causeway). 415 Coronado Dr 33767. Fax: 727/461-3735. **Facility:** 19 units, 15 with efficiency. *Bath:* combo or shower only. 2 stories, exterior corridors. **Terms:** age restrictions may apply, 30 day cancellation notice, weekly rates available. **Amenities:** extended cable TV, hair dryers. **Business Services:** fax. **Cards:** DS, MC, VI. **Special Amenities:** early check-in/late check-out and free newspaper.

SOME UNITS
[symbols] / [symbol] /

HILTON CLEARWATER BEACH RESORT

AAA [SAVE]
♦♦♦♦ Hotel

			Phone: (727)461-3222	106
2/1-4/30	1P: $189-$299	2P: $189-$299		
5/1-8/23	1P: $169-$299	2P: $169-$299		
12/1-1/31 & 8/24-11/30	1P: $159-$299	2P: $159-$299		

Location: Jct SR 60 (Clearwater Pass Bridge); adjacent to the "Fountain". 400 Mandalay Ave 33767. Fax: 727/461-0610. **Facility:** Gulf front locale enhances this resort style property. Upscale furnishings with bright inviting colors in use, most have private balcony with gulf or city views. 425 units. Some suites and whirlpool units. *Bath:* combo or shower only. 9 stories, interior corridors. **Parking:** extra charge or valet. **Terms:** check-in 4 pm, 3 day cancellation notice-fee imposed, weekly & monthly rates available, package plans. **Amenities:** extended cable TV, video games, voice mail, safes, irons, hair dryers. *Some:* irons. **Dining:** 2 restaurants, 6:30 am-10 pm; Sand Bar & Grill, $10-$30, cocktails, entertainment. **Leisure Activities:** 2 heated pools, whirlpool, beach, children's program, recreation program, supervised kids camp, exercise room, volleyball. *Fee:* sailboating, cabanas, hydro bikes, wave runners, spa services, game room. **Guest Services:** [BP] meal plan available, gift shop, valet and coin laundry. *Fee:* massage. **Business Services:** conference facilities, administrative services, fax. *Fee:* PC. **Cards:** AE, DI, DS, MC, VI. **Special Amenities:** free newspaper and preferred room (subject to availability with advanced reservations). *(See ad p 44 & color ad p 852)*

SOME UNITS
[S/D] [symbols] [FEE] [X] [VCR] [FEE] [symbols] /

HOLIDAY INN SUNSPREE RESORT & CONFERENCE CENTER

AAA [SAVE]
♦♦♦ Hotel

			Phone: (727)447-9566	112
12/1-1/2	1P: $149-$199	2P: $149-$199	XP: $10	F19
1/3-11/30	1P: $139-$179	2P: $139-$179	XP: $10	F19

Location: 1 mi s at Clearwater Pass Bridge. 715 S Gulfview Blvd 33767. Fax: 727/446-4978. **Facility:** Gulf front. Many units with balcony and view of inlet. 216 units. Some suites. *Bath:* combo or shower only. 10 stories, interior/exterior corridors. **Terms:** check-in 4 pm, 3 day cancellation notice-fee imposed, package plans. **Amenities:** dual phone lines, voice mail, safes, irons, hair dryers. **Dining:** 2 restaurants, 6:30 am-1 & 5-10 pm; tiki bar, $10-$16, cocktails. **Leisure Activities:** heated pool, wading pool, whirlpool, beach, sun deck, fishing, putting green, children's program, recreation program, social program, activities center, playground, exercise room, shuffleboard, volleyball, game room, lending library. *Fee:* waterskiing, jet skis, parasailing. **Guest Services:** [BP] meal plan available, gift shop, valet and coin laundry. *Fee:* area transportation-trolley, massage. **Business Services:** conference facilities, administrative services, fax. *Fee:* PC. **Cards:** AE, CB, DI, DS, MC, VI. *(See color ad p 856)*

SOME UNITS
[S/D] [FEE] [symbols] [FEE] [symbols] [FEE] [X] [VCR] [symbols] /

(See map p. 796)

HOWARD JOHNSON EXPRESS INN

(AAA) [SAVE]

◆◆◆ ◆◆

Motel

3/1-4/30	1P: $99-$149	2P: $99-$149
12/1-2/28 & 5/1-11/30	1P: $69-$99	2P: $69-$99

Phone: (727)442-6606 98

XP: $10 F16
XP: $10 F16

Location: 0.8 mi s of jct SR 60 (causeway). 656 Bayway Blvd 33767. **Fax:** 727/461-0809. **Facility:** On Intracoastal Waterway. 36 units, 1 with efficiency. 2 stories, exterior corridors. **Amenities:** extended cable TV, safes (fee). *Some:* irons. **Leisure Activities:** heated pool, boat dock, fishing, shuffleboard. **Guest Services:** coin laundry. **Business Services:** fax. **Cards:** AE, DI, DS, MC, VI. **Special Amenities:** free continental breakfast.

SOME UNITS

ISLAND QUEEN RESORT MOTEL

(AAA) [SAVE]

◆◆◆ ◆◆◆

Apartment

2/1-4/20		2P: $72-$98
12/1-1/31		2P: $49-$75
4/21-11/30		2P: $49-$73
4/21-11/30	1P: $54-$67	2P: $54-$67

Phone: 727/442-8068 91

XP: $10 F5
XP: $10 F5
XP: $10 F5
XP: $6 F5

Location: 0.5 mi s on Coronado Dr, just e on Devon Dr, just s. 158 Brightwater Dr 33767. **Fax:** 727/442-2412. **Facility:** On Intracoastal Waterway. 14 units. 3 efficiencies and 11 units with kitchen. Some suites. *Bath:* combo or shower only. 2 stories, exterior corridors. **Terms:** 30 day cancellation notice, weekly & monthly rates available. **Amenities:** extended cable TV, irons. **Leisure Activities:** heated pool, marina, fishing, shuffleboard, sun deck, barbecue. **Guest Services:** coin laundry. **Business Services:** fax. **Cards:** AE, DS, MC, VI.

KOLI-BREE MOTEL/APT

(AAA) [SAVE]

◆◆◆ ◆◆

Apartment

2/1-4/30	1P: $82	2P: $82
12/15-1/31	1P: $62	2P: $62
12/1-12/14 & 5/1-11/30	1P: $56	2P: $56

Phone: (727)461-6223 88

XP: $10 F10
XP: $10 F10
XP: $10 F10

Location: Just n on Pointsettia Dr from jct SR 60 (Cswy). 440 E Shore Dr 33767. **Fax:** 727/298-8712. **Facility:** 10 units with kitchen. *Bath:* combo or shower only. 2 stories, exterior corridors. **Terms:** 2 night minimum stay, 14 day cancellation notice-fee imposed, weekly & monthly rates available. **Amenities:** extended cable TV. *Some:* irons, hair dryers. **Leisure Activities:** sun deck. **Business Services:** fax. **Cards:** AE, CB, DI, DS, MC, VI. SOME UNITS

(See map p. 796)

LEISURE INN & SUITES

AAA [SAVE]

WWW WWW	1/23-4/21		2P: $85-$105	XP: $10	F12
	4/22-9/9		2P: $60-$80	XP: $5	F12
	12/1-1/22		2P: $50-$80	XP: $5	F12
Apartment	9/10-11/30		2P: $50-$70	XP: $5	F12

Phone: (727)441-4902   [97]

Location: 0.5 mi s of roundabout. 445 S Gulfview Blvd 33767. Fax: 727/446-4105. **Facility:** 59 units, 14 with efficiency. Some suites ($70-$105). 4 stories, interior/exterior corridors. **Terms:** age restrictions may apply, 3 day cancellation notice. **Amenities:** extended cable TV, safes (fee). *Some:* irons. **Dining:** tiki bar. **Leisure Activities:** heated pool. **Guest Services:** coin laundry. **Cards:** AE, DI, DS, MC, VI. **Special Amenities:** early check-in/late check-out.

SOME UNITS

[S][D] [†◄] [≈] [DATA PORT] / [✕] [▦] [🖴] /

MANNINGS ON THE BAY

AAA [SAVE]

WWW WWW	2/16-4/30		2P: $85-$149	XP: $8	F11
	12/1-2/15		2P: $59-$104	XP: $8	F11
	5/1-8/31		2P: $51-$91	XP: $8	F11
Apartment	9/1-11/30		2P: $47-$84	XP: $8	F11

Phone: (727)447-6407   [104]

Location: 0.8 mi s of jct SR 60 (causeway). 530 S Gulfview Blvd 33767. Fax: 727/449-8109. **Facility:** On Intracoastal Waterway. 29 units, 22 with efficiency. 2 stories, interior corridors. **Terms:** 10 day cancellation notice, weekly & monthly rates available. **Amenities:** extended cable TV. **Leisure Activities:** heated pool, sun deck, boat dock, fishing. **Guest Services:** [CP] meal plan available. **Cards:** AE, CB, DI, DS, MC, VI.

[†◄] [≈] [🖴]

NEW YORKER MOTEL

AAA [SAVE]

WWW WWW	2/1-4/30	1P: $75-$98	2P: $75-$98	XP: $5	F3
	12/1-1/31	1P: $55-$76	2P: $55-$76	XP: $5	F3
	5/1-11/30	1P: $52-$70	2P: $52-$70	XP: $5	F3

Phone: (727)446-2437   [93]

Location: 0.5 mi s on Coronato Dr, just e on Brightwater Dr. 332 Hamden Dr 33767. Fax: 727/446-5818. **Facility:** 15 units. 8 efficiencies and 7 units with kitchen. Some suites. 2 stories, exterior corridors. **Terms:** 14 day cancellation notice, weekly rates available. **Amenities:** extended cable TV, safes. *Some:* irons, hair dryers. **Leisure Activities:** heated pool, barbecue grill. **Guest Services:** coin laundry. **Business Services:** fax. **Cards:** DS, MC, VI. **Special Amenities:** early check-in/late check-out and free local telephone calls.

[†◄] [≈] [▥] [▭] [▦] [🖴] [DATA PORT]

THE PALM PAVILION INN

AAA [SAVE]

WWW WWW	2/9-4/29	1P: $87-$125	2P: $87-$125	XP: $8	F16
	12/1-2/8 & 4/30-11/30	1P: $59-$89	2P: $59-$89	XP: $8	F16

Phone: (727)446-6777   [85]

Location: 0.6 mi n of SR 60 (causeway). 18 Bay Esplanade 33767. Fax: 727/461-0355. **Facility:** Gulf front view. Home of the oldest operating beach concession in Florida. 29 units, 3 with efficiency. *Bath:* combo or shower only. 1-3 stories, interior/exterior corridors. **Terms:** 14 day cancellation notice, weekly & monthly rates available, package plans. **Amenities:** extended cable TV. **Dining:** restaurant, 9 am-10:30 pm seasonal, seasonal entertainment, $5-$8, cocktails. **Leisure Activities:** heated pool, beach, sun deck. *Fee:* beach chairs, cabanas, umbrellas. **Guest Services:** gift shop. **Business Services:** meeting rooms. **Cards:** AE, DS, MC, VI. *(See color ad below)*

SOME UNITS

[S][D] [†◄] [Y] [≈] [🎥] / [▦] [🖴] /

PELICAN COVE MOTEL

AAA [SAVE]

WWW WWW	2/1-4/22	1P: $52-$82	2P: $52-$82	XP: $10	F3
	12/1-1/31	1P: $42-$72	2P: $42-$72	XP: $10	F3
Apartment	4/23-11/30	1P: $35-$69	2P: $35-$69	XP: $8	F3

Phone: 727/442-3735   [89]

Location: 0.5 mi s on Coronado Dr, just e. 125 Brightwater Dr 33767. Fax: 727/461-2541. **Facility:** On Intracoastal Waterway. 11 units, 2 with efficiency. *Bath:* combo or shower only. 1 story, exterior corridors. **Terms:** 3 night minimum stay, 30 day cancellation notice, One-bedroom apartments, $418-$560. **Leisure Activities:** heated pool, whirlpool, boat dock, fishing, barbecue grill area. **Guest Services:** coin laundry. **Cards:** AE, DS, MC, VI. **Special Amenities:** free local telephone calls.

[†◄] [≈] [▥] [▭] [🖴]

(See map p. 796)

QUALITY INN BEACH RESORT

Phone: (727)442-7171   **119**

AAA SAVE

	2/9-4/21	1P: $159-$199	2P: $159-$199	XP: $20	F17
	4/22-11/30	1P: $129-$169	2P: $129-$169	XP: $10	F17
	12/1-2/8	1P: $125-$159	2P: $125-$159	XP: $10	F17

Motor Inn

Location: 0.8 mi s of jct SR 60 (causeway). 655 S Gulfview Blvd 33767. Fax: 727/446-6177. **Facility:** Gulf view. 93 units. Some suites. 5 stories, interior/exterior corridors. **Amenities:** extended cable TV, voice mail, safes, irons, hair dryers. **Dining:** restaurant, 24 hours, poolside bar, $5-$10, cocktails, entertainment. **Leisure Activities:** heated pool, beach, sun deck, playground. **Fee:** health club privileges, parasailing. **Guest Services:** valet and coin laundry. **Business Services:** meeting rooms, fax. **Cards:** AE, CB, DI, DS, MC, VI. **Special Amenities:** free local telephone calls. (See color ad below)   SOME UNITS

[icons]   FEE

RADISSON SUITE RESORT ON SAND KEY

Phone: (727)596-1100   **126**

AAA SAVE

	1/3-4/30	1P: $269-$310	2P: $269-$310	XP: $10	F17
	12/1-1/2	1P: $219-$299	2P: $219-$299	XP: $10	F17
	5/1-11/30	1P: $229-$269	2P: $229-$269	XP: $10	F17

Suite Hotel

Location: SR 699, just s of Clearwater Pass Bridge. 1201 Gulf Blvd 33767. Fax: 727/595-4292. **Facility:** Bayfront locale, all rooms with balcony overlooking the bay. Beautiful pool area with rocks and waterfall area. Property has several restaurants, shops and boutiques attached by boardwalk. See "Lisa" the blue and gold macaw, always a welcoming site to the property. Rooms have separate living area with wetbar and work area. 220 units. Some whirlpool units. 10 stories, exterior corridors. **Parking:** valet. **Terms:** check-in 4 pm, cancellation fee imposed, weekly rates available, package plans. **Amenities:** video games, voice mail, honor bars, irons, hair dryers. **Dining:** 5 restaurants, deli, 7 am-11 pm; ice cream parlor, donut shop, $9-$20, cocktails, entertainment. **Leisure Activities:** heated pool, wading pool, sauna, whirlpool, fishing, children's program, recreation program, social program, playground, exercise room, sand & water volleyball. **Fee:** bicycles. **Guest Services:** gift shop, coin laundry. **Fee:** area transportation-trolley, massage. **Business Services:** conference facilities, administrative services, fax. **Fee:** PC. **Cards:** AE, CB, DI, DS, MC, VI. (See ad below)   SOME UNITS

[icons]   FEE   FEE

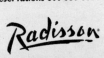

(See map p. 796)

RAMADA INN GULFVIEW

AAA [SAVE]

◇◇◇ ▽▽▽

Hotel

				Phone: (727)447-6461	116
1/18-4/21	1P: $144-$184	2P: $144-$184	XP: $10		F17
4/22-11/30	1P: $119-$169	2P: $119-$169	XP: $10		F17
12/1-1/17	1P: $109-$169	2P: $109-$169	XP: $10		F17

Location: 0.7 mi s of jct SR 60 at jct Hamden. 521 S Gulfview Blvd 33767. Fax: 727/443-5888. **Facility:** Gulf front locale with pool deck overlooking waterway. Each room has private balcony with gulf or harbor/city view. Rooms are bright and cheery with contemporary furnishings, as is the lobby and registration areas. 289 units, 1 with kitchen. Some suites. 9 stories, interior corridors. **Terms:** check-in 4 pm, package plans. **Amenities:** voice mail, safes (fee). *Some:* irons, hair dryers. **Dining:** restaurant, 24 hours, tiki bar, $4-$8, cocktails, entertainment. **Leisure Activities:** heated pool, wading pool, sun deck, game room, electric car rental, hair & nail salon, game room. *Fee:* parasailing, waverunner, health club privileges. **Guest Services:** [BP] meal plan available, gift shop, valet and coin laundry. **Business Services:** meeting rooms, fax. **Cards:** AE, DI, DS, MC, VI. **Special Amenities:** early check-in/late check-out. *(See color ad p 852)*

SOME UNITS
[icons] FEE

RAMADA LIMITED

AAA [SAVE]

◇◇◇ ▽▽

Motel

			Phone: (727)446-2688	101
All Year	1P: $74-$149	2P: $74-$149	XP: $10	F17

Location: 0.8 mi s of jct SR 60 (causeway) via Gulfview. 674 Bayway Blvd 33767. Fax: 727/449-0834. **Facility:** On Intracoastal Waterway. 22 units. Some suites and whirlpool units. 2 stories, exterior corridors. **Terms:** weekly & monthly rates available, package plans. **Amenities:** extended cable TV, safes (fee), hair dryers. *Some:* irons. **Leisure Activities:** heated pool, boat dock, fishing, shuffleboard. *Fee:* boat slips. **Guest Services:** [ECP] meal plan available, coin laundry. **Business Services:** fax. **Cards:** AE, CB, DI, DS, MC, VI. **Special Amenities:** early check-in/late check-out and free continental breakfast.

SOME UNITS
[icons]

SEA CAPTAIN RESORT ON THE BAY

AAA [SAVE]

◇◇◇ ▽▽▽

Apartment

			Phone: 727/446-7550	99
2/15-4/30	1P: $80-$100	2P: $80-$100	XP: $10	F13
12/1-2/14 & 5/1-11/30	1P: $60-$74	2P: $60-$74	XP: $6	F13

Location: Just s of jct SR 60 (causeway) via Coronado. 40 Devon Dr 33767. Fax: 727/298-0100. **Facility:** Contemporary decor in units with many overlooking bay. Room with wood burning fireplace. Designated smoking area. 28 units. 12 efficiencies and 11 units with kitchen. Some suites. 2 stories, exterior corridors. **Terms:** 30 day cancellation notice-fee imposed, weekly & monthly rates available. **Amenities:** extended cable TV. *Some:* irons, hair dryers. **Leisure Activities:** heated pool, whirlpool, sun deck, boat dock, fishing, shuffleboard, picnic area & grills, hammock. *Fee:* boat slips, fishing pier. **Guest Services:** coin laundry. **Business Services:** fax. **Cards:** AE, DS, MC, VI.

SOME UNITS
[icons] FEE

SHEPHARD'S BEACH RESORT

AAA [SAVE]

◇◇◇ ▽▽▽

Motor Inn

				Phone: (727)442-5107	110
2/1-4/30	1P: $129-$159	2P: $129-$159	XP: $10		F17
5/1-8/31	1P: $99-$129	2P: $99-$129	XP: $10		F17
12/1-1/31	1P: $89-$129	2P: $89-$129	XP: $10		F17
9/1-11/30	1P: $89-$119	2P: $89-$119	XP: $10		F17

Location: 1 mi s of jct SR 60 (Cswy). 619 S Gulfview Blvd 33767. Fax: 727/446-4238. **Facility:** Gulf view. 90 units. 4 two-bedroom units and 46 units with kitchen. Some suites ($199-$329) and whirlpool units ($299-$425). 2 stories, interior/exterior corridors. **Terms:** 15 day cancellation notice-fee imposed. **Amenities:** extended cable TV, voice mail, safes, irons, hair dryers. **Dining:** 11 am-11 pm, Sun from 1 pm; tiki bar, cocktails, also, Shephard's Waterfront Restaurant, see separate listing, entertainment. **Leisure Activities:** heated pool, whirlpool, beach, game room. **Guest Services:** gift shop, valet and coin laundry. **Business Services:** meeting rooms. **Cards:** AE, DI, DS, MC, VI. **Special Amenities:** free room upgrade (subject to availability with advanced reservations). *(See color ad below)*

SOME UNITS
[icons] FEE

(See map p. 796)

SHERATON SAND KEY RESORT
Phone: (727)595-1611 `125`

◊◊◊◊ 2/1-4/30 1P: $160-$270 2P: $160-$270 XP: $10 F17
12/1-1/31 & 5/1-11/30 1P: $130-$180 2P: $130-$180 XP: $10 F17

Resort **Location:** 2 mi s on SR 699 at s end of Clearwater Pass Bridge. 1160 Gulf Blvd 33767. Fax: 727/596-8488. **Facility:** Gulf front. Locale enhances this beautifully decorated and landscaped resort property. Bright and cheery rooms welcome the guest and are upscale in appearance. The building has a Mediterranean feel upon approach. 390 units. Some suites ($220-$350). 9 stories, interior corridors. **Parking:** valet. **Terms:** cancellation fee imposed, package plans. **Amenities:** video games, voice mail, safes, irons, hair dryers. **Leisure Activities:** heated pool, wading pool, saunas, whirlpool, beach, fishing, charter fishing, 3 lighted tennis courts, children's program in summer, playground, game room. *Fee:* paddleboats, sailboating, windsurfing, bicycles. **Guest Services:** gift shop, valet and coin laundry. *Fee:* area transportation, massage. **Business Services:** conference facilities, administrative services, PC, fax. **Cards:** AE, CB, DI, DS, MC, VI.

SOME UNITS

(ASK) (S⃝) ⊞ ⊞ ⊠ ⊞ ⊞ ⊞ ⊞ ⊞ ⊞ ⊞ ⊞ DATA PORT / ⊠ VCR ⊞ ⊞ /
FEE   FEE   FEE FEE   FEE   FEE

TRAVELODGE BEACHVIEW RESORT
Phone: (727)446-8305 `122`

◊◊ (SAVE) 3/1-4/30 2P: $99-$158 XP: $8 F16
12/1-2/28 & 5/1-9/17 2P: $60-$99 XP: $5 F16
◊◊◊◊ 9/18-11/30 2P: $59-$99 XP: $5 F16

Apartment **Location:** 0.5 mi s of jct SR 60 (causeway). 401 S Gulfview Blvd 33767. Fax: 727/447-5293. **Facility:** Some motel units. 53 units, 44 with efficiency. Some suites. *Bath:* combo or shower only. 4 stories, exterior corridors. **Terms:** 3 day cancellation notice, weekly & monthly rates available. **Amenities:** safes (fee). *Some:* irons, hair dryers. **Leisure Activities:** heated pool, beach access. **Cards:** AE, DS, MC, VI. **Special Amenities:** free newspaper and preferred room (subject to availability with advanced reservations).

SOME UNITS

(S⃝) ⊞ ⊞ DATA PORT / ⊠ ⊞ ⊞ ⊞ /

TROPICAL BREEZE MOTEL
Phone: (727)442-6865 `95`

◊◊ (SAVE) 2/1-4/23 2P: $80-$95 XP: $8 F5
4/24-9/6 2P: $60-$70 XP: $5 F5
◊◊◊◊ 12/1-1/31 2P: $55-$70 XP: $5 F5
9/7-11/30 2P: $55-$65 XP: $5 F5

Apartment **Location:** 0.5 mi s of jct SR 60 (causeway) on Coronado, just on Brightwater. 333 Hamden Dr 34630. Fax: 727/443-4371. **Facility:** 20 units, 16 with kitchen. 2 stories, exterior corridors. **Terms:** 15 day cancellation notice-fee imposed, weekly & monthly rates available. **Amenities:** extended cable TV, safes (fee). *Some:* irons, hair dryers. **Leisure Activities:** heated pool, boat dock, fishing, shuffleboard, gas barbecue grills. **Guest Services:** coin laundry. **Business Services:** fax. **Cards:** AE, DI, DS, MC, VI. **Special Amenities:** free room upgrade and preferred room (each subject to availability with advanced reservations).

⊞ ⊞ ⊠ ⊞ ⊞ ⊞ ⊞

───── **WHERE TO DINE** ─────

BIG BEN BRITISH RESTAURANT & PUB
Lunch: $7-$16 **Phone:** 727/446-8809 `102`

◊ **Location:** 1 mi s of jct SR 60 (causeway) via Gulfview Blvd; in Bay Bazaar. 731 Bayway Blvd 33767. **Hours:** 9 am-2 pm. **Features:** casual dress; early bird specials; carryout; cocktail lounge; beer & wine only. Authentic British pub feel invites one to this restaurant. Menu is traditional with Lords roast, fish-n-chips, cornish pastry, bangers-n-mash, sheperd's pie, kidney pie to choose. Menu also has sandwiches, salad, steak,
English chops, desserts and side dishes. **Cards:** AE, CB, DI, DS, MC, VI. ⊠

BOB HEILMAN'S BEACHCOMBER
Lunch: $5-$15 **Dinner:** $13-$30 **Phone:** 727/442-4144 `99`

◊◊◊ **Location:** Just n of jct SR 60. 447 Mandalay Ave 33767. **Hours:** 11:30 am-midnight, Sun noon-10 pm. **Reservations:** suggested. **Features:** casual dress; children's menu; early bird specials; carryout; cocktails & lounge; entertainment; valet parking; a la carte. Seafood specialties head the menu with steak and
Seafood chops. Grouper five ways and back-to-back farm fried chicken are favorites. Meals are served in a spacious, well-lighted dining room beside a cozy, intimate lounge area. Excellent desserts round out the meal. **Cards:** AE, DI, DS, MC, VI. ⊠

BONSAI JAPANESE CUISINE-SUSHI BAR
Lunch: $6-$8 **Dinner:** $11-$18 **Phone:** 727/446-9452 `111`

◊ **Location:** 0.8 mi s of jct SR 60 (causeway). 656 S Gulfview Blvd 33767. **Hours:** noon-10 pm, Sat & Sun from 4 pm. Closed: Mon. **Features:** casual dress; children's menu; beer & wine only. If you like sushi, you will find an extensive selection of choices featuring ikura, kappamaki, tekka maki, temaki, salmon, skin roll, sake,
Japanese hamachi, unagi, hotategemi, ebi, saba and amaebiare. Entree choices are limited, but you will enjoy the basic but comfortable surroundings. **Cards:** AE, DI, DS, MC, VI.

COLUMBIA RESTAURANT
Lunch: $6-$10 **Dinner:** $13-$20 **Phone:** 727/596-8400 `116`

◊◊ **Location:** On SR 669, just s of Clearwater Pass Bridge. 1241 Gulf Blvd 33767. **Hours:** 11:30 am-10 pm. **Reservations:** suggested; evenings. **Features:** casual dress; children's menu; carryout; cocktails & lounge; a la carte. This very elegant Spanish eatery overlooks Tampa Bay and specializes in Cuban
Spanish favorites like chicken and rice with black beans. The cigar bar and the cocktail bar are perfect for relaxing after a leisurely meal overseen by a gracious, professional staff. **Cards:** AE, CB, DI, DS, MC, VI. ⊠

COOTERS RAW BAR & RESTAURANT
Lunch: $6-$14 **Dinner:** $6-$14 **Phone:** 727/462-2668 `96`

◊ **Location:** Just n of jct SR 60 (causeway). 423 Poinsettia Ave 33767. **Hours:** 11:30 am-10:30 pm, Fri & Sat-1 am. **Features:** casual dress; children's menu; carryout; cocktails & lounge; a la carte. Rustic sea shanty look to this popular local spot. Menu has good variety of choices - salad, gumbo, chowder, grouper sandwiches,
Seafood po'boy, burgers, several entrees from grouper mahi mahi, shrimp, snow crab, crab cakes to New York strip ribeye and baby back ribs. **Cards:** MC, VI. ⊠

(See map p. 796)

FRENCHY'S CAFE
◇◇◇◇

Seafood

Lunch: $5-$8   **Dinner:** $5-$8   **Phone:** 727/446-3607 ⑨⑦
Location: 0.4 mi n on Mondalay Ave from jct SR 60 (causeway), just e. 41 Baymont St 33767. **Hours:** 11:30 am-11 pm, Fri & Sat-midnight, Sun from noon. Closed: 11/22, 12/25. **Features:** casual dress; children's menu; carryout; beer & wine only; a la carte. Key West style theme with this beach type establishment. Very casual and laid back atmosphere. Menu has great variety of sandwiches, burgers, a few entrees and appetizers available. Deck dining available. **Cards:** AE, MC, VI.

FRENCHY'S ROCKAWAY GRILL & BEACH CLUB
◇◇◇◇

American

Lunch: $5-$8   **Dinner:** $6-$13   **Phone:** 727/446-4844 ⑨⑧
Location: Jct SR 60 (cswy), 0.4 mi n on Mandalay Ave, just w. 7 Rockaway St 33767. **Hours:** 11 am-midnight, Fri & Sat-1 am. Closed: 11/22, 12/25. **Features:** casual dress; children's menu; carryout; cocktails & lounge; a la carte. A variety of salads, burgers, sandwiches and seafood with Caribbean flair is offered in a festive beachfront setting. Pleasant servers bring entrees in plastic baskets with french fries and coleslaw. Try the stuffed grouper with crabmeat. **Cards:** AE, MC, VI.

❌

FRENCHY'S SALTWATER CAFE
◇◇◇◇

Seafood

Lunch: $6-$10   **Dinner:** $6-$10   **Phone:** 727/461-6295 ⑪③
Location: Just n of jct Clearwater Pass Bridge (SR 60). 419 Poinsetta Ave 33767. **Hours:** 11 am-11 pm, Sun from noon. Closed: 11/22, 12/25. **Features:** casual dress; children's menu; cocktails; a la carte. You'll get the feeling you're at a Key West fish camp in this casual cafe, which offers indoor and outdoor dining areas with mainly picnic table seating. Fresh catches, boiled shrimp and Key lime pie are yummy, but the saltwater taffy is a special treat. **Cards:** AE, MC, VI.

❌

GONDOLIER PIZZA AND ITALIAN RESTAURANT
◇◇◇

Italian

Lunch: $6-$19   **Dinner:** $6-$19   **Phone:** 727/441-3353 ⑩④
Location: 0.9 mi s of jct SR 60 (causeway). 674 S Gulfview Blvd 34630. **Hours:** 7 am-midnight. **Features:** casual dress; children's menu; carryout; beer & wine only; a la carte. Casual atmosphere with Italian theme and decor. Pleasant wait staff is ready to serve some one hundered items from extensive menu of specialty and standard items. **Cards:** AE, DS, MC, VI.

LEGENDS STEAKHOUSE
◇◇◇◇ ◇◇◇◇

American

Lunch: $8-$16   **Dinner:** $8-$16   **Phone:** 727/445-1755 ⑩⑨
Location: Just s of jct SR 60 (causeway). 309 S Gulfview Blvd 34630. **Hours:** 11:30 am-10 pm. **Features:** casual dress; children's menu; cocktails & lounge; entertainment; a la carte. Across from beach with great views of the gulf; cozy seating indoors or deckside dining outdoors. Menu offers variety of appetizers, salad, pasta dishes, seafood entrees, sandwiches and steak. **Cards:** MC, VI.

LEVEROCK'S OF CLEARWATER BEACH
◇◇◇◇ ◇◇◇◇

Seafood

Lunch: $6-$21   **Dinner:** $9-$21   **Phone:** 727/446-5884 ⑪⑤
Location: N end of Clearwater Pass Bridge. 551 Gulf Blvd 34630. **Hours:** 11:30 am-10 pm. Closed: 11/22, 12/25. **Features:** casual dress; Sunday brunch; children's menu; early bird specials; carryout; cocktails & lounge. Well-established and centrally located near the end of the Clearwater Pass Bridge, it offers a wide range of choices such as seafood Martinique, a puffed pastry filled with shrimp and fish in a creamy sauce. Hot honey wheat bread makes a nice appetizer. **Cards:** AE, DI, DS, MC, VI.

❌

POST CORNER PIZZA
◇◇◇

American

Lunch: $5-$15   **Dinner:** $5-$15   **Phone:** 727/461-7795 ⑩
Location: 0.5 mi s of jct SR 6 (Causeway). 431 Gulfview Blvd 34630. **Hours:** 7 am-midnight. **Features:** casual dress; children's menu; beer & wine only; a la carte. Contemporary decor accents this local favorite. Nice view of the beach and gulf. Menu offers many items, Greek, pizza, chicken, steak, burgers, sandwiches, omelettes and grinders. **Cards:** MC, VI.

SEAFOOD & SUNSETS AT JULIE'S CAFE
◇◇◇ ◇◇◇

Seafood

Lunch: $6-$17   **Dinner:** $6-$17   **Phone:** 727/441-2548 ⑪②
Location: 0.5 mi s of jct SR 60 (causeway). 351 S Gulfview Blvd 33767. **Hours:** 11 am-10 pm. Closed: 11/22. **Features:** casual dress; children's menu; carryout; beer & wine only. Tropical Key West style theme with deck dining also available, restaurant is directly across from beach and gulf so enjoy the sunset with many entrees to choose such as shellfish, fish, steak, chicken, or pork, surf and turf, pasta and other goodies to choose. **Cards:** AE, MC, VI.

❌

SHEPHARD'S WATERFRONT RESTAURANT
ⒶⒶⒶ

◇◇◇ ◇◇◇

American

Lunch: $8   **Dinner:** $18   **Phone:** 727/441-6875 ⑪④
Location: 1 mi s of jct SR 60; in Shephard's Beach Resort. 601 S Gulfview Blvd 33767. **Hours:** 8-11 am, 11:30-3 & 4-10 pm. **Features:** casual dress; Sunday brunch; children's menu; early bird specials; carryout; salad bar; cocktails & lounge; entertainment; buffet, a la carte. Known for its seafood and prime rib buffet, the waterfront family restaurant offers views of the sparkling Gulf of Mexico from nearly every seat. A colorful and casual atmosphere is enhanced by live entertainment with a Caribbean flavor. **Cards:** AE, DI, DS, MC, VI.

❌

WATERFRONT RESTAURANT
◇◇◇

American

Lunch: $5-$8   **Dinner:** $7-$24   **Phone:** 727/442-3684 ⑨⑤
Location: 0.5 mi n of jct Clearwater Pass Bridge (SR 60). 490 Mandalay Ave 33767. **Hours:** 7 am-11 pm. **Features:** casual dress; children's menu; cocktails. This basic style restaurant offers a variety of appetizers, soup, salad, sandwiches and pasta dishes for lunch; an expansive breakfast menu; and a dinner menu which also offers steak, pork chops, chicken, ribs and seafood choices. **Cards:** AE, MC, VI.

DADE CITY pop. 5,600

———— **WHERE TO STAY** ————

RAINBOW FOUNTAIN MOTEL
ⒶⒶⒶ SAVE

◇◇◇

Motel

			Phone: 352/567-3427	
12/1-4/30	1P: $40-$52	2P: $40-$56	XP: $6	D12
5/1-11/30	1P: $30-$40	2P: $30-$42	XP: $6	D12

Location: 2 mi n on US 301 and 98. 16210 N Hwy 301 33523. **Facility:** Budget choice for the value-oriented. 21 units. *Bath:* combo or shower only. 1 story, exterior corridors. **Terms:** 4 day cancellation notice, weekly rates available. **Guest Services:** coin laundry. **Cards:** AE, DI, DS, MC, VI. **Special Amenities:** early check-in/late check-out and preferred room (subject to availability with advanced reservations).SOME UNITS

🆂ⓓ 🏊 📺 🛏 🚪 / 🖥 /

———— WHERE TO DINE ————

LUNCH ON LIMOGES
⬥⬥⬥ ⬥⬥⬥
American
Lunch: $9-$12
Phone: 352/567-5685
Location: Center; opposite the Court House; in Williams Department Store. 14139 7th St 33525. **Hours:** 11:30 am-2:30 pm. Closed: Sun, also Mon 6/1-10/31. **Reservations:** suggested. **Features:** casual dress; beer & wine only; minimum charge-$9; street parking. Located in an historic department store near the courthouse, the small cafe features excellent Southern cooking with nice touches like a basket of delectable homemade muffins. The varied menu changes daily, making fine use of market-fresh ingredients. Smoke free premises. **Cards:** AE, CB, DI, DS, MC, VI. ✕

DUNEDIN pop. 34,000 (See map p. 796; index p. 802)

———— WHERE TO STAY ————

BEST WESTERN YACHT HARBOR INN & SUITES
Phone: (727)733-4121 **131**

⬥⬥⬥ (SAVE)	2/1-4/16	1P: $119-$139	2P: $119-$139	XP: $10 F17
	12/1-1/31 & 4/17-11/30	1P: $89-$109	2P: $89-$109	XP: $10 F17

Motor Inn
Location: Jct US Alt 19 and gulf end of Main St, 0.5 mi s of SR 580. 150 Marina Plaza 34698. Fax: 727/736-4365. **Facility:** On Intracoastal Waterway across from marina. 55 units. 1 two-bedroom unit and 36 efficiencies. **Bath:** combo or shower only. 2 stories, exterior corridors. **Terms:** 30 day cancellation notice, in season, weekly rates available. **Amenities:** extended cable TV. *Some:* honor bars. **Dining:** 2 restaurants, 11:30 am-9 pm; marina cafe (seasonal), $12-$15; cocktails, also, Bon Appetit Restaurant, see separate listing. **Leisure Activities:** heated pool, shuffleboard. **Business Services:** meeting rooms. **Cards:** AE, DI, DS, MC, VI. **Special Amenities:** free continental breakfast and free local telephone calls.

SOME UNITS

[icons] 🆚 📺 🍽️ 🍷 ♿ 🅿️ 🏊 💻 / ✕ 🍴

INN ON THE BAY
⬥⬥ ⬥⬥
Motor Inn
Phone: (727)734-7689 **130**
All Year   1P: $74   2P: $74   XP: $10 F17
Location: On US Alt 19; 0.5 mi n of jct SR 580. 1420 Bayshore Blvd 34698. Fax: 727/734-0972. **Facility:** Bayfront. 41 units. 40 efficiencies and 1 unit with kitchen. Some suites ($96-$106). 4 stories, exterior corridors. **Terms:** 7 day cancellation notice, in season, weekly & monthly rates available. **Amenities:** *Some:* irons. **Leisure Activities:** heated pool, boat dock, fishing. *Fee:* bicycles. **Guest Services:** coin laundry. **Cards:** AE, DS, MC, VI.

SOME UNITS

(ASK) 🆚 📺 🍽️ 🏊 ✕ 📹 💻 🛏️ / ✕ 🍴 /

———— WHERE TO DINE ————

BON APPETIT RESTAURANT
⬥⬥ ⬥⬥
Continental
Lunch: $7-$14   **Dinner: $12-$15**   **Phone: 727/733-2151** **133**
Location: Jct US Alt 19 and gulf end of Main St (0.5 mi s of SR 580); in Yacht Harbor Inn and Suites. 148 Marina Plaza 34698. **Hours:** 11:30 am-10 pm. **Reservations:** suggested. **Features:** casual dress; Sunday brunch; early bird specials; carryout; cocktails & lounge; valet parking. Creative bistro cuisine can be found at this restaurant overlooking the Intercoastal Waterway. Dock your boat at the Yacht Harbor Inn and dine in the outdoor cafe where professional service and attentiveness is the key to a grand, enchanting meal. **Cards:** AE, CB, DI, MC, VI. ✕

JESSE'S DOCKSIDE
⬥⬥ ⬥⬥
Seafood
Lunch: $7-$9   **Dinner: $9-$21**   **Phone: 727/736-2611** **130**
Location: SR 586, 0.3 mi w of Alt US 19; at w end of the causeway bridge. 345 Causeway Blvd 34698. **Hours:** 11:30 am-10 pm. Closed: 12/25. **Features:** casual dress; children's menu; carryout; cocktails & lounge. Overlooking marina, this restaurant serves up ample portions of attractively garnished, tasty food, including a spicy fried alligator appetizer, seafood gumbo and fresh gulf seafood. Landlubbers and children may prefer beef, chicken and pasta dishes. **Cards:** AE, DS, MC, VI. ✕

"KELLY'S FOR JUST ABOUT...ANYTHING!"
⬥⬥ ⬥⬥
American
Lunch: $5-$12   **Dinner: $10-$18**   **Phone: 727/736-5284** **131**
Location: Center; just e of jct Alt US 19. 319 Main St 34698. **Hours:** 8 am-3 pm & 5-9 pm, Mon-3 pm. Closed: 12/25. **Reservations:** suggested; dinner. **Features:** casual dress; children's menu; carryout; beer & wine only; street parking. An eclectic menu runs the gamut from simple to sublime, with a dining room decor that is as creative as the food. Professional and attentive service follows an "anything goes" philosophy. Try the grilled chicken sandwich for a light lunch. Smoke free premises. **Cards:** AE, DS, MC, VI. ✕

SEA SEA RIDERS
⬥⬥ ⬥⬥
American
Lunch: $6-$16   **Dinner: $6-$16**   **Phone: 727/734-1445** **136**
Location: Center; jct Main St and US 19 Alt. 221 Main St 34698. **Hours:** 11:30 am-10 pm, Fri & Sat-11 pm. Closed: 11/22, 12/25. **Features:** casual dress; children's menu; carryout; cocktails & lounge. Veranda and inside seating both provide for a pleasant and relaxing experience at this 1906 Florida cracker house. Flavorful coconut shrimp, sauteed chicken and mahi-mahi whet the appetite, while artwork by state denizens adds to the tropical decor. **Cards:** AE, MC, VI. ✕

GULFPORT pop. 11,700 (See map p. 796; index p. 804)

———— WHERE TO DINE ————

CASA CORTES
⬥⬥
Mexican
Lunch: $3-$11   **Dinner: $3-$11**   **Phone: 727/321-6523** **212**
Location: I-275, exit 5 northbound (exit 6 southbound); 4.9 mi w on 22 Ave S, 0.7 mi s on Beach Blvd. 3128 Beach Blvd 33707. **Hours:** 11 am-11 pm; Fri & Sat-midnight. Closed: 11/22, 12/25; also Sun. **Features:** casual dress; children's menu; carryout; cocktails & lounge; street parking; a la carte. This very modest eatery has basic furnishings and a reputation for good, dependable Mexican food, as well as American favorites like hamburgers and fried chicken. A basket of tortilla chips and salsa begin the meal. Feast on plump and tasty burritos. **Cards:** MC, VI. ✕

HOLIDAY pop. 19,400

——— WHERE TO STAY ———

BEST WESTERN-TAHITIAN RESORT
Motor Inn
AAA [SAVE]

All Year   1P: $101   2P: $106   **Phone:** (727)937-4121
    XP: $10   F12
Location: US 19, 3 mi n of jct SR 582, 1.5 mi s of SR 54. 2337 US 19 34691. Fax: 727/937-3806. **Facility:** Nicely landscaped "Tahitian" style grounds. 140 units, 18 with efficiency. 2 stories, exterior corridors. **Terms:** 3 day cancellation notice, in season, weekly & monthly rates available, package plans, pets ($5 extra charge). **Amenities:** extended cable TV. **Dining:** restaurant, 6 am-1 pm & 5-9 pm (seasonal), pool bar, $5-$10, cocktails. **Leisure Activities:** heated pool. **Guest Services:** coin laundry. **Cards:** AE, CB, DI, DS, JC, MC, VI.
Special Amenities: free newspaper and free room upgrade (subject to availability with advanced reservations).
(See color ad below)

SOME UNITS

INDIAN ROCKS BEACH pop. 4,000   (See map p. 796; index p. 802)

——— WHERE TO STAY ———

810 GULFSIDE
Apartment

12/1-4/28 Wkly   1P: $695   **Phone:** (727)596-8063   [140]
4/29-8/25 Wkly   1P: $595
8/26-11/30 Wkly   1P: $495
Location: On SR 699, 0.4 mi n of jct SR 688, entrance to property via Beach Tr, just n of property. 810 Gulf Blvd 33785. Fax: 727/593-9343. **Facility:** Gulf front. 6 units with kitchen. 4 two-bedroom units. *Bath:* combo or shower only. 2 stories, exterior corridors. **Terms:** 30 day cancellation notice-fee imposed, daily rates available. **Amenities:** extended cable TV, irons. **Leisure Activities:** beach, boating, fishing, shuffleboard. **Guest Services:** coin laundry. **Business Services:** fax. **Cards:** MC, VI.

FEE

ANCHOR COURT APARTMENTS
Apartment
AAA [SAVE]

1/1-4/30   1P: $85-$111   2P: $85-$111   **Phone:** 727/595-4449   [138]
    XP: $20   D17
5/1-9/8   1P: $75-$100   2P: $75-$100   XP: $20   D17
12/1-12/31 & 9/9-11/30   1P: $70-$90   2P: $70-$90   XP: $20   D17
Location: On SR 699, 0.5 mi n of SR 688. 940 Gulf Blvd N 33785. **Facility:** Gulf front. 20 units. 4 efficiencies and 16 units with kitchen. 2 stories, exterior corridors. **Terms:** weekly rates available. **Amenities:** extended cable TV. *Some:* irons, hair dryers. **Leisure Activities:** heated pool, beach, off-site tennis privileges, shuffleboard, patio seating on wood deck. **Guest Services:** coin laundry. **Cards:** AE, DS, MC, VI. **Special Amenities: preferred room (subject to availability with advanced reservations).**

GULF TOWERS RESORT MOTEL
Apartment

12/1-4/30 Wkly   1P: $476-$630   2P: $476-$630   **Phone:** 727/595-2563   [141]
    XP: $70
5/1-9/3 Wkly   1P: $343-$476   2P: $343-$476   XP: $70
9/4-11/30 Wkly   1P: $294-$427   2P: $294-$427   XP: $70
Location: On SR 699, just s of jct SR 688. 404 Gulf Blvd 33785. Fax: 727/595-2553. **Facility:** Gulf front. 45 units. 41 efficiencies and 4 units with kitchen. 4 stories, interior corridors. **Terms:** 14 day cancellation notice-fee imposed, daily & monthly rates available. **Amenities:** voice mail, safes. **Leisure Activities:** beach. **Guest Services:** coin laundry. **Cards:** AE, MC, VI.

SOME UNITS

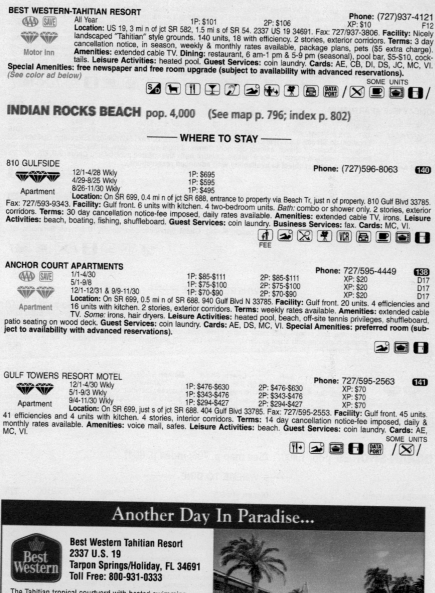

(See map p. 796)

HOLIDAY INN HARBOURSIDE
Phone: (727)595-9484   **142**

(AAA) (SAVE)

Motor Inn

2/1-4/30	1P: $119-$600	2P: $119-$600	XP: $10	F18
5/1-11/30	1P: $92-$172	2P: $92-$172	XP: $10	F18
12/1-1/31	1P: $89-$169	2P: $89-$169	XP: $10	F18

Location: Just e of jct SR 699 on Walsingham Rd, just s. 401 2nd St 33785. Fax: 727/596-4825. **Facility:** On Intracoastal Waterway, Key West style exterior. Rooms with gulf or harbor view. 164 units. 40 efficiencies and 82 units with kitchen. Some suites ($154-$600) and whirlpool units ($154-$600). **Bath:** combo or shower only. 3 stories, exterior corridors. **Terms:** check-in 4 pm, 3 day cancellation notice, package plans. **Amenities:** extended cable TV, voice mail, irons, hair dryers. **Dining:** 2 restaurants, 8 am-10 pm, deli, poolside tiki bar, sundry shop, $6-$23, cocktails. **Leisure Activities:** 2 heated pools, whirlpool, waterslide, beach access, marina, fishing, charter fishing, tennis court, playground, exercise room, volleyball, game room, inline skates, motor scooters. **Fee:** sailboating, windsurfing, boat dock, waterskiing, jet skis, bicycles. **Guest Services:** gift shop, valet and coin laundry. **Business Services:** meeting rooms, fax. **Cards:** AE, CB, DI, DS, JC, MC, VI. **Special Amenities:** free local telephone calls and free newspaper. SOME UNITS

HOLIDAY ISLE APARTMENTS
Phone: 727-596-3488   **137**

(AAA) (SAVE)

Apartment

12/16-4/30	1P: $89-$110	2P: $89-$110	XP: $12	D15
5/1-9/10	1P: $75-$100	2P: $75-$100	XP: $12	D15
12/1-12/15 & 9/11-11/30	1P: $59-$89	2P: $59-$89	XP: $12	D15

Location: On SR 699, 1.3 mi n of jct SR 688. 2200 N Gulf Blvd 33785. Fax: 727/596-0282. **Facility:** Gulf front. 22 units with kitchen. 2 stories, exterior corridors. **Terms:** 3 night minimum stay, 14 day cancellation notice-fee imposed, weekly & monthly rates available. **Leisure Activities:** heated pool, beach. **Cards:** AE, DS, MC, VI.
Special Amenities: preferred room (subject to availability with advanced reservations).

SEA RESORT MOTEL
Phone: 727/595-0461   **143**

Motel

All Year	2P: $60-$100	XP: $10	F16

Location: On SR 699, 0.5 mi s of jct SR 688. 102 Gulf Blvd 33785. Fax: 727/595-2092. **Facility:** Gulf front. 29 units, 14 with efficiency. 2 stories, interior corridors. **Terms:** cancellation fee imposed, weekly rates available. **Leisure Activities:** heated pool, beach, fishing. **Guest Services:** coin laundry. **Business Services:** fax. **Cards:** MC, VI. SOME UNITS

WHERE TO DINE

GUPPY'S ON THE BEACH
Lunch: $6-$28   Dinner: $6-$28   Phone: 727/593-2032   **147**

Seafood

Location: On SR 699 1 mi n of jct SR 688. 1701 N Gulf Blvd 33785. **Hours:** 11:30 am-10:30 pm, Fri & Sat to 11 pm. Closed: 11/22, 12/25. **Features:** casual dress; children's menu; carryout; beer & wine only; a la carte. Enjoy the gulf breeze with patio dining. This diner offers an excellent variety of seafood, steak and sandwich choices with a gorgeous sunset view. The fried shrimp is fresh and served with herbed wild rice and delicate vegetables. **Cards:** AE, DI, DS, MC, VI.

THAI PAN ALLEY & BAMBOO BEACH BAR
Lunch: $6-$8   Dinner: $7-$9   Phone: 727/593-3663   **146**

Thai

Location: SR 699, 1.5 mi n of jct SR 688; in Western Plaza. 2300 Gulf Blvd 33785. **Hours:** 11 am-9 pm, Fri & Sat-10 pm, Sun 4 pm-9 pm. Closed major holidays. **Features:** carryout; cocktail lounge; beer & wine only; a la carte. Hearty portions of rice and noodle dishes coated with sauces from mild to eye-watering spicy characterize the restaurant's cuisine. Dine inside amid Thai decorations that lend the air of the Orient or head out to the colorful beach bar setting. **Cards:** DI, DS, MC, VI.

INDIAN SHORES pop. 1,400   (See map p. 796; index p. 804)

WHERE TO DINE

CHATEAU MADRID
Dinner: $10-$23   Phone: 727/596-9100   **225**

Spanish

Location: 0.8 mi n of Park Blvd Cswy. (SR 694). 19519 Gulf Blvd 33785. **Hours:** 4 pm-10 pm, Fri & Sat-11 pm. **Reservations:** suggested. **Features:** casual dress; children's menu; early bird specials; carryout; cocktails & lounge. A friendly staff serves authentic Spanish cuisine while live entertainment performs on Fridays and Saturdays. Savor the filet mignon with bearnaise sauce for a tender and tasty steak entree. Salads large enough to share are prepared right at your table. **Cards:** AE, DI, MC, VI.

THE HUNGRY FISHERMAN
Lunch: $5-$23   Dinner: $6-$23   Phone: 727/595-4218   **224**

Seafood

Location: 1.3 mi n of Park Blvd Cswy (SR 694). 19915 Gulf Blvd 33785. **Hours:** 11:30 am-10 pm. Closed: 11/22, 12/25. **Features:** casual dress; children's menu; early bird specials; carryout; cocktails & lounge. This local landmark serves peel-and-eat shrimp with a unique cocktail sauce on a bed of lettuce. Try the catfish fillets for a fresh local catch. Seafood and meat specialties complete the menu choices. The service is prompt and pleasant. **Cards:** MC, VI.

THE PUB RESTAURANT & LOUNGE
Lunch: $7-$17   Dinner: $7-$17   Phone: 727/595-3172   **222**

American

Location: On SR 699, 1.2 mi s of jct Walsingham. 20025 Gulf Blvd 33785. **Hours:** 11 am-midnight, Sun from noon. Closed: 11/22, 12/25. **Features:** casual dress; children's menu; early bird specials; cocktails & lounge; entertainment. Great intracoastal waterfront location with beautiful dock views either inside or try the outdoor dining area. Piano bar and dance floor. Menu is extensive with numerous steak, seafood, pasta, rib, burger and sandwiches. Salads, appetizers and desserts. **Cards:** AE, DS, MC, VI.

(See map p. 796)

SALT ROCK GRILL
▼▼▼▼▼
Swiss
Cards: MC, VI.

Dinner: $11-$31   **Phone:** 727/593-7625   (227)
Location: On SR 699, 0.5 mi n of jct CR 694 (Park Blvd). 19325 Gulf Blvd 33785. **Hours:** 5 pm-10 pm.
Features: dressy casual; cocktails & lounge. An extremely trendy and upscale setting awaits the diner here. Beautiful artwork and objects abound and tastefully done decor. The setting is a remake of "Le Pompano". Menu offers open pit citrus and oak fired steaks and seafood prepared by trained chefs.

LARGO pop. 65,700   (See map p. 796; index p. 803)

———— WHERE TO STAY ————

LE VERSAILLES COURTS
◆
Apartment

Phone: (727)391-6045   (150)

12/1-4/30 Wkly		2P: $75-$289	XP: $35 F5
5/1-11/30 Wkly		2P: $38-$220	XP: $35 F5

Location: Just e of jct US Alt 19 (Seminole Blvd). 10464 106th Ave N 33773. **Fax:** 727/559-0322. **Facility:** Located in a quiet residential area, this typical "mom and pop" type establishment has friendly owner and offers basic, but comfortable rooms and decor. Office hours Mon-Sat 9 am-4:30 pm. Smoke free premises. 8 units. 1 two-bedroom unit, 2 efficiencies and 6 units with kitchen. *Bath:* shower only. 1 story, exterior corridors. **Terms:** daily & monthly rates available. **Leisure Activities:** whirlpool, shuffleboard. **Guest Services:** coin laundry.

SOME UNITS

🏊 ✕ ☎ 📋 / 💻 /

———— WHERE TO DINE ————

THE GATHERING RESTAURANT
▼▼▼
American
Cards: AE, CB, DI, MC, VI.

Lunch: $4-$8   **Phone:** 727/593-1600   (155)
Location: SR 688, 1 mi e of jct 699; in Sabala Plaza. 14100 Walsingham Rd 33774. **Hours:** 7 am-2 pm, Sun from 7:30 am. Closed: 11/22, 12/25. **Features:** casual dress; early bird specials; carryout. Bright and airy with lots of room, the restaurant offers up lighter fare, ranging from omelets and eggs Benedict to corned beef sandwiches on rye bread. The Belgian waffles are pretty tasty, too. The servers are polite and prompt.

✕

MADEIRA BEACH pop. 4,200   (See map p. 796; index p. 803)

———— WHERE TO STAY ————

HOLIDAY INN MADEIRA BEACH
🔺🔺🔺 SAVE
▼▼▼▼
Motor Inn

Phone: (727)392-2275   (156)

1/19-4/21	1P: $124-$164	2P: $124-$164	XP: $10
4/22-11/30	1P: $114-$154	2P: $114-$154	XP: $10
12/1-1/18	1P: $109-$149	2P: $109-$149	XP: $10

Location: SR 699, just n of Tom Stuart Cswy. 15208 Gulf Blvd 33708. **Fax:** 727/398-1190. **Facility:** Gulf front locale enhances this property with a tropically landscaped courtyard area overlooking the beach and housing a nice pool area. Rooms are tropically decorated with contemporary accents to furnishings. 148 units. Some suites. *Bath:* combo or shower only. 4 stories, exterior corridors. **Terms:** check-in 4 pm, weekly & monthly rates available, package plans. **Amenities:** extended cable TV, voice mail, safes (fee), irons, hair dryers. **Dining:** restaurant, 6:30 am-11:30 & 5-10 pm; sports bar, tiki bar, $7-$19, cocktails. **Leisure Activities:** heated pool, beach, lighted tennis court, game room. *Fee:* cabana, sailboating, water bikes, health club privileges. **Guest Services:** valet and coin laundry. **Business Services:** meeting rooms, fax. **Cards:** AE, DI, DS, MC, VI. **Special Amenities:** free room upgrade (subject to availability with advanced reservations).
(See color ad below)

SOME UNITS

🅢 🍴 🍽 ☎ 📷 🏊 ✕ 📺 📠 💻 DATA PORT / ✕ 📋 /
FEE   FEE

(See map p. 796)

THE LIGHTHOUSE BED & BREAKFAST MOTEL
♦♦ ♦♦
Bed & Breakfast

1/1-4/30	1P: $80-$95	2P: $80-$95	
12/1-12/31 & 5/1-11/30	1P: $60-$75	2P: $60-$75	

Phone: 727/391-0015 **157**
XP: $10 F12
XP: $10 F12

Location: Just e of jct SR 699 on 134th Ave. 13355 2nd St E 33708. Fax: 727/393-7285. **Facility:** Residential locale, just a block from the Intracoastal Waterway and 3 blocks from the gulf. Faux lighthouse gives nice effect to exterior greeting and nice courtyard area with gazebo. Room decor is of average quality but comfortable. Designated smoking area. 6 units, 3 with efficiency. **Bath:** shower only. 2 stories, exterior corridors. **Terms:** 14 day cancellation notice-fee imposed, pets ($5 extra charge, $50 deposit). **Amenities:** extended cable TV. **Some:** irons. **Leisure Activities:** bicycles. **Guest Services:** [BP] meal plan available, coin laundry. **Cards:** AE, DS, MC, VI.

SOME UNITS

(See map p. 796)

SEA DAWN MOTEL

Phone: (727)391-7500   **162**

AAA SAVE				
	2/1-3/21	2P: $50-$60	XP: $8	F13
	4/1-4/30	2P: $45-$55	XP: $8	F13
	12/1-1/31	2P: $30-$55	XP: $8	F13
	5/1-11/30	2P: $30-$45	XP: $8	F13

Apartment   **Location:** On SR 699, 0.7 mi s of Tom Staurt Cswy. 13733 Gulf Blvd 33708. Fax: 727/391-7500. **Facility:** On Boca Ciega Bay. 8 units. 6 efficiencies and 2 units with kitchen. 2 stories, exterior corridors. **Terms:** 10 day cancellation notice-fee imposed, weekly rates available. **Amenities:** extended cable TV. **Leisure Activities:** small pool, boat dock, fishing, sun deck. **Cards:** MC, VI. **Special Amenities:** free local telephone calls.

SOME UNITS

SHORELINE ISLAND RESORT MOTEL

Phone: (727)397-6641   **161**

AAA SAVE				
	1/27-4/26	1P: $92-$233	2P: $92-$233	XP: $10
	12/18-1/26 & 4/27-11/30	1P: $61-$170	2P: $61-$170	XP: $10
	12/1-12/17	1P: $58-$162	2P: $58-$162	XP: $10

Apartment   **Location:** SR 699; 0.5 mi s of Madeira Beach Cswy. 14200 Gulf Blvd 33708. Fax: 727/393-9157. **Facility:** Gulf front locale enhances this all adult oriented beachfront facility. Most units have private balcony and face the beach. Some motel and apartment units are in separate building located across the street and on waterway. Family owned and operated since 1964 and very welcoming, personable staff. 69 units. 5 two-bedroom units, 47 efficiencies and 12 units with kitchen. 2-5 stories, exterior corridors. **Terms:** age restrictions may apply, 7 day cancellation notice, weekly & monthly rates available. **Amenities:** extended cable TV. *Some:* irons, hair dryers. **Leisure Activities:** heated pool, beach, shuffleboard, complimentary video library. **Guest Services:** coin laundry. **Cards:** AE, DS, MC, VI. *(See color ad p 866)*

SOME UNITS

WITS END MOTEL

Phone: 727/391-6739   **158**

AAA SAVE				
	2/1-4/20	1P: $79-$130	2P: $79-$130	XP: $8
	4/21-9/7	1P: $57-$115	2P: $57-$115	XP: $8
	12/1-1/31	1P: $57-$110	2P: $57-$110	XP: $8
	9/8-11/30	1P: $50-$105	2P: $50-$105	XP: $8

Apartment   **Location:** On SR 699, 0.9 mi s of Tom Stuart Cswy. 13600 Gulf Blvd 33708. Fax: 727/392-4578. **Facility:** Gulf front. Some units in building 1/2 block north. 30 units. 19 efficiencies and 9 units with kitchen. 2 stories, interior/exterior corridors. **Terms:** 30 day cancellation notice. **Amenities:** extended cable TV. **Leisure Activities:** heated pool, beach, shuffleboard. **Cards:** DS, MC, VI. *(See color ad p 866)*

———— **WHERE TO DINE** ————

THE APPLE OF MADEIRA BEACH FAMILY
RESTAURANT & LOUNGE

Lunch: $5-$13   **Dinner:** $7-$18   **Phone:** 727/391-1302   **163**

American   **Location:** Just e of jct SR 699. 100 Madeira Way 33708. **Hours:** 7 am-11 pm. **Features:** casual dress; children's menu; salad bar; cocktail lounge. This local favorite can't be missed sitting at junction of Gulf Blvd and a welcoming beacon to the beach. It offers up such favorites as fresh seafood, steaks and ribs. **Cards:** MC, VI.

FRIENDLY FISHERMAN SEAFOOD RESTAURANT

Lunch: $6-$16   **Dinner:** $6-$16   **Phone:** 727/391-6025   **170**

Seafood   **Location:** At John's Pass Village; 1.4 mi s of jct Madeira Cswy. 150 Johns Pass Boardwalk 33708. **Hours:** 7 am-2 am. Closed: 12/25. **Features:** casual dress; children's menu; early bird specials; carryout; cocktails & lounge. This rustic boardwalk eatery offers an array of seafood choices. Peel-and-eat shrimp is fresh and light. You will be treated to prompt, detail-oriented service during your seafood meal. Enjoy the waterfront view and shop the boardwalk after dinner. **Cards:** AE, DS, MC, VI.

JOHNNY LEVEROCK'S SEAFOOD HOUSE

Lunch: $5-$8   **Dinner:** $9-$23   **Phone:** 727/393-0459   **169**

Steak & Seafood   **Location:** 0.5 mi e of jct SR 699, on Tom Stuart Cswy (SR 666). 565 150th Ave 33708. **Hours:** 11:30 am-10 pm. Closed: 11/22, 12/25. **Features:** casual dress; children's menu; early bird specials; carryout; cocktails & lounge. The crisp, clean dining rooms of this cozy restaurant overlook Boca Ciega Bay. Lots of wood and displays of such items as fishing rods mold a decidedly ocean-themed feeling. The New England clam chowder and onion-crusted salmon are menu favorites. **Cards:** AE, DI, DS, MC, VI.

SCULLY'S BOARDWALK GRILLE

Lunch: $8-$21   **Dinner:** $8-$21   **Phone:** 727/393-7749   **168**

Seafood   **Location:** At Johns Pass Village, 1.4 mi s of jct Tom Stuart Cswy. 190 Johns Pass Boardwalk 33708. **Hours:** 11 am-10 pm. **Features:** casual dress; children's menu; beer & wine only; a la carte. Rustic sea shanty, with nice view of Intracoastal Waterway; boardwalk dining also. Menu has varied choices from seafood to sandwiches and burgers in this comfortable rustic setting with many nautical touches. **Cards:** MC, VI.

VILLAGE LANDING

Lunch: $5-$14   **Dinner:** $5-$14   **Phone:** 727/397-9773   **164**

American   **Location:** On SR 699 at Johns Pass. 13001 Gulf Blvd 33708. **Hours:** 7 am-9:30 pm. **Features:** casual dress; children's menu; carryout; salad bar. Located next to famous shops at Johns Pass, this rustic exterior as well as interior setting offers up a variety of dishes. Try the pork barbecue which has excellent sauce and taste. **Cards:** MC, VI.

NEW PORT RICHEY pop. 14,000

———— WHERE TO STAY ————

COMFORT INN-GATEWAY

[SAVE]

◆◆◆◆

Motel

	2/1-3/31	1P: $89-$99	2P: $99-$109
	12/23-1/31	1P: $79-$89	2P: $89-$99
	12/1-12/22	1P: $69-$79	2P: $79-$89
	4/1-11/30	1P: $59-$67	2P: $64-$74

Phone: (727)842-6800
XP: $10   F18
XP: $10   F18
XP: $10   F18
XP: $10   F18

Location: 0.5 mi n of jct Main St. 6826 US 19 N 34652. Fax: 727/842-5072. **Facility:** Miami art-deco architecture. Convenient to gulf beaches and historical Tarpon Springs. 66 units, 22 with efficiency. 2 stories, exterior corridors. **Terms:** check-in 4 pm, package plans. **Amenities:** extended cable TV. **Leisure Activities:** heated pool, whirlpool, steamroom. **Guest Services:** [CP] meal plan available, coin laundry. **Business Services:** meeting rooms, fax. **Cards:** AE, CB, DI, DS, JC, MC, VI.

SOME UNITS

ECONO LODGE

◆◆◆ [SAVE]

◆◆ ◆◆

Motel

	2/1-4/20	1P: $60-$95	2P: $65-$100
	1/1-1/31	1P: $55-$85	2P: $60-$90
	12/1-12/31	1P: $45-$70	2P: $50-$80
	4/21-11/30	1P: $40-$60	2P: $45-$70

Phone: (727)845-4990
XP: $10   F18
XP: $10   F18
XP: $10   F18
XP: $10   F18

Location: 0.8 mi n of jct Main St. 7631 US 19 34652. Fax: 727/845-4990. **Facility:** 105 units, 11 with efficiency. 1 story, exterior corridors. **Terms:** weekly rates available, small pets only ($10 extra charge). **Amenities:** extended cable TV. *Some:* hair dryers. **Leisure Activities:** heated pool. **Guest Services:** coin laundry. **Business Services:** fax. **Cards:** AE, CB, DI, DS, JC, MC, VI. **Special Amenities:** free continental breakfast and free local telephone calls.

SOME UNITS

RAMADA INN BAYSIDE

◆◆◆ ◆◆◆

Motor Inn

DS, MC, VI.

Phone: 727/849-8551

Property failed to provide current rates

Location: On US 19; 1 mi n of jct SR 54. 5015 US 19 N 34652. Fax: 727/843-0831. **Facility:** 130 units. Some suites. 2 stories, exterior corridors. **Terms:** weekly & monthly rates available. **Amenities:** voice mail. *Some:* irons, hair dryers. **Leisure Activities:** wading pool, boat dock, exercise room, shuffleboard. **Cards:** AE, DI,

SOME UNITS

FEE   FEE

———— WHERE TO DINE ————

CAFE GRAND

◆◆◆ ◆◆◆

American

Lunch: $6-$17   **Dinner:** $9-$17   Phone: 727/848-7098
Location: Just s of Main St. 6238 Grand Blvd 34652. **Hours:** 11 am-9:30 pm, Fri-10 pm, Sat 5 pm-10 pm. Closed: 1/1, 12/25; also Sun. **Features:** dressy casual; cocktails. Located in the historic portion of downtown New Port Richey opposite the theater in two store front sections of a historic building. Operated by California transplants, the cafe uses the freshest of product and ingredients, purchased daily. Interesting pork, chicken, beef, and seafood dishes. Dessert by owner's mother. Artsy, interesting decor.

IRISH COTTAGE CAFE

◆◆◆ ◆◆◆

Irish

Lunch: $5-$15   **Dinner:** $5-$15   Phone: 727/842-5929
Location: US 19, 0.3 mi n of jct SR 54. 4233 US 19 34652. **Hours:** 11 am-midnight, Sat & Sun noon-2 am. Closed: Mon. **Features:** casual dress; early bird specials; carryout; cocktails & lounge; a la carte, a la carte. Traditional dishes like corned beef and cabbage and shepherd's pie are served in an authentic Irish pub setting. Lovely outdoor dining is available with lush gardens and two waterfalls. Enjoy Irish entertainment featured Friday through Sunday. **Cards:** MC, VI.

LEVEROCKS SEAFOOD HOUSE OF NEW PORT RICHEY   **Lunch:** $5-$21   **Dinner:** $9-$21   Phone: 727/849-8000

◆◆◆ ◆◆◆

Seafood

Location: On US 19, 1 mi n of SR 54. 4927 US 19 34652. **Hours:** 11:30 am-10 pm. Closed: 11/22, 12/25. **Features:** casual dress; children's menu; early bird specials; carryout; cocktails & lounge. A nautical restaurant, its large windows and multiple dining levels afford views of the yacht basin from many flattering angles. With its own fleet of fishing boats, this restaurant can boast, "If it's fresher than Leverocks, it's still swimming.". **Cards:** AE, DI, DS, MC, VI.

NORTH REDINGTON BEACH pop. 1,100   (See map p. 796; index p. 803)

———— WHERE TO STAY ————

FAR HORIZONS MOTEL

◆◆ ◆◆

Condominium

	2/2-5/1 Wkly	2P: $588-$637
	5/2-9/1 Wkly	2P: $423-$555
	12/1-2/1 Wkly	2P: $423-$480
	9/2-11/30 Wkly	2P: $388-$455

Phone: 727/393-8791   [172]
XP: $35
XP: $35
XP: $35
XP: $35

Location: On SR 699, 1.5 mi s of jct Park Blvd (SR 694). 17248 Gulf Blvd 33708. Fax: 727/391-3980. **Facility:** Gulf front. 25 units with kitchen. 2 stories, exterior corridors. **Terms:** cancellation fee imposed, weekly & monthly rates available. **Amenities:** extended cable TV. *Some:* irons, hair dryers. **Leisure Activities:** heated pool, beach, shuffleboard. **Guest Services:** coin laundry. **Business Services:** fax. **Cards:** DS, MC, VI.

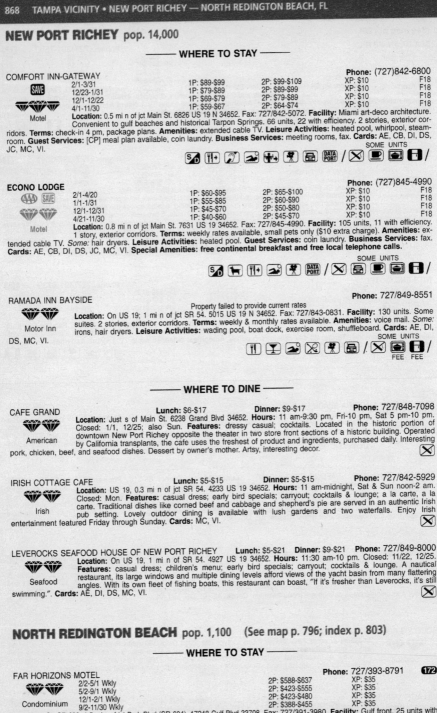

(See map p. 796)

HILTON TAMPA BAY/NORTH REDINGTON BEACH RESORT

[SAVE]

Hotel

2/1-5/31	1P: $160-$260	2P: $160-$260	XP: $25	F18
6/1-11/30	1P: $140-$260	2P: $140-$260	XP: $25	F18
12/1-1/31	1P: $130-$260	2P: $130-$260	XP: $25	F18

Phone: (727)391-4000 [174]

Location: SR 699; 2 mi n of Madeira Beach Cswy. 17120 Gulf Blvd 33708. Fax: 813/932-3322. **Facility:** Gulf front with beautiful beach and bay view. Tropical flair in guest rooms with rattan furnishings and bright colors. Each unit has private balcony. 125 units. Some suites ($450-$1200). 6 stories, interior corridors. **Terms:** 3 day cancellation notice-fee imposed, package plans. **Amenities:** voice mail, honor bars, irons, hair dryers. **Leisure Activities:** heated pool, beach, volleyball. *Fee:* boats, sailboating, windsurfing. **Guest Services:** gift shop, valet laundry. **Business Services:** meeting rooms, fax. **Cards:** AE, CB, DI, DS, MC, VI. *(See ad p 44)*

SOME UNITS

RAMSEA

[AAA] [SAVE]

Condominium

3/10-4/20 Wkly	1P: $1020	2P: $1020
12/1-3/9 Wkly	1P: $570-$720	2P: $570-$720
4/21-9/5 Wkly	1P: $570-$630	2P: $570-$630
9/6-11/30 Wkly	1P: $570	2P: $570

Phone: (727)397-0441 [173]

Location: On SR 699, 1.6 mi s of jct Park Blvd(SR 694). 17200 Gulf Blvd 33708. Fax: 727/397-8894. **Facility:** Gulf front. 68 units with kitchen. 20 two-bedroom units and 40 three-bedroom units. 5-6 stories, exterior corridors. **Terms:** check-in 4 pm, 30 day cancellation notice-fee imposed, daily & monthly rates available, package plans. **Amenities:** safes (fee), irons. **Leisure Activities:** heated pool, whirlpool, beach. *Fee:* cabanas, aquacycles, catamaran, hobiecats, jet skis. **Guest Services:** coin laundry. **Business Services:** fax. **Cards:** AE, MC, VI. **Special Amenities:** free newspaper. *(See color ad below)*

SOME UNITS

SAILS RESORT MOTEL

Apartment

2/1-4/28	1P: $75-$105	2P: $75-$105	XP: $12
12/1-1/31	1P: $55-$85	2P: $55-$85	XP: $10
4/29-5/31	1P: $55	2P: $55	XP: $10
6/1-11/30	1P: $53-$83	2P: $53-$83	XP: $10

Phone: 727/391-6000 [170]

Location: On SR 699, 2 mi n of Tom Stuart Cswy. 17004 Gulf Blvd 33708. Fax: 727/391-6000. **Facility:** Gulf front. Beautifully landscaped, well manicured and maintained property. 24 units. 1 two-bedroom unit, 1 efficiency and 22 units with kitchen. 2 stories, exterior corridors. **Terms:** 21 day cancellation notice-fee imposed. **Amenities:** extended cable TV. **Leisure Activities:** heated pool, beach, shuffleboard. **Guest Services:** coin laundry. **Business Services:** fax. **Cards:** DS, MC, VI.

SOME UNITS

──────── WHERE TO DINE ────────

THE FROG POND

American

Lunch: $6-$11   **Phone:** 727/392-4117 [186]

Location: On SR 699, 2 mi n on Tom Stuart Cswy. 16909 Gulf Blvd 33708. **Hours:** 7 am-2:30 pm, Sun 8 am-2 pm. Closed major holidays. **Features:** casual dress; carryout. Comfortable country decor with bright tropical flair invites you to this local favorite. Select from a wide variety of omelettes, eggs benedict, burgers, sandwiches, soup, salad and various other breakfast favorites. **Cards:** MC, VI.

WINE CELLAR RESTAURANT & CATERING SERVICE

[AAA]

Continental

Dinner: $10-$30   **Phone:** 727/393-3491 [185]

Location: On SR 699, 1.5 mi s of jct Park Blvd (SR 694). 17307 Gulf Blvd 33708. **Hours:** 4:30 pm-11 pm. Closed: 1/1; also 12/24 evening & Mon. **Reservations:** suggested. **Features:** dressy casual; children's menu; early bird specials; cocktails & lounge. Step into an atmosphere of relaxing Old World charm. Rack of lamb, beef Wellington and a variety of fresh seafood are a few of the specialties served with a European flavor. For true gourmands, try Chef Carl's five-course "Culinary Adventure.". **Cards:** AE, DI, DS, MC, VI.

PALM HARBOR pop. 12,100

―――――― WHERE TO STAY ――――――

FOUR POINTS HOTEL TARPON SPRINGS SHERATON
Phone: (727)942-0358

(AAA) [SAVE]
▽▽▽

Motor Inn

1/1-4/30	1P: $109-$135	2P: $109-$135	XP: $10	F12
5/1-11/30	1P: $99-$120	2P: $99-$120	XP: $10	F12
12/1-12/31	1P: $94-$115	2P: $94-$115	XP: $10	F12

Location: On US 19, 3 mi s of jct SR 582. 37611 US 19 N 34684. Fax: 727/938-9826. **Facility:** 99 units. Some suites ($214-$238) and whirlpool units ($135-$150). *Bath:* combo or shower only. 4 stories, exterior corridors. **Terms:** cancellation fee imposed, package plans, pets ($10 extra charge). **Amenities:** voice mail, irons, hair dryers. **Dining:** restaurant, 6:30 am-10:30 pm; tiki bar, $10-$25, cocktails. **Leisure Activities:** heated pool, whirlpool, putting green, exercise room. *Fee:* boating, pontoon. **Guest Services:** [CP] meal plan available, gift shop, valet and coin laundry. **Business Services:** meeting rooms, administrative services, PC, fax. **Cards:** AE, DI, DS, JC, MC, VI. **Special Amenities:** free newspaper.

SOME UNITS

[icons] FEE / FEE FEE

KNIGHTS INN-CLEARWATER/PALM HARBOR
Phone: 727/789-2002

(AAA) [SAVE]
▽▽

Motel

12/1-4/28	1P: $39-$150	2P: $39-$150
4/29-11/30	1P: $40	2P: $40

Location: 1.8 mi n of CR 752 (Tampa Rd). 34106 US 19 N 34684. Fax: 727/784-6206. **Facility:** At-door parking. 114 units, 12 with efficiency. 1 story, exterior corridors. **Terms:** weekly & monthly rates available, small pets only ($5 extra charge). **Leisure Activities:** heated pool. **Guest Services:** coin laundry. **Business Services:** meeting rooms, fax. **Cards:** AE, CB, DI, DS, JC, MC, VI. **Special Amenities:** free local telephone calls.

SOME UNITS

[icons] / [icons]

RED ROOF INN
Phone: (727)786-2529

(AAA) [SAVE]
▽▽▽

Motel

2/1-4/15	1P: $60-$80	2P: $66-$86	XP: $6	F18
12/1-1/31 & 9/1-11/30	1P: $40-$60	2P: $46-$66	XP: $6	F18
4/16-8/31	1P: $30-$50	2P: $36-$56	XP: $6	F18

Location: 0.4 mi s of jct Tampa Rd. 32000 US 19 N 34684. Fax: 727/786-7462. **Facility:** Nicely tended grounds. Lobby and office well separated from the rooms. Adjacent to AAA club office. 100 units, 25 with efficiency. *Bath:* combo or shower only. 2 stories, exterior corridors. **Terms:** 7 day cancellation notice, weekly & monthly rates available, pets ($10 extra charge). **Amenities:** extended cable TV, voice mail. **Leisure Activities:** heated pool. **Business Services:** fax. **Cards:** AE, DI, DS, MC, VI.

SOME UNITS

[icons] / [icons]

THE WESTIN INNISBROOK RESORT
Phone: (727)942-2000

(AAA) [SAVE]
▽▽▽

Condominium

1/13-5/23	1P: $235-$310	2P: $235-$310	XP: $20	F18
9/4-11/30	1P: $199-$285	2P: $199-$285	XP: $20	F18
12/1-1/12	1P: $190-$265	2P: $190-$265	XP: $20	F18
5/24-9/3	1P: $135-$165	2P: $135-$165	XP: $20	F18

Location: US 19; 2.8 mi s of jct SR 582. 36750 US Hwy 19 N 34684. Fax: 727/942-5576. **Facility:** Renowned golf resort complex of 25 buildings on 1,000 acres of manicured grounds. Large units with balcony, many overlooking golf course. 700 units. 67 two-bedroom units and 575 units with kitchen. Some suites and whirlpool units. *Bath:* combo or shower only. 3 stories (no elevator), interior corridors. **Terms:** 3 day cancellation notice-fee imposed, weekly rates available, package plans. **Amenities:** extended cable TV, video games, voice mail, irons, hair dryers. *Some:* honor bars. **Dining:** 6 restaurants, guests & friends only 6 am-midnight, $12-$28, cocktails. **Leisure Activities:** 6 heated pools, saunas, whirlpools, waterslide, fishing, putting green, night driving range, 2 pro shops., children's program, nature trails, recreation program, social program, playground. *Fee:* fishing equipment, golf-72 holes, miniature golf, golf instruction & equipment, 11 tennis courts (7 lighted), racquetball courts, tennis instruction & equipment, bicycles. **Guest Services:** gift shop, area transportation-beach, valet and coin laundry. *Fee:* massage. **Business Services:** conference facilities, administrative services, fax. *Fee:* PC. **Cards:** AE, DI, DS, JC, MC, VI. **Special Amenities:** free newspaper and free room upgrade (subject to availability with advanced reservations).

SOME UNITS

[icons] FEE   FEE   FEE   FEE / [icons]

―――――― WHERE TO DINE ――――――

THE BLUE HERON
Dinner: $17-$26   **Phone:** 727/789-5176

▽▽▽

Seafood

Location: On SR 752 (Tampa Rd), 1 mi e of jct US 19 in Shoppes at Cloverplace. 3285 Tampa Rd 34684. **Hours:** 5 pm-10 pm, Fri & Sat-11 pm, Sun 5 pm-9 pm. Closed major holidays. **Reservations:** accepted. **Features:** dressy casual; children's menu; carryout; cocktails & lounge. Gracious service and elegant, intimate surroundings make entree choices such as snapper, salmon, grouper, duck and chicken that much more enjoyable. All dishes are well-prepared and nicely presented with a salad of mixed greens and bread and butter. **Cards:** AE, DI, DS, MC, VI.

[icon]

SAINT LARRY
Dinner: $12-$21   **Phone:** 727/786-0077

▽▽▽

Steak & Seafood

Location: On US 19 just s of jct Alderman Rd; in the Fountains. 34980 US 19 N 34684. **Hours:** 5-10 pm. Closed: Sun and 12/25. **Features:** casual dress; children's menu; cocktails & lounge. An upscale setting reminiscent of Greenwich Village features original paintings by local artists and a carpet by Salvador Dali. Large portions of certified Angus beef, fresh seafood and quality produce have pleased the local community for over six years. **Cards:** AE, DI, DS, MC, VI.

[icon]

THAI NANA
Lunch: $6-$7   **Dinner:** $8-$17   **Phone:** 727/787-0189

(AAA)

▽▽▽

Thai

Location: US Alt 19 at jct Alderman Rd; in Crystal Beach Plaza. 2880 Alt 19 N 34683. **Hours:** 11 am-3 & 4:30-10 pm, Sat from 4:30 pm, Sun 4 pm-9 pm. **Features:** casual dress; carryout; beer & wine only; a la carte. Spicy, stir-fried dishes are the mainstay of this traditional Thai restaurant. Fresh ingredients can be found in all the entrees, especially try Thai salad with peanut dressing, pad Thai noodle and panang curry. **Cards:** DS, MC, VI.

[icon]

PINELLAS PARK pop. 43,400 (See map p. 796; index p. 803)

──── WHERE TO STAY ────

LA MARK CHARLES MOTEL
AAA [SAVE]

Motel

1/16-4/30	1P: $75-$120	2P: $75-$120
12/1-1/15 & 5/1-11/30	1P: $60-$100	2P: $60-$100

Phone: (727)527-7334 [180]
XP: $5   F12
XP: $5   F12

Location: I-275, exit 15, 1.4 mi w on Gandy Blvd (SR 694), 0.8 mi s on US 19. 6200 34th St N 33781. **Fax:** 727/526-9294. **Facility:** A nice breakfast area with gas burning fireplace is inviting. The exterior style is that of a roadside property with portico adding modern touch. Rooms are comfortable with some dated furnishings. Breakfast area has internet kiosk set-up. Office hours 7 am-10:30 pm. 94 units. 3 two-bedroom units, 18 efficiencies and 17 units with kitchen. 2 stories, exterior corridors. **Terms:** 30 day cancellation notice, pets ($10 fee, $25 deposit). **Leisure Activities:** heated pool, whirlpool. **Guest Services:** coin laundry. **Business Services:** meeting rooms, fax. **Cards:** AE, DS, MC, VI. **Special Amenities: free continental breakfast and free room upgrade (subject to availability with advanced reservations).** *(See color ad below)*

SOME UNITS
[icons] FEE FEE

LA QUINTA INN-PINELLAS PARK
[SAVE]

Motel

All Year	1P: $69-$95	2P: $69-$95

Phone: (727)545-5611 [179]

Location: I-275, exit 15, 1.4 mi s on Gandy Blvd (SR 694), just n. 7500 US Hwy 19N 33781. **Fax:** 727/544-4202. **Facility:** Exterior has a Spanish style appeal with a variety of colorful landscape plants. Inviting public area with fountain and faux fireplace, upscale seating area with pleasant furniture style and many nick nacks for pleasant appeal. 116 units. Some suites. 3 stories, interior/exterior corridors. **Terms:** small pets only. **Amenities:** extended cable TV, video games, voice mail. *Some:* irons, hair dryers. **Leisure Activities:** heated pool. **Guest Services:** [ECP] meal plan available, valet and coin laundry. **Business Services:** meeting rooms, fax. **Cards:** AE, CB, DI, DS, MC, VI. *(See color ad p 829)*

SOME UNITS
[icons] FEE FEE

──── WHERE TO DINE ────

JOHNNY LEVEROCK'S SEAFOOD HOUSE
[icons]

Steak & Seafood

Lunch: $7-$16   **Dinner:** $9-$23   **Phone:** 727/526-9188 [193]
Location: I-275, exit 15, 1.6 mi w on Gandy Blvd (SR 694), just s on US 19. 7000 US 19N 33781. **Hours:** 11 am-10 pm. **Closed:** 11/22, 12/25. **Features:** casual dress; children's menu; early bird specials; carryout; cocktails & lounge. This casual and popular restaurant has an interior rustic shanty theme which teems with the memorabilia of fisherman Johnny Leverock. The crunchy texture of the onion-crusted salmon and the light, sweet taste of the molasses bread are but two of the menu's palate tempters. **Cards:** AE, DI, DS, MC, VI.

[icon]

PLANT CITY pop. 22,800

──── WHERE TO STAY ────

DAYS INN PLANT CITY
AAA [SAVE]

Motor Inn

1/1-1/28	1P: $60-$139	2P: $65-$145	XP: $5 F18
1/29-4/30	1P: $79-$89	2P: $85-$95	XP: $6 F18
12/1-12/31 & 5/1-11/30	1P: $60-$70	2P: $65-$75	XP: $5 F18

Phone: (813)752-0570

Location: I-4, exit 13A, westbound; exit 14 eastbound, just e. 301 S Frontage Rd 33566. **Fax:** 813/754-3422. **Facility:** 175 units. 3 stories, exterior corridors. **Terms:** weekly rates available, package plans, pets ($10 extra charge). **Amenities:** *Some:* irons, hair dryers. **Dining:** restaurant, 6 am-11 pm, $5-$13, cocktails. **Leisure Activities:** playground, shuffleboard, volleyball, picnic area. **Guest Services:** [ECP] meal plan available, coin laundry. **Business Services:** meeting rooms, PC, fax. **Cards:** AE, CB, DI, DS, JC, MC, VI. **Special Amenities: free local telephone calls.**

SOME UNITS
[icons] FEE FEE

PLANT CITY COMFORT INN

Phone: 813/707-6000

SAVE	12/1-2/1	1P: $63-$125	2P: $69-$125	XP: $6	F17

5/2-11/30   1P: $63-$125   2P: $63-$125   XP: $6   F17
2/2-4/30   1P: $125   2P: $125

Motel

Location: I-4, exit 14, just e. 2003 S Frontage Rd 33566. Fax: 813/707-6081. **Facility:** 61 units. Some suites. **Bath:** combo or shower only. 3 stories, interior corridors. **Terms:** weekly & monthly rates available. **Amenities:** voice mail, hair dryers. *Some:* irons. **Leisure Activities:** heated pool, whirlpool. **Guest Services:** [ECP] meal plan available, valet and coin laundry. **Business Services:** meeting rooms, fax. **Cards:** AE, DI, DS, MC, VI.

SOME UNITS

RYSDON HOUSE BED & BREAKFAST

Phone: 813/752-8717

12/1-5/1   2P: $85-$105   XP: $12
5/2-11/30   2P: $65-$85   XP: $12

Historic Bed & Breakfast

Location: I-4, exit 11, 0.8 mi s, 1 mi on US 92. 702 W Reynolds St 33566. Fax: 813/752-8717. **Facility:** Built in 1910 with variety of room types. 2 rooms with fireplace. 1 room with bathroom down hall. Designated smoking area. 4 units. *Bath:* combo or shower only. 3 stories, interior corridors. **Terms:** age restrictions may apply, 4 day cancellation notice-fee imposed, package plans. **Amenities:** extended cable TV. *Some:* irons. **Leisure Activities:** whirlpool. **Guest Services:** [CP] meal plan available, complimentary laundry. **Business Services:** meeting rooms. **Cards:** AE, DS, MC, VI.

-------- **WHERE TO DINE** --------

ABC PIZZA HOUSE

Lunch: $7-$18   Dinner: $7-$18   **Phone: 813/752-5146**

American

Location: Act jct W Reynolds St. 114 N Alexander 33566. **Hours:** 11 am-11 pm, Fri & Sat-midnight. **Features:** casual dress; carryout; beer & wine only; a la carte. Very casual decor to this pizza and sub restaurant. Menu has many pizza choices, grinders, pasta dishes, seafood entrees, sandwiches, gyros and numerous appetizers. **Cards:** MC, VI.

ALL STAR GRILL

Lunch: $5-$16   Dinner: $5-$16   **Phone: 813/719-8187**

American

Location: Just w of jct SR 39; in Lake Walden Sq. 266 W Alexander Rd 33567. **Hours:** 10:45 am-2 am. Closed: 4/15, 11/22, 12/25. **Features:** casual dress; children's menu; early bird specials; carryout; cocktails & lounge; a la carte. Open and airy sports themed restaurant with large screen televisions, many pool tables and game area. Though menu is limited to a few entree items - there are many sandwiches, salad, burgers and appetizers to choose from. **Cards:** AE, MC, VI.

BRANCH RANCH DINING ROOM

Lunch: $6-$9   Dinner: $7-$18   **Phone: 813/752-1957**

American

Location: I-4, exit 10, 0.9 mi n on Branch Forbes Rd, just e. 5121 W Thonotosassa Rd 33565. **Hours:** 11:30 am-9:30 pm. Closed: Mon & Tues. **Features:** casual dress; children's menu; cocktails & lounge. Home-style country cooking has been the trademark of this family diner since 1956. Fried green tomatoes, Southern fried chicken and homemade buttermilk biscuits with orange-pineapple marmalade complement blackboard specials. Extensive country gift shop on site. **Cards:** AE, DS, MC, VI.

BUDDY FREDDY'S RESTAURANT

Lunch: $6-$8   Dinner: $8-$11   **Phone: 813/754-5120**

American

Location: I-4, exit 11, 0.4 mi s on SR 566. 1101 Goldfinch Dr 33566. **Hours:** 6:30 am-9 pm. **Features:** casual dress; children's menu; early bird specials; carryout; salad bar; buffet. This very popular, family-operated establishment offers a congenial atmosphere perfect for home-style cooking. A flexible menu allows for easy substitutions like replacing mashed potatoes with grits. Try the catfish for a real Florida feast. **Cards:** AE, CB, DI, DS, MC, VI.

CHANCY'S CATFISH SHACK

Lunch: $6-$16   Dinner: $6-$16   **Phone: 813/754-3433**

Seafood

Location: I-4, exit 14, just n. 2509 N Park Rd 33566. **Hours:** 11 am-9 pm, Fri & Sat-10 pm. Closed: Sun & Mon. **Features:** casual dress; carryout; beer & wine only. This is a true local favorite with lines out the door just waiting for a taste of the food at this family owned and operated establishment. Bring your hunger as whopping portions served for reasonable prices. Try the catfish filets or how about the fried seamans platter, umm.

HAO HAO'S CHINESE

Lunch: $6-$20   Dinner: $6-$20   **Phone: 813/754-0870**

Chinese

Location: Just s of jct SR 39; in Lake Walden Square. 216 W Alexander St 33567. **Hours:** 11:30 am-9:30 pm, Fri & Sat-10:30 pm, Sun noon-9:30 pm. **Features:** No A/C; casual dress; buffet. Oriental decor with varied decorative items. Buffet bar is available along with main menu which has quite a few choices such as chow mein, beef items, pork, seafood combo platters and house specialty items. **Cards:** MC, VI.

HENRY B'S RESTAURANT

Lunch: $5-$18   Dinner: $5-$18   **Phone: 813/707-9037**

American

Location: Downtown; just e of jct SR 39 on US 92. 110 E Reynolds St 33566. **Hours:** 11 am-9 pm, Fri-10 pm, Sat 3 pm-10 pm. Closed: Sun. **Features:** casual dress; cocktails & lounge; a la carte. Very cozy setting with use of woods and copper fixtures to give a 30s look to restaurant. Menu has choices of pizza, sandwiches, steak, seafood, Italian favorites, pasta dishes, stir-fry, salad, appetizers and dessert. **Cards:** AE, DS, MC, VI.

PESO'S MEXICAN RESTAURANT

Lunch: $7-$11   Dinner: $7-$11   **Phone: 813/752-8841**

Mexican

Location: At jct N Lemon St. 2006 W Reynolds St 33567. **Hours:** 11 am-9 pm. **Features:** casual dress; children's menu; beer & wine only; a la carte. Very basic surroundings. Food is excellent with menu choices including burritos, flautas, fajitas, chimichanga and combination platters. **Cards:** AE, DS, MC, VI.

THE SEA HARVEST RESTAURANT

Lunch: $5-$9   Dinner: $9-$15   **Phone: 813/754-4899**

Seafood

Location: Downtown; 2 mi e of jct SR 39. 1701 S Alexander St 33567. **Hours:** 11:30 am-2:30 pm, Tues-Fri to 9 pm, Sat 4 pm-9 pm. Closed: 1/1, 11/22, 12/25. **Features:** casual dress; children's menu; early bird specials; carryout; beer & wine only. A home-style theme features hospitable servers and basic dishes with seafood, steak, chicken and veal. Cozy surroundings and quick service are a welcome break. The silver-dollar mushrooms are a great starter. **Cards:** AE, DI, DS, MC, VI.

SHANGHAI CHINESE RESTAURANT   **Lunch:** $6-$11   **Dinner:** $6-$11   **Phone:** 813/759-0518
▼▼▼   **Location:** On SR 39 at E Alsobrook St. 805 W Collins St 33566. **Hours:** 11 am-9 pm. **Features:** casual dress; a
      la carte, buffet. Oriental theme with variety of oriental items decorating the walls. Mongolian grill is central
Chinese   to the buffet area which is also available besides the main menu. Buffet is extensive with some 80 items to
      choose from. **Cards:** MC, VI.

WOODY'S BARBECUE   **Lunch:** $5-$8   **Dinner:** $7-$16   **Phone:** 813/754-3229
▼▼▼   **Location:** Just s of jct SR 39; in Lake Walden Square. 203 W Alexander 33566. **Hours:** 11 am-9 pm, Fri & Sat-11
      pm. Closed major holidays. **Features:** casual dress; children's menu; early bird specials; carryout; beer &
American   wine only. Forget the formality of tablecloths and eat with a laid-back attitude. Take in the rustic decor and
      enjoy down-home barbecued chicken, ribs and pork. Hearty portions are coated in a tasty sauce and
served with coleslaw, baked beans, and garlic toast. **Cards:** DS, MC, VI.   🏃 ⊠

**The following restaurant has not been evaluated by AAA
but is listed for your information only.**

SNELLGROVES   **Phone:** 813/752-3652
[fyi]   Not evaluated. **Location:** Downtown; on SR 39. 109 S Collins St 33566. **Features:** Very basic decor and local
      favorite with variety of blue plate type items such as fried chicken, pork chops and liver and onions.

PORT RICHEY pop. 2,500

——— WHERE TO STAY ———

COMFORT INN   **Phone:** (727)863-3336
[SAVE]   2/1-4/15   1P: $72   2P: $72   XP: $6   F17
      4/16-11/30   1P: $62-$67   2P: $62-$67   XP: $6   F17
▼▼▼   12/1-1/31   1P: $65   2P: $65   XP: $6   F17
Motel   **Location:** US 19, just s of jct SR 52. 11810 US 19 34668. **Fax:** 727/863-3336. **Facility:** 98 units. 2 stories, exterior
      corridors. **Terms:** check-in 4 pm, pets ($6 extra charge). **Amenities:** extended cable TV. *Some:* irons, hair
JC, MC, VI.   dryers. **Leisure Activities:** heated pool. **Guest Services:** [ECP] meal plan available. **Cards:** AE, CB, DI, DS,
      SOME UNITS
      [icons] / ⊠ 🖥 🔌 FEE

HOLIDAY INN EXPRESS HOTEL & SUITES   **Phone:** (727)869-9999
▼▼▼   12/1-4/30   1P: $80   2P: $90   XP: $10   F18
      5/1-8/31 & 9/1-11/30   1P: $50-$60   2P: $60-$80   XP: $10   F18
Motel   **Location:** US 19, 1 mi s of SR 52. 10826 US 19 N 34668. **Fax:** 727/861-0941. **Facility:** Modern and impressive
      exterior and public areas. 110 units, 34 with efficiency. Some suites ($100-$160). *Bath:* combo or shower
only. 2 stories, exterior corridors. **Terms:** check-in 4 pm, weekly & monthly rates available, package plans. **Amenities:** video
games, voice mail, irons, hair dryers. **Leisure Activities:** heated pool, whirlpool, steamroom, playground, exercise room. **Guest
Services:** [ECP] meal plan available, gift shop, coin laundry. **Business Services:** meeting rooms, administrative services.
Cards: AE, CB, DI, DS, JC, MC, VI.
      SOME UNITS
      [ASK] [icons] / ⊠ 🖥 🔌 FEE

——— WHERE TO DINE ———

PAPPAS' GAZEBO   **Lunch:** $5-$8   **Dinner:** $7-$14   **Phone:** 727/846-1232
▼▼▼   **Location:** 4.3 mi s of SR 52. 9223 US Hwy 19 34668. **Hours:** 11 am-9 pm, Fri & Sat-10 pm. Closed: 1/1.
      Reservations: suggested; in season. **Features:** casual dress; children's menu; early bird specials;
Greek   carryout; cocktails. Very popular family oriented restaurant. Wide range of food offered with Greek and
      Italian influences. Greek salads, Moussaka, Spanakopita, Dolmades, and Lamb specialties. Low fat, lower
cholesterol alternatives used in preparation. Generous portions. **Cards:** AE, DS, MC, VI.   ⊠

REDINGTON BEACH pop. 1,600   (See map p. 796; index p. 804)

——— WHERE TO STAY ———

EL MOROCCO RESORT MOTEL   **Phone:** 727/391-1675   [187]
[AAA] [SAVE]   2/1-3/31 Wkly   2P: $375-$425   XP: $70   D
      1/1-1/31 Wkly   2P: $325-$395   XP: $70   D
▼   4/1-11/30 Wkly   2P: $295-$395   XP: $70   D
      12/1-12/31 Wkly   2P: $295-$325   XP: $70   D
Apartment   **Location:** On SR 699, 1.3 mi n of Tom Stuart Cswy. 16333 Gulf Blvd 33708. **Fax:** 727/391-1675. **Facility:** Desig-
      nated smoking area. 18 units. 6 efficiencies and 10 units with kitchen. 2 stories, exterior corridors. **Terms:** 14
day cancellation notice, 30 day for monthly rentals-fee imposed, daily & monthly rates available. **Amenities:** extended cable TV.
Some: irons. **Leisure Activities:** sun deck, shuffleboard. **Cards:** MC, VI.   [icons] ⊠ 🔌

LA PLAYA BEACH RESORT   **Phone:** (727)397-0606   [186]
[AAA] [SAVE]   12/24-4/29   1P: $75-$105   2P: $75-$105   XP: $10   F12
      4/30-8/26   1P: $65-$85   2P: $65-$85   XP: $10   F12
▼▼▼   8/27-11/30   1P: $60-$80   2P: $60-$80   XP: $10   F12
      12/1-12/23   1P: $50-$70   2P: $50-$70   XP: $10   F12
Apartment   **Location:** SR 699, 1.3 mi n of jct Tom Stuart Cswy. 16326 Gulf Blvd 33708. **Fax:** 727/397-0606. **Facility:** Gulf front.
      68 units with kitchen. 33 two-bedroom units. 2 stories, exterior corridors. **Terms:** check-in 4 pm, 7 day can-
cellation notice-fee imposed, weekly & monthly rates available. **Amenities:** extended cable TV, voice mail. *Some:* irons, hair
dryers. **Leisure Activities:** whirlpool, beach, fishing, fishing pier, shuffleboard, game room, barbecue grill. **Guest Services:** coin
laundry. **Business Services:** meeting rooms, fax. **Cards:** AE, DI, DS, MC, VI. **Special Amenities:** early check-in/late
check-out and preferred room (subject to availability with advanced reservations).
      SOME UNITS
      [icons] / ⊠

REDINGTON SHORES pop. 2,400 (See map p. 796; index p. 804)

——— WHERE TO DINE ———

THE LOBSTER POT
(AAA)
Seafood

Dinner: $16-$46   **Phone: 727/391-8592** 237
Location: On SR 699; 1 mi s of jct Park Blvd (SR 694). 17814 Gulf Blvd 33708. **Hours:** 4:30 pm-10 pm, Fri & Sat-11 pm, Sun 4 pm-10 pm. Closed: 7/4, 11/22, 12/25. **Reservations:** suggested. **Features:** casual dress; children's menu; early bird specials; cocktails; valet parking. Select from a wide variety of dishes including fresh seafood, lobster and steak. **Cards:** AE, DI, DS, MC, VI.

RIVERVIEW (HILLSBOROUGH COUNTY) (See map p. 805; index p. 810)

——— WHERE TO STAY ———

BIANCHI MOTEL
(AAA) (SAVE)
Motel

Phone: (813)677-1829 95
All Year   1P: $45-$55   2P: $55-$65   XP: $5   D12
Location: I-75, exit 49, 3.1 mi to US 301 southbound; 1.6 mi s northbound exit. 6425 US 301 S 33569. **Facility:** Office hours 8 am-11 pm. Roadside motel with basic furnishings. A local family owned property popular for good rates and yesteryear appeal with modern conveniences. 15 units, 2 with efficiency. **Bath:** shower only. 1 story, exterior corridors. **Terms:** cancellation fee imposed, weekly rates available. **Cards:** DS, MC, VI.

SOME UNITS

——— WHERE TO DINE ———

ABC PIZZA
American

Lunch: $7-$18   **Dinner: $7-$18**   **Phone: 813/677-8465** 100
Location: At jct Bloomingdale. 7210 SR 301 33569. **Hours:** 11 am-11 pm, Fri & Sat-midnight. **Features:** casual dress; carryout; cocktails; a la carte. Very casual decor in this pizza and sub restaurant. Menu has many pizza choices, grinders, pasta dishes, seafood entrees, sandwiches, gyros and numerous appetizers. Casual, but welcoming and capable staff. **Cards:** MC, VI.

BEEF 'O' BRADY'S
American

Lunch: $5-$7   **Dinner: $5-$7**   **Phone: 813/672-9464** 101
Location: On US 301 at jct Gibsonton Rd. 9622 US 301S 33569. **Hours:** 11 am-11 pm, Sun noon-10 pm. Closed: 11/22, 12/25. **Features:** casual dress; children's menu; carryout; cocktail lounge; beer & wine only; a la carte. Dozens of TVs and favorite sports bar foods like burgers, sandwiches and wings make this a locals' hangout. Casual dining from plastic baskets is the norm, so feel free to dress down. Try the Philly cheese steak paired with a hearty order of onion rings. **Cards:** AE, DI, DS, MC, VI.

RUSKIN pop. 6,000

——— WHERE TO STAY ———

BAHIA BEACH ISLAND RESORT & MARINA
Resort

Phone: (813)645-3291
1/1-4/30	1P: $94-$124	2P: $94-$124	XP: $10 F18
5/1-9/30	1P: $84-$114	2P: $84-$114	XP: $10 F18
10/1-11/30	1P: $74-$104	2P: $74-$104	XP: $10 F18
12/1-12/31	1P: $69-$89	2P: $69-$89	XP: $10 F18

Location: 3.5 mi w of US 41 via Shell Point Rd, follow signs. 611 Destiny Dr 33570. Fax: 813/641-1589. **Facility:** Set on several acres in rural locale on Old Tampa Bay with gorgeous views of sunsets and distant panoramic city views of St. Petersburg and water activities. A nice destination spot offering many resort activities for the guests. Units are large with all of the modern conveniences. The restaurant is a local favorite for it's superb seafood buffet. Dock your boat and enjoy the many offerings this place has to offer. 90 units. 20 efficiencies and 12 units with kitchen. **Bath:** combo or shower only. 2 stories, interior/exterior corridors. **Terms:** 3 day cancellation notice, weekly rates available, package plans, small pets only ($15 extra charge, $5 additional days). **Amenities:** extended cable TV. **Some:** irons, hair dryers. **Leisure Activities:** 2 pools (1 heated), wading pool, whirlpool, beach, fishing, 5 lighted tennis courts, playground, basketball, shuffleboard. **Fee:** marina. **Guest Services:** gift shop, coin laundry. **Business Services:** meeting rooms, fax. **Cards:** AE, DI, DS, MC, VI.

SOME UNITS

HOLIDAY INN EXPRESS
Motel

Phone: (813)641-3437
2/1-4/15	1P: $79-$99	2P: $79-$99
12/1-1/31	1P: $59-$79	2P: $59-$79
4/16-11/30	1P: $55-$79	2P: $59-$79

Location: I-75, exit 46A; exit 46 northbound, just w at jct 33rd St SE. 3113 College Ave E 33570. Fax: 813/641-3213. **Facility:** 55 units. **Bath:** combo or shower only. 3 stories, interior corridors. **Terms:** cancellation fee imposed. **Amenities:** extended cable TV, safes, irons, hair dryers. **Guest Services:** [ECP] meal plan available, coin laundry. **Business Services:** meeting rooms, fax. **Cards:** AE, CB, DI, DS, MC, VI.

SOME UNITS

SOUTHERN COMFORT BED & BREAKFAST
Bed & Breakfast

Phone: (813)645-6361
12/1-5/31 & 11/1-11/30	2P: $85-$95	XP: $5
6/1-10/31	2P: $75-$85	XP: $5

Location: From jct US 41, just e on 14 Ave SE, 1.1 mi sw on 1st St, just w on 24th Ave SW, just s. 2409 Ravine Dr W 33570. Fax: 813/645-7375. **Facility:** Access to Little Manatee River. Designated smoking area. 4 units. 1 efficiency and 1 unit with kitchen. Some suites ($125-$145). **Bath:** some combo or shower only. 1 story, interior corridors. **Amenities:** extended cable TV. **Some:** irons, hair dryers. **Leisure Activities:** sauna, whirlpool, sun deck, sun bed, putting green, lighted tennis court, exercise room. **Guest Services:** [ECP] meal plan available, complimentary laundry. **Business Services:** meeting rooms, PC, fax. **Cards:** MC, VI.

SOME UNITS

------ **WHERE TO DINE** ------

BUDDY FREDDY'S COUNTRY BUFFET   **Lunch:** $5-$7   **Dinner:** $5-$8   **Phone:** 813/641-2241

American

Location: I-75, exit 46, northbound; exit 46A southbound, just w; in Sun Point. 3074 College Ave 33570. **Hours:** 11:30 am-7:30 pm. **Features:** casual dress; senior's menu; carryout; buffet. Casual, but congenial atmosphere with contemporary setting. Home-style cooking, all-you-can-eat, with fried chicken, meat loaf, liver, fresh vegetables, homemade mashed potatoes, salad bar fixings, and dessert bar with cake, pie and ice cream. Smoke free premises. **Cards:** AE, DS, MC, VI.

⊠

SAFETY HARBOR pop. 15,100   (See map p. 796; index p. 803)

------ **WHERE TO STAY** ------

SAFETY HARBOR RESORT AND SPA ON TAMPA BAY   **Phone:** (727)726-1161   184

1/5-3/31	1P: $149-$209	2P: $149-$209	XP: $10 F17
12/1-1/4	1P: $129-$199	2P: $129-$199	XP: $10 F17
6/16-11/30	1P: $99-$189	2P: $99-$189	XP: $10 F17
4/1-6/15	1P: $119-$179	2P: $119-$179	XP: $10 F17

Resort

Location: 1.8 mi e on Main St from jct SR 611. 105 N Bayshore Dr 34695. Fax: 727/726-4268. **Facility:** Set on Tampa Bay on extensive, landscaped grounds, this property is world renowned for its extensive spa facilities and fitness center. Facilities include fitness studios, clay and hard tennis courts, cardiovascular and weight training equipment, as well as wellness programs and body composition analysis. 193 units. **Bath:** combo or shower only. 6 stories, interior corridors. **Parking:** valet. **Terms:** check-in 4 pm, 7 day cancellation notice-fee imposed, monthly rates available, package plans, small pets only ($50 deposit). **Amenities:** extended cable TV, dual phone lines, voice mail, irons, hair dryers. **Dining:** 2 restaurants, 7 am-1 am, pool bar, $15-$20, cocktails. **Leisure Activities:** 2 heated pools, saunas, whirlpools, steamrooms, fishing, 9 tennis courts (6 lighted), recreation program, social program, bicycles, basketball, volleyball. *Fee:* tennis & golf academy, driving range, boutique, herbal body wrap, hydrotherapy, mineral springs, salon, spa facilities, theater. **Guest Services:** gift shop, valet and coin laundry. *Fee:* area transportation, massage. **Business Services:** conference facilities, administrative services, fax. *Fee:* PC. **Cards:** AE, DI, DS, MC, VI. **Special Amenities:** early check-in/late check-out and free newspaper. *(See ad below)*   SOME UNITS

$⃝ꜱᴅ ⊞ 🐾 🍴 ⍏ 🐾 ⛷ 🛶 🏊 🏋 ⊠ 🎦 🛢 🗄 ᴅᴀᴛᴀᴘᴏʀᴛ / ⊠ 🕿 /
FEE   FEE

------ **WHERE TO DINE** ------

ENVER'S PARADISE RESTAURANT   **Lunch:** $4-$9   **Dinner:** $4-$9   **Phone:** 727/725-1208   199

American

Location: Center; on SR 590, 1 mi e of jct CR 611. 443 Main St 34695. **Hours:** 7 am-9 pm, Sun 7:30 am-8 pm. **Features:** casual dress; children's menu; carryout; beer & wine only. Warm and friendly, this family-oriented restaurant features an eclectic menu that includes sandwiches, burgers, steak, seafood and such Greek favorites as moussaka and grape leaves. Such desserts as bread pudding and rice pudding are a treat. **Cards:** MC, VI.

⊠

SOUTH PASADENA pop. 5,600   (See map p. 796; index p. 804)

———— WHERE TO DINE ————

HORSE & JOCKEY BRITISH RESTAURANT & BAR   **Lunch:** $5-$7   **Dinner:** $7-$11   **Phone:** 727/345-4995   (230)
▼▼▼ ▼▼▼   **Location:** Just s of jct Gulfport Blvd and Pasadena Ave S; in Pasadena Square. 1155 Pasadena Ave S 33707.
English   **Hours:** 11 am-11 pm, Fri & Sat-11:30 pm, Sun 11 am-10 pm. Closed: 7/4, 12/25. **Features:** casual dress; children's menu; carryout; beer & wine only; a la carte. Fresh British specialties are served along with American favorites in pub-style surroundings. Order the fish 'n' chips in a tasty batter, bangers and mash, or cottage pie. Dine at ease with professional servers who provide knowledgeable, observant care. **Cards:** DS, MC, VI.   [X]

ST. PETE BEACH pop. 9,200   (See map p. 796; index p. 799)

———— WHERE TO STAY ————

ALDEN BEACH RESORT   **Phone:** (727) 360-7081   (29)
(AAA) [SAVE]

1/22-4/22	1P: $164-$249	2P: $164-$249	XP: $10 F12
4/23-9/3	1P: $119-$175	2P: $119-$175	XP: $10 F12
9/4-11/30	1P: $104-$159	2P: $104-$159	XP: $10 F12
12/1-1/21	1P: $116-$149	2P: $116-$149	XP: $10 F12

▼▼▼▼ ▼▼▼▼
Suite Resort   **Location:** SR 699, 2 mi n of Pinellas Bayway. 5900 Gulf Blvd 33706. Fax: 727/360-5957. **Facility:** Gulf front locale enhances this 5 acre property with lush tropical landscaping and inviting public areas. 10 unit types offer a variety of sleeping arrangements. Covered parking a plus. Informational kiosk in lobby. 143 units, 139 with kitchen. 1-6 stories, exterior corridors. **Terms:** check-in 4 pm, cancellation fee imposed, weekly & monthly rates available. **Amenities:** extended cable TV, voice mail, safes, irons, hair dryers. **Dining:** noon-9 pm & Sun 1 pm-9 pm; mini mart, beach bar. **Leisure Activities:** 2 heated pools, whirlpools, beach, charter fishing, 2 lighted tennis courts, playground, basketball, shuffleboard, game room, cook out deck with gas barbeque grills, ping pong, sand volleyball. *Fee:* sailboating, snorkeling equipment, cabanas, kayak, water trikes, parasailing. **Guest Services:** valet and coin laundry. **Business Services:** meeting rooms, fax. **Cards:** AE, CB, DI, DS, MC, VI. **Special Amenities:** free newspaper. *(See color ad below)*

[icons] FEE   FEE   VCR   DATA PORT

BEACH HAVEN   **Phone:** (727) 367-8642   (28)
(AAA) [SAVE]

2/1-4/30	1P: $88-$144	2P: $88-$144	XP: $10
12/1-1/31	1P: $77-$120	2P: $77-$120	XP: $10
5/1-9/7	1P: $65-$107	2P: $65-$107	XP: $10
9/8-11/30	1P: $55-$92	2P: $55-$92	XP: $10

▼▼▼ ▼▼▼
Motel   **Location:** 1 mi n or Pinellas Bayway. 4980 Gulf Blvd 33706. Fax: 727/360-8202. **Facility:** Gulf front. 18 units. 1 two-bedroom unit and 12 efficiencies. Some whirlpool units. *Bath:* combo or shower only. 1 story, exterior corridors. **Terms:** 14 day cancellation notice-fee imposed, weekly & monthly rates available. **Amenities:** extended cable TV. *Some:* irons, hair dryers. **Leisure Activities:** heated pool, beach, horseshoes, beach deck, beach volleyball, croquet & barbecue grills. **Guest Services:** [CP] meal plan available, coin laundry. **Business Services:** fax. **Cards:** MC, VI.   SOME UNITS

[icons] FEE   VCR   DATA PORT   [X]

BEACH HOUSE SUITES BY THE DON CESAR   **Phone:** (727) 363-0001   (30)
(AAA) [SAVE]

2/1-4/30	1P: $325	2P: $393	XP: $15 F15
5/1-9/30	1P: $196-$259	2P: $261-$329	XP: $15 F15
12/1-1/31 & 10/1-11/30	1P: $259	2P: $329	XP: $15 F15

▼▼▼ ▼▼▼
Apartment   **Location:** SR 699, 0.4 mi n of jct Pinellas Bayway. 3860 Gulf Blvd 33706. Fax: 727/367-6952. **Facility:** Gulf front. Each unit with private balcony overlooking gulf. 70 units with kitchen. 6 stories, exterior corridors. **Terms:** check-in 4 pm, 5 day cancellation notice-fee imposed, package plans, $8 service charge. **Amenities:** extended cable TV, voice mail, safes, irons, hair dryers. **Dining:** beach bar 7:30 am-sunset; sundries. **Leisure Activities:** heated pool, whirlpool, beach, sun deck, charter fishing, shuffleboard, hobie cats, picnic area, ping pong, sand volleyball. *Fee:* windsurfing, scuba diving & equipment, banana boat, cabanas, kayaks, sailing lessons. **Guest Services:** area transportation, complimentary laundry. *Fee:* massage. **Business Services:** meeting rooms, fax. **Cards:** AE, CB, DI, DS, JC, MC, VI.   SOME UNITS

[icons] FEE   FEE   DATA PORT   [X]   VCR   FEE

(See map p. 796)

BEST WESTERN BEACHFRONT RESORT

AAA [SAVE]

▼▼▼ Motor Inn

Phone: (727)367-1902 [34]

12/1-2/8	2P: $108-$268	XP: $20	F17
2/9-11/30	2P: $108-$168	XP: $20	F17

Location: SR 699, 2 mi n of Pinellas Bayway. 6200 Gulf Blvd 33706. Fax: 727/367-4422. **Facility:** Gulf front locale with tropically landscaped courtyard area. Expansive grounds with large pool and deck area, overlooking beach and tiki bar. Rooms are comfortably decorated with mahogany finish woods. 102 units. 8 efficiencies and 40 units with kitchen. 2 stories, exterior corridors. **Terms:** check-in 4 pm, 3 day cancellation notice-fee imposed. **Amenities:** extended cable TV, safes (fee), hair dryers. *Some:* irons. **Dining:** 2 restaurants, noon-midnight, $5-$11, cocktails, entertainment. **Leisure Activities:** 2 heated pools, beach, fishing, horseshoes, shuffleboard, volleyball, game room. *Fee:* windsurfing, cabanas, catamarans, jet skis, parasailing, waterbikes & instruction. **Guest Services:** valet laundry. **Business Services:** fax. **Cards:** AE, CB, DI, DS, JC, MC, VI. **Special Amenities:** early check-in/late check-out and free room upgrade (subject to availability with advanced reservations).

SOME UNITS

[icons] /

THE DON CESAR BEACH RESORT & SPA

AAA [SAVE]

▼▼▼ ▼▼▼ Historic Resort

Phone: (727)360-1881 [45]

2/1-4/30	1P: $329-$363	2P: $329-$363	XP: $15	F
12/1-1/31 & 10/1-11/30	1P: $256-$296	2P: $256-$296	XP: $15	F
5/1-9/30	1P: $189-$228	2P: $189-$228	XP: $15	F

Location: On SR 699; at jct Pinellas Bayway. 3400 Gulf Blvd 33706. Fax: 727/367-7597. **Facility:** Lavishly decorated expansive public areas and setting on gulf. Many rooms with gulf view. Numerous specialty boutiques. 46 room types, some of which tend to be small. On the National Register of Historic places. 275 units. 10 two-bedroom units. Some suites ($408-$923) and whirlpool units ($1058-$2178). 10 stories, interior corridors. **Parking:** valet. **Terms:** check-in 4 pm, 5 day cancellation notice-fee imposed. **Amenities:** extended cable TV, voice mail, safes, honor bars, irons, hair dryers. **Dining:** 3 restaurants, poolside grill 7 am-7 pm; ice cream parlor, $6-$15, cocktails, also, Maritana Grille, Sea Porch Cafe, see separate listing, entertainment. **Leisure Activities:** 2 heated pools, sauna, whirlpools, steamroom, beach, water aerobics, charter fishing, children's program, recreation program, aerobic classes, beach volleyball, dancing studio. *Fee:* cabana, paddleboats, sailboating, windsurfing, aqua bikes, catamarans, parasails, waverunners, golf privileges, European spa, yoga classes, dance lessons. **Guest Services:** gift shop, area transportation-golf course & charters, valet laundry. *Fee:* massage. **Business Services:** conference facilities, administrative services, PC, fax. **Cards:** AE, CB, DI, DS, JC, MC, VI.

SOME UNITS

[icons] FEE FEE FEE /

HOLIDAY INN HOTEL & SUITES BEACHFRONT RESORT & CONFERENCE CENTER

▼▼▼ Hotel

Phone: (727)360-1811 [39]

1/25-2/12	1P: $268-$498	2P: $268-$498	XP: $30	F19
2/13-4/12	1P: $168-$388	2P: $168-$388	XP: $20	F19
12/1-1/24	1P: $148-$388	2P: $148-$388	XP: $10	F19
4/13-11/30	1P: $148-$338	2P: $148-$338	XP: $10	F19

Location: On SR 699, 1 mi n of Pinellas Bayway. 5250 Gulf Blvd 33706. Fax: 727/360-1811. **Facility:** Gulf front locale enhances this beachfront property with interesting and inviting circular architecture. Great sunset views from the revolving rooftop restaurant and lounge. Inviting public areas with dark woods, brass and tiles. Dark wood finish to room furnishings; decor is inviting, tastefully done. 156 units. Some suites ($228-$388) and whirlpool units ($338-$498). *Bath:* combo or shower only. 11 stories, interior corridors. **Terms:** check-in 4 pm, 3 day cancellation notice-fee imposed. **Amenities:** extended cable TV, voice mail, safes, irons, hair dryers. **Leisure Activities:** heated pool, beach, snorkeling, charter fishing, exercise room. *Fee:* sailboating, windsurfing, waterskiing, snorkeling equipment. **Guest Services:** gift shop, valet and coin laundry. **Business Services:** meeting rooms, fax. **Cards:** AE, CB, DI, DS, JC, MC, VI.

SOME UNITS

[ASK] [icons] FEE FEE /

(See map p. 796)

HOWARD JOHNSON LODGE ST PETE BEACH RESORT INN
Phone: (727)360-7041 ③⑤
▼▼▼ ▼▼▼
| 2/1-4/30 | 1P: $115 | 2P: $115 | XP: $10 | F18 |
| 12/1-1/31 & 5/1-11/30 | 1P: $90 | 2P: $90 | XP: $10 | F18 |

Motor Inn
Location: SR 699, 1.8 mi n of Pinellas Bayway. 6100 Gulf Blvd 33706. Fax: 727/360-8941. **Facility:** Gulf front locale embraces this property which has a updated exterior look and design. Large pool deck area and neatly done grounds overlook beach. Rooms have contemporary look with whitewash finish to furniture. 133 units. 4 two-bedroom units and 20 units with kitchen. Some suites ($165-$228) and whirlpool units ($120-$140). 5 stories, interior corridors. **Terms:** age restrictions may apply. **Amenities:** extended cable TV, safes (fee), irons, hair dryers. **Leisure Activities:** heated pool, wading pool, beach, shuffleboard, game room. **Guest Services:** coin laundry. **Business Services:** meeting rooms. **Cards:** AE, DI, DS, MC, VI.
SOME UNITS

`ASK` `SD` `TI` `⌽` `⇌` `◄` `▤` `▣` `▨` `⊟` `DATA PORT` `/` `✕` `▦` `/`

ISLAND'S END RESORT
Phone: 727/360-5023 ④⑥
AAA SAVE
| 12/15-5/31 | 1P: $116-$195 | 2P: $116-$195 | XP: $15 |
| 6/1-9/14 | 1P: $99-$195 | 2P: $99-$195 | XP: $15 |
▼▼▼ ▼▼▼
| 9/15-11/30 | 1P: $83-$195 | 2P: $83-$195 | XP: $15 |
| 12/1-12/14 | 1P: $70-$185 | 2P: $70-$185 | XP: $15 |

Cottage
Location: S end of island, in Pass-A-Grille section, 2 mi s of Pinellas Bayway. 1 Pass-A-Grille Way 33706. Fax: 727/367-7890. **Facility:** Bayview. Some units with private deck. Nicely landscaped grounds with pond, deck and gazebo areas. The 3-bedroom unit has its own private pool overlooking bay and barbecue grill on deck area. 6 units with kitchen. and 1 three-bedroom unit. Some whirlpool units. 1 story, exterior corridors. **Terms:** 14 day cancellation notice-fee imposed. **Amenities:** safes. *Some:* irons, hair dryers. **Leisure Activities:** sun deck, boat dock, fishing, private fishing pier, gas barbecue grills. **Guest Services:** [CP] meal plan available, coin laundry. **Business Services:** fax. **Cards:** MC, VI. SOME UNITS

`▣` `VCR` `▣` `▨` `⊟` `/` `▦` `/`
FEE

LAMARA MOTEL APARTMENTS
Phone: (727)360-7521 ②⑤
AAA SAVE
| 2/1-4/30 | | 2P: $65-$75 | XP: $8 | D14 |
| 12/18-1/31 | | 2P: $50-$60 | XP: $8 | D14 |
▼▼▼ ▼▼▼
| 12/1-12/17 & 5/1-11/30 | | 2P: $44-$49 | XP: $8 | D14 |

Apartment
Location: Just w of Gulf Blvd (SR 699). 520 73rd Ave 33706. Fax: 727/363-0193. **Facility:** 16 units. 8 efficiencies and 8 units with kitchen. *Bath:* combo or shower only. 2 stories, exterior corridors. **Terms:** 30 day cancellation notice-fee imposed, weekly rates available. **Amenities:** extended cable TV. *Some:* irons, hair dryers.
Leisure Activities: heated pool, shuffleboard, barbecue grill. **Guest Services:** coin laundry. **Business Services:** fax.
Cards: AE, MC, VI.
SOME UNITS

`TI` `⇌` `▣` `▣` `⊟` `/` `▦` `/`

PALM CREST RESORT MOTEL
Phone: (727)360-9327 ④⓪
AAA SAVE
| 2/1-4/30 | | 2P: $85-$103 | XP: $8 |
| 5/1-9/7 | | 2P: $63-$76 | XP: $6 |
▼▼▼ ▼▼▼
| 12/1-1/31 & 9/8-11/30 | | 2P: $57-$76 | XP: $6 |

Apartment
Location: 0.5 mi n of Pinellas Bayway. 3848 Gulf Blvd 33706. Fax: 727/367-1073. **Facility:** Chalet-style frontage on the gulf. 18 units. 12 efficiencies and 6 units with kitchen. 2 stories, exterior corridors. **Terms:** 10 day cancellation notice-fee imposed, weekly rates available. **Amenities:** extended cable TV. **Leisure Activities:** heated pool, beach, shuffleboard, gas grill. **Guest Services:** coin laundry. **Cards:** AE, DS, MC, VI.

`SD` `TI` `⇌` `◄` `▣` `▦` `⊟`

PASA TIEMPA BED & BREAKFAST
Phone: (727)367-9907 ②⑥
AAA SAVE
| All Year | | 2P: $100-$150 | XP: $25 |
▼▼▼ ▼▼▼

Bed & Breakfast
Location: Jct SR 699 just e on 72nd Ave. 7141 Bay St 33706. Fax: 727/367-9906. **Facility:** Set on Intracoastal Waterway, tastefully decorated rooms and inviting courtyard area. Designated smoking area. 8 units, 1 with kitchen. *Bath:* combo or shower only. 2 stories, exterior corridors. **Terms:** check-in 4 pm, age restrictions may apply, 7 day cancellation notice-fee imposed. **Amenities:** voice mail, irons, hair dryers. **Leisure Activities:** dock patio. **Guest Services:** [ECP] meal plan available. **Business Services:** meeting rooms.
Cards: AE, MC, VI. **Special Amenities:** early check-in/late check-out and free continental breakfast. SOME UNITS

`✕` `▣` `DATA PORT` `/` `VCR` `▣` `⊟` `/`

RITZ MOTEL
Phone: (727)360-7642 ④④
▼▼▼ ▼▼▼
| 12/1-4/30 | | 2P: $66-$85 | XP: $5 | F5 |
| 5/1-11/30 | | 2P: $45-$62 | XP: $5 | F5 |

Apartment
Location: On SR 699, 0.5 mi n of Pinellas Bayway. 4237 Gulf Blvd 33706. Fax: 727/367-6655. **Facility:** On Intracoastal Waterway, some motel units. 14 units, 11 with kitchen. *Bath:* combo or shower only. 2 stories, exterior corridors. **Terms:** weekly & monthly rates available, small pets only. **Amenities:** extended cable TV. *Some:* irons, hair dryers. **Leisure Activities:** heated pool, boat dock, fishing. **Guest Services:** coin laundry. **Cards:** AE, MC, VI. SOME UNITS

`▥` `TI` `⇌` `/` `▣` `▣` `⊟` `/`

TRADEWINDS ISLAND GRAND BEACH RESORT
Phone: (727)367-6461 ③⑦
AAA SAVE
| 1/25-4/30 | 1P: $199-$349 | 2P: $199-$349 | XP: $15 | F12 |
| 12/1-1/24 & 5/1-11/30 | 1P: $169-$279 | 2P: $169-$279 | XP: $15 | F12 |
▼▼▼▼ ▼▼▼▼
Location: SR 699, 1 mi n of Pinellas Bayway. 5500 Gulf Blvd 33706 (PO Box 66307). Fax: 727/562-1214.
Resort
Facility: On gulf. Unique winding waterway with gondolas. Rooms, one-and two-bedroom suites in a six building complex. 577 units. 56 two-bedroom units and 354 units with kitchen. Some suites ($219-$429). 2-7 stories, interior/exterior corridors. **Parking:** valet. **Terms:** check-in 4 pm, package plans, $10 service charge.
Amenities: voice mail, safes, irons, hair dryers. **Dining:** 3 restaurants, deli, 7 am-10 pm ice cream shop, tiki bar, piano bar, pizza shop, $6-$28, cocktails, also, Palm Court Restaurant, see separate listing, nightclub, entertainment. **Leisure Activities:** 4 heated pools, wading pool, sauna, whirlpools, beach, cabanas, paddleboats, charter fishing, water tricycles, putting green. 4 tennis courts, racquetball court, children's program, recreation program, playground, sports court, aerobic instruction, beauty salon, gondola rides. *Fee:* swimming lessons, snorkeling, scuba & snorkeling equipment, golf privileges, tennis lessons, bicycles, tanning salon. **Guest Services:** gift shop, coin laundry. *Fee:* area transportation, massage. **Business Services:** conference facilities, administrative services, PC, fax. **Cards:** AE, CB, DI, DS, MC, VI. *(See color ad p 879)* SOME UNITS

`SD` `⌖` `TI` `▽` `♦` `⌽` `⇌` `✚` `✕` `▣` `▣` `▣` `⊟` `DATA PORT` `/` `✕` `▦` `/`
FEE FEE FEE FEE

(See map p. 796)

TRADEWINDS SANDPIPER HOTEL & SUITES

(AAA) (SAVE)

◆◆◆◆

Suite Hotel

1/25-4/30	1P: $149-$245	2P: $149-$245
12/1-1/24 & 5/1-11/30	1P: $119-$189	2P: $119-$189

Phone: (727)360-5551

XP: $15

XP: $15

36

F12

F12

Location: On SR 699, 1.8 mi n of Pinellas Bayway. 6000 Gulf Blvd 33706. **Fax:** 727/562-1282. **Facility:** Gulf front locale enhances this property which has very inviting and upscale roadside appeal. Trendy architectural design and beautiful landscaping. Rooms are comfortable, most with a great view. A few motel units available. 159 units. 5 two-bedroom units, 39 efficiencies and 115 units with kitchen. *Bath:* combo or shower only. 7 stories, interior/exterior corridors. **Parking:** valet. **Terms:** check-in 4 pm, package plans, $10 service charge. **Amenities:** voice mail, safes, irons, hair dryers. **Dining:** restaurant, 7 am-10 pm; beach bar (kosher kitchen on site), $9-$14, cocktails. **Leisure Activities:** 2 heated pools, beach, fishing, charter fishing, children's program, recreation program, shuffleboard. *Fee:* aquabikes, cabanas, exercise room, trainer avail for appointments. **Guest Services:** gift shop, coin laundry. *Fee:* massage. **Business Services:** meeting rooms, PC, fax. **Cards:** AE, CB, DI, DS, JC, MC, VI. *(See color ad below)*   SOME UNITS

(See map p. 796)

TRADEWINDS SIRATA BEACH RESORT
Phone: (727)367-5100   📱41

AAA (SAVE)

Resort

1/25-4/30	1P: $175-$317	2P: $175-$317	XP: $15 F12
12/1-1/24 & 5/1-11/30	1P: $145-$245	2P: $145-$245	XP: $15 F12

Location: On SR 699, 1.2 mi n of Pinellas Bayway. 5300 Gulf Blvd 33706. **Fax:** 727/367-8082. **Facility:** Gulf front locale and inviting architectural design welcome you to this beachfront property. Inviting public area with contemporary decor in lobby seating area and beautiful use of tile. Rooms are very upscale with pickled finish woods. Computers in 150 units. 380 units. 72 efficiencies and 192 units with kitchen. Some suites ($198-$399). *Bath:* combo or shower only. 3-6 stories, exterior corridors. **Parking:** valet. **Terms:** check-in 4 pm, weekly & monthly rates available, package plans, $10 service charge. **Amenities:** extended cable TV, video games, voice mail, safes, irons, hair dryers. **Dining:** 2 restaurants, 7 am-10 pm, Fri & Sat-11 pm, convenience store, 2 beach bars; Fun center, $7-$17, cocktails, entertainment. **Leisure Activities:** 3 heated pools, whirlpools, beach, sun deck, fishing, charter fishing, miniature golf, playground, exercise room, volleyball. *Fee:* sailboating, windsurfing, boat tours, cabanas, parasailing. **Guest Services:** [BP] meal plan available, gift shop, valet and coin laundry. **Business Services:** conference facilities, administrative services, PC, fax. **Cards:** AE, CB, DI, DS, MC, VI. *(See color ad p 879)*

SOME UNITS

TRAVELODGE ST. PETE BEACH
Phone: (727)367-2711   📱31

AAA (SAVE)

Motor Inn

All Year	1P: $80-$135	2P: $80-$135	XP: $6 F18

Location: SR 699, 2 mi n of Pinellas Bayway. 6300 Gulf Blvd 33706. **Fax:** 727/367-7068. **Facility:** Gulf front locale enhances this property. Large, open design to lobby seating area with rattan furniture and tropical theme. Huge, nicely landscaped courtyard and pool deck area with tiled waterfall overlooking beach. 200 units, 98 with efficiency. 2 stories, exterior corridors. **Terms:** check-in 4 pm, package plans. **Amenities:** extended cable TV, video games, safes (fee). *Some:* irons, hair dryers. **Dining:** restaurant, 8 am-11 & noon-10 pm, Fri & Sat-11 pm; seasonal entertainment, $6-$15, cocktails. **Leisure Activities:** heated pool, wading pool, beach, shuffleboard, volleyball, game room. *Fee:* sailboating, cabanas, parasailing, shelling trips, watertrikes. **Guest Services:** gift shop. **Business Services:** meeting rooms. **Cards:** AE, CB, DI, DS, MC, VI. **Special Amenities:** free local telephone calls and free newspaper. *(See color ad p 877)*

SOME UNITS

WHERE TO DINE

AUNT HEIDI'S ITALIAN RESTAURANT
Lunch: $4-$12   **Dinner:** $6-$12   **Phone:** 727/367-3448   📱34

Italian

Location: On SR 699, 2.2 mi n of Pinellas Bayway. 6340 Gulf Blvd 33706. **Hours:** 11 am-10 pm, Sun & major holidays from 4 pm. Closed: 11/22, 12/25; also Super Bowl Sun. **Features:** casual dress; children's menu; carryout; beer & wine only. Established in 1963, the small, family-oriented restaurant delivers personable service and a tasty selection of entrees that includes many pasta specialties as well as other yummies, such as beef stroganoff, chicken cordon bleu and a turkey club.

BRUNELLO
Dinner: $18-$22   **Phone:** 727/367-1851   📱38

Northern
Italian

Location: 0.3 mi n of Pinellas Bayway. 3861 Gulf Blvd 33706. **Hours:** 5:30 pm-10 pm. Closed: 7/4, 11/22, 12/25; also Sun. **Reservations:** suggested. **Features:** semi-formal attire; carryout; cocktails & lounge; a la carte. A stylishly casual bistro, it offers an extensive wine list that is sure to include the perfect accompaniment to any meal. Enjoy tasty, colorfully presented dishes like the caramelized grilled salmon with vegetables and roasted garlic mashed potatoes. Smoke free premises. **Cards:** AE, MC, VI.

DER EISENHUT
Dinner: $9-$15   **Phone:** 727/367-6495   📱33

German

Location: Just e of SR 699. 357 Corey Ave 33706. **Hours:** 4 pm-10 pm. Closed: 1/1, 12/24, 12/25; also Sun & Mon. **Features:** casual dress; carryout; cocktail lounge; beer & wine only; street parking; a la carte. Relax in the cozy bistro setting and savor an excellent variety of ethnic dishes, ranging from German and French to Hungarian and Russian. European antiques, paintings, crystal chandeliers and assorted imports give this restaurant an air of authenticity. **Cards:** MC, VI.

JOHNNY LEVEROCK'S ON THE BEACH
Lunch: $7-$19   **Dinner:** $7-$19   **Phone:** 727/367-4588   📱30

Steak & Seafood

Location: W end of St. Petersburg Beach Cswy (75th Ave), on Boca Ciega Bay. 10 Corey Ave 33706. **Hours:** 11:30 am-10 pm. Closed: 11/22, 12/25. **Features:** casual dress; children's menu; early bird specials; carryout; cocktails & lounge. An old Florida decor complete with hardwood floors, antiques, nautical memorabilia and big picture windows gives the bayfront restaurant its personality. Grilled mahi coconut shrimp, fresh clam chowder and onion-crusted salmon bring the menu to life. **Cards:** AE, DI, DS, MC, VI.

LA CROISETTE FAMILY RESTAURANT
Lunch: $4-$7   **Dinner:** $10-$19   **Phone:** 727/360-2253   📱31

American

Cards: MC, VI.

Location: On SR 699; at jct Corey Ave. 7401 Gulf Blvd 33706. **Hours:** 7 am-2 & 5-9:30 pm, Mon & Tues 7 am-2 pm. **Features:** casual dress; children's menu; carryout; beer & wine only. Known locally for their hearty breakfasts; this local favorite has an extensive breakfast menu, sandwiches and salads at lunch and a variety of dinner items including French treats and pasta dishes. Decor is basic but still a popular spot.

MARITANA GRILLE
Dinner: $20-$30   **Phone:** 727/360-1882   📱41

American

Location: On SR 699; at jct Pinellas Bayway; in The Don CeSar Beach Resort & Spa. 3400 Gulf Blvd 33706. **Hours:** 5:30 pm-10 pm, Fri & Sat-11 pm. **Reservations:** suggested. **Features:** dressy casual; children's menu; carryout; cocktails & lounge; entertainment; fee for valet parking; a la carte. Resort-casual dining with artistic creations like swirled mashed potatoes that add charm to any plate. A private dining room and chef's table are available. For a light and tasty appetizer, try the lobster spring roll. Smoking is permitted in the bar only. Smoke free premises. **Cards:** AE, CB, DI, DS, JC, MC, VI.

(See map p. 796)

PALM COURT RESTAURANT   **Lunch:** $7-$12   **Dinner:** $16-$25   **Phone:** 727/367-6461   36
Italian
Location: SR 699, 1 mi n of Pinellas Bayway; in TradeWinds Island Grand Beach Resort. 5500 Gulf Blvd 33706. **Hours:** 11:30 am-2 & 5:30-10 pm, Sun from 10 am. **Features:** casual dress; Sunday brunch; children's menu; cocktails; valet parking; a la carte. A quaint atmosphere features indoor and outdoor seating amid resort surroundings. Order the seafood pasta and you will find a thick marinara sauce filled with clams, shrimp, fish, scallops and mussels. The rich raspberry cake is artistically swirled and the chocolate cake is the highlight. Smoke free premises. **Cards:** AE, CB, DI, DS, MC, VI.

SEA CRITTERS CAFE   **Lunch:** $6-$17   **Dinner:** $6-$17   **Phone:** 727/360-3706   42
Seafood
Location: On SR 699, 1 mi s of Pinellas Bayway; at jct 21st Ave. 2007 Pass-A-Grille Way 33706. **Hours:** 11:30 am-9 pm. Closed: 12/24, 12/25; also 12/31 for dinner. **Features:** casual dress; children's menu; carryout; cocktails & lounge; a la carte. Dock your boat and bring a hearty appetite for generous portions of Key West-style food. Experience dockside dining on the Intracoastal Waterway at Vina Del Mar Bridge. The seafood platter gives a sampling of fried clams, shrimp, squid, crab cake grouper nuggets and onion rings. **Cards:** AE, DI, MC, VI.

THE SEAHORSE TAVERN & RESTAURANT   **Lunch:** $5-$11   **Phone:** 727/360-1734   44
Seafood
Location: On SR 699, 1.5 mi s of jct Pinellas Bayway. 800 Pass-A-Grille Way 33706. **Hours:** 8 am-2:30 pm. Closed: Tues. **Features:** casual dress; children's menu; cocktails. A no-frills eatery dating back to 1937, it boasts a breezy courtyard reminiscent of Old Florida homes. Well-seasoned black beans are a signature favorite along with specialty sandwiches such as Cajun chicken and grouper served on grilled Cuban bread. **Cards:** DS, MC, VI.

SEA PORCH CAFE   **Lunch:** $8-$12   **Dinner:** $9-$21   **Phone:** 727/360-1884   39
American
Location: On SR 699; at jct Pinellas Bayway; in The Don CeSar Beach Resort & Spa. 3400 Gulf Blvd 33706. **Hours:** 7 am-11, noon-4 & 5-11 pm. **Reservations:** suggested; for dinner. **Features:** casual dress; children's menu; early bird specials; carryout; cocktails & lounge; entertainment; valet parking; a la carte. Bright and colorful, the decor of the waterfront restaurant is unmistakably tropical. Strong flavor characterizes the rosemary chicken with homemade gravy and the key lime pie. Light, crisp breezes drift across the outdoor boardwalk. **Cards:** AE, CB, DI, DS, MC, VI.

SILAS DENT'S STEAKHOUSE   **Dinner:** $8-$21   **Phone:** 727/360-6961   40
Steak House
Location: On SR 699, 1 mi n of Pinellas Bayway; in Bayside Shores. 5501 Gulf Blvd 33706. **Hours:** 5 pm-10 pm, Fri & Sat-11 pm. **Features:** casual dress; cocktails & lounge. Located on the Intracoastal Waterway with patio dining available. The original Silas Dent was established in 1979 with this newer version carrying on tradition. Much history abounds in conjunction with the name. The menu has a wide variety of salad, seafood, surf and turf, smokehouse items and "steak". **Cards:** MC, VI.

SKIDDER'S RESTAURANT   **Lunch:** $6-$24   **Dinner:** $6-$24   **Phone:** 737/360-1029   32
American
Location: On SR 699, 1 mi n of Pinellas Bayway. 5799 Gulf Blvd 33706. **Hours:** 7 am-11 pm. **Features:** casual dress; children's menu; carryout; cocktails. Very popular local restaurant. Contemporary design and welcoming staff await you. Menu has a great variety of breakfast items as well as numerous lunch and dinner entrees to choose from; omelettes, waffles, croissants, homecooked and Greek specialties as well. **Cards:** AE, DI, DS, MC, VI.

THE SLOPPY PELICAN   **Lunch:** $5-$12   **Dinner:** $5-$12   **Phone:** 727/367-5556   37
Seafood
Location: Just w of jct SR 699. 677 75th Ave 33706. **Hours:** 11 am-midnight. Closed: 11/22. **Features:** casual dress; carryout; cocktails & lounge; a la carte. Nicknamed "the Sloppy" by locals, the name is hardly a commentary on the service or food. Enjoy a relaxed setting on the water as you feast on shrimp, fresh stone crab claws, grouper, and burgers that have a backyard-barbecue flavor. **Cards:** AE, MC, VI.

STARLITE DINER   **Lunch:** $4-$12   **Dinner:** $4-$12   **Phone:** 727/363-0434   35
American
Location: On SR 699, 2.1 mi n of Pinellas Bayway. 5200 Gulf Blvd 33706. **Hours:** 7 am-10 pm, Fri & Sat-11 pm. Closed: 12/25. **Features:** casual dress; children's menu. A '50s-style diner, complete with red vinyl upholstery and vintage signs, features mainly sandwiches, but you'll find selections like pork chops, mashed potatoes and vegetables, too. So put on your poodle skirt and bobby socks and sip on a Coke float. **Cards:** MC, VI.

THE WHARF SEAFOOD RESTAURANT   **Lunch:** $5-$16   **Dinner:** $5-$16   **Phone:** 727/367-9469   43
Seafood
Location: On SR 699, 0.9 mi s of Pinellas Bayway; in Historic Pass-A-Grille. 2001 Pass-A-Grille Way 33706. **Hours:** 11 am-11 pm. **Features:** casual dress; children's menu; cocktails & lounge; a la carte. Very rustic exterior with deck dining and oyster bar. The restaurant sets on the Intracoastal Waterway with great water views. Menu has a nice mix of seafood choices. A rustic, nautical theme decor awaits you. **Cards:** MC, VI.

SUN CITY CENTER pop. 8,300

——————— **WHERE TO STAY** ———————

COMFORT INN-SUN CITY CENTER   **Phone:** (813)633-3318
Motel

1/15-4/21	1P: $79-$89	2P: $89-$99	XP: $10	F12
12/1-1/14	1P: $59-$69	2P: $69-$79	XP: $10	F12
4/22-11/30	1P: $49-$59	2P: $59-$69	XP: $10	F12

Location: I-75, exit 46B; exit 46 northbound, 0.5 mi e on SR 674. 718 Cypress Village Blvd 33573. Fax: 813/633-2747. **Facility:** 74 units, 8 with kitchen. Some suites ($99-$129). *Bath:* combo or shower only. 2 stories, exterior corridors. **Terms:** 7 day cancellation notice, package plans. **Amenities:** extended cable TV. *Some:* irons, hair dryers. **Leisure Activities:** whirlpool. **Guest Services:** [ECP] meal plan available, coin laundry. **Business Services:** fax. **Cards:** AE, CB, DI, DS, MC, VI. **Special Amenities:** free continental breakfast and free local telephone calls.

SOME UNITS

SUN CITY CENTER INN   **Phone:** (813)634-3331

1/16-4/30	1P: $79	2P: $79	XP: $10	F18
12/1-1/15 & 5/1-11/30	1P: $49	2P: $49	XP: $10	F18

Motor Inn   **Location:** I-75, exit 46B; exit 46 northbound, 2.1 mi e on SR 674. 1335 Rickenbacker Dr 33573. Fax: 813/634-2053.
Facility: Located in retirement community. 88 units. *Bath:* combo or shower only. 2 stories, exterior corridors.
Terms: package plans - off season, pets ($7.50 extra charge). **Amenities:** extended cable TV. *Some:* irons, hair dryers. **Leisure Activities:** putting green. *Fee:* golf-72 holes, 6 lighted tennis courts. **Business Services:** meeting rooms. **Cards:** AE, DS, MC, VI.

SOME UNITS

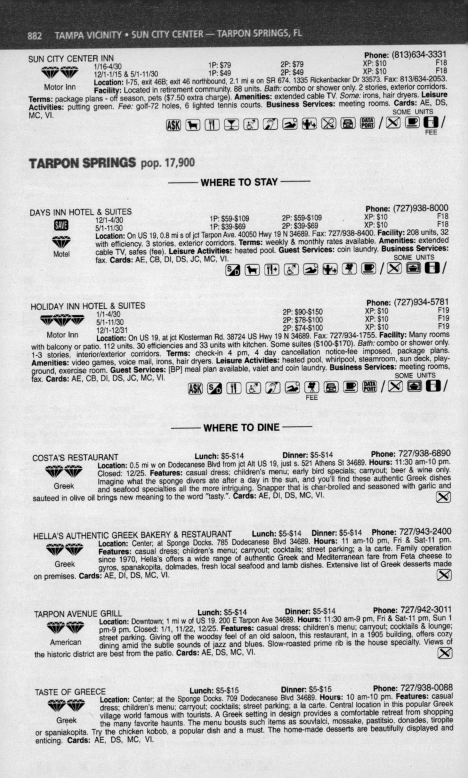

TARPON SPRINGS pop. 17,900

—— WHERE TO STAY ——

DAYS INN HOTEL & SUITES   **Phone:** (727)938-8000

12/1-4/30	1P: $59-$109	2P: $59-$109	XP: $10	F18
5/1-11/30	1P: $39-$69	2P: $39-$69	XP: $10	F18

Motel   **Location:** On US 19, 0.8 mi s of jct Tarpon Ave. 40050 Hwy 19 N 34689. Fax: 727/938-8400. **Facility:** 208 units, 32 with efficiency. 3 stories, exterior corridors. **Terms:** weekly & monthly rates available. **Amenities:** extended cable TV, safes (fee). **Leisure Activities:** heated pool. **Guest Services:** coin laundry. **Business Services:** fax. **Cards:** AE, CB, DI, DS, JC, MC, VI.

SOME UNITS

HOLIDAY INN HOTEL & SUITES   **Phone:** (727)934-5781

1/1-4/30		2P: $90-$150	XP: $10	F19
5/1-11/30		2P: $78-$100	XP: $10	F19
12/1-12/31		2P: $74-$100	XP: $10	F19

Motor Inn   **Location:** On US 19, at jct Klosterman Rd. 38724 US Hwy 19 N 34689. Fax: 727/934-1755. **Facility:** Many rooms with balcony or patio. 112 units. 30 efficiencies and 33 units with kitchen. Some suites ($100-$170). *Bath:* combo or shower only. 1-3 stories, interior/exterior corridors. **Terms:** check-in 4 pm, 4 day cancellation notice-fee imposed, package plans. **Amenities:** video games, voice mail, irons, hair dryers. **Leisure Activities:** heated pool, whirlpool, steamroom, sun deck, playground, exercise room. **Guest Services:** [BP] meal plan available, valet and coin laundry. **Business Services:** meeting rooms, fax. **Cards:** AE, CB, DI, DS, JC, MC, VI.

SOME UNITS

—— WHERE TO DINE ——

COSTA'S RESTAURANT   **Lunch:** $5-$14   **Dinner:** $5-$14   **Phone:** 727/938-6890

Greek   **Location:** 0.5 mi w on Dodecanese Blvd from jct Alt US 19, just s. 521 Athens St 34689. **Hours:** 11:30 am-10 pm. Closed: 12/25. **Features:** casual dress; children's menu; early bird specials; carryout; beer & wine only. Imagine what the sponge divers ate after a day in the sun, and you'll find these authentic Greek dishes and seafood specialties all the more intriguing. Snapper that is char-broiled and seasoned with garlic and sauteed in olive oil brings new meaning to the word "tasty.". **Cards:** AE, DI, DS, MC, VI.

HELLA'S AUTHENTIC GREEK BAKERY & RESTAURANT   **Lunch:** $5-$14   **Dinner:** $5-$14   **Phone:** 727/943-2400

Greek   **Location:** Center; at Sponge Docks. 785 Dodecanese Blvd 34689. **Hours:** 11 am-10 pm, Fri & Sat-11 pm. **Features:** casual dress; children's menu; carryout; cocktails; street parking; a la carte. Family operation since 1970, Hella's offers a wide range of authentic Greek and Mediterranean fare from Feta cheese to gyros, spanakopita, dolmades, fresh local seafood and lamb dishes. Extensive list of Greek desserts made on premises. **Cards:** AE, DI, DS, MC, VI.

TARPON AVENUE GRILL   **Lunch:** $5-$14   **Dinner:** $5-$14   **Phone:** 727/942-3011

American   **Location:** Downtown; 1 mi w of US 19. 200 E Tarpon Ave 34689. **Hours:** 11:30 am-9 pm, Fri & Sat-11 pm, Sun 1 pm-9 pm. Closed: 1/1, 11/22, 12/25. **Features:** casual dress; children's menu; carryout; cocktails & lounge; street parking. Giving off the woodsy feel of an old saloon, this restaurant, in a 1905 building, offers cozy dining amid the subtle sounds of jazz and blues. Slow-roasted prime rib is the house specialty. Views of the historic district are best from the patio. **Cards:** AE, DS, MC, VI.

TASTE OF GREECE   **Lunch:** $5-$15   **Dinner:** $5-$15   **Phone:** 727/938-0088

Greek   **Location:** Center; at the Sponge Docks. 709 Dodecanese Blvd 34689. **Hours:** 10 am-10 pm. **Features:** casual dress; children's menu; carryout; cocktails; street parking; a la carte. Central location in this popular Greek village world famous with tourists. A Greek setting in design provides a comfortable retreat from shopping the many favorite haunts. The menu bousts such items as souvlalci, mossake, pastitsio, donades, tiropite or spaniakopita. Try the chicken kobob, a popular dish and a must. The home-made desserts are beautifully displayed and enticing. **Cards:** AE, DS, MC, VI.

TEMPLE TERRACE pop. 16,400   (See map p. 805; index p. 810)

─── **WHERE TO STAY** ───

EXTENDED STAY OF AMERICA
Phone: 813/989-2264   **88**
All Year   1P: $54-$69   2P: $59-$69
Motel
Location: I-75, exit 55, just w on Fletcher Ave. 12242 Morris Bridge Rd 33617. Fax: 813/989-1184. **Facility:** Office hours 7 am-11 pm. 101 efficiencies. *Bath:* combo or shower only. 3 stories, interior corridors. **Terms:** weekly rates available. **Amenities:** extended cable TV, voice mail. *Some:* irons, hair dryers. **Guest Services:** coin laundry. **Business Services:** fax. **Cards:** AE, CB, DI, DS, JC, MC, VI.
SOME UNITS
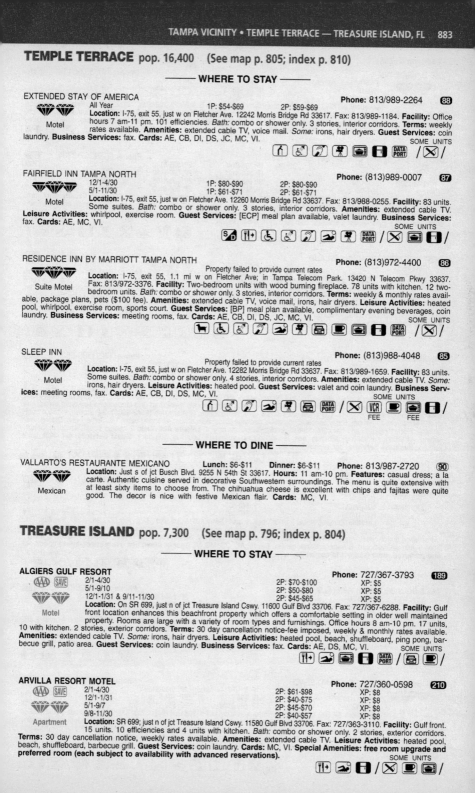

FAIRFIELD INN TAMPA NORTH
Phone: (813)989-0007   **87**
12/1-4/30   1P: $80-$90   2P: $80-$90
5/1-11/30   1P: $61-$71   2P: $61-$71
Motel
Location: I-75, exit 55, just w on Fletcher Ave. 12260 Morris Bridge Rd 33617. Fax: 813/988-0255. **Facility:** 83 units. Some suites. *Bath:* combo or shower only. 3 stories, interior corridors. **Amenities:** extended cable TV.
Leisure Activities: whirlpool, exercise room. **Guest Services:** [ECP] meal plan available, valet laundry. **Business Services:** fax. **Cards:** AE, MC, VI.
SOME UNITS

RESIDENCE INN BY MARRIOTT TAMPA NORTH
Phone: (813)972-4400   **86**
Property failed to provide current rates
Suite Motel
Location: I-75, exit 55, 1.1 mi w on Fletcher Ave; in Tampa Telecom Park. 13420 N Telecom Pkwy 33637. Fax: 813/972-3376. **Facility:** Two-bedroom units with wood burning fireplace. 78 units with kitchen. 12 two-bedroom units. *Bath:* combo or shower only. 3 stories, interior corridors. **Terms:** weekly & monthly rates available, package plans, pets ($100 fee). **Amenities:** extended cable TV, voice mail, irons, hair dryers. **Leisure Activities:** heated pool, whirlpool, exercise room, sports court. **Guest Services:** [BP] meal plan available, complimentary evening beverages, coin laundry. **Business Services:** meeting rooms, fax. **Cards:** AE, CB, DI, DS, JC, MC, VI.
SOME UNITS

SLEEP INN
Phone: (813)988-4048   **85**
Property failed to provide current rates
Motel
Location: I-75, exit 55, just w on Fletcher Ave. 12282 Morris Bridge Rd 33617. Fax: 813/989-1659. **Facility:** 83 units. Some suites. *Bath:* combo or shower only. 4 stories, interior corridors. **Amenities:** extended cable TV. *Some:* irons, hair dryers. **Leisure Activities:** heated pool. **Guest Services:** valet and coin laundry. **Business Services:** meeting rooms, fax. **Cards:** AE, CB, DI, DS, MC, VI.
SOME UNITS
VCR FEE   FEE

─── **WHERE TO DINE** ───

VALLARTO'S RESTAURANTE MEXICANO   **Lunch:** $6-$11   **Dinner:** $6-$11   Phone: 813/987-2720   **90**
Mexican
Location: Just s of jct Busch Blvd. 9255 N 54th St 33617. **Hours:** 11 am-10 pm. **Features:** casual dress; a la carte. Authentic cuisine served in decorative Southwestern surroundings. The menu is quite extensive with at least sixty items to choose from. The chihuahua cheese is excellent with chips and fajitas were quite good. The decor is nice with festive Mexican flair. **Cards:** MC, VI.

TREASURE ISLAND pop. 7,300   (See map p. 796; index p. 804)

─── **WHERE TO STAY** ───

ALGIERS GULF RESORT
Phone: 727/367-3793   **189**
2/1-4/30   2P: $70-$100   XP: $5
5/1-9/10   2P: $50-$80   XP: $5
12/1-1/31 & 9/11-11/30   2P: $45-$65   XP: $5
Motel
Location: On SR 699, just n of jct Treasure Island Cswy. 11600 Gulf Blvd 33706. Fax: 727/367-6288. **Facility:** Gulf front location enhances this beachfront property which offers a comfortable setting in older well maintained property. Rooms are large with a variety of room types and furnishings. Office hours 8 am-10 pm. 17 units, 10 with kitchen. 2 stories, exterior corridors. **Terms:** 30 day cancellation notice-fee imposed. **Amenities:** extended cable TV. *Some:* irons, hair dryers. **Leisure Activities:** heated pool, beach, shuffleboard, ping pong, barbecue grill, patio area. **Guest Services:** coin laundry. **Business Services:** fax. **Cards:** AE, DS, MC, VI.
SOME UNITS

ARVILLA RESORT MOTEL
Phone: 727/360-0598   **210**
2/1-4/30   2P: $61-$98   XP: $8
12/1-1/31   2P: $40-$75   XP: $8
5/1-9/7   2P: $45-$70   XP: $8
9/8-11/30   2P: $40-$57   XP: $8
Apartment
Location: SR 699; just n of jct Treasure Island Cswy. 11580 Gulf Blvd 33706. Fax: 727/363-3110. **Facility:** Gulf front. 15 units. 10 efficiencies and 4 units with kitchen. *Bath:* combo or shower only. 2 stories, exterior corridors. **Terms:** 30 day cancellation notice, weekly rates available. **Amenities:** extended cable TV. **Leisure Activities:** heated pool, beach, shuffleboard, barbecue grill. **Guest Services:** coin laundry. **Cards:** MC, VI. **Special Amenities:** free room upgrade and preferred room (each subject to availability with advanced reservations).
SOME UNITS

(See map p. 796)

THE BAYSIDE INN Phone: 727/367-6456 **217**

2/1-5/1	1P: $59-$400	2P: $79-$540	XP: $15
12/1-1/31	1P: $45-$300	2P: $59-$405	XP: $15
5/2-11/30	1P: $35-$240	2P: $49-$330	XP: $15

Motel **Location:** SR 699, just n of Treasure Island Cswy. 11365 Gulf Blvd 33706. Fax: 727/367-1291. **Facility:** On Boca Ciega Bay. 23 efficiencies. *Bath:* combo or shower only. 2 stories, interior/exterior corridors. **Terms:** 30 day cancellation notice, weekly rates available. **Amenities:** extended cable TV. *Some:* irons. **Leisure Activities:** heated pool, boat dock, fishing, shuffleboard. **Guest Services:** coin laundry. **Cards:** DS, MC, VI.

BEST WESTERN SEA CASTLE SUITES Phone: (727)367-2704 **195**

2/10-4/22	1P: $95-$142	2P: $95-$142	XP: $5	F12
4/23-9/4	1P: $69-$132	2P: $69-$132	XP: $5	F12
9/5-11/30	1P: $63-$105	2P: $63-$105	XP: $5	F12
12/1-2/9	1P: $69-$100	2P: $69-$100	XP: $5	F12

Apartment **Location:** On SR 699; at jct Treasure Island Cswy. 10750 Gulf Blvd 33706. Fax: 727/360-2492. **Facility:** Gulf front. 41 units with kitchen. 2-3 stories (no elevator), exterior corridors. **Terms:** 3 day cancellation notice, weekly rates available. **Amenities:** extended cable TV, hair dryers. **Leisure Activities:** heated pool, beach, fishing, playground, shuffleboard, barbecue grills. **Guest Services:** coin laundry. **Cards:** DS, MC, VI.

SOME UNITS

FEE

BEST WESTERN TREASURE ISLAND Phone: (727)360-6971 **197**

				F18
All Year	1P: $74-$129	2P: $74-$129	XP: $10	F18

Motel **Location:** SR 699, just n of jct Treasure Island Cswy. 11125 Gulf Blvd 33706. Fax: 727/360-9014. **Facility:** Set on Boca Ciega Bay with nice waterfront locale for viewing manatees and dolphins from the dock area. Contemporary decor to rooms with appealing colors. Children's playground is very nice with numerous goodies for the kids. 84 units. *Bath:* combo or shower only. 3 stories, interior corridors. **Amenities:** safes (fee). *Some:* irons, hair dryers. **Leisure Activities:** heated pool, boat dock, fishing, playground. **Guest Services:** coin laundry. **Business Services:** meeting rooms, fax. **Cards:** AE, DI, DS, MC, VI. **Special Amenities:** free local telephone calls and free newspaper. *(See color ad p 877)*

SOME UNITS

BILMAR BEACH RESORT Phone: (727)360-5531 **196**

1/25-4/22	1P: $130-$150	2P: $130-$150	XP: $10	F18
4/23-9/4	1P: $99-$115	2P: $99-$115	XP: $10	F18
12/1-1/24	1P: $85-$113	2P: $113	XP: $10	F18
9/5-11/30	1P: $87-$99	2P: $87-$99	XP: $10	F18

Hotel **Location:** SR 699, jct Treasure Island Cswy. 10650 Gulf Blvd 33706. Fax: 727/360-2362. **Facility:** Gulf front locale enhances this beachside tradition. Pools are set in nicely manicured and landscaped courtyard areas; one overlooks the beach. 171 units. 105 efficiencies and 4 units with kitchen. Some suites ($142-$300). 3-8 stories, exterior corridors. **Terms:** check-in 4 pm, 3 day cancellation notice, package plans. **Amenities:** extended cable TV. *Some:* irons. **Dining:** restaurant, 7 am-10 pm; beach bar cafe, $8-$15, cocktails, entertainment. **Leisure Activities:** 2 heated pools, whirlpool, beach, fishing, jet skiing, parasailing, cabanas, golf, tennis, jogging, volleyball, boutique, sun deck. **Guest Services:** gift shop, valet laundry. **Business Services:** conference facilities, fax. **Cards:** AE, CB, DI, MC, VI.

SOME UNITS

FEE   FEE

FARGO MOTEL Phone: 727/367-3166 **190**

2/1-4/24	1P: $60-$90		XP: $7	F6
12/1-1/31	1P: $45-$65		XP: $6	F6
4/25-9/10	1P: $40-$65		XP: $5	F6
9/11-11/30	1P: $40-$60		XP: $5	F6

Motel **Location:** On SR 699, just n of jct Treasure Island Cswy. 10810 Gulf Blvd 33706. Fax: 727/363-3341. **Facility:** Gulf front. 21 units, 12 with efficiency. *Bath:* combo or shower only. 1-2 stories, exterior corridors. **Terms:** 28 day cancellation notice, weekly rates available. **Amenities:** extended cable TV. *Some:* irons, hair dryers. **Leisure Activities:** heated pool, beach, shuffleboard. **Business Services:** fax. **Cards:** AE, DS, MC, VI. **Special Amenities:** early check-in/late check-out and preferred room (subject to availability with advanced reservations).

SOME UNITS

GULF SOUNDS BEACH RENTALS Phone: (727)363-6114 **191**

			XP: $7
1/11-4/30		2P: $74-$99	XP: $7
12/1-1/10		2P: $59-$79	XP: $7
5/1-11/30		2P: $51-$69	XP: $7

Apartment **Location:** On SR 699, 0.6 mi s of Johns Pass. 12240 Gulf Blvd 33706. Fax: 727/393-4185. **Facility:** 6 units. 2 efficiencies and 4 units with kitchen. 1 story, exterior corridors. **Terms:** 30 day cancellation notice, 7 day off season-fee imposed, weekly & monthly rates available. **Amenities:** *Some:* irons. **Leisure Activities:** beach access, gas barbecue, patio, sun deck. **Guest Services:** coin laundry. **Business Services:** fax. **Cards:** AE, MC, VI.

HOLIDAY INN-TREASURE ISLAND BEACH Phone: (727)367-2761 **200**

12/25-4/18	1P: $110-$149	2P: $110-$149	XP: $10	F19
4/19-11/30	1P: $94-$115	2P: $94-$115	XP: $10	F19
12/1-12/24	1P: $89-$102	2P: $89-$102	XP: $10	F19

Hotel **Location:** SR 699, 0.8 mi n of jct Treasure Island Cswy. 11908 Gulf Blvd 33706. Fax: 727/367-9446. **Facility:** Gulf front locale enhances this property. Spectacular view from the rooftop restaurant. Rooms are nicely decorated with contemporary look and each has a private balcony, many with gulf view. 117 units. 9 stories, interior corridors. **Terms:** check-in 4 pm, package plans - off season. **Amenities:** extended cable TV, irons, hair dryers. **Leisure Activities:** heated pool, whirlpool, beach, exercise room, volleyball, game room. **Guest Services:** [AP] & [BP] meal plans available, gift shop, valet laundry. **Business Services:** fax. **Cards:** AE, CB, DI, DS, JC, MC, VI.

SOME UNITS

FEE   FEE

(See map p. 796)

THE JEFFERSON MOTEL APTS.

AAA SAVE — Apartment

2/1-4/21 Wkly	1P: $679	2P: $679	XP: $12
12/1-1/31 & 4/22-9/3 Wkly	1P: $462	2P: $462	XP: $10
9/4-11/30 Wkly	1P: $427	2P: $427	XP: $10

Phone: 727/360-5826   215

Location: On SR 699, 0.6 mi s of jct Treasure Island Cswy. 10116 Gulf Blvd 33706. Fax: 727/367-9396. **Facility:** Gulf front. 14 units with kitchen. 2-3 stories, exterior corridors. **Terms:** 28 day cancellation notice-fee imposed. **Amenities:** extended cable TV. **Leisure Activities:** heated pool, beach, shuffleboard, volleyball, barbecue grill. **Cards:** MC, VI.

SOME UNITS

JOLLY ROGER MOTEL

Motel

All Year	1P: $45-$100	2P: $45-$100	XP: $10

Phone: 727/360-5571   192
F6

Location: On SR 699, 0.5 mi n of jct Treasure Island Cswy. 11525 Gulf Blvd 33706. Fax: 727/360-4475. **Facility:** On Intracoastal Waterway. 31 units, 18 with kitchen. Some suites. *Bath:* combo or shower only. 2 stories, exterior corridors. **Terms:** 14 day cancellation notice-fee imposed. **Amenities:** extended cable TV. *Some:* irons, hair dryers. **Leisure Activities:** heated pool, boat dock, fishing, shuffleboard. **Guest Services:** coin laundry. **Cards:** MC, VI.

SOME UNITS

MARDI GRAS MOTEL

Apartment

Property failed to provide current rates

Phone: (727)367-1621   212

Location: On SR 699, 0.7 mi n of jct Treasure Island Cswy. 11965 Gulf Blvd 33706. Fax: 727/360-5910. **Facility:** Designated smoking area. 10 units. 1 efficiency and 6 units with kitchen. 2 stories, exterior corridors. **Terms:** 21 day cancellation notice, weekly rates available. **Leisure Activities:** heated pool. **Cards:** DI, MC, VI.

SOME UNITS

PAGE TERRACE MOTEL

AAA SAVE — Apartment

2/1-4/24	1P: $66-$98	XP: $6 F10
12/1-1/31 & 4/25-9/4	1P: $52-$75	XP: $6 F10
9/5-11/30	1P: $45-$65	XP: $6 F10

Phone: (727)367-1997   214

Location: On SR 699, just s of jct Treasure Island Cswy. 10500 Gulf Blvd 33706. Fax: 727/360-7179. **Facility:** Gulf front. 35 units. 24 efficiencies and 6 units with kitchen. 3 stories (no elevator), interior/exterior corridors. **Terms:** 14 day cancellation notice, weekly & monthly rates available. **Amenities:** extended cable TV. *Some:* irons, hair dryers. **Leisure Activities:** heated pool, beach, shuffleboard. **Guest Services:** coin laundry. **Cards:** AE, DS, MC, VI. *(See color ad below)*

SOME UNITS

(See map p. 796)

RAMADA INN TREASURE ISLAND

Phone: (727)360-7051   199

(AAA) (SAVE)

◇◇◇ ◇◇◇
Motor Inn

2/11-4/21	1P: $120-$140	2P: $130-$150	XP: $10	F18
4/22-11/30	1P: $90-$115	2P: $100-$125	XP: $10	F18
12/1-12/31	1P: $90-$110	2P: $100-$120	XP: $10	F18
1/1-2/10	1P: $85-$105	2P: $95-$115	XP: $10	F18

Location: SR 699, 0.8 mi n of jct Treasure Island Cswy. 12000 Gulf Blvd 33706. Fax: 727/367-6641. **Facility:** Gulf front locale enhances their beachfront property. Nice roadside appeal and public areas nicely decorated. Furnishings are contemporary with some new touches. 121 units, 23 with efficiency. Some whirlpool units. 4 stories, interior corridors. **Amenities:** extended cable TV, safes (fee). *Some:* irons, hair dryers. **Dining:** dining room, 7 am-10 pm, tiki bar, $7-$13, cocktails, entertainment. **Leisure Activities:** heated pool, whirlpool, beach, playground, shuffleboard, volleyball, game room, pool table, video rentals. **Guest Services:** gift shop, coin laundry. **Business Services:** meeting rooms. **Cards:** AE, CB, DI, DS, JC, MC, VI.

SOME UNITS

[icons] FEE

ROADSIDE INN

Phone: (727)360-1438   216

(AAA) (SAVE)

◇◇◇ ◇◇◇
Motel

2/1-4/30	1P: $55-$106	2P: $55-$106	XP: $5	F12
12/20-1/31	1P: $50-$91	2P: $50-$91	XP: $5	F12
5/1-11/30	1P: $30-$89	2P: $30-$89	XP: $5	F12
12/1-12/19	1P: $30-$76	2P: $30-$76	XP: $5	F12

Location: On SR 699, 0.5 mi n of Treasure Island Cswy. 11799 Gulf Blvd 33706. Fax: 727/360-6072. **Facility:** Office hours 7:30 am-9 pm. 27 units. 1 two-bedroom unit and 15 units with kitchen. Some suites ($49-$89). *Bath:* combo or shower only. 2 stories, exterior corridors. **Terms:** 30 day cancellation notice-fee imposed, weekly & monthly rates available. **Amenities:** extended cable TV. *Some:* irons. **Leisure Activities:** heated pool, sun deck, shuffleboard. **Guest Services:** coin laundry. **Cards:** MC, VI.

SOME UNITS

[icons]

THE SEA CHEST

Phone: 727/360-5501   205

(AAA) (SAVE)

◇◇◇ ◇◇◇
Apartment

1/24-4/30	1P: $82-$119	2P: $82-$119	XP: $5	
12/19-1/23	1P: $71-$104	2P: $71-$104	XP: $5	
12/1-12/18 & 5/1-11/30	1P: $62-$90	2P: $62-$90	XP: $5	

Location: SR 699, 0.5 mi n of jct Treasure Island Cswy. 11780 Gulf Blvd 33706. Fax: 727/360-8453. **Facility:** Gulf front. Lushly landscaped courtyard area overlooks beach with large pool/sun deck area. 4 motel units available. Office hours 8 am-9:30 pm. 21 units. 1 efficiency and 16 units with kitchen. 2 stories, interior/exterior corridors. **Terms:** 30 day cancellation notice-fee imposed, weekly rates available. **Amenities:** extended cable TV. *Some:* irons, hair dryers. **Leisure Activities:** heated pool, beach, shuffleboard, gas barbecue, ping pong, picnic area. **Guest Services:** coin laundry. **Cards:** AE, MC, VI. **Special Amenities:** free newspaper.

SOME UNITS

[icons]

THUNDERBIRD BEACH RESORT

Phone: (727)367-1961   209

(AAA) (SAVE)

◇◇◇ ◇◇◇
Motel

2/10-4/22	1P: $125-$159	2P: $125-$159	XP: $10	F12
4/23-9/4	1P: $105-$139	2P: $105-$139	XP: $10	F12
12/1-2/9	1P: $89-$115	2P: $89-$115	XP: $10	F12
9/5-11/30	1P: $85-$109	2P: $85-$109	XP: $10	F12

Location: SR 699, at jct Treasure Island Cswy. 10700 Gulf Blvd 33706. Fax: 727/367-1961. **Facility:** Gulf front. 64 units, 32 with kitchen. 2-3 stories (no elevator), exterior corridors. **Terms:** weekly & monthly rates available, package plans - seasonal. **Amenities:** voice mail. **Dining:** restaurant, 7 am-2 pm (seasonal hours); pool bar, cocktails. **Leisure Activities:** heated pool, whirlpool, beach, volleyball. **Business Services:** meeting rooms, PC, fax. **Cards:** AE, CB, DI, DS, MC, VI. *(See color ad below)*

SOME UNITS

[icons]

TRAILS END RESORT MOTEL

Phone: 727/360-5541   207

(AAA) (SAVE)

◇◇◇ ◇◇◇
Motel

2/1-4/30	1P: $75-$103	2P: $75-$103	XP: $10
12/1-1/31 & 5/1-11/30	1P: $47-$70	2P: $47-$70	XP: $10

Location: SR 699, 0.5 mi n of jct Treasure Island Cswy. 11500 Gulf Blvd 33706. Fax: 727/360-1508. **Facility:** Gulf front. 54 units. 17 efficiencies and 12 units with kitchen. *Bath:* combo or shower only. 2 stories, exterior corridors. **Terms:** 14 day cancellation notice. **Amenities:** extended cable TV. **Leisure Activities:** heated pool, beach, fishing, shuffleboard. **Guest Services:** valet laundry. **Cards:** AE, DI, DS, JC, MC, VI.

(See color ad p 885)

SOME UNITS

[icons]

(See map p. 796)

THE TWINS APARTMENTS

Apartment

1/1-4/30 Wkly	2P: $270-$370	XP: $5
5/1-9/4 Dly	2P: $270-$290	XP: $5
12/1-12/31 Wkly	2P: $250-$290	XP: $5
9/5-11/30 Wkly	2P: $250-$270	XP: $5

Phone: 727/360-7420 [198]

Location: On SR 699, 1 mi n of Treasure Island Cswy, just s of John's Pass. 12520 Gulf Blvd 33706. Fax: 727/360-8196. **Facility:** Comfortable property just one-half block from beach. Pool area is very nice with sun deck and gazebo. Rooms have comfortable mix of furnishings with separate living room area. Designated smoking area. 11 units with kitchen. 3 two-bedroom units. 2 stories, exterior corridors. **Terms:** 28 day cancellation notice. **Amenities:** extended cable TV, irons. **Leisure Activities:** heated pool, beach access, shuffleboard. **Guest Services:** coin laundry.

WESLEY CHAPEL pop. 1,300

———— **WHERE TO STAY** ————

COMFORT INN

Motel

12/1-4/30	1P: $65-$75	2P: $70-$80	XP: $5	F17
5/1-7/31 & 11/1-11/30	1P: $50-$60	2P: $55-$65	XP: $5	F17
8/1-10/31	1P: $45-$55	2P: $50-$60	XP: $5	F17

Phone: (813)991-4600

Location: I-75, exit 58, just w. 5642 Oakley Blvd 33544. Fax: 813/991-7733. **Facility:** 68 units. 2 two-bedroom units. Some suites ($90-$140). *Bath:* combo or shower only. 2 stories, interior corridors. **Terms:** pets ($9 extra charge, in smoking rooms). **Amenities:** *Some:* irons, hair dryers. **Leisure Activities:** exercise room. **Guest Services:** [ECP] meal plan available, coin laundry. **Business Services:** meeting rooms, fax. **Cards:** AE, DI, DS, MC, VI. **Special Amenities:** free continental breakfast and free local telephone calls.

SOME UNITS

HOLIDAY INN EXPRESS

Motel

1/26-4/1	2P: $89	XP: $5	F19
12/1-1/25 & 4/2-4/30	2P: $69	XP: $5	F19
5/1-11/30	2P: $65	XP: $5	F19

Phone: 813-907-1379

Location: I-75, exit 58, just w. 27615 SR 54 W 33543. Fax: 813/907-8421. **Facility:** 82 units. Some suites ($120). *Bath:* combo or shower only. 4 stories, interior corridors. **Terms:** weekly rates available. **Amenities:** extended cable TV, safes, irons, hair dryers. **Guest Services:** [CP] meal plan available, valet laundry. **Business Services:** meeting rooms, fax. **Cards:** AE, CB, DI, DS, MC, VI.

SOME UNITS

MASTERS INN TAMPA NORTH

Motor Inn

12/1-4/30	1P: $46	2P: $50	XP: $4 F18
5/1-11/30	1P: $41	2P: $45	XP: $4 F18

Phone: (813)973-0155

Location: I-75, exit 58, just w. 27807 SR 54W 33543. Fax: 813/973-0210. **Facility:** 119 units. 2 stories, exterior corridors. **Terms:** weekly rates available, package plans, pets ($5 extra charge). **Amenities:** extended cable TV. **Dining:** restaurant, 24 hours, $5-$10. **Leisure Activities:** visitors center. **Guest Services:** coin laundry. **Business Services:** meeting rooms. **Cards:** AE, CB, DI, DS, MC, VI. **Special Amenities:** free local telephone calls.

SOME UNITS
FEE FEE

SADDLEBROOK RESORT TAMPA

Resort

1/14-5/11	1P: $307	2P: $370
12/1-1/13 & 10/2-11/30	1P: $257	2P: $320
5/12-10/1	1P: $177	2P: $240

Phone: (813)973-1111

Location: I-75, exit 58, 1.2 mi e on SR 54. 5700 Saddlebrook Way 33543. Fax: 813/973-4504. **Facility:** Clusters of suites with kitchens and large hotel rooms on spacious landscaped grounds. 552 units. 256 two-bedroom units and 419 units with kitchen. Some suites ($202-$660). 2 stories, exterior corridors. **Parking:** valet. **Terms:** 3 day cancellation notice-fee imposed, weekly & monthly rates available, package plans. **Amenities:** dual phone lines, voice mail, honor bars, irons, hair dryers. **Dining:** 3 restaurants, 6 am-10:30 pm; sports bar, $15-$30, cocktails, entertainment. **Leisure Activities:** 3 heated pools, saunas, whirlpools, steamrooms, spa facilities, fishing, putting green, children's program, recreation program, jogging, playground, basketball, volleyball, car rental office, salon. *Fee:* fishing equipment, golf-36 holes, practice range, golf equipment & instruction, 45 tennis courts (5 lighted), tennis equipment & instruction, bicycles. **Guest Services:** gift shop, complimentary laundry. *Fee:* area transportation, massage. **Business Services:** conference facilities, administrative services, fax. *Fee:* PC. **Cards:** AE, CB, DI, DS, MC, VI.

SOME UNITS
FEE   FEE   FEE

SLEEP INN

Motel

1/25-4/15	1P: $55-$90	2P: $55-$90	XP: $6 F18
4/16-11/30	1P: $39-$75	2P: $39-$75	XP: $6 F18
12/1-1/24	1P: $40-$70	2P: $40-$70	XP: $6 F18

Phone: (813)973-1665

Location: I-75, exit 58, just w. 5703 Oakley Blvd 33544. Fax: 813/973-1665. **Facility:** 78 units. Some suites ($80-$149). *Bath:* shower only. 3 stories, interior corridors. **Amenities:** voice mail. *Some:* irons, hair dryers. **Leisure Activities:** heated pool. **Guest Services:** [ECP] meal plan available, valet and coin laundry. **Business Services:** meeting rooms, fax. **Cards:** AE, CB, DI, DS, JC, MC, VI. **Special Amenities:** free continental breakfast and free local telephone calls.

SOME UNITS

——— WHERE TO DINE ———

PEACOCK'S SMOKEHOUSE & GRILL   **Lunch:** $4-$14   **Dinner:** $4-$14   **Phone:** 813/991-9384
▼▼ ▼▼   **Location:** I-75, exit 58, just w. 27531 SR 54 33543. **Hours:** 11 am-10 pm. Closed major holidays.
American   **Features:** casual dress; children's menu; carryout; beer & wine only. Slow-smoked barbecued ribs, blackened or fried catfish and homemade hushpuppies cater to the family crowd at this restaurant. A country theme plays out in the log cabin-style building, decorated throughout with wood and rustic antiques. **Cards:** AE, DI, DS, MC, VI.

ZEPHYRHILLS pop. 8,200

——— WHERE TO STAY ———

BEST WESTERN OF ZEPHYRHILLS   **Phone:** (813)782-5527
▼▼ ▼▼   2/1-4/30   1P: $79-$99   2P: $79-$99   XP: $5   F12
                12/1-1/31 & 11/15-11/30   1P: $69-$89   2P: $69-$89   XP: $5   F12
Motel   5/1-11/14   1P: $59-$79   2P: $59-$79   XP: $5   F12
Location: US 301, 0.5 mi n of jct SR 54. 5734 Gall Blvd 33541. **Fax:** 813/783-7102. **Facility:** 52 units. 2 stories, exterior corridors. **Amenities:** extended cable TV, irons, hair dryers. **Guest Services:** [CP] meal plan available. **Business Services:** meeting rooms, fax. **Cards:** AE, CB, DI, DS, MC, VI.

SOME UNITS

——— WHERE TO DINE ———

BEEF O'BRADY'S   **Lunch:** $5-$7   **Dinner:** $5-$7   **Phone:** 813/780-7931
▼▼ ▼▼   **Location:** On SR 301, just n of jct CR 54; in Merchants Square. 7337 Gall Blvd 33541. **Hours:** 11 am-11 pm, Fri & Sat-11:30 pm, Sun noon-10 pm. **Features:** casual dress; children's menu; carryout; beer & wine only. Big screen TVs keep this spot hopping on game days. A bustling family sports pub that cooks up a variety of traditional burgers, sandwiches, salads and wings. It features terrific Philadelphia cheese steak served with french fries and a pickle spear. **Cards:** DS, MC, VI.

This ends listings for the Tampa Vicinity.
The following page resumes the alphabetical listings of cities in Florida.

TARPON SPRINGS —*See Tampa Bay p. 882.*

TAVARES —*See Orlando p. 703.*

TEMPLE TERRACE —*See Tampa Bay p. 883.*

TEQUESTA pop. 4,500

—— WHERE TO STAY ——

JUPITER WATERFRONT INN
Motel

	2P: $158-$218	XP: $8	F12
12/18-4/24			
12/1-12/17 & 4/25-11/30	2P: $84-$116	XP: $8	F12

Location: 1.5 mi n of SR 811, on US 1. 18903 SE Federal Hwy 33469. Fax: 561/575-3374. **Facility:** Most rooms with view of waterway. Large rooms. Pool area overlooks the waterway. 38 units. Some whirlpool units ($116-$218). 2 stories, exterior corridors. **Terms:** cancellation fee imposed, weekly & monthly rates available. **Amenities:** extended cable TV. **Leisure Activities:** heated pool, whirlpool, fishing. **Guest Services:** [CP] meal plan available, coin laundry. **Cards:** AE, CB, DI, DS, MC, VI.

Phone: (561)747-9085

SOME UNITS

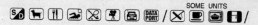

TITUSVILLE pop. 40,000

—— WHERE TO STAY ——

BEST WESTERN SPACE SHUTTLE INN
Motor Inn

	1P: $92-$97	2P: $92-$97	XP: $6	F17
2/1-3/31				
1/1-1/31 & 4/1-11/30	1P: $72-$77	2P: $72-$77	XP: $6	F17
12/1-12/31	1P: $69-$74	2P: $69-$74	XP: $6	F17

Location: I-95, exit 79, just e on SR 50. 3455 Cheney Hwy 32780. Fax: 321/383-4674. **Facility:** 132 units. Some suites ($107-$149) and whirlpool units ($125-$210). 2 stories, exterior corridors. **Terms:** weekly rates available, package plans, small pets only ($5 extra charge). **Amenities:** extended cable TV, hair dryers. **Dining:** restaurant, 11:30 am-10:30 pm, $8-$15. **Leisure Activities:** heated pool, sauna, fishing, playground, exercise room, basketball, sand volleyball, picnic area. **Guest Services:** [ECP] meal plan available, valet and coin laundry. **Business Services:** meeting rooms. **Cards:** AE, CB, DI, DS, MC, VI. **Special Amenities:** free continental breakfast and free newspaper.

Phone: (321)269-9100

SOME UNITS

DAYS INN-KENNEDY SPACE CENTER
Motor Inn

	1P: $69-$129	2P: $74-$135	XP: $6	F18
2/1-3/31				
4/1-11/30	1P: $52-$99	2P: $57-$109	XP: $6	F18
12/1-1/31	1P: $52-$79	2P: $57-$84	XP: $6	F18

Location: I-95, exit 79 (SR 50). 3755 Cheney Hwy 32780. Fax: 321/383-0646. **Facility:** 148 units, 2 with efficiency. Some whirlpool units. 2 stories, exterior corridors. **Terms:** weekly rates available, pets ($10 extra charge). **Amenities:** hair dryers. *Some:* irons. **Dining:** restaurant, 7 am-9 pm, $7-$21, cocktails. **Leisure Activities:** wading pool, exercise room, shuffleboard. **Guest Services:** valet and coin laundry. **Business Services:** meeting rooms. **Cards:** AE, DI, DS, JC, MC, VI. **Special Amenities:** free continental breakfast and free local telephone calls.
(See color ad p 263)

Phone: (321)269-4480

SOME UNITS

HOLIDAY INN-KENNEDY SPACE CENTER
Phone: (321)269-2121

CAAD (SAVE) All Year   1P: $79-$139   2P: $89-$149   XP: $10   F18
Location: US 1, 0.5 mi s of jct SR 50; 1.7 mi n of jct SR 405. 4951 S Washington Ave 32780. Fax: 321/267-4739.
Facility: On Indian River, facing Kennedy Space Center launch sites. 117 units. Some suites ($139-$259).
2 stories, exterior corridors. Terms: 7 day cancellation notice, package plans, small pets only. Amenities: ex-
Motor Inn   tended cable TV, irons, hair dryers. Dining: dining room, 6:30 am-10 & 5-9 pm sports bar, $9-$19, cocktails.
Leisure Activities: wading pool, fishing, exercise room, volleyball. Guest Services: [BP] meal plan available, valet and coin laundry. Business Services: meeting rooms. Cards: AE, CB, DI, DS, MC, VI. Special Amenities: free
newspaper and free room upgrade (subject to availability with advanced reservations). *(See color ad p 889)*

SOME UNITS
(icons) FEE

INDIAN RIVER BED AND BREAKFAST
Phone: (321)269-5945

1/1-3/31   2P: $59   XP: $3   F18
12/1-12/31 & 4/1-11/30   2P: $54   XP: $3   F18
Motel   Location: US 1, 0.8 mi n of jct SR 50. 3810 S Washington Ave 32780. Fax: 321/269-1054. Facility: 105 units. 2
stories, exterior corridors. Terms: weekly rates available. Amenities: extended cable TV. Guest Services:
[ECP] meal plan available, coin laundry. Cards: AE, MC, VI.

SOME UNITS
(icons)

RAMADA INN & SUITES-KENNEDY SPACE CENTER
Phone: (321)269-5510

CAAD (SAVE) 1/1-4/21   1P: $94-$159   2P: $99-$159   XP: $6   F18
12/1-12/31   1P: $89-$98   2P: $93-$106   XP: $6   F18
4/22-11/30   1P: $93   2P: $96   XP: $6   F18
Location: I-95, exit 79, just e on SR 50. 3500 Cheney Hwy 32780. Fax: 321/269-3796. Facility: 124 units, 12 with
Motor Inn   efficiency. Some suites ($119-$199). 2 stories, interior corridors. Terms: monthly rates available.
Amenities: extended cable TV, voice mail. Dining: restaurant, 24 hours, $5-$10, cocktails. Leisure Activities: heated pool, sauna, whirlpool, playground, exercise room. Guest Services: valet and coin laundry. Business Services:
meeting rooms. Cards: AE, CB, DI, DS, MC, VI. Special Amenities: free local telephone calls.

SOME UNITS
(icons) FEE

——— WHERE TO DINE ———

DIXIE CROSSROADS
CAAD   Lunch: $6-$10   Dinner: $10-$14   Phone: 321/268-5000
Location: SR 406; 1 mi w of jct US 1, 2 mi e of jct I-95, exit 80. 1475 Garden St 32796. Hours: 11 am-10 pm.
Closed: 11/22, 12/25. Reservations: accepted. Features: casual dress; children's menu; carryout;
cocktails; a la carte. Stroll through the butterfly garden or stand on the bridge over the fish pond on the
Seafood   grounds of this large and homey family restaurant. Ample servings of such favorites as rock shrimp make
up a menu of mostly seafood and steak choices. Cards: AE, CB, DI, DS, MC, VI. (icon)

PAUL'S SMOKEHOUSE RESTAURANT & LOUNGE
Lunch: $6-$12   Dinner: $10-$18   Phone: 321/267-3663
Location: US 1, 1 mi n of jct US 50. 3665 S Washington Ave 32780. Hours: 11 am-9 pm, Fri & Sat-10 pm.
Closed major holidays; also Mon. Features: casual dress; children's menu; early bird specials; cocktails &
lounge. Witness space shuttle launches from this friendly, waterfront diner on the Indian River. Served in
Steak & Seafood   an Early American decor, the menu leans toward barbecue with prime rib and seafood specialties. Savor
the fresh and flavorful rock shrimp, a local favorite. Cards: AE, CB, DI, DS, MC, VI. (icon)

PUMPERNICKEL'S DELI
Lunch: $4-$10   Dinner: $12-$17   Phone: 321/268-5160
Location: I-95, exit 79, 1 mi e on SR 50; just w of US 1 on SR 50. 2850 S Hopkins Ave 32780. Hours: 8 am-9 pm,
Sat-2 pm. Closed major holidays. Features: casual dress; Sunday brunch; children's menu; carryout; beer
German   & wine only. Authentic style German deli. Moderate prices, senior portions and hot lunch and dinner buffet
bar available. Choose from a variety of German favorites: bratwurst, weisswurst, knackwurst, potato
pancakes, Wiener Schnitzel, Jaeger Schnitzel and homemade pastries and desserts. Cards: AE, CB, DI, DS, MC, VI. (icon)

TREASURE ISLAND *—See Tampa Bay p. 883.*

VALRICO

——— WHERE TO DINE ———

BACKBAY RESTAURANT
Lunch: $6-$16   Dinner: $7-$16   Phone: 813/685-7111
Location: On SR 60; at jct Morningside Dr. 1807 SR 60 E 33594. Hours: 6 am-9:30 pm, Fri & Sat-10 pm.
Closed: 11/22, 12/25. Features: casual dress; children's menu; carryout; beer only; a la carte. Look among
sheltering mature oaks to find home cooking and splendid, easy dining. A menu featuring steak, seafood
Steak & Seafood   and barbecue dishes is highlighted by a homemade specialty sausage. The Backbay House Plate
overflows with seafood, gator and frog legs. Cards: AE, DS, MC, VI. (icon)

FAT WILLIE'S FISH CAMP
Dinner: $9-$16   Phone: 813/685-1940
Location: I-75, exit 51, 4.7 mi e on SR 60, 0.7 mi n on Valrico Rd, 0.3 mi w. 1912 Front St 33595. Hours: 4:30
pm-9:30 pm, Fri & Sat-10 pm, Sun noon-8:30 pm. Closed: 11/22, 12/25; also Mon. Features: casual dress;
Seafood   children's menu; early bird specials; carryout; cocktails; a la carte. Willie didn't get fat sitting in the corner.
He was too busy cooking up great tasting seafood, chicken, steak and ribs over an oak-burning fire.
Specialties such as catfish, gator bites and frog legs fit in perfectly with the tin-roofed shanty setting. Cards: MC, VI. (icon)

WOODY'S BAR BQ

American
MC, VI.

Lunch: $5-$8 **Dinner:** $7-$16 **Phone:** 813/689-7722
Location: SR 60 at jct Valrico Rd; in Valrico Square. 1905 E Hwy 60 33594. **Hours:** 11 am-9 pm, Fri & Sat-10 pm. **Closed:** 12/25. **Features:** casual dress; children's menu; carryout; beer only. Rustic decor gives feel of barbecue shack with the picnic bench seating and replica signs on walls. Menu offers variety of barbecued sandwiches, ribs, beef, turkey, chicken, platters, salad, dessert and side dishes as well. **Cards:** AE, DS,

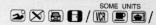

VENICE pop. 16,900

—————— WHERE TO STAY ——————

BANYAN HOUSE HISTORIC BED & BREAKFAST
Bed & Breakfast

12/1-4/30		2P: $99-$129	XP: $20 D10
5/1-11/30		2P: $89-$119	XP: $20 D10

Phone: 941/484-1385

Location: 0.7 mi s of jct Venice Ave. 519 Harbor Dr S 34285. Fax: 941/484-8032. **Facility:** Park-like grounds; beautiful gardens and trees. Home circa 1926 with a lot of history. Nicely furnished and comfortable rooms. One room with gas fireplace. Smoke free premises. 5 units, 3 with efficiency. **Bath:** combo or shower only. 2 stories, interior corridors. **Terms:** age restrictions may apply, 21 day cancellation notice. **Amenities:** extended cable TV, irons, hair dryers. **Leisure Activities:** whirlpool, bicycles. **Guest Services:** [CP] & [ECP] meal plans available, coin laundry. **Cards:** MC, VI.

SOME UNITS

BEST WESTERN AMBASSADOR SUITES
AAA SAVE
Motel

2/1-4/15	1P: $129-$169	2P: $129-$169	
12/15-1/31	1P: $119-$169	2P: $119-$169	
12/1-12/14 & 4/16-11/30	1P: $89-$129	2P: $89-$129	

Phone: (941)480-9898

Location: I-75, exit 35, just w. 400 Commercial Ct 34292. Fax: 941/488-6692. **Facility:** 83 units, 3 with efficiency. Some whirlpool units ($129-$219). **Bath:** combo or shower only. 3 stories, interior corridors. **Terms:** 30 day cancellation notice, package plans. **Amenities:** extended cable TV, irons, hair dryers. **Leisure Activities:** heated pool, exercise room. **Guest Services:** coin laundry. **Business Services:** meeting rooms, administrative services. *Fee:* PC. **Cards:** AE, DI, DS, JC, MC, VI. **Special Amenities: free continental breakfast and free newspaper.** SOME UNITS

BEST WESTERN SANDBAR BEACH RESORT
AAA SAVE
Motor Inn

2/1-4/25	1P: $169-$319	2P: $169-$319	
12/17-1/31	1P: $169-$259	2P: $169-$259	
12/1-12/16 & 4/26-11/30	1P: $109-$179	2P: $109-$179	

Phone: (941)488-2251

Location: On Venice Beach, just n of jct Venice Ave. 811 The Esplanade North 34285. Fax: 941/485-2894. **Facility:** Gulf front. 44 units, 35 with kitchen. **Bath:** combo or shower only. 1-4 stories, exterior corridors. **Terms:** 7 day cancellation notice, package plans in summer. **Amenities:** extended cable TV. *Some:* irons. **Dining:** restaurant, 7 am-2 pm, Sun-noon, wine/beer only. **Leisure Activities:** heated pool, beach, swimming, fishing, shuffleboard, sand volleyball. **Guest Services:** coin laundry. **Cards:** AE, DI, DS, MC, VI. **Special Amenities: free newspaper.**
(See color ad below) SOME UNITS

DAYS INN
AAA SAVE
Motor Inn

2/8-4/17	1P: $112	2P: $112	XP: $10 F16
12/1-1/4	1P: $64-$96	2P: $64-$96	XP: $8 F16
1/5-2/7	1P: $68	2P: $68	XP: $10 F16
4/18-11/30	1P: $64	2P: $64	XP: $8 F16

Phone: (941)493-4558

Location: I-75, exit 35, 2 mi s on Jacaranda Blvd, 3.6 mi w on Center Rd, 0.5 mi s on US 41 bypass. 1710 S Tamiami Tr 34293. Fax: 941/493-1593. **Facility:** 73 units, 11 with efficiency. Some whirlpool units. **Bath:** combo or shower only. 3 stories, exterior corridors. **Terms:** cancellation fee imposed, small pets only ($30 fee). **Amenities:** extended cable TV, voice mail. **Dining:** restaurant, 7 am-4 & 6-9 pm, Fri & Sat-10 pm, $8-$17, cocktails. **Guest Services:** coin laundry. **Business Services:** meeting rooms. **Cards:** AE, DI, DS, MC, VI. **Special Amenities: early check-in/late check-out.**
SOME UNITS
FEE FEE

HAMPTON INN & SUITES

【SAVE】

▽▽▽▽

Motel

Phone: (941)488-5900

12/21-4/15　　　　　　　　1P: $99-$159　　　2P: $99-$159
12/1-12/20 & 4/16-11/30　1P: $75-$99　　　2P: $75-$99

Location: I-75, exit 35, 0.8 mi w on Jacaranda Blvd, 1.3 mi w on Venice Ave, 1.3 mi n on US 41. 881 Venetia Bay Blvd 34292. Fax: 941/488-6746. **Facility:** Pleasant decor in all public areas and rooms. Nice courtyard area for pool setting. 110 units, 36 with kitchen. *Bath:* combo or shower only. 3 stories, interior corridors. **Terms:** cancellation fee imposed. **Amenities:** voice mail, irons. *Some:* hair dryers. **Leisure Activities:** heated pool, whirlpool, jogging, exercise room. **Guest Services:** [ECP] meal plan available, coin laundry. **Business Services:** meeting rooms. **Cards:** AE, CB, DI, DS, MC, VI.

SOME UNITS

🔊 🍴 ♿ 🐕 📷 🏊 📹 🖥 💻 [DATA PORT] / ✕ VCR 🖥 🔌 /

HOLIDAY INN VENICE

【AAA】 【SAVE】

▽▽▽▽

Motor Inn

Phone: (941)485-5411

2/1-4/15　　　　　　　　　1P: $89-$139　　　2P: $89-$139　　XP: $10　　F18
12/21-1/31　　　　　　　　1P: $79-$119　　　2P: $79-$119　　XP: $10　　F18
12/1-12/20 & 4/16-11/30　1P: $69-$99　　　2P: $69-$99　　XP: $10　　F18

Location: I-75, exit 35, 0.8 mi w on Jacaranda Blvd, 3 mi sw on Venice Ave, 0.5 mi n on US 41. 455 US 41 N 34292. Fax: 941/484-6193. **Facility:** 159 units. *Bath:* combo or shower only. 2 stories, interior/exterior corridors. **Terms:** weekly & monthly rates available, package plans. **Amenities:** extended cable TV, irons, hair dryers. **Dining:** restaurant, 6:30 am-10:30 & 4:30-8:30 pm, Sun 10 am-2 & 4-8 pm; dinner theatre, $28, matinees, $22-$23, Tues-Sun in season, $8-$16, cocktails. **Leisure Activities:** heated pool, whirlpool, exercise room, shuffleboard. **Guest Services:** coin laundry. **Business Services:** meeting rooms. **Cards:** AE, CB, DI, DS, JC, MC, VI. **Special Amenities:** early check-in/late check-out and free newspaper. *(See color ad below)*

SOME UNITS

🔊 🍴 📺 ♿ 🐕 📷 🏊 📹 💻 [DATA PORT] / ✕ 🖥 🔌 /
FEE

INN AT THE BEACH RESORT

【AAA】 【SAVE】

▽▽▽▽

Motel

Phone: (941)484-8471

2/9-4/21　　　　　1P: $185-$365　　2P: $185-$365　　XP: $8　　F16
4/22-11/30　　　　1P: $95-$365　　2P: $95-$365　　XP: $8　　F16
12/1-1/1　　　　　1P: $89-$339　　2P: $89-$339　　XP: $8　　F16
1/2-2/8　　　　　　1P: $125-$315　　2P: $125-$315　　XP: $8　　F16

Location: At jct the Esplande. 725 W Venice Ave 34285. Fax: 941/484-0593. **Facility:** Variety of room types across road from beach. Some rooms with beach view. 49 units. 4 two-bedroom units, 21 efficiencies and 28 units with kitchen. Some suites ($149-$365). 1-2 stories, exterior corridors. **Terms:** check-in 4 pm, 10 day cancellation notice, package plans - off season. **Amenities:** extended cable TV, voice mail, safes, irons, hair dryers. **Leisure Activities:** heated pool, whirlpool, beach access. **Guest Services:** coin laundry. **Cards:** AE, DI, DS, MC, VI. **Special Amenities:** free continental breakfast and free newspaper. *(See color ad below)*

SOME UNITS

🔊 🏊 📹 🖥 💻 🖥 🔌 [DATA PORT] / ✕ /

KON-TIKI MOTEL

AAA SAVE
◆◆ ◆◆
Apartment

Phone: 941/485-9696

| All Year | 1P: $60-$120 | 2P: $60-$120 | XP: $15 | F12 |

Location: I-75, exit 35, 0.8 mi w on Jacaranda Blvd, 3.6 mi sw on Venice Ave, 1.7 mi s on US 41 business route. 1487 S Tamiami Tr 34285. **Facility:** Modest facility alongside the Intracoastal Waterway. 10 efficiencies. 1 story, exterior corridors. **Terms:** 7 day cancellation notice, weekly & monthly rates available. **Leisure Activities:** pool heated 12/1-3/31. **Cards:** DS, MC, VI.

SOME UNITS

MOTEL 6 - 364

◆◆ ◆◆
Motel

Phone: 941/485-8255

1/11-4/15	1P: $55-$65	2P: $61-$71	XP: $3	F17
4/16-11/30	1P: $40-$50	2P: $46-$56	XP: $3	F17
12/1-1/10	1P: $38-$48	2P: $44-$54	XP: $3	F17

Fax: 941/488-3005. **Location:** I-75, exit 35, 0.8 mi w on Jacaranda Blvd, 3 mi sw on Venice Ave, just n. 281 US 41 Bypass N 34292. **Facility:** 103 units. *Bath:* shower only. 2 stories, exterior corridors. **Terms:** small pets only. **Leisure Activities:** heated pool. **Guest Services:** coin laundry. **Cards:** AE, CB, DI, DS, MC, VI.

SOME UNITS

QUARTERDECK RESORT CONDOMINIUMS

AAA SAVE
◆◆ ◆◆
Condominium

Phone: (941)488-0449

| 12/1-4/30 Wkly | 2P: $780-$1005 | XP: $8 | F5 |
| 5/1-11/30 Wkly | 2P: $595-$810 | XP: $8 | F5 |

Location: On Venice Beach, 0.4 mi n of jct Venice Ave on The Esplanade, then just w. 1275 Tarpon Center Dr 34285. **Fax:** 941/485-7288. **Facility:** Gulf front. 29 units with kitchen. 24 two-bedroom units. 2 stories, exterior corridors. **Terms:** check-in 4 pm, 30 day cancellation notice, monthly rates available. **Amenities:** extended cable TV, irons. **Leisure Activities:** heated pool, beach, swimming, social program. **Guest Services:** coin laundry. **Cards:** MC, VI. **Special Amenities:** early check-in/late check-out and free local telephone calls.

SOME UNITS

─── WHERE TO DINE ───

THE CROW'S NEST MARINA RESTAURANT

AAA
◆◆ ◆◆ ◆◆
Seafood

Lunch: $5-$13   **Dinner:** $11-$23   **Phone:** 941/484-9551

Location: At S Jetty Venice Inlet, 0.9 mi w of US 41 via Venice Ave, 0.4 mi n on the Esplanade, then 0.5 mi nw. 1968 Tarpon Center Dr 34285. **Hours:** 11:30 am-3 & 5-10 pm, Sun noon-10 pm. Closed: 11/22, 12/25. **Features:** casual dress; children's menu; early bird specials; carryout; cocktails & lounge; a la carte. This bustling restaurant on Venice Inlet gives off a casual ambience. Rich flavors enhance the grouper Key Largo served with scallops, shrimp, crabmeat, mushrooms and hollandaise sauce and the tart key lime pie. The wine cellar is extensive. Smoke free premises. **Cards:** AE, DS, MC, VI.

LUNA RISTORANTE

◆◆
Italian

Lunch: $7-$17   **Dinner:** $7-$17   **Phone:** 941/496-9090

Location: On US 41; in Venice Village Shops. 4191 S Tamiami Tr 34285. **Hours:** 11 am-9 pm, Fri & Sat-10 pm. Closed major holidays. **Features:** casual dress; carryout; beer & wine only; a la carte. After you've eaten one of the specialties, you'll understand the popularity. Hearty portions of chicken, veal, pasta and various baked dishes are loaded onto 16-inch plates. The spicy seafood marinara is full of shrimp, clams, mussels, scallops and fish.

MYAKKA RIVER OYSTER BAR

◆◆
Seafood

Lunch: $4-$7   **Dinner:** $6-$14   **Phone:** 941/423-9616

Location: 12 mi s on US 41, on the northwest bank of the Myakka River, enter via Myakka Dr. 121 Playmore Dr 34293. **Hours:** 11:30 am-9 pm, Fri & Sat-9:30 pm. Closed: 4/15, 11/22, 12/25. **Features:** casual dress; children's menu; early bird specials; carryout; cocktails & lounge; a la carte. Basic but not boring, menu choices include fried and charbroiled seafood, steak, sandwiches, chicken and a great spicy gumbo. Look out onto the scenic Myakka River, home to manatees, osprey and alligators. The atmosphere is fun and lively. **Cards:** AE, DS, MC, VI.

PURPLE'S RESTAURANT

◆◆ ◆◆ ◆◆
American

Lunch: $5-$9   **Dinner:** $12-$18   **Phone:** 941/485-6277

Location: On US 41; at jct of Aldee Farm Rd. 385 US 41 Bypass N 34292. **Hours:** 11:30 am-2 am, Sat & Sun from 4:30 pm. Closed: 12/25. **Features:** casual dress; early bird specials; carryout; cocktails & lounge. The art deco dining room boasts a varied menu of family favorites and sumptuous feasts like the cordon bleu. The smaller lunch menu features sandwiches and salads. Private banquet facilities are available with a state-of-the-art PowerPoint system. **Cards:** AE, DS, MC, VI.

SHARKY'S ON THE PIER

AAA
◆◆ ◆◆ ◆◆
Seafood

Lunch: $6-$8   **Dinner:** $9-$29   **Phone:** 941/488-1456

Location: US 41 business route, 0.5 mi w via Venice Ave, 2 mi s; at the Venice Fishing Pier. 1600 S Harbor Dr 34284. **Hours:** 11:30 am-9:30 pm, Fri & Sat-10 pm, tiki deck Fri & Sat-midnight. Closed: 11/22, 12/25. **Features:** casual dress; children's menu; cocktails; entertainment; a la carte. Fish mounted on the walls and maritime decorations convey a fitting theme in this busy, oceanfront restaurant. Market fresh fish can be broiled, blackened, grilled or fried. Summer treats include children's crab races and calypso sundaes. **Cards:** AE, DS, MC, VI.

VERO BEACH pop. 17,400

———— WHERE TO STAY ————

AQUARIUS OCEAN FRONT RESORT MOTEL

Phone: 561/231-5218

AAA [SAVE]

◆◆◆◆

Apartment

2/1-4/30	2P: $79-$149	XP: $5	F11
12/1-1/31	2P: $69-$115	XP: $5	F11
6/30-11/30	2P: $60-$99	XP: $5	F11
5/1-6/29	2P: $55-$95	XP: $5	F11

Location: 1.8 mi s, just e of SR A1A on south beach, just s of 17th St Causeway Bridge (E Causeway Blvd, SR 656). 1526 S Ocean Dr 32963. Fax: 561/231-5218. **Facility:** Large kitchen units; compact motel rooms. 26 units, 24 with kitchen. 2 stories, exterior corridors. **Terms:** 30 day cancellation notice, weekly rates available. **Amenities:** extended cable TV. **Leisure Activities:** heated pool, beach, swimming, shuffleboard, tiki huts & grills beachside. **Guest Services:** coin laundry. **Cards:** AE, DI, DS, MC, VI.

SOME UNITS

🛎️ 🏊 / 🖥️ /

BEST WESTERN VERO BEACH

Phone: (561)567-8321

AAA [SAVE]

◆◆◆

Motor Inn

12/1-1/19	2P: $65-$85	XP: $10	F18
1/20-4/10	2P: $65-$75	XP: $10	F18
4/11-11/30	2P: $49-$59	XP: $10	F18

Location: I-95, exit 68, (SR 60), 0.5 mi e. 8797 20th St 32966. Fax: 561/569-8558. **Facility:** Older traditional style property. 114 units. 2 stories, exterior corridors. **Terms:** 3 day cancellation notice, package plans. **Amenities:** dual phone lines. *Some:* hair dryers. **Dining:** dining room, 6:30 am-2 & 5-10 pm, $6-$18, cocktails. **Leisure Activities:** heated pool, wading pool. **Guest Services:** coin laundry. **Business Services:** meeting rooms. **Cards:** AE, CB, DI, DS, MC, VI.

SOME UNITS

🍴 🍸 🏊 📽️ 📶 / ✕ 🖨️ /
FEE

COMFORT INN

Phone: (561)569-0900

[SAVE]

◆◆◆

Motel

12/15-4/15	1P: $69-$99	2P: $69-$99	XP: $5	F16
12/1-12/14 & 4/16-11/30	1P: $59-$79	2P: $59-$79	XP: $5	F16

Location: US 1, 1.3 mi s of jct SR 60. 950 Hwy 1 32960. Fax: 561/569-5502. **Facility:** Large to spacious, comfortable rooms with pleasing decor. 66 units. *Bath:* combo or shower only. 2 stories, exterior corridors. **Terms:** 3 day cancellation notice-fee imposed. **Amenities:** *Some:* irons, hair dryers. **Leisure Activities:** heated pool. **Guest Services:** [CP] meal plan available, coin laundry. **Cards:** AE, DI, DS, JC, MC, VI.

SOME UNITS

🅂🄳 🍴 🍸 ♿ 🏊 📽️ 📶 / ✕ 🖨️ 🖥️ 🖥️ /

DAYS INN

Phone: 561/562-9991

◆◆◆

Motor Inn

Property failed to provide current rates

Location: I-95, exit 68, (SR 60), 0.5 mi e. 8800 20th St 32966. Fax: 561/562-0716. **Facility:** 114 units. 2 stories, exterior corridors. **Terms:** check-in 4 pm, small pets only ($10 extra charge). **Guest Services:** coin laundry. **Business Services:** meeting rooms. **Cards:** AE, CB, DI, DS, MC, VI.

SOME UNITS

🛏️ 🍴 🏊 📽️ / ✕ /

DISNEY'S VERO BEACH RESORT

Phone: (561)234-2000

AAA

◆◆◆ ◆◆◆

Complex

12/1-12/31	1P: $145-$965	2P: $145-$965
2/16-6/2	1P: $240-$920	2P: $240-$920
6/3-11/30	1P: $170-$770	2P: $170-$770
1/1-2/15	1P: $170-$670	2P: $170-$670

Location: 7 mi n of Vero Beach; SR A1A, at jct CR 510; from jct I-95, exit 69, 11 mi e via CR 512 and 510. 9250 Island Grove Terrace 32963. Fax: 561/234-2030. **Facility:** Nestled among the sea grass and palm trees along Florida's treasure coast. Impressive Florida-style resort offering a variety of accommodations with balcony or porch, close to Dodger's Spring Training Camp. Designated smoking area. 208 units. 18 two-bedroom units, 6 three-bedroom units and 60 units with kitchen. Some whirlpool units ($230-$920). *Bath:* combo or shower only. 4 stories, interior/exterior corridors. **Terms:** check-in 4 pm, 5 day cancellation notice-fee imposed, package plans. **Amenities:** extended cable TV, voice mail, safes, irons, hair dryers. *Some:* CD players. **Dining:** dining room, restaurant, 7:30-11 am, 11:30-3 & 5-10 pm; pool bar & short order grill, $9-$22, cocktails. **Leisure Activities:** heated pool, sauna, whirlpool, waterslide, beach, swimming, fishing, charter fishing, aqua aerobics, hobie cats, wave runners, miniature golf, 2 lighted tennis courts, children's program, nature program, recreation program, social program, jogging, playground, exercise room, shuffleboard, camp fires, cattle ranch tours, lawn croquet. *Fee:* bicycles. **Guest Services:** gift shop, valet and coin laundry. *Fee:* massage. **Business Services:** meeting rooms, administrative services, PC, fax. **Cards:** AE, DI, DS, JC, MC, VI. *(See color ad p 895)*

SOME UNITS

🍴 🍸 🅿️ 🎾 ♿ 🎧 🏊 ✕ 🖨️ 🖥️ 🖥️ 🖥️ 📶 / ✕ 📼 /
FEE

DOUBLETREE GUEST SUITES

Phone: (561)231-5666

◆◆◆

Suite Motel

2/1-4/30	1P: $235-$265	2P: $235-$265	XP: $10	F18
12/23-1/31	1P: $185-$225	2P: $185-$225	XP: $10	F18
5/1-11/30	1P: $130-$150	2P: $130-$150	XP: $10	F18
12/1-12/22	1P: $125-$145	2P: $125-$145	XP: $10	F18

Location: Just n of SR 60. 3500 Ocean Dr 32963. Fax: 561/234-4866. **Facility:** Spacious one- and two-bedroom suites with balcony. 54 units. 16 two-bedroom units. 5 stories, interior/exterior corridors. **Terms:** 3 day cancellation notice-fee imposed. **Amenities:** extended cable TV, voice mail, irons, hair dryers. **Leisure Activities:** heated pool, wading pool, whirlpool, beach, swimming. **Guest Services:** [BP] meal plan available, coin laundry. **Business Services:** meeting rooms. **Cards:** AE, CB, DI, DS, MC, VI.

SOME UNITS

[ASK] 🅂🄳 🍴 🎧 🌀 🏊 📽️ 📼 🖨️ 🖥️ 🖥️ 📶 / ✕ 🖥️ /
FEE

HOLIDAY INN EXPRESS

Phone: 561/567-2500

◆◆◆

Motel

Property failed to provide current rates

Location: I-95, exit 68. 9400 19th Lane 32966. Fax: 561/567-4979. **Facility:** 65 units. *Bath:* combo or shower only. 3 stories, interior rooms. **Terms:** 10 day cancellation notice-fee imposed. **Amenities:** extended cable TV, irons, hair dryers. **Leisure Activities:** exercise room. **Guest Services:** [ECP] meal plan available, valet laundry. **Business Services:** meeting rooms. **Cards:** AE, CB, DI, DS, MC, VI.

SOME UNITS

🍴 ♿ 🏊 📽️ 🖨️ 📶 / ✕ /

HOWARD JOHNSON EXPRESS INN

Phone: 561/778-1985

(AAA) [SAVE]

Motel

	1P: $69-$99	2P: $69-$99	XP: $8	F17
2/1-4/10	1P: $59	2P: $59	XP: $5	F17
1/1-1/31	1P: $45	2P: $45	XP: $5	F17
12/1-12/31 & 4/11-11/30				

Location: I-95, exit 68 (SR 60), just se. 1985 90th Ave 32966. Fax: 561/778-1998. **Facility:** Traditional rooms, many with curb parking, large truck parking lot. 60 units. 2 stories, exterior corridors. **Terms:** weekly rates available. **Guest Services:** coin laundry. **Cards:** AE, CB, DI, DS, MC, VI. **Special Amenities:** free continental breakfast and preferred room (subject to availability with advanced reservations).

SOME UNITS

HOWARD JOHNSON LODGE-DOWNTOWN

Phone: (561)567-5171

(AAA) [SAVE]

Motel

| 1/1-4/15 | 1P: $48-$75 | 2P: $68-$75 | XP: $8 | F18 |
| 12/1-12/31 & 4/16-11/30 | 1P: $42-$75 | 2P: $54-$75 | XP: $8 | F18 |

Location: 0.3 mi s of jct SR 60. 1725 US Hwy 1 32960. Fax: 561/567-5194. **Facility:** Located in busy commercial area, rooms back from main road. 51 units. 2 stories, interior/exterior corridors. **Amenities:** extended cable TV. **Leisure Activities:** heated pool. **Cards:** AE, DI, DS, MC, VI. **Special Amenities:** free continental breakfast and free newspaper.

SOME UNITS

THE ISLANDER INN

Phone: (561)231-4431

Motel

2/4-4/23	2P: $105-$120	XP: $7	F12
1/14-2/3	2P: $89-$109	XP: $7	F12
12/1-1/13	2P: $79-$99	XP: $7	F12
4/24-11/30	2P: $69-$99	XP: $7	F12

Location: Just s of SR 60. 3101 Ocean Dr 32963. Fax: 561/231-4431. **Facility:** Lovely, quaint property with island feel; lush courtyard with grill, in among shops. 16 units. 2 efficiencies and 1 unit with kitchen. *Bath:* combo or shower only. 2 stories, exterior corridors. **Parking:** street only. **Terms:** 15 day cancellation notice-fee imposed. **Amenities:** extended cable TV. **Cards:** AE, MC, VI.

SOME UNITS

PALM COURT RESORT HOTEL

Phone: (561)231-2800

Motor Inn

| 12/22-4/30 | 1P: $145-$225 |
| 12/1-12/21 & 5/1-11/30 | 1P: $85-$135 |

Location: Just s of SR 60. 3244 Ocean Dr 32963. Fax: 561/231-3446. **Facility:** On the beach, all rooms with balcony, many with full ocean view. 106 units, 8 with efficiency. 5 stories, interior corridors. **Amenities:** extended cable TV, dual phone lines, voice mail, irons, hair dryers. **Leisure Activities:** heated pool, beach, swimming, charter fishing, exercise room. **Guest Services:** coin laundry. **Business Services:** meeting rooms, fax. **Cards:** AE, DI, DS, MC, VI.

SOME UNITS

—— WHERE TO DINE ——

CAFE' DU SOIR
▼▼▼
French
Dinner: $19-$28　　　　　**Phone: 561/569-4607**
Location: 2 mi e of jct US 1 and SR 603 (Indian River Blvd). 21 Royal Palm Blvd 32960. **Hours:** Open 12/1-9/15 & 10/15-11/30; 6 pm-11 pm. Closed: Sun. **Reservations:** suggested. **Features:** semi-formal attire; beer & wine only. The second-floor restaurant, with a terrace that looks out onto the Indian River, is a great place for cozy, romantic dining. Attentive servers often go out of their way to make your experience memorable. Enjoy the snapper for two or the rack of lamb. Smoke free premises. **Cards:** AE, DI, MC, VI.

CHARLEY BROWN'S
▼▼▼
Steak & Seafood
Dinner: $9-$24　　　　　**Phone: 561/231-6311**
Location: SR A1A, 0.3 mi s of jct SR 656. 1410 Hwy A1A 32963. **Hours:** 4:30 pm-9:30 pm, Fri & Sat-10 pm. Closed: 11/22; also Super Bowl Sun. **Reservations:** accepted. **Features:** casual dress; children's menu; early bird specials; carryout; salad bar; cocktails & lounge; a la carte. A popular spot for retirees, this established restaurant is known for well-prepared entrees of fresh fish, steaks, Danish ribs and chicken. The prime rib is slow-cooked and served au jus. The tropical garden setting contributes to the relaxing atmosphere. **Cards:** AE, CB, DI, DS, MC, VI.

CHEZ YANNICK
▼▼▼
French
Dinner: $15-$29　　　　　**Phone: 561/234-4115**
Location: 1.8 mi s, just e of SR A1A on South Beach, just s of 17th St Cswy Bridge (E Causeway Blvd, SR 656). 1601 S Ocean Dr 32963. **Hours:** 6 pm-9:30 pm. Closed: Sun. **Reservations:** suggested. **Features:** casual dress; cocktails & lounge; entertainment; a la carte. Smart, airy dining rooms feature an on-the-ball staff circulating to deliver delicious meals. Select from a great mix of breads, and try the green salad with a most delicate raspberry dressing. For a creative main event, order the tasty veal piccata. **Cards:** AE, MC, VI.

GUYTANO'S ITALIAN BISTRO & BAR
▼▼▼
American
Lunch: $6-$13　　**Dinner: $7-$19**　　**Phone: 561/778-4088**
Location: On SR 60; west end of Indian River Mall. 6200 20th St #394 32966. **Hours:** 11 am-10 pm. Closed: 11/22, 12/25. **Features:** casual dress; carryout; cocktails & lounge. Close your eyes and savor the tastes and smells of Little Italy. All the pasta is handmade. Other specialties include calzone, sandwiches and pizza cooked in an open-flame brick oven. Veal Milanese makes a striking meal presentation. **Cards:** AE, DI, DS, MC, VI.

LOBSTER SHANTY
▼▼▼▼
Seafood
Lunch: $6-$15　　**Dinner: $11-$22**　　**Phone: 561/562-1941**
Location: SR 60; 1 mi w of jct SR A1A. 1 Royal Palm Blvd 32960. **Hours:** 11:30 am-9 pm, Fri & Sat-10 pm. Closed: 11/22. **Reservations:** accepted. **Features:** casual dress; children's menu; early bird specials; carryout; salad bar; cocktails & lounge. When there's a wait, you can guess the reason. Tourists and locals flock to this casual dining room overlooking the Indian River. Chicken, seafood and beef specialties are the best in town, and the salad is one of the crispiest concoctions ever. **Cards:** AE, CB, DI, MC, VI.

OCEAN GRILL
ΔΔΔ
▼▼▼
Steak & Seafood
Lunch: $8-$16　　**Dinner: $15-$30**　　**Phone: 561/231-5409**
Location: E of SR A1A, at end of SR 60. 1050 Sexton Plaza 32963. **Hours:** 11:30 am-2 & 5-10 pm. Closed: 7/4, 11/22; also Super Bowl Sun. **Reservations:** accepted. **Features:** casual dress; children's menu; cocktails & lounge. A dramatic oceanfront view and a rustic dining room serving great food translates to a popular, busy eatery. Broiled salmon with a particularly good dill sauce is definitely worth any wait. A courteous and knowledgeable staff attend your every need. **Cards:** AE, CB, DI, DS, MC, VI.

TANGOS
▼▼▼▼
Regional American
Dinner: $18-$23　　　　　**Phone: 561/231-1550**
Location: Jct A1A and Beachland, just e to Cardinal Dr, then s to Bougainvillea, just e. 925 Bougainvillea Ln 32963. **Hours:** 5:30 pm-10 pm. Closed: 11/22, 12/25; also 9/1-9/30 & Sun. **Reservations:** suggested. **Features:** casual dress; beer & wine only; street parking; a la carte. The chef/owner's creative touch enlivens the cuisine, which include selections of prime cuts of meat, fresh seafood, pasta and breads and desserts made on the premises. Choose from a wide variety of wines, several available by the glass. Smoke free premises. **Cards:** AE, CB, DI, DS, MC, VI.

VILANO BEACH pop. 1,900 (See map p. 739; index p. 741)

—— WHERE TO STAY ——

OCEAN SANDS MOTOR INN
ΔΔΔ [SAVE]
▼▼▼
Motel
Phone: (904)824-1112　[60]
| | | | | XP: $5 | F16 |
2/12-9/4　　　　1P: $69-$99　　2P: $69-$99　　XP: $5　F16
12/1-2/11 & 9/5-11/30　1P: $49-$79　　2P: $49-$79　　XP: $5　F16
Location: 2 mi ne at Vilano Bridge on SR A1A. 3465 Coastal Hwy 32084. Fax: 904/824-1112. **Facility:** Ocean view and marsh view rooms. Private access to beach across street. Many rooms have balcony or patio with comfortable chairs. Short drive to historic area. Designated smoking area. 29 units. Some whirlpool units ($79-$139). *Bath:* combo or shower only. 2 stories, interior corridors. **Amenities:** extended cable TV. **Cards:** AE, DS, MC, VI. **Special Amenities:** free continental breakfast and free local telephone calls. *(See color ad p 749)*

SOME UNITS

—— WHERE TO DINE ——

FIDDLER'S GREEN
ΔΔΔ
▼▼▼
American
Dinner: $9-$18　　　　　**Phone: 904/824-8897**　[40]
Location: Just e of SR A1A where SR A1A turns n, 0.5 mi e of Vilano Beach Bridge. 2750 Anahma Dr 32084. **Hours:** 5 pm-10 pm. Closed: 11/22, 12/19-12/26; also Super Bowl Sun. **Reservations:** suggested. **Features:** casual dress; children's menu; carryout; cocktails & lounge; area transportation. Sink into large rattan chairs and take in the lovely ocean view. Fresh local seafood is used in many of the entrees, including a creative medley of lobster, shrimp and scallops in a white cream sauce. Twice-baked potatoes make a tasty side dish. **Cards:** AE, DI, DS, MC, VI.

WAKULLA SPRINGS

——— WHERE TO STAY ———

WAKULLA SPRINGS LODGE
(Classic Lodge)

All Year — 1P: $69-$90 — 2P: $69-$90 — XP: $5 — F12
Phone: 850/224-5950
Location: At jct SR 61 and 267; in Wakulla Springs State Park. 550 Wakulla Park Dr 32305. Fax: 850/561-7251. **Facility:** Historic. Basic, older-style rooms in 1937 building located on renowned bird and wildlife habitat. National Register of Historic Places. 27 units. 2 stories, interior corridors. **Terms:** 3 day cancellation notice-fee imposed, package plans. **Amenities:** no TVs. **Dining:** The Ball Room, see separate listing. **Leisure Activities:** swimming, nature trails. **Guest Services:** gift shop. **Business Services:** meeting rooms. **Cards:** AE, DS, MC, VI.

SOME UNITS

——— WHERE TO DINE ———

THE BALL ROOM
(Regional American)

Lunch: $6-$12 — **Dinner:** $7-$16 — **Phone: 850/224-5950**
Location: Jct SR 61 and 267; in Wakulla Springs State Park; in Wakulla Springs Lodge. 550 Wakulla Park Dr 32305. **Hours:** 7:30-10 am, 11:30-2 & 6-8:30 pm. **Reservations:** suggested. **Features:** casual dress; children's menu; beer & wine only. Freshly prepared meals with a strong Southern accent, including pecan-crusted grouper, veal chops and excellent fried oysters from Apalachicola Bay, are the key to the restaurant's appeal. Gaze out over lovely and scenic Wakulla Springs. Smoke free premises. **Cards:** AE, DS, MC, VI.

WEEKI WACHEE pop. 50

——— WHERE TO STAY ———

BEST WESTERN WEEKI WACHEE RESORT
(AAA) (SAVE)
(Motel)

12/1-4/30 — 1P: $65-$89 — 2P: $65-$89
5/1-11/30 — 1P: $55-$79
Phone: (352)596-2007
Location: US 19 at jct SR 50 (Cortez Blvd). 6172 Commercial Way 34606. Fax: 352/596-0667. **Facility:** 122 units. 2 stories, exterior corridors. **Terms:** package plans. **Amenities:** extended cable TV, voice mail, hair dryers. **Dining:** cocktails. **Leisure Activities:** wading pool, shuffleboard. **Guest Services:** coin laundry. **Business Services:** meeting rooms, fax. **Cards:** AE, CB, DI, DS, JC, MC, VI. **Special Amenities:** free continental breakfast and free local telephone calls. *(See color ad p 231 & p 785)*

SOME UNITS
FEE

COMFORT INN
(SAVE)
(Motel)
MC, VI.

12/1-4/30 — 1P: $55-$85 — 2P: $60-$85 — XP: $5 — F18
5/1-11/30 — 1P: $50-$70 — 2P: $55-$80 — XP: $5 — F18
Phone: (352)596-9000
Location: SR 50, 0.3 mi e of jct US 19. 9373 Cortez Blvd 34613. Fax: 352/597-4010. **Facility:** 68 units. Some whirlpool units ($80). *Bath:* combo or shower only. 2 stories, exterior corridors. **Terms:** cancellation fee imposed, pets ($10 extra charge). **Amenities:** irons, hair dryers. **Leisure Activities:** exercise room. **Guest Services:** [ECP] meal plan available, coin laundry. **Business Services:** meeting rooms, fax. **Cards:** AE, DI, DS,

SOME UNITS
FEE   FEE

——— WHERE TO DINE ———

NELLIE'S RESTAURANT
(American)

Lunch: $5-$7 — **Dinner:** $5-$11 — **Phone:** 352/596-8321
Location: On SR 50, just e of jct US 19; in Weeki Wachee Village Shops. 6234 Commercial Way 34613. **Hours:** 6 am-9 pm. Closed major holidays. **Features:** casual dress; children's menu; early bird specials; carryout; beer & wine only. A savory Yankee pot roast and homemade mashed potatoes are highlights of this homey eatery. Freshly-prepared dishes of poultry, steaks and seafood complete the menu. Don't leave without a piece of the coconut cream pie and a cup of coffee. **Cards:** MC, VI.

WESLEY CHAPEL —See Tampa Bay p. 887.

WEST MELBOURNE pop. 8,400—See also MELBOURNE.

——— WHERE TO STAY ———

HAMPTON INN MELBOURNE
(AAA) (SAVE)
(Motel)

1/1-4/17 — 1P: $89 — 2P: $94
12/1-12/31 — 1P: $60-$65 — 2P: $69-$74
4/18-11/30 — 1P: $60 — 2P: $69
Phone: 321/956-6200
Location: I-95, exit 71, ne corner. 194 Dike Rd 32904. Fax: 321/956-3230. **Facility:** Designated smoking area. 66 units. Some whirlpool units. *Bath:* combo or shower only. 3 stories, interior corridors. **Terms:** 24 day cancellation notice. **Amenities:** voice mail, irons, hair dryers. **Leisure Activities:** exercise room. **Guest Services:** [ECP] meal plan available, valet and coin laundry. **Business Services:** meeting rooms. **Cards:** AE, CB, DI, DS, MC, VI.

SOME UNITS

HOWARD JOHNSON
(Motel)
MC, VI.

Phone: (321)768-8439
Property failed to provide current rates
Location: I-95, exit 71, just e on SR 192. 4431 W New Haven Ave 32904. **Facility:** 119 units. *Bath:* combo or shower only. 2 stories, exterior corridors. **Terms:** small pets only ($20 extra charge). **Amenities:** extended cable TV, safes. **Guest Services:** coin laundry. **Business Services:** meeting rooms. **Cards:** AE, CB, DI, DS,

SOME UNITS
FEE   FEE

WESTON —See Fort Lauderdale p. 393.

WEST PALM BEACH pop. 67,600   (See map p. 710; index p. 711)—

——— WHERE TO STAY ———

BEST WESTERN PALM BEACH LAKES INN   **Phone: (561)683-8810**   **9**
AAA SAVE   1/15-4/14   1P: $89-$94   2P: $89-$94   XP: $10   F17
    12/1-1/14 & 4/15-11/30   1P: $59-$64   2P: $59-$64   XP: $10   F17
Motel   **Location:** I-95, exit 53, just e. 1800 Palm Beach Lakes Blvd 33401. Fax: 561/478-2580. **Facility:** Landscaped pool courtyard. Facing Palm Beach Mall. 135 units. Some suites ($125-$150). 2 stories, interior/exterior corridors. **Terms:** package plans. **Amenities:** *Some:* irons, hair dryers. **Leisure Activities:** heated pool. **Guest Services:** [ECP] meal plan available, area transportation-within 4 mi, valet laundry. **Business Services:** meeting rooms. *Fee:* fax. **Cards:** AE, DI, DS, MC, VI. **Special Amenities: free continental breakfast and free newspaper.**

SOME UNITS / FEE

COMFORT INN-ON PALM BEACH LAKES   **Phone: 561/689-6100**   **8**
AAA SAVE   1/14-4/14   1P: $99   2P: $119   XP: $10   F18
    12/1-1/13   1P: $69   2P: $99   XP: $10   F18
    4/15-11/30   1P: $59   2P: $89   XP: $10   F18
Motel   **Location:** I-95, exit 53, just w. 1901 Palm Beach Lakes Blvd 33409. Fax: 561/686-6177. **Facility:** Attractive pool area. 162 units. 6 stories, interior corridors. **Terms:** weekly & monthly rates available, package plans, small pets only ($10 extra charge, $25 fee). **Amenities:** video games, safes (fee), irons. **Dining:** No Anchovies! Neighborhood Pastaria, see separate listing. **Leisure Activities:** heated pool. **Guest Services:** [ECP] meal plan available, complimentary evening beverages: Tues-Thurs, coin laundry. **Business Services:** meeting rooms. *Fee:* fax. **Cards:** AE, DI, DS, MC, VI. **Special Amenities: early check-in/late check-out and free room upgrade (subject to availability with advanced reservations).** *(See color ad below)*

SOME UNITS / FEE

COURTYARD BY MARRIOTT-WEST PALM BEACH   **Phone: (561)640-9000**   **2**
VVV   12/1-4/30   1P: $139   2P: $149   XP: $10   F18
    5/1-11/30   1P: $79   2P: $89   XP: $10   F18
Motel   **Location:** Just w of jct I-95, exit 54 (45th St), on CR 702; in Northpoint Corporate Park. 600 Northpoint Pkwy 33407. Fax: 561/471-0122. **Facility:** Rooms with balcony or patio, some overlooking the courtyard. 149 units. Some suites. *Bath:* combo or shower only. 3 stories, interior corridors. **Terms:** check-in 4 pm. **Leisure Activities:** heated pool, whirlpool, exercise room. **Guest Services:** valet and coin laundry. **Business Services:** meeting rooms. **Cards:** AE, CB, DI, DS, MC, VI. *(See color ad p 242)*

SOME UNITS / FEE

CROWNE PLAZA WEST PALM BEACH   **Phone: (561)689-6400**   **15**
AAA SAVE   1/1-5/6   1P: $144-$164   2P: $154-$174   XP: $10   F18
    10/1-11/30   1P: $109-$129   2P: $119-$139   XP: $10   F18
    12/1-12/31 & 5/7-9/30   1P: $99-$119   2P: $109-$129   XP: $10   F18
Hotel   **Location:** I-95, exit 51, 0.5 mi w at jct Australian Ave. 1601 Belvedere Rd 33406. Fax: 561/683-7150. **Facility:** Modern architecture with atrium lobby. 218 units, 12 with kitchen (no utensils). Some suites. 15 stories, interior corridors. **Parking:** valet. **Terms:** check-in 4 pm, cancellation fee imposed. **Amenities:** dual phone lines, voice mail, irons, hair dryers. **Dining:** restaurant, 6:30 am-2 & 5-10 pm, $12-$18, cocktails. **Leisure Activities:** heated pool, saunas, whirlpool, 2 lighted tennis courts, exercise room. **Guest Services:** gift shop, valet laundry. **Business Services:** conference facilities, administrative services. *Fee:* PC, fax. **Cards:** AE, CB, DI, DS, MC, VI.

SOME UNITS / FEE

(See map p. 710)

DAYS INN AIRPORT NORTH

[SAVE]

Motor Inn

1/16-4/30	1P: $69-$110	2P: $69-$110	XP: $10
12/18-1/15	1P: $59-$110	2P: $59-$110	XP: $10
12/1-12/17 & 5/1-11/30	1P: $49-$79	2P: $49-$79	XP: $10

Phone: 561/689-0450 [5]

F17
F17
F17

Location: On SR 702, (45th St) at jct I-95, exit 54. 2300 45th St 33407. Fax: 561/686-7439. **Facility:** Contemporary room decor. 214 units. *Bath:* combo or shower only. 2 stories, exterior corridors. **Parking:** valet. **Terms:** 7 day cancellation notice-fee imposed, weekly & monthly rates available, package plans, small pets only ($10 extra charge). **Amenities:** extended cable TV, voice mail, safes (fee). *Some:* irons, hair dryers. **Leisure Activities:** heated pool, whirlpool, putting green, shuffleboard. **Guest Services:** coin laundry. **Business Services:** meeting rooms. **Cards:** AE, CB, DI, DS, MC, VI.

SOME UNITS

FAIRFIELD INN BY MARRIOTT

Motel

Property failed to provide current rates

Phone: (561)697-3388 [11]

Location: SR 704, at east side of Florida Tpke, exit 99. 5981 Okeechobee Blvd 33417. Fax: 561/697-2834. **Facility:** Attractive public areas. Rooms with contemporary decor and furnishings. 114 units. *Bath:* combo or shower only. 4 stories, exterior corridors. **Terms:** 7 day cancellation notice, weekly rates available, package plans. **Amenities:** voice mail. **Leisure Activities:** heated pool. **Guest Services:** [ECP] meal plan available, valet and coin laundry. **Business Services:** meeting rooms. **Cards:** AE, CB, DI, DS, MC, VI.

SOME UNITS

HAMPTON INN PALM BEACH/INTERNATIONAL AIRPORT

[SAVE]

Motel

All Year   1P: $71

Phone: 561/471-8700 [13]

Location: I-95, exit 51, 0.3 mi w. 1505 Belvedere Rd 33406. Fax: 561/689-7385. **Facility:** 135 units. 3 stories, exterior corridors. **Terms:** monthly rates available. **Amenities:** extended cable TV, video games, voice mail, irons, hair dryers. **Guest Services:** [ECP] meal plan available, valet laundry. *Fee:* fax. **Cards:** AE, DI, DS, MC, VI.

SOME UNITS

FEE   FEE

HIBISCUS HOUSE BED & BREAKFAST

Historic Bed
& Breakfast

12/1-4/30	1P: $95-$180	2P: $95-$180
5/1-11/30	1P: $65-$110	2P: $65-$110

Phone: (561)863-5633 [7]

Location: 1.2 mi n on Flagler Dr from jct Palm Beach Lakes Blvd, 0.3 mi w. 501 30th St 33407. Fax: 561/863-5633. **Facility:** In restored 1922 home built for the mayor, inviting public rooms are furnished with grace and style. Individually decorated bedrooms have period furnishings and antiques. Secluded tropical garden. Smoke free premises. 4 units. *Bath:* combo or shower only. 2 stories, interior corridors. **Terms:** 14 day cancellation notice-fee imposed, weekly rates available, package plans - off season, small pets only. **Amenities:** extended cable TV. **Leisure Activities:** heated pool. **Guest Services:** [BP] meal plan available. **Business Services:** fax. **Cards:** AE, MC, VI.

SOME UNITS

HILTON PALM BEACH AIRPORT

[SAVE]

Hotel

1/1-4/30	1P: $157	2P: $166	XP: $10
12/1-12/31 & 5/1-11/30	1P: $130	2P: $139	XP: $10

Phone: (561)684-9400 [19]

F18
F18

Location: I-95, exit 50, 0.3 mi w at jct Australian Ave and Southern Blvd. 150 Australian Ave 33406. Fax: 561/689-9421. **Facility:** On landscaped lakeside grounds. Very inviting public areas. 247 units. 10 stories, interior corridors. **Parking:** valet. **Terms:** 3 day cancellation notice, package plans. **Amenities:** dual phone lines, voice mail, irons, hair dryers. *Some:* safes. **Leisure Activities:** heated pool, fishing, 2 lighted tennis courts, exercise room. *Fee:* waterskiing. **Guest Services:** gift shop, valet laundry. **Business Services:** conference facilities, fax. **Cards:** AE, CB, DI, DS, MC, VI. *(See ad p 44)*

SOME UNITS

FEE   FEE

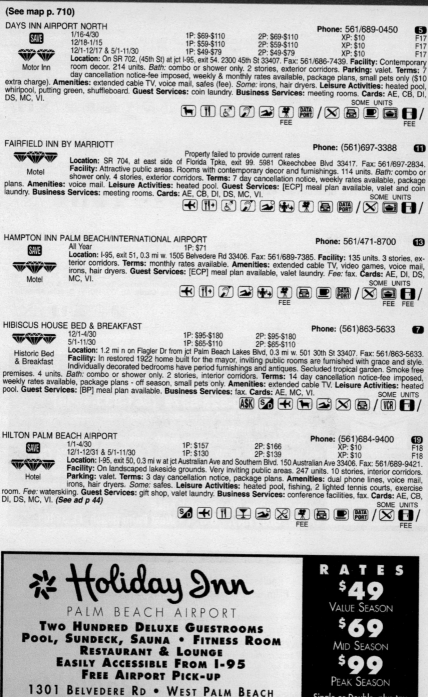

(See map p. 710)

HOLIDAY INN PALM BEACH AIRPORT　　　　　　　　　　　Phone: (561)659-3880　🔞
AAA SAVE　12/21-4/30　　　　1P: $89-$109　　2P: $99-$119　　XP: $10　　F17
　　　　　12/1-12/20 & 5/1-11/30　1P: $59-$79　　2P: $69-$89　　XP: $10　　F17
Motor Inn　**Location:** I-95, exit 51, just w. 1301 Belvedere Rd 33405. Fax: 561/655-8886. **Facility:** Attractive rooms. 199 units.
11 stories, interior corridors. **Terms:** weekly & monthly rates available, package plans. **Amenities:** voice mail,
irons, hair dryers. **Dining:** restaurant, 7 am-2 & 5-10 pm, $8-$17, cocktails. **Leisure Activities:** heated pool,
saunas, exercise room. **Guest Services:** [BP] meal plan available, valet laundry. **Business Services:**
meeting rooms, administrative services. **Fee:** PC, fax. **Cards:** AE, CB, DI, DS, JC, MC, VI. **Special Amenities:** free newspaper
and free room upgrade (subject to availability with advanced reservations). *(See color ad p 899)*　SOME UNITS

HOMESTEAD VILLAGE GUEST STUDIOS　　　　　　　　　　Phone: (561)640-3335　🔟6️⃣
　　　　　1/16-4/30　　　　1P: $90-$110　　2P: $90-$110　　XP: $5　　F18
Extended Stay　12/1-1/15 & 5/1-11/30　1P: $55-$75　　2P: $55-$75　　XP: $5　　F18
Motel　**Location:** I-95, exit 51 (Belvedere Rd), w to Australian Ave, then n to Centrepark Dr, e on Centrepark Dr, straight ahead.
1535 Centrepark Dr N 33401. Fax: 561/640-3374. **Facility:** Office hours, 7 am-9 pm, Sat 9 am-5 pm, Sun
noon-8 pm. Spacious rooms. 137 efficiencies. **Bath:** combo or shower only. 2 stories, exterior corridors.
Amenities: voice mail, irons. **Guest Services:** coin laundry. **Cards:** AE, CB, DI, DS, MC, VI.　SOME UNITS

PARKVIEW MOTOR LODGE　　　　　　　　　　　　　　Phone: (561)833-4644　2️⃣0️⃣
AAA SAVE　1/10-4/16　　　　1P: $70-$80　　2P: $76-$88　　XP: $5　　F17
　　　　　12/19-1/9　　　　1P: $60-$70　　2P: $62-$74　　XP: $5　　F17
Motel　12/1-12/18 & 4/17-11/30　1P: $46-$58　　2P: $48-$60　　XP: $5　　F17
Location: On US 1, 0.5 mi s of US 908 and SR 80. 4710 S Dixie Hwy 33405. Fax: 561/833-4644. **Facility:** Attractively landscaped grounds. Rooms vary in size from small to large. Some small bathrooms. 28 units. 1 two-
bedroom unit. **Bath:** combo or shower only. 1-2 stories, exterior corridors. **Terms:** weekly & monthly rates
available. **Amenities:** extended cable TV. **Guest Services:** valet laundry. **Fee:** fax. **Cards:** AE, DS, MC, VI. **Special Amenities:**
free continental breakfast. *(See color ad below)*　SOME UNITS

(See map p. 710)

RADISSON SUITE INN PALM BEACH AIRPORT

Phone: (561)689-6888 [17]

AAA SAVE

Motor Inn

12/1-4/30 & 11/16-11/30	1P: $119-$139	2P: $119-$139	XP: $10 F18
5/1-11/15	1P: $99-$119	2P: $99-$119	XP: $10 F18

Location: I-95, exit 51, 0.5 mi w on Belvedere Rd, then 0.5 mi n. 1808 Australian Ave S 33409. Fax: 561/683-5783. **Facility:** Well-equipped rooms with sitting area. 174 units. Some suites. 6 stories, interior corridors. **Terms:** cancellation fee imposed, package plans. **Amenities:** voice mail, honor bars, irons, hair dryers. **Dining:** restaurant, 6:30 am-2 & 5-10 pm, Sat & Sun from 7 am, $10-$19, cocktails. **Leisure Activities:** heated pool, sauna, whirlpool, exercise room. **Guest Services:** [CP] meal plan available, gift shop, area transportation-within 5 mi, valet laundry. **Business Services:** meeting rooms. **Fee:** fax. **Cards:** AE, CB, DI, DS, JC, MC, VI.
(See color ad p 900)

SOME UNITS

RED ROOF INN-WEST PALM BEACH

Phone: (561)697-7710 [3]

AAA SAVE

Motel

All Year	1P: $40-$90	2P: $40-$90	XP: $10 F18

Location: On CR 702, just w of jct I-95, exit 54 (45th St); in the Metrocentre Corporate Park. 2421 Metro Center Blvd E 33407. Fax: 561/697-1728. **Facility:** Comfortable functional rooms. 129 units. *Bath:* combo or shower only. 3 stories, interior/exterior corridors. **Terms:** small pets only. **Amenities:** video games, voice mail. **Leisure Activities:** heated pool. **Cards:** AE, CB, DI, DS, MC, VI. **Special Amenities:** free local telephone calls and free newspaper.

SOME UNITS

RESIDENCE INN BY MARRIOTT WEST PALM BEACH

Phone: (561)687-4747 [4]

Apartment

1/16-5/15	1P: $120-$199
12/1-1/15 & 5/16-11/30	1P: $69-$129

Location: I-95, exit 54, just w on 45th St to Metrocenter Corporate Park. 2461 Metrocenter Blvd 33407. Fax: 561/697-3633. **Facility:** Roomy, comfortable rooms with fully-equipped kitchen. 78 efficiencies. 12 two-bedroom units. Some suites. *Bath:* combo or shower only. 3 stories, interior corridors. **Terms:** small pets only ($100 fee). **Amenities:** dual phone lines, voice mail, irons, hair dryers. **Leisure Activities:** heated pool, whirlpool, exercise room, sports court. **Guest Services:** [BP] meal plan available, complimentary evening beverages: Mon-Thurs, valet and coin laundry. **Business Services:** meeting rooms. **Cards:** AE, CB, DI, DS, MC, VI.

SOME UNITS

ROYAL PALM HOUSE B & B

Phone: 561/863-9836 [1]

Bed & Breakfast

12/1-4/30	1P: $75-$125	2P: $75-$125	XP: $15
5/1-11/30	1P: $65-$115	2P: $65-$115	XP: $15

Location: I-95, exit 54 (45th St), 2.4 mi e to Spruce Ave, then 0.7 mi s. 3215 Spruce Ave 33407. Fax: 561/848-1350. **Facility:** Located in the historic district of West Palm Beach. Built in 1925, the rooms take on a personality all their own, homey is a good word to start with. Colors are soft and comfort is another. The pool is soothing, surrounded by fruit trees. A small garden for quiet time too. 5 units. Some whirlpool units ($115-$125). *Bath:* combo or shower only. 2 stories, interior corridors. **Parking:** street only. **Terms:** age restrictions may apply, 14 day cancellation notice. **Amenities:** extended cable TV. **Leisure Activities:** small pool, bicycles. **Guest Services:** [BP] meal plan available. **Cards:** AE, CB, DI, DS, MC, VI.

SOME UNITS

SHERATON HOTEL

Phone: (561)833-1234 [14]

Hotel

1/13-4/13	1P: $169	2P: $169	XP: $10 F17
12/1-1/12 & 10/1-11/30	1P: $149	2P: $149	XP: $10 F17
4/14-9/30	1P: $129	2P: $129	

Location: I-95, exit 52, 0.8 mi e on Okeechobee Blvd E. 630 Clearwater Park Rd 33401. Fax: 561/833-4689. **Facility:** Facing the Kravis Center. Attractive public areas. Large rooms with warm colors. 349 units. 10 stories, interior corridors. **Parking:** valet. **Terms:** small pets only. **Amenities:** dual phone lines, voice mail, irons, hair dryers. *Some:* fax. **Leisure Activities:** heated pool, whirlpool, 2 lighted tennis courts, exercise room. **Guest Services:** gift shop, area transportation, valet laundry. **Business Services:** conference facilities. **Fee:** fax. **Cards:** AE, CB, DI, DS, JC, MC, VI.

SOME UNITS

TROPICAL GARDENS BED & BREAKFAST

Phone: (561)848-4064 [6]

Historic Bed & Breakfast

12/1-4/30 & 11/1-11/30	1P: $75-$125	2P: $75-$125
5/1-10/31	1P: $65-$95	2P: $65-$95

Location: Palm Beach Lakes Blvd, 1.2 mi n on N Dixie Hwy, then just w. 419 32nd St 33407-4809. Fax: 561/848-2422. **Facility:** Attractive pool/courtyard area. Quiet location. Guest rooms and public areas with a Key West tropical flair. Smoke free premises. 4 units. *Bath:* combo or shower only. 1 story. **Terms:** age restrictions may apply, 14 day cancellation notice-fee imposed, weekly rates available. **Amenities:** extended cable TV. *Some:* CD players. **Leisure Activities:** heated pool, bicycles. **Guest Services:** [ECP] meal plan available. **Business Services:** fax. **Cards:** AE, DS, MC, VI.

SOME UNITS

------ **WHERE TO DINE** ------

391ST BOMB GROUP

Lunch: $4-$11 **Dinner:** $12-$29 **Phone:** 561/683-3919 [7]

American

Location: US 98; 2 mi w of jct I-95, exit 50. 3989 Southern Blvd 33406. **Hours:** 11:30 am-3:30 & 4:30-10 pm, Fri-11 pm, Sat noon-11 pm, Sun 10 am-2:30 & 4:30-10 pm. **Closed:** Sat for lunch 6/1-9/30. **Reservations:** suggested. **Features:** casual dress; Sunday brunch; children's menu; early bird specials; cocktails & lounge. The runway lights of the Palm Beach International Airport create a romantic mood in this dining room. World War II memorabilia decorates the walls, and the wait staff serves up scrumptious meals like the cheese beer soup with a Reuben sandwich. **Cards:** AE, CB, DI, DS, MC, VI.

(See map p. 710)

GREAT TEXAS LAND & CATTLE CO.
American
Dinner: $9-$23   **Phone:** 561/840-1511   ①
Location: On SR 809 (Military Tr), 0.5 mi n of jct 45th St. 6000 N Military Tr 33407. **Hours:** 4:30 pm-9 pm, Fri & Sat-10 pm. Closed: 12/25. **Features:** casual dress; children's menu; early bird specials; carryout; cocktails & lounge. A warm, friendly and casual atmosphere with a touch of the Old West, Great Texas offers a full menu featuring USDA choice steak, prime rib, seafood and pasta dishes. **Cards:** AE, DS, MC, VI.

NO ANCHOVIES! NEIGHBORHOOD PASTARIA
Italian
Lunch: $5-$8   **Dinner:** $9-$17   **Phone:** 561/684-0040   ③
Location: I-95, exit 53, just w; in Comfort Inn-on Palm Beach Lakes. 1901 Palm Beach Lakes Blvd 33409. **Hours:** 11:30 am-2:30 & 4:30-10:30 pm, Sun-10 pm. Closed: 11/22, 12/25. **Features:** casual dress; children's menu; carryout; cocktails & lounge. Featuring specialty pasta and dishes cooked in a wood-burning stove, this modern pastaria sports a lively, casual ambience. The combo pasta lets you pair your favorite pasta with your favorite sauce. Valet parking is available at dinner. **Cards:** AE, MC, VI.

RAIN DANCER STEAK HOUSE
Steak & Seafood
Dinner: $15-$30   **Phone:** 561/684-2811   ④
Location: I-95, exit 53, 0.8 mi w. 2300 Palm Beach Lakes Blvd 33409. **Hours:** 5 pm-10 pm, Fri & Sat-10:30 pm. Closed: 11/22, 12/25. **Features:** dressy casual; children's menu; salad bar; cocktails & lounge. An Old World decor sets the tone in the cozy, rustic restaurant, where servers handle the busy tempo without missing a beat. A balanced selection of wines complement succulent top-grade steaks, such as a juicy 22-ounce porterhouse. **Cards:** AE, CB, DI, DS, MC, VI.

———— *The following restaurant has not been evaluated by AAA* ————
but is listed for your information only.

FLANIGAN'S SEAFOOD BAR & GRILL
[fyi]
Phone: 561/659-3129
Not evaluated. **Location:** 330 Southern Blvd. **Features:** A casual atmosphere that is inexpensive and family friendly. Known for their barbecue baby back ribs, large burgers and fresh local seafood.

WHITE SPRINGS (HAMILTON COUNTY)

———— **WHERE TO DINE** ————

THE TELFORD RESTAURANT Historical
American
Lunch: $5-$8   **Dinner:** $7-$13   **Phone:** 904/397-1915
Location: I-75, exit 84, 3 mi e on CR 136, just right from Suwannee River Bridge. 3 River St 32096. **Hours:** 11 am-2:30 & 5:30-8:30 pm, Sat from 5:30 pm. Closed: 12/25. **Features:** casual dress; Sunday brunch; children's menu; a la carte. Experience the gracious Southern hospitality of yesteryear when you dine at this historic hotel. Dinner features beef tenderloins, marinated chicken, and a nice soup and salad bar. An extensive lunch buffet features Southern foods like fried chicken. **Cards:** AE, DS, MC, VI.

WILLISTON pop. 2,200

———— **WHERE TO STAY** ————

WILLISTON MOTOR INN
Motor Inn
All Year   1P: $33   2P: $33   **Phone:** 352/528-4801
Location: 0.5 mi n on US 27 Alt. 606 W Noble Ave 32696. Fax: 352/528-4650. **Facility:** Older style roadside motel with good sized singles, modest doubles and some contemporary room appointments. 44 units, 4 with kitchen. *Bath:* combo or shower only. 1 story, exterior corridors. **Terms:** weekly & monthly rates available, small pets only ($5 extra charge, $5 deposit). **Amenities:** extended cable TV. **Guest Services:** coin laundry. **Business Services:** fax. **Cards:** AE, DS, MC, VI.
SOME UNITS

WINTER GARDEN —See Orlando p. 703.

WINTER HAVEN pop. 24,700

———— WHERE TO STAY ————

BEST WESTERN ADMIRAL'S INN

Phone: (863)324-5950

(AAA) [SAVE]
◊◊◊◊

Motor Inn

2/13-3/31	1P: $95-$125	2P: $95-$125	XP: $6	F17
4/1-4/30	1P: $77-$107	2P: $77-$107	XP: $6	F17
5/1-11/30	1P: $75-$105	2P: $75-$105	XP: $6	F17
12/1-2/12	1P: $74-$104	2P: $74-$104	XP: $6	F17

Location: SR 540, 3 mi e of jct US 17 (at entrance to Cypress Gardens). 5665 Cypress Gardens Blvd 33884. Fax: 863/324-2376. **Facility:** Within walking distance of Cypress Gardens. 157 units. Some suites ($182-$250) and whirlpool units ($182-$250). 3-5 stories, interior/exterior corridors. **Terms:** weekly rates available, package plans, pets ($15 extra charge). **Amenities:** extended cable TV, voice mail, irons. *Some:* hair dryers. **Dining:** restaurant, 7 am-10 & 5-9 pm, Fri & Sat-10 pm, $13-$22, cocktails, entertainment. **Leisure Activities:** heated pool, whirlpool, exercise room, beauty salon, florist. **Guest Services:** [CP] meal plan available, gift shop, coin laundry. **Business Services:** meeting rooms, administrative services. **Cards:** AE, DI, DS, MC, VI. *(See color ad below)*

SOME UNITS
[S/D] 🐾 🍴 📺 🏊 🎥 🖨 💻 [DATA PORT] / ✖ 🖨 🛗 /

CYPRESS MOTEL

Phone: (863)324-5867

(AAA) [SAVE]
◊◊◊◊

Motel

2/15-3/31	1P: $60-$65	2P: $65-$70	XP: $5	F11
12/1-2/14	1P: $40-$50	2P: $45-$60	XP: $5	F11
4/1-11/30	1P: $40-$45	2P: $45-$50	XP: $5	F11

Location: 6 mi e of jct US 17; 1.8 mi w of jct US 27 on SR 540, 0.5 mi n on SR 540A. 5651 Cypress Gardens Rd 33884. Fax: 863/324-5867. **Facility:** 21 units, 8 with efficiency. **Terms:** cancellation fee imposed, weekly & monthly rates available, small pets only ($10 fee). **Amenities:** extended cable TV. **Leisure Activities:** heated pool, playground. **Guest Services:** [CP] meal plan available, gift shop, coin laundry. **Cards:** AE, DS, MC, VI.

SOME UNITS
[S/D] 🐾 🏊 💻 / ✖ 🖨 🛗 /
FEE FEE

HOLIDAY INN CYPRESS GARDENS-WINTER HAVEN

Phone: (863)294-4451

(AAA) [SAVE]
◊◊◊◊

Motor Inn

MC, VI.

2/25-4/7	1P: $135	2P: $135
12/1-2/24 & 4/8-11/30	1P: $72	2P: $72

Location: 0.8 mi s on US 17. 1150 Third St SW 33880. Fax: 863/293-9829. **Facility:** Nicely landscaped. 226 units. *Bath:* combo or shower only. 2 stories, exterior corridors. **Amenities:** voice mail, irons, hair dryers. **Dining:** restaurant, 6:30 am-2 & 5-8 pm, $5-$10, cocktails. **Leisure Activities:** heated pool, wading pool, golf privileges. **Guest Services:** coin laundry. **Business Services:** meeting rooms. **Cards:** AE, CB, DI, DS, JC,

SOME UNITS
[S/D] 🍴 📺 ♿ 🧺 ✏ 🏊 🎥 🖨 💻 🛗 [DATA PORT] / ✖ /

———— WHERE TO DINE ————

CHRISTY'S SUNDOWN RESTAURANT

(AAA)
◊◊ ◊◊

American

Lunch: $5-$10   **Dinner:** $12-$27   Phone: 863/293-0069

Location: 0.8 mi s on US 17. 1100 3rd St 33882. **Hours:** 11:30 am-10:30 pm. Closed major holidays; also Sun. **Features:** casual dress; children's menu; cocktails & lounge; a la carte. Although the restaurant specializes in prime rib, its menu selections also incorporate seafood, veal, pasta and chicken dishes. The quiet dining room is a favorite of major-league baseball players during spring training. **Cards:** AE, DS, MC, VI.   ✖

WINTER PARK —See Orlando p. 704.

YULEE —See Jacksonville p. 450.

ZEPHYRHILLS —See Tampa Bay p. 888.

The One That Does It All

*F*or years, people have turned to AAA for their emergency road service needs. But AAA is more than just towing. Access to AAA's travel services can give you the world. Its financial services can help you pay for it. And AAA insurance can give you the peace of mind to enjoy the ride. Plus, AAA gives you exclusive Show Your Card & Save® offers, bail bond benefits, and much more.

Discover the ways AAA can simplify your life. Call or stop by your nearest AAA office today. And make AAA the one for you.

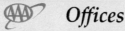 *Offices*

Cities with main offices are listed in **BOLD TYPE** and toll-free member service numbers in *ITALIC TYPE*.
All are closed Saturdays, Sundays and holidays unless otherwise indicated.
The type of service provided is designated below the name of the city where the office is located:
Auto travel services, including books/maps, marked maps and on-demand Triptik maps ✚
Auto travel services, including books/maps, marked maps, but no on-demand Triptik maps ●
Provides books/maps only. No marked maps or on-demand Triptik maps available ■
Travel agency services ▲

FLORIDA

BELLEAIR BLUFFS—AAA AUTO CLUB SOUTH, 100 N INDIAN ROCKS RD, 33770. MON-FRI 8:30-5:30. (727) 584-7678.●▲

BOCA RATON—AAA AUTO CLUB SOUTH, 4400 N FEDERAL HWY #152, 33431. MON-FRI 8:30-5:30. (561) 395-8687.▲

BRADENTON—AAA AUTO CLUB SOUTH, 6210 MANATEE AVE W, 34209. MON-FRI 8:30-5:30. (941) 798-2221.✚▲

BRADENTON—AAA AUTO CLUB SOUTH, 6513 14TH ST W/SARABAY PL, 34207. MON-FRI 8:30-5:30. (941) 756-0606.●▲

BRANDON—AAA AUTO CLUB SOUTH, 415 W ROBERTSON ST, 33511-5009. MON-FRI 8:30-5:30. (813) 681-5761.✚▲

CLEARWATER—AAA AUTO CLUB SOUTH, 2170 RAINBOW DR, 33765. MON-FRI 8:30-5:30. (727) 448-2600.✚▲

DAYTONA BEACH—AAA AUTO CLUB SOUTH, 2525 INTNL SPEEDWAY BLVD, 32114. MON-FRI 8:30-5:30. (904) 252-0531.✚▲

DELRAY BEACH—AAA AUTO CLUB SOUTH, 3075 S FEDERAL HWY, 33483. MON-FRI 8:30-5:30. (561) 278-4711.✚▲

DESTIN—AAA AUTO CLUB SOUTH, 851 HWY 98 E, 32541. MON-FRI 8:30-5:30. (850) 837-8422.■▲

FORT MYERS—AAA AUTO CLUB SOUTH, 2516 COLONIAL BLVD, 33907. MON-FRI 8:30-5:30. (941) 939-6500.✚▲

FORT PIERCE—AAA AUTO CLUB SOUTH, 1971 S US HWY #1, 34950-5147. MON-FRI 8:30-5:30. (561) 461-6972.✚▲

GAINESVILLE—AAA AUTO CLUB SOUTH, 1201 NW 13TH ST, 32601. MON-FRI 8:30-5:30. (352) 373-7801.✚▲

GAINESVILLE—AAA AUTO CLUB SOUTH, 3415 W UNIVERSITY AVE, 32607. MON-FRI 8:30-5:30. (352) 338-7447.●▲

HEATHROW—AAA AUTO CLUB SOUTH, 1000 AAA DR #28, 32746-5080. MON-FRI 8:30-5:30. (407) 444-4240.▲

HEATHROW—AAA AUTO CLUB SOUTH, 1000 AAA DR; MS 53, 32746-5080. MON-FRI 8-5. (407) 444-4597.

HOLIDAY—AAA AUTO CLUB SOUTH, 4740 MILE STRETCH DR, 34690. MON-FRI 8:30-5:30. (727) 938-3794.✚▲

JACKSONVILLE—AAA AUTO CLUB SOUTH, 3718 BEACH BLVD, 32207. MON-FRI 8:30-5:30. (904) 398-0564.✚▲

KISSIMMEE—AAA AUTO CLUB SOUTH, 204 W OAK ST, 34741. MON-FRI 8:30-5:30. (407) 944-0866.✚▲

LADY LAKE—AAA AUTO CLUB SOUTH, 1113 MAIN ST, 32159. MON-FRI 8:30-5:30. (352) 753-2500.●▲

LAKELAND—AAA AUTO CLUB SOUTH, 1457 E MEMORIAL BLVD, 33801. MON-FRI 8:30-5:30. (863) 688-7921.✚▲

LAUDERHILL—AAA AUTO CLUB SOUTH, 4800 N UNIVERSITY DR, 33351. MON-FRI 8:30-5:30. (954) 748-2700.✚▲

LEESBURG—AAA AUTO CLUB SOUTH, 1107 W NORTH BLVD #16, 34748. MON-FRI 8:30-5:30. (352) 787-8800.✚▲

MARY ESTHER—AAA AUTO CLUB SOUTH, 300 MARY ESTHER BLVD #27, 32569. MON-FRI 8:30-5:30. (850) 244-3126.●▲

MELBOURNE—AAA AUTO CLUB SOUTH, 3578 NO HARBOR CITY BLVD, 32935. MON-FRI 8:30-5:30. (321) 253-9100.✚▲

MIAMI—AAA AUTO CLUB SOUTH, 20801 BISCAYNE BLVD #101, 33180. MON-FRI 8:30-5:30. (305) 682-2100.✚▲

MIAMI—AAA AUTO CLUB SOUTH, 6101 SUNSET DR SW, 33143. MON-FRI 8:30-5:30. (305) 661-6131.✚▲

MIAMI—AAA AUTO CLUB SOUTH, 7074 SW 117 AVE, 33183-3806. MON-FRI 8:30-5:30. (305) 270-6450.✚▲

NAPLES—AAA AUTO CLUB SOUTH, 5401 AIRPORT PULLING RD N, 34109. MON-FRI 8:30-5:30. (941) 594-5006.✚▲

OCALA—AAA AUTO CLUB SOUTH, 3033 SW COLLEGE RD, 34474. MON-FRI 8:30-5:30. (352) 237-6251.✚▲

ORANGE PARK—AAA AUTO CLUB SOUTH, 555 BLANDING BLVD, 32073. MON-FRI 8:30-6, SUN 10-4. (904) 272-2010.▲

ORLANDO—AAA AUTO CLUB SOUTH, 4300 E COLONIAL DR, 32803. MON-FRI 8:30-5:30. (407) 894-3333.✚▲

PALM BEACH GARDENS—AAA AUTO CLUB SOUTH, 9123 N MILITARY TRL #110, 33410. MON-FRI 8:30-5:30. (561) 694-9090.✚▲

PALM HARBOR—AAA AUTO CLUB SOUTH, 32050 US HWY 19 N, 34684. MON-FRI 8:30-5:30. (727) 789-7850.✚▲

PENSACOLA—AAA AUTO CLUB SOUTH, 540 BRENT LN, 32503. MON-FRI 8:30-5:30. (850) 477-6860.✚▲

POMPANO BEACH—AAA AUTO CLUB SOUTH, 601 E ATLANTIC BLVD, 33060. MON-FRI 8:30-5:30. (954) 942-5450.✚▲

PONTE VEDRA BEACH—AAA AUTO CLUB SOUTH, 840 A1A N #180, 32082. MON-FRI 8:30-5:30. (904) 280-8181.✚▲

PORT CHARLOTTE—AAA AUTO CLUB SOUTH, 21229-A OLEAN BLVD, 33952. MON-FRI 8:30-5:30. (941) 627-1544.✚▲

PORT RICHEY—AAA AUTO CLUB SOUTH, 10532 DEVCO DR, 34668. MON-FRI 8:30-5:30. (727) 868-9523.✚▲

SARASOTA—AAA AUTO CLUB SOUTH, 3844 BEE RIDGE RD, 34233. MON-FRI 8:30-5:30. (941) 362-2220.✚▲

SARASOTA—AAA AUTO CLUB SOUTH, 258 RINGLING SHOPPING CTR, 34237. MON-FRI 8:30-5:30. (941) 362-2500.✚▲

SEMINOLE—AAA AUTO CLUB SOUTH, 9200 SEMINOLE BLVD, 33772. MON-FRI 8:30-5:30. (727) 398-3120.✚▲

SEMINOLE—AAA AUTO CLUB SOUTH, 12941-A PARK BLVD, 33776. MON-FRI 8:30-5:30. (727) 392-2202.●▲

SPRING HILL—AAA AUTO CLUB SOUTH, 1410 PINEHURST DR, 34606. MON-FRI 8:30-5:30. (352) 683-3446.✚▲

ST. PETERSBURG—AAA AUTO CLUB SOUTH, 800 SECOND AVE S, 33701-4022. MON-FRI 8:30-5:30. (727) 826-3600.✚▲

ST. PETERSBURG—AAA AUTO CLUB SOUTH, 8250 NINTH ST N #2, 33702. MON-FRI 8:30-5:30. (727) 577-5282.●▲

STUART—AAA AUTO CLUB SOUTH, 1610 SE FEDERAL HWY, 34994. MON-FRI 8:30-5:30. (561) 287-5300.✚▲

TALLAHASSEE—AAA AUTO CLUB SOUTH, 1205 APALACHEE PKY, 32301. MON-FRI 8:30-5:30. (850) 878-6000.✚▲

TAMPA—AAA AUTO CLUB SOUTH, 1515 N WESTSHORE BLVD, 33607. MON-FRI 8:30-5:30. (813) 289-5000.✚▲

TAMPA—AAA AUTO CLUB SOUTH, 2335 E FOWLER AVE, 33612. MON-FRI 8:30-5:30. (813) 971-4900.✚▲

TAMPA—AAA AUTO CLUB SOUTH, 14755 N DALE MABRY, 33618. MON-FRI 8:30-5:30. (813) 963-2121.✚▲

VENICE—AAA AUTO CLUB SOUTH, 2100 S TAMIAMI TRL, 34293. MON-FRI 8:30-5:30. (941) 493-2100.✚▲

VERO BEACH—AAA AUTO CLUB SOUTH, 6620 20TH ST, 32966. MON-FRI 8:30-5:30. (561) 770-3400.▲

WINTER HAVEN—AAA AUTO CLUB SOUTH, 601 W CENTRAL AVE, 33880. MON-FRI 8:30-5:30. (863) 293-3151.■▲

FLORIDA

DRIVING DISTANCES

100 MILES IN US

2:00 AVERAGE TIME (EXCLUDING STOPS)

© AAA

3650-H

Know Your Future

Bed & Breakfast Lodgings Index

Some bed and breakfasts listed below might have historical significance. Those properties are also referenced in the Historical index. The indication that continental [CP] or full breakfast [BP] is included in the room rate reflects whether a property is a Bed-and-Breakfast facility.

FLORIDA
ACCOMMODATIONS

Country Inns Index

Some of the following country inns can also be considered as bed-and-breakfast operations. The indication that continental [CP] or full breakfast [BP] is included in the room rate reflects whether a property is a Bed-and-Breakfast facility.

FLORIDA
ACCOMMODATIONS

Historical Lodgings & Restaurants Index

Some of the following historical lodgings can also be considered as bed-and-breakfast operations. The indication that continental [CP] or full breakfast [BP] is included in the room rate reflects whether a property is a Bed-and-Breakfast facility.

FLORIDA
ACCOMMODATIONS

HISTORICAL LODGINGS & RESTAURANTS (CONT'D)

RESTAURANTS

Resorts Index

Many establishments are located in resort areas; however, the following places have extensive on-premises recreational facilities:

FLORIDA

ACCOMMODATIONS

Points of Interest Index

Index Legend

NB.	national battlefield	NR.	national river
NBP.	national battlefield park	NS.	national seashore
NC.	national cemetery	NWR.	national wildlife refuge
NF.	national forest	PHP.	provincial historic(al) park
NHM.	national historic(al) monument	PHS.	provincial historic(al) site
NHP.	national historic(al) park	PP.	provincial park
NHS.	national historic(al) site	SF.	state forest
NL.	national lakeshore	SHM.	state historic(al) monument
NME.	national memorial	SHP.	state historic(al) park
NMO.	national monument	SHS.	state historic(al) site
NMP.	national military park	SME.	state memorial
NP.	national park	SP.	state park
NRA.	national recreation area	SRA.	state recreation area

⬩ GEM: Points of Interest Offering a *Great Experience for Members*

SAVE *Attraction Admission Discount Index*

Comprehensive City Index

Here is an alphabetical list of all cities appearing in this TourBook® guide. Cities are presented by state/province. Page numbers under the POI column indicate where points of interest text begins. Page numbers under the L&R column indicate where lodging and restaurant listings begin.

COMPREHENSIVE CITY INDEX (CONT'D)

Photo Credit Index

Photo Credit Index (cont'd)

Rules of the Road Can Change at State Borders

*S*peed limits are usually posted at state lines, but adherence to less known traffic regulations also is important for safe and enjoyable travel between states. To assist the traveling motorists, AAA published the *Digest of Motor Laws* – a comprehensive description of the laws that govern motor vehicle registration and operation in the United States and Canada.

Examples of laws that differ include:

• In 33 jurisdictions, police can only cite motorists for not wearing seat belts if they are stopped for another infraction. In the remaining 18 jurisdiction, police can stop motorists solely for failure to wear a seat belt.

• Drivers with Learner's Permit are allowed to drive in their own states, subject to their state restrictions. 15 other states impose no additional restrictions while traveling in their respective states. 29 states impose additional restrictions and the remaining 7 jurisdictions prohibit vehicle operation by holders of out-of-state learner's permit.

• While use of cellular telephones is permitted in all states, there may be local ordinances. Florida and Massachusetts have restrictions.

To obtain a copy of the *Digest of Motor Laws*, contact your local AAA club or AAA's National Office at the Traffic Safety Department, 1000 AAA Drive, Heathrow, FL 32746-5063. This glove-compartment-size book retails for $10.95.

Savings for all Seasons

Hertz rents Fords and other fine cars.
® REG. U.S. PAT. OFF. © HERTZ SYSTEM INC., 1999/2006-99.

No matter the season, Hertz offers AAA members exclusive discounts and benefits.

With a fleet of more than 550,000 vehicles and over 6,500 rental locations worldwide, Hertz makes traveling more convenient and efficient wherever and whenever you go. Hertz offers AAA members discounts up to 20% on car rentals worldwide.

To receive your exclusive AAA member discounts and benefits, mention your AAA membership card at time of reservation and present it at time of rental.

For reservations and program details, call your AAA travel office or the Hertz/AAA Desk at **1-800-654-3080**.

Show Your Card & Save

AAA. Every Day.

exactly.

Every ten minutes someone traveling in America loses their cash.* If American Express® Travelers Cheques are lost or stolen, they can be replaced, usually within 24 hours. Cash can't. And they're available at no fee for AAA members at AAA offices.

*1998 US Statistical Abstract
© 2000 American Express. Payment methods vary from club to club.

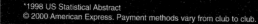